HELP FOR THE SHOPPER
Here is a list of equivalents of many everyday foods.

Coffee, regular grind . . . . 1 lb. (5 cups) . . . . about 45 cups
   instant . . . . 2 oz. (1 cup) . . . . about 25 cups
Tea, regular . . . . 4 oz. (about 1½ cups) . . . about 250 cups

Cornmeal, white or yellow . . . . . 1-lb. 8-oz. pkg. . . . . 4½ cups
Macaroni, elbow or shell . . . . . . 8-oz. pkg. . . . . 2 to 2¼ cups
Noodles . . . . 8-oz. pkg. . . . . 3 to 3½ cups
Rice, uncooked . . . . 1 lb. . . . . 2¼ to 2⅜ cups
Spaghetti . . . . 1-lb. pkg. . . . . about 4 cups

Butter . . . . 1 lb. . . . . 2 cups, 48 squares
Cheese, Cheddar, shredded . . . . . 1 lb. . . . . 4 cups
Eggs (with shells), large . . . . . . 1 lb. 7 or 8 eggs
   medium . . . . 1 lb. 9 or 10 eggs
   small . . . . 1 lb. . . . . 11 or 12 eggs
Milk, evaporated . . . . 14½-oz. can . . . . 1⅔ cups
   instant nonfat dry . . . . 9½-oz. pkg. . . . . 3 quarts fluid
   sweetened condensed . . . . 14-oz. can . . . . 1¼ cups

Flour, all-purpose, sifted . . . . . . 1 lb. . . . . 4 to 4½ cups
Flour, cake, sifted . . . . 1 lb. . . . . 4¾ to 5 cups
Flour, whole wheat, unsifted . . . 1 lb. . . . . about 3½ cups

Margarine . . . . 1 lb. . . . . 2 cups
Vegetable shortening . . . . 1 lb. . . . . 2½ cups

Dates, whole, unpitted, cut . . . . 1 lb. . . . . 3 cups
Prunes, medium, cooked . . . . . . 1 lb. . . . . 4 cups
Raisins, seedless . . . . 15-oz. pkg. . . . . 3 cups

Apples, pared, sliced . . . . 1 lb. (3 or 4 medium) . . . . 3 cups
Bananas, mashed . . . . 1 lb. (3 or 4 medium) . . . . about 2 cups
   sliced . . . . 1 lb. (3 or 4 medium) . . . about 2½ cups
Cherries, pitted . . . . 1 lb. . . . . 2 to 2½ cups
Lemons . . . . 3 lbs. (12 medium) . . about 2 cups juice
                            1 medium . . . . . 2 to 3 tablespoons juice
Oranges . . . . 6 lbs. (12 medium) . . about 1 quart juice
Peaches, peeled, sliced . . . . 1 lb. (3 or 4 medium) . . . . 2 to 2½ cups
Strawberries, hulled . . . . 1 pt. . . . . about 1½ cups

Almonds (in the shell) . . . . 2 lbs. . . . . 2½ to 3 cups nutmeats
Pecans (in the shell) . . . . 2 lbs. . . . . 4 to 4½ cups nutmeats
Walnuts (in the shell) . . . . 2 lbs. . . . . 3 to 3¼ cups nutmeats

Almonds, blanched whole . . . . . . 1 lb. . . . . about 3¼ cups
Peanuts, halves . . . . 1 lb. . . . . about 3¼ cups
Pecans, halves . . . . 1 lb. . . . . about 4¼ cups
   chopped . . . . 1 lb. . . . . about 3¾ cups
Walnuts, halves . . . . 1 lb. . . . . 4¼ to 4½ cups
   chopped . . . . 1 lb. . . . . 3⅔ cups

Sugar, brown . . . . 1- and 2-lb. pkgs. . . . . about 2¼ cups
                                         (packed) per pound
Sugar, confectioners' . . . . 1- and 2-lb. pkgs. . . . . 3 to 4 cups
                                         (unsifted) per pound
Sugar, granulated . . . . 1-, 2-, 5-, 10-lb. pkgs. . . . . about 2¼ cups
                                         per pound

Beans, dried, navy . . . . 1 lb. (2⅛ cups) . . . . 6 cups, cooked
Coconut, flaked . . . . 3½-oz. can . . . . 1⅓ cups
Coconut, shredded . . . . 4-oz. can . . . . 1½ cups
Gelatin, unflavored . . . . 1 env. . . . . about 1 tablespoon

The New
WORLD ENCYCLOPEDIA
of
COOKING

The New
WORLD

ENCYCLOPEDIA
of
COOKING

Edited by the Staff of
CULINARY ARTS INSTITUTE

CONSOLIDATED BOOK PUBLISHERS
CHICAGO

Library of Congress Catalog Card Number: 72-5575

International Standard Book Number: 0-8326-0540-9

Library of Congress Cataloging in Publication Data
    Main entry under title:

    The New World encyclopedia of cooking.

        1. Cookery. I. Culinary Arts Institute.
    II. Title: Encyclopedia of cooking. III. Title:
    World encyclopedia of cooking.
    TX715.N533   641.5   72-5575
    ISBN 0-8326-0540-9

FIRST EDITION

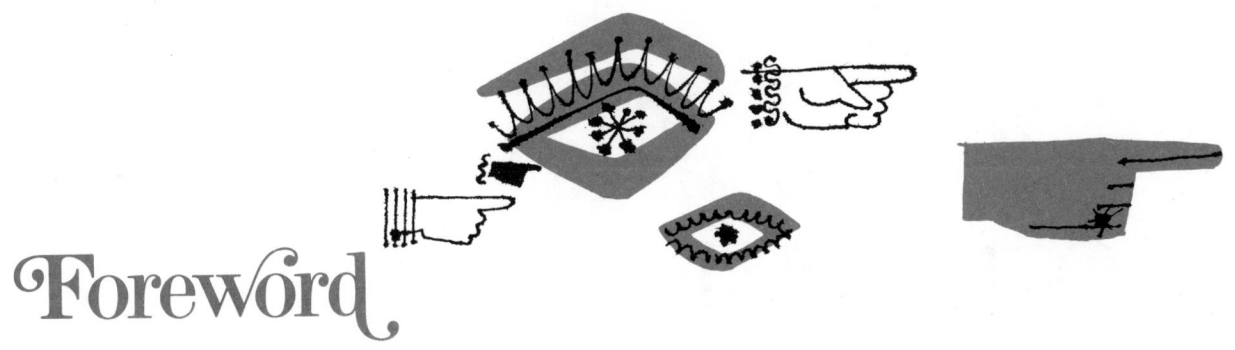

Foreword

THE AMERICAN HOMEMAKER has a unique opportunity to provide her family with new culinary experiences. Using *The New World Encyclopedia of Cooking*, she can borrow from the culinary traditions of cultures all over the world. This new collection contains robust recipes from Scandinavia making generous use of energizing foods; recipes for traditional French cuisine long recognized as some of the finest in the world; Italian recipes for dishes as diverse as the sections of Italy where they originated; recipes for fascinating and savory Hungarian dishes with surprise seasonings; recipes for hearty German and Viennese cooking developed in the kitchens of *hausfrauen* who borrowed ideas from their central European neighbors. These foreign specialties, excitingly unique and distinctive in flavor and eye-appeal, are all adaptable to a variety of tastes and occasions.

But this is not only a book of foreign cookery. Regional American dishes are represented by Pennsylvania Dutch favorites, the fine Creole cooking born in the deep South, the highly seasoned, colorful foods of the Southwest, and recipes for the hearty, satisfying dishes of New England.

Besides the great variety of international, national, and regional recipes, *The New World Encyclopedia of Cooking* offers help in making uncommon dishes from familiar ingredients—creative ways to prepare ground meat, recipes that use cheeses to add zest to a meal, distinctive salads that give a fresh touch to a favorite main dish. And *The New World Encyclopedia of Cooking* provides many new and creative solutions to the problems every cook faces—meals to please the children, cool dishes for hot days, easy and interesting suppers for Sunday night. Also included are helpful hints and recipes for entertaining, menus for special American holidays, suggestions for planning and preparing foods for dieters, directions and recipes for successful preservation of foods, hints on outdoor cookery, and much more.

For the homemaker who wants to bring new interest to family and company meals, *The New World Encyclopedia of Cooking* will be a gratifying and rewarding addition to her cookbook repertory. Conscientious cooks dream of creating memorable specialties—delectable main dishes, vegetables skillfully cooked to produce subtly blended flavors, and distinctive cakes, pies, and other glamorous desserts. Accomplishing this will be easy for the cook who uses *The New World Encyclopedia of Cooking* because in this book even the most complicated recipes are written with clarity and in such detail as to be within the capabilities of both beginners and experienced cooks.

Acknowledgments

Many industries and organizations contributed the excellent photographs that appear in this book. We wish to acknowledge and thank especially those which contributed the beautiful full-page color photographs: American Dairy Association (*opposite pages 65, 544 and 540*); Brussels Sprout Marketing Program/Brussels Sprout Shippers of California (*opposite pages 64 and 193*); California Avocado Advisory Board (*opposite page 385*); California Strawberry Advisory Board (*opposite page 641*); Diamond Walnut Growers, Inc. (*opposite pages 256 and 449*); Massachusetts Seafood Council (*opposite page 289*); National Cherry Growers & Industries Foundation (*opposite pages 449 and 545*); National Live Stock and Meat Board (*opposite page 192*); National Macaroni Insitute (*opposite page 384*); Spanish Green Olive Commission (*opposite pages 257 and 288*).

The following organizations kindly contributed many of the more than 600 black-and-white photographs which appear throughout the book: American Can Company, American Dairy Association, American Honey Institute, American Institute of Baking, American Lamb Council, American Meat Institute, Arm & Hammer Baking Soda, R. C. Bigelow, Inc., Blueberry Cooperative Association, Blueberry Institute, Borden, Inc., Brussels Sprout Marketing Program, Brussels Sprout Shippers of California, California Avocado Advisory Board, California Dried Fruit Research Institute, California Foods Research Institute, California Prune Advisory Board, California Raisin Advisory Board, California Strawberry Advisory Board, Campbell Soup Company, Can Manufacturers Institute, Canada Dry Ginger Ale, Cereal Institute, Commonwealth Edison Co., Corning Glass Works, Delaware State Poultry Commission, Evaporated Milk Association, Florida Citrus Commission, Fresh Cranberry Institute, Fruit Dispatch Co., General Foods Corporation, Glenmore Distilleries Co., H. J. Heinz Co., Hunt-Wesson Foods, Inc., Idle Wild Farms, Kellogg Company, Kraft Foods, Kretschmer Wheat Germ, Lever Bros., Louisiana Yam Commission, Mexican Foods Institute, Michigan Blueberry Growers Association, Minute Maid Fresh Frozen Juices, National Apple Institute, Nabisco, Inc., National Canners Association, National Cherry Growers and Industries Foundation, National Cranberry Association, National Dairy Council, National Fisheries Institute, National Kraut Packers Association, National Live Stock and Meat Board, National Pickle Packers Association, The Nestle Co. Inc., New Jersey Apple Institute, New Jersey Peach Industry, Norwegian Canners Association, Ocean Spray Cranberries, Inc., Oregon Washington California Pear Bureau, Pacific Kitchen, Pan-American Coffee Bureau, Pickle Packers International, Inc., Pineapple Growers Association, Poultry and Egg National Board, The Pump Room, The Quaker Oats Company, R.J.R. Foods, Rockwood Chocolate Co., Sealtest Consumer Service, Shrimp Association of the Americas, South African Rock Lobster Association, Southern Shellfish Company, Spanish Green Olive Commission, Standard Brands, Inc., Sugar Information, Inc., Sunkist Growers, Inc., Swift & Company, Tea Council of the U.S.A., Inc., United Fruit Co., United Fresh Fruit and Vegetable Association, U.S. Brewers Foundation, Universal Foods Corporation, Washington State Fruit Commission, Western Beet Sugar Producers Inc., Western Growers Association, Western Iceberg Lettuce, Wheat Flour Institute, William Underwood Company and Wine Institute.

Contents

THERE'S NO SUBSTITUTE FOR ACCURACY

Read recipe carefully. Assemble all ingredients and utensils. Select pans of proper kind and size. Measure inside, from rim to rim.

Use standard measuring cups and spoons. Use measuring cups with subdivisions marked on sides for liquids. Use graduated nested measuring cups for dry or solid ingredients.

Check liquid measurements at eye level.

Level dry or solid measurements with straight-edge knife or spatula.

Preheat oven at required temperature.

FOR THESE RECIPES— WHAT TO USE

Baking Powder—double-action type.

Bread Crumbs—two slices fresh bread equals about 1 cup soft crumbs or cubes. One slice dry or toasted bread equals about ½ cup dry cubes or ¼ to ⅓ cup fine dry crumbs.

Buttered Crumbs—soft or dry bread or cracker crumbs tossed in melted butter or margarine. Use 1 to 2 tablespoons butter or margarine for 1 cup soft crumbs or 2 to 4 tablespoons butter or margarine for 1 cup dry crumbs.

Chocolate—unsweetened baking or cooking chocolate. A general substitution for 1 oz. (1 sq.) unsweetened chocolate is 3 to 4 tablespoons cocoa plus 1 tablespoon fat.

Chocolate (no melt)—1-oz. packets or envelopes chocolate-flavored product or ingredient.

Cornstarch—thickening agent having double the thickening power of flour.

Cream—light, table or coffee cream containing not less than 18 to 20% milk fat.

Dairy Sour Cream—commercially soured cream containing 18 to 20% milk fat.

Dressed Fish—fish with head, tail, fins and entrails removed.

Flour—all-purpose flour. When substituting for cake flour, use 1 cup minus 2 tablespoons all-purpose flour for 1 cup cake flour.

Garlic Buttered Crumbs—cut 1 clove garlic into halves. Add to hot melted butter and allow to stand until butter has absorbed garlic flavor. Remove garlic and proceed as for buttered crumbs.

Grated Peel—whole citrus fruit peel finely grated through colored part only.

Ground Poppy Seed—freshly ground by grocer using special grinder or ground at home in electric blender. If using electric blender, put into blender container about ½ cup whole poppy seed at one time. Cover container, turn on motor and grind until poppy seed is very finely ground. (½ lb. whole poppy seed—about 1⅔ cups, whole—about 2½ cups, ground.)

Heavy or Whipping Cream—cream containing 30 to 40% milk fat.

Herb Bouquet (bouquet garni)—a bunch of aromatic herbs used to flavor soups, stews, braised dishes and sauces. Usually made with 3 or 4 sprigs of parsley, 1 sprig thyme and ½ bay leaf, tied neatly together. Enclose fine, dry herbs in a cheesecloth bag.

Instant Nonfat Dry Milk—creamy-white, free-flowing particles which dissolve readily in water.

Julienne—vegetables, meats or cheeses cut into matchlike strips.

Monosodium Glutamate—crystalline cereal or vegetable product that enhances the natural flavor of foods.

Non Caloric Sweetening Agents—available in solution (liquid), granulated or tablet form. Be sure tablets are completely dissolved; crush and dissolve in some liquid ingredient of recipe.

Oil—salad or cooking type. Use olive oil only when recipe so directs.

Peppercorns—the dried berries of the pepper plant; used ground (in pepper grinder) or whole.

Shortening—vegetable shortening, all-purpose shortening, butter or margarine. Use lard or oil when specified.

Skim Milk—commercial skim milk or reconstituted nonfat dry milk (reconstitute following directions on package).

Sour Milk—sweet milk soured artificially by the addition of vinegar or lemon juice. (To prepare 1 cup of sour milk, put 1 tablespoon cider vinegar or lemon juice into a measuring cup for liquids, and fill the cup with milk to the 1-cup line; stir.)

Spices and Herbs—ground unless recipe specifies otherwise.

Stuffed Olives—pimiento-stuffed olives.

Sugar—granulated (cane or beet).

Vinegar—cider vinegar. Use other vinegars when specified.

HOW TO DO IT

Baste—spoon liquid over cooking food to add moisture and flavor; or use baster.

Blanch Nuts—the flavor and crisp texture of nuts are best maintained when nuts are allowed to remain in water the shortest possible time during blanching. Therefore, blanch only about ½ cup at a time; repeat process as many times as necessary for larger amounts. Bring to a rapid boil enough water to cover the shelled nuts. Drop nuts into water. Turn off heat and allow nuts to remain in water about 1 min.; drain or remove with slotted spoon or fork. Place between folds of absorbent paper; pat dry. Squeeze nuts between thumb and fingers to remove skins; or peel. Place on dry absorbent paper; to dry thoroughly, shift frequently to dry spots on paper.

Boil—cook in liquid in which bubbles rise continually and break on the surface. Boiling temperature of water at sea level is 212°F.

Clean Celery—trim off root end and cut off leaves. Leaves may be chopped and used for added flavor in soups and stuffings; leaves may be left on inner stalks when serving as a relish. Separate stalks, remove blemishes and wash.

Clean Garlic—separate into cloves and remove thin, papery outer skin.

Clean Green Pepper—rinse and slice away from pod and stem; trim off any white membrane; rinse away seeds; cut into strips, dice or prepare as directed in recipe.

Clean and Slice Mushrooms—wash quickly under running cold water, wipe with paper toweling and cut off tips of stems; slice lengthwise through stems and caps.

Clean Onions (dry)—cut off root end and a thin slice from stem end; peel and rinse.

Cook Macaroni—heat 3 qts. water and 1 tablespoon salt to boiling in a large saucepan. Add gradually 2 cups (8-oz. pkg.) uncooked macaroni (elbows, shells or tubes broken into 1-in. pieces). Boil rapidly, uncovered, 10 to 15 min., or until tender. Test tenderness by pressing a piece against side of pan with fork or spoon. Drain macaroni by turning it into a colander or large sieve.

Cream—work shortening (alone or with other ingredients) by stirring, rubbing or beating with spoon or electric mixer until soft and creamy.

Cut Uncooked Dried or Candied Fruits or Marshmallows—cut with kitchen shears dipped frequently in water to avoid stickiness.

Dice—cut into small cubes.

Fill and Seal Jars—ladle hot mixture into hot jars to within ½ in. of top. Clean rim with damp clean cloth or paper towel. Drain covers; seal jars at once, following manufacturer's directions. Cool away from drafts.

Flake Fish—separate canned or cooked fish into flakes (layerlike pieces) with a fork.

Remove bony tissue from crab meat; salmon bones are edible.

Flame—ignite with a match until flames appear.

Flute Edge of Pastry—press index finger on edge of pastry, then pinch pastry with thumb and index finger of other hand. Lift fingers and repeat procedure to flute entire edge.

Fold—Slip a flexible spatula down side of bowl to bottom. Turn bowl quarter turn. Lift spatula through mixture along side of bowl with blade parallel to surface. Turn spatula over so as to fold lifted material across the surface. Cut down and under again; turn bowl and repeat process until material is blended to desired degree. With every fourth stroke, bring spatula up through center.

Grate Nuts or Chocolate—use a rotary-type grater with hand-operated crank. Follow manufacturer's directions. Grated nuts or chocolate should be fine and light; do not use an electric blender for grating or grinding nuts unless called for in recipe.

Grind Cooked Meat—put boneless meat (fat trimmed) through medium blade of food chopper.

Grind Nuts—put nuts through medium blade of food chopper.

Marinate—allow food to stand in liquid (usually oil and acid) to impart additional flavor.

Measure Brown Sugar—pack firmly into dry measuring cup; sugar should hold shape of cup when turned out.

Measure Granulated Brown Sugar—see manufacturer's substitution table before pouring into measuring cup.

Melt Chocolate—heat unsweetened chocolate over simmering water and sweet or semisweet chocolate over hot (not simmering) water just until melted.

Mince—cut or chop into very small pieces.

Parboil—boil uncooked food until partially cooked. The cooking is usually completed by another method.

Peel Tomatoes—dip into boiling water about ½ min. to loosen skins then into cold water to chill. Peel and refrigerate. Cut out stem ends and prepare as directed in recipe.

Pound Meat—increase tenderness in less tender cuts of meat; place meat on flat working surface and repeatedly pound meat on one side with meat hammer, turn meat and repeat process until of desired thickness.

Prepare Crumbs—place cookies, crackers, zwieback or dry bread on a long length of heavy waxed paper. Loosely fold paper around them, tucking open ends under. With rolling pin, gently crush to make fine crumbs. Or place cookies or crackers in a plastic bag and gently crush with rolling pin. Or prepare crumbs using an electric blender.

Prepare Decorating Chocolate—melt semisweet chocolate (over hot water or over very low heat, stirring constantly), then cool it enough so it can be piped through decorating tubes (if chocolate is too thin, stir in a bit of confectioners' sugar).

Prepare Double-Strength Coffee Beverage—prepare coffee in usual manner (method and grind of coffee depending upon type of coffee maker) using 4 measuring tablespoons coffee per ¾ standard measuring cup of water.

Prepare Quick Chicken Broth—dissolve 1 chicken bouillon cube in 1 cup boiling water.

Prepare Quick Meat Broth—dissolve 1 beef bouillon cube or ½ teaspoon concentrated meat extract in 1 cup boiling water.

Prepare Quick Coffee—put 1 rounded teaspoon instant coffee into each cup. Add boiling water and stir until coffee is completely dissolved. For 1 cup of double-strength coffee increase instant coffee to 1 tablespoon.

Prepare Quick-Cooking Rice—follow directions on package of precooked rice.

Reduce Liquid—continue cooking the liquid until the amount is sufficiently decreased, thus concentrating flavor and sometimes thickening the original liquid. Simmer when wine is used; boil rapidly for other liquids.

Rice—force through ricer, sieve or food mill.

Salt Nuts—toast nuts, using fat before or after toasting; sprinkle with salt.

Scald Milk—heat in top of double boiler over simmering water or in a heavy saucepan over direct heat just until a thin film appears.

Sieve—force through sieve or food mill.

Simmer—cook in a liquid just below boiling point; bubbles form slowly and break below surface.

Steep—allow a substance to stand in a very hot liquid in order to extract color and flavor.

Sterilize Jars or Glasses—put rack or folded dish towel in bottom of large kettle. Set clean jars or glasses and covers on it, pour boiling water into and around them, and boil 15 min., keeping them covered with water at all times. Remove from water one at a time with long-handled tongs, when ready to fill, drain thoroughly, and set right side up on a cooling rack covered with a towel.

Toast Nuts—place nuts in a shallow baking dish or pie pan and, if desired, brush lightly with butter, margarine or cooking oil. Heat in a 350°F oven until delicately browned; move and turn occasionally. Or put nuts into a heavy skillet in which butter, margarine or oil (about 1 tablespoon per cup of nuts) has been heated. Heat until nuts are lightly browned, moving and turning constantly.

Whip Cream—beat thoroughly chilled heavy (whipping) cream in a chilled bowl with a chilled beater; beat until cream stands in peaks when beater is slowly lifted upright.

A CHECK LIST FOR SUCCESSFUL BAKING

Read again "It's Smart To Be Careful—There's No Substitute for Accuracy" (page 9).

Place oven rack so top of product will be almost at center of oven. Stagger pans so no pan is directly over another and they do not touch each other or walls of oven. Place single pan on rack so that product is as near center of oven as possible.

Prepare pan for cake with shortening and for torte, grease bottom of pan only; line with waxed paper; grease the waxed paper. Or grease pan, sprinkle with flour, shake to coat pan evenly, then invert pan and tap out excess flour. If cake (plain or frosted) is to be cut and stored in pan, omit waxed paper. For cake without shortening (sponge-type), do not grease or line pan. For both yeast breads and quick breads, grease pan or baking sheet. For cookies, lightly grease cookie sheets if so directed. If recipe directs "set out pan," do not grease or line pan.

Have all ingredients at room temperature unless recipe specifies otherwise.

Sift (before measuring) all-purpose flour if indicated in recipe. When using instant-type flour, follow package directions and recipes. Level flour in cup with straight-edged knife or spatula. Spoon, without sifting, whole-grain types of flour into measuring cup.

Cream butter or margarine (alone or with flavorings) by stirring, rubbing or beating with spoon or electric mixer until softened. Add sugar gradually, creaming thoroughly. Thorough creaming helps to insure a fine-grained cake.

Beat whole eggs until thick and piled softly when recipe calls for well-beaten eggs.

Beat egg whites as follows: *Frothy*—entire mass form bubbles; *Rounded peaks*—peaks turn over slightly when beater is slowly lifted upright; *Stiff, not dry, peaks*—peaks remain standing when beater is slowly lifted upright.

Beat egg yolks until thick and lemon-colored when recipe calls for well-beaten egg yolks.

When dry and liquid ingredients are added to batters, add alternately, beginning and ending with dry. After each addition, beat only until smooth (do not overbeat). Scrape spoon or beater and bottom and sides of bowl during mixing. If using an electric mixer, beat mixture at a low speed when alternately adding liquid and dry ingredients.

Fill cake pans one-half to two-thirds full.

Tap bottom of cake pan sharply with hand or on table to release air bubbles before placing in oven.

Apply baking tests when minimum baking time is up. For cake or torte, touch lightly at center; if it springs back, cake is done. Or insert a cake tester or wooden pick in center; if it comes out clean, cake is done.

Cool butter-type cake 5 to 10 min., torte 15 min., in pan on cooling rack after removing from oven; or cool as recipe directs.

Remove butter-type cake or torte from pan after cooling. Run spatula gently around inside of pan. Cover with cooling rack. Invert and remove pan. Turn right side up immediately after peeling off waxed paper. When using pans with removable bottoms, loosen edges with spatula and carefully cut layers away from bottoms of pans; cool right side up. Or remove from pan as recipe directs. Cool cake or torte completely before frosting.

To cool sponge-type cake, after removing tubed cake from oven immediately invert pan on tubed end and let hang in pan until completely cooled. If cake is higher than tube, invert between two cooling racks so top of cake does not touch any surface. Hot-milk or hot-water sponge cake baked in layer cake pans should be cooled 5 to 10 min. on cooling racks before removing from the pans.

Remove sponge-type cake from pan when completely cooled. Cut around tube with paring knife to loosen cake. Loosen sides with spatula and gently remove cake.

To fill layer cake or torte, spread filling or frosting over bottom of bottom layer. Cover with the second layer. Repeat procedure if more layers are used. If necessary, hold layers in position with wooden picks; remove when filling is set.

To frost filled layer cake or torte, frost sides first, working rapidly. Be sure that frosting touches plate all around bottom, leaving no gaps. Pile remaining frosting on top of cake and spread lightly.

Test for lukewarm liquid (80°F to 85°F) by placing a drop on wrist; it will feel neither hot nor cold.

Knead dough by folding opposite side over toward you. Using heels of hands, gently push dough away. Give it one-quarter turn; always turn the dough in the same direction. Repeat process rhythmically 5 to 8 min. until dough is smooth, elastic and shows small blisters under surface when dough is drawn tight; use as little additional flour as possible.

Remove rolls, bread, and cookies from pans as they come from the oven, unless otherwise directed. Set on cooling racks to cool.

Keep tops of yeast loaves and rolls soft by immediately brushing with butter or margarine as they come from the oven.

OVEN TEMPERATURES

Very Slow . . . . .250°F to 275°F
Slow .300°F to 325°F
Moderate . . . . .350°F to 375°F
Hot . . . . .400°F to 425°F
Very Hot . . . . .450°F to 475°F
Extremely Hot . . . . .500°F to 525°F

Use a portable oven thermometer to double-check oven temperature.

WHEN YOU BROIL

Set temperature control of range at Broil. Distance from top of food to source of heat determines the intensity of heat upon food.

WHEN YOU DEEP-FRY

A deep-frying thermometer is an accurate guide for deep-frying temperatures. If a thermometer is not available, the following bread cube method may be used as a guide. A 1-in. cube of bread browns in:

60 seconds at . . . . .350°F to 375°F

When using an automatic deep fryer, follow manufacturer's directions for amount of fat and timing.

WHEN USING
THE ELECTRIC BLENDER

To grind or chop, put enough food into blender container at one time to cover blades. Cover, turn on motor and grind or chop to desired degree of fineness. (Turning motor on and off helps to throw food back on blades.) Empty container and grind or chop next batch of food. Or follow manufacturer's directions.

WHEN YOU COOK CANDY
OR SYRUP

A candy thermometer is an accurate guide to correct stage of cooking. Put the thermometer into syrup mixture after sugar is dissolved and boiling starts. A 3-inch depth of syrup is advisable to take an accurate thermometer reading; if necessary, tip pan to obtain this depth. If thermometer is cold, heat it in warm water before plunging it into the hot syrup.

Syrup Stages and Temperatures

Thread (230°F to 234°F)—spins 2-in. thread when allowed to drop from fork or spoon.

Soft Ball (234°F to 240°F)—forms a soft ball in very cold water; it flattens when removed from water.

Firm Ball (244°F to 248°F)—forms a firm ball in very cold water; it does not flatten when removed from water.

Hard Ball (250°F to 266°F)—forms a ball which is pliable yet hard enough to hold its shape in very cold water.

Soft Crack (270°F to 290°F)—separates into threads which are hard but not brittle in very cold water.

Hard Crack (300°F to 310°F)—separates into threads which are hard and brittle in very cold water.

WHAT DOES IT MEAN?

à la, au, aux—prepared in a certain style; "with" or "in," depending on use.

à la Carte—a menu term meaning "according to the menu"; each item is ordered separately.

à la King—served in a cream sauce with mushrooms, pimiento and sometimes sherry along with chicken or turkey.

à la Mode—literally "in style"; examples: pie à la mode (with ice cream) or beef à la mode (braised beef with vegetables and gravy).

al dente—a term for not-quite tender pasta; in Italian, it literally means "to the tooth."

Antipasto—an Italian first course usually served cold.

Apèritif—a drink, such as sherry, served before a meal in order to stimulate the appetite.

au Gratin—a browned or toasted surface, produced by baking with a topping of crumbs or grated cheese, or both.

au Jus—served with natural meat juices.

Beignet—deep-fried batter or dough; French for "fritter."

Bisque—a rich cream soup frequently containing shellfish.

Blini—appetizer-sized Russian buckwheat pancakes.

Bouchée—a filled small pastry shell.

Bouillabaisse—a soup containing a combination of fish and shellfish.

Bouillon—a clear, seasoned stock or broth usually made from browned beef; a quick substitute is 1 beef bouillon cube or ½ teaspoon concentrated meat extract dissolved in 1 cup boiling water.

Bourguignonne, à la—cooked in a red wine sauce along with mushrooms and onions.

Brioche—a round soft yeast roll with a "top hat."

Cacciatore—food, usually chicken, prepared in a spicy tomato sauce; literally "hunter" in Italian.

Café au Lait—hot strong coffee usually in equal proportion with hot milk.

Caffè Espresso—an especially strong Italian coffee prepared by forcing steam under pressure through pulverized coffee; this moisture falls into the cup and condenses to form the beverage.

Cannelloni—pasta in tubes with a filling, usually meat or poultry, with sauce and cheese on top.

Cannelon—meat stuffed, rolled and roasted or braised.

Cannoli—a Sicilian deep-fried pastry filled with ricotta cheese, pudding or whipped cream.

Capers—the flower-bud of a Mediterranean caper bush; it is pickled and used for flavoring or garnish.

Capocollo—cooked boneless pork butt that has been rolled in pepper and other spices and is served in thin slices.

Cappelletti—moist stuffed pasta usually served in soup; said to resemble "little hats."

Cappucino—a blend of espresso coffee and hot milk with a cinnamon stick stirrer.

Chapon—a slice or crust of French bread rubbed well with garlic and tossed with a green salad.

Chasseur, à la—cooked with mushrooms, shallots and white wine.

Chaud-froid—a cold cream sauce with gelatin added which is used to coat chilled foods, especially molded main-dish salads and poultry.

Chiffonade—a garnish of julienne strips of vegetable, usually for soup or salad.

Chorizo—a highly seasoned Mexican and Spanish pork sausage.

Cocotte—a covered casserole of earthenware or porcelain; small cocottes generally are used for baked (shirred) eggs and larger sizes for chicken or other entrées.

Consommé—clear, concentrated stock or broth made from one or a combination of two or more kinds of meat, such as beef, veal and poultry; a quick substitute is 1 chicken bouillon cube dissolved in 1 cup boiling water.

Crêpe—light, thin French pancake.

Croissant—a light, flaky crescent-shaped yeast roll the dough for which has been rolled with butter, following a special procedure.

Croquettes—chopped food in a thick sauce, shaped, coated with egg and crumbs and often deep-fried.

Croustade—hollowed-out toast case or pastry shell used as a container for filling.

Croûte—a large piece of slightly dry bread toasted, or browned in butter or oil.

Croûtons—slices or cubes of bread, toasted and browned in butter, or just toasted.

Daube—braised meat or poultry in an herbed wine sauce.

Demitasse—a small cup of strong black coffee served after dinner.

Ditalini—a tubular-shaped pasta about ¼ in. in both diameter and length and often served in soup.

Duchesse (potatoes)—seasoned mashed potatoes beaten with egg yolk, piped through pastry bag and tube for a border, and browned in the oven.

Eclair—a finger-shaped choux pastry shell filled with pastry cream or whipped cream and spread with chocolate glaze.

Entrée—small prepared dish served between heavy courses at a formal dinner; at informal meals, the main dish of main course.

Escargot—"snail" in French.

Farce—stuffing.

Farci—stuffed.

Fettucine—"noodles" in Italian.

Filé—a powder of ground sassafras leaves mixed into gumbo just before serving.

Filet—a piece of lean boneless meat or fish.

Filet Mignon—a slice of beef tenderloin about 1 in. thick that weighs 6 to 8 ounces.

Fines Herbes—a mixture of finely chopped herbs: chervil, chives, parsley and tarragon.

Finocchio—an anise-flavored celery-like vegetable; also known as fennel.

Florentine, à la—a dish, usually egg or fish, with spinach.

Foie Gras—goose liver; prepared pâté is a paste made from this liver.

Frenched—cut lengthwise into halves and then crosswise, as for green beans.

Fricassee—a dish usually containing browned chicken cooked in a seasoned broth or sauce.

Gâteau—"cake" in French.

Gaufre—wafer-like French cookie.

Gelato—"frozen" in Italian; refers to ice cream or sherbet.

Gnocchi—Italian dumpling often made with potatoes.

Jardinère, à la—an accompaniment of fresh vegetables.

Julienne—matchlike pieces of fruit, meat or vegetables.

Kartoffeln—"potatoes" in German.

Kuchen—"cake" in German; often refers to coffee cake.

Leek—a long bulb with flavor like that of an onion, but milder and sweeter.

Linguine—a narrow, flat pasta about ⅛ in. wide; literally "little tongues" in Italian.

Macchinetta—Italian coffee maker.

Manicotti—a thin, rectangular-shaped pasta stuffed with ricotta cheese mixture.

Noisette—a small, round piece of meat sliced from a filet, such as beef or lamb.

Okra—a green vegetable pod used in gumbos or vegetable dishes.

Pain—"bread" in French.

Pane—"bread" in Italian.

Papillote, en—food wrapped, cooked and served in parchment, waxed paper or aluminum foil.

Parmigiana—prepared using Parmesan cheese.

Pasta—a dough composed chiefly of flour, water and sometimes eggs, and made into many shapes and sizes such as spaghetti, macaroni and noodles.

Pâte—a paste or dough.

Pâté—a pie or patty with a filling of meat or fish, or spiced meat paste such as pâté de foie.

Petits Fours—individual small fancy cakes or pastries of various shapes; frosting is poured on and decorations added.

Petits Pains—"rolls" in French.

Petits Pois—"green peas" in French.

Pièce de Résistance—the main dish, often roasted meat, but also poultry or game served with accompanying sauces and stuffings.

Pizzaiola—"pizza style" in Italian; suggests piquancy and sharpness.

Plum Tomato—Italian tomato, shaped like a plum and slightly stronger flavored than an ordinary tomato; use in any recipe calling for tomatoes.

Polenta—corn meal mush often served with sausage gravy.

Potage—"soup" in French.

Profiterole—a choux paste shell (cream puff) often with a cream filling and chocolate glaze.

Prosciutto—a dry-cured Italian-style ham.

Provençale, à la—a dish containing garlic, olive oil and usually tomatoes.

Purée—sieved fruit or vegetable; smooth thick soup; pounded and sieved fish.

Ragoût—a thick, highly seasoned stew.

Ravioli—thick, square-shaped pasta stuffed with meat or a mixture of meat and spinach or cheese and served with a hot tomato sauce.

Reine, à la—served in a rich sauce, usually containing mushrooms along with chicken.

Roulade—a thin piece of meat, stuffed or not, rolled up and cooked.

Roux—a blended mixture of flour and fat used to thicken sauces and gravies.

Saffron—an orange-colored, sweet-smelling, but strong-flavored spice derived from the stigmas of the saffron plant and used to add color and flavor to white, bland foods such as rice.

Sauté—to cook lightly and quickly in a small amount of hot fat, turning frequently.

Scaloppine—usually refers to veal scaloppine or "pieces" (scallops) of veal.

Shallot—a small pear-shaped reddish onion.

Soufflé—a light, fluffy baked dish containing a sauce with egg yolks, a flavoring mixture and beaten egg whites which cause the mixture to puff during baking. Some soufflés contain gelatin and are chilled before serving.

Spätzle—a noodle made by forcing a dough through a colander and cooking in boiling salted water.

Spumone—an Italian ice cream.

Table d'Hôte—a menu term meaning the price of a complete meal is determined by the entrée selected.

Tournedo—a slice of beef tenderloin about 1 in. thick that weighs 3 to 5 ounces.

Trifle—a dessert with layers of cake soaked with wine, brandy or rum, custard, whipped cream and fruit; garnished with nuts.

Truffle—a black, edible fungus of the mushroom family, delicate in flavor and aroma; available in cans or jars.

Tutti-frutti—preserved mixed chopped fruits often mixed with ice cream.

Vermicelli—pasta shaped into long thin strings thinner than regular spaghetti.

Vinaigrette—a seasoned vinegar and oil sauce.

Wiener Schnitzel—thin slices of veal with egg and bread crumb coating browned in butter.

Appetizers

In the original sense of the word, appetizers were foods meant to stimulate, not satisfy, the appetite. Hors d'oeuvre, the French equivalent for appetizers, literally refers to a quite hearty food which is served in France, instead of soup, as a start to a noon meal. In Italy it is called antipasto, in Sweden, smörgasbord and in Russia, zakdusky. In our country, hors d'oeuvres include a wide variety of "finger foods" served at a cocktail party or before a dinner. Hors d'oeuvres are usually colorful, attractive, bite-size morsels which are easy to eat, preferably with the fingers. An hors d'oeuvre tray often includes canapés—savory bits of foods (or highly seasoned spreads) on a base of toast rounds or crackers. Appetizers also include cocktails served as the first course of a sit-down luncheon or dinner.

DIPS AND DUNKS

AVOCADO DUNK

Wash, cut into halves, pit, peel, and cut into chunks

1 large ripe avocado

Put into an electric blender container with

2 tablespoons mayonnaise
1 tablespoon lemon or lime juice
1 teaspoon salt
Slice onion

Cover and blend until thoroughly mixed.
To keep dunk from darkening over a period of time, place a thin layer of mayonnaise over the top. When ready to serve, mix thoroughly.

About 1 cup dunk

To vary—Add any one of the following: **1 small tomato**, cubed; pitted **ripe olives**; crisp **bacon; few drops Tabasco; ⅛ teaspoon curry powder** or **1 pkg. (8 oz.) softened cream cheese**.

GUACAMOLE I

South of the border, Guacamole turns up in many guises—as salad, sauce, garnish, or as a tortilla filling. But Americans like it best as a dip to be eaten with crisp crackers, potato chips or corn chips.

Rinse and dip into boiling water for a few seconds to loosen skin

1 tomato

Peel, cut out stem end and chop tomato

Rinse, cut into halves and remove pit from

1 large ripe avocado

Carefully scoop out pulp, reserving the shells to use as containers for serving the dip. Put the pulp into a bowl and mash well with a fork. Blend in the chopped tomato and

2 teaspoons grated onion
1 teaspoon olive oil
1 teaspoon lemon juice
¾ teaspoon salt
⅛ teaspoon pepper
1 clove garlic, minced

Blend until ingredients are thoroughly mixed. Cover bowl. Set in refrigerator to chill and to allow flavors to blend.

To serve, spoon the dip into the avocado shells.

About 1¼ cups dip

AVOCADO COTTAGE CHEESE DIP

Force through a sieve or food mill and set aside

1 cup cream-style cottage cheese

Rinse, cut into halves and remove pit from

1 large ripe avocado

Carefully scoop fruit from shells, reserving the shells to use as containers for serving the dip. Put the avocado into a bowl and mash well with a fork. Blend in

2 teaspoons lemon juice

Mix in the sieved cottage cheese and

3 tablespoons minced parsley
2 teaspoons grated onion
½ teaspoon salt
½ teaspoon monosodium glutamate
¼ teaspoon pepper
1 clove garlic, minced

Blend until ingredients are thoroughly mixed. Spoon the dip into the reserved shells. Set in refrigerator to chill.

Before serving, sprinkle with

Paprika

Accompany with slices and pieces of assorted **fresh vegetables, potato chips** or **crackers**.

Arrange all attractively on an hors d'oeuvre tray and garnish with a few **sprigs of parsley**.

About 2 cups dip

Note: For a smooth dip, beat the avocado with an electric mixer. Gradually add cottage cheese and seasonings, beating until smooth.

TANGY CHEESE DIP

Thin slices of pumpernickel or rye bread make perfect "dippers."

Prepare and mix in a bowl

3 cups (about ¾ lb.) shredded sharp Cheddar cheese
⅓ cup (about 1¼ oz.) crumbled Roquefort or blue cheese

Add gradually, stirring constantly until mixture is smooth

¾ cup beer (measured without foam)

Blend in

1 tablespoon butter or margarine, softened
1½ teaspoons grated onion
¾ teaspoon dry mustard
½ teaspoon Worcestershire sauce
2 drops Tabasco

Cover and chill thoroughly in refrigerator.

About 2 cups dip

PIQUANT DIP

Hard-cook and finely chop

1 egg

Beat together until fluffy

1 pkg. (3 oz.) cream cheese, softened
1 cup dairy sour cream

Mix in the egg and

¼ cup minced green pepper
1 tablespoon ketchup
1½ teaspoons prepared horseradish
1 teaspoon Worcestershire sauce
½ small clove garlic, minced

Stir in a blend of

½ teaspoon dry mustard
½ teaspoon salt

Cover and refrigerate at least 2 hrs. to chill and blend flavors.

Serve as a dip with crisp **crackers** or **potato chips**.

About 1½ cups dip

Guacamole I

SNAPPY DUNK

Put into an electric blender container
½ cup dairy sour cream
Cover and turn on motor.

Add, by pieces
6 oz. sharp Cheddar cheese food, smoked or with garlic, cut into chunks
Blend until smooth.

Sprinkle with chopped **chives** before serving. Use **cocktail crackers** as dippers.
About 1 cup dunk

BEAN OLIVE DUNK

Beat together until fluffy
6 oz. cream cheese, softened
1 teaspoon grated lemon peel
1 to 2 teaspoons lemon juice
Mix in
1 can (10½ oz.) condensed black bean soup
Stir in
⅔ cup chopped ripe olives
Chill thoroughly. *About 2 cups dunk*

PRETZEL DUNK

This dunk goes well with the saltiness of pretzels.

Beat in a small bowl
1 pkg. (3 oz.) cream cheese
Add
½ cup drained crushed pineapple
Beat until well mixed. *About 1 cup dunk*

RED TOMATO DUNK

▲ *Base Recipe*

Rinse and dip, one at a time, into boiling water for a few seconds
2 ripe tomatoes
Immediately peel tomatoes and cut away stem end. Cut into pieces and put into an electric blender container (being sure all juice is in the container).

Add to blender container
1 pkg. (8 oz.) cream cheese, cut in pieces
½ teaspoon salt
Slice onion
Sliver garlic
Few drops Tabasco
Cover and blend until smooth.
About 1½ cups dunk

—SOUR CREAM TOMATO DIP

Follow ▲ Recipe. Substitute **1 can (6 oz.) tomato paste** for tomatoes and **1 cup dairy sour cream** for cream cheese.

CHEESE HAM DUNK

Put into an electric blender container in order
½ cup mayonnaise
1 pkg. (8 oz.) cream cheese, cut in pieces
⅓ cup (3-oz. can) deviled ham or liver sausage
½ teaspoon salt
¼ teaspoon Worcestershire sauce
Few grains pepper
1 slice onion
Cover and blend until smooth.

Add
2 strips pimiento
Blend only until pimiento is chopped.

Serve with **potato chips.** *About 2 cups dunk*

DEVILED HAM TOMATO DIP

Mix together until well blended
1 can (6 oz.) tomato paste
1 can (2¼ oz.) deviled ham
½ cup chopped celery
¼ cup chopped onion
½ teaspoon salt
⅛ teaspoon cayenne pepper
Chill thoroughly and serve with **crackers.**
About 1 cup dip

CAMEMBERT BACON DIP

Put into an electric blender container
6 slices Panfried Bacon (page 190), crumbled
¼ cup cream or milk
1 pkg. (8 oz.) cream cheese, cut in pieces
4 oz. Camembert cheese, cut in pieces
Slice onion
Cover and blend until smooth.
About 2 cups dip

EXOTIC OLIVE DIP

Beat together until cheese is softened and mixture is fluffy
2 pkgs. (3 oz. each) cream cheese
1 can (10½ oz.) condensed black bean soup

Devilish Cheese Dip

Stir in
½ cup chopped ripe olives
Serve as dip for **potato chips** or as a spread on **crackers.** *About 2½ cups dip*

CLAM APPETIZER DIP

▲ *Base Recipe*

Drain, reserving ¼ cup liquid
1 can (10 oz.) clams
Put reserved liquid into an electric blender container with
6 oz. cream cheese
1 tablespoon lemon juice
1 teaspoon Worcestershire sauce
½ teaspoon salt
⅛ teaspoon freshly ground pepper
1 sliver garlic
Cover and turn on motor. Add clams; blend.
About 2 cups dip

—DEVILISH CHEESE DIP

Follow ▲ Recipe. Omit clams and clam liquid. Increase cream cheese to 8 oz. Add **2¼-oz. can deviled ham** and **½ cup mayonnaise.**

HORSERADISH DUNK

Put into a small mixer bowl
1 pkg. (8 oz.) cream cheese
¼ cup milk or cream
2 tablespoons prepared horseradish
1 teaspoon Worcestershire sauce
Beat with electric beater until smooth.
About 1 cup dunk

ROQUEFORT OR BLUE CHEESE DIP

▲ *Base Recipe*

Roquefort or blue cheese gives the zip to this mild-looking dip.

Crumble onto waxed paper and set aside
4 oz. Roquefort or blue cheese

Beat together in small bowl
1 pkg. (3 oz.) cream cheese
1 teaspoon lemon juice
½ teaspoon salt

Add gradually, beating until thoroughly mixed
  ½ cup milk or cream
Add crumbled cheese. Beat until smooth.
  About 2 cups dip

—ROQUEFORT WINE DIP

Follow ▲ Recipe. Substitute ¼ cup port wine for milk or cream. Omit lemon juice.

GARLIC CHEESE DIP

The happy owner of a blender can whisk this together in a jiffy, but it can be hand-mixed.

Put into an electric blender container
  1 pkg. (3 oz.) cream cheese
  **1¼ oz. (1 pkg.) Roquefort or
    blue cheese, crumbled**
  ⅓ cup dairy sour cream
  2 tablespoons pineapple juice
  ½ teaspoon Worcestershire sauce
  5 drops Tabasco
  1 sprig parsley
  ⅓ clove garlic
Cover and turn on motor. Blend until just smooth.

Serve as a dip with crisp **crackers** or **potato chips.**
  About 1 cup dip

SPECIAL BLENDER CHEESE DIP

An electric blender puts this special dip on your appetizer tray in no time at all. You'll love the subtle blend of provocative flavors.

Put into blender container
  ¼ lb. blue cheese, crumbled
  1 pkg. (3 oz.) cream cheese
  ¼ cup dairy sour cream
  2 tablespoons pineapple juice
  2 teaspoons Worcestershire sauce
  ½ teaspoon monosodium glutamate
  1 drop Tabasco
  4 or 5 sprigs parsley
  1 slice onion
Cover and turn on motor. Blend until smooth.
  About 1½ cups dip

TEMPTING TUNA DIP

Beat together until fluffy
  **1 pkg. (3 oz.) cream cheese,
    softened**
  1 cup dairy sour cream
Add to mixture
  **1 cup (7-oz. can) tuna, drained
    and flaked**
  2 tablespoons chopped chives
  2 teaspoons prepared horseradish
  1 teaspoon Worcestershire sauce
  ¼ teaspoon salt
Blend gently but thoroughly. Cover and let stand in refrigerator at least 2 hrs. to chill and blend flavors.

Serve as a dip with crisp **crackers** or **potato chips.**
  About 2 cups dip

FISH DIP

  ▲ *Base Recipe*

Put into an electric blender container
  1 cup cream-style cottage cheese
  ¼ cup dairy sour cream
  1 tablespoon lemon juice
  Few drops Tabasco
  4 sweet pickle slices
Cover and turn on motor.

Add
  **1 cup flaked (page 9) cooked salmon,
    tuna or crab meat**
Blend until thoroughly mixed.
  About 2 cups dip

—SARDINE OR ANCHOVY DIP

Follow ▲ Recipe. Substitute **4 or 5 sardines or anchovy fillets** for cooked fish.

COTTAGE CHEESE DIPS

Put into an electric blender container
  1 cup cream-style cottage cheese
  **¼ cup mayonnaise or dairy sour
    cream**
Cover and turn on motor.

Add any one of the following
  ¼ cup pecans
  ¼ cup pitted olives, ripe or green
  2 tablespoons chives
  2 slices onion
  Green pepper strips
  Pimiento strips
  ½ cup Swiss or Cheddar cheese cubes
  4 oz. Roquefort or blue cheese
  1 tablespoon prepared horseradish
  ¼ cup parsley
Blend until smooth. *About 1½ cups dip*

DILL CHEESE DIP

Put into an electric blender container
  1 cup cream-style cottage cheese
  2 teaspoons dill
Cover and blend until consistency is creamy. Let stand in refrigerator overnight.

Serve with **tomato wedges** and **potato chips.**
  About 1 cup dip

BRAZIL NUT DIP

Put into an electric blender container
  1 cup cream-style cottage cheese
  ½ cup dairy sour cream
  **1 pkg. (3 oz.) cream cheese, cut in
    pieces**
  ¼ teaspoon salt
  Few drops Tabasco
Cover and blend until well mixed.

Add
  ½ cup (about 2½ oz.) Brazil nuts
Blend only until nuts are chopped.
  About 2 cups dip

SHRIMP DIP FOR VEGETABLES

Put into an electric blender container
  **1 cup (8 oz.) cream-style cottage
    cheese**
  ½ lb. fresh cooked shrimp
  3 tablespoons chili sauce
  2 green onions, sliced
  1 tablespoon lemon juice
  ⅛ teaspoon Worcestershire sauce
  ¼ cup cream
Blend until creamy and smooth.

Accompany with crisp raw vegetables such as **celery, carrot and cucumber sticks, radish roses, green onions** and **cauliflowerets.**
  1½ cups dip

WATERCRESS DIP

Rinse and drain well
  1 bunch watercress

Put into an electric blender container in order
  ¼ cup dairy sour cream
  **1 pkg. (8 oz.) cream cheese, cut in
    pieces**
  ¼ teaspoon salt
  Slice of onion
  Sliver of garlic
Cover and blend until smooth.

Add watercress and blend until watercress is finely chopped. *About 2 cups dip*

SHRIMP WALNUT DIP

Combine in a bowl and blend well
  ¾ cup chopped cooked shrimp
  ¼ cup chopped ripe olives
  ¼ cup finely chopped walnuts
  **3 tablespoons salad dressing or
    mayonnaise**
  1 tablespoon lemon juice
  Dash thyme
Chill thoroughly. Serve as a dip or spread.
  About 1½ cups dip

LIVER SAUSAGE DIP

Finely chop
  2 sweet pickle slices
  1 slice onion
Put into a small mixer bowl with
  ¾ cup liver sausage
  ¼ cup mayonnaise
  ¼ teaspoon salt
  ⅛ teaspoon pepper
Beat thoroughly with electric beater
  About 1 cup dip

HOT CHEESE DUNKING SAUCE

Combine in a saucepan
    ½ cup shredded Cheddar cheese
    ¾ cup milk
    3 tablespoons condensed cream of
        mushroom soup
Set over low heat and stir constantly until
cheese is melted. Mix in
    ⅛ teaspoon pepper
    1½ teaspoons Worcestershire sauce
    2 tablespoons prepared horseradish
Serve hot in a chafing dish with **crackers** or
French bread, cut in 1-in. cubes (toasted, if
desired).   *About 1½ cups sauce*

HOT CRAB MEAT DIP

Heat in a chafing dish blazer or double boiler
top over direct heat
    2 tablespoons butter or margarine
Stir in
    3 tablespoons all-purpose flour
    ½ teaspoon salt
Heat until mixture bubbles. Add gradually,
stirring constantly
    1 cup milk
Bring to boiling; cook 1 to 2 min., stirring
constantly. Blend in
    ¼ cup shredded Cheddar cheese
Set over hot water.

Combine in a bowl
    ½ cup mayonnaise
    2 tablespoons tomato paste
    ¼ teaspoon Worcestershire sauce
Blend in some of the hot mixture. Stir into
remaining hot mixture with
    1 cup flaked crab meat
Keep warm while serving as a dip for **crackers,**
toast rounds or **potato chips.**
                          About 1½ cups dip

SPREADS

ANCHOVY BUTTER SPREAD
FOR CANAPES

Cream together in a small bowl
    ½ cup butter or margarine
    1 teaspoon lemon or lime juice

Blend in
    1 tablespoon anchovy paste
    ¼ teaspoon paprika
Cover bowl tightly and store in refrigerator for
several hours to allow flavors to blend. Cream
again or allow to stand at room temperature
before using.

Spread on bases such as **crackers** or slices of
fancy-cut **bread** or **toast.** Top with rolled
anchovy fillets and **parsley sprig.**
                          About ½ cup spread

PLANTATION CHEESE LOG

Put through medium blade of food chopper
    1 cup (about 4 oz.) pecans
    2 cloves garlic

Put into a bowl and blend thoroughly
    6 oz. cream cheese, softened
    ⅛ teaspoon Worcestershire sauce
    ⅛ teaspoon Maggi's seasoning
    ⅛ teaspoon salt
    4 drops Tabasco
Blend in the pecan-garlic mixture. Shape into
a roll about 7 in. long and 1½ in. in diameter.

Sprinkle evenly over a sheet of waxed paper
    1½ teaspoons chili powder
Roll the log in the chili powder, coating it
evenly. Wrap tightly in waxed paper or moisture-vaporproof material. Chill in refrigerator
until cheese log is firm and flavors are blended,
about 4 hrs.

Serve with crisp **crackers.**   *One cheese log*

PARTY SPREAD

Cream in a bowl until well blended
    1 pkg. (8 oz.) cream cheese
    ¼ cup butter or margarine, softened
Blend in
    1 teaspoon paprika
    ¼ teaspoon dry mustard
    ½ teaspoon onion salt
    1½ teaspoons caraway seed
    2 teaspoons capers, drained
    1 teaspoon prepared mustard
    2 teaspoons minced onion
Chill several hours to blend flavors.

Spread on thinly sliced **pumpernickel or rye**
bread or **crackers.**   *About 1⅛ cups spread*

CREAM CHEESE "LIPTAUER" SPREAD
(Liptói Turó [Hamis] Krém Sajtból)

*Liptauer Cheese is a sharp, fat cheese made
from the milk of sheep in the Carpathian
Mountains in northern Hungary. Some Hungarians claim that they can actually taste in
the cheese the fresh mountain herbs on which
the sheep feed.*

*Usually the cheese is mixed with butter, cara-
way seeds, paprika, capers, anchovy fillets,
onions and mustard. Sometimes, caviar or sardines are used instead of anchovy fillets. It is
even a common practice to add beer to the mixture for added zest. The cheese mixture is spread
on pumpernickel or rye bread and is eaten as
an appetizer or as a snack with beer or wine. It
is sometimes used as a stuffing for celery.*

*Since Liptauer cheese is not readily avail-
able in this country, we cannot duplicate this
famous Hungarian cheese mixture. But we can
make a very similar cheese spread with cream
cheese or cottage cheese. Even those who have
tasted a genuine Liptauer cheese spread will
enjoy the flavor of this American version.*

Cream together in a bowl until well blended
    1 pkg. (8 oz.) cream cheese
    ½ cup butter or margarine
    3 tablespoons dairy sour cream

Mash together with mortar and pestle or with
fork and add to cheese mixture
    2 anchovy fillets
    1 teaspoon capers
Add to cheese mixture and blend ingredients
thoroughly
    1 tablespoon finely chopped onion or
        chives
    1 tablespoon prepared mustard
    1½ teaspoons paprika
    1 teaspoon caraway seed
    ½ teaspoon salt
Transfer mixture to a serving plate and shape
into a smooth mound. Make slight indentations
in mound with tines of a fork. Sprinkle with
    Paprika
Insert wooden picks into about
    10 stuffed and rolled anchovy fillets
Place on mound. Chill slightly in refrigerator.

Garnish by arranging **parsley sprigs** around

Cream Cheese "Liptauer" Spread

mound. Serve with **crackers, pumpernickel** or **rye bread.** *1¾ cups spread*

—COTTAGE CHEESE "LIPTAUER" SPREAD
(Liptói Turó [Hamis] Tehén Turóból)

Follow ▲ Recipe. Substitute **1 cup (about ½ lb.) cream-style cottage cheese,** drained, for cream cheese. Press cottage cheese through a ricer or fine sieve.

GUACAMOLE II

Rinse and dip into boiling water for a few seconds to loosen skin
1 medium ripe tomato
Peel, cut out stem end, remove seeds and chop tomato.

Rinse, cut into halves, remove pit and peel
2 large ripe avocados
Put avocado pieces into a bowl and finely chop. Blend in the chopped tomato and
2 to 3 teaspoons lemon juice
½ teaspoon salt
3 tablespoons minced onion
Mix thoroughly. Cover and chill in refrigerator.

Serve on **leaf lettuce.** Garnish each serving with a thin slice of **salami** or **cervelat sausage.**
6 servings

EGG SPREAD FOR CANAPES

▲ *Base Recipe*

Prepare, peel, chop and set aside
6 Hard-Cooked Eggs (page 133)

Put into a small bowl and beat with an electric beater
½ cup mayonnaise
½ teaspoon salt
½ teaspoon paprika
¼ teaspoon dry mustard
⅛ teaspoon pepper
Add chopped eggs and
2 strips green pepper, minced
1 slice onion, minced
Beat until of spreading consistency.

Spread on bases such as **crackers** or slices of fancy-cut **bread** or **toast.** Top with **olive slices.**
About 1½ cups spread

—BACON 'N' EGG SPREAD

Follow ▲ Recipe. Prepare **6 slices Panfried Bacon** (page 190); crumble and add to mixture with chopped eggs.

HAWAIIAN SPREAD

Blender-grind (page 11) enough to make ¾ cup
Cooked ham

Put into a small bowl with
½ cup well drained, crushed pineapple
3 tablespoons salad dressing
2 teaspoons brown sugar

Beat until well mixed and of spreading consistency. *About 1½ cups spread*

HAM CANAPE SPREAD

▲ *Base Recipe*

Grind (page 10) enough cooked ham to yield
1 cup ground cooked ham
Combine with ham and mix thoroughly
½ cup (about 2 oz.) salted roasted peanuts, finely chopped
½ cup well-drained chopped sweet pickle
Moisten to spreading consistency with about
½ cup mayonnaise
Spread on canapé bases. *About 1½ cups spread*

—HAM AND EGG SPREAD

Follow ▲ Recipe. Omit peanuts. Reduce pickle to 2 tablespoons. Mix in **2 Hard-Cooked Eggs** (page 133), chopped, and **1 to 2 teaspoons prepared mustard.**

—HAM PINEAPPLE SPREAD

Follow ▲ Recipe. Substitute **¼ cup drained crushed pineapple** for chopped pickle.

—HAM WATERCRESS SPREAD

Follow ▲ Recipe. Substitute **⅓ cup finely chopped watercress** for chopped pickle and about **½ cup cream** for mayonnaise. **Add 1 teaspoon prepared mustard** with cream.

FABULOUS CHEESE MOUSSE

▲ *Base Recipe*

Set out a fancy 1-pt. mold. Place a small bowl and a rotary beater in refrigerator to chill.

Pour into a small saucepan
¼ cup cold water
Sprinkle evenly over cold water
1 env. unflavored gelatin
Set the saucepan over low heat and stir constantly until gelatin is completely dissolved. Set aside.

Force through a fine sieve
3 pkgs. (1¼ oz. each) Roquefort cheese
2 pkgs. (1⅓ oz. each) Camembert cheese
Blend in until mixture is smooth
1 egg yolk, slightly beaten
1 tablespoon sherry
1 teaspoon Worcestershire sauce
Add dissolved gelatin to cheese mixture, blending thoroughly.

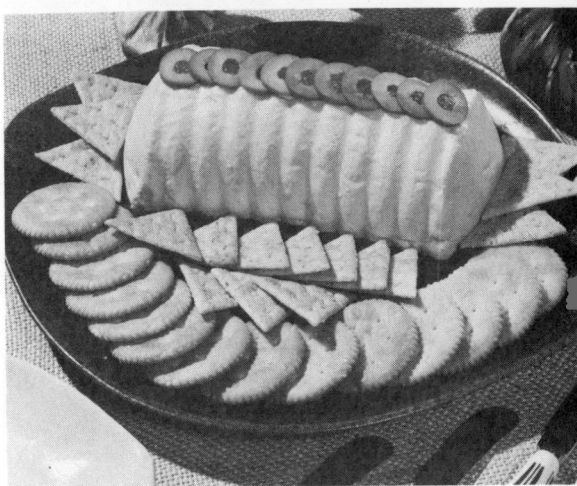

Fabulous Cheese Mousse

Beat until rounded peaks are formed
1 egg white
Beat in chilled bowl with chilled beater until cream is of medium consistency (piles softly)
½ cup chilled whipping cream
Fold whipped cream and egg white into the cheese mixture. Turn into the mold. Chill in refrigerator until firm.

Unmold (page 374) onto chilled serving plate. Garnish with
Pimiento-stuffed olive slices
Serve with **crackers.** *One 1-pt. mold*

—CRUNCHY CHEESE MOUSSE

Follow ▲ Recipe. Fold in **¼ cup chopped toasted blanched almonds** (pages 9 and 10) and **3 tablespoons chopped green olives** with cream mixture.

CHICKEN LIVER SPREAD

Set out a 10-in. skillet and a wooden bowl or cutting board.

Rinse with cold water and drain on absorbent paper
½ lb. chicken livers
Heat in the skillet over low heat
1 tablespoon chicken fat, butter or margarine
Add livers and cook over medium heat 5 to 10 min., or until lightly browned, turning occasionally. Remove skillet from heat and set aside to cool.

Meanwhile, clean, finely chop and set aside
½ lb. mushrooms (about 2 cups, chopped)
Remove cooled livers with slotted spoon to bowl or cutting board; reserve the drippings. Finely chop livers and set aside in a bowl.

Almond Tuna Salad Spread, Hawaiian Spread and Egg Salad Spread for Canapés

Heat in the skillet over low heat
¼ cup butter or margarine
Add mushrooms and cook slowly over medium heat, occasionally moving and turning with a spoon, until mushrooms are lightly browned. Remove from skillet and add to chicken livers.

Combine
¼ cup reserved drippings
1 teaspoon onion juice
½ teaspoon salt
¼ teaspoon monosodium glutamate
¼ teaspoon paprika
Few grains pepper
2 or 3 drops Tabasco
Combine with chicken liver mixture, blending thoroughly. (If necessary, add enough additional drippings until mixture is of spreading consistency.) Chill in refrigerator for about 4 hrs. to allow flavors to blend.

For Canapés—Spread mixture on
Toast rounds or crackers
Sprinkle over top
Finely sieved Hard-Cooked Eggs (page 133)
Crumbled Panfried Bacon (page 190)
Allow about 1 tablespoon Chicken Liver Spread per canapé. *About 1½ cups spread*

POULTRY LIVER PASTE
(Pâté de Foie de Volaille)

Heat until very hot
2 tablespoons salt pork fat

Then add
1 cup uncooked duck or chicken livers
1 teaspoon salt
¼ teaspoon thyme
¼ teaspoon freshly ground pepper
1 bay leaf
Cook 3 to 4 min. Remove bay leaf. Rub livers through a sieve. Blend sieved liver well with
¼ cup brandy or sherry
About 1 cup paste

LIVER PASTE
(Leverpastej)

A smörgasbord favorite.

Grease an 8½x4½x2½-in. loaf pan.

Cut away tubes and outer membrane, if necessary, from
1½ lbs. liver (beef, veal or pork)
Put liver into skillet with
1 cup hot water
Cover and simmer 5 min. Drain and cool.

Meanwhile, combine and mix lightly
2 eggs, slightly beaten
1 cup cream
and a mixture of
¼ cup sifted all-purpose flour
2 teaspoons salt
¼ teaspoon white pepper
⅛ teaspoon cloves
⅛ teaspoon ginger
Few grains nutmeg
Force the cooled liver through the medium blade of a food chopper with
3 slices bacon
4 anchovy fillets, drained
1 slice onion

Mix lightly with the egg mixture, blending thoroughly. Pack into the greased loaf pan.

Bake at 350°F 1½ to 2 hrs.

Cool completely on cooling rack.

When ready to serve, loosen meat gently from sides of pan with spatula. Invert onto platter. Cut into thin slices and garnish with
Pickled Beets (page 422)
10 to 12 servings

LIVER CANAPE SPREAD

▲ *Base Recipe*

Grind (page 10) enough cooked liver to yield
1 cup ground, cooked liver (pork, beef, lamb or veal)
Combine with liver and mix thoroughly
1 Hard-Cooked Egg (page 133), chopped
3 tablespoons finely chopped celery
2 tablespoons minced onion
1 teaspoon prepared mustard
½ teaspoon salt
¼ teaspoon monosodium glutamate
Moisten to spreading consistency with about
¼ cup ketchup
Spread on canapé bases. *About 1½ cups spread*

—LIVER AND BACON SPREAD

Follow ▲ Recipe. Substitute **4 slices Panfried Bacon** (page 133), crumbled, for egg. Omit celery and ketchup. Moisten with **3 tablespoons cream.**

—BOLOGNA SPREAD

Follow ▲ Recipe. Substitute **1 cup (½ lb.) ground bologna** (casing removed) for liver. Substitute **¼ cup mayonnaise** for ketchup.

SHRIMP SPREAD

An electric blender will be needed.

Cook
½ lb. fresh shrimp with shells (see Cooked Shrimp, page 294)
Put into blender container
2 tablespoons mayonnaise
1 tablespoon lemon juice
½ teaspoon Worcestershire sauce
¼ teaspoon salt
1 thin slice onion
Add a few shrimp, cover container and turn on motor. Add shrimp, a few at a time, and blend just to a smooth paste. *About ¾ cup spread*

SALMON NUT SPREAD

An electric blender will be needed.

Prepare, peel and cut into quarters
3 Hard-Cooked Eggs (page 133)
Set aside.

Flake (page 9) and set aside
1 can (7¾ oz.) salmon, drained

Put into an electric blender container
½ cup butter or margarine, softened
¼ cup walnuts
1 tablespoon lemon juice
¼ teaspoon salt
4 sweet pickle slices

Cover and turn on motor. Add egg pieces, blending only until chopped. Add flaked salmon and blend just until mixed.

Empty contents into serving bowl and garnish with chopped **parsley**. Serve with **rye bread slices**.
About 2 cups spread

ALMOND TUNA SALAD SPREAD

Flake (page 9) and set aside
1 can (7 oz.) tuna, drained

Chop and set aside
⅓ cup (about 2 oz.) blanched almonds, toasted (pages 9 and 10)

Put into a bowl and mix using low speed of an electric beater
⅓ cup mayonnaise
¼ cup coarsely chopped sweet pickle
1 teaspoon lemon juice
½ teaspoon monosodium glutamate
½ teaspoon salt
⅛ teaspoon onion salt
Few grains pepper

Continuing on low speed, add chopped nuts and tuna; blend until ingredients are well mixed and mixture is of spreading consistency.
About 2 cups spread

CANAPES

ANCHOVY CANAPES I

Mix in a bowl
1 cup dairy sour cream
1 teaspoon anchovy paste
½ teaspoon onion salt

Spread over canapé bases and top with
Rolled anchovies
About 1 cup spread

ANCHOVY CANAPES II
(Canapés d'Anchois)

Hard-cook and finely chop
1 egg

Combine chopped egg with
1 medium tomato, peeled and finely chopped
6 anchovy fillets, mashed
2 tablespoons flaked tuna
2 tablespoons chopped green pepper

Blend in
2 tablespoons mayonnaise

Spread mixture onto
12 thin slices bread, cut in 2-in. shapes

Sprinkle with
Few drops Worcestershire sauce
12 canapés

CREAM CHEESE BITS
(Canapés de Fromage à la Crème)

Mash together
1 pkg. (3 oz.) cream cheese
1 tablespoon minced fresh mint
1 tablespoon brandy
¼ teaspoon salt

Blend well. Spread onto
24 crackers
24 canapés

CLAM-CREAM CHEESE BITS

Set aside to drain
1 can (8 oz.) minced clams

Blend thoroughly
1 pkg. (3 oz.) cream cheese, softened
1 teaspoon onion juice
½ teaspoon Worcestershire sauce
⅛ teaspoon salt
1 drop green food coloring

Mix in the drained clams.

To serve, spread on
Buttered toast rounds

Garnish each with
Ripe olive slice
About 2½ doz. canapés

Note: For added glamour, cut pitted ripe olives crosswise into halves and put one of the halves in center of each canapé. Using a pastry bag and No. 27 star decorating tube, pipe onto each olive half a rosette of cream cheese.

CANAPE WEDGES

Carefully trim bottom crust from
1 large round loaf pumpernickel bread

Cut 3 slices, each about ½ in. thick, from loaf to use as layers.

Spread 2 layers with
Pasteurized process cheese food

Put slices together, spread-side up. Top with third layer. Blend together
1 can (3 oz.) deviled ham
1 or 2 tablespoons ketchup

Mix thoroughly. Spread mixture over third layer. Top with wedge-shaped slices of **cheese**. Chill in refrigerator until serving time.

Following outline of cheese wedges, cut loaf into wedge-shape servings. *About 16 servings*

BRAUNSCHWEIGER CANAPES

Beat with a fork until soft
½ cup Braunschweiger (smoked liver sausage)

Mix in thoroughly
1 to 2 teaspoons grated onion

Spread mixture on
Buttered toast rounds

Garnish with
Caviar
Sieved hard-cooked egg yolk
About 1 doz. canapés

LIVER SAUSAGE WITH CAVIAR

Beat **liver sausage** with a fork until soft. Blend in **caviar** to taste (the more the better). Blend in **whipped heavy cream** (just enough to make mixture fluffy). Spread on **toast fingers**. Garnish with **caviar** and **hard-cooked egg white cutouts**.

SMOKED SALMON CANAPES

For Lemon Butter—Cream until softened
½ cup firm butter

Blend in
1 tablespoon lemon juice

Spread the Lemon Butter on diamond-shape pieces of **toast**. Top with thin slices of **smoked**

Canapé Wedges

salmon to cover diamonds. Spoon **caviar** onto center of salmon. Garnish both ends of diamonds with **hard-cooked egg white cutouts.**

Or, omit caviar and egg white cutouts. Pipe **softened cream cheese** through a pastry bag and a No. 27 decorating tube onto edge of salmon. Garnish center with a **walnut slice.**

CLAM AND CHEESE CANAPES

Drain and set aside
   1 can (8 oz.) minced clams

Rub inside surfaces of a bowl with cut side of
   Garlic clove
Cream thoroughly in bowl
   1 pkg. (3 oz.) cream cheese, softened
   2 teaspoons lemon juice
   ¼ teaspoon salt
   ¼ teaspoon monosodium glutamate
   ⅛ teaspoon pepper
   5 drops Tabasco
Blend in minced clams. Spread on canapé bases. Garnish with slivers of **pimiento, ripe olives** and **stuffed olives.**

About 1 cup spread

SHRIMP CANAPES I

Prepare and cook (page 294)
   1 lb. fresh shrimp with shells
Marinate shrimp 1 hr. in
   French Dressing (page 410)

For Horseradish Butter—Cream until softened
   ½ cup firm butter
Blend in
   2 tablespoons prepared horseradish
   1 teaspoon lemon juice
Spread on **toast rounds.** Sprinkle Horseradish Butter with sieved **hard-cooked egg yolk.** Top each round with a whole shrimp.

Spoon onto the shrimp
   Caper Mayonnaise (see Lobster Canapés, on this page)
Sprinkle with **finely chopped chives.**

About 24 canapés

SHRIMP CANAPES II
(Canapés de Crevettes)

Have ready
   18 canned, or cooked and peeled shrimp
Reserve and chill in refrigerator 12 shrimp. Finely chop remaining 6; add and blend in well
   2 tablespoons butter

Hard-cook
   1 egg
Meanwhile, finely chop and set aside
   1 tablespoon parsley
Force egg yolk through sieve and set aside.

Spread shrimp butter onto
   12 crisp crackers
Dip the whole shrimp into
   ¼ cup mayonnaise or French Dressing

Place on shrimp-buttered crackers. Sprinkle over shrimp about ¼ teaspoon each of sieved egg yolk and chopped parsley.   *12 canapés*

SARDINE CANAPES

Cream until softened
   ¼ cup butter or margarine
Blend in a mixture of
   1½ teaspoons lemon juice
   1½ teaspoons prepared mustard
Spread **toast strips** with the butter mixture. Top each strip with
   1 chilled sardine, well drained
Garnish each with a thin strip of **pimiento.**

LOBSTER CANAPES

For Caper Mayonnaise—Blend together
   1 cup mayonnaise
   ¼ cup chopped capers
   1 tablespoon lemon juice
   ½ teaspoon sugar
   ¼ teaspoon Worcestershire sauce
   Few grains white pepper
Set in refrigerator to chill.

Prepare (page 290) and chill
   1 live lobster, about 1¼ lbs.

Finely chop the lobster meat, reserving claw meat and put into a bowl. Mix lightly with 5 tablespoons of the Caper Mayonnaise and
   2 tablespoons chopped salted almonds
   1 teaspoon lemon juice
   Few grains white pepper
Spread **toast rounds** with the lobster mixture. Sprinkle very finely **minced parsley** around edges of canapés. To garnish, place a piece of claw meat on each canapé. If desired, also top with a whole **toasted almond.**

SMOKED TURKEY HAM CANAPES

For Mustard Butter—Cream until softened
   ½ cup firm butter
Blend in
   1 tablespoon prepared mustard
   1 teaspoon lemon juice
Spread Mustard Butter on **toast ovals.** Top

with a thin slice of **ham.** Spread ham thinly with
   Caper Mayonnaise (see Lobster Canapés, on this page)
Top with a thin slice of **smoked turkey.** Spread turkey slice with a thin coating of Caper Mayonnaise and sprinkle with **finely chopped chives.**

WATERCRESS CANAPES

Rinse, drain well and snip enough watercress to yield
   ½ cup snipped watercress
Cream on high speed of electric mixer just until whipped
   ½ cup firm butter
Add the watercress and mix on high speed just until blended. Spread on **toast squares** and garnish each with a **sprig of watercress.**

12 to 18 canapés

NIPPY CHEDDAR SAVORIES

   ▲ *Base Recipe*

For Cheese Butter—Shred
   4 oz. sharp Cheddar cheese (about 1 cup, shredded)
Cream until softened
   ¼ cup butter
Gradually blend in the cheese. Beat until mixture is fluffy. Thoroughly blend in
   2 tablespoons mayonnaise
   1 teaspoon prepared mustard
   1 teaspoon lemon juice
   ¼ teaspoon celery salt
   Few grains white pepper

For Savories—Trim crusts from
   12 thin slices white or whole wheat bread

Flatten slightly with a rolling pin. (Bread slices are easier to roll up, if flattened slightly.) Generously spread each slice with about 1 tablespoon of the Cheese Butter. Roll up tightly and cut each roll into halves. Fasten with wooden picks; place on broiler rack.

Place rack under broiler with tops of savories about 3 in. from heat. Broil about 2 min., or until toasted; turn occasionally.

2 doz. appetizers

—CHEESE SCALLION SAVORIES

Follow ▲ Recipe. Omit mayonnaise, mustard and lemon juice. Blend **1 tablespoon minced scallion** and **½ teaspoon Worcestershire sauce** into the fluffy cheese mixture.

MUENSTER CHEESE BACON CANAPES

Mix in a bowl
> **2 cups (8 oz.) finely shredded Muenster cheese**
> **½ lb. Panfried Bacon (page 190), crumbled**
> **¼ cup finely chopped onion**
> **2 tablespoons prepared mustard**

Set aside.

Toast on one side
> **8 thin slices white bread**

Spread untoasted sides with cheese mixture. Trim crusts and cut each into 8 triangles or fingers. Arrange on a baking sheet.

Broil 3 in. from heat 1 to 2 min., or until lightly browned and bubbly. *64 canapés*

CHEESE PIZZA SNACKS

Mix in a bowl and let stand at least 20 min.
> **1 can (10¾ oz.) condensed tomato soup**
> **1 small clove garlic, crushed**
> **⅛ teaspoon basil leaves**
> **⅛ teaspoon oregano leaves**

Cut into squares and set aside.
> **¾ lb. sliced sharp Cheddar cheese**

Arrange on a baking sheet
> **Saltines (about 48 square crackers)**

Spoon soup mixture onto crackers and top with cheese squares.

Set in a 400°F oven until cheese is melted, 3 to 5 min. *About 4 doz. appetizers*

JIFFY PIZZAS

Blend in a bowl
> **Pie crust mix for a 2-crust pie**
> **½ cup finely chopped walnuts**

Add and mix only until blended
> **5 tablespoons water**

Roll out on a lightly floured surface to ⅛-in. thickness. Cut into 3-in. rounds or squares and place on an ungreased baking sheet.

Bake at 450°F about 10 min., or until golden brown.

Meanwhile, combine in a bowl and blend well
> **½ cup ketchup**
> **1 tablespoon prepared horseradish**
> **1 teaspoon prepared mustard**
> **⅛ teaspoon oregano**
> **⅛ teaspoon dill seed**

Spread about ½ teaspoon of mixture over each baked pastry round or square. Top each with a
> **2-in. square sliced cooked ham**
> **2-in. square sliced pasteurized process cheese**

Sprinkle with **Paprika.**

Heat under broiler until cheese is melted. Serve at once. *18 pizzas*

OLIVE CHEESE QUICHE SQUARES

Prepare
> **Pastry for 2-Crust Pie (page 485)**

On a lightly floured surface, roll dough into a 14x10-in. rectangle. Fit gently into an 11x 7x1½-in. baking pan and flute edges.

Bake at 400°F 10 min.

Meanwhile, scald (page 10)
> **1½ cups light cream or milk**

Stir into a mixture of
> **4 eggs, beaten**
> **¾ teaspoon salt**
> **⅛ teaspoon white pepper**

Mix in
> **1 cup (4 oz.) finely shredded Swiss cheese**

Turn into partially baked shell. Spoon evenly over top
> **¾ cup thinly sliced ripe olives**

Sprinkle with
> **2 tablespoons grated Parmesan cheese**

Bake at 400°F 20 to 25 min., or until set. Cool slightly before cutting into small squares.

About 3 doz. appetizers

CHEESE OLIVE SQUARES

Toast
> **6 slices bread**

Spread one side of each slice with
> **Butter or margarine**

Shred and set aside
> **4 oz. Mozzarella cheese (about 1 cup, shredded)**

Prepare and mix in a bowl
> **½ cup finely chopped ripe olives**
> **2 tablespoons chopped pimiento**

Mix in the shredded cheese and
> **2 tablespoons grated Parmesan cheese**
> **1 clove garlic, minced**

Spread each slice with 3 tablespoons mixture. Arrange slices on broiler rack and place under broiler with tops about 3 in. from heat. Broil 1 to 2 min., or until bubbling hot.

To serve, trim crusts off and cut each slice into 4 squares. *2 doz. appetizers*

CREAMED CHICKEN IN PATTY SHELLS
(Bouchées à la Reine)

Prepare (allowing about 9 hrs.)
> **Vol-au-Vent Shells (page 518; cut pastry into 2-in. rather than 3-in. rounds and rims, reserving centers for covers)**

Prepare and set aside
> **Béchamel Sauce (page 304)**

Wipe with a clean, damp cloth and cut off tips of stems with
> **3 or 4 medium mushrooms**

Chop mushrooms and sauté in
> **1 tablespoon butter**

Mix mushrooms and 3 to 4 tablespoons of Béchamel Sauce (reserve remainder for use in other recipes) with
> **¾ cup finely chopped cooked chicken**
> **2 tablespoons chopped salted almonds**
> **1 teaspoon capers**
> **¼ teaspoon salt**
> **Few grains pepper**

Reheat baked shells and fill each with about 1 tablespoon of the mixture. Top with reserved pastry covers.

Shells may be filled with any other favorite canapé mixture. *16 bouchées*

HOT CRAB MEAT CANAPES

For Crab Meat Mixture—Measure
> **¾ cup milk**

Set aside.

Set out
> **2 cups (about 8 oz.) fresh lump crab meat (bony tissue removed)**
> **1 tablespoon chopped pimiento**

Heat in a heavy 2-qt. saucepan
> **3 tablespoons butter or margarine**

Add
> **1 tablespoon finely chopped green pepper**
> **1 teaspoon finely chopped onion**

Cook over low heat 2 to 3 min., or until partially tender. Blend in
> **3 tablespoons all-purpose flour**
> **½ teaspoon salt**
> **¼ teaspoon monosodium glutamate**
> **¼ teaspoon dry mustard**
> **Few grains white pepper**
> **Few grains cayenne pepper**
> **½ teaspoon Worcestershire sauce**

Heat until mixture bubbles. Remove from heat and add the milk gradually, stirring constantly. Return to heat and bring mixture rapidly to boiling, stirring constantly; cook

1 to 2 min. longer. Vigorously stir about 3 tablespoons hot mixture into

1 egg yolk, slightly beaten

Immediately blend into mixture in saucepan and cook, stirring constantly, about 5 min.

Add crab meat and pimiento to saucepan and mix gently until thoroughly blended. Cook over low heat, stirring gently, 2 to 3 min., or until crab meat is thoroughly heated. Remove from heat and stir in

2 tablespoons sherry

Allow mixture to cool (transferring to a shallow dish will hasten cooling).

To Complete Canapés—Trim crusts from and toast until golden brown

5 slices white bread

Set out

5 teaspoons grated Parmesan cheese
**2½ teaspoons melted butter or
    margarine**

Lightly spread toast with

Butter

Cover toast with crab meat mixture. Top each slice with 1 teaspoon grated cheese and ½ teaspoon of the melted butter. Sprinkle with

Paprika

Cut each toast slice diagonally into four triangles and place on a baking sheet.

Bake at 425°F 8 to 10 min.

Place canapés on broiler rack and place rack under broiler with tops of canapés 2 to 3 in. from heat. Broil 1 to 2 min.

Serve piping hot with **lemon wedges.** If desired, garnish with **sprigs of parsley.**

20 canapés

CRAB CANAPES

Mix in a heavy saucepan

½ cup butter or margarine, melted
¼ cup all-purpose flour

Cook until bubbly. Stir in and bring to boiling, stirring constantly

1 cup milk

Cook 1 to 2 min. Add

**4 oz. pasteurized process Cheddar
    cheese, cut in pieces**

Stir until cheese is melted. Remove from heat.

Remove any bony tissue from

**2 pkgs. (6 oz. each) frozen crab meat,
    thawed**

Mix with sauce. Season to taste with

Salt and pepper

Chill until needed.

To serve, spread crab mixture on

Toast rounds

Place on baking sheet and heat under broiler until lightly browned and bubbly on top.

2½ to 3 doz. canapés

CRAB NIPPIES

▲ *Base Recipe*

Spoon onto small toast rounds

**1 cup (6½-oz. can) crab meat,
    flaked (page 9)**

Sprinkle generously with

**½ cup (2 oz.) shredded sharp
    Cheddar cheese**

Arrange canapés on broiler rack and place under broiler with top of canapés 3 in. from heat. Broil 3 to 5 min., or until cheese is melted and slightly browned. Serve piping hot.

About 20 canapés

—CREAMED CRAB NIPPIES

Follow ▲ Recipe. Blend crab meat with ¼ cup Medium White Sauce (one-fourth recipe, page 304); spread on bases and complete as in ▲ Recipe.

CRISPY HAM BITS

Mix in a bowl

½ cup ground cooked ham
¼ cup shredded Cheddar cheese
¼ cup condensed tomato soup
1 tablespoon minced onion
¼ teaspoon prepared horseradish
¼ teaspoon prepared mustard

Spread on small toast rounds or other shapes.

Arrange canapés on broiler rack and place under broiler with top of canapés 3 in. from heat; broil 3 to 5 min., or until slightly browned. Serve canapés piping hot.   *About 1 cup spread*

PASTRY CANAPES

Roll out **pastry** (page 485) and cut into small strips or shapes. Sprinkle with **grated cheese.** If desired, sprinkle **poppy seeds** or **caraway seeds** over grated cheese. Place on a baking sheet and bake at 425°F 10 to 15 min., or until lightly browned.

SARDINE SNACKS

These flavorful little open-face sandwiches can function as appetite-teasers or appetite-satisfiers, depending on how many you eat. Fine finger foods for absorbed TV-viewers.

Drain and mash

2 cans (3¼ oz. each) sardines

Add and blend well

2 tablespoons ketchup
1 tablespoon prepared mustard
2 teaspoons sweet pickle relish

With sharp knife, trim crusts from

6 slices white bread

Arrange bread on broiler rack or a baking sheet, and place under broiler with tops of slices 2 in. from heat. Toast until golden brown on one side. Remove from broiler.

Spread untoasted sides of bread lightly with

Softened butter or margarine

Spread sardine mixture over butter, covering the bread completely. Cut each slice into 3 fingers.

Return to broiler with top of snacks about 3 in. from heat. Broil for 3 min., until thoroughly heated.

To serve, garnish snacks with

Pimiento strips

Arrange hot snacks on serving plate with **pimiento-stuffed olives.** Garnish plate with **parsley** or **watercress.** Serve at once.

1½ doz. snacks

HOT SARDINE CANAPES

Here's a curtain-raiser that may steal the show. Better set a limit on encores.

Set aside to drain

2 cans (3¼ oz. each) sardines

For Sauce—Heat in a saucepan

2 tablespoons butter or margarine

Blend in

1 tablespoon all-purpose flour

Heat until mixture bubbles. Add gradually, stirring constantly until smooth

½ cup milk
⅓ cup mayonnaise

Remove from heat and mix in

1 tablespoon chopped stuffed olives
1 tablespoon chopped sweet pickles
1 teaspoon chopped onion
2 teaspoons capers
½ teaspoon cider vinegar

Keep sauce hot until ready to use.

For Canapés—Trim crusts from

6 slices white bread

Toast the bread on one side only. Cut each slice into thirds and spread the untoasted sides with

Butter or margarine, melted

Arrange one drained sardine on each oblong. Spoon hot sauce over the sardine and sprinkle over top

Paprika

Arrange canapés on broiler rack and place rack under broiler with tops of canapés 3 in. from heat; broil about 5 min., or until heated and slightly browned.

Serve piping hot. *18 canapés*

HORS D'OEUVRES

APPETIZER PIES

For Fillings—Prepared, peel, cut into quarters and set aside
6 Hard-Cooked Eggs (page 133)

Meanwhile, put into an electric blender container
**½ cup cream-style cottage cheese
¼ cup sweet pickle slices
2 tablespoons dairy sour cream
¼ teaspoon salt
Dash pepper
1 slice onion**
Cover and blend until well mixed.

Empty container. Put into blender container
**½ cup Blender Mayonnaise (page 413)
½ teaspoon salt
½ teaspoon paprika
¼ teaspoon dry mustard
⅛ teaspoon pepper
1 slice onion**
Cover and turn on motor. Add, by pieces
4 stalks celery, rinsed and cut into pieces
Add eggs and blend only until eggs are chopped.

Empty container and prepare
Crispy Ham Bits (page 22; spread only, do not broil)
Place fillings in refrigerator until ready to use.

For Assembling Pies—Cut top and bottom crusts from
1 large round loaf pumpernickel
Slice bread crosswise into four ½-in. thick slices. Spoon cottage cheese mixture onto center of each bread slice and pat down with back of spoon. Spread ham-cheese spread in a ring around cheese mixture. Spoon egg filling around outer edge forming a border. Pat down with back of spoon.

Garnish with several **pickle slices**. Chill in refrigerator several hours.

To serve, cut each slice into small wedges.
4 appetizer pies

PECANWICHES

Blend
**3 tablespoons cream cheese, softened
2 tablespoons anchovy paste**
Chill mixture thoroughly.

Meanwhile, toast and salt
1½ cups (about 60) large pecan halves
Spread the cream cheese mixture on one half

**Assorted Canapés
and Hors d'Oeuvres**

of the pecans, allowing about ½ teaspoon per pecan. Top with remaining pecan halves and press together. *About 2½ doz. appetizers*

EGGS STUFFED WITH CHICKEN LIVER PATE

Prepare
5 Hard-Cooked Eggs (page 133)

Meanwhile, rinse with cold water and drain on absorbent paper
¼ lb. chicken livers
Put livers into a saucepan and add
Hot water to barely cover
Cover saucepan and simmer 15 to 20 min., or until liver is tender when pierced with a fork. Drain and set aside to cool.

Fry until crisp
4 slices bacon
Crumble bacon and set aside.

Force chicken livers through a sieve or food mill and set aside.

Cut each egg into halves lengthwise. Remove egg yolks to a bowl and mash with a fork. Mix into egg yolks the liver, crumbled bacon and
**1 tablespoon very finely minced parsley
1½ teaspoons minced chives
½ teaspoon salt
¼ teaspoon very finely minced onion
¼ teaspoon tarragon leaves, finely crushed
¼ teaspoon pepper
Few grains cayenne pepper**
Stir in, moistening mixture to a thick, paste-like consistency
1½ to 2 tablespoons mayonnaise
Pack mixture into the egg whites. Cut into bite-size pieces and sprinkle with
**Paprika
Finely minced parsley**
Chill thoroughly in refrigerator.

To serve, insert a wooden pick into each piece.
About 5 doz. appetizers

MEAT AND DILL SLICES

▲ *Base Recipe*

Meat-filled pickles add interest to a relish tray.

Cut ends from
3 large dill pickles, 5 to 6 in. long
Cut crosswise into halves. Hollow out centers with apple corer and set pickles aside to drain thoroughly.

Grind enough cooked beef to yield
¾ cup ground cooked beef
Mix lightly with beef
**1 Hard-Cooked Egg (page 133), finely chopped
1 tablespoon minced parsley
1 teaspoon Worcestershire sauce
¼ teaspoon monosodium glutamate
¼ teaspoon salt
Few grains cayenne pepper**
Moisten to a heavy paste with
2 tablespoons ketchup
Pack meat mixture into pickles. Place in refrigerator to chill.

Cut crosswise into ½-in. slices.
30 to 36 slices

—MEATY BEETS

Follow ▲ Recipe. Omit pickles. With the tip of a sharp knife or melon baller, hollow out centers of **10 drained tiny pickled beets**. Add **1 teaspoon prepared horseradish** with seasonings in filling mixture. Fill beets with meat mixture. Omit slicing.

—MEAT-STUFFED CELERY STICKS

Follow ▲ Recipe. Omit pickles. Wash and trim **5 crisp stalks celery**. Fill stalks with meat mixture and cut them into 2-in. crosswise pieces.

—MEAT TOASTIES

Follow ▲ Recipe. Omit pickles. Increase ketchup to 3 tablespoons so mixture is of spreading consistency. Set aside. Trim crusts from **16 thin slices bread.** Roll gently with a rolling pin to flatten. Spread bread with **seasoned butter.** Then spread each slice with meat mixture and roll. Secure with wooden picks. Arrange rolls on broiler rack and brush with one half of **¼ cup melted butter or margarine.** Place under broiler with tops of rolls about 3 in. from heat; broil about 2 to 3 min., or until rolls are golden brown. Turn, brush with remaining melted butter and broil about 2 to 3 min. longer.

VEAL PICKS

▲ Base Recipe

These distinctive, delicious tidbits will be the first to disappear from the appetizer tray.

Grind and set aside enough cooked veal to yield
>   **½ cup ground cooked veal**

Grind and set aside
>   **¼ cup pecans (about ¼ cup, ground)**

Cream together in a large bowl
>   **1 pkg. (3 oz.) cream cheese, softened**
>   **2 tablespoons (about ½ oz.) crumbled blue cheese**

Combine with cheese and veal and mix thoroughly
>   **1½ teaspoons Worcestershire sauce**
>   **Few grains paprika**

Shape into balls about ¾ in. in diameter. Coat with ground pecans. Insert cocktail or wooden picks and place in refrigerator to chill.

About 1 doz. appetizers

—VEAL-PARSLEY PICKS

Follow ▲ Recipe. Omit blue cheese. Substitute **¼ cup minced parsley** for pecans. Roll balls in parsley before inserting picks.

SHRIMP ON A PICK

Prepare
>   **2 lbs. fresh shrimp with shells**
>   **(see Cooked Shrimp, page 294)**

Chill thoroughly in refrigerator before serving.

Prepare and chill
>   **Cocktail Sauce for Seafood (double recipe, page 37)**

Remove the shrimp from refrigerator. Insert wooden picks. Arrange shrimp on a chilled serving platter. Spoon sauce into small individual cups; arrange cups on a tray and serve with the shrimp.

TINY TOMATO TOPPERS

▲ Base Recipe

Rinse, cut into halves and set aside
>   **18 cherry tomatoes**

Beat until fluffy
>   **1 pkg. (3 oz.) cream cheese, softened**

Blend in thoroughly
>   **⅓ cup minced cooked chicken**
>   **¼ cup finely chopped walnuts**
>   **1½ tablespoons finely chopped apple**
>   **1½ teaspoons lemon juice**
>   **½ teaspoon Worcestershire sauce**
>   **½ teaspoon grated onion**

Using about ½ teaspoon of cream cheese mixture for each, spoon onto tomato halves.

Chill in refrigerator before serving.

3 doz. appetizers

—TINY TOMATO TOPPERS WITH SOUR CREAM

Follow ▲ Recipe. Blend in **2 tablespoons dairy sour cream.**

—TOMATO TOPPERS WITH SHERRY

Follow ▲ Recipe. Blend in **2 teaspoons sherry.**

BLINI
(Russian Raised Griddlecakes)

Though there is no sour cream in the little dollar-size griddlecakes themselves, the sour cream and caviar that are served with them are a most important part of this unique appetizer.

Set out a griddle or heavy skillet.

Soften
>   **½ teaspoon (¼ pkg.) active dry yeast**

in
>   **1 tablespoon warm water, 105°F to 115°F (Or if using compressed yeast, soften ¼ cake in 1 tablespoon lukewarm water, 80°F to 85°F.)**

Set aside.

Scald
>   **½ cup milk**

Put into a bowl
>   **¾ teaspoon sugar**
>   **⅛ teaspoon salt**

Pour scalded milk into the bowl. When cooled to lukewarm, stir mixture and thoroughly blend into it a mixture of
>   **¼ cup buckwheat or rye flour**
>   **2 tablespoons all-purpose flour**

Stir the softened yeast and add, mixing well. Cover bowl with waxed paper and a clean towel and set aside in a warm place (about 80°F) 1½ hrs., or until light.

Add to yeast mixture and beat until smooth
>   **¼ cup sifted all-purpose flour**

Blend until thick and lemon-colored
>   **1 egg yolk**

Blend into the batter. Beat until stiff, not dry, peaks are formed
>   **1 egg white**

Gently fold into the batter.

Cover bowl with waxed paper and towel and set aside in a warm place (about 80°F) 20 min.

Meanwhile, set the griddle over low heat. Test temperature; it is hot enough for baking when drops of water sprinkled on surface dance in small beads. Lightly grease griddle if manufacturer so directs.

Spoon into griddle enough batter (about 2 teaspoons) to form small pools about 1 in. in diameter, leaving at least 1 in. between cakes. Spread batter out slightly. Turn as they become puffy and full of bubbles, and brown other side. Turn only once. As Blini are cooked, transfer to a warm platter and set in a warm oven (about 250°F) until all are done.

Serve immediately, accompanied by bowls of
>   **Dairy sour cream**
>   **Caviar**
>   **Minced onion**
>   **Sieved hard-cooked egg yolk**
>   **Sieved hard-cooked egg white**

Arrange platter and bowls so each person may serve himself as desired.   *2 doz. Blini*

FILLED PASTRY MORSELS

These delicious morsels of pastry with savory fillings are hot appetizers you will serve with pride. For the custard-like Swiss cheese filling, use only the tart shells; the chicken and crab meat fillings may be baked either in tarts or in little pastry cornucopias.

Twenty-four 1¾-in. muffin-pan wells (1 in. deep) will be needed for the tarts; use baking sheets for the cornucopias.

Prepare and roll (half of dough at a time)
>   **Pastry for 2-Crust Pie (page 485)**

For Tarts—Roll pastry 1/16 to 1/8 in. thick; cut 3-in. rounds and fit carefully into the muffin-pan wells so that dough is not stretched. Press edges neatly against rims with a fork. Fill with Swiss Cheese Filling.

Bake at 375°F 15 min., or until a silver knife inserted into center of filling comes out clean; remove carefully to warm serving plates and serve piping hot.

Or fill with Chicken or Crab Meat Filling and bake at 400°F 30 min., or until pastry is delicately browned.   *About 2 doz. tarts*

For Cornucopias—Prepare one half pastry recipe; roll pastry 1/16 to 1/8 in. thick and cut 2-in. rounds. Place 1/2 to 3/4 teaspoon Chicken or Crab Meat Filling on center of each pastry round and moisten two thirds of outer edge of the round. Bring moistened edges together. Pinch, tapering one end, and leaving other open to form a cornucopia.

Place on baking sheets and bake at 375°F 12 to 15 min., until pastry is delicately browned. Remove to warm serving plates and serve piping hot.   *About 2½ doz. cornucopias*

For Swiss Cheese Filling—Shred and set aside
> **2 oz. Swiss cheese (about 1/2 cup, shredded)**

Prepare
> **2 tablespoons finely chopped onion**

Heat in a skillet over low heat
> **1½ teaspoons butter or margarine**

Add the onion and cook over medium heat until the onion is tender, stirring occasionally. Add to the shredded cheese and blend thoroughly. Divide mixture among the tart shells (about 1 teaspoon each). Set aside.

Blend thoroughly
> **1 egg, slightly beaten**
> **1/3 cup dairy sour cream**
> **1/2 teaspoon prepared mustard**
> **1/8 teaspoon salt**
> **Few grains cayenne pepper**

Spoon 1 teaspoonful of the mixture into each tart shell. Dot tops of tarts with
> **Butter (about 1 tablespoon for all)**

Sprinkle lightly with
> **Nutmeg**
>   *1¼ cups filling*

For Crab Meat Filling—Lightly toss together
> **1 cup crab meat (bony tissue removed)**
> **2 tablespoons dairy sour cream**
> **2 tablespoons mayonnaise**
> **2 teaspoons lime or lemon juice**
> **2 teaspoons minced pimiento**
> **1 teaspoon grated onion**
> **1/4 teaspoon Worcestershire sauce**
> **1/4 teaspoon dry mustard**
> **Few grains pepper**

Sprinkle over crab meat mixture in tart shells or on pastry rounds before shaping cornucopias
> **Grated Parmesan cheese**
> **Paprika**
>   *1½ cups filling*

For Chicken Filling—Lightly toss together
> **1/2 cup finely chopped cooked chicken**
> **1/4 cup finely chopped celery**
> **2½ tablespoons dairy sour cream**
> **2 tablespoons finely chopped toasted almonds**
> **1 tablespoon mayonnaise**
> **1/8 teaspoon salt**
> **Few grains white pepper**
> **Few grains nutmeg**
>   *1 cup filling*

HOT CAMEMBERT MORSELS

A deep saucepan or an automatic deep fryer will be needed.

Force through a fine sieve into a heavy 2-qt. saucepan
> **3 pkgs. (1⅓ oz. each) Camembert cheese**
> **1 pkg. (3 oz.) cream cheese**

Blend in until smooth
> **3/4 cup milk**
> **1/4 cup sifted all-purpose flour**
> **2 tablespoons softened butter**
> **1/4 teaspoon salt**
> **1/4 teaspoon monosodium glutamate**
> **1/4 teaspoon Worcestershire sauce**
> **5 drops Tabasco**

Cook over moderate heat, stirring constantly, until mixture is thick and smooth. Cool slightly; cover and chill in refrigerator 6 hrs. or overnight.

About 20 min. before deep-frying, fill the saucepan or deep fryer with **fat** and heat to 365°F.

Shape chilled mixture into balls about 3/4 in. in diameter. Roll in
> **Fine dry bread crumbs**

Dip in a mixture of
> **1 egg, slightly beaten**
> **2 teaspoons water**

Roll again in the bread crumbs.

Deep-fry cheese balls in heated fat. Fry only as many cheese balls at one time as will float uncrowded one layer deep in fat. Deep-fry 1 to 2 min., or until balls are lightly browned. Lift out with slotted spoon and drain cheese balls over fat for a second before removing to absorbent paper. Insert a wooden pick into each ball; serve immediately.
>   *3½ to 4 doz. cheese balls*

CHEDDAR SPRITZ STICKS

Set out baking sheets.

Blend until smooth
> **6 oz. (1 roll) pasteurized process sharp Cheddar cheese food**
> **1/2 cup butter or margarine, softened**

Set aside for 30 min. to allow flavors to blend.

Meanwhile, sift together and set aside
> **1½ cups sifted all-purpose flour**
> **1/4 teaspoon salt**
> **1/8 teaspoon dry mustard**

Brussels Sprouts with Sour Cream Dipping Sauce

Add gradually to the cheese mixture, stirring in
> **1/4 cup beer (measured without foam)**
> **1/2 teaspoon Worcestershire sauce**

Mixing until well blended after each addition, add dry ingredients in fourths to beer-cheese mixture.

Fill a cookie press about two-thirds full with the dough. Using the disk to form bars, press dough onto baking sheets in 8- to 10-in. strips.

Bake at 400°F about 7 min., or until delicately browned at edges.   *About 1 doz. sticks*

SNAPPY COCKTAIL SPRITZ

Cayenne pepper gives these tangy morsels a pleasing bite. They'll keep beautifully, but seldom is there a chance to prove it.

Finely shred into a bowl
> **1/2 lb. New York Herkimer cheese or any sharp Cheddar cheese**

Cover and set aside overnight.

Set out a baking sheet.

Sift together and set aside
> **1 cup sifted all-purpose flour**
> **3/4 teaspoon paprika**
> **1/4 teaspoon cayenne pepper**

Cream until softened
> **1/4 cup butter or margarine**

Thoroughly mix in the shredded cheese. Mixing until well blended after each addition, add dry ingredients in fourths.

Using pastry bag and No. 7 star tube, squeeze 1½- to 2-in. lengths of mixture onto baking sheet. Or squeeze into any spritz cookie shape.

Bake at 375°F 10 to 15 min., or until delicately browned.   *About 2 doz. cheese sticks*

BRUSSELS SPROUTS WITH SOUR CREAM DIPPING SAUCE

Set out a fondue bourguignonne set or a decorative saucepan (see photo).

For Brussels Sprouts—Heat in a saucepan until boiling
> **2¼ cups Chablis or Sauterne, or**
> **2¼ cups quick meat broth (page 10)**

Add and cook (page 313) 8 to 12 min., or until just tender

1½ lbs. Brussels sprouts, or 3 pkgs. (10 oz. each) frozen Brussels sprouts, cooked following package directions

Drain and keep warm.

For Sour Cream Dipping Sauce—Heat in the bourguignonne pan over direct heat

2 tablespoons butter or margarine

Blend and stir in

1 tablespoon all-purpose flour
1 teaspoon salt
½ teaspoon caraway seed
¼ teaspoon cayenne pepper

Heat until mixture bubbles; remove from heat. Add gradually, stirring constantly

1 cup milk

Return mixture to heat and bring rapidly to boiling, stirring constantly; cook 1 to 2 min. Reduce heat. Stir in, a small amount at a time, and heat thoroughly

1½ cups dairy sour cream

Keep dipping sauce warm; *do not boil.*

Spear a Brussels sprout with a fondue fork; dunk and twirl in the sauce.   *12 servings*

TERIYAKI, MAINLAND STYLE

About 2 doz. skewers will be needed.

Cut into small cubes

1 lb. beef top round or sirloin, cut ¾ in. thick

Put into a shallow dish. Set aside.

Drain, reserving ½ cup syrup

1 can (20 oz.) pineapple chunks

Set pineapple chunks aside.

Mix pineapple syrup with

¼ cup soy sauce
1 clove garlic, finely chopped
1 teaspoon chopped fresh gingerroot or ¾ teaspoon ground ginger

Pour over meat. Allow to stand at least 1 hr.; turn meat occasionally.

Alternately thread meat pieces and pineapple chunks onto skewers. Reserve soy sauce mixture.

Drain

1 small jar pimiento-stuffed olives

Put an olive onto the end of each threaded skewer. Arrange skewers on rack of a broiler pan. Brush with some of the soy sauce mixture. Broil 3 in. from heat 10 to 12 min., turning once and brushing with soy sauce mixture. Serve hot.   *About 2 doz. appetizers*

Note: If using fresh gingerroot, wash and pare, then chop it.

PETITE BURGERS

Set out a baking sheet.

Place on a flat working surface

4 to 6 slices bread (white, whole wheat or rye)

Cut into 1½-in. rounds using a small cookie cutter or a knife and a waxed paper pattern. Arrange in a single layer on baking sheet and toast in a 300°F oven about 15 to 20 min., or until lightly browned. Turn to brown both sides.

Meanwhile, measure and set aside

5 teaspoons ketchup

Combine and mix lightly

½ lb. ground beef
1 egg yolk, beaten
1 tablespoon minced onion

and a mixture of

½ teaspoon salt
½ teaspoon monosodium glutamate
Few grains pepper

Shape into balls about ¾ in. in diameter. Place on toast rounds and flatten meat to edges of toast. Make an indentation in the center of each burger; fill with ¼ teaspoon ketchup. Set burgers on broiler rack and place under broiler with top of meat about 3 in. from heat. Broil about 4 min., or until done.

About 20 appetizers

EXOTIC APPETIZER BALLS

Set out a large heavy skillet.

Combine and set aside to soften

2 teaspoons instant minced onion
2 teaspoons water

Mix in a bowl

1 egg, fork beaten
1 tablespoon instant powdered coffee
1 teaspoon onion salt
⅛ teaspoon pepper
½ teaspoon Worcestershire sauce
8 drops Tabasco

Blend into egg mixture the softened onion and

½ cup chopped water chestnuts

Lightly mix in

1 lb. ground beef

Form into 1-in. balls.

Heat in the skillet over low heat

2 tablespoons butter or margarine

Brown the meat balls in hot butter over medium heat, shaking pan frequently to obtain even browning and round balls.

To serve, spear balls with fancy wooden picks and serve hot. Or, if desired, serve from a chafing dish.   *About 5½ doz. balls*

CORNED BEEF HASH BALLS

Mash with a fork in a bowl

1 cup canned corned beef hash

Add and mix well

¼ cup fine dry bread crumbs
¼ cup mayonnaise
1 tablespoon ketchup
1 teaspoon horseradish mustard
⅛ teaspoon onion salt

Shape into small balls.

Beat slightly in a bowl

1 egg
Salt and pepper to taste

Coat balls with beaten egg and roll in

Fine dry bread crumbs

Arrange in a shallow baking pan. Set under broiler with tops about 3 in. from heat about 5 min., turning once. Accompany with picks.

About 2 doz. appetizers

BRAUNSCHWEIGER BEEF BALLS

Combine in a bowl

2 eggs, beaten
1 pkg. (8 oz.) Braunschweiger (smoked liver sausage)

Mix in lightly and thoroughly

½ lb. lean ground beef
1 cup fine dry bread crumbs
¼ cup ketchup
½ teaspoon seasoned salt

Shape into 1-in. balls.

Heat in a large skillet

¼ cup butter or margarine

Add meat balls and cook until evenly browned, turning as necessary.

Combine

1½ cups hot water
1 env. dry onion soup mix

Pour over meat balls. Cover skillet and cook slowly 15 min. Serve hot with picks.

About 4 doz. appetizers

SMALL HOT PATTIES
(Petits Pâtés Chauds)

Prepare (allowing about 9 hrs.)

Puff Pastry (page 518)

For Filling—Chop finely

¾ cup leftover meat or fish (or use finely shredded cheese)

Add and blend in

2 tablespoons finely chopped nuts, mushrooms or truffles
2 tablespoons grated onion
1 teaspoon chopped parsley
⅛ teaspoon salt
Few grains pepper

Moisten with

2 to 3 tablespoons bouillon or milk

Set aside.

For Patties—Roll puff dough ⅛ in. thick. With a cookie cutter, cut about 24 rounds 3 in. in diameter. On each of 12 rounds cut 3 or 4 tiny slits to allow steam to escape. Set aside.

Lay the remaining 12 on a baking sheet which has been rinsed in cold water and drained. Dampen edges of rounds.

Put about 1 tablespoon of filling onto each pastry round. Cover with the slit rounds. Press edges together with a fork to seal.

Lightly brush onto pastry tops
Slightly beaten egg

Bake at 450°F 8 to 12 min. Serve hot.
1 doz. appetizers

BACON-WRAPPED CHICKEN LIVERS

▲ *Base Recipe*

Rinse with cold water and drain on absorbent paper
½ lb. chicken livers
Cut into bite-size pieces and put in bowl with
⅓ cup cream
Cover and allow to stand about 30 min., turning the pieces from time to time in the cream. Remove chicken livers from cream and set aside on absorbent paper to drain thoroughly.

Meanwhile, cut into halves or thirds, (depending upon length needed to just wrap around liver piece)
9 slices bacon
Wrap one piece around each piece of liver; secure each with a wooden pick.

Arrange chicken livers on broiler rack. Place in broiler with top of livers about 2 in. from heat. Broil 5 min.

Carefully turn chicken livers with tongs. Broil second side 5 min., or until bacon is cooked.

Place appetizers on a warm platter. Garnish and serve immediately.
About 1½ doz. appetizers

—BACON-WRAPPED OYSTERS

Follow ▲ Recipe. Omit chicken livers and cream. Drain **1 pt. (about 1½ doz.) oysters.** Remove any shell particles. Dip in **French Dressing** (page 410) before wrapping in bacon.

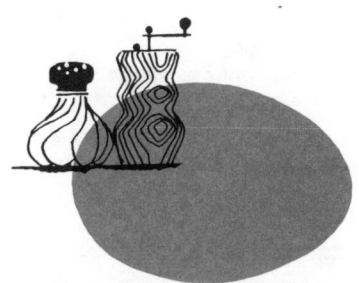

COCONUT CHICKEN TIDBITS

Fill a deep saucepan or an automatic deep-fryer one half to two thirds full with
Vegetable shortening, all-purpose shortening, lard or cooking oil for deep-frying
Heat fat slowly to 325°F.

Rinse and pat dry with absorbent paper
2 whole chicken breasts, boned
Remove skin from chicken. Cut chicken into 1-in. squares. Sprinkle with
1½ teaspoons seasoned salt
¼ teaspoon seasoned pepper
Set aside.

Set out
2 cups flaked coconut
Combine and beat well
1 egg
½ cup milk
Add gradually, beating until smooth
½ cup all-purpose flour
Coat chicken pieces with batter and then coconut.

Deep-fry a few pieces at a time in heated fat until browned on all sides. (Remove any coconut from bottom of pan with a slotted spoon.) Lift out tidbits with slotted spoon and drain on absorbent paper.

Meanwhile, combine in a small saucepan and heat thoroughly
¼ cup butter or margarine, melted
½ cup chopped chutney
Serve as a dip with the chicken tidbits. Accompany with picks. *About 3 doz. appetizers*

PETITE PUFFS OF HAM

Dainty, crisp shells filled with an appetizing creamed ham mixture.

Lightly grease a baking sheet.

For Puffs—Sift together and set aside
½ cup sifted all-purpose flour
½ teaspoon dry mustard

Bring to boiling in a heavy saucepan
½ cup hot water
¼ cup butter or margarine
¼ teaspoon salt
Add dry ingredients all at one time. Beat vigorously with a wooden spoon until mixture leaves sides of pan and forms a smooth ball (about 3 min.). Remove from heat. Immediately add and stir until melted
2 tablespoons grated Parmesan cheese
Quickly beat in, one at a time, beating until smooth after each addition
2 eggs
Continue beating until mixture is smooth and glossy. Drop by teaspoonfuls 2 in. apart onto baking sheet.

Bake at 450°F 10 min. Reduce heat to 350°F and bake about 5 min. longer or until golden in color. Remove to cooling rack to cool completely.

For Filling—Grind and set aside enough cooked ham to yield
½ cup ground cooked ham
Prepare in the top of a double boiler
½ cup Thin White Sauce (one-half recipe, page 304)

Add to sauce the ground ham and
1 tablespoon capers
2 teaspoons minced onion
1 teaspoon lemon juice
Heat mixture thoroughly in top of double boiler over simmering water. Cut top off each puff and fill with ham mixture. Replace top. Serve immediately. *About 2 doz. appetizers*

HAM-STUFFED EGGS
(Töltött Tojás Sonkával)

▲ *Base Recipe*

Prepare
6 Hard-Cooked Eggs (page 133)
Cut each egg into halves lengthwise. Remove egg yolks to a bowl and mash them with a fork or press through ricer or sieve into a bowl. Set egg whites aside. Mix egg yolks with
⅓ cup very finely chopped cooked ham
and a mixture of
¾ teaspoon dry mustard
½ teaspoon salt
¼ teaspoon pepper
Stir in, moistening to a thick, pastelike consistency
3 to 4 tablespoons dairy sour cream
Fill the egg whites with egg yolk mixture, leaving tops rounded and rough. Serve chilled or hot.

To heat, arrange egg halves, filled-side up, in a buttered 8-in. square baking dish. Brush eggs lightly with about
1 tablespoon butter, melted
Sprinkle eggs with
Paprika
Place in 375°F oven about 5 min., or until heated thoroughly.

To serve, cut egg halves into smaller pieces and insert a wooden pick into each.
6 to 8 servings

—ANCHOVY-STUFFED EGGS
(Töltött Tojás Szárdellával)

Follow ▲ Recipe. Substitute **4 or 5 anchovy fillets,** very finely chopped, for the ham and omit salt.

—MUSHROOM-STUFFED EGGS
(Töltött Tojás Gombával)

Follow ▲ Recipe. Omit the ham and decrease sour cream to 2 to 3 tablespoons. Clean (page 9; do not slice) and very finely chop **¼ lb. mushrooms.** Cook slowly in a small skillet in **2 to 3 tablespoons butter or margarine,** stirring gently until lightly browned and tender. Stir into egg yolk mixture.

DEVILED LAMB FOLD-UPS

Mix in a large bowl
> ½ lb. lean lamb shoulder, ground twice
> ¾ cup finely shredded extra sharp Cheddar cheese
> ¾ teaspoon salt
> ⅛ teaspoon seasoned pepper
> 2 tablespoons *each* chopped toasted pecans, finely chopped parsley and prepared mustard
> 1 tablespoon prepared horseradish
> 2 teaspoons Worcestershire sauce

Divide into two equal portions. Set aside.

Have ready in refrigerator
> 2 pkgs. (8 oz. each) refrigerated fresh dough for crescent rolls

Remove 1 package of dough from refrigerator, open and unroll dough. Separate into 8 triangles; cut each triangle into 3 pieces to make 24 triangles (they will be of different shapes). Spread 1 rounded teaspoon lamb mixture over center of each dough triangle. Fold up 2 or 3 ends to center; pinch firmly and twist or roll ends. Arrange on ungreased baking sheet.

Bake at 375°F 10 to 15 min., or until golden brown. Repeat procedure with remaining half of lamb mixture and package of dough.

4 doz. appetizers

TINY LAMB KABOBS

Poultry pins or 3-in. skewers and a broiler pan will be needed.

Have ready
> 1 lb. boneless lean lamb (shoulder or leg), cut in ½-in. cubes
> 1 jar (3½ oz.) cocktail onions, drained
> 2 medium green peppers, cut in ½-in. squares

Alternately thread lamb cubes, onions and green pepper squares on poultry pins or skewers. Brush kabobs generously with
> Bottled brown bouquet sauce

Arrange kabobs on rack of broiler pan.

Broil with tops 3 to 4 in. from heat about 3 min. on each side.

Meanwhile, combine in a saucepan
> 1 can (8 oz.) tomato sauce
> 2 tablespoons prepared mustard
> 2 tablespoons honey
> 1 teaspoon bottled brown bouquet sauce

Heat to serving temperature, stirring occasionally. Pour into a bowl and serve as a dip for lamb kabobs.   *About 3 doz. appetizers*

GOLDEN MUSHROOM AND TOMATO APPETIZERS

Have ready
> 18 small fresh mushrooms, cleaned (page 9) or 1 can (6 or 8 oz.) whole mushrooms, drained

Combine in a small plastic bag
> ⅓ cup corn flake crumbs
> ½ teaspoon Italian seasoning
> ¼ teaspoon salt
> Few grains cayenne pepper

Dip mushrooms into
> Milk (about ¼ cup)

Shake mushrooms, a few at a time, in the bag with crumb mixture. Place on a baking sheet.

Bake at 350°F 15 min., or until golden brown.

To serve, impale warm mushrooms and **cherry tomatoes** on picks.   *18 appetizers*

PIQUANT RICE-STUFFED MUSHROOMS

Heat in a small skillet
> 1 tablespoon butter or margarine

Add and cook until tender
> 1½ tablespoons minced onion

Remove from heat and mix in
> ½ cup cooked rice
> ¼ cup chopped nuts
> 1½ teaspoons chili sauce
> 1½ teaspoons lemon juice
> ½ teaspoon salt
> Few grains pepper

Shape mixture into 12 balls. Set aside.

Place, rounded side up, on rack of a broiler pan
> 12 large fresh mushroom caps

Brush with
> Melted butter or margarine

Set under broiler about 3 in. from heat about 3 min. Turn caps. Sprinkle with
> Salt and pepper

Place a rice ball in each mushroom cap. Drizzle with **melted butter or margarine.** Broil with tops about 3 in. from heat until golden brown.

12 appetizers

BROILED MUSHROOMS

▲ *Base Recipe*

Set out
> 3 slices bacon

Cut each piece crosswise into 16 strips.

Clean
> 2 doz. mushrooms with 1- to 2-in. caps

Remove stems from caps. Set caps aside. Chop stems finely.

Heat in a skillet over low heat
> 5 tablespoons butter or margarine

Add chopped mushroom stems and
> ¼ cup finely chopped onion

Cook about 5 min., stirring occasionally. Add and toss gently a mixture of
> 2 tablespoons finely chopped pitted ripe olives
> 2 tablespoons finely chopped capers
> ½ teaspoon salt
> ¼ teaspoon monosodium glutamate
> ⅛ teaspoon pepper

Remove mixture with a slotted spoon to a bowl, allowing butter to drain back into skillet. Add to chopped mixture and mix
> 2 tablespoons cream

Set mixture aside.

Add mushroom caps to skillet and cook slowly, turning occasionally and moving gently with a spoon. Add butter when necessary. Cook until caps are lightly browned and tender. Remove from skillet. Fill caps with the prepared mixture and set them on a baking sheet. Sprinkle with a mixture of
> 2 tablespoons grated Parmesan cheese
> 1 tablespoon fine dry bread crumbs

Top each mushroom cap with 2 strips of the bacon.

Place filled mushroom caps under broiler with tops of mushrooms about 3 in. from heat. Broil about 4 min., or until bacon is lightly browned.

Serve immediately.   *6 to 8 servings*

—CHEESE-STUFFED MUSHROOM CAPS

Follow ▲ Recipe. Omit olive-caper mixture. Blend mushroom stem-onion mixture with **6 tablespoons grated Parmesan cheese** and **3 tablespoons fine dry bread crumbs** and use to stuff caps. Top with bacon pieces and broil.

MINIATURE MUSHROOM HORNS

Prepare and shape into 2 balls (do not roll out or bake)
> Pastry for 2-Crust Pie (page 485)

Wrap in waxed paper and set in refrigerator until ready to use.

For Filling—Prepare
> 1 Hard-Cooked Egg (page 133)

Finely chop egg and set aside.

Have ready
> 1 tablespoon cooked rice

Set aside.

Prepare
> ½ cup (¼ lb.) finely chopped mushrooms
> 2 tablespoons finely chopped onion

Heat in a small skillet over low heat
> 2 tablespoons butter or margarine

Add mushrooms and onion; cook slowly, moving and turning with a spoon or fork, until mushrooms and onion are tender. Using a slotted spoon, remove mushrooms and onion to a medium-size bowl. Toss lightly with the

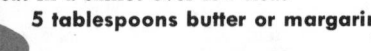

egg and rice. Add a blend of
¼ teaspoon salt
⅛ teaspoon pepper
Few grains cayenne pepper
Add and thoroughly blend in
3 tablespoons dairy sour cream
Set aside.

To Complete Horns—Remove pastry from refrigerator. Using one ball at a time, flatten on a lightly floured surface. Roll from center to edge into a round about ⅛ in. thick. With knife or spatula, loosen pastry from surface wherever sticking occurs; lift pastry slightly and sprinkle flour underneath.

From waxed paper, cut a round pattern 1½ in. in diameter. Using the waxed-paper pattern and a sharp knife, or a lightly floured 1½-in. cookie cutter, cut out pastry rounds. Place ½ to ¾ teaspoon filling on center of each pastry round and moisten two thirds of outer edge of the rounds. Bring moistened edges together. Pinch, tapering the end, to form a cornucopia. (Leave opposite end open.) Place the filled pastry horns on a baking sheet. Brush with a mixture of
1 egg yolk, slightly beaten
1 tablespoon cream

Bake at 400°F 10 to 15 min., or until horns are lightly browned.

Serve immediately.   *5 doz. appetizers*

CHINESE-STYLE BARBECUED RIBS

Put into a large shallow dish
2 lbs. spareribs
Mix in a bowl
¼ cup sugar
2 teaspoons salt
½ teaspoon monosodium glutamate
¼ teaspoon pepper
¼ cup chicken broth
2 tablespoons ketchup
2 tablespoons soy sauce
½ teaspoon bead molasses
Pour over ribs in dish. Cover and refrigerate at least 8 hrs., basting occasionally.

About 2 hrs. before ready to serve, set out a large baking pan with rack. Pour about a cup of cold water into pan to prevent smoking during roasting. Remove meat from refrigerator, transfer to rack in pan and baste with sauce.

Roast ribs in a 350°F oven about 45 min., basting occasionally with sauce. Turn ribs, baste with sauce and roast 45 min. longer, or until meat is tender.

Cut into single-rib portions to serve.
                    6 to 8 servings

OLIVE BITES

Set out a baking sheet.

Set out
25 pitted ripe olives

Stuff olives with
2 to 3 tablespoons finely minced green onion
Set olives aside.

Shred
4 oz. sharp Cheddar cheese (about 1 cup, shredded)
Sift together into a bowl
½ cup sifted all-purpose flour
¼ teaspoon salt
⅛ teaspoon dry mustard
Mix in the cheese. Stir in a mixture of
3 tablespoons butter or margarine, melted and slightly cooled
1 teaspoon milk
1 or 2 drops Tabasco
Using about a teaspoon of dough for each, shape dough around olives, completely covering them. Place on baking sheet.

Bake at 400°F 10 to 12 min.   *25 appetizers*

OLIVE HAM APPETIZERS

Grind enough cooked ham to yield
¾ cup ground cooked ham
Combine with ham and mix thoroughly
½ cup chopped ripe olives
1 tablespoon dairy sour cream
1 teaspoon prepared mustard
1 teaspoon Worcestershire sauce
Set aside.

Set out
1 tablespoon caraway seed
Prepare
Pastry I for 1-Crust Pie (page 485)
Divide pastry dough into 6 equal portions; roll each portion into a 5x3-in. rectangle. Sprinkle about ½ teaspoon caraway seed over each rectangle. Spread one sixth of the ham mixture evenly over each rectangle to edges. Starting with long edge of each rectangle, roll up and pinch long edge to seal (do not pinch ends of roll). Place on baking sheet, sealed edge down.

Bake at 450°F 10 to 12 min., or until lightly browned.

Slice rolls; serve with **radish roses** and **ripe olives** threaded with **carrot sticks.**
                    About 30 appetizers

SAUSAGE ROLL-UPS

Set out a shallow baking pan.

Trim crusts from
12 thin slices bread
Flatten slices with a rolling pin and cut into halves. Spread with
Horseradish mustard (about 2 tablespoons)
Set out
1 pkg. brown and serve sausages
Cut sausages into halves. Place a sausage half on each bread piece, roll up and secure with a pick. Arrange in baking pan. Brush with
Melted butter or margarine

Olive Bites and Cheese Olive Squares

Set in a 400°F oven about 20 min., or until lightly browned.   *2 doz. appetizers*

APPETIZER KABOBS

Whether cooked on the spot in a smart Japanese hibachi (as pictured) or trotted off to the kitchen for cooking, these novel hors d'oeuvres are fun to assemble and eat.

Skewers will be needed.

Set out to drain
1 can (9 oz.) pitted ripe olives
Meanwhile, blend
1 jar (5 oz.) pasteurized process sharp cheese spread
2 teaspoons prepared horseradish
1 teaspoon chili powder
1 teaspoon prepared mustard
¼ teaspoon salt
2 drops Tabasco
Using the point of a small knife, fill each olive with cheese mixture.

For Kabobs—Set out in small bowls the stuffed olives and
Pickled onions
Cocktail sausages
Pineapple chunks
Cooked shrimp
Thread any combination on skewers.

Arrange kabobs on broiler rack. Set under broiler with tops of kabobs about 2 in. from heat. Turning frequently, broil about 5 min., or until thoroughly heated. If using the hibachi, follow manufacturer's directions.

Appetizer Kabobs

TUNA SNACKS

Line a baking sheet with aluminum foil and set aside.

Drain and flake (page 9)

1 can (6½ or 7 oz.) tuna

Set aside.

Put into a bowl

¾ cup soft bread crumbs

Drizzle with

2 tablespoons butter or margarine

Add and mix well

2 tablespoons finely chopped onion
¼ teaspoon salt
⅛ teaspoon pepper
⅛ teaspoon oregano
¼ cup mayonnaise
1 teaspoon lemon juice

Toss in the tuna and

¼ cup finely shredded sharp Cheddar cheese

Shape into 1-in. balls. Coat with

Corn flake crumbs

Place on foil-lined baking sheet.

Bake at 375°F 10 min., or until lightly browned.   *About 2½ doz. appetizers*

DEEP-FRIED SARDINE BALLS

Fill a deep saucepan or an automatic deep-fryer one half to two thirds full with

Vegetable shortening, all-purpose shortening, lard or cooking oil for deep-frying

Heat fat slowly to 375°F.

Cook (page 313) until tender

1 medium potato

Peel potato and mash well in a bowl.

Drain and mash sardines from

2 cans (3¾ oz. each) sardines

Mix sardines with potato and

⅓ cup mayonnaise
2 tablespoons horseradish mustard
Few grains cayenne pepper

Shape into balls. Roll in

Beaten egg

Coat with

Fine bread crumbs (about ⅔ cup)

Deep-fry in heated fat only as many balls at one time as will float one layer deep. Fry 2 to 3 min., or until golden brown. Lift out with slotted spoon and drain on absorbent paper. Accompany with picks.

About 2 doz. appetizers

SEAFOOD-FILLED APPETIZER CREPES

Prepare and set aside

Seafood Filling (below)

Beat together in a bowl until just moistened (batter should be slightly lumpy)

½ cup pancake mix
¾ cup milk
1 egg
1 tablespoon butter or margarine, melted

Lightly grease a griddle or skillet and heat until a drop of water sputters on surface. Drop batter by spoonfuls, forming 3½-in. rounds. Turn crêpes when edges appear dry. Brown second side. Repeat until all of batter is baked.

Spoon about 1 tablespoon Seafood Filling onto center of each crêpe and roll up jelly-roll fashion. Secure with a pick. Arrange on a lightly greased baking sheet.

Heat under broiler with tops 3 to 4 in. from heat 1 to 2 min.   *About 14 appetizers*

For Seafood Filling—Mix in a bowl

¾ cup flaked cooked crab meat, lobster or shrimp
¼ cup chopped ripe olives
3 tablespoons mayonnaise
¼ teaspoon lemon juice
Salt and pepper to taste

Refrigerate until needed.   *About 1 cup filling*

PIGS IN BLANKETS

Set out a broiler pan.

Have ready

12 large oysters, freshly shucked and drained
1 pimiento, cut in 12 strips
12 slices bacon

Season oysters with a mixture of

½ teaspoon salt
⅛ teaspoon pepper
⅛ teaspoon paprika

Put a pimiento strip on each seasoned oyster, wrap in a bacon slice, and secure with a wooden pick. Arrange on broiler pan.

Broil with tops 4 to 5 in. from heat about 5 min., or until bacon is crisp; turn once.

1 doz. appetizers

PUFF SHRIMP WITH ORANGE GINGER SAUCE

Prepare and cool

Orange Ginger Sauce (below)

Fill a deep saucepan or automatic deep fryer one-half to two-thirds full with

Fat for deep frying

Heat slowly to 375°F.

Shell and devein

2 lbs. medium raw shrimp (20 to 25 per lb.)

Set aside.

Beat together in a bowl until smooth

3 egg yolks
½ cup white wine
¾ cup all-purpose flour
1 teaspoon salt
¼ teaspoon pepper

Beat until stiff, not dry, peaks are formed

3 egg whites

Fold egg whites into egg yolk mixture.

Dry shrimp thoroughly and dip into batter, coating well.

Deep-fry one layer deep in heated fat 2 to 3 min. on each side, or until golden brown. Remove from fat with a slotted spoon. Drain on absorbent paper. Be sure temperature of fat is 375°F before frying each layer. Serve shrimp hot accompanied with the Orange Ginger Sauce for dipping.   *40 to 50 appetizers*

—ORANGE GINGER SAUCE

Combine in a saucepan

1 cup orange marmalade
2 tablespoons soy sauce
¼ cup sherry
1 piece whole gingerroot
1 clove garlic, minced

Stir over low heat until mixture bubbles. Remove from heat. Cool. Remove ginger before serving.   *About 1¼ cups sauce*

BACON-WRAPPED SHRIMP APPETIZERS

For Chili Dip—Prepare and chop

1 Hard-Cooked Egg (page 133)

Add and mix thoroughly with egg

¾ cup mayonnaise
3 tablespoons chopped sweet pickle
1 tablespoon chopped stuffed olives
1½ teaspoons grated onion
1 tablespoon chili powder

Cover and set aside in refrigerator 1 to 2 hrs.

For Shrimp—Prepare (page 294)

1 lb. fresh shrimp with shells

For Butter Sauce—Combine in a saucepan

½ cup butter or margarine
1½ teaspoons chili powder
1 clove garlic, minced

Set over low heat, stirring occasionally, until butter is melted and heated thoroughly. Remove from heat and set aside.

Bacon-Wrapped Shrimp Appetizers

To Complete Appetizers—Cut into halves

8 slices bacon

Wrap one half-slice around each cooked shrimp and secure with a wooden pick.

Arrange shrimp on broiler rack. Brush with the butter sauce. Place under broiler with tops of shrimp about 3 in. from heat. Broil 5 min., brushing once with sauce. Carefully turn shrimp; brush with sauce and broil second side 5 min., or until bacon is cooked, brushing once again during cooking.

Arrange appetizers on a warm platter. If desired, garnish with **lemon wedges** and **parsley.** Serve immediately with the Chili Dip.

About 16 appetizers

BACON-WRAPPED WATER CHESTNUTS

Set out

18 canned water chestnuts (about two 5-oz. cans, drained)

Cut into thirds

6 slices bacon

Wrap one piece around each water chestnut and secure with a wooden pick.

Arrange water chestnuts on broiler rack. Place under broiler with tops of appetizers about 3 in. from heat. Broil 4 min. Carefully turn and broil second side 4 min., or until bacon is cooked.

Serve piping hot.   *About 1½ doz. appetizers*

RELISHES FOR THE COCKTAIL HOUR

Some relishes may be eaten easily with the fingers; others need "stems" which can be wooden or plastic picks. If these appetizers are firm, they may be attractively arranged on a serving tray. Or insert them on picks and insert the picks into a holder of your choice. Make a holder from a molded cheese such as Edam, or use grapefruit, oranges, apples, a small head of red or green cabbage, a melon, eggplant, cucumber or a cauliflower. If necessary, level base by removing a thin slice from the under side.

STUFFED BEETS

Use the tiniest of **canned or pickled beets.** Drain. Hollow out each beet with a spoon or melon ball cutter. Cut off thin slices at bases of beets so they will stand upright on serving dish. Fill centers with **well-seasoned meat or cheese mixture.**

BISCUIT BITES

Spread **toasted bite-size shredded wheat biscuits** with **peanut butter.** Insert picks and on each end of biscuit secure a **thin slice of sweet pickle.**

SMOKED CHEESE TEMPTERS

Soften **smoked cheese** and combine with chopped **pimiento, sweet pickle** and **crisp bacon,** crumbled. Roll into small balls and chill in refrigerator. Or pack into a small pan, chill and cut into squares. Insert picks.

MEAT 'N' CHEESE PINUPS

With a round cutter, cut 2½- to 3-in. rounds from ¼-in. thick slices of **ham, canned luncheon meat or a ready-to-serve meat, bologna** or **other sausage.** Repeat the process with ¼-in. thick slices of **Swiss or Cheddar cheese.** Stack alternate meat and cheese rounds, using five in all. Wrap in waxed paper and chill in refrigerator until ready to serve. Cut stacks into ¾-in. wedge-shaped pieces. Insert picks.

DRIED BEEF TASTERS

Flavor **cream cheese** with a small amount of **prepared horseradish.** Roll into small balls. Then roll and press balls in **minced dried beef.** Insert wooden or plastic picks.

OLIVE TEASERS

Coat large **pimiento-stuffed olives** with **cream cheese.** Roll in **finely chopped nuts.** Chill in refrigerator and insert picks.

PECAN SANDWICHES

Finely shred **Swiss cheese** and mix with **cream** until of spreading consistency. Lightly brush large **pecan halves** with **butter or margarine** and spread in pie pan or on baking sheet. Toast lightly at 350°F. Spread one pecan half with cheese mixture and top with second half. Press gently together.

ANTIPASTO

The leader in the parade of foods included in an elaborate Italian dinner is the antipasto or "before the meal" course. Varying from region to region and from season to season, this starter course is a challenge to an adventurous cook. It may vary from a few crisp vegetables to a vast number of bite-size appetizers, including fish, meats, eggs, cheese and pickled vegetables. Whether foods are dipped in wine vinegar or olive oil, the antipasto offers a diversified introduction to a dinner or luncheon.

SUGGESTED FOODS FOR AN ANTIPASTO TRAY

From six to sixty various items—this tray can be just as plain or as elegant as you desire. The decision is yours as to whether you want one or ten different meats, vegetables, fish, greens and cheese.

Meats—**Salami,** sliced thin; **prosciutto,** sliced thin; **capocollo,** sliced thin.

Vegetables—**Mushrooms,** pickled; **peppers,** pickled or raw; **tomatoes,** sliced or with **olive oil; radishes; celery; finocchio** (fennel); **pimiento; pickled vegetables** (carrots, eggplant, zucchini); **olives,** green or ripe; **artichokes,** pickled or with **lemon.**

Eggs—Hard-cooked, sliced.

Fish—**Sardines; tuna,** pieces or chunks; **anchovies** around **capers** or around **stuffed olives.**

Greens—**Lettuce,** head or leaf; **romaine; chicory; endive.**

Cheese—**Mozzarella,** sliced; **Provolone,** sliced; **Gorgonzola,** sliced.

—NORTHERN ITALY ANTIPASTO TRAY

The North prepares slightly more elaborate things for the tray and uses pork products.

Salami, sliced thin, **prosciutto,** sliced thin; **artichokes,** pickled or with lemon; **pickled mushrooms; anchovies** around **capers** or around **olives; tuna,** pieces or chunks; **lettuce; Hard-Cooked Eggs** (page 133).

—SOUTHERN ITALY ANTIPASTO TRAY

The South uses many of its vegetables and fresh cheeses for the tray.

Salami, sliced thin; **sardines; anchovies; peppers,** raw; **celery** and **fennel; olives; pimiento; pickled vegetables; radishes; lettuce; cheese** (Mozzarella, Provolone or Gorgonzola).

Antipasto

ANCHOVIES AND CAPERS
(Acciughe e Capperi)

▲ *Base Recipe*

Wrap
   6 anchovy fillets
around
   6 capers

—ANCHOVIES AND STUFFED OLIVES
(Acciughe e Olive)

Follow ▲ Recipe. Substitute **6 pimiento-stuffed olives** for the capers.

ARTICHOKES IN LEMON
(Carciofi con Limone)

Drain and place in refrigerator to chill
   1 jar (13 oz.) artichoke hearts

Meanwhile, combine
   3 tablespoons lemon juice
   2 tablespoons olive oil
   1 clove garlic, finely chopped
   ¼ teaspoon salt
   ⅛ teaspoon pepper
Chill in refrigerator.

When ready to serve, stir lemon-olive oil mixture and pour over artichoke hearts.

PICKLED CARROTS
(Carote con Olio e Aceto)

Set out 1-pt. screw-top jar.

Wash, pare and cut into strips
   6 to 8 medium carrots
Cook carrots (page 313) and drain. Cool carrots and put into jar. Set aside.

Combine
   2 tablespoons olive oil
   1 clove garlic, cut in halves
   1 hot green pepper
   ½ teaspoon salt
Pour over carrots and cover with
   Wine vinegar
Screw cap onto jar and store jar in refrigerator at least 24 hrs. Serve cold.

PICKLED EGGPLANT
(Melanzane con Olio e Aceto)

Set out 1-qt. screw-top jar.

Wash, pare and slice very thin
   1 small (about 1 lb.) eggplant
Put eggplant slices into the jar and set aside.

Combine
   ⅔ cup wine vinegar
   4 cloves garlic, quartered
   2 hot green peppers
Pour this mixture over eggplant and cover with
   Olive oil
Screw cap onto jar and store jar in refrigerator at least 24 hrs. Serve cold.

PICKLED MUSHROOMS
(Funghi con Olio e Aceto)

Set out 1-pt. screw-top jar.

Clean (page 9; do not slice)
   1 lb. mushrooms with ½-in. caps
Place mushrooms in saucepan and cover with equal amounts of
   White vinegar
   Hot water
Bring mixture to boiling, and cook for 5 min. Drain liquid from mushrooms. When mushrooms are cool, pack in the jar with mixture of
   ¼ cup olive oil
   2 teaspoons salt
   2 teaspoons peppercorns
   2 cloves garlic, quartered
   1 teaspoon mace
Cover mushrooms with
   White vinegar
Screw cap onto jar and store jar in refrigerator for 2 days. Serve cold.

TOMATOES IN OIL
(Pomodori all'Olio)

Wash, remove stem ends and slice lengthwise
   6 plum tomatoes (or 2 tomatoes may be substituted)
Set aside.

Combine
   3 tablespoons olive oil
   1 clove garlic, sliced thin
   ¼ teaspoon salt
   ¼ teaspoon oregano
   ⅛ teaspoon pepper
Pour olive oil mixture over tomatoes and serve.

PICKLED ZUCCHINI
(Zucchini con Olio e Aceto)

Set out 1-pt. screw-top jar.

Wash and trim off ends of
   3 to 4 zucchini
Cut zucchini crosswise into ¼-in. slices.

Heat in skillet
   3 tablespoons olive oil
Add zucchini and cook slowly until browned. Drain on absorbent paper. Cool and place in jar.

Meanwhile, combine
> **2 tablespoons olive oil**
> **2 cloves garlic, quartered**
> **½ teaspoon oregano**
> **¼ teaspoon salt**
> **1 bay leaf**

Pour mixture over zucchini and cover with
> **Wine vinegar**

Screw cap onto jar and store jar in refrigerator at least 24 hrs. Serve cold.

COCKTAILS

CHOPPED CHICKEN LIVERS
(Csirke Máj)

Set out a heavy 10-in. skillet and a wooden bowl or cutting board.

Prepare and set aside
> **2 Hard-Cooked Eggs (page 133)**

Meanwhile, rinse with cold water and drain on absorbent paper
> **1 lb. chicken livers**

Melt in the skillet over low heat
> **2 tablespoons chicken fat or butter**

Add livers; turning occasionally, cook 5 to 10 min., or until lightly browned. Remove from heat and set aside until livers are cool.

Remove livers with slotted spoon to bowl or cutting board; reserve drippings. Finely chop chicken livers, eggs and
> **1 small onion**
> **3 or 4 sprigs parsley**

Put ingredients into a bowl, mix thoroughly and set aside.

Combine the reserved drippings and
> **¼ cup cream**

Blend in a mixture of
> **1 teaspoon salt**
> **½ teaspoon dry mustard**
> **½ teaspoon paprika**
> **¼ teaspoon nutmeg or marjoram**
> **⅛ teaspoon freshly ground pepper**

Combine with liver mixture, mixing thoroughly. Chill in refrigerator for about 4 hrs. to allow flavors to blend.

Garnish servings with **sprigs of parsley.** (Allow about ¼ cup of Chopped Chicken Livers per serving.) Serve with crisp dry **toast.**

10 to 12 servings

FRUIT CUP COMBINATIONS

Try these combinations: **Dark sweet cherries** and **pineapple chunks** in **pineapple** and **lime juice**; **pineapple chunks, sweetened chopped cranberries** and **apple cubes** in **orange juice**; **prunes** in **orange juice** or with **orange sections**; **grapefruit sections** and **strawberries** or **maraschino cherries** in **citrus juice**; **watermelon, cantaloupe** or **honeydew melon cubes** or **balls** in **pineapple juice**; **apricots** and **grapefruit sections** and **plums** in **citrus juice**; **crushed strawberries** or **raspberries** and **diced pears**; **blueberries** and **sliced peaches** sprinkled with **confectioners' sugar.**

The possible combinations are endless and provide a means of using fruits left over from the making of pies, cakes, other desserts and fruit salads or cocktails. For extra special touch, add **chopped dates** and/or **diced marshmallows; maple syrup;** and **coconut** for a Fruit Ambrosia. A dash of **cinnamon** and **nutmeg** and some **brown sugar** will make a wonderful spicy fruit cup.

BROILED GRAPEFRUIT

> ▲ *Base Recipe*

Wash and cut into halves
> **1 grapefruit**

With a grapefruit knife or a sharp paring knife, loosen each section by cutting down and along either side of dividing membranes and around outer skin. Do not remove fibrous center.

Sprinkle each half with
> **1 tablespoon sugar (brown, maple or**
> **granulated) or 2 tablespoons finely**
> **crushed peppermint-stick candy, or**
> **spoon over 1 tablespoon honey**
> **or maple syrup**
> **Few grains salt**

Dot each half with
> **½ teaspoon butter or margarine**

Arrange grapefruit halves on broiler rack.

Place under broiler 4 in. from heat for 8 to 10 min., or until grapefruit is heated through and very lightly browned around edges. (Overcooking may cause a bitter taste.)

The center of grapefruit half may be garnished with fresh **strawberries, cherries, berries** or **mint sprigs.** Serve at once. *2 servings*

—RUBY GRAPEFRUIT

Follow ▲ Recipe for cutting grapefruit. Omit all other ingredients. Spoon **2 to 3 tablespoons sweetened strawberry, raspberry** or **cherry juice** over each half. Omit broiling and serve garnished with about **8 maraschino cherries** or **grape halves** arranged into center resembling a cluster of grapes. Use a **mint sprig** for stem and leaves at upper end of cluster.

BAKED GRAPEFRUIT

Cut into halves and loosen the sections of
> **1 grapefruit**

Sprinkle with
> **Sugar**

Let stand 30 min.

Sprinkle again with
> **Sugar**

Let stand 30 min.

Place grapefruit halves in a pan. Sprinkle with **sugar.** Pour over each grapefruit half
> **1 tablespoon Jamaica rum**

Heat in a 400°F oven 15 to 20 min.

Add to juice in pan
> **2 tablespoons Jamaica rum**

Serve over grapefruit. *2 servings*

MELON AND PROSCIUTTO
(Antipasto di Prosciutto e Melone)

> ▲ *Base Recipe*

The contrasting flavors of ham and subtle melon combine in this colorful, simple and strictly Italian appetizer. A native of northern Italy will place ham slices between slices of melon. His southern cousin prefers his portion of melon whole, side by side on the plate with the prosciutto.

Wash, cut into halves, and remove seedy center from
> **1 cantaloupe, chilled**

Chopped Chicken Livers and Melon and Prosciutto

Cut each cantaloupe half into 4 wedges. Serve with

8 thin slices prosciutto

8 servings

—FIG AND PROSCIUTTO
(Antipasto di Prosciutto e Fichi)

Follow ▲ Recipe. For cantaloupe, substitute **16 skinned fresh figs or canned figs,** drained and chilled. Cut figs lengthwise.

FRUIT COCKTAIL WITH AVOCADO TOPPING

Drain, reserving syrup
1 can (30 oz.) fruit cocktail
Combine in saucepan ¾ cup reserved syrup and

½ cup sugar
1 teaspoon grated lime peel
3 tablespoons lime juice
Bring to boiling; reduce heat and simmer 5 min. Cool and mix with fruit cocktail. Chill.

Cut in half and remove pit and peel from
1 medium avocado
Mash avocado and blend with
½ cup dairy sour cream
¼ teaspoon salt
Spoon fruit cocktail and syrup into sherbet glasses; top with avocado mixture.

About 6 servings

CITRUS MINT CUP

▲ *Base Recipe*

With a sharp knife, remove peel and white membrane from
4 large oranges or 2 grapefruit
Remove sections by cutting on either side of dividing membranes; remove section by section, over bowl, to save the juice. Carefully mix with fruit sections and juice in bowl

3 tablespoons confectioners' sugar
1 tablespoon lemon or lime juice
Short strips of fruit peel
Crushed fresh mint leaves
Chill 1 hr. or longer in refrigerator.

Serve garnished with sprigs of **fresh mint leaves** and slices of **fresh strawberry.**

4 to 6 servings

—CITRUS BOWL

Follow ▲ Recipe. Omit crushing mint leaves and set them aside. Arrange fruit sections in a pile in shallow serving dish. Tuck mint leaves between fruit sections around edge at base. Slice **2 strawberries** and overlap slices at top of fruit sections to form a petal arrangement. Omit mint sprigs.

FRESH FRUIT CUP

Using a fork, gently but thoroughly mix
2 cups (about 3 medium) rinsed, peeled and diced tangerines
1 cup (about 1 medium) peeled and diced banana
½ cup grapes, rinsed
1 large pear, rinsed, pared, cored and diced

Cover tightly and chill in refrigerator.

4 servings

HERRING BITS IN SOUR CREAM

▲ *Base Recipe*

Drain
1 jar (16 oz.) herring fillets
Mix and pour over herring
1 cup dairy sour cream
3 tablespoons (about 1 lemon) lemon juice
1 large onion, thinly sliced
1 tablespoon peppercorns
1 teaspoon salt
¼ teaspoon monosodium glutamate
Stir carefully with a fork to evenly coat all pieces. Let stand in refrigerator at least 2 hrs. before serving.

Serve garnished with **lemon slices** and **paprika.**

About 3 cups

—HERRING AND APPLES IN SOUR CREAM

Follow ▲ Recipe. Whip chilled sour cream before blending in remaining ingredients. Avoid overwhipping. Omit peppercorns. Wash, quarter, core and dice ½ **lb. (about 1½) apples.** Stir into herring mixture before chilling.

PICKLED HERRING
(Inlagd Sill)

The herring of Scandinavia are truly the harvest of the sea. As the season for them approaches, fishermen gather on the shores ready for action. When the clouds of gulls which announce the run are sighted, men and boats take to the sea for the hard toil of gathering one of the most important "crops" of Scandinavia.

Pour into a large bowl
3 qts. cold water

Put into the water
2 salt herring, cleaned and cut into fillets
(See Herring Salad, page 399, *To Prepare Herring.*) Set aside to soak 3 hrs.

Clean and thinly slice
1 large onion
Separate onion slices into rings.

Mix
1 cup cider vinegar
1 cup water
1 tablespoon peppercorns
1 bay leaf
Drain herring and cut into 2-in. square pieces. Put a layer of herring into a shallow bowl and top with some of the onion rings. Repeat layers of herring and onion. Pour over the vinegar-water mixture. Chill thoroughly in refrigerator several hours or overnight to blend flavors.

When ready to serve, drain off liquid. Toss herring and onion lightly to mix and put into a serving bowl. Garnish with **sprigs of parsley.**

10 to 12 servings

LOMI SALMON

Set out
1 lb. smoked salmon
Soak salmon in cold water about 3 hrs. Change water at least once. Drain. Remove skin and small bones. Shred the salmon and combine with

3 large ripe tomatoes, peeled and sliced
Mash with a fork. Stir in
¼ cup ice water
12 green onions with tops, finely chopped
Salt to taste
Chill thoroughly. Serve in individual bowls.

6 to 8 servings

Note: There are other versions of this fish preparation, some of them using raw salmon instead of smoked.

Clams Casino

MARINATED FISH COCKTAIL
(Seviche)

Remove skin from
> **1 lb. fresh firm-fleshed boneless white fish**

Cut fish into pieces and put into a deep bowl.

Combine
> **¾ cup lemon juice**
> **1 teaspoon salt**

Pour over fish. Cover and refrigerate 1 to 2 hrs., tossing fish gently several times.

Add to fish and mix thoroughly
> **3 canned green chiles, seeded and chopped**
> **2 medium ripe tomatoes, peeled and chopped**
> **2 small onions, thinly sliced**
> **2 teaspoons coriander**
> **⅓ cup olive oil**
> **2 tablespoons vinegar**

Chill. Serve in shells or cocktail glasses. If desired, garnish with **avocado slices**.

About 6 servings

CLAMS CASINO

Set out a 15x10x1-in. pan and fill ¼-in. deep with **coarse salt.**

Open (see Oysters on the Half Shell, below)
> **2 doz. clams**

Remove clams from the half shell and drain juice from shells.

Blend thoroughly
> **¼ cup butter**
> **1 teaspoon anchovy paste**

Spoon a small amount of the mixture into each shell. Cover with the clams. Sprinkle clams with
> **Lemon juice**

Spoon over the clams a mixture of
> **¼ cup minced green pepper**
> **¼ cup finely chopped onion**
> **2 teaspoons finely chopped pimiento**

Season with
> **Salt**
> **Pepper**

Cut into small pieces
> **3 slices bacon**

Top each clam with a few pieces of bacon. Place shells in the pan, pushing them down into the salt to keep shells from tipping.

Bake at 450°F 15 to 20 min., or until bacon is thoroughly cooked. *4 to 6 servings*

OYSTERS ON THE HALF SHELL

To Open Oysters—Wash well in cold water
> **2 doz. shell oysters**

Place flat side of shell up and carefully open by inserting knife between edges of shell opposite hinges. (If necessary, break off the thin edges of the shell before inserting tip of knife.) Cut the muscle from the top shell and remove shell. Cut the lower part of the same muscle from the deep half of the shell, leaving the oysters in the shell. Discard the top shells.

To Serve—Arrange oysters-in-the-shell on individual plates. Garnish with
> **Sprigs of parsley**

Serve with
> **Cocktail Sauce for Seafood (page 37)**
> **Lemon wedges**

4 servings

OYSTERS ROCKEFELLER I

▲ *Base Recipe*

Legends are many and recipes numerous for Oysters Rockefeller, a specialty of a famous New Orleans restaurant. These two are typical.

Set out a shallow baking dish and fill ¼ in. deep with rock salt.

Prepare
> **2 cups Medium White Sauce (page 304)**

Remove thickened sauce from heat and vigorously stir about 3 tablespoons hot sauce into
> **1 egg, slightly beaten**

Immediately return to mixture in saucepan and cook over low heat 1 to 2 min., stirring constantly. Set sauce aside and keep it warm.

Thaw partially and cook (page 313) in a heavy saucepan
> **2 pkgs. (10 oz. each) frozen chopped spinach**

Meanwhile, place flat side of shell up and carefully open (by inserting the tip of an oyster knife between edges of shell opposite hinges)
> **2 doz. shell oysters**

Loosen the oysters from the top shell and place on the deep half of the shell. Arrange shells in the prepared baking dish. Discard the top shells. (If shell oysters are not available, use 1 pt. oysters and clam shells, which can be purchased.) Sprinkle over oysters, about ¼ teaspoon on each
> **2 tablespoons sherry**

Set baking dish aside.

Heat in a heavy skillet over low heat
> **2 tablespoons butter or margarine**

Add and cook over medium heat until onion is tender
> **1 tablespoon finely chopped onion**

Meanwhile, thoroughly drain the cooked spinach. Blend spinach with 2 tablespoons of the sauce and
> **1 tablespoon minced parsley**
> **½ teaspoon Worcestershire sauce**
> **6 drops Tabasco**

and a mixture of
> **¼ teaspoon salt**
> **¼ teaspoon monosodium glutamate**
> **Few grains nutmeg**
> **Few grains pepper**

Mix with onion in skillet and heat mixture 2 to 3 min. Spoon the spinach mixture over the oysters; then spoon remaining sauce over spinach mixture. Sprinkle over sauce
> **Grated Parmesan cheese**

Oysters Rockefeller II

Bake at 375°F 15 to 20 min., or until lightly browned.

Serve immediately. *4 to 6 servings*

—OYSTERS ROCKEFELLER II

Follow ▲ Recipe. Omit Medium White Sauce and egg. Blend **2 tablespoons cream** with the cooked spinach. Top spinach mixture with **¾ cup buttered fine dry bread crumbs**, then sprinkle with **cheese**.

SHRIMP APPETIZERS

Prepare
> **1 lb. fresh shrimp with shells (see Cooked Shrimp, page 294)**

Prepare one of the following
> **Horseradish Sauce (page 36)**
> **East Indian Sauce (page 37)**
> **Mustard Shrimp Sauce (page 37)**

Pour over shrimp in a shallow bowl. Put into Refrigerator to marinate (page 10) 3 to 4 hrs., turning shrimp occasionally.

For each serving, spoon 4 or 5 shrimp with sauce onto
> **Crisp lettuce leaves**

Serve as appetizer course at dinner.

(Shrimp and sauce can be chilled separately in refrigerator. Sauce should then be served as a dunking sauce for shrimp. Serve as an hors d'oeuvre.) *4 to 6 servings*

Oysters on the Half Shell

Shrimp Cocktail and Triple Seafood Cocktail

SHRIMP COCKTAIL

▲ *Base Recipe*

Wash in cold water
1½ lbs. fresh shrimp with shells
Drop shrimp into a boiling mixture of
3 cups water
3 tablespoons lemon juice
1 tablespoon salt
1 bay leaf
Cover tightly. Simmer 5 min., or until shrimp are pink and tender. Drain shrimp and cover with cold water to chill. Drain shrimp again. Remove tiny legs. Peel shells from the shrimp. Cut a slit along back (outer curved surface) of shrimp to expose the black vein. With knife point, remove vein in one piece. Rinse the shrimp quickly under running cold water. Drain them on absorbent paper. Store in refrigerator until ready to use.

Serve shrimp on **lettuce** or **curly endive** with **Peppy Cocktail Sauce** (page 37).

About 3 cups shrimp

—HOT SHRIMP APPETIZER

Follow ▲ Recipe. Arrange shrimp on broiler rack. Brush with a mixture of **½ cup butter or margarine**, melted, and **3 tablespoons lemon juice**. Place under broiler about 2 in. from heat for 3 to 5 min., or until shrimp are thoroughly heated. Insert wooden picks. Serve immediately with **Peppy Cocktail Sauce.**

TRIPLE SEAFOOD COCKTAIL

A cocktail for those who know that the only thing better than seafood is more seafood.

Chill 8 cocktail glasses.

Prepare
1 lb. fresh shrimp with shells (see Cooked Shrimp, page 294)
1 live lobster, about 1¼ lbs. (see "Boiled" Lobster, page 290)

Meanwhile, drain and remove any bony tissue from and put into a bowl
2 cups (about 8 oz.) fresh lump crab meat
Reserve 8 large shrimp for garnish and coarsely chop the remaining shrimp and the lobster. Put into the bowl with the crab meat. Chill the seafood thoroughly in refrigerator.

When ready to serve, arrange in each cocktail glass a small leaf of **lettuce.**

Lightly pile seafood mixture into each glass. Perch one of the reserved whole shrimp on rim of each glass. Garnish each serving with
Sprigs of parsley
Serve with
Lemon wedges
Cocktail Sauce for Seafood (page 37)

8 servings

SHRIMP REMOULADE

For a Sunday night supper in hot weather—or any time of the year if you are a real shrimp fan—serve chilled shrimp with a bowl of remoulade sauce, and let guests help themselves. Appetizer and appetite-satisfier in one, this is a fine main dish to team with a long loaf of French bread, coffee steaming hot or tinkling with ice, and a frosty dessert.

For Shrimp—Cook
2½ lbs. fresh shrimp with shells (see Cooked Shrimp, page 294)
After removing shells, chill shrimp thoroughly in the refrigerator.

For Sauce—Prepare
Remoulade Cocktail Sauce (page 37)

To Serve—Heap cracked ice into a large serving bowl. Arrange chilled shrimp over the ice.

Accompany with a bowl of the chilled Remoulade Cocktail Sauce.

4 or 5 servings

SHRIMP AND AVOCADO COCKTAIL

Cook
1½ lbs. fresh shrimp with shells (see Cooked Shrimp, page 294)
Chill in refrigerator until ready to serve.

Prepare and chill in refrigerator
Peppy Cocktail Sauce (page 37)

Just before serving, rinse, peel, cut into halves and remove and discard pit from
1 small avocado
Dice and mix with the shrimp.

Arrange in 6 chilled sherbet glasses
Lettuce or curly endive
Arrange the shrimp and avocado in the glasses. Top each serving with some of the Peppy Cocktail Sauce. Serve with
Lemon wedges

6 servings

SNAILS BURGUNDY
(Escargots à la Bourguignonne)

Set out a large shallow baking dish and fill ¼-in. deep with **coarse salt.**

For Snail Butter—Cream together until thoroughly blended
½ cup butter, softened
1 tablespoon minced parsley
1 teaspoon minced onion
1 clove garlic, minced
½ teaspoon white wine
¼ teaspoon Worcestershire sauce
Chill in refrigerator until ready to use.

For Snails—Drain, reserving the liquid
1 can (2-oz.) snails (about 24)
Spoon ⅛ teaspoon into each snail shell
Reserved liquid
Spoon ¼ teaspoon of the Snail Butter into each shell. Place one snail in each shell. Fill with the remaining Snail Butter. Place shells, open side up, in the baking dish, pushing shells down into the salt to keep standing upright.

Bake at 375°F 5 to 7 min., or until snails are thoroughly heated.

Serve immediately.

2 doz. snails

Note: Snails usually come packed with shells.

COCKTAIL SAUCES

HORSERADISH SAUCE

Clean and chop
1 medium onion (about ½ cup, chopped)
2 stalks celery
Set aside.

Blend in order
  ¼ cup prepared French-style mustard
  2 teaspoons prepared horseradish
  ¼ cup tarragon vinegar
and a mixture of
  1 tablespoon paprika
  2 teaspoons salt
Mix in chopped vegetables with
  2 tablespoons finely chopped parsley
Add gradually, beating well after each addition
  ½ cup salad oil
Store, covered, in refrigerator until thoroughly chilled. *About 1 cup sauce*

COCKTAIL SAUCE FOR SEAFOOD

Combine in a bowl and blend thoroughly
  ½ cup ketchup
  1 tablespoon prepared horseradish
  1 tablespoon lemon juice
  1½ teaspoons brown sugar
  ½ teaspoon onion juice
  ½ teaspoon Worcestershire sauce
  ¼ teaspoon salt
  ⅛ teaspoon monosodium glutamate
  3 drops Tabasco
Chill before serving. *About ¾ cup sauce*

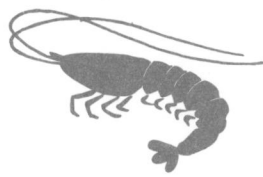

PEPPY COCKTAIL SAUCE

Combine and mix
  1 cup ketchup
  1 tablespoon sugar
  1 tablespoon prepared horseradish
  1 tablespoon lemon juice
  1 teaspoon Worcestershire sauce
  1 teaspoon onion juice
  ½ teaspoon salt
  ¼ teaspoon monosodium glutamate
  Few drops Tabasco
About 1¼ cups sauce

MUSTARD SHRIMP SAUCE

Prepare
  2 Hard-Cooked Eggs (page 133)
Finely chop egg whites and set aside. Reserve egg yolks.

Finely chop and set aside
  1 stalk celery
  1 small scallion or green onion

Mash reserved egg yolks with a fork in a small bowl. Blend in, in order
  ¼ cup prepared mustard
  ½ cup tarragon vinegar
and a mixture of
  1 tablespoon paprika
  1 teaspoon salt
  ¼ teaspoon monosodium glutamate
  ⅛ teaspoon cayenne pepper

Add gradually, beating well after each addition
  1 cup olive oil
Thoroughly mix in chopped egg whites, chopped vegetables and
  1 clove garlic, finely minced
Store, covered, in refrigerator until thoroughly chilled. *About 2 cups sauce*

Note: The electric blender may be used for mixing the Mustard Shrimp Sauce. Pour the olive oil and vinegar into the blender container; add egg yolks, prepared mustard and seasonings. Cover container, turn on motor and blend until well mixed. Add egg whites, vegetables, cut in pieces, and garlic clove. Blend until vegetables are finely chopped.

EAST INDIAN SAUCE

Blend
  2 cups mayonnaise
  2 tablespoons minced scallion or green onion
  1 tablespoon minced green pepper
  1 tablespoon minced parsley
  1 tablespoon chopped capers
  4 anchovy fillets, drained and finely chopped
  1 tablespoon curry powder
  ⅛ teaspoon cayenne pepper
Mix in
  1 can (6 oz.) tomato paste
Put into a container, cover and chill in refrigerator for several hours to allow flavors to blend.

Force the chilled mixture through a fine sieve into a bowl. Blend in
  2 egg yolks, slightly beaten
Chill thoroughly and serve over shrimp.
About 2½ cups sauce

REMOULADE COCKTAIL SAUCE

Blend
  2 cups mayonnaise
  1 tablespoon prepared mustard
  1 tablespoon finely chopped sweet pickle
  1 tablespoon chopped capers
  1 tablespoon minced parsley
  1 teaspoon finely crushed chervil
  1 teaspoon tarragon leaves, finely crushed
  ½ teaspoon anchovy paste
  1 or 2 drops Tabasco
Store, covered, in refrigerator until thoroughly chilled. *About 2 cups sauce*

APPETIZER BEVERAGES

MINTED APPLE JUICE

Mix **2 cups apple juice, 1 cup pineapple juice** and **2 teaspoons lemon juice**. Add a

sprig of **fresh mint leaves,** bruised slightly. Chill in refrigerator. Before serving, remove mint leaves and garnish serving glasses with **sprigs of fresh mint.**

FOUR-FRUIT REFRESHER

Combine
  2 cups apple juice
  1 cup cranberry juice cocktail
  1 cup orange juice
  2 tablespoons lemon juice
  1 teaspoon vanilla extract
Add and stir until completely dissolved
  2 tablespoons sugar
Chill thoroughly.

When ready to serve, add and stir to blend
  1 cup chilled gingerale
Pour into small glasses. Top each serving with a **small scoop of lemon or pineapple sherbet.**
About 5 cups beverage

CRANBERRY SPRITZER

In a tall pitcher combine equal parts of
  Chilled cranberry juice cocktail
  Chilled sparkling white grape juice
Mix lightly. If desired, add
  Few drops red food coloring
Serve at once.

CRANBERRY COCKTAIL

Rinse, pare (be sure to remove white membrane) and cut into pieces
  2 large juice oranges
Cut oranges over and into a bowl to save juice. Set aside.

Put into an electric blender container
  2 cups (16-oz. can) cranberry sauce
  ¼ cup lemon juice
Cover and turn on motor.
Gradually add orange pieces and
  4 ice cubes, one at a time
Blend until mixed.

Serve immediately.
About 3½ cups or seven 4-oz. servings

FRUIT JUICE COCKTAIL

Blend **cranberry juice cocktail** or **apricot, peach or pear nectar** with equal parts **lemon or lime carbonated beverage.** Pour over **crushed ice** in juice glasses. Garnish with **orange, lemon or lime slices,** or **fruit kabobs.**

FRUIT SHRUB

Fill 4- to 6-oz. glasses with icy cold **fruit juice** (or a mixture of juices). If desired, spark with a dash of **carbonated water.** Float a small scoopful of **sherbet** (complementary or contrasting in flavor) on each serving.

—ORANGE SHRUB

Use **orange juice** with **orange sherbet.**

—PINEAPPLE SHRUB

Use **unsweetened pineapple juice** with **lime sherbet.**

—APRICOT SHRUB

Use **apricot nectar** with **lemon or pineapple sherbet.**

BEEF FIZZ

Combine in a tall pitcher
> **2 cans (10½-oz. each) condensed beef broth**
> **1 cup chilled ginger ale**
> **2 tablespoons lemon juice**

Pour over ice in glasses.   *6 to 8 servings*

ORANGE TOMATO COCKTAIL

Put into an electric blender container
> **1½ cups chilled tomato juice**
> **1 cup chilled orange juice**
> **1 tablespoon lemon juice**
> **½ teaspoon salt**
> **1 slice onion**

Cover and blend about 30 sec., or until thoroughly mixed.

Add, one at a time
> **4 ice cubes**

Blend only until mixed.
About 3 cups or six 4-oz. servnigs

TANGY COCKTAIL

Blend
> **1 can (10½ to 11 oz.) condensed beef broth**
> **1 can (12 oz.) cocktail vegetable juice**

Mix in
> **1 teaspoon grated onion**
> **1 teaspoon Worcestershire sauce**
> **2 drops Tabasco**

Chill thoroughly. Garnish with **lemon wedges.**

If desired, mixture may be heated thoroughly and served hot.   *About 6 servings*

CITRUS VEGETABLE COCKTAIL

Put into an electric blender container
> **2 cups water**
> **1 cup diced carrots**

Blend until carrots are liquefied. Add
> **1 stalk celery, cut in pieces**
> **½ cup diced cucumber**
> **1 cup orange juice**
> **2 tablespoons lime juice**
> **2 tablespoons sugar**
> **2 thin slices lemon with peel**
> **Salt to taste**

Blend thoroughly. Chill.   *About 8 servings*

TOMATO COCKTAIL

Mix together
> **3 cups chilled tomato juice**
> **1½ tablespoons lemon or lime juice**
> **2 teaspoons sugar**
> **¼ teaspoon salt**
> **9 drops Tabasco**

Pour into chilled glasses. Garnish with **lemon or lime slices.**   *6 servings*

TOMATO CUKE COCKTAIL

Wash, cut into 1½-in. slices and set aside
> **½ medium cucumber**

Put into an electric blender container
> **2 cups tomato juice**
> **2 tablespoons lemon juice**
> **1 slice onion**
> **1 or 2 drops Tabasco**
> **Dash salt**

Cover and turn on motor. Add cucumber by pieces.

Add, one at a time
> **4 ice cubes**

Blend only until mixed.
About 2½ cups or five 4-oz. servings

Note: From the remaining half of the cucumber, cut sticks. These make unique stirrers for your appetizer drink.

TANGY TOMATO JUICE

Put into an electric blender container
> **2 cups tomato juice**
> **¼ teaspoon salt**
> **1 slice onion**
> **Few rinsed celery leaves**
> **Few drops Tabasco**
> **Few grains pepper**

Cover and blend about 30 sec., or until thoroughly blended.

Add, one at a time
> **4 ice cubes**

Blend only until mixed.
About 3 cups or six 4-oz. servings

SAUERKRAUT TOMATO COCKTAIL

Put into an electric blender container, in order
> **2 cups tomato juice**
> **¾ cup firmly packed sauerkraut**
> **¼ teaspoon prepared horseradish**
> **Dash salt**

Cover and blend about 45 sec., or until thoroughly blended.

Add, one at a time
> **6 ice cubes**

Blend until mixed. Garnish with a **sprig of parsley** or a **twist of lemon peel.**
About 3 cups or six 4-oz. servings

TOMATO LIME COCKTAIL ON THE ROCKS

Mix in a pitcher
> **3½ cups tomato juice**
> **2 tablespoons lime juice**
> **1 teaspoon Worcestershire sauce**
> **¼ teaspoon Angostura bitters**
> **8 drops Tabasco**
> **4 teaspoons sugar**
> **½ teaspoon seasoned salt**

Chill thoroughly.

Serve over **ice cubes** in 6-oz. glasses. Garnish each serving with a **thin slice of lime.**
About 1 qt. cocktail

HERB-BUTTERED HOT TOMATO JUICE

Combine in a saucepan
> **1½ qts. tomato juice**
> **1 teaspoon Worcestershire sauce**
> **½ teaspoon salt**
> **¼ teaspoon marjoram, crushed**
> **¼ teaspoon oregano, crushed**
> **4 whole cloves**
> **¼ to ⅓ cup butter or margarine**

Place over low heat until butter is melted, stirring to blend; *do not boil.* Remove cloves and serve at once.   *About 6 cups*

Soups

Warm and delicious or cooling and refreshing, soups play an important role in family meals all over the world. Soup varieties are infinite and many countries have specialties for which they are known. In the United States, everything from the appetite-stimulating clear soups and bouillons to the thick, hearty appetite-satisfying varieties are considered enhancing additions to family meals. Unlike old-fashioned soups which were cooked for hours (sometimes all day long) on top of the kitchen "stove," modern soups usually require much shorter cooking times and are easy to prepare.

SOUP GARNISHES

CROUTONS

Heat over low heat in a large heavy skillet
   2 or 3 tablespoons butter
Meanwhile, if desired, trim crusts from
   2 slices toasted bread
Cut bread into ¼- to ½-in. cubes. Put into skillet and turn and toss cubes until all sides are coated; remove from heat. If desired, sprinkle with **grated Parmesan cheese.** Spoon Croutons onto soup just before serving.

About 1¼ cups Croutons

CHEESE NUGGETS

Dainty but replete with nutrition, these tangy nuggets can carry clear broths, vegetable and cream soups along the way to becoming main-dish luncheon attractions.

Prepare
   ⅓ cup (1 slice) fine dry bread crumbs
   ¼ cup finely shredded sharp cheese
Set aside.

Beat together slightly in a small bowl
   1 egg
   ¼ teaspoon salt
   ¼ teaspoon dry mustard
   ⅛ teaspoon paprika
Mix in the bread crumbs and shredded cheese. Blend until mixture is the consistency of a thick paste.

Drop by teaspoonfuls into simmering soup. Cook 2 or 3 min. Serve immediately.

About 24 nuggets

CHEESE "CROUTONS"

Float "croutons" on soups, toss with a green salad or use as nibblers—they're delicious!

Melt over low heat in a medium-size skillet
   3 tablespoons butter or margarine
Add
   1½ cups bite-size shredded wheat biscuits
Heat for 5 min., constantly turning biscuits with a spoon. Remove from heat. Add, tossing gently to coat biscuits
   ½ cup (2 oz.) grated Parmesan cheese

Serve warm or cool. Store in tightly covered jar in refrigerator.   *1½ cups "croutons"*

VIENNA "PEAS"
   (Wiener Erbsen)

Set out a deep saucepan or automatic deep fryer (page 11) and heat **fat** to 375°F.

Sift together into a bowl
   ¾ cup sifted all-purpose flour
   ¼ teaspoon salt
Make a well in center and set aside.

Beat together
   1 egg
   2 tablespoons milk

Add all at one time to the dry ingredients. Beat until well blended and smooth.

Drop batter by ¼ teaspoonfuls into the hot fat. Deep-fry only as many balls at one time as will float uncrowded one layer deep. Fry 1 to 2 min., or until balls are golden brown. Lift from fat with slotted spoon, drain over fat a few seconds and remove to absorbent paper.

Float some of the "peas" in each plate of clear soup.   *About 2 cups "peas"*

CUSTARD CUBES

A delicately seasoned broth—clear or flecked with vegetables julienne—is the happiest setting for custard cubes. Introduced to consommé, this garnish confers on it the title Royale and transforms it into a truly aristocratic soup.

Heat water to boiling for baking custard.

Scald (page 10)
   ⅓ cup milk

Beat together slightly
   1 egg
   ¼ teaspoon sugar
   ⅛ teaspoon salt
   ⅛ teaspoon paprika
   Few grains pepper
Pour scalded milk slowly into the egg mixture, beating constantly. Strain the custard into a shallow baking pan (about 5-in. square). Set the pan into a deep pan and place on oven rack. Pour boiling water into deep pan to level of mixture in baking pan.

Bake at 325°F about 30 min., or until a metal knife inserted halfway between center and edge of pan comes out clean. Cool.

Cut custard into ½-in. cubes or fancy shapes and slip into hot soup just before serving.

4 or 5 servings

DUMPLINGS FOR SOUP
   (Boller)

Bring to a rolling boil
   1 cup water
   ¼ cup butter
   ¼ teaspoon salt
Add, all at one time
   1 cup sifted all-purpose flour
Beat vigorously with a wooden spoon until mixture leaves sides of pan and forms a smooth ball. Remove from heat. Quickly beat in, one at a time, beating until smooth after each addition
   2 eggs
Continue beating until smooth and thick.

Heat to boiling in a large saucepan
   2 qts. water
   2 teaspoons salt
Drop dumpling dough by rounded teaspoonfuls into water. (Dough will drop more readily from a spoon moistened in the boiling water.) Cook only as many dumplings at one time as will

float, uncrowded, one layer deep. Cook 3 to 5 min., or until dumplings rise to surface of water. Remove dumplings with a slotted spoon. Put several dumplings in each soup plate and spoon or ladle soup over them.

About 3 doz. dumplings

LIVER DUMPLINGS

▲ *Base Recipe*

Set out a skillet with a tight-fitting cover.

Prepare in a deep saucepan and set aside
> **1 qt. quick meat broth (four times recipe, page 10)**

Combine and set aside
> **1 cup fine cracker crumbs**
> **¾ cup milk**

Cut away tubes and outer membrane, if necessary, from
> **½ lb. liver (beef, lamb, veal or calf's) sliced ¼ to ½ in. thick**

Put into skillet with
> **1 cup hot water**

Cover skillet and simmer about 5 min. Drain. Cool liver slightly and put through medium blade of food chopper with
> **1 small onion, quartered**

Using a fork, blend liver with a mixture of
> **½ cup sifted all-purpose flour**
> **1 teaspoon chopped parsley**
> **½ teaspoon salt**
> **¼ teaspoon marjoram**
> **⅛ teaspoon pepper**

Set aside.

Mix cracker mixture with
> **1 egg, well beaten**

Make a well in meat mixture; add egg mixture all at one time. Mix with a fork until evenly blended.

Bring meat broth to boiling. Drop dumplings by rounded teaspoonfuls into broth. (Dumplings drop more readily from a moist spoon.) Drop only enough to lie uncrowded one layer deep. Cover and cook 3 to 5 min., or until dumplings rise to surface of broth. Remove dumplings with slotted spoon. Place on a baking sheet and set in a 250°F oven while cooking remaining dumplings.

Serve several in meat broth or any desired soup.

About 2 doz. dumplings

—BURGER DUMPLINGS

Follow ▲ Recipe. Substitute **1 cup any ground cooked meat** for liver.

MEAT PUFF SURPRISES

Set out a large heavy skillet.

Prepare and set aside
> **⅓ cup fine dry bread crumbs**

Grind (page 10) enough cooked beef to yield
> **1 cup ground cooked beef**

Combine with beef and mix lightly
> **⅓ cup (about 1½ oz.) grated Parmesan cheese**
> **1 teaspoon finely chopped parsley**
> **1 teaspoon chopped chives**
> **2 egg yolks, well beaten**

and a mixture of
> **¼ teaspoon salt**
> **⅛ teaspoon monosodium glutamate**

Beat until rounded peaks are formed
> **2 egg whites**

Gently fold into meat mixture. Shape into balls about ¾ in. in diameter. Coat with the bread crumbs.

Heat in the skillet
> **3 tablespoons fat**

Add meat balls to the skillet and brown them on all sides, turning occasionally. Remove the meat balls from skillet to absorbent paper to drain thoroughly.

Add to
> **Quick meat broth (page 10)**

Or add to any desired hot soup just before serving.

About 1½ doz. meat puffs

Note: For best flavor, meat puffs should be cooked until very brown.

GARNISH MEAT BALLS

▲ *Base Recipe*

Set out a large skillet.

Combine in a small bowl and set aside
> **⅓ cup (about 1 rusk) rusk crumbs**
> **¼ cup water**

Mix lightly in a bowl
> **¼ lb. ground beef**
> **¼ lb. ground pork**
> **1 egg, well beaten**
> **1 teaspoon lemon juice**
> **2 teaspoons chopped onion**

and a mixture of
> **½ teaspoon salt**
> **¼ teaspoon thyme**

Blend in rusk mixture. Shape into balls about ¾ in. in diameter.

Heat in the skillet over medium heat
> **1 tablespoon fat**

Add meat balls and brown on all sides, turning occasionally.

Meanwhile, bring to boiling
> **1½ qts. quick meat broth (six times recipe, page 10)**

Remove meat balls from skillet to absorbent paper and drain. Add to meat broth. Cover and simmer about 20 min.

Little Sausage Balls and French Toast

Serve several meat balls in each bowl of soup.

About 2 doz. meat balls

—LITTLE SAUSAGE BALLS

Follow ▲ Recipe. Lightly grease the skillet. Substitute **½ lb. bulk pork sausage** for beef and pork. Add **1 tablespoon chopped parsley** with the onion. During browning of meat balls, pour off fat as it collects. Serve piping hot with **French toast.**

MEAT BALLS

Add a few of these miniature meat balls to individual servings of clear broth or vegetable soup.

Set out a large heavy skillet with a tight-fitting cover.

Prepare and set aside
> **⅓ cup (1 slice) fine dry bread crumbs**

Blend
> **1 egg, slightly beaten**
> **¼ cup cream**
> **1 teaspoon lemon juice**
> **1 slice onion, minced**
> **½ teaspoon salt**
> **¼ teaspoon thyme**

Add the bread crumbs and
> **½ lb. ground beef**

Mix lightly. Shape into balls about ¾ in. in diameter.

Heat in the skillet
> **1 tablespoon butter**

Add meat balls and brown over medium heat. Shake pan frequently to secure an even browning and to keep balls round. Reduce heat, cover skillet, and continue to cook about 10 min., shaking pan occasionally.

Place meat balls in individual soup bowls and pour the soup or broth over them.

About 2 doz. Meat Balls

MAYONNAISE GARNISH FOR SOUP

Put into a small bowl
> **⅓ cup Blender Mayonnaise (page 413)**
> **½ teaspoon minced parsley**
> **¼ teaspoon lemon juice or vinegar**

Beat with an electric beater.

Drop by heaping tablespoonfuls onto bowls of hot or cold soup.   *4 or 5 servings*

To vary—Give Mayonnaise Garnish for Soup extra special flavor by adding one of the following: **½ teaspoon prepared horseradish**, **½ to 1 teaspoon curry powder**, **3 or 4 drops Tabasco**, **¼ teaspoon garlic salt** or **grated lemon peel**.

HOT SOUPS

POT-ON-THE-FIRE
(Pot-au-Feu)

▲ *Base Recipe*

Bouillon is a French favorite. It is served piping hot, usually as a separate course. Strained and cooled, it may be stored to use as Brown Stock in soups or sauces. Hence, this Pot-on-the-Fire is often called the Stock Pot.

Put into a marmite or large soup kettle
1 soup bone, cracked
3 lbs. lean beef (chuck or plate), cut in 1-in. pieces

Add
3 qts. cold water
1½ tablespoons salt
Cover and bring slowly to boiling. Skim. Cover and simmer about 4 hrs. Skim as necessary.

Then add
5 carrots, cut in large pieces
2 turnips, cut in large pieces
4 leeks (white part only), sliced
1 large onion, sliced
Herb bouquet (page 9)

Insert
2 whole cloves
in
1 medium onion
Add onion to kettle. Cover and bring to boiling. Simmer about 1½ hrs. longer. Strain through fine sieve. Allow to stand until cold, and fat hardens on surface. Remove fat. Cover bouillon and store in refrigerator for future use. Or reheat and serve with crisp slices of toast.

The meat and vegetables strained from stock may be served as desired.
                    About 2½ qts. stock

—BROWN STOCK
(Fonds Bruns)

Follow ▲ Recipe. Cut meat from soup bone and brown meat with beef in **¼ cup fat** before cooking. Add to kettle with bone and proceed as in ▲ Recipe.

—WHITE STOCK
(Fonds Blancs)

Follow ▲ Recipe, substituting **veal shank and breast** for beef. Add one half of a disjointed ready-to-cook **chicken.**

—CONSOMME

Follow recipe for White Stock. In a large kettle, mix and stir into cold stock **2 egg whites,** slightly beaten, crushed shells of the eggs and **4 teaspoons cold water.** Heat slowly to boiling, stirring constantly. Remove from heat and let stand 25 min. Strain through two thicknesses of cheesecloth.

—BOUILLON

Follow recipe for Consommé. Substitute **Brown Stock** for White Stock.

FRENCH ONION SOUP
(Soupe à l'Oignon)

The most famous and universally popular of all French soups, this one is a tradition in the artists' quarters in Montparnasse. The originator, however, was a king, Louis XV, who returned late one night to his hunting lodge and found only onions, butter and champagne on hand. So hungry and weary was he that he simply mixed them together. Voila—French onion soup!

Peel, rinse and cut into thin slices
5 medium (about 1 lb.) onions

Heat in a 3-qt. heavy saucepan over low heat
3 tablespoons butter
Add the onions. Cook slowly, stirring, until golden in color, about 10 min.

Blend in gradually
1½ qts. Bouillon (on this page)
Season with
½ teaspoon salt
⅛ teaspoon pepper
Bring to boiling. Cover saucepan and simmer about 15 min.

Meanwhile, set temperature control at Broil. Arrange on broiler rack
6 slices French Bread (page 65)
Place in broiler with tops of bread 3 in. from heat. Toast one side only. Remove and spread untoasted sides with about
1 to 2 tablespoons butter
Cut slices into halves; place on broiler rack.

Cut into fine pieces
¼ cup (1 oz.) Gruyère or Cheddar cheese
Sprinkle about 1 teaspoon cheese onto each slice. Set in broiler about 3 in. from heat. Toast until cheese is melted. Pour soup into tureen, hot soup plates or earthenware bowls. Float a toast slice on the top of each serving.

Bread may be toasted lightly, floated on top of soup, and cheese sprinkled over toast. Additional cheese may be served in a bowl.
                    6 servings

BEEF BROTH
(Marhahus Leves)

Set out a large kettle with a tight-fitting cover.

Have ready
1½ lbs. lean beef (boneless chuck or plate)
1 beef soup bone, cracked
1 veal soup bone, cracked
Put meat and soup bones into kettle with
2 qts. water
1 tablespoon salt
8 peppercorns
Bring water to boiling. Reduce heat immediately. Cover kettle and simmer 2 hrs., skimming off and discarding foam as necessary.

Then add to broth
4 medium carrots, washed and scraped or pared
3 medium (about 1 lb.) potatoes, washed and pared
1 large onion
1 medium green pepper
¼ small head (about ½ lb.) cabbage, rinsed
3 12-in. stalks celery (including leaves), cut in pieces
10 sprigs parsley
Pour into kettle
Hot water (enough to cover vegetables)
Cover kettle and simmer 2 hrs. longer, or until meat is tender when pierced with a fork. Remove meat and vegetables with slotted spoon to a serving platter. Cover platter and

French Onion Soup

keep them warm. Remove and discard soup bones. Strain the broth through fine sieve into tureen; discard peppercorns.

Cut meat into serving-size pieces and serve with the vegetables after serving the broth. If desired, serve the broth with **Liver Dumplings** (page 40) or **Noodles** (page 152).

6 to 8 servings

GRANDMA'S CHICKEN BROTH

Set out a 4-qt. kettle with a tight-fitting cover.

Clean, rinse and disjoint
1 stewing chicken, 4 to 5 lbs., ready-to-cook weight
Put chicken into kettle and cover with
2 qts. cold water
Cover and heat slowly to boiling. Remove foam. Add
2 or 3 stalks celery with leaves
2 carrots
1 medium onion
2 teaspoons salt
1 teaspoon monosodium glutamate
2 or 3 peppercorns
1 bay leaf
3 parsley sprigs
Cover and simmer 2 to 3 hrs., or until thickest pieces of chicken are tender when pierced with a fork. Remove chicken for use in salads or creamed dishes.

Strain liquid through fine sieve; set aside to cool. When cool, put into refrigerator to chill. Remove hardened layer of fat from chilled broth.

To clarify broth, stir into cold stock
1 egg white, slightly beaten
Crushed shell of the egg
1 tablespoon cold water
Heat slowly to boiling, stirring constantly. Boil gently, stirring constantly, 7 to 10 min. Remove from heat and let stand 25 min. Strain through 2 thicknesses of cheesecloth. Reheat the strained broth and serve it very hot. If desired, add to clear broth before serving
2 cups cooked rice (page 165)

About 1 qt. chicken broth

CHICKEN BROTH
(Brodo di Pollo)

Clean, disjoint, cut into pieces and rinse
4- to 5-lb. stewing chicken
Rinse with cold water
Giblets (gizzard, heart, liver)
and neck
Refrigerate the liver.

Put chicken, gizzard, heart and neck into a large kettle and add
1¼ qts. hot water
2 teaspoons salt
1 teaspoon monosodium glutamate
5 3-in. pieces celery with leaves
3 small carrots, washed and scraped
2 medium onions
1 large tomato, rinsed and quartered
Cover and bring to boiling. Uncover and remove foam. Cover tightly. Simmer 2 to 3 hrs.; during the last 15 min. of cooking time, add the liver. Chicken is done when thickest pieces are tender when pierced with a fork.

Take chicken and giblets from broth, cool slightly and remove skin. Remove meat from bones. Cut meat into pieces as directed in other recipes.

Strain broth and cool slightly. Remove fat that rises to surface. Refrigerate fat and use in other recipes. Unless using meat and broth immediately, cool, cover and place in refrigerator. If broth seems to be too condensed, add more water.

About 1 qt. broth

NEW ORLEANS BOWL

Combine in a saucepan
1 can (10½ to 11 oz.) condensed chicken gumbo
1 can (10½ to 11 oz.) condensed chicken with rice soup
2 soup cans water
Mix in
2 cups cooked shrimp, cut in small pieces
1 cup cooked cut green beans
Dash cayenne pepper
Heat to serving temperature.   *4 to 6 servings*

ROMAN EGG SOUP
(Stracciatella)

▲ *Base Recipe*

Prepare
1 qt. Chicken Broth (on this page)
Bring to boiling.

Meanwhile, beat until thick and piled softly
4 eggs
Mix together well, add to eggs and beat until thoroughly combined
1½ tablespoons semolina or flour
1½ tablespoons grated Parmesan cheese
⅛ teaspoon salt
⅛ teaspoon pepper
Slowly pour egg mixture into boiling broth, stirring constantly. Continue stirring and simmer 5 min.

Serve in bouillon cups. Top with
Chopped parsley

4 servings

—ROMAN EGG SOUP WITH SPINACH
(Stracciatella con Spinaci)

Follow ▲ Recipe. Add ½ **lb. cooked chopped fresh spinach** to broth before adding beaten egg mixture.

—ROMAN EGG SOUP WITH NOODLES
(Stracciatella con Pasta)

Follow ▲ Recipe. Add **1 cup cooked noodles** to broth before adding beaten egg mixture.

LITTLE HAT SOUP
(Cappelletti in Brodo)

Prepare and set aside
2 qts. quick chicken broth (page 10)
or Chicken Broth (on this page; add 1 qt. water)

*New Orleans Bowl and
"The Virginian" Sandwich (page 115)*

Combine

> ½ cup (about ¼ lb.) Ricotta or
>   cottage cheese
> ½ cup finely chopped cooked chicken,
> 2 tablespoons grated Parmesan
>   cheese
> 1 egg, slightly beaten
> ⅛ teaspoon salt
> Few grains nutmeg
> Few grains pepper

Set aside.

Prepare

> **Basic Noodle Dough (one-half recipe,
>   page 152)**

Roll dough about ¹⁄₁₆ in. thick. Cut into rounds with a 2½-in. round cookie cutter. Place ½ teaspoon cheese-chicken mixture in center of each round of dough. Fold each round in half, covering the mounds of filling. Dampen edges of pasta with water and press together to seal. Bring two extreme ends together. Dampen and press together to seal.

Bring broth to boiling and add pasta.

Cook about 20 to 25 min., or until pasta is tender. Test tenderness by pressing a piece against side of pan with fork or spoon. Serve with broth.   *About 30 cappelletti, 8 servings*

MULLIGATAWNY SOUP

Heat in a Dutch oven

> ¼ cup fat

Add and cook until lightly browned, stirring occasionally

> 1 cup diced uncooked chicken
> ¼ cup chopped onion
> ¼ cup chopped celery
> ¼ cup diced carrots
> 2 tart apples, quartered, cored, pared
>   and sliced

Stir in a blend of

> ¼ cup all-purpose flour
> 1 teaspoon curry powder

Add gradually, stirring constantly

> 6 cups chicken broth

Stir in

> 1 cup drained canned tomatoes, cut in
>   pieces
> ½ green pepper, finely chopped
> 1 teaspoon minced parsley
> 2 whole cloves

Mix in a blend of

> 1 teaspoon salt
> 1 teaspoon sugar
> ⅛ teaspoon pepper
> ⅛ teaspoon mace

Cook, covered, over low heat until chicken is tender.

Remove and reserve chicken. Discard cloves. Strain soup, forcing vegetables through a sieve or food mill (or purée in an electric blender). Return strained soup to Dutch oven, mix in chicken and heat to serving temperature. If desired, mix in **1 cup cooked rice** before serving.   *8 servings*

GUMBO FILE

Gumbos are the most characteristic dishes of old New Orleans. The Choctaw Indians of Louisiana first introduced to Creole markets a powder made from dried sassafras leaves called Filé. Because the Indian word for sassafras was "kombo," the Creole adopted "gumbo" to describe the slippery smoothness of their soups when filé powder was added. Since cooked okra gives the same results, many okra dishes are also called "gumbos."

Set out a 3-qt. heavy saucepot or kettle with a tight-fitting cover.

Disjoint, cut into serving-size pieces and rinse

> 1 stewing chicken, 4 to 5 lbs.,
>   ready-to-cook weight

(If chicken is frozen, thaw according to directions on package.) Refrigerate the liver. Put chicken, gizzard, heart and neck into the saucepot and add

> Hot water to cover
> 2 teaspoons salt
> 1½ teaspoons monosodium glutamate
> 1 small onion
> 3 sprigs parsley
> 2 3-in. pieces celery with leaves
> 1 bay leaf
> 2 or 3 peppercorns

Cover and bring water to boiling. Remove foam. Cover saucepot tightly and simmer 2 to 3 hrs., or until thickest part of drumstick is easily pierced with a fork. Add the liver about 15 min. before end of cooking time.

Remove chicken and giblets from broth. Strain broth and cool slightly. Remove fat that rises to surface. (Refrigerate fat for use in other food preparation.) Cool chicken slightly and remove skin. Remove meat from bones, dice chicken meat and set aside.

Drain, reserving liquor

> 1 pt. oysters

Pick over oysters and remove any shell particles. Set aside in refrigerator until ready to use.

Wash the saucepot and the cover.

Dice and set aside

> ½ lb. cooked ham (about 1 cup, diced)

Clean, chop and set aside

> 2 medium onions (about 1 cup,
>   chopped)

Heat in the saucepot over low heat

> 2 tablespoons reserved chicken fat,
>   butter or margarine

Add to saucepot ham and onion and cook over low heat until the onion is tender. Add to the saucepot strained chicken broth, reserved oyster liquor, diced chicken meat and

> ½ teaspoon salt
> ⅛ teaspoon pepper
> ⅛ teaspoon cayenne pepper
> ⅛ teaspoon chili powder

Cover and simmer for about 1 hr.

Meanwhile, prepare

> **Perfection Boiled Rice (page 165)**

About 10 min. before serving, add oysters to saucepot and cook until edges of oysters begin to curl. Remove saucepot from heat. Remove about ½ cup liquid and mix thoroughly with

> 2 tablespoons filé powder

Return mixture to saucepot and blend thoroughly.

Serve gumbo over mounds of rice.

   6 to 8 servings

Note: Filé powder should always be added *after* the soup has been removed from the heat. If cooked, the gumbo will become stringy and unpalatable.

BEAN SOUP

Set out a large heavy saucepot with a tight-fitting cover.

Heat to boiling in the saucepot

> 7 cups water

Meanwhile, sort and wash thoroughly

> 2⅓ cups (about 1 lb.) dried navy or
>   pea beans

Add beans gradually to water so boiling will not stop. Boil 2 min. and remove saucepot from heat. Cover; set aside for 1 hr.

Add to undrained beans

> 5 cups water
> 1 large ham bone (with meat adhering
>   to it)
> 2 teaspoons salt
> ½ teaspoon pepper

Cover saucepot and simmer 2 hrs., stirring once or twice during cooking.

Meanwhile, wash, pare and cook (page 313)

> 3 medium (about 1 lb.) potatoes

Cook 25 to 35 min., or until potatoes are tender when pierced with a fork. Drain. Mash or rice potatoes thoroughly and set aside.

While potatoes are cooking, clean and finely chop

> 3 medium onions
> 2 stalks celery
> 3 sprigs parsley
> 1 clove garlic

Mix potatoes and vegetables with contents of saucepot. Continue to simmer for 1 hr.

Remove bone from soup. Remove any meat from bone, cut it into small pieces and mix into soup.   *8 to 10 servings*

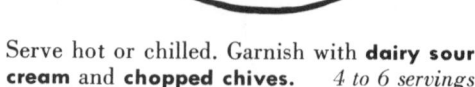

NAVY BEAN SOUP

▲ Base Recipe

Heat to boiling in a large saucepan with a tight-fitting cover

1 qt. water

Meanwhile, wash thoroughly and discard imperfect beans from

1¼ cups dried navy or pea beans

Gradually add beans to water so boiling will not stop. Boil 2 min. and remove from heat. Cover and set aside to soak 1 hr.

Remove and discard rind from and dice

¼ lb. salt pork

Add to undrained beans with

1½ cups water
½ cup (about 1 medium) diced onion
½ teaspoon salt
¼ teaspoon monosodium glutamate
¼ teaspoon pepper

Return to heat, cover and simmer until beans are tender, about 1½ hrs.; stir once or twice during cooking. *5 or 6 servings*

—CREAMY BEAN SOUP

Follow ▲ Recipe. When beans are tender, force mixture through sieve or food mill. Blend in **½ cup milk** and reheat.

NAVY BEAN SOUP WITH MEAT

Bring to boiling in a saucepot or kettle

2½ qts. water

Add

1 lb. dried navy or pea beans

Bring to boiling; boil 2 min. Cover; remove from heat. Allow to stand about 1 hr.

Bring undrained beans to boiling. Put into saucepot

1 cup diced salt pork
2 smoked pork hocks
1 onion, diced
¼ teaspoon pepper
½ teaspoon ginger
1 bay leaf

Cover saucepot, bring to boiling and simmer until beans are almost tender, about 2 hrs.

Remove pork hocks; discard skin, fat and bones. Cut meat into pieces and put into soup with

½ cup diced carrots
½ cup diced potatoes
½ cup chopped celery

Cover, bring to boiling and cook until vegetables are tender, about 40 min.

Mix in

2 or 3 frankfurters, cut in ½-in. slices

Heat thoroughly. Discard bay leaf.

If desired, top bowls of hot soup with **chopped chives or parsley, dairy sour cream, garlic croutons, sliced pimiento-stuffed olives** or **grated Parmesan cheese.** *6 to 8 servings*

PINTO BEAN SOUP

Bring to boiling in a large saucepot or kettle

3 qts. water

Add

1 lb. dried pinto beans, washed

Bring to boiling; boil 2 min. Cover; remove from heat. Allow to stand about 1 hr.

Mix into undrained beans

1½ teaspoons salt
½ lb. boneless lean beef, cut in cubes
¼ cup butter or margarine
1 carrot, diced
1 medium onion, chopped
3 whole cloves
¼ teaspoon mace

Cover and simmer about 2 hrs., or until beans are tender.

Remove and reserve meat. Discard cloves. Force beans through a food mill or sieve. Return beans and liquid to saucepot; mix in cooked meat and

¼ cup sherry

Heat thoroughly.

Have ready

3 hard-cooked eggs, sliced
1 lemon, thinly sliced

Turn soup into a tureen. Top with the egg and lemon slices. Sprinkle with **paprika.**

About 8 servings

BLENDER BORSCH

Set out a 1½-qt. saucepan.

Put into an electric blender container

2 cups (16-oz. can, undrained) beets
½ cup water
1 thin slice lemon with peel
1 slice onion
1 tablespoon vinegar
1 teaspoon sugar
¾ teaspoon salt
⅛ teaspoon pepper
4 or 5 spears of chives

Cover. Blend until beets are coarsely chopped.

Pour into saucepan and stir in

2½ cups (two 10½- to 11-oz. cans) condensed consommé

Bring slowly to boiling; reduce heat and simmer 3 to 5 min.

Serve hot or chilled. Garnish with **dairy sour cream** and **chopped chives.** *4 to 6 servings*

CARAWAY SOUP
(Köménymagos Leves)

▲ Base Recipe

Melt over low heat in a 2-qt. saucepan with a tight-fitting cover

⅓ cup butter

Blend in a mixture of

⅓ cup all-purpose flour
1½ tablespoons caraway seed
1½ teaspoons salt
⅛ teaspoon freshly ground pepper

Heat until mixture bubbles and is lightly browned, stirring constantly. Remove from heat. Blend in

¾ teaspoon paprika

Add gradually, stirring constantly

1½ qts. water

Return to heat and bring rapidly to boiling, stirring constantly. Cover and simmer 15 min.

Meanwhile, prepare and set aside

Croutons (1½ times recipe, page 39)

Remove soup from heat. Vigorously stir about 3 tablespoons of the hot soup into

2 egg yolks, slightly beaten

Immediately blend into hot soup. Stirring constantly, cook over low heat 2 to 3 min. (Do not overcook or allow soup to boil.) Remove soup from heat at once. Pour through sieve; discard caraway seed. Serve with Croutons.

About 6 servings

—CREAMED CARAWAY SOUP
(Krémes Köménymagos Leves)

Follow ▲ Recipe. Just before serving, blend into soup **¾ cup heavy cream.**

LEMON SOUP
(Citrom Leves)

Bring to boiling in a 2-qt. saucepan with a tight-fitting cover.

1 qt. water
½ cup sugar
¼ teaspoon salt
1 piece stick cinnamon

Stir occasionally until sugar dissolves. Cover saucepan and simmer 15 min. Remove from heat; remove and discard cinnamon. Vigorously stir about ⅓ cup hot soup gradually into

4 egg yolks, slightly beaten

Immediately blend into hot soup. Stirring constantly, cook over low heat 3 to 5 min. (Do not overcook or allow soup to boil.) Remove immediately from heat. Add gradually, stirring constantly

⅓ cup (about 2 lemons) lemon juice

Cover saucepan to keep soup warm; set aside.

Make a meringue by beating until frothy

2 egg whites

Add gradually, beating well

2 tablespoons sugar

Beat until stiff peaks are formed. Beat in with few final strokes

2 teaspoons grated lemon peel

Pour soup into individual soup bowls. Top each serving with a spoonful of the meringue. Serve immediately. *4 to 6 servings*

LENTIL SOUP WITH FRANKFURTERS
(Linsensuppe mit Würstchen)

Prepare in a saucepot or kettle with a tight-fitting cover

2 qts. quick meat broth (page 10)

Rinse, sort and add to saucepot

1½ cups (about ½ lb.) dried lentils

Add to pot

1 ham bone, cracked

Cover saucepot and bring broth slowly to boiling.

Meanwhile, prepare

2 stalks celery, sliced
2 carrots, washed, pared or scraped and sliced

Skim foam from broth; add the vegetables with

1 teaspoon salt
½ teaspoon monosodium glutamate
¼ teaspoon pepper
3 sprigs chervil or parsley

Cover and bring to boiling; reduce heat and simmer 2 hrs., or until lentils are tender and soft enough to mash easily. Remove from heat and remove ham bone. Force soup mixture through a coarse sieve or food mill and return to saucepot. Set aside.

Heat in a skillet

2 tablespoons butter

Add and cook over medium heat, occasionally moving and turning with a spoon

2 medium onions, thinly sliced
6 frankfurters, cut diagonally into ½-in. slices

Cook until the onions are tender and frankfurter slices are lightly browned.

Add the onions and frankfurter slices to the soup. Heat soup about 10 min., or until very hot. *About 2 qts. soup*

YELLOW PEA SOUP WITH PORK
(Ärter med Fläsk)

Every Thursday, by a custom whose origin is lost, golden pea soup is served throughout Sweden, from fisher's cottage to Royal Palace. In the other Scandinavian countries it is prepared often enough to be regarded as a typically Scandinavian dish.

Rinse, sort (discarding imperfect peas) and put into a large saucepan

1⅔ cups dried yellow peas

Pour over the peas

2½ qts. cold water

Cover and set peas aside to soak overnight.

The next day, set out

1 piece (1 lb.) smoked shoulder roll

Put into a large saucepot with

3 qts. water
¾ cup coarsely chopped onion

Simmer 1½ to 2 hrs., or until meat is tender.

Remove meat and set aside. Skim off fat from liquid, leaving about 2 tablespoons. Drain the peas and add to the broth with

1 teaspoon salt
1 teaspoon thyme leaves
½ teaspoon monosodium glutamate
¼ teaspoon sugar

Simmer 1½ to 2 hrs., or until peas are tender. If necessary, skim off shells of peas as they come to the surface.

Serve soup with thin slices of the meat. *About 2½ qts. soup*

EASY TOMATO BOUILLON

▲ Base Recipe

Combine in a 1½-qt. saucepan

2½ cups (18-oz. can) tomato juice
2½ cups (two 10½- to 11-oz. cans) condensed beef broth

Stir in

¼ teaspoon celery seed
¼ teaspoon sugar
¼ teaspoon monosodium glutamate
⅛ teaspoon pepper

Bring just to boiling. *5 or 6 servings*

—TOMATO SOUP WITH POTATOES

Follow ▲ Recipe. Gradually add soup to 1½ cups whipped potatoes, stirring constantly. Heat thoroughly in saucepan.

—TOMATO CORN SOUP

Follow ▲ Recipe. Combine **1 tablespoon chopped onion** and **¼ cup chopped green pepper** and cook until vegetables are tender in **1 tablespoon butter or margarine.** Mix into **2 cups (17-oz. can) cream-style corn** and blend into remaining ingredients before heating.

RED HOT TOMATO BOUILLON

▲ Base Recipe

Set out a 2-qt. saucepan.

Put into an electric blender container

1 cup water
2 beef bouillon cubes or 1 teaspoon concentrated meat extract
1 slice onion
½ medium green pepper
1 slice lemon

Cover and blend. Empty contents of blender container into saucepan. Stir in

3 cups tomato juice
1 teaspoon Worcestershire sauce
1 teaspoon sugar
½ teaspoon salt
½ teaspoon monosodium glutamate
⅛ teaspoon cloves
Few grains pepper

Simmer 5 to 7 min.

Serve immediately or add

½ clove garlic

Cool and chill in refrigerator about 3 hrs. Remove garlic clove before serving. *4 servings*

—JELLIED TOMATO BOUILLON

Follow ▲ Recipe. While bouillon is simmering, soften **1 env. unflavored gelatin** in ⅓ cup cold water. Stir into hot bouillon. Cool and place in refrigerator until set (about 5 hrs.). Lightly beat with a fork before serving.

SOUP WITH MEAT BALLS
(Sopa de Albóndigas)

Set out a large saucepan with a tight-fitting cover and a large skillet.

Prepare and pour into the saucepan

1 qt. quick meat broth (page 10)

Force through sieve or food mill enough canned tomatoes to yield

4 cups sieved tomatoes

Add tomatoes to the broth with

¼ cup minced onion
1 teaspoon chili powder
1 teaspoon salt
½ teaspoon pepper

Set over high heat and bring to boiling. Reduce heat and simmer about 30 min.

Meanwhile, combine and set aside

⅓ cup fine dry bread crumbs
¼ cup water

Potato Soup

Mix lightly in a bowl

¼ lb. ground beef
¼ lb. ground pork
1 egg, beaten
2 teaspoons minced onion
1 teaspoon lemon juice

and a mixture of

½ teaspoon chili powder
½ teaspoon salt
¼ teaspoon thyme

Blend in bread crumb mixture. Shape into balls about ¾ in. in diameter.

Heat in the skillet over medium heat

1 tablespoon fat

Add meat balls and brown on all sides, turning occasionally. Remove from skillet to absorbent paper to drain.

Add to the broth the meat balls and

1 sprig mint

Cover and simmer about 20 min. Remove mint.

Serve several meat balls in each bowl of soup.

About 8 servings

BLACK MUSHROOM WINE SOUP

▲ Base Recipe

The dark midnight hue of this delicious and unusual soup comes from the dried mushrooms which are black. Many connoisseurs know these mushrooms as the dried Italian variety.

Set out a heavy 3-qt. saucepan with a cover.

Prepare and set aside

2 qts. quick meat broth (page 10)

Coarsely chop enough onions to yield

¾ cup (about 1½ medium) chopped onion

Set aside.

Heat in the saucepan

⅓ cup butter

Add the onion to the butter with

2 oz. (about 1 cup) dried mushrooms, broken in small pieces
½ cup chopped celery
1 medium garlic clove, minced
2 bay leaves
10 peppercorns
Few sprigs parsley

Cook about 10 min. over moderate heat, stirring occasionally, or until onion and celery become almost black. Remove from heat. Slowly pour in broth, stirring constantly, and

¾ teaspoon monosodium glutamate
¾ teaspoon Worcestershire sauce

Return to heat. Bring to boiling; reduce heat and simmer, partially covered, about 50 min.

Shortly before end of cooking period, blend until smooth

3 tablespoons cornstarch
½ cup cold water

Gradually add cornstarch mixture to the soup, stirring constantly. Bring to boiling and cook 3 min. longer. Remove from heat and strain soup through sieve or colander, lightly pressing mushrooms against sieve with back of spoon to extract as much soup as possible. Discard contents of sieve. Mix into strained soup

¾ cup sauterne

6 to 8 servings

—FRESH MUSHROOM WINE SOUP

Follow ▲ Recipe. Clean and chop **1 lb. fresh mushrooms.** Substitute for the dried mushrooms.

POTATO SOUP
(Kartoffelsuppe)

Set out a heavy 3-qt. saucepan or saucepot with a tight-fitting cover.

Wash, pare and cut into ¼-in. slices

6 medium (about 2 lbs.) potatoes

Put into the saucepan with

5 cups cold water

Cover and bring to boiling. Reduce heat to medium and add

1 carrot, washed, pared or scraped, and cut in pieces
1 leek, washed thoroughly and thinly sliced (white part only)
1 stalk celery, cut into pieces
1 medium onion, sliced
2 teaspoons salt
½ teaspoon monosodium glutamate
¼ teaspoon white pepper
¼ teaspoon thyme
¼ teaspoon marjoram
1 bay leaf

Cover and cook about 1 hr., or until vegetables are tender.

Remove the carrot, leek, celery, onion and bay leaf with a slotted spoon and discard.

Remove 1 cup of the potato broth; add to it

1 beef bouillon cube

Force remaining potato mixture through a fine sieve into a saucepan.

Heat over low heat

2 tablespoons butter

Blend in

3 tablespoons all-purpose flour

Heat until mixture bubbles. Stir the 1 cup of potato broth and gradually add to the butter-flour mixture, stirring constantly. Pour into the soup and blend well. Return to heat; bring to boiling. Reduce heat and simmer gently 5 to 10 min., or until soup is thoroughly heated.

Garnish with

Finely chopped parsley

About 2½ pts. soup

VEGETABLE SOUP, COUNTRY STYLE

Combine in a saucepan

1 can (10¾ oz.) condensed vegetable soup
1 can (11½ oz.) condensed bean with bacon soup
1½ soup cans water

Bring to boiling; simmer about 5 min. If desired, top servings of hot soup with crumbled **crisp bacon.** *4 to 6 servings*

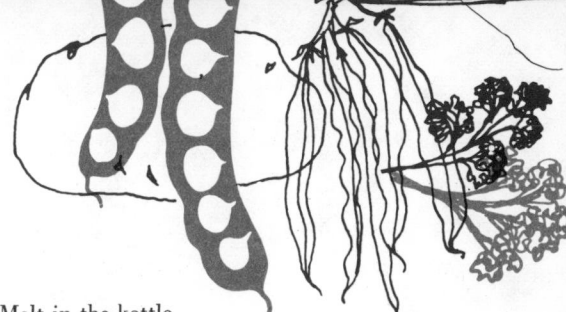

VEGETABLE SOUP
(Gemüsesuppe)

Many German homemakers like to roast marrow bones until the marrow is done, then scoop out the marrow and spread it on tiny rounds of crisp toast to float on vegetable soup.

Put into a large saucepot or kettle with a cover

1 soup bone, cracked

Add to pot

3 qts. cold water
1 tablespoon salt

Cover and bring to boiling, reduce heat and simmer 1½ hrs. During cooking, occasionally remove foam that forms on top.

Meanwhile, prepare

1 lb. potatoes (3 medium), washed, pared and diced
1 lb. green beans, washed, ends cut off and beans cut in halves
3 small carrots, washed, pared or scraped and cut in quarters lengthwise
2 medium onions, chopped (about 1 cup)
2 stalks celery, cut in ½-in. pieces
2 tablespoons minced parsley

After 1½ hrs., add vegetables to soup with

2 tablespoons sugar
2 teaspoons salt
1½ teaspoons monosodium glutamate

Simmer 30 min., or until vegetables are tender.

Just before vegetables are tender, force through a sieve or food mill contents of

2 cans (28 oz. each) tomatoes (about 6 cups, sieved)

Set aside.

Heat in a saucepan

2 tablespoons shortening

Blend in

¼ cup all-purpose flour

Add and cook over low heat, stirring constantly

¼ cup finely chopped onion

Cook until mixture bubbles and is lightly browned. Remove from heat and add gradually, stirring constantly, 1 cup of the soup stock. Cook 1 to 2 min., or until smooth. Blend into soup with the sieved tomatoes. Bring to boiling, reduce heat and simmer 5 to 10 min., or until soup is slightly thickened. Remove soup bone. Serve steaming hot.   *8 to 10 servings*

NORWEGIAN VEGETABLE SOUP
(Fersk Suppe I)

▲ Base Recipe

The base recipe is traditional and very old. The variation dates from the 19th-century acceptance of the tomato as a safe and wholesome food.

Set out

2 lbs. beef short ribs
1 lb. soup bone

Put into a large saucepot with

3 qts. cold water
1 tablespoon salt

Bring to boiling; reduce heat and simmer 2½ hrs. During cooking, occasionally remove foam that forms on top.

Prepare

1½ cups (3 medium) coarsely chopped onion
1¼ cups (3 medium) coarsely chopped carrots
1 small head (1 lb.) cabbage, cut in pieces

After simmering soup 1 hr. add the chopped onion. Continue to simmer 1 hr. longer. Add the carrots and cabbage. Simmer another ½ hr.

Skim fat from soup, leaving about 2 tablespoons. Add

1 whole nutmeg

Simmer 15 min. longer. Remove the short ribs and soup bone to a bowl. Remove and discard the nutmeg. Stir in until bouillon cubes are dissolved

2 beef bouillon cubes
2½ teaspoons salt
1 teaspoon monosodium glutamate
¼ teaspoon pepper

Remove 2 cups of the broth. Stir into the remaining soup

½ cup finely chopped parsley

Keep soup hot while preparing sauce for meat.

Prepare

2 cups Medium White Sauce (double recipe, page 304; substitute the broth for the milk; stir into sauce 4 teaspoons sugar, 2 tablespoons vinegar and 2 tablespoons prepared horseradish)

Add the meat and cook over low heat until heated thoroughly.

Serve soup first. Then serve meat and sauce.
8 to 10 servings

—VEGETABLE SOUP WITH TOMATOES
(Fersk Suppe II)

Follow ▲ Recipe. Rinse **4 medium tomatoes.** Cut out stem ends and cut tomatoes into six pieces. Add tomatoes with bouillon cubes.

SQUARE-MEAL VEGETABLE BEEF SOUP

▲ Base Recipe

Set out a 6-qt. kettle with a tight-fitting cover.

Set out

1 lb. lean beef (chuck or plate), cut in 1-in. pieces

To coat meat evenly, shake 2 or 3 pieces at a time in a plastic bag containing a mixture of

½ cup sifted all-purpose flour
½ teaspoon salt
¼ teaspoon monosodium glutamate
⅛ teaspoon pepper

Melt in the kettle

2 to 3 tablespoons fat

Add meat to kettle and brown on all sides. Remove remaining fat.

Put into kettle

1 large soup bone, cracked
½ cup (about 1 medium) chopped onion

Add to kettle

2 qts. boiling water

Cover kettle and bring water again to boiling over high heat. Lower heat and simmer 2 to 3 hrs., or until meat is almost tender. Remove bone. Add to kettle

2 cups diced raw potatoes
1 cup sliced raw carrots
1 cup chopped celery (1-in. pieces)
¼ teaspoon monosodium glutamate

Cover and simmer 30 min. Remove from heat and let stand until cold and fat rises to surface. Remove fat.

Meanwhile, force through a sieve

2½ cups canned tomatoes

Stir tomatoes into soup with

¼ cup chopped parsley

Reheat soup and serve hot.   *2½ to 3 qts. soup*

—VEGETABLE NOODLE SOUP

Follow ▲ Recipe. Cook vegetables 20 min. and add ½ cup uncooked noodles. Continue cooking 10 min., or until vegetables and noodles are tender. Cool and add tomatoes and parsley as in ▲ Recipe.

—VEGETABLE RICE SOUP

Follow ▲ Recipe. Cook vegetables 10 to 15 min. and add ⅔ cup uncooked rice. Continue cooking 15 to 20 min., or until vegetables and rice are tender. Cool and add tomatoes and parsley as in ▲ Recipe.

Square-Meal Vegetable Beef Soup

Minestrone

OVEN-COOKED VEGETABLE SOUP

Heat in a saucepot
¼ cup butter or margarine
Mix in
½ cup diced white turnip
½ cup diced carrot
½ cup chopped celery
1 small onion, chopped
Cook until delicately browned.

Add to saucepot and stir to mix
1½ cups diced raw potatoes
4 cups broth or water
2 teaspoons salt
Pepper to taste
Cover and set in a 250°F oven about 2 hrs., or until vegetables are tender.

Stir in
1 to 2 tablespoons chili sauce
Serve hot.   *6 servings*

MINESTRONE

Derived from the Latin "to hand out," this soup was a staple in the days when the monks kept it always on the fire to be ready for sojourners or travelers. Even today, it is a favorite, especially in Sicily where it comes into its own on St. Joseph's Day, served in the public square or piazza accompanied by bread shaped to represent various religious symbols.

Set out a small skillet.

Heat to boiling in a large saucepan
6 cups water

Meanwhile, wash thoroughly and discard imperfect beans from
1¼ cups (about ½ lb.) dried navy or pea beans
Gradually add beans to water so boiling will not stop. Boil 2 min. and remove from heat. Cover and soak 1 hr. Add to beans
¼ lb. salt pork
Return to heat and simmer 1 hr., stirring once or twice.

Meanwhile, heat in skillet until onion and garlic are lightly browned and set aside
3 tablespoons olive oil
1 small onion, chopped
1 clove garlic, chopped

Wash, cut into ½-in. slices and set aside
2 stalks celery
2 small carrots, scraped

Wash, pare and dice
1 medium potato
Set aside.

Wash in cold water and remove coarse outer leaves from
¼ head cabbage
Shred finely.

Add all vegetables and onion-garlic mixture to beans, with
1 tablespoon chopped parsley
½ teaspoon salt
¼ teaspoon pepper
Pour in slowly
1 qt. hot water
Simmer about 1 hr., or until beans are tender.

Meanwhile, cook, following package directions
¼ cup packaged precooked rice
About 10 min. before beans are done, add the cooked rice and
½ cup frozen green peas
When peas are tender, stir in
¼ cup tomato paste
Simmer about 5 min.

Serve sprinkled with
Grated Parmesan cheese
                      About 6 servings

ALMOND SOUP

Toasted nut flavor—unusual in soup!

Set out a 2-qt. saucepan.

Put into an electric blender container
1 cup blanched, toasted and salted almonds (pages 9 and 10)
1 cup water
4 egg yolks
3 chicken bouillon cubes
½ slice onion
½ teaspoon sugar
½ teaspoon monosodium glutamate

Cover and blend until almonds are finely ground. Pour into saucepan and stir in
2 cups water
Cook over low heat 10 to 15 min., or until thickened, stirring constantly. *Do not boil.*

Stir in
1 cup cream
Heat thoroughly without boiling.

Serve immediately. Garnish with **grated orange peel.**   *5 or 6 servings*

AVOCADO CHICKEN SOUP

An electric blender will be needed.

Put into a 1½-qt. saucepan
1¼ cups (10½-to 11-oz. can) condensed cream of chicken soup
Add gradually, stirring constantly
1¼ cups water
Heat to boiling, stirring frequently.

Wash, cut into halves, remove pits and peel
2 medium ripe avocados
Cut one avocado half into ½-in. cubes. Put cubes into a small bowl and sprinkle over
2 to 3 tablespoons lemon juice

Put remaining avocado halves into electric blender container with
1 cup milk
1 thin slice onion
1 stalk celery, cut in several pieces
3 or 4 sprigs parsley, rinsed
½ teaspoon salt
Few grains pepper
Cover and blend until smooth.

Add blended mixture to hot soup and heat quickly to boiling, stirring frequently.

Just before serving, add avocado cubes and
1 to 2 tablespoons sherry
Serve at once.   *4 or 5 servings*

BRUSSELS SPROUT SOUP

Set out a large saucepot or Dutch oven and a saucepan.

Set out to thaw partially
4 pkgs. (10 oz. each) frozen Brussels sprouts

Prepare and set aside
5 cups quick chicken broth (page 10; use 7 bouillon cubes)

Fry in saucepot or Dutch oven
8 slices bacon, diced
2 cloves garlic, minced
Add 3 cups of the broth to saucepot with
6 cups milk
¾ cup uncooked rice
and a mixture of
1 teaspoon oregano leaves, crushed
2 teaspoons salt
½ teaspoon pepper
Bring to boiling, reduce heat and simmer cov-

ered 15 min. Add to saucepot contents of

1 pkg. (10 oz.) frozen peas and carrots

Bring to boiling, reduce heat and simmer about 10 min., or until vegetables are tender.

Meanwhile, coarsely chop the partially thawed Brussels sprouts. Combine in saucepan the remaining 2 cups of broth and

1 teaspoon salt
2 cups water

Bring to boiling and add the chopped Brussels sprouts. Return to boiling and simmer uncovered 10 min., or until tender. Add Brussels sprouts with their cooking liquid to rice mixture. Stir in

¾ cup shredded Parmesan cheese

Accompany with **assorted crackers.**

About 20 servings

CREAM OF CELERY SOUP

▲ *Base Recipe*

Set out a 1½-qt. saucepan.

Clean, finely dice and set aside

4 or 5 stalks celery, with leaves

Prepare and set aside

2 tablespoons chopped onion
2 tablespoons chopped parsley

Set out

2½ cups milk

Heat in the saucepan over low heat

1 tablespoon butter or margarine

Add the onion and cook over medium heat, occasionally stirring with a spoon, until onion is tender. Blend in

2 tablespoons all-purpose flour
1 teaspoon salt
½ teaspoon monosodium glutamate
Few grains pepper

Heat until mixture bubbles. Remove from heat.

Add gradually, stirring in, 1 cup of the milk. Cook rapidly, stirring constantly, until sauce thickens. Cook 1 to 2 min. longer. Stir in the celery, parsley and the remaining 1½ cups of milk. Bring to boiling, stirring constantly. Reduce heat and simmer 5 to 8 min., stirring occasionally.

About 4 servings

—CREAM OF CAULIFLOWER SOUP

Follow ▲ Recipe. Substitute **1 cup cooked cauliflower,** chopped, for the celery. Omit parsley. Garnish bowls of soup with **nutmeg** or **paprika.**

—CREAM OF CARROT SOUP

Follow ▲ Recipe. Substitute **1 cup cooked diced carrots** for the celery.

—CREAM OF ASPARAGUS SOUP

Follow ▲ Recipe. Substitute **1 cup cooked asparagus or canned asparagus tips,** cut in pieces, for the celery. Omit onion and parsley. Mix ⅛ **teaspoon dry mustard** with seasonings.

—CREAM OF BROCCOLI SOUP

Follow ▲ Recipe. Substitute **1 cup cooked chopped broccoli** for the celery. Omit parsley and onion. Add ⅛ **teaspoon celery salt,** ⅛ **teaspoon thyme** and a **few grains cayenne pepper** with seasonings.

—CREAM OF SPINACH SOUP

Follow ▲ Recipe. Substitute **2 cups chopped washed spinach** for the celery. Omit parsley. Add a **few grains nutmeg** with seasonings.

—FRESH TOMATO SOUP

Cut out and discard stem ends from **4 large firm tomatoes.** Cut tomatoes into quarters and put into the saucepan with ⅓ **cup finely chopped onion,** ½ **teaspoon salt,** ½ **bay leaf,** **3 whole cloves** and **2 tablespoons sugar.** Cover and simmer for 10 min. Remove bay leaf and cloves; force mixture through a sieve or food mill. Set aside. Follow ▲ Recipe. Omit celery, onion and parsley. Set out only **2 cups milk.** Prepare sauce, substituting the **tomato liquid** for the milk. Stirring constantly, add the hot tomato mixture to the 2 cups of milk. Return soup to saucepan. Heat rapidly, stirring occasionally; do not boil.

CHEESE SOUP

Prepare

⅔ cup (about 2 stalks) finely chopped celery
½ cup (about 2 small) finely diced carrots
⅓ cup (1 small) finely chopped onion

Heat in a 3-qt. saucepan with a tight-fitting cover

6 tablespoons butter

Add vegetables. Cover tightly and cook over very low heat until vegetables are tender.

Meanwhile, dissolve

2 beef or chicken bouillon cubes (or 1 teaspoon concentrated meat extract)

in

2 tablespoons very hot water

Set aside.

Unwrap, slice and set aside

2 6-oz. rolls natural cheese food

When vegetables are tender, carefully remove from butter with a slotted spoon, allowing butter to drain back into saucepan. Set vegetables aside; keep warm.

Scald (page 10)

1 quart milk

Set the saucepan over low heat and blend into the butter

¼ cup sifted all-purpose flour
1 teaspoon salt

Heat until mixture bubbles. Remove from heat. Add gradually while stirring constantly

2 cups milk

Add the scalded milk; return saucepan to heat and bring mixture rapidly in boiling, stirring constantly. Cook 1 to 2 min. longer. Remove from heat. Gently stir in the vegetables and bouillon. Add the cheese all at one time; stir gently and constantly until cheese is melted. Serve immediately.

Garnish with

Crumbled crisp panbroiled bacon

Serve soup hot with garnishes such as slivered, toasted **almonds;** sieved **hard-cooked egg;** chopped **onion,** chopped **green pepper** and **pimiento;** and **popcorn.**   *10 to 12 servings*

GOLDEN CHICKEN CHOWDER

Set out a saucepot or a large saucepan with a tight-fitting cover.

Chop enough cooked chicken to yield

2 cups coarsely chopped cooked chicken

Drain, reserving liquid

1 can (12 oz.) whole kernel corn

Clean, slice thinly and set aside

3 medium onions

Cheese Soup

Golden Chicken Chowder

Remove rind from and dice

2 oz. salt pork (about ¼ cup, diced)

Put into the saucepot and cook over medium heat, occasionally moving and turning with a spoon, until salt pork is crisped and browned. Using a slotted spoon, remove salt pork and set aside to drain on absorbent paper. Add sliced onions to the saucepot; cook, moving and turning frequently with a spoon, until the onions are tender. Using a slotted spoon, remove onion slices and set aside.

Add to the fat in the saucepot and heat

2 tablespoons butter

Blend in

3 tablespoons all-purpose flour
1 teaspoon monosodium glutamate
1 teaspoon salt
¼ teaspoon white pepper
¼ teaspoon savory

Heat until mixture bubbles. Remove from heat. Add the reserved corn liquid gradually, stirring constantly, and

1½ qts. milk

Stir in the onions, corn and chicken pieces. Cover and return to heat for 15 min., or until chicken is thoroughly heated; do not boil.

Pour into a heated tureen and add the crisp salt pork. *About 1½ qts. chowder*

CHICKEN RICE SOUP

▲ *Base Recipe*

Prepare

1 cup Fluffy Rice (about one-third recipe, page 164)

Put into an electric blender container

1 cup water
⅔ cup cooked chicken, cut in chunks
1 egg yolk
2 tablespoons butter or margarine
1 chicken bouillon cube
1 stalk celery with leaves, rinsed and cut in several pieces
1½ teaspoons salt
½ teaspoon monosodium glutamate
⅛ teaspoon pepper

Cover and blend until smooth.

Turn into saucepan and stir in the cooked rice and

3 cups milk

Bring to boiling, stirring frequently. Simmer about 5 min.

Sieve **hard-cooked egg yolk** over soup for a garnish. *6 to 8 servings*

—CURRIED CREAM OF CHICKEN SOUP

Follow ▲ Recipe. Add the cooked rice to blender mixture and blend until smooth. Add **½ to 1 teaspoon curry powder** with rice. Garnish with **slivered toasted almonds.**

—TURKEY RICE SOUP

Follow ▲ Recipe. Substitute **cooked turkey** for chicken.

CREAM OF CHICKEN TOMATO SOUP

In a saucepan, bring to boiling

2 cups water

Stir in

1 pkg. (2½ oz.) tomato vegetable soup mix

Cover and simmer about 10 min.

Add gradually, blending until smooth

1 can (10½ oz.) condensed cream of chicken soup

Stir in

2½ cups milk
⅛ teaspoon savory

Heat thoroughly, stirring constantly. If desired, serve with one of the following: crumbled **blue cheese**, chopped **peanuts**, crumbled crisp **bacon**, chopped **chives**, cubes of **Cheddar cheese**, croutons, bite-size wheat biscuits or pimiento-stuffed olive slices.

About 6 servings

CHICKEN ASPARAGUS SOUP

Blend in a saucepan

1 can (10½ oz.) condensed cream of chicken soup
1 can (10½ oz.) condensed cream of asparagus soup

Gradually add, stirring constantly

2 cups milk

Heat to serving temperature. Garnish with snipped parsley. If desired, serve with **Orange-Buttered Toast** (below). *About 6 servings*

—ORANGE-BUTTERED TOAST

Beat until fluffy

¼ cup butter or margarine, softened
1 cup confectioners' sugar
1 tablespoon grated orange peel
1 tablespoon orange juice

Spread on untoasted side of

Bread slices (toasted on one side)

Heat under broiler until bubbly.

CREAM OF CORN SOUP

Set out a heavy 2-qt. saucepan.

Force through a sieve and set aside

2 cans (17 oz. each) cream-style corn

Combine and scald (page 10)

1 qt. milk
1 large onion, grated
¼ cup chopped celery
¼ cup chopped carrot
1 sprig parsley

Melt in saucepan over low heat

5 tablespoons butter

Blend in

¼ cup all-purpose flour
1 teaspoon salt
½ teaspoon monosodium glutamate
¼ teaspoon pepper

Stirring constantly, heat until mixture bubbles. Remove from heat. Strain the scalded milk and add it gradually to butter-flour mixture, stirring constantly. Return to heat and stir until mixture is thickened. Stir in sieved corn.

Heat to serving temperature over very low heat; do not boil.

Top each bowl of soup with a small amount of **Garlic or Parsley Popcorn** (below). *8 servings*

For Garlic Popcorn—Pop

¼ cup popcorn

Cook together for 5 min.
>   **3 tablespoons butter**
>   **1 glove garlic, finely chopped**

Strain butter over popcorn and stir popcorn well to coat evenly.

For Parsley Popcorn—Follow recipe for Garlic Popcorn. Substitute **2 tablespoons finely chopped parsley** for the garlic.

MUSHROOM SOUP
(Gomba Leves)

▲ *Base Recipe*

Set out a large kettle or saucepot with a tight-fitting cover and a heavy 10-in. skillet with a tight-fitting cover.

Have ready
>   **1 veal soup bone, cracked**

Put soup bone into kettle with
>   **1½ qts. water**
>   **1½ teaspoons salt**
>   **3 or 4 sprigs parsley**
>   **2 or 3 peppercorns**

Bring water to boiling. Skim off and discard foam. Cover kettle and simmer soup about 1 hr., skimming as necessary.

Shortly before end of cooking period, cut off and discard tops, wash, pare or scrape and cut into ¼-in. slices.
>   **4 medium carrots (about 1 cup, sliced)**

Add carrots to kettle, cover and simmer 15 to 20 min., or until carrots are tender.

Meanwhile, clean and slice
>   **1 lb. fresh mushrooms**

Melt in the skillet
>   **½ cup butter or margarine**

Add mushrooms with
>   **1 small onion, chopped**
>   **2 tablespoons chopped parsley**
>   **1 teaspoon paprika**
>   **½ teaspoon salt**

Cook slowly, stirring gently, 5 to 8 min., or until mushrooms and onions are lightly browned and tender; set aside.

Prepare and set aside
>   **Croutons (1½ times recipe, page 39)**

Remove kettle from heat. Remove and discard bone, peppercorns and parsley sprigs. Blend contents of skillet into soup. Vigorously stir ⅓ cup of the hot soup gradually into
>   **4 egg yolks, slightly beaten**

Immediately blend into hot soup. Stirring con-

stantly, cook over low heat 2 to 3 min. (Do not overcook or allow soup to boil.) Remove immediately from heat and cover.

Combine in a bowl
>   **1 cup dairy sour cream**
>   **1 teaspoon lemon juice**

Add gradually, stirring vigorously, about 1 cup hot soup to sour cream mixture. Immediately blend into remaining hot soup. Heat thoroughly; do not boil. Serve with the Croutons.

6 or 7 servings

—SWEET CREAM MUSHROOM SOUP
(Gomba Leves Tejföllel)

Follow ▲ Recipe. Substitute **1 cup heavy or light cream** for the dairy sour cream, adding it directly to the soup. Omit the lemon juice.

CREAM OF MUSHROOM SOUP

Set out a 1½-qt. saucepan, a large skillet and an electric blender.

Clean and slice (page 9)
>   **½ lb. mushrooms**

Heat in skillet
>   **¼ cup butter**

Add mushrooms to skillet with
>   **2 tablespoons chopped onion**

Cook over medium heat, stirring frequently, until mushrooms are tender and lightly browned. Cool and put into electric blender container with
>   **1 cup water**
>   **2 beef bouillon cubes or 1 teaspoon concentrated meat extract**
>   **2 tablespoons all-purpose flour**
>   **½ teaspoon monosodium glutamate**
>   **¼ teaspoon salt**
>   **⅛ teaspoon pepper**
>   **Few grains mace**

Cover and blend until ingredients are blended but mushrooms are not too finely chopped.

Pour into saucepan and stir in
>   **2 cups milk**

Bring to boiling. Reduce heat and simmer about 5 min.

Meanwhile, put into the blender container
>   **2 egg yolks**

Cover and blend 1 or 2 seconds. Add 3 or 4 tablespoons hot soup gradually by tablespoonfuls to egg yolks, covering and blending after each addition. Return to hot soup mixture and cook over low heat, stirring constantly, 3 to 5 min.

About 4 servings

ONION AND BACON CHOWDER

▲ *Base Recipe*

Set out a 1½-qt. saucepan and an electric blender.

Prepare
>   **2 slices Panfried Bacon (page 190)**

Set aside.

Put into fat in skillet and cook until tender
>   **3 medium onions, sliced**

Put contents of skillet into electric blender container with
>   **1 cup milk**
>   **2 tablespoons all-purpose flour**
>   **1½ teaspoons salt**
>   **½ teaspoon monosodium glutamate**
>   **½ teaspoon Worcestershire sauce**

Cover and blend until onion is partially blended. Pour into saucepan; stir in bacon and
>   **2 cups milk**

Bring to boiling, stirring constantly; cook 1 to 2 min. longer.

Serve garnished with **toast strips** dipped first in **melted butter**, then in **grated Parmesan cheese**.

4 or 5 servings

—CORN AND BACON CHOWDER

Follow ▲ Recipe. Use only ½ medium onion. Blend **2 cups (17-oz. can) cream-style corn** with onion.

—LIMA BEAN AND BACON SOUP

Follow ▲ Recipe. Substitute **1¾ cups (16-oz. can, drained) lima beans** for onions. Do not cook lima beans in skillet. Add **1 onion slice** and **2 tablespoons ketchup** to blender container.

GREEN ONION SOUP PARMESAN

Melt in a saucepan
>   **3 tablespoons butter or margarine**

Add
>   **2 cups sliced green onions with tops**

Cook gently until onions are partially cooked but not browned. Add
>   **2 cups water**
>   **3 beef bouillon cubes, crushed**

Bring to boiling; reduce heat and simmer about 5 min. Stir in
>   **2 cans (14½ oz. each) evaporated milk**
>   **Salt and pepper to taste**

Heat thoroughly.

Meanwhile, spread one side of
>   **6 slices French bread (small loaf)**

with
>   **Butter or margarine**

Sprinkle with
>   **½ cup shredded Parmesan cheese**

Place under broiler until cheese is lightly browned. Top each bowl of hot soup with a slice of Parmesan bread.

About 6 servings

RIPE OLIVE SOUP

▲ Base Recipe

Set out a 1½-qt. saucepan and its cover.

Put into an electric blender container
  1 cup water
  ¾ cup pitted ripe olives
  2 stalks celery, cut in several pieces
  1 slice onion
  3 tablespoons butter or margarine
  2 tablespoons all-purpose flour
  ¾ teaspoon salt
  ½ teaspoon garlic salt
  ⅛ teaspoon pepper
Cover and blend until mixture is smooth and flecked with olives.

Pour into saucepan and stir in
  2 cups milk
  ½ cup undiluted evaporated milk
Bring to boiling, stirring constantly. Reduce heat, cover and simmer 5 min., stirring frequently.

Meanwhile, slice into wide, lengthwise strips
  6 or 7 large pitted ripe olives
Add olive strips to soup and serve.
                                4 or 5 servings

—TOMATO-RIPE OLIVE SOUP

Follow ▲ Recipe. Substitute **tomato juice** for milk. Garnish with **chopped parsley.**

—PIMIENTO-STUFFED GREEN OLIVE SOUP

Follow ▲ Recipe. Substitute **pimiento-stuffed green olives** for ripe olives. Slice pimiento-stuffed green olives crosswise for garnish.

CREAM OF ONION SOUP

Heat in a large saucepan
  3 cups water or chicken broth
Add
  3 large onions, sliced

Bring to boiling; cook, covered, about 20 min. Add
  2 potatoes, pared and sliced
Bring to boiling; cook, covered, 20 min., or until potatoes are tender.

Sieve contents of saucepan, or purée in an electric blender. Return to saucepan.

Meanwhile, heat in a small saucepan
  ½ tablespoon butter or margarine
Mix in
  1 onion, chopped
Cook until lightly browned. Mix into purée in saucepan. Set aside.

Heat in the small saucepan
  1 tablespoon butter or margarine
Mix in
  1 tablespoon all-purpose flour
Heat until mixture bubbles. Add gradually, stirring constantly
  1 cup cream
Bring to boiling; stir and cook 1 to 2 min. Blend into mixture in large saucepan. Season to taste with **salt** and **pepper**. Heat thoroughly, stirring occasionally.

Serve topped with **croutons**.   *6 servings*

ONION WINE SOUP

Heat in a large saucepan
  ¼ cup butter or margarine
Mix into butter and cook 5 min.
  5 large onions, chopped
Add to saucepan
  5 cups broth or bouillon
  ½ cup celery leaves
  1 large potato, sliced
Bring to boiling; simmer, covered, 30 min.

Sieve mixture or purée in an electric blender.

Return mixture to saucepan. Blend in
  1 cup dry white wine
  1 tablespoon vinegar
  2 teaspoons sugar
Bring to boiling, reduce heat and simmer 5 min. Stir in
  1 cup light cream
  1 tablespoon minced parsley
  Salt and pepper to taste
Heat thoroughly; do not boil.   *6 to 8 servings*

GREEN PEA SOUP WITH SOUR CREAM
(Erbsensuppe mit Saurer Sahne)

Prepare in a large heavy saucepan or saucepot
  6 cups quick meat broth (page 10)
To retain their delicate flavor, rinse and shell just before using
  2 lbs. fresh green peas
Add peas to boiling broth, cover and cook about 10 min., or until tender. Remove and reserve 1 cup of the broth. Set peas aside.

Meanwhile, heat in a saucepan
  ¼ cup butter
Blend in
  ¼ cup all-purpose flour
  ½ teaspoon salt
  ¼ teaspoon monosodium glutamate
  ⅛ teaspoon white pepper
Heat until mixture bubbles. Remove from heat. Add gradually, stirring in, the cup of reserved broth. Pour mixture gradually into the pea soup, stirring constantly. Bring to boiling. Cook 1 to 2 min.

Beat slightly
  1 egg yolk
Quickly stir about 3 tablespoons of the hot soup into the egg yolk. Immediately return egg-yolk mixture to soup, stirring vigorously.

Reduce heat and cook soup until thoroughly heated, about 5 min., stirring constantly. Do not boil. Remove from heat and force through a sieve. Return to the saucepan.

Stirring vigorously with a French whip, whisk beater, or fork, add to the soup in very small amounts
  ½ cup dairy sour cream
Stir in
  1 tablespoon chopped parsley
Cook soup over low heat, stirring constantly, 3 to 5 min., until well heated; do not boil.

Serve soup garnished with
  Strips of smoked tongue
                                About 3 pts. soup

BUSY DAY SOUP

A minute-saver soup with a delicious, full-bodied flavor.

Blend until smooth
  1¼ cups (11¼-oz. can) condensed green pea soup
  1¼ cups (10¾-oz. can) condensed tomato soup

Add gradually, stirring until smooth

2½ cups milk
½ teaspoon Worcestershire sauce
¼ teaspoon curry powder

Heat just to boiling.   *4 or 5 servings*

GREEN PEA SOUP
(Potage Saint-Germain)

Whenever a Frenchman thinks of good pea soup, he thinks of that suburb of Paris, Saint-Germain, where the peas are exceptionally tender and flavorful.

Put into a heavy saucepan

1 small head lettuce, shredded
2 cups shelled fresh green peas
1 cup water
½ cup chopped leeks (green part only)
2 tablespoons fat
2 teaspoons chopped chervil
1 teaspoon sugar
1 teaspoon salt
¼ teaspoon pepper

Bring quickly to boiling and cook until peas are tender.

Reserve 3 tablespoons peas for garnish. Put remaining mixture through a sieve.

Return sieved mixture to the pan. Reheat with

2 cups Bouillon (page 41)

Just before serving blend in and heat thoroughly

2 cups cream

Garnish with reserved cooked peas.

    5 or 6 servings

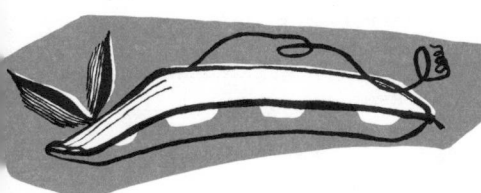

BLENDER PEA SOUP

▲ *Base Recipe*

Set out a 1½-qt. saucepan.

Break apart with a fork and set aside

1 pkg. (10 oz.) frozen green peas

Set out

2 cups milk

Put into an electric blender container in order, 1 cup of the milk and

1 tablespoon all-purpose flour
2 tablespoons butter or margarine
½ teaspoon salt
½ teaspoon monosodium glutamate
½ teaspoon nutmeg
⅛ teaspoon pepper
1 small onion, quartered

Cover, turn on motor and blend. Continue to blend while gradually adding one half of peas.

Use rubber spatula to scrape down sides of container so that ingredients will become evenly mixed. Blend until contents of container are thoroughly mixed. Empty contents of container into saucepan.

Pour second cup of milk into container. Blend while gradually adding remaining peas. Stir contents of container into mixture in saucepan. Bring to boiling, stirring occasionally.

Serve immediately, topped with

Chopped parsley

    4 servings

—MAIN-DISH SOUP

Follow ▲ Recipe. Increase milk to 2½ cups; divide equally for two additions. Gradually add **1 cup cubed cooked ham** with last addition of peas. Sliced frankfurters, added just before heating, may be substituted for ham.

PEANUT BUTTER SOUP

Set out a 1½-qt. saucepan.

Prepare

4 slices Panfried Bacon (page 190)

Crumble and set aside.

Put into an electric blender container

1 cup water
½ cup Blender Peanut Butter (page 114)
1 carrot, washed, pared and diced
1 tablespoon bacon drippings
¼ teaspoon salt
⅛ teaspoon pepper

Cover and blend until smooth.

Pour blended mixture into the saucepan. Stir in bacon and

3 cups milk

Bring to boiling, stirring frequently.

    4 or 5 servings

PIMIENTO CREAM SOUP

Set out a 1½-qt. saucepan.

Put into an electric blender container

1½ cups milk
1 egg
4 pimientos (4-oz. can, undrained)
1 onion slice
3 tablespoons butter or margarine
2 tablespoons all-purpose flour
1 teaspoon salt

Cover and blend until mixture is smooth and flecked with pimiento.

Turn into saucepan and stir in

2 cups milk
2 tablespoons chili sauce

Heat thoroughly, stirring frequently.

Garnish with **chopped parsley**.

    About 4 servings

POTATO BRUSSELS SPROUT CHOWDER

Set out a large saucepan or Dutch oven.

Set out to partially thaw

2 pkgs. (10 oz. each) frozen Brussels sprouts

Pare, dice and set aside

3 large (about 1½ lbs.) potatoes

Put into the saucepan

¼ lb. salt pork (rind removed), diced

Blender Pea Soup and Cheese Rusks (page 125)

Cook over medium heat about 3 min., stirring occasionally. Mix in

1 large onion, halved and sliced

Cook about 7 min., or until pork is lightly browned on all sides and onion is browned.

Cut Brussels sprouts into halves and add to saucepan with diced potato and

2 teaspoons salt
⅛ teaspoon pepper
½ teaspoon basil or marjoram, crushed
1 qt. milk
2 cups boiling water

Bring to boiling and simmer, uncovered, about 10 min., or until vegetables are partially tender.

Blend

⅓ cup cold water
⅓ cup all-purpose flour

Add gradually to hot mixture, stirring constantly. Bring to boiling; stir and cook 3 to 5 min. Serve immediately. *About 12 servings*

POTATO SOUP I

Set out a 2-qt. saucepan with a tight-fitting cover and a heavy 8-in. skillet.

Wash, pare and cut into ½-in. cubes

3 medium (about 1 lb.) potatoes

Put potatoes into the saucepan with

2 cups boiling water
¼ cup chopped onion
2 or 3 leeks, rinsed and chopped
1 stalk celery, rinsed and diced
1 teaspoon salt
½ teaspoon monosodium glutamate
½ teaspoon celery salt
⅛ teaspoon pepper

Cover saucepan; boil at moderate rate about 15 min., or until potatoes are tender.

Meanwhile, fry until crisp in the skillet

4 slices bacon

Remove to absorbent paper and set aside.

When potatoes are almost tender, heat in the same skillet

3 tablespoons bacon drippings

Blend into the drippings

1 tablespoon all-purpose flour

Heat until mixture bubbles. Remove from heat and add gradually, stirring constantly

1 cup milk

Return to heat and bring mixture rapidly to boiling, stirring constantly. Gradually add this mixture to potato mixture, stirring constantly. Crumble bacon into potato mixture. Cover and simmer about 5 min. *4 to 6 servings*

POTATO SOUP II

Set out a large saucepan.

Prepare

4 large potatoes, pared and diced
1 onion, chopped
1 pimiento, finely chopped

Heat in the saucepan

1 tablespoon fat

Mix potato, onion and pimiento into fat. Cook, stirring occasionally, until onion begins to brown. Add to saucepan

4 cups chicken broth
1 tablespoon paprika
½ teaspoon salt
1 tablespoon finely chopped parsley

Stir to mix. Bring to boiling and simmer, covered, about 30 min.

Blend in, a tablespoon at a time

3 tablespoons dairy sour cream

Serve hot garnished with additional chopped parsley. *6 servings*

POTATO BISQUE

▲ Base Recipe

Set out a heavy 3-qt. saucepan or saucepot with a tight-fitting cover.

Wash, pare and cut into ¼-in. slices

4 medium (about 1½ lbs.) potatoes

Put into the saucepan with

4 cups cold water

Cover and bring to boiling. Reduce heat to medium and add

1 stalk celery, finely cut
1 onion, chopped
1 pimiento, minced
1 teaspoon salt
⅛ teaspoon white pepper

Bring to boiling, reduce heat and simmer 1 hr.

Remove saucepan from heat and drain, reserving liquid. Force vegetables through a sieve into the broth. Add and stir until dissolved

2 beef bouillon cubes

Just before serving, put into a bowl

1 cup dairy sour cream

Add gradually, stirring constantly, about 1 cup of the hot soup. Immediately blend into the remaining soup. Cook over low heat just until heated; do not boil.

Serve at once, with a sprinkling of

Chopped fresh dill or parsley

About 1 qt. soup

—LIMA BEAN BISQUE

Follow ▲ Recipe. Omit potatoes. Heat **4 cups water** to boiling. Wash thoroughly and sort **½ lb. (about 1⅓ cups) dried large lima beans.** Add beans gradually to water, so slowly boiling does not stop. Cover and simmer 2 min.; remove saucepan from heat. Set aside and let beans soak 1 hr. Add vegetables and seasonings; cover and simmer 1 to 1½ hrs., or until soft. Drain, reserving liquid. Force vegetables through sieve into broth. Stir in the bouillon cubes. Continue as in ▲ Recipe.

CURRIED POTATO APPLE SOUP

Put into an electric blender container

1 can (10½ oz.) condensed cream of potato soup
1 soup can milk
1 or 2 apples, pared, cored and cut in pieces
½ teaspoon curry powder

Blend until smooth. Pour into a saucepan and heat thoroughly. *4 servings*

POTATO LEEK SOUP

Bring to boiling in a 2-qt. saucepan with a tight-fitting cover

3 cups water

Meanwhile, wash, pare and dice

3 medium (about 1 lb.) potatoes (about 2½ cups, diced)

Add potatoes to boiling water with

¼ cup (2 or 3) thinly sliced leeks (white part only)
1 teaspoon salt
½ teaspoon monosodium glutamate
⅛ teaspoon pepper

Cover saucepan and simmer gently about 15 min., or until potatoes are tender.

Meanwhile, dice and fry until crisp

3 slices bacon

Remove saucepan from heat and drain vegetables, reserving the broth. Force vegetables through food mill, ricer or sieve into broth.

Blend in bacon and

½ cup cream
½ cup milk
2 tablespoons chopped parsley
1 tablespoon butter or margarine

Reheat soup and serve hot. *6 servings*

CREAM OF POTATO LEEK SOUP

Pare and dice

3 medium potatoes

Wash and dice

2 leeks (include some green tops)

Heat to boiling in a saucepan

1 cup chicken broth

Add the potato and leek, bring to boiling and

cook, covered, 20 min., or until vegetables are tender.

Sieve mixture or purée in an electric blender. Return to saucepan, add and stir in
1½ teaspoons butter or margarine
1 teaspoon salt
⅛ teaspoon white pepper
1½ cups light cream
Heat thoroughly, stirring occasionally.

Garnish with
2 tablespoons snipped chives
¼ teaspoon paprika
Serve hot.   *About 4 servings*

CHILI POTATO SOUP

Fry until crisp in a large saucepan
2 slices bacon
Remove bacon, drain on absorbent paper, crumble and set aside.

Add to bacon fat in saucepan
¾ cup chopped onion
Cook until soft, stirring occasionally. Add to saucepan and stir to mix
3 medium potatoes, pared and diced
1½ teaspoons salt
2 cups boiling water
Cover and cook until potatoes are tender.

Purée potato mixture and return to saucepan. Mix in
2½ cups milk
1 teaspoon chili powder
¼ teaspoon oregano
⅛ teaspoon garlic salt
Few grains pepper
Heat thoroughly.

Top each serving with crumbled bacon and
Shredded Parmesan cheese
                                6 servings

GOLDEN PUMPKIN SOUP

Set out a 2-qt. saucepan.

Put into an electric blender container in order
1 cup water
1¾ cups cooked, mashed fresh pumpkin
1 to 2 tablespoons butter or margarine
1 small onion, quartered
2 chicken bouillon cubes

Specialty Cream of Tomato Soup and Picture Puzzle Sandwiches (page 116)

Add
¾ teaspoon salt
½ teaspoon nutmeg
¼ teaspoon Worcestershire sauce
Cover and blend until smooth.

Turn mixture into saucepan and stir in
1⅔ cups milk
⅓ cup heavy cream
Bring to boiling, stirring frequently.

Garnish with **chopped chives.** Serve immediately.   *5 or 6 servings*

For Cooked Fresh Pumpkin—Wash **pumpkin,** cut into halves and scoop out seeds and strings. Cut into 3- or 4-in. pieces and pare off rind. Place in saucepan; cover with small amount of **boiling salted water.** Cover and cook about 25 min., or until tender. Drain off any excess water. Mash until smooth or put through a sieve.

CREAM OF SPINACH SOUP

Cook following package directions
1 pkg. (10 oz.) frozen chopped spinach
Drain, reserving liquid in a 1-qt. measuring cup. Sieve spinach, if desired; set aside. Add to spinach liquid enough to yield 3½ cups liquid
Milk
Set aside.

Heat in a saucepan
¼ cup butter or margarine
Stir into butter
2 tablespoons grated onion
2 tablespoons finely chopped celery

Cook 1 min. Mix in
3 tablespoons all-purpose flour
¾ teaspoon salt
Few grains pepper
Heat until mixture bubbles. Stir in the reserved liquid and
½ cup light cream
1 chicken bouillon cube, crushed
Bring to boiling; stir and cook until thickened. Stir in spinach and heat thoroughly.

Serve hot sprinkled with **paprika.**
                                About 6 servings

SPECIALTY CREAM OF TOMATO SOUP

Children love this rich, colorful soup.

Set out a 1½- or 2-qt. saucepan.

Simmer in a small saucepan for 5 min.
2½ cups canned tomatoes
⅓ cup chopped onion
3 to 4 tablespoons sugar
1 teaspoon salt
½ teaspoon monosodium glutamate
½ bay leaf
Remove and discard bay leaf. Strain, forcing pulp of tomato through sieve. Set aside.

Melt in the large saucepan
2 tablespoons butter or margarine
Blend in
3 tablespoons all-purpose flour
½ teaspoon salt
Heat until mixture bubbles. Remove from heat and gradually stir in hot tomato mixture. Return to heat and bring to boiling, stirring constantly; cook 1 to 2 min. longer.

Slowly stir hot tomato mixture into

2 cups cold milk

Heat rapidly, without boiling. Serve hot. If desired, top with **popcorn** or spoonfuls of **unflavored whipped cream.**   *1 qt. tomato soup*

CREAM OF TOMATO SOUP

Combine in a saucepan

2¼ cups canned tomato juice
1 stalk celery with leaves, cut crosswise into quarters
½ small onion, sliced
2 sprigs parsley
½ bay leaf
6 whole cloves
1½ teaspoons sugar
½ teaspoon salt
Few grains white pepper

Bring to boiling, reduce heat, cover and simmer 10 min.

Meanwhile, prepare in a large saucepan
Sour Cream White Sauce (page 304)
Strain tomato juice mixture. Add it very slowly to the hot white sauce, stirring constantly and vigorously with a wooden spoon; do not boil.

Serve immediately. If desired, drop on top of each serving of soup a teaspoonful of
Whipped Sour Cream Topping (page 482)

About 3½ cups soup

CHEESE TOMATO SOUP

A creamy tomato soup with a tang.

Set out a 1½-qt. saucepan.

Put into an electric blender container
1¼ cups (10½- to 11-oz. can) condensed tomato soup
1 cup water
⅓ cup cream-style cottage cheese, or 1 pkg. (3 oz.) cream cheese (in pieces)
1 teaspoon lemon juice
1 teaspoon prepared horseradish
2 or 3 drops Tabasco
Cover and blend until mixture is smooth and flecked with cottage cheese.

Pour contents of container into saucepan. Heat to boiling. Add hot soup slowly to
1 cup milk
Return to saucepan and heat quickly, stirring frequently.

Serve immediately. Or cool and place in refrigerator to chill 2 or 3 hrs.

About 4 servings

SPICED FRESH TOMATO CREAM SOUP

Put into a large saucepan
8 firm ripe tomatoes, cut in halves
1 onion, quartered
2 tablespoons sugar
1 bay leaf
2 vegetable bouillon cubes
½ teaspoon salt
¼ teaspoon cinnamon
⅛ teaspoon cloves
¼ teaspoon pepper
Bring to boiling, stirring occasionally; simmer, covered, 1 hr.

Strain contents of saucepan through a cheesecloth-lined sieve. Set aside.

Combine in a saucepan
½ cup Thick White Sauce (page 304)
1 cup light cream
Set over low heat, stirring constantly, until smooth and thoroughly heated. Add the sieved tomato mixture gradually while stirring. Heat to serving temperature.

Serve topped with **Croutons** (page 39).

About 4 servings

VEGETABLE CHOWDER

Combine in a saucepan
2 cans (10½ oz. each) condensed cream of celery soup
2 cans (10¾ oz. each) condensed vegetarian vegetable soup
3 soup cans water
Heat until very hot. Garnish with **snipped parsley.**   *About 8 servings*

VEGETABLE MIX-UP CREAM SOUP

Set out a 1½-qt. saucepan with a tight-fitting cover.

Wash, pare or scrape, dice and set aside
2 medium carrots

Clean, cut into crosswise pieces and set aside
2 stalks celery, with leaves

Vegetable Mix-Up Cream Soup

Prepare and set aside
2 tablespoons chopped onion
2 tablespoons chopped parsley

Set out
3 cups milk
Heat in the saucepan
2 tablespoons butter or margarine
Add the onion and cook over medium heat, stirring occasionally with a spoon, until onion is tender.

Blend in
2 tablespoons all-purpose flour
½ teaspoon salt
½ teaspoon monosodium glutamate
Heat until mixture bubbles. Remove from heat. Add gradually, stirring in 1 cup of the milk. Cook rapidly, stirring constantly, until sauce thickens. Cook 1 to 2 min. longer. Stir in the prepared vegetables and the remaining 2 cups of milk. Bring to boiling, stirring constantly. Reduce heat, cover and simmer about 5 min.

Float **celery leaves** and **chopped celery** in the soup for garnish. Serve at once.   *4 servings*

MULTI-VEGETABLE CREAM SOUP

Set out a large saucepan.

Prepare
1 cup sliced raw carrot
1 cup diced raw potato
1 lb. fresh peas, shelled
1 cup raw cauliflowerets
¼ lb. fresh spinach, chopped
Put into the saucepan and bring to boiling
3 cups water
2½ teaspoons salt
Add carrot and potato, bring to boiling and simmer, covered, 10 min.

Stir in peas, cauliflowerets and spinach, bring to boiling and simmer, covered, 10 min.

Set out
> **3 cups milk**

Blend a small amount of milk with
> **2 tablespoons all-purpose flour**

Mix into vegetables along with remaining milk and
> **½ teaspoon chervil**
> **¼ teaspoon pepper**

Bring to boiling; reduce heat and simmer 5 min.

Serve hot sprinkled with **snipped parsley.**

6 to 8 servings

FISH SOUPS AND CHOWDERS

FISH STOCK

Bring to boiling in a large saucepan
> **1 qt. water**
> **1 tablespoon salt**
> **1 lb. fish trimmings (head, bones, skin and tail)**

Cover and simmer 30 min. Strain liquid and use as directed in recipes or for cooking fish.

About 1 qt. stock

SCANDINAVIAN FISH SOUP

The Scandinavians have an inspired way with fish. When they cook this fish soup, they are preparing the main dish at the same time!

Set out a large heavy saucepan or saucepot with a tight-fitting cover.

Rinse in cold water and drain well
> **2 lbs. dressed fish with head**
> **(such as cod, trout or mackerel)**

Using a sharp heavy knife, cut fish crosswise into 1-in. slices. Break through bone by tapping the knife with a hammer.

Put fish slices and head into the saucepan or saucepot with
> **1 qt. water**
> **1 tablespoon salt**

Bring to boiling. Reduce heat, cover and cook 8 to 10 min., or until fish flakes (page 9).

Meanwhile, wash, pare or scrape and dice
> **2 carrots**

Clean and chop
> **1 small onion**

Wash, pare and cut into ½-in. cubes
> **2 medium potatoes**

Cook vegetables (page 313) about 8 min., or until tender. Drain and set aside.

When fish is cooked, remove and discard the head. Ladle out 3 cups of the liquid and set aside. Keep the fish hot.

Beat until thick and piled softly
> **2 eggs**

Stir in
> **1 cup dairy sour cream**
> **2½ teaspoons salt**
> **1 teaspoon monosodium glutamate**

Add the reserved fish liquid very gradually,

stirring constantly. Add the vegetables. Cook over low heat just until heated; do not boil.

Garnish soup with
> **Minced chives**

Serve soup as first course; then drain fish and serve with **parsley potatoes** (boiled potatoes tossed in a mixture of melted butter and chopped parsley).   *About 1½ qts. soup*

MACARONI TUNA SOUP

Set out a large saucepan.

Chop and set aside
> **1 medium onion**

Heat in the saucepan
> **¼ cup butter or margarine**

Stir onion into butter and cook about 2 min. Pour in
> **1 qt. chicken broth**

Bring to boiling. Add gradually so boiling continues
> **4 oz. (about 1¾ cups) rotini or 1 cup elbow macaroni**

Add
> **1 cup diced celery**
> **1 teaspoon salt**
> **¾ teaspoon bouquet garni for soup**
> **Few grains cayenne pepper**

Boil, covered, stirring occasionally, about 10 min., or until macaroni is tender.

Stir in
> **1 cup milk**
> **1 cup light cream**
> **2 cans (6½ or 7 oz. each) tuna, drained and flaked**
> **1 can (3 oz.) chopped broiled mushrooms, undrained**

Heat to serving temperature, stirring occasionally.   *8 to 10 servings*

FISH AND CAPER SOUP

Set out a large saucepan.

Prepare and set aside
> **½ cup chopped celery**
> **½ cup chopped green pepper**
> **½ cup chopped onion**
> **1 or 2 large cloves garlic, crushed**

Cut into 1-in. pieces
> **1 lb. flounder fillets**

Set aside.

Heat in the saucepan
> **¼ cup butter or margarine**

Mix in the celery, green pepper, onion and garlic. Cook about 8 min., or until vegetables are tender; stir occasionally.

Mix in
> **2 tablespoons all-purpose flour**
> **½ teaspoon salt**
> **¼ teaspoon pepper**
> **¼ teaspoon thyme**
> **⅛ teaspoon cayenne pepper**

Heat until mixture bubbles. Stir in
> **3 cups hot chicken broth**

Mix in the flounder pieces. Bring to boiling; cook, covered, over low heat about 10 min., or until fish is tender.

Beat mixture with a fork to break up the fish. Add to the saucepan
> **2 cans (6½ or 7 oz. each) tuna, drained and flaked (page 9)**
> **¼ cup capers**
> **1 tablespoon lemon juice**

Heat, stirring occasionally, to serving temperature.   *6 servings*

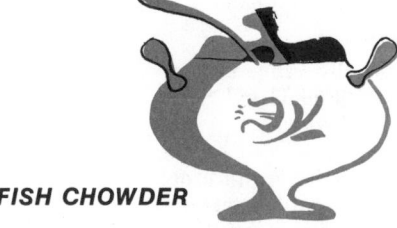

FISH CHOWDER

Set out a saucepot or large saucepan with a cover.

Have ready
> **2 lbs. cod or haddock fillets, cut in 2-in. pieces**

(If using frozen fish fillets, thaw following directions on package.)

Bring to boiling in the saucepot
> **2 cups water**
> **1½ teaspoons monosodium glutamate**

Add the fish pieces. Bring to boiling; reduce heat, cover and simmer 10 to 15 min. Drain fish, reserving liquid, and set aside.

Meanwhile, clean and cut into thin slices and set aside
> **3 medium onions**

Wash, pare and cut into thin slices enough potatoes to yield
> **2 cups thinly sliced potatoes**

Set aside.

Remove rind from and dice
> **2 oz. salt pork (about ¼ cup, diced)**

Put into the saucepot and cook over medium heat, occasionally moving and turning with a spoon, until salt pork is crisped and browned.

Fish Chowder

Remove the salt pork with a slotted spoon and set aside to drain on absorbent paper. Add the sliced onion; cook, moving and turning frequently with a spoon, until the onion is tender. Remove the onion with a slotted spoon and set aside.

Add to the fat in the saucepot and heat
> **2 tablespoons butter**

Blend in a mixture of
> **3 tablespoons all-purpose flour**
> **2 teaspoons salt**
> **⅛ teaspoon white pepper**
> **⅛ teaspoon thyme**
> **⅛ teaspoon finely crushed chervil**

Heat until mixture bubbles. Remove saucepot from heat.

Add gradually, while stirring constantly, the reserved fish liquid and
> **¾ cup water**

Add the potatoes and onion; return to heat. Simmer, stirring mixture occasionally, about 10 min., or until potatoes are tender when pierced with a fork. Stir in
> **½ cup milk**
> **⅓ cup cream**

Simmer about 5 min. longer; do not boil. Remove from heat; stir in the fish pieces and
> **½ cup tomato sauce**

Return to heat; simmer just until fish pieces are thoroughly heated.

Pour into a heated soup tureen and add the crisp salt pork. Serve at once.

About 2 qts. chowder

QUICK SALMON SOUP

Flake (page 9) and put into a saucepan
> **1 can (16 oz.) salmon**

Mix in
> **1 cup cooked fresh or canned tomatoes**
> **2 cups water**
> **1 small onion, thinly sliced**

Bring to boiling; simmer 20 min.

Combine in a saucepan
> **¼ cup all-purpose flour**
> **⅛ teaspoon garlic salt**
> **⅛ teaspoon pepper**

Blend in
> **3 cups milk**

Bring to boiling; cook until thickened, stirring constantly. Stir in salmon mixture and serve at once.

6 servings

CHEESE TUNA CHOWDER

Heat in a saucepan
> **¼ cup butter or margarine**

Mix in and cook 5 min., stirring occasionally
> **1 medium onion, chopped**
> **½ cup chopped celery**
> **¼ cup chopped green pepper**

Stir in a blend of
> **2 tablespoons all-purpose flour**
> **1 teaspoon salt**
> **¼ teaspoon pepper**

Heat until bubbly. Add gradually, stirring constantly
> **3 cups milk**

Bring to boiling; cook until thickened, stirring constantly. Add and stir until melted
> **2 cups shredded sharp Cheddar cheese**

Mix in
> **1 can (6½ or 7 oz.) tuna, drained and flaked**

Heat to serving temperature. Serve at once.

6 servings

SEAFOOD SOUP

Combine in a saucepan and cook 5 min.
> **6 medium blue point oysters with liquor**
> **1 cup diced scallops**
> **10 cherrystone clams**
> **5 or 6 celery leaf sprigs**

Mix in a bowl
> **2 tablespoons quick-cooking tapioca**
> **2 cups chicken broth, cooled**

Let stand 5 min.

Remove seafood from liquid and set aside. Skim liquid if necessary. Stir in tapioca-chicken broth mixture. Bring to boiling over medium heat, stirring frequently.

Meanwhile, beat together
> **2 egg yolks**
> **½ cup light cream**

Add gradually, stirring constantly, to mixture in saucepan. Cook and stir 3 min. Mix in the seafood and
> **Salt and pepper to taste**
> **1 tablespoon butter or margarine**

Heat thoroughly; do not boil.   *6 servings*

CLAM BISQUE

> ▲ *Base Recipe*

Set out a 1½-qt. saucepan.

Drain contents of
> **1 can (8 oz.) clams**

Put clams into an electric blender container with
> **1½ cups tomato juice**
> **2 tablespoons all-purpose flour**
> **1 slice onion**
> **1 teaspoon Worcestershire sauce**
> **½ teaspoon salt**
> **2 or 3 drops Tabasco**

Cover and blend until smooth.

Turn into the saucepan and stir in
> **2½ cups milk or cream**

Heat thoroughly, stirring frequently.

Serve with **Mayonnaise Garnish for Soup** (page 40).   *4 or 5 servings*

—CLAM-MUSHROOM BISQUE

Follow ▲ Recipe. Omit flour. Substitute **1¼ cups (10½- to 11-oz. can) condensed cream of mushroom soup** for 1 cup of the milk.

—SHRIMP BISQUE

Follow ▲ Recipe. Substitute **1½ cups canned shrimp** for the clams. Omit Worcestershire sauce. Add **½ teaspoon dry mustard.**

—LOBSTER BISQUE

Follow ▲ Recipe. Substitute **1 cup (6-oz. can) lobster** for clams.

QUAHOG CHOWDER I
(Hard-Shelled Clam Chowder)

> ▲ *Base Recipe*

Hard-shelled, soft-shelled and surf clams are the market species along the Atlantic Coast. Quahog is the common name for the hard-shelled clam in New England. When purchased in the shell, clams should be alive, that is, the gaping shells should close when handled. Here is a clam chowder, elegant but differing slightly from the usual New England version.

Set out a heavy 3-qt. saucepan.

For Clam Broth—Rinse thoroughly in running cold water
> **12 large hard-shelled clams**

Put clams into a large saucepan and add
> **3 cups water**

Cook over moderate heat until clam shells open completely. Drain the clams, reserving the broth. Set broth aside.

Remove clams from shells, cut off the hard outside of the clam (comb) and mince the clams. Set aside in refrigerator.

For Clam Chowder—Wash, cut off root ends and green tops, peel, rinse and slice thinly enough leeks to yield
> **¼ cup thinly sliced leek (white part only)**

Combine with
> **¼ cup minced onion**
> **¼ cup finely diced green pepper**
> **¼ cup diced celery**

Heat in the saucepan
> **2 tablespoons butter**

Add the vegetables and cook slowly, occasion-

ally moving and turning them with a spoon, 6 to 8 min., or until they are partially tender.

Meanwhile, wash, pare and finely dice enough potatoes to yield
½ cup finely diced potato
Set aside.

Scald (page 10)
1 cup cream
1 cup milk
When vegetables are partially tender, blend in
3 tablespoons all-purpose flour
Cook slowly 3 min. Add gradually, stirring constantly, 2 cups of the clam broth, the scalded cream and milk, potatoes and
½ teaspoon Worcestershire sauce
½ teaspoon monosodium glutamate
½ teaspoon salt
⅛ teaspoon thyme
3 drops Tabasco
Few grains white pepper
Bring to boiling over moderate heat; reduce heat and cook very slowly 35 to 40 min., stirring frequently. Add the minced clams and cook 5 min. longer. Pour soup into a tureen or individual soup bowls. Sprinkle over top
Finely chopped parsley
Serve with **chowder biscuits** or **crackers**.

4 to 6 servings

Note: If desired, 2 cans (8 oz. each) minced clams may be substituted for the fresh clams. Drain and reserve liquid. Substitute the reserved clam liquid for the clam broth. Increase milk in chowder to 1¾ cups.

—QUAHOG CHOWDER II

Follow ▲ Recipe for Clam Broth. Remove rind from and dice **¼ lb. salt pork.** Cook over medium heat in the saucepan, occasionally moving and turning pieces with a spoon, until salt pork is crisped and browned. Remove salt pork with a slotted spoon and set aside to drain on absorbent paper. Continue as in ▲ Recipe for Clam Chowder, cooking vegetables in **salt pork drippings**; omit butter. Add **2 chowder crackers**, crumbled, with minced clams. Omit parsley; add salt pork before serving.

CRAB SHRIMP GUMBO

Set out a large heavy skillet with a tight-fitting cover.

Prepare and set aside in refrigerator
1 lb. fresh shrimp with shells
(see Cooked Shrimp, page 294)

Wash pods, cut off and discard stem ends, slice and set aside
½ lb. okra (about 2 cups, sliced)

Clean, chop and set aside
1 large onion (about ¾ cup, chopped)
1 green pepper (about ½ cup, chopped)
2 stalks celery

Prepare and keep warm
Perfection Boiled Rice (page 165)

While rice is cooking, heat in the skillet over low heat
2 tablespoons butter or margarine
Add to skillet chopped onion, green pepper, celery and
¼ lb. (about ½ cup) diced cooked ham
1 clove garlic, minced
Cook mixture over medium heat until onion is tender.

Meanwhile, wash
6 ripe tomatoes
Dip into boiling water to loosen skins. Peel, cut out and discard stem ends. Chop tomatoes and add to skillet with okra and
1 cup water
1 teaspoon salt
⅛ teaspoon pepper
⅛ teaspoon cayenne pepper
⅛ teaspoon chili powder
⅛ teaspoon thyme
1 teaspoon chopped parsley
½ bay leaf, crushed
Cover and simmer 15 min.

Meanwhile, drain, remove and discard bony tissue and separate contents of
1 can (6½ oz.) crab meat (about ¾ cup)
Add crab meat and cooked shrimp to skillet and cook 10 min., or until okra is tender.

Serve gumbo on mounds of rice.

6 to 8 servings

RICH OYSTER STEW

▲ Base Recipe

Set out a 1-qt. saucepan.

Scald (page 10)
2 cups milk
2 cups cream

Meanwhile, drain, reserving liquor
1½ pts. oysters
Pick over oysters to remove any shell particles. Melt in the saucepan
⅓ cup butter
Add oysters with reserved liquor. Simmer 3 min., or until oysters are plump and edges begin to curl. Stir oyster mixture into scalded milk and cream with
2 teaspoons salt
¼ teaspoon monosodium glutamate
⅛ teaspoon white pepper
Serve at once with **oyster crackers**.

6 servings

Oyster Stew à la Moderne

—OYSTER STEW A LA MODERNE

Reconstitute, following directions on package, **1⅓ cups instant nonfat dry milk**, using **4 cups water**. Follow ▲ Recipe. Substitute reconstituted milk for milk and cream. Increase butter to ½ cup. Before serving sprinkle with **paprika**.

—LOBSTER STEW

Follow ▲ Recipe. Substitute **1 cup cooked lobster meat pieces** (see "Boiled" Lobster, page 290) for oysters. If present, simmer the tomalley (green liver) and coral (bright red roe) in the butter about 7 min. Add the lobster meat and cook over low heat 10 min. Remove from heat and cool slightly. Stirring constantly, gradually add the scalded milk and cream (a mere trickle at a time) to lobster mixture. Stir constantly until stew is a rich salmon color. Omit seasonings. Serve at once; **salt** may be added at the table.

BLENDER OYSTER STEW

Here the electric blender truly comes into its own—for in no other way can the oyster be so easily and so completely chopped and thus compelled to yield up its full rich flavor.

Remove any shell particles from
1 pt. oysters
Heat in a 2-qt. saucepan
¼ cup butter
Add the oysters and the oyster liquor to the saucepan. Cook very slowly until the edges of the oysters begin to curl.

Rich Oyster Stew

Meanwhile, scald (page 10)

2 cups milk

2 cups cream

Put oysters and cooking liquid into blender container with

2 teaspoons salt

½ teaspoon monosodium glutamate

⅛ teaspoon pepper

⅛ teaspoon mace

Cover container and blend 2 or 3 seconds, until oysters are coarsely chopped.

Pour blended mixture into saucepan in which oysters were cooked. Stir in scalded milk and cream. Heat slowly; do not boil.

Place pats of **butter** in serving bowls and pour hot soup over them. Serve immediately.

6 or 7 servings

CRAYFISH BISQUE

Set out a large kettle or saucepot with a tight-fitting cover.

Prepare and set aside in refrigerator

2 8-oz. fresh-frozen crayfish or rock-lobster tails (see Cooked Crayfish Tails, page 290)

Meanwhile, clean, mince and set aside

1 medium onion (about ½ cup)

1 leek, white part only

Wash, pare or scrape, finely chop and set aside

1 medium carrot (about ¼ cup, chopped)

Heat in the kettle over low heat

¼ cup butter or margarine

Blend in a mixture of

¼ cup all-purpose flour

1 teaspoon salt

⅛ teaspoon pepper

Heat until mixture bubbles. Remove from heat. Gradually stir in

5 cups quick chicken broth (page 10)

Few drops Tabasco

Add vegetables and

1 bay leaf

Return to heat; cover kettle and simmer 10 min. Meanwhile, finely chop the cooked crayfish. Add chopped crayfish meat to kettle. Cover and simmer 10 min. Remove bay leaf.

Place a food mill over a large bowl and pour soup mixture through the food mill, forcing through as much crayfish as possible. Return soup to kettle and reheat.

Beat slightly

2 egg yolks

Quickly stir about 3 tablespoons hot soup into egg yolks. Immediately return egg yolk mixture to soup, stirring vigorously. Cook soup until thoroughly heated, about 5 min., stirring constantly; do not boil. Add gradually, stirring constantly

1 cup cream

Add crayfish pieces remaining in food mill to soup. Stirring constantly, heat soup thoroughly.

8 servings

JIFFY LOBSTER BISQUE

Fast-cooking, rich-tasting goodness.

Set out a 2-qt. saucepan.

Drain and break into small pieces, the contents of

1 can (6½ oz.) lobster meat (about 1 cup, drained)

Set lobster aside.

Combine in the saucepan over medium heat

1½ cups milk

1¼ cups (10½-oz. can) condensed cream of mushroom soup

Blend in

1¼ cups (10¾-oz. can) condensed tomato soup

1 teaspoon Worcestershire sauce

4 or 5 drops Tabasco

Few grains cayenne pepper

Add lobster and bring mixture to boiling.

Remove from heat and stir in

1 tablespoon sherry extract

Serve at once. *5 servings*

LOBSTER TOMATO CREAM SOUP

▲ *Base Recipe*

Set out a heavy 3-qt. saucepan.

Prepare

1 live lobster, about 1¼ lbs. (see "Boiled" Lobster, page 290)

Dice the lobster meat and set aside.

Heat in the saucepan over low heat

¼ cup butter

Add and cook until onion is tender

2 tablespoons finely chopped onion

Blend in

¼ cup all-purpose flour

¼ teaspoon salt

¼ teaspoon monosodium glutamate

Few grains pepper

Heat until mixture in the saucepan bubbles. Remove from the heat. Add gradually, stirring in, in order

2 cups tomato juice

1 cup cream

½ cup milk

1½ teaspoons Worcestershire sauce

4 drops Tabasco

Cook rapidly, stirring constantly, until sauce thickens. Add the lobster meat, reserving a few pieces for garnish. Heat but do not boil. Stir in

3 tablespoons sherry

Pour into a soup tureen or individual soup bowls and garnish with the reserved lobster meat and

Whipped cream

6 servings

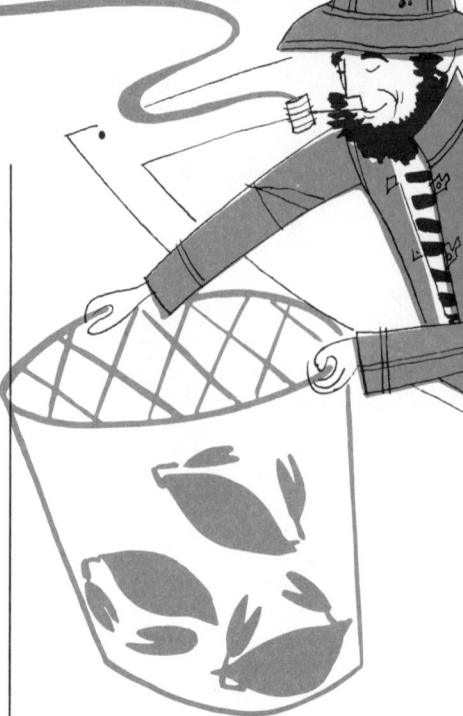

—CRAB TOMATO CREAM SOUP

Follow ▲ Recipe. Substitute **1 cup (4 oz.) fresh lump crab meat** for the lobster. Drain, remove and discard bony tissue.

SHRIMP BISQUE

(Bisque de Crevettes)

Typically French, the bisque is a rich smooth soup. The seafood bisque—shrimp, crab or lobster—is especially worthy of distinction.

Melt in a deep kettle

3 tablespoons butter

Add, cook and stir until onion is tender

½ cup minced onion

⅓ cup minced carrot

1 leek (white part only), minced

Slowly stir in

1 qt. White Stock (page 41)

1 teaspoon salt

⅛ teaspoon pepper

1 bay leaf

Cover and simmer over low heat about 10 min.

Meanwhile, wash in cold water

3 lbs. fresh shrimp with shells

Shrimp Bisque

Shellfish Chowder

Drop shrimp into a boiling mixture of
1 qt. water
1 pt. white wine
4 sprigs parsley
Cover tightly. Simmer 5 min., or only until shrimp are pink and tender. Drain, reserving 1 cup liquid. Cover with cold water to chill.

Drain shrimp again.

To Clean Shrimp—Remove tiny legs. Peel shells from shrimp. Cut a slit to just below surface along back (curved surface) of shrimp to expose the thin black vein. With knife point remove vein in one piece. Rinse shrimp quickly in cold water.

Reserve a few large shrimp for garnish. Mince remainder and stir into simmering soup. Cover and simmer about 10 min. Force mixture through a fine sieve or food mill. Stir in reserved liquid.

Beat slightly
3 egg yolks
Quickly stir about 3 tablespoons hot soup into egg yolks and return to soup, stirring vigorously over direct heat until well blended, about 5 min.

Gradually stir in
1 cup heavy cream
Add whole shrimp. Stirring constantly, heat thoroughly. Serve with **Croutons** (page 39).
8 servings

Note: If substituting 2½ cups canned or frozen shrimp, remove veins if present.

SHELLFISH CHOWDER

Set out
1 cup shucked clams
Drain thoroughly, reserving liquor
1 pt. oysters
Pick over oysters to remove any shell particles.

Dice
½ lb. scallops
Put the reserved oyster liquor into a saucepan. Add clams, oysters and scallops. Heat over medium heat 5 min. Drain, reserving liquid.

Prepare in a large saucepan
3 cups quick chicken broth (page 10)
Add the reserved liquid and
¾ cup cream or milk
Stir into liquid and let stand 5 min.
3 tablespoons quick-cooking tapioca
Bring to boiling, stirring constantly, and cook until soup is thickened. Vigorously stir 3 tablespoons hot soup into
3 egg yolks, slightly beaten
Immediately blend egg yolk mixture into hot soup. Cook 2 to 3 min., stirring constantly; do not boil. Stir in the clams, oysters, scallops and
½ teaspoon monosodium glutamate
¼ teaspoon celery salt
⅛ teaspoon salt
⅛ teaspoon pepper
Heat mixture thoroughly.   *About 6 servings*

CHILLED SOUPS

CHILLED LIMA BEAN SOUP

Heat to boiling in a large heavy saucepan
1 qt. water
Meanwhile, wash thoroughly and sort
½ lb. (about 1¼ cups) dried large lima beans
Add beans gradually to water, so slowly boiling does not stop. Cover and simmer 2 min.; remove saucepan from heat. Set aside and let beans soak 1 hr.

Simmer beans, covered, 1 to 1½ hrs., or until soft. Drain thoroughly.

Prepare
⅓ cup sliced green onion
Heat in a large saucepan over low heat
¼ cup butter or margarine
Add the green onion and cook over medium heat, stirring occasionally with a spoon, until

onion is tender. Remove from heat. Add the drained lima beans and
2 cans (10½ to 11 oz. each) condensed consommé
Return to heat and cook about 10 min.

Set a fine sieve or food mill over a bowl or saucepan and strain soup, forcing the vegetables through. Set aside to cool.

Blend in
1 cup cream
¼ teaspoon salt
⅛ teaspoon monosodium glutamate
Cover and set in refrigerator to chill.

Serve in chilled bowls and garnish with
Chopped chives or parsley
Paprika
10 servings

CRIMSON SOUP

A smooth-as-silk soup that's flecked with nubby bits of tangy beet. It's the perfect curtain-raiser for a salad luncheon.

Set out a large bowl.

Drain, reserving liquid
1 can (16 oz.) diced beets (about 2 cups, drained)
Combine the reserved beet liquid and enough water to make 1 cup. Pour into bowl.

Add and stir until sugar is dissolved
⅓ cup sugar
¼ cup cider vinegar
½ teaspoon salt
Force beets through a coarse sieve or food mill into the liquid mixture. Cover and set in refrigerator to chill. Just before serving, blend in
2 cups chilled cream
Serve in chilled bowls with **saltines.**
About 8 servings

Note: If desired, soup may be served hot.

CHILLED BEET SOUP

A truly elegant soup closely related to that all-time classic, borsch.

Set out a heavy 3-qt. saucepan with a cover.

Rinse, pare, and slice
3 medium fresh beets
Force through the fine blade of a grinder and put into the saucepan with
2 tablespoons minced onion
Pour in and bring to boiling
2½ cups water
Reduce heat, partially cover, and cook slowly for 30 min.

Remove from heat and add gradually, stirring constantly
2 cups cream
Return to heat and bring to boiling; stir in a mixture of
2 teaspoons cornstarch
1 tablespoon water

Cook 2 min. Blend in a mixture of
> **1 egg yolk, slightly beaten**
> **½ cup cream**

Remove from heat and stir in
> **1 tablespoon lemon juice**
> **1 teaspoon Worcestershire sauce**
> **1 teaspoon monosodium glutamate**
> **½ teaspoon salt**
> **½ teaspoon celery salt**

Chill thoroughly in refrigerator. Pour into chilled soup bowls; garnish each serving with
> **Dairy sour cream**

6 servings

CHILLED BORSCH

Set out a large bowl.

Drain, reserving liquid
> **1 can (16 oz.) whole beets**

Put reserved liquid into the bowl and add
> **2¾ cups cold water**

Stir in
> **⅓ cup sugar**
> **3½ tablespoons cider vinegar**
> **¼ teaspoon salt**

Put drained beets through coarse sieve or food mill into the liquid mixture, cover and put into refrigerator to chill.

Serve in chilled bowls, topped with tablespoonfuls of
> **Dairy sour cream**

About 1 qt. soup

MANHATTAN CUP

Combine in a 1-qt. jar
> **2 cans (10½ to 11 oz. each) chilled condensed beef broth**
> **1 soup can icy-cold water**
> **2 to 4 tablespoons lemon juice**
> **½ cup orange juice**
> **½ teaspoon Angostura bitters**
> **½ teaspoon sugar**

Cover jar and shake well. Serve over **ice cubes** in mugs and, if desired, garnish with **orange slices.**

6 to 8 servings

BUTTERMILK SOUP
(Kaernemaelksuppe)

Delicious on hot summer days. It may also be served as a beverage.

Beat until very thick and piled softly
> **3 eggs**

Add gradually, beating thoroughly after each addition
> **½ cup sugar**

Add
> **2 tablespoons grated lemon peel**

Pour over the egg mixture gradually, stirring until blended
> **2 qts. buttermilk**

Chill in refrigerator about 2 hrs.

Serve soup the day it is prepared, preferably soon after chilling.   *About 2½ qts. soup*

CUCUMBER BUTTERMILK SOUP

▲ *Base Recipe*

Set out an electric blender.

Rinse
> **3 medium cucumbers**

Cut eight ⅛-in. slices from one cucumber for a garnish. Place slices in a small bowl of ice and water and set in refrigerator.

Pare remaining cucumbers and cut into small chunks. Put into electric blender container with
> **½ cup milk**
> **2 or 3 green onions, peeled, rinsed and green tops trimmed to within 3 in. of white part**
> **1 teaspoon salt**
> **½ teaspoon monosodium glutamate**
> **⅛ teaspoon pepper**

Cover and blend until smooth.

Stir into
> **2 cups buttermilk**

Place in refrigerator and chill 1 or 2 hrs.

Pour into chilled bowls and garnish with cucumber slices.   *4 or 5 servings*

—CUCUMBER CHICKEN SOUP

Follow ▲ Recipe. Substitute 1¼ cups (10½- to 11-oz. can) condensed cream of chicken soup and 1 cup milk for buttermilk. Put into a saucepan and heat thoroughly.

GAZPACHO

Dashing and colorful as a Spanish dance, this "salad soup" will add excitement to an everyday menu. When made by Spanish cooks, gazpacho is usually served accompanied by minced vegetables in separate bowls.

An electric blender will be needed.

Prepare and set aside to cool
> **2 cups quick meat broth (page 10)**

Combine in a small bowl and set aside
> **3 tablespoons olive oil**
> **1 clove garlic, cut into pieces (impale pieces on wooden pick for easy removal)**

Put into the blender container, cover and blend to make coarse crumbs
> **4 to 6 saltine crackers**

Turn crumbs into a large bowl.

Put cooled broth into blender container with
> **½ onion, sliced**
> **3 stalks celery, cut in pieces**
> **4 sprigs parsley**
> **2 or 3 sprigs watercress**

Cover and blend until coarsely chopped.

Pour over crumbs in bowl. Remove and discard garlic from olive oil and stir oil into vegetable mixture. Add and mix well
> **2 cups tomato juice**
> **2 tablespoons lemon juice**
> **1 teaspoon salt**
> **¼ teaspoon pepper**
> **3 or 4 drops Tabasco**

Set in refrigerator until soup is thoroughly chilled and flavors are blended, about 4 hrs.

Just before serving, rinse, peel, cut out stem end and cut into eighths
> **1 medium ripe tomato**

Rinse and cut into ⅛-in. slices
> **½ small cucumber**

Add tomato and cucumber to soup. Serve in chilled bowls.   *About 6 servings*

LEEK AND POTATO SOUP

Prepare, using about 3½ cups
> **White Stock (page 41, or dissolve 3½ bouillon cubes in 3½ cups boiling water)**

Set aside.

Heat in a 3-qt. saucepan
> **¼ cup chicken fat or butter**

Add and cook over low heat about 5 min.
> **6 to 8 leeks (white part only), finely chopped**
> **¼ cup finely chopped celery**

Wash, pare and thinly slice
> **4 medium potatoes (about 3 cups, sliced)**

Add to saucepan with White Stock and
> **1 teaspoon salt**
> **⅛ teaspoon pepper**

Cover and simmer 15 to 20 min., or until potatoes are tender.

Put mixture through a fine sieve and blend in
2 cups cream
Chill in refrigerator.

Pour soup into a tureen. Sprinkle over the top
1 tablespoon chopped chives

Serve cold, surrounded with crushed ice. This may also be served hot.   *6 servings*

VICHYSSOISE

Although this soup often is considered typically French, it was actually developed by a chef in a popular American hotel.

Set out a 2-qt. saucepan with cover.

Prepare and set aside
3 cups quick chicken broth (page 10)

Wash, pare, dice and set aside
3 medium (about 1 lb.) potatoes

Prepare and set aside
**½ cup (about 1 medium) chopped
   onion**
⅓ cup chopped celery
**¼ cup finely chopped leek
   (white part only)**

Melt in the saucepan over low heat
3 tablespoons butter or margarine
Add the leek and onion and cook over medium heat, stirring occasionally, about 5 min. Remove from heat and add the chicken broth, potatoes, celery and
1 teaspoon salt
⅛ teaspoon pepper
Return to heat, cover and cook about 15 min., or until potatoes are tender when pierced with a fork.

Set a fine sieve or food mill over a bowl or saucepan and strain soup, forcing vegetables through. Set aside to cool. Cover; chill in refrigerator at least 3 hrs.

Shortly before serving, stir in
1 cup chilled cream
Pour into chilled serving bowls and garnish with a sprinkling of
Chopped chives

Vichyssoise

If desired, surround bowls with crushed ice. Serve with crisp salted **crackers**.
                              4 or 5 servings

CALIFORNIA CUP

Combine in a bowl
**1 can (10½ to 11 oz.) condensed
   tomato soup**
**½ soup can *each* cranberry juice
   cocktail and water**
1 teaspoon lemon juice

Chill until serving time. Divide into 3 mugs and swirl **dairy sour cream** (about 2 tablespoons for each serving) through the soup.
                              3 servings

CHILLED WATERCRESS SOUP

Set out a 1½-qt. saucepan.

Wash carefully and thoroughly (remove bruised leaves)
1 bunch watercress
Put watercress into an electric blender container with
2 cups water
2 sprigs parsley
1 sprig celery leaves
3 tablespoons all-purpose flour
2 tablespoons butter or margarine
2 chicken bouillon cubes
½ teaspoon salt
¼ teaspoon monosodium glutamate
⅛ teaspoon pepper
Cover and blend until smooth.

Pour into saucepan and bring to boiling. Reduce heat and simmer 5 min.

Cool; chill in refrigerator at least 3 hrs.

Before serving, stir in
1 cup sweet or dairy sour cream
Serve in chilled bowls. Garnish with thin, crisp slices of **radish** floating on top.
                              4 servings

FRUIT SOUPS

FRESH FRUIT SOUP

Take a tip from Scandinavia and serve the magic taste of summer in a cooling soup.

Set out a large heavy saucepan with a tight-fitting cover.

Rinse, cut into halves and remove pits from
½ lb. peaches
½ lb. plums
Put the fruit into the saucepan and add
1 qt. water
1 cup red wine
1 cup sugar
1 piece (2-in.) stick cinnamon
Cover and simmer about 1 hr., or until fruit is very tender. Force the fruit through a fine-sieve and return to the saucepan.

Blend to make a smooth paste
1 teaspoon cornstarch
2 teaspoons water
Stir into the fruit mixture. Bring to boiling. Reduce heat and cook 3 to 5 min. Cool. Chill in refrigerator.   *3 or 4 servings*

CHERRY SOUP
(Meggy Leves)

▲ *Base Recipe*

Bring to boiling in a 3-qt. saucepan with a tight-fitting cover
1 qt. water
Add to the water, breaking frozen blocks apart with fork
**2 to 2½ lbs. sweetened frozen
   tart cherries, slightly thawed**
½ teaspoon salt
Bring to boiling again. Cover saucepan and simmer cherries 10 min.

Meanwhile, put into a 1-pt. screw-top jar
½ cup cold water
Sprinkle onto it
¼ cup all-purpose flour
Cover jar tightly; shake until ingredients are well blended. Slowly pour flour-water mixture into cherry mixture, stirring constantly. Bring again to boiling. Cook 3 to 5 min., stirring occasionally. Remove from heat. Vigorously stir about ⅓ cup hot soup gradually into
3 egg yolks, slightly beaten
Immediately blend into hot soup. Stirring constantly, cook 2 to 3 min. (Do not overcook or allow soup to boil.) Remove immediately from heat. Gradually add, stirring vigorously, about 1 cup hot soup to
1 cup dairy sour cream
Immediately blend into remaining soup. Cool slightly. Place in refrigerator to chill.
                              About 6 servings

Note: Fresh tart red cherries, pitted, can be substituted for the frozen cherries. Sweeten the soup to taste.

**—CHERRY SOUP WITH SWEET CREAM
(Meggy Leves Más Módon)**

Follow ▲ Recipe. Cook **1 piece (1-in.) stick cinnamon** with cherries: remove and discard cinnamon before adding the flour-water mixture. Substitute **light or heavy cream** for sour cream; add directly to soup, stirring constantly.

**—CHERRY SOUP WITH WINE
(Meggy Leves Borral)**

Follow ▲ Recipe or a variation. Decrease boiling water to 3½ cups. Before chilling soup, stir in **½ cup sherry**.

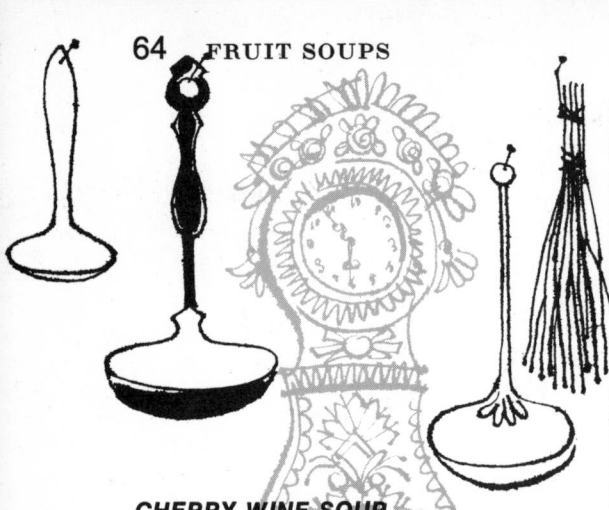

CHERRY WINE SOUP

▲ Base Recipe

Set out a 2-qt. saucepan.

Put through medium blade of food chopper
**2 cups pitted fresh cherries or 1 can
(16 oz.) pitted red tart cherries,
drained**
Put into the saucepan the cherries and
**1 cup liquid (water or syrup from
canned cherries)**
and a mixture of
**¼ cup sugar (more for fresh, or water-
pack cherries)**
2 teaspoons cornstarch
¼ teaspoon salt
¼ teaspoon cinnamon
Cook, stirring constantly, until thickened.

Remove from heat and stir in
**1 cup red wine such as Burgundy or
claret**
1 tablespoon brandy
3 drops almond extract
Chill in refrigerator at least 3 hrs. before serving.   *4 or 5 servings*

—CHERRY ORANGE WINE SOUP

Follow ▲ Recipe. Substitute **½ cup orange
juice** for one half the liquid. Add **¼ teaspoon
grated orange peel** with cherries. Omit almond extract.

NORWEGIAN FRUIT SOUP
(Söt Suppe I)

▲ Base Recipe

*This fragrant soup is usually served warm as a
dessert. It is very popular among Norwegians,
who love fruits and greet each summer with the
fervent hope that it will be kind to the fruit
harvest. The even warmth and long days of the
Norwegian summer favor the perfect maturing
of fruits, and the soups of this type seem to
capture that perfection.*

Bring to boiling in a deep saucepan
1 qt. water
Add to water so boiling will not stop
2 tablespoons rice
(The Rice Industry no longer considers it nec-

essary to wash rice before cooking.) Boil rapidly, uncovered, 15 to 20 min., or until a kernel
is entirely soft when pressed between fingers.
Drain rice, reserving liquid.

Rinse and finely chop enough apple to yield
½ cup finely chopped apple

Put into a bowl
**1 cup pitted dark sweet cherries
and juice**
Add
½ cup red raspberry syrup
¼ cup lemon juice
Return the rice water to the saucepan. Add the
apple and
1 piece (2-in.) stick cinnamon
Cook over medium heat 4 to 5 min., or until
apple is tender. Add the drained rice and the
cherry mixture. Remove the cinnamon. Simmer 5 min.

Blend to form a smooth paste
1 tablespoon cold water
1 teaspoon cornstarch
Blend cornstarch mixture into soup. Bring to
boiling. Continue to cook 3 to 5 min. Cool soup
slightly.

Serve soup warm or cold. If serving soup cold,
garnish with **whipped cream.**
                              About 3½ cups soup

—RAISIN FRUIT SOUP
(Söt Suppe II)

Follow ▲ Recipe. Omit cherries. Increase red
raspberry syrup to 1 cup. Add to the syrup
1 cup (about 5 oz.) dark seedless raisins.

SWEDISH FRUIT SOUP I
(Fruktsoppa I)

▲ Base Recipe

*Deprived of fresh fruits for many months of the
year by the rigors of climate, Swedish homemakers have created miracles with fruit syrups
and dried fruits, both native and imported. This
soup is usually served cold and is equally delicious as the first course or dessert.*

Set out a large saucepot with a tight-fitting
cover.

Set out
1 cup (about 6 oz.) dried apricots
¾ cup (about 3 oz.) dried apples
½ cup (about 3 oz.) dried peaches
½ cup (about 3½ oz.) dried prunes
**½ cup (about 2½ oz.) dark seedless
raisins**
With a sharp paring knife, remove pits from
prunes. Put fruits into the saucepot with
2 qts. water
Cover and soak fruits 2 to 3 hrs., if desired.

Add to the saucepot
¼ cup sugar
3 tablespoons quick-cooking tapioca
1 piece (3-in.) stick cinnamon
1 teaspoon grated orange peel

Bring to boiling; reduce heat, cover and simmer about 20 min., or until fruit is tender.
Remove from heat and stir in
1 cup red raspberry syrup
Chill soup in refrigerator.

Serve soup with
Whipped cream
Slivered blanched almonds
                              About 3 qts. soup

—SWEDISH FRUIT SOUP II
(Fruktsoppa II)

Follow ▲ Recipe. Omit raisins.

DRIED FRUIT SOUP

Set out a 2-qt. saucepan with a cover and an
electric blender.

Rinse well in cold water
1 cup (about 7 oz.) dried prunes
½ cup (about 3 oz.) dried apricots
¼ cup (about 1 oz.) seedless raisins
With a sharp paring knife, remove pits from
prunes. Cover and soak dried fruits for 2 to
3 hrs. in the saucepan with
1 cup orange juice
1 cup grape juice
2 cups water

Remove soaked fruit from liquid with slotted
spoon. Put fruit into electric blender container with
1 cup water
1 apple, washed, quartered and cored
2 tablespoons lemon juice
1 thin slice orange with peel
¼ cup sugar
Cover and blend.

Return blended mixture to saucepan and stir
into liquid in which fruit was soaked. Add
3 tablespoons quick-cooking tapioca
Bring to boiling, stirring constantly; cook
slowly about 20 min. Chill at least 3 hrs.

Serve in chilled bowls.   *6 to 8 servings*

Breads

The warm fragrance of new bread, so legend says, has magic power to dispel the doldrums and lift the spirits. Often called the "staff of life," bread takes on many interesting and delightful forms in the following pages. The quick-to-mix (and equally quick to disappear) breads, as well as yeast breads, hold an important place in this cookbook. You'll find bread recipes for every occasion. Some rich enough to be eaten as desserts, often bursting with candied fruit or flavored with almond, poppy or caraway seeds or ground nuts, the wonderful, hearty foreign breads are famous far beyond the countries of their origin.

YEAST BREADS

ONE-BOWL WHITE BREAD
(CoolRise Method)

Set out an electric mixer. Grease two 8x4x2-in. loaf pans.

Blend thoroughly in large mixer bowl
- **2 cups all-purpose flour**
- **2 tablespoons sugar**
- **1 tablespoon salt**
- **2 pkgs. active dry yeast**

Add to dry ingredients
- **½ cup softened butter or margarine**

Pour in gradually
- **2 cups very hot tap water**

Beat 2 min. at medium speed of electric mixer, occasionally scraping sides of bowl. Add and beat at high speed 2 min., scraping sides of bowl
- **1 cup all-purpose flour (or enough to make a thick batter)**

Mix in enough to make a soft dough
- **3 to 3½ cups all-purpose flour**

Turn out dough onto floured surface and knead dough (page 11) 8 to 10 min. Cover dough with plastic wrap and a towel; let stand 20 min. Punch down dough, divide in halves and shape into loaves. Place in greased pans and brush surface of loaves lightly with
- **Salad or cooking oil**

Cover pans loosely with plastic wrap. Place in refrigerator 2 to 24 hrs.

When ready to bake, remove from refrigerator. Gently remove plastic wrap and let stand 10 min. at room temperature. Prick gas bubbles (if any have formed) with a greased wooden pick or metal skewer.

Bake loaves at 400°F 30 to 40 min., or until bread tests done. Remove from pans to wire racks to cool. If a softer crust is desired, brush loaves lightly with **melted butter or margarine** while warm. *2 loaves bread*

ITALIAN BREAD
(Pane)

▲ Base Recipe

Whether in the round or long, narrow loaf, Italian bread is crusty and easy to prepare, containing only four ingredients. Hard, crunchy bread has been cherished by the Italians for centuries and today often finds its way into the American kitchen.

Lightly grease a 15½x12-in. baking sheet.

Soften
- **1 pkg. active dry yeast**

in
- **¼ cup warm water, 105°F to 115°F (Or if using compressed yeast, soften 1 cake in ¼ cup lukewarm water, 80°F to 85°F.)**

Set aside.

Put into a large bowl
- **1¾ cups warm water**
- **1 tablespoon salt**

Blend in
- **3 cups sifted all-purpose flour**

Stir softened yeast, and add to flour-water mixture, mixing well.

Measure
- **2 to 2½ cups sifted all-purpose flour**

Add about one-half the flour to the yeast mixture and beat until very smooth. Mix in enough remaining flour to make a soft dough. Turn mixture onto a lightly floured surface. Allow to rest 5 to 10 min.

Knead dough (page 11).

Select a deep bowl just large enough to allow dough to double. Shape dough into a smooth ball and place in greased bowl. Turn dough to bring greased surface to top. Cover bowl with waxed paper and towel and let stand in warm place (about 80°F) until dough is doubled, about 1½ to 2 hrs.

Punch down with fist. Knead on a lightly floured surface, about 2 min. Divide into two equal balls. Let stand covered 10 min.

Roll each ball of dough into a 14x8-in. rectangle. Roll up tightly into a long, slender loaf. Pinch ends to seal. Place loaves on prepared baking sheet. Cover loaves loosely with a towel and set aside in a warm place until doubled.

Bake at 425°F 10 min. Reduce temperature to 350°F and bake 1 hr., or until golden brown. To increase crustiness, place a flat pan on bottom of oven and fill with boiling water at beginning of baking period. *2 loaves bread*

—ITALIAN BREAD STICKS
(Grissini)

Follow ▲ Recipe. Grease 3 or 4 baking sheets. Decrease the salt to 2 teaspoons. Lightly roll dough into rectangles ¼ in. thick and about 6 in. wide. Cut dough crosswise with a floured knife into strips 1 in. wide. Use palm of hand to roll strips to pencil thickness, stretching to about 7-in. lengths. Place strips 1 in. apart on baking sheets. Brush lightly with a mixture of **1 egg**, slightly beaten, and **1 tablespoon milk**. Let rise in a warm place (about 80°F) until doubled, about 1 hr. Again brush with egg mixture and sprinkle with **coarse salt**. Bake at 400°F 18 to 20 min., or until sticks are browned and crisp all the way through.
About 4 doz. bread sticks

FRENCH BREAD
(Pain Français)

Here is a recipe for the most typical of French breads—a bread with flavor and fragrance. The long, slender loaf is crisp and golden outside, moist and soft inside.

Lightly butter a 15½x12-in. baking sheet and sprinkle with corn meal or farina.

Soften
- **1 pkg. active dry yeast**

in
- **¼ cup warm water, 105°F to 115°F (Or if using compressed yeast, soften 1 cake in ¼ cup lukewarm water, 80°F to 85°F.)**

Set aside.

Put into a large bowl
- **2 tablespoons butter**
- **1 tablespoon sugar**
- **1½ teaspoons salt**

Pour over ingredients in bowl

¾ cup hot water

Stir until shortening is melted. When mixture is lukewarm, blend in, beating until smooth

½ cup sifted all-purpose flour

Stir softened yeast and add, mixing well.

Measure

3¼ cups sifted all-purpose flour

Add about one-half the flour to yeast mixture and beat until very smooth. Mix in enough remaining flour to make a soft dough. Turn mixture onto a lightly floured surface. Allow to rest 5 to 10 min.

Knead the dough by folding the opposite side toward you. Using heels of hands, gently push dough away. Give dough a quarter turn. Repeat kneading process rhythmically until dough is smooth and elastic, 5 to 8 min., using as little additional flour as possible.

Select a deep bowl just large enough to allow dough to double. Warm it or rinse in hot water and dry; butter lightly. Shape dough into a smooth ball and place in bowl.

Grease surface lightly by turning ball in bottom of bowl. Turn greased side up. Cover with waxed paper and a towel. Let rise in a warm place (about 80°F) until doubled, about 1½ to 2 hrs.

Punch down with fist. Fold edges toward center and turn dough over. Cover. Let rise again until almost doubled, about 45 min. Punch down again; turn onto a lightly floured surface.

Roll dough into a 14x8-in. oblong. Roll up tightly into a long slender loaf. Pinch ends to seal. With palm of hands, gently roll dough back and forth, pulling to lengthen and taper the ends.

Place diagonally on prepared baking sheet. Make diagonal cuts with a sharp knife at 2-in. intervals, ¼ in. deep. Brush with part of a mixture of

1 egg white, slightly beaten
1 tablespoon water

Cover loosely with a towel and set aside in a warm place until doubled.

Brush again with egg white mixture and bake at 425°F 10 min. Brush again and reduce temperature to 375°F. Bake 15 min. Brush again. Continue baking about 20 min., or until bread is golden brown.

To increase crustiness, place a flat pan on bottom of oven and fill with boiling water at beginning of baking period.   *1 loaf bread*

ANADAMA BREAD

Two 9x5x3-in. loaf pans will be needed.

Bring to boiling

2 cups water

Add very gradually, stirring constantly

½ cup yellow corn meal

Remove from heat. Stir in until shortening is melted and ingredients are well blended

½ cup molasses
2 tablespoons shortening
1½ teaspoons salt

Set aside to cool to lukewarm.

Meanwhile, soften

1 pkg. active dry yeast

in

½ cup warm water, 105°F to 115°F
(Or if using compressed yeast, soften 1 cake in ½ cup lukewarm water, 80°F to 85°F.)

Set aside.

When corn meal mixture is lukewarm, stir mixture, and blend in, beating until smooth

1 cup sifted all-purpose flour

Stir softened yeast mixture and add, mixing thoroughly.

Measure

5 cups sifted all-purpose flour

Add about one-half the flour to the yeast mixture and beat until very smooth. Then beat in enough remaining flour to make a soft dough. Turn dough onto a lightly floured surface and allow it to rest 5 to 10 min. before starting to knead.

Knead dough (page 11).

Form dough into a large ball and place it in a greased, deep bowl just large enough to allow dough to double. Turn dough to bring greased surface to top. Cover with waxed paper and towel and let stand in a warm place (about 80°F) until dough is doubled, about 1 hr.

Grease the loaf pans.

Punch down dough with fist and turn onto a lightly floured surface. Divide into two equal portions and form into smooth balls. Cover and allow to rest 5 to 10 min.

To shape into loaves, flatten one portion and form it into a 9x7x1-in. oblong. The width should be about the same as the length of bread pan. Fold narrow ends to center of oblong, overlapping slightly. Press each end down firmly; shape evenly. Seal dough by pinching center fold and ends. Round top of loaf and place, sealed edge down, in prepared pan. Repeat for other portion of dough. Brush tops of loaves with

Melted butter

Cover loaves with waxed paper and towel and let rise again until doubled, about 1 hr.

Bake at 375°F about 45 min., or until bread sounds hollow when tapped lightly. Remove bread from pans. Cool on racks.

2 loaves bread

SWEET RYE BREAD I
(Limpa I)

▲ *Base Recipe*

Soften

2 pkgs. active dry yeast

in

½ cup warm water, 105°F to 115°F
(Or if using compressed yeast, soften 1 cake in ½ cup lukewarm water, 80°F to 85°F.)

Set aside.

Put into a large bowl

½ cup firmly packed brown sugar
⅓ cup molasses
1 tablespoon shortening
1 tablespoon salt
2 teaspoons caraway seed
½ teaspoon ground anise seed

French Bread

Pour over ingredients in bowl and set aside until lukewarm

1¼ cups hot water

When lukewarm, blend in, beating until smooth

1 cup sifted all-purpose flour

Stir softened yeast and add, mixing well.

Measure

4 to 4½ cups sifted all-purpose flour
2 cups rye flour

Add the rye flour and beat until very smooth. Then beat in enough remaining flour to make a soft dough. Turn dough onto a very lightly floured surface. Allow dough to rest 5 to 10 min.

Knead dough (page 11).

Form dough into a large ball and put into a greased, deep bowl. Turn to bring greased surface to top. Cover with waxed paper and a towel and let stand in warm place (about 80°F) until dough is doubled.

Punch down with fist; pull edges in to center and turn dough completely over in bowl. Cover and let rise again until dough is nearly doubled.

Punch down dough and turn out on a lightly floured surface.

Grease a baking sheet.

Divide dough into two portions and shape into balls. Cover and allow to rest 5 to 10 min. Remove to greased baking sheet. Cover and let rise until dough is doubled.

Bake at 375°F 25 to 30 min., or until lightly browned.

Cool completely on cooling racks.

2 loaves bread

—SWEET RYE BREAD II (Limpa II)

Follow ▲ Recipe. Put **1 tablespoon grated orange peel** into bowl with brown sugar.

—SWEDISH RYE BREAD (Ragbröd)

Follow ▲ Recipe. Decrease brown sugar to ¼ cup and molasses to ¼ cup.

CHEESE YEAST BREAD

Two 9x5x3-in. loaf pans will be needed.

Scald (page 10)

2¼ cups milk

Meanwhile, soften

1 pkg. active dry yeast

in

¼ cup warm water, 105°F to 115°F (Or if using compressed yeast, soften 1 cake in ¼ cup lukewarm water, 80°F to 85°F.)

Set aside.

Shred and set aside

10 oz. sharp Cheddar cheese (about 2½ cups, shredded)

Put into a large bowl

2 tablespoons sugar
1 tablespoon shortening
2 teaspoons salt

Immediately pour scalded milk over ingredients in bowl and stir until shortening is melted. When lukewarm, beat in until smooth

1 cup sifted all-purpose flour

Stir softened yeast and add, mixing well.

Measure

4 to 5 cups sifted all-purpose flour

Add about one-half of the flour to yeast mixture and beat until very smooth. Add and mix in the cheese and enough of the remaining flour to make a soft dough. Turn dough onto a lightly floured surface. Let it rest 5 to 10 min.

Knead dough (page 11).

Form dough into a ball and put it into a greased, deep bowl. Turn dough to bring greased surface to top. Cover with waxed paper and a clean towel and let stand in warm place (about 80°F) until dough is doubled.

Grease the loaf pans.

Punch down dough with fist and turn out onto a lightly floured surface. Divide dough into two equal portions. Cover and allow to rest 5 to 10 min. Shape each portion into a loaf and put into greased pan. Brush tops of loaves with

Melted butter or margarine

Cover loaves with waxed paper and towel and let rise again until doubled.

Bake at 375°F about 50 min., or until bread sounds hollow when lightly tapped.

2 loaves bread

YEAST SWEET BREADS AND COFFEE CAKES

BASIC YEAST DOUGH

▲ *Base Recipe*

Scald (page 10)

2 cups milk

Meanwhile, soften

2 pkgs. active dry yeast

in

½ cup warm water, 105°F to 115°F. (Or if using compressed yeast, soften 2 cakes in ½ cup lukewarm water, 80°F to 85°F.)

Set aside.

Put into a large bowl

1 cup butter, softened
½ cup sugar
2 teaspoons salt
2 teaspoons grated lemon peel

Immediately pour scalded milk over ingredients in bowl and stir mixture until butter is completely melted. When mixture has cooled to lukewarm, blend in, beating until smooth

2 cups sifted all-purpose flour

Stir softened yeast and add, mixing well.

Measure

7 to 8 cups sifted all-purpose flour

Add about one-half of the flour to the dough and beat until very smooth.

Add in thirds, beating well after each addition

4 eggs, well beaten

Then beat in enough of the remaining flour to make a soft dough. Turn dough onto a lightly floured surface and allow it to rest 5 to 10 min.

Knead dough (page 11).

Form dough into a large smooth ball and place it in a lightly greased, deep bowl. Turn dough to bring greased surface to top.* Cover with waxed paper and towel; let stand in warm place (about 80°F) until dough is doubled, about 1½ hrs.

Punch down dough with fist and turn out onto a lightly floured surface. Allow dough to rest 10 min. before shaping.

Complete as directed in any of the following variations.

Enough dough for 4 coffee cakes or 4 doz. rolls

*This dough may be kept about 3 days in the refrigerator. Make sure dough is greased and well covered to keep surface of dough moist and elastic. Punch down dough occasionally as it rises. Remove amount of dough needed for a single baking and immediately return remainder to refrigerator. Proceed as directed in the desired variation.

Note: For bread, shape dough into 3 loaves. Place in greased 9x5x3-in. loaf pans. When dough is light, bake at 400°F about 50 min.

—SWEET ROLLS (Buchteln)

To prepare 2 doz. rolls, use one-half of dough in ▲ Recipe. Butter two 11x7x1½-in. pans. Roll dough ⅓ in. thick. Using a sharp knife,

cut dough into twenty-four 3x2-in. rectangles. Spread rectangles almost to edges with **fruit preserves.** Starting with the shorter side, roll up rectangles of dough. Arrange twelve rolls in each pan. Brush generously with **melted butter.** Cover with waxed paper and a towel and let rise in a warm place (80°F) until almost doubled. Bake at 350°F 25 to 30 min., or until rolls are lightly browned. Meanwhile, prepare a glaze by thoroughly blending together ½ **cup sifted confectioners' sugar** and **1 tablespoon milk or cream.** Remove rolls from pans to cooling racks; cool slightly. Using a spoon, drizzle glaze over rolls.

—PLUM COFFEE CAKE
(Pflaumenkuchen)

To prepare 2 rich coffee cakes, decrease ingredients to ½ amounts in ▲ Recipe except decrease milk from 2 cups to ¼ cup, salt from 2 teaspoons to ½ teaspoon, and flour from 9 or 10 cups to 3 cups. Proceed as directed. Lightly grease two 9-in. round layer cake pans. Rinse and remove pits from **25 (about 1¼ lbs.) small Italian plums.** Divide dough in halves; press evenly into pans. Brush with **melted butter.** Arrange plums cut side up on dough to 1 in. from edge of pan. Sprinkle with a mixture of about **1½ cups sugar** (depending on tartness of fruit), **2 tablespoons all-purpose flour** and **2 teaspoons cinnamon.** Dot with ¼ **cup butter.** Cover with waxed paper and a towel and let rise in a warm place (80°F) until almost doubled, about 1 hr. Bake at 375°F 15 min. Then pour a mixture of **4 egg yolks,** beaten, **2 tablespoons sugar** and ¼ **cup cream** over plums. Continue baking 15 to 20 min., or until custard topping is set.

—CINNAMON COFFEE CAKE
(Zimtkuchen)

To prepare 2 coffee cakes, use one-half of dough in ▲ Recipe. Lightly grease two 11x7x 1½-in. pans or two 10-in. round layer cake pans. Divide dough into halves and roll out to fit the pans. Fit into pans. Brush dough with ¼ **cup melted butter;** sprinkle with a mixture of ⅔ **cup sugar** and **2 teaspoons cinnamon.** Cover with waxed paper and a towel and let rise in a warm place (80°F) until almost doubled. Bake at 375°F about 20 min.

—CRUMB COFFEE CAKE
(Streuselkuchen)

Follow recipe for Cinnamon Coffee Cake; omit sugar-cinnamon mixture. Prepare and top with **Streusel Topping** (see Almond-Crumb Coffee Cake, page 71).

—APPLE KUCHEN

To prepare 2 coffee cakes, use one-half of dough in ▲ Recipe. Lightly grease two 9- or 10-in. square pans. Melt ¼ **cup butter;** set aside. Wash, quarter, pare, core and thickly slice **4 cooking apples.** Divide dough in half and evenly press each half into pan. Press apple slices, rounded edge up, into dough forming three rows. Sprinkle each evenly with one half of a mixture of ½ **cup sugar** and ½ **teaspoon cinnamon** and drizzle with 2 tablespoons melted butter. Let rise in a warm place until doubled. Bake at 350°F 40 to 50 min., or until apples are tender and top is well browned. Remove coffee cakes from pans to cooling racks.

—GLAZED COFFEE CAKE

To prepare 2 coffee cakes, use one-half of dough in ▲ Recipe. Lightly grease two 9- or 10-in. round cake pans. Divide dough in half. Roll each half with hands into a long roll about 1 in. in diameter. Coil each roll into pan, beginning at outer edge; press dough lightly with hand to level. Brush tops with **melted butter.** Let rise in a warm place until doubled. Bake at 350°F 30 to 35 min. Remove coffee cakes from pans to cooling racks, and spread with a **confectioners' sugar glaze.**

ALMOND COFFEE CAKE BRAID
(Fonott Kalács Mandulával)

A baking sheet will be needed.

Measure and set aside
    4 to 4¼ cups sifted all-purpose flour

Scald (page 10)
    ¾ **cup milk**

Meanwhile, soften
    1 pkg. active dry yeast
in
    ¼ **cup warm water, 105°F to 115°F**
    (Or if using compressed yeast, soften 1 cake in ¼ cup lukewarm water, 80°F to 85°F.)
Set aside.

Put into a large bowl
    ⅓ **cup sugar**
    ⅓ **cup butter**
    1½ teaspoons salt
Immediately pour the scalded milk over ingredients in bowl. When the milk mixture is lukewarm, stir and add ½ cup of the flour, beating until dough is smooth. Stir the softened yeast and add to dough, mixing well. Add about one-half of the remaining flour and beat until very smooth.

Beat in
    1 egg, well beaten
    ½ **cup (about 2½ oz.) raisins**
    ½ **cup (about 3 oz.) almonds, blanched, toasted and coarsely chopped**
    2 teaspoons grated lemon peel
    1 teaspoon lemon juice
Then beat in enough of remaining flour to make a soft dough. Turn dough onto a lightly floured surface and let stand 5 to 10 min.

Knead dough (page 11).

Form dough into a large ball and put it into a greased bowl. Turn dough to bring greased surface to top. Cover bowl with waxed paper and towel and let stand in warm place (about 80°F) until dough is doubled. Punch dough down with fist; pull edges of dough in to center and turn dough completely over in bowl. Cover; let dough rise again until nearly doubled.

Turn out onto floured surface. Divide dough into halves. Roll each half with palms of hands into a strip 1 in. in diameter and about 26 in. long. To braid, lay one strip horizontally on center of board. Lay other strip vertically on top, crossing at center of first strip. Grasp ends of horizontal strip and reverse positions. Do the same with vertical strip. Repeat until all dough is braided.

Lightly grease the baking sheet.

Place braided dough flat on baking sheet, tucking the ends under the braid. Brush with
    Egg, slightly beaten
Let rise again 30 to 45 min., or until light. Brush again with some of the beaten egg.

Bake at 350°F 45 to 50 min., or until golden

brown. Remove coffee cake to cooling rack. When cool, cut into ½-in. slices.

About 24 slices

COFFEE BREAD
(Vetebröd)

▲ Base Recipe

Two baking sheets will be needed.

Set out
½ cup finely chopped blanched almonds

Scald (page 10)
1 cup milk or cream

Meanwhile, soften
1 pkg. active dry yeast

in
**¼ cup warm water, 105°F to 115°F
(Or if using compressed yeast, soften 1 cake in ¼ cup lukewarm water, 80°F to 85°F.)**

Set aside.

Put into a large bowl
½ cup butter
⅓ cup sugar
1 teaspoon salt

Immediately pour scalded milk over ingredients in bowl. When lukewarm, blend in, beating until smooth
1 cup sifted all-purpose flour

Stir softened yeast and add, mixing well.

Measure
2 to 2½ cups sifted all-purpose flour

Add about one-half the flour to the yeast mixture and beat until very smooth.

Beat in
1 egg, well beaten

Then beat in enough remaining flour to make a soft dough. Turn dough onto a lightly floured surface and allow dough to rest 5 to 10 min.

Knead dough (page 11).

Form dough into a large ball and put it into a greased, deep bowl. Turn dough to bring greased surface to top. Cover with waxed paper and towel and let stand in warm place (about 80°F) until dough is doubled.

Punch down with fist; pull edges of dough in to center and turn dough completely over in bowl. Cover and let rise again until nearly doubled. Punch down and turn dough out onto lightly floured surface. Divide dough into two portions and shape into oblong loaves.

Lightly grease the baking sheets.

Place loaves on baking sheets and brush with
Egg white, slightly beaten

Sprinkle each loaf with one-half of a mixture of chopped almonds and
⅓ cup sugar

Cover and let rise about 45 min., or until dough is doubled.

Bake at 375°F 20 to 25 min.

Cool completely on cooling racks.

2 loaves bread

—CARDAMOM BRAID
(Kardemumma Fläta)

Follow ▲ Recipe. Add to ingredients in bowl **1 teaspoon cardamom**. After second rising, divide dough into 6 equal portions. Roll each portion into a strip about 1 in. thick. Place 3 strips on each greased baking sheet and braid, tucking open ends under. Omit egg white and almond-sugar mixture. Cover and let rise about 45 min., or until doubled. Bake at 375°F about 25 min., or until lightly browned.

—SAFFRON BRAID
(Saffronsbröd)

Follow ▲ Recipe. Crumble very finely into a small cup enough saffron to yield **1 teaspoon saffron**. Pour over the saffron **2 tablespoons boiling water**. Stir and set aside to cool to lukewarm. Beat in with the egg. After second rising, divide dough into 6 equal portions. Roll each portion into a strip about 1 in. thick. Place 3 strips on each greased baking sheet and braid, tucking open ends under. Omit egg white and almond-sugar mixture. Cover and let rise about 45 min., or until doubled. Bake at 375°F about 25 min.

—TWISTS
(Kringlor)

Follow ▲ Recipe. Add to ingredients in bowl **1 tablespoon grated orange peel**. Instead of dividing dough for loaves, break off pieces of dough and roll with hands into strips about 5 in. long and ⅜ in. thick. Shape as in Christmas Rolls. Or hold one end of strip and coil to form a closed spiral, tucking end under securely. Or coil ends of strips in opposite directions until coils are opposite each other. Or coil strips as in Christmas Rolls, but do not place two strips together. Press **1 currant** firmly into the center of each coil. Place rolls on greased baking sheets. Omit egg white and almond-sugar mixture. Cover and let rise until doubled. Bake at 375°F 10 to 15 min.

About 4 doz. rolls

—CHRISTMAS ROLLS
(Julebullar)

Part of the charming ceremony of St. Lucia's Day, Julebullar are offered to family and guests on the morning of December 13, the day that marks the beginning of the Christmas holidays in Sweden. In each household one of the young daughters (or a young maid), dressed in traditional white robe, red girdle and stockings, and wearing a crown of evergreen leaves and lighted candles, brings saffron cakes and coffee to all the bedrooms of the house. She sings a traditional song outside the door, then enters and makes her ceremonial offering.

Follow ▲ Recipe. Instead of dividing dough for loaves, break off pieces of dough and roll with hands into strips 4 in. long and ½ in. thick. Coil each end in to center of strip. Place two coiled strips together so that coils are back to back. Or place two coiled strips at right angles, one on top of the other. Or shape strip into a half circle and coil ends in opposite directions. Press **1 raisin** into the center of each coil. Place rolls on greased baking sheets. Omit egg white and almond-sugar mixture. Cover and let rise until doubled. Bake at 375°F about 15 to 20 min.

About 4 doz. rolls

GOLDEN COFFEE CAKE
(Aranygaluska)

Many sugary balls of dough—raisin dotted and baked in a tubed pan.

A 10-in. tubed pan will be needed.

Measure and set aside
4¾ to 5 cups sifted all-purpose flour

Scald (page 10)
½ cup milk

Meanwhile, soften
2 pkgs. active dry yeast

in
**½ cup warm water, 105°F to 115°F
(Or if using compressed yeast, soften 2 cakes in ½ cup lukewarm water, 80°F to 85°F.)**

Set aside.

Twists

Put into a large bowl

    ½ cup shortening
    ½ cup sugar
    1½ teaspoons salt

Immediately pour the scalded milk over ingredients in bowl. When mixture is lukewarm, mix in ½ cup of the flour, beating until dough is smooth. Stir the softened yeast and add to dough, mixing well. Add about one-half of the remaining flour and beat until very smooth.

Beat in

    2 eggs, well beaten

Then beat in enough of remaining flour to make a soft dough. Turn dough onto a lightly floured surface, cover and allow it to rest 5 to 10 min.

Knead dough (page 11).

Form dough into a large ball and put into a greased bowl. Turn dough over to bring greased surface to top. Cover bowl with waxed paper and towel and let stand in warm place (about 80°F) until dough is doubled.

Punch dough down with fist; pull edges in to center and completely turn dough over in bowl. Cover bowl and let dough rise again until nearly doubled.

Lightly grease the tubed pan.

Mix together in a shallow dish and set aside

    1 cup sugar
    ¾ cup (about 3 oz.) finely chopped
        walnuts
    1½ teaspoons cinnamon

Place in another shallow dish and set aside

    ½ cup butter, melted

Measure and set aside

    ½ cup (about 2½ oz.) raisins

Tear off bits of dough and form into balls about 1¼ in. in diameter. Roll balls first into butter then roll lightly in sugar mixture. Arrange layer of balls in the tubed pan so that they do not touch each other. Sprinkle about one-third of the raisins over balls and slightly press raisins into balls. Continue in this manner until all dough is made into balls and arranged in the pan and all raisins are used. Sprinkle any remaining sugar mixture or butter over top layer of balls. Cover pan with waxed paper and towel and let dough rise again 30 to 45 min., or until light.

Bake at 375°F 35 to 40 min., or until golden brown. Run spatula around sides of coffee cake. Invert onto plate. To serve, break coffee cake apart with two forks.   *8 to 10 servings*

SWEDISH TEA RING
(Krans)

Two baking sheets will be needed.

Scald (page 10)

    1 cup milk or cream

Meanwhile, soften

    1 pkg. active dry yeast

in

    ¼ cup warm water, 105°F to 115°F
        (Or if using compressed yeast,
        soften 1 cake in ¼ cup lukewarm
        water, 80°F to 85°F.)

Set aside.

Put into a large bowl

    ½ cup sugar
    1 teaspoon salt

Pour scalded milk over ingredients in bowl.

When lukewarm, blend in, beating until smooth

    1 cup sifted all-purpose flour

Stir softened yeast and add, mixing well.

Measure

    4 cups sifted all-purpose flour

Add about one-half the flour to the yeast mixture and beat until very smooth. Beat in

    2 eggs, well beaten

Vigorously beat in, 2 to 3 tablespoons at a time

    ½ cup butter, softened

Beat in enough of the remaining flour to make a soft dough.

Turn dough onto a lightly floured surface. Allow dough to rest 5 to 10 min.

Knead dough (page 11).

Form dough into a large ball and put it into a greased, deep bowl. Turn dough to bring greased surface to top. Cover with waxed paper and towel and let stand in warm place (about 80°F) until dough is doubled.

Punch down with fist; pull edges of dough in to center and turn dough completely over in bowl. Cover bowl and let dough rise again until nearly doubled.

Punch down and turn dough out onto lightly floured surface. Divide into two balls. Roll each ball into an 18x9-in. rectangle.

Spread each rectangle with one-half of

    ¼ cup butter, softened

Sprinkle each rectangle with one-half of a mixture of

    ¾ cup firmly packed light brown sugar
    1½ tablespoons cinnamon
    ½ cup (about 2½ oz.) dark seedless
        raisins

Swedish Tea Ring

Beginning with the longer side, roll dough tightly. Press edges to seal.

Lightly grease the baking sheets.

Place uncut roll, sealed edge down, on the greased baking sheet. Pull ends together to form a ring, pressing slightly to seal ends. With scissors, snip at 1-in. intervals through ring almost to center. Turn each cut section on its side. Repeat procedure for the second ring. Brush rings lightly with

    Melted butter

Cover and let rise until doubled.

Bake at 350°F 20 to 25 min.

Meanwhile, blend together (for frosting)

    ½ cup sifted confectioners' sugar
    1 tablespoon milk
    ½ teaspoon vanilla extract

When tea rings are done, remove to cooling racks and frost while still warm.   *2 tea rings*

SOUR CREAM KUCHEN

▲ Base Recipe

This yeast kuchen is rich, sweet, almost as tender as pastry—and if you can hide it from your family, it will keep remarkably fresh and flavorful for several days, if wrapped in aluminum foil or other moisture-vaporproof material.

Two baking sheets will be needed.

Heat in top of double boiler over simmering water until edges become slightly yellow

    1 cup dairy sour cream

(Separation of cream will not affect quality of the product.)

Meanwhile, soften

    2 pkgs. active dry yeast

in

    ½ cup warm water, 105°F to 115°F
        (Or if using compressed yeast,
        soften 2 cakes in ½ cup lukewarm
        water, 80°F to 85°F.)

Set aside.

Sift together

    1 cup sifted all-purpose flour
    2 teaspoons salt
    ¼ teaspoon baking soda

Set aside.

Cream together until butter or margarine is softened

¾ cup butter or margarine
1 tablespoon grated lemon peel

Add gradually, creaming until fluffy after each addition

¾ cup sugar

Add in thirds, beating well after each addition

3 eggs, well beaten

Add and blend in the heated cream. Blend in the dry ingredients, beating until smooth. Stir softened yeast and add, mixing well.

Measure

4 cups sifted all-purpose flour

Add about one-half of the flour to the yeast mixture and beat until very smooth. Then beat in enough of the remaining flour to make a soft dough. Turn dough onto a lightly floured surface and allow it to rest 5 to 10 min.

Knead dough (page 11).

Form dough into a smooth ball and put into a lightly greased, deep bowl. Turn dough to bring greased surface to top. Cover bowl with waxed paper and towel and let stand in warm place (about 80°F) until dough is doubled.

Punch down dough with fist; pull edges in to center and turn dough completely over in bowl. Cover and let rise again until nearly doubled.

Again punch down dough and turn out onto a lightly floured surface. Let rest 5 to 10 min.

Meanwhile, mix together

½ cup sugar
1½ teaspoons cinnamon

Set out

½ cup (about 2½ oz.) dark seedless raisins
¼ cup (about 1½ oz.) slivered citron

Lightly grease the baking sheets.

Divide the dough into halves; roll one-half into a rectangle about 13x10 in. Brush with

Melted butter or margarine

Sprinkle with one-half of the sugar-cinnamon mixture, raisins and citron. Starting with the long side of the dough, roll up tightly and pinch long edge to seal. Place roll, sealed edge down, on a baking sheet. Pull ends together to form a ring, pressing slightly to seal ends.

Repeat procedure for second ring. Make shallow diagonal cuts about 2 in. apart on tops of rings. Cover with waxed paper and a towel and let rise until doubled.

Brush tops of rings lightly with

Milk

Bake at 350°F about 40 min.

Meanwhile, for frosting, blend until smooth

½ cup sifted confectioners' sugar
1 tablespoon milk
½ teaspoon vanilla extract

When kuchens are done, remove to cooling rack. Frost while still warm. If desired, sprinkle **chopped nuts** over frosting. *2 kuchens*

—RAISED LEMON DOUGHNUTS

Follow ▲ Recipe through rising process. Omit sugar, cinnamon, raisins and citron for filling. Omit brushing with butter or margarine. Roll out dough, cut doughnuts, allow to rise and deep-fry according to directions given in recipe for Fluffy Raised Doughnuts (page 84). Shake warm doughnuts in plastic bag containing **sugar or confectioners' sugar.**

ALMOND-CRUMB COFFEE CAKE
(Streuselkuchen mit Mandeln)

▲ *Base Recipe*

Two 8-in. round layer cake pans will be needed.

Blanch (page 9) and set aside
¼ cup (about 1½ oz.) almonds

Prepare dough for
Berlin Doughnuts (Bismarcks, page 84; decrease milk to ½ cup, substitute 1 teaspoon grated lemon peel for the orange juice and omit rum extract)

After the dough has doubled and just before turning dough onto floured surface, lightly grease the pans.

Divide dough into two balls and pat out each in a greased pan. Dough should be ¼ to ½ in. thick. Cover with waxed paper and a towel and let rise 30 to 45 min., or until dough is doubled.

For Streusel Topping—Meanwhile, finely chop the blanched almonds. Blend in

½ cup sifted all-purpose flour
3 tablespoons sugar
1 teaspoon cinnamon
½ teaspoon grated lemon peel

Cut in with a pastry blender or two knives until mixture is size of small peas

3 to 4 tablespoons firm butter

When dough has doubled, brush tops with

Melted butter

Sprinkle dough evenly with the almond-flour mixture.

Bake at 350°F 35 to 40 min., or until coffee cake tests done (page 11).
Two 8-in. round coffee cakes

—QUICK CRUMB COFFEE CAKE
(Streusel Blitzkuchen)

Follow ▲ Recipe. Omit almonds. For the Streusel Topping, omit nuts and lemon peel and, if desired, also omit the cinnamon.

—APPLE CRUMB COFFEE CAKE
(Streuselkuchen mit Apfeln)

Follow ▲ Recipe. After first rising, divide dough into four balls instead of two. Pat out only one ball in each pan and set two balls aside. Lightly brush dough in pans with melted butter. Wash, quarter, core, pare and cut into thin slices **3 medium apples.** Arrange apple slices over the dough in each pan. Lightly

brush apple slices with **melted butter.** Sprinkle with a mixture of ⅓ cup sugar and **2 teaspoons cinnamon.** Pat out remaining two balls of dough and carefully arrange over the apples. Proceed as in ▲ Recipe.

SALLY LUNN

An eighteenth century homemaker of Bath, England, developed a yeast bread recipe which soon became a favorite in her community and was called by her name. It has long been a breakfast favorite of Creoles who insist that Sally Lunn must be baked like a cake, and that it is as good toasted the day after it's baked as when it is fresh from the oven.

Set out a 1½-qt. ring or Turk's-head mold.

Soften

1 pkg. active dry yeast

in

¼ cup warm water, 105°F to 115°F (Or if using compressed yeast, soften 1 cake in ¼ cup lukewarm water, 80°F to 85°F.)

Set aside.

Scald (page 10)
½ cup milk

Meanwhile, put into a large mixer bowl

⅔ cup butter or margarine, softened
2 tablespoons sugar
¾ teaspoon salt

Pour scalded milk over ingredients in bowl. When lukewarm, beat mixture with an electric beater and blend in, beating until smooth

½ cup sifted all-purpose flour

Stir softened yeast and add to mixture, beating well. Add and beat in

¾ cup sifted all-purpose flour

Add and beat until smooth

2 eggs, well beaten

Beat in

¾ cup sifted all-purpose flour

Finally beat thoroughly, at least 5 min. Scrape the dough down from sides of bowl. Cover the bowl with waxed paper and a towel and set aside in a warm place (about 80°F) until dough is doubled, about 45 min.

Lightly grease the ring or Turk's-head mold.

When dough is doubled, beat again with electric beater at least 5 min. and turn into the greased mold. Cover and let the dough rise again until doubled, about 45 min.

Bake at 350°F 25 to 30 min., or until golden brown. Run a knife around inner and outer edges of mold to loosen the loaf. Gently remove to cooling rack.

Serve warm and spread generously with **butter or margarine.** Or toast slices and serve with butter or margarine and **jelly or jam.**

1 Sally Lunn

COFFEE BRAID
(Striezel)

▲ Base Recipe

A baking sheet will be needed.

Bring to boiling

1½ cups water

Add, and again bring water to boiling

1 cup (about 5 oz.) dark seedless raisins

Pour off water and drain fruit on absorbent paper. Set aside.

Set out

1 cup (about 5 oz.) blanched almonds (page 9)

Coarsely chop ¾ cup of the almonds. Very finely chop the remaining ¼ cup of almonds and mix with

2 tablespoons sugar

Set almonds and almond-sugar mixture aside.

Scald (page 10)

1 cup milk

Meanwhile, soften

1 pkg. active dry yeast

in

¼ cup warm water, 105°F to 115°F (Or if using compressed yeast, soften 1 cake in ¼ cup lukewarm water, 80°F to 85°F.)

Set aside.

Put into a large bowl

⅔ cup sugar
½ cup butter, softened
1 teaspoon grated lemon peel
1 teaspoon salt

Immediately pour scalded milk over ingredients in bowl.

When lukewarm, blend in, beating until smooth

1 cup sifted all-purpose flour

Stir softened yeast and add, mixing well.

Measure

3½ to 4½ cups sifted all-purpose flour

Add about one-half the flour to yeast mixture and beat until very smooth. Beat in

2 eggs, well beaten

Add and mix in the raisins and the coarsely chopped almonds.

Beat in enough of the remaining flour to make a soft dough. Turn dough onto a lightly floured surface and allow it to rest 5 to 10 min.

Knead dough (page 11).

Form dough into a large ball and place in a greased deep bowl. Turn dough to bring greased surface to top. Cover with waxed paper and towel and let stand in a warm place (about 80°F) until dough is doubled.

Lightly grease the baking sheet.

Punch dough down with fist. Turn out onto lightly floured surface. Break off one third of dough and divide it into 3 equal parts. Roll each portion with palms of hands into a strip about 14 in. long. Braid the strips together. Place on the baking sheet and tuck under open ends. Divide remaining dough into 2 equal portions. Divide one of the halves into 3 equal portions and roll each into a strip about 12 in. long. Braid the strips together and place on top of the first braid, tucking under open ends. Divide remaining dough into 2 equal parts and roll each into a strip about 10 in. long. Twist together and place on top of the braids, tucking under open ends. Cover with waxed paper and towel and let rise 30 to 45 min., or until doubled.

Brush with

Egg white, slightly beaten

Sprinkle with the almond-sugar mixture.

Bake at 350°F 50 to 60 min., or until lightly browned. Remove coffee cake to cooling rack.

1 large Coffee Braid

—ANISE COFFEE CAKE
(Striezel mit Anis)

Follow ▲ Recipe. Increase the finely chopped almonds to ⅓ cup and mix with ¼ cup sugar.

Omit grated lemon peel and add **1 tablespoon anise seed** with sugar and butter. Omit brushing top of dough with egg white. Just before baking, spread **⅓ cup dairy sour cream** over bread and sprinkle with the almond-sugar mixture.

APRICOT COFFEE CAKE
(Bukta)

An 8-in. square pan will be needed.

Measure and set aside

3 to 3⅓ cups sifted all-purpose flour

Scald (page 10)

⅓ cup milk

Meanwhile, soften

1 pkg. active dry yeast

in

¼ cup warm water, 105°F to 115°F (Or if using compressed yeast, soften 1 cake in ¼ cup lukewarm water, 80°F to 85°F.)

Set aside.

Put into a bowl

¾ cup butter, softened
1 tablespoon sugar
¼ teaspoon salt

Immediately pour the scalded milk over ingredients in bowl and stir until butter is melted. When the milk mixture is lukewarm, blend in ⅓ cup of the flour, beating until dough is smooth. Stir the softened yeast and add to dough, mixing well. Add about one-half of the remaining flour to the dough and beat until very smooth. Blend in

2 egg yolks, well beaten

Then beat in enough of the remaining flour to make a soft dough. Turn dough onto a lightly floured surface and let stand 5 to 10 min.

Knead dough (page 11).

Form dough into a large ball and place in a greased bowl. Turn dough to bring greased

surface to top. Cover bowl with waxed paper and towel and let stand in warm place (about 80°F) until dough is doubled.

Punch dough down with fist; pull edges in to center and turn dough completely over in bowl. Cover and let rise again until nearly doubled.

Lightly grease the pan.

Set out
½ cup thick apricot jam
Roll dough ¼ in. thick. Cut dough into 4x2½-in. rectangles. Spoon 1 teaspoon of the jam onto center of each rectangle. Fold each rectangle into lengthwise halves, pinching the two narrow ends together and leaving center open. Stand pieces open-side up and side by side in the cake pan. Cover pan with towel. Let dough rise again 15 to 25 min., or until light.

Bake at 425°F 15 to 20 min., or until golden brown. Break pieces of coffee cake apart with a fork. Serve warm or cooled.

About 14 pieces

FILLED COFFEE CAKE
(Kringle)

A delicious Danish creation.

Two baking sheets will be needed.

Measure
¼ cup sifted all-purpose flour
Cut in with pastry blender or two knives until well blended
¾ cup butter
Shape mixture into a ball and place on a long length of waxed paper. Cover with another long length of waxed paper and roll into a rectangle, 10x4 in. Chill in refrigerator.

Meanwhile, soften
1 pkg. active dry yeast
in
**¼ cup warm water, 105°F to 115°F
(Or if using compressed yeast, soften 1 cake in ¼ cup lukewarm water, 80°F to 85°F.)**
Set aside.

Beat in a large bowl
1 egg
Beat in until sugar is dissolved
**¾ cup milk
3 tablespoons sugar
1 teaspoon salt**
Blend in, beating until smooth
1 cup sifted all-purpose flour
Stir softened yeast and add, mixing well.

Measure
2 cups sifted all-purpose flour
Add about one-half the flour to the yeast mixture and beat until very smooth. Then beat in enough remaining flour to make a dough which leaves sides of bowl. Turn dough onto a lightly floured surface and roll into a 12-in. square.

Remove chilled flour-butter mixture from refrigerator, peel off waxed paper, and place in the center of the dough. Fold two sides of

Stollen

dough over flour-butter mixture so that sides overlap in center. Turn dough one-quarter way around and roll out again into a 12-in. square. Repeat the folding and rolling two more times, turning dough one-quarter way around each time. Wrap dough in waxed paper. Place in refrigerator to chill thoroughly, overnight if possible.

Meanwhile, bring to boiling
1½ cups water
Add, and again bring to boiling
1½ cups (about ½ lb.) golden raisins
Pour off water and drain raisins on absorbent paper. Set aside.

Cream until butter is softened
**¼ cup butter
1 teaspoon cardamom**
Add gradually, beating thoroughly
2 cups sifted confectioners' sugar
Blend in until the mixture is of spreading consistency
2 to 3 tablespoons cream
Mix in the raisins and set aside.

Set out
⅓ cup finely chopped blanched almonds (page 9)
Lightly grease the baking sheets.

Remove chilled dough from refrigerator and roll into rectangle, 24x12 in. Cut lengthwise with a sharp knife into two strips, 24x6 in. Spread each strip with one-half of the raisin filling. Starting with the long side of dough, roll up each strip tightly and pinch along edge to seal. Carefully stretch dough into a roll 30 in. long, being careful not to tear dough.

Transfer rolls to the greased baking sheets. Form into pretzel shape by overlapping ends so that they touch long side of roll. Gently flatten dough to ½-in. thickness. Brush with
Egg, slightly beaten
Sprinkle with a mixture of the almonds and
⅓ cup sugar

Cover with waxed paper and a clean towel. Let rise in a warm place (about 80°F) until doubled.

Bake at 375°F 20 to 25 min., or until lightly browned. *2 coffee cakes*

STOLLEN

Two 15½x12-in. baking sheets will be needed.

Blanch, toast (pages 9 and 10) and chop
1⅓ cups (about 7 oz.) almonds
Reserve ⅓ cup of the almonds for topping; mix remainder with
**1 cup (about 5 oz.) golden or dark raisins
½ cup (about 3 oz.) currants
1 cup (about 7 oz.) chopped citron
1 tablespoon grated lemon peel**
Set nut-fruit mixture aside.

Scald (page 10)
1 cup milk

Meanwhile, soften
2 pkgs. active dry yeast
in
**½ cup warm water, 105°F to 115°F
(Or if using compressed yeast, soften 2 cakes in ½ cup lukewarm water, 80°F to 85°F.)**
Set aside.

Put into a large bowl
**1 cup sugar
1 cup butter, softened
2 teaspoons salt**
Pour scalded milk over ingredients in bowl and stir mixture until butter is completely melted. When lukewarm, blend in, beating until smooth, a mixture of
**1 cup sifted all-purpose flour
1 teaspoon nutmeg**
Stir softened yeast and add, mixing well.

Measure
6 to 7 cups sifted all-purpose flour

73

Add about one-half the flour to the dough and beat until very smooth. Add in thirds, beating well after each addition

3 eggs, well beaten

Add the reserved nut-fruit mixture and mix thoroughly. Mix in enough of the remaining flour to make a soft dough. Turn dough onto a lightly floured surface and allow it to rest 5 to 10 min.

Knead dough (page 11).

Form dough into a smooth ball and place it in a lightly greased, deep bowl. Turn dough to bring greased surface to top. Cover bowl with waxed paper and towel and let stand in warm place (about 80°F) until dough is doubled, about 2½ hrs.

Punch down dough with fist; pull edges in to center and turn dough completely over in bowl. Cover bowl with waxed paper and towel and let dough rise again until nearly doubled, about 1½ hrs.

Again punch down dough and turn out onto a lightly floured surface. Divide into two portions and shape each into a smooth ball. Let dough rest 5 to 10 min.

Meanwhile, lightly grease the baking sheets.

Roll or pat out each ball of dough into an oval 13 in. long and about 1 in. thick. With rolling pin, flatten and press one lengthwise half of oval about ½ in. thick. Turn unflattened half of dough over flattened half; lightly press edges together. Press the fold down firmly with palm of hand; this helps to prevent dough from springing open during rising. Repeat to shape second oval.

Place one Stollen on each baking sheet. Brush tops with

Melted butter

Cover with waxed paper and towel and let rise in warm place until doubled, about 1½ hrs.

Bake at 325°F about 30 min., or until Stollen are light golden brown.

While Stollen are baking, prepare the frosting by combining

1½ cups sifted confectioners' sugar
¾ teaspoon vanilla extract

Add gradually, blending after each addition

2 to 3 tablespoons milk or cream
(just enough to make frosting of
spreading consistency)

Remove baked Stollen to cooling racks. Immediately spread frosting over tops. Sprinkle reserved almonds over frosting.

2 large Stollen

Note: The addition of a few finely cut candied cherries to the nut-fruit mixture adds a touch of color.

BABA

Regular Creole bakery customers always receive a Baba as a Christmas or New Year's token. Usually it is served with strong, black coffee to holiday guests.

Two 9-in. round layer cake pans will be needed.

Set out

1 cup (about 5 oz.) raisins
1 cup (about 5 oz.) currants

Measure into a small cup or custard cup

⅛ teaspoon saffron

Pour over saffron

1½ teaspoons boiling water

Set aside and cool to lukewarm.

Prepare dough through addition of egg yolks stage

Small Brioches (page 80)

After beating in egg yolks, blend in thoroughly saffron mixture, raisins and currants. Beating in enough to form a soft dough, add about

2 cups sifted all-purpose flour

Beat thoroughly at least 5 min. Turn into a buttered, deep bowl just large enough to allow dough to double. Brush top surface with

Melted butter

Cover with waxed paper and a towel. Let stand in a warm place (about 80°F) until dough is doubled.

Punch down dough with fist. Butter surface of dough and cover again. Set in refrigerator about 12 hrs. or overnight. Punch down dough occasionally as it rises.

Lightly butter the two cake pans.

Remove dough from refrigerator; again punch down dough. Place dough on a lightly floured surface. Divide dough into halves and shape into two flat round loaves about 9 in. in diameter. Place one loaf in each cake pan. Cover with waxed paper and a towel and set aside in a warm place until doubled.

Brush tops lightly with a mixture of

1 egg yolk, slightly beaten
1 tablespoon milk

Bake at 375°F 20 to 30 min., or until loaves are golden brown.

Run spatula around inside of each cake pan and gently lift out Baba. Sprinkle with

Confectioners' sugar

Serve warm. *2 Babas*

FRUIT BREAD, MILAN STYLE
(Panettone)

A holiday favorite—light, fruit-studded bread —that is ordinarily served as a dessert.

Thoroughly grease two 8-in. round cake pans.

Soften

1 pkg. active dry yeast

in

¼ cup warm water, 105°F to 115°F
(Or if using compressed yeast,
soften 1 cake in ¼ cup lukewarm
water, 80°F to 85°F.)

Set aside.

Pour into a large bowl

1 cup butter, melted

Add gradually, beating well after each addition

1 cup sugar
1 teaspoon salt

Have ready

2 cups sifted all-purpose flour
½ cup milk, scalded and cooled to
lukewarm

Beating thoroughly after each addition, alternately add flour in thirds and milk in halves to the butter mixture. Add yeast; beat well.

Beat until thick and piled softly

2 eggs
4 egg yolks

Add the beaten eggs all at one time to yeast mixture and beat well. Beating thoroughly after each addition, gradually add

3½ cups sifted all-purpose flour

Stir in

1 cup dark seedless raisins
¾ cup chopped citron

Measure

½ cup all-purpose flour

Sift one-half of the flour over a pastry canvas or board. Turn dough onto floured surface, cover with waxed paper and let rest 10 min.

Sift remaining flour over dough. Pull dough from edges toward center until flour is worked in. Put dough into a greased large bowl, grease top of dough and cover with waxed paper and a towel. Let stand in warm place (about 80°F) about 2½ hrs.

Punch down dough and pull edges of dough in to center. Let rise in a warm place about 1 hr.

Divide dough into halves and shape each half into a round loaf. Put each loaf into a prepared pan. Brush surfaces generously with a mixture of

1 egg, slightly beaten
1 tablespoon water

Cover; let rise in a warm place, about 1 hr.

Bake at 350°F 40 to 45 min., or until golden brown. Remove loaves from pans to cooling racks to cool. *2 Panettoni*

FESTIVE COFFEE CAKE

Lightly grease 2 baking sheets.

Blanch, toast (pages 9 and 10) and chop
1 cup (about ⅓ lb.) almonds

Scald (page 10)
½ cup milk

Meanwhile, soften
2 pkgs. active dry yeast
in
½ cup warm water, 105°F to 115°F
(Or if using compressed yeast, soften 1 cake in ½ cup lukewarm water, 80°F to 85°F.)

Set aside.

Put into a large bowl
½ cup butter, softened
1 cup sugar
1 teaspoon salt

Immediately pour scalded milk over ingredients in bowl. When lukewarm, stir mixture and blend in, beating until smooth
1 cup sifted all-purpose flour

Stir softened yeast and add, mixing well.

Measure
4 cups sifted all-purpose flour

Add about one-half of the flour to the yeast mixture and beat until very smooth.

Beat until thick and piled softly
2 eggs

Beat into dough. Add and beat in almonds and
½ cup (3 oz.) chopped candied citron
½ cup (3 oz.) chopped candied cherries

Then beat in enough remaining flour to make a soft dough. Turn dough onto a lightly floured surface. Allow it to rest 5 to 10 min.

Knead dough (page 11).

Form dough into a ball and place it in a greased, deep bowl. Turn to bring greased surface to top. Cover with waxed paper and a towel and let stand in warm place (about 85°F) until dough is doubled.

Punch down with fist; pull edges of dough in to center; turn dough completely over in bowl. Cover; let rise again until nearly doubled. Punch down dough and divide into two equal

portions. On a lightly floured surface, shape each portion into a long roll about 2 in. in diameter. Gently twist roll and form it into a circle on baking sheet; press ends together to seal. Cover; let rise until doubled.

Bake at 350°F 30 to 35 min., or until golden brown. Remove coffee cakes to cooling racks. While still warm, drizzle with a **confectioners' sugar glaze** and top with bits of **candied citron**. *2 coffee cakes*

YEAST ROLLS

YEAST ROLLS

▲ Base Recipe

Put into a large mixer bowl
2 pkgs. active dry yeast
2 cups sifted all-purpose flour
½ cup sugar
2 teaspoons salt

Mix at low speed of electric mixer until the ingredients are well blended.

Combine in a saucepan
⅔ cup water
¾ cup milk
6 tablespoons shortening

Set over low heat until liquids are warm. Gradually add heated liquid to dry ingredients in mixer bowl. Beat 2 min. with electric mixer at medium speed. Scrape bowl occasionally.

Measure
3½ to 4½ cups sifted all-purpose flour
Add ½ cup of the flour to yeast mixture and
2 eggs

Beat 2 min. at high speed, scraping bowl occasionally. Then beat in enough remaining flour to make a soft dough. Turn dough onto a lightly floured surface, cover, and let stand 5 to 10 min.

Knead dough (page 11).

Form dough into a ball and place it in a greased, deep bowl. Turn dough to bring greased surface to top. Cover with waxed paper and towel and let stand in warm place (about 80°F) until dough is doubled.

Punch down with fist; pull edges of dough in to center and turn dough completely over in bowl.* Cover and let rise again until nearly doubled. Punch down and turn dough out onto lightly floured surface.

Follow suggestions for shaping rolls (here and on page 76), using amount needed for a single baking. Place rolls on greased baking sheets. Brush with **melted butter or margarine.** If desired, sprinkle with **poppy seed.** Cover with waxed paper and a towel and let rise again 15 to 25 min., or until light.

Bake at 425°F 15 to 20 min.
4¼ to 5 doz. rolls

*This dough may be kept 3 days in the re-

frigerator. Grease top of dough and cover. Punch down occasionally as it rises. Remove amount needed for a single baking and return remainder to refrigerator immediately. When ready to use, shape rolls and let stand at room temperature for 1 hr., or until light.

Parker House Rolls—Roll dough ¼ in. thick; brush with melted butter. Cut into 2½-in. rounds. Use knife handle to make a crease slightly off center; fold larger half over smaller; press edges together.

Cloverleaf Rolls—With hands, shape dough into 1-in. thick rolls. Cut off bits and form into balls about 1 in. in diameter. Place three balls in each muffin-pan well.

Bowknots—Roll dough to ¼-in. thickness. Cut off strips ½ in. wide and 4 to 5 in. long. With hands, roll and stretch into longer strips. Twist dough strips and tie into single or double knots.

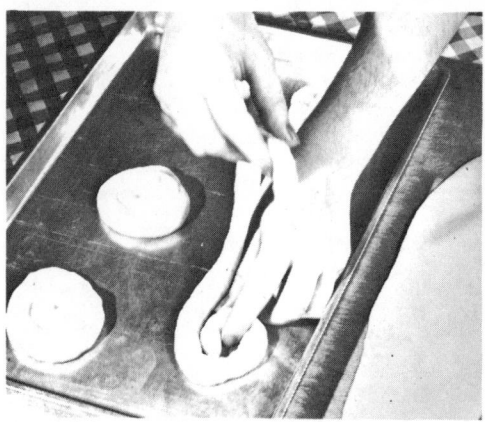

Snails—Roll dough into rectangle ¼ in. thick. Cut off strips ½ in. wide and 4 to 5 in. long. With hands, roll and stretch dough into longer strips. Coil each strip into a closed spiral.

Butterflies—Roll dough into a rectangle 6 in. wide and ¼ in. thick. Brush with melted butter or margarine. Roll dough, starting with long side. Cut into 2-in. pieces. Press with knife handle.

Clothespins—Roll dough into rectangle ¼ in. thick. Cut 6x½-in. strips. With hands, roll and stretch strips. Wrap around greased clothespins. Tuck in ends. When baked, twist out clothespins.

—EIGHTS

Follow ▲ Recipe to shaping process. Shape as for Twists (page 69), but "twist" only once to make figure 8.

—BRAIDS

Follow ▲ Recipe to shaping process. Roll dough into a rectangle 6 in. wide and ¼ in. thick. Brush lightly with **melted butter or margarine.** Cut into ½-in. wide strips. With hands roll and stretch into longer strips. Braid 3 strips together; tuck ends under braid.

—CURLICUES

Follow ▲ Recipe to shaping process. Roll dough into a rectangle ¼ in. thick. Cut into 5x¾-in. strips. With hands, roll and stretch into longer strips. Hold index finger on greased baking sheet and coil one-half of dough strip up to finger; repeat for other half of strip, reversing direction.

—PECAN ROLLS

Follow ▲ Recipe to shaping process. Lightly grease about 2 doz. 2½-in. muffin-pan wells. Set out **2 cups (about ½ lb.) pecan halves.** Coarsely chop 1 cup of the nuts; set the nuts aside. Melt **1⅓ cups butter or margarine.** Put about 2 teaspoons melted butter in each muffin-pan well. Reserve remainder of melted butter. Place the pecan halves in muffin-pan wells, arranging about 5 halves in each well. Set muffin pans aside. Mix together the chopped pecans, **2 cups firmly packed brown sugar** and **1½ tablespoons cinnamon.**

Using one-half of the yeast dough, roll it into a rectangle ½ in. thick and about 24 in. long. Brush dough with reserved melted butter and sprinkle with brown sugar mixture. Beginning with longer side, roll dough and press edges to seal. Cut roll into ¾- to 1-in. slices. Place slices, cut side down, in muffin-pan wells. Brush with melted butter or margarine.

Let rise until doubled. Bake at 350°F 25 to 30 min. Invert pans on cooling racks. Allow to stand a few seconds before lifting off pans. Cool, pecan side up.

POTATO ROLLS

▲ Base Recipe

Some call these Featherbeds because they're so light and fluffy. And don't worry about baking them in quantity. The average healthy appetite can take care of at least a score of them.

For Dough—Wash, pare and cook (page 313)
　　1 small potato
Cook 25 to 35 min., or until tender when pierced with a fork. Drain, reserving ½ cup cooking liquid. Dry potato by shaking pan over low heat. Mash or rice the potato.

Scald (page 10)
　　¼ cup milk

Meanwhile, soften
　　½ pkg. (1⅛ teaspoons) active dry yeast
in
　　2 tablespoons warm water, 105°F to 115°F (Or if using compressed yeast, soften ½ cake in 2 tablespoons lukewarm water, 80°F to 85°F.)
Set aside.

Put into a large bowl
　　¼ cup sugar
　　3 tablespoons shortening
　　¾ teaspoon salt
Pour the scalded milk and the ½ cup of reserved cooking liquid over ingredients in bowl. When lukewarm, stir mixture and blend in, beating until smooth
　　½ cup sifted all-purpose flour
Stir softened yeast and add to mixture, mixing thoroughly.

Measure
　　2½ to 3 cups sifted all-purpose flour

Add about one-half the flour to the yeast mixture and beat until very smooth. Beat in ¼ cup of the mashed potato and
　　1 egg, well beaten
Then beat in enough remaining flour to make a soft dough. Turn dough out onto a lightly floured surface and allow it to rest 5 to 10 min.

Knead dough (page 11).

Form dough into a ball and place it in a greased, deep bowl. Turn dough to bring greased surface to top. Cover with waxed paper and towel and let stand in a warm place (about 80°F) until doubled, about 1 hr.

Punch down dough with fist; pull edges of dough in to center and turn dough completely over in bowl. Cover and let rise again until nearly doubled, about 45 min.

Punch down dough and turn out onto a lightly floured surface. Allow to rest 10 min.

Lightly grease baking sheets.

For Rolls—Roll dough into a 12-in. square, ½ in. thick. With a floured knife, cut into 1-in. squares. With hands, shape each square into a ball about ¾ in. in diameter.

Place on greased baking sheet about 2 in. apart. Cover with waxed paper and towel and let rise until light, about 30 min.

Bake at 425°F about 8 min., or until lightly browned. *About 8 doz. rolls*

—POTATO DOUGHNUTS

Follow ▲ Recipe for dough. About 20 min. before deep-frying, heat **fat** to 365°F. Roll dough into a 13-in. square, ¼ in. thick. Using a sharp knife, cut into 1½-in. squares or diamonds. Cover and let rise on board in a warm place until doubled, about 40 min. When doubled, deep-fry in the heated fat. Fry only as many at one time as will float uncrowded one layer deep in the heated fat. Fry 2 to 3 min., or until lightly browned. Turn doughnuts with a fork as they rise to surface and several times during cooking (do not pierce). Remove with a slotted spoon; drain over fat for a few seconds before removing to absorbent paper. Sprinkle lightly with **sugar,** if desired.

—BAPTIST CAKES

These crisp, tempting morsels got their name, so legend says, "because they were immersed" —in deep fat, that is. But if you prefer, call them "Huffjuffs" (as they do in Maine) or "Holy Pokes" (their Connecticut name).

Follow ▲ Recipe; do not bake rolls. About 20 min. before deep-frying, heat **fat** to 365°F. Divide each ball of dough into halves and stretch each half to a length of 3 in. Deep-fry 1 to 2 min., or until lightly browned. Follow directions in Potato Doughnuts for deep-frying. Serve hot with **butter** and warm **maple syrup.**

CHANGE-ABOUT ROLLS

▲ Base Recipe

Lightly grease baking pans or muffin-pan wells.

Scald (page 10)
   2 cups milk

Meanwhile, soften
   2 pkgs. active dry yeast
in
   **½ cup warm water, 105°F to 115°F
   (Or if using compressed yeast, soften
   2 cakes in ½ cup lukewarm water,
   80°F to 85°F.)**
Set aside.

Put into a large bowl
   **½ cup shortening, softened
   ½ cup sugar
   1½ teaspoons salt**
Pour scalded milk over ingredients in bowl and stir. When lukewarm, blend in, beating until smooth
   1 cup sifted all-purpose flour
Stir softened yeast and add to mixture, beating well.

Measure
   5½ to 6 cups sifted all-purpose flour
Add about one-half the flour to the yeast mixture and beat until very smooth. Beat in
   2 eggs, well beaten
Then beat in enough remaining flour to make a soft dough. Turn dough onto a lightly floured surface and let stand 5 to 10 min.

Knead the dough by folding opposite side over toward you. Using heels of hands gently push dough away. Give dough a quarter turn. Repeat kneading process rhythmically until dough is smooth and elastic, using as little additional flour as possible, 5 to 8 min.

Form dough into a ball and put it into a greased bowl. Turn to bring greased surface to top. Cover bowl with waxed paper and

towel and let stand in warm place (about 80°F) until dough is doubled.

Punch down with fist; pull edges in to center and turn completely over in bowl. Cover and let rise again until nearly doubled.

Turn out onto floured board and shape into desired type of rolls. Place in baking pans or muffin-pan wells. Cover and let rise again 15 to 25 min., or until light.

Bake at 425°F 15 to 20 min. Remove from pans and cool on cooling rack.
About 4 doz. rolls

—CINNAMON ROLLS

Use one-half ▲ Recipe dough. Roll into an 18x 9 in. oblong. Spread with **5 tablespoons softened butter or margarine;** sprinkle with a mixture of **¾ cup brown sugar** and **1½ tablespoons cinnamon.** Beginning with longer side, roll dough tightly. Press edge to seal. Cut roll into 1-in. slices and place cut-side down in a greased pan, or in greased muffin-pan wells. Brush tops with **melted butter.** Cover and let rise until doubled, about 45 min. Bake at 350°F 25 to 30 min.   *1½ to 2 doz. rolls*

—BUTTERSCOTCH WHIRLS

Prepare Cinnamon Rolls. Cover bottom of greased baking pan or muffin-pan wells with a mixture of **½ cup brown sugar, ½ cup melted butter or margarine, 1 teaspoon cinnamon** and **½ cup (about 2 oz.) pecan halves.** Arrange rolls on sugar mixture, cut-side down. Bake at 350°F 25 to 30 min. Turn pan upside down at once on tray or platter. Leave pan over rolls a minute to allow butterscotch to drip down.

—ORANGE ROLLS

Use one-half ▲ Recipe dough. Prepare as for Cinnamon Rolls. For brown sugar mixture, substitute a mixture of **½ cup sugar, ¼ cup orange juice** and **1 tablespoon grated orange peel.**

CRESCENT ROLLS
(Croissants)

Croissants are favorite French rolls, tender and flaky with butter, light with yeast.

Soften
   1 pkg. active dry yeast
in
   **¼ cup warm water, 105°F to 115°F
   (Or if using compressed yeast, soften
   1 cake in ¼ cup lukewarm water,
   80°F to 85°F.)**
Set aside.

Meanwhile, scald (page 10)
   1 cup milk
Pour scalded milk into a large bowl and stir in
   **1 tablespoon sugar
   1 teaspoon salt**
Cool to lukewarm. Stir softened yeast and add with about
   3 cups sifted all-purpose flour
(Use enough flour to make a soft dough.) Turn onto a lightly floured surface and knead until smooth and elastic (see French Bread, page 65. The French hold the dough in one hand and beat it at least 100 times against the pastry board).

Select a deep bowl, just large enough to allow dough to double. Warm it or rinse in hot water and dry; butter lightly.

Shape dough into a smooth ball and place in bowl. Grease surface lightly by turning ball in bottom of bowl. Turn greased side up. Cover with waxed paper and towel. Let rise in a warm place (about 80°F) until doubled.

Punch down with fist. Fold sides toward center. Turn ball smooth-side up and set aside. (Cover and allow to rise again if hard wheat flour was used. Omit this rising if using soft wheat flour.)

Place in a large bowl of cold water and ice cubes or chipped ice
   ¾ cup butter
Work butter with hands. Break it into small portions and squeeze each in water about

Cinnamon Rolls and Butterscotch Whirls

20 times or until butter is pliable and waxy. Remove and wipe off excess water. Divide into three equal portions. Wrap each in waxed paper and chill in refrigerator until firm.

On a lightly floured surface, roll dough into a rectangle ¼ to ½ in. thick. Dot center third of rolled dough with one portion butter, cut in small pieces. Cover butter with right-hand third of dough. Fold left-hand third under butter section. With rolling pin, gently press down and seal the three, upper, open edges. Wrap dough in waxed paper and chill 30 min.

Remove dough from refrigerator and place on lightly floured surface with butter section near top, narrow width toward you. Turn one-quarter way around, to have open edge away from you, and roll to original size. Repeat twice the procedure for folding, sealing and chilling, using second and third portions of butter. Each time place on floured surface, turn and roll as directed.

Butter lightly a 15½x12-in. baking sheet.

Place dough on floured surface and cut into halves. Roll each piece into a round ¼ in. thick. Cut each round into 12 wedge-shaped pieces. Roll up beginning at wide end. Fasten end by brushing tip with part of a mixture of

    1 egg yolk, slightly beaten
    1 tablespoon milk

Crescent Rolls

Place rolls on baking sheet with points underneath. Curve into crescents. Cover lightly with a towel and let rise in a warm place about 1 hr., or until doubled.

Brush with remaining egg mixture and bake at 425°F 15 to 20 min., or until rolls are golden brown. Immediately remove to cooling racks.

24 Crescent Rolls

SOUR CREAM CRESCENTS

    ▲ *Base Recipe*

Heat in top of double boiler over simmering water until edges become slightly yellow

    1 cup dairy sour cream

(Separation of sour cream will not affect quality of the product.)

Meanwhile, soften

    1½ pkgs. active dry yeast

in

    ⅓ cup warm water, 105°F to 115°F
    (Or if using compressed yeast, soften 1½ cakes in ⅓ cup lukewarm water, 80°F to 85°F.)

Set aside.

Put into a large bowl

    1 cup butter or margarine, softened
    ½ cup plus 1 tablespoon sugar
    ½ teaspoon salt

Immediately pour heated sour cream over ingredients in bowl and stir mixture until butter is completely melted. When mixture has cooled to lukewarm, blend in, beating until smooth

    1 cup sifted all-purpose flour

Stir softened yeast and add, mixing well.

Measure

    3 cups sifted all-purpose flour

Add about one-half of the flour to the dough and beat until very smooth.

Add in thirds, beating well after each addition

    2 eggs, well beaten

Then beat in the remaining flour. Knead in the bowl until dough pulls away from sides of bowl. Cover with waxed paper and a towel and put into refrigerator 6 hrs., or overnight.

Grease baking sheets.

Divide dough into four parts. On a lightly floured surface, roll each part into a round ¼ in. thick. Cut each round into 12 wedge-shaped pieces. Roll up each wedge beginning at wide end.

Place rolls on greased baking sheets with points underneath. Curve into crescents. Cover with waxed paper and a towel and let stand at room temperature about 1 hr.

Bake at 375°F 15 to 18 min., or until golden brown.   *4 doz. crescents*

—CINNAMON NUT CRESCENTS

Follow ▲ Recipe. Reduce yeast to 1 pkg. and water to ¼ cup. Add ¼ **teaspoon vanilla extract** with the eggs. Mix together **1 cup**

sugar, **4 teaspoons cinnamon** and ¼ **cup (about 1 oz.) chopped nuts.** Brush each round of dough with **melted butter** before cutting into wedges. Sprinkle evenly on each wedge about 1 teaspoon of filling. Complete as in ▲ Recipe. Sift **confectioners' sugar** over tops after baking.

—CINNAMON CRESCENTS

Follow recipe for Cinnamon-Nut Crescents. Omit nuts from filling.

FAN TAN ROLLS
(No-Knead Type)

About 2 doz. 2¾-in. muffin-pan wells will be needed.

Heat in top of a double boiler over simmering water until tiny bubbles form around edge

    1 cup buttermilk

(Separation of buttermilk will not affect quality of the product.)

Meanwhile, soften

    1 pkg. active dry yeast

in

    ¼ cup warm water, 105°F to 115°F
    (Or if using compressed yeast, soften 1 cake in ¼ cup lukewarm water, 80°F to 85°F.)

Set aside.

Put into a large bowl

    ¼ cup sugar
    2 tablespoons butter or margarine
    1½ teaspoons salt

Pour heated buttermilk over ingredients in the bowl.

When mixture is lukewarm, stir it and blend in, beating until smooth

    1 cup sifted all-purpose flour

Stir softened yeast and add, mixing well.

Measure

    2 to 3 cups sifted all-purpose flour

Add about one-half of the flour to the yeast mixture and beat until very smooth. Then beat in just enough of the remaining flour to make a soft dough.

Form dough into a ball and place it in a greased deep bowl. Brush top surface with

    Melted butter or margarine

Cover with waxed paper and a clean towel and let stand in a warm place (about 80°F) until dough has slightly more than doubled in bulk, about 1½ hrs.

Lightly grease muffin-pan wells.

Punch down dough, turn onto a lightly floured surface and knead dough (page 11) 1 min. Divide into two portions. Roll one portion at a time into a rectangle ¼ in. thick. Brush with

    Melted butter or margarine

Cut dough into strips 1¼ in. wide. Stack 5 or 6 strips together. Cut into 1½ in. sections. Place on end in greased muffin-pan wells.

Fan Tan Rolls

Brush tops with melted butter, cover with waxed paper and towel and let rise until doubled.

Bake at 425°F 12 to 15 min.

About 2 doz. rolls

NO-KNEAD CHEESE ROLLS

Combine in a large mixer bowl and blend thoroughly
1½ cups all-purpose flour
3 tablespoons sugar
1 teaspoon salt
1 pkg. active dry yeast

Measure into a saucepan and heat until liquids are warm
¾ cup milk
½ cup water
3 tablespoons butter or margarine
(It is not necessary for the shortening to be entirely melted.)

Gradually add liquid to the dry ingredients in mixer bowl and beat for 2 min. at medium speed of electric mixer, scraping the bowl occasionally.

Measure
2 cups all-purpose flour
Add 1 cup of flour to mixture and beat at high speed 2 min., scraping the bowl occasionally. Mix in enough of the remaining flour to make a soft dough. (Dough will be slightly sticky.) Put the dough into a greased deep bowl; turn to grease top. Cover with waxed paper and a clean towel and let stand in a warm place (about 80°F) until the dough is doubled, 45 min. to 1 hr.

Generously grease baking sheets.

Grate, cover to prevent drying and set aside
4 oz. sharp Cheddar cheese (about 1 cup, grated)

Melt and set aside
¼ cup butter or margarine

Punch down dough with fist and turn dough out onto a lightly floured surface. Divide dough into two equal portions. Set one portion aside. Roll dough into a 16x8-in. rectangle. Brush with about one-half of melted butter. Sprinkle with about one-half of grated cheese. Cut crosswise

into 8 equal portions. Cut into halves lengthwise. Fold each strip in thirds, lapping each side portion over center third. Place rolls on baking sheet. Repeat for other half of dough.

Beat slightly
1 egg yolk
1 tablespoon milk
Brush tops of rolls with egg yolk mixture. Let rise until doubled.

Bake at 425°F about 8 min., or until rolls are golden brown.   *About 2½ doz. rolls*

CHEESE TRICORN ROLLS

Two baking sheets will be needed.

Soften
1 pkg. active dry yeast
in
¼ cup warm water, 105°F to 115°F
(Or if using compressed yeast, soften 1 cake in ¼ cup lukewarm water, 80°F to 85°F.)
Set aside.

Pour into a large bowl
¼ cup warm water
Blend in
¾ cup sifted all-purpose flour
Stir softened yeast and add, mixing well. Beat until very smooth. Cover bowl with waxed paper and a clean towel and let stand in warm place (about 80°F) 1½ to 2 hrs.

Meanwhile, grate and set aside
4 oz. sharp Cheddar cheese (about 1 cup, grated)

Cream until shortening is softened
¼ cup plus 2 tablespoons shortening
1 tablespoon lemon juice
Add gradually, creaming until fluffy after each addition, a mixture of
½ cup sugar
½ teaspoon salt
Beat until thick
1 egg
1 egg white
Add beaten eggs in thirds to sugar mixture, beating thoroughly after each addition. Add yeast mixture, mixing well.

Measure
2¼ cups sifted all-purpose flour

Add about one-half the flour to yeast mixture and beat until very smooth. Blend in grated cheese, mixing thoroughly. Beat in enough of the remaining flour to make a soft dough. Turn dough onto a lightly floured surface and allow it to rest 5 to 10 min.

Knead dough (page 11).

Form dough into a smooth ball and put it into a greased deep bowl. Turn dough to bring greased surface to top. Cover with waxed paper and a clean towel and let stand in a warm place (about 80°F) until dough is doubled.

Grease the baking sheets.

Punch dough down with fist. Turn out onto a lightly floured surface, cover and allow dough to rest 5 to 10 min.

Roll dough ¼ in. thick. Cut into 3-in. squares. Crease each square diagonally across center by pressing with handle of knife or wooden spoon. Fold squares on creases to form triangles; press edges to seal. Place rolls on baking sheets and brush tops with
Melted butter or margarine
Cover rolls with waxed paper and towel and let rise again until doubled.

Bake at 350°F 40 to 45 min., or until golden brown.   *2 doz. rolls*

ONION-FLAKE ROLLS

▲ *Base Recipe*

A baking sheet will be needed.

Soften
1 pkg. active dry yeast
in
¼ cup warm water, 105°F to 115°F
(Or if using compressed yeast, soften 1 cake in ¼ cup lukewarm water, 80°F to 85°F.)
Set aside.

Put into a large bowl
2 tablespoons sugar
2 tablespoons shortening
1½ teaspoons salt
Pour over ingredients in bowl and stir until sugar is dissolved
1 cup warm water

Blend in, beating until smooth

1 cup sifted all-purpose flour

Stir softened yeast and add, mixing well.

Measure

2½ to 3 cups sifted all-purpose flour

Add about one-half of the flour to the yeast mixture and beat until very smooth. Mix in enough remaining flour to make a soft dough. Turn dough onto a lightly floured surface and let stand 5 to 10 min.

Knead dough (page 11).

Form dough into a ball and put into a greased, deep bowl. Turn dough to bring greased surface to top. Cover bowl with waxed paper and towel and let stand in warm place (about 80°F) until dough is doubled, about 1 hr.

Punch down dough with fist; pull edges in to center and turn completely over in bowl. Cover bowl with waxed paper and towel and let dough rise again until nearly doubled.

Meanwhile, lightly grease the baking sheet and sprinkle evenly with

2 teaspoons yellow corn meal

Melt in small skillet

2 teaspoons butter or margarine

Add and cook over low heat just until soft

2 to 3 tablespoons onion flakes
(Or use 2 to 3 tablespoons onion, sliced very thin and cut into small pieces. Cook until onion is tender.)

Set aside.

Again punch down dough. Form dough into a roll 24 in. long. Cut crosswise into 2-in. pieces. Tuck under ends of each piece to make a smooth, round roll. Place rolls about 1½ in. apart on baking sheet.

Lightly brush each roll with the onion-butter mixture. Cover with waxed paper and a towel and let rise until doubled.

Bake at 425°F 15 to 20 min., or until rolls are golden brown.

Immediately after removing rolls from oven, brush rolls lightly with

Egg white, slightly beaten

Return to oven for about 1 min. to set the egg-white glaze.

1 doz. rolls

—SMALL ONION-FLAKE ROLLS

Follow ▲ Recipe. Divide dough into halves. Form each half into a roll 24 in. long. Cut crosswise into 1-in. pieces and shape as in ▲ Recipe. Bake 15 min., or until lightly browned.

4 doz. rolls

—GLAZED SESAME SEED ROLLS

Follow ▲ Recipe or recipe for Small Onion-Flake Rolls. Omit the onion-butter mixture and the egg-white glaze. Just before baking rolls, beat **2 egg yolks** slightly. Stir in **2 teaspoons milk** and **2 tablespoons sesame seed**. Brush generously on tops of rolls.

SMALL BRIOCHES
(Petites Brioches)

The characteristic little "top hats" lend enchantment to these rich French rolls.

Soften

1 pkg. active dry yeast

in

¼ cup warm water, 105°F to 115°F
(Or if using compressed yeast, soften 1 cake in ¼ cup lukewarm water, 80°F to 85°F.)

Set aside.

Scald (page 10)

½ cup milk

Meanwhile, put into a large bowl

¾ cup softened butter
¼ cup sugar
½ teaspoon salt

Pour scalded milk over butter mixture in bowl. Allow to stand until lukewarm. Mix in thoroughly

½ cup sifted all-purpose flour

Stir softened yeast and add, mixing well. Beat in with large spoon

1½ cups sifted all-purpose flour

Beating well after each addition, add one at a time

3 eggs
4 egg yolks

Beating in enough to form a soft dough, add about

2 cups sifted all-purpose flour

Beat thoroughly at least 5 min. Turn into a deep buttered bowl just large enough to allow dough to double. Brush top surface with

Melted butter

Cover with waxed paper and a towel. Set aside in a warm place (about 80°F) until doubled.

Punch down dough with fist. Butter surface and cover again. Set in refrigerator about 12 hrs. or overnight. Punch dough down occasionally as it rises.

Remove dough from refrigerator. Place dough on lightly floured surface. Shape two-thirds of it into 2-in. balls. Place in buttered 3-in. muffin-pan wells.

Form an equal number of small balls from remaining third of dough. Gently roll each

Onion Flake Rolls

Small Brioches

ball to cone shape between palms of hands. With finger make an impression in center of larger balls. Insert tips of cones. These cone-shape pieces of dough form the "top hats." Cover loosely with towel and set aside in warm place until doubled.

Brush lightly with mixture of

1 egg yolk
1 tablespoon milk

Bake at 425°F 15 to 20 min.

About 18 brioches

ENGLISH MUFFINS

A griddle or heavy skillet will be needed.

Prepare

Yeast Rolls (one-half recipe, page 75; use only 2 tablespoons sugar)

After punching down dough, turn onto lightly floured surface. Roll dough to ½-in. thickness. Cut out muffins, using a 4-in. round waxed-paper pattern.

Sprinkle baking sheet lightly with

Corn meal

With wide spatula, move muffins carefully to baking sheet. Cover and let rise again until nearly doubled.

Set griddle or heavy skillet over low heat. (A low heat is necessary for muffins to cook to complete doneness inside before the outside

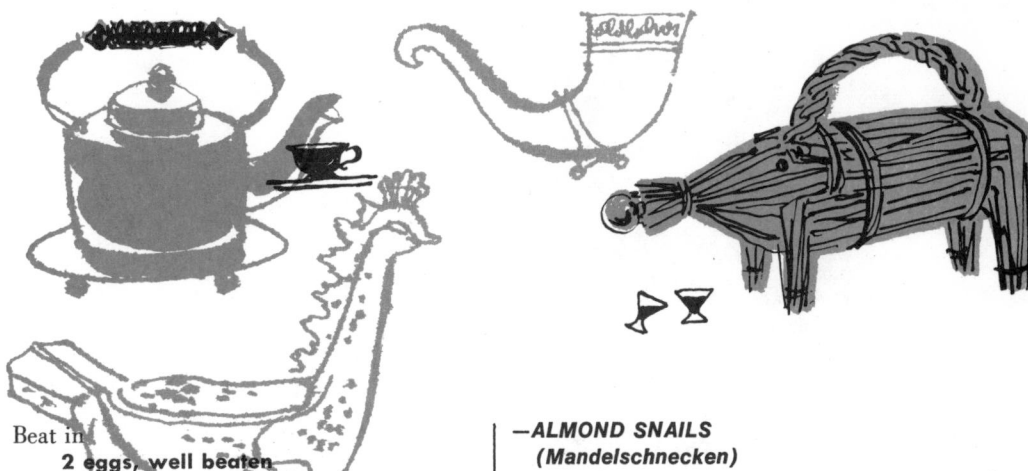

burns. For an even low heat, slip an asbestos mat under griddle.) Test griddle; it is hot enough for baking when drops of cold water dance in small beads on surface. Lightly grease griddle. Transfer muffins carefully to the griddle with a wide spatula. Do not cover the muffins.

Bake muffins on top of range 15 to 20 min. on each side, or until golden brown.

To split muffins for toasting in the electric toaster, cut with a knife; for the broiler, tear apart with a fork. Spread with **butter or margarine** while hot. Serve with **orange marmalade**. *About 8 large muffins*

PECAN SNAILS
(Schnecken)

▲ *Base Recipe*

Twenty-four 2½-in. muffin-pan wells will be needed.

Set out

2 cups (about 7½ oz.) small pecan halves

Coarsely chop 1 cup of the pecans, and set them all aside.

Scald (page 10)

1 cup milk or cream

Meanwhile, soften

1 pkg. active dry yeast

in

¼ cup warm water, 105°F to 115°F (Or if using compressed yeast, soften 1 cake in ¼ cup lukewarm water, 80°F to 85°F.)

Set aside.

Put into a large bowl

½ cup sugar
1 teaspoon salt

Pour scalded milk over ingredients in bowl. Stir until sugar is dissolved. When mixture is lukewarm, blend in, beating until smooth

1 cup sifted all-purpose flour

Stir softened yeast and add, mixing well.

Measure

4 cups sifted all-purpose flour

Add about one-half of the flour to yeast mixture and beat until very smooth.

English Muffins

Beat in

2 eggs, well beaten

Vigorously beat in, 2 to 3 tablespoons at a time

½ cup butter, softened

Beat in enough remaining flour to make a soft dough. Turn dough onto a lightly floured surface. Let stand 5 to 10 min.

Knead dough (page 11).

Form dough into a large ball; place it in a greased deep bowl. Turn dough to bring greased surface to top. Cover with waxed paper and towel and let stand in warm place (about 80°F) until doubled.

Punch down with fist; pull edges of dough in to center and turn completely over in bowl. Cover with waxed paper and towel and let rise again until nearly doubled.

Lightly grease muffin-pan wells.

Meanwhile, melt

⅔ cup butter

Put about 1 teaspoon of melted butter in bottom of each muffin-pan well. Reserve remaining butter for Pecan Snails.

Mix together with chopped nuts

1 cup firmly packed brown sugar
¼ cup currants (omit, if desired)
1 tablespoon cinnamon

Sprinkle 2 teaspoons of this mixture over butter in each muffin-pan well. Gently press 3 or 4 pecan halves onto mixture in each well.

Again punch down dough and form it into two balls. Roll each ball on lightly floured surface into a rectangle ¼ to ⅓ in. thick, 6 to 8 in. wide and 12 in. long. Brush top surface of dough with remaining melted butter and sprinkle evenly with remainder of brown-sugar mixture. Beginning with longer side of rectangle, roll dough tightly into a long roll. Press edges together to seal. Cut each roll into 12 slices. Place one slice in each muffin-pan well, cut side down. Cover muffin pans with waxed paper and a towel and let dough rise until doubled.

Bake at 375°F 15 to 20 min. Invert muffin pans on cooling racks, leaving rolls in pan 1 min. Remove rolls from pans and cool on cooling racks, glazed side up.

2 doz. Pecan Snails

—ALMOND SNAILS
(Mandelschnecken)

Follow ▲ Recipe. Substitute **toasted almonds** for pecan halves.

DANISH PASTRY
(Kaffekage)

Baking sheets will be needed.

Scald (page 10)

¾ cup plus 2 tablespoons milk

Meanwhile, soften

1 pkg. active dry yeast

in

¼ cup warm water, 105°F to 115°F (Or if using compressed yeast, soften 1 cake in ¼ cup lukewarm water, 80°F to 85°F.)

Set aside.

Put into a large bowl

¼ cup sugar
¼ cup butter
¼ teaspoon salt

Immediately pour scalded milk over ingredients in bowl. When lukewarm, blend in, beating until smooth

1 cup sifted all-purpose flour

Stir softened yeast and add, mixing well.

Measure

2 to 2¼ cups sifted all-purpose flour

Add about one-half the flour to the yeast mixture and beat until very smooth. Beat in

1 egg, well beaten

Beat in enough remaining flour to make a soft dough. Cover with waxed paper and a towel and let stand in a warm place (about 80°F) until doubled.

Meanwhile, put into a bowl

½ cup butter
½ cup sugar

Set aside.

Set out

½ cup butter, cut in pieces

Turn dough onto a lightly floured surface. Roll into an 18x13-in. rectangle. Using one-third of the butter, cut in pieces, pat pieces down center third of dough. Cover butter with right-

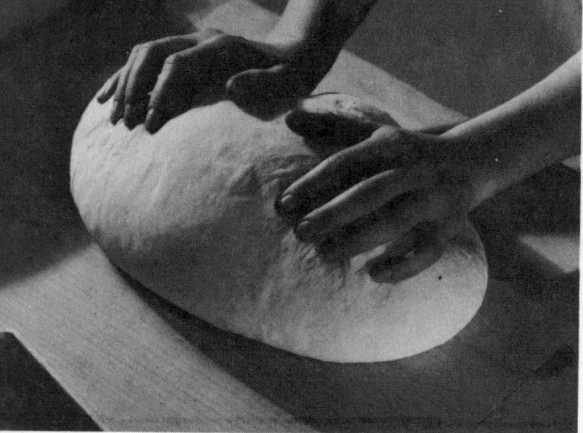

Knead—On a lightly floured board or pastry canvas, knead dough until smooth, elastic and small blisters show when dough is drawn taut. Use as little flour as necessary during kneading.

Punch down—When dough is doubled, punch down dough, then pull edges to center, and turn dough completely over in the bowl. Proceed as directed in recipe.

hand third of dough. Fold left-hand third of dough under butter section. With rolling pin gently press down and seal open edges. Wrap in waxed paper. Chill in refrigerator 20 to 30 min.

Remove from refrigerator and place on board with butter section near top, narrow width toward you. Turn folded dough one-quarter way around, to have open-under edge away from you. Roll to original size. Repeat two times the procedure for folding, sealing and chilling, using second and third portions of butter. Always place dough on floured surface.

Set out baking sheets.

After final chilling, roll dough to original size. Cut into 3-in. squares. Stir the sugar-butter mixture until blended. Place about 1½ teaspoons of the mixture in the center of each square. Fold the opposite corners in to center and press ends to seal. Place on the baking sheets. Cover with waxed paper and a towel. Let rise in a warm place until nearly doubled.

Bake at 450°F 8 to 10 min.

Meanwhile, blend together
½ cup sifted confectioners' sugar
1 tablespoon milk

When pastries are done, remove to cooling racks. Drizzle frosting over warm pastries. If desired, **preserves** may be substituted for the butter-sugar filling.   *2 doz. pastries*

LENTEN BUNS
(Fastelavnsboller)

These delicious buns are served only on the Tuesdays during Lent in Scandinavia. The buns are placed in deep dishes and hot milk flavored with sugar, vanilla extract and chopped almonds is poured over them.

Baking sheets will be needed.

Set out
3 tablespoons chopped blanched almonds

Scald (page 10)
1 cup milk

Meanwhile, soften
1 pkg. active dry yeast
in
**¼ cup warm water, 105°F to 115°F
(Or if using compressed yeast, soften 1 cake in ¼ cup lukewarm water, 80°F to 85°F.)**
Set aside.

Put into a large bowl
½ cup butter
⅓ cup sugar
½ teaspoon salt
Immediately pour scalded milk over ingredients in bowl. When lukewarm, blend in, beating until smooth
1 cup sifted all-purpose flour
Stir softened yeast and add, mixing well.

Measure
2½ to 3½ cups sifted all-purpose flour
Add about one-half the flour to the yeast mixture with the chopped almonds. Beat until very smooth.

Beat in
2 eggs, well beaten
Then beat in enough remaining flour to make a soft dough. Turn dough onto a lightly floured surface and allow it to rest 5 to 10 min.

Knead dough (page 11).

Form dough into a ball and place it in a greased, deep bowl. Turn dough to bring greased surface to top. Cover with waxed paper and towel and let stand in warm place (about 80°F) until dough is doubled.

Punch down with fist; pull edges of dough in to center and turn dough completely over in bowl. Cover and let rise again until nearly doubled. Punch down and turn dough onto lightly floured surface.

Lightly grease the baking sheets.

Shape dough into 24 balls and place on the greased baking sheets. Cover and let rise about 45 min., or until doubled.

Bake at 425°F 15 to 20 min.

Cool buns completely on cooling racks.

Place a bowl and beater in refrigerator to chill.

Force through a sieve enough almond paste to yield
1½ cups sieved almond paste
When buns are cool, cut a triangle ½ in. deep in the top of each. Carefully lift out triangular pieces. Spoon about 1 tablespoon of the almond paste into the cavity of each bun. Set pieces back on buns but without fitting to openings. Sprinkle buns lightly with
**Vanilla Confectioners' Sugar
(page 582)**

Using the chilled bowl and beater, beat until cream stands in peaks when beater is slowly lifted upright
½ cup chilled heavy cream
Force whipped cream through a pastry bag and a No. 27 star tube to decorate around center pieces.   *2 doz. buns*

SHERRY NUTMEG BUNS

Twenty-four 2-in. muffin-pan wells will be needed.

Soften
1 pkg. active dry yeast
in
**¼ cup warm water, 105°F to 115°F
(Or if using compressed yeast, soften 1 cake in ¼ cup lukewarm water, 80°F to 85°F.)**
Set aside.

Scald (page 10)
¾ cup milk

Meanwhile, put into a large bowl
½ cup butter
¼ cup sugar
1¼ teaspoons salt
Immediately pour scalded milk over ingredients in bowl. When mixture is lukewarm, stir it and thoroughly blend in a mixture of
½ cup sifted all-purpose flour
½ teaspoon nutmeg
½ teaspoon mace
Stir the softened yeast and add, mixing well.

Measure
2½ to 3 cups sifted all-purpose flour
Add about one-half the flour to the yeast mixture and beat until very smooth. Beat in
1 egg, well beaten
3 tablespoons sherry
¼ teaspoon vanilla extract
Then beat in enough remaining flour to make a soft dough. Beat thoroughly at least 5 min. Turn into a deep, buttered bowl just large enough to allow dough to double. Brush top surface with
Melted butter
Cover with waxed paper and a towel. Set aside in a warm place (about 80°F) until dough is doubled.

Punch down with fist; butter surface of dough and cover again. Let rise again until dough is nearly doubled.

Lightly grease the muffin-pan wells.

Beat dough thoroughly; drop by spoonfuls into the greased muffin-pan wells, filling about one-half full. Let rise 30 min., or until light.

Bake at 425°F 15 to 20 min., or until buns are lightly browned. *2 doz. buns*

VIRGINIA LEMON RAISIN BUNS

These light, lemony buns may be served in place of biscuits.

Lightly greased baking sheets will be needed.

Put into a sieve placed over a bowl
  ½ cup seedless raisins
Pour over raisins
  Boiling water
Drain raisins, spread on absorbent paper and dry thoroughly. Set aside.

Measure
  3¼ to 3¾ cups sifted all-purpose flour
Mix thoroughly in a large mixer bowl 1 cup of the flour and
  ⅓ cup sugar
  ½ teaspoon salt
  1 pkg. active dry yeast
Put into bowl
  6 tablespoons butter or margarine, softened
Add gradually to dry ingredients, beating constantly
  ¾ cup very hot tap water
Beat at medium speed of electric mixer for 2 min., scraping down bowl occasionally. Add to the bowl
  1 egg (room temperature)
  1 teaspoon lemon extract
Mix in ½ cup of the flour. Beat at high speed 2 min., scraping the bowl occasionally. Work in the raisins and enough of the remaining flour to make a soft dough. Turn onto a lightly floured surface.

Knead dough by folding opposite side over toward you. Using heels of hands, gently push dough away. Give it a quarter turn. Repeat process rhythmically until the dough is smooth and elastic, 8 to 10 min., using as little additional flour as possible. Always turn the dough in the same direction.

Form dough into a ball and put it into a greased deep bowl just large enough to allow dough to double. Turn dough to bring greased surface to top. Cover with waxed paper and clean towel; let rise in a warm place (about 80°F) until dough is doubled, about 1 hr.

Punch down dough and turn onto a lightly floured surface. Divide into 2 equal portions. Roll one-half of dough at a time ½ in. thick. Cut with a lightly floured 2-in. round biscuit cutter. Place buns about 1 in. apart on the lightly greased baking sheets. Cover and let rise in a warm place until doubled, about 1 hr.

Brush rolls lightly with
  Melted butter or margarine

Bake at 400°F 10 to 15 min.
  About 2 doz. buns

CHERRY CHOCOLATE DESSERT ROLLS

▲ Base Recipe

Baking sheets will be needed.

Melt together over low heat and set aside
  1 cup butter or margarine
  ½ cup vegetable shortening or all-purpose shortening

Soften
  1 pkg. active dry yeast
in
  ¼ cup warm water, 105°F to 115°F (Or if using compressed yeast, soften 1 cake in ¼ cup lukewarm water, 80°F to 85°F.)
Set aside.

Measure and set aside
  5 cups sifted all-purpose flour

Set out
  1⅔ cups (14½-oz. can) undiluted evaporated milk

Stir into the melted shortening a mixture of ⅓ cup of the evaporated milk and
  3 egg yolks, slightly beaten
  2 tablespoons sugar
  2 teaspoons salt
  ¼ teaspoon vanilla extract
Blend in, beating until smooth, 1 cup of the flour. Stir softened yeast and add, mixing well.

Beating well after each addition, alternately add the flour in fourths, the milk in thirds to the yeast mixture. Finally beat until smooth.

Knead in the bowl until dough pulls away from sides of bowl. Cover with waxed paper and a clean towel and put into refrigerator for 2 to 3 hrs., or overnight.

Lightly grease the baking sheets.

For filling, mix together
  1 cup (about 4 oz.) walnuts, ground or finely chopped
  1 pkg. (6 oz.) semisweet chocolate pieces
  ½ cup maraschino cherries, cut in quarters and well drained
Set aside.

Mix together
  ½ cup sugar
  2 teaspoons cinnamon
Use this mixture in place of flour for rolling out dough. Sprinkle mixture evenly on board.

Divide dough into two equal parts. Roll each portion of dough into a round about 15 in. in diameter. Cut each round into 16 wedge-shaped pieces. Put 1 teaspoon of the filling on each wedge. Roll up each wedge beginning at wide end. Place rolls on greased baking sheet with points underneath. Cover with waxed paper and a towel and let stand in a warm place (about 80°F) for about 1 hr.

Bake at 350°F 20 to 25 min., or until brown.
  32 rolls

—APRICOT PECAN ROLLS

Follow ▲ Recipe. For filling, substitute **1 cup (about 4 oz.) salted toasted pecans** for the walnuts and **1 cup finely cut dried apricots** for the chocolate pieces and cherries.

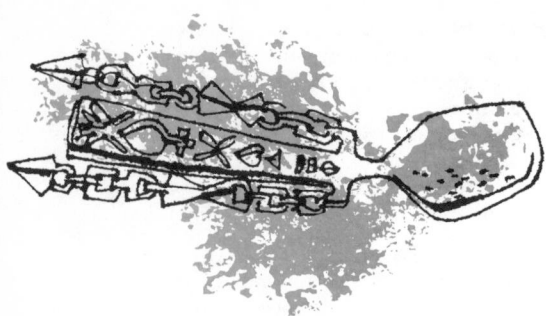

YEAST DOUGHNUTS

FLUFFY RAISED DOUGHNUTS

A deep saucepan or an automatic deep-fryer will be needed.

Heat in top of double boiler over simmering water until edges become slightly yellow

1½ cups dairy sour cream

(Separation of cream will not affect quality of product.)

Meanwhile, soften

3 pkgs. active dry yeast

in

**½ cup warm water, 105°F to 115°F
(Or if using compressed yeast,
soften 3 cakes in ½ cup lukewarm
water, 80°F to 85°F.)**

Set aside.

Turn heated sour cream into a large bowl; add

**½ cup sugar
2 teaspoons salt**

When mixture is lukewarm, add and blend in, beating until smooth

2 cups sifted all-purpose flour

Stir softened yeast and add, mixing well. Add and beat until smooth

**4 eggs, well beaten
¼ cup softened shortening
4 teaspoons vanilla extract
2 teaspoons almond extract
2 teaspoons orange extract**

Beat in, to make a soft dough, about

5 cups sifted all-purpose flour

Turn dough out onto a lightly floured surface and let rest 5 to 10 min.

Knead dough (page 11).

Fluffy Raised Doughnuts

Again let rest for 5 min. Divide dough into halves. Handling very lightly, roll out one-half at a time ½ in. thick and cut with a lightly floured doughnut cutter. Cover doughnuts and "holes" with waxed paper and a towel and let rise in a warm place (about 80°F) until doubled, about 45 min.

About 20 min. before deep-frying, put **fat** into the saucepan or deep-fryer and heat to 365°F.

Deep-fry doughnuts and "holes" in heated fat. Fry only as many at one time as will float uncrowded one layer deep in the fat. Deep-fry about 2 min., until browned. Turn doughnuts with a fork as they brown on the underside, and several times during cooking; do not pierce. Lift from fat with tongs or slotted spoon. Drain over fat for a few seconds before removing to absorbent paper.

While warm, shake 2 or 3 doughnuts at a time in a plastic bag containing a mixture of

**1 cup sugar
1½ teaspoons cinnamon
1 teaspoon nutmeg**

About 2 doz. doughnuts with "holes"

RAISED DOUGHNUTS
(Fánk)

▲ *Base Recipe*

A plump golden doughnut with a flavor all its own.

Measure and set aside

**4¼ to 4½ cups sifted all-purpose
flour**

Scald (page 10)

⅔ cup milk

Meanwhile, soften

1 pkg. active dry yeast

in

**¼ cup warm water, 105°F to 115°F
(Or if using compressed yeast,
soften 1 cake in ¼ cup lukewarm
water 80°F to 85°F.)**

Set aside.

Put into a large bowl

**½ cup sifted confectioners' sugar
¼ cup butter
¼ teaspoon salt**

Immediately pour the scalded milk over ingredients in bowl. When the mixture is lukewarm, mix well and stir in about ½ cup of the flour, beating until dough is smooth. Stir the softened yeast and add to dough, mixing well.

Add about one-half the remaining flour to the dough and beat until very smooth. Add in thirds, beating well after each addition, a mixture of

**6 egg yolks, well beaten
1 teaspoon rum**

Then beat in enough of the remaining flour to make a soft dough. Turn dough onto a lightly floured surface and let it rest 5 to 10 min.

Knead dough (page 11).

Form dough into a large ball and put it into a greased bowl. Turn to bring greased surface to top. Cover bowl with waxed paper and towel and let stand in warm place (about 80°F) until dough is doubled.

Punch down dough with fist; pull edges in to center and turn dough completely over in bowl. Cover bowl and let dough rise again until nearly doubled.

Turn dough out on floured surface and roll about ⅜ in. thick. With spatula, loosen dough from board wherever sticking occurs; lightly sprinkle flour underneath. Cut dough into rounds with a 3-in. lightly floured doughnut cutter (no hole in center). Let dough rise again 15 to 25 min., or until light.

About 20 min. before deep-frying, fill a deep saucepan one-half to two-thirds full with

**Vegetable shortening, all-purpose
shortening, lard or cooking oil**

Heat slowly to 365°F. When using automatic deep-dryer, follow manufacturer's directions for amount of fat and timing.

Deep-fry the doughnuts 2 or 3 min., or until lightly browned. Deep-fry only one layer of doughnuts at a time; do not crowd. Turn doughnuts occasionally with a fork to brown evenly, but do not pierce. Drain doughnuts over fat for a second before removing to absorbent paper; cool slightly.

Soft over doughnuts about

**2 to 3 tablespoons confectioners'
sugar**

About 1½ doz. doughnuts

—JAM-FILLED DOUGHNUTS
(Lekvárral Töltött Fánk)

Follow ▲ Recipe. Make a short slit in side of each cooled doughnut through to the center. Force **½ to 1 teaspoon jam or jelly** into center of each doughnut and close tightly.

BERLIN DOUGHNUTS (Bismarcks)
(Berliner Pfannkuchen)

A deep saucepan for deep-frying or an automatic deep-fryer will be needed.

Scald (page 10)

1 cup milk

Meanwhile, soften

1 pkg. active dry yeast

in

**¼ cup warm water, 105°F to 115°F
(Or if using compressed yeast,
soften 1 cake in ¼ cup lukewarm
water, 80°F to 85°F.)**

Set aside.

Put into a large bowl

**½ cup sugar
⅓ cup butter
1 tablespoon orange juice
2 teaspoons rum extract
1 teaspoon salt**

Immediately pour scalded milk over ingredients in bowl. When lukewarm, blend in, beating until smooth

1 cup sifted all-purpose flour

Stir softened yeast and add, mixing well.

Measure

2½ to 3 cups sifted all-purpose flour

Add about one-half the flour to the yeast mixture and beat until very smooth. Beat in

2 eggs, well beaten

Then beat in enough remaining flour to make a soft dough. Turn dough onto a lightly floured surface and allow it to rest 5 to 10 min.

Knead dough (page 11).

Form dough into a large ball and place in a greased, deep bowl. Turn dough to bring greased surface to top. Cover with waxed paper and towel and let stand in a warm place (about 80°F) until dough is doubled.

Punch down dough with fist. Turn dough out onto lightly floured surface and roll ½ in. thick. Cut dough into rounds with a 3-in. cookie cutter. Cover with waxed paper and let rise on rolling surface, away from drafts and direct heat 30 to 45 min., or until doubled.

About 20 min. before deep-frying, fill the saucepan or fryer with **fat** and heat to 365°F.

Deep-fry doughnuts in heated fat. Fry only as many doughnuts at one time as will float uncrowded one layer deep in the fat. Fry 2 to 3 min., or until lightly browned. Turn doughnuts with a fork or tongs when they rise to the surface and several times during cooking; do not pierce. Lift from fat with tongs or slotted spoon. Drain doughnuts over fat for a few seconds before removing to absorbent paper. Cool completely.

Cut a slit through to the center in the side of each cooled doughnut. Force about **½ teaspoon jam or jelly** into center and press lightly to close slit. (A pastry bag and tube may be used to force jelly or jam into slit.) Shake 2 to 3 Bismarcks at one time in plastic bag containing **sugar**. *About 1½ doz. doughnuts*

CREOLE DOUGHNUTS

Bring into the home a touch of that famed New Orleans French Market where everyone feasts on doughnuts and hot coffee.

A deep saucepan or an automatic deep-fryer will be needed.

Scald (page 10)

2 cups milk

Meanwhile, soften

1 pkg. active dry yeast

in

**¼ cup warm water, 105°F to 115°F
(Or if using compressed yeast, soften 1 cake in ¼ cup lukewarm water, 80°F to 85°F.)**

Set aside.

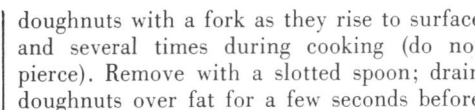

Potato Doughnuts

Put into a large bowl

**½ cup sugar
½ cup cooking oil (not olive oil)
1½ teaspoons salt**

Pour scalded milk over ingredients in bowl. When lukewarm, stir mixture and blend in, beating until smooth

1 cup sifted all-purpose flour

Stir softened yeast and add to mixture, mixing well.

Measure

6½ to 7 cups sifted all-purpose flour

Add about one-half of the flour to yeast mixture and beat until very smooth. Add in thirds, beating well after each addition

2 eggs, well beaten

Mix in enough of the remaining flour to make a soft dough. Turn dough onto a lightly floured surface and allow it to rest 5 to 10 min.

Knead dough (page 11).

Form dough into a smooth ball and place in a lightly greased, deep bowl. Turn dough to bring greased surface to top. Cover bowl with waxed paper and a towel and let stand in a warm place (about 80°F) until dough is doubled, about 1½ to 2 hrs.

Punch down dough with fist. Turn out onto a lightly floured surface. Roll about ¼ in. thick, and using a sharp knife, cut into 2-in. squares or diamonds. Place doughnuts on a floured board; cover and let rise in a warm place until doubled.

About 20 min. before deep-frying, fill a deep saucepan one-half to two-thirds full with

Vegetable shortening, all-purpose shortening, lard or cooking oil for deep-frying

Heat fat slowly to 365°F.

When doughnuts are doubled in size, deep-fry in heated fat. Fry only as many at one time as will float uncrowded one layer deep in the fat. Fry 2 to 3 min., or until lightly browned. Turn

doughnuts with a fork as they rise to surface and several times during cooking (do not pierce). Remove with a slotted spoon; drain doughnuts over fat for a few seconds before removing to absorbent paper.

Shake 2 or 3 doughnuts at one time in a plastic bag containing

Sifted confectioners' sugar (or Vanilla Confectioners' Sugar, (page 313)

Serve warm or store in tightly covered jar.
About 6 doz. doughnuts

POTATO DOUGHNUTS
(Fastnachtsscherben)

Wash, pare and cook (page 322)

3 medium (about 1 lb.) potatoes

Cook 25 to 35 min., or until tender when pierced with a fork. Drain, reserving 1 cup cooking liquid. Dry potatoes by shaking pan over low heat. Cover potatoes and keep warm; set aside.

Soften

2 pkgs. active dry yeast

in

**½ cup warm water, 105°F to 115°F
(Or if using compressed yeast, soften 2 cakes in ½ cup lukewarm water, 80°F to 85°F.)**

Set aside.

When reserved cooking liquid has cooled to lukewarm, pour it into a large bowl. Stir in

2 tablespoons sugar

Stir softened yeast and add to mixture, mixing well. Add and beat until mixture is smooth

2 cups sifted all-purpose flour

Cover bowl with waxed paper and a towel and let stand in a warm place (about 80°F) until very light and bubbly, about 1 hr.

Meanwhile, mash potatoes. Measure 1 cup mashed potatoes. Put into a bowl; beat in

**½ cup softened butter
2 eggs, well beaten**

Add a mixture of
  ½ cup plus 2 tablespoons sugar
  1 tablespoon grated lemon peel
  1½ teaspoons salt
  ¾ teaspoon nutmeg
When yeast mixture becomes very bubbly, stir in potato mixture. Measure
  4 to 5 cups sifted all-purpose flour
Add about one-half of flour to yeast-potato mixture and beat until very smooth. Mix in enough remaining flour to make a soft dough. Turn dough onto a lightly floured surface and allow it to rest 5 to 10 min.

Knead dough (page 11).

Form dough into a smooth ball and place in a greased, deep bowl. Turn dough to bring greased surface to top. Cover bowl with waxed paper and a towel and let stand in a warm place (about 80°F) until dough is doubled, about 1½ to 2 hrs.

Punch down dough with fist. Pull edges in to center and turn completely over in bowl. Cover with waxed paper and towel and let rise again until nearly doubled, about 45 min.

Again punch down dough. Divide dough into two equal parts; turn one part onto a lightly floured surface. Roll about ½ in. thick and cut with lightly floured doughnut cutter. Roll second half about ½ in. thick, and using a sharp knife, cut into 2-in. squares. Place doughnuts and squares on a floured board; cover and let rise in a warm place away from drafts until doubled.

About 20 min. before deep-frying, fill a saucepan or deep-fryer one-half to two-thirds full with **fat** and heat to 365°F.

Deep-fry doughnuts in heated fat. Fry only as many at one time as will float uncrowded one layer deep in the fat. Fry 2 to 3 min., or until lightly browned. Turn doughnuts with a fork when they rise to the surface and several times during cooking; do not pierce. Lift from fat with tongs or slotted spoon. Drain doughnuts over fat for a few seconds before removing to absorbent paper.

Shake 2 or 3 warm doughnuts at a time in a plastic bag containing
  ½ cup sugar
Serve warm or store in tightly covered jar.
  About 3 doz. doughnuts and squares

YEAST GRIDDLECAKES

BUCKWHEAT GRIDDLECAKES

Start this batter the night before to serve delicious, hot Buckwheat Griddlecakes for breakfast in the morning.

Soften
  1 pkg. active dry yeast
in
  3¼ cups warm water, 105°F to 115°F
  (Or if using compressed yeast, soften 1 cake in 3¼ cups lukewarm water, 80°F to 85°F.)
Set aside.

Sift together into a large bowl
  2½ cups sifted buckwheat flour
  1¼ cups sifted all-purpose flour
  1 tablespoon sugar
  1½ teaspoons salt
Stir softened yeast; add gradually to the sifted dry ingredients and mix thoroughly after each addition. Beat until batter is smooth.

Cover bowl with waxed paper and a clean towel. Let mixture stand overnight.

The following morning, set a griddle or heavy skillet over low heat.

Melt and cool
  ¼ cup butter
Mix in
  2 tablespoons brown sugar
  ¾ teaspoon baking soda
Stir batter; quickly blend in the brown sugar mixture. Test griddle; it is hot enough for baking when drops of water sprinkled on surface dance in small beads. Lightly grease griddle if manufacturer so directs.

For each griddlecake spoon about ¼ cup batter onto the heated griddle. Bake slowly until griddlecake is browned on one side. Using a spatula, carefully turn and brown on second side. Repeat procedure for remaining batter.

Serve griddlecakes hot with **butter** and **maple syrup**.   *About 2 doz. griddlecakes*

QUICK TEA BREADS AND COFFEE CAKES

DELECTABLE ALMOND BREAD

A delicate and delicious bread which may be served in thin half-slices and attractively arranged on a tray. Or use it for dainty finger sandwiches, put together with whipped butter.

To Make Pans—Cut a piece of extra heavy aluminum foil 15x9 in. Fold in half to form a rectangle 9x7½ in. Fold, using edge of ruler as a guide, each of 9-in. sides in 2¼ in. toward center. Unfold. Fold, over a ruler, each of the other sides in 2 in. toward the center. Unfold. On the 9-in. sides, cut along the creases 2¼ in., or to where creases make right angles. Draw up the sides to form a box. Secure the flaps on the outside by folding the top edges down and over the flaps ¼ in. Make sure that the corners are sealed and that there are no air pockets. Repeat for the second pan.

For Bread—Set out
  ½ lb. (about 1½ cups) unblanched almonds
Grate (page 10) 1 cup of the almonds. Chop the remaining almonds. Put all of the almonds into a bowl.

Sift together into the bowl
  ½ cup sifted all-purpose flour
  ½ teaspoon baking powder
  ⅛ teaspoon salt
Gently blend mixture and set aside.

Cream together until butter is softened
  ½ cup butter
  2 teaspoons vanilla extract
  ¼ teaspoon almond extract
Add gradually, creaming until fluffy after each addition
  ½ cup plus 2 tablespoons sugar
Add in thirds, beating thoroughly after each addition
  2 eggs, well beaten
Blend in the dry ingredients in fourths, beating until well mixed. Turn batter into pans and carefully spread to corners.

Bake at 325°F 55 to 60 min., or until bread tests done (page 11). Cool bread on cooling rack 15 min. before removing from pans.

Cool bread completely before slicing or storing. To store, wrap tightly in aluminum foil or other moisture-vaporproof material.

  2 small loaves bread

APRICOT NUT BREAD

Prepare (page 10) a 9x5x3-in. loaf pan.

Coarsely cut
1½ cups (½ lb.) dried apricots
Put into a saucepan and add
1 cup water
Bring to boiling, reduce heat and simmer, uncovered, 10 min., or until water is absorbed. Set apricots aside to cool.

Melt and set aside to cool
3 tablespoons butter or margarine

Coarsely chop and set aside
¾ cup (about 3 oz.) nuts

Sift together into a bowl
2½ cups sifted all-purpose flour
¾ cup sugar
4 teaspoons baking powder
1 teaspoon salt
½ teaspoon baking soda
Mix in chopped nuts. Make a well in center of dry ingredients and set aside.

Beat until thick and piled softly
1 egg
Add
1 cup buttermilk
Blend in melted butter and apricots. Add all at one time to the dry ingredients; stir only enough to moisten the dry ingredients. Turn batter into pan and spread to corners.

Bake at 350°F about 1 hr., or until a wooden pick or cake tester comes out clean when inserted in center of bread.

Cool as directed (page 11) and store.
1 loaf bread

EASY BANANA BREAD

Prepare (page 10) an 8x4x2-in. loaf pan.

Measure and set aside
2 cups prepared biscuit mix

Peel, beat or mash and set aside
2 or 3 bananas with all-yellow or brown-flecked peel (or enough to yield 1 cup mashed banana)

Put into a bowl
⅓ cup shortening
Add gradually, creaming until fluffy after each addition
⅔ cup sugar
Add to the creamed mixture in thirds, beating thoroughly after each addition
2 eggs, well beaten
Beating only until smooth after each addition, alternately add the prepared biscuit mix in fourths, the mashed banana in thirds to creamed mixture. Finally beat only until batter is smooth (do not overbeat). Turn batter into the prepared pan.

Bake at 350°F about 1 hr. and 10 min., or until a wooden pick or cake tester inserted in center of bread comes out clean. Immediately remove from pan and set on a cooling rack to cool.

Cool bread completely before slicing or storing. To store, wrap tightly in aluminum foil or other moisture-vaporproof material.
1 loaf bread

To vary—Mix into batter one of the following: **1 cup dark seedless raisins, ½ cup coarsely chopped nuts** or **1 cup finely snipped dates.**

BANANA PARTY BREAD

Prepare (page 10) a 9x5x3-in. loaf pan.

Coarsely chop and set aside
1 cup (3½ oz.) walnuts

Set out
¼ cup chopped candied cherries
¼ cup chopped candied citron
¼ cup chopped candied orange peel
¼ cup chopped candied pineapple

Melt and set aside to cool
¼ cup shortening

Sift together into a large bowl and set aside
2 cups sifted all-purpose flour
¾ cup sugar
1 tablespoon baking powder
½ teaspoon baking soda
½ teaspoon salt

Peel, beat or mash
2 large or 3 small bananas with all-yellow or brown-flecked peel (or enough to yield 1¼ cups mashed banana)
Beat until thick and piled softly
2 eggs
Add to eggs the mashed bananas, cooled shortening and
¼ cup buttermilk
1 teaspoon vanilla extract
Beat until mixture is smooth.

Make a well in center of dry ingredients. Add liquid mixture all at one time with chopped nuts and candied fruits. Stir with spoon only until dry ingredients are moistened. Turn batter into prepared pan and spread to corners.

Bake at 350°F 40 to 45 min., or until bread tests done. Cool as directed (page 11).
1 loaf bread

CORIANDER BANANA NUT BREAD

Prepare (page 10) a 9x5x3-in. loaf pan.

Blend together in a large bowl
1⅔ cups sifted all-purpose flour
¾ cup sugar
1 tablespoon baking powder
½ teaspoon baking soda
½ teaspoon salt
2 teaspoons ground coriander
Mix in and set aside
1½ cups (about 6 oz.) chopped unblanched almonds

Melt and set aside to cool
⅓ cup shortening

Easy Banana Bread

Banana Party Bread

Coriander Banana Nut Bread

Peel, beat or mash and set aside
2 large or 3 small bananas with all-yellow or brown-flecked peel (or enough to yield 1¼ cups mashed banana)

Mix until well blended
1 large egg, well beaten
¼ cup buttermilk
1 teaspoon vanilla extract
Blend in melted shortening and bananas.

Make a well in center of dry ingredients and

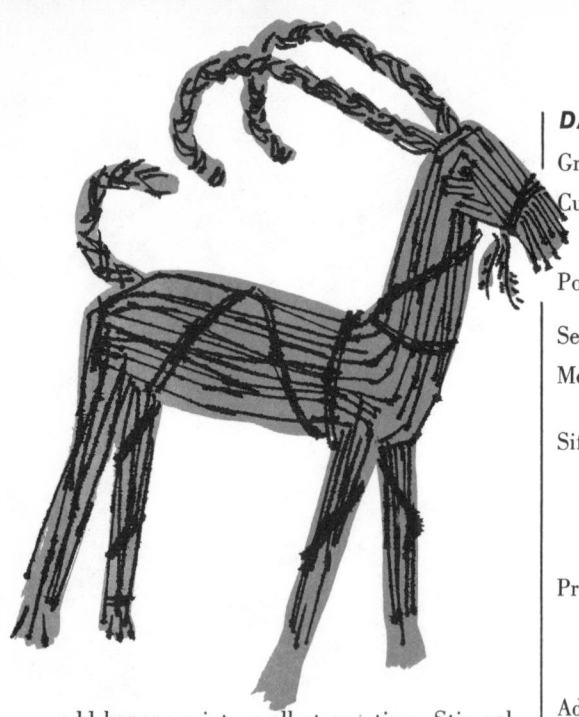

add banana mixture all at one time. Stir only enough to moisten dry ingredients. Turn into pan and spread to corners.

Bake at 350°F about 1 hr., or until a wooden pick or cake tester comes out clean when inserted in center of bread. Immediately remove from pan and set on a cooling rack to cool.

Wrap and store.   *1 loaf bread*

DATE NUT BREAD

Prepare (page 10) a 9x5x3-in. loaf pan.

Melt and set aside to cool
⅓ cup shortening

Sift together into a bowl
2 cups sifted all-purpose flour
2 teaspoons baking powder
1 teaspoon baking soda
1 teaspoon salt
Add and mix in
1 cup whole wheat flour
¾ cup firmly packed light brown sugar
1 cup (about 7 oz.) pitted dates, cut
1 cup (about 4 oz.) chopped nuts
Make a well in center of dry ingredients and set aside.

Mix until blended
1 egg, well beaten
1¼ cups buttermilk
¼ cup molasses
1½ teaspoons vanilla extract
Add and blend in the melted shortening. Add liquid mixture all at one time to the dry ingredients. Stir only enough to moisten dry ingredients. Turn batter into pan and spread to corners.

Bake at 350°F about 70 min., or until a wooden pick or cake tester comes out clean when inserted in center of bread.

Cool as directed (page 11) and store.
1 loaf bread

DATE NUT CHEESE BREAD

Grease bottom of a 9x5x3-in. loaf pan.

Cut finely and put into a bowl
½ lb. pitted dates (about 1½ cups, cut)
Pour over dates
¾ cup very hot water
Set aside to cool.

Melt and set aside to cool
¼ cup shortening

Sift together into a bowl
3 cups sifted all-purpose flour
½ cup sugar
4 teaspoons baking powder
¾ teaspoon salt

Prepare and lightly blend into dry ingredients
1 cup (about 4 oz.) grated sharp Cheddar cheese
¾ cup (about 3 oz.) chopped pecans

Add to the date-water mixture the cooled shortening and
½ cup milk
1 egg, well beaten
1 teaspoon vanilla extract
Mix well.

Make a well in center of dry ingredients and add date-liquid mixture all at one time. Stir only enough to moisten dry ingredients. Turn mixture into pan and spread to corners.

Bake at 350°F about 65 min., or until bread is done. Remove from pan and cool.
1 loaf bread

CALIFORNIA FRUIT NUT BREAD

Prepare (page 10) a 9x5x3-in. loaf pan.

Wash and cut into 8 sections (peel and pulp), removing any seeds
1 medium orange
Set out
1 cup (about 7 oz.) pitted dates
½ cup (about 2 oz.) walnuts
Force orange sections, nuts and dates through the medium blade of a food chopper, reserving juice in a 1-cup measuring cup for liquids.

Melt and set aside to cool
3 tablespoons butter or margarine

Sift together into a large bowl
2½ cups sifted all-purpose flour
¾ cup sugar
1 tablespoon baking powder
1 teaspoon salt
½ teaspoon baking soda
Add to juice from orange mixture
Buttermilk (enough to make 1 cup liquid)
Blend into liquid the melted butter and
1 egg, well beaten

Make a well in center of dry ingredients and add, all at one time, the liquid ingredients and orange-date-nut mixture. Beat until blended. Turn into the pan and spread to corners.

Bake at 350°F about 1¼ hrs., or until bread tests done (page 10).

Cool, wrap and store overnight.   *1 loaf bread*

OATMEAL RAISIN BREAD

Prepare (page 10) a 9x5x3-in. loaf pan.

Sift together into a bowl
2 cups sifted all-purpose flour
½ cup sugar
1 tablespoon baking powder
1½ teaspoons salt
½ teaspoon baking soda
1 teaspoon cinnamon
¼ teaspoon mace or nutmeg
Stir in
1 cup uncooked rolled oats
1 cup (about 5 oz.) raisins
½ cup (about 2 oz.) chopped nuts
Make a well in center and set aside.

Mix and add to dry ingredients, all at one time
1¼ cups sour milk (page 9)
¼ cup firmly packed brown sugar
1 egg, well beaten
3 tablespoons shortening, melted and cooled
Stir only enough to moisten dry ingredients. Turn into pan and spread to corners.

Oatmeal Raisin Bread

California Fruit Nut Bread

Bake at 350°F about 1 hr., or until a wooden pick or cake tester comes out clean when inserted in center of bread.

Cool and store as directed (page 10).

1 loaf bread

ORANGE PECAN BREAD

Prepare (page 10) two 9x5x3-in. loaf pans.

Blender-chop (page 11)
 3 cups (about 11 oz.) pecans
Sift together into a large bowl
 6 cups sifted all-purpose flour
 4 teaspoons baking powder
 1 tablespoon baking soda
 1½ teaspoons salt
Stir in pecans and set aside.

Put into large mixer bowl and beat with electric beater until softened
 1 cup butter or margarine
 2 tablespoons grated orange peel
Add gradually, beating until fluffy after each addition
 2 cups sugar
Continue to beat and add, one at a time, beating well after each addition
 6 eggs, unbeaten
Add and continue to beat until blended
 2½ cups orange juice
Make a well in the center of dry ingredients and add liquid mixture all at one time. Beat just until dry ingredients are moistened.

Turn batter into prepared pans and spread to corners.

Bake at 350°F 55 to 60 min., or until bread tests done.

Cool as directed (page 11). *2 loaves bread*

PEANUT BUTTER BREAD

Prepare (page 10) a 9x5x3-in. loaf pan.

Sift together into a bowl
 2½ cups sifted all-purpose flour
 ¾ cup sugar
 4 teaspoons baking powder
 1 teaspoon salt
Stir in
 ½ cup (about 2 oz.) salted peanuts (skins removed), chopped
Make a well in center and set bowl aside.

Mix until blended
 1 egg, well beaten
 1½ cups milk
Blend gradually into
 1 cup (8 oz.) softened peanut butter
Add to dry ingredients all at one time; stir only until dry ingredients are moistened. Turn into pan and spread to corners.

Bake at 350°F about 1 hr., or until a wooden pick or cake tester comes out clean when inserted in center of bread.

Cool as directed (page 11). *1 loaf bread*

BOSTON BROWN BREAD

Thoroughly grease inside of three 2½-cup size (18- to 20-oz.) cans. Cut aluminum foil or waxed (double thickness) or parchment paper into three 6-in. squares to cover tops and to hang about 1¼ in. over sides of cans. Set out large kettle or steamer and its tight-fitting cover; put trivet or rack in kettle.

Mix together in a bowl
 1 cup rye flour
 1 cup whole wheat flour
 1 cup yellow corn meal
 1½ teaspoons baking powder
 1 teaspoon salt
 ¾ teaspoon baking soda
Make a well in center of the dry ingredients.

Combine
 2 cups buttermilk or sour milk (page 9)
 ¾ cup molasses
Add all at one time to dry ingredients with
 1 cup (about 5 oz.) dark seedless raisins
Stir only enough to moisten all the flour. Pour an equal amount of batter into each can (filling cans not more than two-thirds full). Cover cans tightly by tying on foil or paper with string. Place cans on trivet. Pour boiling water into kettle to no more than one-half the height of the cans. Cover kettle and bring water to boiling. To steam, reduce heat but keep water boiling. If necessary, add more boiling water to keep water level at one-half the height of the cans during steaming. Steam bread 3 hrs.

Remove cans from kettle; remove aluminum foil or paper from cans. Carefully run spatula down and around inside of cans to loosen bread; remove bread from cans and place on cooling rack.

Store cooled loaves wrapped in moisture-vaporproof material in a cool place or in the refrigerator. *3 loaves bread*

BLITZKUCHEN

 ▲ *Base Recipe*

Grease an 8-in. round layer cake pan.

For Topping—Mix together in order and set aside
 ⅓ cup (about 1 oz.) chopped walnuts
 ⅓ cup sugar
 1½ teaspoons cinnamon
 1 tablespoon butter or margarine, melted

Boston Brown Bread

For Cake—Sift together
 1 cup sifted all-purpose flour
 ½ cup sugar
 1½ teaspoons baking powder
 ½ teaspoon salt
Cut in with pastry blender or 2 knives until pieces are size of rice kernels
 ¼ cup shortening
Make a well in center of dry ingredients and add, all at one time, a mixture of
 1 egg, well beaten
 ½ cup milk
Stir, mixing only enough to moisten dry ingredients, about 15 strokes. Turn batter into pan and spread evenly to edges. Sprinkle topping over surface and gently pat down with back of a spoon or fork.

Bake at 375°F about 20 min., or until bread tests done (page 11).

Serve Blitzkuchen hot. *6 servings*

—ORANGE KUCHEN

Follow ▲ Recipe. Substitute **grated orange peel** for cinnamon in topping. For cake, decrease milk to ⅓ cup and add **3 tablespoons orange juice**.

—CARAWAY OR POPPY SEED KUCHEN

Follow ▲ Recipe. Omit topping. Mix in **2 teaspoons caraway or poppy seed** with sifted dry ingredients. Before baking, sprinkle **2 tablespoons sugar** evenly over the batter.

—CRUNCHY KUCHEN

Follow ▲ Recipe. Substitute for topping, **brown sugar** for granulated sugar, **½ cup**

Lazy Man's Coffee Cake

coarsely crushed cereal flakes for nuts and increase butter or margarine to 2 tablespoons.

—FESTIVE COFFEE CAKE

Follow ▲ Recipe for coffee cake. Substitute for topping a mixture of **3 tablespoons sugar, 2 teaspoons cinnamon, ¼ cup (about 1 oz.) chopped nuts** and **⅓ cup chopped candied fruit.**

—APPLE COFFEE CAKE

Follow ▲ Recipe for coffee cake. Substitute the following for topping—Wash, quarter, core, pare and slice **2 medium apples.** Mix together **2 teaspoons cinnamon** and **¼ cup sugar.** Melt **2 tablespoons butter or margarine.** Lightly brush top of batter with some of melted fat. Arrange apple slices on batter, pressing slightly. Sprinkle cinnamon-sugar evenly over apples. Drizzle remaining fat over all.

—PINEAPPLE COFFEE CAKE

Follow ▲ Recipe for coffee cake. Substitute for topping a mixture of **2 tablespoons brown sugar, 2 tablespoons melted butter or margarine** and **½ cup well-drained crushed pineapple.**

LAZY MAN'S COFFEE CAKE

▲ *Base Recipe*

Grease an 8-in. round layer cake pan.

For Sugar Topping—Lightly mix and set aside
  ¼ cup **All-in-One Biscuit Mix (page 93)**
  ¼ cup **firmly packed light brown sugar**
  ½ teaspoon **cinnamon**

For Coffee Cake—Blend thoroughly
  1½ cups **All-in-One Biscuit Mix (page 93)**
  ⅓ cup **sugar**
Beat until thick and piled softly
  1 **egg**
Add and beat until blended
  ¼ cup **milk**

Add liquid to dry ingredients all at one time; mix only enough to moisten dry ingredients. Turn into pan. Spoon sugar mixture over coffee cake batter.

Bake at 375°F about 20 min., or until a cake tester or wooden pick comes out clean when inserted in center of coffee cake.

Cut while warm and serve.   *6 servings*

—COCONUT COFFEE CAKE

Follow ▲ Recipe. Substitute the following for the topping—Cream together ⅓ **cup sugar** and **3 tablespoons butter or margarine.** Blend in **2 tablespoons cream** and ½ **teaspoon cinnamon.** Continue blending until mixture is very soft. Spread over batter; sprinkle with ¾ **cup flaked coconut.**

APPLE MOLASSES COFFEE CAKE

Lightly grease an 8x8x2-in. pan.

For Topping—Blend together in a small bowl and set aside
  ½ cup firmly packed brown sugar
  2 tablespoons butter or margarine, melted
  2 teaspoons cinnamon

Wash and set aside
  1 medium (about ¼ lb.) tart cooking apple

For Coffee Cake—Melt and set aside to cool
  3 tablespoons shortening

Sift together into a large bowl and set aside
  1½ cups sifted all-purpose flour
  2 teaspoons baking powder
  ½ teaspoon salt

Beat until thick and piled softly
  1 egg
Blend into egg the melted shortening and
  ½ cup sugar
  ½ cup milk
  ¼ cup molasses
Make a well in center of dry ingredients and add liquid mixture all at one time. Beat just until dry ingredients are moistened. (Scrape sides of bowl.) Turn into prepared pan and spread evenly.

Quarter, core, pare and thinly slice the apple. Arrange slices on top of batter. Spoon sugar mixture evenly over apples.

Bake at 375°F 30 to 35 min., or until a wooden pick or cake tester comes out clean when inserted in center of cake.

Cut into 2-in. squares and serve immediately.
                                                    16 squares

CORN MEAL BREADS

JOHNNY CAKE I

The name "johnny cake" goes far back into colonial days, when a trip from one settlement to the next was really a "journey"—a full day's jaunt. Then the traveller's good wife would fashion little "journey cakes" of corn meal to fit into his knapsack, so he could break his fast along the way. Over the years the name has been contracted into "johnny cake." Rhode Island folk still like to make theirs (and they drop the "h," by the way) from white corn meal, and to bake them as their many-times-great-grandmothers did, as small cakes in a spider or skillet. Elsewhere in New England yellow corn meal is usually used, and the cakes are baked in the oven—and spelled with the "h."

Grease an 8x8x2-in. pan.

Sift together into a bowl
  1 cup sifted all-purpose flour
  ¼ cup sugar
  1 teaspoon baking powder
  ¾ teaspoon salt
  ½ teaspoon baking soda
Mix in
  1 cup yellow corn meal
Make a well in center of dry ingredients and set aside.

Beat until thick and piled softly
  1 egg
Blend in
  1 cup buttermilk or sour milk
  2 tablespoons butter, melted
  2 tablespoons molasses
Add liquid mixture all at one time to dry ingredients. Beat with rotary beater until just smooth, being careful not to overmix.

Turn batter into pan and spread to corners.

Bake at 425°F about 20 min., or until a wooden pick or cake tester comes out clean when inserted in center.

Break or cut into 2-in. squares. Serve hot with **butter** and warm **maple syrup**.   *16 squares*

JOHNNY CAKE II

Grease an 11x7x1½-in. pan.

Sift together into a bowl
    1 cup sifted all-purpose flour
    ¼ to ½ teaspoon salt
    ½ teaspoon baking soda
Mix in
    1 cup yellow corn meal
    ¾ cup firmly packed brown sugar
Make a well in center of dry ingredients and set aside.

Beat until thick and piled softly
    1 egg
Blend in
    ½ cup buttermilk or sour milk
    ⅓ cup dairy sour cream
Add liquid mixture all at one time to dry ingredients. Beat until just smooth, being careful not to overmix. Turn batter into pan and spread to corners.

Bake at 425°F about 20 min., or until a wooden pick or cake tester comes out clean when inserted in center.

Break or cut into squares. Serve hot with **butter** and warm **maple syrup**.   *15 squares*

FILLED CORN BREAD SQUARES

    ▲ *Base Recipe*

Grease an 8x8x2-in. pan.

Sift together into a bowl
    1 cup sifted all-purpose flour
    2 tablespoons sugar
    1 tablespoon baking powder
    ½ teaspoon salt
Mix in and set aside
    1 cup corn meal

Blend thoroughly
    1 egg, well beaten
    1 cup milk
    3 tablespoons shortening, melted

Make a well in center of dry ingredients and add liquid mixture all at one time. Beat with rotary beater until just smooth, being careful not to overmix. Turn about one-half of batter into pan.

Spoon evenly over batter
    1 cup cherry preserves
Spread remaining batter over cherry preserves. Sprinkle evenly over batter
    1 tablespoon sugar

Bake at 425°F about 20 min., or until a

wooden pick or cake tester comes out clean when inserted gently in center. Cut into squares and serve hot.   *9 servings*

—GOLDEN CORN STICKS

Follow ▲ Recipe. Omit preserves and sugar sprinkled on top of corn bread. Grease and heat thoroughly in oven, 12 corn-stick pan sections. Fill three-fourths full with batter and bake at 425°F 15 to 20 min. Serve hot with **cherry preserves or jam.**

—TOUCH O' BACON CORN BREAD

Follow ▲ Recipe. Omit preserves and sugar sprinkled on top of corn bread. Substitute **bacon drippings** for shortening. Serve topped with **Mustard Sauce** (page 307). Garnish with **Panfried Bacon** (page 190).

RHODE ISLAND JONNY CAKE

Set a griddle or skillet over low heat.

Mix together in a bowl
    2 cups white corn meal
    2 tablespoons sugar
    2¼ teaspoons salt
Make a well in center of dry ingredients and add all at one time
    2 cups milk
Beat only until batter is smooth and thoroughly mixed.

Test griddle; it is hot enough for baking when drops of water sprinkled on surface dance in small beads. Lightly grease griddle.

For each jonny cake, spoon 1 tablespoon of batter onto the heated griddle. Cook until browned on one side. Using a spatula, carefully turn and brown second side. Repeat procedure for the remaining batter.

Serve hot with **butter** and **maple syrup.**
    About 4 doz. jonny cakes

CORN MEAL MUSH

    ▲ *Base Recipe*

Bring to boiling in a saucepan
    3 cups water
    1½ teaspoons salt
Gradually stir in a mixture of
    1 cup corn meal
    1 cup cold water
Continue boiling, stirring constantly, until mixture is thickened. Cover, lower heat, and cook slowly 5 min. or longer for white corn meal, or 10 min. or longer for yellow.

Serve as a hot breakfast cereal.
    6 to 8 servings

—MUSH COOKED IN MILK

Follow ▲ Recipe. Substitute **1 cup milk** for the cold water. Use **1¼ cups milk** and 1½ cups water in place of the 3 cups water.

—SAUTEED MUSH

Follow ▲ Recipe. Pour cooked mush into a greased loaf pan or round containers such as baking powder cans. Cover and chill thoroughly in refrigerator. Remove from mold and cut into ¼-in. slices. To coat, dip slices lightly in ½ cup all-purpose flour. Brown in **1 to 2 tablespoons fat** in a hot skillet, turning once. Fry until crisp and golden brown on both sides. Serve hot with **butter or margarine, syrup, honey, jam** or **brown sugar.**

SOUTHERN BATTER BREAD

Thoroughly grease a 1½-qt. casserole. Heat in oven about 5 min. before pouring in batter.

Mix together in a saucepan
    ½ cup corn meal
    ¾ teaspoon salt
    1 cup cold water
Bring rapidly to boiling. Boil 5 min. (Mixture will be very thick.) Remove from heat. Stirring constantly, thoroughly blend in
    ½ cup milk
    1 tablespoon lard, melted
Beat until thick and piled softly
    2 eggs

Johnny Cake

Golden Corn Sticks

Gradually add corn meal mixture to eggs, beating vigorously. Turn into hot casserole.

Bake at 400°F 45 to 50 min., or until a wooden pick or cake tester comes out clean when inserted gently at center.

Serve immediately with **butter or margarine** and **maple syrup, honey** or **molasses**.

4 servings

SOUTHERN SPOON BREAD

▲ *Base Recipe*

This is veritably the queen of corn breads—light and fluffy as a dream, and so delicate that it must be ladled onto your plate and eaten, dripping butter, with a spoon. Most of the South prefers spoon bread made with white corn meal, and agrees that it must never, never be kept waiting.

Thoroughly grease a 2-qt. casserole.

Scald (page 10) in top of double boiler
   2 cups milk

Meanwhile, beat until thick and lemon-colored
   4 egg yolks
Set aside.

When milk is scalded, add very gradually, stirring constantly
   1 cup white corn meal
Stir until mixture thickens and becomes smooth. Remove double boiler top from simmering water. Quickly and thoroughly blend mixture into the beaten egg yolks with
   ¼ cup butter or margarine
   1 tablespoon sugar
   ½ teaspoon salt

Using clean beater, beat until rounded peaks are formed
   4 egg whites
Spread egg yolk mixture over beaten egg whites and gently fold together. Turn into the casserole.

Bake at 375°F 35 to 40 min., or until a wooden pick or cake tester comes out clean when inserted in center.

Serve at once with **butter or margarine**.

6 to 8 servings

Southern Spoon Bread

—CHEESE SPOON BREAD

Follow ▲ Recipe. Add with the butter, sugar and salt, **1½ cups (about 6 oz.) grated sharp Cheddar cheese.**

BISCUITS AND MUFFINS

BAKING POWDER BISCUITS

▲ *Base Recipe*

Set out a baking sheet.

Sift together into a bowl
   2 cups sifted all-purpose flour
   1 tablespoon baking powder
   1 teaspoon salt
Cut into dry ingredients with a pastry blender or two knives until mixture resembles coarse corn meal
   ½ cup lard, vegetable shortening or
     all-purpose shortening
Make a well in center of mixture and add all at one time.
   ¾ cup milk
Stir with fork until dough follows fork.

Gently form dough into a ball and put onto a lightly floured surface. Knead lightly with fingertips 10 to 15 times. Roll dough ½ in. thick, keeping thickness uniform. Cut with a floured cutter, using an even pressure to keep sides of biscuits straight. Place on baking sheet, close together for soft-sided biscuits or 1 in. apart for crusty sides. Brush tops of biscuits with **milk** or **melted butter.**

Bake at 450°F 10 to 15 min., or until biscuits are golden brown.   *About 1 doz. 2-in. biscuits*

—DROP BISCUITS

Follow ▲ Recipe. Increase milk to 1 cup. Drop unkneaded dough by tablespoonfuls 1 in. apart onto baking sheet. Or drop into muffin-pan wells, filling wells two-thirds full.

—ROLLED SHORTCAKES

Follow ▲ Recipe. Sift **2 tablespoons sugar** with dry ingredients. Cut dough with floured knife into squares or into rounds with 3-in. cutter. Spread one-half of the rounds with **melted butter.** Top with remaining rounds. Place on baking sheet and bake as in ▲ Recipe.

—SEVENTY-FOURS

These interesting biscuits owe their name to the heroic feat of a sailor, who liked them so much he once ate 74 of them at a sitting.

Set out a deep saucepan or automatic deep-fryer and heat **fat** to 360°F. Follow ▲ Recipe. Roll dough ¼ in. thick. Cut with a floured diamond-shaped cutter. Deep-fry only as many Seventy-Fours at one time as will float un-

crowded one layer deep in the fat. Fry 1 to 2 min., or until lightly browned. Turn with a fork as they rise to surface and several times during cooking (do not pierce). Remove with slotted spoon; drain over fat for a few seconds; remove to absorbent paper. Meanwhile, pour **1 cup molasses** into a double boiler top and place over simmering water. Dip the Seventy-Fours into the hot molasses and serve at once.

—TWIN BISCUIT HEARTS

Follow ▲ Recipe. Roll dough to ¼-in. thickness. Cut an even number of hearts. Place one-half of biscuit hearts on baking sheet and brush them with **melted butter or margarine.** Place remaining biscuit hearts on top of buttered hearts and brush tops with **milk.**

TENDER-RICH BUTTERMILK BISCUITS

▲ *Base Recipe*

Set out a baking sheet.

Sift together into a bowl
   2 cups sifted all-purpose flour
   1½ teaspoons baking powder
   1 teaspoon salt
   ½ teaspoon baking soda
Cut in with a pastry blender or two knives until mixture resembles coarse corn meal
   ⅓ cup lard
Make a well in the center of the dry ingredients. Pour in all at one time
   ¾ cup buttermilk
Stir with a fork until dough follows fork. Gently form dough into a ball and put onto a lightly floured surface. Knead lightly with fingertips 10 to 15 times.

Gently roll dough to ½-in. thickness. Cut with a floured cutter or knife, using an even pressure to keep sides of biscuits straight. Place biscuits on baking sheet, close together for soft-sided biscuits, or 1 in. apart for crusty sides.

Lightly brush tops with
  Milk

Bake at 450°F 10 to 15 min., or until biscuits are golden brown.

About 2 doz. 1½-in. biscuits

—TENDER-RICH ROLLED BISCUITS

Follow ▲ Recipe. Omit the baking soda, increase the baking powder to 2 teaspoons and substitute **¾ cup milk** for buttermilk.

—TENDER-RICH DROP BISCUITS

Follow ▲ Recipe or recipe for Tender-Rich Rolled Biscuits. Increase buttermilk or milk to 1 cup. Omit kneading, rolling and cutting. Drop by spoonfuls onto baking sheet.

—BACON BISCUIT SANDWICHES

Panfry **3 slices bacon** until crisp. Cut each slice into 4 pieces and set bacon aside. Follow ▲ Recipe or recipe for Tender-Rich Rolled Biscuits. Roll dough ¼ in. thick. Cut dough with floured cutter and brush biscuit tops lightly with **egg,** slightly beaten. Place one-half of biscuits on baking sheet. Press a piece of bacon on top of each and sprinkle with **½ teaspoon grated Cheddar or Parmesan cheese.** Place remaining biscuits on cheese, egg-side down. Gently press together and bake as in ▲ Recipe.

—TENDER-RICH ROLLED SHORTCAKES

Follow ▲ Recipe or recipe for Tender-Rich Rolled Biscuits. Sift **2 tablespoons sugar** with dry ingredients. Cut dough with floured knife or 3-in. cutter. Or cut dough into halves and roll each portion to fit an 8-in. round layer cake pan. Spread one-half of rounds, or one large round, with **melted butter or margarine.** Top with remaining rounds or round. Place on baking sheet or in layer cake pan and bake as in ▲ Recipe. Split shortcakes and spoon one-half of **Sweetened Crushed Berries** (page 566) over the bottom halves. Replace tops and spoon over remaining berries and top with **Sweetened Whipped Cream** (page 480).

—TENDER-RICH DROP SHORTCAKES

Follow ▲ Recipe or recipe for Tender-Rich Rolled Biscuits. Sift **2 tablespoons sugar** with dry ingredients. Increase milk or buttermilk to 1 cup. Omit kneading, rolling and cutting. Drop by heaping tablespoonfuls onto baking sheet. Serve as suggested in Tender-Rich Rolled Shortcakes.

—CINNAMON OR APPLE ROLLS

Follow ▲ Recipe. Grease baking sheet. Roll dough into rectangle about ¼ in. thick. Brush

Tender-Rich Buttermilk Biscuits

dough with **2 tablespoons melted butter or margarine.** Sprinkle with a mixture of **¼ cup firmly packed brown sugar, ¼ cup (about 1 oz.) finely chopped nuts** and **1 teaspoon cinnamon.** Or, spread dough with a mixture of **1½ cups (about 2 medium) finely chopped apples, ½ cup sugar** and **1 teaspoon cinnamon.** Beginning with long side, roll and press edges together to seal. Cut into 1-in. slices. Do not brush tops with milk. Place flat on baking sheet and bake.

—ORANGE ROLLS

Follow ▲ Recipe. Grease baking sheet. Roll dough into rectangle about ¼ in. thick. Brush with **2 tablespoons butter or margarine.** Reserving 1 tablespoon grated peel, sprinkle dough with mixture of **½ cup sugar** and **¼ cup grated orange peel.** Beginning with long side, roll and press edges together. Cut into 1-in. slices. Do not brush tops with milk. Place flat on baking sheet and bake at 425°F about 15 min. Combine in a saucepan, **½ cup sugar, ¼ cup light corn syrup, 2 tablespoons water** and reserved orange peel. Bring to boiling and cook 2 min., stirring once or twice. Set aside to cool until rolls are removed from oven. Spoon glaze over tops of rolls and serve.

—COCONUT TWISTS

Follow ▲ Recipe or recipe for Tender-Rich Rolled Biscuits. Grease baking sheet. Roll dough into rectangle about ¼ in. thick. Brush dough with **2 tablespoons melted butter or margarine.** Sprinkle lightly with **⅔ cup firmly packed brown sugar** and **1 cup flaked coconut.** Cut dough into 5x1-in. strips. Fold strips in half and twist. Do not brush tops with milk. Place twists on the greased baking sheet and bake about 8 min.

ALL-IN-ONE BISCUIT MIX

Sift together into a large mixing bowl
  8 cups sifted all-purpose flour
  ¼ cup baking powder
  4 teaspoons salt
Cut into dry ingredients with pastry blender

or two knives until mixture resembles coarse corn meal
  2 cups lard, vegetable shortening or all-purpose shortening

Store mix in tightly covered container in a cool place. (Biscuit mix made with lard should be stored in refrigerator.)

About 12 cups biscuit mix

Note: Before measuring for use in recipe, lighten mix by tossing with fork.

QUICK ROLLED BISCUITS

▲ Base Recipe

Set out a baking sheet.

Measure into a mixing bowl
  3 cups All-in-One Biscuit Mix (on this page)
Make a well in center of biscuit mix and add all at one time
  ⅔ cup milk
Stir with a fork until dough follows fork. Gently form dough into a ball. Turn onto lightly floured surface. To knead, fold opposite side of dough over toward you; press lightly with fingertips and turn dough quarter turn. Repeat 10 to 15 times.

Gently roll out dough from center to edge until about ½ in. thick. Cut dough with floured cutter or knife, using an even pressure to keep sides of biscuits straight. Place biscuits on baking sheet. Brush surfaces of biscuits with
  Milk

Bake at 450°F 10 to 15 min.

About 1½ doz. 2-in. biscuits

—QUICK DROP BISCUITS

Follow ▲ Recipe. Increase milk to 1 cup. Omit kneading, rolling and cutting processes. Drop by spoonfuls onto baking sheet.

—ORANGE TEA BISCUITS

Follow ▲ Recipe. Dip a **lump of sugar** in **orange juice.** Press into top of each biscuit before baking. Sprinkle with **grated orange peel.**

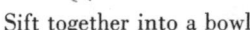

—SCONES

Follow ▲ Recipe. Add **2 tablespoons sugar** to biscuit mix. Decrease milk to ½ cup. Add **1 egg,** well beaten, with milk. Cut biscuits into diamonds, squares or triangles. Sprinkle with **sugar** after brushing with milk.

—QUICK ROLLS

Follow ▲ Recipe. Fill and shape as Cinnamon or Apple Rolls, Orange Rolls, or Coconut Twists (page 93).

—QUICK CHEESE BISCUITS

Follow ▲ Recipe. Blend ½ cup (2 oz.) grated **Cheddar cheese** into biscuit mix. Or, sprinkle **grated Parmesan cheese** over tops of biscuits before baking.

—CHIVE BISCUITS

Follow ▲ Recipe. Add ¼ **cup finely chopped chives** to biscuit mix.

CHEESE FANS

▲ *Base Recipe*

Grease twelve 2½-in. muffin-pan wells.

Grate and set aside
> **4 oz. sharp Cheddar cheese (about 1 cup, grated)**

Cheese Fans

Tender Cheese Biscuit Ring

Sift together into a bowl
> **2 cups sifted all-purpose flour**
> **1 tablespoon baking powder**
> **1 teaspoon salt**

Cut in with a pastry blender or two knives until mixture resembles coarse corn meal
> **½ cup lard, vegetable shortening or all-purpose shortening**

Make a well in center of mixture and add all at one time
> **½ cup milk**

Stir with fork until dough follows fork.

Gently form dough into a ball and put onto a lightly floured surface. Knead it lightly with fingertips 10 to 15 times. Roll dough into a 12x10-in. rectangle about ¼ in. thick. Cut into 5 strips. Spread with
> **Softened butter**

Sprinkle four strips with the grated cheese. Stack the four strips and top with the fifth strip. Cut into 12 equal sections. Place on end in muffin-pan wells. Brush tops with
> **Melted butter**

Bake at 450°F 10 to 15 min., or until biscuits are golden brown.

Serve hot with **butter.**   *1 doz. Cheese Fans*

—CHEESE BISCUITS

Follow ▲ Recipe. Reduce cheese to ¾ cup, grated, and add with the shortening. Roll dough to ½-in. thickness, keeping thickness uniform. Cut with a floured biscuit cutter, using an even pressure to keep sides of biscuits straight. Place on a greased baking sheet, close together for soft-sided biscuits, or 1 in. apart for crusty sides.

—TENDER CHEESE BISCUIT RING

Follow ▲ Recipe; increase recipe one and one-half times. Roll dough into a rectangle ½ in. thick and 8 in. wide. Spread with **2 tablespoons softened butter.** Sprinkle the grated cheese evenly over the dough. Starting at the longer side of dough, roll up and pinch edge to seal (do not pinch ends of roll). Place roll on greased baking sheet, sealed edge down. Bring ends of roll together to form a ring. Brush with **1 tablespoon melted butter.** With scissors or knife, cut at 1½-in. intervals through ring to ¼ in. from center. Turn each section on its side. Bake at 400°F 20 to 25 min., or until ring is light golden brown. Serve immediately with **butter.**

BEATEN BISCUITS

A Southern favorite from 'way back, these are the only biscuits that are properly served cold. Recipes and methods of beating vary from kitchen to kitchen, but the cook who can still turn out good beaten biscuits to pair with ham as sandwiches, or to escort cream soups or chicken salad to the table, may be justly proud.

Set out baking sheets.

Sift together into a bowl
> **4 cups sifted all-purpose flour**
> **2 teaspoons sugar**
> **1 teaspoon salt**

Cut in with pastry blender or two knives until the mixture resembles coarse corn meal
> **½ cup lard**

Stir in about
> **1 cup milk**

Use just enough milk to make a stiff dough. Turn dough out onto a lightly floured surface and knead or beat with a wooden spoon until dough blisters, about 30 min.

Roll dough about ½ in. thick. Cut out biscuits with a floured 1½-in. cutter. Prick with a fork and place on baking sheets.

Bake at 350°F about 30 min., or until very delicately browned.   *About 3 doz. biscuits*

MUFFINS

▲ *Base Recipe*

Grease twelve 2½-in. muffin-pan wells.

Melt and set aside to cool
> **¼ cup butter or margarine**

Sift together into a bowl
> **2 cups sifted all-purpose flour**
> **⅓ cup sugar**
> **1 tablespoon baking powder**
> **½ teaspoon salt**

Make a well in center of dry ingredients and set aside.

Blend thoroughly
> **1 egg, well beaten**
> **1 cup milk**

Blend in melted shortening. Add all at one time to dry ingredients. With not more than 25 strokes, quickly and lightly stir until dry ingredients are barely moistened. The batter will be lumpy and break from spoon. (Too much mixing will result in muffin tunnels.)

Cut against side of bowl with spoon to get enough batter at one time to fill each muffin-pan well two-thirds full. Place spoon in well and push batter off with another spoon or spatula. Fill any empty wells one-half full with water before placing pans in oven.

Bake at 425°F 20 to 25 min., or until muffins are an even golden brown.

Run spatula around each muffin and lift out. If necessary to keep muffins warm before serving, loosen muffins and tip slightly in wells. Keep in a warm place.   *1 doz. muffins*

—CRANBERRY MUFFINS

Follow ▲ Recipe. Wash and drain **1 cup cranberries**; chop coarsely. Mix with **3 tablespoons sugar**. Blend with sifted dry ingredients.

—BLUEBERRY MUFFINS

Follow ▲ Recipe. Rinse and drain **1 cup fresh blueberries**. Gently fold blueberries into batter with final strokes.

—DOUBLE-TOP MUFFINS

Follow ▲ Recipe. Place **1 cooked dried apricot half** in bottom of each greased muffin-pan well. Spoon batter into wells. Top batter with a crumbly mixture of **½ cup firmly packed brown sugar, ½ cup butter or margarine**, softened, **⅓ cup sifted all-purpose flour** and **1 teaspoon cinnamon**.

—QUICK TEA CAKES

Follow ▲ Recipe. Grease bottoms of 3 doz. 1¾-in. muffin-pan wells. Increase sugar to ½ cup and eggs to 3. Reduce milk to ¾ cup. Bake at 425°F about 15 min.

BRAN GEMS
(Bran Muffins)

▲ Base Recipe

Grease 12 muffin-pan wells.

Sift together into bowl
> **1 cup sifted all-purpose flour**
> **2 tablespoons sugar**
> **1 tablespoon baking powder**
> **½ teaspoon salt**

Stir in
> **1 cup whole bran cereal**

Combine
> **1 egg, well beaten**
> **⅔ cup milk**
> **3 tablespoons shortening, melted**

Make a well in dry ingredients and add liquid mixture at one time. With not more than 25 strokes, quickly and lightly stir until flour mixture is barely moistened. Batter will be lumpy and will break from spoon. (Too much mixing will result in muffin tunnels.)

Cut against side of bowl with spoon to get enough batter at one time to fill each muffin-pan well two-thirds full. Place spoon in well and push batter off with another spoon. Fill any empty wells one-half full with water before placing pans in oven.

Bake at 400°F 25 to 30 min.

Run spatula around each muffin and lift out. If necessary to keep muffins warm before serving, loosen muffins and tip slightly in wells. Keep warm.   *1 doz. muffins*

—FRUIT BRAN MUFFINS

Follow ▲ Recipe. Mix into dry ingredients **½ cup (about 2 oz.) raisins or chopped dried prunes.**

CHEESE MUFFINS

An electric blender will be needed. Grease twelve 2½-in. muffin-pan wells.

Melt and set aside to cool
> **3 tablespoons butter or margarine**

Cut into cubes and set aside
> **6 oz. sharp Cheddar cheese (about 1½ cups, cubed)**

Sift together and set aside in a bowl
> **2 cups sifted all-purpose flour**
> **1 tablespoon baking powder**
> **½ teaspoon salt**

Put into the electric blender container
> **1 cup milk**
> **1 egg, unbeaten**
> **1 tablespoon sugar**

Add cooled butter and cheese cubes. Cover and blend a few seconds, or until smooth and well blended.

Make a well in center of dry ingredients. Add blender mixture all at one time. With not more than 25 strokes, quickly and lightly stir until flour mixture is barely moistened.

Fill muffin-pan wells two-thirds full.

Bake at 400°F 25 to 30 min., or until golden brown.   *1 doz. muffins*

CORN MEAL MUFFINS

▲ Base Recipe

Grease twelve 2½-in. muffin-pan wells.

Melt and set aside to cool
> **¼ cup butter or margarine**

Sift together into a bowl
> **½ cup sifted all-purpose flour**
> **1 tablespoon sugar**
> **1 tablespoon baking powder**
> **¾ teaspoon salt**

Mix in
> **1½ cups white corn meal**

Make a well in center of dry ingredients.

Blueberry Muffins

Double-Top Muffins

Bran Gems

Blend together the melted shortening and
> **1 egg, well beaten**
> **1 cup milk**

Add all at one time to dry ingredients. Beat with rotary beater until just smooth, being careful not to overmix. Cut against side of bowl with spoon to get enough batter at one time to fill each muffin-pan well two-thirds full. Place spoon in well and push batter off with another spoon or spatula. Fill any empty wells one-half full with water before baking.

Bake at 425°F 20 to 25 min., or until muffins are an even golden brown.

Run spatula around each muffin and lift out.

Orange Surprise Muffins

If necessary to keep muffins warm before serving, loosen muffins and tip slightly in wells. Keep in warm place. *1 doz. muffins*

—CORN BREAD

Follow ▲ Recipe. Turn batter into a greased 8x8x2-in. pan; spread to corners. Bake about 20 min., or until bread tests done (page 10).

—CRISP CORN STICKS

Follow ▲ Recipe. Grease 12 iron corn-stick pan sections and preheat 15 min. in oven. Spoon batter into sections, filling each three-fourths full. Bake 10 to 15 min.

ORANGE SURPRISE MUFFINS

An electric blender will be needed. Grease twelve 2½-in. muffin-pan wells.

Melt and set aside to cool
  3 tablespoons vegetable shortening or all-purpose shortening

Sift together into a bowl and set aside
  **2 cups sifted all-purpose flour
  1 tablespoon baking powder
  ½ teaspoon salt**

Put into electric blender container in order
  **¾ cup milk
  1 egg, unbeaten
  ½ cup orange marmalade
  3 tablespoons sugar**
Add melted and cooled shortening. Cover and blend until thoroughly mixed.

Make a well in center of dry ingredients. Add blender mixture all at one time. With not more than 25 strokes, quickly and lightly stir until flour mixture is barely moistened.

Fill muffin-pan wells two-thirds full.

Bake at 400°F 30 to 35 min., or until golden brown. *1 doz. muffins*

PEANUT BUTTER MUFFINS

An electric blender will be needed. Grease twelve 2½-in. muffin-pan wells.

Sift together into a bowl and set aside
  **2 cups sifted all-purpose flour
  1 tablespoon baking powder
  ½ teaspoon salt**

Put into electric blender container in order
  **1¼ cups milk
  1 egg, unbeaten
  3 tablespoons sugar
  ½ cup Blender Peanut Butter (page 114) or commercial peanut butter**
Cover and blend until thoroughly mixed.

Make a well in center of dry ingredients. Add blender mixture all at one time. With not more than 25 strokes, quickly and lightly stir until flour mixture is barely moistened.

Fill muffin-pan wells two-thirds full.

Bake at 400°F 25 to 30 min., or until golden brown. *1 doz. muffins*

SPECIALTY QUICK BREADS

CHEESE STICKS

Whether served with a crisp cool salad, a frosty fruit drink or with cocktails, alcoholic or otherwise, these tempting morsels have a tang that sharpens the appetite.

Set out baking sheets.

Sift together into a mixing bowl
  **1⅓ cups sifted all-purpose flour
  ½ teaspoon salt**
Grate and blend into flour
  4 oz. sharp Cheddar cheese (about 1 cup, grated)

Cut in with a pastry blender or two knives until pieces are size of small peas
  ½ cup lard, vegetable shortening or all-purpose shortening
Sprinkle gradually over mixture, a teaspoon at a time, about
  3 tablespoons cold water
Mix lightly with a fork after each addition. Add only enough water to hold pastry together. Work quickly and do not overhandle. Shape into a ball and flatten on a floured surface.

Roll pastry into a rectangle about ½ in. thick. Cut into ½-in. strips. With palms of hands, quickly and gently roll pastry strips until about ½ in. in diameter. Cut into 2½-in. pieces. Arrange on baking sheets.

Bake at 450°F 8 to 10 min.

Serve piping hot or cool.
About 3 doz. Cheese Sticks

PUFF PASTRY CHEESE TWISTS

Preparation of Puff Pastry requires off-and-on attention for 9 hrs.

Prepare and chill
  Puff Pastry (page 518)

Lightly grease two baking sheets.

Grate
  2 oz. Parmesan cheese (about ½ cup, grated)
Set aside.

Divide the dough into 2 equal portions. Return one portion to refrigerator while rolling out the other portion. Roll dough into a rectangle 13½x12 in. Brush dough with
  Egg white, beaten
Sprinkle evenly over surface one-half of the grated Parmesan cheese and one-half of a mixture of
  **¼ teaspoon paprika
  ¼ teaspoon salt**
Cut rectangle into halves to make two 13½x 6-in. pieces. Cut each half into strips, 6x1½ in. Twist each strip. Arrange the strips on one of the greased baking sheets. Set in refrigerator for 15 min. Repeat procedure, using the remaining Parmesan cheese and seasonings with the remaining portion of dough.

Bake at 400°F 15 min. Reduce heat to 300°F and bake about 10 min. longer, or until twists are golden brown. *3 doz. cheese twists*

STAY-POPPED POPOVERS

Grease thoroughly with cooking oil eight 5-oz. heat-resistant glass custard cups or wells of an iron popover pan. Set cups aside; preheat pan 15 min. in oven.

Measure and set aside
  1 cup sifted all-purpose flour

Beat slightly in a small mixing bowl
  3 eggs

Beat in until blended

1 cup milk
2 tablespoons cooking oil
½ teaspoon salt

Add flour to liquid ingredients and beat with rotary beater until batter is smooth. Divide the batter evenly among the custard cups or wells of hot popover pan.

Bake at 400°F 35 to 40 min., or until popovers are a deep golden brown.

Serve hot with **butter.**   *8 popovers*

Note: If a drier interior is desired, make a slit in the side of each baked popover to allow the steam to escape. Return popovers to oven with the heat turned off and allow them to dry for about 10 min.

DEEP-FRIED QUICK BREADS

DOUGHNUTS

About 20 min. before deep-frying, fill a deep saucepan one-half to two-thirds full with

Vegetable shortening, all-purpose shortening, lard or cooking oil for deep-frying

Heat slowly to 365°F. When using an automatic deep-fryer, follow manufacturer's directions for amount of fat and timing.

Sift together and set aside

4 cups sifted all-purpose flour
4 teaspoons baking powder
1 teaspoon salt
1 teaspoon cinnamon
½ teaspoon nutmeg

Beat until thick and piled softly

2 eggs

Add gradually, beating thoroughly after each addition

1 cup sugar

Mix in

2 tablespoons melted shortening
1 tablespoon grated orange peel

Blend in dry ingredients alternately with

1 cup milk

Stir until well blended. Dough will be soft.

Stay-Popped Popovers

If it seems very sticky, measure

½ cup sifted all-purpose flour

Add enough of this flour to make an easily handled but soft dough. Save remainder of flour for rolling process. Chill dough in refrigerator for 1 hr.

Turn dough onto lightly floured surface. Handling very lightly, roll dough ½ in. thick and cut with a lightly floured doughnut cutter.

Deep-fry doughnuts and "holes" in heated fat. Deep-fry only as many doughnuts at one time as will float uncrowded one layer deep in fat. When doughnuts rise to surface, turn with fork or tongs. Do not pierce. Turn doughnuts often. Deep-fry 2 to 3 min., or until lightly browned. Drain doughnuts and "holes" over fat for a second before removing to absorbent paper.

Serve plain or shake 2 or 3 warm doughnuts at a time in a plastic bag containing

½ cup confectioners' or granulated sugar

About 2 doz. doughnuts plus "holes"

SPICY DOUGHNUTS

▲ *Base Recipe*

Doughnuts are never so delectable as when they first emerge—golden-brown, crisp of crust and tender of heart—from the hot fat. Hungry after-the-game teen-agers will love to perch around the kitchen waiting for them—and it will make grown-up appetites young again to eat doughnuts this way. It's easy to serve them hot if you make the dough ahead of time and chill it in the refrigerator until you're ready to start frying.

A deep saucepan or an automatic deep-fryer will be needed.

Sift together and set aside

3⅓ cups sifted all-purpose flour
1 tablespoon baking powder
1 teaspoon cinnamon
1 teaspoon nutmeg
½ teaspoon salt

Beat until thick and piled softly

3 eggs

Add gradually to eggs, beating thoroughly after each addition

⅔ cup sugar

Mix in

2 tablespoons shortening, melted and cooled
½ teaspoon vanilla extract

Measure

⅔ cup milk

Stirring until well blended after each addition, alternately add dry ingredients in fourths, milk in thirds, to egg mixture. Dough will be soft. Chill dough in refrigerator about 1 hr.

About 20 min. before deep-frying, fill the saucepan or deep-fryer one-half to two-thirds full with **fat** and heat to 365°F.

Turn the chilled dough out onto a lightly

Doughnuts

floured surface. Handling very lightly, roll dough ½ in. thick and cut with a lightly floured doughnut cutter.

Deep-fry doughnuts and "holes" in heated fat. Fry only as many at one time as will float uncrowded one layer deep in the fat. Deep-fry 2 to 3 min., or until lightly browned. Turn doughnuts with a fork as they rise to surface (do not pierce) and several times during cooking. Lift from fat with tongs or slotted spoon. Drain doughnuts and "holes" over fat for a few seconds before removing to absorbent paper.

Serve plain or shake 2 or 3 warm doughnuts at a time in a plastic bag containing a mixture of

½ cup confectioners' or granulated sugar
¾ teaspoon cinnamon
½ teaspoon nutmeg

About 2 doz. doughnuts plus "holes"

Note: For drop doughnuts, omit chilling and rolling of dough. Drop dough by spoonfuls into the heated fat.

—ORANGE DOUGHNUTS

Set out **1 cup flaked coconut.** Follow ▲ Recipe. Substitute **2 tablespoons grated orange peel** for vanilla extract and **⅔ cup orange juice** for milk. Add coconut to dough after final addition of dry ingredients and mix thoroughly. Omit spices from sugar mixture.

—FROSTED DOUGHNUTS

Follow ▲ Recipe. Prepare **Glossy Vanilla Icing** (page 478) or **Glossy Chocolate Icing** (page 478). Using a spatula, spread warm doughnuts with frosting, allowing excess to drip down sides of doughnuts. Sprinkle with chopped **pecans or walnuts.**

—CHOCOLATE-FLECKED DOUGHNUTS

Grate with a rotary-type grater with hand-operated crank and set aside ½ cup (about 3 oz.) semisweet chocolate pieces. Follow ▲ Recipe. Add grated chocolate pieces to dough after the final addition of dry ingredients and mix thoroughly. Omit spices from sugar mixture.

BANANA FRITTERS

▲ *Base Recipe*

Peel, cut into 1½-in. crosswise pieces and put into a bowl

4 firm bananas with all-yellow peel

Gently toss banana pieces with a mixture of

3 tablespoons confectioners' sugar
2 tablespoons lemon juice
1½ tablespoons rum or kirsch

Cover bowl and allow banana pieces to marinate 45 min. to 1 hr., turning fruit occasionally.

About 20 min. before deep-frying, fill a deep saucepan one-half to two-thirds full with

Vegetable shortening, or all-purpose shortening, lard or oil for deep-frying

Heat the fat slowly to 365°F. When using an automatic deep-fryer, follow manufacturer's directions for amount of fat and timing.

Meanwhile, sift together into a bowl and set aside

1⅓ cups sifted all-purpose flour
2 tablespoons sugar
1 teaspoon baking powder
½ teaspoon salt

Melt and set aside to cool

1 tablespoon shortening

Drain banana pieces and set aside, reserving liquid for fritter batter.

Beat until thick and lemon-colored

2 egg yolks

Beat in until blended, melted shortening, reserved liquid from bananas and

⅔ cup milk
1 teaspoon vanilla extract

Make a well in center of dry ingredients. Pour in liquid mixture all at one time and blend just until batter is smooth.

Beat until stiff, not dry, peaks are formed

2 egg whites

Gently fold egg whites into batter.

Coat banana pieces by rolling in shallow pan containing

¼ cup all-purpose flour

Banana Fritters

Using a large fork or slotted spoon, dip banana pieces into batter and coat evenly. Drain excess batter from banana pieces before deep-frying. Deep-fry only as many fritters at one time as will float uncrowded one layer deep in the fat. Turn fritters with a fork as they rise to surface of fat and several times during cooking (do not pierce fritters). Deep-fry 2 to 3 min., or until golden brown. Drain fritters over fat for a few seconds before removing to absorbent paper.

Coat the fritters generously with **confectioners' sugar**. Or, if desired, serve with **Mocha Sauce II** (page 580) as a dessert. *5 or 6 servings*

—STRAWBERRY FRITTERS

Follow ▲ Recipe. Substitute for bananas **1 qt. large firm strawberries,** rinsed and hulled. Do not marinate strawberries. Add the rum or kirsch to the batter; omit lemon juice. Increase the confectioners' sugar to ½ cup and roll the strawberries in it (instead of in flour) before dipping into the batter. Increase flour in batter to 1½ cups. Just before serving, sprinkle the fritters with about ¼ **cup Vanilla Confectioners' Sugar** (page 582).

APPLE FRITTERS

▲ *Base Recipe*

Very old, very tasty, and very New England.

Set out a deep saucepan or automatic deep-fryer and heat **fat** to 365°F.

Melt and set aside

1 tablespoon shortening

Sift together into a bowl and set aside

1⅓ cups sifted all-purpose flour
2 tablespoons sugar
1 teaspoon baking powder
¾ teaspoon salt

Wash, core, pare and cut into ¼-in. rings

4 firm apples

Or cut apples into lengthwise wedges ¼ in. thick. Put into a bowl and toss carefully with

3 to 4 tablespoons lemon juice
2 tablespoons confectioners' sugar

Let stand about 5 min.

Blend thoroughly

2 eggs, well beaten
1 cup milk

Blend in the melted shortening.

Make a well in center of dry ingredients. Add liquid mixture all at one time and mix until batter is smooth.

Drain apple pieces. Using a large fork or slotted spoon, dip apple pieces in batter to coat evenly, allowing excess batter to drip into bowl before lowering apple pieces into fat.

Deep-fry only as many fritters as will float, uncrowded, one layer deep in fat. Turn with a fork as they rise to the surface of the fat and

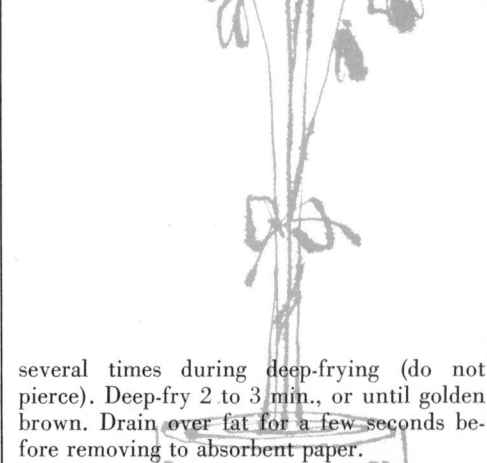

several times during deep-frying (do not pierce). Deep-fry 2 to 3 min., or until golden brown. Drain over fat for a few seconds before removing to absorbent paper.

Serve hot with **maple syrup.** *About 6 servings*

—CORN-GOLD FRITTERS

Follow ▲ Recipe. Omit apples, sugar, lemon juice and confectioners' sugar. Decrease shortening to 1 teaspoon and milk to ⅔ cup. Add **1 teaspoon Worcestershire sauce, ½ teaspoon monosodium glutamate, ⅛ teaspoon pepper** and **1⅓ cups (1 12-oz. can, well drained) whole kernel corn.** Drop by tablespoonfuls into the hot fat.

GLAZED APPLE BALLS

▲ *Base Recipe*

Set out a deep saucepan or automatic deep-fryer and heat **fat** to 365°F about 20 min. before ready to deep-fry.

Melt and set aside to cool

2 tablespoons shortening

Meanwhile, sift together and set aside

2⅔ cups sifted all-purpose flour
2½ teaspoons baking powder
1 teaspoon nutmeg
1 teaspoon cinnamon
½ teaspoon salt

Wash, quarter, core, pare and dice or grate

2 medium apples (or enough to make 1 cup, diced or grated)

Set aside.

In a large mixer bowl, beat with electric beater until thick and piled softly

3 eggs

Add gradually, beating thoroughly after each addition

¾ cup sugar

Beat in cooled shortening and

½ teaspoon vanilla extract

Blend in dry ingredients alternately with

⅔ cup milk

After each addition, beat only until batter is smooth. (*Do not overbeat.*) Stir in apples until evenly blended.

Chill in refrigerator 1 hr.

Drop chilled mixture by teaspoonfuls into fat. Fry only as many apple balls at one time as will float uncrowded in fat. Fry 2 or 3 min., or until lightly browned. Turn with a fork as they rise to surface (do not pierce); turn several times during cooking. Drain over fat for a second before removing to absorbent paper.

While apple balls are still warm, dip in glaze and place on cooling rack to drain.

For Glaze—Measure into a bowl

2 cups sifted confectioners' sugar

Gradually add to sugar, beating constantly

¼ cup hot water
1 tablespoon light corn syrup
1½ teaspoons rum extract
½ teaspoon vanilla extract

Continue beating until smooth. (Glaze should be thin.)   *About 4 doz. apple balls*

—BITTER-CHOCOLATE FLECKED PUFFS

Follow ▲ Recipe. Substitute **3 oz. (3 sq.) unsweetened chocolate,** finely grated, for the apples. Blend chocolate into batter with shortening.

—SUGARED ORANGE BALLS

Follow ▲ Recipe. Substitute **2 teaspoons mace** for nutmeg and cinnamon. Add **1 tablespoon grated orange peel** to egg-sugar mixture. Substitute **orange juice** for milk; omit apples. For glaze, substitute a mixture of **½ cup granulated or confectioners' sugar** and **2 teaspoons grated orange peel.** Put this mixture into a plastic bag and shake warm balls in it.

HUSH PUPPIES

According to a hardy legend, "Hush Puppies" originated at a fish fry when someone dropped corn-bread batter into the kettle of heated fat and tossed the fried cakes to the hungry dogs to quiet their whining. They looked and smelled so tempting that folks, not dogs, have been eating them ever since!

Set out a deep saucepan or automatic deep-fryer and heat **fat** to 375°F.

Mix together

2 cups corn meal
⅓ cup chopped onion
1 tablespoon all-purpose flour
1 teaspoon baking powder
1 teaspoon baking soda
1 teaspoon salt

Blend thoroughly

1 egg, well beaten
1½ cups buttermilk

Make a well in center of dry ingredients and add liquid mixture all at one time. Mix until well blended.

Form into small cakes (about 1 tablespoon for each cake).

Deep-fry only as many cakes at one time as will float uncrowded one layer deep in the hot fat. Fry 3 to 4 min., or until well browned. Turn cakes with tongs or a fork as they rise to the surface and several times during cooking (do not pierce).

Remove cakes with a slotted spoon; drain over fat for a few seconds before removing to absorbent paper.

Serve hot with **fried fish.**

About 2 doz. Hush Puppies

QUICK CALAS

Until recent years, the old Negro woman selling Calas was a daily, early-morning figure on the streets of New Orleans. Upon hearing her cry "Belle Cala, tout chaud!", the Creole cooks would rush out to get fresh hot Calas to serve to their masters and mistresses with their morning coffee. Calas of old New Orleans were leavened with yeast, but here is a modern adaptation of a favorite Creole specialty.

About 20 min. before deep-frying, fill a deep saucepan one-half to two-thirds full with

Vegetable shortening, all-purpose shortening, lard or cooking oil for deep-frying

Heat fat slowly to 360°F.

Prepare and set aside to cool

2 cups Perfection Boiled Rice (two-thirds recipe, page 165)

Meanwhile, sift together and set aside

⅔ cup sifted all-purpose flour
½ cup sugar
1 tablespoon baking powder
½ teaspoon salt
½ teaspoon nutmeg

Beat until thick and piled softly

3 eggs

Thoroughly blend in cooled rice and

¼ teaspoon vanilla extract

Add dry ingredients and mix until well blended.

Drop batter by tablespoonfuls into heated fat. Deep-fry only as many Calas at one time as will float uncrowded one layer deep in the fat. Fry about 2 min., or until golden brown. Turn Calas with a fork as they rise to the surface and

Hush Puppies

several times during cooking (do not pierce). Remove with a slotted spoon; drain over fat a few seconds before removing to absorbent paper.

Sprinkle Calas with

Confectioners' sugar

Serve hot.   *About 20 Calas*

PANCAKES AND WAFFLES

BLENDER PANCAKES

An electric blender will be needed. Heat a griddle or heavy skillet over low heat.

Melt and set aside to cool

2 tablespoons butter or margarine

Sift together and set aside

1¼ cups sifted all-purpose flour
1 teaspoon baking powder

Add to the electric blender container

1 cup milk
1 egg, unbeaten
3 tablespoons sugar
½ teaspoon salt

Add melted shortening and dry ingredients; cover and blend just until batter is smooth.

Test griddle by dropping on it a few drops water; if they dance around in small beads, griddle temperature is right. Lightly grease griddle if manufacturer so directs.

Spoon batter in pools, using about 1½ tablespoons of batter for each pancake. Lightly and carefully spread batter to form a thin pancake, leaving about 1 in. between cakes. Cook over medium heat until golden brown on one side. Turn carefully with spatula or pancake turner and brown other side.

Serve with **butter** and **syrup**.

16 to 18 pancakes

THIN PANCAKES

Heat and lightly grease a 6- or 8-in. heavy skillet.

Sift together
½ cup sifted all-purpose flour
3 tablespoons sugar
½ teaspoon salt

Combine
2 eggs, well beaten
⅔ cup milk
1 tablespoon melted butter or margarine

Add egg mixture all at once to flour. Beat until smooth. Pour about 3 tablespoons batter into hot skillet baking only 1 pancake at a time. Tilt the skillet to spread batter thinly.

When pancake is lightly browned, turn and brown other side. Remove to hot serving plate. Spread with **jelly or jam** and roll. Sprinkle with **confectioners' or granulated sugar.** Or, spread pancakes with jelly or sauce and arrange in stacks. Cut into wedges to serve. *10 pancakes*

SWISS CHEESE PANCAKES

Set out a heavy skillet.

Grate
6 oz. Swiss cheese (about 1½ cups, grated)

Add to cheese, mixing well after each addition
¾ cup dairy sour cream
3 egg yolks, slightly beaten
and a mixture of
2 tablespoons plus 1 teaspoon all-purpose flour
¾ teaspoon salt
Few grains pepper
1½ teaspoons thyme
½ teaspoon dry mustard

Melt in the skillet over low heat
2 tablespoons butter

Drop batter by teaspoonfuls into skillet. Cook over medium heat until lightly browned on bottom. Loosen edges with a spatula, turn and lightly brown other side.

Serve at once with **bacon** or **pork sausage.**

About 2 doz. 3-in. pancakes

NORWEGIAN POTATO PANCAKES
(Lefse)

Wash, pare and cook (page 313)
6 medium (about 2 lbs.) potatoes, cut in halves

Cook about 20 min., or until tender when pierced with a fork. Drain. To dry potatoes, shake pan over low heat.

Mash or rice potatoes thoroughly. Whip into potatoes
¼ cup butter
¼ cup milk
and a mixture of
1½ teaspoons salt
1 teaspoon sugar
¼ teaspoon monosodium glutamate
⅛ teaspoon pepper

Whip potatoes until light and fluffy. Cool potatoes; chill in refrigerator.

Set a griddle or heavy skillet over low heat.

Measure
2½ to 3 cups sifted all-purpose flour

Remove chilled potatoes from refrigerator. Add about one-half the flour and beat until smooth. Beat in enough remaining flour to make a soft dough. Shape dough into a ball and turn onto a lightly floured surface. Roll into a round about ⅛ in. thick. Cut into 6-in. rounds.

Test griddle by dropping on it a few drops cold water; if drops dance around in small beads, griddle temperature is right. Do not grease the griddle.

Place Lefse on griddle and cook until lightly browned. Turn and lightly brown other side. Then, turning frequently, continue cooking until Lefse are browned and dry. Remove to a clean, dry towel. Cool Lefse completely.

Spread cold Lefse with
Butter, softened
Roll loosely and serve.   *About 2½ doz. Lefse*

PANCAKE BALLS
(Ableskiver I)

▲ Base Recipe

Set an ableskiver pan (available in the housewares section of most department stores) over low heat.

Sift together and set aside
2 cups sifted all-purpose flour
2 tablespoons sugar
1 teaspoon baking soda
1 teaspoon cardamom
¾ teaspoon salt

Combine
1 cup dairy sour cream
⅔ cup milk
3 egg yolks, beaten
2 tablespoons melted butter

Make a well in center of dry ingredients. Add liquid mixture all at one time, stirring until well blended.

Beat until stiff, not dry, peaks are formed
3 egg whites
Gently spread batter over egg whites and fold together.

Test ableskiver pan by dropping on it a few drops cold water; if drops dance around in small beads, temperature is right. Grease wells with
Butter (about ½ teaspoon per well)
Pour batter into wells, filling about one-half full. With a fork turn Ableskivers frequently to brown evenly. Do not pierce. Ableskivers are done when a wooden pick inserted in center comes out clean.

Serve immediately sprinkled with
Confectioners' sugar
If desired, accompany with a **tart jam.**

About 4 doz. balls

—APPLE PANCAKE BALLS
(Ableskiver II)

Follow ▲ Recipe. Wash, pare and dice **2 medium apples.** Sprinkle about 1 teaspoon of the diced apples over batter in each well.

BACON PANCAKE
(Ugnspannkaka)

This is a kind of all-in-one pancake, baked in a way that is probably unfamiliar to many American homemakers. The recipe is Swedish and the pancake is usually served as a main dish.

Sift together and set aside
1 cup sifted all-purpose flour
1 tablespoon sugar
½ teaspoon salt

Blend together
2 eggs, slightly beaten
2 cups milk
Gradually add the milk mixture to the dry ingredients, stirring until well blended. Set aside about 1 hr.

Grease well an 11x7x1½-in. baking dish.

Hawaiian Pancake

Prepare
   ½ lb. Panfried Bacon (page 190)
Crumble the bacon. Add to the batter and stir until blended. Pour into the baking dish.

Bake at 400°F 40 to 45 min., or until mixture is browned.

Cut into squares and serve with
   Lingonberry preserves

6 servings

HAWAIIAN PANCAKE

Set out a saucepan and a heavy 10- to 12-in. skillet.

Grate and set aside
   4 oz. sharp Cheddar cheese (about 1 cup, grated)

For Pineapple Topping—Drain, reserving syrup
   1 can (13¼ oz.) pineapple tidbits (about 1 cup, drained)
Put the drained pineapple tidbits into the saucepan; stir in 1 tablespoon of the reserved pineapple syrup and
   1 teaspoon grated lemon peel
   2 teaspoons lemon juice
Set mixture aside.

For Pancake—Put into the skillet
   2 tablespoons butter or margarine
Put skillet into oven and heat oven to 450°F. Remove skillet from oven when butter is melted and skillet is heated.

Meanwhile, sift together into a bowl and set aside
   ⅓ cup sifted all-purpose flour
   ¼ teaspoon salt

Mix together ½ cup of reserved pineapple syrup and
   1 teaspoon lemon juice
Add and mix thoroughly
   3 eggs, beaten
Combine egg mixture with the dry ingredients; beat until smooth. Pour batter into skillet.

Bake at 450°F 12 min., or until pancake is delicately browned and edges draw away from sides of skillet.

While pancake is baking, heat the Pineapple Topping.

When pancake is done, remove from oven.

Sprinkle about one-half of the grated cheese evenly over pancake and carefully roll it up.

Spoon Pineapple Topping over the rolled pancake. Sprinkle remaining cheese over the topping.

Set temperature control of range at Broil.

Place skillet on broiler rack and put in broiler so that pancake is about 3 in. from heat. Broil until cheese is melted and lightly browned.

Remove pancake to a warm serving platter; serve immediately.   *2 servings*

GRIDDLECAKES

▲ Base Recipe

Vermont has a pleasant way of stacking several griddlecakes with butter and shaved maple sugar between them, and serving them, cut in wedges, with maple syrup and puffs of whipped cream—hearty and satisfying.

Set a griddle or heavy skillet over low heat.

Melt and set aside to cool
   2 tablespoons butter

Sift together into a bowl
   1½ cups sifted all-purpose flour
   1 tablespoon sugar
   1½ teaspoons baking powder
   ½ teaspoon salt
Make a well in center of dry ingredients and set them aside.

Beat together
   2 egg yolks
   1⅓ cups milk
Add all at one time to dry ingredients. Beat until well blended and smooth. Blend in the melted butter. Set aside.

Beat until stiff, not dry, peaks are formed
   2 egg whites
Spread beaten egg whites over the batter and gently fold together.

Test griddle; it is hot enough for baking when drops of water sprinkled on surface dance in small beads. Lightly grease griddle if manufacturer so directs. Pour batter onto griddle from a pitcher or large spoon, in small pools about 4 in. in diameter, leaving at least 1 in. between cakes. Turn griddlecakes as they become puffy and full of bubbles. Turn griddlecakes only once.

Serve immediately with **butter** and warm **maple syrup**.   *About 12 Griddlecakes*

—BLUEBERRY GRIDDLECAKES

Follow ▲ Recipe. Rinse and drain **2 cups fresh blueberries.** Gently fold blueberries into batter after folding in beaten egg whites. (If desired, frozen blueberries may be used. Thaw frozen blueberries according to directions on package. Drain thoroughly. Measure 2 cups blueberries.)

—CORN MEAL GRIDDLECAKES

Follow ▲ Recipe. Reduce flour to ¾ cup. Mix **¾ cup yellow corn meal** into dry ingredients.

—BUTTERMILK GRIDDLECAKES

Follow ▲ Recipe. Substitute **½ teaspoon baking soda** for the baking powder and **buttermilk** for the milk. Do not separate eggs. Beat eggs and buttermilk together. Bake griddlecakes as in ▲ Recipe.

—RYE GRIDDLECAKES

Follow recipe for Buttermilk Griddlecakes. Reduce flour to ¾ cup and mix in **¾ cup rye flour.** Blend **3 tablespoons molasses** into the buttermilk-egg mixture.

—CHERRYLAND GRIDDLECAKES

Follow ▲ Recipe. Gently fold **2 cups rinsed, stemmed, pitted ripe red tart cherries** into batter after folding in beaten egg whites.

—BANANA GRIDDLECAKES

Follow ▲ Recipe. Peel and dice **2 bananas** with brown-flecked peel. Fold into batter after folding in beaten egg whites.

—POLKA DOT GRIDDLECAKES

Follow ▲ Recipe. Fold **1 pkg. (6 oz.) semi-sweet chocolate pieces** into batter after folding in beaten egg whites.

OATMEAL GRIDDLECAKES

Mix together
   3 cups buttermilk
   1 cup rolled oats
Cover and set in refrigerator at least 4 hrs., or overnight, stirring once or twice.

Set a griddle or skillet over low heat.

Sift together into a bowl and set aside
   1 cup sifted all-purpose flour
   2 tablespoons sugar
   1 teaspoon baking soda
   1 teaspoon salt

Griddlecakes

Beat

2 eggs

Add the buttermilk mixture and blend thoroughly. Make a well in center of the dry ingredients and add liquid mixture all at one time. Stir only until blended.

Test griddle; it is hot enough for baking when drops of water sprinkled on surface dance in small beads. Lightly grease griddle if manufacturer so directs.

Pour batter from a pitcher or large spoon onto griddle in pools about 3 in. in diameter, leaving at least 1 in. between griddlecakes.

Cook griddlecakes over medium heat until lightly browned on one side. With spatula, carefully turn and brown other side. Turn griddlecakes only once.

About 1½ doz. griddlecakes

CORN GRIDDLECAKES

Set a griddle or heavy skillet over low heat.

Melt and set aside to cool

2 tablespoons butter or margarine

Sift together and set aside

1⅓ cups all-purpose flour
1 tablespoon baking powder
1 tablespoon sugar
¾ teaspoon salt
½ teaspoon celery salt
½ teaspoon monosodium glutamate

Oatmeal Griddlecakes

Corn Griddlecakes

Drain

1 can (12 oz.) whole kernel corn (1½ cups, drained)

Put into a large bowl with

1 egg, well beaten
1 cup milk

Add melted shortening. Mix until corn is evenly distributed throughout mixture. Gradually add dry ingredients, blending well after each addition.

Test griddle; it is hot enough for baking when drops of water, sprinkled on surface, dance in small beads. Lightly grease griddle if manufacturer so directs.

Pour batter from a pitcher or large spoon into pools about 3 in. in diameter, leaving at least 1 in. between griddlecakes. Cook griddlecakes over medium heat about 2 min., or until lightly browned on one side. With spatula, carefully turn and brown other side.

Serve with **butter** and **maple syrup** or **molasses**.   *About 2 doz. 3-in. griddlecakes*

GRIDDLECAKE SANDWICHES

Prepare

Griddlecakes or Buttermilk Griddlecakes (page 101)

Pour batter into pools about 5 in. in diameter, leaving at least 1 in. between. Bake as in griddlecake recipe.

While the griddlecakes are baking, place in a large cold skillet

1 lb. bulk pork sausage

Cook over medium heat, breaking into pieces with fork or spoon. Pour off fat as it collects; cook until browned. Drain on absorbent paper.

Spread hot griddlecake with about ½ cup sausage; top with another griddlecake.

Serve with **butter** and warm **honey, maple syrup** or **melted jelly**.   *6 servings*

APPLE PANCAKES

▲ *Base Recipe*

Set a griddle or heavy skillet over low heat.

Sift together and set aside

2 cups sifted all-purpose flour
4 teaspoons sugar
1 tablespoon baking powder
¾ teaspoon salt

Wash, quarter, core, pare and finely chop enough apples to yield

1½ cups finely chopped apple

Set aside.

Combine

2 eggs, well beaten
1½ cups milk
2 tablespoons melted shortening

Add dry ingredients to egg mixture and beat only until blended.

Griddlecake Sandwiches

Test griddle by dropping on it a few drops cold water; if drops dance around in small beads, griddle temperature is right. Lightly grease griddle if manufacturer directs.

Pour batter from a pitcher into small pools on griddle, leaving at least 1 in. between. Turn pancakes as they become puffy and full of bubbles. Turn and brown other side; turn only once. Before serving, sprinkle tops of pancakes with **granulated or brown sugar**.

2 to 3 doz. pancakes

—ANIMAL GRIDDLECAKES

Follow ▲ Recipe. Omit apples from batter. Working quickly, pour out enough batter for body. Drop bits of batter in correct position for legs, head and ears. Turtles and bunnies are special favorites.

FLANNEL CAKES

Set a griddle or heavy skillet over low heat.

Sift together

2 cups sifted all-purpose flour
1 tablespoon baking powder
1 tablespoon sugar
¾ teaspoon salt

Combine

1 egg, well beaten
1½ cups milk
2 tablespoons melted butter

Make a well in center of dry ingredients. Add liquid mixture all at once, beating only until blended.

Test griddle temperature by dropping on it a few drops of cold water; if drops dance around in small beads, temperature is right. Lightly grease griddle. Pour batter into pools about 4 in. in diameter, leaving about 1 in. between. Turn the cakes when tops are full of bubbles and bake other side until browned. Turn only once.

Serve immediately with **butter** and **maple syrup, honey** or **sugar,** or any desired **fruit** or **fruit preserve,** and accompanied by crisp **bacon, sausages, ham** or **chicken hash**.

About 2 doz. 4-in. cakes

Flannel Cakes

GOLDEN BROWN WAFFLES

▲ *Base Recipe*

Preheat waffle baker. It is hot enough for baking when a drop of cold water "sputters" on surface. (Electric waffle bakers usually have indicators to show correct heat.)

While waffle baker is heating, prepare batter. Sift together

2¼ cups sifted cake flour
1 tablespoon sugar
2½ teaspoons baking powder
¼ teaspoon salt

Combine

3 eggs, well beaten
1¼ cups milk
6 tablespoons melted butter or margarine

Add liquid mixture all at one time to dry ingredients. Beat only until smooth. Pour batter onto center of heated waffle baker, allowing 1 to 2 tablespoons batter for each section.

Lower cover gently and let waffle bake according to manufacturer's directions or until steaming stops (about 5 min.) and waffle is golden brown. Do not raise cover during baking. Lift cover, loosen waffle with fork and serve.

Top waffles with **maple syrup, honey,** any **fruit sauce,** or

Whipped Cream with Fruit—Beat in chilled bowl with chilled rotary beater **1 cup chilled heavy cream;** beat cream until rounded peaks are formed when beater is slowly lifted upright. Blend in **1 cup sliced fresh or canned berries,** well-drained and sweetened with about ⅓ cup sugar. Frozen thawed berries may be used; omit sugar. *6 waffles*

—BLUEBERRY WAFFLES

Follow ▲ Recipe. Fold **1 cup well-drained blueberries** into batter just before baking.

—SOUR MILK WAFFLES

Follow ▲ Recipe. Reduce baking powder to 1½ teaspoons. Add **¾ teaspoon baking soda** to dry ingredients. Substitute **1½ cups sour milk** (page 9) for milk.

BUTTERMILK WAFFLES

▲ *Base Recipe*

Heat waffle baker while preparing waffle batter.

Melt and set aside to cool
½ cup butter or margarine

Sift together into a large bowl and set aside
2 cups sifted all-purpose flour
1 tablespoon sugar
2 teaspoons baking powder
1 teaspoon baking soda
½ teaspoon salt

Beat until thick and lemon-colored
3 egg yolks

Add gradually to the beaten egg yolks the melted butter and
2 cups buttermilk

Continue to beat until well blended. Add liquid mixture all at one time to dry ingredients; mix only until batter is smooth.

Beat until stiff, not dry, peaks are formed
3 egg whites

Spread the beaten egg whites over the batter and gently fold together.

Unless temperature is automatically shown on waffle baker, test heat by dropping a few drops water on baker. It is hot enough for baking when drops of water "sputter" on surface. Pour batter onto center of waffle baker. It's wise to experiment to find out the exact amount of batter your waffle baker will hold; use that same measurement (spoonfuls or cupfuls) in future waffle baking.

Lower cover and allow waffle to bake according to manufacturer's directions, or until steaming stops (4 to 5 min.). Do not raise cover during baking period. Lift cover and loosen waffle with a fork.

Serve immediately with **butter or margarine** and warm **maple syrup.** *About 8 servings*

—SWEET MILK WAFFLES

Follow ▲ Recipe. Omit baking soda and increase baking powder to 1 tablespoon. Substitute **milk** for buttermilk.

—CHEESE WAFFLES

Follow ▲ Recipe. Fold ½ cup (2 oz.) grated **Cheddar cheese** into batter after folding in beaten egg whites.

—CHOCOLATE-DROP WAFFLES

Follow ▲ Recipe. Sprinkle about **¼ cup semi-sweet chocolate pieces** over batter before closing waffle baker.

—POPPY SEED WAFFLES

Follow ▲ Recipe. Add **¼ cup poppy seed** to a skillet with the butter or margarine; heat until butter is melted, stirring occasionally.

—SPICE WAFFLES

Follow ▲ Recipe. Sift **1 teaspoon cinnamon** and **½ teaspoon nutmeg** with dry ingredients. Add **3 tablespoons molasses** with liquid ingredients.

—MAIN-DISH WAFFLES

Follow ▲ Recipe. Sprinkle **2 tablespoons shredded cooked ham** over batter before closing waffle baker. Or, serve a **creamed vegetable, meat, fish or poultry mixture** on waffles.

—DESSERT WAFFLES

Follow ▲ Recipe. Serve waffles immediately with **ice cream** and any one of the suggested **Toppers for Ice Cream** (page 566).

For Shortcake—Spoon **Sweetened Crushed Berries** (page 566) or **sweetened fresh peach slices** over waffle. Spread **Sweetened Whipped Cream** (page 480) over fruit. Top with another waffle and layer of fruit and whipped cream. Sprinkle with **nutmeg.**

RICE WAFFLES

Heat waffle baker while preparing batter.

Prepare and set aside to cool
1 cup Perfection Boiled Rice (page 165; about one-third recipe)

Melt and set aside to cool
½ cup butter or margarine

Special Cheese Waffles

Sift together into a large bowl and set aside
1½ cups all-purpose flour
1 tablespoon sugar
1 tablespoon baking powder
½ teaspoon salt

Beat until thick and lemon-colored
3 egg yolks
Add gradually and blend in
2 cups milk
Thoroughly blend in the melted butter and cooked rice. Add liquid-rice mixture all at one time to dry ingredients; mix only until batter is blended.

Using clean beater, beat until stiff, not dry, peaks are formed
3 egg whites
Spread the beaten egg whites over the batter and gently fold together.

Unless temperature is automatically shown on waffle baker, test heat by dropping a few drops of water on baker. It is hot enough for baking when drops of water sputter on the surface. Pour batter onto center of waffle baker. (It is wise to experiment to find out the exact amount of batter your waffle baker will hold in spoonfuls or cupfuls; use that same measurement in future waffle baking.)

Lower cover and allow waffle to bake according to manufacturer's directions, or until steaming stops (4 to 5 min.). Do not raise cover during baking period. Lift cover and loosen waffle carefully with a fork.

Serve immediately with **butter or margarine** and warm **maple syrup** or **molasses**.
About 8 servings

SPECIAL CHEESE WAFFLES

▲ *Base Recipe*

Heat waffle baker while preparing batter.

Melt and set aside to cool
⅓ cup butter or margarine

Shred and set aside
½ lb. sharp Cheddar cheese (about 2 cups, shredded)

Sift together into a bowl and set aside
1¾ cups sifted all-purpose flour
1½ tablespoons sugar
1 tablespoon baking powder
¾ teaspoon salt
Beat until thick and lemon-colored
2 egg yolks
Blend in the melted butter, cheese and
1¼ cups milk
Add liquid mixture all at one time to dry ingredients; beat only until batter is blended.

Beat until stiff, not dry, peaks are formed
2 egg whites
Spread egg whites over batter and gently fold together.

Unless temperature is automatically shown on waffle baker, test heat by dropping a few drops of water on baker. It is hot enough for baking when the drops of water sputter.

Pour batter onto center of waffle baker. It is wise to experiment to find out the exact amount of batter your baker will hold; use that same measurement (spoonfuls or cupfuls) in future waffle baking.

Lower cover and allow waffle to bake according to manufacturer's directions, or until steaming stops (4 to 5 min.). Do not raise cover during baking period; then lift carefully and loosen waffle with a fork.

Serve immediately with **butter or margarine** and **maple syrup**, accompanied with **sausage links** or **bacon**. Cheese waffles may also be served topped with **creamed eggs, fish, chicken** or **vegetables**. *4 large waffles*

—CHEESE NUT WAFFLES

Follow ▲ Recipe. Fold ½ cup (2 oz.) chopped **nuts** into batter with the egg whites.

—BACON CHEESE WAFFLES

Follow ▲ Recipe. Prepare **8 slices Panfried Bacon** (page 190). Crumble bacon and fold into batter with the egg whites.

SOUR CREAM WAFFLES
(Vafler)

In Norway these tender waffles are served in the afternoon at the sociable coffee hour. Baked in an iron with heart-shaped sections, they are served cold, as if they were cake, and are accompanied by fruit preserves or tissue-thin slices of Norwegian goat cheese.

Heat waffle baker while preparing waffle batter.

Melt and set aside to cool
¼ cup butter

Sift together into a large bowl
1 cup sifted all-purpose flour
2 tablespoons sugar
1 teaspoon baking soda
1 teaspoon cardamom
½ teaspoon salt
Set aside.

Beat until thick and lemon-colored
2 egg yolks
Add the melted butter gradually and
1 cup dairy sour cream
1 cup buttermilk
Continue to beat until well blended. Add liquid mixture all at one time to dry ingredients; beat only until batter is smooth.

Beat until stiff, not dry, peaks are formed
2 egg whites
Spread the beaten egg whites over the batter and gently fold together.

Unless temperature is automatically shown on waffle baker, test baker; it is hot enough for baking when drops of water sprinkled on surface sputter. Pour batter onto center of waffle baker. It is wise to experiment to find out the exact amount of batter your baker will hold;

use that same measurement (spoonfuls or cupfuls) in future waffle baking.

Lower cover and allow waffle to bake according to manufacturer's directions, or until steaming stops (about 5 min.). Do not raise cover during baking period. Lift cover and loosen waffle with a fork. Set waffles aside on a clean towel. As each waffle is baked pile on previous waffles to keep soft.

Serve waffles cold. Spread with
    Butter
If desired, serve with **lingonberry preserves or jam.** *About 4 large waffles*

BROWNIE WAFFLES

▲ *Base Recipe*

Heat waffle baker while preparing batter.

Put into top of double boiler
    1½ pkgs. (9 oz.) semisweet chocolate pieces
    ¾ cup milk
    ½ cup shortening
Heat over simmering water until chocolate and shortening are melted. Remove from heat and blend thoroughly. Set aside to cool.

Meanwhile, chop and set aside
    ½ cup (2 oz.) nuts

Sift together into a large bowl and set aside
    1½ cups sifted cake flour
    ½ teaspoon baking powder
    ½ teaspoon salt

Beat until thick and lemon-colored
    2 egg yolks
Add gradually, continuing to beat
    ⅓ cup plus 1 tablespoon sugar
Beat in chocolate mixture. Add all at one time to dry ingredients; beat until batter is smooth. Mix in the chopped nuts.

Beat until stiff, not dry, peaks are formed
    2 egg whites
Fold beaten egg whites into batter.

Unless temperature is automatically shown on waffle baker, test heat with a few drops of cold water; it is hot enough for baking when the water sputters on the surface. (If temperature is automatically shown, set control at lowest setting.)

Spoon batter onto center of baker, allowing 1 to 2 tablespoons for each section. Lower cover and allow waffle to bake 7 to 8 min., or until steaming stops. Do not raise cover during baking period. Lift cover, loosen waffle with fork and carefully remove one section at a time. Sprinkle with
    Confectioners' sugar
Serve hot or cooled. *About 6 servings*

—BROWNIE WAFFLE SANDWICHES

Follow ▲ Recipe. Spread one-half of waffles with **raspberry jam.** Cover with remaining half. Top with **Sweetened Whipped Cream** (page 480).

—CHERRY BROWNIE WAFFLES

Follow ▲ Recipe. Blend in with nuts ½ **cup (8-oz. jar) maraschino cherries,** drained and quartered.

—BROWNIE WAFFLE SUNDAE

Follow ▲ Recipe. Serve sections of Brownie Waffles topped with **vanilla ice cream** and any **chocolate sauce.**

TOPPINGS FOR PANCAKES AND WAFFLES

HONEY CREAM

Cream until softened
    ½ cup butter or margarine
Add and beat until well blended
    ¼ cup honey
Add gradually, beating until smooth and fluffy
    ½ cup dairy sour cream
If desired, chill.

Serve with **waffles, griddlecakes** or **French toast.** *About 1 cup sauce*

HONEY WHIP

Cream until very soft
    ⅓ cup butter or margarine
    ¼ teaspoon cinnamon, mace or nutmeg
Gradually whip in
    ⅔ cup honey
Continue beating until light and fluffy.

Gently blend in
    ½ cup heavy cream, whipped
Serve with **griddlecakes, waffles** or **French toast.** Store whip in refrigerator if not served immediately. When ready to use, bring to room temperature and whip again.
About 1½ cups whip

SPICY CHERRY SAUCE

Cook 5 min. in a covered saucepan
    4 cups (two 16-oz. cans) pitted red cherries
    3 whole cloves
    1 cinnamon stick (2 in.), broken

Remove from heat and take out cinnamon and cloves. Pour through a sieve or food mill placed over a saucepan. Force cherries through sieve and set aside.

Mix thoroughly
    2 tablespoons cornstarch
    2 tablespoons sugar
    ¼ teaspoon salt

Sour Cream Waffles and Julekake (page 672)

Brownie Waffles

Stir in, in order,
    2 tablespoons cold water
    ⅓ cup corn syrup
Make a smooth paste. Gradually stir into hot cherry mixture. Bring rapidly to boiling, stirring slowly and constantly. Cover and cook gently 3 min. Remove from heat and blend in
    2 tablespoons butter or margarine
    2 teaspoons lemon juice
    ¼ teaspoon almond extract
    2 or 3 drops red food coloring
Serve hot with **griddlecakes, waffles, omelets, cooked cereals, fritters** or **French toast.**
About 2 cups sauce

DUMPLINGS

PLAIN DUMPLINGS
(Klösse)

▲ *Base Recipe*

Prepare in a deep saucepan with a tight-fitting cover
    1 qt. quick meat broth or quick chicken broth (page 10)

Sift together
    2 cups sifted all-purpose flour
    4 teaspoons baking powder
    1 teaspoon salt

Cut in with a pastry blender or two knives until pieces are the size of rice kernels

1 tablespoon shortening

Quickly stir in with a fork until just blended

⅔ cup milk

1 tablespoon chopped parsley

Shape dough into balls about 2 in. in diameter.

Bring broth to boiling. Drop dumplings into the broth. Cook only as many dumplings at one time as will lie uncrowded one layer deep. Cover and simmer 15 min. without removing the cover.

Carefully remove with a slotted spoon and serve with meat or poultry. (If desired, dumplings may be dropped into boiling soup. Serve the dumplings with the soup.)   *12 dumplings*

—HERB DUMPLINGS
(Klösse mit feinen Kräutern)

Follow ▲ Recipe. Add **1 teaspoon marjoram** to dry ingredients.

—PLAIN DUMPLINGS WITH BACON
(Klösse mit Speck)

Follow ▲ Recipe. Prepare **6 slices Panfried Bacon** (page 190); crumble. Stir in with milk.

POTATO DUMPLINGS
(Kartoffelknödel)

Wash, pare and cook (page 313)

6 medium (about 2 lbs.) potatoes

Cook about 30 min., or until potatoes are tender when pierced with a fork. Drain. Dry potatoes by shaking pan over low heat. Mash or rice potatoes thoroughly. Set aside to cool completely.

Meanwhile, melt in a large, heavy skillet over low heat

1 to 1½ tablespoons butter

Cut into ¼- to ½-in. cubes

1 slice toasted bread

Put cubes into the skillet and toss until all sides are coated and browned. Set aside.

Bring to boiling in a large heavy saucepan

2 qts. water

2 teaspoons salt

When potatoes are cooled, whip in until fluffy

1 egg, well beaten

and a mixture of

1 teaspoon salt

¼ teaspoon monosodium glutamate

⅛ teaspoon white pepper

Measure

⅔ to ¾ cup sifted all-purpose flour

¼ cup cornstarch

Mix in cornstarch and one-half the flour. Add enough of the remaining flour to make a soft dough. Break off pieces of the dough and shape into balls about 1 in. in diameter. Poke one of the bread cubes into the center of each ball of dough.

Drop the dumplings into the boiling water. Cook only as many dumplings at one time as will lie uncrowded one layer deep. Cook about 5 min., or until dumplings rise to the surface of the water. Carefully remove with a slotted spoon and drain over the water a few seconds.

Put dumplings into a warm serving dish and serve with

Melted butter

Dumplings may be served with sauerkraut, meat or poultry.   *About 18 dumplings*

SWEDISH POTATO DUMPLINGS
(Kroppkakor)

▲ Base Recipe

Wash, pare, cut in halves and cook (page 313)

6 medium (about 2 lbs.) potatoes

Cook about 20 min., or until potatoes are tender when pierced with a fork. Drain. To dry potatoes, shake pan over low heat. Mash or rice potatoes thoroughly. Whip in until potatoes are fluffy

1 egg yolk, slightly beaten

1½ teaspoons salt

Set potatoes aside.

Have ready

¾ lb. lean salt pork, bacon or ham, cut into cubes or 1-in. pieces

Put into a skillet with

1 medium onion, chopped

Cook over medium heat, moving and turning with a spoon. Pour off fat as it collects. When meat is evenly crisped and browned and onion

is golden brown, remove from skillet and drain on absorbent paper.

Measure

2 to 3 cups sifted all-purpose flour

Add about one-half the flour to the potato mixture, blending thoroughly. Add enough remaining flour to make a soft dough.

Turn out on a floured surface and knead as for bread dough (page 11). Using hands, pat out dough ½ in. thick. Cut into 2-in. rounds using a lightly floured 2-in. round biscuit cutter. Spoon about 2 teaspoons of the bacon-onion mixture into the center of one-half the rounds. Cover with the other rounds. Seal edges securely and shape into balls.

Bring to boiling in a large heavy saucepan

2 qts. water

2 teaspoons salt

Gradually add dumplings to boiling water so that boiling does not stop. Cook only as many dumplings at one time as will float, uncrowded, one layer deep. Cook 15 min. Remove with a slotted spoon; drain over water a few seconds.

Put into a warm serving dish and serve with

Melted butter

About 2 doz. dumplings

—FRIED POTATO DUMPLINGS
(Stekt Kroppkakor)

Follow ▲ Recipe or use leftover dumplings. Heat **3 tablespoons butter** in a skillet. Add the dumplings and cook over medium heat until browned, moving and turning with a spoon to brown evenly.

FISH DUMPLINGS
(Fischklösse)

Bring to boiling in a large heavy saucepan

2 qts. water

1 teaspoon salt

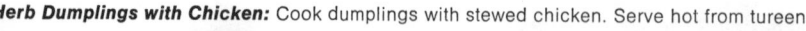
Herb Dumplings with Chicken: Cook dumplings with stewed chicken. Serve hot from tureen.

Put into a large bowl, blend thoroughly and set aside

2 cups (2 slices) soft bread crumbs
1 egg, well beaten
¼ cup milk

Rinse

1 lb. fish fillets (sole, cod or trout)

(If frozen, thaw according to directions on package.) Force through the medium blade of a food chopper.

Heat in a skillet

1 tablespoon butter

Add and cook over medium heat until onion is tender

3 tablespoons chopped onion

Add the fish and the contents of the skillet to the bread crumb mixture with

2 tablespoons grated Parmesan cheese
1 teaspoon finely chopped parsley
1 teaspoon salt
½ teaspoon monosodium glutamate
¼ teaspoon white pepper

Shape pieces of the fish mixture into balls about 1½ in. in diameter. Roll lightly in

¼ cup all-purpose flour

Drop the dumplings into the boiling salted water. Cook only as many dumplings at one time as will lie uncrowded one layer deep. Cook about 6 min., or until dumplings rise to the surface of the water. Remove with a slotted spoon and drain over the water for a few seconds.

Serve immediately with

Mushroom Sauce (page 304).

12 dumplings

BAKERY BREADS

CINNAMON TOAST

▲ *Base Recipe*

For Toaster—Toast

4 slices bread

While bread is still hot, spread with

3 tablespoons butter or margarine, softened

Sprinkle bread with a mixture of

3 tablespoons sugar
1 tablespoon cinnamon

Keep warm in oven until serving time.

For Broiler—Place bread slices on baking sheet. Set temperature control of range at Broil. Place in broiler with tops of bread about 3 in. from heat until browned. Remove from broiler and turn. Using amount of butter in toaster method, butter untoasted side and sprinkle with sugar-cinnamon mixture. Return to broiler and finish toasting. Watch carefully to avoid scorching.

—CINNAMON BUTTER

Follow ▲ Recipe for amounts. Cream the butter until softened. Then slowly beat in the sugar-cinnamon mixture. This butter may be used on either toasted or untoasted bread.

ORANGE SUGAR TOAST

▲ *Base Recipe*

For Orange Sugar—Blend together and set aside

2 tablespoons sugar
1 tablespoon grated orange peel
2 teaspoons orange juice
⅛ teaspoon nutmeg

For Toast—Remove crusts from

4 slices bread

Set temperature control of range at Broil. Place bread slices on broiler rack; place in broiler about 3 in. from heat. When browned, remove toast from broiler and spread untoasted sides of bread with

Butter or margarine

Sprinkle buttered sides with Orange Sugar and return to broiler rack; broil until sugar is melted.

Cut slices into halves, triangles, strips, rounds or other fancy shapes.

—CINNAMON CARAMEL TOAST

Follow ▲ Recipe. Substitute a mixture of **2 tablespoons brown or maple sugar** and **1 teaspoon cinnamon** for Orange Sugar.

—ENGLISH MUFFIN CRISPS

Follow ▲ Recipe for Orange Sugar to make Cinnamon Toast mixture. Cut **English muffins** into halves crosswise and use as bread. Spread with sugar mixture and complete as in ▲ Recipe.

COCONUT QUICK-SWEETS

▲ *Base Recipe*

Lightly grease baking sheets.

Blender-chop (page 11)

¾ cup moist shreaded coconut

Gradually add coconut to blender container and turn off motor immediately after final addition. (Do not finely chop coconut.) Spread on waxed paper and set aside.

Trim crusts from

4 or 5 slices bread, about ½ in. thick

Cut each slice into 1-in. strips and set aside. (If bread slices are large, strips may be cut into halves crosswise.)

Pour into a small, shallow bowl

⅔ cup (about one-half 14-oz. can) sweetened condensed milk

Using a fork, quickly but thoroughly dip bread strip into milk. Then coat bread strip by rolling in the chopped coconut; arrange on baking sheet. Repeat until all bread strips are dipped and coated.

Bake at 350°F 10 to 15 min., or until coconut is lightly toasted. Remove to cooling rack.

About 16 bars

—CHOCOLATE COCONUT QUICKIES

Follow ▲ Recipe. Combine **3 tablespoons cocoa** with the sweetened condensed milk.

FRENCH TOAST

▲ *Base Recipe*

Heat in heavy skillet

1 tablespoon butter

Meanwhile, mix together in a shallow bowl

2 eggs, slightly beaten
1 cup milk
¼ teaspoon salt

Dip into this mixture

6 slices bread

Add two of the slices to hot butter. Lightly brown on one side and turn with spatula to brown other side. Add more butter if necessary to keep slices from sticking.

French Toast

Serve with **jam, jelly, maple syrup** or **honey,** sprinkle with **sugar** and **cinnamon,** or garnish with tiny **sausages.**

Toast may be placed on greased baking sheet and browned in a 450°F oven about 10 min. for each side.   *6 slices French Toast*

—SWEET FRENCH TOAST

Follow ▲ Recipe. Add **2 tablespoons sugar** and **½ teaspoon almond extract** or **1 teaspoon vanilla extract** to egg-milk mixture.

—ORANGE FRENCH TOAST

Follow ▲ Recipe. Substitute **orange juice** for milk. Blend and mix in **3 tablespoons confectioners' sugar** and **2 teaspoons grated orange peel.**

—PEANUT BUTTER FRENCH TOAST

Follow ▲ Recipe. Gradually beat the milk into **¼ cup creamy peanut butter.** Omit salt; add eggs.

—BUTTERMILK FRENCH TOAST

Follow ▲ Recipe. Substitute **buttermilk** for milk.

FRENCH TOAST SANDWICHES

Blend well in a bowl
> **⅓ cup (3-oz. can) deviled ham**
> **¼ cup finely chopped celery**
> **2 tablespoons cream**
> **½ teaspoon Worcestershire sauce**
> **¼ teaspoon dry mustard**

Set out
> **8 slices bread**

Spread deviled ham mixture on 4 of the slices and top with remaining slices. Set aside.

Beat together in a shallow bowl
> **3 eggs, slightly beaten**
> **⅔ cup milk or cream**
> **1 tablespoon sugar**
> **½ teaspoon salt**

Set aside.

Heat in a large skillet
> **3 tablespoons fat**

Carefully dip sandwiches, one at a time, into the egg mixture, coating each side well and allowing excess to drain into bowl. Place as many sandwiches in the hot skillet at one time as will fit easily. Brown on both sides, turning once. If necessary, add more fat to keep sandwiches from sticking.

For sandwich topping, melt, stirring frequently, in a heavy light-colored skillet over low heat
> **3 tablespoons sugar**

Add to skillet
> **4 slices pineapple (8¼-oz. can, drained)**

Heat until pineapple slices are glazed. Top each sandwich with a pineapple slice. Cut sandwiches diagonally into halves and serve hot.   *4 servings*

MAPLE TOAST

Trim crusts from
> **Bread slices**

Put slices onto a baking sheet and set under broiler 3 to 5 in. from heat. Toast until golden brown. Turn slices and brush with
> **Butter or margarine**

Sprinkle generously with
> **Soft maple sugar**

Broil until sugar is melted. Sprinkle with
> **Coarsely chopped walnuts or pecans**

Serve hot.

LOST BREAD
(Pain Perdu)

Creoles relish this crisp-crusted treat as a breakfast bread. This delicacy has much in common with our French toast.

About 20 min. before deep-frying, fill a deep saucepan one-half to two-thirds full with
> **Vegetable shortening, all-purpose shortening, lard or cooking oil for deep-frying**

Heat slowly to 375°F.

While fat is heating, beat slightly in a shallow bowl or pie pan
> **2 eggs**
> **1 cup milk or cream**
> **¼ cup sugar**
> **½ teaspoon salt**
> **¼ teaspoon vanilla extract**

Set mixture aside.

Arrange in three stacks on flat work surface
> **12 slices bread (slightly dry bread produces firmer Pain Perdu)**

If desired, trim off crusts with a sharp knife. Cut stacks of slices into strips or diagonally into halves. Or, spread a few slices at a time out over the working surface and cut them individually into rounds with a large cookie cutter or a knife.

Dip bread pieces one at a time into the egg mixture. Coat each side well. Allow any excess coating to drip off before lowering slice into the heated fat. Deep-fry only as many pieces at one time as will float uncrowded one layer deep in the fat. Fry 1 to 2 min., or until golden brown. Turn pieces with a fork as they rise to surface and several times during cooking. Remove pieces with a slotted spoon; drain over fat for a few seconds before removing to absorbent paper.

Sprinkle pieces with a mixture of
> **¼ cup sifted confectioners' sugar**
> **½ teaspoon nutmeg**

Serve immediately on a warm platter.
6 servings

Note: Orange flower water and brandy are often used as part of the liquid when Pain Perdu is made.

HERB-BUTTERED BREAD I

> ▲ *Base Recipe*

A baking sheet will be needed.

For Herb Butter—Put into a bowl and soften with a wooden spoon
> **½ cup butter or margarine**

Blend in
> **1 teaspoon lemon juice**
> **1 teaspoon caraway seed**
> **1 teaspoon sage**
> **½ teaspoon thyme**
> **Few grains salt**
> **Few grains paprika**

Cover the mixture and set in refrigerator to allow flavors to blend thoroughly (at least 1 hr.). Set out to soften slightly a few minutes before using.

For Bread—Make diagonal cuts about ½ in. apart, almost to bottom of
1 loaf French bread
Spread one side of each bread slice with Herb Butter. Place loaf on baking sheet.

Bake at 350°F 10 to 15 min., or until bread is thoroughly heated.

Serve hot.   *1 loaf Herb-Buttered Bread*

—HERB-BUTTERED BREAD II

Follow ▲ Recipe. Omit caraway seeds, sage, thyme and paprika. Blend in **2 teaspoons chopped parsley, 1 teaspoon crushed sweet basil** and **1 teaspoon crushed tarragon leaves.**

—GARLIC BREAD

Follow ▲ Recipe. Substitute Garlic Butter for Herb Butter. Sprinkle with **paprika, grated cheese** or **poppy seed,** if desired.

For Garlic Butter—Put into a small skillet ⅓ **cup butter or margarine** and **1 clove garlic,** minced. Heat until butter is melted.

SPICY FILLED VIENNA BREAD

▲ *Base Recipe*

Set out a baking sheet.

Cut a thin lengthwise slice from top of
1 loaf Vienna or French bread
Set slice aside. With a small, sharp knife, cut down around edge of loaf, ¾ in. from edges, keeping shell intact. Pull out soft center and set loaf shell aside.

Using bread removed from center of loaf, prepare
2 cups soft bread crumbs
Combine crumbs with
1 lb. ground beef
1 cup Mincemeat (about one-fourth recipe, page 729)
1 cup (4 oz.) grated American cheese
2 tablespoons minced onion
3 tablespoons apple juice
1 egg, beaten

Add a mixture of
1 teaspoon salt
¼ teaspoon pepper
Mix lightly. Pack lightly into bread shell. Set loaf on baking sheet.

Bake at 350°F about 1 hr. To lightly toast slice from top of bread, brush it generously with
Melted butter or margarine
Set it on baking sheet 15 min. before end of baking period.

Fasten toasted bread slice to top of bread loaf with wooden picks. Slice and serve.
8 servings

—INDIVIDUAL BEEF-STUFFED LOAVES

Follow ▲ Recipe. Substitute **6 to 8 large French rolls** for loaf of bread. Bake loaves at 350°F 30 to 45 min. Toast top slices during last 10 min. of baking period. Omit final slicing.

QUICK CHEESE BREAD

Make diagonal cuts almost through
1 small loaf unsliced bread
Insert in cuts
American cheese slices
Set loaf in a greased shallow baking dish. Brush over top and sides of loaf a mixture of
⅓ cup melted butter or margarine
1½ teaspoons caraway seed
1 teaspoon dry mustard

Heat in a 350°F oven 15 to 20 min., or until bread is lightly browned and cheese is melted.

Meanwhile, heat in a small skillet over low heat
2 tablespoons butter or margarine
¼ cup finely chopped anchovies
1 tablespoon lemon juice
Few drops Tabasco
Stir to blend. Spoon over loaf just before serving.   *About 8 servings*

COFFEE CAKE LOAF

Trim crusts from
1 loaf unsliced bread
Cut bread into halves lengthwise. Cut each half into 6 squares, cutting almost through bread. Put onto a greased baking sheet, uncut surface down. Brush tops, sides and cuts with
¼ cup melted butter or margarine
Mix in a bowl
½ cup firmly packed brown sugar
3 tablespoons all-purpose flour
2 teaspoons cinnamon
Cut in with a pastry blender or two knives until mixture resembles coarse corn meal
2 tablespoons butter or margarine
Sprinkle mixture over tops of bread.

Bake at 400°F 12 to 15 min., or until bread is lightly toasted.

To serve, place the halves together to form a loaf. Serve warm.   *About 6 servings*

CHEESE STICKS

Arrange on a baking sheet
3 slices bread (white, whole wheat or rye)
Toast bread slices on one side in a 300°F oven. Turn and spread untoasted side of slices with mixture of
3 tablespoons grated Parmesan cheese
1 egg yolk
2 tablespoons melted butter or margarine
Cut each slice into six strips. Return to oven about 15 to 20 min., or until lightly browned.
18 sticks

ORANGE QUICKIES

Combine in a small saucepan
3 tablespoons sugar
2 tablespoons thawed frozen orange juice concentrate
1 tablespoon butter or margarine
Heat until sugar is dissolved and mixture is blended, stirring constantly. Mix in
⅓ cup flaked coconut

Set on a greased baking sheet
2 doz. brown-and-serve rolls
Spoon glaze over rolls and bake, following directions on package.   *2 doz. glazed rolls*

Herb-Buttered Bread

Quick Cheese Bread

Croustades

Ringlet Shells

Quick Coconut Coffee Bread

QUICK COCONUT COFFEE BREAD

Trim crusts from
1 loaf unsliced bread
Cut loaf diagonally into wedge shapes, cutting almost through bread. Place loaf on a lightly greased baking sheet, uncut surface down. Brush top and sides with
Sweetened condensed milk
Coat top and sides with a mixture of
½ cup flaked coconut
¼ cup (about 1 oz.) chopped nuts

Heat in a 350°F oven about 20 min., or until lightly browned. *About 6 servings*

CROUSTADES

Set out a baking sheet.

Cut into 1¼- to 2-in. thick slices
1 loaf unsliced, dry bread
Remove crusts and cut bread into desired shapes—triangles, squares, diamonds; or cut into rounds or fancy shapes with a large biscuit or cookie cutter. (If cutter is not deep enough, mark with it and finish cutting with the point of a sharp knife.) Following outline of shaped piece, carefully cut out center ¼ to ½ in. from edge, and down to within ¼ to ½ in. of bottom, leaving a neatly cut shell.

Brush outside and inside surfaces of shells with
Melted butter or margarine
Place on baking sheet.

Toast at 325°F 12 to 20 min., or until lightly browned and crisp.

If shells are not used immediately, reheat in oven for a few minutes before filling.

Shell centers and crusts may be toasted or dried, ground and saved for crumbs. Or centers may be toasted and used as a garnish to top filled croustades.

Note: Croustades may be deep-fried (page 11) at 375°F until lightly browned instead of toasted in oven. Drain on absorbent paper.

RINGLET SHELLS

Set on a cutting surface
12 bread slices, about ½ in. thick
Trim off crusts and cut all slices into large squares, rectangles or rounds (making all 12 slices the same shape). Use a cookie or biscuit cutter for the rounds. Set aside four shapes.

With a sharp pointed knife or cookie cutter, trim out centers from the 8 remaining shapes, leaving at least ½-in. rings. Thoroughly brush tops of uncut shapes and both sides of rings with
Milk
Stack 2 rings on each uncut shape. Brush inside and outside with
Melted butter or margarine

Place on a baking sheet and toast in a 325°F oven 12 to 20 min., or until golden brown and crisp. Fill as desired. *4 Ringlet Shells*

TOAST CUPS

Remove crusts from
6 slices bread
Lightly brush both sides of slices with
Melted butter or margarine

Gently press each slice into a muffin-pan well to form a cup.

Toast in a 350°F oven 12 to 15 min., or until lightly browned.

If desired for a dessert, fill with **sweetened fruits.** Serve immediately. *6 Toast Cups*

LOAF BASKET

Neatly trim the crusts from top and sides of
1 loaf unsliced bread
Using a sharp pointed knife, hollow out center leaving about ¾-in. sides and bottom. Brush inside and outside with
Melted butter or margarine

Place on a baking sheet and toast in a 325°F oven 15 to 25 min., or until golden brown and crisp. Fill with any creamed mixture, garnish and serve immediately.

Note: For a cover on the basket, cut a ¾-in. slice from length of loaf before making the basket. Brush both sides with melted butter or margarine. Place on baking sheet with basket and toast.

BREADS FROM MIXES

ONION BREAD

Set out and grease three 7x4x2-in. loaf pans.

Combine in a saucepan, cover and cook over low heat 10 min.
1 env. dry onion soup mix
2 cups boiling water
Measure into a large bowl
1 cup of the soup (use remaining soup as desired)
Cool to lukewarm.

Sprinkle yeast (found in package of roll mix) over soup and stir until dissolved. Beat in
1 pkg. (13¾ oz.) hot roll mix

Turn dough onto a floured surface and knead until smooth and satiny, about 5 min.

Place in greased bowl, turn dough over to bring greased surface to top. Cover and let rise in warm place until doubled, about 1 hr.

Divide dough into 3 equal portions. Roll each into a 7x4-in. rectangle. Roll up jelly-roll fashion, starting with narrow side. Seal edge and ends. Place seam side down in the prepared pans. Let rise in warm place until doubled.

Bake at 375°F about 25 min., or until bread tests done.   *3 small loaves bread*

CRANBERRY STICKY BUNS

Set out a 9x9x2-in. baking pan.

Rinse, drain and chop
1 cup fresh cranberries
Measure
¾ cup firmly packed dark brown sugar
Combine one half of the sugar with the cranberries and
½ cup raisins
Set aside.

Prepare, following package directions
1 pkg. (13¾ oz.) hot roll mix
Turn dough onto lightly floured surface and roll into a 14x12-in. rectangle.

Heat until melted
⅓ cup butter or margarine
Brush rectangle lightly with some of the melted butter. Spread with the cranberry mixture. Roll jelly-roll fashion starting at the 14-in. side.

Combine remaining melted butter, remaining brown sugar and
⅓ cup pecan halves
Spread mixture evenly in bottom of the square pan. Cut the rolled dough into 9 equal slices. Arrange slices, cut side down, on mixture in pan. Cover; let rise in a warm place until doubled.

Bake at 400°F about 30 min., or until rolls are a rich golden brown. Loosen edges with a knife and invert pan onto serving plate. Allow to stand several minutes before lifting off the pan. Separate into individual buns and serve warm.
9 buns

ANISE-FLAVORED NUT BREAD

Set out and generously grease a 9x5x3-in. loaf pan.

Combine in a large bowl
½ cup sugar
1 egg
1¼ cups milk
3 cups biscuit mix
Beat vigorously 30 seconds. (Do not overbeat; batter will be rather lumpy.)

Blend into batter
½ to ¾ teaspoon anise seed

Add, mixing well
½ cup diced mixed candied fruit
½ to ¾ cup chopped nuts (walnuts or pecans)
Turn the batter into prepared loaf pan.

Bake at 350°F about 45 min., or until loaf tests done. Cool the bread before slicing.
1 large loaf bread

BRUNCH CRUNCH

Grease an 8x8x2-in. baking pan.

Combine in a bowl, mixing well
2 cups biscuit mix
⅓ cup sugar
Add a blend of
½ cup water
1 egg
2 tablespoons butter or margarine, melted
Spread the mixture evenly over bottom of the prepared pan.

Toss together lightly using a fork
½ cup firmly packed light brown sugar
1 teaspoon cinnamon
⅓ cup ketchup
⅓ cup coarsely chopped nuts
½ cup coarsely crushed (by hand) corn flakes
2 tablespoons butter or margarine, melted
Spread mixture over top of batter. With a knife, cut down and swirl topping into batter.

Combine, mixing lightly
⅓ cup coarsely crushed (by hand) corn flakes
¼ teaspoon cinnamon
1 tablespoon butter or margarine, melted
Sprinkle evenly over batter.

Bake at 400°F 25 to 30 min. Cool 15 min. before serving.   *9 servings*

HERBED CHEESE BISCUITS

Set out a baking sheet.

Combine in a large bowl
2 cups biscuit mix
¼ teaspoon summer savory
¼ teaspoon crushed tarragon
2 to 3 tablespoons shredded Parmesan cheese

Cut in, using pastry blender or 2 knives
¼ cup butter
Add, stirring gently with a fork
½ cup milk
Shape mixture into a ball and turn onto a lightly floured surface. Knead dough about 10 times and pat or roll ½ in. thick into a round. Cut with a floured 2-in. biscuit cutter and place 2 in. apart on baking sheet. Brush tops of rounds with
1 egg, slightly beaten
Sprinkle with
1 tablespoon sesame seed (or shredded Parmesan cheese)

Bake at 450°F about 10 min., or until lightly browned. Serve at once. *About 1 doz. biscuits*

DEVILED PECAN APPLE BISCUITS

Cover bottom of a 9-in. ring mold with
3 tablespoons butter or margarine, melted
Sprinkle evenly over butter
3 to 4 tablespoons brown sugar
3 tablespoons finely chopped pecans
Set aside.

Combine in a bowl, mixing well
2 cans (4½ oz. each) deviled ham
½ cup finely chopped apple

Measure into a bowl
2 cups biscuit mix
Prepare dough for rolled biscuits, following package directions.

Turn dough onto floured surface and roll into a 14x10-in. rectangle. Cut into 12 squares. Spread each almost to edge with the filling mixture. Roll each from one corner to the diagonally opposite corner. Bring remaining two corners together to enclose the filling and form a ball. Pinch edges to seal. Arrange the balls, sealed side down, on the mixture in the ring mold.

Bake at 400°F about 30 min. Remove from oven and immediately invert ring mold onto serving plate. Allow to stand several minutes before lifting mold from biscuit ring. Serve rolls warm.   *1 doz. biscuits*

Note: If desired, substitute an 8-in. round cake pan for the ring mold and arrange 9 balls around the outside and 3 balls in the center.

CRANBERRY ORANGE MUFFINS

Grease or line with paper baking cups 12 medium-size muffin-pan wells.

Combine in a bowl
2 cups biscuit mix
¼ cup firmly packed brown sugar
Beat together until well mixed
1 large egg (¼ cup)
¾ cup milk or light cream
2 tablespoons cooking oil (or melted shortening)
Stir liquid into biscuit mixture (do not over-mix).

Spoon batter into muffin-pan wells, filling wells about one-third full. Spoon onto center of batter in each well
2 teaspoons cranberry-orange relish (using ½ cup from a 14-oz. jar)
Spoon remaining batter over relish, filling wells about two-thirds full.

Mix thoroughly
⅓ cup firmly packed brown sugar
½ teaspoon cinnamon
Sprinkle the mixture over tops.

Bake at 400°F about 25 min., or until golden brown. Serve muffins hot with **butter or margarine** and **cream cheese**.   *1 doz. muffins*

JAM-FILLED OATMEAL MUFFINS

Set out and grease 12 medium-size muffin-pan wells.

Combine in a large bowl
2 cups biscuit mix
2 tablespoons sugar
⅔ cup quick-cooking rolled oats
Add a blend of
1 egg, slightly beaten
⅔ cup milk or water
Beat vigorously for 30 seconds.

Drop the batter by heaping tablespoonfuls into muffin-pan wells. Spoon onto batter
½ teaspoon grape or plum jam (or jelly)
Top with heaping tablespoons of batter.

Bake at 400°F about 15 min., or until muffins are done. Serve hot.   *1 doz. muffins*

ITALIAN SAUSAGE BISCUIT SQUARES

Topped with a creamy mushroom or cheese sauce, these biscuit squares make a delightful luncheon entrée.

Set out and grease a 9x9x2-in. baking pan.

Prepare
2 Hard-Cooked Eggs (page 133), chopped
⅓ to ½ cup finely chopped onion
½ cup cubed (1 in.) pepperoni

Combine ingredients in a large bowl and add
2 cups biscuit mix
½ teaspoon crushed oregano
¼ teaspoon marjoram
⅛ teaspoon seasoned pepper
⅔ cup milk
Mix only until dry ingredients are moistened. Pat dough evenly in prepared pan. Spread or brush top with
Soft butter or margarine

Bake at 450°F about 20 min., or until lightly browned. Remove from oven and cut into 12 medium or 9 large biscuit squares. Serve warm.
9 to 12 servings

PEEK-A-BOO MUFFINS

Set out and grease 12 medium-size muffin-pan wells.

Combine in a large bowl
1½ cups buttermilk pancake mix
¼ cup sugar
Add to dry ingredients a blend of
1 egg, beaten
1 cup milk
2 tablespoons shortening, melted
Mix only until dry ingredients are moistened.

Turn batter into muffin-pan wells filling each one-third full. Spoon onto batter in each well
1 teaspoon raspberry (or other fruit) preserves
Spoon remaining batter over preserves.

Bake at 425°F about 15 min.   *1 doz. muffins*

HONEY NUT COFFEE CAKE

Prepare, following package directions
1 pkg. (10½ oz.) coffee cake mix
Turn batter into the pan included in the package.

For topping, mix well in a bowl the prepared cinnamon topping and
2 tablespoons finely chopped nuts
Sprinkle mixture over batter.

Bake at 375°F about 25 min. Remove from oven and open the corner folds of aluminum pan. Drizzle over top of warm coffee cake a blend of
1 tablespoon butter or margarine, melted
2 tablespoons honey
Serve warm.   *8 servings*

ORANGE RAISIN COFFEE CAKE

Set out, grease and dust lightly with flour two 8x8x2-in. baking pans.

Prepare and set aside
1 tablespoon grated orange peel

Empty into a bowl contents of
1 pkg. (18½ oz.) yellow cake mix
For topping, measure ⅔ cup of the dry mix

into a small bowl. Add, cutting in with a pastry blender or 2 knives

¼ cup butter

Mix in

1 cup firmly packed brown sugar
½ cup finely chopped nuts

Set topping aside.

Combine in a large bowl

3 eggs, slightly beaten
1½ cups dairy sour cream

Blend in the reserved cake mix (dry), the orange peel and

½ cup seedless raisins

Mix only until dry ingredients are moistened. (Batter will be thick and slightly lumpy.) Turn one half the batter into the prepared pans, spreading batter to corners. Sprinkle with one half of the topping mixture. Spoon equal amounts of the remaining batter evenly over the topping in both pans. Cover with remaining topping mixture.

Bake at 350°F about 45 min., or until coffee cake tests done.   *Two 8-in. coffee cakes*

BUTTER CREATIONS

Butter is usually served in small square pats, cut from a quarter-pound print. But for that extra-special touch on a very special occasion, butter may be served in several attractive ways.

WHIPPED BUTTER

Whip firm **butter,** cut in pieces, using an electric mixer at high speed just until fluffy and of spreading consistency. Whipped butter is excellent for finger sandwiches.

BUTTER PADDLING

Butter paddles are necessary for some of these forms. Scald new butter paddles in boiling water. Each time before using, chill paddles in ice and water about 1 hr. The butter should be firm, but not hard. Before paddling it, chill it in the ice and water with the paddles. While paddling butter, frequently dip paddles into the ice and water long enough to allow them to chill so that butter will not stick. Allow paddled butter to drop back into ice and water while chilling paddles.

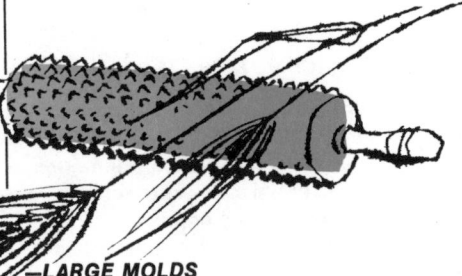

—LARGE MOLDS

Large butter forms are attractive when extra butter is passed at a festive breakfast, brunch, luncheon or dinner.

Butter Roses—Prepare butter balls of uniform size using smooth sides of paddles (see Butter Balls, below). Put into ice and water a few minutes. To form patties for rose petals, place the butter balls, one at a time, on the smooth side of a butter paddle and slap with the smooth side of the other paddle until patties are about ⅛ in. thick. Carefully remove each patty and chill in ice and water with the paddles. Mold one patty to form center of rose, with the bottom closed and slightly flaring at the top. Arrange seven or eight patties around center, overlapping them well at bottom and opening wide at the top. Work quickly so butter will not soften. Put into a bowl of ice and water in refrigerator. When ready to serve, place on a bed of crushed ice and garnish with real rose leaves.

Orange Butter Ball—This is especially attractive and flavorful for breakfast or brunch with waffles, griddlecakes, French toast or muffins. For orange butter, cream **¼ lb. butter** until softened. Blend in **2 tablespoons orange juice** and **1 teaspoon grated orange peel.** Scrape butter together and drop into a bowl of ice and water until firm enough to paddle. Shape into rough balls with paddles. Place on grooved side of one butter paddle. Using the grooved side of the other paddle, work paddles lightly in a rolling motion until a ball is formed. Drop into ice and water. When ready to serve, place ball on absorbent paper. Roll ball in **grated orange peel.** Serve on a bed of crushed ice or on a galax leaf on a chilled serving plate.

Butter Molds—Large butter molds are also attractive on any table. Scald new butter molds in boiling water. Each time before using, chill mold in ice and water about 1 hr. Pull plunger up; force butter (firm but not hard) into mold. Invert the mold and firmly press plunger down. This imprints the design on the butter and forces the butter out of the mold. Chill mold in ice and water before repeating. Butter molds are also available for individual servings.

—INDIVIDUAL MOLDS

Individual molds are an attractive way of serving butter.

Butter Balls—Measure butter by tablespoonfuls (for uniformity) and drop into ice and water. For each ball, place a portion of butter on the grooved side of one paddle. Using the second paddle, grooved side down, work paddles lightly in a rolling motion until a ball is formed. Drop into ice and water. Later pile balls into a serving dish and refrigerate until ready to serve.

Orange Butter Balls—Prepare orange butter (see Orange Butter Ball, above). Proceed as in Butter Balls.

Rosette Butter Pats—Cut butter pats from a quarter-pound print of butter. Place in ice and water to chill. Draw the tip of a teaspoon lengthwise across a quarter-pound print of butter. Divide the butter strip in half and shape each half into a small curl. Put into ice and water to chill. When ready to serve, place three curls on each pat of butter to form a rosette. Garnish with bits of **parsley.**

Butter Curls—Lightly draw a special butter curler (available at most department stores) across a quarter-pound print of butter. Drop each curl into ice and water to chill. Allow several curls for each serving.

Sandwiches

Legend has it that when the Romans conquered England they introduced to the early Britons a food called an offula which resembles today's sandwich. After the Romans left England, the offula was forgotten until the eighteenth century when the Earl of Sandwich, while seated at the gaming table and reluctant to stop even to eat, called for slices of bread with sliced beef between them. Eating this sandwich improvisation with one hand, he continued his gaming. That invention has since undergone many changes until today the sandwich covers a variety of foods used for different occasions . . . everything from the teatime dainties and luncheon creations which vary in sizes, shapes and fillings, to the hearty main-dish sandwiches (hot or cold) which are meals in themselves. Then there's the lunch-box sandwich . . . a real challenge to the busy homemaker who wants to make interestingly different ones each day to avoid monotony and to stimulate appetites.

SANDWICH SPREADS

FRESH HERB BUTTER

▲ *Base Recipe*

Put into a bowl and cream until softened
½ cup butter or margarine
1 teaspoon lemon or lime juice
Thoroughly mix in
1 tablespoon fresh minced herb,
such as chives, dill, parsley, mint
Store in tightly covered container in refrigerator. Cream again or allow to stand at room temperature before using.   *½ cup butter*

—PERKY BUTTERS

Follow ▲ Recipe. Omit fresh herbs. Blend in one of the following: **1 tablespoon anchovy paste** and **¼ teaspoon paprika**; **2 tablespoons grated Parmesan** or crumbled **blue** or **Roquefort cheese**; **1 tablespoon drained chopped capers**; **2 tablespoons chili sauce** and **¼ teaspoon onion** or **garlic salt**; **2 tablespoons prepared horseradish**; **1 tablespoon prepared mustard**; **2 tablespoons minced**

olives; **2 tablespoons minced onion**; **2 tablespoons minced pimiento** and **1 teaspoon well-drained pickle relish**; **¼ cup minced watercress**; **2 tablespoons ground nuts.**

—HERB OR SPICE BUTTERS (DRY)

Follow ▲ Recipe. Omit fresh herbs. Add **½ teaspoon finely crushed dry or ground herbs** or spices such as **caraway seed, cinnamon, dill seed, garlic powder** or **garlic salt, onion powder** or **onion salt,** or **paprika,** or use **¼ teaspoon curry powder, dry mustard, nutmeg, thyme** or **savory.**

—SWEET BUTTERS

Follow ▲ Recipe. Omit fresh herbs. Blend in one or a combination of following: **½ cup honey**; **1 teaspoon grated lemon peel**; **1 tablespoon orange juice** and **½ teaspoon grated orange peel.**

WATERCRESS BUTTER

Rinse, drain well, chop and set aside
½ bunch watercress

Beat in a small bowl until softened
½ cup butter or margarine
Add and mix thoroughly
1 teaspoon lemon juice
⅛ teaspoon salt
Add watercress; beat until watercress is thoroughly blended into butter. *About 1 cup butter*

CHEESE BUTTER

This is a basic cheese butter which can be used with many adaptations.

Cut into pieces and set aside
½ lb. sharp Cheddar or Swiss cheese

Put into an electric blender container
1 cup butter, cut in pieces
½ cup cream
½ teaspoon salt
⅛ teaspoon pepper
Cover and turn on motor.

Gradually add cheese pieces and blend until smooth.   *About 3 cups*

To vary—Add any one of the following: **Worcestershire sauce; mustard; chives; red or green peppers; bologna** or **ready-to-serve meat** and **prepared mustard; crushed pineapple; cubed ham** and **pickle; pimiento; pecans** or **black walnuts;** or **crumbled crisp bacon.**

BLENDER PEANUT BUTTER

▲ *Base Recipe*

Put into blender container about two thirds of
1½ cups (6 to 8 oz.) salted peanuts
(with or without skins—or a combination of both types. Unsalted peanuts may be used; if so, add about ¼ teaspoon salt with last addition of peanuts.)
Cover, turn on motor and blend nuts to a paste. Add remaining peanuts and blend to desired fineness—coarse for chunk-style and very fine for creamy peanut butter. Store in tightly covered jar. *About ¾ cup peanut butter*

Sweet Butter on Easy Banana Bread (page 87)

—CASHEW BUTTER

Follow ▲ Recipe. Substitute **cashew nuts** for salted peanuts.

COLD SANDWICHES

CIRCUS-DAY SANDWICHES

For each sandwich, spread (one side only)
> **2 slices bread**

with about
> **2 teaspoons softened butter or margarine**

Cover 1 slice with
> **1 large crisp lettuce leaf**
> **1 or 2 thin slices tomato**
> **Few grains salt**
> **2 slices crisp bacon**

Spread other slice of bread with
> **2 teaspoons salad dressing or mayonnaise**

Put the slices of bread together. Cut sandwich into 4 triangles.   *1 sandwich*

Note: If desired, the bread may be toasted before spreading with butter or margarine.

TRIPLE DECKER SANDWICHES

Set out
> **12 bread slices**

Spread four slices with
> **Prepared mustard**

Top with thin slices of
> **Swiss or Cheddar cheese**

Spread remaining bread slices with one of the
> **Butters (page 114)**

Top four of the buttered bread slices with thin slices of
> **Cooked ham, tongue, ready-to-eat sausage or canned luncheon meat**

Place on cheese and top with remaining four buttered bread slices.   *4 sandwiches*

SERVE-YOURSELF ONION AND TOMATO-TOPPED SARDINE SANDWICHES

Arrange slices of **sweet Spanish onion** and ripe **tomato** alternately on a bed of **crisp salad greens**. Chill.

Prepare Sardine Butter—Using **2 cans skinless, boneless sardines** (packed in oil), drain off oil and mash sardines with a fork. Blend **½ cup softened butter or margarine** with **2 tablespoons lemon juice, 1 tablespoon prepared mustard** and **¼ to ½ teaspoon white pepper**. Mix thoroughly and turn into a small serving dish. Chill.

At serving time, set out the chilled fresh vegetables and Sardine Butter along with slices of **rye and whole wheat bread**.

To make an open-face sandwich, spread a slice of bread generously with Sardine Butter, then top with onion and tomato slices. Sprinkle vegetables with **lemon pepper marinade** or **seasoned salt**.

LOBSTER LIMELIGHTER

Combine in a bowl and set aside to marinate 1 hr.
> **2 cups cooked lobster, cut in ½-in. chunks**
> **Juice of 1 lime**

Drain lobster and add a mixture of
> **1 cup dairy sour cream**
> **¼ cup mayonnaise or salad dressing**
> **2 tablespoons chopped onion**

Toss together gently and fold in
> **1 cup diced ripe avocado**

Split
> **6 round hard rolls (or sandwich buns)**

Spread halves with
> **Mayonnaise or salad dressing**

Heap the lobster mixture on bottom half of each roll and put top half in place. Garnish or serve with **radish roses, ripe olives** or **carrot sticks**.   *6 sandwiches*

"THE VIRGINIAN" SANDWICH

Have ready
> **8 to 12 slices pumpernickel bread**
> **8 to 12 slices cooked ham (about 8 oz.)**
> **Bibb lettuce**

Combine in a bowl, mixing thoroughly
> **1 jar (5 oz.) pasteurized process cheese spread with pineapple**
> **¼ cup chopped peanuts**

Spread cheese mixture evenly over half of the bread slices. Top with ham, lettuce and remaining bread slices (one side spread with soft butter, if desired).   *4 to 6 sandwiches*

Note: For a luncheon duo, team up "The Virginian" Sandwich with the New Orleans Bowl (page 42).

CHEESE 'N' BACON SANDWICH

Spread **bread slices** with one of the **Sandwich Spreads** (page 114). Place a slice of any desired **cheese** on half of buttered bread slices; top each with **2 slices crisp bacon** and remaining bread slices.

Lobster Limelighter

"THE MIDWESTERNER" SANDWICH

Have ready
> **8 slices rye bread, toasted**
> **Crisp lettuce**
> **Cucumber slices**
> **Radish slices**

Combine in a bowl, mixing well
> **1 pkg. (8 oz.) liverwurst**
> **2 tablespoons ketchup**
> **½ teaspoon dill weed**

Spread 4 slices of the rye toast with
> **¼ cup prepared onion dip**

Top with lettuce, liverwurst mixture and sliced cucumber and radish. Cover with remaining rye toast.   *4 sandwiches*

Note: If open-face sandwiches are desired, use 4 slices of rye toast. Halve the cucumber slices and arrange with radish slices around a mound of liverwurst mixture on each slice of toast. Garnish with parsley sprigs.

SLICED CHICKEN SANDWICH

Spread a mixture of **¼ cup butter or margarine** and **¼ teaspoon Worcestershire sauce** on bread slices. Then spread with **¼ cup cranberry jelly**. Arrange **sliced chicken** on half of buttered bread. Top with remaining slices.

115

Picture Puzzle Sandwiches

PICTURE PUZZLE SANDWICHES

Blend and set aside
   1 pkg. (3 oz.) cream cheese
   2 tablespoons milk or cream

Place on a flat working surface
   8 slices white bread
   8 slices whole wheat bread
With a sharp knife or cutter, cut 3- to 4-in. shapes such as scalloped rounds, squares, diamonds or triangles from the bread. With a fancy cutter or sharp knife cut smaller shapes such as rounds, squares, diamonds, triangles, stars or crescents from the centers of 4 of the whole wheat shapes. Cut identical shapes from the centers of 4 of the white bread shapes. Fit whole wheat cutouts into holes in white shapes, and white cutouts into whole wheat shapes. Spread remaining white and whole wheat shapes (one side only) with
   2 tablespoons butter or margarine
Spread cream cheese mixture evenly over buttered shapes. Over cheese, spread
   ¼ cup jelly
Carefully spread "puzzle pieces" with
   2 tablespoons butter or margarine
Fit "puzzle pieces" over shapes spread with filling. *8 sandwiches*

SHRIMP SALAD IN BUNS

For Shrimp Salad—Prepare
   Cooked Shrimp (page 294)
Reserve 12 whole cooked shrimp for garnish. Chill in refrigerator.

Shrimp Salad in Buns

Coarsely chop remaining shrimp and put into a bowl. Add to the bowl
   ½ cup shredded lettuce
   ¼ cup chopped celery
   2 tablespoons chopped watercress
Blend in lightly a mixture of
   3 tablespoons mayonnaise
   1 tablespoon lemon juice
   2 teaspoons minced onion
   ¼ teaspoon Worcestershire sauce
   ¼ teaspoon salt
Chill thoroughly in refrigerator.

To Assemble Sandwiches — Split almost through
   4 long sandwich buns
Spread with
   Butter or margarine, softened
Fill buns with shrimp salad. Garnish with reserved whole shrimp. *4 servings*

LUNCH-BOX SANDWICHES

As sandwiches often are the mainstay of the carried lunch, make them nutritious, varied and appetizing. Be certain that they serve their purpose as a planned course of a complete meal.

Preparing many sandwich ingredients in advance can be a great aid. Foods that can be prepared, carefully wrapped and stored include: hard-cooked eggs, unpeeled; shredded cheese; chopped or ground nuts; drained or cleaned, canned, dried or fresh fruits and vegetables. Labeling the containers in which these foods are stored is another timesaver. Wrap thin slices of meat, poultry and cheese in waxed paper, plastic wrap or bags, or aluminum foil for storage in refrigerator.

To Prepare Fillings—Assemble all ingredients and blend filling mixtures lightly but thoroughly. Fillings that are too moist do not travel well. Immediately place fillings in shallow container with a cover (or wrap) and return to the refrigerator or freezer until used.

Special Care—Some fillings, such as meat, fish, poultry, eggs, soft cheeses and mayonnaise require special care to prevent growth of food poisoning bacteria. The addition to sandwich fillings of an acid ingredient such as pickles, lemon juice or green olives helps to retain their keeping qualities. It's safest to eat these sandwiches within four hours after removal from refrigerator or freezer. When you use meat leftovers for fillings, subtract the time they have been at room temperature from the safe keeping time—four hours for prepared sandwiches.

Sandwiches made with jelly, peanut butter, hard or semihard cheese and raw vegetables usually are safe for summertime packed lunches when the heat might damage more perishable fillings.

To Assemble—Prepare sandwiches systematically. Line up slices of bread in pairs and spread all of lined-up bread slices with butter or margarine at one time. Use about 1 teaspoon softened (not melted) butter or margarine per

slice; spread to edges of bread with a flexible spatula. (Spreading slices with butter or margarine helps to prevent filling from soaking into bread.) Spread filling to edges of one slice of each pair of lined-up buttered bread slices. Spread all of one kind of filling before going on to the next.

Complete sandwiches and cut into halves, quarters, wedges or other interesting shapes and sizes. For small fry, remember to slice sandwiches into easy-to-handle sections. (They like fancy shapes, too.)

To Wrap—Wrap a whole sandwich or section neatly, securely and separately in waxed paper, plastic wrap or bags or aluminum foil. Never wrap or cover sandwiches with a damp cloth, because it will encourage the growth of some bacteria.

To Refrigerate—Store wrapped sandwiches in refrigerator until the last minute. Sandwiches will keep successfully in the refrigerator at 50°F or below up to 12 hours.

To Freeze—Sandwiches may also be kept in the freezer for two or three weeks. To prepare sandwiches for freezing, wrap in moisture-vaporproof material, seal and label with description and date.

Sandwich fillings that freeze best include sliced or chopped meat or poultry, fish, American Cheddar or cream cheese or peanut butter. Some foods such as lettuce, watercress, cucumbers, radishes, tomatoes, apples and grapes should not be frozen and can be inserted when the sandwich is eaten. Mayonnaise, honey or jelly can also be added at lunchtime since these spreads soak into bread during freezing. Egg salad and sliced egg whites should not be frozen since hard-cooked egg whites toughen. Some nuts may become bitter and discolored.

Put sandwiches into the carried lunch directly from the freezer. They will be thawed by lunchtime (3 to 3½ hours). Do not remove wrapper until ready to eat.

CHEESE FILLINGS

To prepare fillings, shred cheese or set out sliced cheese or cheese spread. Blend remaining ingredients into shredded cheese or cheese spread, or follow directions for sliced cheese fillings. *Enough filling for 4 sandwiches*

DRESSED-UP CHEDDAR CHEESE

▲ *Base Recipe*

¾ cup (3 oz.) shredded Cheddar cheese
3 Hard-Cooked Eggs (page 133), finely chopped
3 to 4 tablespoons salad dressing or mayonnaise
2 tablespoons chopped sweet pickle
1 tablespoon chopped pimiento
1 teaspoon prepared mustard
¼ teaspoon onion salt

—CORNED BEEF AND CHEESE

Follow ▲ Recipe. Substitute ½ **cup finely chopped cooked corned beef** for eggs and **3 tablespoons chili sauce** for salad dressing.

HAM CHEESE

A tempting combination to satisfy husky lunchtime appetites.

Spread one half of bread slices with a mixture of

2 to 3 tablespoons salad dressing or mayonnaise
2 teaspoons prepared mustard
1 teaspoon prepared horseradish

Top each slice with

1 slice cooked ham or bologna
1 slice Swiss cheese

SMOKED CHEESE

½ cup smoked cheese spread
½ cup (about 2 oz.) chopped nuts (walnuts, peanuts, or pecans)
⅓ cup mayonnaise
1 teaspoon Worcestershire sauce

OLIVE CHEESE

▲ *Base Recipe*

1 cup (4 oz.) shredded Cheddar cheese
½ cup chopped pimiento-stuffed olives
2 tablespoons chopped ripe olives
2 tablespoons salad dressing or mayonnaise

—PICKLE CHEESE

Follow ▲ Recipe. Substitute ¼ **cup chopped sweet pickle** for stuffed olives. Omit ripe olives. Blend in **2 tablespoons minced onion**.

ORANGE CHEESE SPREAD

½ cup (2 oz.) shredded Swiss cheese
½ cup orange marmalade
2 tablespoons cream

CREAM CHEESE FILLINGS

To prepare fillings, mash cheese with a fork. Gradually blend in **French Dressing** (page 410), milk, or other liquid suggested in recipe. (In recipes where there is no liquid, cream cheese may be softened at room temperature.) Blend in remaining ingredients.

Enough filling for 4 sandwiches

SPECIAL CHEESE

Put into an electric blender container
¼ lb. blue cheese, crumbled
1 pkg. (3 oz.) cream cheese, cut in pieces
2 tablespoons pineapple juice
2 teaspoons Worcestershire sauce
½ teaspoon monosodium glutamate
1 drop Tabasco
4 or 5 sprigs parsley
1 slice onion

Cover and blend until smooth.

BOSTON BROWN BREAD SPECIAL

1 pkg. (3 oz.) cream cheese
1 tablespoon milk
1 tablespoon grated lemon peel
1 tablespoon lemon juice
¼ teaspoon salt
¼ teaspoon cinnamon

Spread on
Boston Brown Bread (page 89)

CRANBERRY CREAM CHEESE

1 pkg. (3 oz.) cream cheese
¾ cup (about 3 oz.) uncooked cranberries, washed, sorted and chopped
3 tablespoons honey
¼ cup (about 1 oz.) chopped walnuts or pecans
½ teaspoon grated orange peel
2 teaspoons orange juice
Few grains salt

FRUITY

▲ *Base Recipe*

1 pkg. (3 oz.) cream cheese
¼ cup (about 1 oz.) chopped raisins
2 tablespoons peach butter, preserves, or orange marmalade

—PEANUT

Follow ▲ Recipe. Substitute ⅓ **cup peanut butter** for chopped raisins.

DRIED BEEF CREAM CHEESE

1 pkg. (3 oz.) pimiento cream cheese
⅓ cup (about 1 oz.) chopped dried beef
1 tablespoon prepared horseradish
Few drops Worcestershire sauce

LADIES' DAY SPECIAL

1 pkg. (3 oz.) cream cheese
½ cup chopped drained fresh fruit (strawberries, cherries, pineapple, or raspberries)
1 tablespoon confectioners' sugar
½ teaspoon salt
¼ teaspoon lemon juice

IDEAL CHEESE

1 pkg. (3 oz.) cream cheese
¼ cup chopped pimiento-stuffed olives
3 tablespoons crumbled blue or Roquefort cheese
1 to 2 tablespoons French Dressing (page 410)
¼ teaspoon salt

OLIVE PECAN

1 pkg. (3 oz.) cream cheese
⅓ cup chopped green olives
¼ cup (about 1 oz.) salted pecans, finely chopped
1 to 2 tablespoons milk or cream
1 or 2 drops Tabasco
Few grains salt

Date Cottage Cheese, Meat 'n' Cheese, Special Meat, Boston Brown Bread Special and Tuna Salad Fillings

PICKLE OLIVE

1 pkg. (3 oz.) cream cheese
3 tablespoons chopped pimiento-
  stuffed olives
3 sweet pickles, chopped
2 teaspoons finely minced onion
1 to 2 tablespoons pickle juice

PINEAPPLE CREAM CHEESE

1 pkg. (3 oz.) cream cheese
½ cup well-drained crushed pineapple
3 slices crisp bacon, crumbled
1 tablespoon pineapple juice

SUPERMAN'S DELIGHT

1 pkg. (3 oz.) cream cheese
½ cup minced fresh spinach
½ cup (about 2 oz.) salted peanuts
  (skins removed), finely chopped
2 tablespoons milk or cream
½ teaspoon lemon juice

WATERCRESS CREAM CHEESE

1 pkg. (3 oz.) cream cheese
¼ cup finely chopped watercress
3 tablespoons chopped ripe olives
1 tablespoon French Dressing
  (page 410)
¼ teaspoon salt

COTTAGE CHEESE FILLINGS

To prepare fillings, combine cream-style cottage cheese and mayonnaise or salad dressing, blending thoroughly. Mix in remaining ingredients.   *Enough filling for 4 sandwiches*

BACON COTTAGE CHEESE

1 cup (8 oz.) cottage cheese
1 to 3 teaspoons mayonnaise
3 or 4 slices crisp bacon, crumbled
2 tablespoons chopped sweet pickle
½ teaspoon grated onion
Few grains paprika

HAM 'N' CHEESE SUPREME

▲ *Base Recipe*

¾ cup (6 oz.) cottage cheese
⅓ cup (about 3 oz.) deviled ham
¼ cup (about 1 oz.) salted peanuts
  (skins removed), chopped
2 tablespoons salad dressing or
  mayonnaise
1 tablespoon prepared horseradish
1 teaspoon chopped chives

—FRUIT 'N' CHEESE SUPREME

Follow ▲ Recipe. Omit deviled ham, horse-

radish, and chives. Mix in **3 tablespoons fruit preserves.**

DATE COTTAGE CHEESE

1 cup (8 oz.) cottage cheese
¼ cup pitted dates, cut (page 9)
1 tablespoon salad dressing or
  mayonnaise
Few grains salt
Few grains pepper

COTTAGE CHEESE AND RELISH

1 cup (8 oz.) cottage cheese
3 slices crisp bacon, crumbled
2 tablespoons well-drained pickle
  relish
1 tablespoon mayonnaise
½ teaspoon grated onion
Few grains paprika

VEGETABLE COTTAGE CHEESE

1 cup (8 oz.) cottage cheese
¼ cup grated carrot
1 tablespoon mayonnaise
1 teaspoon finely chopped green
  pepper
½ teaspoon chopped pimiento
¼ teaspoon onion salt
Few grains pepper

PEANUT BUTTER FILLINGS

To prepare fillings, blend peanut butter thoroughly with salad dressing, mayonnaise, or liquid specified in recipe. Mix in remaining ingredients.   *Enough filling for 4 sandwiches*

HEARTY PEANUT BUTTER

½ cup (4 oz.) peanut butter
⅓ cup (about 3 oz.) deviled ham
¼ cup finely chopped green pepper
2 tablespoons salad dressing or
  mayonnaise
1 teaspoon minced onion

CITRUS SPECIAL

½ cup (4 oz.) peanut butter
1 teaspoon grated orange peel
¼ cup orange juice
⅓ cup flaked coconut

ROYAL PEANUT BUTTER

▲ *Base Recipe*

¾ cup (6 oz.) peanut butter
⅓ cup (about 1 small) finely chopped
  unpared apple
3 slices crisp bacon, finely crumbled
3 tablespoons cream

—ROYAL PINEAPPLE

Follow ▲ Recipe. Substitute ½ **cup well-drained crushed pineapple** for apple.

—ROYAL OLIVE

Follow ▲ Recipe. Substitute ⅓ **cup chopped olives** for apple.

BANANA PEANUT BUTTER

Spread one half of bread slices with
  ½ cup (4 oz.) peanut butter
Top with slices from
  2 medium bananas with brown-flecked
    peel
Top with buttered bread slices.

SPECIAL PEANUT BUTTER MIX

½ cup (4 oz.) peanut butter
¼ cup grated carrot
2 tablespoons chopped raisins
2 tablespoons salad dressing or
  mayonnaise

MEAT FILLINGS

To prepare fillings with chopped meat and egg or pickle, grind these ingredients in a food chopper. Mix in other ingredients.
     Enough filling for 4 sandwiches

MEAT

Cut into pieces enough to make 1 cup
  **Cooked meat such as beef, pork or
    veal**

Put into an electric blender container in order
    ¼ cup mayonnaise or chili sauce
    1 teaspoon prepared horseradish
    ½ teaspoon salt
    1 slice onion
Add meat; cover and blend until well mixed and meat is finely chopped.

HAM

Cut into pieces enough to make 1½ cups
    Cooked ham

Put into an electric blender container
    ½ cup butter or margarine, cut in pieces
    1 tablespoon prepared mustard
    1 slice onion
Cover and turn on motor. Add ham by pieces and blend until meat is finely chopped.

Serve on **toasted bread.**

HAM RELISH

    ¾ cup minced cooked ham
    ¼ cup pickle relish
    ¼ cup diced celery
    2 to 3 tablespoons mayonnaise
    1 tablespoon minced onion

HUNGRY MAN'S CHOICE

    1 cup (about 8 oz.) minced cooked ham (chopped canned luncheon meat or minced roast beef may be used)
    ¼ cup chopped garlic dill pickle
    2 to 3 tablespoons salad dressing or mayonnaise

DEVILED HAM

    ⅔ cup (about 6 oz.) deviled ham
    2 tablespoons chopped onion
    1 tablespoon mayonnaise
Top with slices of **hard-cooked egg.**

MEAT 'N' CHEESE

Combine and spread on one half of bread slices a mixture of
    ½ cup chive cheese spread
    2 teaspoons prepared mustard
Top with
    Thin slices salami, dried beef, or ham
Cover with remaining bread slices.

SALAMI KIDNEY BEAN

    ½ cup (about 4 oz.) salami, finely chopped
    ½ cup drained canned kidney beans, chopped
    2 to 3 tablespoons chili sauce
    1 teaspoon minced onion
    1 teaspoon prepared mustard

BOLOGNA

    ¾ cup (about 6 oz.) ground bologna (casing removed)
    1 Hard-Cooked Egg (page 133), finely chopped
    2 to 3 tablespoons chili sauce
    2 tablespoons salad dressing or mayonnaise
    1 teaspoon prepared horseradish
    ¼ teaspoon salt
    Few grains pepper

SALAMI

    ¾ cup (about 6 oz.) finely cut salami
    ⅓ cup salad dressing or mayonnaise
    2 tablespoons chopped sweet pickle
    2 tablespoons finely chopped celery
    ½ teaspoon prepared mustard
    ¼ teaspoon onion salt

LAMB SPECIAL

    ▲ Base Recipe

    2 to 3 tablespoons mint, currant, or cranberry jelly (spread on 4 slices buttered bread)
    Thin slices roast lamb

—PORK SPECIAL

Follow ▲ Recipe. Substitute **apple butter** or **applesauce** for jelly and **roast pork** for lamb.

CORNED BEEF

    ▲ Base Recipe
Spread one half of bread slices with
    Butter or margarine
Top with
    Thin slices cooked corned beef
Spread other half of bread slices with
    2 teaspoons prepared mustard
Cover with remaining bread slices.

—TANGY CORNED BEEF

Follow ▲ Recipe. Omit mustard. Substitute a mixture of **2 tablespoons chopped onion, 2 tablespoons chopped dill pickle, 2 tablespoons salad dressing or mayonnaise, and 3 or 4 drops Tabasco.**

—LIVER SAUSAGE SANDWICH

Follow ▲ Recipe. Substitute thin slices of **liver sausage** for corned beef.

Deviled Ham and Salami Fillings

SPECIAL MEAT

    Slices of thuringer sausage
    ⅓ cup drained chutney (or use pickle relish and chopped nuts)

CRISP LIVER

    ▲ Base Recipe

    ¾ cup (about 6 oz.) chopped cooked liver
    4 slices crisp bacon, crumbled
    3 tablespoons salad dressing or mayonnaise
    2 teaspoons minced onion
    1 teaspoon prepared mustard
    ½ teaspoon salt

—EGG AND LIVER

Follow ▲ Recipe. Mix in **1 Hard-Cooked Egg** (page 133), finely chopped.

—PIMIENTO LIVER

Follow ▲ Recipe. Mix in **¼ cup chopped pimiento-stuffed olives.**

Salami Kidney Bean Filling

Braunschweiger Filling: Spread to the edges of bread. Cut sandwich to desired size; wrap in waxed paper.

BRAUNSCHWEIGER

▲ *Base Recipe*

4 oz. (about ½ cup) Braunschweiger (smoked liver sausage)
¼ cup drained pickle relish
2 to 3 tablespoons salad dressing or mayonnaise

—LIVER CHEESE

Follow ▲ Recipe. Mix in **1 to 2 tablespoons minced onion** and **1 pkg. (3 oz.) cream cheese.** *Enough filling for 6 sandwiches*

CHICKEN OR TURKEY FILLINGS

To prepare fillings, chop cooked chicken or turkey. Moisten with mayonnaise, salad dressing, or dairy sour cream. Mix in remaining ingredients.
Enough filling for 4 sandwiches

SPECIAL CHICKEN

▲ *Base Recipe*

1 cup minced cooked chicken
¼ cup finely chopped celery
4 to 6 pitted ripe olives, chopped
2 teaspoons minced parsley
3 tablespoons dairy sour cream
¼ teaspoon salt
Few grains pepper

—SPECIAL CHICKEN PICKLE

Follow ▲ Recipe. Substitute **2 tablespoons chopped sweet pickle** for the olives.

HAWAIIAN CHICKEN

▲ *Base Recipe*

1 cup minced cooked chicken
⅓ cup flaked coconut
¼ cup salad dressing or mayonnaise
2 tablespoons finely chopped celery
½ teaspoon lemon juice
½ teaspoon salt

—CUCUMBER CHICKEN

Follow ▲ Recipe. Omit coconut; add **⅓ cup chopped cucumber** and **3 or 4 pitted ripe olives,** chopped.

CHICKEN MUSHROOM

1 cup minced cooked chicken
½ cup (4-oz. can, drained) mushrooms, chopped
¼ cup (about 1½ oz.) toasted salted almonds, chopped
3 tablespoons salad dressing or mayonnaise
2 tablespoons chopped green olives
¼ teaspoon salt
Few grains paprika

PINEAPPLE CHICKEN

▲ *Base Recipe*

1 cup chopped cooked chicken
½ cup well-drained crushed pineapple
3 tablespoons salad dressing or mayonnaise
3 tablespoons finely chopped celery
½ teaspoon salt

—FRUIT CHICKEN

Follow ▲ Recipe. Substitute for pineapple ½

cup finely chopped unpared apple or seedless grapes, cut in halves.

HEARTY

¾ cup minced cooked chicken giblets
3 slices crisp bacon, crumbled
2 Hard-Cooked Eggs (page 133), finely chopped
¼ cup salad dressing or mayonnaise
1 teaspoon prepared mustard
¼ teaspoon salt

HARD-COOKED EGG FILLINGS

To prepare filling, prepare **Hard-Cooked Eggs** (page 133). Moisten with mayonnaise, salad dressing, or cream. Blend in remaining ingredients, mixing lightly but thoroughly.
Enough filling for 4 sandwiches

BASIC EGG SALAD

▲ *Base Recipe*

4 hard-cooked eggs, finely chopped
3 tablespoons chopped sweet pickle
3 tablespoons salad dressing or mayonnaise
½ teaspoon prepared mustard
¼ teaspoon onion salt
Few grains pepper

—EGG FILLING VARIATIONS

Follow ▲ Recipe. Blend in one of the following: **2 tablespoons finely chopped watercress; 2 tablespoons chopped green pepper; 1 frankfurter,** finely chopped; **2 tablespoons chopped green or ripe olives; ¼ cup finely chopped celery; 1 tablespoon chopped pimiento,** drained; **1 tablespoon chopped chives; 1 tablespoon prepared horseradish.**

EGG AND CHEESE

3 hard-cooked eggs, chopped
½ cup (2 oz.) shredded Swiss cheese
⅓ cup mayonnaise
¼ cup chopped dill pickle
1 tablespoon chili sauce
½ teaspoon salt

Pineapple Chicken Filling

BACON 'N' EGG

4 hard-cooked eggs, chopped
4 slices crisp bacon, crumbled
3 or 4 tablespoons mayonnaise
¼ teaspoon salt
Few grains pepper

Spread on buttered bread.

HAM EGG

Mix together

½ cup coarsely ground cooked ham
4 hard-cooked eggs, chopped
⅓ cup mayonnaise
Few grains paprika

Spread over buttered bread

2 to 3 teaspoons prepared mustard

Spread ham mixture over mustard.

MARINERS' EGG SALAD

4 hard-cooked eggs, finely chopped
4 sardines, drained and mashed
3 tablespoons dairy sour cream
3 tablespoons chopped mustard pickle
1 teaspoon dry mustard
1 teaspoon lemon juice
½ teaspoon salt
Few grains pepper

Best on brown or rye bread.

Enough filling for 6 sandwiches

FISH AND SHELLFISH FILLINGS

To prepare fillings, flake fish (page 9). Moisten with mayonnaise, salad dressing, or other dressing. Mix in remaining ingredients.

Enough filling for 4 sandwiches

FAVORITE FISH

▲ *Base Recipe*

¾ cup cooked fish (salmon, tuna, crab meat, or shrimp)
½ cup finely chopped cabbage
3 tablespoons chopped ripe olives
1 tablespoon olive juice
3 tablespoons salad dressing or mayonnaise
¼ teaspoon paprika
2 or 3 drops Tabasco

—FISH CHEESE

Follow ▲ Recipe. Substitute **2 tablespoons crumbled Roquefort cheese** for olives; omit

---

the olive juice; increase the salad dressing to ¼ cup.

SALMON MIX I

▲ *Base Recipe*

¾ cup flaked cooked salmon (canned or freshly cooked)
¼ cup finely chopped watercress, cucumber, or sweet pickle
3 tablespoons salad dressing or mayonnaise
2 teaspoons grated onion
1 teaspoon lemon juice
¼ teaspoon salt

—SALMON MIX II

Follow ▲ Recipe. Omit onion; for watercress substitute ⅓ **cup finely chopped celery, 1 tablespoon chopped green olives,** and **1 tablespoon chopped ripe olives.**

SARDINE DE LUXE

8 to 10 (3¼-oz. can) sardines, drained and mashed
2 Hard-Cooked Eggs (page 133), finely chopped
3 tablespoons butter or margarine, softened
1 tablespoon Garlic French Dressing (page 410)
1 tablespoon capers, drained
1 teaspoon lemon juice
¼ teaspoon salt
¼ teaspoon paprika

Spread on unbuttered bread.

TUNA SALAD

1 cup (6½- or 7-oz. can) tuna, flaked (page 9)
⅓ cup chopped celery
1 tablespoon chopped sweet pickle
1 tablespoon chopped onion
¼ cup mayonnaise
½ teaspoon salt

FISH AND EGG

¾ cup crab meat or tuna
2 Hard-Cooked Eggs (page 133), chopped
3 tablespoons salad dressing or mayonnaise
2 tablespoons chopped onion
¼ teaspoon salt
Few grains pepper

Liver Sausage and Bacon 'n' Egg Fillings

CRAB MEAT

¾ cup (6½-oz. can, drained) crab meat
½ cup finely chopped cucumber
3 tablespoons salad dressing or mayonnaise
1 tablespoon minced pimiento, drained
1 teaspoon minced chives
1 teaspoon lemon juice
¼ teaspoon salt

SHRIMP AND CREAM CHEESE

¾ cup (5-oz. can, drained) cooked shrimp, finely chopped
1 pkg. (3 oz.) pimiento cream cheese or ⅓ cup pimiento cheese spread
1 to 2 tablespoons chili sauce
1 teaspoon lemon juice
¼ teaspoon salt
2 or 3 drops Tabasco

FRUIT FILLINGS

To prepare fillings, prepare and chop fresh or dried fruits. Moisten with a mayonnaise-type salad dressing and add remaining ingredients, blending lightly but thoroughly.

Enough filling for 4 sandwiches

SPECIAL AVOCADO

▲ *Base Recipe*

1 ripe avocado, peeled and mashed
3 tablespoons minced parsley
2 slices crisp bacon, crumbled
1 tablespoon salad dressing
1 tablespoon lemon or lime juice
Few grains salt
2 or 3 drops Tabasco

—MEAT AVOCADO

Follow ▲ Recipe. Substitute ⅓ **cup finely chopped canned luncheon meat** for bacon.

WALDORF CRESS SALAD

▲ *Base Recipe*

½ cup (about 1 medium) finely
  chopped unpared apple
¼ cup chopped watercress
¼ cup finely chopped celery
¼ cup (about 1 oz.) finely chopped
  walnuts
2 to 3 tablespoons salad dressing
¼ teaspoon salt

—WALDORF HAM

Follow ▲ Recipe. Spread one half of buttered
bread slices with ⅓ **cup (about 3 oz.) deviled
ham.** Top with apple mixture and remaining
bread slices.

BANANA RAISIN

1 cup (about 5 oz.) raisins, chopped
½ cup mashed banana (about 1 small
  banana with brown-flecked peel)
½ teaspoon grated lemon peel
1 teaspoon lemon juice
¼ teaspoon salt

CRANBERRY CRUNCH

½ cup washed, sorted, and chopped
  cranberries
½ cup chopped salted almonds
⅓ cup finely diced apple
¼ cup minced celery
¼ cup sugar
3 to 4 tablespoons salad dressing
Spread on buttered whole wheat bread.

DATE CARROT

½ cup (about 3 oz.) pitted dates, cut
  (page 9)
1 medium carrot, shredded
3 tablespoons salad dressing

PRUNE RAISIN

▲ *Base Recipe*

½ cup (about 4 oz.) dried prunes,
  pitted and cut (page 9)
½ cup (about 3 oz.) raisins, chopped
¼ cup (about 1 oz.) chopped nuts
3 tablespoons salad dressing

—APRICOT RAISIN

Follow ▲ Recipe. Substitute **cooked dried apricots** for prunes; **golden raisins** for raisins.

VEGETABLE FILLINGS

To prepare fillings, prepare and chop or grate
fresh vegetables. Mix in remaining ingredients.
Enough filling for 4 sandwiches

GARDEN VARIETY

¾ cup (about 3 medium) grated carrot
½ cup finely chopped celery
2 tablespoons shredded sharp Cheddar
  cheese
2 tablespoons salad dressing or
  mayonnaise
1 tablespoon finely chopped green
  pepper
1 tablespoon chili sauce
¼ teaspoon salt
Few grains pepper

CARROT RAISIN

▲ *Base Recipe*

Wash, pare or scrape and cut into pieces
  3 medium carrots
Put into an electric blender container
  ¼ cup salad dressing or mayonnaise
  ¼ cup (about 1 oz.) raisins
Cover and turn on motor. Add carrots, piece by
piece. Blend until carrots are finely chopped.
Use as a spread on **whole wheat bread.**

—CARROT PINEAPPLE

Follow ▲ Recipe. Substitute ¼ **cup well-
drained crushed pineapple** for raisins.

SPINACH

▲ *Base Recipe*

1¼ cups finely chopped fresh spinach
2 to 3 tablespoons salad dressing or
  mayonnaise
1 tablespoon chopped pimiento
1 teaspoon lemon juice
¼ teaspoon onion salt

—SPINACH AND EGG

Follow ▲ Recipe. Decrease spinach to ¾ cup.

*Liver Sausage Sandwich, Corned Beef Filling and
Baked Bean Filling with Panfried Bacon (page 190)*

Blend in **2 Hard-Cooked Eggs** (page 133),
finely chopped.

BAKED BEAN

1 cup drained canned baked beans
  in tomato sauce
⅓ cup chopped sweet pickle
2 tablespoons chili sauce or ketchup
1 tablespoon minced onion

GARDEN FRESH

▲ *Base Recipe*

1 cup (about 4 oz.) chopped fresh
  cabbage
⅓ cup grated carrot
2 to 3 tablespoons salad dressing or
  mayonnaise
2 tablespoons chopped peanuts
¼ teaspoon celery salt

—GREEN VEGETABLE

Follow ▲ Recipe. Substitute ½ **cup chopped
watercress** or **chopped cucumber** for the carrot.

OLIVE AND ALMOND

½ cup (about 2½ oz.) finely chopped
  salted almonds
¼ cup finely chopped pimiento-stuffed
  olives
2 tablespoons mayonnaise
Spread on white bread.

CRISPY RADISH

▲ *Base Recipe*

¾ cup finely chopped celery
½ cup finely chopped radishes
3 to 4 tablespoons salad dressing or
  mayonnaise
1 tablespoon chopped chives
¼ teaspoon salt
Few grains pepper

—CUCUMBER VEGETABLE

Follow ▲ Recipe. Decrease celery to ½ cup and add ¼ cup **chopped cucumber.**

LUNCH-BOX TREATS

Fruits—Wash well, drain and dry *fresh fruit.* Wrap loosely in aluminum foil, waxed paper or moisture-vaporproof material and chill until time to carry lunch. Sweet cherries, plums, tangerines, nectarines and grapes are pleasant variations in season from the usual favorites, oranges, pears, bananas and apples.

To prepare oranges for easier lunchtime eating, mark quarter divisions in whole orange by scoring peel; starting at one end, pull back peel leaving it attached at bottom. Loosen sections of orange; replace peel and wrap.

Make your lunch carrier especially happy by tucking in black or red raspberries, strawberries with hulls, blueberries or blackberries. Include a small packet of granulated or confectioners' sugar.

Frozen fruit, such as berries, peaches and strawberries—Pack unthawed fruit in a container with a tight-fitting cover. (An ice pick is helpful for separating lunch portion of frozen fruit.) Since the fruit will be thawed by lunch time, pack a wooden, paper or plastic spoon.

Canned fruit, such as plums, pineapple slices or tidbits and apricot halves—Pack lunch portion in a container with a tight-fitting cover.

Note: For Fruit Cup Combinations of fresh, frozen and canned fruits, see page 33.

Candied fruit, such as candied citrus peel, cherries and kumquats—Wrap carefully to keep out moisture and prevent candied fruit from becoming sticky.

Dried fruit—Wrap and pack dried apricots, prunes, peaches, figs, dates and raisins. Stewed dried fruits may be packed for lunch box according to directions for Canned Fruit.

Vegetables—Clean (page 313) and prepare vegetables as suggested in following paragraphs. Wrap and chill. Send a small container of salt if needed. Or, send along small containers of mayonnaise or French dressing for dunking.

Carrots—Cut pared carrots into narrow strips. Leave young tender carrots whole. Make curls by first cutting them into halves lengthwise. Shave into paper-thin strips with vegetable parer; curl around finger. Fasten each with a wooden pick, and chill in ice and water until curl is set; drain.

Cauliflowerets—See page 418.

Celery—Use crisp, tender center stalks. Split large stalks lengthwise.

Cucumbers—Cut unpared cucumber lengthwise into narrow sticks, about 3 in. long.

Green pepper—Cut green pepper into narrow strips.

Radishes—Prepare crisp, tender radishes or radish roses (page 418).

Tomatoes—Tuck in small (plum) tomatoes with package of salt.

HOT SANDWICHES

BAKED BEAN SANDWICHES

These sandwiches are the inevitable and delicious sequel to a baked bean supper.

Mix and set aside
   2 cups baked beans
   1 cup drained sweet pickle relish
   1 tablespoon minced onion

Cut crosswise into halves and set aside
   4 slices bacon

Set out on a flat working surface
   8 slices white, whole wheat or rye bread
Spread bread slices with
   ¼ cup softened butter or margarine
Spread baked bean mixture over buttered side of bread slices. Top each sandwich with a half slice of the bacon.

Arrange sandwiches on broiler rack. Place under broiler with tops about 3 in. from heat. Broil about 4 min., or until bacon is crisp.

Serve immediately.   *8 open-face sandwiches*

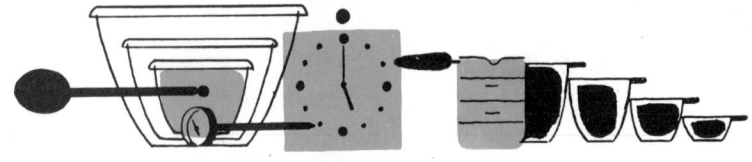

FRENCH TOAST CHEESE SANDWICHES

▲ *Base Recipe*

Set out a heavy skillet.

Beat slightly in a shallow bowl
   2 eggs
Stir in and set aside
   ⅓ cup milk or cream
   ½ teaspoon salt
Set out on a flat working surface
   8 slices white bread
Spread one side of each slice lightly with
   Prepared mustard
Put onto four of the bread slices
   4 slices Swiss or Cheddar cheese
Top cheese with remaining bread slices, buttered side down.

Heat in the skillet
   2 to 3 tablespoons butter or margarine
Dip each sandwich carefully in the egg mixture, coating both sides. Allow excess egg mixture to drain back into bowl. Dip only as many sandwiches at one time as will lie flat in skillet. Cook over low heat until browned. Turn and brown other side.

Repeat procedure for remaining sandwiches. If necessary, add more butter to skillet to prevent sticking.

Or place sandwiches on a well-greased baking sheet and brown in oven at 450°F 8 to 10 min.

Serve at once.   *4 sandwiches*

—CHEESE FRENCH TOAST

Follow ▲ Recipe. Shred **4 oz. Swiss cheese or Cheddar** (about 1 cup, shredded). Add cheese to egg mixture and beat well. Omit mustard and cheese slices. Spread bread slices with egg-cheese mixture and fry as in ▲ Recipe.

GLAMOROUS TRIPLE DECKER SANDWICH

This recipe makes one sandwich. Be sure you have ample ingredients on hand for the demand that's bound to result.

Prepare
   3 slices French toast (see Cheese French Toast recipe, above; omit cheese)

To Assemble Sandwich—Place on top of one slice French toast
   1 slice Swiss cheese
   1 slice cooked ham
Top with second French toast slice.

Spread with a mixture of
   ½ teaspoon dry mustard
   1 teaspoon water
Place on mustard mixture
   Sliced cooked chicken
Top with remaining French toast slice.
      1 sandwich

TOASTED CHEESE SANDWICHES

▲ *Base Recipe*

Set out
   4 slices Cheddar cheese
   2 tablespoons sweet pickle relish (optional)

Spread (one side only)
   4 slices bread
with one half of
   3 to 4 tablespoons softened butter or margarine
Cover two slices of the bread with the cheese and relish. Top with the two remaining bread slices. Spread outsides of sandwiches with remaining butter.

Place sandwiches on broiler rack. Place under broiler with tops of sandwiches 2 to 3 in. from heat. Turn when lightly browned and toast other sides. Cut into halves. Serve immediately.
      2 sandwiches

Saucy Bacon 'n' Tomato Sandwich

—GRILLED CHEESE SANDWICHES

Follow ▲ Recipe. Toast buttered sandwiches in a skillet over low heat, or in a wire broiler over a campfire or grill.

OPEN CHEESE SANDWICHES

Toast on one side only and set aside
   4 slices bread

Panfry (as many slices at one time as will lay flat in skillet)
   8 slices bacon
Cook until bacon is partially cooked. Drain slices on absorbent paper; set aside.

Rinse and cut into 4 slices
   1 medium tomato

Using 1 slice cheese per slice of bread, cover untoasted sides of bread with
   4 slices Cheddar or Swiss cheese
Place slice of tomato on cheese and top each sandwich with 2 slices bacon.

Arrange sandwiches on broiler rack. Place under broiler with tops of sandwiches 2 to 3 in. from heat until cheese is slightly melted and bacon is crisp and browned.

4 open-face sandwiches

SAUCY BACON 'N' TOMATO SANDWICH

Velvety hot Cheddar cheese sauce cascading over a toasted bacon and tomato sandwich adds up to tempting luncheon main-dish fare.

Prepare and keep hot
   Cheddar Cheese Sauce (below)

For each sandwich have ready
   3 thin slices toast (crusts removed)
   2 thick slices tomato
   3 slices crisply cooked bacon
   3 thin slices dill pickle
Spread toast on one side with **mayonnaise.** Place tomato slices on one piece of toast; cover with a second piece, mayonnaise side up. Cover with bacon and dill pickle slices. Top with third slice of toast, mayonnaise side down.

Press gently and transfer to individual serving plate; cut sandwich diagonally into halves. Prepare the desired number of sandwiches before pouring hot cheese sauce (about ½ cup) over each. Garnish each half with a **pimiento-stuffed olive** impaled on a wooden pick. Serve hot.

—CHEDDAR CHEESE SAUCE

Shred and set aside
   4 oz. sharp Cheddar cheese (about 1 cup shredded)

Combine in a heavy saucepan, blending thoroughly
   1 cup milk
   2 tablespoons instant blending flour
   ½ teaspoon salt
   ⅛ teaspoon pepper
Add and bring to boiling, stirring constantly
   2 tablespoons butter or margarine
Cook and stir 1 min. Remove from heat. Blend in
   ½ teaspoon prepared mustard
   ¼ teaspoon prepared horseradish
Add the shredded cheese and stir until melted.

About 2 cups sauce

CHEESE SURPRISE SANDWICHES

Set aside to drain
   1 8¼-oz. can (4 slices) sliced pineapple

Set out
   4 slices Cheddar cheese
   4 slices bacon
Beat together until well blended
   1 pkg. (3 oz.) cream cheese, softened
   ¼ cup (2¼-oz. can) deviled ham
Set out on a flat working surface
   4 slices white or whole wheat bread
Spread cream cheese mixture on bread slices. To make each sandwich, top a slice of bread with 1 slice drained pineapple, 1 slice cheese and 1 slice bacon.

Broil sandwiches about 4 min., or until cheese is melted and bacon is crisp.

Serve immediately. *4 open-face sandwiches*

SAVORY CHEESE SANDWICHES

Shred and set aside
   8 oz. Cheddar cheese (about 2 cups, shredded)

Prepare, chop and set aside
   1 Hard-Cooked Egg (page 133)

Melt in a skillet over low heat
   2 tablespoons butter or margarine
Add and cook until onion is tender
   1 tablespoon chopped onion
Add and stir until blended
   1 tablespoon all-purpose flour
Heat until mixture bubbles. Remove from heat.

Add gradually while stirring constantly
   ½ cup cream
   ¼ teaspoon salt
   2 drops Tabasco
Cook until mixture boils. Cook 1 to 2 min. longer. Remove from heat. Blend in
   2 tablespoons lemon juice
Add to the cream mixture the cheese, egg and
   1 tablespoon chopped pimiento
   1 tablespoon chopped stuffed olives
Mix well and set aside.

Panfry until partially cooked
   12 slices bacon
Spread
   6 slices bread
with
   Butter or margarine, softened
Spread cheese mixture on the bread, allowing ¼ cup for each slice. Top each with 2 of the bacon slices, crossed diagonally.

Arrange sandwiches on broiler rack and place under broiler with tops of sandwiches 3 in. from heat. Broil until cheese mixture is bubbly and slightly browned and bacon slices are crisp.

Serve hot. *6 open-face sandwiches*

BROILED CHEESE OLIVE SANDWICHES

Hard-cook (page 133), peel and slice into a medium-size bowl
   2 eggs
Shred and put into the bowl
   ½ lb. sharp Cheddar cheese (about 2 cups, shredded)
Prepare and add
   1¼ cups chopped ripe olives
   ½ cup chopped green pepper
   ¼ cup chopped onion
Blend
   ⅓ cup ketchup
   2 tablespoons mayonnaise or salad dressing
   2 teaspoons prepared mustard
and a mixture of
   ¼ teaspoon marjoram
   ⅛ teaspoon oregano
   ⅛ teaspoon salt
   Few grains pepper
Add to mixture in bowl and blend. Set aside.

Open Cheese Sandwiches

Split with a sharp knife
   4 sandwich buns
Set buns on broiler rack, cut sides up, and place under broiler with tops of buns 2 in. from heat. Toast until buns are golden brown. Remove broiler rack from broiler and spread toasted sides of buns with
   Butter or margarine
Spread about ⅛ of cheese mixture on buttered side of each bun. Return to broiler with tops of sandwiches 3 in. from heat. Broil until cheese is bubbly.

Serve immediately.　　*8 open-face sandwiches*

HOT 'N' HEARTY CHEESE-PLUS SANDWICHES

Happy youngsters, hungry fathers and hurried mothers—these sandwiches suit everyone's taste and satisfy all appetites.

Prepare any of the sandwiches (below). Arrange sandwiches on broiler rack and put under broiler with tops of sandwiches 3 in. from heat. Broil until cheese is melted and other ingredients are thoroughly heated. Serve sandwiches hot.

OPEN-FACE FRANKFURTER

Spread **bread** with **prepared mustard.** Slice a **frankfurter** in thirds lengthwise and place over the mustard. Top with **1 slice Cheddar cheese, 1 slice tomato, 1 slice pimiento stuffed olive** and **1 onion ring.**

TRIPLE PICKLE

Sprinkle **bread** with a mixture of crumbled crisp **bacon** and finely chopped **onion.** Cover with **1 slice Brick cheese.** Slice **1 dill pickle** crosswise and arrange 3 slices on top of the cheese.

BROILED BEAN

Spread **bread** with **ketchup** or **chili sauce.** Generously cover with **baked beans.** Top with **1 slice Cheddar cheese, 1 thin slice Bermuda onion** and **1 slice pimiento-stuffed olive.**

Hot 'n' Hearty Cheese-Plus Sandwiches

LIVER SAUSAGE

Generously spread **bread** with **butter,** then with **prepared horseradish.** Mash **liver sausage** and spread evenly to edges of bread. Top with **2 or 3 sweet onion slices** and **1 slice Cheddar cheese.**

CROSSED BACON

Spread **bread** with **butter.** Cover with **1 slice cooked ham, 1 or more slices tomato, 1 slice process Cheddar cheese** and **2 slices partially cooked bacon,** crossed diagonally.

CHEESE RUSKS

For each sandwich, partially fry
   2 slices bacon
Set out
   Rusks
Spread each rusk with
   1 tablespoon mayonnaise
Put onto each
   1 slice pasteurized process American cheese
Top with the bacon slices.

Put onto a broiler rack and set under broiler with tops 3 in. from heat. Broil about 4 min., or until cheese is melted. Serve hot.

CHEESE SOUFFLE SANDWICHES

Beat until stiff, not dry, peaks are formed
   3 egg whites
   ½ teaspoon salt
Beat until very thick
   3 egg yolks
   ⅛ teaspoon paprika
   Few grains pepper
   ½ teaspoon Worcestershire sauce
   ½ teaspoon prepared mustard
Stir in
   ½ cup shredded sharp Cheddar cheese
Fold cheese mixture into beaten egg whites until blended.
Spread
   6 slices bread
with
   2 tablespoons butter or margarine
Arrange bread slices on a greased baking sheet. Spoon an equal amount of soufflé mixture over each.

Bake at 350°F about 15 min., or until topping is delicately browned.　*6 open-face sandwiches*

QUICK CHEESE LOAF

A definitely glamorized version of Swiss cheese sandwiches, easy to prepare and a real conversation piece.

Grease a shallow baking dish.

Quick Cheese Loaf

Set out
   1 loaf bread, unsliced
   ½ lb. (8 slices) sliced pasteurized process Swiss cheese
Make 8 diagonal cuts at equal intervals, almost through to bottom of loaf.

Mix in a bowl
   ½ cup butter or margarine, softened
   ⅓ cup minced onion
   3 tablespoons prepared mustard
   1 tablespoon poppy seed
   2 teaspoons lemon juice
Reserve 3 tablespoons of the butter mixture; spread remaining mixture on the cut surfaces of bread.

Sprinkle evenly over the cheese slices
   ½ teaspoon monosodium glutamate
Place 1 slice in each cut. Press bread slices together and place the loaf in the baking dish.

Spread the reserved butter mixture over top and sides of loaf. Arrange on top
   2 or 3 slices bacon, cut in halves
Bake at 350°F about 20 min., or until bacon is cooked and loaf is lightly browned.

Serve immediately.　　*4 to 6 servings*

CHEESE-STUFFED FRANKS IN BUNS

The tangy gold of melting Cheddar gives special zest to ever-popular frankfurters.

Slit almost through lengthwise
   12 frankfurters

"The Astronaut" Sandwich

Mix
  ½ cup sweet pickle relish
  1 tablespoon prepared mustard
Cut into 12 4x½x½-in. strips
  ¾ lb. pasteurized process Cheddar
  cheese
Put one strip of cheese and about 2 teaspoons of the relish mixture into each frankfurter and set aside.

Panfry until partially cooked
  12 slices bacon
Drain. Starting at one end, wrap one slice of bacon around each frankfurter; secure each end with a wooden pick. Arrange the bacon-wrapped frankfurters on the broiler rack with tops 3 in. from heat and broil until bacon is cooked, turning once.

  Serve in
  12 buns, buttered and toasted
                                    12 sandwiches

CHICKEN SHRIMP SANDWICHES

For Sandwich Spread—Mix thoroughly and set aside
  1 cup chopped cooked chicken
  ½ cup chopped cooked shrimp
  ⅓ cup chopped celery
  4 teaspoons grated onion
  4 teaspoons lemon juice
  ⅓ cup mayonnaise
  ¼ teaspoon salt
  ⅛ teaspoon pepper

For Sandwiches—Set out on a flat surface
  4 slices white or whole wheat bread
Spread bread slices with
  ¼ cup softened butter or margarine
Spread each slice of bread with the chicken-shrimp mixture. Sprinkle with
  ¼ cup grated Parmesan cheese

Broil sandwiches about 4 min.

Serve immediately.   *4 open-face sandwiches*

"THE ASTRONAUT" SANDWICH

Have ready
  12 slices white bread
  Butter or margarine
  6 slices cooked ham
  6 slices cooked turkey
  18 cooked asparagus spears
  6 slices Cheddar cheese
  6 deviled egg halves
Toast and butter the bread slices. Top each with a slice of ham, a slice of turkey, 3 asparagus spears, and a slice of cheese. Place sandwiches under broiler heat until cheese is melted. Cover with remaining buttered toast.

Put each sandwich on a serving plate. Spoon over sandwiches
  1 cup hollandaise sauce
Top each with a deviled egg half garnished with a **pimiento strip.**   *6 sandwiches*

"THE LONG ISLANDER" SANDWICH

Have ready
  1 loaf (about ½ lb.) French or Italian
    bread, split lengthwise through
    center, then cut crosswise in halves
  ½ lb. thinly sliced roast beef
  8 tomato slices, halved
  2 hard-cooked eggs, sliced
  1 cup shredded Cheddar cheese
  2 cups finely shredded cabbage
Combine cabbage in a bowl with
  ½ cup bottled coleslaw dressing
  2 tablespoons prepared hot mustard
Toss gently and spoon mixture onto the bread. Top with sliced roast beef, tomato, egg and shredded cheese. Place under broiler about 4 in. from heat until cheese is melted.
                              4 open-face sandwiches

Note: A made-to-order accompaniment for "The Long Islander" is Manhattan Cup (page 62), a delicious chilled soup.

SKY-HIGH BRAUNSCHWEIGER TOWERS

Set out a shallow baking dish.

Cut into 6 slices
  1½ lbs. Braunschweiger (smoked liver
    sausage)

Set out
  6 slices bacon
  6 slices onion
  6 slices tomato
  6 mushroom caps, buttered
  2 tablespoons prepared mustard
Spread about 1 teaspoon of the mustard over top of each slice of sausage. Wrap 1 slice of bacon around each slice of liver sausage; secure bacon with a wooden pick. Arrange in the baking dish in single layer. Place 1 slice of onion on top of each sausage slice; sprinkle onion with
  Paprika
Top each onion slice with 1 slice of tomato and 1 mushroom cap (cavity side down); secure with a wooden pick.

Bake at 350°F about 25 min., or until bacon is cooked.

Toast cut sides of
  6 sandwich buns, split
Spread toasted sides of buns with
  Perky Horseradish Butter Spread
    (see Perky Butters, page 114)
Serve the Braunschweiger towers on the buns, open-face style. Garnish towers with **radish roses** and crisp, colorful **salad greens.**
                                    6 servings

BAR-X SANDWICHES

Hearty, satisfying fare, in high favor with junior cow-hands.

For Bar-X Sauce—Heat in a skillet
  2 tablespoons fat
Add to fat and cook until tender
  ½ cup (about 1 medium) chopped
    onion
Blend into onion
  1¼ cups (10¾-oz. can) condensed
    tomato soup
  2 tablespoons lemon juice
  2 tablespoons brown sugar
  1 teaspoon prepared mustard
  1 teaspoon Worcestershire sauce
and a mixture of
  ¼ teaspoon salt
  ¼ teaspoon monosodium glutamate
  ⅛ teaspoon pepper

Simmer 5 min. Set aside in a warm place.

To Prepare Meat—Heat in a large heavy skillet

3 tablespoons fat

Add to fat, breaking apart with fork or spoon into small pieces

1 lb. ground beef

Brown over moderate heat, turning occasionally. Blend sauce and meat. Simmer 15 min.

Toast

6 hamburger buns, split

Place 2 halves on each of 6 warm plates. Spoon meat mixture over them. If desired, top each serving with

3 or 4 thin onion rings (thinly slice peeled onion; separate into rings)

6 servings

MEXICAN STYLE OPEN-FACE SANDWICHES

Part tacos, part American-style "sloppy joes," sandwich fanciers everywhere will enjoy these gustatory delights.

Heat in a large heavy skillet

1 tablespoon shortening

Add to skillet

1 lb. ground beef
1 cup coarsely chopped onion

Cook over medium heat until meat is crumbly, stirring occasionally with a fork.

Stir in a mixture of

1 tablespoon all-purpose flour
1 teaspoon salt
1½ teaspoons chili powder
¼ teaspoon cinnamon
1½ teaspoons oregano
3 to 4 dashes Tabasco

Blend well and add

1 can (8¾ oz.) tomatoes
¼ cup chili sauce
¼ cup sliced ripe olives

Stir until thoroughly mixed; cover and cook over low heat until thickened, about 20 min.

Spoon about ⅓ cup meat mixture onto

Hot crisp tortillas (or toasted buns)

Top with

Shredded Cheddar cheese (about 1½ cups) or dairy sour cream

If desired, accompany sandwiches with wedges of **ripe avocado.** *8 to 10 open-face sandwiches*

PORK WITH BARBECUE SAUCE

Have ready

12 slices roast pork
6 hamburger buns

Heat in the skillet over low heat

¼ cup butter or margarine

Add and cook over medium heat, stirring occasionally with a spoon

½ cup chopped onion
½ cup chopped celery
1 clove garlic, minced

Cook until onion is tender. Blend in

½ cup water
⅓ cup chili sauce
¼ cup Worcestershire sauce
¼ cup cider vinegar
2 tablespoons brown sugar
¾ teaspoon salt
¾ teaspoon monosodium glutamate
¾ teaspoon chili powder
⅛ teaspoon pepper

Simmer until thoroughly heated, stirring occasionally.

Meanwhile, toast the buns. Spread with

Butter or margarine

Place pork slices on bun halves; spoon some of the sauce over the meat. Serve at once with remaining sauce. *6 servings*

LUNCHEON MEAT SALAD OPEN-FACE SANDWICHES

Combine in a bowl, mixing well

1 can (12 oz.) luncheon meat, chopped
3 hard-cooked eggs, chopped
1 cup finely chopped celery
½ cup piccalilli relish

Add a blend of

½ cup mayonnaise
2 teaspoons prepared horseradish
1½ teaspoons lemon juice
½ teaspoon Worcestershire sauce

Spread **butter or margarine** on cut surfaces of

6 hamburger buns, cut in halves

Place under broiler heat until lightly toasted. Remove from oven and spread salad mixture generously over each half. Sprinkle over top

½ cup shredded Cheddar cheese

Place under broiler and heat until cheese is melted. Serve at once.

12 open-face sandwiches

CHIPPED BEEF AND KIDNEY BEAN BURGERS

Cut (using scissors) into thin strips

5 oz. chipped (or dried) beef

Pork with Barbecue Sauce

Combine in a mixing bowl, tossing until well mixed

1 can (16 oz.) kidney beans, drained
3 tablespoons chopped onion
⅓ cup sweet pickle relish
2 teaspoons prepared mustard
⅓ cup mayonnaise or salad dressing

Split into halves and toast

4 hamburger buns

Spoon beef mixture onto bun halves and top with

¼ cup shredded Cheddar cheese

Arrange on rack in broiler pan and broil about 4 in. from heat until cheese is melted.

Serve immediately. *8 open-face sandwiches*

SALMON TOMATO SANDWICHES

For Garlic Butter—Combine in a saucepan

¼ cup butter or margarine
¼ teaspoon garlic powder

Set over low heat and stir occasionally until butter is melted and mixture is thoroughly heated. Set aside.

For Sandwich Spread—Rinse and cut away stem end from

1 medium tomato

Cut tomato into four slices and set aside.

Drain and flake (page 9) contents of

1 can (7¾ oz.) salmon (about 1 cup, flaked)

Mix thoroughly the flaked salmon and

6 tablespoons chopped sweet pickle
6 tablespoons dairy sour cream
¼ teaspoon salt
⅛ teaspoon pepper
Few grains garlic powder

For Sandwiches—Set out on a flat surface

4 slices white, rye or whole wheat bread

Brush bread slices with half of the Garlic Butter. Spread with salmon mixture. Top each sandwich with a tomato slice. Brush tomato slices with remaining Garlic Butter. Arrange on a broiler rack.

Broil sandwiches about 5 min., or until thoroughly heated.

Serve immediately. *4 open-face sandwiches*

Taste-Teaser Tuna Sandwiches

DEVILED SALMON ROLL-UPS

A cup of hot soup to go with these imaginative roll-ups is all one would need for a satisfying lunch or light supper.

Set out a baking sheet.

Have ready
  1 can (7¾ oz.) salmon, drained and flaked
  12 refrigerated quick parkerhouse rolls
Roll out (using rolling pin) each roll into a thin 5x3-in. rectangle. Spread each rectangle lightly with
  Soft butter or margarine

Beat lightly in a bowl
  1 egg
Remove 1 tablespoon of the egg to use later; add to remaining egg in bowl the flaked salmon and
  1 teaspoon parsley flakes
  ½ teaspoon instant onion flakes
Mix well and spread over the buttered rectangles. Roll up jelly-roll fashion and place on baking sheet. Brush rolls lightly with reserved egg.

Bake in a 375°F oven about 10 min., or until rolls are light golden. Serve hot.   *12 roll-ups*

GRILLED TUNA SALAD SANDWICHES

  ▲ *Base Recipe*

Set out a 10-in. skillet or griddle.

Drain and flake (page 9)
  6½- or 7-oz. can tuna (about 1⅓ cups, drained and flaked)
Set aside.

Shred
  1 oz. pasteurized process cheese food (about ¼ cup, shredded

Combine cheese and tuna with
  1 teaspoon lemon juice
  ¼ teaspoon salt
  ⅛ teaspoon paprika
  3 to 4 tablespoons salad dressing or mayonnaise

Spread (one side only)
  12 slices bread
with about
  ¼ cup softened butter or margarine
Spread tuna mixture on buttered sides of 6 of the bread slices. Top with remaining buttered bread slices. Press sandwiches firmly together and cut diagonally into halves.

Heat in skillet
  2 to 3 tablespoons butter or margarine

Dip each sandwich half into a mixture of
  2 eggs, well beaten
  1 cup milk
Allow excess milk mixture to drain over bowl before placing sandwich in skillet. Dip only as many sandwich halves as will lay flat in skillet. Place sandwiches in skillet and brown over low heat about 5 min. Turn and brown other sides. Add butter or margarine to skillet as necessary.
                                    6 sandwiches

—GRILLED CHICKEN SALAD SANDWICHES

Follow ▲ Recipe. Substitute **minced cooked chicken** for tuna.

—SANDWICH SAILBOATS

Follow ▲ Recipe or variation for filling. Trim thin, long slice off top of each of **4 frankfurter buns.** Using a sharp knife, cut down around insides of buns, ½ in. from edges, being careful not to cut through bottoms of buns. Hollow out with a spoon. Brush these "boats" and the top slices with **melted butter or margarine** and toast in oven at 350°F. Fill boats and cover with toasted caps. Stand a frilly **lettuce leaf** upright, with wooden picks, on top of each sandwich.

"THE SAN FRANCISCAN" SANDWICH

Have ready
  6 slices white bread

Fry in a large heavy skillet until crisp and golden brown
  6 slices bacon
Drain bacon on absorbent paper and pour off all but 1 tablespoon drippings from skillet.

Combine in a bowl, mixing well
  1 can (6½ or 7 oz.) tuna, drained and flaked
  ¼ cup prepared salad and sandwich spread
Spread mixture over half of the bread slices and top each with 2 slices bacon. Cover with remaining bread.

Combine in a shallow bowl
  1 egg, slightly beaten
  ½ cup milk
Dip sandwiches into the mixture, coating both sides. Heat bacon drippings in the skillet. Add sandwiches and brown slowly on both sides. Serve at once.   *3 sandwiches*

Note: California Cup (page 63) is a fine go-along with "The San Franciscan" for a hearty luncheon.

TASTE-TEASER TUNA SANDWICHES

Mix thoroughly and set aside
  1 cup (6½- or 7-oz. can, drained) flaked tuna (page 9)
  8 slices crisp Panfried Bacon (page 190), crumbled
  ¼ cup chopped celery
  2 tablespoons chopped chives
  2 tablespoons chopped green pepper
  3 tablespoons mayonnaise
  ⅛ teaspoon freshly ground pepper

Lightly grease an 8x8x2-in. baking dish.

Arrange in two stacks on a flat working surface
  8 slices white or whole wheat bread
With a sharp knife, trim crusts from slices. Spread one side of each slice with
  Prepared mustard
Spread four slices of bread, mustard side up, with the Tuna Filling. Place in baking dish. Top filling with remaining bread slices, placing them mustard side down.

Spread lavishly over each sandwich
  Pasteurized process cheese spread with pimiento
Blend thoroughly
  3 eggs, well beaten
  1½ cups milk
  ¾ teaspoon salt
Pour the egg mixture over the sandwiches.

Bake at 325°F 40 min., or until golden brown.

Serve sandwiches hot, garnished with
  Sprigs of parsley
Accompany with relishes such as **carrot curls** and **radish fans.**   *4 sandwiches*

CRAB MEAT-STUFFED BUNS

Keep this recipe in mind for a company cook-out. The buns may be stuffed ahead of time, wrapped in foil, stored in refrigerator, and at serving time, heated on an outdoor grill.

Set out a skillet and baking sheet.

Chop finely

2 medium green peppers
1 bunch green onions with tops

Heat in the skillet

½ cup olive oil

Add chopped green peppers and onions to skillet and cook over low heat about 5 min., stirring occasionally. Add

1 can (8 oz.) tomato sauce
½ lb. crab meat or shrimp, cut in pieces
½ cup pimiento-stuffed olives, chopped
1 lb. Cheddar cheese, shredded

Cook and stir over very low heat only until cheese is melted. Remove from heat.

Remove the soft interior from

18 hot dog buns

Fill the cavity with the heated shellfish-cheese mixture. Wrap each roll in aluminum foil and seal ends. Arrange on baking sheet and heat in a 325°F oven about 20 min. *18 sandwiches*

Note: Cut-up cooked ham or chicken may be substituted for shellfish, if desired.

SANDWICHES A LA NAPOLI

Here's an unusual hot sandwich combining bread slices, cheese, shrimp and green beans along with other flavors all contributing to its Italian character.

Set out and grease a 13x9x2-in. baking pan.

Combine in a bowl, mixing well

1 can (16 oz.) cut green beans, drained
½ cup ripe olives, cut in wedges
2 cups ricotta cheese (or drained cottage cheese)
2 tablespoons sliced green onion
½ teaspoon oregano
¼ teaspoon salt

Trim slightly

12 slices sandwich bread

Spread bread on one side with

Soft butter or margarine

Beat well in a bowl

3 eggs

Add, mixing after each addition

1 can (10½ oz.) condensed cream of mushroom soup
½ cup milk
¼ cup ketchup
1 can (4½ oz.) shrimp, drained and cut in pieces

Pour about half the soup-shrimp mixture into the baking pan. Arrange 6 slices bread, buttered side up, in the pan. Spoon bean-cheese mixture over bread. Top with remaining bread, buttered side down. Pour remaining soup mixture over all. Sprinkle over top

Grated Parmesan cheese

Bake in a 350°F oven about 35 min. Let stand 5 min. before serving. If desired, garnish with **parsley sprigs.** *6 sandwiches*

PARTY SANDWICHES

CURRANT CHECKERBOARDS

▲ *Base Recipe*

For Currant Butter—Put into bowl of electric mixer

1 cup firm butter or margarine

Beat on high speed just until butter is whipped. Add

2½ tablespoons currant jelly

Continue beating until blended. Set aside.

For Checkerboards—Arrange in 2 stacks on a flat working surface

6 slices white bread
6 slices whole wheat bread

Trim crusts from bread, trimming so that slices are square. Reserve 3 slices of white bread; spread one side of each of remaining slices with Currant Butter.

Stack 2 whole wheat bread slices and 1 white bread slice, buttered side up, beginning and ending with whole wheat slices. Repeat to form 2 more stacks. Top each stack with one of the reserved white bread slices.

Using a sharp knife, cut each stack into 4 slices. Set 4 slices aside. Spread all remaining slices with Currant Butter. (Each slice will consist of 4 bread strips that are alternately whole wheat and white bread.) Stack two of the slices, buttered side up, so that the white strips of 1 slice are beneath the whole wheat strips of the next slice. Repeat to form 3 more stacks. Top each stack with a slice not spread with the Currant Butter. Wrap each stack in waxed paper, moisture-vaporproof material, or aluminum foil and chill in refrigerator 3 to 4 hrs.

When ready to serve, using a sharp knife, cut each stack into ½-in. slices. Each slice will show a checkerboard pattern.

Arrange attractively on a sandwich tray.
About 2½ doz. sandwiches

—OLIVE CHECKERBOARDS

Follow ▲ Recipe. Substitute for Currant Butter a mixture of **6 oz. cream cheese, 2 to 3 tablespoons milk or cream, ¼ teaspoon lemon juice,** and **½ cup chopped green olives.**

—WATERCRESS CHECKERBOARDS

Follow ▲ Recipe. Substitute for Currant Butter **Watercress Butter** (see Party Pinwheels, page 130).

HAM AND CREAM CHEESE TEA SANDWICHES

Trim crusts and cut ½ in. thick from unsliced sandwich loaves

2 lengthwise slices white bread
1 lengthwise slice whole wheat bread

Flatten bread slices with a rolling pin to ¼-in. thickness. Spread each slice with

Butter or margarine, softened

Set aside.

Combine in a bowl

⅔ cup (two 3-oz. cans) deviled ham
2 tablespoons finely chopped onion
1 tablespoon mayonnaise

Set aside.

Mix in a bowl

1 pkg. (3 oz.) cream cheese
½ cup drained crushed pineapple

Spread the deviled ham mixture over one white bread slice. Cover with the whole wheat slice and spread this with the pineapple-cream cheese mixture. Top with remaining bread slice, buttered side down. Chill thoroughly before serving.

To serve, cut sandwich bar crosswise into six sections, then slice each section in half lengthwise, forming 12 squares. Cut each square diagonally to form triangles.

2 doz. sandwiches

CHILDREN'S DELIGHT

Guests at a party for the small fry will love these eye-appealing and nutritious open-face sandwiches.

Have ready

6 slices white bread
3 ripe bananas
¼ cup chopped maraschino cherries
2 tablespoons chopped nuts

Combine in a bowl, blending thoroughly

2 pkgs. (3 oz. each) cream cheese, softened
2 tablespoons honey

Spread one side of bread slices evenly with the cheese mixture. Cover with banana slices

Children's Delight

(about ½ banana for each slice of bread). Spoon chopped cherries and nuts over banana. Cut sandwich diagonally into halves; serve garnished with **crisp lettuce** and **peach halves.**

6 open-face sandwiches

SPECIAL CHEESE ROLLS

Put into a bowl and blend

4 oz. blue cheese, crumbled
1 pkg. (3 oz.) cream cheese, softened
2 tablespoons pineapple juice
2 teaspoons Worcestershire sauce
½ teaspoon monosodium glutamate
1 tablespoon chopped parsley
1 teaspoon finely chopped onion
1 drop Tabasco

Set aside.

Cut 2 lengthwise slices, each ½ in. thick, from

1 unsliced loaf white sandwich bread

Trim crusts from the slices and reserve remainder of bread for other use.

Flatten bread slices with a rolling pin to ¼-in. thickness. Spread with

Butter or margarine, softened

Spread cheese filling on bread slices. To make cheese rolls, cut each bread slice into four crosswise sections and roll each section up tightly. Place the rolls, overlapping side down, close together on waxed paper, aluminum foil or moisture-vaporproof material. Wrap and chill thoroughly before serving.

To serve, cut each roll into halves and garnish end of roll with

Parsley or watercress sprig

16 sandwiches

FROSTED SANDWICH TREATS

These individual sandwich loaves make a handsome and hearty yet dainty buffet spread.

For Crab Meat Spread—Blend

1⅓ cups (6½-oz. can) drained crab meat, bony tissue removed
¼ cup mayonnaise
2 tablespoons ketchup
1 tablespoon lemon juice
½ teaspoon Worcestershire sauce
¼ teaspoon salt
¼ teaspoon monosodium glutamate
⅛ teaspoon pepper

Frosted Sandwich Treats

Refrigerate until ready to use.

For Almond Olive Spread—Blend

¾ cup (about 4 oz.) toasted almonds (page 10), finely chopped
½ cup (about 3 oz.) chopped pimiento-stuffed olives
2 tablespoons mayonnaise or salad dressing
1 teaspoon prepared mustard

Refrigerate until ready to use.

For Cucumber Spread—Beat until fluffy

1 pkg. (8 oz.) cream cheese, softened
⅔ cup (about 1 small) grated cucumber
¼ teaspoon finely chopped chives
⅛ teaspoon onion salt
⅛ teaspoon salt
⅛ teaspoon pepper
¼ teaspoon monosodium glutamate

Refrigerate until ready to use.

For Avocado Spread—Blend

1 cup (about 1 large) sieved avocado
¼ cup (about 1 oz.) crumbled Roquefort or blue cheese
1 teaspoon lemon juice
¼ teaspoon garlic salt

Refrigerate until ready to use.

For Ham and Horseradish Spread—Blend

2 cups (about ½ lb.) ground cooked ham
¼ cup minced parsley
2 tablespoons dairy sour cream
2 tablespoons prepared horseradish

Refrigerate until ready to use.

For "Frosting"—Beat together until fluffy

1 pkg. (8 oz.) cream cheese, softened
3 tablespoons orange juice
2 drops yellow food coloring

Cover and set aside.

For Sandwiches—Whip at high speed with electric mixer

1 cup butter or margarine

Arrange in several stacks on a flat working surface

42 slices thin-sliced white bread

With a sharp knife, trim off crusts. Spread each slice with the whipped butter. Spread 7 of the bread slices with Crab Meat Spread, 7 with Almond Olive Spread, 7 with Ham and Horseradish Spread, 7 with Cucumber Spread, and 7 with Avocado Spread.

Arrange these slices in 7 stacks, all 5 different fillings in each stack. Top each stack with one of the 7 remaining bread slices, buttered side down. Cut each stack diagonally into halves. Spread top and one side of each triangular stack with the cream cheese "Frosting."

Garnish each triangle with one of the following, impaled on a cocktail pick: **pimiento-stuffed olive, small cooked shrimp, pickled onion** or **rolled anchovy fillet.** Arrange on serving platter (see photo). If desired, garnish with **radish roses** and **parsley.**   *14 servings*

OLIVE ROLL-UPS

Beat until fluffy

2 pkgs. (3 oz. each) cream cheese, softened

Cut 2 lengthwise slices, each ½ in. thick, from

1 unsliced loaf white sandwich bread

Trim crusts from the slices and reserve remainder of bread for other use. Flatten bread slices with a rolling pin to ¼-in. thickness.

Spread bread slices with

Butter or margarine, softened

Spread each slice with the cream cheese.

Set out

20 pimiento stuffed olives

Cut bread slices into halves and arrange a row of five olives along narrow edge of each half slice of bread.

Roll up each half slice of bread like a jelly roll, starting at olive end, being careful to keep first turn firm and olives in place. Place the rolls, overlapping side down, close together on waxed paper, aluminum foil or moisture-vaporproof material. Wrap and chill thoroughly before serving.

To serve, cut each roll into 6 slices.

2 doz. sandwiches

PARTY PINWHEELS

For Pinwheels—Prepare

Cherry Nut Spread and Watercress Butter (page 131)

Set out to soften at room temperature

¼ cup butter or margarine

Set out on a flat working surface and trim crust from

1 loaf unsliced sandwich bread

Cut the loaf into six equal lengthwise slices, each about ½ in. thick. Flatten each slice slightly with a rolling pin. Spread one side of each of three slices with the softened butter. Then spread each slice generously to edges with Cherry Nut Spread. Spread remaining unbuttered slices with Watercress Butter. Starting with the narrow side of bread, roll up each slice tightly, being careful to keep sides even. If necessary, secure ends with wooden picks. Wrap rolls individually in waxed paper, aluminum foil, or moisture-vaporproof material. Twist ends securely. Chill in refrigerator several hours.

When ready to serve, remove wooden picks and, using a sharp knife, cut the chilled rolls crosswise into slices about ½ in. thick. Arrange attractively on a sandwich tray.

About 4 doz. pinwheels

Triple-Ring Sandwiches

For Cherry Nut Spread—Set out to soften at room temperature

2 pkgs. (3 oz. each) cream cheese

Chop and set aside

⅔ cup (about 2 oz.) salted pecans
¼ cup drained maraschino cherries

Add to the softened cream cheese and blend thoroughly, beating until fluffy

2 teaspoons maraschino cherry syrup

Blend in the chopped nuts and cherries.

For Watercress Butter—Rinse, drain well, and finely snip enough watercress to yield

⅔ cup finely snipped watercress

Put into bowl of electric mixer

⅔ cup firm butter

Beat on high speed just until butter is whipped. Add the watercress and mix on high speed just until blended.

SCALLOPED CHICKEN TEA SANDWICHES

Mix in a bowl

1 cup minced cooked chicken
¼ cup finely chopped celery
3 tablespoons dairy sour cream
2 teaspoons minced parsley
¼ teaspoon salt
¼ teaspoon monosodium glutamate
Few grains pepper

Set aside.

Cut 2 lengthwise slices, each ½-in. thick, from

1 unsliced loaf white sandwich bread

Trim crusts from the slices and reserve remainder of bread for other use.

Flatten bread slices with a rolling pin to ¼-in. thickness. Using a 2-in. round scalloped cookie cutter, cut

16 bread rounds

Spread rounds with

Butter or margarine, softened

Spread eight of the bread rounds with chicken spread and cover with the eight remaining rounds, buttered side down. Chill thoroughly before serving.

To serve, cut each sandwich round into halves. If desired, garnish with **watercress sprigs**.

16 sandwiches

TRIPLE-RING SANDWICHES

To Prepare Fillings—Prepare
6 Hard-Cooked Eggs (page 133)

Meanwhile, mix in a bowl

½ cup cream-style cottage cheese
¼ cup finely chopped sweet pickle
2 to 3 tablespoons dairy sour cream
1 tablespoon minced onion
¼ teaspoon salt
Few grains pepper

Set aside.

Finely chop the hard-cooked eggs and put into a bowl. Add a mixture of

½ cup mayonnaise
1 tablespoon minced onion
1 tablespoon prepared mustard
½ teaspoon salt
½ teaspoon paprika
⅛ teaspoon pepper

Blend thoroughly and set aside.

Grind enough cooked ham to yield

1 cup ground cooked ham

Prepare and combine with ham

⅓ cup shredded Cheddar cheese

Add and blend in a mixture of

⅔ cup condensed tomato soup
1 tablespoon minced onion
½ teaspoon prepared mustard
¼ teaspoon prepared horseradish

Cover fillings; chill in refrigerator.

To Assemble Sandwiches—Shortly before serving time, cut thin slices from top and bottom of

1 large round loaf pumpernickel bread

Cut crosswise into four round slices of equal thickness. Trim crust from each slice.

Spoon about 3 tablespoons of the cottage cheese mixture onto the center of each bread slice and gently pat down.

Spread about ½ cup of the ham-cheese mixture in a ring around cottage cheese mixture on each slice.

Spread about ½ cup of the egg filling around ham-cheese mixture on each slice to edges.

Garnish center of each slice with

Sweet pickle slices

To serve, cut each slice into wedges.

3 to 4 doz. sandwich wedges

TUNA KRAUT FOOTBALL PARTY LOAF

Served help-yourself-style on a bread board, this football-shaped sandwich loaf is sure to impress a hungry after-the-game crowd.

Prepare and set aside

Sandwich Fillings (below)

Trim bottom crust from

1 oval loaf rye bread, unsliced

Cut the loaf lengthwise into 5 slices. Set bottom slice on a serving board and spread generously with **butter or margarine**. Spread both sides of remaining 4 slices with **butter or**

Tuna Kraut Football Party Loaf

margarine. Reshaping loaf as each layer is spread, cover bottom layer with Sauerkraut Filling, and second layer with Tuna Filling topped with

Watercress or parsley sprigs

Spread third layer with

Prepared mustard

Cover with

¼ lb. sliced Swiss cheese

Spread fourth layer with Deviled Ham Filling and put top bread slice in place. Set aside.

Combine in a bowl, blending until smooth

1 pkg. (8 oz.) cream cheese, softened
2 to 3 tablespoons cream or milk

Frost the surface of loaf with the cream cheese. Decorate top with **pimiento strips** and **pimiento-stuffed olive slices** to resemble football laces. Chill loaf until ready to serve.

1 sandwich loaf

—SANDWICH FILLINGS

Sauerkraut—Toss **1½ cups well-drained sauerkraut**, snipped, in a bowl with **2 to 3 tablespoons mayonnaise** and **¼ teaspoon celery seed** until well mixed.

Tuna—Drain **1 can (6½ or 7 oz.) tuna**; turn into a bowl and flake with fork. Mix in **2 tablespoons chopped green pepper, 1 tablespoon chopped onion, 1 tablespoon capers**, and **⅓ cup mayonnaise**.

Deviled Ham—Mix **1 can (2¼ oz.) deviled ham** with **1 tablespoon drained sweet pickle relish** in a bowl.

Note: If an unsliced loaf of rye bread is not available, use thinly sliced rye bread. Trim crusts from 2 or 3 slices and put together to form a large slice. Repeat until there are 5 large slices; round off edges on one layer for top of loaf. Proceed as directed.

PARTY SANDWICH LOAF

For Chicken Bacon Filling—Blend

8 slices crisp Panfried Bacon
(page 190), crumbled
1 cup finely chopped cooked chicken
¼ cup mayonnaise
1 tablespoon finely chopped pimiento

Mix in a blend of
    ¼ teaspoon salt
    ¼ teaspoon monosodium glutamate
    ⅛ teaspoon pepper
Refrigerate until ready to use.

For Toasted Pecan Filling—Blend
    1 pkg. (3 oz.) cream cheese, softened
    **1 cup (about 4 oz.) finely chopped
       toasted pecans (page 10)**
    **¾ cup (8¼-oz. can) well-drained
       crushed pineapple (reserve syrup
       for "Frosting")**
Refrigerate until ready to use.

For Shrimp Salad Filling—Blend
    1 Hard-Cooked Egg (page 133), chopped
    **1⅓ cups (7-oz. can) finely chopped
       shrimp**
    ¼ cup finely chopped celery
    ¼ cup chili sauce
    2 tablespoons lemon juice
    ¼ teaspoon salt
    ⅛ teaspoon monosodium glutamate
    Few grains pepper
Refrigerate until ready to use.

For "Frosting"—Beat together until fluffy the reserved pineapple syrup and
    1 pkg. (8 oz.) cream cheese, softened
    1 or 2 drops red food coloring
Cover and set aside.

For Sandwich Loaf—Whip at high speed of electric mixer
    ½ cup butter or margarine
Trim crust from
    1 unsliced loaf sandwich bread
Cut the loaf into four equal lengthwise slices. Flatten each slightly with a rolling pin.

Spread one side of each slice with the whipped butter. Place one bread slice, buttered side up, on a serving platter. Spread evenly with Shrimp Salad Filling. Top with second bread slice and spread evenly with Toasted Pecan Filling. Top with third bread slice and spread evenly with Chicken Bacon Filling. Top with remaining bread slice.

Frost sides and top of loaf with the "Frosting."

Garnish top of loaf with
    Minced parsley
    Pimiento-stuffed olive slices
Set loaf in refrigerator to chill about 1 hr. before serving.

Garnish with crisp greens or decorate platter with huckleberry leaves. To serve, cut loaf into slices.   *8 to 10 servings*

DANISH SANDWICHES
(Smørrebrød)

Danish smørrebrød are open-face sandwiches. Their genealogy is not known, but sometime early in the nineteenth century, the smørrebrød became a reigning favorite of the Danish menu and it has maintained this position to the present. At least once a day and sometimes oftener, practically all the Danes in Denmark are enthusiastically preparing, serving, eating and enjoying the renowned open-face sandwich. Restaurants take pride in the variety they offer and the menus for these sandwiches can run along for a yard or more—like a proud banner. Indeed, the smørrebrød is a custom that foreign visitors joyfully support on trips to the smallest of the Scandinavian countries and remember longingly after they leave.

Virtually all of the produce of land and sea lends itself in some way to the enchantment of the open sandwich, but combinations are not haphazard or merely daring. They are artfully and wisely selected for the perfect mating of flavors. Garnishes and sauces must not mask flavors but accent and enhance them, and by the strictest standards each sandwich must be an object of visual beauty as well as gastronomic appeal. This interesting culinary art has a dual mission: to delight at the same time that it nourishes. Sandwiches may be entertaining, but always within the bounds of good taste—in both meanings of that phrase.

The base of these famed sandwich creations is a single slice of bread, the type depending on what is to compose the sandwich. Danish preference runs to the rye breads. White bread, if it is used, is usually toasted. The kind and amount of butter is also determined by the other ingredients, as are the sauces, garnishes and seasonings. And what then composes the spreads? Virtually anything.

Foremost in popular favor is a sandwich that consists of one slice of lightly buttered **bread** heaped with the prized Danish June **shrimp** or covered with the pink beauties in a pattern so tight that it resembles fish scales. A crisp **lettuce leaf** garnishes this creation. Seasonings for so prized a delicacy are considered superfluous; later in the season, when the shrimp run larger and coarser, **mayonnaise** may be added—and a whisper of **curry**.

In another seafood sandwich **lobster meat**—fresh or canned—is sliced onto bread over a spread of **butter** or **mayonnaise**. Sometimes a ribbon of mayonnaise is run across the lobster and an accent of minced **dill** may be added.

Herring in almost all of its forms—marinated, spiced and kippered—is lavishly used for open sandwiches but rarely combined with anything more than the **onion rings** for which herring seems to have a special affinity. Sometimes a raw **egg yolk**, held in place with a ring of onion, accompanies the herring sandwich, and sliced **hard-cooked egg** is also acceptable.

There are literally hundreds of other kinds of open sandwiches. A sampling of the better-known varieties would include: **ham**, beautifully garnished with chopped cooked **spinach**, **mushrooms** and grilled **tomato**; panfried **bacon**, sliced **tomatoes**, **liver paste**, **jellied meat** and freshly grated **horseradish**; soft **cheese** with a sprinkling of minced **radish** or **celery**; sliced **smoked salmon** on a bed of **scrambled eggs**; **liver sausage** on finely sliced tart **apple**; chopped **ham** with raw **egg yolk** and a bit of chopped **chives**; **roast pork slices** with a **lettuce** cup of cucumber, pickled **beets** or **cabbage relish**; scraped **raw beef** with **smoked salmon** and **caviar** or with a couple of **oysters**, a ribbon of **caviar** and a few **shrimp**; **ham** and **beef slices** with a **lettuce** cup of **mustard pickle**; **sardines** on a bed of sliced **cucumbers** with a ribbon of chopped **radishes** and sieved **hard-cooked eggs**; sliced **tongue** with **macaroni salad**; **lobster** and cooked **asparagus pieces** tossed with **mayonnaise** and laid over a **lettuce leaf**; **herring salad** with a decoration of sliced **hard-cooked egg** or a **fried egg**, sunny-side up; thrifty slices of cold boiled **potato** on **salami** with a ribbon of chopped **chives**.

If Danish sandwiches are to live up to their well-earned reputation a few principles must be observed in making them. They must be prepared immediately or shortly before they are served. Bread must never be soggy; if ingredients are dampish the serviceable lettuce leaf may be used as a shield for the bread. **Seasoned butters** may of course be used but should be carefully chosen to match or pleasantly contrast with other flavors.

Danish Sandwiches

Egg and cheese dishes

Eggs and cheese, great go-togethers, are a perfect blend of flavors, and are cheerful and sunshiny in appearance. Year-round favorites as well as year-round budget beaters, eggs and cheese, together or separately, offer endless possibilities to the imaginative cook.

EGGS

Many associate eggs only with a breakfast menu or perhaps as a meat substitute served at lunch. The fact is, few foods can match them for their versatility. Served alone or in combination with other foods, eggs may be used as the theme of any course, be it for breakfast, lunch or dinner. From the simplest omelet to the most sophisticated soufflé, egg dishes add interest to family menus all over the world.

No guide used for planning well-balanced menus is complete which does not include at least 3 to 5 eggs in the weekly meals. Eggs contain many essential nutrients and are recognized as one of the important sources of protein. Helpful tips about eggs:

Always buy eggs from a refrigerated case and refrigerate them promptly at home, large end up.

Avoid variations in temperature during storage as egg whites become thin.

Use only high-quality clean eggs with sound shells for use in eggnogs, milk shakes or lightly cooked egg dishes.

Cook eggs only at low or moderate temperatures; high temperatures and overcooking toughens eggs.

Color of eggs does not affect the grade, nutritive value, flavor or cooking performance. Eggs with brown shells are just as desirable as those with white shells.

SOFT-COOKED EGGS

Put into a saucepan
4 eggs
Fill with cold or warm water to at least 1 in. above eggs. Cover. Bring rapidly to boiling. Turn off heat. If necessary to prevent further boiling, remove saucepan from heat. Let stand, covered, 2 to 4 min., depending upon firmness desired.   *4 Soft-Cooked Eggs*

HARD-COOKED EGGS

Put into a saucepan
4 eggs
Fill with cold or warm water to at least 1 in. above eggs. Cover. Bring rapidly to boiling. Turn off heat. Let stand covered 20 to 22 min.

Promptly and thoroughly cool eggs in cold water. Immediately crackle shells under water. To loosen shell, roll eggs between hands. When cooled, peel eggs, starting at large end. Prepare as desired.   *4 Hard-Cooked Eggs*

HARD-COOKED EGG DISHES

DEVILED EGGS

Prepare and peel
4 Hard-Cooked Eggs (above)
Chill in refrigerator.

Using a narrow, sharp-pointed knife, mark a sawtooth line lengthwise around each egg. Mark points evenly, ½ in. long. Carefully cut down through marked line to yolk of egg, and carefully remove yolk.

Mash or rice egg yolks and mix with
½ teaspoon dry mustard
1 teaspoon vinegar or lemon juice
¼ teaspoon salt
Few grains cayenne pepper
1 tablespoon softened butter or margarine
About 2 tablespoons milk or cream
Lightly fill egg whites with egg yolk mixture. Sprinkle tops with **paprika**.   *4 servings*

DEVILED EGG TREAT

Prepare
6 Hard-Cooked Eggs (on this page)

While eggs are cooking, prepare
1 cup Cheese Sauce (page 304)
Keep sauce covered and hot. Cut each egg into halves lengthwise. Remove egg yolks and sieve or mash. Mix in
1 teaspoon grated onion
¾ teaspoon dry mustard
½ teaspoon salt
¼ teaspoon pepper
¼ teaspoon tarragon leaves, finely crushed
1 or 2 drops Tabasco
Stir in, moistening to a thick, pastelike consistency
4 to 5 tablespoons mayonnaise
Fill egg whites with egg yolk mixture, leaving tops roughly rounded. To heat, place in a colander over hot water. Cover with towel and leave about 5 min. Using 3 egg halves for each serving, place on hot buttered toasted bread or English muffins, waffles, crisp hot noodles, or in **Toast Cups** (page 110) or **Rice Baskets** (page 165). Serve covered with Cheese Sauce.   *4 servings*

HERB-STUFFED EGGS

▲ *Base Recipe*

Prepare and peel
6 Hard-Cooked Eggs (page 133)

Deviled Eggs: Mark a sawtooth line with a sharp knife lengthwise around each hard-cooked egg. Cut through egg white on marked line, gently pull halves apart and carefully remove egg yolk.

Cut eggs into halves lengthwise. Set egg whites aside.

Finely chop

¼ small onion

Put chopped onion and egg yolks into a small bowl with

2 to 3 tablespoons dairy sour cream or mayonnaise
¾ teaspoon dry mustard
½ teaspoon salt
¼ teaspoon pepper
¼ teaspoon savory or tarragon

(Add enough sour cream or mayonnaise to make a thick paste-like mixture.) Beat until ingredients are thoroughly blended. Spoon mixture lightly into egg whites, leaving tops rounded. Or force mixture through a pastry bag and a No. 7 star tube into egg whites. Sprinkle tops with

Paprika

Chill eggs in the refrigerator.

Serve on a bed of crisp **salad greens**.

4 to 6 servings

—TUNA-STUFFED EGGS

Follow ▲ Recipe, using equal quantities of **ketchup**, about 2 or 3 tablespoons, and sour cream or mayonnaise. Add **¼ cup flaked tuna** with other ingredients.

—ANCHOVY-STUFFED EGGS

Follow ▲ Recipe. Omit salt. Add **4 chopped anchovy fillets** with other ingredients.

—HAM-STUFFED EGGS

Follow ▲ Recipe, using ¼ teaspoon salt. Omit savory or tarragon. Add **¼ cup chopped cooked ham** and **3 chopped sweet pickles** with other ingredients.

CREAMED EGGS

▲ *Base Recipe*

Prepare

2 cups Medium White Sauce (double recipe, page 304)

Slice crosswise into sauce

6 Hard-Cooked Eggs (page 133)

Quickly heat together, stirring gently to avoid breaking egg slices. Add extra salt and pepper, if desired.

Serve on hot buttered toasted **bread** or **English muffin halves, waffles,** or buttered **baking powder biscuits.** *4 or 5 servings*

—SPECIAL CREAMED EGGS

Follow ▲ Recipe. Decrease eggs to 4. Heat any one of the following and add to white sauce before adding eggs: **1 cup any mixture of leftover cooked vegetables,** such as carrots, peas, celery, onions and asparagus; **½ cup cooked vegetable** and **½ cup diced cooked meat, poultry** or **fish;** or **1 cup diced cooked meat, poultry** or **fish.** Serve as suggested in ▲ Recipe or put mixture into greased baking dish (or 4 or 5 individual casseroles). Sprinkle with **¼ cup buttered crumbs** (page 9), and bake at 375°F 10 to 15 min., or until browned. For a pleasing variation, serve egg mixture in individual **Ringlet Shells** or **Toast Cups** (page 110).

—PIQUANT CREAMED EGGS

Follow ▲ Recipe. When sauce is thickened, quickly stir in **2 to 4 tablespoons ketchup** and **1 teaspoon prepared mustard** before adding hard-cooked eggs.

—COUNTRY CREAMED EGGS

Follow ▲ Recipe. Place **2 or 3 slices hot crisp bacon** on each serving of one of the suggested breads. Spoon creamed eggs over bacon. Garnish.

—CREAMED EGG BAKE

Follow ▲ Recipe, using **Mushroom Sauce** (page 304) or **Cheese Sauce** (page 304). Fry together 1 tablespoon chopped **green pepper** and 2 tablespoons chopped **onion** in 2 tablespoons **butter** until the onion is tender. Stir vegetables into sauce with ½ coarsely diced **pimiento.** Crumble **potato chips** (3½- to 4½-oz. pkg.); sprinkle one third of potato chips on the bottom of a buttered 1-qt. casserole. Pour about one half of cooked mixture over

layer. Cover with second third of the chips. Pour in remaining cooked mixture and top with potato chips. Bake at 375°F 10 to 15 min., or until browned.

—OYSTER EGG SCALLOP

Follow ▲ Recipe. Use strained liquor drained from **½ pt. oysters** combined with enough milk to make two cups for liquid in Medium White Sauce. Add **1 teaspoon Worcestershire sauce** and **2 tablespoons finely chopped parsley** to sauce. Carefully stir in 4 of the sliced eggs and the drained oysters. Pour one half of this mixture into greased 1-qt. casserole. Arrange thin slices of remaining eggs on top. Cover with remaining creamed mixture. Top with about **¼ cup buttered crumbs** (page 9). Bake at 375°F 10 to 15 min., or until lightly browned.

EGGS FLORENTINE

▲ *Base Recipe*

Grease 4 ramekins.

Prepare and set aside

6 Hard-Cooked Eggs (page 133)

Prepare and set aside

½ cup buttered bread crumbs (page 9)

Wash and cook (page 313)

1 lb. spinach

While spinach is cooking, prepare

1½ cups Medium White Sauce (1½ times recipe, page 304. Blend in, adding all at one time, ⅓ cup grated Cheddar or Parmesan cheese until melted and 1 teaspoon Worcestershire sauce.)

Drain spinach and chop coarsely. Season with a mixture of

½ teaspoon salt
¼ teaspoon monosodium glutamate
⅛ teaspoon pepper
⅛ teaspoon nutmeg or mace

Divide half of spinach among ramekins. Cut 3 of the eggs into crosswise slices and arrange over spinach. Add to each ramekin ¼ cup sauce and 1 tablespoon crumbs. Cover with remaining spinach. Cut each of remaining eggs into 4 lengthwise sections. Using 3 sections for a ramekin, form attractive petal arrangements. Spoon remaining sauce into centers where "petals" meet.

Sprinkle centers with remaining crumbs and

Paprika

Bake at 350°F 15 to 20 min., or until crumbs are lightly browned and casserole is heated.

4 servings

—SCALLOPED EGGS ON ASPARAGUS

Follow ▲ Recipe. Use a greased 1-qt. casserole. Cut all eggs into slices and prepare 1 cup buttered crumbs. Substitute **1 lb. asparagus** for spinach. Wash and cook (page 313).

Lay one half of asparagus in casserole without cutting stalks. Cover with one half of egg slices, sauce and buttered crumbs; repeat. Bake at 350°F 20 to 30 min. Garnish with a sprig or two of **parsley**.

EGG 'N' CHEESE CASSEROLE

Set out 4 individual casseroles or a 1½-qt. baking dish.

Combine in a large bowl, tossing lightly until well mixed
>   **6 to 8 Hard-Cooked Eggs (page 133), coarsely chopped**
>   **¾ cup finely chopped celery**
>   **⅓ cup chopped pecans**
>   **2 tablespoons finely chopped parsley**
>   **1 teaspoon grated onion**
>   **1 teaspoon salt**
>   **¼ teaspoon pepper**
>   **⅔ cup mayonnaise**

Spoon mixture into the individual casseroles or turn into the baking dish.

Sprinkle top with a mixture of
>   **1 cup shredded sharp Cheddar cheese**
>   **¾ cup coarsely crushed potato chips**

Set in a 375°F oven about 25 min., or until cheese is melted and mixture is thoroughly heated.   *4 servings*

POTATO AND EGG CASSEROLE
(Rakott Burgonya)

Generously butter a 2-qt. casserole.

Prepare
>   **6 Hard-Cooked Eggs (page 133)**

Meanwhile, wash
>   **6 or 7 medium (about 2 lbs.) potatoes**

Cook (page 313) about 25 to 30 min., or until potatoes are tender. Drain potatoes. To dry potatoes, shake pan over low heat. Peel. Cut potatoes and eggs into ¼-in. slices.

Prepare and set aside
>   **⅓ cup fine dry buttered crumbs (page 9)**

Mix
>   **1 cup dairy sour cream**
>   **½ cup butter, melted and cooled**

Reserve one half of the sour cream mixture for top of casserole.

Beginning and ending with potatoes, alternate three layers of potatoes and two layers of eggs in the casserole; spoon about 6 tablespoons sour cream mixture over each egg layer and season with **salt and pepper.**

Cover top layer of potatoes with reserved sour cream mixture. Sprinkle with the buttered crumbs.

Bake at 350°F 20 to 30 min., or until crumbs are browned.   *6 or 7 servings*

CASSEROLE OF CREOLE EGGS

Lightly grease a 1½-qt. casserole.

Prepare
>   **6 Hard-Cooked Eggs (page 133)**

While eggs are cooking, set aside to drain, reserving liquid
>   **1 can (4 oz.) sliced mushrooms (about ½ cup mushrooms)**

Clean and chop
>   **1 medium green pepper (about ½ cup, chopped)**
>   **1 medium onion (about ½ cup, chopped)**
>   **1 stalk celery**

Heat in a skillet over low heat
>   **¼ cup butter or margarine**

Add chopped vegetables and cook over medium heat, stirring occasionally, until onion is tender. Add mushrooms and continue cooking until mushrooms are lightly browned, stirring occasionally.

Add gradually, stirring constantly
>   **2 cups sieved cooked tomatoes**

Simmer 5 min., stirring occasionally.

Meanwhile, melt in a saucepan over low heat
>   **3 to 4 tablespoons butter or margarine**

Blend in a mixture of
>   **6 tablespoons all-purpose flour**
>   **¼ teaspoon salt**
>   **¼ teaspoon monosodium glutamate**
>   **Few grains pepper**

Cook over medium heat, stirring constantly, until mixture bubbles. Remove from heat and gradually add tomato-vegetable mixture while stirring constantly. Return mixture to heat and bring rapidly to boiling, continuing to stir. Cook 1 to 2 min. longer.

Add to the reserved mushroom liquid, enough to make 1 cup liquid
>   **Cold milk**

Pour into a bowl. Stirring constantly, gradually add the hot tomato-vegetable mixture to the milk mixture.

Slice the Hard-Cooked Eggs into the casserole forming layers; pour some of the tomato-milk mixture over each layer of eggs. Finally pour remaining tomato-milk mixture over sliced eggs. Sprinkle over top
>   **1 cup buttered soft bread crumbs (page 9)**

Bake at 350°F 15 to 20 min., or until crumbs are lightly browned and mixture is heated through.

Serve over
>   **Fluffy Rice (page 164)**
>   *6 to 8 servings*

Bran Biscuit Pie

BRAN BISCUIT PIE

Grease a shallow 2-qt. casserole.

Prepare
>   **6 Hard-Cooked Eggs (page 133)**

For Bran Biscuit Topping—Sift together in a bowl
>   **1½ cups all-purpose flour**
>   **2¼ teaspoons baking powder**
>   **¾ teaspoon salt**

Mix in
>   **⅓ cup whole bran cereal**

Cut into dry ingredients with a pastry blender or two knives until pieces are size of coarse corn meal
>   **6 tablespoons lard**

Make a well in center of mixture and add all at one time
>   **½ cup plus 1 tablespoon milk**

Stir with fork until dough follows fork. Gently form dough into a ball and put on a lightly floured surface. Knead lightly with fingertips 10 to 15 times. Roll dough into a rectangle or square; cut about 12 square or round biscuits with floured knife or biscuit cutter. Brush biscuits with
>   **Milk**

Set aside.

For Casserole—Heat slowly in a skillet until onion is soft, stirring frequently
>   **2 tablespoons butter or margarine**
>   **⅓ cup finely chopped onion**

Prepare
>   **2 cups Medium White Sauce (double recipe, page 304)**

Stir in the onion and
>   **2 cups (16-oz. can, drained) peas**
>   **2 teaspoons prepared mustard**
>   **1 teaspoon curry powder**
>   **½ teaspoon lemon juice**

Heat mixture just to boiling. Cut eggs into large pieces; carefully stir into sauce. Immediately turn into casserole. Quickly border casserole with biscuits.

Bake at 450°F 10 to 15 min., or until biscuits are lightly browned.   *4 to 6 servings*

Note: To make an attractive arrangement in a clear glass casserole, cut 3 of the eggs in-

Egg and Nut-Filled Pancakes

Eggs on Noodle Casserole

to crosswise slices; place slices around sides of greased casserole before adding sauce.

EGG AND NUT-FILLED PANCAKES

Delicate pancakes, a filling that's really unique in flavor, and a rich cheese sauce are the components of a distinctive supper dish.

Set out a 6-in. skillet and a shallow baking dish.

For Filling—Prepare
   3 Hard-Cooked Eggs (page 133)
Finely chop and set aside
   ½ cup (about 3 oz.) hazelnuts
Blend
   6 tablespoons mayonnaise
   ¾ teaspoon salt
   ½ teaspoon coriander
   ⅛ teaspoon white pepper
   Few grains paprika
Chop the hard-cooked eggs and add to the mayonnaise mixture with the hazelnuts and
   ½ cup diced celery
Mix thoroughly; cover and set aside.

For Pancakes—Put into a bowl and beat slightly
   3 eggs
Add and beat until smooth
   ¼ cup milk
   2 tablespoons all-purpose flour
   ½ teaspoon salt
Grease the skillet lightly with
   Butter or margarine
Heat the skillet to moderately hot. Spoon about 2 tablespoons batter into the skillet and immediately tilt skillet back and forth to spread batter thinly and evenly. Cook each pancake over medium heat until lightly browned on one side only. (Do not turn.) Carefully remove the pancake from skillet and put on absorbent

paper. Repeat procedure for remaining batter. It should not be necessary to grease the skillet for each pancake.

Spoon about 3 tablespoons of the filling onto each pancake and roll up. Arrange the filled pancake rolls in the baking dish and keep warm in a slow oven.

Prepare
   2 cups Cheese Sauce (double recipe, page 304)
Serve pancakes with the hot Cheese Sauce.
4 or 5 servings

EGGS ON NOODLE CASSEROLE

▲ *Base Recipe*

Grease a shallow 2-qt. casserole or 8 large ramekins.

Prepare
   5 Hard-Cooked Eggs (page 133)

Meanwhile, cook and drain
   8 oz. noodles
Turn noodles into casserole.

Mix in a saucepan and heat
   1⅔ cups undiluted evaporated milk
   1⅓ cups (10¾-oz. can)
   condensed tomato soup
Cook over low heat, stirring occasionally. Set mixture aside.

Cut eggs crosswise into halves. Remove egg yolks and sieve or mash. Mix in
   2 tablespoons anchovy paste
   1 tablespoon minced parsley
   1 teaspoon minced onion
Moisten with about
   2 tablespoons undiluted evaporated milk
   2 to 3 teaspoons lemon juice
Pile mixture into the egg white cavities; leave tops roughly rounded.

Arrange eggs on noodles; pour sauce over.

Prepare (page 9) and sprinkle over casserole
   ½ cup buttered bread crumbs

Bake at 350°F 20 to 25 min., or until crumbs are browned. *8 servings*

—STUFFED EGGS WITH OLIVE SAUCE

Follow ▲ Recipe. Omit anchovy paste. Add **1 teaspoon chopped pimiento** to egg yolks. Add to white sauce **12 green or ripe olives,** pitted and chopped, and **½ teaspoon Worcestershire sauce.**

EGG CUTLETS

Prepare and dice
   4 Hard-Cooked Eggs (page 133)

Meanwhile, prepare
   1 cup Thick White Sauce (page 304. Use 3 tablespoons fat and 4 tablespoons flour to 1 cup milk. Flavor with 1 teaspoon Worcestershire sauce.)

Combine eggs, sauce and
   ⅓ cup fine dry bread crumbs
   ¼ cup shredded cheese
Chill in refrigerator for an hour or longer. Then pat into cutlet-shape patties. Dip in a mixture of
   1 egg, slightly beaten
   1 tablespoon water
Coat well in
   ½ cup (1 to 2 slices) fine dry bread crumbs

Brown evenly over moderate heat in a skillet containing
   2 to 3 tablespoons fat
Serve very hot with either **Mushroom Sauce** (page 304) or **Tomato Sauce** (page 307).
6 servings

EGG CROQUETTES
(Tojás Krokett)

Prepare
   4 Hard-Cooked Eggs (page 133)

Meanwhile, melt over direct heat in top of a double boiler
   ¼ cup butter or margarine
Blend into the butter a mixture of
   ½ cup all-purpose flour
   1 teaspoon salt
   Few grains pepper
Heat until mixture bubbles, stirring constantly. Remove from heat. Add gradually, stirring constantly
   2 cups milk
Return to heat and bring rapidly to boiling, stirring constantly; cook 1 to 2 min. longer. Remove from heat. Vigorously stir about ¼ cup of the hot sauce, 1 tablespoon at a time, into
   3 eggs, slightly beaten
Quickly blend into sauce. Cook over boiling

water 3 to 5 min., stirring slowly to keep it cooking evenly. Remove sauce from water and cool slightly by setting double boiler top in bowl of cold water.

Peel and dice the Hard-Cooked Eggs and gently mix them with the sauce. Cool completely and chill mixture in the refrigerator 1 hr. or longer.

Prepare and keep warm
Mushroom Wine Sauce (see Deep-Fried Eggs with Mushroom Wine Sauce, on this page)

About 20 min. before deep-frying, fill a deep saucepan one-half to two-thirds full with
Vegetable shortening, all-purpose shortening, lard or cooking oil for deep-frying
Heat slowly to 375°F (page 11). When using an automatic deep fryer, follow manufacturer's directions for amount of fat and timing.

Shape cold egg mixture into croquettes (balls or cones), using about ¼ cup of mixture for each. Roll them in
1½ cups (4 to 5 slices) fine dry bread crumbs
Then dip them in a mixture of
1 egg, well beaten
1 tablespoon milk
Again roll them in bread crumbs. Shake off loose crumbs. Deep-fry croquettes 3 to 5 min., or until golden brown. Fry only one layer of croquettes at a time; do not crowd. Turn them occasionally to brown evenly. Remove croquettes with slotted spoon, draining over fat for a second. Remove to absorbent paper.

Serve with the Mushroom Wine Sauce.
12 croquettes

DEEP-FRIED EGGS WITH MUSHROOM WINE SAUCE
(Tojás Bor Mártassal)

These hard-cooked eggs have a new look and new taste. The new look is due to their pancake batter coating and the new taste to a mushroom wine sauce.

For Mushroom Wine Sauce—Set out an 8-in. skillet.

Prepare and set aside
1 cup quick meat broth (page 10)

Clean and slice (page 9)
½ lb. mushrooms

Melt in the skillet over low heat
6 tablespoons butter
Add the mushrooms to the butter with
3 tablespoons finely chopped onion
2 tablespoons finely chopped parsley
Cook slowly, stirring gently, until mushrooms are lightly browned and tender and onions are almost soft. Remove mushroom mixture and the liquid from skillet to a bowl; cover bowl and set aside.

Melt in the skillet
3 tablespoons butter

Blend into butter until smooth
3 tablespoons all-purpose flour
¾ teaspoon salt
⅛ teaspoon pepper
Heat until mixture bubbles and is lightly browned. Remove from heat. Add gradually the reserved broth, stirring constantly. Return to heat and bring rapidly to boiling, stirring constantly; cook 1 to 2 min. longer.

Remove skillet from heat. Add gradually to sauce, stirring constantly
¾ cup dry white wine
Mix the mushrooms and the liquid in bowl with the sauce in skillet; cover skillet and set aside.

For Eggs—About 20 min. before deep-frying, fill a deep saucepan one-half to two-thirds full with
Vegetable shortening, all-purpose shortening, lard or cooking oil for deep-frying
Heat slowly to 365°F (page 11). When using automatic deep fryer, follow manufacturer's directions for amount of fat and timing.

Prepare and remove shells from
10 Hard-Cooked Eggs (page 133)

For Batter—Sift together and set aside
1⅓ cups sifted all-purpose flour
½ teaspoon salt

Combine in a 1-qt. bowl
2 eggs, slightly beaten
¼ cup milk
Add to egg mixture enough of the flour mixture to make a very stiff batter, stirring just until smooth.

Dry Hard-Cooked Eggs thoroughly with absorbent paper. Cut two eggs into halves and wrap in waxed paper; set aside for garnish. Put remaining eggs into batter, a few at a time, to coat thoroughly. Carefully remove eggs from batter with fork or slotted spoon to the heated fat. Deep-fry eggs 3 to 4 min., or until golden

brown. Fry only one layer of eggs at a time; do not crowd. Turn eggs occasionally to brown evenly. Remove eggs with slotted spoon, draining over fat for a second before removing to absorbent paper. Place the eggs on a warm platter. Garnish the platter with the reserved hard-cooked egg halves and **parsley**. Serve with the Mushroom Wine Sauce. *4 servings*

POACHED EGGS

POACHED EGGS

▲ *Base Recipe*

Grease bottom of a small skillet. Add water to 2-in. depth or enough to cover 1 in. above tops of eggs.

Add to water
⅛ to ¼ teaspoon salt
Bring water to boiling and then reduce heat to keep water simmering. Uncover pan.

Break (only one at a time) into a saucer or small dish
4 eggs
Tilting dish toward edge of pan, quickly slip each egg into water; do not crowd. Cook uncovered 3 to 5 min., depending upon firmness desired. Carefully remove eggs with slotted spoon. To drain, hold spoon on folded paper napkin a few seconds.

Serve plain or on hot buttered toasted **bread** or **English muffin halves;** or serve with **vegetables.** Season with **salt and pepper** or **paprika.** *4 servings*

—POACHED EGGS WITH MUSHROOM OR CHEESE SAUCE

Follow ▲ Recipe. Top with **Mushroom Sauce** (page 304) or **Cheese Sauce** (page 304, about ½ cup per serving).

—POACHED EGGS AND GREENS

In individual heat-resistant dishes, make nests of hot finely chopped **well-seasoned spinach,**

Deep-Fried Eggs with Mushroom Wine Sauce

Savory Poached Eggs

Swiss chard or other cooked greens. Shred 2 oz. (½ cup, shredded) Swiss, Parmesan or Cheddar cheese. Sprinkle one half of cheese over greens. Keep hot while proceeding with ▲ Recipe. Place poached egg in each nest of greens. If desired, top with **Medium White Sauce** (page 304, about ¼ cup per serving). Sprinkle with remaining cheese and place on broiler rack. Place under broiler with tops of dishes about 3 in. from heat long enough to melt cheese.

—SAVORY POACHED EGGS

Follow ▲ Recipe. Use **meat or chicken broth or milk** instead of water. Add any additional seasoning desired. Garnish with **crisp bacon slices,** if desired.

—POACHED EGGS AND PATTIES

Brown **Codfish Cakes** (page 276) or rounds of hash in **2 or 3 tablespoons fat.** Keep hot while proceeding with ▲ Recipe. Top servings of hash or cakes with poached eggs and serve with **Mock Hollandaise Sauce** (page 304) or **Cheese Sauce** (page 304, about ¼ cup per serving).

—EGGS BENEDICT

Cover buttered toasted **English muffin halves** with round slices of hot cooked **ham.** Proceed with ▲ Recipe. Place a poached egg on each ham slice and top with **Hollandaise Sauce** (page 306).

Eggs Benedict

EGGS POACHED IN WINE

Combine in a skillet over medium heat
1 tablespoon butter or margarine, melted
½ cup dry white wine
When quite hot carefully slip in, one at a time
4 eggs (yolks whole)
Season to taste with
Salt
Seasoned pepper
Cook gently until whites of eggs are almost "set." Sprinkle eggs with
Roquefort cheese (crumbled), about 2 tablespoons
Cook several minutes longer or until cheese is melted. Serve eggs on buttered **toast rounds.**

4 servings

FRIED EGGS

FRIED EGGS

▲ *Base Recipe*

Heat in a heavy skillet
1 to 2 tablespoons fat (kind of fat used will affect flavor of eggs)

Break into a saucer one at a time and slip into skillet
2 eggs per serving
Reduce heat and cook slowly about 4 min., or until desired stage of firmness. Frequently baste eggs with fat in skillet. Or instead of basting, cover pan, or with spatula turn eggs over once.

—BUTTER-POACHED EGGS

Follow ▲ Recipe. Use just enough butter to cover bottom of skillet. Cook eggs about 1 min., or until edges turn white. Then, for each 2 eggs, add **1 teaspoon water.** Slightly decrease proportion of water for each additional egg. Tightly cover skillet and let the steam which is formed cook the eggs to desired stage of firmness.

EGGS FRIED GASCONY STYLE
(Oeufs aux Aubergines Frittes)

Set out a large skillet with a tight-fitting cover.

Prepare and keep warm
Provençal Sauce (page 308)

Meanwhile, wash and pare enough eggplant for
4 slices eggplant, ¼ in. thick
Coat eggplant slices with mixture of
¼ cup all-purpose flour
⅛ teaspoon salt
Few grains pepper

Heat in skillet
3 tablespoons olive oil

Fried Eggs

Add eggplant and fry about 3 min. on one side.

Break into a saucer, one at a time, as used
4 eggs
Turn each eggplant slice. Immediately and carefully slide one egg onto each eggplant slice. Cover and cook until eggs are done. Remove to a warm serving plate and top with
4 very thin slices cooked ham
and ½ cup hot Provençal Sauce (reserve remainder for future use). Sprinkle with
1 tablespoon chopped parsley

4 servings

BROWN BUTTER EGGS
(Vajas Tojás)

Heat in a heavy 10-in. skillet until lightly browned
⅓ cup butter

Set out
6 eggs
Break one of the eggs into a saucer. Slip egg into the skillet by tilting saucer toward inside edge of the skillet. Add each of the remaining eggs in the same way. Reduce heat. Frequently basting eggs with butter in skillet, cook slowly, about 4 min., or until eggs reach desired stage of firmness. Or, instead of basting, cover pan; or turn eggs over once.

Sprinkle each egg with
Few grains salt
Few grains pepper
Remove eggs to warm platter. Add to remaining butter in skillet and mix well
½ teaspoon vinegar
Pour vinegar-butter mixture over eggs and serve immediately.

4 to 6 servings

SCRAMBLED EGGS

SCRAMBLED EGGS

▲ *Base Recipe*

Set out an 8- to 10-in. skillet.

Put into a bowl

6 eggs
6 tablespoons milk, cream or undiluted evaporated milk
¾ teaspoon salt
⅛ teaspoon pepper

For uniform yellow color, beat egg mixture until thoroughly blended. For streaks, beat only slightly.

Heat skillet until just hot enough to sizzle a drop of water. Melt in skillet

3 tablespoons butter or margarine

Pour in egg mixture and cook slowly over low heat. With a fork or spatula, lift mixture from bottom and sides of skillet as it thickens, allowing uncooked part to flow to bottom. Avoid stirring. Cook slowly until scrambled eggs are thick and creamy throughout but are still moist.

If desired, add **minced parsley or chives** to egg mixture. Serve immediately.   *4 servings*

—EGG AND CHEESE SCRAMBLE

Follow ▲ Recipe. Allow eggs to thicken slightly at first. Then sprinkle with **¼ cup shredded Cheddar cheese**.

—SCRAMBLED EGGS DE LUXE

Follow ▲ Recipe. Beat with the eggs **½ teaspoon Worcestershire sauce**. Scramble with egg mixture, **¼ cup shredded cheese** and **1 medium tomato**, rinsed, stem ends removed, peeled and cubed. Cook until thick and creamy. Stir in **1 cup Croutons** (page 39) just before serving.

—SCRAMBLED EGGS AND MUSHROOMS

Follow ▲ Recipe. Clean and slice (page 9) **6 medium fresh mushrooms**. Cook in skillet about 5 min. in **¼ cup butter or margarine**. Add egg mixture to mushrooms and butter in skillet; cook as in ▲ Recipe.

—SCRAMBLED EGGS WITH HAM OR BACON

Follow ▲ Recipe. Add to skillet with egg mixture **⅓ cup diced cooked ham**. Or add **4 slices crisp fried bacon**, crumbled.

—SCRAMBLED EGGS WITH SAUSAGE

In a skillet, place **½ lb. sausage links** and **2 tablespoons water** and cover tightly. Cook slowly 8 to 10 min. Remove cover and pour off liquid. Brown links, turning occasionally and pouring off fat as it accumulates. Drain on absorbent paper. Keep warm. Follow ▲ Recipe for preparing scrambled eggs. Serve at once with sausage links.

—BACON AND CREAM CHEESE SCRAMBLE

In the top of a double boiler, combine the milk, cream or evaporated milk of the ▲ Recipe with **1 pkg. (3 oz.) cream cheese** and **2 tablespoons butter or margarine**. Heat over simmering water, stirring occasionally, until cheese is softened and ingredients are blended. Remove from heat. Follow ▲ Recipe, decreasing salt to ¼ teaspoon. Add cream cheese mixture gradually to eggs, while beating. Add **½ cup diced panfried bacon** to eggs just before pouring into skillet.

—AVOCADO AND DEVILED HAM SCRAMBLE

Rinse, peel, cut into halves and pit **1 small avocado**. Dice, toss with **1 teaspoon lemon juice** to prevent discoloration, and set aside. Follow ▲ Recipe. When egg mixture is slightly thickened, spoon over it **1 can (4½ oz.) deviled ham** and continue cooking. When eggs are done, quickly fold in the diced avocado.

CREAMY SCRAMBLED EGGS

A delicious luncheon or supper main dish.

Set out an 8- to 10-in. skillet.

Put into a bowl

6 eggs
½ cup dairy sour cream
1 teaspoon prepared mustard
1 teaspoon salt
¼ teaspoon monosodium glutamate
⅛ teaspoon pepper

Beat just until blended with rotary beater. Add to mixture and blend in

2 tablespoons minced onion
2 tablespoons minced parsley

Heat skillet until just hot enough to sizzle a drop of water. Melt in skillet

3 tablespoons butter or margarine

Pour in egg mixture and cook slowly over low heat. With a fork or spoon lift mixture from bottom and sides of pan as it thickens, allowing uncooked part to flow to bottom. Avoid stirring. Cook until eggs are thick and creamy throughout, but still moist.

Serve immediately on hot buttered **toast** or in **Croustades** (page 110).   *4 servings*

SCRAMBLED EGGS WITH ANCHOVIES
(Tojás Szardellával)

Set out an 8-in. skillet.

Blend thoroughly in a mixing bowl

6 eggs, slightly beaten
6 tablespoons dairy sour cream
⅛ teaspoon pepper
2 to 4 anchovy fillets, finely chopped

Heat the skillet until just hot enough to sizzle a drop of water. Melt in the skillet

2 to 3 tablespoons butter or margarine

Pour the egg mixture into the skillet and cook slowly over low heat. With a fork or spatula, lift egg mixture from bottom and sides of skillet as it thickens, allowing uncooked part to flow to bottom; do not stir. Cook until eggs are thick and creamy throughout but still moist. Serve immediately.   *4 servings*

MUSHROOMS WITH SCRAMBLED EGGS
(Gomba Tojással)

Set out a 10-in. skillet.

Clean and slice (page 9)

1 lb. mushrooms

Heat in the skillet

½ cup butter

Add the mushrooms to butter with

¼ cup chopped onion

Cook slowly, stirring occasionally, until onion is almost tender and mushrooms are lightly browned.

Meanwhile, blend thoroughly

2 eggs, slightly beaten
2 tablespoons dairy sour cream
¼ teaspoon salt
Few grains pepper

Creamy Scrambled Eggs: With fork or spoon, lift mixture; uncooked part will flow to bottom. Cook eggs until thick and creamy but still moist. Serve immediately with sausage, ham or bacon.

Banana Omelet

Pour egg mixture into the skillet, mixing with the mushrooms and onions. Cook slowly over low heat; with a fork or spatula lift mixture from bottom and sides of skillet as it thickens, allowing uncooked part to flow to bottom. Avoid stirring. Cook until eggs are thick and creamy throughout but still moist.

4 or 5 servings

OMELETS

QUICK 'N' SURE OMELET

▲ *Base Recipe*

Set out an 8- to 10-in. skillet.

Beat until well blended but not foamy
6 eggs
6 tablespoons water or milk
¾ teaspoon salt
⅛ teaspoon pepper
Heat skillet until just hot enough to sizzle a drop of water. Melt in skillet
3 tablespoons butter or margarine
Pour egg mixture into skillet and reduce heat. As edges of omelet begin to thicken, draw cooked portions toward center with spoon or fork to allow uncooked mixture to flow to bottom of skillet. Shake and tilt skillet as necessary to aid flow of uncooked eggs. Do not stir. When eggs no longer flow but surface is still moist, the heat may be increased to quickly brown the bottom of omelet. Loosen edges carefully and fold in half. Slide onto a warm serving platter. Garnish.

4 to 6 servings

Note: Often omelets to which other ingredients are added are cooked in smaller portions, pancake-fashion, or the larger ones are cut into wedges and served.

—CHICKEN LIVER OMELET

Clean **¼ lb. chicken livers.** Cut into smaller pieces, if desired. Coat evenly by shaking livers in plastic bag containing a mixture of **⅓ cup all-purpose flour, ½ teaspoon salt** and **¼ teaspoon paprika.** Brown livers with **2 tablespoons minced onion** in **3 tablespoons butter or margarine,** turning frequently. Follow ▲ Recipe. Enclose cooked livers in omelet just before serving.

—BANANA OMELET

Follow ▲ Recipe. Peel and slice **2 medium brown-flecked bananas.** Pour **2 teaspoons lemon juice** over slices. Fill omelet with banana slices, reserving about 8 slices for top. Arrange rest of slices on top with a **sprig of parsley** between each slice. Serve with **Pan-fried Bacon** (page 190).

—CHEESE OMELET

Follow ▲ Recipe. Add to egg mixture **1 teaspoon Worcestershire sauce, 3 tablespoons minced parsley** and **¼ cup shredded cheese.** Sprinkle an additional **¼ cup shredded cheese** over omelet while it is cooking.

—CITRUS OMELET

Follow ▲ Recipe. Use **3 tablespoons lemon, orange or grapefruit juice** and **3 tablespoons water** for liquid.

—SWEET OMELET

Prepare Citrus Omelet. Add **¼ cup sugar** to fruit juices. Follow ▲ Recipe.

—BACON OMELET

Cut **8 slices bacon** into small pieces; fry until crisp. Proceed with ▲ Recipe, pouring egg mixture over bacon and using **2 tablespoons bacon fat** in the skillet instead of butter or margarine.

—JAM OR JELLY OMELET

Follow ▲ Recipe. Just before folding omelet in half, spread omelet with **⅓ to ½ cup apricot, strawberry or raspberry jam, orange marmalade, currant or cranberry jelly.**

—CANTONESE OMELET

Panfry in **2 to 3 tablespoons butter or margarine, 2 tablespoons finely chopped onion** and **½ cup sliced mushrooms or drained bean sprouts.** Mix in 1 cup of a combination of cut-up **cooked shrimp** and chopped **cooked pork** and **½ teaspoon soy sauce.** Continue heating for 2 to 3 min. Add **salt** and **pepper** to taste. Keep hot while proceeding with ▲ Recipe. Enclose vegetable-meat combination in folded omelet before serving.

—MUSHROOM OMELET

Drain, reserving liquid, **1 can (6¾ oz.) mushroom pieces and stems** (about ⅔ cup, drained). Cook mushrooms until lightly browned in a small skillet containing **3 tablespoons butter or margarine.** Set aside and keep warm. Follow ▲ Recipe, substituting **mushroom liquid** for milk or water. Spoon mushrooms over top of omelet just before folding.

COTTAGE CHEESE OMELET

Set out a 10-in. skillet.

Beat together until well blended but not foamy
6 eggs
6 tablespoons water or milk
¾ teaspoon salt
⅛ teaspoon pepper
Mix thoroughly and blend into egg mixture
1 cup cream-style cottage cheese
2 tablespoons finely chopped pimiento
1 tablespoon minced chives
Heat skillet until just hot enough to sizzle a drop of water. Heat in skillet
3 tablespoons butter or margarine
Pour egg mixture into skillet and reduce heat. As edges of omelet begin to thicken, draw cooked portions toward center with spoon or fork to allow uncooked mixture to flow to bottom of skillet. Shake and tilt skillet as necessary to aid flow of uncooked eggs. Do not stir.

When eggs no longer flow but surface is still moist, heat may be increased to brown bottom of omelet quickly. Loosen edges carefully and fold in half. Slide omelet onto a warm serving platter.

4 to 6 servings

HUNGARIAN MUSHROOM OMELET
(Gombás Omlette)

▲ *Base Recipe*

Set out an 8-in. skillet and a round 8- or 9-in. shallow baking dish.

Clean and slice (page 9)
¾ lb. mushrooms

Heat in the skillet over low heat
¼ cup butter or margarine
Add mushrooms to the butter and cook them slowly, stirring gently, until lightly browned

Hungarian Mushroom Omelet

and tender. Reserve about 8 mushroom slices for top of omelet. Place remaining mushrooms and liquid into a bowl; cover bowl and set it aside in a warm place. Set the skillet aside.

Melt in a small saucepan over low heat
¼ cup butter or margarine
Blend into the butter until smooth
¼ cup all-purpose flour
½ teapoon salt
⅛ teaspoon pepper
Heat until mixture bubbles. Remove saucepan from heat. Add gradually, stirring constantly
1 cup milk
Return to heat and bring rapidly to boiling, stirring constantly. Remove from heat. Vigorously stir about ⅓ cup of the hot mixture, 1 tablespoon at a time, into
3 eggs, slightly beaten
Immediately blend into remaining hot mixture, stirring until smooth. Cover and set aside.

Place the skillet over low heat.

Meanwhile, measure
4 teaspoons butter or margarine

Test skillet; it is hot enough when drops of water sprinkled on surface dance in small beads. Reduce heat under skillet and melt 1 teaspoon of the butter in the skillet. Pour about one-fourth of the egg mixture into the skillet and cook over low heat until it is lightly browned on bottom and firm but slightly moist on top. Loosen edges carefully with spatula and slide the omelet layer into the baking dish.

Remove about one third of mushrooms with slotted spoon and spread over the omelet layer. Repeat process with remaining egg mixture, alternating omelet and mushroom layers. Top the last omelet layer with reserved mushroom slices.

Bake at 350°F 10 to 15 min., or until omelet is thoroughly heated. Cut omelet into wedges; garnish with **parsley**. *4 servings*

—MUSHROOM OMELET WITH ONIONS
(Gombás Omlette Hagymával)

Follow ▲ Recipe. Combine with sliced mushrooms **½ cup (about 1 medium) chopped onion** and **2 tablespoons chopped green pepper**. Cook until onion is tender, stirring occasionally.

FRENCH OMELET
(Omelette)

▲ Base Recipe

The Frenchwoman prepares her superb omelets in a special omelet pan with a long handle. She never cooks anything else in it and never washes it with water; if she did either, omelets made later might stick to the pan. Instead she cleans it with a towel or, if necessary, with coarse salt.

Set out a 7- or 8-in. skillet.

Combine in a bowl
5 eggs
1 tablespoon cold water
½ teaspoon salt
Few grains cayenne pepper
Beat together until egg whites and egg yolks are well mixed but not frothy.

Heat skillet. Place on end of fork
1 teaspoon butter
Test temperature of skillet by quickly moving butter about skillet. When butter sizzles briskly without browning, desired temperature has been reached. Wipe skillet with soft absorbent paper and repeat test if skillet is too hot or not hot enough.

Spread quickly around the skillet
2 tablespoons butter
Pour in egg mixture, stir once around skillet with fork and then shake skillet by moving it back and forth over medium or low heat until the mixture begins to set. Slowly stir top of mixture until thickened. Without stirring, allow to set about 1 min., or until delicately browned on the bottom. With spatula, loosen edge of omelet, fold in half and slide at once onto a hot serving plate.

If desired, fill with diced or shredded meat or vegetables before folding omelet.

2 or 3 servings

—OMELET WITH SAVORY HERBS
(Omelette aux Fines Herbes)

Follow ▲ Recipe. Add to egg mixture **1 tablespoon minced onion or chives, 1 tablespoon finely chopped parsley, 1 teaspoon chervil** and **1 teaspoon tarragon leaves**, finely chopped.

—SHRIMP OMELET
(Omelette aux Crevettes)

This variation is a specialty of Trouville on the Normandy seacoast.

Have ready **12 canned or cooked, peeled and deveined shrimp**. Cut shrimp into small pieces.

Mix with **¼ cup cream**; set aside. Follow ▲ Recipe. Stir shrimp mixture into egg mixture before pouring into skillet.

—SPINACH OMELET
(Omelette à l'Epinard)

This variation is a specialty of Provence.

Follow ▲ Recipe. Use **½ cup cooked spinach,** (or cook ¼ lb. spinach, page 322). Chop spinach and mix **2 tablespoons hot cream** to moisten. Before folding omelet, spread spinach mixture over top. Serve with **Béchamel Sauce** (page 304) or **Mornay Sauce** (page 305).

CHEESE PUFFY OMELETS

▲ Base Recipe

Start heating oven to 350°F. Set out a griddle or a heavy 10-in. skillet.

Shred and set aside
4 oz. process American cheese (1 cup, shredded)

Beat until thick and lemon-colored
3 egg yolks
Set aside.

Using clean beaters, beat until frothy
3 egg whites
Add to egg whites
3 tablespoons water
½ teaspoon salt
Few grains white pepper
Continue beating egg white mixture until rounded peaks are formed.

French Omelet

Cheese Puffy Omelets

Melt on griddle or in skillet until bubbling hot
1 to 2 tablespoons butter or margarine

Spread egg yolks over egg whites and fold gently together. Slide gently into three equal portions onto hot griddle or as one large omelet into skillet. Cook ½ min.; lower heat and cook slowly about 10 min., or until lightly browned on bottom. Do not stir at any time. Mixture will look moist and puffy on top.

Place griddle with omelets or skillet with omelet into 350°F oven about 5 min. Sprinkle one third of the shredded cheese over the top of each small omelet or all of the cheese over the large omelet.

Return omelets to oven and continue baking until cheese melts. To serve, loosen edges with spatula, make a quick, shallow cut through center and fold one side over. Gently slip onto a warm serving platter. Garnish with
Paprika
Serve immediately. *3 servings*

—FRUIT JUICE OMELETS

Follow ▲ Recipe. Omit cheese. Substitute **orange juice** for water. Or, decrease water to 2 tablespoons and add with **2 teaspoons lemon juice** to egg whites.

—COTTAGE CHEESE OMELETS

Follow ▲ Recipe. Omit cheese. Combine with egg mixture **½ cup cottage cheese, 1 table-spoon finely chopped pimiento** and **2 teaspoons minced chives.**

BAKED EGGS

BAKED (SHIRRED) EGGS

▲ *Base Recipe*

Butter 4 individual casseroles or heat-resistant custard cups.

Break, one at a time, into a saucer or small dish
4 eggs
Slip each egg into a casserole. Sprinkle each with
Few grains salt
Few grains pepper
Top each egg with
1 tablespoon cream
¼ teaspoon butter or margarine

Bake at 325°F, uncovered, 12 to 20 min., depending upon firmness desired.

Garnish and serve in the casseroles.
4 servings

—BAKED EGGS IN BACON RINGS

Allow **1 or 2 slices bacon** for each serving. Partially cook bacon. Line 4 individual baking dishes or muffin-pan wells with the bacon slices. Proceed with ▲ Recipe.

—BAKED EGGS WITH CHEESE

Follow ▲ Recipe. Add **⅛ teaspoon Worcestershire sauce** with each tablespoon cream. In addition to seasonings, sprinkle each egg with **1 tablespoon shredded Swiss or Cheddar cheese** blended with **⅛ teaspoon dry mustard.**

—NESTED BAKED EGGS

For Potato Nests—Lightly spread seasoned hot **whipped or riced potatoes** in buttered shallow baking dish or individual casseroles. Make a hollow in whipped potato for each egg. Put **1 teaspoon ketchup** in each nest and slip in the egg. Season, omitting butter. Lay **1 or 2 slices uncooked bacon** over each nested egg. Bake as in ▲ Recipe.

For Baked Potato Nests—Cut a slice from top of each **baked potato.** (See Baked Filled Potatoes, page 343.) Carefully remove pulp, mash and season. Stuff potato shells two-thirds full. Slip an egg into each. Season. Top with **grated cheese,** if desired. Bake according to ▲ Recipe.

BAKED EGGS WITH SOUR CREAM
(Tojás Tejföllel)

Butter a 1½-qt. casserole.

Set out
1¾ cups dairy sour cream
⅓ cup (1 slice) fine dry bread crumbs
¼ cup butter, cut in small pieces
Put into the casserole 1¼ cups sour cream and one half of butter. Sprinkle over sour cream and butter one half of the crumbs.

Set out
6 eggs
Break one of the eggs into a saucer. Slip the egg onto bread crumbs by tilting saucer toward inside edge of casserole. Add each of the remaining eggs in the same way. Carefully arrange remaining butter, sour cream and crumbs over eggs. Top with
⅓ cup grated Parmesan cheese

Bake at 325°F 25 to 30 min., or until eggs are set. Serve immediately. *4 to 6 servings*

SHIRRED EGGS
(Oeufs sur-le-Plat)

▲ *Base Recipe*

In France these "eggs on-a-dish" are cooked in a special shirrer or cocotte which holds two eggs.

For each person to be served, allow an individual cocotte, custard cup or ramekin.

Arrange cocottes on baking sheet or in shallow pan. Measure into each cocotte
2 teaspoons butter
Set in 350°F oven only until butter is melted and hot. Remove from oven and carefully break into each cocotte, depending upon size
1 or 2 eggs
Season each egg with
⅛ teaspoon salt
Few grains pepper
Dot each egg with
1½ teaspoons butter
Return cocottes to oven for 15 to 20 min., or until the egg whites are set.

Serve the eggs plain or garnished with **cooked chicken livers, kidneys, bacon, tomatoes** or **asparagus tips.** *1 serving*

—EGGS WITH BROWNED BUTTER
(Oeufs au Beurre Noir)

Follow ▲ Recipe. Omit second butter addition. Bake only 2 to 3 min., or until the white is milky in color. Sprinkle with **¼ teaspoon vinegar.** Cover with **Browned Butter** made by slowly heating until very brown, **1½ teaspoons butter** per serving. Return to oven and continue baking 12 to 18 min.

Baked Eggs in Bacon Rings

—EGGS WITH CHICKEN OR TOMATOES
(Oeufs en Cocotte à la Reine ou au Tomates)

Follow ▲ Recipe for preparing cocottes. Put **3 tablespoons chopped cooked chicken or vegetable,** such as tomato or asparagus, into each cocotte before carefully breaking in eggs.

SHIRRED EGGS IN RICE

Grease a shallow 1½-qt. casserole or 6 ramekins.

Prepare
> **Fluffy Rice (page 164)**

Shred and set aside
> **4 oz. Cheddar cheese (1 cup, shredded)**

Meanwhile, prepare
> **2 cups Thin White Sauce (double recipe, page 304)**

Add shredded cheese all at one time with
> **1½ teaspoons prepared mustard**

Stir until cheese is melted.

Carefully blend one half of the sauce with the rice. Turn into casserole. With back of a spoon, make 6 hollows in rice mixture. Break into a saucer, one at a time
> **6 eggs**

Carefully slip each egg into a hollow. Pour remaining sauce around eggs. Sprinkle with
> **⅓ cup buttered crumbs (page 9)**

Bake at 350°F 12 to 15 min., or until eggs reach desired firmness. *6 servings*

SOUFFLES

CHEESE SOUFFLE

▲ Base Recipe

Set out a 2-qt. casserole; do not grease.

Shred and set aside
> **½ lb. sharp process Cheddar cheese (about 2 cups, shredded)**

Melt in a saucepan over low heat
> **6 tablespoons butter or margarine**

Blend in
> **6 tablespoons all-purpose flour**
> **¾ teaspoon dry mustard**
> **½ teaspoon salt**
> **⅛ teaspoon white pepper**
> **⅛ teaspoon paprika**

Heat until mixture bubbles. Add gradually, while stirring constantly
> **1½ cups milk**

Bring rapidly to boiling, stirring constantly; cook 1 to 2 min. longer. Remove from heat. Add the shredded cheese all at one time. Stir rapidly until cheese is melted.

Beat until thick and lemon-colored
> **6 egg yolks**

Slowly spoon sauce into egg yolks while stirring vigorously.

Beat in a bowl just until stiff, not dry, peaks are formed
> **6 egg whites**

Gently spread egg yolk mixture over beaten egg whites. Carefully fold together until just blended. Turn mixture into casserole. Insert the tip of a spoon 1 in. deep in mixture; 1 to 1½ in. from edge; run a line around mixture. (Center part of soufflé will form a "hat.")

Bake at 300°F 1 to 1¼ hrs., or until a metal knife comes out clean when inserted halfway between center and edge of soufflé.

Serve at once, while "top hat" is at its height. *8 servings*

—CHEESE-BACON SOUFFLE

Follow ▲ Recipe. Dice and fry until crisp **5 slices bacon.** Substitute **3 tablespoons bacon fat** for 3 tablespoons butter or margarine. Fold bacon pieces into egg whites with sauce.

—FRESH MUSHROOM SOUFFLE

Follow ▲ Recipe. Decrease cheese to 1 cup. Clean and finely chop **½ lb. mushrooms.** Cook slowly with **¼ cup minced onion** in **2 tablespoons butter or margarine** until the onion is soft and mushrooms are lightly browned and tender; stir frequently. Drain off any excess fat. Blend vegetables into sauce just before folding into egg whites.

—CHEESE SEAFOOD SOUFFLE

Follow ▲ Recipe. Stir **1 cup diced cooked crab meat, shrimp or lobster** into the cheese sauce.

—CRAB SOUFFLE

Follow ▲ Recipe. Omit Cheddar cheese and mustard. Drain, remove and discard bony tissue and flake **1 can (6½ oz.) crab meat** (about 1⅓ cups). Blend crab meat into sauce with **2 tablespoons chopped parsley, 2 tablespoons chopped pimiento, 2 tablespoons grated onion** and **1 tablespoon lemon juice.**

—LITTLE SOUFFLES

Follow ▲ Recipe or variation. Divide soufflé mixture among eight 4- to 4½-in. ungreased individual casseroles. Bake 25 to 30 min., or until soufflés test done.

SOUFFLE WITH MUSHROOM SAUCE
(Svamp Omelett)

▲ Base Recipe

For Soufflé—Set out a 1½-qt. casserole; do not grease. (If necessary, a 1-qt. casserole with straight sides may be used; fold a 2-ft. piece of waxed paper in half lengthwise. Place waxed

Cheddar Cheese Soufflé

paper around casserole, cut-side down, overlapping ends of waxed paper. Secure waxed paper around casserole by tying with a string.)

Prepare
> **2 cups Thick White Sauce (double recipe, page 304)**

Beat until thick and lemon-colored
> **4 egg yolks**

Slowly spoon 1 cup of the sauce into egg yolks, while stirring vigorously. Cool to lukewarm. Set remaining white sauce aside.

Beat in a bowl just until stiff, not dry, peaks are formed
> **4 egg whites**

Gently spread sauce over beaten egg whites. Carefully fold together until just blended. Turn mixture into casserole. Insert the tip of a spoon 1 in. deep in casserole, 1 to 1½ in. from edge; with spoon run a line around mixture to form a circle. (Center part of soufflé will form a "hat.")

Bake at 325°F about 45 to 50 min., or until a metal knife comes out clean when inserted halfway between edge and center of soufflé.

For Sauce—Add to the reserved white sauce, stirring in until blended
> **½ cup milk**

Set aside.

Clean and finely chop
> **½ lb. mushrooms**
> **1 medium onion (about ¼ cup, finely chopped)**

Heat in a skillet
> **2 tablespoons butter**

143

Add the mushrooms and onion to the skillet. Cook over medium heat until onion is tender and mushrooms are lightly browned; with a spoon, move and turn frequently. Add to the white sauce, mixing in thoroughly. Cook over low heat until thoroughly heated.

Serve soufflé immediately with the mushroom sauce. *6 servings*

—SOUFFLE WITH ASPARAGUS SAUCE
(Asparges Omelett)

Follow ▲ Recipe. Substitute asparagus for the mushrooms. Clean, cut into pieces, and cook (page 313) **1½ lbs. asparagus.** Drain asparagus. Mix into sauce with cooked onion.

—SOUFFLE WITH SPINACH SAUCE
(Spenat Omelett)

Follow ▲ Recipe. Substitute spinach for the mushrooms. Clean and cook (page 313) **2 lbs. spinach.** Drain spinach and chop. Mix into sauce with cooked onion.

CHEESE SOUFFLE IN RAMEKINS
(Soufflé au Fromage)

Set out 8 small ramekins.

Melt in a saucepan
¼ cup butter
Stir in until well blended
3 tablespoons all-purpose flour
¼ teaspoon salt
Heat until mixture bubbles. Add gradually, stirring constantly
1 cup milk
Bring mixture rapidly to boiling, stirring constantly; cook 1 to 2 min. longer. Remove from heat.

Cheese Soufflé in Ramekins

Add all at one time and blend in until cheese is melted
1 cup (¼ lb.) finely cut Gruyère or shredded Swiss cheese

Beat until thick and lemon-colored
4 egg yolks
Slowly pour cheese mixture into egg yolks, stirring vigorously.

Beat until stiff, not dry, peaks are formed
4 egg whites

Gently spread sauce mixture over egg whites and fold until blended. Pour into ramekins, filling each about two-thirds full. Set filled ramekins in a large baking pan on oven rack. Pour very hot water into the pan to a 1-in. depth.

Bake at 325°F about 25 min., or until soufflés are delicately browned and a knife comes out clean when inserted halfway between center and edge. Serve at once. *8 servings*

SPINACH WREATH SOUFFLE
▲ *Base Recipe*

Set out a medium-size saucepan and an electric blender. Thoroughly grease a 1½-qt. ring mold.

Remove and discard tough stems, roots and bruised leaves from
1 lb. spinach
Wash leaves thoroughly by lifting up and down several times in a large amount of cold water and lifting leaves out of water each time before pouring off water. When free from sand and gritty material, set spinach aside.

Put into electric blender container
1 cup milk
¼ cup butter or margarine, cut in pieces
3 egg yolks
3 tablespoons all-purpose flour
1 thin slice onion
½ teaspoon salt
½ teaspoon nutmeg
½ teaspoon monosodium glutamate
½ teaspoon paprika
⅛ teaspoon pepper
Add small amount of washed spinach. Cover and blend until spinach is finely chopped; continue to add spinach until all is well blended.

Turn spinach mixture into saucepan, cook rapidly, stirring constantly until sauce thickens. Cook 1 to 2 min. longer. Cool slightly.

While sauce is cooling, beat until rounded peaks are formed
3 egg whites
Spread egg whites over spinach mixture and carefully fold together. Turn into mold. Set mold in a baking pan on oven rack. Pour very hot water into pan to a 1-in. depth.

Bake at 350°F 55 to 60 min., or until a silver knife comes out clean when inserted halfway between center and outer edge of ring.

Remove from oven and unmold by running a spatula around edge of mold to loosen. Invert onto warm serving plate. Gently lift off mold. Serve immediately with **Cheese Sauce** (page 304). *6 servings*

—LAMB SOUFFLE

Follow ▲ Recipe, using a 2-qt. ungreased casserole. Omit paprika and spinach. Use only ⅛ teaspoon nutmeg. Add **2 sprigs parsley** to blender container with remainder of ingredients. Blender-grind (page 11) and set aside enough **cooked lamb** to yield 2 cups ground cooked lamb. Add ground lamb to blended mixture in saucepan.

CARROT SOUFFLE

Place an ungreased 2-qt. casserole in a shallow baking pan and pour boiling water around casserole to depth of 1 inch. Place in a 325°F oven.

Heat in a 1½-qt. saucepan
6 tablespoons butter or margarine
Stir in a mixture of
7 tablespoons all-purpose flour
1 teaspoon salt
¼ teaspoon pepper
½ teaspoon monosodium glutamate
Blend thoroughly and cook over low heat until mixture is bubbly. Blend in gradually
1½ cups milk
Cook and stir until sauce is thickened and set aside to cool slightly.

Meanwhile, grate enough fresh carrots to yield
1 cup grated carrots
Beat in small mixer bowl until very thick
5 egg yolks
Toss with grated carrots
2 tablespoons all-purpose flour

Stir into beaten egg yolks and combine with the cooled white sauce.

Beat in large mixer bowl until stiff, not dry, peaks are formed.
> **7 egg whites (1 cup)**

Adding about ¼ of the cooled white sauce at a time to egg whites, fold in gently but thoroughly after each addition.

Remove hot casserole from oven and turn soufflé mixture into it. Return casserole to pan of hot water and bake in 325°F oven 60 to 70 min., or until a metal knife inserted halfway between center and outside edge comes out clean.

Serve soufflé immediately.   *5 or 6 servings*

CHEESE DISHES

A GUIDE TO CHEESE

Man has been making cheese since recorded history began, and probably longer. In different parts of the world, different kinds of milk and different methods of handling the cheese have produced many different and distinctive types. As people of many races came to the United States, they brought the knowledge of and the taste for native cheeses with them. As a result, many kinds of cheese which originated in many lands are today being produced in this country, and a good many of them are also imported from their native lands and made available to American homemakers. A few, such as Roquefort, blue, Swiss, Parmesan and, most of all, Cheddar, have become so thoroughly domesticated here that almost everyone knows them and has used them at some time.

These cheese varieties are *natural cheeses,* made directly from milk, with or without aging and "ripening" by bacterial action or molds. Natural cheese is purchased in cuts made from the big "wheels" and other forms; it is also available pre-cut in slices, wedges and convenient-shaped pieces and pre-wrapped in airtight packages. Natural cheeses made domestically are often made in loaves or bricks which would not be recognized in the native lands of the cheeses.

Cheese is also available in various other forms:

Pasteurized process cheese is produced from a blend of fresh and aged natural cheeses. The cheeses are shredded, ground together, melted, pasteurized (so no further ripening occurs) and poured into molds lined with moisture-vaporproof packaging material; the packages are sealed and the cheese, virtually sterilized, is cooled in the packages. Process cheese has typically a perfectly smooth consistency and good keeping quality.

Cheese food may be either pasteurized process with certain dairy ingredients added; or cold-pack with the same additions but not pasteur-ized (heated). The process type is perfectly smooth; the coldpack type is somewhat granular and crumbly because it is not homogenized.

Pasteurized process cheese spread is made much like cheese food but contains a stabilizer and has a slightly higher moisture content to produce a more spreadable consistency at room temperature.

A CHECK LIST FOR CHEESE

Cook cheese over low heat to prevent toughening, stringing and separation. Use double boiler or chafing dish when recipe so directs.

Shred cheese with a standard kitchen shredder. Size of perforation to use will depend on kind of cheese and intended use. For garnish, cheese shreds should be long and fluffy.

Grate cheese with a rotary-type grater with hand-operated crank. Follow manufacturer's directions. One-half pound cheese will yield about 2 cups grated or shredded.

Slice cheese with a wire cheese slicer for best results. Or use a sharp, thin-bladed knife.

Soften cream cheese at room temperature until soft enough to handle as required.

Thin cream cheese with milk or cream until of desired consistency. Or use fruit juice for added flavor.

Serve cheeses, except for cottage cheese, Neufchâtel and cream cheese, at room temperature for fullest enjoyment. Remove cheese from refrigerator at least 30 minutes in advance. Serve cottage cheese, Neufchâtel and cream cheese chilled.

Store soft uncured cheeses (cottage, Neufchâtel and cream) in the refrigerator for a short period of time. Cream cheese and Neufchâtel, after opening, should be resealed in the original wrapper, or wrapped in aluminum foil or plastic wrap; cottage cheese should be stored in a covered container.

Store hard cheeses (such as Cheddar and Swiss) in the refrigerator, wrapping tightly in aluminum foil, plastic wrap or plastic bags to prevent drying. Mold development during storage is a normal process. Scrape or cut mold from surface, discard it and use remainder of cheese.

WELSH RABBIT

▲ *Base Recipe*

Set out a double boiler.

Shred
> **1 lb. sharp Cheddar cheese (about 4 cups, shredded)**

Combine in the top of the double boiler the cheese and
> **½ cup milk**
> **½ teaspoon dry mustard**
> **½ teaspoon Worcestershire sauce**
> **Dash cayenne pepper**

Set over simmering water and stir until cheese is melted and mixture is smooth. Remove from simmering water. Pour mixture into a chafing dish blazer and set over pan of simmering water to keep hot.

Serve over
> **Buttered toast points**

If desired, top each serving with a **tomato slice.**
                                    6 servings

—TOMATO-CHEESE RABBIT

Follow ▲ Recipe. Decrease cheese to 2 cups (½ lb.). Substitute **1¼ cups (10¾-oz. can) condensed tomato soup** for milk. Vigorously stir about 3 tablespoons hot mixture into **1 egg,** slightly beaten. Immediately blend with mixture in double boiler. Cook 3 to 5 min. longer over simmering water, stirring constantly.

Welsh Rabbit

CHEESE CHART

NAME	COUNTRY OF ORIGIN	FLAVOR	TEXTURE	COLOR
Soft Unripened	*Uses:* Appetizers, salads, main dishes, desserts			
Cottage Cheese	Uncertain	creamy	soft	white to creamy white
Cream Cheese	United States	buttery	smooth	white
Neufchâtel	France	creamy	smooth	white
Ricotta	Italy	sweet, nutlike	moist or dry	white
Soft Ripened	*Uses:* Appetizers, sandwiches, dessert (cheese and fruit tray)			
Bel Paese	Italy	mild to moderately robust	creamy	interior: creamy yellow; surface: slightly gray or brownish
Brie	France	mild to pungent	smooth, runny	interior: creamy yellow; surface: edible thin brown and white crust
Camembert	France	mild to pungent	smooth, runny	interior: creamy yellow; surface: edible thin white to grayish white crust
Liederkranz	United States	hearty, tangy	smooth, runny	interior: golden; surface: thin brown crust
Limburger	Belgium	strong flavor and aroma	smooth (with holes)	interior: off white; surface: brownish
Semisoft	*Uses:* Appetizers, sandwiches, desserts (cheese and fruit tray)			
Brick	United States	mild to moderately sharp	smooth, waxy	creamy yellow to orange
Monterey (Jack)	United States	mild	smooth, open texture	creamy white
Mozzarella	Italy.	mild, delicate	plastic, slightly firm	creamy white
Muenster	Germany	mild to mellow	smooth, waxy	interior: creamy white; surface: yellow, tan or white
Port du Salut (Oka)	France	mellow to robust	smooth, buttery	interior: creamy yellow; surface: russet
Samsoe	Denmark	mild, nutlike	smooth with small eyes	golden
Scamorze	Italy	mild	smooth	light yellow
Semisoft Blue Veined	*Uses:* Appetizers, salads, salad dressings, sandwiches, dessert			
Blue	France	tangy, spicy	pasty, sometimes crumbly	white, marbled or streaked with blue-green mold
Gorgonzola	Italy	tangy, spicy	pasty, sometimes crumbly	interior: pale yellow, marbled or streaked with blue-green mold; surface light tan
Roquefort	France	sharp, slightly spicy	pasty, sometimes crumbly	white, marbled with blue-green mold
Stilton	England	piquant, milder than Roquefort	flaky, slightly more crumbly than blue	white, marbled with blue-green mold
Hard Unripened	*Uses:* Snacks with dark bread, dessert			
Gjetost	Norway	sweetish, caramel	firm, buttery	golden brown
Mysost	Norway	sweetish, caramel	firm, buttery	light brown
Hard Ripened	*Uses:* Appetizers, sandwiches, cooked dishes, dessert (cheese and fruit tray)			
Caciocavallo	Italy	piquant	firm	interior: off white; surface: tan
Cheddar	England	mild to very sharp	firm, smooth	white to medium yellow-orange
Colby	United States	mild to mellow	softer than Cheddar; more open texture	light yellow to orange
Edam	Holland	mild, nutlike	softer than Cheddar; more open, mealy body	creamy yellow with or without red wax coating
Gouda	Holland	mild, nutlike similar to Edam	similar to Edam	similar to Edam
Gruyère	Switzerland	sweetish, nutlike	firm, small holes	pale yellow
Herkimer	United States	sharp	rather dry and crumbly	pale creamy yellow
Parmesan	Italy	sharp, piquant	granular, very hard	light yellow
Provolone	Italy	mellow to sharp, sometimes smoky	firm, flaky	interior: light golden yellow; surface: light brown or golden yellow
Romano	Italy	sharp, piquant	granular	interior: yellowish white; surface: greenish black
Sapsago	Switzerland	sweetish, with clover leaves	granular (in cones)	light green
Swiss	Switzerland	sweet, nutlike	smooth with large round eyes	light yellow

BAKED CORN AND CHEESE FONDUE

Set out and grease a 2-qt. casserole or baking dish.

Prepare and set aside
**½ lb. sharp Cheddar cheese, shredded
(about 2 cups)
1 cup cooked fresh corn kernels
(3 medium ears)
3 cups soft bread cubes**

Scald (page 10) and pour into a large bowl
1½ cups milk
Add the shredded cheese and
**2 tablespoons grated onion
½ teaspoon salt
½ teaspoon monosodium glutamate
½ teaspoon dry mustard
¼ teaspoon pepper
½ teaspoon paprika
1 or 2 drops Tabasco**
Stir until cheese is melted. Add gradually, stirring constantly
4 egg yolks, beaten until thick
Beat until stiff, not dry, peaks are formed
4 egg whites
Spread egg whites over cheese mixture; add bread cubes and corn. Fold gently until blended and turn mixture into the casserole.

Bake at 350°F 50 to 60 min., or until a metal knife inserted halfway between center and edge comes out clean. Serve at once.

6 servings

BAKED CHEESE FONDUE

Truly satisfying—coffee and delicate cheese fondue, both fragrantly fresh and steaming hot.

Lightly butter a 2-qt. casserole.

Shred and set aside
**¾ lb. sharp Cheddar cheese (about
3 cups, shredded)**
Prepare
**3 cups soft bread cubes (4 to 5
slices bread)**
Toss 1 cup of the bread cubes lightly with
**1 tablespoon melted butter or
margarine
1 teaspoon poppy seed**
Set cubes aside.

Scald (page 10)
2 cups milk
Meanwhile, grate and set aside enough onion to yield
3 tablespoons grated onion
Pour scalded milk into a large mixing bowl.

Add and mix in the 2 cups uncoated bread cubes, shredded cheese, onion and a mixture of
**½ teaspoon salt
¼ teaspoon monosodium glutamate
¼ teaspoon pepper
½ teaspoon dry mustard
¼ teaspoon paprika
1 or 2 drops Tabasco**
Mix lightly but thoroughly until cheese is melted.

Add gradually, stirring constantly
4 egg yolks, well beaten
Beat until rounded peaks are formed
4 egg whites
Spread beaten egg whites over cheese mixture and gently fold together. Turn into the casserole. Top with poppy seed-coated bread cubes. Set casserole in a baking pan. Pour very hot water into pan to a 1-in. depth.

Bake at 375°F 45 to 50 min., or until a metal knife inserted halfway between center and edge comes out clean.

Serve immediately. *About 6 servings*

CHEESE MUSHROOM CASSEROLE

▲ Base Recipe

This can be prepared hours in advance and stored in the refrigerator before baking.

Grease a 1½-qt. casserole.

Set aside to drain, reserving liquid
**1 can (4 oz.) sliced mushrooms
(about ½ cup, drained)**

Cut into ⅛-in. slices
½ lb. sharp Cheddar cheese

Trim crusts from and cut into thirds
6 slices white bread
Arrange some bread fingers on bottom of casserole. Cover with a layer of one half the cheese and mushrooms. Repeat layering; top with remaining bread fingers. Dot with
2 tablespoons butter or margarine

Add to reserved mushroom liquid
**Milk or cream (enough to make
1 cup liquid)**
Beat until thick and piled softly
2 eggs
Beat in the liquid and
**½ teaspoon salt
½ teaspoon paprika
⅛ teaspoon pepper**
Pour over layers in casserole.

Baked Cheese Fondue

Bake at 325°F 30 to 40 min., or until puffed and lightly browned. *About 6 servings*

—CHEESE FRANKFURTER CASSEROLE

Follow ▲ Recipe. Substitute for mushrooms, **3 frankfurters,** cut in pieces ¼-in. thick. Use all milk or cream for the liquid. If desired, use both mushrooms and frankfurters.

POT O' GOLD CHEESE AND EGGS

Toast and trim crusts from
10 slices bread
Butter and cut toast into 1-in. strips. Arrange a portion of the strips in a layer on bottom of a greased 1½-qt. casserole.

Shred
**½ lb. Cheddar cheese (about 2 cups,
shredded)**
Sprinkle a layer of cheese over toast pieces in casserole. Continue adding toast and cheese in layers.

Blend
**4 eggs, well beaten
2 cups milk
¾ teaspoon salt
½ teaspoon monosodium glutamate
½ teaspoon prepared mustard
⅛ teaspoon pepper**
Pour egg mixture over toast and cheese. Cover and refrigerate at least 1 hr.

Bake at 325°F 50 to 60 min.

If desired, sprinkle with
Paprika

5 or 6 servings

BACON TART
(Quiche au Lard)

The quiche is a favorite in Lorraine. Literally in French, it is a "custard with bacon" and can be served as an entrée, a luncheon dish, or for a late evening supper.

Line a 9-in. pie pan with
Pastry for Tarts (page 486)
Flute edge (page 10) and set aside.

Cheese Luncheon Pie

Cut into halves

6 slices bacon or salt pork

(If salt pork is used, parboil, page 10, drain and dry before broiling.)

Arrange bacon on cool broiler rack. Place under broiler 3 to 3½ in. from heat. Turn bacon frequently. Broil about 5 min., or until light brown and crisp. Drain on absorbent paper.

Cut into fine pieces and set aside

6 oz. (1½ cups) Gruyère or Swiss cheese

Scald (page 10)

2 cups milk (or part cream)

Beat slightly

3 eggs
½ teaspoon salt
¼ teaspoon nutmeg
⅛ teaspoon pepper

Gradually add milk, stirring vigorously.

Arrange bacon on pastry. Cover with cheese. Pour egg mixture over all.

Bake at 450°F 10 min. Reduce heat to 350°F. Bake about 25 min. longer, or until a metal knife comes out clean when inserted halfway between center and edge of custard. Serve immediately.

CHEESE LUNCHEON PIE

This is a delightful main dish for a Lenten luncheon, full of flavor and food value—a pleasant surprise at any season. Serve it with a crisp green salad.

Prepare (do not bake)

Pastry I for 1-Crust Pie (page 485; use 9-in. pie pan)

Beat until thick and piled softly

2 eggs

Blend in thoroughly

2 cups (1 lb.) cream-style cottage cheese
2 cups hot mashed potatoes (3 medium potatoes)
¾ cup dairy sour cream
¼ cup finely chopped onion
2 tablespoons chopped pimiento
1 teaspoon salt
⅛ teaspoon white pepper

Turn mixture into the pie shell, spreading evenly. Dot surface with

2 tablespoons butter

Bake at 350°F about 1½ hrs., or until lightly browned. Serve hot or cold.   *8 servings*

ITALIAN-STYLE CHEESE EGG PIE

Prepare (do not bake) and set aside

Pastry I for 1-Crust 9-in. Pie (page 485)

Drain and flake (page 9)

1 can (6½ or 7 oz.) tuna

(Or use 1 cup flaked cooked fish.)

Shred and set aside

½ lb. mozzarella cheese (about 2 cups, shredded)

Beat in a large mixer bowl until thoroughly blended

6 eggs
¼ cup milk

Add a mixture of

¼ teaspoon salt
¼ teaspoon pepper
½ teaspoon basil
½ teaspoon oregano

Mix in tuna and cheese and turn into pie shell.

Bake at 425°F 35 to 40 min., or until pie is lightly browned. Cut pie into wedges and serve at once.   *6 servings*

SWISS CHEESE PIE

A flavorful main dish pie.

Prepare (do not bake) and chill

Pastry I for 1-Crust Pie (page 485; use 8-in. pie pan)

Shred and set aside

8 oz. Swiss cheese (about 2 cups, shredded)

Prepare

8 slices Panfried Bacon (page 190)

Crumble bacon, toss with the cheese and spoon evenly over bottom of pastry shell. Set aside.

Scald (page 10)

1 cup cream
½ cup milk

Meanwhile, beat slightly

3 eggs

Italian-Style Cheese Egg Pie

Add and beat until just blended

½ teaspoon Worcestershire sauce
½ teaspoon salt
Few grains pepper
Few grains cayenne pepper

Stirring constantly, gradually add the scalded cream and milk. Strain mixture into the pastry shell over bacon and cheese.

Bake at 400°F 10 min. Reduce heat to 300°F and bake 25 min. longer, or until metal knife comes out clean when inserted halfway between center and edge of filling.

Serve immediately.   *6 to 8 servings*

CHEESE BREAD PUDDING

Grease a 2-qt. casserole.

Have ready

6 slices bread, cut diagonally in half
¼ cup snipped parsley

Shred and set aside

½ lb. sharp Cheddar cheese (about 2 cups, shredded)

Alternate layers of bread, parsley and cheese in the casserole, ending with bread and cheese.

Beat until light in a mixer bowl

3 eggs

Swiss Cheese Pie

148

Beat in until thoroughly blended

2 cups milk
1 teaspoon seasoned salt
¼ teaspoon thyme
½ teaspoon Tabasco
½ teaspoon Worcestershire sauce
½ teaspoon prepared mustard

Pour mixture over bread and cheese in casserole. Allow to stand at least 30 min.

Bake at 300°F about 1 hr. Serve immediately.
About 6 servings

CHEESE CASSEROLE ROYALE

Grease a shallow 1½-qt. baking dish.

Prepare
1 cup browned buttered soft bread crumbs
Sprinkle crumbs over bottom of baking dish; set aside.

Have ready
¾ cup shredded Swiss cheese
¾ cup finely chopped walnuts

Beat until thick and lemon-colored
4 egg yolks
Add and beat until blended
1 cup dairy sour cream
Mix in the cheese. Turn into the prepared baking dish. Set in a large pan on oven rack. Pour very hot water into pan to a 1-in. depth.

Bake at 375°F 20 min., or until a metal knife inserted near center comes out clean.

Meanwhile, beat until stiff, not dry, peaks are formed
4 egg whites
¾ teaspoon seasoned salt
Fold in the nuts

Remove baking dish from oven and top evenly with the meringue. Return to oven and bake 8 to 10 min., or until meringue is browned.
About 6 servings

BAKED CHEESE SHRIMP DELIGHT

For an attractive supper, fill side dishes of a Lazy Susan (see photo) with cottage cheese with chives, butter balls (for your hot rolls), jam or preserves, and assorted relishes.

Lightly grease a shallow baking dish.

Set out to soften at room temperature
⅓ cup butter

Shred
½ lb. sharp Cheddar cheese (about 2 cups, shredded)
Set aside.

Drain and set aside
2 cans (4½ oz. each) shrimp (about 1¼ cups, drained)

Spread the softened butter on both sides of
8 slices white bread
Arrange in 2 stacks on a flat working surface and cut into 1-in. squares. Arrange one half of the bread squares in the bottom of the

baking dish. Cover well with one half of the shredded cheese and one half of the shrimp. Repeat layering.

Blend and pour over shrimp
3 eggs, slightly beaten
2 cups milk
¼ teaspoon salt
¼ teaspoon celery salt
¼ teaspoon dry mustard
¼ teaspoon paprika
⅛ teaspoon pepper

Bake at 325°F 40 min., or until set. Serve immediately. *About 6 servings*

CHEESE BLINTZES

▲ *Base Recipe*

Set out heavy 6- and 10-in. skillets.

For Filling—Mix thoroughly and set aside in refrigerator
1½ cups cream-style cottage cheese, drained
¼ cup dairy sour cream
1½ tablespoons sugar
½ teaspoon salt

For Pancakes—Melt and set aside to cool
2 tablespoons butter or margarine

Sift together into a bowl and set aside
1½ cups sifted all-purpose flour
3 tablespoons sugar
½ teaspoon salt

Beat until thick and piled softly
2 eggs
Beat in the melted butter and
1¼ cups milk
Combine egg mixture with dry ingredients. With rotary beater, beat until smooth and well blended. Set aside.

Heat the small skillet; it is hot enough when a few drops of water sprinkled on surface dance in small beads. Grease skillet lightly with
Butter or margarine
Pour only enough batter to coat skillet thinly; immediately tilt skillet back and forth to spread batter evenly. Cook pancake over medium heat about 2 min., or until lightly browned on bottom and firm to touch on top. With spatula, remove pancake to a plate, brown side up. Stack pancakes. (It should not be necessary to grease skillet for each pancake.)

For Blintzes—Spoon about 1½ tablespoons filling onto center of brown side of one pancake. Fold two opposite sides of pancake to center. Begin with one of the open sides and roll. Press edge to seal. Repeat for each pancake.

Heat in the large skillet
1 tablespoon butter or margarine
Arrange several blintzes in skillet, sealed sides down. Brown on all sides over medium heat, turning carefully with two spoons or tongs. Remove blintzes from skillet and place on serving platter.

Serve hot with **currant jelly** or **blueberry** or **blackberry jam** and **sour cream.**
About 12 blintzes

—RAISIN CHEESE BLINTZES

Bring to boiling **½ cup water;** add to water **¼ cup dark seedless or golden raisins** and again bring to boiling. Drain raisins thoroughly. Follow ▲ Recipe. Mix raisins with Filling.

—CARAMEL CHEESE BLINTZES

Follow ▲ Recipe. After blintzes are removed from skillet, add **3 tablespoons butter or margarine** to same skillet. Add **1¼ cups firmly packed brown sugar.** Cook over low heat, stirring until sugar is dissolved. Mix in **¼ cup Cointreau.** When sauce is hot, pour over blintzes.

COTTAGE FRITTERS

A deep saucepan or automatic deep fryer will be needed.

To prepare coating batter, sift together into a bowl
1 cup all-purpose flour
½ teaspoon salt
⅛ teaspoon pepper
Make a well in center and add a blend of
⅔ cup milk
1 tablespoon melted butter or margarine
1 tablespoon lemon juice
1 egg yolk
Beat only until smooth. Cover bowl and set batter aside until of room temperature.

Baked Cheese Shrimp Delight

About 20 min. before ready to deep-fry, fill deep saucepan or automatic deep fryer one-half to two-thirds full with

Fat for deep-frying

Heat fat to 370°F.

Shortly before ready to use batter, beat until stiff, not dry, peaks are formed

1 egg white

Fold into batter. Set aside.

Prepare and set aside

2 cups crushed bite-size shredded rice cereal

To make fritter mixture, beat together in a bowl

2 cups dry cottage cheese, sieved
3 egg yolks
2 teaspoons salt
½ teaspoon mace
2 tablespoons all-purpose flour

For each fritter, coat a tablespoonful of the mixture with batter, then roll in the crushed cereal.

Deep-fry a layer of balls at a time in heated fat until golden brown. Remove from fat with a slotted spoon and drain on absorbent paper. Be sure temperature of fat is 370°F before frying each layer.

Serve fritters hot with **Egg Sauce** (page 304).

6 to 8 servings

CREPES IN CHEESE SAUCE

For Filling—Set out a heavy 2-qt. saucepan.

Drain and remove any bony tissue from

½ lb. (about 2 cups) fresh lump crab meat

Set aside.

Scald (page 10)

¾ cup milk

Heat in the saucepan

2 tablespoons butter

Add and cook over medium heat until onion is tender, stirring mixture occasionally with a spoon

¼ cup chopped mushrooms
2 tablespoons minced onion

Blend in

2 tablespoons all-purpose flour
¼ teaspoon salt
¼ teaspoon monosodium glutamate
⅛ teaspoon white pepper

Heat until mixture bubbles. Remove from heat; add the scalded milk gradually, stirring constantly. Mix in

¼ teaspoon Worcestershire sauce
2 drops Tabasco

Bring rapidly to boiling, stirring constantly; cook 1 to 2 min. longer. Remove from heat. Mix in the crab meat and

2 tablespoons sherry
1 teaspoon minced parsley
1 teaspoon chopped pimiento

Cool; place in refrigerator to chill.

For Cheese Sauce—Prepare

1½ cups Cheese Sauce (one and one-half times recipe, page 304)

Cover sauce and set over simmering water to keep warm.

For Crêpes—Lightly butter a 6-in. skillet.

Sift together into a bowl and set aside

½ cup sifted all-purpose flour
2 teaspoons sugar
⅛ teaspoon salt

Beat

2 eggs

Beat in

½ cup milk
1 teaspoon butter, melted

Combine egg mixture with dry ingredients and beat with rotary beater until smooth.

Heat skillet to moderately hot. Pour in just enough batter to cover bottom. Immediately tilt skillet back and forth to spread batter thinly and evenly.

Cook each crêpe over medium heat until lightly browned on bottom and firm to touch on top. Loosen edges with spatula. Turn and brown second side. It should be unnecessary to grease skillet for each crêpe.

As each crêpe is cooked, transfer to a hot platter to keep warm.

To Complete Crêpes—Lightly grease a shallow baking dish with a tight-fitting cover.

Remove filling from refrigerator. Spoon about 2 to 3 tablespoons of the chilled filling onto the center of each crêpe. Fold one edge of crêpe over filling and roll.

Spoon enough Cheese Sauce over bottom of baking dish to make a thin layer. Place filled crêpes in baking dish, with open side down. Spoon remaining sauce over and between crêpes. Sprinkle with

¼ cup grated Parmesan cheese

Cover and bake at 450°F 15 min. Remove from oven and remove cover.

Place baking dish on broiler rack. Place under broiler with top of food 3 to 4 in. from heat and broil 3 to 4 min., or until cheese is lightly browned. Garnish with **sprigs of parsley**.

12 filled crêpes

PIZZA

TOMATO CHEESE PIZZA

▲ *Base Recipe*

Salty anchovies, bland Mozzarella cheese, hot pungent sausage, and tiny mushrooms all lend themselves to the much-varied pizza. A Neapolitan dish, this crisp, tomato-topped bread has become an American favorite.

Lightly grease two large round griddles, two 15-in. pizza pans or two 15½x12-in. baking sheets.

Soften

½ pkg. (1 teaspoon) active dry yeast

in

2 tablespoons warm water, 105°F to 115°F. Or if using compressed yeast, soften ½ cake in 2 tablespoons lukewarm water, 80°F to 85°F.)

Set aside.

Pour into a large bowl

1 cup warm water

Blend in

2 cups sifted all-purpose flour
1 teaspoon salt

Add softened yeast and mix well.

Measure

2 cups sifted all-purpose flour

Add about one half the flour to yeast mixture and beat until very smooth. Mix in enough remaining flour to make a soft dough. Turn mixture onto a lightly floured surface. Allow to rest 5 to 10 min. Knead dough (page 10).

Select a deep bowl just large enough to allow dough to double. Shape dough into a smooth ball and place in greased bowl. Turn dough to bring greased surface to top. Cover with waxed paper and towel and let stand in warm place (about 80°F) until dough is doubled.

Punch down with fist. Fold edge toward center and turn dough over. Divide dough into two equal balls. Grease a second bowl. Place each ball of dough into a greased bowl. Turn greased side up. Cover. Let rise again until almost doubled.

Roll each ball of dough into a 14x10-in. rectangle ⅛ in. thick and place each on prepared baking sheet. Shape edge by pressing dough between thumb and forefinger to make ridge. (For round pizza, roll dough into rounds.)

Sieve

3 cups drained canned tomatoes

Use one half (1½ cups) of sieved tomatoes to cover each pizza.

Sprinkle each pizza with half of a mixture of

1 teaspoon salt
½ teaspoon pepper
2 teaspoons oregano

Top each with half (4 oz.) of

8 oz. mozzarella cheese, thinly sliced

Drizzle each with half of

½ cup olive oil

Sprinkle each with half of
¼ cup grated Parmesan cheese

Bake at 400°F 25 to 30 min., or until crust is browned. Cut into wedges to serve.

6 to 8 servings

—MUSHROOM PIZZA

Follow ▲ Recipe. Before baking, place on each pizza **1 cup (8-oz. can) drained mushrooms.**

—SAUSAGE PIZZA

Follow ▲ Recipe. Before baking, place on each pizza **1 lb. hot Italian sausage**, cut in ¼-in. pieces.

—ANCHOVY PIZZA

Follow ▲ Recipe. Omit mozzarella and Parmesan cheese. Use ¼ **teaspoon oregano.** Top each with **8 anchovy fillets,** cut in ¼-in. pieces.

—MINIATURE PIZZAS

Follow ▲ Recipe. After rolling dough, using a cookie cutter, cut into 3½-in. rounds. Shape edge of rounds as in ▲ Recipe. Using one half the total amount of ingredients in the ▲ Recipe, spread each pizza with 2 tablespoons sieved canned tomatoes. Top with a slice of mozzarella cheese. Sprinkle over cheese ½ teaspoon olive oil, ½ teaspoon grated Parmesan cheese and a few grains salt and pepper. Bake at 400°F 15 to 20 min., or until crust is browned. *About 24 Miniature Pizzas*

SAUERKRAUT SAUSAGE PIZZA

Set out a 12-in. pizza pan.

Have ready
½ lb. sweet Italian sausage
½ cup chopped onion
2 cups drained sauerkraut
6 green pepper rings
½ lb. mozzarella cheese, sliced
¼ cup shredded Parmesan cheese

Prepare, following directions on package for pizza dough
1 pkg. (13¾ oz.) hot roll mix
Divide dough into two equal portions and form each into a ball. Place one ball in center of pizza pan. (Freeze second ball for later use or see note.) Push dough down in center with hand and spread dough with fingers to cover bottom of pan. Shape edge by pressing dough between thumb and forefinger to make a ridge. Brush lightly with
Olive oil
Set aside.

Cut half of the sausage into 12 slices; dice remaining half. Turn the sausage into a skillet with the onion. Cook, stirring occasionally, until the meat is browned, spooning off excess fat as it accumulates. Transfer sliced sausage from skillet to absorbent paper. Add to skillet

the sauerkraut and
2 cans (8 oz. each) tomato sauce with onions
¼ teaspoon basil leaves, crushed
Cook, stirring occasionally, until heated. Remove from heat; turn mixture onto pizza dough and spread evenly to cover surface. Arrange sliced sausage, green pepper rings and mozzarella cheese over sauerkraut mixture. Sprinkle with the Parmesan cheese.

Bake at 450°F 15 to 20 min., or until cheese is melted and crust is browned. Cut into wedges and serve hot. *One 12-in. pizza*

Note: For 2 pizzas, double the filling ingredients.

PARTY PIZZA

Set out a 9-in. pie pan.

Mix in a saucepan and set aside
1 can (8 oz.) tomato sauce
1 can (6 oz.) tomato paste
1 tablespoon sugar
¼ teaspoon salt
Few grains pepper
¼ teaspoon oregano
1 bay leaf

Crush enough round cheese crackers to yield
2 cups cheese cracker crumbs (about 44)
Turn crumbs into a bowl. Mix in with a fork
¼ cup butter or margarine, softened
Add gradually, tossing to mix
3 tablespoons water
Turn crumb mixture into pie pan and press firmly into an even layer on bottom and sides.

Bake at 400°F 5 min. Remove from oven to rack.

Meanwhile, bring the sauce to boiling; simmer 5 min., stirring occasionally. Remove from heat and discard bay leaf. Pour sauce into hot crust. Sprinkle with
1 teaspoon oregano
Cover with
6 oz. mozzarella cheese, thinly sliced
Drizzle with
1 tablespoon olive oil

Bake at 400°F 20 min., or until cheese is lightly browned. *About 6 servings*

Tomato Cheese Pizza

DEEP-DISH PIZZA PIE

▲ *Base Recipe*

Set out a shallow 1½-qt. casserole.

Combine in saucepan
1½ cups (28-oz. can, drained) tomatoes, cut in pieces
¼ cup chopped onion
¼ cup minced green pepper
1 teaspoon sugar
¾ teaspoon salt
½ teaspoon garlic salt
½ teaspoon oregano
⅛ teaspoon pepper
Simmer 10 to 15 min., stirring frequently; cool mixture.

Meanwhile, grate and set aside
¼ lb. Parmesan or sharp Cheddar cheese (1 cup, grated)
Prepare
Baking Powder Biscuit dough (one half recipe, page 92)
Roll about ⅛ in. thick. Fit into bottom and partly up sides of casserole; trim top edge evenly. Brush bottom of dough with
1 tablespoon salad oil
Cover dough with one half the cheese, then with tomato mixture; top with remaining grated cheese.

Bake at 450°F 10 to 15 min. Cut into wedges to serve. *5 or 6 servings*

—PIZZA-BEEF PIE

Follow ▲ Recipe. Brown **¾ lb. ground beef** in **2 tablespoons fat** separating meat into small pieces with fork or spoon. Sprinkle with **½ teaspoon salt.** Spoon evenly onto dough before adding cheese.

Pasta and rice dishes

Pasta and rice play a special role in cuisine. They can be served simply with butter and seasoning or elaborately combined with an unlimited choice of meat, fish, poultry, vegetables, cheese, and sauces or contrasting flavor, texture, or color.

Pasta is an Italian word meaning "paste" and refers to a dough made from semolina or durum wheat flour mixed with water in proper amounts, kneaded, formed into a variety of shapes, and dried. Lasagne, vermicelli, ditalini, ravioli, manicotti, spaghetti, macaroni—all these are only a part of the large family called pasta. Pasta is a low-cost food so bland in flavor it can be combined with all sorts of other ingredients. In Italy it is an integral part of the daily cuisine and favorite dishes from that country have become popular all around the world.

NOODLES

BASIC NOODLE DOUGH
(Pasta)

Sift together into a large bowl
   4 cups sifted all-purpose flour
   ½ teaspoon salt
Make a well in center of flour. Add, one at a time, mixing slightly after each addition
   4 eggs
Add gradually about
   6 tablespoons cold water
Mix well to make a stiff dough. Turn dough onto a lightly floured surface and knead (page 10). Proceed as directed in recipes.

NOODLES
(Gyúrt Tészta)

Sift together into a bowl
   1 cup sifted all-purpose flour
   ½ teaspoon salt
Make a well in center of flour mixture and add
   1 egg, slightly beaten
While blending ingredients, add gradually
   1 to 2 tablespoons water
Dough should be stiff. Turn dough out onto a lightly floured surface. Shape dough into a ball and knead (page 10). Cover dough and let it rest about 5 min.

Roll dough on lightly floured surface to ⅛-in. thickness. If sticking occurs, loosen dough from surface with knife or spatula; sprinkle flour underneath. Turn dough over and continue rolling until paper thin. Allow dough to partially dry about 1 hr.

Cut dough into lengthwise strips, 2½-in. wide, and stack on top of each other. Slice into short strips 1/16- to ⅛-in. wide. Separate noodles and allow to dry thoroughly. (Noodles can be stored in a tightly covered container if not cooked immediately.)   *About ⅓ lb. Noodles*

For Cooking Noodles—Bring to rapid boiling in a 3- or 4-qt. saucepan
   2 qts. water
   2 teaspoons salt
Add noodles gradually to water so that boiling will not stop. Boil noodles uncovered, stirring occasionally with a fork, 6 to 10 min., or until soft when pressed against side of pan. Drain in colander or sieve. Rinse with hot water and drain again.
          About 2½ cups cooked noodles

DROP NOODLES
(Spätzle)

Bring to boiling in a 3- or 4-qt. saucepan
   2 qts. water
   2 teaspoons salt

Meanwhile, sift together and set aside
   2⅓ cups sifted all-purpose flour
   1 teaspoon salt

Combine in a bowl
   1 egg, slightly beaten
   1 cup water
Gradually add flour mixture to egg mixture, stirring until smooth. (Batter should be very thick and break from a spoon instead of pour-

ing in a continuous stream.) Spoon batter into the boiling water by ½ teaspoonfuls, dipping spoon into water each time. Cook only one layer of noodles at one time; do not crowd. After noodles rise to the surface, boil gently 5 to 8 min., or until tender when pressed against side of pan with spoon. Remove from water with slotted spoon, draining over water for a second, and place in a warm bowl.

Toss lightly with noodles
   ¼ cup butter, melted
Serve hot.   *About 5 cups noodles*

GREEN NOODLES
(Pasta Verde)

Grease a 2-qt. casserole and set aside.

Prepare and cook (page 313)
   ¼ lb. spinach
Finely chop cooked spinach and set aside.

Sift together into a large bowl
   3 cups sifted all-purpose flour
   ½ teaspoon salt
Make a well in center of flour. Add, one at a time, mixing slightly after each addition
   3 eggs
Add the chopped spinach and mix well to make a stiff dough. Turn dough onto a lightly floured surface and knead (page 10). Divide dough into halves. Lightly roll each half ⅛ in. thick to form a rectangle. Let stand covered for 1 hr.

Beginning with the narrow end, gently fold over about 2 in. of dough and continue to fold over so that final width will be about 3 in. (Dough must be dry enough so that layers do not stick together.) Beginning at the narrow edge, cut dough into strips ¼ in. wide. Unroll strips and arrange on waxed paper on a flat surface. Let stand about 2½ hrs., or until noodles are dry.

Bring to boiling in a large saucepan
   6 qts. water
   1 tablespoon salt
Gradually add the noodles. Boil rapidly uncovered 8 to 10 min., or until tender.

Set out
   ¾ cup grated Parmesan cheese
   ¼ cup butter
   ½ teaspoon salt
Test tenderness of noodles by pressing a piece

Noodles: Slice the dough into 1/16- to ⅛-in. strips

against side of pan with fork or spoon. Drain by pouring into a colander or large sieve. Place a layer of noodles (about one third of the noodles) into the casserole. Top with one third of cheese and salt. Dot with one third of the butter. Beginning with noodles, repeat layering, ending with grated Parmesan cheese and butter.

Bake at 350°F 15 to 20 min., or until cheese is melted.   *About 8 servings*

BUTTERED NOODLES
(Nudeln)

▲ *Base Recipe*

Heat to boiling in a large saucepan
3 qts. water
1 tablespoon salt
Add gradually
3 cups (about 8 oz.) noodles
Boil rapidly, uncovered, 6 to 10 min., or until tender. Test tenderness by pressing a piece against side of pan with fork or spoon.

Drain noodles by turning them into a colander or large sieve; rinse with hot water to remove loose starch. Turn noodles into a warm serving dish. Using a fork, blend through noodles
3 tablespoons melted butter
                                   6 servings

─NOODLES WITH BREAD CRUMBS
(Nudeln mit gerösteten Semmelbröseln)

Follow ▲ Recipe. Prepare **1 cup buttered bread crumbs** (page 9). Turn noodles into a warm serving dish and sprinkle with crumbs.

SPECIAL NOODLE CASSEROLE

Grease a 1½-qt. casserole and set aside.

For Noodles—Heat to boiling in a saucepan
3 qts. water
1 tablespoon salt
Add gradually
4 oz. fine noodles
Boil rapidly, uncovered, 6 to 10 min., or until tender. Test tenderness by pressing a piece against side of pan with fork or spoon.

Drain noodles by turning them into a colander or large sieve; rinse with hot water to remove loose starch.

To Complete Casserole—Mix
1 cup large-curd cottage cheese, drained
1 cup dairy sour cream
⅓ cup (about 1 small) finely chopped onion
1 clove garlic, minced
1 teaspoon Worcestershire sauce
4 drops Tabasco
Blend in a mixture of
1 to 2 tablespoons all-purpose flour
¼ teaspoon salt
⅛ teaspoon white pepper

Mix with the drained noodles. Turn into the casserole and sprinkle over top
¼ cup buttered fine dry bread crumbs (page 9)

Bake at 350°F about 15 min., or until crumbs are lightly browned.   *About 8 servings*

MEAT CHEESE CASSEROLE

Grease a 2-qt. casserole.

Cook, following directions on package
7 oz. noodles

Using fork, blend through drained noodles
3 tablespoons melted butter or margarine
Set aside in warm place.

Blend thoroughly
1 cup (8 oz.) dairy cottage cheese
6 oz. cream cheese
⅓ cup dairy sour cream
Add
⅓ cup minced onion
2 tablespoons chopped green pepper
1 tablespoon chopped pimiento, drained
1 tablespoon chopped chives
½ teaspoon salt
½ teaspoon monosodium glutamate
Set aside.

Heat in a heavy skillet
1 to 2 tablespoons butter or margarine
Add, breaking into pieces with fork or spoon, and cook over medium heat until lightly browned, stirring occasionally
¾ lb. ground beef
Remove from heat and drain off fat from meat. Stir in
2 cups (two 8-oz. cans) tomato sauce
½ teaspoon salt
½ teaspoon Worcestershire sauce
3 drops Tabasco
Pour small amount of meat sauce into bottom of casserole. Top with one half of noodles. Cover with cheese mixture and remaining noodles. Pour meat sauce over top.

Bake at 350°F 50 to 60 min., or until bubbly.
                                   6 servings

NOODLE FRANKFURTER CASSEROLE

Lightly butter a shallow 2-qt. casserole.

For Noodles—Cook, following directions on package and drain
8 oz. noodles
Using fork, thoroughly blend into the noodles
¼ cup melted butter or margarine
½ teaspoon salt
Set aside to keep warm.

For Frankfurter Mixture—Have ready
1 lb. frankfurters
Cut 5 of the frankfurters into halves lengthwise and reserve for top of casserole. Cut the remaining frankfurters into ¾-in. pieces.

Finely chop enough onion to yield
⅓ cup finely chopped onion
Cut into slices enough ripe olives to yield
½ cup sliced ripe olives
Set aside.

Heat in a large skillet over low heat
3 tablespoons butter or margarine
Add the chopped onion and frunkfurter pieces; cook over medium heat, stirring occasionally, until onion is tender.

Add and mix in
1¼ cups (10¾-oz. can) condensed tomato soup
½ cup hot water
1 teaspoon Worcestershire sauce
¼ teaspoon monosodium glutamate
¼ teaspoon salt
Few grains pepper
Cover and simmer about 10 min.

Meanwhile, shred and set aside
½ lb. sharp Cheddar cheese (about 2 cups, shredded)

To Complete—Remove frankfurter mixture from heat. Mix in the olives and turn the hot mixture into the casserole. Cover the frankfurter mixture evenly with the cheese. Arrange the buttered noodles over the cheese. Top the noodles with the reserved frankfurters.

Put casserole into a 350°F oven for about 15 min., or until thoroughly heated. Remove from oven and garnish with **parsley**.   *6 servings*

ELEGANT NOODLE MUSHROOM CASSEROLE

Set out a 2½-qt. casserole, a large skillet, a large heavy saucepot and a small saucepan.

Prepare and set aside
5 large onions, coarsely chopped
1½ to 2 lbs. fresh mushrooms, cleaned and sliced (page 9)

Cook, following package directions
8 to 10 oz. noodles
Turn drained noodles into a large bowl.

While noodles are cooking, heat in the skillet
3 tablespoons butter or margarine
Add the onion and cook about 5 min., stirring occasionally. Stir in a blend of
½ teaspoon salt
¼ teaspoon seasoned pepper
Cover skillet and cook over low heat about 15 min., stirring occasionally.

Meanwhile, heat in the saucepot
½ cup butter or margarine

Add the mushrooms and cook over low heat until tender, turning occasionally. Stir in a blend of

1½ teaspoons salt
1 teaspoon monosodium glutamate
½ teaspoon nutmeg

Cook, uncovered, over low heat about 15 min. Add the cooked onion and toss lightly. Keep warm.

Meanwhile, heat in the small saucepan

1 cup heavy cream

Stir into the onion-mushroom mixture and heat thoroughly. Add to the drained noodles along with

½ to ¾ cup finely snipped parsley

Toss until well mixed and turn into the casserole. Sprinkle with additional snipped parsley, if desired.

Heat in a 350°F oven 25 to 30 min.

10 to 12 servings

NOODLE VEGETABLE MEDLEY

Prepare and set aside

1 medium onion, thinly sliced
½ cup chopped celery
4 medium zucchini, cut in ½-in. slices
1 small eggplant, cut in thin slices and slices quartered
1 medium green pepper, cut in 1-in. cubes
3 ripe tomatoes, cut in small wedges

Heat in a skillet

2 tablespoons butter or margarine

Add the onion and celery and cook about 3 min., stirring occasionally.

Add a blend of

1 pkg. (1½ oz.) spaghetti sauce mix
1 can (6 oz.) tomato paste
1½ cups water

Simmer over low heat about 5 min.

Meanwhile, heat in a large skillet

⅓ to ½ cup cooking oil

Add the zucchini, eggplant, green pepper and tomatoes and cook until zucchini and eggplant are lightly browned.

Add the hot spaghetti sauce and

½ teaspoon basil
3 oz. mozzarella cheese, shredded

Mix well and cook over low heat 20 min.

Meanwhile, cook, following package directions

8 oz. noodles

When tender, drain noodles and toss with

Melted butter or margarine

When ready to serve, top each serving of buttered noodles with the hot vegetable mixture. Sprinkle with additional shredded mozzarella cheese and serve immediately.

6 to 8 servings

BEEF RIPE OLIVE CASSEROLE

Set out a 1½-qt. casserole or baking dish.

Have ready

2 cups cooked noodles
1½ cups Thin White Sauce (1½ times recipe, page 304)
2 oz. chipped (or dried) beef, cut in pieces
½ cup shredded Cheddar cheese
¾ cup pitted ripe olives, cut in pieces

Turn noodles into the casserole. Pour over noodles a mixture of the Thin White Sauce, chipped beef, cheese and ripe olives. Sprinkle over top

¼ cup buttered dry bread crumbs

Heat in a 350°F oven about 25 min., or until lightly browned on surface. *4 servings*

NOODLE SALMON ROYALE

Set out a 2½-qt. casserole and a heavy saucepan.

Cook, following package directions

12 oz. medium noodles

Turn drained noodles into casserole.

Drain, reserving liquid

2 cans (16 oz. each) salmon

Flake (page 9) salmon and set aside.

Heat in the saucepan

¼ cup butter or margarine

Add and cook 5 min., stirring occasionally

½ cup chopped green onions

Stir in a mixture of

¼ cup all-purpose flour
¾ teaspoon salt
¼ teaspoon paprika
⅛ teaspoon cayenne pepper

Mix well and stir in

3½ cups chicken broth

Bring to boiling; cook and stir until sauce is smooth and slightly thickened. Stir in reserved salmon liquid and

3 tablespoons lemon juice

Stir in salmon and then a mixture of

2 egg yolks
½ cup heavy cream

Cook and stir over low heat about 3 min. (do not boil).

Pour salmon mixture over noodles and toss gently to mix. Sprinkle with

½ cup buttered bread crumbs

Heat in a 350°F oven about 30 min.

8 servings

RAVIOLI

▲ Base Recipe

Prepare (allowing about 4½ hrs.)

Tomato Meat Sauce (page 162)

Set aside.

Heat in skillet

2 tablespoons olive oil

Add, and cook until browned, breaking into small pieces with fork or spoon

¾ lb. ground beef

Meanwhile, prepare and cook (page 313)

½ lb. spinach

Drain well. Mix spinach and ground beef. Add and mix well

2 eggs, well beaten

and a mixture of

1 tablespoon grated Parmesan cheese
¾ teaspoon salt
¼ teaspoon pepper

Set aside.

Prepare

Basic Noodle Dough (page 152)

Divide dough into fourths. Lightly roll each fourth ⅛ in. thick to form a rectangle. Cut dough lengthwise with pastry cutter into strips 5 in. wide. Place 2 teaspoons filling 1½ in. from narrow end in center of each strip. Continuing along the strip, place 2 teaspoons filling 3½ in. apart.

Fold each strip in half lengthwise, covering the mounds of filling. To seal, press the edges together with the tines of a fork. Press gently between mounds to form rectangles about 3½ in. long. Cut apart with a pastry cutter and press the cut edges of rectangles with tines of fork to seal.

Bring to boiling in large saucepan

7 qts. water
2 tablespoons salt

Gradually add the ravioli (cook about one-half the ravioli at one time). Boil rapidly uncovered about 20 min., or until tender. Test tenderness by pressing a piece against side of pan with fork or spoon. Remove with slotted spoon. To drain, hold spoon on folded paper napkin or paper

Ravioli with Tomato Meat Sauce

Lasagne with Tomato Meat Sauce

towel a few seconds. Place ravioli on a warm platter and top with Tomato Meat Sauce. Sprinkle with

Grated Parmesan or Romano cheese
About 3 doz. Ravioli

—RAVIOLI WITH RICOTTA FILLING
(Ripieno di Ricotta per Ravioli)

Follow ▲ Recipe. Substitute **3 cups (about 1½ lbs.) ricotta cheese** for the ground beef. Omit oil and spinach. Add **1½ tablespoons chopped parsley**.

LASAGNE

It is said that on Christmas Eve the grand-mother in an Italian household measures the width of the children's mouths to know how wide to make the lasagne noodles. Here is a combination of Italian cheeses, noodles and tomato sauce you won't want to miss.

Set out an 8x8x2-in. baking dish.

Prepare (allowing about 4½ hrs.)
Tomato Meat Sauce (page 162)

When sauce is partially done, heat to boiling in large saucepan

8 qts. water
¼ cup salt
1 tablespoon olive oil
Gradually add
1 lb. lasagne noodles

Boil rapidly uncovered about 15 min., or until noodles are tender. Test tenderness by pressing a piece against side of pan with fork or spoon.

Heat in skillet
3 tablespoons olive oil
Add and cook until browned, breaking into small pieces with fork or spoon
1 lb. ground beef

Prepare
2 Hard-Cooked Eggs (page 133)

Drain noodles by pouring into a colander or large sieve.

Pour ½ cup of the Tomato Meat Sauce into the baking dish. Top with a layer of noodles (about one third of the noodles) and one half of
¾ lb. mozzarella cheese, sliced

Then add one half of browned ground beef and 1 hard-cooked egg, sliced. Sprinkle with one half of
¼ cup grated Parmesan cheese
½ teaspoon pepper
Top with one half of
1 cup Ricotta cheese
Beginning with sauce, repeat layering, ending with Ricotta cheese. Top Ricotta cheese with ½ cup of sauce. Arrange over this remaining lasagne noodles. Top with more sauce.

Bake at 350°F about 30 min., or until mixture is bubbling. Let stand 5 to 10 min. to set layers.

Cut into 2-in. squares and serve topped with remaining sauce. *6 to 8 servings*

LASAGNETTE

Prepare (allowing about 4½ hrs.)
Tomato Meat Sauce (one half recipe, page 162)

When sauce is partially done, prepare
Basic Noodle Dough (page 152)

Roll lightly ⅛ in. thick to form a rectangle about 12 in. long. Cut dough lengthwise with pastry cutter into strips ½ to ¾ in. wide. Cook strips as for Lasagne (on this page). Drain strips by pouring into a colander or large sieve. Set aside to keep warm.

Put into a saucepan ½ cup Tomato Meat Sauce. Add and mix well
1 cup (½ lb.) ricotta cheese
2 tablespoons grated Parmesan cheese
¼ teaspoon salt
⅛ teaspoon pepper
Cook over low heat until thoroughly heated.

Pour mixture over noodles on warm serving dish. Cover with remaining Tomato Meat Sauce and serve immediately. *About 8 servings*

TURKEY LASAGNE

Set out a shallow 2-qt. casserole.

For Sauce—Break into pieces, using a fork, and put into a cold skillet
¼ lb. bulk pork sausage
Add
1 tablespoon water
Cover and cook 5 min. Remove cover; pour off liquid. Brown sausage over medium heat. Drain off any excess fat from skillet.

Add to the skillet
3½ cups (28-oz. can) tomatoes, drained
2 tablespoons chopped parsley
½ teaspoon salt
1 teaspoon basil leaves
1 teaspoon crushed rosemary
1 bay leaf
1 clove garlic, minced
Simmer, uncovered, over low heat about 30 min., or until sauce is thick.

Cut into pieces enough turkey to yield
1 cup cooked turkey pieces
When sauce is thick, remove the bay leaf, add the turkey and cook 5 min. longer.

For Cottage Cheese Mixture—When sauce is partially done, mix and set aside
1½ cups cream-style cottage cheese
2 eggs, beaten
¼ cup finely chopped parsley
½ teaspoon salt
¼ teaspoon monosodium glutamate
¼ teaspoon pepper

To Cook Noodles—Before preparing Cottage Cheese Mixture, heat to boiling in a large saucepan
3 qts. water
1 tablespoon salt
1½ teaspoons olive oil
Add gradually
½ lb. lasagne noodles
Boil rapidly, uncovered, about 15 min., or until noodles are tender. Test tenderness by pressing a piece against the side of pan with fork or spoon. Drain noodles by turning into a colander or large sieve; rinse with hot water to re-move loose starch.

To Complete Lasagne—Set out
½ cup (about 2 oz.) grated Parmesan cheese
½ lb. Swiss cheese, thinly sliced
Spread one fourth of sauce over bottom of cas-serole. Top with one third of the noodles. Spread noodles with one third of the cottage cheese mixture. Then sprinkle with one third of the Parmesan cheese and arrange one third of the Swiss cheese slices on top. Repeat layer-ing, finishing with sauce on top.

Bake at 350°F about 30 min., or until mixture is bubbling. Let stand 5 to 10 min. to set layers before serving. *8 servings*

MACARONI

MACARONI

▲ Base Recipe

Heat to boiling in a large saucepan
3 qts. water
1 tablespoon salt
Add gradually so water continues to boil
2 cups (8 oz.) uncooked macaroni (tubes broken in 1- to 2-in. pieces, shells, elbows or other small shapes)
Boil, uncovered, 10 to 15 min., or until macaroni is tender; stir occasionally and gently during cooking.

Test tenderness by pressing a piece against side of pan with fork or spoon. Drain macaroni by turning it into a colander or large sieve.

About 4 cups cooked Macaroni

—SPAGHETTI

Follow ▲ Recipe. Substitute for macaroni, an equal amount of **spaghetti**.

MACARONI AND CHEESE I
(Maccheroni al Formaggio)

▲ Base Recipe

Thoroughly grease a 2-qt. casserole.

Melt in skillet
2 tablespoons butter or margarine
Stir in and set aside
2 cups (4 slices) soft bread crumbs
Cook (above)
2 cups (8 oz.) macaroni (tubes broken in 1- to 2-in. pieces; elbows or other small shapes)
Meanwhile, prepare
Thin White Sauce (page 304)
Cool sauce slightly.
Shred
½ lb. pasteurized process cheese food (2 cups, shredded)
Reserving ¼ cup, add cheese all at once to the slightly cooled white sauce with
⅓ cup minced onion
Stir until cheese is melted. Place one half of the macaroni into casserole and cover with one half of the sauce; repeat. Cover top with reserved cheese and buttered crumbs.

Bake at 350°F 20 to 30 min., or until crumbs are lightly browned.

6 to 7 servings

—MACARONI WITH TOMATOES
(Maccheroni al Pomodoro)

Follow ▲ Recipe. Omit buttered bread crumbs. Substitute **1 cup grated Parmesan cheese** for 1 cup of the process cheese food. Rinse, remove stem ends and cut into slices **3 medium (about 1 lb.) tomatoes.** Cover top of cas-

Macaroni and Cheese I

serole mixture with sliced tomatoes. Sprinkle with ¼ cup cheese as in ▲ Recipe.

MACARONI AND CHEESE II

▲ Base Recipe

Grease a 1½-qt. casserole.
Shred
½ lb. sharp Cheddar cheese (about 2 cups, shredded)
Set aside.
Cook (on this page)
2 cups (8 oz.) macaroni (elbows or tubes broken in 2-in. pieces)
Meanwhile, prepare
2 cups Thin White Sauce (page 304)
½ cup buttered fine dry bread crumbs (page 9)
Add the shredded cheese all at one time to the white sauce with
¼ teaspoon dry mustard
Turn one half the macaroni into casserole and pour half the cheese sauce over it. Repeat forming layers. Sprinkle the buttered crumbs over top.

Bake at 350°F 20 to 30 min., or until crumbs are browned. *6 servings*

—SAVORY MACARONI AND CHEESE

Follow ▲ Recipe. Reduce white sauce to 1 cup; omit dry mustard and blend into the sauce **¼ cup chili sauce** and **2 tablespoons Worcestershire sauce.** Proceed as in ▲ Recipe.

—FLAVOR-FILLED MACARONI AND CHEESE

Follow ▲ Recipe. Decrease Cheddar cheese to

6 oz. (about 1½ cups, shredded). Omit dry mustard and blend into white sauce **⅓ cup minced onion** and **½ teaspoon Worcestershire sauce.** Proceed as in ▲ Recipe.

MACARONI ROYAL

Thoroughly grease a shallow 2-qt. casserole.

Cook (on this page)
2 cups (8 oz.) macaroni (use small shapes or tubes broken in 2-in. pieces)
Meanwhile, combine
1¼ cups (10¾-oz. can) condensed tomato soup
½ cup chopped stuffed olives
Few drops Tabasco
and a mixture of
½ teaspoon salt
¼ teaspoon monosodium glutamate
¼ teaspoon dry mustard
Dash paprika
Set aside.

Heat in a skillet
3 to 4 tablespoons fat

Flavor-Filled Macaroni and Cheese

Add and cook about 5 min.

1 cup (8-oz. can, drained) mushrooms
½ cup chopped onion
¼ cup chopped green pepper
1 clove garlic, cut in halves (spear with wooden picks for easy removal after vegetables are cooked)

Blend tomato mixture into vegetables. Cover and simmer 5 min. Place one half of the drained macaroni in casserole and cover with one half of the sauce; repeat.

Cut into ¼-in. slices
½ lb. Cheddar cheese
Overlap cheese slices in a border around top.

Bake at 350°F 25 to 30 min., or until cheese slices are softened and tinged with brown.

6 to 8 servings

FLAVOR-RIGHT BEEF AND MACARONI

A little meat scores a big success in this one-dish meal.

Grease a 2-qt. casserole and set out a large heavy skillet with a tight-fitting cover.

Cook (page 156)
2 cups (8 oz.) macaroni

Meanwhile, heat in the skillet
2 tablespoons fat
Add and cook over medium heat about 5 min., stirring occasionally

1 clove garlic, split (insert wooden picks for easy removal after vegetables are cooked)
½ cup (about 1 medium) chopped onion
¼ cup chopped green pepper
Add and cook until browned, separating into small pieces with fork or spoon
½ lb. ground beef

Add slowly and blend well
2½ cups (two 10¾-oz. cans) condensed tomato soup
½ cup (4-oz. can) mushrooms
1 tablespoon Worcestershire sauce
and a mixture of
1 teaspoon salt
½ teaspoon monosodium glutamate
½ teaspoon dry mustard
¼ teaspoon chili powder
Stir until well blended. Cover; simmer 5 min.

Meanwhile, cut into ¼-in. slices
4 oz. Swiss cheese
Rinse, cut off stem ends and cut into ½-in. slices
4 small (about 1 lb.) tomatoes
Remove garlic from meat mixture. Put one half of the drained macaroni into casserole. Cover with one half of the sauce. Repeat layering. Alternate cheese and tomato slices in a border around top of casserole.

Lightly brush tomato and cheese slices with
1 to 2 tablespoons butter or margarine, melted

Bake at 350°F 20 to 25 min., or until cheese is melted and lightly browned. *6 to 8 servings*

SPECIALTY MACARONI BEEF LOAF

Grease a 9x5x3-in. loaf pan. Set out a small skillet.

Prepare
1 cup (4 oz.) macaroni (one-half recipe, page 156; use tubes broken in 1- to 2-in. pieces)

Meanwhile, prepare and set aside
½ cup quick meat broth (one-half recipe, page 10)

Heat in skillet over medium heat
2 tablespoons fat
Add and cook about 5 min.
¼ cup finely chopped onion
¼ cup finely chopped green pepper
Mix onion and green pepper lightly with broth and
¾ lb. ground beef
¼ lb. bulk pork sausage
2 tablespoons minced pimiento
2 eggs, beaten
and a mixture of
1½ teaspoons salt
½ teaspoon monosodium glutamate
¼ teaspoon pepper
Using a fork, mix in drained macaroni. Pack lightly into loaf pan.

Bake at 350°F about 1 hr.

Meanwhile, prepare
Tomato Cheese Sauce (page 308)
Unmold loaf and serve with sauce.

6 to 8 servings

FRANKFURTER MACARONI

▲ *Base Recipe*

Panfry until browned in large skillet or Dutch oven
4 slices bacon, cut in small pieces

Return to skillet
3 tablespoons fat
Add and cook, stirring occasionally, until onion is tender
1 lb. (8 to 10) frankfurters, cut in ¾-in. pieces
⅓ cup chopped onion
Stir in bacon and
1¼ cups (10¾-oz. can) condensed tomato soup
½ cup boiling water
1 teaspoon Worcestershire sauce
1 teaspoon salt
⅛ teaspoon pepper
Cover and simmer 30 min.

Meanwhile, cook (page 156)
2 cups (8 oz.) macaroni
Carefully stir cooked macaroni into sauce. Simmer 5 min. before serving. *6 servings*

—FRANKFURTER OR HAMBURGER SPAGHETTI

Follow ▲ Recipe or variation. Substitute **spaghetti** for macaroni.

—HAMBURGER MACARONI

Follow ▲ Recipe. Substitute **1 lb. ground beef** for frankfurters. Cook ground beef until browned, separating with fork or spoon.

HAM MACARONI ROLL-UPS

Grease bottom of an 11x7-in. baking dish.

Cook (page 156)
4 oz. tube macaroni

While macaroni is cooking, prepare
2 cups Cheese Sauce (double recipe, page 304; use 14½-oz. can evaporated milk and ⅓ cup water for milk; add 1 teaspoon dry mustard with dry ingredients)

Divide macaroni into 6 bundles. Wrap around

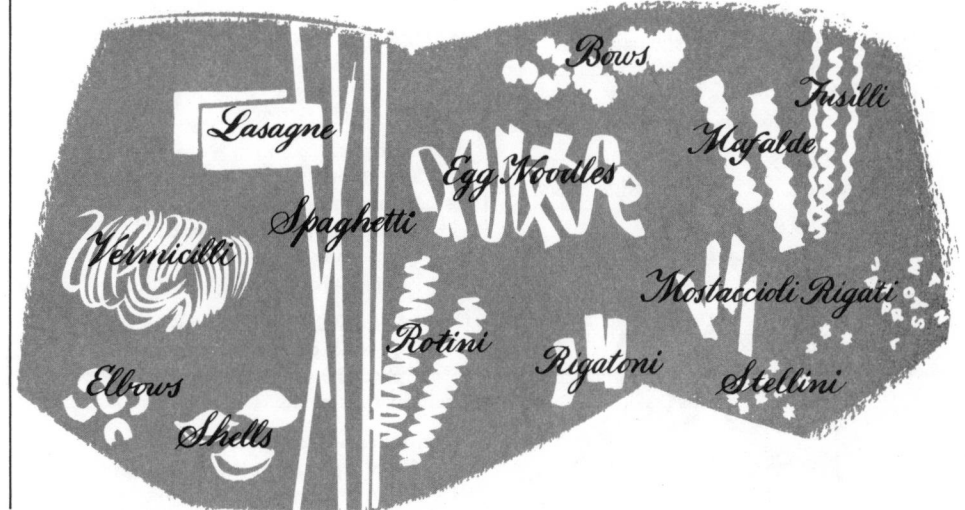

Ham Macaroni Roll-Ups

bundles and secure with wooden picks
6 thin slices cooked ham
Arrange bundles in baking dish; pour hot Cheese Sauce over ham.

Place baking dish under broiler with top of ham about 4 in. from heat; broil about 3 min., or until lightly browned. Remove wooden picks from roll-ups before serving.   *6 servings*

MACARONI AND HAM
(Makkaroniauflauf mit Schinken)

Lightly butter a 1½-qt. casserole.

Cook (page 156)
2 cups (8 oz.) macaroni (elbows or other shapes, or tubes broken in 2-in. pieces)

Meanwhile, prepare and set aside
2 cups Thin White Sauce (double recipe, page 304; mix ¼ teaspoon dry mustard and a dash of paprika with flour before blending into fat; add ½ teaspoon Worcestershire sauce with the milk)

Shred and set aside
4 oz. sharp Cheddar cheese (1 cup, shredded)

Prepare and set aside
¼ cup minced onion

Dice enough cooked ham to yield
1 cup diced cooked ham
Lightly but thoroughly mix the ham, macaroni, sauce, ¾ cup of the cheese and the minced onion. Turn into the buttered casserole. Sprinkle with the remaining cheese.

Bake at 350°F 25 to 30 min., or until top is lightly browned.   *6 to 8 servings*

OYSTER MACARONI TRIUMPH

▲ *Base Recipe*

Grease a 3-qt. casserole.

Drain, reserving liquor, and remove any shell particles from
1 pt. oysters
Set aside in cool place.

Prepare
Macaroni (page 156)

Meanwhile, shred and set aside
10 oz. Cheddar cheese (2½ cups, shredded)

Prepare
3 cups Medium White Sauce (three times recipe, page 000; substitute oyster liquor for part of the milk. Stir in ¼ cup slivered pimiento, ½ cup chili sauce and 2 teaspoons lemon juice.)
Cool sauce slightly.

Add shredded cheese all at one time and stir until cheese is melted. Set sauce aside.

Heat in skillet over medium heat
2 tablespoons butter or margarine
Add to skillet and cook until celery is tender, stirring occasionally
1 cup (3 to 4 stalks) finely diced celery
¼ cup grated onion
Combine vegetables with macaroni and sauce, mixing carefully with a fork; turn mixture into casserole. Make a well in center of macaroni mixture; fill with the oysters.

Bake at 350°F 30 to 35 min.   *8 servings*

—BUFFET OYSTERS

Follow ▲ Recipe. Use shell macaroni. Omit pimiento and chili sauce from sauce. Cut **1 clove garlic** into halves. Heat about 5 min. in butter for sauce. Discard garlic and complete sauce. Combine sauce with macaroni, omitting vegetables and butter. Complete and bake as in ▲ Recipe.

MACARONI VEGETABLE MEDLEY AU VIN

Grease a 2½-qt. casserole.

Have ready
3 oz. fresh mushrooms, chopped
½ cup chopped onion
¼ cup chopped pimiento
1 cup cooked peas
½ lb. Swiss cheese, shredded

Cook, following directions on packages
2 cups (8 oz.) elbow macaroni
1 pkg. (10 oz.) frozen mixed vegetables
Drain and set aside.

Meanwhile, heat in a skillet
2 tablespoons butter or margarine
Mix in the mushrooms and onion. Cook, stir-

ring occasionally, until onion is soft; set aside.

Mix in a large bowl
1 can (10½ oz.) condensed cream of celery soup
1 soup can milk
2 teaspoons Worcestershire sauce
1 teaspoon salt
¼ teaspoon white pepper
1 teaspoon dry mustard
½ cup dry sherry or white wine
Add the pimiento, peas, cheese, mushroom mixture, mixed vegetables, and macaroni; mix well. Turn into the casserole.

Set in a 300°F oven until thoroughly heated, about 30 min.

Garnish with **chopped parsley** and **pimiento strips.**   *About 8 servings*

PEACHES IN PASTA CASSEROLE

Grease a shallow 2½-qt. baking dish.

Have ready
6 to 8 ½ in. thick green pepper rings
¾ lb. sharp Cheddar cheese, shredded
1 can (29 oz.) cling peach halves, drained

Cook (page 156), drain and set aside
1¾ cups (7 oz.) elbow macaroni

Cook the green pepper rings in boiling water 5 min. Drain.

Heat in a large saucepan
¼ cup butter or margarine
Blend in
¼ cup all-purpose flour
1 tablespoon dry mustard
½ teaspoon salt
Heat until bubbly. Add gradually, stirring constantly until smooth
1 cup milk
Bring to boiling; stir and cook 1 to 2 min.

Add the Cheddar cheese and heat, stirring until melted. Mix in the macaroni and
1 can (16 oz.) stewed tomatoes, cut in pieces
Turn mixture into the baking dish. Press pepper rings into mixture and top each with a peach half, rounded side up. Sprinkle with
Grated Parmesan-Romano cheese

Set in a 350°F oven until sauce is bubbly, about 25 min.   *6 to 8 servings*

Buffet Oysters

PARMESAN MACARONI CASSEROLE

Grease a 1½-qt. casserole; set aside.

Have ready
    ½ cup grated Parmesan cheese
    1 can (12 oz.) luncheon meat, diced
    ½ cup sliced celery
    ¼ cup chopped green pepper

Cook (page 156)
    1 cup (4 oz.) elbow macaroni
Drain and turn into a large bowl.

Meanwhile, put into a heavy saucepan over low heat
    1 pkg. (8 oz.) cream cheese
Soften with a spoon. Add
    ½ teaspoon garlic salt
Add gradually, stirring constantly
    1 cup milk
Stir and heat thoroughly. Remove from heat and mix in Parmesan cheese.

Put luncheon meat, celery and green pepper into the bowl with macaroni. Add the sauce and mix well. Turn into the casserole. Generously sprinkle top with additional grated Parmesan cheese.

Set in a 350°F oven about 25 min., or until top is lightly browned. *About 6 servings*

MOSTACCIOLI AND CHEESE
(Mostaccioli al Formaggio)

Set out an 8x8x2-in. baking dish.

Prepare (allowing about 4½ hrs.)
    Tomato Meat Sauce (page 162)

Heat to boiling in saucepot
    4 qts. water
    1 tablespoon salt
Add gradually so boiling continues
    2 cups (8 oz.) mostaccioli
Boil rapidly, uncovered, 12 to 15 min., or until mostaccioli is tender. Test tenderness by pressing a piece against side of saucepot with fork or spoon. Drain by pouring into a colander or large sieve. Return drained mostaccioli to saucepan and mix with 2 tablespoons Tomato Meat Sauce. Put half of mostaccioli into

baking dish. Add in layers
    1 cup chopped mozzarella cheese
    2 tablespoons grated Parmesan cheese
    ¼ teaspoon pepper
Cover with remaining mostaccioli. Cover with Tomato Meat Sauce.

Bake at 350°F 15 to 20 min., or until tomato sauce is bubbling.

Serve with remaining hot Tomato Meat Sauce. Sprinkle with
    Grated Parmesan or Romano cheese
Serve immediately. *4 to 6 servings*

MACARONI MUFFS
(Manicotti)

Set out two 11x7x1½-in. baking dishes.

Prepare (allowing about 4½ hrs.)
    Tomato Meat Sauce (page 162)

When sauce is partially done, heat in skillet
    2 tablespoons olive oil
Add and cook until browned, breaking into small pieces with fork or spoon
    ½ lb. ground beef
Remove browned ground beef from skillet and mix with
    2 cups (about 1 b.) ricotta cheese
    ¼ lb. mozzarella cheese, diced
    2 teaspoons grated Parmesan cheese
    2 eggs, well beaten
    ¾ teaspoon salt
    ¼ teaspoon pepper
Set aside.

Prepare
    Basic Noodle Dough (one half recipe, page 152)
Divide dough into halves. Lightly roll each half ⅛ in. thick to form a rectangle. Cut dough lengthwise with pastry cutter into strips 5 in. wide. Cut strips every 6 in. to form noodles 6x5 in.

Bring to boiling in a saucepot
    5 qts. water
    1 tablespoon salt
Gradually add the noodles. Boil rapidly, uncovered, about 10 to 12 min., or until noodles are tender. Test tenderness by pressing a piece against side of saucepot with fork or spoon. Drain in a colander or large sieve.

Lay noodles out flat on a working surface. About ½ in. from the lengthwise edge of the noodle, place 4 tablespoons filling. Spread the filling from narrow edge to narrow edge so filling is in a ½-in. wide mound. Roll the ½-in. edge of the dough over the filling and continue to roll. Press edges to seal. Place 4 to 6 Manicotti into each baking dish in a single layer. Cover with Tomato Meat Sauce.

Bake at 400°F 15 to 20 min., or until tomato sauce is bubbling hot and Manicotti swells. Serve with remaining Tomato Meat Sauce.
About 8 to 12 Manicotti

MANICOTTI WITH VEAL HAM FILLING

Set out a large heavy skillet and a 2-qt. baking dish with a cover.

Heat in the skillet
    1 tablespoon olive oil
Add and cook over medium heat about 5 min., stirring occasionally
    1 tablespoon finely chopped onion
    ½ lb. ground veal
    ½ lb. ground ham
Turn into a bowl and combine with a blend of
    ½ teaspoon salt
    ¼ teaspoon crushed rosemary
    ¼ teaspoon pepper
    ⅛ teaspoon nutmeg
Mix well and add
    1 egg, slightly beaten
    2 tablespoons Marsala
    1 cup soft white bread crumbs
    2 tablespoons grated Parmesan cheese
Toss until thoroughly mixed and stuff into
    8 pieces (4 in. long) uncooked manicotti
Pour into a 1-qt. measuring cup
    2 cans (15¼ oz. each) or 3 cans (10¼ oz. each) Italian-style marinara sauce
Cover bottom of the baking dish with 1 cup of the sauce. Arrange filled manicotti in a single layer in baking dish, leaving space between them for expansion during baking. Top with remaining sauce and cover baking dish (aluminum foil may be used for a tight seal).

Bake in a 375°F oven 1 hr. Serve with additional grated Parmesan cheese. *4 to 6 servings*

Note: Cannelloni or Stuff-a-roni (4 in. long) may be substituted for manicotti, if desired.

PASTA WITH BROCCOLI
(Pasta con Broccoli)

Heat to boiling in a large saucepot
    4 qts. water
    2 teaspoons salt

Shells with Clam Sauce

Add gradually so boiling continues
4 cups (1-lb. pkg.) ditalini
Boil rapidly, uncovered, about 12 min., or until ditalini is tender. Test tenderness by pressing a piece against side of saucepot with fork or spoon. Reserving 3 cups liquid, drain ditalini in a colander or large sieve. Set aside.

Prepare and cook until just tender (page 313)
1 lb. broccoli
Set aside.

Heat in large saucepan until garlic is lightly browned
¼ cup olive oil
2 cloves garlic, sliced
Add drained broccoli and ditalini with the 3 cups reserved liquid. Season with
⅛ teaspoon pepper
Simmer about 10 min.

Serve topped with
Grated Parmesan or Romano cheese
Serve immediately.   *About 6 servings*

PASTA WITH BEANS
(Pasta con Fagioli)

Heat to boiling in a large saucepan
3 cups water

Meanwhile, wash thoroughly and discard imperfect beans from
1¼ cups (about ½ lb.) navy or pea beans
Gradually add beans to water so boiling continues. Simmer 2 min. and remove from heat. Set aside to soak 1 hr. Add to beans
½ teaspoon salt

Spaghetti with Wine Tomato Sauce

Return to heat and simmer 2 hrs., or until beans are tender, stirring once or twice.

Meanwhile, heat to boiling in large saucepan
2 qts. water
1 teaspoon salt
Add gradually so boiling continues
2 cups (8 oz.) ditalini
Boil rapidly, uncovered, about 12 min., or until ditalini is tender. Test tenderness by pressing a piece against side of pan with fork or spoon. Reserving 1 cup liquid, drain ditalini by pouring into a colander or large sieve. When beans are tender, add the drained ditalini, the 1 cup reserved liquid, and a mixture of
¼ cup tomatoes, sieved
1 tablespoon olive oil
¼ teaspoon pepper
¼ teaspoon oregano

Simmer 10 to 15 min. Sprinkle with
Grated Parmesan cheese
Serve immediately.   *5 or 6 servings*

PASTA WITH PEAS
(Pasta con Piselli)

Heat to boiling in large saucepan
2 qts. water
1 teaspoon salt
Add gradually so boiling continues
2 cups (8-oz. pkg.) ditalini
Boil rapidly, uncovered, about 12 min., or until tender. Test tenderness by pressing a piece against side of pan with fork or spoon. Reserving 2 cups water, drain by pouring into a colander or large sieve. Set aside.

Heat in a large saucepan
¼ cup olive oil
Add and cook slowly until lightly browned
¼ cup chopped onion
Add slowly a mixture of
½ cup tomatoes, sieved
¾ teaspoon salt
⅛ teaspoon pepper
⅛ teaspoon oregano
Simmer about 10 min. Add cooked ditalini, reserved liquid and
3½ cups (2 16-oz. cans) peas
Simmer 10 to 15 min.

Serve topped with
Grated Parmesan or Romano cheese
Serve immediately.   *4 or 5 servings*

SHELLS WITH CLAM SAUCE
(Conchiglie con Salsa alle Vongole)

Cook and drain (page 156)
2 cups (8 oz.) macaroni shells

Meanwhile, prepare
White Clam Sauce (page 164)

Pour sauce over macaroni shells and sprinkle with
1 tablespoon minced parsley
Serve hot.   *4 to 6 servings*

SPAGHETTI

SPAGHETTI WITH MEAT BALLS
(Spaghetti con Polpette)

▲ *Base Recipe*

Prepare (allowing about 4½ hrs.)
Tomato Meat Sauce (page 162)

When sauce is partially done, mix lightly
½ lb. ground beef
½ lb. ground pork
1 cup (2 slices) soft bread crumbs
1 tablespoon grated Parmesan cheese
1 tablespoon minced parsley
1 egg, well beaten
1 teaspoon salt
¼ teaspoon pepper
Shape meat mixture into balls about 1 in. in diameter.

Heat in skillet
2 tablespoons olive oil
1 clove garlic, minced
Add meat balls and brown on all sides, turning occasionally. Pour off fat as it collects. Remove meat balls from skillet. Add meat balls to Tomato Meat Sauce about 20 min. before sauce is done.

Meanwhile, cook (page 156)
8 oz. unbroken spaghetti
Place drained spaghetti on warm platter. Top with Tomato Meat Sauce and sprinkle with
Grated Parmesan or Romano cheese
Surround spaghetti with meat balls.
          4 to 6 servings

—SPAGHETTI WITH WINE TOMATO SAUCE
(Spaghetti con Salsa di Pomodore Vino)

Follow ▲ Recipe. About 30 min. before sauce is done, add **½ cup dry red wine.**

—SPAGHETTI WITH TOMATO SAUCE
(Spaghetti con Salsa di Pomodoro)

Follow ▲ Recipe. Omit meat balls. Top spaghetti with **Tomato Meat Sauce** (page 162) or any of the sauce variations.

—LINGUINE

Omit Tomato Meat Sauce and meat balls. Follow ▲ Recipe, substituting **8 oz. uncooked linguine** for spaghetti. Boil 10 to 15

160

min., or until tender. Serve topped with **Oil and Garlic Sauce** (page 163), any of the sauce variations or **Marinara Sauce** (page 163).

SPAGHETTI, ITALIAN STYLE

Prepare
3 cups Tomato Beef Sauce (page 307)

About 20 min. before sauce is done, prepare
8 oz. unbroken spaghetti (page 156)
Place drained spaghetti into large serving bowl. Top spaghetti with Tomato Beef Sauce and sprinkle with
Grated Parmesan or Romano cheese
Serve with **garlic-buttered French or Italian bread.**   *4 to 6 servings*

Sausage and Spaghetti with Cheese Sauce

SPAGHETTI FEAST

▲ *Base Recipe*

Heat in a large skillet with a tight-fitting cover
2 tablespoons fat
Add and cook over medium heat, stirring occasionally, until onion is tender
½ cup (about 1 medium) chopped onion
¼ cup chopped green pepper
Add and brown, separating into small pieces with fork or spoon
1 lb. ground beef
Blend in
3½ cups (28-oz. can) tomatoes, cut in pieces
and a mixture of
1 teaspoon salt
½ teaspoon monosodium glutamate
¼ teaspoon pepper
¼ teaspoon chili powder
Cover and simmer about 1 hr.

Meanwhile, cook (page 156)
2 cups (8 oz.) spaghetti
Turn hot cooked spaghetti onto warm serving platter and cover with tomato meat sauce. Sprinkle with
¼ cup grated Parmesan cheese
6 servings

—SPAGHETTI AND MEAT BALLS

Follow ▲ Recipe. Combine uncooked meat,

Spaghetti and Meat Balls

onion, green pepper and 1 teaspoon salt. Shape into small balls. Brown in fat and simmer ½ hr. in seasoned tomatoes. Cover cooked spaghetti with meat balls and some of the sauce. Serve with additional sauce and grated cheese.

SAUSAGE AND SPAGHETTI WITH CHEESE SAUCE

Lightly butter a 2-qt. casserole or baking dish.

Lightly brown in skillet and drain off fat
1 lb. smoked pork sausage links
Cut one half of the sausages into ¾-in. pieces; reserve remaining sausages for top of casserole.

For Tomato Mushroom Sauce—Drain, reserving liquid
1 can (4 oz.) sliced mushrooms (about ½ cup, drained)
Finely chop
1 medium onion (about ½ cup, chopped)
Heat in a large skillet over low heat
2½ tablespoons butter or margarine
Add the drained mushrooms and onion; cook over medium heat, frequently moving and turning with a spoon until onion is tender.

Stir in mushroom liquid and
3½ cups (28-oz. can) tomatoes
1 cup (8-oz. can) tomato sauce
2 tablespoons finely chopped parsley
½ teaspoon salt
½ teaspoon monosodium glutamate
¼ teaspoon garlic powder
⅛ teaspoon tarragon, crumbled
⅛ teaspoon rosemary, crumbled
⅛ teaspoon pepper
Cover and simmer about 40 min., stirring occasionally.

For Spaghetti—Prepare and keep warm
Spaghetti (page 156)

For Cheese Sauce—Shred and set aside
4 oz. Cheddar cheese (about 1 cup, shredded)

Set out
¼ cup grated Parmesan cheese
Heat in a saucepan over low heat
2 tablespoons butter or margarine
Blend in
1½ tablespoons all-purpose flour
¼ teaspoon monosodium glutamate
⅛ teaspoon salt
Few grains pepper
Heat until mixture bubbles. Remove from heat.

Add gradually, while stirring constantly
1 cup undiluted evaporated milk
Return to heat and bring to boiling. Cook 1 to 2 min. longer, stirring constantly. Remove from heat. Add the cheeses to the sauce and stir until cheese is melted.

To Complete Casserole—Turn the spaghetti into the casserole. Add the sausage pieces and pour in the Tomato Mushroom Sauce; mix lightly but thoroughly. Spoon the Cheese Sauce over the top. Arrange the remaining sausages in a pattern on top (see photo).

Bake at 375°F 25 min., or until mixture is bubbly and Cheese Sauce is lightly browned.

Remove from oven and serve immediately.
6 servings

SPAGHETTI SALMON AU GRATIN

Set out a 2-qt. casserole or baking dish and a large heavy skillet.

Cook (page 156)
8 oz. thin spaghetti
Turn drained spaghetti into the casserole.

Drain, reserving liquid
1 can (16 oz.) salmon
Flake (page 9) salmon and set aside.

Clean and slice (page 9)
½ lb. fresh mushrooms
Set aside.

Heat in the skillet
¼ cup butter or margarine
Add the mushrooms and cook over medium

161

Tuna Spaghetti

heat 5 min., stirring occasionally. Stir in a mixture of

¼ cup all-purpose flour
¾ teaspoon salt
⅛ teaspoon pepper
¼ teaspoon curry powder

Add gradually, stirring constantly

1 qt. milk

Bring to boiling; cook and stir mixture until thickened. Blend in reserved salmon liquid and

Juice of ½ lemon
2 tablespoons sherry

Mix in salmon and more seasoning, if needed.

Turn most of the mixture in skillet over cooked spaghetti. Toss lightly to mix well, then make a depression in center and fill with remaining salmon-mushroom mixture.

Sprinkle over top a mixture of

¼ cup shredded cheese
½ cup fine soft bread crumbs

Heat in a 350°F oven about 30 min. Garnish with **sprigs of parsley** and serve at once.

6 servings

SPAGHETTI AND TUNA TOSS

Set out a heavy 2-qt. saucepan.

Cook and drain (page 156)

8 oz. spaghetti

Meanwhile, combine in the saucepan

½ cup unsalted butter or margarine
2 cans (6½ or 7 oz. each) tuna, drained and flaked (page 9)
1 can (6 oz.) broiled mushroom crowns
½ cup light cream
½ teaspoon salt
¼ teaspoon pepper
¼ teaspoon tarragon leaves

Heat slowly to serving temperature, stirring gently. Blend in

⅓ cup grated Parmesan or Romano cheese

Toss sauce lightly with the drained hot spaghetti.

4 or 5 servings

TUNA SPAGHETTI

▲ *Base Recipe*

Grease a 3-qt. casserole.

Prepare

Pastry Topping (page 486)

Roll into shape and size of casserole top. Thoroughly prick with fork. Cut pastry into 6 equal wedges with sharp knife, using all of pastry; set aside.

Cook (page 156)

2 cups (about 8 oz.) spaghetti

Drain and set aside.

Shred and set aside

4 oz. sharp cheese (1 cup, shredded)

Prepare

2 cups Medium White Sauce (double recipe, page 304; add 1 cup, 8-oz. can, tomato sauce)

Add the shredded cheese all at one time. Stir sauce rapidly until cheese is melted. Using a fork, gently combine the sauce and spaghetti with

2 cups (two 7-oz. cans, drained) tuna, coarsely flaked (page 9)
2 cups cooked or canned peas
½ teaspoon monosodium glutamate

Turn warm mixture into casserole. Place pastry wedges on top, long points of wedges toward center.

Bake at 425°F 15 to 20 min., or until crust is lightly browned.

8 servings

—HASTY TUNA TREAT

Follow ▲ Recipe. Omit pastry. Top mixture with **¾ cup broken crackers** which have been coated with **melted butter or margarine.** Bake at 350°F 20 to 30 min., or until crackers are lightly browned.

LINGUINE WITH SEAFOOD

Have ready

1 can (6½ oz.) crab meat, drained and flaked
1 can (5 oz.) lobster, drained and flaked
½ lb. cooked shelled shrimp, cut in pieces

Cook, following package directions and drain

1 lb. linguine

Meanwhile, heat in a large heavy skillet until garlic is golden

½ cup butter or margarine
1 clove garlic

Discard garlic and add to butter in skillet

½ cup Chablis
½ cup chicken broth
¼ cup finely snipped parsley
¼ teaspoon basil
¼ teaspoon oregano

Cook over low heat until simmering and add crab meat, lobster and shrimp. Toss to mix well and season to taste with

Salt and pepper

Heat slowly to serving temperature and serve over hot linguine.

About 6 servings

Note: If desired, substitute 1 lb. spaghetti for linguine.

SPAGHETTI SAUCES

TOMATO MEAT SAUCE
(Salsa di Carne al Pomodoro)

▲ *Base Recipe*

Set out a large saucepot with a tight-fitting cover.

Heat in saucepot

¼ cup olive oil

Add and cook until lightly browned

½ cup (about 1 medium) chopped onion

Add to skillet and cook, turning occasionally, until browned

½ lb. beef chuck
½ lb. pork shoulder

Add slowly a mixture of

7 cups canned tomatoes, sieved
1 tablespoon salt
1 bay leaf

Cover saucepot and simmer over very low heat, about 2½ hrs.

Add

¾ cup (6-oz. can) tomato paste

Simmer uncovered over very low heat, stirring occasionally, about 2 hrs., or until thickened. If sauce becomes too thick, add ½ cup water.

Remove meat and bay leaf from sauce. Serve over cooked spaghetti.

About 4 cups sauce

—TOMATO SAUCE WITH GROUND MEAT
(Salsa di Pomodoro e Carne Macinata)

Follow ▲ Recipe. Brown **½ lb. ground beef** in **3 tablespoons olive oil,** separating beef into small pieces with fork or spoon. After remov-

Tomato Sauce with Ground Meat

ing meat from sauce, add ground meat and simmer 10 min. longer.

—TOMATO SAUCE WITH MUSHROOMS
(Salsa di Pomodoro e Funghi)

Follow ▲ Recipe. Clean and slice (page 9) ½ **lb. mushrooms.** Cook slowly in **3 table-spoons melted butter** until lightly browned. After removing meat from sauce, add mushrooms and cook 10 min. longer.

—TOMATO SAUCE WITH CHICKEN LIVERS
(Salsa di Pomodoro e Fegatini di Pollo)

Follow ▲ Recipe. Rinse and pat dry with absorbent paper ½ **lb. chicken livers.** Slice livers and brown in **3 tablespoons olive oil.** After removing meat from sauce, add chicken livers and simmer 10 min. longer.

—TOMATO SAUCE WITH SAUSAGE
(Salsa di Pomodoro e Salsiccia)

Follow ▲ Recipe. Brown about ½ **lb. Italian sausage,** cut in 2-in. pieces, in **1 tablespoon olive oil.** After removing meat from sauce, add sausage and simmer 10 min. longer.

QUICK ITALIAN TOMATO SAUCE
(Salsa di Pomodoro)

Here is an American version of the long-cooking tomato sauce. An ideal, quick sauce for the homemaker in a hurry.

Heat in a large skillet
    2 tablespoons olive oil
Add and cook until lightly browned
    1 clove garlic, minced
    ½ **cup (about 1 medium) chopped onion**
Add and cook over medium heat until browned, separating into small pieces with fork or spoon
    1 lb. ground beef
Stir in slowly
    1¼ **cups (10¾-oz. can) condensed tomato soup**
    1½ **cups (two 6-oz. cans) tomato paste**
    ½ **cup quick coffee (page 10)**

Add a mixture of
    1 teaspoon salt
    ⅛ **teaspoon pepper**
Simmer, uncovered, over very low heat, stirring occasionally, about 30 min., or until thickened.

Stir in
    ½ **cup (4-oz. can, drained) chopped mushrooms**
    ¼ **teaspoon oregano**
Simmer 5 to 10 min. If sauce becomes too thick, blend in ½ cup water. Serve over cooked spaghetti. *4 to 6 servings*

MARINARA SAUCE

Heat in a large saucepan
    ½ **cup olive oil**
Add and cook until browned
    2 medium cloves garlic, sliced
Add slowly, stirring constantly, a mixture of
    3½ **cups canned tomatoes, sieved**
    1¼ **teaspoons salt**
    1 teaspoon oregano
    ¼ **teaspoon chopped parsley**
    ⅛ **teaspoon pepper**
Cook rapidly, uncovered, about 15 min., or until thickened. Stir occasionally.

If sauce becomes too thick, add ¼ to ½ cup water. Serve hot on cooked spaghetti or linguine. *About 4 cups sauce*

BUTTER AND GARLIC SAUCE
(Salsa al Burro e Aglio)

    ▲ *Base Recipe*

Heat in skillet
    ¾ **cup butter or margarine**
Add and cook slowly until lightly browned
    2 cloves garlic, thinly sliced
Add slowly
    ¼ **cup water**
    ½ **teaspoon finely chopped parsley**
Cook about 10 min. and serve over cooked spaghetti. *About 1 cup sauce*

—BUTTER AND CHEESE SAUCE
(Salsa con Burro e Formaggio)

Follow ▲ Recipe. Omit garlic. Mix butter sauce with spaghetti and sprinkle with ¼ **cup grated Parmesan cheese.**

OIL AND GARLIC SAUCE
(Salsa all'Olio e Aglio)

    ▲ *Base Recipe*

Heat in skillet
    ½ **cup olive oil**
Add and cook until browned
    4 cloves garlic, thinly sliced
Stir in
    ½ **cup water**

Quick Italian Tomato Sauce

Add
    1 tablespoon chopped parsley
    ⅛ **teaspoon pepper**
Simmer about 10 min. Serve over cooked spaghetti. *About 1 cup sauce*

—GARLIC SAUCE WITH ANCHOVIES
(Salsa con Aglio e Acciughe)

Follow ▲ Recipe. Add **5 chopped anchovy fillets** with the parsley.

—GARLIC SAUCE WITH WALNUTS
(Salsa con Aglio e Noci)

Follow ▲ Recipe. Add **2 tablespoons chopped walnuts** with the parsley.

—GARLIC SAUCE WITH CAPERS
(Salsa con Aglio e Capperi)

Follow ▲ Recipe. Add **2 tablespoons capers** with the parsley.

—OIL AND ONION SAUCE
(Salsa all'Olio e Cipolla)

Follow ▲ Recipe. Substitute **1 medium onion, very thinly sliced,** for the garlic.

GREEN SAUCE
(Salsa Verde)

The subtle flavors of green herbs combine to make a sauce that lends itself to fish, pasta and vegetables alike.

Mash with a fork or crush in a mortar with pestle to make a smooth paste
    1 tablespoon chopped parsley
    1 tablespoon chopped watercress
    1 tablespoon chopped capers
    ½ **clove garlic, chopped**
    ¼ **teaspoon salt**
    ⅛ **teaspoon pepper**
Add, 1 tablespoon at a time
    6 tablespoons olive oil
Beat vigorously with fork or spoon after each addition. Add slowly while beating
    3 tablespoons lemon juice
Serve with artichokes, cooked spaghetti, shrimp or fried fish. *About ½ cup sauce*

WHITE CLAM SAUCE
(Salsa alle Vongole)

▲Base Recipe

Heat in skillet until garlic is lightly browned
¼ cup olive oil
1 clove garlic, thinly sliced
Stir in slowly
¼ cup water
Stir in
½ teaspoon chopped parsley
½ teaspoon salt
¼ teaspoon oregano
¼ teaspoon pepper
Add slowly
1 cup (8-oz. can) little neck whole clams with juice
Cook until clams are heated through. Serve hot on cooked spaghetti or macaroni.

About 1½ cups sauce

—RED CLAM SAUCE
(Salsa di Vongole al Pomodoro)

Follow ▲ Recipe. Stir in with water **3½ cups tomatoes**, sieved. Simmer about 10 min. Add clams and simmer until clams are heated through.

About 5 cups sauce

GNOCCHI

GNOCCHI

Prepare (allowing about 4½ hrs.)
Tomato Meat Sauce (page 162)

Meanwhile, wash, pare and cook covered in boiling, salted water to cover
3 medium (about 1 lb.) potatoes, cut in quarters
Cook about 20 min., or until tender when pierced with a fork. Drain. To dry potatoes, shake pan over low heat.

Scald with boiling water, potato masher, food mill or ricer. Mash or rice potatoes; keep hot.

Measure into a bowl
1¾ cups sifted all-purpose flour
Make a well in center of flour. Add mashed potatoes. (The mashed potatoes should be added when they are very hot.) Mix well to

make a soft, elastic dough. Turn dough onto a lightly floured surface and knead (page 10).

Break off small pieces of dough and use palm of hand to roll pieces to pencil thickness. Cut into pieces about ¾ in. long. Curl each piece by pressing lightly with the index finger and pulling the finger along the piece of dough toward you. Gnocchi may also be shaped by pressing each piece lightly with a floured fork.

Bring to boiling in a saucepan
3 qts. water
Gradually add the Gnocchi (cook about one-half the Gnocchi at one time). Boil rapidly uncovered 8 to 10 min., or until Gnocchi are tender and come to the surface. Test tenderness by pressing a piece against side of pan with fork or spoon. Drain by pouring into a colander or large sieve. Mix Gnocchi with 2 cups Tomato Meat Sauce and
2 tablespoons grated Parmesan cheese
Top with remaining sauce. Serve immediately.

About 6 servings

SPINACH CHEESE GNOCCHI

Thoroughly grease a 9-in. round baking dish.

Shred and set aside
6 oz. Swiss cheese (about 1½ cups, shredded)

Heat in a small saucepan
1 teaspoon butter or margarine
Add and cook, stirring occasionally until lightly browned
1 tablespoon chopped onion
Set aside.

Prepare and set aside
½ cup well-drained cooked chopped spinach

Bring to boiling in a heavy saucepan
1½ cups milk
1 tablespoon butter or margarine
¼ teaspoon salt
Few grains nutmeg
Add gradually, stirring constantly
¼ cup uncooked farina
Cook over low heat, stirring until mixture becomes very thick and smooth. Mix in the spinach, browned onion, 1 cup of the shredded cheese and
2 eggs, well beaten
Remove from heat and cool slightly. Drop mixture by tablespoonfuls close together in the baking dish. Sprinkle with the remaining ½ cup of cheese.

Beat together
¾ cup milk
1 tablespoon all-purpose flour
1 teaspoon salt
Few grains nutmeg
Pour over spinach mounds.

Bake at 350°F 35 to 40 min., or until topping is golden brown.

About 6 servings

RICE DISHES

Rice, like pasta, has a bland flavor, making it a perfect foil for many other foods. It is a relatively low-cost commodity which is used to feed more than half of the world's population. In fact, it makes up about three fourths of the entire food intake in many countries and is eaten by rich and poor, young and old alike. Today's rice comes in three easily identifiable sizes. Each has its own particular cooking features which make it desirable for certain dishes. There is long grain rice with grains approximately four times as long as they are wide. It cooks tender, with grains separated and each light and fluffy. It is especially good in preparing curries, stews, chicken or meat dishes. Short and medium grain rices have short, plump grains which cook tender and moist. Particles tend to cling together. These varieties are especially good for croquettes, puddings or rice rings. The various types of rice require different cooking directions. It is always a good rule to observe and follow carefully the directions on any package of rice; however, the following general rules may be observed successfully.

Regular milled rice is easy to prepare by adding two cups water and one teaspoon salt to one cup rice and bringing the ingredients to a brisk boil. Cover with a tight fitting lid and simmer for approximately 14 minutes. One cup will yield about three cups of cooked rice.

Parboiled rice has been subjected to a combination of steam and pressure before milling to enable it to retain much of the natural vitamin and mineral content. It takes slightly longer to cook than regular milled rice, and takes 2½ cups of water for each cup of rice. One cup will yield about four cups of cooked rice.

Precooked rice is essentially a dehydrated product which requires a minimum of preparation time and makes it ideal for hurry-up meals or speedy desserts. One cup of precooked rice will yield two to three cups of cooked rice—depending on the brand.

Brown rice requires slightly more cooking time and more liquid than regular milled white rice. One cup will yield about four cups of cooked rice.

FLUFFY RICE

In a heavy 3-qt. saucepan with a tight-fitting cover, combine
1 cup uncooked rice
2 cups cold water
1 teaspoon salt
Bring to boiling over medium heat, stirring several times. Reduce heat to simmer, cover

saucepan and cook rice about 14 min. without removing cover or stirring.

About 3 cups cooked rice

If a drier rice is desired, fluff the rice kernels lightly with a fork and let stand in covered saucepan 5 to 10 min. to steam-dry.

If an extra-soft rice kernel is desired, increase cooking liquid to 2⅓ to 2½ cups and increase cooking time to about 20 min.

To cook rice in oven, use a 3-qt. baking dish or casserole having a tight-fitting cover; bake rice at 350°F about 30 min., or until kernels are of desired tenderness.

Note: Parboiled or brown rice requires more liquid and longer cooking time. To cook, follow directions on package.

To reheat cooked rice, pour liquid into a saucepan to just cover the bottom (or enough to keep rice from scorching); bring to boiling and add the rice. Cover tightly and reduce heat to simmer; steam rice about 5 min., or until of serving temperature.

Note: Hot cooked rice should not be left in saucepan more than 10 min. before serving as it tends to pack.

PERFECTION BOILED RICE

▲ *Base Recipe*

Bring to boiling in a deep saucepan
2 qts. water
1 tablespoon salt
1 teaspoon monosodium glutamate
Add gradually to water so boiling will not stop
1 cup uncooked rice
(The Rice Industry no longer considers it necessary to wash rice before cooking.) Boil rapidly, uncovered, 15 to 20 min., or until a kernel is entirely soft when pressed between thumb and finger.

Drain in colander or sieve and rinse with hot water to remove loose starch. Cover colander and rice with clean towel and set over hot water until kernels are dry and fluffy.

About 3½ cups cooked rice

—BUTTERED RICE

Follow ▲ Recipe. Substitute **1 qt. quick chicken broth** (page 10) for the water. Blend into the cooked rice, tossing lightly, **⅓ cup butter or margarine, ½ teaspoon salt** and **few grains white pepper.**

QUICK RICE RING

Lightly butter a 1-qt. ring mold.

Prepare
3 cups Perfection Boiled Rice (on this page)
Turn cooked rice into prepared mold, packing down gently with a spoon. Invert onto a warm serving platter and lift off mold. Sprinkle rice ring with
Finely chopped parsley
Fill rice ring with a buttered cooked vegetable or any creamed mixture of meat, fish or poultry.

For Jiffy Creamed Chicken Ring—While rice is cooking, prepare
Jiffy Creamed Chicken (page 261, omit bread, butter and baking)
Fill rice ring with creamed chicken mixture.

For Dried Beef in Rice Ring—While rice is cooking, prepare (omit Toast Cups)
Dried Beef in Toast Cups (page 219)
Fill rice ring with dried beef mixture.

4 to 6 servings

RICE BASKETS

Thoroughly oil 6 to 8 3-in. muffin-pan wells or heat-resistant custard cups.

Prepare
Fluffy Rice (page 164)
Cool slightly. Evenly blend into rice
1 egg, well beaten
½ cup (2 oz.) shredded cheese
2 tablespoons butter or margarine, melted
Measure about ½ cup mixture into each muffin-pan well. Press mixture against sides and bottoms until smooth and ¼ in. thick.

Bake at 300°F 15 to 20 min., until shells are set. Cool shells; carefully remove from muffin-pan wells. Fill with any creamed food.

6 to 8 shells

HOT GREEN RICE

Set out 6 individual casseroles or a shallow 2-qt. baking dish.

Have ready
½ cup shredded sharp Cheddar cheese
⅓ cup finely chopped spinach
⅓ cup finely snipped parsley
⅓ cup finely chopped green onions with tops
Scald and set aside
1½ cups milk
Cook, following package directions, using chicken broth for liquid and omitting salt
1½ cups packaged precooked rice
Stir into cooked rice the cheese and
¼ cup butter or margarine
Add spinach, parsley and green onions; mix lightly. Stir in, blending lightly and thoroughly, the hot milk and
2 eggs, well beaten
Spoon into casseroles or turn into baking dish.

Bake at 350°F about 30 min., or until set.

If rice is baked in individual casseroles, unmold each onto a serving plate and garnish with **sprigs of watercress.** If baked in dish, garnish one corner of dish with watercress sprigs.

6 servings

RICE MILANESE
(Risotto alla Milanese)

▲ *Base Recipe*

Set out a heavy 1½-qt. saucepan with a tight-fitting cover.

Melt in saucepan
¼ cup butter or margarine
Add and cook until onion is lightly browned
¼ cup finely chopped onion
Stir in
1 cup uncooked rice
Cook slowly until rice is lightly browned, stirring frequently with a fork. Add slowly, stirring with a fork until mixture boils
3 cups quick chicken broth (page 10) or Chicken Broth (page 42)
½ cup Marsala
1 teaspoon salt
Cover pan. Reduce heat and allow rice to simmer without stirring 18 min. Turn off heat and leave pan in place; do not lift cover as rice must steam.

Meanwhile, dissolve
¼ teaspoon saffron
in
2 tablespoons hot water
In 30 min. water in saucepan should be absorbed and rice tender, fluffy and dry. Add saffron mixture to rice. Mix well using a fork to lift and turn rice.

Serve warm, topped with
¼ cup grated Parmesan cheese
3 to 4 cups rice

—RICE WITH MUSHROOMS
(Risotto con Funghi)

Follow ▲ Recipe, omitting saffron. Increase butter or margarine to 6 tablespoons. Clean and slice ½ **lb. mushrooms** (page 9) and cook with onion until lightly browned.

PAELLA

Set out a large heavy saucepot with a tight-fitting cover, a saucepan and a large casserole.

Paella

For Clams—Wash and scrub well with a brush
   1½ doz. cherrystone clams
Put clams into a bowl; pour over a mixture of
   1 gal. water
   ⅓ cup salt
Set aside for 15 to 20 min.

Drain off salted water and cover with fresh water. Set aside for about 5 min. Drain off water, cover with fresh water and set aside for about 5 min. Drain the clams and set aside.

For Shrimp—Cook
   2 lbs. fresh shrimp with shells
      (see Cooked Shrimp, page 294)

For Chicken—Cut into pieces
   1 frying chicken, 2 to 3 lbs.
      ready-to-cook weight
Rinse, dry, coat and brown chicken as directed in Fried Chicken (page 250; use ¼ cup fat for frying and cook in the saucepot). When chicken is evenly browned, remove from heat and add
   ¼ cup hot water
Cover; cook over low heat about 20 min.

For Rice—Remove saucepot from heat; remove chicken and set aside. Pour off the liquid.

Heat in the saucepot over low heat
   2 tablespoons fat
Add and cook over medium heat, stirring frequently, until rice is golden
   1 cup uncooked rice
   ½ teaspoon saffron
   ½ teaspoon salt
   ⅛ teaspoon pepper

Put into saucepot
   1 qt. hot water
   1¼ cups quick chicken broth (page 10)
   2 teaspoons monosodium glutamate
Return chicken to saucepot. Cook, stirring occasionally, until rice kernels are soft.

For Vegetables—Prepare
   2 cups chopped onion
   1 cup chopped green pepper
Heat in the saucepan over low heat
   2 tablespoons fat
Add the onion, green pepper and
   3 cloves garlic
Cook over medium heat, occasionally stirring mixture with a spoon, until onion is tender. Remove garlic cloves.

To Complete Paella—Carefully mix vegetables into rice-chicken mixture. Turn mixture into casserole. Arrange shrimp and clams attractively over top.

Bake at 450°F 10 min., or until clams open.
About 8 servings

RICE PILAU

Set out a 3-qt. heavy saucepan with a tight-fitting cover.

Cut into small pieces and panfry until brown in the saucepan
   6 slices bacon
Remove bacon from saucepan and drain on absorbent paper. Reserve bacon and bacon drippings.

Meanwhile, chop
   1 large onion (about 1 cup, chopped)
   1 stalk celery
Return to saucepan
   2 tablespoons bacon drippings
Add chopped vegetables. Cook over medium heat, stirring occasionally, until onion is tender. Add to saucepan and stir to mix thoroughly
   2 cups sieved cooked tomatoes
   1½ cups hot water
   2 teaspoons salt
   1½ teaspoons monosodium glutamate
   ⅛ teaspoon pepper
Cover and bring mixture to boiling. So boiling will continue, add gradually to mixture, stirring with a fork
   1 cup rice
(The Rice Industry no longer considers it necessary to wash rice before cooking.) Simmer, covered, 20 min., or until a rice kernel is entirely soft when pressed between fingers and nearly all of the liquid is absorbed. Blend in reserved bacon pieces and serve hot.
4 to 6 servings

PILAFF WITH LAMB

A Dutch oven, a large skillet and a 2-qt. casserole will be needed.

Prepare and set aside
   5 cups quick meat broth (page 10)
Finely chop and set aside
   3 medium onions (about 1½ cups, chopped)

For Lamb Mixture—Set out
   2 lbs. boneless lamb shoulder, cut in 1-in. pieces
Coat the meat pieces evenly by shaking 2 or 3 at a time in a plastic bag containing a mixture of
   ⅓ cup all-purpose flour
   1½ teaspoons salt
   ⅛ teaspoon white pepper
Heat in the Dutch oven
   3 tablespoons butter or margarine
Add about 1 cup of the chopped onion and cook over medium heat, stirring occasionally,

until the onion is tender. (Reserve remaining onion for rice.) Using a slotted spoon, remove the onion to a bowl and set aside. Add the lamb pieces to the remaining butter and slowly brown on all sides.

Remove from heat. Pour off excess fat and add the cooked onion, 1 cup of the broth and
   2 cups (2 8-oz. cans) tomato sauce
Add
   ½ teaspoon salt
   ¼ teaspoon thyme
   Few grains pepper
Cover and bring to boiling. Reduce heat and simmer about 1¼ hrs., or until meat is tender when pierced with a fork.

For Rice—While lamb is cooking, heat in the skillet over low heat
   ½ cup butter or margarine
Add
   2 cups uncooked rice
(The Rice Industry no longer considers it necessary to wash rice before cooking.) Set over medium heat and cook, stirring frequently, until rice is yellow. Remove from heat; add the remaining broth gradually, while stirring constantly. Add the remaining onion and
   ½ teaspoon salt
   ⅛ teaspoon white pepper
Return to heat and bring rapidly to boiling; cook 2 to 3 min. longer.

Turn rice mixture into the casserole.

Cover and cook in a 400°F oven about 15 min., or until a kernel of rice is entirely tender when pressed between thumb and fingers.

To Serve—Spoon rice to form a border on a large heated serving platter. Turn the lamb mixture into the center.
6 servings

GOLDEN PILAFF WITH CHICKEN

Set out a large heavy skillet and a 3-qt. casserole with cover.

For Chicken—Rinse in cold water (do not soak) and pat dry with absorbent paper
   2 lbs. chicken breasts, thighs or legs
(If chicken is frozen, thaw following directions on package.)

Heat in the skillet over low heat
   ¼ cup butter or margarine

Spanish Rice with Beef

Place chicken pieces, meaty side down, in the skillet. To brown chicken pieces on both sides, turn pieces as necessary with tongs or two spoons. When chicken is evenly browned, remove from skillet; set aside to keep warm.

For Rice—Prepare and set aside
  4½ cups quick chicken broth (page 10)
  ⅓ cup finely chopped onion

Heat in the skillet over low heat
  ¼ cup butter or margarine
Add gradually, stirring constantly
  1 cup uncooked rice
(The Rice Industry no longer considers it necessary to wash rice before cooking.) Cook over medium heat until rice is yellow, stirring frequently. Remove from heat. Pour over rice 4 cups of the broth. Add the chopped onion and
  1 teaspoon salt
  ½ teaspoon turmeric
Bring mixture rapidly to boiling. Remove from heat and spoon one half of the rice mixture into the casserole. Arrange chicken pieces over rice. Top with remaining rice mixture. Cover casserole.

Cook in a 350°F oven about 40 min., or until a kernel of rice is soft when pressed between thumb and finger, and chicken is tender.

Meanwhile, put into a small bowl
  1½ cups dairy sour cream
Add the remaining ½ cup chicken broth and blend well. When pilaff is done, remove cover and pour the sour cream mixture over all. Return to oven, uncovered, about 10 min., or until sauce is just heated.

Serve immediately.   *6 to 8 servings*

MEXICAN RICE

Heat in a large heavy saucepan
  3 tablespoons cooking oil
Add to heated oil
  ¼ cup finely chopped onion
  1 small clove garlic, minced
  1 cup uncooked rice
Fry about 3 min., or until rice is golden, stirring occasionally.

Mix in a blend of
  1 teaspoon salt
  ½ teaspoon chili powder
Pour in
  2½ cups water
Stir and cover tightly. Bring to boiling and simmer until rice is tender and liquid absorbed, 15 to 20 min.   *About 8 servings*

SPANISH RICE WITH BACON

▲ *Base Recipe*

Grease a 2-qt. casserole with a cover.

Clean and slice (page 9)
  ½ lb. mushrooms
Set aside.

Panfry until browned, reserving fat
  4 slices bacon, diced
Return to skillet ¼ cup of reserved bacon fat. Add and cook over medium heat, occasionally moving with a spoon, the mushrooms and
  1 cup uncooked rice
  ½ cup (about 1 medium) chopped onion
  ½ cup (about 1 medium) chopped green pepper
Cook until rice is lightly browned.

Stir bacon into rice mixture with
  2½ cups canned tomatoes, cut in pieces
  1½ cups hot water
  1 teaspoon salt
  ¼ teaspoon monosodium glutamate
  ¼ teaspoon pepper
Turn mixture into the casserole and cover.

Cook in a 350°F oven 50 to 60 min., or until rice is tender when a kernel is pressed between fingers; remove cover for last 10 min.
            6 servings

—SPANISH RICE WITH BEEF

Follow ▲ Recipe. Omit bacon. Brown **½ lb. ground beef** with rice mixture.

TURKEY RICE DINNER

▲ *Base Recipe*

Grease a 2-qt. casserole.

Prepare
  Fluffy Rice (page 164)

Meanwhile, blanch (page 9) and sliver
  ½ cup (about 3 oz.) almonds
With fork, toss almonds with
  ½ cup soft bread crumbs
  ¼ cup butter or margarine, melted
Set aside.

Dice and set aside enough cooked turkey to yield
  2 cups diced cooked turkey

Prepare and set aside
  1½ cups Thin White Sauce (1½ times recipe, page 304; if available, use turkey broth for one half of the liquid. Add 2 or 3 drops Tabasco.)

With a fork, gently mix cooked rice and
  12 pimiento-stuffed olives, sliced

Combine diced turkey with
  ½ cup (4-oz. can, drained) sliced mushrooms
Spoon one third of rice mixture into casserole. Add one half the turkey; repeat and top with remaining rice. Pour sauce over all. Sprinkle with crumb-almond mixture.

Heat in a 350°F oven 25 to 30 min., or until top is crusty and golden brown.
            6 to 8 servings

—RICE AND SALMON SCALLOP

Follow ▲ Recipe. Substitute for turkey **2 cups (16-oz. can, drained) salmon**, coarsely flaked (page 9). Add **2 tablespoons lemon juice** and, if desired, **1 teaspoon sherry extract**. Omit bread crumbs. Coarsely crush enough **potato chips** to make 1 cup and sprinkle over casserole mixture. Top with blanched **almonds** tossed in **2 tablespoons melted butter or margarine**.

KEDGEREE

A medley of rice and fish, originally from India and brought to the New England Coast in Clipper days.

Prepare
  2 cups Fluffy Rice (page 164; two thirds recipe)
Flake (page 9) enough fish to yield
  2 cups cold cooked fish (sole, salmon or tuna)
Set fish aside.

Hard-cook (page 133)
   4 eggs
Cool eggs, peel and dice.

Lightly but thoroughly mix rice with the fish, eggs and
   ½ cup cream
   2 tablespoons minced parsley
and a mixture of
   1 teaspoon salt
   ⅛ teaspoon pepper
Turn into top of double boiler. Place over simmering water until thoroughly heated.

About 6 servings

CREOLE-STYLE SHRIMP WITH RICE

Set out a 2-qt. casserole.

For Cooked Shrimp—Wash in cold water
   1½ lbs. fresh or frozen large shrimp with shells
Drop shrimp into a boiling mixture of
   1½ pts. water
   3 tablespoon lemon juice
   1 tablespoon salt
   1 teaspoon monosodium glutamate
   3 or 4 sprigs parsley
   1 clove garlic, peeled and split
   1 bay leaf
   Small piece celery with leaves
Cover tightly. Simmer 5 min., or only until shrimp are pink and tender. Drain and cover with cold water to chill. Drain shrimp again. Remove tiny legs and peel shells from shrimp. Cut a slit to just below surface along back (curved surface) of shrimp to expose black vein. With knife point, remove vein in one piece.* Quickly rinse shrimp in cold water, drain, put into casserole and set aside.

For Casserole Mixture—Heat in skillet
   ¼ cup butter or margarine
Add and cook slowly until onion is tender, stirring occasionally
   1 cup (about 4 stalks) diced celery
   ⅔ cup (about 1½ medium) chopped onion
   ½ cup (about 1 medium) finely chopped green pepper
Thoroughly blend in
   1 cup water
   ¾ cup (6-oz. can) tomato paste
   1 tablespoon minced parsley
   4 or 5 drops Tabasco

Add
   ½ teaspoon salt
   ¼ teaspoon monosodium glutamate
Pour mixture into casserole. Mix gently to distribute shrimp evenly.

Heat in a 350°F oven 30 min.

Meanwhile, prepare
   Fluffy Rice (page 164)
When shrimp mixture is heated thoroughly, serve over hot rice.   *6 servings*

*Veins present in canned shrimp are removed in the same way.

RICE CHEESE PUFFS

A deep saucepan or automatic deep fryer will be needed.

Prepare
   1½ cups Fluffy Rice (page 164; one-half recipe)

To Prepare Cheese Mixture—Set out a medium-size saucepan.

Shred and set aside
   3 oz. sharp Cheddar cheese (about ¾ cup, shredded)

Melt in the saucepan over low heat
   4 teaspoons butter or margarine
Blend in
   4 teaspoons all-purpose flour
   ¼ teaspoon salt
   Few grains pepper
Heat until mixture bubbles. Remove from heat. Add gradually while stirring constantly
   ⅓ cup milk
Return to heat and bring rapidly to boiling, stirring constantly; cook 1 to 2 min. longer.

Add the shredded cheese and stir sauce rapidly until cheese is melted. Blend in
   ½ teaspoon grated onion
   ¼ teaspoon dry mustard
   ¼ teaspoon Worcestershire sauce
   5 drops Tabasco
Mix with cooked rice and place in refrigerator to chill about 1 hr.

About 20 min. before deep frying, fill the saucepan or deep fryer with **fat** and heat to 375°F (page 11).

To Complete Puffs—Shape chilled mixture into 2-in. balls, using about 1 tablespoon of the

mixture for each ball. Dip into a mixture of
   1 egg, slightly beaten
   1 tablespoon milk
Coat balls by rolling in
   ½ cup fine dry bread crumbs (about 1½ slices bread)
Deep fry cheese balls in heated fat. Fry only as many balls at one time as will float un-crowded one layer deep in fat. Turn balls with a fork as they rise to surface and several times during cooking (do not pierce). Fry 1 to 2 min., or until balls are golden brown. Lift them out with a slotted spoon and drain over fat for a few seconds before removing to absorbent paper.

Serve hot with your favorite **tomato sauce** and **buttered green beans.**   *About 12 puffs*

WILD RICE WITH MUSHROOMS

Set out a medium-size skillet.

Bring to boiling in a deep saucepan
   6 cups water
   2 teaspoons salt
Meanwhile, wash in a colander or sieve
   1 cup wild rice
Add rice gradually to water so that boiling continues. Cook, uncovered, 25 to 30 min., or until a kernel of rice is entirely tender when pressed between fingers. Drain rice in a colander or sieve. If necessary, keep rice warm by placing colander over hot water and covering with a folded towel.

While rice is cooking, clean and slice
   ½ lb. mushrooms (page 9)
Heat in the skillet
   ¼ cup butter
Add mushrooms with
   2 tablespoons finely chopped onion
Cook slowly, occasionally turning and moving gently with a spoon, until mushrooms are lightly browned. Remove from heat and re-serve about ¼ cup mushrooms for garnish. Combine remaining mushrooms, onion, wild rice and
   ⅓ cup melted butter
Toss gently until mushrooms and butter are evenly distributed throughout rice. Turn hot mixture into a warm serving dish and garnish with the reserved mushrooms. *6 to 8 servings*

Wild Rice with Mushrooms

Meat

Through the ages meat has been man's most desired food. Prized for its flavor and food value, it holds the center spot in a menu around which the rest of the meal is planned. Most homemakers try to serve meat to their families as often as possible since it satisfies hungry appetites as no other food can. It is also an ideal source of animal protein. Serving it every day does take a large part of the family food dollar, but, fortunately for families on a limited food budget, the less expensive cuts of meat boast the same nutritional value as steaks and roasts. Some people think they taste even better.

BEEF

STANDING RIB ROAST OF BEEF

Set out a shallow roasting pan.

Set out
  1 3- to 4-rib standing rib roast of beef
(Have meat dealer loosen back, chine, bone by sawing across ribs to make carving easier and tie roast.) Place roast in roasting pan, fat side up. Season with
  Salt and pepper
Insert roast meat thermometer in center of thickest part of lean; be sure bulb does not rest on bone or in fat.

Roast at 325°F, allowing 23 to 25 min. per pound for rare; 27 to 30 min. per pound for medium; and 32 to 35 min. per pound for well done. Roast is also done when roast meat thermometer registers 140°F for rare; 160°F for medium; and 170°F for well done.

Carving of the roast will be easier if roast is set aside in a warm place 20 min. It is best to remove roast from oven when thermometer registers 5°F below the desired temperature, since the cooking of the roast continues after removal from the oven. Before carving remove strings from roast and with a sharp knife, remove backbone. Use meat drippings for **Gravy** (page 312), if desired.

Serve roast on a heated platter and garnish with **red horseradish-filled lemon cups.** Accompany with **Choux Paste Fritters** (page 517).

BEEF TENDERLOIN WITH MUSHROOM GRAVY

  ▲ Base Recipe

Set out a shallow roasting pan and rack.

Set out
  1 whole beef tenderloin (4 to 6 lbs.)
Place tenderloin on rack in roasting pan. Insert roast meat thermometer in center of meat so that tip is slightly more than halfway through meat.

Roast, uncovered, at 425°F 45 to 60 min. The roast will be rare when meat thermometer registers 140°F.

Shortly before meat is done, clean and slice (page 9) enough mushrooms to yield
  1 cup sliced mushrooms
Heat in a skillet over low heat
  1 tablespoon butter

Add mushrooms and cook over medium heat, occasionally moving and turning, until lightly browned and tender. Remove the skillet from heat.

When beef tenderloin is done, remove to a warm serving platter.
Add to the drippings in the roasting pan
  1 cup quick meat broth (page 10)
Heat over low heat until very hot, stirring constantly. While stirring, scrape bottom and sides of pan to blend in brown residue. Add the mushrooms and heat thoroughly.

Serve slices of beef tenderloin with gravy spooned over individual servings.

—TENDERLOIN SUPREME IN MUSHROOM SAUCE

Follow ▲ Recipe for roasting beef; omit mushroom gravy. Slice enough beef tenderloin to yield 6 ¼-in. slices (about 1½ lbs.). Prepare Mushroom Sauce; add beef, cover and heat thoroughly.

For Mushroom Sauce—Heat in a skillet **⅓ cup butter.** Add **¾ cup cleaned and sliced mushrooms** (page 9); cook over medium heat until lightly browned and tender. Occasionally move and turn mushrooms with a spoon. Remove mushrooms with a slotted spoon, allowing butter to drain back into skillet; set aside. Add **¾ cup finely chopped onion** to the skillet and cook 3 min. Blend in **1½ tablespoons all-purpose flour, ¾ teaspoon salt, ⅛ teaspoon pepper** and **⅛ teaspoon thyme.** Heat until mixture bubbles. Remove from heat. Gradually add, stirring constantly, **1½ cups quick meat broth** (page 10) **¾ cup red Burgundy** and **1½ teaspoons wine vinegar.** Cook rapidly until sauce thickens. Blend in the mushrooms, **1½ tablespoons tomato paste** and **1½ teaspoons chopped parsley.** Cook about 3 min.

Note: Thin slices of pot roast of beef may be substituted for the beef tenderloin. For an especially good flavor omit heating after adding meat to sauce; marinate (page 10) 24 hrs. in refrigerator. Heat thoroughly before serving.

BEEF WELLINGTON DINNER

Prepare (the day before serving, if desired)
  Beef Tenderloin (page 170)
  Forcemeat (page 170)
  Pastry (page 170)

Roll out three-fourths of the Pastry on a lightly floured surface into an 18-in. square or the size necessary to enclose beef. Place beef on one edge of pastry and cover with the Forcemeat. Moisten the pastry edges with water. Lift pastry up over beef and overlap it under meat; seal edges and ends, enclosing meat. Brush pastry with
  Egg white, lightly beaten
Carefully transfer pastry-encased meat to an ungreased baking sheet.

Roll out remaining pastry and cut into small shapes, using small cookie cutters. Arrange shapes on top of pastry and brush with beaten egg white.

Bake at 425°F 40 min., or until pastry is golden brown. Carefully transfer with two wide spatulas to a heated large serving platter.

Meanwhile, prepare and keep warm
  Parsley-buttered potatoes

Heat in a large saucepan
  ½ cup butter or margarine
Turn into saucepan
  3 pkgs. (10 oz. each) frozen Brussels sprouts

Heat 5 to 10 min., separating with a fork. Stir in

1 cup chicken broth
1 teaspoon salt
¼ teaspoon pepper
½ teaspoon marjoram leaves
2 slices lemon peel (yellow portion only)

Cover, bring to boiling, and simmer 10 min., or until Brussels sprouts are crisp-tender. (If desired, mix in 1½ cups sliced cooked chestnuts for the last 5 min. of cooking.)

Turn Brussels sprouts onto one side of platter with meat and parsley-buttered potatoes to the other side. *12 servings*

Beef Tenderloin—Place on a rack in a shallow roasting pan

1 5- to 6-lb. whole beef tenderloin, trimmed of all fat

Rub meat with cut surfaces of

1 clove garlic, halved

Sprinkle with

Salt and pepper

Insert a roast meat thermometer into center of meat. Cover top with

4 pieces suet

Roast in a 425°F oven 1 hr., or until meat thermometer registers 140°F for rare. Cool meat slightly. Remove suet; wrap roast and chill.

Forcemeat—Clean, chop and set aside

¼ lb. fresh mushrooms

Heat in a saucepan

¼ cup butter or margarine

Add and cook until onion is tender and nuts are toasted

¼ cup chopped onion
½ cup finely chopped filberts

Stir in mushrooms and

¼ cup cognac

Cook, stirring occasionally, 5 to 10 min. over medium heat.

Beat lightly in a large bowl

1 egg

Beat in

¼ cup heavy cream

Add a mixture of

1 teaspoon salt
⅛ teaspoon pepper
¼ teaspoon *each* basil, thyme and rosemary leaves
⅛ teaspoon allspice

Add and mix lightly but thoroughly the mushroom mixture and

½ lb. ground pork
½ lb. ground veal
¼ cup chopped parsley

Cover and chill.

Note: The meat mixture may be shaped into appetizer-size balls, fried in a small amount of butter and served with cocktails or spaghetti in tomato sauce. Or shaped into patties and fried until brown on both sides.

Pastry—Mix in a large bowl

4 cups sifted all-purpose flour
1 teaspoon salt

Cut in with pastry blender or two knives until particles resemble small peas

1 cup chilled butter or margarine, cut in ½-in. pieces
⅔ cup chilled all-vegetable shortening

Sprinkle over flour mixture

10 tablespoons cold water

Work quickly, tossing with a fork until a ball is formed. Sprinkle lightly with

Flour

Wrap in waxed paper and chill.

BEEF TENDERLOIN BOURGUIGNONNE

A princely dish, reflecting the racy traditions of an ancient French duchy.

Set out a heavy 10-in. skillet with a tight-fitting cover.

Peel and rinse

12 small onions

Cook (page 312) 20 to 25 min., or just until tender. Drain and set aside.

Clean and slice (page 9)

12 medium mushrooms

Set aside.

Prepare and set aside

4 cups quick meat broth (page 10)

Set out

2 lbs. beef tenderloin

Using a long sharp-bladed knife, thinly slice tenderloin.

Heat until very hot in the skillet

¼ cup cooking oil

When oil begins to smoke, add one half the sliced tenderloin. Reduce heat and cook until thoroughly browned, 1 to 2 min. Remove from skillet and fry the remaining meat in the same way. Remove the meat from the skillet and add

3 tablespoons finely chopped onion

Fry 1 to 2 min.

Stir in, blending thoroughly

3 tablespoons all-purpose flour
1 teaspoon finely chopped garlic

Add the meat broth gradually, stirring constantly until mixture is smooth. Blend in

¼ cup tomato paste
1 teaspoon Worcestershire sauce
½ teaspoon monosodium glutamate
¼ teaspoon pepper
⅛ teaspoon thyme

Add to skillet the meat and

2 bay leaves

Reduce heat and simmer 5 min. Stir in

1 cup sieved tomatoes
½ cup red Burgundy

Cover and cook over medium heat 25 to 30 min.

Meanwhile, heat in a small skillet

3 tablespoons butter

Add the mushrooms and onions and cook over low heat until lightly browned. Add the contents of the skillet to the meat mixture. Spoon the meat mixture into a casserole or serving dish and sprinkle with

Finely chopped parsley

Serve with

Buttered noodles

6 servings

BEEF FILLETS
(Tournedos aux Champignons)

Suitable for the finest occasion, tournedos are small steaks cut from the smaller part of the beef tenderloin.

Heat in a large heavy skillet

2 to 3 tablespoons butter

Set out

12 3-oz. tournedos or beef tenderloin steaks, cut about 1 in. thick and Frenched (flattened)

Place as many tournedos in the skillet as will lay flat. Brown the tournedos in the butter over medium heat. When browned, turn and season tournedos with one half a mixture of

2½ teaspoons salt
½ teaspoon pepper

Clean, cutting off stems ½ in. from caps of

12 medium mushrooms

Add mushrooms to skillet while meat is browning on second side.

Meanwhile, cut into rounds about the size of the tournedos

6 slices bread

Brown bread on both sides in another skillet in

3 tablespoons butter

Place croutons on warm serving plate. Keep hot. When meat is browned on second side, sprinkle with remaining seasoning mixture. Arrange two tournedos on each crouton and top each tournedos with one mushroom.

Combine in skillet

¼ cup cream
¼ cup red wine

Heat cream-wine sauce and pour over the tournedos. Serve immediately. *6 servings*

BROILED BEEF STEAKS

▲ Base Recipe

Set out

Beef steaks, such as porterhouse, T-bone, sirloin or club, cut about 1 in. thick

Allow about ½ lb. meat per serving.

Arrange beef steaks on broiler rack. Place under broiler with top of steak about 2 in. from heat; broil 8 to 10 min. on each side. (The short cooking time for rare steaks; the longer cooking time for medium-done steaks.)

Meanwhile, for each pound of meat, mix

1 teaspoon salt
½ teaspoon monosodium glutamate
¼ teaspoon pepper

When steaks are browned on one side, sprinkle with one half of seasoning mixture. Turn and broil second side. Test for doneness by cutting a slit along the bone and noting color of meat. Season second side of meat.

Note: For 2-in. steaks, broil with tops of steaks about 3 in. from heat, allowing 15 to 20 min. on each side.

—BROILED LAMB CHOPS

Follow ▲ Recipe. Substitute **shoulder, rib or loin lamb chops** for beef steaks. Broil 5 to 7 min. on each side. Serve with broiled pineapple slices and banana chunks.

—BROILED HAM SLICE

Follow ▲ Recipe. Substitute **¾- to 1-in. thick ham slice** for beef. Omit seasoning mixture. Broil 8 to 10 min. on each side. Serve with **mustard sauce**.

STEAK A LA DIANE

Set out a large heavy skillet. (If using an electric skillet, follow manufacturer's directions.)

Cream until softened

1 cup plus 2 tablespoons butter

Blend in

1 small clove garlic, minced

and a mixture of

¾ teaspoon salt
½ teaspoon monosodium glutamate
¼ teaspoon freshly ground pepper

Cover and chill butter mixture in refrigerator.

Set out

3 sirloin steaks, about 1 lb. each, and cut about ½ in. thick

Cut away bone. Place steaks on a flat working surface and repeatedly pound on one side, then the other, until meat is about ¼ in. thick. (Use flat side of meat hammer.) Cut each steak into two pieces.

Remove butter from refrigerator; put one fourth of it into the skillet. Heat until very hot. Add two of the steak pieces and brown

quickly on one side; turn and brown quickly on second side. Remove steaks and keep warm. Repeat procedure for remaining steaks.

Have ready

1 lemon, rinsed and cut in quarters

Insert prongs of fork through peel of one lemon quarter. Gently rub lemon quarter around sides and bottom of skillet, squeezing some of the lemon juice into the drippings. Repeat procedure with remaining lemon quarters. Add the remaining butter mixture to the skillet with

¾ teaspoon finely chopped chives
½ teaspoon Worcestershire sauce

Set over medium heat until butter begins to brown. Add the steaks and cook 2 to 3 min., or until thoroughly heated; baste continuously with the butter mixture.

Serve immediately with some of the drippings from the skillet. Garnish with

Lemon wedges

6 servings

BEEF WITH GREEN PEPPER

▲ Base Recipe

Set out a large heavy skillet.

Set out

1½ lbs. sirloin steak

Slice into 3x½x⅛-in. strips and set aside.

Prepare and set aside

¾ cup quick meat broth (page 10)

Prepare and set aside

3 cups thinly sliced celery
1 cup thinly sliced onion
1 cup thinly sliced canned water chestnuts

Clean and cut into strips enough green pepper to yield

4 cups green pepper strips

Put green pepper strips into a pan and add

Boiling water to cover

Cook for 2 min. Rinse with cold water and drain. Set aside.

Blend in a small bowl

6 tablespoons sherry
3 tablespoons water
1 tablespoon soy sauce
1½ teaspoons monosodium glutamate
1½ teaspoons sugar
¾ teaspoon finely chopped crystallized ginger
¾ teaspoon sesame seed
1 teaspoon salt
⅛ teaspoon pepper

Heat in the skillet until very hot

3 tablespoons cooking oil

Add and stir in

2 cloves garlic, minced

Add the beef strips, brown and cook quickly. Remove from skillet and set aside.

Add the prepared vegetables and cook over high heat, tossing constantly, for 1 min. Add the soy sauce-sherry mixture to vegetables and

Broiled Sirloin Steak

Broiled Club Steaks

Broiled Lamb Chops

cook 1 min. longer. Add the meat broth and cook 1 min., or until boiling. Do not cover. Remove from heat. Using a slotted spoon, remove vegetables to a bowl and set aside to keep warm.

Combine and blend into liquid mixture in skillet

¾ cup water
3 tablespoons cornstarch
¾ teaspoon soy sauce

Stirring constantly, bring to boiling and boil

171

Beef Stroganoff

3 min., or until mixture thickens. Return meat and vegetables to the skillet and heat thoroughly.   *6 to 8 servings*

—BEEF WITH PEA PODS

Follow ▲ Recipe. Substitute **4 cups pea pods** for the green pepper.

BEEF STROGANOFF

Set out a heavy 10-in. skillet with a tight-fitting cover.

Set out
  2 lbs. boneless beef (tenderloin, sirloin or rib)
Cut into 2x¼x¼-in. strips. To coat the meat evenly, shake 6 to 8 strips at a time in a plastic bag containing a mixture of
  ½ cup all-purpose flour
  1 teaspoon salt
  ½ teaspoon monosodium glutamate
  ⅛ teaspoon pepper
Heat in the skillet over low heat
  ⅓ cup butter or margarine
Add the meat strips and
  ½ cup (1 medium) finely chopped onion
Slowly brown meat on all sides.

Meanwhile, prepare
  2 cups quick meat broth (page 10)
When meat is browned, slowly add the broth. Cover and simmer 20 to 25 min.
Cook, following directions on package
  1⅓ cups packaged precooked rice

Clean and slice (page 9)
  ½ lb. mushrooms
Heat in a skillet over low heat
  3 tablespoons butter or margarine
Add the mushrooms and cook over medium heat until lightly browned and tender.

Blend
  1 cup dairy sour cream
  3 tablespoons tomato paste
  1 teaspoon Worcestershire sauce
When meat is cooked, remove skillet from

heat. Stirring vigorously, add to mixture in the skillet, in very small amounts, the sour cream mixture. Add the mushrooms. Return to heat. Continue cooking over low heat, slowly moving with a spoon, 3 to 5 min., or until thoroughly heated; do not boil.

Spoon the rice into a warm serving dish. Pour the meat mixture into another warm serving dish and sprinkle with
  Finely chopped parsley
Serve immediately.   *6 servings*

FLANK STEAK ROLL-UPS

Set out a large heavy skillet with a tight-fitting cover.

Have ready
  1½- to 2-lb. flank steak
Cut into halves
  1 clove garlic
Rub both sides of flank steak with cut side of the garlic. Season meat with a mixture of
  1 teaspoon salt
  ⅛ teaspoon pepper
Place one of the long sides of the steak near to you and roll up meat. Fasten meat roll at 1-in. intervals with skewers or wooden picks. Cut meat roll between picks into 1-in. slices.

Melt in the skillet
  3 tablespoons fat
Brown meat roll-ups on both sides in the hot fat over medium heat. Add
  ¼ cup water
  1 bay leaf
Cover tightly and cook slowly over low heat about 1½ to 2 hrs., or until tender. If more water is needed, add hot water.

Remove meat from liquid and arrange on platter.   *4 to 6 servings*

FLANK STEAK ROLL-UPS WITH NOODLES

Set out a Dutch oven, or use a heavy sauce-pot with a tight-fitting cover.

Place on a flat working surface
  1½-lb. flank steak
Pound or score the meat. Spread one side with
  3 tablespoons butter or margarine
Sprinkle with a mixture of
  ½ teaspoon thyme
  ¼ teaspoon sage
  ¼ teaspoon basil
Starting at one of the long sides, roll up meat. Tie with cord.

Heat in the Dutch oven over medium heat
  3 tablespoons fat
Add the steak roll and brown on all sides over medium heat. Add
  3½ cups (29-oz. can) tomatoes
  ¾ cup (6-oz. can) tomato paste
  1 cup (about 2 medium) chopped onion
  1 clove garlic, cut into halves

Add a mixture of
  2 teaspoons salt
  1 teaspoon monosodium glutamate
  1 teaspoon chili powder
  ¼ teaspoon pepper
Bring liquid rapidly to boiling; reduce heat, cover and simmer (do not boil) 1½ hrs., or until meat is tender when pierced with a fork.

About 20 min. before meat is tender, cook (page 152)
  4 cups (about 6 oz.) broad noodles

Prepare
  ¼ cup finely chopped parsley
Add one-half of the chopped parsley to the noodles with
  2 tablespoons butter or margarine
Toss lightly to blend thoroughly.

Remove garlic from sauce. Remove steak roll. Insert skewers into meat at 1-in. intervals. Remove cord. Slice between skewers.

Place noodles in center of hot platter. Arrange meat around the noodles. Spoon sauce over all. Garnish with remaining parsley.
                                    4 to 6 servings

GRILLADES

In France grillade means grilled food, but in New Orleans the grillade has nothing to do with a broiler. Creole grillades are pieces of beef or veal round steak prepared in the following manner.

Set out a large heavy skillet with a tight-fitting cover.

Set out
  2 lbs. beef or veal round steak, cut ¾ in. thick
Cut into serving-size pieces, removing and discarding bone.

Heat in the skillet over low heat
  ¼ cup butter or margarine
Add meat and brown well on one side. Turn and sprinkle with one half of a mixture of
  1 tablespoon salt
  1 teaspoon monosodium glutamate
  ¼ teaspoon pepper
Brown well on second side and sprinkle with remaining seasoning mixture.

Meanwhile, clean, chop and set aside
  1 medium onion

When meat is browned, remove from skillet and set it aside.
Heat in the skillet over low heat
  1 tablespoon butter or margarine

Blend in
  1 tablespoon all-purpose flour
Heat until mixture bubbles, stirring constantly. Stir in chopped onion and continue cooking, stirring constantly, until mixture is lightly browned. Remove from heat and blend in
  ½ cup water or tomato juice
Return skillet to heat; add meat pieces and
  1 clove garlic, finely minced

172

Cover tightly and cook slowly over low heat about 1 hr., or until meat is tender. Turn meat occasionally. Add more liquid if necessary.

While meat is cooking, prepare
    Fluffy Rice (page 164)
Serve meat on the hot rice with sauce spooned over meat. *4 to 6 servings*

ESTERHAZY STEAK
(Esterházy Rostélyos)

A dressed-up round steak dating from the days of Hungarian nobility—named in honor of one of the oldest and most prominent families.

Grease an 11x7x1½-in. baking dish; set out aluminum foil and a large heavy skillet.

Set out
    ½ cup all-purpose flour
Have ready and place on a flat working surface or wooden board
    2 lbs. round steak, cut 1 in. thick
Repeatedly pound meat on one side with meat hammer, pounding in about one half of the flour. (Pounding increases tenderness.) Turn meat over and repeat process, using remaining flour. Cut meat into serving-size pieces and coat well with a mixture of
    ¼ cup all-purpose flour
    2 teaspoons salt
    ½ teaspoon pepper
Heat in the skillet
    ⅓ cup fat
Slowly brown meat on both sides. Arrange meat in the baking dish and set aside.

Cook slowly in the skillet 10 min., stirring occasionally
    3 carrots, washed, scraped or pared and thinly sliced
    2 small onions, thinly sliced
    1 parsnip, washed, pared and thinly sliced
    1 stalk celery, chopped

Meanwhile, prepare and set aside to cool to lukewarm
    1 cup quick meat broth (page 10)

Spoon the vegetables over the steak. Add
    1 teaspoon capers

Heat in the skillet
    1 tablespoon fat
Blend into fat
    1 tablespoon all-purpose flour
    ¼ teaspoon salt
    Few grains pepper
Heat until mixture bubbles and is lightly browned, stirring constantly. Remove skillet from heat. Gradually add reserved meat broth, stirring constantly. Return to heat and bring rapidly to boiling, stirring constantly. Remove from heat. Blend in
    ¼ cup dry white wine
Pour sauce over vegetables and meat in baking dish. Cover dish tightly with aluminum foil.

Bake at 350°F 1¼ hrs. Remove aluminum foil.

Spread over vegetables a mixture of
    1 cup dairy sour cream
    1 teaspoon paprika
Return dish to oven, uncovered, and continue to cook about 15 min., or until meat is tender when pierced with a fork. *5 or 6 servings*

BEEF ROLL
(Marhahús Tekercs)

Set out a large heavy skillet with a tight-fitting cover.

Prepare, finely chop and set aside
    2 Hard-Cooked Eggs (page 133)

Set out and spread flat on a wooden board or working surface
    1½ lbs. round steak, sliced ½ in. thick
Cover steak with a mixture of the chopped egg and
    3 slices bacon, cut in 1-in. pieces
    1 teaspoon chopped parsley
    ½ teaspoon capers
    ½ teaspoon salt
    ⅛ teaspoon pepper
Roll up steak lengthwise and tie with a cord or fasten with skewers.

Heat in the skillet
    3 tablespoons fat
Add steak and slowly brown on all sides.

Sprinkle over steak a mixture of
    1 teaspoon paprika
    ¼ teaspoon salt
Slowly pour into the skillet
    1 cup hot water
Cover and simmer 1½ to 2 hrs., or until steak is tender when pierced with a fork. Remove from skillet to serving platter; cover platter and keep steak warm.

For Gravy—Pour drippings from skillet into a bowl, leaving brown residue in skillet. Allow fat to rise to surface of drippings; skim off and reserve fat. Set aside remaining drippings to be used as part of the liquid; cool to lukewarm. Measure 3 tablespoons reserved fat into the skillet. Blend into fat until smooth
    3 tablespoons all-purpose flour
    ¼ teaspoon salt
    ⅛ teaspoon pepper
Heat until mixture bubbles. Remove from heat and add gradually, stirring constantly
    1 cup liquid (drippings or quick meat broth, page 10), cooled to lukewarm
Return skillet to heat and bring rapidly to boiling, stirring constantly. While stirring, scrape bottom and sides of skillet to blend in brown residue. Cook 1 to 2 min. longer. Remove from heat. Stirring gravy vigorously with a French whip, whisk beater, or fork, add in very small amounts
    1 cup dairy sour cream
Heat thoroughly over low heat, 3 to 5 min., stirring constantly; do not boil.

Remove cord or skewers from roll. Slice meat and serve with the gravy. *About 4 servings*

BEEF ROLLS
(Braciola di Manzo)

▲ *Base Recipe*

Set out a large heavy skillet with a tight-fitting cover.

Lay out flat on working surface (meat in one piece)
    1½ lbs. round steak, cut about ½ in. thick
Cover steak with a mixture of
    1 clove garlic, finely sliced
    1 teaspoon grated Parmesan cheese
    1 Hard-Cooked Egg (page 133), chopped
    ½ teaspoon chopped parsley
    2 slices bacon, cut in 1-in. pieces
    ½ teaspoon salt
    ⅛ teaspoon pepper
Roll up steak to enclose mixture and tie securely.

Heat in skillet about 5 min.
    ¼ cup olive oil
    1 small onion, sliced
Add steak roll, and slowly brown on all sides.

Meanwhile, combine
    2½ cups canned tomatoes, sieved
    ½ teaspoon salt
    ¼ teaspoon pepper
    1 bay leaf
Slowly add tomato mixture to browned steak. Cover skillet and simmer about 1½ hrs., or until steak is tender. Remove string and bay leaf. Slice and serve. *4 or 5 servings*

—BEEF ROLLS IN WINE
(Braciola di Manzo con Vino)

Follow ▲ Recipe. Add **½ cup dry red wine** and **a few grains nutmeg** to the tomato mixture.

BEEF CUTS

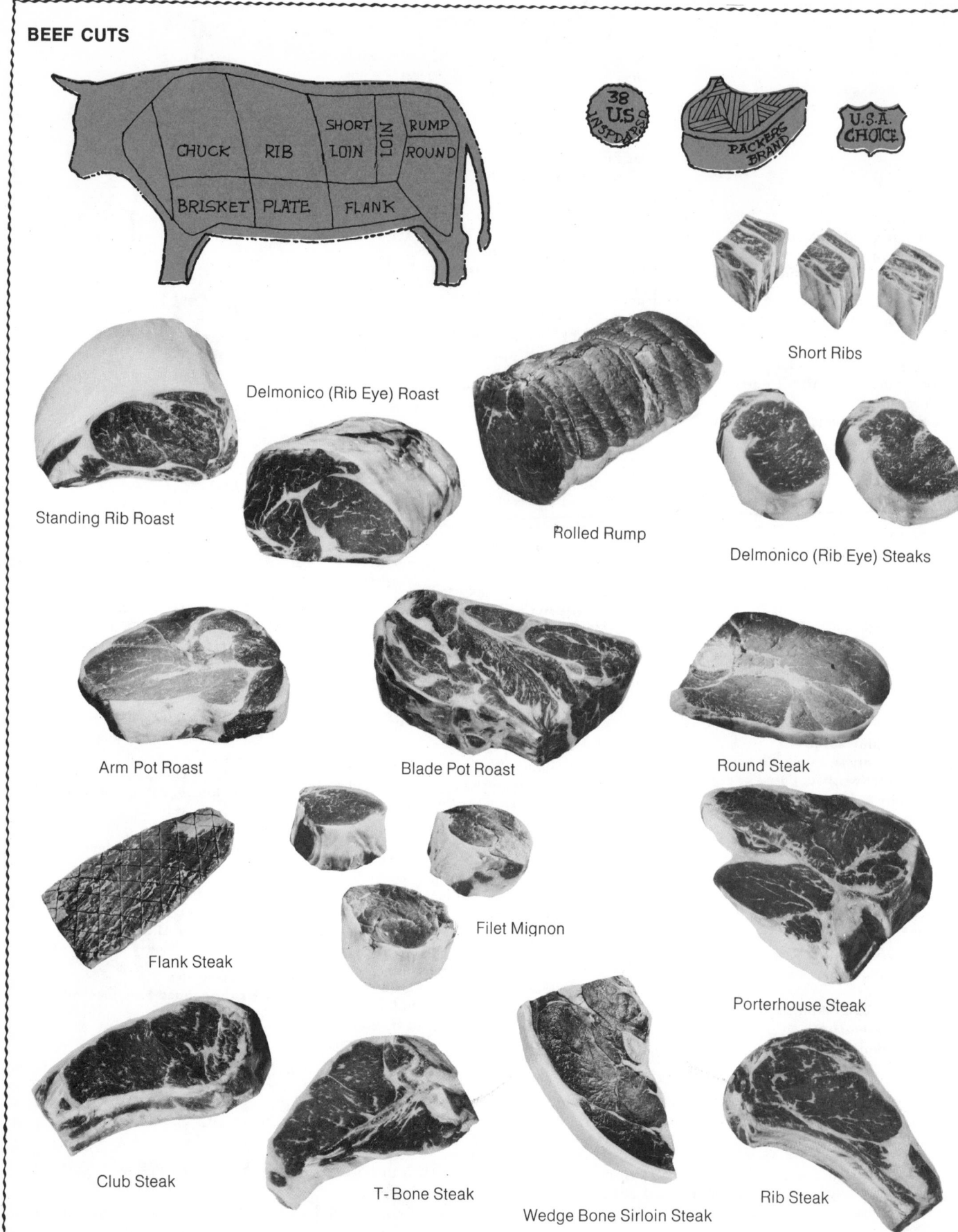

Short Ribs

Delmonico (Rib Eye) Roast

Standing Rib Roast

Rolled Rump

Delmonico (Rib Eye) Steaks

Arm Pot Roast

Blade Pot Roast

Round Steak

Flank Steak

Filet Mignon

Porterhouse Steak

Club Steak

T-Bone Steak

Wedge Bone Sirloin Steak

Rib Steak

PORK CUTS

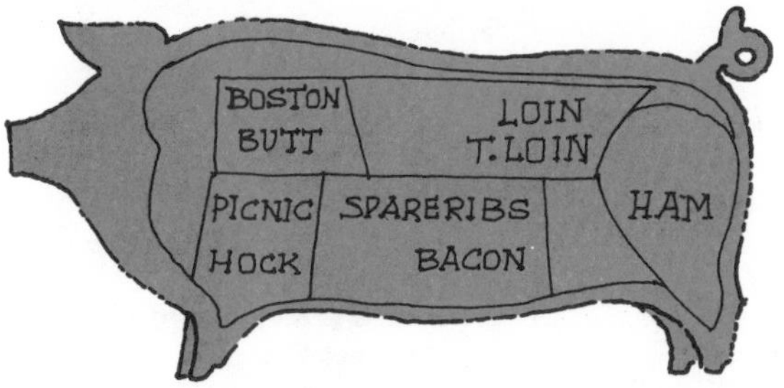

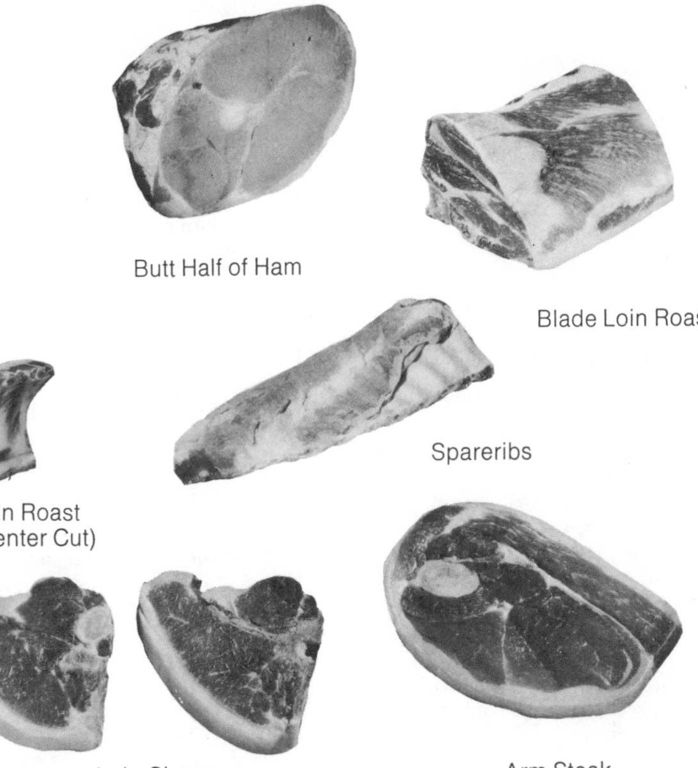

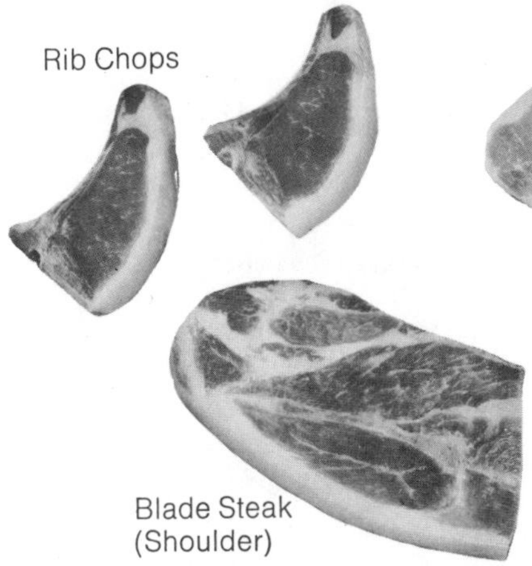

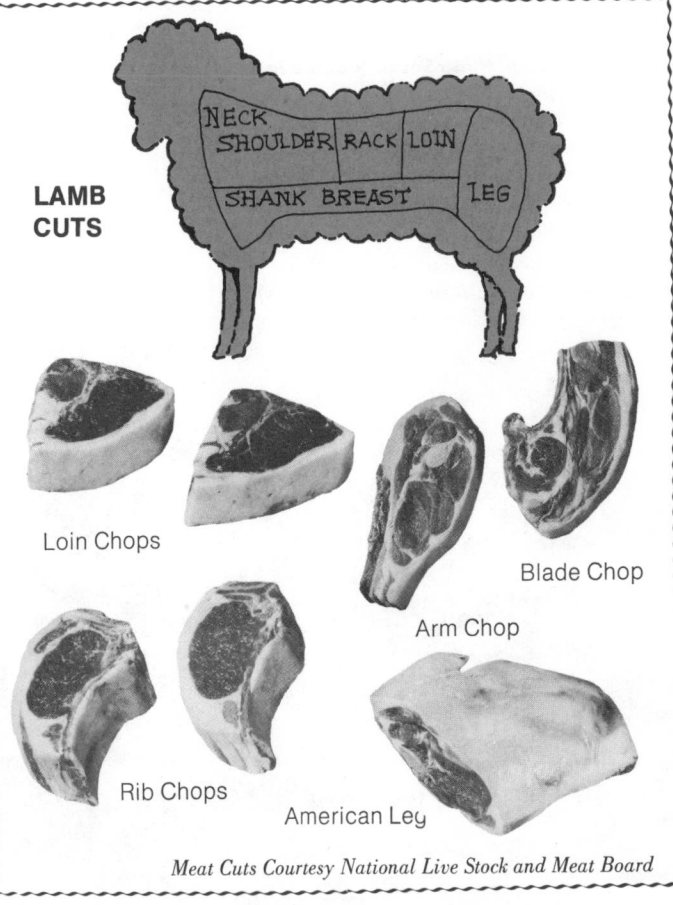

Butt Half of Ham

Blade Loin Roast

Rib Chops

Loin Roast
(Center Cut)

Spareribs

Blade Steak
(Shoulder)

Loin Chops

Arm Steak

VEAL CUTS

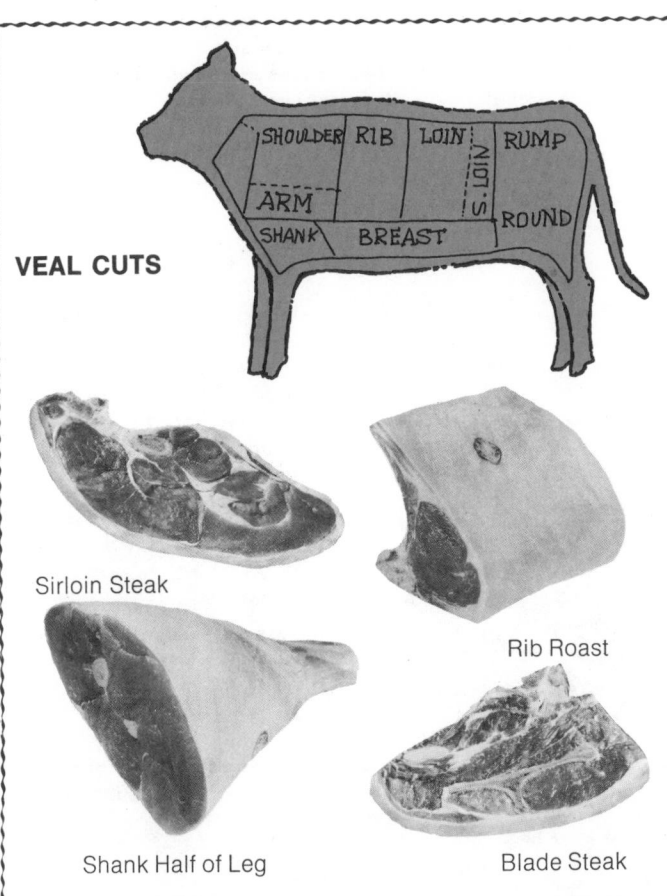

Sirloin Steak

Rib Roast

Shank Half of Leg

Blade Steak

LAMB CUTS

Loin Chops

Blade Chop

Arm Chop

Rib Chops

American Leg

Meat Cuts Courtesy National Live Stock and Meat Board

BEEF ROLL-UPS

The vegetable flavors are baked right into these little rolls of beef.

Grease a 2-qt. casserole with a tight-fitting cover.

Set out
> **1½ lbs. round steak, cut about ½ in. thick**

Coat well with a mixture of
> **½ cup all-purpose flour**
> **¾ teaspoon monosodium glutamate**
> **½ teaspoon salt**
> **⅛ teaspoon pepper**

Pound meat to about ¼-in. thickness. Cut into 6 pie-shape wedges; set aside.
Wash, pare or scrape and cut into 3 pieces each
> **2 small carrots**

Peel, rinse and cut into 6 thin wedges
> **1 small onion**

Clean and cut into 6 lengthwise strips
> **¼ green pepper**

Cut into three pieces each
> **2 slices bacon**

Place a piece of bacon, onion, carrot and green pepper on each beef wedge; roll up, starting at tip of meat. Tuck under ends to keep vegetables inside roll. Insert wooden picks through folded ends and through center of each roll.

Melt in skillet
> **3 tablespoons fat**

Slowly brown meat rolls on all sides. Place meat rolls in casserole.

Prepare in same skillet
> **2 cups Thin White Sauce (double recipe, page 304)**

Stir into completed sauce
> **½ cup (4-oz. can, drained) mushrooms**
> **1 tablespoon minced parsley**
> **1 teaspoon Worcestershire sauce**

Pour sauce over meat.

Cover casserole and cook in a 350°F oven 1 to 1½ hrs., or until meat is tender when pierced with a fork. Remove picks.

6 servings

MARINATED BEEF, PROVENCAL STYLE

(Daube de Boeuf à la Provençale)

Set out a large heavy skillet with a tight-fitting cover.

Cut into 2-in. pieces
> **2½ lbs. beef, round or chuck**

Put into deep bowl with
> **1½ cups thinly sliced onions**
> **1 cup red wine**
> **4 small carrots, sliced**
> **¼ teaspoon thyme**
> **2 cloves garlic, cut in halves**
> **6 peppercorns**
> **3 whole cloves**
> **1 sprig parsley**

Marinate (page 10) 2 to 3 hrs., turning the pieces from time to time in the marinade. Remove beef from marinade and set aside to drain thoroughly.

Place in skillet
> **8 slices bacon, diced**

Cook slowly over low heat, turning frequently. Pour off and set aside fat as it collects. When bacon is evenly crisp and browned, remove and set aside.

Return to skillet and heat over medium heat
> **¼ cup bacon drippings**
> **1 tablespoon olive oil**
> **1 tablespoon lard**

Brown meat on all sides in the hot fat. Add the carrots and onion from the marinade, the bacon pieces and
> **2 medium tomatoes, peeled and chopped**

Heat the marinade, strain and pour over the meat. Add
> **1 cup red wine**

Cover and simmer about 2 hrs., or until meat is tender. Serve meat and sauce over
> **3 cups cooked macaroni**

6 servings

BROCCOLI WITH BEEF

Set out a large heavy skillet with a tight-fitting cover.

Remove and discard outer leaves and cut off tough ends of stalks from
> **2 lbs. broccoli**

Wash thoroughly and drain.

Set out
> **2 lbs. lean boneless beef (round or chuck)**

Cut into pieces about 4x½x⅛ in. and set aside.

Prepare and set aside
> **3 cups quick chicken broth (page 10)**

Set aside to drain
> **2 cans (16 oz. each) bean sprouts (about 2⅔ cups, drained)**

When the broccoli has been drained, cut it into pieces about 2½ in. long and ¼ in. thick. Set aside.

Heat in the skillet until very hot
> **4 teaspoons cooking oil**

Add the beef, brown and cook quickly. Remove from skillet and set aside.

Add to skillet
> **3 tablespoons cooking oil**

Add the broccoli pieces and cook over high heat, tossing constantly for ½ min. Add the chicken broth, cover and cook 3 min. Remove from heat.

Using a slotted spoon, remove broccoli to a bowl and set aside to keep warm.

Blend and add gradually, stirring constantly, to the contents of the skillet
> **¼ cup cold water**
> **4 teaspoons cornstarch**
> **1 tablespoon salt**
> **2 teaspoons monosodium glutamate**
> **2 teaspoons soy sauce**

Bring to boiling and boil 3 min., or until mixture thickens. Mix in bean sprouts; return beef and broccoli to skillet. Heat thoroughly.

8 servings

BURGOO

This native Kentucky dish—a rich, meaty stew—is traditionally cooked out of doors for crowds on Derby Day. Kentuckians like it so well that they reduce the recipe for home use—but never reduce the cooking time, which is four to seven hours! The stew must be watched and stirred to prevent scorching, especially at the end, when it begins to thicken lusciously.

Set out a large heavy saucepot or kettle with a cover.

Cut into pieces
> **1 lb. boneless beef (chuck or rump)**
> **¼ lb. boneless lamb shoulder**

Set out
> **1 beef soup bone, cracked**

Rinse in cold water (do not soak)
> **1 lb. chicken breasts, thighs or legs**

Put meat, soup bone and chicken into pot with
> **2 qts. water**
> **4 teaspoons salt**
> **¾ teaspoon pepper**
> **¼ teaspoon cayenne pepper**

Cover pot and bring to boiling; reduce heat and simmer about 2 hrs. Skim off any foam.

Meanwhile, prepare the vegetables. Remove husks, corn silk and blemishes and carefully cut kernels from enough ears of corn to yield
1½ cups cut corn
Shell, and rinse enough lima beans to yield
1⅓ cups green lima beans
Wash, pare and dice enough potatoes to yield
1 cup diced potatoes
Clean and chop enough to yield
1 cup chopped onion
½ cup chopped green pepper
Wash, pare and dice enough carrots to yield
½ cup diced carrots
Add vegetables to saucepot and simmer, covered, 2 hrs. longer. Stir occasionally to prevent sticking.

Meanwhile, wash, cut off stem ends and slice enough okra to yield
1 cup (about ¼ lb.) sliced okra
Have ready
2½ cups canned tomatoes
1 clove garlic, minced
Add the okra, tomatoes and garlic and simmer 1 hr. longer, stirring occasionally.

Meanwhile, prepare
½ cup chopped parsley

Remove pot from heat; remove soup bone and chicken bones and skin. Return pot to heat and cook, stirring constantly to prevent sticking, about 10 min. longer or until thickened. Remove from heat; stir in parsley.
About 3 qts. Burgoo

BEEF, BURGUNDY STYLE
(Boeuf à la Bourguignonne)

This gastronomical masterpiece is typical of a cookery designed to play up the wines for which Burgundy is so famous.

Set out a large heavy skillet with a tight-fitting cover.

Prepare and cool
1 cup Bouillon (page 41)

Blend to a paste with
3 tablespoons all-purpose flour
1 tablespoon tomato paste
1 teaspoon bottled meat glaze
Set aside.

Set out
2 lbs. lean beef, round or chuck, cut in 3-in. pieces

Heat in skillet
3 tablespoons bacon drippings
Add meat and brown on all sides. Remove from skillet and set aside.

Stir into skillet
2 tablespoons sherry
Add and cook about 5 min., stirring occasionally
1½ cups chopped onion
Blend in tomato paste mixture. Bring rapidly to

boiling, stirring constantly. Then stir in
1 cup Burgundy or other red wine
Herb bouquet (page 9)
Replace beef. Cover and simmer over low heat 2½ to 3 hrs., or until meat is tender.

Meanwhile, clean and slice (page 9)
12 medium mushrooms

Heat in a small skillet
¼ cup butter
Sauté mushrooms until lightly browned. Add to meat about 15 min. before meat is done.

Complete cooking, remove and discard Herb Bouquet, and turn meat into a casserole or serving dish. Sprinkle with **parsley.**
4 servings

CARAWAY BEEF STEW PIE

▲ *Base Recipe*

Set out a 3-qt. top-of-range casserole with a tight-fitting cover.

Set out
1½ lbs. round or sirloin steak, cut in 1-in. pieces
To coat evenly, shake a few pieces at a time in a plastic bag containing a mixture of
½ cup all-purpose flour
2 teaspoons monosodium glutamate
2 teaspoons salt
¼ teaspoon pepper

Melt in casserole over medium heat
¼ cup fat
Add meat to hot fat and brown slowly on all sides. When nearly browned, add
2 medium (about ½ lb.) onions, sliced
Finish browning meat. Slowly add
3 cups hot water
1 bay leaf
Cover casserole and simmer 1½ hrs. If necessary, add more hot water as meat cooks.

Meanwhile, wash, break off ends and cut into julienne strips
½ lb. (about 1½ cups) green beans

Wash, scrape or pare, and slice
3 to 4 (about ½ lb.) carrots
Add beans and carrots to casserole with
3 large (about 1 lb.) onions, quartered
Cover casserole and simmer 15 to 25 min. longer, or until vegetables are tender when pierced with a fork. Remove bay leaf.

Meanwhile, prepare
Pastry Topping (one half recipe, page 486; blend 2 teaspoons caraway seed into sifted dry ingredients)
Cut rolled pastry into strips 1-in. wide. Twist strips and loosely arrange parallel strips across top of casserole, leaving ½ in. between. Trim strips so ends extend about ½ in. beyond edge of casserole; turn ends under and seal.

Bake at 425°F 15 to 18 min., or until pastry strips are lightly browned.
8 servings

Beef Stew with Limas

—BEEF STEW WITH LIMAS

Follow ▲ Recipe. Omit pastry. Substitute **1 pkg. (10 oz.) frozen lima beans** for green beans and carrots.

—BEEF STEW WITH GREEN PEAS

Follow ▲ Recipe. Omit pastry. Use **celery stalks** sliced diagonally into 1-in. pieces (about 1 cup). Substitute **1 pkg. (10 oz.) frozen peas** for green beans and **½ lb. small whole onions** for quartered onions. Wash, pare and cut **2 medium potatoes** into chunks; add with the other vegetables.

ROLLED POT ROAST WITH SOUR CREAM GRAVY

Melt in a Dutch oven
3 tablespoons fat
Brown slowly on all sides in fat
4-lb. rolled pot roast of beef

Meanwhile, cut off root end and a thin slice from stem end of
1 medium onion
Peel, rinse, cut into quarters and set aside.

Season browned meat with a mixture of
1 teaspoon salt
½ teaspoon monosodium glutamate
⅛ teaspoon pepper
Add the onion and
¼ cup water
1 bay leaf
Cover tightly and cook slowly over low heat about 3 hrs. If necessary, add more water during cooking period. Liquid surrounding meat should at all times be simmering, not boiling.

For Noodles—About 15 min. before meat is tender, heat to boiling in a large saucepan
2 qts. water
1½ teaspoons salt
Gradually add, stirring with a fork
1½ cups (about 4 oz.) noodles
Boil rapidly, uncovered, 6 to 10 min. Test tenderness by pressing a piece against side of pan with fork or spoon.

Drain in colander or large sieve; rinse with hot

water to remove loose starch. Using a fork, blend through noodles

3 tablespoons melted butter

Serve buttered noodles in warm serving bowl or on platter with the pot roast.

For Gravy—When meat is tender, remove from liquid and keep warm. Strain liquid and return it to Dutch oven. Set over medium heat.

Put into a 1-pt. screw-top jar

½ cup water

Sprinkle onto it

1 tablespoon all-purpose flour

Cover tightly and shake until mixture is well blended. Gradually stir into liquid in Dutch oven. Bring rapidly to boiling, stirring constantly; cook 3 to 5 min. longer.

Remove Dutch oven from heat. Stirring vigorously with a French whip, whisk beater or fork, add to mixture in Dutch oven in very small amounts, a mixture of

1½ cups dairy sour cream
1½ tablespoons lemon juice
1½ teaspoons grated lemon peel
¾ teaspoon sugar

Place over low heat and stir constantly, until thoroughly heated, about 3 to 5 min., but do not boil.

Serve with pot roast and noodles.

About 8 servings

CRANBERRY POT ROAST

Melt in a Dutch oven

3 tablespoons fat

Have ready

4-lb. beef pot roast (blade or arm)

Brown meat slowly on all sides in fat.

Meanwhile, wash, sort and cook together in a saucepan until skins pop

2 cups (about ½ lb.) cranberries
1 cup water

Season browned meat with a mixture of

1 teaspoon salt
½ teaspoon monosodium glutamate
⅛ teaspoon pepper

Pour cranberries over meat and add

¼ cup water
2 whole cloves

Cover tightly and cook slowly over low heat about 3 hrs. Add more water during cooking period if necessary. Liquid surrounding meat should at all times be simmering, not boiling.

When meat is tender, remove from liquid and keep warm. Strain liquid and return it to Dutch oven. Set over medium heat. Stir in

2 tablespoons sugar

Put into 1-qt. screw-top jar

½ cup water

Sprinkle onto it

1 tablespoon all-purpose flour

Cover tightly and shake until mixture is well blended. Gradually stir into liquid in Dutch oven. Bring rapidly to boiling, stirring constantly until thickened. Cook 3 to 5 min.

Serve as a gravy with pot roast.   *8 servings*

YANKEE POT ROAST

Set out a heavy saucepot or Dutch oven with a tight-fitting cover.

Have ready

3- to 4-lb. beef pot roast (blade, round, rump or chuck)

Coat evenly with a mixture of

⅓ cup all-purpose flour
2 teaspoons salt
½ teaspoon monosodium glutamate
⅛ teaspoon pepper

Heat in the saucepot or Dutch oven

¼ cup pork drippings

Brown meat slowly in the fat over medium heat, turning to brown on all sides.

When meat is well browned, add

½ cup water
1 bay leaf, crushed

Cover; reduce heat and cook over low heat for 2 hrs. If necessary add more water during cooking period. Liquid surrounding meat should at all times be simmering, not boiling.

Meanwhile, wash and pare

8 to 10 small potatoes
8 to 10 small carrots
1 medium turnip

Clean

8 to 10 small onions

When meat has simmered 2 hrs., slice the turnip and add with other vegetables to the saucepot. Continue to simmer, covered, about 1 hr. longer, or until meat and vegetables are tender when tested with a fork.

Remove meat and vegetables from saucepot and arrange on a warm serving platter; keep warm. Strain liquid and add, enough to make 1½ cups liquid

Quick meat broth (page 10)

Return to saucepot and thicken as for gravy. Serve with the pot roast.   *About 8 servings*

DAUBE

The famous Creole pot roast.

Set out a Dutch oven or a heavy saucepot with a tight-fitting cover.

Clean

5 medium (about 1 lb.) onions

Finely chop 1 onion and mix thoroughly with

1 clove garlic, finely minced
1 teaspoon salt
¼ teaspoon pepper
¼ teaspoon thyme
¼ teaspoon cayenne pepper

Set seasoning mixture aside.

Set out

3- to 4-lb. beef pot roast (chuck, blade, round or rump)

Cut slits several inches apart all over surface.

Cut crosswise into thin strips

3 slices salt pork or bacon

Insert strips and seasoning mixture in slits. Set meat aside.

Heat in the Dutch oven over low heat

¼ cup butter or margarine

Slice 2 of the onions and add to heated fat; cook until lightly browned. Put meat into Dutch oven and place onion slices on top of meat. Cover and slowly brown meat.

Meanwhile, wash, pare or scrape and cut into small pieces

3 carrots
1 turnip

Finely chop the remaining onions. When browning second side of meat, add vegetables to Dutch oven with

2 tablespoons finely chopped parsley
1 bay leaf, crushed

Turn vegetables several times while meat is browning.

When meat is well browned, add

½ cup sherry or Madeira

Cover tightly and cook slowly over low heat about 3 hrs., or until tender. If necessary add more wine or water during cooking period. Liquid surrounding meat should at all times be simmering, not boiling.

When meat is tender, remove from liquid. Liquid may be strained and used for gravy.

Serve Daube cutting meat into thin slices across grain of meat.   *6 to 8 servings*

DAUBE GLACE

The jellied meats, a Creole favorite, are highly seasoned. This modern version uses gelatin instead of simmering veal shanks, pigs' or calves' feet with the meat as the Creoles do.

A 10x5x3-in. loaf pan will be needed.

Prepare

Daube (on this page; add 1 teaspoon crushed red pepper with parsley and bay leaf)

Cook Daube 3½ to 4 hrs., or until meat is very tender. (The meat should be easily removed from bone, if there is one.) Remove meat from Dutch oven. Cut away excess fat, remove and discard bone (if there is one) and set meat aside to cool.

Strain liquid through a fine sieve or cheesecloth (several thicknesses). Reserve liquid Remove fat that rises to surface. Refrigerate fat and use in other food preparation.

Wash and pare or scrape

3 small carrots

Cut into slices with a fancy cutter. Cook (page 312) 15 to 20 min., or until just tender.

Meanwhile, put cooled meat through medium blade of food chopper. Set ground meat aside.

Lightly oil the loaf pan with salad or cooking

oil (not olive oil). Invert the pan and set it aside to drain.

Drain cooked carrots and set aside to cool.

Meanwhile, put into a small bowl
½ cup cold water
Sprinkle evenly over cold water
2 env. unflavored gelatin
Let stand until softened.

add to reserved liquid, enough to make 3 cups liquid
Quick meat broth (page 10)
Mix in
¼ teaspoon cayenne pepper
¼ teaspoon pepper
Heat mixture until very hot. Remove from heat; immediately add softened gelatin, stirring until gelatin is completely dissolved.

Stir in
½ cup sherry or Madeira
Pour a small amount of gelatin mixture (enough to make a thin layer) into bottom of prepared loaf pan. Chill in refrigerator until slightly set. Chill remaining gelatin mixture in refrigerator or in a pan of ice and water until mixture is slightly thicker than consistency of thick unbeaten egg white. If mixture is placed over ice and water, stir frequently; if placed in refrigerator, stir occasionally.

When gelatin in loaf pan is slightly set, remove from refrigerator. Arrange carrot slices in slightly set gelatin.

Blend the ground meat into thickened gelatin. Turn thickened meat-gelatin mixture onto gelatin-carrot layer. (Both layers should be of almost same consistency to avoid separation of layers when unmolded.) Put into refrigerator and chill until firm.

Unmold on a platter. Garnish with
Parsley sprigs
Chili peppers
Cut into thin slices.   *8 to 10 servings*

BEEF A LA MODE
(Boeuf à la Mode)

Characteristic of French meat cookery is the use of the larding needle. For Lardoons (Lardons) the needle is threaded with slender strips of fat pork and drawn through the lean of uncooked meat to give it added flavor and richness. Such needles are usually available in large department or hardware stores.

For Lardoons—Cut pork fat (salt or fresh) into thin strips the length of the roast and about ¼ in. wide. These pieces of fat are *Lardoons* and are used in meat lacking fat of its own, especially veal or lean beef. Thread strips into a larding needle. Draw lengthwise through the roast, from cut end to cut end, at 1½-in. intervals.

For Beef—Set out a deep kettle with a tight-fitting cover.

Set out
4-lb. boneless beef pot roast (rump, round, chuck)
Lard roast as in *Lardoons*, above.

Put the larded meat into a deep bowl. Add a mixture of
2 cups red wine
½ cup chopped onion
2 cloves garlic, quartered
2 whole cloves
1 bay leaf
¼ teaspoon pepper
⅛ teaspoon nutmeg
Herb bouquet (page 9)
Marinate meat 2 to 3 hrs., turning occasionally. Drain meat and dry thoroughly. Strain and reserve marinade.

Coat meat evenly with mixture of
¼ cup all-purpose flour
2 teaspoons salt
¼ teaspoon pepper
Heat in the deep kettle
¼ cup fat
Brown meat on all sides in the hot fat. Drain off fat. Add the marinade and
1 veal knuckle
2 cups red wine
2 cups Bouillon (page 41), or just enough to cover the meat
3 shallots, sliced, or ¼ cup chopped onion

Cover tightly and bring to boiling. Reduce heat and simmer over low heat about 3½ hrs. Remove meat from broth and skim off fat. Strain broth.

Clean kettle and return meat and broth with
8 medium carrots, quartered
8 small onions
½ teaspoon salt
Cover and bring to boiling. Reduce heat and cook slowly about 40 min., or until meat is tender. Remove meat to a warm platter. Take out veal bone, skim any fat from liquid.

If desired, thicken the cooking liquid with a mixture of **½ cup cold Bouillon** and **2 tablespoons all-purpose flour.**

Arrange vegetables attractively around meat and pour sauce over both.   *8 servings*

POT ROAST OF BEEF WITH WINE
(Gedämpfter Rindsbraten)

Have ready
3- to 4-lb. boneless beef pot roast (rump, chuck or round)
Put the meat into a deep bowl. Add
2 cups red wine
2 medium onions, chopped
3 medium carrots, washed, pared and sliced
1 clove garlic
1 bay leaf
¼ teaspoon pepper
4 sprigs parsley
Cover and put into refrigerator to marinate 12 hrs., or overnight. Turn meat occasionally. Drain the meat, reserving marinade, and pat meat dry with absorbent paper.

Coat meat evenly with a mixture of
¼ cup all-purpose flour
2 teaspoons salt
½ teaspoon monosodium glutamate
¼ teaspoon pepper
Heat in a Dutch oven or large heavy saucepot
3 tablespoons butter
Brown the meat slowly on all sides in the butter. Drain off the fat. Add the marinade and
2 cups red wine
Cover and bring to boiling. Reduce heat and simmer slowly 2½ to 3 hrs., or until meat is tender. Remove meat to a warm platter.

Strain the liquid. Return the strained liquid to the Dutch oven.

Pour into a screw-top jar

1 cup cold water

Sprinkle onto water

¼ cup all-purpose flour

Cover jar tightly and shake until mixture is well blended.

Stirring constantly, slowly pour one half of the blended mixture into liquid in Dutch oven. Bring to boiling. Gradually add only what is needed of the remaining blended mixture for consistency desired. Bring gravy to boiling after each addition. Cook 3 to 5 min. longer.

Serve meat with gravy, buttered carrots and **Potato Dumplings (page 106)**

8 to 10 servings

HOT PICKLED BEEF
(Savanyu Marhahus)

A spicy variation of the familiar pot roast.

A heavy 4-qt. kettle with a tight-fitting cover will be needed. Set out a deep 3- or 4-qt. bowl with a tight-fitting cover.

Have ready

3- to 4-lb. boneless beef pot roast (rump, chuck, blade or round)

Place meat into the bowl and cover with a mixture of equal parts of

Vinegar

Water

Add

1 teaspoon salt

10 peppercorns

10 juniper berries

2 bay leaves

1 small onion, coarsely chopped

1 lemon, washed and cut in ¼-in. slices

Cover bowl and put into refrigerator. Marinate meat 2 to 3 days, turning meat over once a day.

Set out the kettle and cover.

Remove meat from marinade and drain thor-

oughly. Strain and reserve marinade; discard seasonings.

Melt in the kettle over medium heat

2 tablespoons butter

Add meat to butter and brown on both sides. Cover meat with a mixture of equal parts of

Reserved marinade

Hot water

Bring liquid to boiling. Reduce heat, cover kettle tightly and simmer 3 to 4 hrs., or until meat is tender when pierced with a fork. Remove meat to a warm deep platter; cover and keep meat warm. Pour off cooking liquid and set aside.

For Gravy—Melt in the kettle

¼ cup butter

Thoroughly blend into butter

¼ cup all-purpose flour

Heat until mixture bubbles and is lightly browned, stirring constantly. Remove from heat and add gradually, stirring constantly

3 cups reserved cooking liquid

Return to heat and bring rapidly to boiling, stirring constantly; cook 1 to 2 min. longer. Slice meat and pour the gravy over it.

6 to 8 servings

MARINATED BEEF
(Sauerbraten)

▲ Base Recipe

A heavy 4-qt. kettle or Dutch oven with a tight-fitting cover will be needed. Set out a deep 3- or 4-qt. bowl.

Have ready

4-lb. beef blade pot roast (any beef pot roast may be used)

Put the meat into the bowl. Set aside.

Combine in a saucepan and heat without boiling

2 cups vinegar

2 cups water

1 large onion, sliced

¼ cup sugar

2 teaspoons salt

10 peppercorns

3 whole cloves

2 bay leaves

Pour hot mixture over meat in bowl and allow to cool. Add

1 lemon, rinsed and cut into ¼-in. slices

Cover and set in refrigerator. Marinate for 4 days, turning meat over once each day.

Set out the kettle and a tight-fitting cover.

Remove meat from marinade and drain thoroughly. Strain and reserve marinade.

Heat in the kettle over low heat

2 to 3 tablespoons butter

Add the pot roast and brown slowly on all sides over medium heat. Slowly add 2 cups of the reserved marinade (reserve remaining marinade for gravy). Bring liquid to boiling. Reduce heat; cover kettle tightly and simmer 2½ to

Marinated Beef with Raisins

3 hrs., or until meat is tender when pierced with a fork. Add more of the marinade, if necessary. Liquid surrounding meat should at all times be simmering, not boiling.

Remove meat to a warm platter and keep warm. Pour cooking liquid from kettle and set aside for gravy.

For Gravy—Melt in the kettle

¼ cup butter

Blend in

¼ cup all-purpose flour

Heat until butter-flour mixture bubbles and is golden brown, stirring constantly. Remove kettle from heat.

Add gradually, stirring constantly

3 cups liquid (reserved cooking liquid and enough reserved marinade or hot water to equal 3 cups liquid)

Return to heat. Bring to boiling; cook rapidly, stirring constantly, until gravy thickens. Cook 1 to 2 min. longer. Remove from heat. Stirring vigorously with a French whip, whisk beater, or fork, add to kettle in very small amounts

½ cup dairy sour cream

Cook mixture over low heat about 3 to 5 min., stirring constantly, until thoroughly heated; do not boil.

Serve meat and gravy with

Potato pancakes

8 to 10 servings

—MARINATED BEEF WITH NOODLES
(Sauerbraten mit Nudeln)

Follow ▲ Recipe. Omit gravy and potato pancakes. Serve with **Buttered Noodles** (page 153).

—MARINATED BEEF WITH RAISINS
(Sauerbraten mit Rosinen)

Follow ▲ Recipe. Stir into gravy with the sour cream ½ cup (about 3 oz.) **dark seedless raisins**.

—MARINATED BEEF WITH GARLIC
(Sauerbraten mit Knoblauch)

Follow ▲ Recipe. Before marinating the beef, rub the surface all over with the cut surfaces of **1 clove garlic**.

BEEF IN RED WINE

A Dutch oven or a large heavy saucepot will be needed.

Have ready
  4-lb. boneless beef pot roast
    (rump, chuck or round)
Put meat into a deep bowl. Add
  1 cup quick meat broth (page 10)
  1 cup red wine
  1 teaspoon salt
  ½ teaspoon monosodium glutamate
  ¼ teaspoon pepper
  ¼ teaspoon celery salt
  2 small bay leaves
  2 whole cloves
  1 medium onion, sliced
  2 slices lemon
  1 clove garlic, minced
Cover and put into refrigerator to marinate 24 hrs., turning meat occasionally.

Drain the meat, reserving marinade, and pat meat dry with absorbent paper.

Heat in the Dutch oven over low heat
  1 tablespoon butter or margarine
Brown meat slowly on all sides. Add the marinade to the meat. Cover and bring to boiling. Reduce heat and simmer slowly 2½ to 3 hrs., or until meat is tender. Liquid surrounding meat should at all times be simmering, not boiling.

When meat is tender, remove from liquid. Liquid may be strained and used for gravy. Whole cooked **carrots** and **onions** may be served with the meat. *12 servings*

GOULASH
(Gulyás)

The popularity of Goulash probably began about 1000 years ago when the Magyars were migrating across the Great Plains. This hearty meat dish was prepared in large copper kettles over open fires and it easily satisfied outdoor appetites. Through the years, the popularity of Goulash has spread to all parts of the world. Goulash has become one of the most famous contributions to international cookery.

Set out a Dutch oven or a heavy 3-qt. saucepot with a tight-fitting cover.

Set out on wooden board and cut into 1½-in. pieces
  1½ lbs. boneless beef pot roast,
  chuck or blade
Prepare
  2 cups quick meat broth (double recipe, page 10)
Set aside.

Dice and put into the saucepot
  4 slices bacon
Cook slowly, stirring and turning frequently, until bacon is lightly browned. Remove bacon with slotted spoon from saucepot to small bowl and set aside.

Add to the bacon fat in the saucepot and cook over medium heat until onion is almost tender, stirring occasionally
  1½ cups (about 3 medium) chopped onion

Goulash

Remove onion with slotted spoon to bowl containing bacon and set aside.

Add meat to the bacon fat and slowly brown on all sides, stirring occasionally. Sprinkle evenly over the meat a mixture of
  1 tablespoon paprika
  1½ teaspoons salt
  ¼ teaspoon freshly ground pepper
  ⅛ teaspoon marjoram
Stir in the bacon-onion mixture with
  ¼ cup (about 1 small) chopped green pepper
Slowly pour in the reserved meat broth and
  ¾ cup dry white wine
Bring to boiling. Reduce heat, cover saucepot and simmer 2 to 2½ hrs., or until meat is tender when pierced with a fork. Remove meat with slotted spoon to hot serving dish. Thicken cooking liquid, if desired.

To Thicken Cooking Liquid—Pour into 1-pt. screw-top jar
  ½ cup water
Sprinkle onto the liquid
  ¼ cup all-prupose flour
Cover jar tightly and shake until mixture is well blended. Slowly pour about half of the mixture into the saucepot, stirring constantly. Bring to boiling. Gradually add only what is needed of remaining flour-water mixture for consistency desired. Bring to boiling after each addition. After final addition, cook 3 to 5 min. longer.

Melt in a small skillet
  1 tablespoon butter
Remove from heat. Blend in
  ½ teaspoon paprika
Stir in
  1 tablespoon water
Immediately add to liquid in saucepot, stirring until well blended. Pour this sauce over meat.

Serve immediately. *6 to 8 servings*

—GOULASH WITH POTATOES
(Gulyás Burgonyával)

Follow ▲ Recipe. Use a 4-qt. saucepot or kettle. About ½ hr. before end of cooking time, add **6 medium (2 lbs.) potatoes**, washed, pared and quartered.

181

Vegetable Dinner Pies

—GOULASH WITH CARAWAY SEEDS
(Gulyás Köményaggal)

Follow ▲ Recipe. Add **1 teaspoon caraway seed** with other seasonings.

—GOULASH WITH GARLIC
(Gulyás Foghagymával)

Follow ▲ Recipe. Decrease onion to ¾ cup. Combine onion and green pepper with **1 clove garlic**, minced.

—GOULASH WITH TOMATOES
(Gulyás Paradicsommal)

Follow ▲ Recipe. Substitute **1 cup (one half 16-oz. can) tomatoes**, sieved, for one half of the beef broth.

—GOULASH WITH CARROTS
(Gulyás Sárgarepával)

Follow ▲ Recipe. About ½ hr. before end of cooking time, add to the saucepot **4 medium carrots**, washed, scraped or pared and cut into ½-in. pieces.

VEGETABLE DINNER PIES

Grease 6 small casseroles or ramekins. Set out a kettle or Dutch oven.

Set out
2 lbs. boneless beef (brisket, plate, chuck, flank or round)
Cut meat into 1½-in. pieces. To coat meat evenly, shake two or three pieces at a time in a plastic bag containing a mixture of
⅓ cup all-purpose flour
2 teaspoons salt
½ teaspoon monosodium glutamate
⅛ teaspoon pepper

Melt in the kettle or Dutch oven
3 tablespoons fat
Slowly brown beef pieces on all sides in hot fat, turning occasionally. Pour off excess fat.

While meat is browning, cut off root end and a thin slice from the stem end of
1 medium onion
Peel, rinse, chop onion and set aside.

Slowly pour into the kettle or Dutch oven
1 qt. hot water
Add to kettle the chopped onion and
1 tablespoon salt
1 teaspoon Worcestershire sauce
1 teaspoon lemon juice
2 bay leaves
½ teaspoon pepper
½ teaspoon monosodium glutamate
Few grains ground cloves
Cover and bring water to boiling over high heat. Reduce heat and simmer over low heat about 1½ hrs., or until meat is almost tender.

About 15 min. before adding vegetables to stew, cut off root ends and a thin slice from the stem ends of
12 small onions
Peel, rinse onions and set aside.

Wash, scrape and cut into pieces
8 medium carrots
Add prepared vegetables to kettle. Cover and simmer 30 to 45 min., or until meat and vegetables are tender.

Prepare
Pastry Topping (page 486)
Turn dough out onto a lightly floured surface and roll to ⅛-in. thickness. Cut 6 strips of pastry 1-in. wide. Cut remaining pastry into strips ½-in. wide. Set strips aside.

Just before removing meat and vegetables from stew, if desired, dissolve in a small amount of hot water
2 teaspoons concentrated meat extract
With slotted spoon, remove meat and vegetables to hot dish. Discard bay leaves.

Stir the dissolved concentrated meat extract into the cooking liquid.

To Thicken Cooking Liquid—Put into a 1-pt. screw-top jar
¾ cup cold water
Sprinkle evenly onto water
6 tablespoons all-purpose flour
Cover tightly and shake until mixture is well blended. Slowly pour one-half of mixture into cooking liquid, stirring constantly. Bring to boiling. Gradually add only what is needed of remaining flour-water mixture for consistency desired. Bring mixture to boiling after any additions. Cook 3 to 5 min. Return meat and vegetables to kettle and heat thoroughly. Turn heated stew into casseroles.

Moisten rims of casseroles with water. Place one 1-in. pastry strip around inside edge of each casserole. Press strip onto edge. Carefully arrange strips to form lattice pattern.

To make the lattice top, cross two strips over the pie at the center. Working out from center to edge of pie, add the remaining strips one at a time, weaving the strips under and over each other in crisscross fashion; leave about ¼ in. between the strips. Trim strips so ends extend about ¼ in. beyond edge of casserole. Fold the ends of the strips over the pastry on edge of casseroles; press to seal.

Bake at 425°F 25 to 30 min., or until pastry is lightly browned.   *6 servings*

BEEF STEW

Set out a large heavy saucepot with a tight-fitting cover or a Dutch oven.

Set out
2 lbs. beef for stewing (chuck, round or brisket)
Cut meat into 1½-in. pieces. Coat meat evenly by shaking a few pieces at a time in a plastic bag containing a mixture of
⅓ cup all-purpose flour
2 teaspoons salt
½ teaspoon monosodium glutamate
⅛ teaspoon pepper

Heat in the saucepot
3 tablespoons fat
Add meat and brown on all sides over medium heat, occasionally moving and turning pieces. When meat is browned, pour off the excess fat.

While meat is browning, clean and chop
1 medium onion (about ½ cup, chopped)
Slowly pour into the saucepot
1 qt. hot water
Add the chopped onion and
1 tablespoon salt
1 teaspoon Worcestershire sauce
1 teaspoon lemon juice
½ teaspoon pepper
½ teaspoon monosodium glutamate
2 bay leaves
Few grains cloves
Cover saucepot and bring liquid rapidly to boiling. Reduce heat; simmer (do not boil) about 1½ hrs.

Meanwhile, clean
12 small onions
Wash, scrape and cut into pieces
8 medium carrots
When meat has cooked 1½ hrs., put prepared vegetables into saucepot. Cover and simmer 30 to 45 min. longer, or until meat and vegetables are tender when pierced with fork

Force through sieve or food mill contents of
1 can (16 oz.) tomatoes
With slotted spoon, remove meat and vegetables from saucepot to hot serving dish.

Blend the sieved tomatoes into the cooking liquid. To thicken liquid, put into a 1-pt. screw-top jar, cover tightly and shake until blended
½ cup cold water
¼ cup all-purpose flour
Slowly pour one half of mixture into cooking liquid while stirring constantly. Bring to boiling. Gradually add only what is needed of remaining flour-water mixture for consistency desired. Bring to boiling after each addition. After final addition, cook 3 to 5 min. longer. Return meat and vegetables to saucepot and add
¼ cup chopped green pepper
Heat stew thoroughly. *8 to 10 servings*

BEEF AND POLENTA PIE

Lightly grease a 2-qt. casserole. Set out a double boiler and a large heavy skillet with a tight-fitting cover.

Set out
1½ lbs. beef for stewing (chuck, round or brisket)
Cut into 1-in. pieces. Coat meat evenly by shaking several pieces at a time in a plastic bag containing a mixture of
⅓ cup all-purpose flour
1 teaspoon salt
⅛ teaspoon pepper
Set pieces aside.

Heat in the skillet over low heat
3 tablespoons fat
Put beef pieces into the skillet with
½ cup (1 medium) chopped onion
1 clove garlic, minced
Cook over medium heat until meat is browned, occasionally moving and turning mixture with a spoon. Drain off excess fat.

Mix and pour slowly into the skillet
1¼ cups (10¾-oz. can) condensed tomato soup
1 cup hot water
2 teaspoons chili powder
2 drops Tabasco
Cover skillet tightly and bring mixture to boiling over high heat. Reduce heat and simmer (do not boil) 1 to 1½ hrs., or until meat is tender when pierced with a fork.

Meanwhile, mix
1 cup yellow corn meal
1 teaspoon salt
Mix in thoroughly
1 cup cold milk
Set mixture aside.

Prepare in top of the double boiler
3 cups quick meat broth (page 10)
Bring rapidly to boiling over direct heat. Reduce heat to medium and add the corn meal mixture gradually, stirring constantly. Con-

tinue cooking, stirring occasionally, until mixture is thickened. Place over simmering water. Cover; continue cooking about 30 min., stirring occasionally. Remove double boiler from heat and set corn meal mixture aside to cool. Drain and set aside.
1 can (16 oz.) kidney beans (about 1½ cups, drained)
When meat is tender, mix in the kidney beans.

If necessary to thicken liquid, put into a 1-pt. screw-top jar
½ cup water
Sprinkle evenly onto it
¼ cup all-purpose flour
Cover jar tightly; shake until flour and water are well blended. Slowly pour one half of the mixture into the skillet, stirring constantly.

Bring to boiling. Gradually add only what is needed of remaining mixture for consistency desired; bring to boiling after each addition. After final addition, cook 3 to 5 min. longer.

Turn cooled corn meal mixture into the prepared casserole and spread evenly in a 1-in. layer over bottom and around sides. Spoon meat mixture into the casserole.

Bake at 350°F 30 min. *6 to 8 servings*

Beef and Polenta Pie

and pour in
2 cups hot water
Add the sliced onion. Cover tightly and bring water to boiling over high heat. Reduce heat and simmer (do not boil) about 1½ hrs., or until meat is almost tender (at which time vegetables should be added). Add hot water as necessary.

Before time to add vegetables to ribs, wash and cut off stem ends from
½ lb. green beans

SHORT RIBS OF BEEF WITH VEGETABLES

▲ *Base Recipe*

Set out a large heavy kettle or saucepot with a tight-fitting cover, or use a Dutch oven.

Have ready
3 lbs. beef short ribs
Cut into serving-size pieces. Coat meat evenly with a mixture of
⅓ cup all-purpose flour
2 teaspoons salt
1 teaspoon monosodium glutamate
⅛ teaspoon pepper
Heat in the kettle over medium heat
⅓ cup fat
Add the meat pieces and brown on all sides over medium heat.

While meat is browning, thinly slice and set aside
1 medium onion

When meat is brown, remove kettle from heat

Set beans aside.

Wash, pare, and cut into halves
6 medium (about 2 lbs.) potatoes
Add prepared vegetables to kettle with
1 teaspoon salt
⅛ teaspoon pepper
Cover kettle and continue to simmer.

Meanwhile, clean
12 stalks celery
Cut crosswise into 3-in. pieces and put into kettle. Cover and simmer about 35 min., or until meat and vegetables are tender when pierced with a fork. With a slotted spoon, remove meat and vegetables from kettle to hot serving platter; keep warm. Thicken cooking liquid for gravy; use **¼ cup water** and **2 tablespoons all-purpose flour.** *6 servings*

—SPICY SHORT RIBS OF BEEF WITH FRUIT

Follow ▲ Recipe. Omit vegetables. When ribs

have simmered 1 hr., add **1 cup (about 5 oz.) dried apricots** and **1 cup (about 5 oz.) pitted prunes.** Remove about 1 cup cooking liquid. Blend into liquid a mixture of ½ cup sugar, ½ teaspoon cinnamon, ½ teaspoon allspice and ¼ teaspoon ground cloves. Blend in **3 tablespoons vinegar.** Pour mixture over ribs. Continue to simmer 30 min., or until meat and fruit are tender. Serve with cooking liquid.

BEEF ITALIANO

Thinly slice enough cooked beef to yield
    8 slices cooked beef, cut about ⅛ in. thick

Mix
    ⅓ cup fine dry bread crumbs (about 1 slice bread)
    ¼ cup (about 1 oz.) grated Parmesan cheese

Mix in a bowl
    1 egg, well beaten
    2 tablespoons milk
    1 teaspoon salt
    1 teaspoon dry mustard
    ½ teaspoon monosodium glutamate
    ⅛ teaspoon pepper

Heat in a skillet
    ¼ cup shortening
Dip beef slices (coat both sides) in the egg mixture. Allow excess egg mixture to drain back into bowl. Dip in crumb mixture, coating both sides. Dip only as many slices at one time as will lie flat in skillet. Put into skillet and brown over low heat. Turn and brown other side. Repeat procedure for remaining slices. If necessary, add more shortening to skillet to prevent meat from sticking.

Return all slices to skillet. Arrange over the meat
    8 slices (8 oz.) pasteurized process American cheese
Spoon over cheese
    1 can (6 oz.) tomato paste
Cover and cook over low heat about 15 min.
        4 servings

BEEF IN LEMON SAUCE

Give a transforming lift to leftover beef with a lemony sour cream sauce.

Set out a small saucepan and a 10-in. skillet with a tight-fitting cover.

Cut into ½-in. cubes and set aside enough cooked beef to yield
    3 cups cooked beef cubes

Prepare and set aside to cool to lukewarm
    ½ cup quick meat broth (page 10)

Dice and put into the cold skillet
    4 slices bacon
Cook slowly, frequently moving and turning pieces with a spoon until bacon is lightly browned. Remove bacon with slotted spoon and set aside. Add the beef to the bacon drippings in the skillet. Cover skillet and cook over low heat 7 to 10 min., or until meat is thoroughly heated.

Meanwhile, heat in the saucepan
    1 tablespoon fat
Blend in
    1 tablespoon all-purpose flour
Heat until mixture bubbles, stirring constantly. Remove from heat and gradually add the reserved broth, stirring constantly. Return to heat and bring rapidly to boiling, stirring constantly; cook 1 to 2 min. longer.

Remove saucepan from heat. Stirring vigorously with a French whip, whisk beater or fork, add to contents of saucepan in very small amounts
    1 cup dairy sour cream
Blend into sauce
    1 teaspoon grated lemon peel
    1 tablespoon lemon juice
    ½ teaspoon sugar
Pour sauce over the meat. Return bacon to skillet. Place the mixture over low heat, keeping it moving with a spoon, until thoroughly heated, 3 to 5 min.; do not boil.

Serve hot.   *About 4 servings*

CORNED BEEF HASH WITH TOMATO

  ▲ *Base Recipe*

Grease a 1½-qt. casserole.

Cook (page 312) and dice enough potatoes to yield
    1½ cups diced cooked potatoes
Set aside.

Dice finely or chop enough cooked corned beef to yield
    2½ cups finely diced or chopped cooked corned beef
Mix lightly with potatoes and set aside.

Melt in a large skillet
    3 tablespoons butter or margarine
Add and cook slowly until onion is tender, stirring frequently
    ¼ cup finely chopped onion
    2 tablespoons finely chopped green pepper

Using a fork, stir into potato-corned beef mixture the onion, green pepper and a mixture of
    ⅓ cup milk
    1 teaspoon salt
    ½ teaspoon monosodium glutamate
    ¼ teaspoon pepper
Spoon mixture lightly into casserole.

Wash and cut into ½-in. slices
    2 medium (about ½ lb.) tomatoes
Spread one side of each slice with
    Prepared mustard
Arrange slices on top of hash, mustard-side down; sprinkle with
    ½ cup buttered crumbs (page 9)
    ¼ teaspoon garlic salt

Bake at 350°F 30 to 35 min., or until crumbs are lightly browned.   *4 or 5 servings*

—CORNED BEEF HASH WITH POACHED EGGS

Follow ▲ Recipe. Use 4 large or 6 small ramekins. Omit tomatoes. Spoon hash into ramekins; hollow centers slightly. Heat in 350°F oven while poaching eggs.

For Poached Eggs—Add water to shallow pan or heavy skillet to depth of 2 in., or enough to rise 1 in. above tops of eggs. Heat water to boiling; reduce heat to allow for constant simmering. Break into a saucer and slip into water, one at a time (tilt saucer toward edge of pan), **4 (or 6) eggs.** Cook 3 to 5 min., depending upon firmness desired. Carefully remove with slotted spoon or pancake turner; hold spoon on absorbent paper a few seconds to drain before placing egg in hallowed center of hash. Season each egg with **salt** and **1 or 2 drops Tabasco.**

—TURKEY HASH

Follow ▲ Recipe. Substitute **cooked turkey for** corned beef. Heat **½ cup (4-oz. can, drained) mushrooms** with onion. Substitute **quick chicken broth** (page 10) or thinned leftover turkey gravy for milk. Omit mustard. Sprinkle tomato slices with **grated sharp Cheddar cheese.** Complete as in ▲ Recipe or variation.

NEW ENGLAND "BOILED" DINNER

  ▲ *Base Recipe*

This favorite old recipe of New England families has been handed down from generation to generation. Actually, it is misnamed because the meat should never be boiled, but simmered slowly to juicy tenderness.

Set out a large saucepot, Dutch oven or kettle with a tight-fitting cover.

Have ready
    4- to 6-lb. solid piece of corned beef
Put meat into the saucepot and cover with
    Water

Cover saucepot tightly and bring water just to boiling over high heat. Reduce heat and simmer (do not boil) 3 to 5 hrs. (allow 40 to 50 min. per pound), or until meat is tender.

About an hour before meat is tender, prepare beets. Leave on 1- to 2-in. stem and the root end (this helps beets to retain red color) and cut leaves from

6 medium (about 1 lb.) beets

Scrub beets thoroughly. Cook covered in boiling salted water to cover 30 to 45 min., or until beets are just tender.

While beets are cooking, wash and scrape or pare

6 medium (about 1½ lbs.) carrots

Clean

6 small onions

Wash and pare

6 medium (about 2 lbs.) potatoes
3 medium turnips

Skim off any excess fat from cooking water in saucepot. Put the potatoes, turnips, onions and carrots into the saucepot with meat. Cover and continue to simmer.

When vegetables have cooked about 20 min., remove outer wilted leaves and any blemishes from

1 small head cabbage

Wash thoroughly and cut from top to bottom into wedges. Remove core and heavy ribs of outer leaves. Put cabbage into saucepot about 8 to 12 min. before end of cooking period. Cook, loosely covered, just until tender.

When the beets are tender, drain, peel off and discard skins, stems and root ends. Add to beets

2 tablespoons butter

Keep beets warm while arranging meat platter.

When vegetables and meat are tender, remove the meat from cooking liquid and place on a warm large platter. Surround with the vegetables. Sprinkle **chopped parsley** over potatoes. Serve immediately.   *6 to 8 servings*

—RED FLANNEL HASH

The thrifty New England homemaker prepares hash from meat and vegetables left over from New England "Boiled" Dinner.

Use ingredients saved over from ▲ Recipe or prepare meat and vegetables. Set out a large heavy skillet. Combine **3 cups finely chopped cooked potatoes, 1 cup finely chopped cooked beets, 1 cup finely chopped cooked corned beef** and **⅓ cup finely chopped onion.** Lightly toss chopped vegetables and meat together. Blend in **1 teaspoon Worcestershire sauce, 1 teaspoon salt, ⅛ teaspoon pepper** and about **6 tablespoons milk or cream** (enough to hold mixture together). Heat **¼ cup butter** in the skillet. Add the hash mixture, pressing into an even layer. Cook over low heat until a brown crust is formed on bottom. Loosen edges and bottom of hash; shake

skillet back and forth occasionally to prevent burning while hash is browning. When hash is done, lightly fold in half and serve.

—CORNED BEEF HASH

Follow recipe for Red Flannel Hash. Omit the beets. Increase corned beef to 2 cups.

OXTAIL STEW
(Ochsenschwanz-Eintopf)

Set out a 3-qt. top-of-range casserole with a tight-fitting cover.

Have ready

3 oxtails (about 1 lb. each), disjointed

Coat pieces evenly by shaking 2 or 3 at a time in a plastic bag containing a mixture of

½ cup all-purpose flour
1 teaspoon salt
1 teaspoon monosodium glutamate
¼ teaspoon pepper

Prepare

1½ cups (about 3 medium) chopped onion

Heat in the casserole over low heat

3 tablespoons butter

Add the onion and cook over medium heat until almost tender, occasionally moving and turning with a spoon. Remove onion with a slotted spoon and set aside. Put meat into casserole and brown on all sides.

Meanwhile, drain, reserving liquid

1 can (28 oz.) tomatoes

Cut tomatoes into pieces; set aside.

Return onion to casserole. Add the reserved tomato liquid and

1½ cups hot water

Cover tightly and simmer 2½ to 3 hrs., until meat is nearly tender when pierced with a fork.

When meat has cooked 2 hrs., wash and pare

4 medium (about 1½ lbs.) potatoes

Rinse and pare or scrape

6 medium carrots

Using a ball-shaped cutter, cut the potatoes and carrots into small balls.

Rinse and shell

2 lbs. fresh peas

When meat is almost tender, add the potato and carrot balls, peas, and a mixture of

1 tablespoon paprika
1 teaspoon salt
¼ teaspoon pepper

Cover and simmer 20 min. longer, or until vegetables are nearly tender. Add the tomatoes and cook 10 min. longer, or until meat and vegetables are tender. Remove meat and vegetables to a warm dish.

Pour into a screw-top jar

¼ cup water

Sprinkle onto the liquid

2 tablespoons all-purpose flour

Cover jar tightly and shake until mixture is well blended. Slowly pour half of the mixture into cooking liquid, stirring constantly. Bring to boiling. Gradually add only what is needed of remaining flour mixture for consistency desired. Bring to boiling after each addition. After final addition, cook 3 to 5 min. longer. Return meat and vegetables to casserole and heat thoroughly.   *6 to 8 servings*

New England "Boiled" Dinner

PORK

ROAST LOIN OF PORK WITH PRUNES
(Fläskkarre)

Set out a roasting pan with a rack.

Have ready
  3-lb. pork loin roast
Rub meat with a mixture of
  1 teaspoon salt
  ½ teaspoon monosodium glutamate
  ¼ teaspoon pepper
Place pork roast on rack in roasting pan. Insert meat thermometer in top center of pork loin, being sure that bulb rests in center of the loin and not on bone or in fat.

Roast pork uncovered at 325°F until internal temperature reaches 170°F. The total roasting time should be 1½ to 1¾ hrs. Allow 30 to 35 min. per pound.

Meanwhile, bring to boiling in a large saucepan
  2 cups water
Add
  1½ cups (about 9 oz.) dried prunes
Cover and simmer about 15 min., or until prunes are partially tender. Drain prunes and cut into halves. Remove and discard pits.

About ½ hr. before roast is done, arrange prunes around pork loin. Continue roasting for ½ hr.

Remove pork loin from oven; cool completely. Remove thermometer from meat.

When ready to serve, slice the meat and arrange on a serving platter. Garnish with the prunes and
  Apple slices

8 to 10 servings

PORK TENDERLOIN STUFFED WITH PRUNES
(Morbra)

  ▲ *Base Recipe*

Set out a large heavy skillet with a tight-fitting cover.

For Meat—Set out
  1½ lbs. pork tenderloin, in one piece
Trim off any excess fat. Using a sharp knife cut meat lengthwise about two-thirds through.

Set out
  12 (about 3 oz.) dried prunes
Using a sharp knife, remove pits from prunes. Arrange the prunes in the pork tenderloin and fasten with skewers.

Heat in the skillet
  2 to 3 tablespoons butter
Add the pork tenderloin and cook slowly, turning to brown all sides evenly. When meat is browned, sprinkle over
  1 teaspoon salt
Cover and cook slowly about 1½ hrs., or until meat is tender when pierced with a fork. During cooking, add a small amount of
  Water
When meat is tender, remove to a heated platter and carefully remove skewers.

For Gravy—Leaving brown residue in pan, pour into a bowl
  Drippings
Allow fat to rise to surface; skim off fat and reserve. Remaining drippings are meat juices which should be used as part of the liquid in making gravy.

Measure into roasting pan
  3 tablespoons fat
Blend in until smooth
  3 tablespoons all-purpose flour
  ¼ teaspoon salt
  ⅛ teaspoon pepper
Stirring constantly, heat until mixture bubbles. Remove from heat and slowly blend in, stirring constantly and vigorously
  1½ cups milk
  ½ cup drippings
Return to heat and bring to boiling, stirring constantly. Cook 1 to 2 min. While stirring, scrape bottom and sides of pan to blend in brown residue.

Serve gravy with the meat. *4 servings*

—PORK TENDERLOIN STUFFED WITH PARSLEY
(Morbra med Persille)

Follow ▲ Recipe. Omit prunes. Rinse and remove stems from **about 1 cup parsley.** Stuff meat with the parsley.

RICE AND PORK STEAK CASSEROLE

Grease a 2-qt. casserole with a tight-fitting cover.

Set out
  4 pork steaks (arm or blade), cut about ½ in. thick, and each steak cut in 3 pieces
Brown meat in a large heavy skillet. Maintain a medium temperature which allows juices to evaporate rather than collect in pan. With too low heat, meat will simmer in its own juices and become dry and less tender. Turn meat occasionally for even browning. Pour off fat as it collects.

For each pound of meat, mix
  1 teaspoon salt
  ½ teaspoon monosodium glutamate
  ¼ teaspoon pepper
When meat is lightly browned on one side, turn and sprinkle half of seasoning mixture over tops. Brown other side. Remove meat from skillet; sprinkle with remaining seasoning mixture; set aside in warm place.

Heat in same skillet
  3 tablespoons meat drippings, butter or margarine
Add to skillet
  1 cup uncooked rice
  ¾ cup (about 1 large) thinly sliced onion
  1 cup (8-oz. can, drained) mushrooms, sliced
  ¼ cup chopped green pepper
  2 whole cloves
  1 bay leaf
Cook over medium heat, stirring constantly, until rice is lightly browned. Remove and discard bay leaf and cloves. Stir in
  2½ cups canned tomatoes, cut in pieces
  1½ cups boiling water
  2 teaspoons sugar
  1 teaspoon salt
  ¼ teaspoon monosodium glutamate
  ¼ teaspoon pepper
Pour into casserole. Cover with pork pieces; press down slightly.

Cover casserole and cook in a 350°F oven 50 to 60 min., or until rice is tender when a kernel is pressed between fingers, and meat shows no pink color when cut near bone. Uncover last 10 min. of baking. *6 servings*

BUTTERFLY PORK CHOPS

▲ *Base Recipe*

Heat in a large heavy skillet
1 tablespoon lard

Have ready
6 butterfly pork chops, cut ¾ to 1 in. thick
Rub pork chops with the cut surfaces of
1 garlic clove, cut in half
Place chops in the skillet and brown on both sides. Pour off drippings.

For each pound of meat mix together and sprinkle over chops
1 teaspoon salt
⅛ teaspoon pepper
Add to skillet
¼ cup water
Cover tightly and simmer 45 to 60 min., or until meat is tender and well done. *6 servings*

—SPANISH-STYLE PORK CHOPS

Follow ▲ Recipe. Substitute **¼ cup tomato juice** for water. Add **¼ teaspoon crushed oregano**, **2 tablespoons minced onion** and **¼ cup minced green pepper** with the tomato juice. Spoon sauce over meat before serving.

—BARBECUED PORK CHOPS

Follow ▲ Recipe. Marinate chops overnight in **Wine Barbecue Sauce** (page 310). Substitute marinade for water. Spoon sauce over meat before serving.

—CELERY PORK CHOPS

Follow ▲ Recipe. Substitute **rib or loin chops** for butterfly chops. Add **¾ cup chopped celery** and **2 tablespoons chopped onion**. Spoon sauce over meat before serving.

NEAPOLITAN PORK CHOPS
(Costatelle di Maiale alla Napoletana)

Heat in large heavy skillet with a tight-fitting cover
2 tablespoons olive oil
Add and cook until lightly browned
1 clove garlic, minced

Meanwhile, set out
6 pork rib or loin chops, cut about ¾ to 1 in. thick
Season with a mixture of
1 teaspoon salt
½ teaspoon monosodium glutamate
¼ teaspoon pepper

Place in skillet, and slowly brown chops on both sides.

While chops brown, clean and slice (page 9)
1 lb. mushrooms
Set aside.

Clean and chop
2 green peppers

When chops are browned, add the mushrooms and peppers. Stir in slowly a mixture of
½ cup canned tomatoes, sieved
3 tablespoons dry white wine
Cover skillet and cook over low heat 1 to 1½ hrs., depending on thickness of chops. Add small amounts of water as needed. Test the chops for tenderness by piercing with a fork.
6 servings

BRAISED PORK CHOPS (BREADED)

▲ *Base Recipe*

Set out a large heavy skillet with a tight-fitting cover.

Set out
4 pork chops (loin, rib or blade), cut about ¾ to 1 in. thick
Coat chops with a mixture of
½ cup sifted all-purpose flour
1 teaspoon salt
½ teaspoon monosodium glutamate
¼ teaspoon pepper

Heat in the skillet
2 tablespoons fat

Meanwhile, dip the chops in a mixture of
1 egg, slightly beaten
2 tablespoons milk or water
Coat the chops with
1 cup fine dry bread or cracker crumbs
Place chops in skillet and brown on both sides. Remove from heat and pour off remaining fat. Slowly add to skillet
½ cup tomato juice or water
Cover skillet and cook over low heat 1 to 1½ hrs., depending on thickness of chops. Add small amounts of liquid as needed.

Pork always should be cooked until well done and meat is gray in color. Test for doneness by cutting near bone. *4 servings*

—BRAISED PORK CHOPS

Follow ▲ Recipe. Omit dipping in egg mixture and coating with crumbs.

—BRAISED VEAL CHOPS (BREADED)

Follow ▲ Recipe. Substitute **veal chops or cutlets** for pork. Serve meat with a Tomato Sauce—Melt **2 tablespoons butter or margarine**. Blend in **2 tablespoons all-purpose flour** and cook until mixture bubbles. Remove from heat and gradually stir in **1 cup tomato juice** heated with **⅓ cup chopped onion**, **½ teaspoon salt**, **⅛ teaspoon pepper** and **a few**

Butterfly Pork Chops

grains cayenne pepper. Return to heat and cook sauce rapidly until thickened, stirring constantly. Cook 1 to 2 min.

STUFFED PORK CHOPS

Try serving these flavorful stuffed chops with a spicy barbecue sauce—delicious! And remember that like all good foods, these are enhanced by steaming cups of dark, fragrant coffee.

Set out a large shallow baking dish and aluminum foil to cover.

Set out
8 pork chops, cut 1 to 1¼ in. thick (Have meat dealer cut a pocket for stuffing.)

Wash, quarter, core, pare and dice
1 medium apple (about 1 cup, diced)
Sprinkle with
2 teaspoons lemon juice
Mix with
2 cups (about 2 slices) soft bread crumbs
and a mixture of
1 teaspoon salt
1 teaspoon celery seed
¼ teaspoon monosodium glutamate
⅛ teaspoon pepper
Set aside.

Stuffed Pork Chops

Heat in a saucepan over low heat

¼ cup butter or margarine

Add and cook over medium heat, occasionally moving with a spoon

½ cup (about 1 medium) chopped onion

Turn contents of saucepan into apple and bread crumb mixture. Toss lightly with

¼ cup apple cider (use only enough to barely moisten bread)

Fill pocket of each chop with stuffing.

Heat in a large heavy skillet over medium heat

2 teaspoons fat

Place chops in skillet and brown on both sides. Remove chops to baking dish.

Cover dish with aluminum foil and cook in a 350°F oven 1 hr., or until pork is tender and *thoroughly* cooked. To test for doneness, cut a slit near bone; no pink color should be visible.

8 servings

PORK CHOP CASSEROLE

Grease a shallow 2-qt. casserole with a tight-fitting cover.

Set out

6 pork rib or loin chops, cut ¾ to 1 in. thick

Coat with a mixture of

½ cup all-purpose flour
1 teaspoon salt
½ teaspoon monosodium glutamate
¼ teaspoon pepper

Brown pork chops on both sides in a lightly greased heavy skillet.

While chops brown, set out a mixture of

½ cup firmly packed brown sugar
1 teaspoon salt

Wash, pare and cut into ⅛-in. slices

4 medium (about 1⅓ lbs.) sweet potatoes

Wash, quarter, core, pare and cut into ½-in. slices

3 medium (about 1 lb.) tart apples (about 3 cups, sliced)

Arrange browned chops in casserole. Arrange one half of potatoes in a layer over pork chops. Sprinkle with part of brown sugar mixture. Top with one half of apples and sprinkle again with sugar. Repeat layers. Pour over

½ cup apple cider or apple juice

Cover casserole and cook in a 350°F oven 1 to

1½ hrs., depending upon thickness of pork chops. Remove cover for last 15 min. of cooking. Test for doneness by cutting near bone of pork chops. No pink color should be visible.

6 servings

PORK CHOP DINNER
(Schweinekotletten und Würstchen mit Äpfeln und Zwiebeln)

Set out a 3-qt. saucepan and 2 large skillets, each with a tight-fitting cover.

Have ready

6 pork chops, cut about 1 in. thick

Heat in one of the skillets over medium heat

1 teaspoon fat

Put chops into skillet and brown lightly on both sides. Season chops with a mixture of

¼ teaspoon monosodium glutamate
¼ teaspoon salt
Few grains pepper

Add

½ cup hot water

Cover and cook over low heat about 1 hr., or until meat is tender.

Meanwhile, clean and slice

2 medium (about ½ lb.) onions

Wash, pare and cut into cubes

6 medium (about 2 lbs.) potatoes

Wash, quarter, core, pare and cut into cubes

4 large (about 1½ lbs.) tart apples

Put the onions, potatoes and apples into the saucepan; add

2½ cups (2 10½-oz. cans) condensed beef consommé
1 teaspoon monosodium glutamate
¾ teaspoon salt
Few grains pepper

Cover and cook 30 to 35 min.

Put into the second skillet

12 (about ¾ lb.) link sausages

Add

2 tablespoons water

Cover and cook slowly 8 to 10 min. Remove cover and pour off fat. Brown links over medium heat, turning as necessary (do not pierce links with fork). Remove links to absorbent paper to drain.

When potatoes are tender, drain off consommé. Spoon potato mixture onto center of heated serving platter. Arrange pork chops and link sausages around potatoes. Serve hot.

6 servings

SWEET-SOUR PORK CHOPS

Set out a large shallow baking dish or a 2-qt. casserole with a tight-fitting cover.

Have ready

4 pork chops, cut about 1 in. thick

Coat chops with a mixture of

¼ cup all-purpose flour
½ teaspoon salt
½ teaspoon monosodium glutamate
¼ teaspoon pepper

Pork Chop Dinner

Heat in a large heavy skillet

1 teaspoon fat

Put chops into skillet and brown on both sides over medium heat. Remove to baking dish. Pour over the chops a mixture of

⅓ cup water
2 tablespoons cider vinegar
1½ teaspoons sugar

Add

1 bay leaf

Cover and cook in a 350°F oven about 1 hr., or until chops are tender and thoroughly cooked. To test for doneness, cut a slit near the bone; no pink color should be visible. Remove dish from oven. Spread over chops

¾ cup dairy sour cream

Cover and cook about 15 min. longer.

Serve at once.   *4 servings*

PINEAPPLE PORK

About 20 min. before ready to deep-fry, put **fat** into a deep saucepan or an automatic deep-fryer and heat to 360°F (page 11).

Set out

3 lbs. boneless pork shoulder

Cut meat into ¾-in. cubes and set aside.

Set aside to drain, reserving syrup

1 can (20 oz.) pineapple chunks (about 2 cups, drained)

Prepare and set aside

4 cups (about 8 medium) chopped green pepper
1⅓ cups (about 2 large) chopped onion
2½ cups quick chicken broth (page 10)

Mix

1⅓ cups all-purpose flour
4 teaspoons salt
2 teaspoons monosodium glutamate

Beat slightly

3 eggs

Coat pork with flour mixture, then dip in the egg mixture and again coat with flour mixture.

Deep-fry only as many pieces as will float uncrowded one layer deep in fat. Fry until browned and thoroughly cooked, about 3 min.; with a slotted spoon, turn several times during cooking. Remove with slotted spoon and drain over fat for a few seconds before removing to absorbent paper. Set aside to keep warm.

Mix in a skillet

½ cup sugar

4 teaspoons cornstarch

Add the pineapple syrup and chicken broth gradually, stirring constantly. Mix in

2 tablespoons ketchup

4 teaspoons soy sauce

Bring to boiling and cook rapidly 3 min., or until slightly thickened, stirring constantly. Add the green pepper, onion and pineapple chunks; cover and cook 4 min. Add the pork and heat thoroughly.

Serve immediately in a warm serving dish.

About 8 servings

SZEKELY GOULASH
(Székely Gulyás)

Fare fit for a banquet—chunks of pork in creamy delectable kraut.

Set out a 4-qt. saucepot or a Dutch oven with a tight-fitting cover.

Put onto wooden board and cut into 1½-in. cubes

1½ lbs. lean leg of pork or pork shoulder

To coat meat evenly, shake cubes in a plastic bag containing a mixture of

2 tablespoons all-purpose flour

2 teaspoons paprika

1½ teaspoons salt

Set aside.

Cook in the saucepot over medium heat, stirring occasionally, until onion is soft

2 tablespoons fat

2 tablespoons finely chopped onion

Add contents of plastic bag to saucepot; brown meat on all sides, turning occasionally. Add

2 or 3 tablespoons hot water

Cover saucepot and simmer 1 hr., stirring occasionally; add small amounts of water as needed.

Shortly before end of one-hour cooking period, drain

1 can (27 oz.) sauerkraut (about 3½ cups, firmly packed)

If desired, rinse sauerkraut in cold water, so that the goulash will have a milder flavor; drain again. Mix sauerkraut with the meat; add

2 cups hot water

Bring to boiling; cover and simmer ½ hr. longer, or until meat is tender when pierced with a fork. Remove saucepot from heat. Gradually blend about 1½ cups cooking liquid into

1½ cups dairy sour cream

Blend into hot mixture. Stirring constantly, cook over low heat, 3 to 5 min., until heated

thoroughly; do not boil. Serve in small bowls.

6 to 8 servings

CHINATOWN CHOP SUEY

Heat in a Dutch oven or large heavy skillet with a tight-fitting cover

3 to 4 tablespoons fat

Cut into strips, combine and brown in the fat

1¼ lbs. pork

1 lb. beef

¾ lb. veal

Use moderate heat and turn meat frequently to brown on all sides. Cover and cook 1 hr.

Meanwhile, blanch, toast (pages 9 and 10) and set aside

⅓ cup (about 2 oz.) almonds

Set aside to drain, reserving liquid

1 can (16 oz.) bean sprouts (about 2 cups, drained)

1 can (8 oz.) mushrooms (about 1 cup, drained)

Prepare

1 cup shredded cauliflower leaves

Remove outer leaves of cauliflower and cut narrow strips 3 to 4 in. long from thick stalk of leaf. Also cut strips of green leaf.

Prepare and combine with cauliflower leaves

1½ cups (about 2 large) coarsely chopped onion

3 cups (about 1 medium bunch) diced celery (cut celery crosswise into narrow pieces)

Add drained bean sprouts and mushrooms and stir in

1 cup mushroom and bean sprout liquid

Add vegetable mixture to meat, cover and cook 20 to 30 min. longer.

Meanwhile, blend

¼ cup cornstarch

1 teaspoon monosodium glutamate

¼ cup soy sauce

¼ cup molasses

¼ cup water

Thoroughly blend into meat mixture and cook about 15 min.

Serve chop suey on **hot fluffy rice** or **crisp noodles;** top with **almonds.**

10 to 12 servings

Note: If cauliflower leaves are not available, substitute sliced canned water chestnuts.

SPARERIBS AND SAUERKRAUT
(Rippchen mit Sauerkraut)

▲ *Base Recipe*

Set out a large saucepot or kettle with a tight-fitting cover.

Have ready

3 lbs. spareribs, cracked through center

Chinatown Chop Suey

Cut into serving-size pieces. Put spareribs into the saucepot with

Water to barely cover

½ teaspoon salt

Add

1 can (27 oz.) sauerkraut (about 3½ cups)

Cover and bring liquid rapidly to boiling. Reduce heat and simmer 1½ to 2 hrs., or until meat is tender. Drain slightly and remove to a heated platter. Serve spareribs with the sauerkraut and with

Boiled potatoes and Quick Pickled Beets (page 422)

About 6 servings

—SPARERIBS AND SAUERKRAUT WITH CARAWAY SEED

Follow ▲ Recipe. Add and mix in with the sauerkraut before cooking **1 teaspoon caraway seed.**

ORIENTAL BARBECUED SPARERIBS

▲ *Base Recipe*

Set out a large saucepot or kettle.

To Cook Spareribs—Set out

4 lbs. spareribs, cracked through center

Cut into serving-size pieces and put into the saucepot. Add

Water to cover

189

Cover and bring to boiling; reduce heat and simmer the meat about 1 hr. Meanwhile, prepare the sauce.

To Prepare Sauce—Put into a bowl in order, mixing after each addition

- **2 tablespoons cornstarch**
- **⅔ cup firmly packed light brown sugar**
- **⅔ cup soy sauce**
- **¼ cup cider vinegar**
- **6 tablespoons finely chopped crystallized ginger**
- **2 cloves garlic, minced**

To Barbecue Spareribs—Drain spareribs. Dip each piece into the sauce to coat thoroughly.

Place pieces on broiler rack. Put rack under broiler with tops of ribs about 3 in. from heat. Broil about 5 min., or until richly browned, brushing two or three times with sauce. Turn ribs and brush with remaining sauce. Broil second side until richly browned, about 3 min., brushing once or twice with sauce.

Arrange ribs on serving platter. Accompany with hot fluffy **rice.**   *6 to 8 servings*

—BARBECUED SPARERIBS WITH PINEAPPLE

Follow ▲ Recipe. Substitute **honey** for brown sugar; omit cornstarch. Add **½ cup orange juice**, **1 lemon**, thinly sliced, and **1 can (8¼ oz.) crushed pineapple** (about 1 cup) to the sauce, and mix well. Add the drained, cooked spareribs to the sauce and marinate (page 10) ½ hour before broiling.

BARBECUED SPARERIBS

A shallow roasting pan will be needed.

Set out

- **4 lbs. spareribs, cracked through center**

Cut into serving-size pieces. Put ribs into the roasting pan, meaty side up.

Mix

- **¾ cup soy sauce**
- **¼ cup sugar**
- **¼ cup thick sweetened applesauce**
- **1 teaspoon salt**
- **4 cloves garlic, minced**

Pour soy sauce mixture over ribs. Cover and set in refrigerator for several hours, basting occasionally.

Basting occasionally with the sauce, roast at 350°F about 1½ hrs., or until meat is tender and thoroughly cooked.   *8 servings*

BRAISED SPICY SPARERIBS (Gewürzte Schweinsrippchen)

Set out a heavy skillet and a roasting pan with a tight-fitting cover.

For Ribs—Have ready

- **2 sections (about 4 lbs.) spareribs, cracked through center**

Cut into serving-size pieces. Coat meat evenly with a mixture of

- **⅓ cup all-purpose flour**
- **2 teaspoons salt**
- **¼ teaspoon pepper**

Melt in the heavy skillet

- **3 tablespoons fat**

Add ribs to fat and brown slowly on both sides.

While meat is browning, prepare

- **1½ cups quick meat broth (page 10)**

Mix into meat broth

- **¼ cup ketchup**
- **3 tablespoons Worcestershire sauce**
- **2 tablespoons vinegar**
- **½ teaspoon celery salt**
- **⅛ teaspoon cayenne pepper**
- **3 whole cloves**
- **3 whole allspice**
- **½ bay leaf**
- **½ clove garlic, minced**

Clean and finely chop

- **1 medium onion**

Put meat into the roasting pan. Pour broth mixture over browned ribs. Add chopped onion. Cover and put in 350°F oven for about 1½ hrs., or until ribs are tender.

With a slotted spoon, remove meat from pan to a warm serving platter. Set aside to keep warm while preparing sauce.

For Sauce—If necessary, skim excess fat from cooking liquid. Strain the liquid and pour into a small saucepan.

Put into a 1-pt. screw-top jar

- **¼ cup cold water**

Sprinkle onto it

- **2 tablespoons all-purpose flour**

Cover jar tightly and shake until mixture is well blended.

Bring liquid in saucepan to boiling; stirring constantly, slowly pour one half of the flour mixture into cooking liquid. Bring to boiling. Gradually add only what is needed of the remaining flour mixture for consistency desired.

Bring sauce to boiling after each addition. Cook 3 to 5 min.

Spoon or pour about one half of the hot sauce over spareribs on the platter. Serve remaining sauce in a gravy boat, if desired.
          4 to 6 servings

PANFRIED BACON

Place in a cold skillet

- **½ lb. bacon slices**

Cook slowly, over low heat, turning bacon frequently. If desired, spoon off fat as it collects. When bacon is evenly crisped and browned, remove from skillet and drain on absorbent paper.   *10 to 12 slices bacon*

TIPS ABOUT BACON COOKERY

Easy ways to cook bacon:

Panfry (above)

Bake—An especially convenient method to use when cooking a large quantity of bacon. Arrange slices on rack in shallow baking pan with fat edge of one strip overlapping lean of the next strip. Bake at 400°F 12 to 15 min. No turning of bacon or draining off of fat is necessary.

Broil—Place slices on rack of broiler pan. Place under broiler about 3 in. from heat and broil 2 to 2½ min. on each side, turning once. Use kitchen tongs to turn bacon as it cooks. *To make bacon curls*, cook strips of bacon until partially done but still soft and pliable. Insert tines of fork in one end of each strip and wind it around fork in the pan, using a second fork as a guide. Remove the fork and let bacon curl finish browning.

Cook a batch of bacon pieces at one time for future use in crisp salads or to garnish vegetable dishes. To prepare, use kitchen shears or a sharp knife to cut slices into 1-in. pieces. Cook in a skillet, turning occasionally. When pieces are brown and the drippings foam, remove pieces with slotted spoon and spread on absorbent paper to drain. Store in covered container in refrigerator.

When ready to use, reheat amount of bacon needed at one time in a skillet over direct heat (1 or 2 min.) or under broiler heat until the pieces are crisp. One pound bacon slices makes about 1½ cups crisp pieces.

Allow bacon drippings to cool and settle before pouring them into a container for future use. Keep in refrigerator or freezer.

Suggested Uses for Bacon Drippings

Cocktail frankfurters—Heat **cocktail frankfurters** in a small amount of **bacon drippings.** Serve with dunking sauce. Combine in a chafing dish or skillet contents of **1 jar (6 oz.) currant jelly** and **2 tablespoons prepared mustard.** Heat and stir until jelly is melted.

Fondue oil—Heat one part **bacon drippings** with three parts **peanut oil** for deep-frying strips of **fresh pork or beef.**

Corn popping—Heat ¼ cup **bacon drippings**

in a large heavy skillet. When hot add **⅓ cup popcorn.** Cover skillet tightly and shake constantly over medium-high heat to make the corn pop vigorously. Sprinkle with **salt** and eat while hot.

Cereal topping (for cooked vegetables)—Combine **½ cup crushed cereal flakes, 1 tablespoon liquid bacon drippings** and **⅛ teaspoon salt.** Spoon over hot vegetables just before serving. If desired, substitute coarse cracker or bread crumbs for the cereal.

Baked potatoes—For flavorful, soft skins on baked potatoes, brush **bacon drippings** on **potatoes** before baking.

PANBROILED CANADIAN-STYLE BACON

▲ *Base Recipe*

Arrange in a cold skillet
  8 slices (⅔ lb.) Canadian-style bacon (each slice about ¼ in. thick)

Cook slowly, turning when one side is browned. Pour off any fat that collects during cooking.

Serve with **Fried Eggs** (page 138) fried in same skillet and apple rings.

For Glazed Apple Rings—Melt **¼ cup butter** and **¼ cup brown sugar** in another skillet over low heat. Add **4 apple rings** (½-in. each) and fry until rings are coated with syrup and tender. *4 servings*

—GRILLED SWEETBREADS AND CANADIAN-STYLE BACON

Since sweetbreads do not keep well, precook immediately when brought from market. Using **2 pairs lamb or veal sweetbreads,** cover with **cold water** containing **1 teaspoon salt** and **1 tablespoon vinegar** to 1 qt. water. Simmer covered 20 min. Drain and immediately cover with cold water. Drain again and remove membranes and tubes.

Follow ▲ Recipe for panbroiling Canadian-style bacon, browning one side only. Split pairs of sweetbreads crosswise (making 8 halves). With a sharp knife, shave through **4 slices drained pineapple,** cutting into 8 rings. Arrange 1 ring on each bacon slice and top with sweetbreads. Brush sweetbreads with melted **butter or margarine** and arrange on broiler rack. Place under broiler with top of meat 3 to 4 in. from heat; broil 3 to 5 min., or until sweetbreads are lightly browned.

GOURMET CANADIAN-STYLE BACON

▲ *Base Recipe*

Lightly grease 4 ramekins.

Separate into flowerets, clean and cook (page 313)
  1 large head cauliflower

Meanwhile, arrange in a cold skillet (brushed with melted fat)
  8 slices (about ⅔ lb.) Canadian-style bacon (each slice about ¼ in. thick)

Cook slowly, browning on each side. Pour off any fat that collects during cooking. Place 2 slices in each ramekin.

Shred and set aside
  8 oz. pasteurized process American cheese (2 cups, shredded)

Prepare
  2 cups Medium White Sauce (double recipe, page 304. Add three fourths of the shredded cheese all at one time and stir until blended. Add 1 tablespoon onion juice and ½ teaspoon paprika.)

Divide cauliflower evenly among ramekins. Cover each with about ½ cup sauce.

Set in a 350°F oven 10 min.

Sprinkle over ramekins remaining cheese and
  ½ cup buttered crumbs (page 9)
Return to oven and heat 10 min. longer.
4 servings

—FLOWERETS AND HAM

Follow ▲ Recipe. Omit Canadian-style bacon. Spoon **1½ cups ground cooked ham** around flowerets in ramekins before adding sauce.

GLAZED CANADIAN-STYLE BACON

▲ *Base Recipe*

Place on a rack in a shallow baking pan
  1½ lbs. Canadian-style bacon (in one piece)

Insert
  10 to 12 whole cloves
Cover surface with a mixture of
  ¼ cup firmly packed brown sugar
  1½ tablespoons dry mustard

Roast uncovered at 300°F 30 min.

Pour over meat
  ½ cup cider or apple juice
Basting occasionally, continue cooking 15 to 25 min. longer, or until tender. *6 servings*

—BAKED HAM SLICE

Follow ▲ Recipe. Substitute **1 ham slice,** ¾ to 1 in. thick, for Canadian-style bacon. Place ham in shallow baking dish without rack. Sprinkle ham slice with brown sugar mixture. Pour **cider or apple juice** over ham slice. Bake 1 hr., basting ham slice occasionally.

Broiled Canadian-Style Bacon

CRANBERRY GLAZED CANADIAN-STYLE BACON

▲ *Base Recipe*

Arrange in an 11x7x2-in. baking dish
  10 slices (about 1 lb.) Canadian-style bacon, cut about ¼ in. thick
Sprinkle slices with a mixture of
  1 tablespoon grated orange peel
  ½ teaspoon sugar
  ⅛ teaspoon cloves
  Dash nutmeg
Spread over bacon slices
  1 cup whole cranberry sauce

Bake uncovered at 350°F about 25 min.

Serve with sauce spooned over bacon slices.
5 servings

—BROILED CANADIAN-STYLE BACON

Follow ▲ Recipe for amount of Canadian-style bacon. Arrange bacon slices on broiler rack. Place in broiler with top of meat 3 in. from heat. Broil about 10 min., or until browned, turning slices once. Spoon about **½ cup whole cranberry sauce** into cavities of **5 canned peach halves** and place on broiler rack when bacon is turned. Arrange bacon around peaches on platter.

Note: Any jelly may be used to glaze Canadian-style bacon or to fill cavities of peaches.

PANBROILED BULK PORK SAUSAGE

Shape into 5 or 6 flat patties
  1 lb. bulk pork sausage
(Or place in skillet and break into pieces with fork.) Place in a cold skillet and add
  3 tablespoons cold water

191

Cover and cook slowly 5 min. Remove cover. Pour off fat. Brown, turning as necessary. Pour off fat as it collects. Cook 15 to 20 min., or until browned. Remove to absorbent paper to drain.

5 or 6 sausage patties

PANBROILED CHAURICE PATTIES

▲ *Base Recipe*

This is an adaptation of chaurice—the peppery sausage sold by meat dealers in southern Louisiana for hearty Creole breakfasts.

Set out a large heavy skillet.

Lightly mix in a bowl

1½ lbs. bulk pork sausage
½ cup (about 1 medium) minced onion
½ clove garlic, finely minced

and a mixture of

¼ teaspoon thyme
⅛ teaspoon allspice
⅛ teaspoon chili powder
½ bay leaf, crushed

Shape sausage mixture into 6 or 8 flat patties.

Place patties in the cold skillet. Add

¼ cup water

Cover and cook over medium heat 5 min. Remove cover; pour off liquid.

Continue cooking sausage patties, uncovered, over medium heat 15 to 20 min., or until brown. Turn as necessary to brown both sides evenly. Remove from skillet and drain on absorbent paper.

6 to 8 servings

—PANBROILED LINK SAUSAGE

Follow ▲ Recipe. Substitute **24 pork sausage links** (about 1½ lbs.) for bulk pork sausage. Omit onion, garlic and seasonings. Decrease water to 2 tablespoons. Keep skillet covered 8 to 10 min., cooking slowly. Proceed as in ▲ Recipe. Cook links only until brown, turning as necessary (do not prick links with a fork).

SAUSAGE SCALLOP

Set out a large heavy skillet.

Prepare and set aside

½ cup (about 2 stalks) chopped celery
2 tablespoons minced onion

Sausage Scallop

Put into cold skillet, breaking into pieces with fork or spoon

1 lb. bulk pork sausage

Add

3 tablespoons cold water

Cover and simmer 5 min. Remove cover; pour off water and fat. Add celery and onion. Cook over medium heat, moving and turning with a fork or spoon, until sausage is well browned. Pour off fat as it collects; reserve 2 tablespoons fat. Remove sausage and vegetables from skillet and set aside.

Return reserved fat to skillet. Blend in

3 tablespoons all-purpose flour
½ teaspoon monosodium glutamate
¼ teaspoon salt
¼ teaspoon paprika

Heat until mixture bubbles. Remove from heat. Add gradually, while stirring constantly

1½ cups milk

Return to heat and bring rapidly to boiling, stirring constantly. Cook 1 to 2 min. longer. Add sausage mixture and heat to boiling.

Serve in

Whipped Potato Ring (page 239)

Or serve over baked potatoes or hot toast.

4 to 6 servings

SAUSAGE, APPLE AND ONION BAKE

Grease a 2-qt. casserole with a tight-fitting cover.

Clean and cut into ¼-in. crosswise slices

3 medium (about ½ lb.) onions

Put into a saucepan and cover well with boiling water. Add

1 teaspoon salt
¼ teaspoon monosodium glutamate

Bring to boiling and boil 5 min. Drain and set aside.

Shape into small patties

1 lb. bulk pork sausage

Panbroil (page 191) until lightly browned.

Meanwhile, wash, cut into halves, core and cut into ¼-in. crosswise slices

3 medium (about 1 lb.) tart apples

Mix gently with onions. Arrange one half in bottom of casserole. Sprinkle with one half of a mixture of

⅓ cup firmly packed brown sugar
1 teaspoon salt
½ teaspoon nutmeg

Cover with remaining onions, apples and brown sugar mixture. Drizzle over apples and onions

2 tablespoons orange juice

Arrange panbroiled sausage patties on top of casserole.

Cover and cook in a 350°F oven 25 min. Uncover and bake 15 to 20 min. longer, or until apples are tender when pierced with a fork.

6 servings

SAVORY SAUSAGE CUTLETS

▲ *Base Recipe*

Set out a large heavy skillet and an 11x7x2-in. baking pan.

Prepare

1 cup Fluffy Rice (one third recipe, page 164)

Meanwhile, put into cold skillet

1 lb. bulk pork sausage

Cook over medium heat, breaking into pieces with fork or spoon. Pour off fat as it collects, reserving 4 tablespoons. When sausage is lightly browned, remove to absorbent paper and set aside.

Using reserved fat, prepare

1 cup Thick White Sauce (page 304)

Cool slightly.

Shred

1 oz. Cheddar cheese (about ¼ cup, shredded)

Add all at one time to white sauce and stir until cheese is melted and well blended. Mix into sauce the sausage, rice and

2 tablespoons minced parsley

Put into refrigerator to chill 1 to 2 hrs.

Divide chilled mixture into 6 portions. Put onto waxed paper. To form cutlets, pat each portion into a ½ in. thick round. Coat cutlets by dipping into

⅔ cup fine dry bread crumbs

Dip cutlets into a mixture of

1 egg, slightly beaten
2 tablespoons milk or water

Coat again in remaining bread crumbs. Put into baking dish.

Set in a 350°F oven 25 to 30 min., or until lightly browned. If desired, serve with

Apple Sour Cream Sauce (page 310)
or Mustard Sauce I (page 307)

6 servings

—CRANBERRY SAUSAGE CUTLETS

Follow ▲ Recipe. Pour **2 cups (16-oz. can) whole cranberry sauce** into bottom of baking pan. Arrange breaded cutlets over sauce and brown as in ▲ Recipe.

Standing Rib Roast of Beef, Cran‑
Ported Apples and Choux Paste Fr‑

ACORN SQUASH ENTREE

▲ Base Recipe

Set out a skillet with a cover and a shallow baking dish.

With a sharp heavy knife, split into crosswise halves
>**2 medium (about 1½ lbs. each) acorn squash**

Cut a thin slice from bottom of each half so that halves will stand upright. Remove seedy centers. Place squash, cavity-side down, in baking dish. Pour into baking dish
>**Boiling water to ¼-in. level**

Bake at 400°F 25 to 30 min.

Meanwhile, mix lightly and shape into 4 patties about ¾ in. thick
>**1 lb. bulk pork sausage**
>**⅔ cup fine dry bread crumbs**
>**½ cup undiluted evaporated milk**
>**1 egg, beaten**

Put patties into cold skillet; add
>**2 tablespoons water**

Cover skillet and cook slowly 5 min. Remove cover; pour off liquid. Lightly brown patties over medium heat, turning frequently to brown both sides, and pouring off fat as it collects. Remove patties to absorbent paper. Drain any remaining fat from skillet and wipe skillet with absorbent paper.

Blend in skillet
>**1 cup whole cranberry sauce**
>**¼ cup firmly packed brown sugar**
>**1 tablespoon vinegar**

Heat slowly, stirring to blend. Bring to boiling. Cook 2 to 3 min., stirring constantly.

Remove squash from oven; reduce temperature to 350°F. Turn squash cavity-side up. Brush inside of squash with part of cranberry mixture. Press a sausage patty into each squash half. Spoon a small amount of remaining cranberry mixture over each patty. Return to oven and bake 25 to 30 min., or until squash is tender.

Serve with cranberry sauce.   *4 servings*

—ACORN SQUASH WITH SAUSAGE STUFFING

Follow ▲ Recipe through first baking process

of squash. With spoon, scoop squash from shells; do not break skin. Omit bread crumbs, evaporated milk, egg and water. Brown sausage in skillet, breaking into small pieces with a fork or spoon as it browns. Add to skillet ½ cup (about 1 medium) chopped onion. Cook until the onion is tender. Mix squash, 3 tablespoons undiluted evaporated milk, ½ teaspoon salt and ¼ teaspoon thyme with sausage-onion mixture. Pile mixture lightly into squash shells. Bake at 350°F 10 to 15 min., or until squash is lightly browned.

CASSEROLE SAUSAGES

A thrifty one-dish meal for brunch, lunch or supper.

Grease a 1½-qt. casserole.

Cook (page 313) and slice enough carrots to yield
>**2½ cups (about 1 lb.) sliced cooked carrots**

Set carrots aside.

Meanwhile, cook, following package directions
>**1½ cups broad noodles**

Put drained noodles into casserole; blend in with fork
>**3 tablespoons butter or margarine**

Panbroil (page 192)
>**¾ lb. (about 12) pork sausage links**

When sausages begin to brown, add
>**1 cup (about 2 medium) coarsely chopped onion**

Continue to cook, stirring occasionally, until onion is tender and sausages are browned. Add the sliced carrots.

Mix and pour in
>**½ cup water**
>**⅓ cup molasses**
>**⅓ cup ketchup**
>**½ teaspoon Worcestershire sauce**

Simmer 5 min. Turn mixture into casserole over the noodles.

Set in a 350°F oven about 15 min.

Sprinkle with
>**2 tablespoons finely chopped parsley**

Serve at once.   *5 or 6 servings*

SWEET-SOUR SAUSAGE LINKS
(Bratwurst in süss-saurer Tunke)

The excellent sausages of Germany are often served in a provocative sweet-sour sauce.

Put into a cold large skillet
>**16 pork sausage links (about 1 lb.)**

Add
>**2 tablespoons cold water**

If skillet will not hold entire amount of sausage, cook one half at a time. Cover and cook slowly 8 to 10 min. Remove cover and pour off liquid. Brown links over medium heat, turning

Acorn Squash with Sausage Stuffing

as necessary (do not prick links with fork). Pour off fat as it collects; reserve fat.

Meanwhile, clean and chop
>**1 medium onion**

When sausage links are browned, remove from skillet. Drain on absorbent paper. Set aside to keep warm.

Put onion into hot skillet containing
>**2 tablespoons reserved sausage drippings**

Cook over medium heat until onion is soft. Blend in
>**2 tablespoons all-purpose flour**

Heat until mixture bubbles. Remove from heat and add gradually, stirring constantly
>**1 cup hot water**
>**2 tablespoons vinegar**
>**2 tablespoons brown sugar**
>**¼ teaspoon salt**
>**⅛ teaspoon pepper**

Bring to boiling. Reduce heat and cook 1 to 2 min. Return sausages to the sauce and cook over low heat 10 min., or until thoroughly heated.   *4 servings*

LINK SAUSAGE AND APPLE RINGS

Festive-looking, yet so easy to make.

Place in a cold large skillet
>**16 pork sausage links (about 1 lb.)**

Add
>**2 tablespoons cold water**

If skillet will not hold entire amount of sausage, cook one half at a time. Cover and cook slowly 8 to 10 min. Remove cover and pour off liquid. Brown links over medium heat, turning as necessary (do not prick links with a fork). Pour off fat as it collects; reserve fat.

Link Sausage and Apple Rings

Meanwhile, wash and core

4 medium (about 1⅓ lbs.) apples

Cut each apple crosswise into about 5 slices (½ to ¾ in. thick).

When sausage links are browned, remove from skillet. Drain on absorbent paper. Set aside to keep warm while cooking apple slices.

Place apple slices flat in hot skillet containing

3 tablespoons reserved sausage drippings

Cook over low heat 5 to 8 min., or until apple rings are almost tender when pierced with a fork; turn carefully.

Sprinkle apple rings with a mixture of

⅓ cup firmly packed brown sugar
½ teaspoon nutmeg

Cook gently until sugar is completely melted.

Serve with sausage links.   *4 to 6 servings*

POLENTA
(Polenta con Salsiccia)

Here is a corn meal mush so unusual that a holiday is celebrated in its honor! On the Friday before Lent, the people of Ponti, Italy, celebrate the feast of Polentine. The town's best cooks combine their efforts in preparing a huge dish of polenta said to weigh a thousand pounds. The day is celebrated by a parade and merrymaking in honor of the polenta. At the end of this day, the polenta is distributed to the poor.

Set out a large heavy skillet.

Remove casing if necessary and separate into pieces with a fork or spoon

1 lb. Italian sausage

Clean and slice (page 9)

1 lb. mushrooms

Heat in skillet

2 tablespoons olive oil

Add mushrooms and sausage to skillet. Cook slowly, stirring occasionally, until mushrooms and sausage are lightly browned. Slowly stir in a mixture of

2½ cups canned tomatoes
1 teaspoon salt
¼ teaspoon pepper

Simmer 20 to 30 min.

Meanwhile, bring to boiling in a saucepan

3 cups water
1½ teaspoons salt

Gradually stir in a mixture of

1 cup yellow corn meal
1 cup cold water

Continue boiling, stirring constantly, until mixture is thickened. Cover, lower heat, and cook slowly 10 min. or longer. Transfer cooked corn meal to a warm platter and top with the tomato mixture. Sprinkle with

Grated Parmesan or Romano cheese

Serve immediately.   *6 to 8 servings*

SAUSAGE WITH CABBAGE
(Kolbász Káposztával)

Some Hungarian-American grocers make and sell their own sausage which is similar to that which is made in their native country. This sausage, usually flavored with garlic, is excellent for this recipe, but it is not readily available. Thuringer sausage, though somewhat different from the typical Hungarian product, can be substituted to enhance the flavor of shredded cabbage in tomato sauce.

Set out a 4-qt. saucepot with a tight-fitting cover.

Remove and discard wilted outer leaves, rinse, cut into quarters (discarding core) and coarsely shred

1 head (about 2 lbs.) cabbage (about 2 qts., shredded)

Place cabbage in saucepot and add

1 qt. boiling water
1 teaspoon salt

Cook cabbage, uncovered, over medium heat 10 min. Stir in

2½ cups canned tomatoes

Place on top of cabbage

10 (about 2 lbs.) thuringer sausage links

Cover saucepot and cook 15 to 20 min., or until sausage is heated. Remove ½ cup cooking liquid from saucepot and set aside to cool to lukewarm.

Meanwhile, make a thickening mixture by melting in a small skillet over low heat

⅓ cup fat

Add to the fat and cook until almost tender, stirring occasionally

1 tablespoon chopped onion

Blend in

⅓ cup all-purpose flour

Stirring constantly, cook until mixture bubbles and is lightly browned. Remove from heat. Add gradually, stirring constantly, a mixture of the ½ cup reserved cooking liquid and

½ cup water

Remove the sausage from the saucepot to serving platter. Immediately blend contents of skillet into liquid in saucepot. Bring mixture rapidly to boiling, stirring constantly; cook 1 to 2 min. longer.

Serve sausage with some of cabbage mixture.

5 or 6 servings

CRISP SALT PORK IN MILK GRAVY

Set out a large heavy skillet.

Have ready

1 lb. salt pork (streaked with lean)

Slice pork into slices ¼ in. thick. Pour boiling water over pork slices and set aside to drain.

Dry with absorbent paper. Dip pork slices in

⅓ cup corn meal

Heat in the skillet

2 tablespoons lard or salt pork drippings

Add the salt pork slices. Cook over low heat until crisp and golden brown, turning slices occasionally to brown evenly. Drain on absorbent paper; set aside and keep warm.

Pour salt pork drippings from skillet. Measure ¼ cup of the drippings and return to the skillet. Blend in

3 tablespoons all-purpose flour

Cook until mixture bubbles. Remove from heat. Add gradually, stirring constantly

2 cups milk

Cook rapidly, stirring constantly, until sauce thickens. Cook 1 to 2 min. longer.

Serve crisp salt pork slices with the hot gravy.

4 to 6 servings

HAM

SAVORY ROAST HAM

▲ Base Recipe

Ham that is baked the day before is just right for cutting neat, thin slices to be served cold for Sunday evening supper. Garnish serving platter with spiced peaches.

For Ham—Set out a shallow roasting pan with a rack.

Follow directions on wrapper for roasting or roast as directed below

10-lb. smoked whole ham

Place ham fat side up on rack. Insert roast meat thermometer in thickest part of lean, being sure bulb does not rest on bone or in fat.

Roast uncovered at 300°F 2½ hrs.

Meanwhile, prepare Glaze and Fruit Garnish.

For Glaze and Fruit Garnish—Mix in a small bowl

1 cup firmly packed brown sugar
1 tablespoon all-purpose flour
1 teaspoon dry mustard

Add and stir in to form a smooth paste

2 tablespoons cider vinegar

Set aside.

Drain (reserving syrup for use in other food preparation) and set aside

1 can (8¼ oz.) pineapple tidbits
(about ⅔ cup, drained)

Rinse

1 orange

With a sharp knife, cut away peel through colored part only (white is bitter). Cut peel into desired shapes for decorating; set aside.

Thoroughly drain

8 maraschino cherries

Cut two cherries into thin slices and remainder into halves. Set aside.

To Glaze and Garnish Ham—Remove ham

Cider Roast Ham

from oven after it has roasted 2½ hrs. Remove rind (if any), being careful not to remove fat. Making diagonal cuts, score fat surface of ham to make diamond pattern; or use scalloped cookie cutter to make flower pattern. Spread about one half of Glaze over ham. Arrange pineapple tidbits, whole and sliced maraschino cherries, and pieces of orange peel on ham in an attractive design, and press firmly into glaze. Carefully spread remainder of Glaze over fruit. Return ham to oven and continue roasting about 45 min., or until internal temperature of ham reaches 160°F. (The total roasting time is about 3 hrs., allowing 18 to 20 min. per pound.)

Remove ham from oven; remove thermometer. Keep ham hot. Allow to stand 15 to 20 min. before serving. This helps to make meat easier to carve.

For Pineapple Garnish—Drain, reserving syrup for use in other food preparation

1 can (20 oz.) pineapple slices
(10 slices)

Place slices on broiler rack or a baking sheet. Brush tops with

Melted butter or margarine

Sprinkle with

Brown sugar

Place under broiler with tops of pineapple slices 3 in. from heat. Broil 5 to 6 min., or until brown sugar is melted and pineapple slices are lightly browned.

Garnish ham platter with the pineapple and

Sprigs of parsley

About 20 servings

—SAVORY ROAST HALF HAM

Follow ▲ Recipe. Substitute **5-lb. smoked half ham** for the whole ham. Allow 22 to 25 min. per pound for roasting. Prepare and apply one half of the Glaze and Fruit Garnish.

About 10 servings

CIDER ROAST HAM

Set out a shallow roasting pan with rack.

Have ready

10-lb. smoked whole ham

Follow directions on wrapper for roasting or place ham fat side up on rack. Insert roast meat thermometer in center of thickest part of lean; bulb should not rest on bone or in fat.

Roast, uncovered, at 300°F for 2½ hrs.

Meanwhile, prepare Glaze.

For Glaze—Blend

¾ cup firmly packed brown sugar
2 tablespoons maple syrup
½ teaspoon dry mustard

When ham has roasted 2½ hrs., remove from oven. Remove rind (if any), being careful not to remove the fat. Cut fat surface into diamond pattern or use a scalloped cutter to make a flower design. Insert in centers of patterns

Whole cloves

Spread the glaze over ham. Return ham to oven and continue roasting about 45 min., or until internal temperature reaches 160°F. (Total roasting time is about 3 hrs., allowing 18 to 20 min. per pound.) Occasionally baste ham using

¾ cup apple cider

Garnish as desired.

About 20 servings

COOKED WHOLE COUNTRY HAM

▲ Base Recipe

Country hams, usually sugar-cured, hickory-smoked and aged right on the farm, are found mostly in the South. They are scarce, often high-priced—and worth, say connoisseurs, every penny of the price. The finest of country hams are aged a year or more, hanging in the farmer's smokehouse. They require thorough scrubbing, long soaking, and long slow cooking, after which there is no more delicious meat in this world. And don't discard the cooking liquid! It makes unequalled seasoning for all kinds of greens and beans.

Scrub thoroughly with warm water, rinse and put into a large kettle with a tight-fitting cover

Country-style ham, 14 to 16 lbs.

(If a large kettle is not available, whole ham may be cut into halves and each piece cooked separately until done.)

Cover ham completely with cold water, cover kettle, and bring to boiling. Pour off water and again cover ham with cold water. Cover and bring to boiling. Reduce heat and simmer, covered, 4 to 6 hrs., or until internal temperature reaches 170°F. Internal temperature is obtained by inserting roast meat thermometer into center of thickest part of lean at this time, being sure bulb does not rest on bone or in fat.

Remove ham from kettle. Allow to stand 15 or 20 min. before slicing. This allows meat to set and become easier to slice. Serve ham either hot or cold, cut into thin slices.

If desired, cook only half of ham; store uncooked half in refrigerator for future use.

—BAKED COUNTRY HAM

Follow ▲ Recipe. Remove ham from kettle about ½ hr. before done. Remove rind (if any), being careful not to remove fat. Making diagonal cuts, score fat surface of ham to form a diamond pattern. Place **whole cloves** in centers of diamonds. Place ham, fat side up, on a rack in a shallow roasting pan. Spread glaze over ham and bake at 300°F 30 to 40 min., or until ham tests done with a meat thermometer and glaze is set.

For Glaze—Mix in a small bowl **1 cup firmly packed brown sugar, 1 tablespoon all-purpose flour** and **1 teaspoon dry mustard.** Blend in **2 tablespoons vinegar** until smooth. Spread on ham.

ROAST BUFFET HAM WITH APRICOT GLAZE

A shallow roasting pan will be needed.

Put into a bowl

8 oz. dried apricots, cut in pieces

Pour over apricots

1⅓ cups apple cider

Cover tightly and refrigerate overnight.

Purée apricot mixture in an electric blender or force through a food mill. Stir in a mixture of

6 tablespoons light brown sugar
½ teaspoon cinnamon
½ teaspoon allspice
¼ teaspoon cloves

Set aside.

Remove excess gelled substance from

1 canned ham (about 3 lbs.), sliced and tied

Set ham in roasting pan. Spread apricot mixture generously over ham.

Heat in a 325°F oven about 1 hr. 15 min. or the length of time recommended by the packer. Transfer ham to a serving platter. Cut and carefully remove cord. Decorate top, if desired. Surround ham with **watercress** or **parsley.**

Heat remaining sauce and serve with the ham.

About 8 servings

Note: Ham and sauce may be served cold.

HAM BAKED IN PASTRY SHELL
(Jambon en Croûte)

Excellent for festive occasions and the buffet table, ham wrapped in pastry is native to Morvan and popular in many other sections of France.

Remove the wrapper from a

10- to 12-lb. ham

Place ham, fat-side up, on rack in a shallow open roasting pan. Insert roast meat thermometer so that the bulb will reach the center of the thickest portion of lean but not rest in fat or on bone.

Roast at 300°F 3 to 4 hrs., until meat thermometer registers 160°F (allow about 18 min. per pound).

One hour before ham is done, remove from oven and pour off drippings from pan. If rind has not been removed, trim off, leaving ½-in. thickness of fat.

For Glaze—Pour by spoonfuls over fat surface about one half of

1 cup Madeira, champagne or other white wine

Sprinkle with

½ cup confectioners' sugar

Carefully spoon remaining wine over sugar. Return ham to oven and baste every 20 min. until well glazed and browned. Remove from oven. Drain ham on absorbent paper.

Set oven temperature regulator at 425°F.

Meanwhile, prepare

Pastry for Meat Pies (three times recipe, page 487)

To Encase Ham—On well-floured surface, roll the prepared pastry ½ in. thick and shape to size large enough to enfold the ham. Place the ham, glazed side down, on the pastry. Wrap quickly and carefully. Moisten the edges of the pastry with cold water or milk. Pinch them together tightly. Turn the ham over and put it onto a clean rack in a clean roasting pan with the sealed side down.

If desired, cut fancy shapes such as leaves and flowers from the trimmings of the dough. Moisten underside of each with cold water and arrange in a design on dough-encased ham.

Brush onto the pastry a mixture of

1 egg, slightly beaten
2 tablespoons cold water

Cut a few slits in the dough to allow steam to escape. Return ham to oven 15 to 18 min., or until pastry is golden brown. Allow ham to stand at least 30 min. before carving.

To serve, remove the crust and serve pieces with ham slices. Accompany the ham, as the French do, with **purée of spinach** or with **small green peas.**

About 20 servings

HAM WITH CREAMY FROSTING

Have ready

1 chilled canned ham, 8 to 10 lbs.

Pour into a small cup or custard cup

1 tablespoon cold water
1 tablespoon wine vinegar

Sprinkle over liquid

1½ teaspoons unflavored gelatin

Dissolve gelatin completely over hot water.

Meanwhile, mix

1½ cups dairy sour cream
3 tablespoons mayonnaise
¼ teaspoon sugar
¼ teaspoon garlic salt

Blend in a mixture of

¼ teaspoon dry mustard
¼ teaspoon water

Add the dissolved gelatin gradually, stirring until thoroughly blended. Chill until mixture begins to gel (becomes slightly thicker).

When gelatin mixture is of desired consistency, blend in thoroughly

½ cup snipped watercress

Spread frosting over the sides and top of the ham.   *1 frosted ham (about 1¾ cups frosting)*

BAKED HAM SLICE I

▲ Base Recipe

Place in an 11x7x2-in. baking dish

1 smoked ham slice, cut 1½ in. thick

Allow ⅓ to ½-lb. meat per serving.

Insert in ham slice at 1-in. intervals

Whole cloves

Sprinkle evenly over ham a mixture of

2 tablespoons brown sugar
2 tablespoons fine dry bread crumbs
2 tablespoons raisins
½ teaspoon dry mustard

Slowly pour over ham slice

1 cup orange juice

Bake at 300°F 45 min.; occasionally baste ham slice with liquid in baking dish.

Blend thoroughly

½ cup orange juice
1 teaspoon cornstarch

Remove ham from oven and pour orange juice mixture over ham surface. Return to oven about 20 min., or until liquid is thickened and clear. Remove cloves from ham before serving.

—FROSTED HAM SLICE

Follow ▲ Recipe. For brown sugar mixture, substitute the following mixture: **1½ cups milk**, scalded (page 10), **1 cup fine dry bread crumbs**, **1½ tablespoons finely chopped onion**, **½ teaspoon cinnamon** and **½ teaspoon salt**. Spread mixture evenly over ham

slice. Sprinkle with **3 tablespoons brown sugar.** Omit orange juice and cornstarch. Bake at 300°F 45 to 50 min.

—APPLE BAKED HAM SLICE

Follow ▲ Recipe. Omit whole cloves and raisins. Substitute **apple juice** for orange juice. Serve with **applesauce.**

BAKED HAM SLICE II

▲ Base Recipe

Juicy and tender—good-with-fruit flavor.

Place in an 11x7x2-in. baking dish
    1 smoked ham slice, cut about ½ in. thick
Allow ⅓ to ½ lb. meat per serving.

Insert in ham slice at 1-in. intervals
    Whole cloves
Sprinkle over ham a mixture of
    2 tablespoons brown sugar
    2 tablespoons fine dry bread crumbs
    1 teaspoon grated orange peel
    ½ teaspoon dry mustard

Rinse and cut into ¼-in. slices
    1 orange
Arrange slices on ham over sugar mixture. Garnish with
    Maraschino cherries, cut in rings
Carefully pour over top of ham slice
    ¾ cup orange juice

Bake at 300°F about 40 min. Remove cloves from ham slice before serving.

—PINEAPPLE BAKED HAM SLICE

Follow ▲ Recipe. Substitute **lemon peel** for orange peel, **canned pineapple juice** for orange juice and **3 canned pineapple slices** for the orange slices.

—GINGER BAKED HAM SLICE

Follow ▲ Recipe. Substitute **lemon peel** for orange peel and **ginger ale** for orange juice. Omit orange and cherry garnish.

—PLUM BAKED HAM SLICE

Follow ▲ Recipe. Substitute syrup drained from **1 can (17 oz.) purple plums** for orange juice. Arrange plums around ham slice. Omit orange and cherry garnish.

SPICY CIDER BAKED HAM SLICE

Set out a shallow baking pan.

Cut through fat at 1-in. intervals on outside edges of
    1 smoked ham slice, 1 to 1½ in. thick
Rub meat with
    1 teaspoon allspice

Place ham slice in the baking pan and pour over
    2 cups apple cider
Cover pan and place in refrigerator 1 hr., spooning the cider over ham several times.

Remove cover and bake at 350°F 35 to 40 min., basting several times during baking period.

Meanwhile, drain, reserving syrup
    1 can sliced pineapple (about 4 slices)
Cut one pineapple slice into halves to form 2 thin slices. Set aside. (Remaining pineapple slices and syrup may be used in other food preparation.)

When ham is done, remove from oven and arrange pineapple slices on top. Spoon over
    Melted butter
Sprinkle with about
    1 tablespoon brown sugar
Place in centers of pineapple slices
    2 maraschino cherries
Place baking pan on broiler rack. Place under broiler with tops of pineapple slices 3 to 4 in. from heat. Broil 5 min., or until pineapple slices are golden brown. *6 servings*

STUFFED HAM SLICES

Set out a 13x9x2-in. baking dish.

Set out
    2 smoked ham slices, cut about ½ in. thick
Place one ham slice in the baking dish.

Mix
    4 cups soft bread cubes
    ½ cup (about 2½ oz.) raisins
    ¼ cup firmly packed brown sugar
    ½ teaspoon dry mustard
Lightly toss bread mixture with
    ⅓ cup butter or margarine, melted
Lightly spoon stuffing evenly over ham slice in dish. Top stuffing with second ham slice. Insert around edge of top slice of ham
    Whole cloves
Drain, reserving syrup
    1 can (20 oz.) sliced pineapple (about 10 slices)
Place two slices of pineapple in each corner of baking dish. Cut the two remaining pineapple slices into wedges and arrange wedges to resemble flower petals on top of ham. Brush top ham slice with reserved pineapple syrup.

Bake, uncovered, at 300° to 325°F about 1½ hrs. Brush top ham slice with pineapple syrup several times during baking.

Garnish ham slices with **parsley** and serve.
    6 to 8 servings

FRIED COUNTRY HAM SLICES

Ham and eggs—perfect for breakfast.

Place in a large heavy skillet
    4 country-style ham slices, cut ¼ in. thick

Stuffed Ham Slices

Cover with cold water. Bring to boiling and pour off water. Fry ham over low or medium heat using the same skillet, without adding extra fat. Cook about 15 min., or until done, turning frequently.

Serve immediately or keep hot while preparing eggs. *4 servings*

"FRIED" HAM WITH RED GRAVY

▲ Base Recipe

A ham slice "fried" in this manner is really panbroiled, and produces just enough drippings to make the flavorful "red" gravy dear to all Southerners. To give the palate a real surprise, try using hot coffee instead of water to make the gravy, as some cooks do down South.

Heat a large heavy skillet over medium heat.

Set out
    1 smoked ham slice, cut ¼ in. thick
Allow ⅓ to ½ lb. meat per serving.

Rub hot skillet with piece of fat trimmed from ham. Place ham slice in skillet and cook over medium heat. Maintain a temperature which allows juices to evaporate rather than collect in pan. With too low heat, meat will simmer in its own juices and become dry and less tender when cooked. Turn meat occasionally for even browning. Remove ham slice to warm serving plate; set aside. Remove skillet from heat and add
    ½ cup hot water
Bring liquid to boiling, stirring and scraping bottom of skillet to loosen all drippings. Simmer until some of the water evaporates. Pour gravy over ham or serve with the ham.

—"FRIED" HAM WITH COFFEE GRAVY

Follow ▲ Recipe. Substitute 1 cup **coffee beverage** for the water.

GYPSY-STYLE FRIED HAM SLICES

Lightly grease a heavy 10- or 12-in. skillet.

Cut through fat at 1-in. intervals on edges of
    2 smoked ham slices, cut ¼ to ½ in. thick

197

Be careful not to cut through the lean. Place ham in the skillet and cook slowly over medium heat 10 to 12 min., turning occasionally, until lightly browned on both sides.

Meanwhile, prepare and set aside to cool to lukewarm

1½ cups quick meat broth (one and one half times recipe, page 10)

Remove ham to a heated platter, cover and set aside in warm place.

Pour off and reserve fat from skillet. Return to skillet

2 tablespoons reserved fat

Stir into fat and brown lightly, stirring constantly

3 tablespoons (1½ slice) fine dry bread crumbs

Remove skillet from heat and gradually add a mixture of the reserved broth and

4 teaspoons vinegar
1 teaspoon sugar
Few grains pepper

Bring mixture to boiling, stirring constantly. Blend in

1 tablespoon chopped parsley

Pour sauce over ham slices and serve immediately.   *4 or 5 servings*

HAM STEAK ORIENTAL

Set out a large shallow baking dish.

Mix

¼ cup soy sauce
¼ cup chili sauce
¼ cup light corn syrup
¼ cup lemon juice

Put into the baking dish

1 cooked smoked ham slice, cut 1 in. thick (about 1½ lbs.)

Pour soy sauce mixture over ham. Allow to stand about 1 hr. at room temperature; spoon sauce over ham occasionally.

Meanwhile, prepare

1 green pepper, cut in 1-in. squares

Top the ham with green pepper squares and spoon sauce over all.

Heat in a 325°F oven about 25 min., basting occasionally. Remove from oven and add

1 banana, sliced diagonally in 1-in. pieces

Baste with sauce. Return to oven and heat 5 min. Serve individual portions of ham topped with green pepper, banana and sauce.

4 servings

Note: If desired, cut cooked ham into 2½-in. strips; allow to stand in soy sauce mixture 1 hr. Turn into a large skillet with green pepper; heat thoroughly. Mix in banana; cook until banana is slightly soft.

HAM SWEET POTATO CASSEROLE

▲ *Base Recipe*

Grease a 2-qt. casserole.

Prepare

Whipped sweet potatoes (see Golden Glow Sweet Potatoes, page 338. Use one half recipe; omit marshmallows.)

Meanwhile, cube and set aside enough cooked ham to yield

3 cups cubed cooked ham

Heat in a skillet

2 tablespoons butter or margarine

Add to skillet and cook slowly about 5 min., stirring frequently

⅓ cup chopped green pepper
2 tablespoons chopped onion

Stir in the cubed ham and

1¼ cups (10½-oz. can) condensed cream of mushroom soup
½ cup milk
2 teaspoons prepared mustard
⅛ teaspoon pepper

Bring mixture to boiling. Turn mixture into casserole; lightly spoon whipped potatoes in a ring around top of casserole.

Bake at 350°F 15 to 20 min., or until potatoes are lightly browned.   *6 servings*

—BUTTERED SWEET POTATO HAM CASSEROLE

Follow ▲ Recipe. Cook potatoes but do not mash; slice and lightly brown in **3 tablespoons fat.** Place a ring of overlapping slices around top of casserole. Bake until casserole mixture is heated thoroughly.

HAM-STUFFED PEPPERS

Set out a shallow 2-qt. baking dish and a medium-size saucepan.

Rinse and cut into halves lengthwise

4 large green peppers

With a knife remove stem, white fiber and seeds. Rinse cavities. Drop pepper halves into boiling salted water to cover and simmer 5 min. Remove peppers from water and invert. Set aside to drain.

While peppers are cooking, cut finely and set aside enough cooked ham to yield

2 cups cooked ham

Have ready

1½ cups tomato juice

To Cook Rice—Bring to boiling in a saucepan

⅔ cup water
¼ teaspoon salt
⅓ cup rice

(The Rice Industry no longer considers it necessary to wash rice before cooking.) Bring to boiling, stirring once or twice. Reduce heat, cover tightly, and cook about 14 min., or until rice is tender. (Cooked rice prepared from packaged precooked rice may be used if directions on the package are followed carefully for amounts and timing.)

To Prepare Filling—Cut into 8 slices

¼ lb. Cheddar cheese

Set aside.

Heat in the saucepan

½ cup butter or margarine

Add ham and toss lightly with a fork to blend. Mix in rice and

2 tablespoons minced onion

Mix and blend in

¼ teaspoon dry mustard
¼ teaspoon garlic salt
¼ teaspoon monosodium glutamate
⅛ teaspoon pepper

To Complete Stuffed Peppers—Lightly fill peppers with ham-rice mixture, heaping slightly. Place one slice of cheese on top of each pepper. Place peppers in baking dish. Pour the tomato juice around peppers.

Bake at 350°F about 20 min. Increase heat to 400°F and bake 10 min. longer, or until cheese is lightly browned.

If desired, spoon the hot tomato juice over stuffed peppers.   *4 servings*

HAM MUSHROOM CASSEROLE

Grease a 2-qt. casserole.

Have ready
    4 oz. sharp Cheddar cheese, shredded
    1 lb. fresh mushrooms, cleaned and
        sliced (page 9)
    3 cups (about 1 lb.) julienne strips
        cooked ham (page 12)

Cook, following directions on package, and drain
    2 pkgs. (10 oz. each) frozen cut green
        beans

Meanwhile, heat in a skillet over low heat
    ¼ cup butter or margarine
Add the sliced mushrooms and
    1 tablespoon minced onion
Cook, stirring occasionally, until mushrooms are delicately browned. Blend in a mixture of
    ⅓ cup all-purpose flour
    1 teaspoon salt
    ¼ teaspoon dry mustard
Heat until mixture bubbles. Add gradually, stirring constantly
    2 cups milk
    1 cup cream
Bring to boiling; stir and cook 1 to 2 min. Mix in ham strips, drained beans and
    ¼ cup pimiento strips
Turn into the casserole. Sprinkle the shredded cheese and **paprika** over the top.

Heat in a 350°F oven 20 min., or until cheese is golden brown.   *6 servings*

HAM IN ORANGE SAUCE

Set out a large skillet.

Have ready
    1 cup chopped celery
    ½ cup chopped green pepper
    ½ cup chopped onion
    1 can (13½ oz.) pineapple chunks,
        drained (reserve ⅓ cup syrup)
    1 can (6 oz.) frozen orange juice
        concentrate, thawed
    1 lb. cooked ham, cut in strips

Heat in the skillet
    ½ cup butter or margarine
Add the celery, green pepper and onion. Cook about 10 min., or until vegetables are crisp-tender; stir occasionally. Set aside.

Combine the reserved pineapple syrup and
    1 tablespoon cornstarch
Mix with vegetables in skillet. Add the orange juice concentrate, pineapple chunks and
    1 tablespoon soy sauce
Heat thoroughly, stirring occasionally. Mix in ham, cover skillet and heat thoroughly.

Meanwhile, cook, following package directions
    1 cup packaged precooked rice

Add to cooked rice and toss lightly
    ¼ cup butter or margarine
    ¼ cup grated Parmesan cheese

Turn into a heated serving dish. Spoon the hot ham mixture over rice. If desired, accompany with a bowl of **grated Parmesan cheese.**
            About 6 servings

HAM A LA CRANBERRY

Set out a large saucepan.

Have ready
    1 lb. (about 4 cups) cranberries, washed
    2 teaspoons grated lemon peel
    6 cups cubed cooked ham or luncheon
        meat
    ½ cup seedless raisins (optional)

Combine in the saucepan the cranberries and
    2 cups sugar
    ¼ teaspoon salt
    2 cups water
Heat to boiling, stirring until sugar is dissolved. Boil, uncovered, 5 min., or until berries pop open.*

Stir in the grated lemon peel, ham and raisins, if used. Heat until mixture begins to bubble, stirring occasionally. Serve over **toast triangles, patty shells** or **hot biscuits.**
            8 to 10 servings

*Cooked cranberry sauce may be sieved before blending in remaining ingredients.

HAM 'N' ONION TURNOVERS

Set out a small skillet and a baking sheet.

Have ready
    ½ cup finely chopped onion
    1 cup finely chopped cooked ham

Heat in the skillet
    1 tablespoon butter or margarine
Add onion and cook until onion is soft, about 5 min., stirring occasionally. Mix in the ham and
    1 tablespoon sweet pickle relish
    1 tablespoon prepared mustard

Open and separate dough into triangles
    1 pkg. (8 oz.) refrigerated fresh dough
        for crescent rolls
Spoon ham mixture equally onto four of the triangles. Spread to within ¼ in. of the edges. Top with remaining triangles and press edges with a fork to seal. Place on baking sheet. Brush tops lightly with
    1 egg yolk, slightly beaten
Sprinkle with **sesame** or **caraway seed.**

Bake at 375°F about 13 min., or until golden brown. Serve immediately.   *4 servings*

HAM STRUDEL
(Sonkás Rétes)

Try the ever-popular Strudel transformed into a meat dish! Serve it Hungarian-style as a snack or American-style as the main course of a meal.

Ham à la Cranberry

Prepare
    Strudel Dough (page 519)

While dough is resting 30 min., thinly slice and finely chop enough cooked ham to yield
    3 cups finely chopped cooked ham
Mix ham with
    ¼ cup dairy sour cream
    ¼ to ½ teaspoon pepper
Set ham mixture aside.

After Strudel Dough is stretched and slightly dried, sprinkle evenly over the dough
    ¼ cup (about 1 slice) fine dry bread
        crumbs

Spoon ham mixture in small mounds evenly over the dough. Spread mounds carefully with spatula.

Roll, bake and slice as in Apple Strudel (page 519; do not sprinkle with confectioners' sugar). Serve Ham Strudel warm.   *8 to 10 servings*

HAM 'N' YAMS IN RAISIN CARAMEL SAUCE

Set out a large skillet.

Have ready
    6 cooked ham slices (about ½ lb.),
        cut in halves
    6 canned yams or sweet potatoes, cut
        lengthwise in halves
    ½ cup golden raisins

Heat in the skillet
    3 tablespoons butter or margarine
Add the raisins and
    1 cup packed light brown sugar
Stir until smooth, about 10 min.

Remove from heat; add very slowly, stirring until blended
    ½ cup cream
Return to heat and cook 1 min. Add ham and yams and spoon sauce over all. Heat thoroughly. Blend in a small amount of cream if necessary to thin sauce.   *6 servings*

199

Ham Asparagus Roll-Ups

CRANBERRY HAM ROLLS

Grease a large shallow baking dish.

Prepare and set aside

1¾ cups Perfection Boiled Rice (one-half recipe, page 165; omit salt; use quick meat broth, page 10, for liquid)

Set out

6 slices cooked ham, cut ⅛ in. thick

1 can (16 oz.) jellied cranberry sauce

Measure 1 cup of the cranberry sauce into a bowl and mash with a fork. Add and mix

¼ cup firmly packed brown sugar

¼ teaspoon nutmeg

Few grains mace

Set cranberry sauce mixture aside.

Heat in a skillet over low heat

⅓ cup butter or margarine

Add and cook over medium heat, occasionally moving and turning with a spoon

½ cup finely chopped onion

½ cup finely chopped celery

Cook until onion and celery are tender. Season with a blend of

½ teaspoon salt

½ teaspoon dry mustard

⅛ teaspoon pepper

Add the rice and mix well. Spoon about ½ cup of rice mixture onto each ham slice. Fold slice around rice mixture to form a roll; secure with a wooden pick. Place rolls, pick side down, in baking dish. Spoon the cranberry sauce mixture over center of ham rolls.

Bake at 350°F 15 to 20 min., or until heated thoroughly. *6 servings*

HAM ASPARAGUS ROLL-UPS

For Roll-Ups—Cook, following directions on package

3 pkgs. (10 oz. each) frozen asparagus spears

Set out

8 slices cooked ham, cut about ⅛ in. thick

When asparagus is tender, drain, if necessary. Place 4 or 5 cooked asparagus spears in the center of each ham slice. Fold slice around asparagus to form a roll (see photo); secure

with a wooden pick. Place roll-ups on a baking sheet and heat in a 325°F oven 10 to 15 min., or until ham is thoroughly heated.

For Sauce—While ham is heating, melt in a double-boiler top over low heat

2 tablespoons butter or margarine

Blend in

2 tablespoons all-purpose flour

¼ teaspoon salt

Few grains white pepper

Heat until mixture bubbles. Remove from heat. Add gradually, stirring constantly

⅔ cup quick chicken broth (page 10)

⅓ cup milk

Return to heat and bring rapidly to boiling, stirring constantly; cook 1 to 2 min. longer. Remove from heat and vigorously stir about 3 tablespoons of hot mixture into

2 egg yolks, slightly beaten

Immediately blend into mixture in double boiler and cook over simmering water 3 to 5 min. Stir constantly to keep mixture cooking evenly. Cool slightly. Add all at one time and stir until thoroughly blended in

¼ cup (1 oz.) shredded sharp Cheddar cheese

Blend in thoroughly

1 tablespoon lemon juice

Carefully transfer roll-ups from baking sheet to a warm serving platter and remove wooden picks. Spoon or pour sauce over them.

Sprinkle with

Paprika

Garnish with **parsley** and serve. *8 servings*

LAMB

ROAST LEG OF LAMB

▲ *Base Recipe*

Set out a shallow roasting pan with rack.

Have ready

5- to 6-lb. leg of lamb

Do not remove the fell (thin, papery covering).

Roast Leg of Lamb

Rub lamb with a mixture of

2 teaspoons salt

1 teaspoon monosodium glutamate

¼ teaspoon pepper

Place lamb skin side down on rack in pan. Insert roast meat thermometer in center of thickest part of meat, being sure that bulb does not rest on bone or in fat.

Roast at 300°F about 3 hrs., allowing 30 to 35 min. per pound. Meat is medium done when thermometer reaches 175°F and well done at 180°F.

Place paper frill around end of leg bone. Serve on warm platter. Garnish with **parsley** or **mint leaves**. *About 10 servings*

—MINTED-STUFFED LAMB

Heat **⅓ cup butter** in a large skillet. Add **2 tablespoons finely chopped celery** and **2 tablespoons finely minced onion**. Cook over low heat until onion is almost tender. Add **½ cup finely chopped mint leaves** and **½ cup water**. Simmer about 5 min. Mix in **2 cups soft bread crumbs** and a mixture of **1 teaspoon salt, ½ teaspoon monosodium glutamate** and **¼ teaspoon pepper**. Follow ▲ Recipe. Substitute **4- to 5-lb. cushion shoulder roast of lamb** for leg of lamb. Lightly fill pocket with stuffing; sew or skewer opening to hold stuffing inside. Roast as in ▲ Recipe about 2½ hrs., allowing 30 to 35 min. per pound. Remove skewers or thread and serve.

ROAST LEG OF LAMB, ITALIAN STYLE
(Agnello al Forno)

Set out a shallow roasting pan with rack.

Set out
5- to 6-lb. leg of lamb
Do not remove fell (thin, papery covering). Cut several small slits in surface. In each slit, insert
1 slice garlic
Place lamb skin-side down on rack in pan. Insert roast meat thermometer in center of the thickest part of meat, being sure the bulb does not rest in fat or on bone.

Brush meat with
⅓ cup olive oil
Sprinkle meat with
1 tablespoon grated lemon peel
Combine and sprinkle over meat
1½ teaspoons salt
1 teaspoon dried rosemary
¼ teaspoon pepper

Roast at 300°F 2½ to 3½ hrs., allowing 30 to 35 min. per pound. Meat is medium done when roast meat thermometer registers 175°F and well done at 180°F. Serve on warm platter.

About 10 servings

ROAST LEG OF LAMB, FRENCH STYLE
(Rôti d'Agneau)

Set out a roasting pan with rack.

Set out a
5- to 6-lb. leg of lamb (do not have fell removed)
Rub meat with mixture of
2 teaspoons salt
¼ teaspoon pepper
Cut several small slits in surface of meat. In each slit insert
1 sliver of garlic
Melt
3 tablespoons butter
Use butter to brush meat frequently during roasting.

Place meat skin-side down on rack in roasting pan. Insert roast meat thermometer in thickest part of meat, being sure that bulb does not rest in fat or on bone.

Roast Leg of Lamb, French Style

Roast at 300°F 2½ to 3½ hrs., allowing 30 to 35 min. per lb. Meat is medium done when thermometer registers 175°F and well done at 180°F.

Remove meat from pan to a warm platter and pour off fat from drippings in pan.

For Gravy—Stir into drippings in pan
1 cup cold Bouillon (page 41) or water
Bring to boiling, stirring constantly.

Season with mixture of
½ teaspoon salt
¼ teaspoon pepper

10 to 12 servings

STUFFED LAMB SHOULDER ROAST WITH HONEY CHUTNEY GLAZE

Set out a shallow roasting pan with rack.

For Lamb Shoulder Roast—Have ready
4- to 5-lb. boned lamb shoulder
Rub lamb with a mixture of
2 teaspoons salt
¼ teaspoon pepper
Spread inside surface with
2 tablespoons chutney
Top chutney with
1 medium onion, sliced
2 cloves garlic, slivered
Roll meat as for jelly roll and secure with cord, tying in parallel lines.

Place roast, seam side down, on rack in pan. Insert roast meat thermometer so the bulb reaches the center of the thickest part of the meat, being sure that bulb does not rest in fat or in stuffing. Do not add water or cover.

Roast at 325°F allowing about 40 to 45 min. per lb. When meat has roasted about 1¾ hrs., pour off fat drippings and reserve.

Mix and spoon over roast
¼ cup honey
¼ cup water
2 tablespoons chutney
Continue roasting until meat has reached the desired degree of doneness, basting occasionally. Meat is medium done when thermometer reaches 175°F and well done at 180°F. Remove thermometer and transfer meat to a warm serving platter; keep hot while preparing gravy.

Do not remove cord before carving or roast will fall apart. When carving, sever and discard each cord as it is reached.

For Gravy—Leaving the brown residue in pan, pour the honey mixture into a bowl and allow fat to rise to surface. Skim off fat and add enough of the reserved fat drippings, if necessary, to make
3 tablespoons fat
Add to honey mixture and set aside
Water (enough to make 2 cups liquid)
Put the 3 tablespoons fat into the roasting pan. Blend in until smooth
3 tablespoons all-purpose flour
¼ teaspoon salt

Stirring constantly, heat until mixture bubbles. Remove from heat and slowly blend in, stirring constantly, the honey-water mixture. Return to heat and boil 1 to 2 min. While stirring, scrape bottom and sides of pan to blend in brown residue. Season to taste. Serve hot with roast.

8 servings

Note: Serve roast with hot, well-seasoned asparagus spears, small whole onions and carrots.

LAMB WITH DILL
(Dillkött Lamm)

For Lamb—Set out
3 lbs. lamb shoulder
Put lamb into a Dutch oven or a large heavy saucepot with a tight-fitting cover. Add
2 qts. water
1 tablespoon salt
Few sprigs fresh dill or 1 teaspoon dill seed
Bring to boiling. Skim foam from liquid, reduce heat, cover and simmer slowly 1 to 1½ hrs., or until lamb is tender.

When meat is tender, remove to a warm serving platter and allow to stand 15 to 20 min. before carving.

For Sauce—Prepare
1 cup Medium White Sauce (page 304; substitute 1 cup lamb broth for the milk)

Remove sauce from heat and stir in
2 tablespoons vinegar
2 teaspoons sugar
2 tablespoons finely chopped fresh dill or ½ teaspoon ground dill seed
Vigorously stir about 3 tablespoons of the hot mixture into
1 egg yolk, slightly beaten
Blend into sauce and immediately place over simmering water. Cook 3 to 5 min.

When ready to serve, slice lamb thinly and garnish with
Sprigs of dill
Serve with the sauce.

6 servings

LAMB CROWN ROAST WITH RICE RAISIN STUFFING

Set out a shallow roasting pan with a rack.

Have ready
4- to 6-lb. crown roast of lamb
Sprinkle meat with
Seasoned salt and pepper
Place roast, rib ends down, on rack in roasting pan.

Roast in a 325°F oven about 1 hr.

Remove from oven and turn roast, rib ends up. Insert a meat thermometer in center of the thickest part of meat. Return to oven and roast 1½ to 2½ hrs., or until thermometer registers 175°F.

Meanwhile, prepare
Rice Raisin Stuffing (below)
About 1 hr. before end of roasting time, spoon half of the Rice Raisin Stuffing into center of roast. Cover with aluminum foil and return to oven.

Spoon remaining stuffing into a 1-qt. casserole. Set in oven with the roast. Heat, uncovered, stirring occasionally with a fork until roast is done.

Transfer roast to a serving platter. Garnish with **parsley**.   *6 to 8 servings*

—RICE RAISIN STUFFING

Prepare, following directions on package and using 2¼ cups water
1 pkg. (6 oz.) curry-seasoned rice

Meanwhile, put into a hot skillet
1 lb. ground lamb
Brown meat, separating into pieces with a spoon. Mix cooked rice with browned lamb and
½ cup diced green pepper
⅓ cup golden raisins
½ cup chicken broth
2 tablespoons lemon juice
Lightly mix in a blend of
½ teaspoon seasoned salt
½ teaspoon salt
⅛ teaspoon pepper
(Use half as a stuffing for Lamb Crown Roast and remaining half for an accompanying casserole.)

Lamb Crown Roast with Rice Raisin Stuffing

MUTTON, SAINT-MENEHOULD STYLE
(Mouton Saint-Menehould)

The procedure used here, original to Saint-Menehould, is unusual in that it requires three cooking methods. Mutton is specified, for, like champagne, it is one of the choicest products of the region.

Set out a large skillet with a tight-fitting cover.

Prepare and set aside
3 cups Bouillon (page 41)

Melt in skillet
¼ cup butter

Set out a
3-to 4-lb. mutton shoulder, boned and cut in serving-size pieces
Place in the hot butter in skillet and brown meat on all sides. Sprinkle meat evenly with a blend of
1½ teaspoons salt
¼ teaspoon pepper
Remove meat to warm dish.

Cook in skillet, until vegetables are tender, stirring occasionally
¾ cup (about 3 small) sliced carrots
1 cup (about 2 medium) thinly sliced onions
1 leek (white part only), sliced
4 peppercorns
2 sprigs parsley
1 bay leaf
¼ teaspoon thyme
Return meat to skillet and add Bouillon. Cover and bring just to boiling. Reduce heat and simmer 2 to 2½ hrs., or until meat is tender. Remove meat from skillet and drain. Cool slightly.

Remove herbs and peppercorns from liquid remaining in the skillet. Reduce liquid to about one half by boiling and serve as sauce with the meat.

Meanwhile, roll pieces of meat in
1 cup (about 3 slices) fine dry bread crumbs
Dip meat in a mixture of
2 eggs, slightly beaten
2 tablespoons water
Roll meat again in crumbs.

Arrange meat on broiler rack. Place under broiler with top of meat 3 in. from heat, turning to brown evenly.   *5 or 6 servings*

Panbroiled Lamb Chops

PANBROILED LAMB CHOPS

▲ *Base Recipe*

Heat a heavy 10-in. skillet.

Set out
4 lamb chops, cut about ¾ in. thick
Cut through fat at 1-in. intervals on outside edges of each lamb chop. Be careful not to cut through the lean.

Place chops in skillet and brown meat slowly over medium heat. Maintain a temperature which allows juices to evaporate rather than collect in pan. With too low heat, the meat will simmer in its own juices and become dry and less tender when cooked. If necessary, turn meat occasionally for even browning and pour off fat as it accumulates.

For each pound of meat mix
1 teaspoon salt
½ teaspoon monosodium glutamate
¼ teaspoon pepper

When chops are browned on one side, turn and sprinkle one half of seasoning mixture over top. Sprinkle remaining seasoning over other side just before serving. Allow 10 to 12 min. for complete panbroiling time. Test for doneness by cutting a slit along the bone and noting color of meat.   *4 servings*

—PANBROILED BEEF STEAKS

Follow ▲ Recipe for panbroiling **porterhouse, sirloin, rib or tenderloin steaks.** Allow 10 to 20 min., depending on degree of doneness desired. If steaks are more than 1 in. thick, broil instead of panbroil.

—PANBROILED HAM SLICES

Follow ▲ Recipe for panbroiling **½ to 1 in. thick ham slices.** Allow 13 to 20 min. cooking time. Omit seasoning mixture.

LAMB CHOPS HAWAIIAN

Set out a shallow baking dish.

Prepare and set aside to keep warm
> **1 cup Mornay Sauce (one half recipe, page 305)**

Set aside to drain, reserving syrup for use in other food preparation
> **1 can (8¼ oz.) sliced pineapple (about 4 slices)**

Set out
> **4 lamb loin or rib chops, cut about 1 in. thick**

Season lamb chops with a mixture of
> **½ teaspoon salt**
> **¼ teaspoon ginger**
> **¼ teaspoon monosodium glutamate**
> **⅛ teaspoon pepper**

Heat in a heavy skillet
> **2 tablespoons butter**

Add the lamb chops and cook slowly on one side about 5 to 7 min. Turn and cook about 5 to 7 min. longer. Arrange the lamb chops in the baking dish and set aside.

Add to the skillet
> **1 tablespoon butter**

Add the pineapple slices and cook until golden brown on both sides. Arrange the pineapple slices over lamb chops and pour over the Mornay Sauce. Sprinkle with
> **Grated Parmesan cheese**
> **Paprika**

Place baking dish on broiler rack. Place under broiler with top of food 2 to 3 in. from heat and broil 3 to 4 min., or until sauce is lightly browned. *4 servings*

BROILED LAMB CHOPS GRATINE

Set out a broiler pan with rack.

Have ready
> **1¼ to 1¾ cups coarse dry bread crumbs**
> **¼ cup chopped parsley**

Clean
> **18 medium mushrooms**

Remove stems from mushrooms and chop them. Sprinkle inside of caps with
> **Monosodium glutamate**

Set aside.

Brush
> **6 lamb rib chops, cut about 1½ in. thick**

with
> **Cooking oil**

Set chops on rack of broiler pan. Broil 6 to 7 in. from heat 10 to 12 min. on each side, or until desired degree of doneness is reached. After turning chops, season with
> **Salt and lemon pepper marinade**

Meanwhile, heat in a skillet
> **¼ cup butter or margarine**

Mix in chopped mushroom stems and
> **1 large clove garlic, minced**

Cook about 5 min., stirring occasionally. Add
> **¼ cup butter or margarine**

Stir until butter is melted. Mix in bread crumbs and parsley until crumbs are well coated. Fill mushroom caps and top broiled chops with crumb mixture.

Set caps on broiler rack with chops. Broil 2 to 3 min., or until crumbs are golden brown. Transfer chops and mushrooms to a heated serving plate. *6 servings*

LAMB CHOPS PIQUANT

Set out a large skillet.

Have ready
> **5 lamb shoulder chops, cut ¾ in. thick**

Heat in the skillet
> **2 tablespoons butter or margarine**

Add the lamb chops and brown on both sides.

Blend
> **½ cup sweet pickle liquid**
> **½ cup tarragon vinegar**
> **¼ cup water**

and a mixture of
> **4 teaspoons sugar**
> **2 teaspoons dry mustard**
> **1 teaspoon salt**
> **½ teaspoon pepper**

Pour over chops in skillet. Cover and cook over low heat 40 min., or until lamb is tender. Baste chops occasionally, adding a small amount of hot water if necessary during cooking.

When meat is tender, pour off excess liquid. Mix
> **2 tablespoons capers**
> **6 tablespoons caper liquid**
> **6 tablespoons water**

Pour over chops and heat thoroughly. *5 servings*

GOLDEN LAMB SHOULDER CHOPS

Set out a large skillet.

Have ready
> **5 lamb shoulder chops, cut ¾ in. thick**
> **1 can (29½ oz.) sliced pineapple, drained (reserve syrup)**

Broiled Lamb Chops Gratiné

Heat in the skillet
> **2 tablespoons butter or margarine**

Add the lamb chops and brown on both sides. Sprinkle browned chops with
> **1 teaspoon salt**
> **½ teaspoon monosodium glutamate**

Place one pineapple slice on each chop. Pour ⅓ cup of the pineapple syrup over chops. Cover and cook over low heat 40 min., or until lamb is tender when pierced with a fork. Baste occasionally; add hot water if necessary during cooking.

When lamb chops are tender, remove to a heated serving plate.

Mix 1 tablespoon of the pineapple syrup and
> **2½ teaspoons cornstarch**

Pour off liquid from skillet and return 2 tablespoons to the skillet. Blend in the cornstarch mixture and remaining pineapple syrup. Bring to boiling, stirring until thickened. Spoon sauce over chops. Serve immediately. *5 servings*

LAMB CHOP BRUNCH GRILL

▲ Base Recipe

Pretty as a picture for your party mood.

Panfry
> **¼ lb. bacon slices (see Panfried Bacon, page 190)**

Set aside in warm place.

Prepare
> **Apple rings (one half recipe, see Link Sausages and Apple Rings, page 193)**

Keep warm.

Meanwhile, mix for each pound of meat to be used (weight of lamb chops and chicken livers)
> **1 teaspoon salt**
> **½ teaspoon monosodium glutamate**
> **¼ teaspoon pepper**

Rinse with cold water, pat dry with absorbent paper and set aside
> **4 to 8 chicken livers**

Put onto rack of a broiler pan
> **4 lamb chops, 1 in. thick**

203

Lamb and Peach-Crowned Rice Casserole

Place under broiler with top of chops 2 in. from heat. In 6 or 7 min., or when chops are browned on one side, sprinkle with seasoning mixture and turn.

Place livers on broiler rack with chops and brush with

2 to 3 tablespoons melted butter or margarine

When partially cooked, season and turn livers. Brush again with butter. Broil chops 6 to 7 min., or until second side of meat is lightly browned.

Test chops for doneness by cutting a slit along the bone and noting color of meat. Sprinkle remaining seasoning mixture over top.

While meat is broiling, prepare
Scrambled Eggs (page 139)

Remove meat to warm serving plate. Arrange attractively around it the bacon, apple rings and scrambled eggs. *4 servings*

—LAMB CHOP PINEAPPLE GRILL

Follow ▲ Recipe. Omit apple rings. Place **4 slices pineapple** on broiler rack with chicken livers. Brush with **butter or margarine.** Turn when slightly browned.

LAMB CHOPS BURGUNDY

▲ Base Recipe

Put into a shallow dish
8 loin or rib lamb chops, cut 1½ to 2 in. thick

Combine in a screw-top jar and shake to blend
½ cup Burgundy
¼ cup olive oil
⅔ cup chopped red onion
½ clove garlic, minced
¼ teaspoon salt
3 peppercorns, crushed
½ teaspoon cumin seed, crushed
Pour marinade over meat. Cover and set in refrigerator to marinate about 2 hrs., turning chops occasionally.

Remove chops from marinade and place on broiler rack. Set under broiler with tops of chops 3 to 5 in. from heat. Broil 18 to 22 min., or until meat is of desired degree of doneness.

When chops are browned on one side, turn and brown other side. Occasionally brush with remaining marinade. To test doneness, slit meat near bone and note color of meat. *8 servings*

—MINTED LAMB CHOPS

Stir together **½ cup water, ¼ cup lemon juice, 12 fresh mint leaves,** crushed, **2 split cloves garlic, 2 tablespoons chopped onion** and **1 teaspoon rosemary,** crushed. Let stand overnight. Follow ▲ Recipe. Omit marinade. During broiling, brush chops frequently with the mint sauce.

—CHEF'S CHOICE LAMB CHOPS

Follow ▲ Recipe. Omit marinade. During broiling, brush chops frequently with a sauce of **3 tablespoons melted butter** thoroughly blended and heated with **2 teaspoons bottled exotic steak sauce.**

SWEET AND SOUR LAMB CHOPS

Set out a large skillet.

Have ready
4 lamb shoulder chops, cut ¾ in. thick
1 can (8¾ oz.) pineapple tidbits, undrained

Heat in the skillet
1 tablespoon cooking oil
Add chops and brown on both sides. Pour off excess fat.

Mix
½ cup firmly packed brown sugar
1 teaspoon dry mustard
½ cup vinegar
½ cup water
¾ cup ketchup
1 tablespoon soy sauce
Pour over chops and add pineapple tidbits.

Cover skillet, bring to boiling and simmer until chops are tender, about 45 min.; basting occasionally. Skim fat from sauce.

Serve with **hot cooked rice,** if desired.
4 servings

LAMB AND PEACH-CROWNED RICE CASSEROLE

Set out a large skillet and a shallow 2-qt. casserole.

Prepare
6 Panbroiled Lamb Chops (page 202)

Have ready
½ cup chopped onion
1 clove garlic, minced
2¼ cups canned chicken broth
¼ cup golden raisins

Drain, reserving ¼ cup syrup
1 can (16 oz.) sliced cling peaches

Heat in the skillet
⅓ cup butter or margarine
Add onion and garlic and cook until onion is soft, stirring occasionally. Add gradually, stirring constantly
1 cup uncooked rice
Cook 2 to 3 min. Add the broth, raisins and a blend of
½ teaspoon salt
¼ teaspoon allspice
¼ teaspoon cinnamon
Mix well. Cover skillet and cook over low heat until rice is tender.

Mix the reserved peach syrup with rice and turn into the casserole. Arrange lamb chops and peach slices over top of rice mixture. Brush the peaches lightly with **melted butter or margarine.** Tightly cover casserole with lid or aluminum foil.

Set in a 350°F oven until thoroughly heated.
6 servings

BROILED LAMB SIRLOIN CHOPS WITH OLIVES

A broiler pan with rack will be needed.

Put into a shallow dish
4 lamb sirloin chops, cut 1 in. thick
Mix
¼ cup cooking oil
3 tablespoons lemon juice
⅓ cup chopped pimiento-stuffed olives
1 clove garlic, minced
and a blend of
½ teaspoon salt
⅛ teaspoon pepper
¼ teaspoon oregano leaves
¼ teaspoon basil leaves
Pour over lamb chops. Marinate in refrigerator 2 to 3 hrs.; turn chops over once.

Remove chops from marinade and arrange on broiler rack.

Broil with top 3 to 4 in. from heat about 6

min. on each side, or until desired degree of doneness.

Meanwhile, heat olive marinade in a small saucepan. Spoon over chops before serving.

4 servings

LAMB CHOPS WITH DILL SAUCE
(Bécsi Báránykottlet Kapormártással)

For Chops—Melt in a large heavy skillet with a tight-fitting cover

3 tablespoons fat

Add to fat and, stirring occasionally, cook slowly about 5 min.

½ cup (about 1 medium) chopped onion

Remove onion from skillet with slotted spoon to small dish and set aside.

Have ready

4 lamb shoulder chops, cut ½ in. thick

Cut through fat on outside edges about every inch. Be careful not to cut through lean. Place chops in skillet; slowly brown both sides.

Meanwhile, mix

2 tablespoons water
1 tablespoon vinegar
1 teaspoon salt
¼ teaspoon pepper
1 bay leaf

Slowly add this mixture to the browned lamb. Return onion to skillet. Cover skillet and simmer 25 to 30 min., or until lamb is tender when pierced with a fork. If needed, add small amounts of water as lamb cooks.

For Sauce—When meat is almost tender, prepare and set aside to cool to lukewarm

½ cup quick meat broth (one half recipe, page 10)

Melt in small skillet over low heat

2 tablespoons butter or margarine

Blend into butter until smooth

2 tablespoons all-purpose flour
¼ teaspoon salt
Few grains pepper

Heat until mixture bubbles and is lightly browned. Remove skillet from heat. Add gradually, stirring constantly, a mixture of the reserved broth and

1 tablespoon chopped fresh dill

Bring rapidly to boiling, stirring constantly; cook 1 to 2 min. longer. Remove sauce from heat and gradually add, stirring constantly

½ cup dry white wine, such as Chablis or sauterne
2 tablespoons vinegar

Serve the sauce over lamb chops. *4 servings*

LAMB CHOPS EN BROCHETTE

A broiler pan with rack will be needed.

Have ready

6 lamb round-bone shoulder chops, cut 1½ to 2 in. thick

Rub chops with cut surfaces of

1 clove garlic, halved

Put chops into a shallow dish along with

12 shelled Brazil nuts
18 tomato wedges or cherry tomatoes
12 large mushrooms, cleaned

Pour over all

1½ cups bottled Italian salad dressing

Marinate in refrigerator several hours; baste occasionally.

Remove chops from marinade and thread onto long skewers. Put onto broiler rack and brush with marinade. Broil about 5 in. from heat about 22 min., turning several times and brushing frequently with marinade.

Cut into halves

6 slices bacon

Wrap nuts in bacon and thread alternately with tomatoes and mushrooms onto three long skewers. Brush with marinade.

Broil vegetable kabobs about 10 min., turning and brushing frequently with the marinade.

6 servings

LAMB CHOPS AND VEGETABLES ON SKEWERS

A broiler pan with rack will be needed.

Put into a large shallow dish

6 lamb round-bone shoulder chops, cut about 1½ in. thick

Combine

¼ cup lemon juice
1 clove garlic, minced
¼ teaspoon *each* marjoram leaves, crushed, rosemary leaves, crushed, tarragon leaves, crushed, and thyme
⅛ teaspoon onion powder
¾ cup cooking oil

Mix well and pour over chops. Marinate in refrigerator several hours; turn chops over occasionally.

Remove chops from marinade (reserve for brushing) and thread 2 chops on each of 3 long skewers. Put onto broiler rack. Broil about 4 in. from heat about 18 min., or until desired degree of doneness; turn frequently and brush with marinade. Season with **lemon pepper marinade.**

Meanwhile, prepare

1 pkg. (10 oz.) frozen cauliflower, partially cooked and drained
Green pepper squares (about 1½ in.)
Tomato wedges

Alternately thread vegetable pieces on long skewers. Put onto broiler rack and brush generously with marinade. Broil until of desired doneness, turning and brushing with marinade. Sprinkle with **salt.**

To serve, remove meat and vegetables from skewers. *6 servings*

LAMB KABOBS

▲ Base Recipe

For the most tantalizing flavor, marinate lamb or kidney at least 24 hours in advance.

Set out

1½ lbs. boned lamb shoulder or leg

Cut into 1½-in. cubes. Cover lamb with marinade and set in refrigerator for at least 24 hrs., turning meat several times.

For Marinade—Mix thoroughly

¾ cup tarragon vinegar
⅓ cup salad oil
2 teaspoons salt
¾ teaspoon monosodium glutamate
½ teaspoon pepper
1 bay leaf
½ clove garlic

For Kabobs—Set out six 8-in. skewers.

Clean, cut into halves from top to base and set aside

6 small (about 1 lb.) onions

Clean (page 9, do not slice), remove stems and set aside

12 large mushrooms

(Mushroom stems may be used in other recipes as desired.)

Set out

6 chicken livers

Cut into halves and wrap around chicken livers

3 slices bacon

Thread onto each skewer in the following order: lamb, onion half, mushroom and liver; repeat, ending with mushroom. Do not crowd pieces on skewer.

Brush meat and vegetables generously with

Melted butter or margarine

Arrange skewers on broiler rack.

Place broiler rack in broiler with tops of kabobs about 3 in. from heat. Broil 15 to 20 min., turning kabobs several times and brushing with melted butter or margarine. Test for doneness by cutting a slit in lamb cubes and noting color of meat.

Beef Kabobs and Kidneys en Brochette

Sprinkle kabobs with a mixture of

1 teaspoon salt
¼ teaspoon monosodium glutamate
⅛ teaspoon pepper

Serve at once.   *6 servings*

—LIVER KABOBS

Follow ▲ Recipe. Substitute **veal or calf's liver** for lamb; cut into ¾-in. cubes. Omit marinade and chicken livers. Thread the bacon, liver, onions and mushrooms alternately on skewers as desired. Broil about 10 min., or until liver is browned.

—BEEF KABOBS

Follow ▲ Recipe. Substitute tender **beef** for lamb. Omit chicken livers. Thread beef, bacon and vegetables alternately on skewers.

—SCALLOP KABOBS

Follow ▲ Recipe. Substitute **scallops** for lamb. Omit marinade, chicken livers and onions. Rinse, remove and discard stem end and cut into fourths **3 small tomatoes**. Thread the scallops, tomatoes, bacon and mushrooms alternately on skewers. Broil 5 to 10 min., or until scallops are lightly browned.

—OUT-OF-CUPBOARD KABOBS

Follow ▲ Recipe. Substitute for lamb and chicken livers, **1 can (12 oz.) luncheon meat,** cut in cubes. Omit marinade and bacon. Alternate meat cubes and vegetables on skewers.

—KIDNEYS EN BROCHETTE

Follow ▲ Recipe, using only **lamb kidneys** and omitting lamb, vegetables, chicken livers

and bacon. Split and remove membrane (unless this has been done at market). Using scissors, remove tubes. Rinse kidneys with cold water. Marinate at least 24 hrs. Insert skewer through lamb kidneys. Broil 10 to 15 min., or until kidneys are tender. Serve with **Tomato Sauce** (page 304).

LEMON LAMB SHANKS

Set out a Dutch oven or large heavy skillet.

Have ready
4 to 6 lamb shanks

Cut into small pieces
½ clove garlic
Make a gash in each lamb shank and insert a piece of garlic. Season shanks with
1 teaspoon salt
½ teaspoon pepper
Coat evenly with a blend of
3 tablespoons all-purpose flour
1 teaspoon paprika

Heat in the Dutch oven
2 tablespoons shortening
Add shanks and brown slowly, turning as necessary. Add to the Dutch oven
½ cup water
1 bay leaf, crushed
4 peppercorns
2 tablespoons grated lemon peel
½ cup lemon juice
Cover and simmer 2 to 2¼ hrs., or until meat is fork tender; turn meat occasionally and baste. Add a small amount of water if necessary. Serve with lemon wedges, if desired.
4 to 6 servings

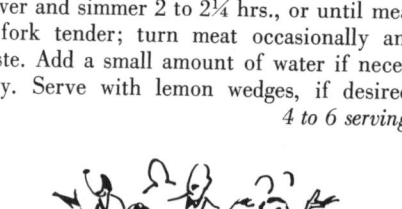

LAMB CASSEROLE

Set out a 2-qt. top-of-range casserole with a tight-fitting cover.

Prepare (page 9) and set aside
½ cup garlic buttered bread crumbs

Set out
1½ lbs. boneless lamb shoulder, cut in 1-in. pieces
Brown the lamb on all sides in casserole in
2 tablespoons hot melted fat
Add gradually
2½ cups water
Add
1½ teaspoons salt
½ teaspoon curry powder
⅛ teaspoon pepper
Cover casserole and simmer 1¼ hrs.

Meanwhile, clean and cut into crosswise thin slices
1 medium bunch (about ½ lb.) celery
Clean, pare or scrape and slice
1 lb. carrots (about 2½ cups)
Mix with carrots and celery
½ cup (about 1 medium) chopped onion
¼ cup chopped green pepper
Mix vegetables with meat in casserole. Cover casserole and cook over medium heat 20 to 25 min., or until vegetables are tender.

Meanwhile, cook
1½ cups noodles (one half recipe, page 152)
Stir noodles into casserole; simmer 10 min.

Meanwhile, pour into a screw-top jar
½ cup cold water
Sprinkle evenly over water
¼ cup all-purpose flour
Cover jar and shake until mixture is well blended. Stirring constantly, slowly add to casserole. Cook rapidly, still stirring, and bring sauce to boiling. (Sauce should be thickened.) Cook 3 to 5 min. longer.

Top with garlic buttered bread crumbs. Place casserole under broiler with top of casserole 4 in. from heat. Broil until crumbs are lightly browned.   *6 to 8 servings*

LAMB IN CABBAGE
(Faar i Kaal)

Set out
1½ lbs. boneless lamb shoulder, cut in 1-in. cubes
Put into a large saucepan with a tight-fitting cover. Add
3 cups water
Cook over medium heat 20 to 30 min., or until just tender.

Meanwhile, remove and discard wilted outer leaves, rinse and cut into 1-in. pieces (discarding core)
1 head (about 2 lbs.) cabbage

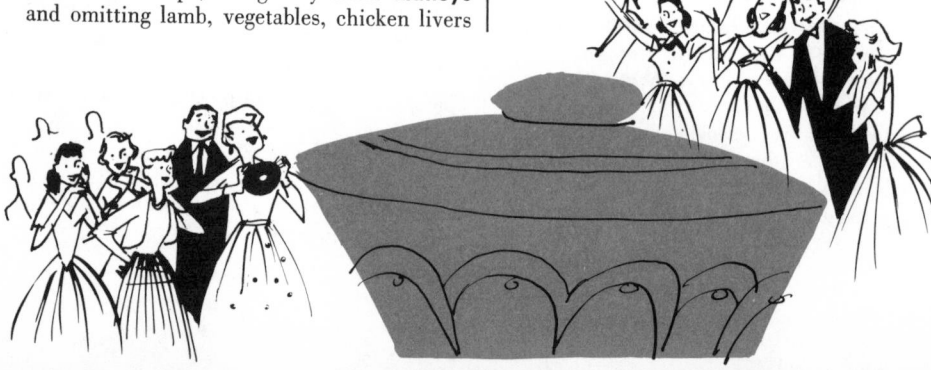

When meat is just tender, drain, reserving liquid. Put one half cabbage into saucepan.

Set out a mixture of
3 tablespoons all-purpose flour
1½ teaspoons salt
1½ teaspoons peppercorns

Sprinkle one half of mixture over cabbage. Put the meat into the saucepan in an even layer over the cabbage. Add the remaining cabbage and sprinkle remaining half of flour mixture over all. Pour over cabbage 2⅓ cups of the reserved liquid. Cover and cook over low heat about 1½ hrs., or until meat and cabbage are very tender.
6 servings

SWEET SOUR RAISIN LAMB

Set out a shallow baking pan.

Have ready
1 2-lb. lean breast of lamb, cut in 4 pieces (by meat dealer)

Slice and set aside
1 medium onion
1 lemon

Arrange lamb in the baking pan. Season with
1 teaspoon seasoned salt
½ teaspoon ginger
Put onion and lemon slices over lamb.

Set in a 450°F oven 20 to 25 min. Remove from oven and drain off excess fat. Turn oven control to 350°F.

Combine in a saucepan
½ cup seedless raisins
1 cup ketchup
1 cup dry red or white wine
2 tablespoons wine vinegar
¼ cup packed brown sugar
2 teaspoons Worcestershire sauce
Heat to boiling, stirring occasionally. Pour over meat and cover pan with aluminum foil. Return to oven and cook about 1 hr.
4 servings

Saucy Lamb Stew

SAUCY LAMB STEW

Set out a Dutch oven or large saucepan.

Have ready
1 medium onion, halved and thinly sliced
3 lbs. boneless lamb shoulder, cut in large cubes
1 can (16 oz.) cut green beans, drained; reserve liquid
Herb bouquet*
4 large carrots, cut in 1-in. pieces
1 cup diagonally sliced celery
1 lb. potatoes, pared and cut in large pieces
½ lb. large fresh mushrooms, thickly sliced

Heat in the Dutch oven
¼ cup butter or margarine
Stir in the onion and cook, stirring occasionally, until golden. Add lamb and cook over medium heat, stirring occasionally, until lightly browned, about 10 min.

Lower heat. Add reserved bean liquid, herb bouquet and
1 cup boiling water
1 can (8 oz.) tomato sauce
1 teaspoon salt
⅛ teaspoon pepper
Simmer, covered, 20 min. Add carrots, celery, potatoes and mushrooms. Continue to simmer, covered, 40 min., or until vegetables are tender.

Put into a jar
¼ cup water
Add
1 tablespoon all-purpose flour
Cover tightly and shake vigorously to blend. Bring stew to boiling and quickly stir in flour blend. Cook 1 to 2 min., continuing to stir. Mix in beans and
1 cup dairy sour cream
Heat to serving temperature (do not boil). Remove herb bouquet before serving and, if desired, sprinkle stew with chopped parsley.
6 to 8 servings

*For herb bouquet, wrap **celery leaves, parsley sprigs, 1 bay leaf, ⅛ teaspoon thyme leaves** and **⅛ teaspoon rosemary leaves** in a small square of cheesecloth; tie securely.

VEGETABLE LAMB NECK STEW

Set out a Dutch oven.

Set out
4 lbs. lamb neck slices

Have ready
2 cups diced white turnips
1 cup sliced carrots
12 small white onions
1 medium green pepper, cut in 1-in. strips

Heat in the Dutch oven
2 tablespoons cooking oil

Add the lamb neck slices and brown well. Pour off excess fat. Add to Dutch oven
1 can (13¾ oz.) chicken broth
2 cups water
1 clove garlic, minced
and a blend of
2 teaspoons salt
¼ teaspoon pepper
2 teaspoons oregano leaves
½ teaspoon thyme leaves
½ teaspoon nutmeg
Cover and simmer about 45 min. Add the vegetables and cook, covered, about 20 min., or until vegetables are almost tender.

Pour into a jar
¼ cup water
Add
2 tablespoons all-purpose flour
Cover tightly and shake vigorously to blend. Pour flour blend into stew and mix in
1 can (8 oz.) whole kernel corn, undrained
Bring to boiling; cook, uncovered, about 10 min., stirring occasionally. Sprinkle with **chopped chives** before serving.
About 6 servings

LAMB STEW

A favorite of long standing in New England where lamb has always been popular.

Set out a large kettle or Dutch oven with a tight-fitting cover.

For Stew—Have ready
2 lbs. boneless lamb (shoulder)
Cut meat into 2-in. cubes. Coat meat evenly

by shaking two or three pieces at a time in a plastic bag containing a mixture of

⅓ cup all-purpose flour
2 teaspoons salt
½ teaspoon monosodium glutamate
⅛ teaspoon pepper

Heat in the kettle or Dutch oven

3 tablespoons fat

Add the meat cubes to the kettle. Brown meat on all sides over medium heat, turning occasionally. Pour off excess fat. Remove from heat and slowly pour into kettle

1 qt. hot water

Cover kettle and bring to boiling. Reduce heat and simmer about 1½ hrs., or until meat is almost tender.

Meanwhile, prepare and leave whole

6 small onions
6 to 8 small carrots, washed and scraped or pared

About 45 min. before end of cooking period, add the vegetables to the kettle with

1½ teaspoons salt
½ teaspoon monosodium glutamate
¼ teaspoon marjoram
⅛ teaspoon pepper
1 bay leaf

About 25 min. before end of cooking period, add to the stew

½ cup fresh or frozen lima beans

Meanwhile, prepare Dumplings.

For Dumplings—Sift together into a bowl

2 cups sifted all-purpose flour
4 teaspoons baking powder
1 teaspoon salt

Cut in with pastry blender or two knives until mixture resembles rice kernels

1 tablespoon shortening

Quickly stir in with a fork until just blended

⅔ cup milk

Bring stew to boiling. Drop batter by spoonfuls on top of stew. Dumplings should rest on meat and vegetables; if they settle down into liquid, they may become soggy. If necessary pour off excess liquid to prevent this. Cover kettle tightly and cook over medium heat 20 min. Do not remove cover while dumplings are cooking.

Remove cooked dumplings, meat and vegetables and keep warm while thickening liquid.

To Thicken Cooking Liquid—Pour into a screw-top jar

½ cup cold water

Sprinkle onto it

¼ cup all-purpose flour

Cover jar tightly and shake until mixture is well blended. Slowly pour one half of the mixture into cooking liquid while stirring constantly. Bring to boiling. Gradually add only what is needed of remaining flour-water mixture for consistency desired. Bring mixture to boiling after each addition. After final addition cook 3 to 5 min. longer.

To Complete—Return meat and vegetables to kettle and heat thoroughly.

Turn stew mixture into a warm serving dish or tureen. Arrange dumplings attractively with stew. Garnish stew with **chopped parsley.**

8 to 10 servings

LAMB WITH GREEN BEANS
(Bárányhús Zöldbabbal)

▲ Base Recipe

Set out a heavy 10-in. skillet with a tight-fitting cover.

Put on a wooden cutting board and cut into 1-in. cubes

2 lbs. boneless lamb shoulder

Put into the skillet

4 slices bacon, diced

Cook slowly, moving and turning frequently, until bacon is lightly browned. Remove bacon with slotted spoon to a small dish and set aside.

Add to the bacon fat in skillet

½ cup (about 1 medium) chopped onion

Cook slowly, stirring occasionally, until onion is almost tender. Remove onion with slotted spoon to dish containing the bacon and set aside.

Add the meat to the bacon fat and brown slowly on all sides. Sprinkle over meat a mixture of

2 teaspoons salt
1 teaspoon caraway seed
1 teaspoon paprika

Remove skillet from heat and slowly pour in

2 cups quick meat broth (double recipe, page 10)

Return bacon and onion to skillet. Cover skillet and simmer 1½ to 2 hrs., or until meat is tender when pierced with a fork.

About an hour before meat is tender, wash, remove ends, cut into 1-in. pieces and cook (page 313) about 15 min., or until just tender

1 lb. (about 3 cups) green beans

If necessary, drain beans (reserving any cooking liquid) and set aside. Cool the cooking liquid.

Pour into a small screw-top jar

½ cup liquid (reserved bean cooking liquid plus water)

Sprinkle onto the liquid

¼ cup all-purpose flour

Cover jar tightly and shake until mixture is

well blended. Bring contents of skillet to boiling. Slowly pour the flour mixture (shaking again if necessary) into skillet while stirring constantly. Bring this gravy to boiling, stirring constantly; cook 3 to 5 min. longer. Remove from heat and vigorously stir about ½ cup of the gravy, 1 tablespoon at a time, into

½ cup dairy sour cream

Pour the mixture gradually into the skillet, stirring constantly. Gently mix in the green beans. Cook ingredients over low heat, moving mixture gently, 3 to 5 min., until heated thoroughly; do not boil.   *5 to 7 servings*

—BEEF WITH GREEN BEANS
(Marhahus Zoldbabbal)

Follow ▲ Recipe. Substitute **lean beef** for lamb.

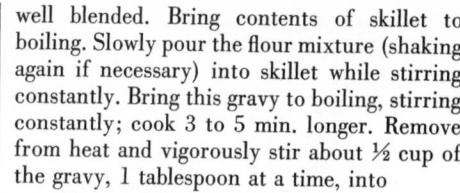

VEAL

VEAL CHOPS PIZZAIOLA
(Scaloppine alla Pizzaiola)

▲ Base Recipe

Set out a large heavy skillet with a tight-fitting cover.

Heat in skillet

¼ cup olive oil

Put into heated oil in skillet and slowly brown on both sides

6 veal rib or loin chops, cut about ½ in. thick

Meanwhile, combine

3½ cups (28-oz. can) tomatoes, sieved
2 cloves garlic, sliced
1 teaspoon oregano
1 teaspoon salt
½ teaspoon pepper
½ teaspoon chopped parsley

Slowly add tomato mixture to browned veal. Cover skillet and cook slowly for 45 min., or until meat is tender when pierced with a fork.

6 servings

—BEEFSTEAK PIZZAIOLA
(Bistecca alla Pizzaiola)

Follow ▲ Recipe. Substitute **2 lbs. beef round steak,** cut about ¾ in. thick, for the veal chops. Cook slowly about 1½ hrs.

VEAL CHOPS EN PAPILLOTE
(Côte de Veau en Papillote)

Cooking in paper (en papillote) is one of the oldest of French culinary customs. It is used for fish, and lamb, mutton and veal chops.

Set out a 1-qt. casserole with a cover.

Set out

8 thin veal chops

Puffy Veal Cutlets and American Style Wiener Schnitzel

—AMERICAN-STYLE WIENER SCHNITZEL

Follow recipe for Veal Cutlets with Fried Eggs. Omit fried eggs. Melt over low heat **2 tablespoons butter.** Stir in **6 anchovy fillets,** mashed, and **1 tablespoon lemon juice.** Pour over the cutlets. Garnish with **parsley.**

BREADED VEAL CUTLETS
(Wiener Schnitzel)

About 20 min. before deep-frying, fill a deep saucepan one half to two thirds full with **lard.** Heat lard to 375°F (page 11).

Put onto a cutting board or other flat working surface
   **2 lbs. veal round steak (cutlet),
      cut ½ in. thick**
Pound meat on one side with meat hammer. Turn and repeat process until meat is about ¼ in. thick. Cut into 6 serving-size pieces. Coat cutlets with a mixture of
   **⅓ cup all-purpose flour
   1½ teaspoons salt
   1 teaspoon monosodium glutamate
   ¼ teaspoon pepper**
Dip cutlets into
   3 eggs, slightly beaten
Carefully coat (not too heavily) with
   1½ cups French bread crumbs*
Let stand 5 to 10 min. to "seal" coating.

Deep-fry only as many cutlets at one time as will lie uncrowded one layer deep in the fat. Fry until browned on both sides, about 3 or 4 min.; with a long fork or tongs, turn slices several times during cooking (do not pierce). Remove cutlets with tongs or slotted spoon

---

Put meat into casserole with
   1 cup olive oil
Cover and let stand in refrigerator 12 hrs. to marinate. Turn chops occasionally if not entirely covered with oil.

Cut large enough to wrap around each chop and allow a margin for overlapping
   8 pieces parchment-type paper
Lightly butter one side of paper.

Mix together
   **⅓ cup chopped mushrooms
   ¼ cup chopped onion
   2 teaspoons chopped parsley
   2 teaspoons chopped olives**
Place heaping tablespoon of mixture on buttered side of each paper. Place a chop on top. Dot each chop with
   ¼ teaspoon butter
Draw the paper tightly around each chop and gather excess paper at top and tie with string. Or fold the paper over each chop and tie so no steam or juice will escape.

Put onto a baking sheet and bake at 300°F 30 to 40 min. Remove papers. Season chops with
   **1 teaspoon salt
   ⅛ teaspoon pepper**

8 servings

PUFFY VEAL CUTLETS
(Panierte Kalbsschnitzel)

▲ *Base Recipe*

Set out a large heavy skillet with a tight-fitting cover.

Have ready
   **1½ lbs. veal round steak (cutlet),
      cut about ½ in. thick**
Cut into 4 serving-size pieces. Coat cutlets with a mixture of
   **¼ cup all-purpose flour
   1½ teaspoons monosodium glutamate
   1 teaspoon salt
   ⅛ teaspoon pepper**
Set aside.

Beat until thick and lemon-colored
   1 egg yolk
Set aside.

Heat in the skillet over low heat
   3 or 4 tablespoons butter

Meanwhile, using a clean beater, beat until rounded peaks are formed
   1 egg white
Spread the egg yolk over the egg white and gently fold together.

Coat cutlets on one side with the egg mixture. Put cutlets into skillet, egg-coated side down. Cook until lightly browned, about 15 min.

Spoon remaining egg mixture onto cutlets, being sure to cover tops, and turn. Cover and cook over low heat about 20 min., or until meat is tender when pierced with a fork.

4 servings

—VEAL CUTLETS WITH FRIED EGGS
(Schnitzel Holstein)

Follow ▲ Recipe. Do not separate egg; beat slightly and mix with **1 tablespoon milk.** After flouring cutlets, dip into the egg mixture and then coat with **1 cup (3 to 4 slices) fine dry bread crumbs.** Cook; keep warm while preparing fried eggs. Heat **1 to 2 tablespoons butter** in a heavy skillet over low heat. Break into a saucer, one at a time, and slip into the skillet, **4 eggs.** Reduce heat and cook slowly about 4 min., or to desired stage of firmness. Baste eggs frequently with butter in skillet.

Arrange fried eggs on top of cutlets. Garnish platter with **vegetables** and diamonds of **crisp toast** topped with **smoked salmon, caviar** and cutouts of **hard-cooked egg white.**

Veal Cutlets with Fried Eggs

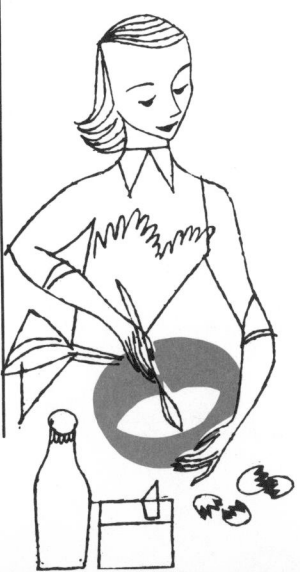

and drain over fat for a few seconds before removing to absorbent paper.

Serve with

Lemon wedges

6 servings

*Sour French bread crumbs may be used.

VEAL CUTLET IN WINE WITH OLIVES

Set out

1½ lbs. veal round steak (cutlet), cut about ¼ in. thick

To increase tenderness, place meat on flat working surface and repeatedly pound with meat hammer. Turn meat and repeat process. Cut into six serving-size pieces. Coat with a mixture of

¼ cup all-purpose flour
1 teaspoon salt
½ teaspoon monosodium glutamate
¼ teaspoon pepper

Heat in a skillet over low heat

2 to 3 tablespoons butter or margarine

Brown meat over medium heat. Add

⅓ cup Marsala
⅓ cup sliced green olives

Cover skillet and cook over low heat about 1 hr., or until meat is tender when pierced with a fork.   *About 6 servings*

VEAL BIRDS

▲ Base Recipe

Set out a large heavy skillet with a tight-fitting cover.

For Bread Stuffing—Mix

⅓ cup melted butter
1 teaspoon salt
½ teaspoon sage (or ¼ teaspoon each of thyme, rosemary and marjoram
⅛ teaspoon pepper

Lightly toss butter mixture with

1 qt. soft bread cubes (about 6 slices bread)
⅓ cup milk
¼ cup chopped celery with leaves
2 tablespoons chopped onion

Set aside.

For Veal Birds—Have ready

2 lbs. veal round steak (cutlet), cut about ¼ in. thick

To increase tenderness, place meat on a flat working surface and repeatedly pound meat on one side with meat hammer. Turn meat and repeat process. Cut into eight serving-size pieces.

Season with a mixture of

1½ teaspoons salt
¾ teaspoon monosodium glutamate
½ teaspoon basil
½ teaspoon tarragon
¼ teaspoon pepper

Spoon 2 to 3 tablespoons of stuffing onto center of each piece of veal. Roll meat around stuffing and fasten securely with skewer or wooden picks. Coat evenly by rolling in

All-purpose flour

Heat in the skillet over low heat

3 tablespoons butter

Add the veal rolls and brown on all sides over medium heat. Remove from heat and slowly pour into the skillet

1 cup hot water

Cover skillet and cook over low heat about 45 min., or until meat is tender when pierced with a fork.

Remove veal birds from skillet to hot serving platter. Set aside to keep warm.

For Sour Cream Gravy—Put into a small screw-top jar

¼ cup cold water

Sprinkle onto the water

2 tablespoons all-purpose flour

Cover jar tightly and shake until mixture is well blended. Bring contents of skillet to boiling. Slowly pour the flour mixture (shaking again if necessary) into skillet while stirring constantly. Again bring to boiling; cook 3 to 5 min. longer.

Remove from heat and with French whip, whisk beater or fork, vigorously stir into the hot mixture, 1 tablespoon at a time

1 cup dairy sour cream

Cook gravy over low heat, stirring constantly, 3 to 5 min., or just until heated; *do not boil.*

Remove skewers or picks from veal birds before serving. Serve with the sour cream gravy; if desired, garnish with **parsley**.   *8 servings*

—VEAL CHOPS WITH SOUR CREAM GRAVY

Follow ▲ Recipe for Sour Cream Gravy only. Heat **2 tablespoons butter** in a large skillet. Add **6 veal chops** cut ¾ in. thick and brown on both sides over medium heat. Season browned chops with a mixture of **1 teaspoon salt**, **⅛ teaspoon pepper** and **1 bay leaf**, crushed. Slowly add **¼ cup hot water** to skillet. Cover, reduce heat and simmer until tender. Remove chops to warm serving platter. Prepare gravy and spoon over chops.

Veal Rollettes

VEAL ROLLETTES
(Rosolini di Vitella)

Grease a 2-qt. casserole with a tight-fitting cover.

Combine and set aside

2 cloves garlic, chopped
1 tablespoon grated Parmesan cheese
2 teaspoons chopped parsley
½ teaspoon salt
¼ teaspoon pepper

Set out on a wooden board and cut into approximately 4x3-in. rectangular pieces

1½ lbs. veal round steak (cutlet), cut about ½ in. thick

Place on each piece of meat

1 slice mozzarella cheese

Top each with 1 teaspoon garlic-cheese mixture. Roll each piece of meat to enclose mixture and fasten with wooden picks or skewers or tie securely. Set aside.

Heat in skillet

3 tablespoons olive oil

Place rolled meat into skillet and brown slowly on all sides. Place meat in casserole. Pour over meat a mixture of

½ cup melted butter or margarine
¼ cup water

Cover casserole and cook in a 300°F oven about 1 hr., or until meat is tender when pierced with a fork. Remove wooden picks or string.   *About 4 servings*

VEAL PAPRIKA

Set out a heavy 10-in. skillet with a tight-fitting cover.

To Cook Veal—Set out

2 lbs. veal round steak, cut about 1 in. thick

Coat veal steak with a mixture of

¼ cup all-purpose flour
1 tablespoon paprika
1 teaspoon salt
½ teaspoon monosodium glutamate
Few grains cayenne pepper
Few grains pepper

Reserve remaining flour mixture.

Clean and thinly slice

2 medium onions

Veal Birds

Heat in the skillet

3 tablespoons butter

Add the onions and cook over medium heat until tender. Using a slotted spoon, remove onions from skillet and set aside. Add the veal steak and slowly brown on one side; turn and brown second side. Place onions on the veal steak.

Pour into a screw-top jar

1 cup water

Sprinkle onto the liquid the reserved flour mixture. Cover jar tightly and shake until mixture is well blended. Slowly pour mixture over the veal steak, stirring constantly; cover and simmer about 1 hr., or until meat is tender.

For Noodles—About 30 min. before meat is tender, chop and set aside

½ cup (about 3 oz.) blanched, toasted almonds (pages 9 and 10)

Meanwhile, heat to boiling in a large saucepan

3 qts. water
1 tablespoon salt

Add gradually

3 cups (about 8 oz.) noodles

Boil rapidly, uncovered, 6 to 10 min. Test tenderness by pressing a piece against side of pan with fork or spoon. Drain noodles by turning into colander or large sieve. Put into a large bowl. Add to the noodles the almonds and

2 tablespoons butter
1 tablespoon poppy seed
½ teaspoon paprika

Toss lightly until butter is melted and mixture thoroughly combined. Set aside; keep warm until meat is tender.

When ready to serve, place veal steak on a warm serving platter. Spoon noodles around veal steak. Slice and arrange on veal steak

4 pimiento stuffed olives

Keep warm while preparing gravy.

For Gravy—Stirring vigorously, add to the mixture in the skillet in very small amounts

1 cup dairy sour cream

Blend in

2 tablespoons sherry
¼ teaspoon oregano

Heat thoroughly; do not boil. Serve gravy with veal steak. *6 servings*

VEAL PARMESAN

▲ *Base Recipe*

The Italian title for this delectable dish is Scaloppine di Vitella alla Parmigiana.

Set out an 11x7x2-in. baking dish.

Prepare (allowing about 4½ hrs.)

Tomato Meat Sauce (one half recipe, page 162)

When the sauce is partially cooked, remove from refrigerator

1½ to 2 lbs. veal round steak (cutlet), cut about ½ in. thick

To increase tenderness, place meat on a flat working surface and repeatedly pound meat on one side with meat hammer. Turn meat and repeat process. Cut into six serving-size pieces. Set aside.

Mix and set aside

1⅓ cups fine dry bread crumbs (about 4 slices bread)
⅓ cup grated Parmesan cheese

Mix

3 eggs, beaten
1 teaspoon salt
¾ teaspoon monosodium glutamate
¼ teaspoon pepper

Heat in a skillet

⅓ cup olive oil

Dip meat pieces (coat both sides) in egg mixture. Allow excess egg mixture to drain back into bowl. Dip piece into crumb mixture (coat both sides). Dip only as many pieces at one time as will lie flat in skillet. Put in skillet and brown on both sides over low heat.

Repeat procedure for remaining pieces. If necessary, add more oil to skillet to prevent sticking. Arrange browned pieces in baking dish. Pour the Tomato Meat Sauce over them. Top with

6 slices (3 oz.) mozzarella cheese (1 slice per piece)

Bake at 350°F 15 to 20 min., or until cheese is melted and lightly browned. *6 servings*

—LIGHT VEAL PARMESAN

Follow ▲ Recipe. Brown veal lightly and place in baking dish. Pour over it ¼ **cup melted butter**; sprinkle with ¼ **cup grated Parmesan cheese.** Omit tomato sauce and mozzarella cheese.

VEAL MARSALA

(Scaloppine di Vitella al Marsala)

Set out a large heavy skillet with a tight-fitting cover.

Heat in skillet until garlic is lightly browned

1 clove garlic, sliced thin
¼ cup olive oil

Set out on a wooden board, pound and cut in six pieces

1½ to 2 lbs. veal round steak (cutlet), cut about ½ in. thick

Coat veal with a mixture of

¼ cup all-purpose flour
¾ teaspoon monosodium glutamate
½ teaspoon salt
⅛ teaspoon pepper

Add veal to garlic and olive oil and slowly brown on both sides.

While veal is browning, combine

¼ cup Marsala
¼ cup water
¼ teaspoon chopped parsley
⅛ teaspoon salt
⅛ teaspoon pepper

Slowly add Marsala mixture to browned veal. Cover skillet and simmer very slowly for about 20 min., or until veal is tender. If mixture tends to become too thick, add a small amount of water. *6 servings*

VEAL SCALOPPINE

(Scaloppine di Vitella)

▲ *Base Recipe*

Set out a large heavy skillet with a tight-fitting cover.

Set out on a wooden board and pound with a meat hammer

1 lb. veal round steak (cutlet), cut about ½ in. thick

Cut veal into 1-in. pieces. To coat veal evenly, shake 2 or 3 pieces at a time in a plastic bag containing a mixture of

½ cup all-purpose flour
¾ teaspoon monosodium glutamate
½ teaspoon salt
⅛ teaspoon pepper

Set aside.

Heat in skillet until garlic is lightly browned

1 clove garlic, sliced thin
¼ cup olive oil

Add veal to garlic and olive oil and slowly brown on both sides.

While veal is browning, combine

1¾ cups tomatoes, sieved
½ teaspoon salt
¼ teaspoon chopped parsley
¼ teaspoon oregano
⅛ teaspoon pepper

Slowly add tomato mixture to browned veal.

Veal Scaloppine

Cover skillet and simmer about 25 min., or until veal is tender. If mixture tends to become too thick, add a small amount of water.

3 or 4 servings

—VEAL SCALOPPINE WITH MUSHROOMS AND PEPPERS
(Scaloppine di Vitella con Funghi e Peperoni)

Follow ▲ Recipe. Prepare **1 green pepper** and ½ **lb. fresh mushrooms.** Cook mushrooms and green pepper in **3 tablespoons butter or margarine** until mushrooms are lightly browned. Add to browned veal with tomato mixture.

VEAL RICE CASSEROLE
(Borjuhus Rizzsel)

Grease a 2-qt. casserole; set out a large heavy skillet with a tight-fitting cover.

Have ready

    1 lb. veal round steak (cutlet), cut
        ¼ **in. thick**

Cut veal into 1-in. pieces and set aside.

Heat in the large skillet over low heat

    ¼ **cup butter or margarine**

Stir in

    1 tablespoon paprika

Place meat in skillet and brown over medium heat, stirring occasionally. Add

    ¼ **cup hot water**
    1 teaspoon salt

Cover skillet and simmer about 45 min., or until meat is tender when pierced with a fork.

Meanwhile, bring to boiling in a deep saucepan

    2 qts. water
    1 tablespoon salt

So boiling will not stop, add gradually to water

    1 cup uncooked rice

(The Rice Industry no longer considers it necessary to wash rice before cooking.) Boil rapidly, uncovered, 15 to 20 min., or until a rice kernel is entirely soft when pressed between fingers. Drain rice in colander or sieve and rinse with hot water to remove loose starch. Cover colander and rice with towel and set over hot water until kernels are dry and fluffy.

Meanwhile, clean and slice (page 9)

    ½ **lb. mushrooms**

Melt in an 8-in. skillet over low heat

    2 or 3 tablespoons butter or margarine

Add the mushrooms to the butter. Stirring

gently, cook over low heat until mushrooms are lightly browned and tender. Put contents of skillet into a bowl. Add the rice and gently mix with a fork. Set aside.

Wash and cut off and discard stem ends from

    1 large or 2 small firm tomatoes

Cut tomatoes into ½-in. slices and set aside.

Place one half of meat into the casserole. Top with one half rice-mushroom mixture and all of tomato slices. Repeat layering of meat and mushroom-rice mixture; top with a layer of

    1½ cups dairy sour cream

Sprinkle over the sour cream

    ¼ **cup grated Parmesan cheese**

Bake at 350°F about 15 to 20 min., or until thoroughly heated. Serve immediately.

6 servings

VEAL, HUNTER STYLE
(Sauté de Veau Chasseur)

The province of Ile-de-France first applied the term "chasseur" to cookery. Now it is understood as the preparation of any kind of meat, game or poultry in a sauce of white wine, mushrooms and shallots.

Set out a large skillet and butter a 2-qt. casserole with a tight-fitting cover.

Heat in skillet

    3 tablespoons butter

Put into skillet

    1½ to 2 lbs. veal round steak (cutlet), cut about ½ in. thick and cut in 6 portions

Cook slowly 6 to 7 min. on each side without allowing meat to brown. Remove to casserole.

Clean and slice (page 9)

    8 medium mushrooms

Add mushrooms to skillet with

    6 shallots, chopped

Cook 3 to 5 min., stirring occasionally, without browning. Turn into casserole.

Heat in the skillet

    1 cup white wine
    1 cup Bouillon or Brown Stock (page 41)

Pour over the meat. Add

    1 teaspoon salt
    ¼ **teaspoon pepper**
    Herb bouquet (page 9)

Cover and cook in a 325°F oven 1 to 1½ hrs., or until meat is tender, basting occasionally. Remove and discard Herb Bouquet. Remove about 1 cup of the liquid and return casserole to oven to keep warm.

Stir the 1 cup liquid vigorously into

    2 egg yolks, slightly beaten

Pour into a small saucepan. Cook and stir about 5 min., or until slightly thickened. Stir into mixture in casserole.

Meanwhile, prepare and slice

    2 Hard-Cooked Eggs (page 133)

Use as a garnish with

    Croutons (page 39)
    1 teaspoon minced parsley
    1 teaspoon chopped tarragon

About 6 servings

VEAL IN CREAMY IVORY SAUCE
(Blanquette de Veau)

Since blanc means white, a blanquette is a dish notable for its whiteness. Hence, a blanquette is made with veal, lamb or white meat of poultry —covered with a white or creamy sauce.

Set out a 3-qt. saucepan with a tight-fitting cover.

Set out

    2 lbs. veal (breast or boneless shoulder), cut in 2-in. pieces

Put meat into saucepan with

    1 onion, cut in halves
    1 carrot, cut in quarters
    Herb bouquet (page 9)

Add

    Water just to cover
    1 tablespoon salt
    ¼ **teaspoon pepper**

Cover and simmer about 2 hrs.

Meanwhile, clean and slice (page 9)

    ½ **lb. mushrooms**

Stirring constantly, add mushrooms to skillet with

    3 tablespoons butter
    ½ **cup sliced onion**

Cook about 5 min.

Strain veal, reserving stock. Set mushrooms, onion and veal aside.

Melt in same saucepan

    ¼ **cup butter**

Stir in

    ¼ **cup all-purpose flour**

Heat until mixture bubbles. Remove from heat. Gradually stir in 2 cups of liquid in which veal was cooked. Return to heat and bring rapidly to boiling, stirring constantly; cook 2 to 3 min. longer.

Remove from heat and vigorously stir about 2 tablespoons of the sauce into

    2 egg yolks, slightly beaten

Immediately return the egg mixture to the sauce and stir constantly over low heat about 3 to 5 min. Add the cooked onion, mushrooms and meat.

Just before serving, blend in

    1 tablespoon butter
    1 tablespoon lemon juice

Garnish with **chopped parsley** and serve.

6 servings

VEAL IN CURRY SAUCE

Set out a 3-qt. saucepan with a tight-fitting cover.

Set out

**1 lb. boneless veal shoulder, cut in
1-in. cubes**

Put meat into the saucepan with

**2 cups water
1 teaspoon salt**

Cover and simmer over low heat for 1 hr.

Meanwhile, wash, scrape or pare and cut into quarters

3 medium carrots

Rinse and remove ends from

½ lb. green beans

Clean and cut into ½-in. slices

2 large stalks celery

When meat has cooked 1 hr., add vegetables to the meat. Cover and simmer over low heat 1 hr., or until meat is tender when pierced with a fork.

When meat is tender, remove meat and vegetables with a slotted spoon and set aside to keep warm. Reserve cooking liquid.

Heat in the saucepan

3 tablespoons butter or margarine

Blend in

**2 tablespoons all-purpose flour
½ teaspoon curry powder
¼ teaspoon salt**

Heat until mixture bubbles. Remove from heat. Add the reserved cooking liquid gradually, stirring constantly. Return to heat and bring rapidly to boiling, stirring constantly; cook 1 to 2 min. longer.

Add the cooked vegetables and meat cubes; mix well. Heat thoroughly, stirring occasionally. If desired, keep warm in a chafing dish blazer over the pan of simmering water.

Serve with

Fluffy Rice (page 164)

6 servings

BROWNED VEAL
(Borju Pörkölt)

Richly browned cubes of veal, delightfully flavored, are stars on the culinary stage. If the cubes were cooked in true Hungarian-style, the
rich brown would border on "scorched" or "singed"—a literal translation of Pörkölt.

Put into a heavy 10- or 12-in. skillet with a tight-fitting cover

**8 slices bacon, diced
½ cup (about 1 medium) chopped onion
¼ cup chopped green pepper
1½ teaspoons paprika**

Cook slowly, stirring frequently, until bacon is lightly browned.

Meanwhile, cut into 1-in. cubes

1½ lbs. boneless veal shoulder

Coat meat by shaking it in a plastic bag containing a mixture of

**¼ cup all-purpose flour
1 teaspoon salt
¼ teaspoon pepper**

With slotted spoon, remove bacon mixture to small dish, leaving bacon fat in the skillet. Add meat to skillet and brown meat slowly on all sides.

Return bacon mixture to skillet with

⅓ cup hot water

Cover skillet and simmer, stirring occasionally and adding small amounts of water as needed, 45 to 60 min., or until meat is tender when pierced with a fork. Transfer the meat and liquid to warm platter or bowl and garnish with **parsley**.

4 to 6 servings

VEAL AND GREEN BEAN STEW
(Kalbsragout mit grünen Bohnen)

Set out a saucepot or kettle with a cover.

Have ready

1½ lbs. boneless veal shoulder

Cut into 1-in. cubes. Put into saucepot with

**3½ cups cold water
1½ teaspoons salt
1 teaspoon monosodium glutamate**

Cover saucepot and bring water slowly to boiling. Reduce heat and simmer 1 hr.

Meanwhile, wash, cut off and discard ends from and cut into 1-in. pieces

1½ lbs. green beans

Add beans to saucepot, cover loosely and cook 25 min. longer, or until beans are tender.

Dissolve

1 chicken bouillon cube

in

½ cup very hot water

Set aside.

Remove saucepot from heat and drain, reserving stock. Return the veal and beans to saucepot and set aside.

Heat in a small saucepan

3 tablespoons butter

Blend in

**¼ cup all-purpose flour
1 tablespoon sugar
1½ teaspoons salt
1 teaspoon monosodium glutamate**

Heat until mixture bubbles. Remove from heat. Add gradually, stirring in, the reserved stock, chicken broth and

2 tablespoons vinegar

Cook rapidly, stirring constantly, until sauce thickens. Cook 1 to 2 min. longer. Blend in a mixture of

**2 tablespoons minced parsley
¼ teaspoon savory
⅛ teaspoon pepper**

Add to the saucepot and mix carefully, with the veal and beans. Heat about 10 min., or until meat is thoroughly heated.

About 6 servings

VEAL PAPRIKA WITH WILD RICE

Set out a 2-qt. top-of-range casserole with a tight-fitting cover; rub with cut surface of

½ clove garlic

Set out

1½ lbs. boneless veal shoulder, cut in 1-in. cubes

Coat evenly by shaking a few cubes at a time in a plastic bag containing a mixture of

**½ cup all-purpose flour
¾ teaspoon monosodium glutamate
1 teaspoon salt
⅛ teaspoon pepper**

Melt in casserole over medium heat

3 tablespoons fat

Veal and Green Bean Stew

Add veal and brown slowly on all sides.

Meanwhile, clean and chop
> **1 medium onion**
> **½ medium green pepper**

Add vegetables to casserole with
> **1½ cups water**

Cover casserole and simmer 1½ to 2 hrs., or until meat is tender.

Meanwhile, cook, uncovered, 30 min.; drain
> **1 cup wild rice**
> **6 cups boiling water**
> **1 teaspoon salt**

Using a fork, stir into drained rice
> **3 tablespoons butter or margarine**

Set aside.

Drain meat and vegetables, reserving stock.

Prepare
> **2 cups Thin White Sauce (double recipe, page 304; use 1 cup reserved stock and 1 cup cream for liquid. Add 1 tablespoon paprika with seasonings. Add 1 tablespoon chopped parsley to completed sauce.)**

Stir meat and vegetables into sauce. Cover bottom of casserole with one half of the rice.

Add one half of the meat mixture. Repeat layers. Sprinkle over top
> **½ cup canned crisp noodles**

Heat in a 350°F oven 25 to 30 min.

6 servings

JELLIED VEAL
(Kalv Sylta)

Set out a 9x5x3-in. loaf pan.

Set out
> **2 lbs. veal shank**
> **1 lb. veal shoulder**

Put meat into a large heavy saucepot with
> **2 qts. boiling water**

Calf's Liver with Bacon

Add
> **1 tablespoon salt**
> **10 peppercorns**
> **1 bay leaf**

Bring to boiling. Skim off any foam. Cover, reduce heat and simmer slowly about 2 hrs., or until meat is tender. Remove meat from broth and set aside.

Strain the broth and return it to the saucepot. Bring to boiling and boil rapidly, uncovered, until 1 qt. liquid remains.

Meanwhile, remove the meat from the bone. Put through the medium blade of a food chopper. Add the meat to the broth with
> **¾ teaspoon ginger**
> **¼ teaspoon pepper**

Turn into the loaf pan and set aside to cool.

Chill in refrigerator until firm.

When ready to serve, unmold onto a chilled serving plate. Slice and serve with
> **Lingonberry preserves or**
> **Pickled Beets (page 422)**

10 to 12 servings

VARIETY MEATS

SAVORY PANFRIED LIVER

Set out a large heavy skillet.

Cut away, if necessary, tubes and outer membrane from
> **4 slices (about 1 lb.) veal or calf's liver (about ½ in. thick)**

Coat slices evenly with a mixture of
> **¼ cup all-purpose flour**
> **1 teaspoon monosodium glutamate**
> **¾ teaspoon salt**
> **½ teaspoon dry mustard**
> **¼ teaspoon pepper**
> **¼ teaspoon chili powder**

Heat in skillet over medium heat
> **2 tablespoons butter or margarine**

Put liver slices into the skillet and brown on both sides; do not overcook. Place on a warm serving platter; garnish with
> **Sprigs of celery leaves (from inner stalks)**

4 servings

CALF'S LIVER WITH BACON

Panfry (page 190)
> **8 slices (about ⅓ lb.) bacon**

Set aside to keep hot.

For Panbroiled Liver—If necessary, remove tubes and outer membrane from
> **4 slices (about 1 lb.) veal or calf's liver (about ½ in. thick)**

Coat slices evenly with a mixture of
> **⅓ cup all-purpose flour**
> **1 teaspoon monosodium glutamate**
> **¾ teaspoon salt**
> **¼ teaspoon pepper**

Return to skillet and heat
> **3 tablespoons reserved bacon drippings**

Place liver slices in skillet and brown both sides; do not overcook. Place on warm serving plate with bacon slices.

4 servings

LIVER AND ONIONS, ITALIAN STYLE
(Fegato con Cipolla)

▲ Base Recipe

Set out a large heavy skillet.

Cut away tubes and outer membrane, if necessary, from
> **1½ lbs. liver (beef, lamb, veal or calf's), about ¼ to ½ in. thick**

Cut liver into serving-size pieces.

Coat liver with a mixture of
> **½ cup all-purpose flour**
> **1 teaspoon salt**
> **½ teaspoon monosodium glutamate**
> **⅛ teaspoon pepper**

Set aside.

Heat in skillet
> **⅓ cup olive oil**

Add and cook slowly until tender
> **2 medium (about ½ lb.) onions, thinly sliced**

Remove onions from skillet and add liver. Brown liver on both sides over medium heat; do not overcook.

Replace onions in skillet with liver and add
> **½ cup Marsala**

Bring to boiling, cook 1 min. and serve.

4 or 5 servings

—LIVER AND ONIONS WITH MUSHROOMS
(Fegato con Cipolla e Funghi)

Follow ▲ Recipe. Add **1 cup (8-oz. can) mushrooms**, drained, with Marsala.

Liver and Onions, Italian Style

SMOTHERED LIVER WITH ONIONS

▲ Base Recipe

Grease a 1½-qt. casserole with a cover.

Cut away tubes and outer membrane, if necessary, from
1 lb. liver (beef, lamb, veal or calf)
Cut into serving-size pieces. Coat with a mixture of
⅓ cup all-purpose flour
½ teaspoon salt
½ teaspoon monosodium glutamate
Few grains pepper
Heat in a large heavy skillet
2 tablespoons bacon drippings
Add liver to skillet and brown on both sides over medium heat; place liver in casserole. Heat in same skillet
¼ cup butter or margarine
Add to skillet and cook until onions are tender
5 medium onions, thinly sliced
1 cup (8 oz. can, drained) sliced mushrooms
¼ cup chopped green pepper
Pour vegetable mixture over liver.

Prepare
1½ cups Thin White Sauce (1½ times recipe, page 304; use 2 tablespoons flour, and use tomato juice for liquid. Add 1 teaspoon sugar and ⅛ teaspoon chili powder with seasonings.)
Remove sauce from heat and blend in
1 tablespoon lemon juice
2 teaspoons Worcestershire sauce
Pour over meat and vegetables.

Cover and bake at 350°F 25 to 30 min.
4 servings

—LIVER AND RICE PIQUANT

Prepare **2 cups Fluffy Rice (page 164; use ⅔ cup rice)**. Follow ▲ Recipe. With a fork, blend rice with cooked onion, green pepper and mushrooms. Spoon over liver and top with sauce.

LIVER IN WINE SAUCE

▲ Base Recipe

Cooking with wine gives liver a subtle elegance.

Set out a large heavy skillet.

Cut away tubes and outer membrane, if necessary, from
1 lb. liver (veal or calf's)
Cut liver into strips about ½ in. wide. Coat with a mixture of
⅓ cup all-purpose flour
1 teaspoon salt
½ teaspoon paprika
Few grains pepper
Heat in the skillet over low heat
3 tablespoons butter or margarine
1 small clove garlic, minced

Add the liver to the skillet. Cook over medium heat, turning with a fork until strips of liver are browned on all sides, about 3 min.

Remove liver to a hot platter and keep warm. Add to skillet
½ cup sherry or sauterne
Stir until brown residue is loosened from skillet. Remove from heat and with French whip, whisk beater or fork, vigorously stir into hot mixture, 1 tablespoon at a time
¾ cup dairy sour cream
Heat sauce thoroughly; do not boil.

Return liver strips to sauce and toss lightly; serve at once. If desired, garnish with **chopped parsley** and serve with **noodles**. *4 servings*

—CHICKEN LIVERS IN WINE SAUCE

Follow ▲ Recipe. Substitute **1 lb. chicken livers** for the liver. (Rinse with cold water and drain on absorbent paper. Properly cleaned chicken livers have no trace of gall, the green substance which may cause a bitter taste.) If livers are large, cut into halves. Decrease garlic to ½ clove and use sherry.

DEEP-FRIED LIVER

A deep saucepan or automatic deep fryer will be needed.

Cut away tubes and outer membrane, if necessary, from
1 lb. veal or calf's liver slices (about ¼ in. thick)
Marinate (page 10) slices about 30 min. in
2 cups French Dressing I (page 410)
Turn slices several times.

About 20 min. before deep-frying, fill the deep saucepan one-half to two-thirds full with
Vegetable shortening, all-purpose shortening, lard or cooking oil for deep-frying
Heat fat to 360°F (page 11).

Drain liver thoroughly and coat slices evenly with a mixture of
⅓ cup all-purpose flour
1 teaspoon monosodium glutamate
¾ teaspoon salt
¼ teaspoon pepper

Deep-fry only as many slices at one time as will lie uncrowded one layer deep in the fat. Fry until browned on both sides; with a large fork or tongs, turn slices several times during cooking (do not pierce). Remove slices and drain over fat for a few seconds before removing to absorbent paper.

Serve liver hot with
French Fried Onions (page 336)
4 servings

SMOKED BEEF TONGUE
(Rökt Tunga)

Put into a large kettle or a saucepot with a tight-fitting cover
3- to 4-lb. smoked beef tongue
Add enough boiling water to cover the tongue. Cover and simmer 3 to 4 hrs., or until tender. (If necessary, add more boiling water to keep the tongue covered during cooking period.) Or follow cooking directions on the wrapper.

When tongue is tender, slit skin on underside of tongue and peel it off. Cut away roots and gristle. (Plunging tongue into cold water after cooking helps to loosen the skin.) Return tongue to cooking liquid to complete cooling. Drain and chill in refrigerator.

Cut chilled tongue into thin slices and arrange on a serving platter. Garnish with
Whole apple and celery leaves
9 to 12 servings

BEEF TONGUE WITH TOMATO SAUCE
(Nyelv Paradicsom Mártással)

▲ Base Recipe

A heavy 10-in. skillet with a tight-fitting cover will be needed.

Place in a 4-qt. kettle or saucepot with a tight-fitting cover
3- to 4-lb. fresh beef tongue, rinsed
Add to kettle
Hot water (enough to cover tongue)
1 tablespoon salt
2 or 3 bay leaves
1 stalk celery, including leaves, cut in pieces
1 small onion
1 teaspoon peppercorns
Cover kettle and simmer 3 to 4 hrs., or until tongue is tender when pierced with a fork. Place tongue on platter. When cool enough to handle, remove skin, cut away roots, gristle and small bones at thick end. Diagonally cut tongue into ¼-in. thick slices. Put tongue slices into the skillet and set aside.

For Tomato Sauce—Mix
1½ cups (two 6-oz. cans) tomato paste
1¼ cups (10¾-oz. can) condensed tomato soup
½ to ¾ cup water
¼ to ½ teaspoon thyme
Pour the sauce over tongue, cover skillet and simmer about 20 min.

Meanwhile, prepare

Spätzle (see Chicken Paprika with
Spätzle, page 255)

Serve tongue and sauce with the noodles.

9 to 12 servings

—SLICED TONGUE WITH ANCHOVY SAUCE (Nyelv Szárdella Mártással)

Follow ▲ Recipe. Omit tomato sauce. Serve slices of hot tongue with the following anchovy sauce: Put **4 teaspoons anchovy paste** into a small bowl and gradually add **½ cup dairy sour cream**, stirring constantly. Blend anchovy mixture with **1½ cups dairy sour cream** and **⅓ cup chopped parsley** in top of double boiler. Heat thoroughly over simmering water, stirring occasionally. Put sauce into serving bowl and garnish with about **2½ tablespoons buttered fine dry bread crumbs** (page 9).

PICKLED FRESH TONGUE

Set out a large kettle or saucepot with a tight-fitting cover.

Wash thoroughly in warm water

1 fresh beef tongue, 3 to 4 lbs.

Put into the kettle. Add to tongue

Water to cover
2 tablespoons vinegar
1 tablespoon salt
½ teaspoon monosodium glutamate
4 whole cloves
3 bay leaves

Simmer covered 3 to 4 hrs., or until tender.

Remove from liquid and slit skin on underside of tongue; peel it off. Cut away roots and gristle.

Return to liquid to complete cooling. Drain and chill in refrigerator.

Cut tongue into thin slices. Serve cold. Or spread slices with **guava** or **blackberry jelly**. Heat thoroughly in a 375°F oven.

9 to 12 servings

TONGUE AND GREENS

To Cook Tongue—Wash thoroughly in warm water

1 fresh beef or veal tongue

Cover and simmer, in water to cover, with

2 teaspoons salt
½ teaspoon monosodium glutamate
1 onion

Cook (about 1 hr. per lb.) until tender. Slit skin on under side of tongue and peel it off.

Cut away roots and gristle. Cool tongue in cooking liquid if not used immediately; drain. Store in refrigerator.

For Casserole—Grease a 1½-qt. casserole. Slice enough of the cooked tongue (¾ to 1 lb.) to line bottom and sides of casserole. Line casserole with tongue and set casserole aside.

Wash, cook (page 313) and chop

2 lbs. greens such as spinach, chard or tender beet tops

(Or use two 10-oz. pkgs. frozen spinach; cook following directions on package.)

Meanwhile, prepare, reserving drippings

4 slices Panfried Bacon (page 190)

Crumble and set aside.

Heat slowly in skillet until onion is tender, stirring occasionally

2 tablespoons bacon drippings
¼ cup finely chopped onion

Using a fork, gently combine greens, onion, crumbled bacon and

½ cup heavy cream
1 tablespoon prepared horseradish
Dash pepper

Lightly pile greens in tongue-lined casserole. Sprinkle over top

½ cup buttered bread crumbs (page 9)

Bake at 350°F 20 to 25 min., or until crumbs are browned. *6 servings*

Note: If smoked tongue is substituted for fresh tongue, prepare following directions on wrapper. Leftover tongue should be tightly covered and stored in refrigerator.

HEART WITH APPLE RAISIN STUFFING

Set out a 2-qt. top-of-range casserole with a tight-fitting cover.

Cut arteries, veins and any hard parts from

2 lbs. heart (beef, lamb, veal or pork)

Wash in warm water. Drain on absorbent paper. Cut into 1-in. cubes. To coat evenly, shake cubes in a plastic bag containing

½ cup all-purpose flour
2 teaspoons salt
1 teaspoon monosodium glutamate
½ teaspoon pepper

Melt in casserole

3 tablespoons fat or drippings

Add meat and brown on all sides over medium heat, stirring occasionally. Add gradually

1 cup hot water
1 lemon, sliced
8 whole cloves
1 bay leaf

Cover casserole tightly. Simmer 1½ to 2½ hrs., or until meat is tender. If necessary, add additional hot water during cooking period.

Meanwhile, wash, quarter, core, pare and dice

3 medium (1 lb.) tart apples

Melt in a large skillet

¼ cup fat or bacon drippings

Add apples and

½ cup (about 1 medium) chopped onion
½ cup firmly packed brown sugar
½ cup raisins
2 tablespoons water

Cover and simmer 5 min., stirring occasionally.

Drain meat; remove lemon, cloves and bay leaf. Lightly mix apple mixture, meat and

1 qt. (4 to 6 slices) bread cubes
½ cup milk
2 tablespoons melted butter or margarine
½ teaspoon salt

Spoon mixture into casserole.

Bake at 350°F 15 to 20 min., or until browned.

6 or 7 servings

SIMMERED HEART

Set out a kettle or saucepot with a tight-fitting cover.

Cut arteries, veins and any hard parts from

1 small beef heart, 2 veal hearts, 3 pork hearts or 4 lamb hearts

Wash in warm water. Drain heart on absorbent paper.

Put heart into kettle. Add water to cover and

2 teaspoons salt
1 teaspoon celery salt
¾ teaspoon marjoram
½ teaspoon thyme
½ teaspoon pepper
½ teaspoon monosodium glutamate

Simmer covered 2½ hrs., or until tender. (Add ½ to 1 hr. for beef heart.) Drain and chill in refrigerator.

Slice for a cold meat platter or use in sandwiches. *6 to 8 servings*

Heart with Apple Raisin Stuffing

KIDNEY KABOBS

▲ *Base Recipe*

Set out four 8-in. skewers.

Remove membrane (unless this has been done at market) and split horizontally through centers only of

8 lamb kidneys

Using scissors, remove cores and tubes. Rinse clean with cold water.

Put into a bowl and pour in

½ cup French dressing

Turn each piece of kidney to coat well. Cover bowl and let kidneys marinate in refrigerator at least 1 hr.

Wipe caps and stems with a clean damp cloth and cut off stems of

12 medium mushrooms

(Mushroom stems may be used in other recipes as desired.)

Cut into halves

8 slices bacon

Wrap each kidney piece in a bacon slice. Insert skewer through bacon end. Then insert skewer through center of a mushroom. Continue in same way, alternately threading four bacon-wrapped kidney pieces and three mushrooms. Put mushrooms and kidneys close together but do not crowd.

Brush mushrooms lightly with

**1 to 2 tablespoons softened butter or
    margarine**

Place kabobs on broiler rack. Place under broiler with tops of kabobs 3 in. from heat. Broil 10 to 15 min., or until bacon is crisp and kidneys are tender. Turn to brown other sides.

Remove from broiler and sprinkle with a mixture of

½ teaspoon salt
¼ teaspoon monosodium glutamate
⅛ teaspoon pepper

Serve kabobs on the skewers. Serve with **Fluffy Rice (page 164).**   *4 servings*

—VEAL KIDNEY KABOBS

Follow ▲ Recipe. Substitute 4 **veal kidneys** for 8 **lamb kidneys.** Clean as directed and cut each kidney into 4 pieces.

BEEF AND KIDNEY PIE

Set out a 2-qt. top-of-range casserole with a tight-fitting cover.

Remove membrane (unless this has been done at the market) and split horizontally through center of

1 beef kidney

Remove cores and tubes. Rinse clean with cold water. Cut into ¾- to 1-in. cubes. Put into a bowl and pour in

½ cup French dressing

Turn each piece of kidney to coat well. Cover

---

bowl and let kidney marinate at least 1 hr. Turn pieces occasionally; drain.

Set out

**1 lb. beef for stewing (chuck, brisket
    or rump), cut in 1-in. pieces**

Coat kidney and beef with mixture of

⅔ cup all-purpose flour
1½ teaspoons salt
1 teaspoon monosodium glutamate
¼ teaspoon paprika
¼ teaspoon pepper

Heat in casserole over medium heat

3 tablespoons bacon drippings

Add meat and

¼ cup chopped onion

Brown meat, stirring and turning occasionally. Combine and pour slowly into casserole

**2½ cups (two 10¾-oz. cans)
    condensed tomato soup**
1 cup hot water
1 tablespoon Worcestershire sauce

If necessary, add more hot water to allow liquid to cover meat. Add

1 bay leaf
¼ teaspoon basil

Cover casserole tightly; simmer 1 to 1½ hrs., or until meat is tender.

Meanwhile, prepare and set aside
Pastry Topping (page 486)

Heat in a saucepan

3 tablespoons butter or margarine

Add and cook about 5 min., stirring and turning frequently

1 cup (8 oz. can, drained) mushrooms

Remove bay leaf from casserole. Stir mushrooms into casserole.

If necessary to thicken liquid, put into a 1-pt. screw-top jar

¾ cup water

Sprinkle evenly onto it

6 tablespoons all-purpose flour

Cover jar tightly; shake until flour and water are well blended. Slowly pour one half of the mixture into casserole, stirring constantly. Bring to boiling. Gradually add only what is needed of remaining mixture for consistency desired; bring to boiling after each addition. Cook 2 to 3 min. longer. Arrange rolled pastry

---

Beef and Kidney Pie

on casserole. Press edges of pastry to casserole to seal; flute (page 9).

Bake at 425°F 15 to 20 min., or until pastry is browned.   *6 servings*

SWEETBREADS WITH MUSHROOMS
(Borju-mirigy Gombával)

Set out a 2-qt. saucepan with a tight-fitting cover and a heavy 10-in. skillet.

As soon as possible when purchased, rinse with cold water and put into saucepan

2 pairs lamb or veal sweetbreads

Immediately cover with

Cold water

Add for each quart of water

1 tablespoon vinegar or lemon juice
1 teaspoon salt

Cover saucepan and simmer 20 min. Drain sweetbreads; immediately cover with cold water. Drain sweetbreads again. (Cool and refrigerate now if sweetbreads are not to be used immediately.) Remove membrane. Separate sweetbreads into smaller pieces; set aside.

Cook, following directions on package

1 pkg. (10 oz.) frozen peas

Meanwhile, prepare and set aside

**2 cups quick meat broth (double
    recipe, page 10)**

Clean and slice (page 9)

½ lb. mushrooms

Heat in the skillet

⅓ cup butter or margarine

217

Pot o' Dried Beef and Macaroni

Add mushrooms to butter and cook slowly, stirring gently until lightly browned and tender. Push mushrooms to one side.

Heat in skillet

3 tablespoons butter or margarine

Thoroughly blend into butter a mixture of

3 tablespoons all-purpose flour

½ teaspoon salt

⅛ teaspoon pepper

Heat until mixture bubbles and is lightly browned, stirring constantly. Remove from heat and gradually add reserved broth, stirring constantly. Blend in mushrooms. Return to heat and bring rapidly to boiling, stirring constantly. Cook 1 to 2 min. longer. Vigorously stir about ⅓ cup hot mixture, 1 tablespoon at a time, into

4 egg yolks, slightly beaten

Immediately and thoroughly blend into mixture in skillet, stirring constantly. Cook 2 to 3 min. over low heat, stirring constantly. Mix in the drained peas and sweetbreads. Heat thoroughly; do not boil. Serve immediately.

4 or 5 servings

SWEETBREADS AND DRIED BEEF

▲ *Base Recipe*

Grease a shallow 1½-qt. casserole.

As soon as possible when brought from market, rinse with cold water

2 pairs lamb or veal sweetbreads

Cover with cold water. Add for each quart of water

1 tablespoon vinegar or lemon juice

1 teaspoon salt

Cover and simmer 20 min. Drain; immediately cover sweetbreads with cold water. Drain again. (Cool and refrigerate now if sweetbreads are not to be used immediately.) Remove membrane and tubes. Separate sweetbreads into smaller pieces; set sweetbreads aside in a cool place.

Blanch (page 9)

½ cup (about 3 oz.) almonds

Cut into coarse slivers. Coat almonds with

1 tablespoon melted butter or margarine

Sprinkle lightly with

Salt

Set almonds aside.

Melt in a large skillet over medium heat

¼ cup butter or margarine

Add sweetbreads to skillet with

1 cup (two 4-oz. cans, drained) sliced mushrooms

1 cup (about 2½ oz.) dried beef, shredded

Cook over low heat, stirring frequently, until edges of beef are curled and sweetbreads are lightly browned. Set skillet aside in a warm place while preparing sauce.

Prepare

2 cups Medium White Sauce (double recipe, page 304; use 1 cup cream for half of the liquid. Omit salt.)

Blend sauce, sweetbread mixture and

2 tablespoons lemon juice

Turn mixture into casserole. Sprinkle over top

Paprika

Arrange buttered almond slivers around edge of casserole.

Set in a 350°F oven 20 to 30 min., or until almonds are lightly toasted. *6 to 8 servings*

—POT O' DRIED BEEF AND MACARONI

Follow ▲ Recipe. Omit almonds, sweetbreads and lemon juice. Increase dried beef to 1½ cups. Decrease butter to 2 tablespoons and brown mushrooms and 1 cup of the dried beef in the butter. Reserve remaining dried beef for topping. Shred **about 6 oz. Cheddar cheese** (1½ cups, shredded). Increase sauce to 3 cups. Add shredded cheese to sauce all at one time, stirring until cheese is melted. Cook and drain (page 156) enough shell macaroni to yield **3 cups cooked macaroni.** Reserve 1 cup of sauce and 1 cup of macaroni. Mix remaining sauce and macaroni. Put into casserole. Top with buttered mushrooms and dried beef. Arrange reserved macaroni over dried beef and pour reserved sauce over all. Tuck pieces of dried beef into sauce in an attractive pattern on top of casserole. Sprinkle with paprika and heat thoroughly as in ▲ Recipe.

FRITTO MISTO
(Mixed Fry)

An excellent way to use variety meats and left-over vegetables in a typically Roman fashion.

Set out a deep saucepan or automatic deep fryer for deep-frying (page 11) and heat fat to 360°F.

Wash in cold water

½ lb. brains

Simmer brains gently 20 min. in

2 cups water

1½ teaspoons vinegar or lemon juice

½ teaspoon salt

Drain brains and drop into cold water. Drain again and remove membranes. Separate into small pieces and set aside.

Prepare and coat with flour mixture, (see Liver and Onions, Italian Style, page 214)

½ lb. liver (beef, lamb, veal or calf's), about ¼ to ½ in. thick

Cut liver into serving-size pieces and set aside.

Drain

6 artichoke hearts, canned in water

Set aside.

Wash, trim off ends and cut crosswise into 1-in. slices

2 zucchini squash

Set aside.

Clean and cut into 3-in. pieces

3 stalks celery

Set aside.

Meanwhile, sift together

2 cups all-purpose flour

1 teaspoon salt

¼ teaspoon pepper

Set aside.

Combine

1½ cups milk

3 eggs, well beaten

2 tablespoons melted shortening

Gradually add dry ingredients, beating until smooth. Dip each vegetable and piece of meat into batter.

218

Dried Beef en Croustades

Deep-fry as many vegetables or meats as will float uncrowded one layer deep in fat. Fry about 5 min., or until vegetables and meats are golden brown, turning occasionally during frying time. Drain over fat before removing to absorbent paper. Serve on a warm platter.

6 servings

READY-TO-EAT MEATS

DRIED BEEF IN TOAST CUPS

Prepare
> **4 Hard-Cooked Eggs (page 133)**
> **6 Toast Cups (page 110)**

Meanwhile, prepare and keep hot
> **2 cups Medium White Sauce (double recipe, page 304)**

Force egg yolks through a sieve or ricer and set aside for a garnish.

Chop egg whites and set aside.

Drain
> **1 can (4 oz.) sliced mushrooms (about ½ cup, drained)**
Stir mushrooms and chopped egg whites into sauce with
> **1 cup (about 2½ oz.) dried beef, shredded**
> **¼ cup chopped parsley**
Cook mixture a few minutes to heat thoroughly, stirring occasionally. Spoon into Toast Cups. Sprinkle sieved egg yolks over tops.

Serve immediately. *6 servings*

DRIED BEEF EN CROUSTADES

For Croustades—Set out a baking sheet.

Cut into 1¼- to 2-in. thick crosswise slices
> **1 loaf unsliced, dry bread**
Remove crusts and cut each slice into halves. Following outline of rectangle, cut out center ¼ to ½ in. from edge, and down to within ¼ to ½ in. of bottom, leaving a neatly cut shell. Brush outside and inside of shells with
> **Melted butter or margarine**

Place on baking sheet.

Toast in oven at 325°F 12 to 20 min., or until lightly browned and crisp.

For Creamed Dried Beef—Prepare
> **Sour Cream White Sauce (one and one half times recipe, page 304; add ¾ teaspoon dry mustard with the seasonings)**

Stir in
> **2 cups (about 5 oz.) dried beef, shredded**
To serve, spoon the Creamed Dried Beef into warm Croustades. Garnish as desired.
8 servings

HASH-STUFFED ZUCCHINI

Set out a large shallow baking dish.

Wash and remove stem ends from
> **4 large zucchini**
Cut into halves lengthwise. Scoop out pulp, chop it and set aside for filling.

Generously oil with **cooking oil** the outside of zucchini shells and arrange, cut side up, in the baking dish. Sprinkle with
> **Monosodium glutamate**
Set aside.

Turn into a bowl
> **1 can (15 oz.) roast beef hash**
Mix in zucchini pulp and
> **1 tablespoon bottled steak sauce**
> **1 tablespoon instant minced onion**
> **¼ teaspoon garlic powder**
> **½ cup shredded Cheddar cheese**
Spoon into shells. Sprinkle with **snipped parsley.**

Bake at 350°F about 30 min., or until zucchini is crisp-tender. *8 stuffed zucchini halves*

HASH DISTINCTIVE

▲ *Base Recipe*

Just a few trimmings, and corned beef hash is ready for a party.

Remove both ends from can and push out
> **1 can (15 oz.) corned beef hash**
Cut hash evenly into 4 rounds. Place on broiler rack and brush tops with
> **2 teaspoons melted butter or margarine**
Place broiler rack under broiler with top of meat 3 in. from heat; broil 3 to 5 min., or until browned.

Shred and set aside
> **2 oz. Cheddar cheese (about ½ cup, shredded)**

Turn hash rounds and spread tops thinly with
> **2 teaspoons prepared horseradish**

Rinse, remove and discard stem end and cut into four slices
> **1 medium tomato**

Place one slice on each hash round. Brush tomato slices with
> **Melted butter or margarine**
Sprinkle shredded cheese over tomato slices. Sprinkle with a mixture of
> **½ teaspoon salt**
> **¼ teaspoon monosodium glutamate**
> **Few grains pepper**
Broil about 5 min. longer. *4 servings*

—HASH DELECTABLE WITH PINEAPPLE TOPPING

Follow ▲ Recipe. Omit horseradish-tomato topping. Turn hash rounds and top each round with **1 canned pineapple slice.** Spread with a mixture of ⅔ cup firmly packed brown sugar and ¼ cup softened butter or margarine. Broil about 5 min., or until pineapple is glazed. Serve immediately; garnish with **parsley.**

—SUNNY-SIDE CORNED BEEF HASH

Cut **1 can (15 oz.) corned beef hash** into rounds as in ▲ Recipe. Lightly and evenly coat rounds with ⅓ cup all-purpose flour. In a heavy skillet, brown both sides of rounds in **2 to 3 tablespoons hot fat.** Top servings with **Poached Eggs** (page 137) or **Fried Eggs** (page 138), yolk-sides up. Top with **Mock Hollandaise Sauce** (page 304) or **Cheese Sauce** (page 304). Garnish with **paprika.**

—CORNED BEEF HASH BISCUIT ROLL

Prepare **Baking Powder Biscuit dough** (page 92). Before adding liquid, blend into flour mixture **¼ teaspoon paprika, 1 tablespoon finely chopped parsley** and **1 tablespoon minced green pepper.** Roll into a rectangle ¼ in. thick. Mix **1 can (15 oz.) corned beef hash** with **¼ cup chili sauce** and **⅛ teaspoon pepper.** Spread evenly over biscuit dough. Roll and bake at 400°F 15 to 25 min. Serve with **gravy, Mushroom Sauce** or **Cheese Sauce** (page 304). *4 to 6 servings*

—CORNED BEEF HASH PATTIES

Thoroughly mix **1 can (15 oz.) corned beef hash** with **1 tablespoon prepared mustard, 2 tablespoons chili sauce, 2 tablespoons minced onion** and a **few grains cayenne pepper.** Blend in **1 egg,** well beaten. Shape into 4

Hash Delectable with Pineapple Topping

flat patties. Chill in refrigerator 1 hr. or longer. In a heavy skillet, over low heat, brown both sides of patties in **2 to 3 tablespoons hot fat.**

4 servings

—ISLAND CORNED BEEF HASH

Grease 1-qt. casserole. Drain and reserve syrup from **1 can (8¾ oz.) pineapple tidbits.** Thoroughly mix 2 tablespoons reserved syrup with **1 can corned beef hash, 2 tablespoons capers or chopped sweet pickle, 2 tablespoons chopped onion** and **1 tablespoon lemon juice.** Spoon lightly into casserole. Press pineapple tidbits lightly into surface of hash. Dot top with **2 tablespoons butter or margarine** and sprinkle with **3 tablespoons brown sugar.** Set in a 350°F oven 20 to 30 min., or until surface is lightly browned.

HASH ON A BUN

Set out an 8-in. skillet.

Remove both ends from can and push out
1 can (15 oz.) corned beef hash
Mix lightly, but thoroughly, with a mixture of
¼ cup pickle relish, drained
¼ cup chopped onion
2 teaspoons prepared horseradish
½ teaspoon salt
½ teaspoon monosodium glutamate
⅛ teaspoon pepper
Shape into 4 patties.

Heat in the skillet
2 tablespoons butter or margarine
Add patties and brown slowly on both sides.

Meanwhile, prepare
Cheese Sauce (page 304)
Serve patties on halves of **buttered toasted buns.** Top with sauce and remaining toasted bun halves.

4 servings

SPEEDY DILL PICKLE BEEF STEW

Clean and quarter
½ lb. fresh mushrooms
Heat in a large skillet
2 tablespoons butter or margarine

Add mushrooms and cook, stirring occasionally until tender. Put into skillet
2 cans (1½ lbs. each) beef stew
¼ cup chili sauce
¼ cup dill pickle liquid
¾ cup sliced dill pickles
Stir to mix. Heat thoroughly, stirring occasionally. Serve in soup bowls.

6 to 8 servings

DEVILED HAM CUSTARD

▲ *Base Recipe*

If it rates an A— in appearance, it is sure to rate A+ in flavor. The whole family will relish second servings.

Grease a 1½-qt. casserole.

Shred and set aside
6 oz. Cheddar cheese (1½ cups, shredded)

Scald (page 10)
2 cups milk

Meanwhile, toast (on both sides) until very crisp and brown
5 slices bread
Spread with
2 tablespoons butter or margarine
Cut into 1-in. cubes. Arrange a layer of cubes in casserole. Alternate layers of remaining cubes with shredded Cheddar cheese. Set bread cubes for one layer aside. Set casserole aside.

Mix thoroughly
2 eggs, slightly beaten
⅓ cup (about 3-oz. can) deviled ham
1 teaspoon Worcestershire sauce
½ teaspoon chili powder
Slowly blend in milk, stirring vigorously, pour into casserole. Top mixture with remaining bread cubes.

Bake at 300°F about 40 min., or until a metal knife comes out clean when inserted halfway between center and edge of casserole. Serve immediately.

4 or 5 servings

—LUNCHEON CUSTARD

Follow ▲ Recipe. Omit deviled ham. Grind

6 oz. cubed-canned luncheon meat; stir into egg mixture. Substitute **1 tablespoon prepared mustard** for chili powder.

RODEO STUFFED FRANKFURTERS

▲ *Base Recipe*

Mix
½ cup (2 oz.) coarsely shredded Cheddar cheese
3 tablespoons sweet pickle relish
⅛ teaspoon monosodium glutamate
⅛ teaspoon salt
Few grains cayenne pepper

Split lengthwise, not quite through
8 frankfurters
Stuff frankfurters with cheese mixture. Wrap each with one slice of
8 slices bacon
Fasten ends of bacon with wooden picks.

Arrange frankfurters on broiler rack. Place under broiler 3 in. from heat to tops of frankfurters. Broil 5 to 8 min., turning to brown all sides.

8 servings

—RODEO BREAD-STUFFED FRANKFURTERS

Follow ▲ Recipe for broiling. Spread split frankfurters thinly with **ketchup.** Lightly cover with a mixture of **2 cups soft bread crumbs (about 2 slices bread), ⅓ cup minced onion, ½ teaspoon salt, ½ teaspoon monosodium glutamate, ⅛ teaspoon pepper, ¼ cup melted butter or margarine** and **2 tablespoons milk.** Insert picks. Broil 8 to 10 min.

—RODEO RED HOTS

Follow ▲ Recipe. Omit cheese stuffing. Spread between split frankfurters a mixture of **½ cup sweet pickle relish** and **1 tablespoon prepared mustard.**

—OUTDOOR GRILLED FRANKFURTERS

Follow ▲ Recipe using **sliced cheese.** Place cheese, cut in 1-in. wide strips, into each frankfurter and top with relish mixture. Place on a long-handled fork and roast over an outdoor fire. Or, place on a grill, turning to brown all sides.

FRILLY FRANKFURTERS

▲ *Base Recipe*

Set out an 11x7x2-in. baking dish.

Prepare
1 cup Fluffy Whipped Potatoes (one half recipe, page 339)

Mix thoroughly with
¼ cup finely chopped onion
¼ cup chopped sweet pickle
3 tablespoons chopped pimiento

Set aside.

Make a lengthwise slit almost through
6 frankfurters

Open slit frankfurters and spread cut surfaces with
¼ cup prepared mustard

Arrange frankfurters in baking dish; pile potato mixture lightly over top.

Bake at 350°F 20 min.

Or, for broiling, arrange frankfurters on broiler rack. Pile whipped potato mixture on frankfurters.

Place under broiler with top of potatoes 4 to 5 in. from heat; broil 7 to 8 min., or until lightly browned.   *6 servings*

—FRANKS WITH CHEESE FRILLS

Follow ▲ Recipe. Omit chopped ingredients. Blend the Whipped Potatoes with **¾ cup (3 oz.) shredded Cheddar cheese.** Bake or broil.

FRANKFURTER BEAN FARE

Chop finely enough onion to yield
½ cup (about 1 medium) onion

Turn into casserole
2 cans (16 oz. each) pork and beans

Mix in the onion. Top with a mixture of
¼ cup molasses
¼ cup ketchup
2 teaspoons prepared horseradish
1 teaspoon dry mustard

Arrange over top of casserole
6 frankfurters

Brush frankfurters thoroughly with about
1 tablespoon melted butter or margarine

Set in a 350°F oven 20 to 30 min., or until thoroughly heated.   *6 servings*

FRANKFURTER SUPPER BAKE

Lightly grease a 1½-qt. casserole. Set out a large skillet.

Prepare
1 cup diagonally sliced celery
3 tablespoons minced parsley

Have ready
2 cans (8 oz. each) tomato sauce with onions
1 lb. frankfurters

Make diagonal slits at 1-in. intervals almost to bottom of each frankfurter. Set aside.

Toast, cut into ½-in. cubes and set aside
8 slices bread

Mix
½ cup cooking oil
1 large clove garlic, minced

Pour about half of it into the skillet. Heat thoroughly. Add about half of the toast cubes

and toss until all sides are coated and browned. Turn into a large bowl. Repeat heating oil; brown remaining toast cubes and turn into bowl. Mix in celery and 2 tablespoons of the parsley.

Beat slightly in a bowl
1 egg
Salt and pepper to taste

Stir in 1 can of tomato sauce. Pour over crouton mixture and toss lightly. Turn half of the mixture into the casserole. Put half of the frankfurters onto the mixture. Brush with a small amount of tomato sauce from remaining can. Repeat layers and brushing.

Heat in a 350°F oven about 45 min.

Pour remaining tomato sauce into a small saucepan and heat thoroughly. Pour evenly over heated casserole mixture. Top with remaining parsley.   *6 servings*

TANGY FRANKFURTERS

Set out a large skillet.

Have ready
1 lb. frankfurters

Make a 3-in. lengthwise slit almost through each frankfurter. Set aside.

Heat in the skillet
3 tablespoons butter or margarine

Add and cook, stirring occasionally, until soft
¼ cup coarsely chopped onion

Blend in
½ cup water
½ cup ketchup
¼ cup vinegar
4 teaspoons Worcestershire sauce
1 teaspoon prepared mustard
4 teaspoons sugar
¼ teaspoon salt
⅛ teaspoon pepper

Bring to boiling. Add the frankfurters and baste with sauce. Heat thoroughly. *4 servings*

TOASTED FRANKFURTER ROLLS

▲ Base Recipe

Cream together thoroughly and set aside
¼ cup butter or margarine
1 tablespoon prepared mustard
1 teaspoon prepared horseradish

Trim crusts from
8 slices bread

Spread bread slices with creamed mixture. Place diagonally on bread slices
8 frankfurters

Pin free corners of bread together around frankfurters with wooden picks. Arrange on broiler rack. Brush tops with
Melted butter or margarine

Place under broiler with tops of rolls 4 to 5 in. from heat; broil until browned. Or, bake at 400°F about 20 min.

Frankfurter Biscuits

Fasten on the ends of the wooden picks
8 tiny sweet gherkins

Serve immediately.   *8 frankfurter rolls*

—FRANKFURTER BISCUITS

Follow ▲ Recipe. Omit bread slices. Prepare **biscuit dough** (Quick Rolled Biscuits, page 93). Roll ¼ in. thick and spread with creamed mixture. Cut dough into wedge-shape pieces. Wrap wedges around frankfurters, starting with wide end. Place on baking sheet with points of wedges underneath. Brush dough with **milk.** Bake at 425°F about 12 min., or until biscuit rolls are golden brown.

FRANKFURTERS WITH GREEN PEPPER AND TOMATOES
(Lecsó)

▲ Base Recipe

Heat in a large heavy skillet with a tight-fitting cover
¼ cup butter

Add to butter and cook until onion is almost tender, stirring occasionally
4 medium green peppers, cut in lengthwise strips
2 medium onions, thinly sliced

Cheese Dinner Pie

Meanwhile, rinse, cut out and discard stem ends and blemishes from, and cut into slices

4 large, ripe tomatoes (or use 1½ cups, 16-oz. can, drained, tomatoes)

Add tomatoes to the skillet. Sprinkle over the vegetables a mixture of

1½ teaspoons salt
¼ teaspoon paprika
⅛ teaspoon freshly ground pepper

Cover skillet and simmer 15 min.

Meanwhile, cut into 1-in. pieces

8 frankfurters

Add frankfurters to skillet and mix gently with the vegetables; cover skillet and cook about 10 min., or until frankfurters are heated.

6 or 7 servings

—EGG, GREEN PEPPER AND TOMATO SCRAMBLE (Lecsó Tojással)

Follow ▲ Recipe. Omit frankfurters. After simmering vegetables 15 min., add **6 eggs,** slightly beaten. Cook slowly over low heat, gently stirring occasionally with a fork or spatula, until eggs are thick and creamy throughout, but moist.

CHEESE DINNER PIE

Set out a 1½-qt. casserole and a baking sheet.

Prepare

Pastry Topping (double recipe, page 486)

Divide pastry and shape into two balls, one about twice the size of the other. Roll larger portion ⅛ in. thick; fold and place in casserole. Unfold; gently pat to fit over bottom and up sides of casserole (avoid stretching pastry), allowing edges to extend about ¾ in. over sides of casserole. Fold edges under; flute (page 9). Prick entire surface with tines of fork.

Roll remainder of dough to size and shape of casserole top. Using a pastry wheel, cut evenly into three pie-shape wedges. Place wedges on baking sheet; prick thoroughly with fork.

Bake shell and wedges at 450°F about 10 min., or until lightly browned.

Cook (page 313) enough vegetables to yield

1 cup cooked cauliflower
½ cup sliced cooked carrots
½ cup cooked green beans

Meanwhile, dice

½ lb. bologna (about 2 cups, diced.)

Heat in a large skillet

¼ cup butter or margarine

Add bologna and

½ cup (about 1 medium) chopped onion

Cook over medium heat, stirring occasionally, until onion is tender. With a slotted spoon, lift bologna and onion from skillet to a bowl, allowing butter to drain back into skillet. Add to skillet additional butter or margarine necessary to prepare

2 cups Medium White Sauce (double recipe, page 304; add ¼ teaspoon Worcestershire sauce with milk)

Meanwhile, shred

6 oz. Cheddar cheese (1½ cups, shredded)

Add the cheese to sauce all at one time. Stir sauce rapidly until cheese is melted. Gently mix sauce, bologna, onion and other vegetables. Turn mixture into baked pastry shell; top with pastry wedges.

Bake at 350°F 15 to 20 min., or until heated thoroughly.

Garnish center with **sprigs of parsley.** Serve immediately.

6 servings

BAKED BOLOGNA

Set out a shallow roasting pan with a rack.

Leaving piece whole, carefully remove skin, if necessary, from

3-lb. roll of bologna

Making diagonal cuts, score surface of bologna to form diamond pattern. If desired, insert a **whole clove** in each diamond. Place bologna on the rack.

Bake at 350°F about 1½ hrs., or until thoroughly heated. Brush several times with

Pineapple or other fruit juice

To serve, place bologna on a heated platter and surround with **scrambled eggs.** Cut bologna into slices.

About 12 servings

SPICY ORANGE BOLOGNA ROLL

Set out a shallow baking dish.

Mix in a heavy saucepan

¼ cup firmly packed brown sugar
¼ cup instant minced onion
¼ teaspoon dry mustard
⅛ teaspoon cloves
¼ teaspoon Worcestershire sauce
1 can (8 oz.) tomato sauce
1½ teaspoons grated orange peel
½ cup orange juice
½ cup water

Bring to boiling, stirring until sugar is dissolved. Simmer, uncovered, about 15 min., stirring occasionally.

Meanwhile, set out

1 bologna roll (1½ lbs.)

Score surface of bologna roll to form a diamond pattern. Put bologna into baking dish. Pour hot sauce over it.

Set in a 350°F oven 45 min., or until thoroughly heated, basting occasionally with the sauce.

Garnish with **quartered slices of orange.**

About 6 servings

PEACH-CROWNED LUNCHEON MEAT BAKE

Grease a 1½-qt. baking dish.

Have ready

6 canned cling peach halves

Cook (page 313), peel and cut into cubes

4 medium potatoes

Turn into the baking dish.

Meanwhile, prepare

1 can (12 oz.) luncheon meat, shredded
2 medium onions, chopped
⅔ cup diced celery
⅓ cup slivered green pepper

Add to the potatoes and mix gently. Pour in

1 cup beef broth

Set in a 400°F oven 30 min.

Remove from oven and top with the peach halves. Brush generously with **butter or margarine** and sprinkle with **brown sugar.** Return to oven and continue heating 15 min.

About 6 servings

Ground meat cookery

Quiz an American on his food preferences and you will uncover a lover of hamburger, that succulent ground-meat patty in a bun. But ground meats are more than hamburgers, for they have a versatility all their own. They can be combined deliciously with pastry, cereal, or with fruits and vegetables. Piled into molds or shaped into loaves, balls, or patties, they are adaptable to the skillet, the casserole, the oven, or the open fire. Ground meats of all kinds merit top place on family menus. They can start the day, gratify lunchtime cravings, stimulate the dinner appetite or satisfy it altogether.

A CHECK LIST FOR GROUND MEAT COOKERY

Purchase ground beef that has been freshly ground, either regular (contains not more than 25% fat) or lean (contains not more than 12% fat). Or buy a cut of beef such as chuck, round, flank, plate, brisket, shank or neck meat and have it ground. If the cut is quite lean, have 2 ounces of suet per pound of beef ground with the meat. A coarse single grind helps to insure extra-juicy patties.

Purchase pork that has been freshly ground or have pork shoulder meat ground.

Purchase lamb that has been freshly ground or have lamb shoulder meat or boneless stew meat ground.

Store ground meat uncovered or lightly covered in the refrigerator. Use within two days of purchase.

Store frozen ground meat in the freezer, wrapped in freezer wrapping material.

Separate ground meat block with a fork or spoon when meat is added to the skillet. Brown over medium heat. For small pieces, move and turn with a fork or spoon at beginning of browning process. For larger pieces, brown slightly before moving and turning meat.

Shape balls, burgers and loaves with a light touch. (Excessive handling results in a compact and less juicy product.)

Cook pork until well done. It should be grayish white in color with no tinge of pink.

Place oven products on oven rack so top of product will be almost at center of oven. Stagger pans so no pan is directly over another and they do not touch each other or walls of oven.

Let meat loaves stand 5 to 10 min. after removing from oven for easier slicing.

Unmold meat loaves. With spatula loosen meat gently from sides of pan. Pour off excess juices; invert loaf on platter and remove pan. Or, for meat loaves with topping, pour off excess juices and lift onto platter with two wide spatulas.

GROUND BEEF

TENDERFOOT HAMBURGERS

▲ *Base Recipe*

Combine and mix lightly
- **1 lb. ground beef**
- **1 cup fine cracker or fine dry bread crumbs**
- **½ cup finely chopped onion**
- **½ cup tomato juice**
- **1 egg, well beaten**
- **½ teaspoon salt**
- **¼ teaspoon pepper**

Lightly shape meat mixture into patties ¾ to 1 in. thick.

Arrange patties on broiler rack. Place under broiler with tops of patties about 3 in. from heat. Broil 10 to 12 min. Turn and brown other sides of patties. Serve on split and toasted **hamburger buns.**   *6 servings*

—TENDERFOOT CHEESEBURGERS

Follow ▲ Recipe. Use tomato juice or **milk.** After second side of each patty is browned, cover with **1 thin slice Cheddar cheese.** Broil until cheese is slightly melted.

—TENDERFOOT BARBECUES

Follow ▲ Recipe. Substitute **milk** for tomato juice. Make a sauce by combining **2 tablespoons brown sugar, 1 tablespoon Worcestershire sauce, 2 tablespoons lemon juice** and **1 cup ketchup.** Heat thoroughly. Place patties on toasted buns. Pour sauce over patties.

HAMBURGER FAVORITES

▲ *Base Recipe*

Set out a large heavy skillet.

Mix lightly
- **1½ lbs. ground beef**
with a blend of
- **1½ teaspoons salt**
- **¾ teaspoon monosodium glutamate**
- **¼ teaspoon pepper**

Shape into 6 patties about ¾ in. thick or 8 patties about ½ in. thick.

Heat in skillet
- **1 tablespoon fat**

Put patties in skillet and cook over medium heat until brown on one side. Turn and brown other side. Allow 10 to 15 min. for cooking thick patties and 6 to 10 min. for cooking thin patties. Remove from skillet to warm serving platter; garnish with **parsley.**   *4 to 6 servings*

—BROILER BURGERS

Follow ▲ Recipe. Arrange ¾ in. thick patties on broiler rack. Put under broiler with top of patties about 3 in. from heat. Broil 6 to 8 min. When patties are browned on one side, turn and broil second side about 6 to 8 min.

Hamburger Favorites

Garlic-Flavored Burgers and Man-Size Burgers

—CHEESEBURGERS

Follow ▲ Recipe or Broiler Burgers recipe. After second sides of patties are browned, cover each patty with **1 thin slice Cheddar cheese.** Cook 2 min. longer, or until cheese is slightly melted.

—GARLIC HAMBURGER FAVORITES

Follow ▲ Recipe. Blend in **1 egg,** beaten, and **1 clove garlic,** slivered.

—GARLIC-FLAVORED BURGERS

Follow ▲ Recipe or Broiler Burgers recipe. While patties are cooking, brush with **garlic-flavored French dressing.**

For Garnish—Place **6 well-drained peach halves,** cut-side down, in skillet or on broiler rack. Brush with **garlic-flavored French dressing.** Cook 2 to 3 min. and turn. Spoon **1 teaspoon brown sugar** into hollow in each peach half. Brush with more garlic-flavored French dressing and cook until brown sugar is melted. Arrange burgers on warm platter. Garnish peach halves with **parsley.**

BIG-FELLOWS

▲ Base Recipe

Mix lightly
 1½ lbs. ground beef
 ⅓ cup minced onion
 ⅓ cup ketchup
 1 egg, beaten
 1½ teaspoons prepared horseradish
and a blend of
 1½ teaspoons salt
 ¾ teaspoon monosodium glutamate
 Few grains pepper
Set aside.

Slice into halves
 6 hamburger buns
Spread generously with
 Butter or margarine
Spread each bun half with about ¼ cup meat mixture. Spread mixture carefully to edges to prevent edges of bun from becoming too brown. Dot with
 3 to 4 teaspoons butter or margarine

Arrange the buns on broiler rack, meat-side up. Put under broiler with top of meat about 5 in. from heat. Broil about 6 min., or until meat is cooked. *6 to 8 servings*

—BIG-FELLOWS WITH CHEESE

Follow ▲ Recipe. Spread untoasted sides of bun halves with **prepared mustard** before spreading with meat mixture. At end of broiling period, put **1 slice sharp Cheddar cheese** on each burger. Return to broiler for 2 or 3 min., or until cheese is melted slightly. Or mix **¾ cup (3 oz.) shredded Cheddar or Swiss cheese** with the meat mixture before broiling.

MAN-SIZE BURGERS

▲ Base Recipe

Set out a large heavy skillet.

Combine and mix lightly
 1½ lbs. ground beef
 ¼ cup minced onion
 2 tablespoons ketchup
and a blend of
 1 teaspoon dry mustard
 1½ teaspoons salt
 ¾ teaspoon monosodium glutamate
 ¼ teaspoon pepper
Shape into 4 large patties, about 1 in. thick.

Heat in skillet
 1 tablespoon fat
Put patties in skillet and cook over medium heat until brown on one side. Turn and brown other side. Allow 12 to 16 min. for cooking. Remove burgers from skillet to warm serving platter and keep warm. Place in same skillet
 6 slices pineapple, drained and cut in halves
Brown both sides over medium heat, turning occasionally.

Serve burgers and pineapple slices with **green peas** and buttered **finger sandwiches;** garnish with **parsley.** *4 servings*

—RELISH BURGERS

Follow ▲ Recipe. Shape meat mixture into 12 thin patties. Set out **¾ cup sweet pickle relish.** Put about 2 tablespoons pickle relish onto each of 6 patties. Top with remaining patties. Press edges together with tines of fork and cook as in ▲ Recipe. Omit pineapple.

—BLUE CHEESE BURGERS

Follow ▲ Recipe. Shape meat mixture into 12 thin patties. Crumble **3 oz. blue cheese** (about ¾ cup, crumbled). Mix with **2 tablespoons mayonnaise.** Put about 2 tablespoons cheese mixture onto each of 6 patties. Top with remaining patties. Press edges together with tines of fork and cook as in ▲ Recipe. Omit pineapple.

TRIPLE DECK BURGERS

▲ Base Recipe

Juicy meat, flavorful stuffing, tangy sauce— a praise-winning combination!

Set out a small skillet and grease a 10x6x2-in. baking dish.

Prepare and set aside to keep warm
 2 cups Quick Tomato Sauce (page 307; increase water to ¾ cup)

For Stuffing— Heat in the skillet
¼ cup butter or margarine
Add and cook until onion is tender, stirring gently
¼ cup finely chopped onion
Pour contents of skillet over
1 qt. (4 to 6 slices) soft ½-in. bread cubes
Add to bread cubes and mix gently with a fork
3 tablespoons minced celery leaves
and a blend of
½ teaspoon salt
⅛ teaspoon pepper
Set aside.

Beat together in a small bowl
1 egg, beaten
⅓ cup milk
Gently blend egg mixture into bread mixture. Shape stuffing into 6 patties. Set aside.

For Meat Patties—Prepare
Hamburger Favorites (page 223; add ¼ teaspoon allspice with seasonings)
Shape meat into 12 thin patties. Arrange 6 of the meat patties in bottom of baking dish; cover each with a stuffing patty. Top with remaining meat patties. Pour tomato sauce over patties.

Bake at 350°F 40 to 50 min. Baste patties occasionally during cooking period.

6 servings

—CORN-STUFFED BURGERS

Follow ▲ Recipe. Decrease bread cubes to 3 cups and blend in 1½ cups (12-oz. can, drained) whole kernel corn with stuffing.

BEEF BURGERS WITH WINE BARBECUE SAUCE

▲ Base Recipe

A shallow baking dish will be needed.

Heat and keep warm
¾ cup Wine Barbecue Sauce (page 310)
Mix lightly
1 lb. lean ground beef
1 teaspoon salt
½ teaspoon monosodium glutamate
⅛ teaspoon pepper
Shape into four patties about ¾ in. thick.

Heat a medium-size skillet over medium heat. Put patties in skillet and cook until brown on one side. Turn and brown other side. Allow 6 to 10 min. for cooking patties. When patties are browned, place in the baking dish. Pour the sauce over the patties.

Place in a 350°F oven 10 to 15 min. Baste patties occasionally with the sauce.

Serve patties with the sauce. *4 servings*

—SANDWICH-STYLE HAMBURGERS

Follow ▲ Recipe. Omit barbecue sauce. Shape meat into eight thin patties. Spread four patties with a mixture of **2 teaspoons olive oil** and **8 teaspoons softened Roquefort or blue cheese.** Top with remaining patties and press edges together. Arrange patties on broiler rack. Set temperature control of range at Broil. Place in broiler with top of patties about 3 in. from heat. Broil 5 to 8 min. on each side.

—WATER CHESTNUT BEEF BALLS

Follow ▲ Recipe. Omit barbecue sauce. Decrease salt to ¼ teaspoon; mix **1 tablespoon soy sauce** and **⅔ cup shredded water chestnuts** with meat. Shape mixture into eight balls. Heat **1 tablespoon butter or margarine** in a large heavy skillet. Add balls and brown over medium heat, turning occasionally to brown all sides; continue cooking to desired doneness.

—ALMOND BEEF BALLS

Follow recipe for Water Chestnut Beef Balls. Substitute **½ cup toasted slivered almonds** for the water chestnuts.

CHEESEBURGERS WITH OLIVES

Really hearty snacktime fare for hungry teenagers or their dads. These fill the hollow within produced by an active evening of bowling.

Cut into crosswise slices and set aside
16 large pimiento-stuffed olives
Mix lightly
1½ lbs. ground beef
1 cup (3 slices) fine dry bread crumbs
½ cup (about 1 medium) chopped onion
3 tablespoons olive liquid
3 tablespoons water
1 egg, beaten

Add a blend of
¾ teaspoon monosodium glutamate
½ teaspoon salt
⅛ teaspoon pepper
Divide mixture into 8 portions. Lightly shape each portion into a round patty.

Arrange patties on broiler rack. Put rack under broiler with tops of patties about 3 in. from heat. Broil about 7 min. Turn patties and broil until browned, about 5 min.

Spread with
Prepared mustard
Arrange olive slices over mustard and top with
8 slices (8-oz. pkg.) pasteurized process Swiss cheese
Return to broiler and broil 3 min. longer, or until cheese is melted and tinged with brown.

Serve with **hamburger buns** which have been split, buttered and toasted. *8 servings*

SPICY BEEF BURGERS

Set out a large heavy skillet.

Blend
⅓ cup ketchup
1 tablespoon prepared horseradish
2 teaspoons Worcestershire sauce
½ teaspoon salt
½ teaspoon monosodium glutamate
⅛ teaspoon pepper
2 or 3 drops Tabasco
Combine with seasonings and mix lightly
2 lbs. ground beef
Shape into 8 patties about ¾ in. thick.

Heat in skillet
1 to 2 tablespoons fat
Put meat patties into skillet and cook over medium heat until browned on one side. Turn and brown on other side. Allow 10 to 15 min. for cooking patties. Pour off fat as it collects.

Serve with thin slices of onion and
Quick Tomato Sauce (page 307)
6 to 8 servings

BEEF LINDSTROM
(Biff à la Lindstrom)

Wash and scrub with a vegetable brush
3 medium potatoes (about 1 lb.)

Cheeseburgers with Olives

Beef Patties

Cook (page 313) 30 to 35 min., or until potatoes are tender when pierced with a fork.

Meanwhile, finely dice enough pickled beets to yield

    ½ cup finely diced Pickled Beets
        (page 422)

Mix in a bowl

    1½ lbs. beef, ground twice
    2 egg yolks, beaten
    ¼ cup cream
    2 tablespoons chopped onion
    1 tablespoon capers

and a blend of

    1 teaspoon salt
    ½ teaspoon monosodium glutamate
    ¼ teaspoon pepper

Drain the potatoes. To dry potatoes, shake over low heat. Peel potatoes and set aside to cool. When potatoes are cooled, finely dice and blend into the meat mixture with the beets. Chill in refrigerator 1 to 2 hrs. to allow flavors to blend thoroughly.

Shape the meat mixture into patties about ½ in. thick.

Heat in a heavy skillet

    3 tablespoons butter

Put the meat patties into the skillet and cook over medium heat until browned on one side. Turn and brown other side. Allow 10 to 15 min. for cooking patties. Serve immediately.

6 to 8 servings

BEEF PATTIES

    ▲ *Base Recipe*

Set out a large heavy skillet.

Combine and mix lightly

    1½ lbs. ground beef
    ⅓ cup fine dry bread crumbs
    ¼ cup grated onion
    1½ teaspoons Worcestershire sauce

and a blend of

    1½ teaspoons salt
    ½ teaspoon monosodium glutamate
    ¼ teaspoon pepper

Wash, quarter, core, pare and shred

    2 medium apples (about 1½ cups,
        shredded)

Mix lightly and thoroughly with meat. Shape into 6 patties, about ¾ in. thick.

Heat in skillet

    1 to 2 tablespoons fat

Add patties and brown both sides over medium heat, turning occasionally. Allow 10 to 15 min. for cooking. Drain off any excess fat as it accumulates.

6 servings

—FORK-TENDER STEAK

Follow ▲ Recipe. Omit shredded apple. Add **1 egg,** well beaten, with bread crumbs and seasonings. Place meat mixture on broiler rack and pat into a large oval about 1½ in. thick. Place broiler rack under broiler with top of meat 3 in. from heat; broil 12 to 15 min. When browned on one side, carefully turn and broil 8 to 10 min. on second side. Serve with **Panfried Bacon** (page 190).

—BACON-WRAPPED BEEF PATTIES

Follow recipe for Fork-Tender Steak. Shape meat mixture into 6 patties. Wrap **1 slice bacon** around each patty and secure with a wooden pick. Broil, allowing about 10 min. on first side and 8 min. on second side.

—APRICOT LAMB PATTIES

Cut **4 slices bacon** into ¼-in. pieces and panfry until crisp. Meanwhile, follow ▲ Recipe. Omit shredded apple. Substitute **ground lamb** for ground beef. Add **1 egg,** well beaten, with bread crumbs and seasonings. Divide mixture into 6 portions. Stuff **6 large cooked apricot halves** with bacon pieces. Place an apricot half on each meat portion; gently shape patty around apricot. Cook as in ▲ Recipe. Garnish lamb patties with **sprigs of mint.**

GROUND BEEF PARMESAN
(Manzo alla Parmigiana)

Mix thoroughly

    1½ lbs. ground beef
    1 egg, well beaten
    1 medium onion, chopped
    1 teaspoon salt
    ½ teaspoon monosodium glutamate
    ⅛ teaspoon pepper

Shape meat mixture into a large square about ¾ in. thick. Cut into 6 equal portions. Arrange

Ground Beef Parmesan

portions on broiler rack. Place under broiler with top of meat 2 in. from heat.

Broil on first side 10 min., turn and spread with mixture of

    ¾ cup (6-oz. can) tomato paste
    1 tablespoon grated Parmesan cheese

Top portions with

    6 slices (3 oz.) mozzarella cheese
        (1 slice per portion)

Broil until cheese is melted and lightly browned.

6 servings

GROUND MEAT TOWERS

The meat patties for this sumptuous hamburger feast may be prepared ahead of time, stacked with waxed paper between them, and stored in the refrigerator until just before supper. The sauce may be made in advance, too, for quick last-minute preparation.

For Sauce—Heat in a saucepan

    ⅓ cup butter or margarine

Add and cook until the onion is tender, moving and turning mixture with a fork

    1 cup thinly sliced onion
    ¼ cup chopped green pepper

Add

    1 can (16 oz.) tomatoes, whole pieces
        cut small
    1 can (4 oz.) mushroom pieces
    2 whole cloves
    1 bay leaf
    1 teaspoon salt
    ½ teaspoon thyme
    ¼ teaspoon pepper

Cover and simmer about 20 min., stirring occasionally.

For Stuffing—Heat in the skillet

    ¼ cup butter or margarine

Add and cook until the onion is tender, stirring gently

    ¼ cup finely chopped onion

Pour contents of skillet over

    1 qt. soft ½-in. bread cubes (4 to 6
        slices bread)

Add to bread cubes and mix gently with a fork

    3 tablespoons minced celery leaves
    ½ teaspoon salt
    ⅛ teaspoon pepper

Beat together in a small bowl
> **1 egg, beaten**
> **⅓ cup milk**

Lightly blend egg mixture into bread mixture. Shape stuffing into 6 patties. Set aside.

For Meat Patties—Mix lightly
> **2 lbs. ground beef**
> **½ cup (1 medium) finely chopped onion**
> **¼ cup finely chopped green pepper**
> **2 eggs, beaten**

and a blend of
> **2 teaspoons salt**
> **1 teaspoon monosodium glutamate**
> **1 teaspoon Worcestershire sauce**
> **½ teaspoon garlic salt**
> **¼ teaspoon pepper**

Shape into 12 flat patties.

Heat in a large skillet over medium heat
> **¼ cup fat**

Brown in fat as many patties at one time as will lie flat in the skillet. When evenly browned, turn and brown on other side. Remove patties to absorbent paper and brown remaining patties.

Lightly grease a 13x9x2-in. baking dish.

Place 6 meat patties in the baking dish. Put a stuffing patty on each, and top with the remaining meat patties. Pour sauce over and around the "towers."

Bake at 350°F about 25 min., or until heated thoroughly.   *6 servings*

MEAT MUFFINS

▲ *Base Recipe*

Grease twelve 2½-in. muffin-pan wells.

Combine, tossing lightly
> **1¼ lbs. ground beef**
> **½ lb. ground pork**
> **2 cups soft bread crumbs**
> **1 cup milk**
> **1 egg, beaten**
> **1 teaspoon Worcestershire sauce**

Add a blend of
> **2 teaspoons salt**
> **1 teaspoon monosodium glutamate**
> **½ teaspoon thyme**
> **¼ teaspoon pepper**

Divide mixture into 12 equal portions. Pack meat mixture lightly into muffin wells.

Layered Loaf

Bake at 350°F about 40 min.

Meanwhile, thoroughly mix
> **⅓ cup firmly packed brown sugar**
> **⅓ cup ketchup**

Set aside.

After 20 min. of baking time, spoon about 2 teaspoons ketchup mixture on top of each meat muffin and continue baking. Unmold.
12 Meat Muffins

—BEEF AND PORK LOAF

Follow ▲ Recipe. Pack meat mixture lightly into greased 9x5x3-in. loaf pan instead of muffin-pan wells. Bake about 1½ hrs. Cover top of loaf with ketchup mixture after first hour of baking period. Unmold. Surround loaf with **Brussels sprouts** and garnish with **parsley**.

—MEAT RING

Follow ▲ Recipe. Pack meat mixture lightly into a greased 1½-qt. ring mold instead of muffin-pan wells. Bake about 1½ hrs. Omit ketchup and brown sugar. Unmold and fill center of meat ring with **potato balls** shaped with a ball-shape cutter. Garnish with **parsley**.

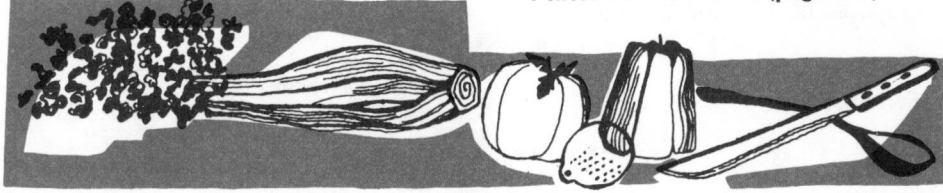

—PETITE RINGS

Follow ▲ Recipe for preparing meat mixture. Omit ketchup and brown sugar. Grease 8 individual ring molds. Divide meat mixture into 8 equal portions and pack lightly into the molds. Bake 30 to 35 min. Unmold and place a spoonful of colorful cooked **vegetable** in center of each ring.

—LAYERED LOAF

Follow ▲ Recipe for meat mixture. Increase ground beef to 1¾ lbs., ground pork to 1 lb.; decrease thyme to ¼ teaspoon. Add ¼ **cup chopped onion**, ¼ **cup chopped parsley**, 1 **tablespoon brown sugar** and **1 tablespoon wine vinegar** to combined ingredients before mixing. Grease a 10x5x3-in. loaf pan.

For Rice Mixture—Bring to boiling in a saucepan 1½ **cups water**. Add 1⅓ **cups packaged precooked rice**, 1 **tablespoon chopped onion**, ½ **teaspoon salt**, ½ **teaspoon monosodium glutamate** and a **few grains pepper**. Mix just until rice is moistened. Cover saucepan and remove from heat. Let stand about 5 min. without removing cover to allow rice to steam. Mix in **1 tablespoon chopped parsley** and **1 slightly beaten egg**. Lightly pack one third of meat mixture into pan. Top with one half

Meat Ring

of rice mixture. Repeat layers and top with remaining meat mixture. Bake at 350°F about 1½ hrs. Omit brown sugar and ketchup. Unmold loaf onto a serving plate. Garnish with **parsley**.   *About 8 servings*

BEEF ROLY POLY

Grease a 9x9x2-in. baking dish.

For Stuffing—Prepare, reserving 3 tablespoons bacon fat
> **4 slices Panfried Bacon (page 190)**

Put on absorbent paper to drain; crumble and set aside.

Drain
> **1 can (12 oz.) whole kernel corn (about 1½ cups, drained)**

Using a fork, toss bacon, corn and reserved bacon fat with
> **1½ cups soft bread crumbs**
> **2 tablespoons minced onion**
> **3 tablespoons water**

and a blend of
> **½ teaspoon salt**
> **¼ teaspoon marjoram**
> **⅛ teaspoon pepper**

Set aside.

For Meat Roll—Combine, mixing lightly and thoroughly
> **½ lb. ground beef**
> **½ lb. ground veal**
> **¼ lb. ground pork**
> **2 tablespoons minced celery leaves**
> **1 egg, beaten**
> **2 tablespoons water**

and a blend of
> **1 teaspoon salt**
> **¾ teaspoon monosodium glutamate**
> **¼ teaspoon garlic salt**
> **⅛ teaspoon pepper**

Turn meat mixture onto a large sheet of waxed

Drumsticks

paper. Pat into a rectangle ½ in. thick. Spoon stuffing over meat and pat into an even layer, covering meat. Lift waxed paper along one long side of meat rectangle. Using paper as a guide, gently push meat into a firm roll. Lift waxed paper and roll carefully to baking dish; slide roll off paper into baking dish, open edge of roll on bottom to prevent unrolling during baking.

Bake at 350°F about 1 hr. With large spatulas or spoons, lift roll onto warm platter.

6 to 8 servings

DRUMSTICKS

Set out eight 6-in. wooden skewers and a large heavy skillet.

Mix lightly
   2 lbs. ground beef
   2 eggs, beaten
   ½ cup (about 1 medium) finely chopped onion
   2 teaspoons prepared mustard
   1 teaspoon Worcestershire sauce
and a blend of
   2 teaspoons salt
   1 teaspoon monosodium glutamate
   Few grains pepper
Divide meat mixture into 8 portions. Shape each portion around one of the skewers. Roll drumsticks in
   1 cup (about 3 slices) fine dry bread crumbs
Heat in the skillet about
   6 tablespoons fat
Place drumsticks in skillet. Cook over moderate heat, turning carefully to brown all sides. Reduce heat and continue to cook slowly about 15 min., turning occasionally.

Serve on warm platter or plates. Garnish with **parsley.**

8 servings

BEEF BALLS PAR EXCELLENCE

Set out a large heavy skillet with a tight-fitting cover.

Combine and toss lightly
   1 lb. ground beef
   ½ cup crushed corn flakes
   ¼ cup minced onion
   ¼ cup milk
and a blend of
   1 teaspoon salt
   ½ teaspoon monosodium glutamate
   ¼ teaspoon pepper
Shape into balls about 1 in. in diameter. Coat by rolling meat balls in
   ⅓ cup all-purpose flour
Heat in skillet
   3 tablespoons fat
Add meat balls to skillet and brown over medium heat, turning occasionally to brown on all sides. Remove meat balls to absorbent paper and set aside.

Prepare
   Sauce Par Excellence (page 306)
Add meat balls to sauce and heat slowly to simmering.

Serve on **buttered noodles.**   *About 6 servings*

POTLUCK MEAT BALLS

Set out a large heavy skillet.

Combine in a large bowl
   1 lb. ground beef (chuck or round)
   1 egg, beaten
   ½ cup milk
   1 cup fine soft bread crumbs
   1 tablespoon instant minced onion
   1 tablespoon minced parsley
   ¾ cup finely chopped toasted walnuts

Add a blend of
   1 teaspoon chili con carne seasoning
   1 teaspoon seasoned salt
   ⅛ teaspoon seasoned pepper
Toss with a fork until thoroughly mixed. Shape mixture into 1-in. balls.

Heat in the skillet
   1 tablespoon (about) cooking oil or other fat
Add meat balls to hot oil and brown them on all sides over medium heat, shaking skillet occasionally to keep meat balls as round as possible. When balls are cooked to desired doneness, remove them from skillet and keep warm until ready to serve.

To serve, dip warm balls in **Guacamole I** (page 13) or **Spicy Ketchup Dip** (below) and in **finely chopped toasted walnuts.**

About 3 doz. small meat balls

To vary—For surprise meat balls, shape the meat mixture around small cubes of **cheese,** pieces of **pimiento, pickle,** canned **green chile, ripe** or **green stuffed olives,** or any other filling that appeals to you.

Spicy Ketchup Dip—Combine in a bowl and mix well **3 tablespoons brown sugar, ½ teaspoon dry mustard, ½ teaspoon ginger, 1 cup ketchup, 2 tablespoons soy sauce** and **1 tablespoon garlic-flavored wine vinegar.**

About 1¼ cups dip

DANISH MEAT BALLS
   (Frikadeller)

Combine in a large bowl
   1 lb. beef, ground twice
   ½ lb. pork, ground twice
   1 tablespoon finely chopped onion
and a mixture of
   ½ cup sifted all-purpose flour
   1 teaspoon salt
   ½ teaspoon monosodium glutamate
   ¼ teaspoon pepper
Add gradually, mixing vigorously
   1 cup milk
   ¼ cup water
   1 egg, beaten
Beat vigorously until mixture is smooth and well blended.

Heat in a heavy skillet
3 tablespoons butter

Using a tablespoon (not measuring spoon), drop the meat mixture by rounded tablespoonfuls into the skillet. (Meat will drop more readily from a spoon dipped in melted butter). Cook over medium heat until browned. Using a slotted spoon turn meat balls to brown evenly. Allow about 8 to 10 min. to cook meat balls.

Serve with browned potatoes and
Sweet-Sour Red Cabbage II (page 325)
About 3 doz. small balls

KOENIGSBERG MEAT BALLS
(Königsberger Klops)

Set out a 2-qt. saucepan.

Put into a large bowl
1 cup soft bread crumbs
¼ cup milk
Clean and chop
1 medium onion
Heat in a skillet
2 tablespoons butter
Add the onion and cook over medium heat until the onion is golden, moving and turning with a spoon. Add the contents of the skillet to the bowl with
1 lb. beef, ground twice
¼ lb. veal, ground twice
4 anchovy fillets, mashed
1 egg, beaten
and a blend of
1 teaspoon salt
½ teaspoon monosodium glutamate
¼ teaspoon pepper
Combine lightly and thoroughly. Shape into balls about 2 in. in diameter.

Bring to boiling in the saucepan
3 cups water
2 tablespoons chopped onion
1 bay leaf
1 whole clove
2 peppercorns
¼ teaspoon salt
Carefully put the meat balls into the liquid. Bring to boiling; reduce heat and simmer 20 min. Remove the balls with a slotted spoon and set aside to keep warm.

Strain the liquid. Heat in the saucepan
2 tablespoons butter
Blend in
2 tablespoons all-purpose flour
Heat until mixture bubbles. Remove from heat. Gradually add 2 cups of the liquid and
2 tablespoons lemon juice
1 tablespoon capers, chopped
Bring rapidly to boiling, stirring constantly.

Cook 1 to 2 min. longer. Return the meat balls to the sauce and heat thoroughly.

Serve with **Buttered Noodles** (page 153), allowing 2 or 3 balls to each serving.
6 to 8 servings

NORWEGIAN MEAT BALLS AND GRAVY
(Kjötkaker)

For Meat Balls—Heat in a large heavy skillet
2 tablespoons butter
Add and cook over medium heat until onion is golden yellow, stirring occasionally
6 tablespoons finely chopped onion
Combine and mix lightly the onion and
1 lb. ground beef
¼ lb. ground lean pork
½ cup soft bread crumbs
½ cup milk
1 egg, beaten
and a blend of
2 teaspoons sugar
1¼ teaspoons salt
½ teaspoon nutmeg
¼ teaspoon allspice
Shape meat mixture into 1-in. balls.

Heat in the skillet over low heat
2 tablespoons butter
Add the meat balls and brown over medium heat. Shake pan frequently to obtain an even browning and to keep balls round. When thoroughly cooked, remove meat balls to warm serving dish; keep warm while preparing gravy.

For Gravy—Add to the fat in the skillet a mixture of
3 tablespoons all-purpose flour
1 teaspoon sugar
½ teaspoon salt
¼ teaspoon pepper
Heat until mixture bubbles and flour is lightly browned.

Remove from heat; add gradually, stirring in, a mixture of
1 cup water
1 cup cream
Cook rapidly, stirring constantly, until mixture thickens; do not boil. Cook 1 to 2 min. longer. Pour gravy over meat balls in dish.

Serve at once.   *6 servings*

NORWEGIAN MEAT BALLS
(Karbonader)

Put into a large bowl
¼ cup (about ¾ slice) fine dry bread crumbs
Pour over the crumbs
1 cup milk
Stir until blended.

Add to the bowl
1 lb. round steak, ground twice
1 egg, beaten
3 tablespoons grated onion

Add a blend of
1 teaspoon salt
½ teaspoon monosodium glutamate
¼ teaspoon nutmeg
⅛ teaspoon pepper
Mix lightly until thoroughly blended. Shape into patties 2½ in. in diameter and ¼ in. thick.

Heat in a large skillet with a tight-fitting cover
3 tablespoons butter
Add the patties to the skillet and cook over medium heat until patties are well browned. Turn to brown second side. Set patties aside in the skillet to keep warm.

Prepare and set aside
½ cup quick meat broth (page 10)

Clean and cut into thin slices
1 large onion
Heat in a small skillet
2 tablespoons butter
Add the onion and cook over medium heat until lightly browned. Remove onion from the skillet and set aside. Drain off any fat. Add to the skillet
1 tablespoon sugar
Stirring constantly with the back of a wooden spoon, heat until sugar is melted. Add the meat broth gradually and
2 tablespoons butter
Stir until well blended. Pour over the meat balls. Cover meat with the onion slices. Cover skillet and simmer 10 min.   *4 or 5 servings*

Note: Norwegian Meat Balls may be served on the smörgåsbord.

SWEDISH MEAT BALLS I
(Köttbullar I)

▲ *Base Recipe*

Most widely known of all Swedish dishes, these tiny succulent balls typify the Scandinavian homemaker's genius in ground-meat cookery. Some cooks add a pinch of sugar, dash of paprika or chopped mushrooms to the gravy.

Set out a large heavy skillet with a tight-fitting cover.

Swedish Meat Balls I

Meat Balls with Tomato Sauce

Porcupine Beef Balls

Set out

    1 cup (3 slices) fine dry bread crumbs

Combine in a large bowl ½ cup bread crumbs and

    1 lb. ground round steak
    ½ lb. ground pork
    ½ cup mashed potatoes
    1 egg, beaten

and a blend of

    1 teaspoon salt
    ½ teaspoon monosodium glutamate
    ½ teaspoon brown sugar
    ¼ teaspoon pepper
    ¼ teaspoon allspice
    ¼ teaspoon nutmeg
    ⅛ teaspoon cloves
    ⅛ teaspoon ginger

Shape mixture into balls about 1 in. in diameter. Roll balls lightly in remaining crumbs.

Heat in the skillet over low heat

    3 tablespoons butter

Add the meat balls and brown on all sides. Shake pan frequently to brown evenly and to keep balls round. Cover and cook about 15 min., or until meat balls are thoroughly cooked.

Keep meat balls hot for the smörgåsbord.

About 3 doz. meat balls

—SWEDISH MEAT BALLS II (Köttbullar II)

To serve meat balls for dinner, follow ▲ Recipe. Prepare **1 cup quick meat broth** (page 10). Remove meat balls from skillet after browning. Blend **2 tablespoons all-purpose flour, ¼ teaspoon salt,** and **a few grains pepper** into the contents of the skillet. Heat until mixture bubbles. Stirring constantly, gradually add **1 cup cream** and the meat broth. Return the meat balls to the skillet and cover. Simmer 30 min. Serve the meat balls in the gravy.

6 servings

MEAT BALLS WITH TOMATO SAUCE

Set out a large heavy skillet with a cover.

For Meat Balls—Combine in a large bowl and mix thoroughly

    1 lb. ground round steak
    ½ lb. ground lean pork
    1 egg, beaten
    ½ cup fine dry bread crumbs

Add a blend of

    1½ teaspoons salt
    1 teaspoon dry mustard
    ¼ teaspoon white pepper

Shape mixture into small balls, about 1½ in. in diameter.

Heat in the skillet over low heat

    3 tablespoons butter

Add the meat balls and cook over medium heat, turning frequently, until they are browned on all sides. Add

    2 to 3 tablespoons water

Cover skillet and cook over low heat about 20 min., turning meat balls occasionally. Remove to warm serving dish or platter and keep warm.

For Tomato Sauce—Prepare in the skillet

    1 cup quick meat broth (page 10)

Add and stir until blended a mixture of

    ⅓ cup tomato paste
    1 tablespoon all-purpose flour
    1 teaspoon Worcestershire sauce

Heat to boiling, stirring constantly. Boil 1 to 2 min. longer. Remove from heat. Add about ½ cup of the mixture, stirring vigorously, to

    1 cup dairy sour cream

Blend into remaining mixture. Cook over low heat, stirring constantly, about 5 min., or until sauce is just heated; do not boil.

Pour sauce around meat balls and serve immediately.

5 servings

LEMON MEAT BALLS

Set out a large heavy skillet with a tight-fitting cover.

Shred

    2 oz. Cheddar cheese (about ½ cup, shredded)

Combine with cheese and mix lightly

    1 lb. ground beef
    ½ lb. ground pork
    ½ cup (about 1 slice) fine dry bread crumbs
    1 tablespoon chopped parsley
    1 tablespoon grated lemon peel
    1 tablespoon lemon juice
    1 egg, beaten

and a blend of

    1 teaspoon salt
    ½ teaspoon monosodium glutamate
    ¼ teaspoon pepper

Shape into balls about 2 in. in diameter. Coat by rolling meat balls in

    3 tablespoons all-purpose flour

Heat in skillet

    3 tablespoons fat

Add meat balls to skillet and brown over medium heat, turning occasionally to brown on all sides. Remove from heat and add slowly, blending well

    1½ cups tomato juice
    1¼ cups hot water

Return to heat, cover and simmer about 40 min. Turn meat balls occasionally.

6 to 8 servings

PORCUPINE BEEF BALLS

    ▲ *Base Recipe*

Lightly grease a 2½-qt. casserole with a tight-fitting cover.

Prepare and set aside

    2 cups Quick Tomato Sauce (page 307; add ½ cup water)

Meanwhile, combine and mix lightly

    1 lb. ground beef
    ½ cup uncooked rice
    ¼ cup minced onion

and a blend of

    1 teaspoon salt
    ½ teaspoon monosodium glutamate
    ⅛ teaspoon pepper

Shape into 1½-in. balls and put into casserole. Pour tomato sauce over meat balls.

Cover and cook in a 350°F oven about 1 hr., or until rice is tender when pressed lightly between fingers.

To serve, garnish with **parsley.**

4 to 6 servings

—PORCUPINE BEEF BALLS WITH MUSHROOMS

Follow ▲ Recipe. Substitute a mixture of **1¼ cups (10½-oz. can) condensed cream of mushroom soup** and **1 cup water** for the Quick Tomato Sauce.

—PORCUPINE BEEF BALLS WITH CELERY

Follow ▲ Recipe. Add ½ teaspoon celery salt with the seasonings in beef balls. Substitute a mixture of **1½ cups (10½-oz. can) condensed cream of celery soup** and **1 cup water** for the Quick Tomato Sauce.

SAVORY MEAT LOAF

▲ Base Recipe

Set out a 9x5x3-in. loaf pan.

Toast in a 325°F oven
2 cups (about 2 slices) soft bread crumbs
Mix bread crumbs lightly with
1 lb. ground beef
½ lb. ground pork
1 egg, well beaten
1 cup milk
¼ cup minced onion
and a blend of
1½ teaspoons salt
½ teaspoon monosodium glutamate
¼ teaspoon pepper
Pack mixture lightly in pan. Cover top with
½ cup chili sauce or ketchup

Bake at 350°F 1½ hrs.   *8 servings*

—LITTLE MEAT LOAVES

Follow ▲ Recipe. Pack and shape meat lightly in 8 heat-resistant custard cups. Spoon **1 tablespoon chili sauce or ketchup** on top of each. Bake 50 to 60 min.

—HAM LOAF

Follow ▲ Recipe or prepare Little Meat Loaves. Substitute 1½ **lbs. ground smoked ham** for beef. Decrease salt to ¼ teaspoon and add **½ teaspoon dry mustard** with seasonings. Omit onion and ketchup.

—LIVER LOAF

Follow ▲ Recipe. Substitute **1 lb. liver** and **½ lb. smoked ham**, ground, for beef and pork. Cook liver slowly 5 min. on both sides in a small amount of **fat**. Grind liver with **1 small onion**. Decrease milk to ¾ cup. Omit ketchup.

—SURPRISE MEAT LOAF

Follow ▲ Recipe or a variation. Lightly pack one half of meat mixture in pan. Place on meat, end to end, **3 or 4 Hard-Cooked Eggs** (page 133). Add remaining meat and shape loaf.

LAYERED MEAT LOAF

▲ Base Recipe

Grease a 9x5x3-in. loaf pan.

Lightly mix
1 lb. ground beef
½ lb. bulk pork sausage
1 cup fine dry bread crumbs
½ cup (about 2 oz.) grated Parmesan cheese
¼ cup finely chopped onion
2 tablespoons chopped parsley
½ cup milk
1 egg, beaten

Add a blend of
2 teaspoons salt
½ teaspoon monosodium glutamate
¼ teaspoon pepper
Lightly pack one half of mixture into loaf pan. Thoroughly blend and spread evenly over meat in pan
¾ lb. (about 1½ cups) ricotta cheese
1 egg, beaten
1 tablespoon chopped chives
Top with remaining meat mixture, smoothing evenly to corners.

Bake at 350°F about 1½ hrs.

About 6 servings

—MOZZARELLA-LAYERED MEAT LOAF

Follow ▲ Recipe. Omit ricotta cheese mixture. Hard-cook **4 eggs**. Slice and arrange over meat mixture in pan. Cover with **6 slices (3 oz.) mozzarella cheese**. Continue as in ▲ Recipe.

WALNUT MEAT LOAF

Grease a 8x4x2-in. loaf pan.

Mix lightly together
1 lb. ground beef
½ lb. ground veal
½ cup chopped walnuts
½ cup dry red wine
¼ cup milk
¼ cup (about 1 small) chopped onion
1 tablespoon chopped parsley
1 egg, fork beaten
Add and mix in a blend of
1 teaspoon salt
½ teaspoon monosodium glutamate
¼ teaspoon paprika
¼ teaspoon marjoram, crushed
⅛ teaspoon ground thyme
⅛ teaspoon pepper
Pack meat mixture lightly into loaf pan.

Bake at 350°F about 1½ hrs.

To unmold, loosen meat gently from sides of pan with a spatula. Pour off excess juices; invert onto platter and remove pan. Garnish meat loaf with **radish roses** and **parsley sprigs**, or as desired.   *8 servings*

BEST-EVER STUFFED MEAT LOAF

Wheat germ imparts a pleasantly different flavor to both the meat and stuffing layers.

Grease a 9x5x3-in. loaf pan. Set out a large heavy skillet.

For Wheat Germ-Bread Stuffing—Toast and cut into cubes
6 slices bread (about 4 cups cubes)
Set aside.

Prepare and set aside
1 cup quick meat broth (page 10)
Rinse, drain and finely chop enough celery stalks to yield
1 cup chopped celery (2 large stalks)
Set aside.

Melt over low heat in the skillet
¼ cup butter or margarine
Add the toasted bread cubes. Turn occasionally until they are coated evenly on all sides with butter and are golden brown in color. Remove skillet from heat. To bread cubes in

skillet, add one half the meat broth (reserving remainder for meat-wheat germ mixture), the chopped celery and
¼ cup wheat germ
¼ cup finely chopped green pepper
¼ cup minced onion
1 egg, beaten
and a blend of
¼ teaspoon salt
¼ teaspoon monosodium glutamate
⅛ teaspoon freshly ground pepper
Mix lightly with a fork. Set aside.

For Tomato Topping—Put into a small bowl
1 can (6 oz.) tomato paste (⅔ cup)
Blend in
⅓ cup firmly packed brown sugar
1 teaspoon prepared mustard
½ teaspoon Worcestershire sauce
Set aside.

Best-Ever Stuffed Meat Loaf

Planked Ground Meat Dinner

For Meat-Wheat Germ Layers—Put into a large bowl

2 lbs. ground beef
½ cup wheat germ
2 tablespoons minced onion

and a mixture of the reserved meat broth and

2 teaspoons salt
⅛ teaspoon thyme
⅛ teaspoon freshly ground pepper

Lightly mix with a fork.

Divide meat-wheat germ mixture into two equal portions. Lightly pack one portion into loaf pan. Spread Wheat Germ-Bread Stuffing evenly over top of meat layer. Lightly pack remaining meat-wheat germ mixture evenly over stuffing. Spread Tomato Topping evenly over top of loaf.

Bake at 350°F about 1 hr.

Unmold the meat loaf onto a warm serving platter. Garnish with **radish roses** and **sprigs of parsley.** Slice and serve. *8 servings*

PLANKED GROUND MEAT DINNER

To Season a New Plank—Brush a hardwood plank with unsalted fat. Heat in a 250°F oven for 1 hr. Cool and store until used.

For Vegetables—Prepare and set aside to keep warm

Fluffy Whipped Potatoes (page 339)

Cut off roots and a thin slice from each stem end of

6 medium (about 1½ lbs.) onions

Peel, rinse and cook (page 313) 20 to 30 min., or just until tender. Drain the onions; set aside and keep warm.

Rinse and cut off stem ends from

2 large (about 1 lb.) tomatoes

Cut into halves crosswise and set aside.

For Meat—Mix lightly

1 lb. ground beef
¼ cup milk or water
2 teaspoons Worcestershire sauce

and a blend of

1 teaspoon salt
½ teaspoon monosodium glutamate
⅛ teaspoon pepper

Put meat mixture on broiler rack and pat into a large oval about 1½ in. thick, or shape to resemble a steak.

Grease the seasoned plank with unsalted fat. Heat in oven while broiling meat.

Put meat under broiler with top of meat about 3 in. from heat. Broil 10 to 12 min. When meat is browned on one side, remove from broiler and place meat, browned side down, in center of the heated plank. Surround with the cooked whole onions and tomato halves. Force whipped potatoes through a pastry bag and a No. 7 star tube to form a border around meat and vegetables. Cover exposed plank as completely as possible.

Brush onions, tomatoes and potatoes with

Melted butter or margarine

Place plank under broiler with top of meat about 3 in. from heat. Broil about 8 min., or until meat is browned and potatoes are lightly browned.

Meanwhile, prepare

3 slices Panfried Bacon (page 190)

Remove plank from oven and set on a serving tray. Arrange bacon on top. *4 servings*

RANCH SHORTCAKE

▲ *Base Recipe*

Set out a baking sheet and a large heavy skillet with a cover.

Prepare

2 Hard-Cooked Eggs (page 133)

Chop and set aside.

Prepare and bake

Baking Powder Biscuits (page 92; roll dough to ⅓-in. thickness and use a 2½-in. cutter)

Meanwhile, heat in the skillet

1 to 2 tablespoons fat

Add and cook, stirring occasionally, until tender

1 medium onion, thinly sliced

Remove onion with slotted spoon and set aside.

Add to skillet, separating into small pieces with fork or spoon

1 lb. ground beef

Cook over medium heat until browned. Mix in the onion and add slowly, stirring in

2 cups (two 8-oz. cans) tomato sauce
1 teaspoon Worcestershire sauce

and a blend of

1 teaspoon salt
⅛ teaspoon pepper

Cover and simmer about 5 min.

Cook and drain

1 pkg. (10 oz.) frozen green peas

Add cooked peas and chopped eggs to skillet. Cook 3 to 5 min. longer, or until heated thoroughly.

Cut or tear biscuits into halves. Spoon sauce over half of biscuits and top with remaining halves. *4 to 6 servings*

—CHEESE RANCH SHORTCAKE

Follow ▲ Recipe. *For Baking Powder Biscuits*—Shred **3 oz. Cheddar cheese** (about ¾ cup, shredded). Cut cheese into dry ingredients for biscuits with **lard.**

—UPSIDE-DOWN RANCH SHORTCAKE

Follow ▲ Recipe. Prepare meat and vegetable sauce first; cover and simmer while preparing Baking Powder Biscuit dough. Roll dough into a round to fit top of skillet. Bring mixture to boiling and place dough on top of meat mixture in skillet. Put skillet into oven and bake at 450°F 10 to 15 min., or until biscuit topping is golden brown. Cover with warm serving plate. Invert and remove skillet.

BEEF AND GREEN BEAN CARAWAY STEW

Set out a large heavy skillet with a tight-fitting cover.

Prepare and set aside

2 cups quick meat broth (double recipe, page 10)

Cut into ½-in. pieces

4 slices bacon

Put bacon into skillet with

½ cup (about 1 medium) chopped onion

Place over medium heat until bacon is par-

tially cooked, moving and turning the mixture with a spoon or fork. Add and cook over medium heat until browned, separating into pieces with a fork or spoon

1½ lbs. ground beef

Remove from heat and blend in the meat broth and a mixture of

1½ teaspoons salt
1 teaspoon caraway seed
1 teaspoon paprika

Cover skillet and simmer 30 min.

Meanwhile, wash, remove and discard ends and cut into 1-in. pieces

1 lb. (about 3 cups) green beans

Cook (page 313) about 15 min., or until just tender. Drain, if necessary, reserving cooking liquid and set aside. Cool cooking liquid.

Pour into a 1-pt. screw-top jar

½ cup liquid (cooled bean cooking liquid plus water)

Add

¼ cup all-purpose flour

Cover tightly and shake until mixture is well blended. Bring contents of skillet to boiling. Shake flour mixture and add slowly to skillet, stirring constantly. Bring to boiling; cook 3 to 5 min. longer. Remove from heat and vigorously stir about ½ cup of the mixture, 1 tablespoon at a time, into

½ cup dairy sour cream

Pour the mixture gradually into the skillet while stirring constantly. Gently mix in green beans. Cook over low heat, moving mixture gently, 3 to 5 min., until heated thoroughly; do not boil. *5 to 7 servings*

BARLEY BEEF STEW WITH TOMATO DUMPLINGS

An easy-on-the-budget meal in the form of a hearty, vegetable-rich stew under fluffy rosy-red dumplings.

Set out a large heavy skillet and a 6-qt. sauce-pot with a tight-fitting cover.

Wash, scrape or pare and cut into lengthwise strips

4 medium carrots
2 medium turnips

Peel, rinse and quarter

3 medium onions

Wash, trim ends and cut into 1-in. pieces

⅓ lb. green beans (about 1 cup pieces)

Set vegetables aside.

Bring to boiling in saucepot

1 qt. quick meat broth (4 times recipe, page 10)
2 cups water

Stir in

¼ cup pearl barley
2 stalks celery with leaves, cut in quarters
1 bay leaf
¼ teaspoon thyme

Bring to boiling, cover and cook 30 min.

Meanwhile, heat in skillet

1 or 2 tablespoons fat

Add and cook over medium heat, separating into pieces with fork or spoon, until browned

1 lb. ground beef

Remove bay leaf from barley mixture. Add beef and vegetables to barley mixture with a blend of

1 teaspoon salt
½ teaspoon monosodium glutamate
⅛ teaspoon pepper

Bring to boiling, cover and cook 20 min.

For Dumplings—Sift together into a bowl

1½ cups sifted all-purpose flour
2 teaspoons baking powder
¾ teaspoon salt

Make a well in center of dry ingredients. Pour in all at one time

¾ cup plus 1 tablespoon tomato juice

Stir until dry ingredients are moistened.

Bring stew to boiling. Drop batter by heaping tablespoonfuls onto stew. (Batter will drop more readily from a moist spoon.) Dumplings should rest on vegetables; if dumplings settle down into the liquid, they may become soggy. Cover tightly and cook over low heat 20 min. without removing cover. *About 8 servings*

LIMA BEAN CASSEROLE

Set out a large heavy skillet and grease a 1½-qt. casserole.

Cook

1 pkg. (10 oz.) frozen lima beans

Meanwhile, combine in a large bowl

2½ cups (3½ slices) soft bread crumbs
¼ cup milk

Add and mix lightly

1 lb. ground beef
1 egg, beaten
1 small clove garlic, finely chopped

Blend in

1 teaspoon salt
½ teaspoon monosodium glutamate
¼ teaspoon pepper

Shape into balls about 1 in. in diameter.

Heat in the skillet

1 tablespoon fat

Add meat balls and brown over medium heat, turning occasionally to brown on all sides. Pour off fat as it collects. Remove meat balls from skillet and put into casserole. Pour over meat balls

¼ cup water

Drain lima beans and season with a mixture of

1½ teaspoons salt
½ teaspoon pepper
¼ teaspoon monosodium glutamate

Add and mix thoroughly

3 tablespoons butter or margarine

Cover meat balls with beans.

Bake at 350°F about 30 min. Remove from oven and spread with

1 cup dairy sour cream

Return to oven and bake, uncovered, 5 min. longer.

Serve immediately. *About 4 servings*

CHILI CON CARNE WITH SPAGHETTI

Here's a dish that keeps hot beautifully. Give it glamour by serving from a chafing dish, or accentuate its down-to-earth qualities by serving it in the kitchen.

Heat in a large heavy skillet

3 tablespoons fat

Add and cook about 3 min., occasionally moving and turning with a spoon

¾ cup (about 1 large) chopped onion

Add and cook until browned, separating into small pieces with fork or spoon

1½ lbs. ground beef

Add and stir in

3½ cups (28-oz. can) tomatoes, cut in pieces
1½ cups (16-oz. can, drained) kidney beans

and a blend of

1 tablespoon chili powder
1½ teaspoons salt
1 teaspoon sugar
¼ teaspoon monosodium glutamate
¼ teaspoon pepper

Cover and simmer 45 min.

When chili has simmered 15 min., bring to boiling in a large saucepan

3 qts. water
1 tablespoon salt

Add gradually

1 cup (4 oz.) uncooked spaghetti (broken in 2-in. pieces)

Boil rapidly, uncovered, 10 to 15 min., or until spaghetti is tender. Test tenderness by pressing a piece against side of pan with fork or spoon. Drain spaghetti by turning into a colander or large sieve; rinse with hot water to remove starch.

Add to cooked chili mixture and simmer until thoroughly heated, gently keeping mixture moving with a spoon. *6 to 8 servings*

Chili con Carne

Tamale Casserole

CHILI CON CARNE

Who can resist! South-of-the-border charm in a speedy main dish.

Heat in a large skillet
1 tablespoon fat
Add and cook over medium heat until browned, separating into small pieces with a fork or spoon
1 lb. ground beef

Meanwhile, heat in a saucepan, over medium heat, stirring occasionally
2 cups (16-oz. can, drained) kidney beans
1¼ cups (10¾-oz. can) condensed tomato soup
⅓ cup hot water
Blend in a mixture of
1 tablespoon chili powder
1 teaspoon salt
½ teaspoon monosodium glutamate
⅛ teaspoon pepper

Stir into sauce
1 cup (about 2 medium) chopped onion
¼ cup chopped green pepper
Continue cooking sauce over medium heat while meat browns. Combine sauce with meat in skillet. Bring to boiling and simmer 10 min., stirring frequently.   *5 or 6 servings*

CHILI CON CARNE BAKE

▲ *Base Recipe*

Melt in a 2-qt. top-of-range casserole with a tight-fitting cover
2 tablespoons meat drippings or fat

Lima Bean Chili con Carne

Add and cook over medium heat until meat is browned, separating into pieces with fork or spoon
1 lb. ground beef
½ cup (1 medium) chopped onion
¼ cup green pepper, cut in strips
Season with a blend of
1 tablespoon chili powder
1 teaspoon salt
1 teaspoon sugar
¼ teaspoon monosodium glutamate
⅛ teaspoon pepper
Add
2½ cups canned tomatoes, cut in pieces
2 cups (16-oz. can) red kidney beans, drained
1 bay leaf
Cover and simmer 20 to 25 min., stirring occasionally.

Meanwhile, prepare topping.

For Corn Bread Topping—Sift into a bowl
½ cup sifted all-purpose flour
2 teaspoons sugar
1½ teaspoons baking powder
¼ teaspoon salt
Mix in
½ cup corn meal

Blend thoroughly
1 egg, well beaten
½ cup milk
1 tablespoon melted shortening
Make a well in center of dry ingredients. Add liquid mixture all at one time. Beat with a rotary beater just until smooth; do not overmix. Remove bay leaf from hot mixture. Immediately spoon topping over hot mixture; spread evenly.

Set in oven and bake, uncovered, at 400°F 20 to 25 min., or until a wooden pick comes out clean when inserted in center of topping.
6 servings

—LIMA BEAN CHILI CON CARNE

Follow ▲ Recipe. Substitute **lima beans** for kidney beans. Add **2 cups (16-oz. can) corn**, drained, and **⅓ cup coarsely chopped celery**. Mix **¼ teaspoon celery seed** and **⅛ teaspoon savory** with other seasonings. Omit bay leaf and topping. Cover casserole and simmer gently about 1 hr. Add water, bean liquid or tomato juice if mixture requires more liquid.

TAMALE CASSEROLE

There's authentic South-of-the-border flavor in this hearty casserole.

Grease a 2-qt. casserole.

Put into a large heavy skillet with a tight-fitting cover
¼ lb. bulk pork sausage
Cut into pieces with fork or spoon. Add
1½ teaspoons cold water
Cover and cook slowly 8 to 10 min.

Meanwhile, prepare
1 cup (about 2 medium) finely chopped onion
½ cup finely chopped celery
⅓ cup finely chopped green pepper

Remove cover from skillet; pour off fat. Add
1 lb. ground beef
Cut into small pieces with fork or spoon. Brown meat over medium heat, occasionally moving with a spoon. Pour off fat as it collects. When meat begins to brown, add chopped vegetables. Cook until meat is well browned.

Add and stir in
2½ cups canned tomatoes, sieved
1¼ cups (12-oz. can, drained) whole kernel corn
1 tablespoon salt
2 teaspoons chili powder
½ teaspoon monosodium glutamate
¼ teaspoon pepper
Cover and bring mixture to boiling over high heat. Reduce heat and simmer about 15 min.

Meanwhile, prepare and set aside
1 cup sliced ripe olives
¾ cup (about 3 oz.) shredded sharp Cheddar cheese

Mix thoroughly
1 cup cold water
½ cup yellow corn meal
Bring mixture in skillet to boiling; gradually add corn meal mixture while stirring constantly. Cook over medium heat, stirring slowly, until mixture is thickened. Mix in the sliced olives. Turn mixture into the casserole.

Bake at 350°F about 1 hr.

Remove casserole from oven and sprinkle the

shredded cheese over top. Return casserole to oven and bake about 5 min. longer, or until cheese is bubbly. *8 servings*

MEAT 'N' CHEESE BLINTZES

Set out heavy 6- and 10-in. skillets.

For Filling—Combine, mix lightly and set aside
1 cup (½ lb.) ground cooked beef
¾ cup (4 oz.) cottage cheese, drained
¼ cup finely chopped celery
1 tablespoon sugar
1 teaspoon grated lemon peel
and a mixture of
½ teaspoon salt
¼ teaspoon monosodium glutamate

For Pancakes—Melt and set aside to cool
2 tablespoons butter or margarine

Sift together into a bowl and set aside
1 cup sifted all-purpose flour
2 tablespoons sugar
½ teaspoon salt

Beat until thick and piled softly
3 eggs
Beat in the melted butter and
1 cup milk
Combine egg mixture with dry ingredients. Beat with rotary beater until smooth and well blended. Set aside.

Heat the small skillet; it is hot enough when drops of water sprinkled on surface dance in small beads. Grease skillet *very* lightly. Pour in only enough batter from pitcher or large spoon to thinly cover bottom of skillet; immediately tilt skillet back and forth to spread batter evenly. Cook pancake over medium heat until lightly browned on one side. With spatula, remove pancake to a plate, brown-side up. Stack pancakes. (It should not be necessary to grease skillet for each pancake.)

For Blintzes—Spoon about 2 tablespoons meat mixture onto the center of one pancake. Fold two opposite sides of pancake to center. Begin with one of the open sides and roll. Press edges to seal. Repeat for each pancake.

Heat in the large skillet
1 tablespoon butter or margarine
Arrange several blintzes in skillet, sealed-sides down. Brown on all sides over medium heat, turning carefully with two spoons or tongs. Remove blintzes from skillet and place on serving platter. Serve hot with **jam** and/or **dairy sour cream.** *About 8 servings*

CHEESE MEAT PIES

Set out a large skillet.

Prepare and bake in six 3½-in. tart pans
Pastry for Little Pies and Tarts (one-half recipe; page 485)
Set aside.

Meanwhile, heat in the skillet
1 tablespoon fat
Add and cook about 3 min.
¼ cup finely chopped onion
Add and cook over medium heat, separating into small pieces with fork or spoon
½ lb. ground beef
¼ lb. bulk pork sausage
Pour off fat as it collects. When meat begins to brown, add and cook until celery and green pepper are tender
½ cup (about 2 stalks) finely diced celery
¼ cup chopped green pepper
Add a blend of
¾ teaspoon salt
⅛ teaspoon basil
Few grains cayenne pepper
Remove from heat and mix in
¾ cup tomatoes, sieved
1½ teaspoons Worcestershire sauce
Simmer, uncovered, about 10 min., occasionally moving and turning mixture with a fork or spoon.

Meanwhile, set out
½ lb. pasteurized process cheese food
Shred about one fourth of cheese food (about ½ cup, shredded). Cut remaining cheese into six slices. Put one cheese slice in bottom of each baked pie shell. Fill with meat mixture. Sprinkle with the shredded cheese.

Bake at 350°F 15 to 20 min. *6 servings*

BEEF AND CHEESE PIE

Set out a large heavy skillet.

Prepare (but do not bake) in 8-in. pie pan
Pastry for 1-Crust Pie (page 485)

Heat in the skillet
1 to 2 tablespoons fat
Add and cook over medium heat until lightly browned, separating into small pieces with fork or spoon
¾ lb. ground beef
Remove from heat and slowly blend in
1 cup (8-oz. can) tomato sauce
½ teaspoon Worcestershire sauce
¼ teaspoon salt
2 drops Tabasco

Simmer for 5 min. Set aside.

Put into a small bowl and beat with fork until softened
1 pkg. (3 oz.) cream cheese
Blend one half of the softened cream cheese with
½ cup (4 oz.) dry cottage cheese
¼ cup dairy sour cream
2 tablespoons minced onion
1 tablespoon chopped green pepper
1 tablespoon chopped drained pimiento
½ teaspoon monosodium glutamate
¼ teaspoon salt
Carefully spread remaining softened cream cheese over pastry in pie pan. Turn cottage cheese mixture into pie pan over cream cheese layer and spread to edges. Cover with meat mixture.

Bake at 425°F 10 min.; reduce heat to 325°F and bake 30 min. *About 6 servings*

MEAT-CRUSTED CORN PIE

▲ *Base Recipe*

A newcomer to the popular pie family is a colorful corn and tomato filling in a well-seasoned meat shell.

Set out a 9-in. pie pan.

Heat in a large skillet
2 tablespoons butter or margarine
Add and cook about 3 min.
½ cup (about 1 medium) chopped onion
Drain
1 can (16 oz.) whole kernel corn (about 1¾ cups, drained)

Cheese Meat Pies

Meat-Crusted Corn Pie

Add to the skillet, mixing with fork or spoon, the corn and

 1¼ cups (10¾-oz. can) condensed
  tomato soup

and a blend of

 1 teaspoon salt
 ½ teaspoon marjoram
 ¼ teaspoon chili powder

Simmer, uncovered, about 10 min.

Meanwhile, mix lightly

 ¾ lb. ground beef
 ¼ lb. ground pork
 ½ cup uncooked brown granular wheat
  cereal
 1 egg, beaten
 ½ cup milk
 3 tablespoons minced onion
 1 tablespoon Worcestershire sauce

and a blend of

 1 teaspoon salt
 ½ teaspoon monosodium glutamate
 ⅛ teaspoon pepper

Turn into pie pan. Gently pat mixture to evenly cover bottom, sides and rim of pan. Pour corn mixture into shell.

Bake at 350°F. 35 to 45 min.

Garnish with **green pepper rings.**

About 6 servings

—MEAT-CRUSTED LIMA BEAN PIE

Follow ▲ Recipe. Substitute for corn, **1 can (16 oz.) lima beans,** drained (about 1½ cups).

CARAWAY BEEF AND ONION PIE

Set out a shallow 1½-qt. casserole and a large heavy skillet.

Prepare

 **Baking Powder Biscuit dough
  (page 92)**

Roll dough to ⅛-in. thickness on a lightly floured surface. Fit into bottom and up sides of casserole; allow dough to extend about ¾ in. over sides. Flute (page 10) edge of dough and set aside.

Prepare

 4 slices Panfried Bacon (page 190)

Remove bacon from skillet, crumble and set aside.

Return 3 tablespoons bacon drippings to skillet. Add and cook about 5 min.

 **1½ cups (about 3 medium) chopped
  onion**

Add and cook over medium heat until browned, separating into small pieces with a spoon

 ¾ lb. ground beef

Mix bacon with cooked onion and meat; spread evenly over biscuit dough.

Beat thoroughly

 **2 eggs
 1½ cups dairy sour cream**

and a blend of

 **1 teaspoon salt
 ¼ teaspoon monosodium glutamate
 ⅛ teaspoon pepper**

Pour over meat mixture. Sprinkle lightly over the top

 2 teaspoons caraway seeds

Bake at 425°F 20 to 25 min., or until a knife comes out clean when inserted halfway between center and edge of casserole.

6 to 8 servings

DEEP-FRIED PIES

Tender, flaky crust encasing a spicy meat filling is extra delicious for the main dish.

Prepare

 **Pastry for Little Pies and Tarts
  (page 485)**

Shape into a ball, wrap in waxed paper, and place in refrigerator while preparing filling.

For Meat Filling—Set out a large skillet with a tight-fitting cover.

Prepare

 **⅓ cup finely chopped green pepper
 ¼ cup finely chopped carrot
 ¼ cup finely chopped celery
 ¼ cup (about 1 small) finely chopped
  onion
 ¼ cup (about 1 small) finely chopped
  green onion**

Add

 **1 tablespoon (about 1 medium)
  chopped hot red pepper
 1 tablespoon chopped parsley
 1 tablespoon chopped raisins
 1 tablespoon chopped green olives
 1 tablespoon capers**

Rinse and plunge into boiling water about ½ min. to loosen skin

 1 medium ripe tomato

Plunge tomato into cold water. Carefully remove and discard skin and stem end. Cut tomato into small pieces and add to chopped vegetable mixture.

Mix lightly

 ¾ lb. ground beef

and a blend of

 **1 teaspoon salt
 ¼ teaspoon pepper
 ¼ teaspoon monosodium glutamate
 ⅛ teaspoon cayenne pepper**

Heat in the skillet over medium heat

 **2 tablespoons shortening
 1½ teaspoons olive oil**

Add meat and cook until browned, separating into small pieces with a fork or spoon. Add vegetable mixture and blend well. Stir into hot mixture

 **¼ cup water
 2 or 3 drops Tobasco**

Cover and cook over low heat 30 min.

About 20 min. before deep-frying, fill a deep saucepan one-half to two-thirds full with

 **Vegetable shortening, all-purpose
  shortening, lard or cooking oil
  for deep-frying**

Heat slowly to 375°F (page 11).

Remove pastry from refrigerator and shape into two balls. Roll pastry to about ⅛-in. thickness (as in Pastry for Little Pies and Tarts). Using a lightly floured cookie cutter or a knife, cut into rounds about 4 in. in diameter. Place about 2 tablespoons filling onto each round. Moisten edges with cold water, fold pastry over, and press edges together. Flute (page 10) or press edges with a fork. Be certain seal is tight.

Stuffed Cabbage Rolls I

Deep-fry only as many pies at one time as will lie flat and uncrowded one layer deep in fat. Deep-fry about 3 min., or until golden brown.

Turn pies as they rise to surface and several times during cooking (do not pierce). Drain over fat for a few seconds before removing to absorbent paper. *About 16 pies*

CRUSTY CROQUETTES

▲ *Base Recipe*

Prepare and set aside to cool
1½ cups Thick White Sauce (1½ times recipe, page 304)

Meanwhile, grind (page 10) enough cooked meat to yield
2 cups ground cooked beef, veal or lamb

Put through medium blade of food chopper
2 medium carrots, washed and pared or scraped
2 stalks celery with leaves, cut in pieces
1 medium onion, quartered

Combine sauce, meat and vegetables; mix lightly. Mix in a blend of
½ teaspoon salt
¼ teaspoon monosodium glutamate
¼ teaspoon marjoram

Put into refrigerator to chill 1 hr.

Allowing about ⅓ cup mixture for each, shape into rolls, balls or cones. Roll in a shallow pan containing
1 cup (about 3 slices) fine dry bread crumbs

Dip into mixture of
1 egg, slightly beaten
2 tablespoons milk or water

Roll again in crumbs. Return to refrigerator to chill about 40 min. longer.

About 20 min. before deep-frying, fill a deep saucepan one-half to two-thirds full with
Vegetable shortening, all-purpose shortening, lard or cooking oil for deep-frying

Heat slowly to 375°F (page 11).

Deep-fry only as many croquettes at one time as will lie flat and uncrowded, one layer deep

in fat. Turn frequently to brown evenly. Deep-fry 5 to 7 min., or until golden brown; drain over fat before removing to absorbent paper.

Serve immediately accompanied with
Tomato Cheese Sauce (page 308)
5 servings

—OVEN CROQUETTES

Follow ▲ Recipe. Omit deep-frying. Set coated, chilled croquettes in a shallow, greased baking pan. Brush croquettes with **3 to 4 tablespoons butter or margarine,** melted. Bake at 400°F 20 to 25 min., or until golden brown.

STUFFED CABBAGE ROLLS I

▲ *Base Recipe*

Grease a shallow 2-qt. top-of-range casserole with a tight-fitting cover. Set out a large saucepan with a tight-fitting cover and a medium-size skillet.

From a head of cabbage, remove and wash
8 large cabbage leaves

Pour boiling water into the large saucepan to 1-in. level. Add cabbage leaves and
½ teaspoon salt

Cover and simmer 2 to 3 min., or until leaves begin to soften; drain.

Meanwhile, heat in skillet
2 to 3 tablespoons butter or margarine

Add and cook until tender
1 cup (about 2 medium) finely chopped onion

Remove from heat and mix in thoroughly
⅔ lb. ground beef (separate into small pieces with fork or spoon)
⅔ cup packaged precooked rice

and a blend of
¾ teaspoon salt
½ teaspoon Worcestershire sauce
¼ teaspoon monosodium glutamate
⅛ teaspoon pepper

Place about ¼ cup of the mixture in center of each cabbage leaf. Roll each leaf, tucking ends in toward center. Fasten securely with wooden picks; place in casserole. Pour over cabbage rolls a mixture of
3½ cups (28-oz. can) tomatoes, sieved
1 bay leaf
1 clove garlic, uncut (insert wooden pick for easy removal)
½ teaspoon salt
Few grains pepper

Cover and simmer 45 to 60 min., or until rolls are tender. Place rolls in warm serving dish. Remove wooden picks, garlic and bay leaf. Spoon sauce over rolls. *4 servings*

—LAMB-STUFFED CABBAGE ROLLS

Follow ▲ Recipe. Substitute **⅔ lb. ground lamb** for beef.

GROUND PORK

ENCHILADAS

Time was when every homemaker made her own tortillas, the traditional corn meal pancakes which are the foundation of enchiladas. Today, almost everyone buys these labor-consuming little items bakery-made, or packed in cans, and no one deplores this time-saving practice.

Rinse and cut into quarters
2 doz. hot red peppers

Remove stem, fiber and seeds with spoon or knife; rinse. Put peppers into a bowl and cover with
1 qt. warm water

Allow peppers to soak 1 hr. While peppers are soaking, prepare Chorizo (meat filling).

For Chorizo—Mix lightly
1½ lbs. ground pork
3 tablespoons cider vinegar
3 cloves garlic, minced

and a blend of
1½ tablespoons chili powder
1½ teaspoons salt

Heat in a large heavy skillet
1 tablespoon fat

Add meat mixture and cook over medium heat until browned, separating into small pieces with fork or spoon. Remove contents of skillet to a small bowl and set aside.

For Sauce—Turn the peppers and water into a sieve or food mill placed over a bowl. Force peppers through. Blend in
1 tablespoon oregano

Mix thoroughly in a skillet with
½ cup cooking oil

Bring mixture rapidly to boiling, stirring constantly. Reduce heat and simmer gently, stirring occasionally, about 15 min., to allow flavors to blend.

Stir in
1 tablespoon salt
⅛ teaspoon cumin seed

Remove from heat.

To Complete Enchiladas—While sauce is cooking, set out a large shallow baking dish and
18 tortillas (or use canned tortillas)

Shred and set aside
1½ lbs. Cheddar cheese (about 6 cups, shredded)

Clean, finely chop and set aside
> **6 medium onions (about 3 cups, chopped)**

Melt in the skillet in which the meat was browned
> **1 teaspoon fat**

Using a slotted spoon or fork, dip the tortillas into the sauce one at a time. Fry tortillas in skillet, 1 or 2 at a time, until lightly browned on both sides. Add more fat as needed. As the tortillas brown, remove from skillet and place in the baking dish.

Generously spoon Chorizo, chopped onion and one half the shredded cheese over tortillas. Roll up tightly and fasten with wooden picks. Turn so that fastened side is down. Pour remaining sauce over top of enchiladas and sprinkle with remaining cheese.

Bake at 375°F 10 to 15 min., or until cheese is bubbly and lightly browned. Place on a warm serving platter and garnish with
> **Sprigs of parsley**
> **Radishes**

Serve immediately.   *8 to 10 servings*

Note: Canned hot red peppers may be substituted for fresh peppers. Drain peppers and reserve liquid. Omit soaking. Combine the reserved liquid with the warm water, using only enough water to make 1 qt. liquid.

MEXICAN PANCAKE ROLLS

Grease a large shallow baking pan.

Shred and set aside
> **4 oz. sharp Cheddar cheese (about 1 cup, shredded)**

For Meat Sauce—Prepare
> **½ cup finely chopped onion**

Heat in a large heavy skillet
> **¼ cup fat**

Add the onion; cook over medium heat, stirring occasionally, until onion is tender.

Add and cook until browned, separating into small pieces with a fork or spoon and turning occasionally
> **1 lb. ground pork**

Stir in
> **2½ cups canned tomatoes**
> **1 cup (8-oz. can) tomato sauce**
> **1½ teaspoons chili powder**
> **1 teaspoon salt**
> **½ teaspoon monosodium glutamate**
> **⅛ teaspoon garlic powder**
> **Few grains pepper**

Simmer mixture, uncovered, about 30 min., stirring occasionally.

Meanwhile, prepare pancakes.

For Pancakes—Set a griddle or heavy skillet over low heat. Set temperature control of range at 400°F; put baking pan into oven to heat.

Melt and set aside to cool
> **¼ cup butter or margarine**

Sift together into a bowl
> **⅔ cup sifted all-purpose flour**
> **2 teaspoons baking powder**
> **1½ teaspoons salt**
> **¾ teaspoon baking soda**

Stir in
> **1⅓ cups yellow or white corn meal**

Make a well in center of dry ingredients and set aside.

Beat together
> **2 eggs, well beaten**
> **1⅔ cups buttermilk**
> **½ cup milk**

Blend in the melted butter or margarine. Add all at one time to dry ingredients. Beat until well blended and smooth. Set aside.

Test griddle or skillet; it is hot enough for baking when drops of water sprinkled on surface dance in small beads. Lightly grease griddle if manufacturer so directs. Pour about ½ cup batter onto the griddle. Cook slowly until lightly browned on one side. With spatula, carefully turn and brown other side. Repeat procedure, using remaining batter.

To Complete Rolls—Spoon about ¼ cup Meat Sauce onto each pancake. Sprinkle about 1 tablespoon of the shredded cheese over the sauce. Roll pancake tightly and put into the heated baking pan.

Spoon remaining sauce over the pancake rolls in the baking pan; sprinkle with the remaining shredded cheese.

Bake at 400°F about 8 min., or until cheese is melted.

Serve at once.   *8 to 10 servings*

PORK BROWN SAUCE ON SWEET POTATO BISCUITS

▲ *Base Recipe*

For Sweet Potato Biscuits—Set out a baking sheet.

Wash, scrub with a vegetable brush and cook covered in boiling salted water to cover
> **1 medium sweet potato**

Cook 35 to 45 min., or until potato is tender when pierced with a fork.

Pork Brown Sauce in Whipped Potato Ring

Meanwhile, sift together
> **1¼ cups sifted all-purpose flour**
> **1 tablespoon baking powder**
> **1 tablespoon sugar**
> **1 teaspoon salt**

Cut into dry ingredients with a pastry blender or two knives until mixture resembles coarse corn meal
> **½ cup lard, vegetable shortening or all-purpose shortening**

When sweet potato is cooked, drain, peel and mash. Add ¾ cup of the mashed sweet potato to flour-lard mixture; blend in thoroughly. Make a well in center of mixture and add all at one time
> **½ cup milk or cream**

Stir with a fork until just blended. Drop by large spoonfuls onto baking sheet, forming 8 large biscuits.

Bake at 400°F 20 to 30 min., or until lightly browned.

For Pork Brown Sauce—Set out a large heavy skillet with a tight-fitting cover.

Prepare
> **2 cups quick meat broth (double recipe, page 10)**

Blend in and set aside
> **1 tablespoon molasses**
> **2 teaspoons soy sauce**
> **½ teaspoon salt**
> **½ teaspoon monosodium glutamate**
> **¼ teaspoon paprika**
> **⅛ teaspoon pepper**

Prepare and set aside
> **¾ cup (1 to 2 medium) washed, pared or scraped and sliced carrots**
> **½ cup (about 1 medium) chopped onion**
> **¼ cup finely chopped green pepper**

Heat in the skillet
> **1 teaspoon fat**

Add and cook over medium heat, separating into pieces with fork or spoon
> **1 lb. ground pork**

Pork 'n' Apple Balls with Noodles

Pour off fat as it collects.

Meanwhile, drain

1 can (3¼ oz.) sliced mushrooms (about ⅓ cup, drained)

As the pork begins to brown, add chopped vegetables and mushrooms. Cook until meat is well browned, occasionally moving and turning mixture with a fork or spoon. Remove from heat and slowly pour in meat broth mixture. Cover and simmer about 15 min.

Meanwhile, put into a 1-pt. screw-top jar

½ cup water
¼ cup all-purpose flour

Cover jar tightly and shake until well blended. Bring contents of skillet to boiling. Shake contents of jar again and slowly pour into skillet while moving and turning mixture with a fork or spoon. Bring mixture to boiling and cook 3 to 5 min. Cover and simmer about 10 min. longer.

Split sweet potato biscuits into halves; serve with meat sauce between halves.

4 to 6 servings

—PORK BROWN SAUCE IN WHIPPED POTATO RING

Follow ▲ Recipe. Omit Sweet Potato Biscuits. Prepare **Whipped Potato Ring** (page 340). Pour Pork Brown Sauce into center of ring. Garnish with **parsley** and **carrot flowers.**

PORK 'N' APPLE BALLS WITH NOODLES

Set out a large heavy skillet with a tight-fitting cover and a large saucepan.

For Pork Balls—Coarsely grate

1 medium pared apple (about ⅔ cup, grated)

Combine with apple and mix lightly

1 lb. ground pork
½ cup soft bread crumbs
2 teaspoons minced onion
1 egg yolk, beaten

and a blend of

½ teaspoon monosodium glutamate
¼ teaspoon mace
¼ teaspoon nutmeg
⅛ teaspoon salt
⅛ teaspoon pepper

Shape into balls about 1½ in. in diameter.

Coat pork balls by rolling in

¼ cup all-purpose flour

Heat in skillet

2 tablespoons fat

Put pork balls into skillet and brown over medium heat, turning them occasionally to brown on all sides. Remove skillet from heat and add

¼ cup hot water

Return to heat, cover and simmer about 30 min., turning occasionally.

For Raisins and Noodles—Bring to boiling

⅓ cup water

Add, and again bring to boiling

⅓ cup raisins or currants

Pour off water and put raisins on absorbent paper. Set aside.

Heat to boiling in a large saucepan

1½ qts. water
1½ teaspoons salt

Add gradually, stirring with a fork

1½ cups (about 4 oz.) noodles

Boil rapidly, uncovered, 6 to 10 min., or until noodles are tender. Test tenderness by pressing a piece against side of pan with fork or spoon.

Drain by turning noodles into colander or large sieve; rinse with hot water to remove loose starch. Put drained noodles in a warm serving bowl. Using fork, blend through the noodles, the raisins and

2 tablespoons butter or margarine

For Gravy—Prepare and set aside

2 cups quick meat broth (double recipe, page 10)

When meat balls are cooked, remove them from skillet with slotted spoon; arrange them over noodles and set aside to keep warm.

Pour off fat in skillet and return 2 tablespoons of the fat to skillet. Blend in

3 tablespoons all-purpose flour
½ teaspoon salt
⅛ teaspoon pepper

Heat until mixture bubbles. Remove from heat and gradually add the meat broth, stirring constantly. Return to heat and bring rapidly to boiling, stirring constantly. Cook 1 to 2 min. longer. Pour into a warm gravy server.

Serve with pork balls and noodles.

4 to 6 servings

ALL-AMERICAN CHOP SUEY

▲ Base Recipe

This almond-topped version of chop suey features both ground pork and ground veal.

Set out a heavy 10-in. skillet with a cover.

Prepare and set aside

4½ cups Perfection Boiled Rice (one and one half times recipe, page 165)

Prepare and set aside

1 cup (about 4 stalks) diced celery (cut celery crosswise into narrow pieces)
¾ cup (about 1½ medium) coarsely chopped onion
⅔ cup (6-oz. can, drained) sliced water chestnuts

Spread out in shallow pan and heat in a 350°F oven until lightly toasted

⅓ cup slivered almonds

Heat in skillet

1 tablespoon fat

Add and cook over medium heat until lightly browned, separating into pieces with a fork or spoon

1 lb. ground pork
½ lb. ground veal

Pour off fat as it collects.

Meanwhile, drain, reserving 1 cup liquid.

1 can (16 oz.) bean sprouts (about 2 cups, drained)
1 can (4 oz.) mushrooms (about ½ cup, drained)

Add reserved liquid, bean sprouts, mushrooms and vegetables to meat. Cover and cook 20 to 30 min.

Meanwhile, thoroughly blend, in order

3 tablespoons cornstarch
1 teaspoon salt
1 teaspoon monosodium glutamate
3 tablespoons soy sauce
3 tablespoons water
3 tablespoons molasses

Pour gradually into meat mixture, stirring constantly. Bring rapidly to boiling, continuing to stir; cook 3 min. longer. Cover and cook over low heat about 15 min., moving and turning mixture occasionally with a fork or spoon. Sprinkle almonds over chop suey.

Serve with rice. *8 to 10 servings*

—ALL-AMERICAN CHOP SUEY WITH GREEN PEPPER

Follow ▲ Recipe. Clean **1 medium green pepper**; cut into narrow strips. Add to Chop Suey when other vegetables are added. Serve over rice in large bowl.

—ALL-AMERICAN CHOW MEIN

Follow ▲ Recipe. Substitute **2 cans (5 oz. each) chow mein noodles** for rice.

STUFFED CABBAGE
(Töltött Káposzta)

Set out an 8-qt. kettle with a tight-fitting cover.

Have ready
½ lb. beef short ribs
Put ribs into the kettle with
½ teaspoon salt
Water to cover
Bring quickly to boiling; skim foam from liquid and discard. Reduce heat; cover and simmer 30 min., skimming as necessary.

Meanwhile, remove and discard wilted outer leaves, rinse and cut one half the core from
2 medium (about 2 lbs. each) heads cabbage
Place cabbage in a large bowl and cover with
Boiling water
Let stand 1 to 2 min. Take cabbage out of the water; drain. One by one, carefully remove leaves that can be taken off easily; be careful not to tear leaves. Return remainder of cabbage to the water for 1 to 2 min. and repeat process. Remove a total of 18 to 20 leaves. Carefully trim down the thick, heavy part of each leaf. Set leaves aside. Store remainder of cabbage in refrigerator for use in other cooking.

Blend
2 eggs, well beaten
1½ teaspoons salt
¼ teaspoon paprika
⅛ teaspoon freshly ground pepper
Mix egg lightly and thoroughly with
1½ lbs. ground lean pork, such as shoulder
⅛ lb. ground smoked pork shoulder roll
1 small onion, slivered
1½ cloves garlic, minced
¼ cup uncooked rice
(The Rice Industry no longer considers it necessary to wash rice before cooking.)

To stuff the cabbage leaves, place on the center of each leaf about ¼ cup of the meat mixture. Roll each leaf tucking the ends in toward center. If desired, use wooden picks to fasten the leaves securely. Set aside.

Cover ribs in kettle with one half
1 can (27 oz.) sauerkraut (total yield is about 3½ cups firmly packed sauerkraut plus juice)
Lay stuffed cabbage carefully on top of the layer of sauerkraut. Cover stuffed cabbage with remaining sauerkraut. Pour over sauerkraut
1 cup (8-oz. can) tomato sauce
Water (enough to cover contents of kettle)
Bring to boiling. Reduce heat; cover and simmer about 2 hrs.

Remove stuffed cabbage, sauerkraut and ribs with slotted spoon to a large bowl. Cover to keep warm and set aside. Remove from kettle and set aside to cool to lukewarm
1 cup cooking liquid
Melt in a small skillet
2 tablespoons fat
Add to fat and cook until almost tender, stirring frequently
1 tablespoon finely chopped onion

Thoroughly blend in a mixture of
2 tablespoons all-purpose flour
1 teaspoon paprika
Stirring constantly, heat until mixture bubbles. Remove from heat. Gradually add the 1 cup of reserved cooking liquid, stirring constantly until smooth. Blend into liquid in kettle and bring rapidly to boiling; cook 1 or 2 min. longer. Pour sauce over stuffed cabbage. Serve with sauerkraut and ribs.   *8 servings*

GROUND HAM

HAM AND PINEAPPLE TURNOVERS

▲ *Base Recipe*

Set out a baking sheet.

Prepare
Pastry for 2-Crust Pie (page 485)
Roll each ball of pastry into a square ⅛ in. thick and cut each into quarters. Set aside.

Cut into thin slices and set aside
3 to 4 oz. Cheddar cheese

Thoroughly mix
1½ cups (¾ lb.) ground cooked ham
1 cup (13½-oz. can, well drained) crushed pineapple
¼ cup cream or undiluted evaporated milk
2 tablespoons finely chopped onion
and a mixture of
1 tablespoon brown sugar
1 teaspoon dry mustard

So pastry square can be folded diagonally to form a triangle, place an equal amount of cheese slices on each pastry square to one side of diagonal. Divide meat mixture into 8 portions. Spoon over cheese.

Using about ½ teaspoon for each, dot fillings with
Butter or margarine
Moisten edges of squares with water. Form triangles by folding one half of each square of dough over filling; press gently to seal edges

Stuffed Cabbage: Combine egg mixture, ground meat, uncooked rice and seasonings for stuffing. Place meat filling on center of cabbage leaf. Roll, tucking ends in. Fasten with wooden pick.

Ham Balls with Spiced Cherry Sauce

and flute (page 10). Prick tops to allow steam to escape. Place on baking sheet. Brush tops lightly with

Milk

Bake at 425°F 15 to 25 min.   *8 turnovers*

—BEEF PASTIES

Follow ▲ Recipe. Substitute **2 cups cooked ground beef** for ham, **½ cup cooked diced carrots** for pineapple and **¼ cup ketchup** for cream. Increase onion to **¼ cup** and cook with **2 tablespoons finely chopped green pepper** in **2 tablespoons fat** about 3 min. Omit sugar.

HAM BALLS WITH SPICED CHERRY SAUCE

Set out a large heavy skillet with a tight-fitting cover.

Grind (page 10) enough cooked ham to yield
　　2 cups ground cooked ham
Combine with ham and mix thoroughly
　　⅓ cup fine dry bread crumbs
　　1 egg, beaten
　　¼ cup milk
　　¼ teaspoon pepper
Shape into balls about 1½ in. in diameter.

Heat in skillet
　　¼ cup fat
Add ham balls to skillet and brown over medium heat, turning occasionally to brown on all sides. Remove from heat and add
　　¼ cup hot water
Return to heat, cover skillet and simmer about 30 min., turning balls occasionally.

Meanwhile, prepare
　　Spiced Cherry Sauce (page 308)
Remove ham balls from skillet to a serving plate and pour sauce over them.

About 10 ham balls

TEASER HAM ROLLS

Set out a baking sheet.

Grind (page 10) enough cooked ham to yield
　　1 cup ground cooked ham
Peel and mash
　　1 medium banana with all-yellow or green-tipped peel (about ½ cup, mashed)
Combine with ham and mix lightly, the mashed banana and
　　2 teaspoons minced onion
　　½ teaspoon prepared mustard
　　Few grains cayenne pepper
Set aside.

Prepare
　　Baking Powder Biscuit dough (page 92)
Roll dough into a square about ¼ in. thick. Cut into 3-in. squares. Spread about 2 tablespoons ham mixture evenly over each square. Roll up each square, pinching long edge to seal (do not pinch ends of roll). Put rolls on baking sheet, sealed edges down; brush with
　　Melted butter or margarine

Bake at 400°F 20 to 30 min., or until rolls are lightly browned.

Meanwhile, prepare and set aside
　　1 cup Mushroom Cheese Sauce (one half recipe, page 306)

Serve ham rolls topped with Cheese Mushroom Sauce.   *About 4 servings*

HAM CROQUETTES

A deep saucepan or automatic deep fryer will be needed.

Prepare and set aside to cool
　　1½ cups Thick White Sauce (one and one half times recipe, page 304; add ¼ teaspoon marjoram with seasonings)

Wash, pare or scrape and cut into thirds
　　2 medium (about ⅔ lb.) carrots
Cook (page 313) 15 to 20 min., or until just tender.

Meanwhile, put through medium blade of food chopper enough cooked ham to yield
　　2 cups ground cooked ham
Set aside.

Clean, finely chop and set aside
　　2 stalks celery with leaves
　　1 medium onion (about ½ cup, chopped)

Drain carrots and finely chop. Lightly mix together ground ham, chopped vegetables and cooled white sauce. Place mixture in refrigerator to chill.

About 20 min. before ready to deep fry, fill the saucepan or automatic deep fryer one-half to two-thirds full with
　　Vegetable shortening, all-purpose shortening, lard or cooking oil for deep frying
Heat fat slowly to 375°F (page 11).

Place in a shallow pan or dish and set aside
　　1 cup (about 3 slices) fine dry bread crumbs
Allowing about ⅓ cup·mixture for each croquette, shape chilled mixture into rolls, balls or cones. Coat by rolling croquettes in the bread crumbs. Dip croquettes into a mixture of
　　1 egg, slightly beaten
　　2 tablespoons milk or water
Roll again in the crumbs. Deep-fry in the heated fat only as many croquettes at one time as will lie flat and uncrowded one layer deep in the fat. Fry 5 to 7 min., or until golden brown, turning occasionally during frying time to brown evenly. Remove with a slotted spoon; drain over fat for a few seconds before removing to absorbent paper. Keep warm.

Serve croquettes with
　　Cheese Sauce (page 304)
　　　　　　　　　　5 servings

Note: Any cooked meat such as beef, veal or lamb may be substituted for the ham.

HAWAIIAN HAM AND JOHNNIE CAKE

Hungry folks cheer when these two old favorites get together for a spirited taste appeal.

In an 8-in. skillet or baking pan melt
　　3 tablespoons butter or margarine
Sprinkle in evenly
　　6 tablespoons brown sugar
Drain and cut crosswise to make 6 slices
　　3 slices pineapple
Arrange the 6 pineapple rings attractively on sugar mixture. Over pineapple rings spread
　　2 cups ground cooked ham

Prepare
　　Johnnie Cake I batter (page 90)

Ham Croquettes

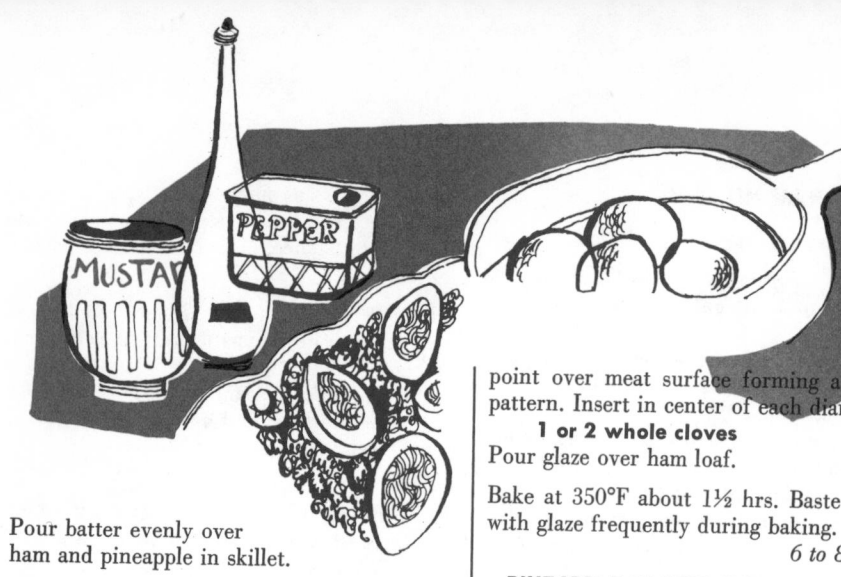

Pour batter evenly over ham and pineapple in skillet.

Bake at 425°F 20 to 30 min., or until a wooden pick or cake tester comes out clean when inserted gently in center. With a spatula, loosen sides of cake. Invert onto a warm serving plate. Allow to stand 5 min. before lifting skillet or baking pan. *9 servings*

GLAZED HAM LOAF

▲ *Base Recipe*

Set out a shallow baking pan.

For Ham Glaze—Mix thoroughly to form a smooth paste and set aside

1 cup firmly packed brown sugar
¼ cup vinegar
¼ cup water
1 teaspoon dry mustard

For Ham Loaf—Grind (page 10) enough ham to yield

2 cups ground cooked ham
Combine with ground ham and mix lightly
1 lb. ground pork
1 cup fine dry bread crumbs
1 teaspoon Worcestershire sauce
1 cup milk
2 eggs, beaten
and a blend of
1 teaspoon dry mustard
¼ teaspoon salt
¼ teaspoon pepper
Put meat mixture into baking pan and shape to resemble a ham. To score ham, draw knife

point over meat surface forming a diamond pattern. Insert in center of each diamond
1 or 2 whole cloves
Pour glaze over ham loaf.

Bake at 350°F about 1½ hrs. Baste (page 9) with glaze frequently during baking.
6 to 8 servings.

—PINEAPPLE-GLAZED HAM LOAF

Follow ▲ Recipe. Substitute **1 cup (8¼-oz. can) crushed pineapple** for vinegar and water.

—PINEAPPLE UPSIDE-DOWN HAM LOAF

Follow ▲ Recipe. Use a 9x5x3-in. loaf pan instead of baking pan. Omit glaze. Spread in bottom of loaf pan a mixture of ⅔ cup firmly packed brown sugar, ¼ cup vinegar and 2 teaspoons dry mustard. Set out **3 pineapple slices.** Cut two into halves. Arrange slices over sugar mixture in an attractive pattern (as pictured). Pack ham mixture lightly into pan. After baking, pour off excess liquid and unmold. Serve garnished with **sprigs of parsley** and **radish roses.**

—ORANGE UPSIDE-DOWN HAM LOAF

Follow recipe for Pineapple Upside-Down Ham Loaf. Omit pineapple slices. Cut **3 or 4 ¼-in. unpeeled orange slices** into halves. Arrange slices over sugar mixture.

—CRANBERRY UPSIDE-DOWN HAM LOAF

Follow recipe for Pineapple Upside-Down Ham Loaf. For brown sugar mixture, substitute a mixture of **1 cup whole cranberry sauce, ⅛ teaspoon cloves** and **⅛ teaspoon allspice.** Spread in loaf pan. Omit pineapple slices. Pack ham mixture lightly into pan.

HAM AND VEAL LOAF

Grease a 9x5x3-in. loaf pan. Set out a small skillet.

Grind (page 10) enough cooked meat to yield
2 cups ground cooked ham
2 cups ground cooked veal
Combine with ground meats and mix lightly
1 cup cracker crumbs
¼ cup minced onion
¼ cup minced green pepper
2 eggs, beaten
2 cups milk
½ teaspoon salt
⅛ teaspoon pepper

Pack lightly into loaf pan.

Bake at 350°F about 1½ hrs.

Meanwhile, prepare
Vegetable Sauce (page 308)

Unmold meat loaf and top with sauce. Garnish with **carrot curls, pearl onions** and **parsley sprigs.** *6 to 8 servings*

HAM LOAF

A slice of Ham Loaf and a cup of hot coffee for brunch or luncheon pleasure!

Set out a baking sheet.

Prepare and peel
5 Hard-Cooked Eggs (page 133)
Slice three eggs and reserve for garnish.

For Ham Mixture—Coarsely chop remaining two eggs and put them into a large bowl. Grind (page 10) enough cooked ham to yield
2 cups ground cooked ham
Mix thoroughly
½ can (10½-oz. can) condensed cream of mushroom soup (Pour remaining ½ can soup into a saucepan and reserve for sauce.)
¼ cup milk
2 teaspoons grated onion
and a blend of
½ teaspoon celery salt
½ teaspoon dry mustard
⅛ teaspoon marjoram
Few grains pepper
Add to ground ham mixture and blend well. Set aside.

For Loaf—Arrange in several stacks on a flat working surface
12 slices whole wheat bread
Trim crusts from slices. (One loaf of whole wheat sandwich bread, unsliced, may also be used. Trim crusts and cut four equal lengthwise slices from loaf.)

Place three slices of bread side by side lengthwise (or one lengthwise slice of loaf) on a baking sheet and spread with one third of ham mixture. Arrange three more bread slices on top of mixture and continue to alternate layers of ham mixture and bread until there are three

Pineapple Upside-Down Ham Loaf

Ham Loaf

Ham Pinwheel Ring

layers of ham and four layers of bread. Brush top of loaf with

1½ tablespoons melted butter or margarine

Bake at 375°F about 20 min., or until thoroughly heated.

Meanwhile, prepare Quick Mushroom Sauce or **Mushroom Sauce I (page 303)**

For Quick Mushroom Sauce—Stir into reserved soup in saucepan

2 tablespoons milk
1 tablespoon butter or margarine
1 teaspoon chopped chives
¼ teaspoon salt
Few grains pepper

Put saucepan over low heat and stir occasionally until mixture is thoroughly heated.

Using a broad spatula, remove ham loaf from baking sheet and place on a serving platter. Top with hot sauce. If sliced bread was used, pour sauce over loaf at places where bread slices join. Garnish with reserved egg slices. Slice loaf and serve. *6 servings*

HAM RING

Grease a 1½-qt. ring mold.

Grind (page 10) enough cooked ham to yield
4 cups ground cooked ham

Measure into a small bowl
2 teaspoons dry mustard
Stir in to make a smooth paste, about 2 tablespoons milk from
1 cup milk
Stir in the remaining milk.

Combine with ground ham and mix lightly, the milk mixture and
1 lb. ground veal
2 cups soft bread crumbs
¼ cup minced onion
3 eggs, beaten
¼ teaspoon pepper

Pack lightly into the prepared mold.

Bake at 350°F about 1½ hrs.

Unmold the ring. Garnish with **pineapple**

slice, **crab apples** and **parsley**. If desired, accompany with
Horseradish Sour Cream Sauce (page 310)

10 to 12 servings

HAM PINWHEEL RING

▲ *Base Recipe*

Set out a baking sheet.

Grind (page 10) enough cooked ham to yield
1½ cups ground cooked ham
Combine with ham and mix lightly
⅓ cup sweetened condensed milk
¼ cup pickle relish
2 tablespoons minced parsley
2 teaspoons prepared mustard

Set aside.

Prepare
Baking Powder Biscuit dough (page 92)
Roll dough into a rectangle about ¼ in. thick on a lightly floured surface. Spread ham mixture evenly over biscuit dough. Starting with long side of dough, roll up and pinch long edge to seal. (Do not pinch ends of roll.) Place roll on baking sheet, sealed-edge down. Bring ends of roll together to form a ring. Brush ring lightly with
1 to 2 tablespoons melted butter or margarine
With scissors or sharp knife, make cuts at 1 in. intervals around outside of ring to within ¼ in. of center. Slightly pull out and twist each section so that cut sides rest almost flat on baking sheet.

Bake at 400°F 20 to 30 min., or until ring is golden brown.

Meanwhile, prepare
Sauce Par Excellence (one half recipe, page 306)

Serve ring with Sauce Par Excellence. Garnish with **parsley**. *6 to 8 servings*

—BEEF PINWHEEL RING

Follow ▲ Recipe. Substitute **1½ cups ground cooked beef** for ham. Add **1 teaspoon salt** and **⅛ teaspoon pepper** to meat mixture. Substitute **Tomato Cheese Sauce** (one half recipe, page 308) for Sauce Par Excellence.

—LUNCHEON MEAT PINWHEEL RING

Follow ▲ Recipe. Substitute **1½ cups ground luncheon meat** for ham.

—HAM CRESCENTS

Follow ▲ Recipe. Omit Mushroom-Cheese Sauce. Divide biscuit dough into halves. Roll each half into a round about ¼ in. thick. Spread each round with one half of the ham mixture and cut each into 8 wedges. Roll each wedge, beginning at wide end. Put rolls on

baking sheet with pointed edges down. Curve slightly to form crescents. Bake as in ▲ Recipe.

GROUND LAMB

LAMB BURGERS

▲ *Base Recipe*

Combine and mix lightly
1½ lbs. ground lamb
3 tablespoons minced parsley
1 egg, beaten
and a blend of
1 teaspoon salt
½ teaspoon monosodium glutamate
¼ teaspoon allspice
Shape into 5 patties about 1 in. thick.

Arrange patties on broiler rack. Put under broiler with top of patties about 3 in. from heat. Broil about 9 min. When browned on one side, turn and broil second side about 9 min.

Meanwhile, toast and butter
Hamburger bun halves
Put broiled burgers on bun halves. Top with
Onion rings
Arrange on platter alternately with **buttered whole carrots**. Garnish with **parsley**. Serve with chilled sour cream or
Horseradish Sour Cream Sauce (page 310)

5 servings

—BACON RING LAMB BURGERS

Follow ▲ Recipe. Set out **5 slices bacon**. Before broiling patties, wrap 1 bacon slice

Lamb Burgers

around edge of each patty. Fasten ends of bacon slice to patty with wooden pick.

—MINTED LAMB BURGERS

Follow ▲ Recipe. Set out **2 tablespoons mint jelly.** When lamb burgers are cooked, place about 1 teaspoonful of jelly on each patty. Broil 2 or 3 min. longer, or until jelly is melted and heated.

—LAMB BUNS WITH TOMATOES

Follow ▲ Recipe. Add **½ cup sieved drained tomatoes** to ground lamb with the other ingredients and mix lightly. Shape mixture into 6 patties. Split, toast, and butter **3 hamburger buns.** Place one patty on each bun half. Set on a baking sheet. Bake at 350°F about 30 min., or until meat is cooked.

CURRIED LAMB WITH APPLE

Set out a large heavy skillet.

Prepare
   1½ cups Fluffy Rice (one-half recipe, page 164)

Meanwhile, heat in the skillet
   1 tablespoon fat
Add and cook over medium heat until lightly browned, separating into small pieces with a fork or spoon
   1 lb. ground lamb
Pour off fat as it collects in skillet.

Add to skillet
   ¼ cup finely chopped celery
   3 tablespoons finely chopped onion
Cook slowly, moving and turning mixture occasionally, until celery is tender.

Meanwhile, prepare
   2 cups quick chicken broth (double recipe, page 10)
Add to lamb mixture and simmer.

Put into a 1-pt. screw-top jar
   ½ cup water
Sprinkle evenly onto water a mixture of
   ¼ cup all-purpose flour
   1½ teaspoons salt
   1 teaspoon curry powder
   ½ teaspoon monosodium glutamate
   ¼ teaspoon ginger
   ⅛ teaspoon nutmeg
   Few grains cayenne pepper

Cover jar tightly; shake until well blended. Bring lamb mixture to boiling; shake flour mixture and pour slowly into the skillet; keep mixture moving with a fork or spoon. Bring to boiling. Cook 3 to 5 min.

Wash, quarter, core, pare and slice
   1 medium apple (about 1 cup, sliced)
Add to lamb mixture. Thoroughly mix the lamb mixture and rice and turn into a warm serving bowl. Sprinkle top with
   ½ cup moist flaked coconut
Serve immediately.   *6 to 8 servings*

SAVORY LAMB AND CARROT BALLS

Set out a large heavy skillet with a tight-fitting cover.

Wash, scrape or pare and put through medium blade of food chopper
   3 medium carrots (about ¾ cup, ground)
Combine with carrots and mix lightly
   1 lb. ground lamb
   ¼ cup finely chopped celery
   2 tablespoons finely chopped celery leaves
   1 tablespoon minced onion
   1 egg, beaten
and a blend of
   1 teaspoon salt
   ½ teaspoon monosodium glutamate
   ¼ teaspoon pepper
   ⅛ teaspoon sage
Shape into balls about 1½ in. in diameter.

Heat in skillet
   3 tablespoons fat
Put lamb balls into skillet and brown over medium heat, turning occasionally to brown on all sides. Cover skillet and cook over low heat about 10 min., turning balls occasionally. Add more fat if necessary.   *4 to 6 servings*

FROSTED LAMB LOAF

   ▲ **Base Recipe**

Glamorous, delicious combination that will please the "meat 'n' potatoes" crowd.

Grease a 9x5x3-in. loaf pan.

Mix lightly
   1½ lbs. ground lamb
   ¾ cup uncooked rolled oats
   ½ clove garlic, finely minced
   ¼ cup minced onion
   2 tablespoons minced parsley
   1¼ cups (10¾-oz. can) condensed tomato soup
   2 eggs, beaten
   1½ teaspoons salt
   ¾ teaspoon monosodium glutamate
   ¼ teaspoon pepper
Pack lightly into loaf pan.

Bake at 350°F about 1½ hrs.

While loaf bakes, prepare
   Fluffy Whipped Potatoes (page 339)
Unmold loaf onto heat-resistant platter or baking pan. Spread whipped potatoes over top and sides of loaf. Brush with
   Melted butter or margarine
Return to oven for 15 to 20 min., or until potatoes are lightly browned.

Remove loaf from oven and sprinkle over top
   2 tablespoons chopped chives
For an attractive platter, serve loaf with **carrots** sliced with a fancy cutter for preparing lattice vegetables, cooked and glazed. Serve immediately.   *6 to 8 servings*

—CRUSTY INDIVIDUAL LAMB LOAVES

Follow ▲ Recipe. Lightly grease a shallow baking pan instead of the loaf pan. Divide unbaked mixture into 6 portions and shape each into a small loaf. Gently roll loaves in **1 cup crushed corn flakes.** Place loaves in the baking pan and bake at 350°F about 45 min. Omit potatoes, chives and second baking.

GROUND LAMB SCALLOP

Grease a 2-qt. casserole.

Heat in a large skillet
   2 tablespoons fat or meat drippings
Add and cook over medium heat until browned, separating into small pieces with a spoon
   2 lbs. ground uncooked lamb
When lightly browned, add and continue cooking about 5 min.
   2 tablespoons chopped onion
   1 small green pepper, chopped

Frosted Lamb Loaf

Meanwhile, mix

1 egg, well beaten
1 cup dairy sour cream
2 tablespoons minced parsley

and a blend of

1½ teaspoons salt
1 teaspoon monosodium glutamate
¼ teaspoon pepper
⅛ to ¼ teaspoon marjoram

Pour over browned lamb and mix well. Turn one half of mixture into casserole. Top with

1 cup coarsely grated carrot

Cover with remaining meat.

Peel, rinse and cut into thin slices

1 medium onion

Separate slices into rings. Using a fork, blend with

3 to 4 tablespoons melted butter or margarine

Arrange onion rings over meat (reserving remaining butter).

Bake at 350°F 35 to 45 min. After 15 min. of baking, drizzle remaining butter over onions.

6 servings

LAMB SOUFFLE

▲ *Base Recipe*

Set out a 1½-qt. casserole.

Grind (page 10) and set aside enough cooked lamb to yield

2 cups ground cooked lamb

Prepare and cool slightly

1 cup Thick White Sauce (page 304); add ½ teaspoon onion salt and ⅛ teaspoon nutmeg with seasonings

Mix ground lamb into white sauce.

Beat until very thick and lemon-colored

4 egg yolks

Slowly spoon sauce into beaten egg yolks, while beating vigorously with a spoon. Mix or blend in

3 tablespoons minced parsley

Beat until rounded peaks are formed and egg whites do not slide when bowl is partially inverted

4 egg whites

Gently spread sauce over beaten egg whites. Carefully fold together until just blended. Turn mixture into casserole. Set casserole in a baking pan on oven rack. Pour very hot water into pan to a 1-in. depth.

Bake at 350°F 40 to 50 min., or until a metal knife comes out clean when inserted halfway between center and edge of casserole.

Serve at once. *6 to 8 servings*

—TONGUE SOUFFLE

Follow ▲ Recipe. Substitute **ground cooked tongue** for lamb. Omit nutmeg in seasonings for white sauce. Shred **2 oz. cheese** (½ cup, shredded). Add all at one time to slightly cooled sauce, blending until cheese is melted.

GROUND VEAL

VEAL BALLS WITH SOUR CREAM
(Borjuhus Tejföllel)

Prepare
Noodles (page 152)

Shortly before noodles are dry, set out a heavy 10-in. skillet with a tight-fitting cover.

Lightly mix

1 lb. ground veal
¾ cup milk
½ cup (about 1½ slices) fine dry bread crumbs
½ cup (about 1 medium) chopped onion
2 tablespoons chopped parsley
1 egg, well beaten
1 teaspoon salt
¼ teaspoon pepper

Form veal mixture into medium (2-in.) or small (1-in.) balls. Heat in the skillet

¼ cup fat

Add veal balls to fat; brown over medium heat, turning balls occasionally. Add

½ cup (4-oz. can) sliced mushrooms

Cover skillet and simmer 30 to 45 min., or until veal balls are done, turning balls occasionally and adding water if needed.

Meanwhile, cook the noodles (page 152) and drain.

Prepare
½ cup quick meat broth (one half recipe, page 10)

Set broth aside to cool to lukewarm.

When veal balls are done, remove skillet from heat. Drain cooking liquid from the meat into a cup; set skillet aside.

Put into top of a double boiler
1 cup dairy sour cream

Add gradually to sour cream, stirring constantly, the liquid drained from skillet and the reserved broth. Cook sauce over simmering water, stirring occasionally, until heated thoroughly.

Turn noodles into serving bowl, top with contents of skillet and sour cream sauce. Serve immediately. *6 servings*

POTATO BURGERS

▲ *Base Recipe*

Make excellent use of leftover potatoes in these luscious burgers.

Set out a large heavy skillet with a cover.

Mix lightly

½ lb. ground veal
½ lb. ground pork
1 cup whipped potato
⅓ cup fine dry bread crumbs
¼ cup minced onion
¼ cup milk
1 egg, well beaten

and a blend of

½ teaspoon celery salt
½ teaspoon monosodium glutamate
½ teaspoon salt
⅛ teaspoon pepper

Shape meat mixture into patties about 2½ in. in diameter.

Heat in skillet
2 to 3 tablespoons fat

Put patties into skillet and brown over medium heat, turning occasionally to brown on both sides. Add

2 to 3 tablespoons water

Cover and cook over low heat 20 to 25 min., turning occasionally. *4 to 6 servings*

—SWEET POTATO HAM BURGERS

Follow ▲ Recipe. Substitute **1 cup whipped sweet potatoes or yams** for white potato and **1 cup ground cooked ham** for veal. Omit celery salt. Add **½ teaspoon dry mustard** with the seasoning mixture and **¼ cup well-drained crushed pineapple** with the meat.

—POTATO BALLS

Follow ▲ Recipe. Substitute **1 cup grated raw potato** (about 2 medium) for mashed potatoes. Shape meat into balls about 1½ in. in diameter. Serve with **buttered carrots** and **buttered green beans**.

—BEEF 'N' POTATO BALLS

Follow Potato Balls recipe. Substitute **1 lb. ground beef** for pork and veal.

Cheese-Filled Veal Rolls

CHEESE-FILLED VEAL ROLLS

Delicious accompaniments for these veal rolls with their melting hearts of gold are fruits which are as beautiful as they are good. Choose whatever the season or your canned fruit cupboard offers.

Set out a large heavy skillet.

Slice into quarters lengthwise
¼ lb. (4 slices) sliced pasteurized process American cheese
Mix lightly
1 lb. ground veal
¼ cup finely chopped onion
and a blend of
¾ teaspoon salt
⅛ teaspoon pepper
Few grains cayenne pepper
Divide meat mixture into 8 equal portions. Shape each portion into a rectangle about 4 in. long and ¼ in. thick. Stack 2 strips of cheese and place on the center of a rectangle of meat. Fold meat around cheese to form a roll enclosing it completely.

Heat in skillet
2 tablespoons butter or margarine
Put veal rolls into skillet and cook over medium heat, turning carefully to brown all sides. Allow about 25 min. for cooking.

Serve hot with
Fluffy Rice (page 164)

About 4 servings

VEAL POT PIE

Set out a 1½-qt. casserole and a large heavy skillet.

Prepare
Baking Powder Biscuit dough (one-half recipe, page 92; add 1 teaspoon celery salt and 1½ teaspoons paprika to dry ingredients)
Roll dough into a round ½ in. thick on a lightly floured surface. Using an even pressure to keep sides of biscuits straight, cut into rounds with a floured 2-in. cutter. Set aside.

Wash, pare, thinly slice and set aside
2 medium carrots

Prepare
½ cup (about 1 medium) chopped onion
¼ cup chopped green pepper
Heat in the skillet
1 to 2 tablespoons fat
Add and cook over medium heat, separating into small pieces with a fork or spoon
¾ lb. ground veal
When meat begins to brown, add vegetables and cook until carrots are tender, frequently moving and turning with fork or spoon. When carrots are tender, mix in
1¼ cups (10½-oz. can) condensed cream of mushroom soup
½ cup milk
2 tablespoons minced parsley
and a blend of
½ teaspoon salt
¼ teaspoon monosodium glutamate
¼ teaspoon pepper
Simmer about 5 min. Bring just to boiling; turn into casserole. Arrange biscuits over top.

Bake at 450°F 10 to 15 min., or until biscuits are lightly browned. *About 6 servings*

VEAL MUSHROOM TIMBALES

▲ *Base Recipe*

Set out an 8-in. skillet, a double boiler and 8-heat-resistant custard cups.

Cut into thin crosswise strips
1 whole canned pimiento
Arrange 2 or 3 pimiento strips in bottom of each custard cup. Set aside.

Clean and slice (page 9)
½ lb. mushrooms
Heat in skillet
2 to 3 tablespoons butter or margarine
Add mushrooms to skillet with
2 tablespoons minced onion
Cook over medium heat, occasionally moving and turning with a spoon or fork until mushrooms are lightly browned. Set aside.

Grind (page 10) and set aside enough cooked veal to yield
2 cups ground cooked veal

Combine in top of the double boiler
1½ cups milk
⅓ cup fine dry bread crumbs
Place over simmering water until milk is scalded (page 9). Remove from simmering water. Mix in veal, onion, mushrooms and
2 tablespoons butter or margarine
and a blend of
1 teaspoon salt
½ teaspoon monosodium glutamate
⅛ teaspoon paprika
Add gradually, vigorously stirring mixture into
3 eggs, well beaten
Fill custard cups two-thirds full with mixture. Set filled cups in a baking pan on oven rack. Pour very hot water into pan to a 1-in. depth.

Bake at 350°F 20 to 30 min., or until a metal knife comes out clean when inserted in center of timbale. Run a spatula around inside of cups to loosen timbales. Unmold onto hot serving plates.

While timbales bake, prepare
Tomato Cheese Sauce (page 308)
Serve sauce over unmolded timbales.

4 servings

—SPINACH VEAL TIMBALES

Follow ▲ Recipe. Substitute **1 cup cooked spinach** (page 313), well drained and finely chopped, for mushrooms and onion. Omit browning in butter or margarine.

STUFFED CABBAGE ROLLS II
(Kaldolmar)

Set out a large saucepot or kettle with a tight-fitting cover.

For Cabbage—Remove and discard wilted outer leaves, rinse and cut core from
1 large head (3 to 3½ lbs.) cabbage
Put cabbage into the saucepot and add
Boiling water to cover
1 teaspoon salt
Cover and simmer about 5 min., or until leaves are softened. Carefully separate cabbage leaves and set aside on absorbent paper to drain.

For Filling—Mix lightly in a bowl
1 lb. veal, ground four times
1 lb. beef, ground four times
1¼ cups milk
⅔ cup fine dry bread crumbs
4 teaspoons grated onion
2½ teaspoons salt
1 teaspoon nutmeg

For Cabbage Rolls—Place a small cabbage leaf in the center of a large leaf. Drop about ½ cup of the meat mixture onto the center of each small leaf. (Meat mixture will drop more readily from a moist spoon or cup.) Roll each leaf,

Stuffed Cabbage Rolls II

tucking ends in toward center. Fasten securely with wooden picks or tie with clean string.

Bring to boiling in the saucepot
Water to cover
Salt (1 teaspoon per quart of water)
Add the cabbage rolls one at a time so that water continues to boil. Reduce heat, cover and cook 20 min., or until tender. Carefully remove rolls with a slotted spoon. Remove wooden picks or string. Place rolls in a serving dish and serve with Cream Gravy.

For Cream Gravy—Heat in a saucepan
3 tablespoons butter
Blend in
3 tablespoons all-purpose flour
¾ teaspoon salt
½ teaspoon cardamom
Heat until mixture bubbles. Remove from heat. Add gradually, while stirring constantly
2 cups milk
Return to heat and bring rapidly to boiling, stirring constantly. Cook 1 to 2 min. longer.
About 15 cabbage rolls

VEAL OYSTER LOAF

Grease a 9x5x3-in. loaf pan.

Drain, remove any bits of shell and chop finely
½ pt. oysters
Combine with oysters and mix lightly
1 lb. ground veal
1¼ cups crushed corn flakes
½ cup (about 1 medium) minced onion
¾ cup undiluted evaporated milk
1 egg, beaten
and a blend of
¾ teaspoon salt
½ teaspoon monosodium glutamate
¼ teaspoon paprika
¼ teaspoon marjoram
⅛ teaspoon thyme
Pack lightly into loaf pan.

Bake at 350°F about 1½ hrs.

Unmold the loaf and serve with **Swiss cheese slices**. Garnish with **parsley sprigs**.

JELLIED VEAL LOAF

A cooling, refreshing answer to the hot-weather meat course problem.

Set out a 9x5x3-in. loaf pan or a 1½-qt. ring mold.

Prepare and chill
1 Hard Cooked Egg (page 133)

Prepare in small saucepan
1¾ cups quick meat broth (page 10)
Add to broth
½ cup (about 1 medium) chopped onion
½ teaspoon celery seed
3 or 4 peppercorns
Simmer over low heat about 8 min.

Meanwhile, empty into a small bowl
1 pkg. (3 oz.) lemon-flavored gelatin
Strain broth and pour over gelatin; stir until gelatin is completely dissolved. Stir in
1 tablespoon prepared horseradish
1 teaspoon salt
½ teaspoon monosodium glutamate
Cool; chill gelatin mixture in refrigerator. Or chill in a pan of ice and water until gelatin is slightly thicker than consistency of thick un-beaten egg white. (If mixture is placed over ice and water, stir frequently; if placed in refrigerator, stir occasionally.)

Meanwhile, grind (page 10) and set aside enough cooked veal to yield
2 cups ground cooked veal

Cut the Hard-Cooked Egg into three slices and arrange in bottom of prepared pan. Spoon a small amount of the slightly thickened gelatin mixture (enough to make a thin layer covering egg slices) in bottom of pan. Chill in refrigerator until slightly set.

Blend into remaining gelatin mixture, the ground veal and
¼ cup finely chopped parsley
When first layer in mold is slightly set, immediately turn veal mixture onto first layer. (Both layers should be of almost same consistency to avoid separation of layers when unmolded.) Chill in refrigerator until firm.

Unmold as for gelatin. Garnish with **parsley** and notched **carrot slices**.   *8 servings*

GROUND VARIETY MEATS

BACON-WRAPPED LIVER PATTIES

Heat in a large skillet
2 tablespoons fat
Add to skillet
1 lb. sliced beef liver
Cook slowly about 5 min., turning once. Remove from skillet and cool slightly. Force liver through the medium blade of a food chopper into a bowl. Mix in
3 tablespoons finely chopped onion
1 egg, beaten
and a mixture of
1 tablespoon all-purpose flour
¾ teaspoon salt
⅛ teaspoon pepper
Divide mixture into four portions and shape into patties.

Have ready
4 slices bacon
Put one patty onto each bacon slice; bring ends of bacon over top and fasten each with a wooden pick. Put into a large skillet. Cook over low heat until browned. Remove picks; turn and brown second side.

Serve hot garnished with **parsley sprigs**.
4 servings

Jellied Veal Loaf

LIVER BALLS IN ONION GRAVY

Set out a large skillet and a small skillet with tight-fitting covers.

Cut away tubes and outer membrane, if necessary, from
½ lb. sliced liver (beef, lamb, pork or veal)
Heat in the small skillet
1 tablespoon fat
Add liver and cook slowly 5 min., turning once. Set liver aside.

Meanwhile, prepare in the large skillet, reserving fat
4 slices Panfried Bacon (page 190)
While bacon is cooking, mix in a large bowl
1 egg, beaten
¼ cup milk
¼ cup chopped onion
3 tablespoons well-drained chopped sweet pickle
⅓ cup fine dry bread crumbs
and a blend of
½ teaspoon salt
¼ teaspoon monosodium glutamate
⅛ teaspoon pepper
Crumble bacon and mix with crumb mixture.

Grind (page 10) the liver. Combine with bacon mixture and mix lightly. Shape into balls about 1½ in. in diameter.

Return reserved bacon fat to skillet and heat. Brown liver balls in skillet over medium heat, turning occasionally to brown on all sides.

Meanwhile, prepare and set aside
2 cups quick meat broth (double recipe, page 10)
Remove browned liver balls from skillet with slotted spoon and set aside to keep warm.

Melt in skillet
½ cup butter or margarine
Add and cook about 5 min.
¼ cup chopped onion
3 tablespoons chopped carrot
1 bay leaf
Blend into mixture in skillet
4½ tablespoons all-purpose flour
Heat until mixture bubbles, stirring constantly with a spoon. Remove from heat.

Gradually add the meat broth while stirring constantly. Return to heat and bring rapidly to boiling, stirring constantly; cook 1 to 2 min. longer. Add meat balls and simmer about 30 min. Remove bay leaf.

Meanwhile, heat in the small skillet
   2 tablespoons butter or margarine
Add and cook until tender
   1 small onion (about ⅓ lb.) peeled, washed and sliced thinly

Garnish meat balls and gravy with onion slices.
About 4 servings

LIVER LOAF

Grease an 8x4x3-in. loaf pan. Set out a large skillet with a tight-fitting cover.

Cut away tubes and outer membrane, if necessary, from
   1 lb. sliced beef liver
Heat in the skillet
   2 tablespoons fat
Add liver and cook slowly 5 min., turning once. Set liver aside.

Combine and cook over medium heat until lightly browned
   ½ lb. bulk pork sausage
   ¼ cup chopped onion
   ¼ cup chopped green pepper
Pour off drippings, cool, and combine with
   2 eggs, beaten
   ½ cup tomato juice
   1½ cups soft bread crumbs
   ¼ cup ketchup
   2 teaspoons Worcestershire sauce
and a blend of
   1 teaspoon salt
   ½ teaspoon chili powder
   ⅛ teaspoon black pepper
Grind (page 10) the liver. Mix lightly with the sausage mixture. Pack into loaf pan.

Bake at 350°F about 1 hr.

Unmold.   *6 to 8 servings*

HEART PATTIES WITH GRAVY

Set out a large heavy skillet with a cover.

Mix in a small bowl and set aside
   1 egg, well beaten
   ⅓ cup milk
   1 cup soft bread crumbs

Grind (page 10) enough cooked heart to yield
   2 cups ground cooked heart
Put through medium blade of food chopper
   1 medium onion, peeled, rinsed and quartered
   2 slices bacon
   1 large stalk celery, cut in pieces
Mix lightly and blend in bread mixture, heart and a blend of
   1½ teaspoons salt
   ½ teaspoon monosodium glutamate
   ⅛ teaspoon pepper

Shape into 8 thin patties. Coat by dipping patties in
   ⅓ cup all-purpose flour
Heat in skillet
   2 to 3 tablespoons fat
Put patties into skillet and brown over medium heat, turning occasionally to brown both sides. Cover and cook over low heat about 20 min., turning occasionally.

For Gravy—Prepare and set aside
   1½ cups quick meat broth (one and one-half times recipe, page 10)

When heart patties are cooked, remove to warm place and keep warm.

Pour fat from skillet and return 2 tablespoons of the fat to the skillet. Blend in
   3 tablespoons all-purpose flour
   ¼ teaspoon salt
   ¼ teaspoon monosodium glutamate
   Few grains pepper
Cook until mixture bubbles. Remove from heat and gradually add the meat broth, stirring constantly. Return to heat and bring rapidly to boiling, stirring constantly. Cook gravy 1 to 2 min. longer.

Serve gravy with heart patties.
About 4 servings

GROUND READY-TO-EAT MEATS

SWEET-SOUR MEAT BALLS

Easily made meat balls in a sauce with just-right flavor.

Set out a heavy skillet.

Grind
   1 can (12 oz.) luncheon meat
Mix thoroughly with
   ⅔ cup uncooked rolled oats
   2 tablespoons all-purpose flour
   ¼ cup milk
   1 egg, well beaten
   1½ tablespoons prepared mustard
   1 teaspoon Worcestershire sauce
Shape into 6 balls.

Heat in the skillet
   1 tablespoon butter or margarine
Add balls and brown over medium heat, turning occasionally.

Meanwhile, prepare Sweet-Sour Sauce. Pour over balls in skillet. Stir constantly, basting

balls. Cook until sauce thickens. Serve ham balls with sauce.

For Sweet-Sour Sauce—Blend
   ⅓ cup firmly packed brown sugar
   1 tablespoon all-purpose flour
Stir in
   ½ cup water
   ¼ cup vinegar
   1 tablespoon light corn syrup
   6 whole cloves
Remove cloves before serving.   *6 servings*

BAKED LUNCHEON MEAT FAVORITES

Set out an 8x8x2-in. baking dish.

Grind (page 10)
   1 can (12 oz.) luncheon meat (1½ to 2 cups, ground)
Combine with meat and mix lightly
   ½ cup soft bread crumbs
   ¼ cup (about 1 oz.) finely chopped nuts
   1 egg, beaten
and a blend of
   2 teaspoons brown sugar
   1 teaspoon dry mustard
   ¼ teaspoon paprika
Set aside.

Drain, reserving ⅓ cup syrup
   1 can (8¼ oz.) sliced pineapple (4 slices pineapple)
Lay slices flat in bottom of baking dish.

Shape meat mixture into 4 patties the same size as pineapple slice. Put a patty on each pineapple slice.

Mix reserved pineapple syrup with
   2 tablespoons lemon juice
   2 tablespoons brown sugar
Spoon syrup mixture over patties.

Bake at 350°F 35 to 45 min. Baste patties with syrup mixture three or four times during cooking period.   *4 servings*

GOLDEN CORN FRITTERS

About 20 min. before deep-frying, fill a deep saucepan one-half to two-thirds full with
   Vegetable shortening, all-purpose shortening, lard or cooking oil for deep-frying
Heat slowly to 365°F (page 11).

Grind (page 10)
   1 can (12 oz.) luncheon meat
Set aside.

Melt and set aside to cool

1 tablespoon fat

Sift together into a bowl and set aside

1¼ cups sifted all-purpose flour
1 teaspoon baking powder
1 teaspoon salt
⅛ teaspoon paprika
⅛ teaspoon pepper

Beat together

2 eggs, well beaten
½ cup milk

Make a well in center of dry ingredients. Pour in egg mixture and melted fat all at one time. Stir until smooth. Gently blend in meat and

1½ cups (12-oz. can, drained) whole kernel corn

Drop batter by spoonfuls into the hot fat. (Batter will more readily leave a spoon which has been dipped in the hot fat). Deep-fry only as many fritters at one time as will lie flat and uncrowded, one layer deep in the fat. Turn as they rise and frequently during frying. Fry 2 to 3 min., or until golden brown. Drain over fat before removing to absorbent paper.

Serve hot with **cranberry sauce** or **gravy**.

6 servings

CORN BREAD-CROWNED MEAT AND BEAN PIE

A peek under the golden, tender crust reveals a steaming, appetite-satisfying meat dish.

Grease a 2-qt. casserole. Set out a large skillet.

Grind (page 10)

1 can (12 oz.) luncheon meat (about 1½ cups, ground)

Heat in the skillet

1 tablespoon fat

Add ground luncheon meat and cook over medium heat, gently moving and turning occasionally, until lightly browned. Add

4 cups (two 16-oz. cans) baked beans in tomato sauce
½ cup (about 1 medium) chopped onion
½ cup tomato juice
¼ cup molasses
¼ cup ketchup
1 teaspoon dry mustard

Mix thoroughly. Simmer 8 to 10 min.

No-Bake Pickle Ham Loaf

For Topping—Sift together into a bowl

½ cup sifted all-purpose flour
2 teaspoons sugar
1½ teaspoons baking powder
¼ teaspoon salt

Mix in

½ cup yellow corn meal

Blend thoroughly

1 egg, well beaten
½ cup milk
1 tablespoon shortening, melted

Make a well in center of dry ingredients and add liquid mixture all at one time. Stir vigorously only until dry ingredients are moistened, being careful not to overmix. Bring bean mixture to boiling. Turn into casserole. Immediately drop corn bread batter by spoonfuls evenly over top. (Corn bread will spread together during baking to form a topping.)

Bake at 400°F 20 to 25 min., or until a wooden pick or cake tester comes out clean when inserted gently in center of corn bread.

6 to 8 servings

GROUND "FRANK" LOAF

An electric blender will be needed. Grease a 9x5x3-in. loaf pan.

Cut into pieces and set aside

1½ lbs. frankfurters

Have ready

1 large onion, quartered
1 large green pepper, cut in pieces

Toast well and break into pieces

3 bread slices

Put toast pieces into electric blender container, cover and prepare crumbs. Empty into a bowl.

Set out

1 cup milk

Put into blender container ½ cup of the milk, a quarter of the frank pieces and

2 eggs

Cover and blend; remove cover and continue to add franks, onion, green pepper and remaining milk while blending until entire mixture is smooth. Empty one half of the mixture into the bowl with the crumbs to allow remaining ingredients to be blended until smooth. Empty into bowl with crumbs and mix thoroughly. Turn into prepared loaf pan.

Bake at 350°F 45 min. Put onto a cooling rack and let stand about 5 min. Unmold loaf onto a platter and spread top with

¼ cup chili sauce

Garnish top of loaf and platter with **parsley sprigs**.

About 8 servings

NO-BAKE PICKLE HAM LOAF

An electric blender will be needed.

Line a 9x5x3-in. loaf pan with waxed paper, cutting paper long enough to cover bottom and ends of pan and to extend far enough to cover

Golden Corn Fritters

mixture in pan while chilling. Cut a second piece of waxed paper large enough to cover bottom and sides of pan and to overlap mixture.

Set out

8 midget sweet gherkins

Cut 6 gherkins into halves lengthwise; cut 2 crosswise into slices. Set aside.

Have ready

2 cans (12 oz. each) chopped ham or luncheon meat, cut in chunks
3 canned pineapple slices, drained (reserve 1 tablespoon syrup) and halved
½ cup sweet pickle relish

Turn into a bowl and set aside

1 can (about 16 oz.) lima beans, drained
1 cup finely chopped celery

Grind meat in electric blender, following manufacturer's directions. Set aside.

Blend reserved pineapple syrup and

¼ teaspoon dry mustard

Mix with

⅔ cup mayonnaise

Turn into blender container and add pickle relish. Blend. Turn into the bowl with limas and celery; mix well.

On waxed paper in bottom of loaf pan, arrange 2 half-slices of pineapple with the pickle slices. Cover with about 2 cups of the ham, pressing firmly over the pickle-pineapple design. Arrange remaining pineapple and pickle slices at sides of pan. Carefully pack remaining ham into pan. Chill well.

Lift upper covering of waxed paper, and unmold the loaf onto a serving platter. Gently peel off paper.

8 servings

Poultry and stuffings

Poultry has almost universal appeal. In fact, many of us have never fully recovered from an early conviction that no special occasion can be properly observed without chicken for dinner. Years ago, except on the coastal plains, duckling and game birds were considered quite a luxury. These, along with turkey and goose, usually were served only for holiday meals. Today, due to modern methods of poultry production and freezer storage, poultry in some form is available throughout the year. A budgetwise homemaker can count on chicken, and often turkey, as an economical source of high quality protein and other nutrients important for her family's well-being. With all the imaginative and novel ways of cooking poultry today, it can be served frequently without losing its popular appeal.

CHICKEN

FRIED CHICKEN

▲ Base Recipe

Most parts of the South love chicken better fried than any other way—but there the agreement among them ends. The pieces may be floured and fried in shallow fat in a skillet or in deep fat; they may be dipped in a well-seasoned batter and deep-fried; or they may be floured, browned in shallow fat, smothered in cream or milk, and baked slowly in the oven. The way a Southerner likes it best depends on what part of the South he came from; but most Northerners find no fault with any method of cooking "Southern fried chicken."

Set out a large heavy skillet with a tight-fitting cover, or a Dutch oven.

Set out
> **1 broiler-fryer chicken, 2 to 3 lbs. ready-to-cook weight**

Disjoint chicken and cut into serving-size pieces. (If chicken is frozen, thaw, following directions on package.) Rinse and pat dry with absorbent paper.

Coat chicken evenly by shaking 2 or 3 pieces at a time in a plastic bag containing a mixture of
> **½ cup all-purpose flour**
> **1 teaspoon paprika**
> **1 teaspoon salt**
> **½ teaspoon monosodium glutamate**
> **¼ teaspoon pepper**

Heat in the skillet over medium heat
> **Fat or cooking oil to at least ½-in. depth**

Put the chicken pieces, meaty ones first, skin-side down in skillet. Add less meaty pieces as others brown. To brown all sides, turn pieces as necessary with tongs or two spoons.

When chicken is evenly browned, reduce heat and add
> **1 to 2 tablespoons water**

Immediately cover skillet. Cook slowly 25 to 40 min., or until thickest pieces of chicken are tender when pierced with a fork. Uncover the last 10 min., if desired.   *2 to 4 servings*

—MARYLAND FRIED CHICKEN

Coat chicken pieces with seasoned flour (omit paprika) as in ▲ Recipe. Dip them into a mixture of **2 eggs** beaten with **3 tablespoons water**. Roll pieces in 1½ cups fine dry bread crumbs, corn meal, fine cracker crumbs or fine crushed corn flakes. Let stand 5 to 10 min. to "seal" coating. Cook as in ▲ Recipe.

—CREAM-SMOTHERED CHICKEN

Follow ▲ Recipe through browning process. Arrange pieces of chicken one layer deep in roasting pan or casserole. Blend ½ **cup milk** with ⅓ cup remaining flour-coating mixture. Gradually blend into it 1½ **cups hot thin cream or milk**. Add ½ **cup canned sliced mushrooms**. Pour mixture over chicken. Cover and bake in oven at 325°F 1 to 1½ hrs., or until chicken is tender when pierced with a fork. Turn once during baking period.

—BATTER-FRIED CHICKEN

Follow ▲ Recipe, dipping pieces of chicken into the following batter instead of coating in flour mixture:

For Batter—Sift together **1 cup sifted all-purpose flour, 1½ teaspoons paprika, 1 teaspoon salt** and **1 teaspoon monosodium glutamate**. Combine **1 egg**, slightly beaten, ⅔ **cup milk** and **1 tablespoon melted shortening**. Mix with rotary beater and add slowly to dry ingredients. Beat until smooth.

—FRIED YOUNG TURKEY

Follow ▲ Recipe using **1 frying turkey, 4 lbs. ready-to-cook weight**. After browning turkey, add water and cover tightly. Cook 50 to 60 min., on top of the range, or bake in oven 1¼ to 2 hrs., or until tender when pierced with a fork. The variations given for chicken may be used for turkey.

FARMER BROWN'S FRIED CHICKEN I

▲ Base Recipe

Set out a large heavy skillet and a shallow baking pan.

Rinse and pat dry with absorbent paper
> **1 broiler-fryer chicken, 2 to 3 lbs. ready-to-cook weight**

Disjoint and cut into serving-size pieces. (If chicken is frozen, thaw, following directions on package.)

Fried Chicken

To coat chicken evenly, shake 2 or 3 pieces at a time in a plastic bag containing a mixture of

½ cup sifted all-purpose flour
1 teaspoon salt
½ teaspoon monosodium glutamate
½ teaspoon pepper

Heat in the skillet over medium heat
Fat or cooking oil to at least
½-in. depth

Starting with meaty pieces of chicken, place them skin-side down in skillet. Put in less meaty pieces as others brown. To brown all sides, turn pieces as necessary with two spoons or tongs. When chicken is evenly browned, place in the shallow baking pan one layer deep.

Combine
½ cup milk or cream
2 tablespoons melted butter or
margarine

Pour butter mixture over chicken and bake uncovered at 325°F 45 to 60 min., or until thickest pieces of chicken are tender when pierced with fork.

To crisp evenly turn chicken once and if it appears dry, drizzle on a small amount of milk or cream. *4 servings*

—**FARMER BROWN'S FRIED CHICKEN II**

Follow ▲ Recipe for preparing and browning chicken. Cover skillet tightly, reduce heat and cook slowly on top of range 25 to 40 min., or until tender. Uncover last 10 min. of cooking period to crisp skin.

HUNGARIAN-STYLE FRIED CHICKEN
(Kirántott Csirke)

Springtime is fried chicked time in Hungary. Don't wait for Sunday in Spring; treat your family often to this delicious fried chicken.

Set out a Dutch oven or a heavy 12-in. skillet with a tight-fitting cover.

Rinse and pat dry with absorbent paper
1 broiler-fryer chicken, 2 to 3 lbs.
ready-to-cook weight

(If chicken is frozen, thaw, following directions on package.) Disjoint and cut into serving-size pieces. Cut away and discard tough lining from gizzard. Slit heart; remove blood vessels. Refrigerate the liver. (For cooking of giblets and neck, see Chicken Paprika with Spätzle, page 255.)

To coat chicken evenly, shake 2 or 3 pieces at a time in a plastic bag containing a mixture of

¾ cup all-purpose flour
1½ teaspoons salt
½ teaspoon pepper

Dip chicken pieces into a mixture of
1 egg, slightly beaten
1 tablespoon water

Roll chicken pieces in
1 cup (about 3 slices) fine dry bread
crumbs

Let stand 5 to 10 min. to "seal" coating.

Meanwhile, heat in the skillet over medium heat
Fat or cooking oil to at least
½-in. depth

Starting with meaty pieces of chicken, brown skin sides first. Put in less meaty pieces as others brown. To brown all sides, turn pieces as necessary with two spoons or tongs. When chicken is evenly browned, reduce heat and add
1 to 2 tablespoons water

Cover skillet and cook slowly 25 to 40 min., or until thick pieces are tender when pierced with a fork; uncover last 10 min., if desired. Serve on a warm platter. *3 or 4 servings*

PARMESAN FRIED CHICKEN

▲ *Base Recipe*

A Dutch oven or a large heavy skillet with a tight-fitting cover will be needed.
Thaw, following directions on package
2 to 3-lb. (1 pkg.) frozen
ready-to-cook frying chicken

(Or use two 1-lb. pkgs. frozen pieces.) Rinse chicken and pat dry with absorbent paper.

Mix and set aside
⅔ cup grated Parmesan cheese
⅓ cup fine dry bread crumbs

Coat chicken evenly by shaking 2 or 3 pieces at a time in a plastic bag containing a mixture of
⅓ cup all-purpose flour
¾ teaspoon salt
¼ teaspoon poultry seasoning
Few grains pepper

Beat slightly
2 eggs
3 tablespoons milk

Dip the floured chicken pieces into the beaten egg mixture; then roll in the cheese-bread crumb mixture. Let stand 5 to 10 min.

Heat in the skillet over medium heat
Fat (or cooking oil) to at least
½-in. depth

Starting with the meaty pieces of chicken, place them skin-side down in the skillet. Put in less meaty pieces as others brown. To brown all sides, turn pieces as necessary with tongs or two spoons.

When chicken is evenly browned, reduce heat and add
1 to 2 tablespoons water

Immediately cover skillet. Cook slowly 25 to 40 min., or until thickest pieces of chicken are tender when pierced with a fork. Uncover the last 10 min., if desired. *About 4 servings*

A GUIDE FOR ROASTING POULTRY

The poultry listed below is thawed, stuffed at home, and roasted. Time indications are approximate but should be helpful guides. Decrease total cooking time if poultry is not stuffed.

Kind	Ready-to-Cook Weight (Pounds)	Oven Temperature Constant	Approximate Total Roasting Time (Hours)	Internal Temperature of Bird
Chicken	1½ to 2	400°F	1 to 1¼	
	2 to 2½	400°F	1½ to 1¾	
	2½ to 3	375°F	1¾ to 2¼	
	3 to 4	375°F	2¼ to 2¾	
Capon	5 to 6	325°F	2½	
Turkey	6 to 8	325°F	3 to 3½	180°-185°F
	8 to 12	325°F	3½ to 4½	180°-185°F
	12 to 16	325°F	4½ to 5½	180°-185°F
	16 to 20	325°F	5½ to 6½	180°-185°F
	20 to 24	325°F	6½ to 7	180°-185°F
Duckling	4 to 5	325°F	2½ to 3	
Goose	4 to 8	325°F	2¾ to 3½	
	8 to 12	325°F	3½ to 4¼	
	12 to 14	325°F	4¼ to 4¾	
Rock Cornish Game Hens	About 1	400°F	1	

251

—CRACKLING GOOD ALMOND FRIED CHICKEN

Follow ▲ Recipe. Omit the cheese-bread crumb mixture. Finely chop **1½ cups (about 8 oz.) blanched almonds** (page 9). After dipping the chicken pieces in the egg mixture, roll in the chopped almonds.

—FRIED CHICKEN WITH ZIPPY BARBECUE SAUCE

Follow ▲ Recipe. Omit the cheese-bread crumb mixture. Prepare **Zippy Barbecue Sauce** (page 686). Pour the hot sauce over the hot chicken and serve.

FRIED CHICKEN, ITALIAN STYLE
(Pollo Fritto)

Set out a large heavy skillet with a tight-fitting cover and fill to ½-in. depth with
> **Olive oil**

Set out
> **1 broiler-fryer chicken, 2 to 3 lbs. ready-to-cook weight**

(If chicken is frozen, thaw, following directions on package.) Disjoint and cut into serving-size pieces. Rinse and pat dry with absorbent paper.

To coat chicken evenly, shake 2 or 3 pieces at a time in a plastic bag containing a mixture of
> **½ cup all-purpose flour**
> **1½ teaspoons salt**
> **¼ teaspoon pepper**

Combine
> **2 eggs, well beaten**
> **¼ cup milk**
> **1 tablespoon chopped parsley**

Set prepared skillet with oil over medium heat. When oil is almost heated, dip each piece of chicken into egg mixture. Roll pieces in
> **½ cup grated Parmesan cheese**

Starting with meaty pieces of chicken, place them skin-side down in skillet. Put in less meaty pieces as others brown. To brown all

sides, turn pieces as necessary with two spoons or tongs. When chicken is evenly browned, reduce heat and add
> **1 to 2 tablespoons water**

Cover tightly and cook slowly 25 to 40 min., or until thick pieces of meat are tender when pierced with fork; uncover last 10 min., if desired.　　　　　*3 or 4 servings*

CHICKEN CACCIATORE, NAPLES STYLE
(Pollo alla Cacciatora)

▲ *Base Recipe*

A universal Italian favorite, whether served with plain tomato sauce or smothered with fresh mushrooms and green peppers.

Heat in a large heavy skillet until garlic is lightly browned
> **½ cup olive oil**
> **2 cloves garlic, thinly sliced**

Meanwhile, prepare and coat with flour mixture as in recipe for Fried Chicken, Italian Style (on this page)
> **1 broiler-fryer chicken, 2 to 3 lbs. ready-to-cook weight**

Starting with meaty pieces of chicken, place them, skin-side down, in skillet containing oil and garlic. Add less meaty pieces of chicken as others brown. To brown all sides, turn as necessary with tongs or two spoons.

While chicken is browning, combine
> **3½ cups (28-oz. can) tomatoes, sieved**
> **1¼ teaspoons salt**
> **1 teaspoon oregano**
> **½ teaspoon pepper**

Slowly add tomato mixture to browned chicken with
> **1 teaspoon chopped parsley**

Cook slowly 25 to 30 min., or until thickest pieces of chicken are tender when pierced with a fork. If mixture tends to become too thick, add a small amount of water.
　　　　　About 4 servings

—CHICKEN CACCIATORE WITH MUSHROOMS
(Pollo alla Cacciatora con Funghi)

Follow ▲ Recipe. Clean and thinly slice **1 small onion** and **½ lb. mushrooms.** Cook in **3 tablespoons butter or margarine** in a skillet until onion and mushrooms are lightly browned. Add to browned chicken with tomato mixture.

—CHICKEN CACCIATORE WITH MUSHROOMS AND PEPPERS
(Pollo alla Cacciatora con Funghi e Peperoni)

Follow ▲ Recipe. Clean and dice **1 green pepper** and clean and slice (page 9) **½ lb. mushrooms.** Cook in **3 tablespoons butter or margarine** until mushrooms are lightly

Chicken Cacciatore, Naples Style

browned. Add to browned chicken with tomato mixture.

BREAST OF CHICKEN ENCHANTÉE

Set out a 10-in. skillet with a tight-fitting cover.

Set out
> **1 cup pineapple juice**
> **½ cup orange juice**

Cut into ½-in. cubes and set aside enough cooked ham to yield
> **1 cup (about ½ lb.) cubed cooked ham**

Clean and slice (page 9) enough fresh mushrooms to yield
> **1 cup sliced fresh mushrooms**

Set mushrooms aside.

Rinse in cold water (do not soak) and pat dry with absorbent paper
> **4 chicken breasts (about 1½ lbs.)**

(If chicken is frozen, thaw, following directions on package.)

Coat chicken evenly, by shaking 1 piece at a time in a plastic bag containing a mixture of
> **½ cup all-purpose flour**
> **1 teaspoon salt**
> **⅛ teaspoon pepper**

Heat in the skillet over low heat
> **¼ cup butter or margarine**

Place chicken breasts skin-side down in the skillet. To brown chicken breasts on both sides, turn pieces as necessary with tongs or two spoons. When chicken is evenly browned, remove from skillet; set chicken breasts aside to keep warm. Add mushrooms to the skillet and cook slowly, turning occasionally and moving with a spoon. Cook until mushrooms are lightly browned. Add to the mushrooms in the skillet the cubed ham and a mixture of ¾ cup of the pineapple juice, 6 tablespoons of the orange juice, and
> **1 clove garlic, minced**

Add the browned chicken pieces to the skillet, cover, and simmer 25 to 30 min., or until the pieces of chicken are tender when pierced with a fork. Occasionally spoon sauce over the chicken breasts.

Meanwhile, cook, following directions on package

1 pkg. (10 oz.) frozen cut green beans

Gently break block of beans apart with a fork or spoon while cooking. When beans are tender, drain, if necessary.

When chicken is tender, remove from skillet to a warm serving dish. Add the beans to mixture remaining in skillet. Gently mix to coat beans thoroughly. Spoon mixture over the chicken; set aside to keep warm.

Pour into the skillet the remaining ¼ cup pineapple juice and the 2 tablespoons orange juice. Heat thoroughly. Stirring vigorously with a French whip, whisk beater, or fork, blend in

½ cup dairy sour cream

Cook over low heat 3 to 5 min., or until thoroughly heated; do not boil. Pour mixture into serving dish.   *4 servings*

CHICKEN WITH VEGETABLES

Set out a large heavy skillet with a tight-fitting cover.

Set out

¾ lb. lean pork

Rinse and pat dry with absorbent paper

4 chicken breasts (about 1½ lbs.)

(If chicken is frozen, thaw, following directions on package.) Remove skin and using a very sharp knife, remove meat from breast bone. Cut the chicken and the pork into strips about 3x½x⅛ in. and set aside.

Prepare and set aside

3 cups quick chicken broth (page 10)
3 cups thinly sliced Chinese cabbage (celery cabbage)
3 cups thinly sliced celery
1½ cups sliced mushrooms
1½ cups sliced canned bamboo shoots
¾ cup sliced canned water chestnuts

Blend 2 tablespoons of broth and

3 tablespoons cornstarch
1 tablespoon monosodium glutamate
1 tablespoon soy sauce
1½ teaspoons salt

Set aside.

Heat in the skillet until very hot

3 tablespoons cooking oil

Add and stir in

2 cloves garlic, minced

Add the chicken and pork strips, brown and cook quickly. Remove from skillet; set aside.

Mix in the skillet

3 tablespoons soy sauce
1 tablespoon sugar
¾ teaspoon sesame seed
⅛ teaspoon pepper

Add the prepared vegetables and cook over high heat, tossing constantly, for 3 min. Add the chicken broth. Cover and cook 2 min. Remove from heat. Using a slotted spoon, remove vegetables to a bowl and set aside to keep warm.

Blend the cornstarch mixture into the contents of the skillet, stirring constantly. Bring to boiling and boil 3 min., or until mixture thickens. Return meat and vegetables to the skillet and heat just until thoroughly heated.

6 to 8 servings

HERB CHICKEN WITH MUSHROOMS

Rinse and pat dry with absorbent paper
1 broiler-fryer chicken, 2½ lbs. ready-to-cook weight, cut in quarters

Heat in a large skillet or chicken fryer
2 tablespoons butter or margarine
Place chicken pieces, skin side down, in skillet and brown on all sides.

Meanwhile, combine
¾ cup cider vinegar
¼ cup water
Pour over
1 cup (about 3 oz.) sliced mushrooms
Let stand 10 min.; drain.

When chicken is evenly browned, transfer to a shallow baking dish. Sprinkle over chicken a mixture of
1 tablespoon finely chopped parsley
1 tablespoon finely chopped chives
1 teaspoon crushed tarragon
½ teaspoon thyme, crushed
½ teaspoon salt
¼ teaspoon pepper
Spoon drained mushrooms over the top.

Pour over all
1½ cups quick meat broth (page 10; use 2 bouillon cubes)
½ cup sherry

Bake at 325°F. 1 hr., or until tender.
About 4 servings

SPICY CHICKEN WITH FRUIT

Set out a large heavy skillet with a tight-fitting cover, or a Dutch oven.

Cut into serving-size pieces
1 broiler-fryer chicken, 2 to 3 lbs. ready-to-cook weight
Rinse, dry, coat and brown chicken as directed in Fried Chicken (page 250; omit paprika and add 1 teaspoon allspice and 1 teaspoon cin-

namon). When evenly browned, reduce heat and add
1 cup orange juice
Sprinkle with
4 teaspoons brown sugar
Immediately cover skillet. Cook slowly 25 to 40 min., or until thickest pieces of chicken are tender when pierced with a fork. (Or bake covered at 350°F 30 to 40 min.)

Meanwhile, rinse
2 medium oranges
Using a sharp knife, cut away peel. Remove sections by cutting on either side of dividing membrane, working over a bowl to save juice. About 10 min. before chicken is done, add orange sections and juice. Cover; continue to cook until chicken is done.

Arrange chicken on platter. Garnish with ripe **avocado slices** and **grapes**. *About 4 servings*

CHICKEN MARENGO
(Poulet Sauté à la Marengo)

At the time of the battle of Marengo in 1800, so the story goes, Napoleon's chef was unable to obtain butter for dinner. So he sautéed his chicken in olive oil and added whatever else was at hand. Napoleon was delighted and so have been the French ever since. Veal Marengo is a pleasing variation.

Set out a large heavy skillet with a tight-fitting cover.

Set out
1 broiler-fryer chicken, 2 to 3 lbs. ready-to-cook weight
Disjoint chicken and cut into serving-size pieces. Rinse and pat dry with absorbent paper.

To coat chicken evenly, shake 2 or 3 pieces at a time in a plastic bag containing a mixture of
⅓ cup all-purpose flour
1 teaspoon salt
¼ teaspoon pepper

Heat in a large skillet
¼ cup olive oil
Brown chicken in the hot oil. Add
1 clove garlic, crushed
3 tablespoons chopped onion
4 tomatoes, quartered
1 cup white wine
Herb bouquet (page 9)
Cover and simmer over low heat about ½ hr., or until thickest pieces of chicken are tender when pierced with a fork.

Sauté in small skillet
2 tablespoons butter
1 cup (about 4 oz.) sliced mushrooms
Add to chicken with
½ cup sliced olives

Chicken Sauté à la Creole

To Thicken the Liquid—Put into a screw-top jar

> ½ cup cold Consommé (page 41)

Sprinkle over consommé

> 2 tablespoons all-purpose flour

Cover and shake well.

Remove chicken from skillet and discard Herb Bouquet. Gradually add consommé-flour liquid to mixture in skillet, stirring constantly. Boil 3 to 5 min. until mixture thickens.

Return chicken to sauce, cover and simmer 10 min. Arrange chicken on a hot platter. Cover with the sauce.   *4 or 5 servings*

CHICKEN SAUTÉ À LA CREOLE

▲ *Base Recipe*

Set out a large heavy skillet with a tight-fitting cover.

For Chicken—Disjoint and cut into serving-size pieces

> 1 broiler-fryer chicken, 2 to 3 lbs. ready-to-cook weight

(If chicken is frozen, thaw, following directions on package.) Quickly rinse pieces in cold water and pat dry with absorbent paper.

To coat chicken evenly, shake 2 or 3 pieces at a time in a plastic bag containing a mixture of

> ¾ cup all-purpose flour
> 1½ teaspoons salt
> 1 teaspoon monosodium glutamate
> ½ teaspoon pepper

Heat in the skillet over medium heat

> Fat or cooking oil (not olive oil) to at least ½-in. depth

Starting with meaty pieces of chicken, place them skin-side down in the skillet. Put in the less meaty pieces as others brown. To brown

chicken on all sides, turn pieces as necessary with tongs or two spoons. When chicken is evenly browned, remove from skillet; set aside and keep it warm. Pour off fat and reserve.

For Sauce—Return to the skillet and set over heat until hot

> 2 tablespoons reserved chicken drippings

Add to skillet and cook over low heat until onion is tender

> 1 cup (2 medium) chopped onion
> ½ cup (about 1 medium) chopped green pepper

Stir in

> 2 cups sieved cooked tomatoes
> 1 clove garlic, finely minced
> ¼ teaspoon basil

To Complete—Add chicken pieces to sauce, cover and simmer 30 to 40 min., or until thickest pieces of chicken are tender when pierced with fork. Stir sauce occasionally.

When chicken is tender, add to sauce and heat thoroughly

> 1 cup pitted ripe olives, cut in halves

Serve chicken with sauce spooned over pieces.
      4 or 5 servings

—DEVILED CHICKEN

Follow ▲ Recipe for chicken. Return 2 tablespoons chicken drippings to the skillet. Blend in a mixture of **2 tablespoons all-purpose flour, 1½ teaspoons dry mustard** and **dash cayenne pepper.** Heat until mixture bubbles. Remove from heat. Gradually stir in **1 cup quick chicken broth** (page 10) and **2 teaspoons Worcestershire sauce.** Cook rapidly, stirring constantly, until sauce thickens. Blend in **1 cup white wine.** Add chicken, cover and simmer 30 to 40 min., or until chicken is tender. Serve sauce spooned over chicken.

CHICKEN WITH RICE
(Arroz con Pollo)

Set out a large heavy skillet with a tight-fitting cover, or a Dutch oven.

Set out

> 1 broiler-fryer chicken, 2 to 3 lbs. ready-to-cook weight

Disjoint chicken and cut into serving-size pieces. (If chicken is frozen, thaw, following directions on package.) Rinse and pat dry with absorbent paper.

Heat in the skillet over medium heat

> ¼ cup fat

Add and cook until onion is tender, occasionally moving with a spoon

> ½ cup (about 1 medium) chopped onion
> 1 clove garlic, minced

Remove onion with slotted spoon; set aside.

Put chicken pieces, meaty ones first, skin-side down in skillet. Add less meaty pieces as others brown. To brown all sides, turn pieces as necessary with tongs or two spoons.

Meanwhile, rinse, cut out stem end, and chop

> 1 large tomato

When chicken pieces are well browned on all sides, add tomato and onion to skillet with

> 3 cups hot water
> 1 cup uncooked rice
> 1 tablespoon minced parsley
> 2 teaspoons salt
> ½ teaspoon paprika
> ¼ teaspoon pepper
> ¼ teaspoon saffron
> 1 bay leaf

(The Rice Industry no longer considers it necessary to wash rice before cooking.)

Cover and cook over low heat 45 to 60 min. or until thickest pieces of chicken are tender when pierced with a fork.   *6 to 8 servings*

BASQUE CHICKEN WITH OLIVES

Set out a Dutch oven and a skillet.

Rinse and pat dry with absorbent paper

> 1 broiler-fryer chicken, 3½ lbs. ready-to-cook weight

Sprinkle body and neck cavities with

> Salt

Set aside.

Clean, slice (page 9) and set aside

> ¼ lb. fresh mushrooms

Chop and set aside

> 1 medium onion

Set out

> ½ cup small pimiento-stuffed olives

Heat in the Dutch oven

> 2 tablespoons olive oil
> 1 tablespoon butter

Add the chicken to hot fat. Fry until golden on all sides, turning with two wooden spoons. Remove chicken from Dutch oven and set aside.

Add the mushrooms and onion to hot fat and stir occasionally until lightly browned. Stir in

> 2 cans (8 oz.) tomato sauce
> ½ cup dry white wine or chicken broth
> 10 small whole onions, peeled
> 2 sprigs parsley

Return chicken to Dutch oven. Sprinkle with

> ½ teaspoon salt
> ⅛ teaspoon pepper

Simmer, covered, 1 hr., or until chicken is tender, basting occasionally; add olives 15 min. before end of cooking time.

Transfer chicken to a large platter and tuck in neck skin; keep warm.

Simmer sauce uncovered 5 min.

Meanwhile, prepare

- **2 medium tomatoes, peeled and cut in wedges**
- **1 medium green pepper, cut in strips**

Heat in the skillet

- **1 tablespoon olive oil**

Add green pepper and cook, stirring occasionally, about 2 min. Gently mix in tomato wedges and heat thoroughly. Arrange green pepper strips and tomato wedges around chicken. Using a slotted spoon, lift olives, onions and mushrooms from sauce and arrange on platter.

Serve with hot **cooked rice** and remaining sauce. *4 to 6 servings*

CHICKEN PAPRIKA

Set out a deep heavy 10-in. skillet with a tight-fitting cover, or use a Dutch oven.

Rinse and pat dry with absorbent paper

- **1 broiler-fryer chicken, 2 to 3 lbs. ready-to-cook weight**

Disjoint and cut into serving-size pieces. (If chicken is frozen, thaw, following directions on package.) Cut away and discard tough lining from gizzard. Slit heart; remove blood vessels. Refrigerate chicken and liver. Put cleaned gizzard, heart and neck in a saucepan and add

- **1 qt. hot water**
- **1 small onion**
- **3 sprigs parsley**
- **2 teaspoons salt**
- **2 or 3 peppercorns**

Bring water to boiling. Skim off any foam. Cover saucepan tightly and simmer 1 hr., or until giblets and neck meat are tender when pierced with a fork.

Meanwhile, coat chicken evenly by shaking 2 or 3 pieces at a time in a plastic bag containing a mixture of

- **½ cup all-purpose flour**
- **1½ teaspoons salt**
- **1½ teaspoons paprika**

Heat in the skillet over low heat

- **½ cup butter or margarine**

Starting with meaty pieces of chicken, place chicken pieces, skin side down, in the skillet.

Put in less meaty pieces as others brown. To brown chicken on both sides, turn pieces as necessary with tongs or two spoons. When chicken is evenly browned, reduce heat. Add cooked gizzard, heart and neck to the skillet with 1 to 2 tablespoons of the giblet broth. (Strain remainder of broth; reserve 1 cup and cool to lukewarm.) Cover skillet tightly and cook slowly 25 to 40 min., or until thick pieces are tender when pierced with a fork. Add liver to skillet 10 to 15 min. before end of cooking.

Meanwhile, heat in a saucepan over low heat

- **2 tablespoons butter or margarine**

Blend in

- **2 tablespoons all-purpose flour**

Heat until mixture bubbles, stirring constantly. Remove from heat and add gradually, stirring constantly, the reserved chicken broth and

- **1 cup (8-oz. can) tomato sauce**

(If giblets are not being used, substitute 1 cup quick chicken broth, page 10, for giblet broth.) Return saucepan to heat and bring mixture rapidly to boiling, stirring constantly; cook 1 to 2 min. longer. Mix in

- **1½ teaspoons paprika**

When thoroughly heated, remove saucepan from heat. Stirring vigorously with a French whip, whisk beater or fork, add to the sauce, 1 tablespoonful at a time

- **1 cup dairy sour cream**

Pour the sauce into the skillet over the chicken. Heat 3 to 5 min.; do not boil. Serve immediately. *About 4 servings*

CHICKEN PAPRIKA WITH SPÄTZLE
(Csirke Paprikás Galuskával)

Set out a deep heavy 10-in. skillet or a Dutch oven with a tight-fitting cover.

Rinse and pat dry with absorbent paper

- **1 broiler-fryer chicken, 2 to 3 lbs. ready-to-cook weight**

Disjoint and cut into serving-size pieces. (If chicken is frozen, thaw, following directions on package.)

Cook gizzard, heart and neck as in Chicken Paprika (on this page), adding to the hot water

- **1 bay leaf**

Shortly before end of cooking period, dice and put into the skillet

- **8 slices bacon**

Cook slowly, stirring and turning frequently, until bacon is slightly crisp and browned. Add

- **¼ cup finely chopped onion**

Stirring occasionally, cook until onion is almost tender.

Meanwhile, coat chicken evenly by shaking 2 or 3 pieces at a time in a plastic bag containing a mixture of

- **¾ cup all-purpose flour**
- **1½ teaspoons salt**
- **1½ teaspoons paprika**

With slotted spoon, remove bacon and onion from skillet, leaving bacon fat in skillet. Set aside.

Slightly increase heat under the skillet. Starting with meaty pieces of chicken, brown skin sides first. Put in less meaty pieces as others brown. To brown on all sides, turn chicken pieces as necessary with two spoons or tongs. When chicken is lightly and evenly browned, reduce heat.

Add cooked gizzard, heart and neck to the skillet with 1 to 2 tablespoons of the giblet broth. (Strain remainder of broth; reserve 1 cup and cool to lukewarm.) Cover skillet tightly. Add liver to skillet 10 to 15 min. before end of cooking time. Cook chicken *slowly* 25 to 40 min., or until thick pieces are tender when pierced with a fork.

Meanwhile, heat in a saucepan over low heat

- **2 tablespoons fat**

Blend into the fat

- **2 tablespoons all-purpose flour**

Heat until mixture bubbles, stirring constantly. Remove from heat and add gradually, stirring constantly

- **1 cup reserved giblet broth**

(If giblets are not being used, substitute 1 cup quick chicken broth, page 10, for giblet broth.) Return saucepan to heat and bring mixture rapidly to boiling, stirring constantly; cook 1 to 2 min. longer. Gradually add to sauce, stirring constantly

- **⅔ cup milk**
- **1 to 1½ tablespoons paprika**

When thoroughly heated, remove saucepan from heat. Stirring vigorously with a French whip, whisk beater, or fork, add to the sauce in very small amounts

- **1½ cups dairy sour cream**

Chicken Paprika with Spätzle

Flavor-full Broiled Chicken

Mix in the bacon and onion. Pour the sauce into the skillet over each piece of chicken. Cook the mixture over low heat, stirring sauce and turning chicken frequently, 3 to 5 min., until thoroughly heated; do not boil. Cover skillet tightly; turn off heat under chicken and let stand about 1 hr. Baste twice with sauce.

After setting chicken and sauce aside, prepare
Drop Noodles (Spätzle, page 152)
Toss hot noodles lightly with
¼ cup butter or margarine, melted

Just before serving, reheat chicken and sauce. Place chicken on a platter, leaving room at one end of platter for noodles. Cover chicken with sauce; sprinkle with **paprika.** Arrange noodles on platter. Garnish with **parsley.**

4 to 6 servings

TOMATO-SAUCED CHICKEN

Set out a Dutch oven.

Have ready
6 lbs. broiler-fryer chicken pieces
Coat chicken pieces with a mixture of **flour, salt** and **seasoned pepper.**

Heat in the Dutch oven
3 to 4 tablespoons cooking oil
Add some of the chicken pieces and brown slowly on all sides. Remove chicken as it browns and keep warm while browning remaining chicken. Add more oil as needed.

When all chicken is browned, add to the oil remaining in Dutch oven
1 onion, chopped
1 green pepper, chopped
1 clove garlic, crushed or minced
Cook about 5 min., stirring occasionally.

Stir in a blend of
4 cans (8 oz. each) or 2 cans (15 oz. each) tomato sauce with tomato bits
2 teaspoons curry powder
½ cup water
Return chicken to Dutch oven and spoon sauce over it. Bring to boiling, reduce heat and continue cooking slowly until chicken is tender, basting occasionally with the sauce. Arrange chicken on large serving platter and spoon sauce overall. Garnish with **snipped**

parsley. Accompany with a bowl of **hot fluffy rice** tossed with **plump seedless raisins** and sprinkled with **toasted slivered almonds.**

About 8 servings

CHICKEN MEXICANA

Rinse and pat dry with absorbent paper
2 broiler-fryer chickens, 2½ to 3 lbs. each ready-to-cook weight, cut in pieces
Add chicken to hot **cooking oil** in a large heavy skillet and brown well.

Meanwhile, set out
1 can (13¼ oz.) chicken broth
Combine in a saucepan ¾ cup of the broth and
2 cans (8 oz. each) tomato sauce
2 tablespoons (½ env.) dry onion soup mix
¾ cup chopped onion
1 clove garlic, minced
Heat thoroughly, stirring constantly. Pour sauce over chicken in skillet. Simmer, covered, 20 min.

Mix until smooth the remaining broth and
6 tablespoons chunk-style peanut butter
½ cup cream
Stir into the skillet with
½ teaspoon chili powder
¼ cup dry sherry
Heat thoroughly. Serve chicken with **cooked rice.**

About 6 servings

CHICKEN KIEV

▲ *Base Recipe*

Put into a bowl and allow to soften at room temperature
½ lb. unsalted butter
Blend into the softened butter a mixture of
⅛ teaspoon salt
⅛ teaspoon pepper
Chill in refrigerator until butter is firm but not hard.

Rinse and pat dry with absorbent paper
2 broiler-fryers, about 3 lbs. each, ready-to-cook weight
Using a very sharp knife, cut along ridge of breast bone completely through meat, working from the tip, to divide breast meat into halves. Breast half must be removed in one piece with wing attached. Cut away from breast bone toward wing and side of chicken, cutting close to ribs to remove all of the meat and cutting through tendon which holds wing in place. Using a meat cleaver or heavy knife, cut off the upper portion of the wing between the two wing joints, but leaving about 2 in. of the wing

bone attached to the breast. Set aside. Remove second half of breast and repeat procedure for second chicken.

(Remaining chicken and giblets should be refrigerated for use in other food preparation.)

To prepare each breast half, carefully remove all skin from breast and wing bone. Cut the small "fillet" or loose flap of meat from the breast and carefully cut away the white sinew running the length of it. Using a smooth-surfaced meat hammer or a rolling pin, flatten each breast and "fillet," cut side up, to about ¼ in. thick, being careful not to tear meat.

Remove the butter from the refrigerator and divide into four portions. Shape each portion into a roll about ¾ to 1 in. thick. Place roll lengthwise on each breast half. Cover with the small "fillet." Roll each breast so that the butter is completely enclosed and the wing joint is smoothly covered. Wrap in waxed paper or aluminum foil and chill in refrigerator 1 to 2 hrs.

Set out a deep saucepan or automatic fryer for deep-frying (page 11) and heat **fat** to 375°F.

Combine in a bowl
1 egg, slightly beaten
2 tablespoons milk
Set out
1½ cups cracker meal
Remove chicken breasts from refrigerator. To coat evenly, roll each breast in some of the cracker meal. Dip each breast into the egg-milk mixture. To coat evenly, again roll chicken breasts generously in the cracker meal. Chicken breasts must be well sealed to keep butter in breast. Let stand 5 to 10 min. to "seal" coating.

Deep-fry chicken breasts two at one time. Fry 5 to 6 min., or until golden brown, turning once during frying time. Drain over fat for a few seconds; remove to absorbent paper to drain thoroughly.

Place chicken breasts in a baking dish and bake at 350°F 10 to 12 min., or until chicken is tender.

To serve, place on warm serving plates. Make a small incision in the bottom of each breast and slip a paper frill onto the wing bone.

4 servings

—CHICKEN KIEV À LA ALEXIS
Follow ▲ Recipe. Shred ¼ lb. Swiss cheese and blend with the softened butter.

—CHICKEN KIEV ELEGANTE
Follow ▲ Recipe. Blend **4 teaspoons pâté pe foie gras** with the softened butter.

Potluck Meatballs
Spicy Ketchup Dip and Guacam

FLAVOR-FULL BROILED CHICKEN

Young broiler-fryer chickens of any weight may be broiled. The popular size is 2½ pounds and under. Chicken may be split in half lengthwise, quartered, or favorite parts may be broiled. Have meat dealer remove backbone, neck and keel bone. Reserve giblets for use in other food preparation. If chicken is frozen, thaw following directions on package.

Rinse with cold water (do not soak) and pat dry with absorbent paper
> **2 ready-to-cook broiler-fryer chickens, cut in halves**

Prepare **Herb Garlic Butter, Lemon Butter, Rosemary Butter,** or **Tarragon Butter** (below).

Spread chicken halves generously with one of the butters, brush some of the butter between skin and meat. Place, skin side down, in a shallow pan or broiler pan without rack. Place pan in broiler so that surface of chicken is 7 to 9 in. from heat. Broil 25 to 30 min., regulating the distance or the heat so that surface of chicken just begins to brown after 15 min., brushing occasionally with the butter. Turn and broil, continuing to brush, 20 min. or until tender.

4 servings

—FLAVOR-FULL BUTTERS FOR CHICKEN

Herb Garlic Butter—Blend together
> ½ cup butter or margarine, softened
> 1 clove garlic, minced
> ¾ teaspoon thyme, crushed
> ¼ teaspoon curry powder

Lemon Butter—Blend together
> ¼ cup butter or margarine, melted
> ¼ cup cooking or salad oil
> 3 tablespoons lemon juice
> ¼ teaspoon seasoned salt
> ¼ teaspoon Tabasco

Rosemary Butter—Blend together
> ½ cup butter or margarine, softened
> 1½ teaspoons rosemary leaves, crushed
> 2 tablespoons snipped chives

Tarragon Butter—Blend together
> ½ cup butter or margarine, softened
> 1½ teaspoons tarragon leaves, crushed

BROILED CHICKEN

Rinse and pat dry with absorbent paper
> **1 broiler-fryer, 1½ lbs. ready-to-cook weight**

(Have your meat dealer split bird into halves lengthwise and remove backbone, neck and keel bone. If chicken is frozen, thaw, following directions on package.) Arrange chicken pieces skin-side down in broiler pan (not on rack). Bring wing tips onto backs under shoulder joint. Press down.

Prepare
> ½ cup reconstituted nonfat dry milk (use double amount of milk solids)

Brush chicken thoroughly with the milk. Sprinkle with a mixture of
> **1 teaspoon salt**
> **½ teaspoon monosodium glutamate**
> **½ teaspoon pepper**

Place under broiler so that surface of chicken is 7 to 9 in. from heat. Broil 40 to 50 min., turning and brushing pieces with the milk every 15 min. Chicken is done when browned and when drumstick moves easily. *2 servings*

GOURMET BAKED CHICKEN

Rinse and pat dry with absorbent paper
> **1 broiler-fryer, 3 lbs. ready-to-cook weight, cut in serving-size pieces**
Fill a skillet to ¼-in. depth with
> **Butter or margarine**
Heat until a drop of water sputters. Add chicken pieces and brown evenly. Cover and cook over low heat until tender, about 15 min.

Transfer to a shallow baking pan; sprinkle with
> **Salt, pepper and paprika**
Pour over chicken
> **1½ cups heavy cream**

Bake at 300°F for 30 to 45 min., or until cream thickens; baste occasionally. *About 4 servings*

AVOCADO CHICKEN CASSEROLE

A 1-qt. shallow baking dish will be needed. Set out a large skillet with a tight-fitting cover.

For Chicken—Rinse in cold water (do not soak) and pat dry with absorbent paper
> **2 chicken breasts, split**
(If chicken is frozen, thaw, following directions on package.)

Coat chicken evenly by shaking one piece at a time in a plastic bag containing a mixture of
> **¼ cup all-purpose flour**
> **¾ teaspoon salt**
> **⅛ teaspoon white pepper**
Heat in the skillet
> **2 tablespoons butter or margarine**
Place chicken breasts skin-side down in skillet. Brown on all sides, turning pieces as necessary with tongs or two spoons. When chicken is evenly browned, remove skillet from heat and add
> **6 tablespoons hot water**
Cover skillet tightly.

Broiled Chicken

Set in a 325°F oven for 1 to 1½ hrs., or until chicken is tender when pierced with a fork. If necessary, add more water during cooking.

When chicken tests done, remove from oven. Cool slightly; carefully remove skin and bones and cut chicken meat into slices.

For Noodles—Prepare and keep warm
> **Noodles (one third recipe, page 152; use 1 cup [about 2 oz.] wide noodles)**

For Avocado—Rinse, peel, cut into halves, and remove and discard pit from
> **1 small ripe avocado**
Cut into slices ¼ to ½ in. thick. Put slices into a bowl and brush with
> **1 tablespoon lemon juice**
Set aside.

For Cheese Sauce—Shred and set aside
> **4 oz. sharp Cheddar cheese (about 1 cup, shredded)**

Heat in a saucepan over low heat
> **¼ cup butter or margarine**
Blend in
> **5 tablespoons all-purpose flour**
> **½ teaspoon salt**
> **⅛ teaspoon white pepper**
Heat until mixture bubbles. Remove from heat. Add gradually, while stirring constantly
> **1½ cups cream**
> **¾ cup milk**
Return to heat and cook rapidly, stirring constantly, until sauce thickens. Cook 1 to 2 min. longer. Remove from heat and cool a few moments. Add the shredded cheese all at one time to the slightly cooled sauce and stir until cheese is melted. Remove 1 cup of the sauce and set aside. Mix noodles with the remaining sauce.

To Complete Casserole—Lightly grease the baking dish. Arrange the chicken slices over bottom. Spoon the noodle mixture over the chicken. Arrange the avocado over the noodles and spoon the reserved sauce over all. Sprinkle lightly with
> **Paprika**
Bake at 350°F about 25 min. *4 servings*

FAVORITE CHICKEN CASSEROLE

▲ Base Recipe

A traditional and Italian favorite.

Grease a 2-qt. casserole with a tight-fitting cover. Set out a large heavy skillet.

Set out
- **1 broiler-fryer chicken, 2 to 3 lbs. ready-to-cook weight**

(If chicken is frozen, thaw, following directions on package.) Disjoint chicken and cut into serving-size pieces. Rinse and pat chicken pieces dry with abosrbent paper.

To coat chicken evenly, shake 2 or 3 pieces at a time in plastic bag containing a mixture of
- **½ cup all-purpose flour**
- **1½ teaspoons salt**
- **1 teaspoon monosodium glutamate**
- **¼ teaspoon pepper**
- **¼ teaspoon red pepper**

Starting with meaty pieces of chicken, place them skin-side down in hot skillet containing
- **Cooking oil and melted butter or margarine to at least ½-in. depth**

Put in less meaty pieces of chicken as others brown. To brown all sides, turn as necessary with tongs or two spoons. When chicken is evenly browned, remove chicken to casserole.

Heat in a skillet
- **2 tablespoons butter or margarine**

Add and cook until onion is tender, stirring occasionally
- **1 medium onion, sliced**
- **½ cup finely chopped green pepper**
- **1 clove garlic, minced**

Force through a sieve into the same skillet
- **3½ cups (28-oz. can) tomatoes**

Stir into skillet mixture
- **2 tablespoons chopped parsley**
- **½ teaspoon oregano**

Bring mixture to boiling; pour over chicken.

Cover and bake at 350°F 30 to 35 min. Uncover and bake 15 to 20 min., or until chicken is tender. Garnish with **sprigs of parsley.**

4 or 5 servings

—CHICKEN CASSEROLE AND NOODLES

Follow ▲ Recipe; use a 3-qt. casserole. Prepare **Noodles** (page 152) and put into casserole. Arrange browned chicken pieces on noodles. Pour seasoned tomatoes over all.

—CHICKEN CASSEROLE WITH MUSHROOMS

Follow ▲ Recipe. Clean and slice (page 9) **½ lb. mushrooms.** Increase butter to 4 tablespoons and stir mushrooms into onion mixture; cook until mushrooms are lightly browned and tender.

CHICKEN VESUVIO
(Pollo alla Vesuviana)

Named after the volcano, the rim of this casserole is topped with deep-fried potatoes and seems to be erupting flavorful fried chicken.

Set out a large heavy skillet and a large shallow baking dish.

Prepare and coat with flour mixture as in Fried Chicken, Italian Style (page 252)
- **1 broiler-fryer chicken, 2 to 3 lbs. ready-to-cook weight**

Heat in skillet
- **½ cup olive oil**

Starting with meaty pieces of chicken, place them skin-side down in skillet. Add less meaty pieces of chicken as others brown. To brown all sides, turn as necessary with tongs or two spoons. When browned, place chicken one layer deep in baking dish. Set aside.

Heat in skillet until garlic is lightly browned
- **2 tablespoons olive oil**
- **1 clove garlic, sliced**

Stir in
- **2 tablespoons Marsala**
- **½ teaspoon chopped parsley**

Pour this mixture over chicken in baking dish.

Bake at 325°F about 45 min., turning once, or until thickest pieces of chicken are tender when pierced with a fork.

Meanwhile, prepare and place in the oven to keep warm
- **French-Fried Potatos (page 345)**

To serve, place French-Fried Potatoes around rim of baking dish to form "volcano."

4 servings

CHICKEN A SEVILLE

Set out a shallow baking dish.

Have ready
- **3 lbs. broiler-fryer chicken pieces, rinsed and patted dry**
- **½ lb. fresh mushrooms, halved lengthwise**

Heat in a large heavy skillet
- **3 tablespoons butter or margarine**

Add the mushrooms and cook until lightly browned. Remove mushrooms from skillet and set aside.

Heat in the skillet
- **3 to 4 tablespoons olive oil**

Coat chicken pieces with a mixture of **flour, salt** and **pepper.** Add to the heated oil and brown on all sides. Remove chicken and keep warm.

Chicken à Seville

Add to oil remaining in the skillet
- **1 cup uncooked long grain white rice**
- **1 large clove garlic, minced or crushed**

Stir in
- **1 cup chicken broth**

Turn contents of skillet into baking dish. Arrange browned chicken and mushrooms over rice. Put into the dish
- **12 very small white onions**
- **1 cup small pimiento-stuffed olives**

Pour over all
- **1 cup chicken broth**
- **1 cup dry white wine**

Sprinkle with
- **¾ teaspoon oregano**

Cover and bake at 375°F about 45 min., or until rice is tender. Remove from oven and top with
- **½ cup toasted blanched almonds, sliced**

About 6 servings

CHICKEN IN THE POT
(Poule-au-Pot)

This famous method of cooking chicken comes from Bearn, one of two small provinces once comprising the kingdom of Navarre. The "good king," Henry IV, was its last monarch before he ascended the throne of France and unified the nation. This dish is sometimes called "Our Henry's Soup." Its origin perhaps may be found in the statement King Henry is said to have made, "I wish that every Sunday my peasants may have 'la poule au pot'."

Set out a kettle with a tight-fitting cover.

Clean, cut off neck at body, leaving skin, and thoroughly wash in cold water, body cavity of
- **1 stewing chicken, 4 to 5 lbs. ready-to-cook weight**

Drain and pat dry with abosrbent paper. Set aside.

Thoroughly clean heart, liver and gizzard. Trim thick skin from gizzard. Grind these giblets with
- **¼ lb. ham (½ cup, ground)**

Mix ham-giblet mixture with
- **5 cups buttered soft bread crumbs (page 9)**
- **1 teaspoon chopped parsley**
- **1 clove garlic, minced**

Blend well with mixture of
2 eggs, well beaten
1 tablespoon brandy
1 teaspoon salt
¼ teaspoon pepper
¼ teaspoon nutmeg
Rub cavity of chicken with
1 teaspoon salt
Stuff the chicken lightly with ham mixture, reserving ¾ cup.

To truss—Insert skewers across cavity opening and lace shut with cord. Tie drumsticks together and then tie securely to tail. Bring wing tips onto back shaping into "akimbo" style. Fasten neck skin to back with skewer.

Put chicken into kettle and add
1¼ qts. hot Consommé (page 41)
Bring to boiling and remove foam. Cover and simmer. Skim as necessary.

Meanwhile, to prepare cabbage rolls, put into a bowl
6 large cabbage leaves
Cover with boiling water and let stand about 1 min., or until wilted. Drain.

Fill each leaf with 2 tablespoons reserved dressing. Roll and secure with wooden picks. (Before serving, remove picks.)

When chicken has simmered 2 hrs., add cabbage rolls and
¾ lb. cooked ham, cut in strips
Continue cooking 1 hr., or until chicken is tender. Chicken is done when meat on thickest part of drumstick is easily pierced with a fork. Serve with freshly boiled **potatoes.**

5 or 6 servings

STEWED CHICKEN WITH NOODLES
(Huhn mit Nudeln)

▲ *Base Recipe*

Set out a kettle with a tight-fitting cover.

Rinse
1 stewing chicken, 4 to 5 lbs.
ready-to-cook weight
(If frozen, thaw, following directions on package.) Disjoint and cut into serving-size pieces. Rinse chicken pieces and giblets. Refrigerate the liver. Put chicken, gizzard, heart and neck into the kettle. (If desired, brown

Chicken Fricassee

chicken pieces in a skillet with hot fat. Pieces may be coated with seasoned flour.) Add
Hot water to barely cover
Add to the water
1 small onion
3 sprigs parsley
2 pieces (3 in. each) celery with leaves
1 bay leaf
2 or 3 peppercorns
2 teaspoons salt
1½ teaspoons monosodium glutamate
Bring water to boiling; remove foam. Cover kettle tightly, reduce heat, and simmer chicken 1 hr., skimming foam from surface as necessary. Continue cooking chicken 1 to 2 hrs. longer, or until thickest pieces are tender when pierced with a fork. During last 15 min. of cooking time, add liver to kettle. About 30 min. before chicken is tender, prepare
Buttered Noodles (page 153; use
broad noodles)
Arrange noodles on a warm serving platter. Remove chicken from broth and arrange on the noodles; keep warm. Strain broth and cool slightly; skim fat from surface.

For Gravy—Heat in a saucepan over low heat
3 tablespoons butter or chicken fat
Blend in
3 tablespoons all-purpose flour
Heat until mixture bubbles. Remove from heat. Add gradually, stirring in
3 cups cooled chicken broth
2 teaspoons lemon juice
(Remaining chicken broth may be used in other food preparation.) Cook rapidly, stirring constantly, until mixture thickens. Cook 1 to 2 min. longer.

Pour over the chicken. Garnish with **parsley.**

About 6 servings

—CHICKEN FRICASSEE
(Hühnerfricassee)

Follow ▲ Recipe. Add **¼ teaspoon thyme** with seasonings. Omit noodles. Clean and slice (page 9) **¼ lb. fresh mushrooms.** Cook mushrooms in **2 tablespoons butter,** moving and turning them with a spoon, until mushrooms are lightly browned. For gravy, use only 2 cups of the cooked chicken broth and **1 cup cream.** Blend the lemon juice into thickened gravy and add cooked mushrooms slices.

—CHICKEN AND DUMPLINGS
(Suppenhuhn mit Mehlnockerln)

Follow ▲ Recipe. Omit noodles. Prepare **Plain Dumplings** (page 105) or **Herb Dumplings**

(page 106) about 30 min. before chicken is tender. Add liver to kettle and mix in **1½ cups (16-oz. can, drained) peas.** Drop dumpling batter by spoonfuls on top of chicken pieces. Dumplings should rest on top of chicken; if dumplings settle down into liquid, they may become soggy. If necessary, pour off excess liquid to prevent this. Cover tightly and continue cooking over medium heat 20 min. without removing cover. Remove dumplings and chicken to a warm serving dish; keep warm. Continue as in ▲ Recipe; reserve peas when broth is strained. Return only 1½ cups peas to gravy, reserving about ½ cup for garnish.

BRUNSWICK STEW

Set out a large heavy saucepot with a tight-fitting cover, or a Dutch oven.

Set out
2 broiler-fryer chickens, 2 to 3 lbs.
each, ready-to-cook weight
(If frozen, thaw, following directions on package.) Rinse chickens and giblets. Pat liver dry with absorbent paper and place in refrigerator until ready to use.

Place chickens, breasts down, in the saucepot. Add gizzards, hearts and necks. Add
Hot water (enough to barely cover
chickens)
Add to water
1 tablespoon salt
Bring to boiling. Skim any foam from surface. Reduce heat, cover saucepot and simmer about 45 min., or until chicken meat is quite tender and will come readily from bones. About 15 min. before end of cooking time, add liver to the saucepot.

While chickens are cooking, clean and chop
2 medium onions (about 1 cup,
chopped)
Cut into pieces and set aside
¼ lb. ham, bacon or salt pork
Set out
1 can (16 oz.) tomatoes
1 can (8½ oz.) whole kernel corn
1 pkg. (10 oz.) frozen lima beans
1 pkg. (10 oz.) frozen okra

When the chickens are tender, remove chickens and giblets from broth. Cool chickens slightly and remove meat from bones. Return chicken meat to broth. Add the onion, ham, tomatoes, corn, lima beans and okra, and
1¼ teaspoons Tabasco
½ teaspoon salt
¼ teaspoon thyme
⅛ teaspoon pepper
Set over low heat and simmer about 1 hr., stirring occasionally.

Meanwhile, finely chop and set aside
1 small green pepper

Heat in a small saucepan
3 tablespoons butter or margarine

Blend in

¼ cup all-purpose flour

Heat, stirring constantly, until mixture bubbles and is lightly browned.

Stir the flour mixture gradually into the stew and cook over medium heat, stirring constantly, until broth is slightly thickened. Reduce heat and simmer about 10 min. longer. Add green pepper and serve at once.

About 16 servings

CHICKEN WITH CORN MEAL DUMPLINGS

Set out a Dutch oven or saucepot with a tight-fitting cover.

Disjoint and cut into serving-size pieces

1 stewing chicken, 4 to 5 lbs. ready-to-cook weight

(If frozen, thaw, following directions on package.) Rinse and pat pieces and giblets dry with absorbent paper. Refrigerate liver.

To coat chicken and giblets evenly, shake 2 or 3 pieces at a time in a plastic bag containing a mixture of

**¾ cup all-purpose flour
2 teaspoons salt
1½ teaspoons monosodium glutamate
½ teaspoon pepper**

Heat in the Dutch oven over medium heat, enough to make a thin layer

Fat or cooking oil (not olive oil)

Starting with meaty pieces of chicken, place them skin-side down in the skillet. Put in less meaty pieces as others brown. To brown chicken on all sides, turn pieces as necessary with tongs or two spoons.

When chicken is evenly browned, remove Dutch oven from heat and add

**1 qt. hot water
1 small onion, quartered
3 sprigs parsley
2 pieces (3 in. each) celery with leaves
1 bay leaf
2 or 3 peppercorns**

Return Dutch oven to heat. Cover, and bring water to boiling. Remove foam. Cover tightly and simmer 2 to 3 hrs., or until thickest pieces are tender when pierced with a fork.

During last 20 min. of cooking time, add liver to Dutch oven. Also at this time add Corn Meal Dumplings. Dumplings should rest on top of chicken; if dumplings settle down into liquid, they may become soggy. If necessary, pour off excess liquid to prevent this. Cover tightly and continue cooking over medium heat 20 min. without removing cover.

Remove dumplings and chicken to a warm serving dish. Thicken cooking liquid, if desired.

For Corn Meal Dumplings—Sift together

**1 cup sifted all-purpose flour
1 tablespoon baking powder
½ teaspoon salt**

Stir into dry ingredients

1 cup corn meal

Cut in with a pastry blender or two knives until pieces are the size of peas

3 tablespoons shortening

Beat together

**1 egg, well beaten
¾ cup milk**

With a fork, stir egg-milk mixture into flour mixture until just blended. Drop batter by tablespoonfuls into hot chicken mixture.

6 to 8 servings

CHICKEN IN A COOP
(Chicken Pie)

▲ *Base Recipe*

Set out a 4-qt. kettle with a tight-fitting cover.

Rinse, disjoint and cut into pieces

1 stewing chicken, 4 to 5 lbs. ready-to-cook weight

(If chicken is frozen, thaw, following directions on package.) Place in kettle. Add

**1 qt. hot water
1 small onion
2 pieces (3 in. each) celery with leaves
2 teaspoons salt
1 teaspoon monosodium glutamate
3 parsley sprigs
2 or 3 peppercorns
1 bay leaf**

Cover kettle and bring water to boiling. Remove foam. Cover tightly and simmer 2 to 3 hrs., or until thickest pieces of chicken are tender when pierced with a fork. Remove

chicken from broth, cool slightly and remove meat from bones. Cut meat into 1-in. pieces. Set aside.

Strain broth and allow to cool. Remove fat that rises to surface. Heat broth to boiling.

Add and cook, covered, about 20 min., or until tender

**4 medium potatoes, washed, pared and quartered
4 carrots, scraped and sliced
3 stalks celery, cut in 1-in. pieces
2 small onions
¼ teaspoon monosodium glutamate**

Prepare and set aside biscuits.

For Biscuits—Sift together

**1½ cups sifted all-purpose flour
2¼ teaspoons baking powder
¾ teaspoon salt**

Cut into dry ingredients with a pastry blender or two knives until pieces are size of coarse corn meal

6 tablespoons lard, chilled vegetable shortening, or all-purpose shortening

Make a well in center of mixture and add all at one time

6 tablespoons milk

Stir with fork until dough follows fork.

Gently form dough into ball and put onto lightly floured surface. Knead lightly with fingertips 10 to 15 times. Roll lightly ½ in. thick.

Cut out chickens or other desired shapes with a floured cutter. Brush tops lightly with

½ cup milk

Chicken in a Coop

In each chicken cutout insert a clove for the eye. Set aside.

Lightly grease a 2-qt. casserole.

Put into a screw-top jar

½ cup water

Add to water

¼ cup sifted all-purpose flour

Cover and shake until well blended.

Pour flour-water mixture into broth. Stirring constantly, quickly bring to boiling and cook 3 to 5 min. longer. Remove from heat and add chicken. Return to heat and bring quickly to boiling. Immediately turn into casserole and quickly top with prepared biscuits.

Bake at 425°F 15 to 20 min., or until biscuits are lightly browned. *6 to 8 servings*

—CHICKEN WITH DUMPLINGS

Follow ▲ Recipe for preparation of chicken and vegetables. Instead of turning mixture into a casserole, heat in kettle to boiling point and top with Dumplings.

For Dumplings—Sift together **2 cups sifted all-purpose flour, 4 teaspoons baking powder, 1 teaspoon salt.** Cut in **1 tablespoon shortening.** Combine **1 egg** well beaten, and **⅔ cup milk.** With a fork, stir egg-milk mixture quickly into flour mixture until just blended. Drop by tablespoonfuls on top of boiling stew. Cover tightly and cook over moderate heat 20 min. without removing cover. Serve at once with hot stew.

CREAMED CHICKEN

Set out a kettle with a tight-fitting cover.

Have ready

1 stewing chicken, 4- to 4½-lbs. ready-to-cook weight

Disjoint and cut into serving-size pieces. Rinse chicken pieces under running cold water. Put chicken into kettle and add

Hot water to barely cover

2 teaspoons salt

1½ teaspoons monosodium glutamate

Bring to boiling and remove foam. Cover and simmer 1 hr., skimming foam from surface as necessary.

Place in kettle with chicken

2 carrots, cut in halves

1 small onion, cut in halves

1 stalk celery, cut in pieces

4 peppercorns

Continue cooking chicken 1 to 2 hrs., or until tender. Chicken is done when thickest part of drumstick is easily pierced with a fork. Remove chicken from stock to a warm platter. Keep hot.

For Sauce—Blanch (page 9) and sliver

½ cup (about 3 oz.) almonds

Remove pits and sliver

8 to 10 green or ripe olives

Heat in a saucepan

1 tablespoon butter or margarine

Add slivered almonds to saucepan and brown almonds lightly, stirring constantly. Remove almonds from saucepan. Set them aside.

In same saucepan, prepare

3 cups Medium White Sauce (three times recipe, page 304. Substitute 2 cups strained chicken stock and 1 cup cream for milk.)

When sauce is thickened, blend in olives and

2 teaspoons lemon juice

½ teaspoon paprika

Remove from heat and keep hot over simmering water.

Remove bones from cooled chicken and cut meat into size of pieces desired. Stir into sauce. Serve on hot **rusks, waffles, crisp noodles** or in **Toast Cups** (page 110) or **pastry shells.** Garnish with the almonds.

6 to 8 servings

JIFFY CREAMED CHICKEN

Grease a 1½-qt. casserole or a 10-in. pie pan.

Cut with a small chicken-shape cookie cutter, or cut into cubes

3 slices bread

Toss bread cubes in, or brush cutouts with

2 to 3 tablespoons melted butter or margarine

Set aside.

Drain, reserving liquid, and put into a large saucepan

1 can (16 oz.) peas (about 1½ cups, drained)

Blend in and heat thoroughly

Boned chicken (13-oz. can), cut in pieces

1¼ cups (10½-oz. can) condensed cream of mushroom soup

⅓ cup reserved pea liquid

½ teaspoon salt

½ teaspoon monosodium glutamate

⅛ teaspoon pepper

Turn into the casserole or pie pan. Top with buttered bread.

Bake at 400°F 15 min., or until bread is browned. *6 servings*

Note: If mixture seems too thick, gradually add some of the remaining reserved liquid.

CREAMED CHICKEN IN POTATO CUPS

▲ *Base Recipe*

Wash, pare and cook, covered, in boiling, salted water

4 medium (about 1⅓ lbs.) potatoes, cut in halves

Cook 20 to 30 min., or until tender when pierced with a fork. Drain. To dry potatoes, shake pan over low heat.

Creamed Chicken

While potatoes are cooking, heat in a saucepan

¼ cup butter or margarine

Stir in all at once

¼ cup sifted all-purpose flour

1 teaspoon salt

¾ teaspoon monosodium glutamate

Heat until mixture bubbles. Remove from heat and gradually stir in

1 cup quick chicken broth (page 10)

1 cup milk

Return to heat and bring rapidly to boiling, stirring constantly; cook 1 to 2 min. longer. Stir in

2 cups diced cooked chicken

Cover and keep warm.

Pour boiling water over potato masher, food mill or ricer and bowl to heat thoroughly. Mash or rice potatoes into bowl. Add to potatoes

⅓ to ½ cup warm milk

1 tablespoon butter or margarine

½ teaspoon salt

⅛ teaspoon pepper

Whip potato mixture until light and fluffy.

To make "cups," spoon potatoes onto warm plates. Make a well in center of each "cup" and spoon hot creamed chicken into each well. Garnish with

Grated raw carrot or chopped parsley

6 servings

—CHICKEN À LA KING

Follow ▲ Recipe. Omit potatoes. Clean and slice ½ lb. mushrooms (page 9). Cook mushrooms and ¼ cup chopped green pepper in **2 or 3 tablespoons butter or margarine** until mushrooms are lightly browned and tender. Add chicken, mushrooms and pepper to sauce and stir in **2 tablespoons chopped pimiento.** Serve hot on split **biscuits, toast points** or fluffy **rice.**

Creamed Chicken Treat

CREAMED CHICKEN TREAT

▲ *Base Recipe*

This easy-to-prepare chicken dish is perfect for luncheon, supper, brunch or even a hearty Sunday morning breakfast. Cups of steaming, fragrant coffee are the ideal accompaniment.

Chop enough cooked chicken to yield
2 cups chopped cooked chicken

Prepare
Savory Sour Cream Sauce (page 304; use chicken broth)
Blend the chicken with the sauce and set aside too keep hot.

Prepare
Buttermilk French Toast (one half recipe, page 108)
Cut French toast slices diagonally into halves. Spoon the chicken mixture into a serving dish. Top with the hot French toast (see photo).

Serve immediately. *4 to 6 servings*

—CREAMED TURKEY TREAT

Follow ▲ Recipe. Substitute **2 cups chopped cooked turkey** for the chicken.

—CREAMED CHICKEN WITH ALMONDS

Follow ▲ Recipe. Prepare **1 cup (5½ oz.) toasted blanched almonds** (pages 9 and 10). Mix into the sauce with the chicken.

CHICKEN 'N' BROCCOLI DINNER

▲ *Base Recipe*

Grease a shallow 2-qt. casserole.

Cut large leaves and any woody stalks from
2 lbs. broccoli
(If frozen broccoli is used, follow directions on package.) Wash well and cook (page 313). Boil loosely covered 8 to 15 min., or until stalks are barely tender.

Meanwhile, prepare
2 cups Medium White Sauce (double recipe, page 304; if available, substitute 1 cup chicken broth for 1 cup of milk)
Remove sauce from heat and stir in
2 tablespoons lemon juice
2 teaspoons Worcestershire sauce
Set sauce aside.

Arrange in casserole about
2½ cups thickly sliced cooked chicken

Set out
½ cup (2 oz.) grated Parmesan cheese
When broccoli is tender, drain thoroughly; arrange over chicken in casserole. Sprinkle one half of cheese over broccoli. Turn sauce into casserole. Mix remaining cheese with
½ cup crushed cereal flakes
Cover casserole with this mixture.

Bake at 350°F 20 to 25 min., or until topping is lightly browned and mixture is heated.
6 servings

—CHICKEN AND ASPARAGUS DINNER

Follow ▲ Recipe. Substitute **1½ lbs. asparagus** for broccoli. Clean and cook asparagus (page 313). Substitute **coarsely chopped nuts** for cheese in cereal mixture. Toss nuts and crushed cereal with **2 tablespoons melted butter or margarine.**

CHICKEN CURRY WITH RICE

Serve it elegantly from a chafing dish, accompanied by fluffy, steaming-hot rice in a covered bowl, curry condiments, and the hot tea its slightly Oriental character demands. It makes a wonderful late-supper dish for after the theatre.

Heat in a heavy 3-qt. saucepan over low heat
⅔ cup butter or margarine
Add and cook over medium heat until lightly browned, occasionally moving and turning with a spoon
6 tablespoons chopped onion
6 tablespoons chopped celery
6 tablespoons chopped green apple
24 peppercorns
2 bay leaves
Blend in a mixture of
⅔ cup sifted all-purpose flour
5 teaspoons curry powder
1 teaspoon monosodium glutamate
½ teaspoon sugar
¼ teaspoon nutmeg
Heat until mixture bubbles. Remove from heat and add gradually, stirring constantly
5 cups milk

Return to heat and bring rapidly to boiling. Stirring constantly, cook until mixture thickens; cook 1 to 2 min. longer. Remove from heat; add and stir in
4 teaspoons lemon juice
1 teaspoon Worcestershire sauce
Strain mixture through a fine sieve, pressing vegetables against sieve to extract all sauce. Set sauce aside.

Cube enough cooked chicken to yield
6 cups cubed cooked chicken

Reheat the curry sauce and blend in
½ cup cream
¼ cup sherry
½ teaspoon Worcestershire sauce
Add cubed chicken and cook over medium heat 2 to 3 min., or until mixture is thoroughly heated.

Serve with
Perfection Boiled Rice (page 165)
Preserved kumquats
Chutney
Shredded coconut
Finely chopped roasted peanuts
8 servings

CHICKEN CHEESE SAUCER PIES

Chicken and "store cheese" are featured in this adaption of the popular New England main dish pie. ("Store cheese" in New England designates an aged Cheddar.)

Set out 4 small individual pie pans and a large skillet.

Prepare dough for
Pastry for 2-Crust Pie (one and one half times recipe, page 485)
Make one pastry ball slightly larger than the other. Roll out larger ball and cut into four 8½-in. rounds. Fit into pans. Roll out remaining ball for top crusts and cut into four 6½-in. rounds. Cover with waxed paper and set aside.

Prepare and set aside to cool
Quick chicken broth (page 10; use only ½ cup hot water)

For Filling—Dice enough chicken to yield
2 cups diced cooked chicken
Set aside.

Drain and set aside
1 can (4 oz.) sliced mushrooms (about ½ cup, drained)
Heat in the skillet over medium heat
¼ cup butter
Add and cook until almost tender, occasionally moving and turning with a spoon
¼ cup chopped onion
Blend in a mixture of
3 tablespoons all-purpose flour
½ teaspoon monosodium glutamate
¼ teaspoon salt
¼ teaspoon garlic salt
¼ teaspoon pepper
Heat until mixture bubbles. Remove from heat

and add gradually while stirring constantly, the chicken broth and

1 cup cream
½ teaspoon Worcestershire sauce

Return to heat and stir constantly until thickened and thoroughly blended. Add chicken and mushrooms and mix gently. Set aside to cool.

To Complete—Shred

1 oz. sharp Cheddar cheese (about)
¼ cup, shredded)

Put one fourth of the cooled filling into each pastry shell. Sprinkle the shredded cheese over the filling.

Complete pies as directed in Pastry for 2-Crust Pie (page 485).

Bake at 450°F 15 to 20 min., or until pies are delicately browned. *4 chicken pies*

INDIVIDUAL PASTRY-TOPPED CHICKEN PIES

Set out 4 individual casseroles.

For Pastry Topping—Prepare but do not roll out

Pastry I for 1-Crust Pie (page 485)

Cover and set aside in refrigerator.

For Chicken Filling—Drain, slice lengthwise, and set aside

1 can (8 oz.) mushrooms (about 1 cup, drained)

Prepare and set aside

3 cups cooked chicken, cut in pieces
¾ cup sliced celery

Prepare and set aside

1 cup quick chicken broth (page 10)

Heat in a saucepan

6 tablespoons butter or margarine

Add the mushrooms and celery; cook over medium heat, frequently moving and turning with a spoon, until mushrooms are lightly browned. Using a slotted spoon, remove vegetables to a bowl and set aside.

Blend into remaining butter in saucepan

¼ cup all-purpose flour
½ teaspoon onion salt
½ teaspoon monsodium glutamate
¼ teaspoon salt
⅛ teaspoon white pepper

Heat until the mixture bubbles, then remove it from the heat.

Add gradually, while stirring constantly, the broth and

1 cup milk

Cook rapidly, stirring constantly, until sauce thickens. Cook 1 to 2 min. longer.

Blend into the sauce the chicken pieces, vegetables and

2 tablespoons minced parsley
1 teaspoon lemon juice

Spoon the hot mixture into casseroles.

To Complete Pies—Roll pastry as directed in Pastry for 1-Crust Pie. Cut into strips about ½ in. wide. Moisten casserole rims with water. To make lattice top, weave strips crisscross over the pie, leaving about ½ in. between. Trim strips so ends extend ¼ in. beyond edge. Turn ends under; press to rims to seal.

Bake at 425°F 25 to 30 min., or until pastry is lightly browned. *4 servings*

CHICKEN PIE DE LUXE

▲ *Base Recipe*

Set out a shallow 2-qt. casserole.

Slice thickly, enough chicken to yield about

3 cups sliced cooked chicken

Set aside.

Prepare

Pastry Topping (one and one half times recipe, page 486)

Roll dough to shape of casserole and about 2 in. larger than casserole top; fold dough and lay it in casserole. Unfold; gently pat to fit over bottom and up sides of casserole, allowing dough to extend about 1 in. over sides of dish. Fold under; flute (page 10) and prick thoroughly on bottom and sides of dough.

Bake at 425°F 15 to 20 min., or until shell is lightly browned.

Meanwhile, cover with boiling salted water and cook covered over medium heat about 10 min. in deep saucepan

2 medium-size (about ⅓ lb.) onions, quartered
¾ cup (about 3 stalks) coarsely cut celery

Add and cook 10 to 12 min. longer, or until vegetables are tender

1 pkg. (9 oz.) frozen cut green beans

Meanwhile, prepare

2 cups Medium White Sauce (double recipe, page 304; substitute 1 cup quick chicken broth, page 10 for one half of milk)

Chicken Cheese Saucer Pies

Drain vegetables; blend into sauce mixture with sliced chicken. Heat thoroughly. Turn into pastry shell.

Garnish with **pimiento strips.** Serve immediately. *6 servings*

—GOLDEN FLUFF PIE

Follow ▲ Recipe; omit Pastry Topping and pimiento strips. Force **whipped potatoes** (sweet, or white, page 339) through a pastry bag and a No. 7 star tube, or lightly spoon into a border around casserole mixture. Brush with melted **butter or margarine.** Bake 10 to 15 min., or until potatoes are lightly browned. Garnish dish with sliced **Hard-Cooked Eggs** (page 133) and **sprigs of parsley.**

CHICKEN CROQUETTES

▲ *Base Recipe*

Mix lightly and set aside.

2 cups finely chopped or ground cooked chicken
1 tablespoon finely chopped parsley
1 tablespoon lemon juice
½ teaspoon onion juice
½ teaspoon salt
½ teaspoon monosodium glutamate
¼ teaspoon celery salt

Golden Fluff Pie

263

Prepare
1½ cups Thick White Sauce (page 304)
Combine with the chicken mixture. Chill in refrigerator.

About 20 min. before deep-frying, fill a deep saucepan one half to two thirds full with **fat or oil** for deep-frying (page 11). Heat slowly to 375°F.

Shape chilled chicken mixture into balls, cones or cylinders. Roll in
1 cup fine dry bread crumbs
Dip in a mixture of
1 egg, slightly beaten
1 tablespoon milk
Again coat in bread crumbs, shaking off loose crumbs.

Deep-fry the croquettes, turning frequently to brown evenly. Drain on absorbent paper. Serve immediately.   *6 servings*

—FISH CROQUETTES

Follow ▲ Recipe. Substitute cooked flaked (page 9) **fish** for chicken.

ELEGANT CHICKEN LOAF

▲ *Base Recipe*

Grease bottom of a 9x5x3-in. loaf pan.

Put through food chopper (using fine blade) enough to yield
2¼ cups ground (about 1 lb. 5 oz.) cooked chicken
1¼ cups ground (about 7 oz.) mushrooms
1¼ cups ground (about 7 oz.) toasted almonds (page 10)
Set aside.

Prepare
1½ cups Medium White Sauce (one and one half times recipe, page 304)
Vigorously stir about 3 tablespoons of hot sauce into
3 egg yolks, slightly beaten
Immediately return egg yolk mixture to sauce, stirring vigorously.

Stir into sauce the chicken, mushrooms, almonds and
1½ cups soft bread crumbs (about 2½ slices bread)
¼ cup finely chopped pimiento, well drained

Add a mixture of
2 teaspoons salt
½ teaspoon monosodium glutamate
½ teaspoon pepper
½ teaspoon paprika
Beat until rounded peaks are formed
3 egg whites
Spread beaten egg whites over chicken mixture and fold together. Turn mixture into pan.

Set pan in a larger pan and pour very hot water into larger pan to a 1-in. depth.

Bake at 350°F. about 1 hr. 10 min.

To unmold, loosen loaf gently from sides of pan with spatula. Invert onto warm serving plate and remove pan.

Serve at once with mushroom sauce and additional **toasted** almonds.   *About 8 servings*

Note: Chicken, mushrooms, almonds and bread crumbs may be prepared in an electric blender. Follow manufacturer's directions.

—HOT SALMON LOAF

Follow ▲ Recipe. Substitute finely flaked (page 9) **salmon** for ground chicken. Omit mushrooms. Garnish with **parsley** and **lemon**.

CHICKEN LIVERS WITH APPLES AND ONIONS I

▲ *Base Recipe*

Set out a large skillet.

Clean, slice thinly and set aside
1 medium onion

Rinse with cold water and drain on absorbent paper
12 chicken livers
(Properly cleaned chicken livers should have no trace of green gall, the substance which might cause a bitter taste.) Coat livers evenly with a mixture of
3 tablespoons all-purpose flour
½ teaspoon salt
¼ teaspoon monosodium glutamate
⅛ teaspoon cayenne pepper
Set aside.

Wash and remove cores from
2 medium cooking apples
(To core, insert corer in stem end and push halfway through toward blossom end. Remove

corer and insert in opposite end. Make a complete turn with corer in both ends, removing all the core.) Cut apples into ½-in. slices.

Melt in the skillet over low heat
1½ tablespoons butter
Add the apple rings and cook, covered, over medium heat until lightly browned. Turn slices carefully and sprinkle with
¼ cup sugar
Cook uncovered over low heat until lightly browned. Remove from skillet and set aside to keep warm.

Heat in the skillet over low heat.
¼ cup butter
Put chicken livers into skillet. Separate onion slices into rings and add to skillet. Cook over medium heat, occasionally moving and turning mixture with a spoon, until livers are lightly browned. Transfer to a warm serving platter. Serve with the apple rings.   *4 servings*

—CHICKEN LIVERS WITH APPLES AND ONIONS II

Follow ▲ Recipe. Omit coring apples and cutting into rings. Instead, quarter, core, pare and slice them. Omit the 1½ tablespoons butter and the sugar. Add the apple slices to the skillet and cook with the chicken livers and onion rings.

CHICKEN LIVERS AND MUSHROOMS

Rinse with cold water and drain on absorbent paper
2 lbs. chicken livers
(Properly cleaned chicken livers should have no trace of green gall, the substance which might cause a bitter taste.) Place livers in a deep dish and cover with
1 cup cream
Place in refrigerator 12 hrs., or overnight to marinate (page 10). Turn chicken livers several times.

To Prepare Chicken Livers—Set out a large heavy skillet and a small skillet.

Drain cream from the chicken livers. To coat evenly, shake the chicken livers in a plastic bag containing a mixture of
½ cup all-purpose flour
1 teaspoon salt
¼ teaspoon white pepper
¼ teaspoon monosodium glutamate
Heat in the large skillet over low heat
½ cup butter
Place chicken livers in skillet. Occasionally moving and turning them with a spoon, cook about 10 min., or until the chicken livers are lightly browned.

Meanwhile, clean and slice (page 9)
12 medium mushrooms
Heat in the small skillet
3 tablespoons butter
Add the mushrooms and cook slowly, moving

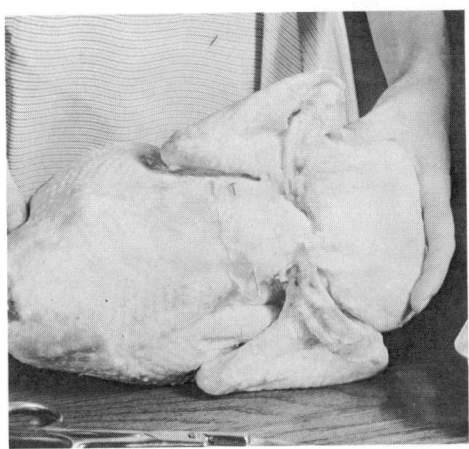

Roast Turkey: Fasten neck skin to the back with a skewer. Bring wing tips onto the back.

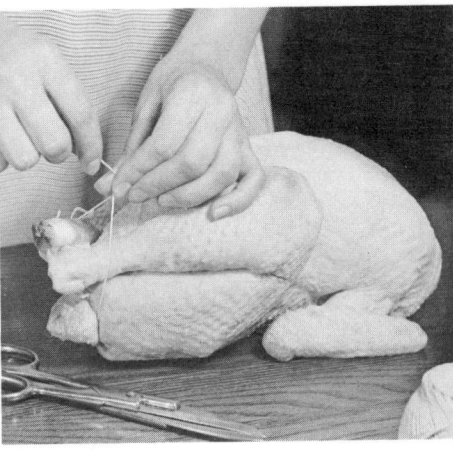

Tie the drumsticks of the turkey to the tail with cord. Brush the skin thoroughly with melted fat.

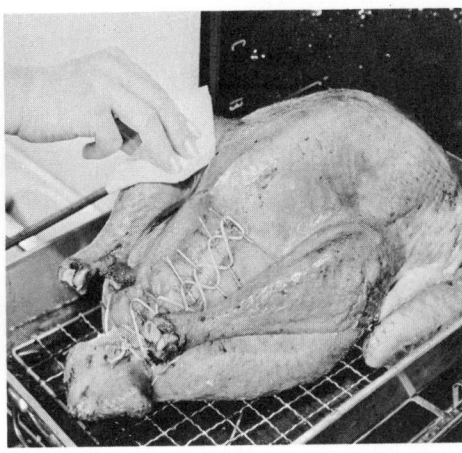

Test turkey for doneness; thickest part of the drumstick feels soft when pressed with fingers.

and turning them gently with a spoon until lightly browned and tender.

When livers are browned, arrange on a warm serving platter. Top with the mushrooms and sprinkle with

Finely chopped parsley

Serve immediately. *6 servings*

ROAST CAPON

Prepare for stuffing (see Roast Turkey, on this page)

5- to 8-lb. capon

Rub body and neck cavities with

Salt

Fill cavities lightly with

Stuffing (your favorite recipe or a packaged stuffing mix)

Fasten neck skin to back with a skewer and bring wing tips onto back. Push drumsticks under band or skin at tail, or tie with cord. Place breastside up on rack in shallow roasting pan. Brush with

Melted fat

Roast at 325°F 2½ to 3½ hrs., or until thickest part of drumstick feels soft when pressed with fingers, basting frequently with melted fat or pan drippings.

When capon is two-thirds done, cut band of skin or cord at drumsticks. Roast until done. After removal from oven, allow capon to stand about 20 min. to make carving easier.

Meanwhile, prepare gravy from drippings, if desired. *1 stuffed capon*

TURKEY

ROAST TURKEY

▲ *Base Recipe*

Set out a shallow roasting pan with a rack.

Clean and cut off neck at body (leaving on neck skin) of

1 turkey, 10 to 12 lbs. ready-to-cook weight

(If turkey is frozen, thaw, following directions on package.) Rinse turkey; pat dry with absorbent paper. Set turkey aside. Reserve giblets and neck for stuffing or gravy.

Prepare

Herb Stuffing (page 273) or Oyster Stuffing (page 273)

Rub neck and body cavities of turkey with a mixture of

1 to 2 teaspoons salt
½ teaspoon monosodium glutamate

Lightly fill body and neck cavities with stuffing. To close body cavity, sew or skewer and lace with cord. Fasten neck skin to back with skewer. Push drumsticks under band of skin at tail, if present, or tie them to tail. Bring wing tips onto back. Place breast-side up on rack on roasting pan. Brush thoroughly with

Melted fat

If meat thermometer is used, place it in center of inside thigh muscle. (When done, meat thermometer will register 180°-185°F.)

Roast uncovered at 325°F 3½ to 4½ hrs. When two-thirds done, cut cord of band of skin at

drumsticks. Continue roasting until thickest part of drumstick feels soft when pressed with fingers; protect fingers with cloth or paper napkin. If desired, baste or brush occasionally with butter or pan drippings.

Remove turkey from oven. Remove roast meat thermometer and keep turkey hot. Allow to stand about 20 min. before serving.

Remove cord and skewers. Serve turkey on a heated platter. Garnish with **parsley** and serve with **Spicy Cranberry Sauce** (page 670). If desired, put paper frills on drumsticks.

About 16 servings

For Paper Frills—Select a sheet of white paper twice as wide as desired for length of frills; fold lengthwise. With fold toward you, make parallel cuts through fold ⅛ in. apart to within ½ in. of opposite side. Cut paper desired length; turn inside out. Wind around drumsticks. Fluff fringed ends with fingers. Fasten in place with cellulose tape.

—ROAST HALF TURKEY

Follow ▲ Recipe; use half or quarter turkey, 3½ to 5 lbs., ready-to-cook weight. Rub cut side with one half salt mixture. Skewer skin along cut sides to prevent shrinking. Tie leg to tail and wing flat against breast. Place skin-side up on rack. Roast at 325°F about 2 hrs. Meanwhile, prepare Herb or Oyster Stuffing (see note). Remove turkey from rack. Spoon stuffing onto a piece of aluminum foil and place on rack. Cover stuffing with half turkey. Roast 1 to 1½ hrs. longer, or until thickest part of drumstick feels soft when pressed with fingers. (Protect fingers with cloth or paper napkin.) *About 8 servings*

—ROAST CHICKEN

Follow ▲ Recipe. For turkey, substitute **1 roasting chicken,** 3 to 4 lbs., ready-to-cook weight. For rubbing cavities, reduce salt to ¼ to ½ teaspoon and monosodium glutamate.

to ⅛ teaspoon. Use one third recipe of stuffing. Chicken may be placed breast-side up or down. If placed down, turn breast side up when about three-quarters done. Roast at 375°F about 2¼ to 2¾ hrs.

TURKEY CORONET IN PINEAPPLE SHELLS

Set out a baking sheet and a 1½-qt. saucepan.

Cut into halves lengthwise through the crowns
2 large or medium fresh pineapples
Cut out and discard core sections. With a grapefruit knife or sharp paring knife, carefully remove and reserve the fruit from pineapple halves; leave the shells about ½ in. thick. Place shells on baking sheet, cover with aluminum foil (tucking it in around the crowns) and set in a 300°F oven to heat while preparing the filling. Dice enough of the reserved pineapple to make 1 cup.

Prepare and set aside
2 cups diced cooked turkey
½ cup (2 oz.) coarsely chopped salted almonds
¼ cup chopped green pepper

Drain; reserve liquid in a 2-cup measuring cup
1 can (4 oz.) sliced mushrooms
Prepare and add to the mushroom liquid
¾ cup chicken broth (dissolve
1 chicken bouillon cube in ¾ cup boiling water)
Fill measuring cup to 2-cup line with
Milk (about 1 cup)
Heat in the saucepan
¼ cup butter or margarine
Add the mushrooms and
2 tablespoons finely chopped onion
Cook over medium heat about 3 min. Blend in
⅓ cup all-purpose flour
½ teaspoon salt
½ teaspoon monosodium glutamate
⅛ teaspoon pepper
Cook and stir until mixture is bubbly. Remove from heat and add the liquid mixture gradually, stirring constantly. Continue cooking until sauce thickens; cook 1 to 2 min. longer. Add the turkey, almonds and green pepper. Cook until turkey is thoroughly heated. Remove from heat and add the diced pineapple.

Spoon the hot mixture into the heated pineapple shells. Sprinkle over the filling
2 tablespoons grated Parmesan cheese
Cover only the spiny crowns of the pineapple shells with aluminum foil.

Set in 450°F oven 15 to 20 min., or until filling is bubbly and cheese is lightly browned.

For Garnish—Cut crown shapes from scooped-out **orange halves**. Impale a **maraschino cherry** on the highest point of each "crown." After transferring filled pineapple shells to a serving platter, top each with a "crown" and sprinkle **moist shredded coconut** inside the "crown." Serve immediately.   *4 to 6 servings*

TURKEY L'ORANGE

Have ready
White meat of cooked turkey, thinly sliced (enough for 6 servings)

Combine in a large skillet
1 can (6 oz.) frozen orange juice concentrate, thawed
⅓ cup water
1 tablespoon lemon juice
Stir in a mixture of
2 tablespoons brown sugar
½ teaspoon ginger
¼ teaspoon marjoram
¼ teaspoon poultry seasoning
½ teaspoon salt
Cover skillet and cook over low heat about 15 min., stirring occasionally.

Remove cover and bring to boiling; stir in a blend of
1 teaspoon cornstarch
1 tablespoon cold water
Cook and stir about 3 min. Add
1 tablespoon butter or margarine
and the sliced turkey. Continue cooking until thoroughly heated.
Allowing 2 slices of turkey for each serving, arrange on plates and garnish with
Piquant Orange Cartwheels (below)
  6 servings

—PIQUANT ORANGE CARTWHEELS

Pare and cut crosswise into thin slices
3 medium oranges
Toss slices gently with a mixture of
1 tablespoon sugar
1 tablespoon wine vinegar
2 teaspoons instant minced onion
Store, covered, in refrigerator until ready to use.

SAUCED TURKEY IN BUNS

Have ready
3 cups diced cooked turkey

Combine in a saucepan
¾ cup ketchup
1 cup currant jelly
¼ cup finely chopped onion
2 tablespoons Worcestershire sauce
1 teaspoon salt
¼ teaspoon garlic salt
Cook over low heat about 20 min. Stir in the turkey. Heat thoroughly and spoon onto
Toasted buttered hamburger buns
  8 to 10 servings

TURKEY MEDITERRANEAN

Set out a shallow baking dish.

Prepare
Rich White Sauce (below)
½ cup julienne cooked ham
1½ cups sliced fresh mushrooms
4 cups julienne cooked turkey

Heat in a skillet
¼ cup butter or margarine
Add the ham and mushrooms and cook until mushrooms are tender, stirring occasionally. Combine turkey, ham and mushrooms with the sauce; heat thoroughly and keep hot.

Prepare **Spaghetti Parmesan** (below). Turn into the baking dish; push spaghetti to edge forming a ring. Stir into hot turkey mixture
¼ cup dry sherry
Turn into center of spaghetti. Top with
2 tablespoons shredded Parmesan cheese
2 tablespoons butter or margarine, melted
Pitted ripe olives
Green pepper strips
Set under broiler about 3 in. from heat until cheese is lightly browned.   *6 servings*

—RICH WHITE SAUCE

Heat in a saucepan
¼ cup butter or margarine
Stir in a blend of
¼ cup all-purpose flour
½ teaspoon salt
½ teaspoon monosodium glutamate
2 teaspoons paprika
Cook and stir until bubbly. Blend in
2 cups milk
1 cup cream
Cook and stir until boiling; cook 1 to 2 min. and remove from heat. Stir several tablespoons of the hot mixture into
2 egg yolks, slightly beaten
Immediately return to saucepan and cook gently 3 to 5 min. stirring occasionally.

—SPAGHETTI PARMESAN

Cook following package directions
8 oz. thin spaghetti
Drain thoroughly and toss with
2 tablespoons butter or margarine
2 tablespoons shredded Parmesan cheese
1 tablespoon cream
1 tablespoon sherry

PERKY TURKEY DINNER

Have ready
2 cups diced cooked turkey

Heat in a large skillet
3 tablespoons butter or margarine
Add and cook about 5 min., stirring occasionally
**1 medium green pepper, cut in thin
strips**
Blend in a mixture of
**2 tablespoons all-purpose flour
½ teaspoon seasoned salt
¼ teaspoon onion salt**
Cook and stir until bubbly. Remove from heat and slowly stir in
**1 bottle (7 oz.) lemon-lime
carbonated beverage**
Cook and stir until boiling; cook 1 or 2 min. Stir in
**1¼ teaspoons Worcestershire sauce
1 tablespoon pimiento strips**
Add the diced turkey and heat thoroughly.

Serve over crisp **chow mein noodles.**

4 servings

TURKEY CRANBERRY FRITTERS

Set out a deep saucepan (or an automatic deep fryer).

Have ready
Fat for deep frying (page 11)

Prepare and set aside
1½ cups finely chopped turkey

Put into a saucepan with enough water to cover
1 cup fresh cranberries
Tie together in a cheesecloth bag and add to berries
**1 whole allspice
1 whole clove
½ in. stick cinnamon**
Cover saucepan and cook over medium heat until cranberries burst, about 5 min. Remove spice bag and stir in
1¼ cups sugar
Blend thoroughly and cook until mixture becomes clear, stirring occasionally. Drain berries and reserve syrup; set berries aside to cool.

Start heating fat for deep frying to 365°F.

Combine in a mixing bowl, mixing thoroughly
**2 cups all-purpose flour
1¼ teaspoons baking powder
½ teaspoon salt
¼ teaspoon cinnamon
¼ teaspoon nutmeg**

Mix thoroughly
**2 eggs, beaten
¾ cup milk
1½ teaspoons grated lemon peel**
Add to flour mixture, beating only until batter is smooth.

Season chopped turkey to taste with **salt** and stir with the cranberries into batter. Drop

batter by tablespoonfuls into the hot fat. Deep-fry only as many fritters at one time as will float uncrowded one layer deep in the fat. Fry 3 to 4 min., or until golden brown and well puffed, turning several times to brown evenly. Remove with a slotted spoon; drain on absorbent paper. Serve immediately with the reserved hot cranberry syrup as a sauce.
About 40 fritters

CURRIED TURKEY AND WILD RICE

Set out and grease a 2½-qt. casserole.

Have ready
**4 cups diced cooked turkey
4 Hard-Cooked Eggs (page 133), diced**

Heat to boiling in a large saucepan
**6 cups water
2 teaspoons salt**
Meanwhile, wash in a colander or sieve
1½ cups wild rice (see note)
Add rice to water gradually, so boiling continues. Boil rapidly, covered, 25 to 30 min., or until rice is tender when pressed between fingers. Drain.

Meanwhile, combine in a large mixing bowl the turkey, eggs and
**½ to 1 cup chopped parsley
5 tablespoons butter or margarine,
melted**
Add rice and sprinkle with a mixture of
**1 tablespoon curry powder
1½ teaspoons salt**
Toss lightly until well mixed. Turn into the casserole. Pour over all
1¼ cups undiluted evaporated milk
Sprinkle top generously with
Paprika

Heat in 350°F oven 30 to 35 min.   *8 servings*

Note: White rice may be substituted for the wild rice.

LEFTOVER SPECIAL

▲ *Base Recipe*

Wonderful with turkey, just as good with other kinds of poultry and better than ever when served with cups of steaming coffee.

Set out a baking sheet and a 1-qt. saucepan.

Prepare dough for
**Quick Rolled Biscuits (page 93; blend
¼ teaspoon marjoram into dry ingredients)**
Roll biscuit dough into a rectangle ¼-in. thick. Set aside while preparing filling.

Leftover De Luxe

For Filling—Have ready and set aside
**2 cups diced turkey
1¾ cups leftover gravy
2 tablespoons chopped onion**

Heat in saucepan ¾ cup of the leftover gravy. Vigorously stir about 3 tablespoons hot gravy into
1 egg yolk, slightly beaten
Immediately blend into hot gravy and cook 2 to 3 min. Blend in 1 cup of the diced turkey, chopped onion and
**¼ teaspoon monosodium glutamate
Salt and pepper to taste (depending
upon amount of seasoning in
gravy)**
Spread filling on biscuit dough. Starting with long side of dough, roll; pinch ends to seal. Place on baking sheet.

Bake at 450°F 10 to 15 min.

Meanwhile, heat together in a saucepan remaining turkey and gravy. Serve over roll.
6 servings

—LEFTOVER DE LUXE

Follow ▲ Recipe. While turkey roll is baking, prepare **Fried Mushrooms (page 334)**. Stir into turkey-gravy mixture to be served over roll.

TURKEY À LA KING

▲ *Base Recipe*

Waffles, delicate and crisp, are a fine foundation for any creamed or à la king dish—but so are golden-brown toast points or croustades, toasted rusks or English muffins, tender hot biscuits, crunchy fried noodles or noodle baskets.

Set out a chafing dish or a large skillet.

Cut into chunks and set aside enough cooked turkey to yield
3 cups cooked turkey pieces

Prepare and set aside

1½ cups quick chicken broth (page 10; use 2 chicken bouillon cubes)

Set out

1 cup cooked peas

Clean and slice (page 9)

½ lb. mushrooms

Heat in the chafing dish blazer or the skillet over direct heat

⅓ cup butter or margarine

Add the mushrooms and

¼ cup finely chopped onion

Cook, occasionally moving and turning with a spoon, until the onion is tender and mushrooms are lightly browned and tender. With slotted spoon remove mushrooms, allowing fat to drain back into pan; set mushrooms aside.

Blend into butter in pan

¼ cup all-purpose flour

and a mixture of

1 teaspoon salt

1 teaspoon paprika

½ teaspoon white pepper

½ teaspoon monosodium glutamate

Heat until mixture bubbles, stirring constantly. Remove from heat. Add gradually, stirring in, the chicken broth and

1½ cups cream

Return mixture to heat and bring rapidly to boiling, stirring constantly; cook 1 to 2 min. longer. Add the turkey, peas, mushrooms and

¼ cup (2-oz. jar or can, drained) pimiento strips

Cook mixture slowly until turkey is thoroughly heated.

Serve over

Buttermilk Waffles (page 103)

About 6 servings

—TURKEY SWEETBREAD CASSEROLE

Follow ▲ Recipe. Grease a 1½-qt. casserole. Omit peas and pimiento strips. Reduce turkey to 1 cup cooked turkey. Cook (below) **½ lb. sweetbreads,** cut into pieces and set aside. Meanwhile, prepare **½ cup (about 2½ oz.) toasted blanched almonds** (pages 9 and 10). Reduce chicken broth and cream to 1 cup each. Blend the sweetbreads, turkey, mushrooms and almonds into the sauce mixture. Turn into casserole. Sprinkle evenly over top

Creamed Oysters and Turkey

½ cup buttered bread crumbs (page 9). Bake at 350°F 10 to 15 min., or until crumbs are browned and mixture is thoroughly heated.

To Cook Sweetbreads—Put **½ lb. sweetbreads** into a saucepan with **2 cups water, 1½ teaspoons cider vinegar or lemon juice** and **½ teaspoon salt.** Simmer, uncovered, for about 15 min. Drain and cover with cold water, changing water until sweetbreads are cool. Remove and discard membrane.

—TURKEY AND HAM EN CREME

Follow ▲ Recipe. Omit onion, peas and pimiento strips. Decrease mushrooms to ¼ lb. Reduce turkey to 1½ cups cooked turkey. Cut into pieces enough cooked ham to yield **1 cup cooked ham.** Reduce chicken broth to 1 cup. Substitute **½ teaspoon dry mustard** for the paprika. Vigorously stir about 3 tablespoons of the hot sauce mixture into **2 egg yolks,** slightly beaten. Immediately and thoroughly blend into mixture in pan, stirring constantly. Cook 2 to 3 min. over low heat, stirring constantly. Mix in the ham, turkey and **¾ teaspoon grated lemon peel.** Heat thoroughly. Do not boil.

—TURKEY AND HAM AMANDINE

Follow recipe for Turkey and Ham en Crème. Omit grated lemon peel. Add **¾ cup (about 4½ oz.) salted (page 10) almonds.**

—CREAMED TURKEY AND HAM WITH OLIVES

Follow recipe for Turkey and Ham en Crème. Add **¾ cup coarsely chopped ripe olives** with the ham and turkey.

—CREAMED TURKEY WITH OLIVES

Follow ▲ Recipe. Omit peas and pimiento strips. Mix in **¾ cup coarsely chopped ripe olives** with turkey and mushrooms.

Note: Chicken may be substituted for turkey in the ▲ Recipe or any of the variations.

TURKEY AND OYSTER PIE

Butter a 1½-qt. casserole.

Cut into cubes enough cooked turkey to yield

3 cups cubed cooked turkey

Drain, reserving liquor, and remove any shell particles from

1 pt. oysters

Set turkey and oysters in refrigerator until ready to use.

Prepare dough for

Pastry I for 1-crust Pie (page 485)

Flatten ball of dough on a lightly floured surface. Roll dough in all directions from center to edges about ⅛ in. thick and about 1 in. larger than overall size of casserole top. With

knife or spatula, loosen pastry from surface whenever sticking occurs; lift pastry slightly and sprinkle flour underneath. Cut a simple design near center of pastry to allow steam to escape during baking. Set aside.

Prepare

2 cups Medium White Sauce (double recipe, page 304; use reserved oyster liquor and milk for liquid and increase salt to ¾ teaspoon)

Meanwhile, put oysters and turkey into casserole. Dot with

2 tablespoons butter

Pour White Sauce over all. Moisten rim of casserole with cold water.

Loosen one half of pastry and fold over other half. Lift pastry gently and place loosely over hot mixture in casserole; unfold. Trim edge of pastry with scissors about ¾ in. beyond rim of casserole. Fold extra pastry under at edge and gently press edges to moistened rim of casserole. Flute (page 10) or press edges together with a fork.

Bake at 425°F 20 to 25 min., or until pastry is lightly browned. *About 6 servings*

CREAMED OYSTERS AND TURKEY

Cut into chunks, enough turkey to yield

2 or 3 cups cooked turkey

Set in refrigerator until ready to use.

Prepare in chafing dish or saucepan

3 cups Medium White Sauce (three times recipe, page 304; use milk or cream for liquid)

Mix into sauce, in order

1 can (2¼ oz.) deviled ham

1 pt. oysters (shell particles removed)

Add cooked turkey. Heat thoroughly.

Meanwhile, prepare toast cups.

For Toast Cups—Trim or cut the crusts from

8 slices bread

Lightly brush both sides of slices with

Melted butter or margarine

Gently press each slice into muffin-pan well to form shell. Toast in 350°F oven 12 to 15 min., or until toast cups are lightly browned. Fill toast cups with creamed mixture. Serve at once.   *8 servings*

DAY-AFTER TURKEY AND STUFFING

▲ *Base Recipe*

Grease a shallow 3-qt. casserole with a cover.

Toast and cut into cubes
   4 to 6 slices bread (6 cups cubes)
Set aside.

Boil in a covered saucepan in a small amount of salted water 15 to 20 min., or until tender
   ¾ cup chopped celery
Drain, reserving liquid.

Meanwhile, drain and remove any shell particles from
   ½ pt. oysters
Cut into small pieces with scissors; set aside.

Slice thinly and set aside enough cooked turkey to yield
   3 cups sliced cooked turkey

Heat slowly in a skillet until onion is tender. stirring occasionally
   ⅓ cup butter or margarine
   ¼ cup finely chopped onion
Turn into a bowl the onion (with excess butter), celery, oysters, toast cubes and
   2 tablespoons chopped parsley
and mixture of
   1½ teaspoons salt
   ½ teaspoon monosodium glutamate
   ½ teaspoon thyme or marjoram
   ⅛ teaspoon paprika
Mix with a fork. Drizzle over mixture
   ⅓ cup reserved celery liquid
(If a more moist stuffing is desired, add extra liquid.) Then gently mix in
   1 egg, well beaten
Cover bottom of casserole with one third of stuffing; do not pack down. Arrange one half of sliced turkey over stuffing. Repeat these two layers and top with remaining stuffing.

Cover and bake at 350°F 20 min. Remove cover and bake 10 to 15 min. longer.

For Sauce—Mix and heat thoroughly
   1¼ cups (10½-oz. can) condensed cream of mushroom soup
   ½ cup milk
   2 tablespoons chopped parsley
Serve casserole mixture with sauce. *8 servings*

—TURKEY WITH CRANBERRY STUFFING

Follow ▲ Recipe. Omit onion, parsley and oysters. Chop **1½ cups (about 6 oz.) cranberries,** washed and sorted; mix with **6 tablespoons sugar.** Decrease thyme or marjoram to ⅛-teaspoon. Melt **butter or margarine** and mix with toast cubes, cranberry mixture and seasonings.

Roast Duckling with Broiled Orange Slices

DUCKLING

ROAST DUCKLING

Orange rice stuffing is the distinguishing feature of this roast duckling recipe.

Set out a shallow roasting pan with rack.

Clean and cut off necks at bodies (leaving on skin) from
   2 ducklings, 4 lbs. each, ready-to-cook weight
(If ducklings are frozen, thaw following directions on package.) Rinse and pat ducklings dry with absorbent paper. Set aside.

Prepare and cool
   Orange Rice Stuffing (page 274)
Rub cavities of ducklings with
   1 to 2 teaspoons salt
Lightly fill body and neck cavities with stuffing. To close body cavity, sew or skewer and lace with cord. Fasten neck skin to back and wings to bodies with skewers. Place ducklings breast-side up on rack in roasting pan.

Roast uncovered at 325°F.

Set out
   1 cup orange juice
After 30 min. of roasting, brush ducklings with juice; brush them with juice frequently thereafter. Roast 3 hrs., or until ducklings test done. To test doneness, move leg gently by grasping end of bone; drumstick-thigh joint moves easily. (Protect fingers with cloth or paper.)

Remove skewers and cord from ducklings. Serve ducklings on heated platter. Garnish with paper frills (see page 265) on drumsticks, **endive** and **Broiled Orange Slices.**

For Broiled Orange Slices—Arrange on broiler rack
   10 orange slices
Sprinkle over slices
   1¼ teaspoons sugar
Place under broiler with top of slices about 3 in. from heat about 3 min., or until edges are slightly browned.

ROAST DUCKLING À L'ORANGE

Set out a shallow roasting pan with rack. Cord and skewers will be needed.

Prepare and set aside
   Apricot Stuffing (page 273)

Clean and cut off necks at bodies (leaving on skin) from
   2 ducklings, 4 lbs. each, ready-to-cook weight
(If ducklings are frozen, thaw, following directions on package.) Rinse and pat ducklings dry with absorbent paper. Rub cavities of ducklings with
   1 to 2 teaspoons salt
Set ducklings aside.

Put into a small saucepan
   1 cup orange juice
   2 tablespoons butter
Place over low heat, stirring occasionally until butter is melted. Remove from heat. Using a pastry brush, brush cavities of ducklings with the orange juice mixture.

Lightly fill body and neck cavities with the cooled stuffing. To close body cavities, sew or skewer and lace with cord. Fasten neck skin to backs and wings to bodies with skewers. Place ducklings breast-side up on rack in roasting pan. Brush with orange juice mixture.

Roast uncovered at 325°F. Frequently brush ducklings with orange juice mixture during roasting period. Pour drippings and fat from roasting pan into a bowl as they accumulate; reserve for gravy preparation. Roast 2½ to 3 hrs., or until ducklings test done. To test doneness, move leg gently by grasping end bone; drumstick-thigh joint moves easily when duckling is done. (Protect fingers from heat with paper napkin.)

Place ducklings on a heated platter; remove skewers and cord. Keep ducklings warm while preparing Orange Gravy.

For Orange Gravy—Leaving brown residue in roasting pan, pour into the bowl containing the reserved drippings and fat, the remaining drippings. Allow fat to rise to surface; skim off fat and reserve. Remaining drippings are meat juices and orange juice which should be used as part of the liquid in the gravy.

Measure into roasting pan 3 tablespoons of the reserved fat. Blend in

3 tablespoons all-purpose flour
¼ teaspoon salt
⅛ teaspoon pepper

Stirring constantly, heat until mixture bubbles. Remove from heat. Add slowly, stirring constantly and vigorously

2 cups liquid (drippings plus orange juice)

Return to heat and cook rapidly, stirring constantly, until gravy thickens. Cook 1 to 2 min. longer. While stirring, scrape bottom and sides of pan to blend in brown residue. Add and stir until well blended

⅓ cup orange marmalade

Remove from heat; pour into gravy boat and serve hot.

Slip paper frills onto drumsticks and garnish ducklings with

Broiled Orange Slices (page 269)
Sprigs of parsley

Serve immediately. *6 to 8 servings*

Note: For a brown, crisp skin, place ducklings on broiler pan and broil 5 to 7 min., or until skin is well browned and crisp.

GLAZED DUCKLING GOURMET

Rinse, pat dry and quarter

2 ready-to-cook ducklings, 4 lbs. each

Skin duckling pieces (do not use wings, necks and backs) and remove excess fat. Rub pieces with a mixture of

1½ teaspoons salt
¼ teaspoon nutmeg

Heat in a large skillet over medium heat

3 to 4 tablespoons butter or margarine
1 clove garlic, minced

Add duckling pieces and brown well on all sides. Sprinkle over duckling

1½ teaspoons rosemary, crushed
1½ teaspoons thyme

Add a blend of

1½ cups Burgundy
2 teaspoons red wine vinegar
⅓ cup currant jelly

Bring to boiling, cover skillet, lower heat and cook gently until duckling is tender, about

45 min. Remove duckling to a heated platter and keep warm.

Combine, blending well

2 tablespoons cold water
2 teaspoons cornstarch

Stir into liquid in skillet and bring to boiling. Cook and stir 1 to 2 min. Add and mix lightly until thoroughly heated

1½ cups halved seedless green grapes

Pour the hot sauce over duckling; garnish platter with sprigs of **watercress**.

6 to 8 servings

ROAST DUCKLING WITH OLIVES

Set out a large heavy saucepot or deep skillet.

Rinse, pat dry and cut into quarters

1 ready-to-cook duckling, 4 lbs.

Remove any excess fat from pieces.

Heat in saucepot or skillet

⅓ cup olive oil or other cooking oil

Add duckling and cook over medium heat until well browned on all sides. Remove pieces from saucepot and keep warm.

Add to the saucepot

2 medium carrots, coarsely chopped
1 large onion, coarsely chopped
½ teaspoon salt
⅛ teaspoon seasoned pepper
¼ teaspoon rosemary
⅛ teaspoon savory
2 small stalks celery, chopped
3 sprigs parsley, chopped
1 small bay leaf

Continue cooking until carrots and onions are lightly browned. Drain off excess fat in skillet. Return duck to skillet and pour over it

⅓ cup cognac

Ignite and when flaming ceases add a blend of

2 tablespoons tomato paste
2 cups hot chicken broth
⅓ cup dry white wine

Cover saucepot or skillet and set in a 350° F oven about 1½ hrs., or until duckling is tender.

Remove to heated serving platter and keep warm. Strain remaining mixture in skillet into a saucepan and add

16 whole pitted green olives

Heat until sauce is very hot and pour over duckling. *4 servings*

DUCKLING IN CASSEROLE NORMANDY STYLE
(Caneton à la Normandie)

Typical of apple-rich Normandy, this famous dish also may be prepared with partridge, pheasant or chicken.

Butter a 3-qt. casserole with a tight-fitting cover.

Clean

1 duckling, 4 lbs., ready-to-cook weight

Disjoint duckling and cut into serving-size pieces. Rinse and pat dry with absorbent paper. Cut away and discard excess fat.

Heat in a large skillet

2 tablespoons butter

Sprinkle pieces of duckling with mixture of

¾ teaspoon salt
⅛ teaspoon pepper

Add duckling to skillet and brown on all sides, turning with tongs. Pour off fat as it collects.

Wash, quarter, core, pare and slice

6 medium (about 2 lbs.) apples

Melt in a deep saucepan

3 tablespoons butter

Toss apple slices in melted butter. Put a thin layer of buttered apple slices on bottom of casserole. Arrange duckling over apples, plumpest pieces on top. Surround with remaining apple slices.

Discard fat from skillet and add to same skillet

½ cup apple brandy

Stir over low heat to loosen particles. Heat until steaming. Pour over the duckling.

Duckling in Casserole, Normandy Style

Cover and bake at 350°F 1½ to 2 hrs., or until duckling is tender. Serve in casserole.

About 3 servings

Note: If duck is used instead of duckling, additional cooking may be necessary.

GOOSE

ROAST GOOSE

Set out a shallow roasting pan with rack.

Clean (and cut off neck at body, leaving skin)
    1 goose, 10 to 12 lbs. ready-to-cook weight
(If goose is frozen, thaw, following package directions.) Rinse and pat goose dry with absorbent paper. Set aside.

Prepare and cool
    Apple Stuffing for Poultry (page 664)

Rub cavity of goose with mixture of
    1 to 2 teaspoons salt
    ½ teaspoon monosodium glutamate
Lightly fill body and neck cavities with stuffing. To close body cavity, sew or skewer and lace with cord. Fasten neck skin to back with skewer. Loop cord around legs and tighten slightly. Place goose breast down on rack in roasting pan.

Roast at 325°F for 3¾ to 4¼ hrs. or until goose tests done. Allow about 25 min. per pound. To test for doneness, move leg gently by grasping end of bone; the thigh joint should move easily. (Protect fingers with cloth or paper.) During roasting period, spoon off fat occasionally as it accumulates. This fat may be used in other cooking.

Remove skewers and cord. Serve goose on heated platter. Garnish with **parsley.**

About 8 servings

ROAST GOOSE WITH SAUERKRAUT STUFFING

Singe and clean (remove any large layers of fat from body and neck cavities)
    1 goose, 10 to 12 lbs. ready-to-cook weight
Rinse thoroughly, drain and pat dry with absorbent paper; set aside.

Heat in a skillet
    1 tablespoon butter or margarine
Add and cook 3 to 5 min.
    2 large onions, chopped

Meanwhile, combine in a large bowl and toss lightly
    6½ cups drained sauerkraut, snipped
    2 medium apples, quartered, cored and diced
    1 carrot, pared and shredded
    2 medium potatoes, shredded (about 1½ cups)

Add the onion and
    ½ cup dry white wine
    2 tablespoons brown sugar
    2 teaspoons caraway seed
    ½ teaspoon seasoned pepper
Continue tossing until thoroughly mixed. Rub body and neck cavities of goose with
    Salt
Lightly spoon stuffing into cavities. Truss goose and set, breast side up, on a rack in a shallow roasting pan.

Roast Goose with Prune Apple Stuffing

Roast, uncovered, in a 325°F oven about 3½ hours, or until goose tests done. Remove stuffing to a serving dish and serve with roast goose.

2 qts. stuffing

Note: Put leftover stuffing into a shallow casserole or baking dish. Sprinkle with brown sugar. Overlap thinly sliced apples over top and sprinkle again with brown sugar. Set in oven about 1 hr. before goose is finished roasting, or heat stuffing alone in a 350°F oven 45 min.

ROAST GOOSE WITH PRUNE APPLE STUFFING
(Gefüllter Gänsebraten)

▲ *Base Recipe*

Roast goose is a traditional Christmas Day dish and is often served with red cabbage. In some parts of Germany, potato pancakes or noodles are also part of the holiday menu.

Set out a shallow roasting pan with rack.

Have ready
    2 cups pitted cooked prunes
Reserve about 8 to 10 prunes for garnish.

Clean and remove any layers of fat from body cavity and opening of
    1 goose, 10 to 12 lbs. ready-to-cook weight
Cut off neck at body, leaving on neck skin. (If goose is frozen, thaw, following directions on package.) Rinse and pat dry with absorbent paper. (Reserve giblets for use in gravy or other food preparation.) Rub body and neck cavities of goose with
    Salt
Wash, quarter, core and pare
    6 medium (about 2 lbs.) apples
Lightly fill body and neck cavities with the apples and prunes. To close body cavity, sew or skewer and lace with cord. Fasten neck skin to back with skewer. Loop cord around legs and tighten slightly. Place breast-side down on rack in roasting pan.

Roast uncovered at 325°F 3 hrs. Remove fat from pan is it accumulates during this period. Turn goose breast side up. Roast 1 to 2 hrs.

longer, or until goose tests done. To test for doneness, move leg gently by grasping end of bone; drumstick-thigh joint should move easily. (Protect fingers with paper napkin.) Allow about 25 min. per pound to estimate total roasting time.

To serve, remove skewers and cord. Place goose on heated platter. Remove some of the apples from goose and arrange on the platter. Garnish with the reserved prunes and **watercress**. For an attractive garnish, place cooked **prunes** on top of cooked **apple rings** if desired.   *8 servings*

—ROAST GOOSE
WITH POTATO STUFFING
(Gänsebraten mit Kartoffelfulle)

Follow ▲ Recipe. Omit apples and prunes. Prepare and lightly fill body and neck cavities with **Potato Stuffing** (page 274).

ROAST GOOSE WITH PRUNE STUFFING
(Oie Rôti aux Pruneaux)

The town of Agen in old Guyenne, now known as Bordelais, is the source of this recipe.

Set out a shallow roasting pan with rack, a saucepan, and a skillet with cover.

Clean, cut off neck at body, leaving skin, and thoroughly wash in cold water, body and neck cavities of

1 goose, 10 to 12 lbs. ready-to-cook weight

Drain and pat dry with absorbent paper. Set goose aside.

Roast Goose with Prune Stuffing

Put into the saucepan

1 cup large dried prunes
2 cups water

Cover saucepan; bring to boiling and simmer prunes about 20 min., or until plump and tender. Slit prunes with a sharp knife and carefully remove pits. Set prunes aside.

Meanwhile, heat in the skillet

1 tablespoon fat

Add

1 lb. lean pork, coarsely ground
½ cup chopped onion

Cook and stir over medium heat until meat is lightly browned. Season with

1 teaspoon salt
½ teaspoon pepper

Cover skillet and cook over low heat about 20 min.

Remove from heat and stir in

1 egg yolk, slightly beaten

Remove ¼ cup of pork stuffing and combine with

¼ cup chopped green olives

Fill prunes with this mixture and gently mix prunes with remaining stuffing.

Rub cavity of goose with

Salt

Lightly fill body and neck cavities with stuffing. To close body cavity, sew or skewer and lace with cord. Fasten neck skin to back with skewer. Loop cord around legs and tighten slightly. Place breast-side down on rack in roasting pan.

Roast uncovered at 325°F for 3 hrs. Remove fat from pan several times during this period. Turn goose breast-side up. Roast 1 to 2 hrs. longer, or until it tests done. (Allow about 25 min. per pound for total roasting time.) To test for doneness, move leg gently by grasping end of drumstick; thigh joint should move easily.

Remove skewers and cord. Serve on heated platter. Garnish as desired.   *8 servings*

CASSEROLE OF GOOSE OR DUCK

Grease a 1½-qt. casserole with a tight-fitting cover.

Slice and set aside enough cooked goose or duck to yield

2½ to 3 cups sliced cooked goose or duck

Wash, quarter, core and cut into ½-in. wedges

3 medium (about 1 lb.) tart apples

Place in a shallow dish. Pour in a mixture of

1 cup orange juice
½ cup currant jelly, melted

Cover and allow apples to stand in orange juice mixture about 30 min.; turn apples occasionally.

Meanwhile, clean and slice thickly (page 9)

½ lb. mushrooms

Heat in a skillet

3 to 4 tablespoons butter or margarine

Add mushrooms to skillet and heat slowly about 5 min., moving and turning occasionally, with

2 tablespoons minced onion

Line bottom of casserole with one half of sliced goose or duck. Drain apples (reserving marinade); arrange apple wedges over goose. Cover with mushrooms and onion. Sprinkle with a mixture of

½ teaspoon salt
¼ teaspoon monosodium glutamate
⅛ teaspoon basil
⅛ teaspoon nutmeg
Dash ginger
Few grains pepper
2 tablespoons finely chopped parsley

Arrange remaining goose slices over top.

Spoon into casserole

½ cup marinade

Top with a mixture of

½ cup fine buttered bread crumbs (page 9)
1 teaspoon grated orange or lemon peel

Cover and cook in a 350°F oven 20 to 25 min., or until apples are almost tender. Remove cover and cook 10 to 12 min. longer, or until crumbs are lightly browned.   *6 to 8 servings*

ROCK CORNISH GAME HENS

ROCK CORNISH GAME HENS

▲ Base Recipe

Set out a shallow roasting pan with a rack.

Prepare and set aside for stuffing

Wild Rice with Mushrooms (one half recipe, page 168; add all mushrooms to rice)

Have ready

4 Rock Cornish game hens, about 1 lb. each, thawed if frozen

Rinse and pat game hens dry with absorbent paper. Rub cavities of the four hens with

2 teaspoons salt

Lightly fill body cavities with the stuffing. To close body cavities, sew or skewer and lace with cord. Fasten neck skin to backs and wings to bodies with skewers. Place game hens breast-side up on rack in roasting pan.

Set out

¼ cup unsalted butter, melted

Brush each hen with about 1 tablespoon of the butter.

Roast uncovered at 350°F. Roast 1 to 1½ hrs., or until hens test done. Frequently baste hens during roasting period with drippings from roasting pan.

Roast Rock Cornish Game Hens

To test doneness, move leg gently by grasping end bone; drumstick-thigh joint moves easily when hens are done. (Protect fingers from heat with paper napkin.)

Place game hens on a heated platter; keep warm while preparing gravy. Before serving, remove skewers and garnish hens with

Sprigs of watercress

For Gravy—Prepare and set aside to cool
½ cup quick meat broth (page 10)
Leaving brown residue in roasting pan, pour the drippings into a bowl. Allow fat to rise to surface; skim off fat and reserve. Remaining drippings are meat juices which should be used as part of the liquid in the gravy. Measure into roasting pan 1½ tablespoons of the reserved fat. Blend in

1½ tablespoons all-purpose flour
¼ teaspoon monosodium glutamate
⅛ teaspoon salt
⅛ teaspoon pepper

Stirring constantly, heat until mixture bubbles. Remove from heat and add slowly, stirring constantly and vigorously, the broth and
½ cup liquid (drippings)
Return to heat and cook rapidly, stirring constantly, until gravy thickens. Cook 1 to 2 min. longer. While stirring, scrape bottom and sides of pan to blend in brown residue. Remove from heat and stir in

2 tablespoons Madeira

Pour into a gravy boat and serve hot.

4 servings

—ROAST SQUAB

Follow ▲ Recipe. Substitute **4 squabs, ¾ to 1 lb. each,** ready-to-cook weight, for the Rock Cornish game hens.

LIME-GLAZED ROCK CORNISH GAME HENS

Thaw, following directions on package
4 frozen Rock Cornish game hens,
1 to 1¼ lbs. each

Blend and set aside
½ cup butter, melted
2 tablespoons brown sugar
2 to 4 tablespoons lime juice
2 teaspoons soy sauce

Rinse game hens and pat dry with absorbent paper. Rub cavities with
2 teaspoons salt

Brush cavities with some of butter mixture. Close cavities. Fasten neck skin to backs and wings to bodies with skewers. Place game hens breast-side up on rack in shallow roasting pan. Brush hens with butter mixture.

Roast uncovered at temperature and for time given on package. Baste hens frequently with drippings from roasting pan and any remaining butter mixture. Roast until hens test done.

Arrange on a warm serving platter and garnish with **Spicy Minted Prunes** (page 421).

4 servings

ROCK CORNISH GAME HENS, SPIT ROASTED

Thaw, rinse and pat dry
4 frozen Rock Cornish game hens,
1 to 1¼ lbs. each

Melt in a skillet over medium heat
¼ cup butter or margarine
Add and cook 3 to 5 min.
½ cup chopped celery
3 tablespoons chopped onion

Combine in a large bowl
3½ cups ¼-in. bread cubes
¼ teaspoon salt
¼ teaspoon poultry seasoning
½ cup seedless raisins

Add the celery-onion mixture and toss ingredients gently to mix thoroughly. (If a more moist stuffing is desired, add 3 to 4 tablespoons water to mixture.) Spoon stuffing into cavities of hens, truss and arrange securely on a spit.

Roast hens on rotisserie about 1 hr., or until well browned and tender, brushing occasionally with **melted butter.** *4 servings*

STUFFINGS

HERB STUFFING

Mix
¾ cup melted butter
2 teaspoons salt
1 teaspoon sage (or ½ teaspoon
each of thyme, rosemary and
marjoram)
¼ teaspoon pepper
In a large bowl, lightly toss mixture with
2 qts. soft bread cubes
¾ cup milk
⅓ cup chopped celery with leaves
⅓ cup chopped onion

Spoon stuffing into neck and body cavities of turkey—do not pack. Stuff the turkey just before roasting. Extra stuffing may be placed in greased, covered baking dish or wrapped in aluminum foil and baked with turkey the last hour of roasting time. *Stuffing for 10-lb turkey*

Note: Immediately after meal is served, remove stuffing from turkey. Store stuffing in a covered dish in refrigerator. If only one side of turkey has been carved, wrap remainder in waxed paper or aluminum foil. If more than one half of the meat has been carved off, remove remainder of meat from bone. Store covered in refrigerator.

This stuffing may also be used for chicken, goose or duckling. Allow about 1 cup bread cubes per pound of ready-to-cook weight of birds; if weight is 10 lbs. or less, subtract 1 cup from total; if weight is more than 10 lbs., subtract 2 cups from total. Proportionately decrease or increase the remaining ingredients in recipe. Mix diced apple with the stuffing before filling cavity of goose or duckling. Use ½ teaspoon marjoram instead of sage.

APRICOT STUFFING

Prepare
Perfection Boiled Rice (page 165)

Meanwhile, finely chop enough dried apricots to yield
1 cup (about 5 oz.) finely chopped
dried apricots
Set aside.

Mix in a large bowl
¼ cup Cointreau
¼ cup butter, melted
½ teaspoon salt
¼ teaspoon pepper
¼ teaspoon monosodium glutamate
⅛ teaspoon thyme
⅛ teaspoon nutmeg
⅛ teaspoon cloves
Add the rice, apricots and
¼ cup finely chopped onion
¼ cup finely chopped celery
2 tablespoons finely chopped parsley
Toss lightly until thoroughly combined.

About 5 cups stuffing

OYSTER STUFFING

Cut into cubes
24 slices dry bread
Put cubes into a large bowl and set aside.

Finely chop enough turkey giblets to yield
⅔ cup finely chopped giblets
Heat in a heavy skillet
½ cup butter

Add giblets; cook over medium heat 20 min., occasionally moving and turning with a spoon.

Meanwhile, drain
> **1 pt. oysters**

Pick over to remove any shell particles. Coarsely chop oysters and set in refrigerator.

Clean and chop enough to yield
> **2½ cups (about 1 lb.) finely chopped celery**
> **1 cup (about 2 medium) finely chopped onion**

Wash, pare and grate enough apple to yield
> **1½ cups (about 2 medium) grated apples**

Heat in a large skillet
> **½ cup butter**

Add chopped vegetables and apple and cook over medium heat until celery is crisp-tender, occasionally moving with a spoon.

Meanwhile, pour over bread cubes
> **½ cup water**

Sprinkle over bread cubes a mixture of
> **2½ teaspoons salt**
> **1 teaspoon sage**
> **½ teaspoon sugar**
> **¼ teaspoon pepper**

Toss gently with a fork. Add and mix lightly
> **2 eggs, beaten**

Blend in oysters, giblets, vegetables and apple. (See Herb Stuffing, page 273, for directions for stuffing turkey.)   *Stuffing for 15-lb. turkey*

ORANGE RICE STUFFING

Melt in a heavy 2-qt. saucepan
> **3 tablespoons butter or margarine**

Add and cook about 5 min.
> **1 cup diced celery with leaves**
> **2 tablespoons chopped onion**

Add to saucepan and bring to rapid boiling
> **1½ cups water**
> **1 cup orange juice**
> **2 tablespoons thinly sliced orange peel (colored part only)**
> **1½ teaspoons salt**
> **½ teaspoon monosodium glutamate**
> **⅛ teaspoon thyme**
> **⅛ teaspoon marjoram**

Add gradually to mixture so boiling will continue
> **1 cup uncooked rice**

Stir to blend thoroughly. Cover saucepan tightly, reduce heat to very low and cook

about 25 min. without removing cover. Cool slightly.   *Stuffing for two 4-lb. ducklings*

Note: Stuff bird with rice mixture. Bake extra stuffing in greased casserole or wrap stuffing loosely in aluminum foil and bake with bird during last hour of roasting time.

ORANGE FILBERT STUFFING

Have ready
> **4 cups white bread cubes**

Prepare
> **2 cups chopped pared apple**
> **1 cup chopped celery**
> **½ cup chopped onion**
> **2 cups chopped toasted filberts (page 10)**
> **2 teaspoons finely shredded orange peel**
> **1½ teaspoons finely shredded lemon peel**

Put bread cubes, apple, celery, onion and filberts into a large bowl with the shredded peels. Drizzle with
> **¼ cup butter or margarine, melted**

Toss lightly

Beat until frothy
> **2 eggs**

Stir in
> **½ cup orange juice**
> **2 tablespoons lemon juice**
> **1 teaspoon seasoned salt**
> **½ teaspoon pepper**
> **½ teaspoon thyme**
> **¼ teaspoon nutmeg**

Pour over mixture in bowl and toss lightly.

Spoon into body cavities of poultry or into a greased 2-qt. casserole. Truss poultry and roast at 325°F, or cover casserole and bake stuffing at 325°F 1 hr.   *About 2 qts. stuffing*

POTATO STUFFING
(Kartoffelfülle)

Wash, pare and cook (page 313)
> **3⅓ lbs. (about 10 medium potatoes)**

Cook about 30 min., or until potatoes are tender when pierced with a fork. Drain. Dry potatoes by shaking pan over low heat.

Meanwhile, prepare
> **1 cup (about 2 medium) chopped onion**
> **⅔ cup chopped celery**

Heat in a skillet
> **½ cup fat**

Add the onion and celery and cook over medium heat until vegetables are tender, occasionally moving and turning them with spoon. Remove skillet from heat; set aside.

Force potatoes through a food mill or ricer into a large bowl. Add cooked vegetables and
> **4 cups (about 6 slices) soft bread crumbs**

Mix thoroughly; toss with a mixture of
> **2 eggs, beaten**
> **1 tablespoon poultry seasoning**
> **2 teaspoons salt**
> **1½ teaspoons monosodium glutamate**
> **¼ teaspoon pepper**

Spoon stuffing into neck and body cavities of goose; do not pack. Stuff the goose just before roasting. Extra stuffing may be placed in greased baking dish and baked with goose the last hour of baking.
> *Stuffing for a 10- to 12-lb. goose*

CRAN-PRUNE STUFFING FOR TURKEY

Combine in a large mixing bowl
> **2 pkgs. (8 oz. each) herb-seasoned stuffing croutons**
> **1½ cups fresh cranberries, rinsed and drained**
> **1 cup diced pitted prunes**
> **1 cup diced celery**
> **1 large onion, chopped**
> **½ cup butter or margarine, melted**
> **1½ cups orange juice**

Toss ingredients lightly but thoroughly.
> *Stuffing for 12- to 15-lb. turkey*

WINE STUFFING FOR TURKEY

Combine in a large bowl and toss to mix
> **3 qts. ½-in. bread cubes**
> **2 cups chopped blanched almonds**
> **4 cups diced celery**
> **2 cups chopped celery leaves**

Heat in a skillet until melted
> **¼ cup butter or margarine**

Add and cook 3 to 5 min., stirring occasionally
> **2 cloves, garlic, minced**
> **½ cup finely chopped green onions**

Toss with the mixture in bowl. Combine and pour over bread-cube mixture.
> **3 eggs, slightly beaten**
> **1 tablespoon salt**
> **¼ teaspoon cracked black pepper**
> **½ teaspoon nutmeg**
> **½ teaspoon mace**
> **½ cup dry red wine**

Continue to toss lightly until thoroughly mixed.

Spoon stuffing lightly into body and neck cavities of 18- to 20-lb. turkey.
> *Stuffing for 18- to 20-lb. turkey*

Note: Turn any extra stuffing into a well-greased baking dish with cover or wrap in heavy-duty aluminum foil and heat in oven during last hour of roasting bird.

Fish and shellfish

Thanks to modern transportation and methods of preservation (canning, drying, freezing, and packing in ice), bounty from the lakes, rivers, streams and sea, for many years foods available only along the coastlines, can now be enjoyed by everyone. Salt-water fish, shellfish, and fresh-water fish make a handsome meal when served whole, when combined with other foods in salads or casseroles, or as the dominant ingredient in sauces to accompany rice or pasta. Fish is a high-quality protein food with an abundance of the vitamins and minerals that contribute to good health and energy. For the "dieter," fish is generally low in calories and water-retaining salt. For the budget-conscious meal planner, there is a wide variety of reasonably priced canned and frozen fish available in the markets. A wise homemaker will serve this excellent food to her family several times a week.

FISH

PANFRIED FISH FILLETS

Set out a large skillet.

Set out
2 lbs. fish fillets

(If using frozen fish fillets, allow additional time for thawing. Thaw, following directions on package.) Cut into serving-size pieces and set fillets aside.

Mix in a shallow pan and set aside
1 cup fine dry bread crumbs
1 tablespoon grated Parmesan cheese
2 teaspoons salt
1 teaspoon monosodium glutamate
⅛ teaspoon pepper

Beat slightly in a shallow dish
2 eggs
1 or 2 tablespoons milk

Heat in the skillet enough to make a layer ¼ in. deep
Olive oil

Add
½ clove garlic, crushed

Dip fillets into egg mixture, then coat with crumb mixture. When oil is hot, panfry fish over moderate heat. Cook one side until crisp and browned. Turn carefully with spatula or pancake turner and brown other side. Allow 8 to 12 min. total cooking time, depending upon thickness of fillets.

Serve with
Maître d'Hôtel Butter (page 309)
6 servings

FRESH TROUT WITH SAUCE SUPREME

▲ Base Recipe

For Fish—Remove heads and fins, if desired; rinse quickly under running cold water and pat dry with absorbent paper
6 cleaned fresh trout, 8 to 10 oz. each

Rub inside of fish with a cut
Lemon

Season with a mixture of
¼ teaspoon salt
⅛ teaspoon pepper

Heat in a large skillet over medium heat
6 tablespoons butter or margarine

Add trout to skillet and cook 5 to 8 min. on each side, or until lightly browned and fish flakes easily. If desired, remove bones from fish. Transfer trout to a heated serving platter and garnish with **watercress** or **parsley sprigs.**

For Sauce Supreme—Add to the butter in skillet
¼ cup finely chopped onion
1 large clove garlic, cut in half

Cook until onion is golden, stirring occasionally. Remove and discard the garlic. Gradually add, stirring constantly
1 cup heavy cream
3 tablespoons tomato paste
¼ cup chopped pimiento-stuffed olives
¼ to ½ teaspoon salt

Heat thoroughly. Serve sauce hot with the trout.
6 servings

—TROUT AMANDINE

Follow ▲ Recipe. Omit sauce. Melt **½ cup butter** over low heat; add **1 cup slivered blanched almonds** and cook, stirring constantly, until almonds are evenly browned. Remove from heat and stir in **1 teaspoon salt** and **½ teaspoon lemon juice.** Spoon over the trout.

BROWNED FISH FILLETS

▲ Base Recipe

Set out a large skillet.

Thaw, following directions on package
2 lbs. frozen fish fillets

Cut into serving-size pieces. Long thin fillets may be rolled and secured with wooden picks or skewers.

To coat fish evenly, shake 1 piece at a time in a plastic bag containing a mixture of
½ cup yellow corn meal, fine cracker crumbs or all-purpose flour
2 teaspoons salt
1 teaspoon monosodium glutamate
⅛ teaspoon pepper

Heat in large skillet enough to make a layer ¼ in. deep
Bacon or salt pork drippings

When fat is hot, panfry fish over moderate heat. Cook one side until crisp and browned. Turn with spatula or pancake turner and brown other side. Allow 8 to 12 min. total cooking time, depending upon thickness of fillets. Sprinkle with
Paprika

Serve with **lemon wedges** or **Tomato Sauce** (page 307).
6 servings

—FILLETS AMANDINE

Follow ▲ Recipe for preparing fish fillets. Substitute **butter or margarine** for bacon or salt pork drippings. Prepare Amandine Sauce by heating in a skillet **½ cup butter or margarine** and **½ cup slivered blanched almonds** (page 9). Cook slowly, stirring constantly, until nuts are delicately browned. Remove from heat and blend in **2 tablespoons lemon**

Fillets Mornay and Broiled Tomatoes

juice and ½ teaspoon salt. Place fish on serving platter and pour hot sauce over.

—FILLETS MORNAY AND BROILED TOMATOES

Prepare **Mornay Sauce** (page 305). Follow ▲ Recipe to prepare 4 fish fillets, substituting **butter or margarine** for bacon or salt pork drippings. Surround fish with hot Mornay Sauce. Rinse, cut out stem ends and cut **2 firm tomatoes** into halves. Sprinkle halves with a mixture of ½ teaspoon salt, ¼ teaspoon pepper and ¼ teaspoon monosodium glutamate. Dot halves with **2 teaspoons butter or margarine,** allowing ½ teaspoon per serving. Sprinkle with **2 teaspoons chopped parsley.** Set seasoned tomato halves around fish in skillet. Toss **½ cup (about 2½ oz.) blanched almonds** (page 9) over fish and into sauce. Place skillet under broiler with top of tomatoes 2 in. from heat. Broil about 5 min., or until nuts are lightly browned and mixture is piping hot.

—PANFRIED SMELTS

Clean **2 to 2½ lbs. smelts** by drawing a sharp knife over the skin to remove scales. Remove head and tail. Make a slit in underside and pull out entrails. Rinse smelts with cold **water** and dry with absorbent paper. Split open by cutting through backbone almost to skin. Proceed as in ▲ Recipe.

FRIED KIPPERS IN CREAM

▲ *Base Recipe*

Cover with cold water and bring to boiling
  4 kippered herring
Drain and dry well with absorbent paper. Set aside.

Heat in a skillet
  3 to 4 tablespoons butter or margarine
Add and cook onions until tender, turning occasionally
  3 medium onions, cut into ¼-in. slices and separated in rings

Remove onions and keep warm.

Place herring in skillet. Brown over low heat about 5 min. on each side.

Scald (page 10)
  1¼ cups cream
Slowly pour one half of cream into skillet with herring and simmer 2 min. Add remaining cream and simmer 3 min. longer.

Serve immediately, without cream. (Cream may be reserved for use in a white sauce, Mock Hollandaise, or Cheese Sauce, page 304.) Garnish with onion rings.   *4 servings*

—FRIED KIPPERS

Follow ▲ Recipe. Omit onions and cream.

CODFISH BALLS

▲ *Base Recipe*

A deep saucepan or automatic deep fryer will be needed.

Set out
  1 lb. salt codfish
Cover with cold water to freshen. Let stand in cold water at least 4 hrs. Change water 3 or 4 times during that period. (Or follow directions on package.) Drain fish and remove any pieces of bone. Flake (page 9).

About 20 min. before ready to deep-fry, heat fat to 365°F (page 11).

Wash, pare and cut into pieces
  4 to 6 medium (about 2 lbs.) potatoes
Combine fish and potatoes in a saucepan. Cook covered in boiling water to cover about 20 min., or until potatoes are tender when pierced with a fork.

Thoroughly drain and mash potatoes and fish. Whip in until potatoes are fluffy.
  2 tablespoons butter
and a mixture of
  2 eggs, beaten
  ½ teaspoon paprika
  ⅛ teaspoon pepper
Deep-fry by dropping spoonfuls of the mixture into the hot fat. Drop only as many at one time as will float uncrowded one layer deep in the fat. Turn balls as they brown, cooking each 2 to 5 min., or until golden brown. Remove from fat with a slotted spoon, draining over fat for a few seconds before removing to absorbent paper.

Serve with **Egg Sauce** (page 304).
    About 6 servings

—CODFISH CAKES

Follow ▲ Recipe. Omit deep-frying procedure. Heat enough **shortening** in a large heavy skillet to make a layer about ¼ in. deep. Shape fish mixture into cakes about ½ in. thick. Fry cakes until crisp and browned. Turn and brown the second side. Serve with **Tomato Sauce** (page 307).

FISH BALLS (Fiskekroketer)

Set out a deep saucepan or automatic deep fryer (page 11) and heat fat to 350°F.

Heat over low heat in a saucepan
  2 tablespoons butter
Blend in
  ¼ cup sifted all-purpose flour
  1 teaspoon salt
  ⅛ teaspoon pepper
Heat until mixture bubbles. Add gradually, stirring constantly
  1 cup cream
Cook rapidly, stirring constantly, until mixture thickens. Remove from heat; cool.

Meanwhile, flake finely (page 9) enough cooked fish to yield
  3 cups flaked cooked fish (cod, trout, fillet of sole, whitefish)

When sauce is cool, blend in the fish and
  1 egg yolk, beaten
Shape mixture into balls 1 in. in diameter. Dip balls into
  2 eggs, slightly beaten
To coat evenly, roll balls in
  1 cup fine dry bread crumbs
Deep-fry Fish Balls in heated fat. Deep-fry only as many balls at one time as will float uncrowded one layer deep in the fat. Turn balls often. Deep-fry 2 min., or until lightly browned. Drain; remove to absorbent paper.
    About 5 doz. Fish Balls

COD ALLA MARINARA (Baccalà alla Marinara)

▲ *Base Recipe*

Grease a 1½-qt. casserole.

Thaw, if frozen
  2 lbs. cod steaks, about 1 in. thick
Place cod in casserole and set aside.

Combine in a saucepan
  2 cups canned tomatoes, sieved
  ¼ cup pitted and chopped green olives
  2 tablespoons capers
  1 tablespoon parsley
  1 teaspoon salt
  ½ teaspoon pepper
  ½ teaspoon oregano
Bring to boiling and pour over cod in casserole.

Bake at 350°F 25 to 30 min., or until the fish flakes when gently pierced with a fork.
    4 servings

—HALIBUT ALLA MARINARA
(Pesce alla Marinara)

Follow ▲ Recipe. Substitute **halibut steaks** for the cod.

FISH AU GRATIN
(Fiskgratin)

Classic in its simplicity and popular everywhere.

Butter a shallow 1½-qt. baking dish.

Set out
1½ lbs. fish fillets (cod, haddock, flounder or pike)
(If using frozen fish fillets, thaw according to directions on package.) Put fillets into the baking dish and sprinkle with
1 teaspoon salt
½ teaspoon pepper
3 tablespoons lemon juice
Dot with
1 tablespoon butter
Cover baking dish with aluminum foil or parchment paper and bake at 350°F 20 to 25 min., or until fish flakes (page 9).

Meanwhile, prepare and keep hot
2 cups Medium White Sauce (double recipe, page 304; use cream for liquid; after cooking sauce, remove from heat and blend in until smooth 2 egg yolks, slightly beaten, and 2 tablespoons butter)

Remove fish from oven and drain off any excess liquid. Pour the sauce over the fish and sprinkle with
2 tablespoons grated cheese

Place baking dish on broiler rack. Place broiler rack under broiler with top of baking dish 4 to 5 in. from heat. Broil 1 to 2 min., or until lightly browned. *4 or 5 servings*

BAKED HADDOCK WITH OYSTERS

▲ Base Recipe

Oysters lend glamor here to the modest haddock.

Grease a shallow baking dish.

Have ready
2 haddock fillets, about 1 lb. each

(If frozen, thaw, following directions on package.) Place one fillet in baking dish.

Drain, reserving liquor for use in other food preparation
½ pt. oysters
Pick over oysters to remove shell particles.

Prepare
1½ cups cracker or bread crumbs
Reserve ½ cup for topping. Mix remaining 1 cup of crumbs with
1 tablespoon chopped parsley
½ teaspoon salt
⅛ teaspoon pepper
Lightly toss crumb mixture with
2 tablespoons butter, melted
Coat oysters evenly with the crumb mixture. Lightly spoon oyster mixture evenly over fillet in dish. Drizzle with
2 tablespoons lemon juice
Top with second fillet. Fasten edges together with wooden picks or metal skewers.

Brush top surface with
Melted butter
Sprinkle reserved ½ cup crumbs over buttered surface of fish. Dot with
2 tablespoons butter

Bake at 350°F 30 to 40 min., or until fish flakes (page 9) easily. *5 or 6 servings*

—BAKED HALIBUT WITH OYSTERS

Follow ▲ Recipe. Substitute **2 halibut steaks,** cut ½ in. thick, for the haddock fillets.

FISH DINNER

Grease a 2-qt. casserole. Set out a small saucepan.

Blanch, toast (pages 9 and 10) and set aside
½ cup (about 2¾ oz.) almonds
Shred
4 oz. sharp Cheddar cheese (about 1 cup, shredded)
Set aside.
Drain, reserving liquid in a 2-cup measuring cup
1 jar (3 oz.) pimiento-stuffed olives (about ½ cup)
Cut each olive crosswise into about 4 slices. Set olives and reserved liquid aside.

Cut off root end and a thin slice from stem end of
1 medium onion
Peel, rinse, finely chop onion and set aside.

Cut into 1-in. pieces and, if necessary, remove any small bones from
2 lbs. fish fillets (such as ocean perch, haddock or flounder)
Place one half of the fish in an even layer in casserole and set remaining fish aside.

Heat in the saucepan over low heat
¼ cup butter or margarine

Add the onion and cook about 5 min., stirring occasionally. Blend in
¼ cup all-purpose flour
½ teaspoon salt
½ teaspoon monosodium glutamate
Few grains pepper
Heat until mixture bubbles. Remove from heat.

Add to olive liquid
1¼ cups milk (or enough to make 1½ cups liquid)

Add gradually, stirring constantly, the flour mixture. Bring to boiling, stirring constantly; cook 1 to 2 min. longer. Remove from heat and set aside.

Wash, pare, slice thinly and set aside
3 to 4 medium (about 1½ lbs.) potatoes

Sprinkle about one half of the shredded cheese evenly over fish in casserole. Add the toasted almonds to make a layer. Cover with a layer of the remaining fish, and then a layer of the remaining cheese. Top with a layer of the sliced olives. Pour over about two thirds of the sauce. Cover with overlapping layers of the potato slices and the remaining sauce.

Bake at 375°F about 60 min., or until potatoes are tender. *About 8 servings*

FISH PUDDING
(Fiskepudding)

Butter a 1-qt. casserole.

Set out
2 lbs. fish fillets (haddock, cod)
Force fish through the medium blade of a food chopper.

Mix in
2 teaspoons salt
½ teaspoon pepper
⅛ teaspoon nutmeg
Blend to form a smooth paste
1½ tablespoons cornstarch
2 tablespoons water
Add gradually, stirring in
1 cup cream
Blend with fish mixture. Turn into casserole.

Set in a large baking pan and pour very hot water into pan to a 1-in. depth.

Fish Dinner

Bake at 350°F 40 to 50 min., or until a metal knife comes out clean when inserted halfway between center and edge of casserole.

Serve with

Mushroom Sauce II (page 304)

6 servings

FISH POTATO CASSEROLE
(Hal Burgonyával)

▲ *Base Recipe*

Butter an 11x7x2-in. baking dish. Set out a large heavy skillet.

Wash, pare and cut into halves

6 medium (about 2 lbs.) potatoes

Cook potatoes (page 313) 20 to 30 min., or until tender when pierced with a fork.

A few minutes before the potatoes are tender, set out

2 lbs. fish fillets, such as pike or trout

(If fish is frozen, thaw, following directions on package.) Cut into serving-size pieces. Sprinkle fish with a mixture of

1 teaspoon salt
¼ teaspoon pepper

Set aside.

Heat in the skillet over low heat

¼ cup butter or margarine

Place fish in skillet and lightly brown on both sides; carefully turn only once. Cook 8 to 10 min., or until fish flakes (can be separated with a fork into thin, layer-like pieces).

Drain potatoes. To dry potatoes, shake pan over low heat. Mash or rice potatoes. Whip into the potatoes

¼ cup butter or margarine

Add gradually, whipping in a mixture of

⅓ cup hot milk
1 teaspoon salt
1 teaspoon paprika
⅛ teaspoon pepper

Whip potato mixture until light and fluffy. Spread in bottom of baking dish.

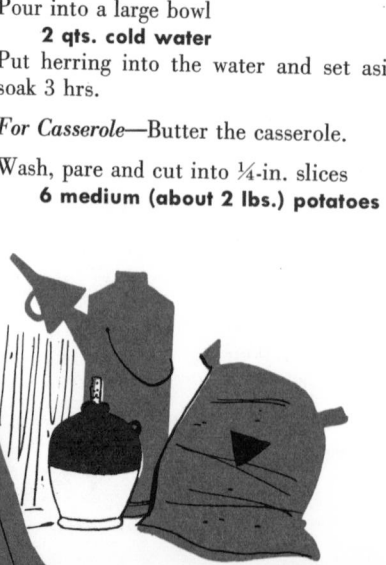

Set out

1¼ cups dairy sour cream
¼ cup (about 1 slice) fine dry bread crumbs

Spread one third of the sour cream over potatoes. Add a layer of

3 tablespoons finely chopped onion

Sprinkle onion with 3 tablespoons of the bread crumbs. Arrange fish in layers on top of crumbs. Sprinkle with remaining crumbs and

2 tablespoons grated Parmesan cheese

Spread remaining sour cream over cheese. Sprinkle with

Paprika

Bake at 350°F 20 to 30 min., or until thoroughly heated. Serve immediately. *6 servings*

—SAUSAGE POTATO CASSEROLE
(Kolbász Burgonyával)

Follow ▲ Recipe. Substitute **10 (about 2 lbs.) thuringer sausage links** for fish. To prepare sausage links, cook covered, in water to cover, over medium heat about 15 min.

BAKED HERRING CASSEROLE
(Heringsauflauf)

▲ *Base Recipe*

A favorite fish dish of northern Germany.

A 2-qt. casserole will be needed.

To Prepare Herring—With a sharp knife, cut off and discard heads of

2 salt herring

Slit along underside of the fish from head to tail. Remove entrails and scrape insides well. Cut off tails and fins. Rinse thoroughly in cold water. Cut off and discard a ½-in. strip along each underside edge of fish. Make a slit along backbone just to the bone. Using a sharp knife, carefully pull and scrape the blue skin from the flesh. Be careful not to tear fish. Then cut along backbone through bone and flesh to remove one side of fish. Repeat for the second side. Remove as many of the small bones as possible without tearing fish.

Pour into a large bowl

2 qts. cold water

Put herring into the water and set aside to soak 3 hrs.

For Casserole—Butter the casserole.

Wash, pare and cut into ¼-in. slices

6 medium (about 2 lbs.) potatoes

Baked Stuffed Fish

Cook (page 313) about 10 min., or until potatoes are nearly tender. Drain potatoes and set aside.

Clean and chop

2 medium onions

Drain the herring, cut into small pieces and mix with the onion. Arrange a layer of potatoes in the casserole. Top with a layer of the fish-onion mixture. Repeat layers of potatoes and fish-onion mixture, ending with potatoes.

Beat until thick and lemon-colored

2 egg yolks

Stir in until blended a mixture of

1 cup dairy sour cream
1 teaspoon salt
¼ teaspoon monosodium glutamate
⅛ teaspoon pepper

Pour over the potatoes. Top with

⅓ cup buttered bread crumbs (page 9)

Bake at 350°F 35 to 40 min., or until lightly browned. *6 servings*

—FRESH HADDOCK, HAMBURG STYLE
(Schellfisch nach Hamburger Art)

Follow ▲ Recipe. Omit salt herring. Cut into small pieces **2 lbs. dressed haddock**. Combine with the onion.

BAKED FISH STEAKS

▲ *Base Recipe*

Set out a bake-and-serve platter or shallow baking dish.

Wash, coarsely chop, mix and line platter or baking dish with equal quantities of

Parsley
Celery leaves
Onion (outer skin removed)

Have ready

2 lbs. fish steaks, cut about 1 in. thick (such as cod, haddock, halibut, salmon or tuna)

(If using frozen steaks, thaw following directions on package.)

Sprinkle on both sides of steaks a mixture of
  1½ teaspoons curry powder
  ½ teaspoon salt
  ⅛ teaspoon pepper
Arrange on parsley mixture. On each steak, place a slice of
  Bacon

Bake uncovered at 350°F 25 to 30 min., or until fish flakes (page 9) when gently pierced with a fork.

Serve with **Maître d'Hôtel Butter** (page 309).
6 servings

—BAKED FILLETS

Follow ▲ Recipe. Substitute **fillets** such as cod, perch, trout or flounder for steaks. Substitute **tarragon** for curry powder.

—BAKED STUFFED FISH

Follow ▲ Recipe. Substitute **3 lbs. dressed fish** such as snapper, halibut, trout or whitefish for steaks. Wash and dry thoroughly. Omit curry powder. Loosely fill fish cavity with **Herb Stuffing** (one half recipe, page 273). To close cavity, skewer and lace with cord. Bake 40 to 60 min., or until fish flakes easily when pierced with a fork. Remove skewers and cord before serving.

FILLET OF SOLE IN WHITE WINE
(Filetti di Sogliole al Vino)

Grease a shallow 2-qt. casserole with a cover.

Thaw, if frozen, and place in casserole
  2 lbs. fillet of sole
Pour over fillets a mixture of
  ½ cup dry white wine
  ½ cup (1 medium) chopped onion
  3 tablespoons melted butter or margarine
  2 bay leaves, crushed
  1 teaspoon chopped parsley
  ½ teaspoon salt
  ¼ teaspoon pepper

Cover casserole and bake at 375°F for 25 min., or until the fish flakes when gently pierced with a fork.
6 servings

POMPANO EN PAPILLOTE

Set out a shallow baking dish and four 12x9-in. pieces parchment paper.

To Prepare Filling—Set out
  ½ cup coarsely chopped cooked shrimp
  ½ cup coarsely chopped cooked lobster meat
Prepare
  1 cup Thick White Sauce (page 304; use cream for liquid)
Stir into cooked sauce
  ¼ cup white wine

Mix in the chopped shrimp and lobster meat. Cool mixture and chill in refrigerator.

To Make Papillotes—Fold the pieces of parchment paper into halves crosswise. From other paper make a pattern of a half heart that is as wide and long as the folded parchment paper. Place straight edge of pattern on folded edge of parchment paper, trace and cut out heart shapes. Set papillotes aside.

To Fill Papillotes—Set out
  4 fresh pompano fillets, about 6 oz. each
Cut each fillet into halves crosswise, keeping halves of the same fillet together. (If frozen, thaw fillets completely.)

Brush inside of each paper heart with **cooking or salad oil** (not olive oil). On one half of each paper heart lay fillet half, skin-side down.

Sprinkle the four halves with one half of a mixture of
  1 teaspoon salt
  ½ teaspoon monosodium glutamate
  ⅛ teaspoon pepper
Remove filling from refrigerator and divide into fourths. Place one fourth on each fillet half; pat with back of spoon over fish. Place matching fillet half over filling, skin-side up. Sprinkle all four with remaining seasoning mixture. Fold top half of paper heart over fillets. (Top half will not meet edge of bottom paper half.)

To Seal Papillotes and Complete—Starting at top end of paper heart, fold small portion of bottom edge over top and crease; hold folded portion down with one hand while folding and creasing next portion, overlapping it on folded portion. Repeat, following outline of heart, folding and creasing. At end, twist paper. Repeat with remaining papillotes. Place papillotes in the baking dish.

Bake at 375°F about 30 min., or until papers are puffed and golden brown.

Cut a cross in top of paper with scissors just before ready to serve.
4 servings

BAKED KIPPERS
(Bakt Nedlagt Röket Sild)

Butter a 2-qt. casserole.

Wash, pare and cut into ¼-in. slices
  4 medium (about 1¼ lbs.) potatoes
Cook (page 313) about 10 min., or until potatoes are partially tender. Drain the potatoes and set them aside.

Clean and cut into ¼-in. slices
  2 medium onions
Drain on absorbent paper
  4 cans (3¼ oz. each) Norway kippers
Cover bottom of casserole with a layer of the partially cooked potatoes. Brush with
  3 tablespoons melted butter
Cover with a layer of the onion slices. Top onions with a layer of kippers. Repeat layers of potatoes, onions and kippers.

Beat slightly
  4 eggs
Add gradually, stirring constantly
  2 cups milk
  1 teaspoon salt
  ¼ teaspoon pepper
Pour over the fish in the casserole. Set casserole in a large baking pan and pour very hot water into pan to a 1-in. depth.

Bake at 350°F 40 min., or until a metal knife comes out clean when inserted halfway between center and edge of casserole.

Garnish with **sprigs of parsley** and serve immediately.
6 to 8 servings

PERCH WITH PARSLEY AND DILL
(Abbore)

Dill comes from an old Norse word meaning "to lull." But here it adds a lively touch to fish.

Butter a 1½-qt. baking dish.

Have ready
  8 medium perch, dressed
Season fish with a mixture of
  1 teaspoon salt
  ½ teaspoon pepper

Baked Kippers

Cover bottom of baking dish evenly with
¼ cup finely chopped parsley
Arrange the fish in the baking dish. Top with
2 tablespoons finely chopped parsley
2 tablespoons chopped fresh dill
or 1 teaspoon dill seed
Pour around the fish
¼ cup hot water

Bake at 350°F 20 to 25 min., or until fish flakes (page 9).

Carefully transfer fish to a warm serving platter and garnish with
Sprigs of parsley
Sprigs of dill
Lemon wedges

4 servings

ALSATIAN SALMON PATE
(Pâté Chaud de Saumon)

The making of pâtés is practically an institution in Alsace, which boasts 42 traditional recipes! Surprisingly, as many of these are made with fish as with goose livers. Other interesting pâtés may be prepared by substituting pike or trout for the salmon.

Butter a 2-qt. casserole with a tight-fitting cover.

Clean, remove scales and bones from
2 lbs. salmon
Rinse salmon with cold water and cut into 1-in. pieces. (If fish is frozen, thaw following directions on package.) Marinate (page 10) salmon at least 3 hrs., turning occasionally, in
1 cup dry white wine

About 30 min. before end of marinating period, clean, remove scales and bones, and rinse with cold water
½ lb. fresh cod
Finely chop cod and blend thoroughly with
⅓ cup (about 1 slice) fine dry bread crumbs
2 large truffles (page 12), finely chopped
2 egg yolks, well beaten
1 tablespoon butter or margarine, melted

Add
½ teaspoon salt
⅛ teaspoon pepper
Stir in the wine in which the salmon has been marinated. Blend mixture thoroughly.

Arrange one half of the salmon pieces on bottom of baking dish; cover with one half of the cod mixture. Repeat layering.

Cover and bake at 350°F about 50 min. Remove cover and bake 10 min. longer, or until lightly browned.

8 to 10 servings

CURRIED TUNA BASKETS

Thoroughly grease 4 large ramekins or individual casseroles.

Cut off tops, wash, pare or scrape and cut into small thin strips
4 medium carrots
Put into a saucepan with
½ cup chopped onion
1 teaspoon salt
¼ teaspoon monosodium glutamate
Cover with boiling water and cook covered 10 to 20 min., or until vegetables are just tender; drain well, reserving liquid.

Meanwhile, prepare
Baking Powder Biscuit dough (page 92)
Roll dough to ¼-in. thickness; cut into 2-in. biscuits. Line sides of ramekins with overlapping biscuit border. Set ramekins aside.

Blend thoroughly
1¼ cups (10½-oz. can) condensed cream of celery soup
1 cup (7-oz. can, drained) tuna, coarsely flaked (page 9)
½ cup reserved vegetable liquid
1½ teaspoons lemon juice
½ teaspoon curry powder

Stir in cooked vegetables. Bring mixture to boiling. Immediately pour into ramekins. Fold biscuits over filling.

Bake at 450°F 10 to 15 min., or until biscuits are lightly browned.

4 servings

Curried Tuna Baskets

Rice-Stuffed Peppers

TUNA-STUFFED PEPPERS

▲ *Base Recipe*

A special kind of main dish that's easy to serve and easy to eat.

Grease a 2-qt. baking dish.

Rinse and slice stem ends from
4 large green peppers
With a knife or spoon, remove and discard white fiber and seeds. Rinse cavities. Drop into boiling salted water to cover and simmer 5 min. Remove peppers from water and invert. Set aside to drain.

Meanwhile, prepare
1 cup Medium White Sauce (page 304; use cream for milk)
Blend into sauce and set aside
1 teaspoon lemon juice
½ teaspoon paprika

Drain and flake (page 9) with a fork
1 can (7 oz.) tuna or 1 can (7¾ oz.) salmon
Combine with sauce; spoon mixture into peppers. Place in baking dish.

Bake at 350°F about 15 min.

Just before serving, sprinkle with
¼ cup (1 oz.) grated Parmesan or Cheddar cheese

Other kinds of fish may be used, or combinations of several kinds.

4 servings

—RICE-STUFFED PEPPERS

Follow ▲ Recipe. Substitute **Tomato Sauce** (page 307) for Medium White Sauce. Substitute **½ lb. ground beef** for tuna. Brown ground beef in **2 tablespoons shortening**, breaking it into small pieces with a fork or spoon. Prepare **⅔ cup packaged precooked rice** following directions on package. Mix with sauce and browned meat. Heap mixture into peppers and bake as in ▲ Recipe.

BROILED FISH STEAKS

▲ Base Recipe

Grease a broiler rack.

Have ready

2 lbs. fish steaks such as cod, halibut or salmon

(If using frozen steaks, thaw according to directions on package.) If possible, bring horseshoe ends of each steak together and fasten with a small skewer to give oval shape. Arrange steaks on the greased broiler rack. Brush tops of steaks with one half of a mixture of

¼ cup butter or margarine, melted
1 tablespoon chopped parsley or chives

Place under broiler with top of steaks 2 in. from heat; broil 5 to 8 min. (depending upon thickness of steaks). Season steaks with one half of a mixture of

1 teaspoon salt
½ teaspoon monosodium glutamate
⅛ teaspoon pepper

Turn steaks carefully and brush second side with remaining butter mixture. Broil 5 to 8 min. longer, or until fish flakes (page 9) easily. Sprinkle second side with remaining seasoning mixture. Remove carefully to warm serving platter.

Serve with **lemon wedges** or **Hollandaise Sauce** (page 306).   *6 servings*

—BROILED FISH FILLETS

Follow ▲ Recipe. Substitute **fish fillets** for steaks. Place skin-side down on greased rack. Broil 10 to 12 min. without turning. Brush fillets with **butter or margarine** during broiling.

Broiled Fish Fillets

POMPANO FLORENTINE

▲ Base Recipe

Prepare and keep warm over simmering water
2 cups Mornay Sauce (page 305)

Meanwhile, cook in a heavy saucepan, following package directions
1 pkg. (10 oz.) frozen chopped spinach

Grease a broiler rack.

Have ready
4 pompano fillets, about 6 oz. each
(If frozen, thaw completely.) Place fillets skin-side down on the greased broiler rack. Brush fillets with one half of a mixture of
¼ cup butter or margarine, melted
2 tablespoons lemon juice

Place under broiler with tops of fillets 2 in. from heat. Broil about 8 min., or until fish flakes (page 9). Brush fillets with remaining butter mixture during broiling

When spinach is tender, drain in sieve, pressing spinach firmly against sieve with back of spoon to remove water thoroughly. Blend spinach into 1 cup of the Mornay Sauce; keep mixture hot.

When fillets flake, sprinkle with a mixture of
1 teaspoon salt
½ teaspoon monosodium glutamate
⅛ teaspoon pepper
Spoon about ¾ cup of the Mornay Sauce over fillets. Broil 2 to 3 min., or just until sauce is lightly browned.

Arrange spinach mixture in four servings on a warm serving platter. Carefully place fillets over spinach. Pour remaining Mornay Sauce around fillets.

Garnish serving platter with
Parsley sprigs
Fancy-cut lemons
Turnip Roses (page 419)
Serve immediately.   *4 servings*

—POMPANO WITH GARDEN FRESH SPINACH

Follow ▲ Recipe. Substitute **1½ lbs. fresh spinach** for frozen spinach. Remove and dis-

card tough stems, roots and bruised leaves from spinach. Wash leaves thoroughly by lifting up and down several times in a large amount of cold water. Lift leaves out of water each time before pouring off water. When free from sand and gritty material, transfer spinach to a large heavy saucepan. Cook (page 313) 3 to 10 min. When spinach is tender, drain as in ▲ Recipe. Finely chop spinach and drain again; combine with sauce.

BROILED TROUT

Green and speckled trout from Louisiana waters are relished by Creoles for breakfast.

Grease a broiler rack.

Set out
4 small, cleaned and scaled trout, about 10 oz. each
(If using frozen trout, thaw, following directions on package.) Do not cut off tails or heads; game fish are usually served with the head and tail on. Arrange trout on the greased broiler rack. Brush with one half of a mixture of
¼ cup butter or margarine, melted
1 tablespoon lemon juice

Place under broiler with top of trout 2 in. from heat; broil 5 to 8 min. (depending upon thickness of trout).

Season trout with one half of a mixture of
2 teaspoons salt
1 teaspoon monosodium glutamate
½ teaspoon paprika
¼ teaspoon pepper
Turn trout carefully and brush second side with remaining butter mixture. Broil 5 to 8 min. longer, or until fish flakes (page 9) easily. Sprinkle second side with remaining seasoning mixture. Remove carefully to a warm serving platter. Garnish with **parsley**.

Serve trout with **lemon wedges**.   *4 servings*

BROILED FISH CALIFORNIAN

▲ Base Recipe

Grease a broiler rack.

Broiled Fish Californian

Set out

> **6 dressed small whole fish (such as sea bass, sea trout or yellow perch), 8 to 10 oz. each**

(If fish is frozen, thaw, following directions on package.)

Brush cavities of fish with a mixture of

> **¼ cup lemon juice**
> **1 teaspoon salt**
> **1 teaspoon monosodium glutamate**
> **¼ teaspoon pepper**
> **⅛ teaspoon nutmeg**

Place fish on greased broiler rack. Brush with one half of

> **¼ cup butter or margarine, melted**

Place under broiler with tops of fish 3 in. from heat. Broil 5 to 8 min. (depending upon thickness of fish). Turn fish carefully and brush second side with remaining melted butter or margarine. Broil 5 to 8 min. longer, or until fish flakes (page 9) easily.

While fish is broiling, prepare
> **Raisin Sauce II (page 308)**

Remove fish carefully to a warm serving platter. Pour hot sauce over fish. Garnish with **lemon wedges** and **sprigs of mint**. Serve immediately.

6 servings

—FISH AMANDINE

Follow ▲ Recipe. Substitute Amandine Sauce for the Raisin Sauce.

For Amandine Sauce—Heat ½ cup butter or margarine and 1 cup (about 5½ oz.) blanched

Broiled Swordfish

(page 9) slivered almonds. Cook slowly, stirring constantly until almonds are delicately browned. Remove from heat and blend in **1 teaspoon salt, ½ teaspoon monosodium glutamate** and ½ **teaspoon lemon juice.**

BROILED SCROD

▲ *Base Recipe*

A scrod is a young cod which has been cut open, the head, tail and bones removed, and thus is ready to cook.

Prepare
> **Maître d'Hôtel Butter (page 309)**

Set aside.

For Broiled Scrod—Set out on a cutting surface
> **2 cod, 1 to 2 lbs. each**

Split the fish down the back and remove backbone.

Set out
> **¼ cup melted butter**
> **1 teaspoon salt**
> **½ teaspoon pepper**

Grease a broiler rack.

Place the fish on the broiler rack, skin side down. Brush with some of the butter and season with some salt and pepper. Place under broiler with top of fish 2 in. from heat; broil 5 to 8 min. Turn fish, brush with remaining butter and season with salt and pepper. Broil 5 to 8 min. longer, or until fish flakes (page 9) easily.

Pour drippings over fish and serve with Maître d'Hôtel Butter. *4 to 6 servings*

—BROILED MACKEREL

Follow ▲ Recipe. For cod, substitute **1 mackerel**, about 2 lbs. Increase broiling time to about 10 min. on each side, or until skin is brown and crisp.

—BROILED SWORDFISH

Follow ▲ Recipe. For Maître d'Hôtel Butter, substitute the following Lemon Butter Sauce: combine **½ cup melted butter, ¼ cup lemon juice** and **1 tablespoon chopped parsley.** For cod, substitute **slices of swordfish**, cut about ¾ in. thick (1 slice for each serving).

FISH POACHED IN COURT BOUILLON
(Poisson Poché au Court Bouillon)

The French improve the flavor of fish and shellfish by poaching them in Court Bouillon. They serve the fish with an appropriate sauce—made with cream, eggs or white wine—to enhance its goodness.

For Court-Bouillon—Heat in a large kettle
> **1 qt. water**

Add
> **½ cup vinegar**
> **1 carrot, sliced**
> **2 small onions, sliced**
> **3 or 4 shallots, minced (optional)**
> **½ lemon, sliced**
> **1 teaspoon salt**
> **Herb bouquet (page 9)**

When the mixture comes to boiling, reduce heat, cover and simmer 20 min. Add
> **4 peppercorns**

Cook 10 min. longer. Strain. *About 1 qt. stock*

To Poach Fish—Tie any cleaned **fish** in cheesecloth to prevent breaking. Place in skillet. Cover with stock and poach, covered, over low heat. Allow about 8 min. per pound of fish or until fish flakes. Drain. Remove cheesecloth. Serve hot with **melted butter** or **Hollandaise Sauce** (page 306) or **Bercy Sauce** (page 305).

If the fish is to be served cold, let it remain in the Court Bouillon until completely cool. This will prevent drying. Remove cheesecloth. Serve.

Servings depend upon variety and size of fish

ROLLED FISH FILLETS
(Rullet Fiske Filet)

Prepare and chill in refrigerator
> **Sauce for Lobster (page 311)**

Set out
> **1½ lbs. fish fillets (sole, cod, halibut, haddock)**

(If using frozen fish fillets, thaw following directions on package.) Cut fillets with a sharp knife into strips 10x1-in. Starting with the narrow end, roll fillets tightly and fasten with a wooden pick. Put fish rolls into a saucepan with
> **3 cups water**
> **1½ teaspoons salt**

Bring to boiling. Reduce heat and simmer 6 to 8 min., or until fish flakes (page 9). Carefully remove fish rolls from liquid with a slotted spoon. Drain on absorbent paper. Chill in refrigerator.

When ready to serve, remove wooden picks and arrange fish rolls on a serving platter. Cover with the sauce. Garnish with
> **Pimiento**
> **Sprigs of parsley**

About 2 doz. fish rolls

POACHED FISH WITH HORSERADISH SAUCE
(Hal Torma Mártással)

For special tang and zip—typically Hungarian, too—when available, grate fresh horseradish root into sauce.

Set out a 10-in. skillet with a tight-fitting cover. Also have ready a large square of cheesecloth.

For Poached Fish—Set out

1½ lbs. fish fillets, such as perch or bass

(If fish is frozen, thaw following directions on package.) Tie fish loosely in cheesecloth to prevent breaking; place into skillet. Add in order

Boiling water (enough to just cover fish)
½ cup dry white wine
1 small onion, chopped
2 tablespoons chopped parsley
1 teaspoon salt
⅛ teaspoon pepper

Cover skillet and simmer about 10 min., or until fish flakes (can be separated with a fork into thin, layer-like pieces). Meanwhile, prepare sauce.

For Horseradish Sauce—Blend well

1 cup dairy sour cream
2 to 3 tablespoons prepared horseradish
2 tablespoons grated lemon peel

Pour sauce into serving dish; set aside.

Drain fish; remove cheesecloth. Place fish onto warm platter. Serve with sauce.

4 servings

FINNAN HADDIE
(Röket Kolje)

Have ready

2 lbs. finnan haddie (smoked haddock)

Put fish on a length of cheesecloth and tie ends securely. Lower fish into a large saucepot or kettle and add

3 qts. water
2 teaspoons salt

Bring to boiling. Reduce heat and simmer 10 to 15 min., or until fish flakes (page 9).

Meanwhile, prepare

2 Hard-Cooked Eggs (page 133)

Chop one of the peeled eggs finely and set aside. Cut the other peeled egg into slices crosswise and set aside.

When fish flakes, carefully lift from the saucepot or kettle. Remove the cheesecloth and lift fish onto a warm serving platter.

Melt over low heat

¼ cup butter

Remove from heat; add the finely chopped egg and pour over the fish. Garnish with the egg slices and

Sprigs of parsley
Lemon wedges

6 servings

SALT FISH DINNER
(Cape Cod Turkey)

▲ Base Recipe

The codfish enjoys a unique place in the history, the cooking traditions and the esteem of coastal New England. Originally referring to cod prepared in this way, Cape Cod Turkey now is a nickname for any cooked fish.

Set out

1½ lbs. salt codfish

Tear or cut into serving-size pieces. Cover cod with cold water to freshen. Let stand for about 4 hrs., changing water 3 to 4 times.

About 1 hour before dinner is to be served, prepare beets. Leave on 1- to 2-in. stem and the root end (this helps beets to retain red color) and cut off leaves from

6 medium (about 1 lb.) beets

Wash and cook covered in boiling salted water to cover 30 to 45 min., or until beets are just tender. When beets are tender, drain. Peel off and discard skins, stems and root ends. Add to beets

2 tablespoons butter

Set aside to keep warm.

Drain fish and remove any pieces of bone. Cover again with fresh, cold water and bring slowly to boiling. Reduce heat, cover and simmer about 20 min., or until fish flakes (page 9). Drain.

Meanwhile, wash, pare and cook (page 313)

6 medium (about 2 lbs.) potatoes

Cook about 25 to 35 min., or until tender. Drain. Shake pan over low heat to dry potatoes. Add to potatoes

2 tablespoons butter

While potatoes and fish cook, prepare

Egg Sauce (page 304)

Remove rind and cut into thin slices

¼ lb. salt pork

Place pork slices in a skillet and fry over low heat until pork slices are crisp and lightly browned. Remove from fat with a slotted spoon to absorbent paper. Reserve pork drippings for use in other food preparation.

To serve, arrange fish pieces in center of a large, warm platter. Garnish fish with the salt pork slices. Spoon the egg sauce over top. Place cooked buttered potatoes along one side of the platter and cooked buttered beets along the other side.

About 6 servings

—RED SALT FISH HASH

Use ingredients saved over from ▲ Recipe or prepare vegetables and fish. Combine **2 cups cold flaked fish, 2 cups diced cold cooked beets, 2 cups diced cold cooked potatoes,** and **1 tablespoon minced onion.** Season with **¼ teaspoon pepper.** Beat and mix in **1 egg.** Heat in a skillet enough **fat** to make 3 tablespoons (or use salt pork drippings). Add the hash mixture, pressing into an even layer. Cook over low heat until a brown crust is formed on the bottom. Loosen edges and bottom of hash; shake skillet back and forth occasionally to prevent burning while hash is browning. When hash is done, lightly fold in half and serve on a warm platter.

—SALT FISH HASH

Follow recipe for Red Salt Fish Hash. Omit the beets.

FISH PAPRIKA
(Hal Paprikás)

Fish Paprika is sometimes called Fish Soup or Fisherman's Soup (Szegedi Halászlé). It is prepared by fishermen over open fires along Hungary's riverbanks, especially along the Tisza.

Fishermen who know the art of preparing this dish claim that it must be prepared immediately after the fish are caught and it must be made of many different kinds of fish, both small and large. Carp, bass and sterlet are always included. The fish are scaled, cleaned and cut into broad strips. Some of the small fish are put into a deep kettle or bogracs first, followed by alternate layers of onion slices, carp and bass. The choicest fish, usually the sterlet, are placed on top. Salt, paprika and water are added. While the Szegedi Halaszlé is cooking, the fishermen shake the kettle from time to time instead of stirring. This prevents the fish from breaking apart.

Only the best fish from the top layers are eaten. The small fish on the bottom of the pan serve merely to enrich the flavor.

By using at least three different kinds of fresh water fish, we can prepare a soup similar to that of the Hungarian fishermen. We cook it indoors, though some fishermen might prefer to use an open fire for their fresh "catch."

Set out a 4-qt. kettle with a tight-fitting cover.

Clean and wash in cold salted water
   3 to 4 lbs. assorted fresh water fish (such as trout, pike and bass)
(If fish is frozen, thaw, following directions on package.) Cut into 2-in. pieces.

Cut into slices ¼ in. thick
   2 or 3 large (1 to 1½ lbs.) onions
Cover bottom of kettle with one layer of onion slices; add a layer of fish. Alternate in layers, remaining onion slices and fish. Add to the kettle
   2 qts. water (or enough to cover contents)
Bring to boiling; reduce heat to simmer and season fish with
   1 tablespoon paprika
   2 teaspoons salt
Cover kettle and simmer 30 to 40 min., or until fish flakes (can be separated with a fork into thin, layer-like pieces). Shake pan gently from time to time during cooking; do not stir. Remove fish from kettle with slotted spoon to large serving bowl or soup tureen. Strain the broth over fish. Serve hot in bowls.

About 8 servings

FISH STEW WITH RED WINE
(Matelote au Vin Rouge)

Several kinds of fresh water fish are required to make a typical matelote, although occasionally just one variety is used. If so, the dish is garnished with seafood, such as mussels, shrimp, or even a crayfish cooked in Court Bouillon. Eels are traditional to the dish, but pike, perch and haddock may be used. Red wine is most common but even champagne is used in its home province, and cider in apple-rich Normandy.

Set out a large heavy skillet with a tight-fitting cover.

Clean, wash, dry and cut into thick slices
   2 lbs. fish
Put fish into skillet and add
   2 cups red wine
   1 carrot, sliced
   1 onion, minced
   2 cloves garlic, cut in halves
   1 teaspoon salt
   ¼ teaspoon pepper
   Herb bouquet (page 9)
Bring to boiling.

Heat in a small saucepan
   3 tablespoons brandy
Ignite brandy and immediately pour over the

fish. When the flame has burned out, cover the pan. Cook fish slowly 15 to 20 min., or until the fish flakes when pierced with a fork. Remove fish to a warm serving dish. Keep hot. Strain and reserve cooking liquid.

Blend thoroughly in same skillet
   3 tablespoons melted butter
   2 tablespoons all-purpose flour
Cook over low heat until mixture bubbles. Remove from heat; gradually stir in cooking liquid. Cook rapidly; stir constantly until sauce thickens. Boil 1 to 2 min. longer. Pour sauce over the fish.

Serve with **Croutons** (page 39) browned in garlic butter. Garnish with tiny **cooked onions, sautéed mushrooms** or cooked **shrimp.**

4 servings

CREOLE BOUILLABAISSE

Frenchmen use the fish and shellfish of the Mediterranean for their fish stew. The Creoles have a similar method of cooking fish, using red snapper and redfish from the Gulf waters.

Set out a deep 10-in. heavy skillet with a tight-fitting cover. (Skillet should be large enough to allow fish fillets to lie only one layer deep, or cook one half of the fish at one time.)

Set out
   1 lb. red snapper fillets
   1 lb. redfish fillets
(If fish is frozen, thaw, following directions on the package.) Thoroughly rub into fish fillets a mixture of
   2 teaspoons minced parsley
   1 teaspoon salt
   ¾ teaspoon thyme
   ½ teaspoon allspice
   ⅛ teaspoon pepper
   2 bay leaves, finely crushed
   1 clove garlic, finely minced
Set fillets aside.

Clean and chop
   1 large onion (about ¾ cup, chopped)
Heat in the skillet over low heat
   2 tablespoons olive oil
Add chopped onion and fillets. Cover and cook over low heat 10 min., turning fillets once.

Meanwhile, wash
   3 large ripe tomatoes
Dip into boiling water for about 1 min. to loosen skins. Peel tomatoes, cut out and dis-

card stem ends. Cut tomatoes into ¼-in. slices and set aside.

Remove fish fillets from skillet, set aside and keep warm.

Pour into the skillet, stirring well
   1 cup white wine
Add tomato slices and bring mixture to boiling. Add
   3 or 4 lemon slices
   1 cup hot Fish Stock (page 57) or hot water
   ¾ teaspoon salt
   ⅛ teaspoon pepper
   Dash cayenne pepper
Simmer about 25 min., or until liquid is reduced almost one half.

Add the fish fillets to skillet and continue cooking 5 min. longer.

Meanwhile, blend several tablespoons of the liquid in which the fish is cooking with
   Pinch of saffron
When fish has cooked 5 min., spread saffron mixture over fillets. Remove fillets from sauce and place on
   6 slices buttered toasted bread
Pour sauce over fish.

Serve at once. *6 servings*

"BOILED" SALMON
(Kokt Lakse)

There is an old story in Norway that servants sometimes set the terms of their service on the understanding that they should not be fed salmon too often. This superb game fish, prized by gourmets, exists in unbelievable abundance in Norwegian waters.

Set out a large saucepot with a tight-fitting cover and a rack.

Have ready
   4- to 6-lb. piece salmon, dressed
Place salmon on a length of cheesecloth and tie ends securely.

Bring to boiling in the saucepot
   3 qts. water
   ¼ cup lemon juice
   3 tablespoons salt
Lower the fish carefully into the saucepot so that it rests on the rack. Cover and simmer

Chilled Salmon Steaks

10 to 15 min., or until fish flakes (page 9). Carefully lift fish from saucepot. Place on a large platter or baking sheet to cool. Chill in the refrigerator.

Meanwhile, prepare
   Sauce for Salmon (page 311)

When ready to serve, remove fish carefully from cheesecloth and place on a serving platter. Scrape off skin (if any). Garnish with
   Sprigs of parsley
   Lemon wedges
Serve with the sauce.   *10 to 12 servings*

CHILLED SALMON STEAKS

Prepare in a large kettle with a cover
   3 cups quick meat broth (page 10)
Add to the broth and bring broth to boiling
   2 teaspoons lemon juice
   2 teaspoons mixed pickling spice
   1 teaspoon monosodium glutamate
   ½ teaspoon salt
   1 stalk celery, with leaves, cut in pieces
   1 sprig parsley

Set out
   4 salmon steaks, ¾ to 1 in. thick
(If using frozen salmon, thaw following directions on package.) Arrange the salmon steaks on a large square of cheesecloth. Pull up corners of cheesecloth and tie together. Lower salmon into the kettle. Cover and simmer 10 to 12 min., or until salmon flakes easily (page 9) but is firm and whole. Remove kettle from heat; do not unwrap salmon or remove from liquid. Cool; chill in refrigerator.

Meanwhile, prepare
   Special Hot Sauce (page 310)

Rinse and cut into halves
   2 limes or lemons
Using a sharp knife, remove one half of pulp section from each lime or lemon half. Fill with the Special Hot Sauce.
A few minutes before serving, drain salmon in cheesecloth over liquid. (Liquid may be strained for later use in making sauces or as a base for soups.) Carefully remove salmon from

cheesecloth, pat dry with absorbent paper and arrange on serving platter with the lime or lemon cups. Garnish with
   Sprigs of watercress
   Onion slices
   Green pepper rings
Serve with remaining sauce.   *4 servings*

CREAMED KIPPERS AND MUSHROOMS
(Nedlagt Röket Sild
med Chompineon i Hvit Saus)

Drain on absorbent paper
   4 cans (3¼ oz. each) Norway kippers
Cut into 1-in. pieces and set aside.
Prepare
   3 cups Mushroom Sauce II (three times recipe, page 304)
Add the kippers and heat thoroughly.

Turn into a warm serving dish or casserole and garnish with
   Sprigs of parsley
Serve with
   Toast triangles
                              6 servings

CREAMED FINNAN HADDIE

   ▲ *Base Recipe*

In the top of a double boiler or in a covered saucepan, soak for 1 hour
   2 lbs. finnan haddie (smoked haddock)
in
   Milk to cover
Heat slowly 20 min. Drain, reserving milk for sauce. Set aside.
Prepare
   2 Hard-Cooked Eggs (page 133)
Cool peeled eggs and coarsely chop.

Melt in top of double boiler over low heat
   3 tablespoons butter
Blend in
   3 tablespoons all-purpose flour
   1 teaspoon monosodium glutamate
Heat until mixture bubbles. Remove from heat and add gradually, stirring constantly, the milk "stock" from the fish. (If "stock" measures less than 1½ cups liquid, add enough cream to make this amount.) Return to heat.

Cook rapidly, stirring constantly, until sauce thickens. Remove from heat and vigorously stir about 3 tablespoons of the sauce into
   3 egg yolks, slightly beaten
Immediately return mixture to double boiler. Cook over simmering water 3 to 5 min. Stir slowly and constantly to keep mixture cooking evenly. Remove from simmering water; cool slightly.

Remove bones and skin from fish. Break fish into pieces and combine with the sauce. Gently stir in the chopped eggs. Place over simmering water until thoroughly heated.

Turn into a warm serving dish. Garnish with **parsley** and serve at once with **baked potatoes**.
                              About 6 servings

—CREAMED CODFISH

Follow ▲ Recipe. Substitute **codfish** for finnan haddie. If cod is salted, cover with water and heat slowly to boiling. (If dry and/or very salty, drain and again cover with water and bring to boiling.) Drain, cover with milk and proceed as in ▲ Recipe.

—CREAMED FINNAN HADDIE WITH CRACKER TIPS EN CASSEROLE

Follow ▲ Recipe. Add **3 tablespoons capers** with the chopped eggs. Pour fish mixture into a greased 2-qt. casserole. Insert into mixture at a slant **10 to 12 crisp thin crackers**, lightly buttered (leave about half of each cracker exposed). Set casserole in a 375° oven 10 to 12 min., or until crackers are lightly browned. Garnish with **parsley**.

Note: Codfish may be substituted for the finnan haddie. Soak as in Creamed Codfish.

Creamed Finnan Haddie and Creamed Codfish with Cracker Tips en Casserole

Mushroom-Stuffed Sole Distingué

SALMON CHEESE CAKES
(Syrinki)

These delicate pancakes make a nourishing main dish for a quick lunch.

Set out a griddle or heavy skillet.

Drain, reserving liquid for sauce
1 can (16 oz.) salmon
Combine in a bowl
1 egg, beaten
1 lb. cream-style cottage cheese
Beat to blend thoroughly; mix in the flaked salmon and
¼ cup all-purpose flour
½ teaspoon dill weed (optional)
¼ teaspoon salt
Freshly ground black pepper
Drop mixture by tablespoonfuls onto a hot well-greased griddle, forming 3- to 3½-in. cakes. Flatten slightly with a spatula and cook slowly about 5 min. on each side, or until golden.

Serve hot with **Sour Cream Sauce** (below).
About 8 cakes

—SOUR CREAM SAUCE

Combine
Reserved salmon liquid
1 cup dairy sour cream
1 teaspoon lemon juice
Serve cold or heated slightly over hot water.

MUSHROOM-STUFFED SOLE DISTINGUE

Mornay sauce completes this fillet of sole dish.

Set out a skillet and a shallow baking dish or casserole; grease the baking dish.

Have ready
6 fillets of sole

Heat in skillet
2 tablespoons butter or margarine
Add and cook over medium heat until lightly browned, stirring occasionally
1½ cups chopped mushrooms
2 tablespoons chopped onion
Add and mix well
½ cup finely chopped toasted walnuts
¼ cup chopped parsley
¼ teaspoon salt
⅛ teaspoon dill weed
Drizzle the sole with
Juice of 1 lemon
Sprinkle with
Salt and pepper
Place a spoonful of mushroom mixture on the skin side of each fillet and roll up. Place in baking dish. Brush fish with **melted butter or margarine.**

Bake at 350°F 25 to 30 min., or until fish flakes easily when tested with a fork.

While fish is baking, prepare **Mornay Sauce** (page 305). To serve, pour hot sauce over fish and garnish with **walnut halves.**   *6 servings*

FRIED FILLETS WITH ORIENTAL-STYLE SAUCE

Set out a large heavy skillet.

Have ready
1 lb. sole or other fish fillets

Combine in a saucepan and bring to boiling
1½ cups flaked coconut
1½ cups water
Strain, pressing coconut to extract all of the liquid; reserve ½ cup of the coconut to use for garnish (see Toasted Coconut, below). Return strained coconut liquid to the saucepan and set aside.

Soak until softened, following package directions
1 pkg. (2 oz.) dried Japanese mushrooms
Drain soaked mushrooms, reserving the liquid. Reserve 8 or 9 mushrooms for garnish. Slice remaining mushrooms and set aside.

Coat the fish fillets with
Cornstarch
Then dip in
1 egg, slightly beaten
Dip again in cornstarch, coating all sides. Heat in the skillet **butter or margarine** to cover bottom. Add fillets and fry on both sides until lightly browned and fish flakes easily when tested with a fork. Arrange fish on a heated platter and keep warm.

Blend 2 tablespoons of the mushroom liquid into
2 teaspoons cornstarch
Add mixture to the coconut liquid in saucepan. Blend well and add the sliced mushrooms along with
1 scallion, sliced
¼ cup sugar
¼ to ½ teaspoon salt
3 to 4 teaspoons lemon juice
Cook and stir until boiling; continue cooking until thickened and smooth.

Spoon sauce over fish and garnish with reserved whole mushrooms heated in some of their liquid and the Toasted Coconut.   *About 4 servings*

—TOASTED COCONUT

Lightly brown the ½ cup drained coconut in
1 tablespoon butter or margarine in a skillet, stirring occasionally to brown evenly.

SHELLFISH

STEAMED CLAMS

To the true New Englander, participation in a steamed clam dinner is a gustatory rite requiring special vestments in the form of large napkins tucked under the chin, and special preparation of the appetite, which should be equal to consuming an average of twenty succulent soft-shelled clams almost without pause!

Preparation of Clams—Pick over **clams** to remove any open ones, or those which are too large (over 2½ inches) or too small (under 2 inches). Thoroughly scrub and rinse clams. Put into a large kettle with about ½ inch **boiling water** in the bottom, covered with a tight-fitting cover, and steamed just until all

are open, with an occasional stir to insure that the heat reaches them all. (Discard any clams which do not open.)

To Serve Steamed Clams—Heap clams in a big heated bowl or on a platter. Accompany with cups of **clam broth** (which has been strained through two or three thicknesses of clean cheesecloth to remove any sand) and with small warm dishes of **melted butter.**

To Eat Clams—Remove the clam from its shell with an oyster or dinner fork (experienced Yankees often prefer to use their fingers), and remove the black cap with the trailing "veil" or "beard" from the head. Then dip the whole clam first into the clam broth and then into the melted butter, and devour it without further ceremony.

FRIED CLAMS

Fill a deep saucepan or automatic deep fryer with

**Vegetable shortening, all-purpose
    shortening or oil for deep-frying**
Heat slowly to 350°F.

Drain and set aside
1 qt. fresh clams, shucked
Combine

**2 eggs, beaten
2 tablespoons milk
2 teaspoons salt
Few grains pepper**
Set out

3 cups dry bread crumbs
Dip clams in egg mixture and roll in crumbs. Fry (using a wire basket if available) in heated fat 1 to 2 min., or until brown. Drain on absorbent paper. Repeat procedure, being sure that temperature of fat is 350°F before each frying.

Serve hot with **tartar sauce.**

About 6 servings

CLAM CORN CASSEROLE

Grease a 1½-qt. casserole.

Have ready
**1 cup canned cream-style corn
½ cup cracker crumbs**
Drain
1 can (10 oz.) clams
Strain liquid and add
Milk (enough to make 1 cup liquid)
Rinse clams under running cold water. Combine the clams, liquid, corn, cracker crumbs and

**3 eggs, beaten
1 tablespoon butter or margarine, melted
2 tablespoons chopped onion
2 tablespoons chopped pimiento
½ teaspoon salt
Few grains cayenne pepper**
Turn mixture into the casserole.

Bake at 350°F about 1 hr., or until set.

4 or 5 servings

CLAM PIE

Hard-shelled clams (quahogs, as they're called in New England) or sea clams may be used for this pie. It is an excellent dish to serve to company.

Set out an 8-in. pie pan.

Wash and cook (page 313)
2 medium (about ⅔ lb.) potatoes
Cook about 25 to 35 min., or until potatoes are tender when pierced with a fork. Drain. Dry potatoes by shaking pan over low heat. Peel, dice and set aside.

Drain, reserving clam liquid
1 to 1½ pts. shucked clams
Finely chop the clams and set aside.

Heat in a large skillet
3 tablespoons butter
Add and cook until onion is almost tender, occasionally moving and turning with a spoon
**½ cup (about 1 medium) chopped
    onion**

Blend in a mixture of
**2 tablespoons all-purpose flour
¼ teaspoon monosodium glutamate
¼ teaspoon salt
Few grains pepper**
Heat until mixture bubbles. Remove from heat.

Add gradually, stirring constantly, ¼ cup of the reserved clam liquid and
¼ cup milk
Return to heat and bring rapidly to boiling, stirring constantly. Cook 1 to 2 min. longer.

Remove from heat; add the diced cooked potatoes and chopped clams. Turn into the pie pan.

Prepare and roll as directed
Pastry for 1-Crust Pie (page 485)
Cut a simple design near center of pastry to allow steam to escape during baking. Loosen one half of pastry and fold over other half. Moisten edge of pie pan with cold water. Lift pastry gently and place over hot mixture in pie pan; unfold. Trim edge so pastry extends about ¾ in. beyond edge of pie pan. Fold extra pastry under edge and gently press edges to seal to moistened rim of pie pan. Flute (page 9) or press with a fork.

Bake at 450°F about 20 min., or until pastry is lightly browned.   *4 to 6 servings*

NEW ENGLAND CLAMBAKE

The oldest eating tradition along New England's rocky shore line is the clambake, a legacy from the Indian tribes who greeted the white man. In the three centuries that the tradition has been honored by New Englanders the form and method of the bake have remained essentially unchanged. Basically it consists of green corn, clams and fish closely covered and steamed in seaweed over white-hot stones to a medley of goodness that has not its equal this side of paradise.

The modern clambake is apt to include foods not known to the Indians—sweet potatoes, chicken, sausages, butter for the clams, coffee for the follow-up—and such latterday trappings as cheesecloth, paper bags or wire baskets to confine the separate foods, but fundamentally the clambake has withstood the advances of civilization and mechanization.

Every bakemaster has his own opinion on how to conduct the preliminary stages of a clambake, but the general working procedure shapes up to something like this: A fire of wood is burned in a shallow pit over layers of stones about the size of cabbages. When the stones are crackling hot (after about an hour of exposure to intense heat), embers and ashes are swept away and a layer of wet seaweed or rockweed is laid atop the stones to a depth of several inches. Ingredients follow in this approximate order—well-scrubbed clams (a dozen or two per serving) followed by a second layer of seaweed; unpared white or sweet potatoes or both; ears of corn stripped to the inner husks and cleaned of silk; fish, preferably bluefish, in paper bags; sausages similarly encased; vivacious lobsters (one per serving) arranged side by side in a large square of cheesecloth securely tied; broiler chickens, if you must, also tied in cheesecloth. Four to six inches of seaweed are now laid snugly over the food and the imposing heap is closely shrouded with a clean wet canvas. The edges of the canvas are weighted down with stones and the tiniest apertures are plugged with seaweed. For an hour (some experts allege a longer time is allowable) the pungent steam of seaweed and clam penetrate the edibles. The tantalizing aroma slowly seeps through the containing canvas with stimulating effect on the taste buds of the waiting company. Appetites may be appeased with relishes—sliced cucumbers, tomatoes and onions—bread, and cups of clam broth. Then with the ceremonial lifting of the canvas the banquet is ready. Tin plates are piled high. Melted butter daubs unheeding chins. The feast is on!

For small family-size clambakes variations on the standard procedure are permitted, and a barrel or a washboiler is an acceptable container for the bake. A wooden-hooped barrel is recommended and a lining of sheet-metal scraps will prevent the hot stones from igniting its sides. For best results the barrel must be sunk in sand, the deeper the better. The washboiler clambake is an admittedly weak facsimile of the genuine article. The traditional foods are layered atop a rack placed in the bottom of the boiler over an inch or so of water.

287

Patio Crab Casserole

Crab Meat Ramekins

The lid must fit tightly. Cooking is over an open fire. And to be certain that everyone will have as many steamed clams as he wants, it is best to prepare an auxiliary supply (see Steamed Clams, page 286).

FRIED SOFT-SHELLED CRABS

The crab is most highly esteemed by epicures in its soft-shelled stage, just after it has shed its hard shell and before the new one grows. Crabs may be broiled and served with seasoned melted butter, or deep-fried, but many New England homemakers prefer to pan-fry them, believing that this best preserves their elusive flavor.

Set out a large heavy skillet.

Kill, by inserting a sharp-pointed, narrow-bladed knife into the body between the eyes

12 soft-shelled crabs

Wash, cut off the pointed apron on underside and cut off spongy material beneath points at each end of shell. Turn the crab and cut off the face.

Coat crabs evenly with a mixture of

½ cup all-purpose flour
½ teaspoon salt
¼ teaspoon pepper

Shake off excess flour. Set crabs aside.

Heat in the skillet over low heat

½ cup butter

Fry only as many crabs at one time as will lie flat in the pan. Cook until crabs are browned and crisp on the edges. Turn and brown second side.

Serve crabs hot with **brown butter.**

4 to 6 servings

PATIO CRAB CASSEROLE

Grease a 3-qt. shallow baking dish.

Have ready

2 cups chopped onion
1 lb. frozen or 2 cans (7½ oz. each)
Alaska king crab, drained and sliced
1½ cups shredded extra sharp
Cheddar cheese

Heat in a skillet

¼ cup butter or margarine

Add onion and cook until tender, stirring occasionally. Mix in the crab and

½ cup snipped parsley
2 tablespoons capers
2 tablespoons snipped chives
2 pimientos, diced

Heat, stirring occasionally.

Meanwhile, put into a bowl

1½ cups corn muffin mix
⅛ teaspoon salt
1 egg, fork beaten
½ cup milk
1 cup canned cream-style corn

Stir just until moistened (batter should be lumpy). Turn into the baking dish and spread evenly to edges. Spoon hot crab mixture over batter and then spread with

2 cups dairy sour cream

Sprinkle cheese over all.

Bake at 400°F 25 to 30 min. If desired, garnish top with **watercress.** *About 12 servings*

CRAB MEAT RAMEKINS

▲ *Base Recipe*

Grease 6 ramekins or individual casseroles.

Prepare in top of double boiler

Thin White Sauce (page 304)

Remove from heat and vigorously stir 3 tablespoons sauce into

2 egg yolks, slightly beaten

Immediately stir into hot sauce in double boiler and cook over simmering water 3 to 5 min.; stir slowly to keep mixture cooking evenly. Remove from heat; add gradually, stirring in

1 tablespoon lemon juice
1½ teaspoons onion juice
¼ cup minced green pepper

Remove bony tissue from

2 cups (two 7-oz. cans) crab meat

Add to sauce, mixing gently with a spoon.

Turn mixture into ramekins. Top with

¾ cup buttered dry bread crumbs (page 9)

Bake at 350°F 20 to 25 min., or until crumbs are lightly browned. *6 servings*

—CRAB MEAT AND TOMATO SAUCE

Follow ▲ Recipe. Prepare **Medium White Sauce** (page 304) instead of Thin White Sauce, substituting **tomato juice** for liquid. Decrease crumbs to ½ cup and combine with ¼ cup (1 oz.) grated Parmesan cheese.

CREAMED CRAB MEAT AND MUSHROOMS

Prepare

6 Croustades (page 110)

Remove and discard bony tissue and set aside to drain

1 can (6½ oz.) crab meat (about 1⅓ cups, drained)

Clean

½ lb. mushrooms

Remove stems from caps. Slice the stems and caps separately. Set caps aside.

Put stems into a small saucepan and add

Cold water (to barely cover)

Bring slowly to boiling, reduce heat and simmer 15 min. Remove from heat and drain stems, reserving liquid in a 1-cup measuring cup for liquids. Set aside.

Heat in top of a double boiler over low heat

5 tablespoons butter or margarine

Add sliced mushroom caps, drained mushroom stems and

1 tablespoon minced onion
1 tablespoon chopped chives
1 tablespoon chopped parsley

Cook over medium heat, occasionally moving and turning vegetables with a spoon, until mushrooms are lightly browned and tender. Remove vegetables with a slotted spoon to a small bowl and set aside.

Add to the mushroom liquid and set aside

Milk (enough to make 1 cup liquid)

Marinated Shrimp and Ol

Blend into butter in double boiler top

6 tablespoons all-purpose flour
1 teaspoon salt
Few grains cayenne pepper
Few grains nutmeg

Heat until mixture bubbles. Remove from heat. Add liquid mixture gradually while stirring constantly. Return to heat and cook, stirring constantly, until mixture thickens. Cook 1 to 2 min. longer.

Remove from heat and vigorously stir about 3 tablespoons of hot mixture into

3 egg yolks, slightly beaten

Immediately return mixture to double boiler top and cook over simmering water 3 to 5 min., stirring slowly to keep mixture cooking evenly. Add the crab meat and vegetable mixture. Stirring occasionally, cook 10 to 12 min., or until thoroughly heated. Remove from heat.

Stirring vigorously with a French whip, whisk beater or fork, add to the sauce in small amounts

2 cups dairy sour cream

Add and stir in

¼ cup sherry

Serve immediately. *6 servings*

BAKED CRAB MEAT DELICIOUS

Grease a 1-qt. shallow baking dish.

Have ready

1½ slices dry white bread, finely crumbled (about 1 cup crumbs)
1 Hard-Cooked Egg (page 133), mashed
1½ tablespoons minced pimiento
1½ tablespoons minced green pepper
1 tablespoon minced parsley
1 lb. cooked crab meat, flaked and bony tissue removed

Lightly toss bread crumbs with

1 tablespoon butter, melted

Add and toss together the mashed egg, minced pimiento, green pepper, parsley and

2 tablespoons Worcestershire sauce
2 tablespoons mayonnaise
1 egg, slightly beaten
¼ teaspoon salt
Few grains pepper

Add the crab meat and toss gently. Turn into the baking dish. Mix and spoon over top

3 tablespoons mayonnaise
1 tablespoon cream

Set in a 350°F oven about 20 min., or until thoroughly heated. *4 to 6 servings*

CRAB CAKES

Have ready

¾ cup finely chopped onion
1 cup soft bread crumbs
1 lb. crab meat, flaked and bony tissue removed

Heat in a skillet

3 tablespoons butter or margarine

Add onion and cook about 3 min., stirring occasionally. Remove from heat and stir in bread crumbs and then the flaked crab meat.

Mix

3 eggs, beaten
¾ teaspoon salt
1 teaspoon dry mustard
⅛ teaspoon paprika
1 teaspoon Worcestershire sauce
3 tablespoons chopped parsley

Combine with crab meat mixture and add enough to hold together

Cream (1 to 2 tablespoons)

Shape into about twelve 2½-in. cakes. Coat with

All-purpose flour (about ½ cup)

Heat in a large skillet a ¼-in. layer of

Butter, margarine or cooking oil

Add cakes and fry until golden brown, about 3 min. per side. Serve with **lemon wedges.**

4 to 6 servings

ELEGANT PARTY CRAB CREPES

Set out a heavy saucepan and a large shallow baking dish.

Prepare 16 to 18 crêpes (use your favorite recipe); keep warm until ready to use.

Have ready

3 pkgs. (6 oz. each) thawed frozen or
2 cans (7½ oz. each) drained
Alaska king crab, sliced

Heat in saucepan

1 tablespoon butter or margarine

Add and cook until lightly browned

4 to 6 mushrooms, sliced through caps and stems
2 tablespoons minced onion

Remove mushrooms with a slotted spoon and keep warm.

Add to the saucepan

6 tablespoons butter or margarine

Blend in

⅓ cup all-purpose flour
1 teaspoon rosemary leaves, crushed
½ teaspoon seasoned salt
Few grains pepper

Gradually add, stirring constantly

1½ cups chicken broth

Cook and stir until boiling; cook about 2 min. and remove from heat.

Stir in, a small amount at a time

1½ cups dairy sour cream

Mix in the mushrooms, the crab meat and

1 tablespoon snipped parsley

Spoon about ¼ cup filling along center of

Elegant Party Crab Crêpes

each crêpe and roll up. Arrange, overlapping side down, in a single layer in the baking dish. Top with

1 cup shredded Swiss cheese

Sprinkle with

Paprika

Heat in 350°F oven 10 to 15 min., or until cheese is melted and crêpes are thoroughly heated. Garnish with **sprigs of parsley.**

16 to 18 crab-filled crêpes

CRAB CROQUETTES

A deep saucepan or an automatic deep fryer will be needed.

Prepare and set aside to cool

1 cup Thick White Sauce (page 304)

Mix

2 cups (about 9 oz.) fresh, frozen or drained canned crab meat (bony tissue removed)
1 tablespoon chopped parsley
½ teaspoon onion juice

and a mixture of

½ teaspoon salt
¼ teaspoon dry mustard
Few grains white pepper

Lightly mix in the cooled white sauce. Put mixture into refrigerator to chill.

About 20 min. before deep-drying, put **fat** into the pan or fryer and heat to 375°F (page 11).

Allowing ⅓ cup mixture for each croquette, shape chilled mixture into rolls, balls or cones. Put into a shallow pan

1 cup (about 3 slices) fine dry bread crumbs

Roll the croquettes in the bread crumbs. Dip in a mixture of

1 egg, slightly beaten
2 tablespoons milk or water

Roll again in the crumbs.

Fry croquettes in heated fat. Fry only as many croquettes at one time as will lie uncrowded one layer deep in fat. Fry 3 to 4 min., or until golden brown. Lift out with slotted spoon and drain croquettes over fat for a second before removing to absorbent paper.

About 4 servings

Bouillabaisse

AFRICAN ROCK LOBSTER-ASPARAGUS EN CASSEROLE

Set out a 2- to 2½-qt. casserole or shallow baking dish.

Drop into **boiling salted water** in a large kettle

6 frozen South African rock lobster tails (3 oz. each)

Return water to boiling, reduce heat and cook gently 3 min. Remove cooked lobster tails and place under cold water until cool enough to handle. With scissors, cut along each edge of bony membrane on the underside of shell. Remove meat. Dice half of the meat and cut remainder into chunks; set aside.

Cook, following package directions

1 or 2 pkgs. (10 oz. each) frozen asparagus spears
1 pkg. (8 oz.) spaghetti

Meanwhile, heat in saucepan

¼ cup butter or margarine
Stir in and cook until bubbly
¼ cup all-purpose flour
Add and blend thoroughly
2 cups chicken broth

Cook and stir until sauce comes to boiling; cook 2 min. or until thickened and smooth.

Immediately blend 3 tablespoons sauce into

2 egg yolks, slightly beaten
Stir into the hot sauce. Cook about 3 min. longer, stirring constantly. Blend in

½ cup light cream
2 to 3 teaspoons Worcestershire sauce
1 teaspoon dry mustard (blended with 1 tablespoon cold water)

Stir in the diced lobster and heat thoroughly.

Arrange drained asparagus spears in bottom of the casserole. Season with **monosodium glutamate.** Cover with hot cooked spaghetti and pour over the hot lobster sauce. Sprinkle generously with

Shredded Parmesan or Romano cheese
Top with lobster chunks and
¼ cup toasted slivered almonds

If desired, place under broiler heat several minutes to lightly brown the top.   *6 servings*

COOKED CRAYFISH OR ROCK LOBSTER TAILS

The crayfish or spiny lobster is found in the Gulf waters. Only the tails of the crayfish are found in the retail market and are available under such names as South African lobster tails, Langoosta, rock lobster, or spiny lobster tails. They may be purchased in the frozen state.

Bring to boiling in a large kettle or saucepot

2 to 3 qts. water
¼ cup lemon juice
1 tablespoon salt
½ cup (1 medium) chopped onion
½ cup chopped celery with leaves
1 clove garlic, finely minced

Add to boiling water

2 fresh-frozen crayfish or rock lobster tails (8 oz. each)

Cover, bring water again to boiling, lower heat and simmer 11 min., or until meat is completely white and opaque. (If tails were thawed before cooking, simmer 9 min.)

Drain and cover with cold water; drain again. With scissors cut through and remove thin shell on underside; remove vein. Gently pull meat from shell. (Shells may be saved for serving crayfish.)

Chill crayfish meat in refrigerator. Chop or dice and use in recipes as directed.

About 2 cups crayfish meat

"BOILED" LOBSTER
(Kokt Hummer)

Fresh dill garnishes the smörgåsbord lobster.

Fill a large deep kettle or saucepot with a tight-fitting cover about ⅔ full (or enough to cover the lobster) with

Hot salted water (1 tablespoon salt per qt. water)

Bring water rapidly to boiling. Grasp by the back and plunge head first into the water

1 live lobster, about 1½ lbs.

Cover, bring water again to a rolling boil. Reduce heat and simmer 15 to 20 min. Drain and cover with cold water to chill. Drain again. Place shell-side down on a cutting board.

Twist off the two large claws, the smaller ones and the tail. With a pair of scissors cut or with a sharp knife slit the bony membrane on the underside of tail. Remove and discard the intestinal vein. Using a sharp knife, cut completely through tail crosswise into 1½ in. pieces. With a sharp knife, cut lobster into halves; cut completely through entire length of body and through shell. Remove and discard the intestinal vein running lengthwise through center of body. Remove and discard stomach

(a small sac which lies in the head) and spongy lungs (which lie in upper body cavity between meat and shell).

If present, remove and reserve the tomalley (green liver) and the coral (bright red roe) to be used along with the lobster meat or as a garnish. Using a sharp knife, cut the body crosswise into 1½-in. pieces.

Chill pieces of lobster and the claws in refrigerator. When ready to serve on the smörgåsbord, arrange pieces of lobster and claws on a platter, shell-side up, to resemble a whole lobster. Garnish lobster with

Fresh dill or parsley
Serve with
Sauce for Lobster (page 311)
About 8 to 10 servings

Note: To use cooked lobster meat in food preparation, do not cut lobster into pieces. Spread tail shell apart and remove meat in one piece; remove meat from body shell. Disjoint the large claws and crack with a nutcracker. A nut pick may be helpful in removing meat from small joints and claws. Chill in refrigerator, cut and use as desired.   *1¼ cups lobster meat*

BROILED LOBSTER

Purchase for each serving
1 live lobster, about 1½ lbs.
(Live lobsters may be killed at the market.)

To Kill and Clean Lobster—Place lobster on a cutting board with back or smooth shell up. Hold a towel firmly over head and claws. Quickly insert the point of a sharp heavy knife into center of the small cross on the back of the head. This kills the lobster by severing the spinal cord. Before removing knife, bear down heavily, cutting through entire length of body and tail. Pull halves apart; remove and discard the stomach (a small sac which lies in the head) and the spongy lungs (which lie in upper body cavity between meat and shell). Remove and discard the dark intestinal vein running through center of body. Crack claws with a nutcracker.

Place lobster, shell-side down, on preheated broiler pan. Brush meat generously with
Melted butter

Place in broiler with top of lobster 3 to 4 in. from heat. Broil about 10 min., basting frequently with butter.

Serve with additional melted butter and
Lemon wedges

LOBSTER FRA DIAVOLO
(Aragosta alla Diavola)

Prepare
Marinara Sauce (page 163)

While sauce is cooking, fill large deep kettle, with a cover, about ⅔ full with water. Bring to a rapid boil and plunge head first into boiling water (one at a time)
2 live lobsters, about 1½ lbs. each
Cover and boil about 8 min. (Lobsters will turn pink.) Remove with tongs. Slit underside lengthwise and remove stomach, lungs and vein. Set lobsters aside and keep warm.

When sauce is cooked, stir in
½ cup red wine
Few grains cayenne pepper
Bring sauce to boiling and pour over lobsters. Serve immediately.   *2 servings*

LOBSTER THERMIDOR

▲ *Base Recipe*

Purchase
3 live lobsters, about 1½ lbs. each
Live lobsters may be killed at the market. (Or see Broiled Lobster, page 290, *To Kill and Clean Lobster*.) Cut completely through shell to divide lobsters into halves; disjoint large and small claws.

Heat in a large heavy skillet with a tight-fitting cover
6 tablespoons butter
Add halves of lobster, meat-side down, to skillet. Place large and small claws on top. Cover; cook slowly 12 to 15 min., or until tender. (Lobster meat cooked at a high temperature becomes tough and is difficult to remove from shell.)

Meanwhile, prepare
1½ cups Medium White Sauce (one and one half times recipe, page 304; stir into sauce 3 tablespoons heavy cream after removing from heat)
Set aside.

Clean and chop enough mushrooms to yield
⅔ cup chopped mushrooms
Heat in a saucepan
3 tablespoons butter
Add the mushrooms and
2 tablespoons chopped shallots or onion

Cook over medium heat until mushrooms are tender and lightly browned and onion is soft. Occasionally move and turn mixture with a spoon. Remove from heat.

Blend into one half of the white sauce
3 tablespoons heavy cream
2 tablespoons white wine
1 teaspoon finely chopped chervil or parsley
½ teaspoon Worcestershire sauce
and a mixture of
½ teaspoon dry mustard
¼ teaspoon salt
⅛ teaspoon cayenne pepper
Add to the mushroom-onion mixture. Cook over low heat, until thoroughly heated, moving and turning mixture gently with a spoon.

When lobster is done, starting at tail, with first and second fingers, gently pry lobster meat from shells, reserving shells. Remove meat from large claws. Place the shells, cavity side up, on a baking sheet and heat at 325°F about 7 min., or until shells are heated.

Meanwhile, cut the lobster meat into 1-in. pieces and blend into the sauce.

Remove shells from oven and sprinkle over interior of each
White wine (about ¼ teaspoon per shell)
Fill the lobster shells with the lobster mixture.

Pour remaining white sauce into the top of a double boiler. Stir over low heat until heated. Vigorously stir about 3 tablespoons sauce into
1 egg yolk, slightly beaten
Immediately return mixture to top of double boiler. Stirring constantly, cook over simmering water 3 to 5 min. Remove from heat and blend in
2 tablespoons whipped cream
Spoon over lobster mixture in the shells.

Set out
2 tablespoons grated Parmesan cheese
Sprinkle 1 teaspoon of the cheese over each of the filled shells.

Place baking sheet on broiler pan with tops of food 2 to 3 in. from heat. Broil 2 to 3 min., or until lightly browned.   *6 servings*

—ROCK LOBSTER THERMIDOR

Follow ▲ Recipe. Substitute **6 rock lobster tails (8 oz. each)** for the whole lobsters. Bring **3 qts. water, 1 tablespoon salt,** and **1 teaspoon monosodium glutamate** to boiling in a

Rock Lobster Thermidor

large heavy saucepot or kettle. Add the lobster tails and again bring to boiling. (Lobster tails may be cooked frozen or thawed.) Reduce heat and cook 9 to 11 min., or until lobster meat is tender. Drain and rinse with cold water. Using scissors or a sharp knife, cut through and remove thin shell on underside of each lobster tail. Insert fingers under meat and carefully pull meat out. If desired, omit the grated Parmesan cheese and browning. Reheat filled shells thoroughly in 325°F oven.

CURRY OF LOBSTER

▲ *Base Recipe*

Set out a heavy 3-qt. saucepan.

Prepare and set aside
Curry Sauce (page 306)

Prepare
2 live lobsters, about 1¼ lbs. each (see "Boiled" Lobster, page 290)
Cut the lobster meat into pieces and set aside.

Reheat Curry Sauce in the saucepan. Blend in
¼ cup cream
2 tablespoons sherry
¼ teaspoon Worcestershire sauce
Add the cut lobster meat and cook over medium heat 2 to 3 min., or until mixture is thoroughly heated.

Serve with
Perfection Boiled Rice (page 165)
Preserved kumquats
Chutney
Shredded coconut
Finely chopped roasted peanuts
                    4 servings

—CURRY OF FRESH CRAB MEAT

Follow ▲ Recipe. Substitute **3 cups (about 12 oz.) fresh lump crab meat** (bony tissue removed) for the lobster.

—CURRY OF FRESH SHRIMP

Follow ▲ Recipe. Omit the lobster. Prepare **2 lbs. fresh shrimp with shells** (see Cooked Shrimp, page 294). Heat **½ cup butter** in a skillet. Add the shrimp and cook over medium

Lobster in Ramekins

heat, moving and turning gently with a spoon until shrimp are lightly browned. Pour contents of the skillet into the Curry Sauce.

—CURRY OF CHICKEN

Follow ▲ Recipe. Substitute **3 cups cubed cooked chicken** for the lobster.

—CURRY OF CHICKEN LIVERS

Follow ▲ Recipe. Rinse **2 lbs. chicken livers** in cold water and drain on absorbent paper. Heat **¼ cup butter** in a skillet, add the chicken livers and cook over medium heat, moving and turning gently with a spoon until browned on both sides. Drain chicken livers on absorbent paper and substitute for the lobster.

—CURRY OF LAMB

Follow ▲ Recipe. Substitute **3 cups cubed cooked lamb** for the lobster.

LOBSTER IN RAMEKINS

This subtle blend of delicate lobster and cheese, served with fragrant coffee, is a gastronomic experience you will remember fondly.

Set out 6 shell-shaped ramekins or individual casseroles.

Drain and remove any bits of shell and bony tissue from
    3 cans (6 oz. each) lobster meat (about 3 cups)
Set aside 6 pieces of claw meat for garnish. Cut remaining meat into small pieces. Set aside.

Shred and set aside
    2 oz. Gruyère cheese (about ½ cup, shredded)

Heat in a saucepan
    ¼ cup butter

Blend in
    ¼ cup sifted all-purpose flour
    1 teaspoon salt
    ¼ teaspoon paprika
    ⅛ teaspoon nutmeg
Heat until mixture bubbles. Remove from heat and add gradually, stirring in
    2 cups cream
Return to heat. Cook rapidly, stirring constantly, until mixture thickens. Cook 1 to 2 min. longer. Mix in the lobster meat and heat thoroughly. Remove from heat and blend in
    2 tablespoons sherry
Spoon mixture into ramekins. Sprinkle with the shredded cheese. Garnish each ramekin with a piece of lobster claw meat.

Put ramekins under broiler with tops of ramekins 2 to 3 in. from heat. Broil 5 min., or until cheese is bubbly.

Garnish with **parsley sprigs**. *6 servings*

LOBSTER NEWBURG

▲ Base Recipe

Born in "foreign parts," i.e. New York, this recipe was adopted by New England.

Cut into 1-in. pieces and set aside
    2 cups cooked lobster meat (see "Boiled" Lobster, page 290)

Melt in the top of a double boiler
    ¼ cup butter
Blend in
    2 cups cream
    ¾ teaspoon salt
    ¼ teaspoon monosodium glutamate
    ⅛ teaspoon pepper
    ⅛ teaspoon nutmeg
Bring just to boiling. Stir in lobster and cook over low heat until lobster is thoroughly heated. Vigorously stir about 3 tablespoons of hot mixture into
    4 egg yolks, slightly beaten
Immediately blend into hot mixture. Place over simmering water and cook 3 to 5 min., or just until mixture thickens. Stir slowly to keep mixture cooking evenly. (Do not overcook as sauce will curdle.) Remove immediately from heat. Blend in about
    2 tablespoons sherry
Serve on **toast points** or **cooked rice**.
About 6 servings

—CRAB MEAT NEWBURG

Follow ▲ Recipe. Substitute **2 cups cooked crab meat** for the lobster. Remove and discard bony tissue from meat.

SAVORY OYSTERS

Grease a 2-qt. casserole.

Prepare coarse crumbs from
    6 slices crisp toast (2 cups crumbs)
Set aside.

Heat slowly about 5 min. in a large skillet, stirring occasionally
    ½ cup butter or margarine
    1 cup (8-oz. can, drained) mushrooms, finely sliced
    ⅓ cup chopped green pepper
    ½ clove garlic, (insert wooden pick for easy removal)
Remove skillet from heat; discard garlic. Stir in toast crumbs, blending well. Set aside.

Drain thoroughly, reserving liquor
    1 qt. oysters
Remove any shell particles. Combine
    ¼ cup reserved oyster liquor
    ¼ cup cream or milk
    1 teaspoon Worcestershire sauce
Set aside oysters and liquid.

Mix
    1 teaspoon salt
    1 teaspoon paprika
    ½ teaspoon monosodium glutamate
    ⅛ teaspoon mace
    Dash of cayenne pepper
Line bottom of casserole with one third of crumb mixture. Top with layers of one half of oysters, one half of seasonings and one third of crumb mixture. Repeat oyster and seasoning layers. Spoon liquid over oysters before topping with remaining mixture of crumbs.

Bake at 375°F 20 to 30 min., or until crumbs are golden brown. *6 to 8 servings*

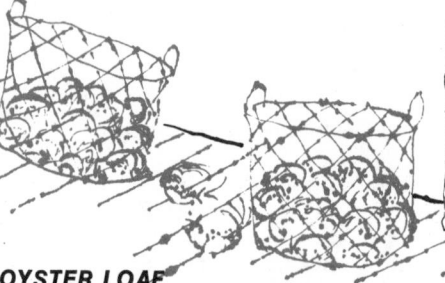

OYSTER LOAF

Called the "peace maker" in Creole homes.

Set out a baking sheet.

Cut a thin lengthwise slice from the top of
    1 loaf French Bread (page 65)
With a small, sharp knife, cut down around edge of loaf, ¾ in. from edges, keeping shell intact. Pull out soft center (reserve for use in other food preparation). Brush inside of bread shell and cut-side of top slice generously with
    Melted butter or margarine
Place bread shell and top slice, cut-side up, on the baking sheet.

Bake at 350°F 12 to 15 min., or until lightly browned.

Meanwhile, prepare
    Deep-Fried Oysters (page 294)
Place oysters in the bread shell and cover with top slice. Hot cream may be poured over oysters.

Serve loaf hot, broken or cut into slices.
6 to 8 servings

CREAMED OYSTER LOAF

▲ Base Recipe

Set out a baking sheet.

Cut a thin lengthwise slice from top of
1 loaf Vienna bread
With a small, sharp knife, cut down around
edge of loaf, ¾ in. from edges, keeping shell
intact. Pull out soft center. Prepare ½ cup
soft bread crumbs; reserve remaining bread for
use in other food preparation. Brush inside of
bread shell and cut-side of top slice, and toss
the bread crumbs with
Melted butter or margarine
Place bread shell, top slice, buttered side up,
and bread crumbs on the baking sheet.

Bake at 350°F 12 to 15 min., or until lightly
browned, turning bread crumbs once or twice.

Meanwhile, drain, reserving liquor
1 qt. oysters
Pick over to remove any shell particles. (If
oysters are frozen, thaw following directions
on package.)

Heat in a saucepan over low heat
½ cup butter or margarine
Add oysters with reserved oyster liquor, and
simmer 3 min., or until oysters are plump and
edges begin to curl. Remove from heat and
stir in the bread crumbs and
½ cup cream
2 tablespoons minced celery
2 teaspoons salt
⅛ teaspoon white pepper
2 drops Tabasco
Turn the oyster mixture into the bread shell
and cover with top slice.

Return loaf to oven and bake about 15 min.
About 6 servings

—INDIVIDUAL OYSTER LOAVES

Follow ▲ Recipe. Substitute **French rolls** for
the loaf of bread.

SOUTHERN OYSTER LOAF

▲ Base Recipe

Set out a baking sheet.

Prepare and keep warm
6 Hard-Cooked Eggs (page 133)
Cut a thin lengthwise slice from top of
1 loaf unsliced white bread
With a small, sharp knife, cut down around
edge of loaf, ¾ in. from edges, keeping shell
intact. Remove soft center all in one piece and
cut into small cubes. Using a star-shaped
cookie cutter, cut 4 stars from the lengthwise
top slice. Brush inside of bread shell and the
stars, and toss bread cubes with
Melted butter or margarine
Place bread shell, stars and cubes on the
baking sheet.

Toast in 350°F oven 15 min., or until lightly
browned, turning bread cubes occasionally to
brown evenly. Set aside.

Meanwhile, drain, reserving liquor
1 qt. oysters
Pick over to remove any shell particles. (If
oysters are frozen, thaw according to directions
on package.) Heat in a saucepan
⅓ cup butter or margarine
Add oysters with reserved liquor. Simmer 3
min., or until oysters are plump and edges
begin to curl. Set aside.

Heat in the top of a double boiler
⅓ cup butter or margarine
Add
**½ cup (about 1 medium) chopped
green pepper**
Cook over medium heat, occasionally moving
and turning with a spoon, until tender. Blend
in
3 tablespoons all-purpose flour
¾ teaspoon salt
½ teaspoon monosodium glutamate
¼ teaspoon rosemary
Few grains pepper
Heat until mixture bubbles. Remove from heat.
Gradually add in order, stirring constantly
¾ cup milk
1 cup (8-oz. can) tomato sauce
Cook rapidly, stirring constantly, just until
sauce thickens. Set double boiler top over
simmering water. Add gradually, blending well
1½ cups dairy sour cream
Add the oysters and heat thoroughly. Mix in
the toasted bread cubes.

Place the toasted bread shell on a serving
platter and pour the oyster mixture into it.
Top with toasted bread stars. Arrange the hard-
cooked eggs, cut in halves lengthwise, around
the loaf. *About 8 servings*

—CREAMED SWEETBREAD LOAF

Prepare bread shell and cubes as in ▲ Recipe.
Prepare **Creamed Sweetbreads** (page 676) in
double boiler instead of chafing dish. Fold in
toasted bread cubes and serve in bread shell.

Southern Oyster Loaf

—CREAMED HAM LOAF

Follow recipe for Creamed Sweetbread Loaf;
fill bread shell with **Creamed Ham** (page 676).

SCALLOPED OYSTERS

▲ Base Recipe

Butter a 2-qt. shallow casserole.

Drain, reserving liquor
1 qt. oysters
Pick over oysters and remove any shell particles. Set oysters aside.

Set out
¾ cup butter
Place a long length of heavy waxed paper
half of
48 crackers (2 in. each)
Loosely fold paper around crackers, tucking
under open ends. With a rolling pin, gently
crush crackers to make fine crumbs. Repeat
with remaining crackers to make about 3 cups
crumbs. Set aside 2 cups crumbs. Melt 2 to
4 tablespoons of the butter; add remaining 1
cup crumbs and toss lightly. Set aside.

Prepare and set aside
⅓ cup finely chopped onion
Add to reserved oyster liquor
**Cream or milk (enough to make 2
cups liquid)**
Stir into liquid
1 teaspoon salt
⅛ teaspoon pepper
Use about 1 cup of the unbuttered crumbs to
form a layer in bottom of casserole. Arrange
about 2 cups of oysters on the crumbs. Pour
1 cup of liquid mixture over all. Sprinkle with
one half the chopped onion and dot with one
half the butter or margarine. Repeat layering,
using the remaining unbuttered crumbs and
oysters. Pour over the remaining liquid. Top
with buttered crumbs.

Bake at 350°F 20 to 25 min., or until mixture
is thoroughly heated. *6 to 8 servings*

—SCALLOPS IN CASSEROLE

Follow ▲ Recipe. For oysters, substitute **2 lbs.**

Fried Scampi

scallops. Wash scallops with cold water and drain on absorbent paper. Cut scallops into halves crosswise.

DEEP-FRIED SCALLOPS

▲ Base Recipe

Set out a deep saucepan or automatic deep-fryer (page 11) and heat **fat** to 365°F.

Set out

2 lbs. scallops

(If using frozen scallops, thaw following directions on package.) Rinse scallops in cold water. Set aside to drain on absorbent paper.

Put into a shallow pan or dish and set aside

1 cup (about 3 slices) fine dry bread crumbs or corn meal

Mix in a bowl

2 eggs, slightly beaten
2 tablespoons milk
2 tablespoons paprika
1 teaspoon salt
¼ teaspoon pepper

Coat scallops, one at a time, by rolling in bread crumbs, dip in egg mixture and then coat again with bread crumbs.

Deep-fry in the heated fat only as many scallops at one time as will lie uncrowded one layer deep in the fat. Fry 2 or 3 min., or until brown. Turn scallops as they rise to surface and several times during cooking. Remove scallops with a slotted spoon; drain over fat for a few seconds before removing them to absorbent paper.

Serve hot with

Tartar Sauce (page 311)
Lemon wedges

6 to 8 servings

—DEEP-FRIED OYSTERS

Follow ▲ Recipe. Heat fat to 375°F. Substitute **1 qt. large oysters** for the scallops. Drain and pick over to remove any shell particles. (Reserve liquor for use in other food preparation.)

—DEEP-FRIED CLAMS

Follow ▲ Recipe. Heat fat to 375°F. Substitute **1 qt. shucked clams** for the scallops.

SCALLOPS BAKED IN SHELLS
(Coquilles Saint-Jacques)

The origin of the French name for scallops is supposedly connected with St. James of Compostela, known as Saint-Jacques. Legend has it that one day a bridegroom was tossed by his horse into the sea. His miraculous rescue was believed to be due to the intervention of St. James. The groom was converted to Christianity on the spot. When he returned to the shore, he was covered with scallop-edged shells. His friends believed the shells to be a sign from St. James and thereupon gave them his name.

Butter 6 baking shells or ramekins.

Heat in a saucepan

2 cups dry white wine
Herb bouquet (page 9)

Wash in cold water and drain

2 lbs. (1 qt.) scallops

Add to wine with

½ teaspoon salt

Cover and simmer about 10 min., or until tender. Remove herb bouquet, drain scallops, and reserve the liquid. Cut the scallops into fine pieces and set aside.

Clean and chop

½ lb. mushrooms

Add mushrooms to a saucepan with

6 shallots or ¼ cup minced onion
1 tablespoon minced parsley
3 tablespoons butter
2 tablespoons water
1 teaspoon lemon juice

Cover and simmer 5 to 10 min. Strain liquid into seasoned wine. Add vegetable mixture to scallops. Set aside.

Make a *roux* by blending in a saucepan

¼ cup melted butter
¼ cup all-purpose flour

Cook over low heat until mixture bubbles. Remove from heat and gradually stir in wine-vegetable liquid. Return to heat and bring rapidly to boiling, stirring constantly; cook 1 to 2 min. longer.

Remove sauce from heat and add gradually, stirring vigorously, to a mixture of

2 egg yolks, slightly beaten
¼ cup heavy cream

Then stir in the scallop mixture. Fill shells or ramekins, piling high in center. Sprinkle with about

⅓ cup (1 slice) buttered dry bread crumbs (page 9)

To brown, set shells on a baking sheet and place in oven at 450°F 8 to 10 min., or place under broiler 3 to 4 in. from heat to top of the creamed mixture. Serve when browned.

6 servings

FRIED SCAMPI
(Scampi Fritti)

In Italian, scampi means prawns and is the name for a class of shrimplike shellfish.

Set out deep saucepan or automatic deep fryer for deep-frying (page 11) and heat **fat** to 360°F.

Wash in cold water

3 lbs. fresh prawns or large shrimp with shells

Remove tiny legs. Peel shells from prawns. Cut a slit to just below surface along back of prawns (outer curved surface) to expose the black vein. Remove vein with knife point. Rinse prawns quickly in cold water. Drain on absorbent paper.

Fry only as many prawns as will float uncrowded one layer deep in the fat. Fry 3 to 5 min., or until golden brown. Drain over fat before removing to absorbent paper. Turn fried prawns onto a warm platter.

Heat in skillet

½ cup olive oil

Add and cook until garlic is lightly browned

4 cloves garlic, minced
1 teaspoon salt
½ teaspoon oregano
¼ teaspoon pepper

Pour oil sauce over prawns on platter, and sprinkle with

1 teaspoon chopped parsley

About 6 servings

Note: Prawns and oil sauce can be put into a casserole and baked at 375°F 15 min.

COOKED SHRIMP

Wash in cold water

1 lb. fresh shrimp with shells

Drop shrimp into a boiling mixture of

1 pt. water
3 tablespoons lemon juice
1 tablespoon salt

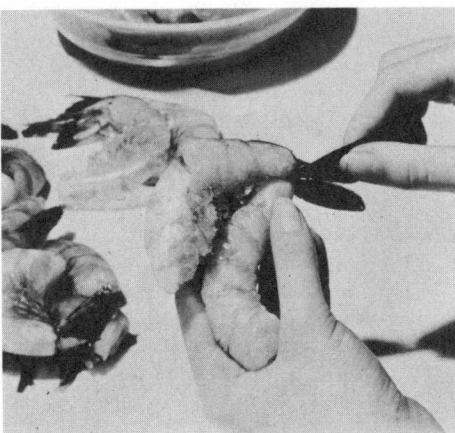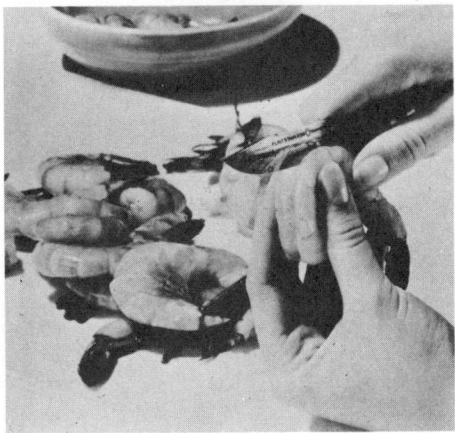

Cooked Shrimp: Drop shrimp with shells into boiling mixture. Remove tiny legs. Peel shells from shrimp. Cut slit along back to expose black vein.

Cover tightly. Simmer 5 min., or only until shrimp are pink and tender. Drain and cover with cold water to chill. Drain shrimp again. Remove tiny legs. Peel shells from shrimp. Cut a slit to just below surface along back (curved surface) of shrimp to expose the black vein. With knife point remove vein in one piece. Rinse quickly in cold running water.

Serve cooked shrimp in creamed mixtures, shrimp salad, or as an appetizer with
   Peppy Cocktail Sauce (page 37)
                    ½ lb. Cooked Shrimp

Note: Veins present in canned or frozen shrimp are removed in the same way.

DEEP-FRIED SHRIMP

Bread crumbs and an egg mixture form the coating.

About 20 min. before ready to deep-fry, fill a deep saucepan or automatic deep fryer one-half to two-thirds full with
   Vegetable shortening, all-purpose shortening, lard or cooking oil for deep-frying
Heat fat slowly to 350°F (page 11).

Peel, remove vein (see Cooked Shrimp, page 294) and set aside
   2 lbs. fresh shrimp with shells

Put into a shallow pan or dish and set aside
   1 cup (3 slices) fine dry bread crumbs

Mix in a bowl
   2 eggs, slightly beaten
   2 tablespoons milk
   2 tablespoons paprika
   1 teaspoon salt
   1 teaspoon monosodium glutamate
   ¼ teaspoon pepper
   ⅛ teaspoon cayenne pepper
Dip shrimp into egg mixture and then coat shrimp by rolling in bread crumbs.

Deep-fry in the heated fat only as many shrimp at one time as will lie uncrowded one layer deep in the fat. Fry shrimp 2 to 3 min., or until brown. Turn shrimp as they rise to surface and several times during cooking. Remove shrimp with a slotted spoon; drain over fat for a few seconds before removing them to absorbent paper.

Serve hot with **lemon wedges** and **melted butter** or **chili sauce**.   *6 to 8 servings*

SHRIMP, LOUISIANA STYLE

Cook
   **1 lb. fresh shrimp with shells
      (see Cooked Shrimp, page 294)**
Cut shrimp into pieces; if desired, reserve several whole shrimp for a garnish.

Heat in a large heavy skillet
   ¼ cup fat
Add and cook over medium heat, occasionally moving with a spoon, until onion and green pepper are tender
   ¾ cup (about 1 large) finely chopped onion
   ¾ cup (about 1 large) finely chopped green pepper
Mix in
   2½ cups canned tomatoes, sieved
   1 teaspoon Worcestershire sauce
   1 bay leaf
   1½ teaspoons salt
   ½ teaspoon sugar
   ½ teaspoon oregano
   ¼ teaspoon pepper
Bring mixture to boiling; reduce heat and simmer, uncovered, stirring occasionally. Cook about 15 min., or until thickened. Stir in the shrimp pieces and cook over low heat until heated thoroughly.

Serve with
   Perfection Boiled Rice (page 165)
Garnish with the reserved whole shrimp.
                    About 4 servings

SHRIMP, VIENNESE-STYLE
(Skampi auf wienerische Art)

To Cook Shrimp—Wash in cold water
   2 lbs. fresh shrimp with shells
Drop shrimp into a boiling mixture of
   1 qt. water
   ¼ cup lemon juice
   1 tablespoon salt
   1 bay leaf
Cook, drain and clean as in Cooked Shrimp (page 294).

To Complete—Heat in a skillet
   ¼ cup butter
Add the shrimp and
   2 tablespoons chopped green onion
Cook over medium heat about 3 min.

Remove from heat and blend in a mixture of
   ½ cup white wine
   1 tablespoon tomato paste
   ¼ teaspoon sugar
   ½ teaspoon salt
   ¼ teaspoon monosodium glutamate
   Few grains cayenne pepper

Cooked Shrimp, Deep-Fried Shrimp and Shrimp, Louisiana Style

Return to heat and simmer 15 min. Remove the shrimp and set aside.

Heat in a saucepan
1 tablespoon butter
Blend in
1 tablespoon all-purpose flour
Heat until mixture bubbles. Remove from heat. Add gradually 3 tablespoons of the shrimp sauce, stirring constantly. Immediately blend into the sauce in the skillet. Bring to boiling. Cook 1 to 2 min.

Add the shrimp and cook over medium heat 5 min., or until thoroughly heated. Serve hot.

6 servings

MARINATED SHRIMP WITH MUSHROOMS AND OLIVES

Combine in a large saucepan
1 lb. fresh mushrooms, quartered
1 cup water
½ cup Italian salad dressing
2 tablespoons lemon juice
2 cloves garlic, halved
1¼ teaspoons salt
½ teaspoon thyme leaves
½ teaspoon peppercorns
⅛ teaspoon nutmeg
2 bay leaves
Bring to boiling, reduce heat, cover and simmer 5 min.

Put into a large bowl
2 lbs. medium shrimp, cooked and deveined
¾ cup small pimiento-stuffed olives
Pour hot mixture into bowl and toss lightly to mix; cool. Refrigerate, covered, 6 to 8 hrs., or overnight before serving.

To serve, pile generous amounts of the mixture with some of the marinade onto crisp **salad greens** on luncheon plates. Serve as a luncheon or supper entrée.

6 servings

SHRIMP DE JONGHE

Butter 4 large clam shells or individual casseroles. Set out a medium-size heavy skillet.

For De Jonghe Butter—Prepare
⅓ cup fine dry bread crumbs

Curried Shrimp on Toast Petals

Mix ¼ cup of the crumbs, reserving remainder for topping, with
½ teaspoon salt
¼ teaspoon pepper
Set mixture aside.

Cream together until butter is softened
½ cup butter
2 cloves garlic, minced
Thoroughly blend in the crumb mixture and
1 tablespoon finely chopped parsley
1½ teaspoons finely chopped chives
1 teaspoon minced onion
¼ teaspoon Worcestershire sauce
Wrap mixture in waxed paper and put into refrigerator until ready to use.

For Shrimp De Jonghe—Prepare
1 lb. fresh shrimp with shells (see Cooked Shrimp, page 294)
Heat in the skillet over low heat
1 tablespoon butter
Add the cooked shrimp and cook over medium heat 1 to 2 min., or until shrimp are heated thoroughly and coated with the butter. Turn shrimp occasionally. Remove skillet from heat.

Arrange shrimp in prepared shells (about six shrimp in each). Sprinkle over shrimp
¼ cup sherry
Pour drippings from skillet over shrimp. Remove De Jonghe Butter from refrigerator and cut off small pieces about ¼ in. thick. Place on shrimp, spreading butter slightly over shrimp. Sprinkle over butter and shrimp, the reserved bread crumbs and
Paprika
Bake at 400°F 20 to 25 min., or until crumbs are lightly browned.

Serve Shrimp De Jonghe immediately in shells or casseroles.

4 servings

CREAMY CURRIED SHRIMP

A pleasurable eating experience.

Set out a 2-qt. saucepan.

Prepare and keep hot
3 cups Perfection Boiled Rice (page 165)
Meanwhile, drain, reserving liquid
1 can (4 oz.) sliced mushrooms (about ½ cup, drained)
2 cans (5 oz. each) shrimp (about 1½ cups, drained)
Remove black veins from shrimp (see Cooked Shrimp, page 294). Set mushrooms and shrimp aside.

Add to mushroom and shrimp liquids enough to make 2 cups liquid
Milk
Set aside.

Dice enough cooked ham to yield
1½ cups (about ¾ lb.) diced cooked ham
Set aside.

Melt in the saucepan over low heat
¼ cup butter or margarine
Add and cook over medium heat about 5 min., stirring occasionally
¼ cup finely chopped onion
¼ cup finely chopped celery
Blend in a mixture of
¼ cup all-purpose flour
1 teaspoon curry powder
½ teaspoon salt
½ teaspoon monosodium glutamate
⅛ teaspoon pepper
Heat until mixture bubbles, stirring constantly. Remove from heat. Add gradually and stir liquid into mixture. Return to heat and bring mixture rapidly to boiling, stirring constantly. Cook until sauce thickens.

Blend mushrooms, shrimp and ham into sauce.

Cook a few minutes longer until shrimp and ham are heated keeping mixture moving gently with a spoon.

Serve over hot rice on a warm serving platter.

4 servings

SHRIMP ON TOAST PETALS

▲ *Base Recipe*

Set out a 10-in. pie pan.

For Garlic Butter—Soften
½ cup butter or margarine
Thoroughly crush in mortar with pestle (or use garlic press to crush garlic)
1 clove garlic
⅛ teaspoon salt
Blend thoroughly into softened butter. Let the mixture stand at room temperature for about 1 hr.

Prepare
1½ lbs. fresh shrimp, with shells (see Cooked Shrimp, page 294, use 3 cups water)
Store in refrigerator until ready to use.

To Prepare Toast Petal Crust—Stack and trim crusts from
12 slices bread
Generously spread garlic butter on bread slices. To form petal crust, completely cover the bottom and sides of pie pan with the bread slices, overlapping them around the edge to form the pointed petal design.

Bake the bread slices at 350°F 15 to 20 min., or until bread is lightly browned.

To Prepare Sauce—Meanwhile, melt in a saucepan over low heat
3 tablespoons butter or margarine
Blend in
3 tablespoons all-purpose flour
¼ teaspoon salt
Few grains pepper
Heat until mixture bubbles. Remove from heat. Gradually stir in
2 cups milk
½ cup condensed tomato soup

Return to heat and bring rapidly to boiling, stirring constantly; cook 1 to 2 min. longer. Cool sauce slightly and add all at one time

    ¼ cup (1 oz.) grated Parmesan cheese

Stir sauce rapidly until cheese is melted.

Blend in one half the cooked shrimp and

    ½ cup (4-oz. can) sliced mushrooms, drained

Pour mixture into toast crust. Arrange remaining shrimp in circle around edge of sauce.

Return to oven for 3 to 4 min., or until sauce is bubbling hot.   *6 servings*

—CURRIED SHRIMP ON TOAST PETALS

Follow ▲ Recipe. Increase grated Parmesan cheese to ½ cup. Use 2 tablespoons of the grated cheese to sprinkle over the bread which has been spread with garlic butter. Omit tomato sauce and prepare **Medium White Sauce** (double recipe, page 304, adding **2 teaspoons curry powder** and **⅛ teaspoon ginger** to dry ingredients). Stir ¼ cup cheese into slightly cooled white sauce. After arranging shrimp around outer edge of toast petal crust, sprinkle with remaining cheese and return to oven for about 5 min.

SHRIMP JAMBALAYA

Although many believe jambalaya received its name from the French word "jambon" meaning "ham," others believe it had a more colorful origin. Some Creoles say that many years ago a distinguished guest stopped unexpectedly at a New Orleans inn. The proprietor, having nothing left from dinner to serve him, said to his cook Jean, "Balayez" (blend good things together). The visitor was pleased with the unusual dish offered him and suggested that it be called "Jean Balayez," which has since been shortened to Jambalaya.

Set out a 3-qt. saucepan with a tight-fitting cover.

Prepare, coarsely chop and set aside

    1 lb. fresh shrimp with shells (see Cooked Shrimp, page 294)

Clean and finely chop

    1 large onion (about ¾ cup, chopped)

Heat in the saucepan over low heat

    2 tablespoons butter or margarine

Add onion to saucepan and

    ½ lb. (about 1 cup) diced cooked ham
    1 clove garlic, finely minced

Cook over medium heat until the onion is tender. Add to saucepan and blend

    3 cups quick meat broth (page 10)
    2 cups sieved cooked tomatoes
    2 tablespoons chopped parsley
    1 teaspoon salt
    ¼ teaspoon thyme
    ⅛ teaspoon pepper
    ⅛ teaspoon cayenne pepper
    ⅛ teaspoon chili powder
    ½ bay leaf, crushed

Cover and bring to boiling. Remove cover. So boiling will continue, add gradually, stirring with a fork

    1 cup rice

(The Rice Industry no longer considers it necessary to wash rice before cooking.)

Simmer, covered, about 20 min., or until a rice kernel is entirely soft when pressed between fingers.

Add cooked shrimp pieces and simmer about 5 min. longer.

Serve jambalaya hot.   *6 to 8 servings*

Note: Any shellfish, such as crab or lobster, may be substituted for shrimp.

MIXED SEAFOOD DISHES

BOUILLABAISSE
(Bouillabaisse)

This rich and savory stew may be found in one form or another in every French seaport bordering on the Mediterranean. The most famous version is that made in Marseilles, where it is said to have been created in a convent to give variety to Friday's meatless meals.

    Since most of the fish used there can be found only in the waters of the Mediterranean, we cannot duplicate the native recipe. Yet we can get fairly comparable results by using three kinds of fish plus seafood, and by including tomatoes, garlic, saffron and olive oil. The blending of these particular ingredients gives Bouillabaisse its characteristic flavor.

Set out a 3-qt. kettle.

Bouillabaisse

Clean, remove bones and wash in cold salted water

    1½ lbs. bass
    1 lb. perch
    1 lb. cod

Cut into pieces 1½ to 2 in. thick; set aside.

Remove tiny legs, shells and black veins from

    1 lb. fresh shrimp

Rinse quickly in cold water; set aside.

Rinse in cold water and set aside

    1 lb. sea scallops (fresh or thawed frozen)

Kill and clean (page 290)

    1 lobster (1½ to 2 lbs.)

Cut into 1½- to 2-in. pieces; set aside.

Heat in kettle

    ¼ cup olive oil

Add and cook in kettle about 5 min.

    ⅔ cup chopped onion
    2 leeks, chopped (white part only)
    1 clove garlic, crushed

Add

    1 can (16 oz.) tomatoes
    1 tablespoon minced parsley
    ½ bay leaf
    ½ teaspoon savory
    ½ teaspoon fennel
    ⅛ teaspoon saffron

Add lobster and bass and just enough water to cover. Season with

    1½ teaspoons salt
    ¼ teaspoon pepper

Bring rapidly to boiling. Simmer 10 min. Add perch and cod. Continue to simmer 10 min., or until fish are almost tender. Add shrimp and scallops; cook 5 min. longer.

Meanwhile, drain, reserving liquor
1 pt. oysters
Pick over to remove any shell particles. Simmer in reserved liquor 3 min., or until edges begin to curl. Add to fish mixture.

Line a deep serving dish with
6 slices French bread, toasted
Cover with fish and pour sauce in which fish has been cooked over all. Serve at once.

6 to 8 servings

DEVILED SEAFOOD WITH PECANS

Deliciously seasoned for taste-tempting appeal!

Rub 6 ramekins or large clam shells thoroughly with cut-side of
½ clove garlic, peeled
Grease ramekins.

Prepare and set aside
3 Hard-Cooked Eggs (page 133)

Shred onto waxed paper
4 oz. sharp Cheddar cheese (1 cup, shredded)
Mix ¼ cup of shredded cheese with
1 cup (3 to 4 slices) fine dry bread crumbs, buttered (page 9)
½ cup (about 2 oz.) chopped pecans
Set crumb mixture aside. Fold waxed paper around remaining cheese to prevent drying and set aside for sauce.

Prepare
2 cups Medium White Sauce (double recipe, page 304. Add ¼ cup minced onion to butter and cook about 5 min.; blend into flour mixture. Add 1½ teaspoons dry mustard and few grains cayenne pepper with seasonings.)
Add the shredded cheese to sauce all at one time with
1 teaspoon Worcestershire sauce

Deviled Seafood with Pecans

Add
3 or 4 drops Tabasco
Stir sauce rapidly until cheese is melted.

Force cooked eggs through ricer or sieve. Gently mix eggs into sauce with
1 cup (7-oz. can, drained) flaked (page 9) or diced seafood, such as crab, lobster, tuna or shrimp (if desired, reserve 6 whole shrimp for garnish)
2 tablespoons chopped parsley
Turn one half of mixture into ramekins; sprinkle each with about 2 tablespoons of crumb mixture. Add remaining seafood mixture; top with remaining crumbs.

If whole shrimp were reserved, dip in
Melted butter or margarine
Place one shrimp on each ramekin.

Bake at 375°F 20 to 25 min., or until crumbs are lightly browned.

6 servings

FILLET OF SOLE MARGUERY

See how even this culinary masterpiece can be enhanced by the addition of Worcestershire sauce and mustard.

Lightly grease 6 fish-shaped individual casseroles or a shallow baking dish.

Set out
2 lbs. English fillet of sole

Pick over and remove any shell particles from
1 pt. oysters
Put the oysters and their liquor into a saucepan with
1 tablespoon butter
Heat slowly until edges just curl. Drain and set aside to keep warm.

Prepare
½ lb. fresh shrimp with shells (see Cooked Shrimp, page 294)
Bring to boiling in a large heavy skillet with a tight-fitting cover
1 cup sauterne or other white table wine
1 cup water
Add the fillet of sole, cover and reduce heat. Simmer very gently 3 to 4 min., or until fish flakes (page 9). Carefully remove fish from liquid. Reserve ½ cup of the liquid. Set fish aside to keep warm.

Prepare
2 cups Medium White Sauce (double recipe, page 304; add with seasonings ¼ teaspoon dry mustard and ¼ teaspoon paprika; substitute ½ cup cream and reserved fish liquid for 1 cup of the milk; add ½ teaspoon Worcestershire sauce and ½ teaspoon lemon juice with the liquid)
Stir into the sauce
2 tablespoons sherry

Arrange the fillets in the casseroles or baking

Fillet of Sole Marguery

dish. Top with the oysters and the shrimp. Pour sauce over seafood. Sprinkle with
Paprika

Place casseroles or baking dish on broiler rack. Place broiler rack under broiler with top of casseroles or baking dish 3 to 4 in. from heat. Broil 4 to 5 min., or until sauce is lightly browned.

Serve immediately.

6 servings

SEAFOOD IN RAMEKINS

Grease 6 ramekins and set aside.

Mix and set aside
1 cup fine dry bread crumbs, buttered (page 9; 3 to 4 slices bread)
¼ cup (about 1 oz.) shredded sharp Cheddar cheese

Drain, remove and discard bony tissue and separate
1 can (6½ oz.) crab meat (about 1⅓ cups)
Drain and, if desired, cut into halves lengthwise
1 can (5½ oz.) shrimp (about 1 cup)

Prepare
3 cups Sour Cream White Sauce (double recipe, page 304; add ¼ cup minced onion to butter or margarine and cook until the onion is tender. Add 1½ teaspoons dry mustard and few grains cayenne pepper with seasonings)
2 tablespoons chopped parsley
Mix the crab meat, shrimp and parsley into the sauce. Turn one half of mixture into the ramekins; sprinkle each with about 2 tablespoons of crumb mixture. Spoon remaining mixture into ramekins and top with remaining crumbs.

Bake at 375°F 20 to 25 min., or until crumbs are lightly browned.

6 servings

SEAFOOD POTPOURRI

▲ Base Recipe

Grease a 2-qt. casserole.

Prepare

    3 Hard-Cooked Eggs (page 133)

Meanwhile, combine gently with a fork

    1 cup (7-oz. can, drained) tuna, coarsely flaked (page 9)

    1 cup (6- to 7-oz. can, drained) crab meat, bony tissue removed

    ⅔ cup (5-oz. can, drained) shrimp, black veins removed, if necessary, and discarded and shrimp cut in halves

Drain, reserving liquid

    1 cup (8-oz. can) sliced mushrooms

Set aside.

Shred and set aside

    4 oz. Cheddar cheese (1 cup, shredded)

Prepare

    2 cups Thin White Sauce (double recipe, page 304; substitute reserved mushroom liquid for part of milk)

Add the shredded cheese all at one time. Stir sauce rapidly until cheese is melted.

Blend in

    3 tablespoons finely chopped chives

    10 ripe olives, pitted and sliced

Arrange one half of the seafood in casserole. Slice the eggs and arrange one half of the slices on seafood. Add mushrooms and one half of the sauce. Add, in order, layers of remaining eggs and seafood. Cover with remaining sauce and

    ½ cup coarsely crushed potato chips

Bake at 350°F 20 to 30 min., or until well browned. *8 servings*

—SEAFOOD AND BISCUITS

Follow ▲ Recipe. Omit potato chips. Prepare **Baking Powder Biscuit dough** (one half recipe, page 92; if desired, add 1 tablespoon finely chopped parsley to flour-lard mixture. Cut 1-in. square biscuits.) Arrange casserole layers. Bake at 425°F 10 min. Remove from oven and arrange biscuits in diagonal lines across casserole; leave spaces between biscuits.

Seafood and Biscuits

Increase oven temperature to 450°F and bake 10 to 15 min. longer, or until biscuits are lightly browned. Garnish with additional parsley.

CREAMED SHRIMP AND LOBSTER OVER CAULIFLOWER
(Hummer og Reker i Hvit Saus over Blomkaal)

Drain, reserving liquids separately

    1 can (6 oz.) lobster meat (about 1 cup)

    1 can (4½ oz.) shrimp (about 1 cup)

Remove any bony tissue from the lobster and cut lobster into pieces. Cut the shrimp into halves lengthwise. Set aside.

Prepare, soak and cook (page 313)

    1 medium head cauliflower

Meanwhile, prepare

    1 cup Medium White Sauce (page 304)

Stir into the sauce the shrimp, lobster and

    3 tablespoons reserved lobster liquid

    1 tablespoon reserved shrimp liquid

Cook over medium heat until mixture is thoroughly heated.

Drain cauliflower and put into a serving bowl. Pour the sauce over the cauliflower and serve immediately. *4 or 5 servings*

FROG LEGS

FROG LEGS WITH LEMON BUTTER SAUCE

Wash

    8 pairs large skinned frog legs

Soak frog legs in salted water (1 tablespoon per 2 qts. water) 15 min.; drain.

Meanwhile, prepare Lemon Butter Sauce.

For Lemon Butter Sauce—Heat together

    1 cup butter

    ¼ cup lemon juice

    ¼ teaspoon salt

    ¼ teaspoon paprika

    ⅛ teaspoon pepper

    ¼ cup chopped parsley

Marinate (page 10) frog legs about 30 min., turning several times. Drain, reserving marinade.

To Broil Frog Legs—Set baking sheet under the broiler with tops of frog legs 2 in. from heat. Turning frequently and brushing several times with reserved marinade, broil frog legs 12 to 15 min., or until tender.

To Grill Frog Legs—Place the frog legs on greased grill. Grill about 3 in. from coals, about 5 min. on each side, or until tender. Baste often with marinade.

Serve with hot Lemon Butter Sauce.

4 servings

Fried Frog Legs

FRIED FROG LEGS IN CREAM SAUCE

▲ Base Recipe

Set out a large heavy skillet.

Wash

    8 pairs large skinned frog legs

Soak frog legs in salted water (1 tablespoon per 2 qts. water) 15 min.; drain. Coat frog legs evenly by shaking 2 or 3 at a time in a plastic bag containing a mixture of

    ½ cup all-purpose flour

    1 teaspoon salt

    ¼ teaspoon monosodium glutamate

    ⅛ teaspoon pepper

Heat in the skillet over low heat

    ¼ cup butter or margarine

Add frog legs and cook over medium heat about 20 min., or until frog legs are golden brown and tender when pierced with a fork.

To brown all sides, turn frog legs as necessary with two spoons or tongs. Drain frog legs on absorbent paper; set aside and keep them warm while preparing Cream Sauce.

For Cream Sauce—Return to the skillet

    1 tablespoon drippings

Blend in

    1 tablespoon all-purpose flour

    ¼ teaspoon salt

    ¼ teaspoon monosodium glutamate

    Few grains pepper

Heat until mixture bubbles, stirring constantly. Remove skillet from heat. Add gradually, stirring constantly

    1 cup cream

Mix in

    1 tablespoon finely minced onion

    1 tablespoon finely chopped parsley

Return skillet to heat; cook rapidly, stirring constantly, until sauce thickens. Add frog legs to sauce and cook 1 to 2 min. longer.

4 servings

—FRIED FROG LEGS

Follow ▲ Recipe. Omit Cream Sauce. Blend into ½ cup mayonnaise 2 teaspoons each of **chopped chervil, chives, tarragon leaves and parsley.** Serve frog legs with mayonnaise mixture and **lemon wedges.**

Game and game birds

The term game in America means any wild bird or animal commonly used as food. It also encompasses partially wild birds which have been domesticated for table use, including quail, pheasant, turkey, partridge, and pigeons, to name only a few. Game is considered one of the luxuries of the dinner table. The widespread taste for it is not new but is actually part of our American heritage because it offered our early New England colonizers a food for survival. Game is healthful, savory, and easy to digest, yet no branch of the art of cookery demands more knowledge and care on the part of the cook. The most important points to remember about cooking game are that it should be exactly the right degree of doneness, and it should be served sizzling hot. Wine used both in the preparation of and served with game, adds to its enjoyment.

RABBIT STEW

Set out a large kettle or saucepot with a tight-fitting cover.

Heat to boiling in a large saucepan
2½ cups water
Meanwhile, sort and wash thoroughly
1 cup (about ½ lb.) dried large lima beans
Add beans gradually to water so boiling will continue. Simmer 2 min. and remove saucepan from heat. Cover saucepan; set beans aside to soak 1 hr.

Meanwhile, clean, cut into thin slices and set aside
2 medium (about ½ lb.) onions

Finely chop enough ham to yield
¼ cup chopped cooked ham
Set aside.

Rinse and cut into serving-size pieces
1 rabbit, 2½ to 3 lbs., ready-to-cook weight
Set aside.

Heat in the kettle over low heat
2 tablespoons butter or margarine
Add the onion slices and cook over medium heat until just tender. Add the rabbit pieces, chopped ham and
Hot water (enough to half cover the rabbit)

Add
1 tablespoon salt
1 teaspoon monosodium glutamate
¼ teaspoon pepper
⅛ teaspoon thyme
1 clove garlic, finely minced
1 bay leaf, crushed
Cover and simmer 45 min.

Meanwhile, wash, scrape or pare and slice
1 lb. carrots (about 2½ cups, sliced)

Drain lima beans and add with sliced carrots to kettle. Continue cooking about 45 min., or until rabbit and vegetables are tender. Add more boiling water as needed.

During last 15 min. of cooking time, add
2 green peppers, sliced in rings
Thicken cooking liquid, if desired.

To Thicken Cooking Liquid—Pour into a screw-top jar
½ cup water
Add to the liquid
¼ cup all-purpose flour
Cover jar tightly and shake until mixture is well blended. Slowly pour one half of the mixture into cooking liquid, stirring constantly. Bring to boiling. Gradually add only what is needed of remaining flour-water mixture for consistency desired. Bring to boiling after each addition. After final addition, cook 3 to 5 min. longer. *6 to 8 servings*

MARINATED RABBIT STEW
(Hasenpfeffer)

Traditional German recipe for preparing hare.

A Dutch oven or a large heavy saucepot with a tight-fitting cover will be needed.

Clean and cut into serving-size pieces
1 rabbit, 2½ to 3 lbs., ready-to-cook weight
Put rabbit pieces into a deep bowl and cover with a mixture of
3 cups red wine vinegar
3 cups water
½ cup sugar
1 medium onion, sliced
2 carrots, washed, pared and cut into pieces
1 tablespoon salt
1 teaspoon pickling spices
¼ teaspoon pepper
Cover and put into refrigerator 2 to 3 days to marinate (page 10). Turn rabbit pieces often.

Drain rabbit pieces, reserving marinade. Dry on absorbent paper. Strain the marinade. Coat rabbit pieces evenly by shaking two or three at a time in a plastic bag containing a mixture of
⅓ cup all-purpose flour
1 teaspoon salt
½ teaspoon monosodium glutamate
¼ teaspoon pepper
Heat in the Dutch oven or saucepot
3 tablespoons fat
Add the rabbit pieces and brown slowly, turning to brown evenly. Remove from heat. Gradually add 2 cups of the marinade. Cover and simmer 45 to 60 min., or until meat is tender.

Pour into a screw-top jar ½ cup of the reserved marinade. Add
¼ cup all-purpose flour
Cover jar tightly and shake until mixture is well blended. Slowly pour one half of the mixture into cooking liquid, stirring constantly. Bring to boiling. Gradually add only what is needed of remaining mixture for consistency desired. Bring to boiling after each addition. After final addition, cook 3 to 5 min.

Arrange the rabbit pieces on a serving platter. Pour some of the gravy over the rabbit and serve with the remaining gravy. *6 servings*

Rabbit Stew

JUGGED HARE, SOLOGNE STYLE
(Civet de Lièvre à la Sologne)

Set out a heavy 10- or 12-in. skillet with a tight-fitting cover and an 8-in. skillet.

Prepare and set aside
2 cups Bouillon (page 41)

Rinse thoroughly, disjoint and cut into serving-size pieces
1 cleaned and table-dressed rabbit (preferably young)
Set aside.

Reserve cleaned liver and set in refrigerator until ready to use. (It should be clear and dark red in color, firm and free from spots.)

Cook in the larger skillet, stirring and turning occasionally
½ lb. bacon, diced
When bacon is crisp, place on absorbent paper to drain.

Add to bacon fat and cook about 5 min., stirring occasionally
½ cup coarsely chopped onion
Remove onion and set aside.

Remove skillet from heat.

Shake together in a plastic bag
¾ cup all-purpose flour
1 teaspoon salt
¼ teaspoon pepper
Put two pieces of rabbit in bag at a time and shake to coat pieces. Return skillet to heat and brown meat on both sides.

Pour prepared bouillon over rabbit with
2 cups red wine
Bring just to boiling. Add bacon pieces, cooked onion and
Herb bouquet (page 9)
Cover tightly and simmer 1½ to 2 hrs., or until meat is tender.

Meanwhile, clean and slice (page 9)
1 lb. mushrooms
Melt in smaller skillet
¼ cup butter
Add mushrooms and
Rabbit liver, coarsely chopped
Heat about 5 min., stirring occasionally. Add to rabbit about 20 min. before end of cooking period. Remove rabbit and mushrooms to warm serving plate and keep hot. Remove herb bouquet and pour liquid into bowl.

To Make Sauce—Prepare a *roux* by blending in the smaller skillet
½ cup melted butter
½ cup all-purpose flour
Cook over low heat until mixture bubbles. Remove from heat and gradually stir in liquid. Return to heat and bring rapidly to boiling, stirring constantly; cook 1 to 2 min. longer. Pour sauce over rabbit.

Heat in a small saucepan
⅓ cup brandy
Ignite brandy and pour over rabbit and sauce. Serve immediately. *4 servings*

BARBECUED VENISON

Set out a large heavy skillet, a large shallow baking dish and a saucepan.

Trim, removing fat from
3 lbs. venison steaks or chops

Heat in skillet
Fat or meat drippings (or fry salt pork and use rendered fat)
½ cup chopped onion
½ clove garlic, crushed
Add the venison steaks and cook over medium heat about 2 min. on each side. Transfer to baking dish.

Meanwhile, combine in saucepan
1 cup ketchup
2 tablespoons tarragon vinegar
1 teaspoon monosodium glutamate
3 tablespoons bottled steak sauce
Dash Tabasco
¼ cup chili sauce
3 slices lemon
Salt, if needed
Cook and stir over medium heat until boiling. Pour sauce over venison. Cover baking dish.

Cook in a 350°F oven about 1½ hrs., or until meat is tender. *About 4 servings*

ROAST PHEASANT

Set out a shallow roasting pan.

Clean and remove any pin feathers from
Pheasant, 2 to 3 lbs.

Brush the cavity with
2 teaspoons lemon juice
Salt
Spoon into cavity a mixture of
1 cup coarsely chopped celery
1 cup coarsely chopped onion
Put bird into roasting pan and brush skin with
Melted butter or margarine
Spread over top
4 slices bacon
Pour into roasting pan
1 cup boiling water
½ cup dry white wine

Set in 350°F oven and roast, covered, 50 to 60 min. for a 2-lb. bird. (Allow 25 min. per lb. for roasting.) Baste with liquid in bottom of pan every 15 min. Remove cover and the bacon slices during last 20 min. of roasting.

When tender, remove pheasant to heated serving platter. Keep hot while preparing gravy from liquid in pan. Thicken the basting liquid with enough **flour** or **cornstarch** mixed with several tablespoons **cold water** to make a thin gravy. Cook and stir 3 to 5 min. and serve with the pheasant. *2 to 4 servings*

Note: Pheasant meat is quite dry so frequent basting of the bird during roasting is necessary. The addition of bacon strips or sliced salt pork also adds to the succulence.

WILD DUCK WITH RAISIN-NUT STUFFING

Have ready
2 wild ducks (about 2½ lbs. each), dressed
Rub cavities of birds with
Salt
Set aside.

Heat in a skillet until melted
3 tablespoons butter or margarine
Add and cook 3 to 5 min., stirring occasionally
1 cup finely chopped celery with leaves
¼ cup chopped onion

Put celery mixture into a large bowl and toss with
½ to ¾ cup seedless raisins
½ cup chopped pecans
4 cups soft bread crumbs
¼ teaspoon marjoram
¼ teaspoon rosemary
½ teaspoon salt
Add a mixture of
⅓ to ½ cup hot water
1 egg, beaten
Fill body cavities of birds with the stuffing, leaving cavities open. Place birds, breast up, on rack in shallow roasting pan. Spread over breast of each bird
3 slices bacon

Roast, uncovered, in 450°F oven 15 min. for very rare, 20 min. for medium rare, and 25 min. for medium-well done. Baste duck frequently with a blend of
½ cup ketchup
1 to 2 tablespoons Worcestershire sauce
1 tablespoon bottled steak sauce
2 tablespoons chili sauce
When ready to serve, place duck on heated serving platter; garnish with **orange slices** and **parsley sprigs.**

Skim the fat from liquid left in roasting pan and serve liquid in gravy boat with ducks. *4 or 5 servings*

PHEASANT MULLIGAN WITH DUMPLINGS

Clean, rinse, cut into serving portions, and put into a saucepot

2 young pheasants

Add water to cover and bring to boiling over medium heat. Add

2 cups diced carrots
1 cup coarsely chopped onion
Salt and pepper to taste

Cover and bring to boiling; lower the heat and simmer until pheasant is almost tender, about 30 min.

Add

2 cups diced potatoes
1 cup finely shredded cabbage
2 to 3 tablespoons fat or drippings
Salt and pepper, if needed

Continue cooking until meat and vegetables are tender.

While vegetables are cooking, prepare dumpling batter.

Mix thoroughly in a bowl

2 cups all-purpose flour
3 teaspoons baking powder
½ teaspoon salt

Add to dry ingredients a blend of

1 egg, well beaten
¾ cup milk

Mix only until dry ingredients are moistened (do not overmix). Add more milk, if needed, to make a drop batter. Drop by tablespoons onto the hot stew; cover saucepot tightly and cook dumplings 15 min.   *6 to 8 servings*

BROILED SQUAB

Succulent dainties for an epicurean feast.

Clean

4 squabs, ¾- to 1-lb. each, ready-to-cook weight

Rinse and pat squabs dry with absorbent paper.

Cut squabs into halves lengthwise. Brush squab halves with

2 to 3 tablespoons unsalted butter, melted

Sprinkle over squab halves a mixture of

1 teaspoon salt
½ teaspoon monosodium glutamate
¼ teaspoon pepper

Place squab halves in broiler pan, skin-sides down. Place under broiler with top of squabs 7 to 9 in. from heat. Turn squab and brush with unsalted butter two or three times during broiling period. Broil slowly 20 to 30 min. Squabs are done when nicely browned and drumstick twists easily out of thigh joint.

Serve squab halves on

Slices of toast

Garnish with **watercress**.   *4 servings*

SQUAB WITH PEAS
(Pigeons aux Petits Pois)

Set out a large heavy skillet or saucepot.

Clean and truss

4 small or 2 large squab

Heat in skillet or saucepot

3 tablespoons butter or margarine

Add the birds and brown well on all sides. Remove from skillet and keep hot. Add to skillet and cook until browned

4 thick slices lean bacon, diced

Remove bacon and set aside.

Stir into skillet and cook until lightly browned

3 tablespoons all-purpose flour

Add, stirring constantly

2 cups chicken broth
Salt and pepper to taste
Herb bouquet (page 9)

Cook and stir 2 to 3 min., or until thickened. Return bacon to sauce, cover and cook over low heat about 10 min. Add to skillet, cover and cook about 2 min.

2 pkgs. 10 oz. each frozen green peas, partially thawed

Return the browned squab to skillet and continue cooking 20 to 30 min., or until birds are tender.

To serve, place squab on a heated platter. Remove the bouquet garni and spoon the sauce with peas around the squab.   *4 servings*

PARTRIDGE WITH WILD RICE STUFFING

Set out and grease a deep casserole or baking dish with tight-fitting cover.

Rinse, pat dry, and set aside

4 ready-to-cook partridges (thaw if frozen)

Prepare a wild rice or bread stuffing (your favorite recipe or see page 273). Spoon the stuffing lightly into cavities of partridges.

Arrange birds in casserole, topping each with a strip of **salt pork**. Add a small amount of hot water to barely cover the bottom of the casserole (about ¼ cup).

Place in a 350°F oven 15 min. Pour over birds

½ cup dry white wine

Cover casserole and continue cooking until birds are tender, about 30 min. Serve with **Grapefruit Sauce**.   *4 servings*

For Grapefruit Sauce—Combine in a small saucepan ⅓ **cup sugar, 1 tablespoon corn-starch** and a **dash salt**. Add and stir until smooth ⅓ **cup cold water**. Blend in ½ **tea-spoon grated grapefruit peel** and **1 cup fresh or frozen grapefruit juice**. Bring to boiling over medium heat, stirring constantly. Cook and stir 2 to 3 min. If desired, add several drops **red food coloring**. Before serving, add peeled sections from **1 grapefruit**. Heat sauce until hot.   *About 1 cup sauce*

PARTRIDGE AU VIN

Set out a heavy saucepot or deep heavy skillet.

Rinse and pat dry

4 ready-to-cook partridges

Heat in saucepot or skillet

2 tablespoons butter, margarine or cooking oil

Add and cook about 2 min., stirring occasionally

½ cup chopped onion
¼ cup chopped celery leaves

Add partridges and brown on all sides over medium heat. Pour over birds

½ cup dry sherry

Cover sauce pot and cook slowly about 15 min. Add a blend of

1¾ cups cooked or canned tomatoes
2 whole cloves
½ bay leaf
½ teaspoon salt
⅛ teaspoon lemon pepper marinade

Cover and continue cooking gently about 1½ hrs., or until birds are tender. Serve immediately with **cooked wild rice**.   *4 servings*

Sauces and gravies

A sauce is a liquid or semiliquid adjunct which complements or defines the food it accompanies. A well-chosen sauce should offer pleasing contrasts in color, flavor, and consistency and add nutritive values to the food. Just the right sauce can often glamorize an otherwise ordinary dish. Included in this chapter are sauces for meat, fish, poultry, and vegetables—white and brown, rosy and orange, hot and cold, bland and piquant, thick and thin, aromatic, herb laden and laced with wine. The distinction between sauces and gravies cannot be easily made. Gravies generally depend for their flavor upon stock and drippings left after meat or poultry has been cooked. This chapter includes a basic gravy for meat or poultry, as well as several other types.

BROWN ROUX OR PASTE
(Roux Brun)

Used for thickening brown sauces, this paste can be made in advance and kept in the refrigerator until needed.

Melt in a heavy saucepan or skillet
1 cup fat or meat drippings
Blend in with a fork
1½ cups all-purpose flour
Place over low heat. Stir constantly to distribute heat evenly. The roux is cooked when the mixture acquires a light brown color.

Cover and store in refrigerator.
About 2 cups roux

BORDELAISE SAUCE

Set out a heavy 2-qt. saucepan.

Prepare and set aside
1 cup quick meat broth (page 10)

Clean and finely chop eonugh mushrooms to yield
¼ cup finely chopped mushrooms
Heat in the saucepan
2 tablespoons butter

Add the mushrooms and
1 tablespoon finely chopped onion
1 slice garlic, minced
Cook over medium heat until mushrooms and onion are tender. Add gradually, stirring constantly
½ cup dry red wine
Simmer until liquid is reduced to one-half the quantity. Add the meat broth gradually, stirring constantly; bring rapdily to boiling. Reduce heat and simmer 8 to 10 min., stirring occasionally. Remove from heat and add
2 teaspoons finely chopped parsley
About 1 cup sauce

MUSHROOM SAUCE I

Glorify ground meat dishes with this smooth sauce studded with flavorful slices of rich, tender mushrooms.

Set out a large heavy skillet.

Prepare and set aside
2 cups quick meat broth (double recipe, page 10)

Clean and slice (page 9)
½ lb. mushrooms

Heat in the skillet
⅓ cup butter or margarine
Add mushrooms and cook slowly, gently moving and turning them with a fork or spoon, until mushrooms are lightly browned and tender. Remove to a small bowl and set aside.

Melt in the skillet
1 to 2 tablespoons butter or margarine
Blend in
3 tablespoons all-purpose flour
½ teaspoon salt
¼ teaspoon monosodium glutamate
⅛ teaspoon pepper
Cook until mixture bubbles and is slightly browned, stirring constantly.

Remove from heat and gradually add the quick meat broth while stirring constantly. Return to heat and bring rapidly to boiling, stirring constantly; cook 1 to 2 min. longer. Vigorously stir about 3 tablespoons of this hot mixture into
4 egg yolks, slightly beaten
Immediately blend into mixture in skillet. Cook over low heat 2 to 3 min., stirring constantly. Do not boil. Blend in mushrooms and heat thoroughly. *About 2½ cups sauce*

ONION SAUCE
(Zwiebel Sosse)

▲ Base Recipe

This favorite sauce adds flavor to ground beef patties, panbroiled round steak or leftover roast beef; and it takes the place of gravy.

Prepare and set aside
2 cups quick meat broth (page 10)

Melt in a skillet
½ cup butter
Add and cook about 5 min.
¼ cup chopped onion
3 tablespoons (about 1 small) chopped carrot
1 bay leaf
Blend into mixture in skillet
4¼ tablespoons all-purpose flour
Heat until mixture bubbles, stirring constantly.

Remove from heat. Gradually add the meat broth while stirring constantly. Return to heat and bring rapidly to boiling, stirring constantly; cook 1 to 2 min. longer. Remove bay leaf.
About 2 cups sauce

—MUSHROOM ONION SAUCE
(Champignon Zwiebel Sosse)

Follow ▲ Recipe. Omit carrot. Clean and slice (page 9) **½ cup mushrooms.** Add with the onion to butter in skillet; cook until onion and mushrooms are lightly browned and tender, occasionally moving and turning with a spoon. After mushrooms are browned, remove with a slotted spoon and set aside. Return to skillet after sauce has thickened. Heat thoroughly.

MEDIUM WHITE SAUCE

▲ Base Recipe

Heat in a saucepan over low heat
2 tablespoons butter or margarine
Blend in
2 tablespoons all-purpose flour
¼ teaspoon salt
¼ teaspoon monosodium glutamate
Few grains pepper
Heat until mixture bubbles. Remove from heat. Add gradually, stirring in
1 cup milk
Cook rapidly, stirring constantly, until sauce thickens. Cook 1 to 2 min. longer.

Use for gravies and creamed mixtures.

About 1 cup sauce

Note: Quick chicken broth (page 10) may be substituted for the milk.

—THICK WHITE SAUCE

Follow ▲ Recipe. Use 3 to 4 tablespoons flour and 3 to 4 tablespoons butter or margarine. Use in preparation of soufflés and croquettes.

THIN WHITE SAUCE

Follow ▲ Recipe. Use 1 tablespoon flour and 1 tablespoon butter or margarine. Use as a base for cream soups. For a rich cream soup, substitute cream for milk.

—MOCK HOLLANDAISE SAUCE

Follow ▲ Recipe, using a double boiler top instead of a saucepan. When sauce is thickened, vigorously stir about 3 tablespoons of hot mixture into **2 egg yolks**, slightly beaten. Return to sauce and cook over simmering water 3 to 5 min. Stir slowly to keep mixture cooking evenly. Stir in **1 tablespoon lemon juice** and **2 tablespoons butter or margarine**.

—TOMATO SAUCE

Follow ▲ Recipe. Cook **1 tablespoon finely chopped onion** in the butter before adding flour mixture. Substitute **tomato juice** for milk. Blend in **1 teaspoon Worcestershire sauce** with tomato juice.

—CHEESE SAUCE

Follow ▲ Recipe. Blend in **¼ teaspoon dry mustard** and **a few grains cayenne pepper** with flour and seasonings. Cool sauce slightly. Add all at one time, **¼ cup (1oz.) grated Parmesan, sharp Cheddar or Swiss cheese**. Heat slowly, stirring constantly, until cheese is melted.

—EGG SAUCE

Follow ▲ Recipe. Coarsely chop **2 Hard-Cooked Eggs** (page 133) and mix into the hot sauce.

—MUSHROOM SAUCE II

Follow ▲ Recipe. Clean and slice (page 9) **½ lb. mushrooms.** Heat in a skillet **¼ cup butter or margarine.** Add mushrooms and **1 tablespoon minced onion.** Cook slowly, moving and turning with a spoon until mushrooms are tender. Do not brown. Stir into sauce. (Or ½ cup drained canned mushrooms may be substituted for fresh mushrooms, and mushroom liquid may be used for part of milk.)

SOUR CREAM WHITE SAUCE

▲ Base Recipe

Rich, smooth sour cream white sauce gives a fine, zestful flavor to well-cooked vegetables without any added seasoning at all; but the addition of herbs and spices can contribute just that difference that will make your creamed vegetables unique. For creamed peas or peas and carrots, try stirring a half-teaspoonful of crushed dried mint leaves into white sauce; or add a pinch or two of savory, marjoram or rosemary. Cauliflower responds delightfully to a touch of mace or tarragon; thyme, basil or nutmeg is especially congenial to delicate boiled onions. Try a little curry powder in the cream sauce with asparagus; season creamed turnips with dill or caraway seed; and see how ginger, thyme or tarragon blends with creamed mushrooms. Use seasonings with a light hand; it's easy to add more but impossible to subtract— and what you want to do is complement, not disguise, the natural flavor of the vegetable.

Heat in a saucepan over low heat
2 tablespoons butter or margarine
Blend in
2 tablespoons all-purpose flour
¼ teaspoon salt
¼ teaspoon monosodium glutamate
Few grains pepper
Heat until mixture bubbles. Remove from heat. Add gradually, stirring in
¾ cup milk
Cook rapidly, stirring constantly, until sauce thickens. Remove from heat. Stirring vigorously, add in very small amounts
¾ cup dairy sour cream
Cook 2 or 3 min. longer, stirring constantly until sauce is just heated. Serve at once.

About 1½ cups sauce

—SAVORY SOUR CREAM SAUCE

Follow ▲ Recipe. Add **1 tablespoon grated onion, ½ teaspoon dry mustard** and **⅛ to ¼ teaspoon marjoram** to the butter. Substitute **¾ cup quick meat or chicken broth** (page 10) for the milk.

VELVET SAUCE
(Sauce Veloute)

▲ Base Recipe

A relative of white sauce, Velvet Sauce is

wonderful with croquettes, baked fish or eggs. When served with fish, it is made with White Stock which has been prepared from fish or fish trimmings, and is called Fish Veloute. For chicken or Veal Veloute, vary the basis of the stock using chicken or veal.

Heat in a saucepan over low heat
3 tablespoons butter
Stir in until well blended a mixture of
3 tablespoons all-purpose flour
¼ teaspoon salt
⅛ teaspoon white pepper
Heat until mixture bubbles. Remove from heat and gradually stir in
½ cup cold White Stock or Consommé (page 41)
Return to heat and bring rapidly to boiling, stirring constantly; cook 1 to 2 min. longer. Blend in gradually
1 cup cold White Stock
Boil 1 to 2 min., stirring constantly, until thick and smooth. Stir in
½ teaspoon nutmeg
Serve hot.

About 1½ cups sauce

—BECHAMEL SAUCE
(Sauce Bechamel)

This sauce is named for its originator, Louis de Bechamel, Lord Steward of the Household in the Court of King Louis XIV.

Follow ▲ Recipe. Substitute **¾ cup cream** for ¾ cup of the stock. Stir in **1 tablespoon minced onion.** Serve hot on vegetables, fish, hard-cooked eggs or poultry.

—NORMANDY SAUCE
(Sauce Normande)

The flavor of almost any vegetable may be

enhanced with this sauce. Use it freely with these—celery, carrots, cauliflower, asparagus, green peas or salsify—all typical of Normandy.

Follow ▲ Recipe. Substitute **½ cup cream** and **1 cup cider** for stock. Blend in **¼ teaspoon lemon juice** with nutmeg.

WINE-MERCHANT OR BERCY SAUCE
(Sauce Bercy)

Cook slowly without browning, stirring occasionally
>   **2 tablespoons butter**
>   **¼ cup chopped shallots**

Blend in
>   **1 cup white wine**
>   **1 cup fish stock**

Simmer until reduced to one third the quantity. Stir in
>   **⅔ cup (Velvet Sauce, page 304;**
>   **use fish stock for White Stock)**

Continue slow cooking about 5 min., or until sauce is clear. Strain.

Just before serving, stir in ½ teaspoon at a time
>   **½ cup butter**

Blend in
>   **2 tablespoons chopped parsley**
>   **1½ tablespoons lemon juice**

Serve hot with poached fish (Fish Poached in Court-Bouillon, page 282).

About 1¾ cups sauce

GREEN HERB SAUCE
(Sauce Ravigote)

The name for this sauce comes from the word "ravigoter," meaning "to revive." This indicates that it will whet the appetite. Although used most often with poultry or eggs, variety meats and leftovers also benefit from its flavor.

Simmer in a saucepan
>   **½ cup white wine**
>   **¼ cup tarragon or wine vinegar**
>   **1 shallot, minced**

When the liquid is reduced to less than one-half, add
>   **2 cups Velvet Sauce (page 304)**

Heat.

Just before serving, thoroughly blend in
>   **2 tablespoons butter**
>   **1 teaspoon minced chervil**
>   **1 teaspoon minced tarragon**
>   **1 teaspoon chopped chives**

Serve hot   *About 2¼ cups sauce*

A LA KING SAUCE

Set out a double boiler.

Drain, reserving ½ cup of liquid
>   **1 can (16 oz.) green peas (about 1¾**
>   **cups, drained)**

Set aside.

Heat in top of double boiler over low heat
>   **¼ cup butter or margarine**

Blend in
>   **¼ cup all-purpose flour**
>   **½ teaspoon salt**
>   **¼ teaspoon dry mustard**
>   **⅛ teaspoon pepper**

Heat until mixture bubbles. Remove from heat. Stirring constantly, gradually add the reserved pea liquid and
>   **1½ cups milk**

Return to heat and bring rapidly to boiling, stirring constantly. Cook 1 to 2 min. longer. Blend in the peas and
>   **½ cup (4-oz. can) sliced mushrooms,**
>   **drained,**
>   **2 tablespoons chopped pimiento**

Cook over low heat, gently stirring occasionally, until mixture is heated thoroughly.

To keep sauce warm, cover and place over simmering water.   *About 2½ cups sauce*

QUICK CHEESE SAUCE

Melt in double boiler top over simmering water
>   **½ lb. pasteurized process Cheddar**
>   **cheese**

Add and stir until smooth
>   **¼ cup milk**
>   **1½ teaspoons Worcestershire sauce**
>   **1 teaspoon prepared mustard**
>   *About 1½ cups sauce*

PARMESAN CHEESE SAUCE

Cook asparagus, broccoli or cauliflower until just tender. Arrange in a greased baking dish, top with this sauce, then sprinkle with fine dry bread crumbs. Whisk it under the broiler for a few minutes, and what have you done? You've made the elegance in vegetables emerge.

Heat in top of a double boiler over low heat
>   **2 tablespoons butter**

Blend in
>   **1 tablespoon all-purpose flour**

Heat until mixture bubbles. Remove from heat and add very gradually, stirring in
>   **1 cup dairy sour cream**

Cook over simmering water, stirring constantly, 1 to 2 min. longer. Remove from heat and vigorously stir about 3 tablespoons of the hot sauce into
>   **1 egg yolk, slightly beaten**

Immediately return mixture to double boiler. Cook over simmering water 3 to 5 min. Stir slowly to keep mixture cooking evenly. Remove from heat and add (all at one time)
>   **¼ cup (about 1 oz.) grated Parmesan**
>   **cheese**

Blend thoroughly.   *About ¾ cup sauce*

MORNAY SAUCE

Prepare and set aside.
>   **¾ cup quick chicken broth (page 10)**

Heat in top of double boiler over low heat
>   **3 tablespoons butter**

Stir in until well blended
>   **3 tablespoons all-purpose flour**

Heat until mixture bubbles. Remove from heat and gradually stir in the chicken broth and
>   **¾ cup cream**

Return to heat and bring rapidly to boiling, stirring constantly; cook 1 to 2 min. longer. Remove from heat and vigorously stir about 3 tablespoons sauce into
>   **2 egg yolks, slightly beaten**

Immediately return mixture to double boiler. Cook over simmering water 3 to 4 min. Stir slowly to keep mixture cooking evenly. Cool slightly. Add at one time and blend in until cheese is melted
>   **⅓ cup grated Parmesan or finely cut**
>   **Gruyére cheese**
>   **1 tablespoon butter**

Serve hot.   *About 2 cups sauce*

Note: This elegant sauce may be used for Brussels sprouts, asparagus, broccoli, green beans, cauliflower or for fish, vegetables, poultry or other mixtures which are to be browned in the oven. If desired, sauce may be sprinkled with grated cheese before browning. If a very brown color is desired, reserve a few table-spoons of the sauce and fold in 1 tablespoon whipped cream. Spread over the top before browning.

Chives   Basil   Bay   Thyme   Parsley   Savory

Hollandaise Sauce: Beat egg yolks and cream in the top of the double boiler with a wire whisk. Remove double broiler from heat; beat butter, ½ teaspoon at a time, into thickened mixture.

SOUR CREAM HOLLANDAISE SAUCE

Beat until thick and lemon-colored
3 egg yolks
Add and beat until blended
¾ cup dairy sour cream
1 tablespoon lemon juice
½ teaspoon dry mustard
¼ teaspoon salt
2 or 3 drops Tabasco
Pour into top of a double boiler; set over hot (not boiling) water. (Bottom of double boiler top should not touch water.) Cook over low heat, stirring constantly, until sauce is heated and has consistency of thick cream.

Remove from heat and serve immediately. Especially good with asparagus, broccoli, artichokes or green beans. *About 1 cup sauce*

HOLLANDAISE SAUCE
(Sauce Hollandaise)

▲ Base Recipe

Set out a small double boiler.

In the top of the small double boiler, beat with a wire whisk until thickened and light-colored
2 egg yolks
2 tablespoons cream
Blend in
¼ teaspoon salt
Few grains cayenne pepper
Place top of double boiler over hot (not boiling) water. (Bottom of double boiler top should not touch water.)

Add gradually, beating constantly
2 tablespoons lemon juice or tarragon vinegar
Cook over low heat, beating constantly with the whisk until sauce is the consistency of thick cream. Remove double boiler from heat, leaving top in place.

Add, beating constantly, ½ teaspoon at a time
½ cup butter
Beat with whisk until butter is thoroughly melted and blended into mixture. Serve immediately with vegetables, fish or eggs.

If necessary, this sauce may be kept warm 15 to 30 min. by setting it over hot water. Stir occasionally. Cover tightly. *1 cup sauce*

—BEARNAISE SAUCE
(Sauce Bearnaise)

Follow ▲ Recipe. Crush **1 peppercorn** and add with the salt. Blend in, after the butter, **3 tablespoons finely chopped fresh herbs** such as tarragon, chervil, shallots (or green onion or chives) and parsley.

LEMON SAUCE

Heat in a saucepan over low heat
1½ tablespoons butter or margarine
Blend in
2 tablespoons all-purpose flour
½ teaspoon salt
⅛ teaspoon pepper
Heat, stirring constantly, until mixture bubbles. Remove saucepan from heat. Add gradually, stirring well after each addition
¾ cup boiling water
¾ cup undiluted evaporated milk
Return to heat and bring rapidly to boiling, stirring constantly; cook 1 to 2 min. longer.

Vigorously stir about 3 tablespoons of hot mixture into
2 egg yolks, slightly beaten
Immediately blend into mixture in saucepan. Continue to stir and cook 2 to 3 min. Stir in
¼ cup lemon juice
Serve hot with fish. *About 1¾ cups sauce*

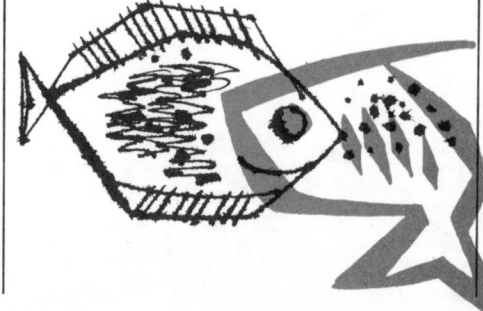

CURRY SAUCE

A sauce of distinction!

Heat in a heavy 2-qt. saucepan
⅓ cup butter
Add and cook over medium heat until lightly browned, stirring occasionally
3 tablespoons chopped onion
3 tablespoons chopped celery
3 tablespoons chopped green apple
12 peppercorns
1 bay leaf
Blend in a mixture of
⅓ cup sifted all-purpose flour
2½ teaspoons curry powder
½ teaspoon monosodium glutamate
¼ teaspoon sugar
⅛ teaspoon nutmeg
Heat until mixture bubbles. Remove from heat and add gradually, stirring constantly
2½ cups milk
Return to heat and bring rapidly to boiling. Stirring constantly, cook until mixture thickens. Cook 1 to 2 min. longer. Remove from heat and stir in
2 teaspoons lemon juice
½ teaspoon Worcestershire sauce
Strain mixture through a fine sieve, pressing vegetables against sieve to extract all sauce.
About 2 cups sauce

MUSHROOM CHEESE SAUCE

Set out a medium-size saucepan.

Shred and set aside
1 oz. Cheddar cheese (about ¼ cup, shredded)
Heat in the saucepan over low heat
¼ cup butter or margarine
Blend in
¼ cup all-purpose flour
½ teaspoon salt
¼ teaspoon monosodium glutamate
¼ teaspoon dry mustard
Few grains cayenne pepper
Heat until mixture bubbles. Remove from eat.

Add gradually while stirring constantly
2 cups milk
Return to heat and bring rapidly to boiling, stirring constantly; cook 1 to 2 min. longer. Blend in
½ cup (4-oz. can) sliced mushrooms, drained
Cool sauce slightly and add the shredded cheese all at one time. Blend sauce rapidly until cheese is melted and well blended.

To keep sauce warm, cover and place over simmering water. *About 2 cups sauce*

SAUCE PAR EXCELLENCE

Clean and slice (page 9) and set aside
½ lb. mushrooms
Heat in skillet
⅓ cup fat

Add mushrooms and cook slowly, gently moving and turning with a fork or spoon, until mushrooms are lightly browned and tender.

Blend thoroughly.

1¼ cups (10½-oz. can) condensed cream of chicken soup

2 tablespoons milk

1 teaspoon Worcestershire sauce

Add slowly to skillet, moving mixture constantly. Simmer, moving mixture constantly, until mixture is bubbling hot.

Remove from heat; add in very small amounts, blending vigorously after each addition

1 cup dairy sour cream

Cook over low heat, moving mixture constantly, until mixture is heated thoroughly. Do not boil. *About 2½ cups sauce*

MUSTARD SAUCE I

Scald in top of double boiler over simmering water

¾ cup cream or undiluted evaporated milk

Meanwhile, blend in a small saucepan

¼ cup sugar

2 tablespoons dry mustard

2 teaspoons cornstarch

½ teaspoon salt

Add, stirring well

¼ cup cream or undiluted evaporated milk

Gradually add the scalded milk while stirring constantly. Stirring gently and constantly, bring cornstarch mixture rapidly to boiling over direct heat and cook for 3 min.

Wash double boiler top to remove scum.

Pour mixture into double boiler top and place over simmering water. Cover and cook 5 min., stirring occasionally.

Remove cover and vigorously stir about 3 tablespoons of this hot mixture into

1 egg yolk, slightly beaten

Immediately blend into mixture in double boiler. Cook over simmering water 3 to 5 min. Stir slowly to keep mixture cooking evenly. Remove from heat. Add gradually and stir in

¼ cup vinegar

Serve sauce hot with

Glazed Ham Loaf (page 242)

Or serve with other meat.

About 1¼ cups sauce

MEXICAN BARBECUE SAUCE

A truly "hot" meat sauce.

Set out a large heavy skillet with a tight-fitting cover.

Prepare and mix

1½ cups (about 3 medium) chopped onion

¾ cup (about 1 large) chopped green pepper

Heat in the skillet

2 tablespoons fat

Add the chopped vegetables and cook, moving and turning mixture with a spoon, until onion is tender.

Add and cook over medium heat until browned, breaking into small pieces with fork or spoon

1 lb. ground round steak

Meanwhile, blend

2½ cups canned tomatoes

1¼ cups (12-oz. bottle) chili sauce

1 cup (8-oz. can) tomato sauce

¾ cup (6-oz. can) tomato paste

3 tablespoons brown sugar

3 tablespoons cider vinegar

2 tablespoons Worcestershire sauce

2 tablespoons oregano

1 tablespoon prepared mustard

2 teaspoons cumin

2 teaspoons thyme

1½ teaspoons salt

1 teaspoon basil

1 teaspoon cloves

½ teaspoon crushed red peppers

¼ teaspoon pepper

2 cloves garlic, minced

1 bay leaf

Set aside.

Heat in a small saucepan over low heat

2 tablespoons butter or margarine

Add and cook over medium heat, moving and turning mushrooms with a spoon until lightly browned

1 can (8-oz.) whole mushrooms, drained

Add the mushrooms and the tomato mixture to the browned meat and bring to boiling, stirring constantly. Reduce heat, cover and simmer about 2½ hrs., stirring occasionally to prevent sticking or burning.

Remove cover and simmer 1 hr. longer, stirring occasionally. Sauce should be thick, if it becomes thicker than desired, add

Boiling water

Remove bay leaf before serving.

About 2 qts. sauce

Note: If Spanish red chili sauce is used, omit crushed red peppers.

QUICK TOMATO SAUCE

Heat in a small skillet

2 tablespoons butter or margarine

Add

¼ cup coarsely chopped celery

¼ cup coarsely chopped green pepper

2 tablespoons finely chopped onion

Cook, stirring frequently, until celery and green pepper are tender. Remove from heat and add slowly while stirring constantly

1¼ cups (10¾-oz. can) condensed tomato soup

⅓ cup water

2 tablespoons lemon juice

1 teaspoon Worcestershire sauce

2 tablespoons brown sugar

1 teaspoon dry mustard

½ teaspoon salt

Few grains pepper

Simmer, uncovered, about 5 min., or until sauce is heated thoroughly.

About 2 cups sauce

TOMATO SAUCE

Combine in a saucepan and simmer 10 to 12 minutes

2½ cups cooked or canned tomatoes

2 tablespoons chopped onion

2 teaspoons sugar

½ teaspoon salt

½ teaspoon monosodium glutamate

⅛ teaspoon pepper

Force through a sieve to remove tomato seeds and onion pieces. Set aside.

Heat in a skillet

2 tablespoons butter

Blend in

2 tablespoons all-purpose flour

Heat until mixture bubbles. Remove from heat. Add gradually, stirring in, the tomato mixture and

⅛ teaspoon Worcestershire sauce

Cook rapidly, stirring constantly until sauce thickens. Cook 1 to 2 min. longer.

About 2 cups sauce

TOMATO BEEF SAUCE

▲ *Base Recipe*

Heat in a large heavy skillet

2 tablespoons fat

Add and cook over medium heat, stirring occasionally, about 3 min.

½ cup (about 1 medium) chopped onion

1 clove garlic, minced

Add and cook over medium heat until browned, breaking into small pieces with fork or spoon

½ lb. ground beef

Add slowly and stir in

2½ cups cooked or canned tomatoes, sieved

¾ cup (6-oz. can) tomato paste

¼ cup finely chopped parsley

1 tablespoon Worcestershire sauce

1¼ teaspoons salt

½ teaspoon monosodium glutamate

¼ teaspoon basil

⅛ teaspoon pepper

Few grains cayenne pepper

Simmer uncovered, stirring occasionally, about 30 min., or until thickened.

Blend in
½ cup (4-oz. can) sliced mushrooms, drained
Simmer 5 to 10 min. If sauce is too thick, blend in ½ cup water. *About 3 cups sauce*

—OLIVE 'N' TOMATO BEEF SAUCE

Follow ▲ Recipe. Substitute **½ cup pitted and sliced green or ripe olives** for mushrooms.

—BEEF BARBECUE SAUCE

Follow ▲ Recipe. Stir in **¾ cup chili sauce, ⅓ cup lemon juice** and **2 or 3 drops Tabasco** along with the tomatoes. Add **2 tablespoons brown sugar** and **1 teaspoon dry mustard**.

—VEGETABLE SAUCE

Follow ▲ Recipe. Omit ground beef, parsley and mushrooms. Add **½ cup chopped celery, ¼ cup finely chopped green pepper, 2 tablespoons chopped ripe olives** and **2 or 3 drops Tabasco** along with tomatoes.

TOMATO CHEESE SAUCE

Set out a large skillet.

Shred and set aside
2 oz. Cheddar cheese (about ½ cup, shredded)

Drain and chop
1 can (4 oz.) mushrooms (about ½ cup, drained)
Put mushrooms into skillet with
2½ cups (two 10¾-oz. cans) condensed tomato soup
Simmer about 10 min., or until mixture is bubbling hot, stirring occasionally.

Add cheese all at one time. Stir sauce rapidly until cheese is melted and well blended.

Serve sauce hot. *About 3 cups sauce*

PROVENCAL SAUCE
(Sauce Provencale)

Wash and place in boiling water 1 min.
6 medium tomatoes
Peel, remove seeds and chop.

Heat in a saucepan
2 tablespoons olive oil
½ clove garlic, crushed
Add the tomatoes and
1 teaspoon chopped parsley
½ teaspoon salt
⅛ teaspoon pepper
Cook gently 30 min.

Serve hot over sliced cooked meat or croquettes. *1½ cups sauce*

SPICED CHERRY SAUCE

Combine in a small saucepan
1 cup cherry preserves
2½ tablespoons lemon juice
¾ teaspoon cinnamon
¼ teaspoon cloves
Place over low heat and bring just to boiling, stirring occasionally.

Serve hot. *1 cup sauce*

SPICY RAISIN SAUCE

A flavorful sauce guaranteed to impart a Southwestern touch to any meat it's served with.

Heat in a large heavy skillet over low heat
2 tablespoons butter or margarine
Add and cook over medium heat, occasionally moving with a spoon, until onion and green pepper are tender
⅓ cup chopped onion
⅓ cup chopped green pepper
1 clove garlic, minced
Add to the skillet
1 cup (8-oz. can) tomato sauce
1 cup water
⅔ cup sliced pitted ripe olives
½ cup (about 3 oz.) dark seedless raisins
1 tablespoon sherry
1½ teaspoons chili powder
1 teaspoon sugar
½ teaspoon salt
½ teaspoon monosodium glutamate
3 drops Tabasco
Cook over medium heat, stirring frequently, 10 min. Remove from heat and cool. Chill, covered, in refrigerator about 24 hrs. to allow flavors to blend.

To serve, heat sauce thoroughly.
About 2 cups sauce

RAISIN SAUCE I

This spicy sauce is a perfect accompaniment for ham and tongue.

Mix in a saucepan
¾ cup firmly packed brown sugar
1 tablespoon cornstarch
¼ teaspoon cloves
Add gradually, stirring in
1½ cups broth from ham or tongue (if none is available, use water; and ¼ teaspoon salt)
¾ cup dark seedless raisins
Put over high heat and bring rapidly to boiling. Stirring constantly, cook until mixture is

thickened, about 3 min. Remove from heat and stir in
1 tablespoon lemon juice
1 tablespoon butter
Serve hot. *About 2 cups sauce*

RAISIN SAUCE II

This pleasantly sweet-sour version of a favorite sauce is perfect with any baked or broiled fish.

Heat in a saucepan over low heat
¼ cup butter or margarine
Blend in
½ cup firmly packed brown sugar
¼ cup all-purpose flour
1 teaspoon monosodium glutamate
1 teaspoon salt
½ teaspoon grated orange peel
Heat and stir until thoroughly blended. Remove from heat.

Add gradually, stirring in
1 cup water
½ cup lemon juice
½ cup orange juice
Cook rapidly, stirring constantly until sauce thickens. Add and stir in
1 cup (about 5 oz.) golden raisins
Cook 1 to 2 min. longer.
About 2¾ cups sauce

CREAMED BACON AND ONION
(Bonddoppa)

▲ *Base Recipe*

Clean and dice
2 large onions (about 2 cups, diced)
Cut into 1-in. pieces
½ lb. bacon
Put the bacon and onion into a skillet. Cook over medium heat, moving and turning frequently with a spoon until onion is golden brown and bacon is evenly crisped and browned. Pour off excess fat as it collects.

Meanwhile, put into a screw-top jar
2 cups milk
Add to milk
3 tablespoons all-purpose flour
½ teaspoon salt
⅛ teaspoon pepper
Cover jar tightly; shake until well blended.

When bacon and onion are done, remove skillet from heat. Stirring constantly, slowly pour the milk-flour mixture into the skillet. Return to heat and bring to boiling. Reduce heat and simmer 3 to 5 min., keeping mixture moving gently with a spoon.

Serve over
Boiled potatoes
4 servings

—CREAMED SALT PORK AND ONION
(Gron Salted Flask)

Follow ▲ Recipe. Substitute **½ lb. salt pork,** diced, for the bacon.

BROWN BUTTER

▲ Base Recipe

In a heavy saucepan melt **1 tablespoon butter** for each serving. Heat butter slowly over low heat until it becomes browned. Pour over cooked vegetable and serve immediately.

—BROWN ONION BUTTER

Follow ▲ Recipe. Heat with each tablespoon butter ½ **teaspoon grated onion.**

—MEUNIERE BUTTER

Follow ▲ Recipe. Stir into browned butter ⅛ to ¼ **teaspoon lemon juice** and **1 teaspoon chopped parsley** for each tablespoon butter.

MAITRE d'HOTEL BUTTER

Cream until blended
    ½ **cup softened butter**
    2 tablespoons lemon juice
    2 teaspoons chopped parsley
    ¼ **teaspoon salt**
    ⅛ **teaspoon pepper**
Serve with fish.   *About ½ cup butter*

MINT BUTTER

▲ Base Recipe

Put into small mixer bowl
    1 cup butter or margarine
    1 tablespoon cream
    2 teaspoons lemon juice
    4 or 5 sprigs fresh mint leaves, finely chopped
Whip until smooth. Cover and store in refrigerator.

Allow to stand at room temperature before using. Serve with meats, vegetables or quick breads.   *About 1½ cups butter*

—CHIVE BUTTER

Follow ▲ Recipe. Substitute **8 to 10 chive spears** for the mint leaves.

DEVILED BUTTER FOR VEGETABLES

Cream in a small bowl
    ½ **cup butter**
    2 Hard-Cooked Eggs (page 133), sieved
    1½ tablespoons white vinegar
    1 teaspoon lemon juice
    1 teaspoon prepared mustard

Season to taste with **cayenne pepper.** Serve over green vegetables such as spinach or green beans.   *⅔ cup butter*

PARMESAN BUTTER FOR VEGETABLES

A nice flavor accent for asparagus spears.

Heat in a small saucepan over low heat
    ¼ **cup butter or margarine**
Stir in until cheese is partially melted
    ½ **cup shredded Parmesan cheese**
    ½ **teaspoon monosodium glutamate**
    ⅛ **teaspoon pepper**
Pour over hot cooked vegetable in a serving dish. Serve immediately.   *About ½ cup butter*

PARSLEY ONION BUTTER FOR VEGETABLES

Especially good with French-style green beans.

Heat in a small saucepan
    2 tablespoons butter or margarine
Add and cook until just tender, stirring occasionally
    2 tablespoons minced celery
Blend in and simmer 10 min.
    ⅓ **cup instant minced onion**
    ¼ **cup minced parsley**
    ½ **clove garlic, minced**
    ½ **teaspoon salt**
    ⅛ **teaspoon rosemary, crushed**
    ⅛ **teaspoon sweet basil, crushed**
Add parsley mixture to hot cooked vegetable and toss lightly to thoroughly mix. Serve immediately.   *About ½ cup butter*

RIPE OLIVE BUTTER FOR VEGETABLES

Heat in a saucepan about 5 min. over low heat
    ⅓ **cup butter**
    ½ **clove garlic, minced**
Mix in and heat thoroughly
    2 teaspoons lemon juice
    Few grains pepper
    ¼ **cup ripe olive rings**
    Seasoned salt
Spoon over hot cooked green vegetable in a serving dish. Serve immediately.
    About ½ cup butter

ROQUEFORT BUTTER FOR GREEN VEGETABLES

Heat in a skillet over low heat ⅓ **cup butter.** When butter is heated, stir in **2 tablespoons** crumbled Roquefort cheese and **1 tablespoon cider vinegar.** Pour over cooked vegetable in a serving dish.   *About ½ cup butter*

GRIBICHE SAUCE
(Sauce Gribiche)

Hard cook (page 133)
    3 eggs
Separate egg whites from egg yolks and set aside.

Force egg yolks through ricer or sieve. Blend into egg yolks, making a paste
    1 teaspoon prepared mustard
    ½ **teaspoon salt**
    ⅛ **teaspoon pepper**
Beat in, 1 teaspoon at a time, gradually increasing amounts of each addition
    1½ cups olive oil
When smooth, gradually beat in
    ½ **cup vinegar**
Stir in
    3 sweet gherkins, chopped fine
    2 teaspoons chopped parsley
    2 teaspoons chopped chervil
    2 teaspoons chopped chives or tarragon

Cut whites of the hard-cooked eggs into thin strips and blend into the sauce. Serve with cold fish.   *About 2 cups sauce*

VINAIGRETTE SAUCE I

Combine in a medium-size bowl
    ½ **cup olive oil**
    ¼ **cup cider or wine vinegar**
Blend in
    2 teaspoons finely chopped parsley
    2 teaspoons finely chopped chives
    2 teaspoons finely chopped pimiento
    1 teaspoon chopped chervil
    1 teaspoon chopped capers
    1 teaspoon salt
    ½ **teaspoon dry mustard**
    ⅛ **teaspoon pepper**
Serve hot or cold.   *1 cup sauce*

VINAIGRETTE SAUCE II

Mix thoroughly
    1 tablespoon minced green pepper
    1 teaspoon minced chives
    1 teaspoon minced parsley
    ½ **teaspoon minced fresh basil or**
        ⅛ **teaspoon crushed dried basil**
    1½ teaspoons minced capers
    1 tablespoon chopped pickles
    ½ **cup French dressing**
Serve with lamb or beef.   *About ⅔ cup sauce*

BARBECUE SAUCE

Like wine, this tangy, hot sauce improves with age.

Put into an electric blender container
- **1 cup ketchup**
- **¼ cup lemon juice**
- **2 tablespoons brown sugar**
- **1 tablespoon soy sauce**
- **1 tablespoon prepared horseradish mustard**
- **1½ teaspoons salt**
- **½ teaspoon monosodium glutamate**
- **½ teaspoon pepper**
- **¼ teaspoon oregano, marjoram or thyme**
- **½ teaspoon Tabasco**
- **¼ teaspoon cayenne pepper**
- **2 slices onion**

Cover and blend until thoroughly mixed and onion slices are finely chopped.

Pour blended mixture into saucepan. Add
- **1 clove garlic**

Simmer over low heat at least 10 min. Remove garlic. Use immediately or store in refrigerator. Stir before using. *About 1½ cups sauce*

WINE BARBECUE SAUCE

Add to a screw-top jar
- **1 cup dry red wine**
- **½ cup salad or cooking oil**
- **½ cup red wine vinegar**
- **1 tablespoon Worcestershire sauce**
- **½ cup finely chopped onion**
- **1 clove garlic, minced**
- **5 tablespoons sugar**
- **½ teaspoon salt**
- **½ teaspoon seasoned pepper**
- **1 tablespoon finely chopped parsley**
- **½ teaspoon crushed rosemary**
- **¼ teaspoon crumbled bay leaves**
- **6 whole cloves**

Cover; shake to blend. Store in the refrigerator. Shake before using. *About 2½ cups sauce*

SPECIAL HOT SAUCE

Combine thoroughly in a small bowl
- **½ cup chili sauce**
- **2 tablespoons minced onion**
- **½ teaspoon Worcestershire sauce**
- **½ teaspoon capers**
- **¼ teaspoon brown sugar**
- **¼ teaspoon monosodium glutamate**
- **5 drops Tabasco**

About 2 cups sauce

APPLE SOUR CREAM SAUCE

▲ Base Recipe

Blend
- **1 cup dairy sour cream**
- **⅓ cup prepared horse radish**
- **1 tablespoon grated lemon peel**

Add
- **¾ teaspoon salt**
- **⅛ teaspoon white pepper**

Wash, quarter, core and chop
- **1 medium red apple**

Add chopped apple to sour cream mixture and mix thoroughly.

Chill in refrigerator until ready to serve. *About 2 cups sauce*

—HORSERADISH SOUR CREAM SAUCE

Follow ▲ Recipe: omit chopped apple.

BUTTERMILK SAUCE

Blend thoroughly
- **1 cup buttermilk**
- **1 cup dairy sour cream**
- **1 teaspoon salt**
- **½ teaspoon paprika**
- **2 tablespoons chopped pimiento-stuffed olives**
- **½ teaspoon capers**
- **¼ cup chopped parsley**

Chill until ready to use. Serve with fried fish. *About 2 cups sauce*

CUMBERLAND-STYLE SAUCE

A peppery sauce—wonderful with roast ham (cold or hot) or assorted cold meats!

Rinse and very finely chop
- **3 green onions or scallions**

Put into a bowl and mash with a fork
- **⅓ cup red currant jelly**

Mix in the green onion and
- **1 tablespoon grated orange peel**
- **2 teaspoons grated lemon peel**
- **¼ cup orange juice**
- **1 tablespoon lemon juice**
- **½ teaspoon prepared mustard**
- **⅛ teaspoon ginger**
- **⅛ teaspoon cayenne pepper**

Mix thoroughly.

Serve cold or hot. *About ¾ cup sauce*

CAPER SAUCE

Blend in a bowl
- **½ cup mayonnaise**
- **Few grains salt**
- **Few grains paprika**
- **⅛ teaspoon dry mustard**
- **3 tablespoons caper liquid**
- **1 teaspoon anchovy paste**

Beat until soft peaks are formed
- **½ cup chilled heavy cream**

Fold whipped cream into mayonnaise mixture until blended. Pile into a serving bowl and chill. Garnish with **capers**. Serve with chilled meat from cooked rock lobster tails. *About 1½ cup sauce*

CRANBERRY CHANTILLY SAUCE

Sauce cold sliced ham or turkey with this creamy pink blend.

Crush with a fork
- **1 cup jellied cranberry sauce**

Mix in
- **⅔ cup (5 oz. jar) prepared horseradish**
- **2 tablespoons confectioners' sugar**
- **½ teaspoon salt**

Chill thoroughly.

When ready to serve, beat until soft peaks are formed
- **1 cup chilled heavy cream**

Fold cranberry mixture into whipped cream. *About 3 cups sauce*

CUCUMBER SAUCE I

Rinse and cut into pieces
- **1 large cucumber**

Put into an electric blender container
- **1 cup mayonnaise**
- **½ teaspoon salt**
- **¼ teaspoon pepper**
- **⅛ teaspoon anchovy paste**
- **2 slices onion**

Add cucumber pieces, cover and blend until cucumbers are chopped. Chill. Serve with fish. *About 2 cups sauce*

CUCUMBER SAUCE II

▲ Base Recipe

Wash, pare and finely chop
- **1 medium cucumber**

Drain thoroughly.

Mix the chopped cucumber and
- **1 cup mayonnaise**
- **2 tablespoons lemon juice**
- **1 tablespoon minced parsley**

Chill in refrigerator until ready to serve. *About 2 cups sauce*

—SOUR CREAM CUCUMBER SAUCE I

Follow ▲ Recipe. Substitute **1 cup dairy sour cream** for the mayonnaise.

CUCUMBER SAUCE III

▲ *Base Recipe*

Rinse, trim and discard stem end from
1 medium cucumber
Pare, if desired, chop and set aside.

Put into a small bowl
1 cup mayonnaise
Blend in
2 teaspoons grated onion
½ teaspoon salt
½ teaspoon monosodium glutamate
¼ teaspoon pepper
Stir in the chopped cucumber. Spoon sauce into a serving dish, cover and refrigerate until chilled and flavors are blended.

Before serving, sprinkle over sauce
1 tablespoon diced sweet pickle
1 tablespoon diced pimiento
Serve sauce as a complement to fish.
About 2 cups sauce

—SOUR CREAM CUCUMBER SAUCE II

Follow ▲ Recipe. Decrease mayonaisse to ½ cup and add **½ cup dairy sour cream**.

LEMON CUCUMBER SAUCE

A delightful sauce that takes honors when served with baked ham slices, ready-to-serve meats or fish.

Pare and finely chop enough cucumber to yield
½ cup finely chopped cucumber
Put into a bowl
1½ cups mayonnaise
¼ cup lemon juice
2 tablespoons prepared horseradish
2 tablespoons chili sauce
1 teaspoon finely chopped chives
½ teaspoon salt
⅛ teaspoon curry powder
Add cucumber and mix thoroughly. Cover and chill in refrigerator before serving.

Serve garnished with **paprika**.
About 2 cups sauce

HORSERADISH CREAM

Ham Mousse Imperial and this Horseradish Cream are friendly companions.

Place a bowl and a rotary beater in refrigerator to chill.

Blend until thoroughly mixed
1 cup mayonnaise
3 tablespoons prepared horseradish
1 tablespoon tarragon vinegar
1 tablespoon lemon juice
¼ teaspoon prepared mustard
Few grains cayenne pepper
Few grains salt
Few grains sugar
Using the chilled bowl and beater, whip until cream is of medium consistency (piles softly)
1 cup chilled heavy cream

Spread mixture over whipped cream and fold together.
About 3 cups sauce

HORSERADISH SAUCE

Chill in refrigerator, a bowl, beater and
1 cup dairy sour cream
Using chilled bowl and beater, whip about 5 min., or until of medium consistency (piles softly).

Blend in
3 tablespoons prepared horseradish
2 tablespoons grated lemon peel
Serve with fish.
About 2 cups sauce

MUSTARD SAUCE II

Put into a bowl
1 cup chilled heavy cream
1 tablespoon prepared horseradish
1 tablespoon vinegar
2½ teaspoons dry mustard
½ teaspoon monosodium glutamate
¼ teaspoon salt
Combine all ingredients and chill in refrigerator. After mixture is well chilled, whip until mixture is of medium consistency (piles softly).
About 2 cups sauce

FISH SAUCE SUPREME

The extra flavor touch that will make your quick fish dinner extra successful.

Blend in a bowl
½ cup mayonnaise
¼ cup pickle relish
2 tablespoons chopped parsley
1 tablespoon lemon juice
1 teaspoon prepared horseradish
¼ teaspoon salt
2 drops Tabasco
Put into refrigerator to chill and allow flavors to blend.
About 1 cup sauce

TARTAR SAUCE

Combine in a small bowl
1 cup mayonnaise
3 tablespoons chopped sweet pickle
3 tablespoons chopped green olives
2 tablespoons drained capers
2 teaspoons minced onion
Stir until well blended. Store in a tightly covered jar in refrigerator and use as needed.
About 1½ cups sauce

SAUCE FOR LOBSTER
(Saus for Hummer)

Blend thoroughly
1 cup mayonnaise
¼ cup lemon juice
1 tablespoon sugar
Chill in refrigerator.
1¼ cups sauce

SAUCE FOR SALMON
(Saus for Lakse)

Blend thoroughly
½ cup dairy sour cream
1 teaspoon prepared horseradish
¼ teaspoon salt
¼ teaspoon sugar
Chill thoroughly in refrigerator
About ½ cup sauce

PUFFY SAUCE

Mix together
¼ cup mayonnaise
2 tablespoons finely chopped green olives
½ teaspoon prepared horseradish
Few grains cayenne pepper

Beat until rounded peaks are formed
1 egg white
Fold mayonnaise mixture into beaten egg white.

When broiling fish steaks, the last 2 min. of broiling, top fish steaks with sauce. Broil until topping is puffy and golden brown.
½ to 1 cup sauce

RAVIGOTE SAUCE

▲ *Base Recipe*

Hard-cook (page 133) and chill
1 egg

Put into a small bowl and blend until mixed thoroughly
1 cup mayonnaise
2 tablespoons finely chopped shallots
2 teaspoons chopped parsley
2 teaspoons chopped chives
2 teaspoons finely crushed chervil
1 teaspoon tarragon leaves, finely crushed
⅛ teaspoon salt
Few grains freshly ground pepper
Chop hard-cooked egg and blend into mixture. Cover and set in refrigerator 1 to 2 hrs. to chill and allow flavors to blend.

Pour sauce into a serving bowl. If desired garnish with **sieved hard-cooked egg yolk**.
About 1 cup sauce

—TOMATO RAVIGOTE SAUCE

Follow ▲ Recipe. Blend **¼ cup ketchup** into the sauce before adding the chopped egg.

TOMATO MAYONNAISE SAUCE

Put into an electric blender container
1 cup mayonnaise
¼ cup tomato paste
¼ teaspoon pepper
2 or 3 sprigs parsley
1 strip pimiento
Cover and blend until pimiento is finely chopped. Chill. Serve with fish or vegetables.
About 1½ cups sauce

MAYONNAISE WITH GARLIC
(Sauce Aioli)

This sauce, one of the glories of Provencal cookery, is served most often with fish or vegetables.

Peel
>**2 cloves garlic**

Crush to a fine paste in a small bowl with
>**½ teaspoon salt**

Add, mixing well
>**1 egg yolk**
>**1 tablespoon lemon juice**
>**½ teaspoon dry mustard**

Beat thoroughly with rotary beater.

Add 1 teaspoon at a time, at first
>**½ cup salad oil**

Gradually increase amounts of additions. Beat vigorously after each addition. Alternately beat in a little at a time
>**½ cup salad oil**
>**2 tablespoons lemon juice**

If mayonnaise should separate because oil is added too rapidly, add mayonnaise gradually, beating constantly, into 1 egg yolk.

About 1½ cups sauce

GRAVY

▲ Base Recipe

Method 1—Remove roasted meat or poultry from roasting pan. Leaving brown residue in pan, pour into bowl
>**Drippings**

Allow fat to rise to surface; skim off fat and reserve. Remaining drippings are meat juices which should be used as part of the liquid.

Measure into roasting pan
>**3 tablespoons fat**

Blend in until smooth
>**3 tablespoons all-purpose flour**
>**¼ teaspoon salt**
>**⅛ teaspoon pepper**

Stirring constantly, heat until mixture bubbles. Brown slightly, if desired. Remove from heat and slowly blend in, stirring constantly and vigorously
>**2 cups liquid, warm or cool**
>**(drippings, water, quick meat or**
>**chicken broth, page 10, or milk)**

Return to heat and cook rapidly, stirring constantly, until sauce thickens. Cook 1 to 2 min. longer. While stirring, scrape bottom and sides of pan to blend in brown residue.

Serve hot with meat or poultry.

6 to 8 servings

Note: Other fats may be melted in skillet and blended with flour is pan drippings are not available.

Method 2—Bring to boiling
>**2 cups chicken or meat broth (from**
>**which the fat has been skimmed)**

Drippings from roasted meats may be substituted for part of broth; if necessary, add milk or water to drippings to make 2 cups liquid.

Meanwhile, put into a 1-pt. screw-top jar
>**½ cup water**

Sprinkle evenly over water
>**¼ cup all-purpose flour**

Cover jar tightly; shake until well blended. Stirring broth or liquid constantly, slowly pour one half of the flour-water mixture into broth. Bring to boiling. Gradually add only enough remaining flour-water mixture for consistency desired; bring to boiling after each addition.

Season with
>**¼ teaspoon salt**
>**⅛ teaspoon pepper**
>**⅛ teaspoon monosodium glutamate**

Cook gravy 3 to 5 min. longer.

—GIBLET GRAVY

Follow Method 1 or 2 of ▲ Recipe. Use chicken or giblet broth. Add **cooked chopped giblets** (see Stewed Chicken with Noodles, page 259) to completed gravy and bring to boiling to thoroughly heat giblets.

GOLDEN GRAVY

It's truly amazing how taste-tempting leftovers become when served with a delicious gravy.

Set out a large skillet.

Combine
>**1 cup boiling water**
>**2 chicken bouillon cubes**
>**½ teaspoon monosodium glutamate**
>**½ teaspoon Worcestershire sauce**
>**⅛ teaspoon salt**

Stir until bouillon cubes are dissolved. Set aside to cool slightly.

Put into the skillet over low heat
>**3 tablespoons meat drippings**

Blend in until smooth a mixture of
>**3 tablespoons all-purpose flour**
>**¼ to ½ teaspoon dry mustard**
>**⅛ teaspoon freshly ground pepper**

Stirring constantly, heat until mixture bubbles and browns slightly. Add broth mixture gradually, stirring constantly. Blend in thoroughly.
>**1 cup milk**

Bring to boiling, stirring constantly, until gravy thickens. Cook 1 to 2 min.

About 2 cups gravy

SOUR CREAM GRAVY

Heat in a skillet
>**2 tablespoons pan drippings (from**
>**meat or poultry)**

Add and cook 2 min.
>**2 tablespoons minced onion**
>**1 tablespoon minced parsley**

Stir in a mixture of
>**2 tablespoons all-purpose flour**
>**¼ teaspoon salt**
>**Few grains cayenne pepper**

Blend in
>**1½ cups dairy sour cream**

Cook and stir just until boiling. Serve hot with beef, ham, veal or poultry. *1½ cups*

HORSERADISH GRAVY

Add to pan drippings in roasting pan (after removing the roast)
>**2 tablespoons all-purpose flour**
>**1 teaspoon salt**
>**½ teaspoon paprika**

Stir well and add
>**½ cup prepared horseradish**
>**½ cup water**
>**⅓ cup cream or milk**

Cook and stir until thickened. Pour a small amount of the hot mixture into
>**2 egg yolks, slightly beaten**

Stir into gravy mixture and cook 1 to 2 min.

About 1½ cups

CELESTINE GRAVY

Have ready
>**Chicken pan stock***
>**2 peeled and diced ripe tomatoes**
>**½ lb. mushroom caps**

Heat the pan stock in a heavy skillet. Add tomatoes and mushrooms and cook 10 min., stirring occasionally.

Stir in and mix well
>**1 cup dry white wine**
>**2 tablespoons bottled concentrated**
>**meat sauce**
>**2 tablespoons brandy**

Heat to boiling and season with
>**Salt and pepper**
>**Few grains cayenne pepper**

Cover and simmer 10 min. Skim off excess fat from gravy and stir in.
>**1 tablespoon *each* minced parsley**
>**and chives**
>**½ clove garlic, crushed**

Simmer until reduced to about 1½ cups.

1½ cups

*This liquid remains after frying 3 broiler-fryer chickens (using about ⅓ cup fat).

Vegetables

How fortunate we are to live in a country that is so big and that has so many changes of climate and varieties of soil that we produce just about every type of commonly known vegetable in great abundance. Contrary to yesteryear's homemaker who considered them as a mere accompaniment to a meal, the homemaker of today knows that vegetables are an essential part of our diet as a valuable source of vitamins and minerals. The appearance of spring's first-of-the-season vegetables, such as "new" potatoes or fresh asparagus, used to be a cause for rejoicing. Now, almost all family favorites are available all year in some form—garden fresh, fresh-frozen, or canned.

GARDEN FRESH VEGETABLES

Buy vegetables that are blemish-free and firm —and keep them fresh. Store less perishable vegetables in a cool place without beforehand washing. Wash other vegetables before storing, drain thoroughly and place into refrigerator in vegetable compartment or plastic bags, or wrap tightly in moisture-vaporproof material such as plastic wrap or aluminum foil.

Do not soak vegetables when washing them. If necessary, crisp them by placing them for a short time in icy cold water.

Leave edible peel on the vegetable or use vegetable parer or sharp paring knife to keep parings thin.

Artichokes—Prepare for cooking (page 314).
Asparagus—Prepare for cooking (page 314).
Beans, green—Prepare for cooking (page 319).
Beets—Prepare for cooking (page 322).
Broccoli—Prepare for cooking (page 323).
Brussels sprouts—Trim stem ends and wash well.
Carrots—Scrub with a vegetable brush; scrape or pare. *Chopped or Diced*—Cut lengthwise into quarters or halves; hold on flat surface and slice with French knife. *Shredded or Grated*—Use vegetable shredder or medium-blade grater.
Cauliflower—Discard outside leaves and woody base. Trim any blemishes from head. Rinse, drain and dry.
Flowerets—Break apart clusters of the head.
Celery—Clean. *Chopped*—Split wide stalks lengthwise one or more times. Line up several stalks on a flat surface; cut desired length, slicing through all stalks at once.
Corn—Remove husks and silk just before cooking.

Cucumber—Rinse and dry; cut off and discard seedless ends; pare, if desired. *Diced*—Lay on flat surface; cut into cubes with French knife. *Fluted Slices*—Draw tines of a fork lengthwise over entire surface of cucumber. Cut into thin slices.
Eggplant—Wash, pare and slice or dice; for shells, see recipe, page 331.
Mushrooms—Clean and slice (page 9).
Okra—Prepare for cooking (page 334).
Onions (*dry*)—Clean. *Chopped or Minced*— Slice into halves crosswise. Score surface of onion by cutting into small squares; slice thin pieces off scored surface. Or hold thin onion slices on cutting surface and chop into small pieces, extra-fine for minced onion. *Grated*—See Grated Carrots; use finest blade of grater. *Juice*—Scrape cut surface of onion with sharp knife.
Peas—Prepare for cooking (page 337).
Peppers (*green*)—Clean. *Chopped*—Cut pepper lengthwise into narrow strips and then cut crosswise into small pieces. *Slivers*—cut pepper lengthwise into thin short strips. *Rings*—Cut thin slice from stem end of whole pepper. Carefully remove all white fiber and seeds; slice crosswise keeping rings intact.
Potatoes, sweet and white—Wash and scrub well.
Radishes—Scrub firm red or white radishes with a brush; gently scrape or trim away any discolored spots; trim roots and stems leaving a short piece of stem and a tiny, fresh leaf or two. *Roses*—With a sharp knife, mark petals on firm red radishes. Pare each petal thinly from tip almost to stem. Chill in ice and water until petals spread apart. Drain before serving.
Scallions (*green onions*)—Cut off roots and

trim green top to 2 to 3 in., discarding any wilted or bruised parts. Peel and rinse. *Chopped* —Split large bulbs. Hold several scallions on a flat surface and chop with a French knife; include the green as well as the bulb if desired.
Squash, summer—Prepare for cooking (page 349).
Squash, winter—Prepare for cooking (page 349).
Tomatoes—Rinse and pat dry. With tip of a sharp knife, cut out stem end and any blemishers. To peel, rinse tomatoes and put into boiling water about ½ min., or until skin loosens. Peel, remove stem ends and chill. *Sliced or Cut into Wedges*—Place firm tomato on flat surface; cut crosswise slices about ¼ in. thick, or cut lengthwise into six or eight wedges.
Turnips—Remove stem and roots; scrub and pare. *Diced*—Stack several thin slices on flat surface; cut into small cubes with a French knife. *Sticks*—Cut thick slices into strips.

HOW TO COOK VEGETABLES

Baking—Bake such vegetables as potatoes, tomatoes and squash without removing skins. Pare vegetables for oven dishes, following directions given with recipes.
Boiling—Have water boiling rapidly before adding vegetables. Add salt at beginning of cooking period (¼ teaspoon per cup of water). After adding vegetables, again bring water to boiling as quickly as possible. If more water is needed, add boiling water. Boil at a moderate rate and cook vegetables until just tender.

In general, cook vegetables in a covered pan, in the smallest amount of water possible and in the shortest possible time. Exceptions for amounts of water or for covering are:
Potatoes—cooked in water to cover.
Green vegetables (*peas, green or lima beans*)— loosely covered.
Spinach—covered pan with only the water which clings to leaves after final washing.
Asparagus—arranged in tied bundles with stalks standing in bottom of a double boiler containing water to cover lower half of spears; cover with inverted double-boiler top.
Broccoli—boil broccoli 5 min. in an uncovered skillet containing boiling salted water to a depth of 1 in. Cover and cook until tender, 5 to 10 min.; drain.

A desirable boiled vegetable is free from excess water, retains its original color and is well seasoned. Pieces are uniform and attractive.
Broiling—Follow directions with recipes.
Frying and Deep Frying—Follow directions with specific recipes.
Panning—Finely shred or slice vegetables. Cook slowly until just tender in a small amount of fat, in a covered heavy pan. Occasionally move with spoon to prevent sticking and burning.
Steaming—Cooking in a pressure saucepan is a form of steaming. Follow directions given with saucepan because overcooking may occur in a matter of seconds.

Note: Some saucepans with tight-fitting covers may lend themselves to steaming vegetables in as little as 1 teaspoon water, no water or a small amount of butter, margarine or shortening.

Canned vegetables—Reduce liquid from can to one half of the original amount by boiling rapidly. Add the vegetables; heat thoroughly and quickly.

Home-canned vegetables—Boil 10 min. (not required for tomatoes or sauerkraut.)

Dried (dehydrated) vegetables—Soak and cook as directed in specific recipes.

Frozen vegetables—Do not thaw before cooking unless indicated on package. Use the specified amount of boiling salted water, separate the frozen vegetables with a fork and bring to boiling. Follow directions on the package for length of cooking time.

COOKED ARTICHOKES
(Globe or French)

▲ *Base Recipe*

Set out a large saucepot or kettle.

With a sharp knife cutting straight across, cut off 1 in. of the tops from

4 artichokes

Cut off stems about 1 in. from base and remove outside lower leaves. With scissors, clip off tips of uncut leaves and discard. Rinse artichokes under cold water and stand them upright in the saucepot. Add boiling water to a depth of 1 in. and

1 tablespoon lemon juice
1 teaspoon salt

Cook, covered, 35 to 45 min., or until a leaf can be easily pulled from artichoke. (Cooking time will depend upon size of artichokes.) If more water is needed during cooking, add boiling water.

Remove artichokes and drain upside down so all the water can run out. Cut off remainder of artichoke stem.

Serve immediately standing upright on serving platter. Garnish with

Lemon slices
Parsley sprigs

Accompany with individual servings of

Hot melted butter or margarine

or individual servings of

Hollandaise Sauce (page 306)

How to Eat Artichokes—Pull off each leaf and dip in melted butter or sauce. Eat only the tender part of leaf by drawing it between teeth. Discard less tender tip. Continue with each leaf until choke or fuzzy part in center is reached. Remove choke with knife and fork and discard. The heart or base may be eaten by cutting it with a fork and dipping each piece into the melted butter or sauce.   *4 servings*

—CHILLED ARTICHOKES

Follow ▲ Recipe. Drain artichokes and chill in refrigerator until ready to serve. Chilled artichokes are usually served as a salad on individual serving plates. Accompany with individual servings of **mayonnaise, French Dressing I** (page 410) or any of its variations.

STUFFED ARTICHOKES SICILIAN
(Carciofi Imbottiti alla Siciliana)

▲ *Base Recipe*

Set out a 10-in. skillet with a tight-fitting cover.

Remove outside lower leaves and cut off stems from

4 medium artichokes

Cover with cold water. Add

1 teaspoon salt

Let stand 5 to 10 min. Drain upside down.

Meanwhile, mix

⅔ cup (2 slices) fine dry bread crumbs
1 clove garlic, sliced thin
1 teaspoon grated Parmesan cheese
1 teaspoon chopped parsley
1 teaspoon salt
¾ teaspoon pepper

Set aside.

Spread leaves of artichokes open slightly and place in each artichoke

3 slices garlic

Sprinkle crumb mixture between leaves and over top of artichokes. Sprinkle with

1 tablespoon chopped parsley

Place artichokes close together in skillet so they will remain upright during cooking. Add

2 cups boiling water

Drizzle artichokes with

2 tablespoons olive oil

Cover and cook about 30 min., or until artichoke leaves are tender.

To eat artichokes, pull out leaves, one by one.
4 servings

—ARTICHOKES WITH ANCHOVY DRESSING
(Carciofi Imbottiti con Acciughe)

Follow ▲ Recipe. When preparing artichokes, cut off the top of the leaves and cut out the choke from the center. Discard choke. Add to stuffing **4 anchovy fillets**, chopped. Fill center and between leaves with the stuffing.

ASPARAGUS PIEMONTAIS

"Piemontais" signifies a dish born at the foot of the Alps where they step into Italy—a country where folks like more than a soupcon of garlic, and believe that the brisk tang of Parmesan cheese makes any good food better.

Break off and discard lower parts of stalks (as far down as they will snap) from

1½ lbs. asparagus

Wash remaining portions of stalks thoroughly. If necessary, remove scales to dislodge any sand. Cook (page 313) 10 to 20 min., or until

asparagus is tender; drain. (If using frozen asparagus, cook following directions on package.)

Meanwhile, heat over low heat in a saucepan

6 tablespoons butter

Add and cook over medium heat until lightly browned

2 cloves garlic

Remove garlic and add to the butter

1 teaspoon nutmeg

Cook 1 min. longer.

Place cooked asparagus on a warm serving platter. Pour the sauce over the asparagus and sprinkle with

3 tablespoons grated Parmesan cheese

Serve immediately.   *About 6 servings*

ASPARAGUS WITH ROQUEFORT BUTTER

Break off and discard lower part of stalks (as far down as they will snap) from

1½ lbs. asparagus

Wash remaining portion of stalks thoroughly. If necessary, remove scales to dislodge any sand. Cook (page 313) 10 to 20 min., or until asparagus is just tender. (Or cook two 10-oz. pkgs. frozen asparagus.)

Just before asparagus is tender, heat in a small saucepan over low heat

⅓ cup butter or margarine

Add and stir until cheese is melted

2 tablespoons crumbled Roquefort cheese
1 tablespoon cider vinegar

When asparagus is tender, drain and transfer to a warm serving dish. Pour the Roequefort sauce over asparagus and serve at once.

About 6 servings

Asparagus with Cheese Sauce

ASPARAGUS WITH CHEESE SAUCE

▲ Base Recipe

Break off and discard lower parts of stalks, as far down as they will snap, from

3 lbs. asparagus

Wash remaining portions of stalks thoroughly. If necessary, remove scales to dislodge any sand. Cook (page 313; add 1½ teaspoons monosodium glutamate to cooking water) 10 to 20 min., or until asparagus is tender. (Or cook three 10-oz. pkgs. frozen asparagus.)

Meanwhile, prepare

2 cups Cheese Sauce (page 304)

Keep sauce warm by setting it over hot water. Cover tightly.

Toast

6 slices bread

Spread one side of each slice with

Butter or margarine

When asparagus is tender, drain if necessary. Arrange servings of asparagus on slices of toast. Spoon hot sauce over asparagus. Sprinkle each serving with

Few grains paprika

Serve immediately.   *About 8 servings*

—ASPARAGUS WITH BEARNAISE SAUCE

Follow ▲ Recipe. Substitute **Bearnaise Sauce** (page 306) for Cheese Sauce. Omit toast. When ready to serve, arrange asparagus on a serving platter (see photo). Top with sauce and garnish with **pimiento strips.**

ASPARAGUS POLONAISE

Break off and discard lower parts of stalks as far down as they will snap from

1½ lbs. asparagus

Wash remaining portions of stalks thoroughly. If necessary, remove scales to dislodge any sand. Cook (page 313) 10 to 20 min., or until asparagus is tender. (If using frozen asparagus, substitute two 10-oz. pkgs. Cook, following directions on package. Gently break blocks

apart with a fork or spoon while asparagus is cooking.)

Meanwhile, prepare Polonaise Topping.

For Polonaise Topping—Prepare

½ cup (1 to 2 slices) fine soft or dry bread crumbs

Melt in a small skillet over low heat

2 to 3 tablespoons butter

Add the bread crumbs and cook over medium heat until bread crumbs are lightly browned, turning and moving mixture gently with a spoon.

Remove skillet from heat and mix in

½ Hard-Cooked Egg (page 133), finely chopped

⅛ teaspoon salt

Few grains pepper

Polonaise Topping may also be served over other cooked vegetables such as broccoli, green beans or cauliflower.

When asparagus is tender, drain; place on a warm serving platter. Brush asparagus with a mixture of

2 tablespoons melted butter

¼ teaspoon lemon juice

Spoon Polonaise Topping over asparagus.

About 6 servings

ASPARAGUS WITH SOUR CREAM
(Spárga Tejföllel)

Break off and discard lower parts of stalks as far down as they will snap from

2 lbs. asparagus

Wash asparagus thoroughly. If necessary, remove scales to dislodge any sand. Cook (page 313) 10 to 20 min., or until asparagus is just tender.

Meanwhile, for sauce, prepare and set aside

½ cup quick meat broth (one half recipe, page 10)

Melt in a small skillet over low heat

1 tablespoon butter

Blend into the butter until smooth

1 tablespoon all-purpose flour

½ teaspoon salt

¼ teaspoon pepper

Heat until mixture bubbles, stirring constantly. Remove skillet from heat. Gradually add the broth, stirring constantly. Return to heat and bring rapidly to boiling, stirring constantly; cook 1 to 2 min. longer. Remove sauce from heat. Vigorously stir about 3 tablespoons of hot sauce into

1 egg yolk, slightly beaten

Immediately blend into hot mixture. Stirring sauce constantly, cook slowly 2 to 3 min. (Do not overcook or allow sauce to boil.) Remove from heat. Stirring vigorously with a French whip, whisk beater or fork, add to sauce in

Asparagus with Béarnaise Sauce

very small amounts

1 cup dairy sour cream

Cook sauce over low heat, stirring constantly, 3 to 5 min., until heated thoroughly. Do not boil sauce; remove immediately from heat. Cover saucepan and set sauce aside.

Drain asparagus and cut stalks into 3 or 4 pieces; put into bowl. Pour sauce over asparagus and mix lightly.   *6 to 8 servings*

BACON-BUNDLED ASPARAGUS

Set out an ovenproof platter.

Partially fry and drain

6 slices bacon

Meanwhile, drain and arrange in 6 groups

2 cans (14½ oz. each) green asparagus spears

Brush with

2 tablespoons butter or margarine, melted

Sprinkle spears with

¼ teaspoon salt

¼ teaspoon monosodium glutamate

Wrap each group of spears with a bacon strip and arrange on the platter. Sprinkle bacon-asparagus bundles with

2 tablespoons shredded Parmesan cheese

Broil 4 to 5 in. from heat 3 min., or until lightly browned.   *6 servings*

ASPARAGUS ALLA MILANESE

Set out and butter 6 individual casseroles.

Break off and discard lower part of each stalk as far down as it snaps easily from

2 lbs. asparagus

Wash remaining portions of stalks thoroughly. If necessary, remove scales to dislodge any sand. Cook (page 313) 10 to 20 min., or just until tender. Divide asparagus equally and place in the individual casseroles.

Break one at a time into a saucer or small dish

6 eggs

Slip one egg onto each bed of asparagus.

Top each egg with

1 teaspoon butter or margarine

Asparagus alla Milanese

Sprinkle with
Few grains salt
Few grains pepper
Shredded Parmesan cheese

Bake at 350°F 10 to 20 min., depending upon firmness desired. If desired, garnish each casserole with a **sprig of parsley**. Serve immediately. *6 servings*

ASPARAGUS PARMESAN
(Asparagi alla Parmigiana)

Grease a 1½-qt. casserole.

Break off and discard lower parts of stalks as far down as they will snap from
1½ lbs. asparagus
Wash remaining portions of stalks thoroughly. If necessary, remove scales to dislodge any sand. Cook (page 313) 10 to 20 min., or until asparagus is tender.

Meanwhile, melt in small saucepan and add to casserole
½ cup butter or margarine
Place cooked asparagus in casserole and sprinkle with a mixture of
½ cup (about 2 oz.) grated Parmesan or Romano cheese
1 teaspoon salt
½ teaspoon pepper

Set in a 450°F oven 5 to 10 min., or until cheese is melted. *About 6 servings*

BAKED BEANS

▲ Base Recipe

New Englanders say about their baked-bean-and-brown-bread supper—"We like it."

A 2-qt. casserole with a tight-fitting cover will be needed.

Heat to boiling in a large saucepan
1½ qts. water

Meanwhile, sort and wash thoroughly
1 lb. (2⅓ cups) dried navy or pea beans
Add beans gradually to water so boiling will continue. Boil beans 2 min. and remove saucepan from heat. Cover; set beans aside to soak for 1 hr.

Remove rind from and cut into narrow strips
¼ lb. salt pork
Add pork strips to beans with
2 teaspoons salt
Return saucepan to heat and simmer 45 min., stirring once or twice. Drain beans, reserving liquid. Turn beans and salt pork strips into greased casserole. Set aside while making sauce.

Mix in the saucepan 2½ cups of the reserved bean liquid and
⅓ cup firmly packed brown sugar
¼ cup molasses
1 tablespoon cider vinegar
2 teaspoons onion juice
¾ teaspoon dry mustard
½ teaspoon monosodium glutamate
Bring to boiling. Pour sauce over beans.

Cover and bake at 300°F about 2½ hrs. If necessary, add more liquid to just cover beans during baking. Remove cover and cook ½ hr. longer to brown pork and beans.

Serve with **Boston Brown Bread** (page 89). *About 8 servings*

Note: Some New England homemakers embed 1 whole cleaned onion in the beans. Others use maple syrup in place of the molasses and brown sugar.

—BAKED LIMA BEANS

Follow ▲ Recipe. Substitute **1 lb. dried lima beans** for navy beans.

COMPANY BAKED BEANS

Proper Bostonians might not acknowledge these as authentic, but would surely recognize them as delicious with the rich spiciness of ketchup permeating the whole dish. Perfect for serving a good-sized crowd on Sunday night.

A 4-qt. casserole with a tight-fitting cover will be needed.

Sort and wash thoroughly
3 lbs. (about 7 cups) dried navy or pea beans
Put beans into a large saucepot and pour in
3 qts. boiling water
Boil 2 min.; remove from heat. Cover and set beans aside 1 hr.

Bring the undrained beans to boiling. Simmer, covered, 1 hr. Skim off any foam.

Meanwhile, grease the casserole.

Remove and discard rind from and cut into thin slices
1 lb. salt pork

Drain beans, reserving the liquid.

Set out
1½ cups firmly packed brown sugar
Put one third of the beans into the casserole; sprinkle over beans ½ cup of the brown sugar and lay over top one third of the salt pork slices. Repeat layering ending with salt pork.

Pour over casserole a mixture of 2 cups of the reserved bean liquid and
1¾ cups ketchup
2 tablespoons dry mustard
1 tablespoon salt

Cover and bake at 275°F 5 to 6 hrs. If necessary, add a mixture of 1 cup reserved bean liquid and 1 cup ketchup if beans become dry during baking. Cover may be removed during last ½ hr. of baking to brown pork and beans.

Serve with **Boston Brown Bread** (page 89). *About 20 servings*

FLAVOR-RICH BEAN CASSEROLE

▲ Base Recipe

Grease a 2-qt. casserole with cover.

Heat to boiling in a large heavy saucepan
1½ qts. water
Wash thoroughly, sort and discard imperfect beans from
1 lb. (2⅓ cups) dried navy or pea beans
Add beans gradually to water so boiling will not stop. Simmer 2 min. and remove saucepan from heat. Set beans aside to soak 1 hr.

Remove rind and cut into 1-in. chunks
½ lb. salt pork
Add pork chunks to beans with
½ cup chopped celery
1 medium onion, chopped
1 teaspoon salt
1 teaspoon monosodium glutamate
Return saucepan to heat and simmer 45 min., stirring once or twice. Drain beans, reserving liquid and turn beans and salt pork chunks into casserole. Set aside while making sauce.

For Sauce—Mix in a saucepan
1 cup reserved bean liquid
¼ cup ketchup
¼ cup molasses

Flavor-Rich Bean Casserole

316

Baked

Add a mixture of

2 tablespoons brown sugar
1 teaspoon dry mustard
½ teaspoon pepper
¼ teaspoon ginger

Bring to boiling. Pour sauce over beans.

Cover casserole and bake at 300°F about 2½ hrs. If necessary, add more liquid during baking. Remove cover and bake ½ hr. longer.

About 8 servings

—LIMA BEANS IN BARBECUE SAUCE

Follow ▲ Recipe. Substitute **1 lb. dried lima beans** for navy beans. Omit celery and onion. Cook beans with **1 bay leaf** and **1 clove garlic,** minced. Cook **2 cups chopped onion** in ¼ cup **butter or margarine** until onion is tender. Drain beans. Remove bay leaf. Pour one half of beans into casserole and cover with onion and salt pork. Pour in remaining beans. Substitute **1 teaspoon chili powder** for ginger. If more liquid is needed during baking, use heated **canned tomatoes.**

QUICK BAKED BEANS

Lightly grease a 2-qt. casserole.

Remove rind from and cut into pieces
¼ lb. salt pork

Put into a skillet and cook over moderate heat until browned, occasionally moving and turning pieces with a spoon. Remove from skillet with a slotted spoon; set aside to drain on absorbent paper.

Empty into a bowl
3 cans (16 oz.) baked beans
(about 6 cups)

Add to beans and mix in thoroughly
6 tablespoons molasses
6 tablespoons ketchup
3 tablespoons brown sugar
2¼ teaspoons prepared horseradish
1 teaspoon monosodium glutamate
¾ teaspoon dry mustard

Turn into prepared casserole. Top with salt pork pieces.

Bake at 375°F 20 to 30 min., or until beans are thoroughly heated.

Serve with **Boston Brown Bread** (page 89) and **pickle relish.** *6 to 8 servings*

BAKED BEAN MIX-UP

▲ *Base Recipe*

Set out a large heavy skillet with a tight-fitting cover.

Prepare, crumble and set aside
4 slices Panfried Bacon (page 190)

Heat in same skillet
2 tablespoons bacon drippings

Add and cook until onion is tender, stirring occasionally
½ cup (about 1 medium) chopped onion
½ clove garlic, minced

Remove from heat and blend in a mixture of
1¼ cups (10¾ oz. can) condensed tomato soup
1 tablespoon sugar
2 teaspoons prepared mustard

Stir in bacon and
4 cups (two 16-oz. cans) baked beans
10 ripe olives, pitted and sliced
1 dill pickle, finely chopped

Cover and heat over low heat 10 to 12 min., or until flavors are well blended. *6 servings*

—SAVORY LIMAS

Follow ▲ Recipe. Substitute for the baked beans, **2 pkgs. (10 oz. each) frozen lima beans** cooked following package directions. Or substitute **2 cans (10 oz. each) lima beans (4 cups).** Omit olives and pickle and stir in ½ **teaspoon Worcestershire sauce.**

—BEANS 'N' FRANKS

Follow ▲ Recipe. Omit bacon. Substitute **butter or margarine** for drippings. Cut **3 frankfurters** into ¼-in. slices; heat with onion.

GLORIFIED BAKED BEANS

Put into a skillet
½ lb. bulk pork sausage

Cook, separating meat into small pieces with a fork or spoon. Pour off excess fat.

Meanwhile, drain
1 can (16 oz.) apricot halves (about 20 halves)

Reserve six halves and combine remaining halves with sausage and
2 cans (16 oz. each) baked beans

Blend in a mixture of
⅓ cup firmly packed brown sugar
1 teaspoon dry mustard

Turn mixture into casserole. Press reserved apricot halves into surface, cut-side up. Fill each apricot half with
Brown sugar

Dot apricot halves with
Butter or margarine

Bake at 350°F 20 to 30 min., or until thoroughly heated. *8 servings*

DOUBLE-QUICK BAKED BEANS

Hearty family fare to satisfy even the hungriest.

Heat four individual casseroles in oven.

Heat in a skillet
1 tablespoon butter or margarine

Add and cook over medium heat until soft, stirring occasionally
¼ cup chopped onion

Blend in
¼ cup ketchup
2 tablespoons molasses
2 drops Tabasco
2 tablespoons brown sugar
½ teaspoon salt
½ teaspoon dry mustard
¼ teaspoon monosodium glutamate

Bring to boiling. Stir in
2 cups (16-oz. can) baked beans

Turn mixture into casseroles.

Cut crosswise into pieces
4 slices bacon

Put several pieces on top of bean mixture in each casserole.

Bake at 375°F about 20 min., or until bacon is cooked.

Serve with **Boston Brown Bread.** (page 89).

4 servings

BAKED BEAN SAVORY

Heat in a large skillet
1 to 2 tablespoons salad oil

Add to skillet
¾ cup (about 1 large) sliced onion
½ clove garlic, minced

Quick Baked Beans and Double-Quick Baked Beans

Gourmet Baked Beans

Cook until onion is tender, stirring occasionally.

Remove from heat and stir in
- **1¼ cups (10¾-oz. can) condensed tomato soup**
- **1 tablespoon sugar**
- **2 teaspoons prepared mustard**
- **10 ripe olives, pitted and sliced**
- **1 dill pickle, finely chopped**

Bring mixture to boiling.

Remove from heat and stir in
- **2 cans (16 oz. each) baked beans**

Turn mixture into casserole. Top with
- **4 slices bacon, cut in halves**

Bake at 350°F 15 to 20 min., or until bacon is cooked. *6 servings*

GOURMET BAKED BEANS

Grease a 1½-qt. casserole.

Pour into a 1-cup measuring cup for liquids
- **1 tablespoon cider vinegar**

Add and blend thoroughly
- **Undiluted evaporated milk (enough to make 1 cup liquid)**

Mix in a bowl
- **⅓ cup firmly packed brown sugar**
- **¼ cup all-purpose flour**
- **1 teaspoon dry mustard**
- **½ teaspoon salt**

Add the evaporated milk mixture gradually. Blend thoroughly. Blend in
- **1 tablespoon molasses**
- **¼ teaspoon Worcestershire sauce**
- **2 drops Tabasco**

Add
- **2 cans (16 oz. each) molasses-style baked beans (about 4 cups)**

Mix gently but thoroughly. Turn into the casserole.

Bake at 350°F 35 to 40 min., or stirring 2 or 3 times during baking.

Garnish with **onion rings**, if desired.
6 to 8 servings

BROWN BEANS
(Bruna Bönor)

A favorite Swedish dish, this recipe is prized for its interesting flavor. Brown beans are frequently included with the smörgasbord.

Heat to boiling in a large heavy saucepan with a tight-fitting cover
- **1½ qts. water**

Wash and sort
- **1 lb. (2⅓ cups) dried brown beans or pinto beans**

Add beans gradually to water so boiling will continue. Reduce heat, cover and simmer 2 min. Remove saucepan from heat and set the beans aside for 1 hr.

Return saucepan to heat, cover and simmer about 1¾ hrs., stirring once or twice, until beans are tender. If necessary, add hot water to keep beans covered with liquid.

When beans are tender, add to the saucepan
- **1 cup dark corn syrup**
- **¼ cup cider vinegar**
- **1 tablespoon salt**

Blend thoroughly and cook uncovered over medium heat 45 min., or until sauce has thickened.

Serve hot with fried salt pork or
Swedish Meat Balls (page 230)
6 servings

RED BEANS WITH RICE

A favorite dish of Creole families—traditionally served on "Wash-day Monday."

Heat to boiling in a large heavy saucepan
- **1½ qts. water**

Sort and wash thoroughly
- **1 lb. (2½ cups) dried red kidney beans**

Add beans gradually to water so boiling will continue. Simmer 2 min. and remove saucepan from heat. Set beans aside to soak 1 hr.

Chop or dice
- **1 medium onion (about ½ cup, chopped)**
- **1 medium carrot, washed and pared or scraped**

Add chopped vegetables to beans with
- **¼ cup meat drippings, butter or margarine**
- **1 bay leaf**
- **1 teaspoon salt**
- **¼ teaspoon monosodium glutamate**
- **⅛ teaspoon pepper**

Simmer about 45 min., or until beans are tender. Remove bay leaf and drain beans.

While beans are cooking, prepare
Perfection Boiled Rice (page 165)
Serve red beans with rice. *8 servings*

CASSEROLE OF RED BEANS

Set out a 2-qt. casserole.

Wash, soak and cook until tender (see Red Beans with Rice, on this page; omit carrot).
- **1 lb. (2½ cups) dried red kidney beans**

Remove bay leaf. Drain beans.

Meanwhile, thoroughly drain and with a spoon cut into pieces
- **1 can (28 oz.) tomatoes (about 2 cups pieces)**

Mix tomatoes and cooked beans with
- **1 tablespoon molasses**

and a mixture of
- **1 teaspoon dry mustard**
- **1 teaspoon salt**
- **¼ teaspoon pepper**

Turn mixture into casserole. Top with, in order
- **½ cup (2 oz.) shredded American cheese**
- **6 slices bacon**

Bake at 350°F 15 to 20 min.

Place casserole under broiler with top of casserole about 3 in. from heat. Broil about 5 min., or until bacon is evenly crisped and browned. *8 servings*

BARBECUED LIMA BEANS

The Southwest favors beans and flavor, and this dish combines the two: large, plump lima beans baked in a barbecue sauce which is wonderfully flavorful and delicious.

Grease and set aside a 2-qt. casserole.

Heat to boiling in a large saucepan
- **5 cups water**

Meanwhile, sort and wash thoroughly
- **2 cups dried large lima beans**

Add beans to water gradually so boiling will continue. Simmer 2 min. and remove saucepan from heat. Set beans aside to soak 1 hr.

Meanwhile, remove rind from
- **¼ lb. salt pork (about ½ cup, diced)**

Dice the salt pork and add to saucepan. Cover the pan and bring water to boiling over high heat. Reduce heat and simmer about 1 hr., stirring occasionally.

Meanwhile, heat over low heat
- **¼ cup fat**

Add and cook over medium heat, occasionally moving and turning with a spoon
- **½ cup (about 1 medium) chopped onion**
- **¼ cup chopped green pepper**
- **1 clove garlic, minced**

Cook about 5 min., or until onion and green pepper are tender. Remove from heat and add, mixing well

**1¼ cups (10¾-oz. can) condensed
    tomato soup**
⅓ cup cider vinegar
2 teaspoons Worcestershire sauce
1½ teaspoons dry mustard
1 teaspoon salt
¾ teaspoon chili powder
⅛ teaspoon cayenne pepper

Cook slowly 10 min.

Drain lima beans and salt pork, reserving liquid. Blend liquid into tomato soup mixture. Turn one half of the lima beans and salt pork into the casserole; cover with one half of the tomato soup mixture. Repeat layering.

Bake at 350°F 20 to 30 min., or until beans are tender.   *6 to 8 servings*

MEXICAN BEANS
(Frijoles)

▲ Base Recipe

In the Southwest, cooked beans, usually of the pinto variety, appear on most tables at least once a day. Southwesterners far from home think of them as nostalgically as a New Englander of his native bean pot.

Heat to boiling in a large heavy saucepan
3 cups water
Meanwhile, sort and wash thoroughly
1 cup dried pinto beans
Add beans to water gradually so boiling will continue. Simmer 2 min. and remove saucepan from heat. Set beans aside to soak 1 hr.

Add to saucepan
1 teaspoon salt
Cover pan tightly and bring mixture to boiling over high heat. Reduce heat and simmer 2 hrs., or until beans are tender, stirring occasionally.

Heat in a large, heavy skillet over low heat
**2 tablespoons bacon drippings or
    other fat**

Barbecued Lima Beans

Add and cook over medium heat until onion is tender, occasionally moving with a spoon
¾ cup chopped onion
1 clove garlic, minced
Add the cooked beans, the cooking liquid and
1½ teaspoons chili powder
¼ teaspoon pepper
Mash the bean mixture in the skillet. Continue cooking over medium heat, stirring occasionally, until mixture is thick.   *4 servings*

—REFRIED BEANS
(Frijoles Refritos)

Use ingredients saved from ▲ Recipe or prepare Frijoles. Heat in a skillet **3 tablespoons butter or margarine** per cup of Frijoles. Add Frijoles and cook, stirring occasionally, about 6 min., or until mixture is dry.

GREEN BEANS
(Zöldbab)

Wash, cut off ends and cut into 1-in. pieces
1 lb. green beans
Cook (page 313) 15 to 20 min., or until beans are tender.

Meanwhile, prepare and set aside to cool to lukewarm
1 cup quick meat broth (page 10)

Melt in a small skillet over low heat
3 tablespoons butter
Blend into butter
3 tablespoons all-purpose flour
Heat until mixture bubbles and is lightly browned, stirring constantly. Remove skillet from heat. Gradually add the reserved broth, stirring constantly. Return to heat and bring rapidly to boiling, stirring constantly; cook 1 to 2 min. longer. Remove skillet from heat. Stir into sauce
2 tablespoons vinegar or lemon juice
1 to 2 tablespoons sugar
Cover skillet and set sauce aside.

When beans are tender, pour sauce over beans and simmer 5 min. Turn beans and sauce into bowl and sprinkle with
¼ teaspoon paprika
                                About 4 servings

GREEN BEANS IN SAUCE
(Fagiolini al Sugo)

▲ Base Recipe

Set out large skillet with a tight-fitting cover.

Wash, cut off ends and cut into crosswise pieces
1 lb. green beans

Cook (page 313) 15 to 20 min., or until tender. Drain immediately.

While beans are cooking, heat in the skillet until garlic is lightly browned
2 tablespoons olive oil
1 clove garlic, chopped
Add slowly
2½ cups canned tomatoes, sieved
1 cup boiling water
Stir in a mixture of
½ teaspoon salt
⅛ teaspoon pepper
⅛ teaspoon oregano
Add
2 teaspoons chopped parsley
Bring to boiling and simmer covered about 20 min., stirring occasionally.

Pour sauce over beans and serve.   *4 servings*

—GREEN BEANS WITH ONIONS
(Fagiolini con Cipolla)

Cut beans lengthwise into fine strips. Cook as in ▲ Recipe. While beans are cooking, prepare **8 to 12 small whole onions**. Cook onions (page 313) 15 to 20 min., or until tender. Drain and set aside. Heat garlic and oil as in ▲ Recipe. Omit tomatoes, water, parsley and oregano. Add green beans and onions to olive oil and cook 5 to 10 min., or until thoroughly heated, stirring occasionally. Season with a mixture of **salt** and **pepper**.

TART GREEN BEANS WITH BACON

Green beans are in good company here.

Wash, cut off ends and cut into crosswise pieces
1 lb. green beans
Cook (page 313) 15 to 20 min., or until tender. (Frozen or canned green beans may be substituted for fresh beans. Follow directions on package or container for cooking.)

Meanwhile, fry in a skillet until lightly browned
4 slices bacon, cut in ½-in. pieces

Add to skillet
⅓ cup finely chopped onion
2 tablespoons vinegar
2 tablespoons water
2 tablespoons sugar
¼ teaspoon salt
¼ teaspoon monosodium glutamate
Dash pepper
Bring to boiling.

Drain cooked beans. Pour bacon mixture over beans and toss lightly together.   *4 servings*

GREEN BEANS, COUNTRY STYLE

Rinse, cut off ends and cut into lengthwise strips
   1 lb. green beans
Cook, covered, in small amount of boiling salted water 15 to 20 min., or until tender.

Meanwhile, prepare
   3 slices Panfried Bacon (page 190)
Return to skillet
   2 tablespoons bacon fat
Cook in skillet until tender
   ½ cup (about 1 medium) chopped onion

Drain beans thoroughly. Mix onion with bacon and beans. Keep hot.

Combine and heat (do not boil)
   ½ cup cream
and a mixture of
   ½ teaspoon salt
   ¼ teaspoon monosodium glutamate
   ¼ teaspoon pepper
   ¼ teaspoon nutmeg
Pour cream mixture over beans and serve immediately.

6 servings

STRING BEANS WITH BACON

The South likes its green beans, more often called string beans or snap beans, cooked for a long time with salt pork, ham hock or jowl bacon. In these vitamin-conscious days, however, Southern cooks get the same flavor without cooking away the precious vitamins (and green beauty) by cooking the bacon first and adding the beans to the "pot likker" for just long enough to make them tender and delicious.

Put into a saucepan
   ½ lb. piece bacon
Add and bring to boiling
   1 qt. cold water
Reduce heat, cover and simmer about 1 hr. If necessary, add boiling water during cooking.

Meanwhile, wash, cut off ends and cut into 1-in. pieces
   2 lbs. green beans
When bacon has cooked 1 hr., add the green beans and
   ⅛ to ¼ teaspoon salt
Cook 15 to 20 min., or until beans are tender.

Serve beans in individual sauce dishes with some of the cooking liquid. Slice the bacon and serve with beans.   *About 8 servings*

GREEN BEANS WITH ALMONDS AND MUSHROOMS

Wash, cut off ends and cut diagonally
   1½ lbs. (about 5 cups) green beans
Cook (page 313) 15 to 20 min., or until tender. (Or cook two 9-oz. pkgs. frozen green beans.)

Coarsely chop and set aside
   ¼ cup (about 1½ oz.) toasted blanched almonds (pages 9 and 10)

Clean and slice (page 9)
   ¼ lb. mushrooms
Heat in a skillet
   2 tablespoons butter or margarine
Add mushrooms and cook slowly, occasionally moving and turning with a spoon, until mushrooms are lightly browned and tender.

When beans are tender, drain if necessary.

Add almonds and mushrooms to cooked green beans and toss with a mixture of
   3 tablespoons melted butter or margarine
   ½ teaspoon salt
   ¼ teaspoon monosodium glutamate
   ¼ teaspoon lemon juice
   ¼ teaspoon rosemary or savory
Serve immediately.   *6 to 8 servings*

SPECIAL GREEN BEANS

Green beans au gratin take sophisticated flavor from a well-seasoned, creamy-rich sauce.

Set out a shallow 1-qt. baking dish.

Cook until just tender
   1 pkg. (9 oz.) frozen French-style green beans

Meanwhile, shred
   2 oz. sharp Cheddar cheese (about ½ cup, shredded)
Set aside.

Heat in a saucepan
   2 tablespoons butter
Add and cook over medium heat, occasionally moving with a spoon
   ¼ cup minced onion
Cook until the onion is tender. Remove from heat and blend in
   2 tablespoons all-purpose flour
   1 teaspoon salt
   ¼ teaspoon pepper
   ¼ teaspoon dry mustard
   ¾ teaspoon Worcestershire sauce

Special Green Beans

Heat until mixture bubbles. Remove from heat. Add gradually, stirring constantly
   1 cup dairy sour cream
Cook over low heat, stirring constantly just until mixture is thicker; cook 2 or 3 min. longer, stirring constantly; *do not boil.*

When beans are just tender, drain, if necessary, and add to sauce. Toss gently until well-coated with sauce. Turn into the baking dish. Sprinkle with the shredded cheese.

Bake at 350°F 10 to 15 min.   *4 servings*

GREEN BEANS IN CHEESE SAUCE

   ▲ *Base Recipe*

A flavor and color triumph.

Grease a 1-qt. casserole.

Combine in the top of a double boiler
   1⅓ cups (½ lb.) diced Cheddar cheese
   ⅔ cup milk
   1 tablespoon finely chopped pimiento
   1 teaspoon Worcestershire sauce
   ¼ teaspoon monosodium glutamate
   ⅛ teaspoon salt
   Dash cayenne pepper
Cook over simmering water, stirring occasionally, until sauce is smooth and well blended.

Meanwhile, prepare
   3 slices Panfried Bacon (page 190)
   ¾ cup buttered crumbs (page 9)
Crumble bacon and mix with crumbs.

Put into casserole
   2 cups (16-oz. can, drained) green beans
Cover with sauce and top with bacon-crumb mixture.

Bake at 350°F 20 to 30 min., or until crumbs are browned.   *4 servings*

—CAULIFLOWER IN CHEESE SAUCE

Follow ▲ Recipe. Substitute **1 small head (about 1 lb.) cauliflower**, cooked (page 313), for green beans. Separate into flowerets before cooking.

—ASPARAGUS SPEARS IN CHEESE SAUCE

Follow ▲ Recipe. Substitute **1 lb. asparagus,** cooked (page 313), for green beans. Cut into about 2-in. pieces before cooking. Omit pimiento from sauce and add ½ **cup sliced pimiento-stuffed olives.** Reserve a few slices for garnish.

—ONION AND CELERY IN CHEESE SAUCE

Remove leaves, trim off discolored spots and thoroughly wash about **1 lb. celery.** Cut into 1-in. pieces, splitting wide stalks. Peel, rinse and coarsely chop **2 (about 1 lb.) Bermuda onions.** Cover onions and celery with boiling salted water. Cover partially and boil gently 15 to 20 min., or until tender. Drain. Proceed as in ▲ Recipe, substituting the celery and onions for green beans. Serve garnished with thin **green pepper rings.**

GREEN BEANS, LYONNAISE STYLE
(Haricots Verts à la Lyonnaise)

Set out a large heavy skillet.

Rinse, cut off ends and cut lengthwise into fine strips
1 lb. green beans
Place beans in saucepan with
½ **cup boiling water**
½ **teaspoon salt**
Cook loosely covered 15 min., or until tender.

Meanwhile, heat in a skillet
3 tablespoons butter
Add and cook until tender, stirring occasionally
1 cup (about 2 medium) thinly sliced onions

Drain beans and add to skillet with
½ **teaspoon salt**
¼ **teaspoon pepper**
¼ **teaspoon nutmeg**
Sauté 5 min.

Add
3 tablespoons butter
1 tablespoon lemon juice
1 tablespoon minced parsley
Toss well and serve.   *4 servings*

CREAMY CURRIED GREEN BEANS

Combine in a saucepan with a tight-fitting cover
2 tablespoons butter
1 tablespoon water
½ **teaspoon salt**
Few grains pepper
1 pkg. (9 oz.) frozen cut green beans, partially thawed
Cover and heat to steaming over medium heat; reduce heat and cook until beans are tender,

Blend
¼ **to** ½ **teaspoon curry powder**
½ **cup dairy sour cream**

Toss beans with sour cream until well coated. Serve immediately. If desired, sprinkle with additional **curry powder.**   *4 servings*

FRENCH-STYLE GREEN BEANS IN MUSTARD SAUCE

▲ Base Recipe

Wash, break off ends and French (cut lengthwise into fine strips)
1½ lbs. (about 5 cups) green beans
Cook (page 313) 15 to 20 min., or until tender. (Or use two 9-oz. pkgs. frozen French-style green beans. Break apart gently with a fork or spoon while cooking. Follow directions on package for time and amount of water.) Drain immediately and, if necessary, keep beans warm.

While beans are cooking, prepare
Mustard Sauce I (page 307)
Put beans into hot serving dish. Pour sauce over beans and serve immediately.
4 or 5 servings

—FRENCH STYLE GREEN BEANS AND ONIONS

Follow ▲ Recipe. Omit Mustard Sauce. Prepare **8 to 12 small whole onions.** Cook (page 313) 15 to 25 min., or until tender. Drain and combine with cooked green beans. Pour over vegetables a mixture of ¼ **cup melted butter or margarine,** ½ **teaspoon salt,** ¼ **teaspoon pepper** and ¼ **teaspoon monosodium glutamate.** Toss gently. Heat slowly 5 min., or until thoroughly heated.

—HERB-BUTTERED GREEN BEANS

Follow ▲ Recipe. Omit Mustard Sauce. Add to cooked green beans a mixture of **3 tablespoons melted butter or margarine,** ½ **teaspoon salt,** ¼ **teaspoon lemon juice** and ¼ **teaspoon rosemary or savory.** Toss gently.

GREEN BEANS SUPREME

Set out a medium-size saucepan and a shallow 1-qt. baking dish.

Shred and set aside
4 oz. pasteurized process cheese food (about 1 cup, shredded)

Wash, cut off ends and French (cut lengthwise into fine strips)
1 lb. (about 3 cups) green beans
Cook (page 313) 15 to 20 min., or until just tender. (If using frozen green beans, substitute two 9-oz. pkgs. frozen French-style green beans. Cook following directions on package.)

Heat in the saucepan over low heat
2 tablespoons butter
Add and cook over medium heat until onion is tender
2 tablespoons minced onion

Green Beans Supreme

Remove from heat and blend in
1 tablespoon all-purpose flour
½ **teaspoon salt**
½ **teaspoon paprika**
¼ **teaspoon dry mustard**
¼ **teaspoon monosodium glutamate**
½ **teaspoon Worcestershire sauce**
Heat until mixture bubbles. Remove from heat. Add gradually, stirring constantly
1 cup heavy cream
Return to heat and bring rapidly to boiling, stirring constantly; cook 1 to 2 min. longer.

When beans are tender, drain if necessary, and add to sauce. Toss mixture gently with a spoon until blended. Spoon into the baking dish. Sprinkle with the shredded cheese food and
2 tablespoons fine dry bread crumbs

Place baking dish on broiler rack. Place under broiler with the top of the mixture 2 to 3 in. from heat. Broil 5 min., or until bread crumbs are lightly browned and cheese is melted.
4 to 6 servings

CREOLE STRING BEANS

Thoroughly grease a 1-qt. casserole.

Wash, cut off ends and cut into 1-in. pieces
1 lb. green beans (about 3 cups, pieces)
Cook (page 313) 15 to 20 min., or until just tender. Drain beans.

While beans are cooking, heat in a skillet over low heat
2 tablespoons butter or margarine
Add and cook over medium heat until onion is tender
1 tablespoon chopped onion
1 tablespoon chopped green pepper

Mix the cooked onion, green pepper, green beans and

1⅓ cups (28-oz. can, drained) cooked tomatoes

and a mixture of

¾ teaspoon salt

¼ teaspoon monosodium glutamate

⅛ teaspoon pepper

Turn into casserole. Sprinkle over top

½ cup cracker crumbs

2 tablespoons grated American or Parmesan cheese

Set in a 350°F oven 15 to 20 min., or until topping is lightly browned. *6 servings*

HARVARD BEETS

▲ Base Recipe

Set out a 2-qt. saucepan with a tight-fitting cover.

Leaving on 1- to 2-in. stem and the root end (this helps beets to retain red color), cut off leaves from

1 lb. (about 5 medium) beets

Wash and cook covered in boiling salted water to cover 30 to 45 min., or until just tender. When beets are tender, drain if necessary and reserve liquid in a measuring cup. Set aside.

Plunge beets into running cold water. Peel off and discard skin, stems and root ends. Dice or slice beets and set aside.

Mix in the saucepan

2 tablespoons sugar

1 tablespoon cornstarch

½ teaspoon salt

¼ teaspoon monosodium glutamate

Pour into reserved beet liquid

Cold water (enough to make ¾ cup liquid)

Stirring constantly, gradually add liquid to mixture in saucepan with

3 tablespoons cider vinegar

Stirring constantly, bring rapidly to boiling and cook 3 min. Add the beets and

2 tablespoons butter

Keeping mixture moving with a spoon, bring again to boiling; cover and simmer 8 to 10 min.

Serve immediately. *4 servings*

Note: Canned whole, sliced or diced beets may be substituted for fresh beets. Use drained 16-oz. can; beet liquid may be substituted for water in the sauce.

—BEETS IN MUSTARD SAUCE

Follow ▲ Recipe. Add **1½ to 2½ teaspoons dry mustard** and **a few grains cloves** with the seasonings. Serve with ham.

BEETS IN SOUR CREAM

Set out a saucepan.

Drain

1 can or jar (16 oz.) small whole beets

Shred beets and set aside.

Heat in the saucepan

2 tablespoons butter or margarine

Blend in

1 tablespoon all-purpose flour

Heat until mixture is bubbly. Stir in

2 tablespoons sugar

2 tablespoons cider vinegar

Mix in the shredded beets. Heat thoroughly. Add and stir in

½ cup dairy sour cream

Heat thoroughly, stirring occasionally; do not boil. Turn into a heated serving dish.

6 servings

SWEET-SOUR BEETS
(Sursöte Rödbeter)

Caraway seed gives an unexpected accent of flavor to this Norwegian version of beets.

Leaving on 1- to 2-in. stem and root end, cut off leaves from

2 lbs. (about 10) medium beets

Scrub beets thoroughly. Cook (page 313) in a large saucepan in water to cover 30 to 45 min., or until tender.

When beets are tender, drain and reserve liquid in a measuring cup. Plunge beets into running cold water. Peel off and discard skin, stem and root end from beets. Cut beets into thin slices and set aside.

Meanwhile, mix in a saucepan

2 cups reserved beet liquid

¼ cup vinegar

¼ cup sugar

1 teaspoon salt

½ teaspoon caraway seed

10 whole cloves

8 drops red food coloring

Blend thoroughly

1 tablespoon cornstarch

¼ cup water

Blend into the mixture in the saucepan. Bring rapidly to boiling. Reduce heat and cook 3 to 5 min., or until thickened. Add the sliced beets and cook until heated thoroughly, stirring occasionally.

Serve hot or cold. *6 servings*

BEETS IN ORANGE SAUCE

▲ Base Recipe

Set out a 1-qt. casserole.

Drain, reserving liquid

1 can (16 oz.) sliced beets (about 2 cups, drained)

Place drained beets in casserole and set aside.

Melt in a saucepan

2 tablespoons butter or margarine

Remove from heat; stir in

1 tablespoon sugar

1 tablespoon cornstarch

½ teaspoon salt

¼ teaspoon monosodium glutamate

⅛ teaspoon paprika

Cook over low heat until mixture bubbles. Remove from heat; gradually stir in

½ cup reserved beet liquid

Cook rapidly, stirring constantly, until mixture thickens. Remove from heat. Blend in

½ cup orange juice

1 teaspoon lemon juice

Pour over beets.

Bake at 350°F 15 to 20 min.

If desired, garnish with

Hard-Cooked Egg (page 133), chopped

Serve immediately. *4 servings*

—CRISPY CRESTED BAKED BEETS

Follow ▲ Recipe. Omit garnish. Before baking, top prepared beets with a mixture of **½ cup buttered crumbs** (page 9), **1 tablespoon brown sugar** and **1 teaspoon grated orange peel**. Bake about 20 min., or until crumbs are browned.

GINGERED BEETS

Set aside to drain

1 can (16 oz.) sliced beets (about 2 cups, drained)

Mix in a saucepan

½ cup sugar

1 tablespoon cornstarch

¾ teaspoon ginger

¼ teaspoon salt

Blend in

½ cup cider vinegar

Stirring constantly, bring rapidly to boiling and cook 3 min.

Add to sauce the beets and

2 tablespoons butter or margarine

Cover and simmer over low heat about 10 min., or until beets are thoroughly heated, moving and turning occasionally.

Transfer to warm serving dish. Sprinkle with

Chopped parsley

4 servings

BROCCOLI WITH HORSERADISH CREAM

Set out a double boiler.

Prepare and cook (page 313)

2 lbs. broccoli

Meanwhile, mix in top of double boiler

¾ cup dairy sour cream
½ teaspoon prepared horseradish
½ teaspoon prepared mustard
⅛ teaspoon salt
⅛ teaspoon monosodium glutamate

Cook over simmering water, stirring constantly, 3 to 5 min., or until thoroughly heated.

When broccoli is tender, arrange in a heated serving dish. Pour sauce over the broccoli and serve immediately. *8 servings*

ONION-BUTTERED BROCCOLI

▲ *Base Recipe*

Set out a deep saucepan.

Remove and discard outer leaves and cut off tough ends of stalks from

1 lb. broccoli

Rinse well. Split heavy stalks lengthwise, about ½ in. thick. Cook (page 313) broccoli in saucepan and drain.

Meanwhile, heat in a small skillet

¼ cup butter or margarine

Add and cook until onion is tender

2 tablespoons finely chopped onion

Mix in

½ teaspoon monosodium glutamate
⅛ teaspoon pepper

Pour onion mixture over broccoli. Serve immediately. *3 servings*

—ALMOND-BUTTERED BROCCOLI

Follow ▲ Recipe. Omit onion and seasonings. Increase butter or margarine to ⅓ cup. When butter is hot, stir in ½ cup (about 2 oz.) **toasted almonds** (page 10), slivered. Remove from heat. Pour over broccoli in serving dish.

—ALMOND-BUTTERED ASPARAGUS

Wash **asparagus** and cook (page 313). Drain and serve as for Almond-Buttered Broccoli.

Broccoli San Vincente

BROCCOLI SAN VINCENTE

Set out an ovenproof platter.

Prepare and cook (page 313)

2 lbs. broccoli

When broccoli is tender, arrange on the platter (see photo).

Combine and spoon over broccoli

1 cup dairy sour cream
½ cup finely shredded American cheese
1 tablespoon lemon juice
½ teaspoon grated lemon peel
¼ teaspoon salt
Few grains pepper

Sprinkle with

¼ cup toasted, slivered almonds

Place under broiler about 5 in. from heat. Broil 3 min., or until cheese begins to melt.

Serve immediately. *8 servings*

BROCCOLI WITH FLUFFY SAUCE

Set out a deep saucepan and a shallow baking dish.

For Broccoli—Remove and discard outer leaves and cut off tough ends of stalks from

2 lbs. broccoli

Rinse and cook (page 313) broccoli in the saucepan. When tender, drain. (Or cook two 10-oz. pkgs. frozen broccoli.)

Meanwhile, prepare Fluffy Sauce.

For Fluffy Sauce—Blend

½ cup mayonnaise
3 tablespoons pickle relish
2 tablespoons minced pimiento
1 teaspoon lemon juice
¼ teaspoon celery salt
Few grains cayenne pepper

Beat until rounded peaks are formed

2 egg whites

Fold mayonnaise mixture into beaten egg whites.

Arrange broccoli in the baking dish. Spoon the sauce over broccoli and sprinkle with **paprika**.

Set baking dish on broiler rack. Place under broiler with top of sauce 3 to 4 in. from heat and broil about 1 min., or until surface is golden brown. *6 servings*

BROCCOLI FLORENTINE
(Broccoli alla Fiorentina)

▲ *Base Recipe*

Set out a deep saucepan. (Top of a double boiler or a deep coffeepot may be used.)

Remove and discard outer leaves and cut off tough ends of stalks from

1 lb. broccoli

Split the heavier stalks (over ½ in. thick) lengthwise through the stems up to the flowerets (buds). Tie stalks together securely and stand in deep saucepan. Fill saucepan with boiling salted water up to flowerets. Boil loosely covered 10 to 20 min., or until broccoli is tender.

Meanwhile, heat in skillet

2 tablespoons olive oil

Add to skillet and cook until lightly browned

2 cloves garlic, sliced thin

Drain broccoli and add to skillet. Cook 10 to 15 min., stirring occasionally. Season with a mixture of

¼ tablespoon salt
¼ teaspoon pepper

Serve hot. *4 servings*

Broccoli with Fluffy Sauce

—BROCCOLI ROMAN STYLE
(Broccoli alla Romana)

Follow ▲ Recipe. Omit cooking of broccoli in boiling water. Cook the broccoli in olive oil for only 5 min. Add **1½ cups dry red wine** and cook, covered, over low heat, stirring occasionally, about 20 min., or until broccoli is tender.

—SPINACH SAUTEED IN OIL
(Spinaci Saltati all 'Olio)

Follow ▲ Recipe for cooking in oil and seasonings. Substitute **2 cups (about 1 lb. fresh) chopped cooked spinach** for the broccoli. Add **1 tablespoon chopped pine nuts or almonds** and **1 tablespoon raisins** to olive oil mixture with spinach.

BEST-EVER BRUSSELS SPROUTS

This full-flavored creation more than deserves its name.

Set out a large saucepan.

Wash thoroughly
2 lbs. Brussels sprouts
Shred the Brussels sprouts.

Heat in the saucepan over low heat
1 cup butter or margarine
Add the shredded Brussels sprouts; cook, constantly moving and turning pieces with a fork or spoon, about 5 min., or until just tender.

Add a mixture of
½ cup heavy cream
1½ teaspoons salt
1½ teaspoons sugar
½ teaspoon monosodium glutamate
⅛ teaspoon pepper
Cook 2 to 3 min. longer, or until thoroughly heated, keeping mixture moving with a fork or spoon. *About 8 servings*

BRUSSELS SPROUTS WITH CHESTNUTS

Grease a 1-qt. casserole.

Wash and cook (page 313)
2 cups (about ½ lb.) Brussels sprouts

Meanwhile, wash, make a slit on two sides of each shell and put into a saucepan
½ lb. chestnuts
Cover with boiling water and boil about 20 min. Peel off shells and skins. Return blanched nuts to saucepan and cover with boiling salted water. Cover and simmer 8 to 20 min., or until chestnuts are tender; drain.

Prepare and set aside
¼ cup buttered crumbs (page 9)

Drain the Brussels sprouts, reserving liquid. Measure ½ cup of hot liquid. Add to liquid
1 beef bouillon cube or ½ teaspoon concentrated meat extract
Set aside.

Combine the whole chestnuts with Brussels sprouts. Arrange in two layers in casserole; sprinkle each layer with
Salt
Pepper
Nutmeg
¼ teaspoon monosodium glutamate
Dot each layer generously with
Butter or margarine
Pour the reserved beef broth into casserole. Sprinkle buttered crumbs over casserole.

Set in a 350°F oven 15 to 20 min., or until crumbs are lightly browned.
4 servings

BRUSSELS SPROUTS IN HERB BUTTER

Cook following package directions
2 pkgs. (10 oz. each) frozen Brussels sprouts

Meanwhile, put into a saucepan
3 tablespoons butter or margarine
½ tablespoon grated onion
½ tablespoon lemon juice
¼ teaspoon salt
⅛ teaspoon thyme, crushed
⅛ teaspoon marjoram, crushed
⅛ teaspoon savory, crushed
Set saucepan over low heat until butter is melted, stirring to blend in the herbs and seasonings.

When Brussels sprouts are tender, drain thoroughly and turn into a warm serving dish. Pour the seasoned butter mixture over the Brussels sprouts and toss gently to coat evenly and thoroughly. *6 servings*

CABBAGE STRUDEL
(Káposztás Rétes)

Set out a 3-qt. saucepan.

Remove and discard wilted outer leaves, rinse, cut into quarters (discarding core) and finely shred
1 head (about 3 lbs.) cabbage (about 3 qts., shredded)
Put cabbage into a large bowl and mix with
2 tablespoons salt
Let stand ½ hr., mixing occasionally.

Meanwhile, prepare
Strudel Dough (page 519)

While Strudel Dough is resting 30 min., melt in the saucepan
¼ cup butter
Squeeze cabbage, a small amount at a time, discarding the juice; put cabbage into the saucepan. Cook uncovered over medium heat, stirring frequently, 10 to 15 min., or until just tender. Remove cabbage from heat and mix in
¾ to 1 teaspoon pepper
Set cabbage aside.

After Strudel Dough is stretched and slightly dried, spoon over entire surface in small mounds
¼ cup dairy sour cream
Carefully spread mounds of cream with spatula. Sprinkle over the sour cream
¼ cup (about 1 slice) fine dry bread crumbs
Spoon cabbage in small mounds over the bread crumbs. With spatula spread mounds carefully.

Roll, bake and slice as in Apple Strudel (page 519; do not sprinkle with confectioners' sugar). Serve warm. *12 slices strudel*

COMPANY CABBAGE

Combine in a large heavy saucepan
5 cups finely shredded cabbage
1 cup finely shredded carrot
½ cup chopped green onion, including some of the green tops
½ teaspoon salt
⅛ teaspoon pepper

Mix together until cube is dissolved
1 beef bouillon cube
¼ cup boiling water
Add to vegetables in saucepan and toss with a fork to blend thoroughly. Cover and cook over low heat for 5 min., stirring once during cooking. Drain if necessary; turn into a warm serving dish. Set aside and keep warm.

Melt in a small saucepan over low heat
¼ cup butter or margarine
Stir in and heat thoroughly
1 teaspoon prepared mustard
⅓ cup chopped pecans
Pour over vegetables and sprinkle with
¼ teaspoon paprika

Serve immediately. *6 servings*

CABBAGE WITH CARAWAY SEEDS
(Káposztá Köménymaggal)

Set out a heavy 3-qt. saucepan with a tight-fitting cover.

Remove and discard wilted outer leaves, rinse, cut into quarters (discarding core) and coarsely shred
1 head (about 2 lbs.) red or green cabbage (about 2 qts., shredded)
Melt in the saucepan
¼ to ⅓ cup butter
Add the cabbage to butter with a mixture of
1 teaspoon caraway seed
1 teaspoon salt
⅛ teaspoon pepper
Cover the saucepan and cook over low heat,

stirring frequently, 10 to 15 min., or until cabbage is just tender. Stir into the cabbage mixture

1 to 2 tablespoons vinegar

Cover saucepan and cook 5 min. longer.

About 6 servings

RED CABBAGE AND WINE
(Rotkohl mit Wein)

Set out a heavy 3-qt. saucepan with a tight-fitting cover.

Remove and discard wilted outer leaves from

1 head (about 2 lbs.) red cabbage

Rinse, cut into quarters (discarding core) and coarsely shred (about 2 qts., shredded). Put cabbage into the saucepan with

1 cup red wine
⅓ cup firmly packed brown sugar
1 teaspoon salt
Few grains cayenne pepper

Rinse, quarter, core and pare

4 medium apples

Add the apples to the saucepan.

Cover and simmer over low heat 20 to 30 min., or until cabbage is tender. Add to the cabbage

¼ cup cider vinegar
¼ cup butter

Toss together lightly until butter is melted.

6 servings

SWEET-SOUR RED CABBAGE I
(Rotkohl)

▲ *Base Recipe*

Set out a heavy 3-qt. saucepan.

Remove and discard wilted outer leaves from

1 head (about 2 lbs.) red cabbage

Rinse, cut into quarters (discarding core) and coarsely shred (about 2 qts., shredded). Put cabbage into the saucepan and add

Boiling salted water to cover (1 teaspoon salt per quart of water)
⅓ to ½ cup firmly packed brown sugar
¾ teaspoon allspice
4 whole cloves

Cover loosely and boil at a moderate rate 8 to 12 min., or until cabbage is just tender.

Remove from heat; drain. Add to cabbage

½ cup vinegar
¼ cup butter

Toss together lightly to mix. *6 servings*

—RED CABBAGE WITH APPLES
(Rotkohl mit Äpfeln)

Follow ▲ Recipe. Wash, quarter, core, pare

and chop **3 apples.** Add to saucepan with cabbage. Cook until apples and cabbage are just tender.

SWEET-SOUR RED CABBAGE II
(Rödkal)

Set out a heavy 3-qt. saucepan.

Remove and discard wilted outer leaves from

1 head (about 2 lbs.) red cabbage

Rinse, cut into quarters (discarding core), and coarsely shred (about 2 qts., shredded). Put cabbage into the saucepan and add

Boiling salted water to cover (1 teaspoon salt per quart of water)
⅓ to ½ cup firmly packed brown sugar
1 tablespoon caraway seed

Cook (page 313) 8 to 12 min., or until cabbage is just tender. Remove from heat and drain.

Add to cabbage

½ cup vinegar
¼ cup butter

Toss together lightly to mix.

Serve immediately. *6 servings*

BUTTERED CARROTS

Wash, pare or scrape

12 medium carrots

Using a fancy fluted cutter, cut carrots crosswise into slices ¼ in. thick.

Cook carrots (page 313) about 15 min., or until just tender when pierced with a fork. Drain, if necessary. Toss with carrots

¼ cup softened butter

Season with

1 teaspoon sugar
½ teaspoon salt

Turn carrots into a warm serving dish and garnish with

Minced parsley

Serve immediately. *About 8 servings*

CARROTS COOKED IN BUTTER
(Párolt Sárgarépa)

Set out a heavy 2-qt. saucepan with a tight-fitting cover.

Cut off and discard tops; wash, pare or scrape, and cut into ¼-in. slices

8 medium carrots (about 2 cups, sliced)

Melt in the saucepan over low heat

¼ cup butter or margarine

Add the carrots to butter with

2 teaspoons finely chopped parsley
1 teaspoon sugar
½ teaspoon salt

Cover saucepan and cook about 20 min., or until carrots are just tender, stirring occasionally to coat evenly and prevent scorching.

Meanwhile, prepare and set aside

1 cup quick meat broth (page 10)

Put into a small screw-top jar

¼ cup water

Add to the water

2 tablespoons all-purpose flour

Cover jar tightly and shake until ingredients are well blended. Set aside.

Remove carrots from saucepan with slotted spoon to a warm bowl; cover bowl.

Pour reserved broth into the saucepan in which carrots were cooked. Return saucepan to heat. Again shake jar containing flour-water mixture and gradually add mixture to the broth stirring constantly. Bring broth rapidly to boiling, stirring constantly; cook 3 to 5 min. longer. Pour this sauce over the carrots.

4 to 6 servings

CANDIED CARROTS

▲ *Base Recipe*

Set out a small baking dish.

Wash and pare or scrape

6 medium (about 1½ lbs.) carrots

Cook (page 313) whole carrots 15 to 25 min., or until just tender.

Meanwhile, combine in a small saucepan

¾ cup firmly packed brown sugar
6 tablespoons water
3 tablespoons butter or margarine

Stirring constantly, cook over medium heat until sugar is dissolved. Drain carrots and place in baking dish. Cover with sugar mixture.

Bake at 350°F about 10 min., or until carrots are completely glazed; baste occasionally.

6 servings

—GLAZED CARROTS

Follow ▲ Recipe. Prepare whole carrots or cut lengthwise into sticks. Omit brown sugar mixture. Drain cooked carrots and dry thoroughly on absorbent paper. Melt **1½ tablespoons butter or margarine** in skillet. Stir in **3 tablespoons sugar.** With skillet over low heat, turn carrots in mixture until coated.

Glazed Carrots

PINEAPPLE GLAZED CARROTS

Set out a 1½-qt. saucepan.

Drain, reserving liquids
> **1 can (16 oz.) sliced carrots (about 2 cups, drained)**
> **1 can (8½ oz.) pineapple tidbits (about ⅔ cup, drained)**

Combine in the saucepan
> **2 teaspoons cornstarch**
> **½ teaspoon salt**

Mix and add gradually to cornstarch mixture, stirring constantly
> **⅔ cup reserved carrot liquid**
> **⅓ cup reserved pineapple syrup**

Bring to boiling. Stirring constantly, cook about 3 min., or until the liquid is thick and clear. Stir in
> **1 tablespoon butter or margarine**

Add carrots and pineapple. Heat thoroughly.

4 or 5 servings

CRISPY-COATED CARROTS

Carrots decked in new attire.

Cut off tops, wash and pare or scrape
> **8 whole, small carrots**

Put carrots into a saucepan with
> **½ teaspoon salt**
> **¼ teaspoon monosodium glutamate**

Pour in boiling water to almost cover and cook, covered, 15 to 25 min., or until just tender.

Drain carrots and roll in
> **3 tablespoons melted butter or margarine**

Coat carrots with a mixture of
> **1 cup corn flakes, crushed fine**
> **½ teaspoon salt**
> **¼ teaspoon pepper**
> **⅛ teaspoon paprika**

Place carrots on broiler rack. Place under broiler with tops of carrots about 2 in. from heat. Carefully turn as necessary to brown all sides.

4 servings

GOLDEN CARROT CASSEROLE

Thoroughly grease a 1-qt. casserole with a tight-fitting cover.

Prepare in blender (page 11) and set aside
> **⅓ cup fine dry bread crumbs**

Pineapple Glazed Carrots

Blender-chop (page 11) and set aside
> **½ cup (2¾ oz.) blanched almonds (page 9)**

Melt and set aside
> **¼ cup butter or margarine**

Wash, pare or scrape and cut into pieces
> **6 large carrots**

Put into an electric blender container
> **½ cup cream**
> **1 slice onion**
> **1 teaspoon salt**
> **⅛ teaspoon pepper**

Cover and turn on motor. Add carrots by pieces and blend until carrots are coarsely chopped. Turn mixture into greased casserole.

Thoroughly mix chopped nuts, bread crumbs and melted butter. Sprinkle nut mixture evenly over carrot mixture in casserole.

Cover and bake at 350°F about 35 min., or until carrots are tender. Uncover and heat 10 min., or until top is crisp and golden brown.

6 servings

CARROT SPECIALTY

Wash, pare or scrape, notch* and cut into ¼-in. crosswise slices
> **10 medium carrots**

Cook carrots (page 313) about 15 min., or just until tender.

Meanwhile, melt in a small saucepan
> **½ cup butter or margarine**

Stir in
> **¼ cup finely chopped parsley**
> **½ teaspoon monosodium glutamate**
> **⅛ teaspoon finely crushed chervil**

Keep mixture warm.

When carrots are tender, drain immediately, if necessary. Add carrots to the butter mixture and turn and toss to coat carrots thoroughly. Turn into a warm serving dish. Serve immediately.

6 to 8 servings

*To notch carrots make 3 or 4 lengthwise cuts at evenly spaced intervals around the carrot and remove small wedge-shaped strips before slicing.

BAKED CAULIFLOWER
(Karfiol)

Lightly grease a 1½-qt. casserole.

Remove leaves and cut off all the woody base from
> **1 large head cauliflower**

Trim off any blemishes. Carefully break into flowerets and allow cauliflower to stand in salted cold water for a few minutes to remove dust or small insects. Rinse cauliflower and cook (page 313) 20 to 30 min., or until tender but still firm.

Mix and set aside
> **½ cup (about 1½ slices) buttered fine dry bread crumbs (page 9)**
> **½ cup grated Parmesan cheese**

Mix in a bowl
> **2 egg yolks, slightly beaten**
> **2 tablespoons all-purpose flour**

Blend into egg yolk mixture
> **2 cups dairy sour cream**

Beat until stiff, not dry, peaks are formed
> **2 egg whites**

Fold egg whites into sour cream mixture. Set sauce aside.

Drain cauliflower; arrange one half on bottom of casserole. Spoon over cauliflowerets
> **1 cup cubed cooked ham**

Pour one half of the sauce over ham. Arrange remaining cauliflower over sauce; then add sauce. Sprinkle crumb mixture over top.

Bake at 350°F 20 to 30 min., or until top is lightly browned.

6 to 8 servings

CAULIFLOWER AU FINES HERBS

Set out a saucepot and a saucepan. Heat a serving platter.

Rinse and remove blemishes from
> **1 medium head cauliflower**

Brush cauliflower with
> **Melted butter or cooking oil**

Tie head in square of cheesecloth and place in saucepot. Cover with boiling water and add
> **1 teaspoon salt**
> **1 teaspoon monosodium glutamate**

Cook over medium heat until cauliflower is tender (but not soft). Lift from boiling water and remove cheesecloth. Place cauliflower on heated platter and keep warm. While cauliflower is cooking, prepare butter sauce.

Combine in saucepan
> **3 tablespoons butter or margarine, melted**
> **1 tablespoon *each* finely chopped green onion, mushrooms and parsley**
> **½ tablespoon *each* finely chopped shallots and mild-flavored onion**

Cook over low heat about 7 min., stirring occasionally. Pour over cauliflower and sprinkle with **shredded Parmesan or Cheddar cheese**.

About 6 servings

CAULIFLOWER WITH ANCHOVY SAUCE

Remove leaves, cut off all the woody base and trim any blemishes from
   1 medium head cauliflower
Rinse and cook (page 313) the cauliflower 20 to 30 min., or until tender but still firm, adding to water
   1 tablespoon lemon juice
   Few grains mace

Just before cauliflower is tender, blend thoroughly
   ½ cup softened butter or margarine
   1 teaspoon lemon juice
   ½ to ¾ teaspoon anchovy paste
When cauliflower is tender, drain and transfer to warm serving dish. Cover with the butter mixture and sprinkle with
   Chopped chives
Serve immediately.   *5 or 6 servings*

CAULIFLOWER CHEESE SENSATION

Set out four individual casseroles.

Prepare and cook (page 313)
   1 medium head cauliflower

Meanwhile, put through medium blade of food chopper
   4 frankfurters
Set aside.

Melt in a small skillet
   2 tablespoons butter or margarine
Stir in and set aside
   ⅓ cup fine dry bread crumbs
Shred and set aside
   ½ lb. pasteurized process American cheese (2 cups, shredded)
Prepare
   1½ cups Medium White Sauce (one and one half times recipe, page 304; add
   1 teaspoon dry mustard with the flour)
Remove sauce from heat; cool slightly. Add three fourths of the shredded cheese all at one time. Stir sauce rapidly until cheese is melted.

Cauliflower Cheese Sensation

To keep sauce warm, cover and set over simmering water.

Drain cauliflower when it is tender and separate into flowerets. Spoon ¼ cup of cheese sauce into each casserole. Arrange flowerets in the casseroles. Sprinkle the ground frankfurters over flowerets. Spoon remaining cheese sauce over the cauliflower and ground frankfurters. Sprinkle tops with the buttered crumbs and remaining shredded cheese.

Bake at 350°F 10 min., or until cheese melts.

Serve immediately.   *4 servings*

CAULIFLOWER WITH MUSTARD SAUCE
(Blumenkohl mit Senfsosse)

For Cauliflower—Remove leaves, cut off all the woody base and trim any blemishes from
   1 medium head cauliflower
Rinse and cook (page 313) the cauliflower 20 to 25 min., or until tender but still firm.

For Mustard Sauce—Meanwhile, set out
   1 cup heavy cream
Scald (page 10) in top of double boiler ¾ cup of the cream.

Mix thoroughly in a small saucepan
   ¼ cup sugar
   2 tablespoons dry mustard
   2 teaspoons cornstarch
   ½ teaspoon salt
Add, stirring well, the remaining ¼ cup cream. Gradually add the scalded cream; stir constantly. Stirring gently and constantly, bring cornstarch mixture rapidly to boiling over direct heat and cook for 3 min.

Wash double-boiler top to remove scum.

Pour mixture into double-boiler top and place over simmering water. Cover and cook 5 min., stirring occasionally. Remove cover and vigorously stir about 3 tablespoons of this hot mixture into
   1 egg yolk, slightly beaten
Immediately blend into mixture in double boiler. Cook over simmering water 3 to 5 min. Stir slowly to keep mixture cooking evenly. Remove from heat. Add gradually, stirring in
   ¼ cup cider vinegar
Drain the cauliflower and serve on platter with **Veal Cutlets with Fried Eggs** (page 209) or on a separate plate; pour the sauce over cauliflower.   *4 servings*

CAULIFLOWER A LA MOUSSELINE*
(Blumenkohl à la Mousseline)

For Cauliflower—Remove leaves, cut off all woody base and trim any blemishes from
   1 large head cauliflower
Separate the head into flowerets and cook (page 313) 8 to 10 min., or until just tender. Drain and set aside to keep warm.

For Sauce—In the top of a small double

boiler, beat with a whisk beater until thickened and light-colored
   2 egg yolks
   2 tablespoons cream
Blend in a mixture of
   ½ teaspoon salt
   ½ teaspoon monosodium glutamate
   ½ teaspoon sugar
   ¼ teaspoon paprika
Set over hot (not boiling) water; bottom of double-boiler top should not touch water. Add gradually, beating constantly
   2½ tablespoons lemon juice
Cook over low heat, beating constantly with the whisk beater, until sauce has the consistency of thick cream. Remove double boiler from heat, leaving top in place. Beating constantly, add to egg yolk mixture, ½ teaspoon at a time
   ¼ cup butter
Beat with whisk beater until butter is thoroughly blended ito the mixture. Remove top of double boiler from bottom.

Beat until rounded peaks are formed
   2 egg whites
Fold egg whites into the sauce. Arrange cauliflower on platter or in serving dish and spoon sauce over flowerets. Sprinkle with
   Paprika
          6 servings

*True mousseline sauce is made by folding whipped cream into hollandaise sauce; but as here, beaten egg white may be used if preferred.

CAULIFLOWER CASSEROLE

Butter a 1½-qt. casserole.

Remove leaves, cut off all the woody base and trim off any blemishes from
   1 large head cauliflower
Wash cauliflower thoroughly and carefully separate into flowerets. Cook (page 313) in boiling salted water 8 to 10 min., or until tender but still firm.

Meanwhile, shred and set aside
   4 oz. sharp Cheddar cheese (about
   1 cup shredded)

Cauliflower Casserole

Heat in a skillet

3 tablespoons butter

Add to skillet, tossing to coat evenly

¾ cup small bread cubes

When bread cubes are lightly browned, remove from heat and set aside.

When cauliflower is cooked, turn into colander and set aside to drain thoroughly.

For Sauce—Melt in top of a double boiler over direct heat

¼ cup butter

Add and cook until onion is tender

¼ cup minced onion

Blend in

3 tablespoons all-purpose flour
½ teaspoon salt
Few grains pepper

Heat until mixture bubbles. Remove from heat. Add gradually, stirring in

1⅔ cups undiluted evaporated milk
⅔ cup water

Return to heat and cook rapidly, stirring constantly, until sauce thickens. Cook 1 to 2 min. longer. Vigorously stir about 3 tablespoons of sauce into

2 egg yolks, slightly beaten

Immediately return mixture to double boiler. Cook over simmering water 3 to 5 min. Stir slowly to keep mixture cooking evenly. Remove from simmering water and cool sauce lightly.

Add all at one time and blend in

½ cup grated Parmesan cheese

Blend in

1 tablespoon lemon juice

Arrange one half of cauliflowerets in casserole. Cover with one half of sauce. Top with remaining cauliflowerets and sauce. Sprinkle the shredded cheese over top. Arrange bread cubes in a border around top of casserole.

Bake at 350°F about 30 min., or until lightly browned and thoroughly heated.

About 6 servings

CAULIFLOWER A LA ROMAGNA
(Cavolfiore alla Romagna)

Prepare and cook (page 313)

1 head cauliflower

Meanwhile, set out deep saucepan or auto-

matic deep fryer for deep-frying (page 11) and heat **fat** to 365°F.

Drain cauliflower, separate into flowerets and set aside to cool.

Mix

⅔ cup fine dry bread crumbs
1 teaspoon grated Parmesan cheese
½ teaspoon salt
¼ teaspoon pepper

Set aside.

Combine in a small deep bowl

2 eggs, slightly beaten
¼ cup milk

Coat flowerets with egg mixture and then roll in crumb mixture. Fry only as many flowerets as will float uncrowded one layer deep in the fat. Fry 2 to 4 min., or until golden brown, turning occasionally during frying time. Drain over fat before removing to absorbent paper.

About 4 servings

DEEP-FRIED CAULIFLOWER WITH SOUR CREAM SAUCE
(Kirántott Karfiol Tepfölös Mártással)

▲ Base Recipe

Remove leaves, cut off all the woody base and trim off any blemishes from

1 medium head cauliflower

Carefully break into 5 or 6 large flowerets. Allow cauliflower to stand in cold salted water a few minutes to remove dust or small insects. Rinse cauliflower and cook (page 313) 20 to 30 min., or until tender but still firm.

Meanwhile, prepare sauce.

For Sour Cream Sauce—Mix in top of double boiler

2 egg yolks, slightly beaten
1 cup dairy sour cream
2 teaspoons lemon juice
½ teaspoon salt
¼ teaspoon paprika
¼ teaspoon pepper

Cook over simmering water, stirring constantly, 3 to 5 min., or until sauce is thoroughly heated. Set aside and keep sauce warm.

About 20 min. before deep-frying, fill a deep saucepan one-half to two-thirds full with

Vegetable shortening, all-purpose shortening, lard or cooking oil for deep-frying

Heat slowly to 365°F (page 11). When using automatic deep-fryer, follow manufacturer's directions for amount of fat and timing.

Drain cauliflower and set aside to cool slightly.

Meanwhile, mix and set aside

⅔ cup fine dry bread crumbs
½ teaspoon salt
¼ teaspoon pepper

Blend

2 eggs, slightly beaten
¼ cup milk

Dip flowerets into the egg mixture and then

into the crumb mixture. Deep-fry only one layer of flowerets at one time; do not crowd. Fry them 2 to 4 min., or until golden brown, turning occasionally. Drain flowerets over fat for a few seconds before removing to absorbent paper. Place cauliflowerets into bowl and top with the Sour Cream Sauce. Serve immediately.

4 to 6 servings

—BATTER-FRIED CAULIFLOWER
(Kirántott Karfiol Máskép)

Follow ▲ Recipe: omit egg and bread crumb mixtures. Beat together **1 cup all-purpose flour, ¾ cup milk, 1 egg** and **¼ teaspoon salt** for a batter coating. Dip cooked cauliflowerets into the batter and deep-fry.

CELERY IN ALMOND SAUCE
(Céleri Amandine)

Blanch, toast (pages 9 and 10) and sliver

1 cup (about 5½ oz.) almonds

Set almonds aside.

Trim roots and cut off leaves from

1 lb. celery

(Leaves may be used for added flavor in soups and stuffing; inner leaves may be left on stalk when serving as a relish.) Separate celery stalks, remove blemishes and wash. Slice celery crosswise into ¾- to 1-in. thick pieces.

Melt in a heavy 2-qt. saucepan with a tight-fitting cover

¼ cup butter
½ teaspoon salt
¼ teaspoon white pepper

Add celery pieces to saucepan, cover and cook over low heat about 20 min., or until celery is tender. Uncover saucepan once during cooking and stir in

1½ tablespoons finely grated onion
1 tablespoon finely chopped chives

When celery is tender, stir in a mixture of

1 tablespoon all-purpose flour
1 teaspoon salt
⅛ teaspoon white pepper

Heat until mixture bubbles. Remove from heat and add gradually, stirring constantly

1 cup cream
½ cup double strength consommé
(dissolve 1 chicken bouillon cube in ½ cup hot water)

Return to heat and bring rapidly to boiling, stirring constantly; cook 1 to 2 min. longer. Stir in the slivered almonds. *4 to 6 servings*

BRAISED CELERY

Set out a 1½-qt. casserole or baking dish.

Peel, thinly slice, and spread evenly in bottom of the casserole
2 large Spanish onions
Sprinkle with
Salt and pepper
2 tablespoons chopped parsley

Heat in a saucepan or skillet
¼ cup butter or margarine
Add and cook over medium heat until lightly browned, stirring occasionally
4 cups diagonally sliced celery, cut ½ in. thick

Prepare in a saucepan
2 cups quick meat broth (page 10)
Combine to form a smooth paste
2 tablespoons water
1 tablespoon cornstarch
Stir into the broth, cooking over high heat until mixture comes to boiling. Cook and stir 3 to 5 min., or until sauce is thickened and smooth. Combine with the partially cooked celery. Spoon over the onions in casserole and bake in a 325°F oven about 1 hr.

6 to 8 servings

CORN IN SOUR CREAM

Heat in a heavy 1½-qt. saucepan
3 tablespoons butter or margarine
Add and cook over medium heat about 5 min., stirring occasionally.
½ cup chopped onion
½ cup chopped green pepper
Stir in a mixture of
2 tablespoons all-purpose flour
1 teaspoon salt
½ teaspoon monosodium glutamate
Add, stirring constantly
1 cup water
Cook and stir until mixture comes to boiling and is thickened. Reduce heat to low and blend in
1 cup dairy sour cream
2 cups drained corn kernels (canned or frozen, cooked)
Continue cooking until thoroughly heated (do not boil).

5 or 6 servings

FRIED CORN

Set out a skillet or 1½-qt. saucepan.

Cut from ears of cooked sweet corn enough to yield
4 cups corn kernels
Combine corn in a bowl with
¼ cup chopped green pepper
2 tablespoons chopped onion
½ teaspoon salt
⅛ teaspoon pepper

Heat in the skillet
¼ cup butter or margarine
Add corn mixture and cook over medium heat about 20 min.; stirring occasionally. *6 servings*

MEXICAN CORN

Heat over low heat in a medium-size saucepan with a tight-fitting cover
¼ cup butter or margarine
Add and cook until onion is tender, occasionally moving and turning with a spoon
¼ cup finely chopped onion
¼ cup chopped green pepper
Add
1 pkg. (10 oz.) frozen corn (or 17-oz. can whole kernel corn, drained)
Cook corn, covered, over low heat about 10 min., or until tender. With a fork or spoon gently break corn apart while cooking. During last few minutes of cooking, mix in
¼ cup diced pimiento
Season with a mixture of
1 teaspoon salt
½ teaspoon monosodium glutamate
¼ teaspoon pepper
Mix gently. If desired, garnish with
Sweet red pepper slices

4 servings

SOUTHERN CORN PUDDING

Grease bottom and sides of a 1-qt. baking dish or casserole.

Cut kernels from fresh corn ears to yield
3 cups uncooked corn kernels
Combine thoroughly in a bowl with
3 eggs, beaten
2 teaspoons grated onion
1 teaspoon salt
⅛ teaspoon pepper
3 tablespoons fat, melted
3 tablespoons sugar
1 cup plus 2 tablespoons scalded milk
Turn into baking dish.

Bake at 325°F 30 to 40 min., or until pudding is "set." *About 6 servings*

PLANTATION CORN PUDDING

▲ *Base Recipe*

Grease a 1½-qt. casserole.

Scald (page 10)
1¾ cups milk
Add
1 tablespoon butter or margarine

While milk scalds, beat slightly
4 eggs
Blend eggs with
2 cups (16-oz. can) cream-style corn
2 tablespoons slivered pimiento
2 tablespoons finely chopped green pepper
2 tablespoons grated onion
and a mixture of
1 teaspoon sugar
1 teaspoon salt
¼ teaspoon pepper
Stirring vigorously, gradually add the milk to the corn mixture; pour into casserole. Place

Plantation Corn Pudding and Mexican Corn

in a large baking pan. Pour very hot water into pan to a 1-in. depth.

Bake at 300°F 45 to 60 min., or until a metal knife comes out clean when inserted halfway between center and edge of casserole. Serve immediately. *6 servings*

—CORN AND SAUSAGE PUDDING

Follow ▲ Recipe; use a 10-in. shallow bake-and-serve dish. Decrease milk to ½ cup and eggs to 2. Substitute for pimiento and green pepper, **½ cup (4-oz. can, drained) sliced mushrooms**. Stir **¼ cup fine dry bread crumbs** into corn mixture. Bake pudding, without the pan of hot water, at 375°F 20 min.; remove from oven. Arrange **Vienna sausages** (two 4-oz. cans, drained) attractively around edge of casserole; push ends of sausages into mixture. Bake 15 min. longer. Garnish with **green pepper strips.**

CORN PUDDING

Flecks of green pepper and scarlet pimiento give this golden corn pudding a piquant flavor and gay color that make it a star attraction.

Grease a 2-qt. casserole.

Remove husks, corn silk and blemishes from
6 or 7 fresh ears of corn
Carefully cut kernels of corn from cob. Chop finely enough corn to yield 2 cups, chopped.

Set out
2¾ cups milk
Scald (page 10) 1 cup of the milk in the top of a double boiler. Put the corn into a saucepan and pour in the scalded milk. Stirring frequently, cook covered over low heat about 10 min., or until just tender.

While corn is cooking, wash double-boiler top to remove scum; scald the remaining 1¾ cups milk. Add
1 tablespoon butter or margarine
While milk scalds, beat slightly
4 eggs
Blend eggs with the cooked corn and
2 tablespoons slivered pimiento
2 tablespoons finely chopped green pepper
2 tablespoons grated onion
and a mixture of
1 teaspoon sugar
1 teaspoon salt
½ teaspoon monosodium glutamate
¼ teaspoon pepper
Stirring vigorously, gradually add the milk to the corn mixture; pour into the casserole. Set in a large baking pan. Pour very hot water into pan to a 1-in. depth.

Bake at 300°F 45 to 50 min., or until a metal knife comes out clean when inserted halfway between center and edge of casserole. Serve at once.   *About 8 servings*

SCALLOPED CORN

Grease a 1-qt. shallow baking dish.

Combine in a bowl
3 cups uncooked kernels cut from fresh ears of sweet corn
2 tablespoons coarsely chopped pimiento
2 eggs, well beaten
½ teaspoon salt
⅛ teaspoon pepper

Prepare
¾ cup coarse cracker crumbs
Place alternate layers of the corn mixture and crumbs in baking dish ending with crumbs.

Dot each crumb layer with
Butter or margarine (using 3 to 4 tablespoons)
Pour over top
1 cup milk

Bake in a 325°F oven about 30 min., or until mixture is "set" and top is lightly browned.
4 to 6 servings

PURE-GOLD SCALLOPED CORN

▲ *Base Recipe*

Grease a 1-qt. casserole.

Combine
2½ cups canned cream-style corn
½ cup milk
3 tablespoons butter or margarine melted
Thoroughly blend in
1 cup fine dry bread crumbs
3 tablespoons minced onion
3 tablespoons minced green pepper
2 tablespoons brown sugar
and a mixture of
1 teaspoon salt
¼ teaspoon monosodium glutamate
¼ teaspoon pepper
Turn into casserole. Dot with
2 teaspoons butter or margarine

Bake at 350°F 30 min., or until browned.
6 servings

—SCALLOPED CORN AND TOMATOES

Follow ▲ Recipe. Substitute **whole kernel corn** for cream-style corn. Substitute **1¾ cups (one half of a 28-oz. can) tomatoes**, cut in pieces, for milk.

DEVILED CORN CASSEROLE

Set out and grease a 1½-qt. shallow baking dish or casserole.

Heat in a heavy saucepan
¼ cup butter or margarine
Blend in a mixture of
¼ cup all-purpose flour
½ teaspoon dry mustard
1 teaspoon salt
Mix thoroughly, then stir in
1½ cups milk
2 teaspoons Worcestershire sauce

Cook and stir over medium heat until sauce comes to boiling. Cook and stir several minutes longer until thickened and smooth.

Combine in a mixing bowl
1 can (17 oz.) cream-style corn
1 egg, well beaten
Add the sauce, mix well and turn into baking dish.

Toss together lightly
1 cup coarse cracker crumbs
2 tablespoons melted butter or margarine
Top casserole with crumbs.

Set in 350°F oven about 30 min., or until crumbs are browned.   *About 6 servings*

CORN "OYSTERS"

Put into a large heavy skillet or saucepan and heat to 365°F
Fat for frying (to about 1-in. depth)

Meanwhile, sift together into a mixing bowl
1 cup all-purpose flour
1 teaspoon baking powder
1 teaspoon sugar
1 teaspoon monosodium glutamate
½ teaspoon salt
¼ teaspoon paprika
Stir in
2 teaspoons dill weed, crushed
Add a mixture of
2 cups fresh corn kernels cut from cob (about 4 ears)
6 tablespoons milk
2 egg yolks, beaten
Mix thoroughly and fold in
2 stiffly beaten egg whites
Drop mixture by the teaspoonful into hot fat. Fry uncrowded until golden on both sides, turning once. Lift out of fat with slotted spoon and drain on absorbent paper-lined baking sheet. Serve hot.   *About 2½ cups batter*

CORN AND PEPPER FRITTERS

Set out a large heavy skillet.

Combine in a mixing bowl
2 cups cooked corn kernels (cut from cooked corn ears or well-drained canned corn)
2 tablespoons sugar
½ teaspoon salt
¼ teaspoon onion salt
⅛ teaspoon pepper
½ cup cream
2 eggs, beaten
¼ cup chopped green pepper
Sift together
1½ cups all-purpose flour
1½ teaspoons baking powder

Add to corn mixture, beating thoroughly.

Heat in the skillet

> **Shortening (enough to cover bottom of skillet)**

Drop the corn mixture (using a tablespoonful for each fritter) into fat and cook slowly until puffed and browned. Turn and brown reverse side. Serve with **tomato sauce.**   *6 servings*

BRAISED CUCUMBER STICKS

Set out a heavy 8-in. skillet with a tight-fitting cover.

Wash, score, cut off ends and cut into 4-in. lengthwise sticks

> **2 medium cucumbers**

Meanwhile, heat in the skillet

> **1 tablespoon olive oil**
> **1 tablespoon butter or margarine**

Add cucumber sticks and lightly brown over medium heat, stirring occasionally

Dissolve

> **1 chicken bouillon cube, crushed**

in

> **2 tablespoons boiling water**

Add to skillet. Cover tightly and cook over low heat about 5 min., or until cucumber is crisp-tender. Season to taste with **seasoned salt** and **pepper.** Top with snipped **parsley.** Serve immediately.   *6 servings*

HAM-STUFFED EGGPLANT

Set out a large, shallow baking dish and a 2-qt. saucepan with a tight-fitting cover.

Wash and cut into halves lengthwise

> **1 large (about 1½ lbs.) eggplant**

Scoop out pulp with spoon, leaving shells ¼ to ½ in. thick. Place shells in baking dish, cut-sides up, and set aside.

Cut pulp into small pieces and put in the saucepan with

> **½ cup boiling water**
> **¼ cup finely chopped onion**
> **¼ cup finely chopped green pepper**

Cover and cook about 15 min., or until eggplant is tender.

Meanwhile, grind (page 10) and set aside enough cooked ham to yield

> **2 cups ground cooked ham**

Prepare and set aside

> **1 cup fine cracker crumbs**

Drain eggplant; add meat, one half of cracker crumbs and

> **1 cup (8-oz. can) tomato sauce**

Mix lightly. Spoon mixture into eggplant shells.

Blend remaining cracker crumbs with

> **¼ cup (1 oz.) grated cheese**
> **2 tablespoons melted butter**

Spoon mixture over tops of stuffed eggplant

halves. Pour around the eggplant in the baking dish

> **1 cup boiling water**

Bake at 350°F 15 to 20 min., or until crumbs are golden brown.

Serve immediately.   *4 to 6 servings*

EGGPLANT WITH SHRIMP STUFFING

> ▲ *Base Recipe*

Set out a shallow 2-qt. baking dish and a skillet.

Prepare

> **1 lb. fresh shrimp with shells (see Cooked Shrimp, page 294)**

Chop shrimp and set aside.

For Eggplant Shells—Wash and cut into halves lengthwise

> **1 large (1½ to 2 lbs.) eggplant**

Cook covered in a small amount of boiling salted water about 10 min., or until just tender. Remove eggplant from water.

With a spoon scoop out pulp, leaving a ½-in. thick shell. Set the shells aside. Finely chop pulp and reserve for stuffing.

For Shrimp Stuffing—Heat in the skillet over low heat

> **2 tablespoons butter or margarine**

Add and cook over medium heat until onion is tender

> **½ cup chopped (about 1 medium) onion**
> **2 tablespoons chopped green pepper**
> **1 clove garlic, finely minced**

Mix chopped shrimp, reserved eggplant pulp and chopped vegetables with

> **1 cup soft bread crumbs**

and a mixture of

> **½ teaspoon salt**
> **¼ teaspoon monosodium glutamate**
> **⅛ teaspoon pepper**

Spoon mixture into eggplant shells, heaping slightly. Place in baking dish. Cover tops with

> **1 cup buttered soft bread crumbs (page 9)**

Bake at 375°F 20 to 25 min., or until crumbs are browned.   *6 to 8 servings*

—PEPPERS WITH SHRIMP STUFFING

Follow ▲ Recipe; substitute **6 large green peppers** for eggplant. Rinse green peppers, cut off tops (reserving for Shrimp Stuffing), remove and discard white fiber and seeds from peppers. Rinse cavities. Drop peppers into boiling salted water to cover and simmer 5 min. Remove from water; invert and set aside to drain.

For Shrimp Stuffing—Substitute **1¾ cups Perfection Boiled Rice (one half recipe, page 165)** for eggplant pulp and bread crumbs. Heat **2 cups (two 8-oz. cans) tomato sauce** and **½ teaspoon Worcestershire sauce** in a saucepan until mixture bubbles. Blend with shrimp-

rice-vegetable mixture. Spoon into green pepper shells. Omit bread crumb topping. Pour **½ cup boiling water** into baking dish with peppers. Bake peppers at 350°F about 30 min.

EGGPLANT CASSEROLE

Set out a large heavy skillet; butter a 2-qt. casserole with a tight-fitting cover.

For Eggplant Slices—Set out

> **1 cup fine dry bread crumbs (3 to 4 slices bread)**

Wash, pare and cut crosswise into ½-in. slices

> **2 medium eggplants (about 1 lb. each)**

Mix in a shallow bowl

> **1 egg, slightly beaten**
> **¼ cup milk**
> **½ teaspoon salt**

Dip eggplant slices into egg mixture. Then coat with bread crumbs, coating evenly on both sides.

Set out

> **½ cup butter**

Heat ¼ cup of the butter in the skillet over low heat. Add as many eggplant slices at one time as will lie flat in skillet. Cook over medium heat until lightly browned; turn and brown other side. Add the extra butter as necessary. Set slices aside and keep them warm.

While eggplant slices are browning, shred and set aside

> **6 oz. sharp Cheddar cheese (about 1½ cups, shredded)**

For Tomato Sauce—Heat in the skillet

> **3 tablespoons butter**

Add and cook over medium heat until onion is tender

> **¼ cup finely chopped onion**
> **2 tablespoons minced green pepper**

Blend in contents of

> **1 can (6 oz.) tomato paste**

and

> **1½ cups water**
> **1 teaspoon salt**
> **¼ teaspoon pepper**

Remove from heat.

Eggplant Casserole

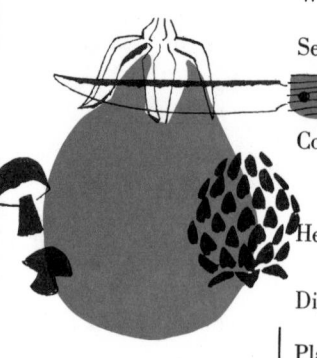

Eggplant with Cheese

Wash, pare and cut into ½-in. thick slices
1 eggplant (about 1 lb.)
Set aside.

Combine
2 eggs, slightly beaten
¼ cup undiluted evaporated milk

Heat in skillet
3 tablespoons olive oil

Dip eggplant in egg mixture, then in
⅔ cup (2 slices) fine dry bread crumbs
Place eggplant in skillet and slowly brown on
both sides.

Meanwhile, shred and set aside
**4 oz. pasteurized process cheese food
(1 cup, shredded)**

Put one third of the drained noodles into the
casserole. Top with one third of the eggplant
slices. Pour into casserole 1 cup Tomato Meat
Sauce. Top with one half of the shredded
cheese. Repeat layers (including sauce and
cheese) ending with eggplant topped with
**6 slices (3 oz.) pasteurized process
cheese food**

Cover casserole and bake at 350°F about 20
min. Remove cover and bake 10 to 15 min.
longer, or until cheese is lightly browned.
Serve with remaining Tomato Meat Sauce.
4 to 6 servings

—EGGPLANT PARMESAN
(Melanzane alla Parmigiana)

Follow ▲ Recipe. Substitute **grated Parmesan
cheese** for shredded cheese food. Substitute
Mozzarella cheese slices for sliced cheese
food.

GREEN PEPPERS
WITH HAM RICE STUFFING

▲ Base Recipe

Set out a shallow 2-qt. baking dish and a
medium-size saucepan.

Rinse and cut into halves lengthwise
4 large green peppers
With a knife remove stem, white fiber and
seeds. Rinse cavities. Drop pepper halves into
boiling salted water to cover and simmer 5
min. Remove peppers from water and invert.
Set aside to drain.

While peppers are cooking, grind (page 10)
enough cooked ham to yield
2 cups ground cooked ham

Prepare
**1 cup Perfection Boiled Rice
(one third recipe, page 165)**

Meanwhile, cut into 8 slices and set aside
¼ lb. Cheddar cheese

Melt in the saucepan
½ cup butter or margarine

For Casserole—Arrange a layer of eggplant
slices in bottom of casserole. Pour some of
sauce over slices and sprinkle with part of
cheese. Repeat layering, ending with cheese.

Cover casserole and bake at 325°F 20 min.
Remove cover and bake about 5 min. longer,
or until eggplant is golden brown and cheese
is bubbly.   *6 to 8 servings*

BLUE CHEESE EGGPLANT
EN CASSEROLE

Grease a 2-qt. casserole.

Rinse, pare and dice
1 large eggplant (about 1½ lbs.)
Combine in a saucepan with
⅔ cup (about 1 large) chopped onion
Cook (page 313) 7 to 10 min., or until eggplant
is just tender when pierced with a fork. Drain
immediately.

Meanwhile, set out
**1 cup fine dry bread crumbs (about
3 slices bread)**
Toss together the vegetables, ¾ cup of the
bread crumbs and
**½ cup (about 2 oz.) crumbled blue
cheese**
1 egg, well beaten
⅛ teaspoon marjoram
Turn into casserole. Top with the remaining
bread crumbs and dot with
3 tablespoons butter

Bake at 350°F 30 to 35 min.   *8 servings*

FRIED EGGPLANT

▲ Base Recipe

Set out a large heavy skillet.

Wash, pare and cut into ¼-in. slices
1 medium (about 1 lb.) eggplant
Dip slices in a mixture of
1 egg, slightly beaten
1½ teaspoons salt
¼ teaspoon pepper

Coat with
¾ cup fine cracker crumbs
Heat in skillet over medium heat
¼ cup fat
Add as many eggplant slices at one time as
will lie flat in skillet. Cook about 15 min.,
or until crisp and browned, turning several
times. Add extra fat when necessary.
6 servings

—FRIED EGGPLANT AND TOMATOES

Follow ▲ Recipe. Wash **4 firm ripe or green
tomatoes**; remove stem ends. Cut into ½-in.
slices. Coat with a mixture of ½ cup all-purpose flour, 1 teaspoon salt, ¼ teaspoon
monosodium glutamate and ⅛ teaspoon
pepper. Remove eggplant to warm platter when
browned; keep hot. Add tomatoes to skillet
and brown lightly on both sides; serve on
eggplant.

EGGPLANT WITH CHEESE
(Melanzane con Formaggio)

▲ Base Recipe

Grease a 2-qt. casserole with a tight-fitting
cover.

Prepare (allowing about 4½ hrs.) and set
aside
Tomato Meat Sauce (page 162)

Heat to boiling in a large saucepan
4 qts. water
1 tablespoon salt
Gradually add, stirring with a fork
3 cups (about 8 oz.) noodles
Boil rapidly uncovered, 10 to 15 min., or
until noodles are tender. Test tenderness by
pressing a piece against side of pan with fork
or spoon. Drain by pouring into a colander or
large sieve. Set aside.

Add ham and toss lightly with a fork to blend. Blend in rice and

    2 tablespoons minced onion

Mix and blend in

    ¼ teaspoon dry mustard
    ¼ teaspoon garlic salt
    ¼ teaspoon monosodium glutamate

Lightly fill peppers with ham-rice mixture, heaping slightly. Place one slice of cheese on top of each pepper. Place peppers in the baking dish. Pour around peppers

    1½ cups tomato juice

Bake at 350°F about 20 min. Increase heat to 400°F and bake 10 min. longer, or until cheese is lightly browned.

If desired, spoon the hot tomato juice over stuffed peppers.

4 servings

—HAM CORN-STUFFED PEPPERS

Follow ▲ Recipe, omit butter, rice and seasonings. Mix lightly with the ham and onion, **1½ cups (one 12-oz. vacuum can, drained) whole kernel corn**, **½ cup (about ½ slice) soft bread crumbs**, **¼ teaspoon salt** and **few grains pepper**. Gently mix in with a fork **2 well-beaten eggs**. Omit cheese. Cut **4 slices bacon** into halves and place a half slice on top of each filled pepper. Water may be substituted for tomato juice.

STUFFED PEPPERS
(*Peperoni Imbottiti*)

Set out a 2-qt. baking dish.

Rinse and cut a thin slice from stem ends of

    4 green peppers

Remove white fiber and seeds. Rinse cavities. Drop into boiling salted water to cover and simmer 5 min. Remove peppers from water; invert and set aside to drain.

Meanwhile, cook, following package directions

    ⅔ cup packaged precooked rice

Heat in skillet

    ¼ cup olive oil

Add to skillet and cook until browned, breaking into small pieces with fork or spoon

    1 lb. ground beef

Stir in

    2 tablespoons minced onion
    1 tablespoon minced parsley

Add

    ½ teaspoon salt
    ¼ teaspoon pepper

Mix with cooked rice. Lightly fill peppers with rice-meat mixture, heaping slightly. Set in baking dish. Pour around peppers a mixture of

    1½ cups canned tomatoes, sieved
    ¼ cup water
    ¼ cup minced celery
    1 tablespoon olive oil
    ½ teaspoon salt
    ¼ teaspoon pepper

Place on top of each pepper, strips of

    Mozzarella cheese

Bake at 350°F about 15 min.   *4 servings*

PEPPER SCALLOP-ETTES

    ▲ *Base Recipe*

Lightly grease a shallow 2-qt. casserole.

Prepare

    Perfection Boiled Rice (page 165)

Meanwhile, shred and set aside

    3 oz. Cheddar cheese (¾ cup, shredded)

Chop and set aside

    1 cup salted peanuts

Clean, cutting off stem end and leaving pepper whole

    6 medium (about 1 lb.) green peppers

Cover with boiling salted water. Boil 5 min. Invert and drain on absorbent paper; set aside.

Stir into cooked rice shredded cheese and

    ¼ cup minced onion
    1 teaspoon prepared mustard

With a fork, lightly stir in salted peanuts. Stuff the peppers lightly with the rice; do not pack. Set them in casserole.

Mix and pour into casserole

    1 can (10¾ oz.) condensed tomato soup
    ½ cup water

Baste the peppers with the sauce before baking and twice during baking preiod.

Bake at 350°F 20 to 30 min., or until tops are delicately browned.   *6 servings*

—HOMINY-STUFFED PEPPERS

Follow ▲ Recipe. Substitute **3 cups drained canned hominy** for rice.

HOMINY GRITS

Coarsely ground hominy, known as hominy grits, or just grits, or even, in Charleston, as grist, is one of the beloved cereal foods of the South. In many homes it is served at three meals a day, with butter, syrup or gravy as the time of day dictates.

Set out a large saucepan.

Measure

    1 cup hominy grits

Bring to boiling in the saucepan

    5 cups water
    1 teaspoon salt

Add the grits slowly to the boiling water, stirring constantly. Cover saucepan and cook grits over low heat 25 to 30 min., stirring frequently.

Serve as cereal with **butter** and **sugar** or as a meat accompaniment with **butter** and **gravy**.

About 6 servings

Note: If desired, the grits may be cooked in the top of a double boiler; decrease water to 4 cups and cook about 45 min. over boiling water.

KOHLABI WITH SOUR CREAM

    ▲ *Base Recipe*

Set out a large skillet with a tight-fitting cover.

Trim off leaves and stems, wash and pare

    2 lbs. (about 8 medium) kohlrabi

Cut into ½-in. cubes. Heat in the skillet

    3 tablespoons butter

Add kohlrabi and cook about 2 min., moving and turning pieces with a spoon; then add

    ¼ cup hot water
    ½ teaspoon salt
    ¼ teaspoon monosodium glutamate

Cover tightly and cook at a moderate rate about 10 min., or until tender.

Meanwhile, blend

    1 cup dairy sour cream

and a mixture of

    1 tablespoon all-purpose flour
    ¼ teaspoon monosodium glutamate
    ⅛ teaspoon cayenne pepper

Push kohlrabi to one side of skillet; add the sour cream mixture gradually to the skillet, stirring constantly. Stir in the kohlrabi and cook, constantly moving and turning with a spoon, until sauce becomes thicker. Cook 1 to 2 min. longer.   *6 servings*

—LEEKS WITH SOUR CREAM

Follow ▲ Recipe. Substitute **8 large leeks** for the kohlrabi. Trim off roots and tough part of green tops. Rinse and peel. Rinse again and cut into ¾-in. slices.

LEEKS AU GRATIN
(*Lauch au Gratin*)

Set out a saucepan. Butter a shallow 10x6x2-in. baking dish.

Trim off roots and tough part of green tops and peel

    2 lbs. large tender leeks

Wash and cut lengthwise into halves. Put leeks into a saucepan, cover with boiling water and cook until tender, about 10 min. Drain thoroughly. Arrange in baking dish.

Shred and set aside
> **1 oz. sharp Cheddar cheese (about ¼ cup, shredded)**

Beat together just until blended
> **4 eggs, slightly beaten**
> **3 tablespoons dairy sour cream**
> **¼ teaspoon salt**
> **¼ teaspoon monosodium glutamate**

Pour mixture over leeks. Sprinkle over the top the shredded cheese and
> **2 tablespoons fine dry bread crumbs (page 10)**

Dot with
> **2 tablespoons butter**

Set the baking dish in a large baking pan on oven rack. Pour very hot water into baking pan to a 1-in. depth.

Bake at 350°F 10 to 15 min., or until a metal knife inserted in center of mixture comes out clean. *5 servings*

FRIED MUSHROOMS

Clean and slice (page 9)
> **½ lb. mushrooms**

Heat in a skillet
> **¼ cup butter or margarine**

Add mushrooms to skillet. Cook slowly, occasionally moving and turning gently with a spoon, until mushrooms are tender and lightly browned. Sprinkle with
> **1 teaspoon minced parsley**

Put mushrooms into a warm dish and serve immediately. *2 servings*

MUSHROOM DELIGHT

Clean and slice (page 9)
> **1 lb. mushrooms**

Heat in a skillet over low heat
> **¼ cup butter or margarine**

Add the mushrooms and
> **½ clove garlic, minced**
> **2 tablespoons minced parsley**
> **½ teaspoon salt**
> **⅛ teaspoon pepper**

Cook over medium heat until mushrooms are tender and lightly browned, occasionally moving and turning them with a spoon.

Add to the mushrooms a mixture of
> **1 cup dairy sour cream**
> **1 tablespoon all-purpose flour**

Cook over medium heat, keeping mixture moving constantly, for about 5 min., until sauce is slightly thicker and thoroughly heated. *Do not boil.*

Serve on **croutons** or **toast points**. *6 servings*

MUSHROOMS PARMESAN
(Funghi alla Parmigiana)

▲ *Base Recipe*

Grease a shallow 1½-qt. casserole.

Clean but do not slice
> **1 lb. mushrooms with 1- to 2-in. caps**

Cut off stems from caps. Place caps open-side up in casserole. Set aside. Finely chop mushroom stems.

Heat in skillet
> **2 tablespoons olive oil**

Add mushroom stems and
> **¼ cup chopped onion**
> **½ clove garlic, finely chopped**

Cook slowly until onion and garlic are lightly browned.

Meanwhile, combine
> **⅓ cup (about 1 slice) fine dry bread crumbs**
> **3 tablespoons grated Parmesan cheese**
> **1 tablespoon chopped parsley**
> **½ teaspoon salt**
> **⅛ teaspoon oregano**

Mix in onion, garlic and stems. Pile mixture lightly into inverted caps. Pour into casserole
> **2 tablespoons olive oil**

Bake at 400°F 15 to 20 min., or until mushrooms are tender and tops are browned.
6 to 8 servings

—ANCHOVY STUFFED MUSHROOMS
(Funghi con Acciughe al Forno)

Follow ▲ Recipe. Omit cheese. Mix in **4 anchovy fillets,** finely chopped.

MUSHROOMS, BORDELAISE STYLE
(Cèpes à la Bordelaise)

Clean, cutting off stems ½ in. from caps of
> **½ lb. mushrooms**

Slice through the stems. Season with
> **½ teaspoon salt**
> **¼ teaspoon pepper**

Heat in a skillet
> **¼ cup olive oil**

Add the mushroom caps and stems and
> **1 clove garlic, crushed**

Cook slowly, stirring gently. about 5 min.

Tangy Mushrooms

Immediately add
> **2 shallots, minced**

Continue to sauté about 5 min., stirring constantly. Sprinkle with
> **1 teaspoon minced parsley**

Serve at once in a hot dish. *2 to 4 servings*

TANGY MUSHROOMS

▲ *Base Recipe*

Clean and slice (page 9)
> **½ lb. mushrooms**

Heat in a skillet over low heat
> **2 tablespoons butter**

Add the mushrooms and
> **1 teaspoon grated onion**

Cook over medium heat until mushrooms are tender and lightly browned, occasionally moving and turning with a spoon.

Meanwhile, mix
> **1 cup dairy sour cream**
> **2 teaspoons all-purpose flour**
> **½ teaspoon salt**
> **⅛ teaspoon pepper**

Add to the mushrooms and cook over low heat until slightly thicker; cook 2 or 3 min. longer, keeping mixture moving. Do not boil.

Serve immediately on **toast points**.
4 servings

—MUSHROOMS WITH TARRAGON

Follow ▲ Recipe. Add 1/16 teaspoon tarragon **leaves,** finely crushed, to sour cream mixture.

MUSHROOMS BAKED IN CREAM

▲ *Base Recipe*

Lightly grease a shallow baking dish.

Clean but do not slice
> **1 lb. mushrooms having 1- to 2-in. caps**

Remove stems from caps. Set caps aside. Chop stems finely.

Heat in a skillet
> **¼ cup butter**

Add chopped mushroom stems to skillet with
> **1 tablespoon minced onion**

Cook slowly about 5 min., gently moving and turning with a fork or spoon.

Add and toss gently a mixture of
⅓ cup (about 1 slice) fine dry bread crumbs
½ teaspoon salt
¼ teaspoon monosodium glutamate
¼ teaspoon paprika
⅛ teaspoon pepper
Pile mixture lightly into mushroom caps. Place caps in the baking dish.

Cut into small pieces to top mushroom caps
3 to 5 slices bacon (depending upon size of mushrooms)
Pour around mushrooms a mixture of
1 cup cream
½ teaspoon Worcestershire sauce

Bake at 400°F 15 to 20 min., or until bacon is cooked. *6 to 8 servings*

—MUSHROOM CAPS PAR EXCELLENCE

Follow ▲ Recipe. Sprinkle ¼ teaspoon **grated Parmesan cheese** over each filled cap before topping with bacon.

MUSHROOMS IN SOUR CREAM
(Gomba Fözelék)

Set out a 10-in. skillet.

Clean and slice (page 9) and set aside
1 lb. mushrooms

Prepare and set aside
½ cup quick meat broth (one half recipe, page 10)

Melt in the skillet
6 tablespoons butter
Add the mushrooms to the butter with
1 small onion, sliced
Cook slowly, stirring gently, until mushrooms are lightly browned and tender and onion is soft. Remove from heat and set aside.

Melt in a small saucepan
1 tablespoon butter

Blend into the butter until smooth
1 tablespoon all-purpose flour
½ teaspoon salt
⅛ teaspoon pepper
Heat until mixture bubbles, stirring constantly. Remove from heat. Gradually add the reserved broth, stirring constantly. Return to heat and bring rapidly to boiling, stirring constantly; cook 1 to 2 min. longer; remove from heat. Stirring vigorously with a French whip, whisk beater or fork, add to contents of saucepan in very small amounts
1 cup dairy sour cream
Pour sour cream mixture into the skillet and place over low heat. Stirring constantly, but gently, heat thoroughly 3 to 5 min.; do not boil. Mix in
2 tablespoons finely chopped parsley
Serve immediately. *4 to 6 servings*

OKRA IN TOMATO SAUCE

Set out a large heavy skillet. Grease a 1½-qt. baking dish with a tight-fitting cover.

Wash, cut off stem ends, and cut into ½-in. slices
1½ lbs. okra
Heat in skillet
3 tablespoons butter or margarine
Add and cook over medium heat until lightly browned
1 medium onion, thinly sliced
Add okra and cook about 5 min., stirring frequently. Season with
½ teaspoon salt
⅛ teaspoon pepper
Turn into baking dish and sprinkle with
3 tablespoons chopped parsley
Pour over okra
1¼ cups tomato sauce
Cover baking dish.

Set in a 350°F oven about 30 min.
About 6 servings

GLAZED ONIONS

▲ Base Recipe

Clean
8 small (about 1 lb.) onions
Cook (page 313) 15 to 25 min., or until onions are just tender.

Meanwhile, melt in a skillet
¼ cup butter
Add and stir in
2 tablespoons brown sugar
Stir over low heat until sugar is dissolved. Drain onions thoroughly. Dry onions by shaking pan over low heat. Add to butter-sugar mixture in skillet. Simmer a few minutes, or until onions are glazed. Turn several times to glaze evenly. *4 servings*

—CREAMED ONIONS

Follow ▲ Recipe for cooking onions; omit brown sugar mixture. Prepare **1 cup Thin White Sauce** (page 304); add onions and heat thoroughly.

SCALLOPED ONIONS WITH HAM

▲ Base Recipe

Grease a 1½-qt. casserole and set out a small skillet.

Heat in the small skillet
2 tablespoons butter or margarine

Stir in and set aside
⅓ cup fine dry bread crumbs

Grind (page 10) and set aside enough cooked ham to yield
1 cup ground cooked ham

Clean and cook (page 313)
6 medium (about 1¼ lbs.) onions

Meanwhile, prepare
2 cups Medium White Sauce (double recipe, page 301; add ½ teaspoon dry mustard to flour)

Blend the ground ham into the white sauce. Cover and set aside.

Drain the cooked onions and arrange in bottom of the casserole. Pour white sauce over onions. Sprinkle with buttered bread crumbs.

Bake at 400°F about 15 min., or until sauce is bubbling hot. *6 servings*

—SCALLOPED ONIONS WITH BEEF

Follow ▲ Recipe. Substitute **2 cups Mushroom Cheese Sauce** (page 306; omit mushrooms) for white sauce and **1 cup ground cooked beef** for ham.

HERBED ONIONS

Set out a heavy 8-in. skillet with a tight-fitting cover.

Clean, leaving whole
6 medium onions
Put onions into the skillet and pour over them a mixture of
1 cup quick chicken broth (page 10)
½ teaspoon salt
1 teaspoon sugar
¼ teaspoon oregano, crushed
¼ teaspoon basil, crushed
¼ teaspoon garlic powder
2 whole cloves
1 large sprig parsley
½ small bay leaf
1 tablespoon olive oil
Cover tightly and bring to boiling. Reduce heat and simmer onions until crisp-tender, about 25 min. Drain. Season to taste.

Serve immediately. *6 servings*

STUFFED ONIONS
(Cipolle Imbottite)

Grease a 2½-qt. casserole.

Cut off root end, peel, rinse and cut off ½-in. slice from top of each of
6 large onions
Cook, covered, in several inches of boiling salted water 10 to 15 min., or until slightly tender. Drain well and cool.

Meanwhile, melt in a skillet
2 tablespoons butter or margarine

Stuffed Onions and French Fried Onions

Stir in

1 cup soft bread crumbs

Turn into a small bowl and set aside.

Heat in skillet

2 tablespoons olive oil

With a sharp knife, cut down around onions, about ¼ in. from edge, leaving about three outside layers. With a spoon, scoop out centers. Chop centers and add to olive oil with

¼ lb. ground beef

Separating beef into small pieces with fork or spoon, cook until beef is browned.

Combine beef mixture with

2 cups soft bread crumbs
1 egg yolk
2 teaspoons chopped parsley
1 teaspoon salt
¼ teaspoon pepper
¼ teaspoon marjoram

Lightly fill onions with mixture. Place in casserole. Cover tops with buttered crumbs and sprinkle onions with

2 tablespoons olive oil
1 tablespoon chopped parsley

Bake at 350°F about 1 hr.

6 servings

FRENCH FRIED ONIONS

About 20 min. before ready to deep-fry, fill a deep saucepan one-half full with

Vegetable shortening, all-purpose shortening, lard or cooking oil for deep-frying

Meanwhile, clean and cut into slices ½ in. thick

3 medium (about ½ lb.) onions

Separate slices into rings and set aside.

Melt and set aside to cool

1 tablespoon butter or margarine

Sift together into a bowl and set aside

1¼ cups sifted all-purpose flour
½ teaspoon salt
½ teaspoon monosodium glutamate
⅛ teaspoon pepper

Beat until thick and piled softly

2 eggs

Blend in

¾ cup milk

Blend in butter or margarine. Make a well in center of dry ingredients; add liquid mixture all at one time. Blend just until smooth.

Dip onion rings in batter with fork or slotted spoon to coat evenly. Deep-fry only as many onion rings at one time as will float uncrowded one layer deep in fat. Fry 2 to 3 min., or until golden brown. Turn onion rings with a fork as they rise to surface and several times during cooking. Drain over fat for a few seconds before removing to absorbent paper.

Serve with meats, vegetable plates or as an appetizer. *About 6 servings*

HOPPING JOHN

Originally a native of South Carolina, Hopping John is now relished throughout the South. It is well-known (but not why) that a dish of it eaten on New Year's Day brings good luck all year. But for that matter, blackeye peas are always lucky.

Put into a large saucepan

¼ lb. piece bacon

Add and bring to boiling

6 cups cold water

Reduce heat, cover and simmer 45 min.

Meanwhile, sort and wash thoroughly

1 cup dried blackeye peas

Add peas gradually to water so boiling will con-

tinue. Cover pan and simmer about 1½ hrs., or until peas are almost tender; stir occasionally.

Add gradually so boiling will continue

1 cup uncooked rice
½ teaspoon salt
¼ teaspoon pepper

(The Rice Industry no longer considers it necessary to wash rice before cooking.) Cover and simmer about 30 min., stirring occasionally, or until a kernel is soft when pressed between fingers. If necessary, add more boiling water during cooking.

Remove bacon and drain pea-rice mixture thoroughly in a colander or sieve. Cover colander with a clean cloth and set over hot water until ready to serve.

Meanwhile, slice the bacon and keep warm.

To serve, turn the pea-rice mixture into a warm serving bowl and garnish with **parsley**. Accompany with the sliced bacon.

6 to 8 servings

Note: Salt pork may be substituted for the piece of bacon.

GLAZED PARSNIPS

Set out a heavy saucepan and a large heavy skillet.

Rinse and pare

12 medium parsnips

Put into saucepan with

½ cup water
1 teaspoon salt

Cover tightly and cook over medium heat until boiling; lower heat and cook 20 to 30 min., or until tender. Drain and cut into quarters, lengthwise.

Melt in skillet

¼ cup butter or margarine

Add

¼ cup brown sugar
1 teaspoon grated orange peel
⅓ cup orange juice
1 tablespoon lemon juice
¼ teaspoon nutmeg
½ teaspoon salt

Mix thoroughly and add parsnips. Cook over low heat about 5 min., turning parsnips to coat on all sides.

Serve sprinkled with **chopped parsley**.

6 servings

PEAS IN SOUR CREAM SAUCE

Combine in a heavy saucepan and cook, tightly covered, over medium heat 8 to 10 min., or until peas are just tender

1 pkg. (10 oz.) frozen green peas
1 cucumber, pared and diced
¼ cup water
1 teaspoon salt
½ teaspoon tarragon
¼ teaspoon marjoram

Heat together in the top of a double boiler over simmering water, stirring frequently

½ cup dairy sour cream
½ cup mayonnaise
1 tablespoon lemon juice

Add hot vegetables and serve immediately.

5 or 6 servings

FRENCH PEAS

Set out a saucepan with a tight-fitting cover.

To retain their delicate flavor, rinse and shell just before using, reserving about one third of the pods

3 lbs. fresh peas

Place the pods in a length of cheesecloth and tie securely. Set peas and pea pods aside.

Rinse, shake off excess water, and remove outer leaves, leaving heart of

1 medium head lettuce

(Reserve outside leaves for use in other food preparation.)

Tear lettuce heart into bite-size pieces. Put one half of the lettuce pieces into the saucepan. Set remaining lettuce aside.

Cut off roots and trim green tops to 2 to 3 in., discarding any bruised or wilted parts from

4 scallions or green onions

Peel, rinse and chop. Add the scallions, reserved peas and pea pods to the saucepan with

3 tablespoons butter, cut in pieces
2 teaspoons sugar
1½ teaspoons salt
1 teaspoon monosodium glutamate
¼ teaspoon pepper
½ bay leaf

Cover with the remaining lettuce. Cover the saucepan and cook over low heat about 20 to 25 min., or until peas are tender but still moist. Remove from heat. Remove bay leaf and pea pods and discard.

Toss peas, lettuce and onion with a mixture of

3 tablespoons butter, melted
2 tablespoons finely chopped parsley
2 tablespoons chopped chives

Serve immediately in a warmed serving dish.

4 to 6 servings

PEAS AND ONIONS WITH LEMON BUTTER

Set out a heavy 1½-qt. saucepan.

Cook until tender, following package directions, and drain thoroughly

2 pkgs. (10 oz. each) frozen green peas
2 teaspoons sugar (added to cooking water)

Meanwhile, drain contents of

1 jar (16 oz.) whole white onions

Chop enough drained onions to yield ½ cup chopped. Set remaining onions aside.

Heat in saucepan

3 tablespoons butter or margarine

Add chopped onion and cook over medium heat 5 min. Stir in

1 tablespoon brown sugar
½ teaspoon salt
¾ teaspoon pepper
1 tablespoon lemon juice
¼ cup water

Heat 2 to 3 min., then add cooked peas and remaining whole onions. Toss lightly and continue cooking until thoroughly heated.

About 8 servings

CREAMY PEAS

Drain, reserving liquid

1 can (4 oz.) sliced mushrooms

Dice, panfry and drain

3 slices bacon

Put 2 tablespoons bacon drippings into skillet. Blend in a mixture of

1 tablespoon all-purpose flour
½ teaspoon seasoned salt
½ teaspoon crushed sweet basil

Heat until mixture bubbles. Add gradually stirring constantly, the mushroom liquid and

⅔ cup cream

Bring to boiling, stirring constantly. Mix in

1 teaspoon instant minced onion

Stir and cook 1 to 2 min. Mix in mushrooms and

1 can (16 oz.) green peas, drained
1 teaspoon diced pimiento

Heat thoroughly. Toss with the bacon. Turn into a heated serving dish.   *About 6 servings*

HERBED PEAS

Set out to thaw partially

1 pkg. (10 oz.) frozen green peas

Have ready

4 green onions with tops, thinly sliced
1 tablespoon minced parsley

Heat in a suacepan or skillet

¼ cup butter or margarine

Add onion and cook 5 min., stirring occasionally. Add the peas, parsley and a blend of

½ teaspoon thyme, crushed
¼ teaspoon marjoram, crushed
½ teaspoon sugar
¼ to ½ teaspoon salt

Bring to boiling. Cook, covered, until peas are tender, 5 min., stirring occasionally. Stir in

1 tablespoon chopped pimiento

Turn into a heated serving dish.   *4 servings*

PEAS DISTINCTIVE

Cook, following package directions

1 pkg. (10 oz.) frozen green peas

Add to water before cooking

1 beef bouillon cube

Meanwhile, mix

2 tablespoons butter or margarine, melted
¾ teaspoon sugar
½ teaspoon salt
⅛ teaspoon tarragon leaves, crushed
⅛ teaspoon finely crushed chervil

Drain peas. Add butter mixture and toss lightly to coat peas thoroughly.   *About 4 servings*

CANDIED SWEET POTATOES I

All over the South, "potato" means a sweet potato—or yam, if you prefer. The white ones are usually referred to, with less enthusiasm, as Irish potatoes. The sweetness of the favored variety of tubers is usually reinforced with other sweetness—of sugar or fruit or both.

Set out a large heavy skillet and a large saucepan with a cover.

Scrub and cook in boiling salted water

6 medium (about 2 lbs.) sweet potatoes

Cook, covered 30 to 35 min., or until potatoes are just tender when pierced with a fork. Drain. Shake pan over low heat to dry potatoes. Peel them and set aside.

Heat in the skillet over low heat

⅓ cup butter or margarine

Blend in

⅓ cup firmly packed brown sugar
¼ teaspoon salt

Heat until mixture bubbles. Add potatoes. Cook over medium heat, turning potatoes several times, about 20 min., or until they are well-glazed and thoroughly heated.

6 servings

CANDIED SWEET POTATOES II

Grease a shallow baking pan.

Cook (see Sweet Potatoes in a Basket, page 339)

6 medium (about 2 lbs.) sweet potatoes

While potatoes cook, combine and boil together for 5 min.

1 cup firmly packed brown sugar
⅓ cup water
2 tablespoons butter or margarine
½ teaspoon salt

Peel potatoes and cut into halves lengthwise. Dip potatoes in syrup and place, cut-side down, in baking pan. Add remaining syrup. Dot potatoes with

6 to 8 marshmallows, quartered

Bake at 400°F 20 min., basting occasionally with the syrup.   *6 servings*

BAKED SWEET POTATOES

▲ *Base Recipe*

Wash and scrub with a vegetable brush

6 medium (about 2 lbs.) sweet potatoes or yams

Dry potatoes with absorbent paper. Rub potatoes well with about

1 tablespoon fat

Place potatoes on rack in oven and bake at 375°F 45 to 60 min., or until potatoes are soft when pressed with the fingers (protected from heat by paper napkin).

Remove potatoes from oven. To make each potato more mealy, gently roll potatoes back and forth on a flat working surface.

Cut a small cross in skin of each potato. Squeeze sides of potato until mealy portion is visible. Top each potato with

1 tablespoon butter or margarine

Serve immediately.   *6 servings*

—LEMON-BUTTERED SWEET POTATOES

Follow ▲ Recipe. While potatoes are baking, blend **½ cup butter or margarine**, melted, **2 tablespoons lemon juice, ½ teaspoon salt, ¼ teaspoon monosodium glutamate** and **⅛ teaspoon pepper**. Keep mixture warm. Peel baked sweet potatoes and cut into halves or leave whole. Place in a baking dish and pour lemon-butter mixture over potatoes. Return to oven and bake 5 to 10 min. Spoon lemon-butter (in baking dish) over potatoes several times.

—BAKED FILLED SWEETS

Follow ▲ Recipe. While potatoes are baking, panbroil (page 192) **12 (about ¾ lb.) pork sausage links**. Set aside to drain on absorbent paper and keep warm. Cut large baked potatoes into halves lengthwise. Or cut a thin slice from each small potato. With a spoon, scoop out inside without breaking skin. Mash or rice potatoes thoroughly. Whip in until potatoes are light and fluffy, **½ cup hot orange juice** (adding gradually), **3 tablespoons butter or margarine** and a mixture of **2 tablespoons brown sugar, 1 teaspoon grated orange peel, ¾ teaspoon salt, ½ teaspoon cinnamon** and **¼ teaspoon monosodium glutamate**. Whip potatoes until light and fluffy. Pile mixture lightly into potato shells, leaving surfaces uneven. Top each filled potato with two sausage links. Bake 8 to 10 min. longer, or until potatoes reheat and brown lightly.

GOLDEN GLOW SWEET POTATOES

▲ *Base Recipe*

Grease a 1½-qt. casserole.

Wash and cook covered in boiling salted water to cover

6 medium (about 2 lbs.) sweet potatoes, cut into halves or quarters

Cook about 20 min., or until tender when pierced with a fork. Drain. To dry potatoes, shake pan over low heat. Peel; mash or rice.

Meanwhile, cut into crosswise halves and set aside

12 marshmallows (3 oz.)

Whip in until potatoes are fluffy

3 to 4 tablespoons butter or margarine
⅓ to ½ cup cream or milk

and a mixture of

¼ cup firmly packed brown sugar
¾ teaspoon salt
1 teaspoon nutmeg
½ teaspoon cinnamon

Fold one half of the marshmallow slices into potatoes; pile lightly into casserole.

Bake at 350°F 15 min. Remove from oven and arrange remaining marshmallows around top of casserole. Bake 15 to 20 min. longer, or until marshmallows are lightly browned.

6 servings

—GLAZED GRAPEFRUIT SWEET POTATOES

Follow ▲ Recipe. Omit marshmallows. Wash **1 grapefruit**. With a sharp knife, cut into ¼-in. crosswise slices; cut each into halves. Dip slices into mixture of **¼ cup honey** and **2 tablespoons melted butter or margarine**. Arrange a wheel of overlapping slices over potatoes in casserole. Drizzle remaining honey mixture over top. Bake 20 to 25 min., or until grapefruit is slightly browned.

—PECAN SWEET SQUASH

Follow ▲ Recipe for seasonings. Use **3 pkgs. (10 oz. each) frozen squash**; cook following directions on package. If squash seems dry, moisten with necessary amount of **cream** or **orange juice**. Otherwise, omit cream and whip butter into squash. Turn squash into casserole; top with **½ cup (about 2 oz.) coarsely chopped pecans**. Bake 15 to 20 min., or until heated and nuts are toasted.

MAPLE SWEET POTATOES AND APPLES

Butter a 1½-qt. baking dish.

Wash, scrub and cook (page 313)

6 medium (about 2 lbs.) sweet potatoes

Cook 30 to 35 min., or until tender when pierced with a fork.

Meanwhile, measure into a saucepan

1 cup maple syrup

Maple Sweet Potatoes and Apples

Add

Few grains salt

Wash, quarter, core, peel and thinly slice

4 large apples (about 1½ lbs.)

Add apples to saucepan and cook over low heat until apples are just tender. Carefully turn apple slices to cook evenly. Remove from heat and set aside. Peel the cooked sweet potatoes. Cut into thin, crosswise slices. Arrange one half of the potato slices in the baking dish. Top with one half of the apple slices and syrup. Repeat layers, using remaining potatoes, apples and syrup. Sprinkle with

⅓ cup buttered crumbs (page 9)

Bake at 350°F about 10 min., or until crumbs are lightly browned.   *6 to 8 servings*

SWEET POTATO PONE

Grease a 1½-qt. baking dish.

Wash, pare, cover with cold salted water and set aside

4 medium (about 1½ lbs.) sweet potatoes or yams

Cream until softened

⅔ cup butter or margarine
1 teaspoon grated lemon peel
1 teaspoon grated orange peel
½ teaspoon salt
½ teaspoon nutmeg
½ teaspoon cinnamon
½ teaspoon cloves

Add gradually, creaming until fluffy after each addition

½ cup firmly packed brown sugar

Add in thirds, beating thoroughly after each addition

4 eggs, well beaten

Stir in a mixture of

1 cup milk
⅓ cup molasses

Set aside while grating sweet potatoes.

Drain sweet potatoes and grate using medium-size grater (about 5 cups, grated). Blend grated potatoes into liquid mixture and pour into the baking dish. Set in a large baking pan and pour very hot water into pan to a 1-in. depth.

Bake at 350°F about 1 hr., or until top is crusty and lightly browned.   *6 servings*

ELEGANT APRICOT SWEET POTATOES

A shallow 1-qt. baking dish will be needed.

Put into a heavy saucepan
½ lb. (1½ cups) dried apricots
Add
2 cups water
Bring water to boiling, reduce heat, and cook, covered, about 25 min., or until apricots are plump and tender when pierced with a fork. (Be careful not to overcook the fruit.) Remove saucepan from heat. Cool and drain well, reserving the liquid.

Meanwhile, wash and scrub with a vegetable brush
6 medium (about 2 lbs.) sweet potatoes or yams
Cook (page 313) 30 to 35 min., or until potatoes are tender when pierced with a fork. Drain potatoes and peel; cut into lengthwise slices about ½ in. thick.

Lightly grease the baking dish.

Set out
1 cup firmly packed dark brown sugar
Arrange a layer of the sweet potatoes in the baking dish. Cover with a layer of apricots. Sprinkle with one half of the brown sugar. Repeat layers of sweet potatoes and apricots and sprinkle with remaining sugar.

Blend thoroughly ¼ cup of the reserved apricot liquid and
3 tablespoons melted butter
1 teaspoon grated orange peel
2 teaspoons orange juice
Pour mixture over the layers.

Bake at 375°F 30 to 45 min., basting occasionally with liquid in bottom of baking dish. About 5 min. before sweet potatoes are done, top with
¼ cup (about 1 oz.) pecan halves
6 to 8 servings

SWEET POTATOES WITH ORANGE

Grease a 1½-qt. casserole with a tight-fitting cover.

Scrub
4 medium (about 1⅓ lbs.) sweet potatoes
Cook, covered, in boiling salted water for 10

Elegant Apricot Sweet Potatoes

min. Drain. Shake pan over low heat to dry potatoes. Peel. With a sharp knife, cut into crosswise slices ⅛ in. thick. Set aside.

Mix
¼ cup sugar
4 teaspoons grated orange peel
½ teaspoon salt
¼ teaspoon cinnamon
Wash, cut away peel and cut into crosswise slices ¼ in. thick
2 large oranges
Set out
¼ cup butter
Arrange one half of the potato slices in an even layer in the casserole. Cover with one half of the orange slices and sprinkle with one half of the sugar mixture. Dot with 2 tablespoons of the butter. Repeat layering. Pour over all
½ cup orange juice

Cover; cook in a 375°F oven about 40 min., or until potatoes are tender when pierced with a fork.
About 4 servings

SWEET POTATOES IN A BASKET

Scrub and rinse
4 medium (about 1¾ lbs.) sweet potatoes
Cook, covered, in boiling salted water 30 to 35 min., or until potatoes are tender when pierced with a fork.

While potatoes cook, cut into halves crosswise
3 large oranges
With a spoon or grapefruit knife, remove pulp sections from inside dividing membranes. With scissors or knife trim and remove membranes from orange shells. Set aside orange shells, cut-sides down, to drain thoroughly.

Peel potatoes. Pour boiling water over potato

masher, food mill or ricer and bowl to heat thoroughly. Mash or rice potatoes into bowl.

Add to potatoes the orange pulp and a mixture of
2 tablespoons brown sugar
1 teaspoon salt
¼ teaspoon monosodium glutamate
Whip until light and fluffy. Pile lightly into orange shells. Top each with one of
6 marshmallow halves

Place filled baskets on broiler rack. Place in broiler with tops of marshmallows about 4 in. from heat until marshmallows are browned and slightly melted.
6 servings

WHIPPED SWEET POTATOES

▲ Base Recipe

Wash, scrub and cook covered in boiling salted water to cover
6 medium (about 2 lbs.) sweet potatoes, cut in quarters
Cook about 20 min., or until potatoes are tender when pierced with a fork. Drain and peel sweet potatoes.

To dry potatoes, shake pan over low heat. To heat potato masher, food mill or ricer and a mixing bowl, scald them with boiling water.

Mash or rice potatoes thoroughly. Whip in until potatoes are fluffy
2 tablespoons butter or margarine
¼ to ½ cup hot milk or cream (adding gradually)
½ teaspoon salt
Whip potatoes until light and fluffy. If necessary, keep potatoes hot over simmering water and cover with folded towel until ready to serve. - *About 3 cups whipped potatoes*

—MELLOW SWEET POTATO BAKE

Follow ▲ Recipe. Grease a 1½-qt. baking dish. Substitute **orange juice** for milk or cream. Blend into whipped potatoes a mixture of ½ cup (about 2 oz.) chopped pecans, ⅓ cup firmly packed brown sugar, 1 teaspoon cinnamon and ½ teaspoon nutmeg. Spoon into baking dish. Cut (page 9) **6 marshmallows** into halves; arrange them on top of potatoes. Put baking dish under broiler with top of food 4 in. from heat. Broil until marshmallows are delicately browned and slightly melted.

FLUFFY WHIPPED POTATOES

▲ Base Recipe

Wash, pare and cook (page 313)
6 medium (about 2 lbs.) potatoes
Cook about 25 to 35 min., or until potatoes are tender when pierced with a fork. Drain. Heat potato masher, food mill or ricer and a mixing bowl by scalding them with boiling water. Mash or rice potatoes thoroughly. Whip

in until potatoes are fluffy

3 to 4 tablespoons butter
⅓ to ½ cup hot milk or cream
(adding gradually)

and a mixture of

¾ teaspoon salt
¼ teaspoon monosodium glutamate
¼ teaspoon paprika
¼ teaspoon pepper

Whip potatoes until light and fluffy. If necessary, keep potatoes hot over simmering water and cover with folded towel until ready to serve. *About 6 servings*

—MASHED TURNIPS

Follow ▲ Recipe. Substitute washed, pared and quartered **turnips** for the potatoes. Omit milk or cream and paprika.

—HASHED BROWN POTATOES I

Follow ▲ Recipe for cooking potatoes: do not mash or rice. Dice potatoes and mix with **1 teaspoon salt** and **¼ teaspoon pepper.** Heat ⅓ **cup fat** in a skillet. Add the potatoes, pressing into an even layer. Cook over low heat until a brown crust is formed on the bottom. Loosen edges and bottom of potatoes; shake skillet back and forth occasionally to prevent burning while browning. When potatoes are done, lightly fold in half and serve on a warm platter.

—FRIED PARSNIP CAKES

Follow ▲ Recipe. Substitute washed, pared and quartered **parsnips** for the potatoes. Cook about 30 min., or until tender. Omit paprika and add **2 tablespoons all-purpose flour.** Shape parsnip mixture into flat cakes. Heat about ¼ **cup fat** in a skillet. Cook parsnip cakes over medium heat until golden brown and crisp on one side. Turn cakes and brown second side. Add extra fat when necessary.

—WHIPPED POTATO RING

Follow ▲ Recipe. Spoon whipped potatoes onto warm serving platter to form a ring. Draw tines of fork around ring for patterned effect.

DUCHESS POTATOES
(Pommes de Terre Duchesse)

Wash, pare and cut into quarters

1 lb. (about 3 medium) potatoes

Cover and cook in boiling salted water to cover 15 to 25 min., or until tender. Drain well. Shake saucepan over low heat until dry. Force potatoes through a sieve into a saucepan. Add

1 tablespoon melted butter

Using a wooden spoon, work into potatoes

2 egg yolks (or 1 egg, for softer mixture)

Season with a mixture of

½ teaspoon salt
¼ teaspoon white pepper

If potatoes are to be used later, brush a little butter over top to prevent a crust from forming. If prepared immediately, divide the mixture into small portions. Roll each portion on a floured surface, shaping as desired.

Brown in skillet over medium heat, turning as necessary, in

¼ cup butter

Or brush with melted butter and brown in oven at 450°F.

This mixture is popular also as a garnish. Force through a No. 7 star pastry tube to form spiral-shape patties or a ring around a heat-resistant serving platter. Brown in a 450°F oven.

3 or 4 servings

HEAVENLY POTATO SOUFFLE

Lightly grease a 1½-qt. casserole.

Wash, pare and cook (page 313)

6 medium (about 2 lbs.) potatoes

Cook 25 to 35 min., or until potatoes are tender when pierced with a fork. Drain.

Meanwhile, shred and set aside

2 oz. Cheddar cheese (about ½ cup, shredded)

To dry potatoes, shake pan over low heat. To heat potato masher, food mill or ricer and a mixing bowl, scald them with boiling water. Whip or rice potatoes thoroughly. Whip in, in order, until potatoes are fluffy

¼ cup butter or margarine
2 egg yolks
1 cup hot milk or cream (adding gradually)
3 drops Tabasco
1 teaspoon salt
½ teaspoon dry mustard
¼ teaspoon monosodium glutamate
⅛ teaspoon white pepper

Whip potatoes until light and fluffy. Add the shredded cheese all at one time and beat until cheese is melted. Set aside.

Beat until stiff, not dry, peaks are formed

2 egg whites

Spread beaten egg whites over potato mixture and gently fold together. Turn mixture into the casserole.

Bake at 325°F about 50 min., or until metal knife comes out clean when inserted halfway between center and edge of casserole.

Serve immediately. *About 6 servings*

WHIPPED POTATO PATS

▲ Base Recipe

Grease a large shallow baking pan.

For Whipped Potatoes—Wash, pare and cook covered in boiling salted water

4 medium (about 1⅓ lbs.) potatoes cut in halves

Cook about 20 min., or until potatoes are tender when pierced with a fork. Drain.

To dry potatoes, shake pan over low heat. To heat potato masher, food mill or ricer and a mixing bowl, scald them with boiling water.

Whip or rice potatoes thoroughly. Whip in until potatoes are fluffy

3 to 4 tablespoons butter or margarine
⅓ to ½ cup hot milk or cream (adding gradually)

and a mixture of

¾ teaspoon salt
¼ teaspoon paprika
¼ teaspoon pepper

Whip into potatoes

1 egg, beaten
¼ cup shredded Cheddar cheese

Whip potatoes until light and fluffy.

For Potato Pats—Shape mixture into balls, patties or pyramids.

Brush with

3 to 4 tablespoons softened butter or margarine

Carefully roll in

½ to ¾ cup finely crushed potato chips

Place in baking pan. Make a tiny hollow in top of each patty and dot with

Butter or margarine

Bake at 400°F 15 to 20 min., or until heated thoroughly and browned. *6 servings*

—SWEET POTATO BALLS

Follow ▲ Recipe, using unpared **sweet potatoes.** Peel when tender. Substitute ½ **cup orange juice** for milk. Omit pepper, paprika and cheese. With seasonings, add **1 teaspoon grated orange peel, 2 tablespoons brown sugar** and **½ teaspoon cinnamon.**

WHIPPED POTATOES AND RUTABAGA
(Kartoffelpuree mit gelben Rüben)

Wash, cut into halves and pare
½ lb. rutabaga
Cut rutabaga into cubes or slices; cook (page 313) covered in just enough boiling salted water to cover for 25 to 40 min., or until rutabaga is tender when pierced with a fork. Drain.

Wash, pare and cook (page 313)
4 medium (about 1⅓ lbs.) potatoes
Cook about 25 to 35 min., or until tender when pierced with a fork. Drain.

Dry potatoes and rutabaga by shaking each pan over low heat. Heat potato masher, food mill or ricer and a mixing bowl, by scalding with boiling water. Mash or rice potatoes and rutabaga together thoroughly.

Whip in until fluffy
2 tablespoons butter
¼ to ⅓ cup hot milk or cream (adding gradually)
1 teaspoon salt
¼ teaspoon monosodium glutamate
⅛ teaspoon white pepper
Whip until light and fluffy. If necessary, keep hot over simmering water and cover with folded towel until ready to serve.
6 to 8 servings

PARSLEY NEW POTATOES

Wash and scrub with a vegetable brush
24 (about 3 lbs.) small new potatoes
Cook (page 313) about 20 min., or until potatoes are tender when pierced with a fork.

Meanwhile, melt in a small saucepan
½ cup butter
Stir in
¼ cup finely chopped parsley
1 teaspoon salt
½ teaspoon monosodium glutamate
¼ teaspoon pepper
Keep mixture warm.

Drain potatoes. To dry potatoes, shake pan over low heat. Peel potatoes immediately. Place potatoes in warm serving dish. Pour parsley mixture over potatoes and turn them to coat well. Serve immediately.
6 to 8 servings

PARSLEY POTATO BALLS
(Kartoffelbällchen mit Petersilie)

Set out a large heavy skillet with a tight-fitting cover.

Wash, pare, and cut into balls with a ball-shaped cutter
6 medium (about 2 lbs.) potatoes

(The remaining potato pieces may be used in other food preparation.)

Melt in the skillet
¼ cup butter
Add the potato balls, cover and cook over low heat about 15 to 20 min., or until potatoes are tender when pierced with a fork. Occasionally turn and move balls gently with a spoon to brown all sides slightly.

Toss potato balls with a mixture of
2 tablespoons minced parsley
½ teaspoon salt
Few grains paprika
About 4 servings

PAPRIKA POTATOES I
(Paprikás Burgonya)

Set out a heavy 10-in. skillet with a tight-fitting cover.

Wash, pare and cut into ½-in. cubes
3 or 4 medium (about 1 lb.) potatoes (about 2½ cups, cubed)
Set potatoes aside.

Heat in the skillet
2 tablespoons bacon fat
Add to the bacon fat and cook over low heat, stirring occasionally, until almost tender
¾ cup (about 1 large) chopped onion
Add to onion a mixture of
1 teaspoon paprika
1 teaspoon salt
⅛ teaspoon pepper
Remove skillet from heat and blend into the fat and onion, stirring vigorously
1¼ cups dairy sour cream
Add potatoes to sour cream mixture and mix gently and thoroughly. Cover skillet and cook over very low heat, about 30 min., or until potatoes are just tender; do not boil. Occasionally turn potatoes in sauce. Garnish with
1 tablespoon chopped parsley
4 to 6 servings

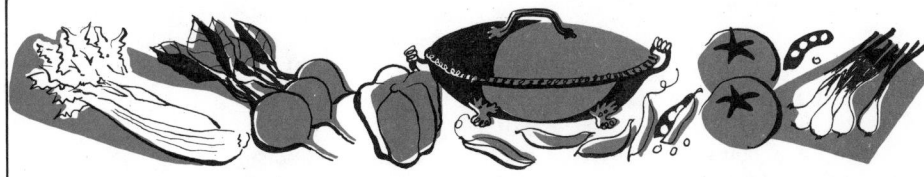

PAPRIKA POTATOES II
(Paprikakartoffeln)

Set out a large heavy skillet.

Prepare and set aside
2 cups quick meat broth (page 10)

Wash and scrub with a vegetable brush
6 medium (about 2 lbs.) potatoes
Cook (page 313) about 30 min., or until potatoes are tender when pierced with a fork. Drain potatoes. Dry potatoes by shaking pan over low heat. Peel potatoes and cut into cubes.

Meanwhile, heat in the skillet
2 tablespoons butter
Add and cook over medium heat until onion is golden yellow in color
¼ cup chopped onion
Blend in
2 tablespoons all-purpose flour
1 teaspoon paprika
½ teaspoon salt
¼ teaspoon monosodium glutamate
Heat until mixture bubbles. Remove from heat. Gradually add the meat broth, stirring constantly. Bring to boiling. Cook 1 to 2 min.

Remove skillet from heat. Stirring vigorously with a French whip, whisk beater or fork, add to contents of skillet in very small amounts, a mixture of
1 cup dairy sour cream
2 tablespoons tomato paste
Gently mix potatoes into the sauce and cook over low heat, moving and turning constantly with a spoon, 3 to 5 min., or until thoroughly heated; do not boil.

Turn into a serving dish and garnish with
Sprigs of parsley
Serve immediately.
6 servings

POTATOES WITH TOMATO
(Burgonya Paradicsommal)

Wash and cook (page 313) 20 to 30 min., or until tender when pierced with a fork
6 medium (about 2 lbs.) potatoes
Drain the potatoes. To dry potatoes, shake pan over low heat. Peel and slice ½ in. thick; set aside in warm place.

Melt over low heat in the saucepan in which potatoes were cooked
¼ cup butter
Add to the butter and cook until almost tender, stirring frequently
¼ cup chopped onion

Mix with the onion and heat to boiling
1 cup (8-oz. can) tomato sauce
1 tablespoon sugar
⅛ teaspoon pepper
Remove saucepan from heat. Stirring vigorously with a French whip, whisk beater or fork, add to contents of saucepan in very small amounts, a mixture of
1 cup dairy sour cream
½ cup milk
Gently mix potatoes into the sauce and cook over low heat, stirring constantly, 3 to 5 min., until heated thoroughly; do not boil.

Garnish with

2 tablespoons chopped parsley

Serve immediately.   *6 to 8 servings*

LEMON CHIVE POTATOES

Potatoes are special with this zesty butter sauce.

Wash and cook covered in boiling salted water to cover

12 (about 1½ lbs.) small new potatoes

Cook about 20 min., or until potatoes are tender whem pierced with a fork.

Meanwhile, melt in a small saucepan

⅓ cup butter or margarine

Stir in

2 tablespoons minced chives
2 teaspoons grated lemon peel
1 tablespoon lemon juice
½ teaspoon salt
¼ teaspoon monosodium glutamate
⅛ teaspoon pepper

Keep mixture warm.

Drain potatoes. To dry them, shake pan over low heat. Peel potatoes immediately and place in warm serving dish. Pour butter mixture over potatoes and turn them to coat well.

Serve immediately.   *4 serivngs*

CREAMED POTATOES

▲ Base Recipe

Wash, pare and cook covered in boiling salted water to cover

6 or 7 medium (about 2 lbs.) potatoes

Cook about 20 min., or until potatoes are tender when pierced with a fork.

Meanwhile, prepare

2½ cups Medium White Sauce (two and one-half times recipe, page 304)

Drain potatoes. Peel and cut into ½-in. cubes. Stir potatoes into sauce, being careful not to break cubes.   *6 servings*

Note: Leftover cooked potatoes may be diced and creamed. If this is done, use 4 cups potatoes to 2 cups Medium White Sauce. Heat together in top of double boiler over simmering water, stirring gently.

—CREAMED POTATOES WITH CHEESE

Follow ▲ Recipe. Add ¼ cup (1 oz.) shredded **Cheddar cheese** to white sauce and stir rapidly, before addition of potatoes.

—BAKED CREAMY POTATOES

Follow ▲ Recipe. Combine potatoes, ½ cup (2 oz.) shredded **cheese** and ¼ cup pimiento **strips** with slightly cooled white sauce. Put into a greased 1½-qt. casserole and cover with **½ cup buttered crumbs** (page 9). If desired,

blend 2 tablespoons of the cheese with the crumbs. Bake uncovered at 400°F 10 to 15 min., or until crumbs are browned.

SPECIAL CREAMED POTATOES

Another way to glamorize an old stand-by.

Shred and set aside

3 oz. sharp Cheddar cheese (about ¾ cup, shredded)

Wash, pare and dice

4 medium (about 1⅓ lbs.) potatoes

Bring to boiling in a saucepan

1 cup water
1 teaspoon salt

Add potatoes with

½ cup (about 1 medium) chopped onion

Cover and cook 10 min. Uncover and continue cooking slowly until almost all the water is evaporated. Turn occasionally and move gently with a spoon.

Remove from heat. Blend in the cheese and

½ cup milk
¼ teaspoon monosodium glutamate
⅛ teaspoon pepper

Heat and stir until cheese is melted.
                                                   6 servings

CREAMED NEW POTATOES AND ASPARAGUS

▲ Base Recipe

Wash, pare and place in a saucepan, in boiling, salted water

6 small whole new potatoes

Cover and cook 20 to 30 min., or until tender.

Meanwhile, break off and discard lower parts of stalks (as far down as they will snap) from

½ lb. asparagus

Wash remaining portions of stalks thoroughly. If necessary, remove scales to dislodge any sand. Tie in bunches and stand upright in deep, narrow pan containing just enough boiling salted water to cover lower half of spears. Cover and cook 10 to 20 min., or until asparagus is tender.

Meanwhile, prepare

Medium White Sauce (page 304)

Drain asparagus thoroughly. Cut asparagus stalks into 3 or 4 sections.

Drain potatoes and shake pan over low heat to dry thoroughly. Put asparagus and potatoes into warm serving dish and cover with hot sauce. Sprinkle with

Nutmeg

                                                   6 servings

Potatoes au Gratin

—CREAMED NEW POTATOES AND PEAS

Follow ▲ Recipe. Substitute **1 lb. fresh peas** for asparagus. Shell just before cooking. Cook peas, loosely covered, in small amount of boiling salted water, 10 to 20 min., or until just tender.

—CREAMED NEW POTATOES AND CARROTS

Follow ▲ Recipe. Substitute **½ lb. carrots** for asparagus. Cut off tops, scrape, rinse and dice carrots. Cook, covered in boiling salted water to almost cover, 15 to 20 min., or until carrots are tender.

SCALLOPED POTATOES I

Butter a 1½-qt. casserole.

Wash and cook (page 313)

6 medium (about 2 lbs.) potatoes

Cook 25 to 35 min., or until potatoes are tender when pierced with a fork. Drain potatoes. Dry them by shaking over low heat. Peel and cut into ¼-in. slices. Arrange slices in neat, close layers in casserole.

While potatoes cook, shred and set aside

2 oz. sharp Cheddar cheese (about ½ cup, shredded)

Heat in a saucepan over low heat

2 tablespoons butter or margarine

Add and cook over medium heat, occasionally moving and turning with a spoon

⅓ cup chopped onion

Blend contents of saucepan with a mixture of

2 eggs, well beaten
1 cup dairy sour cream
1 teaspoon salt
⅛ teaspoon pepper

Spoon sour cream mixture over potatoes in casserole. Top with the shredded cheese.

Bake at 350°F about 35 min.   *6 servings*

SCALLOPED POTATOES II

▲ Base Recipe

Grease a shallow 1½-qt. casserole with a tight-fitting cover.

Wash, pare and thinly slice
**4 to 5 medium (about 1½ lbs.)
potatoes (about 3 cups, sliced)**
Shake potato slices in a plastic bag containing
**1 tablespoon all-purpose flour
2 teaspoons salt
½ teaspoon monosodium glutamate
¼ teaspoon pepper**
Carefully place potato slices in even layers in casserole.

Scald (page 10)
1¾ cups milk
Add
3 tablespoons butter or margarine
Pour over potatoes (milk should barely reach top of potatoes).

Bake at 350°F min., or until potatoes are tender when pierced with a fork. Turn off heat. Cover potatoes and leave in oven 10 min. or more to absorb liquid. *6 servings*

—HAM CHEESE SCALLOP

Follow ▲ Recipe. Decrease salt to ½ teaspoon and omit monosodium glutamate. Sprinkle potato layers with **1 cup ground cooked ham** and **¾ cup (3 oz.) shredded Cheddar cheese.**

—POTATO ONION SCALLOP

Follow ▲ Recipe. Cover first layer of potatoes with **½ cup finely chopped onion.**

—POTATOES AU GRATIN

Follow ▲ Recipe. Distribute **1 cup (4 oz.) shredded pasteurized process cheese** evenly between potato layers and over top.

—POTATO MUSHROOM SCALLOP

Follow ▲ Recipe for potatoes and seasonings. Omit flour. Sprinkle seasoning mixture over potato layers. Dilute **1¼ cups (10½-oz. can) condensed cream of mushroom soup** with **⅔ cup water.** Pour over potatoes in baking dish.

POTATOES ANNA

Butter generously a 2-qt. casserole.

Wash and pare
**6 to 8 medium (2 to 3 lbs.) potatoes
(6 cups, sliced)**
With sharp knife or vegetable slicer, cut into thin uniform crosswise slices. Dry thoroughly with absorbent paper. Arrange even layers of potatoes in casserole, overlapping slices in each layer about ¼ in.

Sprinkle each layer with a mixture of
**Salt
Pepper
Monosodium glutamate**
Dot layers generously with
½ cup butter or margarine

Bake at 425°F 40 to 60 min., or until potatoes are tender and golden brown. To remove from casserole for serving, run spatula around edge to loosen. Invert onto warm serving plate.

6 to 8 servings

FLUFFY CHEESE POTATOES

▲ Base Recipe

Wash and scrub with a vegetable brush
**6 medium (about 2 lbs.) baking
potatoes**
Dry potatoes with absorbent paper and rub with about
1 tablespoon fat
Place potatoes on rack in oven.

Bake at 425°F 45 to 60 min., or until potatoes are soft when pressed with the fingers (protected by paper napkin).

While potatoes bake, shred and set aside
**2 oz. pasteurized process Swiss cheese
(about ½ cup, shredded)**

Remove potatoes from oven. To make each potato mealy, gently roll potatoes back and forth on a flat surface. Cut large potatoes into halves lengthwise or cut a thin lengthwise slice from each smaller potato. With a spoon, scoop out inside without breaking skin. Mash thoroughly or rice. Whip in, in order, until mixture is fluffy
**3 to 4 tablespoons butter or
margarine
⅓ to ½ cup hot milk or cream
(adding gradually)**
and a mixture of
**¾ teaspoon salt
¼ teaspoon paprika
¼ teaspoon pepper**
Mix in the shredded cheese and
**8 slices crisp Panfried Bacon
(page 190), crumbled
1 tablespoon finely chopped onion**
Pile mixture lightly into potato skins, leaving tops uneven.

Return potatoes to oven for 8 to 10 min., or until thoroughly heated.

Sprinkle with
Finely chopped parsley
6 servings

—CHEDDAR CHEESE POTATOES

Follow ▲ Recipe. Substitute **⅓ cup shredded sharp Cheddar cheese** for Swiss cheese.

—CHEDDAR CHEESE-OLIVE POTATOES

Follow ▲ Recipe. Substitute **⅓ cup shredded sharp Cheddar cheese** for the Swiss cheese. Omit the bacon and onion and add **8 to 10 pimiento-stuffed olives,** finely chopped, with the cheese. If desired, omit parsley and top potatoes with **⅓ cup crushed buttered corn flakes or crumbs** before baking.

BAKED POTATOES

Wash and scrub with a vegetable brush
3 medium (about 1 lb.) potatoes
Dry with absorbent paper. Rub skins with
2 teaspoons fat

Place potatoes on rack in oven and bake at 425°F 45 to 60 min., or until soft when pressed with fingers (protected from heat by paper napkin).

Remove potatoes from oven. To make them more mealy, gently roll back and forth on a flat working surface.

Cut small cross through skin on each potato. Squeeze sides until mealy portion is visible.

Season each potato with
**Few grains salt
Few grains pepper**
Serve immediately. Top with **butter or margarine** or **dairy sour cream,** if desired.
3 servings

BAKED FILLED POTATOES

▲ Base Recipe

Wash and scrub with a vegetable brush
**6 medium (about 2 lbs.) baking
potatoes**
Dry potatoes with absorbent paper. Rub potatoes well with about
1 tablespoon fat

Place potatoes on rack in oven and bake at 425°F 45 to 60 min., or until potatoes are soft when pressed with the fingers (protected by paper napkin or potholder).

Remove potatoes from oven. To make each potato more mealy, gently roll potatoes back and forth on a flat working surface. Cut large potatoes into halves lengthwise. Or cut a thin lengthwise slice from each smaller potato. With a spoon, scoop out inside without breaking skin.

Whip and season potatoes as desired.

Also beat in any one of the following combinations
**⅓ to ½ cup minced or deviled ham
3 tablespoons minced parsley**
Or
**⅓ cup (about 1½ oz.) shredded Ched-
dar cheese (2 tablespoons may be
reserved for topping)
8 to 10 pimiento-stuffed olives, finely
chopped**

Baked Filled Potatoes

Or combine

> ½ can (3 oz.) crabmeat, drained, flaked
> and bony tissue removed
> ¼ cup (about 1 oz.) shredded Cheddar
> cheese
> 1 tablespoon minced onion

Pile mixture lightly into potato skins, leaving surfaces uneven. If desired, top with

> ⅓ cup crushed buttered corn flakes or
> crumbs (page 9)

Bake 8 to 10 min. longer, or until potatoes reheat and brown lightly. *6 servings*

—BAKED FILLED SWEET POTATOES

Follow ▲ Recipe using **sweet potatoes.** Whip and season as suggested in recipe for Sweet Potato Balls (page 340).

—BAKED SHRIMP-FILLED POTATOES

Follow ▲ Recipe. Drain and finely chop **1 can (5 oz.) small shrimp.** Reserve several whole shrimp for garnish. Add ⅔ cup (about 3 oz.) **shredded process American cheese** and shrimp to whipped potato mixture instead of suggested combinations; beat thoroughly on high speed. Pile whipped potato mixture lightly into shells, reserving some for topping. Using pastry bag and a No. 7 star tube, force reserved whipped potato mixture onto filled potato shells to decorate. Omit buttered corn flakes or crumbs. Garnish with reserved shrimp.

HAM-STUFFED POTATOES

▲ Base Recipe

Set out a shallow baking dish.

Wash and scrub with a vegetable brush

> 6 medium (about 2 lbs.) baking
> potatoes

Dry potatoes with absorbent paper. Rub well with about

> 1 tablespoon fat

Place potatoes on rack in oven and bake at 425°F 45 to 60 min., or until they are soft when pressed with the fingers (protected from heat by paper napkin).

Meanwhile, prepare and set aside

> 1 cup quick meat broth (page 10)

Force through the medium blade of a food chopper enough cooked ham to yield

> ¾ cup ground cooked ham

Clean and finely chop

> 1 medium onion

Remove potatoes from oven. To make texture more mealy, gently roll them back and forth on a flat working surface. Cut large potatoes into halves lengthwise, or cut a thin lengthwise slice from each small potato. With a spoon, scoop out inside of each potato without breaking skin. Mash or rice thoroughly and whip in until potatoes are fluffy

> ⅔ to ¾ cup dairy sour cream
> 1 egg, beaten
> 2 tablespoons butter or margarine

and a mixture of

> 1 teaspoon salt
> ¼ teaspoon monosodium glutamate
> ⅛ teaspoon pepper

Blend in the ham and onion. Pile mixture lightly into the potato shells, leaving surfaces uneven. Place potatoes in the baking dish and pour the broth around them.

Bake at 350°F 15 to 20 min., or until thoroughly heated and lightly browned.

6 servings

—GLORIFIED BAKED POTATOES

Follow ▲ Recipe for baking potatoes. Cut a small cross through skin on top of each potato. Squeeze sides of each potato until mealy portion is visible. Top with generous portions of **butter.** Serve immediately, topped with **sour cream** and **chopped chives.** Or arrange bowls of sour cream, chopped chives, extra-crisp crumbled **Panfried Bacon** (page 190), and **grated Parmesan cheese** on a tray. When the baked potatoes are served, pass the tray so each person may select the toppings desired.

HASHED BROWN POTATOES

▲ Base Recipe

Set out a large heavy skillet.

Leftover cooked potatoes may be used. Otherwise, wash, cut into halves and cook covered in boiling salted water to cover

> 6 or 7 medium (about 2 lbs.) potatoes

Cook about 20 min., or until potatoes are tender when pierced with a fork.

Drain potatoes. To dry potatoes, shake pan over low heat. Peel potatoes and dice or chop.

Combine potatoes with

> ⅓ cup milk

and a mixture of

> 1 teaspoon salt
> ¼ teaspoon pepper
> ¼ teaspoon paprika

Heat in skillet

> 3 to 4 tablespoons fat

Baked Shrimp-Filled Potatoes

When hot, place potatoes in skillet. Press down. Cook slowly without stirring until crusty and browned on under side. Turn with a pancake turner or spatula, and brown other side. (Add more fat to skillet if necessary.) Quickly turn potatoes onto platter. *6 servings*

—O'BRIEN POTATOES

Follow ▲ Recipe for cooking potatoes. Dice or chop. Heat fat in skillet and add ¼ **cup chopped onion, 2 tablespoons minced pimiento** and **2 tablespoons minced green pepper.** Add potatoes, milk and seasonings. Cook, stirring frequently, until potatoes are lightly browned.

—SKILLET BROWNED POTATOES

Follow ▲ Recipe. Cook **12 small whole potatoes.** Do not dice. Heat fat in skillet. Panfry potatoes, turning them in hot fat until lightly browned and crisp. Sprinkle with seasonings given in ▲ Recipe after frying. Omit milk.

—FRIED SWEET POTATOES

Follow ▲ Recipe. Use **sweet potatoes.** Peel and slice evenly, all crosswise or all lengthwise. Heat fat, add potatoes and season with **1 teaspoon salt** and **1 tablespoon brown sugar.** Omit other ingredients. Panfry over moderate heat, turning pieces frequently and carefully until browned.

COUNTRY FRIED POTATOES

Prepare and drain on absorbent paper

> 6 slices Panfried Bacon (page 190)

Peel and slice

> 6 cold cooked potatoes

Return to the skillet

> ¼ cup bacon drippings

Add potato slices to skillet. Sprinkle with a mixture of

> ¾ teaspoon salt
> ½ teaspoon paprika
> ¼ teaspoon monosodium glutamate
> ⅛ teaspoon pepper

Cook potatoes over medium heat, turning only

occasionally, until potatoes are well browned. Crumble the bacon and mix with potatoes just before serving. *6 servings*

RAW-FRIED POTATOES
(Pfannkuchen aus rohen gebackenen Kartoffeln)

Set out a 6-in. skillet and
⅓ cup butter
Add 1 tablespoon of the butter to the skillet. Melt the remaining butter.

Meanwhile, wash and pare
1 large potato
Cut into ⅛-in. lengthwise slices. Then cut into ⅛-in. strips. Pat dry with absorbent paper.

Heat the skillet. Leaving skillet on heat, arrange potato strips parallel in about a 1-in. layer in the skillet. Pour the melted butter over the layer. Sprinkle over potato strips a mixture of
¼ teaspoon salt
⅛ teaspoon monosodium glutamate
Heat rapidly until butter sizzles. Reduce heat to medium. Cook about 10 min., or until underside of potato layer is browned. Drain off butter and reserve. Using a pancake turner, carefully turn the potatoes without breaking apart the layer. Return about ½ of the butter to skillet. Cook 5 min. longer over medium heat, or until potatoes are browned on second side and tender (butter should be sizzling). Drain off butter. (Reserve for use in other potato dishes.) Serve immediately. *3 or 4 servings*

FRENCH FRIED POTATOES

▲ Base Recipe

Method 1—About 20 min. before ready to deep-fry, fill a deep saucepan one-half to two-thirds full with
Vegetable shortening, all-purpose shortening, lard or cooking oil for deep-frying
Heat fat slowly to 300°F (page 11).

Meanwhile, wash and pare
6 medium (about 2 lbs.) potatoes

Cut potatoes with knife or fancy cutter. Trim off sides and ends to form large blocks. Cut lengthwise into ⅜-in. slices; stack evenly. Cut lengthwise into sticks about ⅜ in. wide. Pat dry with absorbent paper.

Fry about 1 cup at a time in hot fat until potatoes are transparent but not browned. Remove from fat and drain on absorbent paper.

Just before serving, heat fat to 360°F. Return potatoes to fat, frying 1 cup at a time. Fry until crisp and golden brown. Drain on absorbent paper. Sprinkle with
Salt
Serve immediately or keep warm in 300°F oven. *6 servings*

Method 2—Heat fat to 360°F. Prepare potatoes as in Method 1 and deep-fry until tender and golden brown.

—CHEESE FRENCH FRIES

Follow ▲ Recipe. Omit sprinkling with salt. Toss hot potatoes in a mixture of ⅓ cup grated Parmesan cheese, ¼ teaspoon salt and ¼ teaspoon monosodium glutamate. Place on a baking sheet. Sprinkle with **onion or garlic salt,** if desired. Reheat potatoes in a 350°F oven.

—SWEET POTATO CHIPS

Follow ▲ Recipe, Method 2. Substitute **sweet potatoes or yams** for potatoes. Cut sweet potatoes evenly into thin slices; put immediately into a pan of ice and water to prevent discoloring. Deep-fry 2 to 3 min., or until golden brown. Sprinkle with **salt** or **confectioners' sugar.**

—LATTICE POTATOES

Follow ▲ Recipe, Method 2, for frying. Heat fat to 370°F. For lattice effect, cut potatoes with a fancy fluted cutter into thin crosswise slices, turning potato each time to make lattice.

—SHOESTRING POTATOES

Follow ▲ Recipe, Method 2, for frying. Heat fat to 370°F. Cut potatoes into slices ⅛ in. thick, then cut slices into strips ⅛ in. wide.

French Fried Potatoes

GOLD RUSH FRIES

Set out a heavy skillet with a cover.

Wash, pare and cut into extra-thin, crosswise slices
6 to 8 medium (2 to 2½ lbs.) potatoes (6 cups, sliced)
Heat in skillet
⅓ cup butter or margarine
Add potato slices to skillet and sprinkle with a mixture of
1¼ teaspoons salt
¼ teaspoon monosodium glutamate
⅛ teaspoon pepper
Cover and cook slowly, without turning, 10 to 15 min., or until potatoes are golden brown and crisp. Turn potatoes with spatula or turner. Continue to cook slowly, uncovered, about 15 min. longer, or until second side is browned. *6 servings*

CRISPY POTATO CUPS

A deep saucepan or an automatic deep fryer and a wire-mesh mold for making potato cups will be needed.

About 20 min. before deep-frying, put **fat** into saucepan or deep-fryer and heat slowly to 360°F (page 11).

Meanwhile, wash and pare
3 medium (about 1 lb.) potatoes
Evenly slice potatoes as thin as possible; stack slices evenly; cut into strips about ⅛ in. thick. Immediately put strips into a pan of ice and water to prevent discoloring.

When ready to deep-fry, remove potato strips from water, drain and dry thoroughly between pieces of absorbent paper. To form potato cups, cover the inside of the larger basket with the potato strips, making the sides of the potato cups about 2 in. in height and keeping the cups about ¼ in. thick. Place upper basket carefully over potato strips.

Deep-fry 6 to 7 min., or until potato cup is golden brown and crisp. Drain over fat a few seconds.

To remove the potato cup from mold, lift upper basket. Sharply strike top edge with a

knife to release the potato cup onto absorbent paper to drain.

Fill cups with **Creamed Ham** (page 676) or other creamed mixture and serve immediately.
About 8 potato cups

POTATO CROQUETTES

▲ *Base Recipe*

Wash, pare and place in a saucepan, in salted water

4 medium (about 1⅓ lbs.) potatoes, cut in halves

Cover and cook 20 to 30 min., or until tender when pierced with a fork. Drain. To dry potatoes, shake pan over low heat. Using a potato masher, food mill or ricer, thoroughly rice or mash potatoes into a bowl.

Thoroughly whip in until fluffy

1 egg, well beaten
3 tablespoons melted butter or margarine
1 tablespoon grated Parmesan cheese
2 tablespoons finely chopped parsley
2 teaspoons chopped onion

and a mixture of

1 teaspoon salt
½ teaspoon monosodium glutamate
⅛ teaspoon pepper

Chill in refrigerator at least 1 hr.

Shape into balls, cylinders or cones, using about ¼ cup potatoes for each. Roll in

1 cup (3 slices) fine dry bread crumbs

Dip into a mixture of

1 egg, slightly beaten
1 tablespoon milk

Again coat in bread crumbs and shake off loose crumbs.

About 20 min. before deep-frying, fill a deep saucepan one-half to two-thirds full with **fat or oil** for deep-frying (page 11). Heat slowly to 365°F.

Deep-fry croquettes until rich brown. Fry only as many at one time as will float uncrowded on the surface. Turn when underside is lightly browned and brown other side. Remove with slotted spoon and drain on absorbent paper. Serve hot. *About 8 croquettes*

—SWEET POTATO CROQUETTES

Follow ▲ Recipe using **4 medium sweet potatoes**. Add **2 tablespoons brown sugar** with the egg. Omit cheese, parsley and onion.

POTATO PANCAKES
(Reibekuchen)

▲ *Base Recipe*

Baked king-size to serve as a main dish or scaled down for main-dish accompaniments, potato pancakes are a beloved feature of German cuisine.

Combine

2 tablespoons all-purpose flour
1½ teaspoons salt
¼ teaspoon baking powder
⅛ teaspoon pepper

Set aside.

Wash, pare and finely grate

6 medium (about 2 lbs.) potatoes (about 3 cups, grated)

Set aside.

Heat in a heavy skillet over low heat

Fat (enough to make a layer ¼ in. deep)

Combine the flour mixture with

2 eggs, well beaten
1 tablespoon grated onion
1 tablespoon minced parsley

Drain liquid that collects from grated potatoes; add potatoes to egg mixture and beat thoroughly with a spoon.

When fat is hot, spoon about 2 tablespoons of batter for each pancake into fat, leaving about 1 in. between pancakes. Cook over medium heat until golden brown and crisp on one side. Turn carefully and brown other side. Drain on absorbent paper.

Serve with **Sauerbraten** (page 180), or as a main dish accompanied by **applesauce**.
About 20 medium-size pancakes

—POTATO PANCAKES, KING-SIZE
(Grosser Reibekuchen)

Follow ▲ Recipe; use a large heavy skillet. Heat **2 tablespoons fat** in the skillet. Spoon about one third of batter into skillet. Quickly spread batter evenly with spoon to cover bottom, making one large pancake. When golden brown and crisp, turn carefully. Add **2 tablespoons shortening** and brown other side. Repeat for rest of batter. *3 large pancakes*

SAUERKRAUT AND APPLES

Melt in a 2-qt. top-of-range casserole with a cover

¼ cup butter or margarine

Add and cook slowly about 5 min., stirring occasionally

1 cup (8-oz. can, drained) sliced mushrooms

Wash, quarter, core, pare and cut into wedges

3 medium (about 1 lb.) tart apples

Gently mix into casserole with

1 can (27 oz.) sauerkraut, drained

Pour in a mixture of

¼ cup water
1 teaspoon sugar
1 teaspoon caraway seed
¼ teaspoon celery seed
⅛ teaspoon pepper

Mix thoroughly with a fork. Cover and simmer 15 to 25 min., or until apples are tender.
6 servings

SAUERKRAUT WITH CARAWAY SEEDS
(Sauerkraut mit Kümmel)

Drain

1 can (27 oz.) sauerkraut

Put sauerkraut into a large heavy saucepan and pour over it

2 cups boiling water

Cook over low heat about 45 min., or until most of the liquid is absorbed and the sauerkraut is thoroughly heated. Drain the sauerkraut and put into a serving dish.

Toss lightly with a mixture of

2 tablespoons butter, melted
½ teaspoon salt
½ to 1 teaspoon caraway seed
⅛ teaspoon pepper

6 to 8 servings

KRAUT WITH APPLE CIDER

Heat in a large saucepan

2 tablespoons butter or margarine

Add to saucepan and toss to mix

4 cups drained sauerkraut
2 apples, thinly sliced
½ cup apple cider
1 tablespoon brown sugar

Cover and simmer 5 min., or until apples are tender. Garnish with **parsley**.
About 8 servings

SAUERKRAUT CASSEROLE

Set out a shallow 2-qt. casserole or baking dish.

Have ready

2 large onions, chopped
6½ cups drained sauerkraut, snipped
2 medium apples, quartered, cored and diced
1 small carrot, pared and shredded
2 medium potatoes, shredded (about 1½ cups)

Heat in a skillet

1 tablespoon butter or margarine

Add the onion and cook, stirring occasionally, until crisp-tender, 3 to 5 min.

Meanwhile, combine kraut, apple, carrot and potato in a large bowl. Toss until mixed. Add the onion and

½ cup dry white wine
1 to 2 tablespoons brown sugar
2 teaspoons caraway seed
½ teaspoon seasoned pepper

Toss again. Turn into the casserole. Sprinkle generously with **brown sugar.** Overlap **thinly sliced apples** on top. Sprinkle again with brown sugar.

Set in a 350°F oven until thoroughly heated and apples are tender. *10 to 12 servings*

SAUERKRAUT WITH GARLIC

Have ready
   **½ cup chopped onion
   1 clove garlic, minced
   2 cups drained sauerkraut
   1 can (4 oz.) pimiento, drained and diced**
Heat in a large skillet
   ⅓ cup butter or margarine
Add onion and garlic. Cook, stirring occasionally until tender. Add kraut, pimiento and
   **3 tablespoons sugar
   ¼ teaspoon salt
   Few grains pepper**
Toss well. Heat thoroughly. *6 servings*

SAUERKRAUT WITH POTATO

Have ready
   **½ cup chopped onion
   2 cans (16 oz. each) sauerkraut**
Heat in a heavy saucepan
   2 tablespoons butter or margarine .
Add onion and cook, stirring occasionally, about 3 min. Stir in sauerkraut and cook 8 min. Meanwhile, prepare
   1 potato, pared and grated (about ¾ cup)
Mix with sauerkraut the potato and
   1 teaspoon caraway seed
Pour in **boiling water** to cover. Cook, uncovered, over low heat about 30 min. Cover and continue cooking 30 min. *6 to 8 servings*

CREAMED CHOPPED SPINACH
   (Paraj)

   ▲ *Base Recipe*

Thaw partially and cook in a heavy 2-qt. saucepan
   1 pkg. (10 oz.) frozen chopped spinach

Meanwhile, melt in a small saucepan
   2 tablespoons butter or margarine
Blend into the butter until smooth
   **2 tablespoons all-purpose flour
   ¼ teaspoon salt
   ⅛ teaspoon garlic salt
   ⅛ teaspoon freshly ground pepper**
Heat until mixture bubbles, stirring constantly. Remove from heat. Add gradually, stirring constantly
   ¾ cup cream
Return to heat and bring rapidly to boiling, stirring constantly; cook 1 to 2 min. longer.

Remove sauce from heat. Vigorously stir about 3 tablespoons sauce into
   1 egg, slightly beaten
Immediately blend this mixture into hot sauce, stirring until smooth. Cover sauce and set aside in a warm place.

When spinach is tender, drain in sieve, pressing spinach firmly against sieve with back of spoon to remove water thoroughly. Blend spinach into sauce. Serve hot.
About 4 servings

—CREAMED GARDEN FRESH SPINACH
   (Friss Kerti Paraj)

Follow ▲ Recipe. Substitute **1½ lbs. fresh spinach** for frozen spinach. Remove and discard tough stems, roots and bruised leaves from spinach. Wash leaves thoroughly by lifting up and down several times in a large amount of cold water. Lift leaves out of water each time before pouring off water. When free from sand and gritty material, transfer spinach to large heavy saucepan. Add **1 clove garlic.** Cook (page 313) 8 to 10 min. Omit garlic salt in the sauce. When spinach is tender, discard garlic. Drain spinach. Finely chop spinach; drain again; combine with sauce.

CREAMED SPINACH, MOREZ STYLE
   (Epinards à la Mode de Morez)

Although the flavor of this dish suggests that Morez means "more!" it's actually the name of a town in the Jura Mountains.

Set out a large heavy skillet.

Remove and discard tough stems, roots and bruised leaves from
   3 lbs. spinach
Wash leaves thoroughly by lifting up and down several times in a large amount of cold water. Lift leaves out of water each time before pouring off water. When free from sand and gritty material, transfer spinach to a heavy saucepan. Partially cover and cook 8 to 10 min., using only the water clinging to leaves. Drain, chop and set aside.

Heat in large skillet
   3 tablespoons butter
Add and cook until onion is tender, stirring occasionally
   **½ cup chopped onion
   1 clove garlic, minced**
Add the chopped spinach and sprinkle with
   ¼ teaspoon nutmeg

Cook, stirring constantly, until spinach is well heated. Blend in
   ⅓ cup cream
Serve with **sausage** or **fried ham slices.**
6 to 8 servings

SPINACH 'N' EGGS

Remove and discard tough stems, roots and bruised leaves from
   1½ lbs. spinach
Wash leaves thoroughly by lifting up and down several times in a large amount of cold water, and lifting leaves out of water each time before pouring off water. When free from sand and gritty material, transfer spinach to a heavy saucepan. Cook, partially covered, over medium heat 8 to 10 min., using only the water clinging to leaves. Drain and chop spinach fine. Season with mixture of
   **½ teaspoon salt
   ¼ teaspoon monosodium glutamate
   ⅛ teaspoon pepper
   ⅛ teaspoon nutmeg**

Set spinach in warm place while poaching
   4 eggs (see Poached Eggs, page 137)

Form small nests of spinach on individual serving plates. Place one egg in each nest. Dot each with
   Butter or margarine
4 servings

GOURMET SPINACH

   ▲ *Base Recipe*

Remove and discard tough stems, roots, and bruised leaves from
   1 lb. spinach
Wash thoroughly by lifting up and down in cold water. Lift leaves out of water each time. When free from sand and gritty material, place spinach in heavy saucepan. Cook (page 313) 8 to 10 min.

Drain cooked spinach and chop. Return spinach to saucepan. Add and stir to blend
   **¼ cup cream
   2 tablespoons butter or margarine
   1 tablespoon minced onion
   1 teaspoon prepared horseradish**
and a mixture of
   **½ teaspoon salt
   ¼ teaspoon monosodium glutamate
   ⅛ teaspoon pepper**
Return to heat; cook until heated thoroughly.
4 servings

—SPINACH CHEESE RAMEKINS

Set out 6 ramekins or individual baking dishes. Follow ▲ Recipe. Omit cream, onion and horseradish. While spinach is cooking, prepare **Welsh Rabbit** (one half recipe, page 145). Add butter or margarine and seasonings to spinach and spoon equal portions into ramekins. Pour Welsh Rabbit over tops. Sprinkle with **⅔ cup buttered crushed corn flakes.** Bake at 350°F about 10 min.

FLORENTINE SPINACH
(Spinaci alla Fiorentina)

▲ Base Recipe

Thoroughly grease a 9-in. ring mold.

Remove and discard tough stems, roots and bruised leaves from

2 lbs. spinach

Wash leaves thoroughly by lifting up and down several times in a large amount of cold water and lifting leaves out of water each time before pouring off water. When free from sand and gritty material, transfer spinach to a saucepan. Cook (page 313) 8 to 10 min.

Meanwhile, prepare

2 cups Medium White Sauce (double recipe, page 304)

Stirring vigorously to blend, pour white sauce slowly into

3 eggs, slightly beaten

Set aside to cool to lukewarm.

Drain and finely chop spinach. Blend spinach and white sauce-egg mixture with

3 tablespoons minced onion
½ teaspoon salt
½ teaspoon pepper

Pour into mold. Set in a large baking pan and pour very hot water into pan to a 1-in. depth.

Bake at 350°F 45 to 55 min., or until set. Remove from oven and set aside 5 min.

To unmold run tip of knife around top of edge of mold. Invert on warm serving plate. Gently lift off pan. Serve immediately.

6 servings

—SPINACH AND EGGS FLORENTINE
(Spinaci con Uova alla Fiorentina)

Grease 2-qt. casserole instead of ring mold. Follow ▲ Recipe for preparation of spinach and white sauce. Omit beaten eggs. Do not combine sauce and spinach. Add seasonings and onion to spinach. Hard-cook (page 133) **6 eggs.** Place one half of spinach in casserole. Cut eggs into crosswise slices and arrange one half of slices over spinach. Cover with 1 cup sauce. Add remaining spinach and top with remaining egg slices. Cover with remainder of sauce. Bake, omitting the pan of hot water, 15 to 20 min., or until thoroughly heated.

POPEYE SPINACH TIMBALES

Grease or oil 6 heat-resistant custard cups.

Cook (page 313)

2 lbs. spinach

Drain and finely chop spinach. Combine spinach with mixture of

3 eggs, well beaten
1 cup cream or undiluted evaporated milk
½ cup soft bread crumbs
2 tablespoons melted butter or margarine
2 tablespoons minced onion

Add a mixture of

1 teaspoon salt
¼ teaspoon nutmeg
¼ teaspoon monosodium glutamate

Mix well. Fill custard cups two-thirds full with mixture. Set cups in a large baking pan and pour very hot water into pan to a 1-in depth.

Bake at 350°F 30 to 40 min., or until firm.

While timbales are baking, prepare

Medium White Sauce (page 304)

Run a spatula around cups to loosen timbales. Unmold on hot serving plates. Pour on hot white sauce.

If desired, garnish each with

1 or 2 slices Hard-Cooked Egg (page 133)

6 servings

SPINACH ARISTOCRAT

Perfectly seasoned, thoroughly chilled, and blended with rich sour cream, spinach becomes a true aristocrat. Serve on a plate with other colorful foods to create a dramatic effect.

An electric blender will be needed.

Remove and discard tough stems, roots and bruised leaves from

1 lb. spinach

Wash leaves thoroughly by lifting up and down several times in a large amount of cold water, changing water as necessary. Lift leaves out of water each time before pouring off water. When spinach is free from sand and gritty material, transfer to a heavy saucepan. Cook (page 313) 8 to 10 min. Drain; put spinach into blender container. (If using frozen spinach, cook following directions on package.)

Add to blender container

1 cup dairy sour cream
1 teaspoon prepared horseradish
½ teaspoon salt
½ teaspoon lemon juice
¼ teaspoon monosodium glutamate
⅛ teaspoon pepper
2 drops Tabasco

Cover container and flick motor switch on and off several times until mixture is white with flecks of green. Chill several hours.

6 servings

PECAN-CRUSTED SQUASH CASSEROLE

▲ Base Recipe

Lightly grease a 1-qt. casserole.

Coarsely chop and set aside

¾ cup (about 3 oz.) pecans

Cook

2 pkgs. (12 oz. each) frozen squash

Blend thoroughly into squash

3 tablespoons melted butter or margarine
2 tablespoons cream

Add a mixture of

1 tablespoon brown sugar
¼ teaspoon salt
¼ teaspoon pepper
⅛ teaspoon monosodium glutamate
⅛ teaspoon ginger

Blend in ½ cup of the chopped pecans. Turn mixture into casserole.

Combine remaining pecans with

3 tablespoons light corn syrup
2 tablespoons brown sugar
1 tablespoon melted butter or margarine

Lightly drizzle this mixture over squash in casserole.

Bake at 350°F about 20 min., or until the glaze sets to form a crust.   *About 6 servings*

—STUFFED ACORN SQUASH

Follow ▲ Recipe. Substitute **2 medium acorn squash** for frozen squash. Omit pecans. Wash squash and cut into halves lengthwise; remove seeds and fibers. Place cut side down in baking pan. Pour in boiling water to ¼-in. depth in baking pan. Bake squash halves at 350°F 25 min. Turn squash cut side up and bake 25 min. longer, or until tender when pierced with a fork. Carefully scoop out squash with a spoon, without breaking skins. Mash squash and proceed as for ▲ Recipe. Pile mixture lightly into skins. Omit top glaze. Bake 8 to 10 min. longer, or until the squash is reheated and lightly browned.

—MAPLE-FLAVORED SQUASH

Follow directions for preparing squash as in recipe for Stuffed Acorn Squash. Bake as directed 25 min. Meanwhile, prepare stuffing. Heat in a saucepan ¼ cup **butter.** Add **3 tablespoons minced onion** and cook until onion is tender, stirring occasionally. Remove from heat and stir in **3 cups soft bread crumbs** and a mixture of ½ **teaspoon salt,** ¼ **teaspoon monosodium glutamate** and ⅛ **teaspoon pepper.** Remove squash from oven, drain and turn cut side up. Spoon ¼ **cup maple syrup** over squash. Fill squash halves with the stuffing. Return to oven and bake 25 min. longer, or until tender when pierced with a fork.

BAKED ACORN SQUASH

Set out a large shallow baking dish.

Wash, cut into halves crosswise and remove seeds and fibers from
3 medium acorn squash
Place squash, cut side down, in baking dish. Pour into baking dish
Boiling water to ½-in. level

Bake squash at 400°F for 30 min.; turn and put into the squash halves
¼ cup butter or margarine
and a mixture of
1½ tablespoons brown sugar
½ teaspoon salt
¼ teaspoon monosodium glutamate
¼ teaspoon ginger
Continue baking squash until tender when pierced with a fork. *6 servings*

SUMMER SQUASH WITH DILL
(Tökfozelék)

Set out a heavy 3-qt. saucepan with a tight-fitting cover.

Wash, trim off ends and cut into thin cross-wise slices
2 lbs. summer squash
(Choose young, tender squash; it is not neces-sary to pare them. Pare the squash before slicing if the outside seems tough.)

Put squash into the saucepan with
½ cup boiling water
2 teaspoons finely chopped fresh dill or ¼ teaspoon dill seed
½ teaspoon salt
Cover saucepan and simmer squash 15 to 20 min., or until just tender.

Meanwhile, heat thoroughly in top of double boiler over simmering water, stirring con-stantly
1 cup dairy sour cream
1 tablespoon lemon juice
2 teaspoons sugar
½ teaspoon paprika
Carefully mix sauce with the squash.

Serve immediately. *6 servings*

SQUASH WITH ORANGE

Set out a double boiler.

Combine in the top of the double boiler
2 cups mashed cooked squash (Hubbard or butternut)
¼ cup butter or margarine, melted
¼ cup brown sugar
1 teaspoon salt
⅛ teaspoon pepper
1 tablespoon grated orange peel
3 tablespoons orange juice
Mix thoroughly and place over boiling water. Cook until squash is very hot.
4 or 5 servings

STUFFED BUTTERNUT SQUASH

Set out a shallow baking dish or pan.

Wash thoroughly and cut into halves length-wise
2 butternut squash (about 1½ lbs. each)
Scoop out seeds and stringy portion. Invert halves in the baking dish and pour in ¼ in. boiling water. Set in 400°F oven and bake 20 to 30 min., or until squash is tender.

Remove from oven and scoop out squash into a large mixing bowl, leaving two shells intact. (Discard remaining two shells.)

Mash squash and beat in
½ teaspoon salt
⅛ teaspoon pepper
⅛ teaspoon garlic powder
2 tablespoons butter or margarine
1 teaspoon lemon juice
1 cup diced cooked ham
Spoon squash mixture into two halves. Place filled shells in baking dish and set under broiler about 4 in. from heat until squash is lightly browned.

Serve garnished with snipped **parsley**.
4 servings

STUFFED PATTYPAN SQUASH

These delicate summer squash are also known as scalloped squash or cymlings.

Set out a heavy 3-qt. saucepan with a tight-fitting cover, and a baking pan.

Wash and trim off ends of
6 white pattypan squash (about 4 lbs.)
Put squash into the saucepan with
½ cup boiling water
⅛ teaspoon salt
⅛ teaspoon monosodium glutamate

Cover saucepan; simmer squash 35 min., or until they are just tender.

Drain squash and cut a slice off top of each. Carefully scoop out squash with a spoon, with-out breaking shells. Drain squash, put into a bowl and mash.

Blend into the squash
¼ cup butter or margarine
1 tablespoon cream
½ teaspoon grated onion
¼ teaspoon salt
⅛ teaspoon monosodium glutamate
⅛ teaspoon pepper
Pile squash mixture lightly into shells. Sprin-kle over the squash a mixture of
⅓ cup fine dry bread crumbs
1 tablespoon minced parsley
Dot generously with
Butter or margarine
Place squash in the baking pan. Pour boiling water into baking pan to ¼-in. depth.

Bake at 350°F 30 min., or until browned on top. *6 servings*

FRIED TOMATOES

▲ Base Recipe

Set out a large heavy skillet.

Rinse, cut out stem ends and slice ½ in. thick
4 firm ripe or green tomatoes
Mix in a shallow pan or dish
½ cup corn meal
1 teaspoon salt
¼ teaspoon monosodium glutamate
⅛ teaspoon pepper
Coat both sides of slices by dipping in corn meal mixture.

Heat in the skillet over low heat
¼ cup butter or margarine
Add as many slices at one time as will lie flat in skillet. Lightly brown both sides, turning only once. Cook very slowly until tender. Add extra butter or margarine as needed.
4 servings

—CREAMED TOMATOES

Follow ▲ Recipe. Add ½ teaspoon sugar to corn meal mixture. When tomatoes are lightly browned, stir to break up. Cook 5 min. Mix in **2 tablespoons cream.** Serve immediately.

TOMATOES HOLLANDAISE

Set out a shallow baking dish.

Cut a slice from stem end of
6 firm ripe medium tomatoes
Hollow out tomatoes slightly; set aside in dish.

Combine and mix well
2 egg yolks, fork beaten
2 teaspoons prepared mustard
1 teaspoon salt
2 tablespoons lemon juice

Vegetable Plate with Tomato Broil

Add and thoroughly blend to a smooth paste
¼ cup butter, creamed
Divide mixture evenly and spoon into hollowed-out portion of each tomato.

Bake at 400°F about 20 min. Serve hot.

6 servings

SCALLOPED TOMATOES

Grease a 1¼-qt. shallow baking dish.

Toast until very crisp and cut into ½-in. cubes
3 slices bread

Meanwhile, peel, rinse and chop
2 medium (about ½ lb.) onions

Drain and cut into pieces with a spoon
1 can (28 oz.) tomatoes
Mix in the casserole one half the chopped onion, the tomatoes and
⅓ cup cheese cracker crumbs
1 tablespoon parsley flakes
1½ teaspoons sugar
1 teaspoon seasoned salt
Cover with remaining chopped onion. Spoon over the mixture
1 cup dairy sour cream

Toss toast cubes with
2 tablespoons melted butter or margarine
Spoon over sour cream. Sprinkle with **parsley flakes.**

Bake at 325°F 20 min., or until mixture is thoroughly heated.

Serve in sauce dishes. *6 servings*

TOMATO BROIL

▲ *Base Recipe*

Mix and set aside
3 tablespoons fine cracker crumbs
1 teaspoon sugar
¼ teaspoon salt
⅛ teaspoon pepper

Wash, remove stem ends and cut into halves crosswise
2 large tomatoes

Brush with
Melted butter or margarine
Sprinkle with crumb mixture. Arrange on broiler rack.

Place broiler rack under broiler with top of tomatoes about 3 in. from heat. Broil 10 min., or until crumbs are lightly browned.

When broiling meat, add tomatoes when turning meat to brown second side. *4 servings*

—TOMATOES WITH BANANA TOPPER

Follow ▲ Recipe. Omit crumbs, pepper and sugar. Sprinkle **salt** over tomato halves. Peel and slice **1 banana.** Overlap banana slices on buttered tomato halves. Sprinkle ¼ cup (1 oz.) **shredded Cheddar cheese** over bananas. Broil as in ▲ Recipe, or until cheese melts.

—TOMATO BAKE

Follow ▲ Recipe. Place tomato halves in a lightly greased shallow baking dish. Bake at 400°F about 20 min.

BROILED TOMATOES I

▲ *Base Recipe*

Rinse, cut out stem ends and cut crosswise into halves
3 large tomatoes
Arrange tomatoes, cut-side up, on a baking sheet or broiler rack.

Brush cut sides of tomatoes with
1 tablespoon melted butter or margarine (½ teaspoon for each half)
Sprinkle with a mixture of
½ teaspoon salt
¼ teaspoon pepper
¼ teaspoon monosodium glutamate

Place under broiler with tops of tomatoes about 3 in. from heat. Broil about 5 min., or until tomatoes are thoroughly heated. *6 servings*

—BROILED TOMATOES II

Follow ▲ Recipe. For seasonings, substitute the following mixture: Mix ¼ cup **fine cracker crumbs,** 3 tablespoons grated Parmesan cheese, 1½ teaspoons sugar, ½ teaspoon salt and ¼ teaspoon pepper. Broil about 10 min., or until crumbs are lightly browned.

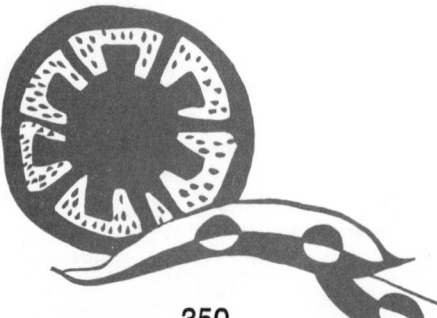

Crusty Tomato Halves, Potatoes and Beans

CRUSTY TOMATO HALVES

▲ *Base Recipe*

Rinse and cut into halves crosswise
6 medium tomatoes
Spread cut surfaces with a mixture of
2 tablespoons softened butter or margarine
1 teaspoon prepared mustard
Sprinkle with mixture of
⅓ cup fine dry bread crumbs
2 tablespoons melted butter or margarine
½ teaspoon salt
¼ teaspoon monosodium glutamate
¼ teaspoon pepper
Place tomatoes, cut-side up, on broiler rack.

Place under broiler with tops of tomatoes about 3 in. from heat, 7 to 10 min., or until lightly browned. *6 servings*

—CRUSTY TOMATO HALVES WITH CHEESE

Follow ▲ Recipe. Combine ¼ cup shredded **Cheddar cheese** with crumb mixture.

STUFFED TOMATOES I

Set out a shallow 2-qt. baking dish and a skillet.

Prepare and keep hot
1 cup Perfection Boiled Rice (one third recipe, page 165)

While rice is cooking, wash and cut off tops of
6 large firm tomatoes
With a spoon, scoop out center pulp from tomatoes. Reserve pulp. Set tomato shells aside.

Heat in the skillet over low heat
2 tablespoons butter or margarine
Add to skillet and cook over medium heat until onion is tender
½ cup (about 1 medium) chopped onion
⅓ cup chopped celery
¼ cup chopped green pepper
⅓ cup (3-oz. can) deviled ham

Meanwhile, drain
1 can (4 oz.) sliced mushrooms

Mix cooked rice, reserved tomato pulp, contents of skillet and mushrooms with

1 teaspoon Worcestershire sauce

and a mixture of

1 teaspoon salt
⅛ teaspoon pepper

Spoon mixture into tomato shells, heaping slightly. Place in the baking dish. Evenly cover tops of stuffed tomatoes with

½ cup buttered soft bread crumbs (page 9)

Bake at 375°F 15 to 20 min., or until crumbs are lightly browned. *6 servings*

STUFFED TOMATOES II
(Pomodori Imbottiti)

Thoroughly grease an 8x8x2-in. baking dish.

Cook (page 10)

1 cup packaged precooked rice

Shred and set aside

4 oz. pasteurized process cheese food (1 cup, shredded)

Heat in skillet

2 tablespoons olive oil

Add and cook until lightly browned

½ clove garlic, chopped

Stir cheese, oil and garlic into rice. Set aside.

Rinse and remove stem ends from

6 large firm tomatoes

Cut a ¼-in. slice from top of each tomato and set aside. With a sharp knife, cut down around inside of tomatoes, about ¼ in. from edges, being careful not to cut through bottom. With a spoon, scoop out center pulp. Sieve tomato pulp and set aside liquid. Sprinkle each tomato with

⅛ teaspoon salt

Lightly fill tomatoes with rice-cheese mixture. Sprinkle 1 tablespoon tomato liquid over each. Replace tops of tomatoes. Place tomatoes in prepared baking dish. Pour over tomatoes

2 tablespoons olive oil

Bake at 375°F 20 to 25 min.

Garnish with **watercress**. *6 servings*

CHEESE RICE-STUFFED TOMATOES I

▲ Base Recipe

Grease an 8-in. square baking dish.

For Filling—Cook

⅔ cup rice (two thirds recipe Perfection Boiled Rice, page 165)

Meanwhile, shred

2 oz. Cheddar cheese (about ½ cup, shredded)

Mix 2 tablespoons of the cheese with

⅓ cup (about ½ slice) soft bread crumbs
2 tablespoons melted butter or margarine

Set prepared crumbs aside.

Heat in skillet

2 tablespoons butter or margarine

Stir in and heat thoroughly

½ cup (4-oz. can, drained) sliced mushrooms

Stir remaining shredded cheese and mushrooms into rice, adding

1 teaspoon Worcestershire sauce

For Tomatoes—Rinse

6 large firm tomatoes

Cut a ¼-in. slice from top of each tomato. With a sharp knife, cut down around inside of tomatoes, about ¼ in. from edges, being careful not to cut through bottoms. With a spoon scoop out center pulp. Sprinkle each tomato with

⅛ teaspoon salt
Few grains monosodium glutamate

Lightly fill tomatoes with rice mixture, heaping slightly. Place in baking dish. Top with buttered crumb mixture.

Bake at 375°F 20 to 25 min. *6 servings*

—TOMATOES STUFFED WITH GREEN PEAS

Follow ▲ Recipe for preparing tomatoes. Cook **2 lbs. fresh peas** (page 313). Substitute peas for rice. Omit Worcestershire sauce. Top with buttered crumbs and cheese.

CHEESE RICE-STUFFED TOMATOES II

▲ Base Recipe

Thoroughly grease a shallow 2-qt. baking dish. Set out a skillet.

Cook, following directions on package

⅓ cup packaged precooked rice (about 1 cup, cooked)

Meanwhile, shred and set aside

½ lb. pasteurized process Swiss cheese (about 2 cups, shredded)

Rinse, cut out and discard stem end from

6 large firm tomatoes

Cut a slice about ¼ in. thick from top of each tomato; reserve. With a spoon, scoop out pulp from tomatoes. Drain excess liquid from pulp; reserve pulp. Set tomatoes aside to drain.

Heat in the skillet

2 tablespoons butter

Add to skillet and cook over medium heat until onion is tender

½ cup chopped onion
¼ cup chopped celery

Mix the rice, contents of the skillet, shredded cheese, tomato pulp and

½ cup (4-oz. can drained) canned sliced mushrooms
1 teaspoon salt
¼ teaspoon marjoram
⅛ teaspoon pepper

Spoon mixture into tomato shells. Replace tops. Place in baking dish.

Bake at 350°F 15 min., or until thoroughly heated.

Garnish centers of tomato tops with

Watercress

Serve immediately. *6 servings*

—STUFFED TOMATOES WITH CHEESE SAUCE

Follow ▲ Recipe. Cut a thin slice from top of each tomato. Omit shredded Swiss cheese from filling. While tomatoes bake, prepare **1 cup Cheese Sauce** (page 304). Serve each tomato topped with 2 or 3 tablespoons of the sauce. Substitute **parsley** for watercress.

TURNIP FLUFF

Grease a 1½-qt. baking dish or casserole.

Cook in boiling salted water until tender and drain thoroughly

2 lbs. turnips, pared and cubed

Mash turnips and mix with

¼ cup cream
1 egg, beaten
2 tablespoons butter or margarine
¼ cup light brown sugar
2 tablespoons uncooked farina
Salt and pepper to taste

Turn mixture into baking dish and set in 350°F oven about 40 min. *6 servings*

ZUCCHINI ITALIAN STYLE

▲ Base Recipe

Sweet Italian squash becomes a sophisticate.

Set out a 2-qt. casserole and a 3-qt. saucepan with a tight-fitting cover.

Cheese Rice-Stuffed Tomatoes II

Wash, trim off ends and cut crosswise into ⅛-in. slices
8 to 10 small (2½ lbs.) zucchini

Heat in the saucepan
3 tablespoons olive oil
Add zucchini with
⅔ cup (about 3 small) coarsely chopped onion
¼ lb. mushrooms, sliced
Cover saucepan and cook zucchini mixture over low heat 10 to 15 min., or until tender, occasionally turning and moving mixture with a spoon.

Meanwhile, set out
⅔ cup (about 3 oz.) grated Parmesan cheese

Remove zucchini mixture from heat; mix in about one half of grated cheese with fork. Pour in a mixture of
1½ cups (two 6-oz. cans) tomato paste
1 teaspoon salt
½ teaspoon monosodium glutamate
½ teaspoon garlic salt or 1 clove garlic, minced
⅛ teaspoon pepper
Blend lightly and thoroughly; turn mixture into casserole. Sprinkle with remaining cheese.

Bake at 350°F 20 to 30 min.   *8 servings*

—EGGPLANT ITALIAN STYLE

Follow ▲ Recipe. Substitute **1 eggplant** (about 1 lb.) for zucchini; wash, pare, and cut into ½-in. cubes. Brown lightly in the oil over low heat. Continue as in ▲ Recipe.

ZUCCHINI WITH TOMATOES

Set out a large heavy skillet. Grease a 1½-qt. baking dish or casserole.

Rinse thoroughly and cut into ¼-in. slices
2 lbs. zucchini

Heat in skillet
3 tablespoons butter or margarine
Add and cook 3 to 5 min., stirring occasionally
¼ cup chopped onion
Add zucchini and cook 5 min., stirring frequently.

Add and cook, covered, 5 min. longer
2 cups cooked or canned tomatoes
½ teaspoon salt
⅛ teaspoon pepper
Turn mixture into baking dish and sprinkle with
¾ cup shredded sharp Cheddar cheese

Set in 375°F oven about 20 min., or until cheese is melted.   *6 to 8 servings*

STUFFED ZUCCHINI

Set out a large shallow baking dish.

Wash, remove stem ends and cut into halves lengthwise
4 large zucchini
Scoop out pulp, chop it and set aside for filling. Generously brush outside of shells with
Cooking oil
Arrange, cut side up, in baking dish and sprinkle zucchini shells with
Seasoned salt

Combine in a mixing bowl with reserved zucchini pulp
1 can (15 oz.) roast beef hash
1 tablespoon bottled steak sauce
1 tablespoon instant minced onion
¼ teaspoon garlic powder
½ cup shredded cheddar cheese
Spoon mixture into zucchini shells and sprinkle with
Chopped parsley

Set in 350°F oven about 30 min., or until zucchini is tender (but not soft).
8 stuffed zucchini halves

DEEP-FRIED ZUCCHINI

About 20 min. before ready to deep fry, put **fat** into a deep saucepan or an automatic deep fryer and heat to 365°F (page 11).

Rinse and pare
6 medium (about 2 lbs.) zucchini
Cut each zucchini lengthwise into ⅜-in. slices; stack evenly. Cut lengthwise into sticks about ⅜ in. wide; cut sticks into halves crosswise. Set aside.

Melt and set aside to cool
1 tablespoon butter or margarine

Sift together into a bowl and set aside
1¼ cups sifted all-purpose flour
1 teaspoon salt
½ teaspoon monosodium glutamate
¼ teaspoon pepper

Beat until thick and piled softly
2 eggs
Blend in
¾ cup milk
1 teaspoon Worcestershire sauce
Blend in the butter or margarine. Make a well in center of dry ingredients; add liquid mixture all at one time. Blend just until smooth.

Dip zucchini pieces into batter with fork or slotted spoon to coat evenly. Allow any excess coating to drip off before lowering zucchini into fat. Deep fry only as many pieces as will

float uncrowded one layer deep in fat. Fry 2 to 3 min., or until golden brown. Turn zucchini pieces with a fork several times during cooking. Drain over fat for a few seconds before removing to absorbent paper.

Sprinkle with **salt**. Serve hot.   *6 servings*

MIXED VEGETABLES

GREEN BEAN-MUSHROOM MEDLEY

Heat in a saucepan over low heat
¼ cup butter or margarine
Add and cook over medium heat until mushrooms are lightly browned, stirring occasionally
½ lb. mushrooms, sliced
1 cup chopped green onion tops
Add and cook over high heat 1 min. (break frozen blocks apart with a fork as they thaw)
2 pkgs. (9 oz. each) frozen cut green beans
1 can (8 oz.) water chestnuts, drained and sliced
1 teaspoon salt
Few grains freshly ground pepper
1 teaspoon crushed savory leaves
Reduce heat to low and cook, loosely covered, 12 to 15 min., or until beans are just tender.
10 servings

VEGETABLE AND HAM CASSEROLE

Butter a 2-qt. casserole.

Remove leaves, cut off all the woody base and trim any blemishes from
1 small head cauliflower
Separate the cauliflower into flowerets; rinse and cook (page 313) 8 to 10 min., or until tender but still firm. Drain the cauliflower and set aside.

Meanwhile, coarsely chop and set aside
¼ lb. cooked ham

Clean and slice (page 9)
¼ lb. mushrooms
Heat in a skillet
2 tablespoons butter or margarine
Add the mushrooms and cook over medium heat until lightly browned and tender, occasionally moving and turning with a spoon.

Set out
¾ cup cooked green peas
¾ cup grated Parmesan cheese
Cream until softened
½ cup butter or margarine

Blend in, in thirds

6 egg yolks, well beaten

Thoroughly blend in a mixture of 2 tablespoons of the Parmesan cheese and

1 cup dairy sour cream
¼ cup sifted all-purpose flour

Beat until stiff, not dry, peaks are formed

6 egg whites

Gently fold egg whites into sour cream mixture. Turn one half of mixture into the casserole. Quickly arrange the ham in an even layer over mixture. Sprinkle with 2 tablespoons of cheese. Top with the green peas and sprinkle with 2 tablespoons of cheese. Cover with the cauliflower and 2 tablespoons of cheese. Add the mushrooms and top with remaining cheese. Turn remaining sour cream mixture into the casserole.

Bake at 325°F 45 to 50 min., or until a metal knife inserted halfway between center and edge of casserole comes out clean.

Serve immediately. *6 servings*

HONEY BAKED CARROTS AND BEANS

▲ Base Recipe

Grease a 1½-qt. casserole with a tight-fitting cover.

Wash, scrape or pare, cut into julienne strips (page 12) and put into casserole

6 or 7 carrots

Peel and rinse

½ lb. (about 15) very small whole onions

Arrange in casserole over carrots; reserve 5 or 6 for garnish.

Wash, break off ends and cut into julienne strips

½ lb. (about 1½ cups) green beans

Cover onions with the beans. Arrange reserved onions in center.

Mix and pour over vegetables

⅓ cup hot water
¼ cup honey
½ teaspoon salt
¼ teaspoon monosodium glutamate

Dot generously with

¼ cup butter or margarine

Cover and bake at 350°F 45 to 60 min., or until

vegetables are tender. Remove cover and bake 10 to 20 min. longer, or until lightly browned. *6 servings*

—MUSTARD BAKED CARROTS AND BEANS

Follow ▲ Recipe. Omit honey and water. Prepare **1½ cups Thin White Sauce** (1½ times recipe, page 304; add 1 tablespoon prepared mustard and 2 teaspoons lemon juice to completed sauce). Pour this sauce over vegetables. Decrease butter to 2 tablespoons.

CABBAGE TOMATO SCALLOP

Grease 6 ramekins.

Crush until fine

3 cups corn flakes

Mix in evenly and set aside

1 cup shredded Cheddar cheese

Remove and discard wilted outer leaves from, wash and shred coarsely

1 head (1 lb.) cabbage (about 4 cups, shredded)

Heat to boiling enough water to cover cabbage. Add for each quart of water

1 teaspoon salt

Boil cabbage, loosely covered, over medium heat about 7 min., or until cabbage is just tender; drain well.

Meanwhile, heat slowly in a large saucepan, stirring frequently

3 tablespoons butter or margarine
½ cup (about 1 medium) chopped onion

Cook onion until tender. Blend in

3 tablespoons all-purpose flour
1 teaspoon salt
⅛ teaspoon pepper

Heat until mixture bubbles. Remove from heat.

Gradually stir in

2½ cups canned tomatoes, cut in pieces
⅓ cup chopped green pepper

Cook rapidly, stirring constantly, until mixture thickens. Pour one third of tomato mixture into ramekins and add one half of cabbage; repeat. Cover with final one third of tomato mixture. Top with cheese and corn flakes.

Bake at 375°F about 25 min. *6 servings*

MONTEREY JACK

Set out a large saucepan.

Panfry (page 190), reserving fat

4 slices bacon, diced

Shred and set aside

½ lb. sharp Cheddar cheese (about 2 cups, shredded)

Clean, chop and set aside

1 medium onion (about ½ cup, chopped)
1 small green pepper (about ½ cup, chopped)

Cabbage Tomato Scallop

Cut into pieces with a spoon

2½ cups canned tomatoes

Set aside.

Heat in the saucepan over low heat 2 tablespoons of the reserved fat. Add the onion and green pepper and cook over medium heat, occasionally moving and turning mixture with a spoon, until onion and green pepper are tender. Add the bacon, tomatoes and

2 cans (16 oz. each) kidney beans (about 3 cups)

and a mixture of

2 tablespoons chili powder
1 teaspoon salt
1 teaspoon monosodium glutamate
⅛ teaspoon pepper

Bring mixture to boiling, reduce heat and simmer about 1 hr., stirring occasionally.

Remove from heat and add the cheese all at one time. Stir carefully until cheese is melted. Serve hot. *8 servings*

SUCCOTASH

Set out a large saucepan.

Shell, discarding pods, and rinse

2 lbs. green lima beans (about 1⅓ cups or ⅔ lb. shelled)

Cook (page 313) 20 to 30 min., or until just tender when pierced with a fork.

Meanwhile, remove husks, corn silk and blemishes from

3 or 4 fresh ears corn

Monterey Jack

Carefully cut kernels from cob (about 1 cup cut corn).

Drain the lima beans, reserving the liquid. Mix the beans and corn; add about ½ cup of the reserved liquid. Cook over low heat, stirring occasionally, until liquid is almost all absorbed. Blend in

¼ cup cream
3 tablespoons butter

and a mixture of

1 teaspoon salt
½ teaspoon sugar
¼ teaspoon pepper

4 to 6 servings

QUICK SUCCOTASH

Drain, reserving liquids

1 can (17 oz.) whole kernel corn
(about 2 cups, drained)
1 can (17 oz.) lima beans (about
2 cups, drained)

Heat in a medium-size saucepan

¼ cup butter

Add vegetables to saucepan and toss lightly to coat evenly with butter. Add ½ cup of reserved liquids and

1½ teaspoons salt
1 teaspoon sugar
½ teaspoon monosodium glutamate
¼ teaspoon pepper

Cover saucepan and cook over low heat until liquid is almost all absorbed. Add and blend in

⅓ cup cream

Heat thoroughly. Serve hot.   *About 8 servings*

OKRA AND CORN

If the South has a typical vegetable, it's okra.

Prepare, reserving fat

4 slices Panfried Bacon (page 190)

Crumble bacon and set aside.

Return 2 tablespoons fat to skillet and add

1 onion, sliced
1 pkg. (10 oz.) frozen okra, thawed
and cut into ¼-in. thick slices
1 pkg. (10 oz.) frozen corn, thawed

Cook, stirring constantly, 10 min. Mix in

1½ cups (about 2 medium) peeled and
diced tomatoes
¼ cup diced green pepper
½ teaspoon salt
⅛ teaspoon pepper

Cook over low heat about 20 min., or until liquid is absorbed.

Turn into warm serving dish and sprinkle the bacon over the top.   *About 8 servings*

OKRA AND TOMATOES

Set out a large skillet with a tight-fitting cover.

Wash, cut off stem ends, slice and set aside

1 lb. okra (about 4 cups, sliced)

Clean, chop and set aside

2 medium (about ½ lb.) onions
(about 1 cup, chopped)
1 green pepper (about ½ cup,
chopped)

Heat in the skillet over low heat

2 tablespoons bacon drippings, butter
or margarine

Add onion and green pepper and cook over medium heat until the onion is tender. Add sliced okra and

2 cups (16-oz. can) cooked
tomatoes, cut in pieces

Stir in a mixture of

½ teaspoon salt
¼ teaspoon monosodium glutamate
⅛ teaspoon pepper
⅛ teaspoon curry powder
⅛ teaspoon thyme

Simmer, covered, 30 to 40 min., or until okra is tender.   *6 servings*

VEGETABLES AMANDINE

Cut crosswise into ¼-in. slices

6 medium carrots, pared

Cook, covered, in a small amount of boiling salted water about 10 min., or until crisp-tender.

Meanwhile, cook following package directions

1 pkg. (10 oz.) frozen cauliflower
1 pkg. (10 oz.) frozen cut green beans

Arrange vegetables in a heated serving dish. Sprinkle with **salt** and

½ cup blanched slivered almonds,
toasted

Pour over all a mixture of

⅓ cup butter or margarine, melted
½ teaspoon lemon juice
½ teaspoon crushed rosemary

About 8 servings

RATATOUILLE WITH SPANISH OLIVES

Set out a large heavy skillet.

Pare and cut into 3x½-in. strips

1 medium eggplant

Wash thoroughly and cut into ¼-in. slices

2 zucchini

Toss the vegetables in a bowl with

1 teaspoon salt

Let stand 30 min. Drain and dry on absorbent paper.

Heat in the skillet

¼ cup olive oil

Add eggplant and zucchini and cook until lightly browned, turning slices occasionally. Remove vegetables with a slotted spoon and set aside.

Heat in the skillet

¼ cup olive oil

Add and cook about 5 min.

2 onions, thinly sliced
2 green peppers, thinly sliced

Stir in

2 cloves garlic, crushed or minced

Top vegetables with

3 tomatoes, peeled and cut in strips

Cover tightly and cook over medium heat 5 min. Gently stir in eggplant, zucchini and

1 cup sliced pimiento-stuffed olives
¼ cup snipped parsley
1 teaspoon salt
¼ teaspoon pepper

Cook, covered, over low heat 20 min. Remove cover and cook 5 min., basting with juices in bottom of skillet.

Serve hot or chilled garnished with parsley.

About 8 servings

VEGETABLE MEDLEY ORIENTALE

Put into a large heavy skillet over low heat

2 pkgs. (10 oz. each) frozen broccoli
spears
1 pkg. (10 oz.) frozen green peas
1 large carrot, sliced with a fancy cutter
1 cup diagonally sliced celery

Sprinkle generously with **monosodium glutamate.** As frozen vegetables heat gently break apart with a fork.

Meanwhile, combine

1 can (10½ oz.) condensed chicken
broth
3 tablespoons soy sauce
2 to 3 tablespoons sugar
¼ teaspoon ginger
1 clove garlic, crushed

Mix well and pour over vegetables in skillet. Cover tightly and bring to boiling; cook about 10 min., or until vegetables are tender (but not soft), basting occasionally.

Cook, following package directions

1 pkg. (7 oz.) frozen Chinese pea pods

Remove cooked vegetables from skillet with a slotted spoon and keep warm over low heat.

Stir into sauce in skillet a blend of

1 tablespoon cornstarch
2 tablespoons cold water

Bring to boiling; cook and stir about 1 min. Transfer cooked, well-drained pea pods to a large heated serving platter. Season with

monosodium glutamate. Spoon some of the sauce over pods. Cover with the hot vegetables and spoon the remaining sauce over all.

About 8 servings

CORN CASSEROLE A LA MEXICALI

Set out a large heavy skillet and a 1½-qt. casserole; grease the casserole.

Cut from fresh corn ears
2 cups corn kernels (3 to 4 ears)
Combine corn in a bowl with
2 tablespoons all-purpose flour
1 teaspoon salt
½ teaspoon chili powder
⅛ teaspoon pepper
Dash cayenne pepper
12 pitted ripe olives, coarsely chopped

Heat in the skillet
1 tablespoon fat
Add and cook about 3 min.
1 medium onion, finely chopped
Add to the corn mixture. Combine and mix with corn
1 cup tomato purée
1 bay leaf, crushed
¼ teaspoon oregano
Turn into casserole and sprinkle with
1 cup shredded sharp Cheddar cheese

Set in a 350°F oven about 15 min., or until cheese is melted. *6 to 8 servings*

SAUTEED CARROTS WITH ONIONS AND GREEN PEPPER

Cook in 1 in. boiling water in a saucepan 10 to 12 min., or until almost tender
3 cups sliced carrots

Meanwhile, heat in a skillet or heavy saucepan
2 tablespoons butter or margarine
Add and sauté over medium heat about 3 min.
½ cup sliced onion, separated in rings
½ cup diced green pepper
Drain parboiled carrots; season with
½ teaspoon salt
Add to skillet; cover tightly and cook until carrots are tender. Sprinkle with
½ teaspoon freshly ground pepper
Serve at once. *4 servings*

CREAMED VEGETABLES IN TOAST CUPS

Prepare
1 cup shredded cabbage
2 cups sliced carrots
2 medium onions, sliced

Combine the vegetables in a heavy saucepan and add only enough boiling salted water to cover bottom of pan. Cover tightly and cook only until carrots are crisp-tender. (Do not overcook vegetables and do not drain them.)

Combine in a jar
1 cup cream or half and half
3 tablespoons all-purpose flour
¼ teaspoon salt
Cover jar and shake to mix ingredients. Stir the mixture into vegetables and liquid in saucepan and stir gently over medium heat until sauce is thickened. Add and mix well
2 tablespoons butter or margarine

Serve in **French Toast Cups** (below).
6 to 8 servings

—FRENCH TOAST CUPS

Scoop out centers of **6 slices French bread** (sliced 2 in. thick). Brush cut surfaces with **melted butter or margarine**. Place on baking sheet and heat in 400° to 425°F oven until lightly toasted.

CELERY CABBAGE CASSEROLE

Set out two 1-qt. saucepans and a 1½-qt. shallow baking dish.

Prepare
3 cups diagonally sliced celery
(cut ¾ in. thick)
2 cups finely shredded green cabbage

Combine in saucepan
1 cup boiling water
1 bouillon cube (beef or vegetable)
Add the sliced celery, cover and cook 10 to 15 min., or until celery is crisp-tender.

While celery is cooking, cook cabbage in ½ cup boiling salted water in a covered saucepan until crisp-tender. Drain thoroughly. Drain

celery and reserve ¾ cup of cooking liquid. Combine liquid with
1 can (10½ oz.) condensed cream of mushroom soup
⅛ teaspoon seasoned pepper
1 tablespoon instant minced onion
Set aside.

Toss together in a large bowl the celery, cabbage and
1 can (5 oz.) water chestnuts, drained and sliced
1 canned pimiento, drained and cut in strips
Mix thoroughly with the soup. Turn into the casserole and sprinkle with
¾ cup shredded sharp Cheddar cheese
Top evenly with
1 can (5 oz.) chow mein noodles

Heat in a 375°F oven 15 to 20 min., or until mixture is bubbly and topping is golden brown.
About 8 servings

STUFFED ZUCCHINI "BOATS"

Set out a large heavy skillet and a shallow baking dish. Grease the baking dish.

Prepare and set aside
½ cup diced onion
½ cup chopped green pepper
1½ cups diced celery
1 large tomato, peeled and chopped

Wash and cut into halves lengthwise
4 or 5 medium zucchini
Scoop out centers and chop the scooped-out portion. Cook zucchini "boats" in boiling salted water about 3 min., or until crisp-tender (do not overcook). Drain and set aside.

Meanwhile, heat in skillet
2 tablespoons butter or margarine
Add the chopped onion and green pepper and cook 3 to 5 min. Stir in
1 pkg. chicken gravy mix
1 teaspoon salt
Add the chopped celery and tomato, the chopped zucchini, and
1 cup shredded Cheddar cheese
Dash pepper
Dash garlic powder

Vegetable Scrapple

Toss to mix well and fill parboiled zucchini "boats" with the mixture. Spread leftover filling mixture in bottom of baking dish. Arrange "boats" on top. Dot with

⅓ cup butter or margarine

Sprinkle "boats" with

½ cup bread crumbs

Bake at 400°F 20 to 25 min. The last 5 min. of baking, garnish "boats" with **ripe olives**.

6 to 8 servings

ALL GREEN VEGETABLE SKILLET

Wash thoroughly and thinly slice

1 lb. zucchini (about 4 cups, sliced)

Cook, following package directions (do not overcook)

1 boil-in-a-bag pkg. (about 9 oz.) diagonally sliced green beans in butter sauce

1 boil-in-a-bag pkg. (about 10 oz.) lima beans in butter sauce

Meanwhile, heat in a large skillet

¼ cup butter or margarine

Add and cook 2 to 3 min.

¼ cup chopped onion

Add zucchini slices. Sprinkle generously with **Monosodium glutamate**

Cover tightly and cook over medium heat about 15 min., stirring occasionally. Mix in the cooked vegetables (with their sauces) and

½ cup snipped parsley

Season to taste with

Seasoned salt or pepper

Spoon into a warm serving dish.

About 8 servings

SAUCY TOMATO BEAN CASSEROLE

Set out a large skillet and a 1½-qt. casserole.

Heat in the skillet

3 tablespoons vegetable oil

Add and cook over medium heat 3 to 5 min.

1 medium onion, chopped

½ cup chopped green pepper

Mix in

2 cans (8 oz. each) or 1 can (15 oz.) tomato sauce with tomato bits

1 pkg (1¼ oz.) chili, chili dog, or sloppy joe seasoning mix

1 can (16 or 17 oz.) lima beans, drained

1 can (16 oz.) cut green beans, drained

½ cup shredded sharp Cheddar cheese

Toss lightly and turn into the casserole. Sprinkle with an additional ½ cup shredded cheese.

Set in a 350°F oven about 35 min., or until mixture is bubbly.

8 to 10 servings

MIXED VEGETABLE CASSEROLE

Set out a shallow 1½-qt. casserole or baking dish.

Cook, following package directions

1 pkg. (10 oz.) frozen mixed vegetables

1 pkg. (10 oz.) frozen cauliflower

1 pkg. (10 oz.) frozen green peas

Meanwhile, heat in a small saucepan

¼ cup butter or margarine

Stir in and cook until bubbly

¼ cup all-purpose flour

Remove from heat and stir in

1 cup cream or half and half

1 cup chicken broth (dissolve 1 chicken bouillon cube in 1 cup boiling water)

Return to heat and bring mixture rapidly to boiling; cook and stir 1 to 2 min.

Blend in

1 teaspoon prepared mustard

1 tablespoon prepared horseradish

4 drops Tabasco

Thoroughly drain the cooked vegetables and toss lightly in the casserole. Pour sauce over all and top with

1½ cups soft bread crumbs

1 cup shredded sharp Cheddar cheese

Heat in a 400°F oven about 20 min., or until cheese is melted and crumbs are lightly browned.

About 8 servings

CHILLED VEGETABLE PLATTER

Chill thoroughly

1 can (14½ oz.) mixed green-tipped and white asparagus spears, drained

1 can (14½ oz.) green asparagus spears, drained

1 jar (16 oz.) small whole beets, drained

Arrange vegetables attractively on a chilled serving plate and serve with **Sour Cream Mayonnaise (page 413)**.

6 to 8 servings

VEGETABLE SCRAPPLE

Lightly grease a 9x5x3-in. loaf pan.

Prepare and set aside

½ cup (about 1 medium) finely chopped onion

⅓ cup (about 1 medium) finely chopped carrot

¼ cup finely chopped green pepper

Pour into top of double boiler

3½ cups boiling water

Add slowly, stirring constantly, a mixture of

1¼ cups yellow corn meal

1 tablespoon salt

⅛ teaspoon pepper

Cook over direct heat until thickened, stirring constantly. Add the chopped vegetables and

2 tablespoons finely chopped pimiento

1 teaspoon monosodium glutamate

Set over simmering water and cook 1 hr.

Meanwhile, chop coarsely

1 cup (about 5 oz.) peanuts

Stir peanuts into cooked corn meal mixture. Pour into the pan, spreading to edges. Chill in refrigerator about 4 hrs.

Remove from refrigerator and cut into slices 1 in. thick.

Heat in a skillet over medium heat

2 tablespoons fat

Arrange slices in skillet. Cook at one time only as many slices as will lie flat in skillet. When lightly browned on one side, turn and brown other side.

Serve warm.

6 to 8 servings

Salads and salad dressings

Because of their crispness, their refreshing flavor, and their eye appeal, salads have become an essential part of our meals. They are family fare because they are packed with the foods everyone needs each day, and they are party fare because they are so beautiful, so flavorful, so satisfying—and so easy to serve. Salads come in many forms. There are first course salads, highly flavored and designed to whet the appetite; main course salads which, if used in place of a hot main dish, should provide comparable food value; salads accompanying the main course, which should be light and simple; and dessert salads, which include fruit gelatins, frozen salads, and assorted fresh fruit plates. With this unlimited variety of salads from which to choose, do not overlook the importance of salad dressings. Complete each of your salad creations with a perfectly blended, distinctively flavorful salad dressing.

SALAD POINTERS

Have all salad ingredients, bowls, and plates thoroughly chilled. With the exception of a very few hot salads, coldness is essential to the appeal of all salads.

Trim and rinse greens under cold running water, handling them carefully to avoid bruising. Shake off the excess moisture and then gently pat them *dry* before putting them into a plastic bag or the vegetable drawer, and into your refrigerator. Wet greens not only make watery salads; they present a surface to which an oil dressing cannot cling.

Allow ample time for chilling. Fine restaurants chill greens and other salad ingredients twenty-four hours before serving salad.

Greens should always be broken or torn, never cut (except in the case of head lettuce which is to be served in wedges or quarters).

Tomatoes may be peeled or not, as your family prefers, for use in salads. Unpeeled tomato shells or tomato cups are sturdier and keep their shape better; peeled ones are easier to cut with a salad fork.

Tomatoes cut in wedges or chunks are delicious additions to many tossed salads, but their juice tends to make the dressing watery unless they are added at the last moment before serving.

Fruits that tend to discolor after peeling or paring (such as avocado, banana, apples, fresh peaches and pears) should be brushed with pineapple or citrus fruit juice unless they are to be tossed immediately with an acid fruit or salad dressing.

The final assembling of ingredients for a salad of fresh fruits, vegetables or greens should be done *just* before serving. Many main dish salads, potato and macaroni salads, and cooked vegetable salads improve in flavor when the mixture is prepared an hour or so ahead of serving time and allowed to stand in the refrigerator to chill and blend the individual flavors. But even these mixtures should be combined with their green garnishes at the last moment.

Avoid unnecessary handling of salad materials. Salads should always have that fresh-from-the-refrigerator look which is so appealing to the eye and tempting to the taste. Arrange the fruits or vegetables on the salad plate if the salad requires it, but don't destroy that carefree look by *rearranging* them.

SALAD ACCOMPANIMENTS

Salads can be made still more tempting by serving them with appealing accompaniments. Often these are crisp and crunchy: **Melba toast, rye wafers, breadsticks** or **cheese pastry straws.** (Vary Melba toast by brushing it lightly with **butter** in which you have delicately browned **sesame seed;** or butter the toast and sprinkle with **poppy seed,** which need no toasting.) Another flavorful variation of Melba toast is made by brushing thin slices of **"icebox" rye bread** with **garlic butter** and oven-toasting them until crisp and slightly browned.

Dainty alternatives to the crisp accompaniments are **finger sandwiches** with an assortment of fillings: **watercress** or **cucumber** with **butter, cream cheese** with **chopped nuts** or **olives** (or both), **peanut butter,** or **jelly. Celery Whirls** (page 421) are a pleasing accompaniment which becomes part of the salad.

GREEN AND VEGETABLE SALADS

SALAD GREEN VARIETIES AND PREPARATION

The many varieties of greens star in the tossed salad and form the background of other salads. Select greens that are fresh, blemish-free and crisp. In general, wash them before storing, drain thoroughly and gently pat dry with a soft, clean towel or absorbent paper. Place in the refrigerator in the vegetable drawer or a plastic bag, or wrap tightly in aluminum foil or other moisture-vaporproof material to prevent wilting.

Never soak greens when washing them. If necessary, crisp them by placing for a short time in ice and water. Before using, remove all moisture left from washing or crisping.

Lettuce—Discard bruised and wilted leaves; rinse, drain and dry. (For *Lettuce Cups,* remove the core from head lettuce with a sharp, pointed knife; let cold water run into the core cavity to loosen the leaves; drain thoroughly; gently pull leaves from head; cut off heavy, coarse ends; pat dry.) The following are types of lettuce: *Head or Iceberg*—firm, compact head with medium-green outside leaves, pale-green heart. *Butterhead or Boston*—loose, lighter-weight head with light-green outside leaves, light-yellow heart; less crisp than iceberg. *Romaine or Cos*—elongated green head with coarser leaves having stronger flavor than iceberg. *Bibb or Limestone*—head similar in size and shape to Boston; deep-green leaves with delicate flavor. *Leaf*—leafy bunches of curly-edged leaves; many varieties are grown commercially and in the home garden. A bright attractive touch for lettuce is achieved by dipping the curly edges of leaves in a paste made of two parts of paprika and one part of water.

Cabbage—Store in a cool place without washing. Discard bruised and wilted outside leaves, rinse, cut into quarters and remove core; chop or shred as directed in the recipe. The following are varieties of cabbage: *Early or new*—pointed heads with light-green leaves. *Danish-type*—staple winter cabbage: compact head having pale-green or white leaves. *Savoy*—round head of yellowish, crimped leaves. *Celery or Chinese*—long, looser head of pale-green to white leaves.

Endive—Discard bruised and wilted leaves; rinse; drain; dry. The following are varieties of endive: *Curly endive* (*often called chicory*)—bunchy head with narrow, ragged-edged curly leaves; dark green outside, pale-yellow heart; pleasantly bitter flavor. *Escarole*—(*broad-leaf endive*)—bunchy head of broad leaves that do not curl at tips; dark-green outer leaves, pale-yellow heart; less bitter than curly endive. *French endive* (*Witloof chicory*)—thin, elongated stalk, usually bleached while growing.
Kale—Curly-leafed member of cabbage family; dark-green; leaves may have slightly browned edges as a result of frost in growing season. Trim off tough stems and bruised or wilted leaves; wash; drain; dry.
Parsley—Discard coarse stems and bruised leaves; wash gently but thoroughly in cold water; drain and shake off excess water; pat dry. Store in tightly covered jar or plastic bag in refrigerator.
Spinach—Discard tough stems, roots and bruised or wilted leaves. Wash leaves thoroughly by lifting up and down several times in a large amount of cold water; lift leaves out completely and pour off water; repeat in several changes of water until all sand and grit are removed. Drain; pat dry.
Watercress—See Parsley. Watercress may be stored without washing, if preferred. Let the tied bunch stand in a jar or bowl containing enough cold water to reach about halfway up the stems. Cover and store in refrigerator. When ready to use, snip off the amount needed, rinse, drain and shake off excess water.
Other greens—*Field salad*—spoon-shaped leaves; *finocchio*—anise-flavored stalk (serve like celery); *Swiss chard and beet, dandelion, mustard and turnip greens*—use tops only.

GREEN SALAD
(Insalata Verde)

▲ Base Recipe

Wash in cold water
  1 large head lettuce
Or use an equal amount, approximately, of another fresh salad green, alone or in combination—curly endive, romaine, small dandelion greens, escarole or chicory. Cut out core of lettuce. Separate lettuce leaves. Remove any thick stalks or bruised leaves. Drain, dry thoroughly and carefully. Tear lettuce into bite-size pieces, put into plastic bag or vegetable freshener. Chill in refrigerator at least 1 hr.

Just before serving, rub a wooden bowl with
  1 clove garlic, cut in halves
Put greens into bowl and pour over
  **6 tablespoons Italian Salad Dressing
    (page 412)**
Using a salad spoon and fork, turn and toss the greens until well coated with dressing and no liquid remains on the bottom of bowl.

About 6 servings, depending upon size of lettuce head

—GREEN SALAD WITH
ANCHOVY DRESSING
(Insalata Verde con Accighue)

Follow ▲ Recipe. Substitute **Anchovy Dressing** (page 412) for Italian Salad Dressing. Add to lettuce in bowl, **2 tomatoes**, cut in wedges, **¼ cup diced celery** and **½ cup diced ripe olives**.

—MIXED SALAD
(Insalata Mista)

Follow ▲ Recipe. Add **¼ cup chopped cucumber**, **¼ cup chopped celery**, **¼ cup sliced radishes** and **¼ cup diced ripe olives**.

GREEN GODDESS SALAD

▲ Base Recipe

Prepare and chill
  **Green Goddess Salad Dressing
    (page 414)**

Rinse, discard bruised leaves, drain and dry
  **Salad greens (such as lettuce, curly
    endive or escarole)**
Using as much of each green as desired, tear into pieces enough greens to yield about 2 qts. Put into a large plastic bag or vegetable freshener. Chill in refrigerator.

When ready to serve, turn salad greens into a chilled bowl. Add the dressing and gently turn and toss until greens are evenly coated.

Serve immediately.   *6 to 8 servings*

—GREEN GODDESS SALAD
WITH CRAB MEAT

Follow ▲ Recipe. Drain, remove and discard bony tissue, and separate **2 cans (6½ oz. each) crab meat** (about 2⅜ cups, drained). Lightly toss crab meat with salad greens.

—GREEN GODDESS SALAD
WITH SHRIMP

Follow ▲ Recipe. Cook **1 lb. fresh shrimp with shells** (see Cooked Shrimp, page 294). Lightly toss shrimp with salad greens.

CHEF'S SPECIAL TOSSED SALAD

Prepare
  2 Hard-Cooked Eggs (page 133)
Put into a small bowl, cover and set in refrigerator to chill.

Discard bruised leaves, cut out core, allow cold water to run into cavity, and drain
  1 medium head lettuce
Dry lettuce carefully. Tear lettuce into pieces and put into a large salad bowl.

Wash, discard bruised leaves from, and dry thoroughly with absorbent paper (using as much of each green as desired)
  Curly endive
  Escarole
  Chicory
  Romaine
  Spinach
Tear greens into pieces. Add to the salad bowl.

Rinse and thinly slice into salad bowl
  1 medium firm cucumber
Put salad bowl into large plastic bag or cover with aluminum foil and set in refrigerator to chill at least 1 hr.

Rinse and dip, one at a time, into boiling water for a few seconds
  2 medium tomatoes
Immediately peel tomatoes and cut away stem ends. Put into small bowl, cover and set in refrigerator to chill.

Meanwhile, prepare
  Croutons (page 39)
Remove salad bowl from refrigerator.

Prepare
  1 small onion

Thinly slice onion and separate into rings; cut the tomatoes into wedges; slice the hard-cooked eggs; add to salad bowl and toss lightly.

Set out
**Blue Cheese Salad Dressing
(page 414)**
Slowly pour dressing over salad while gently turning and tossing; use only enough to coat all ingredients lightly.

Add Croutons and toss quickly, Serve immediately.

CAESAR SALAD

▲ Base Recipe

Set out a skillet and a large salad bowl.

Put into a small screw-top jar
**¼ cup salad oil
¼ cup lemon juice
¼ teaspoon Worcestershire sauce
1 clove garlic, cut in halves**
Cover and shake until mixture is well blended. Chill dressing in refrigerator about 1 hr. to allow flavors to blend.

Wash, discard bruised leaves from, and dry thoroughly with absorbent paper (using as much of each green as desired)
**Curly endive
Lettuce
Romaine
Watercress**
Tear into pieces enough greens to yield about 2 qts. Put into a large plastic bag and chill in refrigerator at least 1 hr.

Meanwhile, prepare croutons. Stack and, if desired, trim crusts from
2 slices toasted bread
Cut bread into ½-in. cubes and set aside.

When the dressing is chilled, remove from refrigerator. Remove and reserve the garlic clove. Return dressing to refrigerator.

Heat in the skillet over low heat
2 tablespoons salad oil
Add to skillet the garlic clove reserved from the salad dressing, toasted-bread cubes and
1 clove garlic, cut in halves
Increase heat and toss until all sides of bread cubes are well coated with oil and are brown. Remove skillet from heat. Discard garlic.

Rub the salad bowl with cut surface of
1 clove garlic, cut in halves
Discard garlic clove. Remove salad greens from refrigerator and put into the salad bowl. Sprinkle over greens a mixture of
**¾ cup grated Parmesan cheese
½ teaspoon salt
½ teaspoon dry mustard
¼ teaspoon pepper**
Shake the dressing and pour over the greens.

Break into a small bowl
1 egg
Add to the seasoned greens. Using salad fork

and spoon, gently turn and toss salad until greens are well coated with salad dressing and no trace of egg remains. Add the croutons and toss lightly to mix thoroughly.

Top with
Anchovy fillets (12 to 15)
Serve at once.   *6 to 8 servings*

—BLUE CHEESE SPECIAL

Follow ▲ Recipe. Substitute ½ cup (about 2 oz.) **crumbled blue cheese** for the Parmesan cheese. Omit dry mustard and anchovy fillets.

FRENCH ENDIVE SALAD WITH MELBOURNE DRESSING

Prepare and chill
Melbourne Salad Dressing (page 412)

Meanwhile, rinse and drain
Leaves of French endive
Put into a plastic bag and set in refrigerator to chill.

Just before serving, arrange leaves of endive on individual salad plates. Shake the dressing well and drizzle over the endive. (Store remaining dressing in a covered container in refrigerator.) Serve immediately.

SHADES O' GREEN SALAD

▲ Base Recipe

One of those enticing arrangements of cool greens that you will want to cast as a star in your repertory of very special salads.

Chill 6 individual salad bowls in refrigerator.

Wash (see Spinach Salad, page 360) and drain thoroughly
3 cups (about 3 oz.) spinach
Use part of the spinach to line the salad bowls. Set remainder aside.

Rinse, discard bruised leaves and pat dry with a clean towel or absorbent paper
½ head lettuce
Set aside.

Coarsely chop or dice
**4 stalks Pascal celery
½ green pepper
1 cucumber, rinsed**

Tear lettuce and reserved spinach into pieces. Toss chopped vegetables lightly with lettuce, spinach and
2 tablespoons chopped chives
Add and toss lightly to coat thoroughly
⅓ cup french dressing
Arrange individual portions of salad in the chilled bowls.

Pit and slice
6 green olives
Rinse, cut into halves, pit, peel and slice
1 small avocado

Caesar Salad

Garnish salads with avocado and olive slices.
6 servings

—ROMAINE SALAD BOWL

Follow ▲ Recipe. Substitute **Tarragon French Dressing** (page 411) for the French Dressing. Substitute **1 head romaine** for the spinach. Omit olive and avocado garnish.

—GREEN AND WHITE SALAD BOWL

Follow ▲ Recipe. Substitute **Roquefort French Dressing** (page 411) for the French Dressing. Lightly toss with salad greens **1 cup raw cauliflowerets** (bite-size), washed and soaked. Omit olive and avocado garnish.

—SURPRISE GREEN SALAD BOWL

Prepare and chill **Roquefort or Blue Cheese Stuffer** (see Celery Whirls, page 421). Stuff **Pascal celery stalks.** Follow ▲ Recipe. Omit olive and avocado garnish. When ready to serve, cut stuffed celery into crosswise pieces and toss lightly with salad greens and dressing.

—CHEF'S SALAD BOWL

Follow ▲ Recipe. Substitute a large bowl for individual bowls. Omit chives, olives and avocado. If desired, substitute or add other salad greens such as **curly endive, romaine, Bibb** or **leaf lettuce.** Hard-cook, chill and slice **3 eggs.** Clean and slice enough radishes to yield **½ cup sliced radishes.** Rinse, peel and chill **2 medium tomatoes.** Cut each tomato into 6 wedges. Cut into thin strips enough cooked chicken and Swiss or Cheddar cheese to yield **1 cup cooked chicken strips** (see Stewed Chicken, page 259) and **1 cup cheese strips.** Cut into thin strips enough cooked **ham, tongue, bologna** or **salami** to yield 1 cup. Canned luncheon meat of cooked meats such as pork, lamb, beef or veal may also

359

be used. When ready to serve, fill the bowl with the salad greens; lightly toss with the prepared vegetables and egg slices. Pour some of the dressing over salad mixture. Toss lightly to coat evenly. Arrange cheese, chicken and meat strips over salad. If desired, granish with **anchovy fillets.**

LETTUCE AND SOUR CREAM SALAD
(Sur Flöte Krem for Salad)

▲ *Base Recipe*

Cut out core and discard bruised leaves, rinse with cold water and drain well
- **1 medium head lettuce**

Chill lettuce in refrigerator.

Blend thoroughly
- **1 cup dairy sour cream**
- **1 tablespoon plus 1 teaspoon sugar**
- **1 tablespoon vinegar**
- **1 tablespoon grated onion**
- **2 teaspoons prepared horseradish**
- **1 teaspoon salt**

Chill thoroughly in refrigerator.

When ready to serve, tear lettuce into bite-size pieces and put into a bowl. Spoon the sour cream mixture over the lettuce and toss lightly to coat thoroughly. Sprinkle around outer edge of salad
- **Finely chopped parsley**

Sprinkle center of salad with
- **Paprika**

Serve immediately. *6 servings*

—LETTUCE AND WHIPPED CREAM SALAD
(Piska Flöta med Salat Blador)

Follow ▲ Recipe. Omit sour cream mixture. Put a bowl, beater and **1½ cups heavy cream** into the refrigerator to chill. When ready to serve salad, beat the cream, using the chilled bowl and beater until it is of medium consistency (piles softly). Beat in with final few strokes **3 tablespoons sugar** and **¼ teaspoon salt.** Gently stir in **1 tablespoon vinegar.** Omit paprika.

SPINACH SALAD

Remove and discard tough stems, roots and bruised leaves from
- **1 lb. spinach**

Wash leaves thoroughly by lifting up and down several times in a large amount of cold water and lifting leaves out of water each time before pouring off water. When free from sand and gritty material, drain; tear leaves into bite-size pieces. Sprinkle and toss with
- **1½ tablespoons salad oil**
- **1½ tablespoons lemon juice**

Cover and set in refrigerator to chill.

Prepare and chill
- **2 Hard-Cooked Eggs (page 133)**

For Dressing (About 1 pt.)—Mix
- **1 egg, slightly beaten**
- **¼ cup ketchup**
- **1½ teaspoons sugar**
- **½ teaspoon Worcestershire sauce**
- **½ teaspoon salt**
- **½ teaspoon paprika**
- **½ teaspoon dry mustard**
- **¼ teaspoon monosodium glutamate**

Measure and set aside
- **1 cup salad oil**

Mix
- **1 to 2 tablespoons cider vinegar**
- **2 tablespoons lemon juice**

Alternately add oil and vinegar mixture in small amounts to egg mixture. Beat constantly with a rotary beater. Add slowly, beating constantly
- **2½ tablespoons warm water**

To serve salad, finely chop the eggs and sprinkle over spinach. Toss lightly. Pour some of the Dressing over spinach mixture and toss to mix thoroughly. Use only enough dressing to coat greens well.

Serve at once. *6 to 8 servings*

Note: Remaining dressing may be covered and stored in refrigerator.

COLORFUL VEGETABLE SALAD

Prepare
- **1 medium cucumber, sliced**
- **¾ cup cooked peas**
- **¾ cup diced cooked carrots**
- **¼ cup chopped green pepper**
- **¼ cup sliced pimiento-stuffed olives**

Rinse, cut out stem end and slice
- **1 medium tomato**

Peel, rinse, cut off green tops to within 3 in. of white part, and slice
- **6 green onions**

Mix the vegetables, tossing lightly.

Blend
- **¾ cup mayonnaise**
- **1 tablespoon chili sauce**
- **1 teaspoon prepared horseradish**

Turn dressing over vegetables and toss lightly. Serve in crisp **lettuce cups.** *6 servings*

FARMER'S CHOP SUEY

Here is a traditional summertime favorite, a crisp, colorful, cooling salad made from some of the most refreshing vegetables yielded by the garden. Sour cream does the work of a dressing, and it does it so provocatively that you will want to put Farmer's Chop Suey high on the list of your serve-often salads.

Set out a salad bowl and put the vegetables into it as they are prepared.

Rinse, pare and cut into small cubes
- **1 large firm cucumber**

Wash, cut off root and stem ends, and thinly slice enough red radishes to yield
- **1 cup sliced red radishes**

Peel, cut off roots, rinse and cut crosswise
- **6 green onions (use some green tops)**

Put salad bowl into a plastic bag or cover tightly and set in refrigerator to chill for at least 1 hr.

Rinse and chill in refrigerator
- **3 medium tomatoes**

Just before serving, remove tomatoes from refrigerator, cut out stem ends, cut tomatoes into chunks and toss gently with vegetables in salad bowl. Season with a mixture of
- **¼ teaspoon salt**
- **⅛ teaspoon pepper**

Pour over the salad and mix lightly
- **1½ cups chilled dairy sour cream**

Serve immediately. *6 servings*

Note: Lettuce, torn into bite-size pieces, and chopped green pepper may be added.

VEGETABLE SALAD BOWL WITH AVOCADO CHEESE DRESSING

Chill a large wooden salad bowl and 6 individual salad bowls.

For Dressing—Rinse, peel, cut in half, pit and force through a sieve or mash with a fork

1 medium ripe avocado

Stir in

1 tablespoon lemon juice

Blend in

1 cup cream-style cottage cheese, sieved

½ cup dairy sour cream

½ teaspoon prepared horseradish

¼ teaspoon Worcestershire sauce

½ teaspoon salt

Few grains cayenne pepper

Cover and chill.   *About 2 cups dressing*

For Salad—Rinse, discard bruised leaves, drain and dry

Salad greens (such as head, Boston, or Bibb lettuce, spinach and romaine)

Using as much of each green as desired, tear into pieces enough greens to yield about 2 qts. Put into a large plastic bag or a vegetable freshener. Chill in the refrigerator.

Rinse, pare, slice and chill

½ medium firm cucumber

Cut into pieces or slices and chill

3 stalks celery

Rinse and chill

2 medium ripe tomatoes

A few minutes before serving, remove tomatoes from refrigerator, cut out stem ends, cut into chunks and set aside.

To Complete Salad—Rub the large salad bowl with the cut surfaces of

1 clove garlic, cut in half

Turn salad greens into the bowl. Arrange on top of greens the cucumber, celery and tomatoes. Serve immediately with dressing spooned over each serving. If desired, toss lightly before serving.   *8 servings*

VEGETABLE PATCH SALAD

At least once a day fresh greens are washed, dried and chilled and the Creole salad bowl is rubbed with garlic. Simple salads with sharply seasoned French dressings are the Creoles' delight. Creoles also hold dearly to the idea of tossing these salads at the table—no salad of greens should wait for the guest.

Cut out core and discard bruised and wilted leaves from

1 large head lettuce

Rinse with cold water, drain and pat dry with a soft clean towel or absorbent paper. Store in a plastic bag or in vegetable compartment in refrigerator.

Other salad greens that can be used, alone or in combination, are chicory, watercress, small dandelion greens, chervil, parsley or curly endive. Wash thoroughly in cold water, drain and pat dry with a soft clean towel or absorbent paper. Store and chill as for head lettuce.

Prepare and chill in refrigerator

French Dressing I or one of the variations (page 410)

(It is a wise idea to prepare several dressings and store them in the refrigerator. Make use of them in other food preparation and for variety in tossed salads.)

Just before serving salad, rub a wooden salad bowl with

1 clove garlic, cut in halves

Tear chilled lettuce or other greens into bite-size pieces. Put into salad bowl. Pour about 6 tablespoons dressing over lettuce. Lightly toss the lettuce until it is well coated with the dressing and no liquid remains on the bottom of the bowl.

Other fresh vegetables such as green pepper strips, tomato chunks, radish, cucumber and onion slices frequently share the limelight with the crisp greens.

Cooked vegetables such as green beans, cauliflower, beets, asparagus or artichokes are used. Sometimes alone, sometimes in combination with cooked or fresh vegetables, the Creoles toss them with their favorite French dressing.
About 6 servings, depending upon size of lettuce head

ROYAL SWISS CHEESE SALAD BOWL

Cut into thin strips

¼ to ½ lb. natural Swiss cheese

Put cheese into a shallow bowl and cover with

French Dressing (page 410)

Marinate (page 10) in refrigerator 1 hr.

Wash, discard bruised leaves from, drain thoroughly and pat dry

Bibb lettuce

Leaf lettuce

Watercress

Arrange Bibb and leaf lettuce in a large salad bowl. Fill center with watercress. Put salad bowl into plastic bag or cover with aluminum foil. Chill in refrigerator at least 1 hr.

Drain marinated cheese strips. Arrange in salad

Vegetable Patch Salad

bowl on both sides of watercress. Serve with additional French dressing.

MAINE SALAD BOWLS

Rinse, drain and pat dry

Romaine or other salad greens

Tear into bite-size pieces, cover and chill in refrigerator at least 1 hr.

Meanwhile, prepare

2 Hard-Cooked Eggs (page 133)

Mix and chill in refrigerator

½ cup mayonnaise

3 tablespoons chili sauce

1 tablespoon minced onion

½ teaspoon prepared horseradish

Set aside to drain

2 cans (3¼ oz. each) sardines

Cut into 8 strips or wedges

¼ lb. sharp Cheddar cheese

Slice the hard-cooked eggs. Line 4 individual salad bowls with the greens. Arrange several sardines and three egg slices in each bowl. Add two cheese strips to each bowl. Serve with the salad dressing.   *4 servings*

ANCHOVY-STUFFED ARTICHOKE SALAD

A creamy stuffing complements artichokes.

Prepare and cook (page 362)

4 medium artichokes

Royal Swiss Cheese Salad Bowl and Maine Salad Bowls

Royal Swiss Cheese Salad Bowl and Maine Salad Bowls

Gourmet Artichoke Salad

Spread artichokes open and pull out center leaves. Using a spoon, remove and discard the choke or fuzzy part in center. Scrape pulpy, edible portion from center leaves and reserve for filling. Chill artichokes in refrigerator until ready to stuff.

Clean and finely chop
6 medium mushrooms
Cream until thoroughly blended
1 pkg. (3 oz.) cream cheese
2 tablespoons anchovy paste
Blend in the mushrooms and reserved artichoke pulp with
1 teaspoon minced onion
Cover and put into refrigerator to chill.

When ready to serve, spoon chilled filling into the "cup" formed by the outer leaves and heart of the artichoke.

Serve the stuffed artichokes on individual salad plates, garnished with **lemon wedges.**

4 servings

GOURMET ARTICHOKE SALAD

With a sharp knife, cutting straight across, trim 1 in. from tops of
4 medium artichokes
Cut off stems about 1 in. from base and remove outside lower leaves. Trim off with scissors and discard the tips of uncut leaves. Let stand in cold salted water for a few minutes to remove any dust or small insects which may have settled in the artichokes. Rinse in clear water and drain upside down.

Cook artichokes, uncovered, in boiling salted water to cover, adding to water
1 tablespoon lemon juice
Cook 25 to 45 min., or until a leaf can be easily pulled from artichoke. (Cooking time will depend upon size of artichokes.) If more water is needed to keep artichokes covered during cooking, add boiling water.

Remove artichokes and drain upside down so that all water can run out. Cut off remainder of the stem. Chill artichokes in refrigerator until ready to serve.

Serve the artichokes on individual salad plates with **mayonnaise.** Garnish with **lemon slices.**

4 servings

Note: To eat artichokes, pull out the leaves, dip in mayonnaise and eat one by one by drawing them between the teeth to remove only the tender portion at the base. Discard the less tender portion. If choke is present, cut it out with knife and fork after leaves are eaten, and discard it. Cut heart or base into pieces and eat with a fork.

MARINATED GREEN BEAN SALAD

▲ Base Recipe

Put into a bowl
3 cups cooked green or wax beans
Combine in a saucepan
1⅓ cups cider vinegar
⅔ cup water
½ cup sugar
1 onion, cut in halves
1 tablespoon mixed pickling spices
Cook, stirring until sugar is dissolved. Bring to boiling. Remove from heat; pour over the green beans. Lightly toss together. Cool. Refrigerate overnight.

To serve, drain beans; remove the onion. Put beans into salad bowl; or serve on lettuce-lined individual salad plates. Garnish with thinly sliced **onion rings** and **pimiento strips.**

About 6 servings

—GREEN BEAN SALAD PARMESAN

Follow ▲ Recipe. Lightly toss **⅓ cup grated Parmesan cheese** and **⅓ cup chopped onion** with beans before serving. Omit onion rings.

GREEN BEAN SALAD I
(Grüner Bohnensalat)

▲ Base Recipe

Wash, cut off and discard ends from, and cut into 1-in. pieces
1 lb. green beans
Cook (page 313) 10 to 15 min., or until beans are tender. Drain thoroughly if necessary, and put beans into a bowl. Keep beans warm.

Meanwhile, clean and cut into slices ⅛ in. thick
2 small onions
Separate onion slices into rings and put into bowl with beans.

Dice and fry until crisp, without pouring off drippings
6 slices bacon
Add to skillet containing bacon
⅓ cup vinegar
2½ tablespoons sugar
½ teaspoon salt
¼ teaspoon monosodium glutamate
Heat mixture to boiling, stirring well. Pour vinegar mixture over beans and onions and toss lightly to coat throughly.

4 servings

—WAX BEAN SALAD
(Wachsbohnensalat)

Follow ▲ Recipe. Substitute **wax beans** for the green beans.

GREEN BEAN SALAD II
(Zöldbab Saláta)

▲ Base Recipe

Cook
1 pkg. (9 oz.) frozen French-style green beans
Drain beans thoroughly and put into a bowl; set aside to cool.

Meanwhile, prepare
Oil-Vinegar Marinade (page 412)
Pour marinade over beans. Gently toss beans until well coated with marinade. Chill beans in refrigerator about 1 hr.; carefully turn beans occasionally.

Shortly before serving, panfry
4 slices bacon
Crumble bacon and set aside.

Green Bean Salad I

Drain beans thoroughly, and put into a bowl. Carefully mix the beans with the bacon.

3 or 4 servings

—GREEN BEAN SALAD WITH ONION
(Zöldbab Saláta Hagymával)

Follow ▲ Recipe. Add **1 tablespoon finely chopped onion** to green bean-bacon mixture.

KIDNEY BEAN SALAD

▲ Base Recipe

Prepare and dice
4 Hard-Cooked Eggs (page 133)

Meanwhile, drain, discarding liquid
1 can (16 oz.) kidney beans (about 2 cups, drained)
Toss lightly with diced eggs and
⅓ cup coarsely chopped sweet pickle
¼ cup finely chopped onion
3 tablespoons sweet pickle liquid or Jiffy French Dressing (page 411)

Blend
½ cup Blender Mayonnaise (page 413)
1 tablespoon pickle liquid
Pour over salad mixture and toss lightly to coat vegetables. Chill if time allows. Serve in crisp **lettuce cups.**

4 servings

—BOLOGNA KIDNEY BEAN SALAD

Follow ▲ Recipe. Reserve and slice Hard-Cooked Eggs for garnish. Omit mayonnaise mixture, if desired. Toss with vegetables **1 cup thinly sliced celery** and **½ cup shredded cabbage.** Wrap individual servings in large, thin slices of **bologna**; secure with **wooden picks.** Arrange on a platter with **hot buttered broccoli** (see How to Cook Vegetables, page 313) and garnish with reserved sliced Hard-Cooked Eggs.

HEARTY KIDNEY BEAN SALAD

Put into a bowl and toss lightly
1½ to 2 cups kidney beans, drained
½ cup (2 oz.) finely diced Cheddar cheese
½ cup chopped sweet pickle
½ cup chopped celery
⅓ cup chopped onion

Bologna Kidney Bean Salad

For Dressing—Mix
½ cup salad dressing
1 teaspoon cider vinegar
1 teaspoon sugar
1 teaspoon cream
¼ teaspoon salt
Few grains pepper
Turn dressing over salad mixture and toss lightly until vegetables are coated.

4 to 6 servings

RED KIDNEY BEAN SALAD
(Insalata di Fagioli)

Drain
1 can (16 oz.) kidney beans (about 1½ cups)
Combine beans with a mixture of
¼ cup wine vinegar
3 tablespoons olive oil
¼ teaspoon oregano
¼ teaspoon salt
⅛ teaspoon pepper
Blend in
¼ cup diced celery
2 tablespoons chopped onion
Chill in refrigerator. Serve in crisp **lettuce cups.**

4 servings

LIMA BEAN SALAD

Lightly toss together
2 cups cooked lima beans
1 tablespoon chopped pimiento
1 tablespoon chopped chives
Mix together
⅔ cup dairy sour cream
1 tablespoon wine vinegar
2 teaspoons lemon juice
and a mixture of
1 teaspoon sugar
¾ teaspoon salt
⅛ teaspoon white pepper
Add sour cream mixture to lima beans and toss lightly together until all beans are coated with dressing. Set in refrigerator to chill for at least 1 hr.

About 4 servings

BROCCOLI SALAD
(Insalata di Broccoli)

▲ Base Recipe

Prepare and cook (page 313) just until tender
1 lb. broccoli
Drain and chill in refrigerator.

When thoroughly chilled, sprinkle over broccoli a mixture of
3 tablespoons olive oil
3 tablespoons lemon juice
1 medium clove garlic, sliced thin
¼ teaspoon salt
⅛ teaspoon pepper

About 3 servings

—CAULIFLOWER SALAD
(Insalata di Cavolfiore)

Follow ▲ Recipe. Prepare and cook (page 313) **1 small potato.** Dice potato and chill in refrigerator. Substitute **1 medium head cauliflower** for broccoli. Separate into flowerets, prepare and cook (page 313) cauliflower. Combine diced potatoes with cauliflower. Substitute **wine vinegar** for the lemon juice and add **¼ teaspoon oregano.**

—GREEN BEAN SALAD
(Insalata di Fagiolini)

Follow ▲ Recipe. Substitute **½ lb. green beans** for the broccoli. Prepare and cook (page 313) green beans. Substitute **wine vinegar** for the lemon juice.

—ASPARAGUS SALAD
(Insalata di Asparagi)

Follow ▲ Recipe. Substitute **1 lb. asparagus** for the broccoli. Prepare and cook (page 313) asparagus.

CABBAGE SALAD

Remove and discard wilted outer leaves, rinse, cut into quarters (discarding core) and finely shred
1 head (about 2 lbs.) cabbage (about 2 qts., shredded)
Put cabbage into a large bowl and toss with
1 tablespoon salt
Let mixture stand 1 hr., tossing occasionally.

Meanwhile, combine in a small screw-top jar and set aside
⅓ cup wine vinegar
3 tablespoons salad oil
1 tablespoon sugar
⅛ teaspoon freshly ground pepper

Squeeze the cabbage, a small amount at a time, and discard the juice. Place cabbage into a salad bowl and add
¼ cup chopped onion
¼ cup chopped green pepper

Shake the dressing until well blended and pour over the salad. Using salad spoon and fork, turn and toss cabbage mixture until well coated with dressing.

Rinse and dip into boiling water for a few seconds
2 medium tomatoes
Peel; cut out and discard stem ends and cut each tomato into eighths. Arrange tomatoes over top of salad.

Chill salad in refrigerator 1 hr. before serving.

6 to 8 servings

CABBAGE AND PEANUT SALAD

Prepare
4 cups (about 1 lb.) shredded cabbage

Put cabbage into a bowl and set in refrigerator to chill.

Blend and set in refrigerator to chill
¾ cup mayonnaise
¼ cup sugar
2 tablespoons cider vinegar
¼ teaspoon monosodium glutamate
Few grains pepper
Shortly before serving, remove cabbage from refrigerator. Pour the chilled dressing over the cabbage. Toss lightly until cabbage is well coated.

Mix in
1 cup (about 5 oz.) salted Spanish peanuts
Serve immediately. *About 8 servings*

CREAMY CABBAGE SLAW I

▲ *Base Recipe*

Discard wilted outer leaves, rinse, cut into quarters and remove core, and chop or shred
1 lb. cabbage (about 4 cups, chopped)
Put cabbage into a bowl, cover and chill in refrigerator.

Blend and chill in refrigerator
⅓ cup mayonnaise
3 tablespoons dairy sour cream
2 teaspoons cider vinegar or lemon juice
1 teaspoon prepared mustard
2 drops Tabasco
and a mixture of
¾ teaspoon sugar
½ teaspoon salt
¼ teaspoon celery seed
⅛ teaspoon pepper

Before serving, pour the dressing over the cabbage. Toss lightly until cabbage is well coated. *About 8 servings*

—CABBAGE SLAW I

Follow ▲ Recipe for preparing cabbage; shred cabbage very finely. Omit mayonnaise mixture; substitute **¼ cup Cooked Salad Dressing** (page 416) mixed with **¼ cup heavy cream**, whipped. If desired, sprinkle completed salad lightly with **cayenne pepper**.

—TART CABBAGE SLAW

Follow ▲ Recipe for preparing cabbage; use 3 cups finely shredded cabbage. Omit mayonnaise mixture; mix **2½ tablespoons cider vinegar, 1 teaspoon grated onion** and a mixture of **1 tablespoon sugar, 1 teaspoon salt,** and **⅛ teaspoon pepper**. Pour over shredded cabbage and toss lightly.

CREAMY CABBAGE SLAW II

▲ *Base Recipe*

Toss together and set aside in a large bowl
4 cups shredded cabbage (about 1 lb. cabbage)
½ cup chopped onion
2 teaspoons celery seed

Put into a small bowl and blend well
½ cup dairy sour cream
2 tablespoons cider vinegar
2 tablespoons sugar
1 teaspoon salt
¼ teaspoon pepper
Pour over cabbage mixture and toss to coat evenly. Chill before serving. Sprinkle with
Paprika
8 servings

—SUNSHINE SLAW I

Follow ▲ Recipe. Toss **½ cup shredded carrot** and **½ cup chopped green pepper** with the cabbage mixture.

—CABBAGE SLAW II

Follow ▲ Recipe. Omit onion and celery seed. Substitute **mayonnaise** for the sour cream; blend in **¼ cup cream** and **2 teaspoons prepared mustard**. Substitute **2 to 3 tablespoons lemon juice** for vinegar.

CREAMY COLE SLAW

▲ *Base Recipe*

Blend thoroughly
½ cup dairy sour cream
½ cup mayonnaise
1 tablespoon lemon juice
2 teaspoons celery seed
1 teaspoon sugar
¼ teaspoon salt
⅛ teaspoon monosodium glutamate
Few grains cayenne pepper
Set in refrigerator to chill.

Prepare
4 cups (about 1 lb.) shredded cabbage
Put cabbage into a bowl and set in refrigerator to chill.

Shortly before serving, remove cabbage from refrigerator and pour over it enough of the chilled dressing to moisten. Toss lightly until cabbage is well coated.

Serve immediately. *6 to 8 servings*

—CREAMY APPLE COLE SLAW

Follow ▲ Recipe. Decrease sour cream to ¼ cup and shredded cabbage to 3 cups (about ¾ lb.). Substitute **pepper** for cayenne pepper. Just before serving, wash, quarter, core and thinly slice **3 red apples**. Lightly toss apple slices with the cabbage.

—TANGY CABBAGE SALAD

Follow ▲ Recipe. Substitute **French dressing** for sour cream. Omit lemon juice and seasonings. Blend in **1 teaspoon dry mustard, ¼ teaspoon curry powder** and **¼ teaspoon salt**. Garnish with **pimiento** and **sprigs of parsley**.

—PINEAPPLE COLE SLAW

Follow ▲ Recipe. Reduce cabbage to ¾ lb. (about 3 cups, shredded). Just before serving time, add to slaw **1 can (8¼ oz.) pineapple tidbits,** drained (about ⅔ cup, drained).

SURE-FIRE CABBAGE SLAW

▲ Base Recipe

Prepare and put into a bowl
3 cups finely shredded cabbage

Blend well
2 tablespoons sugar
1 teaspoon salt
1 teaspoon celery seed
⅛ teaspoon pepper
Sprinkle seasonings over cabbage and mix lightly with a fork. Pour over cabbage
¾ cup Never-Fail Salad Dressing (page 417)

Toss together lightly with fork.

Arrange on serving platter
6 large slices tomato
Heap spoonfuls of slaw on each tomato slice and sprinkle slaw with
Paprika

6 servings

—CONFETTI CABBAGE SALAD

Follow ▲ Recipe. Combine **¼ cup slivered green pepper** and **2 tablespoons chopped drained pimiento** with seasoned cabbage before adding salad dressing.

RED CABBAGE ALMOND SLAW

▲ Base Recipe

Put into a bowl and chill in refrigerator
3 cups (about ¾ lb.) shredded red cabbage
Prepare and set aside
½ cup (about 3 oz.) whole toasted blanched almonds (page 9)
Drain thoroughly, reserving syrup
1 can (8¼ oz.) pineapple tidbits (about ⅔ cup, drained)
Blend and chill 1 tablespoon reserved pineapple syrup and
⅓ cup salad dressing or mayonnaise
Shortly before serving, mix cabbage lightly with almonds and pineapple. Spoon dressing over cabbage mixture and toss lightly.

About 6 servings

—RED 'N' GREEN SLAW I

Follow ▲ Recipe. Decrease red cabbage to 2 cups and add **1 cup shredded green cabbage.** Omit almonds and pineapple. Blend **2 table-spoons cream, 1 tablespoon tarragon vinegar, 1 teaspoon prepared mustard** and **¼ teaspoon garlic salt** into the salad dressing.

SUNSHINE SLAW II

▲ Base Recipe

Wash, shred, toss together and set aside in a large bowl
¾ lb. cabbage (about 3 cups, shredded)
½ lb. carrots, pared or scraped

Set out
½ cup undiluted evaporated milk
Add gradually, stirring constantly
¼ cup lemon juice
2 teaspoons grated onion
Stir in
2 tablespoons sugar
1 teaspoon salt
¼ teaspoon monosodium glutamate
⅛ teaspoon pepper
Pour over cabbage mixture and toss to coat cabbage and carrots well. Chill in refrigerator. Serve on salad greens, if desired.   *6 servings*

—RED 'N' GREEN SLAW II

Follow ▲ Recipe. Substitute **¼ lb. (about 1 cup, shredded) red cabbage** for carrots. Drain **1 can (8¼ oz.) pineapple tidbits** (about ⅔ cup, drained); toss with cabbage.

—APPLE SLAW

Follow ▲ Recipe. Omit carrots. Wash, quarter, core and thinly slice **3 red apples;** toss with cabbage. Add **1 tablespoon celery seed** with the seasonings.

SLAW-FILLED TOMATO ASPIC RING MOLD

▲ Base Recipe

For Tomato Aspic Ring Mold—Set out a 5-cup ring mold. Follow recipe for
Tomato Aspic (page 391)

For Slaw—Wash, finely shred or chop and put into a large bowl and set aside
¾ lb. cabbage (about 3 cups, shredded)

Put into a bowl
¼ cup undiluted evaporated milk
Add gradually, stirring constantly
2 tablespoons lemon juice
1 teaspoon grated onion

Apple Slaw

Stir in
1 tablespoon sugar
1 tablespoon celery seed
1 teaspoon salt
⅛ teaspoon pepper

Pour over cabbage and toss to coat cabbage. Chill in refrigerator.

To Complete—Unmold (page 374) the aspic ring onto chilled plate. Spoon into center of mold the chilled slaw. Garnish slaw with
Parsley
Sliced pimiento-stuffed olives
Arrange around sides of mold
Whole ripe olives
Parsley sprigs
Serve immediately.   *8 servings*

—PEANUT SLAW

Follow ▲ Recipe. Omit aspic. Just before serving, toss with the cabbage **¾ cup (about 3½ oz.) salted Spanish peanuts.**

—GREEN PEPPER SLAW

Follow ▲ Recipe. Omit aspic. Toss with **green pepper strips.**

—SLAW-FILLED TOMATO SHELLS

Follow ▲ Recipe. Omit aspic. Rinse **8 medium**

Slaw-Filled Tomato Aspic Ring Mold

Kraut and Beet Slaw

sized firm tomatoes; dip into boiling water to loosen skins. Peel and cut a slice from tops. Remove and discard pulp with a spoon. Invert the tomato shells and set aside to drain. Chill. To serve, sprinkle inside of shells with **salt and pepper** and lightly fill with slaw.

KRAUT AND BEET SLAW

Drain
1 can (27 oz.) sauerkraut (about 3½ cups, drained)
1 can (16 oz.) diced beets (2 cups, drained)
Combine in a large bowl beets, sauerkraut and
1 tablespoon chopped onion
Set aside.

Blend
1 cup dairy sour cream
1 tablespoon prepared horseradish
and a mixture of
1 tablespoon sugar
½ teaspoon caraway seed
¼ teaspoon salt
Few grains pepper
Add sour cream mixture to sauerkraut mixture. Gently toss until thoroughly blended. Chill salad in refrigerator until ready to serve.

If desired, garnish with **hard-cooked egg white rings** and **parsley sprigs.** *8 servings*

CAULIFLOWER SALAD
(Blumenkohlsalat)

Remove leaves, cut off all the woody base and trim any blemishes from
1 medium head cauliflower
Separate the cauliflower into flowerets; rinse and cook (page 313) 8 to 10 min., or until tender but still firm. Drain the flowerets and set aside to cool. Chill in refrigerator.

Meanwhile, drain
1 can (5 oz.) shrimp
Cut the shrimp into pieces and put into a bowl; chill in refrigerator.

Combine in a screw-top jar
¼ cup vinegar
3 tablespoons salad oil
½ teaspoon salt
⅛ teaspoon white pepper
Shake dressing thoroughly and put into refrigerator to chill.

When ready to serve, put the chilled cauliflower into a bowl with the chilled shrimp and
1 tablespoon chopped parsley
Shake the dressing well and pour over the cauliflower. Toss lightly to coat evenly.

Serve immediately. *6 servings*

DRAMATIC CAULIFLOWER SALAD

A colorful, different-flavored salad that will be an ornament to any salad bar or buffet table. Folks who like avocado are sure to go for this.

Remove leaves, cut off all the woody base and trim any blemishes from
1 medium head cauliflower
Let stand in cold salted water a few minutes to remove any dust or small insects which settle in the cauliflower. Drain. Cook in a loosely covered pan in a large amount of boiling salted water. Cook for 20 to 30 min., or until tender but still firm. Drain.

Put the whole cauliflower into a deep bowl and pour over it
1½ cups French Dressing (one and one half times recipe, page 410)

Set in refrigerator to marinate (page 10) 1 to 2 hrs., turning several times.

Meanwhile, prepare and cut into pieces
2 medium ripe avocados
Force avocado through a sieve or food mill into a bowl. Blend in
2 teaspoons lemon juice
¼ teaspoon salt
¼ teaspoon nutmeg
⅛ teaspoon pepper
Set in refrigerator to chill.

Coarsely chop and set aside
½ cup (about 3 oz.) toasted blanched almonds (pages 9 and 10)

When ready to serve, drain the cauliflower. Arrange on a chilled serving plate
Crisp lettuce leaves

Place drained cauliflower on lettuce. Spread avocado mixture over cauliflower. Top with the chopped almonds. *About 8 servings*

CUCUMBER SALAD I
(Pressgurka)

You'll enjoy the sprightly sweet-sour flavor.

Rinse and pare
1 large cucumber
Score cucumber by pulling the tines of a fork lengthwise through cucumber. Cut cucumber into very thin slices. Put into a shallow bowl.

Mix well
⅓ cup cider vinegar
5 tablespoons water
5 tablespoons sugar
½ teaspoon salt
Few grains white pepper
Pour over the cucumber slices and toss lightly to coat evenly. Cover and put in the refrigerator for several hours to chill and allow flavors to blend.

Garnish cucumbers with
1 tablespoon finely chopped parsley
8 to 10 servings

CUCUMBER SALAD II
(Uborka Saláta)

▲ *Base Recipe*

Slice thinly into a bowl
2 medium (about 1¼ lbs.) cucumbers, washed and pared
Sprinkle over the cucumber slices
2 teaspoons salt
Mix lightly and set cucumbers aside for 1 hr.

Meanwhile, mix and set aside
3 tablespoons vinegar
3 tablespoons water
½ teaspoon sugar
¼ teaspoon paprika
¼ teaspoon pepper
½ clove garlic, minced

Squeeze cucumber slices, a few at a time (discarding liquid), and put into a bowl. Pour the vinegar mixture over the cucumbers and toss lightly together. Sprinkle onto cucumbers
¼ teaspoon paprika
Chill the salad in refrigerator for 1 to 2 hrs. *6 to 8 servings*

—CUCUMBER SALAD WITH SOUR CREAM
(Uborka Saláta Tejföllel)

Follow ▲ Recipe. Blend in **1 cup dairy sour cream** after the vinegar mixture.

—CUCUMBER SALAD WITH ONIONS
(Uborka Saláta Hagymával)

Follow ▲ Recipe or variation. Omit garlic. Cut off root ends from **3 or 4 fresh green onions or scallions.** Trim green tops down to 2 or 3 in., removing any wilted or bruised parts; peel and rinse. Slice onions by holding on hard surface and cutting across all with sharp knife. Add sliced onions to cucumber slices before adding the vinegar mixture.

CUCUMBER SALAD WITH SOUR CREAM II
(Gurkensalat mit saurer Sahne)

Prepare and set aside
1 Hard-Cooked Egg (page 133)

Rinse and pare
1 large cucumber
Score cucumber ⅛ in. deep by pulling the tines of a fork lengthwise; repeat to score entire surface. Cut cucumber into thin slices. Put into a bowl.

Mix
½ cup dairy sour cream
1½ tablespoons vinegar
1 tablespoon chopped chives
¾ teaspoon salt
⅛ teaspoon white pepper
Pour the mixture over the cucumber slices and toss lightly to coat evenly. Chill in refrigerator.

When ready to serve, cut the peeled egg into halves, remove egg yolk and chop finely. (The egg white may be used in other food preparation.) Garnish salad with the chopped yolk.
4 to 6 servings

POTATO SALAD

An easy to prepare salad.

Wash, cut into halves and cook covered in boiling salted water
6 medium (about 2 lbs.) potatoes
Cook about 20 min., or until potatoes are tender when pierced with a fork.

Meanwhile, prepare
2 Hard-Cooked Eggs (page 133)
Cut into eighths and set aside.

Drain potatoes. To dry potatoes, shake pan over low heat. Peel potatoes and cut into cubes (about 4½ cups, cubed). Put potatoes into a bowl and toss lightly with a mixture of
1 teaspoon salt
½ teaspoon monosodium glutamate
⅛ teaspoon pepper

Cucumber Salad with Sour Cream

Mix in the eggs and
¾ cup salad dressing or mayonnaise
2 tablespoons chopped onion
Toss lightly to coat potatoes well with dressing. Place in refrigerator to chill.
4 to 6 servings

ITALIAN POTATO SALAD
(Insalata di Patate)

Prepare and cook (page 313)
2 medium potatoes
Dice potatoes; chill in refrigerator.

Meanwhile, wash and dice
1 stalk celery (about ⅓ cup, diced)

Toss together lightly with a fork the potatoes, celery and
½ cup diced, pared cucumber
½ cup ripe olives, diced
2 tablespoons minced onion
With a fork, thoroughly but carefully blend in a mixture of
¾ cup Italian Salad Dressing (page 412)
¼ teaspoon oregano
Cover salad. Chill in refrigerator about 1 hr. before serving.
About 4 servings

POTATO ONION SALAD
(Burgonya Saláta Hagymával)

▲ Base Recipe

Wash, cook (page 313) 20 to 30 min., or until potatoes are tender when pierced with a fork
6 medium (about 2 lbs.) potatoes
Drain potatoes. To dry potatoes, shake pan over low heat. Set aside to cool.

Meanwhile, thinly slice and separate into rings
1 large onion

Peel potatoes and cut into ¼ in. slices. Arrange potatoes and onion rings alternately in a large shallow dish and add
Oil-Vinegar Marinade (double recipe, page 412)
Chill at least 1 hr. in the refrigerator, carefully turning vegetables occasionally.

Shortly before serving the salad, rinse and remove the stem end of
1 green pepper
Remove all white fiber and seeds from the pepper; rinse the cavity. Cut green pepper crosswise into ⅛ in. rings and set aside.

Pour the marinade off the potatoes and onions before serving. Garnish top of the salad with the green pepper rings. *About 6 servings*

—POTATO ONION SALAD WITH EGGS
(Burgonya Saláta Tojással)

Follow ▲ Recipe. Prepare **2 or 3 Hard-Cooked Eggs** (page 133). Slice eggs and place on top of salad with green pepper rings. Sprinkle lightly with **paprika**.

FIESTA POTATO SALAD

Wash, cut into halves and cook covered in boiling salted water to cover
6 medium (about 2 lbs.) potatoes
Cook about 20 min., or until potatoes are tender when pierced with a fork. Drain potatoes. Dry potatoes by shaking pan over low heat. Peel potatoes, cut into cubes and put into a deep bowl. Sprinkle with a mixture of
1 teaspoon salt
½ teaspoon paprika
¼ teaspoon monosodium glutamate
¼ teaspoon pepper

Meanwhile, prepare
3 Hard-Cooked Eggs (page 133)
Put into a small bowl, cover and chill.

Prepare and add to the potatoes
6 slices Panfried Bacon (page 190), crumbled
⅓ cup finely sliced scallions
2 tablespoons drained slivered pimiento
Add and toss until potatoes are well coated
¼ cup French Dressing I (page 410)
Slice the eggs into the bowl and add
¾ cup mayonnaise or Cooked Salad Dressing (page 416)

Hearty Potato Salad I

Toss lightly to coat potatoes well with dressing. Set in refrigerator to chill.

If desired, garnish with **radishes, tomato wedges,** sliced or whole **olives** or **pickle fans.** Or plan to outline salad bowl with a border of crisp **salad greens.**   *4 to 6 servings*

CURRIED POTATO SALAD

Wash, pare and cut into cubes
**6 medium (about 2 lbs.) potatoes
(about 4 cups, cubed)**
Cook covered in boiling water to cover, with
**1 teaspoon salt
1 teaspoon curry powder**
Cook 8 to 10 min., or until tender when pierced with a fork. Do not overcook. Drain.

Dry potatoes by shaking pan over low heat. Put into a bowl with
**3 tablespoons French dressing
2 tablespoons lemon juice
1 teaspoon garlic salt
½ teaspoon salt
¼ teaspoon curry powder
⅛ teaspoon pepper**
Set in refrigerator to marinate (page 10) 1 to 2 hrs., turning several times.

Meanwhile, prepare and chill
3 Hard-Cooked Eggs (page 133)

Prepare
**1 cup diced celery
½ cup diced green pepper**
Dice the hard-cooked eggs. Add to the potatoes the diced eggs, celery, green pepper and
½ cup mayonnaise
Toss lightly to coat all ingredients evenly. Set in refrigerator to chill thoroughly before serving.   *About 6 servings*

HEARTY POTATO SALAD I

Wash and cook (page 313) 20 to 30 minutes
5 medium (about 1⅔ lbs.) potatoes

Drain potatoes. Dry them by shaking pan over low heat. Set aside to cool.

Peel potatoes; cut into cubes and toss with
**1 onion, thinly sliced
1 tablespoon minced parsley**
Cover and chill in refrigerator.

Meanwhile, to prepare croutons, stack and, if desired, trim crusts from
2 slices toasted bread
Cut bread into ¼-in. cubes. Heat in skillet over low heat
2 tablespoons salad oil
Add the toasted bread cubes and
2 cloves garlic, cut in halves
Increase heat and cook over medium heat, moving and turning gently with a spoon until all sides of bread cubes are lightly coated with oil and are browned. Remove skillet from heat and set croutons aside.

Separate into pieces with a spoon
1 can (4½ oz.) deviled ham
Toss lightly with the chilled potato mixture and a mixture of
**1¼ cups dairy sour cream
¾ teaspoon salt
½ teaspoon monosodium glutamate
¼ teaspoon pepper**
Sprinkle the croutons over the top and mix lightly.   *About 6 servings*

HEARTY POTATO SALAD II

▲ Base Recipe

Cook (page 313) and cube
**4 medium (about 1⅓ lbs.) potatoes
(about 3 cups, cubed)**

Meanwhile, prepare and cut into eighths
3 Hard-Cooked Eggs (page 133)

While eggs and potatoes are cooking, dice and panfry
6 slices bacon

Prepare
**½ cup (about 1 medium) minced onion
½ cup diced cucumber**
Put into a large bowl and toss potatoes, eggs, bacon, onion and cucumber together lightly with a fork. Add a mixture of
**1 teaspoon salt
½ teaspoon monosodium glutamate
¼ teaspoon pepper**
Thoroughly but carefully blend in
**¾ cup Never-Fail Salad Dressing
(page 417)**
Cover salad and store in refrigerator at least 1 hr. before serving.

Sprinkle salad with
Paprika
     6 servings

—POTATO RADISH SALAD

Follow ▲ Recipe. Substitute **sliced radishes** for cucumber. Or use a portion of each.

—POTATO PICKLE SALAD

Follow ▲ Recipe. Substitute **chopped sweet pickle** for cucumber. Or use a portion of each.

POTATO SALAD WITH SOUR CREAM DRESSING
(Burgonya Saláta Telföllel)

Wash and cook (page 313) 20 to 30 min., or until potatoes are tender when pierced with a fork
8 (about 2½ lbs.) medium potatoes
Drain potatoes. To dry potatoes, shake pan over low heat. Peel potatoes, cut into cubes and put into a large bowl. (The cubed potatoes will measure approximately 6 cups.) Add to the potatoes
**¾ cup (about 1½ medium) chopped onion
½ cup chopped celery**
and a mixture of
**⅓ cup vinegar
1½ teaspoons paprika
1 teaspoon salt
⅛ teaspoon pepper**
Toss ingredients together lightly with a fork; let stand 15 min.

Meanwhile, heat in top of a double boiler over simmering water until butter is melted
**2 cups dairy sour cream
¼ cup butter**
Stir until sour cream and butter are well blended and pour over potato mixture, mixing carefully with a fork to blend well. Chill thoroughly in the refrigerator before serving. Garnish with **parsley**   *6 to 8 servings*

SOUR CREAM POTATO SALAD

To make this creamy potato salad even more attractive, serve it colorfully in Green Pepper Shells or Cucumber Boats, either of which will add flavor as well as eye appeal.

Wash
> **6 medium (about 2 lbs.) potatoes**

Cook (page 313). Peel potatoes, cut into cubes and put into a bowl with
> **½ cup French dressing**

Set in refrigerator to marinate (page 10) for about 2 hrs., turning several times.

Meanwhile, prepare and chill
> **3 Hard-Cooked Eggs (page 133)**

Coarsely chop the eggs and add to the potatoes along with
> **1 cup diced cucumber**
> **½ cup chopped celery**
> **⅓ cup finely chopped onion**
> **2 tablespoons chopped chives**
> **2 tablespoons chopped parsley**
> **1 teaspoon salt**
> **½ clove garlic, minced**

Add
> **1 cup dairy sour cream**

Mix lightly until vegetables are well coated. Set in refrigerator to chill thoroughly before serving.

Meanwhile, prepare and chill
> **Green Pepper Shells (page 418)**
> **or Cucumber Boats (page 418)**

To serve, lightly fill with salad mixture.

6 servings

TOMATO SALAD
(Paradicsom Saláta)

▲ Base Recipe

The colors of this salad represent the national colors of Hungary—red, white and green.

Combine in a small screw-top jar; cover tightly and chill in refrigerator
> **¼ cup vinegar**
> **¼ cup olive oil**
> **2 tablespoons sugar**
> **¼ teaspoon salt**
> **⅛ teaspoon pepper**

Rinse and dip into boiling water for a few seconds
> **5 medium tomatoes**

Peel tomatoes, cut out and discard stem ends and chill thoroughly in refrigerator. Cut the tomatoes into small pieces and put into a salad bowl with
> **½ cup (about 1 medium) chopped onion**
> **2 tablespoons chopped parsley**

Shake jar of dressing until well blended and pour over salad; lightly toss together. Serve immediately. *4 or 5 servings*

—TOMATO SALAD WITH GREEN PEPPER
(Paradicsom Saláta Zöldpaprikával)

Follow ▲ Recipe. Substitute for parsley, **1 green pepper** chopped (about ½ cup, chopped).

STUFFED TOMATO SHELLS

▲ Base Recipe

For Tomato Shells—Rinse and cut slice from tops of
> **6 firm tomatoes**

Scoop out centers of tomatoes with a spoon. Invert and set aside to drain.

For Filling—Blend
> **½ cup (¼ lb.) dry cottage cheese**
> **¼ cup chopped cucumber**
> **¼ cup chopped celery**
> **2 tablespoons chopped green pepper**
> **1 tablespoon minced onion**
> **1 tablespoon Mayonnaise (page 412)**
> **½ teaspoon salt**
> **¼ teaspoon monosodium glutamate**
> **Few grains pepper**

Spoon filling into tomato shells. Place into refrigerator and chill until time to serve.

6 servings

—SEAFOOD-STUFFED TOMATOES

Follow ▲ Recipe for preparing tomato shells. Fill with one half recipe of **Seafood Salad** (page 393).

COTTAGE CHEESE-FILLED TOMATOES

▲ Base Recipe

Prepare
> **6 Tomato Shells (page 418)**

Chill in refrigerator until ready to assemble salad.

Thoroughly mix
> **2 cups cream-style cottage cheese**
> **2 tablespoons salad dressing or mayonnaise**

Mix in lightly but thoroughly
> **5 slices crisp Panfried Bacon (page 190), crumbled**
> **2 tablespoons grated onion**
> **4 teaspoons capers**
> **¼ teaspoon pepper**

Chill in refrigerator.

When ready to serve, lightly fill Tomato Shells with cottage cheese mixture. If desired, garnish with **sprigs of parsley**. *6 servings*

—DEVILED COTTAGE CHEESE-FILLED TOMATOES

Follow ▲ Recipe. Omit bacon and capers. Blend ⅓ cup (3-oz. can) deviled ham and ¼ teaspoon curry powder with cheese mixture.

FRUIT SALADS

FRUIT PREPARATION

Apples, pears—Wash fruit. Cut into quarters, remove core and, if desired, pare and cut into lengthwise slices. Toss fruit with pineapple or citrus fruit juice to help prevent discoloration.

Avocados—Rinse avocados, peel, cut into halves lengthwise and remove pits. Brush surfaces with lemon juice to help prevent discoloration.

Bananas—Peel bananas with brown-flecked peel and cut into crosswise slices. Toss slices gently with pineapple or citrus fruit juice to help prevent discoloration.

Blueberries, raspberries—Sort and rinse berries; drain thoroughly.

Cherries—Sort, rinse and drain cherries. Remove stems, cut into halves and remove pits.

Grapes—Rinse and drain grapes thoroughly. Cut large bunches into small clusters.

Melons—Rinse melons and cut into halves. With a knife or spoon, remove seedy center.

For Melon Balls—Using melon-ball cutter, carefully cut balls.

For Melon Bowls—Rinse melons and cut into halves. If a scalloped edge is desired, using a narrow sharp-pointed knife, carefully carve around each melon half. If a sawtooth edge is

desired, do not cut melons into halves. Using a narrow sharp-pointed knife, mark points in a sawtooth line at 1-in. intervals around center of melon. Cut on line between points marked and pull halves apart. With a knife or spoon, remove seedy center from melon halves. Using a spoon or melon-ball cutter, scoop out meat from melon halves keeping surface smooth and leaving shells about ½ in. thick. Chill shells and pieces in refrigerator.

For Melon Rings—Rinse melon and cut into halves, crosswise. With a knife or spoon, remove seedy center. Cut melon into ¾-in. slices, reserving ends. With sharp paring knife, remove the rind from each ring. Using a melon-ball cutter, carefully cut balls from inside of melon ends. Meat removed from the ends may be used in other food preparation. Chill melon rings and balls in refrigerator.

Nectarines—Rinse nectarines, cut into halves and remove pits.

Oranges, Grapefruit—Rinse fruit. With a sharp knife, cut away peel and white membrane from fruit. Remove sections by cutting on either side of the dividing membranes; remove, section by section, over a bowl to collect juice. Discard seeds, if any.

For Grapefruit Baskets—Rinse grapefruit and cut into halves. With a grapefruit knife or a sharp paring knife, loosen each section by cutting down and along either side of dividing membranes. Cut completely around outer skin to loosen membrane from shell. Remove grapefruit sections and reserve for use in food preparation. Remove and discard membrane and fibrous center. To make a handle for basket, about ¼-in. down from top of each half-shell carefully cut through peel and around shell, leaving a 1-in. piece attached at opposite sides of the shell. Bring the strips up together at the center and secure with a small piece of thread or short piece of wooden pick. Decorate center of handle with a sprig of watercress or mint.

Peaches—Rinse peaches; plunge into boiling water to loosen skins. Immediately plunge into cold water; gently slip off skins. Cut peaches into halves; remove pits. Brush cut surfaces with lemon juice to prevent discoloration.

Pineapple—Cut off and discard crown (spiny top) and rinse pineapple. Cut into crosswise slices. With a sharp knife, cut away and discard rind and "eyes" from each slice. Cut away the core and cut the rings into wedges.

For Pineapple Shells—Rinse pineapple. To prepare, cut whole pineapple into halves lengthwise through crown (spiny top). Cut out and discard core. With a grapefruit knife or sharp paring knife, carefully remove and reserve fruit from pineapple halves, leaving shells about ½ in. thick. Cut reserved pineapple into pieces and chill with the pineapple shells.

Strawberries—Sort, rinse, and drain berries. Remove hull or leave on for garnish.

FRESH FRUIT SALADS

Wherever the weather is warm and fresh fruits are abundant, fruit plates are sure to be favorites—with the homemaker because they are so easy to prepare and serve, and with everyone else because they are beautiful, cool, delicious and satisfying.

Simplest of all to make ready is the "serve yourself" salad. In the center of a large serving platter, place a mound or bowl of **seasoned cottage cheese**, topped colorfully with a sprinkling of **paprika**, or of **minced chives or parsley**, or with a **maraschino cherry**. Around the cottage cheese arrange **lettuce cups**, and fill each with a different fruit in season: **orange and grapefruit sections, slices of Japanese persimmon, papaya cubes, avocado cubes or slices, chunks of juicy fresh pineapple, whole ripe strawberries, varicolored melon balls.**

Be sure that the fruits, greens, cottage cheese and the platter are thoroughly chilled. Serve with a **simple syrup** flavored with **lime juice**, or use the **freshly squeezed lime juice** alone.

FRUIT SALAD
(Gyümölcs Saláta)

Put into a small bowl

> **2 cups any mixture of fresh fruits, such as watermelon balls, sliced bananas, peach or pear cubes, berries, pitted cherries, seeded or seedless grapes or orange sections**

(Dip banana, peach and pear pieces into lemon juice to prevent darkening.) Add to fruit and toss gently

> **¼ cup confectioner's sugar**

Chill fruit in refrigerator 1 hr.

Toss salad gently. Spoon individual portions into

> **Lettuce cups**

Serve on chilled salad plates.

Set out

> **4 teaspoons rum, cognac or wine**

Sprinkle 1 teaspoon over each salad. Serve immediately. *4 servings*

FRUIT SALAD SPARKLER

Have ready

> **Honey Lime French Dressing (page 411)**

Cut off and discard crown (spiny top) from

> **1 small fresh pineapple**

Rinse and cut into crosswise slices ¼ to ½ in. thick. With a sharp knife, cut away and discard rind and "eyes" from each slice. Cut

out and discard the core. Cut into small wedges enough of the pineapple to yield 1½ cups pineapple wedges. (Use remaining pineapple in other food preparation.) Put the wedges into a bowl and set aside.

Sort, rinse, drain and hull

> **1 pt. fresh ripe strawberries**

Reserve several whole berries for garnish; chill. Slice the remaining strawberries and add to the pineapple wedges. Pour about ½ cup of the dressing over the fruit and allow to stand covered in the refrigerator at least 1 hr., turning occasionally.

Just before serving, rinse, cut into halves lengthwise, and remove and discard pits from

> **3 chilled large ripe avocados**

Arrange the avocado halves on a chilled serving platter. Brush the cut surfaces with

> **Lime juice**

Spoon about ½ cup of the strawberry-pineapple mixture into the cavity of each avocado half. Garnish the platter with the reserved berries and **curly endive**. *6 servings*

GLAMOUR FRUIT SALAD

Have all fruits thoroughly chilled. Prepare as directed (see Fruit Preparation) and set aside in refrigerator until ready to use

> **Orange sections**
> **Grapefruit sections**
> **Strawberries**
> **Blueberries**
> **Honeydew melon balls**
> **Cantaloupe balls**
> **Peach halves**
> **Nectarine halves**
> **Tokay grapes**
> **Frosted white seedless grapes**

Just before serving, rinse and pat dry with absorbent paper

> **Bibb lettuce**

Arrange lettuce on a chilled platter. Attractively arrange fruit on lettuce.

Serve with **oil** and **lemon**, or **Orange Fruit Salad Dressing** (page 416).

For Frosted White Seedless Grapes—Beat **1 egg white** until frothy. Dip small clusters of **grapes** in beaten egg white. Shake off excess, then dip grapes in a bowl of **sugar**. Set aside to dry. Chill grapes in refrigerator.

SOUTHWESTERN SALAD BOWL

Creamy avocado slices, juicy grapefruit sections and onion rings—mmmm! A perfect pick-up for days when the mercury soars.

Rinse, discarding bruised leaves, pat dry and chill

> **Bibb lettuce or leaf lettuce (enough to line the salad bowl)**

With a sharp knife, cut away peel from

> **1 large grapefruit**

Remove sections by cutting on either side of dividing membrane, working over a bowl to save the juice. Set aside.

Rinse, peel, cut into halves and remove and discard pit from

1 large avocado

Slice into bowl containing the grapefruit juice. Toss slices gently to coat with juice (this helps to prevent discoloring).

Arrange the slices of avocado alternately with grapefruit sections on lettuce in salad bowl. Cover and chill in refrigerator.

Just before serving, garnish with thin **onion rings.** Serve with **French Dressing** (page 410).

4 to 6 servings

WHITE FRUIT SALAD

▲ Base Recipe

Prepare and chill

Orange or Apricot Fruit Salad Dressing (one half recipe, page 416)

Drain thoroughly, reserving pineapple syrup (cherry syrup may be saved for use in other food preparation.)

1 can (20 oz.) pineapple chunks (about 2 cups, drained)

1 can (17 oz.) pitted light sweet cherries (about 1¼ cups, drained)

Put drained fruit into a bowl and set in refrigerator to chill.

Wash, quarter, core, pare and cut into small pieces

3 medium (about 1 lb.) apples

Put apple pieces into a small bowl and pour over them ½ cup of the reserved pineapple syrup. Set in refrigerator to chill thoroughly, 2 to 3 hrs.

Meanwhile, coarsely chop and set aside

¾ cup (about 4 oz.) toasted blanched almonds (pages 9 and 10)

Shortly before serving, cut (page 9) into quarters

16 (¼ lb.) marshmallows

Peel, score (by drawing tines of a fork lengthwise over entire banana), and cut crosswise into ¼-in. slices

2 bananas with brown-flecked peel

Put into a large bowl and drizzle with

2 teaspoons lemon juice

Toss lightly to coat banana slices evenly with the lemon juice.

Remove chilled fruit from the refrigerator. Thoroughly drain the apple pieces; add to the bowl of banana slices with the pineapple chunks, cherries, almonds and marshmallows. Spoon over the fruit as much chilled dressing as desired. Toss lightly to mix thoroughly.

When ready to serve, arrange **curly endive** on chilled salad plates and carefully spoon a portion of the fruit salad onto each serving plate. If desired, garnish with **mint sprigs.**

6 to 8 servings

—OVERNIGHT FRUIT SALAD

Prepare **Dressing for Overnight Fruit Salad** (page 416). From ▲ Recipe, use only pineapple chunks, light sweet cherries and marshmallows, increasing marshmallows to 24 (6 oz.). Prepare and section **4 medium oranges.** Slice ½ **cup maraschino cherries** and set aside on absorbent paper to drain. Add the marshmallows, oranges and maraschino cherries to the bowl with the fruit. Spoon the dressing over the fruit mixture and toss lightly. Cover; chill in refrigerator overnight.

—SOUR CREAM FRUIT SALAD

Follow ▲ Recipe or recipe for Overnight Fruit Salad. Omit the dressing. Add **1 cup dairy sour cream** to the fruit mixture and toss lightly.

DELECTABLE FRUIT SALAD

Rinse in cold water

Bibb lettuce

Separate leaves. Remove any bruised leaves. Drain, dry thoroughly and carefully. Put into a plastic bag or vegetable freshener. Chill in refrigerator at least 1 hr.

Meanwhile, set out in a small bowl

½ cup orange juice

Rinse and plunge into boiling water (to loosen the skins)

6 large (about 2 lbs.) firm ripe peaches

Plunge peaches into cold water. Gently slip off skins. Cut peaches into halves, remove and discard pits. Dip peach halves, one at a time, into the orange juice to coat thoroughly (this helps to prevent peaches from darkening). Put peach halves into a bowl and sprinkle over peaches

3 tablespoons kirsch

Cover and chill in refrigerator at least 1 hr.

Drain, reserving syrup

1 can (17 oz.) pitted dark sweet cherries

Set out

36 (about ¼ cup) blanched almonds (page 9)

Place a blanched almond in each cherry. (Remaining cherries and syrup may be used in other food preparation.) Chill stuffed cherries in refrigerator until ready to serve.

Split and remove seeds from

6 preserved kumquats

Fill each kumquat with

Cottage cheese

Chill filled kumquats in refrigerator until ready to serve.

When ready to serve, arrange the Bibb lettuce on chilled salad plates. Place two peach halves, rounded side down, on each plate. Arrange 3 stuffed cherries on each peach half. Place one of the filled kumquats on each salad plate.

Serve with

Pineapple Salad Dressing (page 416)

6 salads

OVERNIGHT COCONUT FRUIT SALAD

Drain, reserving syrup for use in other food preparation

1 can (11 oz.) mandarin oranges (about 1 cup, drained)

1 can (8¼ oz.) crushed pineapple (about ¾ cup, drained)

Prepare and section enough oranges to yield

1 cup orange sections

Cut (page 9) into quarters

8 marshmallows (2 oz.)

Put the mandarin oranges, pineapple, orange sections and marshmallows into a large bowl with

1 cup (about 4 oz.) moist shredded coconut, cut

Mix

1 cup dairy sour cream

2 tablespoons sugar

Pour over the fruit mixture and toss lightly to mix thoroughly. Cover; chill in refrigerator overnight.

To serve, spoon portions of salad onto chilled serving plates lined with crisp **salad greens.** Garnish with **mint sprigs.**   *About 6 servings*

EMPRESS SALAD

Wash and thoroughly chill salad ingredients before preparing salad. Set out a salad bowl.

Tear into pieces

Escarole

Prepare (using as much as desired of each)

Watermelon chunks

Pear cubes (unpared)

Cucumber cubes (pared)

Put the fruit and cucumber cubes into the salad bowl with the escarole. Pour on (using just enough to coat fruit and greens)

French Dressing I (page 410; use lemon juice)

Toss lightly and serve immediately.

Fruit-Filled Melon Rings

FRUIT PLATES

Arrange chilled **fresh or canned fruit** attractively on a chilled plate lined with cool crisp **salad greens**. Top with a scoop of **Cranberry Sherbet** (page 561) or other sherbet. Garnish the plate with **Cream Cheese Nut Balls** or **Frosted Grapes** (page 370), if desired.

For Cream Cheese Nut Balls—Prepare **chopped pecans** or **chopped toasted almonds**. Beat **1 pkg. (3 oz.) cream cheese** until softened. Form cream cheese into balls and roll in chopped nuts.

FRUIT-FILLED MELON RINGS

Prepare **Melon Rings** (page 370). Fill with available **fresh fruit**; use fruit that harmonizes in color with melon rings. If desired, sprinkle fruit with **lemon or lime juice** or with any desired **liqueur** (crème de menthe, kirsch, Cointreau or curaçao). Garnish with **mint sprigs**. Serve with **Orange Fruit Salad Dressing** (page 416), **Pineapple Salad Dressing** (page 416) or **Enchanting Fruit Dressing I or II** (page 416).

FRESH PEAR LUNCHEON SALAD

Line a chilled serving platter with **crisp lettuce**

Fresh Pear Luncheon Salad

and **watercress**. Arrange chilled **fresh Anjou pear halves**, cut side up, on one side of the platter. Arrange strips of **cheese** and/or cold **cooked chicken or turkey, luncheon meat, ham or roast meat** on the opposite side of the platter. Garnish with **Celery Whirls** (page 421). If desired, serve with **French Dressing I** (page 410).

SALAD-FILLED PINEAPPLE SHELLS

Prepare **Pineapple Shells** (page 370). Shells may be filled with available chilled **fresh fruit, chicken salad** (mix in some of the fresh pineapple pieces, if desired) or a **seafood salad**.

For a dessert salad, mix **chilled fruit** with a small amount of **Syrup for Fruit**; spoon mixture into Pineapple Shells. Top fruit with a small scoop of **sherbet**. Garnish the stem end of each Pineapple Shell with a thin **half slice of lime**. Garnish with **mint sprigs**.

For Syrup for Fruit—Mix **1 cup sugar** and **1 cup water** in a saucepan. Stir over low heat until sugar is dissolved. Cover, bring to boiling and boil 5 min. Cool. Stir in about **1 tablespoon lime juice** or **1 teaspoon vanilla extract**. Store in refrigerator and use as needed.

When sweetening fruit, for a special flavor accent, use **Vanilla Confectioners' Sugar** (page 582).

WALDORF SALAD

▲ *Base Recipe*

Wash, quarter, core and dice
   2 medium (about ⅔ lb.) apples (about 2 cups, diced)
Wash, remove strings from and dice
   3 large stalks celery (about 1 cup, diced)

Combine apples and celery. Stir in
   ½ cup (about 1¾ oz.) walnuts, halves or coarsely chopped
   ¼ cup mayonnaise
Chill thoroughly in refrigerator.

Place on individual salad plates one of
   4 crisp lettuce leaves (cup shape)
Spoon portion of apple-celery mixture onto each lettuce leaf. *4 servings*

—CRISPY APPLE SALAD

Follow ▲ Recipe. Increase mayonnaise to ½ cup. Add ⅓ cup (about 1⅔ oz.) **golden raisins** and ¼ cup seeded halved **Tokay grapes**. Arrange salad on a **bed** of **lettuce and curly endive**.

CANTALOUPE SALAD

Rinse and cut into halves
   2 medium ripe cantaloupes

Remove seedy centers and pare. Cut cantaloupes into ¾-in. cubes, put into a large bowl and set aside.

For Dressing—Mix until well blended
   ½ cup mayonnaise
   ½ cup dairy sour cream
   ½ teaspoon salt
   ⅛ teaspoon pepper
Pour one half of the dressing onto cantaloupe and toss lightly until well mixed. Chill cantaloupe and remaining dressing in the refrigerator for about 1 hr.

Remove from refrigerator and place individual servings on **crisp lettuce** on chilled salad plates. Top each serving with some of remaining dressing. *About 8 servings*

THREE-MEN-IN-A-TUB SALAD

Cut into halves, remove seeds, cover with waxed paper and place in refrigerator to chill
   2 cantaloupes

Drain, reserving syrup
   1 can (20 oz.) pineapple chunks (about 2 cups, drained)
Chill in refrigerator.

Set out
   1 pkg. (8 oz.) cream cheese
Divide and roll cream cheese into 12 1-in. balls. Cover with waxed paper and chill in refrigerator.

Blend
   ¼ cup Never-Fail Salad Dressing (page 417)
   2 tablespoons reserved pineapple syrup
Add reserved pineapple chunks to salad dressing and toss lightly with fork to coat well.

Fill each chilled cantaloupe half with the pineapple mixture. Top each with 3 cream cheese balls. Insert in one cheese ball of each serving, stem down
   Sprig of watercress

4 servings

Crispy Apple Salad

SUNNY CALIFORNIA SALAD

Thoroughly chill salad ingredients. Set out a large plate.

Prepare
  **Fluffy Citrus Salad Dressing
    (page 415)**
Chill in refrigerator.

With a sharp knife, cut away peel and white membrane from
  **5 large oranges
  1 large grapefruit**
Peel and section grapefruit (see Fruit Preparation, page 370). Slice each of the oranges crosswise into 6 slices. Set fruit in refrigerator to chill.

Rinse, peel, cut into halves, remove pit, and cut into thin slices
  1 medium ripe avocado
Add to bowl containing the orange and grapefruit juice. Toss slices very gently to coat with juice.

Arrange on the salad plate
  Crisp salad greens
Place a bowl of Fluffy Citrus Salad Dressing in the center of the plate. Alternately arrange the grapefruit sections and the avocado slices around the bowl. Arrange the orange slices, overlapping (see photo) in a circle around the grapefruit and avocado. Garnish with
  Fresh berries
Serve immediately. *6 to 8 servings*

ORANGE SALAD BOWL

Prepare
  Orange Salad Dressing (below)
Chill in refrigerator.

Put into a large salad bowl
  **1 qt. torn fresh spinach leaves
  1 qt. torn lettuce leaves
  ½ cup sliced radishes**

Toss gently, cover and refrigerate until ready to serve. Peel, slice, cut in thirds and chill
  2 or 3 navel oranges

Before serving, toss orange pieces with chilled greens. Drizzle with Orange Salad Dressing and toss. Garnish center with orange pieces and radish slices. Accompany with dressing.
About 6 servings

—ORANGE SALAD DRESSING

Combine in a jar or bottle
  **½ cup orange juice
  ¼ cup lemon juice
  1 teaspoon seasoned salt
  ⅛ teaspoon seasoned pepper
  ½ teaspoon garlic powder
  ½ teaspoon paprika**
Cover and shake well. Add and shake well
  **⅓ cup salad oil
  ⅓ cup light corn syrup**
Chill thoroughly. Shake well before serving.
About 1½ cups dressing

BLOSSOM SALAD

▲ Base Recipe

Wash
  4 oranges
Beginning at top, make 6 equally spaced cuts through orange peel to pul; slit to within an inch of base. Pull each piece of peel away from pulp, forming 6 petals attached at base. Carefully pull fruit from base. Remove white membrane from fruit. Cut fruit into sections and set aside.

Set aside to drain, reserving syrup.
  **1 can (8¼ oz.) pineapple tidbits
    (about ⅔ cup, drained)**

Peel, quarter lengthwise and dice
  1 banana with brown-flecked peel

Lightly toss orange sections, pineapple tidbits and diced banana together. Fill orange peel shells with fruit mixture.

Blend
  **1 cup (½ lb.) cottage cheese
  2 tablespoons reserved pineapple
    syrup**
Spoon onto fruit. Top salads with
  Sprigs of mint, watercress or parsley
Serve on crisp **salad greens.** *4 servings*

—LOTUS LUNCHEON SALAD

Follow ▲ Recipe. Substitute **grapefruit** for oranges. Cut fruit sections into halves. Cut **6 maraschino cherries** into quarters and toss with fruit.

WESTWARD-HO PEACH SALAD

▲ Base Recipe

For each salad, allow
  1 large crisp lettuce leaf (cup shape)
Place lettuce leaf on individual salad plate and top with
  2 peach halves
Place peach halves close together, rounded sides down. Arrange from center of one peach half to center of the other
  1 large green pepper ring
Inside pepper ring heap, shaping into a mound
  ¼ cup cottage cheese
Circle cheese mound with
  2 or 3 rings green pepper

Sunny California Salad

The peach halves are the brim of the cowboy hat, the cheese forms the crown and pepper rings are bands around the sombrero. If desired, drizzle over top of "hat crown"
  Jiffy French Dressing (page 411)
1 salad

—WESTWARD-HO PEAR OR PINEAPPLE SALAD

Follow ▲ Recipe. Substitute **pear halves** or **pineapple slices** for the peaches.

PEACH BLUSH SALAD

▲ Base Recipe

Drain, reserving syrup, and set aside
  **8 medium canned peach halves
    (17-oz. can)**

Blend in a bowl
  **1 pkg. (3 oz.) cream cheese
  ¼ cup mayonnaise
  ½ teaspoon prepared horseradish
  ¼ teaspoon salt**

Thoroughly mix in
  **¼ cup chopped almonds
  ¼ cup chopped celery
  ¼ cup chopped green pepper**

Orange Salad Bowl

373

press two peach halves together to make a whole peach. Chill if time allows.

Arrange peaches on large plate of
Crisp salad greens

Dilute with water
1 drop red food coloring
Gently brush color on top of each peach.

Blend
⅓ cup dairy sour cream
2 tablespoons cranberry jelly
1½ tablespoons reserved peach syrup
Serve with peaches. *4 servings*

—PEAR BLUSH SALAD

Follow ▲ Recipe. Substitute **canned pears and syrup** for peaches and syrup. Accompany each pear with **maraschino cherry**, cut in eighths from stem end almost to base.

—APRICOT SALAD

Follow ▲ Recipe. Substitute **16 canned apricot halves and syrup** for peaches and syrup. Omit food coloring. Allow two whole apricots for each serving.

FUNNY BUNNY SALAD

On an individual salad plate, arrange a nest of
Endive or shredded lettuce
Place on it, cut side down
1 pear half (well drained if canned)
Make a tail at larger end of pear with
1 marshmallow
The head is the stem end. The tongue or mouth is
½ maraschino cherry
For eyes, insert
2 raisins
And the long ears, growing upright, are
2 blanched and toasted almonds (pages 9 and 10)
1 salad

RING-AROUND SALAD

For each salad, allow
1 crisp lettuce leaf
Place on individual salad plate. In center of lettuce place
1 slice pineapple, well drained
Around pineapple, arrange
6 grapefruit or orange sections
Place in center of pineapple
1 apricot half, cut side up

Fill apricot with
1 teaspoon Jiffy French Dressing (page 411)
6 raisins
1 salad

AVOCADO AND PINEAPPLE SALAD WITH CHUTNEY DRESSING

For Chutney Dressing—Mix in a 1-qt. screw-top jar
1 cup salad oil
⅓ cup vinegar
1 teaspoon salt
½ teaspoon nutmeg
1 clove garlic, finely minced
Finely chop (if large pieces are present) and add to jar
1 cup chutney
Cover jar, shake thoroughly and chill.
About 2⅓ cups dressing

For Salad—Wash, remove bruised spots from leaves and pat dry
Curly endive
Put into refrigerator to chill.

Set aside to drain
1 can (29½ oz.) pineapple (8 slices), chilled

Rinse, peel, cut into halves and remove and discard pits from
2 medium ripe avocados
Cut each avocado half into 8 crosswise slices. Dip slices into a bowl containing
¼ cup water
3 tablespoons lemon juice
To serve, arrange beds of the endive on 8 chilled individual salad plates. Quarter the pineapple slices and arrange pieces alternately with avocado slices to form circles on endive beds. Sprinkle avocado slices with
Paprika
Shake dressing well, pour into a bowl, and serve with the salad. *8 individual salads*

MOLDED SALADS

GELATIN TECHNIQUES

To turn out a salad mold that is shapely and unscarred by removal from the mold, and that has solid ingredients distributed throughout, a few simple techniques should be followed.

Chill gelatin mixtures either by setting the bowl in the refrigerator or by putting it in a container of ice and water. If placed in the refrigerator, stir occasionally; if placed over ice and water (a quicker method), stir frequently. If the gelatin mixture is clear, chill until slightly thicker than consistency of thick unbeaten egg white before adding any solid ingredients. If the mixture contains ingredients which thicken it or make it opaque, chill until it begins to gel (becomes slightly thicker); mix in solid ingredients only after mixture begins to gel.

Unmold gelatin by first running the tip of a knife around the top edge to loosen it and admit air; then invert the mold on a chilled plate. If the mold cannot be lifted off immediately, wet a clean towel in hot water, quickly wring it almost dry, and wrap the hot towel around the mold for a few seconds. Repeat if necessary.

TWO-LAYER WALDORF SALAD

Set out a 1½-qt. fancy mold.

Empty into a bowl
2 pkgs. (3 oz. each) lemon-flavored gelatin
Add and stir until gelatin is dissolved
2 cups boiling water
Stir in
1 cup cold water
¼ cup lime juice
Cool. Pour about one third of the gelatin mixture into the mold. Chill until partially set.

Chill (on this page) remaining gelatin mixture until slightly thicker than consistency of thick unbeaten egg white.

Meanwhile, wash, quarter, core and chop
1 medium red apple
Prepare
½ cup chopped celery
½ cup (about 2 oz.) chopped walnuts
When second gelatin mixture is of desired consistency, blend in
⅔ cup mayonnaise
Add and mix in the apple, celery and walnuts. When first layer in mold is partially set, immediately spoon the fruit-gelatin mixture over it. (Both layers should be of almost the same consistency when combined to avoid separation when unmolded.) Chill in refrigerator until firm.

Unmold (on this page) onto chilled serving plate. Garnish with **crisp curly endive**.
8 to 10 servings

Apple Cider Salad

APPLE CIDER SALAD

▲ Base Recipe

Set out a 1-qt. mold.

Pour into a bowl
½ cup cold water
½ cup apple cider
Sprinkle evenly over cold liquids
2 env. unflavored gelatin
Set aside.

Heat until very hot
1½ cups apple cider
⅛ teaspoon salt
Remove from heat and immediately add to softened gelatin, stirring until gelatin is completely dissolved. Cool; chill (page 374) until slightly thicker than consistency of thick unbeaten egg white.

Just before gelatin mixture is of desired consistency, prepare
2 cups (about 2 medium) diced apple (do not pare)
⅓ cup (about 1½ oz.) chopped walnuts
1 tablespoon finely chopped parsley
When gelatin is of desired consistency, mix in the apples, walnuts and parsley. Turn into the mold. Chill in refrigerator until firm.

Unmold (page 374) onto chilled serving plate.
About 6 servings

—APPLEJACK SALAD

Follow ▲ Recipe. Decrease cider to 1¾ cups. Add **¼ cup apple brandy** to gelatin after it has cooled but before chilling.

LAYERED APPLE CRANBERRY SALAD

It's just as pretty and just as flavorful in June as in December, but the gay red and green layers make it an ideal Christmastime salad.

Set out a 1½-qt. mold.

For Apple Layer—Empty into a bowl
1 pkg. (3 oz.) lime-flavored gelatin
Add and stir until gelatin is completely dissolved
1 cup boiling water

Stir in
1 cup thick sweetened applesauce
½ cup apple juice
Pour into mold. Cool; chill in refrigerator until partially set.

For Cranberry Layer—Empty into a bowl
1 pkg. (3 oz.) cherry-flavored gelatin
Add and stir until gelatin is completely dissolved
1 cup boiling water
Cool; chill (page 374) until gelatin mixture is slightly thicker than consistency of thick unbeaten egg white.

Meanwhile, chop
½ cup (about 2 oz.) pecans
Set out
2 cups (16-oz. can) whole cranberry sauce
When the second gelatin mixture is of desired consistency, stir in the pecans and cranberry sauce.

When first layer in mold is partially set, immediately turn the cranberry mixture into the mold. (Both layers should be of almost the same consistency when combined to avoid separation when unmolded.) Chill in refrigerator until firm.

Unmold (page 374) onto a chilled serving plate.
8 to 10 servings

APRICOT LUNCHEON MOLD

Set out a 1-qt. ring mold. Set a bowl and rotary beater in refrigerator to chill.

Set in freezer until ice crystals form
⅔ cup undiluted evaporated milk

Drain, reserving syrup
1 can (8¾ oz.) apricot halves (7 to 10 halves)
Add to the reserved apricot syrup
Water (enough to make 1 cup liquid)
Heat to boiling.

Empty into a bowl
1 pkg. (3 oz.) lemon-flavored gelatin
Add the boiling liquid and stir until gelatin is completely dissolved. Stir in
2 tablespoons lemon juice
Cool; chill (page 374) until mixture is slightly thicker than consistency of thick unbeaten egg white.

Prepare
½ cup diced celery
½ cup (about 2 oz.) chopped pecans

Apricot Luncheon Mold

When gelatin mixture is of desired consistency, blend in the celery, pecans and
1½ cups cream-style cottage cheese
Using chilled bowl and beater, beat the chilled evaporated milk until very stiff. Gently fold into gelatin mixture. Arrange apricot halves, cut side up, in bottom of mold. Carefully turn the gelatin mixture into the mold and chill in refrigerator until firm.

Unmold (page 374) onto a chilled serving plate. Garnish with **curly endive**. *About 6 servings*

MOLDED AVOCADO KUMQUAT SALAD

▲ Base Recipe

Smooth avocado+tangy kumquat=delightful salad, fit for a party!

Set out a 1-qt. mold.

Empty into a bowl
1 pkg. (3 oz.) lemon-flavored gelatin
Add and stir until dissolved
¾ cup boiling water
Blend in
1¼ cups ginger ale
¼ teaspoon salt
Chill (page 374) until mixture is slightly thicker than consistency of thick unbeaten egg white.

Remove leaves, rinse, drain and thinly slice
1 pt. kumquats (about 2 cups, sliced)
Rinse, peel, cut into halves, remove and discard pits from, and dice
2 small avocados (about 1½ cups, diced)
When gelatin mixture is of desired consistency, mix in the kumquats and avocados. Turn gelatin mixture into the mold and chill in refrigerator until firm.

To serve, unmold (page 374) onto chilled serving plate. If desired, garnish with **curly endive**.
About 6 servings

—MOLDED AVOCADO GRAPEFRUIT SALAD

Follow ▲ Recipe. Increase boiling water to 1½ cups and substitute **½ cup grapefruit juice** for the ginger ale. Substitute **1 cup grapefruit sections** for the kumquat slices. To pre-

Avocado Ring with Blueberries

Cherry Salad Ring

pare grapefruit sections, cut away peel from the garpefruit. Remove sections by cutting on both sides of membranes that divide them, working over a bowl to save juice. Remove and discard the seeds.

AVOCADO RING WITH BLUEBERRIES

Delightful contrast in color, flavor, texture.

Set out a 1-qt. ring mold.

Pour into a small cup or custard cup
  ½ cup cold water
Sprinkle evenly over cold water
  1 env. unflavored gelatin
Let stand until gelatin is softened. Dissolve completely by placing the cup over very hot water. Stir dissolved gelatin and blend in
  1½ teaspoons sugar
  1 teaspoon salt
  ¼ teaspoon monosodium glutamate
  Few grains pepper
  1 cup water
Set aside.

Rinse, cut into halves, remove pits and peel
  2 medium ripe avocados
Cut each into several pieces. Force through a sieve or food mill into a bowl. Blend in
  1 teaspoon grated onion
  ¼ teaspoon grated lemon peel
  ½ teaspoon lemon juice
Blend in the dissolved gelatin mixture and
  1 cup dairy sour cream
  ¼ cup mayonnaise
Turn into the mold. Chill in refrigerator until firm.

Shortly before serving, rinse, sort and drain
  1 pt. blueberries
Unmold (page 374) Avocado Ring onto chilled serving plate. Arrange a ring of blueberries around bottom of mold. Heap remaining berries in center of ring.   *About 8 servings*

BING CHERRY GELATIN SALAD

Set out a 1-qt. mold or 6 individual molds.

Set aside to drain well, reserving syrup
  1 can (17 oz.) Bing cherries (yields about 1½ cups cherries)

Empty into a bowl
  1 pkg. (3 oz.) lemon-flavored gelatin
Add, stirring until the gelatin is completely dissolved
  1 cup boiling water
Blend in a mixture of reserved cherry syrup and
  Cold water (enough to make 1 cup liquid)
  Few drops red food coloring
Pour into a large bowl and set aside to chill (page 374).

Cut cherries into halves and remove pits. Mix cherries into thickened gelatin with
  ½ cup chopped pimiento-stuffed olives
  ½ cup (about 2 oz.) chopped walnuts
Turn mixture into the molds. Chill in refrigerator until firm. Unmold (page 374).

Garnish with
  Curly endive
Top each serving with **mayonnaise.** For individual molds, invert into **lettuce cups** on chilled salad plates.   *6 servings*

BLUE CHEESE SALAD MOLD

Eight ¾-cup individual molds will be needed.

Drain, reserving syrup in a 2-cup measuring cup for liquids
  2 cans (17 oz. each) pitted dark sweet cherries
Cut cherries into halves.

Crumble
  4 oz. blue or Roquefort cheese (about 1 cup, crumbled)
Put cherries and cheese into refrigerator until ready to use.

Add to the reserved syrup
  Water (enough to make 2 cups liquid)
Empty into a large bowl
  2 pkgs. (3 oz. each) cherry-flavored gelatin
Add, stirring until gelatin is dissolved
  2 cups boiling water
When gelatin is completely dissolved, blend in the reserved fruit syrup mixture and
  ¼ cup lemon juice
Chill (page 374) until gelatin mixture is slightly thicker than consistency of thick unbeaten egg white.

When gelatin mixture is of desired consistency, blend in the cherries and cheese and
  ⅓ cup sliced pimiento-stuffed olives
Turn mixture into molds. Chill in refrigerator until firm.

Unmold (page 374) onto chilled salad plates and serve with
  Mayonnaise
      8 servings

Note: A 1½-qt. ring mold may be substituted for the individual molds.

CHERRY SALAD RING

For a luncheon for the girls, fill the center of this pretty ring with Chicken Salad DeLuxe (page 396). Accompany with vegetable relishes and a quick nut bread. It's easy and very good!

Set out a 1-qt. ring mold.

Coarsely chop and set aside on absorbent paper to drain
  ½ cup maraschino cherries
(To avoid a pink tint in the salad, drain cherries thoroughly.)

Drain thoroughly, reserving syrup in a measuring cup
  1 can (20 oz.) crushed pineapple (about 1¾ cups, drained)

Pour into a small saucepan
  ½ cup cold water
Sprinkle evenly over water
  1 env. unflavored gelatin
Set saucepan over low heat and stir until gelatin is completely dissolved.

Remove from heat. Stir in ¾ cup of the pineapple syrup and
  ½ cup water
  ¼ cup lime juice
Arrange about 2 tablespoons maraschino cherries in bottom of the mold. Pour in a small amount of gelatin mixture (just enough to cover the cherries). Chill until partially set.

Chill (page 374) remaining gelatin mixture until slightly thicker than consistency of thick unbeaten egg white.

Meanwhile, beat until fluffy

1 pkg. (8 oz.) cream cheese, softened

Add gradually and beat in the remaining pineapple syrup.

When gelatin mixture is about the same consistency as cheese mixture, stir several tablespoonfuls into the cheese mixture. Continue to add gelatin mixture slowly, beating constantly until well blended. Stir in pineapple and remaining cherries.

When first layer in mold is of desired consistency, spoon the cheese mixture over it, spreading evenly. (Both layers should be of almost the same consistency when combined to avoid separation when unmolded.) Chill in refrigerator until firm.

Unmold (page 374) onto chilled plate; garnish.
6 to 8 servings

CRANBERRY RING-AROUND GRAPEFRUIT MOLD

Set out a 1½-qt. ring mold.

Pour into a small bowl

½ cup cold water

Sprinkle evenly over water

2 env. unflavored gelatin

Let stand until gelatin is softened. Dissolve completely by placing bowl over very hot water.

Meanwhile, combine in a bowl and blend thoroughly

4 cups (two 16-oz. cans) whole cranberry sauce

2 teaspoons grated orange peel

¼ cup orange juice

When gelatin is dissolved, blend into the cranberry mixture. Chill (page 374) until mixture begins to gel (becomes slightly thicker).

Chop and set aside

½ cup (about 2 oz.) pecans

Cut (page 9) into small pieces and set aside

16 marshmallows (¼ lb.)

When gelatin mixture is of desired consistency, stir in the nuts. Spoon one half of the gelatin mixture into the mold. Top with marshmallow pieces. Spoon in the remaining gelatin mixture. Chill in refrigerator until firm.

Unmold (page 374) onto chilled platter. Fill center with

Grapefruit sections

If desired, garnish with few **sprigs of mint.**
8 to 10 servings

MOLDED CRANBERRY SALADS

▲ Base Recipe

Set out eight ¾-cup individual molds.

For Cranberry Relish—Wash and sort

2 cups cranberries

Rinse (do not peel), cut into pieces and, if necessary, remove seeds from

1 medium orange

½ lemon

Put the fruit through the medium blade of a food chopper. Blend in

1 cup sugar

Cover; chill in refrigerator at least 1 hr. to allow flavors to blend.

For Salad—When cranberry relish is chilled, drain, reserving syrup in a 2-cup measuring cup for liquids. Add to the syrup

Water (enough to make 2 cups liquid)

Empty into a large bowl

2 pkgs. (3 oz. each) raspberry- or cherry-flavored gelatin (or use one 3-oz. pkg. of either flavor and one 3-oz. pkg. lemon-flavored gelatin)

Add and stir until gelatin is completely dissolved

2 cups boiling water

Stir in the syrup mixture. Cool; chill (page 374) until gelatin mixture is slightly thicker than consistency of thick unbeaten egg white.

When gelatin mixture is of desired consistency, blend in the cranberry relish. Turn into the molds and chill in refrigerator until firm.

Unmold (page 374) onto chilled individual salad plates lined with crisp **salad greens.**
8 servings

—CRANBERRY APPLE SALAD

Follow ▲ Recipe. Substitute for the one half lemon **1 apple,** rinsed, quartered, cored and coarsely chopped (do not put through food chopper).

—CRANBERRY WALNUT SALAD

Follow ▲ Recipe or recipe for Cranberry Apple Salads. Mix in **½ cup (about 2 oz.) chopped walnuts** with the cranberry relish.

CREAMY CRANBERRY DESSERT SALADS

▲ Base Recipe

Set out eight ½-cup star molds. Chill bowl and beater in refrigerator.

Pour into a small cup or custard cup

2 tablespoons lemon juice

2 tablespoons orange juice

Sprinkle evenly over the juices

1 env. unflavored gelatin

Dissolve gelatin completely by placing cup over very hot water.

Stir gelatin and put into an electric blender container with

1 can (16 oz.) whole cranberry sauce (about 2 cups)

⅔ cup cream-style cottage cheese

½ cup crushed pineapple (including syrup)

1 strip (4 in.) lemon peel (colored part only)

Cover; blend until mixture is creamy and the cranberries are finely chopped. Pour mixture into a bowl.

Cranberry Ring-Around-Grapefruit Mold

Chill until gelatin mixture is slightly thicker than consistency of thick, unbeaten egg white.

Just before mixture is of desired consistency, using chilled bowl and beater, whip

½ cup chilled heavy cream

Gently fold whipped cream into gelatin mixture. Turn into molds.

Chill in refrigerator until firm. Unmold (page 374) onto crisp **lettuce cups.** Garnish with small star cutouts from **jellied cranberry sauce.**
8 servings

—FROZEN CREAMY CRANBERRY SALAD

Follow ▲ Recipe. Set refrigerator control for colder operating temperature. Turn mixture into refrigerator tray (instead of star molds); freeze 3 to 4 hrs.

TWO-TONE SALAD

Set out eight ¾-cup individual molds or a 1½-qt. mold.

For Grape Juice Layer—Set out

2 cups grape juice

Blend thoroughly in a saucepan

2 env. unflavored gelatin

½ cup sugar

Stir in 1 cup of the grape juice. Set saucepan over low heat and stir until gelatin and sugar are dissolved. Remove from heat. Stir in remaining 1 cup of grape juice and

½ cup orange juice

1 teaspoon lemon juice

Pour mixture into molds. Chill until slightly set.

Creamy Cranberry Dessert Salad

Two-Tone Salad

For Cream Cheese Layer—Pour into a small saucepan
   ½ cup cold water
Sprinkle evenly over water
   1 env. unflavored gelatin
Set saucepan over low heat and stir until gelatin is completely dissolved.

Pour dissolved gelatin into an electric blender container. Add in order
   1 cup milk or cream
   9 oz. cream cheese, cut in pieces
   ¼ cup sugar
   1 strip lemon peel (colored part only)
   1 tablespoon lemon juice
   ½ teaspoon salt
Cover and blend until smooth and fluffy.

When grape layer in mold is slightly set, immediately turn cream cheese mixture onto first layer. (Both layers should be of almost same consistency to avoid separation of layers when unmolded.) Chill in refrigerator until firm.

Unmold (page 374) onto **salad greens.** Garnish with **fresh grapes.**   *8 servings*

COLORFUL LAYERED SALAD

Set out a 9x5x3-in. loaf pan.

For Green Layer—Empty into a bowl
   1 pkg. (3 oz.) lime-flavored gelatin
Add and stir until the gelatin is completely dissolved
   1 cup boiling water
Stir into gelatin mixture
   1 cup cold water

Pour into the loaf pan a small amount of the gelatin mixture (enough to make a thin layer). Chill in refrigerator until slightly set.

Chill (page 374) remaining gelatin mixture until slightly thicker than consistency of thick unbeaten egg white. When gelatin mixture in mold is of the desired consistency, arrange in rows in the slightly set gelatin, cut sides up
   ½ cup halved seedless green grapes
Carefully spoon remaining gelatin over grapes. Chill in refrigerator until slightly set.

Meanwhile, prepare Cream Cheese Layer.

For Cream Cheese Layer—Put into a bowl,
   1 cup mayonnaise
Empty into another bowl
   1 pkg. (3 oz.) lemon-flavored gelatin
Add and stir until gelatin is completely dissolved
   1 cup boiling water
Stir into gelatin mixture
   1 cup unsweetened pineapple juice
   1 tablespoon sugar
   ¼ teaspoon salt
Add gelatin mixture gradually to mayonnaise, stirring constantly. Chill (page 374) until mixture begins to gel (becomes slightly thicker).

Meanwhile, beat until of medium consistency
   1 pkg. (3 oz.) cream cheese, softened
When gelatin mixture is of about the same consistency as the cheese, stir several tablespoons of the gelatin mixture into the cheese. Continue to add gelatin mixture slowly, beating constantly until well blended.

When green layer in mold is of the proper consistency, immediately spoon cheese mixture over it, spreading evenly to corners. (Layers should be almost same consistency when combined to avoid separation of layers when unmolded.) Chill in refrigerator until slightly set.

Meanwhile, prepare Red Layer.

For Red Layer—Empty into a bowl
   1 pkg. (3 oz.) raspberry-flavored gelatin
Add and stir until the gelatin is completely dissolved
   1 cup boiling water
Stir into gelatin mixture
   1 cup cold water
   1 teaspoon lemon juice
Chill (page 374) until slightly thicker than consistency of thick unbeaten egg white.

Meanwhile, peel and slice crosswise into ¼-in. thick slices
   1 banana with all-yellow or brown-flecked peel
When gelatin mixture is of desired consistency, fold in banana slices. When cream cheese layer in mold is about the same consistency, turn banana mixture over the cheese layer. Chill in refrigerator until firm.

Unmold (page 374) onto chilled serving plate. Garnish with
   Lettuce leaves
   Red and green maraschino cherries, drained
Cut into ¾-in. slices and serve.
     About 12 servings

CITRUS PECAN MOLD

Set out a 1½-qt. mold.

Pour into a small bowl
   ½ cup lime juice
   ¼ cup orange juice
Sprinkle evenly over juice
   2 env. unflavored gelatin
Set aside.

Heat until very hot
   1 cup orange juice
Remove from heat and immediately stir in softened gelatin until gelatin is completely dissolved. Stir in, in order
   ⅔ cup sugar
   ¼ teaspoon salt
   2 cups ginger ale
Chill (page 374) until gelatin mixture is slightly thicker than consistency of thick unbeaten egg white.

Using a sharp knife, cut away peel and remove sections (by cutting on either side of dividing membrane) from enough oranges to yield
   2 cups orange sections
Remove and discard any seeds.

Coarsely chop
   ⅔ cup (about 2½ oz.) pecans
When gelatin mixture is of desired consistency, mix in the orange sections and pecans. Turn into mold and chill in refrigerator until firm.

To serve, unmold (page 374) onto chilled serving plate.   *About 8 servings*

PEACHES AND CREAM SALAD

Set out a 1-qt. mold.

Drain, reserving syrup
   1 can (29 oz.) sliced peaches (about 2 cups, drained)
Heat 1 cup of the syrup to boiling

Meanwhile, empty into a bowl
   1 pkg. (3 oz.) lemon-flavored gelatin
Add the hot peach syrup and stir until gelatin is completely dissolved. Cool; chill (page 374) until gelatin mixture is slightly thicker than consistency of thick unbeaten egg white.

Set a bowl and rotary beater in refrigerator to chill.

When gelatin mixture is of desired consistency, mix in the peaches and
- **⅔ cup cream-style cottage cheese**
- **½ cup (2 oz.) salted pecans, chopped**

Using the chilled bowl and beater, beat until cream is of medium consistency (piles softly)
- **½ cup chilled heavy cream**

Fold whipped cream into gelatin mixture. Turn into the prepared mold and chill in refrigerator until firm.

Unmold (page 374) and garnish.

6 to 8 servings

PARTY-PERFECT SALAD MOLDS

▲ Base Recipe

Set out six ½ cup individual molds.

Set out to thaw according to directions on package
- **1 pkg. (10 oz.) frozen sliced peaches**

Drain the peaches, reserving syrup in a 1-cup measuring cup for liquids.

Empty into a bowl
- **1 pkg. (3 oz.) orange-flavored gelatin**

If necessary, add to the reserved peach syrup
- **Water (enough to make ¾ cup liquid)**

Heat to boiling and add to bowl containing gelatin. Stir until gelatin is completely dissolved. Stir into gelatin mixture
- **1 cup ginger ale**
- **¼ cup lemon juice**

Chill (page 374) until gelatin mixture is slightly thicker than consistency of thick, unbeaten egg white.

Set out
- **½ cup maraschino cherries, halved**
- **¼ cup (about 1½ oz.) blanched almonds (page 9), chopped**

When gelatin is of desired consistency, blend in the peaches, cherries, and almonds. Turn into molds and chill in refrigerator until firm.

Unmold (page 374) onto chilled salad plates. Garnish with sprigs of **watercress.**

6 servings

—MANDARIN ORANGE MOLD

Follow ▲ Recipe. Use a 1-qt. mold instead of the individual molds. Substitute **2 cans (8½ oz. each) mandarin oranges,** drained, for the peaches and the **orange syrup** for the peach syrup. Increase the syrup and water mixture to 1 cup; omit the lemon juice.

JELLIED PEACH AND CHEESE SALAD

For First Layer—Set out a 2-qt. oval mold.

Empty into a bowl
- **1 pkg. (3 oz.) lemon-flavored gelatin**

Add and stir until the gelatin is completely dissolved
- **1 cup boiling water**

Stir into gelatin mixture
- **1 cup cold water**

Pour a small amount of gelatin mixture (enough to make a thin layer) into bottom of mold. Chill in refrigerator until slightly set. Chill (page 374) remaining gelatin mixture until slightly thicker than consistency of thick unbeaten egg white.

Meanwhile, rinse, peel, cut into halves and pit
- **4 medium (about 1 lb.) firm ripe peaches**

Quickly blot peaches on absorbent paper, if necessary. Cut peaches into slices. Add to peaches and mix lightly
- **1 teaspoon lemon juice**

Set aside.

When gelatin in mold is slightly set, immediately remove from refrigerator. Arrange peach slices in two lengthwise rows in the gelatin layer in mold. Carefully spoon in remaining gelatin mixture. Chill in refrigerator until slightly set.

For Second Layer—Meanwhile, pour into a small saucepan
- **½ cup cold water**

Sprinkle evenly over cold water
- **1 env. unflavored gelatin**

Set saucepan over low heat and stir constantly until gelatin is completely dissolved. Remove from heat.

Put into a bowl and beat until well blended and creamy
- **1 cup cream-style cottage cheese**
- **1 pkg. (3 oz.) cream cheese, softened**
- **½ cup milk**
- **½ cup mayonnaise**
- **1 tablespoon lemon juice**
- **¼ teaspoon salt**

Stir dissolved gelatin and blend it into cheese mixture. When first layer in mold is slightly set, immediately turn cheese mixture onto it and gently spread out in an even layer. (The two layers should be of about the same consistency when combined to avoid separation of layers when unmolded.) Chill in refrigerator until firm.

Unmold (page 374) onto a chilled platter. Garnish with
- **Pineapple slices, cut in halves**
- **Fresh ripe whole strawberries or Bing cherries**
- **Curly endive**

6 to 8 servings

MOLDED PEAR GINGER SALAD

Set out six 4½-in. shallow molds or individual pie pans.*

Empty into a bowl
- **1 pkg. (3 oz.) lemon-flavored gelatin**

Add, stirring until gelatin is dissolved
- **¾ cup boiling water**

Stir until completely dissolved. Blend in
- **1¼ cups ginger ale**

Chill (page 374) until gelatin mixture is slightly

Jellied Peach and Cheese Salad

thicker than consistency of thick unbeaten egg white.

Drain, reserving syrup or use in other food preparation
- **1 can (16 oz.) pear halves (about 6)**

Spoon about 2 tablespoons of slightly thickened gelatin into each mold. Spoon onto center of gelatin in each mold ½ teaspoon chopped ginger. Place one pear half, cavity side down, over the ginger in each mold. Spoon remaining slightly thickened gelatin into molds, covering pears.

Chill in refrigerator until firm.

Unmold (page 374) onto chilled individual salad plates and garnish with **salad greens.** Accompany with **ripe olives** and **Cream Cheese Nut Balls** (page 372). *6 servings*

*An 11x7x1½-in. pan or 9x9x2-in. pan may be substituted for the individual molds. Spoon about one third of the slightly thickened gelatin into the pan and proceed as above, spacing ginger and pears evenly. Arrange pear halves over the ginger. Chill in refrigerator until firm. Cut into squares when ready to serve. Using a wide spatula or pancake turner, transfer to salad plates.

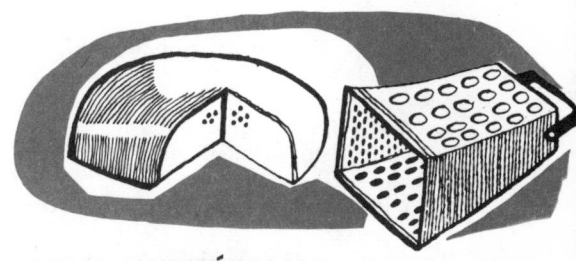

CHEESE SOUFFLÉ SALAD

▲ Base Recipe

Set out a 1-qt. mold.

Set aside to drain, reserving syrup
- **1 can (16 oz.) pear halves (6 to 8 halves)**
- **¾ cup drained canned seedless grapes**

Empty into an electric blender container
- **1 pkg. (3 oz.) lime-flavored gelatin**

379

Pour into blender container

1 cup boiling water

Cover and blend until gelatin is dissolved. Add ½ cup reserved syrup (grape and pear syrups combined) and

½ cup Blender Mayonnaise (page 413)
⅓ cup cream-style cottage cheese
1 tablespoon lime juice
¼ teaspoon salt

Cover and blend until mixture is smooth. Pour into a refrigerator tray.

Set tray in the freezing compartment of refrigerator about 25 min., or until mixture is firm about 1 in. in from edges of tray. (Do not change refrigerator control from normal operating temperature.)

Return the chilled mixture to the blender container and blend until fluffy. Turn off motor. Add the pear halves, grapes and

¼ cup (about 1 oz.) walnuts

Cover and blend just to coarsely chop fruits and nuts. Turn mixture into mold.

Chill in refrigerator until firm. Unmold (page 374) onto crisp **salad greens**.

4 to 6 servings

—GRAPEFRUIT CHEESE SOUFFLÉ SALAD

Follow ▲ Recipe. Substitute **canned grapefruit sections** for pear halves. Omit grapes. Use ½ cup reserved grapefruit syrup instead of the pear-grape syrup mixture. Wash, cut into halves, remove pit and peel **1 small avocado**; cut into pieces. Add avocado to blender container with the cottage cheese and blend until both are smooth.

LIME COTTAGE CHEESE SALAD

Set out a 1½-qt. ring mold or fancy mold.

Set aside to drain, reserving syrup in a 2-cup measuring cup

1 can (8¼ oz.) crushed pineapple (about ⅔ cup, drained)

Empty into a large bowl

2 pkgs. (3 oz. each) lime-flavored gelatin

Add

2 cups boiling water

Stir until gelatin is completely dissolved. Add to reserved pineapple syrup

Cold water, enough to make 1⅔ cups liquid

Blend into dissolved gelatin.

Chill until gelatin mixture is slightly thicker than consistency of thick unbeaten egg white.

Rinse, quarter, core, coarsely chop and set aside

2 pears

Put into a small mixer bowl and beat until creamy and smooth

1 cup cream-style cottage cheese
½ teaspoon ginger

Blend into thickened gelatin mixture with the crushed pineapple and chopped pears. Pour into mold.

Chill in the refrigerator until firm.

Unmold (page 374) onto crisp **salad greens**. Garnish with **fresh fruits** in season.

6 to 8 servings

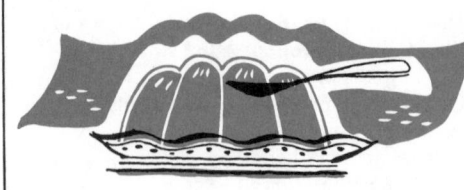

MOLDED CHEESE OLIVE SALAD

Set out six ½-cup salad molds. Place a bowl and rotary beater in refrigerator to chill.

Set out to soften

1 pkg. (3 oz.) cream cheese

Drain, reserving liquid

1 can (8½ oz.) pineapple tidbits (about ⅔ cup, drained)

Set pineapple tidbits aside.

Add to reserved pineapple liquid and set aside

Water (enough to make ½ cup liquid)

Empty into a bowl

1 pkg. (3 oz.) orange-flavored gelatin

Add and stir until gelatin is completely dissolved

1 cup boiling water

Stir in reserved ½ cup liquid and

3 tablespoons lemon juice

Beat the cream cheese until smooth. Stir several tablespoonfuls of the gelatin mixture into the cheese. Continue to add gelatin mixture slowly, beating constantly, until well blended. Chill until mixture is slightly thicker than consistency of thick unbeaten egg white.

When gelatin mixture is of desired consistency, fold in pineapple tidbits and

1 cup shredded sharp Cheddar cheese
½ cup chopped pimiento-stuffed olives

Using chilled bowl and beater, beat until of medium consistency (piles softly) and fold into gelatin mixture

½ cup chilled heavy cream

Turn mixture into molds. Chill in refrigerator until firm.

To serve, unmold (page 374) into **lettuce cups**. Or unmold on **curly endive** and garnish with crisp **bacon strips**.

6 servings

MOLDED PINEAPPLE CHEESE SALAD

Set out a 2-qt. ring mold.

Drain, reserving syrup, and set aside

1 can (20 oz.) crushed pineapple (about 1¾ cups pineapple, drained)

Mix thoroughly in a bowl

2 env. unflavored gelatin
½ cup sugar
½ teaspoon salt

Set aside.

Add to reserved pineapple syrup, if necessary

Water (enough to make 1½ cups liquid)

Heat in a saucepan until very hot. Remove from heat and immediately add to gelatin mixture, stirring until gelatin and sugar are completely dissolved. Mix in

1 cup unsweetened pineapple juice
1 cup orange juice
2 or 3 drops yellow food coloring

Chill (page 374) until mixture is slightly thicker than consistency of thick unbeaten egg white.

Put into a bowl

1 lb. cream cheese

Beat cheese until softened. Add gradually, beating in

2 teaspoons grated lemon peel
3 tablespoons lemon juice

When gelatin mixture is of the same consistency as the cheese mixture, stir several tablespoons of the gelatin mixture into cheese mixture. Continue to add gelatin mixture slowly, beating constantly, until well blended. Mix in crushed pineapple. Turn mixture into mold. Place mold in refrigerator to chill until firm.

Unmold (page 374) onto chilled large serving plate.

If desired, fill center of salad ring with

Honeydew melon balls

Garnish with

Frosted grapes (page 370)
Mint leaves

10 to 12 servings

LAYERED FRUIT CHEESE BUFFET SALAD

▲ *Base Recipe*

This impressive salad mold is as beautiful as it is big, and as good as it is beautiful. It will ornament any party buffet and delight your guests. For the family or for small luncheons, the cherry layer alone is the basis of another appealing salad.

Set out a 3-qt. ring mold.

For Cheese Layer—Drain thoroughly, reserving syrup in a 1-cup measuring cup for liquids

1 can (17 oz.) pitted dark sweet cherries (about 1¼ cups, drained)

Add to the reserved cherry syrup, if necessary

Water (enough to make 1 cup liquid)

Empty into a bowl

1 pkg. (3 oz.) cherry-flavored gelatin

Add and stir until gelatin is completely dissolved

1 cup boiling water

Stir in the reserved liquid. Cool; chill (page 374) until mixture is slightly thicker than consistency of thick unbeaten egg white.

When gelatin mixture is of desired consistency, stir in the cherries. Turn into mold and chill in refrigerator until partially set.

For Cheese Layer—Drain, combining and reserving the syrups

> **1 can (30 oz.) peeled apricot halves (about 2 cups, drained)**
> **1 can (17 oz.) pear halves (about 6 halves)**
> **1 can (17 oz.) sliced peaches (about 1¼ cups, drained)**

Cut the fruit into pieces and put into a bowl. Set aside to use in Mixed Fruit Layer.

Drain, reserving syrup

> **1 can (8¼ oz.) crushed pineapple (about ¾ cup, drained)**

Set the drained pineapple aside.

Stir the pineapple syrup into the mixed fruit syrups and set aside.

Pour into a small cup or custard cup

> **¼ cup cold water**
> **¼ cup reserved fruit syrup**

Sprinkle evenly over water

> **1 env. unflavored gelatin**

Let stand until softened.

Prepare

> **½ cup finely chopped celery**
> **¼ cup (about 1 oz.) finely chopped pecans**
> **2 tablespoons minced green pepper**

Heat 1 cup of the reserved fruit syrup until very hot. Remove from heat and immediately stir in softened gelatin until gelatin is completely dissolved. Cool; chill (page 374) until gelatin mixture is slightly thicker than consistency of thick unbeaten egg white.

Meanwhile, beat until fluffy

> **6 oz. cream cheese, softened**

When gelatin mixture is about the same consistency as the cheese, stir several tablespoonfuls into the cheese. Continue to add gelatin mixture slowly, beating constantly until well blended. Stir in the drained pineapple, celery, pecans and green pepper.

When first layer in mold is partially set, immediately spoon the cheese mixture over it, spreading evenly. (Both layers should be of almost the same consistency when combined to avoid separation when unmolded.) Chill in refrigerator until cheese layer is partially set.

For Mixed Fruit Layer—Empty into a bowl

> **1 pkg. (3 oz.) lemon-flavored gelatin**

Measure remaining fruit syrup; if necessary, add

> **Water (enough to make 2 cups liquid)**

Heat 1 cup of the liquid to boiling; add to bowl and stir until gelatin is completely dissolved. Stir in the remaining liquid. Cool; chill (page 374) until mixture is slightly thicker than consistency of thick unbeaten egg white.

Meanwhile, prepare, section and cut into small pieces

> **2 medium oranges**

Wash, quarter, core and cut into small pieces

> **2 small red apples**

Mix oranges and apples with reserved fruit in the bowl.

When gelatin mixture is of desired consistency, stir in the fruit.

Turn mixture into the mold over the cheese layer. Chill in refrigerator until firm.

Unmold (page 374) onto a chilled serving plate.

14 to 16 servings

—DARK SWEET CHERRY SALAD MOLD

Follow ▲ Recipe for Cherry Layer only. Substitute a 1-qt. mold for the 3-qt. ring mold and **lemon-flavored gelatin** for the cherry-flavored gelatin. Add a **few drops red food coloring** with the syrup mixture. Cut the cherries into halves. Stir in **½ cup sliced pimiento-stuffed olives** and **½ cup (about 2 oz.) chopped walnuts** with the cherries. Chill until firm. Unmold.

6 to 8 servings

FRUIT-FILLED GELATIN SALAD

▲ Base Recipe

For Lemon Mayonnaise—Set a bowl and beater in refrigerator to chill.

Set out

> **1 cup mayonnaise**

Blend in

> **1½ tablespoons lemon juice**

Using the chilled bowl and beater, beat until cream is of medium consistency (piles softly)

> **¼ cup chilled heavy cream**

With few final strokes, beat or blend in

> **2½ tablespoons sifted confectioners' sugar**

Fold into mayonnaise mixture.

For Salad—Drain, reserving syrup in a 2-cup measuring cup for liquids

> **1 can (20 oz.) crushed pineapple (about 1½ cups, drained)**
> **1 can (16 oz.) sliced peaches (about 1¼ cups, drained)**

Rinse

> **2 medium oranges**

With a sharp knife, cut away peel and white membrane. Remove sections by cutting on either side of dividing membranes; remove, section by section, over the measuring cup to collect juice.

Put fruit into a bowl, cover, and put into refrigerator until ready to use.

Add to reserved syrup

> **Orange juice (enough to make 2 cups liquid)**

Empty into a large bowl

> **2 pkgs. (3 oz. each) cherry-flavored gelatin**

Add, stirring constantly

> **2 cups boiling water**

Stir until gelatin is completely dissolved; blend in the reserved fruit juice and

> **¼ cup lemon juice**

Chill in refrigerator or over ice and water until gelatin mixture is slightly thicker than consistency of thick unbeaten egg white. (If mixture is placed over ice and water, stir frequently; if it is placed in the refrigerator, stir occasionally.)

When gelatin is of desired consistency, stir in the pineapple, peaches, and orange sections. Turn mixture into 1-qt. mold. Place in refrigerator to chill until firm.

Unmold (page 374) onto chilled serving platter. Serve with the Lemon Mayonnaise.

About 12 servings

—JEWEL MOLD

Follow ▲ Recipe. Omit fruit. Substitute **2 cups orange juice** for the 2 cups fruit syrup. Pour mixture into a 1-qt. fancy mold and chill until firm.

About 8 servings

FRUITY MARSHMALLOW MOLDS

Set out eight ½-cup individual molds. Chill bowl and beater in refrigerator.

Set aside to drain, reserving syrup

> **1 jar or can (29 oz.) mixed fruits for salad (about 2 cups, drained)**

Heat until very hot

> **½ cup reserved fruit syrup**

Put syrup into an electric blender container with

> **24 marshmallows (6 oz.)**
> **1 tablespoon lemon juice**

Fruity Marshmallow Molds

Cover and blend until smooth. Add drained fruit; cover and blend just until chopped.

Using chilled bowl and beater, whip
1½ cups chilled heavy cream
Add blended mixture to whipped cream and mix gently and thoroughly. Turn into molds. Chill in refrigerator until firm.

Unmold (page 374) on **curly endive**. Garnish each mold with a **sprig of mint** and **maraschino cherry** half. Serve immediately.

8 servings

Note: If using canned fruit cocktail, do not chop in blender. Add drained fruit to whipped cream with blended marshmallows.

To vary—Add a generous dash of **rum or brandy** to fruit before blending.

BEET SALAD MOLD

▲ *Base Recipe*

Set out a 1-qt. mold.

Drain, reserving liquid
1 can (16 oz.) diced beets (about 2 cups, drained)

Empty into a bowl
1 pkg. (3 oz.) lemon-flavored gelatin
Add to bowl and stir until gelatin is completely dissolved
1 cup boiling water
Stir in the reserved beet liquid and
3 tablespoons cider vinegar
½ teaspoon salt
Cool; chill (page 374) until gelatin mixture is slightly thicker than consistency of thick unbeaten egg white.

Dice enough celery to yield
½ cup diced celery

When gelatin mixture is of desired consistency, mix in the diced beets, celery and
2 tablespoons grated onion
1 tablespoon prepared horseradish
Turn into the mold and chill in refrigerator until firm.

Unmold (page 374) onto chilled serving plate.
6 to 8 servings

—CREAMY BEET SALAD MOLD

Follow ▲ Recipe. Decrease vinegar to 1 tablespoon and omit horseradish. Blend **½ cup dairy sour cream** into gelatin mixture with the diced beets.

—BEET AND CUCUMBER SALAD

Follow ▲ Recipe. Decrease beets to 1 cup and vinegar to 2 tablespoons. Omit celery. Rinse and pare **1 small cucumber.** Remove and discard seeds. Dice enough of the cucumber to yield ¾ cup diced cucumber. Mix in the cucumber with diced beets.

MOLDED COTTAGE CHEESE AND OLIVE SALAD

Set out an 8x4x2-in. loaf pan.

Pour into a small bowl
¾ cup cold water
Sprinkle evenly over water
2 env. unflavored gelatin
Let gelatin stand until softened.

Meanwhile, heat until very hot
1¼ cups (10¾-oz. can) condensed tomato soup
Remove from heat, add softened gelatin and stir until gelatin is completely dissolved. Chill (page 374) until gelatin mixture begins to gel (becomes slightly thicker).

Meanwhile, prepare and set aside
1 cup chopped ripe olives
½ cup (about 1 stalk) chopped celery
⅓ cup chopped green pepper
2 tablespoons chopped pimiento
1 tablespoon minced onion

Force through sieve into a bowl
2 cups cream-style cottage cheese
Blend with cheese
⅓ cup mayonnaise
2 tablespoons lemon juice
2 teaspoons Worcestershire sauce
¼ teaspoon monosodium glutamate
Few grains pepper
Blend in vegetables and add to gelatin mixture. Turn into loaf pan. Chill in refrigerator until firm.

Unmold (page 374) onto chilled serving plate. Garnish with
Whole ripe olives
Bits of pimiento
Green pepper strips
About 8 servings

LIME AND COTTAGE CHEESE LOAF

▲ *Base Recipe*

Set out a 9x5x3-in. loaf pan.

Empty into a bowl
1 pkg. (3 oz.) lime-flavored gelatin
Add and stir until gelatin is completely dissolved
1 cup boiling water
Cool; chill (page 374) until mixture is slightly thicker than consistency of thick unbeaten egg white.

Rinse and pare
1 medium cucumber
Cut into halves lengthwise; remove and discard seeds. Dice the cucumber (enough to yield 1 cup, diced). Mix with
1 cup cream-style cottage cheese
½ cup mayonnaise
⅓ cup sliced ripe olives
2 teaspoons grated onion
and a mixture of
½ teaspoon salt
⅛ teaspoon white pepper
When gelatin mixture is of desired consistency, blend in the cottage cheese mixture. Turn into the pan and chill in refrigerator until firm.

Mix and set in refrigerator to chill and to allow flavors to blend
1 pkg. (3 oz.) cream cheese, softened
1 tablespoon salad dressing
¾ teaspoon grated onion
⅛ teaspoon salt
To serve, unmold (page 374) onto a chilled serving plate. Spread cream cheese mixture over top of mold. *About 8 servings*

—LIME AND PINEAPPLE MOLD

Follow ▲ Recipe; use a 1-qt. mold. Drain **1 can (20 oz.) crushed pineapple** and set aside. Omit cucumber, mayonnaise, olives, onion, salt and pepper. When gelatin mixture is of desired consistency, stir in the drained

Molded Cottage Cheese and Olive Salad

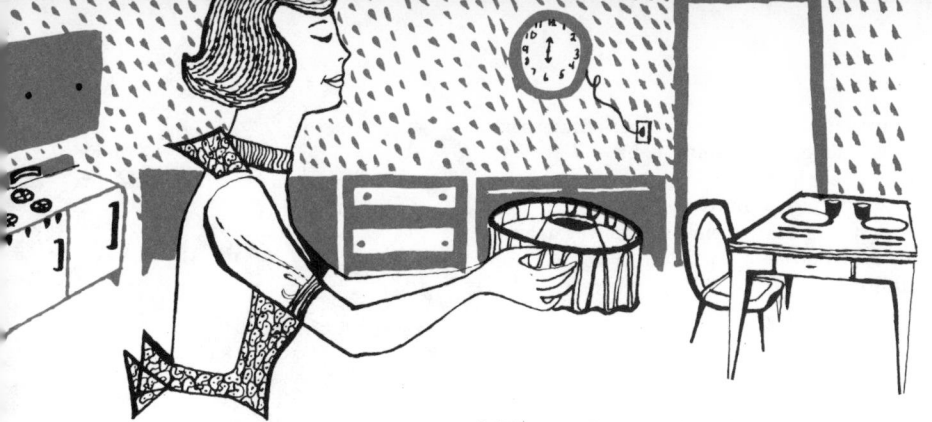

crushed pineapple, **½ cup diced celery** and **½ cup chopped walnuts** and the cottage cheese. Omit cream cheese topping.

—LIME MANGO SALAD

Chill a bowl and rotary beater in refrigerator. Chill **½ cup undiluted evaporated milk** in freezer until ice crystals form. Follow ▲ Recipe; use a 1½-qt. mold. Omit cucumber, mayonnaise, olives, onion, salt and pepper. Rinse, cut into halves, remove and discard pits, peel and dice enough mangoes to yield **2 cups diced mango.** Toss lightly with **3 tablespoons lime juice.** When gelatin mixture is of desired consistency, stir in mango with cottage cheese. Using chilled bowl and beater, beat evaporated milk until very stiff; fold into the gelatin mixture. Omit cream cheese topping.

—HORSERADISH SALAD MOLD

Best when served with cold meat or chicken.

Follow ▲ Recipe; use an 8x8x2-in. pan. Prepare double recipe, but use ⅔ cup mayonnaise and 2 tablespoons grated onion. Omit the cucumber and olives. Add **1 cup cold water** to the dissolved gelatin before cooling, and add **½ cup prepared horseradish** with the cottage cheese. Omit cream cheese topping.

EXQUISITE CUCUMBER MOLD

Set out a 2-qt. fancy mold. Place a bowl and rotary beater in refrigerator to chill.

Pour into a small saucepan
½ cup cold water
Sprinkle evenly over cold water
2 env. unflavored gelatin
Set the saucepan over low heat and stir constantly until gelatin is completely dissolved. Remove from heat.

Rinse and pare
5 medium cucumbers
Cut into halves lengthwise; remove and discard seeds. Finely grind cucumbers in an electric blender making 3 cups of cucumber pulp. (If cucumbers are put through a food chopper using fine blade, pulp will be coarser and texture of mold less smooth.) Set aside.

When gelatin is dissolved, stir it and mix thoroughly with
1½ cups mayonnaise
2½ tablespoons prepared horseradish
2 tablespoons grated onion
¼ teaspoon green food coloring
and a mixture of
1 teaspoon salt
¼ teaspoon white pepper
Blend in the cucumber pulp.

Chill gelatin mixture in refrigerator or over ice and water until mixture begins to gel (becomes slightly thicker). If mixture is placed over ice and water, stir frequently; if placed in refrigerator, stir occasionally.

Shortly before gelatin mixture gels, beat, using the chilled bowl and beater, until cream is of medium consistency (piles softly)
1 cup chilled heavy cream
Gently fold whipped cream into gelatin mixture. Turn into mold. Place in refrigerator to chill until firm.

Just before unmolding the salad, score, by pulling tines of fork down cucumber through peel only
½ medium cucumber, rinsed
Cut into thin slices and cut slices into halves.

Unmold salad (page 374); garnish with the cucumber slices and **watercress.**   *8 servings*

DEVILED EGG SALAD

▲ Base Recipe

Prepare and chill
6 Hard-Cooked Eggs (page 133)

Set out six ½-cup individual molds.

Pour into a small cup or custard cup
¼ cup cold water
Sprinkle evenly over water
1 env. unflavored gelatin
Let stand to soften.

Meanwhile, beat together until fluffy
1 pkg. (3 oz.) cream cheese, softened
½ cup mayonnaise
¼ cup ketchup
2 tablespoons cider vinegar
3 drops Tabasco
Dissolve gelatin completely by placing cup over very hot water. Stir it and add gradually to the cream cheese mixture.

Chop the hard-cooked eggs. Add to the cream

cheese mixture with
¼ cup finely chopped green pepper
¼ cup finely chopped celery
2 tablespoons finely chopped pimiento
1 tablespoon finely chopped parsley
1 teaspoon grated onion
1 teaspoon salt
Mix thoroughly. Turn into the molds and chill in refrigerator until firm.

Unmold (page 374) onto chilled serving plates. If desired, serve with slices of cold **ham;** garnish with **watercress.**   *6 servings*

—EGG SALAD

Follow ▲ Recipe; omit molds. Reserve 1 hard-cooked egg for garnish. Decrease mayonnaise to ¼ cup and ketchup to 2 tablespoons. Omit gelatin, cold water, vinegar and Tabasco. Spoon onto **Bibb lettuce leaves** and top each serving with a slice of egg. Or garnish each serving generously with **minced parsley** before topping with egg slice.

MUSTARD RELISH MOLD
(Senfgelee)

A 1½-qt. mold will be needed.

Pour into a small bowl
1 cup cold water
Sprinkle evenly over cold water
2 env. unflavored gelatin
Let stand until softened.

Beat slightly in top of a double boiler
6 eggs
Blend in a mixture of
1½ cups sugar
1½ tablespoons dry mustard
2 teaspoons monosodium glutamate
1¼ teaspoons salt
Add gradually, stirring constantly
1½ cups vinegar
Cook over simmering water, stirring constantly, until mixture thickens. Remove from simmering water. Stir softened gelatin; add to egg mixture and stir until gelatin is completely dissolved. Cool; chill until mixture begins to gel (becomes slightly thicker).

Mustard Relish Mold

Meanwhile, drain
> **1 can (16 oz.) peas (about 1¾ cups, drained)**

Prepare
> **1 cup (about 2 medium) grated carrot**
> **1 cup chopped celery**
> **1 tablespoon minced parsley**

When gelatin is of desired consistency, blend in the vegetables. Turn into the mold. Chill in refrigerator until firm.

Unmold (page 374) onto chilled serving plate. Garnish with
> **Curly endive or other crisp greens**
> *About 12 servings*

MOLDED PICKLE SALAD

For an easy and fun-to-prepare buffet service, unmold this colorful salad (or any one of your favorite molded salads) onto a piece of cardboard cut to fit the mold and covered with aluminum foil. Place this on a large bread board, and surround it with radiating rows of sliced cold meats and cheeses. Around the mold arrange sprigs of watercress and lettuce leaves with ripe olives nestled among them. Into lettuce cups at the corners of the board, drop crisp radish roses and olives. Garnish all with quarters of hard-cooked eggs. Set the board out on your buffet accompanied by baskets of assorted breads and seasoned butter.

Set out a 1-qt. mold.

Empty into a bowl
> **1 pkg. (3 oz.) lime-flavored gelatin**

Add and stir until gelatin is completely dissolved
> **1 cup boiling water**

Stir in
> **½ cup cold water**
> **½ cup liquid from sweet gherkins**

Chill (page 374) until mixture is slightly thicker than consistency of thick unbeaten egg white.

Meanwhile, prepare
> **¾ cup sliced sweet gherkins**
> **⅔ cup shredded cabbage**
> **⅓ cup grated carrot**
> **¼ cup chopped pimiento**
> **¼ cup chopped green pepper**

Molded Pickle Salad

When gelatin is of desired consistency, beat with a rotary beater until light and frothy. Add and beat in
> **¼ cup mayonnaise**

Mix in the prepared pickles and vegetables. Turn into the mold and chill in refrigerator until firm.

Unmold (page 374) onto the foil-covered cardboard or chilled serving plate. *6 servings*

PERFECTION SALAD SURPRISE

▲ Base Recipe

Set out a 1½-qt. mold.

For Cabbage Layer—Mix thoroughly in a saucepan
> **3 tablespoons sugar**
> **1 env. unflavored gelatin**
> **½ teaspoon salt**

Add to mixture
> **½ cup water**

Set over low heat and stir constantly until gelatin is completely dissolved. Remove from heat and stir in
> **¾ cup cold water**
> **2 tablespoons cider vinegar**
> **1 tablespoon lemon juice**

Cool; chill (page 374) until gelatin mixture is slightly thicker than consistency of thick unbeaten egg white.

Meanwhile, prepare and mix in a bowl
> **1 cup shredded cabbage**
> **½ cup finely chopped celery**
> **⅓ cup shredded carrot**
> **¼ cup sliced pimiento-stuffed olives**
> **¼ cup chopped sweet pickle**
> **3 tablespoons slivered green pepper**

When gelatin mixture is of desired consistency stir in the vegetables. Turn mixture into mold. Chill in refrigerator until slightly set. Meanwhile, prepare Cottage Cheese Layer.

For Cottage Cheese Layer—Pour into a small saucepan
> **¼ cup cold water**

Sprinkle evenly over cold water
> **1 env. unflavored gelatin**

Set saucepan over low heat and stir until gelatin is completely dissolved.

Blend dissolved gelatin thoroughly into a mixture of
> **1 cup cream-style cottage cheese**
> **⅔ cup milk or cream**
> **⅔ cup mayonnaise**
> **1 tablespoon lemon juice**
> **1 tablespoon minced chives**
> **¼ teaspoon salt**
> **⅛ teaspoon paprika**

Chill (page 374) until gelatin mixture begins to gel (becomes slightly thicker).

When first layer of mold is slightly set, immediately turn cottage cheese mixture onto first layer. (Layers should be of almost same consistency to avoid separation when un-

molded.) Chill in refrigerator until firm.

Unmold (page 374) on chilled serving plate. Garnish with
> **Watercress**

Serve with
> **Sour Cream Mayonnaise (page 413)**
> *8 to 10 servings*

—PERFECTION SALAD

Follow ▲ Recipe. Use a 1-qt. mold. Increase cabbage to 1½ cups, celery to ¾ cup and carrot to ½ cup. Omit cottage cheese layer. Complete as in ▲ Recipe.

—JELLIED PINEAPPLE GRAPE SALAD

Follow ▲ Recipe. Use a 1-qt. mold. Omit pickle and olives. Add ½ cup drained crushed pineapple and ½ cup seeded and halved Tokay grapes. Omit cottage cheese layer. Complete as in ▲ Recipe.

MOLDED HAM SALAD

Set out a 2-qt. fancy mold.

Pour into a small bowl
> **1 cup cold water**

Sprinkle evenly over cold water
> **2 env. unflavored gelatin**

Set aside.

Put into a saucepan and heat, stirring, until very hot
> **2½ cups (two 10½-oz. cans) condensed consommé**

Remove from heat and immediately stir in the softened gelatin until it is completely dissolved. Stir in
> **3 tablespoons lemon juice**
> **2 tablespoons prepared horseradish**
> **2 tablespoons minced onion**

Cool; chill (page 374) until mixture is slightly thicker than the consistency of thick unbeaten egg white.

Macaroni Picnic

Meanwhile, cut into cubes enough cooked ham to yield

2 cups cubed cooked ham

Prepare

1 cup diced celery
½ cup diced green pepper

When the gelatin mixture is of desired consistency, blend in the ham, celery, and green pepper. Turn into the mold and place in refrigerator to chill until firm.

Unmold (page 374) onto a chilled serving plate. Garnish top of mold with

Strips of pimiento
Sprigs of parsley

Arrange on the plate around mold

Curly endive

About 8 servings

HAM MOUSSE

Set out a 1½-qt. fancy ring mold and a double boiler. Put a small bowl and rotary beater in the refrigerator to chill.

Pour into a small bowl

½ cup cold water

Sprinkle evenly over water

1 env. unflavored gelatin

Let stand to soften.

Combine and beat together slightly in top of double boiler

2 eggs, slightly beaten
1 cup milk

and a mixture of

1 teaspoon dry mustard
½ teaspoon salt
¼ teaspoon paprika
Few grains cayenne pepper

Place double boiler top over simmering water and cook mixture, stirring constantly and rapidly, until mixture coats a metal spoon.

Remove from simmering water at once. Stir the softened gelatin and immediately stir it into custard mixture until gelatin is completely dissolved. Cool; chill in refrigerator. Or chill over ice and water until gelatin mixture is slightly thicker than consistency of thick unbeaten egg white. (If mixture is placed over ice and water, stir frequently; if placed in refrigerator, stir occasionally.)

Grind (page 10) enough cooked ham to yield

2 cups ground cooked ham

Mix thoroughly and set aside the ham, slightly thickened gelatin mixture and a mixture of

2 tablespoons lemon juice
1 tablespoon minced parsley
2 teaspoons prepared horseradish
1 teaspoon onion juice

Using the chilled bowl and rotary beater, beat until cream is of medium consistency (piles softly)

1 cup chilled heavy cream

Gently fold whipped cream into meat mixture. Turn into mold. Put into refrigerator to chill until firm.

Prepare

Horseradish Sour Cream Sauce (page 310)

Unmold gelatin (page 374) onto chilled serving plate. Garnish with **pineapple slice, crab apples,** and **parsley.** Serve with sauce.

About 6 servings

HAM MOUSSE IMPERIAL

Line twelve 2½-in. muffin-pan wells with paper baking cups. Place a bowl and a rotary beater in refrigerator to chill.

Pour into a small saucepan

1 cup cold water

Sprinkle evenly over water

2 env. unflavored gelatin

Set the saucepan over low heat and stir constantly until gelatin is completely dissolved. Remove from heat.

Stir into the gelatin

1 tablespoon prepared mustard
Few grains cayenne pepper

Set the gelatin mixture aside to cool, then chill in refrigerator. Or chill over ice and water until mixture begins to gel (becomes slightly thicker). If mixture is placed over ice and water, stir frequently; if placed in refrigerator, stir occasionally.

Meanwhile, put through medium blade of a food chopper enough cooked ham to yield

4 cups chopped cooked ham

When gelatin is of desired consistency, mix in the ground ham and

2 tablespoons chopped pimiento
2 tablespoons chopped sweet pickle

Using the chilled bowl and beater, beat until cream is of medium consistency (piles softly)

1 cup chilled heavy cream

Fold whipped cream into ham mixture until thoroughly mixed. Spoon into the baking cups. Chill in refrigerator until firm, 2 to 3 hrs.

When ready to serve, arrange lettuce cups on a platter or tray and invert molds onto lettuce cups, removing paper liners.

Serve with

Horseradish Cream (page 311)

1 doz. ham molds

HAM AND ORANGE SOUFFLE SALAD

▲ Base Recipe

Set out a 1-qt. mold. Set a bowl in refrigerator to chill.

Prepare and set aside

1¼ cups diced cooked ham
¾ cup orange sections, cut
¼ cup (about 1 oz.) chopped walnuts

Empty into a bowl

1 pkg. (3 oz.) orange-flavored gelatin

Add and stir until gelatin is completely dissolved

1 cup boiling water

Ham Mousse Imperial (double receipe)

Add and beat with rotary beater until smooth

½ cup cold water
½ cup mayonnaise
2 tablespoons cider vinegar
1 teaspoon grated onion
¼ teaspoon salt
⅛ teaspoon pepper

Pour mixture into a refrigerator tray and put into freezer 15 to 20 min., or until edges are firm about 1 in. from sides of tray, but center is still soft.

When gelatin mixture is of desired consistency, turn into the chilled bowl and beat with rotary beater *just* until fluffy. Mix in the ham, orange pieces and walnuts. Turn mixture into prepared mold and chill in refrigerator 30 to 60 min., or until firm.

Unmold (page 374); garnish. *4 to 6 servings*

▬COLORFUL SOUFFLE SALAD

Follow ▲ Recipe. Substitute **lemon-flavored gelatin.** Omit vinegar, ham, orange, walnuts and pepper. Blend **3 or 4 drops Tabasco** into the mayonnaise mixture. Mix into the whipped gelatin **1 cup (about ¼ lb.) shredded sharp Cheddar cheese, 2 Hard-Cooked Eggs (page 133),** chopped, **⅓ cup diced celery, 2 tablespoons diced pimiento** and **2 tablespoons diced green pepper.**

CORNED BEEF SALAD

Your electric blender makes preparation of this main-dish salad a snap (of the motor switch).

Set out a 1½-qt. ring mold.

Set out a large bowl.

Prepare

4 Hard-Cooked Eggs (page 133)

Peel, cut into halves, and chill.

Avocado Crab Salad, Paella Style

Corned Beef Salad

Pour into a small cup or custard cup

½ cup cold water

Sprinkle evenly over cold water

1 env. unflavored gelatin

Let stand until softened. Dissolve softened gelatin completely by placing it over very hot water.

Meanwhile, break into pieces with a fork and set aside.

2 cans (12 oz. each) corned beef

Cut into pieces and set aside

2 stalks celery, including leaves
1 small onion
½ cucumber, rinsed and pared
¼ lemon, rinsed and seeds removed

Measure and put into blender container

1¼ cups tomato juice
½ cup mayonnaise
1½ to 2 tablespoons capers
¾ teaspoon salt
5 or 6 peppercorns

Stir dissolved gelatin and add to ingredients in blender container with lemon and onion pieces. Cover and blend until peppercorns are very finely chopped. Turn off motor (adding all ingredients at one time before motor is turned on prevents ingredients from being ground too fine). Add celery, cucumber pieces, and egg halves; cover and blend until vegetables are medium-fine. (If blender container becomes too full, empty a little of blended mixture into bowl before adding all of egg halves.) Empty contents of blender container into large bowl.

Turn on blender motor; add a few pieces at a time, about one fourth of the corned beef and coarsely chop. Empty blender-chopped corned beef into the large bowl. Repeat this until all the corned beef is chopped. Gently mix ingredients. Turn mixture into mold and pack gently. Chill in refrigerator 3 to 4 hrs., or until salad is firm.

Unmold (page 374) and garnish with **ripe olives** and **radish roses**. Place in refrigerator until ready to serve. *8 to 10 servings*

CORNED BEEF CABBAGE MOLD

Set out an 8x8x2-in. pan.

Grind (page 10) and set aside enough cooked corned beef to yield

2 cups ground cooked corned beef

Rinse, finely shred and set aside

½ small head cabbage

Wash, quarter, core, finely dice and set aside

1 small apple

Chop and set aside enough sweet pickle to yield

¼ cup chopped sweet pickle

For Corned Beef Layer—Pour into a small cup or custard cup

½ cup cold water

Sprinkle evenly over water

1 env. unflavored gelatin

Let stand until softened.

Heat until very hot

1 cup quick meat broth (page 10)

Stir softened gelatin and add it to meat broth stirring until gelatin is completely dissolved. Stir in

2 tablespoons lemon juice
1 tablespoon Worcestershire sauce
½ teaspoon salt
¼ teaspoon paprika
2 or 3 drops Tabasco

Chill in refrigerator until gelatin mixture is slightly thicker than consistency of thick unbeaten egg white. Stir mixture occasionally.

For Cabbage Layer—Pour into a small cup or custard cup

½ cup cold water

Sprinkle evenly over water

1 env. unflavored gelatin

Let stand until softened.

Heat until very hot

¾ cup water

Stir gelatin and add it to hot water stirring until gelatin is completely dissolved. Stir in until sugar is dissolved

3 tablespoons sugar
¼ cup vinegar
1 tablespoon lemon juice
½ teaspoon salt

Chill in refrigerator as directed for first layer.

To Complete Mold—Blend

½ cup mayonnaise
¼ cup minced onion

When first gelatin mixture is of desired consistency, blend in mayonnaise mixture and corned beef. Turn into prepared pan and chill.

When second mixture is of desired consistency, blend in cabbage, apple, pickle and

½ teaspoon caraway seed

When meat layer is slightly set, immediately turn cabbage mixture onto first layer. (Both layers should be of almost the same consistency to avoid separation of layers when unmolded.) Put into refrigerator to chill until firm.

Unmold (page 374); garnish as desired.

8 to 10 servings

LAYERED MEAT POTATO SALAD RING

Set out a 1½-qt. ring mold.

Grind (page 10) and set aside enough luncheon meat to yield

1½ cups ground luncheon meat

Wash and cook covered in boiling salted water to cover

3 medium (about 1 lb.) potatoes

Cook about 30 min., or until potatoes are tender when pierced with a fork. Drain. To dry potatoes, shake pan over low heat. Peel immediately, dice and set aside.

Prepare, chop and set aside

2 Hard-Cooked Eggs (page 133)

For Meat Layer—Pour into a small cup or custard cup

¼ cup cold water

Sprinkle evenly over water

1 env. unflavored gelatin

Let stand to soften.

Heat in medium-size saucepan

1 can (8 oz.) tomato sauce
(about 1 cup)

Remove from heat and immediately stir in softened gelatin until gelatin is completely dissolved. Blend in chopped eggs, ground luncheon meat and

2 tablespoons minced onion
2 tablespoons minced sweet pickle

Blend well and mix in

2 tablespoons lemon juice
1 teaspoon prepared mustard
1 teaspoon prepared horseradish
2 or 3 drops Tabasco

Turn gelatin mixture into mold and place in refrigerator to chill until very thick but not completely gelled.

For Potato Salad Layer—Pour into a small cup or custard cup

¼ cup cold water

Sprinkle evenly over water

1 env. unflavored gelatin

Let stand to soften. Dissolve completely by placing over very hot water. When gelatin is completely dissolved, stir and blend it into a mixture of

1 tablespoon vinegar
1 teaspoon salt
¼ teaspoon paprika
⅛ teaspoon pepper

Gently mix the diced potato and

½ cup (about 2 stalks) finely chopped celery
½ cup (about ½ small) pared and diced cucumber
3 tablespoons minced onion
2 tablespoons chopped pimiento
½ cup mayonnaise

Blend in gelatin mixture. When meat layer in mold is slightly set, immediately turn potato salad mixture onto first layer in mold. (Both layers should be of almost same consistency to avoid separation of layers when unmolded.) Put into refrigerator and chill until firm.

Unmold (page 374) gelatin. Garnish with **salad greens.**   *8 to 10 servings*

AVOCADO DELIGHT

Set out a 1½-qt. mold. Place a bowl and rotary beater in refrigerator to chill.

Pour into a small saucepan
1¼ cups cold water
Sprinkle evenly over cold water
2 env. unflavored gelatin
Set the saucepan over low heat and stir constantly until gelatin is completely dissolved. Add to the dissolved gelatin and blend in thoroughly
1½ teaspoons sugar
1 teaspoon salt
¼ teaspoon monosodium glutamate
Few grains pepper

Rinse, cut into halves, peel, remove and discard pit from
1 medium ripe avocado
Cut into several pieces. Force avocado through a food mill or a fine sieve into a large mixing bowl. Add to puréed avocado and stir until evenly mixed
1 teaspoon grated onion
½ teaspoon prepared horseradish
¼ teaspoon grated lemon peel
½ teaspoon lemon juice
Blend in the dissolved gelatin mixture until evenly mixed. Chill in refrigerator or over ice and water until mixture begins to gel (becomes slightly thicker). If placed over ice and water, stir frequently; if placed in refrigerator, stir occasionally.

Chop enough pecans to yield
¼ cup (about 1 oz.) chopped pecans
Gently fold into gelatin the chopped pecans and
1 cup dairy sour cream
1 cup diced cooked chicken
1 cup diced cooked ham
¼ cup mayonnaise
Using the chilled bowl and beater, beat until cream is of medium consistency (piles softly)
½ cup chilled heavy cream
Fold whipped cream into gelatin mixture. Turn into mold; chill in refrigerator until firm.

Unmold (page 374) and garnish with **watercress.**   *8 servings*

MOLDED CHICKEN SALAD

Set out a 1½-qt. mold.

Prepare and set aside
3 Hard-Cooked Eggs (page 133)
Pour into a saucepan
½ cup cold water
Sprinkle evenly over cold water
1 env. unflavored gelatin
Set saucepan over low heat and stir until gelatin is completely dissolved.

Blend the dissolved gelatin thoroughly into a mixture of
1¼ cups (10½ oz. can) condensed cream of chicken soup
½ cup mayonnaise
2 tablespoons prepared horseradish
Chill (page 374) until mixture begins to gel (becomes slightly thicker).

Chop the hard-cooked eggs and prepare
1 cup diced cooked chicken
½ cup chopped celery
½ cup chopped cucumber
½ cup small seedless grapes
When gelatin mixture is of desired consistency, blend in the chicken, celery, cucumber, hard-cooked eggs, grapes and
½ cup (about 2 oz.) pecan halves
Turn into the mold and chill in refrigerator until firm.

Unmold (page 374) onto chilled serving plate. Garnish with **curly endive** or other **greens.**   *About 8 servings*

CHICKEN MOLD

Set out a 1-qt. mold.

Pour into a small saucepan
½ cup cold water
Sprinkle evenly over cold water
1 env. unflavored gelatin
Place saucepan over low heat and stir until gelatin is dissolved. Remove from heat. Add and stir until dissolved
1 chicken bouillon cube, crushed
Stir in
¾ cup water
2 teaspoons prepared horseradish
2 teaspoons lemon juice
1 teaspoon grated onion
½ teaspoon salt
½ teaspoon celery salt
Chill (page 374) until mixture is slightly thicker than consistency of thick unbeaten egg white.

Meanwhile, put through medium blade of food

chopper enough cooked chicken to yield
2 cups ground cooked chicken
When gelatin mixture is of desired consistency, blend in the ground chicken and
½ cup mayonnaise-type salad dressing
¼ cup finely chopped celery
2 tablespoons minced parsley
2 tablespoons minced pimiento
Turn mixture into mold. Chill in refrigerator until firm.

Unmold (page 374) onto chilled serving plate. Garnish with **tomato wedges** and **parsley.**   *8 servings*

CHICKEN SALAD SENSATION

Set out a 1½-qt. mold.

Empty into a bowl
1 pkg. (3 oz.) lemon-flavored gelatin
Add and stir until gelatin is completely dissolved
1 cup boiling water
Blend in
1 cup ginger ale
1 tablespoon lemon juice

Put into a large bowl
1½ cups mayonnaise
Add the gelatin mixture gradually, stirring until blended. Chill (page 374) until mixture begins to gel (becomes slightly thicker).

Prepare and set aside
2 cups cubed cooked chicken
⅔ cup halved and seeded Tokay grapes
½ cup (about 3 oz.) chopped blanched almonds (page 9)
⅓ cup chopped celery
⅓ cup chopped green pepper

When gelatin mixture is of desired consistency, stir in the chicken, grapes, almonds, celery and green pepper. Turn into the mold and chill in refrigerator until firm.

Unmold (page 374) onto chilled serving plate.   *8 to 10 servings*

CHAUD-FROID CHICKEN SALAD MOLD

Set out a 1-qt. fancy mold, a large bowl and a double boiler.

For Salad Dressing—Mix thoroughly in top of the double boiler

¼ cup sugar
1 tablespoon all-purpose flour
½ teaspoon dry mustard
½ teaspoon salt
¼ teaspoon monosodium glutamate
⅛ teaspoon pepper

Add gradually, blending thoroughly

1 cup water

Stirring gently and constantly, bring mixture to boiling over direct heat. Cook 1 to 2 min. longer. Remove from heat. Stir in

¼ cup vinegar

Vigorously stir about 3 tablespoons hot mixture into

4 egg yolks, slightly beaten

Immediately blend into mixture in top of double boiler. Place over simmering water and cook 3 to 5 min., stirring constantly to keep mixture cooking evenly. Remove from heat and blend in

2 tablespoons butter

Set dressing aside to cool; chill in refrigerator.

For Chicken Salad Mold—Put into the bowl

1 cup diced celery

Cut into cubes and add to the bowl enough chicken to yield

3 cups cubed cooked chicken

Rinse, stem, cut into halves and put in bowl

1 cup small white seedless grapes
(or use white grapes cut into
quarters and seeded)

Coarsely chop and put into the bowl

½ cup (about 2 oz.) toasted pecans or
½ cup (about 3 oz.) blanched,
toasted almonds (pages 9 and 10)
½ cup moist shredded coconut

Lightly toss together ingredients in bowl and set bowl aside.

Pour into a small saucepan

¼ cup cold water

Sprinkle evenly over water

1 env. unflavored gelatin

Set the saucepan over low heat and stir constantly until gelatin is completely dissolved. Add the dissolved gelatin gradually to the chilled salad dressing, blending thoroughly. Stir in a mixture of

½ teaspoon salt
¼ teaspoon monosodium glutamate
⅛ teaspoon pepper

Add the gelatin mixture to the chicken mixture and blend thoroughly. Turn into mold and chill in refrigerator several hours until firm.

Meanwhile, cut a piece of cardboard the same size and shape as the mold; completely cover with aluminum foil, smoothing foil out over the cardboard; set aside.

While Chicken Salad Mold is chilling, prepare Chaud-Froid Sauce.

For Chaud-Froid Sauce—Prepare

1 cup Medium White Sauce (page 304;
increase salt to ½ teaspoon; use
white pepper; add 1 or 2 drops
Tabasco)

Set cooked sauce aside and keep it warm.

Pour into a small saucepan

¼ cup cold water

Sprinkle evenly over water

1½ teaspoons unflavored gelatin

Set the suacepan over low heat and stir constantly until gelatin is completely dissolved.

Remove from heat. Add the dissolved gelatin gradually to the white sauce, blending thoroughly. Add slowly, stirring constantly, to

2 tablespoons mayonnaise

Stir in, until desired color is reached, one or more drops

Yellow food coloring

(Sauce must be smooth.) Force sauce through a fine sieve or two thicknesses of cheesecloth. Chill sauce mixture in refrigerator or over ice and water until it is slightly thicker than consistency of thick unbeaten egg white. (If mixture is placed over ice and water, stir frequently; if placed in refrigerator, stir occasionally.)

Meanwhile, prepare Glaze.

For Glaze—Pour into a small cup or custard cup

¼ cup cold water

Sprinkle evenly over water

1 env. unflavored gelatin

Set aside.

Heat until very hot

1 cup water

Remove from heat and immediately add softened gelatin, stirring until gelatin is completely dissolved.

Chill gelatin mixture in refrigerator or over ice and water until it is slightly thicker than consistency of thick unbeaten egg white. (If mixture is placed over ice and water, stir frequently; if placed in refrigerator, stir occasionally.)

Meanwhile, prepare decoration.

For Decoration—Cut into lengthwise strips

Green pepper
Pitted ripe olives

Set aside. (To form a flower, use green pepper

strips for the stem and leaves and the ripe olive strips for petals.)

To Complete the Chaud-Froid Chicken Salad Mold—When chicken salad mold is firm, unmold (page 374) onto the aluminum-foil-covered cardboard. Set on a cooling rack in a jelly roll pan. Set out one pan of ice and water and one of hot water.

When Chaud-Froid Sauce is of consistency which will cling to mold when poured, slowly pour sauce over chicken mold until mold is evenly covered. (If sauce becomes too firm to pour, place over hot water and stir constantly until sauce is thinner. Then place in the pan of ice and water and stir until sauce is of correct consistency.)

Arrange decoration on top of the mold, pressing pieces gently into the sauce.

Chill mold in refrigerator until Chaud-Froid Sauce is set (about 20 min.).

When sauce is firm and glaze is of correct consistency, set mold again on a cooling rack in a clean jelly roll pan. Pour the glaze over the mold, coating it evenly. Chill mold in refrigerator until glaze is firm.

When ready to serve, carefully place mold on a chilled serving platter, keeping mold on the aluminum-foil-covered cardboard. Garnish base of mold with **greens.** Accompany with

Pineapple Salad Dressing (page 416)

6 to 8 servings

CHICKEN MOUSSE AMANDINE

With Chicken Mousse Amandine for the main dish and champagne, of course, for the toast, you have the irresistible combination for a gay celebration. And to make it the kind of party that guests will recall fondly, include Puff Pastry Cheese Twists (page 96) in the menu.

Set out a 1½-qt. fancy mold. Place a small bowl and a rotary beater in refrigerator to chill.

Blanch, toast (page 9) and finely chop
½ cup (about 3 oz.) almonds
Set aside.

Pour into a small cup or custard cup
½ cup white wine, such as sauterne
Sprinkle evenly over wine
2 env. unflavored gelatin
Set aside.

Meanwhile, prepare
1 cup quick chicken broth (page 10)
Beat slightly in top of double boiler
3 egg yolks
Add gradually, stirring constantly
1 cup milk
Stir in the chicken broth gradually. Cook over simmering water, stirring constantly and rapidly until mixture coats a metal spoon. Remove from heat. Stir softened gelatin and immediately stir it into the hot mixture until gelatin is completely dissolved. Cool; chill in refrigerator or over ice and water until gelatin mixture begins to gel (becomes slightly thicker). If mixture is placed over ice and water, stir frequently; if placed in refrigerator, stir occasionally.

Meanwhile, put through medium blade of food chopper enough cooked chicken to yield
3 cups ground cooked chicken
Blend into the chilled custard mixture the finely chopped almonds, ground chicken and
¼ cup mayonnaise
2 tablespoons minced parsley
2 tablespoons chopped green olives
1 teaspoon lemon juice
1 teaspoon onion juice
and a mixture of
½ teaspoon salt
½ teaspoon celery salt
¼ teaspoon monosodium glutamate
Few grains paprika
Few grains cayenne pepper
Using the chilled bowl and beater, beat until cream is of medium consistency (piles softly)
½ cup chilled heavy cream
Fold whipped cream into chicken mixture. Turn into mold. Chill in refrigerator until firm.

Unmold (page 374) onto chilled serving plate and, if desired, garnish with **sprigs of parsley.**
8 servings

Chicken Mousse Amandine

TWO-LAYER CHICKEN CRANBERRY SALAD

Set out a 3-qt. mold.

For Cranberry Layer—Pour into a small saucepan
½ cup cold water
Sprinkle evenly over cold water
1 env. unflavored gelatin
Set saucepan over low heat and stir until gelatin is completely dissolved.

Mix in a large bowl
4 cups (two 16-oz. cans) whole cranberry sauce
1 cup (8¼-oz. can) crushed pineapple
⅓ cup (about 2½ oz.) chopped walnuts

When gelatin is dissolved, stir it and blend into cranberry mixture. Turn mixture into prepared mold. Chill in refrigerator until gelatin mixture is slightly set.

For Chicken Layer—Set out
2 cups cubed cooked chicken
¾ cup finely chopped celery
3 tablespoons chopped parsley

Pour into a small saucepan
½ cup cold water
Sprinkle evenly over cold water
1 env. unflavored gelatin
Set saucepan over low heat and stir until gelatin is completely dissolved.

Meanwhile, blend in a large bowl
1 cup mayonnaise
½ cup undiluted evaporated milk
1 teaspoon monosodium glutamate
½ teaspoon salt
Mix thoroughly. When gelatin is dissolved, stir it and gradually blend into the mayonnaise mixture. Blend in the cubed chicken, chopped celery and chopped parsley.

When first layer in mold is slightly set, turn the chicken mixture onto the first layer. (Both layers should be of almost same consistency to avoid separation when unmolded.) Set in refrigerator to chill until firm.

Unmold (page 374) onto chilled serving plate. If desired, serve with additional mayonnaise.
About 12 servings

TURKEY ALMOND MOUSSE

Set out a 1½-qt. mold. Place a small bowl and beaters in refrigerator to chill.

Blanch, toast (pages 9 and 10) and set aside
1¼ cups (about 7 oz.) almonds

Pour into a small cup or custard cup
½ cup cold water
Sprinkle evenly over water
1 env. unflavored gelatin
Set aside.

Prepare
1 cup quick chicken broth (page 10)

Two-Layer Chicken Cranberry Salad

Immediately stir softened gelatin into hot broth until gelatin is completely dissolved. Blend in well
1 tablespoon lemon juice
½ teaspoon grated onion
½ teaspoon prepared horseradish
½ teaspoon prepared mustard
½ teaspoon salt
Chill (page 374) until gelatin mixture is slightly thicker than consistency of thick unbeaten egg white.

Meanwhile, blender-chop (page 11) the almonds.

Cut into pieces enough turkey to yield
2 cups cooked turkey
Put into blender container
¼ cup mayonnaise
Cover and turn on motor. Gradually add turkey by pieces; blend until mixture resembles a fine paste.

Turn off motor and add
3 or 4 stalks celery, cut in pieces
1 strip pimiento
Blend until celery is chopped. Combine chopped nuts, gelatin mixture and turkey mixture. Mix thoroughly.

Using chilled bowl and beaters, whip
⅔ cup chilled heavy cream
Fold whipped cream into turkey mixture. Turn into mold. Chill in refrigerator until firm.

Unmold (page 374) onto chilled serving plate.
6 servings

SALMON SALAD

▲ *Base Recipe*

Set out a 1½-qt. mold.

Prepare and set aside
Blender Mayonnaise (page 413)

Drain, reserving liquid
2 cans (16 oz. each) salmon (about 4 cups, drained)
Discard the skin. Set salmon aside.

Pour into a small saucepan
½ cup cold water
Sprinkle evenly over water
1 env. unflavored gelatin

Tuna Delight Salad Mold

Set saucepan over low heat and stir until gelatin is dossolved.

Meanwhile, cut into pieces and set aside

2 stalks celery, including leaves
½ cucumber, rinsed and pared
1 small onion
¼ lemon, rinsed and seeds removed

Add to the salmon liquid

Cold water (enough to make ⅔ cup liquid)

Pour liquid into an electric blender container; add the dissolved gelatin, lemon and onion pieces and

1½ to 2 tablespoons capers
¾ teaspoon salt
5 or 6 peppercorns

Cover and blend until the peppercorns are very finely chopped. Turn off motor.

Add celery and cucumber pieces; cover and blend until vegetables are medium fine. Empty contents of blender container into a large bowl.

Cover blender container and turn on motor; add, a few pieces at a time, about one cup of the salmon. Empty blender-chopped salmon into the large bowl. Repeat this process until all of the salmon is chopped. Lightly toss ingredients and turn into mold.

Chill in refrigerator until firm. Unmold (page 374) onto crisp **salad greens.** *6 to 8 servings*

—TUNA SALAD

Follow ▲ Recipe. Substitute **4 cans (6½ or 7 oz. each) tuna** for salmon.

TUNA DELIGHT SALAD MOLD

Food for the gods on a summer Sunday night!

Set out a 9x5x3-in. loaf pah.

For Pineapple Layer—Drain thoroughly, reserving syrup

1 can (8¼ oz.) crushed pineapple (about ⅔ cup, drained)

Add to the reserved pineapple syrup

Water (enough to make ½ cup liquid)

Set aside.

Empty into a bowl

1 pkg. (3 oz.) lime-flavored gelatin

Add to bowl and stir until gelatin is completely dissolved

1 cup boiling water

Blend in the liquid mixture and

2 tablespoons lemon juice

Chill (page 374) until mixture is slightly thicker than consistency of thick unbeaten egg white.

Wash, pare, chop, and set aside enough cucumber to yield

½ cup chopped cucumber

When gelatin mixture is of desired consistency, blend in the pineapple and cucumber. Turn into the pan and set in refrigerator to chill until partially set.

For Tuna Layer—Pour into a small bowl

1 cup cold water

Sprinkle evenly over cold water

2 env. unflavored gelatin

Set aside.

Beat slightly with rotary beater in top of a double boiler

2 eggs

Blend in thoroughly

1 cup undiluted evaporated milk
2 tablespoons lemon juice
1 tablespoon minced onion
½ teaspoon Worcestershire sauce
½ teaspoon salt
½ tesponn monosodium glutamate
Few grains cayenne pepper

Set over simmering water and cook, stirring constantly, until mixture thickens slightly. Remove from heat and immediately add the softened gelatin; stir until the gelatin is completely dissolved. Cool; chill (page 374) until mixture begins to gel (becomes slightly thicker).

Meanwhile, drain, flake (page 9), and set aside

1 can (7 oz.) tuna (about 1 cup)

Prepare and set aside

½ cup finely chopped celery
¼ cup finely chopped green pepper

When the second gelatin mixture is of desired consistency, blend it into

1 cup mayonnaise

Mix in tuna, green pepper, and celery; set aside.

Beat until rounded peaks are formed

2 egg whites

Gently fold into the tuna mixture.

When first layer in mold is partially set, immediately spoon the tuna mixture into the mold. (Both layers should be of almost the same consistency to avoid separation when unmolded.) Set salad in refrigerator to chill until firm.

To Serve—Unmold (page 374) onto a chilled serving platter. Garnish with

Lettuce
Cream Cheese "Pineapples"

10 to 12 servings

For Cream Cheese "Pineapples"—Divide into six equal portions

1 pkg. (8 oz.) cream cheese

Using a knife or spatula, mold each portion in shape of a miniature pineapple. Chill in refrigerator.

Meanwhile, cut into thin slices enough stuffed olives to yield

½ cup pimiento-stuffed olives

Gently press the olive slices onto sides of cream-cheese shapes (see photo). Insert into tops of "pineapples"

Celery pieces

Arrange "pineapples" around mold and serve.

TUNA SALAD MOLD

Set out a 1-qt. mold (fish-shape, if desired).

Pour into a small bowl

½ cup cold water
½ cup cold chicken broth

Sprinkle evenly over water

2 env. unflavored gelatin

Let stand until softened.

Shred and set aside

2 oz. Cheddar cheese (about ½ cup, shredded)

Prepare

½ cup very hot quick chicken broth (page 10)

Stir in softened gelatin until completely dissolved.

Put into a large bowl

1 cup mayonnaise

Add the gelatin mixture gradually, stirring constqntly. Blend in the cheese and

2 tablespoons lemon juice
1 tablespoon minced onion
½ teaspoon Worcestershire sauce

Tuna Salad Mold

Stir in a blend of
½ teaspoon monosodium glutamate
⅛ teaspoon salt
⅛ teaspoon cayenne pepper
Chill (page 374) until mixture begins to gel (becomes slightly thicker).

Prepare and set aside
½ cup (about 3 oz.) slivered and toasted blanched almonds (pages 9 and 10)
½ cup sliced pimiento-stuffed olives

Drain and flake (page 9)
1 can (7 oz.) tuna (about 1 cup, flaked)

When gelatin mixture is of desired consistency, stir in the almonds, olives and tuna (reserve one olive slice if using a fish-shape mold). Turn into the mold and chill in refrigerator until firm.

Unmold (page 374) onto chilled platter. If mold is fish-shape, place reserved olive slice on head of fish for the eye. Garnish with crisp **lettuce leaves.** *6 to 8 servings*

CRAB MEAT MOUSSE

A 1-qt. mold will be needed. Put a bowl and a hand rotary or electric beater into refrigerator to chill.

Break into pieces and set aside
2 cups cooked crab meat (bony tissue removed)

Pour into a small cup or custard cup
½ cup cold water
Sprinkle evenly over cold water
1 env. unflavored gelatin
Let stand until softened.

Meanwhile, blend in a medium-size bowl
¼ cup lemon juice
1 teaspoon salt
¼ teaspoon paprika
Few grains pepper
Dissolve gelatin completely by placing over hot water. Stir into the lemon juice mixture. Chill gelatin mixture in refrigerator or over ice and water until gelatin is slightly thicker than consistency of thick unbeaten egg white. If placed over ice and water, stir frequently; if placed in refrigerator, stir occasionally.

When gelatin is of desired consistency, blend in the crab meat.

Using the chilled bowl and beater, beat until cream is of medium consistency (piles softly)
1 cup chilled heavy cream
Spread whipped cream over crab meat mixture and gently fold together. Turn into mold. Chill in refrigerator until firm, about 3 hrs.

Unmold (page 374) onto chilled serving platter. Serve with
Cucumber Sauce II (page 310) or Sour Cream Cucumber Sauce (page 310)
About 6 servings

ASPICS

TOMATO ASPIC

▲ Base Recipe

Set out a 1-qt. ring mold.

Pour into a suacepan
4 cups tomato juice
Add to tomato juice
⅓ cup chopped celery leaves
⅓ cup chopped onion
2½ tablespoons sugar
1¼ teaspoons salt
½ teaspoon monosodium glutamate
1 bay leaf
Simmer, uncovered, 10 min.

Meanwhile, pour into a small bowl
½ cup cold water
Sprinkle evenly over water
2 env. unflavored gelatin
Let stand to soften.

Remove tomato juice mixture from heat and strain into a large bowl. Immediately add the softened gelatin to hot tomato juice mixture and stir until gelatin is completely dissolved.

Add and stir well
2½ tablespoons cider vinegar
Pour tomato-juice mixture into the mold. Cool; chill in refrigerator until firm.

Unmold (page 374) onto chilled serving plate.
6 to 8 servings

—INDIVIDUAL TOMATO ASPIC MOLDS

Follow ▲ Recipe; use eight ½-cup individual molds instead of the 1-qt. ring mold.

—COTTAGE CHEESE IN TOMATO ASPIC

Follow ▲ Recipe. After adding vinegar to tomato juice mixture, chill (page 374) until mixture is slightly thicker than consistency of thick unbeaten egg white. Meanwhile, mix **1 cup cream-style cottage cheese, 2 tablespoons grated onion, ⅛ teaspoon Worcestershire sauce and ⅛ teaspoon pepper.** When gelatin mixture is of desired consistency, blend in the cottage cheese mixture. Turn into the ring mold and chill in refrigerator until firm.

Tomato Aspic

TOMATO ASPIC CREAM CHEESE SALAD RING

▲ Base Recipe

This very American salad lends a colorful touch to a smörgasbord. It is sometimes seen in American-Scandinavian restaurants.

Two identical 1-qt. ring molds will be needed.

For Salad Ring—Prepare and chill until firm
Tomato Aspic Ring (on this page)
Cream Cheese Ring (below)
When ready for serving, unmold (page 374) the Tomato Aspic onto a chilled plate large enough for the aspic to be expanded to twice its size. Cut aspic into 1-in. slices and spread slices about 1 in. apart.

Unmold (page 374) Cream Cheese Ring onto a second chilled plate. Cut into 1-in. slices. Transfer slices to the alternating spaces between the tomato aspic slices. Arrange so that a perfect ring is formed again.

Place on plate in the center of salad ring a small bowl of
Salad dressing

For Cream Cheese Ring—Pour into a small saucepan
½ cup cold water

Chicken Tomato Aspic Ring

—AVOCADO TOMATO ASPIC RING

The surprising combination of flavors results in a gay red color that will delight you.

Follow ▲ Recipe for Tomato Aspic only; use a 1-qt. mold. Add **3 tablespoons chopped celery leaves, 1 tablespoon sugar** and **½ bay leaf** to tomato juice mixture before heating. Substitute **strawberry-flavored gelatin** for lemon-flavored gelatin; add **1 tablespoon lemon juice.** Cool; chill (page 374) until gelatin mixture is slightly thicker than consistency of thick unbeaten egg white. Meanwhile, prepare **1½ cups diced avocado.** When gelatin mixture is of desired consistency, mix in the diced avocado. Turn into the mold and chill in refrigerator until firm.

Sprinkle evenly over cold water
   1 env. unflavored gelatin
Set the saucepan over low heat and stir constantly until gelatin is completely dissolved. Remove from heat.

Beat until very soft
   3 pkgs. (3 oz. each) cream cheese
Mix in, in order (adding cream gradually and stirring until smooth after each addition)
   2 cups dairy sour cream
   4 teaspoons lemon juice
   1½ tablespoons sugar
   1 teaspoon salt
Blend dissolved gelatin into cream cheese mixture. Turn mixture into the second mold. Place in refrigerator to chill until firm.
About 24 servings

—TOMATO ASPIC SQUARES

Follow ▲ Recipe. Omit salad ring and Cream Cheese Ring. Set out a 13x9x2-in. pan. Pour Tomato Aspic into pan, cool and chill in refrigerator until firm. When ready to serve, cut into 2-in. squares. Beat **1½ oz. (½ pkg.) cream cheese,** softened, and **1 tablespoon milk** until fluffy. Force cream cheese through a pastry bag and No. 27 decorating tube onto center of each square. Arrange squares on a serving tray and garnish with **sprigs of parsley.**
About 2 doz. aspic squares

CHICKEN TOMATO ASPIC RING

▲ *Base Recipe*

Set out a 1½-qt. ring mold.

For Tomato Aspic Layer—Pour into a saucepan
   2 cups tomato juice
Add to tomato juice
   3 tablespoons chopped onion
   ½ teaspoon salt
   ¼ teaspoon monosodium glutamate
   ⅛ teaspoon pepper
   2 or 3 drops Tabasco
Simmer, uncovered, 10 min.

Meanwhile, empty into a bowl
   1 pkg. (3 oz.) lemon-flavored gelatin

Remove tomato juice mixture from heat. Strain into the bowl with gelatin and stir until gelatin is completely dissolved.

Pour into the mold. Cool; chill in refrigerator until partially set.

For Chicken Rice Layer—Meanwhile, cook following directions on package
   ⅔ cup packaged precooked rice
Turn into a large bowl; set aside to cool.

Chop and set aside enough cooked chicken to yield
   1 cup chopped cooked chicken
Prepare
   ½ cup chopped celery
   ¼ cup chopped pimiento-stuffed olives

Pour into a small cup or custard cup
   ¼ cup cold water
Sprinkle evenly over water
   1 env. unflavored gelatin
Let stand to soften. Dissolve completely by placing cup over very hot water.

Stir gelatin and blend into a mixture of
   1 cup mayonnaise
   ½ cup cream
   ½ teaspoon salt
   ¼ teaspoon paprika
   ⅛ teaspoon pepper
   ⅛ teaspoon crushed dried tarragon leaves
Add the chopped chicken, celery, olives and the mayonnaise mixture to bowl containing cooled rice; mix thoroughly.

When first layer in mold is partially set, immediately spoon the chicken-rice mixture into the mold. (Both layers should be of almost the same consistency when combined to avoid separation when unmolded). Chill in refrigerator until firm.

Unmold (page 374) onto chilled serving plate.
8 to 10 servings

—TURKEY TOMATO ASPIC RING

Follow ▲ Recipe. Substitute **cooked turkey** for the chicken.

FISH IN ASPIC
(Fisk i Aspec)

Set out a 1½-qt. mold.

Prepare
   Tomato Aspic (page 391)
Chill in refrigerator or over ice and water until mixture is consistency of thick unbeaten egg white. (If mixture is placed over ice and water, stir frequently; if placed in refrigerator, stir occasionally.)

Meanwhile, cut into 1-in. pieces enough cooked fish to yield
   1½ cups cooked fish pieces (herring, fillet of sole, or trout)
When mixture is of desired consistency, blend in the fish and turn into the mold. Chill in refrigerator until firm.

When ready to serve, unmold (page 374) onto a chilled serving platter and garnish with
   Sprigs of parsley
8 to 10 servings

MAIN-DISH SALADS

BEEF SALAD ACAPULCO

Put into a shallow dish
   3 cups cooked beef strips
Combine in a jar or bottle
   ¾ cup salad oil
   ½ cup red wine vinegar
and a blend of
   1½ teaspoons salt
   ¼ teaspoon pepper
   ⅛ teaspoon cayenne pepper
   1 tablespoon chili powder
Cover tightly and shake vigorously to blend. Pour over beef strips; cover and refrigerate several hours or overnight.

Remove beef from marinade and arrange on chilled salad plates lined with
   Crisp salad greens
Brush with marinade
   Avocado slices

Arrange avocado on greens (see photo) along with

Onion rings
Green pepper rings
Tomato wedges
Ripe olives

Serve the marinade as the dressing.

About 4 servings

ROAST BEEF SALAD

Prepare and chill
1 Hard-Cooked Egg (page 133)

Cut into cubes enough cold roast beef to yield
3 cups cold roast beef cubes
Drizzle over beef, mixing to coat cubes
¼ cup quick meat broth (page 10)
Set in refrigerator to chill.

Cut the hard-cooked egg into halves. Chop the egg white and set aside.

For Dressing—Mash the egg yolk with a fork or force through ricer or sieve. Mix in, in order
1 uncooked egg yolk
1 tablespoon cider vinegar
1 teaspoon dry mustard
Add very gradually while beating constantly
⅓ cup salad oil
Mix in
2 tablespoons chopped parsley
1 tablespoon chopped anchovy fillets
1 teaspoon capers
¾ teaspoon thyme
Pour dressing over beef and toss lightly to mix thoroughly. Garnish with the chopped egg white.

About 4 servings

JEAN LAFITTE SALAD

Set out
1 cup diced chilled cooked meat or poultry
Prepare
½ cup diced cooked potato
½ cup diced cooked carrots
½ cup cut cooked green beans
2 tablespoons chopped sweet pickle
Toss meat and vegetables with a mixture of
½ teaspoon salt
¼ teaspoon monosodium glutamate
⅛ teaspoon pepper

Beef Salad Acapulco

Add and toss until meat and vegetables are well coated
½ cup French Dressing I (page 410)
Chill in refrigerator at least 1 hr.

Meanwhile, prepare and chop
1 Hard-Cooked Egg (page 133)
Add the egg and toss lightly to mix thoroughly.

About 6 servings

MEAT VEGETABLE SALAD

▲ *Base Recipe*

Set out
1½ cups diced chilled cooked meat or poultry
Prepare
½ cup (about 1 medium) grated carrot
⅓ cup chopped celery

Toss diced meat and vegetables lightly with
⅔ to 1 cup cooked peas
¼ cup chopped sweet pickle
6 ripe olives, pitted and chopped
and a mixture of
½ teaspoon salt
¼ teaspoon monosodium glutamate
⅛ teaspoon pepper
Add and toss until vegetables are well coated
¼ cup French Dressing I (page 410)
Place in refrigerator to chill at least 1 hr.

Gently mix in
¾ cup Mayonnaise (page 412)
Chill until ready to serve.

6 servings

—SEAFOOD SALAD

Follow ▲ Recipe. Substitute for meat **1 cup (7-oz. can) tuna, 1 cup (6½-oz. can) crab meat** (bony tissue removed) or **1 cup (7¾-oz. can) salmon.** Drain and separate seafood into chunks with a fork. Add **1 tablespoon lemon juice** with the French Dressing.

LAMB AND DILL SALAD BOWL

Delicious though it is, cold roast lamb seldom appears in salads. This salad is an unusual combination of flavors and textures.

Prepare and put into a bowl
3 cups cold roast lamb cubes
½ cup sliced celery
½ cup diced dill pickle
¼ cup diced green pepper

Wash, quarter, core and dice
1 medium red apple
Add to the bowl with a mixture of
¼ cup French dressing
½ teaspoon garlic salt
¼ teaspoon salt
Few grains pepper
Toss lightly to mix thoroughly. Chill in refrigerator.

Just before serving, prepare
Croutons (see Caesar Salad, page 359; use 2 cloves garlic)
Line a salad bowl with
Crisp salad greens
To serve, turn salad into the salad bowl. Sprinkle croutons over salad and toss lightly.

About 4 servings

MARINATED LAMB SALAD

Prepare and chill
Marinade (below or use ¾ cup chilled bottled herb salad dressing)

Prepare and slice
2 Hard-Cooked Eggs (page 133)

Have ready
Cooked lamb strips, about 3 cups
½ cup sliced pimiento-stuffed olives
2 medium tomatoes, cut in pieces
1 green pepper, cut in strips
Add lamb to bowl with chilled Marinade or salad dressing; toss to coat.

Line a large bowl with
Boston or Bibb lettuce
Arranging in individual piles, spoon the marinated lamb, egg slices, olives, tomatoes and green pepper onto the lettuce. Mix remaining marinade and pour over all.

4 servings

Marinade—Mix in a large bowl ⅓ **cup olive**

Marinated Lamb Salad

Greek-Style Lamb and Olive Salad

oil, ¼ cup lemon juice, 2 tablespoons cider vinegar, 1 tablespoon chopped chives, ½ teaspoon salt, ⅛ teaspoon pepper and ½ teaspoon basil leaves.

GREEK-STYLE LAMB AND OLIVE SALAD

Have ready
> **1½ lbs. roast lamb, trimmed of fat and cut in strips**

Prepare in a large bowl
> **Greek-Style Salad Dressing (below)**

Add lamb strips to bowl with dressing and toss to coat. Refrigerate at least 1 hr., or until thoroughly chilled.

Have ready
> **1 large cucumber, pared and sliced**
> **4 medium tomatoes, sliced and quartered**
> **1 cup pitted ripe olives**

Before serving, toss cucumber, tomatoes and olives with some of the salad dressing.

Line a large salad bowl with
> **Curly endive**

Turn vegetable mixture into bowl. Spoon meat over vegetables and pour dressing over all.
About 6 servings

—GREEK-STYLE SALAD DRESSING

Mix
> **½ cup olive oil or other salad oil**
> **1 cup red wine vinegar**
> **3 to 4 tablespoons honey**
> **1½ teaspoons salt**
> **⅛ teaspoon dry mustard**
> **2 teaspoons crushed dried mint leaves**
> **¼ teaspoon crushed oregano**
> **¼ teaspoon crushed thyme**
> **¼ teaspoon anise seed**
About 1¾ cups dressing

ORIENTAL SALAD

Cut into thin strips enough cold roast pork to yield
> **1½ cups strips of cold roast pork**

Wash, trim off roots, separate stalks, remove any blemishes and slice enough Chinese cabbage to yield
> **2 cups sliced Chinese cabbage (celery cabbage)**

Drain
> **1 can (16 oz.) bean sprouts (about 2 cups, drained)**
> **1 can (5 oz.) sliced water chestnuts**

Combine the Chinese cabbage, pork, bean sprouts, water chestnuts and
> **1¾ cups cooked rice**
> **1 cup cooked peas**

Toss lightly to mix. Chill thoroughly in refrigerator.

Blend and chill thoroughly
> **⅔ cup dairy sour cream**
> **⅓ cup mayonnaise**
> **2 tablespoons soy sauce**
> **1 tablespoon cider vinegar**
> **1 teaspoon celery seed**
> **½ teaspoon monosodium glutamate**
> **¼ teaspoon garlic salt**
> **¼ teaspoon pepper**

Just before serving, pour dressing over salad and toss lightly to mix thoroughly. Serve in a salad bowl; garnish with **pimiento strips** or **green pepper strips.**
About 8 servings

VEGETABLE PORK SALAD

Prepare and put into a bowl
> **2 cups cold roast pork cubes**
> **⅔ cup coarsely shredded pasteurized process American cheese**
> **½ cup diced celery**
> **2 tablespoons sliced pimiento-stuffed olives**

Add and mix lightly
> **1 cup cooked peas**
> **⅓ cup small white cocktail onions**

Blend and add
> **½ cup mayonnaise**
> **1 teaspoon salt**
> **⅛ teaspoon white pepper**

Toss lightly to mix thoroughly. Chill in refrigerator.

Serve on **curly endive.** Garnish with thin strips of **pimiento.**
About 4 servings

COLD MEAT TRAY

Ready-to-serve meats, cheese slices, relishes and a salad all charmingly arranged on a large bread board, gay little bowls of zesty butter spreads and baskets of assorted breads are a deluxe invitation to an informal taste thrill. No long hours of preparation are needed. And it's such fun to compose the tempting array into a picture-pretty meal that can be carried easily to the backyard or to the patio.

Purchase an assortment of sliced
> **Ready-to-serve meats (such as bologna, salami, Braunschweiger liver sausage, Thuringer, pickle and pimiento loaf and veal loaf)**
> **Cheese (such as American and Swiss)**

Cut a cardboard to fit the top of any selected salad mold. Cover the cardboard carefully with aluminum foil.

Prepare and unmold onto aluminum foil covered cardboard
> **Molded salad (any recipe)**

Return salad to refrigerator until ready to use.

Prepare and chill thoroughly
> **4 Hard-Cooked Eggs (page 133)**

Drain and chill
> **Pimiento-stuffed olives, ripe olives and sweet gherkin pickles**

Prepare and chill
> **Radish roses, large head lettuce and watercress**

Place the salad mold in center of a large bread board. Line center of mold (if it is a ring mold) with lettuce leaves and nestle the ripe olives in the lettuce. Radiate from the mold to two opposite corners of the board the sliced meat in alternating colors. Arrange cheese slices radiating to other two corners. Prepare four lettuce cups and place one on each corner of board. Fill two with the radish roses and two with stuffed olives or gherkins.

For garnish, place quarters of the hard-cooked eggs and sprigs of watercress over entire assortment between the rows of meat and cheese. Surround base of mold with sprays of watercress.

Serve accompanied by baskets of assorted **breads** and small bowls of
Fresh Herb Butter (page 114)
Perky Butters (page 114)

CHEF'S FRUIT SALAD

Prepare and chill
Creamy Lemon Celery Seed Dressing (below) or Tarragon Salad Dressing (page 412)

Have ready
Crisp salad green (to line salad bowl)
1 qt. shredded salad greens
6 cups mixed fruit
1½ cups each Swiss cheese strips and cooked ham or turkey strips
Cinnamon Buttered Raisins (below)

Line a salad bowl with the greens. Add the shredded greens. Arrange fruit in bowl. Spoon some of the dressing over all. Top with cheese and ham or turkey strips alternated with Cinnamon Buttered Raisins (see photo). Serve with remaining dressing. *About 6 servings*

—CREAMY LEMON CELERY SEED DRESSING

Blend thoroughly
1½ cups mayonnaise
¼ cup unsweetened pineapple juice
1 teaspoon grated lemon peel
1 tablespoon lemon juice
½ teaspoon celery seed
Few drops Tabasco
Cover and refrigerate 1 hr. to blend flavors. *About 1½ cups dressing*

—CINNAMON BUTTERED RAISINS

Melt in a skillet over low heat
1 tablespoon butter or margarine
Add
½ cup dark seedless raisins
½ cup golden raisins
½ teaspoon cinnamon
Heat and stir 5 min. Cool. *About 1 cup raisins*

CLUB SALAD

▲ Base Recipe

A main dish salad capable of many variations, every one of them handsome to look at and thoroughly satisfactory to eat.

Chill a salad bowl.

For Salad—Wash, discard bruised leaves, and dry thoroughly and carefully
French endive
Lettuce
Bibb lettuce
Romaine
Using as much of each green as desired, tear into bite-size pieces enough greens to yield about 2 qts. Put into a large plastic bag or vegetable freshener. Chill in refrigerator at least 1 hr.

Cut into strips and set aside enough cold cooked chicken and ham to yield
2 cups cooked chicken strips
2 cups cooked ham strips

Dice and set aside enough celery to yield
1 cup diced celery

Remove salad greens from the refrigerator and put them into the chilled salad bowl. Sprinkle over them a mixture of
¼ teaspoon salt
¼ teaspoon monosodium glutamate
⅛ teaspoon pepper
Add diced celery and toss lightly until well mixed. Arrange the strips of chicken over one third of the salad. Arrange the strips of ham over another third. Rinse, peel, cut into halves and remove and discard pit from
1 medium ripe avocado
Slice avocado halves lengthwise and arrange slices on remaining third of salad. Using a pastry brush, brush avocado slices with
1 teaspoon lemon juice

When serving, be sure each person receives a portion of chicken, ham, avocado and the tossed greens.

Serve with Creamy Lemon Mayonnaise.

For Creamy Lemon Mayonnaise—Put a bowl and rotary beater into refrigerator to chill.

Put into a bowl and mix well
1 cup mayonnaise
1 teaspoon grated lemon peel
3 tablespoons lemon juice

Using the chilled bowl and beater, beat until cream is of medium consistency (piles softly)
⅓ cup chilled heavy cream
With few final strokes, beat in
3 tablespoons sifted confectioners' sugar
Fold the whipped cream into the lemon mayonnaise. *6 to 8 servings*

—CHEF'S SALAD

A classic and ever-appealing accompaniment.

Follow ▲ Recipe. Omit chicken and ham. Add to seasoned greens **2 medium firm ripe tomatoes** cut into wedges, **1 peeled sliced medium cucumber**, and **½ cup French Dressing** (page 410). Garnish with the avocado slices. Omit the mayonnaise.

—CLUB SALAD SCANDINAVIAN

Follow ▲ Recipe. Omit avocado. Rinse thoroughly and put into a saucepan **2 cups (about 1 lb.) prunes.** Cover with **1 qt. hot water.** Cover and simmer about 10 min. Drain and cool. Remove and discard pits (these are more easily removed when prunes are slightly warm). Chill pitted prunes in refrigerator. Set 6 prunes aside for garnish. Coarsely chop remaining prunes. Wash and cut 3 thin slices from **1 medium seedless orange.** Cut each slice into halves. Cut away peel and white

Chef's Fruit Salad

membrane from remaining orange and cut orange sections into small pieces. Insert an orange slice into each whole prune, allowing peel to show. Toss the chopped prunes, orange pieces, and **¼ cup toasted blanced almonds** (pages 9 and 10) with the seasoned greens. Arrange strips of chicken over one half of the salad, strips of ham over the other half. Garnish with the stuffed whole prunes.

—CHEESE BOLOGNA CLUB SALAD

Follow ▲ Recipe. Substitute for the chicken strips **½ lb. Cheddar cheese,** cut in strips, and for the ham strips **½ lb. bologna,** cut in strips. Omit avocado and lemon juice. Garnish with **ripe olives**

SPECIAL SALAD BOWL

A large salad bowl will be needed.

Rinse, remove core, discard bruised leaves from and pat dry
1 large head lettuce
1 head curly endive
Finely cut endive with scissors. Tear lettuce into bite-size pieces. Toss greens with
3 finely chopped green onions (peeled, rinsed, green tops cut off to within 3 in. of white part)

Club Salad Scandinavian

Put into a large plastic bag and chill in refrigerator at least 1 hr.

Meanwhile, prepare and set aside
4 Hard-Cooked Eggs (page 133)

Mix in a bowl
1 cup cooked chicken or turkey, cut in thin strips
2 tablespoons tarragon vinegar
Set aside.

Crumble and set aside
4 oz. Roquefort cheese (about 1 cup, crumbled)
Gently mix
¾ cup mayonnaise
3 tablespoons chili sauce
3 tablespoons sweet pickle relish
½ teaspoon celery salt
Mix in the salad bowl the greens, chicken or turkey mixture and the cheese. Pour the dressing over the mixture and toss lightly. Cut the hard-cooked eggs into quarters and arrange on salad.

Serve immediately.   *8 servings*

CHICKEN SALAD DE LUXE

▲ Base Recipe

So elegant, and so very delicious—this chicken salad! And there are so many ways of serving to make it even more appealing. Serve it, for example, heaped into the cavities of avocado halves which have been brushed with lemon juice; or in bright Tomato Shells (page 418). Or spoon it into crisp lettuce cups. And garnish the salad itself with a sprinkling of capers, with perky sprigs of watercress, or with green or ripe olives.

Set a small bowl and rotary beater in refrigerator to chill.

Prepare and put into a large bowl
3 cups cooked chicken cubes
1 cup diced celery
Rinse, drain, add to bowl and mix
½ cup small seedless grapes (or use green grapes cut into halves and seeded)
Set in refrigerator to chill.

Prepare and set aside
½ cup (2 to 3 oz.) toasted pecans or toasted blanched almonds (pages 9 and 10), chopped
¼ cup (1 oz.) moist shredded coconut, cut fine

Before serving, using chilled bowl and beater, beat until of medium consistency (piles softly)
¼ cup chilled heavy cream
Blend the whipped cream into
¾ cup Cooked Salad Dressing (page 416)
Lightly toss nuts and coconut with chicken mixture. Add salad dressing mixture; toss gently to coat evenly.   *About 6 servings*

Note: Cooked Sour Cream Dressing (page 417) or Cooked Marshmallow Dressing (page 416) may be substituted for the salad dressing mixture.

—CHICKEN CURRY SALAD

Follow ▲ Recipe. Blend **½ to 1 teaspoon curry powder** into the salad dressing mixture.

—CHICKEN ROQUEFORT SALAD

Follow ▲ Recipe. Substitute **2 cups shredded lettuce** for celery. Omit grapes and coconut. Increase salad dressing to 1 cup and blend in **1½ oz. Roquefort cheese,** crumbled.

—TURKEY SALAD

Follow ▲ Recipe or any variation. Substitute **cooked turkey** for chicken.

INDIVIDUAL CHICKEN SALADS

▲ Base Recipe

Prepare and set aside
⅓ cup French Dressing I (one half recipe, page 410)

Prepare and set aside
4 Tomato Shells (page 418)

For Chicken Salad—Put into a large bowl
1 cup (about 3 stalks) thinly sliced celery

Add and combine
1 can (6 oz.) cubed boned chicken (about ¾ cup)
½ cup (about 2 oz.) diced Swiss cheese
¼ cup chopped green pepper
Toss lightly with French Dressing I. Chill in refrigerator until ready to serve.

Set out
¼ cup (about 1½ oz.) coarsely chopped salted toasted (page 10) almonds

To Assemble—Sprinkle inside of tomatoes with a mixture of
¼ teaspoon salt
¼ teaspoon monosodium glutamate
⅛ teaspoon pepper

Drain salad mixture and blend in nuts. Lightly fill tomato shells.

Serve with
Blender Mayonnaise (page 413)
Garnish with pitted and sliced **ripe olives.**
    4 servings

—CHICKEN SALAD BOWL

Follow ▲ Recipe. Omit tomato shells. Toss **¼ cup chopped pimiento** and **4 sliced Hard-Cooked Eggs** (page 133) with remaining ingredients. To serve, lightly pile mixture in a salad bowl. Garnish with **watercress** or **parsley.**

—CHICKEN WALDORF SALAD

Follow ▲ Recipe. Omit tomato shells. Decrease celery to ½ cup. Wash, quarter, core and dice 1 medium **apple** (about 1 cup, diced). Substitute **walnuts** for almonds. Lightly toss with remaining ingredients. To serve, lightly pile into **lettuce cups.**

—INDIVIDUAL FISH SALADS

Follow ▲ Recipe or variations. Substitute for chicken, 1 cup (7- to 7¾-oz. can, drained) flaked (page 9) **tuna or salmon.** Substitute **¼ cup chopped cucumber** for green pepper.

CHICKEN AND FRUIT SALAD

Prepare and set in refrigerator to chill
French Dressing I (page 410)

Drain and set aside
1 can (20 oz.) pineapple tidbits (about 1½ cups drained)

Blanch and toast (pages 9 and 10)
½ cup (about 3 oz.) almonds

With a sharp knife, remove peel and white membrane from
2 oranges
Remove sections by cutting on either side of dividing membranes; remove section by section, over bowl, to save the juice. Juice may be added with the French Dressing.

Put the almonds and orange sections into an

electric blender container. Cover container and blend only until coarsely chopped by flicking motor switch on and off. Empty contents of blender container into a large bowl and add the pineapple.

Cover blender container and turn on motor; add, a few pieces at a time, about one cup of

4 cups cooked and boned chicken

Blend only until coarsely chopped. Empty blender-chopped chicken into the fruit mixture in bowl. Repeat this process until all chicken is chopped.

Toss ingredients lightly with the French Dressing. Chill in the refrigerator. Serve very cold spooned onto crisp **salad greens.**

8 to 10 servings

Note: Turkey or duck may be used instead of chicken.

MACARONI SALAD

▲ *Base Recipe*

Set in refrigerator to chill a 1-qt. bowl, a rotary beater and

1½ cups heavy cream

For Macaroni—Heat to boiling in a large saucepot or kettle

3 qts. water
1 tablespoon salt
2 bay leaves

Add gradually, so boiling does not stop

2 cups (8 oz.) uncooked macaroni (elbows, shells, other shapes, or tubes broken into 1-in. pieces)

Boil rapidly, uncovered, 10 to 15 min., stirring occasionally to prevent sticking. Test tenderness by pressing a piece against side of pan with fork or spoon.

Meanwhile, prepare and set aside

½ cup finely chopped celery
2 teaspoons grated onion

Flake (page 9) enough salmon to yield

½ cup flaked canned salmon

Drain macaroni by turning it into a colander or large sieve; rinse with water to remove loose starch; set aside to cool.

While macaroni is cooling, prepare dressing.

For Dressing—Put ¾ cup of the chilled heavy cream into the chilled bowl. (Remaining ¾ cup will be needed for decorating salad.) Using the chilled beater, beat until cream is of medium consistency (piles softly). Blend or beat into whipped cream with few final strokes a mixture of

½ cup mayonnaise
2 teaspoons lemon juice
1 teaspoon sugar
1 teaspoon dry mustard
½ teaspoon salt
⅛ teaspoon white pepper
Few grains cayenne pepper

Return clean bowl and rotary beater to refrigerator to chill.

For Salad—Combine cooled, cooked macaroni, flaked salmon, chopped celery, grated onion and dressing. Mix lightly until all pieces are coated with dressing. Chill salad thoroughly to allow flavors to blend.

Lightly pile salad onto a serving platter.

Just before serving time, put reserved ¾ cup of chilled heavy cream into the chilled bowl. Beat, using chilled beater, until cream stands in peaks when beater is slowly lifted upright. Blend or beat in with few final strokes, a mixture of

2 teaspoons lemon juice
1 teaspoon sugar
½ teaspoon dry mustard
½ teaspoon salt
Few grains cayenne pepper

Force whipped cream mixture through a pastry bag and a No. 7 star tube to decorate top of salad. Make zigzag border around top and straight lines across center within the border.

Garnish with

Pimiento or sweet red pepper

About 8 servings

—CHEF'S MACARONI SALAD

Follow ▲ Recipe. Omit salmon and add **6 pimiento-stuffed olives,** sliced, **¼ lb. Cheddar cheese, ¼ lb. bologna,** cubed, **1 cucumber,** pared and diced. Garnish with **quartered tomatoes.**

MACARONI FRANK SALAD BOWL

Prepare

Macaroni (one half recipe, page 156; add 1 small clove garlic and 1 small onion to the water)

Remove and discard garlic and onion.

Blend with hot macaroni

1 cup dairy sour cream
¼ cup French Dressing I (page 410)
½ teaspoon salt

Set in refrigerator to chill thoroughly.

Rinse, peel, cut into wedges and chill

2 medium tomatoes

Rinse and tear into pieces enough curly endive to yield

2 cups curly endive pieces

Chef's Macaroni Salad

Put into a large salad bowl with

1 cup diced celery
¼ cup thinly sliced radishes
¼ cup sliced green onions
2 frankfurters, sliced

Add the macaroni mixture and tomato wedges to salad bowl and toss lightly to mix thoroughly.

6 to 8 servings

MACARONI PICNIC SALAD

Cook in boiling salted water following directions on package

1 pkg. (16 oz.) elbow macaroni (4 cups)

Drain in colander.

Combine the macaroni in a large bowl with

1 cup *each* sliced radishes, sliced celery and sliced sweet gherkins
2 tablespoons chopped onion

Mix thoroughly in a small bowl

1 cup mayonnaise
⅓ cup sweet pickle liquid
¼ cup spicy brown mustard
1 teaspoon prepared horseradish
1 teaspoon salt
⅛ teaspoon white pepper

Toss dressing with macaroni mixture. Chill.

When ready to serve salad, garnish with **salad greens, radish roses** and **gherkin fans.**

About 8 servings

MACARONI CANTALOUPE SALAD

Bring to boiling in a large saucepan
3 qts. water
Add to boiling water
2 onions, quartered
12 chicken bouillon cubes
1 bay leaf
1½ teaspoons salt
1 tablespoon garlic salt
1 teaspoon seasoned pepper
Add gradually to water so boiling continues
8 oz. (2 cups) elbow macaroni
Cook until macaroni is tender. Drain, reserving broth. Discard onion and bay leaf.

Meanwhile, mix ¼ cup reserved broth with
1 cup mayonnaise
¼ cup bottled Italian salad dressing
Turn macaroni into a large bowl. Add the mayonnaise mixture and toss well. Chill. Before serving, mix in
1 cup sliced filberts
2 cups cantaloupe balls
Garnish with **curly endive.** *About 6 servings*

CHILLED MACARONI SUPPER SALAD

Cook, following package directions, and drain
8 oz. (2 cups) elbow macaroni
Turn macaroni into a large bowl and add
¼ cup bottled Italian salad dressing
Toss lightly and set aside.

Chilled Macaroni Supper Salad

Drain and set aside
1 can (about 14 oz.) asparagus spears
Cut thin strips, enough to alternate with asparagus spears, from
1 can (12 oz.) luncheon meat
Dice remaining meat and set aside.

Blend and pour over macaroni
1 cup mayonnaise
2 tablespoons cider vinegar
1 teaspoon salt
⅛ teaspoon seasoned pepper
1 teaspoon fennel seed
Mix in diced luncheon meat and
1 can (8½ oz.) green peas, drained
1 canned pimiento, diced
Turn mixture into a shallow 2-qt. dish. Alternate the luncheon meat strips and asparagus spears lengthwise on salad mixture (see photo). Brush meat and asparagus generously with **Italian salad dressing.** Chill.

About 6 servings

AUTUMN MACARONI SALAD

Cook, following package directions
7 oz. (about 1¾ cups) elbow macaroni
Drain and turn into a bowl. Add
½ cup Italian salad dressing
Toss until coated. Cover and set aside at room temperature to marinate about 2 hrs., tossing occasionally.

Combine in a bowl
1 cup coarsely shredded carrots
1 cup chopped celery (including tender leaves)
½ cup thinly sliced green onions with tops
¼ cup finely chopped parsley
1 medium green pepper, slivered
½ medium sweet red pepper, slivered (or use well-drained pimiento)
1 can (about 16 oz.) green peas, well drained
Sprinkle with a blend of
½ teaspoon garlic salt
½ teaspoon monosodium glutamate
½ teaspoon salt
⅛ teaspoon pepper
Toss until well mixed. Add and toss again
1 can (12 oz.) luncheon meat, cubed
Refrigerate until ready to use.

Just before serving, toss the chilled vegetable-meat mixture with the macaroni and
⅓ cup mayonnaise or salad dressing
1 tablespoon prepared mustard
2 tablespoons India relish
Turn salad into a salad bowl lined with **crisp lettuce.** *10 to 12 servings*

TOMATO CAVIAR TEMPTATION

Wash
4 large firm tomatoes
Dip into boiling water to loosen skins. Peel, cut out and discard stem ends. Put tomatoes into refrigerator to chill thoroughly.

For Stuffed Eggs—Set out
12 rolled anchovy fillets

Prepare
4 Hard-Cooked Eggs (page 133)
Reserve one egg for the Cheese Spread. Cut the remaining eggs into halves lengthwise. Remove egg yolks to a bowl and mash with a fork or press through ricer or sieve into the bowl. Mix in until thoroughly blended
2 tablespoons dairy sour cream
1 tablespoon salad dressing
¼ teaspoon grated onion
1 or 2 drops Tabasco
⅛ teaspoon garlic salt
⅛ teaspoon celery salt
Few grains monosodium glutamate
Few grains white pepper
Lightly fill the egg whites with the egg yolk mixture. Poke two of the anchovy fillets into each stuffed egg. Chill in refrigerator.

For Cheese Spread—Shred
4 oz. sharp Cheddar cheese (about 1 cup, shredded)
Set aside.

Finely chop the reserved egg or press through ricer or sieve into a bowl. Mix in the shredded cheese with
½ teaspoon prepared horseradish
½ teaspoon Worcestershire sauce
1 or 2 drops Tabasco
¼ teaspoon salt
⅛ teaspoon dry mustard
⅛ teaspoon pepper
⅛ teaspoon monosodium glutamate

Macaroni Cantaloupe Salad

Blend in
¼ cup dairy sour cream
3 tablespoons salad dressing
Put into refrigerator to chill thoroughly.

For Cottage Cheese Filling—Lightly mix
1½ cups (about ½ lb.) cream-style cottage cheese
⅓ cup finely chopped sweet pickle, well drained
1 tablespoon salad dressing
¼ teaspoon monosodium glutamate
⅛ teaspoon salt
⅛ teaspoon onion salt
Few grains pepper
Put into refrigerator to chill thoroughly.

Dice and panfry until very crisp
8 slices bacon
Drain on absorbent paper.

Just before serving salad, lightly mix into the cottage cheese mixture.

To Complete Salad—Wash well in cold water, discard bruised leaves from, and dry thoroughly
Salad greens (such as lettuce or curly endive)
Arrange on 6 chilled individual salad plates.

Cut the chilled tomatoes into 12 slices about ½ in. thick. Place one slice on each salad plate. Spoon Cottage Cheese Filling over slices, allowing about ¼ cup for each slice. Top with remaining tomato slices. Spread tomato slices with the Cheese Spread. Place Stuffed Egg halves, filling-side down, on Cheese Spread. Spoon over eggs a mixture of
Dairy sour cream
Caviar
If desired, top salad with more caviar.

Sprinkle over lettuce leaves around salad
French Dressing I (page 410)
Serve with **melba toast** or crusty **hard rolls.**
6 servings

SARDINE-STUFFED TOMATOES

Rinse, cutting out and discarding stem ends from
6 medium tomatoes
Cut a thin slice from top of each tomato. With a spoon, scoop out pulp. Invert shells and set aside to drain; chill.

Prepare
4 Hard-Cooked Eggs (page 133)

Mash with a fork
1 can (3¾ oz.) sardines, drained
Chop the hard-cooked egg whites and mash the egg yolks. Mix eggs with the sardines and
1 cup chopped watercress
1 teaspoon chopped chives
1 teaspoon capers
1 tablespoon prepared mustard
1 tablespoon lemon juice
½ teaspoon salt
Few grains pepper
1 tablespoon olive oil
To serve, sprinkle tomato shell slightly with

salt. Lightly fill with sardine mixture. Garnish each with a **sprig of watercress.** *6 servings*

DILLY MACARONI-STUFFED TOMATOES

Cook, following package directions
1⅓ cups elbow macaroni
Drain and set aside.

Remove and store in refrigerator eight frilly outer leaves from
1 head iceberg lettuce, cored, rinsed and drained
Cut the head into quarters. Using one quarter at a time, place a cut side down on chopping board and using a sharp knife, finely cut enough lettuce to measure 3 cups.

In a large bowl, beat
¾ cup pasteurized process blue cheese spread
¾ cup mayonnaise
2 teaspoons grated onion
2 teaspoons dill weed
½ teaspoon monosodium glutamate
⅛ teaspoon garlic powder
Mix in the macaroni and lettuce. Chill.

Rinse and remove stem ends from
8 firm ripe tomatoes
Turn stem ends down. Starting from center of blossom end, cut each tomato into quarters (do not cut all the way through; see photo). Sprinkle cut surfaces lightly with **salt.**

Place tomatoes on the frilly lettuce leaves and fill with macaroni mixture. Serve with sandwiches, if desired. *8 servings*

HERRING SALAD
(Sillsalat)

What beans are to Boston and ambrosia to the gods, herring is to many Scandinavians. It appears in a hundred different guises, and this salad is one of the finest.

Pour into a large bowl
2 qts. cold water
Put into the water
1 salt herring, cleaned and cut into fillets
Set aside to soak 3 hrs.

Dilly Marcaroni-Stuffed Tomatoes

To Prepare Herring—With a sharp knife cut off and discard head. Slit along underside of the fish from head to tail. Remove entrails and scrape insides well. Cut off tail and fins. Rinse thoroughly in cold water. Cut off a strip about ½ in. wide along each of cut edges. Discard strips. Make a slit along backbone just to the bone. Using a sharp knife, carefully pull and scrape the blue skin from the flesh. Be careful not to tear fish. Then cut along backbone through bone and flesh to remove one side of fish. Repeat for the second side. Remove as many of the small bones as possible without tearing fish.

For Salad—Set out
½ lb. boneless veal for stew, cut in ½-in. cubes
Put into a saucepan with
3 cups water
Cook over medium heat about 1 hr., or until meat is tender. Drain, chill in refrigerator.

Meanwhile, leaving on 1- to 2-in. stem and the root end, cut off leaves from
1 lb. (about 5) medium beets
Scrub beets thoroughly. Cook (page 313) 30 to 45 min., or until just tender. When beets are tender, drain. Plunge beets into running cold water; peel off and discard skin, stem and root end. Cut beets into slices ¼ in. thick. Cut slices into strips ¼ in. wide. Set in refrigerator to chill.

While beets cook, wash and scrub with a vegetable brush
2 small (about ½ lb.) potatoes
Cook (page 313) about 20 min., or until the potatoes are tender when pierced with a fork. Drain potatoes. To dry potatoes, shake pan over low heat. Peel potatoes and dice. Chill in refrigerator.

Prepare
3 Hard-Cooked Eggs (page 133)
Cut 2 of the peeled eggs into halves lengthwise. Finely shop the egg whites and egg yolks separately and set aside. Cut the remaining peeled egg into slices crosswise. Set aside.

Put a bowl and beater in refrigerator to chill.

Clean and finely chop
2 medium onions

Drain the herring, dry on absorbent paper, and cut into ½- to ¾-in. pieces. Put the herring, veal, potatoes, and onion into a large bowl with

1 large apple, rinsed and diced

Pour over ingredients in bowl a mixture of

1½ tablespoons white vinegar
½ teaspoon sugar
½ teaspoon salt
Few grains pepper

Toss lightly to coat evenly.

Using the chilled bowl and beater, beat until cream is of medium consistency (piles softly)

1 cup chilled heavy cream

Turn the whipped cream over the herring mixture and toss lightly until thoroughly combined. Add the beets and mix thoroughly, being careful not to break the strips. Turn into a serving bowl and chill thoroughly in refrigerator. If desired, turn Herring Salad into a 2-qt. mold. Pack lightly. Chill thoroughly.

When ready to serve, spoon the chopped egg white around the edge of the salad, the chopped egg yolk over center. Arrange the hard-cooked egg slices in a circle between the chopped egg white and egg yolks. Complete the garnish with **sprigs of parsley.** Place a cruet of **white vinegar,** colored with beet juice, and a cruet of **cream** on the table so that each person may sour the salad to his own taste.

10 to 12 servings

SALMON SALAD IN GRAPEFRUIT BASKETS

Garnish each salad-filled grapefruit basket with a "wreath" of minced parsley or watercress leaves which have been stripped from the stems.

Prepare Grapefruit Baskets (page 370), reserving and draining pulp, from

2 medium grapefruit

Drain, flake (page 9) and put out into a bowl

1 can (16 oz.) salmon (about 2 cups, flaked)

Add drained grapefruit pulp to the salmon with

½ cup diced celery

Toss together lightly.

Blend and pour over salad mixture

½ cup mayonnaise
¼ cup chili sauce
1 teaspoon grated onion
½ teaspoon monosodium glutamate

Toss lightly to mix thoroughly. Chill in refrigerator to allow flavors to blend.

When ready to serve, heap salad carefully into the grapefruit shells. *4 servings*

SALMON CUCUMBER SALAD

Drain, flake (page 9) and put into a bowl

1 can (16 oz.) salmon (about 2 cups, drained)

Coarsely chop or dice and add to salmon

1 medium size cucumber, pared
4 stalks celery

Add to mixture

¼ cup mayonnaise
2 tablespoons lemon juice
1 to 2 tablespoons capers
1 tablespoon grated onion
1 teaspoon monosodium glutamate
Few grains pepper

Mix lightly until all pieces are coated with dressing. Chill mixture thoroughly to allow flavors to blend.

When ready to serve, pile lightly on a serving platter. Garnish with

Melon balls
Watercress

Serve with **Creamy Celery Seed Dressing** (page 414) *4 to 6 servings*

SARDINE EGG SALAD

Prepare and chill

5 Hard-Cooked Eggs (page 133)

Prepare and chill

5 Tomato Shells (page 418)

Drain, remove tails and cut into pieces

1 can (3¼ oz.) sardines

Dice the hard-cooked eggs and add to the sardines. Prepare and add

¼ cup chopped celery
¼ cup chopped green pepper

Mix lightly.

Blend and add to salad mixture

½ cup mayonnaise
½ teaspoon salt

Toss lightly to mix well. Chill thoroughly in refrigerator.

To serve, lightly fill Tomato Shells with the egg mixture. If desired, serve with **lemon wedges.** *5 servings*

TUNA SALAD

▲ Base Recipe

Drain well, separate into small chunks and put into a bowl

2 cans (7 oz. each) tuna (about 2 cups, drained)

Prepare and mix lightly with the tuna

1 cup sliced celery
¼ cup sliced radishes
2 tablespoons chopped green pepper

Blend and add

½ cup salad dressing or mayonnaise
1 tablespoon lemon juice
1 tablespoon minced onion
¼ teaspoon pepper

Toss lightly to mix thoroughly. Chill mixture thoroughly in refrigerator.

To serve, arrange on a chilled serving plate

Crisp salad greens

Spoon the tuna salad in the center. Garnish with strips of **pimiento.** *About 4 servings*

—TUNA CHEESE SALAD

Follow ▲ Recipe. Omit celery and radishes. Toss tuna lightly with 1½ cups (about 6 oz.) shredded Swiss cheese. Increase salad dressing to about 1 cup. Before serving, add ⅔ cup coarsely chopped cashew nuts and toss.

—TUNA SALAD PIQUANT

Follow ▲ Recipe. Omit celery, radishes and onion. Toss tuna lightly with ½ cup small white cocktail onions. Blend ¼ cup chili sauce with salad dressing mixture.

—TUNA APPLE SALAD

Follow ▲ Recipe. Omit radishes and salad dressing mixture. Mix 2 cups (about 2 medium) diced red apple, unpared, with the tuna. Toss salad lightly with about ⅔ cup Mayonnaise (page 412); season with curry powder.

GREEN SALAD BOWL WITH TUNA

Cook, following directions on packages

1 pkg. (10 oz.) frozen lima beans
1 pkg. (9 oz.) frozen cut green beans
1 pkg. (9 oz.) frozen artichoke hearts

Drain and separate into chunks

3 cans (6½ or 7 oz. each) tuna

Pour over drained vegetables and tuna

1 cup French dressing

Cool and toss occasionally; cover and chill.

Salmon Cucumber Salad

Tuna Cheese Salad with Chive Dressing

Reserving a few leaves for lining salad bowl, tear into pieces

5 oz. fresh spinach (about 6 cups, loosely packed)
1 head Boston lettuce

Put the greens into a large salad bowl with

3 green onions with tops, sliced
3 oz. blue cheese, crumbled

Line edge of bowl with reserved spinach. Top with the vegetables and tuna.   *8 servings*

TUNA CHEESE SALAD WITH CHIVE DRESSING

Chill a large salad bowl and 6 individual bowls.

For Dressing—Combine in a pint jar with a tight-fitting cover and shake to blend

½ cup undiluted evaporated milk
½ cup salad oil
3 tablespoons cider vinegar
1 teaspoon salt
¼ teaspoon pepper
1 teaspoon sugar
2 tablespoons chopped chives

Chill thoroughly.   *About 1 cup dressing*

For Salad—Rinse, discarding bruised leaves, drain and dry thoroughly

Salad greens (such as lettuce, curly endive or escarole)

Using as much of each green as desired, tear into pieces enough greens to yield about 1 qt. Put into a large plastic bag or vegetable freshener. Chill in the refrigerator.

To Complete Salad—Turn chilled salad greens into the large bowl.

Drain, separate into small chunks and put into the bowl

1 can (6½ or 7 oz.) chunk-style tuna, chilled (about 1 cup, drained)

Arrange over tuna

4 slices American cheese, cut in thin strips

Serve immediately with dressing spooned over each serving. If desired, toss before serving.   *4 servings*

TRIO SALAD PLATE

For Tart Shells—Prepare and bake

Corn Meal Pastry for Tarts (one half recipe, page 485)

Set aside to cool.

For Salad Plates—Have ready

12 crisp lettuce cups

Just before serving time, set out 6 luncheon plates. Remove tart shells from pans and set one in center of each plate. Arrange two lettuce cups on each plate.

Lightly pile the fruit salad into one lettuce cup and the vegetable salad into the other.

Combine the tuna salad with its dressing and lightly pile a serving into the tart shell on each plate. Sprinkle with **paprika**. Serve with Watercress Butter Sandwiches.

For Tuna Salad—Drain and separate into small chunks

1 can (7 oz.) tuna (about 1 cup, drained)

Put tuna chunks into a large shallow bowl and cover with

French dressing

Marinate (page 10) in refrigerator 1 to 2 hrs.

Lightly toss together in a bowl

⅓ cup diced celery
⅓ cup seedless grapes (or use green grapes cut into halves and seeded)

Cover bowl and set in refrigerator to chill.

Chop coarsely and set aside

¼ cup (about 1½ oz.) toasted (page 10) almonds

Set out

⅓ cup cooked salad dressing

Drain tuna. Combine tuna and almonds with the grapes and celery; add salad dressing and toss gently to coat evenly.

For Vegetable Salad—Remove outside leaves and stalk from

1 small head cauliflower

Wash cauliflower thoroughly and carefully separate into small flowerets.

Rinse and dip into boiling water to loosen skin

1 firm tomato

Peel, cut out stem end and chill. Cut lengthwise into 6 wedges.

Lightly toss together the cauliflowerets and

⅔ cup cooked peas
⅔ cup cooked carrots, cut in ¼-in. slices
⅔ cup cooked green beans

Cover vegetable mixture with

French dressing

Marinate in refrigerator 1 to 2 hrs.

Lightly toss together the marinated vegetables and the tomato wedges.

For Fruit Salad—Choose several well-chilled fresh fruits in season, selecting them for an appealing harmony of colors and flavors. For example: **Cantaloupe and honeydew melon balls, strawberries, grapes, orange sections, peach slices, fresh pineapple** and **apple wedges.** Toss them together very lightly with a sprinkling of **Cointreau, kirsch,** or **curaçao** and heap into the crisp lettuce cups.

For Watercress Butter Sandwiches—Rinse, drain and finely cut enough watercress to yield

⅔ cup finely cut watercress

Set out

⅔ cup firm butter

Beat on high speed of electric mixer just until butter is whipped. Add the watercress and mix on high speed just until blended.

Spread onto thin slices of **bread;** prepare sandwiches; trim crusts and cut into fingers.   *6 servings*

AVOCADO CRAB SALAD, PAELLA STYLE

Paella—a colorful melange of seafoods, meat and rice along with other flavorful ingredients —was the inspiration for this cold salad adaptation of that famous hearty Spanish hot dish.

Drain and remove bones from

2 cans (5 oz. each) lobster (or use fresh lobster, see below)

Cook gently in boiling salted water to cover until the shells open

2 doz. small clams*

Remove clams and cook, covered, in the same liquid 3 to 5 min.

¾ lb. fresh shrimp

Chill the shellfish, strain and measure 2½ cups of the fish broth into a medium saucepan. Add

1 clove garlic, crushed
1 tablespoon butter or margarine
2 tablespoons dry sherry
¼ teaspoon saffron, crushed
Dash pepper

Bring to boiling and add

1¼ cups uncooked rice

Cover and cook over low heat about 15 min., or until rice kernels are soft and broth is absorbed.

Shell the chilled shrimp. (If using freshly cooked lobster, shell and cut meat into pieces; reserve 2 claws for garnish.)

Combine rice, clams, shrimp and lobster in a large mixing bowl. Add

¾ cup small pimiento-stuffed olives

Mix lightly with a fork and chill thoroughly.

When ready to serve, peel, halve, remove seeds and brush lightly with lemon juice

2 ripe avocados

Turn salad mixture into serving bowl and arrange avocado, cut in wedges, over top. (Garnish with lobster claws, if available.)

Serve the salad with **olive oil, herbed mayonnaise, salad dressing** or **tartar sauce,** as desired. *6 to 8 servings*

Note: If using fresh lobster meat, cook lobsters (about 1¼ lbs. each) in 3 qts. boiling water and 3 tablespoons salt. Cover pot and cook lobsters over low heat about 20 min. Remove lobsters and use the same liquid to cook the clams and shrimp (one shellfish at a time). Reserve the cooking liquid.

*If desired, 1 doz. mussels may be substituted for 1 doz. small clams.

CRAB MEAT SALAD

▲ *Base Recipe*

It adds a touch of elegance to any meal—and is something special at luncheon or supper.

Drain, remove and discard bony tissue, and separate

2 cans (6½ oz. each) crab meat (about 2⅔ cups, drained)

Prepare and mix with crab meat

½ cup diced celery

Mix and add

⅔ cup mayonnaise
⅛ teaspoon pepper

Toss lightly to mix thoroughly. Chill in refrigerator.

When ready to serve, pile salad lightly in lettuce cups. Serve with

Lemon or lime wedges
About 4 servings

—CURRIED CRAB MEAT SALAD

Follow ▲ Recipe. Mix ½ **cup chopped ripe** olives and/or ⅔ **cup coarsely chopped toasted blanched almonds** (pages 9 and 10), with the celery. Omit pepper, increase mayonnaise to 1 cup and blend in **2 teaspoons lemon juice** and **1 teaspoon curry powder.** If desired, while salad is chilling, prepare and chill **4 Tomato Shells** (page 418). When ready to serve, lightly fill the shells with salad mixture.

CRAB-STUFFED ARTICHOKE SALAD

Prepare and cook

4 medium artichokes (page 362)

Drain artichokes upside down so all the water can run out. Cut off remainder of stem. Open leaves of artichokes and pull out center leaves. Using a spoon, remove and discard the choke or fuzzy part in center. Scrape pulp from center leaves and reserve for stuffing. Chill in refrigerator until ready to stuff.

For Crab Stuffing—Drain, remove and discard bony tissue and separate

1 can (6½ oz.) crab meat (about ¾ cup)

Lightly toss together until crab meat is well coated with mayonnaise, crab meat, reserved artichoke pulp and

¼ cup chopped celery
½ cup chopped pimiento-stuffed olives
¼ cup minced onion
¼ cup mayonnaise
½ teaspoon salt
½ teaspoon monosodium glutamate
¼ teaspoon pepper
2 or 3 drops Tabasco

Cover; put into refrigerator to chill about 1 hr.

Carefully spoon chilled stuffing into "cup" formed by outer leaves and heart of artichoke.

Serve stuffed artichokes on individual salad plates. Spoon mayonnaise into lettuce cups and serve with salad. Or accompany with individual portions of **French Dressing** (page 410) in which to dip the artichoke leaves. Top artichokes, one slice on each, with

4 lemon slices

For directions on how to eat artichokes see Cooked Artichokes (page 362). *4 servings*

CRAB PARFAIT SALAD

Layer two salads—crab and tomato aspic.

Four 6- to 7-oz. parfait or cocktail glasses will be needed.

Drain and chill thoroughly

1 can (7½ oz.) Alaska king crab or ½ lb. thawed frozen Alaska king crab

Set out

2 cups tomato juice

Blend in a saucepan

1 env. unflavored gelatin
1 tablespoon sugar

Mix in 1 cup of the tomato juice. Stir over low heat until gelatin and sugar are dissolved.

Remove from heat. Blend in remaining tomato juice and

2 teaspoons Worcestershire sauce
1 tablespoon prepared horseradish
2 teaspoons grated onion
1 teaspoon grated lemon peel
1 teaspoon lemon juice

Chill until set.

Meanwhile, combine

⅓ cup mayonnaise
¼ cup dairy sour cream
1 tablespoon capers
2 tablespoons finely chopped green pepper
2 tablespoons finely chopped celery

Slice crab, reserving 4 pieces for garnish; mix remainder with the mayonnaise. Chill.

Spoon ¼ cup of the tomato aspic into each glass. Form a layer with ¼ cup crab mixture, then with another ¼ cup tomato aspic. Garnish with reserved crab pieces and **parsley**.
4 servings

CRAB MEAT POTATO SALAD

Combine in a large heavy skillet

2 pkgs. (9 oz. each) or 1 pkg. (16 oz.) frozen crinkle-cut French fries
¼ cup Italian salad dressing

Set over low heat until potatoes are thawed, tossing occasionally. Cover and cook 4 min. Cool; chill potatoes thoroughly.

Prepare, coarsely chop and set aside

2 Hard-Cooked Eggs (page 133)

Blend and set aside

1 cup dairy sour cream
¼ cup chili sauce
1 tablespoon lemon juice
1 teaspoon salt

Toss together the chopped eggs and

1 can (6½ oz.) crab meat, drained
1 cup sliced celery
½ cup sliced radishes
⅓ cup thinly sliced green onion
2 tablespoons minced parsley

Crab Parfait Salad

Add chilled French fries (reserve some for garnish) and the dressing; toss until well mixed. Chill thoroughly.

Before serving, arrange reserved chilled French fries in spoke-fashion on top of salad.

About 6 servings

LOBSTER PARADISE

Crab meat or shrimp may be substituted for part or all of the lobster meat, or the pineapple shell may be filled with a mixture of crab meat, shrimp and lobster meat.

Prepare and chill
   Russian Dressing (page 413)

For two servings, have ready two serving bowls (each large enough to hold crushed ice and a pineapple half) and
   2 cups (two 6-oz. cans) chilled lobster meat, cut into pieces (or use cooked fresh lobster meat)
   1 medium fresh pineapple, chilled
   Crushed ice

Prepare **Pineapple Shells** (page 370). Cut part of the fruit into small, thin slices. Reserve remaining pineapple for use in other food preparation.

Prepare and set aside
   4 Carrot Curls (page 418)
   2 green pepper rings
   2 thin lemon or lime slices
   4 teaspoons finely chopped celery
   4 thin strips of pimiento
   ¼ teaspoon chopped pimiento
   ¼ teaspoon chopped ripe olives

Set out
   2 teaspoons capers

Toss the lobster meat lightly with some of the pineapple pieces. Spoon mixture into shells. Arrange the remainder of the pineapple pieces around the lobster mixture.

Fill the bowls with crushed ice. Arrange the filled shells on the ice beds. Garnish the lobster mixture with the green pepper rings. Spoon the celery into the green pepper rings and top with the capers. Lay the pimiento strips crosswise over the rings. Put the lemon or lime slices at the base of each pineapple crown and garnish slices with the chopped pimiento and olive. Arrange on the ice beds, at both ends of each pineapple shell, carrot curls and
   Ripe or green olives
Just before serving, garnish dressing with
   1 teaspoon caviar
Serve the salad immediately with the dressing.

2 servings

LUSCIOUS ROCK LOBSTER SALAD

Prepare (page 290)
   3 frozen rock lobster tails, 6 to 8 oz. each (or use three 6-oz. cans rock lobster meat)

If using canned lobster, chill in the cans in refrigerator. Drain and cut into chunks when ready to prepare salad.

To Complete Salad—Prepare
   1 cup diced celery
   ½ cup slivered unblanched almonds
   1 tablespoon minced scallions or onion
Put into a large bowl, reserving about 2 tablespoons of the almonds for garnish.

Blend
   ¾ cup mayonnaise
   2 tablespoons cream
   2 tablespoons lemon juice
   ¼ teaspoon sugar
   ¼ teaspoon salt
   ¼ teaspoon tarragon leaves, finely chopped
   ⅛ teaspoon white pepper
Add to the ingredients in the bowl, with the lobster meat; toss lightly but thoroughly.

Line a chilled serving dish or salad bowl with
   Crisp salad greens
Fill with the lobster mixture and garnish with the reserved almonds and
   Ripe olives
Serve salad immediately.

6 servings

SHRIMP IN AVOCADO HALVES

Prepare
   Cooked Shrimp, page 294 (or use three 5-oz. cans shrimp, drained)
Put shrimp into a bowl and pour over them
   ½ cup French Dressing (page 410)
Toss lightly to coat evenly with dressing. Cover and set in refrigerator to chill and to marinate (page 10). Toss shrimp occasionally.

Just before serving time, rinse, cut into halves lengthwise, and remove pits from
   3 medium ripe avocados, chilled
Brush cut surfaces with
   Lemon juice
Pile shrimp into the avocado halves and garnish with sprigs of
   Watercress

Luscious Rock Lobster Salad

If desired, set avocado halves on a bed of crushed ice. Accompany with
   Ravigote Sauce or Tomato Ravigote Sauce (page 311)
   Melba toast

6 salads

SHRIMP SLAW

Cook and cut into pieces
   1 lb. fresh shrimp with shells (see Cooked Shrimp, page 294)
Prepare and toss lightly with the shrimp
   2 cups shredded cabbage
   1 cup chopped celery
Set in refrigerator to chill.

For Dressing—Blend thoroughly and chill in refrigerator
   ⅔ cup mayonnaise
   2 tablespoons tarragon vinegar
   2 tablespoons cream
   2 tablespoons finely chopped parsley
   2 tablespoons minced onion
and a mixture of
   ½ teaspoon celery seed
   ½ teaspoon basil
   ½ teaspoon salt
   ¼ teaspoon monosodium glutamate
   ¼ teaspoon pepper
To serve, pour dressing over shrimp mixture. Toss lightly to mix thoroughly.

About 6 servings

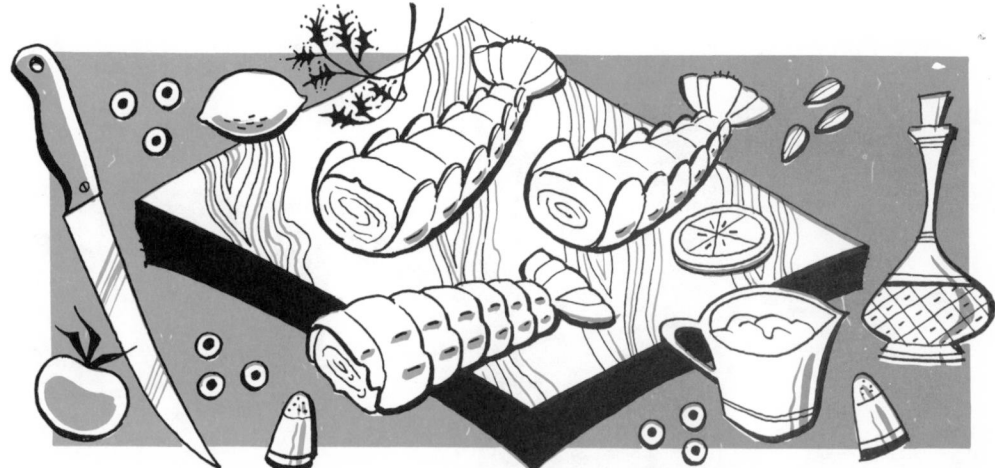

SHRIMP ARTICHOKE SALAD

Prepare **Coral Dressing** (below) and chill desired amount of **cooked shrimp** and **canned artichoke hearts.** When ready to serve, line a chilled salad bowl with **crisp lettuce.** Heap with the shrimp and artichoke hearts. Spoon Coral Dressing over salad.

—CORAL DRESSING

Mix until smooth
> 1 can (10¾ oz.) condensed tomato
>   soup
> 1 cup mayonnaise

Blend in
> 2 teaspoons sugar
> 1½ tablespoons lemon juice
> 1 tablespoon white wine vinegar
> 6 to 8 drops Tabasco
> 1 small clove garlic, minced

Chill thoroughly.   *2¼ cups dressing*

PINEAPPLE SEABREEZE SALAD

Set a salad bowl in refrigerator to chill.

Drain, reserving ½ cup syrup
> 1 can (30 oz.) pineapple chunks

Prepare and chill
> **Spicy Tomato Dressing (below)**

Thoroughly chill
> 2 cups shredded crisp salad greens
> Crisp romaine leaves
> 2 cups cooked shrimp
> 2 cups grapefruit segments
> 1 cucumber, pared and sliced

To assemble salad, line bottom of chilled salad bowl with shredded greens and put romaine around edge. Arrange pineapple, shrimp, grapefruit and cucumber in the bowl. Serve with the chilled salad dressing.   *6 servings*

—SPICY TOMATO DRESSING

Pour into a bottle the reserved ½ cup pineapple syrup and
> ¼ cup light corn syrup
> ¼ cup wine vinegar

Pineapple Seabreeze Salad

Add a blend of
> ½ teaspoon seasoned salt
> ½ teaspoon pepper
> ½ teaspoon dry mustard
> ½ teaspoon celery seed

Cover and shake well. Add
> ¼ cup ketchup
> ¼ cup salad oil

Shake vigorously to blend. Chill at least 1 hr. Shake well before using.

About 1½ cups dressing

BUFFET SALAD

A new idea for your next Sunday night supper. Let guests help themselves to this colorful springtime salad, making sure they dip deep enough to get some of the dressing-coated vegetables and salad greens.

Prepare and chill
> **French Dressing I (page 410)**

Chill a large salad bowl. Prepare ingredients and chill separately in the refrigerator until ready to assemble salad, or at least 1 hr.

Carefully rinse, drain, pat dry and chill
> **Lettuce leaves**
> **Curly endive**

Wash, pare and cut into balls with a melon-ball cutter
> **6 medium (about 2 lbs.) potatoes**

Cook potato balls (page 313) about 15 min., or until tender when pierced with a fork. Drain thoroughly. Dry potatoes by shaking pan over low heat. Put warm potato balls into a shallow dish and pour the French dressing over them. Cover and set in refrigerator; marinate (page 10) for at least 1 hr., turning several times.

Cook and clean
> **1 lb. fresh shrimp with shells (see Cooked Shrimp, page 294)**

Set in refrigerator to chill.

Wash and trim, leaving a bit of stem on each
> **8 radishes**

With a sharp knife, cut each radish into 3 equal-sized petal-shaped sections almost to stem around a triangular center. Make another parallel cut in each section to form smaller petals. Chill radishes in bowl of ice and water until petals spread apart.

Wash, pare or scrape, and grate
> **1 medium carrot (about ½ cup, grated)**

Buffet Salad

Clean and cut crosswise into ¼-in. slices
> **3 or 4 stalks celery**

Clean and coarsely chop
> **1 medium green pepper**

Clean and slice
> **1 large onion**

Rinse
> **1 small cucumber**

Score by pulling tines of a fork down the cucumber lengthwise. Repeat until entire surface is scored. Cut cucumber into ¼-in. slices.

Rinse, remove stem ends and, if desired, remove peel from
> **3 medium (about 1 lb.) tomatoes**

Cut into ½-in. slices.

When ready to assemble salad, line the chilled salad bowl with the chilled greens.

Drain the potato balls, reserving the French dressing. Toss the grated carrot, celery slices, green pepper, and onion rings to mix. Spoon evenly over the salad greens. Pour about one half of the reserved dressing over the tossed vegetables in the salad bowl.

Arrange the tomato slices, potato balls, cucumber slices and shrimp over the tossed vegetable mixture in the salad bowl (see photo). Pour the remaining dressing over the vegetables and shrimp. Garnish with radish roses. Sprinkle over the potato balls

Finely chopped parsley

Serve immediately.   *6 to 8 servings*

SEAFOOD-STUFFED AVOCADOS I

Cool, colorful and delicious are stuffed avocados, a delightful main-dish salad for a warm Sunday evening. Either of the salad mixtures in this recipe will yield enough to fill two medium avocados—four halves, and each half a serving.

Set in refrigerator to chill

2 medium avocados

Prepare either of the following salad mixtures, or prepare one half of each. Set in refrigerator to chill and allow flavors to blend.

For Lobster Salad—Drain

2 cans (5 oz. each) lobster meat (about 1½ cups, drained)

Cut into pieces and put into a bowl, reserving claw meat for garnish.

Clean and dice enough celery to yield

1 cup diced celery

Put into bowl with lobster meat.

Cut off and discard crown (spiny top) and rinse

1 small ripe pineapple

Cut into crosswise slices ¼ to ½ in. thick. With a sharp knife, cut away and discard rind and "eyes" from each slice. Cut out and discard the core. Cut slices into bite-size wedges of uniform size. Put 1 cup of the pineapple wedges into the bowl with the lobster. (Remaining pineapple may be reserved for use in other food preparation.)

Add to the bowl a mixture of

¼ cup mayonnaise
½ teaspoon salt
¼ teaspoon soy sauce
⅛ teaspoon pepper
Few grains cayenne pepper

Toss lightly until thoroughly mixed.

For Crab Meat Salad—Drain, remove and discard bony tissue, and separate

1 can (6½ oz.) crab meat (about 1⅓ cups, drained)

Clean and dice enough celery to yield

1¼ cups diced celery

Put into a bowl with the crab meat. Add

¼ cup diced green pepper

Add a mixture of

6 tablespoons dairy sour cream
4 teaspoons lemon juice
1 teaspoon salt
¼ teaspoon pepper

Toss lightly until thoroughly mixed.

To Complete Salad—Just before serving time, rinse, cut into halves lengthwise, and remove and discard pits of the chilled avocados.

Brush the cut surfaces with

Lemon juice

Arrange avocado halves on a chilled serving platter. Pile chilled salad into them. Garnish the crab meat salad with **green pepper strips,** the lobster salad with the reserved claw meat.

4 servings

SEAFOOD-STUFFED AVOCADOS II

Perfect partners—tall glasses of sparkling iced coffee and a delightful seafood salad!

Prepare, reserving four pieces of claw meat for garnish

1 live lobster, about 1¼ lbs. (see "Boiled" Lobster, page 290)

Cut lobster meat into pieces.

Prepare

1 lb. fresh shrimp with shells (see Cooked Shrimp, page 294)

Reserve two whole shrimp for garnish; cut remainder into pieces.

Drain and remove bony tissue from

1 cup (about 4 oz.) fresh lump crab meat

Put seafood into a bowl and pour over it

½ cup French Dressing I (page 410)

Toss lightly to coat evenly with dressing. Cover and set in refrigerator to chill and to marinate (page 10). Toss occasionally.

Meanwhile, blend

1 teaspoon tarragon vinegar
¼ teaspoon salt
¼ teaspoon dry mustard
¼ teaspoon sugar

Blend into

¼ cup mayonnaise
¼ cup dairy sour cream

Put into refrigerator until ready to use.

Just before serving time, rinse, cut into halves lengthwise, and remove pits from

3 medium chilled ripe avocados

Brush cut surfaces with

Lemon juice

Seafood-stuffed Avocados II

Mound the seafood mixture into the avocado halves. Spoon some of the mayonnaise mixture over each. Sprinkle with

1 tablespoon finely chopped chives

Garnish two of the filled avocado halves with the reserved whole shrimp; the remaining halves with the reserved lobster claw meat.

Arrange the avocado halves on a platter with

Tomato slices
Cucumber slices

Serve with the remaining mayonnaise mixture.

6 servings

SEAFOOD MEDLEY

An elegant and hearty main-dish salad—perfect for a small buffet or a large luncheon party.

Drain, remove and discard bony tissue, and separate

1 can (6½ oz.) crab meat (about 1⅓ cups, drained)

Drain

2 cans (6 oz. each) lobster meat (about 1½ cups, drained)
1 can (5 oz.) shrimp (about ¾ cup, drained; remove black veins if present)

Cut lobster and shrimp into pieces. Combine in a bowl with crab meat and chill in refrigerator.

Prepare and chill

3 Hard-Cooked Eggs (page 133)

Prepare and put into a large salad bowl

1 qt. (about ½ head) shredded lettuce
1 cup diced celery
¼ cup sliced radishes
¼ cup sliced green onions

Set in refrigerator to chill at least 1 hr.

Shortly before serving, prepare and cut into cubes

1 medium ripe avocado

Coat pieces with

2 tablespoons lemon juice

Add to the salad bowl. Dice the hard-cooked eggs and add to the salad bowl, together with the seafood. Coarsely chop and add

½ cup (about 2 oz.) walnuts

Rinse, cut out stem ends, dice and add
2 medium tomatoes, chilled
Toss all ingredients together thoroughly.

Blend
1 cup mayonnaise
¼ cup cream
1 teaspoon salt
¼ teaspoon pepper
Add to salad bowl and toss lightly.

About 12 servings

Note: If desired, reserve lobster meat from claws or use some shrimp to garnish. Or top with capers, green pepper strips or ripe olives. Cooked Sour Cream Dressing (page 417) or Cooked Marshmallow Dressing (page 416) may be substituted for the mayonnaise.

SEAFOOD SALAD SUPREME

Drain, remove and discard bony tissue from and separate
1 can (6½ oz.) crab meat (about 1⅓ cups, drained)
Drain
1 can (5 oz.) shrimp (about ¾ cup)
1 can (6 oz.) lobster (about ¾ cup)
1 can (6½ or 7 oz.) tuna (about 1 cup)
Cut shrimp and lobster into pieces and separate tuna into small chunks. Combine in a bowl, cover and set in refrigerator.

Put into a large salad bowl
2 qts. (1 head) shredded lettuce
1 cup diced celery
½ cup (about 2 oz.) chopped walnuts
⅓ cup sliced radishes
¼ cup sliced green onions

Rinse, peel, cut into halves, remove and discard pit and dice
1 medium ripe avocado
Sprinkle with
3 tablespoons lemon juice
Toss lightly to coat thoroughly. Turn into salad bowl. Refrigerate at least 1 hr.

Prepare and chill
3 Hard-Cooked Eggs (page 133), finely diced
2 medium tomatoes, diced

When ready to serve, mix
1 cup mayonnaise
¼ cup cream
1 teaspoon salt
¼ teaspoon pepper
Add dressing to salad bowl with the seafood, diced eggs and tomatoes; toss lightly until all ingredients are coated with dressing.

Serve heaped lightly into crisp **lettuce cups.**

6 to 8 servings

FROZEN SALADS

FROZEN WALDORF SALAD

Set out an 8-in. square pan.

Drain, reserving syrup
1 can (8½ oz.) crushed pineapple

Mix in a saucepan
2 eggs, slightly beaten
½ cup sugar
¼ cup lemon juice
⅛ teaspoon salt
Blend in the reserved pineapple syrup. Cook, stirring constantly, until mixture is slightly thickened. Remove from heat; cool.

Mix in a bowl the drained pineapple and
2½ cups diced unpared apples (2 medium apples)
½ cup diced celery
½ cup coarsely chopped walnuts

Beat until soft peaks are formed
½ cup chilled heavy cream
Fold whipped cream into cooled sauce. Combine with fruit and toss lightly to mix thoroughly. Turn into the pan. Freeze until firm.

To serve, cut into squares. *9 servings*

FROZEN BANANA STRAWBERRY SALAD

Line a 9x5x3-in. loaf pan with aluminum foil; set aside.

Chill in a tray in freezer until ice crystals begin to form around edge
⅔ cup undiluted evaporated milk
Beat until softened
1 pkg. (8 oz.) cream cheese
Beat in
½ cup sugar
⅓ cup mayonnaise
Mix in
½ cup chopped walnuts
½ pt. fresh strawberries, rinsed, hulled and sliced
Peel and slice
2 ripe bananas
Gently mix bananas into strawberry mixture. Combine the icy evaporated milk and
2 tablespoons lemon juice
Beat until very stiff. Fold in the fruit-nut mixture. Turn into the lined loaf pan. Freeze

until firm. Soften salad slightly before slicing. Serve on **crisp salad greens.** *8 to 10 servings*

FROZEN SWEET CHERRY SALAD

Refrigerator trays will be needed.

Drain
1 can (17 oz.) pitted light sweet cherries
1 can (17 oz.) pitted dark sweet cherries
1 can (13½ oz.) pineapple tidbits
Combine fruit with
1 pt. yogurt
2 tablespoons lemon juice
¼ teaspoon salt
Turn mixture into trays. Sprinkle over top
Toasted slivered almonds
Freeze until firm.

Cut into serving-size pieces. *9 servings*

FRUITY FROZEN SALAD

A 9x5x3-in. loaf pan, a fancy shallow 2-qt. mold, individual molds or circular cartons will be needed.

Drain, reserving syrup separately
1 can (13½ oz.) pineapple tidbits
1 can (8¾ oz.) apricot halves
Cut apricot halves into pieces. Set fruit aside. Add enough apricot syrup to pineapple syrup to make 1 cup; set aside.

Melt in a saucepan
½ cup butter or margarine
Blend in a mixture of
2 tablespoons all-purpose flour
Few grains salt
Cook, stirring constantly until mixture bubbles. Add the fruit syrup gradually, stirring constantly, and cook until thick and smooth. Stir in
2 tablespoons sugar
Stir several tablespoons hot mixture into
1 egg, slightly beaten
Immediately blend into mixture in saucepan. Cook, stirring constantly, about 3 min. Remove from heat. Stir in
2 tablespoons lemon juice
Cool and chill.

In a bowl, toss together the fruit pieces and
¾ cup orange sections, cut in ½-in. pieces
½ cup maraschino cherries, drained and cut in quarters
¼ cup chopped pecans
1 cup miniature marshmallows
½ cup packaged grated coconut
Beat until soft peaks are formed
1½ cups chilled heavy cream
Blend whipped cream, chill fruit sauce and
¼ cup mayonnaise
Combine with fruit mixture until well blended. Turn into mold and freeze until firm.

Remove from freezer and soften slightly before serving on chilled plates. *About 16 servings*

Frozen Sweet Cherry Salad

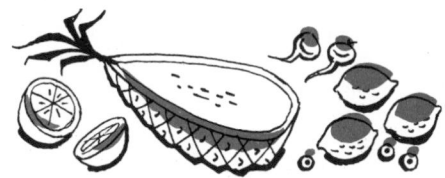

FROZEN FRUIT SALAD

▲ Base Recipe

Set a bowl and rotary beater in refrigerator to chill. Set out a 1½-qt. mold or large refrigerator tray.

Blanch, toast and salt (page 9 and 10)
½ cup (about 3 oz.) almonds
Chop coarsely and set aside.

Set out to drain, reserving syrup
**1 can (20 oz.) crushed pineapple
(about 1¾ cups, drained)**

Cut into quarters and set aside on absorbent paper to drain
½ cup maraschino cherries
(To avoid a pink tint in the mixture, drain cherries thoroughly.)

Cut (page 9) into slivers and set aside
½ cup (about 3 oz.) pitted dates

Cut (page 9) into eighths and set aside
24 marshmallows (6 oz.)

Beat until well blended 3 tablespoons of the reserved pineapple syrup and
1 pkg. (8 oz.) cream cheese, softened
Mix in
¼ cup mayonnaise
Gently mix in nuts, fruits and marshmallows.

Using the chilled bowl and beater, beat until cream is of medium consistency (piles softly)
1 cup chilled heavy cream
Lightly spread over cheese mixture and fold together. Turn into mold or refrigerator tray. Freeze until firm, about 4 hrs.

Unmold (page 374) onto chilled serving plate and garnish base with **fruit** and sprigs of **mint** or **watercress.** Or serve slices or wedges of the salad on chilled individual salad plates.

Serve with
Pineapple Salad Dressing (page 416)
8 to 10 servings

Note: If desired, turn salad mixture into two 29-oz. cans or three 16-oz. cans, washed and drained. Freeze until firm.

—FROZEN TROPICAL SALAD

Follow ▲ Recipe. Substitute **pecans** for almonds and **¾ cup diced banana** for the dates.

FROZEN FRUIT HARMONY

This is a fine main dish at Sunday night supper for "the girls," who love sweet salads. Serve it with flavorful Easy Banana Bread (page 87). The menfolks will like it better as an accompaniment salad for the main course, or even for dessert.

Set in refrigerator to chill a large refrigerator tray, a bowl, a rotary beater and
1 cup heavy cream

Cut into small pieces and set aside
**1 cup drained apricot halves
1 cup drained peach halves
1 cup drained pineapple chunks
¼ cup drained maraschino cherries**

Chop and set aside
¼ cup (about 1 oz.) salted pistachio nuts

Pour into a small saucepan
½ cup cold water
Sprinkle evenly over cold water
1 env. unflavored gelatin
Set saucepan over low heat and stir until gelatin is completely dissolved.

Measure into a large bowl
1 cup mayonnaise
When the gelatin is dissolved, stir in and blend into the mayonnaise. Blend in thoroughly
**½ cup sugar
3 tablespoons lemon juice**
Chill (page 374) until mixture begins to gel (becomes slightly thicker). When mixture is of desired consistency, blend in fruit and nuts thoroughly.

Using the chilled bowl and beater, beat the chilled cream until it is of medium consistency (piles softly). Blend into the fruit-gelatin mixture. Turn into a large refrigerator tray and freeze until firm.

To serve, cut into squares and place on chilled individual salad plates. Garnish with
Crisp lettuce or curly endive
About 10 servings

FROZEN FRUIT SALAD DELICIOUS

A delightful dessert for any occasion; and if you choose to serve it as a dessert-salad to the ladies of your club or bridge circle, you'd better have copies of the recipe on hand for them to take home!

Line ten 2½-in. muffin-pan wells with paper baking cups.

Prepare and set aside
**⅓ cup (about 1 oz.) coarsely chopped walnuts
3 tablespoons finely chopped maraschino cherries, well drained**

Drain, reserving syrup for use in other food preparation
**1 can (8¼ oz.) crushed pineapple
(about ¾ cup, drained)**
Mix
**2 cups dairy sour cream
¾ cup sugar
2 tablespoons lemon juice
⅛ teaspoon salt**
Blend in the pineapple, walnuts and cherries.

Pear and Frozen Cheese Salad

Peel and dice
1 medium banana with brown-flecked peel
Mix in the diced banana. Spoon mixture into the baking cups. Freeze until firm.

Before serving, remove paper cups. Allow salads to stand at room temperature for a few minutes to soften very slightly. *10 servings*

PEAR AND FROZEN CHEESE SALAD

▲ Base Recipe

For Frozen Roquefort or Blue Cheese Cubes—
Set a bowl and rotary beater in refrigerator to chill.

Crumble into a bowl
**4 oz. Roquefort or blue cheese
(about 1 cup, crumbled)**
Set aside.

Prepare and set aside
½ cup chopped celery
Beat until fluffy
1 pkg. (3 oz.) cream cheese, softened
Mix in, stirring until thoroughly blended after each addition
**¼ cup mayonnaise
1 tablespoon lemon juice
¼ teaspoon salt
⅛ teaspoon pepper**
Stir in the crumbled cheese and chopped celery. Set mixture aside.

Using the chilled bowl and beater, beat until cream is of medium consistency (piles softly)
½ cup chilled heavy cream
Gently fold into cheese mixture. Turn into a refrigerator tray. Freeze until firm.

When ready to serve, cut frozen cheese mixture into 1-in. cubes.

For Bartlett Pear Salad—Rinse, cut into halves and core
   4 chilled ripe Bartlett pears
Brush cut sides of pears with
   Lemon juice
Place on each of 8 chilled salad plates
   **Curly endive, watercress, or other
      salad greens**
Put one pear half, cut side up, on each plate. Place two or three Frozen Roquefort or Blue Cheese Cubes in hollow of each pear half. Or arrange greens, pear halves and cheese cubes on a large chilled serving plate. Serve immediately with
   French dressing

8 servings

—PEAR CABBAGE CHEESE CUBE SALAD

Follow ▲ Recipe for Frozen Roquefort or Blue Cheese Cubes. Add **1½ cups chopped cabbage** with crumbled cheese and celery, and mix well. Substitute **⅛ teaspoon paprika** for the pepper. Increase heavy cream to 1 cup. Complete as in ▲ Recipe.

FROZEN PEPPERMINT DESSERT SALAD

Like many frozen fruit salads, this one may be served as the dessert course of a women's luncheon. Its rosy hue is particularly appealing for a birthday celebration, shower or Valentine party.

Put into a large bowl
   **1 can (20 oz.) crushed pineapple
      (about 2½ cups)**
   **1 pkg. (3 oz.) strawberry-flavored
      gelatin**
   **1 pkg. (10½ oz.) miniature
      marshmallows**
Add to bowl
   **¼ cup (about 2 oz.) cinnamon
      candies**
Mix well, cover and chill overnight.

Set a bowl and rotary beater in refrigerator to chill.

Using the chilled bowl and beater, beat (one cup at a time) until cream is of medium consistency (piles softly)
   2 cups chilled heavy cream
Fold whipped cream into pineapple mixture with
   ¼ lb. soft butter mints, crushed
Turn into refrigerator trays or a 10-in. tubed pan. Freeze until firm. *About 20 servings*

Note: The strawberry-flavored gelatin is used for flavor and color rather than for gelling the mixture.

GREENGAGE PLUM SALAD

Roquefort, blue cheese or any other desired dressing may be served with this salad to enhance its flavor.

Cut into halves, remove and discard pits, and force through a sieve or food mill
   **2½ cups canned greengage plums
      and syrup (about 2¼ cups,
      sieved)**
Prepare and mix in
   1 cup chopped celery
   ½ cup (about 2 oz.) chopped walnuts
Turn into a refrigerator tray. Freeze until mixture is firm, about 4 hrs., stirring 2 or 3 times.

6 to 8 servings

NIPPY CHEESE FREEZE SALAD

▲ Base Recipe

Flavorful frozen cheese cubes add variety of temperature as well as flavor and texture to a tossed green salad. Of course the salad must be served at once and eaten promptly.

For Nippy Cheese Freeze—Chop
   8 to 10 pimiento-stuffed olives
Set aside.

Put into a small bowl and mash with a fork
   3 oz. natural cheese food
Add gradually, blending until mixture is smooth
   ½ cup dairy sour cream
Blend in the chopped olives and
   1 teaspoon lemon juice
   ¼ teaspoon monosodium glutamate
   3 drops Tabasco
Turn mixture into a 1-qt. refrigerator tray. Freeze until mixture is firm.

For Tossed Salad—Rinse, discarding bruised leaves, drain and dry thoroughly
   Lettuce
   Curly endive
   Romaine
   Watercress
Using as much of each green as desired, tear into pieces enough greens to yield about 2 qts. Put into a large plastic bag or vegetable freshener. Chill in refrigerator at least 1 hr.

When ready to serve, rub a salad bowl with cut surface of
   1 clove garlic, cut in halves
Cut the frozen cheese mixture into small cubes.

Put the chilled greens into the salad bowl and toss lightly with **French dressing**. Add the cheese cubes and toss just enough to distribute the cubes evenly throughout the greens. Serve immediately. *6 to 8 servings*

—GARLIC COTTAGE CHEESE FREEZE

Follow ▲ Recipe. Use two refrigerator trays. Substitute **ripe olives** for stuffed olives and **2 cups sieved cream-style cottage cheese** for cheese food. Blend in **1 clove garlic**, minced.

CUCUMBER ICE SALAD

Chill a bowl in the refrigerator.

For Cucumber Ice—Heat together in top of a double boiler, stirring occasionally, until marshmallows are melted
   16 marshmallows (¼ lb.), cut
   ⅓ cup lemon juice

Meanwhile, rinse, pare, cut into halves lengthwise and remove seeds from
   2 medium cucumbers
Grate cucumbers and mix with
   1 teaspoon grated onion
   ½ teaspoon salt
   3 drops green food coloring
   Few grains cayenne pepper
Remove marshmallow imxture from simmering water; blend in cucumber mixture. Pour into a refrigerator tray. Freeze until mixture is mushy in consistency.

Beat until frothy
   2 egg whites
Add and beat until rounded peaks are formed
   1 tablespoon sugar
Turn frozen mixture into the chilled bowl and beat with rotary beater. Spread egg whites over cucumber mixture and fold together. Immediately return mixture to refrigerator tray and freeze until firm, about 4 hrs.

To Complete Salad—Meanwhile, rinse and cut ½-in. slices from tops of
   8 medium tomatoes
Remove pulp with a spoon. Invert the shells and place in refrigerator to drain and chill while cucumber mixture is freezing.

To serve, fill the tomato shells with Cucumber Ice and serve at once on chilled salad plates.

8 servings

HOT SALADS

HOT SLAW

Set out a heavy 2-qt. saucepan.

Shred coarsely
   1 medium head green cabbage
Cook in saucepan over low heat until crisp
   6 slices bacon, cut in 1-in. pieces

German Potato Salad

Remove bacon pieces to absorbent paper.

Add to bacon drippings in saucepan
½ teaspoon celery seed
¼ cup packed brown sugar
½ teaspoon dry mustard
¼ cup vinegar
½ teaspoon salt

Blend well, cook until heated, and add shredded cabbage. Cook and toss until cabbage is well coated with the hot dressing. Remove from heat and sprinkle with bacon pieces.

4 to 6 servings

WILTED CABBAGE

Prepare
6 slices Panfried Bacon (page 190)

Reserve bacon fat. Set bacon pieces and skillet aside.

Remove and discard wilted outer leaves, rinse thoroughly and cut into pieces (discarding core)
½ medium head (about 1½ lbs.) cabbage

Turn on an electric blender and gradually *but quickly* add about one-fourth of the cabbage; blend only until coarsely chopped. Turn off motor and empty contents of blender container into a large bowl. Repeat process until all the cabbage is coarsely chopped. Set aside.

Prepare
French Dressing I (page 410), using the reserved bacon fat and enough salad oil to make ¾ cup)

Pour the dressing into the skillet in which the bacon was cooked. Heat to boiling, stirring occasionally. Pour over cabbage and lightly toss together.

Spoon into salad bowl; garnish with bacon pieces.

4 to 6 servings

WILTED LETTUCE SALAD
(Kopfsalat)

▲ Base Recipe

Using a sharp-pointed knife, remove core from
1 small head lettuce

Rinse with cold water and drain well. Gently pat dry. Tear lettuce into pieces. Put into a bowl. Cover and chill in refrigerator.

Prepare
1 Hard-Cooked Egg (page 133)

Cut egg into slices crosswise and set aside.

Combine in a small skillet
¼ cup cider vinegar
¼ cup salad oil
2 tablespoons sugar
½ teaspoon salt
⅛ teaspoon pepper

Heat mixture to boiling, stirring well. Immediately pour vinegar mixture over the lettuce and toss lightly to coat lettuce thoroughly.

Garnish with the hard-cooked egg slices.

6 servings

—WILTED LETTUCE WITH BACON (Kopfsalat with Speck)

Follow ▲ Recipe. The egg may be omitted. Dice **6 slices bacon**; fry until crisp without pouring off fat. Substitute the **bacon fat** for the salad oil. Omit salt and pepper.

GERMAN POTATO SALAD
(Warmer Kartoffelsalat)

Wash and cut into halves
6 medium (about 2 lbs.) potatoes

Cook (page 313) about 20 min., or until potatoes are tender when pierced with a fork. Drain potatoes. Dry potatoes by shaking pan over low heat. Peel and cut into ¼-in. slices.

Meanwhile, dice and panfry, reserving bacon drippings
12 slices bacon

Set aside.

Clean and chop
3 medium onions (about 1½ cups, chopped)

Put 6 tablespoons of the bacon drippings into a saucepan. Add the onion and cook until it is tender, occasionally moving and turning with a spoon. Stir in
¾ cup vinegar
2½ tablespoons sugar
2 teaspoons salt
¾ teaspoon monosodium glutamate
¼ teaspoon pepper

Heat mixture to boiling. Add the diced bacon to the onion-vinegar mixture. Pour over the hot potato slices and toss lightly to coat evenly.

6 to 8 servings

Note: To prepare thuringer sausage links (shown in photo), cook covered, in water to cover, about 15 min. over medium heat.

HOT POTATO SALAD I

Wash
6 medium (about 2 lbs.) potatoes

Cook covered in boiling salted water to cover

Hot Potato Salad

20 to 30 min., or until potatoes are tender when pierced with a fork. Drain. Dry potatoes by shaking pan over low heat. Peel, cut into ¼-in. slices, put into a bowl and add
1 cup (about 2 medium) finely chopped onion
3 tablespoons finely chopped parsley

and a mixture of
1½ teaspoons monosodium glutamate
1¼ teaspoons salt
¼ teaspoon pepper

Toss together lightly and set aside.

Stir together in a small saucepan and heat to boiling
⅔ cup cider vinegar
⅓ cup water
1½ teaspoons sugar

Beat slightly
1 egg

Continue beating while gradually adding the vinegar mixture. Add gradually, while beating constantly
⅓ cup salad oil

Pour dressing over potato mixture and toss lightly to coat evenly. Turn salad into a large skillet and set over low heat for 10 to 15 min., or until potatoes are heated. Keep mixture moving gently with a spoon.

Serve immediately.

About 6 servings

HOT POTATO SALAD II
(Varm Potetes Salad)

Wash, pare and cook (page 313)
12 medium (about 4 lbs.) potatoes, cut in halves

Cook about 20 min., or until tender when pierced with a fork. Drain.

To dry potatoes, shake pan over low heat. To heat potato masher, food mill or ricer and a mixing bowl, scald them with boiling water. Mash or rice potatoes thoroughly. If necessary, keep potatoes hot over simmering water.

Meanwhile, cream until softened

2 tablespoons butter

Blend in thoroughly

4 egg yolks, beaten
¼ cup cream
4 teaspoons cider vinegar

and a mixture of

1 tablespoon salt
2 teaspoons sugar
1 teaspoon pepper

Stir in

¼ cup chopped parsley
¼ cup chopped onion

Add the hot mashed potatoes and mix until thoroughly blended. Turn into a warm serving dish. Garnish with

Sprigs of parsley
Pickled Beets (page 422), cut in strips
Lemon slices

8 to 10 servings

BAKED FRANKFURTER AND POTATO SALAD

▲ Base Recipe

Grease a 1½-qt. casserole.

Wash and cook covered in boiling salted water to cover

4 medium (about 1¼ lbs.) potatoes

Cover and cook over medium heat about 20 min., or until potatoes are tender when pierced with a fork. Drain. To dry potatoes, shake pan over low heat. Peel potatoes, cut into ½-in. cubes and put into casserole with

2 tablespoons diced pimiento
¼ teaspoon celery seed

Heat in a small skillet

2 tablespoons fat or bacon drippings

Add to skillet and cook about 5 min.

¼ cup finely chopped onion
¼ cup chopped green pepper

Meanwhile, put into a 1-pt. screw-top jar

⅓ cup water
¼ cup vinegar
1 tablespoon sugar
1½ teaspoons all-purpose flour
1 teaspoon salt
¼ teaspoon pepper

Cover jar and shake until ingredients are thoroughly blended.

Remove skillet from heat. Stir in flour mixture; return to heat. Cook rapidly, stirring constantly, and bring sauce to boiling. Boil 3 to 5 min. stirring constantly. (Sauce should be thickened.) With fork, lightly mix sauce with potatoes.

Set out

4 frankfurters

Wrap with

4 slices bacon

Secure ends of bacon with wooden picks. Arrange on the potato salad.

Bake at 400°F 15 to 20 min., or until bacon is cooked. Turn frankfurters to cook bacon evenly.

Garnish salad with

Sprigs of parsley or minced green onion tops

4 servings

—QUICK FRANKFURTER AND POTATO SALAD

Follow ▲ Recipe; use top-of-range casserole and do not grease it. Do not set cubed potatoes, pimiento and celery seed aside in casserole. Panfry bacon, crumble and set aside. Increase bacon drippings to ¼ cup. Cut frankfurters into bite-size pieces and heat in casserole with onion and pepper. Mix in bacon and remaining ingredients. Mix in potato mixture. Heat thoroughly.

SALAD DRESSINGS

In a broad sense, salad dressings are sauces which enhance salads. The general types are oil and vinegar, creamy, including mayonnaises, and cooked dressings, both hot and cold.

OIL-AND-VINEGAR DRESSINGS

FRENCH DRESSING I

▲ Base Recipe

Combine in a jar with a tight cover

¾ cup salad oil or olive oil
¼ cup lemon juice or cider vinegar
1 tablespoon sugar
¾ teaspoon salt
¼ teaspoon paprika
¼ teaspoon dry mustard
¼ teaspoon pepper

Cover jar tightly and shake vigorously to blend well. Store in covered container in refrigerator. Shake well before using. *About 1 cup dressing*

—ANCHOVY FRENCH DRESSING

Follow ▲ Recipe. Use lemon juice. Omit salt and add **4 minced anchovy fillets.** Shake well.

—CHIFFONADE FRENCH DRESSING

Follow ▲ Recipe. Add **1 Hard-Cooked Egg** (page 133), chopped, **2 tablespoons finely chopped ripe olives,** and **4 teaspoons finely chopped parsley.** Shake well.

—CREAMY FRENCH DRESSING

Follow ▲ Recipe. Add **¼ cup dairy sour cream** and blend well.

—CREOLE FRENCH DRESSING

Prepare **2 Hard-Cooked Eggs** (page 133). Meanwhile, follow ▲ Recipe. Mash egg yolks with a fork and blend with completed dressing. Chop egg whites and use as a garnish for dressing or salad.

—CURRIED FRENCH DRESSING

Follow ▲ Recipe. Add **¼ teaspoon curry powder** and shake well.

—FRUIT JUICE FRENCH DRESSING

Follow ▲ Recipe. Substitute **orange or pineapple juice** for the lemon juice or vinegar, or use 2 tablespoons of each fruit juice.

—GARLIC FRENCH DRESSING

Follow ▲ Recipe. Cut into halves **1 clove garlic;** add to completed dressing. Chill dressing about 12 hours before using to allow flavors to blend. Remove garlic before serving, or when flavor of dressing is sufficiently strong.

—FRENCH DRESSING WITH HERBS

Follow ▲ Recipe. Add **1 tablespoon mixture of chopped parsley, tarragon, chervil and chives.**

—HONEY FRENCH DRESSING

Follow ▲ Recipe. Use lemon juice. Blend in **½ cup honey** and **¼ teaspoon grated lemon peel.** For added flavor, add **½ teaspoon celery seed** and shake well.

—HONEY LIME FRENCH DRESSING

Follow ▲ Recipe. Substitute **lime juice** for the lemon juice or vinegar. Blend in **½ cup honey** and **¼ teaspoon grated lime peel.**

—TANGY FRENCH DRESSING

Follow ▲ Recipe. Add **3 to 4 tablespoons prepared horseradish** and shake well.

—ITALIAN DRESSING

Follow ▲ Recipe. Use olive oil. Omit lemon juice or vinegar and add **6 tablespoons wine vinegar.** Reduce salt to ½ teaspoon. Omit sugar, paprika and dry mustard. Shake well.

—LORENZO FRENCH DRESSING

Follow ▲ Recipe. Add **¼ cup finely chopped watercress** and **2 tablespoons chili sauce.** Shake well.

—OLIVE FRENCH DRESSING

Follow ▲ Recipe. Add **½ cup chopped pimiento-stuffed olives** and shake well.

—ONION FRENCH DRESSING

Follow ▲ Recipe. Add **½ cup (1 medium minced onion** and blend with completed dressing.

—ROQUEFORT FRENCH DRESSING

Follow ▲ Recipe. Blend until smooth **3 oz. (about ¾ cup) crumbled Roquefort cheese** and **2 teaspoons water.** Add dressing slowly to cheese, blending after each addition.

—TARRAGON FRENCH DRESSING

Follow ▲ Recipe. Use olive oil. Substitute **tarragon vinegar** for lemon juice or cider vinegar. Decrease sugar to 1 teaspoon. Add **1 clove garlic,** cut in halves, **¼ teaspoon Worcestershire sauce** and **⅛ teaspoon thyme.** Shake well.

—TOMATO FRENCH DRESSING

Follow ▲ Recipe. Add **2 tablespoons ketchup** and **1 teaspoon Worcestershire sauce** with seasonings. Finely chop **¼ green pepper** and blend with completed dressing.

—TOMATO SOUP FRENCH DRESSING

Follow ▲ Recipe. Add **⅔ cup (about one-half 10¾-oz. can) condensed tomato soup, 1 tablespoon chopped onion** and **½ teaspoon marjoram.** Shake well.

—VINAIGRETTE FRENCH DRESSING

Follow ▲ Recipe. Add **2 tablespoons finely chopped dill pickle, 2 teaspoons chopped chives** and **1 Hard-Cooked Egg** (page 133), chopped. Shake well.

FRENCH DRESSING II

This dressing achieves its utmost perfection when tossed with generous amounts of crisp mixed salad greens.

Combine in a jar with a tight cover
¾ cup olive oil
¼ cup tarragon or cider vinegar
¼ teaspoon Worcestershire sauce
1 clove garlic, cut into halves
1 teaspoon sugar
¼ teaspoon salt
½ teaspoon paprika
¼ teaspoon dry mustard
⅛ teaspoon pepper
⅛ teaspoon thyme
Shake well. Chill in refrigerator.

Before serving remove garlic and beat or shake dressing thoroughly.   *About 1 cup dressing*

JIFFY FRENCH DRESSING

Blend well
1 tablespoon sugar
1 teaspoon paprika
1 teaspoon dry mustard
1 teaspoon salt
⅛ teaspoon pepper

Put into a 1-pt. screw-top jar with
1 cup salad oil
¼ cup vinegar or lemon juice
Cover jar tightly and shake vigorously to blend. Store in refrigerator. Shake well before using.
1¼ cups dressing

AROMATIC FRENCH DRESSING

Combine in a jar with a tight cover
⅔ cup salad oil
¼ cup lemon juice
2 tablespoons water
2 tablespoons ketchup
1 teaspoon sugar
1 teaspoon salt
1 teaspoon aromatic bitters
½ teaspoon dry mustard
½ teaspoon oregano
½ teaspoon paprika
3 drops Tabasco
Few grains pepper
Cut into halves and put into the jar
1 clove garlic
1 very small onion
Cover jar tightly and shake well. Store in covered container in refrigerator. Shake well before using.   *About 1 cup dressing*

Note: Remove and discard garlic and onion halves before serving, or when flavor of dressing is sufficiently strong.

AVOCADO DRESSING

Serve with citrus fruits for a new twist to a favorite combination.

Prepare and cut into pieces
1 medium ripe avocado
Force avocado pieces through a sieve or food mill into a bowl. Add very gradually while beating constantly
½ cup salad oil
Continue beating while adding gradually
2 tablespoons lemon juice
Blend in
2 tablespoons minced onion
½ teaspoon salt
1 drop Tabasco
Few grains white pepper
Chill in covered container in refrigerator. Serve the same day.   *About 1 cup dressing*

BLUE CHEESE DRESSING

Crumble into a bowl
4 oz. (about 1 cup) blue cheese
Blend in until smooth
2 tablespoons wine vinegar
1 tablespoon lemon juice
½ teaspoon Worcestershire sauce

Add and stir until blended a mixture of
½ teaspoon sugar
½ teaspoon dry mustard
½ teaspoon paprika
¼ teaspoon salt
⅛ teaspoon pepper
Add gradually, beating constantly
⅔ cup salad oil
Store in covered container in refrigerator. Mix well before using.

About 1¼ cups dressing

ITALIAN SALAD DRESSING

▲ *Base Recipe*

Combine in a screw-top jar
6 tablespoons olive oil
3 tablespoons wine vinegar
1 clove garlic, crushed
¼ teaspoon salt
⅛ teaspoon pepper
Shake well. Chill in refrigerator. Before serving, beat or shake thoroughly.

About ½ cup dressing

—ANCHOVY DRESSING

Follow ▲ Recipe. Add to ingredients in jar **1 teaspoon prepared mustard** and **2 anchovy fillets,** finely chopped.

FAVORITE SALAD DRESSING

Put through fine blade of food chopper
1 medium green pepper
1 medium onion
Combine in a screw-top jar with
⅓ cup orange juice
¼ cup salad oil
3 tablespoons lemon juice
2 tablespoons cider vinegar
2 tablespoons sugar
½ teaspoon salt
¼ teaspoon pepper
1 clove garlic, cut in halves
Cover jar tightly and shake well. Store in refrigerator. Shake well before serving.

About 1½ cups dressing

Note: Remove and discard garlic halves before serving, or when flavor of dressing is sufficiently strong.

MELBOURNE SALAD DRESSING

A piquant dressing for salad greens.

Combine in a jar with a tight cover
⅔ cup lemon juice
¼ cup olive oil
¼ cup Worcestershire sauce
3 tablespoons plus 1 teaspoon sugar
Cover jar tightly and shake vigorously to blend well. Store in covered container in refrigerator. Shake well before using. Serve icy cold.

About 1¼ cups dressing

RUM-FLAVORED DRESSING

Add surprising and sophisticated flavor to the delicate goodness of avocado.

Combine in a jar with a tight cover
3 tablespoons olive oil
4 teaspoons lime juice
4 teaspoons rum
2 teaspoons brown sugar
¼ teaspoon salt
Few grains pepper
Cover jar tightly and shake vigorously to blend well. Store in covered container in refrigerator. Shake well before using.

About ⅔ cup dressing

POPPY SEED MUSTARD DRESSING

Put into a small bowl
¼ cup honey
¼ cup cider vinegar
2 tablespoons prepared mustard
2 tablespoons poppy seed
4 teaspoons grated onion
¼ teaspoon salt
Beat with rotary beater until thoroughly mixed. Add very gradually while beating constantly
⅔ cup salad oil
Continue beating until mixture is of desired consistency.

Chill thoroughly in covered container in refrigerator. Shake well before using.

About 1⅓ cups dressing

CELERY SEED DRESSING

Set out
4½ tablespoons cider vinegar
Mix in a bowl
½ cup sugar
1 teaspoon dry mustard
1 teaspoon salt
¼ teaspoon monosodium glutamate

Blend in 2 tablespoons of the vinegar and
1 teaspoon grated onion
Add very gradually while beating constantly
1 cup salad oil
Beat until thick and light. Slowly beat in the remainder of the vinegar. Add and mix well
1 tablespoon celery seed
Store in covered container in refrigerator. Shake well before using.

About 1⅔ cups dressing

TARRAGON SALAD DRESSING

Put into a small bowl
¼ cup sugar
¼ cup light corn syrup
¼ cup tarragon vinegar
1½ teaspoons celery seed
1 teaspoon dry mustard
1 teaspoon salt
½ teaspoon grated onion
Few grains white pepper
Beat with rotary beater until thoroughly mixed. Add gradually (about ½ teaspoon at a time) while beating constantly
¾ cup salad oil
Continue beating until mixture is of desired consistency. (It is very important to add oil gradually and in very small amounts, to avoid separation of salad dressing.) Chill thoroughly in refrigerator. Shake chilled dressing well just before serving. *About 1⅛ cups dressing*

OIL-VINEGAR MARINADE
(Olaj-Ecet Pác)

Put into a small screw-top jar
½ cup vinegar
2 tablespoons olive oil
1 tablespoon sugar
1 teaspoon salt
½ teaspoon freshly ground pepper
Cover tightly and shake jar until ingredients are well blended.

If marinade is not used immediately, store in refrigerator and beat or shake thoroughly before using. *About ⅔ cup*

CREAMY DRESSINGS

MAYONNAISE

▲ *Base Recipe*

Creamy-smooth mayonnaise is capable of any number of delectable variations to suit your salad. Make it fluffy for a sweet salad by folding in whipped cream—sweetened or not; add zest with lemon or orange juice and a bit of grated peel; give extra sweetness by stirring in honey or marshmallow cream. Sherry and unsweetened whipped cream lend a touch of sophistication to the mayonnaise for a freshfruit salad. And you can give an exotic flavor

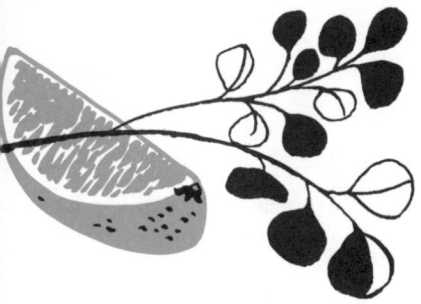

to meat or fish salad by blending curry powder, lemon juice, a dash of Worcestershire sauce and a bit of mustard into the mayonnaise. Let imagination and your own taste inspire you!

Put into a small bowl and beat with a rotary beater until well blended

2 egg yolks
1 tablespoon cider vinegar
½ teaspoon dry mustard
½ teaspoon salt
¼ teaspoon sugar
⅛ teaspoon white pepper
Few grains cayenne pepper

Measure

1 cup salad oil

Add oil, 1 teaspoon at a time at first, beating vigorously after each addition. Gradually increase amounts added until one half of the salad oil has been used.

Alternately beat in small amounts of remaining salad oil and (a few drops at a time)

1 tablespoon lemon juice

(If mayonnaise separates because oil has been added too rapidly, beat it slowly and thoroughly into 1 egg yolk, 1 tablespoon cold water, small quantity of vinegar or small portion of good mayonnaise.) Store in covered container in refrigerator. *About 1½ cups Mayonnaise*

—ELEGANT MAYONNAISE

Follow ▲ Recipe. Blend into 1 cup chilled Mayonnaise **1 teaspoon lemon juice, 1 teaspoon curry powder** and **a few grains salt.** Using a chilled bowl and beater, beat ⅓ **cup chilled heavy cream** until cream is of medium consistency (piles softly). With few final strokes, beat or blend in **2 tablespoons plus 1 teaspoon confectioners' sugar.** Fold whipped cream into Mayonnaise mixture.

—THOUSAND ISLAND DRESSING

Follow ▲ Recipe. Mix into ½ cup Mayonnaise **1 or 2 Hard-Cooked Eggs (page 133),** sieved or finely chopped, **2 tablespoons chili sauce, 2 tablespoons finely chopped scallions** (with tops), **2 tablespoons chopped sweet pickle, 1 tablespoon chopped green olives** and ½ **teaspoon paprika.**

—RUSSIAN DRESSING

Follow ▲ Recipe. Blend into ½ cup Mayonnaise **3 tablespoons chili sauce, 1 tablespoon minced onion** and ½ **teaspoon prepared horseradish.**

MIXER MAYONNAISE

Put into a small mixer bowl

2 eggs
½ cup vinegar or lemon juice
1½ teaspoons salt
1 teaspoon sugar
1 teaspoon dry mustard
1 teaspoon paprika
¾ teaspoon monosodium glutamate
4 drops Tabasco

Beat thoroughly on medium speed.

Continue beating while pouring very slowly into center of ingredients

3 cups salad oil

Continue beating mayonnaise on medium speed until it reaches proper consistency, (about 10 min). (If mayonnaise separates because oil is added too rapidly, beat it slowly and thoroughly into 1 egg yolk.)

Store in covered jar in refrigerator.

About 1 qt. mayonnaise

BLENDER MAYONNAISE

▲ Base Recipe

See page 11 for using an electric blender.

Put into blender container in order

1 egg, unbeaten
2 tablespoons cider vinegar or lemon juice
¼ teaspoon salt
¼ teaspoon sugar
¼ teaspoon monosodium glutamate
¼ teaspoon dry mustard
¼ teaspoon paprika
2 or 3 drops Tabasco

Cover and blend thoroughly. Continue blending while pouring very slowly into center of ingredients

½ to ¾ cup salad oil

Add oil just until it begins to layer on surface; mayonnaise then will be proper consistency. (If mayonnaise separates because oil is added too rapidly, beat mixture slowly and thoroughly into 1 egg yolk, 1 tablespoon cold water, small quantity of vinegar or small portion of good mayonnaise.)

Store in covered container in refrigerator.

About 1 cup mayonnaise

—BLENDER RUSSIAN DRESSING

Follow ▲ Recipe. Put ¼ onion, ⅓ cup chili sauce and **1 teaspoon prepared horseradish** into blender container with mayonnaise. Blend until ingredients are thoroughly mixed.

—BLENDER THOUSAND ISLAND DRESSING

Follow ▲ Recipe. Add to blender container containing mayonnaise ¼ **cup chili sauce, ¼ cup pimiento-stuffed olives, ¼ cup sweet pickle relish, 2 or 3 green onions** (with tops), cut into pieces, and ½ **teaspoon paprika.** Cover and turn on motor. Add by quarters **1 Hard-Cooked Egg (page 133),** peeled and quartered. Blend only until egg is chopped.

SHAKER SALAD DRESSING

This quickly made, smooth-textured dressing is both sharp and sweet.

Combine in a jar with a tight cover

⅔ cup sweetened condensed milk
¼ cup salad oil
3 tablespoons lemon juice or cider vinegar
1 tablespoon minced parsley
1 teaspoon prepared mustard
½ teaspoon salt
Few grains cayenne pepper

Cover jar tightly and shake well. Store in covered container in refrigerator. Shake well before using. *About 1 cup dressing*

SOUR CREAM MAYONNAISE

▲ Base Recipe

Blend

2 teaspoons cider vinegar
1 teaspoon sugar
½ teaspoon dry mustard

Blend into a mixture of

½ cup mayonnaise
½ cup dairy sour cream

About 1 cup dressing

Blue Cheese Salad Dressing

—CREAMY CELERY SEED DRESSING

Follow ▲ Recipe. Omit vinegar, sugar and mustard; add **2 tablespoons ketchup**, **½ teaspoon Worcestershire sauce**, **½ teaspoon celery seed** and **¼ teaspoon monosodium glutamate**.

DRESSING FOR VEGETABLE SALADS

Combine in a jar with a tight cover
- **½ cup salad oil**
- **½ cup undiluted evaporated milk**
- **3 tablespoons cider vinegar or lemon juice**
- **4 teaspoons sugar**
- **1¼ teaspoons paprika**
- **1 teaspoon dry mustard**
- **½ teaspoon salt**
- **⅛ teaspoon pepper**
- **1 teaspoon grated onion**

Cover jar tightly and shake vigorously to blend well. Store in covered container in refrigerator. Shake well before using.

About 1¼ cups dressing

BUTTERMILK SALAD DRESSING

Mix
- **½ cup buttermilk**
- **4 teaspoons prepared horseradish**
- **1 teaspoon sugar**
- **⅛ teaspoon dry mustard**
- **⅛ teaspoon salt**
- **Few grains pepper**

Chill thoroughly. *About ½ cup dressing*

EXTRA-SPECIAL ANCHOVY DRESSING

Here's a salad dressing that's real magic with those crisp greens in your salad bowl.

Drain, reserving oil in a 1-cup measuring cup for liquids
- **1 can (2 oz.) anchovy fillets**

Add to the anchovy oil
- **Salad oil (enough to make ⅓ cup oil)**

Pour into a screw-top jar. Add
- **1 clove garlic, cut in halves**

Mash the anchovy fillets and add to oil with
- **½ cup undiluted evaporated milk**
- **3 tablespoons cider vinegar**
- **1 teaspoon lemon juice**
- **1 teaspoon finely chopped chives**
- **½ teaspoon salt**
- **⅛ teaspoon pepper**
- **⅛ teaspoon crushed dried tarragon leaves**

Cover jar tightly and shake well. Set in refrigerator about 2 hrs. to chill and to allow flavors to blend.

Remove the garlic halves. Store dressing in covered container in refrigerator. Beat or shake well before using.

About 1¼ cups dressing

GREEN GODDESS SALAD DRESSING

Blend thoroughly
- **1 cup mayonnaise**
- **½ cup dairy sour cream**
- **3 tablespoons tarragon vinegar**
- **1 tablespoon lemon juice**
- **⅓ cup finely chopped parsley**
- **3 tablespoons finely chopped onion**
- **3 tablespoons mashed anchovy fillets**
- **1 tablespoon chopped chives**
- **2 teaspoons chopped capers**
- **1 clove garlic, minced**
- **⅛ teaspoon salt**
- **⅛ teaspoon pepper**

Cover bowl tightly and chill in refrigerator 3 to 4 hrs.

Serve on **Green Goddess Salad** (page 358) or other green salad.

About 2½ cups dressing

CHEDDAR CHEESE DRESSING

▲ *Base Recipe*

Shred
- **4 oz. sharp Cheddar cheese (about 1 cup, shredded)**

Blend in
- **1 cup dairy sour cream**

Mix in
- **1 tablespoon minced parsley**
- **1 tablespoon prepared mustard**
- **1 tablespoon grated onion**
- **½ teaspoon lemon juice**
- **½ teaspoon salt**
- **½ teaspoon Worcestershire sauce**
- **⅛ teaspoon pepper**

Store in covered container in refrigerator.

If desired, thin with cream before using.

About 1½ cups dressing

—BACON CHEESE DRESSING

Follow ▲ Recipe. Omit lemon juice. Mix in **½ cup crumbled Panfried Bacon. (page 190)**

—ROQUEFORT CHEDDAR CHEESE DRESSING

Follow ▲ Recipe. Omit prepared mustard. Mix in **¼ cup (about 1 oz.) crumbled Roquefort cheese.**

—GARLIC CHEESE DRESSING

Follow Recipe for Roquefort Cheddar Cheese Dressing. Omit grated onion. Blend in **½ clove garlic,** minced.

ZESTFUL BLUE CHEESE DRESSING

▲ *Base Recipe*

Crumble into a bowl
- **2 oz. blue cheese (about ½ cup, crumbled)**

Add and blend
- **1 cup mayonnaise**
- **¼ cup dairy sour cream**
- **2 tablespoons cider vinegar**
- **1 tablespoon sugar**
- **½ clove garlic, minced**
- **Few grains salt**

Beat until mixture is fluffy. Store in covered container in refrigerator.

About 1½ cups dressing

—PIMIENTO BLUE CHEESE DRESSING

Follow ▲ Recipe. Mix in **3 tablespoons chopped pimiento.**

BLUE CHEESE SALAD DRESSING

Mix in a small bowl
- **½ cup cream**
- **1 teaspoon prepared mustard**
- **¾ teaspoon paprika**
- **½ teaspoon Worcestershire sauce**
- **¼ teaspoon salt**
- **⅛ teaspoon coarsely ground pepper**
- **2 or 3 drops Tabasco**

Add, about 1 teaspoon at a time, while beating constantly with a rotary beater
- **¾ cup salad oil or olive oil**

Continue beating while adding gradually
- **2 tablespoons wine vinegar or cider vinegar**

Add to dressing

1 cup (about 4 oz.) crumbled blue cheese

Blend just until mixed. Store dressing in a screw-top jar in refrigerator.

Shake well before using.

About 2 cups dressing

DAIRYLAND SALAD DRESSING

Put into a bowl

1 cup (½ lb.) cream-style cottage cheese
½ cup dairy sour cream
2 teaspoons Worcestershire sauce
½ teaspoon monosodium glutamate
¼ teaspoon salt
2 drops Tabasco

Beat with rotary beater until well blended. Add and mix thoroughly

½ cup (about 2 oz.) crumbled blue cheese
2 tablespoons minced onion
2 tablespoons coarsely chopped pimiento

About 2 cups dressing

SWEET CREAM CHEESE DRESSING

▲ *Base Recipe*

Put into small mixer bowl

2 pkgs. (3 oz. each) cream cheese, softened
⅓ cup currant jelly
1½ teaspoons lemon juice
1 teaspoon grated lemon peel

Beat until smooth and fluffy. Add a small amount of milk, if necessary, to produce consistency desired.

Serve chilled as a topping for fruit salads.

About 1 cup dressing

—TART CREAM CHEESE DRESSING

Follow ▲ Recipe. Substitute **buttermilk** for jelly and **½ to 1 teaspoon Worcestershire sauce** for lemon. Serve with egg, meat or fish salads.

GOURMET SALAD DRESSING

▲ *Base Recipe*

Crumble into a bowl

3 oz. (about ¾ cup) Roquefort cheese

Blend in until smooth

1 pkg. (3 oz.) cream cheese, softened

Add and blend until creamy

1 cup dairy sour cream
⅓ cup sherry
1 tablespoon grated onion
½ teaspoon salt
¼ teaspoon paprika
1 or 2 drops Tabasco

Store dressing covered in refrigerator.

About 2 cups dressing

—VARIETY SALAD DRESSING

Follow ▲ Recipe. Omit Roquefort cheese. Blend with the cream cheese **5 oz. (1 jar) process cheese spread with blue cheese.** Decrease sherry to ¼ cup. Omit Tabasco.

ROQUEFORT CREAM DRESSING

▲ *Base Recipe*

Crumble into a bowl

2 oz. (about ½ cup) Roquefort or blue cheese

Mix in to form a smooth paste

2 tablespoons water

Blend in

1 cup dairy sour cream
3 tablespoons chopped chives
½ teaspoon salt

Store in covered container in refrigerator.

About 1½ cups dressing

—ROQUEFORT MAYONNAISE DRESSING

Follow ▲ Recipe. Substitute **¾ cup mayonnaise** and **⅓ cup cream** for sour cream.

FLUFFY CITRUS SALAD DRESSING

Set a bowl and rotary beater in refrigerator to chill.

Just before serving, blend

3 tablespoons honey
2 to 3 teaspoons lemon, lime or orange juice

Using the chilled bowl and beater, beat until cream is of medium consistency (piles softly)

½ cup chilled heavy cream

Beat the honey mixture into cream with final few strokes.

Serve with fruit salads.

About 1¼ cups dressing

MINT SALAD DRESSING

Chill a bowl and rotary beater in refrigerator.

Drain thoroughly

1 can (8¼ oz.) crushed pineapple (about ¾ cup, drained)

Rinse and chop or cut with scissors enough fresh mint leaves to yield

¼ cup chopped mint leaves

Just before serving, using the chilled bowl and beater, beat until mixture piles softly

1 cup chilled dairy sour cream
2 tablespoons lemon juice
2 tablespoons sugar
½ teaspoon monosodium glutamate
¼ teaspoon salt
Few grains pepper

Gently fold the drained pineapple and mint leaves into the sour cream mixture. If desired, garnish with additional chopped mint leaves.

Serve dressing with fruit salads.

About 2½ cups dressing

YOGURT SALAD DRESSING

▲ *Base Recipe*

Blend

¾ cup yogurt
2 tablespoons mayonnaise
2 tablespoons brown sugar
4 teaspoons ketchup
½ teaspoon salt

Chill thoroughly. *About 1 cup dressing*

—PIQUANT YOGURT SALAD DRESSING

Follow ▲ Recipe. Omit ketchup. Decrease brown sugar to 1 tablespoon. Mix in **½ cup chili sauce, 2 tablespoons minced onion** and **2 tablespoons minced green pepper.**

—YOGURT FRUIT SALAD DRESSING

Follow ▲ Recipe. Omit ketchup. Blend in **4 teaspoons lemon juice.**

—CRUNCHY YOGURT DRESSING

Follow recipe for Yogurt Fruit Salad Dressing. Mix in **¼ cup chopped toasted blanched almonds.**

CRUNCHY SESAME SEED DRESSING

For Dressing—Mix

¼ cup finely chopped green pepper
¼ cup finely diced pared cucumber
2 tablespoons minced onion

Drain, if necessary. Mix

1 cup dairy sour cream
½ cup mayonnaise
1 tablespoon tarragon vinegar
1 tablespoon sugar
1 teaspoon salt
Few grains pepper
1 clove garlic, minced

Add to vegetables and mix well. Chill thoroughly in refrigerator.

For Sesame Seed Topping—While dressing chills, heat in a skillet

1 tablespoon butter

Add and heat over medium heat until delicately browned, stirring constantly

½ cup sesame seed

Remove from heat and add

¼ cup (1 oz.) grated Parmesan cheese

Toss until well blended. Cool.

Serve the chilled dressing with cooked or raw vegetable salads, or with mixed greens or seafood salads. Sprinkle the seed topping generously over the dressing.

About 2 cups dressing

COOKED DRESSINGS

COOKED SALAD DRESSING

▲ *Base Recipe*

Mix thoroughly in the top of a double boiler

¼ cup sugar
1 tablespoon all-purpose flour
½ teaspoon dry mustard
½ teaspoon salt
¼ teaspoon monosodium glutamate
⅛ teaspoon pepper

Blend in gradually

1 cup water

Set over direct heat. Stirring gently and constantly, bring mixture to boiling. Cook 1 to 2 min. longer. Add and stir in

¼ cup cider vinegar

Vigorously stir about 3 tablespoons of the hot mixture into

4 egg yolks, slightly beaten

Immediately blend into mixture in top of double boiler. Place over simmering water and cook 3 to 5 min., stirring slowly to keep mixture cooking evenly. Remove from heat and stir in

2 tablespoons butter

Cool; store in covered container in refrigerator. Before using, thin to desired consistency with cream, fruit juice or cider vinegar.

About 1½ cups dressing

—DRESSING FOR OVERNIGHT FRUIT DRESSING

Follow ▲ Recipe for method only. Use **2 tablespoons sugar, ⅛ teaspoon salt, ⅛ teaspoon monosodium glutamate, 2 tablespoons cider vinegar** and **2 tablespoons pineapple syrup.** Bring mixture only to boiling. Substitute **3 egg yolks** and **1 tablespoon butter** and complete as in ▲ Recipe. When dressing is cooled, beat **1 cup chilled heavy cream** until it is of medium consistency (piles softly). Fold the cooled dressing into the whipped cream.

About 2 cups dressing

ENCHANTING FRUIT DRESSING I

▲ *Base Recipe*

Put into a small saucepan with a tight-fitting cover

½ cup water
½ cup honey
8 mint leaves
⅛ teaspoon whole cardamom seed (contents of 3 cardamom pods), crushed

Bruise the mint with the back of a spoon. Set over low heat and stir until mixed. Cover saucepan and bring rapidly to boiling. Boil gently 5 min. Remove from heat and stir in

¼ teaspoon salt

Set aside to cool.

When mixture is cool, strain it and blend in

½ cup sherry, Madeira or port
1 tablespoon lemon juice

About 1⅓ cups dressing

—ENCHANTING FRUIT SALAD II

Follow ▲ Recipe. Omit fresh mint. Stir in **¼ teaspoon crushed dried mint** with the crushed cardamom.

COOKED MARSHMALLOW DRESSING

Scald in top of double boiler over simmering water, just until thin film appears

½ cup milk
½ cup cream

Beat until thick and lemon-colored

2 egg yolks
¼ cup sugar
2 tablespoons all-purpose flour
½ teaspoon dry mustard
¼ teaspoon salt
⅛ teaspoon white pepper

Add, stirring well

¼ cup cider vinegar
1 tablespoon plus 1 teaspoon lemon juice
2 teaspoons lime juice

Vigorously stir a small amount of scalded milk and cream into egg yolk mixture. Immediately blend into milk and cream in double boiler top. Mix in

16 marshmallows (¼ lb.), cut in quarters (page 9)

Cook over simmering water 10 to 12 min., or until mixture thickens. Stir slowly to keep mixture cooking evenly. Cool. Store in covered container in refrigerator.

About 2 cups dressing

ORANGE FRUIT SALAD DRESSING

▲ *Base Recipe*

Set out

½ cup orange juice

Combine in the top of a double boiler ¼ cup of the orange juice and

¼ cup sugar
⅛ teaspoon salt

Stirring constantly, heat mixture over medium heat until sugar is dissolved and mixture simmers. Place over simmering water. Vigorously stir about 3 tablespoons of the hot mixture into

2 egg yolks, slightly beaten

Immediately blend into mixture in top of double boiler. Place over simmering water and cook 3 to 5 min., stirring slowly to keep mixture cooking evenly. Remove from heat.

Beat until frothy

2 egg whites

Add gradually, beating well after each addition

2 tablespoons sugar

Beat until rounded peaks are formed. Blend beaten egg whites into orange mixture. Heat remaining orange juice to lukewarm with

1 tablespoon lemon juice

Stirring constantly, gradually add to mixture in top of double boiler. Cook over simmering water until thick and smooth, about 10 min., stirring constantly.

Add and stir until melted

1 tablespoon butter

Remove from heat and set aside to cool. Set in refrigerator to chill.

Set a bowl and rotary beater in refrigerator to chill.

Just before serving, using the chilled bowl and beater, beat until cream is of medium consistency (piles softly)

¼ cup chilled heavy cream

Gently fold whipped cream into orange mixture. Spoon into serving dish. Sprinkle over top

½ teaspoon grated orange peel

About 2½ cups dressing

—RASPBERRY FRUIT SALAD DRESSING

Follow ▲ Recipe. Substitute **raspberry fruit syrup** for the orange juice. Decrease the ¼ cup sugar to 2 tablespoons. Increase lemon juice to 3 tablespoons and omit the grated orange peel.

—APRICOT FRUIT SALAD DRESSING

Follow ▲ Recipe. Omit the orange juice and add **1 cup plus 2 tablespoons apricot nectar.** Increase lemon juice to 1½ tablespoons and omit the grated orange peel.

PINEAPPLE SALAD DRESSING

Set out

1½ cups pineapple juice

Mix thoroughly in top of a double boiler

½ cup sugar
1 tablespoon cornstarch
⅛ teaspoon salt

Stir in ½ cup of the pineapple juice. Stirring gently and constantly, bring mixture rapidly to boiling over direct heat and cook for 3 min. Place over simmering water. Vigorously stir about 3 tablespoons of the hot mixture into

2 egg yolks, slightly beaten

Immediately blend into mixture in double boiler. Cook over simmering water 3 to 5 min. Stir slowly to keep mixture cooking evenly. Remove double boiler from heat.

Beat until frothy

2 egg whites

Add gradually, beating well after each addition

2 tablespoons sugar

Beat until rounded peaks are formed. Gently blend into mixture in top of double boiler.

Heat the remaining 1 cup pineapple juice to lukewarm. Stirring constantly, gradually add to egg white mixture.

Cook over simmering water until thick and smooth, stirring constantly, about 10 min. Add and stir until melted

2 tablespoons butter

Remove from heat and set aside to cool. Set in refrigerator to chill.

Meanwhile, set a bowl and rotary beater in refrigerator to chill.

When pineapple mixture is chilled, using the chilled bowl and beater, beat until cream is of medium consistency (piles softly)

¾ cup chilled heavy cream

Gently fold whipped cream into pineapple mixture. *About 4 cups dressing*

SOUR CREAM SALAD DRESSING

Set out a double boiler.

Blend in the top of the double boiler

1 tablespoon all-purpose flour
½ teaspoon dry mustard
½ teaspoon salt

Stir in

¼ cup water
¼ cup vinegar
2 tablespoons sugar

Place over direct heat. Stirring constantly, bring rapidly to boiling and cook 1 to 2 min. Immediately stir about 2 tablespoons of the hot mixture into

2 egg yolks, fork beaten

Immediately blend into mixture in double-boiler top and place over boiling water. Cook 3 to 5 min., stirring constantly. Remove from heat. Blend in

1 tablespoon butter

Set aside to cool.

Beat until of medium consistency (piles softly)

1 cup dairy sour cream

Fold into cooled dressing.

About 2 cups dressing

COOKED SOUR CREAM DRESSING

Mix thoroughly in the top of a double boiler

⅔ cup sugar
2 tablespoons all-purpose flour
½ teaspoon salt
⅛ teaspoon monosodium glutamate

Add gradually, blending until smooth

½ cup cider vinegar or lemon juice

Set over direct heat. Stirring gently and constantly, bring mixture to boiling. Cook 1 or 2 min. longer. Remove from heat and vigorously stir about 3 tablespoons of the hot mixture into

3 eggs, slightly beaten

Immediately blend into mixture in top of the double boiler. Place over simmering water and cook 3 to 5 min., stirring slowly to keep mixture cooking evenly. Remove from heat and add very gradually, stirring until well blended

1 cup dairy sour cream
2 teaspoons prepared mustard

Cool. Store in covered container in refrigerator.

If desired, thin with cream before using.

About 2½ cups dressing

HOT SOUR CREAM DRESSING FOR GREENS

Panfry, reserving fat

4 slices bacon, cut in ¼-in. pieces

Return ¼ cup of the fat to skillet and add

¼ cup chopped onion

Cook until the onion is tender, moving and turning occasionally with a spoon. Blend in

2 tablespoons sugar
2 teaspoons all-purpose flour
¾ teaspoon salt

Heat until mixture bubbles. Remove from heat. Stirring vigorously, add in very small amounts

1 cup dairy sour cream

Cook over medium heat, stirring constantly, until slightly thicker; cook 2 or 3 min. longer keeping the sauce moving constantly. *Do not boil.*

Remove from heat. Mix in the bacon and

2 tablespoons cider vinegar

Pour hot dressing over crisp **salad greens** (leaf lettuce, curly endive, raw spinach, or a mixture of such greens). Toss lightly and serve at once. *About 1¼ cups dressing*

NEVER-FAIL SALAD DRESSING

Blend in a saucepan

⅓ cup all-purpose flour
1 teaspoon sugar
1 teaspoon salt
½ teaspoon dry mustard
Few grains cayenne pepper

Gradually blend in

1 cup cold water
¼ cup vinegar or lemon juice

Stir constantly over moderate heat until mixture boils. Continue stirring and cook about 2 min. Remove from heat and stir in

1 tablespoon butter or margarine

Beat slightly with rotary beater

1 egg

Slowly pour cooked mixture into beaten egg, beating constantly. Continue beating while very gradually adding

1 cup salad oil

About 2⅓ cups dressing

SNAPPY SALAD DRESSING

Mix in a saucepan

¼ cup butter or margarine
¼ cup ketchup
3 tablespoons cider vinegar
3 tablespoons sugar
1¼ teaspoons Worcestershire sauce
¼ teaspoon salt
¼ teaspoon paprika

Set over direct heat. Stirring gently and constantly, bring to boiling. Remove from heat and stir in

¼ teaspoon Tabasco

Set aside to cool. Set in refrigerator to chill.

About ¾ cup dressing

TANGY SALAD DRESSING

Beat together in a bowl

2 egg yolks
2 tablespoons cider vinegar
2 tablespoons lemon juice
1 tablespoon sugar
1 teaspoon salt
½ teaspoon dry mustard
Few grains cayenne pepper
¾ cup salad oil

Set aside.

Heat in a saucepan until melted

3 tablespoons butter or margarine

Stir in and cook, mixing well, until bubbly

¼ cup all-purpose flour

Remove from heat and gradually add, stirring constantly

1 cup water

Return to heat and cook until boiling, stirring constantly. Cook and stir abuto 3 min. longer.

Gradually spoon cooked mixture into egg mixture, beating with a rotary beater until thick and smooth. Cool. Store in covered container in refrigerator.

If desired, thin to desired consistency with cream before using. *About 2 cups dressing*

Relishes, garnishes, accompaniments

Relishes are a wide variety of distinctively flavored foods which are served with other food to add special enhancement. This chapter contains an intriguing assortment of recipes for fruit and vegetable relishes . . . hot and cold . . . tart and sweet . . . to complement the flavor of meat, poultry, and fish dishes. Garnishes, too, add extra appeal. Inexpensive and easy-to-make garnishes may include interestingly shaped vegetables and fruits which add flavor, color, and texture contrast to the foods they accompany. Use edible garnishes wherever possible, since they add both eye appeal and nutritional value.

There are many foods which require certain traditional garnishes or accompaniments to complete them. A fish platter, for example, almost demands lemon or lime wedges to complete it. Pork calls for apple rings, whole baked apples, or applesauce. Lamb needs mint sprigs or jelly for a garnish. The English accompany roast beef with Yorkshire pudding, and so on. Garnishes are often hearty enough to double for salad, as exemplified by the horseradish and other gelatin molds which follow. Also included are baked bananas, pickled and deviled eggs, and other accompaniments.

RAW VEGETABLE RELISHES

Use raw vegetables for colorful, easy-to-prepare relishes. Select only those that are in prime condition—crisp, fresh, preferably young and tender. Clean them thoroughly; with a sharp knife trim ends, when necessary, and cut the vegetables into varied shapes as suggested. Chill thoroughly before serving.

Carrot Circles—Using an apple corer, remove centers of large cleaned **carrots.** Fill with a firm **cheese spread.** Chill. Slice before serving.

Carrot Curls—Cut tender cleaned **carrots** into halves lengthwise. Using a vegetable parer, shave into paper-thin strips. Curl around finger. Fasten with wooden pick and chill in **ice** and **water.** Drain and remove pick before serving.

Carrot Sticks—Cut tender cleaned **carrots** into narrow strips about 3 in. long. Chill in the refrigerator. If desired, carrot sticks may be drawn through **pitted ripe olives.**

Cauliflowerets—Remove outside leaves and stalk from **cauliflower head.** Separate cauliflower into flowerets. Immerse, if desired, in **cold salted water** a few minutes to remove any dust or small insects which settle in the cauliflower. Rinse, drain and chill in refrigerator.

Double Celery Curls—Cut tender cleaned **celery** into 2½-to 3-in. lengths. Slit each into narrow parallel strips from either end almost to center. Chill in **ice** and **water** until curled. Drain before serving.

Fluted Cucumber Slices—Draw tines of a fork lengthwise over entire surface of rinsed **cucumbers.** Cut into thin slices.

Green Pepper Strips—Rinse **whole green peppers** and cut into halves lengthwise. Carefully remove all white fiber and seeds; slice lengthwise into strips. For rings, slice cleaned whole green peppers crosswise.

Radish Fans—Wash firm **red or white radishes.** Remove root ends. Cut thin lengthwise parallel slices almost to end. Chill in **ice and water** until slices spread apart. Drain.

Radish Roses—Wash firm **red radishes.** Cut off root ends. On each, leave a bit of stem and a fresh leaf or two for garnish. With a sharp knife, cut petals. Chill in **ice** and **water** until petals spread apart. Drain before serving.

Tomato Wedges—Rinse firm **tomatoes** and put into **boiling water** about ½ min., or until skin loosens. Peel, cut out stem ends and chill. Place chilled tomato on flat surface and cut lengthwise into six or eight wedges.

Turnip Sticks—Cut cleaned **turnips** into narrow strips about 3 in. long. Chill in the refrigerator. If desired, turnip sticks may be drawn through **pitted ripe olives.**

VEGETABLE BOATS, BOWLS AND SHELLS

Cabbage Bowl—Rinse firm **green or red cabbage** head. If necessary, level base by cutting a thin slice from core end. Form the bowl by cutting out center of cabbage head. Shred the cabbage removed from the head for cabbage salads or slaw. Spoon completed salad into bowl and serve. Cabbage bowls also make attractive containers for other salads.

Cucumber Boats—Rinse (do not pare) firm **cucumbers.** Cut into halves lengthwise. Using a spoon, scoop out centers. Chill in refrigerator.

Green Pepper Shells—Rinse and cut a thin slice from stem end of **green peppers.** Remove seeds; using edge of spoon, cut away white fiber. Rinse cavities. Invert the shells and set aside to drain. Chill in refrigerator.

Tomato Shells—Rinse firm **tomatoes** and peel if desired. Chill in refrigerator. Cut a slice from top of each tomato. Using a spoon, remove pulp. Invert shells and set aside to drain. Chill and sprinkle lightly with **salt** before filling.

VEGETABLE FLOWERS FOR GARNISH

Carved vegetable flowers give a gourmet touch when arranged on a cold meat platter, appetizer

Raw Vegetable Relishes

tray or impressive main dish for that very special occasion.

Turnip Rose—Select a firm round **turnip** that is the size of the rose desired. Cut off and discard stem and root ends. Pare turnip, being sure that surface is smooth. If necessary to form a flat base for rose, cut a thin slice from stem end of turnip. Using the tip of a sharp paring knife, lightly outline the shapes of about five rounded petals evenly spaced around turnip. Following outline of petals and keeping each slice thin, cut each petal completely away from the turnip down to about ¼ in. from base. Continue around turnip until all five petals are formed. Pare inside of turnip, just within petals, to again make a smooth surface. Lightly outline petal-shapes, spacing each one between two outside petals. Cut petals thinly.

Continue working as for outer petals, smoothing the surface before outlining petals. Cut as many layers as desired, forming as many petals as desired from each layer. Work toward center as far as possible. Cut the center piece of turnip down and round it to form the center of the rose.

Set out a bowl of **cold water.** Add enough **food coloring** to tint carved rose desired color. Put rose upside down in water and allow it to remain until enough color has been absorbed. (Turnips differ in the amount of time required to tint them.) Carved vegetable flowers will keep for several weeks in water in refrigerator. Omit food coloring if a white rose is desired.

Turnip Water Lily—Follow the same technique used in carving turnip rose, making petals more pointed. When center is reached, cut out the center piece of turnip. Put into a bowl of cold water in refrigerator if not used at once.

Cut a **cucumber** into halves. Scoop out center. Shape leaves for water lily from cucumber peel. Using pieces of wooden picks, fasten leaves to lily. Return lily to water. Just before using lily, sieve a little **hard-cooked egg yolk** into the center.

Other Flowers—Thin crosswise slices of pared **carrot** or **turnip** may be used to make other flowers such as daisies, dogwood blossoms, narcissi, cosmos or wild roses. Using scissors, shape petals of correct number and size from each slice. For stems use **chives** or **parsley stems.** Tint as for turnip rose.

GARNISHES FOR MAIN DISHES

Bacon—Crisp slices, chips, curls (insert fork in partially cooked bacon, wrap and curl around fork; remove fork and carefully cook until crisp).

Beets, cooked, pickled—Diced, thin discs, cutouts, tiny balls, hollowed-out cups to hold other foods.

Capers

Carrots, cooked and uncooked—Thin rounds, latticed, curls and sticks (page 418), glazed (cooked, brushed with brown sugar syrup, baked in moderate oven, basted occasionally; or turned in melted brown or granulated sugar over direct heat).

Celery—Small whole stalks with leaves, curls, and stuffed.

Cheese—Coarse shreds, strips, small flat shapes.

Chives—minced.

Cottage Cheese—Small portions in cucumber boats, tomato or beet cups.

Cranberry Sauce, whole or jellied—Jellied molds, sliced cutouts or cubes.

Cream Cheese—Shaped into balls or sticks, rolled in finely chopped parsley, chives, pimiento, nuts.

Cucumbers, raw—Thin, green-bordered slices, notched slices (tines of fork drawn lengthwise down entire surface of unpared cucumber), 3-in. hollowed-out boats to hold other foods.

Dates—Stuffed with cream cheese, slivered cherries or pineapple, chopped nuts.

Eggs, hard-cooked—Wedges, rings, sieved, slices, stuffed halves, sawtooth-edged cups of whites to hold other foods.

Endive, curly—Sprigs, minced.

Fruit, cooked or uncooked (hot with hot food)—Sections, slices, halves of such fruits as apricots, peaches or pears centered with bright-colored jam or jelly, small fruits such as cherries or strawberries with hull or stem, pickled, frosted (see Cherries).

Grapefruit, fresh (hot with hot food—Sections, half slices with peel, cups with decorative edges to hold other foods.

Horseradish—Served in tiny tomato, beet or egg cups.

Lemon—Thin slices or wedges dipped in minced parsley, decorative cups to hold other foods.

Lettuce—Bibb, leaf or colorful leaves of head.

Lime—See Lemon.

Mushrooms, slices or caps—Cooked in butter or margarine.

Olives, green or ripe—Slivers, arranged attractively, coarsely chopped, rings of pitted olives, pimiento-stuffed olive slices.

Onions—Raw or parboiled rings, small whole, pickled, small whole cooked in butter or margarine and coated with minced parsley, fresh garden onions.

Orange—Sections, whole or half slices with peel, cups with decorative edges to hold other foods, grated peel.

Paprika

Parsley—Sprigs, chopped.

Pepper, green or red, parboiled or raw—Finely chopped, narrow strips, flat shapes, rings.

Pickles—Fans of sweet gherkins (3 or 5 slices cut lengthwise from top almost to bottom and gently spread apart).

Pimiento—Small, flat shapes, strips, minced.

Pineapple—Plain, panfried or broiled whole or half slices, chunks, **Pineapple Shells** (page 370).

Prunes—Stuffed with cheese (cottage, cream, grated), peanut butter, chopped or whole pitted cherries or nuts.

Radishes—Fans or roses (page 418) plain with 1 or 2 crisp leaves.

Relish, vegetable—In boats of beets, tomatoes, whites of hard-cooked eggs.

Tangerine—Sections.

Tomato, raw—Slices, wedges, lilies (petals marked and peeled part way down and gently spread apart), hollowed-out cups to hold other foods.

Watercress—Sprigs, chopped.

GARNISHES FOR FRUITS OR DESSERTS

Berries, whole—Centered or used in a border around larger fruits.

Cherries, whole or slivered—Center or border arrangement, frosted (coated with slightly beaten egg white, dipped in confectioners' or granulated sugar, dried on waxed paper); maraschino or minted cherries—with or without stems, with or without a nut protruding, acorn style.

Coconut, shredded or grated—Delicately colored (placed on waxed paper, sprinkled with few drops of food coloring mixed with few drops water, shaken and dried on the paper), toasted in slow oven.

Gelatin, fruit flavored—Bright colored cubes.

Grapes, small clusters—Brushed with salad oil for glossiness, frosted (see Cherries).

Ices or sherbets—Small scoops of contrasting colors.

Jelly, melted—Bright colors, drizzled over cooked or uncooked fruits.

Kumquats—Sliced, frosted whole (see Cherries), oiled clusters with leaves, flowers (petals marked and peeled part way down. Arranged in clusters, or singly with leaves).

Leaves, large and decorative (such as galax)—Used under fruits or on serving plate as a doily.

Mint leaves—Fresh sprigs, frosted (see Cherries), sprinkled with confectioners' sugar.

Melon—Tiny balls, small slices with rind, decorative cups to hold fruits.

Nuts, plain, toasted or salted—Chopped, ground, slivered, whole, dipped in cinnamon sugar (see Cherries).

Syrup, simple (1 cup sugar to 1 cup water, stirred until boiling begins, covered and boiled 5 min.)—Tinted a delicate color and poured over fruits.

Whipped cream, plain or tinted a delicate color—Force through a pastry bag and tube to form decorative patterns or shapes.

SWEETS FOR THE RELISH TRAY

These, like Relishes for the Cocktail Hour (page 31), may be eaten with the fingers or speared with a pick. The same holders and arrangements may be used.

APPLE SANDWICHES

Wash and core but don't pare **small apples.** Cut crosswise into thin slices. Dip in **lemon, orange or pineapple juice** to prevent darkening. Spread **peanut butter** or **cheese** between two rings. Cut into thirds.

FILLED APRICOT HALVES

Fill **canned or soaked dried apricot halves** with any desired **cheese mixture.** Top with **blanched salted peanut halves.**

BANANA BITS

Cut **bananas** once lengthwise, then into ¾-in. pieces. Dip in **mayonnaise** thinned with a small amount of **cream.** Dip in **finely chopped nuts.** Insert picks.

NO-FUSS SWEETS

Grapefruit, tangerine, orange—Remove peel and all of white part. Carefully break apart sections, leaving on separating membranes. Spear small or one-half sections on pick.

Grapes—Separate bunches of grapes into tiny clusters. Brush with **salad oil** for a gloss.

Pineapple chunks or wedges—Drain and dry. Dip in **confectioners' sugar,** if desired. Insert picks.

Strawberries or cherries—Serve attractive whole fresh fruit with hulls or stems.

FIG TREATS

Grind together **figs** and a smaller amount of **salted peanuts.** Season with **lemon juice.** Roll into balls and chill in refrigerator. Or pack into a small pan, chill and cut into squares. Insert picks.

FRUIT AND HAM "KABOBS"

Spear cubes of **cooked ham** or **canned luncheon meat** alternately with **seedless grapes** or **cubes of melon or pineapple.**

MELON BALLS

With a ball-shape cutter, scoop out balls of **melon** such as cantaloupe, honeydew or watermelon. Insert a pick into balls of varied flavors and colors.

MELON BLOSSOMS

Prepare **Pineapple Shells** (page 370) for buffet-style servers. Insert wooden picks in **pineapple cubes,** and in **melon balls** of contrasting colors and flavors. Heap centers of bowls with fruit, picks upright. Sprinkle **2 or 3 tablespoons lime juice** over fruit.

PINEAPPLE CHEESE CUBES

On a pick alternate **cubes of pineapple** and flavorful **cheese.**

STUFFED PRUNES OR DATES

Pit and dry plump soaked prunes and pit **dates.** Stuff with a tangy **cheese.** If desired, add **chopped nuts, crushed drained pineapple** or **maraschino cherries** to cheese.

MINT APPLES

▲ *Base Recipe*

Wash and set aside
6 medium (2 lbs.) apples

Combine in a deep saucepan and bring to boiling, stirring until sugar is dissolved.
2 cups sugar
1 cup water

Meanwhile, core and pare (leaving whole) only as many apples as will fit uncrowded in the saucepan.

Stir into syrup
¼ teaspoon green food coloring
5 drops peppermint extract

Add apples to syrup; cover and cook slowly just until tender (about 15 min.). Turn carefully several times to obtain an even color. With a slotted spoon, carefully remove apples from syrup; allow excess syrup to drain into saucepan. Core, pare and repeat cooking process for any remaining apples.

Garnish with **mint leaves** and serve warm or chilled with meat.   *6 servings*

—MINT APPLE SALAD

Follow ▲ Recipe. Chill apples in refrigerator. Fill core hole with a mixture of **softened**

cream cheese and **chopped nuts.** Serve on crisp lettuce leaves.

CRANBERRY PORTED APPLES

Combine in a large saucepan
1 cup cranberry juice cocktail
¾ cup port wine
1 tablespoon lemon juice
1½ cups sugar
½ teaspoon red food coloring
1 cinnamon stick

Bring to boiling, stirring until sugar is dissolved. Cover and simmer 5 min.

Add to boiling syrup
8 small whole apples, pared (cored, if desired)

Cover and cook about 10 min. over very low heat, turning apples once or twice and basting frequently with syrup. Uncover and cook 5 to 10 min. longer, or until apples are tender, continuing to turn and baste. Cool in syrup.

8 servings

Note: If the saucepan is not large enough to hold 8 apples, cook 4 apples at a time.

BROILED BANANAS

Peel
6 firm bananas having all-yellow or slightly green-tipped peel

Arrange bananas on broiler rack. Brush generously with
Melted butter or margarine

Minted Apples

Sprinkle with

Few grains salt

Place under broiler with tops of bananas 3 in. from heat for 5 min., or until bananas are lightly browned and tender.

Serve on warm serving plate; garnish with **sprigs of parsley.** *6 servings*

REFRIGERATOR FRUIT COMPOTE

Set out a large casserole or a 1 qt. jar with a cover.

Wash thoroughly

1 pkg. (12 oz.) mixed dried fruits or ¾ cup (¼ lb.) dried peaches, ¾ cup (about ⅓ lb.) dried prunes and ½ cup (2 to 3 oz.) dried apricots

Put into casserole or jar, allowing space for expansion of fruits. Cover with

Boiling water

Stir in

½ cup sugar
3 tablespoons lemon juice
2 teaspoons grated orange or lemon peel
3 pieces (3 in. each) sticks cinnamon, broken

Cover casserole or jar; allow fruits to cool.

Let stand in refrigerator at least 48 hrs. for fruits to soften and flavors to blend. Add more sugar if you wish sweeter fruit. *5 or 6 servings*

CRANBERRY ORANGE RELISH

Rinse and set aside

2 cups (about ½ lb.) fresh cranberries

Rinse, cut into eighths and remove seeds from

1 orange

Wash, quarter, core and cut into eighths

1 apple

Force cranberries, orange pieces and apple pieces through medium blade of food chopper. Mix with

1 cup sugar

Spoon relish into a container.

Cover and set in refrigerator to chill at least 1 hr. to allow flavors to blend.

About 2 cups relish

Note: A pear may be substituted for the apple. Or add half a lemon (cut in pieces) with the orange. Or omit the apple entirely.

CINNAMON SPICED PEACHES

▲ *Base Recipe*

Set out a shallow baking dish with a cover.

Set aside to drain thoroughly, reserving syrup

1 can (16 oz.) peach halves (about 5)

Break into ¼-in. pieces

4 in. stick cinnamon

Cut 3 tiny slits in rounded side of each peach

half. Insert in each slit a piece of stick cinnamon.

Place peaches in baking dish, cut side down. Pour into dish ¼ cup of the reserved peach syrup and

2 tablespoons lemon juice

Cover and heat in a 350°F oven 15 to 20 min.

Serve hot or chilled. Or serve as a meat garnish. *5 servings*

—CLOVE SPICED PEACHES

Follow ▲ Recipe. Substitute **whole cloves** for the cinnamon pieces.

SPICED PINEAPPLE

Drain, reserving syrup, and put into a 1-qt. jar with a cover

2½ cups (20-oz. can) pineapple chunks

Combine syrup in a saucepan with

½ cup sugar
¼ cup vinegar
½ teaspoon grated lemon peel
10 whole cloves
1 stick cinnamon

Simmer about 10 min. Strain and pour over pineapple chunks. Cover, cool and store in refrigerator.

Serve chilled. *2½ cups pineapple chunks*

SPICY MINTED PRUNES

Set out a medium-size saucepan with a tight-fitting cover.

Rinse and put into the saucepan

1 lb. (about 2½ cups) dried prunes

Cover prunes with

1 qt. water

Add to saucepan

¼ cup cider vinegar
1 piece (3 in.) stick cinnamon
4 whole cloves

Bring mixture to boiling, reduce heat and simmer, uncovered, 10 to 20 min.

Remove saucepan from heat. Add and mix in

¼ cup firmly packed brown sugar
¼ teaspoon mint extract

Allow prunes to cool in the liquid. Turn them into a jar, cover tightly, and store in refrigerator at least 8 hrs. before serving.

Before serving, drain prunes; remove cinnamon and cloves.

About 3½ cups Spicy Minted Prunes

CELERY WHIRLS

▲ *Base Recipe*

Clean

1 medium bunch celery

Set aside to drain on absorbent paper while preparing one of the cheese stuffings.

Cranberry Orange Relish

To Complete Whirls—Fill full-length crisp stalks of celery with one of the stuffers. Rearrange filled stalks into natural shape of celery bunch. Wrap bunch tightly in waxed paper, moisture-vaporproof material, or aluminum foil and put into refrigerator to chill for several hours.

Cut into crosswise slices ¼ to ½ in. thick. Arrange on appetizer tray to serve.

About 1½ doz. whirls

For Roquefort or Blue Cheese Stuffer—Crumble and set aside

4 oz. Roquefort or blue cheese (about 1 cup, crumbled)

Thoroughly blend

3 oz. cream cheese, softened
1 tablespoon mayonnaise

Add crumbled cheese and beat until mixture is smooth and creamy. Blend in

2 teaspoons lemon juice
1 teaspoon onion juice

and a mixture of

¼ teaspoon garlic salt
⅛ teaspoon monosodium glutamate
Few grains cayenne pepper

Beat until smooth and thoroughly mixed.

For Cheddar Cheese Stuffer—Shred and set aside

4 oz. Cheddar cheese (about 1 cup shredded)

Thoroughly blend

3 oz. cream cheese, softened
3 tablespoons milk or cream

Add shredded cheese and beat until mixture is creamy. Blend in a mixture of

1½ teaspoons dry mustard
½ teaspoon salt
¼ teaspoon monosodium glutamate
Few grains pepper

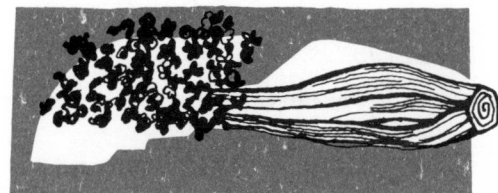

421

Stir in
Few drops Tabasco
Mix thoroughly.

—STUFFED CELERY SPEARS

Follow directions in ▲ Recipe for preparing and filling celery stalks. Stuff celery stalks with one of the stuffers, cut into 2-in. lengths, and serve on appetizer or relish tray.

PICKLED BEETS
(Inlagd Rödbetor)

Leaving on 1- to 2-in. stem and the root end, cut off leaves from
1 lb. (about 5) medium beets
Scrub beets thoroughly. Cook (page 313) in water to cover 30 to 45 min., or until just tender. When beets are tender, drain, reserving liquid in a measuring cup for liquids.

Plunge beets into running cold water; peel off and discard skin, stem and root end. Cut beets into slices ¼ in. thick.

Clean and thinly slice
1 medium onion
Separate the onion slices into rings.

Put a layer of beets into a shallow bowl. Cover with some of the onion rings. Repeat layers of beets and onions, ending with the beets. Pour over a mixture of
¾ cup cider vinegar
¾ cup reserved beet liquid
1 whole clove
Cover and chill thoroughly in refrigerator several hours or overnight to blend flavors.
8 to 10 servings

QUICK PICKLED BEETS
(Süss-saure rote Rüben)

Drain
1 can (16 oz.) sliced beets or small whole beets (about 2 cups, drained)
Clean, slice very thinly and separate into rings
2 medium onions
Lightly mix the beets and onions. Set aside.

Mix in a saucepan
1 cup vinegar
½ cup sugar
½ teaspoon salt
Bring to boiling; pour over beets and onions. Cool; chill in refrigerator 1 hr. or longer.
About 6 servings

BEET RELISH

▲ Base Recipe

Drain, reserving liquid
1 can (16 oz.) sliced beets (about 2 cups, drained)

Put the beets into a 1-qt. bowl and add a mixture of
½ cup vinegar
¼ cup reserved beet liquid
2 tablespoons sugar
1½ teaspoons salt
1 teaspoon caraway seed
⅛ teaspoon freshly ground pepper
Toss beets lightly in this salad marinade. Cover bowl and place in refrigerator to marinate (page 10) 1 or 2 days; carefully turn beets occasionally.

Serve beets with some of the marinade.
4 or 5 servings

—BEET RELISH WITH HORSERADISH

Follow ▲ Recipe. Add **1 or 2 tablespoons freshly grated horseradish** or **¼ cup prepared horseradish** to beets with the seasonings.

MINTED CUCUMBER RELISH

▲ Base Recipe

Rinse (do not pare) and coarsely shred
1 medium cucumber
Blend
1 cup dairy sour cream
1 teaspoon finely chopped fresh mint leaves or ½ teaspoon crushed dried mint leaves
1 clove garlic, minced
½ to ¾ teaspoon salt
Few grains white pepper
Mix in the shredded cucumber. Set in refrigerator to chill thoroughly.   *4 to 6 servings*

—MINTED PEA RELISH

Follow ▲ Recipe. Substitute **2 cups chilled cooked peas** for the cucumber.

CUCUMBERS IN CREAMY SWEET-SOUR DRESSING

Slice thinly into a bowl and set aside
2 medium (about 1¼ lbs.) cucumbers, rinsed and, if desired, pared

Put into a small bowl
½ cup cream
Add gradually, stirring constantly
2 tablespoons cider vinegar
Stir in
2¼ teaspoons sugar
¾ teaspoon salt
⅛ teaspoon pepper
Pour dressing over cucumbers and toss to coat evenly. Chill thoroughly.   *4 to 6 servings*

MARINATED MUSHROOM CAPS

▲ Base Recipe

Set aside to drain
2 cans (3 oz. each) mushroom caps

Meanwhile, prepare
Garlic French Dressing or Curried French Dressing (page 410)
Put mushroom caps into a shallow dish. Pour the dressing over the mushrooms. Set dish in refrigerator and allow to marinate (page 10) several hours, carefully turning mushrooms from time to time.

Serve as a garnish on a cold meat platter.
4 to 6 servings

—MARINATED BEETS

Follow ▲ Recipe. Substitute **1 can (16 oz.) small whole beets** (about 2 cups, drained) for the mushroom caps. Marinate in **Fruit Juice French Dressing** (page 410; use orange juice).

—MARINATED CUCUMBER SLICES

Follow ▲ Recipe. Substitute **1 cucumber**, rinsed and sliced, for the drained mushroom caps. Marinate in **Creamy French Dressing** (page 410).

CHILLED MINTED PEAS

Cook following package directions
2 pkgs. (10 oz. each) frozen green peas
Drain thoroughly and chill.

Combine in a bowl
2 tablespoons vinegar
⅓ cup salad oil
½ teaspoon paprika
¼ teaspoon salt
Few grains white pepper
1 teaspoon minced mint leaves
Add chilled peas and toss together lightly. Refrigerate several hours to marinate, tossing several times.   *6 to 8 servings*

PICKLED PEPPER RELISH

Combine
2 tablespoons olive oil
2 tablespoons wine vinegar
¼ teaspoon pepper
¼ teaspoon oregano
⅛ teaspoon salt

Toss with

2 cups sliced pickled red peppers
¾ cup chopped celery
½ cup ripe olives, pitted and sliced
8 anchovy fillets, chopped

Serve very cold.   *6 to 8 servings*

BRANDIED TOMATOES I

▲ *Base Recipe*

Rinse, peel and chill

4 medium tomatoes

Cut chilled tomatoes into thin vertical slices. Put tomato slices into a shallow dish and cover with a mixture of

¼ cup brandy
½ teaspoon salt
⅛ teaspoon pepper

Set in refrigerator to marinate (page 10) about 2 hrs., carefully turning several times.

When ready to serve, arrange tomato slices in a chilled bowl. Pour brandy marinade over tomatoes. Garnish with

Chopped parsley

Serve at once.   *About 6 servings*

—BRANDIED TOMATOES II

Follow ▲ Recipe. After marinating, drain and reserve brandy marinade. Put tomato slices into a chilled bowl. Mix **1 tablespoon olive oil** and **1 tablespoon cider vinegar** with the reserved marinade and pour over tomato slices. Lightly toss together. Garnish with thin **onion rings** and **chopped parsley.**

STUFFED EGGS
(Fyllda Ägg)

Prepare

6 Hard-Cooked Eggs (page 133)

Cut peeled eggs into halves lengthwise. Remove egg yolks to a bowl. Set egg whites aside.

Force egg yolks through sieve or ricer, or mash with fork. Stir in a mixture of

¾ teaspoon dry mustard
½ teaspoon salt
¼ teaspoon pepper
¼ teaspoon monosodium glutamate

Blend in

1 tablespoon finely chopped onion
1 tablespoon lemon juice

Stir in, moistening egg yolk mixture to a smooth, thick consistency

2 to 3 tablespoons dairy sour cream
**   or mayonnaise**

Spoon mixture lightly into egg whites, leaving tops rounded. Or force mixture through a pastry bag and a No. 7 decorating tube into egg whites. Garnish center of egg with

Pimiento

Chill eggs   *12 stuffed egg halves*

For Variety—Blend in one of the following: **¼ teaspoon savory or tarragon; 1 table-** spoon prepared horseradish; 1 tablespoon chopped parsley or chives.

PICKLED EGGS

Set out two 1-qt. screw-top jars and their lids.

Prepare

1 doz. Hard-Cooked Eggs (page 133)

Put into a saucepan

1½ cups white vinegar
½ cup water
2 tablespoons brown sugar
1 teaspoon salt
1 clove garlic, cut in halves
⅛ teaspoon celery seed
3 peppercorns
2 whole cloves
Small piece whole mace

Set over medium heat and bring to boiling. Reduce heat; simmer about 5 min. Strain. Put 6 eggs into each jar and pour into each one half of the hot vinegar mixture. Cover, cool, and set in refrigerator.

Let eggs stand several hours or overnight to acquire flavor. Before serving, insert a few **whole cloves** into each egg.

1 doz. Pickled Eggs

SPICY GELATIN GARNISH

Eighteen 1½-in. muffin-pan wells will be needed.

Pour into a small cup or custard cup

¼ cup cold tomato juice

Sprinkle evenly over juice

1 env. unflavored gelatin

Let stand until softened.

Meanwhile, heat to boiling in a small saucepan a mixture of

1 cup quick meat broth (page 10)
½ cup chili sauce

Lightly oil the muffin-pan wells and set aside to drain.

Remove broth mixture from heat and immediately stir in softened gelatin until gelatin is completely dissolved. Pour into muffin wells. Cool and then place in refrigerator to chill until firm. To unmold, run tip of knife around each well. Cover with baking sheet. Invert and remove muffin pan.   *About 18 rounds*

HORSERADISH MOLD I

▲ *Base Recipe*

Best when served with cold meat or poultry.

Set out an 8x8x2-in. pan.

Empty into a bowl

2 pkgs. (3 oz. each) lime-flavored
**   gelatin**

Pour over gelatin, stirring until gelatin is completely dissolved

1 cup very hot water

Blend in

2 cups cold water

Chill (page 374) until gelatin mixture is slightly thicker than consistency of thick unbeaten egg white.

Meanwhile, blend until well mixed

2 cups cream-style cottage cheese
⅔ cup mayonnaise
½ cup prepared horseradish
2 tablespoons grated onion

When gelatin is of desired consistency, blend in horseradish mixture. Pour into pan. Chill in refrigerator until firm.

Unmold (page 374) onto a chilled serving plate and serve as an accompaniment to cold **chicken, veal** or **tongue.** If desired, cut mold into cubes to serve.

—HORSERADISH MOLD II

Follow ▲ Recipe. Omit mayonnaise.

YORKSHIRE PUDDING

Pour into an 11x7x2-in. baking dish and keep hot

¼ cup hot drippings from roast beef

Beat until thick and piled softly

2 eggs

Add to beaten eggs and beat with rotary beater until smooth

1 cup milk
1 cup sifted all-purpose flour
½ teaspoon salt

Pour mixture over hot meat drippings.

Bake at 400°F 30 to 40 min., or until puffed and browned.

Cut into squares and serve immediately with **Standing Rib Roast of Beef** (page 169).

About 6 servings

APPLE CHUTNEY

Put into a large saucepan
   2 cups coarsely chopped tart apples
   1 small onion, chopped
   ½ cup chopped green pepper
   ½ lb. seedless raisins
   ½ cup firmly packed brown sugar
   ½ cup dark corn syrup
   ¾ cup cider vinegar
   ½ teaspoon grated lemon peel
   1½ teaspoons lemon juice
   1½ teaspoons mustard seed
   1½ teaspoons ginger
   ¾ teaspoon salt
   1 clove garlic
Mix well and bring to boiling, stirring constantly. Simmer, uncovered, 35 to 40 min., stirring occasionally, until mixture thickens.

Remove from heat and discard garlic. Cool.

Serve as a meat or curry accompaniment.
About 3 cups chutney

TOMATO MINT CHUTNEY

Toss together in a bowl
   1 cup firmly packed fresh mint leaves, finely chopped, or ¼ cup dried mint leaves
   1 cup finely chopped onion
   1 ripe tomato, finely chopped
   ¼ cup lemon juice
   ½ teaspoon salt
   4 drops Tabasco
   ¼ to ½ teaspoon mustard seed
Allow to stand at room temperature at least 1 hr. to blend flavors.   *About 1⅔ cups chutney*

CELERY ROOT RELISH

Wash, cut off ends and pare
   1- to 1½-lb. celery root
Cut into crosswise slices ½ in. thick. Put into a saucepan with
   1 lemon, sliced
Pour in enough boiling water to cover slices. Cover; bring to boiling and cook 5 to 7 min., or

until just tender. Drain; cool slightly.

Cut slices into sticks about ⅜ in. thick and 2½ in. long. Put sticks into a shallow dish. Add enough to coat evenly
   French dressing
Chill about 2 hrs., turning occasionally.

Meanwhile, blend
   1 cup mayonnaise
   1 teaspoon prepared mustard
   1 teaspoon paprika
   7 teaspoons sherry
Chill.

Just before serving, drain celery root sticks and toss lightly with mayonnaise mixture.
About 6 servings

SWEET-TART BEAN SPROUT RELISH

This is an excellent topper for hamburgers.

Combine in a saucepan
   1 can (16 oz.) bean sprouts, undrained
   ½ cup diagonally sliced celery
   2 tablespoons brown sugar
Bring rapidly to boiling; reduce heat and simmer about 1 min. Drain thoroughly through a colander or sieve. Turn into a bowl and set aside to cool slightly.

Meanwhile, mix
   ⅓ cup wine vinegar
   2 tablespoon olive oil or other salad oil
   2 tablespoons sugar
   ¼ to ½ teaspoon salt
   ¼ teaspoon seasoned pepper
Pour mixture over sprouts in bowl. Add and toss in
   1 canned pimiento, cut in strips
Refrigerate at least overnight before serving.
About 1 pt. relish

CUCUMBER RELISH

Prepare
   3½ cups thinly sliced pared cucumber
   1 cup 1½-in. green pepper strips
   ½ cup sliced onion

Bring to boiling in a saucepan
   1 cup water
Add cucumber slices, bring to boiling and cook about 5 min., or until just tender. Immediately drain thoroughly. Turn into a bowl and toss with the green pepper strips and sliced onion. Set aside.

Blend in a small bowl
   ½ teaspoon salt
   ½ teaspoon ginger
   ⅛ teaspoon cayenne pepper
Add and beat until blended
   1 clove garlic, minced
   2 tablespoons vinegar
   2 tablespoons salad oil
Pour marinade over vegetables and let stand 2 hrs., tossing vegetables frequently.

Chill thoroughly before serving.
About 3 cups relish

SAUERKRAUT RELISH

The sweet-tart flavor of this relish becomes increasingly better if allowed to chill at least several days.

Combine in a bowl
   1 can (16 oz.) sauerkraut, thoroughly drained
   1 cup coarsely chopped Spanish onion (1 large onion)
   ½ cup coarsely chopped green pepper
   1 jar (2 oz.) pimientos, drained and chopped
   1 cup sugar
   1 cup cider vinegar
Toss lightly until well blended. Store mixture in a tightly covered 1-qt. jar in refrigerator at least 24 hrs. before serving.   *About 1 qt. relish*

SHRIMP COCONUT RELISH

Here's a sharp relish to accent dishes such as macaroni and cheese, Spanish rice and cheese soufflé.

Chill thoroughly
   1 cup finely chopped cooked shrimp
   ½ cup packaged grated coconut
   1 apple (¾ cup, finely chopped)
   ¼ cup lemon juice
   Watercress or lettuce (¾ cup, snipped)
Finely chop unpared apple and snip watercress. Put into a chilled bowl with shrimp, coconut, lemon juice and
   1 tablespoon grated onion
   ¼ teaspoon Tabasco
Toss well. Serve immediately.   *2 cups relish*

VEGETABLE RELISH

Jars with lids will be needed.

Have ready
   2 cans (28 oz. each) tomatoes, drained and quartered
   2 cups chopped green pepper
   2 cups chopped onion
Put into a saucepan
   1 cup firmly packed brown sugar
   1 tablespoon monosodium glutamate
   1 teaspoon seasoned salt
   1 cup cider vinegar
Stir over medium heat until sugar is dissolved. Mix in vegetables. Bring to boiling and simmer 15 min.

Remove from heat and cool completely. Ladle into jars and cover tightly. Store in refrigerator.
2½ pts. relish

Cakes and tortes

An attractive, delicious cake (or its first cousin, a torte) is a work of art and gives pleasure to its creator. More than any other culinary achievement, a cake can create a festive atmosphere and give a festive air to a birthday party or other special-occasion celebration. For many years, the art of cake making remained unchanged. There were two basic types of cakes—the so-called butter-type cakes and the egg-leavened cakes without butter of the sponge-type varieties. Through the years, however, quite different methods of mixing have given us other intriguing types. In this book will be found recipes for plain and scrumptious cakes using both the standard methods of mixing and the more time-saving methods now commonly used. So, homemakers, obey that creative impulse—bake a cake or luscious torte and give to that family meal, picnic, or celebration an air of festivity which only a cake can give.

WHAT YOU SHOULD KNOW ABOUT CAKES AND TORTES

Basically, there are only two types of cakes: butter-type (made with shortening) and sponge-type (made without shortening). Chiffon cakes and some others, however, fall on the border-line between the two classifications.

The butter-type cake contains fat (butter, margarine, all-purpose shortening, vegetable shortening or lard) and a chemical leavening agent (baking powder or baking soda). Any of three methods of mixing may be used for butter-type cakes.

In the *conventional method,* fat is creamed with the flavoring extract and then with sugar; eggs or egg yolks are beaten into the creamed mixture; dry and liquid ingredients are added alternately and beaten in; and finally, egg whites, if used, are beaten and folded in.

The *conventional sponge method* is similar, except that part of the sugar is beaten with the egg whites and folded in last.

The *quick, quick-mix,* or *one-bowl method* is used only in recipes specially developed for this method. Dry ingredients and shortening are put into the mixing bowl, and eggs and liquid are added according to directions; all are then beaten by hand or electric mixer for a specified time.

The sponge-type cake contains beaten whole eggs, egg yolks or egg whites and flour, sugar and flavorings, which may be beaten or folded in. A cake of this type which is made with egg yolks or whole eggs is a sponge cake; one made with egg whites only is an angel food cake. A true sponge or angel food cake contains no fat, baking powder or baking soda; it is leavened only by expanding air and steam. Some sponge-type variations may contain a small amount of butter or baking powder.

The chiffon cake is a special type which has the lightness of a sponge-type cake and the richness of a butter-type cake, without following the rules for mixing either. It contains a cooking or salad oil and baking powder in addition to eggs, flour, sugar and flavorings.

All the cakes described are essentially New World developments. The light, airy, tender confection which we know as "cake" is not familiar on the Continent, in England or in the East. The Old World's "cakes" are almost always tortes, and many of the torte recipes found on these pages are naturalized versions of classic Old World favorites. Others are native American tortes.

Tortes as a class are cake-like desserts, made light with eggs and often enriched with nuts. Bread crumbs, cracker or cookie crumbs, or grated nuts may take, wholly or in part, the place of flour. Ingredients are handled similarly to those in cakes. The texture of tortes differs from that of cake, depending upon the ingredients used. In general, tortes are coarse in texture rather than delicate like cakes, and unlike a good cake, they may be compact rather than light and fluffy.

WHEN YOU STORE CAKES AND TORTES

Cakes, except fruitcakes, are at their best the day they are made. But if stored properly, most cakes will remain fresh for several days.

Plain or frosted cakes—Store in a cake keeper, or invert a large, deep bowl over the cake on its serving plate.

Whipped cream cakes (filled, or filled and frosted, with whipped cream)—Assemble shortly before the cake is to be served. Refrigerate the complete cake until it is served; if it is kept in the refrigerator more than an hour, it may become soggy. Place any leftover cake in the refrigerator immediately after the meal.

Fruitcakes—Wrap cake in aluminum foil or other moisture-vaporproof material as soon as it is completely cooled. Store it in a cool place to age for several weeks before serving. If desired, unwrap cakes once or twice a week and, using a pastry brush, paint them with rum, brandy or any desired liqueur, or with fruit juice. Then rewrap and store again.

Tortes—Store like plain or frosted cakes or like whipped cream cakes, depending on the filling or frosting used.

425

AN IMPERFECT CAKE

May have this fault . . .   *For these reasons . . .*

	A BUTTER-TYPE CAKE	A SPONGE-TYPE CAKE
Coarse grain.	Use of all-purpose instead of cake flour Excess of leavening Not enough creaming Undermixing Baking temperature too low	Use of all-purpose instead of cake flour Omission of cream of tartar (in angel food cake) Undermixing
Heaviness or compactness.	Excess of liquid, shortening or eggs Not enough leavening or flour Overmixing Baking temperature too high	Underbeating of egg yolks or overbeating of egg whites Overmixing
Heavy, soggy layer at bottom of cake.	Excess of liquid Shortening too soft Underbeating of eggs Undermixing Baking time too short	Excess of eggs or egg yolks Underbeating of egg yolks Undermixing Failing to bake batter promptly after turning into pan
Hard top crust.	Baking temperature too high Baking time too long	Baking temperature too high Baking time too long
Cracked or humped top.	Excess of flour Not enough liquid Overmixing Uneven spreading of batter Baking temperature too high	Excess of flour or sugar Baking temperature too high
Sticky top crust.	Excess of sugar Baking time too short	Excess of sugar Baking time too short
Falling.	Excess of sugar, liquid, leavening or shortening	Excess of sugar Overbeating of egg whites Incomplete mixing
Tough crumb.	Not enough sugar Not enough shortening Excess of flour Excess of eggs Baking temperature too high Overmixing	Not enough sugar Underbeating of egg yolks or overbeating of egg whites Omission of cream of tartar (in angel food cake) Baking temperature too high Baking time too long
Crumbling or falling apart.	Excess of leavening, sugar or shortening Undermixing Incorrect preparation of pan Incorrect cooling	
Falling out of pan before cooling is complete.		Baking time too short Excess of sugar Greasing of pan
One side higher.	Uneven spreading of batter Pan warped Range or oven rack not level Pan too close to wall of oven Uneven oven heat	Range or oven rack not level Pan warped
Pale top crust.	Baking temperature too low Not enough sugar or shortening Excess of flour Pan too large Overmixing	Baking temperature too low Not enough sugar Excess of flour
Dry crumb.	Excess of flour Not enough shortening or liquid Overbeating of egg whites Baking time too long	Excess of flour Overbeating of egg whites Baking time too long

Note: Failure of some cakes may be caused by failure to beat and add egg whites and egg yolks separately (where recipe so directs). Adding whole eggs, no matter how thoroughly beaten, may produce different results.

BUTTER-TYPE CAKES

WHITE LAYER CAKE
(Quick-Method)

▲ *Base Recipe*

Prepare (page 10) two 8-in. round layer cake pans.

Sift together into large mixer bowl
>**2 cups sifted cake flour**
>**1¼ cups sugar**
>**1 tablespoon baking powder**
>**¾ teaspoon salt**

Add to sifted dry ingredients
>**⅔ cup milk**
>**½ cup vegetable shortening or all-purpose shortening**
>**2 teaspoons vanilla extract**
>**¼ teaspoon rum extract**

Beat on medium speed of electric mixer for 2 min., scraping sides of bowl several times during beating.

Add to batter
>**4 egg whites, unbeaten**
>**⅓ cup milk**

Beat on medium speed for 2 min., scraping bowl while beating. Pour batter into pans.

Bake at 350°F 30 to 35 min., or until cake tests done (page 11).

Cool and remove from pans as directed for butter-type cakes (page 11).

Two 8-in. round layers

—CHERRY NUT LOAF CAKE

Prepare a 9x5x3-in. loaf pan instead of layer cake pans. Finely chop **1 cup (3¾ oz.) pecans,** **¾ cup (6 oz.) red candied cherries** and **¼ cup (2 oz.) candied citron.** Set aside. Follow ▲ Recipe. Substitute **1 teaspoon almond extract** for vanilla extract. Fold in finely chopped pecans, cherries and citron. Pour batter into pan. Bake at 350°F 55 min., or until cake tests done.

—PINK MARBLE CAKE

Follow ▲ Recipe. Pour two-thirds of batter into prepared pans. To remaining one-third batter, blend in **⅛ teaspoon almond extract.** Tint to desired color with **1 or more drops red food coloring.** Divide tinted batter equally and pour over batter in pans. Gently lift white batter through tinted batter to produce marbled effect.

—SILVER CUPCAKES

Line with paper baking cups or grease 18 2½-in. muffin-pan wells, instead of layer cake pans. Follow ▲ Recipe. Fill baking cups or muffin wells one-half full. Bake at 400°F 18 to 20 min., or until cakes test done.

Eighteen 2½-in. cupcakes

WHITE CAKE SQUARES

▲ *Base Recipe*

Prepare (page 10) a 9x9x2-in. pan.

Sift together and set aside
>**2 cups sifted cake flour**
>**1 tablespoon baking powder**
>**¾ teaspoon salt**

Cream until softened
>**⅔ cup vegetable shortening, all-purpose shortening, butter or margarine**
>**1 teaspoon vanilla extract**

Add gradually, creaming until fluffy after each addition
>**½ cup sugar**

Measure
>**⅔ cup milk**

Alternately add dry ingredients in thirds and milk in halves to creamed mixture, beating only until smooth after each addition; finally beat until batter is smooth (do not overbeat).

Beat until frothy
>**4 egg whites**

Add gradually, beating well after each addition
>**½ cup sugar**

Continue beating until rounded peaks are formed. Gently slide beaten egg whites over batter and fold together. Turn batter into pan and spread evenly.

Bake at 350°F 30 to 35 min., or until cake tests done (page 11).

Meanwhile, spread over bottom of a shallow pan
>**½ cup flaked coconut**

Remove cake to cooling rack and place pan of coconut in oven. Heat 10 to 15 min., or until lightly toasted; stir occasionally.

Meanwhile, cool cake and remove from pan as directed (page 11).

Prepare
>**Chocolate Butter Frosting II (page 478)**

When cake is completely cooled, frost (page 11) sides and top with frosting. Sprinkle top of frosted cake with the toasted coconut.

One 9-in. square cake

—MARBLE CAKE

Follow ▲ Recipe, first melting (page 10) **1½ oz. (1½ sq.) unsweetened chocolate** and setting it aside to cool. Turn two thirds of batter into pan. Fold into remaining batter a mixture of the cooled chocolate, **1 tablespoon sugar, 2 tablespoons hot water** and **¼ teaspoon baking soda.** Spoon over batter in pan. Gently lift white batter through chocolate batter until marbled effect is produced. Omit coconut.

—NUT LOAF CAKE

Follow ▲ Recipe. Prepare a 9x5x3-in. loaf pan, instead of 9x9x2-in. pan. Fold in after egg white addition, **1 cup (about 4 oz.) finely chopped nuts** and **¼ cup (about 2 oz.) finely chopped well-drained maraschino cherries.** For Chocolate Butter Frosting substitute **Lemon Butter Frosting** (page 478). If desired, sprinkle top of cake with **finely chopped nuts** and **maraschino cherries.** Omit coconut.

BLENDER WHITE CAKE

▲ *Base Recipe*

Prepare (page 10) two 9-in. round layer cake pans.

Sift together into bowl and set aside
>**3 cups sifted cake flour**
>**4 teaspoons baking powder**
>**¾ teaspoon salt**

Put into an electric blender container in order
>**1 cup milk**
>**⅔ cup vegetable shortening or all-purpose shortening**
>**1 cup sugar**
>**1 teaspoon vanilla extract**
>**1 teaspoon almond extract**

Cover and blend 2 min. Scrape down sides of container and blend a few seconds longer.

Add gradually, stirring after each addition, two-thirds of blended mixture to sifted dry ingredients. Stir until well blended (total strokes, about 100). Add remaining blended mixture all at one time; mix until smooth. Set aside while beating egg whites.

Beat until frothy
   5 egg whites
Add gradually, beating well after each addition
   ½ cup sugar
Continue to beat until stiff peaks are formed.

Spread egg whites over batter and gently fold together. Turn into pans.

Bake at 350°F 25 to 30 min., or until cake tests done (page 11).

Cool and remove from pans as directed for butter-type cakes (page 11).

Two 9-in. round layers

—BLENDER ORANGE CAKE

Follow ▲ Recipe. Substitute **fresh orange juice** for milk and **1 teaspoon orange extract** for vanilla and almond extracts. Add **1 strip (about 1-in. square) orange peel** (colored part only) to blender container with extract.

—CHOCOLATE-FLECKED WHITE CAKE

Grind **1 pkg. (6 oz.) semisweet chocolate pieces** in blender (should be powdery). Follow ▲ Recipe. Reduce almond extract to ½ teaspoon. Sprinkle ground chocolate over batter; then spread egg whites over chocolate and fold together. Bake at 350°F 30 to 35 min., or until cake tests done.

Note: If the blender-liquid mixture looks "curdled" when blending, don't be alarmed. It blends in smoothly with the dry ingredients.

SHOWER CAKE

Delicate whipped cream takes the place of shortening in this cake of sheer elegance.

Prepare (page 10) two 9-in. round layer cake pans. Set a bowl and rotary beater in refrigerator to chill.

Shower Cake

Prepare and set in refrigerator to chill
   Pineapple Cream Filling (page 484)

Set out
   1½ cups sugar
Sift ½ cup of the sugar with
   2 cups sifted cake flour
   1 tablespoon baking powder
   ½ teaspoon salt
Set mixture aside.

Using chilled bowl and beater, beat until cream stands in soft peaks when beater is slowly lifted upright
   1 cup chilled heavy cream
Beat in ¼ cup of the sugar. Set in refrigerator while beating egg whites.

Using clean beater, beat until frothy
   4 egg whites
Add the remaining ¾ cup sugar gradually, beating well after each addition. Beat until rounded peaks are formed. Fold in the whipped cream together with
   ¾ teaspoon almond extract
Measure
   ½ cup water
Folding only until blended after each addition, alternately add dry ingredients in thirds and water in halves to whipped cream mixture. Finally, fold only until blended. Turn batter into pans.

Bake at 350°F 30 min., or until cake tests done (page 11).

Cool and remove from pans as directed for butter-type cakes (page 11). Cool completely.

Fill (page 11) with the Pineapple Cream Filling. Frost sides and top of cake with
   Seven-Minute Frosting (page 474) or
   White Mountain Frosting (page 474)
Reserve ½ cup frosting for decorating.

For Shower Decoration—If necessary, add **1 to 2 tablespoons confectioners' sugar** to the reserved frosting to give it a decorating-frosting consistency. Blend in **red food coloring**, a drop at a time, until frosting is a delicate pink color. Set frosting aside.

To make umbrella, cut a piece of heavy aluminum foil into a wedge shape, 4 in. wide at base and 4 in. long. Curve wedge to form umbrella top (see photo). Using a spatula, spread pink frosting over both sides of umbrella, using lengthwise strokes on the outside to simulate umbrella spokes. Allow frosting on umbrella to set, keeping curved position. At one side of the frosted cake form the shaft and curved handle of the umbrella by forcing remaining pink frosting through a pastry bag and No. 2 decorating tube. Make the shaft about 4 in. long. Using same decorating tube, form small droplets over top of cake (see photo). Set umbrella top in place.

One 9-in. round layer cake

BRIDE'S CAKE

It's traditional and it's fun to add to the bride's-

---

cake batter the trinkets that foretell the future of the guests who find them in their portions of cake: a penny for wealth, a horseshoe for luck, a ring for the next bride, a thimble for the spinster and a button for the bachelor. Fold them into the batter with the egg whites, and be sure to divide them among the three layers.

For Cake Layers—Prepare (page 10) two 8-in. round layer cake pans, one 12x2-in. round layer cake pan and two 6x2-in. round layer cake pans. Grease sides of 12-in. pan and line with parchment paper cut ½ in. wider than sides of pan. Lightly grease paper.

Prepare one recipe of batter for 12-in. layer and another for 8- and 6-in. layers.

Sift together
   3 cups sifted cake flour
   1 tablespoon baking powder
   ½ teaspoon salt
Set aside.

Cream until softened
   ¾ cup butter
   1 tablespoon vanilla extract
   ¼ teaspoon almond extract
Add gradually, creaming until fluffy after each addition
   1 cup sugar
Measure and combine
   ½ cup water
   ½ cup milk
Beating only until smooth after each addition, alternately add dry ingredients in fourths and liquid in thirds to creamed mixture; do not overbeat.

Beat until frothy
   6 egg whites
Add gradually, beating well after each addition
   ¾ cup sugar
Beat until rounded peaks are formed. Spread beaten egg whites over batter and gently b t thoroughly fold together. Turn batter into the 12-in. pan.

Bake at 350°F 50 to 55 min., or until cake tests done (page 11).

Cool and remove from pan as directed for butter-type cakes (page 11).

Repeat recipe for 6- and 8-in. layers. Fill 8-in. pans two-thirds full. Divide remaining batter equally in 6-in. pans.

Bake at 350°F 30 to 35 min. for 6- and 8-in. layers, or until cakes test done.

Cool and remove from pans as directed.

Prepare
   Bride's Butter Frosting (page 478)

To Frost and Decorate Cake—Spread sides and tops of cooled cake layers with a thin coating of frosting. (This coating prevents crumbs from getting in the final frosting and also helps keep the cake moist and fresh.) Put the 6-in. layers together. *Do not put other layers together.* Cover well with waxed paper, tucking paper under racks.

The next day, when ready to start decorating, prepare

**Bride's Butter Frosting (one and one
half times recipe, page 478)**

Cut two rounds of thin cardboard, one about 8 in., the other 5 in. in diameter. Cover with aluminum foil. (Cardboard merely prevents knife from cutting into lower layers.)

Place 12-in. layer on cake plate. In the center of the layer, spread a thin layer of frosting the size of the larger cardboard round. Press cardboard firmly into the frosting. Cover with one of the 8-in. layers, frosted surface up. Spread top with frosting; cover with the other 8-in. layer.

In the center of the top layer, spread a thin layer of frosting the size of the smaller cardboard. Press cardboard firmly into the frosting. Cover with 6-in. layer, frosted side up.

Frost sides of all three tiers (layers), completely covering the cake.

Dip spatula in hot water and smooth frosting. Frost exposed top of each tier. Decorate cake by forcing frosting through cake decorator or pastry bag and tube, using shell, rosette, or star tube. Make a fluting of frosting around base and edge of each tier.

Tiny icing flowers and other decorations may be used to decorate cake.

The traditional bride and groom dolls may be affixed to the top with frosting. Or top the cake with a miniature of the bride's bouquet.

To Serve a Three-Tiered Bride's Cake—Hold knife vertically and cut through the bottom layer around outside of middle layer. Slice part of bottom layer that extends beyond middle layer into serving-size pieces. Repeat with middle layer, cutting through middle layer around outside of top layer only to top of bottom layer. (See illustration.)

The top layer may be removed and placed on a small serving plate on the table. Remainder of cake may be removed to the kitchen for slicing. Serve on individual plates or from one large plate. It is best to wipe crumbs and frosting from the knife frequently. Dipping the knife in hot water also aids in cutting the cake.

50 to 60 servings

LADY BALTIMORE CAKE

For Cake—Prepare (page 10) three 8-in. round layer cake pans.

Sift together and set aside.
**3 cups sifted cake flour
1½ tablespoons baking powder
1 teaspoon salt**

Cream until softened
**1 cup butter
1½ teaspoons vanilla extract**
Add gradually, creaming until fluffy after each addition
¾ cup sugar
Measure
1 cup milk
Beating only until smooth after each addition, alternately add dry ingredients in fourths and milk in thirds to creamed mixture; do not overbeat.

Beat until frothy
6 egg whites
Add gradually, beating well after each addition
¾ cup sugar
Continue beating until rounded peaks are formed. Spread beaten egg whites over batter and gently fold together. Turn batter into prepared pans.

Bake at 350°F 30 to 35 min., or until cake tests done (page 11).

Cool; remove from pans as directed (page 11) and spread with hot glaze.

For Glaze—Shortly before cake is done, combine in a saucepan
**1 cup sugar
½ cup water**
Stir over low heat until sugar is dissolved. Increase heat and bring mixture to boiling. Cover saucepan and boil gently 5 min. Uncover pan and put a candy thermometer in place so that the bulb does not touch bottom or side of pan. Cook, stirring occasionally, until thermometer registers 230 to 234°F (or until syrup spins a thread when dropped from spoon; remove pan from heat while testing). Using pastry brush dipped in water, wash down sides of pan from time to time during cooking.

Bride's Cake

Remove from heat, remove candy thermometer and stir in
**1 teaspoon vanilla extract
½ teaspoon almond extract**
Spread hot glaze over cake layers after removing them from the pans. Set layers aside to cool completely.

When cake is almost cool, prepare Lady Baltimore Frosting.

For Lady Baltimore Frosting—Prepare
**⅓ cup (about 2 oz.) chopped dried
light figs
¼ cup (about 2 oz.) chopped dark
seedless raisins
¼ cup (about 1 oz.) chopped pecans
or walnuts**
Combine and mix well in top of a double boiler
**1½ cups sug
⅓ cup water
1 tablespoon light corn syrup
⅛ teaspoon salt
2 egg whites, unbeaten**

Set over boiling water and immediately beat with hand rotary beater or electric mixer 7 to 10 min., or until mixture holds stiff peaks. Remove from heat and beat in

2 teaspoons vanilla extract
½ teaspoon almond extract

Fold fruit and nuts into one third of the frosting and use for the filling. Immediately fill and frost (page 11) cake.

One 8-in. 3-layer cake

KISS AND TELL CAKE

Prepare (page 10) a 13x9x2-in. cake pan.

Sift together and set aside

3 cups sifted cake flour
1½ tablespoons baking powder
¾ teaspoon salt

Cream until softened

⅔ cup butter, margarine, vegetable
shortening or all-purpose shortening
2 teaspoons almond extract

Add gradually, creaming until fluffy after each addition

1⅓ cups sugar

Measure

1¼ cups milk

Alternately add dry ingredients in fourths and milk in thirds to creamed mixture. After each addition, beat only until smooth; do not overbeat.

Beat until frothy

5 egg whites

Add gradually, beating well after each addition

⅓ cup sugar

Continue beating until very stiff peaks are formed. Spread beaten egg whites over batter and gently fold together. Turn batter into pan.

Bake at 375°F 25 to 30 min., or until cake tests done (page 11). Cool and remove from pan as directed (page 11).

When cake is cooled, prepare
Seven-Minute Frosting (page 474)
Divide frosting into two portions. Blend into one portion
1 or more drops green food coloring

Blend into remaining frosting about
1 or more drops yellow food coloring
Reserve about ⅓ cup yellow tinted frosting for decoration. Frost sides and top of one half of the cake with green tinted frosting and the other half with yellow tinted frosting.

Mark off 12 squares in the yellow frosting and place a flower, such as a daisy, in each square. Mark off 12 diagonal sections in green frosting. Spoon a small mound of reserved yellow frosting onto each diagonal piece.

About 24 servings

MARASCHINO CHERRY CAKE

Prepare (page 10) two 9-in. round layer cake pans.

Sift together and set aside

3 cups sifted cake flour
4 teaspoons baking powder
¾ teaspoon salt

Drain, reserving syrup
1 bottle (8 oz.) maraschino cherries
Finely chop cherries (about ⅔ cup, chopped) and set aside.

Beat together
⅔ cup shortening
1 teaspoon almond extract
Add gradually, creaming until fluffy after each addition

1 cup sugar

Combine
⅔ cup milk
⅓ cup reserved cherry syrup
Alternately add dry ingredients in fourths and milk mixture in thirds to creamed mixture. After each addition beat only until smooth. Finally, beat only until batter is smooth (do not overbeat). Stir in chopped cherries.

Beat until frothy
5 egg whites
Add gradually, beating well after each addition
½ cup sugar
Continue beating until rounded peaks are formed. Spread beaten egg whites over batter and gently fold together. Turn batter into cake pans.

Bake at 350°F 30 to 35 min., or until cake tests done (page 11).

Cool and remove from pans as directed (page 11).

Meanwhile, preare
Butter Frosting (one and one half
times recipe, page 473)

When cake is completely cooled, fill and frost (page 11). *One 9-in. round layer cake*

MARBLEIZED CAKE

▲ Base Recipe

The ladies of New England used to make both a marble cake and a marbled or marbleized one. The first was so easy that a child could do it —you just dropped into the pan alternate spoonfuls of light and dark batter. The second required an artist's touch, because you put in all the light batter and then all the dark, and swirled them together with the spoon to form graceful veinings like marble all through the cake. A sort of personalized cake that's a joy to make, to behold, and to eat at teatime.

Prepare (page 10) an 8x8x2-in. cake pan.

Melt (page 10)
1½ oz. (1½ sq.) unsweetened
chocolate
Set aside to cool.

Sift together
2 cups sifted cake flour
2 teaspoons baking powder
½ teaspoon salt
Set aside.

Cream until softened
½ cup butter
2 teaspoons vanilla extract
Add gradually, creaming until fluffy after each addition
1 cup sugar
Measure
¾ cup milk
Beating only until smooth after each addition, alternately add dry ingredients in thirds and milk in halves to creamed mixture; do not overbeat.

Beat until stiff, not dry, peaks are formed
3 egg whites
Spread beaten egg whites over batter and gently fold together. Turn one half of batter into cake pan. Blend into remaining batter a mixture of cooled chocolate and
2 tablespoons hot water
1 tablespoon sugar
½ teaspoon baking soda
Spoon chocolate batter on top of batter in pan. Gently lift white batter through chocolate batter until swirled effect is produced.

Luscious Pistachio Cake

Bake at 350°F 40 to 45 min., or until cake tests done (page 11).

Cool; remove from pans as directed (page 11).
One 8-in. square cake

—MARBLEIZED CHOCO-MINT CAKE

Follow ▲ Recipe. Add to the white portion of batter ¼ to ½ teaspoon peppermint extract and **3 drops red or green food coloring,** and blend thoroughly. Proceed as in ▲ Recipe.

—MOCHA CAKE

Follow ▲ Recipe, but bake in a 9x9x2-in. cake pan. Do not divide batter. Sift ⅓ cup **instant powdered coffee** with the flour. Reduce chocolate to ½ oz. (½ sq.); omit hot water, sugar and baking soda mixture. Blend the melted chocolate with the creamed shortening-sugar mixture.

LUSCIOUS PISTACHIO CAKE

Prepare (page 10) two 9-in. round layer cake pans.

Sift together and set aside
 3 cups sifted cake flour
 3½ teaspoons baking powder
 ¾ teaspoon salt

Cream until softened
 ⅔ cup butter
 2 teaspoons almond extract
Add gradually, creaming until fluffy after each addition
 1½ cups sugar
Measure
 1¼ cups milk
Beating only until batter is smooth after each addition, alternately add dry ingredients in fourths and milk in thirds to creamed mixture.

Finally, beat only until batter is smooth (do not overbeat).

Beat until frothy
 5 egg whites
Add gradually, beating well after each addition
 ½ cup sugar
Continue beating until very stiff peaks are formed. Spread beaten egg whites over batter and gently fold together. Turn batter into pans.

Bake at 350°F 25 to 30 min., or until cake tests done (page 11).

Cool and remove from pans as directed (page 11).

Prepare
 Pistachio Cream Filling (page 484)
 Seven-Minute Pistachio Frosting (page 474)
Fill and frost cake (page 11).
One 9-in. round layer cake

POPPY SEED CAKE

Addition of poppy seed to a white-cake batter gives the cake a delicate nutlike flavor.

Prepare (page 10) two 9-in. round layer cake pans.

Put into a small bowl
 ¾ cup milk
Add and allow to soak 2 hrs.
 ½ cup (about 2½ oz.) poppy seed

Sift together and set aside
 2¼ cups sifted cake flour
 2 teaspoons baking powder
 ½ teaspoon salt

Cream until softened
 ¾ cup butter
 1½ teaspoons vanilla extract
 ¼ teaspoon grated lemon peel
 Few drops almond extract
Add gradually, creaming until fluffy after each addition
 1½ cups sugar
Beating only until smooth after each addition, alternately add dry ingredients in fourths and poppy seed and milk mixture in thirds to creamed mixture. Finally, beat only until smooth (do not overbeat).

Beat until stiff, not dry, peaks are formed
 4 egg whites
Carefully spread beaten egg whites over batter and gently fold together. Turn batter into pans.

Bake at 350°F 30 to 35 min., or until cake tests done (page 11).

Cool and remove from pans as directed for butter-type cakes (page 11).

When cake is completely cooled, prepare
 White Mountain Frosting (page 474)
Fill and frost cake (page 11). Sprinkle **poppy seed** over top. *One 9-in. round layer cake*

YELLOW CAKE

Prepare (page 10) two 8-in. round layer cake pans.

Sift together and set aside
 2½ cups sifted cake flour
 2½ teaspoons baking powder
 ¾ teaspoon salt

Put into large mixer bowl and cream until butter is softened
 ⅔ cup butter or margarine
 2 teaspoons vanilla extract
Add gradually, creaming thoroughly after each addition
 1½ cups sugar
Continue to beat and add one at a time, beating thoroughly after each addition
 3 eggs

Measure
 1 cup milk
Beating only until smooth after each addition, alternately add dry ingredients in fourths, milk in thirds to creamed mixture. Turn batter into pans.

Bake at 350°F 30 to 35 min., or until cake tests done (page 11).

Cool and remove from pans as directed for butter-type cakes (page 11). Frost sides and top with **Magic Glossy Chocolate Frosting** (page 476). *Two 8-in. round layers*

BLENDER YELLOW CAKE

A tender, fine-grained cake is the result.

Prepare (page 10) two 8-in. round layer cake pans. An electric blender will be needed.

Sift together into a large bowl and set aside
 2 cups sifted cake flour
 1 tablespoon baking powder
 ½ teaspoon salt

Put into the blender container
 2 eggs, unbeaten
Cover and blend for a few seconds. Turn off motor and add to blender container in order
 ½ cup vegetable shortening or all-purpose shortening
 1¼ cups sugar
 1½ teaspoons vanilla extract
 ½ teaspoon almond extract
 1 cup milk

Poppy Seed Cake

Cover and blend 2 min.

Using a rubber spatula, scrape down sides of container. Blend a few seconds longer. Gradually add two thirds of blended mixture to the sifted dry ingredients, stirring after each addition. Stir until well blended (total strokes, about 100). Add remaining mixture all at one time; mix until smooth. Turn batter into pans.

Bake at 350°F 25 to 30 min., or until cake tests done (page 11).

Cool and remove from pans as directed for butter-type cakes (page 11).

Two 8-in. round layers

TWO-EGG CAKE

▲ *Base Recipe*

Prepare (page 10) a 9x9x2-in. cake pan.

Sift together and set aside
1¾ cups sifted cake flour
2 teaspoons baking powder
¼ teaspoon salt

Cream until softened
⅔ cup butter
1½ teaspoons vanilla extract
Add gradually, creaming until fluffy after each addition
1 cup sugar
Add, one at a time, beating thoroughly after each addition
2 eggs
Measure
½ cup milk
Beating only until smooth after each addition, alternately add dry ingredients in thirds and milk in halves to creamed mixture. Finally, beat only until smooth (do not overbeat). Turn batter into the pan.

Bake at 350°F 35 to 40 min., or until cake tests done (page 11).

Cool and remove from pan as directed for butter-type cakes (page 11).

One 9-in. square cake

—EASY MARBLE CAKE

Follow ▲ Recipe. Divide batter into halves. Blend **1 oz. (1 sq.) unsweetened chocolate**, melted (page 10) and cooled, into one portion. Spoon batters into prepared pan, alternating spoonfuls of light and dark. Bake as in ▲ Recipe.

—BROILER CAKE

Follow ▲ Recipe for baking cake. Set cake on cooling rack while preparing Broiler Topping.

For Broiler Topping—Measure **1 cup flaked coconut** and chop **¼ cup nuts**; set aside. Cream **⅓ cup butter or margarine** until softened. Add **⅔ cup firmly packed brown sugar** gradually, creaming until fluffy after each addition. Blend in **¼ cup cream**. Stir in the coconut and nuts. Lightly spread topping over the cake after it has cooled in pan 10 to 15 min. Place cake on broiler rack and put under broiler so top is about 4 in. from heat. Broil about 2 min., or until topping bubbles. Watch closely to avoid scorching.

—COTTAGE PUDDING

Follow ▲ Recipe. To serve, cut cake into squares and pour **Vanilla, Lemon or Butterscotch Sauce** over each serving.

For Vanilla Sauce—Mix thoroughly in a saucepan **1 cup sugar, 2 tablespoons cornstarch** and **¼ teaspoon salt**. Add **2 cups boiling water** gradually, stirring constantly. Continuing to stir, bring to boiling; simmer 5 min. Remove from heat and blend in **¼ cup butter or margarine** and **2 teaspoons vanilla extract**. Serve warm or cold.

For Lemon Sauce—Follow the recipe for Va-

nilla Sauce. Substitute **3 tablespoons lemon juice** and **2 teaspoons grated lemon peel** for the vanilla extract.

For Butterscotch Sauce—Melt over low heat in a saucepan **1 tablespoon butter or margarine**. Add a mixture of **⅔ cup firmly packed brown sugar** and **5 tablespoons all-purpose flour**, stirring constantly until blended. Gradually add **2 cups milk**, stirring until blended. Bring to boiling; boil 1 min., stirring constantly. Remove from heat. Blend in **1 teaspoon vanilla extract**. Cool slightly before serving.

—CUPCAKES

Follow ▲ Recipe; line eighteen to twenty 2½-in. muffin-pan wells with paper baking cups, or lightly grease bottoms of wells. Fill each about two-thirds full. Bake at 350°F 18 to 20 min.

For Chocolate Cupcakes—Blend in **3 oz. melted unsweetened chocolate** after eggs. Bake 16 to 18 min.

GOLD CAKE
(Quick Method)

▲ *Base Recipe*

Prepare (page 10) two 8-in. round layer cake pans.

Sift together into a large bowl
2 cups sifted cake flour
1¼ cups sugar
2½ teaspoons baking powder
½ teaspoon salt
Measure
1 cup milk
Add ⅔ cup of the milk to dry ingredients with
½ cup vegetable shortening or
all-purpose shortening
1 teaspoon lemon extract
½ teaspoon vanilla extract
Stir only enough to moisten. Beat 200 strokes by hand or 2 min. on electric mixer at medium speed. Scrape sides of bowl several times during beating. Add remaining milk and
4 egg yolks, unbeaten
Beat 200 strokes or 2 min. on electric mixer, scraping sides of bowl several times. Pour batter into pans.

Bake at 350°F 25 to 30 min., or until cake tests done (page 11).

Cool and remove from pans as directed for butter-type cakes (page 11).

Two 8-in. round layers

—LORD BALTIMORE-STYLE CAKE

Prepare two 9-in. round layer cake pans. Prepare one and one-half times ▲ Recipe. Sift **½ teaspoon nutmeg** with dry ingredients. Omit vanilla extract and increase lemon extract to 1½ teaspoons. When cake is cool, prepare **Lord Baltimore Frosting** (page 475); fill and frost as directed (page 11). Cake layers may be split.

—SPICE CAKE

Follow ▲ Recipe. Sift **1 teaspoon cinnamon,** **½ teaspoon nutmeg** and **¼ teaspoon cloves** with dry ingredients. Omit extracts. Substitute **2 eggs** for the 4 egg yolks.

BROWN AND GOLD CAKE

Prepare (page 10) two 8-in. round layer cake pans.

Sift together and set aside
- **2½ cups sifted cake flour**
- **2½ teaspoons baking powder**
- **1 teaspoon salt**

Cream until softened
- **⅔ cup butter**
- **1¼ teaspoons vanilla extract**
- **¼ teaspoon orange extract**
- **½ teaspoon yellow food coloring (optional)**

Add gradually, creaming thoroughly after each addition
- **1½ cups sugar**

Add in thirds, beating thoroughly after each addition
- **3 eggs, well beaten**

Measure
- **1 cup milk**

Alternately add dry ingredients in fourths and milk in thirds to creamed mixture. After each addition, beat only until smooth. Finally, beat only until batter is smooth (do not overbeat). Turn batter into pans.

Bake at 350°F 30 to 35 min., or until cake tests done (page 11).

Cool; remove from pans as directed (page 11).

When cake is cool, prepare
- **Glossy Chocolate Frosting (double recipe, page 476)**

Frost cake (page 11) with frosting.

One 8-in. round layer cake

BANANA CAKE ROYALE

For Cake Layers—Prepare (page 10) three 8-in. round layer cake pans.

Set out
- **6 bananas with all-yellow or brown-flecked peel**

Sift together and set aside
- **2 cups sifted all-purpose flour**
- **1 tablespoon baking powder**
- **1 teaspoon salt**
- **½ teaspoon baking soda**

Prepare crumbs (page 10) from
- **14 to 16 graham crackers (or enough to yield 1 cup crumbs)**

Or use an electric blender (page 11) to prepare crumbs. The graham cracker crumbs for this cake should be granular (like corn meal) not fine and powdery (like flour). Mix with dry ingredients and set aside.

Peel and mash 3 to 4 of the bananas (or enough to yield 1⅓ cups mashed banana). Reserve the remaining bananas for filling and garnish.

Put into 1-cup measuring cup for liquid
- **1 teaspoon lemon juice**

Add, up to ⅓-cup line
- **Milk**

Mix with mashed bananas; set mixture aside.

Beat together
- **⅔ cup shortening**
- **2 teaspoons vanilla extract**

Add gradually, creaming until fluffy after each addition
- **⅔ cup sugar**

Add in thirds, beating thoroughly after each addition
- **3 egg yolks, well beaten**

Beating only until smooth after each addition, alternately add dry ingredients in fourths and banana-milk mixture in thirds to the creamed mixture. Finally, beat only until the batter is smooth (do not overbeat).

Beat until frothy
- **3 egg whites**

Add gradually, beating well after each addition
- **½ cup sugar**

Continue beating until very stiff peaks are formed. Spread beaten egg whites over the batter and gently fold together. Turn batter into the prepared pans.

Bake at 350°F 30 to 35 min., or until cake layers test done (page 11).

Cool; remove from pans as directed (page 11).

For Whipped Cream—While cake is cooling, chill a bowl and rotary beater in refrigerator.

Chop and set aside
- **½ cup (about 2 oz.) walnuts**

When ready to serve cake, using chilled bowl and beater, prepare
- **Sweetened Whipped Cream (page 480)**

To Complete Cake—Peel the remaining bananas and cut into slices. Dip slices into
- **Pineapple juice**

Place one cooled cake layer on a serving plate. Spread about one third of the whipped cream over the cake layer. Arrange one third of banana slices over whipped cream. Top with the second layer and repeat procedure. Top with third layer, spread remaining whipped cream over the top, and arrange banana slices and chopped nuts, as in photo.

Serve immediately. *One 8-in. round layer cake*

BLENDER BANANA CAKE

Prepare (page 10) two 8-in. round cake pans.

Sift together into bowl and set aside
- **2 cups sifted cake flour**
- **1½ teaspoons baking powder**
- **½ teaspoon baking soda**
- **½ teaspoon salt**

Banana Cake Royale

Purée in an electric blender (enough to make 1 cup) and set aside
- **2 to 3 all-yellow or brown-flecked bananas**

Put into blender container
- **2 eggs, unbeaten**

Cover and blend a few seconds. Turn off motor and add in order
- **½ cup vegetable shortening or all-purpose shortening**
- **1 cup sugar**
- **2 teaspoons vanilla extract**

Add bananas, cover and blend 2 min. Scrape down sides of container and blend few seconds longer.

Add gradually, stirring after each addition, two-thirds of blended mixture to sifted dry ingredients. Stir until well blended (total strokes, about 100). Add remaining blended mixture all at once; mix until smooth. Pour into cake pans.

Bake at 350°F 30 to 35 min., or until cake tests done (page 11).

Cool and remove from pans as directed for butter-type cakes (page 11).

Two 8-in. round layers

Buttermilk Layer Cake

BUTTERMILK LAYER CAKE

▲ *Base Recipe*

Prepare (page 10) two 9-in. round layer cake pans.

Sift together and set aside

3 cups sifted cake flour
2 teaspoons baking powder
¾ teaspoon baking soda
¼ teaspoon salt

Cream until softened

½ cup butter
1½ teaspoons vanilla extract

Add gradually, creaming until fluffy after each addition

1½ cups sugar

Add, one at a time, beating thoroughly after each addition

2 eggs

Measure

1½ cups buttermilk

Beating only until smooth after each addition, alternately add dry ingredients in fourths and buttermilk in thirds to creamed mixture. Finally, beat mixture only until smooth (do not overbeat). Turn batter into pans.

Bake at 350°F 25 to 30 min., or until cake tests done (page 11).

Cool; remove from pans as directed (page 11).

Fill and frost (page 11) as desired.

Two 9-in. round layers

—LEMON LAYER CAKE

Follow ▲ Recipe. Decrease vanilla extract to 1 teaspoon and add **½ teaspoon lemon extract.**

CARAWAY CAKE

▲ *Base Recipe*

Prepare (page 10) a 10x6x2-in. pan.

Sift together into a bowl

1½ cups sifted all-purpose flour
1 cup sugar
2 teaspoons baking powder
¼ teaspoon salt

Mix in

2 tablespoons caraway seed

Cut in with pastry blender or two knives until mixture resembles coarse corn meal

¼ cup lard

Blend

¾ cup milk
½ teaspoon vanilla extract
1 egg, beaten

Make a well in center of dry ingredients. Pour milk mixture in all at one time. Mix until all ingredients are moistened. Turn batter into pan. Sprinkle over top

2 tablespoons sugar

Bake at 375°F 30 min., or until cake tests done (page 11).

Cool in pan on cooling rack. Cut into squares.

One 10x6-in. cake

—CARAWAY ALMOND CAKE

Follow ▲ Recipe. Sift **⅛ teaspoon mace** with the dry ingredients. Substitute **¼ teaspoon almond extract** for the vanilla extract.

MARBLE CAKE
(Marmorkuchen)

Prepare (page 10) two 9-in. round layer cake pans.

Sift together and set aside

3½ cups sifted cake flour
1 tablespoon baking powder
½ teaspoon salt

Cream until softened

1 cup butter
1 teaspoon almond extract

Add gradually, creaming until fluffy after each addition

1½ cups sugar

Add in thirds, beating thoroughly after each addition

4 eggs, well beaten

Measure

1 cup milk

Beating only until smooth after each addition, alternately add dry ingredients in fourths and milk in thirds to creamed mixture. Finally, beat only until smooth (do not overbeat). Divide the batter into two equal portions. Divide one portion into the two prepared cake pans.

Blend thoroughly

¼ cup sugar
¼ cup cocoa
3 tablespoons rum

434

Gently blend cocoa mixture into remaining batter. Turn one half of the chocolate batter over the yellow batter in each pan. With a spatula, gently lift yellow batter through chocolate batter to produce marbled effect, but do not overblend.

Bake at 350°F 35 to 40 min., or until cake tests done (page 11).

Cool and remove from pans as directed (page 11).

When cake is cooled, prepare
Creamy Rum Filling (page 484)
Bittersweet Velvet Frosting (page 479)
Fill and frost as directed (page 11).

One 9-in. round layer cake

GOLDEN HONEY CAKE

Prepare (page 10) two 8-in. round layer cake pans.

Sift together into a large bowl

2 cups sifted cake flour
⅔ cup sugar
2 teaspoons baking powder
1 teaspoon salt
¼ teaspoon baking soda

Measure

¾ cup sour milk (page 9)

Add one half of milk to dry ingredients with

½ cup honey
½ cup vegetable shortening or all-purpose shortening
1 teaspoon vanilla extract

Stir only enough to moisten dry ingredients. Beat 200 strokes, or 2 min. on electric mixer on medium speed. Scrape sides of bowl several times during beating.

Add remaining milk and

4 egg yolks (about ⅓ cup), unbeaten

Beat 200 strokes, or 2 min. on electric mixer. Scrape sides of bowl several times. Turn into cake pans.

Bake at 350°F about 30 min., or until cake tests done (page 11).

Cool and remove from pans as directed (page 11).

Meanwhile, prepare
Lemon Cream Cheese Frosting (one and one half times recipe, (page 479)

When cake is completely cooled, fill and frost (page 11). *One 8-in. round layer cake*

GRAHAM CRACKER CAKE

An old-fashioned favorite, light and luscious, with a distinctive flavor and texture.

Prepare (page 10) two 9-in. round layer cake pans.

Prepare and chill
Vanilla Cream Filling (page 482)

Sift together and set aside
½ cup sifted cake flour
2 teaspoons baking powder
¼ teaspoon salt

Set out
24 graham crackers (or enough to yield 2 cups crumbs)
Prepare crumbs (page 10). Add to dry ingredients with
¾ cup (about 3 oz.) chopped pecans
Mix together and set aside.

Cream until softened
1 cup butter or margarine
1½ teaspoons vanilla extract
Add gradually, creaming until fluffy after each addition
1 cup sugar
Add in thirds, beating thoroughly after each addition
3 egg yolks, well beaten
Measure
1 cup milk
Beating only until smooth after each addition, alternately add dry ingredients in fourths and milk in thirds to the creamed mixture. Finally, beat only until batter is smooth (do not overbeat).

Using clean beater, beat until frothy
3 egg whites
Add gradually, beating well after each addition
⅓ cup sugar
Beat until rounded peaks are formed. Spread egg whites over the batter and gently fold together. Turn batter into pans.

Bake at 350°F 30 to 35 min., or until cake layers test done (page 11).

Cool and remove from pans as directed for butter-type cakes (page 11).

Spread the chilled filling over one layer of cooled cake. Cover with second layer. Sift evenly over the top
Confectioners' sugar
One 9-in. round layer cake

MAPLE SYRUP CAKE

▲ Base Recipe

Maple syrup in the cake, maple sugar in the frosting and a crown of butternuts are combined here to perfection. This is a rich cake, the kind that Vermonters are specially partial to.

Prepare (page 10) two 9-in. round layer cake pans.

Sift together
2⅔ cups sifted cake flour
1 tablespoon baking powder
¾ teaspoon salt
Set aside.

Cream until softened
¾ cup butter
Add gradually, creaming until fluffy after each addition
⅔ cup firmly packed light brown sugar

Set mixture aside.

Beat until thick and lemon-colored
7 egg yolks
Add to creamed mixture in thirds, beating thoroughly after each addition.

Measure and blend together
⅔ cup milk
⅔ cup maple syrup
Beating only until smooth after each addition, alternately add the dry ingredients in fourths, liquid in thirds to the creamed mixture. Finally, beat only until batter is smooth (do not overbeat). Turn batter into pans.

Bake at 350°F 35 to 40 min., or until cake tests done (page 11).

Cool; remove from pans as directed (page 11).

When layers are cooled, prepare
Maple Sugar Frosting (page 477)
Fill and frost cake (page 11).

Sprinkle around outside edge of top
½ cup (about 2 oz.) coarsely chopped butternuts or walnuts
One 9-in. round layer cake

—MAPLE BUTTERNUT CAKE

Coarsely chop ½ cup (about 2 oz.) butternuts (or walnuts). Follow ▲ Recipe. Blend in nuts just before turning batter into pan.

GOLDEN ORANGE CRUNCH CAKE

▲ Base Recipe

Set out a 9-in. tubed pan.

For Crunch Topping—Have ready
1½ cups very finely chopped walnuts, filberts or unblanched almonds
Melt in a small saucepan over low heat
⅓ cup butter
Mix thoroughly the nuts, melted butter and
¾ cup fine dry bread crumbs
½ cup firmly packed brown sugar
¼ teaspoon salt
¼ teaspoon cinnamon
Using the back of a spoon, press nut mixture very firmly into an even layer on bottom and sides of tubed pan. Set aside.

For Cake—Sift together and set aside
2¾ cups sifted cake flour
2 teaspoons baking powder
½ teaspoon salt

Cream until softened
1 cup butter
1 tablespoon grated orange peel
1 teaspoon vanilla extract
Add gradually, creaming until fluffy after each addition
1½ cups sugar
Add in thirds, beating thoroughly after each addition
4 eggs, well beaten
Measure
½ cup undiluted evaporated milk

Combine with
¼ cup orange juice
Beating only until smooth after each addition, alternately add dry ingredients in fourths and liquid in thirds to creamed mixture. Finally, beat only until smooth (do not overbeat). Turn batter into pan.

Bake at 375°F about 65 min., or until cake tests done (page 11).

Remove cake from oven and place on a cooling rack. Allow cake to cool in pan 30 min. Cover with cake plate, carefully invert and remove pan. Cool thoroughly before cutting.
One 9-in. tubed cake

—LEMON CRUNCH CAKE

Follow ▲ Recipe. Substitute **1½ teaspoons grated lemon peel** for the orange peel, and **2 tablespoons lemon juice** and **2 tablespoons water** for the orange juice.

—PINEAPPLE CRUNCH CAKE

Follow ▲ Recipe. Substitute **½ teaspoon pineapple extract** for the grated orange peel. Fold **⅓ cup well-drained crushed pineapple** into the batter and substitute **syrup** drained from pineapple for the orange juice.

PINEAPPLE UPSIDE-DOWN CAKE

▲ Base Recipe

Set out an 8x8x2-in. cake pan.

For Pineapple Topping—Drain, reserving syrup
1 can (20 oz.) pineapple slices (about 10 medium slices)
Heat in a saucepan over low heat
¼ cup butter or margarine
Add and blend in thoroughly
⅔ cup firmly packed brown sugar
Turn mixture into cake pan and spread evenly. Arrange the drained pineapple slices on top of the brown sugar mixture. Set aside.

For Cake—Sift together and set aside
1½ cups sifted cake flour
2 teaspoons baking powder
½ teaspoon salt

Cream until softened
½ cup butter or margarine
1 teaspoon vanilla extract
Add gradually, creaming until fluffy after each addition
½ cup sugar
Add and beat thoroughly
1 egg, well beaten
Measure ½ cup of the reserved pineapple syrup. (Remaining syrup may be used in other food preparation.)

Beating only until smooth after each addition, alternately add dry ingredients in fourths and pineapple syrup in thirds to creamed mixture. Finally, beat only until smooth (do not overbeat). Turn batter over pineapple slices and spread evenly to edges of pan.

Bake at 350°F about 50 min., or until cake tests done (page 11).

Remove from oven; let stand 1 to 2 min. in pan on cooling rack. To remove from pan, run spatula gently around sides. Cover with a serving plate and invert; allow pan to remain over cake 1 or 2 min. Lift pan off. Serve cake warm or cool.   *One 8-in. square cake*

—CRANBERRY UPSIDE-DOWN CAKE

Follow ▲ Recipe. Substitute Cranberry Topping for Pineapple Topping. Substitute ½ **cup milk** for the pineapple syrup in cake batter.

For Cranberry Topping—Heat **¼ cup butter or margarine** over low heat. Add **⅔ cup sugar**, **1 tablespoon grated orange peel** and **½ teaspoon vanilla extract**; blend in thoroughly. Spread mixture evenly in the cake pan. Wash and coarsely chop **2 cups cranberries**. Mix thoroughly with **⅓ cup sugar**. Spread over mixture in pan.

SUGAR CAKE
(Sockerkaka)

Butter a 2-qt. fancy tubed mold or a form cake mold.

Sift together and set aside
1½ cups sifted all-purpose flour
2 teaspoons baking powder
⅛ teaspoon salt

Burnt-Sugar Cake

Measure
½ cup boiling water
Add to the water and set aside to cool
¼ cup butter
Beat until very thick and piled softly
3 eggs
Add gradually, beating thoroughly after each addition
1 cup less 1 tablespoon sugar
Stir in
2 teaspoons grated lemon peel
Sift dry ingredients over mixture, about one-fourth at a time; gently fold until just blended after each addition. Add the water-butter mixture all at one time and quickly mix just until smooth. Turn into the prepared mold.

Bake at 325°F 1 hr., or until cake tests done (page 11).

Cool completely; run a small sharp knife around tube and sides; remove cake from mold.

Sprinkle cake generously with
Vanilla Confectioners' Sugar
(page 582)
Or serve plain with fruit or ice cream.
          1 tubed cake

BURNT-SUGAR CAKE

▲ Base Recipe

Prepare (page 10) a 9x9x2-in. cake pan.

For Burnt-Sugar Syrup—Melt in a heavy, light-colored skillet (a black skillet makes it difficult to see the color of the syrup) over low heat
2 cups sugar
With back of wooden spoon, gently keep sugar moving toward center of skillet until it is melted. Heat until syrup is a rich brown (darker than for caramel syrup) and until foam appears. Remove from heat and add gradually, a very small amount at a time, stirring constantly
1½ cups boiling water
(Be careful that steam does not burn hand.)
Return to low heat and continue to stir until bubbles are the size of dimes (about 5 min.). Set aside to cool completely.

For Cake—Sift together and set aside
2½ cups sifted cake flour
2½ teaspoons baking powder
½ teaspoon salt
Mix
½ cup water
½ cup Burnt-Sugar Syrup (part of remainder to be used for Burnt-Sugar Frosting)
Cream until softened
½ cup shortening
1 teaspoon vanilla extract
Add gradually, creaming until fluffy after each addition
½ cup sugar
Add in thirds, beating thoroughly after each addition
2 egg yolks, well beaten

Beating only until smooth after each addition, alternately add dry ingredients in thirds and liquid in halves to creamed mixture; do not overbeat.

Using clean beater, beat until frothy
2 egg whites
Add gradually, beating thoroughly after each addition
¼ cup sugar
Beat until rounded peaks are formed. Spread beaten egg whites over batter and gently fold together. Turn batter into pan.

Bake at 350°F 35 to 40 min., or until cake tests done (page 11).

Cool and remove from pan as directed for butter-type cakes (page 11).

When cake is completely cool, prepare
Burnt-Sugar Frosting (page 478)
Frost sides and top of cake (page 11). Sprinkle top with
Chopped toasted pecans
          One 9-in. square cake

Note: Burnt-Sugar Syrup may be stored in a tightly covered jar for future use.

—BURNT-SUGAR LAYER CAKE

Follow ▲ Recipe. Use two 8-in. round layer cake pans. Bake at 350°F 25 to 30 min.

WHIPPED CREAM CAKE

Prepare (page 10) two 8-in. round layer cake pans. Set a bowl and rotary beater in refrigerator to chill.

Sift together and set aside
1½ cups sifted cake flour
1 cup sugar
2 teaspoons baking powder
¼ teaspoon salt

Using chilled bowl and beater, beat until cream stands in soft peaks when beater is lifted upright
1 cup chilled heavy cream
Set in refrigerator while beating eggs.

Beat until thick and piled softly

2 eggs

Fold the whipped cream and beaten eggs together with

1½ teaspoons vanilla extract
¼ teaspoon lemon extract

Sift dry ingredients, about one fourth at a time, over mixture; gently fold until just blended after each addition. Finally, fold only until blended. Turn batter into pans.

Bake at 350°F 30 min., or until cake tests done (page 11).

Cool and remove from pans as directed for butter-type cakes (page 11). Cool completely.

Two 8-in. round layers

TURBAN CAKE
(Napfkuchen)

▲ Base Recipe

Butter a 2-qt. fluted tube mold.

Sift together and set aside

2 cups sifted all-purpose flour
2¼ teaspoons baking powder

Cream until softened

½ cup butter
1 tablespoon grated lemon peel
1 teaspoon vanilla extract

Add gradually, creaming until fluffy after each addition

½ cup sugar

Add in thirds, beating well after each addition

4 egg yolks, well beaten

Measure

¾ cup milk

Beating only until smooth after each addition, alternately add dry ingredients in fourths and milk in thirds to creamed mixture. (Do not overbeat.)

Using clean beaters, beat until frothy

4 egg whites

Add gradually, beating well after each addition

½ cup sugar

Beat until very stiff peaks are formed. Fold beaten egg whites into the batter. Turn batter into the mold.

Bake at 350°F about 55 min., or until cake tests done (page 11).

Invert pan on tube end and let cake hang in pan 1 hr. If cake is higher than tube, invert

between two cooling racks so top of cake does not touch any surface.

Remove from pan by running a paring knife or small spatula carefully around tube and around edge of cake. Serve slightly warm, if desired.

Sprinkle cake generously with

Vanilla Confectioners' Sugar
(page 582)

8 to 10 servings

—CHOCOLATE-GLAZED CAKE
(Napfkuchen mit Schokoladenglasur)

Follow ▲ Recipe. Partially melt over hot (not simmering) water, being careful not to overheat, **¼ lb. semisweet candymaking chocolate** and **¼ cup butter**. Remove from the hot water and stir until chocolate is completely melted. Quickly spread over the cake while mixture is still warm. Let chocolate cool completely before serving.

—POPPY SEED CAKE
(Napfkuchen mit Mohn)

Follow ▲ Recipe. Set out ½ cup (about 1½ oz.) freshly ground poppy seed. Just before first addition of dry ingredients, blend in the poppy seed.

POUND CAKE

▲ Base Recipe

Prepare (page 10) a 9x5x3-in. loaf pan or a star-shape (about 1½-qt.) mold.

Sift together

2 cups sifted all-purpose flour
¾ teaspoon baking powder
¼ teaspoon salt
¼ teaspoon mace

Set aside.

Cream until softened

1 cup butter
2 teaspoons grated lemon peel
1½ teaspoons vanilla extract
½ teaspoon almond extract

Add gradually, creaming until fluffy after each addition

1 cup plus 2 tablespoons sugar

Add in thirds, beating well after each addition

4 eggs, well beaten

Blend in dry ingredients in fourths. After each addition, beat only until smooth. Finally, beat only until batter is smooth.

Turn batter into pan. With spatula, draw batter from center toward edges of pan.

Bake at 325°F 1 hr. 10 min., or until cake tests done (page 11).

Cool and remove from pan as directed (page 11).

If desired, the Star Cake may be frosted with **White Velvet Frosting** (page 478).

One 9x5-in. loaf cake or 1 Star Cake

—LAMB CAKE

Thoroughly mix **2 tablespoons shortening** and **1 tablespoon all-purpose flour**; brush both sides of lamb mold. Follow ▲ Recipe. Substitute **cake flour** for flour. Turn batter into face-side of mold, filling it level. Spoon a small amount of batter into back-side of mold, being careful to fill ears. Cover face-side with back-side. Set on baking sheet. Bake at 375°F 50 to 55 min. Remove from oven and carefully remove top of mold. Let stand in mold 10 min.; turn out on rack. When cooled, frost with **Seven-Minute Frosting** (page 474) and sprinkle with **flaked coconut**. Use **raisins** for eyes and nose and **candied cherry** for mouth.

—CARAWAY POUND CAKE

Follow ▲ Recipe. Fold in **1 teaspoon caraway seed** with the last addition of flour.

—PARTY-COLOR POUND CAKE

Follow ▲ Recipe. Divide batter into three equal portions. Leave one portion uncolored; tint second portion green and third portion pink, adding only enough **green and red food coloring** (one drop at a time) to tint very delicately. Spoon the three portions alternately into the pan; draw spoon through batter once or twice to swirl three colors together.

—CHERRY-NUT POUND CAKE

Follow ▲ Recipe. Fold in **½ cup finely chopped candied cherries**, **¼ cup finely chopped candied citron** and **¼ cup chopped walnuts** with the last addition of flour. Fruit may first be marinated in just enough **brandy** or **rum** to cover.

APPLESAUCE CAKE

Prepare (page 10) a 9x9x2-in. cake pan.

Set out

¾ cup (about 4 oz.) raisins

Sift together and set aside

2 cups sifted cake flour
1 teaspoon baking soda
½ teaspoon salt
1 teaspoon cinnamon
½ teaspoon cloves

Cream until softened
½ cup butter or margarine
Add gradually, creaming until fluffy after each addition
1 cup firmly packed brown sugar
Add in thirds, beating well after each addition
2 eggs, well beaten
Measure and blend
1 cup applesauce
⅔ cup undiluted evaporated milk
2 tablespoons cider vinegar
Beating only until smooth after each addition, alternately add dry ingredients in fourths, applesauce mixture in thirds, to creamed mixture. Finally, beat only until smooth (do not overbeat). Add and stir in the raisins. Turn batter into the prepared pan.

Bake 350°F 40 min., or until cake tests done (page 11). Set cake on cooling rack while preparing frosting.

For Frosting—Coarsely chop and set aside
½ cup (about 3 oz.) blanched, toasted almonds (pages 9 and 10)

Cream until softened
2 tablespoons butter or margarine
Add gradually, creaming until fluffy after each addition
½ cup firmly packed brown sugar
Blend in
2 tablespoons undiluted evaporated milk
Stir in the chopped almonds.

Lightly spread frosting over the cake after it has cooled in pan 10 to 15 min. Place under broiler with top of cake about 4 in. from heat. Broil about 1 min., or until frosting bubbles. Watch closely to avoid scorching.

One 9-in. square cake

APPLE UPSIDE-DOWN CAKE

▲ ***Base Recipe***

Set out an 8x8x2-in. cake pan.

Melt in the cake pan
¼ cup butter or margarine
Meanwhile, mix
⅔ cup firmly packed brown sugar
1 teaspoon cinnamon
Stir in
2 tablespoons chopped walnuts
Blend sugar mixture into the melted butter or margarine and spread evenly.

Wash, quarter, core, pare and slice
1 medium apple
Arrange apple slices on the brown sugar mixture. Brush with
2 teaspoons lemon juice
Set aside.

Sift together
1½ cups sifted cake flour
1 teaspoon baking powder
¼ teaspoon baking soda
¼ teaspoon salt
¾ teaspoon cinnamon
¼ teaspoon nutmeg
¼ teaspoon allspice
Set aside.

Cream until softened
⅓ cup butter or margarine
½ teaspoon vanilla extract
Add gradually, creaming until fluffy after each addition
¾ cup firmly packed brown sugar
Add gradually, beating thoroughly after each addition
1 egg, well beaten
Measure
½ cup buttermilk
Beating only until smooth after each addition, alternately add dry ingredients in thirds and buttermilk in halves to creamed mixture. Finally beat only until smooth (do not overbeat). Turn batter over apple slices.

Bake at 350°F 40 to 45 min., or until cake tests done (page 11).

Using a spatula, loosen cake from sides of pan and invert immediately on serving plate. Let pan remain over cake a few seconds, so that syrup will drain onto cake. Remove pan.

Serve warm, with
Whipped Sour Cream Topping (page 482)

One 8-in. square cake

—PEAR UPSIDE-DOWN CAKE

Follow ▲ Recipe. Reduce butter or margarine in bottom of pan to 2 tablespoons, brown sugar to ⅓ cup; substitute **2 medium pears** for apple and **¼ teaspoon nutmeg** for the 1 teaspoon cinnamon. In the cake batter, omit cinnamon, nutmeg and allspice, and substitute **½ cup sugar** for the brown sugar.

GINGERBREAD

Prepare (page 10) a 9x9x2-in. cake pan.

Sift together and set aside
2½ cups sifted all-purpose flour
1 teaspoon baking soda
½ teaspoon baking powder
½ teaspoon salt
1 teaspoon cinnamon
1 teaspoon ginger
½ teaspoon nutmeg
¼ teaspoon cloves
¼ teaspoon allspice

Combine and set aside
1 cup molasses
1 cup boiling water

Put into a bowl
½ cup shortening
Add gradually, creaming until fluffy after each addition
½ cup sugar
Add in halves, beating thoroughly after each addition
1 egg, well beaten
Beating only until smooth after each addition, alternately add dry ingredients in fourths and liquid in thirds to creamed mixture. Finally, beat only until batter is smooth (do not overbeat). Turn batter into pan.

Bake at 350°F 50 to 60 min., or until gingerbread tests done (page 11).

Cool; remove from pans as directed (page 11).

To serve, cut into 3-in. squares and top each serving with **Sweetened Whipped Cream** (page 480) or **Vanilla Hard Sauce** (page 581)

9 servings

BUTTERMILK NUT GINGERBREAD

Prepare (page 10) a 9x9x2-in. cake pan.

Coarsely chop and set aside
¾ cup (about 3 oz.) pecans or walnuts

Sift together and set aside
2 cups sifted all-purpose flour
1¼ teaspoons baking soda
½ teaspoon salt
1 teaspoon ginger
1 teaspoon cinnamon
½ teaspoon allspice
¼ teaspoon cloves

Cream until softened
⅓ cup butter

Add gradually, creaming until fluffy after each addition
⅔ cup firmly packed brown sugar
Add gradually, beating well after each addition, a mixture of
1 egg, well beaten
½ cup molasses

Gingerbread

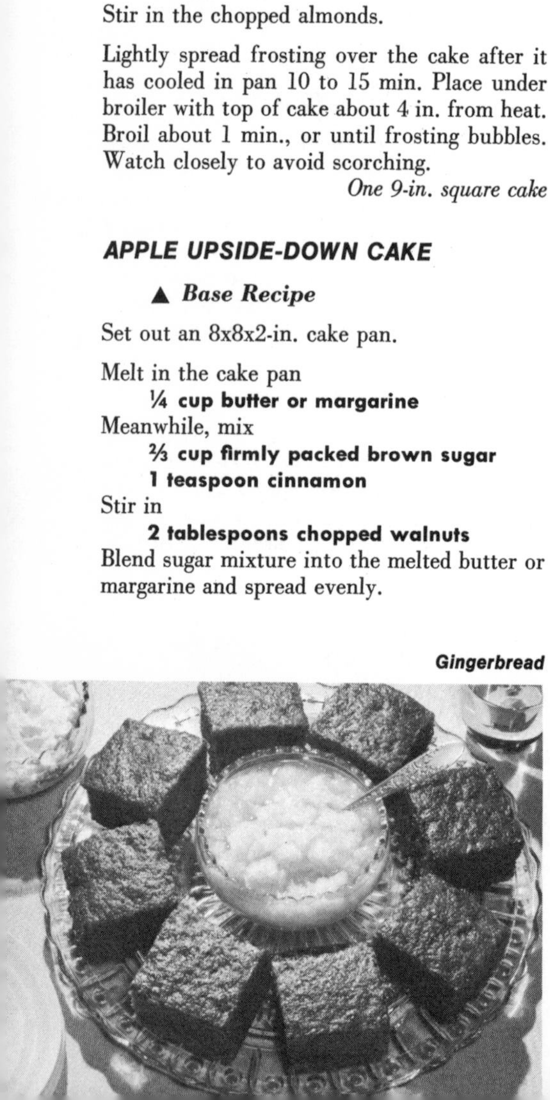

Buttermilk Nut Gingerbread

Measure

¾ cup buttermilk

Beating only until smooth after each addition, alternately add dry ingredients in thirds and buttermilk in thirds to creamed mixture. Finally, beat only until smooth (do not overbeat). Blend in the nuts. Turn batter into pan.

Bake at 350°F 35 to 45 min., or until cake tests done (page 11).

Cool; remove from pan as directed (page 11).

To serve, cut into 3-in. squares. If desired, top each serving with **Vanilla Cream Topping** (page 482). *9 servings*

TOPSY-TURVY GINGERBREAD

Melt in an 8-in. square cake pan

¼ cup butter or margarine

Evenly blend in

⅓ cup firmly packed brown sugar

Arrange on brown sugar mixture

9 halves cooked pears, apricots or peaches, cut-side up

Set aside.

Sift together

1½ cups sifted all-purpose flour
1 teaspoon baking powder
¾ teaspoon baking soda
¼ teaspoon salt
1½ teaspoons cinnamon
½ teaspoon ginger
½ teaspoon nutmeg

Blend

2 eggs, slightly beaten
¾ cup sour milk or buttermilk
½ cup firmly packed brown sugar
⅓ cup molasses
¼ cup melted shortening

Gradually add flour mixture, stirring until blended. Turn batter into pan over fruit-sugar mixture.

Bake at 350°F 30 to 40 min. Loosen cake from sides of pan and invert immediately on serving plate. Let pan rest over cake a few seconds so syrup will drain on cake.

One 8-in. square cake

JAM CAKE

Prepare (page 10) two 8x8x2-in. cake pans.

Prepare and set aside

1 cup (about 5 oz.) dark seedless raisins, chopped (page 9)
1 cup (about 4 oz.) coarsely chopped pecans

Sift together and set aside

2½ cups sifted cake flour
2 teaspoons baking powder
1 teaspoon baking soda
½ teaspoon salt
1 teaspoon cinnamon
½ teaspoon nutmeg
⅛ teaspoon cloves

Set out

1 cup raspberry or blackberry jam

Cream until softened

½ cup butter or margarine
1 tablespoon vanilla extract

Add gradually, creaming until fluffy after each addition

1 cup firmly packed light brown sugar

Add in thirds, beating thoroughly after each addition

3 eggs, well beaten

Blend the jam with

⅔ cup dairy sour cream

Beating only until smooth after each addition, alternately add dry ingredients in fourths and jam mixture in thirds to creamed mixture. Finally, beat only until smooth (do not overbeat). Stir in the chopped pecans and raisins. Turn batter into pans.

Bake at 375°F 30 to 35 min., or until cake tests done (page 11).

Cool; remove from pans as directed (page 11).

Cut into squares. If desired, serve with **Vanilla Cream Topping** (page 482), or lightly sift **confectioners' sugar** over each serving.

Two 8-in. square cakes

MARASCHINO DATE NUT CAKE

▲ Base Recipe

Prepare (page 10) a 13x9x2-in. cake pan.

Sift together and set aside

2 cups sifted all-purpose flour
2 teaspoons baking powder
¼ teaspoon salt
1 teaspoon allspice
1 teaspoon cinnamon

Drain, slice and set aside on absorbent paper

1½ cups (about 12 oz.) maraschino cherries

(A few pats with the paper will absorb excess moisture.)

Coarsely chop

2 cups (about 8 oz.) pecans

Cut (page 9) into small pieces enough pitted dates to yield

1 cup (about 7 oz.) date pieces

Put fruits and nuts into a large bowl with

¼ cup sifted all-purpose flour

Mix well and set aside.

Grate (page 10) and set aside

2 oz. (2 sq.) unsweetened chocolate

Cream until softened

¾ cup butter or margarine
½ teaspoon vanilla extract

Add gradually, creaming until fluffy after each addition

2 cups sugar

Add in thirds, beating thoroughly after each addition

4 egg yolks, well beaten

Add and beat until well blended the grated chocolate and

1 cup unseasoned mashed potatoes

Measure

½ cup milk

Beating only until blended after each addition, alternately add dry ingredients in thirds and milk in halves to creamed mixture; do not overbeat. Pour batter over fruit-nut mixture and mix thoroughly.

Beat until rounded peaks are formed

4 egg whites

Spread beaten egg whites over batter and fold together. Turn batter into pan and spread evenly to edges.

Bake at 275°F about 2 hrs., or until cake tests done (page 11) with cake tester.

Cool and remove from pan as directed for butter-type cakes (page 11). *One 13x9-in. cake*

—DATE NUT CAKE

Follow ▲ Recipe; use two 8x8x2-in. cake pans. Omit maraschino cherries and chocolate. Increase date pieces and pecans to 3 cups each.

Bake at 350°F 50 min., or until cake tests done.

—DATE NUT CUPCAKES

Follow ▲ Recipe or recipe for Date Nut Cake. Use twenty-four 2½-in. muffin-pan wells lined with paper baking cups, or with bottoms greased. Bake at 350°F about 20 min.

CRUMB CAKE

Prepare (page 10) a 13x9x2-in. cake pan.

Coarsely chop and set aside
    1 cup (about 4 oz.) pecans

Sift together into a large bowl
    3 cups sifted all-purpose flour
    2 cups sugar
Cut in with pastry blender or two knives until pieces are size of small peas
    1 cup butter or margarine
Measure 1 cup of the crumb mixture and set aside.

To crumb mixture remaining in bowl, add and mix in until well blended a mixture of
    2 tablespoons cinnamon
    1 teaspoon nutmeg
    ⅛ teaspoon cloves
    4 teaspoons cocoa
    1 teaspoon baking soda
    ½ teaspoon baking powder
    ⅛ teaspoon salt
Mix in pecans and
    **1 cup (about 5 oz.) dark seedless
      raisins**
Make a well in center of dry ingredients and add all at one time
    2 cups buttermilk
Stir until just blended.

Turn batter into pan and sprinkle top with the reserved crumb mixture.

Bake at 350°F 1 hr., or until cake tests done (page 11).

Cool; remove from pan as directed (page 11).
One 13x9-in. cake

NUTMEG CAKE

Prepare (page 10) two 9-in. round layer cake pans.

Sift together
    2 cups sifted cake flour
    2½ teaspoons nutmeg
    1 teaspoon baking powder
    ½ teaspoon baking soda
    ¼ teaspoon salt
Set aside.

Cream until softened
    ½ cup butter
    1 teaspoon vanilla extract
Add gradually, creaming until fluffy after each addition
    1½ cups sugar
Add in thirds, beating thoroughly after each addition
    3 eggs, well beaten
Measure
    1 cup buttermilk
Beating only until smooth after each addition, alternately add the dry ingredients in fourths and buttermilk in thirds to the creamed mixture; do not overbeat. Turn batter into the prepared pans and spread evenly.

Bake at 350°F about 30 min., or until cake layers test done (page 11).

Cool; remove from pans as directed (page 11).

Fill and frost cake (page 11) with
    **Lemon Cream Cheese Frosting
      (page 479)**
If desired, sprinkle with **nutmeg.**
One 9-in. round layer cake

SPICE CAKE

Prepare (page 10) a 13x9x2-in. cake pan.

Sift together and set aside
    3 cups sifted cake flour
    1½ teaspoons baking powder
    ¾ teaspoon baking soda
    ¾ teaspoon salt
    1½ teaspoons cinnamon
    ¾ teaspoon nutmeg
    ½ teaspoon allspice
    ½ teaspoon cloves

Cream until softened
    ¾ cup butter

Add gradually, creaming until fluffy after each addition
    1 cup firmly packed brown sugar
    1 cup sugar
Add in thirds, beating thoroughly after each addition
    3 eggs, well beaten
Measure
    **1½ cups buttermilk or sour milk
      (page 9)**
Beating only until smooth after each addition, alternately add dry ingredients in fourths and liquid in thirds to creamed mixture. Finally, beat only until smooth (do not overbeat).

Turn batter into pan.

Bake at 350°F 55 to 60 min., or until cake tests done (page 11).

Cool; remove from pan as directed (page 11).
One 13x9-in. cake

WALNUT CAKE

Lightly grease a 10-in. tubed pan. Line bottom with waxed paper cut to fit pan. Lightly grease paper.

Put into a bowl
    **2 cups (about 10 oz.) dark seedless
      raisins**
Pour over the raisins
    ⅔ cup sherry
Set aside.

Sift together and set aside
    4 cups sifted all-purpose flour
    2 teaspoons baking powder
    ¼ teaspoon salt
    1 teaspoon nutmeg

Chop and set aside
    4 cups (about 1 lb.) walnuts

Cream until softened
    1¼ cups butter or margarine
    2 teaspoons grated orange peel
Add gradually, creaming until fluffy after each addition
    2 cups sugar
Add gradually, beating thoroughly after each addition
    6 eggs, well beaten
Set aside.

Drain raisins, reserving liquid. Mix liquid with
    ⅔ cup orange juice
    ½ cup molasses
Beating only until smooth after each addition, alternately add dry ingredients in fourths and liquid in thirds to creamed mixture. Finally, beat only until smooth (do not overbeat). Blend in the raisins and walnuts. Turn batter into pan, spreading evenly to edges.

Bake at 275°F 2½ hrs., or until cake tests done (page 11).

Cool completely on cooling rack and remove from pan. *One 10-in. tubed cake*

CHOCOLATE CAKE

Prepare (page 10) two 8-in. round layer cake pans.

Melt (page 10) and set aside to cool
    2 oz. (2 sq.) unsweetened chocolate

Sift together and set aside
    2 cups sifted cake flour
    1 teaspoon baking powder
    ½ teaspoon baking soda

Beat together
    ⅔ cup shortening
    1½ teaspoons vanilla extract

Chocolate Cake

Add gradually, creaming until fluffy after each addition

1⅓ cups firmly packed brown sugar

Add in thirds, beating thoroughly after each addition

2 eggs, well beaten

Mix and set aside

1 cup milk
1 tablespoon vinegar or lemon juice

Blend melted chocolate into batter. Alternately add dry ingredients in fourths and liquid in thirds to creamed mixture. After each addition, beat only until smooth. Finally, beat only until batter is smooth (do not overbeat). Turn batter into pans.

Bake at 375°F 25 min., or until cake tests done (page 11).

Cool and remove from pans as directed (page 11).

When cake is cool, prepare
Chocolate Butter Frosting II (page 478)
Frost sides and top of cake. Arrange around sides of cake
½ cup (1¾ oz.) walnut halves
One 8-in. round layer cake

FAVORITE CHOCOLATE CAKE

Prepare (page 10) two 9-in. round layer cake pans.

Melt (page 10) and set aside to cool
3 oz. (3 sq.) unsweetened chocolate

Sift together and set aside
2½ cups sifted cake flour
1 teaspoon baking soda
¾ teaspoon salt

Cream together
¾ cup lard
2 teaspoons vanilla extract

Add gradually, creaming until fluffy after each addition
2 cups sugar

Beat until thick and lemon-colored
5 egg yolks

Add egg yolks to creamed mixture in thirds, beating thoroughly after each addition. Blend in melted chocolate.

Measure
1 cup sour milk (page 9)

Alternately add dry ingredients in fourths and sour milk in thirds to creamed mixture. After each addition, beat only until smooth. Finally, beat only until batter is smooth (do not overbeat).

Beat until stiff, not dry, peaks are formed
5 egg whites

Fold egg whites into batter. Turn batter into pans.

Bake at 375°F 30 to 35 min., or until cake tests done (page 11).

Cool and remove from pans as directed (page 11).   *Two 9-in. round layers*

BLENDER CHOCOLATE CAKE

▲ Base Recipe

Prepare (page 10) two 8-in. round layer cake pans. An electric blender will be needed; see manufacturer's directions.

Melt (page 10) and set aside to cool
2 oz. (2 sq.) unsweetened chocolate

Sift together into a bowl and set aside
2 cups sifted cake flour
1 tablespoon baking powder
½ teaspoon salt

Put into blender container
2 eggs, unbeaten

Cover and blend a few seconds. Turn off motor and add in order
½ cup vegetable shortening or all-purpose shortening
1¼ cups sugar
1½ teaspoons vanilla extract
1 cup milk

Add melted chocolate, cover and blend 2 min. Scrape down sides of container and blend few seconds longer.

Add gradually, stirring after each addition, two thirds of blended mixture to sifted dry ingredients. Stir until well blended (total strokes, about 100). Add remaining blended mixture all at one time; mix until smooth. Turn into cake pans.

Bake at 350°F about 25 min., or until cake tests done (page 11).

Cool and frost as directed (page 11).
Two 8-in. round layers

—CHOCOLATE CUPCAKES

Follow ▲ Recipe; use eighteen to twenty 2½-in. muffin pan wells instead of 8-in. round

layer cake pans. Line with paper baking cups or grease bottoms of wells. Fill each one-half full. Bake at 400°F 18 to 20 min., or until cakes test done. Cool and frost as suggested in ▲ Recipe.

Or, cool cakes slightly in pans on cooling rack; top with **Broiler Nut Frosting** (below). Place muffin pans under broiler with tops of cakes about 4 in. from heat. Broil 2 to 3 min., or until topping bubbles. (Watch closely.)
18 to 20 cupcakes

For Broiler Nut Frosting—Mix **1 cup firmly packed brown sugar, 3 tablespoons butter or margarine**, melted, and 1 tablespoon **cream** or **undiluted evaporated milk**. Spread lightly on tops of warm cakes; sprinkle with **½ cup (about 2 oz.) coarsely chopped nuts.**

FEATHERLIGHT CHOCOLATE CAKE

Prepare (page 10) two 9-in. round layer cake pans.

Combine and stir until chocolate is melted
1½ oz. (1½ sq.) unsweetened chocolate
½ cup boiling water
Set aside to cool.

Sift together
2¼ cups sifted cake flour
1 teaspoon baking powder
1 teaspoon baking soda
¼ teaspoon salt
Set aside.

Cream until softened
½ cup butter or margarine
1 teaspoon vanilla extract

Favorite Chocolate Cake

Add gradually, creaming until fluffy after each addition

2 cups firmly packed light brown sugar

Add in thirds, beating thoroughly after each addition

2 eggs, well beaten

Stir in cooled chocolate mixture.

Measure

½ cup buttermilk

Beating only until smooth after each addition, alternately add dry ingredients in thirds and buttermilk in halves to creamed mixture. Finally, beat only until smooth (do not overbeat). Blend in with final few strokes

1 teaspoon red food coloring

Turn batter into pans.

Bake at 350°F 30 to 35 min., or until cake tests done (page 11).

Cool; remove from pans as directed (page 11).

Fill and frost as desired (page 11).

Two 9-in. round cake layers

CREOLE CHOCOLATE CAKE

Spread the chocolate layers with creamy vanilla filling and swirl chocolate frosting around and over the cake—a chocolate temptation!

Prepare (page 10) three 9-in. round layer cake pans. Set out double boiler.

Prepare (page 10)

1½ cups quick coffee beverage

Combine in top of double boiler coffee beverage and

6 oz. (6 sq.) unsweetened chocolate, grated

Cook over simmering water, stirring constantly, until chocolate is melted and mixture thickens. Set aside to cool.

Sift together and set aside

4 cups sifted cake flour
1½ teaspoons baking soda
1 teaspoon baking powder
1 teaspoon salt

Cream until softened

1 cup butter or margarine
2½ teaspoons vanilla extract

Add gradually, creaming until fluffy after each addition

3 cups firmly packed brown sugar

Add in thirds, beating thoroughly after each addition

4 eggs, well beaten

Measure

⅔ cup sour milk (page 9)

Beating only until smooth after each addition, alternately add dry ingredients in fourths and milk in thirds to creamed mixture. Stir in chocolate mixture. Finally, beat only until batter is smooth (do not overbeat). Turn batter into pans.

Bake at 375°F 30 to 35 min., or until cake tests done (page 11).

Cool and remove from pans as directed (page 11).   *Three 9-in. round layers*

FLOWER GARDEN CHOCOLATE CAKE

Bring an air of spring to your table with this festive flower cake!

Prepare (page 10) 13x9x2-in. cake pan.

Combine in top of double boiler and heat over simmering water until milk is scalded (page 10) and chocolate is melted

⅔ cup milk
4 oz. (4 sq.) unsweetened chocolate

Stir until well blended.

Vigorously stir about 3 tablespoons hot mixture into

1 egg yolk, slightly beaten

Immediately blend into mixture in double boiler. Cook 2 to 3 min., stirring constantly. Add and stir until dissolved

1 cup minus 2 tablespoons sugar

Cook over simmering water, stirring constantly, about 5 min. Remove from simmering water and set aside to cool.

Sift together

2⅔ cups sifted cake flour
1 tablespoon baking powder
½ teaspoon baking soda
½ teaspoon salt

Set aside.

Cream until softened

⅔ cup butter
⅓ cup almond paste
2 teaspoons vanilla extract
Few drops red food coloring

Add gradually, creaming until fluffy after each addition

¾ cup firmly packed brown sugar

Add in thirds, beating thoroughly after each addition

4 egg yolks, well beaten

Blend in the chocolate mixture and set aside.

Mix

⅓ cup water
3 tablespoons milk

Alternately add dry ingredients in thirds and liquid in halves to creamed mixture. After each addition, beat only until smooth. Finally, beat only until batter is smooth (do not overbeat).

Beat until frothy

3 egg whites

Add gradually, beating well after each addition

⅓ cup sugar

Beat until stiff peaks are formed. Spread beaten egg whites over blended batter and fold together. Turn batter into pan.

Bake at 375°F 35 to 40 min., or until cake tests done (page 11).

Cool and remove from pan as directed (page 11).

Flower Garden Chocolate Cake

When cake is cooled, prepare
  Seven-Minute Frosting (page 474)
Frost sides and top of cake. Spread evenly.

Mark cake into serving-size pieces, then sprinkle with colored sugar. Decorate with fresh garden flowers. Wrap stem of each flower with aluminum foil and place one blossom on each serving. Colored wooden picks or cocktail picks inserted to form "X's" on the top of outer edge of cake form a colorful border for Flower Garden Cake. *18 to 24 servings*

FABULOUS CHOCOLATE PARTY CAKE

Prepare (page 11) three 11x7x2-in. cake pans.

Combine in top of double boiler and heat over simmering water until milk is scalded (page 10) and chocolate is melted
  **1 cup milk
  7 oz. (7 sq.) unsweetened chocolate**
Stir until well blended.

Vigorously stir about 3 tablespoons hot mixture into
  2 egg yolks, slightly beaten
Immediately blend into mixture in double boiler. Cook 2 to 3 min., stirring constantly. Add and stir until dissolved
  1¼ cups sugar
Cook over simmering water, stirring constantly, about 5 min. Remove from simmering water and set aside to cool.

Sift together and set aside
  **4 cups sifted cake flour
  1 tablespoon plus 1 teaspoon baking powder
  1 teaspoon salt
  ½ teaspoon baking soda**

Cream until softened
  **1 cup butter
  ⅔ cup almond paste
  1 tablespoon vanilla extract
  ¼ teaspoon red food coloring**
Add gradually, creaming until fluffy after each addition
  1¼ cups firmly packed brown sugar
Add in thirds, beating thoroughly after each addition
  4 egg yolks, well beaten
Stir in the cooled chocolate mixture.

Combine
  **½ cup water
  ¼ cup milk**
Alternately add dry ingredients in fourths and liquid in thirds, to creamed mixture. After each addition, beat only until smooth; do not overbeat.

Beat until frothy
  4 egg whites
Add gradually, beating well after each addition
  ½ cup sugar

Beat until very stiff peaks are formed. Fold beaten egg whites into batter. Turn batter into pans.

Bake at 375°F 20 to 25 min., or until cake tests done (page 11).

Cool and remove from pans as directed (page 11).

While cake is cooling, prepare
  Mocha Butter Cream Frosting (page 474)
Frost (page 11) cake.

Prepare
  Sweetened Whipped Cream (page 480)
Spoon whipped cream into pastry bag having a No. 3 star tube. Force through tube to decorate top and sides of cake.

If desired, garnish with
  **Finely chopped nuts
  Maraschino cherries**
Serve immediately or store in refrigerator until serving time. *36 servings*

THREE-LAYER CHOCOLATE CAKE

Prepare (page 10) three 9-in. round layer cake pans.

Combine in top of double boiler
  **6 oz. (6 sq.) unsweetened chocolate
  1½ cups boiling water**
Cook over simmering water, stirring constantly, until chocolate is melted and mixture thickens. Set aside to cool.

Sift together and set aside
  **4 cups sifted cake flour
  1½ teaspoons baking soda
  1 teaspoon baking powder
  1 teaspoon salt**

Beat together
  **1 cup vegetable shortening or all-purpose shortening
  2½ teaspoons vanilla extract**
Add gradually, creaming until fluffy after each addition
  3 cups sugar
Add in thirds, beating thoroughly after each addition
  4 eggs, well beaten
Measure
  ⅔ cup sour milk (page 9)
Alternately add dry ingredients in fourths and sour milk in thirds to creamed mixture. After each addition, beat only until smooth. Stir in chocolate mixture. Finally, beat only until batter is smooth (do not overbeat). Turn batter into pans.

Bake at 350°F 30 to 35 min., or until cake tests done (page 11).

Cool and remove from pans as directed (page 11).

When cake is cool, prepare
  Seven-Minute Chocolate Frosting (one and one half times recipe, page 474)
Fill and frost (page 11).

One 9-in. 3-layer cake

Three-Layer Chocolate Cake

TOPSY-TURVY CHOCOLATE CAKE

▲ *Base Recipe*

Set out an 8-in. square cake pan.

Thaw, drain thoroughly and set aside
  2 pkgs. (12 oz. each) frozen sliced peaches (about 2 cups, drained)

Melt (page 10) and set aside to cool
  2 oz. (2 sq.) unsweetened chocolate

Meanwhile, melt in the baking pan
  ¼ cup butter or margarine
Sprinkle over the butter
  ½ cup firmly packed brown sugar
Arrange the sliced peaches evenly over the sugar. Set pan aside.

Sift together into a large bowl
  **1 cup sifted cake flour
  ¾ cup sugar
  1 teaspoon baking powder
  ¼ teaspoon salt**
Add to sifted dry ingredients
  ½ cup butter or margarine, softened
Set aside.

Combine and beat with rotary beater to blend
  **1 egg, well beaten
  ⅓ cup milk
  1 teaspoon vanilla extract**
Add the milk mixture to flour mixture. Blend; beat vigorously about 200 strokes, or beat with electric mixer on medium speed for 2 min. Scrape sides of bowl occasionally. Add the chocolate. Beat as above 100 strokes or for 1 min. Turn batter into pan over the peaches.

Bake at 350°F 45 to 50 min., or until cake tests done (page 11). Immediately loosen cake from sides of pan. Invert on serving plate. Let pan rest over cake a few seconds so syrup will drain on cake; lift off pan. Serve warm. Garnish with **Sweetened Whipped Cream** (page 480).

One 8-in. square cake

—TOPSY-TURVY PECAN CAKE

Follow ▲ Recipe. Substitute 1½ cups (about 5½ oz.) **pecan halves** for the peaches.

Sour Cream Chocolate Cake

SOUR CREAM CHOCOLATE CAKE

▲ *Base Recipe*

Prepare (page 10) two 8-in. round layer cake pans or one 9x9x2-in. pan.

Combine and heat until chocolate is melted (page 10)

3 oz. (3 sq.) unsweetened chocolate
½ cup double-strength coffee beverage (page 10)

Blend thoroughly. Set aside to cool.

Sift together and set aside

2 cups sifted cake flour
1 teaspoon baking soda
½ teaspoon salt

Mix

1½ cups sugar
1 cup dairy sour cream
2½ teaspoons vanilla extract

Add in thirds, beating thoroughly after each addition

2 eggs, well beaten

Add chocolate mixture and mix well. Beating only until smooth after each addition, add dry ingredients in fourths to sour cream mixture. Finally, beat only until smooth (do not overbeat). Turn batter into pans.

Bake at 350°F 35 min., or until cake tests done (page 11).

Cool; remove from pans as directed (page 11).

Meanwhile, prepare
Sour Cream Chocolate Frosting (page 479)

Chocolate Potato Cake

Frost (page 11) cake. Garnish (see photo) with
Walnut halves

> *One 8-in. round layer cake or one 9-in. square cake*

—BLACK WALNUT CHOCOLATE CAKE

Follow ▲ Recipe. Stir in ⅔ cup (about 2 oz.) **chopped black walnuts** with final strokes.

VELVET COLA CAKE

Prepare (page 10) two 8-in. round layer cake pans.

Melt (page 10) and set aside to cool
2 oz. (2 sq.) unsweetened chocolate

Sift together and set aside
1¾ cups sifted cake flour
1 teaspoon salt
1 teaspoon baking powder
½ teaspoon baking soda

Cream until softened
½ cup butter
Add gradually, creaming well after each addition
1¼ cups sugar
Add in thirds, beating thoroughly after each addition
2 eggs, well beaten
Blend in the cooled chocolate.
Measure
1 cup carbonated cola beverage
Beating only until smooth after each addition, alternately add dry ingredients in thirds and liquid in halves to creamed mixture. Finally, beat only until smooth (do not overbeat). Turn batter into prepared cake pans.

Bake at 350°F 30 min., or until cake tests done (page 11).

Cool and remove from pans as directed for butter-type cakes (page 11).

Frost with **Cola Butter Frosting** (below).

> *Two 8-in. round layers*

Cola Butter Frosting—Cream **¼ cup butter** until softened. Gradually add **2 cups confectioners' sugar**, beating well after each addition. Stir in **1 tablespoon carbonated cola beverage**. Beat until of spreading consistency.

CHOCOLATE POTATO CAKE

Prepare (page 10) two 9-in. round layer cake pans.

Wash, pare and cook, covered, in boiling, salted water to cover
2 medium (about ⅔ lb.) potatoes
Cook 20 to 30 min., or until tender.

Melt (page 10) and set aside to cool
1 oz. (1 sq.) unsweetened chocolate

Sift together and set aside
2 cups sifted cake flour
2 teaspoons baking powder
½ teaspoon salt

Drain potatoes and shake pan over low heat to dry thoroughly. Force hot cooked potatoes through ricer or sieve. Packing lightly, measure
1 cup sieved potatoes
Set aside to cool.

Beat together
1 cup vegetable shortening or all-purpose shortening
2 teaspoons grated lemon peel

Add gradually, creaming until fluffy after each addition
2 cups sugar
Add in thirds, beating thoroughly after each addition
4 eggs, well beaten
Stir in the cooled chocolate.

Blend potatoes with
½ cup milk
Alternately add dry ingredients in thirds and potato mixture in halves to creamed mixture. After each addition, beat only until smooth. Finally, beat only until batter is smooth (do not overbeat). Turn batter into pans.

Bake at 350°F 40 to 45 min., or until cake tests done (page 11).

Cool and remove from pans as directed (page 11). *Two 9-in. round layers*

Note: Grated raw potatoes may be substituted for the cooked ones; grate them just after adding the eggs to the creamed mixture.

DEVIL'S FOOD CAKE

▲ *Base Recipe*

Its rich, red color makes this definitely devil's food, not chocolate cake.

Prepare (page 10) two 8-in. round layer cake pans.

Melt (page 10) and set aside to cool
3 oz. (3 sq.) unsweetened chocolate

Sift together and set aside
2 cups sifted cake flour
1 teaspoon baking soda
½ teaspoon salt

Cream until softened
½ cup butter
1½ teaspoons vanilla extract
Add gradually, creaming until fluffy after each addition
1½ cups sugar or firmly packed light brown sugar
Add in thirds, beating thoroughly after each addition
2 eggs, well beaten
Stir in cooled chocolate.

Measure
1 cup milk
Beating only until smooth after each addition, alternately add dry ingredients in thirds and milk in halves to creamed mixture. Finally, beat

only until smooth (do not overbeat). Blend in with few final strokes

½ teaspoon red food coloring

Turn batter into pans.

Bake at 350°F 30 to 35 min., or until cake tests done (page 11).

Cool and remove from pans as directed for butter-type cakes (page 11).

Two 8-in. round layers

Note: Red food coloring or an excess of baking soda will produce a red color. The excess soda also imparts a distinctive flavor.

—DEVIL'S FOOD CUPCAKES

Follow ▲ Recipe. Use 2 doz. 2½-in. muffin-pan wells lined with paper baking cups, or with bottoms greased. Fill each about two-thirds full. Bake at 350°F about 20 min.

—DEVIL-MINT CAKE

Follow ▲ Recipe. Fill and frost cake (page 11) with **Peppermint Butter Frosting** (page 480). Sprinkle crushed **peppermint-stick candy** over top of cake.

SPICED DEVIL'S FOOD CAKE

Prepare (page 10) two 9-in. round layer cake pans.

Combine and stir until chocolate is melted

1½ oz. (1½ sq.) unsweetened chocolate
½ cup boiling water

Set aside to cool.

Sift together and set aside

2¼ cups sifted cake flour
1 teaspoon baking powder
1 teaspoon baking soda
½ teaspoon salt
1 teaspoon cinnamon
½ teaspoon allspice
¼ teaspoon cloves

Cream until softened

½ cup butter
1 teaspoon vanilla extract

Add gradually, creaming until fluffy after each addition

2 cups firmly packed light brown sugar

Add in thirds, beating thoroughly after each addition

2 eggs, well beaten

Stir in cooled chocolate mixture.

Measure

½ cup buttermilk or sour milk (page 9)

Beating only until smooth after each addition, alternately add dry ingredients in thirds and buttermilk in halves to creamed mixture. Finally, beat only until batter is smooth (do not overbeat). Turn batter into prepared pans.

Bake at 375°F 30 to 35 minutes, or until cake tests done (page 11).

Cool; remove from pans as directed (page 11).

Fill and frost (page 11) as desired.

Two 9-in. round layers

FUDGE CAKE

Prepare (page 10) two 8-in. round layer cake pans.

Combine in top of double boiler

3 oz. (3 sq.) unsweetened chocolate, grated
¾ cup boiling water

Cook over simmering water, stirring constantly, until chocolate is melted and mixture thickens. Set aside to cool.

Sift together and set aside

2 cups sifted cake flour
¾ teaspoon baking soda
½ teaspoon baking powder
½ teaspoon salt

Cream until softened

½ cup lard
1½ teaspoons vanilla extract
1 teaspoon rum extract

Add gradually, creaming until fluffy after each addition

1½ cups sugar

Add in thirds, beating thoroughly after each addition

2 eggs, well beaten

Add and stir in the cool chocolate mixture.

Measure

⅓ cup buttermilk or sour milk

Beating only until smooth after each addition, alternately add dry ingredients in thirds and liquid in halves to creamed mixture. Finally, beat only until smooth (do not overbeat). Turn batter into pans.

Bake at 350°F 25 to 30 min., or until cake tests done (page 11).

Cool and remove from pans as directed for butter-type cakes (page 11).

Two 8-in. round layers

SOUR CREAM FUDGE CAKE
(Quick Method)

You just can't get this special richness without sour cream. It's the easy one-bowl method.

Prepare (page 10) two 8-in. round layer cake pans.

Combine and stir until well blended and thick

3 oz. (3 sq.) unsweetened chocolate, melted (page 10)
¼ cup boiling water

Set aside to cool.

Sift together into a large bowl

2 cups sifted cake flour
1¼ cups sugar
1 teaspoon baking powder
½ teaspoon baking soda
½ teaspoon salt

Add to dry ingredients

1 cup dairy sour cream
⅓ cup vegetable shortening or all-purpose shortening

Stir only enough to moisten. Beat 200 strokes by hand or 2 min. on electric mixer at medium speed. Scrape sides of bowl several times during beating. Add cooled chocolate mixture and

2 eggs, unbeaten
1¼ teaspoons vanilla extract

Beat 200 strokes or 2 min. on electric mixer, scraping sides of bowl several times. Pour batter into pans.

Bake at 350°F about 30 min., or until cake tests done (page 11).

Cool and remove from pans as directed for butter-type cakes (page 11).

Two 8-in. round layers

QUICK HONEY FUDGE CAKE

Prepare (page 10) a 13x9x2-in. cake pan.

Melt (page 10) and set aside to cool

3 oz. (3 sq.) unsweetened chocolate

445

Coarsely chop and set aside
¾ cup (about 3 oz.) nuts

Sift together into large bowl
2 cups sifted cake flour
1 teaspoon baking soda
½ teaspoon salt
Add to sifted dry ingredients
¾ cup firmly packed brown sugar
½ cup vegetable shortening or
all-purpose shortening

Combine and beat with rotary beater to blend
1 cup milk
¾ cup honey
2 teaspoons vanilla extract
Add one half of the milk mixture to flour mixture. Beat vigorously about 200 strokes, or beat with electric mixer on medium speed for 2 min. Scrape sides of bowl occasionally. Add the cooled chocolate, remaining milk mixture and

2 eggs, unbeaten
Beat as above with about 200 strokes or for 2 min. Stir in the chopped nuts. Pour batter into prepared pan.

Bake at 375°F about 30 min., or until cake tests done (page 11).

Cool and remove from pan as directed (page 11).   *One 13 x 9-in. cake*

WELLESLEY FUDGE CAKE

This is the luscious dark fudge cake which became famous in the favorite village haunt of Wellesley undergraduates.

Prepare (page 10) two 8x8x2-in. cake pans.

Combine and set over simmering water
4 oz. (4 sq.) unsweetened chocolate
½ cup hot water
When chocolate is melted, blend thoroughly. Add and stir until dissolved
½ cup sugar
Set aside to cool.

Meanwhile, sift together and set aside
2 cups sifted cake flour
1½ teaspoons baking powder
½ teaspoon baking soda
½ teaspoon salt

Cream until softened
½ cup butter
2 teaspoons vanilla extract
Add gradually, creaming until fluffy after each addition
1¼ cups sugar
Add in thirds, beating thoroughly after each addition
4 eggs, well beaten

Mix in the cooled chocolate mixture.

Measure
⅔ cup milk
Beating only until smooth after each addition, alternately add dry ingredients in thirds and milk in halves to creamed mixture. Finally, beat only until smooth (do not overbeat). Turn batter into prepared pans.

Bake at 350°F 25 to 30 min., or until cake tests done (page 11).

Cool; remove from pans as directed (page 11).

Meanwhile, prepare
Fudge Frosting (page 475)
Fill and frost (page 11) cake.
                One 8-in. square layer cake

COCOA CAKE

▲ *Base Recipe*

Prepare (page 10) two 8-in. round layer cake pans.

Sift together and set aside
2 cups sifted cake flour
⅔ cup cocoa
1 teaspoon instant powdered coffee
1 teaspoon baking powder
½ teaspoon baking soda
½ teaspoon salt

Cream until softened
½ cup butter or margarine
1 teaspoon vanilla extract
Add gradually, creaming until fluffy after each addition
1⅓ cups sugar
Add in thirds, beating thoroughly after each addition
2 eggs, well beaten
Measure
1 cup buttermilk or sour milk
Beating only until smooth after each addition, alternately add dry ingredients in fourths and liquid in thirds to creamed mixture. Finally, beat only until smooth (do not overbeat). Turn batter into pans.

Bake at 350°F 25 to 30 min., or until cake tests done (page 11).

Cool and remove from pans as directed for butter-type cakes (page 11).
                Two 8-in. round layers

—DUTCH-COCOA CAKE

Follow ▲ Recipe. Substitute ⅔ **cup Dutch process cocoa** for the cocoa in the recipe and omit the coffee.

PARTY COCOA CAKE

▲ *Base Recipe*

Prepare (page 10) two 9-in. round or two 8-in. square cake pans.

Mix in a saucepan
¾ cup firmly packed brown sugar
¾ cup cocoa
½ cup hot water
Bring to boiling and then cook slowly for 3 min., or until mixture is slightly thickened; stir constantly. Set aside to cool.

Sift together
2 cups sifted cake flour
1½ teaspoons baking powder
½ teaspoon baking soda
½ teaspoon salt
Set aside.

Beat together
⅔ cup shortening
1½ teaspoons vanilla extract
Add gradually, creaming until fluffy after each addition
1 cup sugar
Add in thirds, beating thoroughly after each addition
3 eggs, well beaten
Stir in cooled cocoa mixture.

Measure
¾ cup milk
Alternately add dry ingredients in thirds and milk in halves to creamed mixture. After each addition, beat only until smooth. Finally, beat only until batter is smooth (do not overbeat). Turn batter into pans.

Bake at 375°F 25 to 30 min., or until cake tests done (page 11).

Cool and remove from pans as directed (page 11).

When cake is cooled, prepare
Bittersweet Velvet Frosting (page 479)
Using one half of frosting, spread over top of one cake layer.

Cut (page 9) into halves
32 (about ½ lb.) marshmallows
Press marshmallows into frosting on cake. Top with second cake layer.

Cut into eighths and blend into remaining frosting
8 marshmallows

Party Cocoa Cake

Spread frosting over top of second cake layer. Garnish cake corners with

2 marshmallows, cut in halves

Two 9-in. round or 8-in. square layers

—PARTY MOCHA CAKE

Follow ▲ Recipe. Substitute **½ cup double-strength hot coffee beverage** (page 10) for the hot water.

QUICK COCOA CAKE

This ring of light-as-a-sunbeam chocolate cake around servings of ice cream is easy to create and always exciting.

Grease bottom of 2-qt. ring mold or prepare (page 10) 8-in. square cake pan.

Sift together into a large bowl

1⅓ cups sifted cake flour
1 cup sugar
½ cup cocoa
1 teaspoon baking powder
½ teaspoon baking soda
¼ teaspoon salt

Add to sifted dry ingredients

6 tablespoons vegetable shortening or all-purpose shortening

Beat with rotary beater to blend and add to flour mixture

2 eggs, well beaten
¼ cup milk
1½ teaspoons vanilla extract

Quick Cocoa Cake

Blend; beat vigorously about 200 strokes, or beat with electric mixer on medium speed for 2 min. Scrape sides and bottom of bowl occasionally.

Blend and add to batter

½ cup milk
2 teaspoons vinegar

Beat as above about 100 strokes or for 1 min. Pour batter into mold or pan.

Bake at 350°F about 30 min. for ring and 35 min. for square or until cake tests done (page 11).

Cool and remove from mold or pan as directed (page 11).   *One ring-shape cake or one 8-in. square cake*

MELTAWAY WHIPPED CREAM CAKE

Prepare (page 10) two 9-in. round layer cake pans. Set a bowl and rotary beater in refrigerator.

Sift together and set aside

2 cups sifted cake flour
1½ cups sugar
½ cup cocoa
1 tablespoon baking powder
½ teaspoon salt

Using the chilled bowl and beater, beat until cream stands in peaks when beater is slowly lifted upright

1 cup chliled heavy cream

Beat until stiff, not dry, peaks are formed

3 egg whites

Gently but thoroughly fold together whipped cream and beaten egg whites. Sift over this mixture the dry ingredients in fourths, alternately folding in with a mixture of

½ cup milk
2 teaspoons vanilla extract

Turn into pans.

Bake at 350°F 25 to 30 min., or until cake tests done (page 11).

Cool and remove from pans as directed (page 11).   *Two 9-in. round layers*

COCOA-MALLOW CAKE

Prepare (page 10) two 9-in. round layer cake pans.

Combine in top of double boiler

20 (about ⅓ lb.) marshmallows, cut in quarters (page 9)
⅔ cup cocoa
½ cup hot water

Set over boiling water and heat until marshmallows are melted, stirring constantly. Set aside to cool.

Sift together

2 cups sifted cake flour
1 teaspoon baking powder
1 teaspoon salt
½ teaspoon baking soda

Set aside.

Cream until softened

⅔ cup shortening
2 teaspoons vanilla extract

Add gradually, creaming until fluffy after each addition

1 cup sugar

Add in thirds, beating thoroughly after each addition

3 eggs, well beaten

Stir in cooled cocoa mixture.

Measure

¾ cup dairy sour cream

Beating only until smooth after each addition, alternately add dry ingredients in thirds and sour cream in halves to creamed mixture. Finally, beat only until smooth (do not overbeat). Turn batter into pans.

Bake at 350°F 30 to 35 min., or until cake tests done (page 11).

Cool, remove from pans as directed (page 11).

Fill and frost (page 11) as desired.
Two 9-in. round layers

CHOCOLATE APPLESAUCE CAKE

Set out 10-in. tubed pan having removable bottom.

Coarsely chop and set aside

¾ cup (about 3 oz.) nuts

Sift together and set aside

3 cups sifted cake flour
¾ cup cocoa
1 tablespoon baking powder
½ teaspoon baking soda
¾ teaspoon salt
1½ teaspoons cinnamon
¾ teaspoon nutmeg
½ teaspoon cloves

Beat together

½ cup vegetable shortening or all-purpose shortening
½ cup butter

Add gradually, creaming until fluffy after each addition

1½ cups sugar

Add in thirds, beating thoroughly after each addition

2 eggs, well beaten

Combine and blend thoroughly

1 cup thick sweetened applesauce
¾ cup sour milk (page 9)

Alternately add dry ingredients in fourths and applesauce-sour milk mixture in thirds to creamed mixture. After each addition, beat only until smooth. Finally, beat only until batter is smooth (do not overbeat). Stir in the chopped nuts. Turn batter into pan.

Bake at 350°F about 1 hr., or until cake tests done (page 11).

Remove cake from oven and place on cooling rack. Allow cake to cool in pan 15 min. Remove tubed section of pan and the cake from the sides of the pan and place on cooling rack. When cake is cooled, with paring knife cut around tube to loosen cake. Loosen cake from bottom. Gently remove cake.

One 10-in. tubed cake

CHOCOLATE BUTTERMILK CAKE

Prepare (page 10) two 8-in. round layer cake pans.

Mix in a saucepan

½ cup cocoa
½ cup sugar

Add gradually, blending until smooth

½ cup double-strength coffee beverage (page 10)

Bring to boiling. Boil 1 min., stirring constantly. Set aside to cool.

Sift together and set aside

2 cups sifted cake flour
1 teaspoon baking soda
½ teaspoon salt

Cream until softened

½ cup butter or margarine
1 teaspoon vanilla extract

Add gradually, creaming until fluffy after each addition

1 cup sugar

Add in thirds, beating thoroughly after each addition

2 eggs, well beaten

Blend in cooled cocoa mixture.

Measure

⅔ cup buttermilk

Beating only until smooth after each addition, alternately add dry ingredients in thirds and buttermilk in halves to creamed mixture. Finally, beat only until smooth (do not overbeat). Turn batter into pans.

Bake at 350°F 30 to 40 min., or until cake tests done (page 11).

Cool; remove from pans as directed (page 11).

Fill and frost (page 11) as desired.

Two 8-in. round layers

DOUBLE-QUICK CHOCOLATE PRUNE CAKE

Prepare (page 10) two 8-in. round layer cake pans.

Remove pits, cut into small pieces and set aside

1 lb. uncooked dried prunes

Sift together into a bowl

2 cups minus 2 tablespoons sifted all-purpose flour
1 cup plus 2 tablespoons sugar
½ cup cocoa
1 tablespoon baking powder
½ teaspoon baking soda
¾ teaspoon nutmeg
¾ teaspoon allspice
½ teaspoon cinnamon

Add to sifted dry ingredients and set aside

½ cup vegetable shortening or all-purpose shortening

Combine and beat with rotary beater to blend

3 eggs, well beaten
¾ cup milk
1½ teaspoons vanilla extract

Add one half of the milk mixture to flour mixture. Blend; beat vigorously about 200 strokes, or beat with electric mixer on medium speed for 2 min. Scrape sides of bowl occasionally. Add remaining milk mixture and beat as above 100 strokes or for 1 min. Stir in the prunes. Turn batter into pans.

Bake at 375°F 30 to 35 min., or until cake tests done (page 11).

Cool; remove from pans as directed (page 11).

Serve hot or cold, topped with **Sweetened Whipped Cream** (page 481) or any desired sauce. *Two 8-in. round layers*

SEMISWEET CHOCOLATE CAKE

Prepare (page 10) two 9-in. round layer cake pans.

Melt (page 10) and set aside to cool

9 oz. semisweet chocolate

Sift together and set aside

2¾ cups sifted cake flour
1 tablespoon baking powder
½ teaspoon baking soda
½ teaspoon salt

Cream until softened

1 cup butter or margarine
1 teaspoon vanilla extract

Add gradually, creaming until fluffy after each addition

1 cup sugar

Add in thirds, beating thoroughly after each addition

4 eggs, well beaten

Stir in cooled chocolate.

Measure

⅔ cup water

Alternately add dry ingredients in thirds and water in halves to creamed mixture. After each addition, beat only until smooth. Finally, beat only until batter is smooth (do not overbeat). Turn batter into pans.

Bake at 350°F 30 to 35 min., or until cake tests done (page 11).

Cool and remove from pans as directed (page 11).

Frost with **Mocha Cocoa Frosting** (page 479).

Two 9-in. round layers

GRANDMOTHER'S SWEET CHOCOLATE CAKE

Prepare (page 10) two 8-in. round layer cake pans.

Combine and melt (page 10)

3 oz. sweet chocolate
½ cup boiling water

Blend thoroughly. Set aside to cool.

Sift together and set aside

2 cups sifted cake flour
1 teaspoon baking soda
½ teaspoon salt

Beat together

½ cup shortening
1 teaspoon vanilla extract

Add gradually, creaming until fluffy after each addition

1 cup sugar
½ cup firmly packed brown sugar

Add in thirds, beating thoroughly after each addition

2 eggs, well beaten

Cherry Fruitcak

Milk Chocolate Cake

Stir chocolate and blend in; mix well.

Measure
⅔ cup buttermilk
Alternately add dry ingredients in thirds and buttermilk in thirds to creamed mixture. After each addition, beat only until smooth. Finally, beat only until batter is smooth (do not overbeat). Turn batter into pans.

Bake at 375°F 25 to 30 min., or until cake tests done (page 11).

Cool and remove from pans as directed (page 11).   *Two 8-in. round layers*

MILK CHOCOLATE CAKE

Prepare (page 10) two 8-in. round layer cake pans.

Combine and stir until chocolate is melted
5 oz. milk chocolate, cut in small pieces
½ cup boiling water
Set aside to cool.

Sift together and set aside
2 cups sifted all-purpose flour
2 teaspoons baking powder
½ teaspoon salt
¼ teaspoon baking soda

Cream until softened
½ cup butter or margarine
1 teaspoon vanilla extract
Add gradually, creaming until fluffy after each addition
1 cup firmly packed brown sugar
Add in thirds, beating thoroughly after each addition
2 eggs, well beaten
Stir chocolate mixture and blend into creamed mixture.

Measure
½ cup sour milk or buttermilk (page 9)
Alternately add dry ingredients in thirds and liquid in halves to creamed mixture. After each addition, beat only until smooth. Finally, beat only until batter is smooth (do not overbeat). Turn batter into pans.

Bake at 375°F 25 to 30 min., or until cake tests done (page 11).

Cool and remove from pans as directed (page 11).   *Two 8-in. round layers*

Walnut Torte, Chocolate Eggnog Pie and
Chocolate Walnut Roll

YEAST CHOCOLATE CAKE

Mixed today and baked tomorrow, this chocolate yeast cake will win everyone's highest approval.

Have available for tomorrow's baking two 8-in. round layer cake pans.

Melt (page 10) and set aside to cool
2 oz. (2 sq.) unsweetened chocolate

Sift together and set aside
2 cups sifted cake flour
1 teaspoon salt

Put into a bowl
½ cup shortening
Add gradually, creaming until fluffy after each addition
1⅓ cups sugar
Add in thirds, beating thoroughly after each addition
2 eggs, well beaten
Set aside.

Soften
1 pkg. active dry yeast
in
¼ cup warm water, 105°F to 115°F
(Or if using compressed yeast, soften
1 cake in ¼ cup lukewarm water,
80°F to 85°F.)
Let stand about 5 min. Stir softened yeast and blend into creamed mixture with the cooled chocolate.

Measure
⅔ cup milk
Alternately add dry ingredients in thirds and milk in halves to creamed mixture. After each addition, beat only until blended. Finally, beat only until batter is smooth (do not overbeat). Cover bowl and place batter in refrigerator for at least 6 hrs. or overnight.

Remove batter from refrigerator and set aside.

Prepare (page 10) the two 8-in. round layer cake pans and set aside.

Mix until baking soda is dissolved
¾ teaspoon baking soda
2 tablespoons warm water
Immediately blend soda mixture into the batter with
1½ teaspoons vanilla extract
Turn batter into pans, spreading to edges.

Bake at 350°F 25 to 35 min., or until cake tests done (page 11).

Cool and remove from pans as directed (page 11).   *Two 8-in. round layers*

ELECTION DAY YEAST CAKE

About a century ago, Election Day in New England was a great event with its own food traditions. After a trip to the polls, large groups met to celebrate victory or defeat. These Election Day guests were served a rich yeast cake, which originated in Hartford. This was

Election Day Yeast Cake

always accompanied by punch or eggnog. The traditional supper menu might also include homemade sausages, fried green apples, hot biscuits and blueberry conserve.

Grease bottom only of a 9-in. tubed pan.

Scald (page 9) and cool to lukewarm
½ cup milk

Meanwhile, soften in a bowl
2 pkgs. active dry yeast
in
½ cup water, 108°F to 115°F (Or if
using compressed yeast, soften 2
cakes in ½ cup lukewarm water,
80°F to 85°F).
Set aside.

Add the lukewarm milk to softened yeast. Add gradually, beating well after each addition
1½ cups sifted all-purpose flour
Beat until mixture is smooth. Cover bowl with waxed paper and a clean towel and let rise in a warm place (80°F) until very light and bubbly, about 45 min.

Meanwhile, sift together and set aside
1¾ cups sifted all-purpose flour
1 teaspoon salt
1½ teaspoons cinnamon
½ teaspoon mace
½ teaspoon nutmeg
¼ teaspoon cloves

Chop and set aside
1 cup (3¾ oz.) pecans
3 oz. candied citron (about ½ cup,
chopped)

Cream until softened
½ cup butter
Add gradually, creaming until fluffy after each addition
¾ cup sugar

449

Add in thirds, beating thoroughly after each addition

3 eggs, well beaten

Blend in yeast mixture. Beating until smooth after each addition, gradually add dry ingredients. Add the pecans and citron and mix well. Turn mixture into prepared pan.

Cover with waxed paper and towel and let rise in a warm place away from drafts until pan is almost full, about 2 hrs.

Bake at 350°F 50 to 55 min. Remove from oven to cooling rack and cool 10 min. in pan.

Cut around tube with paring knife to loosen cake. Loosen sides with spatula; invert on cooling rack and lift off pan. Cool completely before slicing.   *One 9-in. tubed cake*

Light Fruitcake

FRUITCAKES

LIGHT FRUITCAKE

▲ *Base Recipe*

Prepare (page 10) two 8x4x2-in. loaf pans.

Bring to boiling

2 cups water

Add, and again bring to boiling

½ lb. (about 1½ cups) golden raisins

3 oz. chopped dried apricots (about ½ cup, chopped)

Pour off water and drain fruit on absorbent paper. Set aside.

Sliver and set aside

2 cups (about 11 oz.) toasted (page 10) almonds

Place in a large bowl

½ cup sifted all-purpose flour

Chop and combine with flour

9 oz. candied pineapple (about 1½ cups, chopped)

6 oz. red candied cherries (about 1 cup, chopped)

6 oz. green candied cherries (about 1 cup, chopped)

3 oz. candied citron (about ½ cup, chopped)

3 oz. candied orange peel (about ½ cup, chopped)

3 oz. candied lemon peel (about ½ cup, chopped)

3 oz. pitted dates (about ½ cup, chopped)

3 oz. dried figs (about ½ cup, chopped)

Add well-drained raisins and apricots, slivered almonds and

1½ cups flaked coconut

Set aside.

Sift together and set aside

1½ cups sifted all-purpose flour

1½ teaspoons baking powder

1 teaspoon salt

Cream until softened

1 cup butter

1 teaspoon lemon juice

Add gradually, creaming until fluffy after each addition

1 cup sugar

Add in thirds, beating thoroughly after each addition

5 eggs, well beaten

Beat vigorously about 150 strokes. Blend in dry ingredients alternately with

½ cup orange juice

Add dry ingredients in thirds and liquid in halves to creamed mixture, beating only until smooth after each addition. Finally, beat only until batter is smooth (do not overbeat). Pour batter over fruit and mix thoroughly.

Place a shallow pan containing 2 cups water on bottom rack of oven during baking time.

Turn batter into pans, spreading to edges.

Bake at 275°F 2 to 2½ hrs., or until cake tests done (page 11).

Cool cakes on cooling racks before removing from pans. Wrap tightly in waxed paper or aluminum foil and store in cool place to age for several weeks before serving. Once or twice a week, using a pastry brush, paint cake with rum and store again. Before serving, brush glaze lightly over cakes.

For Glaze—Combine in a saucepan

¼ cup light corn syrup

2 tablespoons water

1 tablespoon orange juice

Bring to boiling and boil for 1 min.

After brushing glaze over cake, sprinkle cake with

Grated toasted almonds

Decorate with candied cherries and candied citron; brush these with glaze. When glaze is dry, slice cake and serve.

About 6 lbs. fruitcake

—BITE-SIZE FRUITCAKES

Follow and prepare one-half ▲ Recipe. Brush about 6 doz. 1¼-in. paper soufflé cups with salad oil or melted shortening. Fill with about 1 tablespoon of batter. Decorate with bits of **red or green candied cherries.** Arrange, with space between cups, on baking sheet on which double thickness of wet paper toweling has been placed. Bake at 300°F about 30 min., or until cakes test done. Glaze before serving.

—MINIATURE FRUITCAKES

Follow ▲ Recipe. Brush about 4 doz. 2½-in. paper baking cups with **salad oil** or **melted shortening.** Fill two-thirds full of batter. Decorate tops of cakes with strips of **candied cherries, a whole candied cherry,** or **whole blanched** (page 9) **almonds.** Place cups in muffin-pan wells and bake as in ▲ Recipe. Bake at 300°F about 45 min., or until cakes test done. Glaze before serving.

DARK FRUITCAKE

Prepare (page 10) two 9x5x3-in. loaf pans.

Bring to boiling

2 cups water

Add and let stand 5 min.

½ lb. (about 1½ cups) dark seedless raisins

5 oz. (about 1 cup) currants

Drain fruit; dry on absorbent paper. Set aside.

Put into a large bowl

½ cup sifted all-purpose flour

Coarsely chop and put into the bowl

½ lb. pitted dates (about 1⅓ cups, chopped)

½ lb. walnuts (about 2 cups, chopped)

½ lb. pecans (about 2 cups, chopped)

¼ lb. candied citron (about ⅔ cup, chopped)

¼ lb. candied pineapple (about ⅔ cup, chopped)

2 oz. candied orange peel (about ⅓ cup, chopped)

2 oz. candied lemon peel (about ⅓ cup, chopped)

Add to the bowl the drained raisins and currants and

½ lb. candied cherries, sliced (about 1⅓ cups, sliced)

Mix until coated with flour; set aside.

Sift together and set aside

**2½ cups sifted all-purpose flour
1 teaspoon baking powder
¾ teaspoon salt
1 teaspoon cinnamon
¼ teaspoon nutmeg
¼ teaspoon allspice
⅛ teaspoon mace**

Cream until softened

1 cup butter or margarine

Add gradually, creaming until fluffy after each addition

**1 cup sugar
1 cup firmly packed brown sugar**

Add in thirds, beating thoroughly after each addition

4 eggs, well beaten

Blend in

½ cup grape jelly

Measure

½ cup grape juice

Beating only until smooth after each addition, alternately add dry ingredients in thirds and grape juice in halves to creamed mixture. Turn batter over fruit and nuts and mix thoroughly. Turn into pans, spreading to edges.

Place a shallow pan containing 2 cups water on bottom rack of oven during baking time.

Bake at 275°F 2 to 2½ hrs., or until cake tests done (page 11) with cake tester.

Cool completely, remove from pans, wrap and store (page 11).

Once or twice a week, unwrap cakes and paint them with **brandy, sherry, orange juice** or **grape juice,** using a pastry brush. Rewrap and store again. *About 6½ lbs. fruitcake*

CHERRY FRUITCAKE

Grease two 9x5x3-in. loaf pans; line with aluminum foil, allowing a 2-in. overhang; grease the foil.

Sift into a large mixing bowl

**1½ cups sifted all-purpose flour
1½ cups sugar
1 teaspoon baking powder
1 teaspoon salt**

Add to flour mixture and toss until coated

**2 pkgs. (7¼ oz. each) pitted dates
1 lb. diced candied pineapple
2 jars (16 oz. each) red maraschino cherries, drained
18 oz. (about 5½ cups) pecan halves**

Beat in a bowl until thick

6 eggs

Blend in

½ cup dark rum

Pour over fruit mixture and toss until thoroughly mixed. Turn into prepared loaf pans, pressing mixture with spatula to pack tightly.

Bake at 300°F about 1¾ hrs., or until wooden pick inserted in center of loaves comes out clean.

Remove from oven to cooling rack and allow to cool 15 min. before removing loaves from pans. Peel off foil and while still warm brush loaves with

½ cup light corn syrup

Cool thoroughly before serving or storing.

2 loaves fruitcake

PECAN DATE FRUITCAKE

▲ Base Recipe

This luscious, fruit and nut laden cake is so simple to bake! A cake of holiday cheer—at its best when servings are straight from the refrigerator.

Prepare (page 10) 9x5x3-in. loaf pan.

Sift together

**¾ cup sifted all-purpose flour
¾ cup sugar
½ teaspoon baking powder**

Grate (page 10)

1 oz. (1 sq.) unsweetened chocolate

Mix with dry ingredients and set aside.

Place in a large bowl

**3 cups (about ¾ lb.) salted pecan halves
2 cups (about 14 oz.) pitted dates
1 cup (about 8 oz.) maraschino cherries, well drained**

Add dry ingredients to mixture in bowl; mix lightly until fruit and nuts are well coated.

Beat until thick and piled softly

**3 eggs
1¼ teaspoons vanilla extract
¼ teaspoon almond extract
¼ teaspoon orange extract**

Blend beaten eggs into fruit-nut mixture until well mixed. Turn batter into pan and spread batter to corners.

Bake at 300°F 1 hr. and 45 min., or until cake tests done (page 11). Cool cake in pan on cooling rack 15 min. before removing from pan.

Wrap in aluminum foil or moisture-vaporproof material and store in refrigerator.

One 9x5-in. fruitcake

—HAZELNUT FRUITCAKE

Follow ▲ Recipe. Omit chocolate. Substitute **3 cups unblanched whole hazelnuts** for salted pecan halves.

REGAL FRUITCAKE

Lightly grease bottom of 9x5x3-in. loaf pan. Line bottom and sides with parchment paper cut to fit pan. Lightly grease paper.

Coarsely chop and set aside

2 cups (about 8 oz.) walnuts

Cut (page 9) into small pieces and set aside enough pitted dates to yield

1 cup (about 7 oz.) date pieces

Drain, slice and set aside on absorbent paper

1 cup (about 8 oz.) maraschino cherries

(A few pats with the paper will absorb the excess moisture from cherries.)

Sift together and set aside
1½ cups sifted all-purpose flour
1 teaspoon baking powder
½ teaspoon salt

Beat until thick and piled softly
3 eggs
Add gradually, beating well after each addition
¾ cup sugar
Thoroughly blend in fruits, nuts and
1 pkg. (6 oz.) semisweet chocolate pieces

Mixing only until blended after each addition, add dry ingredients in thirds to egg-fruit mixture. Finally, mix only until blended. Turn batter into pan, spreading to edges.

Place a shallow pan containing 2 cups water on bottom rack of oven during baking period.

Bake at 300°F 1 hr. 45 min., or until cake tests done (page 11).

Cool cake on cooling rack 10 min. before removing from pan. Run spatula gently around sides of pan. Cover with cooling rack. Invert. Turn right side up immediately after peeling off parchment paper.

Using a pastry brush, paint cake with **brandy** or **apple cider**. Cool thoroughly and wrap tightly in waxed paper, aluminum foil or moisture-vaporproof material. Store in cool place to age for 10 days before serving.
One 9x5-in. fruitcake

ELEGANT LOAF CAKE

Prepare (page 10) 9x5x3-in. loaf pan.

Coarsely chop and set aside
½ cup (about 2 oz.) walnuts

Chop very finely and set aside
1 cup (3¾ oz.) walnuts
¾ cup (6 oz.) candied cherries (page 9)
¼ cup (2 oz.) candied citron (page 9)

Sift together and set aside
2 cups sifted cake flour
2½ teaspoons baking powder
¾ teaspoon salt

Cream until softened
⅔ cup butter, margarine, vegetable shortening or all-purpose shortening
1 teaspoon almond extract
½ teaspoon vanilla extract
Add gradually, creaming until fluffy after each addition
½ cup sugar
Add in thirds, beating thoroughly after each addition
2 egg yolks, well beaten

Measure
⅔ cup milk
Alternately add dry ingredients in thirds and liquid in halves to creamed mixture. After each addition, beat only until smooth. Finally, beat only until batter is smooth. (Do not overbeat.) Stir in chopped cherries and citron with the 1 cup finely chopped nuts.

Beat until frothy
4 egg whites
Add gradually, beating well after each addition
¼ cup sugar
Beat until rounded peaks are formed. Gently fold beaten egg whites into batter. Turn batter into pan.

Bake at 350°F 1 hr. 10 min., or until cake tests done (page 11).

Cool and remove from pan as directed (page 11).

Prepare
Glossy Vanilla Icing (page 478)
Top cake with icing and decorate with the coarsely chopped nuts.   *One 9x5-in. loaf cake*

CHOCOLATE FRUITCAKE

An exciting, new, chocolate version of the always popular fruitcake.

Elegant Loaf Cake

Two 1½-qt. molds will be needed.

Mix in a bowl
½ lb. (about 1¼ cups) diced assorted candied fruits
½ lb. candied red cherries, cut in quarters (page 9); about 1¼ cups, quartered
5 oz. (about 1 cup) golden raisins
Pour over the fruit a mixture of
⅓ cup water
⅓ cup rum
Cover tightly and allow to stand 8 hrs. or overnight.

Thoroughly grease molds and set aside.

Coarsely chop and set aside
2¼ cups (about ¾ lb.) toasted salted almonds (pages 9 and 10)

Melt (page 10) and set aside to cool
4 oz. (4 sq.) unsweetened chocolate

Sift together and set aside
2 cups sifted all-purpose flour
1 teaspoon baking powder

Beat until thick and lemon-colored and set aside
6 egg yolks

Cream until softened
¾ cup butter
Add gradually, creaming until fluffy after each addition
1 cup sugar
Add the beaten egg yolks in thirds, beating thoroughly after each addition.

Stir melted chocolate into creamed mixture. Alternately add dry ingredients in fourths and fruit mixture in thirds to creamed mixture. After each addition, beat only until batter is blended. Finally, beat only until batter is well blended (do not overbeat). Then mix in the chopped nuts.

Beat until frothy
6 egg whites
Add gradually
½ cup sugar
Continue beating until rounded peaks are formed. Spread beaten egg whites over batter and gently fold together. Turn into prepared molds.

Bake at 250°F 2 hrs. to 2 hrs. 15 min., or until cake tests done (page 11). Cool com-

pletely on cooling rack before removing from pans. Wrap tightly in aluminum foil and store in cool place to age for several weeks before serving. Once or twice a week, using a pastry brush, paint cakes with **rum** and store again.

Two 2½-lb. fruitcakes

SPONGE AND ANGEL FOOD CAKES

SPONGE CAKE

▲ Base Recipe

The distinguishing characteristic of a true sponge cake is its leavening agent, which is air rather than baking powder. The true sponge cake contains no shortening.

Set out a 9-in. tubed pan.

Measure and set aside
   1 cup sifted cake flour

Combine and beat until very thick and lemon-colored
   5 egg yolks
   ½ cup sugar
   1 teaspoon grated lemon or orange peel
   2 tablespoons lemon or orange juice
   1 teaspoon vanilla extract
Set aside.

Using clean beater, beat until frothy
   5 egg whites
   ½ teaspoon salt
Add gradually, beating well after each addition
   ½ cup sugar
Beat until rounded peaks are formed and egg whites do not slide when bowl is partially inverted. Spread the egg yolk mixture over beaten egg whites and gently fold together. Sift about one fourth of the flour at a time over surface. Fold together gently after each addition. Turn batter into pan.

Bake at 325°F 60 to 65 min., or until cake surface springs back when lightly touched.

Cool and remove from pan as directed for sponge-type cakes (page 11).

One 9-in. tubed cake

—PINEAPPLE-FILLED SPONGE CAKE

Follow ▲ Recipe. Split cake into layers. Fill with a mixture of **Sweetened Whipped Cream** (page 480), **well-drained crushed pineapple** and **quartered marshmallows.** Spoon additional filling onto individual servings.

—ORANGE CREAM CAKE

Follow ▲ Recipe, using orange juice and orange peel. Substitute two 9-in. round layer cake pans for tubed pan and bake 30 to 35 min. While cake is cooling, prepare Orange Filling. Spread one half of filling over each layer. Place in refrigerator for at least 1 hr. (Filled

cake may stand in refrigerator overnight.) About 1 hr. before ready to serve, prepare **Sweetened Whipped Cream** (one and one-half times recipe, page 480). Spread one layer, filling side up, with about one third of whipped cream. Place second layer, filling side up, on top of cream. Cover sides and top with remaining whipped cream. Place in refrigerator until ready to serve.

For Orange Filling—Mix **¾ cup orange juice, ½ cup sugar** and **1 tablespoon grated orange peel**; set aside. Beat **2 egg whites** until frothy. Add **¼ cup sugar** gradually, beating well after each addition; beat until stiff, not dry, peaks are formed. Fold orange mixture into beaten egg whites.

BUTTER SPONGE CAKE
(Gâteau Génoise)

▲ Base Recipe

Butter bottom of a 15x10x1-in. pan. Line pan bottom with waxed paper cut to fit exactly; butter waxed paper.

Melt over hot water and set aside to cool
   3 tablespoons butter

Put into top of a 3-qt. double boiler
   5 eggs
   1 cup less 1 tablespoon sugar
Set over simmering water. Beat constantly until mixture is thick and piles softly (about 10 min. with electric mixer or 20 to 25 min. with hand rotary beater). Remove from heat and continue beating until mixture is cold.

Blend in
   ¼ teaspoon vanilla extract
   ⅛ teaspoon almond extract

Divide into four portions
   1¼ cups sifted cake flour
Sift one portion at a time over egg mixture and gently fold in until just blended. Gradually add melted butter, folding only until blended. Turn batter into pan; spread evenly.

Bake at 325°F about 25 min., or until cake springs back when lightly touched at center. Loosen edges with a spatula and remove immediately from pan. Carefully peel off paper. Cool on rack, top-side up.

For Three-Layer Cake—Line and butter, as for sheet cake, three 8-in. round layer cake pans. Bake layers at 325°F 30 to 35 min., or until cakes spring back when lightly touched at centers. Remove from oven to cooling racks; cool slightly. Loosen edges with spatula and remove from pans. Peel off paper immediately. When cake layers are completely cooled, fill and frost as desired.

—SMALL FANCY CAKES
(Petits Fours)

Follow ▲ Recipe; prepare sheet cake. (Will yield about 150 1-in. squares and rounds.)

When cool, trim cake edges and cut cake into tiny squares, diamonds, rounds or other fancy shapes. Use the shapes whole or split. Split shapes may be hollowed out and filled or spread with filling and gently pressed together. Fill with **Chantilly Cream** (page 481), **French Pastry Cream** (page 482) or **Almond Pastry Cream** (page 483). Remove any loose crumbs. Frost as directed in **Fondant Glaze** (page 610). Remove cakes with spatula and trim glaze from bottom edges with sharp knife. Decorate as desired with **chocolate shot, finely chopped nuts, coconut,** or **candied cherries.** Or force **Decorating Frosting** (page 478) through cake decorator or pastry tube to form flowers, leaves and borders (see page 473).

Tray of Assorted French Pastries—Guests and family are sure to welcome trays of assorted French pastries served at teatime, at parties or as a meal-time dessert. To tempt the eye before pleasing the palate, the pastries must be kept small and be arranged neatly and simply on the tray. A delightful assortment can be assembled from **Small Fancy Cakes, French Pastries, Napoleons** (page 453), **Eclairs** (page 517), **Cream Puffs** (page 517) or **Meringue Mushrooms** (page 526).

—FRENCH PASTRIES
(Petits Gâteaux)

Follow ▲ Recipe; prepare sheet cake. (Will yield 6 rectangles, 4 squares, 6 rounds, and 6 ovals or diamonds.) When cool, trim edges from cake and cut into pairs of 1¾x3-in. rectangles, 2-in. squares, 2¼-in. rounds, and 3-in. ovals or diamonds. Spread one half of shapes thinly with raspberry, strawberry, or apricot jam, and then with **Chocolate Butter Frosting** (page 476) or **Butter Cream Frosting** (page 476). Top with remaining shapes. Frost sides

Small Fancy Cakes

and tops with same frosting as in center. Cover sides of pastries with **flaked toasted almonds, ground pistachios** or **toasted nuts.** Decorate tops with **frosting swirls, chocolate curls, chocolate shot, candied cherries, flaked** or **chopped nuts.**

HOT-MILK SPONGE CAKE

▲ Base Recipe

You can do so much with extra-tender hot-milk sponge. Try it all these ways, or with sauce as a cottage pudding, or with ice cream.

Set out two 9-in. round layer cake pans.

Sift together and set aside
   1 cup sifted cake flour
   1 teaspoon baking powder
   ¼ teaspoon salt

Beat until very thick and piled softly
   3 eggs
Add gradually, beating well after each addition
   1 cup sugar
   2 or 3 teaspoons lemon juice
Heat thoroughly (do not boil) over low heat
   6 tablespoons milk
Sift dry ingredients over egg mixture about one fourth at a time; gently fold in until just blended after each addition. Add hot milk all at one time and quickly mix just until smooth. Pour batter into pans.

Bake at 375°F about 15 min., or until cake surface springs back when lightly touched.

Cool and remove from pans as directed for sponge-type cakes (page 11).
   Two 9-in. round layers

—WASHINGTON PIE

Follow ▲ Recipe. When ready to serve, spread **raspberry jam or jelly** over bottom layer; cover with second layer. Sift **¼ cup confectioners' sugar** over top of cake.

—BOSTON CREAM PIE

Follow ▲ Recipe. While cake is baking, prepare **Vanilla Cream Filling** (page 482). When thoroughly chilled, spread filling over bottom layer of cake. Cover with second layer. Sift ¼

Boston Cream Pie

cup confectioners' sugar over top of cake. To make a lacy design, sift confectioners' sugar over a lacy paper doily on top of cake; carefully remove doily.

—CHOCOLATE CREAM PIE

Follow Recipe for Boston Cream Pie. Substitute the following Fudge Glaze for the confectioners' sugar topping: Melt (page 10) and set aside **2 oz. (2 sq.) unsweetened chocolate** and **3 tablespoons butter.** Heat **¼ cup cream.** Mix in **1¼ cups confectioners' sugar** and **⅛ teaspoon salt.** Add the melted chocolate and butter and stir vigorously until glaze is smooth. Spread over top of cake and part way down sides.

—PEACH TEMPTATION

Follow ▲ Recipe. Thaw **2 pkgs. (10 oz. each) frozen sliced peaches** (or use sweetened sliced fresh peaches). When ready to serve, place one cake layer on serving plate. Top with about one third of the sliced peaches. Place second layer on top of peaches. Pile remaining peaches over top of cake. Top with **Sweetened Whipped Cream** (page 480). Serve immediately.
   10 to 12 servings

ITALIAN SPONGE CAKE
(Pan di Spagna)

Set out a 9-in. tubed pan.

Combine and beat well
   5 egg yolks
   ½ cup sugar
   1 teaspoon grated lemon peel
   2 tablespoons lemon juice
   1 teaspoon vanilla extract
Set aside.

Beat until frothy
   5 egg whites
   ½ teaspoon salt
Add gradually, beating well after each addition
   ½ cup sugar
Beat until stiff peaks are formed. Gently fold egg yolk mixture into beaten egg whites. Fold in until well blended, sifting in about one-fourth at a time
   1 cup sifted cake flour
Turn batter into pan.

Bake in a 325°F oven for 60 to 65 min., or until cake springs back when lightly touched in center or when a cake tester or wooden pick inserted in the center of the cake comes out clean.

Invert and leave hanging in pan until cold. Remove cake from pan after cooling. Run spatula gently around sides of pan. Cover with cooling rack. Invert and remove pan. Turn right side up immediately. Cool cake completely before frosting.

For Zuppa Inglese (page 509)—Unlike the

Peach Temptation

regular sponge cake, this sponge cake batter is baked in three 11x7x1½-in. cake pans for 30 to 35 min. for the Zuppa Inglese. This gives the Zuppa three layers which are each about 1 in. in height—exactly what is needed to prepare the Zuppa.

SPONGE CAKE LOAF

Set out a 9x5x3-in. loaf pan.

For Cake—Measure and set aside
   ¾ cup sifted cake flour

Combine and beat until very thick and lemon-colored
   3 egg yolks
   6 tablespoons sugar
   1 tablespoon cold water
   1 teaspoon grated lemon peel
   2 teaspoons lemon juice
Gently fold flour into egg yolk mixture until blended. Set aside.

Using clean beater, beat until frothy
   3 egg whites
   ¼ teaspoon salt
Add and beat slightly
   ¼ teaspoon cream of tartar
Add gradually, beating well after each addition
   6 tablespoons sugar
Beat until rounded peaks are formed and egg whites do not slide when bowl is partially inverted. Spread egg yolk mixture over surface of egg whites and carefully fold together until blended. Turn batter into pan.

Bake at 325°F 35 to 40 min., or until cake surface springs back when lightly touched.

Cool and remove from pan as directed for sponge-type cakes (page 11).

Meanwhile, prepare Caramel Topping.

For Caramel Topping—Melt in a heavy, light-colored skillet (a black skillet makes it difficult to see color of syrup) over low heat
   ½ cup sugar
With back of wooden spoon, gently keep sugar

moving toward center of skillet until completely melted. Heat until syrup is of an amber color (lighter than for burnt-sugar syrup). Remove from heat and add gradually, a very small amount at a time, stirring constantly

¼ cup boiling water

(Be careful that steam does not burn hand.) Return to low heat and continue to stir until small bubbles form. Set syrup aside to cool completely.

Cream until softened

¼ cup butter or margarine

Add gradually, creaming until fluffy after each addition

¾ cup confectioners' sugar

Add the cooled syrup gradually, beating well after each addition. Blend in

1 to 2 tablespoons cream

Add only enough cream to produce correct consistency (mixture runs slightly). Beat until smooth and creamy.

Pour topping over cake. Let a small amount run over sides of cake. Sprinkle over top

½ cup (about 2 oz.) chopped nuts

8 to 10 servings

SPONGE CAKE RING DESSERT

Set out a 1½-qt. ring mold.

For Sponge-Cake Ring—Sift together and set aside

½ cup sifted cake flour
⅛ teaspoon salt

Combine and beat until very thick and lemon-colored

3 egg yolks
¼ cup sugar
2 tablespoons water
1 teaspoon vanilla extract

Gently fold dry ingredients into egg yolk mixture until blended. Set aside.

Using clean beater, beat until frothy

3 egg whites

Add and beat slightly

¼ teaspoon cream of tartar

Add gradually, beating well after each addition

3 tablespoons sugar

Beat until rounded peaks are formed and egg whites do not slide when bowl is partially

Sponge Cake Loaf

inverted. Gently spread egg yolk mixture over egg whites and carefully fold together until blended. Turn batter into the mold.

Bake at 325°F about 30 min., or until cake surface springs back when lightly touched.

Cool and remove from pan as directed for sponge-type cakes (page 11).

When ready to serve, place the cooled cake ring on a serving plate. Prepare Coffee Butterscotch Glaze and brush over top of cake. Fill center of cake ring with scoops of **coffee** or **vanilla ice cream.** Drizzle **Fudge Sauce Café** (page 579) over the ice cream. Pour remaining sauce into a pitcher and serve with the dessert.

6 to 8 servings

For Coffee Butterscotch Glaze—Mix in a small saucepan

⅓ cup firmly packed light brown sugar
⅓ cup double-strength coffee beverage (page 10)

Set over medium heat and bring to boiling, stirring constantly. Continue to stir and boil 8 to 10 min., or until slightly thickened.

Remove from heat and blend in

2 tablespoons butter

Cool slightly before brushing on cake.

EGG YOLK APRICOT CAKE

For Apricot Purée—Put into a saucepan

½ lb. (1½ cups) dried apricots

Add

2 cups water

Boil uncovered until apricots are tender, about 15 min. Remove from heat. Drain. Purée by putting apricots into an electric blender container and blending until thick and smooth; or by pressing through strainer or food mill. Set aside.

For Cake—Set out a 10-in. tubed pan.

Sift together and set aside

3¼ cups sifted cake flour
4 teaspoons baking powder
1 teaspoon salt

Put into large mixer bowl

1 cup (about 12) egg yolks
1 cup sugar
1 teaspoon almond extract

Add a mixture of

¾ cup warm apricot purée
½ cup hot water

Beat (about 12 to 15 min.) until very thick and lemon colored. Continue beating and gradually add

1 cup sugar

Add flour mixture about one-fourth at a time, blending well after each addition. Frequently scrape sides of bowl. (*Do not overbeat.*) Turn batter into the pan.

Bake at 325°F 1 hr., or until cake tests done (page 11).

Sponge Cake Ring Dessert

Immediately invert cake on tubed end on cooling rack and let hang in pan until cold. (If cake is higher than pan, invert between two cooling racks so top of cake does not touch any surface.)

10-in. tubed cake

BLUEBERRY UPSIDE-DOWN CAKE

▲ *Base Recipe*

A heavy 10-in. skillet will be needed.

For Topping—Rinse and drain

2 cups firm fresh blueberries

Heat in the skillet over low heat

⅓ cup butter or margarine

Add and mix thoroughly

½ cup sugar
⅛ teaspoon salt

Remove from heat. Turn blueberries into the skillet and spread evenly. Set aside.

For Cake—Sift together and set aside

1¾ cups sifted cake flour
1 teaspoon baking powder
½ teaspoon salt

Beat until thick and lemon-colored

3 egg yolks

Add gradually, beating thoroughly after each addition

½ cup sugar

and

⅓ cup orange juice
2 tablespoons lemon juice

Sift dry ingredients, about one fourth at a time, over egg yolk mixture; gently fold until just blended after each addition. Set aside.

Using clean beater, beat until frothy
3 egg whites
Add gradually, beating well after each addition
½ cup sugar
Beat until rounded peaks are formed and egg whites do not slide when bowl is partially inverted.

Spread egg yolk mixture over the egg whites and gently fold together until blended. Turn batter into the skillet over the fruit, spreading evenly to edge of skillet.

Bake at 350°F 45 to 50 min., or until cake surface springs back when lightly touched.

Loosen cake by running a spatula carefully around sides. Cover skillet with a large serving plate; invert. Let skillet remain over cake a few seconds so all the syrup will drain onto cake. Lift skillet off.

Serve cake warm. If desired, serve with
Sweetened Whipped Cream (page 480)

8 to 12 servings

—FRESH PEACH UPSIDE-DOWN CAKE

Follow ▲ Recipe. Substitute **4 medium (about 1 lb.) firm ripe peaches**, peeled and sliced, for the blueberries. Use **light brown sugar** with the melted butter or margarine.

—STRAWBERRY UPSIDE-DOWN CAKE

Follow ▲ Recipe. Substitute **1 qt. ripe fresh strawberries**, rinsed, hulled and sliced, for the blueberries. Use **light brown sugar** with the melted butter or margarine.

CHOCO-MINT SPONGE CAKE

Set out a 10-in. tubed pan.

Sift together 4 times and set aside
3¾ cups sifted cake flour
1 tablespoon baking powder

Combine and beat until very thick
12 egg yolks (about 1 cup)
1 teaspoon salt
1 teaspoon vanilla extract
1½ teaspoons lemon extract
Measure
2 cups sugar
1 cup hot water
Add sugar and water alternately in four por-

tions each, beating until very thick after each addition. Sift one-fourth of the flour mixture at a time over surface; fold gently after each addition. Turn into pan.

Bake at 350°F 55 to 60 min., or until cake tests done (page 11). Invert cake and cool.

Frost with **Choco-Mint Frosting** (below).
One 10-in. tubed cake

For Choco-Mint Frosting—While cake is cooling, melt (page 10) **4 oz. (4 sq.) unsweetened chocolate** and **½ cup butter or margarine** in top of a double boiler. Stir in **2⅔ cups confectioners' sugar, 1 egg, 6 tablespoons water, 2 teaspoons vanilla extract, 2 or 3 drops peppermint extract,** and **⅛ teaspoon salt.** Place top of double boiler in a bowl of ice and water. Beat with electric mixer 5 min., or until frosting is of spreading consistency. *About 3 cups frosting*

FEATURE COCOA SPONGE CAKE

Set out 10-in. tubed pan.

Blend and set aside
¾ cup sifted cake flour
⅓ cup cocoa

Combine and beat until thick and lemon-colored
6 egg yolks
¾ cup sugar
¼ cup water
1½ teaspoons vanilla extract
Set aside.

Beat until frothy
6 egg whites
Beat in
½ teaspoon cream of tartar
¼ teaspoon salt
Add gradually, beating well after each addition
½ cup sugar
Beat until very stiff peaks are formed. Spread the egg yolk mixture over entire surface of beaten egg whites and gently fold together until mixture is completely blended. Sift about one fourth of the flour at a time over surface. Fold together gently after each addition. Turn batter into pan.

Bake at 350°F about 45 min., or until cake tests done (page 11). Immediately invert pan on tubed end on cooling rack until cake is cold. (If cake is higher than pan, invert between two cooling racks so top of cake does not touch any surface.) When cake is cool, with paring knife cut around tube to loosen cake. Loosen sides with spatula and gently remove cake from pan.
One 10-in. tubed cake

DAFFODIL CAKE

Set out a 10-in. tubed pan.

Measure and pour into a large bowl
1¼ cups (about 10) egg whites
Allow to stand at room temperature at least 1

hr. before beating. This will help to insure greater volume.

Put into a bowl
4 egg yolks
Meanwhile, sift together and set aside
1¼ cups sifted cake flour
½ cup sugar
Add to egg whites
¾ teaspoon salt
Beat with wire whisk, hand rotary beater or electric mixer until frothy. Beat in
1½ teaspoons cream of tartar
Continue beating just until rounded peaks are formed and egg whites do not slide when bowl is partially inverted. Sprinkle over surface of egg whites and fold in, 2 tablespoons at a time
1 cup sugar
Sift about 4 tablespoons of flour mixture over egg white mixture; fold gently together. Repeat until all the flour mixture is folded in.

Add to egg yolks
1½ teaspoons grated orange peel
2 tablespoons orange juice
¼ teaspoon almond extract
Beat until very thick and lemon-colored. Fold one third of egg white mixture into egg yolk mixture.

Add to remaining egg white mixture and fold in with a minimum number of strokes
½ teaspoon vanilla extract
Immediately turn alternate layers of yellow and white batters into pan, ending with white batter on top. Cut through batter in several places with knife or spatula to break large air bubbles. Lift white batter through yellow batter to produce a marbled effect.

Bake at 375°F 35 min., or until cake surface springs back when lightly touched.

Cool and remove from pans as directed for sponge-type cakes (page 11).
One 10-in. tubed cake

SUNNY ORANGE SPONGE CAKE

Fresh orange juice and grated peel give this big, beautiful sponge cake a sunny color and a wonderful fresh-fruit flavor.

Set out a 10-in. tubed pan.

Sift together and set aside
1¾ cups sifted cake flour
2 teaspoons baking powder
¼ teaspoon salt

Measure and pour into a large bowl
1 cup (about 12) egg yolks
Beat until thick and lemon-colored. Add gradually, beating well after each addition
1 tablespoon grated orange peel
⅔ cup orange juice
2 tablespoons warm water
Add gradually, beating well after each addition
1¼ cups sugar
Sift dry ingredients, about one fourth at a time,

over egg yolk mixture; gently fold until just blended after each addition. Turn batter into pan.

Bake at 325°F about 55 min., or until cake surface springs back when lightly touched.

Cool and remove from pan as directed for sponge-type cakes (page 11).

One 10-in. tubed cake

SPICY PECAN SPONGE CAKE

Set out a 10-in. tubed pan.

Finely chop and set aside
½ cup (about 2 oz.) pecans

Sift together and set aside
1 cup sifted cake flour
½ teaspoon baking powder
½ teaspoon salt
1 teaspoon cinnamon
¼ teaspoon cloves

Beat until very thick and lemon-colored
1 cup (about 12) egg yolks
¼ cup warm water
1 teaspoon vanilla extract
Add gradually, beating well after each addition
1 cup sugar
Sift dry ingredients, about one fourth at a time, over egg yolk mixture; gently fold until just blended after each addition. Set mixture aside.

Using clean beater, beat until rounded peaks are formed
3 egg whites
Spread egg whites over egg yolk mixture and carefully fold together until blended. Fold in the pecans; turn batter into pan.

Bake at 325°F about 55 min., or until cake surface springs back when lightly touched.

Cool and remove from pan as directed for sponge-type cakes (page 11).

One 10-in. tubed cake

PINEAPPLE SPONGE CAKE

Set out a 10-in. tubed pan.

Sift together and set aside
1½ cups sifted cake flour
1 teaspoon baking powder

Mix in a large bowl
1½ cups sugar
½ cup pineapple juice
1 tablespoon lemon juice
Add to sugar mixture
6 egg yolks
Beat until very thick and lemon-colored.

Folding in until just blended after each addition, add dry ingredients in fourths.

Using a clean beater, beat until frothy
6 egg whites
Add
¼ teaspoon salt
Beat until rounded peaks are formed and egg

whites do not slide when the bowl is partially inverted. Spread egg yolk mixture over egg whites and carefully fold together until blended. Turn batter into pan.

Bake at 325°F 50 to 60 min., or until cake surface springs back when lightly touched.

Remove from oven. Immediately invert pan on tube end and let hang in pan until completely cooled. If cake is higher than tube, invert between two cooling racks so top of cake does not touch any surface.

When cake is completely cooled, cut around tube with paring knife to loosen cake. Loosen sides with spatula and gently remove cake.

Prepare
Pineapple Cream Filling (page 484)
Using a sharp knife, split cake into two layers. Place bottom layer of the cake on a serving plate. Spread about three fourths of the filling over the cake layer. Cover with the top layer and sift over top of cake
Confectioners' sugar
Top each serving with a small spoonful of the remaining filling.   *One 10-in. tubed cake*

ANGEL FOOD CAKE

▲ Base Recipe

Set out a 10-in. tubed pan.

Measure and pour into a large bowl
1½ cups (about 12) egg whites
Allow egg whites to stand at room temperature at least 1 hr. before beating. This will help to insure greater volume.

Meanwhile, sift together 4 times and set aside
1 cup sifted cake flour
¾ cup sugar

Add to the egg whites
½ teaspoon salt
Beat with whisk beater, hand rotary beater, or electric mixer until frothy. Beat in
1½ teaspoons cream of tartar
Continue beating just until rounded peaks are formed and egg whites do not slide when bowl is partially inverted. Sprinkle over surface of the egg whites, 2 tablespoons at a time, and carefully fold in after each addition (do not stir)
¾ cup sugar
Blend in
1 teaspoon vanilla extract
½ teaspoon almond extract

Angel Food Cake

Sift about 4 tablespoons of flour mixture over surface of meringue (egg white mixture) and fold gently together. Repeat procedure until all of the flour mixture has been folded in. Carefully slide batter into pan, turning pan as batter is poured. Cut through batter with knife or spatula to break large air bubbles.

Bake at 350°F about 45 min., or until cake surface springs back when lightly touched.

Cool and remove from pan as directed for sponge-type cakes (page 11).

One 10-in. tubed cake

—ANGEL FOOD CAKE VARIETIES

Follow ▲ Recipe for preparing batter. *For Miniatures*—Use 16 individual tubed pans for large pan. Bake at 350°F 15 to 20 min. *For Loaves*—Use two 9x5x3-in. loaf pans for tubed pan. Bake at 350°F about 30 min., or until done. *For Party-Pink Cake*—Fold in **½ cup finely chopped nuts** and **¼ cup finely chopped well-drained maraschino cherries** with last addition of flour. *For Toasty-Coconut Cake*—Fold in **1 cup toasted flaked coconut** with last addition of flour.

—BANANA ANGEL FOOD CAKE

Follow ▲ Recipe. Decrease vanilla extract to ½ teaspoon, almond extract to ¼ teaspoon, and add **2 teaspoons banana extract**.

—CHOCOLATE-FLECKED ANGEL FOOD CAKE

Follow ▲ Recipe. Fold **½ cup chocolate shot** or **1 oz. (1 sq.) unsweetened chocolate**, grated, into batter with last flour addition.

Chocolate-Glazed Angel Food Cake

—CHOCOLATE-GLAZED ANGEL FOOD CAKE

Follow ▲ Recipe. Melt (page 10) together, stirring constantly, **1 pkg. (6 oz.) semisweet chocolate pieces** and **½ cup butter or margarine.** Remove from simmering water; stir until smooth and slightly cooled. Quickly spread over cake while mixture is still warm.

—COCOA ANGEL FOOD SPICE CAKE

Follow ▲ Recipe. Sift with flour and sugar **¼ cup cocoa, 1 teaspoon cinnamon, ½ teaspoon nutmeg, ½ teaspoon allspice** and **¼ teaspoon cloves.** Fold 1 cup sugar into beaten egg whites. Omit almond extract.

—BURNT SUGAR ANGEL FOOD CAKE

Prepare ½ cup Burnt-Sugar Syrup (page 436). Finely chop ½ cup (about 2 oz.) pecans; set aside. Follow ▲ Recipe. Increase cake flour to 1½ cups and the sugar sifted with flour to 1 cup. Increase the sugar folded into the egg whites to 1 cup and the vanilla extract to 1½ teaspoons; omit almond extract. Fold in the pecans and 2 tablespoons Burnt-Sugar Syrup after last addition of flour mixture. Complete as in ▲ Recipe.

—MOCHA ANGEL DESSERT

A tawny-crowned beauty with the rich, dark, mysterious flavor that only coffee can give.

Follow ▲ Recipe. Substitute four 9-in. round

Mocha Angel Dessert

layer cake pans for the individual tubed pans. Lightly grease bottoms and line with waxed paper. Divide batter equally among the pans. Bake at 325°F 25 to 30 min., or until layers test done. Invert pans on cooling racks; allow to cool completely. Loosen sides with spatula, cover with cooling rack, invert and remove pan. Turn right side up immediately after peeling off waxed paper. Substitute Mocha-Mallow Cream for the Seven-Minute Frosting. Place 1 cake layer on serving plate; spread about ¼ of the Cream over top. Cover with the second layer; repeat procedure with remaining Cream and layers. Chill thoroughly in refrigerator. If desired, top with chocolate curls made by pulling **½ oz. (½ sq.) unsweetened chocolate** across a shredder.

For Mocha-Mallow Cream—Put a bowl, rotary beater and **2 cups heavy cream** into refrigerator to chill. Heat **24 marshmallows (6 oz.),** cut (page 9) in quarters, and **½ cup double-strength coffee beverage** (page 10) together in top of double boiler over simmering water. Stir occasionally until marshmallows are melted. Cool; chill in refrigerator until mixture thickens. Using the chilled bowl and beater, beat 1 cup of the heavy cream at a time until cream is of medium consistency (piles softly). Fold the whipped cream into marshmallow mixture.

COCOA ANGEL FOOD CAKE

Set out 10-in. tubed pan.

Measure into a large bowl
1½ cups (about 12) egg whites
Allow to stand at room temperature about 1 hr. before beating. This will insure greater volume.

Meanwhile, sift together 4 times and set aside
1 cup minus 2 tablespoons sifted cake flour
½ cup sugar
⅓ cup cocoa

Measure and set aside
1 cup sugar

Add to egg whites
½ teaspoon salt
Beat with wire whisk, hand rotary beater or electric mixer until frothy. Beat in
1¼ teaspoons cream of tartar
Continue beating until rounded peaks are

formed. Add the 1 cup sugar by sprinkling about 3 tablespoons at a time over egg whites and folding only until blended after each addition.

Blend in
1½ teaspoons vanilla extract
Gradually sift flour mixture, about 3 tablespoons at a time, over beaten egg whites. Gently fold in dry ingredients after each addition. Slide batter into the pan, turning pan as batter is poured. Cut through batter with knife or spatula to break large air bubbles.

Bake at 350°F about 45 min. Cake is done if top springs back when lightly touched at center. Immediately invert pan on tubed end on cooling rack until cake is cold. (If cake is higher than pan, invert between two cooling racks so top of cake does not touch any surface.) When cake is cool, with paring knife cut around tube to loosen cake. Loosen sides with spatula and gently remove cake from pan.

One 10-in. tubed cake

CAKE ROLLS

JELLY ROLL I

▲ *Base Recipe*

Prepare (page 10) a 15x10x1-in. jelly roll pan.

Beat until very thick
4 egg yolks
½ cup sugar
¼ cup water
1½ teaspoons vanilla extract
Fold in until just blended
1 cup sifted cake flour

Chocolate Mint Roll

Beat until frothy
4 egg whites
½ teaspoon cream of tartar
¼ teaspoon salt
Add gradually, beating constantly
½ cup sugar
Continue beating until stiff peaks are formed. Fold in the egg yolk mixture until blended. Turn into pan and spread evenly to edges.

Bake at 350°F 15 to 20 min., or until cake surface springs back when lightly touched.

Immediately loosen edges with a sharp knife. Turn cake out onto a clean towel sprinkled generously with
Sifted confectioners' sugar
Remove paper and cut off any crisp edges of cake. To roll, begin with near edge of cake, using towel as a guide. Tightly grasp near edge of towel and quickly pull it over beyond opposite edge. Cake will roll itself as you pull. Wrap cake roll in towel and set on cooling rack to cool (about ½ hr.).

When ready to fill, carefully unroll cake. Spread with
Jelly or jam (about 1 cup)
Carefully reroll. Sift over top
2 tablespoons confectioners' sugar
1 Jelly Roll

—JELLY ROLL II

Follow ▲ Recipe. When cake is cool, unroll and spread with **Orange Filling I** (page 483) and sprinkle with **1 cup semisweet chocolate pieces.** Reroll and sprinkle top with **¼ cup sifted confectioners' sugar.**

—ICE CREAM CAKE ROLL

Follow ▲ Recipe. Substitute **1 qt. softened vanilla ice cream** for jelly or jam. Serve immediately or put into freezer section of refrigerator until ice cream is firm. Serve with a thick **fudge sauce.**

—CREAMY CAKE ROLL

Follow ▲ Recipe. Omit jelly or jam and confectioners' sugar. Prepare **Butter Cream Frosting** (page 474) or any variation. Use about one half of frosting as filling for the roll. Spread some of the frosting over roll and decorate roll by forcing remainder through a pastry bag and No. 3 star tube. (If desired, Butter Cream Frosting may be tinted with a few drops of food coloring.) Sprinkle with **chopped toasted almonds** or **slivered unblanched almonds.**

—WHIPPED CREAM CAKE ROLL

Follow ▲ Recipe. Substitute **Sweetened Whipped Cream** (page 480) or any variation for the jelly or jam. If desired, fold crushed **peppermint-stick candy** or **peanut brittle** into the whipped cream.

CHOCOLATE MINT ROLL

Prepare (page 10) a 15x10x1-in. jelly roll pan.

Sift together and set aside
¾ cup sifted cake flour
5 tablespoons cocoa
¼ teaspoon salt

Beat until very thick and lemon-colored
4 egg yolks
½ cup sugar
¼ cup water
1½ teaspoons vanilla extract
Fold in dry ingredients. Set aside.

Beat until frothy
4 egg whites
Add and beat slightly
½ teaspoon cream of tartar
Add gradually, beating well after each addition
½ cup sugar
Beat until rounded peaks are formed and whites do not slide when bowl is partially inverted. Spread egg yolk mixture over egg whites and gently fold together. Turn batter into pan and spread evenly to edges.

Bake at 325°F 30 min., or until cake tests done (page 11). Loosen edges with a sharp knife. Turn immediately onto a towel sprinkled with
Sifted confectioners' sugar
Remove waxed paper and cut off any crisp edges of cake.

To roll, begin rolling nearest edge of cake. Using towel as a guide, tightly grasp nearest edge of towel and quickly pull it over beyond opposite edge. Cake will roll itself as you pull. Wrap roll in towel and set on cooling rack to cool (about ½ hr.).

When ready to fill, carefully unroll cooled cake and spread with
Seven-Minute Peppermint Frosting (one-half recipe, page 474)
Reroll and sift over top of roll
2 to 4 tablespoons confectioners' sugar
1 Chocolate Mint Roll

CHOCOLATE WALNUT ROLL

Set out a 15x10x1-in. pan. Line with greased waxed paper. To prevent sticking and for a slightly heavier crust, sprinkle greased paper with
2 tablespoons fine dry bread crumbs
Prepare
1 cup walnuts, ground

Sift together
¼ cup sifted cake flour
¼ cup unsweetened cocoa
1 teaspoon baking powder
½ teaspoon salt
¼ cup sugar
Combine with walnuts, mixing well.

Separate
4 eggs
Beat egg whites in large mixer bowl until foamy with
¼ teaspoon cream of tartar
Beating constantly, add gradually until very stiff peaks are formed
½ cup sugar
Using same beater, beat the 4 egg yolks until thick; beat in
2 tablespoons coffee beverage

Blend in the walnut-flour mixture. Turn batter over beaten egg whites and fold gently with spatula until no streaks of white remain. Turn into the baking pan and spread batter evenly into corners.

Bake at 400°F 10 min. Turn out onto sheet of waxed paper sprinkled with **granulated sugar** (about 2 tablespoons). Carefully peel off paper from cake. Cover cake with the pan and cool.

Meanwhile, prepare Walnut Cream Filling. Combine in small mixer bowl
1 cup heavy cream, chilled
2 tablespoons sugar
Beat until stiff peaks are formed; blend in
½ teaspoon vanilla extract
1 tablespoon brandy

459

Fold in

¼ cup chopped walnuts
¼ cup chopped candied cherries
(half red and half green)

Spread cooled cake with the filling and roll up lengthwise. Place roll on serving plate.

Prepare Chocolate Glaze. Melt over hot water

2 oz. (2 sq.) semisweet chocolate
2 teaspoons vegetable shortening

Remove from heat and stir in

2 teaspoons light corn syrup

Cool slightly, then spread over top and sides of cake roll. Decorate with **walnut halves** and **candied red cherries**.   *1 cake roll*

MINCEMEAT CAKE ROLL

Grease bottom of a 15x10x1-in. pan; line with waxed paper cut to fit bottom of pan; grease again.

Sift together and set aside

1 cup sifted cake flour
¼ teaspoon salt

Beat until very thick and lemon-colored

4 egg yolks
½ cup sugar
¼ cup water
1½ teaspoons vanilla extract

Gently fold in dry ingredients until well blended. Set aside.

Beat until frothy

4 egg whites

Add and beat slightly

½ teaspoon cream of tartar

Add gradually, beating thoroughly after each addition

½ cup sugar

Continue beating until very stiff peaks are formed. Gently spread egg yolk mixture over egg whites and carefully fold together until blended. Turn batter into pan and spread evenly to edges.

Bake at 350°F 20 to 25 min., or until a wooden pick or cake tester inserted in center of cake comes out clean.

Immediately loosen edges of cake with a sharp knife; turn onto clean towel sprinkled with

Sifted confectioners' sugar

Carefully remove paper and cut off any crisp

Marbleized Chiffon Cake

edges of cake. To roll, begin rolling nearest edge of cake. Using towel as a guide, tightly grasp nearest edge of towel and quickly pull it over beyond opposite edge. Cake will roll itself as you pull. Wrap cake in towel and set on cooling rack to cool (about ½ hr.).

Shortly before ready to serve, unroll cake and spread with

1¾ cups Mincemeat (½ recipe,
page 729)

Carefully reroll cake. Cut filled cake roll into crosswise pieces and serve.   *1 cake roll*

CHIFFON CAKES

MARBLEIZED CHIFFON CAKE

Set out a 10-in. tubed pan.

Measure and pour into a large bowl

1 cup (7 to 8) egg whites

Allow to stand at room temperature at least 1 hr. before beating. This will help to insure greater volume.

Put into a small bowl

5 egg yolks

Mix together and set aside to cool

⅓ cup cocoa
¼ cup sugar
¼ cup boiling water
⅛ teaspoon red food coloring

Sift together into a bowl

2 cups sifted cake flour
1 cup sugar
1 teaspoon baking powder
¾ teaspoon salt

Make a well in center of dry ingredients; add

½ cup cooking or salad oil

Add in order the 5 egg yolks and

¾ cup water
2¼ teaspoons vanilla extract

Beat until smooth. Set aside.

Using clean beater, beat the egg whites until frothy. Beat in

½ teaspoon cream of tartar

Add gradually, beating well after each addition

½ cup sugar

Beat until rounded peaks are formed and egg whites do not slide when bowl is partially inverted. Slowly pour egg-yolk mixture over entire surface of egg whites. Gently fold together until just blended. *Do not stir.* Turn one half of batter into another bowl. Pour cocoa mixture gradually over it, gently folding until blended. Immediately turn alternate layers of dark and light batter into pan, rotating pan as you pour. Cut through batter in several places with knife or spatula to break air bubbles. Lift light batter through dark batter to give a marbled effect.

Bake at 325°F 55 min., then at 350°F 10 to 15 min., or until cake surface springs back when lightly touched.

Cocoa Chiffon Cake

Cool and remove from pan as directed for sponge-type cakes (page 11).

One 10-in. tubed cake

COCOA CHIFFON CAKE

▲ *Base Recipe*

Set out a 10-in. tubed pan.

Measure and pour into a large bowl

1 cup (7 to 8) egg whites

Allow to stand at room temperature at least 1 hr. before beating. This will help to insure greater volume.

Put into a small bowl and set aside

7 egg yolks

Mix and set aside to cool

½ cup cocoa
¾ cup boiling water

Sift together into a bowl

1¾ cups sifted cake flour
1 cup sugar
1 tablespoon baking powder
¾ teaspoon salt

Make a well in center of dry ingredients; add

½ cup cooking or salad oil

Add in order the egg yolks, cooled cocoa mixture and

2 teaspoons vanilla extract

Beat until smooth. Set aside.

Using clean beater, beat the egg whites until frothy. Beat in

½ teaspoon cream of tartar

Add gradually, beating well after each addition

¾ cup sugar

Beat until rounded peaks are formed and egg whites do not slide when bowl is partially inverted. Slowly pour egg-yolk mixture over entire surface of egg whites. Gently fold together until just blended. *Do not stir.* Turn batter into pan.

Bake at 325°F 55 min., then at 350°F 10 to 15 min., or until cake surface springs back when lightly touched.

Cool and remove from pan as directed for sponge-type cakes (page 11).

One 10-in. tubed cake

—PECAN COCOA CHIFFON CAKE

Finely chop **1 cup (about 4 oz.) pecans.** Follow ▲ Recipe. Pour egg yolk mixture over egg whites, then sprinkle pecans over surface. Gently fold together.

—COCOA MINT CHIFFON CAKE

Follow ▲ Recipe. Substitute **1 teaspoon peppermint extract** for vanilla extract. Frost sides and top of cooled cake with **Peppermint Seven-Minute Frosting** (page 474).

LEMON CHIFFON CAKE

▲ Base Recipe

Set out a 10-in. tubed pan.

Measure and pour into a large bowl
1 cup (7 to 8) egg whites
Allow to stand at room temperature at least 1 hr. before beating. This will help to insure greater volume.

Put into a small bowl
5 egg yolks
Sift together into a bowl
2¼ cups sifted cake flour
1 cup sugar
1 tablespoon baking powder
¾ teaspoon salt
Make a well in center of dry ingredients; add
½ cup cooking or salad oil
Add in order the 5 egg yolks and
¾ cup water
1 teaspoon grated lemon peel
1 tablespoon lemon juice
Beat until smooth. Set aside.

Using clean beater, beat the egg whites until frothy. Beat in
½ teaspoon cream of tartar
Add gradually, beating well after each addition
½ cup sugar
Beat until rounded peaks are formed and egg whites do not slide when bowl is partially inverted. Slowly pour egg yolk mixture over entire surface of egg whites. Gently fold together until just blended. *Do not stir.* Turn batter into pan.

Bake at 325°F 55 min., then at 350°F 10 to 15 min., or until cake surface springs back when lightly touched.

Cool and remove from pan as directed for sponge-type cakes (page 11).
One 10-in. tubed cake

—RUM CHIFFON CAKE

Follow ▲ Recipe. Substitute **4 teaspoons rum extract** for lemon juice and peel. Frost with **Raisin Rum Butter Frosting** (page 478).

—BANANA PECAN CHIFFON CAKE

Follow ▲ Recipe. Omit water and lemon peel. Finely chop **1 cup (about 4 oz.) pecans**. Peel and force through sieve or food mill enough bananas (2 or 3) with brown-flecked peel to yield **1 cup sieved bananas**. Mix with the

lemon juice; add after the egg yolks. Sprinkle pecans over egg yolk mixture before folding. Continue as in ▲ Recipe.

—PINEAPPLE CHIFFON CAKE

Follow ▲ Recipe. Substitute **unsweetened pineapple juice** for the water. Omit lemon juice and lemon peel.

ORANGE CHIFFON CAKE

Set out a 9x9x2-in. cake pan or 9x5x3-in. loaf pan.

Measure and pour into a large bowl
½ cup (4 to 5) egg whites
Allow to stand at room temperature at least 1 hr. before beating. This will help to insure greater volume.

Put into a small bowl
2 egg yolks

Sift together into a bowl
1 cup plus 2 tablespoons sifted cake flour
½ cup sugar
1½ teaspoons baking powder
½ teaspoon salt
Make a well in center of dry ingredients; add
¼ cup cooking or salad oil
Add in order the 2 egg yolks and
1 tablespoon grated orange peel
⅓ cup orange juice
Beat until smooth. Set aside.

Using clean beater, beat the egg whites until frothy. Beat in
¼ teaspoon cream of tartar
Add gradually, beating well after each addition
¼ cup sugar
Beat until rounded peaks are formed and egg whites do not slide when bowl is partially inverted. Slowly pour egg yolk mixture over entire surface of egg whites. Gently fold together until just blended. *Do not stir.* Carefully turn batter into pan.

Bake square cake at 350°F 30 to 35 min., loaf cake at 325°F 50 to 55 min., or until cake surface springs back when lightly touched.

Cool and remove from pan as directed for sponge-type cakes (page 11).
One 9-in. square or 9x5-in. loaf cake

CUPCAKES

AMBROSIA CAKES

▲ Base Recipe

If ambrosia is truly the food of the gods, then these delicious orange-saturated cakes are aptly named. Served flambée, they are a dramatic and impressive dessert as well as a delectable one. Yet, wrapped snugly in moisture-vaporproof material, they can be kept for days without losing freshness—a most practical quality!

Grease bottoms of sixteen 2¼-in. muffin-pan wells.

Coarsely chop and set aside
½ cup (about 2 oz.) pecans

Cut into small pieces (page 9) and add to nuts
4 oz. pitted dates (about ⅔ cup, cut)

Sift together and set aside
1 cup sifted cake flour
½ teaspoon baking soda
¼ teaspoon baking powder
¼ teaspoon salt

Cream until softened
¼ cup butter
1½ teaspoons grated orange peel
½ teaspoon vanilla extract
Add gradually, creaming until fluffy after each addition
½ cup sugar

Orange Chiffon Cake

461

Add in thirds, beating thoroughly after each addition

1 egg, well beaten

Measure

½ cup dairy sour cream

Beating only until smooth after each addition, alternately add dry ingredients and sour cream to creamed mixture. Finally, beat only until smooth (do not overbeat). Mix in the chopped nuts and date pieces. Spoon mixture into the muffin-pan wells, filling each about half-full. (Fill any empty wells half-full with water.)

Bake at 350°F 30 to 40 min., or until cakes test done (page 11).

Meanwhile, mix and set aside

⅔ cup sugar

½ cup orange juice

2½ tablespoons Cointreau

Stir occasionally to dissolve sugar.

When cakes are done, remove from oven and immediately drizzle orange juice mixture over hot cakes (about 1 tablespoon to each).

When the orange juice mixture has been absorbed (about 3 min.), run spatula gently around sides of each muffin-pan well.

Remove each cake and set on cooling racks to cool completely.

Serve plain or with **Vanilla Cream Topping** (page 482).   *16 cupcakes*

—AMBROSIA CAKES FLAMBEE

Follow ▲ Recipe. Omit Cointreau and increase orange juice to ⅔ cup. To set aflame, heat ½ **cup brandy** in a small pan. Ignite brandy with a match and pour flaming brandy over top of each cake, at the table. Serve at once.

WEE CHARM CAKES

▲ *Base Recipe*

Line with paper baking cups or grease bottoms of 36 small muffin-pan wells.

Melt (page 10) and set aside to cool

2 oz. (2 sq.) unsweetened chocolate

Sift together and set aside

1½ cups sifted cake flour

2 teaspoons baking powder

¼ teaspoon salt

Cream until shortening is softened

½ cup shortening

1½ teaspoons vanilla extract

Add gradually, creaming until fluffy after each addition

1 cup sugar

Add in thirds, beating thoroughly after each addition

2 eggs, well beaten

Blend in melted chocolate.

Measure

½ cup milk

Alternately add dry ingredients in thirds and milk in halves to creamed mixture. After each addition, beat only until smooth. Finally, beat only until batter is smooth. Fill muffin wells two-thirds full.

Bake at 350°F 15 to 20 min., or until cakes test done (page 11).

Cool and remove from pans as directed (page 11).   *36 small cupcakes*

—COCOA CAKES

Follow ▲ Recipe. Omit chocolate. Sift in **6 tablespoons cocoa** with dry ingredients.

—COCONUT BALLS

Follow ▲ Recipe or Cocoa Cakes recipe. Frost sides and tops with **white or chocolate frosting** and, while moist, roll in **moist shredded coconut**, cut.

MINCEMEAT CUPCAKES

Generously butter 2 doz. 2½-in. muffin-pan wells.

For Topping—Combine in a saucepan

¼ cup butter or margarine

¾ cup firmly packed brown sugar

Cook over low heat until well blended, stirring constantly. Remove the mixture from heat and blend in

1¾ cups Mincemeat (one half recipe, page 729)

½ cup (about 2 oz.) chopped nuts

Put 1 to 2 tablespoons of this mixture in each muffin-pan well. Set aside.

For Cake—Sift together and set aside

2 cups sifted cake flour

1 tablespoon baking powder

¾ teaspoon salt

Beat together

⅔ cup vegetable shortening, all-purpose shortening, butter or margarine

½ teaspoon orange extract

Add gradually, beating until fluffy after each addition

½ cup sugar

Measure

⅔ cup milk

Alternately blend dry ingredients in thirds and milk in halves into creamed mixture, beating only until smooth after each addition. Finally beat only until batter is smooth (do not overbeat).

Beat until frothy

4 egg whites

Add gradually, beating well after each addition

½ cup sugar

Continue beating the meringue until very stiff peaks are formed. Gently slide beaten egg whites over batter and fold together.

Spoon batter into muffin-pan wells over mincemeat mixture. Fill each well one-half to two-thirds full.

Bake at 350°F about 20 min., or until cake tester or wooden pick inserted in center of cupcake comes out clean or until cakes spring back when lightly touched at center. Invert muffin pans onto cooling racks. Remove pans.

Serve cupcakes with **unsweetened whipped cream**.   *2 doz. cupcakes*

"MO"-LASSES CUPCAKES

Line with paper baking cups or grease bottoms of 2 doz. 2½-in. muffin-pan wells.

Sift together and set aside

2½ cups sifted cake flour

1 tablespoon baking powder

½ teaspoon salt

1 teaspoon cinnamon

Beat until blended

½ cup shortening

1½ teaspoons vanilla extract

Add gradually, creaming until fluffy after each addition

1 cup sugar

Add in thirds, beating thoroughly after each addition

2 eggs, well beaten

Blend in

½ cup molasses

Measure

¾ cup milk

Alternately blend dry ingredients in thirds and milk in halves into molasses mixture, beating only until smooth after each addition. Finally, beat until batter is smooth (do not overbeat). Fill muffin cups or wells one-half full.

"Mo"-Lasses Cupcakes

Bake at 350°F 25 to 30 min., or until cakes test done (page 11).

Cool and remove from muffin wells as directed (page 11).

Meanwhile, prepare
Lemon Butter Frosting (page 478)

When cupcakes are completely cooled, frost (page 11). *2 doz. cupcakes*

MOHRENKOPFE

Attractive little cream-filled cakes—a favorite German dessert.

Grease bottoms of 1 doz. 2½-in. muffin-pan wells.

For Cakes—Measure and set aside
1 cup sifted cake flour

Combine and beat until very thick and lemon-colored
4 egg yolks
⅓ cup sugar
1 teaspoon grated lemon peel
Set aside.

Using clean beater, beat until frothy
4 egg whites
Add gradually, beating well after each addition
⅓ cup sugar
Beat until rounded peaks are formed. Spread egg yolk mixture over surface of egg white mixture and gently fold together. Sift about one fourth of the flour at a time over egg mixture. Fold together gently after each addition. Turn batter into muffin-pan wells, filling each about two-thirds full.

Bake at 325°F 18 min., or until delicately browned.

Cool slightly; run spatula gently around sides of cakes. Lift out cakes and set on cooling racks to cool completely.

For Glaze—Partially melt over hot (not simmering) water, being careful not to overheat
3 oz. semisweet candymaking
chocolate
3 tablespoons butter or margarine
Remove from the hot water and stir until completely melted.

For Filling—Prepare
Sweetened Whipped Cream
(one-half recipe, page 480)

To Complete Dessert—Cut a thin slice from bottom of each cake. Carefully hollow out the cakes, working from cut end. Fill with the whipped cream and invert onto the cake slices. Spoon the glaze over tops of cakes, allowing excess to drip over sides. *6 servings*

SPICE CUPCAKES

▲ *Base Recipe*

Line sixteen 2½-in. muffin-pan wells with paper baking cups. or grease bottom of wells.

Sift together and set aside
2 cups sifted cake flour
1 teaspoon baking powder
½ teaspoon baking soda
½ teaspoon salt
1 teaspoon cinnamon
½ teaspoon nutmeg
¼ teaspoon allspice
¼ teaspoon cloves
Cream until softened
½ cup butter or margarine
Add gradually, creaming until fluffy after each addition
½ cup sugar
½ cup firmly packed brown sugar
Add in thirds, beating thoroughly after each addition
2 eggs, well beaten
Measure
⅔ cup buttermilk or sour milk
Beating only until smooth after each addition, alternately add dry ingredients in thirds and liquid in halves to creamed mixture. Finally, beat only until smooth (do not overbeat).

Spoon mixture into the prepared muffin-pan wells, filling each about one-half full. (Fill any empty wells one-half full with water.)

Bake at 350°F about 20 min., or until cakes test done (page 11).

Cool and remove from muffin-pan wells as directed for butter-type cakes (page 11).

Serve with
Maple Whipped Cream (page 481)
16 cupcakes

—FAVORITE SPICE CAKE

Follow ▲ Recipe. Substitute for the muffin-pan wells two 8-in. round layer cake pans. Prepare the pans (page 10). Bake at 350°F 25 min., or until cake tests done.

TORTES

SPICY APPLESAUCE TORTE

Prepare (page 10) two 8-in. round layer cake pans.

Set out
16 gingersnaps (or enough to yield
1 cup fine crumbs)
Prepare crumbs (page 10).

Sift together
1 cup sifted cake flour
4 teaspoons baking powder
½ teaspoon salt
1 teaspoon cinnamon
½ teaspoon nutmeg
¼ teaspoon cloves
Mix crumbs with the dry ingredients; set aside.

Finely chop and set aside
½ cup (about 2 oz.) walnuts

Cream until softened
⅓ cup butter or margarine
Add gradually, creaming until fluffy after each addition
¾ cup sugar
Add in thirds, beating well after each addition
2 eggs, well beaten
Measure
1 cup thick unsweetened applesauce
Beating only until smooth after each addition, alternately add dry ingredients in thirds and applesauce in halves to creamed mixture. Finally, beat only until smooth (do not overbeat). Blend in the chopped nuts. Turn batter into pans and spread to edges.

Bake at 350°F 35 to 40 min., or until torte layers test done (page 11).

Cool and remove from pans as directed for tortes (page 11).

Fill and frost (page 11) as desired.
Two 8-in. round torte layers

BLITZ TORTE
(Blitztorte)

Prepare (page 10) two 8-in. round layer cake pans.

Prepare and chill
Vanilla Cream Filling (page 482)

Prepare and set aside
½ cup (about 3 oz.) blanched
(page 9), slivered almonds

Mix and set aside
1 tablespoon sugar
½ teaspoon cinnamon

Sift together and set aside

1 cup sifted cake flour
1 teaspoon baking powder
⅛ teaspoon salt

Cream until softened

½ cup butter
1 teaspoon vanilla extract

Add gradually, creaming until fluffy after each addition

½ cup sugar

Add in thirds, beating well after each addition

4 egg yolks, well beaten

Measure

3 tablespoons milk

Mixing only until well blended after each addition, alternately add dry ingredients and milk to creamed mixture, beginning and ending with dry ingredients. Turn batter into pans, spreading to edges.

Beat until frothy

4 egg whites

Add 2 tablespoons at a time, beating well after each addition

¾ cup sugar

Continue beating until very stiff peaks are formed. Carefully spread one half of meringue over batter in each pan. Sprinkle each layer with half of the slivered almonds and half of the sugar-cinnamon mixture.

Bake at 325°F 1 hr., or until meringue is delicately browned. Cool torte layers in pans on cooling racks.

After cooling, loosen sides with a spatula. Remove one torte layer from pan, peel off waxed paper and place layer, meringue side up, on a serving plate. Spread with all the filling. Remove second layer from pan, peel off waxed paper and place, meringue side up, on top of filling.   *About 10 servings*

APRICOT TORTE

For Sieved Apricots—Rinse thoroughly and put into a saucepan

1½ cups (about ½ lb.) dried apricots

Add

2 cups water

Cover the saucepan tightly and cook the apricots over heat to simmer 25 to 35 min., or until fruit is plump and tender when pierced

with a fork. Remove from heat; drain. Force apricots through a food mill or sieve. Add and stir until dissolved

⅓ cup sugar

Set aside.

For Torte—Set out an 8-in. tubed springform pan.

Grate (page 10)

1 cup (about 4 oz.) walnuts (about 1¾ cups, grated)

Set out

20 saltine crackers (or enough to yield 1 cup fine crumbs)

Prepare crumbs (page 10). Mix thoroughly the walnuts, crumbs and

½ teaspoon nutmeg

Divide into four portions by marking with a spatula; set aside.

Beat until very thick and lemon-colored

5 egg yolks
½ cup sugar

Beat 2 tablespoons of sieved apricots into egg yolk mixture with final few strokes. Set aside. (Reserve remaining apricots for topping.)

Using a clean beater, beat until frothy

5 egg whites

Add gradually, beating well after each addition

½ cup sugar

Beat until rounded peaks are formed and egg whites do not slide when bowl is partially inverted. Gently spread egg yolk mixture over beaten egg whites. Spoon one portion of the walnut-crumb mixture over surface and gently fold with a few strokes until batter is only *partially* blended. Repeat with second and then third portions of walnut-crumb mixture. Spoon remaining portion over batter and gently fold until *just* blended. *Do not overmix!* Carefully turn batter into pan and spread to edges.

Bake at 350°F 45 to 50 min., or until torte tests done (page 11).

Immediately invert pan and cool as directed for sponge-type cakes (page 11).

To Complete Torte—While torte is cooling, chill a bowl and rotary beater in refrigerator.

When torte is completely cooled, cut around

Cherry Torte

tube with paring knife to loosen torte; loosen sides with spatula. Remove sides from the bottom of the pan; cut torte away from pan bottom. Place on serving plate. Spread remaining sieved apricots over top of torte.

Using the chilled bowl and beater, prepare

Sweetened Whipped Cream (page 480)

Spread whipped cream over apricots. Serve immediately.   *About 12 servings*

CHERRY TORTE
(Cseresznye Torta)

Set out deep 9-in. springform pan.

Blanch (page 9)

1 cup (about ⅓ lb.) almonds

Grate (page 10) ⅔ cup of the blanched almonds (about 1⅔ cups, grated); mix with

2 tablespoons fine dry bread crumbs

Divide almond-crumb mixture into four portions and set aside. Toast (page 10) and coarsely chop the remaining almonds; mix with

2 tablespoons sugar

Reserve almond-sugar mixture for topping.

Wash, cut into halves and remove pits from

1 lb. dark sweet cherries (about 2¼ cups, pitted)

Drain cherries and set aside.

Beat in a large bowl until very thick and lemon-colored

6 egg yolks
3 tablespoons sugar
3 tablespoons lemon juice

Set egg yolk mixture aside.

Beat until frothy

6 egg whites
⅛ teaspoon salt

Add gradually to egg whites, beating well after each addition

3 tablespoons sugar

Continue beating until very stiff peaks are formed. Gently spread egg yolk mixture over beaten egg whites. Spoon one portion of the almond-crumb mixture over egg mixture and gently fold with a few strokes until batter is only *partially* blended. Repeat with second and then third portions of almond-crumb mixture. Spoon remaining one fourth of almond-crumb

mixture over batter and gently fold *just* until blended. Do not overmix! Gently turn batter into pan and spread to edges. Gently place cherries evenly over top of batter.

Bake at 350°F 30 to 40 min., or until torte tests done (page 11). Set torte onto cooling rack. Cool torte in pan 15 min. Remove the rim from the bottom of the pan and, if desired, cut away torte from pan bottom and return to rack. When torte is completely cooled, set on a baking sheet.

For Meringue—Beat until frothy
3 egg whites
Add gradually to egg whites, beating well after each addition
6 tablespoons sugar
Continue beating until stiff peaks are formed. Completely cover sides and top of torte with the meringue. Sprinkle the toasted almond mixture evenly over the top of the meringue.

Bake at 350°F 10 to 15 min., or until meringue is delicately browned. Cool torte and transfer to a cake plate. Before cutting first serving of torte, dip knife blade into hot water. To cut remainder of torte (for each cut), wipe meringue off knife blade and dip knife blade into hot water. *12 to 16 servings*

SACHER TORTE
(Sacher Torta)

Prepare (page 10) an 11x7x1½-in. cake pan.

Measure, divide into four portions and set aside
1 cup plus 2 tablespoons sifted all-purpose flour

Grate (page 10) and set aside
4 oz. semisweet candymaking chocolate

Cream until *very* soft and fluffy
½ cup unsalted butter
Add gradually, creaming until fluffy after each addition
⅓ cup sugar
Add one at a time, beating until very well blended and fluffy after each addition
6 egg yolks
Set egg yolk mixture aside.

Beat until frothy
7 egg whites
Add gradually, beating well after each addition
⅓ cup sugar
Continue beating until very stiff peaks are formed. Gently spread beaten egg whites over egg yolk mixture. Spoon the grated chocolate evenly over the egg whites. Sift one portion of the flour over the chocolate; gently fold with a few strokes until batter is only *partially* blended. Repeat with second and then third portions of flour. Sift remaining fourth of flour over batter and gently fold *just* until blended. Do not overmix! Gently turn batter into pan and spread to edges.

Bake at 350°F 25 to 30 min., or until torte

tests done (page 11). Cool and remove from pan as directed (page 11). When torte is cooled, split into two layers. Spread evenly over top of one layer (cut-side up)
⅓ cup strawberry preserves
Place second layer (cut-side down) on top of preserves and spread with
⅓ cup strawberry jelly

Prepare Chocolate Frosting.

For Chocolate Frosting—Partially melt (page 10), being careful not to overheat
3 oz. semisweet candymaking chocolate
Remove chocolate from the simmering water and stir until completely melted. Add
½ cup unsalted butter
Stir until butter is melted. Cool frosting slightly and pour onto torte; spread evenly over sides and top. Chill torte until frosting is firm.
About 12 servings

CHOCOLATE TORTE
(Schokoladentorte)

▲ *Base Recipe*

Prepare (page 10) three 9-in. round layer cake pans.

Blanch (page 9) and grate
½ lb. almonds (about 3½ cups, grated)
Sift together
1¼ cups cocoa
1 teaspoon cinnamon
Mix almonds and cocoa mixture together. Turn onto a piece of waxed paper. Using a spatula, mark into four portions, and set aside.

Cream until softened
1 cup unsalted butter
1½ teaspoons vanilla extract
Add gradually, creaming until fluffy after each addition
⅔ cup sugar
Add one at a time, beating until well blended and fluffy after each addition
8 egg yolks, unbeaten
Beat an additional 2 min. after addition of last yolk. Set mixture aside.

Using clean beater, beat until frothy
8 egg whites
Add about 2 tablespoons at a time, beating well after each addition
⅔ cup sugar
Beat the meringue until very stiff peaks are formed.

Gently spread beaten egg whites over egg yolk mixture. Sprinkle one portion of the cocoa mixture over egg whites; gently fold with a few strokes until batter is only *partially* blended. Repeat with second and then third portions. Spoon remaining mixture over batter and gently fold until *just* blended. *Do not overmix!* Gently turn batter into pans and spread evenly to edges.

Bake at 350°F 30 to 35 min., or until torte layers test done (page 11).

Cool; remove from pans as directed (page 11). When completely cooled, fill and frost torte layers (page 11) with
Chocolate Mocha Butter Cream Frosting (page 474)
Place in refrigerator until ready to serve.
12 to 16 servings

Note: Butter Cream Frosting (page 474) or any variation except the Hazelnut may be used.

—PICTURE-PRETTY CHOCOLATE TORTE

Follow ▲ Recipe for baking and frosting torte layers. Cover sides of torte with **chocolate shot.** Set Chocolate Rolls radiating from center (but allowing a space at center) slightly over edge around entire top surface of frosted torte. Break several of the Rolls into pieces and scatter over center of torte. Sift **Vanilla Confectioners' Sugar** (page 582) over the broken chocolate.

For Chocolate Rolls—Mark 3-in. squares on waxed paper on baking sheet. Melt (page 10) **semisweet chocolate.** Spread 1 teaspoon melted chocolate within borders of each 3-in. square. Cool at room temperature, then set in refrigerator to harden. To roll, set out at room temperature for a few minutes. As chocolate softens and becomes pliable, roll

Sacher Torte

it by slowly folding the waxed paper over itself, loosening chocolate as you roll it. Chill.

COFFEE TORTE

From Scandinavia, where luscious rich tortes take the place of our frosted layer cakes, comes this delectable creation.

Grease bottoms and sides of two 9-in. round layer cake pans. Line bottoms with waxed paper; grease waxed paper. Cut two lengths of parchment paper 2 in. wide and 30 in. long. Line sides of pans with the parchment paper, pressing paper against sides of pans. Fasten ends with cellulose tape.

Grate (page 10)

> **2 cups (about ½ lb.) pecans (about 3½ cups, grated)**

Thoroughly mix with pecans

> **2 to 3 tablespoons instant powdered coffee**

Divide into four portions by marking with a spatula; set aside.

Beat until very thick and lemon-colored

> **7 egg yolks**
> **1 cup sugar**

Set aside.

Beat until rounded peaks are formed and egg whites do not slide when bowl is partially inverted

> **7 egg whites**
> **⅛ teaspoon salt**

Gently spread egg yolk mixture over beaten egg whites. Spoon one portion of the pecan-coffee mixture over surface and gently fold with a few strokes until batter is only *partially* blended. Repeat with second and then third portions. Spoon remaining portion of pecan-coffee mixture over batter and gently fold until *just* blended. *Do not overmix!* Carefully turn batter into pans and spread to edges.

Bake at 350°F 25 to 30 min., or until torte layers test done (page 11).

Cool and remove from pans as directed for tortes (page 11).

When torte is cooled, prepare

> **Mocha-Mallow Whipped Cream Frosting (page 480)**

Fill and frost (page 11) and place in refrigerator until ready to serve.   *12 to 16 servings*

FARINA TORTE

Grease bottom of a 9-in. springform pan.

Grate (page 10)

> **½ cup (about 3 oz.) blanched almonds (about 1¼ cups, grated)**

Add to almonds a mixture of

> **1 cup uncooked farina**
> **1 teaspoon baking powder**
> **½ teaspoon salt**

Mix and set aside.

Beat together until thick and lemon-colored

> **6 egg yolks**
> **⅔ cup sugar**
> **½ teaspoon grated lemon peel**
> **¼ teaspoon almond extract**

Beating very thoroughly after each addition, add the almond-farina mixture in fourths to the beaten egg yolks.

Using a clean beater, beat until frothy

> **6 egg whites**

Add gradually, beating well after each addition

> **⅓ cup sugar**

Beat until rounded peaks are formed and egg whites do not slide when bowl is partially inverted. Gently spread beaten egg whites over the batter and fold together until just blended. Turn into the pan and spread evenly to edges.

Bake at 350°F about 45 min., or until torte tests done (page 11).

Cool and remove from pan as directed for tortes (page 11).

Serve with a topping of **Sweetened Whipped Cream** (page 480).   *One 9-in. torte*

MARZIPAN TORTE

For Torte—Grease bottom of a 7-in. spring-form pan. Set aside.

Measure

> **1¼ cups sifted all-purpose flour**

Divide into four portions by marking with a spatula; set aside.

Measure

> **1 cup almond paste**

Force almond paste through a sieve. Set aside.

Combine and beat until very thick and lemon-colored

> **12 egg yolks**
> **⅓ cup sugar**
> **4 teaspoons grated orange peel**
> **1 tablespoon grated lemon peel**
> **¼ teaspoon almond extract**

Add in small amounts, beating thoroughly after each addition, the sieved almond paste and

> **⅓ cup sugar**

Beat an additional 2 min. after last addition of sugar.

Measure and combine

> **¼ cup orange juice**
> **2 tablespoons lemon juice**

Beating only until smooth after each addition, alternately add flour in thirds and liquid in halves to egg yolk mixture. Finally, beat only until smooth (do not overbeat). Turn batter into pan. Cut through batter with knife or spatula to break large air bubbles.

Bake at 300°F about 1 hr. 10 min., or until torte tests done (page 11) with cake tester.

Cool and remove from pan as directed for tortes (page 11). When torte is completely cooled, cut into four equal layers.

For Filling and Frosting—Set a bowl and rotary beater in refrigerator to chill.

Chop and set aside enough fruit to yield

> **2 tablespoons finely chopped pitted dates**
> **2 tablespoons finely chopped dark seedless raisins**
> **2 tablespoons finely chopped dried figs**
> **2 tablespoons finely chopped candied cherries**

Grate (page 10) and set aside

> **¼ cup (about 1½ oz.) blanched toasted almonds (about ⅔ cup, grated)**

Just before serving, using the chilled bowl and beater, prepare

> **Sweetened Whipped Cream (one and one half times recipe, page 480; beat only one half of cream at a time)**

Put about 2 cups of the whipped cream into a second bowl and fold in the chopped fruit. Fill torte layers (page 11) with this mixture. Fold the grated almonds into the remaining whipped cream. Spread over the top layer.

Serve immediately.   *10 to 12 servings*

GALA TORTE

Here's a surprising and novel combination of flavors which is really terrific, worthy of the most gala occasions!

For Torte—Prepare (page 10) two 9-in. round layer cake pans.

Grate (page 10)

**1 cup (about 5 oz.) hazelnuts (about
1¾ cups, grated)**

**1 cup (about 4 oz.) walnuts (about
1¾ cups, grated)**

Combine nuts and mix well with

2 tablespoons all-purpose flour

Divide into four portions by marking with a
spatula; set aside.

Beat until very thick and lemon-colored

6 egg yolks
½ cup sugar

Set aside.

Using clean beater, beat until frothy

6 egg whites
¼ teaspoon salt

Add gradually, beating well after each addition

½ cup sugar

Beat until rounded peaks are formed and egg
whites do not slide when bowl is partially inverted. Spread egg yolk mixture over beaten
egg whites. Spoon one portion of the nut-flour
mixture over surface and gently fold with a
few strokes until batter is only partially
blended. Repeat with second and then third
portions. Spoon remaining portion of nut-flour
mixture over batter and gently fold until *just*
blended. *Do not overmix!* Gently turn batter
into pans and spread to edges.

Bake at 350°F about 50 min., or until torte
layers test done (page 11).

Cool and remove from pans as directed for
tortes (page 11). When torte is completely
cooled, prepare frosting.

For Frosting—Partially melt in double-boiler
top over hot (not simmering) water, being
careful not to overheat

**4 oz. semisweet candymaking
chocolate**

Remove chocolate from the hot water and
stir until completely melted. Blend in

½ cup milk

Set aside to cool.

Cream until softened

¾ cup butter
½ teaspoon vanilla extract

Add gradually, creaming until light and fluffy
after each addition

¾ cup sugar
¼ teaspoon salt

Add in thirds, beating thoroughly after each
addition

2 egg yolks, well beaten

Blend in the cooled chocolate mixture; set
aside.

To Complete Torte—Split torte layers into
halves, forming four equal layers. Set out

¾ cup raspberry or strawberry jam

Spread ¼ cup over each of three layers. Spread
some of the frosting over the jam-covered
bottom layer; cover with second layer, jam
side up. Spread with more of the frosting; repeat with third layer. Place remaining layer
on top; frost torte (page 11) with remaining

*Hazelnut Torte à la Glamour and
Picture- Pretty Chocolate Torte*

frosting. If desired, sprinkle **finely chopped
nuts** over top of torte. *12 to 16 servings*

HAZELNUT TORTE I
(Haselnusstorte)

▲ *Base Recipe*

Grease bottoms of two 9-in. round layer cake
pans with removable bottoms or prepare
(page 10) two 9-in. round layer cake pans.

Grate (page 10)

**1½ cups (about ½ lb.) hazelnuts
(about 4⅓ cups, grated)**

Sift together

½ cup sifted all-purpose flour
**½ teaspoon instant powdered
coffee**
**½ teaspoon cocoa or Dutch process
cocoa**

Thoroughly blend hazelnuts with flour mixture.
Turn onto a piece of waxed paper and with a
spatula mark into four portions; set aside.

Combine and beat until very thick and lemon-
colored

6 egg yolks
½ cup sugar
1 teaspoon grated lemon peel
1 teaspoon rum
½ teaspoon vanilla extract

Set egg yolk mixture aside.

Using clean beater, beat until frothy

6 egg whites
¼ teaspoon salt

Add gradually to egg whites, beating well after
each addition

½ cup sugar

Beat the meringue until very stiff peaks are
formed.

Gently spread egg yolk mixture over beaten
egg whites. Spoon one portion of the flour-
hazelnut mixture over egg mixture and gently
fold with a few strokes until batter is only
partially blended. Repeat with second and then
third portions. Spoon remaining mixture over

batter and gently fold *just* until blended. *Do not
overmix!* Gently turn batter into pans and
spread to edges.

Bake at 350°F 25 to 30 min., or until torte
layers test done (page 11).

Cool and remove from pans (page 11).

When torte is cooled, prepare
**Hazelnut Butter Cream Frosting
(page 474)**

Cut one of the torte layers into halves forming
2 equal layers. Fill and frost all three torte
layers (page 11), placing bottom side of split
layer next to plate. Put into refrigerator until
ready to serve. *12 to 16 servings*

—HAZELNUT TORTE A LA GLAMOUR
(Garnierte Haselnusstorte)

Follow ▲ Recipe for preparing and splitting
torte layers. Grate ½ cup (about 2½ oz.)
hazelnuts (about 1½ cups, grated). Set aside.
Prepare **Butter Cream Frosting** (page 474; using
7 egg yolks, ¾ cup plus 2 tablespoons sugar,
¾ teaspoon cornstarch, ¾ cup plus 2 tablespoons cream and 1½ cups butter). Remove
and reserve 1 cup of the frosting. Blend
the grated nuts into the remaining frosting;
fill and frost torte layers (page 11). Force
some of the remaining frosting through a
pastry bag and a No. 1 star tube to make a
border around outer edge of top layer. Using a
No. 26 decorating tube and remaining frosting,
pipe a zigzag decoration from center to border;
allow one decoration for each serving. Use No.
26 decorating tube, form rosettes around base.

HAZELNUT TORTE II
(Hassel Nöt Tarta)

▲ *Base Recipe*

Set out two 8-in. round layer cake pans.

Grate (page 10)

**1 cup (about 4¾ oz.) hazelnuts
(about 1¾ cups, grated)**

467

Sift together

2 tablespoons sifted all-purpose flour
2 teaspoons baking powder

Blend flour mixture and grated nuts together and set aside.

Beat until thick and piled softly

3 eggs

Gradually blend in

¾ cup sugar

Gently fold nut-flour mixture into the egg mixture. Turn batter into the pans.

Bake at 350°F 20 min., or until torte tests done (page 11). Invert pans and let layers hang until cool. (If torte is higher than pan, invert between two cooling racks so that top of torte does not touch any surface.)

When torte is cooled, remove from pans as directed (page 11). Sift over tops of layers

¼ cup confectioners' sugar

12 to 16 servings

—FILLED HAZELNUT TORTE
(Fyllda Hassel Nöt Tarta)

Follow ▲ Recipe. Prepare **Sweetened Whipped Cream** (page 480); refrigerate until needed. Fill the cooled torte (page 11) with the whipped cream. Sprinkle top of torte with **confectioners' sugar**.

DOBOS TORTE
(Dobos Torta)

▲ *Base Recipe*

Delicate layers, velvety rich chocolate filling and a crown of crunchy caramel glaze were the inspiration of a Hungarian pastry chef named Dobos. This torte is a special celebration treat for Hungarians.

Six 8-in. round layer cake pans or six 8-in. round layer cake pans with removable bottoms will be needed. (If necessary, three cake layers may be baked at one time and the same three pans reused for the remaining three layers.)

For Frosting—Put into a shallow baking dish

8 hazelnuts

Set in a 400°F oven 3 to 5 min., or until skins are loosened and nuts are lightly toasted. Remove from oven and cool slightly; discard skins. Finely chop or crush hazelnuts; set aside.

Melt (page 10) and set aside to cool

4 oz. (4 sq.) unsweetened chocolate

Cream in a large bowl until butter is light and fluffy and set bowl aside

1 cup firm unsalted butter
1 teaspoon vanilla extract

Mix in a small saucepan with a tight-fitting cover

1 cup sugar
¼ cup water

Bring to boiling, stirring gently until sugar is dissolved. Cover saucepan and boil syrup gently 5 min. to help wash down any crystals that might have formed on sides of saucepan. Uncover saucepan and continue cooking syrup to thread stage (230°F to 234°F), or until syrup spins a 2-in. thread when allowed to drop from fork or spoon. (Remove from heat while testing.) Set syrup aside.

Meanwhile, beat until thick and lemon-colored

6 egg yolks

Beating constantly with rotary beater, pour the hot syrup very gradually in a thin stream into egg yolks. (Do not scrape syrup from bottom and sides of saucepan.) Beat egg yolk mixture until very thick and of same consistency as the creamed butter. Cool completely. Beat egg yolk mixture, about 2 tablespoons at a time, into the butter until *just* blended. Gradually mix in the chocolate and the hazelnuts. Set frosting in the refrigerator to chill.

For Torte—Prepare (page 10) the six 8-in. round layer cake pans, or grease bottoms of the six 8-in. round layer cake pans with removable bottoms.

Measure and set aside

1 cup sifted all-purpose flour

Put into a large bowl and beat until very thick and lemon-colored

6 egg yolks
¼ cup sugar

Set egg yolk mixture aside.

Beat until frothy

6 egg whites
⅛ teaspoon salt

Add gradually to egg whites, beating well after each addition

¼ cup sugar

Continue beating until very stiff peaks are formed. Gently spread egg yolk mixture over beaten egg whites.

Divide the sifted flour into four portions. Sift one portion at a time over egg mixture and gently fold just until blended after each addition. Spoon equal amounts of batter into cake pans and spread ¼ in. thick. Stagger pans in oven (page 10).

Bake at 350°F about 15 min., or until lightly browned. Remove torte layers to cooling racks. If using waxed paper lined pans, carefully and quickly remove layers from pans. Beginning at center, tear paper and gently pull it off in small pieces. (Allow layers in removable bottom pans to stand in pans 2 min.; loosen edges with spatula and carefully cut layers away from bottoms of pans.) Carefully place on cooling racks right-side up and cool completely.

Beat the chilled frosting until fluffy. Spread frosting ⅛ in. thick on four of the torte layers, placing one layer on top of another. Add fifth layer, but do not frost top. Thinly spread frosting on sides of torte. Put the five layers and remainder of frosting into refrigerator.

Meanwhile, place the sixth layer, which will be the top of torte, onto a shallow baking sheet. With back of knife blade, make 16 to 18 wedge-shape indentations on top of layer, but do not cut wedges apart. Grease a small area of baking sheet around torte layer (so that caramel topping will not stick to baking sheet if it runs off).

For Caramel Topping—Melt in heavy, light-colored, small skillet over low heat, stirring constantly

¾ cup confectioners' sugar

Occasionally remove skillet from heat and press out lumps of sugar with back of spoon. Cook sugar until smooth and golden brown.

Remove from heat and *quickly* pour onto top layer of torte. Spread caramel topping evenly over layer with a spatula, working rapidly before sugar hardens. With back of knife blade, make wedge-shape indentations over the ones made previously in the torte layer. With blade of knife, cut wedges apart.

Remove the layers and frosting from refrigerator. Beat frosting until fluffy. Spread frosting ⅛ in. thick on top of fifth layer and arrange caramel-topped wedges on top of it. Frost sides of sixth layer. Using a pastry bag and a No. 6 decorating tube, pipe a border of frosting around top edge of torte. Chill torte in refrigerator until frosting is firm. Cut servings with knife, blade of which has been dipped into hot water.

16 to 18 servings

—PISCHINGER TORTE

Follow ▲ Recipe for torte layers. For frosting, substitute the following: cream until light and fluffy ½ cup unsalted butter and 1½ tablespoons lemon juice. Add gradually, creaming well after each addition, **1 cup confectioners' sugar**. Mix in ½ cup (about 2 oz.) grated hazelnuts (page 10) and **2 oz. (2 sq.) grated unsweetened chocolate**. Frost (page 11) torte. Omit Caramel Topping.

Note: When available, use 7 Karlsbader or Oblaten wafers instead of these torte layers. Fill and frost with Pischinger frosting. No baking is required with these wafers.

ROCKY-ROAD NUT TORTE

Snowy bits of marshmallow in the unusual topping are the tender "rocks" which give this torte its name.

Dobos Torte

Rocky-Road Nut Torte

For Torte—Prepare (page 10) an 8x8x2-in. pan.

Grate (page 10)

    1 cup (about 5 oz.) hazelnuts (about 1¾ cups, grated)

Set out

    24 vanilla wafers (or enough to yield 1 cup crumbs)

Prepare crumbs (page 10).

Sift together

    ¼ cup sifted all-purpose flour
    1 teaspoon baking powder
    ¼ teaspoon salt
    ½ teaspoon cinnamon

Mix nuts, crumbs and dry ingredients. Divide into four portions by marking with a spatula; set aside.

Beat until very thick and piled softly

    3 eggs
    ⅔ cup sugar

Spoon one portion of the nut mixture over beaten eggs and gently fold with a few strokes until batter is only *partially* blended. Repeat with second and then third portions. Spoon remaining portion of nut mixture over batter and gently fold until *just* blended. *Do not overmix!* Carefully turn batter into pan and spread to edges.

Bake at 350°F 35 to 40 min., or until torte tests done (page 11).

Cool and remove from pan as directed for tortes (page 11). While torte is cooling, prepare topping.

For Topping—Set a small bowl and a rotary beater in refrigerator to chill.

Have ready

    ¾ cup (about 2 oz.) miniature marshmallows*
    ½ cup (about 2½ oz.) coarsely chopped hazelnuts

Pour into a small cup or custard cup

    ¼ cup cold water

Sprinkle evenly over the cold water

    1½ teaspoons unflavored gelatin

Set aside.

Combine in the top of a double boiler

    ¾ cup milk
    ¼ cup sugar
    ⅛ teaspoon salt
    1 oz. (1 sq.) unsweetened chocolate

Heat over simmering water, stirring occasionally, until chocolate is melted.

Vigorously stir about 3 tablespoons of the hot mixture into

    1 egg yolk, slightly beaten

Immediately blend into mixture in double boiler. Cook over simmering water 3 to 5 min., stirring constantly to keep mixture cooking evenly.

Immediately remove from heat. Add softened gelatin and stir until gelatin is completely dissolved. Cool; chill gelatin mixture in refrigerator or over ice and water until mixture begins to gel (gets slightly thicker). If placed over ice and water, stir frequently; if placed in refrigerator, stir occasionally.

Return the cooled torte to its pan.

Using chilled bowl and beater, beat until cream is of medium consistency (piles softly)

    ¼ cup chilled heavy cream

Beat in with few final strokes

    ¼ teaspoon vanilla extract

Set in refrigerator while beating egg white.

Using clean beater, beat until stiff, not dry, peaks are formed

    1 egg white

When gelatin mixture is of desired consistency, fold in the beaten egg white, whipped cream, marshmallows and hazelnuts. Spread evenly over the cooled torte. Chill in refrigerator until topping is set. Cut into squares.

About 9 servings

*Or cut 8 (2 oz.) marshmallows into sixths.

ORANGE CREAM TORTE

Tender, perfect sponge cake is transformed into a truly superb dessert when topped with a special filling to give the cake a piquant touch of golden orange moistness.

Set out two 9-in. round layer cake pans.

Combine in a large bowl and beat until very thick and lemon-colored (10 min. with an electric mixer on medium-high speed)

    5 egg yolks
    ½ cup sugar
    1 teaspoon grated orange peel
    2 tablespoons orange juice
    ½ teaspoon lemon extract

Set aside.

Beat until frothy

    5 egg whites
    ½ teaspoon salt

Add gradually, beating thoroughly after each addition

    ½ cup sugar

Beat meringue until very stiff peaks are formed when beater is lifted upright.

Gently spread egg yolk mixture over beaten egg whites and gently fold together.

Fold in, sifting in about one-fourth at a time

    1 cup sifted cake flour

Carefully turn batter into pans.

Bake at 325°F 30 to 35 min., or until cake tests done (page 11). Invert so edge of pan rests on edges of two cooling racks and let hang in pans until cold.

Loosen with spatula to remove from pans.

While cake is cooling, prepare
    Orange Filling II (page 483)

Spread one half of filling over each layer. Place in refrigerator for at least 1 hr. (Torte may stand in refrigerator overnight.)

Orange Cream Torte

About an hour before ready to serve, prepare **Sweetened Whipped Cream (one and one half times recipe, page 480)** Spread one layer with part of whipped cream. Place second layer, with filling side up, on top of cream. Cover sides and top with remaining whipped cream.

Place in refrigerator until ready to serve.

About 12 servings

OLD-WORLD TORTE

Prepare (page 10) four 8-in. round layer cake pans.

For Torte Layers—Grate (page 10)
3 cups (about ¾ lb.) pecans (about 5¼ cups, grated)
Divide into four portions by marking with a spatula; set aside.

Beat until very thick and lemon-colored
8 egg yolks
1⅓ cups sugar
2 teaspoons vanilla extract
½ teaspoon salt
Set aside.

Using a clean beater, beat until frothy
8 egg whites
Add gradually, beating well after each addition
⅔ cup sugar
Beat until rounded peaks are formed and egg whites do not slide when bowl is partially inverted. Gently spread beaten egg whites over the egg yolk mixture. Spoon one portion of the pecans over surface and gently fold with a few strokes until batter is only *partially* blended. Repeat with second and then third portions. Spoon remaining portion of pecans over batter and gently fold until *just* blended. *Do not overmix!* Gently turn batter into pan and spread to edges.

Bake at 350°F 25 to 30 min., or until torte layers test done (page 11).

Cool and remove from pans as directed for tortes (page 11).

For Filling—While torte layers are cooling, cream until softened
⅔ cup butter
1 teaspoon vanilla extract

Add gradually, beating well after each addition
2 cups confectioners' sugar
⅔ cup cocoa

To Complete Torte—When torte layers are completely cooled, fill with the prepared filling. Generously sift over top of torte
Confectioners' sugar

12 to 16 servings

LINZER TORTE
(Linci Torta)

Prepare (page 10) two 9-in. round layer cake pans.

Measure, divide into four portions and set aside
2¼ cups sifted all-purpose flour

Cream until *very* soft and fluffy
1 cup unsalted butter
Add gradually, creaming until fluffy after each addition
⅔ cup sugar
Add one at a time, beating until very well blended and fluffy after each addition
8 egg yolks
Beat an additional 2 min. after addition of final egg yolk. Set egg yolk mixture aside.

Beat until frothy
8 egg whites
Add 2 tablespoons at a time, beating well after each addition
⅔ cup sugar
Continue beating until very stiff peaks are formed. Gently spread beaten egg whites over egg yolk mixture. Sift one portion of the flour over egg whites; gently fold with a few strokes until batter is only `partially` blended. Repeat with second and then third portions of flour. Sift remaining one fourth of flour over batter and gently fold *just* until blended. Do not overmix! Gently turn batter into pans and spread to edges.

Bake at 350°F 30 to 35 min., or until torte tests done (page 11).

Cool and remove from pans as directed (page 11).

Meanwhile, blanch (page 9) and set aside
12 to 16 almonds

When torte is cooled, spread evenly over top of one layer
⅓ cup thick raspberry preserves
Place second layer on top; set torte aside. Prepare and frost sides and top of torte with
Chocolate Frosting (see Sacher Torte, page 465)
Before frosting becomes firm, garnish top edge of torte with the almonds.   *12 to 16 servings*

RASPBERRY WHIPPED CREAM TORTE
(Tejszinhabos Málna Torta)

Set out a 4-qt. double boiler or a 4-qt. heat-resistant bowl and a large kettle.

Prepare (page 10) two 9-in. round layer cake pans.

Measure, divide into four portions and set aside
1⅓ cups sifted all-purpose flour

Melt over simmering water and set aside to cool
3 tablespoons unsalted butter

Put into top of the double boiler
6 eggs
4 egg yolks
1½ cups sifted confectioners' sugar
Set over simmering water, making sure the bottom of double boiler top does not touch water. (Or, use the 4-qt. bowl set over the large kettle containing simmering water, making sure that bottom of bowl does not touch water.) With rotary beater, beat egg mixture constantly for about 5 min., or until mixture is slightly heated.

Remove double boiler top from simmering water and beat egg mixture until thick, piled softly and completely cooled. Sift one portion of the flour over egg mixture and gently fold with a few strokes until batter is only *partially* blended. Repeat with second and then third portions of flour. Sift remaining one fourth of flour over batter and gently fold *just* until blended. Gradually add melted butter, folding *just* until blended. Do not overmix! Gently turn batter into pans and spread to edges.

Bake at 350°F 25 to 30 min., or until torte tests done (page 11).

Cool and remove from pans as directed (page 11).

While torte is cooling, rinse and thoroughly drain
2 cups red raspberries
Select 16 berries for garnish and place in refrigerator.

Cut remaining raspberries and mix with
1 teaspoon rum
Set fruit aside.

For Sweetened Whipped Cream—Chill in refrigerator two 1-qt. bowls, a rotary beater and
2 cups heavy cream

Set out
½ cup confectioners' sugar

Linzer Torte

Raspberry Whipped Cream Torte

Pour 1 cup of chilled cream into each bowl. Beat until cream stands in peaks when beater is slowly lifted upright. With few final strokes, beat one half the sugar into each portion of whipped cream. Place one half in refrigerator.

To Assemble Torte—Fold the cut raspberries into the second portion of whipped cream and spread evenly over one of the torte layers. Top with second layer; using spatula, cover sides and then top of torte with the reserved whipped cream.

Roll reserved berries in about
    2 teaspoons sugar
Arrange raspberries in a circle around top edge of torte. Set in refrigerator until ready to serve. To avoid sogginess, chill torte no longer than 1 hr.   *10 to 12 servings*

FLAVORFUL RYE TORTE

Arrange on a baking sheet
    Rye bread slices (about ¼ lb.)
Place in 325°F oven until bread is completely dry and crisp. Remove from oven and cool.

Meanwhile, grate (page 10)
    1 oz. blanched almonds (about ½ cup, grated)
    1 oz. (1 sq.) unsweetened chocolate
When dried bread is cool, prepare 1 cup crumbs (page 10; the crumbs for this torte should be slightly coarser than corn meal). Add to almonds and chocolate with
    ¼ teaspoon cinnamon
    ⅛ teaspoon cloves
Mix well; divide into four portions by marking with a spatula; set aside.

Grease bottom of a 9-in. springform pan and dust it lightly with very fine rye bread crumbs.

Combine and beat until very thick and lemon-colored
    5 egg yolks
    ½ cup sugar
    2 tablespoons water
    1 teaspoon vanilla extract
Stir in
    2 tablespoons finely chopped citron
    2 tablespoons finely chopped candied orange peel
Using clean beater, beat until frothy
    5 egg whites

Add gradually, beating thoroughly after each addition
    ½ cup sugar
Beat until rounded peaks are formed and egg whites do not slide when bowl is partially inverted. Gently spread egg yolk mixture over the beaten egg whites. Spoon one portion of the bread-crumb mixture over surface and gently fold with a few strokes until batter is only *partially* blended. Repeat with second and then third portions. Spoon remaining portion over batter and gently fold until *just* blended. *Do not overmix!* Turn batter into the pan and spread to edges.

Bake at 350°F 1 hr., or until torte tests done (page 11).

Cool and remove from pan as directed (page 11). Sift **confectioners' sugar** over top.
    One 9-in. torte

WALNUT TORTE I
(Walnusstorte)

Set out a 7-in. springform pan.

Grate (page 10)
    1 cup (about 3½ oz.) walnuts (about 1¾ cups, grated)
Thoroughly mix walnuts with
    1 cup fine dry bread crumbs (about 3 slices bread)
Turn onto a piece of waxed paper. With a knife divide into four portions and set aside.

Beat until very thick and lemon-colored
    5 egg yolks
    ½ cup sugar
Beat in with final few strokes and set aside
    2 tablespoons rum

Using clean beater, beat until frothy
    5 egg whites
Add 2 tablespoons at a time, beating well after each addition
    ½ cup sugar
Beat until very stiff peaks are formed. Gently spread egg yolk mixture over beaten egg whites. Spoon one portion of the walnut-bread crumb mixture over egg mixture and gently fold with a few strokes until batter is only *partially* blended. Repeat with second and then third portions of walnut-crumb mixture. Spoon remaining portion over batter and gently fold *just* until blended. *Do not overmix!* Gently turn batter into pan and spread to edges.

Bake at 350°F 40 to 45 min., or until torte tests done (page 11). Set torte on cooling rack. Cool in pan 15 min. Remove the sides from the bottom of the pan and, if desired, cut away torte from pan bottom. Return torte to cooling rack to cool completely.

Meanwhile, prepare
    Creamy Rum Filling (page 484)
Chop finely and set aside
    ½ cup (2 oz.) walnuts
When torte is completely cooled, split into two layers. Place bottom half on a serving plate,

cut side up. Spread with about one half of the filling. Cover with second layer, cut side down. Spread remaining filling over top of torte. Sprinkle with the finely chopped walnuts.
    One 7-in. torte

WALNUT TORTE II
(Gateaux aux Noix)

Butter bottom of a 9x5x3-in. loaf pan. Line pan bottom with waxed paper cut to fit exactly; butter waxed paper.

Mix and set aside
    ⅓ lb. (about 1½ cups) finely chopped walnuts
    ⅔ cup (2 slices) fine dry bread crumbs
    ¼ teaspoon salt
    ¼ teaspoon mace
    ⅛ teaspoon cloves
(The electric blender is excellent for finely chopping nuts and preparing bread crumbs.)

Beat 3 min. on electric mixer at medium speed
    5 egg yolks
    1 cup sugar
    1 teaspoon grated lemon peel
    1½ teaspoons lemon juice
Blend in nut mixture.

Beat until stiff, not dry, peaks are formed
    5 egg whites
Carefully fold into batter. Turn batter into pan.

Bake at 350°F 40 to 45 min. Cake is done if top springs back when lightly touched at center. Allow cake to cool in pan 10 min. Loosen sides with a spatula and turn onto a cake rack. Remove paper from bottom, turn right side up and cool completely. Wrap in waxed paper. *Flavor is improved if this cake is stored a day before serving.* Just before serving, cut the cake into lengthwise slices.

Beat (1 cup at a time) in a chilled bowl with chilled rotary beater until cream stands in peaks when beater is slowly lifted upright
    3 cups chilled heavy cream
With few final strokes, beat in
    ½ cup confectioners' sugar
Reshape cake into a loaf, spreading whipped cream between each slice and generously over top of cake.

Walnut Torte II with Sugared Roses

Walnut Torte with Butter Frosting

For Sugared Roses—Brush slightly beaten egg white onto natural roses with a small brush; sprinkle the surfaces of the roses generously with granulated sugar; allow roses to dry before placing on cake. *10 to 12 servings*

WALNUT TORTE WITH BUTTER FROSTING
(Diós Torta Vajas Mázzal)

▲ Base Recipe

Grease bottoms of two 9-in. round layer cake pans with removable bottoms or prepare (page 10) two 9-in. round layer cake pans.

Sift together and set aside
½ cup sifted all-purpose flour
½ teaspoon instant powdered coffee
½ teaspoon cocoa or Dutch process cocoa

Grate (page 10)
2 cups (about ½ lb.) walnuts (about 3½ cups, grated)
Thoroughly combine walnuts with flour mixture, divide into four portions and set aside.

Beat until very thick and lemon-colored
6 egg yolks
½ cup sugar

Mix gently into egg yolk mixture
1 teaspoon grated lemon peel
1 teaspoon rum
½ teaspoon vanilla extract
Set egg yolk mixture aside.

Beat until frothy
6 egg whites
⅛ teaspoon salt
Add gradually to egg whites, beating well after each addition
½ cup sugar
Continue beating until very stiff peaks are formed. Gently spread egg yolk mixture over beaten egg whites. Spoon one portion of the flour-walnut mixture over egg mixture and gently fold with a few strokes until batter is only *partially* blended. Repeat with second and then third portions. Spoon remaining one fourth of flour-walnut mixture over batter and gently fold *just* until blended. Do not overmix! Gently turn batter into pans and spread to edges.

Bake at 350°F 25 to 30 min., or until torte tests done (page 11).

Cool and remove from pans as directed (page 11).

When torte is cooled, prepare the frosting. Frost (page 11) torte and place in refrigerator until ready to serve.

For Butter Frosting—Grate (page 10) and set aside
½ cup (about 2 oz.) walnuts (about ¾ cup, grated)

Cream together until mixture is light and fluffy
1½ cups firm unsalted butter
½ teaspoon vanilla extract
½ teaspoon rum
Add, one at a time, beating thoroughly after each addition
2 egg yolks
Set aside.

Combine in a small saucepan with a tight-fitting cover
1 cup plus 2 tablespoons sugar
⅓ cup water
Bring to boiling over medium heat, stirring gently until sugar is dissolved. Cover saucepan tightly and boil syrup gently 5 min. to help wash down any crystals that might have formed on the sides of saucepan. Uncover saucepan and continue cooking syrup to thread stage (230°F to 234°F), or until syrup spins a 2-in. thread when allowed to drop from spoon. (Remove pan from heat while testing.)

Meanwhile, beat until stiff, not dry, peaks are formed
2 egg whites
Continue beating egg whites and pour the hot syrup in a thin stream into beaten egg whites. (Do not scrape syrup from bottom and sides of pan.) Continue beating a few minutes just until egg white mixture is very thick (piles softly) and of same consistency as the butter mixture. Cool completely. Beat egg white mixture, about

2 tablespoons at a time, into butter mixture until *just* blended. Gradually blend the grated walnuts into frosting. If necessary, chill frosting in refrigerator until firm enough to spread.
12 to 16 servings

CREAM FILLED WALNUT TORTE

Set out and grease three 8-in. layer cake pans; line bottoms with circles of waxed paper, foil, or greased brown paper.

Grate (page 10)
1½ cups walnuts
Combine nuts in a bowl with
¾ cup superfine sugar
¾ cup sifted cake flour
Mix thoroughly and set aside.

Combine in a large mixer bowl, beating until foamy
9 egg whites
1 teaspoon cream of tartar
½ teaspoon salt
Beating constantly, add gradually
1½ cups superfine sugar
Continue beating until very stiff peaks are formed. Add
1½ teaspoons vanilla extract
Fold in the walnut mixture, mixing gently until blended. Divide batter equally in the prepared pans; spread evenly.

Bake in 325°F oven 40 min. Remove from oven to cooling racks. When cool, loosen sides of cake layers with spatula and remove from pans. Peel off waxed paper immediately.

Combine in a heavy saucepan
1 pkg. (about 3½ oz.) lemon pie filling
2 teaspoons grated orange peel
1¾ cups liquid (juice of 1 large orange plus water)
Blend thoroughly and stir in
2 egg yolks, slightly beaten
Cook and stir over medium heat until mixture comes to a full boil. Cover and set aside to cool.

Beat until soft peaks are formed
1 cup heavy cream, chilled
Fold into cooled filling. Spread the filling evenly on top of each and stack layers. Refrigerate several hours before serving.
One 9-in. torte

Note: If desired, decorate torte with Meringue Mushrooms. To prepare, remove about ⅔ cup of the meringue before folding in the walnut-flour mixture in the torte. Cover a baking sheet with foil and spoon 6 rounds about 1¼ inches in diameter on the foil. Spoon onto foil 6 tiny rounds to use for mushroom stems. Dust tops of larger mounds with unsweetened cocoa. Set aside while baking meringue layers. When layers are removed from oven reset temperature control to 275°F. Place "mushrooms" in oven and bake 1¼ hrs. Turn off heat and let mushrooms remain in oven until cold. Stack large mounds on smaller ones and arrange on torte just before serving.

472

Frosting Roses—Use a No. 103 flower tube. First pipe a small amount of frosting onto cake to form a compact center for the rose. Hold tube parallel to top of cake, with narrow end of tube-opening pointing up. With tube touching side of rose's center, make first petal by gently forcing frosting through tube; working around center, first raise tube slightly, then lower it, releasing pressure on bag as tube is lowered. Repeat for other petals, overlapping them; make petals wider as rose gets larger. For outside petals of fully opened rose, tip tube-opening away from flower center. Finish rose with one or two green leaves, using a No. 66 leaf tube.

COOKED FROSTINGS

BUTTER FROSTING

Grate (page 10) and set aside
½ cup (about 2 oz.) walnuts (about ¾ cup, grated)

Cream together until mixture is light and fluffy
1½ cups firm unsalted butter
½ teaspoon vanilla extract
½ teaspoon rum
Add one at a time, beating thoroughly after each addition
2 egg yolks
Set aside.

Combine in a small saucepan with a tight-fitting cover
1 cup plus 2 tablespoons sugar
⅓ cup water
Bring to boiling over medium heat, stirring gently until sugar is dissolved. Cover saucepan tightly and boil syrup gently 5 min. to help wash down any crystals that might have formed on the sides of saucepan. Uncover saucepan and continue cooking syrup to thread stage (230°F to 234°F), or until syrup spins a 2-in. thread when allowed to drop from spoon. (Remove pan from heat while testing.)

Meanwhile, beat until stiff, not dry, peaks are formed
2 egg whites
Continue beating egg whites while pouring the hot syrup in a thin stream into beaten egg whites. (Do not scrape syrup from bottom and side of pan.)

Continue beating a few minutes just until egg white mixture is very thick (piles softly) and

Frosting and fillings

A plain cake without frosting, filling, or any other form of embellishment could be quite acceptable but, somehow, cakes seem to come into their glory only when decked in the swirled coat of sweetness known as frosting. Frostings may be plain or fancy, chocolaty brown or soft pink in color, laced with essence of fruits or flecked with fragments of nuts or candy. They may be prepared in many ways, but they are designed to beautify and delight. The frostings in this chapter are of both the cooked and uncooked varieties and use different types of sugar as their main ingredient. The chapter also includes a recipe for decorative frosting to be used with pastry bag and tubes to decorate special-occasion cakes. In addition are offered fillings appropriate for a variety of cakes and other goodies.

CAKE DECORATING

Your cakes can bloom with flowers and other festive decorations. All you need is a cake decorating set including a pastry bag or gun (or use a bag you can make yourself from parchment paper), several tubes for producing the various decorative forms, and lots of practice. Get your practice before you start decorating your first cake. You can use actual frosting, making the decorations on waxed paper or on the back of a clean cake pan, so you can scrape the frosting off and re-use it; or you can practice with shortening or lard. Fill the pastry bag or gun only two-thirds full of frosting. If you're using a bag, be sure to close the top by twisting it securely. The tubes you will use most frequently are:

THE STAR TUBE
(small star tube No. 27,
or larger star tubes Nos. 1 to 3)

B
THE WRITING TUBE
(Nos. 1 to 3)

The star tube makes *rosettes*, the writing tube is used for *script and stems*, and the leaf tube is used for *leaves*. Master these before experimenting with others. Almost any decorating tube can produce an attractive border. The more you practice, the easier decorating will become. Once you learn to control pressure, you need only guide the tube in the right direction. Variations in pressure and direction produce the forms you want.

THE LEAF TUBE
(Nos. 65 to 67)

is of same consistency as the butter mixture. Cool completely. Beat egg white mixture, about 2 tablespoons at a time, into butter mixture until *just* blended. Gradually mix the grated walnuts into frosting. If necessary, chill frosting in refrigerator until firm enough to spread.

Enough to frost sides and tops of two 9-in. cake layers

BUTTER CREAM FROSTING

▲ Base Recipe

In top of a double boiler, beat until thick and lemon-colored

6 egg yolks

Add gradually, beating constantly, a mixture of

¾ cup sugar
½ teaspoon cornstarch

Add gradually and stir until well blended

¾ cup cream

Set over simmering water and cook, stirring constantly, until thickened, about 17 min. Remove from heat and stir in

2 teaspoons vanilla extract

Cover; cool slightly. Set in refrigerator to chill.

When mixture is chilled, put into a large bowl

1½ cups firm unsalted butter

Beginning with medium speed of an electric mixer, and as soon as possible increasing to high, beat until butter is fluffy. Gradually add the chilled mixture to the creamed butter, beating after each addition just until blended. If necessary, set frosting over ice and water until firm enough to spread. If frosting should curdle, beat again until just smooth.

This frosting will keep several days, tightly covered, in the refrigerator. Beat just until smooth before using. *Enough to frost sides and tops of three 9-in. cake layers*

—HAZELNUT BUTTER CREAM FROSTING

Grate ½ cup (about 2½ oz.) hazelnuts (about 1½ cups, grated). Follow ▲ Recipe. Blend the grated nuts into the frosting after blending in the egg yolk mixture.

—MOCHA BUTTER CREAM FROSTING

Put **1¾ teaspoons instant powdered coffee** into a small cup; add **1 teaspoon boiling water** and stir until coffee is dissolved. Set aside to cool. Follow ▲ Recipe. Omit vanilla extract. Blend cooled coffee into the butter.

—CHOCOLATE MOCHA BUTTER CREAM FROSTING

Melt (page 10) and set aside to cool **1½ oz. (1½ sq.) unsweetened chocolate.** Follow recipe for Mocha Butter Cream Frosting; gradually blend chocolate into whipped butter after adding coffee.

—RUM BUTTER CREAM FROSTING

Follow recipe for Mocha Butter Cream Frosting. Whip **1½ teaspoons rum extract** with the butter.

WHITE MOUNTAIN FROSTING

Set out a candy thermometer and a medium-size saucepan with a tight-fitting cover.

Combine in the saucepan

2 cups sugar
¾ cup water
2 tablespoons light corn syrup
⅛ teaspoon salt

Stir over low heat until sugar is dissolved. Cover saucepan and bring to boiling. Boil gently 5 min. Uncover and set candy thermometer in place. During cooking, wash sugar crystals from sides of pan with a pastry brush dipped in water. Cook without stirring until thermometer registers 244°F (firm ball stage, page 11; remove from heat while testing).

Beat until stiff, not dry, peaks are formed

½ cup (about 4) egg whites

Continue beating egg whites while pouring the hot syrup over them in a steady thin stream. (Do not scrape syrup from bottom and sides of pan.) After all the hot syrup is added, continue beating 2 or 3 min., or until frosting forms rounded peaks (holds shape). Fold in with minimum number of strokes

2 teaspoons vanilla extract
½ teaspoon almond extract

Frost (page 11) cake immediately.

Enough to frost sides and tops of two 8- or 9-in. cake layers

SEVEN-MINUTE FROSTING

▲ Base Recipe

Combine and mix well in top of a double boiler

1½ cups sugar
⅓ cup water
1 tablespoon light corn syrup
⅛ teaspoon salt
2 egg whites, unbeaten

Place over boiling water and immediately

Peppermint Seven-Minute Frosting

beat with rotary beater 7 to 10 min., or until mixture holds stiff peaks.

Remove from heat and beat in

1 teaspoon vanilla extract

Enough to frost sides and tops of two 9-in. cake layers

Note: Mixture may be tinted by gently stirring in one or more drops food coloring.

—PISTACHIO SEVEN-MINUTE FROSTING

Follow ▲ Recipe. Substitute **½ to 1 teaspoon pistachio extract** for vanilla extract. Blend in **1 or 2 drops green food coloring,** if desired.

—PEPPERMINT SEVEN-MINUTE FROSTING

Follow ▲ Recipe. Fold in **½ cup finely crushed peppermint-stick candy** and about **2 drops red food coloring.**

—BEIGE SEVEN-MINUTE FROSTING

Follow ▲ Recipe. Decrease sugar to **¾ cup** and add **¾ cup firmly packed brown sugar.**

—CHOCOLATE SEVEN-MINUTE FROSTING

Melt (page 10) **3 oz. (3 sq.) unsweetened chocolate** and set aside to cool. Follow ▲ Recipe.

Chocolate Seven-Minute Frosting

Blend in chocolate when mixture holds stiff peaks.

—GREEN VALLEY FROSTING

Follow ▲ Recipe. Substitute a **few drops peppermint extract** for vanilla extract. Blend in about **2 drops green food coloring.**

LORD BALTIMORE-STYLE FROSTING

Arrange on a baking sheet and put into a 325°F oven for 15 min., or until dry
   3 almond macaroons (or enough to yield ¼ cup crumbs)

Prepare crumbs (page 10) and set aside.

Chop and set aside
   ⅓ cup (2 oz.) candied cherries
   ¼ cup (1½ oz.) unblanched almonds
   ¼ cup (about 1 oz.) pecans
Prepare
   Seven-Minute Frosting (page 474)
Fold macaroon crumbs, cherries and nuts into one half of frosting with
   1 tablespoon sherry extract
   2 teaspoons lemon juice
Use to fill cake. Frost sides and top of cake with remaining frosting.
   Filling and frosting for one 3-layer cake

COCONUT FROSTING

Set out a candy thermometer.

Have ready
   ½ cup flaked coconut

Combine in a saucepan
   ½ cup water
   1½ cups sugar
Bring to boiling, stirring until sugar is dissolved. Boil, covered, 5 min. Uncover; set candy thermometer in place. Continue cooking without stirring until thermometer registers 230°F.

Using pastry brush dipped in water, wash down crystals from sides of saucepan as needed during cooking; change water each time.

Beat until stiff, not dry, peaks are formed
   2 egg whites
   ½ teaspoon cream of tartar
Continue beating egg whites while pouring the hot syrup over them in a steady thin stream. (Do not scrape saucepan.) After all the syrup is added, continue beating 2 to 3 min., or until frosting is very thick. If desired, blend in drops of food coloring, tinting frosting to the desired color. Fold in the coconut.
   Enough to frost sides and tops of two 8- or 9-in. cake layers

CARAMEL FROSTING

Melt in a 10-in. skillet over low heat
   ½ cup butter

Blend in
   1 cup firmly packed brown sugar
   ¼ cup cream
Bring to boiling, stirring constantly, and cook for 1 min., or until sugar is dissolved. Remove from heat and cool to lukewarm (110°F).

Add gradually
   1½ cups confectioners' sugar
Beat until thick enough to spread.
   Enough to frost sides and tops of two 8- or 9-in. cake layers

BROWNIE CARAMEL FROSTING

Combine and bring to boiling, stirring constantly
   1¼ cups sugar
   ⅔ cup cream
Boil to 238°F (soft ball stage, page 11; remove from heat while testing).

Melt in a heavy skillet
   ¾ cup firmly packed brown sugar
Stir melted brown sugar rapidly into the syrup. Boil again to soft ball stage. Remove from heat and add
   1 teaspoon vanilla extract
Cool to warm (110°F) and beat until creamy and stiff enough to spread. Place frosting over hot water if it becomes too stiff while spreading on cake.
   Enough to frost sides and tops of two 8-in. cake layers or 2 doz. cupcakes

SEA FOAM FROSTING

Combine in the top of a double boiler
   2 egg whites
   1½ cups firmly packed dark brown sugar
   Few grains salt
   ⅓ cup water
Beat 1 min. until thoroughly blended.

Place over boiling water and beat constantly about 7 min., or until frosting will stand in stiff peaks; stir frosting up from bottom and sides occasionally during cooking.

Remove from water and add
   1 teaspoon vanilla extract
Beat until thick enough to spread.
   Enough to frost sides and tops of two 9-in. cake layers

BUTTERMILK FUDGE FROSTING

Set out a candy thermometer.

Combine in a heavy 3-qt. saucepan
   ¾ cup butter
   1 cup buttermilk
   2 cups sugar
   1 teaspoon baking soda
Stir over low heat until sugar is completely dissolved. Increase heat and bring mixture to boiling. Set candy thermometer in place. Cook, stirring constantly, until thermometer registers 232°F. Remove from heat and put onto top of frosting
   2 tablespoons butter
Cool to 110°F; do not disturb during cooling.

When cool, stir in
   1 teaspoon vanilla extract
Beat until creamy and of spreading consistency. If frosting becomes too thick to spread smoothly, mix in a few drops of hot water.
   Enough to frost sides and tops of two 9-in. cake layers

FUDGE FROSTING

   ▲ Base Recipe

Set out a candy thermometer.

Combine in a 3-qt. saucepan
   4 oz. (4 sq.) unsweetened chocolate, cut in small pieces
   3 cups sugar
   1 cup milk
   ½ cup butter
   2 tablespoons light corn syrup
Stir over low heat until sugar is dissolved. Increase heat and bring mixture to boiling. Set thermometer in place. During cooking, wash any crystals from sides of pan with pastry brush dipped in water; move thermometer to one side and wash down crystals that may have formed under the thermometer. Cook, stirring occasionally, until thermometer registers 234°F (stage at which a few drops of syrup form a soft ball in cold water; remove pan from heat while testing). Remove from heat. Set aside to cool to 110°F, or until just cool enough to hold pan on palm of hand. Do not disturb frosting during cooling.

When cool, blend in
   1 tablespoon vanilla extract
Beat until creamy and of spreading consistency.
   Enough to frost sides and tops of two 8- or 9-in. cake layers

—MALLOW NUT FROSTING

Follow ▲ Recipe. Add **1½ cups (about 6 oz.) chopped nuts** and **8 marshmallows,** cut in pieces (page 9), after first minute of beating.

Glossy Chocolate Frosting

CHOCOLATE BUTTER FROSTING I
(Crème au Beurre Chocolat)

▲ *Base Recipe*

Put into a heavy saucepan and set over low heat until chocolate melts
   6 oz. semisweet chocolate
   ¼ cup strong coffee beverage
Remove from heat; blend well. Set aside to cool.

Cream until light and fluffy and set aside
   1½ cups firm unsalted butter
   1½ teaspoons vanilla extract

Boil gently to 230°F to 234°F (thread stage, page 11; remove from heat while testing)
   ¾ cup light corn syrup

Meanwhile, beat until thick and lemon-colored
   4 egg yolks
Beating constantly with a rotary beater, pour syrup very slowly into egg yolks. Beat until mixture is very thick and of same consistency as the whipped butter. Cool completely. Beat egg yolk-corn syrup mixture, about 2 tablespoons at a time, into butter until just blended. Gradually blend in chocolate mixture.

If tightly covered, this frosting may be stored for several days in refrigerator.
Enough to frost sides and tops of two 8- or 9-in. cake layers

—BUTTER CREAM FROSTING
(Crème au Beurre Vanille)

Follow ▲ Recipe. Omit chocolate and coffee.

—LIQUEUR BUTTER FROSTING
(Crème au Beurre au Liqueur)

Follow ▲ Recipe or prepare Butter Cream Frosting. Substitute for vanilla extract **1 tablespoon liqueur** such as kirsch, curaçao or Cointreau.

GLOSSY CHOCOLATE FROSTING

▲ *Base Recipe*

Mix thoroughly in a 1-qt. saucepan
   ½ cup sugar
   2 tablespoons cornstarch

Stir in
   ½ cup boiling water
   1 oz. (1 sq.) unsweetened chocolate, cut in pieces
   ¼ teaspoon salt
Cook over medium heat until mixture thickens, stirring frequently. Remove from heat. Stir in
   2 tablespoons butter or margarine
   1 teaspoon vanilla extract
Spread on cake while frosting is hot.
Enough to frost tops of two 9-in. cake layers

—GLOSSY NUT FROSTING

Follow ▲ Recipe. Sprinkle **1 cup (4 oz.) chopped nuts** on top and sides of frosted cake.

—GLOSSY CRUNCH FROSTING

Follow ▲ Recipe. Crush **¼ lb. peanut or almond brittle.** Stir into frosting before spreading on cake.

—GLOSSY COCONUT FROSTING

Follow ▲ Recipe. Finely chop **1 cup moist shredded coconut.** Stir into frosting before spreading on cake.

—GLOSSY PEPPERMINT FROSTING

Follow ▲ Recipe. Crush **6 to 8 small sticks peppermint candy.** Stir into frosting before spreading on cake.

MAGIC GLOSSY CHOCOLATE FROSTING

Blender-grind (page 11)
   2 oz. (2 sq.) unsweetened chocolate
Put into the top of a double boiler with
   1¼ cups (14-oz. can) sweetened condensed milk
   1½ tablespoons water
   ⅛ teaspoon salt
Place over boiling water. Using low speed of electric beater, beat constantly until frosting is of spreading consistency, about 10 min. Remove from heat and beat in
   1 teaspoon vanilla extract
   ½ teaspoon almond extract
Spread on cooled cake.
Enough to frost sides and tops of two 8-in. round cake layers

HONEY CHOCOLATE FROSTING

Combine in top of double boiler and place over boiling water
   ½ cup sugar
   2 oz. (2 sq.) unsweetened chocolate, cut in pieces
   ⅓ cup honey
   ¼ cup cream or top milk
   ¼ cup butter or margarine
   ⅛ teaspoon salt

When chocolate is melted, blend well with rotary beater. Vigorously stir about 3 tablespoons of the hot mixture into
   2 egg yolks, slightly beaten
Mix thoroughly and then combine with the mixture in double boiler. Cook over boiling water, stirring constantly. When slightly thickened (about 2 min.), remove from heat; place in bowl of ice and water and beat frosting until of spreading consistency.
Enough to frost sides and tops of two 8-in. cake layers

CHOCOLATE MARSHMALLOW FROSTING

Cut (page 9) into eighths and set aside
   8 marshmallows

Blend well and set aside
   1 cup confectioners' sugar
   2 egg yolks, unbeaten
   ⅛ teaspoon salt

Melt in a saucepan and stir until smooth
   3 oz. (3 sq.) unsweetened chocolate
   2 tablespoons butter or margarine
Blend thoroughly and add slowly to melted chocolate mixture
   2½ tablespoons cornstarch
   ⅓ cup cold milk
Immediately stir in egg yolk-sugar mixture. Cook, stirring constantly, until mixture thickens. Remove from heat and stir in
   2 teaspoons vanilla extract

When cool, blend in
   1½ cups confectioners' sugar
   Cream, 1 tablespoon at a time, until easy to spread
Remove about one half of frosting, blend in marshmallows and frost tops of layers. Use plain frosting for sides.
Enough to frost sides and tops of two 8- or 9-in. cake layers

JELLY FROSTING

Put into the top of a double boiler
   1¼ cups jelly
   2 egg whites
   ⅛ teaspoon salt
Cook over boiling water, beating constantly on medium speed. Continue beating until mixture stands in rounded peaks. Remove from heat.
Enough to frost sides and tops of two 8- or 9-in. cake layers

Honey Chocolate Frosting

476

MOCHA BUTTER CREAM FROSTING

Combine in a small saucepan with a tight-fitting cover

1¾ cups sugar
½ cup water

Bring to boiling over medium heat, stirring gently until sugar is dissolved. Cover saucepan tightly and boil syrup gently 5 min. to help wash down any crystals that might have formed on the sides of saucepan. Uncover and continue cooking syrup to 230°F to 234°F (thread stage, page 11; remove from heat while testing). Remove from heat and set aside.

Beat until stiff, not dry, peaks are formed

3 egg whites

Continue beating egg whites and pour the hot syrup in a thin stream into beaten egg whites. (Do not scrape syrup from bottom and sides of pan.) Continue beating a few minutes just until egg white mixture is very thick (piles softly). Cool completely.

Cream until softened and fluffy

2 cups firm unsalted butter

Beat in

1 tablespoon Dutch process cocoa
2 teaspoons instant powdered coffee
1 teaspoon vanilla extract

Beat in, one at a time, blending well after each addition

3 egg yolks

Add about 2 tablespoons egg white mixture at a time, to butter, beating until *just* blended.

Chill in refrigerator until frosting is firm enough to spread.

Enough to frost sides and top of
Fabulous Chocolate Party Cake

MAPLE SUGAR FROSTING

▲ Base Recipe

Set out a candy thermometer.

Combine in a medium-size saucepan

1 cup sugar
1 cup firmly packed maple sugar
1 cup dairy sour cream

(If maple sugar is available only in solid form, grate, using a fine grater, before using. Or heat over simmering water until sugar is softened, then force through a fine sieve.) Set over low heat and stir until sugar is dissolved. Increase heat and bring to boiling. Hang candy thermometer in pan so bulb does not touch bottom or side of pan. Continue cooking without stirring. During cooking, wash sugar crystals from sides of pan occasionally with pastry brush dipped into water. Cook to 238°F (soft ball stage: a few drops of mixture form a soft ball in very cold water). Remove from heat while testing.

Remove saucepan to a cooling rack and cool to lukewarm (about 110°F) without stirring or moving the pan.

Beat vigorously with wooden spoon or electric mixer until mixture begins to lose its gloss and is of spreading consistency.

Spread on cake immediately. If frosting becomes too thick to spread, beat in a few drops **cream or milk.**

Enough to frost sides and tops
of three 8-in. cake layers

—BROWN SUGAR FROSTING

Follow ▲ Base Recipe. Substitute **1 cup firmly packed light brown sugar** for the maple sugar. Add **1 teaspoon vanilla extract** just before beating.

UNCOOKED FROSTINGS

CONFECTIONERS' SUGAR FROSTING

▲ Base Recipe

Combine

1 cup confectioners' sugar
½ teaspoon vanilla extract

Add just enough

Milk or cream

to make a frosting that will hold its shape when forced through a pastry bag and tube.

About ½ cup frosting

Note: Mixture may be tinted by stirring in one or more drops of food coloring.

—CONFECTIONERS' SUGAR GLAZE

Follow ▲ Recipe. Thin frosting to a spreading consistency with additional milk or cream (about 2 tablespoons). Drizzle over hot breads such as Stollen, sweet rolls or coffee cake.

CREAMY VANILLA FROSTING

Combine and heat in top of double boiler over boiling water just until butter is melted, stirring constantly

½ cup sugar
½ cup dairy sour cream
1 tablespoon light corn syrup
1 tablespoon butter or margarine
⅛ teaspoon salt

Remove from heat and gradually blend in

3⅓ cups confectioners' sugar
2½ teaspoons vanilla extract

If frosting is too stiff to spread, blend in additional dairy sour cream.

Enough to frost sides and tops of
two 8- or 9-in. cake layers

WHITE VELVET FROSTING

▲ Base Recipe

Cream together until softened

¼ cup butter or margarine
1½ teaspoons vanilla extract
⅛ teaspoon salt

Add gradually, beating until smooth after each addition

3 cups confectioners' sugar

Blend in

1 egg yolk

Add slowly to blended mixture

3 tablespoons milk or cream

Add only enough milk or cream to make frosting the consistency for spreading.

Enough to frost sides and tops of
two 8- or 9-in. cake layers

—BROWN VELVET FROSTING

Follow ▲ Recipe. Melt (page 10) and cool **2 oz. (2 sq.) unsweetened chocolate;** mix in after egg yolk addition.

—CHOCOLATE MOCHA FROSTING

Follow ▲ Recipe. Decrease sugar to 2⅔ cups; sift with ⅓ cup cocoa. Substitute **double-strength coffee beverage** (page 10) for the milk or cream.

—CREAMY ORANGE FROSTING

Follow ▲ Recipe. Substitute **orange juice** for

milk or cream. Add **2 or 3 drops orange food coloring**. Sprinkle **grated orange peel** over top of frosted cake.

WHITE VELVET FROSTING, BLENDER METHOD

▲ *Base Recipe*

Put into a bowl and set aside
2 cups sifted confectioners' sugar

Put into an electric blender container in order
3 tablespoons milk or cream
¼ cup butter or margarine
1 egg yolk
1½ teaspoons vanilla extract
⅛ teaspoon salt
1 cup sifted confectioners' sugar
Cover and blend until smooth. Turn blended mixture into bowl with confectioners' sugar. Beat until smooth. If too thin for spreading, add more sifted confectioners' sugar; if too thick for spreading, add more cream.
Enough to frost sides and tops of two 8- or 9-in. layers

—MOCHA-SCOTCH FROSTING, BLENDER METHOD

Double ▲ Recipe. Substitute **½ cup double-strength coffee beverage** (page 10) for milk or cream. Add **1 cup brown sugar** with confectioners' sugar in blender container.
Enough to frost sides and tops of four 8- or 9-in. layers

—BROWN VELVET FROSTING, BLENDER METHOD

Melt (page 10) **2 oz. (2 sq.) unsweetened chocolate;** cool. Follow ▲ Recipe. Add chocolate to ingredients in container.

—CHOCOLATE MOCHA FROSTING, BLENDER METHOD

Follow ▲ Recipe. Decrease sugar added to blender container to ⅔ cup and sift with ⅓ cup cocoa. Substitute **3 tablespoons double-strength coffee beverage** (page 10) for milk or cream.

—RAISIN NUT FROSTING, BLENDER METHOD

Follow ▲ Recipe. After blending mixture in container until smooth, add **½ cup (about 2 oz.) raisins** and **½ cup (about 2 oz.) walnuts** to blender mixture. Blend only until raisins and nuts are chopped.

—CREAMY ORANGE FROSTING, BLENDER METHOD

Follow ▲ Recipe. Substitute **orange juice** for milk or cream. If desired, tint frosting with **1 or more drops orange food coloring**. Sprinkle **grated orange peel** over top of frosted cake.

GLOSSY VANILLA ICING

▲ *Base Recipe*

Combine and cook in top of double boiler over boiling water, stirring until butter is melted
½ cup sugar
½ cup cream
1 tablespoon light corn syrup
1 tablespoon butter or margarine
Remove from heat and gradually blend in
3⅓ cups confectioners' sugar
2½ teaspoons vanilla extract
If frosting is too stiff to spread, blend in
Several drops cream

With spatula, spread frosting on top of cake allowing some frosting to drip slightly down sides of cake. *Enough to frost top of loaf cake or tops of two 8- or 9-in. cake layers*

—GLOSSY CHOCOLATE ICING

Follow ▲ Recipe. Melt **1 oz. (1 sq.) unsweetened chocolate** with butter mixture.

—GLOSSY RUM ICING

Follow ▲ Recipe. Substitute **1½ teaspoons rum extract** for vanilla extract.

BASIC BUTTER FROSTING

▲ *Base Recipe*

Cream together until softened
¼ cup butter
1 teaspoon vanilla extract
Add gradually, beating well after each addition
2 cups confectioners' sugar
Stir in and beat to spreading consistency
1 tablespoon milk or cream
Enough to frost sides and tops of two 8-in. cake layers or 2 doz. cupcakes

—LEMON BUTTER FROSTING

Follow ▲ Recipe. Substitute **lemon juice** for milk and add **1 teaspoon grated lemon peel**. If desired, add a **few drops yellow food coloring**.

—MOCHA BUTTER FROSTING

Follow ▲ Recipe. Mix **1 teaspoon instant powdered coffee** with the confectioners' sugar. Melt (page 10) and cool **2 oz. (2 sq.) unsweetened chocolate**.

—CHOCOLATE BUTTER FROSTING II

Melt (page 10) and cool **2 oz. (2 sq.) unsweetened chocolate**.

Follow ▲ Recipe. Blend chocolate in after adding sugar.

—BURNT-SUGAR FROSTING

Follow ▲ Recipe. After adding sugar, blend in **5 tablespoons Burnt-Sugar Syrup** (page 436) and **few grains salt;** increase cream to 1½ tablespoons.

—RAISIN RUM BUTTER FROSTING

Follow ▲ Recipe. Decrease vanilla extract to ¼ teaspoon and add ¾ teaspoon rum. Increase milk to about 2 tablespoons and add **1 drop red food coloring** and **3 tablespoons finely chopped golden raisins**.

—ORANGE BUTTER FROSTING

Follow ▲ Recipe. Substitute **1 teaspoon grated orange peel** for the vanilla extract and **1 to 2 tablespoons orange juice** for the milk.

BRIDE'S BUTTER FROSTING

▲ *Base Recipe*

Cream together until softened
⅔ cup butter
1½ teaspoons vanilla extract
¼ teaspoon almond extract
Add gradually, creaming until fluffy after each addition
6 cups (about 1¾ lbs.) confectioners' sugar
Add and continue creaming until smooth
1 egg white, unbeaten
Blend in gradually, a tablespoonful at a time, until frosting is of spreading consistency
3 to 6 tablespoons cream
Enough to frost sides and top of Bride's Cake

—RUM BUTTER FROSTING

Follow ▲ Recipe. Omit almond extract. Add **1½ teaspoons rum** with the vanilla extract.
Enough to frost and decorate a Zuppa Inglese

DECORATING FROSTING

Cream together until softened
2 tablespoons butter or margarine
½ teaspoon vanilla extract

Thoroughly blend in, in order
1½ cups confectioners' sugar
1 tablespoon warm cream
Tint as desired with about
1 drop food coloring
Use for decorating Petits Fours (page 453).
About ¾ cup frosting

CINNAMON CANDY FROSTING

Combine in a small saucepan
2 tablespoons red cinnamon candies
2 tablespoons water
Heat until candies are melted. Add gradually
to hot mixture
1½ cups confectioners' sugar
Blend until smooth. Mix in until frosting is
of spreading consistency
Cream (about 2 tablespoons)
About 1 cup frosting

CHOCOLATE BUTTER FROSTING III

Melt (page 10) and set aside to cool
2½ oz. (2½ sq.) unsweetened chocolate

Measure and set aside
1 cup confectioners' sugar

Cream until softened
¼ cup butter
½ teaspoon vanilla extract
Add gradually one half of confectioners' sugar
and beat well after each addition. Add the
cooled chocolate and remaining confectioners'
sugar and beat until fluffy.
Enough to decorate 36 small cookies

SOUR CREAM CHOCOLATE FROSTING

Melt (page 10) and cool slightly
1 pkg. (12 oz.) semisweet chocolate pieces
Blend melted chocolate into
1 cup dairy sour cream
Add and blend in
1 teaspoon vanilla extract
¼ teaspoon almond extract
⅛ teaspoon salt
Enough to frost sides and tops of two 8- or 9-in. cake layers

CREAMY CHOCOLATE FROSTING

Melt (page 10) over simmering water and stir
until smooth
1 pkg. (6 oz.) semisweet chocolate pieces
Add
⅔ cup sweetened condensed milk
Cook over low heat 10 min., stirring frequently. Remove from heat. Add and beat until of
spreading consistency
2 teaspoons hot water
1 teaspoon vanilla extract
Enough to frost sides and tops of two 8-in. cake layers or one 8-in. square cake

BITTERSWEET VELVET FROSTING

Melt (page 10) together and stir until smooth
4 oz. (4 sq.) unsweetened chocolate
3 tablespoons butter or margarine
Remove from heat and add
2½ cups confectioners' sugar
½ cup milk or cream
1 teaspoon vanilla extract
Beat until of spreading consistency.
Enough to frost sides and tops of two 8- or 9-in. cake layers

FUDGE GLAZE

Melt (page 10) and set aside
2 oz. (2 sq.) unsweetened chocolate
3 tablespoons butter or margarine
Heat
¼ cup cream
Mix in
1¼ cups confectioners' sugar
⅛ teaspoon salt
Vigorously stir in the melted chocolate until
frosting is smooth. *Enough to glaze top of one 9-in. cake layer*

BROILER FUDGE FROSTING

Have ready a hot cake in an 8-in. square pan.
Coarsely chop and set aside
½ cup (about 2 oz.) nuts
Cream until fluffy
2 tablespoons butter or margarine, softened
½ cup firmly packed brown sugar
2 tablespoons cocoa
Add and continue creaming
2 tablespoons cream
Stir in the chopped nuts. Spread lightly over
the cake after it has cooled in pan 10 to 15
min.
Place cake under broiler with top of frosting
about 4 in. from heat. Broil about 1 min. or
until frosting bubbles. Watch closely to avoid
scorching. *Enough to frost top of 8-in. square cake*

CHOCOLATE BAR FROSTING

Immediately upon removing cake layers from
pans and while cake is warm, place on top of
each layer, one half of
5 semisweet or milk chocolate bars (about 2 oz. each)
As the chocolate melts, quickly spread it
around sides and over top of cake layers.
Enough to frost sides and tops of two 8-in. cake layers

DUSKY CREAM CHEESE FROSTING

Soften
1 pkg. (3 oz.) cream cheese
Blend in
½ teaspoon vanilla extract
Sift together and add gradually
1 cup confectioners' sugar
3 tablespoons cocoa
Blend thoroughly. If too stiff to spread, add,
1 teaspoon at a time, milk or cream until easy
to spread. *Enough to frost one 8- or 9-in. cake layer*

LEMON CREAM CHEESE FROSTING

▲ *Base Recipe*

Blend
2 pkgs. (3 oz. each) cream cheese, softened
½ teaspoon grated lemon peel
1½ teaspoons lemon juice
Add gradually and blend in
4 cups confectioners' sugar
If frosting is too stiff to spread, blend in, 1
teaspoonful at a time, until easy to spread
Milk or cream
Enough to frost sides and tops of two 9-in. cake layers

—ORANGE CREAM CHEESE FROSTING

Follow ▲ Recipe. Omit lemon juice and lemon
peel. Blend with the cream cheese **2 tablespoons plus 2 teaspoons thawed frozen
orange juice concentrate.** Chill frosting in
refrigerator until of spreading consistency
(about 30 min.).

—CHOCOLATE CREAM CHEESE FROSTING

Melt (page 10) and set aside to cool **2 oz. (2
sq.) unsweetened chocolate.** Follow ▲ Recipe.
Omit lemon juice and peel. Blend with the
cream cheese **1 teaspoon vanilla extract.** After
sugar has been added, blend in the chocolate.

MOCHA COCOA FROSTING

▲ *Base Recipe*

Sift together
3 cups confectioners' sugar
½ cup cocoa
Make a well in center. Add and beat until
smooth
½ cup butter or margarine, softened

Blend in

**3 tablespoons double-strength coffee
beverage (page 10)**

Add and beat well

2 egg yolks or 1 whole egg

Spread between layers and on sides and top of cake. *Enough to frost sides and tops of two 9-in. cake layers*

—CHOCOLATE CREAM FROSTING

Follow ▲ Recipe. Substitute for coffee, **¼ cup cream or milk.**

—TOASTED ALMOND CHIP FROSTING

Follow ▲ Recipe. Sprinkle **1 cup (about 5½ oz.) sliced toasted almonds** on top and sides of frosted cake.

—SUNSHINE CHOCOLATE FROSTING

Follow ▲ Recipe. Substitute for coffee, **1 or 2 tablespoons lemon juice or orange juice** with **1 teaspoon grated peel.**

MOCHA-MALLOW WHIPPED CREAM FROSTING

Set in refrigerator a bowl, rotary beater and
2 cups heavy cream

Heat together in top of double boiler over boiling water, stirring occasionally, until marsh-mallows are melted.

16 (4 oz.) marshmallows
⅓ cup quick coffee beverage (page 10)

Remove from heat. Cool; chill in refrigerator.

When mixture is chilled, whip the cream, using the chilled bowl and beater. Whip 1 cup at a time until cream is of medium consistency (piles softly). Fold whipped cream into chilled mixture. *Enough to fill and frost one 9-in. cake*

GLOSSY ORANGE FROSTING

Melt and set aside

1 tablespoon butter or margarine

Beat slightly in a bowl

1 egg white

Beat in

1½ cups confectioners' sugar

Add the melted butter and

⅛ teaspoon salt
1 teaspoon vanilla extract
¼ teaspoon orange extract

To tint orange, blend in a drop at a time

Orange food coloring (mix about 2 drops red and 6 drops yellow)

Beat until smooth. If frosting is thin, beat in more confectioners' sugar.

About 1 cup frosting

SATINY PEANUT BUTTER FROSTING

Have ready

1 cup (about half a 16-oz. can) ready-to-spread vanilla-flavored frosting

Mix in a bowl until blended

¼ cup peanut butter
¼ cup cream

Spoon in the frosting while continuing to mix.

About 1½ cups frosting

CREAMY PEANUT BUTTER FROSTING

Cream in a bowl until blended

6 tablespoons butter
1½ tablespoons peanut butter
¾ teaspoon vanilla extract

Add gradually, beating well after each addition

2½ cups confectioners' sugar

Beat in

1 egg yolk

Beat in until of spreading consistency

1½ tablespoons milk (about)

About 1½ cups frosting

PEPPERMINT BUTTER FROSTING

Cream together until softened

½ cup butter
½ teaspoon peppermint extract
⅛ teaspoon salt

Add gradually, beating until smooth after each addition

3½ cups confectioners' sugar

Beat in thoroughly

1 egg

If necessary, blend in

1 to 2 tablespoons milk or cream

Beat until frosting is of spreading consistency. Tint to desired color with

Red food coloring

Enough to frost sides and tops of two 9-in. cake layers

TOASTED PECAN FROSTING

Stir constantly in skillet over medium heat until pecans are toasted

1 cup (about ¼ lb.) coarsely chopped pecans
¼ cup butter

Remove from heat. Stir in, in order

½ cup cream
1½ teaspoons vanilla extract
⅛ teaspoon salt
3 cups confectioners' sugar

Blend until smooth enough to spread on cake.

Enough to frost sides and top of one 8- or 9-in. square cake

TOPPINGS

SWEETENED WHIPPED CREAM

▲ *Base Recipe*

Place a rotary beater and a 1-qt. bowl in refrigerator to chill.

Using chilled bowl and beater, beat until cream stands in peaks when beater is slowly lifted upright

1 cup chilled heavy cream

Beat into whipped cream with few final strokes until blended

¼ cup confectioners' sugar
1 teaspoon vanilla extract

Set in refrigerator if not used immediately.

About 2 cups whipped cream

Note: Mixture may be tinted by gently stirring in one or more drops of food coloring.

—CRUNCHY WHIPPED CREAM

Follow ▲ Recipe. Fold in about **1 cup crushed peanut brittle** or **1 cup chopped nuts.**

—DUTCH COCOA WHIPPED CREAM

Follow ▲ Recipe. Sift **3 tablespoons Dutch process cocoa** with the sugar.

—MOCHA WHIPPED CREAM

Follow ▲ Recipe. Sift **1 teaspoon instant powdered coffee** with the sugar.

—ALMOND WHIPPED CREAM

Blanch (page 9), sliver and toast (page 10) **½ cup (about 3 oz.) almonds** and set aside.

Follow ▲ Recipe. Substitute ¼ teaspoon **almond extract** for vanilla extract. Fold the almonds into the whipped cream after blending in the sugar and the extract.

—FRUITY WHIPPED CREAM

Follow ▲ Recipe. Fold into whipped cream desired amount of **diced bananas, sweetened fresh or frozen peaches or berries.** Use as a topping or filling.

—MAPLE WHIPPED CREAM

Follow ▲ Recipe. Add few grains **salt** to cream. Substitute **¼ cup maple syrup** for sugar, adding gradually to the whipping cream while beating constantly; omit vanilla extract.

—RUM WHIPPED CREAM

Follow ▲ Recipe. Substitute **1 to 1½ tablespoons rum** for vanilla extract.

—SPICY WHIPPED CREAM

Follow ▲ Recipe. Mix with confectioners' sugar and beat in with few final strokes **1 teaspoon cinnamon, ½ teaspoon nutmeg** and **⅛ teaspoon cloves.**

COCOA WHIPPED CREAM

Place a rotary beater in refrigerator to chill.

Mix in a bowl in order
- **5 tablespoons sugar**
- **3 tablespoons cocoa**
- **¼ teaspoon salt**
- **1 cup heavy cream**
- **2 teaspoons vanilla extract**

Chill in refrigerator 2 hrs. or longer.

Whip with chilled beater until cream stands in peaks when beater is slowly lifted upright.

About 2 cups whipped cream

COFFEE WHIPPED CREAM

Place a rotary beater and a bowl in refrigerator to chill.

Pour into a small saucepan
- **2 tablespoons cold double- or triple-strength coffee beverage (page 10)**

Sprinkle evenly over cold coffee
- **1 teaspoon unflavored gelatin**

Set saucepan over low heat and stir constantly until the gelatin is completely dissolved. Set aside to cool.

Using the chilled bowl and rotary beater, beat only until frothy
- **1 cup chilled heavy cream**

Stir cool gelatin. *Very* gradually add gelatin to cream and continue to beat after each addition until cream is of medium consistency (piles softly). Work quickly. When all gelatin has been added, beat into whipped cream with

few final strokes until blended
- **⅓ cup confectioners' sugar**

Beat until cream stands in peaks when beater is slowly lifted upright.

Filling for 24 Miniature Puffs

Note: The use of gelatin in the whipped cream helps to stabilize the cream or to hold its volume and shape. Therefore, when the stabilized whipped cream is used to decorate molds or used as a filling or frosting, it should hold its shape for hours, if necessary.

ORANGE WHIPPED CREAM

Chill a rotary beater and a 1-qt. bowl.

Blend and set aside
- **2 tablespoons orange juice**
- **4 drops yellow food coloring**
- **1 drop red food coloring**

Using chilled bowl and beater, beat until soft peaks are formed when beater is slowly lifted upright
- **1 cup chilled heavy cream**

Beat into whipped cream until blended
- **4 teaspoons sugar**
- **1½ teaspoons grated orange peel**

With final strokes gradually beat in orange mixture. *About 2 cups whipped cream*

CHANTILLY CREAM
(Crème Chantilly)

The name of this well-known garnish for cakes and desserts came from the especially good, thick cream once produced at a model dairy. French royalty operated this dairy in Chantilly, a suburb of Paris.

Pour into a chilled bowl and beat with chilled rotary beater
- **1 cup chilled heavy cream**

Beat until cream stands in peaks when beater is slowly lifted upright.

Fold or beat into whipped cream with few final strokes until blended
- **3 tablespoons confectioners' sugar**
- **1½ teaspoons vanilla extract, coffee beverage, fruit essences or fine liqueur**

About 2 cups whipped cream

Mocha Ginger Cream

MOCHA GINGER CREAM

▲ Base Recipe

Combine in a 1-qt. saucepan
- **1 cup sugar**
- **½ cup double-strength coffee beverage (page 10)**

Cook slowly, over low heat, stirring until sugar is dissolved. Increase heat and bring mixture to boiling. Cover saucepan and boil gently for 5 min. (This will help to dissolve any crystals that may have formed on sides of saucepan.) Uncover and continue cooking, stirring occasionally, to 234°F (soft ball stage, page 11). Using a pastry brush dipped in water, wash down any crystals from sides of saucepan from time to time during cooking.

Beat until thick and lemon-colored
- **3 egg yolks**

Gradually pour syrup over beaten egg yolks, beating constantly. Continue beating until very stiff. Chill in refrigerator.

Chill a bowl, beater and
- **1 cup heavy cream**

Just before serving, using chilled bowl and beater, beat on high speed until cream stands in peaks when beater is slowly lifted upright.

Fold whipped cream into chilled mixture with
- **½ cup (3 oz.) candied ginger, blender-chopped (page 11)**

Spread part of sauce between split squares of **gingerbread.** Serve topped with sauce.

About 1 qt. sauce

—MOCHA MAPLE CREAM

Follow ▲ Recipe. Add **3 tablespoons maple syrup** to ingredients in saucepan before cooking. Fold in with whipped cream, **½ teaspoon maple extract.** Omit ginger.

PEACH WHIP TOPPING

Have ready
- **1 container (4½ oz.) frozen whipped dessert topping, thawed**
- **1 can (5 oz.) diced cling peaches**
- **¼ cup chopped salted nuts**

Turn the thawed topping into a bowl. Gently fold in the peaches with syrup. Mix in nuts until just blended.

Spoon onto squares of **warm gingerbread or cake** and garnish with **chopped maraschino cherries.** *About 2 cups topping*

SEAFOAM TOPPING

An excellent topping for chocolate cake, angel food cake or ice cream.

Combine in the top of a double boiler
2 eggs, well beaten
½ cup light corn syrup
2 tablespoons sugar
¼ teaspoon salt
1 tablespoon lemon juice
Cook over boiling water, stirring constantly, until thickened, about 10 min. Remove from water and set aside to cool. Chill about 1 hr.

Set a bowl and rotary beater in refrigerator to chill.

Chop and set aside
½ cup (about 2 oz.) pistachio nuts

When ready to serve, using the chilled bowl and beater, beat until of medium consistency
1 cup chilled heavy cream
With final few strokes, blend in a mixture of
1 teaspoon vanilla extract
⅛ teaspoon almond extract
5 drops green food coloring
Gently fold the chilled mixture and nuts into the whipped cream. *About 3½ cups topping*

WHIPPED SOUR CREAM TOPPING

▲ Base Recipe

Dairy sour cream, when it is chilled and whipped in a chilled bowl with a chilled beater like sweet heavy cream, does not become stiff, but takes on a softly piling fluffiness that is very pleasing; and it almost doubles in volume. Garnish it attractively, whether sweetened or not, with a sprinkling of sieved brown sugar, or with chopped pecans or toasted almonds or black walnuts, *or with chopped drained maraschino cherries, or crushed peppermint stick candy, or finely shaved curls of chocolate.*

Chill a bowl and rotary beater in refrigerator.

Using the chilled bowl and beater, beat until cream piles softly
½ cup chilled dairy sour cream
Serve on **gingerbread, spice cake,** or **puddings.** *About ¾ cup topping*

—VANILLA CREAM TOPPING

Follow ▲ Recipe. Beat in **3 tablespoons confectioners' sugar** and **½ teaspoon vanilla extract** with few final strokes.

FILLINGS

VANILLA CREAM FILLING

▲ Base Recipe

Two saucepans will be needed.

Measure
1½ cups cream
Pour ½ cup of the cream into a saucepan and heat just until a thin film appears; reserve remaining ½ cup cream.

Meanwhile, mix thoroughly in a saucepan
⅓ to ½ cup sugar
2½ tablespoons all-purpose flour
¼ teaspoon salt
Blend in the reserved cream; add the scalded cream gradually while stirring. Bring rapidly to boiling, stirring gently and constantly; cook 3 min.

Vigorously stir 3 tablespoons of the hot mixture into
3 egg yolks, slightly beaten
Immediately blend into mixture in saucepan. Cook 2 to 3 min., stirring constantly to keep mixture cooking evenly. Remove from heat.

Blend in
1 tablespoon butter or margarine
2 teaspoons vanilla extract
¼ teaspoon almond extract
Cover, cool slightly and chill in refrigerator.
About 1½ cups filling

—CHOCOLATE CREAM FILLING I

Follow ▲ Recipe. Add **1½ oz. (1½ sq.) unsweetened chocolate** to cream; heat until cream is scalded and chocolate is melted.

—CHERRY CREAM FILLING

Follow ▲ Recipe. Blend **1 to 2 tablespoons maraschino cherry syrup** into filling with the sour cream. Fold in **½ cup chopped maraschino cherries.**

—PINEAPPLE CREAM FILLING I

Follow ▲ Recipe. Drain **1 can (8¼ oz.) crushed pineapple** (about ⅔ to ¾ cup, drained) and fold pineapple into filling.

—BLACK WALNUT FILLING

Follow ▲ Recipe. Blend **¾ cup (about 3 oz.) coarsely chopped black walnuts** into filling before spreading onto cake layer.

Note: If a sour cream filling is desired, follow ▲ Recipe or variation; decrease cream to 1 cup and blend in ½ cup dairy sour cream with the butter. If desired, omit almond extract.

FRENCH PASTRY CREAM
(Crème Pâtissière)

▲ Base Recipe

This exquisite cream filling for pastries is an elegant dessert in itself. Serve in pots de crème cups garnished with chocolate curls.

Scald (page 10) and set aside
1½ cups milk

Blend in a double boiler top
3 tablespoons all-purpose flour
6 tablespoons sugar
¼ teaspoon salt
Add, stirring well
½ cup cold milk
Gradually stir in scalded milk. Place over direct heat. Stirring gently and constantly, bring milk mixture rapidly to boiling over direct heat and cook 2 min.

Place over boiling water and immediately stir about 3 tablespoons of this hot mixture into
4 egg yolks, slightly beaten
Immediately blend into mixture in double boiler.

482

Cook over boiling water 3 to 5 min. Stir slowly to keep mixture cooking evenly. Remove from heat and strain into a bowl. Add and stir until blended

1 teaspoon vanilla extract

Cover and cool, stirring occasionally. Chill in refrigerator until ready to use.

About 2 cups pastry cream

—SAINT-HONORE CREAM
(Crème Saint-Honoré)

Follow ▲ Recipe. Sprinkle **1 env. unflavored gelatin** over ¼ cup cold water. Dissolve gelatin in completed hot French Pastry Cream, stirring constantly. Cool completely. Beat **6 egg whites** until frothy and gradually add **3 tablespoons sugar**, beating well after each addition; beat until rounded peaks are formed. Fold beaten egg whites into cooled cream. Use to fill Saint-Honoré Cake (page 519) or Cream Puffs (page 517).

About 5 cups Saint-Honoré Cream

ALMOND PASTRY CREAM
(Crème Pâtissière d'Amandes)

Grind fine

⅓ lb. (about 1 cup) blanched almonds (page 9)

Mix in

½ cup confectioners' sugar

Set aside.

Cream until softened

3 tablespoons butter

Beat in, one at a time

1 tablespoon rum or kirsch
2 egg yolks

Beat until well blended. Blend in almond-sugar mixture. This paste may be used in Napoleons (page 519).

1 cup paste

CHOCOLATE CREAM FILLING II

▲ Base Recipe

Put into a saucepan and heat until milk is scalded (page 10) and chocolate melted

¾ cup milk
1 oz. (1 sq.) unsweetened chocolate

Meanwhile, put into a saucepan and mix thoroughly

½ cup sugar
2 tablespoons all-purpose flour
¼ teaspoon salt

Stir in and blend well

¼ cup cold milk

Gradually add hot milk mixture, stirring constantly. Bring chocolate mixture to boiling, stirring gently and constantly, and cook about 3 min.

Vigorously stir about 3 tablespoons of the hot mixture into

2 egg yolks, slightly beaten

Immediately blend into mixture in saucepan. Cook 2 to 3 min., stirring gently and constantly. Remove from heat.

Add and stir until butter is melted

1 tablespoon butter or margarine
1 teaspoon vanilla extract

Cover, cool and chill in refrigerator.

About 1 cup filling

—COCOA CREAM FILLING

Follow ▲ Recipe. Omit chocolate. Blend **3 tablespoons cocoa** with dry ingredients.

—RUM CHOCOLATE FILLING

Follow ▲ Recipe. Blend in **2 teaspoons rum extract** with the vanilla extract.

CHOCOLATE FILLING

Set out a double boiler.

Melt (page 10) and set aside to cool

2 oz. (2 sq.) unsweetened chocolate

Bring just to boiling

¾ cup water

Combine in top of double boiler

1 cup sugar
¼ cup cornstarch
½ teaspoon salt

Stir in and blend well

¼ cup cold water

Gradually add boiling water. Stirring gently and constantly bring mixture rapidly to boiling over direct heat and cook 3 min. Place over boiling water; cover and cook 5 min., stirring three or four times. Remove from heat and stir in melted chocolate and

¼ cup butter or margarine
2 teaspoons vanilla extract

Cool filling slightly. *About 1 cup filling*

LEMON FILLING

Combine in double boiler top and beat slightly with rotary beater

3 egg whites
1 cup sugar
1 teaspoon grated lemon peel
3 tablespoons lemon juice

Place over boiling water. Cook about 5 min., or until thickened, stirring constantly.

Vigorously stir about 3 tablespoons of hot mixture into

3 egg yolks, slightly beaten

Immediately blend into mixture in double boiler. Cook over boiling water 5 min.; stir slowly to keep mixture cooking evenly. Remove from heat and cool thoroughly before using.

About 1 cup filling

MALLOW FILLING

Heat in a saucepan until melted

32 marshmallows (about ½ lb.), cut in quarters (page 9)
1 oz. (1 sq.) unsweetened chocolate

Meanwhile, prepare and set aside

¼ cup (about 1 oz.) raisins, cut in pieces (page 9)
¼ cup (about 1 oz.) chopped nuts
½ teaspoon grated orange or lemon peel

Remove melted marshmallows and chocolate from heat and stir in

1 tablespoon cream

Blend in the raisins, nuts and grated peel. Stir until filling is of spreading consistency. (Omit chocolate is white filling is desired.)

About 1½ cups filling

ORANGE FILLING I

Mix in top of a double boiler

½ cup sugar
2½ tablespoons cornstarch
⅛ teaspoon salt

Add gradually, stirring in

½ cup water
½ cup orange juice

Stirring gently and constantly, bring rapidly to boiling over direct heat and cook for 3 min. Cover and cook over boiling water 5 min., stirring three or four times.

Vigorously stir about 2 tablespoons hot mixture into

1 egg yolk, slightly beaten

Immediately blend into mixture in double boiler. Cook over boiling water 3 to 5 min., stirring slowly and constantly to keep mixture cooking evenly.

Remove from heat and blend in

1 tablespoon lemon juice
1 tablespoon grated orange peel
2 teaspoons butter or margarine

Cool filling before spreading on cake.

About 1 cup filling

ORANGE FILLING II

Mix and set aside

1 tablespoon grated orange peel
¾ cup orange juice
½ cup sugar

Beat until frothy

2 egg whites

Add 1 tablespoon at a time, beating well after each addition

¼ cup sugar

Beat until stiff, not dry, peaks are formed (peaks remain standing when beater is slowly lifted upright).

Gently blend orange mixture into egg whites.
Enough to fill Orange Cream Torte

PISTACHIO CREAM FILLING

▲ *Base Recipe*

Two saucepans will be needed.

Coarsely chop and set aside

¾ cup (about 3 oz.) pistachio nuts

Set out

1½ cups cream

Scald (page 10) 1 cup of the cream in a saucepan, reserve remainder.

Put into a saucepan and mix thoroughly

⅓ to ½ cup sugar
2½ tablespoons all-purpose flour
¼ teaspoon salt

Blend in the reserved cream; add gradually and stir in the scalded cream. Bring mixture rapidly to boiling, stirring gently and constantly; cook 3 min.

Vigorously stir about 3 tablespoons of the hot mixture into

3 egg yolks, slightly beaten

Immediately blend into filling mixture in saucepan. Cook 2 to 3 min., stirring slowly and constantly to keep mixture cooking evenly. Remove from heat.

Add and stir until butter is melted

1 tablespoon butter
1 teaspoon vanilla extract
½ teaspoon pistachio extract

Tint filling to desired color by mixing in one to three drops

Green food coloring

Cool the filling slightly; mix in the chopped pistachio nuts. Cover and chill thoroughly in refrigerator.

When thoroughly chilled, stir the filling to blend and spread evenly on one cake layer and top with second layer.
About 1⅔ cups filling

—CREAMY RUM FILLING

Follow ▲ Recipe. Omit vanilla extract, pis-

tachio extract and green food coloring. Blend in **2 tablespoons rum** with the butter.

PINEAPPLE CREAM FILLING II
(Crema d'Ananasso)

▲ *Base Recipe*

Scald (page 10) in top of double boiler

1½ cups milk

Meanwhile, mix in a saucepan

½ cup sugar
2 tablespoons cornstarch
⅛ teaspoon salt

Add, stirring well

½ cup cold milk

Gradually stir in scalded milk.

Stirring gently and constantly, bring cornstarch mixture rapidly to boiling over direct heat and cook for 3 min. Pour into double boiler and place over boiling water. Cover and cook about 5 min., stirring three or four times.

Vigorously stir about 3 tablespoons hot mixture into

3 eggs, slightly beaten

Immediately blend into mixture in double boiler. Cook over boiling water 3 to 5 min. Stir slowly to keep mixture cooking evenly. Remove from heat. Cover and cool.

Stir in

1½ cups (20-oz. can, drained) crushed pineapple
1 teaspoon vanilla extract

Chill in refrigerator.   *About 3 cups filling*

—CHOCOLATE CREAM FILLING III

Follow ▲ Recipe. **Add 1½ oz. (1½ sq.) unsweetened chocolate** to milk and heat to scalding. Beat smooth with rotary beater. Increase sugar to ⅔ cup. Omit pineapple.

CREAMY PINEAPPLE FILLING

Mix in top of a double boiler

½ cup sugar
2 tablespoons cornstarch
¼ teaspoon salt

Add gradually, stirring constantly

1 cup pineapple juice

Bring rapidly to boiling over direct heat, stirring constantly; cook 3 min. Cover and cook over boiling water about 5 min., stirring three or four times.

Vigorously stir about 3 tablespoons hot mixture into

3 egg yolks, slightly beaten

Immediately blend into mixture in the double boiler top. Cook over boiling water 3 to 5 min. Stir slowly to keep mixture cooking evenly. Remove from heat. Cover and cool slightly. Blend in.

½ cup well-drained crushed pineapple

Cover; set in refrigerator to chill.

Set a small bowl and a rotary beater in refrigerator to chill.

Just before serving, using the chilled bowl and beater, beat until cream is of medium consistency (piles softly)

½ cup chilled heavy cream

Gently fold whipped cream into pineapple mixture.   *About 2¼ cups filling*

TOPPERS FOR CAKES

Add distinction to a plain cake by giving it a baked or broiled topping; or dress up individual servings with quickly made sauces.

To Decorate with Confectioners' Sugar—Place a lacy paper doily on top of cake and sift **confectioners' sugar** over doily; carefully remove doily from cake.

SAUCY TOPPERS

Try **Soft Custard** (page 528) with an added ½ teaspoon sherry or rum extract; **Fudge Sauce** (page 579), **Chocolate Sauce** (page 578), **Butterscotch Sauce** (page 577), **Coffee Sauce** (page 700), **Red Cherry Sauce** (page 578) or

Orange Sauce—Combine in top of double boiler **2 egg yolks,** slightly beaten, **⅓ cup sugar** and **¼ cup orange juice.** Cook over boiling water, stirring constantly, until thickened. Set in bowl of ice and water to chill quickly. Fold in **1 tablespoon grated orange peel** and **1 cup whipped cream.**   *About 1½ cups sauce*

BAKE-QUICK TOPPERS

Place cake on baking sheet and spread with Honey Topping or Meringue Nut Topping. Bake at 425°F 8 to 10 min.

Honey Topping—Mix ⅓ cup honey, 2 tablespoons softened butter or margarine and ½ cup flaked coconut.

Meringue Nut Topping—Prepare **Meringue** (see Jiffy Lemon Pie, page 495) and spread over cake. Sprinkle with **chopped nuts.**

BROIL-QUICK TOPPERS

Place cake on broiler pan. Cover cake with Nut Topping or Coconut Topping. Place broiler pan under broiler with top of cake 3 in. from heat; broil about 3 min., or until lightly toasted.

Nut Topping—Generously spread cake or cake slices with **butter or margarine.** Sprinkle with a mixture of **cinnamon, sugar or brown sugar,** and **chopped salted nuts.**

Coconut Topping—Cream **3 tablespoons butter or margarine** with **2 tablespoons peanut butter.** Mix in ⅓ cup firmly packed brown sugar and 2 tablespoons cream; spread over cake. Sprinkle with **flaked coconut.**

Pies

Pastry making is part of our American heritage and was introduced into our country by the Pilgrims. Real pastry, however, was not to be developed to its high-quality, present-day standard until early in the nineteenth century. Pie is now probably our most popular dessert and is an important item in the American diet. Pies offer an endless variety of textures and flavors in both their crusts and fillings. Included in this chapter are masterpieces of creativity and imagination which will win the highest praises of family and guests . . . recipes for delectable fruit, cream, custard, and chiffon pies, as well as tarts and turnovers.

PASTRY AND PIE SHELLS

PASTRY I FOR 1-CRUST PIE

▲ Base Recipe

Set out an 8- or 9-in. pie pan or plate.

Sift together into a bowl
1 cup sifted all-purpose flour
½ teaspoon salt
Cut in with pastry blender or two knives until pieces are size of small peas
⅓ cup lard, vegetable shortening or all-purpose shortening
Sprinkle gradually over mixture, about 1 tablespoon at a time
2 to 3 tablespoons cold water
Mix lightly with fork after each addition. Add only enough water to hold pastry together. Work quickly; do not overhandle. Shape into a ball and flatten on lightly floured surface.

Roll from center to edge into a round about ⅛ in. thick and about 1 in. larger than overall size of pan. With knife or spatula, loosen pastry whenever sticking occurs; lift pastry slightly and sprinkle flour underneath.

Loosen one half of pastry from surface with spatula and fold over other half. Loosen remaining pastry and fold in quarters. Gently lay in pan and unfold pastry, fitting it to the pan so that it is not stretched.

Trim edge with scissors or sharp knife to overlap ½ in. Fold extra pastry under at edge and flute (page 10) or press edges together with a fork. Thoroughly prick bottom and sides of shell with a fork. (Omit pricking if filling is to be baked in shell.)

Bake at 450°F 10 to 15 min., or until crust is light golden brown. Cool on cooling rack.
One 8- or 9-in. pastry shell

—10-IN. PASTRY SHELL

Follow ▲ Recipe. Increase flour to 1⅓ cups, shortening to ½ cup, salt to ¾ teaspoon and water to about 3 tablespoons.

—PASTRY FOR 2-CRUST PIE

Double ▲ Recipe. Divide pastry into halves and shape into two balls. Roll each ball as in ▲ Recipe. For top crust, roll out one ball of pastry and cut 1 in. larger than pie pan. Slit pastry with knife in several places to allow steam to escape during baking. Gently fold in half and set aside while rolling bottom crust. Roll second ball of pastry and gently fit pastry into pie pan; avoid stretching. Trim pastry with scissors or sharp knife around edge of pan. Do not prick. Fill as desired. Moisten edge with water for a tight seal. Carefully arrange top crust over filling. Gently press edges to seal. Fold extra top pastry under bottom pastry. Flute (page 10) or press edges together with a fork. Bake as directed for type of filling used:

—PASTRY FOR LITTLE PIES AND TARTS

Double ▲ Recipe. Roll pastry ⅛ in. thick and cut about ½ in. larger than overall size of pans. Carefully fit rounds into pans without stretching, fold excess pastry under at edge and flute (page 10) or press together with a fork. Prick bottoms and sides of shells with fork. (Omit pricking if filling is to be baked in pastry shells.) Bake at 450°F 8 to 10 min., or until light golden brown. Cool. Carefully remove pastry from pans. *Six 6-in. pies, twelve 3½-in. tarts or eighteen 1½-in. tarts*

—PASTRY FOR ROSE PETAL TARTS

Double ▲ Recipe. Roll pastry ⅛ in. thick. Cut pastry into rounds, using a 2½-in. cookie cutter. Place one pastry round on bottom of each 2¾-in. muffin-pan well. Fit 5 pastry rounds around sides of well, overlapping edges. Press all edges together. Prick bottom and sides well with fork. Bake at 450°F 8 to 10 min., or until light golden brown. Carefully remove from pan and cool on cooling rack.
Six 3½-in. tarts

—CORN MEAL PASTRY FOR TARTS

Double ▲ Recipe. Set out twelve 3½-in. tart pans. Stir **⅓ cup yellow corn meal** into sifted flour and salt. Roll pastry ⅛ in. thick and cut about ½ in. larger than overall size of pans. Carefully fit rounds into pans without stretching, fold excess pastry under at edge and flute (page 10) or press together with a fork. Prick bottoms and sides of shells with fork. Bake at 450°F 8 to 10 min., or until light golden brown. Cool. Carefully remove tarts from pans.
Twelve 3½-in. tarts

—PASTRY FOR LATTICE-TOP PIE

Double ▲ Recipe. Divide pastry into halves and shape into two balls. Follow directions in ▲ Recipe for rolling pastry. Roll one ball for bottom crust allowing for overhang; fit gently into pie pan. Roll the second ball into a rectangle ⅛ in. thick and at least 10 in. long. Cut pastry with a sharp knife or pastry wheel into strips about ½ in. wide. Fill pastry shell as directed in specific recipe.

To Make Lattice Top—Cross two strips over the pie at the center. Working out from center to edge of pie, add the remaining strips one at a time, weaving the strips under and over each other in crisscross fashion; leave about 1 in. between the strips. Trim the strips even with

485

the edge of the pastry. Moisten edge of the pastry shell with water for a tight seal. Fold edges of bottom crust over ends of strips. Flute (page 10) or press edges together with a fork. Bake as directed in specific recipe.

—BRAIDED EDGE

Prepare **Pastry for 1-Crust Pie (page 485)**, but do not flute edge. Set aside. *For Braided Edge Only*—Follow ▲ Recipe using ½ cup sifted flour, 3 tablespoons shortening, ¼ teaspoon salt and about 1½ tablespoons water. Roll pastry into a rectangle about ⅛ in. thick, 3 in. wide and 14 in. long. Cut 9 strips, ⅓ in. wide. Carefully braid three strips. Brush rim of pastry with water and place braid on rim. Braid next three strips; brush rim of pastry with water and place braid on rim. Overlap ends of braids and press together. Repeat to complete braided edge.

—PASTRY CUTOUTS

Follow ▲ Recipe. Roll pastry trimmings ⅛ in. thick. Prepare in one of the ways given below. Prick with a fork. Bake on an ungreased baking sheet at 450°F 10 to 15 min., or until lightly browned. Cool; arrange on baked pie or tarts.

Fancy Shapes—Hatchets, pumpkins, animals, hearts, shamrocks, Santa Claus, stars, bells and witch cutouts may be made by using a cookie cutter or a knife and a waxed-paper pattern. Sprinkle cutouts with **Colored Sugar** (page 582) as desired.

—PASTRY TOPPING

Follow ▲ Recipe. Roll dough to about ⅛-in. thickness and about 1 in. larger than overall size of casserole top. Cut a design in pastry to allow steam to escape during baking. Place pastry on mixture in casserole and fold overhang under; flute or press edge with a fork. Bake as directed.

—PLAIN PASTRY PINWHEELS

Prepare one-half ▲ Recipe. Roll pastry into rectangle and set aside. Combine **2 tablespoons melted butter, 1 tablespoon sugar, ½ teaspoon cinnamon, ⅛ teaspoon salt** and **¼ cup walnuts**, grated. Spread over pastry. Roll lengthwise and cut into ¼-in. slices.

PASTRY II FOR 1-CRUST PIE

Set out an 8- or 9-in. pie pan or plate.

Measure into a bowl
   1¼ cups Perfect Pastry Mix (below)
Sprinkle gradually over mixture, about 1 tablespoon at a time
   2 to 3 tablespoons cold water
Mix lightly with a fork after each addition. Add only enough water to hold pastry together. Work quickly; do not overhandle. Shape into

a ball and flatten on a lightly floured surface. (If dough is not to be used immediately, wrap in waxed paper, moisture-vaporproof material or aluminum foil and place in refrigerator.)

Roll dough in all directions from center to edge to about ⅛-in. thickness and about 1 in. larger than overall size of pan. With knife or spatula, loosen pastry from surface whenever sticking occurs; lift pastry slightly and sprinkle flour underneath.

Loosen one half of pastry from surface with spatula and fold over other half. Loosen remaining pastry and fold in quarters. Gently lay pastry in pan and unfold, carefully fitting it to the pan so that it is not stretched.

Trim edge with scissors or sharp knife to overlap ½ in. Fold extra pastry under at edge and flute (page 10) or press edges together with a fork. Prick bottom and sides of shell thoroughly with a fork. (Omit pricking if filling is to be baked in shell.)

Bake at 450°F 10 to 15 min., or until crust is light golden brown. Cool on cooling rack.

One 8- or 9-in. pastry shell

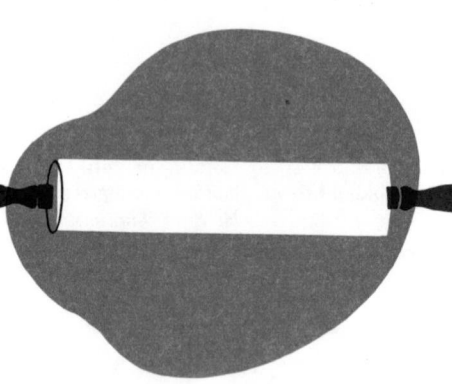

PERFECT PASTRY MIX

Sift together into a large bowl
   6 cups sifted all-purpose flour
   1 tablespoon salt
Cut in with pastry blender or two knives until pieces are size of small peas
   2 cups (1 lb.) lard, vegetable
      shortening or all-purpose shortening
Store in covered bowl or container in refrigerator and use as needed. Will keep at least 1 month.   *About eight 8-in. or*
six 9-in. pie shells

HOW TO USE PERFECT PASTRY MIX

Before measuring for recipe, lighten mix by tossing with fork. Lightly pile mix into measuring cup. Level with straight-edge knife.

For 1-Crust Pies—Use 1 cup pastry mix with 2 to 3 tablespoons water for 8-in. pie shells. Use 1¼ cups mix with 2 to 3 tablespoons water for 9-in. pie shells.

For 2-Crust Pies—Use 2 cups pastry mix with 3 to 5 tablespoons water for 9-in. 2-crust pie.

PASTRY FOR TARTS
(Pâte Brisée)

Sift together into a bowl
   1¾ cups sifted all-purpose flour
   1 tablespoon sugar
   ¼ teaspoon salt
Cut in with pastry blender or two knives until pieces are size of small peas
   ½ cup butter
Sprinkle, about 1 tablespoon at a time, over dry ingredients
   4 to 6 tablespoons cold water
Mix with fork after each addition until dough can be gathered easily into a ball. Cut dough into halves. Shape each into a ball. (Part or all may be wrapped in waxed paper and stored in refrigerator until ready to use.)

Roll one ball of dough at a time on floured surface. Flatten and roll ⅛ in. thick, keeping shape round. With knife or spatula, loosen pastry from surface whenever sticking occurs; lift pastry slightly and sprinkle flour under it.
   Pastry for about twelve 4-in. tarts, two 9-in.
   pastry shells or one 2-crust pie

For Small Tarts—Invert small tart pan over dough and cut rounds about 1 in. larger than pan. Gently fit pastry rounds over outside of pans; avoid stretching. Trim off excess pastry. Gently press to pan. Prick entire surface with fork. Place inverted pan on baking sheet. Bake at 450°F 8 to 12 min. Cool on rack and fill with any of the following
   French Pastry Cream (page 482)
   French Applesauce (page 568)
   Any favorite chocolate or glazed
      fruit filling

For Pastry Shells—Roll pastry 2 in. larger than pie pan. Fold and transfer to pan. Fit in loosely and gently pat to fit; avoid stretching. Trim edges to overlap about ½ in. Fold excess pastry under at edge and flute (page 10) or press edges together with a fork. Prick bottom and sides of shell with a fork. Bake at 450°F 12 to 15 min., or until crust is light golden brown.

Note: Omit pricking if filling is to be baked in shell.

For 2-Crust Pie—For top crust, roll out one half of dough and cut 1 in. larger than pie pan. Slit pastry with knife in several places to allow steam to escape during baking. Gently fold in half and set aside while rolling bottom crust. Roll second half of dough and gently fit pastry into pie pan; avoid stretching. Trim pastry with scissors or sharp knife around edge of pan. Do not prick. Fill as desired. Moisten edge with water for a tight seal. Carefully arrange top crust over filling. Gently press edges to seal. Fold extra top pastry under bottom pastry. Flute (page 10) or press edges together with fork. Bake as directed for type of filling used.

For Pastry Topping—Mix **½ cup (about 3 oz.) chopped, blanched almonds** (page 9) with **2 teaspoons confectioners' sugar** and sprinkle over top crust before baking.

CHEESE PASTRY FOR 2-CRUST PIE

▲ *Base Recipe*

Set out an 8- or 9-in. pie pan or plate.

Sift together into a bowl
    2 cups sifted all-purpose flour
    1 teaspoon salt
Shred and mix into flour mixture
    4 oz. Cheddar cheese (about 1 cup, shredded)
Cut in with pastry blender or two knives until pieces are size of small peas
    ⅔ cup lard, vegetable shortening or all-purpose shortening
Sprinkle over mixture, 1 tablespoon at a time, about
    5 tablespoons cold water
Mix lightly with a fork after each addition. Add only enough water to hold pastry together. Work quickly and do not overhandle. Divide dough into halves and shape each into a ball.

For bottom crust, flatten one ball of pastry on a lightly floured surface. Roll from center to edge into a round about ⅛ in. thick and about 1 in. larger than overall size of pan. With knife or spatula, loosen pastry from surface whenever sticking occurs; lift pastry slightly and sprinkle flour underneath. Loosen one half of pastry and fold over other half; loosen remaining pastry and fold into quarters. Gently lift pastry into pan and unfold it, fitting it to the pan without stretching. Trim pastry around rim of pan with a sharp knife. Do not prick.

Roll second ball of pastry for upper crust. Slit it with knife in several places to permit escape of steam during baking. Fold in half.

Fill pie as desired.

Moisten edge of bottom crust with water for a tight seal. Carefully lay top crust over filling and unfold. Trim with scissors about ½ in. beyond edge of rim. Fold extra top pastry under edge of bottom pastry and flute (page 10) or press edges together with a fork.

Bake as directed.   *Pastry for one 8- or 9-in. 2-crust pie*

—CHEESE PASTRY FOR 1-CRUST PIE

Follow ▲ Recipe. Reduce Cheddar cheese to 2 oz. (½ cup, shredded), flour to 1 cup, salt to ½ teaspoon, shortening to ⅓ cup and water to about 2½ tablespoons. Roll out full amount of pastry for bottom crust, gently fit into pan without stretching and trim with scissors ½ in. beyond edge of pan. Fold extra pastry under at edge and flute (page 10) or press with a fork. Thoroughly prick bottom and sides of pastry shell with a fork. (Omit pricking if filling is to be baked in shell.) Bake at 450°F 10 to 15 min., or until crust is light golden brown. Cool on cooling rack before filling.

—CHEESE PASTRY FOR 1-CRUST 10-IN. PIE

Follow recipe for Cheese Pastry for 1-Crust Pie, but use 3 oz. cheese (¾ cup, shredded), 1⅓ cups flour, ¾ teaspoon salt, ½ cup shortening and about 3 tablespoons water. Fit into a 10-in. pie pan.

SPICE PASTRY FOR 1-CRUST PIE

Set out an 8- or 9-in. pie pan or plate.

Sift together into a bowl
    1 cup sifted all-purpose flour
    2 tablespoons sugar
    ½ teaspoon salt
    ¼ teaspoon cinnamon
    ⅛ teaspoon ginger
    ⅛ teaspoon cloves
Cut in with pastry blender or two knives until pieces are size of small peas
    ⅓ cup lard, vegetable shortening or all-purpose shortening
Sprinkle gradually over mixture, 1 tablespoon at a time
    2 to 3 tablespoons orange juice
Mix lightly with fork after each addition. Add only enough orange juice to hold pastry together. Work quickly and do not overhandle. Shape into a ball and flatten on a lightly floured surface.

Roll from center to edge into a round about ⅛ in. thick and about 1 in. larger than overall size of pan. With knife or spatula, loosen pastry from surface whenever sticking occurs; lift pastry slightly and lightly sprinkle flour underneath.

Loosen one-half from surface with spatula and fold over other half. Loosen remaining pastry and fold in quarters. Gently lay in pan and unfold pastry, fitting it to the pan so that it is not stretched.

Trim edge with scissors or sharp knife to overlap ½ in. Fold overlapping pastry under at edge and flute (page 10) or press edges together with a fork. Prick bottom and sides of shell with a fork. (Omit pricking if filling is to be baked in shell.)

Bake at 450°F 10 to 15 min. Cool pastry on cooling rack.   *One 8- or 9-in. pastry shell*

SWEET PASTRY
(Pâte Sucrée)

Sift onto a pastry board
    1 cup sifted all-purpose flour

Make a well in center, and in well work to a creamy mixture
    ¼ cup softened butter
    ¼ cup sugar
    ¼ teaspoon salt
    1 egg
Quickly and thoroughly mix with the flour. Form into a large ball and wrap in waxed paper. Set aside in a cool place for at least 3 hrs.

Roll out as for Pastry for Tarts (page 485). Fit into a 9- or 10-in. pie pan. Complete and bake as directed in recipe used.

Or, prick and bake at 450°F 12 to 15 min., or until lightly browned.
   Pastry for 9- or 10-in. pastry shell

FILBERT PASTRY

Set out a 9-in. pie pan.

Sift together into a bowl
    1⅓ cups sifted all-purpose flour
    ½ cup toasted filberts (page 10), finely chopped
    ¾ teaspoon salt
Cut in with pastry blender or 2 knives until mixture is crumbly
    ½ cup all-vegetable shortening
Sprinkle, a small amount at a time, over dry ingredients
    ¼ cup cold water
Mix lightly with a fork after each addition until a dough is formed. Proceed as directed in Pastry I for 1-Crust Pie (page 485), rolling pastry 1½ in. larger than pan. Fit pastry into pan and flute edge. Line inside of the shell with a sheet of aluminum foil or waxed paper. Half fill with dried beans or rice.

Bake at 425°F 10 min. Remove beans and foil. Sprinkle shell lightly with
    Sugar
Bake 5 min. longer, or until pastry is lightly browned. Cool.   *One 9-in. pastry shell*

PASTRY FOR MEAT PIES

Sift together and set aside
    1¾ cups sifted all-purpose flour
    1 teaspoon salt

Cream until softened
    ⅓ cup butter
Work in
    2 tablespoons olive oil

Add and work in

1 egg yolk

Cut butter into sifted dry ingredients with pastry blender or two knives; blend until pieces are size of small peas. Stirring with a fork after each addition, add gradually to form a dough that will hold together, about

3 tablespoons water

Gather dough in waxed paper and gently squeeze into a ball. Store in refrigerator if not ready to use.

Remove paper and set dough on floured surface. To blend ingredients, knead (page 11) gently several times or until smooth. Cut ball into halves. Roll each half ⅛ in. thick to proper size and shape on well-floured surface.

With spatula loosen pastry from surface whenever sticking occurs; lift pastry slightly and sprinkle flour underneath.

Crust for 9- or 10-in. two-crust pie

For Meat Pie—Use a deep 9- or 10-in. pie pan. Proceed as for 2-Crust Pie (page 485). Fill shell with any desired mixture of meat, poultry, fish or vegetables. Bake at 425°F 10 min. Reduce heat to 375°F and bake 20 to 25 min., or until crust is lightly browned.

For a Designed Top—Cut top-crust pastry into interesting shapes such as stars, diamonds and crescents, using a sharp-pointed knife or cookie cutter. Arrange shapes in design on pie filling.

For Croustades—Cut all of rolled pastry into rounds large enough to line 3-in. muffin pan wells. Line, prick bottoms and sides with fork and flute edges. Bake at 450°F 10 to 15 min.

8 Croustades

GRAHAM CRACKER CRUMB CRUST

▲ *Base Recipe*

Set out a 9-in. pie pan or plate.

Place on a long length of heavy waxed paper or in a plastic bag

20 graham crackers

Loosely fold paper around crackers, tucking under open ends. With rolling pin, gently crush crackers to make fine crumbs (about 1½ cups). Turn crumbs into a bowl. Stir in

¼ cup sugar

⅛ teaspoon salt

Graham Cracker Crumb Crust

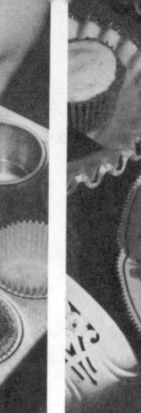

Graham Cracker Crumb Tart Shells

Using a fork or pastry blender, evenly cut in

¼ cup softened butter or margarine

Press crumb mixture evenly over bottom and sides of pie pan; press with spoon until firm.

Bake at 375°F 8 min.   *One 9-in. pie shell*

Note: For a 10-in. pie shell, use 1⅔ cups crumbs, 5 tablespoons sugar and 5 tablespoons butter or margarine.

—GRAHAM CRACKER CRUMB TART SHELLS

Follow ▲ Recipe; use 8 muffin-pan wells. Line with paper baking cups. Press mixture into paper cups. Bake at 375°F 6 min. Cool. Carefully remove paper baking cups from shells.

—COOKIE CRUMB CRUST

Follow ▲ Recipe. Substitute **gingersnaps, vanilla, lemon or chocolate wafers** (about twenty-four 2⅛-in. cookies) for graham crackers. Omit sugar. Bake chocolate crumb shell at 325°F 10 min.

—NUT CRUMB CRUST

Follow ▲ Recipe. Decrease graham cracker crumbs to 1 cup and mix in ⅓ **cup finely chopped nuts.**

—ZWIEBACK CRUMB CRUST

Follow ▲ Recipe. Substitute 1⅓ **cups zwieback crumbs** (about eighteen 3½x1½-in. zwieback) for graham crackers.

—COFFEE-FLAVORED CRUMB CRUST

Follow Cookie Crumb Crust recipe, using vanilla or chocolate wafers. Add **2 teaspoons instant powdered coffee** to crumbs with the butter. Bake chocolate crumb crust at 325°F 10 min.

CEREAL PEANUT BUTTER CRUST

Butter a 9-in. pie pan.

Mix in a bowl

⅓ cup peanut butter

⅓ cup light corn syrup

Add

2 cups oven-toasted rice cereal

Mix until well coated. Turn mixture into pie pan and press firmly and evenly on bottom and sides. Chill until firm.   *One 9-in. pie shell*

CHOCOLATE CORN FLAKE CRUST

▲ *Base Recipe*

Butter an 8-in. pie pan.

Melt over hot, not boiling, water

1 pkg. (6 oz.) semisweet chocolate pieces

2 tablespoons butter or margarine

Remove from heat and mix in

2 cups presweetened corn flakes

Stir until corn flakes are well coated. Turn mixture into pie pan and press firmly and evenly on bottom and sides. Set in a cool place until firm.

Fill with desired cream filling.

One 8-in. pie shell

—RICE CEREAL CHOCOLATE CRUST

Follow ▲ Recipe. Use a 9-in. pie pan. Substitute **2 cups oven-toasted rice cereal**, slightly crushed, for the corn flakes.

CHOCO-COCONUT PIE SHELL

Set out an 8- or 9-in. pie pan.

Melt in top of double boiler over simmering water

2 oz. (2 sq.) unsweetened chocolate

3 tablespoons butter or margarine

1 teaspoon vanilla extract

Blend ingredients well and remove from simmering water. Add, stirring constantly

¼ cup sweetened condensed milk

Blend in well, in order

½ cup confectioners' sugar

2 cups moist shredded coconut, cut

Press coconut mixture firmly into an even layer onto bottom and up sides of pie pan.

Wrap in waxed paper, aluminum foil or moisture-vaporproof material. Chill in refrigerator about 1 hr., or until firm.

One 8- or 9-in. pie shell

FRUIT PIES

FAVORITE APPLE PIE

▲ *Base Recipe*

Prepare and set aside
Pastry for 2-Crust Pie (page 485; use a 9-in. pie pan)

Wash, quarter, core, pare and thinly slice
6 to 8 (2 to 3 lbs.) tart cooking apples (about 6 cups, sliced)
Brush apple slices with
1 tablespoon lemon juice
Lightly toss apple slices with a mixture of
1 cup sugar
3 to 3½ tablespoons all-purpose flour
1 teaspoon cinnamon
¼ teaspoon nutmeg
⅛ teaspoon salt
Fill pastry shell with apple slices. Dot evenly with
2 tablespoons butter
Cover apples with pastry and complete pie as directed in Pastry for 2-Crust Pie.

Bake at 450°F 10 min. Reduce heat to 350°F and bake about 40 min. longer, or until crust is lightly browned.

Serve warm or cold.   *One 9-in. pie*

—CREAMY APPLE PIE

New England farm wives have always known a thing or two about what to do with cream. Here it is flooded into a hot apple pie. You'll want deep dishes or bowls to serve this steamy creamy delicious dessert.

Follow ▲ Recipe. Flute bottom crust as directed in Pastry I for 1-Crust Pie (page 485); do not prick. Fill with apple mixture. From pastry rolled for upper crust, cut a round to fit over apples just to fluted edge and put it over apples. Immediately on removal of pie from oven, lift the top crust, pour in **½ cup heavy cream** and replace crust. Serve warm.

—CRANBERRY APPLE PIE

Follow ▲ Recipe. Reduce apples to 4 or 5 medium cooking apples (about 3½ cups, sliced).

Wash and sort **3 cups cranberries.** Coarsely chop cranberries and mix with apples. Increase sugar to 1 cup. Trim bottom crust ½ in. beyond rim of pie pan. Make lattice top (page 485). Bake as in ▲ Recipe.

—APPLE CHEESE PIE

Follow ▲ Recipe. Cut **1 cup (4 oz.) finely shredded Cheddar cheese** into pastry with shortening. For filling, shred **4 oz. sharp Cheddar cheese** (about 1 cup, shredded). Place one third of apples in pastry; top with one half of shredded cheese. Repeat layers. Top with remaining apples.

—RED 'N' HOT PIE

Follow ▲ Recipe for preparing pastry and apple slices. For filling, combine in large saucepan **1 cup sugar, ⅛ teaspoon salt, ½ cup red cinnamon candies** and **1 cup water.** Cook until candies dissolve, stirring occasionally. Add apple slices and simmer until apples are desired color. Drain. Cool syrup. Blend **2 tablespoons all-purpose flour** and **1 tablespoon lemon juice** with ½ cup syrup. Fill pastry shell with apple slices and pour syrup mixture over them. Complete pie with top crust as in ▲ Recipe. Bake at 450°F 10 min. Reduce heat to 350°F and bake 15 min.

—CHERRY PIE

Follow ▲ Recipe. Substitute for the apples, **3 cups (two 16-oz. cans) drained pitted red tart cherries.** Omit cinnamon and nutmeg. Blend **½ cup cherry juice** with dry ingredients. If using fresh tart cherries, increase sugar to 1¼ cups.

—LATTICED APPLE TARTS

Follow ▲ Recipe. Prepare **Pastry for Little Pies and Tarts** (double recipe, page 485). Roll one half of pastry and fit into six 3½-in. tart pans; reserve remaining pastry. Do not flute or bake pastry shells. Set out **1½ cups apricot preserves.** Fill each shell with about ½ cup apple mixture. Spoon about ¼ cup apricot preserves over apples. Roll remaining pastry into a rectangle. Cut pastry with a sharp knife or pastry wheel into strips about ½ in. wide. Moisten edge of pastry shell with water for a tight seal. Carefully arrange strips to form lattice pattern over filling. Gently press edges to seal. Press edges together with a fork or flute edges (page 10). Brush with slightly beaten egg yolk. Bake at 450°F 8 min. Reduce heat to 350°F and bake 15 to 20 min., or until apples are tender.

—LATTICED CHERRY TARTS

Prepare **Pastry for Little Pies and Tarts** (double recipe, page 485). Roll one half of pastry and fit into tart pans, reserving remainder. Do not flute or bake. Prepare Cherry

Pie filling. Fill each pastry shell with about ½ cup filling. Roll remaining pastry into rectangle. Proceed as in Latticed Apple Tarts.

APPLE MINCE PIE

Prepare (but do not bake) in a 9-in. pie pan
Pastry I for 1-Crust Pie (page 485)
Line pan with rolled pastry; flute (page 10) edges of pastry.

Wash, quarter, core, pare and chop
1 large apple (about 1¼ cups, chopped)
Put into saucepan with
3½ cups Mincemeat (page 729; if using packaged condensed mincemeat, prepare according to package directions)
1 teaspoon grated lemon peel
1 tablespoon lemon juice
Heat mixture thoroughly. Cool slightly. Fill pastry shell with mincemeat mixture.

Bake at 400°F 30 to 35 min. Cool pie on cooling rack.

Meanwhile, prepare
Brandy Hard Sauce (page 581)
Force hard sauce through pastry bag and No. 27 star decorating tube onto cooled mincemeat pie, in long strips forming a lattice pattern. Serve immediately.   *One 9-in. pie*

Apple Mince Pie

Favorite Apple Pie

TOPPINGS FOR APPLE PIE

CREAM CHEESE TOPPING

Beat until very fluffy
   6 oz. cream cheese
Add gradually to cream cheese, beating until fluffy after each addition
   1 cup confectioners' sugar
Add and beat until smooth
   5 tablespoons milk or cream
   ½ teaspoon almond extract
Cover mixture and put into the refrigerator to chill thoroughly.

Serve in a chilled serving bowl as a topping for warm **apple pie.**   *About 1⅓ cups topping*

EDAM CHEESE TOPPING

Set out to soften at room temperature
   1 Edam cheese (about 1 lb.)

Meanwhile, coarsely chop and set aside
   ¼ cup (about 1 oz.) pecans

When cheese is softened, cut a thin slice from the top, through the wax coating. Hollow out the cheese, leaving a ¼-in. shell. Set cheese shell aside.

Crumble the cheese into a bowl. Cover with
   1 cup cream
Beat until fluffy. Mix in the chopped pecans. Spoon the mixture into the cheese shell. Garnish with
   Pecan halves
Serve as an accompaniment to **apple, mince** or **pumpkin pie.**   *About 2½ cups topping*

Note: If you prefer a larger Edam cheese for your centerpiece, soften only part of the cheese with cream and refill shell. If there is any sauce remaining after serving, scrape it away, rewrap cheese and store.

RICH CHEESE SAUCE

Put in top of double boiler
   6 oz. pasteurized process sharp
   Cheddar cheese food
Place over simmering water and stir constantly until cheese begins to melt. Add gradually while stirring constantly
   ½ cup milk
Continue to stir constantly until cheese is melted and mixture is smooth.

Serve piping hot over **apple pie**
                              About 1 cup sauce

FRENCH APRICOT TART

For a stylish dessert that's typically French and incomparably flavorful serve this delicate tart. It's fancy; it's fabulous; and it's made in practically no time at all.

For Pastry—Set out a 9-in. pie pan or tart pan.

Sift together into a bowl
   ¾ cup plus 2 tablespoons sifted
      all-purpose flour
   1½ teaspoons sugar
   ⅛ teaspoon salt
Cut in with pastry blender or two knives until pieces are the size of small peas
   ¼ cup butter
Sprinkle, about 1 teaspoonful at a time, over dry ingredients
   2 to 3 tablespoons cold water
Blend with fork after each addition until dough can be gathered easily into a ball. Shape into a ball and flatten on a lightly floured surface. (Dough may be wrapped and stored in refrigerator until ready to use.)

Roll out pastry on a floured surface. Flatten and roll ⅛ in. thick, keeping shape round, and about 2 in. larger than overall size of pan. With a knife or spatula, loosen pastry from surface wherever sticking occurs; lift pastry slightly and sprinkle flour under it. Fold and transfer to pan. Fit it loosely and gently pat to fit; avoid stretching. Trim edges to overlap about ½ in. Fold excess pastry under at edges and flute (page 10) or press edges together

with a fork. Prick bottom and sides of shell thoroughly with a fork.

Bake at 450°F 10 to 12 min., or until crust is light golden brown. Remove from oven and set aside to cool.

For Apricot Filling—Set aside to drain, reserving syrup
   2 cans (30 oz. each) whole peeled
      apricots
Carefully remove and discard pits, leaving apricots intact.

Melt in a small saucepan over low heat, 1 tablespoon of the reserved apricot syrup and
   ¼ cup strawberry preserves
   2 drops red food coloring
Set aside to cool slightly. (Remaining apricot syrup may be reserved for use in other food preparation.)

When pastry shell is cooled, spread carefully in bottom of pastry
   1 cup apricot preserves
Place whole apricots on preserves in the pastry shell. Spoon glaze over apricots; set in refrigerator to chill and to allow red glaze to thicken slightly before serving.
                                One 9-in. tart

LUSCIOUS BLUEBERRY PIE

Set out
   1 baked 9-in. pastry shell (page 485)

Drain, reserving syrup,
   2 cans (16 oz. each) blueberries
      (about 2½ cups, drained)
Set blueberries aside.

Combine in a saucepan and stir with a spoon until thoroughly blended
   3 tablespoons cornstarch
   1 cup reserved blueberry syrup
Stirring constantly, bring rapidly to boiling. Continue stirring and cooking until thickened. Stir in
   6 tablespoons sugar
Remove from heat and mix in
   2 tablespoons lemon juice
   1½ tablespoons butter or margarine
   ⅛ teaspoon salt
Gently mix in the blueberries. Set pan in bowl of ice and water to chill quickly. Pour cooled filling into pie shell.

Serve with **ice cream.**   *One 9-in. pie*

CHERRY CUTOUT PIE

   ▲ *Base Recipe*

Prepare
   Pastry for 2-Crust Pie (page 485)
Line bottom of 9-in. pie pan with rolled pastry. Roll pastry for top crust and cut into a round 9 in. in diameter. Cut round into six equal wedges. Using a thimble, cut out three small rounds from each wedge along curved edge (as pictured). The round openings represent

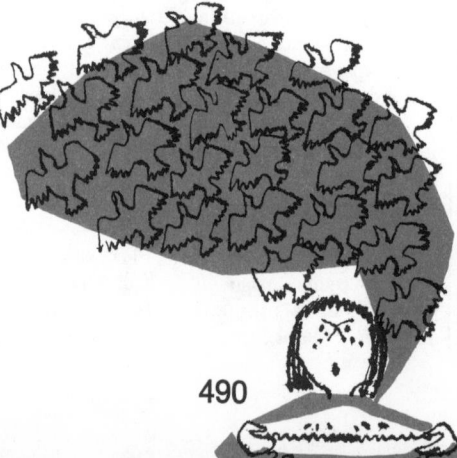

cherries. With sharp knife, cut stems and leaves in each wedge as pictured. Carefully place wedges on baking sheet.

Bake pie shell and wedges at 450°F 8 to 10 min., or until pastry is a golden brown. Remove pastry wedges to a cooling rack and set aside to cool.

For Filling—Drain, reserving liquid
    2 cans (16 oz. each) pitted red tart cherries (about 3 cups cherries)

Put into a saucepan
    3 tablespoons cornstarch
Add gradually and stir in
    Reserved cherry liquid
Mix well and bring rapidly to boiling, stirring constantly, until mixture is thickened. Stir in until dissolved
    ¾ cup sugar
Remove from heat and mix in
    1 teaspoon lemon juice
    ½ teaspoon almond extract
    ¼ teaspoon salt
(For brighter color, stir in a few drops of red food coloring.) Gradually mix in cherries. Cool filling.

Spoon cooled filling into cooled pastry shell. Arrange pastry wedges on filling to form top crust. Decorate with two maraschino cherries with stems and two green leaves.

One 9-in. pie

—CHERRY ROSE PETAL TARTS

Prepare and bake **Pastry for Rose Petal Tarts** (page 485) instead of Pastry for 2-Crust Pie. Follow ▲ Recipe for filling. Fill Rose Petal Tarts with filling and cool.

FABULOUS CHERRY PIE

    ▲ *Base Recipe*

If there is any way to improve the classic perfection of cherry pie, it is to serve it—warm or cold—under a brandy hard sauce.

Prepare (do not bake)
    Pastry I for 1-Crust Pie (page 485; use a 9-in. pie pan)
Set aside.

For Filling—Rinse, drain, stem, cut into halves, and remove and discard pits from enough cherries to yield
    4 cups pitted fresh red tart cherries
Toss gently with a mixture of
    1½ cups sugar
    5 tablespoons all-purpose flour
    ⅛ teaspoon salt
Turn cherry mixture into the pastry shell and sprinkle with
    ¼ teaspoon almond extract
Dot with
    2 tablespoons butter or margarine

Bake at 450°F 10 min. Reduce heat to 375°F and bake about 45 min. longer. Remove to cooling rack and allow to cool thoroughly.

Prepare
    Brandy Hard Sauce (page 580)

When pie is cool, force hard sauce through pastry bag and No. 7 star decorating tube, forming a crisscross design over top of pie. At points where lines cross, make small rosettes with same decorating tube. *One 9-in. pie*

—HEAVENLY CHERRY PIE

Follow ▲ Recipe. Substitute **Almond Hard Sauce** (page 581) for Brandy Hard Sauce. Omit almonds.

GRAPE ARBOR PIE

Prepare and set aside
    Pastry for Lattice-Top Pie (page 485; use an 8-in. pie pan)

Sort, rinse and stem enough grapes to yield
    3 cups Concord grapes
Slip skins from grapes. Chop skins; set aside. Put the pulp into a small saucepan and bring to

boiling; reduce heat and simmer 5 min., or until seeds are loosened. Drain pulp, reserving juice. Force the pulp through a fine sieve or food mill to remove the seeds. Add the chopped grape skins to the pulp. Set aside.

Blend thoroughly in a saucepan
    1 cup sugar
    3 tablespoons cornstarch
    ¼ teaspoon salt
Gradually add the reserved grape juice, stirring well. Stirring gently and constantly, bring cornstarch mixture rapidly to boiling over direct heat; cook until thickened. Remove from heat. Stir in the pulp and skins with
    1 tablespoon lemon juice
    2 teaspoons grated orange peel
    1 tablespoon orange juice
Turn grape filling into pastry shell. Complete as in Pastry for Lattice-Top Pie.

Bake at 450°F 10 min. Reduce heat to 350°F and bake 20 to 25 min. longer, or until pastry is light golden brown.

Cool on cooling rack. *One 8-in. pie*

MINCEMEAT PIE

Mix in a saucepan
    3½ cups Mincemeat (page 729; if using packaged condensed mincemeat, prepare according to package directions)
    1 teaspoon grated lemon peel
    1 tablespoon lemon juice
Heat mixture thoroughly. Set aside to cool slightly.

Meanwhile, prepare
    Pastry for 2-Crust Pie (page 485; use a 9-in. pie pan)
Fill pastry shell with mincemeat mixture. Complete as in Pastry for 2-Crust Pie.

Bake at 450°F 10 min. Reduce heat and bake at 350°F 40 min. longer, or until crust is light golden brown.

Cool on cooling rack. *One 9-in. pie*

Cherry Cutout Pie and Cherry Rose Petal Tarts

Peanut Butter Mincemeat Pie

PEANUT BUTTER MINCEMEAT PIE

Set out a 9-in. pie plate.

Have ready
½ cup finely chopped salted peanuts
Put into a bowl
Pie crust mix for a 2-crust pie
Mix in the chopped nuts. Following package directions, prepare pastry for a 2-crust 9-in. pie; roll out and line pie plate.

Mix
1 jar (28 oz.) mincemeat
½ cup chunk-style peanut butter
Turn filling into pastry-lined pie plate. Cut steam slits in top crust (see photo); place over filling. Seal edge and flute.

Bake at 425°F 35 to 40 min., or until lightly browned.
One 9-in. pie

CREAMY PEAR PIE

▲ *Base Recipe*

Prepare and set aside
Pastry for Lattice-Top Pie (page 485; use an 8-in. pie pan)

Thoroughly drain
1 can (29 oz.) sliced pears
Set aside.

Mix in a bowl
¾ cup sugar
1 tablespoon cornstarch
¼ teaspoon cinnamon
⅛ teaspoon nutmeg
Few grains salt
Add gradually, blending until smooth
½ cup cream
2 tablespoons lemon juice
Gently mix in the sliced pears. Turn filling into pastry shell. Complete as in Pastry for Lattice-Top Pie.

Bake at 425°F 30 to 35 min., or until pastry is light golden brown.

Serve warm or cool.
One 8-in. pie

—FRESH PEAR PIE

Follow ▲ Recipe. Use Pastry for 2-Crust Pie (page 485). Wash, quarter, core, pare and slice enough fresh Anjou pears to yield **4 cups sliced pears.** Omit the canned pears, cinnamon and cream. Increase cornstarch to 3 tablespoons and nutmeg to ½ teaspoon. Sprinkle lemon juice over pears and mix lightly; toss gently with dry ingredients. Dot with **2 tablespoons butter or margarine.** Complete as in Pastry for 2-Crust Pie. Sprinkle top of crust with **sugar.** Bake at 450°F 10 min. Reduce heat to 350°F and bake 30 to 35 min. longer, or until crust is light golden brown.

HOLIDAY PEAR AND CRANBERRY PIE

Set out a 9-in. pie plate.

Prepare
Pastry I for 1-Crust Pie (page 485)
Line pie plate with half of pastry. Cut out a pear-tree shape with pears and a partridge (see photo) from remaining pastry. Set aside.

Rinse, sort and set aside
1½ cups cranberries

Wash, quarter, core, slice (do not pare) and set aside
3 fresh winter pears (about 3½ cups, sliced)

Combine cranberries and
1 cup sugar
2 teaspoons grated orange peel
⅛ teaspoon salt
2 tablespoons quick-cooking tapioca
Mix in pears. Spoon filling into pastry-lined pie plate. Carefully place pear tree, pears and partridge cutouts over the filling.

Bake at 400°F 40 min., or until fruit is tender and pastry is golden brown.
One 9-in. pie

PEACH 'N' CHERRY GINGER PIE

Set out a 9-in. pie pan or six 5-in. tart pans.

Crush enough ginger snaps to yield
2 cups ginger snap crumbs (about 34 cookies)
Turn crumbs into a bowl and mix thoroughly with
½ cup butter or margarine, melted
Turn mixture into the pie pan or tart pans. Press crumbs firmly into an even layer over bottom and up sides of pan, building rim up slightly.

Holiday Pear and Cranberry Pie

Bake at 375°F about 8 min. Set on a rack to cool. Chill thoroughly.

Drain, reserving syrup in a measuring cup for liquids
1 jar (8 oz.) red maraschino cherries
Halve cherries and set aside.

Mix in a saucepan
2 tablespoons cornstarch
3 tablespoons light brown sugar
Add enough water to reserved cherry syrup to yield ½ cup. Blend with cornstarch mixture. Bring to boiling, stirring constantly; cook 2 min.

Remove from heat and turn into a large bowl. Stir in
2 tablespoons lemon juice
Mix in the cherries.

Pare and slice enough ripe peaches to yield
6 cups sliced peaches
Add peaches to cherry mixture and mix well. Turn into the crumb crust and chill.

Using a pastry bag with a star decorating tube, pipe **Sweetened Whipped Cream** (page 480) around edge of pie.
One 9-in. pie

PINEAPPLE DELIGHT PIE

Prepare and set aside
Pastry for Lattice-Top Pie (page 485; use an 8-in. pie pan)

Drain, reserving syrup (will be about 1½ cups)
1 can (29½ oz.) crushed pineapple (about 2 cups, drained)

Peach 'n' Cherry Ginger Pie

Mix in a saucepan
½ cup sugar
3 tablespoons cornstarch
¼ teaspoon salt
Add the reserved pineapple syrup gradually, stirring until smooth. Stirring constantly, bring cornstarch mixture to boiling; cook 3 min. Remove from heat. Mix in the drained pineapple and
3 tablespoons butter or margarine
2 teaspoons grated lemon peel
1 tablespoon lemon juice
1 tablespoon orange juice
Turn filling into unbaked pastry shell. Complete as in Pastry for Lattice-Top Pie.

Bake at 425°F 25 to 30 min., or until pastry is light golden brown. Cool on a rack.

One 8-in. pie

LEMON RAISIN PIE

Prepare, bake and set aside to cool
Pastry I for 1-Crust Pie (page 485; use a 9-in. pie pan)

Put into a heavy saucepan
2 cups seedless raisins
2 cups water
Bring to boiling; simmer 10 min.

Blend thoroughly
½ cup sugar
3 tablespoons all-purpose flour
¼ teaspoon salt
½ teaspoon cinnamon
¼ teaspoon cloves
Mix into hot raisins. Bring to boiling; cook and stir until thickened.

Stir a small amount of hot mixture into
2 eggs, beaten
Immediately blend with remaining hot mixture in saucepan. Cook and stir 3 min. over medium heat.

Remove from heat. Stir in
2 tablespoons butter or margarine
1 teaspoon grated lemon peel
3 tablespoons lemon juice

Turn filling into baked pastry shell. Sprinkle in a circle on top
¼ cup chopped walnuts
Serve cool, garnished with a border of **Sweetened Whipped Cream** (page 480).

One 9-in. pie

RHUBARB PIE

▲ *Base Recipe*

Delightful announcement of Spring's arrival.

Prepare and set aside
Pastry for 2-Crust Pie (page 485; use a 9-in. pie pan)

Wash, trim off ends of stems and leaves, and cut into 1-in. pieces enough rhubarb to yield
6 cups fresh rhubarb

Sift together
1¾ cups sugar
½ cup sifted all-purpose flour
¼ teaspoon salt
Sprinkle one third of the dry ingredients over bottom of the pastry shell.

Mix with remaining dry ingredients
1 teaspoon grated orange peel
Turn rhubarb into pastry shell, heaping slightly at center. Sprinkle with remaining dry ingredients. Dot with
2 tablespoons butter
Complete as in Pastry for 2-Crust Pie.

Bake at 425°F 10 min. Reduce heat to 350°F and bake 40 to 45 min. longer, or until crust is light golden brown.

Cool on cooling rack. *One 9-in. pie*

—BLACKBERRY PIE

Follow ▲ Recipe. Substitute **6 cups fresh blackberries,** washed and sorted, for the rhubarb, and sprinkle over them **2 teaspoons lemon juice.** Reduce the sugar to 1½ cups. Mix with dry ingredients **½ teaspoon cinnamon.** Add to blackberries and toss gently together before filling pie.

—BLUEBERRY PIE

Follow ▲ Recipe. Substitute **6 cups fresh**

Lemon Raisin Pie

blueberries, washed and sorted, for rhubarb, and sprinkle over them **2 tablespoons lemon juice.** Reduce sugar to 1 cup plus 2 tablespoons, flour to ⅓ cup, and blend with sugar-flour mixture **¾ teaspoon cinnamon, ½ teaspoon nutmeg,** and **¼ teaspoon salt.** Add to blueberries and toss gently together before filling pie.

GLAZED STRAWBERRY PIE

Set out
1 baked 9-in. pastry shell (page 485)
1 qt. strawberries, rinsed (discarding imperfect berries) and hulled
Set aside 2 cups whole berries. Crush remaining berries with fork and set aside.

Mix in a saucepan in order
¼ cup plus 2 tablespoons sugar
1½ tablespoons cornstarch
¼ cup plus 2 tablespoons water
Stirring gently and constantly, bring rapidly to boiling and cook for 3 min., or until mixture is clear. Stir in the crushed berries and blend in
1 teaspoon lemon juice
3 or 4 drops red food coloring
Cool mixture slightly with pan set in bowl of ice and water. Cover and set aside.

Beat together until blended
1 pkg. (3 oz.) cream cheese
1 tablespoon orange juice
Spread over bottom of pie shell; cover with

whole berries. Pour cooled strawberry mixture over berries. Chill in refrigerator.

Top with
Sweetened Whipped Cream (page 480)

One 9-in. pie

—GLAZED STRAWBERRY TARTS

Prepare pastry for six 3½-in. tarts using **Pastry for Little Pies and Tarts** (page 485). Follow ▲ Recipe for glaze. Place several whole berries in each tart. Spoon about 3 tablespoons cooled glaze over berries. Chill until ready to serve.

For Toasted Coconut—Coarsely chop and spread over bottom of shallow pan
½ cup moist shredded coconut
Set pan in 350°F oven 10 to 15 min., or until coconut is lightly toasted. Sprinkle 1 tablespoon coconut around edge of each tart.

Or prepare
Sweetened Whipped Cream (one half recipe, page 480)
Decorate tarts by forcing sweetened whipped cream through pastry bag and No. 27 star decorating tube.   *6 tarts*

CREAM PIES

DE LUXE CREAM PIE OR TARTS

▲ *Base Recipe*

Prepare and bake in an 8-in. pie pan
Pastry I for 1-Crust Pie (page 485)
or
Pastry for six 3½-in. tarts (see Pastry for Little Pies and Tarts, page 485)
Cool on cooling rack.

Scald (page 10)
1½ cups milk

Meanwhile, mix thoroughly in a heavy saucepan
⅔ cup sugar
¼ cup sifted all-purpose flour
¼ teaspoon salt
Add, stirring well
½ cup cold milk
Gradually stir in scalded milk.

Stirring gently and constantly, bring the mixture rapidly to boiling, reduce the heat and cook about 3 min.

Vigorously stir about 3 tablespoons of the hot mixture into
3 egg yolks, slightly beaten

Immediately blend into hot mixture in saucepan. Cook 2 to 3 min., stirring constantly. Remove from heat. Add and stir until butter is melted
2 tablespoons butter or margarine
2 teaspoons vanilla extract
Cover and set filling aside to cool slightly, stirring occasionally; set in refrigerator to cool to lukewarm. Spoon lukewarm filling into cooled pastry or tart shells, allowing about ⅓ cup for each tart. Cool completely except when topping with Meringue (see below).

Just before serving, garnish with **maraschino cherries** or top with **Sweetened Whipped Cream** (page 480); prepare one-half recipe for the tarts and whole recipe for 8-in. pie).

Or, prepare a Meringue (makes enough for tarts or 8- or 9-in. pie).

Beat until frothy
3 egg whites
Gradually add, beating after each addition
6 tablespoons sugar
Beat until rounded peaks are formed. With final strokes, beat in
¼ teaspoon vanilla extract
Pile meringue onto lukewarm filling and seal meringue to crust.

Bake at 350°F 10 to 15 min., or until meringue is delicately browned. Cool on cooling racks.
One 8-in. pie

—BANANA CREAM PIE OR TARTS

Follow ▲ Recipe. Slice **2 bananas** about ⅛ in. thick into large shell before adding filling; for tart shells, cut about 10 slices into each.

Chocolate Cream Pie

—BUTTERSCOTCH CREAM PIE OR TARTS

Follow ▲ Recipe. Decrease sugar to ⅓ cup and add ⅓ cup firmly packed brown sugar. Increase butter to 3 tablespoons.

—CHOCOLATE CREAM PIE OR TARTS

Follow ▲ Recipe. **Add 2 oz. (2 sq.) unsweetened chocolate** to milk and heat until milk is scalded and chocolate is melted. Sprinkle about **3 teaspoons grated chocolate** over the whipped cream or meringue-topped pie or about ½ teaspoon over each tart. Or, garnish filled pie shell with mounds of the whipped cream. Arrange **semisweet chocolate pieces** on each mound.

—CHOCOLATE CREAM PUDDING

Follow recipe for Chocolate Cream Pie or Tarts. Pour into 6 individual serving dishes. When cool, serve with **cream**.

—LEMON CREAM PIE OR TARTS

Follow ▲ Recipe. Increase sugar to ¾ cup and flour to 6 tablespoons. Omit vanilla extract; add with the butter ¼ cup lemon juice, 2 teaspoons grated lemon peel and 3 to 6 drops yellow food coloring. Just before serving, garnish with **maraschino cherries** or **Plain Pastry Pinwheels** (page 486).

—LIME CREAM PIE OR TARTS

Follow recipe for Lemon Cream Pie or Tarts. Substitute **lime juice** for lemon juice, ½ **teaspoon lime peel** for lemon peel and **2 to 4 drops green food coloring** for yellow. Garnish with **maraschino cherries**.

—MOCHA CHOCOLATE CREAM PIE

Follow ▲ Recipe. Substitute **1 cup double-strength coffee beverage** for 1 cup milk.

—COCOA CREAM PIE

Follow ▲ Recipe. Substitute **½ cup cocoa** for chocolate. Mix cocoa with dry ingredients.

CHOCOLATE MINT PIE

Prepare and bake in a 9-in. pie pan
   Pastry I for 1-Crust Pie (page 485)
Set aside to cool on cooling rack.

Meanwhile, melt (page 10) and set aside
   1 oz. (1 sq.) unsweetened chocolate

Cream until softened
   ½ cup butter or margarine
Add gradually, creaming until fluffy after each addition
   ¾ cup sugar
Blend in cooled chocolate and
   2 or 3 drops peppermint extract
Add one at a time, beating 5 min. after each addition
   2 eggs, unbeaten
Pour filling into cooled pie shell. Chill in refrigerator 2 to 3 hrs.

Just before serving, prepare and pile onto top of pie
   **Sweetened Whipped Cream
   (page 480)**
Garnish with
   **¼ cup (about 1 oz.) blanched and
   toasted (pages 9 and 10) almonds,
   slivered**
   **½ oz. (½ sq.) unsweetened chocolate,
   grated**

One 9-in. pie

HONEY CHOCOLATE PIE

Prepare and bake in a 9-in. pie pan
   Pastry I for 1-Crust Pie (page 485)
Set aside on cooling rack to cool.

Heat in a saucepan until milk is scalded (page 10) and chocolate melted
   2 cups milk
   2 oz. (2 sq.) unsweetened chocolate

Meanwhile, combine in a heavy saucepan
   ⅓ cup all-purpose flour
   ½ teaspoon salt
Add, stirring well, a mixture of
   ½ cup cold milk
   ½ cup honey
Gradually add scalded milk and chocolate, stirring until blended.

Stirring gently and constantly, bring the mixture to boiling, reduce the heat and cook 3 min. Vigorously stir about 3 tablespoons hot mixture into
   3 egg yolks, slightly beaten
Immediately blend into hot mixture in saucepan. Cook 2 to 3 min. Stir slowly to keep mixture cooking evenly. Remove from heat. Add and stir until butter is melted
   2 tablespoons butter or margarine
   1 teaspoon vanilla extract
Cover and cool to lukewarm.

Prepare a meringue by beating in a bowl until frothy
   3 egg whites
   ⅛ teaspoon salt
Add gradually and beat well after each addi-

tion finally beating until rounded peaks are formed and egg whites do not slide when bowl is partially inverted
   6 tablespoons sugar

Pour lukewarm filling into cooled pastry shell; pile meringue onto filling and seal meringue to crust.

Bake at 350°F 10 to 15 min., or until meringue is delicately browned. Cool.

Melt (page 10) and set aside to cool
   ½ oz. (½ sq.) unsweetened chocolate

Streak cooled meringue with melted chocolate.

One 9-in. pie

COCONUT CREAM PIE

   ▲ *Base Recipe*

Prepare, bake and set aside to cool
   **Pastry I for 1-Crust Pie (page 485; use
   an 8-in. pie pan)**
Set out
   2 cups milk
Scald (page 10) 1½ cups of the milk; reserve remainder.

Meanwhile, mix thoroughly in a heavy saucepan
   ⅔ cup sugar
   ¼ cup all-purpose flour
   ¼ teaspoon salt
Blend in the reserved milk; add gradually and stir in the scalded milk. Bring rapidly to boiling, stirring gently and constantly; cook 3 min. Remove from heat.

Vigorously stir about 3 tablespoons of the hot mixture into
   3 egg yolks, slightly beaten
Immediately blend into hot mixture in saucepan. Cook 2 to 3 min. Stir slowly to keep mixture cooking evenly. Remove from heat. Add and stir until butter is melted
   2 tablespoons butter or margarine
   2 teaspoons vanilla extract
Cool to lukewarm in the refrigerator, stirring occasionally.

Set out
   1 cup flaked coconut
When filling is lukewarm, fold in the coconut and turn the filling into the pastry shell. Cool completely.

If desired, before serving spread over top and swirl with back of spoon
   Sweetened Whipped Cream (page 480)
Garnish with
   Flaked coconut

One 8-in. pie

Honey Chocolate Pie

JIFFY LEMON PIE

   ▲ *Base Recipe*

Tart lemon filling topped with meringue.

Set out
   1 baked 8-in. pastry shell (page 485)

Blend thoroughly
   **1¼ cups (14-oz. can) sweetened
   condensed milk**
   1½ teaspoons grated lemon peel
   ⅔ cup lemon juice
   2 egg yolks, slightly beaten
Pour into shell and set aside.

For Meringue—Beat until frothy
   2 egg whites
   ⅛ teaspoon salt
Add gradually, beating well after each addition
   ¼ cup sugar
Beat until rounded peaks are formed and egg whites do not slide when bowl is partially inverted. Pile meringue lightly onto filling and seal meringue to crust.

Bake at 350°F 10 to 12 min., or until meringue is delicately browned. Set aside to cool until ready to serve.

One 8-in. pie

—JIFFY LIME PIE

Follow ▲ Recipe. Substitute **½ teaspoon
lime peel** and **⅓ cup each lime juice and
orange juice** for lemon. Blend in **1 or 2 drops
green food coloring**, if desired.

Jiffy Lemon Pie

Mocha Cream Pie

KEY LIME PIE

Prepare, bake and set aside to cool
> **Pastry I for 1-Crust Pie (page 485; use a 9-in. pie pan)**

Blend just until well mixed
> **1¼ cups (14-oz. can) sweetened condensed milk**
> **⅔ cup lime juice**
> **3 egg yolks, slightly beaten**
> **1 or 2 drops green food coloring**

Pour into pastry shell. Beat until frothy
> **3 egg whites**

Add gradually, beating well after each addition
> **⅓ cup sugar**

Continue beating until rounded peaks are formed. Pile meringue lightly over pie filling, sealing to edge of crust.

Bake at 450°F about 5 min., or until meringue is delicately browned. Cool.   *One 9-in. pie*

MOCHA CREAM PIE WITH CRUNCHY PEANUT BUTTER TOPPING

Prepare, bake and cool
> **Pastry I for 1-Crust Pie (page 485; use a 9-in. pie pan)**

Put into a bowl
> **½ cup chunk-style peanut butter**
> **¾ cup confectioners' sugar**

Using a pastry blender or fork, blend peanut butter and sugar until pieces resemble small peas. Spread two thirds of mixture over bottom of pastry shell; reserve remaining mixture.

Combine in a heavy saucepan
> **½ cup sugar**
> **2 teaspoons flour**
> **⅛ teaspoon salt**
> **1 tablespoon instant powdered coffee**

Blend in
> **1 can (14½ oz.) evaporated milk**

Bring mixture to boiling, stirring constantly. Cook and stir 2 min.

Stirring constantly, gradually add about a third of hot mixture to
> **2 eggs, fork beaten**

Immediately blend into hot mixture. Cook and stir 5 min.

Remove from heat and mix in
> **2 tablespoons butter or margarine**
> **½ teaspoon vanilla extract**

Turn filling over crumb mixture in pastry shell. Sprinkle remaining crumb mixture on filling to form a border (see photo). Chill pie before serving. If desired, serve with a **whipped dessert topping** or **Sweetened Whipped Cream** (page 480).   *One 9-in. pie*

CHOCOLATE RAISIN PIE

Prepare (do not bake) and set aside
> **Pastry I for 1-Crust Pie (page 485; use a 9-in. pie pan)**

Coarsely chop
> **1½ cups dark seedless raisins**

Put raisins into a heavy saucepan with
> **1 cup heavy cream**
> **2 oz. sweet chocolate**
> **¼ cup butter or margarine**

Set over low heat and stir until chocolate and butter are melted.

Remove from heat. Mix in extract. Stir in a blend of
> **¾ cup sugar**
> **3 tablespoons cornstarch**
> **½ teaspoon instant powdered coffee**
> **⅛ teaspoon salt**
> **⅛ teaspoon cinnamon**

Beat until foamy
> **2 eggs**

Stir eggs into raisin mixture. Turn into unbaked pastry shell and spread evenly to edges.

Bake at 375°F 25 min., or until set. Cool completely on a rack.

Spread **Sweetened Whipped Cream** (page 480)

over top of pie. Garnish with **dark seedless raisins** forming daisies (see photo).

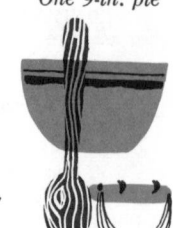

One 9-in. pie

DUCHESS STRAWBERRY CREAM PIE

▲ *Base Recipe*

Set out a 9-in. pie pan.

Prepare (do not bake) and set aside
> **9-in. pastry shell (page 485)**

Sort, rinse, drain, hull and halve if large
> **2½ cups ripe strawberries**

Turn berries into the pastry shell.

Measure into a bowl
> **1 cup dairy sour cream**

Add gradually to the sour cream, blending well
> **1 cup sugar**
> **¼ cup all-purpose flour**
> **¼ teaspoon salt**

Pour mixture over strawberries. Sprinkle over surface a mixture of
> **2 tablespoons fine dry bread crumbs**
> **2 tablespoons sugar**
> **1 tablespoon melted butter**

Bake at 425°F 15 min. Reduce heat to 350°F and bake 30 min. longer, or until topping is lightly browned.

Cool on cooling rack.   *One 9-in. pie*

—BLACKBERRY CREAM PIE

Follow ▲ Recipe. Substitute **4 cups fresh whole blackberries** for the halved strawberries.

—RASPBERRY CREAM PIE

Follow ▲ Recipe. Substitute **4 cups fresh red or black raspberries** for the strawberries.

Chocolate Raisin Pie

CUSTARD PIES

BLACK BOTTOM PIE I

▲ Base Recipe

A queen of pies—handsome and rich.

Prepare and bake in a 10-in. pie pan
Pastry I for 1-Crust Pie with Braided Edge (page 486)
Set aside on cooling rack to cool.

Melt (page 10) and set aside to cool
1½ oz. (1½ sq.) unsweetened chocolate

Pour into a small cup or custard cup
¼ cup cold water
Sprinkle evenly over the water
1 env. unflavored gelatin
Let stand until softened.

For Custard Filling—Beat slightly in a small bowl and set aside
4 egg yolks

Scald (page 10) in double boiler top
1½ cups milk

Blend thoroughly in a heavy saucepan
½ cup sugar
4 teaspoons cornstarch
Add and blend in well
½ cup cold milk
Stir hot milk into cornstarch mixture. Bring rapidly to boiling over direct heat, stirring gently and constantly. Cook 3 min. Pour into double boiler top.

Vigorously stir about 3 tablespoons of hot mixture into egg yolks. Immediately blend into cooked mixture, stirring constantly. Cook over simmering water 3 to 5 min. until mixture thickens, or coats a metal spoon. Remove from heat. Remove 1 cup cooked filling mixture from double boiler and set aside.

Add softened gelatin to mixture in double boiler. Stir until gelatin is completely dissolved. Set aside. Cool until the mixture sets slightly. If it becomes too stiff, soften over simmering water. Cool again.

For Chocolate Filling—Stir melted chocolate into the 1 cup of reserved filling with
2 teaspoons vanilla extract
Cool completely. Pour into pie shell and spread evenly over bottom. Chill until set.

To Complete Pie—Meanwhile, beat until frothy
4 egg whites
¼ teaspoon salt
Add and continue to beat egg whites slightly
¼ teaspoon cream of tartar
Add gradually, beating well after each addition
½ cup sugar
Continue beating until very stiff peaks are formed. Fold beaten egg whites into cooled plain filling. Blend in
1 tablespoon rum extract
Pour over set chocolate filling in pie shell. Chill until firm.

Set a rotary beater and bowl in refrigerator to chill.

When ready to serve, use chilled bowl and beater and whip until cream stands in peaks when beater is slowly lifted upright
1 cup chilled heavy cream
Spread on pie. Top with chocolate curls made by pulling across a shredder
½ oz. (½ sq.) unsweetened chocolate
Chill until ready to serve. *One 10-in. pie*

—BLACK BOTTOM PIE II

Follow ▲ Recipe. Omit chocolate. Add vanilla extract after removing filling from heat. While pie shell is still warm, place **2 or 3 milk chocolate bars**, broken in pieces, or **1 pkg. (6 oz.) semisweet chocolate pieces** in shell. When cool and set, pour filling mixture over chocolate. Chill. Top as directed.

LEMON BUTTERMILK PIE

▲ Base Recipe

A custard pie that is distinctively different.

Set out a 9-in. pie pan.

Prepare (do not bake) and set aside
9-in. pastry shell (page 485)

Melt and set aside to cool
3 tablespoons butter or margarine

Beat slightly
3 egg yolks
Blend in a mixture of
½ cup sugar
2 tablespoons all-purpose flour
¼ teaspoon salt
Stir in the melted butter and
1½ cups buttermilk
½ teaspoon grated lemon peel
3 tablespoons lemon juice

Using a clean beater, beat until frothy
3 egg whites
Add gradually and continue beating until very stiff peaks are formed
¼ cup sugar
Spread over buttermilk mixture and fold together. Turn into pastry shell.

Bake at 450°F 10 min. Reduce heat to 350°F and bake 20 to 25 min. longer, or until a metal knife comes out clean when inserted halfway between center and edge of filling. Cool on cooling rack. *One 9-in. pie*

—VANILLA BUTTERMILK PIE

Follow ▲ Recipe. Omit lemon peel and juice. Decrease sugar in egg yolk mixture to 6 or 7 tablespoons and increase buttermilk to 1⅔ cups; add **1½ teaspoons vanilla extract**.

Black Bottom Pie II

DE LUXE CARAMEL PECAN PIE

Prepare (do not bake) in an 8-in. pie pan
Pastry I for 1-Crust Pie (page 485)
Set aside.

Combine
1 cup milk
2 egg yolks, slightly beaten
2 tablespoons butter or margarine, melted
1 teaspoon vanilla extract
Stir in a mixture of
½ cup sugar
½ cup firmly packed brown sugar
2 tablespoons all-purpose flour
Set aside.

Beat until rounded peaks are formed
2 egg whites
Fold gently into egg yolk mixture. Pour into pastry shell.

Bake at 450°F 10 min. Quickly reduce heat to 350°F and bake 25 to 30 min. longer, or until a metal knife inserted halfway between center and edge of filling comes out clean.

Top cooled pie with **Glossy Chocolate Frosting** (page 476) and **pecan halves**.
One 8-in. pie

PEACHES AND CREAM PIE

Peaches and Cream Pie—lovely to see and magnificent to eat—its goodness emphasized by glasses of refreshing iced coffee.

Set aside to drain thoroughly
1 can (30 oz.) peach halves (about 7)

Prepare and bake in 9-in. pie pan
Pastry I for 1-Crust Pie (page 485)

Set aside to cool on cooling rack.

Mix
¼ cup sugar
¼ cup all-purpose flour
½ teaspoon cinnamon
Sprinkle two thirds of dry ingredients evenly over bottom of pastry shell. Place thoroughly drained peach halves in pastry shell. cut-side up; do not overlap. Sprinkle remaining dry

ingredients over peaches. Spread evenly over peaches a mixture of

2 cups dairy sour cream
1 teaspoon vanilla extract

Mix and sprinkle over cream

2 tablespoons sugar
½ teaspoon cinnamon

Swirl with back of spoon for decorative effect.

Bake at 450°F 20 min. Remove from oven and set on cooling rack. Serve pie slightly warm.

One 9-in. pie

CHESS PIE I

▲ Base Recipe

The jelly-like filling is shallow because it is so very rich. We recommend small servings!

Prepare (do not bake) and set aside

Pastry I for 1-Crust Pie (page 485; use an 8-in. pie pan)

Cream together until softened

½ cup butter
2 teaspoons vanilla extract

Add gradually, creaming until fluffy after each addition

1½ cups sugar

Add in thirds, beating well after each addition

4 egg yolks, well beaten

Turn into the pastry shell.

Bake at 425°F 10 min. Reduce heat to 325°F and bake 40 to 45 min. longer, or until a metal knife comes out clean when inserted halfway between center and edge of filling. Serve warm or cool. *One 8-in. pie*

—CHESS PIE II (OSGOOD PIE)

Follow ▲ Recipe. Decrease butter to ⅓ cup, vanilla extract to 1 teaspoon and sugar to 1 cup. Use **2 eggs** instead of the egg yolks. Blend in ¼ cup cream. Stir in **1 cup (about 4 oz.) chopped pecans** and **1 cup (about 5 oz.) dark seedless raisins**. Bake at 450°F 10 min. Reduce heat to 350°F and bake 30 min. longer.

PECAN PIE

One of the richest and most delicious of all the rich, delicious Southern traditional pies.

Prepare (do not bake) and set aside

Pastry I for 1-Crust Pie (page 485; use a 9-in. pie pan)

Set out

½ cup (about 2 oz.) pecan halves
½ cup (about 2 oz.) chopped pecans

Melt

3 tablespoons butter

Combine in a bowl

3 eggs
¾ cup sugar
⅛ teaspoon salt
1 cup dark corn syrup
1 teaspoon vanilla extract

Add the melted butter to mixture in bowl and beat with a rotary beater until blended. Mix in the chopped pecans. Turn filling into the pastry shell.

Bake at 450°F 10 min. Arrange pecan halves on top of pie filling. Reduce heat to 350°F and bake 30 to 35 minutes longer, or until a metal knife comes out clean when inserted halfway between center and edge of filling.

Cool on cooling rack. *One 9-in. pie*

CRUNCHY PECAN-TOPPED PUMPKIN PIE

▲ Base Recipe

Prepare in a 9-in. pie pan

Pastry I for 1-Crust Pie (page 485)

Meanwhile, mix

1 can (16 oz.) pumpkin
⅔ cup firmly packed brown sugar

Add a blend of

1 teaspoon cinnamon
½ teaspoon ginger
½ teaspoon nutmeg
⅛ teaspoon cloves
½ teaspoon salt

Mix in

2 eggs, slightly beaten

Gradually add, stirring until mixture is smooth

2 cups cream, scalded

Pour into pastry shell.

Bake at 400°F about 50 min., or until a metal knife comes out clean when inserted halfway between center and edge. Cool on cooling rack. While pie is cooling, prepare

Crunchy Coated Pecans (below)

When pie is cool, arrange coated pecans, rounded side up, over the top in an attractive design. Place under broiler about 3 in. from heat. Broil 1 to 2 min.

Serve warm or cold with

Sweetened Whipped Cream (page 480)

One 9-in. pie

For Crunchy Coated Pecans—Melt in small skillet over low heat

3 tablespoons butter

Add

1 cup (about 4 oz.) pecan halves

Occasionally turn pecans until thoroughly coated with butter. Turn nuts into a bowl containing

¼ cup firmly packed brown sugar

Toss to coat thoroughly.

—GLAZED PUMPKIN PECAN PIE

Follow ▲ Recipe. Omit Crunchy Coated Pecans. While pie is baking, using a pastry blender or two knives, cut **⅓ cup softened butter** into **1 cup firmly packed brown sugar** until mixture is crumbly. Spoon mixture evenly over top of hot baked pie. Decorate top of pie with **1 cup (about 4 oz.) pecan halves**. Place pie under broiler with top 3 in. from heat. Broil about 1 min., or until butter-sugar mixture bubbles.

—SQUASH PIE

Follow ▲ Recipe. Substitute **thawed frozen squash** for the pumpkin.

Pecan Pie and Pumpkin Pecan Tarts

Almond-Topped Pumpkin Pie and Sour Cream Pie with Pecans

—ALMOND-TOPPED PUMPKIN PIE

Follow ▲ Recipe. Omit Crunchy Coated Pecans. Spread top of cooled pie with **Sweetened Whipped Cream** (page 480) and sprinkle with **½ cup chopped toasted (page 10) almonds.**

—PUMPKIN PECAN TARTS

Follow ▲ Recipe. Substitute **Pastry for Little Pies and Tarts** (two-thirds recipe, page 485) for Pastry I for 1-Crust Pie. (Prepare 8 3½-in. tart shells.) Pour ½ cup filling into each tart. Top with Crunchy Coated Pecans as in ▲ Recipe or glaze as for Glazed Pumpkin Pecan Pie. Bake at 450°F 10 min.; then at 350°F 20 min.

SWEET POTATO PIE

What pumpkin pie is to the northern part of the country, sweet potato pie is to the South— and some folks can hardly tell the difference.

Prepare (do not bake) and set aside
　　Pastry I for 1-Crust Pie (page 485; use a 9-in. pie pan)

Set out
　　1½ cups sieved cooked sweet potatoes or yams

Scald (page 10)
　　1½ cups milk

Add to the sweet potatoes
　　2 tablespoons melted butter
　　1 teaspoon grated orange peel
and a mixture of
　　½ cup firmly packed brown sugar
　　1 teaspoon cinnamon
　　½ teaspoon ginger
　　½ teaspoon nutmeg
　　¼ teaspoon cloves
　　½ teaspoon salt

Beat well. Add in thirds, beating well after each addition
　　2 eggs, beaten
Blend in scalded milk. Turn into pastry shell.

Bake at 450°F 10 min. Reduce heat to 350°F and bake 30 to 35 min. longer, or until metal knife comes out clean when inserted halfway between center and edge of filling. Cool on cooling rack.

Before serving, spread over top of pie
　　Sweetened Whipped Cream (use one half recipe, page 480)
Sprinkle with
　　2 tablespoons chopped pecans
　　　　　　　　　　　　　　One 9-in. pie

SOUR CREAM PIE WITH PECANS

Set out a 10-in. pie pan.

Prepare (do not bake) and set aside
　　10-in. pastry shell (page 485)

Mix
　　1½ cups firmly packed light brown sugar
　　2 tablespoons all-purpose flour
　　⅛ teaspoon salt
Blend
　　3 eggs, beaten
　　1½ cups dairy sour cream
　　1 teaspoon vanilla extract
Add sugar mixture; stir until blended. Mix in
　　1½ cups (about 6 oz.) small pecan halves
Turn mixture into pastry shell.

Bake at 450°F 10 min. Reduce heat to 350°F and bake about 30 min., or until a metal knife comes out clean when inserted halfway between center and edge of filling. Cool on cooling rack.　　*One 10-in. pie*

SOUR CREAM RAISIN PIE

Prepare (do not bake) and set aside
　　Pastry I for 1-Crust Pie (page 485; use a 9-in. pie pan)

Mix
　　½ cup sugar
　　2 tablespoons all-purpose flour
　　½ teaspoon cinnamon
　　¼ teaspoon nutmeg
　　¼ teaspoon salt
Blend
　　1 egg, well beaten
　　1½ cups dairy sour cream
Add dry ingredients to the sour-cream mixture and blend thoroughly. Mix in
　　1⅓ cups (about 7 oz.) seedless raisins
Turn into the pastry shell.

Bake at 450°F 10 min. Reduce heat to 350°F and bake 20 to 25 min. longer, or until a metal knife comes out clean when inserted halfway between center and edge of filling.

Place on cooling rack to cool slightly.

Serve warm.　　　　　　*One 9-in. pie*

SOUR CREAM APPLE PIE

Prepare
　　9-in. Graham Cracker Crumb Crust (page 488)

For Filling—Put into a saucepan
　　2½ cups (20 oz. can) sliced apples (sweetened)
　　½ cup firmly packed brown sugar
Toss gently and place over medium heat until mixture bubbles. Reduce heat and cook 5 min., occasionally moving mixture with a spoon. Remove from heat and set aside.

Blend until smooth
　　1 egg, well beaten
　　2 cups dairy sour cream
and a mixture of
　　3 tablespoons brown sugar
　　2 tablespoons all-purpose flour
　　½ teaspoon cinnamon
　　⅛ teaspoon nutmeg
　　⅛ teaspoon mace
　　⅛ teaspoon salt
Turn about one half of the sour cream mixture into the pie shell; spread evenly. Spoon the apple slices in an even layer over the sour cream mixture; top with remaining sour cream mixture, spreading evenly.

Bake at 400°F 10 to 12 min., or until sour cream mixture is set.

Cool on cooling rack; chill pie thoroughly in refrigerator before serving.　*One 9-in. pie*

CHEESE PIES

LEMON CHEESE PIE

For Crust—Prepare (do not bake)
　　Graham Cracker Crumb Crust (page 488; use an 8-in. pie pan. Reserve 2 tablespoons crumb mixture for topping.)

For Filling—Mix in a bowl until thoroughly blended
　　9 oz. cream cheese, softened
　　2 tablespoons butter or margarine
　　½ teaspoon vanilla extract

Add in order, blending until smooth after each addition

½ cup sugar
1 egg, slightly beaten
2 tablespoons all-purpose flour
⅔ cup milk
2 tablespoons grated lemon peel
¼ cup lemon juice

Turn filling into prepared pie shell. Sprinkle reserved crumb mixture over top of pie to form a decorative pattern.

Bake at 325°F 35 min. Remove from oven and cool on cooling rack.

Chill in refrigerator until ready to serve.

One 8-in. pie

Note: For interesting flavor variation, omit crumb garnish on top and spread baked pie with dairy sour cream.

COTTAGE CHEESE PIE A L'ARISTOCRATE

Prepare and bake 10 min.
10-in. Pastry Shell (page 485)
Set aside.

For Filling—Crumble enough cake to yield
3 cups cake crumbs
Set crumbs aside.

Cream together until softened
½ cup butter
1 teaspoon grated lemon peel
¾ teaspoon cinnamon
½ teaspoon nutmeg
¼ teaspoon salt

Plum-Glazed Cheese Pie

Add gradually, creaming until fluffy after each addition
½ cup sugar
Add gradually, beating well after each addition
2 egg yolks
Add and beat until curds are slightly broken
1 cup firmly packed dry cottage cheese
Stir cake crumbs into creamed mixture.

Add in order, mixing well after each addition
3 tablespoons sherry
3 tablespoons brandy
1 cup cream (adding gradually)
Beat until stiff, not dry, peaks are formed
4 egg whites

Spread beaten egg whites over cottage-cheese mixture and fold together. Turn mixture into the cooled pastry shell.

Bake at 350°F about 50 min., or until filling is set.

Serve pie slightly warm. *One 10-in. pie*

PLUM-GLAZED CHEESE PIE

▲ *Base Recipe*

Set a bowl and rotary beater in refrigerator to chill.

Prepare (page 488)
10-in. Graham Cracker Crumb Crust

For Filling—Put into a bowl
1 pkg. (8 oz.) cream cheese, softened
Add gradually and blend in thoroughly
½ cup sweetened condensed milk
2 tablespoons lemon juice
1 teaspoon grated lemon peel
¼ teaspoon vanilla extract
Using the chilled bowl and beater, beat until cream is of medium consistency (piles softly)
½ cup chilled heavy cream

Fold the whipped cream into the cream-cheese mixture. Turn into the pie shell and set in refrigerator to chill.

For Glaze—Wash thoroughly and drain
1 lb. fresh Italian plums
Cut into halves; remove and discard pits. Set plums aside.

Combine in a saucepan
1 cup sugar
¾ cup water
Set over medium heat; stir until sugar is dissolved. Bring to boiling. Cover and boil gently 5 min. Add the plum halves to the syrup and cook slowly until just tender. Remove from heat; cool plum halves in syrup. Using a slotted spoon, carefully remove plums to a shallow dish or pan. Reserve the syrup.

Put into a small saucepan.
1½ teaspoons cornstarch
Add gradually, blending in, ½ cup of the reserved syrup. Stirring gently and constantly, bring rapidly to boiling and cook until mixture is thickened. Set aside to cool.

Arrange the cooled plum halves, cut sides down, on top of the filling (see photo). Spoon the glaze (cooled syrup mixture) over plums and filling. Set in refrigerator to chill thoroughly before serving. *One 10-in. pie*

—ORANGE BANANA CHEESE PIE

Follow ▲ Recipe for crust and filling. Using a sharp knife, cut away peel from **1 orange**. Remove sections by cutting on each side of dividing membrane, working over a bowl to save juice. Remove and discard seeds, if any. Peel **2 bananas** with brown-flecked peel. Score by pulling tines of fork down the bananas lengthwise. Repeat until entire surface is scored. Cut the scored bananas, on a slant, into ¼-in. slices. Brush with **lemon juice** to prevent darkening. To prepare a glaze, mix in a saucepan **6 tablespoons sugar** and **2 teaspoons cornstarch**. Stir in **3 tablespoons orange juice, 2 tablespoons water** and **2 teaspoons lemon juice**. Stirring gently and constantly, bring mixture rapidly to boiling and cook until mixture is thickened. Set aside to cool.

On top of the chilled filling, arrange 3 of the banana slices, slightly overlapping, from edge toward center of pie. Place an orange section next to slices, parallel to them. Repeat process, alternating the orange sections and banana slices around the pie to form a fruit ring. Spoon the cooled glaze over the fruit and filling. Set in refrigerator to chill thoroughly before serving. Garnish with **mint sprigs.**

—STRAWBERRY-GLAZED CHEESE PIE

Follow ▲ Recipe for crust and filling. Thaw **1 pkg. (16 oz.) frozen strawberries.** Drain strawberries thoroughly, reserving syrup. Put **2 teaspoons cornstarch** into a small saucepan. Gradually add ¾ cup of the reserved strawberry syrup, stirring until smooth. Stirring gently and constantly, bring rapidly to boiling and cook until mixture is thickened. Set aside to cool for about 10 min. Gently blend in the strawberries. Spoon glaze over pie and set in refrigerator to chill.

RICOTTA PIE
(Torta di Ricotta)

Set out 9-in. round layer cake pan.

For Pastry—Sift together into a bowl
>**2 cups all-purpose flour**
>**½ teaspoon salt**

Cut in with pastry blender until pieces are size of small peas
>**1 cup shortening**

Sprinkle gradually over mixture, 1 teaspoon at a time
>**2 egg yolks, slightly beaten**
>**1 to 2 tablespoons cold water**

Mix lightly with fork after each addition. Add only enough water to hold dough together. Mix until egg is thoroughly combined and completely blended.

Shape pastry into a ball and flatten on lightly floured surface. Lightly flour rolling pin. Roll from center to edge into a round about ⅛ in. thick and about 1 in. larger than overall size of pan. With knife or spatula, loosen pastry from surface whenever sticking occurs; lift pastry slightly and sprinkle flour underneath.

Loosen one half from surface with spatula and fold over other half. Loosen remaining half and fold into quarters. Place dough in pan and gently unfold. (Dough must be handled very carefully because it is rich and breaks easily.) Fit dough to pan.

Trim dough with scissors or sharp knife, allowing a ½-in. border. Pinch dough between index finger and thumb to make it stand about ¼ in. high around edge of cake pan. Set aside.

For Filling—Combine
>**3 cups (1½ lbs.) ricotta cheese**
>**¼ cup all-purpose flour**
>**2 tablespoons grated orange peel**
>**2 tablespoons grated lemon peel**
>**1 tablespoon vanilla extract**
>**⅛ teaspoon salt**

Beat until foamy
>**4 eggs**

Add gradually, beating until eggs are thick and piled softly
>**1 cup sugar**

Stir beaten eggs into ricotta mixture until well blended and smooth. Pour ricotta filling into pastry.

Bake at 350°F 50 to 60 min., or until mixture is firm and pastry is golden brown. Remove from oven and place on cooling rack.

Before serving, sprinkle with
>**2 tablespoons sifted confectioners' sugar**

8 to 10 servings

CHIFFON PIES

APRICOT CHIFFON PIE

▲ *Base Recipe*

For Apricot Purée—Put into a saucepan
>**¾ lb. (2¼ cups) dried apricots**

Add
>**2 cups water**

Cook uncovered until apricots are tender, about 15 min. Remove from heat. Put into an electric blender container; cover and blend until smooth and same consistency throughout. Keep purée hot.

Place a bowl and beater in refrigerator to chill.

For Pie—Prepare and bake
>**9-in. pastry shell (page 485)**
>**or Graham Cracker Crumb Crust or one of its variations (page 488)**

Shortly after puréeing apricots, pour into a small cup or custard cup
>**¼ cup cold water**

Sprinkle evenly over water
>**1½ teaspoons unflavored gelatin**

Set aside.

Remove about 1 cup hot Apricot Purée to a large bowl and set aside.

Put into blender container with remaining hot Apricot Purée, the softened gelatin and
>**½ cup sugar**
>**1 pkg. (3 oz.) lemon-flavored gelatin**

Cover and blend until gelatin is completely dissolved, stopping motor and scraping down sides of container several times.

Pour into bowl with reserved purée; stir until ingredients are evenly mixed. Chill until mixture begins to gel (gets slightly thicker).

Just before gelatin is of desired consistency, whip, using chilled bowl and beater
>**½ cup chilled heavy cream**

Set whipped cream in refrigerator while egg whites are beaten.

Using a clean beater, beat until frothy
>**2 egg whites**
>**⅛ teaspoon salt**

Gradually add, beating after each addition
>**¼ cup sugar**

Beat until stiff peaks are formed.

Fold beaten egg whites and reserved whipped cream into gelatin mixture until mixture is uniform in color. Turn into pie shell.

Chill in refrigerator 30 to 40 min., or until mixture is firm.

Top servings with **whipped cream.**

One 9-in. pie

—CRANBERRY CHIFFON PIE

Follow ▲ Recipe; omit Apricot Purée. For Cranberry Purée, wash **3 cups (¾ lb.) firm cranberries.** Put cranberries into saucepan containing **1½ cups boiling water.** Cook

cranberries uncovered over medium heat without stirring until skins pop. Put into blender container and blend until smooth and same consistency throughout. Keep purée hot. Soften 2 teaspoons (instead of 1½ teaspoons) unflavored gelatin in **½ cup orange juice;** omit the cold water. Meanwhile, pour hot purée through a sieve; discard skins. Reserve 1 cup hot purée; return remainder to blender container; use ¾ to 1 cup sugar, depending on tartness of cranberries. Proceed as directed. (The unchilled cranberry-gelatin mixture is much thinner than the apricot; it should be chilled until it is slightly thicker than consistency of thick unbeaten egg white.)

AVOCADO ORANGE CHIFFON PIE

Place a bowl and a rotary beater in refrigerator to chill.

Prepare, bake in a 9-in. pie pan and set aside
>**Pastry I for 1-Crust Pie (page 485)**

Pour into a small cup or custard cup
>**2 tablespoons lemon juice**
>**2 tablespoons water**

Sprinkle evenly over liquids
>**1 env. unflavored gelatin**

Let stand until softened.

Heat until very hot
>**¾ cup orange juice**

Remove the juice from heat and immediately add the softened gelatin, mixing until the gelatin is completely dissolved. Add and stir until dissolved
>**⅓ cup sugar**
>**¼ teaspoon salt**

Stir in
>**¼ teaspoon grated orange peel**
>**½ cup orange juice**

Blueberry Chiffon Pie

Chill in refrigerator or in pan of ice and water until gelatin mixture is slightly thicker than the consistency of thick unbeaten egg white. (If placed over ice and water, stir frequently; if placed in refrigerator, stir occasionally.)

Meanwhile, wash, cut into halves, remove pit and peel from

    1 large ripe avocado

Force through strainer or food mill enough to make 1 cup avocado. Set aside.

Using chilled bowl and rotary beater, beat until cream is of medium consistency (piles softly)

    1 cup chilled heavy cream

Blend avocado and whipped cream into chilled gelatin mixture. Turn into cooled pie shell.

Chill in refrigerator until firm.   *One 9-in. pie*

BLUEBERRY CHIFFON PIE

Prepare and bake in a 9-in. pie pan

    Pastry I for 1-Crust Pie (page 485)

Set aside to cool on cooling rack.

Rinse, discarding imperfect berries, and drain

    2 cups ripe blueberries

Put ¼ cup berries in refrigerator until needed for garnish. Gently crush 1 cup berries with a fork; combine with remaining ¾ cup whole berries and

    ¾ cup plus 2 tablespoons sugar

Let stand about 20 min.

Meanwhile, pour into small cup or custard cup

    ¼ cup cold water

Sprinkle evenly over water

    1 env. unflavored gelatin

Let stand until softened.

Meanwhile, pour into a saucepan and heat until very hot

    ½ cup water

    ¼ cup orange juice

Remove from heat and immediately stir in softened gelatin until gelatin is completely dissolved. Stir in

    1 teaspoon lemon juice

    1 teaspoon grated orange peel

Add to blueberries and mix well. Place mixture

over pan of ice and water or in refrigerator and chill until mixture begins to gel (becomes slightly thicker). (If mixture is placed over ice and water, stir frequently; if placed in refrigerator, stir occasionally.)

Beat until stiff, not dry, peaks are formed

    2 egg whites

    ⅛ teaspoon salt

Gently spread beaten egg whites over blueberry mixture and fold together. Spoon into cooled pie shell. Place in refrigerator to chill.

Meanwhile, place a bowl and rotary beater in refrigerator to chill.

When ready to serve, using chilled bowl and beater, prepare

    Sweetened Whipped Cream

    (page 480)

Gently pile whipped cream in mounds around top of pie. Garnish with reserved blueberries.

One 9-in. pie

BANANA CHOCOLATE MALLOW PIE

    ▲ *Base Recipe*

Set a rotary beater and a bowl in refrigerator to chill.

Prepare and bake in an 8-in. pie pan

    Pastry I for 1-Crust Pie (page 485)

    or Cookie Crumb Crust or Graham

    Cracker Crumb Crust (page 488)

Set aside on cooling rack to cool.

Combine in top of double boiler

    16 (about 4 oz.) marshmallows

    ½ cup milk

    1 oz. (1 sq.) unsweetened chocolate,

    cut in pieces

Heat over simmering water until marshmallows and chocolate are melted, stirring occasionally. Remove from heat; let stand until cool but not set.

Meanwhile, arrange in an even layer over bottom of baked pie shell

    3 all-yellow or brown-flecked

    bananas, cut in ¼-in. slices

Using chilled rotary beater and bowl, beat until of medium consistency (piles softly)

    1 cup chilled heavy cream

Fold whipped cream into the cooled marshmallow mixture. Turn filling into pie shell and spread evenly over bananas. Put pie into refrigerator and chill until set, about 1½ to 2 hrs.   *One 8-in. pie*

—BANANA COCOA MALLOW PIE

Follow ▲ Recipe. Omit grated chocolate. Combine **¼ cup cocoa** and **2 tablespoons water**; cook over low heat, stirring constantly, until mixture is smooth. Add to hot marshmallow mixture and blend well.

VELVET CHOCOLATE PIE

    ▲ *Base Recipe*

Prepare and bake

    10-in. Pastry Shell (page 485)

Set aside on cooling rack to cool.

Pour into small cup or custard cup

    ¼ cup cold water

Sprinkle evenly over water

    1 env. unflavored gelatin

Let stand until softened.

Meanwhile, blend well in top of double boiler and cook over boiling water, stirring constantly and rapidly, until mixture coats a metal spoon

    3 egg yolks, slightly beaten

    1½ cups milk

    ¼ cup sugar

    ⅛ teaspoon salt

Remove from simmering water and blend in softened gelatin, stirring until gelatin is completely dissolved. Stir in until chocolate is melted

    1 pkg. (6 oz.) semisweet chocolate

    pieces

    1 teaspoon vanilla extract

Chill in refrigerator or in pan of ice and water until mixture begins to gel (becomes slightly thicker). (If mixture is placed over ice and water, stir frequently; if placed in refrigerator, stir occasionally.)

Beat until frothy

    3 egg whites

Add gradually, beating well after each addition

    ½ cup sugar

Velvet Chocolate Pie

Continue beating until stiff peaks are formed. Fold beaten egg whites into cooled gelatin mixture. Pour into baked pie shell and chill in refrigerator until filling is set, about 2 hrs.

One 10-in. pie

—CHOCOLATE VELVET TARTS

Follow ▲ Recipe. Prepare and bake 24 to 30 1½ in. tarts (1½ times recipe, page 485). Fill each cooled tart shell with about 2½ tablespoons filling. Top with **Sweetened Whipped Cream** (page 480) and **1 semisweet chocolate piece** for each tart.

CHOCOLATE EGGNOG PIE

Set out a double boiler and a 9-in. pie pan.

Prepare and bake
9-in. pastry shell (page 485)

Prepare and set aside
1 cup finely chopped toasted walnuts (see note)

Combine in top of double boiler, mixing thoroughly
¼ cup sugar
1 env. unflavored gelatin
⅛ teaspoon salt
⅛ teaspoon mace or nutmeg
Stir in
1 cup milk
1 oz. (1 sq.) unsweetened chocolate, cut fine
Heat over hot water until chocolate is melted.

Separate
4 eggs
Beat egg yolks slightly. Using same beater, beat milk-chocolate mixture until smooth. Blend in the egg yolks and continue cooking over simmering water until slightly thickened, stirring occasionally. Remove from heat and cool.

When mixture is completely cold and begins to gel, beat egg whites until foamy. Beating constantly, add gradually
¼ cup sugar
Continue beating meringue until very stiff peaks are formed. Using same beater, beat until soft peaks are formed
½ cup heavy cream, chilled
Fold the meringue, whipped cream, and walnuts into gelatin mixture along with
2 tablespoons brandy or light rum

Continue folding gently until well mixed and turn into baked pie shell. Refrigerate several hours to chill thoroughly.

When ready to serve, whip
½ cup heavy cream, chilled
Swirl over pie and decorate with **walnut halves, chocolate candies** and **cherries.**

One 9-in. pie

Note: To toast walnuts, drop kernels into rapidly boiling water; boil 2 min. and drain. Spread in shallow baking pan and heat in 350°F oven 15 min., or until golden, stirring often.

COCOA CHIFFON PIE

▲ Base Recipe

Prepare and bake in an 8-in. pie pan
Pastry I for 1-Crust Pie (page 485)
Set aside on cooling rack to cool.

Meanwhile, mix thoroughly in top of a double boiler
1 env. unflavored gelatin
⅓ cup sugar
⅓ cup cocoa
¼ teaspoon salt

Beat together in a bowl until thoroughly blended
4 egg yolks
1 cup milk
Blend into the gelatin mixture in top of the double boiler. Set over boiling water in the bottom of double boiler and cook, stirring occasionally, about 5 min., or until gelatin is completely dissolved.

Blend in
1 teaspoon vanilla extract
Chill in refrigerator or in a pan of ice and water until mixture mounds slightly when dropped from a spoon. (If mixture is placed over ice and water, stir frequently; if placed in refrigerator, stir occasionally.)

When mixture begins to thicken, beat until frothy
4 egg whites
Add gradually, beating well after each addition
⅓ cup sugar
Continue to beat until very stiff peaks are formed. Gently fold a small amount of the beaten egg whites into chilled chocolate mixture. Spoon about one half of the chocolate mixture over the remaining egg whites and fold until blended. Fold in remaining chocolate mixture. Turn into pastry shell and chill in refrigerator until set.

Serve topped with **Sweetened Whipped Cream** (page 480). If desired, sprinkle lightly over whipped cream topping about ¼ **cup toasted shredded or flaked coconut** or **finely chopped pecans** or **chocolate cookie crumbs.**

One 8-in. pie

—CHOCOLATE CHIFFON PIE

Follow ▲ Recipe. Substitute **2 oz. (2 sq.)**

unsweetened chocolate, grated for cocoa. Increase each sugar measurement to ½ cup.

—BRAZIL NUT CHIFFON PIE

Follow ▲ Recipe using cocoa or chocolate. Fold in ½ **cup heavy cream,** whipped, before turning into pastry shell. Top with shaved curled **Brazil nuts.**

COCONUT CHIFFON PIE

Everyone will be thrilled with this colorful dessert—a delicious pie garnished with crimson stars cut from jellied cranberry sauce.

Prepare and bake
9-in. pastry shell (page 485)
Set aside to cool.

Mix thoroughly in top of a double boiler
1 env. unflavored gelatin
½ cup sugar
¼ teaspoon salt
Beat slightly in a mixing bowl
4 egg yolks
Blend in
1¼ cups milk
Add to the gelatin mixture and place over boiling water in lower part of double boiler. Cook, stirring constantly, until gelatin is completely dissolved, about 5 min. Remove from the heat and set aside to cool slightly. Then place in refrigerator to chill. Or chill the mixture in a bowl of ice and water, stirring occasionally, until it mounds when dropped from a spoon.

Blend in
⅔ cup flaked coconut
1½ teaspoons vanilla extract
Spread evenly in pie shell and set aside
½ cup jellied cranberry sauce

Beat until frothy
4 egg whites
Add gradually, beating well after each addition
¼ cup sugar
Beat until very stiff peaks are formed. Spread lightly over gelatin mixture and gently fold together. Turn into sauce-lined pastry shell. Sprinkle with
¼ cup flaked coconut
Chill pie in refrigerator until firm.

Just before serving, cut a few stars with small cutter from
Jellied cranberry sauce, cut into
¼-in. slices
Garnish top of pie with stars.   *One 9-in. pie*

ORANGE MARLOW REFRIGERATOR PIE

For Crust—Prepare (reserving 2 tablespoons of mixture for topping), bake and cool

9-in. Graham Cracker Crumb Crust (page 488)

For Pie Filling—Set a small bowl and beater in refrigerator to chill.

Heat together in the top of a double boiler over simmering water, stirring occasionally, until marshmallows are melted

32 marshmallows (½ lb.)
1 cup orange juice
1 tablespoon lemon juice

Cool mixture slightly and set it in refrigerator to chill until it becomes slightly thicker.

A few minutes before marshmallow mixture is of desired consistency, using the chilled bowl and beater, beat until cream is of medium consistency (piles softly)

½ cup chilled heavy cream

Blend the whipped cream with the marshmallow mixture. Pour into the prepared pie shell. Sprinkle the reserved crumb mixture over top of pie to form a decorative pattern. Set pie in refrigerator to chill until firm.

One 9-in. pie

LIME CHIFFON PIE

▲ Base Recipe

Prepare, bake and set aside to cool

Pastry I for 1-Crust Pie (page 485; use a 9-in. pie pan)

Mix thoroughly in the top of a double boiler

⅔ cup sugar
1 env. unflavored gelatin
¼ teaspoon salt

Beat together

4 egg yolks
½ cup lime juice (about 6 limes)
¼ cup water

Blend into mixture in double boiler top. Set over boiling water and cook, stirring constantly, until gelatin is dissolved, about 5 min. Remove from water and stir in

2 teaspoons grated lime peel

Tint the gelatin mixture to desired color by blending in thoroughly

1 or 2 drops green food coloring

Lemon Chiffon Pie

Cool the gelatin mixture, then chill (page 374) until mixture mounds slightly when dropped from a spoon.

When gelatin is of desired consistency, beat until frothy

4 egg whites

Add 1 tablespoon at a time, beating well after each addition

½ cup sugar

Beat until rounded peaks are formed. Spread over gelatin mixture and gently fold together. Turn into pastry shell and chill in refrigerator just until firm.

If desired, serve with **Sweetened Whipped Cream** (page 480). *One 9-in. pie*

—LEMON CHIFFON PIE

Follow ▲ Recipe. Substitute **Graham Cracker Crumb Crust** (page 488) for pastry shell. Substitute **½ cup lemon juice** for lime juice and **2 teaspoons grated lemon peel** for lime peel. Omit food coloring.

ORANGE-BLOSSOM CHIFFON PIE

Prepare, bake and cool

Pastry I for 1-Crust Pie (page 485; use a 9-in. pie pan)

Set out to thaw partially

1 can (6 oz.) frozen orange juice concentrate

Pour into the top of a double boiler

⅓ cup cold water

Sprinkle over water

1 env. unflavored gelatin

Beat together and blend into gelatin

2 egg yolks
1 cup water
¼ teaspoon salt

Cook over boiling water, stirring constantly, until gelatin is dissolved and mixture is slightly thickened, about 5 min. Immediately remove from heat and add orange juice concentrate; stir until blended. Chill, stirring occasionally, until mixture mounds when dropped from a spoon.

Meanwhile, whip until soft peaks are formed

1 cup chilled heavy cream

Beat in with final few strokes

2 tablespoons confectioners' sugar
1 teaspoon vanilla extract

Set in refrigerator.

Orange-Blossom Chiffon Pie

Using a clean beater, beat until frothy

2 egg whites

Add gradually, continuing to beat until rounded peaks are formed

¼ cup sugar

Fold beaten egg whites and whipped cream into gelatin mixture. Turn into the baked pastry shell. Using the back of a spoon, swirl top. Chill thoroughly.

Decorate pie with **orange sections** or **orange sections** and **pastry cutouts** (see photo).

One 9-in. pie

FRUIT CHEESE CHIFFON PIE

Place a bowl and beater in refrigerator to chill.

Prepare, bake and set aside to cool

9-in. pastry shell (page 485),
Graham Cracker Crumb Crust or Zwieback Crumb Crust (page 488)

Set aside to drain thoroughly

1 can (16 oz.) pear halves (6 or 7 halves)

(Sweetened Bing cherries, cut into halves and pitted may be substituted for pear halves.)

Mix thoroughly in the top of a double boiler

1 env. unflavored gelatin
¼ cup sugar

Beat together

2 egg yolks
½ cup water
2 tablespoons lemon juice

Stir egg yolk mixture into gelatin mixture. Cook over boiling water, stirring constantly until gelatin is dissolved, about 5 min.

Pour gelatin mixture into an electric blender container with

1½ cups (12 oz.) cream-style cottage cheese
1 piece (3 in.) lemon peel (colored part only)

Cover and blend until mixture is smooth.

Pour mixture into a mixing bowl. Chill until mixture begins to gel (gets slightly thicker).

When gelatin mixture is of desired consistency, whip, using chilled bowl and beater

1 cup chilled heavy cream

Set in refrigerator while egg whites are beaten.

Using a clean beater, beat until frothy
2 egg whites
⅛ teaspoon salt
Add gradually, beating after each addition
¼ cup sugar
Continue to beat on high speed until rounded peaks are formed.

Fold beaten egg whites and reserved whipped cream into gelatin mixture.

Arrange pear halves or Bing cherries cut side down over crust. Pour filling over fruit.

Chill in refrigerator about 1 hr., or until firm. *One 9-in. pie*

COCONUT PEACH PIE

▲ *Base Recipe*

A blend of apricot preserves, peach syrup and sherry imparts a distinctive flavor to peaches.

Prepare in a 9-in. pie pan
Choco-Coconut Pie Shell (page 488)
Wrap in waxed paper, aluminum foil or moisture-vaporproof material and set in refrigerator to chill.

Meanwhile, set aside to drain thoroughly, reserving syrup
1 can (30 oz.) peach halves (about 7 halves)

Pour into a small cup or custard cup
¼ cup cold water
Sprinkle evenly over water
1 env. unflavored gelatin
Let stand until softened.

Mix in a saucepan and heat until very hot, stirring occasionally
1 cup reserved peach syrup
½ cup apricot preserves
¼ cup sugar
⅛ teaspoon salt
Remove from heat and stir in softened gelatin until gelatin is completely dissolved. Chill over ice and water or in refrigerator until mixture is slightly thicker than consistency of thick unbeaten egg white. (If mixture is placed over ice and water, stir frequently; if placed into refrigerator, stir occasionally.)

When gelatin mixture is cool, but before it thickens, blend in
¼ cup dry sherry
Pour one half of thickened gelatin mixture into pie shell. Place drained peach halves into gelatin mixture in pie shell, cut-side down. Spoon remaining mixture over peach halves.

Chill in refrigerator until firm. *One 9-in. pie*

—BLUSHING PEAR PIE

Follow ▲ Recipe. Substitute **canned pear halves** and **pear syrup** for peaches. Add **1 or more drops red food coloring** to a few drops of water. Using this coloring, delicately tint larger end of each pear half with "blush."

PINEAPPLE VOLCANO CHIFFON PIE

Prepare, bake and cool
Graham Cracker Crumb Crust (page 488; use a 9-in. pie pan)

Have ready
1 can (20 oz.) crushed pineapple
1 can (8¼ oz.) crushed pineapple, drained

Mix in the top of a double boiler
¼ cup sugar
2 env. unflavored gelatin
¼ teaspoon salt
Beat together
3 egg yolks, fork beaten
½ cup water
Stir egg yolk mixture into gelatin mixture along with the undrained pineapple. Set over boiling water. Cook, stirring constantly, about 5 min., or until gelatin is dissolved.

Remove from water and mix in
¼ teaspoon grated lemon peel
1 tablespoon lemon juice
Chill, stirring occasionally, until mixture mounds slightly when dropped from a spoon.

Beat until frothy
3 egg whites
Add gradually, beating until stiff peaks are formed
¼ cup sugar
Fold beaten egg whites into gelatin until blended. Turn filling into pie shell. Chill.

Garnish pie with generous mounds of **whipped dessert topping**. Spoon drained pineapple onto mounds to resemble "volcanoes" (see photo). *One 9-in. pie*

PRUNE CHIFFON PIE

Prepare, bake and cool
Pastry I for 1-Crust Pie (page 485; use a 9-in. pie pan)

Prepare
1 cup chopped plumped prunes*
Mix in a heavy saucepan the chopped prunes and
⅓ cup bottled prune juice
2 tablespoons grated orange peel

Beat in a bowl
3 eggs
Add a mixture of
½ cup packed light brown sugar
¼ cup sugar
1 env. unflavored gelatin
½ teaspoon salt
Beat well. Blend in
1 cup dairy sour cream
Stir into the prune mixture. Cook, stirring constantly, over medium heat about 10 min., or until thickened. Cool the mixture to lukewarm.

Whip until soft peaks are formed
½ cup chilled heavy cream
Fold whipped cream into prune mixture. Turn filling into pastry shell. Chill until firm.

Pineapple Volcano Chiffon Pie

Just before serving, force **Sweetened Whipped Cream** (page 480), **meringue,** or **whipped dessert topping** through pastry bag and star decorating tube to form a border of rosettes on pie. *One 9-in. pie*

Note: For decorative edge as in photo, trim pastry even with rim, moisten pastry with water and overlap small leaf-shaped pastry cutouts around edge.

*To plump—Put dried prunes into a colander and set over boiling water 30 min., or until well plumped.

PUMPKIN CHIFFON PIE

Prepare, bake and set aside
9-in. pastry shell (page 485)

Mix thoroughly in a heavy saucepan
1 env. unflavored gelatin
½ cup sugar
½ teaspoon salt
2 teaspoons cinnamon
½ teaspoon ginger
¼ teaspoon nutmeg

Beat together
3 egg yolks
½ cup cream
¼ cup water
1⅓ cups canned pumpkin

Stir pumpkin mixture into gelatin mixture in saucepan. Cook over medium heat, stirring constantly until gelatin is dissolved and mixture is thoroughly heated, about 10 min. Remove from heat.

Chill until mixture mounds slightly when dropped from a spoon.

Prune Chiffon Pie

Pumpkin Chiffon Pie and Sherry Almond Chiffon Pie

When gelatin mixture is of desired consistency, beat until frothy

3 egg whites

Add gradually, beating after each addition

½ cup sugar

Continue beating until stiff peaks are formed. Carefully fold beaten egg whites into pumpkin mixture. Turn into pastry shell. Chill about 2 hrs., or until firm.

Serve topped with

Sweetened Whipped Cream (one half recipe, page 480)

Garnish with **blanched almonds,** if desired.

One 9-in. pie

SHERRY ALMOND CHIFFON PIE

Here is a delicate and delicious wine-flavored pie to go with your after-dinner cup of coffee.

Chill a bowl and a rotary beater in refrigerator.

Prepare, bake and set aside to cool

Pastry I for 1-Crust Pie (page 485; use a 9-in. pie pan)

Chop coarsely and set aside

¼ cup (about 1½ oz.), toasted blanched almonds (pages 9 and 10)

Mix thoroughly in the top of a double boiler

⅓ cup sugar
1 env. unflavored gelatin
½ teaspoon salt

Beat slightly in a bowl

3 egg yolks

Beat in until blended

1¾ cups milk

Pineapple Pie

Add the milk mixture gradually to gelatin mixture in double boiler top, stirring constantly until blended.

Set over boiling water and cook, stirring constantly, until gelatin is completely dissolved, about 5 min.

Remove the gelatin mixture from heat. Cool; chill in refrigerator or over ice and water until the mixture mounds when dropped from a spoon. (If mixture is placed over ice and water, stir frequently; if placed in refrigerator, stir occasionally.)

Using the chilled bowl and beater, beat until of medium consistency (piles softly)

½ cup chilled heavy cream

Set whipped cream in refrigerator while preparing the meringue.

Using a clean beater, beat until frothy

3 egg whites

Add gradually, beating well after each addition

¼ cup sugar

Beat until stiff peaks are formed. Fold the meringue and whipped cream into custard mixture with

3 tablespoons sherry
½ teaspoon almond extract

Fold in the chopped toasted almonds. Turn into cooled pie shell.

Chill in refrigerator 2 to 3 hrs., or until firm. When ready to serve, top with chocolate curls made by pulling across a shredder

1 oz. (1 sq.) unsweetened chocolate

One 9-in. pie

STRAWBERRY RHUBARB PIE

▲ *Base Recipe*

Prepare and set aside

10-in. Graham Cracker Crumb Crust (page 488)

Wash, cut into 1-in. pieces and put into a large saucepan

1 lb. fresh rhubarb (yields about 4 cups)

Stir in

¾ cup sugar
2 teaspoons lemon juice

Cover and simmer until just tender. (Or, cook 2 16-oz. pkgs. frozen rhubarb according to

directions on package.) Remove from heat. Drain well, reserving syrup. Set aside to cool.

Empty into a bowl

1 pkg. (3 oz.) strawberry-flavored gelatin

Mix in

¼ cup sugar
¼ teaspoon salt

Add, stirring until gelatin is completely dissolved

1 cup boiling water

Blend into gelatin mixture, enough to make 1 cup liquid, a mixture of

Reserved syrup
Cold water

Stir in cooked rhubarb, and beat gelatin mixture until frothy. Chill until gelatin mixture is slightly thicker than consistency of thick unbeaten egg white.

Prepare

Sweetened Whipped Cream (page 480)

Fold whipped cream into frothy gelatin mixture. Turn into pie shell. Chill in refrigerator until firm.

One 10-in. pie

—PINEAPPLE PIE

Follow ▲ Recipe. Substitute for crumb pie shell, a **10-in. pastry shell (page 485)**. Substitute for cooked rhubarb, **1½ cups (20-oz. can, drained) crushed pineapple,** reserving syrup. Substitute **lemon-flavored gelatin** for strawberry.

YAM CHIFFON PIE

Prepare, bake and cool

10-in. Pastry Shell (page 485)

Have ready

1½ cups puréed peeled cooked yams (about 3 medium)

Mix in a heavy saucepan

¾ cup firmly packed brown sugar
1 env. unflavored gelatin
1 teaspoon cinnamon
¼ to ½ teaspoon allspice
½ teaspoon salt

Beat until blended

3 egg yolks
¾ cup milk

Add to mixture in saucepan and blend well. Cook over medium heat, stirring constantly, until gelatin and sugar are dissolved and mixture is slightly thickened, about 5 min.

Remove from heat and blend in puréed yams. Chill, stirring occasionally, until mixture mounds when dropped from a spoon.

Beat until frothy

3 egg whites

Add gradually, continuing to beat just until stiff peaks are formed

¼ cup sugar

Fold in the yam mixture and

½ cup thawed frozen whipped dessert topping

Turn filling into the baked pastry shell. Swirl top of pie using the back of a spoon. Chill thoroughly.

Garnish with additional **whipped dessert topping** and **mixed candied fruit.**

One 10-in. pie

TARTS AND TURNOVERS

LITTLE LEMON TARTS

Set out

8 small baked pastry or crumb tart shells

Little Lemon Tarts

For Lemon Curd Filling—Rinse, discard imperfect berries, drain and set aside

½ cup blueberries

Mix in the top of a double boiler

2 eggs, slightly beaten
½ cup sugar
⅓ cup butter or margarine
1 tablespoon grated lemon peel
¼ cup lemon juice

Cook over boiling water, stirring constantly, until mixture is thickened. Set over ice and water to chill quickly; stir occasionally.

Fill tart shells with cooled mixture; top with blueberries.   *8 tarts*

LUSCIOUS LEMON TARTS

▲ *Base Recipe*

Prepare six 3½-in. tart shells, bake and set aside to cool as in

Pastry for Little Pies and Tarts (page 485)

Combine and mix until thoroughly blended in a heavy saucepan

1½ cups sugar
⅓ cup cornstarch
⅛ teaspoon salt

Add, stirring well

½ cup cold water

Gradually stir in

1 cup boiling water

Stirring gently and constantly, bring the mixture rapidly to boiling, reduce the heat and cook 10 min. Vigorously stir about 3 tablespoons hot mixture into

3 egg yolks, slightly beaten

Immediately blend into mixture in saucepan. Cook 2 to 3 min. Stir slowly to keep mixture cooking evenly. Remove from heat. Add and stir until butter is melted

1½ tablespoons grated lemon peel
¼ cup lemon juice
2 tablespoons butter or margarine

Set aside to cool to lukewarm.

Spoon about ⅓ cup lukewarm filling into each pastry shell.

Prepare

Meringue (see De Luxe Cream Pie, page 494)

Pile meringue onto filling and seal to edge.

Bake at 350°F 10 to 15 min., or until meringue is delicately browned. Cool on cooling racks.

6 tarts

—*TREASURE TARTS*

Follow ▲ Recipe. Omit meringue. Place **a red and green maraschino cherry** in each filled tart. Sprinkle edge of tart with **Toasted Coconut** (see Glazed Strawberry Tarts, page 494).

BLUSHING PEAR TARTS

▲ *Base Recipe*

Extra special if filled with a cream filling.

Prepare six 3½-in. tart shells, bake and set aside to cool as in

Pastry for Little Pies and Tarts (page 485)

Meanwhile, drain, reserving syrup

1 can (16 oz.) pears (about 6 halves)

Combine and mix until thoroughly blended in a heavy saucepan

⅓ cup sugar
1½ tablespoons cornstarch
⅛ teaspoon salt

Add, stirring well

2 tablespoons cold water

Heat in saucepan until very hot

1 cup reserved pear syrup

Stirring constantly, add gradually to cornstarch mixture. Stirring gently and constantly, bring cornstarch mixture rapidly to boiling and cook 3 min. Remove from heat. Add and stir until blended

⅛ teaspoon grated lemon peel
2 teaspoons lemon juice
1½ teaspoons butter or margarine
2 or 3 drops yellow food coloring
1 or 2 drops red food coloring

Set mixture aside to cool.

Meanwhile, set out

Few drops red food coloring
Few mint leaves

Apply blush to rounded sides of pears by brushing with small amount of food coloring. Spoon about 1 tablespoon cooled glaze into each tart shell and place one pear, rounded-side up, in each shell. Garnish with mint. Spoon about 3 tablespoons cooled glaze over each pear. Sprinkle edges of tarts with

Toasted Coconut (see Glazed Strawberry Tart recipe, page 494)

6 tarts

—*PEACH TARTS*

Follow ▲ Recipe. Substitute **1 can (16 oz.) peach halves** (about 6 halves) for pears and peach syrup for pear syrup. Omit brushing peaches with red food coloring. Place peach, cut-side up, in pastry shell. Spoon about 1½ teaspoons glaze over each peach. Omit coconut. Cover and store remaining glaze in refrigerator for future use.

Apple Triangles and Little Princess Fried Pies

APPLE TRIANGLES

Set out a baking sheet.

Prepare
> **Spice Pastry for 1-Crust Pie (page 487)**

Roll pastry into rectangle ⅛ in. thick on lightly floured surface. Cut into 4-in. squares. Set aside.

Mix and set aside
> **2 tablespoons sugar**
> **½ teaspoon cinnamon**
> **⅛ teaspoon cloves**

Wash, quarter, core, pare and thinly slice into a 2-qt. bowl
> **2 or 3 cooking apples (2 cups, sliced)**

Toss apple slices with a mixture of one half of sugar-spice mixture and
> **2 tablespoons water**

Place a mound of apple slices (about 1 tablespoon) on one half (diagonally) of each pastry square. Dot each with
> **Butter or margarine (about 1 teaspoon for each pastry)**

Fold pastry diagonally in half over apple slices to form triangles. Press edges of pastry together to seal. Prick tops several times with fork. Place apple triangles on baking sheet.

Brush tops of triangles with
> **Egg white, slightly beaten**

Sprinkle with remaining sugar-spice mixture.

Bake at 350°F 30 to 35 min., or until lightly browned. Cool on cooling rack.   *6 servings*

LITTLE PRINCESS FRIED PIES

▲ *Base Recipe*

Prepare, shape into 2 balls (do not roll) and set aside
> **Cheese Pastry for 2-Crust Pie (page 487, double recipe; no pie pan will be needed)**

Set out a 2-qt. saucepan with a tight-fitting cover and a heavy 10-in. skillet.

Wash, quarter, core, pare and coarsely dice
> **6 medium (about 2 lbs.) cooking apples (about 6 cups, diced)**

Put apples into the saucepan with
> **⅓ cup hot water**

Cover and simmer, moving and turning apple pieces occasionally, 5 to 10 min., or until apples are just tender when pierced with a fork. Drain thoroughly.

While the apples are cooking, shred
> **4 oz. Cheddar cheese (about 1 cup, shredded)**

Mix with cheese and set aside
> **½ to ⅔ cup sugar (depending upon tartness of apples)**
> **1½ teaspoons cinnamon**
> **½ teaspoon nutmeg**

Add to the drained cooked apples
> **2 tablespoons butter**
> **4 teaspoons lemon juice**

Add the cheese mixture and stir only enough to mix ingredients evenly. Set aside.

Flatten one ball of pastry on a lightly floured surface. Roll from center to edge into a round about ⅛ in. thick. Loosen pastry from surface whenever sticking occurs; lift pastry slightly and sprinkle flour underneath.

Cut out 6-in. rounds, using a saucer or a waxed paper pattern as a guide. Spoon about 2 tablespoons of the apple filling onto one half

of each round. Moisten the edge of one half of the round with water to help form a tight seal and fold other half of round over the filling. Press edges together with a fork. Be certain that the seal is tight and pastry unbroken to avoid leaking of filling.

Repeat with the remaining ball of pastry.

Heat in the skillet over medium heat
> **3 to 4 tablespoons lard, vegetable shortening or all-purpose shortening**

Carefully put into the skillet as many pies as will fit in without crowding. Fry pies on one side about 5 min., or until golden brown. Turn and fry until other side is golden brown. Add more shortening to skillet if necessary to keep pies from sticking.

Serve warm with slices of **sharp cheese**, a dip of **ice cream** or a mound of **whipped cream**; or sift **confectioners' sugar** over the pies.

12 to 14 pies

—FRIED PIES A LA ROBERTA

Follow ▲ Recipe; prepare **Pastry for 2-Crust Pie** (page 485) instead of cheese pastry. Omit cheese in filling.

PASTRY TURNOVERS

Prepare
> **Pastry I for 1-Crust Pie (page 485)**

Roll dough into a rectangle about ⅛ in. thick. Cut into 4-in. squares. Place in center of each square, 1 tablespoon of
> **Mincemeat (page 729; if using packaged condensed mincemeat, follow directions on package)**

Fold in half diagonally, pressing edges together with floured fork. Prick tops in several places with fork.

Bake at 450°F about 15 min., or until turnovers are golden brown.

Thick sweetened **applesauce**, **jam or jelly** may be used to fill turnovers.   *7 turnovers*

Pastry Turnovers

Desserts and dessert sauces

Desserts are the ultimate magic of memorable meals, and choosing just the right one to conclude the meal is an art. A wisely chosen dessert should complement the other foods in the menu. Thus, a hearty main course calls for a light dessert while a light meal leaves room for a filling dessert. A soup-and-salad lunch often needs a robust pudding or cake dessert to satisfy hearty appetites. Flavorwise, seafood main dishes are complemented with citrus desserts. Everyday family meals call for eye-appealing as well as nourishing milk-rich desserts to meet the needs of growing children. Hot weather calls for cooling and refreshing desserts such as fruit ices, ice creams, sherbets, and fluffy gelatin mixtures. In this chapter are recipes for desserts suitable for every occasion . . . for family and company meals, sole refreshments at a party, an afternoon tea or bridge game, and many more.

CAKE DESSERTS

ALMOND CAKE
(Fyrstekake)

Set out an 8-in. round layer cake pan.

Sift together into a bowl
> **1½ cups sifted all-purpose flour**
> **½ cup sugar**
> **1 teaspoon baking powder**

Cut in with a pastry blender or two knives until well blended
> **½ cup butter**

Blend in thoroughly
> **1 egg, beaten**

Chill dough in refrigerator.

Meanwhile, grate (page 10)
> **⅔ cup (about 3 oz.) blanched almonds**

Thoroughly mix with almonds
> **⅔ cup confectioners' sugar**

Blend in
> **1 egg, beaten**

Remove chilled dough from refrigerator and divide into two balls. Put one ball in the cake pan and return remaining ball to refrigerator. Using hands, work dough in pan to cover bottom and sides. Turn almond mixture into the cake pan, spreading evenly over surface of dough. Remove dough from refrigerator. Cut off pieces of dough and roll with hands into rolls about ½ to ¾ in. thick. Arrange four strips parallel to each other across filling. Arrange four strips at right angles, weaving over and under to form a lattice. Roll remaining dough into a thin roll and arrange around edge of cake, pressing ends together to seal. If dough becomes too sticky to handle, return to refrigerator for about 10 min.

Bake at 375°F 25 to 30 min., or until lightly browned.

Set on a cooling rack to cool completely. With a spatula, loosen sides of cake from pan and cut into wedges. Or loosen sides of cake from pan and carefully remove cake from pan.

6 to 8 servings

BUTTERSCOTCH PEACH CAKE

Set out a 13x9x2-in. baking pan.

Drain
> **2 cans (29 oz. each) sliced cling peaches**

Reserve 9 peach slices for garnish; chop remaining slices. Distribute chopped peaches over the bottom of the pan. Sprinkle with a mixture of
> **½ cup chopped nuts**
> **2 tablespoons brown sugar**

Set aside.

Blend in a bowl
> **1 pkg. (about 18 oz.) yellow cake mix**
> **1 teaspoon pumpkin pie spice**

Add
> **1 egg, fork beaten**
> **½ cup butter or margarine, melted**

Stir until just blended, but not smooth (batter will be very thick). Spoon batter over peach mixture and spread evenly.

Bake at 375°F about 35 min., or until browned. Cool in pan on wire rack.

To serve, cut into pieces and spoon into dessert dishes. Top each serving with a dollop of **whipped dessert topping** and reserved peach slice. *9 servings*

ZUPPA INGLESE

Zuppa Inglese, which means English soup, probably has more variations and stories about its origin than any other Italian food, including macaroni. That a rum-soaked cake should be called English soup has given much cause for comment on the origin of this wrongly named delicacy. Perhaps the most logical explanation has been that the name was given to tease the English about their love of rum, and the first Zuppa was so rum-soaked that it had to be eaten with a soup spoon. Some stories say that this Zuppa was first served to Lord Nelson and Lady Hamilton in the 18th century.

Prepare
> **Italian Sponge Cake (page 454; in**
> **11x7x2-in. cake pans; see note)**

Prepare and chill in refrigerator
> **Pineapple Cream Filling (page 484)**
> **Chocolate Cream Filling III (page 484)**

Combine and set aside
> **½ cup rum**
> **2 tablespoons cold water**

Trim each of the three sponge cake layers placing one at a time' on an 8x11½-in. oval platter and trimming the cake to fit the platter.

Set two layers aside. Save all leftover pieces cut from cake.

Sprinkle first layer of cake with one third of rum mixture, and spread with Pineapple

Zuppa Inglese

Cream Filling. Top with second layer and sprinkle with one third of rum mixture. Spread with Chocolate Cream Filling. Top with third layer and sprinkle with remaining rum mixture. Cover cake with waxed paper. Place in refrigerator for several hours to chill.

From leftover pieces of cake, make a square, diamond or heart shape for top of Zuppa.

For frosting sides and top of cake and for decorating, use one of these

   **Sweetened Whipped Cream (page 480),
   Seven-Minute Frosting (page 474)
   or Butter Frosting (page 473)**

To decorate, force frosting or whipped cream through pastry bag and a No. 27 star decorating tube. Garnish with

   Candied cherries

Store Zuppa Inglese in refrigerator until ready to serve.   *16 to 20 servings*

SPONGE PUFF DESSERT
(Indiáner)

Flavored whipped cream tucked into tender, light cake and topped with rich chocolate.

Cover baking sheets with unglazed paper and draw 2½-in. circles on it, spacing them about 2 in. apart.

Measure and set aside
   1⅓ cups sifted all-purpose flour

Put into a 1½-qt. bowl and beat until very thick and lemon-colored
   **5 egg yolks
   3 tablespoons sugar
   1 tablespoon water**
Sift one half of the flour, about 2½ tablespoons at a time, over egg yolk mixture and fold just until blended after each addition; set aside.

Beat until frothy
   **8 egg whites
   ⅛ teaspoon salt**
Add gradually to egg whites, beating well after each addition
   3 tablespoons sugar
Continue beating until very stiff peaks are formed. Gently spread egg yolk mixture over egg whites and fold until blended. Lightly sift one half remaining flour over egg mixture and fold just until flour is blended. Sift remaining flour over batter and fold. Do not overmix!

Using drawn circles on the unglazed paper as a guide, quickly and gently spoon batter onto

baking sheets in peaked mounds. Keep mounds as uniform as possible.

Bake at 325°F 15 to 20 min., or until slightly browned. With spatula, cut puffs away from paper and allow to cool on cooling rack. Hollow out centers from tops of one half of puffs and from bottoms of remaining one half. Tear portions taken from centers into small pieces; set aside.

Prepare (but do not spoon into sherbet glasses)
   **Rum Whipped Cream (page 481),
   Mocha Whipped Cream (page 480)
   or Cocoa Whipped Cream
   (page 481)**

Set 1 cup of the whipped cream dessert into the refrigerator; reserve for garnish. Fold the pieces taken from the puffs into remaining whipped cream and spoon into the hollows in the puffs. Use puffs having flat bottoms as bases. Top with remaining puffs so that the cream in base and cream in top puff come together. Place puffs flat onto cooling rack having waxed paper underneath. Set aside.

Partially melt over simmering water, being careful not to overheat
   **¾ lb. milk chocolate or semisweet
   candymaking chocolate**

Remove chocolate from simmering water and stir until completely melted. Spoon chocolate onto puffs, allowing excess chocolate to drip onto waxed paper. Spread chocolate evenly over tops, if necessary. (Scrape together and wrap excess chocolate; store for future use.)

When chocolate is firm, place puffs on individual plates. Using pastry bag and a No. 27 decorating tube, pipe reserved whipped cream around base of each puff. Serve immediately.
                          10 to 12 servings

CHERRY BANANA SPONGE CAKE

Prepare and cool
   Hot-Milk Sponge Cake (page 454)

Drain, reserving syrup in a measuring cup
   1 can (17 oz.) dark sweet cherries
Set cherries aside. Add enough **water** to cherry syrup to yield 1 cup. Put into a saucepan

   **2 tablespoons cornstarch
   ⅛ teaspoon salt**

Blend in cherry syrup and
   3 tablespoons apricot preserves
Bring to boiling and cook 3 min., stirring constantly. Remove from heat and stir in cherries (reserve about 12 for garnish) and
   ¼ teaspoon grated lemon peel
Chill in refrigerator.

Just before assembling cake, whip until soft peaks are formed
   1 cup chilled heavy cream
With final few strokes, beat in
   **¼ cup confectioners' sugar
   ½ teaspoon vanilla extract
   ½ teaspoon almond extract**
Refrigerate until ready to use.

Peel
   4 medium all-yellow bananas
Cut 3 bananas in half crosswise. Slice each half lengthwise into 3 or 4 petals; drizzle with
   2 tablespoons orange juice
Slice remaining banana into ¼-in. slices and mix with cherry filling.

Place one cake layer on serving plate and spoon on the filling. Top with second cake layer. Arrange banana petals around top edge of cake and pile whipped cream in the center. Form a ring of reserved cherries around whipped cream.   *One 9-in. filled layer cake*

DOUBLE-RICH FUDGE PUDDING

   ▲ *Base Recipe*

A rich cake with a creamy sauce underneath.

Grease a deep 8-in. round cake pan.

Sift together into a bowl and set aside
   **1¼ cups sifted cake flour
   ¾ cup sugar
   ½ teaspoon baking soda
   ¼ teaspoon salt**
Melt (page 10) and set aside
   **1 oz. (1 sq.) unsweetened chocolate
   2 tablespoons butter or margarine**

Pour into a measuring cup
   2 tablespoons vinegar
Add
   **6 tablespoons milk (or enough to
   make ½ cup liquid)**
Stir milk-vinegar mixture (soured milk) into melted chocolate mixture with
   1 teaspoon vanilla extract
Add chocolate-milk mixture, all at once, to dry ingredients. Stir until thoroughly blended. Add
   1 cup (3¾ oz.) salted pecan halves
Blend just until pecan halves are evenly distributed. Turn batter into pan. Sprinkle over batter and set aside
   1 cup firmly packed brown sugar

Combine
   **1½ cups boiling water
   2 oz. (2 sq.) unsweetened chocolate**
Stir until chocolate is melted and thoroughly blended with water. Pour over top of batter.

Double-Rich Fudge Pudding

Bake pudding at 350°F 45 to 50 min. Serve warm with **heavy cream, whipped cream** or **vanilla ice cream.** *8 to 10 servings*

—DOUBLE FUDGE PUDDING

Follow ▲ Recipe. Substitute **2 teaspoons baking powder** for baking soda. Omit vinegar and increase milk to ½ cup. Omit salted pecan halves. Reduce brown sugar to ½ cup and combine with it **½ cup granulated sugar** and **2 tablespoons cocoa.** Omit chocolate (which is poured over top) and reduce boiling water to 1 cup. Bake and serve as in ▲ Recipe.

—MOCHA FUDGE PUDDING

Follow ▲ Recipe or Double Fudge Pudding. Add **2 teaspoons instant powdered coffee** with the brown sugar. Batter may be spooned into individual heat-resistant custard cups, sprinkled with topping and the hot water poured over each pudding.

DUTCH SOMERSAULT CAKE-PIE

Sometimes known as a "funny-cake pie," this is an old Pennsylvania Dutch recipe. The sauce, which is poured over the cake batter, turns up as a spicy, creamy layer underneath the delicate feathery cake—and the pastry shell makes the whole thing twice as interesting as an ordinary upside-down pudding, and easier to serve, too.

Set out a 9-in. pie pan.

For Pastry—Prepare (do not bake) and set aside
1 9-in. pie shell (page 485)

For Sauce—Mix
⅔ cup sugar
1 tablespoon all-purpose flour
½ teaspoon salt
½ teaspoon cinnamon
¼ teaspoon ginger
⅛ teaspoon cloves

Beat until thick and piled softly
1 egg
Blend in
⅔ cup dairy sour cream
⅓ cup molasses
Add the dry ingredients and mix thoroughly.

For Cake—Sift together and set aside
1¼ cups sifted cake flour
1 teaspoon baking powder
½ teaspoon salt
¼ teaspoon baking soda

Cream until softened
¼ cup butter
½ teaspoon vanilla extract
Add gradually, creaming until fluffy after each addition
½ cup sugar
Add gradually, beating well after each addition
1 egg, well beaten
Measure
½ cup buttermilk
Beating only until smooth after each addition, alternately add dry ingredients in thirds and buttermilk in halves to creamed mixture. Finally, beat only until smooth (do not overbeat). Turn batter into pastry shell. Stir sauce and carefully pour over cake batter. (Sauce will sink to bottom.)

Bake at 350°F 40 min., or until cake tests done.

Serve warm. *6 to 8 servings*

CHOCOLATE FUNNY CAKE-PIE

▲ Base Recipe

For Pastry—Prepare (do not bake) and set aside
1 9-in. pastry shell (Use your favorite recipe or a mix.)

For Chocolate Sauce—Put into a saucepan
½ cup water
1½ oz. (1½ sq.) unsweetened chocolate
Stir constantly over low heat until chocolate is melted. Add
⅔ cup sugar
Stirring constantly, bring to boiling; remove from heat and stir in
¼ cup butter or margarine
1½ teaspoons vanilla extract
Set aside.

For Cake—Finely chop and set aside
1 cup (about 4 oz.) walnuts
Sift together into a large bowl
1¼ cups sifted cake flour
¾ cup sugar
1¼ teaspoons baking powder
¼ teaspoon salt

Add to sifted dry ingredients
½ cup milk
¼ cup vegetable shortening or all-purpose shortening
1½ teaspoons vanilla extract
Beat until dry ingredients are just mixed. Add
1 egg, unbeaten
Beat 200 strokes by hand, or 2 min. on electric mixer at medium speed. Scrape sides of bowl several times during beating.

Add nuts and beat 100 strokes, or 1 min. on electric mixer. Turn batter into pastry shell. Stir sauce and carefully pour over cake batter. (Sauce will sink to bottom.)

Bake at 350°F 50 to 55 min., or until cake tests done (page 11).

Serve warm. Top with **whipped cream.**
6 to 8 servings

—APRICOT FUNNY CAKE-PIE

Follow ▲ Recipe for Pastry and Cake. Substitute Apricot Sauce for the Chocolate Sauce.

For Apricot Sauce—Rinse and put into a saucepan **⅓ lb. (about 1 cup) dried apricots.** Cover apricots with **1½ cups water.** Cover pan and simmer apricots for 40 min., or until fruit is plump and tender. Drain cooked apricots, reserving liquid in a 1-cup measuring cup for liquids. Force apricots through a sieve or food mill into a saucepan. Add water, if necessary, to the reserved apricot liquid to make ⅔ cup liquid. Add the liquid to the sieved apricots with **½ cup sugar.** Stirring constantly, bring to boiling; cook 1 min. Remove from heat; stir in **3 tablespoons butter or margarine.**

PINEAPPLE GINGERBREAD

▲ Base Recipe

Butter bottoms of 6 individual casseroles. Put a bowl and rotary beater in refrigerator to chill for preparation of topping.

Drain, reserving syrup
1 can (29½ oz.) sliced pineapple (8 slices pineapple)
Place one slice in each casserole. Cut remaining two slices finely; reserve for topping.

Pineapple Gingerbread

For Sauce—Mix in a saucepan

　⅔ cup water
　1½ tablespoons quick-cooking tapioca
　⅛ teaspoon salt

Bring quickly to boiling. Boil 1 min., stirring constantly. Remove from heat and stir in

　⅓ cup reserved pineapple syrup

Pour sauce over pineapple slices in casseroles.

For Gingerbread—Sift together and set aside

　1½ cups sifted all-purpose flour
　½ teaspoon salt
　½ teaspoon baking powder
　½ teaspoon baking soda
　½ teaspoon ginger
　½ teaspoon cinnamon
　½ teaspoon nutmeg
　¼ teaspoon cloves

Prepare

　½ cup double-strength coffee beverage
　(page 10)

Put into a bowl

　⅓ cup shortening

Add gradually, creaming until light and fluffy after each addition

　½ cup firmly packed brown sugar

Add in thirds, beating thoroughly after each addition

　1 egg, well beaten

Combine with the hot coffee beverage and blend in

　½ cup molasses

Add dry ingredients all at one time. Beat until smooth. Turn batter into casseroles, filling each two-thirds full.

Bake at 350°F 25 to 30 min., or until wooden pick or cake tester comes out clean when inserted in center of cake.

For Topping—Using chilled bowl and beater, beat until cream stands in peaks when beater is slowly lifted upright

　½ cup chilled heavy cream

Fold reserved pineapple into whipped cream.

Serve sauce on warm gingerbread. *6 servings*

—SPICY PLUM CAKE

Follow ▲ Recipe. Use a shallow 2-qt. casserole. Butter bottom of casserole. Substitute **1 can (17 oz.) purple plums** for pineapple; drain, reserving syrup. Cut plums into halves, remove and discard pits, and arrange plum halves in casserole. Substitute plum syrup for pineapple syrup in sauce. Bake at 375°F 45 to 55 min., or until cake tests done. Substitute **Vanilla Hard Sauce** (page 581) for whipped cream topping. Serve Spicy Plum Cake warm.

STRAWBERRY SHORTCAKE SUPREME

▲ Base Recipe

Set out one 8-in. round layer cake pan.

Sort, rinse and drain

　1 qt. fresh strawberries

Set aside in refrigerator about 14 strawberries (with hulls) for garnishing. Hull remaining berries. Slice larger berries and leave smaller ones whole. Sprinkle hulled berries with

　½ cup sugar

Mix lightly; allow to stand about 1 hr., or until juice collects.

For Shortcake—Sift together into a bowl

　2 cups sifted all-purpose flour
　2 tablespoons sugar
　1 tablespoon baking powder
　½ teaspoon salt

Cut into dry ingredients with a pastry blender or two knives until mixture resembles coarse corn meal

　½ cup lard, vegetable shortening, or
　all-purpose shortening

Make a well in center of mixture and add, all at one time

　¾ cup cream

Stir with a fork until dough follows fork.

Gently form dough into a ball and put onto a lightly floured surface. Knead dough by folding opposite side over toward you. Using fingertips gently push dough away. Give it a quar-

ter turn. Repeat process rhythmically 10 to 15 times, until dough is just smooth. Always turn dough in same direction, using as little additional flour as possible.

Divide dough into halves, Gently roll each half into a round about ½ in. thick to fit an 8-in. round layer cake pan. Place one round in cake pan, brush top with

　Melted butter

Cover with other round. Brush top with

　Melted butter

Sprinkle lightly with

　Sugar

Bake at 425°F 15 to 18 min., or until lightly browned.

Immediately remove from pan. Split shortcake while hot into two layers and spread each split side with

　Softened butter

Place bottom layer on serving plate. Cover with one half of the sweetened berries. Place top layer over berries. Top with remaining berries. Garnish with reserved whole berries.

Serve with lots of

　Sweetened Whipped Cream
　(page 480) or heavy cream

　　　　　　　　　　　　　　　6 servings

—PEACH SHORTCAKE SUPREME

Follow ▲ Recipe for shortcake. Substitute **2 pkgs. (10 oz. each) frozen sliced peaches**, thawed, or **sweetened sliced fresh peaches** for strawberries. Complete as in ▲ Recipe.

—BANANA ORANGE SHORTCAKE

Follow ▲ Recipe for shortcake. Substitute a mixture of **orange sections** and **sliced bananas** for strawberries. Sweeten with **confectioners' sugar**.

For Butterscotch Peach Shortcake—This mixture baked onto the shortcake, gives a unique flavor to the peach shortcake. After shortcake dough is rolled and cut (do not brush with butter or milk), place on a baking sheet and spread with a butterscotch mixture made by creaming until smooth **¼ cup butter or margarine** and **⅔ cup firmly packed brown sugar**. Complete using **peaches** for the fruit.

For Sunshine Shortcake—A mixture of **orange sections, sliced bananas** and **confectioners'**

Strawberry Shortcake Supreme

Individual Strawberry Shortcakes

sugar makes an interesting fruit shortcake. The beauty of this shortcake lies in the year-round availability of the fruits used.

—INDIVIDUAL STRAWBERRY SHORTCAKES

Follow ▲ Recipe. Roll out all the dough at one time and cut into rounds with a 3-in. cutter. Use even pressure to keep sides straight. Put one half of the rounds on a baking sheet; brushed with **melted butter or margarine.** Top with remaining rounds; brush tops with **milk.** Bake as for ▲ Recipe.

CHEESE CAKES

OLD-FASHIONED CHEESE CAKE

Every bit as good as Grandmother used to make!

Set out a 9-in. springform pan.

For Crust—Set out
    18 zwieback (or enough to yield
      1½ cups crumbs)
Prepare crumbs (page 10); turn crumbs into a bowl and stir in
    1 tablespoon sugar
Using fork or pastry blender, blend in
    ¼ cup butter or margarine, softened
With fingers or back of spoon, press crumb mixture very firmly into an even layer on bottom of pan.

Bake at 375°F 5 min. Cool.

For Filling—Blend
    1 lb. cream cheese, softened
    2 teaspoons vanilla extract
Add gradually, blending until smooth after each addition
    ½ cup sugar
    2 tablespoons all-purpose flour
    ⅛ teaspoon salt
Add, one at a time, beating thoroughly after each addition
    4 egg yolks, unbeaten
Blend in
    1 cup cream
Beat until rounded peaks are formed
    4 egg whites

Spread beaten egg whites over cheese mixture and gently fold together. Turn into the pan.

Bake at 325°F 1 hr.

Remove to cooling rack to cool completely (about 2 hrs.).

Chill in refrigerator several hours or overnight.
About 12 servings

CHEESE CAKE
(Käsekuchen)

Set out a 9-in. springform pan.

For Crust—Sift together into a bowl
    1 cup sifted all-purpose flour
    2 tablespoons sugar
    ¼ teaspoon salt
Make a well in center of flour, and in well work to a creamy mixture
    ¼ cup softened butter
    1 egg, slightly beaten
Quickly and thoroughly mix with the flour. Shape dough into a ball and wrap in waxed paper. Set in refrigerator to chill about 2 hrs.

Put dough out onto a lightly floured surface and flatten. Roll from center to edge into a round about ¼ in. thick. With a knife or spatula, loosen pastry from surface whenever sticking occurs; lift pastry slightly and sprinkle flour under it.

With spatula, loosen pastry from surface and fold it in half, then in quarters. Gently lay it in pan and unfold pastry without stretching, fitting it to bottom of pan only.

Bake at 450°F 10 min.

Set aside on cooling rack to cool.

For Filling—Grate (page 10) and set aside
    2¼ cups (about 12 oz.) blanched
      almonds (page 9); about 5⅓
      cups, grated

Set aside to drain thoroughly
    1 can (16 oz.) pitted red tart cherries

Force through a sieve or food mill into a bowl and set aside
    1 lb. (2 cups) dry cottage cheese

Cream until softened
    1 cup butter
    2 teaspoons grated lemon peel
Add gradually, creaming until fluffy after each addition
    1 cup sugar
Beat until thick and lemon-colored
    7 egg yolks
Add the beaten egg yolks in thirds to the creamed mixture, beating thoroughly after each addition. Beat in the cheese and the grated almonds. Set aside.

Lightly butter the sides of the springform pan.

Using clean beater, beat until frothy
    7 egg whites
Add gradually, beating well after each addition
    ¾ cup sugar
Continue beating until very stiff peaks are formed. Gently fold into the cheese mixture.

Arrange the well-drained cherries in an even layer over the cooled crust. Gently turn the cheese mixture into the pan; spread evenly.

Bake at 300°F about 1 hr. and 30 min. Let stand in oven 1 hr. longer. Remove to cooling rack to cool completely, about 4 hrs. Set in refrigerator to chill.

Carefully run a spatula around inside of pan from top to bottom to loosen cake. Remove sides of pan. If desired, sprinkle edges of Cheese Cake with sifted **confectioners' sugar.**
About 16 servings

APRICOT CHEESE CAKE

Set out a 7-in. springform pan. Put a bowl and rotary beater into refrigerator to chill.

Drain, reserving syrup
    1 can (30 oz.) apricot halves
Set 4 apricot halves aside in refrigerator.

513

Measure 1 cup of the reserved apricot syrup into a small saucepan. Sprinkle evenly over the syrup to soften

2 env. unflavored gelatin

Set saucepan over low heat and stir constantly until gelatin is completely dissolved. Remove from heat and set aside.

Meanwhile, force remaining apricots through a coarse sieve or food mill. Force through the sieve or food mill and blend with the apricots

2 cups (1 lb.) cream-style cottage cheese

Stir into the cheese-apricot mixture

1 cup dairy sour cream
½ cup sugar
¼ cup lemon juice
1 teaspoon salt
¼ teaspoon almond extract

Blend thoroughly; add and blend in the gelatin.

Using the chilled bowl and beater, beat until cream is of medium consistency (piles softly)

1 cup chilled heavy cream

Fold into cheese mixture. Turn into springform pan and chill in refrigerator several hours, or until firm.

Meanwhile, prepare crumbs (page 10) from

6 graham crackers (or enough to yield ½ cup crumbs)

Turn crumbs into a small bowl and mix with

¼ cup (about 1 oz.) chopped nuts
¼ cup melted butter

Carefully run a spatula around inside of pan from top to bottom, to loosen cake. Remove sides of pan; do not remove cake from bottom of pan. Place on chilled serving plate. Sprinkle crumb-nut mixture over top of cake. Arrange reserved apricot halves around cheese cake; place a **maraschino cherry** in each half.

8 to 10 servings

Apricot Cheese Cake

DRAMATIC COTTAGE CHEESE CAKE

▲ Base Recipe

Set out a 7-in. springform pan. Put a bowl and rotary beater in refrigerator to chill.

For Crust—Set out

½ lb. chocolate wafers (or enough to yield 2¼ cups crumbs)

Prepare crumbs (page 10). Reserve 1¼ cups crumbs to coat cake. Turn remaining 1 cup crumbs into a bowl; add and stir in

¼ cup confectioners' sugar

Using a fork or pastry blender, blend in

¼ cup butter or margarine, softened

With fingers or back of spoon, press crumb mixture very firmly into an even layer on bottom of pan. Set aside.

For Filling—Force through a food mill or a sieve into a bowl and set aside

1 lb. (about 2 cups, firmly packed) dry cottage cheese

Pour into a small cup or custard cup

¼ cup cold water

Sprinkle evenly over water

1 env. unflavored gelatin

Let gelatin stand to soften.

Meanwhile, blend well in top of double boiler

3 egg yolks, slightly beaten
⅔ cup sugar
¼ cup cream

Cook over simmering water, stirring constantly and rapidly, until mixture thickens. Remove from heat and strain into a bowl. Immediately blend in softened gelatin, stirring until gelatin is completely dissolved. Add the cottage cheese all at one time and blend thoroughly. Mix in

2 teaspoons grated lemon peel
1½ teaspoons vanilla extract

Using the chilled bowl and beater, beat until cream is of medium consistency (piles softly)

½ cup chilled heavy cream

Fold into cottage cheese mixture.

Beat until frothy

3 egg whites

Add gradually, beating well after each addition

½ cup sugar

Continue beating until rounded peaks are formed. Spread beaten egg whites over cheese mixture and gently fold together.

Spoon filling evenly over crust. Spoon one half of reserved crumbs over top. Refrigerate 10 to 12 hrs., or until firm.

Carefully run a spatula around inside of pan, from top to bottom, to loosen cake. Remove sides of pan. Do not remove cake from bottom of pan. Turn remaining crumbs onto a long sheet of waxed paper. Set cake on paper next to crumbs. With wide spatula or spoon, toss crumbs onto sides of cake, coating completely. Return to refrigerator until serving time.

If desired, decorate by forcing **Sweetened Whipped Cream** (page 480) through a pastry bag and No. 27 star tube.   *12 to 14 servings*

—LEMON COTTAGE CHEESE CAKE

Follow ▲ Recipe. Substitute **lemon wafers** for chocolate wafers.

—RASPBERRY COTTAGE CHEESE CAKE

Sort, rinse, drain and crush **1 pt. fresh red raspberries; mix with ¼ cup sugar.** Set aside until sugar is completely dissolved; stir occasionally. Force the berries through a sieve or food mill. Set aside. Follow recipe for Lemon Cottage Cheese Cake. Increase cold water to ⅓ cup and gelatin to 1½ env. Substitute ¼ cup of the raspberries for the cream. Omit lemon peel and vanilla extract. After adding the softened gelatin, blend in the remaining raspberries and **1 tablespoon lemon juice.**

BLENDER CHOCOLATE CHEESE CAKE

▲ Base Recipe

Though a blender makes it easier, the cake is just as delicious when prepared by hand.

For Crumb Crust—Butter bottom and sides of a 9-in. springform pan.

Set out

32 to 36 graham crackers (or enough to yield 3 cups crumbs)

Prepare fine crumbs in an electric blender. Return about one half of the crumbs to container and add

½ cup butter or margarine
2 tablespoons sugar
¼ teaspoon salt

Cover and blend a few seconds until ingredients are well blended. Add the remaining crumbs; cover and blend only until ingredients are mixed together. Reserve ½ cup of the crumb mixture for topping. Spoon remainder of crumb mixture into the springform pan. Using back of spoon, press crumb mixture very firmly into an even layer on bottom and around sides of pan.

Bake at 325°F 5 min. (Prebaking tends to prevent a soggy crust.) Set aside on a cooling rack to cool.

For Filling—While crust is cooling, wash and dry blender container; put into it

1 pkg. (6 oz.) semisweet chocolate pieces

514

Blender Cheese Cake

Luscious Lemon Cheese Cake

Cover blender and grind until pieces are very fine. Empty blender container and set ground chocolate aside.

Wash blender container and put into it
- **4 egg yolks**
- **1 cup dairy sour cream**
- **¼ cup sugar**
- **¼ cup all-purpose flour**
- **2 cups (1 lb.) cream-style cottage cheese**
- **2 teaspoons vanilla extract**
- **1 teaspoon almond extract**
- **¼ teaspoon salt**

Cover and blend about 30 sec. Scrape sides of blender container. Cover and blend 30 sec. longer, or until mixture is smooth and well blended. Empty contents of blender container into a large bowl. Gently fold in the ground chocolate and set aside.

Beat until frothy
- **4 egg whites**

Add gradually, beating well after each addition
- **¼ cup sugar**

Continue beating until very stiff peaks are formed. Gently fold the beaten egg whites into the cottage cheese mixture. Turn into pan. Sprinkle the reserved crumb mixture over top.

Bake at 325°F 1¼ hrs., or until a metal knife inserted in center of the cake comes out clean.

Remove to cooling rack and allow to cool thoroughly, 4 to 6 hrs.

Chill in refrigerator several hours before serving. *16 to 20 servings*

—BLENDER CHEESE CAKE

Follow ▲ Recipe. Omit semisweet chocolate pieces. Sprinkle reserved crumb mixture around edges. Bake as directed. When ready to serve, garnish center with **pineapple chunks** and **fresh strawberries.**

LUSCIOUS LEMON CHEESE CAKE

Accompany it with cups of fragrant, steaming coffee for a distinguished dessert treat.

Butter bottom and sides of a 9-in. spring-form pan.

For Crust—Prepare crumbs (page 10) from
- **24 slices (6 oz.) zwieback (or enough to yield 2⅔ cups crumbs)**

Turn crumbs into a bowl. Stir in
- **½ cup confectioners' sugar**
- **1½ teaspoons grated lemon peel**

Using a fork or pastry blender, blend in
- **½ cup butter or margarine, softened**

Reserve ¾ cup of mixture for topping; turn remainder into the springform pan. With fingers or back of spoon, press crumbs very firmly into an even layer on bottom of pan and up around sides to the rim; set aside.

For Filling—Put into a large bowl and beat together
- **2½ lbs. cream cheese, softened**
- **1½ teaspoons grated lemon peel**
- **½ teaspoon vanilla extract**

Add gradually, beating until smooth after each addition
- **1¾ cups sugar**
- **3 tablespoons all-purpose flour**

Beat together and add gradually to cream cheese mixture, beating thoroughly after each addition
- **5 eggs**
- **2 egg yolks**

Blend in
- **¼ cup heavy cream**

Turn into the pan. Spread evenly. Sprinkle reserved crumb mixture evenly over top.

Bake at 250°F 1 hr. Turn off heat. Let stand in oven 1 hr. longer. Remove to cooling rack to cool completely, 4 to 6 hrs.

Chill in refrigerator several hours or overnight.
16 to 20 servings

BLUEBERRY ORANGE CHEESE CAKE

Set out a 9-in. springform pan.

To prepare crust, combine in a small bowl
- **2 tablespoons sugar**
- **½ teaspoon cinnamon**
- **½ teaspoon nutmeg**

Stir in
- **6 tablespoons butter, melted**

Press the mixture on bottom and about three-fourths up sides of the springform pan. Chill crust while preparing the filling.

Drain (reserving the cream)
- **4 cups cream-style cottage cheese**

Press through a coarse sieve and set aside.

Measure reserved cream in a measuring cup for liquids and fill to 1-cup level with
- **Heavy cream**

In a large mixing bowl, beat until very thick
- **6 eggs**

Add, beating until light and fluffy
- **1½ cups sugar**

Blend in the sieved cottage cheese, the cream and
- **½ cup all-purpose flour**
- **3 tablespoons thawed frozen orange juice concentrate**
- **1 teaspoon vanilla extract**
- **⅛ teaspoon salt**

Mix well and turn filling into crumb-lined pan.

Bake in 350°F oven 1 hr. and 10 to 20 min. (Cheese cake is done when a metal knife inserted near center comes out clean.)

While cake is baking, prepare topping. Combine in a small bowl
- **1 cup dairy sour cream**
- **2 tablespoons confectioners' sugar**
- **1 cup dry-pack frozen blueberries, thawed**

When cake tests done, turn off heat. Open oven door and gently spread cake with topping mixture. Cool in oven until cake is of room temperature. Chill. *One 9-in. cheese cake*

Note: Syrup-pack canned or frozen blueberries, drained, may be used in topping.

PINEAPPLE CHEESE CAKE

Butter bottom and sides of one 9-in. round layer cake pan with removable bottom.

For Crust—Prepare crumbs (page 10) from
- **24 graham crackers (or enough to yield 1¾ cups crumbs)**

Turn crumbs into a bowl. Stir in
- **¼ cup sugar**

Strawberry-Glazed Cheese Cake

Using a fork or pastry blender, blend in
½ cup butter or margarine, softened
Using back of spoon, press crumb mixture very firmly into an even layer on bottom and sides of the pan. Bake at 375°F 5 min. Cool.

For Filling—Drain, reserving syrup for use in other food preparation
1 can (15¼ oz.) crushed pineapple (about 1½ cups, drained)
Put into a bowl and blend
12 oz. cream cheese, softened
½ teaspoon vanilla extract
Add in order, blending until smooth after each addition
½ cup sugar (adding gradually)
⅛ teaspoon cinnamon
2 eggs, slightly beaten
Gently blend in the crushed pineapple. Turn filling into the crumb crust in pan.

Bake at 325°F 35 min.

Meanwhile, mix
1 cup dairy sour cream
3 tablespoons sugar
1 teaspoon vanilla extract
Spread sour cream mixture on top of cake. Cool completely. Chill thoroughly before serving. *About 12 servings*

ORANGE CHEESE CAKE

Lightly butter bottom and sides of a 9-in. round layer cake pan with removable bottom.

For Crust—Set out
24 graham crackers (or enough to yield 1¾ cups crumbs)
Prepare crumbs (page 10); turn crumbs into a bowl and mix in
¼ cup sugar
Using fork or pastry blender, blend in
⅓ cup butter or margarine, softened
Using back of spoon, press crumb mixture very firmly into an even layer on bottom and sides of pan.

Bake at 375°F 5 min. Cool.

For Filling—Put into a bowl and beat together
12 oz. cream cheese, softened
½ teaspoon vanilla extract

Add in order, beating until smooth after each addition
½ cup sugar (adding gradually)
2 eggs, slightly beaten
Blend in
1 can (6 oz.) frozen orange juice concentrate, thawed
Turn filling into crumb crust.

Bake at 375°F 20 min. Remove from oven and place on cooling rack for 15 min.

Meanwhile, mix
2 cups dairy sour cream
⅓ to ½ cup sugar
2 to 3 teaspoons vanilla extract
Spoon mixture gently and evenly over cake.

Return to oven and bake at 375°F 10 min. Cool completely.

Chill in refrigerator overnight.
About 12 servings

STRAWBERRY-GLAZED CHEESE CAKE

▲ *Base Recipe*

Lightly butter bottom and sides of a 7-in. springform pan.

For Crust—Set out
16 slices (4 oz.) zwieback (or enough to yield 1¾ cups crumbs)
Prepare crumbs (page 10); turn crumbs into a bowl and stir in
⅓ cup confectioners' sugar
1 teaspoon grated lemon peel
Using a fork or pastry blender, blend in
⅓ cup butter or margarine, softened
With fingers or back of spoon, press crumbs very firmly into an even layer on bottom of pan and up around sides to the rim; set aside.

For Filling—Beat together
2 lbs. cream cheese, softened
1 teaspoon grated lemon peel
½ teaspoon vanilla extract

Add gradually, beating until smooth after each addition
1 cup plus 6 tablespoons sugar
2 tablespoons plus 1 teaspoon all-purpose flour
Beat together and add gradually to cream cheese mixture, beating thoroughly
4 eggs
1 egg yolk
Blend in
3½ tablespoons heavy cream
Turn into pan and spread evenly.

Bake at 250°F 70 to 75 min. Turn off heat. Let stand in oven 1 hr. longer. Remove to cooling rack to cool completely, 4 to 6 hrs.

Chill several hours or overnight.

For Strawberry Glaze—When cheese cake is thoroughly chilled, sort, rinse, drain and hull
1 qt. fresh ripe strawberries
Crush enough berries to make ½ cup crushed strawberries. Set remaining strawberries in refrigerator to chill.

Mix in a saucepan
½ cup sugar
1 tablespoon cornstarch
Add gradually, stirring until blended, the crushed berries and
¼ cup water
Stirring constantly, bring rapidly to boiling. Continue stirring and boil about 2 min. Remove from heat and stir in
2 teaspoons butter or margarine
8 drops red food coloring
Strain the glaze and set aside to cool slightly.

Meanwhile, carefully arrange the strawberries on the cheese cake (if very large berries are used, cut them into halves and arrange on cake cut side down). Spoon the cooled glaze carefully over the berries. Chill in refrigerator.
12 to 16 servings

—PINEAPPLE-GLAZED CHEESE CAKE

Follow ▲ Recipe. Omit Strawberry Glaze. Prepare **Pineapple Glaze**; spoon cooled glaze over cake and chill in refrigerator.

For Pineapple Glaze—Drain, reserving syrup,
1 can (8½ oz.) pineapple tidbits. If desired, cut the tidbits into halves; set aside. Blend ⅔ cup syrup with **2 teaspoons cornstarch** in a small saucepan. Stirring constantly, bring rapidly to boiling. Continue stirring and boil about 3 min. Set aside to cool slightly. Stir in pineapple. Cool completely before spooning glaze over cake.

PASTRY DESSERTS

CREAM PUFF OR CHOUX PASTE
(Pâte à Choux)

▲ *Base Recipe*

Since this pastry puffs up in baking, it is used in many interesting ways by French pastry cooks. A popular use is for cream puffs and éclairs which are delightful in taste and appearance. These crisp, hollow shells also may be filled with a salad mixture or any hot creamed food. To insure crispness, fill just before serving.

Bring to rolling boil
> **1 cup hot water**
> **½ cup butter**
> **1 tablespoon sugar**
> **½ teaspoon salt**

Add, all at once
> **1 cup sifted all-purpose flour**

Beat vigorously with a wooden spoon until mixture leaves sides of pan and forms a smooth ball. Remove from heat. Quickly beat in, one at a time, beating until smooth after each addition

> **4 eggs**

Continue beating until mixture is thick and smooth. Dough may be shaped and baked at once, or wrapped in waxed paper and stored in refrigerator overnight.

Complete as directed in any one of the following variations or Saint-Honoré Cake (page 519).

> *1 doz. large or 4 doz.*
> *miniature puffs or éclairs*

—CREAM PUFFS
(Choux à la Crème)

Prepare ▲ Recipe. Force dough through a pastry bag or drop by tablespoonfuls 2 in. apart onto a lightly greased baking sheet. Bake large puffs at 450°F 15 min. Lower heat to 350°F and bake 20 to 25 min. longer, or until golden in color. Bake small puffs at 450°F 10 min. Lower heat to 350°F and bake 5 min. longer, or until golden in color. Remove to rack and cool. Cut off tops and fill shells with **Saint-Honoré Cream**

(page 483) or **Chantilly Cream** (page 481). Replace tops and sprinkle with sifted confectioners' sugar.

—CHOUX PASTE FRITTERS
(Beignets Soufflés)

These whisper-light fritters were originated over two centuries ago at Beaume-les-Dames Abbey (in old Franche-Comte). They are often referred to as Pets-de-Nonne.

Fill a deep saucepan about two-thirds full with **fat or oil** for deep-frying. Heat to 360°F, or until a 1-in. bread cube browns in 1 min. Follow ▲ Recipe omitting sugar. Add **2 teaspoons grated lemon peel** and **2 teaspoons lemon juice** with butter. Do not chill batter; use immediately. Drop batter by half-teaspoonfuls, a few at a time, into hot fat. Fry until uniformly brown, about 6 min. Drain well on absorbent paper. Serve hot, sprinkled with sifted **confectioners' sugar** or **Vanilla Confectioners' Sugar** (page 582).
> *10 doz. Choux Paste Fritters*

—MINIATURE CREAM PUFFS
(Profiteroles au Chocolat)

Follow ▲ Recipe to baking, shaping cream puffs into small balls. Bake miniature puffs at 450°F 10 min. Reduce heat to 350°F and bake 10 min. longer, or until golden in color. Remove to racks to cool completely. Cut off tops and fill shells with **Vanilla Cream Filling** (page 482), **Sweetened Whipped Cream** (page 480) or **ice cream.** Replace tops and pile Profiteroles on a serving plate pyramid-fashion. Top with hot **Fudge Sauce Café** (page 579).

—ECLAIRS
(Eclairs de Crème au Chocolat)

Follow recipe for Cream Puffs, forming dough into oblongs 1x4½ in. When cool, cut small opening at one end and force filling into éclair. Fill with **French Pastry Cream** (page 482). Frost with Glaze.

For Chocolate Glaze (Cooked)—Melt 1 oz

Bring the butter-water mixture to a rolling boil.

Add flour and beat until a smooth ball is formed.

Beat thoroughly after the addition of each egg.

Drop by tablespoonfuls onto greased baking sheet.

Cream Puffs

Eclairs

(1 sq.) unsweetened chocolate. Mix in heavy saucepan ¾ cup confectioners' sugar, 1 teaspoon dark corn syrup, 1 tablespoon cream, melted chocolate, 2 teaspoons boiling water and 1 teaspoon butter. Place over low heat and stir constantly until butter melts. Remove from heat and add ½ teaspoon vanilla extract. Cool slightly. Spread over tops of éclairs.

For Chocolate Glaze (Uncooked)—Blend 1½ cups confectioners' sugar into 1 egg white. Add ¾ teaspoon vanilla extract and 1½ oz. (1½ sq.) unsweetened chocolate, melted. Mix thoroughly and spread over tops of éclairs.

—COFFEE-GLAZED CREAM PUFFS

A coffee duet—ravishing cream puffs with a mocha glaze and an elegant coffee whipped cream filling.

Follow recipe for Cream Puffs. Shortly before ready to serve, cut off tops and fill shells with **Coffee Whipped Cream** (page 481) or **Mocha Whipped Cream** (page 480). Replace tops and frost with Coffee Glaze.

For Coffee Glaze—Measure into mixing bowl
   3¾ cups confectioners' sugar
Add and mix thoroughly
   ¼ cup plus 2 tablespoons warm
     triple-strength coffee beverage
   1½ teaspoons rum extract

–ST. JOSEPH'S DAY CREAM PUFFS

Follow ▲ Recipe. When mixture is smooth and glossy, add, mixing thoroughly, 1 teaspoon grated orange peel and 1 teaspoon grated lemon peel. Shape and bake as in recipe for Cream Puffs. Cut a slit in each puff and fill

with **Sweetened Whipped Cream** (page 480), **Ricotta Filling** (See Ricotta Pie, page 501), or **Pineapple Cream Filling** (page 484). If desired, top with hot **Fudge Sauce** (page 579).

PUFF PASTRY
(Pâte Feuilletées)

▲ Base Recipe

Place into a large bowl of cold water and ice cubes or chipped ice
   1 cup butter
Work butter with hands. Break it into small portions and squeeze each in water about 20 times, or until butter is pliable and waxy. Remove and wipe off excess water. Reserve ¼ cup of this butter. Pat remainder ½ in. thick, divide into five equal portions, wrap each in waxed paper. Chill in refrigerator until firm.

Sift together into a bowl
   2 cups sifted all-purpose flour
   ½ teaspoon salt
With two knives or pastry blender, cut in the ¼ cup butter until pieces are the size of small peas. Gradually stir in with a fork about
   7 tablespoons ice water
When blended, gather into a ball and knead on lightly floured surface until elastic and smooth (page 11). Cover with bowl and let ripen about 30 min.

Roll on a floured surface to form a rectangle ¼ in. thick. Keep corners square, gently pulling dough into shape where necessary.

Remove one portion of chilled butter and cut into small pieces. Quickly pat pieces down center third of dough. Cover butter with right-hand third of dough. Fold left-hand third under butter section. With rolling pin gently press down and seal the open edges. Wrap pastry in waxed paper. Chill in refrigerator about 1 hr.

Remove from refrigerator and place on the board with butter section near top, narrow width toward you. Turn folded dough one-quarter way around, to have open edge away from you. Roll to original size. Repeat four times the procedure for folding, sealing and chilling, using second, third, fourth and fifth portions of butter. Each time place dough on floured surface, turn and roll as directed.

With last rolling, fold four sides toward center. Gently press down with rolling pin. Fold in

half. Wrap dough in waxed paper. Cover with a damp towel. Chill in refrigerator about 2 hrs. before using.

To store for several days, wrap dough in waxed paper and place in refrigerator.
   Puff Pastry for Saint-Honoré Cake, page 519; 12 Napoleons or 6 Vol-au-Vent Shells

—VOL-AU-VENT SHELLS (Patty Shells)
(Croûtes de Vol-au-Vent)

For Individual Vol-au-Vent—Follow ▲ Recipe. Roll pastry ⅛ in. thick. With a sharp knife or 3-in. cookie cutter, cut out rounds. With 2-in. cookie cutter cut centers from half the 3-in. rounds. Remove centers, leaving ½-in. rims. Moisten ½-in. edges of solid 3-in. rounds with cold water. Fit rims on top. Thoroughly prick through rims and bases with a fork. Gently and evenly press rims down. Transfer to baking sheet which has been rinsed with cold water and well drained.

Roll the 2-in. centers to ¼-in. thickness. These are used as covers and may be cut into shapes such as stars or scalloped rounds. Transfer to baking sheet. Prick well. Chill shells and covers in refrigerator for 30 min.

Bake at 450°F 8 min. Reduce heat to 350°F and bake about 20 min. longer. If browning is too rapid, cover with a sheet of unglazed paper. Remove to rack to cool. Reheat before filling with hot creamed mixture.

For Large Vol-au-Vent—Divide pastry into two portions. Roll each into a round or oval of the same size to ⅛-in. thickness. From one, cut out center, leaving a rim about ¾ in. wide. Moisten ¾-in. edge of solid round with cold water. Transfer it to one end of ungreased baking sheet covered with three thicknesses of unglazed paper. Place rim over round. Prick well. Gently and evenly press rim down.

Roll remaining center to ¼-in. thickness. Transfer it to other end of baking sheet. Prick well. Chill in refrigerator 30 min.

Bake as individual Vol-au-Vent Shells. Reheat before filling with hot creamed mixture. Use baked center as a cover.

St. Joseph's Day Cream Puffs and Coffee-Glazed Cream Puffs

—NAPOLEONS
(Petites Mille-Feuilles)

Follow ▲ Recipe and divide pastry into three portions. Immediately return two portions to refrigerator. Roll remaining portion into a rectangle ⅛ in. thick. Cut into even 3x5-in. strips. Trim ends so all strips are equal. Transfer to baking sheet rinsed with cold water and drained thoroughly. Prick well. Repeat process with each remaining portion of pastry. Chill in refrigerator 30 min.

Bake at 425°F 10 min. Reduce temperature to 325°F and bake 20 min., or until golden brown. Remove to racks. When cold, split each slice lengthwise. Let stand about 30 min. to dry.

Fill one split slice with **Almond Pastry Cream** (page 483). Gently press together. Spread more filling over top and cover with one half of another slice, cut-side down. Spread top with more filling and cover with remaining half of slice. This completes one Napoleon, excepting the glaze.

For Napoleon Glaze—Mix in a heavy saucepan **¾ cup confectioners' sugar, 1 tablespoon hot water, 1 teaspoon light corn syrup** and **2 teaspoons butter.** Place over low heat, stirring constantly until butter melts. Add ½ **teaspoon vanilla extract.** Spread evenly over tops of Napoleons.

SAINT-HONORE CAKE
(Gâteau Saint-Honoré)

Named for the patron saint of bakers, Saint-Honoré Cake is a dessert for special occasions. The gâteau shell is prepared from Puff and Choux Pastes and decorated with miniature cream puffs. Usually it is filled with a French cream.

Prepare (allowing about 9 hrs.) and chill in refrigerator
Puff Pastry (page 518)

Roll out pastry ¼ in. thick. With a sharp knife, cut one 9-in. round. (Cake pan may be used as a guide.) Cover ungreased baking sheet with three thicknesses of unglazed paper. Place pastry round on center of paper and prick well with fork. Chill the pastry in refrigerator 30 min. or longer.

Meanwhile, prepare
Cream Puff or Choux Paste (one half recipe, page 517)
Use a pastry bag with about a ½-in. opening. Fill one-half to two-thirds full of Choux Paste. Gently squeezing bag, pipe a continuous border of paste around top of pastry round ½ in. in from edge. Set aside bag containing the remaining paste.

Bake "Le gâteau" at 450°F 15 min. Cover with two thicknesses of unglazed paper. Reduce temperature to 350°F and bake about 20 min., or until the whole surface is lightly browned. Remove paper covering from "Le gateau" and

carefully transfer from baking sheet to a rack. Set aside to cool.

Force remaining Choux Paste onto a greased baking sheet into about 8 miniature decorative puffs. When gâteau is removed from oven, increase temperature to 450°F and bake puffs 10 min. Reduce temperature to 350°F and bake about 5 min. longer. Cool on rack.

Meanwhile, melt over low heat in light-colored heavy skillet
½ cup sugar
Stir constantly until golden brown, and foam appears. Remove from heat. Gradually add
6 tablespoons boiling water
Return to heat. Stir until a smooth syrup is formed. Cook syrup until bubbles are size of a dime. Cool.

Carefully cut off top of each puff and fill with
**Saint-Honoré Cream (page 483) or
Chantilly Cream (page 481)**
Replace tops. Lightly spread syrup around top surface of "Le gâteau" rim. Dip bottom of each cream puff into syrup and arrange on rim. Fill center of "Le gâteau" with remaining Saint-Honoré Cream.

If desired, top each tiny puff with about 1 teaspoon of a mixture of
**3 tablespoons Chantilly Cream
  (page 481)
1 tablespoon chopped candied
  cherries
1 tablespoon chopped walnuts**

To make an unusual birthday cake, insert candles in an appropriate number of the small puffs.   *8 servings*

APPLE STRUDEL
(Apfelstrudel)

Generously butter 2 baking sheets.

For Strudel Dough—Put into a large bowl and make a well in center
**3 cups sifted all-purpose flour
½ teaspoon salt**
Add and mix well
**1 egg, beaten
1 tablespoon cooking oil**

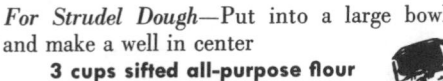

Napoleon

Stirring constantly to keep mixture a smooth paste, add gradually
1 cup lukewarm (80°F to 85°F) water
Mix until a soft dough is formed (the dough will be sticky). Turn dough out onto a lightly floured pastry board. Hold dough high above board and hit it hard against the board about 100 to 125 times, or until the dough is smooth and elastic and leaves the board easily. (After 15 or 20 times it will no longer stick.)

Knead (page 11) slightly and pat into a round. Lightly brush top of dough with
Cooking oil (not olive oil)
Cover dough with an inverted bowl and allow it to rest 30 min.

Meanwhile, see filling recipe; prepare apples, bread crumbs, nuts and sugar mixture.

Melt and set aside to cool
1 cup butter

Cover a table (about 48x30 in.) with a clean cloth, allowing cloth to hang down, and sprinkle with approximately
½ cup all-purpose flour (most in center of cloth)
Place dough on center of cloth and roll into a 12-in. square. If necessary, sprinkle more

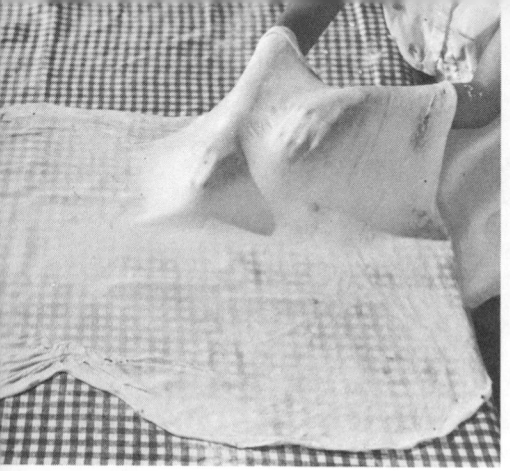

Strudel Dough: Stretch dough until it is as thin as paper. Cover dough with filling and fold the edges over.

flour under dough so it does not stick. Keep dough square. Using a soft brush, lightly brush off any flour on top and brush top with

Cooking oil (not olive oil)

(The oil aids in preventing formation of holes during stretching.)

With palms of hands down, reach under the dough to its center (dough will rest on backs of hands) and lift slightly, being careful not to tear dough. To stretch dough, gently and steadily pull arms in opposite directions. Lower dough to table as you walk slowly around table, pulling one side and another, but not too much in one place. Keep dough close to table. (Dough should not have any torn spots. If some should appear, do not try to patch them.) Keep pulling and stretching dough, draping it over edge of table. Continue until dough is as thin as tissue paper and hangs over edges of table on all sides. With kitchen shears, trim off thick outer edges. Allow stretched dough to dry 10 min. Avoid drying too long as it becomes brittle.

Drizzle dough with about ¼ cup of the cooled melted butter. Sprinkle the bread crumbs over dough as directed in recipe for filling. Cover dough with remaining ingredients for the filling.

For Rolling and Baking—Fold overhanging dough on three sides over the filling. Drizzle the filling with ½ cup of the cooled melted butter. Beginning at narrow folded end of

dough, grasp the cloth with both hands, holding it taut; slowly lift cloth and roll dough over filling. Pull cloth toward you; again lift cloth and, holding it taut, slowly and loosely roll dough. Cut Strudel into halves, and lifting each half on cloth, gently roll onto the baking sheets. Brush off excess flour from the roll; cut off ends of roll. Brush top and sides of Strudel with some of the melted butter.

Bake at 350°F 35 to 45 min., or until Strudel is golden brown. Baste and brush about 4 times during baking with melted butter. When Strudel makes a crackly sound on touching it is done. (Strudel should not be smooth.)

Remove to cooling rack; cool slightly. Sift over top of Strudel

Confectioners' sugar or Vanilla
Confectioners' Sugar (page 582)

Remove to a cutting board. Cut Strudel into 2-in. slices and serve warm with

Sweetened Whipped Cream
(page 480)

12 slices

For Filling—Wash, quarter, core and pare

4 medium (about 1½ lbs.)
cooking apples

Cut apples into slices about ⅛ in. thick and put into a bowl with

2 tablespoons vanilla extract
2 tablespoons brown sugar

Toss lightly to coat slices evenly. Set aside for at least 30 min., tossing occasionally.

Mix

2 tablespoons sugar
1½ teaspoons cinnamon
½ teaspoon allspice

Blend in and set aside

2 tablespoons brown sugar

Chop finely and set aside

1 cup (about 4 oz.) walnuts

Grate (page 10) and set aside

2 teaspoons grated lemon peel

Heat a skillet over medium heat. Add and melt quickly

2 tablespoons butter

Toss in the butter until browned and thoroughly coated

¾ cup (about 2 slices) fine dry
bread crumbs

Sprinkle the bread crumbs evenly over one-half the stretched and slightly dry dough.

Drain the apples and cover crumbs evenly with the slices. Sprinkle lemon peel over apples. Toss evenly over apples the nuts and

2 tablespoons dark seedless raisins
3 tablespoons currants

Sprinkle sugar mixture over nuts and fruit. Drizzle mixture with melted butter.

APPLE-FILLED PASTRY
(Almás Píte)

▲ *Base Recipe*

For Pastry—Set out a 15x10x1-in. jelly roll pan.

Sift together into a large bowl

5 cups sifted all-purpose flour
¼ cup sugar
1½ teaspoons salt

Work into dry ingredients, by pressing against bottom and sides of bowl with a fork

1¼ cups butter, chilled and cut in pieces

Add gradually to the ingredients in the bowl, mixing with a fork after each addition, a mixture of

4 egg yolks, slightly beaten
½ cup dairy sour cream

(Mixture will be crumbly.) Gather dough into a ball. Turn out onto lightly floured surface. Work with hands, squeezing dough until well blended. Shape into a smooth roll with palms of hands. Cut off one third of dough for top pastry; wrap in waxed paper and place it in refrigerator. Roll remaining dough into a rectangle to fit bottom of pan. Place in pan; with a fork, prick dough at 1-in. intervals.

Bake at 450°F 10 min. Remove pan from oven to cooling rack; reduce oven heat to 350°F. Sprinkle evenly over the baked pastry

¼ cup (about 1 slice) fine dry bread
crumbs

Set aside.

For Filling—Wash, quarter, core, pare and

Apple Strudel

thinly slice into a bowl
4 medium (about 1½ lbs.) cooking apples (4½ to 5 cups, sliced)
Immediately toss apples with a mixture of
2 teaspoons grated lemon peel
1 tablespoon lemon juice
and lightly toss with a mixture of
½ cup (about 2½ oz.) raisins
⅓ to ½ cup sugar (depending upon tartness of apples)
1½ teaspoons cinnamon
Set apple mixture aside.

Beat until frothy
3 egg whites
Add gradually to egg whites, beating well after each addition
6 tablespoons sugar
Continue beating until very stiff peaks are formed. Gently place beaten egg whites onto apple mixture and fold. Set the filling aside.

For Completing Pastry—Remove remaining pastry from refrigerator and roll into a rectangle ½ in. larger than the pan. With fork, prick top pastry at 2-in. intervals. With spatula loosen pastry.

Spoon apple filling evenly over the bread crumbs on bottom pastry.

Fold top pastry in half; lift gently and place on apple mixture; unfold. Gently press edges of top pastry against sides of pan to seal. Brush top of pastry with
Egg, slightly beaten

Bake at 350°F 25 to 30 min., or until pastry is golden brown and apples are tender when pierced with a fork. Remove pan from oven; set on cooling rack and cut pastry into 2½-in. squares. Sprinkle onto the pastry squares
2 to 3 tablespoons confectioners' sugar

Serve warm or cold. *2 doz. squares*

—APPLE-FILLED PASTRY WITH NUTS
(Almás Pite Dióval)

Follow ▲ Recipe. Substitute **1 cup (about 4 oz.) coarsely chopped walnuts** for raisins.

APPLE TORTE
(Epleterte)

Set out a 9-in. pie pan.

Measure into a bowl
1¼ cups sifted all-purpose flour
Cut in with pastry blender or two knives until well blended
½ cup butter, softened
Cover and set aside overnight (in a cool place but *not* in refrigerator).

The next day, cut in with a pastry blender or two knives until well blended
½ cup butter, softened

Add and blend thoroughly
6 tablespoons sifted all-purpose flour
Chill in refrigerator.

Put into a heavy 3-qt. saucepan
½ lb. (about 2 cups) dried apples
3 cups water
Cook over medium heat 30 min. Stir in
¾ cup sugar
¾ teaspoon cinnamon
Cook 15 min. longer. Cool completely.

Remove pastry from refrigerator. Divide into two balls. Set each ball on a length of waxed paper. Cover with another length of waxed paper. Roll from center to edge into a round about ⅛ in. thick and about 1 in. larger than overall size of pan. Chill in refrigerator.

Set out
½ cup (about 2 oz.) blanched almonds (page 9), split in half
When pastry is chilled, remove a layer from refrigerator and peel off waxed paper. Place pastry in pie pan and press evenly over bottom and sides of pan. Turn the apple mixture into the pie pan. Remove the second pastry layer from refrigerator and place on top of apple mixture. Gently press edges to seal. Fold extra pastry under bottom pastry. Flute (page 10) or press edges together with a fork. With the tines of a fork, pierce top in several places. Arrange the almond halves in a decorative pattern over top of torte.

Sprinkle evenly over top of torte
¼ cup sugar
Bake at 375°F 45 to 50 min., or until browned.

Cool completely on cooling rack. To serve, cut into wedges. *6 to 8 servings*

MAZARIN CAKE
(Mazarintårta)

Lightly butter an 8-in. cake pan with removable bottom.

Prepare and chill in refrigerator
Raspberry Sauce (page 580)

For Pastry—Measure and set aside
¾ cup sifted all-purpose flour

Cream until softened
¼ cup butter
Add gradually, creaming until fluffy after each addition
¼ cup sugar
Blend in
1 egg yolk, slightly beaten
Add the flour in halves, blending well after each addition. Chill pastry in refrigerator.

For Filling—Meanwhile, grate (page 10)
½ lb. (about 1½ cups) blanched almonds (page 9)
Blend in
⅓ cup confectioners' sugar
Set aside.

Cream until softened
½ cup butter
Blend in
4 egg yolks, well beaten
Blend in the almond-sugar mixture until smooth. Set filling aside.

To Complete Cake—Remove pastry from the refrigerator and place on a lightly floured surface. Roll ¼ in. thick and about 1 in. larger than overall size of pan. With knife or spatula, loosen pastry from surface wherever sticking occurs; lift pastry slightly and sprinkle flour underneath.

With spatula, loosen pastry and fold in half and then in quarters. Gently lay pastry in pan and unfold, fitting it to the pan so that it is not stretched.

Trim edge with scissors or sharp knife, leaving ½ in. overlap. Fold extra pastry under at edge and flute (page 10) or press edges together with a fork. Spread the Raspberry Sauce evenly over the pastry at bottom of pan. Carefully spread almond mixture over the Raspberry Sauce being careful to cover sauce completely.

Bake at 325°F 35 to 40 min., or until lightly browned.

Cool completely on a cooling rack.

Meanwhile, blend
¼ cup sifted confectioners' sugar
1½ teaspoons milk
When ready to serve, carefully remove cake from pan to cake plate. Spread confectioners' sugar glaze over top of cake. Or omit glaze and sprinkle cake with **confectioners' sugar**.
One 8-in. cake

SUET PASTRY
(Hájas Tészta)

▲ Base Recipe

Set out 2 shallow baking sheets with 4 sides.

Have ready
½ lb. beef suet
Break suet into small pieces, removing and discarding the membrane which coats it.

Sift together onto pastry board
1 cup sifted all-purpose flour
½ teaspoon salt
Press suet into flour with heel of hand until well blended. Shape suet mixture into a rectangle 2 in. thick; wrap in waxed paper and set aside in refrigerator.

Measure and set aside
1¾ to 2 cups sifted all-purpose flour

Scald (page 10)
¼ cup milk

Meanwhile, soften

1 pkg. active dry yeast

in

¼ cup warm water, 105°F to 115°F
(Or if using compressed yeast, soften
1 cake in ¼ cup lukewarm water,
80°F to 85°F.)

Set aside.

Put into a bowl

1 tablespoon sugar
½ teaspoon salt

Immediately pour the scalded milk over ingredients in bowl. When mixture is lukewarm, blend in ¼ cup of the flour, beating until smooth. Stir the softened yeast and add, mixing well. Add about one half of the remaining flour to the dough and beat until very smooth. Beat in

1 egg yolk
1 tablespoon lemon juice

Then beat in enough of the remaining flour to make a soft dough. Turn dough onto a lightly floured surface and let stand 5 to 10 min. Knead dough (page 11). Cover dough with inverted bowl and let rest about 15 min. in warm place.

Lightly flour rolling pin. Roll dough on a lightly floured surface into a rectangle ½ in. thick around edges, leaving center slightly thicker. Keep corners square, gently pulling dough into shape where necessary. With knife or spatula, loosen pastry from surface wherever sticking occurs; lift pastry slightly and sprinkle flour underneath.

Remove suet mixture from refrigerator; place on center of rolled dough. Fold edges of dough over suet mixture. Turn the dough upside down. Flatten with rolling pin, pressing down heavily while rolling. Make a rectangle about 14 in. long and 24 in. wide. Fold right third of dough over middle section. Fold left third over the right third. Let dough rest 5 min. Turn dough one quarter way around to have overlapping open edge away from you. Turn dough upside down. Again roll dough into rectangle about 14 in. long and 24 in. wide. Repeat folding, resting, turning one quarter way around, and turning dough upside down. Follow directions for shaping dough into Crescents, Squares or Biscuits. Place pastries onto baking sheets. Brush each pastry with

Egg, slightly beaten

Set pastry aside 15 min.; brush again with some of remaining egg.

Bake at 350°F 20 to 30 min., or until golden brown.   *About 3 doz. crescents or squares; about 2 doz. biscuits*

—SUET PASTRY CRESCENTS
(Hájas Kifli)

After second folding process in ▲ Recipe, roll dough into 3-in. squares. Set out ⅔ cup thick jam such as apricot or strawberry. Spoon about ¾ teaspoon jam diagonally across center of each square. Starting at one of the corners, roll each square and turn ends slightly toward middle to form crescents. Press ends slightly with fingers to completely seal in jam. Place crescents, with overlapping edges underneath, about 1 in. apart onto baking sheets.

—SUET PASTRY SQUARES
(Hájas Béles)

Follow recipe for Suet Pastry Crescents, but place jam at center of each square. Bring four corners of the square up toward center, pressing points together slightly with fingers to seal at the mid-point. Place squares about 1 in. apart onto baking sheets.

—SUET PASTRY BISCUITS
(Hájas Pogácsa)

After second folding process in ▲ Recipe, roll dough into a rectangle ½ in. thick. Score top of biscuit dough with sharp long-bladed knife by starting at upper left corner of rectangle and making diagonal cuts ⅛ in. deep and ¼ in. apart across dough. Repeat, starting at upper right corner. Cut biscuits with a lightly floured 2-in. biscuit cutter using an even pressure to keep sides of biscuits straight. Place biscuits about 1 in. apart onto baking sheets. Gather remaining dough by pushing pieces together without stacking. Avoid over-handling dough. Make top smooth with rolling pin. Make diagonal cuts across top of dough as before and cut out additional biscuits. Place on baking sheets.

Note: Caraway seed may be sprinkled onto top of biscuits just before baking.

CREAM ROLLS
(Cannoli)

It is said that in many Italian homes a thin broomstick is quickly converted to Cannoli "tubes" by cutting the broomstick into 6-in. lengths and scrubbing until the sticks are clean and smooth.

Set out six 6-in. aluminum tubes (about ¾-in. in diameter).

For Filling—Combine and beat until smooth

Cream Rolls

(about 10 min. with an electric mixer on medium-high speed)

3 cups (about 1½ lbs.) ricotta cheese
1¼ cups sugar
2 teaspoons vanilla extract

Stir in, mixing thoroughly

½ cup finely chopped candied citron
¼ cup semisweet chocolate pieces

Place mixture in refrigerator to chill.

For Shells—Sift together into a bowl

3 cups all-purpose flour
¼ cup sugar
1 teaspoon cinnamon
¼ teaspoon salt

Cut in with pastry blender until pieces are size of small peas

3 tablespoons shortening

Stir in

2 eggs, well beaten

Blend in, a tablespoon at a time

2 tablespoons white vinegar
2 tablespoons cold water

Turn dough onto a lightly floured surface and knead (page 11). Wrap in waxed paper and chill in refrigerator for 30 min.

Set out deep saucepan or automatic deep fryer for deep-frying (page 11) and heat **fat** to 360°F.

From cardboard, cut out an oval pattern (6x 4½-in.).

Blanch (page 9), finely chop and set aside

¼ to ½ cup (2 oz.) pistachio nuts

Roll chilled dough ⅛ in. thick on floured surface. With cardboard pattern and pastry cutter, cut ovals from dough.

Wrap dough loosely around tubes just lapping over opposite edges. Seal edges by brushing with

Egg white, slightly beaten

Press edges together to seal.

Fry only as many Cannoli shells as will float uncrowded one layer deep in the fat. Fry about 8 min., or until golden brown, turning occasionally during frying time. Drain over fat before removing to absorbent paper. Cool slightly and remove tubes. Cool completely.

When ready to serve, fill with ricotta filling. Sprinkle ends of Cannoli with chopped nuts and dust shells with

Sifted confectioners' sugar

16 to 18 Cannoli

HONEY CLUSTERS
(Strufoli)

Tiny balls—deep-fried and honey-coated— arranged in cone and cluster shapes and often used as a centerpiece on Christmas Day.

Set out deep saucepan or automatic deep fryer for deep-frying (page 11) and heat **fat** to 365°F.

Meanwhile, place in a large bowl
2 cups sifted all-purpose flour
¼ teaspoon salt
Make a well in center of flour. Add, one at a time, mixing slightly after each addition
3 eggs
Add
½ teaspoon vanilla extract
Mix well to make a soft dough.

Turn dough onto a lightly floured surface and knead (page 11). Divide dough into halves. Lightly roll each half ¼ in. thick to form a rectangle. Cut dough with a pastry cutter into strips ¼ in. wide. Use palm of hand to roll strips to pencil thickness. Cut into pieces about ¼ to ½ in. long.

Fry only as many pieces of dough as will float uncrowded, one layer deep in the fat. Fry 3 to 5 min., or until lightly browned, turning occasionally during frying time. Drain over fat before removing to absorbent paper.

Meanwhile, cook in skillet over low heat about 5 min.

1 cup honey
1 tablespoon sugar
Remove from heat and add deep-fried pieces. Stir constantly until all pieces are coated with honey-sugar mixture. Remove Strufoli with a

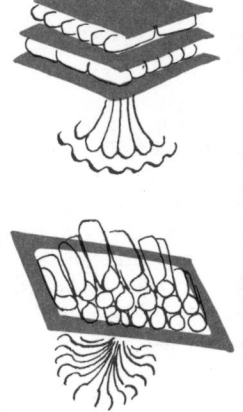

Honey Clusters

slotted spoon and set in refrigerator to chill slightly. Remove to a large serving platter and arrange in a cone-shape mound. Sprinkle with

1 tablespoon tiny multicolored candies
Chill in refrigerator. Serve by breaking off individual pieces. *8 to 10 servings*

STEAMED SWEET DUMPLINGS
(Dampfnudeln)

Set out a heavy 10-in. skillet with a tight-fitting cover.

Scald (page 10)
½ cup milk
Meanwhile, soften
½ pkg. (1 teaspoon) active dry yeast
in
2 tablespoons warm water, 105°F to 115°F (Or if using compressed yeast, soften ½ cake in 2 table-spoons lukewarm water, 80°F to 85°F.)
Set aside.

Put into a large bowl
¼ cup butter
⅓ cup sugar
¼ teaspoon salt

Immediately pour scalded milk over ingredients in bowl. When lukewarm, blend in, beating until smooth
1 cup sifted all-purpose flour
Stir softened yeast and add, mixing well.

Measure
2 to 2½ cups sifted all-purpose flour
Add about one half the flour to the yeast mixture and beat until very smooth. Beat in
2 eggs, well beaten

Then beat in enough of the remaining flour to make a soft dough. Turn dough onto a lightly floured surface and let rest 5 to 10 min.

Knead (page 11). Form dough into a large ball and place in a greased deep bowl. Turn dough to bring greased surface to top. Cover with waxed paper and a towel and let stand in warm place (about 80°F) until dough is doubled.

Punch down and turn dough out onto lightly floured surface. Shape dough into balls about 1 in. in diameter. Cover with waxed paper and a towel and let rise on rolling surface until balls are doubled.

Put into the skillet
1½ cups milk
1 tablespoon butter
1 tablespoon sugar
Put about eight of the balls into the skillet. Do not set them too close together. Cover and cook over high heat until steam appears. Reduce heat and cook 30 min., or until steaming stops. Do not remove cover during cooking!

Carefully remove dumplings with a slotted spoon to serving dishes and serve with
Cherry Sauce II (page 578) or Wine Sauce (page 576)

About 24 dumplings

COTTAGE CHEESE PLUM DUMPLINGS
(Pflaumenknödel aus Topfenteig)

Force through a food mill or sieve into a bowl
½ lb. (about 1 cup, firmly packed) dry cottage cheese

Honey Clusters: Cut dough into strips ¼ in. thick with a pastry cutter on a lightly floured surface. Cut dough strips (rolled to thickness of a pencil) into pieces one-fourth to one-half inch in length.

Sift together and set aside
  1 cup sifted all-purpose flour
  ¼ teaspoon salt

Prepare (page 10) and set aside
  3 cups (4 to 5 slices) soft bread crumbs

Cream until softened
  2 tablespoons butter
Add in thirds, beating well after each addition
  2 eggs, well beaten
Blend in the cottage cheese and the bread crumbs. Add the dry ingredients, beating thoroughly. Set in refrigerator 1 hr.

Meanwhile, rinse, cut almost into halves and remove pits from
  4 small blue plums
Set out
  4 cubes of loaf sugar
Insert one of the cubes of sugar into each plum.

When dough is chilled, divide into four portions. Shape one portion of the dough around each plum, being sure the plum is completely sealed in.

Heat to boiling in a large heavy saucepan
  2 qts. water
Carefully drop the dumplings into the boiling water. Cook about 10 min., or until dumplings rise to the surface. Remove carefully with a slotted spoon and serve with
  Vanilla Sauce III (page 576)

4 servings

DESSERT PANCAKES

SWEDISH PANCAKES
(Plättar)

▲ Base Recipe

Set out a griddle or large heavy skillet. A Swedish platt pan (available at most department stores) may be used for these pancakes.

Sift together into a large bowl and set aside
  1½ cups sifted all-purpose flour
  3 tablespoons sugar
  ½ teaspoon salt

Beat in a bowl until thick and piled softly
  3 eggs
Beat in until blended
  2 cups milk
  2 tablespoons melted butter

Add to dry ingredients and beat until smooth.

Heat griddle over low heat; it is hot enough when drops of water sprinkled on surface dance in small beads. Lightly grease with
  Butter

For each pancake, spoon about 1 tablespoon batter onto griddle or skillet (pancakes should be about 2½ to 3 in. in diameter). Cook each pancake over medium heat until lightly browned on bottom. Loosen edges with a spatula, turn, and lightly brown second side. As each pancake is cooked, transfer to a heated plate. Arrange pancakes in a circle, slightly overlapping each other. In center, set a bowl of
  Lingonberry preserves

5 doz. 3-in. pancakes

—APPLE PANCAKE CAKE
(Pannkakstårta)

Follow ▲ Recipe. Prepare six 8-in. pancakes. As each pancake is cooked, transfer it to a platter; spread with **¼ cup thick sweetened applesauce.** Do not spread applesauce on top pancake. (Remaining batter may be used for plättar.) Chill. Prepare **Sweetened Whipped Cream** (page 480; use 1 cup chilled heavy cream). Frost pancake stack with cream. Chill in refrigerator until ready to serve. Cut into wedges.

6 to 8 servings

FILLED PANCAKES
(Palacsinta)

▲ Base Recipe

For Filling—Prepare and set aside
  Ground walnuts or roasted almonds, grated semisweet chocolate, vanilla granulated sugar, and/or set out
  1 to 1½ cups thick jam, such as apricot or peach

For Batter—Set out a 6-in. skillet.

Sift together into a bowl
  1 cup sifted all-purpose flour
  1½ teaspoons sugar
  ⅛ teaspoon salt

Mix
  1 egg, slightly beaten
  1 cup milk
  ½ teaspoon vanilla extract
Make a well in center of the dry ingredients and add milk mixture. Beat mixture with rotary beater until smooth.

Heat the skillet until moderately hot. Test skillet; it is hot enough when drops of water dance in small beads on surface. Lightly butter skillet. Remove skillet from heat; pour in 2 to 2½ tablespoons batter, or just enough batter to cover bottom of skillet. Immediately tilt skillet back and forth to spread batter thinly and evenly. (Batter should be *very thin* at all times so that it will spread easily. Stir in a small amount of additional milk from time to time because batter thickens on standing.)

Fry pancake over medium heat until lightly browned on bottom. Loosen edges with spatula. Turn pancake and brown second side; invert onto a warm plate. Repeat with remainder of batter, buttering skillet lightly for each pancake.

While one pancake is frying, spread baked pancake with 2 tablespoons filling; roll. Transfer to warm platter and keep pancakes warm by placing in a 350°F oven. Serve pancakes warm, sprinkle with
  Confectioners' sugar

14 to 16 pancakes

—PANCAKES BAKED WITH SOUR CREAM
(Palacsinta Tejföllel)

Follow ▲ Recipe. Omit confectioners' sugar. Place rolled and filled pancakes one layer deep in buttered shallow baking dish about 13x9x2 in. Spoon **2 cups dairy sour cream** evenly over them. Bake uncovered at 350°F 25 to 30 min., or until thoroughly heated.

CREAM CHEESE CREPES

Melt in a 6-in. skillet and set aside to cool
  1 tablespoon butter

Sift together into a bowl and set aside
  1 cup sifted all-purpose flour
  2 tablespoons sugar
  ¼ teaspoon salt

Beat until fluffy
  6 oz. cream cheese
Blend in until smooth
  3 eggs, well beaten
  1½ cups milk
Beat in the melted butter and
  1 teaspoon grated orange peel
Combine egg mixture with dry ingredients and beat with rotary beater until smooth.

Heat skillet; it is hot enough when a few drops cold water dropped on it dance rapidly in small beads. Pour in about 2 tablespoons batter for each crêpe. Immediately tilt skillet back and forth to spread batter thinly and evenly. Cook each crêpe over medium heat until lightly browned on bottom and firm to touch on top. Loosen edges with spatula. Turn and brown second side. (It should be unnecessary to grease the skillet for each crêpe.)

As each crêpe is cooked transfer it to a hot platter. Roll up the crêpes and set them in oven to keep warm.

When all are cooked, sift over tops
Confectioners' sugar

6 to 8 servings

APPLE PANCAKES
(Apfelpfannkuchen)

Set out a 10-in. skillet.

Wash, quarter, core and pare
3 small firm cooking apples (about 2½ cups, sliced)
Thinly slice the apples. Heat in the skillet over low heat
¼ cup butter
Add apple slices, cover and cook over medium heat until apples are almost tender, moving and turning slices with a spoon several times during cooking. When apple slices are almost tender, sprinkle over them and gently blend in a mixture of
2 tablespoons sugar
1 teaspoon cinnamon
Continue cooking, uncovered, until apples are *just* tender. Turn apple mixture into a bowl and set aside to keep warm.

Sift together into a bowl and set aside
½ cup sifted all-purpose flour
1 tablespoon sugar
¼ teaspoon salt

Beat until thick and piled softly
4 eggs
Beat in
⅓ cup milk
Combine egg mixture with dry ingredients and beat with rotary beater until smooth. Set aside.

Set out
6 tablespoons butter
Add 3 tablespoons of the butter to the skillet and heat until moderately hot.

Spoon in enough batter to cover bottom of skillet. Spoon about one half of apple mixture evenly over batter. Spoon in more batter, to just cover apples. Cook pancake over medium heat until golden brown on bottom. Loosen edges with spatula. Carefully turn and brown other side.

When pancake is cooked, remove skillet from heat and brush pancake generously with
Melted butter
Roll up pancake and transfer to a warm platter. Sift over top
Confectioners' sugar
Keep pancake hot. Repeat procedure.

2 Apple Pancakes

SOUR CREAM APPLE ROLL-UPS

▲ **Base Recipe**

Set out a 6-in. skillet.

Melt and set aside to cool
2 tablespoons butter or margarine

Sift together into a bowl and set aside
1½ cups sifted all-purpose flour
3 tablespoons sugar
2 teaspoons baking powder
½ teaspoon salt

Beat until thick and piled softly
1 egg
Beat in the cooled butter and
1½ cups milk
Combine egg mixture and dry ingredients. With rotary beater, beat until smooth and well blended.

Wash, quarter, core, pare and chop finely
1 large apple
Add the apple to batter and blend until apple is evenly distributed.

Heat the 6-in. skillet; it is hot enough when drops of water sprinkled on surface dance in small beads. Grease skillet lightly with
Butter or margarine
Spoon about ¼ cup batter into skillet. Quickly spread batter evenly with spoon. Cook pancake over medium heat until lightly browned; turn and brown second side. Repeat until all batter is used.

To keep pancakes warm, stack pancakes and place in 300°F oven while remaining pancakes are cooking. (It should not be necessary to grease skillet for each pancake.)

Set out
3 cups dairy sour cream
Fill pancakes with the sour cream, reserving remainder of cream. Wrap pancakes around filling to form rolls.

Before serving, sift over roll-ups
1 tablespoon confectioners' sugar
Serve with reserved sour cream.

About 12 pancake roll-ups

—SOUR CREAM RASPBERRY ROLL-UPS

Prepare **Raspberry Sauce** (page 580). Follow ▲ Recipe. Decrease sour cream to 1 cup and fold 1 cup of the sauce into the sour cream.

STRAWBERRY PANCAKES
(Palacsinta Földieperrel)

These large, fluffy pancakes are served as a main dish. Their delicate flavor is enhanced by the natural sweetness of the ripe strawberries. Savory pancakes topped and filled with dewy-fresh berries are certain to make a hit when served as dessert too!

Set out a griddle or a heavy 10-in. skillet.

Wash and remove blemishes from
1 qt. fully ripe strawberries

Sour Cream Apple Roll-Ups

Set 18 berries aside to garnish serving plates; hull and slice remaining berries, place them in refrigerator.

Sift together into a bowl and set aside
1¼ cups sifted all-purpose flour
⅛ teaspoon salt

Beat with rotary beater to blend
2 eggs, well beaten
½ cup milk
½ teaspoon vanilla extract

Set griddle over low heat.

Make a well in center of dry ingredients. Add egg mixture, stirring batter only until blended; set batter aside.

Beat until frothy
2 egg whites
Add gradually, beating well after each addition
4 teaspoons sugar
Beat until stiff peaks are formed. Carefully fold egg whites into batter.

Test griddle; it is hot enough for baking when drops of water sprinkled on surface dance in small beads. Lightly grease griddle if manufacturer so directs. For each pancake, pour about 1 cup of the batter onto griddle. Immediately tilt griddle back and forth to spread batter evenly. If necessary, use spatula to spread batter. Cook until pancake is puffy, full of bubbles and golden brown on underside. Turn only once and brown other side. Transfer pancakes to a warm platter and keep them warm by placing between folds of absorbent paper in a 350°F oven.

Strawberry Pancake

525

When all the pancakes are cooked, remove strawberries from refrigerator. Mix one half of the sliced berries with

2 tablespoons sugar

Spoon about ½ cup of the sweetened strawberries onto each pancake and roll. Place pancakes onto individual plates. Sprinkle each with

Confectioners' sugar

Arrange remaining sliced strawberries over the top of pancakes. Garnish plates with the whole strawberries. Serve immediately.   *3 servings*

EMPEROR'S DESSERT
(Kaiserschmarren)

▲ Base Recipe

For Pancakes—Lightly butter a 6-in. skillet.

Melt

2 tablespoons butter

Sift together into a bowl

1 cup sifted all-purpose flour
¼ cup sugar
¼ teaspoon salt

Beat until thick and piled softly

3 eggs

Beat in the melted butter and

1 cup milk

Combine egg mixture with dry ingredients and beat with rotary beater until smooth.

Heat skillet moderately hot. Pour in just enough batter to cover bottom. Immediately tilt skillet back and forth to spread batter thinly and evenly.

Cook over medium heat until light brown on bottom and firm to touch on top. Loosen edge with spatula. Turn and brown second side. It should be unnecessary to grease skillet for each pancake.

As each pancake is cooked, transfer to a hot platter. When all are cooked, set platter in warm oven to keep pancakes warm.

For Sauce—Melt over low heat in a saucepan

¾ cup butter

Stir in

½ cup golden raisins
½ teaspoon cinnamon

Add and mix very lightly

¾ to 1 cup sugar

Do not stir sugar too much. It should not be dissolved in the butter.

To Complete Dessert—Tear pancakes with two forks into 1-in. pieces. Mix into the sauce.

8 to 10 servings

—EMPEROR'S DESSERT WITH NUTS
(Kaiserschmarren mit Nüssen)

Follow ▲ Recipe. Stir into sauce ¾ **cup toasted flaked almonds or other nuts**, chopped.

MERINGUE DESSERTS

SAVOY MERINGUES
(Meringues de Savoie)

▲ Base Recipe

Line bottom of baking sheet with unglazed paper.

Beat until frothy

2 egg whites

Add and beat slightly

1 teaspoon vanilla extract
½ teaspoon cream of tartar
¼ teaspoon salt

Add gradually, beating well after each addition

½ cup sugar

Beat until stiff peaks are formed when beater is slowly lifted upright.

Drop 6 large or 18 small mounds from spoon onto baking sheet, allowing 2 in. between mounds. Hollow out centers to form meringue shells or nests. (Or, force meringue through pastry bag and a No. 7 star tube to form shells.) Sprinkle each with about

½ teaspoon sifted confectioners' sugar (use less for smaller shells)

Bake at 250°F about 1 hr., or until dry to touch.

Carefully remove meringues at once with a spatula and turn upside down onto same paper-lined pan. (If meringues are difficult to remove

from paper, raise paper from baking sheet. Lightly moisten underside of paper directly under each meringue; carefully remove them at once with a spatula. This makes it necessary to re-line baking sheet with dry paper.)

Return to oven 5 min. to complete drying. Cool on rack.

Fill with **ice cream, sherbet, cream filling** or **fruit**; garnish with **fruit, whipped cream** or **chopped nuts**.

6 large or 18 small meringue shells

—MERINGUE MUSHROOMS
(Meringues Garnies)

Follow ▲ Recipe only to the directions for shaping. For mushroom caps, force one half the mixture through a pastry bag and a No. 7 plain tube into small (about 2 in.) low, rounded mounds on lined baking sheet. For stems, force remaining mixture through tube into an equal number of small pyramids. Bake and remove from paper as directed.

With a pointed knife carefully make a small hollow in bottom of each cap. Fill caps with **Chantilly Cream** (page 481) or **Almond Pastry Cream** (page 483) and join to stems. Sprinkle caps lightly with grated **unsweetened chocolate**.   *About 1 doz. Meringue Mushrooms*

Savoy Meringues

CHOCOLATE-TOPPED MERINGUE

Mix in the top of a double boiler
> ½ cup sugar
> ¼ cup cocoa
> ¼ teaspoon salt

Add and stir until smooth
> ¾ cup milk

Continue stirring and add
> 1 cup milk

Place over direct heat. Stir constantly and gently while bringing rapidly to boiling. Place over boiling water.

Vigorously stir about 3 tablespoons of hot mixture into
> 3 egg yolks, slightly beaten

Immediately blend egg yolk mixture into hot mixture in double boiler. Stir constantly and rapidly. Cook over boiling water until mixture coats a metal spoon. Remove from heat. Stir in
> 1 tablespoon butter
> 2 teaspoons vanilla extract

Pour into bowl. Cover. Chill in refrigerator.

Before serving, prepare a meringue by beating until frothy
> 3 egg whites
> ⅛ teaspoon salt

Add gradually and beat well after each addition
> ⅓ cup sugar

Continue beating until very stiff peaks are formed. Heap meringue lightly into serving dishes. Top with chilled chocolate custard.

5 servings

MERINGUE TORTE
(Schaumtorte)

Grease bottoms only of two 9-in. round layer cake pans with removable bottoms, or line two 9-in. round layer cake pans with unglazed paper cut to fit pan bottoms.

Beat until frothy
> 6 egg whites

Add and beat slightly
> 2 teaspoons vinegar
> 1 teaspoon vanilla extract
> ½ teaspoon almond extract
> ¼ teaspoon salt

Add about 2 tablespoons at a time, beating well after each addition
> 2 cups sugar

Continue beating until very stiff peaks are formed. Turn equal amounts of meringue into the pans and spread evenly to edges.

Bake at 300°F 40 min. Turn off oven and open oven door about 1 or 2 in. Allow torte layers to dry out in oven 30 min. with door partially open. Completely cool torte layers on cooling racks before removing from pans. Remove from pans as directed (page 11) for torte layers. (It is likely that top surface may become slightly cracked when torte is being removed from pans.)

Just before serving, prepare
> Sweetened Whipped Cream
> (three-fourths recipe, page 480)

(If desired, sweetened berries or other fruit may be folded into the whipped cream.) Place one torte layer on a serving plate. Spread the whipped cream evenly over it. Top with second torte layer. Fresh berries arranged on the plate around the torte make an attractive dessert.

12 servings

LEMON OR ORANGE ANGEL PIE

▲ Base Recipe

Steaming black coffee is the perfect accompaniment to this heavenly dessert with alluring beauty and freshness.

Lightly grease a 9-in. pie pan or pie plate.

For Meringue Pie Shell—Beat until frothy
> 4 egg whites

Add and beat slightly
> ½ teaspoon cream of tartar

Add 2 tablespoons at a time, beating well after each addition
> 1 cup sugar

Continue beating meringue until very stiff peaks are formed.

Spread a 1-in. thick layer of meringue on bottom of pie pan. Pile remaining meringue around edge of pan and swirl with spatula to form sides of shell.

Bake the meringue shell at 275°F for 1½ hrs. Turn off oven heat and leave meringue in oven

1 hr. (Do not open oven door at any time.) Remove meringue shell from the oven, place on a cooling rack and cool completely in pan. Gently remove the shell from pie pan and if not used immediately store it in an airtight container so meringue will not absorb moisture and become soft.

The meringue shell should be crisp, dry and have a very fine texture.

For Lemon or Orange Pie Filling—Set out a small double boiler.

Spoon into a small cup or custard cup
> 4 teaspoons cold water

Sprinkle evenly over cold water
> 1 teaspoon unflavored gelatin

Set aside to soften.

Beat together in a bowl until thick and piled softly
> 4 egg yolks
> 2 eggs
> 1 cup sugar

Mix, add gradually to egg yolk mixture and stir until well blended
> 2 tablespoons grated lemon peel or
> orange peel
> ⅓ cup lemon juice or orange juice
> ⅓ cup water

Pour into top of double boiler and place over boiling water. Cook, stirring constantly, until thick. Remove top of double boiler from simmering water. Immediately stir in softened gelatin until it is completely dissolved. Chill in refrigerator or over ice and water until mixture is partially set.

When mixture is of desired consistency, spoon into meringue shell. Place in refrigerator to chill just until mixture is completely set. (Filled meringue shells tend to become soggy if chilled too long.)

Put a rotary beater and small bowl in refrigerator to chill.

A few minutes before serving, beat using the chilled bowl and beater, until cream stands in peaks when beater is lifted slowly upright
> 1 cup chilled heavy cream

Spread whipped cream over lemon filling.

Serve immediately with cups of fragrant, delicious coffee.

About 8 servings

Lemon Angel Pie

Chocolate Angel Pie Sensation

—PINEAPPLE ANGEL PIE

Follow ▲ Recipe. Omit peel and ⅓ cup water. Reduce lemon juice to 2 tablespoons and mix with ⅔ **cup pineapple juice.**

—RASPBERRY ANGEL PIE

Follow ▲ Recipe. Omit peel and ⅓ cup water. Reduce lemon juice to 1 tablespoon and sugar to ½ cup. Thaw and drain **2 pkgs. (10 oz. each) frozen red raspberries.** Mix ⅔ cup of the raspberry juice with the one tablespoon lemon juice before mixing into egg yolk mixture in filling. Use drained raspberries for topping; fold them into the whipped cream before spreading over pie.

—CHOCOLATE ANGEL PIE SENSATION

Here is a dusky beauty, flavored with the magic that only chocolate and rum can give. It's called an angel pie for the simple reason that it is hard to imagine a more heavenly dessert this side of paradise.

Follow ▲ Recipe for Meringue Pie Shell. Omit Lemon or Orange Pie Filling. Spoon Chocolate Filling into shell. Put pie into refrigerator just until thoroughly chilled.

For Chocolate Filling—Put a bowl and a rotary beater into refrigerator to chill.

Melt (page 10) and set aside to cool
4 oz. sweet chocolate

Using the chilled bowl and beater, beat until cream is of medium consistency (piles softly)
1 cup chilled heavy cream
Blend into the cooled chocolate
3 tablespoons rum
½ teaspoon vanilla extract
Spread the chocolate mixture over the whipped cream and gently fold together. Turn into the cooled meringue shell.

CREAMY PEACHES

▲ Base Recipe

Butter a 1½-qt. casserole.

Cut into 1-in. squares, cover and set aside
5 slices sponge or pound cake, ½ in. thick

Set out to drain
1 can (17 oz.) sliced peaches (1½ cups)

For Custard—Scald (page 10)
2 cups milk

Meanwhile, separate egg yolks from egg whites of
4 eggs
Put whites of 2 eggs in a medium-size bowl; set aside for use in meringue. (Cover and refrigerate extra egg whites for future use.)

Beat egg yolks slightly and blend in
¼ cup sugar
⅛ teaspoon salt
Gradually pour milk into egg mixture, stirring vigorously at first; strain through a fine sieve into top of double boiler. Cook over boiling water, stirring constantly and rapidly, until mixture coats a metal spoon. Remove from water at once; blend in
1 teaspoon vanilla extract
½ teaspoon almond extract

For Casserole—Arrange one third of cake squares over bottom of casserole; sprinkle with
2 to 3 tablespoons chopped nuts
Cover with 1 cup of drained peaches. Repeat and top with remaining cake squares. Pour in cool custard sauce. Set aside to cool.

For Meringue—Add to the 2 reserved egg whites
⅛ teaspoon salt
Beat until frothy. Add
½ teaspoon almond extract or vanilla extract

Add gradually, beating well after each addition
¼ cup sugar
Beat until stiff peaks are formed. Pile meringue lightly over cooled pudding.

Bake at 350°F 10 to 15 min., or until meringue is delicately browned. *6 servings*

—BANANA CREAM DESSERT

Follow ▲ Recipe. Substitute **3 (about 1 lb.) bananas** having all-yellow or brown-flecked peel, sliced, for peaches. Increase vanilla extract to 1½ teaspoons. Omit almond extract.

CUSTARDS AND PUDDINGS

SOFT CUSTARD

▲ Base Recipe

Scald (page 10) in top of double boiler
2 cups milk

Meanwhile, beat slightly
4 egg yolks
Blend in
¼ cup sugar
⅛ teaspoon salt
Gradually stir hot milk into eggs. Strain and return to double boiler. Cook over simmering water, stirring constantly and rapidly until mixture coats a metal spoon. Remove from heat at once. Blend in
2 teaspoons vanilla extract
Pour immediately into 6 sherbet glasses. Set aside to cool until lukewarm and immediately chill in refrigerator.

Sprinkle with **chopped nuts,** if desired.
6 servings

—CUSTARD WITH BRITTLE

Follow ▲ Recipe. Crush ½ **cup nut brittle.** Spoon ¼ cup into sherbet glasses. Pour in Soft Custard and top with the remaining ¼ cup crushed nut brittle.

—MINTY CUSTARD

Follow ▲ Recipe. Just before serving, prepare **Sweetened Whipped Cream** (one half recipe, page 480). Add **1 or 2 drops peppermint extract** with vanilla extract. Alternate layers of custard and whipped cream in sherbet glasses, ending with whipped cream.

—BROWNIE CUSTARD

Follow ▲ Recipe. Put ½ **cup brownie crumbs** into sherbet glasses. Pour custard over crumbs. Sprinkle a few crumbs over the top.

—FRUIT CUSTARD

Follow ▲ Recipe. Pour custard over **orange sections** or **well-drained fruit.**

—DATE CUSTARD

Follow ▲ Recipe. Cut **8 pitted dates** into slivers. Reserving a few date slivers for garnish, place remaining dates in sherbet glasses. Pour in Soft Custard; garnish servings with reserved dates.

—FLOATING ISLAND

Follow ▲ Recipe. Beat **3 egg whites** until frothy. Add **¼ teaspoon salt** and **½ teaspoon vanilla extract**. Gradually add **6 tablespoons sugar**, beating well after each addition and continuing to beat until rounded peaks are formed. Drop by tablespoonfuls into simmering (not boiling) water in a large saucepan. Cover. Cook about 5 min., or until set. Remove meringues and drain on absorbent paper. Float on chilled Soft Custard just before serving.

BLANCMANGE

▲ Base Recipe

Set out a 1-qt. mold.

Scald (page 10)
1½ cups milk

Meanwhile, mix in a saucepan
⅓ cup sugar
3 tablespoons cornstarch
⅛ teaspoon salt
Stir in
½ cup cold milk
Gradually add scalded milk, stirring constantly. Stirring gently and constantly, bring mixture rapidly to boiling over direct heat. Cook 3 min.

Wash double boiler top to remove scum.

Pour mixture into double boiler top; place over simmering water. Cover and cook about 7 min., stirring three or four times.

Remove cornstarch mixture from heat. Cool slightly.

Blancmange

Meanwhile, beat until rounded peaks are formed
4 egg whites
Blend into cornstarch mixture
1 teaspoon vanilla extract
Spread beaten egg whites over mixture and fold together. Turn into mold and chill in refrigerator until firm.

When ready to serve, unmold (page 374) and serve with fruit or
Sweetened Whipped Cream (page 480)

4 to 6 servings

—COCONUT BLANCMANGE

Follow ▲ Recipe. With extract, blend in **1 cup finely chopped shredded coconut.**

—FRUIT BLANCMANGE

Follow ▲ Recipe. Blend in **1 cup well-drained canned or sweetened fresh fruit** with extract.

ZABAIONE

An international favorite, this rich wine dessert has many adapted variations using many different ingredients. Here is an Italian version containing egg yolks, sugar, and Marsala beaten to a light foam.

Set out a double boiler.

Beat until thick and lemon-colored
6 egg yolks
½ cup sugar
Stir in
1 cup Marsala
Pour mixture into top of double boiler, and set over simmering water. Beat constantly with rotary beater until mixture is very light and begins to thicken. When mixture begins to rise, remove from heat.

Serve either hot or cold in sherbet glasses.

6 servings

TIPSY SQUIRE

Chill a bowl and rotary beater in refrigerator.

Have ready
Hot-Milk Sponge Cake (page 454; use one layer and reserve remainder for other use)

Blanch (page 9) and split into halves lengthwise
½ cup (about 3 oz.) almonds
Set aside.

Prepare and cool
Soft Custard (page 528)
Put the cake into a casserole or serving dish. Poke almonds upright into cake. Pour over all
1 cup sherry
Pour custard over the cake.

Using chilled bowl and beater, beat until cream is of medium consistency (piles softly)
1 cup chilled heavy cream

Floating Island

Beat into whipped cream with final few strokes
2 tablespoons sherry
1 tablespoon confectioners' sugar
Spread whipped cream over the custard; chill thoroughly.
8 to 10 servings

DATE VANILLA CREAM

▲ Base Recipe

Chop and set aside
⅓ lb. pitted dates (about 1 cup, chopped)

Scald (page 10) in double boiler top
1¾ cups milk

Meanwhile, mix in a saucepan
⅔ cup sugar
3 tablespoons cornstarch
¼ teaspoon salt
Stir in
¼ cup cold milk
Gradually add scalded milk, stirring constantly.

Stirring gently and constantly, bring mixture rapidly to boiling over direct heat. Cook the mixture 3 min.

Pour mixture into double boiler top; place over simmering water. Cover and cook about 5 min., stirring three or four times.

Vigorously stir about 3 tablespoons hot mixture into
3 egg yolks, slightly beaten

Immediately blend into mixture in double boiler. Cook over simmering water 3 to 5 min.; stir slowly to keep mixture cooking evenly. Remove from heat and stir in the chopped dates and

3 tablespoons butter
2 teaspoons vanilla extract

Cool slightly.

Pour into serving dishes. Cover and chill in refrigerator until ready to serve.

Top with

Sweetened Whipped Cream
(page 480)

o servings

—MAPLE CREAM PUDDING

Follow ▲ Recipe. Substitute **1 cup maple syrup** for sugar and heat with milk. Omit dates and vanilla extract. Top servings with ⅓ cup **(about 2 oz.) coarsely chopped hazelnuts.**

SMALL VANILLA CUSTARDS
(Petits Pots de Crème à la Vanille)

▲ Base Recipe

The French were so proud of this dessert that they designed special, little, handleless cups for serving it.

Set out 6 *petits pots* or individual custard cups.

Scald (page 10)
2 cups milk or cream
1 piece vanilla bean, 1 in. long

Meanwhile, beat slightly
6 egg yolks
Stir in
6 to 8 tablespoons sugar

Slowly add scalded milk, stirring vigorously and constantly. Strain. Pour into the little French earthenware pots. Set filled pots in a large baking pan. Pour very hot water into pan to a 1-in. depth.

Bake at 325°F 30 to 45 min., or until a metal knife comes out clean when inserted in custard halfway between center and edge of cup. Chill in refrigerator before serving.

Serve with **Macaroons** (page 587) or other crisp cookies.

6 servings

—SOFT VANILLA CUSTARDS
(Crème Anglaise)

Follow ▲ Recipe. Chill six French earthenware pots or custard cups. Pour strained custard mixture into top of double boiler. Stir constantly and rapidly over simmering water until mixture is thickened and coats a metal spoon. Pour into chilled cups. Cover. Chill in refrigerator before serving.

—COFFEE CUSTARDS
(Crème Anglaise au Moka)

Follow ▲ Recipe or prepare Soft Vanilla Custards. Omit vanilla bean and add **1 tablespoon strong coffee beverage.**

—SOFT CHOCOLATE CUSTARDS
(Crème Anglaise au Chocolat)

Follow recipe for Soft Vanilla Custards. Add **2 oz. (2 sq.) unsweetened chocolate** to milk. Heat until chocolate is melted.

POTS DE CREME CHOCOLAT

▲ Base Recipe

Choice custard, soft or baked, a memorable chocolate treat of historic importance.

Set out 6 heat-resistant custard cups.

Heat over simmering water until milk or cream is scalded (page 10) and chocolate melted
3 cups milk or cream
2½ oz. (2½ sq.) unsweetened chocolate
Set aside.

Beat slightly
5 egg yolks
Stir in
¾ cup sugar

Add hot chocolate mixture slowly, stirring vigorously and constantly. Strain. Blend in
1 tablespoon vanilla extract

Pour into custard cups. Set the filled custard cups in a large baking pan. Pour very hot water into pan to a 1-in. depth.

Bake at 325°F 30 to 40 min., or until a metal knife inserted in custard comes out clean.

6 servings

—CREME AU CHOCOLAT

Follow ▲ Recipe. Pour strained custard mixture into top of double boiler and continue to cook over simmering water, stirring constantly and rapidly, until mixture coats a metal spoon. Remove from heat at once. Cool. Blend in vanilla extract. Pour into custard cups or serving dish. Mixture will be the consistency of heavy cream. Chill in refrigerator. Serve with **Sweetened Whipped Cream** (page 480).

SPECIAL BAKED CUSTARD

▲ Base Recipe

Set out a 1½-qt. casserole.

Scald (page 10)
2 cups milk
1½ cups cream or milk

Meanwhile, beat slightly
5 eggs (or 10 egg yolks)
Blend in
6 tablespoons sugar
1 tablespoon vanilla extract
¼ teaspoon salt

Gradually add milk, stirring vigorously and constantly; stir until sugar is dissolved. Strain through a fine sieve into casserole. Sprinkle with

Nutmeg

Set casserole in a baking pan. Pour very hot water into pan to a 1-in. depth.

Bake at 325°F 40 to 50 min., or until a metal knife comes out clean when inserted in custard halfway between center and edge of casserole. Remove from water to cooling rack. Chill in refrigerator until time to serve. *6 or 7 servings*

—HIDDEN SURPRISE HONEY CUSTARD

Follow ▲ Recipe. Substitute ½ **cup honey** for sugar. Omit vanilla extract. Arrange over bottom of 2-qt. casserole **2 cups well-drained canned sliced peaches;** sprinkle with **3 tablespoons ground nuts.** Cut **8 marshmallows** into quarters and arrange them over nuts and peaches. Pour custard over marshmallows. Omit nutmeg. Bake at 325°F about 1 hr.

—CUSTARD BRULEE

Follow ▲ Recipe; use a shallow 1½-qt. casserole. Omit nutmeg. Cool the baked custard and chill it in the refrigerator. When chilled, sift ⅔ **cup firmly packed brown sugar** evenly over top of custard. Place custard under broiler with top of custard 3 in. from heat; broil until sugar is bubbly. Watch carefully so sugar will not burn. Cool and then chill in refrigerator several hours before serving.

CREME BRULEE

Set out a 1-qt. baking dish.

Scald (page 10)
2 cups heavy cream
Meanwhile, beat slightly
4 egg yolks
Blend in
¼ cup sugar

Stirring constantly, gradually add hot cream to egg yolk mixture. Stir until sugar is dissolved. Blend in
2 teaspoons vanilla extract

Strain the mixture into the baking dish. Set in a large baking pan and pour very hot water into pan to a 1 in. depth.

Bake at 325°F 50 min., or until a metal knife comes out clean when inserted in custard halfway between center and edge.

Remove from the water. Set on a cooling rack until lukewarm. Chill thoroughly in refrigerator.

When chilled, remove from refrigerator and sift evenly over top

**½ cup firmly packed maple sugar
or brown sugar**

Place chilled crème under broiler with top 5 in. from heat; broil until sugar is bubbly. Watch carefully so sugar will not burn. Cool and place in refrigerator to chill.

6 to 8 servings

FLAN
(Baked Custard)

▲ *Base Recipe*

Set out a 1-qt. baking dish or mold.

Scald (page 10)

2 cups milk

Meanwhile, beat slightly

3 eggs

Mix in

¼ cup sugar

Stirring constantly, gradually add hot milk to the egg mixture. Stir until sugar is dissolved. Blend in

1 teaspoon vanilla extract

Strain the mixture into the baking dish. Set in a large baking pan and pour very hot water into pan to a 1-in. depth.

Bake at 325°F 55 to 60 min., or until a metal knife comes out clean when inserted in custard halfway between center and edge. Remove carefully from the water. Set on a cooling rack until lukewarm. Chill thoroughly in refrigerator.

6 servings

—CARAMEL CUSTARD

Prepare **Caramelized Sugar** (below). Pour it into the baking dish. Quickly tilt baking dish until bottom is evenly coated. Set aside. Follow ▲ Recipe. When ready to serve, unmold by running a knife around inside edge of baking dish; invert onto a chilled serving dish. Top of mold will be caramel-coated and excess coating will run down sides to form a sauce at base of custard.

For Caramelized Sugar—Put **½ cup sugar** into a heavy light-colored skillet (a black skillet makes it difficult to see the color of the syrup) over low heat. With back of a wooden spoon keep sugar moving constantly in skillet until sugar is completely melted, and of a golden-brown color (caramelized).

LIME SPONGE

▲ *Base Recipe*

Set out six 6-oz. custard cups.

Mix together until thoroughly blended

**3 egg yolks
1 to 2 teaspoons grated lime peel
¼ cup lime juice
1 tablespoon butter or margarine,
melted
⅓ cup sugar**

Stir in

1 cup milk

Blend in a bowl

**2 tablespoons all-purpose flour
⅛ teaspoon salt**

Blend egg-milk mixture with flour.

Beat until stiff, not dry, peaks are formed

3 egg whites

Fold beaten egg whites into egg-milk mixture. Turn into the custard cups. Set filled cups in a large baking pan. Pour very hot water into pan to a 1-in. depth.

Bake at 350°F 35 to 40 min., or until puffed and golden brown and a metal knife comes out clean when inserted halfway between center and edge of custard. Serve immediately, or cool and chill in the refrigerator. *6 servings*

—LEMON SPONGE

Follow ▲ Recipe. Substitute **lemon peel and juice** for lime peel and juice.

TAPIOCA CREAM

▲ *Base Recipe*

Set out a 1-qt. saucepan.

Beat until frothy

2 egg whites

Caramel Custard

Add gradually, beating well after each addition

¼ cup sugar

Beat until very stiff peaks are formed.

Put into the saucepan

2 egg yolks, slightly beaten

Mix in

**2 cups milk
⅓ cup quick-cooking tapioca
⅓ cup sugar
¼ teaspoon salt**

Let stand 5 min. Set over medium heat and bring mixture to a full boil, stirring constantly. Do not overcook.

Remove from heat and stir a small amount of hot tapioca mixture gradually into egg whites. Then quickly blend in remaining mixture and

**1 cup dairy sour cream
2 teaspoons vanilla extract**

Cool, stirring once after 15 to 20 min. Spoon into serving dishes. Chill.

If desired, serve with fresh fruit.

About 6 servings

—PEPPERMINT TAPIOCA CREAM

Follow ▲ Recipe. Add **½ cup crushed peppermint stick candy** with the sour cream.

SNOW PRINCESS TAPIOCA CREAM

▲ *Base Recipe*

Beat with rotary beater until frothy

2 egg whites

Add gradually and beat until rounded peaks are formed

¼ cup sugar

Set aside.

Put into a saucepan

2 egg yolks, slightly beaten

Stir in

3 cups milk

Add, stirring well

**⅓ cup quick-cooking tapioca
¼ to ⅓ cup sugar
¼ teaspoon salt**

Let stand 5 min. Place over medium heat and bring mixture to a full boil (5 to 8 min.), stirring constantly. Do not overcook.

Remove from heat and blend a small amount

Snow Princess Tapioca Cream

of hot tapioca mixture gradually into egg whites. Then quickly blend in remaining tapioca mixture.

Cool slightly and add
1½ teaspoons vanilla extract
Serve warm or chilled. Garnish as desired.

8 servings

—PEACH TAPIOCA CREAM

Follow ▲ Recipe. Arrange **sliced peaches** in dishes. Top with chilled tapioca cream.

—CHOCOLATE TAPIOCA CREAM

Follow ▲ Recipe. Add **2 oz. (2 sq.) unsweetened chocolate,** cut in pieces, after milk addition.

BAKED COCONUT TAPIOCA CREAM

Butter a 1-qt. casserole.

Scald (page 10)
2 cups milk
Add gradually to milk and vigorously stir in a mixture of
1 egg, slightly beaten
⅓ cup sugar
1 teaspoon vanilla extract
½ teaspoon almond extract

Mix and stir in
1 cup (about 3 oz.) moist shredded coconut
¼ cup quick-cooking tapioca
¼ teaspoon salt
Pour mixture into casserole.

Bake at 375°F 20 min.; stir after first 5 min. and again after 10 min. (Use back-and-forth motion of fork, bringing tines across bottom of casserole.) Remove casserole from oven; sprinkle top with
½ cup moist shredded coconut
Return to oven; bake 10 to 15 min. longer, or until coconut is toasted. Serve warm or chilled.

5 or 6 servings

CHOCOLATE BREAD PUDDING

▲ *Base Recipe*

Grease a 1½-qt. casserole.

Chop and set aside
½ cup (1¾ oz.) walnuts

Heat until milk is scalded (page 10) and chocolate is melted
3 cups milk
2 oz. (2 sq.) unsweetened chocolate

Blend chocolate and milk with rotary beater. Stir in chopped walnuts and
3 cups (about 3 slices) soft ½-in. bread cubes
Combine and add to bread mixture
2 eggs, slightly beaten
½ cup firmly packed brown sugar
1 teaspoon vanilla extract
½ teaspoon salt
Blend gently and turn into casserole.

Bake at 350°F 45 min., or until metal knife inserted halfway between center and outer edge of pudding comes out clean. Serve with cream or pipe **Sweetened Whipped Cream** (page 480) on top.

8 servings

—SPICED BREAD PUDDING

Follow ▲ Recipe. Add ½ teaspoon cinnamon and ⅛ teaspoon ginger to egg mixture.

CHOCOLATE FLUFF PUDDING

▲ *Base Recipe*

Melt (page 10)
2 oz. (2 sq.) unsweetened chocolate
Add
1¼ cups (14-oz. can) sweetened condensed milk
Stir over rapidly boiling water until mixture thickens. Remove from heat. Stir in
½ cup water
½ teaspoon almond extract
Let cool for about 5 min.

Beat until rounded peaks are formed
2 egg whites

Fold egg whites into chocolate mixture. Fill sherbet glasses. Chill in refrigerator.

6 servings

Note: This pudding can be used as a filling for an 8-in. pie shell.

—SHERRY FLUFF PUDDING

Follow ▲ Recipe. Fold in **1 teaspoon sherry extract** with beaten egg whites.

HOLIDAY BREAD PUDDING

Butter a shallow 2-qt. casserole.

Scald (page 10)
3 cups milk

Meanwhile, toast until very crisp enough bread slices to make
4 cups bread cubes (5 to 6 slices)
Cut toast into ½-in. cubes; put into casserole. Turning cubes lightly with a fork, drizzle over
3 tablespoons melted butter or margarine
Add gradually and mix thoroughly with fork
½ cup (3 oz.) mixed candied fruits
½ cup (about 3 oz.) golden raisins
½ cup (about 2 oz.) coarsely chopped black walnuts
8 to 10 maraschino cherries, quartered and well drained
Set aside.

Blend
3 eggs, slightly beaten
½ cup sugar
½ teaspoon nutmeg
½ teaspoon cinnamon
½ teaspoon allspice
Add milk gradually, stirring constantly and vigorously. Pour over bread cube mixture; turn with fork to blend well.

Bake at 325°F 35 to 45 min., or until a metal knife comes out clean when inserted in pudding halfway between center and edge.

Meanwhile, prepare
Custard sauce (see Custard in Creamy Peaches, page 528. Use 2 eggs; do not separate.)
Serve pudding warm with warm custard sauce and sprinkle with
Nutmeg

Serve immediately.

7 or 8 servings

DESSERT SUPERB

Prepare (page 10) a 15x10x1-in. jelly roll pan; cut the waxed paper long enough to extend 1 in. beyond ends of pan. Set aside.

Put into top of a double boiler
½ lb. sweet chocolate (in pieces)
7 tablespoons double-strength coffee beverage (page 10)
Set over simmering water until chocolate is

melted. Remove from water; set aside to cool.

Beat with an electric beater until very thick
- **½ cup (6 or 7) egg yolks**
- **¾ cup sugar**
- **1 teaspoon vanilla extract**

Set aside.

Beat until frothy using a clean beater
- **1 cup (7 or 8) egg whites**
- **¼ teaspoon salt**

Add gradually, beating until stiff peaks form
- **¼ cup sugar**

Stir the cooled chocolate and blend into egg yolk mixture. Gently stir in egg whites. Turn into the lined pan; spread evenly.

Bake at 350°F 20 min. Set on a cooling rack until slightly cool.

Sift over a clean towel
- **2 tablespoons Dutch process cocoa**

Cut around edge of pan to loosen dessert; turn out onto the towel. Carefully remove paper. If desired, let stand about 30 min. to absorb cocoa flavor. Cover with waxed paper until ready to serve. Just before serving, prepare
- **Sweetened Whipped Cream (page 480)**

Cut dessert into 16 portions. Transfer 8 to plates. Spoon whipped cream onto each. Top with remaining portions, cocoa side up.

8 servings

TOP O' RANGE DATE FUDGE PUDDING

Set out heavy 3-qt. saucepan or skillet with a tight-fitting cover.

Melt (page 10) and set aside to cool
- **2 oz. (2 sq.) unsweetened chocolate**

Chop and set aside
- **½ cup (about 2 oz.) nuts**

Cut in pieces (page 9) and set aside
- **½ cup pitted dates**

Sift together and set aside
- **1 cup sifted all-purpose flour**
- **2½ teaspoons baking powder**
- **1½ teaspoons cinnamon**
- **½ teaspoon salt**

Beat together until blended
- **⅓ cup shortening**
- **1 teaspoon vanilla extract**

Add gradually, creaming until fluffy after each addition
- **¼ cup sugar**

Blend in the melted chocolate. Add dry ingredients alternately with
- **½ cup milk**

Blend well after each addition. Fold nuts and dates into batter and set aside.

Bring to boiling in the saucepan, stirring until chocolate is melted, a mixture of
- **2 cups water**
- **½ cup sugar**
- **1 oz. (1 sq.) unsweetened chocolate**
- **1 teaspoon vanilla extract**

Drop heaping tablespoonfuls of batter into hot chocolate mixture. Cover tightly and cook over low heat 35 to 40 min. Serve immediately.

6 servings

BIRD'S NEST PUDDING

The origin of the odd name seems lost in antiquity, but several versions of this pudding flourish in New England. All of them have one thing in common: apples.

Set out a shallow 1½-qt. baking dish.

Wash and set aside
- **6 medium (about 2 lbs.) apples**

Combine in a deep saucepan and bring to boiling, stirring until sugar is dissolved
- **2 cups sugar**
- **1 cup water**

Meanwhile, core and pare (leaving whole) only as many of the apples as will fit uncrowded in the saucepan.

Stir into the syrup
- **¼ teaspoon red food coloring**

Add apples to syrup; cover and cook slowly until barely tender (about 7 min.), turning carefully several times to obtain an even color.

With a slotted spoon, carefully remove apples from syrup, allowing excess syrup to drain into the saucepan. Place them in the baking dish. Core, pare and cook any remaining apples; place in baking dish.

While apples are cooking, scald (page 10)
- **2 cups cream**

Meanwhile, beat slightly
- **3 eggs**

Blend in
- **¼ cup sugar**
- **2 teaspoons vanilla extract**
- **⅛ teaspoon salt**

Gradually add hot cream, stirring vigorously and constantly; stir until sugar is dissolved. Strain mixture through a fine sieve over and around apples in baking dish. Set filled baking dish in a large baking pan and pour very hot water into pan to a 1-in. depth.

Bake at 325°F 50 to 60 min., or until a metal knife comes out clean when inserted halfway between center and edge of baking dish.

6 servings

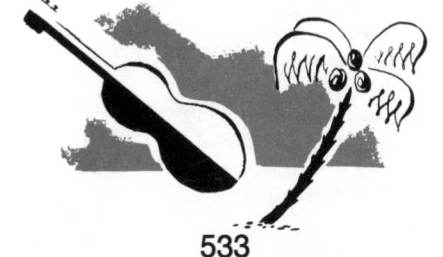

Rice Raisin Pudding

RICE RAISIN PUDDING

Scald (page 10) in top of double boiler
- **5 cups milk**

Measure
- **1 cup rice**

(The Rice Industry no longer considers it necessary to wash rice before cooking.)

Add to scalded milk the rice and
- **6 tablespoons sugar**
- **1 teaspoon salt**

Cover and cook over simmering water 1 hr. 10 min. During cooking, stir rice occasionally.

Stir in
- **¾ cup (about 4 oz.) dark seedless raisins**

Cover and cook over simmering water 15 min. longer, or until rice is entirely soft when a kernel is pressed between fingers and mixture is very thick and creamy. Remove from heat.

Spoon into individual serving dishes and sprinkle each serving lightly with
- **Cinnamon**

Serve warm.

4 to 6 servings

BAKED RICE PUDDING

Grease a 2-qt. casserole.

Prepare
- **1½ cups Fluffy Rice (one half recipe, page 164)**

Scald (page 10)
- **4 cups milk**

Gradually pour milk, stirring constantly, into a mixture of
- **4 eggs, slightly beaten**
- **¾ cup sugar**
- **2 teaspoons vanilla extract**

Stir in rice and
- **1 cup (about 5 oz.) raisins**

Pour into casserole. Sprinkle over top a mixture of
- **1 teaspoon nutmeg**
- **1 teaspoon cinnamon**

Set filled casserole in a large baking pan and pour very hot water into pan to a 1-in. depth.

Bake uncovered at 350°F. After 15 min. of baking, stir pudding with fork, using back-

and-forth motion, bringing tines across bottom of casserole. Bake 25 to 30 min. longer, or until a metal knife comes out clean when inserted halfway between center and edge of custard.

Serve warm or cold. If desired, top each serving with **heavy cream.** *6 servings*

DESSERT RICE AND APRICOTS

▲ *Base Recipe*

Butter a 1½-qt. casserole.

Scald (page 10) in top of double boiler
>   **2½ cups milk**

Stir in
>   **½ cup uncooked rice**
>   **½ teaspoon salt**
>   **½ teaspoon nutmeg**

(The Rice Industry no longer considers it necessary to wash rice before cooking.) Cover and cook over simmering water about 1 hr., or until most of milk is absorbed and rice is entirely soft when a kernel of rice is pressed between fingers.

Meanwhile, force through a sieve or food mill
>   **1½ cups (about 8 oz.) cooked dried apricots, drained**

Set apricots aside.

Mix thoroughly, in order
>   **2 eggs, slightly beaten**
>   **½ cup sugar**
>   **¾ cup milk or cream**
>   **2 teaspoons grated lemon peel**
>   **1½ teaspoons vanilla extract**

Gradually and vigorously stir 3 to 4 tablespoons hot rice into egg mixture. Blend in remaining rice and apricot purée. Pour mixture into casserole.

Bake at 350°F 40 to 50 min.

Serve warm or chilled, with or without **cream.** *6 servings*

—DUSKY DESSERT RICE

Follow ▲ Recipe. Mix until smooth ⅓ **cup quick chocolate-flavored milk mix** and ¼ **cup cold water;** thoroughly blend into scalded milk before adding rice. Substitute **cinnamon** for nutmeg. Omit apricots and lemon peel. Bake as in ▲ Recipe.

Indian Pudding

RICE AND APPLE PUDDING
(Reisauflauf mit Apfeln)

A 2-qt. baking dish will be needed.

Put into the top of a double boiler
>   **3 cups milk**
>   **½ cup rice**
>   **¼ teaspoon salt**

(The Rice Industry no longer considers it necessary to wash rice before cooking.) Cover and cook over simmering water 1¾ to 2 hrs., or until rice is entirely soft when a kernel is pressed between fingers and the mixture is quite thick.

Butter the baking dish.

Just before rice is thick, cream together until butter is softened
>   **½ cup butter**
>   **1 tablespoon grated lemon peel**

Add gradually, creaming until fluffy after each addition
>   **⅓ cup sugar**

Blend in, in thirds, beating thoroughly after each addition
>   **4 egg yolks, well beaten**

Blend in the rice and
>   **¼ cup dark seedless raisins**

Set aside.

Wash, quarter, core and pare
>   **3 medium apples**

Cut into very thin slices. Set aside.

Beat until stiff, not dry, peaks are formed
>   **4 egg whites**

Gently fold beaten egg whites into the rice mixture. Turn one half of the mixture into the greased baking dish. Arrange apples on top of rice mixture. Sprinkle with
>   **1 to 2 tablespoons sugar (depending upon tartness of apples)**

Turn remaining rice mixture into baking dish.

Bake at 325°F 60 to 65 min., or until lightly browned.

Sprinkle with
>   **Confectioners' sugar**

Serve warm. *6 to 8 servings*

INDIAN PUDDING

▲ *Base Recipe*

Thoroughly butter a 1½-qt. casserole.

Scald (page 10) in top of double boiler
>   **3 cups milk**

Remove from heat. Stirring constantly, slowly blend into a mixture of
>   **½ cup yellow corn meal**
>   **¼ cup sugar**
>   **1 teaspoon salt**
>   **1 teaspoon cinnamon**
>   **½ teaspoon ginger**

Vigorously stir about 3 tablespoons of the hot mixture into a mixture of
>   **1 egg, well beaten**
>   **½ cup molasses**

Coffee-Flavored Indian Pudding

Blend into the hot corn meal mixture. Cook over boiling water about 10 min., or until very thick; stir constantly. Beat in
>   **2 tablespoons butter**

Turn mixture into casserole. Pour over top
>   **1 cup cold milk**

Bake at 300°F about 2 hrs., or until the top is browned.

Serve pudding warm with **cream, whipped cream, Vanilla or Maple Ice Cream Superbe** (page 560), or **Vanilla or Brandy Hard Sauce** (page 581). *About 6 servings*

—COFFEE-FLAVORED INDIAN PUDDING

Follow ▲ Recipe. Decrease the 3 cups of milk to 2½ cups. Blend ½ **cup cold double-strength coffee beverage** into molasses-corn meal mixture. Serve warm pudding with **coffee ice cream.**

NEW ENGLAND PUMPKIN PUDDING

Butter a 1½-qt. casserole.

Mix well
>   **¾ cup firmly packed brown sugar**
>   **¾ teaspoon salt**
>   **1 teaspoon cinnamon**
>   **½ teaspoon nutmeg**
>   **½ teaspoon ginger**
>   **¼ teaspoon cloves**

Blend thoroughly into

2 cups (16-oz. can) pumpkin

Add and stir in a mixture of

3 eggs, slightly beaten
1 cup heavy cream
¾ cup milk

Pour pumpkin mixture into casserole.

Bake at 350°F about 1 hr., or until a metal knife comes out clean when inserted in custard halfway between center and edge of casserole. Cool slightly.

Decorate top of pudding by forcing **Sweetened Whipped Cream** (page 480) or **Vanilla Hard Sauce** (page 581) through a pastry bag and No. 27 tube to form a lattice design.

6 to 8 servings

SPICED PRUNE CHEESE PUDDING

▲ *Base Recipe*

Butter a shallow 1½-qt. casserole.

Put into a saucepan

¾ cup (about ⅓ lb.) dried prunes
1½ cups water

Cover; bring to boiling and simmer 10 to 20 min., or until tender; drain. Remove pits and chop prunes coarsely. Set aside.

Lightly blend with fork

½ cup vanilla wafer crumbs
3 tablespoons melted butter or margarine

Set crumbs aside.

Chop coarsely and set aside

⅓ cup (about 1 oz.) walnuts

Sift together

⅓ cup sugar
1 tablespoon all-purpose flour
¼ teaspoon salt
¼ teaspoon cinnamon
¼ teaspoon nutmeg
⅛ teaspoon cloves

Set aside.

Put through a sieve

1½ cups cottage cheese

Combine cottage cheese with

2 eggs, well beaten
½ cup cream or undiluted evaporated milk
½ teaspoon grated lemon peel
1 teaspoon lemon juice

Stir in the sugar mixture and chopped walnuts and prunes. Turn mixture into casserole; top with wafer crumbs.

Bake at 350°F 35 to 50 min., or until a metal knife inserted halfway between center and edge of casserole comes out clean. Serve pudding warm. *4 to 6 servings*

—CASSEROLE COTTAGE CHEESE CAKE

Follow ▲ Recipe; omit prunes, spices and nuts.

Press crumbs firmly on bottom of casserole. Bake at 325°F 5 min. Cool. Increase flour to 3 tablespoons. Add **½ teaspoon vanilla extract** with lemon juice. Increase eggs to 4; separate egg yolks from egg whites. Beat the egg yolks until very thick and substitute them for the whole eggs. Beat the egg whites until rounded peaks are formed. Carefully fold them into pudding before turning mixture into casserole. Sprinkle top of mixture with **nutmeg**. Bake at 325°F 1 to 1½ hrs., or until cake tests done. Serve warm, with or without **Sweetened Whipped Cream** (page 480).

FARINA PUDDING
(Griesauflauf)

▲ *Base Recipe*

Butter a 2-qt. casserole.

Scald (page 10) in top of double boiler

2 cups milk

Add and stir in

2 tablespoons butter
1½ teaspoons grated lemon peel
¼ teaspoon salt

Add gradually, stirring constantly

⅓ cup farina

Cook over boiling water 20 min., or until thick, stirring constantly. Remove from boiling water and turn mixture into a medium-size bowl. Cool to lukewarm, stirring occasionally.

Beat until thick and lemon-colored

4 egg yolks

Blend into cooled mixture and set aside.

Beat until frothy

4 egg whites

Add gradually, beating well after each addition

¼ cup sugar

Continue to beat until very stiff peaks are formed. Spread beaten egg whites over farina mixture and gently fold together. Turn mixture into casserole. Set filled casserole in a large baking pan and pour very hot water into pan to a 1-in. depth.

Bake at 325°F 1 hr. 35 min., or until surface is lightly browned and a metal knife inserted in pudding halfway between center and edge of casserole comes out clean.

Serve at once. *6 to 8 servings*

—FARINA PUDDING WITH APRICOTS
(Griesauflauf mit Aprikosen)

Follow ▲ Recipe. Before turning mixture into casserole, arrange over bottom of casserole **¼ lb. dried apricots** which have been cooked until just tender, following package directions; drain if necessary.

LEMON DUFF

▲ *Base Recipe*

Set out a 1½-qt. casserole.

Chop and set aside

½ cup (about 2 oz.) pecans or black walnuts

Cut finely and set aside

½ cup (2 to 3 oz.) pitted dates

Mix and set aside

2 teaspoons grated lemon peel
¼ cup lemon juice

Stir together

1 cup sugar
¼ cup sifted all-purpose flour
¼ teaspoon salt

Blend and stir into dry ingredients

2 egg yolks, well beaten
1 cup milk
2 tablespoons melted butter or margarine

Mix in the lemon peel and juice, chopped nuts and dates. Set aside.

Beat until frothy

2 egg whites
⅛ teaspoon salt

Add gradually, beating well after each addition

2 tablespoons sugar

New England Pumpkin Pudding

Beat until rounded peaks are formed. Gently and quickly fold into batter. Turn into the casserole. Set filled casserole in a large baking pan and pour very hot water into pan to a 1-in. depth.

Bake at 375°F 35 to 45 min., or until a metal knife comes out clean when inserted in pudding halfway between center and edge.

Serve warm or cold, with or without **Sweetened Whipped Cream** (page 480). *6 servings*

—SWEET CHERRY DUFF

Follow ▲ Recipe. Decrease sugar to ¾ cup. Use only 1 tablespoon lemon juice and add **milk** or **cherry syrup** to make ¼ cup liquid. Substitute **1 cup finely chopped canned dark sweet cherries** for dates.

SWEDISH CHRISTMAS PORRIDGE
(Risgrynsgröt)

This rice porridge is served at Christmastime. According to Swedish custom the person who finds the almond will marry within the next year. When the porridge is served, each person makes up a rhyme as he takes a spoonful. This continues around the table until all the porridge is eaten. At other times of the year the porridge is served only with a fruit sauce and the almond is omitted.

Put into the top of a double boiler
> **6 cups milk**
> **1 cup rice**
> **3 tablespoons sugar**
> **½ teaspoon salt**

(The Rice Industry no longer considers it necessary to wash rice before cooking.) Cover and cook over simmering water 2½ to 3 hrs., or until rice is entirely soft when a kernel is pressed between fingers and mixture is quite thick. Remove cover for last 10 min. if mixture is not thick enough.

Mix in just before serving
> **1 whole blanched almond (page 9)**

Serve with
> **Cool milk**
> **Sugar**
> **Cinnamon**

Or serve with a **fruit sauce.** *6 servings*

STEAMED PUDDINGS

DARK PLUM PUDDING

Grease two 1-qt. molds, one 2-qt. mold or 2 1-lb. coffee cans. Grease tight-fitting covers. (Aluminum foil, parchment paper or two layers of waxed paper cut larger than mold may be used if a cover is not available. Grease before using.)

Chop and set aside
> **1 cup (about 4 oz.) nuts**

Sift together and set aside
> **1¼ cups sifted all-purpose flour**
> **1 teaspoon baking soda**
> **1 teaspoon salt**
> **½ teaspoon allspice**
> **½ teaspoon nutmeg**
> **½ teaspoon cinnamon**
> **¼ teaspoon cloves**

Break apart, discarding membrane which coats it, and finely chop
> **3 oz. suet (about ¾ cup, chopped)**

Mix thoroughly with
> **2 eggs, well beaten**
> **1¼ cups fine dry bread crumbs (page 9)**
> **⅔ cup sugar**
> **⅓ cup apple cider**

Combine and stir in
> **1 cup molasses**
> **1 cup buttermilk**

Thoroughly mix with nuts and add
> **1½ cups (about 8 oz.) raisins**
> **¼ cup finely chopped candied citron**

Blend in dry ingredients. Turn into molds, filling each two thirds full. Cover tightly with greased cover or tie on aluminum foil, parchment paper or waxed paper.

Place mold on trivet or rack in steamer or deep kettle with tight-fitting cover. Pour boiling water into kettle to no more than one-half the height of the mold. Cover kettle and bring water to boiling. To steam, reduce heat but keep water boiling. Quickly add more boiling water as necessary to keep water level at one-half the height of mold throughout steaming. Steam pudding about 4 hrs.

Remove from steamer and unmold. Immediately place on hot serving dish and garnish as

Dark Plum Pudding

desired. Serve with **Almond Hard Sauce** (page 581) or **Cherry Sauce I** (page 577).

If pudding is to be stored several days before serving, unmold onto cooling rack. Let stand until cold. Wrap in aluminum foil and store in cool place. Steam thoroughly about 1 to 2 hrs., before serving. *About 16 servings*

Note: To flame a plum pudding, heat desired amount of brandy in a small saucepan. Ignite brandy with match and pour over top of pudding. Serve when the flaming stops.

SPICY STEAMED BUTTERMILK PUDDING

Grease a 1½-qt. mold and a tight-fitting cover. (Aluminum foil, parchment paper or two layers of waxed paper cut larger than the top of the mold may be used if cover is not available. Grease before using.) Set out steamer or large kettle with tight-fitting cover; put trivet or rack in kettle.

Put into a bowl
> **1 cup fine dry bread crumbs (about 4 slices bread)**

Pour over crumbs
> **1½ cups buttermilk**

Let stand 30 min.

Meanwhile, chop and set aside
> **½ cup (about 2 oz.) pecans**

Sift together and set aside
> **½ cup sifted all-purpose flour**
> **1 teaspoon baking soda**
> **½ teaspoon salt**
> **½ teaspoon cinnamon**
> **½ teaspoon allspice**
> **½ teaspoon nutmeg**
> **⅛ teaspoon cloves**

Cream until softened
> **¼ cup butter or margarine**

Add gradually, creaming until fluffy after each addition
> **⅔ cup firmly packed brown sugar**

Add and blend well
> **2 tablespoons molasses**

Add dry ingredients, buttermilk-crumb mixture, nuts and
> **¾ cup (about 4 oz.) dark seedless raisins**

FOOD FESTIVAL

Stir only enough to blend thoroughly. Turn into the mold. Cover tightly with greased cover, or tie on aluminum foil, parchment paper or waxed paper with string.

Set mold on trivet. Pour boiling water into kettle to no more than one-half the height of the mold. Cover kettle and bring water to boiling. To steam, reduce heat but keep water boiling. Quickly add more boiling water as necessary to keep water level at one-half the height of the mold throughout steaming. Steam pudding 3 hrs.

Remove mold from kettle; remove cover from mold. Carefully run spatula down along sides of mold to loosen pudding; unmold onto cooling rack.

Serve warm with **Vanilla Cream Topping** (page 482).

If a portion of the pudding is to be stored for a day or longer before serving, wrap it when thoroughly cooled in aluminum foil and store in a cool place. Reheat before serving by replacing in mold and steaming 1 to 2 hrs.

About 10 servings

STEAMED CHOCOLATE PUDDING

▲ *Base Recipe*

Grease a 1½-qt. mold.

Melt (page 10) and set aside to cool
   3 oz. (3 sq.) unsweetened chocolate

Sift together and set aside
   1½ cups sifted all-purpose flour
   1½ teaspoons baking powder
   ½ teaspoon salt

Cream until softened
   ⅔ cup butter
   2 teaspoons vanilla extract

Add gradually, creaming until fluffy after each addition
   ¾ cup plus 2 tablespoons sugar

Add in thirds, beating well after each addition
   2 eggs, well beaten

Add chocolate and blend well.

Measure
   ¾ cup milk

Alternately add dry ingredients in thirds and milk in halves to creamed mixture. After each addition, beat only until blended. Finally, beat

Spicy Steamed Buttermilk Pudding

only until batter is smooth (do not overbeat). Turn batter into mold. Cover mold tightly with greased lid or tie on aluminum foil, parchment paper or 2 layers of waxed paper.

Place on trivet or rack in steamer or deep kettle with tight-fitting cover. Pour boiling water into bottom of steamer (enough to continue boiling throughout entire steaming period if possible. Quickly add more boiling water if necessary during cooking period.) Mold should be above the water level. Tightly cover steamer and steam the pudding 1½ hrs., keeping the water boiling at all times.

Remove pudding from steamer. Immediately loosen edges of pudding with spatula. Unmold onto serving plate. If desired, garnish with **raisins, pecan halves** and **candied cherries.**

Serve hot with **Sweetened Whipped Cream** (page 480) or **Chocolate Marshmallow Sauce I** (page 578). *6 to 8 servings*

—CHOCOLATE NUT PUDDING

Follow ▲ Recipe. Add and blend in **½ cup (about 2 oz.) coarsely chopped nuts** before turning batter into mold.

—RAINBOW PUDDING

Follow ▲ Recipe. Omit chocolate. Divide batter into 3 parts and put into separate bowls. To one part add **2 or 3 drops red food coloring** and **½ teaspoon almond extract;** to the second add **1 oz. (1 sq.) melted and cooled unsweetened chocolate;** to the third add **2 or 3 drops yellow or green food coloring,** or no coloring. Stir each mixture until blended. Pour batter into mold in 3 layers. For swirled effect, gently draw a spoon through the layers about 3 times after layers are in mold.

SPICY STEAMED CRANBERRY PUDDING

Lightly oil a 1½-qt. mold.

Drain and set aside, reserving syrup
   1 can (16 oz.) whole cranberry sauce (about 1 cup, drained)

Sift together and set aside
   1½ cups sifted all-purpose flour
   1 teaspoon baking soda
   1 teaspoon baking powder
   ½ teaspoon salt
   ¼ teaspoon cinnamon
   ¼ teaspoon cloves

Put into a large mixer bowl
   ¼ cup shortening

Add gradually, beating thoroughly
   ½ cup sugar

Add, one at a time, beating well after each addition
   2 eggs

Blend in gradually
   ½ cup molasses

Blend in dry ingredients alternately with
   ⅓ cup reserved cranberry syrup

After each addition beat *only* until well blended. (*Do not overbeat.*) Blend in drained whole cranberries. Turn batter into the mold.

Cover mold tightly with greased lid or tie on aluminum foil, parchment paper or waxed paper cut larger than mold. Place mold on trivet or rack in steamer or deep kettle with tight-fitting cover. Pour boiling water into bottom of steamer (enough to continue boiling throughout entire steaming period if possible; quickly add more boiling water if necessary during cooking period).

Tightly cover steamer and steam 2 hrs. Keep water boiling at all times.

Unmold and serve warm with **Vanilla Hard Sauce** (page 581). Garnish with a few **candied cherries.** *6 to 8 servings*

SUET PUDDING

Grease two 1-qt. molds, one 2-qt. mold or 2 1-lb. coffee cans. Grease tight-fitting covers. (Aluminum foil, parchment paper or two layers of waxed paper cut larger than mold may be tied on if a cover is not available. Grease well before using.)

Chop and set aside
   1 cup (about 4 oz.) nuts

Spicy Steamed Cranberry Pudding

Suet Pudding

Sift together and set aside

    3 cups all-purpose flour
    1 teaspoon baking soda
    1 teaspoon cinnamon
    1 teaspoon ginger
    ¾ teaspoon nutmeg
    ¼ teaspoon cloves

Break apart, discarding membrane which coats it, and finely chop

    4 to 5 oz. suet (1 to 1¼ cups, chopped)

Mix suet thoroughly with

    1 cup molasses
    1 cup milk

Thoroughly mix with nuts and

    ½ cup (about 2½ oz.) dark seedless raisins

Blend in dry ingredients. Turn into molds, filling each two-thirds full. Cover tightly with greased cover or tie on aluminum foil, parchment or waxed paper.

Place molds on trivet or rack in steamer or deep kettle with tight-fitting cover. To steam, see Boston Brown Bread (page 89). Cover steamer and steam pudding about 3 hrs.

Remove pudding from steamer and unmold. Immediately place on hot serving dish and garnish as desired. Serve with **Vanilla or Brandy Hard Sauce** (page 581) or **Maple Whipped Cream** (page 480).

If pudding is to be stored several days before serving, unmold onto cooling rack. Let stand until cool. Wrap in aluminum foil and store in a cool place. Reheat thoroughly before serving by steaming 1 to 2 hrs.

About 12 servings

DESSERT SOUFFLES

VANILLA SOUFFLE
(Soufflé à la Vanille)

    ▲ *Base Recipe*

Butter the bottom of a 1½-qt. soufflé dish or casserole and sift over it

    1 tablespoon confectioners' sugar

Melt in a saucepan

    ¼ cup butter

Stir in all at one time

    3 tablespoons all-purpose flour

Cook until mixture bubbles. Remove from heat and add gradually, stirring in

    1 cup milk

Return to heat and bring rapidly to boiling, stirring constantly; cook 1 to 2 min. longer. Cool slightly.

Beat until thick and lemon-colored

    4 egg yolks
    ½ cup sugar
    1 tablespoon vanilla extract

Beating vigorously with rotary beater, pour sauce slowly into egg yolk mixture. Cool to lukewarm.

Beat until stiff, not dry, peaks are formed

    4 egg whites

Spread egg yolk mixture over egg whites and gently fold together. Turn into the dish and set in a large baking pan. Pour very hot water into pan to a depth of 1 in.

Bake at 400°F 15 min., reduce heat to 375°F and bake 30 to 40 min., or until a metal knife comes out clean when inserted halfway between center and edge. Serve immediately from soufflé dish. Serve with **Apricot Sauce** (page 577), or a **purée of strawberries or raspberries.**

6 to 8 servings

HAZELNUT SOUFFLE

    ▲ *Base Recipe*

Butter bottom of a 2-qt. casserole. Sift evenly over bottom of casserole

    1 tablespoon confectioners' sugar

Chop finely and set aside

    1 cup (about 4¾ oz.) hazelnuts

Melt in a saucepan

    ¼ cup butter or margarine

Stir in all at one time

    ¼ cup all-purpose flour

Heat until mixture bubbles; remove from heat and gradually stir in

    1 cup milk

Return to heat and bring rapidly to boiling, stirring constantly; cook 1 to 2 min. longer. Cool slightly.

Beat until very thick and lemon-colored

    4 egg yolks
    ½ cup sugar
    1 teaspoon vanilla extract

Stirring vigorously to blend, pour sauce slowly into egg yolk mixture. Mix in the chopped hazelnuts. Cool to lukewarm.

Beat until rounded peaks are formed

    4 egg whites

Spread egg yolk mixture over egg whites; carefully fold together. Turn into casserole and set filled casserole in a large baking pan. Pour very hot water into pan to a 1-in. depth.

Bake at 350°F about 60 min., or until a metal knife comes out clean when gently inserted in soufflé halfway between center and edge of casserole.

Meanwhile, prepare sauce.

For Caramel Custard Sauce—Scald (page 10)
    2 cups milk

Melt in a heavy skillet over low heat

    ½ cup sugar

Stir constantly until sugar is golden brown and a foam appears. Carefully add to skillet

    2 tablespoons hot water

Stir and cook to make a foamy syrup. Remove from heat. Add gradually, stirring constantly, to scalded milk. Add gradually to milk

    2 eggs, slightly beaten
    ⅛ teaspoon salt

Stir vigorously at first. Strain through a fine sieve into top of double boiler. Cook over simmering water, stirring constantly and rapidly, until mixture coats a metal spoon. Remove from simmering water at once. Blend in

    1 teaspoon vanilla extract

Serve soufflé immediately with warm sauce.

6 servings

—CHOCOLATE NUT SOUFFLE

Follow ▲ Recipe. Melt (page 10) **2 oz. (2 sq.) unsweetened chocolate;** stir into sauce before blending into egg yolk mixture. Substitute **Sweetened Whipped Cream** (page 480) for Caramel Custard Sauce.

CHOCOLATE SOUFFLE

Grease bottom of a 2-qt. casserole.

Heat in top of double boiler over simmering water until chocolate is melted and milk scalded (page 10)

2 oz. (2 sq.) unsweetened chocolate
1½ cups milk

Blend with rotary beater and set aside.

Combine

½ cup sugar
⅓ cup all-purpose flour
¾ teaspoon salt

Gradually stir in

½ cup cold milk

Add to mixture in double boiler. Cook over simmering water until thickened, stirring constantly. Continue cooking 5 to 7 min., stirring occasionally.

Meanwhile, beat until thick and lemon-colored

4 egg yolks

Remove about 3 tablespoons chocolate mixture and stir vigorously into beaten egg yolks. Return to mixture in double boiler and cook 3 to 5 min., stirring constantly. Remove from heat and blend in

2 tablespoons butter or margarine
2 teaspoons vanilla extract

Set aside.

Beat until rounded peaks are formed

4 egg whites

Fold chocolate mixture quickly into beaten egg whites. Turn into the casserole and set in a large baking pan. Pour very hot water into pan to a 1-in. depth.

Bake at 350°F 1 hr., or until a metal knife inserted in soufflé halfway between center and edge comes out clean. Serve immediately with **Chocolate Marshmallow Sauce I** (page 578) or with **cream.**   *8 servings*

POPPY SEED SOUFFLE
(Mák Koch)

Grease bottom of a 1-qt. baking dish.

Finely chop

¼ cup (about 1 oz.) blanched (page 9) almonds

Mix almonds with

½ cup (about 2 oz.) freshly ground poppy seed

Chocolate Nut Soufflé

Set mixture aside.

Put into a bowl and cream until softened

¼ cup butter or margarine

Add gradually, creaming until fluffy after each addition

¼ cup sugar

Add in thirds, beating thoroughly after each addition

4 egg yolks, well beaten

Mix in the poppy seed-almond mixture and

¼ cup (about 1 slice) fine dry bread crumbs
¼ cup milk

Beat until stiff, not dry, peaks are formed

4 egg whites

Slide egg whites onto poppy seed mixture; quickly and gently fold together. Turn batter into the baking dish and set filled dish in a large baking pan. Pour very hot water into pan to a 1-in. depth.

Bake at 350°F 45 to 50 min., or until a metal knife inserted halfway between center and edge comes out clean. Serve immediately.
5 or 6 servings

GELATIN DESSERTS

SPANISH CREAM

▲ Base Recipe

Set out a 1½-qt. mold.

Mix in a heavy saucepan

¼ cup sugar
1 env. unflavored gelatin
¼ teaspoon salt

Blend

3 egg yolks, slightly beaten
2¼ cups milk

Add gradually to gelatin mixture in saucepan, stirring to blend. Set over low heat and cook, stirring constantly, until gelatin is completely dissolved. Remove from heat.

Cool to lukewarm by setting pan in larger pan of cold water. Blend in

1½ teaspoons vanilla extract

Chill (page 374) until mixture begins to gel (becomes slightly thicker).

Just before gelatin mixture is of desired consistency, beat until frothy

3 egg whites

Add gradually, beating well after each addition

¼ cup sugar

Beat until rounded peaks are formed. Spread over gelatin mixture and fold together. Turn into mold; chill until firm.

Unmold (page 374) onto chilled serving plate.
About 8 servings

—CREAMY PUDDING

Follow ▲ Recipe. Use a 1-qt. fluted mold. Pour ½ cup **cold water** into a bowl. Sprinkle the gelatin evenly over water. Stir in ¾ **cup**

Chocolate Soufflé

boiling water until gelatin is completely dissolved. Omit milk and both amounts of sugar. Beat egg yolks until thick. Stir in ⅔ **cup sweetened condensed milk,** the vanilla extract and salt. Blend dissolved gelatin into egg yolk mixture. Chill until mixture begins to gel (becomes slightly thicker). Beat egg whites until rounded peaks are formed. Spread over slightly thickened gelatin mixture and fold together. Turn into mold and chill until firm. Unmold.   *4 to 6 servings*

JELLIED CREAM

Set out six custard cups.

Scald (page 10) in the top of a double boiler

1 cup cream

Meanwhile, pour into a small bowl

¼ cup cold water

Sprinkle evenly over cold water

2 teaspoons unflavored gelatin

Set aside.

When cream is scalded, remove from heat and add softened gelatin, stirring until gelatin is completely dissolved. Mix in

¾ cup sugar

Chill until mixture is slightly thicker than consistency of thick unbeaten egg white.

Fold in

1 cup dairy sour cream
¼ teaspoon salt
½ teaspoon vanilla extract

Turn mixture into the cups. Chill in refrigerator until firm.

Creamy Pudding

Minted Chocolate Fluff

To serve, unmold (page 374) into sherbet glasses and spoon crushed **fresh strawberries** or **raspberries** over mold, if desired.

6 servings

MINTED CHOCOLATE FLUFF

▲ *Base Recipe*

Combine in top of double boiler
1 pkg. (6 oz.) semisweet chocolate pieces
1 cup milk
Set over hot (not simmering) water and heat, stirring occasionally, until chocolate is melted.

Meanwhile, pour into a small bowl or cup
¼ cup cold water
Sprinkle evenly over the water
1½ teaspoons unflavored gelatin
Let stand to soften.

Meanwhile, beat until thick and lemon-colored
4 egg yolks
Pour chocolate mixture slowly into beaten egg yolks, stirring constantly. Return to top of double boiler and cook, stirring constantly, over simmering water 5 min. Remove from heat; add softened gelatin, stirring until gelatin is completely dissolved. Set aside to cool.

Beat until frothy
4 egg whites
Add gradually, beating well after each addition
½ cup sugar

Beat until very stiff peaks are formed. Fold beaten egg whites into chocolate mixture with
1 teaspoon vanilla extract
½ teaspoon peppermint extract
Pour into sherbet glasses. Chill in refrigerator.
About 6 servings

—MINTED CHOCOLATE CREAM FLUFF

Follow ▲ Recipe. Omit egg whites. Using chilled bowl and beater whip **1 cup chilled heavy cream** until of medium consistency (piles softly). Beat in **½ cup sugar**. Fold into chocolate mixture with flavoring extracts.

MOCHA DATE NUT MOLD

An attractive special-occasion dessert with a novel and unusually pleasing blend of flavors.

Set out a 1½-qt. fancy mold. Chill a bowl and rotary beater in refrigerator.

For Mold—Mix thoroughly in a heavy saucepan
2 env. unflavored gelatin
⅔ cup sugar
6 tablespoons instant cocoa
1 teaspoon salt
Set aside.

Heat until very hot
2½ cups double-strength coffee beverage (page 10)
Remove from heat and immediately stir into the gelatin-sugar mixture. Place over very low heat and continue stirring until gelatin and sugar are completely dissolved.

Cool; chill (page 374) until mixture is slightly thicker than consistency of thick unbeaten egg white.

Meanwhile, set out
1¾ cups (about 9 oz.) pitted dates
Beginning and ending with dates, alternately put through medium blade of food chopper 1⅛ cups of the dates and
½ cup (about 2 oz.) walnuts
Reserve about ½ cup of date-nut mixture and the remaining whole dates for Stuffed Dates.

Mocha Date Nut Mold

When gelatin mixture is of desired consistency, add the remaining date-nut mixture and stir until blended.

Using the chilled bowl and beater, beat until cream is of medium consistency (piles softly)
1 cup chilled heavy cream
Gently fold whipped cream into the gelatin mixture with
2 teaspoons vanilla extract
Turn into the prepared mold. Chill in refrigerator until firm.

To serve, unmold (page 374) onto a chilled serving platter. Garnish mold (see photo) with
Stuffed Dates (below)
Sweetened Whipped Cream (page 480)

6 to 8 servings

For Stuffed Dates—Spread open the reserved whole dates. Blend in a small bowl
2 tablespoons marshmallow cream
1 teaspoon double-strength coffee beverage (page 10)
Mix in the reserved date-nut mixture. Generously fill dates with mixture. Roll the stuffed dates in **sugar**.

MOLDED MOCHA PUDDING

Set out six 4- to 5-oz. molds.

Pour into a small bowl
½ cup cold water
Sprinkle evenly over cold water
1 env. unflavored gelatin
Set aside.

Blend in the top of a double boiler
6 tablespoons sugar
3 tablespoons cocoa
2 teaspoons cornstarch
⅛ teaspoon salt
Stir in
1½ cups water
Place over direct heat. Stirring constantly, bring rapidly to boiling and cook 3 min. Stir in
1 tablespoon instant powdered coffee
Immediately stir about 3 tablespoons of the hot mixture into
2 egg yolks, fork beaten
Immediately blend into mixture in double-

540

boiler top and place over boiling water. Cook 3 to 5 min., stirring constantly. Remove from heat.

Stir in softened gelatin and
  ¾ teaspoon vanilla extract
  ¼ teaspoon almond extract
Chill until mixture mounds slightly when dropped from a spoon.

Beat until stiff, not dry, peaks are formed
  2 egg whites
When gelatin mixture is of desired consistency, spread mixture over beaten egg whites and fold together. Turn pudding into the molds. Cover and chill in refrigerator until firm.

Unmold (page 374) onto chilled serving dishes. If desired, serve with **Soft Custard** (page 528). *6 servings*

WITCHES' SNOW
(Hexenschnee)

A 2-qt. mold will be needed.

Pour into a small cup or custard cup
  ½ cup cold water
Sprinkle evenly over cold water
  1 env. unflavored gelatin
Let stand until softened.

Meanwhile, mix in a large bowl
  2 cups (16-oz. can) thick sweetened applesauce
  ¾ cup sugar
  ½ cup apricot preserves
  2 tablespoons rum
  1 teaspoon lemon juice
Dissolve gelatin completely by placing over very hot water. Stir gelatin into applesauce mixture. Stir until sugar is completely dissolved.

Chill in refrigerator or over ice and water until mixture begins to gel (becomes slightly thicker). (If mixture is placed over ice and water, stir frequently; if placed in refrigerator, stir occasionally.)

When mixture is of desired consistency, add
  2 egg whites
Beat with electric mixer or rotary beater until

mixture is very thick and piles softly (about 14 min.). Turn into the mold.

Chill in refrigerator until firm, about 4½ hrs.

When ready to serve, unmold (page 374) onto chilled serving plate. Garnish base of mold with any **fresh fruit** in season.
8 to 10 servings

SNOW PUDDING
(Sne Pudding)

Set out a 2½-qt. fancy mold.

Prepare
  Vanilla Sauce I (page 576)

Mix thoroughly in a saucepan
  2 env. unflavored gelatin
  1¼ cups sugar
  ⅛ teaspoon salt
Stir in
  2½ cups water
Set the saucepan over low heat and stir constantly until gelatin and sugar are completely dissolved. Remove the saucepan from heat.
Mix in
  ⅓ to ½ cup strained lemon juice
Chill in refrigerator or over ice and water until mixture is slightly thicker than consistency of thick unbeaten egg white. (If mixture is placed over ice and water, stir frequently; if placed in refrigerator, stir occasionally.)

When gelatin is of desired consistency, beat until rounded peaks are formed and egg whites do not slide when bowl is partially inverted
  6 egg whites

Beat gelatin mixture with a rotary or electric beater until frothy. Gently but thoroughly fold gelatin mixture into beaten egg whites. Turn into prepared mold. Chill in refrigerator until firm, at least 4 hrs.

When ready to serve, unmold (page 374) onto chilled serving plate.

Serve with Vanilla Sauce I. *8 to 10 servings*

LEMON SNOW

Set out a 1½-qt. ring mold.

Pour into a small bowl
  1 cup cold water
Sprinkle evenly over water
  2 env. unflavored gelatin
Set aside.

Pour into large mixer bowl
  1½ cups hot water
Add softened gelatin and stir until completely dissolved. Stir in
  ½ cup sugar
  ½ teaspoon grated lemon peel
  ½ cup lemon juice
  ⅛ teaspoon salt
Chill gelatin mixture until slightly thicker than consistency of thick unbeaten egg white.

When gelatin is of desired consistency, beat until frothy
  3 egg whites
Add gradually, beating after each addition
  ½ cup sugar
Continue beating until stiff peaks are formed. Beat gelatin mixture until frothy. Gently, but thoroughly, fold beaten egg whites into gelatin mixture. Turn into mold. Chill in refrigerator until firm.

When ready to serve, unmold (page 374) onto serving plate. Fill center with **Blender Applesauce** (page 567). Sprinkle top with **nutmeg**; garnish edge of serving plate with **candied lemon slices** and **candied red cherries**, cut in halves. *6 servings*

LIME CHIFFON CANTALOUPE CUPS

Set a bowl and beater in refrigerator to chill.

Rinse and set in refrigerator to chill
  3 medium cantaloupes

Pour into a small refrigerator tray
  1 can (6 oz.) evaporated milk (⅔ cup)
Set in freezer until ice crystals form around edge of tray.

Empty into a large bowl
  1 pkg. (3 oz.) lime-flavored gelatin
Add, stirring until gelatin is dissolved
  1 cup boiling water
Add and stir until sugar is completely dissolved
  ½ cup sugar
Blend in
  2 tablespoons lime juice
  1½ tablespoons lemon juice
Cool; chill (page 374) until gelatin mixture is slightly thicker than consistency of thick unbeaten egg white.

While gelatin mixture is chilling, use a narrow sharp-pointed knife to mark 1-in. points in a sawtooth line around the center of each cantaloupe. Carefully cut through marked lines to center. Pull the melon halves apart. With a knife or spoon, remove seedy centers and drain cavity thoroughly. For a flat base, cut a thin slice from bottom of each cantaloupe. Cover and set in refrigerator until ready to fill.

When gelatin mixture is of desired consist-

Lemon Snow

Creamy Orange Ring

ency, use the chilled bowl and beater to beat the chilled evaporated milk until of medium consistency (piles softly).

Peel and dice
2 bananas with all-yellow or brown-flecked peel
Fold the whipped evaporated milk and diced banana into the gelatin mixture. Spoon the mixture into the chilled cantaloupe halves, heaping slightly.

Cover and set in refrigerator to chill until firm. When ready to serve, place each half on serving plate. Garnish each serving with
Mint leaves

6 servings

CREAMY ORANGE RING

A 1½-qt. ring mold will be needed.

Set out to thaw
1 can (6 oz.) frozen orange juice concentrate

Pour into a small bowl
½ cup cold water
Sprinkle evenly over cold water
1½ env. unflavored gelatin
Let stand 5 min. to soften.

Scald in top of a double boiler
1 cup milk

Beat slightly
2 egg yolks
Blend in
¼ cup sugar
Add the scalded milk gradually, stirring until blended.

Strain mixture into double-boiler top. Cook over simmering water, stirring constantly and rapidly, until mixture coats a metal spoon. Remove from simmering water and immediately stir in the softened gelatin until gelatin is completely dissolved. Cool slightly. Blend in the thawed orange juice concentrate.

Cool; chill (page 374) until mixture begins to gel (becomes slightly thicker).

When gelatin mixture is of the desired consistency, blend in
1 cup dairy sour cream

Beat until frothy
2 egg whites
¼ teaspoon salt
Add gradually, beating well after each addition
2½ tablespoons sugar
Spread beaten egg whites over gelatin mixture and gently fold together. Turn into the mold. Chill in refrigerator until firm.

To serve, unmold (page 374) onto chilled serving plate. *About 8 servings*

PEACH MACAROON MOLD

A 2-qt. mold will be needed. Set a bowl and rotary beater in refrigerator to chill.

Set out
1 doz. dry 2-in. macaroons
(If necessary, dry macaroons on a baking sheet in 325°F oven 15 min.; cool.)
Prepare crumbs (page 10; about ¾ cup crumbs).

Drain, reserving syrup
1 can (29 oz.) cling peach halves (about 2 cups, drained)
Dice and set aside enough of the peach halves to yield 1½ cups diced peaches. Reserve and chill remaining peach halves for garnishing serving plate.

Pour into a small bowl
1 cup cold water
Sprinkle evenly over cold water
2 env. unflavored gelatin
Set aside.

Add to the reserved peach syrup
Water (enough to make 1½ cups liquid)
Heat liquid until very hot. Remove from heat; immediately stir in the softened gelatin until completely dissolved. Add and stir in
1 tablespoon lemon juice
½ teaspoon almond extract
Cool; chill (page 374) until slightly thicker than consistency of thick unbeaten egg white.

When gelatin mixture is of desired consistency, beat until frothy
2 egg whites
⅛ teaspoon salt
Add gradually, beating well after each addition
½ cup sugar
Continue beating until rounded peaks are formed. Spread beaten egg whites over thickened gelatin mixture and gently fold together. Fold in the diced peaches and macaroon crumbs.

Using chilled bowl and beater, beat until cream is of medium consistency (piles softly)
1 cup chilled heavy cream
Gently fold whipped cream into gelatin mixture. Turn into mold. Chill until firm.

Unmold (page 374) onto chilled serving plate. Garnish with reserved peach halves and
Frosted Grapes (below)

8 to 10 servings

For Frosted Grapes—Beat **1 egg white** until frothy. Dip small clusters of rinsed and thoroughly drained **grapes** in beaten egg white. Shake off excess, then dip grapes into **sugar.**

ROYAL PINEAPPLE DESSERT

Set out a 1-qt. mold. Place a bowl and rotary beater in refrigerator to chill.

Mix thoroughly in a small saucepan
1 env. unflavored gelatin
½ cup sugar
Stir in
½ cup water
Place saucepan over low heat and stir until gelatin and sugar are dissolved. Remove from heat and stir in
½ cup milk
Chill until mixture is slightly thicker than consistency of thick unbeaten egg white.

Meanwhile, pour into chilled bowl
1 cup heavy cream
Using the chilled beater, beat until cream is of medium consistency (piles softly). Set aside in refrigerator.

Using clean beater, beat until stiff, not dry, peaks are formed
1 egg white
When gelatin mixture is of desired consistency, blend in
½ cup drained crushed pineapple
½ cup sliced strawberries
1 cup chopped walnuts
Spread the egg white and whipped cream over the gelatin mixture and fold together. Turn mixture into mold. Chill until firm.

Unmold (page 374) onto chilled serving plate.
8 servings

PINEAPPLE MACAROON CREAM

Set out a 1½-qt. mold. Set a bowl and a rotary beater in refrigerator to chill.

Finely crush and set aside
12 2-in. dry macaroons (about ¾ cup crumbs)

Drain, reserving syrup in a 2-cup measuring cup for liquid
1 can (29½ oz.) sliced pineapple (8 slices)

Peach Macaroon Mold

542

Pineapple Macaroon Cream

Set aside 4 slices for garnish. Cut remaining pineapple slices into small wedge-shaped pieces and set aside.

Pour into reserved pineapple syrup in measuring cup

Water (enough to make 1½ cups liquid)

Set aside.

Pour into a saucepan

1 cup cold water

Sprinkle evenly over cold water

2 env. unflavored gelatin

Set saucepan over low heat and stir constantly until gelatin is completely dissolved. Remove from heat. Stir in the reserved liquid and

1 teaspoon grated lemon peel

2 tablespoons lemon juice

Chill (page 374) until gelatin mixture is slightly thicker than consistency of thick unbeaten egg white.

When gelatin mixture is of desired consistency, beat until frothy

2 egg whites

⅛ teaspoon salt

Add gradually, beating well after each addition

½ cup sugar

Continue beating until rounded peaks are formed. Spread beaten egg whites over thickened gelatin mixture and gently fold together. Fold in pineapple pieces and macaroon crumbs.

Using chilled bowl and beater, beat until cream is of medium consistency (piles softly)

1 cup chilled heavy cream

Fold whipped cream into gelatin mixture. Turn into the mold. Chill until firm.

Unmold (page 374). Cut 3 reserved pineapple slices into halves; place around base of mold alternately with

Frosted Mint Leaves (below)

Garnish the mold with the remaining pineapple slice and

Fresh ripe strawberries

Set in refrigerator until ready to serve.

8 servings

For Frosted Mint Leaves—Beat **1 egg white** until frothy. Dip **mint leaves** in beaten egg white. Shake off excess, then sprinkle leaves with **sugar**. Chill in refrigerator until ready to use.

PRUNE DELIGHT IN RICE RING
(Turban d'Agen)

The French title of this delicious dessert comes from the town of Agen in southern France, famous for its prunes.

Set out a 3-qt. ring mold.

Combine in a heavy saucepan

3 cups boiling water

3 cups milk, scalded (page 10)

4 teaspoons vanilla extract

1 teaspoon salt

Bring to boiling and add gradually, stirring with a fork

1 cup uncooked rice

Continue to stir 1 min. Cover and cook over low heat 15 min. to 1 hr., stirring occasionally until almost all of the liquid is absorbed and a rice kernel is soft when pressed between the fingers.

Meanwhile, measure into a small bowl

½ cup cold water

Sprinkle evenly over water

4 teaspoons unflavored gelatin

Add softened gelatin to the hot cooked rice along with

1 cup sugar

Stir with fork until completely dissolved. Cool.

Fold into cold rice a mixture of

3 cups chilled heavy cream, beaten, one half at a time, to medium consistency (piles softly)

1 tablespoon vanilla extract

Press gently into mold. Chill in refrigerator until firm.

Meanwhile, prepare a compote of prunes.

For Compote—Put into a saucepan

½ lb. (about 1 cup) dried prunes

1 cup red wine

1 cup water

Cover. Bring to boiling; reduce heat and simmer 20 to 25 min., or until prunes are tender and liquid is reduced to about 1 cup. If desired, remove pits from prunes.

Blend the prune liquid into a mixture of

3 tablespoons apricot jam

1 teaspoon lemon juice

Combine with prunes and chill in refrigerator.

When ready to serve, loosen the edges of rice ring and turn it out onto a round serving platter. Fill center with chilled prune compote.

12 to 16 servings

Note: A compote is a simple French dessert made of one or more fruits cooked whole or in pieces in a rich sugar syrup and chilled before serving. In Normandy, cooking is done with cider. Elsewhere, as at Agen, it is done with wine.

RASPBERRY BAVARIAN CREAM

Set out a 1-qt. mold. Place a bowl and rotary beater in refrigerator to chill.

Mix thoroughly in the top of a double boiler

1½ env. unflavored gelatin

½ cup sugar

Few grains salt

Beat together

2 egg yolks

2¼ cups milk

Stir milk mixture into gelatin mixture. Set over boiling water. Cook, stirring constantly until gelatin is dissolved, about 5 min. Remove from heat. Chill until mixture begins to gel (gets slightly thicker).

Meanwhile, pour into chilled bowl

½ cup heavy cream

Using the chilled beater, beat until cream is of medium consistency (piles softly). Set aside in refrigerator.

Using clean beater, beat until frothy

2 egg whites

Danish Rum Pudding III

Add gradually, beating until stiff peaks are formed

¼ cup sugar

When gelatin mixture is of desired consistency, blend in

1 cup raspberries
1 teaspoon lemon juice

Spread the egg whites and whipped cream over the gelatin mixture and fold together. Turn mixture into mold. Chill until firm.

Unmold (page 374) onto chilled serving plate.

8 servings

DANISH RUM PUDDING I
(Rom Budding I)

Set out 6 custard cups.

Pour into a small cup or custard cup

¼ cup cold water

Sprinkle evenly over cold water

2 teaspoons unflavored gelatin

Set aside.

Blend well in top of double boiler

4 egg yolks, slightly beaten
2 cups heavy cream
½ cup sugar
¼ teaspoon salt

Cook over simmering water, stirring constantly and rapidly, until egg yolk mixture coats a metal spoon.

Remove from heat and strain into a bowl. Immediately blend in softened gelatin, stirring until gelatin is completely dissolved. Set aside to cool, stirring occasionally.

Add and stir until thoroughly blended

3 tablespoons rum

Pour mixture into the custard cups and set in refrigerator to chill, about 2 hrs.

When ready to serve, unmold desserts by carefully running a knife around inside edges of cups; invert onto serving dishes.

Serve with

Lingonberries or Raspberry Sauce
(page 580)

6 servings

Note: For a more delicate gel, use only 1 teaspoon gelatin.

DANISH RUM PUDDING II
(Rom Budding II)

Danish fondness for the flavor of rum was acquired in the days when Denmark held possessions in the West Indies.

Set out a 2½-qt. fancy mold.

Pour into a small saucepan

½ cup cold water

Sprinkle evenly over water

1½ env. unflavored gelatin

Set saucepan over low heat and stir constantly until gelatin is completely dissolved. Remove from heat.

Beat until thick and lemon-colored

6 egg yolks

Add gradually, beating in

1 cup sugar

Mix in

6 tablespoons rum
2 tablespoons lemon juice

Stir the dissolved gelatin and blend into the egg yolk mixture.

Beat until rounded peaks are formed and egg whites do not slide when bowl is partially inverted

6 egg whites

Spread egg yolk mixture over beaten egg whites. Gently but thoroughly fold together. Rinse the mold with cold water. Turn mixture into the mold and set in refrigerator to chill until firm.

When ready to serve, unmold (page 374) onto a chilled serving plate. Garnish with

Sweetened Whipped Cream
(page 480)

Arrange around the pudding

Sweetened whole strawberries

Serve with the pudding so that each person may help himself

Raspberry Sauce (page 580)

8 to 10 servings

DANISH RUM PUDDING III
(Rom Budding III)

Set out a 2½-qt. mold.

Pour into a small bowl

½ cup cold water

Sprinkle evenly over cold water

2 env. unflavored gelatin

Set aside.

Beat with rotary or electric beater until thick and lemon-colored

6 egg yolks

Add gradually, beating constantly

½ cup sugar

Add gradually to egg yolk mixture, stirring until well blended

2 cups milk
½ cup cream

Pour into top of double boiler and place over simmering water. Cook, stirring constantly, until mixture coats a metal spoon. Remove top of double boiler from heat and simmering water. Immediately stir in softened gelatin until gelatin is completely dissolved.

Chill in refrigerator or over ice and water until mixture begins to gel (becomes slightly thicker). (If placed over ice and water, stir frequently; if placed in refrigerator, stir occasionally.)

Blend in

6 tablespoons rum

Beat until rounded peaks are formed

6 egg whites

Spread beaten egg whites over mixture and gently fold together. Rinse mold with cold water. Turn mixture into the mold. Chill in refrigerator until firm.

When ready to serve, unmold (page 374) onto a chilled serving plate and serve with

Raspberry Sauce (page 580) or
lingonberry preserves

10 to 12 servings

Blueberry Orange Cheese C

SHERRY WINE JELLY

Beautiful—sophisticated—elegant—delicious!

Set out a 1½-qt. fancy mold.

Combine in a saucepan
½ cup sugar
3 env. unflavored gelatin
Stir in
1 cup boiling water
Set over low heat and stir constantly until sugar and gelatin are dissolved. Add
2 cups boiling water
1 cup sugar
Continue heating and stirring until sugar is completely dissolved. Remove the saucepan from heat.

Blend in
1 cup plus 2 tablespoons sherry
¾ cup strained orange juice
⅓ cup strained lemon juice
9 drops red food coloring
Pour mixture into the prepared mold and chill in refrigerator until firm.

Unmold (page 374) onto a chilled serving plate.

Serve with
Sweetened Whipped Cream (page 480)
6 to 8 servings

SHERRY ELEGANCE

▲ *Base Recipe*

A shimmering, sophisticated appearance and a subtle, smooth flavor are molded together into a dessert of elegant perfection.

Set out a 1½-qt. fancy mold.

Combine and blend thoroughly in a medium-sized heavy saucepan
1½ cups sugar
3 env. unflavored gelatin
Blend in
2 cups water
Set over low heat and stir constantly until sugar and gelatin are completely dissolved.

Remove from heat. Add
1 cup cold water
Blend in
1 cup plus 2 tablespoons sherry
¾ cup strained orange juice
⅓ cup strained lemon juice
Add, a drop at a time, until the desired color is reached
Red food coloring
Pour mixture into the prepared mold and chill in refrigerator until firm.

Unmold (page 374) onto a chilled dessert plate.

Serve with
**Sweetened Whipped Cream
(page 480)**
6 to 8 servings

—SWEET CHERRY ELEGANCE

Follow ▲ Recipe. Drain, reserving syrup, **2 cans (17 oz. each) dark sweet cherries** (about

2 cups, drained). Reduce sugar to 1 cup. Substitute **port** for the sherry and reserved **cherry syrup** for the orange juice. Omit red food coloring. Chill gelatin (page 374) until slightly thicker than consistency of thick unbeaten egg white. When of desired consistency, fold in the cherries. Turn into the mold and set in refrigerator to chill until firm.

ELEGANT STRAWBERRY CREAM

▲ *Base Recipe*

Set out a 1-qt. fancy mold.

Set out to thaw
**1 pkg. (16 oz.) frozen sliced
strawberries (about 2 cups)**

Meanwhile, pour into a small bowl
½ cup cold water
Sprinkle evenly over the water
1½ env. unflavored gelatin
Let stand until softened.

Scald (page 10)
1 cup cream
Remove from heat. Immediately add the softened gelatin, stirring until gelatin is completely dissolved. Add and stir until sugar is dissolved
¾ cup sugar
½ teaspoon vanilla extract
¼ teaspoon salt
Cool; chill (page 374) until mixture begins to gel (gets slightly thicker).

When gelatin mixture is of desired consistency, whip with rotary beater until light and fluffy. Add and stir lightly until blended, the strawberries and
1 cup dairy sour cream
Turn into the mold and chill in refrigerator until firm.

Unmold (page 374) onto chilled serving plate.
About 6 servings

—RASPBERRY CREAM

Follow ▲ Recipe. Substitute **2 pkgs. (10 oz. each) frozen red raspberries** for the strawberries.

Strawberry Bavarian Cream

STRAWBERRY BAVARIAN CREAM

Set out a 1½-qt. heart-shape mold. Place rotary beater and bowl in refrigerator to chill.

Set out to thaw
**2 pkgs. (10 oz. each) frozen sliced
sweetened strawberries (about 2
cups)**

Meanwhile, pour into a small bowl
½ cup cold water
Sprinkle evenly over the water
1½ env. unflavored gelatin
Let stand until the gelatin is softened. Dissolve completely by placing over very hot water.

When gelatin is dissolved, stir it and blend into a mixture of thawed strawberries and
6 tablespoons sugar
1½ tablespoons lemon juice
1 teaspoon almond extract
Stir until well blended. Chill in refrigerator or over ice and water until gelatin mixture is slightly thicker than consistency of thick unbeaten egg white. If mixture is placed over ice and water, stir frequently; if placed in refrigerator, stir occasionally.

Meanwhile, using chilled bowl and beater.

Cherry Filbert Sundae Pie

Trifle

beat about one half of cream at a time until of medium consistency (piles softly)

1¾ cups chilled heavy cream

Combine the two portions of whipped cream.

Fold into whipped cream, 3 drops at a time, until desired color is reached

10 to 12 drops red food coloring

Fold whipped cream into slightly thickened strawberry mixture. Turn into prepared mold. Chill in refrigerator until firm.

Meanwhile, wash rotary beater and bowl and return to refrigerator to chill.

When Strawberry Bavarian Cream is firm, unmold (page 374).

Using chilled bowl and beater, beat until cream stands in peaks when beater is slowly lifted upright

¼ cup chilled heavy cream

Decorate top of Bavarian with whipped cream forced through pastry bag and No. 27 decorating tube for border and a No. 6 decorating tube for flower.   *8 to 10 servings*

REFRIGERATOR DESSERTS

TRIFLE

Set small bowl and rotary beater into refrigerator to chill.

Blanch, sliver, toast (pages 9 and 10) and set aside

½ cup (about 3 oz.) almonds

Set aside.

Cut into 1-in. pieces

1 lb. day-old pound cake

Place cake pieces in bowl and pour over them

½ cup brandy or rum

Cover and set aside.

Combine and blend thoroughly in top of a double boiler

¼ cup sugar
1 env. unflavored gelatin
⅛ teaspoon salt

Beat in a bowl until thoroughly blended

5 egg yolks
1¾ cups milk

Combine with the gelatin mixture in top of the double boiler. Set over boiling water in the bottom of double boiler and cook, stirring occasionally, about 5 min., or until the gelatin is completely dissolved. Remove from heat and stir in

1 teaspoon vanilla extract

Chill in refrigerator or over ice and water until mixture mounds slightly when dropped from a spoon. (If mixture is placed over ice and water, stir frequently; if placed in refrigerator, stir occasionally.)

When the gelatin mixture is of desired consistency, prepare whipped cream. Beat in the chilled small bowl with chilled rotary beater until cream piles softly

¼ cup chilled heavy cream

Beat until frothy

3 egg whites

Add gradually, beating thoroughly after each addition

¼ cup sugar

Continue to beat until very stiff peaks are formed.

Blend egg whites and whipped cream into gelatin mixture. Carefully fold in cake mixture. Turn into serving dish. Chill in refrigerator until firm.

About 1 hr. before serving, place a bowl and rotary beater in refrigerator to chill.

Just before serving, prepare, using the chilled bowl and beater

Sweetened Whipped Cream (page 480)

Force whipped cream through a pastry bag and No. 27 star decorating tube, forming a border around Trifle. Garnish top of Trifle with the slivered almonds, **pieces of angelica** and a **red candied cherry.**   *12 servings*

BROWN-EDGE WAFER ROLL

▲ *Base Recipe*

Prepare

Creamy Chocolate Frosting (page 479)

Spread a thin layer of frosting on each of

27 brown-edge wafers

Turn wafers on end and press together to form one long roll made up of alternate layers of wafers and filling. Cover outside of roll with remaining filling.

Chill in refrigerator 2 to 3 hrs. Cut into diagonal slices about 1 in. thick.

6 to 8 servings

—CHOCOLATE WAFER ROLL

Follow ▲ Recipe. Substitute for the Creamy Chocolate Frosting, **1 cup Sweetened Whipped Cream** (page 480). Substitute **Crispy Rolled Wafers** (page 604) or commercial chocolate wafers for the brown-edge wafers.

—PARTY LOAF

Double Chocolate Wafer Roll recipe. Prepare 9 rolls of alternate wafers and filling, each made of 6 wafers. Place rolls on end close together on serving dish to form loaf 3 rolls long and 3 rolls wide. Cover entire loaf with remaining filling. Top with **moist shredded coconut.** Slice straight across loaf.

About 12 servings

DRAMATIC CHERRY DELIGHT I

▲ *Base Recipe*

The dark sweet cherries of deep summer give rich color and a special lusciousness to this dessert—perfect when your guest list is doubled.

Set out a 10-in. tubed springform pan. Chill a bowl and rotary beater in refrigerator.

Have ready

Jelly Roll I (page 458; about one half of roll will be needed)

Empty into a large bowl

2 pkgs. (3 oz. each) cherry-flavored gelatin

Add

2 cups boiling water

Stir until gelatin is completely dissolved.

Stir in

1 cup cold water
1 tablespoon lemon juice

Chill (page 374) until gelatin mixture is slightly thicker than consistency of thick unbeaten egg white.

Brown-Edge Wafer Roll: Form wafers and frosting into a roll and, after chilling, slice diagonally.

Party Loaf

Meanwhile, rinse, drain, stem, cut into halves and remove and discard pits from

**3 cups dark sweet cherries (about
2½ cups, halved and pitted)**

Put cherries into a bowl and mix in

⅓ cup granulated sugar

When gelatin mixture is of desired consistency, using the chilled bowl and beater, beat (one cup at a time) until cream is of medium consistency (piles softly)

2 cups chilled heavy cream

Beat in with few final strokes

**¼ cup confectioners' sugar
½ teaspoon almond extract**

Set whipped cream in refrigerator while beating gelatin.

Using a rotary beater, beat the gelatin until light and frothy. Spread the whipped cream over gelatin, add the cherry halves and gently fold together.

Cut 8 crosswise slices about ½ in. thick from jelly roll, reserving any remaining jelly roll for other use. Arrange the jelly-roll slices around the sides of the tubed springform pan. Turn the gelatin mixture into the pan, being careful to keep jelly-roll slices in place. Set in refrigerator to chill until gelatin mixture is firm, at least 4 hrs.

To serve, carefully run a spatula around inside of pan and tube, from top to bottom, to loosen dessert. Remove sides of pan. Do not remove dessert from bottom of pan. Place on chilled serving plate. *16 servings*

—DRAMATIC CHERRY DELIGHT I

This version can be made any time of the year.

Prepare one half ▲ Recipe; use a 7-in. springform pan. Substitute **1 can (17 oz.) pitted dark sweet cherries** for the fresh cherries; drain the cherries, reserving the syrup, and cut into halves. Substitute **½ cup cherry syrup** for the cold water. (Reserve remaining cherry syrup for other use.) Use only 3 tablespoons granulated sugar. Use only 3 slices of jelly roll. Cut each slice into halves crosswise and arrange slices cut side down around the sides of the springform pan.

CHOCOLATE REFRIGERATOR CAKE

Place a small bowl and a rotary beater in refrigerator to chill.

Line bottom and sides of 9-in. springform pan with

Ladyfingers or vanilla or chocolate wafers (about 3 doz. for entire cake)

Melt (page 10)

6 oz. sweet chocolate

in

⅓ cup water

Stir and set aside to cool.

Chop and set aside

½ cup (2 oz.) nuts

Beat with rotary beater until thick and lemon colored

**4 egg yolks
3 tablespoons sugar**

Blend in thoroughly the cooled chocolate and

1 teaspoon vanilla extract

Chill mixture in refrigerator.

Using chilled bowl and beater, beat until of medium consistency (piles softly)

1 cup chilled heavy cream

Beat until rounded peaks are formed

4 egg whites

Gently fold whipped cream and egg whites into chocolate mixture. Pour one-half into prepared pan. Cover with remaining ladyfingers or wafers. Pour remainder of chocolate mixture over top.

Refrigerate about 8 hrs., or until set. If desired, garnish top with **whipped cream** and **chopped nuts.** *10 to 12 servings*

ALMOND CHOCOLATE REFRIGERATOR CAKE

Set out an 8x8x2-in. pan. Set a bowl and a rotary beater in refrigerator to chill.

Put into top of a double boiler

**1¼ cups (14-oz. can) sweetened condensed milk
2 oz. (2 sq.) unsweetened chocolate**

Set over simmering water and cook, stirring

frequently, until mixture is thick and smooth. Remove from heat.

Meanwhile, pour into a small saucepan

½ cup cold water

Sprinkle evenly over cold water

1 env. unflavored gelatin

Set saucepan over low heat and stir constantly until gelatin is completely dissolved. Remove from heat.

Pour gelatin into chocolate mixture and blend thoroughly. Set aside to cool.

Meanwhile, line bottom of the pan with waxed paper. Split into halves lengthwise

12 ladyfingers

Line bottom and sides of the pan with the ladyfingers, cut sides in.

When chocolate mixture is cool, stir into it

**⅔ cup fine dry macaroon crumbs
½ teaspoon almond extract**

Using the chilled bowl and beater, beat until of medium consistency (piles softly)

½ cup chilled heavy cream

Fold into chocolate mixture. Spoon mixture into prepared pan, being careful to keep ladyfingers in place. Chill in refrigerator until firm, about 3 hrs.

To serve, cover with a serving plate; invert and remove pan and waxed paper.
About 8 servings

CHIFFON REFRIGERATOR CAKE

Place a rotary beater and a bowl in refrigerator.

Set in freezer until ice crystals form

1⅓ cups undiluted evaporated milk

Line bottom and sides of a 9-in. springform pan with

Ladyfingers (about 36)

Set aside.

Pour into a small bowl or custard cup

¼ cup cold water

Sprinkle evenly over the water

1 env. unflavored gelatin

Let stand 5 min. to soften.

Combine in top of double boiler

**1 pkg. (12 oz.) semisweet chocolate pieces
1 cup cream
½ cup sugar
¼ teaspoon salt**

Cook over simmering water; stir constantly until chocolate melts and mixture is blended. Remove from heat at once. Vigorously stir about 6 tablespoons hot mixture into

6 egg yolks, slightly beaten

Immediately blend into mixture in double boiler. Cook over simmering water, stirring constantly, 3 to 5 min., or until mixture thickens. Remove from heat at once; add softened gelatin and stir until gelatin is completely dissolved. Add and blend well

**4 teaspoons rum extract
2 teaspoons vanilla extract**

Cool and chill in refrigerator or over ice and water until consistency of thick unbeaten egg white. (If mixture is placed over ice and water, stir frequently; if placed in refrigerator, stir occasionally.)

Beat until frothy

6 egg whites

Add gradually, beating well after each addition

½ cup sugar

Beat until rounded peaks are formed. Spread thickened gelatin mixture over beaten egg whites and fold together gently.

Using chilled bowl and beater, blend icy cold evaporated milk and

2 tablespoons lemon juice

Whip until stiff.

Gently fold into gelatin mixture. Turn into prepared pan. Chill about 8 hrs., or until set.

10 to 12 servings

CHOCALINDA

Set out an 8-in. square pan.

Sliver and set aside

½ cup (3 oz.) blanched, toasted and salted almonds (pages 9 and 10)

Finely crush

8 graham crackers (about ⅔ cup, crushed)

Sprinkle the crushed graham crackers evenly over bottom of pan.

Put into a bowl

2 cups confectioners' sugar
½ cup cocoa
½ cup butter or margarine, softened
2 eggs
1 teaspoon vanilla extract

Beat with electric mixer until smooth, creamy, light in color and mixture stands in peaks. Do not overbeat. Using spoon or rubber spatula, take portions of mixture and place carefully in each corner and in middle of graham cracker crumb-lined pan. Gently spread mixture to cover entire pan. Sprinkle the almonds over the mixture. Using back of spoon, gently press almonds onto mixture. Chill in refrigerator 12 hrs. Serve thoroughly chilled.

8 servings

Mocha Refrigerator Dream Cake

MOCHA REFRIGERATOR DREAM CAKE

Set out an 8-in. springform pan. Put a bowl and hand rotary or electric beater in refrigerator to chill.

Pour into a small cup or custard cup

½ cup cold water

Sprinkle evenly over cold water

1 env. unflavored gelatin

Let stand until softened.

Pour

¾ cup very hot water

over

4 teaspoons instant powdered coffee

Stir coffee and immediately add the softened gelatin, stirring until gelatin is completely dissolved. Add, stirring until dissolved

¼ cup sugar
¼ teaspoon salt

Chill in refrigerator or over pan of ice and water until mixture is slightly thicker than consistency of thick unbeaten egg white. If mixture is placed over ice and water, stir frequently; if placed in refrigerator, stir occasionally.

Meanwhile, set out

2 doz. chocolate wafers

Put 14 of the wafers on a long length of heavy waxed paper. Loosely fold paper around wafers, tucking under open ends. With a rolling pin, gently crush to make fine crumbs. Or put cookies in a plastic bag and crush gently. Set aside.

Line the sides of the springform pan with the remaining whole cookies and set aside.

When coffee-gelatin mixture is of desired consistency, using the chilled bowl and beater, beat until cream is of medium consistency (piles softly)

1 cup chilled heavy cream

Gently fold into the coffee-gelatin mixture.

Spoon one half of the whipped cream mixture into the pan. Sprinkle with one half the cookie crumbs. Repeat, using remaining whipped cream mixture and then remaining crumbs. Chill in refrigerator until cake is firm.

Chill a bowl and beater in refrigerator.

A few minutes before ready to serve, using the chilled bowl and beater, beat until cream stands in peaks when beater is slowly lifted upright

½ cup chilled heavy cream

Beat into whipped cream with few final strokes just until blended

2 tablespoons confectioners' sugar
¼ teaspoon almond extract

Remove cake from refrigerator. Remove rim from bottom of pan and place on chilled serving plate. Decorate cake by forcing whipped cream through a pastry bag and No. 27 decorating tube. If desired, garnish with

Slivered, toasted, blanched almonds

Place in refrigerator until ready to serve.

About 6 servings

LUSCIOUS CHOCOLATE RUM CAKE

Set out a 10-in. springform pan.

Stirring occasionally, cook in top of a double boiler until mixture is smooth

4 oz. (4 sq.) unsweetened chocolate
½ cup sugar
¼ cup water

Vigorously stir a small amount into

8 egg yolks, well beaten

Blend into mixture in double boiler top and set over gently boiling water; cook about 5 min., stirring constantly. Remove from heat and cool.

Blend in

3 to 4 tablespoons rum

Cream together until light and fluffy

2 cups butter
1 lb. confectioners' sugar

Blend in the chocolate mixture. Set aside.

Line sides and bottom of springform pan with

18 split ladyfingers, rounded side up

Beat as for a meringue

8 egg whites
½ cup sugar

Fold into chocolate mixture. Spoon over ladyfingers. Chill at least 24 hrs. Serve with whipped cream.

One 10-in. cake

NEW ORLEANS HOLIDAY PUDDING

Tempting cups of hot coffee accompany New Orleans Pudding to make a memorable treat.

Set out a 9- or 10-in. tubed pan and a 3-qt. saucepan with a cover.

Chill in refrigerator a bowl, rotary beater and

1½ pts. heavy cream

Meanwhile, pour into the saucepan

3 cups water

Add to the water

1¼ cups (about ½ lb.) prunes
1 cup (about 6 oz.) dried apricots

Bring to boiling; cover and simmer about 20 min., or until fruit is tender.

Bring to boiling in a small saucepan

2 cups water

Add and bring water again to boiling

    1½ cups (about 7½ oz.) golden raisins

Drain raisins and put into a large bowl with

    1 lb. (about 2¼ cups) candied cherries

    ⅓ cup (about 2 oz.) diced candied citron

    ⅓ cup (about 2 oz.) diced candied lemon peel

Set fruit mixture aside.

Turn prune-apricot mixture into colander or large sieve to drain. Reserve liquid in a measuring cup (add water if needed to yield 1½ cups liquid); set aside to cool. Pit prunes.

Force prune-apricot mixture through sieve or food mill into the saucepan to make a purée. Stir in until sugar is dissolved a mixture of

    1 cup sugar

    1 teaspoon cinnamon

    1 teaspoon nutmeg

    1 teaspoon allspice

Blend into candied fruit mixture with

    1 cup orange juice

    3 tablespoons brandy

Cover and set aside for about 1½ hrs., stirring occasionally.

Coarsely chop and set aside

    1½ cups (about 6 oz.) walnuts

Pour into a heavy saucepan

    1½ cups cold reserved prune-apricot liquid

Sprinkle evenly over liquid

    3 env. unflavored gelatin

Set saucepan over low heat and stir constantly until gelatin is completely dissolved. Blend the dissolved gelatin into the fruit mixture. Mix in the chopped walnuts. Set mixture in refrigerator while whipping cream.

Pour one third of chilled heavy cream into the chilled bowl. Beat with the chilled rotary beater until cream is of medium consistency (piles softly). Turn whipped cream onto fruit-gelatin mixture.

Beat remaining heavy cream as above and turn onto previously whipped cream. Gently fold together, blending thoroughly. Carefully spoon into prepared pan. Chill in refrigerator until firm. Unmold (page 374) onto a large serving plate.

This dessert will keep for several days in the refrigerator. *20 to 24 servings, depending upon size of tubed pan*

For Festive Topping (see photo)—Cover bottom of pan with chopped nuts. Reserve 12 cherries and arrange in clusters of three, moving nuts to let cherries touch bottom of pan. When spooning mixture over nuts and cherries, gently press mixture over nuts to cover entirely.

FRUIT CHARLOTTE

Set out a 1-qt. fancy mold. Put a bowl and beater in refrigerator to chill.

Cook, following package directions

    ¾ cup (about ¼ lb.) dried apricots

Drain, reserving ¼ cup of the cooking liquid. Set aside.

Blend in a small saucepan

    ¼ cup sugar

    1 env. unflavored gelatin

    ⅛ teaspoon salt

Stir in the reserved apricot cooking liquid and

    ¼ cup cold water

Stir over low heat until gelatin and sugar are dissolved. Remove from heat and mix in

    1 can (8¼ oz.) crushed pineapple, undrained

    ½ cup (2½ oz.) golden raisins

Chill until mixture is slightly thickened.

Meanwhile, prepare and set aside

    ½ cup (about 3 oz.) slivered and toasted blanched almonds (pages 9 and 10)

Drain well and cut into quarters

    ⅓ cup maraschino cherries (half red and half green)

Cut into strips enough of the drained cooked apricots to yield ½ cup strips.

Line the sides of the mold with

    ½ doz. ladyfingers, split

Arrange several of the apricot strips and a few of the maraschino cherry pieces in bottom of mold. Set aside.

When gelatin mixture is of the desired consistency, using the chilled bowl and beater, beat until soft peaks are formed

    1 cup chilled heavy cream

Fold whipped cream, almonds, apricot strips and cherry pieces lightly and thoroughly into the gelatin mixture. Spoon into the prepared mold, being careful to keep ladyfingers in position. Chill until firm. Unmold onto a chilled serving plate. *About 8 servings*

PEPPERMINT STICK DELIGHT

▲ *Base Recipe*

Set out an 8x8x2-in. pan. Put a bowl and rotary beater into refrigerator to chill.

Set out

    ¼ lb. vanilla wafers (or enough to yield 1 cup crumbs)

Prepare crumbs (page 10). Turn crumbs into a large bowl. Stir in

    2 tablespoons sugar

Add gradually, stirring in with a fork

    3 tablespoons butter or margarine, melted

New Orleans Holiday Pudding

Using back of spoon, press crumb mixture firmly into an even layer on bottom of the pan. Set aside.

Coarsely crush and set aside

    5 small (about 1½ oz.) sticks peppermint candy

Coarsely chop and set aside

    ½ cup (about 2 oz.) walnuts

Cut into quarters (page 9)

    16 marshmallows (4 oz.)

Using the chilled bowl and beater, beat (about one half of the cream at a time) until cream is of medium consistency (piles softly)

    1½ cups chilled heavy cream

Fold the nuts, candy and marshmallows into the whipped cream. Turn into pan. Chill in refrigerator about 12 hrs. *8 servings*

—CHOCOLATE PEPPERMINT FLUFF

Follow ▲ Recipe. Substitute ½ lb. chocolate wafers (2¼ cups crumbs) for the vanilla wafers. Omit sugar and melted butter. Mix 1 cup of chocolate crumbs with ¼ cup confectioners' sugar and ¼ cup softened butter. Press on bottom of the pan. Sprinkle remaining crumbs evenly over top of fluff before chilling.

PINEAPPLE SWIRL TRIFLE

Set out a 9-in. springform pan.

Drain thoroughly

    1 can (20 oz.) pineapple slices

Have ready

    Jelly roll (commercial or see recipes, page 458), cut in 12 slices

Pour into a small bowl

    ½ cup cold milk

Pineapple Swirl Trifle

Sprinkle over milk

1 env. unflavored gelatin

Set aside.

Set out

3 cups milk

Prepare, following directions on package and using the 3 cups milk

2 pkgs. (about 3 oz. each) vanilla pudding and pie filling

Remove from heat. Immediately add the softened gelatin and stir until gelatin is dissolved. Mix in

1 tablespoon vanilla extract

Cool thoroughly.

Line the sides of the springform pan with 4 pineapple slices alternated with 4 jelly roll slices (see photo).

Prepare, following directions on package

2 env. (2 oz. each) dessert topping mix

Fold whipped topping into pudding. Spoon a third of the pudding into pan. Arrange a layer of jelly roll slices over pudding. Repeat layers, ending with the pudding. Top with the remaining pineapple slices. Chill until set, about 5 hrs.

To serve, remove rim of pan and cut dessert into wedges. *About 10 servings*

PINEAPPLE PARTY CAKE

▲ *Base Recipe*

Set out a 9x5x3-in. loaf pan. Place a medium-size bowl and a rotary beater in refrigerator to chill.

Set aside to drain thoroughly reserving syrup

1 can (20 oz.) sliced pineapple

Pour into a small cup or custard cup

¼ cup cold water
¼ cup reserved pineapple syrup

Sprinkle evenly over top

1 env. unflavored gelatin

Let stand until softened.

Mix thoroughly in top of double boiler

1 cup sugar
2 tablespoons cornstarch

Add gradually and blend in thoroughly

¾ cup reserved pineapple syrup

Stirring constantly, bring mixture rapidly to boiling over direct heat and cook for 3 min.

Beat until thick and piled softly

2 eggs

Gradually add about 3 tablespoons of hot mixture to eggs, stirring vigorously. Immediately blend into mixture in double boiler, while stirring constantly. Cook over simmering water 3 to 5 min. until mixture thickens. Remove from heat and immediately add softened gelatin, stirring until gelatin is completely dissolved.

Chill in refrigerator or over ice and water until mixture begins to gel (becomes slightly thicker). If mixture is placed over ice and water, stir frequently; if placed in refrigerator, stir occasionally.

Meanwhile, set out

2 doz. ladyfingers (or use sponge cake cut in 4x1½x1-in. pieces)

Line bottom and sides of the loaf pan with ladyfingers. Set aside loaf pan and remaining ladyfingers.

Shortly before gelatin mixture is slightly thicker, beat, using the chilled bowl and beater, until cream is of medium consistency (piles softly)

½ cup chilled heavy cream

Gently fold whipped cream into gelatin mixture with

1½ teaspoons grated lemon peel
2 teaspoons lemon juice

Return the bowl and beater to refrigerator.

Pour one half of the whipped cream-pineapple mixture into the ladyfinger-lined pan. Cover with reserved ladyfingers. Pour remaining half of mixture over ladyfingers. Chill until firm, about 2 hrs.

Just before serving, unmold by running tip of a knife around top edge of mold to loosen. If necessary, dip mold into hot water for a few seconds. Invert onto a chilled plate.

Using the chilled bowl and beater, beat until cream stands in peaks when beater is slowly lifted upright

1 cup chilled heavy cream

Spread whipped cream evenly over top of cake. Slice two pineapple rings into halves. Arrange the pineapple halves on top of cake with

5 maraschino cherries, well drained

Serve immediately. *8 to 10 servings*

—PINEAPPLE PARTY ELEGANCE

For loaf pan substitute a 7-in. springform pan. Double ▲ Recipe for filling; use 3 doz.

ladyfingers. Omit pineapple slices and maraschino cherries. To decorate, remove a small amount of whipped cream to each of two small bowls. Blend into one bowl **1 or more drops red food coloring** to tint cream pink. Blend into remaining bowl **1 or more drops green food coloring** to tint cream a delicate green. Force untinted whipped cream through a pastry bag and No. 27 star tube to form rosettes between ladyfingers at base of serving plate. Swirl remaining untinted whipped cream over top. Using a No. 103 flower decorating tube, force pink whipped cream through pastry bag and tube to form roses. Using a No. 66 leaf decorating tube force green whipped cream through a pastry bag and tube to form leaves. Set in refrigerator if not served immediately.

CHOCOLATE-CROWNED RICE ROYALE

Lightly butter a 2-qt., shallow baking dish.

Prepare

Fluffy Rice (page 164)

Meanwhile, prepare

Custard (see Custard in Creamy Peaches, page 528; reduce eggs to 3 and do not separate them. Increase vanilla extract to 1 tablespoon. Omit almond extract.)

Toss cooked rice lightly with

¼ cup firmly packed brown sugar

Mix custard into rice. Turn into baking dish. Set aside to cool.

Meanwhile, combine and place over simmering water until chocolate is melted

⅓ cup milk
1 pkg. (6 oz.) semisweet chocolate pieces

Set out

½ cup salted pecan halves

Pineapple Party Cake

Cut in pieces (page 9)

8 marshmallows

Toss pecan halves and marshmallow pieces over rice-custard mixture. Stir chocolate and pour evenly over entire surface. Cover with waxed paper, aluminum foil or moisture-vaporproof material and place in refrigerator to chill.

Just before serving, prepare

Sweetened Whipped Cream (page 480)

Top individual servings with whipped cream. *About 8 servings*

TOFFEE DESSERT

▲ *Base Recipe*

Butter an 8-in. square pan.

Melt (page 10) and set aside to cool

2 oz. (2 sq.) unsweetened chocolate

Crush to fine crumbs

¼ lb. vanilla wafers

Blend in

1 cup (about 4 oz.) chopped nuts

Set aside.

Cream together

½ cup butter or margarine, softened

1 cup confectioners' sugar

2 teaspoons vanilla extract

Beat until thick and lemon-colored and blend into creamed mixture

3 egg yolks

Stir in melted chocolate

Beat until rounded peaks are formed and fold into chocolate mixture

3 egg whites

Spread one third crumb mixture in the pan. Cover with one half the chocolate mixture, pressing firmly into crumbs. Repeat, ending with crumb layer. Chill overnight. *8 servings*

—RUM TOFFEE DESSERT

Follow ▲ Recipe. Substitute **2 teaspoons rum extract** for vanilla extract.

FROZEN DESSERTS

WHAT YOU SHOULD KNOW ABOUT FROZEN DESSERTS

Frozen desserts—This term includes a number of mixtures that can be frozen—in the refrigerator or in an ice-cream freezer. Some frozen desserts should be agitated during freezing to break up large ice crystals while they are forming. The smaller the ice crystals, the smoother and creamier-seeming will be the texture of the frozen dessert. Therefore, when the dessert is frozen to a mushy consistency it should be removed from the refrigerator and beaten or stirred until smooth. The whipped

cream used in mousses prevents formation of large ice crystals by incorporating air into the mixture. Any substance, such as gelatin, eggs, flour, cornstarch or rennet, which increases the viscosity (resistance to pouring) of the mixture tends to separate the crystals and prevent them from growing.

Stirring (agitation) during freezing process— *American ice cream*—mixture of cream, sugar and flavoring. Cream that can be whipped is highly desirable since the incorporation of air during whipping gives a smooth texture to the ice cream. Whipping also distributes the fat evenly, creating added smoothness as the mixture freezes. Because heavy cream is expensive, recipes have been developed which use thin cream, evaporated milk, or milk thickened with gelatin, flour, eggs or marshmallows for part or all of the heavy cream. *French ice cream*—a rich mixture of eggs, cream, sugar and flavorings; virtually a frozen custard. *Philadelphia ice cream*—uncooked mixture of cream, sugar and flavorings; never with gelatin or other binder added. *Frozen custard*—mixture with a custard base; also a frozen product, in the wholesale and retail trade, too low in butterfat content to be legally called ice cream. *Water ice*—diluted fruit juice, sweetened with sugar, syrup or honey; coarse texture, melts easily. *Granité*—water ice frozen with little stirring; rough and icy in texture. *Frappé*—water ice frozen to a mushy consistency. *Sherbet*—water ice (the base of which may be fruit juice or pulp) with beaten egg white or gelatin added—this decreases the size of crystals and gives a smoother product; milk sherbet uses milk as part of liquid. *Sorbet*—sherbet made of several kinds of fruit. *Coupe*—frozen cup composed of fruit and ice cream; garnished with whipped cream, candied fruits and peels, chopped nuts, mint leaves or fresh fruit; originally served in a special glass similar to the "champagne coupe."

Little or no stirring during freezing process— The following are ice creams made of heavy cream with or without eggs: *Parfait*—made by pouring a hot thick syrup over beaten egg whites or beaten egg yolks, adding flavoring and folding in whipped cream. *Biscuit*—parfait or similar mixture, partially frozen, then packed in small individual paper cases and

frozen until firm. *Bombe*—two or more frozen mixtures packed in a melon-shaped or round mold and refrozen. *Mousse*—flavored whipped cream mixture; may contain gelatin.

FROZEN BOMBE
(Bombe Glacé)

A truly French innovation, the bombe once was prepared in a bomb-shape mold. Now it may be molded in a melon mold or other fancy form and served at the most festive occasion.

Chill in refrigerator a 2-qt. mold or two 1-qt. molds.

For Pâté à Bombe—Combine in a saucepan with a tight-fitting cover

2 cups sugar

1 cup water

¼ teaspoon cream of tartar

Stir over low heat until sugar is dissolved. Increase heat to medium and bring mixture to boiling. Cover saucepan and boil mixture gently 5 min. Uncover and continue cooking to 232°F (thread stage, page 11; remove from heat while testing).

Beat until thick and lemon-colored

8 egg yolks

Beating constantly, gradually pour a very fine stream of syrup into beaten egg yolks. Cook over simmering water, stirring constantly, until mixture is smooth and thick. Cool over ice and water, beating constantly until cold. Blend in any one of the following

2 teaspoons almond extract, 1 tablespoon vanilla extract, 2 tablespoons liqueur or 1 cup puréed fruit

Beat (1 cup at a time) in a chilled bowl with a chilled rotary beater until cream is of medium consistency (piles softly)

2 cups chilled heavy cream

Fold into egg yolk mixture.

For Preparation of Bombe—Rinse chilled mold with cold water and, working rapidly, line with a layer ¾ to 1 in. thick of

1 qt. frozen fruit ice

Pack the *Pâté à Bombe* inside the fruit ice. Fill mold level with top. Any leftover pâté may be put into refrigerator tray and frozen. Cover mold with waxed paper. Seal with its cover, with foil, or several more thicknesses of waxed paper tied over the top of mold.

Bury mold in mixture of

4 parts crushed ice

1 part rock salt

Freeze 3 to 4 hours.

At end of freezing period, carefully rinse the salt from the mold with cold water and remove covering. Loosen sides of mold with a cold knife. Dip quickly into lukewarm water, dry and unmold.

Garnish Frozen Bombe with **whipped cream** or fancy **glacé fruits.** *12 to 14 servings*

MOUSSE DELICIEUSE

Set out a 2-qt. fancy mold, two 1-qt. molds, or 10 to 12 individual molds.

Mix in the top of a double boiler
¾ cup sugar
2 env. unflavored gelatin
¼ teaspoon salt
Beat together until well blended
2 egg yolks
2 cups milk
Stir into gelatin mixture. Cook and stir over boiling water until gelatin is dissolved, about 5 min.

Remove from heat and stir in
3 tablespoons brandy
1 tablespoon vanilla extract
Chill until mixture mounds when dropped from a spoon.

Beat until frothy
2 egg whites
Add gradually, beating until stiff peaks are formed
¼ cup sugar
Whip until soft peaks are formed
2 cups chilled heavy cream
Fold beaten egg whites into whipped cream until well blended. Fold in the chilled mixture. Turn into the mold or molds. Cover with aluminum foil and freeze.

Before serving, allow sufficient time (1 or more hours if necessary) for mold to soften slightly in the refrigerator. Unmold onto a chilled serving plate. Serve with a **strawberry sauce.**   *10 to 12 servings*

CHOCOLATE MOUSSE I

Set a rotary beater and a bowl in refrigerator to chill.

Pour into a small cup or custard cup
2 tablespoons cold water
Sprinkle evenly over water
1½ teaspoons unflavored gelatin
Let stand until softened.

Heat until milk is scalded (page 10) and chocolate melted
1 cup milk
2 oz. (2 sq.) unsweetened chocolate
Remove from heat. Blend in softened gelatin, stirring until gelatin is completely dissolved. Stir in
¾ cup sugar
½ teaspoon salt
Blend well until sugar and salt are dissolved. Cool. Stir in
1 teaspoon vanilla extract

Using chilled bowl and beater, whip one cup at a time until of medium consistency (piles softly)
2 cups chilled heavy cream
Fold into gelatin mixture. Turn into refrigerator tray and freeze until firm, 3 to 4 hrs.

Set mousse in refrigerator and allow to soften slightly before serving.   *5 servings*

CHOCOLATE MOUSSE II

▲ *Base Recipe*

Set out a fancy 1½-qt. mold. Place a rotary beater and a bowl in refrigerator to chill.

Put into top of double boiler and place over direct heat, stirring until sugar is completely dissolved
⅔ cup sugar
¼ cup water
Place over simmering water; add and heat until chocolate is melted
4 oz. (4 sq.) unsweetened chocolate
Remove from heat and set aside to cool.

Meanwhile, pour into a small cup or custard cup
¼ cup cold water
Sprinkle evenly over cold water
1½ teaspoons unflavored gelatin
Let stand until softened, then dissolve completely by placing cup over very hot water.

Rinse the mold with cold water and set aside to drain.

Using the chilled bowl and rotary beater, beat 1 cup at a time until cream is of medium consistency (piles softly)
2 cups chilled heavy cream
Beat into whipped cream with few final strokes until blended
½ cup confectioners' sugar
1 teaspoon vanilla extract
Stir dissolved gelatin into chocolate mixture and gently mix chocolate into whipped cream

until mixture is thoroughly blended. Spoon into mold.

Freeze about 3 hrs., or until firm.

Chill a rotary beater and a bowl in refrigerator.

Drain, reserving syrup
1 can (20 oz.) pineapple tidbits

Using the chilled bowl and rotary beater, beat until cream stands in peaks when beater is slowly lifted upright
½ cup chilled heavy cream

When firm, unmold mousse. To unmold, loosen top edge of mold with a knife. Wet a clean towel in hot water and wring it almost dry. Invert mold onto chilled serving plate. Wrap hot towel around mold for a few seconds only. (If mold does not loosen, repeat.)

Force whipped cream through a pastry bag and a No. 27 star tube, to decorate center and sides of mold. Garnish whipped cream with pineapple tidbits and
Maraschino cherries
(Reserve pineapple syrup and remaining pineapple tidbits for use in other cooking.)

Serve immediately.   *One 1½-qt. mold*

—MOUSSE CAFE

Follow ▲ Recipe. Omit sugar and water. Omit chocolate. Prepare **2 cups double-strength coffee beverage** (page 10). Immediately add softened gelatin (do not dissolve gelatin over hot water) and stir until gelatin is completely dissolved. Chill in refrigerator or over ice and water until gelatin is slightly thicker than consistency of thick unbeaten egg white. (If placed over ice and water, stir frequently; if placed in refrigerator, stir occasionally.) When mixture is of desired consistency, blend in the sweetened whipped cream. Increase confectioners' sugar to ¾ cup.

GINGER YAM MOUSSE

Spices are blended with yams in this dessert ring.

Set out a 6½-cup ring mold.

Prepare
1½ cups mashed cooked yams (about 3 medium yams)

Mix in a heavy saucepan
1 cup sugar
2 teaspoons ginger
1 teaspoon nutmeg
½ teaspoon cinnamon
Few grains salt
Mix in the yams and
3 egg yolks, fork beaten
2 cups milk
Cook over medium heat, stirring constantly, until mixture is thick. Remove from heat when mixture comes just to boiling. Cool, stirring occasionally.

Ginger Yam Mousse

Blend into cooled yam mixture

½ teaspoon grated lemon peel
½ teaspoon lemon juice
½ cup light cream or half and half

Beat until frothy

3 egg whites

Add gradually, beating until stiff peaks are formed

¼ cup sugar

Fold beaten egg whites into completely cooled yam mixture. Turn into the mold and spread evenly. Freeze until firm.

Allow mousse to soften slightly at room temperature before unmolding. Unmold onto a chilled plate. Spoon **sweetened whipped cream** into center and sprinkle with **toasted slivered almonds**. Arrange clusters of **seedless green grapes** around edge of plate.

6 to 8 servings

PARFAIT
(Parfait Glacé)

Mix in a saucepan

½ cup sugar
¼ cup water
⅛ teaspoon cream of tartar

Boil 5 min.

Beat until thick and lemon-colored

2 egg yolks

Beating constantly, gradually pour a very fine stream of the sugar syrup into beaten egg yolks. Cook in top of double boiler over simmering water, stirring constantly, until mixture is smooth and thick. Cool over ice and water, beating constantly until cold. Blend in

1 teaspoon vanilla extract

Beat until rounded peaks are formed

2 egg whites

Beat in a chilled bowl with a chilled rotary beater until cream is of medium consistency (piles softly)

1 cup chilled heavy cream

Fold beaten egg whites and whipped cream together, then fold into egg yolk mixture. Pour into 1-qt. refrigerator tray. Freeze until firm, about 3 to 4 hrs., without stirring.

6 servings

BLACKBERRY PARFAIT

Chill 8 parfait glasses.

Mix in a saucepan

½ cup sugar
¼ cup water
⅛ teaspoon cream of tartar

Set over low heat and stir until sugar is dissolved. Increase heat and bring rapidly to boiling; boil 5 min.

Beat until thick and lemon-colored

2 egg yolks

Beating constantly, gradually pour a very fine stream of the sugar syrup into beaten egg yolks. Cook in top of a double boiler over simmering water, stirring constantly, until mixture is smooth and thick. Cool over ice and water, beating constantly, until cold. Blend in

1 teaspoon vanilla extract

Beat until rounded peaks are formed

2 egg whites

Beat in a chilled bowl with a chilled beater until cream is of medium consistency (piles softly)

1 cup chilled heavy cream

Fold beaten egg whites and whipped cream together; fold into egg yolk mixture. Pour into 1-qt. refrigerator tray. Freeze until firm, 3 to 4 hrs., without stirring.

Sort, rinse, drain, and put into a bowl

1 pt. fresh ripe blackberries

Mix with berries

½ to ¾ cup sugar (depending on sweetness of berries)

Cover bowl, set in refrigerator, and allow berries to stand until sugar has dissolved and syrup has formed.

Shortly before serving, set out the berries and the firm parfait. Beginning and ending with the parfait, spoon alternate layers of parfait and berries into the chilled glasses. Serve at once.

8 servings

CHOCOLATE PARFAIT

▲ *Base Recipe*

Set a rotary beater and a bowl in refrigerator to chill.

Melt (page 10) and set aside to cool

2 oz. (2 sq.) unsweetened chocolate

Mix in saucepan

1 cup sugar
1 cup water

Cook to 238°F (soft ball stage, page 11; remove from heat while testing).

Shortly before syrup is cooked, beat until rounded peaks are formed

3 egg whites

Pour syrup in fine stream over egg whites, beating constantly until mixture is cool.

Using chilled bowl and beater, whip one cup at a time until of medium consistency (piles softly)

2 cups chilled heavy cream

Blend melted chocolate and whipped cream into cooled egg white mixture with

1½ tablespoons vanilla extract

Pour into refrigerator trays or molds and freeze 3 to 4 hrs.; or pour into mold to overflowing, cover with waxed paper, and press cover down tightly over paper. Pack in a mixture of one part ice and four parts rock salt. Freeze 3 to 4 hrs.

1¼ qts. parfait

—PEPPERMINT PARFAIT

Follow ▲ Recipe. Add **1 cup crushed peppermint stick candy** or **½ teaspoon peppermint extract** when folding ingredients into cooled egg white mixture.

CAFE PARFAIT

Place a rotary beater and a 1-qt. bowl in refrigerator to chill. Set out a fancy 1½-qt. mold.

Combine in a small heavy saucepan

½ cup sugar
¼ to ⅓ cup double-strength coffee beverage (page 10)

Stir over low heat until sugar is dissolved. Increase heat to medium and bring mixture to boiling. Cook to 234°F (thread stage, page 11; remove from heat while testing).

Beat until very thick and lemon-colored

4 egg yolks
¼ teaspoon vanilla extract

Beating constantly with electric mixer or a hand rotary beater, pour hot coffee syrup in a fine stream into beaten egg yolks. After all hot syrup is added, continue beating 8 to 10 min., or until mixture is piled softly and cooled. Set aside.

Rinse mold with cold water and set aside to drain.

Using chilled bowl and rotary beater, beat until cream is of medium consistency (piles softly)

1½ cups chilled heavy cream

Gently fold whipped cream into coffee-egg mixture. Pour mixture into the mold; freeze 8 hrs. or overnight.

Just before unmolding, prepare

Coffee Whipped Cream (page 480)

When firm, unmold parfait. To unmold, loosen top edge of mold with a knife. Wet a clean towel in hot water and wring it almost dry. Invert mold onto chilled serving plate. Wrap hot towel around mold for a few seconds only. (If mold does not loosen, repeat.)

To decorate mold, force Coffee Whipped Cream through a pastry bag and a No. 27 star tube in an attractive design over mold.

Sprinkle generously with
  Pistachio nuts, blanched and finely chopped
Set in refrigerator until ready to serve.
                                        8 to 10 servings

BLACKSTONE PUDDING

Set bowl and rotary beater in refrigerator to chill. Six individual molds will be needed.

Set aside to drain
  ¼ cup crushed pineapple

Finely chop and set aside
  ½ cup (about 1¾ oz.) walnuts
  ¼ cup maraschino cherries, drained

Soften in bowl by working with spoon
  1 pt. vanilla ice cream
  2 tablespoons rum
Blend pineapple, walnuts and cherries into ice cream with
  ¼ cup currants

Using the chilled bowl and rotary beater, beat until cream is of medium consistency (piles softly)
  1 cup chilled heavy cream
Fold whipped cream into ice cream mixture. Turn into refrigerator tray and freeze 2 to 3 hrs., stirring 2 or 3 times.

Remove pudding from freezing compartment when it is firm but still soft enough to spoon into individual molds. Rinse individual molds with cold water and drain just before filling. Pack pudding mixture into molds. Replace filled molds into freezing compartment and freeze 1 to 2 hrs., or until firm.

Meanwhile, prepare
  Rum Sauce (page 581)

To unmold, loosen top edge of mold with a knife. Wet a clean towel in hot water and wring it almost dry. Invert mold onto chilled serving plate. Wrap hot towel around mold for a few seconds only. (If mold does not loosen, repeat.) Serve topped with sauce.   *6 servings*

NESSELRODE PUDDING

American version of a famed European dessert. The original was created by a court chamberlain in Belgium many years ago.

Set out a 9x5x3-in. loaf pan. Put a medium-size bowl and a rotary beater into refrigerator to chill.

Set out
  1½ doz. single ladyfingers (or use sponge cake cut in 4x¾x½-in. pieces)
Line sides of the loaf pan with the ladyfingers and set aside.

Put into a large bowl and beat until very thick and lemon-colored
  2 egg yolks
Add gradually, beating well after each addition
  ½ cup sugar
Add gradually, beating constantly
  ¼ cup (2 oz.) sherry
Set egg yolk mixture aside.

Using the chilled bowl and beater, beat until cream is of medium consistency (piles softly)
  1¾ cups chilled heavy cream (beat only one half at a time)
Beat into whipped cream with few final strokes
  ⅓ cup confectioners' sugar
  1¼ teaspoons vanilla extract
Set in refrigerator while beating egg whites.

Using clean beater, beat until stiff, not dry, peaks are formed
  2 egg whites
  ⅛ teaspoon salt
Blend into the egg yolk mixture
  1 jar (10 oz.) Nesselrode mixture (about 1¼ cups)
Spread the whipped cream and egg whites over the egg yolk mixture and gently fold together. Turn mixture into the prepared pan and spread evenly.

Freeze until firm, about 12 hrs.
                                        About 8 servings

Note: If desired, omit ladyfingers and freeze mixture in refrigerator trays.

FROZEN CHERRY CREME

Set out a 1½-qt. soufflé dish (straight-sided casserole).

Mix and set aside
  ⅓ cup chopped toasted blanched almonds (pages 9 and 10)
  ⅓ cup (about 4) finely crushed short-bread cookies*

Frozen Cherry Crème

Have ready
  ¾ cup chopped red candied cherries

Beat until frothy
  2 egg whites
Add gradually, beating until stiff peaks are formed
  ¼ cup sugar
Set aside.

Whip
  2 cups chilled heavy cream
Add gradually, beating until soft peaks are formed
  ¼ cup sugar
Blend in about half of the nut-crumb mixture and
  2 tablespoons cognac
Fold in cherries and beaten egg whites. Turn mixture into the soufflé dish. Form a border with remaining nut-crumb mixture; press lightly. Garnish center with whole **toasted blanched almonds** and **candied cherries**. Freeze until firm.

Before serving, allow crème to soften slightly at room temperature.   *About 12 servings*

*Almond macaroons may be substituted.

FROZEN CHERRY CREAM MAGNIFIQUE

Set out a 1½-qt. fancy mold.

Prepare and set aside
  2 cups quartered dark sweet cherries

Mix in a heavy saucepan
  1 cup sugar
  1 env. unflavored gelatin
  Few grains salt
Stir in
  2 cups heavy cream
Set over low heat and stir occasionally until gelatin is completely dissolved, about 10 min.

Pour into a bowl and chill until mixture is partially set, stirring occasionally.

Mix

2 cups dairy sour cream
1½ teaspoons vanilla extract
¼ teaspoon almond extract

Blend with partially set gelatin and

½ teaspoon red food coloring

Stir in cherries. Turn into the mold, cover with aluminum foil and freeze until firm.

Before serving, allow time for mold to soften slightly in refrigerator. Unmold onto a chilled serving plate.   *10 to 12 servings*

FROZEN CRANBERRY WHIP

Place a bowl and a rotary beater in refrigerator to chill.

Wash, sort and cook in a saucepan until cranberry skins pop

2 cups (½ lb.) cranberries
1 cup water

Meanwhile, heat in top of double boiler over simmering water until marshmallows are melted, stirring occasionally

24 (about 6 oz.) marshmallows, cut in quarters (page 9)
½ cup orange juice
½ cup pineapple juice

Force cooked cranberries through a sieve or food mill to make a smooth pulp. Immediately add and stir until sugar is dissolved

⅔ cup sugar
2 tablespoons lemon juice

Remove marshmallow mixture from simmering water and blend thoroughly into cranberry pulp. Pour into refrigerator tray. Place in freezer and freeze until mixture is mushlike in consistency.

Using chilled bowl and rotary beater, beat until of medium consistency (piles softly)

1 cup chilled heavy cream

Gently fold whipped cream and chilled cranberry mixture together until blended. Turn into a fancy 1-qt. mold which has been rinsed in cold water and drained. Freeze about 4 hrs., or until firm.   *About 1 qt. whip*

FROZEN LEMON CUSTARD

▲ Base Recipe

Set in freezer until ice crystals form

1 cup undiluted evaporated milk

Set bowl and rotary beater in refrigerator to chill.

Beat slightly in top of double boiler

3 egg yolks

Stir in

½ cup sugar
⅓ cup lemon juice

Cook over simmering water until mixture thickens, stirring constantly. Cool.

Stir in

1 teaspoon grated lemon peel

Beat until rounded peaks are formed

3 egg whites

Fold in lemon mixture. Whip icy cold milk in chilled bowl with chilled rotary beater until very stiff. Fold in lemon-egg white mixture lightly but thoroughly. Pour at once into cold freezing trays and freeze.   *1 qt. frozen custard*

—FROZEN COCONUT CUSTARD

Follow ▲ Recipe. Fold **½ cup flaked coconut** into custard mixture with whipped milk.

FROZEN ORANGE CREME

Set a bowl and a rotary beater into refrigerator to chill.

Set out to thaw

1 can (6 oz.) frozen orange juice concentrate

Combine in a small bowl and stir until sugar is dissolved

½ cup sugar
⅓ cup lemon juice
1 tablespoon curaçao

Stir in thawed orange juice.

Using the chilled bowl and beater, beat until cream is of medium consistency (piles softly)

2 cups chilled heavy cream (beat one cup at a time)

Fold whipped cream into orange mixture. Turn into refrigerator tray. Freeze until firm, 2 to 3 hrs.

Coarsely chop

¾ cup (about 3 oz.) nuts

Serve dessert in chilled sherbet glasses; garnish with chopped nuts.   *6 servings*

FROZEN TANGERINE CREME

Set out to thaw

1 can (6 oz.) frozen tangerine juice concentrate

Combine in a small bowl and stir until sugar is dissolved

⅓ cup sugar
⅓ cup lemon juice
1 tablespoon curaçao

Frozen Lemon Custard

Mix in tangerine juice.

Whip

2 cups chilled heavy cream

Fold whipped cream into tangerine mixture. Turn into refrigerator tray. Freeze until firm.

Serve in chilled sherbet glasses.   *6 servings*

FROZEN COCOA MARLOW

▲ Base Recipe

Set a rotary beater and a bowl in refrigerator to chill.

Cut into quarters (page 9) and set aside

32 (½ lb.) marshmallows

Blend

½ cup cocoa
2 cups milk

Combine with marshmallows and heat over simmering water, stirring occasionally until well blended. Stir in

1½ teaspoons vanilla extract
Few grains salt

Cool until slightly stiffened. Using chilled bowl and beater, whip until of medium consistency (piles softly) and combine with marshmallow mixture

1 cup chilled heavy cream

Pour into refrigerator tray. Freeze about 4 hrs.
          6 to 8 servings

—FROZEN CHOCO-MINT MARLOW

Follow ▲ Recipe. Add **¼ teaspoon peppermint extract** with vanilla extract. Or **¼ cup crushed peppermint stick candy** with the whipped cream.

RASPBERRY MARLOW

▲ Base Recipe

Set a bowl and a rotary beater into refrigerator to chill.

Thaw and drain, reserving syrup

2 pkgs. (10 oz. each) frozen raspberries

Melt over simmering water

32 (½ lb.) marshmallows, cut in quarters (page 9)

Add, stirring occasionally
1 cup reserved raspberry syrup
¼ cup lemon juice
Remove from heat, cool and put into refrigerator to chill. When chilled, blend in drained raspberries.

Using the chilled bowl and beater, beat until cream is of medium consistency (piles softly)
2 cups chilled heavy cream (beat
one cup at a time)
Fold whipped cream into raspberry mixture. Pour into 1-qt. refrigerator tray. Freeze until firm, 4 to 6 hrs. Serve in chilled sherbet glasses. *8 servings*

—CHOCOLATE MARLOW

Follow ▲ Recipe. Omit raspberries and lemon juice. Substitute **1 cup milk** for raspberry syrup. Melt **2 oz. (2 sq.) unsweetened chocolate** over simmering water with milk and marshmallows.

TROPICAL MARLOW

Put a bowl and rotary beater into refrigerator to chill.

Drain, reserving syrup
1 can (20 oz.) crushed pineapple
(about 1½ cups, drained)
Prepare and set aside
32 marshmallows (about 8 oz.), cut
(page 9) into quarters
½ cup (about 3 oz.) dates, cut
(page 9) into small pieces
⅓ cup (about 1½ oz.) chopped pecans

Put the reserved pineapple syrup and the marshmallows into the top of a double boiler and place over simmering water, stirring occasionally, until marshmallows are melted. Remove marshmallow mixture from simmering water; cool.

Add gradually to cooled mixture and blend in
1 cup milk
Set in refrigerator to chill.

When mixture is chilled, blend in the crushed pineapple, dates and pecans.

Mint Gelato

Using chilled bowl and beater, beat until cream is of medium consistency (piles softly)
1 cup chilled heavy cream
Gently fold whipped cream into the pineapple mixture. Turn into refrigerator trays and freeze until firm, about 4 hrs.

Serve in chilled sherbet glasses.
About 1½ qts. marlow

MINT GELATO

▲ Base Recipe

A delicate, cooling dessert that has a flavor as refreshing as springtime.

Pour into a saucepan
½ cup cold milk
Sprinkle evenly over cold milk
1 env. unflavored gelatin
Place saucepan over low heat and stir until gelatin is dissolved. Remove from heat and stir in

3½ cups milk
2 cups instant nonfat dry milk
1 cup sugar
2 teaspoons vanilla extract
½ teaspoon mint extract
Pour into refrigerator trays and freeze until firm, 2 to 3 hrs.

Spoon the amount of gelato to be served into a bowl; allow it to soften slightly and whip until smooth, using an electric beater.

To serve, spoon whipped gelato into chilled stemmed glasses and, if desired, swirl tops (see photo). Serve immediately. *12 servings*

—AVOCADO GELATO

Follow ▲ Recipe. Substitute **1½ cups mashed ripe avocado** and **2 tablespoons lemon juice** for the extracts.

—VANILLA GELATO

Follow ▲ Recipe. Omit mint extract and increase vanilla extract to 1 tablespoon. If desired, serve with **Hot Wine Jelly Sauce** (page 580).

SPUMONE

Frozen desserts date back to days of ancient Rome when they were frozen with snow and ice brought down from the mountains by slaves.

For centuries Italians have been masters of the art of making frozen desserts—including ices, frozen custards, and fancy, molded ice creams, all said to have originated in Italy. Multi-colored and multiflavored Spumone, is one of the most popular Italian ice creams. Usually prepared commercially, here is a surprisingly easy spumone to delight your family and entice your friends.

Chill a bowl, rotary beater and 1-qt. mold.

Scald in top of double boiler (page 10)
1 cup milk
Stir in
½ cup sugar
⅛ teaspoon salt
Vigorously stir about 3 tablespoons of hot mixture into
3 egg yolks, slightly beaten
Immediately blend into mixture in top of double boiler. Cook over simmering water, stirring constantly, about 5 min., or until mixture coats a metal spoon. Remove from heat and cool.

Meanwhile, melt (page 10) and set aside
½ oz. (½ sq.) unsweetened chocolate

Stir into egg mixture
1 cup heavy cream
Divide mixture equally into two bowls.

Add melted chocolate to mixture in one bowl, mixing thoroughly. Place in refrigerator.

Add to remaining bowl, mixing well
2 teaspoons rum extract

Pour mixture into refrigerator tray. Freeze until mushy. Turn into chilled bowl and beat with chilled rotary beater until mixture is smooth and creamy. Spoon into chilled mold and freeze until firm.

Beat in a chilled bowl with a chilled rotary beater until cream stands in peaks when beater is slowly lifted upright
½ cup chilled heavy cream
Fold or beat into whipped cream with few final strokes until blended
1 tablespoon sugar
⅛ teaspoon pistachio extract
To tint whipped cream desired color, fold in, a drop at a time (about 2 drops)
Green food coloring
Spoon whipped cream mixture over firm rum ice cream. Return mold to freezer until firm.

When pistachio cream becomes firm, place

on top of cream in center

**1 maraschino cherry, drained and
chilled**

Return to freezer.

Beat in a chilled bowl with a chilled rotary beater until cream stands in peaks when beater is slowly lifted upright

½ cup chilled heavy cream

Fold or beat into whipped cream until blended

1 tablespoon sugar
**6 unblanched almonds, finely
chopped**
¼ teaspoon almond extract

Spoon whipped cream mixture over firm pistachio cream. Freeze until firm.

When almond cream is firm, pour chocolate ice cream mixture into refrigerator tray. Freeze until mushy. Turn into a chilled bowl and beat with a chilled rotary beater until mixture is smooth and creamy. Spoon mixture over firm whipped cream. Cover mold with waxed paper. Freeze 6 to 8 hrs., or until Spumone is very firm.

To remove from mold, quickly dip mold into warm water.   *6 to 8 wedge-shape servings*

BISCUIT TORTONI

Set out ten 2-in. paper baking cups. Chill a small bowl and rotary beater.

Using the electric blender (page 11), grind enough Italian Macaroons (page 587) to make

**½ cup plus 2 tablespoons fine dry
macaroon crumbs**

Set aside.

Beat in chilled bowl with chilled rotary beater until cream stands in peaks when beater is slowly lifted upright

1 cup chilled heavy cream

Fold into whipped cream ½ cup macaroon crumbs and

⅓ cup confectioners' sugar
1 egg white, stiffly beaten
1 tablespoon rum or sherry

Spoon mixture into paper baking cups and sprinkle with remaining macaroon crumbs.

Place in refrigerator tray. Freeze until firm, about 3 to 4 hrs.   *10 servings*

SEMISWEET CHOCOLATE TORTONI

Set 2 bowls and a rotary beater in refrigerator to chill. Place eight 2-in. paper baking cups in muffin-pan wells.

Finely crush (page 10) enough macaroons to yield

½ cup fine macaroon crumbs

Set crumbs aside.

Using the chilled bowl and beater, beat until cream is of medium consistency (piles softly)

1 cup chilled heavy cream

Beat in with few final strokes

2 tablespoons sugar
1½ teaspoons vanilla extract

Fold in the macaroon crumbs.

Beat until frothy

1 egg white

Add gradually, beating well after each addition

2 tablespoons sugar

Continue beating until rounded peaks are formed. Fold into the whipped cream mixture, turn into refrigerator tray and set in freezer about 1½ hrs., or until mixture is firm about ½ in. from sides of tray.

Meanwhile, melt over hot water

**½ pkg. (3 oz.) semisweet chocolate
pieces**
2 teaspoons shortening

Turn frozen mixture into the chilled bowl. Beat until smooth but not melted. While stirring constantly and rapidly, gradually pour the melted chocolate in a thin stream into the cream mixture. (The chocolate forms fine, firm pieces as it is blended into the cold mixture.) Immediately spoon mixture into the paper baking cups. Freeze until firm.

8 servings

FAVORITE VANILLA ICE CREAM

▲ Base Recipe

These ice cream recipes may be prepared in a dasher-type freezer or in refrigerator.

If using the dasher-type freezer, clean and scald cover, container and dasher. Chill before using.

If using a refrigerator, set control for colder operating temperature if necessary, and chill a large bowl and rotary beater in refrigerator.

Scald (page 10)

2 cups milk

Combine and then gradually stir into milk

1 cup sugar
1 tablespoon all-purpose flour
¼ teaspoon salt

Stir constantly and cook over direct heat 5 min. Remove from heat and vigorously stir about 3 tablespoons of hot mixture into

3 egg yolks, slightly beaten

Spumone

Immediately stir into hot mixture in top of double boiler. Return to heat and cook over simmering water 10 min., stirring constantly until mixture coats a metal spoon. Remove from heat and cool. Stir in

2 cups cream
2 teaspoons vanilla extract

Chill in refrigerator.

For Dasher-Type Freezer—Fill chilled container two thirds full with ice cream mixture. Cover tightly. Set into freezer tub and, alternating layers, fill with

8 parts crushed ice
1 part rock salt

Turn handle slowly 5 min. Turn rapidly until handle becomes very difficult to turn (about 15 min.). Remove dasher. Pack down ice cream and cover with waxed paper. Put lid on top again and fill opening for dasher with cork.

Repack freezer in ice using

4 parts crushed ice
1 part rock salt

Cover with heavy paper or cloth. Let ripen 2 to 3 hrs.

For Refrigerator—Pour the chilled mixture into refrigerator trays and place in freezer compartment of refrigerator. When mixture becomes mushy, turn into chilled bowl and beat with chilled rotary beater. This helps to form fine crystals and to give a smooth creamy mixture. Return mixture to trays and set in freezer until mixture is firm.

About 1½ qts. ice cream

—FRENCH VANILLA ICE CREAM

Follow ▲ Recipe. Omit flour and increase egg

Semisweet Chocolate Tortoni

557

yolks to 5. Substitute **2 cups heavy cream** for cream.

—CHOCOLATE ICE CREAM

Follow ▲ Recipe. Add **2 oz. (2 sq.) unsweetened chocolate** to milk and heat until milk is scalded and chocolate is melted, in top of double boiler.

—CHOCOLATE CHIP ICE CREAM

Follow ▲ Recipe. Just before freezing, add **2 oz. semisweet chocolate**, grated.

—BUTTERED PECAN ICE CREAM

Follow ▲ Recipe. Melt in a skillet **3 tablespoons butter**. Add about **1 cup (about 3¾ oz.) chopped pecans** and heat to golden brown, stirring occasionally. Stir into mixture just before freezing.

—BERRY ICE CREAM

Follow ▲ Recipe. Just before freezing, blend in **2 cups crushed strawberries or raspberries**, sweetened.

—PEACH ICE CREAM

Follow ▲ Recipe. Substitute **1 teaspoon almond extract** for vanilla extract. Just before freezing, blend in **1 tablespoon lemon juice** and **1½ cups crushed fresh peaches**, sweetened.

PHILADELPHIA ICE CREAM

▲ *Base Recipe*

Set out refrigerator trays. Place two 2-qt. bowls and rotary beater in refrigerator to chill.

Scald (page 10)
> **2 cups cream**

Remove from heat and stir in
> **¾ cup sugar**
> **⅛ teaspoon salt**

Set aside to cool.

Stir in
> **1 teaspoon vanilla extract**

Pour into refrigerator trays and freeze until mushy.

Using chilled bowl and rotary beater, beat (1 cup at a time) until of medium consistency (piles softly)
> **2 cups chilled heavy cream**

Scrape mushy ice cream mixture into a thoroughly chilled bowl and beat until smooth.

Fold in whipped cream. Return to refrigerator trays and freeze until firm.

> *About 2 qts. ice cream*

Note: After whipped cream has been added, ice cream may be spooned into 24 individual 2-in. paper baking cups set in muffin pan wells. Top each with a rosette made by forcing whipped cream through a pastry bag and a No. 27 star tube. Freeze until firm.

—STRAWBERRY ICE CREAM

Rinse (discarding imperfect berries), drain, and hull **3 cups ripe strawberries**. Crush berries. Stir **¾ cup sugar** and **1½ teaspoons lemon juice** into crushed berries. Let mixture stand about 15 min., or until juice collects. Prepare ice cream as in ▲ Recipe; omit vanilla extract. Stir strawberry mixture into ice cream before first freezing.

—BANANA ICE CREAM

Follow ▲ Recipe. Peel **6 all-yellow or brown-flecked bananas**. Force through a sieve or food mill into a bowl. Stir in **1 tablespoon lemon juice**. Stir banana mixture into ice cream before first freezing.

BUTTERMILK ICE CREAM

Chill a bowl and rotary beater and 2 large refrigerator trays in refrigerator.

Mix until sugar is dissolved
> **1 qt. buttermilk**
> **2 cups cream**
> **1 cup sugar**
> **2 tablespoons vanilla extract**
> **¼ teaspoon salt**

Pour mixture into refrigerator tray and freeze until mushy.

When mixture becomes mushy, turn into the chilled bowl and beat with chilled beater until smooth. Return to refrigerator trays and again freeze until mushy.

Meanwhile, chill the bowl and beater. When mixture becomes mushy, again beat until smooth. Return to refrigerator trays and freeze until firm.
> *About 1½ qts. ice cream*

AVOCADO ICE CREAM

Have refrigerator trays ready.

Set out to soften slightly
> **2 pts. vanilla ice cream**

Halve, pit and peel
> **3 fully ripe avocados**

Force avocado through a food mill or fine sieve into a bowl. Mix in
> **⅓ cup lime juice**
> **½ cup sugar**

Combine avocado mixture with ice cream and beat until smooth. Turn into refrigerator trays. Freeze until firm.

To serve, allow to soften slightly at room temperature before spooning into dessert dishes.
> *About 1½ qts. ice cream*

CARAMEL ICE CREAM

Spoon Caramel Ice Cream into chilled sherbet glasses and garnish with a very generous sprinkling of coarsely chopped pecans—beautiful and delicious!

Chill a bowl, a rotary beater, and a 1-qt. refrigerator tray in refrigerator.

For Caramel Syrup—Melt in a heavy light-colored skillet (a black skillet makes it difficult to see the color of the syrup) over low heat
> **¾ cup sugar**

With back of wooden spoon, gently keep sugar moving toward center of skillet until sugar is completely melted and of a golden-brown color (lighter than for burnt-sugar syrup).

Remove from heat and gradually add (a very small amount at a time)
> **¾ cup boiling water**

(Be careful that steam does not burn hands.)

Return to low heat and continue to stir until bubbles are size of dimes.

Set aside to cool while preparing ice cream.

For Ice Cream—Scald (page 10) in top of double boiler
> **2 cups milk**

Remove from heat and stir in a mixture of
> **⅔ cup sugar**
> **2 tablespoons all-purpose flour**
> **¼ teaspoon salt**

Cook mixture over direct heat 5 min., stirring constantly.

Remove from heat and vigorously stir about 3 tablespoons of hot mixture into

2 egg yolks, slightly beaten

Immediately stir into hot mixture in top of double boiler. Cook over simmering water 10 min., stirring constantly until mixture thickens and coats a metal spoon. Remove from simmering water and cool.

Blend in the Caramel Syrup and

1¼ teaspoons vanilla extract

Set in refrigerator while beating egg whites.

Beat until stiff, not dry, peaks are formed

2 egg whites

Spread beaten egg whites over egg yolk mixture and gently fold together.

Pour mixture into refrigerator tray and freeze until mushy.

When mixture becomes mushy, turn into chilled bowl and beat with chilled beater until smooth. This helps to form fine crystals and to give a smooth creamy mixture. Return mixture to tray and freeze until firm.

About 1 qt. ice cream

CHERRY NUT ICE CREAM

Set a small bowl, a rotary beater and a 1-qt. refrigerator tray into refrigerator to chill. Set out a double boiler.

Coarsely chop and set aside

2 oz. walnuts or pecans (about ½ cup, chopped)

Rinse, drain, stem and pit about

1½ cups fresh dark sweet cherries

Coarsely chop and set aside enough of the cherries to yield 1 cup chopped cherries. Reserve the remaining whole cherries for garnish.

Cut into quarters (page 9)

24 (6 oz.) marshmallows

Put into top of double boiler over simmering water with

3 tablespoons lemon juice

Stir occasionally until the marshmallows are melted. Remove from simmering water. Stir mixture until smooth. Set aside on cooling rack to cool slightly.

Blend into cooled mixture

1 cup chilled cream or evaporated milk

Mix in the chopped cherries, nuts and

1 teaspoon grated lemon peel

Using the chilled bowl and beater, beat until cream is of medium consistency (piles softly)

1 cup chilled heavy cream

Turn the whipped cream onto the cherry mixture and fold gently together. Turn into the chilled refrigerator tray. Freeze until the mixture is mushy.

Meanwhile, chill a large bowl in refrigerator.

Turn mushy ice cream mixture into the chilled bowl and beat until smooth. Return to refrigerator tray and freeze until firm.

Serve ice cream, garnished with the reserved whole cherries, in chilled sherbet glasses.

About 1 qt. ice cream

FREEZER CHOCOLATE ICE CREAM

This mixture may be frozen in a crank freezer or in refrigerator. If using crank freezer, clean and scald cover, container and dasher. Cool before using. If using a refrigerator, set freezer control for colder temperature. Set a large bowl and a rotary beater in refrigerator.

Heat in top of double boiler until milk is scalded (page 10) and chocolate melted

1½ cups milk
3 oz. (3 sq.) unsweetened chocolate

Set aside.

Mix thoroughly

1 cup sugar
¼ cup all-purpose flour
¼ teaspoon salt

Add and blend well

½ cup cold milk

Stir sugar mixture into hot milk and chocolate. Stirring constantly, bring rapidly to boiling over direct heat. Cook until mixture is thickened. Place over simmering water and cover; cook 7 min., stirring occasionally. Vigorously stir about 3 tablespoons of hot mixture into

2 eggs, slightly beaten

Immediately return to cooked mixture. Stirring constantly and rapidly, cook 3 to 5 min. Remove from heat. Cool.

Stir in

4 cups heavy cream
3 tablespoons vanilla extract

For Dasher-Type Freezer—Fill chilled container two-thirds full with ice cream mixture. Cover tightly. Set in freezer tub. (For electric freezer, follow manufacturer's directions.) Fill tub with alternate layers of

8 parts crushed ice
1 part rock salt

Turn handle slowly 5 min. Turn rapidly until handle becomes difficult to turn (about 15 min.).

Wipe lid well and remove dasher. Pack down ice cream and cover with waxed paper. Again put lid on top and fill opening for dasher with cork. Repack freezer container in ice using

4 parts crushed ice
1 part rock salt

Cherry Nut Ice Cream

Cover with heavy paper or cloth. Let ripen 2 to 3 hrs.

For Refrigerator—Pour ice cream mixture into refrigerator trays. When mixture becomes mushy, turn into chilled bowl and beat with chilled beater. Beating helps to form fine crystals and give a smooth, creamy mixture. Return to trays and freeze until firm.

2 qts. ice cream

BUDGETWISE CHOCOLATE ICE CREAM

Set a large bowl and rotary beater in refrigerator to chill.

Pour into a small cup or custard cup

2 tablespoons cold water

Sprinkle evenly over water

2 teaspoons unflavored gelatin

Let stand to soften.

Heat over simmering water until chocolate is melted

1½ oz. (1½ sq.) unsweetened chocolate
¾ cup water

Remove hot melted chocolate from heat and add softened gelatin. Stir until gelatin is completely dissolved. Cool.

Beat until thick and lemon-colored

2 egg yolks
6 tablespoons sugar
¼ cup light corn syrup

Freezer Chocolate Ice Cream

Budget-Wise Chocolate Ice Cream

Blend in cooled gelatin mixture and
   1½ cups undiluted evaporated milk
   2 teaspoons vanilla extract
Pour into a refrigerator tray and chill in the freezer.

When fairly firm, beat with rotary beater until frothy
   2 egg whites
Add gradually, beating well after each addition
   2 tablespoons sugar
Beat until rounded peaks are formed.

Turn mixture into chilled bowl and beat with chilled rotary beater until fluffy. Fold in egg whites and return mixture to refrigerator tray; freeze until firm, 2½ to 3 hrs.

5 or 6 servings

CITRUS ICE CREAM

Have refrigerator tray ready.

Beat thoroughly
   ⅔ cup (one half 14-oz. can) sweetened condensed milk
   ½ cup orange or tangerine juice
   ½ teaspoon grated lemon peel
   1½ tablespoons lemon juice
   ⅛ teaspoon salt
Place in refrigerator to chill.

Meanwhile, whip
   1 cup chilled heavy cream
Fold whipped cream into chilled mixture. Turn into refrigerator tray. Freeze until mushy.

Meanwhile, set a large bowl and beaters into refrigerator to chill. When mixture is mushy, remove to chilled bowl. Beat with chilled beaters until mixture is smooth and fluffy. Return to tray and freeze until firm.

1 qt. ice cream

LEMON CHEESE ICE CREAM

▲ Base Recipe

Put a bowl, rotary beater and refrigerator tray into refrigerator to chill.

Beat until fluffy
   2 pkgs. (3 oz. each) cream cheese
Add gradually, creaming after each addition
   ⅔ cup sugar
Add gradually, mixing thoroughly
   2 cups chilled cream
and
   1 teaspoon grated lemon peel
   2 tablespoons lemon juice
   ¼ teaspoon vanilla extract
Turn into refrigerator tray and freeze until mushy.

Turn mixture into the chilled bowl and beat with chilled beater until smooth. Return to refrigerator tray and freeze until firm.

About 1 qt. ice cream

—VANILLA ALMOND ICE CREAM

Follow ▲ Recipe. Omit lemon juice and grated peel. Increase vanilla extract to 1 tablespoon. Mix in ½ cup (3 oz.) coarsely chopped toasted almonds (page 10) before turning into refrigerator tray.

—MARASCHINO CHERRY SPECIAL

Follow ▲ Recipe. Omit lemon peel. Decrease lemon juice to 2 teaspoons and increase vanilla extract to 1 teaspoon. Mix in ½ cup coarsely chopped maraschino cherries, well drained, before turning into refrigerator tray.

FRESH PEACH ICE CREAM SUPERBE

▲ Base Recipe

Wash and scald cover, container and dasher of a 4-qt. ice cream freezer. Chill thoroughly before using.

Dip into boiling water for 3 to 4 min.
   12 medium (about 3 lbs.) ripe peaches
Gently slip off skins; cut into halves and remove pits. Force peaches through sieve or food mill into a bowl. Stir into peaches
   2¾ cups sugar
   1 tablespoon lemon juice
Let peach mixture stand 15 to 20 min.

Blend
   1½ qts. cream, chilled
   1 teaspoon vanilla extract
   1 teaspoon almond extract
   ¼ teaspoon salt
Blend into peach mixture.

Fill freezer container two-thirds full with ice cream mixture. Cover tightly. Place in freezer tub. (For electric freezer, follow manufacturer's directions.) Fill tub with alternate layers of
   8 parts crushed ice
   1 part rock salt
Turn handle slowly 5 min. Turn rapidly until handle becomes difficult to turn, about 15 min. Add ice and salt as necessary. Carefully wipe cover and remove dasher. Pack down ice cream and cover with waxed paper. Replace cover and fill opening for dasher with cork. Repack freezer in ice using
   4 parts ice
   1 part rock salt
Cover with heavy paper or cloth. Let ripen 2 to 3 hrs.

About 3 qts. ice cream

—CHOCOLATE ICE CREAM SUPERBE

Follow ▲ Recipe. Omit peaches and lemon juice. Decrease sugar to 1¾ cups. Melt (page 10) **3 oz. (3 sq.) unsweetened chocolate** in cream. Omit almond extract. Cool and place in refrigerator to chill. Pour mixture into ice cream freezer container.

—VANILLA ICE CREAM SUPERBE

Follow ▲ Recipe. Omit peaches and lemon juice. Decrease sugar to 1¼ cups. Increase vanilla extract to 3 tablespoons. Omit almond extract.

—STRAWBERRY ICE CREAM SUPERBE

Follow ▲ Recipe. Substitute **1½ qts. fresh strawberries**, rinsed and hulled, for peaches. Force strawberries through sieve or food mill. Combine crushed berries with sugar and lemon juice. Omit almond extract.

—APRICOT ICE CREAM SUPERBE

Follow ▲ Recipe. For peaches, substitute **1 lb. (about 3 cups) dried apricots**. Put apricots into saucepan with **4 cups water**. Cover and simmer 25 min., or until tender. Force apricots through a sieve or food mill. Decrease sugar to 1¾ cups. Stir sugar and lemon juice into apricots. Cool. Chill in refrigerator. When chilled, blend into cream mixture.

Apricot Ice Cream Superbe

—MAPLE ICE CREAM SUPERBE

Pour 1½ cups maple syrup into a saucepan. Bring to boiling and boil 5 min. (until quantity is reduced to 1¼ cups). Remove from heat and set aside to cool. Follow ▲ Recipe. Omit almond extract. Blend maple syrup with cream mixture.

PUMPKIN ICE CREAM

Have a 1-qt. refrigerator tray ready.

Melt over simmering water in the top of a double boiler

10 marshmallows, diced
1 tablespoon boiling water

Meanwhile, beat until thoroughly mixed

1 cup canned pumpkin (about one-half 16-oz. can)
⅓ cup firmly packed brown sugar
2 tablespoons orange juice
1 teaspoon cinnamon
½ teaspoon ginger
½ teaspoon nutmeg
½ teaspoon salt

Blend mixture thoroughly with marshmallows. Cook over boiling water, stirring constantly, about 10 min.

Whip

1 cup chilled heavy cream

Fold into chilled pumpkin mixture. Pour into refrigerator tray. Freeze until firm. *6 servings*

APPLESAUCE SHERBET

Set a bowl and a rotary beater in refrigerator to chill. Set out a heavy saucepan.

For Applesauce—Wash, quarter, core and pare

6 medium (about 2 lbs.) tart cooking apples

Put apples into the saucepan with

¼ cup water

Bring to boiling. Cover and simmer, stirring occasionally, 15 to 20 min., or until apples are soft and somewhat transparent. Add and stir until sugar is dissolved

½ cup sugar

Stir in

¼ teaspoon lemon juice

Cool applesauce. Place in refrigerator to chill completely.

For Sherbet—Blend thoroughly with chilled applesauce

2 cups chilled buttermilk
1 cup sugar
2 tablespoons lime juice

Stir until sugar is dissolved.

To tint sherbet desired color, mix in one or more drops

Green food coloring

Pour sherbet into refrigerator trays. Freeze until sherbet is mushy.

Turn into chilled bowl and beat thoroughly with chilled rotary beater. Return sherbet to refrigerator trays. Freeze until firm.

Coarsely chop

½ cup (about 2 oz.) Brazil nuts

Sprinkle nuts over each serving.

About 8 servings

CRANBERRY SHERBET

Set a large bowl and a rotary beater in refrigerator to chill.

Wash, sort, and put into a saucepan

4 cups (about 1 lb.) cranberries

Add

2 cups boiling water

Cover and cook over medium heat until cranberry skins burst, about 10 min.

Meanwhile, set out

¾ lb. marshmallows (about 48)

Cut (page 9) into quarters and put in top of double boiler with

1 cup orange juice

Heat over simmering water until marshmallows are melted but still fluffy, stirring occasionally. Remove from heat and set aside.

When cranberry skins have all burst, force cranberries and liquid through a food mill or sieve. Immediately add to the hot sieved berries, stirring until sugar is dissolved

¼ cup sugar
2 tablespoons lemon juice

Add marshmallow mixture to cranberry mixture together with

1 teaspoon grated orange peel

Blend well and turn into refrigerator trays. Freeze until mixture is mushy.

When mixture is mushy, turn out into the chilled bowl and beat with the chilled beater *just* until smooth but not melted. Return mixture to refrigerator tray and freeze until firm.

About 1 qt. sherbet

GRAPE SHERBET

Set a large bowl in refrigerator to chill.

Combine in a saucepan

2 cups water
¾ cup sugar

Bring to boiling and boil for 5 min.

Meanwhile, pour into a small cup or custard cup

¼ cup cold water

Sprinkle evenly over water to soften

1 env. unflavored gelatin

Add softened gelatin to hot syrup and stir until completely dissolved. Cool slightly. Blend in

2 cups grape juice
1 tablespoon grated lemon peel
¼ cup lemon juice
¼ teaspoon salt

Mix until thoroughly blended. Pour liquid mixture into refrigerator tray and freeze until mushy, stirring 2 or 3 times.

When mixture is mushy, beat until frothy

2 egg whites

Add gradually, beating thoroughly after each addition

¼ cup sugar

Continue beating until stiff peaks are formed.

Remove grape mixture to chilled bowl and beat until smooth. Add beaten egg whites and then beat again until smooth. Return to refrigerator tray and freeze until firm. *About 1½ qts. sherbet*

CREAMY LEMON SHERBET

▲ *Base Recipe*

Set a rotary beater and a bowl in refrigerator to chill.

Blend in a large bowl, in order

1¼ cups sugar
2 teaspoons grated lemon peel
½ cup lemon juice
⅛ teaspoon salt
2 cups cream
Few drops yellow food coloring

Stir until sugar is dissolved. Pour into the refrigerator tray and set in freezer until mixture is mushy.

Turn mixture into the chilled bowl and beat

Applesauce Sherbet

with the chilled beater until smooth but not melted. Immediately return mixture to refrigerator tray. Set in freezer; freeze until firm.

1½ pts. sherbet

—CREAMY LIME SHERBET

Follow ▲ Recipe. Substitute **lime peel and lime juice** for the lemon peel and lemon juice. Substitute **green food coloring** for yellow food coloring.

—GRAPEFRUIT SHERBET

Follow ▲ Recipe. Decrease sugar to ½ cup. Substitute **2 teaspoons grapefruit peel** for lemon peel and **1¼ cups grapefruit juice** for lemon juice. Decrease cream to 1¾ cups. Substitute **2 drops red food coloring** for yellow food coloring.

—CREAMY ORANGE SHERBET

Follow ▲ Recipe. Omit lemon peel. Use only 2 tablespoons lemon juice. Add **½ cup orange juice**. Substitute **orange food coloring** for yellow food coloring.

—CREAMY TANGERINE SHERBET

Follow ▲ Recipe. Substitute **2 teaspoons grated tangerine peel** for lemon peel. Use only 2 tablespoons lemon juice. Add **½ cup tangerine juice**. Substitute **2 to 3 drops orange food coloring** for yellow food coloring.

LIME SHERBET

Set a bowl and beater in refrigerator to chill.

Pour into a small cup or custard cup
    ½ cup cold water
Sprinkle evenly over water
    1 env. unflavored gelatin
Set aside.

Meanwhile, heat until very hot
    2¾ cups water
Remove from heat and immediately stir in softened gelatin until gelatin is completely dissolved. Add and stir until sugar is dissolved
    1¾ cups sugar
    ¾ cup lime juice
    2 teaspoons grated lemon peel
    2 tablespoons lemon juice

To tint sherbet mixture desired color, mix in one or more drops at a time
    Green food coloring
Set aside to cool.

Pour cooled sherbet mixture into refrigerator trays. Freeze until sherbet is mushy, stirring 2 or 3 times.

When mixture is mushy, beat until frothy
    2 egg whites
Add gradually, beating well after each addition
    ¼ cup sugar
Beat until stiff peaks are formed.

Remove sherbet mixture to chilled bowl and beat with chilled beater until smooth. Add beaten egg whites and then beat again until smooth.

Return to refrigerator tray and freeze until firm.

1 qt. sherbet

PEACH LIME SHERBET

Have an electric blender and refrigerator trays ready.

Set out
    1 can (29 oz.) sliced cling peaches
Using electric blender as manufacturer directs, chop peaches in syrup. Set aside.

Mix in a bowl
    1½ to 2 cups sugar
    1½ teaspoons grated lime peel
    ⅓ cup lime juice
Add gradually, stirring until sugar is dissolved
    2 cups milk
Blend in, a drop at a time
    Green food coloring (about 4 drops)
Mix in the chopped peaches in syrup. Turn mixture into the trays and set in freezer, stirring occasionally until partially frozen.

Meanwhile, chop
    1 cup salted almonds or pecans
    (page 10)
Press nuts onto partially frozen surface. Freeze until firm.

About 2 qts. sherbet

FRESH PINEAPPLE SHERBET

Set out refrigerator tray. Chill a 2-qt. bowl and rotary beater in refrigerator.

Cut off and discard crown (spiny top) from
    1 small fresh pineapple
Rinse and cut into crosswise slices ¼ to ½ in. thick. With a sharp knife, cut away and discard rind and "eyes" from each slice. Cut out and discard the core. Finely dice enough of the pineapple to yield 2 cups diced pineapple.

Combine
    2 cups chilled buttermilk
    1 cup sugar
    1 teaspoon vanilla extract
Stir until sugar is dissolved. Add the diced pineapple and mix well. Pour mixture into refrigerator tray. Freeze until mixture is mushy.

Turn mixture into chilled bowl and beat with chilled beater until smooth. Return to refrigerator tray and freeze until firm.

About 1 qt. sherbet

ORANGE BANANA SHERBET

▲ Base Recipe

Put a bowl, rotary beater and a 1-qt. refrigerator tray in refrigerator to chill.

Pour into a small cup or custard cup
    ½ cup cold water
Sprinkle evenly over cold water
    1 env. unflavored gelatin
Let stand until softened. Place cup over very hot water and stir constantly until the gelatin is completely dissolved.

Mix
    1 tablespoon grated orange peel
    1½ cups orange juice
    1½ cups buttermilk
    ¾ cup sugar
    2 tablespoons lemon juice
Stir until sugar is dissolved. Blend in the dissolved gelatin. Pour into refrigerator tray. Freeze until mixture is mushy.

Turn into chilled bowl and beat with chilled beater. Peel, dice and mix in
    1 medium banana with brown-flecked peel
Immediately return sherbet to tray. Freeze until firm.

About 1 qt. sherbet

—ORANGE SHERBET

Follow ▲ Recipe. Omit the banana.

—AMBROSIA SHERBET

Follow ▲ Recipe. Mix in **1 cup flaked coconut** with the banana pieces.

LEMON WATERMELON ICE

Remove seeds and rind, cut into pieces and sieve enough watermelon to yield
    2½ cups sieved watermelon
Add to the watermelon and stir in
    1 can (6 oz.) frozen lemonade concentrate, thawed

Stir in
> ¾ **cup water**
> **2 teaspoons grated lemon peel**

Pour mixture into refrigerator tray and freeze until mushy, stirring 2 or 3 times.

Set a large bowl in refrigerator to chill.

Beat until rounded peaks are formed
> **2 egg whites**
> ⅛ **teaspoon salt**

Turn watermelon mixture into chilled bowl and beat just until smooth, but not melted.

Add beaten egg whites and beat until smooth. Return to refrigerator tray and freeze until firm, 2 to 3 hrs.

Serve in chilled sherbet glasses.   *1 qt. ice*

LIME ICE

▲ *Base Recipe*

Pour into a small cup or custard cup
> ¼ **cup cold water**

Sprinkle evenly over water
> **2 teaspoons unflavored gelatin**

Let stand until softened.

Meanwhile, heat until very hot
> **3 cups water**

Remove from heat and immediately stir in softened gelatin until gelatin is completely dissolved. Add, stirring until sugar is dissolved
> **2 cups sugar**

Blend into gelatin mixture
> ¾ **cup lime juice**
> **2 teaspoons grated lemon peel**
> **2 tablespoons lemon juice**

To tint desired color, mix in a drop at a time
> **Green food coloring**

Cool. Pour into a refrigerator tray. Freeze until firm (3 to 4 hrs.), stirring 2 or 3 times.

Serve in chilled sherbet glasses.   *1 qt. ice*

—LEMON ICE

Follow ▲ Recipe. Omit lime juice. Increase lemon juice to ¾ cup; substitute **yellow food coloring** for green.

—ORANGE ICE

Follow ▲ Recipe. Decrease hot water to 2 cups and sugar to 1¼ cups. Substitute **orange peel** for lemon peel and **2 cups orange juice** for lime juice. Use **orange food coloring.**

—APRICOT ICE

Follow ▲ Recipe. Decrease hot water to 1½ cups and sugar to 1 cup. Substitute **2 cups apricot nectar** for lime juice and **orange juice** for lemon juice. Omit food coloring.

—RASPBERRY ICE

Follow ▲ Recipe. Decrease hot water to 2 cups and sugar to ¾ or 1 cup. Omit lime juice, lemon peel and food coloring. Force through fine sieve **1 pt. rinsed, sorted and drained raspberries.** Blend sieved raspberries into gelatin mixture with lemon juice.

—MOCHA ICE

Follow ▲ Recipe. Increase hot water to 3½ cups. Decrease sugar to 1 cup. Omit lime and lemon juices, lemon peel and food coloring. Mix **2 tablespoons instant powdered coffee** with sugar and blend into hot mixture. Top with **Sweetened Whipped Cream** (page 480).

PAPAYA ICE

Combine in a saucepan
> ½ **cup sugar**
> **2 teaspoons unflavored gelatin**

Stir in
> **1 cup boiling water**

Set over low heat and stir constantly until gelatin and sugar are dissolved. Stir in
> ¾ **cup boiling water**
> ½ **cup sugar**

Continue heating and stirring until sugar is dissolved. Remove from heat.

Blend into gelatin mixture
> **2 cups papaya nectar**
> **2 teaspoons grated lime peel**
> **2 tablespoons lime juice**

Cool. Pour into a refrigerator tray. Freeze until firm (3 to 4 hrs.), stirring 2 or 3 times.

Serve Papaya Ice in chilled sherbet glasses and garnish with
> **Sprigs of mint**
>   *1 qt. ice*

STRAWBERRY ICE
(Gelato di Fragole)

Wash, hull and force through food mill or sieve
> **1 pt. ripe strawberries**

Set aside.

Heat until very hot
> **1 cup water**

Remove from heat and add, stirring until dissolved
> ¾ **cup sugar**

Set aside to cool.

Combine strawberry purée with cooled sugar syrup and
> **2 tablespoons lemon juice**
> **1 tablespoon orange juice**

Pour into refrigerator tray. Freeze until firm.
About 6 servings

ICE CREAM DESSERTS

DRAMATIC PECAN RING

Serve this when you want to startle and delight your guests! Even without the flaming sugar-cube garnish, it's a superlatively good dessert.

Thoroughly butter a 2-qt. ring mold.

Have ready
> **1 qt. French vanilla ice cream**

For Pecan Ring—Butter a large mixing bowl. Mix in the bowl
> **8 cups (8 oz.) corn flakes, finely crushed**
> **1½ cups (about 6 oz.) coarsely chopped pecans**

Set aside.

Put into a saucepan, set over low heat and stir until sugar is entirely dissolved and evenly blended with butter
> **2 cups firmly packed light brown sugar**
> ¾ **cup butter**

Bring to boiling and cook, stirring constantly, about 2 min. Remove from heat. Stir in
> ½ **teaspoon almond extract**

Tossing corn flakes and pecans lightly and quickly, gradually pour hot syrup over them.

When corn flakes and pecans are thoroughly coated, turn them into the ring mold. Press firmly into mold, leaving no air spaces. Put into refrigerator to chill until serving time.

To Assemble Dessert—Set aside to drain, reserving syrup for use in other food preparation
> **1 can (8¼ oz.) pineapple slices (4 slices)**

To unmold ring, loosen top edges with a knife. Cover with chilled serving plate. Invert and lift mold off ring.

Arrange around mold, on serving plate
> **4 galax leaves**

Put one drained pineapple slice on each leaf. Arrange fresh berries between pineapple slices.

Just before serving, fill center of ring with scoops of the ice cream.

Quickly dip
> **4 cubes of loaf sugar**

into
> **Lemon extract**

Place a sugar cube in center of each pineapple slice. Ignite the sugar cubes with matches. Serve immediately.   *About 8 servings*

INDIVIDUAL BAKED ALASKAS

Prepare or purchase
> **1½ pts. chocolate, strawberry or vanilla ice cream**

Put into refrigerator to chill about 3 hrs.
> **1 can (29½ oz.) sliced pineapple (8 slices pineapple)**

Individual Baked Alaskas: For meringue—beat egg whites until stiff peaks are formed.

Completely cover ice cream with the meringue. Serve Individual Baked Alaskas immediately.

Drain pineapple slices thoroughly, reserving syrup for other use.

Beat until frothy

5 egg whites
1 teaspoon vanilla extract
¼ teaspoon salt

Add about 2 tablespoons at a time, beating well after each addition

¾ cup sugar

Beat the meringue until very stiff peaks are formed.

Set out a thick wooden board.

Pat the pineapple slices dry with absorbent paper. Arrange them on the board. Quickly place 1 scoop of very firm ice cream in center of each slice. Completely cover ice cream with meringue, spreading evenly. Be careful to completely seal bottom edge to pineapple slice.

Place in 450°F oven for about 4 min., or until meringue is lightly browned.

Remove to serving tray, and serve immediately.
8 servings

BAKED ALASKA

▲ Base Recipe

Chill a 2-qt. mold. Cover baking sheet with two sheets heavy paper or set out wooden board.

Line chilled mold with

Chocolate Ice Cream Superbe
(one third recipe, page 560,
or 1 qt. commercial ice cream)

Pack ice cream firmly against sides of mold.

Fill center of mold, packing firmly, with

Berry Ice Cream (one third recipe,
page 558; or use 1 qt. commercial
ice cream)

Freeze strawberries until very firm.

Meanwhile, prepare and cool

Pound Cake (page 437)

Split cake into two layers and trim one layer about ½ in. larger than mold. Place cake slice on baking sheet or wooden board. Set aside.

Prepare meringue by beating with rotary beater until frothy

5 egg whites
½ teaspoon vanilla extract
¼ teaspoon salt

Add about 2 tablespoons at a time, beating well after each addition

¾ cup sugar

Beat until very stiff peaks are formed.

To unmold, loosen top edge of mold with a knife. Wet a clean towel in hot water and wring it almost dry. Invert mold onto center of cake. Wrap hot towel around mold for a few seconds only. (If mold does not loosen, repeat.)

Working quickly, completely cover ice cream and cake with meringue, spreading evenly and being careful to completely seal bottom edge. With spatula, quickly swirl meringue into an attractive design and, if desired, garnish with

Maraschino cherries

Place in 450°F oven 4 to 5 min., or until meringue is lightly browned.

Using two broad spatulas, quickly slide Baked Alaska onto a chilled serving plate. Slice and serve immediately.
12 to 16 servings

—BAKED ALASKA LOAF

Follow ▲ Recipe. Substitute a **1-qt. brick com-** mercial ice cream for molded ice cream. Prepare Pound Cake (loaf, page 437) or substitute purchased oblong pound cake. Slice ½-in. layer from bottom of cake and cut layer about ½ in. larger than length and width of brick of ice cream to be used. Omit cherries.

ICE CREAM CHERRY PYRAMID

Drain, reserving syrup

3 cans or jars (17 oz. each) pitted
dark sweet cherries

Set out

3 qts. vanilla ice cream

Arrange scoops of ice cream, pyramid fashion, on a serving plate (see photo). Set in freezer until serving time.

Meanwhile, blend in a heavy saucepan

3 tablespoons cornstarch
1 tablespoon sugar
2 tablespoons grated lemon peel

Stir in the reserved cherry syrup. Bring mixture to boiling, stirring constantly; cook 3 min. Mix in the cherries and heat, stirring occasionally.

To serve, pour cherry sauce over ice cream pyramid. Place a **sugar cube** soaked with **lemon extract** on top and ignite it. Pass additional sauce.
14 to 16 servings

FROZEN CHERRY EASTER EGG

Set out a 1½-qt. melon mold.

Set out to soften

3 pts. vanilla ice cream

Prepare and mix into the softened ice cream

1½ cups chopped red candied cherries
¾ cup chopped toasted filberts (page 10)
¼ cup finely chopped flaked coconut

Mix in

3 tablespoons maraschino cherry syrup
1 tablespoon vanilla extract

Rinse the mold with cold water and pack ice cream mixture into it. Cover and freeze until firm.

Invert the mold on a chilled plate. Dip a clean towel in hot water, quickly wring it almost dry and wrap it around the mold for a few seconds;

Baked Alaska Loaf

Ice Cream Cherry Pyramid

lift off mold. If mold cannot be lifted off immediately, repeat procedure. If necessary, set in freezer before frosting.

Prepare, following directions on package
1 env. (2 oz.) dessert topping mix
Frost the egg with the whipped topping. Decorate using a cake decorating set or your favorite **decorating frosting** and pastry bag with decorating tubes. Pipe frosting onto frozen egg in an attractive design (see photo). Garnish with **red candied cherries.** Set in freezer until ready to serve. *10 to 12 servings*

CANDLELIGHT PINEAPPLE BOMBE

Set out a deep 7-cup mold.

Chop and set aside
½ cup toasted pecans (page 10)

Put into a heavy saucepan
1 can (20 oz.) crushed pineapple, undrained
⅛ teaspoon salt
3 cups miniature marshmallows
2 teaspoons vanilla extract
1 teaspoon almond extract
Set over low heat, stirring occasionally, until marshmallows are melted.

Frozen Cherry Easter Egg

Remove from heat and cool. Stir in the nuts. Turn into a refrigerator tray and freeze until sufficiently set to spoon into bombe.

Thoroughly chill the mold by filling it with ice and water; set aside.

Set out to soften slightly
2 qts. vanilla ice cream

When ready to use mold, pour out ice and water and quickly line the mold with two thirds of the ice cream. Turn thickened pineapple mixture into center and spread remaining ice cream over the top. Cover with aluminum foil; freeze overnight.

Shortly before ready to serve, wrap a hot towel around mold for a few seconds only, and run a knife around edge. Invert mold on a chilled serving plate. If mold does not lift off, repeat the hot towel procedure. Decorate the bombe (see photo) with rosettes of **tinted whipped cream, stemmed maraschino cherries** and **canned pineapple chunks.** *8 to 10 servings*

PEAR MELBA FLAMBEE

Drain, reserving syrups
1 pkg. (10 oz.) frozen raspberries, thawed
1 can (16 oz.) sliced pears
Mix thoroughly in a saucepan
1 tablespoon cornstarch
2 tablespoons sugar
Blend in the reserved syrups. Add
1 piece (1 in.) stick cinnamon
Dash nutmeg
Bring to boiling, stirring constantly; cook until thickened. Mix in the raspberries, pears and
1 teaspoon grated lemon peel
1 tablespoon lemon juice
Heat to simmering. Discard cinnamon.

Heat
2 tablespoons rum
Ignite and pour over fruit. When flame has burned out, spoon sauce over **vanilla ice cream.** *6 to 8 servings*

Note: If flaming is not desired, substitute 1 teaspoon rum extract for rum.

SERVE-YOURSELF SUNDAES

A delightfully informal conclusion to a Sunday night supper: the "makin's" of everyone's favorite dessert! Let your guests' own calorie-consciences be their guides as they dip into the homemade ice cream you provide, and top it with luscious homemade sauces, fruits, nuts, whipped cream—one or all. For those who like cake with their ice cream, provide that too—and whoever chooses may add a foundation of cake to his personal dessert creation, or enjoy it as an accompaniment.

Chill the center bowl of a Lazy Susan.

Fill some of the Lazy Susan's side dishes with

Candlelight Pineapple Bombe

an assortment of sauces; for example, **Butterscotch Sauce** (page 577), chilled **Ginger Sauce** (page 580) and **Mocha Sauce I** (page 580); and don't forget to heap one of the dishes with **Sweetened Whipped Cream** (page 480) or one of its flavor-variants. Into others put fruits (fresh or frozen), such as sliced or crushed sweetened **strawberries,** sliced **peaches, bananas** cut lengthwise into finger lengths and dipped into **pineapple** or **lemon juice,** and **maraschino cherries;** add bowls of **nuts,** moist shredded **coconut,** and perhaps jewel-red **pomegranate seeds** when in season, for garnishing.

When the side dishes are all filled and in place, remove the chilled center bowl from the refrigerator and fill it with scoops of **ice cream**— rich, delicious homemade **Philadelphia Ice Cream** (page 558), for instance, or its strawberry variation. Put it in place and rush the whole array to the table.

Cakes take gracefully to the serve-yourself treatment. Choose one such as **Angel Food Cake** (page 457), **Velvet Cola Cake** (page 444), **Golden Orange Crunch Cake** (page 435), or **pound cake.** Or perhaps you'd prefer an assortment. They're delicious accompaniments for the ice cream, as well as pleasing foundations for the desserts.

Serve-Yourself Sundaes

Strawberry Queen Ice Cream Pie

ICE CREAM BALLS

Pack into deep refrigerator tray and freeze hard

1 qt. ice cream

Prepare

**1 cup Crumbs for Cookie Crust
(page 604)**

Form ice cream balls with a scoop rinsed each time in hot water. Roll each ball in crumbs until thickly coated.

Place balls in shallow refrigerator tray and freeze until serving time. *6 to 8 servings*

SNOWBALLS ADRIFT

Ice cream goodness, enhanced by chewy coconut and flavorful chocolate makes an exciting combination.

Ice cream of any desired flavor may be used for snowballs. It must be firm before shaping balls.

Spread in a chilled shallow pan

1 cup moist shredded coconut

With a scoop, rinsed each time in hot water, quickly form 6 to 8 balls of ice cream from

1 qt. ice cream

After forming each ball, roll immediately in the coconut. Place snowballs in chilled refrigerator tray and cover with waxed paper. Before serving, spoon **chocolate syrup** into individual dishes and in each one float a snowball. *6 to 8 servings*

CHERRY FILBERT SUNDAE PIE

Prepare and chill
Cherry Morency Sauce (page 577)

Prepare, bake and set aside to cool
Filbert Pastry (page 487)

Just before serving pie, scoop into pie shell
1 qt. vanilla ice cream
Sprinkle with

**¼ cup toasted filberts, coarsely
chopped**
Pour ½ cup of the Cherry Morency Sauce over top. Serve immediately with remaining sauce.
One 9-in. pie

STRAWBERRY QUEEN ICE CREAM PIE

Prepare and bake in a 9-in. pie pan
**Graham Cracker Crumb Crust
(page 488)**
Sort, rinse, drain, hull and slice
1 pt. fresh ripe strawberries
Gently mix fresh berries with
¼ cup sugar
(A 10-oz. pkg. frozen sliced strawberries, thawed, may be substituted for fresh berries. Omit sugar.)

Set out to soften slightly
**1 qt. Vanilla Ice Cream Superbe (page
560) or commercial ice cream**
Spoon about one fourth of the ice cream onto bottom of cooled crust; spread ice cream into an even layer. Cover with one half of the strawberries and then with remainder of ice cream. Top with remaining strawberries. Freeze until firm. *About 6 servings*

PEACHY STRAWBERRY ICE CREAM PIE

▲ *Base Recipe*

Prepare (page 560)
**1½ qts. Strawberry Ice Cream Superbe
(or purchase commercial ice cream)**
Keep ice cream solidly frozen.

Thaw, following directions on package
1 pkg. (10 oz.) frozen sliced peaches

Prepare and bake in 9-in. pie pan
Pastry I for 1-Crust Pie (page 485)
Cool pastry shell thoroughly.

Spoon Strawberry Ice Cream into pastry shell. Top with sliced peaches. Serve immediately.
One 9-in. pie

—BANANA CHOCOLATE ICE CREAM PIE

Substitute **Banana Ice Cream** (page 558) for strawberry ice cream and **Fudge Sauce Café** (page 579) for peaches. Or omit sauce and top ice cream with **chocolate curls** (pull ½ oz.-chocolate across a shredder to make curls).

FROSTY COOKIE CRUMB PIE

▲ *Base Recipe*

Set out on 8- or 9-in. pie pan

Blend
**1⅓ cups Crumbs for Cookie Crust
(page 604)**
¼ cup softened butter or margarine
Using back of a spoon, press firmly on bottom and sides of the pan.

Bake at 325°F 10 min. Cool thoroughly before adding filling.

Fill crust with
1 qt. vanilla ice cream
Top with **grated chocolate, nuts, coconut,** crushed **peppermint stick candy** or any **chocolate sauce.** Serve at once or freeze. *6 servings*

—FROSTY GRAHAM CRACKER PIE

Follow ▲ Recipe. Substitute **graham cracker crumbs** (about 16 to 18 crackers) for the cookie crumbs. Blend in ¼ cup sugar, **¼ lb. finely chopped milk or semisweet chocolate** and ½ teaspoon cinnamon.

TOPPERS FOR ICE CREAM

Top purchased ice cream with any of the following; shaved **maple sugar; maple syrup; honey; applesauce,** sprinkled with **cinnamon; fresh peaches; whipped cream,** flavored with **peppermint extract; toasted macaroon crumbs;** or:

Chocolate Curls—Pull **chocolate squares** across a shredder.

Colored Coconut—Place **flaked, shredded or grated coconut** on waxed paper and sprinkle with a mixture of **a few drops each food coloring** and **water.** Toss well, dry and toast in a slow oven.

Frozen Fruit—Thaw partially.

Sweetened Crushed Berries—Rinse, discard imperfect berries and hull **1 qt. strawberries.** Reserve ½ cup berries for garnish, if desired. Crush remaining berries slightly and sweeten with about **1 cup sugar.** Cover and set in refrigerator to chill thoroughly. Gently mix fruit occasionally. **Raspberries, blackberries** or **blueberries** may be substituted for strawberries.

MAGIC COCONUT NESTS

Butter six 2½-in. muffin-pan wells.

Cook in top of double boiler, stirring frequently, over rapidly boiling water
⅔ cup sweetened condensed milk
1 oz. (1 sq.) unsweetened chocolate
When mixture is thick (about 10 min.) turn into large bowl. Add and blend well
1 teaspoon vanilla extract
2 cups moist shredded coconut
Place about ¼ cup of mixture in each muffin well. Pack firmly around bottom and sides. Let mixture extend ½ in. above rim of pans.

Bake at 350°F until top edges are browned and

Magic Coconut Nests

firm (about 20 min.). Loosen edges and lift carefully from pans. Cool on rack. Just before serving, fill nests with **vanilla ice cream.** Top with **Peppermint Fudge Sauce Superb** (page 579).

6 nests

FRUIT DESSERTS

FRUIT PARFAIT

▲ *Base Recipe*

Set a bowl and rotary beater in refrigerator to chill.

Chill in refrigerator
1 cup fruit, cut in small pieces

Place on a sheet of heavy waxed paper about
20 cookies (vanilla wafers, graham crackers, ginger snaps, butter or chocolate cookies)
Loosely fold paper around cookies, tucking open end under. With rolling pin, gently crush cookies to make fine crumbs (about 1½ cups crumbs). Set aside.

Prepare
Sweetened Whipped Cream (page 480)

Set out 6 chilled individual sherbet or parfait glasses. Spoon a layer of crumbs in each glass, next a layer of fruit and then a layer of whipped cream; repeat layering. Serve immediately or chill in refrigerator until serving time.

6 parfaits

—BUTTERSCOTCH PARFAIT

Follow ▲ Recipe. Substitute **1 cup butterscotch sauce** for fruit and decrease sugar to 2 tablespoons. Use vanilla wafers for cookie crumbs. Top each serving with a maraschino cherry.

—CHOCOLATE GRAHAM PARFAIT

Follow ▲ Recipe. Substitute **1 cup chocolate syrup** for fruit. Use graham crackers for crumbs.

—PINEAPPLE PARFAIT

Follow ▲ Recipe. Use **crushed or chunk-style pineapple** for the fruit and ginger snaps for

Fruit Plate

the crumbs. Top each serving with a **maraschino cherry.**

—RASPBERRY PARFAIT

Follow ▲ Recipe. Substitute **1 cup raspberry syrup** for fruit. Use butter cookies for crumbs.

—BANANA PARFAIT

Follow ▲ Recipe. For the fruit, slice **3 all-yellow or brown-flecked bananas;** reserve 12 slices. Mix remaining banana slices with ¼ cup **moist shredded coconut** and ¼ cup **orange juice.** Use chocolate cookies for the crumbs. Top each serving with 2 of the reserved banana slices.

FRUIT PLATE
(Frutta)

▲ *Base Recipe*

Chill large serving plate.

Drain and chill in refrigerator
7 peach halves (29-oz. can)

Wash and chill in refrigerator
½ lb. grapes

Arrange peach halves in the center of the chilled serving plate.

Pare and cut each into 6 wedges
½ chilled cantaloupe
½ chilled honeydew melon
Arrange wedges around peaches on plate, with clusters of grapes between melon sections. Garnish with
Mint leaves

6 servings

—SICILIAN FRUIT PLATE
(Frutta alla Siciliana)

Follow ▲ Recipe. Substitute **2 peeled and quartered oranges or mandarines** (a variety of oranges with a loose peel and sweet juice) for the peaches.

COUPE ST. JACQUES

Have ready
Lime, Orange and Raspberry Ice (page 563)

Prepare (see below) and put into a large bowl
2 cups fresh pineapple wedges
1 cup orange pieces
1 cup fresh peach pieces
½ cup white seedless grapes, cut in halves
¼ cup fresh blueberries
Sprinkle over fruit
1 cup sifted confectioners' or granulated sugar
Gently mix fruits thoroughly. Pour over fruit
⅓ cup kirsch
Set bowl in refrigerator to chill fruits.

Before serving add to bowl
¼ cup fresh raspberries
Gently mix fruit. Spoon into chilled serving dishes, spooning some of the fruit juices over fruit. Top each serving with 1 scoop each of the three ices. Serve immediately.

For Pineapple Preparation—Cut off and discard crown (spiny top) of pineapple and rinse pineapple. Cut into crosswise slices ¼ to ½ in. thick. With a sharp knife, cut away and discard rind and "eyes" from each slice. Cut away the core and discard. Cut slices into wedges (keep bite-size and uniform in shape).

For Orange Preparation—With a sharp knife, remove peel and white membrane from orange. Remove sections, cutting on either side of dividing membranes over the bowl to save juice. Remove and discard seeds, if any. Cut sections into halves, if desired.

For Peach Preparation—Rinse, pare, cut into halves and pit peaches. Slice and cut into bite-size pieces (keeping uniform in shape). To keep peach slices from darkening, toss to coat with orange, lemon, or pineapple juice.

For Berry Preparation—Rinse and thoroughly drain blueberries and raspberries.

For Grape Preparation—Rinse, stem and drain thoroughly white seedless grapes. Cut grapes into halves.

10 to 12 servings

BLENDER APPLESAUCE

▲ *Base Recipe*

The happy owner of an electric blender will be delighted with this delicious, double-quick method for preparing applesauce. Try the cranberry variation for a luscious, yet easy-to-prepare fruit combination.

Wash, quarter, core and pare
3 or 4 medium (about 1 lb.) cooking apples
Put into blender container
¼ cup pineapple juice
¼ cup sugar

Cover and turn on motor. While motor is running, gradually add apple pieces and blend until the consistency is the same throughout (thick and sauce-like). Use rubber spatula to scrape down sides of container several times.

Pour applesauce into saucepan and bring to boiling, stirring occasionally. (If served immediately, omit heating.) Serve either hot or chilled.   *About 2 cups applesauce*

—CRANBERRY APPLESAUCE

Follow ▲ Recipe. Increase pineapple juice to ½ to ⅔ cup. Increase sugar to ½ or ⅔ cup and reserve. Add to blender container **1 cup washed and sorted cranberries**, after addition of apples. Bring mixture to boiling; add sugar, stirring until sugar is dissolved.

QUICK APPLESAUCE WHIP

Combine and set aside
Blender Applesauce (page 567), or
1 can (16 oz.) applesauce
½ teaspoon grated lemon peel
2 teaspoons lemon juice
½ teaspoon cinnamon

Put into a small mixer bowl and beat until frothy
3 egg whites
⅛ teaspoon salt
Add gradually, beating after each addition
6 tablespoons sugar
Continue beating on high speed until stiff peaks are formed.

Fold beaten egg whites into applesauce mixture. Sprinkle each serving with **nutmeg** and serve immediately.   *6 servings*

SPICED APPLESAUCE

▲ Base Recipe

Wash, quarter and core
8 large (about 4 lbs.) cooking apples
Put into large saucepan with
¾ cup water
Cover and simmer 15 to 20 min., or until apples are tender when pierced with a fork. Stir occasionally. Add more water if necessary. Press through a strainer or food mill.

Stir in
½ cup firmly packed brown sugar
1 teaspoon cinnamon
½ teaspoon nutmeg
2 teaspoons lemon juice
Heat over low heat until sugar is dissolved.

Serve hot or cold. Use a dessert or as a topping for waffles and griddlecakes.
          8 to 10 servings

—ROSY PINK APPLESAUCE

Follow ▲ Recipe. Substitute **½ cup granulated sugar** for brown sugar. Add **½ cup**

(about 4 oz.) red cinnamon candies and stir until blended. Omit nutmeg and lemon juice.

—FRUIT JUICE APPLESAUCE

Follow ▲ Recipe. Before serving, blend in **2 tablespoons orange juice or pineapple juice.**

ROSY APPLESAUCE

▲ Base Recipe

Set out a 2-qt. saucepan with a tight-fitting cover.

Wash, quarter and core
8 large (about 3 lbs.) apples
Immediately put apples into saucepan with
½ cup water
Cover. Simmer 15 to 20 min., or until tender when peirced with fork. Stir occasionally; add water if needed to keep from scorching.

Press apples through a coarse strainer or food mill. Add to hot mixture
½ cup sugar
1 tablespoon lemon juice
1 or more drops red food coloring
Stir until sugar dissolves. Serve hot or cold.
          6 servings

—SPICY APPLESAUCE

Follow ▲ Recipe. Substitute **brown sugar** for granulated sugar and blend in **¼ teaspoon cinnamon or mace.** Omit food coloring.

FRENCH APPLESAUCE
(Purée de Pommes)

▲ Base Recipe

Wash, quarter, pare and core
8 medium (2 to 3 lbs.) tart cooking apples
Heat in a heavy saucepan with
3 tablespoons water
2 tablespoons butter
½ teaspoon grated lemon peel
Stirring occasionally, cover and simmer 15 to 25 min., or until apples are soft and somewhat

---

transparent. Stir in
½ cup sugar
Stir over low heat until sugar is dissolved.

This thick sauce may be sprinkled with **confectioners' sugar** and served hot.

To serve applesauce cold, in true French style, heat over low heat
½ cup Apricot Sauce (page 577) or
½ cup currant jelly
2 tablespoons water
Pour over cold applesauce just before serving.
          6 servings

—APPLE CHARLOTTE
(Charlotte de Pommes)

A typically French dessert, the charlotte consists of a cooked fruit—apples, peaches, pears or apricots—enclosed in a shell of bread. The fruit mixture must be very thick to keep the shell crisp.

Follow ▲ Recipe for cooking apples. Omit granulated sugar. Add **1-in. piece stick cinnamon** and **¼ cup confectioners' sugar** with the butter. When apples are soft, remove cinnamon. Butter a 1-qt. mold or casserole. Remove crusts from **6 to 8 thin slices white bread.** Melt **¼ cup butter.** Brush both sides with melted butter. To form the shell, line bottom of mold with part of the bread. Cut remaining slices to the height of the sides of the mold. Arrange slightly overlapping slices against sides of mold. Fill mold with applesauce, piling high in center. Bake at 375°F about 30 min., or until bread tips are lightly browned. Loosen sides with spatula, invert and turn onto serving plate. Serve at once with **Apricot Sauce** (page 577).

SWEDISH APPLECAKE WITH VANILLA SAUCE
(Applekaka med Vaniljsas)

Butter bottom and sides of a 1-qt. baking dish.

Prepare
Vanilla Sauce I (page 576)

Place on a long length of heavy waxed paper
16 (about 7 oz.) rusks
Loosely fold paper around rusks, tucking under open ends. With a rolling pin, gently crush rusks to make fine crumbs (about 2 cups crumbs). Or place rusks in a plastic bag and gently crush. Turn crumbs into a bowl. Stir in
¼ cup sugar

Melt in a saucepan over low heat
⅓ cup butter
Pour butter evenly over the crumb mixture and toss lightly to coat crumbs evenly.

Put one third of the crumbs into the baking dish and firmly press into an even layer on bottom and sides of baking dish.

Set out
2½ cups thick sweetened applesauce
¼ cup butter
Spoon one half the applesauce into the baking

Baked Apples with Meringue

dish. Dot with one half of the butter. Sprinkle with one half the remaining crumbs. Repeat layering, ending with remaining crumbs.

Bake at 350°F 25 to 30 min.

Cool completely; chill in refrigerator several hours.

When ready to serve, sift over top of cake to form a decorative pattern*

    ¼ cup confectioners' sugar

Serve applecake with the Vanilla Sauce.

        8 servings

*To form a pattern place a paper doily on top of the cake. Sift the confectioners' sugar over the doily. Carefully lift doily off the cake. The confectioners' sugar will form the decorative pattern.

ENCORE BAKED APPLES

    ▲ *Base Recipe*

Set out a 2-qt. casserole with a tight-fitting cover.

Select

    **6 medium (about 2 lbs.) firm
      cooking apples**

Wash, core and pare upper fourth of each apple. Place in casserole.

Mix

    **¾ cup firmly packed brown sugar
    2 teaspoons cinnamon**

Fill center cavity of each apple with about 2 tablespoons cinnamon-sugar mixture. Allowing ½ teaspoon for each apple, dot tops with

    1 tablespoon butter or margarine

Pour in casserole

    **Water, to a depth of ½ in. (unsweet-
      ened fruit juice may be used as
      part of liquid)**

Cover and bake at 350°F 45 to 50 min., or until apples are tender when gently pierced with a fork. Or bake uncovered and baste frequently with liquid from bottom of casserole.

        6 servings

—GLAZED BAKED APPLES

Prepare apples as in ▲ Recipe. Sprinkle one half of sugar-cinnamon mixture on tops and in centers of apples. Cover and bake until apples are tender. Remove from oven. Sprinkle apples with remaining sugar mixture and dot with butter. Baste with liquid. Place casserole under broiler so tops of apples are 4 in. from heat. Broil 5 to 10 min., basting frequently, until apples are glazed.

—VARIETY BAKED APPLES

Follow ▲ Recipe for preparing apples. In center cavity of each apple, place one of the following mixtures: **2 tablespoons mincemeat** mixed with **1 teaspoon orange juice; 1 tablespoon finely chopped nuts** mixed with **1 tablespoon granulated or brown sugar; 2 tablespoons mixed chopped nuts, raisins, chopped dates or figs;** or **2 tablespoons thick cranberry sauce** or **jelly.** Finish preparation and baking as in ▲ Recipe.

—BAKED APPLES WITH MERINGUE

Follow ▲ Recipe. Instead of water, use a syrup made by boiling **¾ cup sugar** and **1 cup water** for 5 min. Bake apples uncovered 30 to 40 min., or until almost tender, basting frequently with syrup. Remove from oven and cool in syrup. Pile meringue on apples. Bake at 350°F 10 to 15 min., or until meringue is delicately browned.

For Meringue—Beat **2 egg whites** until frothy; gradually beat in **¼ cup sugar;** beat until very stiff peaks are formed.

FLAMING APPLES WITH ALMONDS

Butter a large shallow baking dish with a tight-fitting cover.

Blanch (page 9) and set aside

    1¼ cups (about 6 oz.) almonds

Wash, cut into crosswise halves and core

    **4 large (about 2 lbs.) baking
      apples**

Cut small slits in spoke design in cut surfaces of apples. Cut away a thin wedge from each slit and place an almond lengthwise in each groove. Arrange apples cut-side up in baking dish.

Flaming Apples with Almonds

Mix and fill cavities of apple halves with equal portions of

    **½ cup Mincemeat (page 729; or
      use bottled mincemeat)
    ⅓ cup butter or margarine, softened
    1 teaspoon cinnamon
    ¾ teaspoon nutmeg**

Pour around apple halves

    1 cup water

Cover and bake at 350°F 35 to 45 min., or until tender.

Meanwhile, set out to drain

    8 maraschino cherries

Garnish apple halves with cherries. Before serving, heat thoroughly in a small saucepan

    **¼ cup rum
    ¼ cup brandy**

Flame (page 10) and pour over baked apples. Serve immediately.   *8 servings*

DEEP-DISH CHEESE APPLE SCALLOP

    ▲ *Base Recipe*

Butter a 2-qt. casserole.

Thoroughly blend

    **¾ cup firmly packed brown sugar
    3 tablespoons all-purpose flour
    ½ teaspoon salt
    1 teaspoon cinnamon
    ¼ teaspoon nutmeg**

Cut in with pastry blender or two knives until mixture is in coarse crumbs

    **3 tablespoons butter or margarine
    1 teaspoon grated orange peel**

Shred and mix in

    **3 oz. Cheddar cheese (¾ cup,
      shredded)**

Wash, quarter, core, pare and cut into ⅛-in. slices

    **6 to 7 medium firm tart cooking
      apples (6 cups, cut)**

Arrange one half of the apple slices in casserole. Sprinkle with one half of sugar-cheese mixture; repeat. Sprinkle over top

    ¼ cup orange juice

Cover surface with mixture of

    **1½ cups corn flakes, coarsely crushed
    ¼ cup firmly packed brown sugar**

Bake at 375°F 35 to 40 min., or until apples

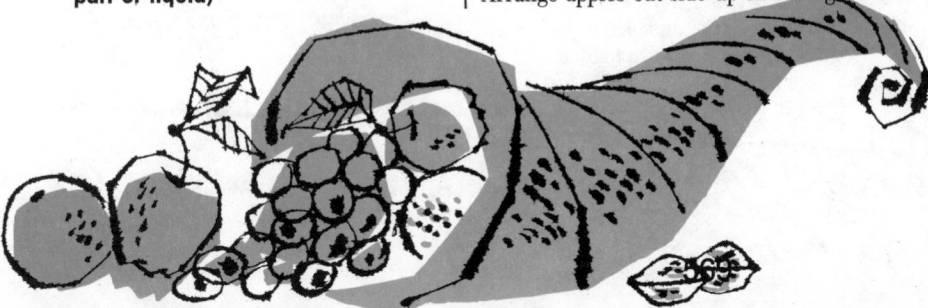

Mincemeat Betty

are tender when pierced with a fork. Cool pudding slightly and serve with heavy cream.

6 to 8 servings

—HIS FAVORITE APPLE PUDDING

Follow ▲ Recipe; butter a casserole with a cover. Toast until very crisp **5 slices white bread.** Butter both sides of each slice. Place ⅓ of apples on bottom of casserole; sprinkle ⅓ of sugar-cheese mixture over apples and cover with one half of whole and part slices toast. Repeat. Top with remaining apples and sugar-cheese mixture. Pour orange juice over top. Omit corn flake-brown sugar topping. Arrange ½ **cup buttered soft bread cubes** (page 9) over top. Cover casserole and bake at 425°F 30 min. Uncover and bake 10 min. longer.

APPLE GRAHAM BETTY

▲ Base Recipe

Butter a 1½-qt. casserole.

Blend

**2 cups (about 24 crackers) coarse
    graham cracker crumbs**
¼ **cup firmly packed brown sugar**
⅓ **cup melted butter or margarine**
1 teaspoon grated lemon peel

Wash, quarter, core, pare and cut into thin slices

**4 medium (about 1⅓ lbs.) tart
    apples (about 3 cups, sliced)**

Spread one third of crumb mixture evenly and lightly over bottom of casserole. Cover with one half of the apples. Repeat. Top with remaining crumb mixture. Drizzle over top a mixture of

¼ **cup orange juice**
2 tablespoons lemon juice

Bake at 375°F 30 to 40 min., or until apples are tender when pierced with a fork.

Serve warm with

½ **cup chilled heavy cream, beaten
    until cream stands in peaks
    (add ½ teaspoon cinnamon and
    ½ teaspoon grated lemon peel with
    vanilla extract)**

5 or 6 servings

—MINCEMEAT BETTY

Follow ▲ Recipe. Use one half of the apples; chop apples coarsely and mix with 1½ cups **Mincemeat** (page 729; or use packaged condensed mincemeat, prepared following directions). Substitute **granulated sugar** for brown sugar, and **coarse dry bread crumbs** for graham cracker crumbs. If desired, omit cinnamon and lemon peel from whipped cream; garnish whipped cream with **slivered maraschino cherries,** drained.

APPLE PANDOWDY

Apples in pandowdy are almost as irresistible as they were in the Garden of Eden.

Grease a 1½-qt. casserole.

Blend

½ **cup sugar**
½ **teaspoon salt**
1 teaspoon cinnamon
¼ **teaspoon nutmeg**

Cut in pastry blender or two knives until mixture is in coarse crumbs

3 tablespoons butter

Set aside.

Prepare dough for

Pastry for 1-Crust Pie (page 485)

Roll dough ⅛ in. thick and 1 in. larger than overall size of casserole top. Cut a simple design near center of pastry to allow steam to escape during baking. Set aside.

Wash, quarter, core, pare and slice

**6 to 7 medium (about 2 lbs.) tart
    cooking apples (about 6 cups, sliced)**

Arrange one half of apples in the casserole. Sprinkle one half of the sugar mixture over them. Repeat with remaining apples and sugar.

Moisten rim of casserole with cold water. Lift pastry carefully and lay over apples. Trim edge of pastry with scissors, allowing ½ in. to hang over. Fold extra width under and press edges gently all around to seal to moistened rim of casserole. Flute edge (page 10) or press with a fork.

Bake at 425°F 30 min. Remove casserole from oven; reduce heat to 350°F. With a spoon, break up the crust and mix down into the apples. Return to oven and bake 10 to 15 min. longer, or until apples are tender.

6 to 8 servings

OLD-FASHIONED APPLE PAN

Butter a 12x8x2- or 13x9x2-in. baking dish.

Mix in a saucepan

1 cup packed light brown sugar
2 tablespoons all-purpose flour
¼ **teaspoon salt**

Add and stir until smooth

1 cup water
2 teaspoons vinegar
2 teaspoons lemon juice

Bring to boiling; cook 2 to 3 min., stirring until thickened. Remove from heat. Mix in

2 tablespoons butter
1 teaspoon vanilla extract
¼ **teaspoon cinnamon**
⅛ **teaspoon nutmeg**

Cover and set sauce aside.

Quarter, pare and slice enough apples to yield

5 cups cooking apple slices

Spread apple slices evenly in the baking dish. Pour sauce over apples.

Bake at 375°F 40 min., or until apples are tender. Serve warm accompanied with **whipped dessert topping.** *About 6 servings*

SPICY APRICOT COBBLER

Set out a shallow 1-qt. baking dish.

Drain, reserving 1 cup syrup

2 cans (16 oz. each) apricots

Cut apricots into quarters and put into the baking dish. Set aside.

Blend in a saucepan

½ **cup firmly packed brown sugar**
2 tablespoons cornstarch
⅛ **teaspoon salt**
⅛ **teaspoon cinnamon**
⅛ **teaspoon cloves**

Stir in the reserved apricot syrup and

2 tablespoons cider vinegar
1 tablespoon butter or margarine

Bring mixture to boiling, stirring frequently; cook until clear and thickened, about 10 min. Pour over apricots and set in a 400°F oven.

Combine in a bowl

1 cup biscuit mix
½ **cup finely shredded sharp
    Cheddar cheese**

Stir in with a fork to form a soft dough

¼ **cup milk**
**2 tablespoons butter or margarine,
    melted**

Remove dish from oven and drop dough by heaping tablespoons onto top of hot apricots. Return to oven and bake 20 min., or until crust is golden brown. Serve warm. *6 servings*

ORANGE BAKED BANANAS

▲ Base Recipe

In season the year around, bananas make an unusual hot dessert at any time.

Thoroughly grease a large shallow baking dish.

For Orange Sauce—Mix in a saucepan
  ½ cup firmly packed brown sugar
  1 tablespoon cornstarch
  ⅛ teaspoon cinnamon
  Few grains salt
Add gradually, blending in
  ¾ cup boiling water
Bring rapidly to boiling and cook about 5 min., or until sauce is thickened, stirring constantly.

Remove from heat and blend in
  1½ teaspoons grated orange peel
  ¼ cup orange juice
  1 teaspoon lemon juice
  2 tablespoons butter or margarine

To Complete—Peel and cut into halves lengthwise
  6 bananas with all-yellow or green-tipped peel
Arrange halves cut side down in baking dish.

Brush with about
  2 tablespoons melted butter or margarine
Sprinkle over bananas
  ½ teaspoon salt
Pour Orange Sauce over bananas.

Bake at 375°F 10 to 20 min.

Serve hot, spooning sauce over bananas.

6 servings

—SOUTH SEA BANANAS

Follow ▲ Recipe. Omit from sauce the cinnamon, orange juice and peel, lemon juice and butter or margarine. After removing sauce from heat, stir in **¼ cup rum, Cointreau** or **any desired liqueur.**

BLUEBERRY CRISP

Set out a 9-in. square baking dish.

Rinse and set aside
  4 cups fresh blueberries

Mix in a bowl
  1 cup sifted all-purpose flour
  ½ cup firmly packed brown sugar
  1 teaspoon cinnamon
Cut in with pastry blender or two knives until mixture is crumbly
  ½ cup butter

Brunch Grapefruit Dessert

Turn the blueberries into the baking dish and spoon crumb mixture evenly over top.

Bake at 350°F 40 to 45 min., or until top is lightly browned.

Serve warm or cold.

6 to 8 servings

BLUEBERRY CREAM SURPRISE

Set out a 10x6x1½-in. dish.

Turn into a saucepan
  1 can (15 oz.) blueberries
Heat to boiling.

Meanwhile, trim crusts from
  4 slices white bread
Spread slices with
  3 tablespoons softened butter or margarine
Cut slices into halves and arrange in dish. Pour the hot blueberries over bread. Cool, cover and set in refrigerator to chill thoroughly.

When ready to serve, spread over all
  1½ cups dairy sour cream
Sprinkle with
  2 tablespoons sugar or light brown sugar

4 servings

BRUNCH GRAPEFRUIT DESSERT

Prepare as in Broiled Grapefruit (page 33)
  2 large grapefruit
Notch peel with sharp knife if fancy effect is desired. Sprinkle grapefruit halves with
  2 teaspoons sugar
Chill grapefruit halves in refrigerator.

Before serving, top each half with a scoop of
  Raspberry sherbet
Garnish with
  sprigs of fresh mint

4 servings

MELON SERVICE

For a Large Party—Cut a large chilled **watermelon** into unequal lengthwise halves. From the larger half cut a thin slice to form a base so the melon will stand squarely. Cut pink meat into balls with a ball-shaped cutter. Put balls into a large bowl and set in refrigerator to chill. Pour juice from shell. Scoop out any ragged bits of melon, leaving a fairly even inner surface. Scallop edges attractively. Place in refrigerator to chill. Also cut balls from other varieties of chilled melons; pale-green **honeydews,** salmon-colored **cantaloupes,** orange-pink **Persians.** Add all balls to the large

bowl and pour over them a **flavored sugar syrup.** Toss to coat and mix balls. Heap into the chilled melon bowl and drizzle additional syrup over all. Serve on a platter and arrange galax or grape leaves around melon, placing a cluster of **Frosted Grapes** (page 370) on each leaf. Garnish melon balls with sprigs of **mint.**

For Individual Service—Cut into halves and scoop out seedy centers from **cantaloupes, honeydews, Persian melons, Cranshaws, honeyballs** or **other melons.** Fill with an assortment of chilled and sweetened fresh fruit: **strawberries, raspberries, grapes,** sliced **peaches,** cubes of **pineapple,** and **melon balls,** which have been tossed together with a **flavored sugar syrup** (see below). Or fill partially with fruit and top with any desired **fruit ice** or **sherbet.** Or fill melon bowls with ball-shaped scoops of **ice cream** which have been quickly rolled in flaked or shredded **coconut.** Or fill with **ginger ale ice** and top with clusters of **Frosted Grapes** (page 370). Serve unadorned halves on individual plates with a garnish of **mint sprigs** and **lime** or **lemon wedges.**

For Flavored Sugar Syrup—Bring to boiling **1 part water** and **1 part sugar.** Remove from heat, add a few bruised **mint leaves,** and cool. Strain and add **lemon or lime juice,** or any desired **liqueur** (crème de menthe, kirsch, Cointreau or curaçao). Chill syrup thoroughly.

MINTED CANTALOUPE BALLS

Set out
  1 large ripe cantaloupe
Using a melon-ball cutter, cut out balls (about 3 cups) from cantaloupe. Put into a bowl, and cover and chill thoroughly.

Mix in a saucepan
  ½ cup sugar
  1½ teaspoons cornstarch
  Few grains salt
Blend in
  ¾ cup water
Add
  12 fresh mint leaves
Bruise mint by pressing with back of spoon

Frosty Berry Melon Dessert

against side of pan. Bring to boiling, stirring constantly, and cook until mixture is slightly thickened.

Remove from heat; cool slightly and strain. Mix in
   1 tablespoon butter or margarine
   2 drops green food coloring
Chill in refrigerator.

To serve, turn chilled melon balls into a chilled serving bowl and pour sauce over them. Garnish with **mint sprigs.**   *About 6 servings*

FROSTY BERRY MELON DESSERT

Chill 4 serving plates in refrigerator

Rinse, cut into halves and remove seeds from
   1 medium cantaloupe
Place in refrigerator to chill.

Rinse (discarding imperfect berries) and set aside to drain
   1 pt. fresh blueberries
Put blueberries into a bowl and mix in
   ¼ cup sugar
   1 tablespoon Cointreau
Cover. Place in refrigerator to chill 1 hr.

Cut chilled cantaloupe into 4 ¾-in. slices, reserving ends. With a sharp paring knife, cut along inside of rind to loosen melon ring. Cut melon rings into wedges, keeping rind and sections intact in ring form. Cover with waxed

Banana Ambrosia

paper and place in refrigerator to chill.

Scoop out the inside of the melon ends with a melon baller to form melon balls. Put melon balls into a bowl, cover and set in refrigerator to chill.

Just before serving, peel, mark sides of banana with tines of fork and cut into ¼-in. slices
   1 banana with all-yellow or brown-flecked peel
Put into a bowl and sprinkle with
   1 tablespoon Cointreau
   1 teaspoon lemon juice
Gently toss banana slices.

Arrange on chilled plates
   Galax leaves
Place chilled melon rings on leaves and fill center with blueberries. Alternate melon balls and banana slices on top of melon ring. Place additional melon balls around each slice.

Generously sprinkle dessert with
   Cointreau
Garnish with
   Sprigs of fresh mint
                                    4 servings

FRESH FRUIT-FILLED CANTALOUPE

Rinse, cut into halves and remove seeds from
   3 cantaloupes

Rinse
   2 cups fresh blueberries
   2 cups fresh raspberries or strawberries
Toss berries with
   ¼ cup grenadine
   2 tablespoons lime juice
   ⅓ cup confectioners' sugar
Spoon fruit into cantaloupe cavities. Chill at least 1 hr. before serving. Garnish with **fresh mint leaves.**   *6 servings*

AMBROSIA

   ▲ *Base Recipe*

All over the South, ambrosia is a traditional Christmas dessert. When available, fresh coconut is used, and the dish is often prepared a day ahead of time and kept in the refrigerator to chill and blend the flavors.

With a sharp knife, cut away peel and white membrane from
   3 medium oranges
Separate sections by cutting on either side of dividing membranes, working over a bowl to save the juice; or cut into thin crosswise slices, removing any seeds, and cut slices into halves.

Coarsely chop
   ⅔ cup (about 3 oz.) moist shredded coconut
Arrange orange sections in two or three layers in a crystal serving dish, sprinkling each layer with the coconut and with
   Sugar

Chill in refrigerator at least 1 hr.   *4 servings*

—PINEAPPLE AMBROSIA

Follow ▲ Recipe. Substitute about ¾ **cup diced fresh pineapple** or **drained pineapple chunks** for 1 of the oranges.

—BANANA AMBROSIA

Follow ▲ Recipe. Peel and slice about ¼ in. thick **2 bananas** with brown-flecked peel. Alternate orange, coconut and banana layers in bowl; just before serving, garnish with additional banana and orange slices.

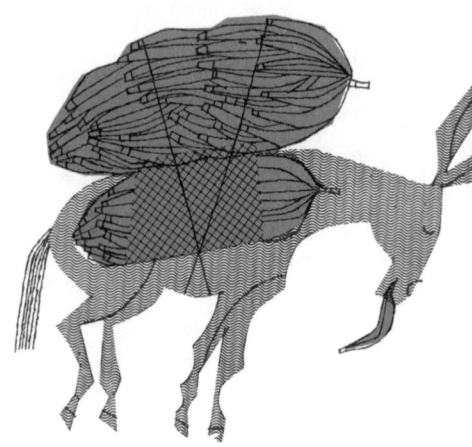

GOLDEN FRUIT

   ▲ *Base Recipe*

Set a small bowl and rotary beater in refrigerator to chill.

Rinse, peel, section and cut into small pieces
   3 oranges
Carefully combine with
   2 all-yellow or brown-flecked bananas, sliced
   2 pineapple slices, cut in small pieces
   6 to 8 marshmallows, quartered (page 9)
Sprinkle fruit with
   2 teaspoons orange or pineapple juice
Chill in refrigerator.

Using the chilled bowl and beater, beat until cream stands in peaks when beater is slowly lifted upright
   ½ cup chilled heavy cream

Spoon fruit into 4 chilled dishes and top with whipped cream.   *4 servings*

—GOLDEN FRUIT MOLD

Follow ▲ Recipe. Use canned (not fresh) pineapple. Empty into a bowl **1 pkg. (3 oz.) cherry or raspberry-flavored gelatin.** Add, stirring until dissolved, **1 cup boiling water.** Stir until completely dissolved and then stir in **1 cup cold water.** Chill in refrigerator, stirring

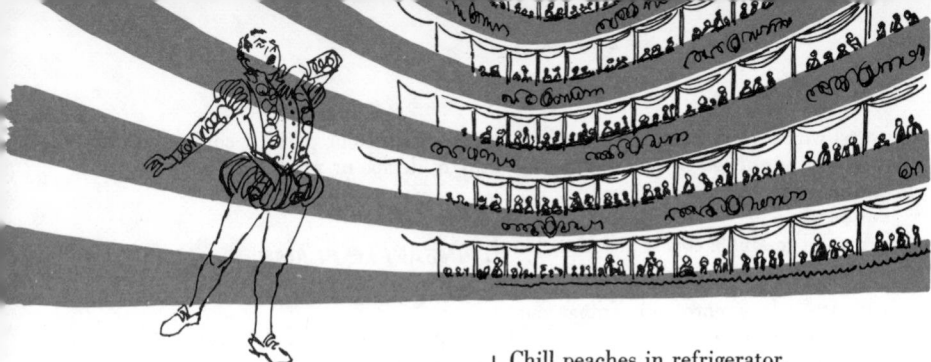

occasionally, or over ice and water, until gelatin mixture is slightly thicker than consistency of thick unbeaten egg white. (If mixture is placed over ice and water, it will have to be stirred frequently.)

Set out 6 individual molds. Fold fruit into slightly thickened gelatin, turn into molds, and chill in refrigerator until firm. To unmold, run tip of knife around top edge of mold to loosen. Dip mold into hot water for a few seconds. Invert onto chilled plate. Top with whipped cream.

BAKED SPICED PEACHES

Set out 4 small individual baking dishes or a shallow baking dish.

Drain, reserving syrup
1 can (29 oz.) peach halves
Arrange peaches, cut-side up, in baking dishes. Pour over peaches a mixture of
¼ cup reserved peach syrup
¼ cup firmly packed brown sugar
½ teaspoon cinnamon
¼ teaspoon nutmeg

Bake 350°F 10 min., basting two or three times. Remove from oven. Increase oven temperature to 400°F. Sprinkle over peaches a mixture of
¼ cup coarsely crushed corn flakes
2 tablespoons finely chopped pecans
2 tablespoons butter or margarine, melted

Return to oven and bake 5 min. longer.

Serve peaches warm with **cream.**   *4 servings*

PEACH A L'OPERA

Mix in a saucepan
1 cup sugar
1 cup water
Place over medium heat and bring to boiling, stirring constantly. Cover and boil 5 min. Remove from heat and stir in
1 teaspoon vanilla extract
Rinse, pare, cut into halves, and pit
3 large (about 1 lb.) firm ripe peaches
Quickly blot peaches on absorbent paper.

Set syrup over medium heat. Add peaches, two halves at one time, and simmer 3 min. With a slotted spoon, carefully remove peaches from syrup; allow excess syrup to drain into saucepan. Repeat for the remaining peach halves.

Chill peaches in refrigerator.

Meanwhile, rinse, drain, and force through coarse sieve or food mill
2 cups (1 pt.) ripe red raspberries
Stir in
¼ cup sugar
Chill in refrigerator.

To serve, spoon some of the raspberry sauce into each of 6 individual serving dishes. Place one chilled peach half cut side up in each dish. Spoon a blob of **whipped cream** into each. Serve with remaining raspberry sauce.
6 servings

STUFFED PEACHES
(Pesche Ripiene)

Set out 10x6x1½-in. baking dish.

Blanch (page 9), finely chop and set aside
½ cup (2¾ oz.) almonds

Using the electric blender (page 11), grind enough Italian Macaroons (page 587) to make
½ cup macaroon crumbs
Set crumbs aside.

Wash, pare and cut into halves
6 large firm peaches
Remove pit and a small portion of the pulp around cavity.

Combine and mix macaroon crumbs, chopped almonds and
2 tablespoons sugar
1 tablespoon chopped candied orange peel
Lightly fill peach halves with mixture. Put two halves together and fasten with wooden picks. Place in baking dish.

Pour over peaches
⅓ cup sherry or Marsala
Sprinkle over peaches
2 tablespoons sugar

Bake at 350°F 15 min. and serve either hot or cold.   *6 servings*

RICE FRUIT DESSERT
· (Rizs Gyümölccsel)

Set a 1-qt. bowl and rotary beater in refrigerator to chill.

Bring to boiling in a saucepan
1 qt. water
1½ teaspoons salt
So boiling will not stop, add gradually to water
½ cup uncooked rice
(The Rice Industry no longer considers it

necessary to wash rice before cooking.) Boil rapidly, uncovered, 15 to 20 min., or until a kernel is entirely soft when pressed between fingers. Drain rice in colander or sieve and rinse with hot water to remove loose starch. Cool rice completely.

When rice is completely cooled, gently mix and set aside
1 cup sliced peaches
1 cup sliced strawberries
3 to 4 tablespoons sugar (depending upon tartness of fruit)

Using the chilled bowl and beater, beat until cream stands in peaks when beater is slowly lifted upright
1 cup chilled heavy cream
Beat in with final few strokes
¼ cup Vanilla Confectioners' Sugar (page 582)
Fold whipped cream into cooled rice.

Arrange alternate layers of rice mixture and fruit in serving bowl, beginning and ending with rice mixture. Chill several hours.
About 6 servings

MINTED PEARS

▲ *Base Recipe*

Set out an 11x7x2-in. baking dish.

Drain, reserving syrup
8 medium canned pear halves (17-oz. can)
Place in the baking dish, cut-side up.

Mix in a bowl
1 cup reserved pear syrup
1 teaspoon grated lemon peel
2 tablespoons lemon juice
Pour over pears. Place in core cavities
8 chocolate-coated mint patties

Bake at 375°F 8 to 10 min., or until patties are softened. Serve warm with the syrup.
4 servings

—MERINGUE PEAR MOUNDS

Follow ▲ Recipe. While Minted Pears are baking, prepare **Meringue** (see Jiffy Lemon Pie,

Baked Spiced Peaches

page 495). Spoon into mounds over softened patties. Return to oven and bake 8 to 10 min. longer, or until meringue is lightly browned. Serve hot.

—HOLIDAY PEARS

Follow ▲ Recipe. Substitute **½ cup currant or cranberry jelly** for mint patties. Bake until jelly melts. Beat **1 pkg. (3 oz.) cream cheese** with **3 tablespoons milk** until light and fluffy. Spoon onto each serving.

BLUSHING PEARS

▲ *Base Recipe*

Set out an 8-in. shallow baking dish with a cover.

Wash, cut into halves, core and pare
> **2 large or 4 small pears**

Cut three tiny slits in full part of each rounded side. Insert in each slit
> **1 small red cinnamon candy**

Place pears in baking dish, cut-side down. Pour into dish
> **¼ cup water**
> **2 tablespoons lemon juice**

Cover and bake at 350°F 30 to 50 min. (depending upon size and variety of pears), or until pears are tender when gently pierced with a fork.

Remove pears from oven. Turn pears and fill (in order) the center of each half with
> **1 tablespoon sugar, brown or granulated**
> **½ teaspoon grated lemon peel**
> **¼ teaspoon butter or margarine**
> **Sprinkling of cinnamon or nutmeg**

Return baking dish to oven uncovered and leave until pears are glazed.

Serve hot or chilled. Or serve as a meat garnish, if desired.   *4 servings*

Note: For variety, substitute for sugar and spices in each pear center 2 teaspoons colorful tart jelly such as currant, mint or cranberry, or orange marmalade.

—BLUSHING PEACHES

Follow ▲ Recipe. Substitute **2 large or 4 small peaches** for pears. Bake 15 to 20 min. before turning fruit. In place of the spices, try **1 or 2 drops almond extract** in each center. Sprinkle each peach half with **1 teaspoon moist shredded coconut**. Omit second baking period.

FLAMING PEARS

▲ *Base Recipe*

Butter a large shallow baking dish with a tight-fitting cover.

Work together by pressing against bottom and sides of bowl with a fork
> **⅓ cup firmly packed brown sugar**
> **2 tablespoons butter or margarine, softened**

(Mixture should resemble coarse crumbs.) Set mixture aside.

Rinse, cut into halves, core and arrange cut-side up in baking dish
> **4 medium pears**

Fill cavities of pear halves with equal portions of brown sugar mixture.

Mix and pour over pear halves
> **¾ cup water**
> **¼ cup brandy**
> **1 teaspoon grated lemon peel**
> **2 tablespoons lemon juice**

Cover and bake at 350°F about 30 to 40 min., or until tender.

Meanwhile, toast (page 10) and coarsely chop
> **⅓ cup (about 2 oz.) walnuts**

Garnish baked pear halves with the walnuts. Before serving, heat thoroughly in a small saucepan
> **½ cup brandy**

Flame (page 10) and pour over baked pears. Serve immediately.   *4 servings*

—PEARS A LA ELEGANCE

Follow ▲ Recipe. Omit flaming and thoroughly chill baked pear halves. Omit walnuts. Serve on **vanilla ice cream** and top with **Fudge Sauce Café** (page 579).

SUGARED FRESH PINEAPPLE

▲ *Base Recipe*

Cut into crosswise slices about ½ in. thick
> **1 medium ripe pineapple**

Pare each slice, removing eyes. Remove core sections with a small biscuit cutter or sharp knife, leaving rings which may be used decoratively. Or cut wedges after removing core. Arrange pineapple slices or wedges in layers in a bowl, sprinkling between and over them
> **1 cup sugar**

Cover and let stand several hours until juicy and sugar is dissolved.   *5 or 6 servings*

—HALF-AND-HALF PINEAPPLE

Follow ▲ Recipe for preparing pineapple wedges; decrease sugar to ½ cup. Combine one-half of pineapple pieces with **1 cup frozen or fresh strawberries or raspberries**, sweetened. Combine other half of pineapple pieces with a **cup (about 1) diced banana** and ½ **½ cup** moist shredded **coconut**.

—PINEAPPLE FINGER SPEARS

Make pineapple finger spears by cutting down around "eyes" of pineapple with apple corer or sharp knife. Draw out sections and serve with **confectioners' sugar**. Remaining pineapple may be prepared according to directions in ▲ Recipe or variation.

PINEAPPLE FLAMBEE

▲ *Base Recipe*

Vanilla ice cream is a flattering flavor-complement to any of these elegant mixtures.

Cut off and discard stem and rinse
> **1 whole fresh pineapple**

Cut into crosswise slices about ½ in. thick. With a sharp knife, cut away and discard the rind and "eyes" from each slice. Cut away the core and cut slices into wedges.

Put into skillet over medium heat and stir until butter is melted and sugar is dissolved
> **¼ cup firmly packed brown sugar**
> **2 tablespoons butter**

Mix in
> **¼ cup Cointreau**
> **1 or 2 tablespoons lemon juice**

Add pineapple wedges and
> **¼ cup kirsch**

Mix gently until the liqueurs are thoroughly heated. Flame (page 10). Serve immediately.
          8 servings

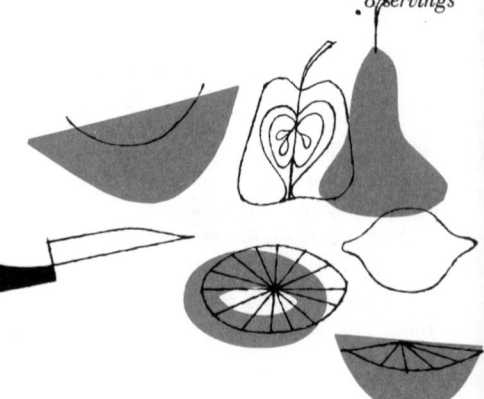

—PEACH FLAMBEE

Follow ▲ Recipe. Substitute **4 medium (about 1 lb.) ripe peaches** for pineapple. Rinse, pare, cut into halves and pit. Cut into large pieces. Continue as in ▲ Recipe.

—CHERRY FLAMBEE

Follow ▲ Recipe. Substitute **1 lb. fresh Bing cherries** for pineapple. Rinse, drain, and remove and discard the cherry stems and pits. Continue as in ▲ Recipe, reducing the lemon juice to 1 tablespoon.

RHUBARB COBBLER

▲ *Base Recipe*

Set out a 1½-qt. casserole.

Wash and cut off stem ends and leaves from
> **1 lb. rhubarb**

Peel stalks only if skin is tough. Cut into 1-in. pieces. Put one half of rhubarb in casse-

Tea Cream for Strawberries

role. Sprinkle with one half of a mixture of

> **1 cup sugar**
> **1 teaspoon grated lemon peel**
> **½ teaspoon cinnamon**

Drizzle over rhubarb one-half of

> **1 tablespoon lemon juice**

Dot with

> **Butter or margarine**

Add remaining rhubarb to casserole and top with remaining sugar mixture, drizzle with lemon juice and dot with butter or margarine.

Bake at 350°F 20 min.

Meanwhile, prepare

> **Drop Biscuit dough (one half recipe, page 92; sift 1 tablespoon sugar with flour mixture)**

Remove rhubarb from oven; set temperature control of oven at 450°F. Drop spoonfuls of biscuit dough over top of hot rhubarb. Return casserole to oven.

Bake at 450°F 10 to 15 min. longer, or until biscuits are lightly browned.

Serve warm with **cream.**   *6 servings*

—BLUEBERRY COBBLER

Follow ▲ Recipe. Substitute **2 cups fresh blueberries,** rinsed, for rhubarb. Decrease sugar to ½ cup.

—CHERRY COBBLER

Follow ▲ Recipe. Substitute **4 cups (two 16-oz. cans) tart red cherries,** drained, for rhubarb. Decrease sugar to ¾ cup and mix in **2 tablespoons all-purpose flour.**

STEWED RHUBARB

Here is sparkling springtime itself in delicately pink rhubarb. Served frosty cold or pleasantly warm, it spells real eating zest.

Set out a 2-qt. saucepan with a tight-fitting cover.

Wash, cut off stem ends and leaves of

> **1 lb. rhubarb**

Peel stalks only if skin is tough. Cut into 1-in. pieces (3 to 4 cups, cut) and place in saucepan.

Combine and mix with rhubarb

> **¾ cup sugar**
> **1 teaspoon grated lemon peel**
> **½ teaspoon cinnamon**

Drizzle with

> **2 teaspoons lemon juice**

Place over low heat. Stir until sugar dissolves, forming a syrup. Cover and cook slowly about 15 min., or until rhubarb is tender.

If rhubarb is not as pink as desired, carefully stir in

> **Few drops red food coloring**

Serve hot or cold.   *4 or 5 servings*

Note: If your yen for rhubarb happens to fall on "baking day," this recipe may also be prepared in a casserole in the oven, with other goodies. Prepare the rhubarb the same way, but put it in a casserole instead, cover the casserole and bake the rhubarb at 325°F about 25 min., or until it is tender when pierced with a fork.

QUINCE OR CRAB APPLE CREAM FOR STRAWBERRIES

Beat together in a bowl until blended

> **¼ cup quince jelly**
> **1 tablespoon confectioners' sugar**

(Or use **¼ cup crab apple jelly** and **1 tablespoon honey.**) Add and whip to soft peaks

> **1 cup chilled heavy cream**

Serve with **fresh strawberries** (sliced, if desired) sweetened with **sugar** to taste.

TEA CREAM FOR STRAWBERRIES

Put into a bowl

> **1 tablespoon black tea**
> **1 2-in. slice orange peel**
> **½ cinnamon stick**
> **1 whole nutmeg**
> **4 whole cloves**

Add

> **3 tablespoons boiling water**

Allow to stand at room temperature 1 hr.

Strain brew through a fine sieve or a sieve lined with cheesecloth into a bowl. Mix in

> **2 cups heavy cream**

Allow to stand 30 min.

Meanwhile, hull, slice and put into a bowl

> **2 pts. fresh strawberries**

Sprinkle with

> **Brown or granulated sugar to taste**

Chill 15 to 30 min.

Stir into the tea cream (whip, if desired)

> **¼ cup sugar**

Serve the cream with sugared berries.

About 6 servings

CHEESE PINEAPPLE DESSERT PLATTER

Wash and cut into halves lengthwise through the crown (spiny top)

> **1 whole pineapple**

Using a sharp knife, cut out and discard core sections. Remove pineapple from shells with a grapefruit knife or sharp paring knife. Cut pineapple into bite-size chunks and set aside.

Blend

> **2 jars (5 oz. each) pasteurized process cheese spread with pineapple**
> **3 tablespoons milk**
> **2 tablespoons finely chopped maraschino cherries, drained**

Pile half of filling into each pineapple shell.

Cut into wedges

> **1 "Baby" Gouda cheese**

To Arrange Platter—Place filled pineapple shells, end to end, in center of platter. Spear pineapple chunks with wooden or cocktail picks, and arrange around sides of cheese filling. Following edge of platter, arrange overlapping, to form a border

> **Swiss cheese slices**

Arrange Gouda cheese wedges in overlapping rows around pineapple shells. Serve with crisp **crackers.**

Cheese Pineapple Dessert Tray

Cheese and Fruit Dessert Tray

CHEESE AND FRUIT FOR DESSERT

A dessert tray of cheese, fruit and crackers has everything—beauty, subtlety of flavor, gourmet elegance and scope for personal choice. It is the easiest of desserts to prepare and serve, yet few more elaborate ones can equal its appeal and its universal suitability.

Choose your handsomest tray to display the cheeses. Select both familiar and unusual cheeses with a variety of flavors and textures. Let them stand at room temperature for an hour or two before serving, to regain their full flavor and their natural texture (refrigeration hardens all cheese somewhat).

Classic choices for this type of service are soft **cream cheese,** usually served in the piece; gay red **Edams** or **Goudas** served whole with the top cut off, to be scooped out as desired, making a striking centerpiece for the tray; slim wedges of tangy **Roquefort,** luscious big triangles of pungent **Camembert,** thick slices of delicate **Swiss,** cubes or paper-thin slices of mild dark **goats'-milk cheese,** mild or sharp **Cheddar** in slices, fingers or triangles.

Arrange pieces of fruit on the same tray with the cheese (see photo); or heap whole fruit in a separate crystal bowl or on another tray or plate to accompany the cheese tray. Polished red and green **apples,** juicy **pears,** rich red or purple or green **grapes,** all glowing like jewels, are particularly pleasing in their season. A charming and unusual type of fruit service to match the dramatic appeal of the cheese tray is fruit kabobs: ready-to-eat fruits —hulled fresh **strawberries,** fresh or canned **pineapple chunks,** seedless green **grapes,** **cantaloupe** and **honeydew melon** balls, sweet

dark **cherries**—threaded on little metal skewers and arranged attractively on a nest of cracked ice in your loveliest crystal bowl. Smaller bowls of sparkling **fruit preserves** or especially interesting **jelly,** such as bar-le-duc, are appealing accompaniments for cheese and crackers when fresh fruits are not available; **candied fruits** and **peels** and **dried fruits** may also be used.

Be sure to serve plenty of crisp **crackers**— both salted and unsalted crackers, without competing flavors, to suit all tastes.

So that your guests may conveniently serve themselves, have a stack of your prettiest dessert plates at hand. Provide cheese cutters and scoops for any cheeses that you put out in the whole piece; butter spreaders will be needed by all who choose Camembert or cream cheese, and sharp fruit knives by those who wish to cut their own fruit.

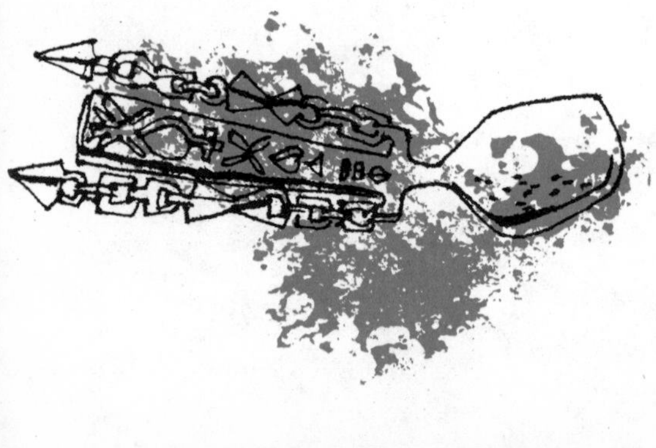

DESSERT SAUCES

Sauces can do much to glamorize desserts by adding pleasing flavor and color contrasts. Here is a variety of delightful sauces to go with desserts of all types. They will often transform everyday desserts into gourmet treats.

VANILLA SAUCE I
(Vaniljsas)

Cream until softened
   ⅓ cup butter
Add gradually, creaming until fluffy after each addition
   ½ cup sugar
Add gradually, blending in
   6 egg yolks, slightly beaten
Add *very* gradually, stirring in
   ¾ cup boiling water
Put mixture in top of double boiler and cook over simmering water, stirring constantly, until thickened.

Remove from heat and blend in
   1 teaspoon vanilla extract
Cool; chill in refrigerator.   *About 2 cups sauce*

VANILLA SAUCE II

   ▲ *Base Recipe*

Mix in a saucepan
   1 cup sugar
   2 tablespoons cornstarch
   ¼ teaspoon salt
Add gradually, stirring constantly
   2 cups boiling water
Continue to stir, bring to boiling and simmer 5 min.

Remove from heat and blend in
   ¼ cup butter or margarine
   2 teaspoons vanilla extract
                              About 2 cups sauce

—LEMON SAUCE

Follow ▲ Recipe. Substitute 3 tablespoons **lemon juice** and 2 teaspoons grated **lemon peel** for vanilla extract.

—BRANDY SAUCE

Follow ▲ Recipe for recipe for Lemon Sauce, decreasing lemon juice to 1 tablespoon. Stir in **3 tablespoons brandy.**

VANILLA SAUCE III
(Vanillesosse)

   ▲ *Base Recipe*

Mix in the top of a double boiler
   1 cup sugar
   2 tablespoons cornstarch
   ¼ teaspoon salt
Add, stirring well
   2 cups boiling water
Stirring gently and constantly, bring mixture rapidly to boiling over direct heat and cook for 3 min. Place over simmering water. Cover and cook about 5 min., stirring three or four times. Vigorously stir about 3 tablespoons of the hot mixture into
   1 egg yolk, slightly beaten
Immediately blend into mixture in double boiler. Cook over simmering water 3 to 5 min. Stir slowly to keep mixture cooking evenly. Remove from heat and blend in
   ¼ cup butter
   2 teaspoons vanilla extract
   ¼ teaspoon nutmeg
                              About 2 cups sauce

—WINE SAUCE
(Chaudeau Creme)

Follow ▲ Recipe. Omit nutmeg. Cool sauce and add gradually, stirring in, **½ cup white wine.**

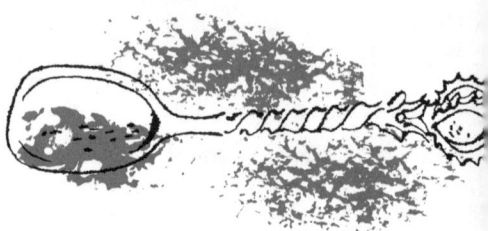

BUTTERMILK CUSTARD SAUCE

Delightfully different in flavor wherever custard sauce is called for.

Scald (page 10) in top of a double boiler
   1 cup milk

Meanwhile, beat slightly
   3 eggs
Blend into eggs
   ¼ cup sugar
   ¼ teaspoon salt

Stirring constantly, add scalded milk gradually to egg mixture.

Wash double-boiler top to remove scum.

Strain mixture into double-boiler top. Cook over simmering water, stirring constantly and rapidly until mixture coats a metal spoon. Remove from simmering water at once. Adding gradually, blend in a mixture of

1 cup buttermilk
2 teaspoons vanilla extract

Cover and chill sauce in refrigerator.

About 2½ cups sauce

APRICOT SAUCE
(Sauce Abricot)

Because of the blandness of many favorite desserts served in French homes, a fruit sauce such as this is a frequent accompaniment. It is delicious with puddings.

Heat in a saucepan

1½ cups apricot jam

Stir in gradually

½ cup water
2 tablespoons sugar

Heat to the boiling point. Then cook over low heat 5 to 10 min., stirring to prevent scorching. Strain. Stir in

1 tablespoon apricot brandy

Serve hot or cold.

For Storage—Store in covered jar in a cold place. Before covering, top with

1 or 2 tablespoons liqueur

1¾ cups sauce

DE LUXE APRICOT SAUCE

▲ *Base Recipe*

Have ready a double boiler with a tight-fitting cover.

Put into a 1-qt. bowl

1 small pear, washed, quartered, cored and diced (about ½ cup, diced)
1 small all-yellow or brown-flecked banana, peeled and diced (about ½ cup, diced)
8 large strawberries, washed, hulled and sliced (about ⅓ cup, sliced)

Using fork, gently but thoroughly combine fruit with

2 tablespoons lemon juice

Place in refrigerator to chill.

Meanwhile, mix thoroughly in top of double boiler

⅔ cup sugar
3 tablespoons cornstarch
¼ teaspoon salt

Add gradually, blending in

2½ cups apricot nectar

Stirring gently and constantly bring starch mixture rapidly to boiling over direct heat and cook for 3 min. Place over simmering water. Cover and cook about 5 min., stirring three or four times.

Remove from heat and blend in

2 tablespoons butter or margarine

Cool. When cool blend in fruit mixture. Chill in refrigerator. Just before serving, stir in

¼ cup apricot brandy

About 3½ cups sauce

—APRICOT WHIPPED CREAM SAUCE

Prepare one half of ▲ Recipe. Just before serving, fold **½ cup chilled heavy cream,** whipped into sauce. *About 3 cups sauce*

BUTTERSCOTCH SAUCE I

Combine in a 3-qt. saucepan

1 cup firmly packed brown sugar
1 cup sugar
1 cup cream or undiluted evaporated milk
½ cup butter or margarine
¼ cup light corn syrup
¼ teaspoon salt

Cook slowly over low heat, stirring constantly, until sugar is dissolved. Increase to medium heat and bring mixture to boiling. Cook, stirring occasionally, to 230°F, the thread stage (spins 2-in. thread when allowed to drop from fork or spoon). Using a pastry brush dipped in water, wash down crystals from sides of saucepan from time to time during cooking.

Remove mixture from heat and add

1½ teaspoons vanilla extract

Cool to warm (110°F to 115°F).

Beat about 1 min.

Serve sauce cold with ice cream or puddings.

About 1¾ cups sauce

BUTTERSCOTCH SAUCE II

Put into a small heavy saucepan

1 cup firmly packed light brown sugar
⅓ cup butter or margarine
⅓ cup cream
Few grains salt

Stir over low heat until sugar is dissolved and butter is melted. Increase heat to medium and

bring mixture to boiling, stirring occasionally.

Boil 5 min. without stirring. Remove from heat and beat sauce about 1 min.

Serve warm. *About 1¼ cups sauce*

BUTTERSCOTCH SAUCE III

Combine and bring to boiling in a heavy saucepan

1 cup firmly packed brown sugar
1 cup light corn syrup
⅓ cup cream
⅓ cup water
2 tablespoons butter or margarine

Stir only until sugar is dissolved. Cook until a candy thermometer registers 230°F. Serve sauce warm. *About 1½ cups sauce*

CARAMEL SAUCE

Heat in the top of a double boiler over simmering water

½ lb. vanilla caramels
⅓ cup milk

Stir until smooth. *About 1¼ cups sauce*

CHERRY MORENCY SAUCE

Drain, reserving syrup in a measuring cup

1 jar (8 oz.) red maraschino cherries

Measure ⅓ cup of the cherries. Halve remaining cherries. Set aside.

Add enough water to syrup to make ½ cup. Put syrup and the ⅓ cup of cherries into an electric blender container. Cover; blend about 20 sec. Turn into a small saucepan and blend in

1½ teaspoons cornstarch

Add

½ cup red currant jelly

Stir over medium heat until jelly melts and sauce comes to boiling; boil 1 min. Stir in the halved cherries and

1 tablespoon lemon juice

Chill. *About 1⅛ cups sauce*

CHERRY SAUCE I

Combine in saucepan

1 cup sugar
½ cup water
1 tablespoon light corn syrup

Bring to boiling, stirring constantly. Cover and cook 5 min. Cool.

Blend in thoroughly until desired color is reached

10 to 15 drops red food coloring

Stir in thoroughly, in order

⅓ cup brandy
½ cup finely chopped candied cherries

Serve over plum pudding.

About 1½ cups sauce

CHERRY SAUCE II
(Kirschsosse)

The wine-like flavor of cherry in a spicy sauce.

Cook 5 min. in a covered saucepan
> **1 can (16 oz.) pitted red tart cherries**
> **2 whole cloves**
> **2-in. piece stick cinnamon**

Remove from heat; take out and discard cinnamon and cloves. Pour through a sieve or food mill placed over a saucepan. Force cherries through and set aside.

Mix thoroughly in a small bowl
> **4 teaspoons sugar**
> **4 teaspoons cornstarch**
> **¼ teaspoon salt**

Stir in, in order, until mixture is smooth
> **4 teaspoons cold water**
> **3½ tablespoons light corn syrup**

Add gradually, stirring into hot cherry mixture. Bring rapidly to boiling, stirring gently 3 min.

Remove from heat and blend in
> **4 teaspoons butter**
> **1½ teaspoons lemon juice**
> **¼ teaspoon almond extract**
> **1 drop red food coloring**

Serve hot with **Steamed Sweet Dumplings** (page 523). *About 1½ cups sauce*

RED CHERRY SAUCE

Mix in a saucepan
> **⅔ cup sugar**
> **2 tablespoons cornstarch**
> **⅛ teaspoon salt**

Drain, reserving liquid
> **1 can (16 oz.) pitted tart red cherries**
> **(about 1½ cups cherries)**

Gradually stir in reserved liquid. Stirring constantly, bring to boiling over medium heat.

Pear Sundaes with Chocolate Miracle Sauce

Cover and simmer 3 min. Remove from heat. Stir in drained cherries and
> **1 tablespoon butter or margarine**
> **¼ teaspoon almond extract**

Serve warm. *About 3 cups sauce*

MARASCHINO SAUCE

Mix in a saucepan
> **⅓ cup sugar**
> **1½ tablespoons cornstarch**
> **⅛ teaspoon salt**

Drain, reserving syrup
> **1 jar (8 oz.) maraschino cherries**

Gradually stir in reserved syrup and
> **1 cup water**

Stirring constantly, bring to boiling; simmer 3 min. Stir in cherries, cut in halves.
> *About 2½ cups sauce*

CHOCOLATE SAUCE

Heat in the top of a double boiler over hot (not boiling) water until chocolate is melted
> **1 pkg. (6 oz.) semisweet chocolate pieces**
> **½ cup milk**

Stir in
> **¼ teaspoon vanilla extract**
> **¼ teaspoon almond or peppermint extract**

Serve warm. *About 1 cup sauce*

CHOCOLATE MIRACLE SAUCE

▲ Base Recipe

A sauce triumph which is chocolate ambrosia.

Cook in double boiler top 5 min., or until smooth
> **5 oz. (5 sq.) unsweetened chocolate**
> **1½ cups sugar**
> **1½ cups water**
> **¼ teaspoon salt**

Add and stir in
> **1¼ cups (14-oz. can) sweetened condensed milk**

Cook over hot water until mixture coats a metal spoon. *About 3 cups sauce*

—MIRACLE SEMISWEET SAUCE

Follow ▲ Recipe. Substitute **1 pkg. (6 oz.) semisweet chocolate pieces** for chocolate.

BITTERSWEET CHOCOLATE SAUCE I

Heat together in the top of a double boiler over hot (not simmering) water, stirring frequently until sauce is smooth
> **12 oz. semisweet chocolate**
> **2 oz. (2 sq.) unsweetened chocolate**
> **1 cup heavy cream**
> **¾ cup sugar***
> **1 teaspoon vanilla extract**

Serve hot over ice cream for sundaes.

The sauce may be stored, covered, in the refrigerator and reheated. *2 cups sauce*

*Use only if a sweet sauce is desired; dissolve in the cream before adding cream to chocolate.

BITTERSWEET CHOCOLATE SAUCE II

▲ Base Recipe

Heat in top of double boiler until chocolate is melted and milk scalded (page 10)
> **4 oz. (4 sq.) unsweetened chocolate**
> **¾ cup milk**

Stir well. Blend in thoroughly
> **1 cup sugar**
> **¼ teaspoon salt**

Remove double boiler top and place over direct heat. Cook about 2 min., stirring constantly, to dissolve sugar and thicken sauce. Remove from heat and blend in
> **¼ cup butter or margarine**
> **½ teaspoon almond extract**

Serve hot or cold. *About 2 cups sauce*

—CHOCO-ALMOND TOPPING

Follow ▲ Recipe. Stir in with the butter **½ cup (about 2½ oz.) blanched and toasted (pages 9 and 10) almonds**, slivered.

—CHOCO-RAISIN TOPPING

Follow ▲ Recipe. Stir in ½ cup (about 2 oz.) **raisins** with the butter.

—CHOCOLATE WHIPPED CREAM SAUCE

Follow ▲ Recipe and thoroughly chill sauce. Fold **1 cup heavy cream**, whipped, into sauce before serving. *About 4 cups sauce*

CHOCOLATE MARSHMALLOW SAUCE I

Melt (page 10)
> **3 oz. (3 sq.) unsweetened chocolate**

Stir in
> **⅓ cup cream**

When well blended, add
> **16 (¼ lb.) marshmallows**

Continue heating, stirring occasionally, until marshmallows are melted and sauce is thoroughly blended. Serve cold. *1½ cups sauce*

CHOCOLATE MARSHMALLOW SAUCE II

Cut (page 9) into quarters and put into the top of a double boiler

16 (¼ lb.) marshmallows

Add

1 cup light corn syrup
2 oz. (2 sq.) unsweetened chocolate
⅛ teaspoon salt

Heat over simmering water, stirring occasionally until marshmallows and chocolate are melted. Remove double boiler top from heat and blend in

1 tablespoon butter or margarine
1 teaspoon vanilla extract

Serve hot over ice cream. *About 2 cups sauce*

HONEY CHOCOLATE DESSERT SAUCE

Flavor-rich and easy to prepare, this fluffy sauce is especially delicious served with ice cream for sundaes.

Melt in a heavy 1-qt. saucepan

¼ cup butter or margarine

Blend in a mixture of

¼ cup unsweetened cocoa
1 tablespoon cornstarch
¼ teaspoon salt

Mix until smooth and add

½ cup honey
½ cup water

Cook and stir over low heat until thickened and smooth. Remove from heat and add

6 large marshmallows

Stir until marshmallows are melted.

About 1½ cups sauec

ORANGE CHOCOLATE SAUCE

Melt (page 10)

1 oz. (1 sq.) unsweetened chocolate

Meanwhile, mix thoroughly in top of a double boiler

½ cup sugar
⅓ cup instant nonfat dry milk
1 tablespoon cornstarch
⅛ teaspoon salt

Add gradually, stirring until smooth

1 cup water

Blend in melted chocolate. Stirring gently and constantly, bring rapidly to boiling over

---

direct heat. Reduce heat; cook and stir for 3 min. Place over simmering water. Cover and cook about 5 min., stirring 3 or 4 times. Remove from simmering water. Blend in

1 teaspoon grated orange peel
2 tablespoons orange juice
1 tablespoon butter or margarine

Cool and chill in refrigerator. Serve cold.

About 1½ cups sauce

BLENDER CHOCOLATE RUM SAUCE

Put into electric blender container in order listed

⅓ cup warm water
½ cup sugar
4 teaspoons instant nonfat dry milk
2 oz. (2 sq.) unsweetened chocolate,
  cut in small pieces
1 tablespoon butter or margarine
¼ teaspoon rum extract
⅛ teaspoon salt

Cover, turn on motor and blend ingredients about 1 min. Turn off motor. Scrape down sides of container with rubber spatula so ingredients will become evenly mixed. Cover and blend about 3 min. more, or until sauce is smooth, creamy and thick. Store in covered jar in refrigerator. *¾ cup sauce*

FUDGE SAUCE

Heat in the top of a double boiler over boiling water until chocolate is melted

2 oz. (2 sq.) unsweetened chocolate
2 tablespoons butter or margarine
⅔ cup hot water

Add

1¾ cups sugar
¼ cup light corn syrup
¼ teaspoon salt

Stir until sugar is dissolved. Bring mixture just to boiling over direct heat, stirring constantly. Simmer over low heat 5 min. Remove from heat. Stir in

1 teaspoon vanilla extract

Serve hot. *About 1½ cups sauce*

For Marbled Sauce—Cut **8 marshmallows** into small pieces and simmer with fudge mixture. Stir slightly.

FUDGE SAUCE SUPERB

▲ *Base Recipe*

Combine in saucepan

2 cups firmly packed brown sugar
1 cup cream
3 oz. (3 sq.) unsweetened chocolate
3 tablespoons butter or margarine

Cook gently, stirring occasionally, to 234°F (soft ball stage, page 11; remove from heat while testing). Add

1 teaspoon vanilla extract

Beat 1 min. Serve hot or cold.

About 1½ cups sauce

Fudge Sauce Superb on Baked Apples

—COCOA FUDGE SAUCE SUPERB

Follow ▲ Recipe. Substitute ¾ **cup cocoa** for the chocolate; mix with brown sugar before adding butter and cream.

—PEPPERMINT FUDGE SAUCE SUPERB

Follow ▲ Recipe. Stir in **2 or 3 drops peppermint extract** with the vanilla extract.

—PEANUT FUDGE SAUCE SUPERB

Follow ▲ Recipe. Stir in ¼ **cup peanut butter** or ¼ **cup (1 oz.) finely chopped peanuts** after removing from heat.

FUDGE SAUCE CAFE

Mix in a small heavy saucepan

½ cup sugar
½ cup double-strength coffee beverage
  (page 10)
2 oz. (2 sq.) unsweetened chocolate,
  broken in pieces
1 tablespoon cream
⅛ teaspoon salt

Place over low heat, Cook, stirring constantly, until sauce becomes slightly thickened. Remove from heat and blend in

1 tablespoon butter or margarine
½ teaspoon vanilla extract

Serve sauce warm or cool. *1 cup sauce*

QUICK COFFEE SAUCE

Mix in a saucepan

⅓ cup sugar
2 to 3 teaspoons instant powdered
  coffee
1 tablespoon cornstarch
⅛ teaspoon salt

Gradually stir in

1½ cups cream

Stirring constantly, bring to boiling over me-

579

dium heat. Cover and simmer 3 min. Remove from heat and stir in

½ teaspoon vanilla extract
1 tablespoon butter or margarine

Serve warm.   *About 1½ cups sauce*

MOCHA SAUCE I

▲ *Base Recipe*

Here's a dessert sauce that's not too sweet. Delightful when served warm, it becomes pleasingly thick and smooth when chilled. You'll like it both ways—on ice cream, on cake or on waffles.

Combine in top of a double boiler

6 oz. sweet chocolate, cut in pieces
1 oz. (1 sq.) unsweetened chocolate, cut in pieces
½ cup double-strength coffee beverage (page 10)
Few grains salt

Heat over simmering water until chocolate is melted; stir occasionally. Serve warm or chilled.   *About 1 cup sauce*

—TOFFEE MOCHA SAUCE

Follow ▲ Recipe. Crush enough English toffee to yield **¼ cup crushed English toffee.** Add to sauce after chocolate is melted.

MOCHA SAUCE II

▲ *Base Recipe*

Prepare and set aside about

2 cups double-strength coffee beverage (page 10)

Melt in a heavy light-colored skillet over low heat, stirring constantly

1 cup sugar

Heat until sugar is completely melted and smooth. Add slowly, stirring constantly, 1½ cups of the double-strength coffee beverage.

Mix thoroughly and stir into coffee-sugar mixture

2 tablespoons cornstarch

Add 3 tablespoons cold double-strength coffee beverage. Stirring constantly, bring sauce to boiling. Continue to cook, stirring constantly, 3 to 5 min., or until mixture thickens. Remove from heat and add

3 tablespoons butter or margarine
1 teaspoon vanilla extract

Stir until butter or margarine is completely melted and sauce is well blended. Serve sauce hot over **Banana Fritters** (page 98).
                              About 2 cups sauce

—MOCHA WHIPPED CREAM SAUCE

Prepare one half of ▲ Recipe and thoroughly chill sauce in refrigerator. Fold **½ cup chilled heavy cream,** whipped, into chilled sauce just before serving.

GINGER SAUCE

Chop and set aside enough crystallized ginger to yield

¾ cup finely chopped crystallized ginger

Mix in a saucepan

1 cup sugar
1 cup water
Few grains salt

Stir over low heat until sugar is dissolved. Increase heat and bring to boiling; cover and boil gently 5 min. Remove from heat and add the ginger.

Serve warm or chilled.   *About 1¾ cups sauce*

HOT WINE JELLY SAUCE

Put into a small heavy saucepan

¾ cup red raspberry jelly

Melt jelly over low heat. Stir in

6 tablespoons dry white wine

Mix together until thoroughly blended

2 tablespoons dry white wine
½ tablespoon cornstarch

Stirring constantly, blend into jelly mixture.

Bring rapidly to boiling, continuing to stir. Cook 2 to 3 min. Remove from heat and stir in

1 tablespoon butter or margarine
¼ teaspoon grated lemon peel

Serve hot over baked custard or ice cream.
                                   ¾ cup sauce

LEMON DESSERT SAUCE

Put into a bowl

⅔ cup (one-half 14-oz. can) sweetened condensed milk
2 teaspoons grated lemon peel
¼ cup lemon juice
1 tablespoon warm water
2 teaspoons rum

Beat until ingredients are well blended. Chill in refrigerator until ready to serve.

Serve as a topping for cake.
                              About 1 cup sauce

MINT SYRUP (FOR PARFAITS)

Mix in a small saucepan with a tight-fitting cover

1½ cups sugar
1 cup water
2 tablespoons light corn syrup

Set over medium heat and stir until sugar is dissolved and mixture begins to boil. Cover and boil 3 min. Remove cover and continue boiling 5 min. Remove from heat and set aside to cool.

When syrup is cooled completely, mix in

¼ teaspoon mint extract
¼ teaspoon green food coloring

Serve with parfaits or as a sauce for sundaes.
                              About 1½ cups syrup

ORANGE SHERRY SAUCE

Mix in a saucepan

2 tablespoons grated orange peel
1 cup orange juice
⅔ cup sugar
Few grains salt

Stir over low heat until sugar is dissolved. Increase heat and bring to boiling; cover and boil gently 5 min.

Remove from heat and add

¼ cup sherry

Serve warm.   *About 1¼ cups sauce*

QUICK RASPBERRY ICE CREAM SAUCE

Heavenly spooned over angel food or sponge cake; elegant when served over white cake.

Set an electric blender container in refrigerator to chill.

Partially thaw

1 pkg. (10 oz.) frozen sweetened raspberries

Cut partially thawed block into chunks. Put several chunks into chilled blender container. Cover and turn on motor.

Add by spoonfuls

1 pt. vanilla ice cream, softened

(Use rubber spatula to scrape down sides of container, as this is a thick mixture.)

Add remainder of raspberries and blend thoroughly.   *About 3 cups sauce*

RASPBERRY SAUCE

▲ *Base Recipe*

Set out a heavy 1-qt. saucepan.

Sort, rinse and drain thoroughly

2 cups fresh raspberries

Force berries through a sieve or food mill into the saucepan. Blend in

½ cup sugar

Set berry mixture aside.

Blend to make a smooth paste

1 tablespoon cold water
1½ teaspoons cornstarch

Thoroughly blend into berry mixture. Stirring gently and constantly, bring rapidly to boiling. Continue stirring and boil over medium heat about 3 min. Set aside to cool. Cover and chill in refrigerator.   *About 1 cup sauce*

—STRAWBERRY SAUCE

Follow ▲ Recipe. Substitute **2 cups rinsed, drained and hulled strawberries** for raspberries.

CURRANT RASPBERRY SAUCE

Mix in a saucepan
⅓ cup sugar
1 teaspoon cornstarch
⅛ teaspoon salt
Mash
1 cup fresh red raspberries
Stir raspberries into mixture in saucepan with
½ cup currant jelly
Stirring constantly, bring to boiling over medium heat. Cover and simmer 3 min. Remove from heat. Stir in
½ teaspoon vanilla extract
1 tablespoon butter or margarine
Strain cooked sauce. Cool and serve with peach ice cream.   *About 1½ cups sauce*

RUM SAUCE

Place a bowl and rotary beater in refrigerator to chill.

Set out
1 cup milk
Scald (page 10) in top of double boiler ¾ cup of the milk; reserve remainder.

Meanwhile, mix in a saucepan
⅓ cup sugar
2 tablespoons cornstarch
Blend in the reserved ¼ cup milk; add gradually and stir in the scalded milk. Bring rapidly to boiling over direct heat, stirring gently and constantly; cook 3 min. Remove saucepan from heat.

Pour mixture into double boiler top and place over simmering water. Cover and cook about 5 min., stirring three or four times.

Vigorously stir about 3 tablespoons of the hot mixture into
1 egg, slightly beaten
Immediately blend into mixture in double boiler. Cook over simmering water 3 to 5 min., stirring slowly and constantly to cook evenly.

Remove from heat, cover, and cool to lukewarm. Blend in
2 to 3 tablespoons rum
Chill in refrigerator.

Shortly before serving, beat, using the chilled bowl and rotary beater, until cream is of medium consistency (piles softly)
1 cup chilled heavy cream
Gently fold whipped cream into sauce mixture. Serve cold.   *About 3 cups sauce*

RHUBARB SAUCE

Set out 1½-qt. saucepan with a tight-fitting cover.

Cut off and discard leaves and stem end from
1 lb. rhubarb (3 to 4 cups, cut)
Cut remainder into 1-in. pieces. Put rhubarb into saucepan and add
¾ cup sugar
Heat and stir until sugar dissolves. Cover and cook slowly about 15 min. Serve hot or cold.
4 servings

STRAWBERRY-RHUBARB SAUCE

Set out a 2-qt. saucepan with a tight-fitting cover.

Sort, rinse, drain, hull and cut into halves
1 pt. fresh ripe strawberries
Set aside.

Cut off and discard leaves and stem ends from
1 lb. rhubarb
Rinse and cut into 1-in. pieces (3 to 4 cups pieces). Put rhubarb into saucepan and add
¾ cup sugar
¼ teaspoon salt
Stirring occasionally, heat until sugar dissolves and mixture boils. Cover and cook slowly about 10 min., stirring occasionally.

Gently mix strawberries with the rhubarb. Cover pan and continue to cook mixture slowly 3 to 5 min., or until rhubarb is tender.

Remove from heat and mix in
2 tablespoons butter or margarine
2 teaspoons grated orange peel
Set aside to cool.

Serve over vanilla ice cream.   *3 cups sauce*

ALMOND HARD SAUCE

▲ *Base Recipe*

Cream until softened
⅔ cup butter or margarine
½ teaspoon almond extract
Add gradually, creaming until fluffy
2 cups confectioners' sugar
⅛ teaspoon salt
Beat in
2 teaspoons cream

Blend in
½ cup (about 2¾ oz.) finely chopped almonds
With back of spoon, press sauce evenly into an 8-in. square pan to about ½-in. thickness. Chill until firm. (Or, if desired, pile sauce into a serving bowl before chilling.)

Using a cookie cutter or a waxed-paper pattern and a knife, cut into fancy shapes.

Serve with plum pudding.   *1½ cups sauce*

—BRANDY HARD SAUCE

Follow ▲ Recipe. Substitute **¼ cup brandy** for almond extract. Increase confectioners' sugar if necessary. Omit cream and almonds.

—VANILLA HARD SAUCE

Follow ▲ Recipe. Substitute **2 teaspoons vanilla extract** for almond extract. Omit almonds. Pile sauce into a bowl.

CONGO HARD SAUCE

▲ *Base Recipe*

Melt (page 10) and set aside to cool
⅓ pkg. (2 oz.) semisweet chocolate pieces
Cream until softened
¼ cup butter or margarine
½ teaspoon vanilla extract
⅛ teaspoon salt
Cream in gradually
⅔ cup confectioners' sugar
Blend in chocolate and stir until smooth and well mixed. Add and blend thoroughly
⅓ cup confectioners' sugar
More sugar may be added if a stiffer hard sauce is desired.   *About ⅔ cup sauce*

—CHOCOLATE HARD SAUCE

Follow ▲ Recipe. Substitute **1 oz. (1 sq.) melted unsweetened chocolate** for semisweet pieces. Add ½ teaspoon rum or brandy extract.

—COCOA HARD SAUCE

Follow ▲ Recipe. Omit semisweet chocolate pieces. Sift ⅓ cup cocoa with all of the confectioners' sugar. Increase butter or margarine to ⅓ cup.

Cookies

Though the origin of the cookie is unknown, the early Dutch settlers are credited with introducing to Americans a sweetmeat made of honey and nuts called koejke ("little cake") from which came the word cookie. As more and more Europeans arrived, they brought with them their treasured recipes, including many wonderful cookie delicacies. Often their recipes were memorized rather than written, and it was left for creative homemakers to record them and adapt them to American ingredients and techniques. On these pages are cookie recipes from many countries, including simple wholesome everyday varieties appropriate for filling the family cookie jar and the rich, colorful creations for entertaining and gift giving.

VANILLA CONFECTIONERS' SUGAR

A subtly flavored sugar for cookies, cakes, waffles, griddlecakes and doughnuts.

Set out a 1- to 2-qt. container with a tight-fitting cover. Fill with

Confectioners' sugar

Wipe with a clean, damp cloth and dry

1 vanilla bean, about 9 in. long

Cut vanilla bean into quarters lengthwise; cut quarters crosswise into thirds. Poke pieces of vanilla bean down into the sugar at irregular intervals. Cover container tightly and store.

Note: The longer sugar stands, the richer will be the vanilla flavor. If tightly covered, sugar may be stored for several months. When necessary, add more sugar to jar. Replace vanilla bean when aroma is gone.

CINNAMON SUGAR

Mix thoroughly

¼ cup sugar

2 teaspoons cinnamon

Use to sugar cookies, doughnuts or toast.

¼ cup sugar

COLORED SUGAR

Mix

3 drops food coloring

3 drops water

Put into a bowl

¼ cup sugar

Pressing and stirring with a teaspoon, work in, a drop at a time, enough dissolved food coloring for desired color. Put through fine sieve to obtain even color.

¼ cup sugar

BARS AND SQUARES

FANCY SCOTCH SHORTBREAD

▲ Base Recipe

Set out a 15x10x1-in. pan.

Cream until softened

1 cup butter

Add gradually, creaming until fluffy after each addition

½ cup sugar

Add gradually, beating until well blended (mixture will be crumbly)

3½ cups sifted all-purpose flour

Turn dough into pan. Using a spatula, carefully spread, press and level cookie dough to fit pan.

Bake at 325°F 45 min., or until light golden brown. Remove from oven and immediately cut with cookie cutter into crescents or other interesting shapes. (Shortbread must be cut into shapes while hot.) Cool cookies in pan placed on cooling racks. When cool, remove from pan and sprinkle the shapes lightly with

Sifted confectioners' sugar

2 to 3 doz. cookies

Note: For fancy shapes, patterns can be prepared from a piece of waxed paper. After shortbread is baked, remove from oven, lay waxed paper pattern over shortbread, and with a sharp knife cut carefully around the pattern.

—ALMOND-GLAZED SHORTBREAD

Follow ▲ Recipe. Bake shortbread 35 min. Meanwhile, prepare glaze. Mix **2 tablespoons almond paste, 1 tablespoon brown sugar** and **2 drops lemon extract**. Add gradually and stir in enough **egg white** to make a thin paste. Remove shortbread from oven and drop ¼ teaspoon or less of glaze at intervals onto baked dough. (Space so that the glaze will add a flavorful and decorative touch at the center of each cookie.) Spread glaze slightly. Place in oven again; bake 10 to 12 min., or until glaze is crisp and shortbread is light golden brown. Remove from oven and cut into fancy shapes. Cool as directed in ▲ Recipe.

—SHORTBREAD SENSATIONS

Follow ▲ Recipe. Bake 25 min. Meanwhile, prepare dough for **Frosted Almond Leaf Cookies** (page 603). Remove shortbread from oven. Put **semisweet chocolate pieces** about 2 in. apart on top of shortbread. Force almond cookie mixture through pastry bag and No. 27 star decorating tube into rings around chocolate pieces. Place in oven again; bake 18 to 20 min., or until almond ring is slightly browned and shortbread is light golden brown. Cut into fancy clover shapes, so that a chocolate piece is in the center of each cookie. Cool as directed in ▲ Recipe.

FROSTED SHORTBREAD SQUARES

Set out 15x10x1-in. pan.

Mix thoroughly

2 cups sifted all-purpose flour

½ cup firmly packed brown sugar

Cut in with pastry blender or two knives until mixture resembles coarse corn meal

¾ cup butter

Press firmly into ungreased pan.

Bake at 325°F 25 to 28 min.

Fancy Scotch Shortbread

582

Frosted Shortbread Squares

A few minutes before removing shortbread from oven, melt (page 10)

1 pkg. (6 oz.) semisweet chocolate pieces

Spread quickly over hot baked cookie dough. Sprinkle over top and gently press into chocolate

⅔ cup (about 3 oz.) chopped nuts

Cut shortbread into 1½-in. squares while warm.

70 cookies

BELGIAN CHRISTMAS COOKIES

Grease a 15x10x1-in. pan; set aside.

Sift together and set aside

1⅔ cups sifted all-purpose flour
1½ teaspoons baking powder
½ teaspoon salt

Beat together in a bowl until softened

⅔ cup butter or margarine
1 teaspoon almond extract

Add, beating constantly until thoroughly blended

1 cup firmly packed dark brown sugar

Beat in, one at a time

2 eggs

Continue beating until light and fluffy. Add flour mixture in thirds, mixing only until blended after each addition. Turn into greased pan and spread evenly to edges (layer will be thin). Sprinkle over batter a mixture of

½ cup unblanched almonds, finely chopped
½ teaspoon cinnamon
2 teaspoons *each* red and green decorative sugar

With the back of a spoon, gently pat onto batter.

Bake at 375°F 10 to 12 min. Remove from oven to cooling rack. While still warm, cut into 1½-in. squares.   *About 5 doz. cookies*

CHEWY BUTTERSCOTCH BARS

Generously grease a 15x10x1-in. pan; set aside.

Prepare and set over simmering water
Topping (below)

Sift together and set aside
1⅓ cups sifted cake flour
2 teaspoons baking powder
1 teaspoon salt

Beat together in a bowl
2 cups firmly packed brown sugar
½ cup corn oil
2 teaspoons vanilla extract

Beat in, one at a time
2 eggs

Continue beating until thoroughly blended. Beat in the dry ingredients and

1 cup pecans, coarsely chopped
1 cup flaked coconut

Mix only until blended and turn batter into greased pan; spread evenly into corners. Drizzle hot Topping over entire surface.

Bake at 350°F about 30 min. Remove from oven to cooling rack. Cool at least 30 min. before cutting into bars and removing from pan.

About 2½ doz. cookies

For Topping—Set out a candy thermometer. Combine in top of a double boiler or in a saucepan

¾ cup firmly packed brown sugar
2 tablespoons butter or margarine
3 tablespoons cream or evaporated milk
¼ cup dark corn syrup

Cook over medium heat, stirring occasionally, until thermometer registers 234°F (soft ball stage, page 11). Remove from heat and stir in

1 teaspoon vanilla extract

About ⅔ cup

APRICOT BUTTER BARS

Set out a 9x9x2-in. pan.

Put into a heavy saucepan with a tight-fitting cover

1 cup (about 5 oz.) dried apricots

Add to saucepan
1 cup water

Bring to boiling, reduce heat, cover and simmer apricots 3 to 5 min. Remove from heat, drain and set aside to cool.

Sift together into a bowl
1 cup sifted all-purpose flour
¼ cup sugar

Cut in with a pastry blender or two knives until pieces are size of small peas

½ cup butter

Using the back of a spoon, firmly press flour mixture into an even layer on the bottom of the pan.

Bake at 350°F about 25 min., or until lightly browned.

Meanwhile, chop the cooled apricots and
½ cup (about 2 oz.) pecans
Set aside.

Sift together and set aside
⅓ cup sifted all-purpose flour
½ teaspoon baking powder
½ teaspoon salt

Beat slightly
2 eggs
1 teaspoon vanilla extract

Add and beat until thoroughly blended
1 cup firmly packed brown sugar

Stir in the flour, apricots and pecans.

When the first layer is lightly browned, remove from oven and spread the apricot mixture evenly over it. Return to oven and bake 30 min. longer.

Cool completely on a cooling rack before cutting into 2½x1½-in. bars.   *2 doz. cookies*

SURPRISE BARS

Grease an 8x8x2-in. pan; set aside.

Melt and set aside to cool
1 oz. (1 sq.) unsweetened chocolate

Combine in a bowl, tossing to blend well
½ cup graham cracker crumbs
2 tablespoons butter or margarine, melted
Set aside.

Sift together and set aside
¾ cup sifted all-purpose flour
⅛ teaspoon baking soda
⅛ teaspoon salt

Beat together in a bowl until softened
½ cup butter or margarine
1 teaspoon vanilla extract

Add gradually, beating until light and fluffy
½ cup sugar
Beat in thoroughly
1 egg
Blend in the dry ingredients with
¼ cup dairy sour cream

Mix only until blended and divide batter in half. Stir melted chocolate into one portion and turn into the greased pan; spread evenly. Cover with the buttered crumbs and press lightly.

Stir into remaining half of batter
¾ cup walnuts, coarsely chopped

Drop batter by spoonfuls over crumbs and gently spread to cover evenly.

Bake at 375°F 25 min. Remove to cooling rack. While still warm, cut into bars.

2½ doz. cookies

COCOA ALMOND BARS SUPREME

Lightly grease an 8x8x2-in. pan.

Blanch, toast (pages 9 and 10), chop coarsely and set aside
1 cup (about 5½ oz.) almonds

Marbled Brownies

Sift together and set aside

 ⅔ cup sifted all-purpose flour
 ⅓ cup Dutch process cocoa
 ½ teaspoon baking powder
 ¼ teaspoon salt

Cream until thoroughly blended

 ½ cup shortening
 ¼ cup almond paste
 1½ teaspoons vanilla extract
 ½ teaspoon almond extract

Add gradually, creaming until fluffy after each addition

 ¾ cup sugar

Beat vigorously

 1 egg
 1 egg yolk

Add in thirds to creamed mixture, beating thoroughly after each addition. Blend in the dry ingredients in halves, mixing well after each addition. Stir in ½ cup of the chopped almonds (reserve other ½ cup). Mix thoroughly. Spread in pan and set aside.

Beat until frothy

 1 egg white
 ¼ teaspoon cream of tartar

Add gradually and beat well after each addition

 ¼ cup sugar

Continue beating until stiff peaks are formed. Fold in reserved almonds. Spread mixture over batter in pan.

Bake at 350°F 35 to 40 min., or until meringue is lightly browned and wooden pick inserted in center of baked dough comes out clean. Cut into 2x1-in. bars when thoroughly cooled.

2½ doz. cookies

Brownie Sandwiches

COCOA DREAM BARS

Set out an 11x7x1½-in. pan.

Mix in a bowl

 1 cup sifted all-purpose flour
 ½ cup cocoa
 ¼ cup firmly packed brown sugar
 ¼ teaspoon salt

Blend in with pastry blender until a soft dough is formed

 ½ cup butter

Turn into the pan and press evenly and firmly to cover bottom.

Bake at 375°F 10 min. Cool slightly.

Meanwhile, coarsely chop and set aside

 1 cup (about 4 oz.) nuts

Set out

 1½ cups (about 4 oz.) flaked coconut

Beat slightly

 2 eggs

Beat in until very thick

 1 cup sugar
 1 teaspoon vanilla extract

Mix thoroughly the chopped nuts, coconut and a blend of

 3 tablespoons all-purpose flour
 ½ teaspoon salt
 1 teaspoon baking powder

Combine egg and flour mixtures and blend well; spread over the partially cooled crust.

Bake at 350°F 25 to 30 min. Cut into bars while warm. Cool thoroughly in pan.

About 20 cookies

FUDGE BROWNIES

▲ Base Recipe

Grease an 8x8x2-in. pan.

Melt (page 10) and set aside to cool

 2 oz. (2 sq.) unsweetened chocolate

Sift together

 1 cup sifted cake flour
 ½ teaspoon baking powder
 ½ teaspoon salt

Chop, mix into dry ingredients and set aside

 1 cup (about 4 oz.) nuts

Cream until well blended

 ½ cup shortening
 ½ teaspoon vanilla extract

Add gradually, creaming until fluffy after each addition

 1 cup sugar

Add, one at a time, beating thoroughly after each addition

 2 eggs

Stir in chocolate. Blend in dry ingredients. Spread in pan.

Bake at 350°F about 25 min. Cut into 2-in. squares while warm and cool in pan.

16 cookies

—PEANUT BUTTER BROWNIES

Follow ▲ Recipe. Cream ¼ **cup peanut butter** with the shortening. Use only ¼ cup (about 1¼ oz.) peanuts for nuts.

—BROWNIE SANDWICHES

Follow ▲ Recipe, substituting ½ **pkg. (3 oz.) semisweet chocolate pieces** for chocolate. Cool baked dough in pan, but do not cut into squares.

For Filling—blend **1 tablespoon softened butter, 1 cup confectioners' sugar, 1 tablespoon milk** and **2 or 3 drops peppermint extract.** When brownies are cool, carefully remove from pan and cut into fourths. Split each fourth; set the top halves aside; spread filling over remaining lower halves. Place brownie tops over filling to form a sandwich. Cut into bar shapes.

—COCONUT TOASTIES

Follow ▲ Recipe. While brownies bake, blend ½ **cup moist shredded coconut, 2 tablespoons softened butter or margarine, 2 tablespoons milk or cream** and ½ **teaspoon cinnamon.** Spread on baked brownies as soon as they are done. Place under broiler about 4 in. from heat for 2 min., or until topping bubbles. Watch closely to avoid scorching. Cool slightly. Cut into squares.

—BROWNIES A LA MODE

Follow ▲ Recipe. Bake in greased 9-in. pie pan. Cut into six wedges; cool. Serve topped with **vanilla ice cream** and **chocolate sauce.**

MARBLED BROWNIES

The aristocrat of brownies—a perfect match for iced coffee.

Cream until softened

 1½ tablespoons butter or margarine

Add gradually, creaming until fluffy after each addition

 3 tablespoons sugar

Blend in, in order, and set aside

 2 teaspoons cornstarch
 ⅔ cup dry cottage cheese
 1 egg, well beaten
 1 tablespoon milk
 ½ teaspoon vanilla extract
 ⅛ teaspoon salt

Prepare

 Fudge Brownies (on this page; omit nuts)

Grease 9x9x2-in. pan and spread one half of brownie dough in bottom of pan. Spread cheese mixture over chocolate layer. Spread remaining half of dough over cheese. Draw spoon through layers until marbled effect is produced.

Bake at 350°F about 35 min., or until wooden pick inserted in center comes out clean. Cool in pan and cut into squares. *16 cookies*

Quick-Mix Brownies

QUICK-MIX BROWNIES

▲ Base Recipe

For Mix—Sift together three times into a large bowl

3 cups sifted all-purpose flour
3 cups sugar
1½ teaspoons baking powder
1½ teaspoons salt

Cut in with pastry blender or two knives until pieces are size of small peas

1½ cups shortening

Store mix in tightly covered container in a cool place; mix made with lard should be stored in refrigerator. Before measuring for recipe, lighten mix by tossing with fork.

About 7½ cups mix (enough for three recipes of Brownies)

For Brownies—Grease an 8x8x2-in. pan.

Chop and set aside

1 cup (about 4 oz.) nuts

Melt (page 10) and set aside to cool

2 oz. (2 sq.) unsweetened chocolate

Measure into bowl

2½ cups mix

Add in thirds, beating thoroughly after each addition

2 eggs, well beaten
1 teaspoon vanilla extract

Add cooled chocolate and stir until well blended. Stir in chopped nuts. Spread in pan.

Bake at 350°F 25 to 30 min., or until a wooden pick or cake tester comes out clean when inserted in center. Set pan on cooling rack. Cut into 2-in. squares when slightly cooled. Frost, if desired. *16 cookies*

—MINT FROSTED BROWNIE CAKES

Follow ▲ Recipe; use 18 2½-in. muffin-pan wells instead of 8x8x2-in. pan. Line with paper baking cups or grease wells. Fill each one-half full. Bake at 350°F 20 to 25 min., or until brownie cakes test done. Place **1 chocolate mint patty** on the top of each baked cake. Return cakes to oven about 3 min., or until the patties are softened. Remove cakes to cooling racks and spread mint patty to cover tops of cakes.

FUDGIES

Grease and set aside a 9x9x2-in. pan.

Melt (page 10) and set aside to cool

2 oz. (2 sq.) unsweetened chocolate

Sift together

¾ cup sifted all-purpose flour
½ teaspoon salt

Coarsely chop and mix with dry ingredients

1 cup (about 4 oz.) pecans

Combine and beat until well blended

1¼ cups firmly packed light brown sugar
¼ cup dairy sour cream
1 teaspoon vanilla extract

Add, one at a time, beating well after each addition

2 eggs

Stir in the chocolate. Blend in the dry ingredients. Turn batter into pan and spread evenly.

Bake at 350°F about 30 min., or until wooden pick inserted in center comes out clean. Remove pan to cooling rack.

Cut into 3x1½-in. bars while still warm; cool completely in pan. *About 1½ doz. cookies*

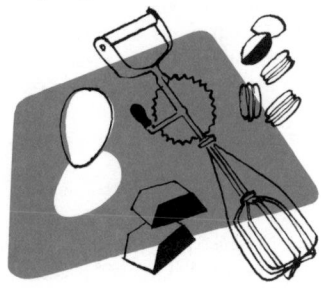

DATE NUT BARS

Grease a 9x9x2-in. baking pan.

Snip and set aside

1 cup (6 oz.) pitted dates

Chop finely and set aside

1 cup nuts

Sift into a mixing bowl

¾ cup sifted all-purpose flour
1 cup sugar
¼ teaspoon baking powder
¼ teaspoon salt

Make a well in center of dry ingredients and add in order

½ cup salad or cooking oil
2 eggs
1 teaspoon vanilla extract

Beat mixture with wooden spoon until smooth (do not overbeat). Stir in the nuts and dates, mixing well. Turn batter into prepared pan.

Bake at 350°F 30 to 35 min.

Set on cooling rack to cool slightly before cutting into bars. While still warm, dust bars with **confectioners' sugar.** *2 doz. cookies*

TEATIME DATE FINGERS

▲ Base Recipe

Invert a 9x9x2-in. pan onto piece of waxed paper. Using a knife, mark around pan to form outline without cutting through paper. Set aside the waxed paper. Turn pan right-side up, grease bottom of pan and set aside.

For Filling—Coarsely chop and set aside

½ cup (2 oz.) nuts

Combine in a saucepan and cook over medium heat, stirring occasionally

¾ lb. pitted dates, cut in pieces (page 9)
1 cup hot water
½ cup orange juice

Cook about 15 min., or until of paste consistency. Stir in chopped nuts and set aside.

For Dough—Sift together and set aside

1½ cups sifted all-purpose flour
¾ teaspoon baking soda
¼ teaspoon salt

Cream until softened

¾ cup butter or margarine
1 teaspoon orange juice
⅛ teaspoon almond extract

Add gradually, creaming until fluffy after each addition

⅔ cup firmly packed brown sugar

Mix in dry ingredients. Add gradually and mix thoroughly after each addition

1¼ cups uncooked rolled oats

Pat one half the mixture into the pan.

Spread filling over dough to within ¼ in. of sides of pan.

Pat remainder of dough over the marked-off square of waxed paper. Invert waxed paper onto top of filling, pressing down gently. Carefully peel off waxed paper.

Bake at 400°F about 35 min., or until browned. Remove from oven and loosen sides with spatula. Cool on cooling rack. Cut into 1½x¾-in. date "fingers" and remove from pan. Sprinkle with

2 tablespoons sifted confectioners' sugar

Decorate with pink rosettes and green leaves.

For Pink Rosettes—Prepare

Glossy Vanilla Icing (page 478; reserve one half of the icing for green leaves)

Tint icing with one or more drops

Red food coloring

Using a pastry bag and No. 27 star decorating tube, pipe frosting onto center of each date "finger" to form a rosette.

For Green Leaves—Tint remaining Glossy Vanilla Icing with one or more drops

Green food coloring

Using a pastry bag and No. 66 leaf decorating tube, pipe frosting onto opposite sides of each rosette to form leaves.

About 6 doz. decorated cookies

—EXOTIC DATE DESSERT

Follow ▲ Recipe. Cut baked cookie dough into 3-in. squares. Omit frosting decorations. Prepare **Sweetened Whipped Cream** (page 480) and top each serving. *9 servings*

HONEY CAKES
(Lebkuchen)

Grease a 15x10x1-in. pan.

Finely chop and set aside
¾ cup (about 4 oz.) unblanched almonds
2 oz. candied orange peel (about ⅓ cup, chopped)
2 oz. candied lemon peel (about ⅓ cup, chopped)

Sift together and set aside
3 cups all-purpose flour
¼ teaspoon baking soda
1 teaspoon cinnamon
½ teaspoon allspice
½ teaspoon nutmeg
½ teaspoon cloves

Beat until thick and piled softly
2 eggs
1 cup sugar

Beat in
½ cup honey

Gently fold in the dry ingredients in thirds. Mix in the almonds and candied peel. Turn batter into pan, spreading to corners.

Bake at 350°F 25 to 30 min., or until a wooden pick or cake tester comes out clean when inserted in center. Set pan on cooling rack.

Meanwhile, blend
⅓ cup confectioners' sugar
1 tablespoon water
1 teaspoon lemon juice

When Lebkuchen is slightly cooled, spread

mixture evenly over top and cut into 3x1½-in. bars. Remove to cooling rack.

About 2½ doz. cookies

MINCEMEAT TRIANGLES

▲ Base Recipe

Grease a 15x10x1-in. pan.

Sift together and set aside
2⅔ cups sifted all-purpose flour
¾ teaspoon baking soda
½ teaspoon salt
¾ teaspoon cinnamon
½ teaspoon nutmeg

Measure into mixing bowl
¾ cup shortening

Add gradually, beating until fluffy after each addition
1¼ cups firmly packed brown sugar
¼ cup sugar

Add, one at a time, beating thoroughly after each addition
2 eggs

Beat in the dry ingredients, then mix in
¾ cup thick mincemeat (if using packaged condensed mincemeat, follow directions on package)

Turn batter into pan and spread to corners.

Bake at 375°F 20 to 25 min., or until a wooden pick comes out clean when inserted in center. Cool slightly in pan on cooling rack before cutting; mark and cut 4 rows across and 6 rows lengthwise. Make diagonal cuts across pan so that each square is cut into two triangles. Remove to cooling racks. *4 doz. cookies*

—APRICOT NUT SQUARES

Follow ▲ Recipe. Substitute **2 teaspoons baking powder** for baking soda. Omit mincemeat; substitute **1¼ cups cooked finely chopped dried apricots** and **½ cup (about 2 oz.) chopped pecans**. Mark and cut 5 rows across and 8 rows lengthwise.

—HONEY DATE TRIANGLES

Follow ▲ Recipe; increase flour to 3 cups. Decrease sugars to ½ cup plus 2 tablespoons brown and 3 tablespoons granulated sugar. After sugar additions, gradually add **¾ cup honey**, beating constantly. Omit mincemeat and mix in **1¼ cups (about 7 oz.) pitted finely chopped dates**.

—APPLESAUCE CURRANT COOKIES

Follow ▲ Recipe. Add **¼ teaspoon cloves** to dry ingredients. Omit mincemeat; instead use **1¼ cups thick applesauce** and **½ cup currants**.

—FULL-OF-PRUNES COOKIES

Follow ▲ Recipe. Substitute **2 teaspoons baking powder** for baking soda. Omit mince-

meat; substitute **1½ cups pitted and finely chopped dried prunes**.

MINCEMEAT BARS

Lightly grease an 11x7x1½-in. pan.

Prepare and set aside
1¾ cups Mincemeat (one half recipe, page 729)

Sift together
1½ cups sifted all-purpose flour
1 teaspoon baking soda
½ teaspoon salt
½ teaspoon nutmeg
¼ teaspoon mace

Mix in
1¾ cups uncooked rolled oats

Beat together
½ cup shortening
¼ teaspoon lemon extract

Add gradually, creaming until fluffy after each addition
1 cup firmly packed brown sugar

Measure
⅓ cup cream

Mix in one half of dry ingredients; mix in cream. Finally add remaining dry ingredients and mix until well blended. (Mixture will be crumbly.)

Divide dough into two portions. Firmly press one portion into pan. Spread mincemeat over dough in pan in an even layer. Top with remaining dough, patting until smooth.

Bake at 350°F about 30 min.

Remove pan to cooling rack. Cut into bars about 2¼x1-in. *About 3 doz. cookies*

CHIP-FILLED OAT BARS

Lightly grease a 10x6x1½-in. pan.

Chop and set aside
1 cup (about 3½ oz.) walnuts

Cream until softened
⅔ cup butter or margarine
1 teaspoon vanilla extract

Add gradually, creaming until fluffy after each addition
1 cup firmly packed brown sugar

Sift together and mix in
1½ cups sifted all-purpose flour
¼ teaspoon salt

Mix in thoroughly
1¼ cups uncooked rolled oats

Press one half of this stiff, dry mixture into pan. Sprinkle with the chopped walnuts and
1 pkg. (6 oz.) semisweet chocolate pieces

Cover with remaining mixture. Spread and press until flat and firm.

Bake at 375°F 35 to 40 min. Cut into 3x1-in. bars while warm. Cool in pan.

20 cookies

FUDGE OATMEAL SQUARES

Lightly grease an 8x8x2-in. pan.

Coarsely chop
½ cup (about 2 oz.) nuts
Reserve 2 tablespoons of the chopped nuts for topping. Set aside.

Melt (page 10)
2 oz. (2 sq.) unsweetened chocolate
⅓ cup butter or margarine
Remove from heat. Mix thoroughly in order
¼ cup light corn syrup
2 teaspoons vanilla extract
¼ teaspoon salt
⅔ cup sugar
Mix in the chopped nuts and
2 cups uncooked rolled oats
Spread the thick mixture into pan and sprinkle top with the reserved chopped nuts.

Bake at 400°F 12 min. Remove the soft, bubbling mixture from oven. Cut into 2x1-in. bars while warm. Cool thoroughly in pan. Store covered in cool place.   *32 cookies*

PEANUT BUTTER BARS

Set out 15x10x7-in. pan.

Sift together and set aside
1¼ cups sifted all-purpose flour
2 teaspoons baking powder
¼ teaspoon salt
Cream until thoroughly blended
½ cup butter or margarine
½ cup (4 oz.) peanut butter
1½ teaspoons vanilla extract
Add gradually, creaming until fluffy after each addition
½ cup firmly packed brown sugar
½ cup sugar
Add and beat thoroughly
1 egg
Thoroughly blend in dry ingredients. Turn into pan and spread evenly.

Bake at 375°F about 20 min. Cut into 3x1½-in. bars while warm. Remove to cooling rack.
2½ doz. cookies

DROP COOKIES

LACY ALMOND CRISPS

Grease and lightly flour cookie sheets.

Melt and set aside to cool
¼ cup butter or margarine

Grate and put into a bowl
⅓ cup (about 2 oz.) blanched almonds (page 9)
Mix in
¼ cup sugar
2 teaspoons all-purpose flour
1 tablespoon milk
Blend in the melted and cooled butter or mar-

garine. Drop by teaspoonfuls about 4 in. apart onto cookie sheets.

Bake at 350°F 8 to 10 min., or until golden brown. Cool slightly and remove carefully with a spatula. (If desired, place them over a rolling pin to obtain a curved shape.)
About 25 cookies

ALMOND FROSTIES

The rum in these cookies gives a subtle, yet distinctive flavor.

Set out cookie sheets.

Sift together into a bowl
2 cups sifted all-purpose flour
½ cup confectioners' sugar
¼ teaspoon salt
Grate and mix in
½ cup unblanched almonds (about 1¼ cups, grated)
Using a pastry blender or two knives, cut in until mixture becomes a soft dough (requires working beyond the stage when mixture resembles coarse corn meal)
1 cup butter or margarine, chilled and cut in pieces
Stir in, adding a tablespoon at a time
¼ cup rum
Drop by tablespoonfuls about 2 in. apart onto the cookie sheets.

Bake at 350°F 20 to 25 min. Remove cookies to cooling racks. When cooled, roll in
Vanilla Confectioners' Sugar (page 582)
About 5 doz. cookies

ALMOND TILES
(Tuiles aux Amandes)

Set out a cookie sheet.

Blanch (page 9)
1½ cups (about ½ lb.) almonds
Shave and reserve broad slices from about ½ cup of the almonds. Finely chop remaining almonds and set aside.

Sift together and set aside
1 cup sifted all-purpose flour
⅛ teaspoon salt
Mix thoroughly in a large bowl
6 egg whites
1½ cups sugar
1 teaspoon vanilla extract
Melt, cool to lukewarm and stir into sugar mixture
1 cup butter
Add sifted dry ingredients with the finely chopped almonds. Beat well. Drop by tablespoonfuls 5 in. apart onto cookie sheet. Sprinkle shaved almond slices over tops.

Bake at 350°F about 10 min., or until golden brown. Remove one at a time and quickly curve it over a rolling pin or a glass and set aside on a cooling rack. If cookies harden before molding, return to oven a few seconds to soften.
About 5 doz. cookies

Macaroons

ITALIAN MACAROONS
(Amaretti)

Cover the bottom of a cookie sheet with unglazed paper.

Blanch (page 9)
¾ cup (¼ lb.) almonds
Using the electric blender or nut grinder, grind blanched almonds. Set aside.

Beat until frothy
2 egg whites
¼ teaspoon salt
Add, one tablespoon at a time, beating thoroughly after each addition
1 cup sugar
Beat until stiff peaks are formed. Fold in ground almonds with
½ teaspoon almond extract
Drop by teaspoonfuls about 1 in. apart onto the unglazed paper. Keep small and uniform.

Bake at 350°F about 20 min., or until very lightly browned.   *About 3 doz. Macaroons*

FRENCH MACAROONS
(Macarons de Nancy)

Line bottom of a cookie sheet with unglazed paper.

Force through a coarse sieve, a little at a time
½ lb. almond paste
Add gradually and stir until smooth with each addition
⅓ cup (about 3) egg whites (Slightly more or less egg white may be needed, depending on moisture of almond paste.)

Blend in
¾ teaspoon vanilla extract
¼ teaspoon yellow food coloring
Mix
½ cup sugar
½ cup confectioners' sugar
Blend a little at a time into almond paste mixture. Mix thoroughly. The mixture should be thick enough to hold its shape but must not be stiff. Drop by teaspoonfuls onto cookie

sheet. Flatten top of each macaroon. Sprinkle lightly with

Sifted confectioners' sugar

Bake at 300°F about 25 min. Remove from oven and slightly moisten underside of paper directly under each macaroon. Remove macaroons to rack. *About 3 doz. cookies*

FLORENTINES I
(Echte Florentiner)

▲ *Base Recipe*

These delicate, delicious cookies, favorites of old Vienna—so rich, so sweet, so full of fruit and nuts—are almost like candy!

Butter cookie sheets. Sprinkle lightly with flour; shake off excess flour.

Blanch (page 9), sliver and set aside
4 oz. (about ¾ cup) almonds (about 1 cup, slivered)

Chop finely and set aside
3 oz. candied orange peel (about ½ cup, chopped)

Sift together and set aside
¾ cup sifted cake flour
¼ teaspoon salt

Rub through a coarse sieve
⅓ cup firmly packed light brown sugar
Cream until softened
¼ cup butter
Add sugar gradually, creaming until light and fluffy after each addition. Add gradually, beating in
2 tablespoons honey
2 tablespoons light corn syrup
1 tablespoon heavy cream
Add the almonds and chopped candied peel and mix well. Add dry ingredients and blend thoroughly. Drop by level tablespoonfuls onto the cookie sheet about 3 in. apart and spread into 2-in. rounds.

Bake at 350°F 7 min., or until cookies are delicately browned. The cookies will be about 3 in. in diameter with a slightly lacy appearance.

Remove cookie sheets to cooling racks and let cool 2 to 3 min. (Cookies must be warm to be removed.) Carefully remove cookies with a spatula (they may stick slightly to pan); place flat side up on cooling racks to cool.

When cookies are cooled, heat over hot (not simmering) water until chocolate is partially melted, being careful not to overheat
6 oz. (6 sq.) semisweet candymaking chocolate
6 tablespoons butter
Remove from the hot water and stir until chocolate is completely melted. Cool mixture to lukewarm.

Carefully spread about 1½ teaspoons of chocolate mixture over flat side of each cookie, spreading to edges. Let stand until chocolate is

almost set. Using a fork, carefully draw wavy lines through the chocolate.
About 26 cookies

—FLORENTINES II
(Florentiner II)

Follow ▲ Recipe. Decrease almonds to 1½ oz. (¼ cup) and grate (about ¾ cup, grated). Omit candied orange peel. Decrease flour to ¼ cup plus 2 tablespoons. Cream **2 teaspoons grated lemon peel** and **½ teaspoon almond extract** with butter. Blend in the almonds before addition of dry ingredients. Drop by heaping teaspoonfuls about 3 in. apart onto cookie sheets. Bake at 350°F 10 min., or until cookies are golden brown. The cookies should be very thin, about 4 in. in diameter, and have a lacy appearance. Decrease chocolate to 5 oz. (5 sq.) and butter to 5 tablespoons. Spread about 2 teaspoons chocolate mixture on flat side of each cookie.

ANISE DROPS
(Anisscheiben)

Generously grease cookie sheets.

Sift together and set aside
1½ cups sifted all-purpose flour
¼ teaspoon baking powder

Put into a liquid measuring cup
2 eggs
Add, if necessary
Water (enough to make ½ cup liquid)
Put into a mixing bowl with
1 cup sugar
¼ teaspoon anise flavoring
Beat until very thick and piled softly. Fold in the dry ingredients, sifting in about one fourth at a time. Drop by teaspoonfuls about 2 in. apart onto the cookie sheets. Set cookie sheets aside in a cool place (not in refrigerator) 8 to 10 hrs., or overnight. Do not cover cookies and do not disturb!

Bake at 350°F 5 to 6 min.

Remove to cooling racks to cool completely. Cookies form a cakelike layer on the bottom with a crisp "frosting" on the top.
About 4 doz. cookies

LUSCIOUS CHOCOLATE CRISPIES

Generously grease cookie sheets.

Coarsely chop and set aside
1¼ cups (about 5 oz.) nuts

Put into a saucepan and cook over low heat, stirring constantly, 3 min.
¾ cup firmly packed brown sugar
¼ cup butter
Remove from heat. Stir in chopped nuts and
½ pkg. (3 oz.) semisweet chocolate pieces
Cool slightly (about 5 min.).

Add to chocolate mixture and mix well
1 egg, well beaten
1 teaspoon vanilla extract
¼ teaspoon almond extract

Drop by ½ teaspoonfuls onto cookie sheets.

Bake at 375°F 8 to 10 min. Let cookies cool until easy to remove. *About 3 doz. cookies*

COCOA DROPS

Lightly grease cookie sheets.

Sift together and set aside
1½ cups sifted cake flour
¾ cup cocoa
¼ teaspoon salt

Cream until softened
1 cup butter or margarine
1 teaspoon vanilla extract
Add gradually, creaming until fluffy after each addition
¾ cup sugar
Add, one at a time, beating thoroughly after each addition
2 eggs
Stir in dry ingredients in halves, mixing well after each addition. Drop by teaspoonfuls about 2 in. apart onto the cookie sheets.

Bake at 375°F 12 to 15 min. Remove to cooling racks. *About 7 doz. cookies*

CHOCOLATE-DROP DELIGHTS

▲ *Base Recipe*

Grease cookie sheets.

Sift together and set aside
2¼ cups sifted cake flour
1 teaspoon baking soda
¾ teaspoon salt

Cream until softened
1 cup butter or margarine
2½ teaspoons vanilla extract
Add gradually, creaming until fluffy
1¼ cups sugar
Add, one at a time, beating well after each addition
2 eggs
Blend in about
1 teaspoon hot water

Choco-Nut Mounds

Stir in dry ingredients. Mix in

1 pkg. (12 oz.) semisweet chocolate pieces

Drop by teaspoonfuls about 2 in. apart onto cookie sheets.

Bake at 375°F 10 to 12 min. Remove to cooling racks. *About 8 doz. cookies*

—ORANGE CHOCOLATE-DROP COOKIES

Follow ▲ Recipe. Decrease vanilla extract to 2 teaspoons; add **1 teaspoon orange extract** or **2 teaspoons (slightly thawed) frozen orange juice concentrate (undiluted)** to the creamed butter.

CHOCOLATE BANANA DROPS

Set out cookie sheets.

Melt (page 10) and set aside to cool

1 pkg. (6 oz.) semisweet chocolate pieces

Prepare and set aside

Cinnamon Sugar (page 582)

Sift together and set aside

2¼ cups sifted all-purpose flour
2 teaspoons baking powder
¾ teaspoon salt
¼ teaspoon baking soda

Mash, beat or force through a food mill

2 to 3 all yellow or brown-flecked bananas (enough to make 1 cup mashed bananas)

Set aside.

Cream until well blended

⅔ cup shortening
1 teaspoon lemon extract
1 teaspoon vanilla extract

Add gradually, creaming until fluffy after each addition

1 cup sugar

Add, one at a time, beating thoroughly after each addition

2 eggs

Blend in melted chocolate. Stir in dry ingredients alternately with mashed bananas, adding dry ingredients in thirds, bananas in halves. Drop by teaspoonfuls about 1½ in. apart onto cookie sheets. Sprinkle with Cinnamon Sugar.

Bake at 400°F 12 to 15 min. Remove to cooling racks. *About 5 doz. cookies*

MELTAWAY CHOCOLATE COOKIES

Set out cookie sheets.

Sift together and set aside

1 cup sifted cake flour
⅓ cup sifted confectioners' sugar
2 tablespoons cocoa
¼ teaspoon salt

Cream until softened

½ cup butter
1 teaspoon vanilla extract

Beating until smooth after each addition, add dry ingredients in halves.

Drop dough by teaspoonfuls about 2 in. apart onto the cookie sheets. Flatten each to about ⅛-in. thickness with tines of a fork, dipped frequently in water. Form a crisscross pattern.

Bake at 300°F 12 to 15 min.

Remove cookies from cookie sheets. Place close together on waxed paper. Generously sift **confectioners' sugar** over warm cookies.
About 4 doz. cookies

CHOCO-NUT MOUNDS

▲ Base Recipe

Lightly grease cookie sheets.

Chop and set aside

½ cup (about 2 oz.) nuts

Melt (page 10) and set aside to cool

3 oz. (3 sq.) unsweetened chocolate

Sift together and set aside

1¾ cups sifted cake flour
½ teaspoon salt
½ teaspoon baking soda

Cream until well blended

½ cup shortening
1 teaspoon vanilla extract

Add gradually, creaming until fluffy after each addition

1 cup firmly packed brown sugar

Add, one at a time, beating thoroughly after each addition

2 eggs

Stir in the melted chocolate.

Measure

½ cup buttermilk or sour milk

Alternately add dry ingredients in thirds, buttermilk in halves, to creamed mixture.

After each addition, beat until smooth. Finally beat only until batter is smooth (do not overbeat). Stir in chopped nuts. Drop by teaspoonfuls 2 in. apart onto cookie sheets.

Bake at 350°F 10 to 12 min. Cool on racks.

When cool, frost with **Chocolate Butter Frosting** (page 479). If desired, top with **chopped nuts.** *2½ doz. cookies*

—CHOCO MOUNDS

Follow ▲ Recipe. Omit chopped nuts in recipe. Top each cookie with a **walnut half** before baking. Omit frosting.

FROSTED CHOCOLATE NUT DROPS

▲ Base Recipe

Nut-filled drops are twice as good when chocolate is double featured.

Lightly grease cookie sheets.

For Cookies—Melt (page 10) and set aside to cool

4 oz. (4 sq.) unsweetened chocolate

Coarsely chop and set aside

2 cups (7 oz.) black walnuts

Sift together and set aside

3 cups sifted all-purpose flour
½ teaspoon salt
½ teaspoon baking soda
½ teaspoon baking powder

Cream until softened

1 cup butter or margarine
2 teaspoons vanilla extract

Add gradually, creaming until fluffy after each addition

2 cups sugar

Add, one at a time, beating thoroughly after each addition

3 eggs

Stir in cooled chocolate.

Measure

1 cup sour milk (page 9)

Alternately add dry ingredients in fourths, sour milk in thirds, to creamed mixture. After each addition, beat until smooth. Finally beat only until batter is smooth (do not overbeat).

Frosted Chocolate Nut Drops

Mix in nuts. Drop by tablespoonfuls onto greased cookie sheets.

Bake at 350°F 12 to 15 min.

Remove cookies to cooling racks immediately and set aside to cool.

Melt (page 10) in double boiler top

3 to 4 oz. (3 to 4 sq.) unsweetened chocolate
½ cup butter or margarine

Stir into the melted chocolate mixture

2⅔ cups confectioners' sugar

Then stir in

1 egg
6 tablespoons water
2 teaspoons vanilla extract
⅛ teaspoon salt

Place the double boiler top in a bowl of ice and water. Beat with electric mixer about 5 min., or until frosting is of spreading consistency. If using a hand rotary beater, allow more beating time. Spread frosting on the cooled cookies, allowing about 1 tablespoon frosting for each cookie. *About 4 doz. cookies*

—CHOCOLATE FRUIT DROPS

Follow ▲ Recipe. Replace 1 cup of nuts with an equal amount of **raisins or chopped dates.**

—CANDY CHOCOLATE DROPS

Follow ▲ Recipe. Substitute **1½ cups gum drops,** cut in pieces, for nuts. Try many colored ones or use candy orange slices only.

POLKA DOT DROPS

Lightly grease cookie sheets.

Coarsely chop and set aside

½ cup (about 2 oz.) nuts

Sift together and set aside

1¼ cups sifted all-purpose flour
½ teaspoon baking soda
¼ teaspoon baking powder
¼ teaspoon salt

Cream until softened

¼ cup butter
¾ teaspoon vanilla extract

Add gradually, creaming until fluffy after each addition

¾ cup firmly packed brown sugar

Add to the creamed mixture and beat until thoroughly blended

1 egg

Measure

½ cup dairy sour cream

Mixing until well blended after each addition, alternately add dry ingredients in thirds, sour cream in halves to creamed mixture. Stir in the chopped nuts and

1 pkg. (6 oz.) semisweet chocolate pieces

Drop by heaping teaspoonfuls about 2 in. apart onto cookie sheets.

Bake at 375°F 10 to 12 min. Remove to cooling racks. *About 4½ doz. cookies*

SEMISWEET CHOCOLATE FAVORITES

▲ *Base Recipe*

Lightly grease 2 cookie sheets.

Chop and set aside

1 cup (about 3¾ oz.) pecans

Sift together and set aside

2½ cups sifted cake flour
¾ teaspoon baking soda
½ teaspoon salt

Cream until well blended

1 cup shortening
1 teaspoon vanilla extract

Add gradually, creaming until fluffy after each addition

¾ cup sugar
¾ cup firmly packed brown sugar

Add in thirds, beating well after each addition

2 eggs, well beaten

Blend in

2 tablespoons hot water

Mix in dry ingredients. Stir in pecans and

1 pkg. (6 oz.) semisweet chocolate pieces

Drop by teaspoonfuls about 2 in. apart onto cookie sheets.

Bake at 375°F 10 to 12 min. Remove to cooling racks. *About 4 doz. cookies*

—SEMISWEET CHOCOLATE BARS

Grease a 15x10x1-in. pan. Follow ▲ Recipe. Spread batter in pan and bake at 350°F 15 to 20 min. Cool completely; cut into 56 bars about 2x1½ in.

—ORANGE SEMISWEET COOKIES

Follow ▲ Recipe. Add **1 teaspoon grated orange peel** to the creamed shortening. Substitute **orange juice** for water.

Semisweet Chocolate Favorites

—SEMISWEET CHOCOLATE DIAMONDS

Grease a 15x10x1-in. pan. Follow ▲ Recipe. Spread batter in pan and bake at 350°F 15 to 20 min. Meanwhile, melt (page 10) a second package of **semisweet chocolate pieces** with **2 tablespoons butter;** stir occasionally. Quickly spread evenly over baked cookies. If desired, sprinkle with **chopped pecans.** Cool completely; cut into diamond or wedge shapes.

GLAZED COCONUT DATE DELIGHTS

Lightly grease cookie sheets.

Chop finely and set aside

1 cup walnuts or pecans

Snip and set aside

1 pkg. (6½ oz.) pitted dates (about 1 cup)

Sift together and set aside

2⅔ cups sifted all-purpose flour
½ teaspoon salt
1 teaspoon baking soda

Cream until butter is softened

1 cup butter or margarine
1½ teaspoons vanilla extract

Add gradually, creaming until fluffy after each addition

1¼ cups firmly packed brown sugar

Add one at a time, beating thoroughly after each addition

2 eggs

Beating only until blended after each addition, add dry ingredients in thirds. Beat in

2 tablespoons water

Stir in the nuts, dates and

1 cup flaked coconut

Drop batter by heaping teaspoonfuls about 2 in. apart onto the cookie sheets.

Bake at 375°F about 8 min., or until cookies are lightly browned. Remove cookies to cooling racks. Dribble glaze over cookies while they are still warm. *6½ to 7 doz. cookies*

Note: If desired, substitute 1 cup golden raisins for the dates.

Glaze—Heat **½ cup butter or margarine** in a small heavy skillet or saucepan until golden brown. Stir in until smooth **1 cup confectioners' sugar** and **1 teaspoon vanilla extract.**

CHOCOLATE MACAROONS

▲ Base Recipe

Cover the bottom of a cookie sheet with unglazed paper.

Melt (page 10) and set aside to cool
1½ oz. (1½ sq.) unsweetened chocolate

Beat until frothy
2 egg whites

Add and beat slightly
1 teaspoon vanilla extract
¼ teaspoon salt

Add, one tablespoon at a time, beating well after each addition, finally beating until stiff peaks are formed
1 cup sugar

Fold in chocolate and
1½ cups moist shredded coconut

Drop by teaspoonfuls onto unglazed paper. Keep macaroons small and uniform.

Bake at 350°F 20 to 25 min. Remove to cooling rack. *15 to 20 cookies*

—CRUNCHY NUT MACAROONS

Follow ▲ Recipe. Decrease coconut to ½ cup. Add **1 cup cereal** such as corn or wheat flakes and **¼ cup (about 1 oz.) chopped nuts.**

—FILBERT SWEETSTUFFS

Follow ▲ Recipe. Substitute **chopped filberts** for coconut.

COCONUT CRISPS

▲ Base Recipe

Lightly grease cookie sheets.

Sift together and set aside
3 cups sifted all-purpose flour
1½ teaspoons baking powder
1 teaspoon salt

Chop and set aside
1 cup moist shredded coconut
¼ cup maraschino cherries, well drained

Cream until well blended
1 cup shortening
2 teaspoons vanilla extract

Add gradually, creaming until fluffy after each addition
1½ cups sugar

Beat together
1 egg
1 egg yolk
3 tablespoons cream or undiluted evaporated milk

Add egg mixture in halves to creamed mixture, beating thoroughly after each addition. Add dry ingredients gradually, mixing thoroughly. Blend in chopped coconut and maraschino cherries.

Drop by teaspoonfuls 1½ in. apart onto cookie

sheets. Flatten slightly with spatula or back of spoon.

Bake at 400°F 8 to 10 min., or until cookies are very lightly browned. Cool on cooling rack and store in tightly covered container.
5 to 5½ doz. cookies

—FRUIT CRISPS

Follow ▲ Recipe. Substitute **1 cup diced candied fruit** or **1 cup chopped dried figs** for coconut and cherries.

—LEMON SUGAR COOKIES

Follow ▲ Recipe. Decrease vanilla extract to 1 teaspoon. Add with it **2 teaspoons grated lemon peel** and **1 teaspoon lemon extract.** Omit coconut and cherries. Sprinkle cookies with **plain or colored sugar** before baking.

—CHOCOLATE ALMOND COOKIES

Follow ▲ Recipe. Omit coconut and cherries. Add **½ teaspoon almond extract** with vanilla extract. Blend **2 oz. (2 sq.) unsweetened chocolate**, melted (page 10) and cooled, into creamed mixture after addition of eggs. With last addition of dry ingredients, add **½ cup finely chopped toasted blanched almonds,** (pages 9 and 10).

OATMEAL DROP COOKIES

▲ Base Recipe

Set out cookie sheets.

Chop and set aside
1 cup (about 4 oz.) nuts
3 oz. candied citron (about ½ cup, chopped)

Sift together into a bowl
2 cups sifted all-purpose flour
1 cup sugar
1 teaspoon baking soda
1 teaspoon cinnamon
½ teaspoon salt

Cut in with pastry blender or two knives until pieces are size of rice kernels
1 cup shortening

Mix in the chopped nuts, citron and
2½ cups uncooked rolled oats
1½ cups (about 8 oz.) raisins
½ teaspoon grated lemon peel

Oatmeal Nut Drops

Add in thirds, mixing thoroughly after each addition
3 eggs, well beaten

Thoroughly mix in
½ cup milk

Drop by teaspoonfuls about 2 in. apart onto cookie sheets.

Bake at 375°F about 10 min., or until delicately browned. Remove cookies to cooling racks.
About 7½ doz. cookies

Note: If desired, mix 2 tablespoons instant nonfat dry milk with dry ingredients and substitute water for milk.

—CHOCOLATE OATMEAL DROPS

Follow ▲ Recipe. Substitute **1 pkg. (6 oz.) semisweet chocolate pieces** for raisins and citron.

—OATMEAL NUT DROPS

Follow ▲ Recipe. Omit citron and raisins. Increase nuts to 2 cups. Sliver **¾ cup (about 3 oz.) pitted dates.** Press several date slivers into each cookie and bake.

—PINEAPPLE OATMEAL DROPS

Follow ▲ Recipe. Omit citron and raisins. Drain **1 can (20 oz.) crushed pineapple.** Chop **½ cup (about 2 oz.) nuts.** Make an indentation with tip of spoon in center of each cookie. Fill with pineapple and sprinkle with chopped nuts. Bake as directed.

Pineapple Oatmeal Drops

Oatmeal Freckles and Four-Stripers

OATMEAL COOKIES

Lightly grease cookie sheets.

Sift together into a bowl
¾ cup sifted all-purpose flour
½ cup sugar
1 teaspoon cinnamon
½ teaspoon baking soda
½ teaspoon salt
¼ teaspoon allspice
¼ teaspoon cloves
Stir in
½ cup firmly packed brown sugar
Add to the bowl and beat in thoroughly (about 2 min. with electric mixer on medium speed)
½ cup shortening, softened
1 egg
3 tablespoons water
1 teaspoon vanilla extract
Mix in
1½ cups uncooked rolled oats
Drop by teaspoonfuls about 2 in. apart onto cookie sheets.

Bake at 375°F about 9 min., or until browned. Cool on racks. *About 4 doz. cookies*

BUTTERSCOTCH OATMEAL DROPS

Lightly grease cookie sheets.

Sift together and set aside
2 cups sifted all-purpose flour
2½ teaspoons baking powder
½ teaspoon salt

Coarsely chop and set aside
1⅓ cups nuts

Cream until well blended
1⅓ cups shortening
2 teaspoons vanilla extract

Add gradually, creaming until fluffy after each addition
2 cups firmly packed brown sugar
Beat until thick and piled softly
2 eggs
1 egg yolk
Add in thirds to sugar mixture; beat until fluffy after each addition. Stir in dry ingredients and
1⅓ cups uncooked rolled oats
Mix in the chopped nuts.

Drop by teaspoonfuls about 2 in. apart onto cookie sheets. Top cookies with about
½ pkg. (3 oz.) semisweet chocolate pieces

Bake at 400°F 7 to 10 min., or until lightly browned. Cool on racks. *About 5 doz. cookies*

OATMEAL FRECKLES

▲ *Base Recipe*

Lightly grease cookie sheets.

Chop and set aside
½ cup (about 2 oz.) nuts

Sift together into bowl
¾ cup sifted all-purpose flour
½ cup sugar
1 teaspoon cinnamon
½ teaspoon baking soda
½ teaspoon salt
Stir in
½ cup firmly packed brown sugar
Add and beat together thoroughly (2 min. with electric mixer on medium speed)
½ cup shortening, softened
1 egg
3 tablespoons water
1 teaspoon vanilla extract
Mix in the chopped nuts and
1 pkg. (6 oz.) semisweet chocolate pieces
1½ cups uncooked rolled oats
Drop by teaspoonfuls onto cookie sheets.

Bake at 375°F about 12 min. Remove to cooling racks. *About 6 doz. cookies*

—HONEY OATMEAL FRECKLES

Follow ▲ Recipe. Omit brown sugar. Add ½ **cup honey** with shortening. Decrease water to 1 tablespoon.

GEORGIA PECAN KISSES

Line cookie sheets with unglazed paper.

Chop and set aside
1 cup (about 4 oz.) pecans

Beat until frothy
2 egg whites
¼ teaspoon salt
Add gradually, beating well
1 cup firmly packed light brown sugar
Continue beating until stiff, not dry, peaks

are formed. Carefully fold in pecans and
½ teaspoon maple flavoring
Drop by teaspoonfuls onto unglazed paper. Keep cookies small and uniform.

Bake at 300°F 25 to 30 min. Working quickly and carefully, remove cookies to cooling racks. If necessary, slightly moisten underside of paper directly under each cookie to loosen. *About 4 doz. cookies*

BUTTER PECAN DROPS

Set out cookie sheets.

Set out
½ cup pecan halves

Chop coarsely and set aside
½ cup pecans

Measure and set aside
1 cup sifted all-purpose flour

Cream until butter is softened
½ cup butter or margarine
1 teaspoon vanilla extract
Add gradually, creaming until fluffy after each addition
⅔ cup firmly packed brown sugar
Add and beat thoroughly
1 egg
Mixing until well blended after each addition, add flour in halves. Mix in the chopped pecans.

Drop by rounded teaspoonfuls about 2½ in. apart onto the cookie sheets. Top each cookie with a pecan half.

Bake at 375°F about 10 min. Immediately remove cookies to cooling racks. *About 3 doz. cookies*

SOUTHERN CREAM DROPS

Lightly grease cookie sheets.

Sift together and set aside
2 cups sifted all-purpose flour
½ teaspoon baking powder
½ teaspoon baking soda
½ teaspoon nutmeg
¼ teaspoon salt

Cream until softened
½ cup butter or margarine
½ teaspoon vanilla extract
Add gradually, creaming until fluffy after each addition
1 cup firmly packed light brown sugar
Add in halves, beating well after each addition, a mixture of
1 egg, well beaten
½ cup dairy sour cream
Mixing until well blended after each addition, add dry ingredients in fourths to creamed mixture. Drop by teaspoonfuls about 2 in. apart onto cookie sheets.

Bake at 350°F about 12 min., or until lightly browned. Using a spatula, immediately remove to cooling racks to cool. *About 4 doz. cookies*

SOUR CREAM COOKIES

Lightly grease cookie sheets.

Chop and set aside
¾ cup (about 3 oz.) walnuts

Sift together and set aside
2 cups all-purpose flour
½ teaspoon baking powder
½ teaspoon baking soda
½ teaspoon cinnamon
¼ teaspoon salt

Cream until softened
½ cup butter
1 teaspoon vanilla extract
Add gradually, creaming until fluffy
1 cup sugar
Add, beating well after each addition
1 egg
½ cup dairy sour cream
Mix in dry ingredients until well blended. Stir in walnuts. Drop by teaspoonfuls about 2 in. apart onto cookie sheets.

Bake at 350°F about 12 min., or until lightly browned. Transfer to cooling racks and cool.
About 4 doz. cookies

HERMITS

Lightly grease cookie sheets.

Bring to boiling
2 cups water
Add and again bring water to boiling
1 cup (about 5 oz.) dark seedless raisins
Pour off water and drain raisins on absorbent paper. Coarsely chop raisins and set aside.

Chop and set aside
1 cup (about 4 oz.) walnuts

Sift together and set aside
2½ cups sifted all-purpose flour
¾ teaspoon baking soda
½ teaspoon salt
1 teaspoon cinnamon
½ teaspoon nutmeg
⅛ teaspoon cloves

Cream until softened
¾ cup butter
Add gradually, creaming until fluffy after each addition
1½ cups firmly packed brown sugar
Add, one at a time, beating thoroughly after each addition
3 eggs

Mixing until well blended after each addition, add dry ingredients in halves to creamed mixture. Mix in the raisins and walnuts. Drop mixture by teaspoonfuls about 2 in. apart onto the cookie sheets.

Bake at 400°F about 7 min. Remove to cooling racks.
About 8 doz. cookies

SPICE DROPS

▲ *Base Recipe*

Lightly grease cookie sheets.

Blend in a mixing bowl
3 cups All-in-One Biscuit Mix (page 93)
1 cup firmly packed brown sugar
1½ teaspoons cinnamon
½ teaspoon allspice
½ teaspoon nutmeg
¼ teaspoon cloves
Beat until blended
2 eggs, well beaten
3 tablespoons milk
1½ teaspoons vanilla extract
¼ teaspoon orange extract
Make a well in center of dry ingredients and add liquid mixture all at one time. Beat until batter is smooth. Carefully scrape around sides and bottom of bowl several times during mixing. Drop dough by teaspoonfuls about 2 in. apart onto cookie sheets.

Bake at 375°F about 10 min. Remove to cooling racks.
About 5½ doz. cookies

—OATMEAL DROPS

Follow ▲ Recipe. Omit orange extract and spices except for cinnamon. When batter is smooth, stir in **½ cup uncooked rolled oats**, **½ cup (about 2 oz.) chopped nuts** and **½ cup flaked coconut.**

—PEANUT BUTTER CHECKS

Follow ▲ Recipe. Cut **⅓ cup softened peanut butter** into mix. Substitute **granulated sugar** for brown. Omit spices and orange extract. Flatten cookies with floured fork, making criss-cross marks on top.

—CHOCOLATE DROPS

Follow ▲ Recipe. Melt (page 10) and cool **1 oz. (1 sq.) unsweetened chocolate.** Substitute **granulated sugar** for brown. Omit spices and orange extract. When batter is smooth, blend in melted chocolate. Press **1 walnut half** onto each before baking.

—SEMISWEET DROPS

Follow ▲ Recipe. Omit spices and orange extract. Blend in **1 pkg. (6 oz.) semisweet chocolate pieces** and **½ cup (about 2 oz.) chopped nuts.**

—GUMDROP CHEWS

Follow ▲ Recipe. Omit spices. Blend in **1½ cups chopped gumdrops** (do not use licorice-flavored gumdrops).

REFRIGERATOR COOKIES

REFRIGERATOR COOKIES

▲ *Base Recipe*

Cookie sheets will be needed.

Melt (page 10) and set aside to cool
2 oz. (2 sq.) unsweetened chocolate

Sift together and set aside
3 cups sifted all-purpose flour
2 teaspoons baking powder
½ teaspoon salt

Cream until well blended
1 cup shortening
2 teaspoons vanilla extract
Add gradually, creaming until fluffy
1 cup sugar
Add, one at a time, beating thoroughly after each addition
2 eggs
Add the dry ingredients in halves, mixing thoroughly after each addition. Divide dough into halves. To one half the dough, stir in melted chocolate and
1 tablespoon milk
Wrap each half of dough in waxed paper and chill in refrigerator until easy to handle. Shape both white and chocolate dough into 2 rolls, each 2 in. in diameter. Again wrap in waxed paper and chill. Cut into ⅛-in. slices. Place on ungreased cookie sheets.

Bake at 400°F 5 to 9 min. Remove to cooling racks.
10 doz. cookies

—COCOA REFRIGERATOR COOKIES

Follow ▲ Recipe. Substitute **½ cup cocoa** for chocolate; sift cocoa in with the dry ingredients decreasing flour to 2½ cups. Blend in after the flour mixture **½ cup (2 oz.) chopped nuts** (or **½ cup [2¾ oz.] toasted slivered almonds**).

Cocoa Refrigerator Cookies

—ORANGE REFRIGERATOR COOKIES

Follow ▲ Recipe. Substitute **orange juice** for milk and add **1 teaspoon grated orange peel.**

—VARIETY TRAY

Follow ▲ Recipe using one third of each dough for plain cookies. Make up remaining two thirds in Pinwheels and Stripers.

—PINWHEELS

Follow ▲ Recipe. After chilling dough enough to handle, divide each dough into three portions. Roll one third of the chocolate and one third of the white dough into rectangular sheets, 8x6x⅛-in. Place chocolate sheet on top of white sheet and roll up tightly into a roll. Repeat process, forming two additional rolls.

—STRIPERS

Follow ▲ Recipe. Divide each dough into six portions. Roll two portions of the chocolate dough into 2 squares, ¼ in. thick. Roll two portions of the white dough in the same way. Line a flat pan with waxed paper. Stack layers in pan alternating colors and brushing each layer with **slightly beaten egg white** before putting on the next. Repeat process, forming two additional stacks. Wrap waxed paper around blocks of dough. Chill. Remove from pan and unwrap. Cut into slices and bake as in ▲ Recipe.

BROWN 'N' WHITE CHIPS

Here you get two crisp, delicious cookies from a single recipe, just by dividing the dough and adding chocolate to one half. Arrange both brown and white cookies on your serving plate or tray, for color contrast that appeals to the eye as the flavor contrast appeals to the taste.

Melt (page 10) and set aside to cool
2 oz. (2 sq.) unsweetened chocolate

Sift together and set aside
4 cups sifted all-purpose flour
1½ teaspoons baking powder
¼ teaspoon baking soda
½ teaspoon salt

Cream until softened
1 cup butter or margarine
2 teaspoons vanilla extract

Add gradually, creaming until fluffy after each addition
1 cup sugar
Add in halves, beating thoroughly after each addition, a mixture of
2 egg yolks, well beaten
½ cup dairy sour cream
Mixing until well blended after each addition, add dry ingredients in fourths to creamed mixture.

Divide dough into halves. Stir into one half of the dough the cooled melted chocolate, and
1 tablespoon dairy sour cream
Wrap each half of dough in waxed paper and chill in refrigerator until firm enough to handle easily. Shape each half of dough into 2 rolls 1½ in. in diameter. Wrap each roll in waxed paper and chill several hours or overnight in refrigerator.

Set out cookie sheets.

Remove rolls from refrigerator as needed. Cut into ⅛-in. slices. Place 1 in. apart on the cookie sheets.

Bake at 400°F 6 to 8 min. With a spatula, remove to cooling racks.
About 12 doz. cookies

Note: These two differently colored doughs may be shaped into pinwheels, checkerboards or ribbon cookies. Addition of chopped nuts or chopped candied fruits to the dough gives extra flavor and touches of color.

COCONUT BUTTER COOKIES

Line bottom and sides of a 9x5x3-in. loaf pan with waxed paper. Cookie sheets will be needed.

Cut into short lengths and set aside
1 cup (4 oz.) moist shredded coconut

Measure and set aside
2 cups sifted all-purpose flour

Cream until softened
1 cup butter
1 tablespoon vanilla extract
Add and cream until fluffy
⅓ cup confectioners' sugar
Beating until smooth after each addition, add the sifted flour in halves. Blend in the coconut. Press dough into loaf pan in an even layer.

Cover and chill in refrigerator several hours.

Set out cookie sheets.

Using a sharp knife, cut dough crosswise into ten strips. Cut lengthwise forming four rows of 10 pieces each. Holding waxed paper, lift dough from pan. Roll each piece of dough in palms of hands to form a ball. Place balls about 1 in. apart on cookie sheets, pressing slightly to flatten.

Bake at 275°F about 25 min.

Remove to cooling racks. Sift **confectioners' sugar** over cooled cookies.
About 3½ doz. cookies

LEMON WAFERS

Cookie sheets will be needed.

Sift together and set aside
1½ cups sifted all-purpose flour
½ teaspoon salt
½ teaspoon baking soda

Cream until well blended
½ cup shortening
1½ teaspoons grated lemon peel
1½ tablespoons lemon juice
Add gradually, creaming until fluffy after each addition
1 cup firmly packed brown sugar
Add and beat well
1 egg
Blending thoroughly after each addition, add dry ingredients in halves.

Shape into rolls 1 in. in diameter. Roll in waxed paper. Chill several hours or overnight in refrigerator.

Lightly grease cookie sheets.

Remove roll from refrigerator and cut into thin slices. Place slices on cookie sheets. If dough becomes too soft to slice, chill again in refrigerator.

Bake at 400°F 8 to 10 min. Remove cookies immediately from sheets and cool on cooling racks.
About 4 doz. cookies

WALNUT WAFERS

Chop and set aside
½ cup (about 1¾ oz.) walnuts

Sift together and set aside
3 cups sifted all-purpose flour
1 teaspoon salt
1 teaspoon baking soda

Cream until well blended
1 cup shortening
1 teaspoon vanilla extract
Add gradually, creaming until fluffy after each addition
2 cups firmly packed brown sugar
Add, one at a time, beating thoroughly after each addition
2 eggs

Walnut Wafers and Spritz Cookies

Stir in chopped walnuts. Blend in sifted dry ingredients. Shape into rolls, 1½ in. in diameter. Roll in waxed paper. Chill in refrigerator several hours or overnight.

Lightly grease cookie sheets.

Remove roll from refrigerator and cut into thin slices. Place slices on cookie sheets.

Bake at 400°F 8 to 10 min.
About 8 doz. cookies

SHAPED COOKIES

NUT-FILLED CRESCENTS
(Diós Kifli)

▲ *Base Recipe*

Lightly grease cookie sheets.

For Nut Filling—Mix thoroughly and set aside
2 cups (about ½ lb.) walnuts, ground (page 10)
½ cup sugar
3 egg whites, slightly beaten
2 tablespoons milk

For Dough—Put into a large bowl
3 cups sifted all-purpose flour
Work into flour by pressing against bottom and sides of bowl with a fork
1 cup unsalted butter, chilled and cut in pieces
Add gradually to ingredients in the bowl, mixing thoroughly with a fork, a mixture of
3 egg yolks, slightly beaten
1½ tablespoons cream
2 teaspoons grated lemon peel
(Mixture will be crumbly.) Gather dough into a ball. Turn out onto lightly floured surface. Work with hands, squeezing dough until well blended. With palms of hands, shape dough into a smooth roll. Slice into 48 pieces. (If dough is too soft and sticky to handle, chill for a short time.) Shape pieces into balls.

For Crescents—Lightly sprinkle a small area of working surface with
Confectioners' sugar
Roll one ball at a time into a circle about 1/16 in. thick. Spread dough with 2 teaspoons of the filling. Gently lifting nearest edge, roll; shape into crescent by curving ends of roll slightly. Place crescent on cookie sheet with overlapping edge underneath. In this way, make other crescents, lightly sprinkling confectioners' sugar onto working surface each time. Brush crescents with
Egg, slightly beaten

Bake at 375°F 15 to 20 min., or until lightly browned. Remove to cooling racks.

Just before serving crescents, sprinkle with
2 tablespoons Vanilla Confectioners' Sugar (page 582)
Shake off excess sugar. *4 doz. cookies*

—POPPY SEED CRESCENTS
(Mákos Kifli)

Follow ▲ Recipe. Substitute **Poppy Seed Filling** for Nut Filling.

For Poppy Seed Filling—Combine in a heavy 1½-qt. saucepan **3 cups (about ⅔ lb.) freshly ground poppy seed, 1¼ cups sugar, ¾ cup milk** and **½ cup butter.** Cook over low heat, stirring constantly, about 5 min., or until mixture is slightly thickened. Remove from heat and cool. (If, on standing, filling becomes too thick to spread easily, stir in a small amount of milk.)

SPRITZ COOKIES
(Spritsar)

▲ *Base Recipe*

Generations-old, spritz cookies are traditionally baked in "S" or ring shapes.

Set out cookie sheets.

Measure and set aside
2½ cups sifted all-purpose flour

Cream until softened
1 cup butter
1 teaspoon vanilla extract
Add gradually, creaming until fluffy after each addition
½ cup sugar
Thoroughly beat in, one at a time
2 egg yolks
Add flour in halves, thoroughly blending in after each addition.

Fill a cookie press about two-thirds full with dough. According to manufacturer's directions, form cookies of varied shapes directly onto cookie sheets.

Bake at 350°F 12 to 15 min., or until cookies are golden yellow. With spatula, carefully remove cookies to cooling racks; cool completely.
About 6 doz. cookies

For Variety—(*Jelly*) Before baking make a small depression at center of some round cookies and spoon **¼ to ½ teaspoon jelly** onto centers of cookies. (*Nuts*) Lightly brush slightly **beaten egg white** over unbaked cookies and sprinkle each with about **½ teaspoon finely chopped pistachios.** (*Confectioners' Sugar*) Lightly sift **confectioners' sugar** over baked and cooled cookies. (*Maraschino Cherries*) Press **¼ maraschino cherry** onto center of round cookies before baking. (*Colored Sugar*) Lightly sprinkle unbaked cookies with **red or green colored sugar.** (*Chocolate-Dipped*) Partially melt over simmering water **semisweet candy-making chocolate** or **semisweet chocolate pieces.** Remove from heat and stir until it is melted. Stir in **butter** (1 tablespoon butter for 2 oz. chocolate) until butter is melted and blended in. Immediately coat ends of some cookies by dipping in chocolate mixture. Immediately dip coated ends of some cookies into **chocolate shot.** Set coated cookies on cooling rack over a piece of waxed paper.

—CHOCOLATE SPRITZ COOKIES

Put **6 tablespoons cocoa** into a small bowl. Add gradually, blending until smooth, **¼ cup boiling water.** Set aside to cool. Follow ▲ Recipe. Blend in the cooled cocoa mixture after addition of the egg yolks.

ALMOND SPRITZ COOKIES
(Mandelspritsar)

Set out cookie sheets.

Sift together and set aside
4¾ cups sifted all-purpose flour
½ teaspoon baking powder

Grate (page 10) and set aside
1 cup (about ⅓ lb.) blanched almonds (page 9)

Cream until softened
2 cups butter
½ teaspoon almond extract
Add gradually, creaming until fluffy after each addition
1 cup sugar
Add and beat well
1 egg
Blend in the grated nuts. Mixing well after each addition, blend in dry ingredients in fourths.

Fill a cookie press about two-thirds full with dough. Following manufacturer's directions, form cookies of varied shapes directly onto cookie sheets.

Bake at 350°F 12 to 15 min., or until cookies are golden yellow.

With spatula, carefully remove cookies to cooling racks; cool completely.
About 10 doz. cookies

BUTTER-PECAN COOKIES

What could be more distinctively Southern than butter-rich cookies with nut-sweet pecans!

Set out cookie sheets.

Set out
   ½ cup (about 2 oz.) pecan halves

Sift together and set aside
   2 cups sifted all-purpose flour
   ¼ teaspoon salt

Cream until softened
   1 cup butter
   1½ teaspoons vanilla extract
   ½ teaspoon almond extract
Add gradually, creaming until fluffy after each addition
   1 cup confectioners' sugar
Blending thoroughly after each addition, add dry ingredients in halves to creamed mixture.

Shape dough into 1-in. balls. Place about 2 in. apart on cookie sheets. Using back of spoon or spatula, flatten balls to form cookie rounds.

Blend thoroughly
   2 egg yolks, slightly beaten
   1 tablespoon cream
Brush lightly over tops of cookies. Press one pecan half onto center of each cookie.

Bake at 400°F 10 to 12 min., or until very lightly browned.

Using a spatula, immediately remove cookies to cooling racks; cool completely.
   About 3½ doz. cookies

DREAMS
   ### (Drömmar)

Set out cookie sheets.

Set out
   36 (about 1½ oz.) whole blanched almonds (page 9)

Sift together and set aside
   2 cups sifted all-purpose flour
   1 teaspoon baking powder

Cream until softened
   1 cup butter
   2 teaspoons vanilla extract
Add gradually, creaming until fluffy after each addition
   ¾ cup sugar
Mixing well after each addition, blend in dry ingredients in halves. Shape dough into small

balls about 1 in. in diameter. Place on the cookie sheets. Press one whole almond onto the center of each cookie.

Bake at 325°F 20 to 25 min., or until cookies are golden brown.

Remove to cooling racks to cool completely.
   About 3 doz. cookies

QUEEN'S BISCUITS
   ### (Biscotti di Regina)

Lightly grease two cookie sheets.

Sift together into a bowl
   4 cups sifted all-purpose flour
   1 cup sugar
   1 tablespoon baking powder
   ¼ teaspoon salt
Cut in with pastry blender or two knives until pieces are size of small peas
   1 cup shortening
Stir in to make a soft dough
   2 eggs, slightly beaten
   ½ cup milk (1 tablespoon at a time)
Mix thoroughly.

Break dough into small pieces and roll each piece between palms of hands to form rolls about 1½ in. in length. Flatten rolls slightly, and roll in
   ¼ lb. (about ⅔ to ¾ cup) sesame seed
Place about ¾ in. apart on cookie sheets.

Bake at 375°F 12 to 15 min., or until cookies are lightly browned. Remove to cooling racks.
   About 6 doz. cookies

BERLIN WREATHS I
   ### (Berlinerkranser)

Prepare
   3 Hard-Cooked Eggs (page 133)
While eggs are cooking, cream together until butter is softened
   1 cup butter
   ½ teaspoon vanilla extract
Add gradually, creaming until fluffy after each addition
   ½ cup sugar
Cut the hard-cooked eggs into halves; remove egg yolks to a bowl. Mash them with a fork. Add, one at a time, blending in thoroughly
   2 egg yolks
Add the egg mixture to the creamed mixture and beat thoroughly.

Measure
   2 cups sifted all-purpose flour
Add the sifted flour in halves, beating thoroughly after each addition. Chill dough in refrigerator.

Set out cookie sheets.

Cut off a small amount of dough and roll with hands into a strip about 4 in. long and ¼ in. thick. The ends of the strip should be slightly pointed. Overlap ends about ¼ in., forming a wreath. Brush with
   Egg white, slightly beaten

Sprinkle lightly with
   Sugar
Place cookies on cookie sheets.

Bake at 350°F 10 to 12 min., or until cookies are golden yellow.

With spatula, carefully remove cookies to cooling racks; cool completely.
   About 5 doz. cookies

BERLIN WREATHS II

Lightly grease cookie sheets.

Sift together into a large bowl
   3¾ to 4 cups sifted all-purpose flour
   ½ teaspoon baking soda
   ⅛ teaspoon salt
Cut in with a pastry blender or two knives until pieces are size of small peas
   1 cup butter or margarine
Set aside.

Beat until thick and lemon-colored
   4 egg yolks
Add gradually, beating well after each addition
   1 cup sugar
Blend into the egg mixture
   ½ cup dairy sour cream
   1 teaspoon vanilla or almond extract
Add the sour cream mixture to the flour mixture and mix well. Chill dough until firm enough to handle.

Break off small pieces of dough. Roll with hands on a lightly floured surface into rolls about 6 in. long and ¼ in. thick. Form into wreaths or bowknots, or twist into pretzels. Brush top of each cookie with
   Egg white, slightly beaten
Dip each cookie into
   Crushed loaf sugar

Bake at 350°F about 10 min., or until firm and very lightly browned. Remove to cooling racks.
   About 8 doz. cookies

ALMOND COOKIES I

   ▲ *Base Recipe*

Set out cookie sheets.

Set out
   1 cup (about 5½ oz.) blanched almonds (page 9)
Grate ⅔ cup of the almonds (about 2 cups, grated). Toast (page 10) the remaining almonds and set aside for garnish.

Measure
   1 cup sifted all-purpose flour
Mix flour and grated almonds.

Cream until softened
   ½ cup butter
Add gradually, creaming until fluffy after each addition
   ½ cup firmly packed light brown sugar
Mixing until well blended after each addition,

add dry ingredients in fourths. Wrap tightly in waxed paper or moisture-vaporproof material and chill in refrigerator until easy to handle.

Shape dough into 1-in. balls. Place balls on cookie sheet about 2 in. apart and flatten each until about ½ in. thick. Press a toasted almond onto top of each cookie.

Bake at 325°F 10 to 15 min., or until light golden brown.

Using a spatula, immediately remove cookies to cooling racks; cool completely.

About 2½ doz. cookies

—ALMOND COOKIES II

Follow ▲ Recipe. Substitute **very finely chopped almonds** for grated almonds and **granulated sugar** for brown sugar.

SAND TARTS
(Sandbakkelse)

Set out sandbakkelse molds and cookie sheets.

Measure and set aside
    2 cups sifted all-purpose flour

Chop *very finely* and set aside
    ⅓ cup (about 2 oz.) blanched almonds (page 9)

Cream until softened
    1 cup butter
    ¼ teaspoon almond extract
Add gradually, creaming just until blended
    ¾ cup sugar
Beat in
    1 egg
Add the flour in halves, blending well after each addition. Blend in the chopped almonds. Chill dough in refrigerator.

Remove a portion of the dough from refrigerator and return remaining dough to continue

chilling. Place about 2 teaspoons dough in each mold. Using the thumb, firmly press dough into each mold, coating the bottom and sides evenly. Place molds on the cookie sheets. Repeat with the remaining dough.

Bake at 375°F 6 to 8 min., or until sand tarts are golden brown.

Immediately invert molds onto a smooth surface. Cool slightly. To remove sand tart from mold, hold the mold in the hand and tap lightly but sharply with the back of a spoon. Remove pan and place sand tarts on a smooth surface to cool completely.

Serve sand tarts inverted. Or turn sand tarts right side up and fill with **jam, jelly,** or **whipped cream.**

About 5 doz. cookies

REGAL ALMOND TARTLETS

▲ Base Recipe

Muffin pans having 1¾x1-in. wells will be needed (about 24 wells).

For Miniature Tart Shells—Prepare
    Pastry for 2-Crust Pie (page 485)
Using scalloped cookie cutter, cut pastry about 1 in. larger than overall size of well. Gently fit pastry into wells, reserving remaining pastry. Prick entire surface with fork.

Bake at 450°F 10 to 12 min., or until delicately browned. Cool in muffin pans on cooling racks.

For Filling—Meanwhile, sift together and set aside
    ½ cup sugar
    2 tablespoons sifted all-purpose flour

Mix together and set aside
    1¼ cups (about 7 oz.) ground almonds (page 10)
    2 tablespoons orange juice
    ½ teaspoon almond extract

Meanwhile, beat until thick and piled softly
    2 eggs
Gradually add sugar-flour mixture, beating well after each addition. Blend in
    2½ tablespoons softened butter or margarine
Thoroughly blend in almond mixture.

Spread over bottom of each baked pastry shell
    ½ teaspoon raspberry jelly
Fill each tart shell three-fourths full with filling mixture.

From reserved pastry, cut small cross-strips with sharp knife and place on each tart.

Bake at 350°F about 15 min., or until delicately browned. Cool slightly before removing from muffin wells. Cool on cooling racks.

2 doz. tarts

—HAZELNUT TARTLETS

Follow ▲ Recipe. Substitute **1¼ cups (about 5 oz.) ground hazelnuts** for almonds. Omit almond extract.

FINNISH COFFEE FINGERS
(Mördegspinnar)

Set out cookie sheets.

Set out a mixture of
    ½ cup very finely chopped blanched almonds (page 9)
    3 tablespoons sugar

Measure and set aside
    1¼ cups sifted all-purpose flour

Cream until softened
    ½ cup butter
    1 teaspoon almond extract
Add gradually, creaming until fluffy after each addition
    2 tablespoons sugar
Add the flour in fourths, thoroughly blending in after each addition. Chill in refrigerator.

Cut off small pieces of chilled dough and roll with the hands about ¼ in. thick and 2½ in. long to resemble fingers. Brush cookies with
    Egg white, slightly beaten
Roll fingers in the almond mixture. Carefully place cookies on the cookie sheets.

Bake at 350°F 10 to 12 min., or until cookies are golden yellow.

With a spatula, carefully remove cookies to cooling racks to cool completely.

About 5 doz. cookies

ANISE ALMOND CRISPS
(Biscotti)

These unique slices make a perfect duo with coffee for a morning brunch or an afternoon cup of tea.

Set out a cookie sheet.

Sift together and set aside
    3½ cups sifted all-purpose flour
    1 tablespoon baking powder
    ½ teaspoon salt

Assorted Scandinavian Cookies

Coffee Butter Cookies

Chop finely and set aside

    1 cup almonds (blanched or unblanched)

Cream until butter is softened

    ½ cup butter or margarine
    2 or 3 drops anise oil (or 1 teaspoon anise extract)

Add gradually, beating only until well mixed

    1 cup sugar

Add one at a time, beating well after each addition

    3 eggs

Stir in the dry ingredients and the nuts. Turn dough onto a floured surface and knead only until smooth. (Avoid overhandling of dough.) Divide into halves and shape into two long narrow rolls 1½ in. in diameter. Place side by side on cookie sheet.

Bake at 350°F about 30 min., or until loaves are firm to the touch.

Remove from oven and cool slightly. While still warm cut crosswise into ¾-in. slices. Arrange slices, cut side down, on cookie sheet and return to oven 10 min. to toast slightly. If a golden brown surface is desired, brush slices lightly with **melted butter** about 5 min. before removing from oven. Turn slices once to brown both sides. Sift **confectioners' sugar** over the slices while warm, turning to coat both sides. When completely cooled, store in a tightly covered container. *3 doz. cookies*

ANISE TEA COOKIES

Set out a cookie sheet.

Sift together into a mixing bowl

    2½ cups sifted all-purpose flour
    ½ teaspoon salt

Chop finely

    ¼ cup walnuts, pecans, or other nuts

Add to dry ingredients along with

    1 tablespoon anise seed
    ⅔ cup cooking or salad oil

Beat only until blended.

Combine

    ¾ cup confectioners' sugar
    2 tablespoons orange juice
    1 teaspoon vanilla extract

Add to mixture in bowl and mix only until blended. (Mixture will be rather dry and crumbly.) Shape with hands into small rolls 2 in. long and ¾ in. in diameter. Arrange on cookie sheet. If desired, curve each roll to form a crescent shape.

Bake at 350° F 20 to 25 min., or until lightly browned.

Remove from oven and while warm, roll cookies in **confectioners' sugar**.

About 2½ doz. cookies

BROWN SUGAR COOKIES
(Brunekager)

Set out cookie sheets.

Measure and set aside

    2 cups sifted all-purpose flour

Cream until softened

    1 cup butter

Add gradually, creaming until fluffy after each addition

    ¾ cup firmly packed brown sugar

Blend in thoroughly

    1 egg yolk

Add the flour in fourths, mixing thoroughly after each addition. Shape dough into balls about ½ to ¾ in. thick. Place about 2 in. apart on the cookie sheets. Using the back of a fork, flatten cookies with crisscross marks.

Set out

    Pecan or walnut halves

Press a nut half onto the top of each cookie.

Bake at 375°F 8 to 10 min.

Cool cookies about 2 min. on cookie sheets. With spatula, remove cookies to cooling racks to cool completely. *6 to 7 doz. cookies*

COFFEE BUTTER COOKIES

A twin coffee treat—rich coffee-flavored cookies served with iced coffee!

Set out cookie sheets.

Sift together and set aside

    1 cup sifted all-purpose flour
    ½ cup confectioners' sugar
    ½ cup cornstarch
    1 tablespoon instant powdered coffee
    ⅛ teaspoon salt

Cream until softened

    1 cup butter
    ¼ teaspoon vanilla extract

Mixing until well blended after each addition, add dry ingredients in fourths to creamed mixture. Chill in refrigerator about 1 hr.

Shape dough into balls about 1 in. in diameter. Place about 1½ in. apart on the cookie sheets. With a lightly floured fork, slightly flatten cookies, forming a crisscross pattern.

Bake at 300°F 20 to 25 min.

Set cookie sheets on cooling racks about 10 min. Carefully remove cookies to racks to cool.

About 2½ doz. cookies

FOUR-STRIPERS

Lightly grease cookie sheets.

Sift together and set aside

    1¼ cups sifted flour
    ¾ teaspoon baking soda
    ½ teaspoon baking powder
    ½ teaspoon salt

Cream until thoroughly blended

    ½ cup shortening
    ½ cup peanut butter
    2 teaspoons vanilla extract

Add gradually, creaming until fluffy after each addition

    1 cup firmly packed brown sugar

Beat in vigorously

    1 egg

Blend in dry ingredients in fourths. Mix well after each addition. Chill dough in refrigerator until firm. Pinch off small pieces and roll into balls. Place on cookie sheets. Melt (page 10)

    ½ pkg. (3 oz.) semisweet chocolate pieces

Dip tines of fork into melted chocolate and flatten each cookie with chocolate-dipped fork.

Bake at 350°F 10 to 12 min. Remove to cooling racks. *4 to 5 doz. cookies*

THIMBLE COOKIES

Lightly grease two large cookie sheets.

Chop finely and set aside

    1½ cups nuts

Sift together and set aside

    2¼ cups sifted all-purpose flour
    1½ teaspoons baking powder
    ½ teaspoon salt

Cream until butter is softened

    ¾ cup butter or margarine
    1 teaspoon vanilla extract

Add gradually in order, beating until fluffy after each addition

    ⅔ cup firmly packed brown sugar
    ⅓ cup dark corn syrup

Add, beating well after each addition

    1 egg
    1 egg yolk

Beat in dry ingredients alternately with

    1 tablespoon milk

Beat only until well mixed. (Dough will be

rather soft). Refrigerate the dough until firm enough to handle, overnight if necessary.

Shape into 1-in. balls, keeping hands moist to prevent sticking.

Combine in a small bowl
1 egg white, slightly beaten
2 tablespoons water
Dip balls into mixture, then roll in the chopped nuts. Place 1 in. apart on cookie sheets.

Bake at 375°F 5 min. Remove from oven. Working quickly, make a small depression in top of each cookie and fill with
Jam or jelly (about ¼ teaspoon in each)
Return to oven and bake cookies about 10 min. longer.

When done, remove cookies to cooling racks immediately. *About 6 doz. cookies*

CARAMEL PUDDING COOKIES

▲ *Base Recipe*

Line with paper cups or lightly grease bottoms of 3 doz. small (about 1¾-in.) muffin-pan wells.

Melt and set aside to cool
3 tablespoons butter or margarine

Finely chop and set aside
1 cup (3¾ oz.) pecans

Sift together and set aside
⅓ cup sifted all-purpose flour
¼ teaspoon baking soda
¼ teaspoon salt

Beat with hand rotary or electric beater until thick and piled softly
2 eggs
¼ cup firmly packed brown sugar
¼ cup sugar
Blend in cooled butter and
2 tablespoons milk
1 teaspoon vanilla extract
Add dry ingredients and blend in quickly.

Assorted German Cookies

Stir in chopped pecans. Fill paper cups or muffin wells one-half full.

Bake at 375°F 10 to 12 min., or until tops spring back when touched lightly. Immediately remove from muffin wells and set on cooling racks.

When cooled, decorate tops with
Chocolate Butter Frosting (page 479)
Sprinkle with **finely chopped pistachio nuts.**
3 doz. cookies

—CHOCOLATE PECAN MINIATURES

Follow ▲ Recipe. Decrease butter or margarine to 2 tablespoons. Melt **1 oz. (1 sq.) unsweetened chocolate** with butter.

HAZELNUT BALLS
(Haselnuss Bällchen)

Lightly grease cookie sheets.

Grate (page 10) and set aside
1½ cups (about 6 oz.) hazelnuts

Beat until frothy
2 egg whites
Add about 2 tablespoons at a time, beating well after each addition
1 cup sugar
Continue beating the meringue until stiff peaks are formed.

Fold the hazelnuts into the meringue mixture. Shape dough into balls about ½ in. in diameter. Place on the cookie sheets.

Bake at 300°F 25 min.

With a spatula, carefully remove cookies from cookie sheets to cooling racks.
About 4 doz. cookies

COCONUT CLASSICS

Finely chop in electric blender (page 11) and set aside
3½ cups moist shredded coconut

Sift together and set aside
2 cups sifted all-purpose flour
½ teaspoon baking soda

Cream until softened
1 cup butter or margarine
½ teaspoon vanilla extract
Add gradually, creaming until fluffy after each addition
1 cup sugar
Add and beat thoroughly
1 egg
Blend in 2 cups of the chopped coconut. Mix thoroughly. Stir in dry ingredients. Knead lightly with fingertips 5 to 10 times or until mixture holds together.

Spread remaining coconut onto waxed paper. Form dough into 6 rolls about 1 in. in diameter. Coat rolls with the coconut. Wrap in waxed paper and chill in refrigerator for at least 3 hrs.

Meanwhile, measure and set aside
1½ cups (6 oz.) pecan halves

Lightly grease cookie sheets.

With sharp knife, slice crosswise into ½-in. slices. Place on cookie sheets ¾ in. apart.

Mix and brush cookie tops with
1 egg yolk
1 tablespoon cream
Press a pecan half on top of each cookie.

Bake at 325°F about 20 min., or until very lightly browned. Remove to cooling racks.

Heat until warm
½ cup light corn syrup
Glaze pecan and cookie by brushing with warm corn syrup. *About 10 doz. cookies*

CRACKLE-TOP MOLASSES COOKIES

Set out cookie sheets.

Melt, pour into bowl and set aside to cool slightly
¾ cup shortening

Sift together and set aside
2¼ cups sifted all-purpose flour
2 teaspoons baking soda
2 teaspoons instant powdered coffee
1 teaspoon cinnamon
½ teaspoon salt
½ teaspoon ginger
¼ teaspoon cloves

Beat into cooled shortening, in order
1 cup firmly packed brown sugar
¼ cup molasses
1 egg, well beaten
Add dry ingredients, beating only until well blended.

Shape into 1-in. balls. Place balls about 2 in. apart on cookie sheets.

Bake at 375°F 10 to 12 min. Remove to cooling racks to cool. *About 5 doz. cookies*

DAINTY TEA COOKIES

Lightly grease cookie sheets.

Finely chop and set aside
  1¼ cups (about 4¾ oz.) pecans

Sift together and set aside
  2½ cups sifted all-purpose flour
  2¼ teaspoons cinnamon
  1½ teaspoons baking powder

Cream until butter is softened
  1 cup butter or margarine
  1½ teaspoons vanilla extract

Add gradually, creaming until fluffy after each addition
  1½ cups sugar

Add one at a time, beating well after each addition
  3 egg yolks

Add the sifted dry ingredients to the creamed mixture and mix until well blended.

Shape dough into ¾-in. balls. Roll balls in the chopped pecans. Place balls about 2 in. apart on cookie sheets.

Bake at 350°F 10 to 12 min. Remove to cooling racks.   *6 doz. cookies*

GINGERSNAPS

Lightly grease cookie sheets.

Sift together and set aside
  2 cups sifted all-purpose flour
  2 teaspoons baking soda
  ½ teaspoon salt
  1 teaspoon cinnamon
  1 teaspoon ginger
  ½ teaspoon cloves

Cream until softened
  ¾ cup shortening

Add gradually, creaming until fluffy after each addition
  1 cup sugar

Add and beat thoroughly
  1 egg, well beaten

Blend in
  ¼ cup molasses

Mixing until well blended after each addition, add dry ingredients in halves to creamed mixture

Form dough into 1-in. balls and roll in **sugar.** Place balls about 3 in. apart on the cookie sheets.

Bake at 350°F 12 to 15 min. Transfer from cookie sheets to cooling racks.
                    About 5 doz. cookies

PEANUT BUTTER COOKIES

Set out two cookie sheets.

Sift together and set aside
  1⅔ cups sifted all-purpose flour
  1½ teaspoons baking powder
  ¼ teaspoon salt

Beat together until blended
  ½ cup butter or margarine
  ½ cup creamy or chunk-style peanut butter
  1 teaspoon vanilla extract

Add gradually, beating until fluffy after each addition
  ½ cup firmly packed brown sugar

Beat in until well blended
  ⅓ cup dark corn syrup

Add, beating until blended
  1 egg, well beaten

Mix in the dry ingredients, beating only until blended. (Do not overbeat.)

Shape dough into 1-in. balls and place about 2 in. apart on cookie sheets; flatten balls slightly using tines of a fork. Top with
  Peanut butter (about ½ teaspoon for each ball)

Bake at 350°F 15 to 17 min., or until lightly browned. Remove to cooling racks.
                    About 3½ doz. cookies

Note: The flavor improves with storage.

MADELEINES
(Madeleines de Commercy)

Butter and lightly flour 12 madeleine molds (designed to give shell-shape cakes).

Melt and set aside to cool
  ¼ cup butter

Sift together
  ½ cup sifted all-purpose flour
  Few grains salt

Beat until thick and piled softly
  2 eggs
  ¼ cup sugar
  1 teaspoon lemon juice, vanilla extract or brandy
  ½ to 1 teaspoon grated lemon peel

Sift dry ingredients over mixture and slowly fold in until just blended. Gradually add cooled butter and continue folding until blended. Fill pans two-thirds full.

Bake at 325°F about 15 min., or until madeleines are a delicate brown. Cake is done if top springs back when lightly touched at center. Set on cooling rack to cool 5 min. Remove from molds and invert on cooling rack until cool.
                    About 30 Madeleines

LADYFINGERS

Dainty double ladyfingers are intriguing on the tea table or when they are served with a frozen dessert.

Line cookie sheets with unglazed paper.

To make cardboard patterns, cut 4x1-in. rectangle for large ladyfingers, and 2½x¾-in. rectangle for small ones. Round corners of rectangles, and gradually taper at center to ¾-in. width for large and ½-in. width for small fingers. Trace patterns onto unglazed paper.

Sift together and set aside
  ⅓ cup sifted cake flour
  ⅛ teaspoon salt

Combine and beat with hand rotary or electric beater until thick and lemon-colored
  2 egg yolks
  ½ cup confectioners' sugar

Fold dry ingredients into egg yolk-sugar mixture.

Beat until rounded peaks are formed and egg whites do not slide when bowl is partially inverted
  2 egg whites

Fold the egg whites into the egg yolk-flour mixture with
  ½ teaspoon vanilla extract

Force mixture through pastry bag onto prepared cookie sheets, using guide lines to shape ladyfingers. Use decorating tube No. 10 for small ladyfingers and pastry bag coupling for large ladyfingers.

Sprinkle lightly with confectioners' sugar.

Bake at 325°F for 12 to 18 min., or until delicately browned.

With spatula, remove at once to cooling rack.
                About 2 doz. large Ladyfingers,
                or 3 doz. small Ladyfingers

Note: For double ladyfingers, brush bottom-sides of baked fingers with slightly beaten egg white and press together in pairs.

ROLLED COOKIES

BIG FELLOW SUGAR COOKIES

  ▲ *Base Recipe*

Watch eyes light up when your cookie-jar raiders discover these old favorites.

Sift together and set aside
  2 cups sifted all-purpose flour
  1 teaspoon baking powder
  ½ teaspoon salt

Cream until softened
  ⅔ cup butter or margarine
  1 teaspoon vanilla extract

Add gradually, creaming until fluffy after each addition
  ¾ cup sugar

Add in halves, beating thoroughly after each addition
  1 egg, well beaten

Gradually stir in dry ingredients and blend well. Chill thoroughly in refrigerator.

Lightly grease cookie sheets.

Roll dough ⅛ in. thick on lightly floured surface. Cut dough with a floured large cookie cutter. Sprinkle tops of cookies with **sugar**. Place cookies on cookie sheets.

Bake at 375°F 10 to 12 min. Remove immediately to rack to cool.   *1½ doz. large cookies*

—FIG BARS

Follow ▲ Recipe. Mix in a saucepan **½ cup sugar** and **2 tablespoons all-purpose flour**. Gradually blend in **¾ cup water** and **2 tablespoons lemon juice**. Heat to boiling. Stir in **1 cup chopped dried figs** (approximately ⅓ lb.) and **2 teaspoons grated lemon peel**. Cook over low heat stirring occasionally until thickened (5 min.). Divide chilled dough into halves. Roll each into a rectangle ⅛ in. thick. Cut into long strips 3 in. wide. Spread half of each strip lengthwise with fig filling and cover with remaining half. Pinch edges together with fork. Place on cookie sheets and bake about 20 min. at 350°F. Cut strips immediately into 2-in. lengths.   *2 doz. Fig Bars*

—GINGER COOKIES

Follow ▲ Recipe. Reduce baking powder to ½ teaspoon. Sift **¼ teaspoon baking soda**, **1½ teaspoons ginger**, **½ teaspoon cinnamon** and **¼ teaspoon allspice** with flour mixture. Decrease sugar to ½ cup and blend **6 tablespoons molasses** into creamed mixture. Omit vanilla extract.

—BUTTERSCOTCH COOKIES

Follow ▲ Recipe. Reduce sugar to ¼ cup. Add **½ cup firmly packed brown sugar**. Increase shortening 2 tablespoons.

—SPICED SUGAR COOKIES

Follow ▲ Recipe. Sift ½ **teaspoon cinnamon**,

¼ **teaspoon mace** and ¼ **teaspoon nutmeg** with flour.

—CHOCOLATE SUGAR COOKIES

Follow ▲ Recipe. Melt (page 10) **2 oz. (2 sq.) unsweetened chocolate** and set aside to cool. Blend in after addition of egg.

—LEMON OR ORANGE SUGAR COOKIES

Follow ▲ Recipe. Substitute **1½ teaspoons lemon or orange juice** for vanilla extract. Add **1 tablespoon grated lemon peel** or **2 tablespoons grated orange peel**.

—COCONUT SUGAR COOKIES

Follow ▲ Recipe. Blend in **1 cup (4 oz.) moist shredded coconut** after addition of dry ingredients.

DECORATED SUGAR COOKIES

Set out cookie sheets and cookie cutters.

Sift together and set aside
   2½ cups sifted all-purpose flour
   ¼ teaspoon baking powder
   ¼ teaspoon salt

Cream until butter is softened
   1 cup butter or margarine
   1¼ teaspoons vanilla extract
Add gradually, creaming until fluffy after each addition
   1 cup confectioners' sugar
Mixing until well blended after each addition, add dry ingredients in fourths to creamed mixture.

Put one third of the dough on a lightly floured surface. Roll about ¼ in. thick. Cut out cookies with lightly floured cookie cutters. Transfer cookies to cookie sheets. Repeat for remaining dough. Set aside.

Beat together until blended
   1 egg yolk
   2 teaspoons cream
Brush over cookies. Sprinkle with
   Sugar, colored sugar, chocolate sprinkles or finely chopped nuts

Bake at 350°F 12 to 15 min. With spatula remove cookies to cooling racks.
          4 to 5 doz. cookies

ALMOND WREATHS
(Mandelkränzchen)

Set out cookie sheets.

Finely chop and set aside
   1 cup (5½ oz.) blanched almonds

Measure and set aside
   2 cups sifted all-purpose flour

Cream until softened
   ¾ cup butter

Add gradually, creaming until fluffy after each addition
   ¼ cup sugar
Beat in thoroughly
   1 egg
Add the flour in fourths, blending well after each addition. Chill dough in refrigerator several hours.

Remove one half the dough from refrigerator and turn onto a lightly floured surface. Roll ¼ in. thick. Cut rounds with a lightly floured 1¾-in. round cookie cutter. Using a lightly floured ¾-in. round cookie cutter, cut out centers of the cookies. Brush cookies lightly with
   Egg yolk, slightly beaten

Sprinkle cookies with the chopped almonds. Carefully transfer to the cookie sheets.

Bake at 350°F 10 to 15 min.

With a spatula, carefully remove cookies to cooling racks.

Repeat above procedure for remainder of dough.   *About 6 doz. cookies*

DANISH COOKIES
(Smaakager)

Set out cookie sheets.

Sift together and set aside
   2 cups sifted all-purpose flour
   ¼ teaspoon hartshorn (ammonium carbonate which is obtainable at any drugstore)

Cream until softened
   ¾ cup butter
Add gradually, creaming until fluffy after each addition
   ½ cup sugar
Beat in thoroughly
   1 egg yolk
Add the dry ingredients in fourths, mixing thoroughly after each addition. Set aside.

Meanwhile, prepare a meringue by beating until frothy
   1 egg white
   ⅛ teaspoon salt
Add gradually, beating well after each addition
   1¼ cups confectioners' sugar
Continue beating until very stiff peaks are formed. Cut dough into halves and set one half aside. Roll one half of the dough ⅛ in. thick on a lightly floured surface. Using a sharp knife, cut strips 1 in. wide. Cut each strip into diamond-shaped pieces by making diagonal cuts 1 in. apart. Place cookies on the cookie sheets and lightly spread cookies with the meringue. Repeat with the second half of the dough.

Bake at 375°F 10 min., or until lightly browned.

Cool cookies on cookie sheets about 2 min. Using a spatula, carefully remove cookies to cooling racks to cool completely.
          About 6 doz. cookies

Assorted Hungarian Cookies

ALMOND STICKS
(Mandulás Rud)

▲ *Base Recipe*

Lightly grease cookie sheets.

Grate (page 10) and set aside
¾ cup (about ¼ lb.) almonds

Put into bowl and cream until softened
½ cup unsalted butter

Add gradually to the butter, creaming until fluffy after each addition
1 cup confectioners' sugar

Add to the butter mixture, stirring just until the ingredients are blended, a mixture of the almonds and
1 cup sifted all-purpose flour

Gather dough into a ball. Turn dough out onto lightly floured surface and roll into a rectangle ½ in. thick, keeping edges straight. Cut dough into strips 2½x½-in. and place strips 1 in. apart onto cookie sheets.

Bake at 350°F 20 to 25 min., or until cookies are lightly browned. Immediately remove to cooling racks. When cooled, roll in
½ cup Vanilla Confectioners' Sugar (page 582)

About 3 doz. cookies

—HAZELNUT STICKS
(Mogyorós Rud)

Follow ▲ Recipe. Substitute **1 cup plus 2 tablespoons (about 5 oz.) hazelnuts** (about 2 cups, grated) for almonds.

MEDALLION COOKIES
(Medaljakager)

Set out cookie sheets.

Prepare and chill
Vanilla Cream Filling (page 482)

Measure and set aside
4½ cups sifted all-purpose flour

Cream until softened
2 cups butter

Add gradually, creaming just until blended
¾ cup plus 2 tablespoons confectioners' sugar

Beat in thoroughly
1 egg

Add the flour in fourths, blending thoroughly after each addition. Set aside for 20 min. (not in refrigerator).

Place one third of the dough on a lightly floured surface. Roll about ¼ in. thick. Cut out cookies with a lightly floured 2-in. round cookie cutter. Place cookies on cookie sheets. Repeat for remaining dough.

Bake at 375°F about 10 min., or until cookies are lightly browned at edges.
With spatula, carefully remove cookies to cooling racks. Cool completely.

Meanwhile, combine
1 cup confectioners' sugar
½ teaspoon vanilla extract
Add
Milk or cream (about 1 tablespoon or enough to make a frosting that will hold its shape)

When cookies are cooled completely, spoon about ¾ teaspoon of the filling onto one half the cookies. Top with the remaining cookies. Spread filled cookies with the confectioners' sugar mixture.

Cookies should be filled shortly before ready to serve. Fill only as many as will be needed. Refrigerate filled cookies if they are to be kept for any length of time before serving.

About 5 doz. cookies

DANISH SADDLE COOKIES
(Krumkager)

Set out cookie sheets. Wash and scrub a wooden stick about 1 in. in diameter and 12 to 18 in. long. Dry it thoroughly.

Mix and set aside
½ cup finely chopped blanched almonds (page 9)
¼ cup sugar

Measure and set aside
2¼ cups sifted all-purpose flour

Cream until softened
1 cup butter

Add gradually, creaming until fluffy after each addition
1 cup plus 2 tablespoons sugar

Add the flour in fourths, mixing well after each addition.

Mix and set aside
2 egg yolks, beaten
1 tablespoon water

Place a small amount of dough at one time on a lightly floured surface and roll about ¼ in. thick. Cut into rectangles 3x1½-in. Place only

6 cookies at one time on the cookie sheet. Brush tops of cookies with the egg-yolk mixture and sprinkle cookies with the almond-sugar mixture.

Bake at 375°F 8 to 10 min., or until delicately browned.

Cool cookies slightly. Using a spatula, quickly remove cookies from cookie sheet and bend lengthwise over the stick. Cool (all six at one time) on stick; carefully remove cookies from the wooden stick. Repeat procedure until all of remaining dough is baked.

About 7 doz. cookies

LINZER WREATH COOKIES
(Linczi Koszorúk)

Lightly grease cookie sheets.

Mix and set aside
¼ cup (about 1 oz.) finely chopped walnuts
¼ cup sugar

Sift together into a large bowl
2 cups sifted all-purpose flour
½ cup confectioners' sugar
¼ teaspoon baking soda

Work into the dry ingredients by pressing against bottom and sides of bowl with a fork
½ cup unsalted butter, chilled and cut in pieces

Gradually add to the ingredients in the bowl, mixing with a fork after each addition, a mixture of
2 egg yolks, slightly beaten
¼ teaspoon vanilla extract
¼ teaspoon grated lemon peel

(Mixture will be crumbly.) Gather dough into a ball. Turn dough out onto lightly floured surface. Work with hands, squeezing dough until well blended. Shape into smooth ball with palms of hands. If dough becomes too soft, chill slightly in refrigerator.

Roll dough ⅛ to ¼ in. thick. With lightly floured 2-in. scalloped cookie cutter, cut dough into rounds. Place one half of the rounds onto cookie sheets. Using a thimble dipped in flour, cut ½-in. holes in centers of remaining rounds, forming rings. Brush all the rounds and rings with
Egg, slightly beaten

Dip top surface of rings into the nut-sugar mixture.

Place rings, coated-side up, on cookie sheets (not on top of cookie rounds).

Bake at 350°F 15 to 20 min., or until lightly browned. Remove cookies to cooling racks.

Set out
¼ cup thick jam, such as apricot or strawberry

Spread ½ to ¾ teaspoon of the jam onto each plain cookie round. Top each with a nut-topped cookie ring. Sprinkle onto cookies
2 tablespoons confectioners' sugar

About 1½ doz. cookies

602

LOVE LETTERS
(Szerelmes Levél)

Love Letters are an unusually rich pastry specialty. Tender pastry squares become "letters," each with a cinnamon-nut surprise sealed inside.

Lightly grease baking sheets.

For Dough—Sift together into a large bowl
2 cups sifted all-purpose flour
2 tablespoons sugar
¼ teaspoon salt
Work into dry ingredients by pressing against bottom and sides of bowl with a fork
¾ cup butter, chilled and cut in pieces
Add gradually to butter-flour mixture, blending ingredients with a fork
4 egg yolks, slightly beaten
(Mixture will be crumbly.) Gather dough into a ball. Turn out onto lightly floured surface. Work with hands, squeezing dough until well blended. Shape into smooth ball with palms of hands. Divide dough into halves; wrap in waxed paper and place in refrigerator for about 1 hr. Shape dough in a very cool kitchen.

After 45 min., prepare filling.

For Filling—Mix and set aside
½ cup (about 2 oz.) coarsely chopped walnuts
1 teaspoon grated lemon peel

Beat until frothy
2 egg whites
Add gradually to egg whites, beating well after each addition, a mixture of
¼ cup sugar
½ teaspoon cinnamon
Beat until very stiff peaks are formed. Gently fold nut mixture into the egg whites.

To Form Love Letters—Remove one half of dough from refrigerator. Place dough on lightly floured surface and roll into rectangle ⅟₁₆ in. thick. Work quickly to prevent dough from becoming too soft. With knife or spatula, gently loosen dough from board wherever sticking occurs; lift dough slightly and sprinkle flour underneath. Trim off uneven edges of rectangle. Gather trimmings into a ball; wrap in waxed paper and place in refrigerator.

Cut rectangle into 3-in. squares. Place about 2 teaspoons of the filling onto center of each square. To make "letters," bring opposite corners together, overlapping slightly at center. Repeat with other two corners. Place on baking sheet. In this way, continue to make Love Letters and place 1 in. apart on baking sheet. Brush Love Letters with
Egg, slightly beaten

Bake at 350°F 20 to 30 min., or until lightly browned. Carefully remove Love Letters from baking sheets to cooling racks.

When cooled, sift over them a mixture of
2 to 3 tablespoons confectioners' sugar
½ to 1 teaspoon cinnamon

About 2½ doz. Love Letters

FLAKY LAYERS
(Blätterteig Pastetchen)

Luscious cookies that separate into layer upon layer of tender, leaflike flakes. One cookie calls for more. For best results, be very sure all the ingredients are thoroughly chilled.

Wash and scrub with a vegetable brush
2 small (about ½ lb.) potatoes
Cook (page 322) about 30 min., or until tender when pierced with a fork. Drain. Dry potatoes by shaking pan over low heat. Set potatoes aside to cool completely.

Meanwhile, sift together into a bowl
2 cups sifted all-purpose flour
¼ cup confectioners' sugar
Cover tightly and set in refrigerator to chill.

Peel cold potatoes and force through a sieve or food mill. Measure 1 cup of the sieved potato. Remove flour mixture from refrigerator and add potato. Using a fork, gently mix together. Cut in with pastry blender or two knives until pieces are size of small peas
1 cup firm butter
Sprinkle gradually over mixture, a few drops at a time.
1 teaspoon vanilla extract
Mix lightly with a fork after each addition. Dough should be crumbly. Shape into a ball, wrap in waxed paper, and chill in refrigerator several hours.

Set out two cookie sheets.

Remove dough from refrigerator and divide into two balls. Return one ball to refrigerator. Put other ball on a lightly floured surface. Roll dough ¼ in. thick. Cut out rounds with a cookie cutter 1¾ in. in diameter. Using a cookie cutter ¾ in. in diameter, cut out centers from one half of the cookie rounds so that a ring shape is formed. Place rounds, rings, and centers on one of the cookie sheets. Bake at 400°F 10 to 15 min.

With spatula, remove cookies to cooling racks. Cool completely.

Repeat above procedure for remainder of dough, using second cookie sheet.

When all the cookies are cooled, set out
Currant jelly (or another jelly)
Spread jelly thinly on cookie rounds. Top with rings. Fill centers of rings with a small amount of jelly. Top with centers.

About 2 doz. cookies

FROSTED ALMOND LEAF COOKIES

Unique, intriguing, the conversation piece of the cookie assortment—a crisp, thin leaf with a flavor combination of almond and chocolate.

Generously grease cookie sheets.

For Cookies—Sift together and set aside
1¼ cups sifted all-purpose flour
1 cup confectioners' sugar
¼ teaspoon salt

Measure and force a little at a time through a sieve into a bowl
¾ cup (6 oz.) almond paste
Add gradually and work in with back of wooden spoon
3 tablespoons cold water
⅛ teaspoon almond extract
Mix in
1 egg white, unbeaten
Mixing until blended, add dry ingredients in fourths to almond paste mixture.

Turn out onto a pastry cloth sprinkled with
Sifted confectioners' sugar
Roll dough about ⅛ in. thick. Cut out cookies with leaf-shaped cookie cutter or with sharp knife around waxed paper pattern. (Leaf should be 4½x2½ in.) With a spatula, remove to cookie sheets.

Bake at 350°F 5 to 6 min., or until cookies are delicately browned.

With a spatula, immediately remove cookies to cooling rack; cool completely.

Meanwhile, prepare Chocolate Frosting.

For Chocolate Frosting—Melt (page 10)
1 oz. (1 sq.) unsweetened chocolate
Remove from simmering water; add and mix in thoroughly
¾ cup confectioners' sugar
1 tablespoon cream
2 teaspoons boiling water
1 teaspoon dark corn syrup
1 teaspoon butter
Place over low heat and stir until butter melts. Remove from heat and stir in
½ teaspoon vanilla extract

Spread thinly on leaf cookies. Let frosting partially set and with the point of a knife mark veins in leaves. If necessary, place in refrigerator just long enough to set chocolate.

About 2½ doz. frosted cookies

SHORT'NIN' BREAD

It's no wonder "Mammy's little baby" loved these delectably rich and tender cookies!

Set out cookie sheets.

Press through a sieve
1 cup firmly packed light brown sugar
Mix thoroughly with
4 cups sifted all-purpose flour
Add and work in until a smooth dough is formed
1 lb. softened butter
Turn onto a lightly floured surface and pat to ½-in. thickness. (If necessary, chill dough for easier handling.) Cut into desired shapes and transfer to cookie sheets.

Bake at 325°F about 25 min., until very delicately browned.

Remove sheets to cooling racks 5 min. before transferring cookies to racks to cool thoroughly.
3 to 4 doz. cookies, depending on size and shape

SWEET CHOCOLATE COOKIES

Lightly grease cookie sheets.

Grate (page 10)
¾ cup unblanched almonds (about 2 cups, grated)

Sift together into a bowl
1¾ cups sifted all-purpose flour
¾ teaspoon baking powder
½ teaspoon cinnamon
¼ teaspoon cloves
⅛ teaspoon nutmeg
¼ teaspoon salt
Mix the grated almonds with the dry ingredients and set aside.

Melt (page 10) and set aside to cool
4½ oz. sweet chocolate

Cream together in a bowl until thoroughly blended
½ cup butter or margarine
1½ teaspoons grated lemon peel
2 teaspoons lemon juice
Add gradually, creaming until fluffy after each addition
½ cup sugar
Add and beat thoroughly
1 egg
Blend in the cooled chocolate. Beating until well blended after each addition, add dry ingredients in fourths. Cover and refrigerate several hours, or until thoroughly chilled.

Remove dough from refrigerator, separate amount needed for a single rolling, and return remainder to refrigerator. Roll dough ¼ in. thick on lightly floured surface. Cut with a lightly floured 2-in. round cookie cutter. Using a spatula, place cutouts on cookie sheet. Brush lightly with
Egg white, slightly beaten
Sprinkle over tops
Sugar
Bake at 350°F 6 to 8 min.

Immediately remove cookies to cooling racks.

Repeat procedure, using remaining dough.
About 8 doz. cookies

CRISPY ROLLED WAFERS

▲ *Base Recipe*

Set out cookie sheets.

Melt (page 10) and set aside to cool
4 oz. (4 sq.) unsweetened chocolate

Sift together three times and set aside
2¼ cups sifted all-purpose flour
1½ teaspoons baking powder
½ teaspoon baking soda
¼ teaspoon cinnamon

Cream until well blended
½ cup shortening
1 tablespoon vanilla extract
Add gradually, creaming until fluffy
1 cup sugar
Add, one at a time, beating well after each addition
2 eggs
Blend in melted chocolate and
1 tablespoon cream
Add dry ingredients in halves, beating until smooth after each addition.
Roll dough thin on lightly floured surface. Cut with 3-in. cookie cutter or cut into squares. With spatula lift gently onto ungreased cookie sheet.

Bake at 400°F 5 to 7 min. Remove to cooling rack at once.
4 doz. cookies

—CRUMBS FOR COOKIE CRUST

Follow ▲ Recipe. Roll dough thin on waxed paper cut to fit cookie sheet. Lift paper to cookie sheet; invert onto cookie sheet and gently remove paper from dough. Bake at 400°F 5 to 7 min. Remove to cooling rack at once. When cool, roll into crumbs and store in covered jar or container. Use for **Frosty Cookie Crumb Pie** (page 566).
About 3¼ cups crumbs

—MINT-FILLED WAFERS

Follow ▲ Recipe. Place an **after-dinner mint patty** on an unbaked cookie cut slightly larger than mint. Cover with another unbaked cookie. Press edges together with tines of a fork. Bake at 400°F 5 to 7 min. Remove to cooling rack at once.

—TEATIME TEMPTATIONS

Follow ▲ Recipe. Use small fancy-shape cookie cutter. Spread baked wafers with filling and press pairs together.

For Filling—Work together until smooth and blended thoroughly **1 pkg. (3 oz.) cream cheese, 2¼ cups confectioner's sugar, 3 tablespoons orange juice** and **1 teaspoon grated orange peel.**

COFFEE CRISPS

It's coffee that brings out the wonderful flavor of these frosted crunchy cookies!

For Cookies—Sift together and set aside
3 cups sifted all-purpose flour
1 teaspoon baking powder
½ teaspoon baking soda
¼ teaspoon salt

Cream until softened
1 cup butter or margarine
½ teaspoon orange extract
¼ teaspoon vanilla extract
Add gradually, creaming until fluffy after each addition
1 cup sugar
Stir in
¼ cup orange juice

Blend in dry ingredients in thirds, mixing well after each addition. Refrigerate 1 hr.

Grease cookie sheets.

Place chilled dough on a lightly floured surface and roll ¼ in. thick. Cut with a 2-in. floured crescent cookie cutter. Place cookies on greased cookie sheets.

Bake at 350°F 8 min., or until lightly browned. Cool on cooling racks.

For Topping—Coarsely chop and set aside
1 cup (about 4 oz.) walnuts

Combine in a saucepan
1 cup sugar
¾ cup quick coffee (page 10)
½ cup honey
Bring to boiling; simmer 5 min.

Brush tops of cookies with syrup. Sprinkle the chopped walnuts over the cookies. Remove to cooling racks to cool completely.
7 doz. cookies

COCONUT JEWELS

▲ *Base Recipe*

Southern cookie jars are often filled (but not for long) with scrumptious coconut cookies.

Set out cookie sheets.

Prepare (but do not roll) and set aside to chill, dough for
Vanilla Tea Rounds (page 607)

Chop very fine
2 cups moist shredded coconut (yields 2½ cups, very finely chopped)
Put chopped coconut into a 2-qt. saucepan with
⅔ cup (about 6) egg whites, unbeaten
1 cup sugar
1 tablespoon cornstarch
¼ teaspoon almond extract
Mix thoroughly. (If mixture is too heavy, add a little more egg white.) Place over very low heat and stir constantly, being careful to keep temperature of mixture below 150°F.

Remove mixture from heat and cool to room temperature.

Meanwhile, remove amount of chilled dough needed for a single rolling and return remainder to refrigerator. Roll dough about ¼ in. thick and with a 2-in. fluted cookie cutter, cut out the dough. Place cookies on ungreased cookie sheets.

Cut into halves and set aside
21 (about 1½ oz.) candied cherries
When coconut mixture is cooled, force mixture through pastry bag and a No. 7 star tube to form a ring on fluted cookie rounds. Place cherry half in center of each coconut ring.

Bake at 350°F 20 to 25 min., or until delicately browned. Remove with spatula to cooling racks.
About 3½ doz. cookies

—COCONUT MACAROONS DE LUXE

Follow ▲ Recipe. Cover cookie sheets with unglazed paper. Omit the dough for Vanilla Tea Rounds. Force coconut mixture through pastry bag and tube or drop by teaspoonfuls

directly onto unglazed paper. Top with cherry half and bake as directed.

DATE-FILLED COOKIES

Set out cookie sheets.

Shred and set aside
4 oz. sharp Cheddar cheese (about 1 cup, shredded)

Sift together and set aside
1¼ cups sifted all-purpose flour
⅛ teaspoon salt

Cream until softened
½ cup butter or margarine
½ teaspoon vanilla extract
Blend in the shredded cheese. Mixing well after each addition, add dry ingredients in halves. Wrap dough in waxed paper and chill until easy to handle.

Meanwhile, prepare
½ cup (about 3 oz.) finely cut dates (page 9)
¼ cup (about 1 oz.) finely chopped pecans
Put dates into a saucepan with
3 tablespoons brown sugar
3 tablespoons water
Cook over low heat, stirring constantly, until thick and blended, about 5 min. Stir in nuts. Set filling aside to cool.

Put chilled dough on a lightly floured surface. Roll dough into a 16x12-in. rectangle about ⅛ in. thick. Cut dough into halves. Spread one half of dough with cooled filling and top with remaining dough. Cut into 2-in. squares. Transfer to cookie sheets. Press all edges of cookies with a fork to seal.

Bake at 350°F about 12 to 15 min., or until edges are light brown. *About 2 doz. cookies*

ISCHL COOKIES
(Isli Tea Sütemény)

These chocolate-coated hazelnut cookies were highly favored by Francis Joseph, former emperor-king of Austria-Hungary. They were named in honor of a summer resort in the Austrian Alps where Francis Joseph liked to spend his leisure hours.

Lightly grease cookie sheets.

Grate (page 10) and set aside
½ cup (about 3 oz.) hazelnuts (about 1 cup, grated)

Sift together and set aside
1½ cups sifted all-purpose flour
¼ teaspoon cinnamon
¼ teaspoon cocoa

Cream until softened
¾ cup unsalted butter
1 teaspoon grated lemon peel
½ teaspoon lemon juice

Add gradually, creaming until fluffy after each addition
¾ cup confectioners' sugar
Blend in the ground nuts.

Add the dry ingredients to creamed mixture in thirds, mixing until blended after each addition. Cover bowl with waxed paper and let dough rest 15 min. Roll dough on lightly floured surface to ¼-in. thickness. Cut into rounds with a lightly floured 1½-in. cookie cutter. Place rounds about 1 in. apart onto cookie sheets.

Bake at 350°F 15 to 20 min., or until lightly browned; remove cookies to cooling racks.

While cookies are cooling, set out about
¼ cup thick jam, apricot or strawberry
¼ cup whole blanched almonds (page 9)
When cookies are cool, turn one half of the cookies upside down and spread about ½ teaspoon jam on each. Make cookie sandwiches by placing remaining cookies on top of jam; set aside. Set almonds aside to be used as a garnish for the cookies.

Set out two cooling racks, each over a piece of waxed paper.

Partially melt over simmering water, being careful not to overheat
¾ lb. semisweet candymaking chocolate
Remove chocolate from the simmering water and stir until completely melted. Dip top of sandwich cookies into chocolate. Place cookies, chocolate-side up, onto one of the cooling racks; let excess chocolate drip off cookies onto the waxed paper. (Scrape together and wrap excess chocolate; store for future use.) Immediately top each cookie with one of the reserved almonds; cool cookies until chocolate coating is firm. Refrigerate if necessary.
About 2 doz. cookies

CRISP ORANGE COOKIES

Cookie sheets will be needed.

Thaw
1 can (6 oz.) frozen orange juice concentrate, undiluted

Sift together and set aside
3 cups sifted all-purpose flour
¼ teaspoon salt
½ teaspoon baking soda

Beat in a large bowl until softened
1 cup butter or margarine
Add gradually, creaming until fluffy after each addition
1 cup sugar
Add the orange juice concentrate all at one time and beat until mixture is well blended.

Gradually add dry ingredients, beating until thoroughly mixed.

Wrap dough in waxed paper and thoroughly chill in the refrigerator (2 hrs.).

Meanwhile, cut (page 9) and set aside

Candied orange peel
Candied cherries

Remove one-fourth of chilled dough from re-frigerator; return remainder of dough to re-frigerator immediately. Roll dough about ⅛ in. thick on lightly floured surface. Cut with light-ly floured, scalloped 2-in. cookie cutter. Gently lift cookies onto cookie sheets with spatula. Decorate cookies as desired with candied peel and cherries.

Bake at 400°F about 6 min., or until lightly browned. Let stand on cookie sheet a few sec-onds, then remove to cooling rack.

About 9 doz. cookies

JAM POCKETS

Set out and grease a cookie sheet.

Prepare and chill

1 hard-cooked egg yolk*

Press the chilled egg yolk through a sieve into a bowl. Stir in

1 tablespoon lemon juice

Combine in a bowl, blending well

⅔ cup all-purpose flour
2 tablespoons sugar
½ cup finely grated blanched almonds

Stir in the sieved egg yolk. Using pastry blender or 2 knives, cut in

¼ cup chilled unsalted butter

Working quickly, knead dough gently into a smooth ball; wrap and chill thoroughly 1 hr. or longer.

Roll dough ⅛ in. thick on a floured surface (preferably a pastry canvas). Cut into 3-in. squares. Spoon on each

1 rounded teaspoon grape (or other fruit) jam

Fold over dough to form a triangle and press edges together to seal. Place triangles on prepared cookie sheet.

Brush lightly with a blend of the reserved egg white beaten until foamy and

1 tablespoon water

Bake at 350°F about 20 min., or until golden brown. Remove from cookie sheet to wire rack to cool. While slightly warm, sift **confectioners' sugar** over the "pockets."

About 1 doz. cookies

*To hard-cook egg yolk, separate egg (reserve egg white), drop yolk gently into simmering water, simmer 10 min., and drain.

SWEDISH JELLY SLICES

Grease two cookie sheets.

Chop finely and set aside

⅓ cup toasted blanched almonds

Sift together and set aside

1¾ cups sifted all-purpose flour
1½ teaspoons baking powder
½ teaspoon salt

Beat until softened in a large bowl

¾ cup butter

Add gradually, beating until fluffy

¾ cup sugar

Beat in, blending thoroughly

1 egg
1 teaspoon grated lemon peel
1 teaspoon coriander
½ teaspoon cardamom

Add dry ingredients, beating only until just blended. (Do not overbeat.) Refrigerate dough until thoroughly chilled. Divide into halves and return one half to refrigerator.

Roll dough on floured surface (preferably a pastry canvas) into an 8x6-in. rectangle. Cut into 6 strips 1 in. wide and arrange 4 in. apart on cookie sheet. Make a depression ¼ in. deep and ¼ in. wide lengthwise down center of each strip of dough. Fill depression with

Cherry jelly (10-oz. jar)

Repeat process with remaining chilled dough.

Bake at 375°F 12 min.

Meanwhile, beat together in a small bowl until very thick

1 egg yolk
2 teaspoons water
¼ cup sugar

After 12 min. remove strips from oven and quickly brush tops with the egg yolk mixture, then sprinkle with chopped almonds. Bake 4 to 6 min. longer. Cool on cookie sheet 5 min., then cut each strip into 1-in. diagonal slices. Remove from cookie sheets to cooling racks.

7 doz. cookies

SPECIAL EASTER COOKIES

Grease cookie sheets.

Chop and set aside

½ cup (about 4 oz.) candied lemon or orange peel
¼ cup blanched almonds

Sift together and set aside

2 cups sifted all-purpose flour
¼ teaspoon baking soda
½ teaspoon cinnamon
¼ teaspoon nutmeg
⅛ teaspoon cloves
⅛ teaspoon salt

Put into a saucepan and bring to boiling

1 cup honey
1 tablespoon sugar

Boil 5 min., stirring occasionally. Stir in chopped almonds; boil 5 min. Cool.

Blend into cooled mixture

2 tablespoons butter or margarine
1 tablespoon rum or sherry
¾ teaspoon grated lemon peel

Mixing until well blended after each addition, add dry ingredients in fourths. Mix in the candied peel. Refrigerate dough 1 to 2 hrs., or until thoroughly chilled.

Put one third of the dough on a lightly floured surface. Roll ¼ to ½ in. thick. Cut into 2x1-in.

bars. Transfer to cookie sheets. Repeat for remaining dough.

Bake at 300°F 20 min. With spatula, remove cookies to cooling racks. While still warm, sprinkle with **sugar**. *4 to 5 doz. cookies*

Note: These cookies keep well stored in a tightly covered container with a slice of apple to keep them moist. Replace the apple slice when it dries out.

SPICY CINNAMON TOWERS

▲ *Base Recipe*

Build tempting little towers of flavor and fra-grance—these Spicy Cinnamon Towers.

Sift together and set aside

2¼ cups sifted all-purpose flour
1½ teaspoons baking powder
1 teaspoon cinnamon
¼ teaspoon salt

Cream until butter or margarine is softened

½ cup butter or margarine

Add gradually, creaming until fluffy after each addition

¾ cup sugar

Add and beat well

1 egg, beaten
1 tablespoon milk

Add dry ingredients gradually, blending thor-oughly after each addition. Chill in refrigerator several hours, or until dough is firm enough to roll easily.

Set out cookie sheets.

Remove amount of dough needed for a single rolling and return remainder to refrigerator. Roll dough on a lightly floured surface, not more than ¼ in. thick. Using lightly floured fluted cookie cutters that are 2 in., 1¼ in. and ¾ in. in diameter, cut out an equal number of cookies of the three varying sizes. Place cookies of one size on the same cookie sheet.

Bake at 425°F 5 to 7 min.

Using a spatula, immediately and carefully remove cookies to a cooling rack. Cool them completely.

Note: Keeping cookies of one size together speeds up the job of assembling cookie towers.

Set out

¼ to ⅓ cup apple butter

Use largest cookies for the base of cookie towers. Spoon ¼ to ½ teaspoon apple butter onto center. Top with medium-size cookies. Spoon apple butter onto centers and top with smallest cookies.

Set cookie towers onto waxed paper. Sift lightly over all cookies

Confectioners' sugar

About 2½ doz. cookie towers

—ALMOND-STRAWBERRY TOWERS

Follow ▲ Recipe. Cut an equal number of cookies with 2-in. fluted cookie cutter and with 1¼-in. round cookie cutter; omit the ¾-in. cookies. Sprinkle smaller unbaked cookies with **crushed rock candy.** Bake as directed. Substitute **strawberry jelly** for apple butter. Place a dot of jelly on center of each candy-sprinkled cookie; top with **whole blanched almond.**

—VANILLA TEA ROUNDS

Follow ▲ Recipe. Decrease flour to 2 cups. Omit cinnamon. Add **1 teaspoon vanilla extract** to butter or margarine and cream together. Cut out cookies with fluted cookie cutters. Serve plain or sprinkle with **sifted confectioners' sugar.** Or assemble cookies into towers, if desired.

JOE FROGGERS

These big, soft, fat molasses cookies, known as Joe Froggers in New England, Bolivars in New York, are a happy inheritance from the Gay Nineties.

Cookie sheets will be needed.

Sift together and set aside

5 cups sifted all-purpose flour
1½ teaspoons salt
1 teaspoon baking powder
1 teaspoon baking soda
1½ teaspoons ginger
¼ teaspoon cloves

Put into a bowl

¾ cup shortening

Add gradually, creaming until fluffy after each addition

1 cup firmly packed brown sugar

Joe Froggers

Combine

1 cup molasses
½ cup water

Mixing until well blended after each addition, alternately add dry ingredients in fourths, molasses mixture in thirds, to creamed mixture. Finally blend until well mixed Wrap dough in waxed paper and chill in refrigerator 1½ hrs.

Lightly grease the cookie sheets.

Remove amount of dough needed for a single rolling. Roll ¼ in. thick on a lightly floured surface. Cut with a floured 3-in. cookie cutter. Using a pancake turner, place cookies about 2 in. apart on cookie sheets.

Bake at 375°F about 10 min. Remove cookies from sheets and set on cooling racks to cool.

About 2 doz. large cookies

PEPPERNUTS
(Pfeffernüsse)

These spicy cookies are very hard when they are cooled. Store in tightly covered containers with a piece of apple.

Grease cookie sheets.

Grate (page 10)

½ cup (2½ oz.) blanched almonds (page 9)

Sift together into a bowl

4 cups sifted all-purpose flour
2 teaspoons cinnamon
½ teaspoon nutmeg
½ teaspoon allspice
½ teaspoon cloves
¼ teaspoon mace
¼ teaspoon salt
¼ teaspoon pepper

Stir in the almonds and set aside.

Chop and set aside

3 oz. candied citron (about ½ cup, chopped)

Beat until thick and piled softly

4 eggs

Add gradually, beating thoroughly after each addition

2 cups sugar

Add the flour-almond mixture in fourths, blending thoroughly after each addition. Mix in the citron. Turn about one half the dough onto a lightly floured surface and roll ½ in. thick. Cut with a lightly floured 1-in. round cookie cutter. Transfer cookies to the cookie sheets.

Set out

2¼ teaspoons brandy

Put a drop on the center of each cookie.

Bake at 350°F 15 to 20 min., or until cookies are lightly browned.

Remove to cooling racks, cool and store.

About 11 doz. cookies

GINGERBREAD MEN

Sift together and set aside

4½ cups sifted all-purpose flour
1 tablespoon cinnamon
1 teaspoon salt
1 teaspoon baking soda
1 teaspoon ginger
½ teaspoon cloves

Cream until softened

½ cup butter or margarine

Add gradually, creaming until light and fluffy after each addition

½ cup firmly packed brown sugar

Add and beat thoroughly

1 egg

Add gradually while beating

1 cup molasses
2 teaspoons vinegar

Stir in dry ingredients.

Wrap dough in moisture-vaporproof material and chill in refrigerator 8 hrs. or overnight.

Lightly grease cookie sheets.

Roll one portion of chilled dough at a time, ¼ in. thick, on a lightly floured surface. Cut dough with gingerbread-man cookie cutter, or lay a cardboard pattern over dough and cut with sharp knife carefully around pattern. Using pancake turner, transfer cookies to cookie sheets.

Bake at 350°F about 10 min. When cool, add fancy decorations with frosting or candies.

About 1½ doz. Gingerbread Men or 2½ doz. round cookies

ANISE COOKIES
(Springerle)

A quaintly carved springerle rolling pin or mold, available in most department stores, gives these cookies an Old World charm.

Sift together and set aside

4½ cups sifted cake flour
1 teaspoon baking powder

Beat until thick and piled softly

4 eggs

(One-fourth teaspoon oil of anise added to the eggs at this time can be substituted for the anise seed that is to be sprinkled on the cookie sheets.) Add gradually, beating until thoroughly mixed.

3½ cups (1 lb.) sifted confectioners' sugar

4 teaspoons grated lemon peel

Beat in dry ingredients in fourths, mixing thoroughly. Chill dough in refrigerator until firm enough to handle easily (about 1 hr.).

Lightly grease cookie sheets and sprinkle with

Anise seed

Roll dough ½ in. thick on lightly floured surface. Press lightly floured springerle rolling pin into dough, rolling carefully to make clear designs; or press mold down firmly. Brush surface gently with soft brush to remove excess flour. Cut cookies apart. With a spatula, gently lift them onto the cookie sheets. Cover with waxed paper and let them stand overnight.

Bake at 350°F 30 min., or until very slightly browned.

With a spatula, remove at once to cooling racks. When thoroughly cooled, store in a tightly covered jar for 1 or 2 weeks before using. (Storage period develops flavor and characteristic consistency. Cookies will keep for months.)   *About 2½ doz. cookies*

SWEDISH GINGERSNAPS
(Pepparkakor)

The tangy fragrance of these cookies is part of the wonderful smell of a Swedish Christmas. They should be rolled as thin as parchment.

Set out cookie sheets.

Set out

Whole blanched almonds (page 9; about 10)

Sift together and set aside

1½ cups sifted all-purpose flour

1 teaspoon baking soda

1½ teaspoons ginger

1 teaspoon cinnamon

¼ teaspoon cloves

Cream until softened

½ cup butter

Add gradually, creaming until fluffy after each addition

¾ cup sugar

Add gradually, beating thoroughly after each addition

1 egg, well beaten

1½ teaspoons dark corn syrup

Blend in dry ingredients in fourths, mixing thoroughly after each addition. Chill in refrigerator several hours.

Remove some of the chilled dough and place on a lightly floured surface. Roll about 1/16 in. thick. Cut with lightly floured cookie cutters into various shapes. Cut almonds into small pieces and place one piece in the center of each cookie. Transfer cookies to cookie sheets. Repeat with remaining chilled dough.

Sand Tarts, Dreams, Swedish Gingersnaps, Danish Cookies and Rosettes

Bake at 375°F 6 to 8 min.

Carefully remove cookies to cooling racks to cool completely.   *About 7 doz. cookies*

DEEP FRIED AND SPECIALTY COOKIES

ROSETTES
(Struvor)

A deep saucepan or automatic deep fryer and a rosette iron will be needed.

Beat very slightly with a fork

2 eggs

1½ teaspoons sugar

¼ teaspoon salt

Add and beat just until smooth

1 cup milk

1 cup sifted all-purpose flour

Set out a deep saucepan or automatic deep fryer (page 11) and heat **fat** to 365°F. Heat iron in fat before dipping it into batter.

When iron is hot enough, dip into batter to within ¼ in. of top of iron. Return to hot fat, covering iron entirely, for 20 to 35 sec., or until delicately browned. When browned, drain over fat a few seconds. Using the tip of a sharp knife, carefully remove rosette from iron. Drain on absorbent paper.

Sprinkle with

Vanilla Confectioners' Sugar (page 582)

If necessary, sprinkle again before serving. Or rosettes may be topped with sliced fresh strawberries and garnished with whipped cream.
    About 3½ doz. Rosettes

Note: If rosette is difficult to remove from the iron, it has not been fried long enough. If fat blisters are present, eggs have been beaten too long. If batter drops from iron, it is not deep enough in fat or iron is too hot. If rosette is not crisp, it has been fried too fast.

TINY DOUGHNUT COOKIES
(Jortitog)

A deep saucepan or automatic deep fryer will be needed.

Sift together and set aside

3½ cups sifted all-purpose flour

½ teaspoon hartshorn (ammonium carbonate which is obtainable at any drugstore)

Cream until softened

½ cup butter

Add gradually, creaming until fluffy after each addition

1 cup sugar

Add gradually, blending in thoroughly

4 eggs, slightly beaten

Add the dry ingredients in fourths, mixing well after each addition. Chill in refrigerator.

Cut off pieces of the chilled dough and place one at a time on a lightly floured surface. Press each piece ¼ in. thick with the fingers. Cut dough into 2x¼ in. strips. Roll each strip with the hands to about 5 in. in length. Bring ends together to form a ring and press together to seal. Place rings on a baking sheet. Using a sharp knife, make 3 slanted cuts, about ¼ in. long, at equal intervals around each ring.

Set out a deep saucepan or automatic deep fryer (page 11) and heat **fat** to 375°F.

Deep-fry only about 4 cookies at one time. Deep-fry 1 to 2 min., or until lightly browned, turning once to brown evenly. Drain cookies over fat for a second before removing to absorbent paper.   *About 6 doz. cookies*

DEEP-FRIED COOKIES
(Csörege)

About 20 min. before deep-frying, fill a deep saucepan one-half to two-thirds full with

Vegetable shortening, all-purpose shortening, lard or cooking oil for deep-frying

Heat slowly to 365°F (page 11). When using

an automatic deep fryer, follow manufacturer's directions for amount of fat and timing.

Meanwhile, sift together into a bowl

2 cups sifted all-purpose flour
1 tablespoon sugar
½ teaspoon salt

Make a well in center of dry ingredients and pour in a mixture of

3 egg yolks, slightly beaten
½ cup dairy sour cream
½ teaspoon vanilla extract

Blend ingredients until all the flour is moistened. Let dough rest 1 or 2 min. Turn dough out onto lightly floured surface and knead (page 10), only until ingredients are well blended. Shape dough into a smooth ball; roll dough on lightly floured surface into a rectangle ⅛ in. thick. (If space will not permit, roll only one half the dough at a time.) With spatula, loosen dough from board wherever sticking occurs; lift dough slightly and sprinkle a little flour underneath. With floured knife, cut dough into diamond-shape pieces 2 in. wide at center and 6 in. long. (A cardboard pattern may be used.) Make a 1-in. lengthwise cut in the center of each diamond; pull one end through slit, twisting slightly.

Deep-fry only one layer of cookies at one time; do not crowd. Turn cookies with fork as they rise to surface and several times during cooking, but do not pierce. Fry about 3 min., or until lightly browned. Drain cookies over fat for a second before removing to absorbent paper. Sprinkle cookies with

2 to 3 tablespoons confectioners' sugar (or Vanilla Confectioners' Sugar, page 582)

2½ doz. cookies

POOR MAN'S COOKIES
(Fattigmands Bakkelse)

Rich man or poor man—these "poor man's cookies" are a holiday treat for Norwegians.

A deep saucepan or automatic deep fryer will be needed.

Sift together and set aside

5 cups sifted all-purpose flour
1 teaspoon cardamom

Beat until mixture is thick and lemon-colored

10 egg yolks
2 egg whites
¾ cup sugar
3 tablespoons brandy

Add slowly, stirring in

1 cup heavy cream

Blend in flour mixture, about ½ cup at a time, to make a soft dough. Wrap dough in waxed paper and chill overnight in refrigerator.

Set out a deep saucepan or automatic deep fryer (page 11) and heat to 365°F to 370°F

Lard

Meanwhile, roll dough, a small portion at a time, to 1⁄16-in. thickness on a lightly floured surface. Cut into diamond shapes, 5x2-in. (A pattern may be used as a guide around which to cut with a floured knife.) Make a lengthwise slit in the center of the diamond and pull one tip end through it and tuck back under itself.

Deep-fry only as many cookies at one time as will float uncrowded one layer deep in fat. Deep-fry 1 to 2 min., or until golden brown, turning once during deep-frying time. Drain over fat a few seconds before removing to absorbent paper. Sprinkle with

Confectioners' sugar

Store in tightly covered containers.

About 6 doz. cookies

ROLLED WAFERS
(Gaufres)

The marchand de gaufre is a familiar sight in French public gardens. He bakes his product on a sizzling hot gaufrier (irons held together with long handles). His recipe is one of the oldest, dating back to the 12th century when gaufres were served at great religious festivals.

Set out gaufrier (wafer or krumkake iron).

Sift together into a bowl

1¾ cups sifted all-purpose flour
⅔ cup sugar
⅛ teaspoon salt

Blend well with rotary beater

3 eggs
2 cups milk
1 teaspoon vanilla extract

Make a well in center of dry ingredients and add liquid. Beat until smooth. Beat in

½ cup melted butter

Set batter aside about 30 min.

Heat gaufrier until a drop of water "sputters" on its hot surface. Pour a small amount of batter into hot iron. Close the gaufrier and cook wafer a few seconds on each side, or until browned. Roll gaufre immediately around the handle of a wooden spoon. Sprinkle with sifted confectioners' sugar before serving.

About 36 small Gaufres

NORWEGIAN CONES
(Krumkaker)

▲ Base Recipe

Set out a krumkake iron (usually available in the housewares section of a department store).

Sift together into a bowl

1½ cups sifted all-purpose flour
½ cup cornstarch
1½ teaspoons cardamom

Cream until softened

1 cup butter

Add gradually, creaming until fluffy after each addition

1¼ cups sugar

Beat in, one at a time, until thoroughly blended

3 egg yolks

Add the dry ingredients in fourths, mixing well after each addition.

Beat until stiff, not dry, peaks are formed

3 egg whites
⅛ teaspoon salt

Spread the beaten egg whites over batter and gently fold together.

Heat krumkake iron until a drop of water "sputters" on its hot surface. Spoon about 1½ to 2 teaspoons batter onto hot iron. Close the krumkake iron and cook on each side for a few seconds or until lightly browned. Immediately remove wafer with a spatula and roll into a cone. Cool completely.

Serve cones plain.

About 4 doz. cones

—FILLED NORWEGIAN CONES
(Fylda Krumkaker)

Follow ▲ Recipe. Fill cones with **sweetened fresh berries** or **Sweetened Whipped Cream** (page 480). If desired, garnish whipped cream with strips of **candied orange peel.**

Candies and confections

Candymaking is one of the most fascinating forms of cooking. Until the beginning of the nineteenth century, the art of making "sweet-meats" was practiced chiefly by physicians and apothecaries who used their concoctions, usually made of sugar and honey, to conceal the disagreeable taste of medicines. Today's creations are a far cry from those simple confections, and for the hostess, the ability to make fine candies is an aid to popularity. The hostess who can serve homemade candies when she entertains is greatly admired for her ingenuity. And for gift giving, no offering is more appreciated than a box of beautifully made candy. One might add that candymaking represents a happy blend of art and science—or beauty and delectability.

To insure success in making candy, there are some general rules to follow. Among them are:
Use only ingredients of the highest quality and freshness.
Before starting to cook candy, assemble all ingredients and equipment needed.
Be exact in weighing or measuring ingredients.
Have a candy thermometer ready. It is the only accurate way of measuring temperature. Test the thermometer before each use as follows:

Place the bulb in water 3 inches deep in a saucepan and bring rapidly to boiling; boil 3 minutes and take a reading. Water boils at 212°F at sea level but will vary with altitude and atmospheric pressure (2° per 1000 feet). Humidity as well as mechanical discrepancies affect the reading. If your thermometer registers 210° in the boiling water; you should cook your candies 2° lower to allow for the difference because all degrees given in the recipes are for 212° boiling. At no time plunge a cold thermometer into boiling liquid or a hot thermometer into cold liquid.
How to use a thermometer—Put the thermometer into syrup mixture after sugar is dissolved and candy starts boiling. Syrup depth should be at least 3 inches. To read the thermometer, hold it in an upright position with the mercury bulb completely under the boiling syrup. The eyes should be level with mercury.

When the mixture has reached the correct temperature, remove pan from heat immediately. If mixture is to be cooled in the saucepan, set pan in cold water for a minute to cool the pan quickly. When finished with the thermometer, place in a pan of hot water. *When a thermometer is not available,* test syrup in cold water (see page 11). Remove syrup from heat and use a clean spoon each time a test is made.
In hot, humid weather allow candy mixtures to cook 2° higher than specified in recipe, as candy absorbs some moisture from the air while cooling.
To avoid graininess in candy, stir sugar mixtures at beginning of cooking period over low heat until sugar is completely dissolved and mixture begins to boil. Stir gently so sugar crystals do not adhere to sides of saucepan.
Covering sugar and water mixtures (such as fondant) for the first few minutes of cooking helps to soften the sugar crystals adhering to pan. After removing the cover, wipe down crystals as they form with a pastry brush dipped in hot water or with dampened cheesecloth wrapped around tines of a fork.
Cook candy mixtures containing milk, cream or molasses without a cover to avoid boiling over. Cook over medium heat until mixture thickens, then reduce heat and cook slowly. Sugar and water mixtures may be cooked more rapidly.
Allow candy to cool before beating unless otherwise specified.
Store candy in tightly covered containers in a cool place.

FONDANT

▲ Base Recipe

Originally meaning "melting," the word fondant has come to suggest "that which melts in the mouth" or "luscious," a true description of this creamy confection.

Set out a large platter or marble slab. (Surface must be smooth and level.)

Combine in a 3-qt. heavy saucepan with a tight-fitting cover
1 cup water
3 cups sugar
⅛ teaspoon cream of tartar
Stir over low heat until sugar is dissolved. Increase heat to medium and bring mixture to boiling. Cover saucepan and boil mixture gently 5 min. (This will dissolve any crystals that may have formed on sides of saucepan.) Uncover and continue cooking without stirring. Using pastry brush dipped in water, wash down crystals from sides of saucepan from time to time during cooking. Cook to 238°F (soft ball stage, page 11; remove from heat while testing).

Wipe platter or slab with damp cloth. Immediately pour fondant onto its surface. Do not scrape pan. Without stirring, cool just enough to hold platter on palm of hand, or to warm (about 100°F). Pour onto fondant
1 teaspoon vanilla extract
With wide spatula or wooden spoon, work fondant in circles from edges to center until white and creamy. Pile into a ball, cover with bowl and allow to rest 20 to 30 min.

With hands, work fondant (in a kneading motion) until soft and smooth.

Ripen at least 24 hrs. in a tightly covered jar. Shape into small candies or use in following recipes. *About 1¼ lbs. fondant*

—FONDANT GLAZE
(Glace au Fondant)

Follow ▲ Recipe. Place ripened fondant in double boiler top. Place over simmering water. Stirring as necessary, melt fondant, heating to 130°F (no higher temperature). Blend in, to taste, any desired **flavoring** or **liqueur.** To tint, blend in **1 or 2 drops food coloring.** If fondant is not thin enough to pour over Petits Fours (or to coat fruits and nuts) gradually stir in hot water, 1 teaspoonful at a time, until fondant is of pouring consistency. Use for coating nuts, dates and other fruits. Or frost French Pastries or Petits Fours by quickly pouring melted fondant over the cake pieces set on a rack over a tray lined with waxed paper. Collect fondant from tray, remelt and use again.

For Chocolate Fondant Glaze—When melting fondant, add **4 oz. (4 sq.) unsweetened chocolate,** cut in pieces. When temperature reaches 130°F (no higher temperature), stir in hot water, 1 tablespoon at a time, (will take about 4 tablespoons) until thin enough to pour.

—BONBONS

No one could quarrel with this French name which, literally translated, repeats "Good! Good!"

Reserve about one third ▲ Recipe for dipping. Divide remaining two thirds into three or more portions. Color and flavor each portion differently. Work into one portion less than a drop **green food coloring** and several drops **pistachio or lime flavoring**. In another portion use **vanilla extract or almond extract**. Use **rose extract** and **red coloring** for remainder. For a different flavor, grate about **1 teaspoon citrus fruit peel**, allow to stand 2 to 3 min. in citrus juice; drain peel and add it to the fondant.

If adding chopped nuts, coconut, candied fruits, dates, figs or raisins, work in with fingers only until blended. (Use alone or in any combination.)

Shape into 1-in. rolls. Cut into small uniform pieces and shape into balls or ovals; slightly flatten one side. Keep small; dipping increases size. Allow all fondant centers to stand on racks or trays covered with waxed paper. Dry several hours before dipping.

Melt reserved fondant as in Fondant Glaze. Add desired flavoring and less than 1 drop food coloring. Test for proper coating consistency by dipping a test center.

Lower a center, rounded side down, into fondant and cover completely with fondant. Immediately remove with fork or candy dipper. Scrape bonbon on edge of pan to remove excess fondant.

Place flat side down onto waxed paper. Make fancy swirl on top by twirling fork or dipper. (Fondant may be reheated to proper dipping consistency.)

Yield will vary according to shapes made

—FONDANT PATTIES
(Petits Pâtés Fondants)

Follow ▲ Recipe. Fondant can be used for making patties about an hour after working fondant with hands (short ripening period). Prepare space for pouring patties by covering a flat surface with waxed paper.

Stirring as necessary, melt fondant over simmering water, heating fondant to 130°F (no higher temperature). Add desired colorings and flavorings. If fondant is not the consistency of thick cream, thin it with hot water, stirring in a small amount at a time. Pour fondant in pools (about the size of quarters) from measuring cup or small pan having a sharp lip. (Warm measuring cup or pan with hot water and dry before filling with fondant.)

As soon as patties are firm, remove from waxed paper and stack patties upright, side by side.

About 60 patties

BLUEBERRY PASTEL CREAMS

Combine in top of a double boiler
¼ cup butter or margarine
2 tablespoons milk
Heat until butter is melted and stir in
1 pkg. vanilla frosting mix
Place over rapidly boiling water; cook 5 min., stirring occasionally.

Cool mixture and divide in half. Tint one half to desired color with **green food coloring** and blend in
4 drops peppermint extract
Tint other half to desired color with **yellow food coloring** and blend in
⅛ teaspoon lemon extract
Form each portion into a roll ¾ in. in diameter. Thinly slice rolls. Using the bottom of a glass, flatten each slice. Place a blueberry in center of each; fold up edges and lightly press against blueberry.   *About 1 lb. candy*

Note: Small pieces of green or yellow candied pineapple, green or red candied cherries or other candied fruits may be substituted for blueberries.

ALMOND CREAMS

▲ *Base Recipe*

Place a sheet of waxed paper on a baking sheet.

Finely chop and set aside
¾ cup (about 3 oz.) nuts

Put into a bowl
2 tablespoons butter
Beat in until thoroughly blended
¼ cup cream
1 teaspoon almond extract
Add gradually, beating constantly
3½ cups (1 lb.) sifted confectioners' sugar
Beat until mixture is smooth and creamy.

Shape into 1-in. balls. Roll in the chopped nuts. Place on waxed paper-lined baking sheet.

Store candy in a cool dry place.

About 40 creams

—STUFFED DATES

Follow ▲ Recipe. Substitute **vanilla extract** for almond extract. Remove pits from **60 dates** and roll in **sugar**. Fill cavities of dates with cream candy.

—HAZELNUT CREAMS

Follow ▲ Recipe. Substitute **vanilla extract** for almond extract. Omit chopped nuts. Mold cream candy around **hazelnuts.**

—CHOCOLATE PECAN PATTIES

Follow ▲ Recipe. Substitute **vanilla extract** for almond extract. Omit chopped nuts. Roll candy pieces in **¾ cup (3 oz.) grated unsweet-** ened chocolate. Flatten slightly and place each piece between **2 salted pecan halves.**

—CHERRY SURPRISES

Follow ▲ Recipe. Omit chopped nuts. Drain **60 maraschino cherries** with stems. Form cream candy around cherries, keeping stems uncovered for "handles."

ALMOND CARAMEL FUDGE

Set out a large heavy light-colored skillet and a heavy 4-qt. saucepan. Butter an 8-in. square pan. A candy thermometer will be needed.

Have ready
2 cups unblanched almonds, toasted and chopped
Place the skillet over low heat and add
2 cups sugar
With back of a wooden spoon gently keep sugar moving toward center until it melts and turns golden brown; keep warm.

Combine in the saucepan
4 cups sugar
2 cups milk
Stir over low heat until sugar is dissolved. Increase heat and bring mixture to boiling. Add the melted sugar very slowly, stirring constantly. Wash down sides of pan with a pastry brush dipped in water. Set candy thermometer in place. Cook, stirring occasionally to prevent scorching, until thermometer registers 234° to 236°F (soft ball stage, page 11); wash down crystals from sides of pan as necessary and change water after each washing. Remove from heat. Cool to lukewarm (about 110°F); do not jar pan or stir.

Add to the cooled fudge
2 teaspoons vanilla extract
Beat vigorously until mixture begins to lose its gloss. With few strokes, stir in the almonds. Quickly turn mixture into the prepared pan and spread evenly. Cool completely before cutting into 1½-in. squares.

About 2¾ lbs. fudge

CHOCOLATE FUDGE

▲ *Base Recipe*

Butter a 9-in. square pan.

Combine in a heavy 3-qt. saucepan
1⅓ cups milk
4 oz. (4 sq.) unsweetened chocolate
Stir over low heat until chocolate is melted. Do not allow mixture to boil. Stir in
4 cups sugar
2 tablespoons light corn syrup
½ teaspoon salt
Cook slowly, stirring until sugar is dissolved. Increase heat to medium and bring mixture to boiling.

Cook, stirring occasionally, to 234°F (soft ball stage, page 11; remove from heat while testing).

Butter Pecan Fudge

Using a pastry brush dipped in water, wash down the crystals from sides of saucepan from time to time during cooking. Remove mixture from heat and cool to lukewarm (about 110°F) without stirring or jarring the saucepan. Then add

**¼ cup butter or margarine
4 teaspoons vanilla extract**

Beat vigorously until mixture is dull in color. Quickly turn into the buttered pan without scraping bottom and sides of saucepan and spread evenly. Set aside to cool. When firm, cut into 1½-in. squares.   *About 2¼ lbs. fudge*

—PEANUT BUTTER FUDGE

Follow ▲ Recipe. Substitute ½ **cup peanut butter** for butter.

—COCOA FUDGE

Follow ▲ Recipe. Substitute ¾ **cup cocoa** for chocolate. Blend cocoa with sugar before adding milk.

—PECAN FUDGE

Follow ▲ Recipe. Before pouring, add **2 cups (about 8 oz.) chopped pecans.**

—TUTTI-FRUTTI FUDGE

Follow ▲ Recipe. Before pouring, add ⅓ cup each: **candied cherries, candied pineapple, raisins.**

—MARSHMALLOW FUDGE

Follow ▲ Recipe. Stir **32 (½ lb.) marshmallows, quartered,** into cooled fudge along with butter and extract.

QUICK CHOCOLATE FUDGE

▲ *Base Recipe*

Butter an 8-in. square pan.

Melt (page 10) and set aside to cool
4 oz. (4 sq.) unsweetened chocolate
Coarsely chop and set aside
¾ cup (about 3 oz.) nuts

Beat until fluffy
2 pkgs. (3 oz. each) cream cheese, softened
Add gradually, beating until fluffy after each addition
4¼ cups sifted confectioners' sugar
Blend in thoroughly the cooled chocolate and
1 tablespoon vanilla extract
Stir in the nuts. Turn into the buttered pan. Chill in refrigerator until firm.

Cut into 1½-in. squares.   *About 2 lbs. fudge*

—COCONUT FUDGE

Follow ▲ Recipe. Substitute ¾ **cup moist shredded coconut,** cut, for the nuts.

—BUTTER PECAN FUDGE

Follow ▲ Recipe. Omit chocolate. Use **pecans** for the nuts, increase amount to 1 cup and toast (page 10) before chopping.

SOUR CREAM CHOCOLATE FUDGE

▲ *Base Recipe*

Sour cream gives fudge a different, delicious flavor-tang that will set folks guessing.

Butter an 8-in. square pan. Set out a candy thermometer.

Chop and set aside
¾ cup (about 3 oz.) walnuts or pecans

Mix in a heavy 2-qt. saucepan
**2 cups sugar
1 cup dairy sour cream
2 tablespoons light corn syrup
¾ teaspoon salt
2 oz. (2 sq.) unsweetened chocolate, broken in pieces**
Stir over low heat until sugar is dissolved. Increase heat and bring mixture to boiling. Set candy thermometer in place. During cooking wash any crystals from sides of pan with a pastry brush dipped in water; move candy thermometer to one side and wash down crystals that may have formed under the thermometer.

Cook mixture until thermometer registers 236°F (stage at which a few drops form a soft ball in cold water; remove pan from heat while testing). Remove from heat and set aside until just cool enough to hold pan on hand. Do not jar pan or stir mixture.

When cool, add
**2 tablespoons butter or margarine
1 tablespoon vanilla extract**
Beat vigorously until mixture begins to lose its gloss. Beat in the nuts. When mixture loses its gloss, quickly turn into the buttered pan without scraping bottom and sides of saucepan, and spread evenly. Set aside to cool.

When firm, cut into squares. Top each square with a nut half.   *About 1½ lbs. fudge*

Sour Cream Chocolate and Black Walnut Fudge

—BLACK WALNUT FUDGE

Follow ▲ Recipe. Omit the chocolate. Substitute **black walnuts** for the pecans.

—BROWN SUGAR FUDGE

Follow ▲ Recipe. Decrease sugar to 1½ cups; add **1 cup firmly packed light brown sugar.** Omit corn syrup and chocolate. (Black walnuts add extra flavor.)

QUICK FOUR-WAY FUDGE

▲ *Base Recipe*

Butter an 8-in. square pan, line with waxed paper cut to fit bottom; butter again.

Melt (page 10)
2 pkgs. (6 oz. each) semisweet chocolate pieces
Blend in
1¼ cups (14-oz. can) sweetened condensed milk
Remove from heat and stir in
2 teaspoons vanilla extract
Pour into pan and sprinkle top with
½ to 1 cup (2 to 4 oz.) chopped nuts
Chill in refrigerator about 4 hrs., or until firm.

When firm, cut into 1-in. squares.
   About 1¼ lbs. fudge

—FUDGE PATTIES

Follow ▲ Recipe, omitting chopped nuts. Shape cooled (not chilled) squares into small balls. Flatten; gently press a nut half onto center of each.

—FUDGE MINIATURES

Follow ▲ Recipe. Set out a baking sheet in place of the square pan and line with waxed paper. With vanilla add 3 cups of any one or any mixture of these: **crisp rice cereal, corn flakes, seedless raisins, unsalted chopped nuts** or **moist shredded coconut.** Drop by teaspoonfuls onto waxed paper and put in cool place to set.

—FUDGE BALLS

Follow ▲ Recipe. With vanilla extract add 2 cups of any one or any mixture of these: **seedless raisins, unsalted chopped nuts** or **moist shredded coconut.** Turn into pan and cool. When firm enough to handle, cut into squares. Shape into small balls and roll in **finely chopped coconut or nuts.**

PANOCHA

Lightly butter an 8-in. square pan. Set out a candy thermometer and a heavy 3-qt. saucepan.

Chop and set aside
  ½ cup (about 2 oz.) pecans

Combine in the saucepan
  2 cups firmly packed brown sugar
  ¾ cup undiluted evaporated milk
  2 tablespoons butter or margarine
  1 tablespoon light corn syrup
  Few grains salt
Stir over low heat until the sugar is dissolved. Hang candy thermometer on pan so the bulb does not touch side or bottom of pan.

Increase heat to medium and bring mixture to boiling. Cook, stirring constantly, until thermometer registers 234 to 240°F (or a small amount of syrup forms a soft ball in cold water; remove pan from heat while testing). During cooking wash down any crystals from sides of pan with pastry brush dipped in water; move candy thermometer to one side and wash down any crystals that may have formed on side of pan under the thermometer.

Remove mixture from heat and cool to lukewarm (about 110°F) without stirring the candy or jarring the saucepan. Then remove candy thermometer and add the pecans and
  1 teaspoon vanilla extract

Beat vigorously until mixture loses its gloss. Quickly turn into the buttered pan without scraping bottom and sides of saucepan; spread evenly. Set aside to cool.

When candy is firm, cut into 1½-in. squares.
  24 pieces Panocha

DIVINITY

▲ Base Recipe

Lightly butter a baking sheet. Set out a candy thermometer.

Heat in saucepan over medium heat, stirring only until mixture begins to boil
  2 cups sugar
  ⅔ cup water
  ½ cup light corn syrup
  ¼ teaspoon salt
Cover and cook 5 min. (This helps to dissolve any crystals that may have formed on sides of pan.) Remove cover and set candy thermometer (page 11) in place. Boil mixture without stirring. During cooking, wash any crystals from sides of pan with a pastry brush dipped in water.

Shortly before syrup reaches 252°F (hard ball stage, page 11), beat in large mixer bowl until stiff, not dry, peaks are formed
  3 egg whites

When the syrup reaches 252°F, immediately pour syrup in a fine stream onto stiffly beaten egg whites, beating constantly on high speed. When mixture begins to lose its gloss, turn off motor and lift beater. In the early stage, the mass flows down from beater in a continuous ribbon. Continue beating until mixture no longer flows but holds its shape (about 35 min.). At this point, quickly blend in
  1 teaspoon vanilla extract
Drop by teaspoonfuls onto baking sheet.

Store in a cool place in tightly covered container. *About 48 pieces Divinity*

—SEAFOAM DIVINITY

Follow ▲ Recipe. Decrease sugar to ¾ cup and blend in 1¼ cups **firmly packed brown sugar.**

Blend in with the vanilla **1 cup chopped nuts.**

—CHOCOLATE DIVINITY

Melt (page 10) **2 oz. (2 sq.) unsweetened chocolate** and set aside. Follow ▲ Recipe. Cook and beat as directed. When mixture holds its shape, quickly blend in the melted chocolate and extract.

CHOCOLATE CARAMELS
(Caramels Mous au Chocolat)

▲ Base Recipe

The name of these delicious candies is said to have come from Viscount Caramel.

As a French candymaker does, butter lightly a marble slab on which a buttered 8-in. frame is placed. If this is not available, lightly butter an 8-in. square pan. Set out a heavy 3-qt. saucepan and its cover.

Melt (page 10) and set aside
  4 oz. (4 sq.) unsweetened chocolate

Set out
  3 cups heavy cream
  2 tablespoons butter

Pour one cup of cream into the saucepan. Add
  2 cups sugar
  1 cup light corn syrup
  ¼ teaspoon salt
Stir gently until sugar is dissolved. Cover pan and bring mixture to boiling over medium heat. Cook 5 min. (This will dissolve any crystals that may have formed on sides of pan.) Remove cover; reduce heat to very low and cook mixture, stirring frequently, until it reaches 234°F. (soft ball stage, page 11; remove from heat while testing).

Stirring constantly, gradually add another cup of the cream to saucepan, so that boiling will not stop. Continue cooking over very low heat, stirring frequently, to 234°F.

Stirring constantly, gradually add remaining cream and the butter to saucepan so that boiling will not stop. Stirring frequently, cook to 244°F (firm ball stage). Remove mixture from heat. Immediately add the melted chocolate to saucepan with
  1 tablespoon vanilla extract
Stir just until well blended. Immediately pour hot mixture into the buttered pan, but do not scrape bottom and sides of saucepan. To cool, set aside on cooling rack.

When completely cooled (several hours or overnight), turn out upside down onto a board. Using a sharp, long-bladed knife, cut with a sawing motion into 1-in. square caramels. Wrap each caramel in waxed paper or plastic wrap.
  64 caramels

—VANILLA CARAMELS
(Caramels Mous à la Vanille)

Follow ▲ Recipe. Omit chocolate.

Hasty Chocolate Caramels and Almond Filled Caramels

—NUT CARAMELS
(Caramels Mous aux Noisettes)

Follow ▲ Recipe or recipe for Vanilla Caramels. Stir in **½ cup (about 2 oz.) chopped nuts** with vanilla extract.

HASTY CHOCOLATE CARAMELS

Set out a candy thermometer. Butter an 8-in. square pan.

Heat in heavy saucepan over lowest heat
3 oz. (3 sq.) unsweetened chocolate
1¼ cups (14-oz. can) sweetened condensed milk
½ cup light or dark corn syrup
⅛ teaspoon salt

Set candy thermometer (page 11) in place. Stirring constantly, cook mixture (about 20 min.) to 235°F (this particular mixture tends to form a firm ball rather than the usual soft ball at 235°F; remove from heat while testing). The consistency of the ball will be the consistency of the finished product. Cook longer, if desired. The higher the temperature reached, the firmer the candy. Candy cooked beyond 244°F will be too brittle.

Stir in one tablespoon at a time
3 tablespoons butter or margarine
Mix in
½ cup (about 2 oz.) chopped nuts such as almonds, blanched (page 9)
2 teaspoons vanilla extract

Turn into buttered pan without scraping bottom or sides of saucepan. Cool until lukewarm.

Loosen sides and turn candy onto cutting board. Cut into 6 strips. Work each strip with hands into roll. Cut each roll into 1-in. pieces. Wrap in waxed paper or plastic wrap and store in a tightly covered container.

About 4 doz. caramels

ALMOND-FILLED CARAMELS

Butter a 15x10x1-in. pan.

Blanch, toast (pages 9 and 10), salt and set aside
24 (about ¼ cup) whole almonds

Heat together in a saucepan
1 cup sugar
¾ cup molasses
½ cup cream
⅓ cup butter

Stir over low heat until sugar is dissolved. Increase heat and cook rapidly, stirring constantly. Set a candy thermometer in place. During cooking, wash any crystals from sides of pan with a pastry brush dipped in water; move thermometer and wash down any crystals that may have formed on sides of pan under the thermometer. Cook mixture until thermometer registers 250°F (hard ball stage, page 11; remove from heat while testing). Remove saucepan from heat and stir in
1½ teaspoons vanilla extract

Pour into prepared pan, without scraping bottom or sides of saucepan. Cool until lukewarm.

Cut caramels into 2½-in. squares. Place a whole almond in center of each square. Keeping almond in center, roll caramel over almond. Wrap caramels in waxed paper or plastic wrap.

About 2 doz. caramels

NOUGAT
(Nougat de Montélimar)

Thoroughly butter inside of an 8-in. square pan. Set out a candy thermometer.

Blanch (page 9) and chop
½ cup (about 2 oz.) pistachios
Blanch, toast (page 10) and chop
1 cup (about 5½ oz.) almonds
Set nuts aside.

Combine in a heavy saucepan with a tight-fitting cover
2 cups sugar
1 cup water
2 tablespoons light corn syrup

Stir over low heat until sugar is dissolved. Increase heat to medium and bring mixture to boiling. Cover saucepan and boil mixture gently 5 min. (This will dissolve any crystals that may have formed on sides of saucepan.) Remove cover and set candy thermometer (page 11) in place. Continue cooking without stirring. Using pastry brush dipped in water, wash down crystals from sides of saucepan from time to time during cooking.

Shortly before thermometer registers 290°F (soft crack stage, page 11; remove from heat while testing), beat in a 4-qt. mixer bowl until stiff, not dry, peaks are formed
4 egg whites

When the syrup reaches 290°F, immediately pour syrup in a fine stream onto stiffly beaten egg whites. Using electric mixer, beat at a high speed constantly until mixture is thick and bowl is warm (about 100°F) to touch.

Meanwhile, wash thermometer. Combine in saucepan and set thermometer in place (mixture must cover thermometer bulb)
1 cup honey
2 tablespoons light corn syrup

Cook over medium heat until thermometer registers 270°F (soft crack stage). (To keep bubbles from rising above top of pan during cooking, pat bubbles down with back of wooden spoon.)

At once pour a fine stream into egg white mixture, beating constantly at a medium speed until mixture has lost some of its gloss. (The longer the mixture is beaten the shorter will be the drying period over boiling water.)

Transfer mixture to double boiler top and place over boiling water. Using a wooden spoon constantly stir and turn mixture until it no longer appears moist (at least 25 min.). Nougat is done when a small amount, removed on a spoon and cooled, is no longer sticky. (Nougat on spoon should not stick to finger when finger is pressed on it.) Mix in
2 teaspoons vanilla extract

Gradually stir in the nuts. Turn into pan and set on a cooling rack for 10 min. Press down firmly with hand. When completely cool, cover pan tightly.

Set aside to ripen at least 24 hrs. Loosen sides and shake well to remove block of candy from pan to cutting board. Cut into 1½-in. oblong pieces. Wrap each in waxed paper or plastic wrap.

About 40 pieces Nougat

ITALIAN NOUGAT
(Torrone)

Oil two 8-in. square pans.

Toast (page 10)
2⅓ cups (⅔ lb.) whole unblanched hazelnuts
Set aside.

Pour into top of double boiler over boiling water and stir with wooden spoon one hour
1 cup honey
Remove honey from heat.

Beat until stiff, not dry, peaks are formed
2 egg whites
Add beaten egg whites to honey, 1 tablespoon at a time, beating well with wooden spoon after each addition. Set aside.

Combine in a light-colored skillet
1 cup sugar
2 tablespoons water
Bring to boiling over medium heat and cook, stirring occasionally, until caramelized.

Add caramelized sugar to honey mixture, a tablespoon at a time, mixing well after each addition.

Turn mixture into a heavy saucepan. Stirring constantly, cook over direct heat to 240°F (soft ball stage), or until a small amount forms a soft ball in cold water. Remove from heat while testing. Add, all at once, hazelnuts and
2 cups (⅔ lb.) whole unblanched almonds
Mix well and quickly pour into prepared pans. Cool 20 min.

Cut nougat into 2x1-in. pieces and wrap in waxed paper or plastic wrap.

32 pieces nougat

CHOCOLATE NOUGAT

Line an 11x7-in. pan with aluminum foil and butter it; set aside. A candy thermometer will be needed.

Have ready
½ cup candied cherries, chopped
¾ cup toasted blanched almonds, chopped
Combine in a saucepan
2 cups sugar
⅔ cup light corn syrup
⅓ cup water
Stir until sugar is moistened. Wash down crystals from sides of pan with a pastry brush dipped in water. Cover and bring to boiling over medium heat. Uncover, wash down crystals and set candy thermometer in place. Boil mixture without stirring until thermometer registers 270°F (soft crack stage, page 11).

Melt and set aside
2 oz. (2 sq.) unsweetened chocolate

Italian Nougat

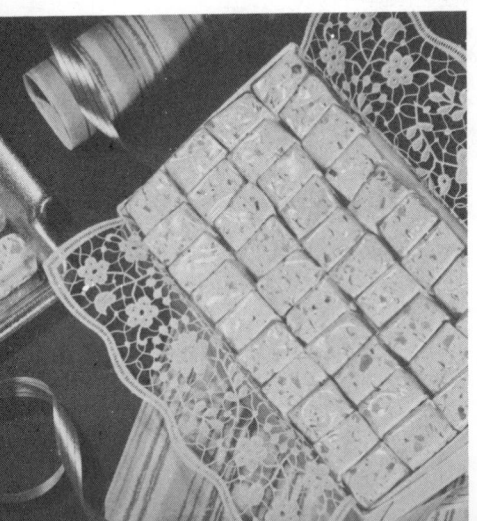

Beat in a bowl until stiff, not dry, peaks are formed
½ cup (about 2) egg whites
⅛ teaspoon salt
When syrup reaches 270°F, remove from heat and set aside until bubbles subside. Remove thermometer. Then pour syrup over egg whites in a steady stream, beating constantly with electric beater until all syrup is added. Using a wooden spoon, stir in the melted chocolate, cherries, nuts and
½ teaspoon almond extract
Beat with the spoon until mixture falls in large chunks.

Turn into prepared pan and level mixture. Cover with waxed paper or foil, pressing it down firmly. Let stand overnight. Cut nougat into squares and wrap in waxed paper.

About 1½ lbs. nougat

Note: If nougat or rice paper is available, place a sheet on a board and enclose an 8x7-in. space with caramel bars. Use a similar sheet to place on top of nougat as soon as it is enclosed in prepared space.

CRACKLE PEANUT BRITTLE

Butter two baking sheets.

Combine in a heavy 3-qt. saucepan with a tight-fitting cover
2 cups sugar
1 cup light corn syrup
1 cup water
Stir over low heat until sugar is dissolved. Increase heat to medium and bring mixture to boiling. Cover saucepan and boil mixture gently 5 min. (This will dissolve any crystals that may have formed on sides of saucepan.)

Uncover and continue cooking, without stirring, to 235°F (soft ball stage, page 11; remove from heat while testing). Using pastry brush dipped in water, wash down crystals from sides of saucepan from time to time during cooking. Mix in
2 cups (about ¾ lb.) unroasted peanuts
2 teaspoons butter
Cook over low heat to 300°F to 304°F (hard crack stage, page 11), stirring frequently.

Remove from heat and add, mixing well
2 teaspoons baking soda
1 teaspoon vanilla extract
Pour onto the baking sheets, spreading as thinly as possible. As soon as candy is cool enough to handle, wet hands in water and stretch candy as thin as desired. Turn candy over and cool completely. When cool and firm, break candy into medium-size pieces. Store in tightly covered container.

About 2 lbs. peanut brittle

PECAN CRUNCH

Butter a 9-in. square pan. Set out a candy thermometer.

Finely chop and reserve ½ cup
1 cup (about 4 oz.) pecans
Mix the remaining nuts with
1 cup (about 4 oz.) coarsely chopped pecans
1 teaspoon baking soda
Set mixture aside.

Prepare a syrup by combining in a heavy saucepan
2¼ cups sugar
1¼ cups butter or margarine
½ cup water
1 tablespoon cider vinegar
1 teaspoon salt
Cook slowly, stirring constantly, until sugar is dissolved.

Set candy thermometer (page 11) in place. Boil, without stirring, to 290°F (soft crack stage, page 11, if a candy thermometer is not available; remove from heat while testing). Add pecan-soda mixture to syrup stirring just enough to blend. Pour into buttered pan and cool on cooling rack.

When cooled, melt
3 oz. milk chocolate
Spread the melted chocolate over candy and sprinkle with the reserved pecans.

Turn candy out of pan when chocolate is set. Cut into pieces. Store in tightly covered container between waxed paper layers.

About 1½ lbs. crunch

TOFFEE

Kitchen magic—when nuts are ground on an electric blender for this butter-rich candy.

Set out a candy thermometer. Lightly butter a 9-in. square pan.

Blanch (page 9) and set aside
6 oz. (about 1 cup) nuts such as almonds or Brazil nuts (or use pecans or walnuts)

Melt in heavy 2-qt. saucepan over medium heat
1 cup butter or margarine
Add and stir until mixture begins to boil
1 cup sugar
3 tablespoons water
¼ teaspoon salt

Set candy thermometer (page 11) in place. Stirring occasionally to prevent scorching, cook syrup slowly to 310°F (hard crack stage, page 11; remove from heat while testing).

Meanwhile, using electric blender, grind the nuts. When syrup is done, remove from heat and blend in only ¾ cup ground nuts and

1 teaspoon vanilla extract

Quickly pour into prepared pan and spread to corners. Mark candy quickly into squares with a sharp knife before it cools. Cool.

Meanwhile, melt

5-oz. milk chocolate bar or 1 pkg. (6 oz.) semisweet chocolate pieces

Spread melted chocolate evenly over cooled candy. Sprinkle remaining nuts over top.

When candy is hard, break into pieces. Store in tightly covered container between layers of waxed paper, aluminum foil or moisture-vapor-proof material. Texture improves after storing for one day.

About 1½ lbs. Toffee

MOLASSES WALNUT CRACKLE

Generously butter a 15x10x1-in. pan; set aside. A candy thermometer will be needed.

Melt in a heavy saucepan

2 tablespoons butter or margarine

Mix in

1 cup light molasses
⅓ cup sugar

Cook and stir over low heat until mixture comes to boiling. Increase heat and set candy thermometer in place. Cook to 270°F (soft crack stage, page 11), stirring to prevent scorching.

Stir in

½ cup walnuts, broken in small pieces
Few grains salt

Pour into prepared pan. When cool, mark into squares. When cold, break into pieces.

About ¾ lb. candy

MOLASSES-PECAN KISSES

Butter a 15x10x1-in. pan. Set out a candy thermometer.

Set out

48 (about 1 cup) pecan halves

Mix in a heavy 3-qt. saucepan

1 cup firmly packed brown sugar
1 cup cream
½ cup light molasses
2 tablespoons butter

Stir over low heat until sugar is dissolved. Increase heat and bring mixture to boiling. Set candy thermometer in place. Cook, stirring constantly, until thermometer registers 250 to 266°F (or until a small amount of syrup forms a ball which is pliable yet hard enough to hold its shape in very cold water; remove pan from heat while testing). During cooking wash any crystals from sides of pan with a pastry brush dipped in water; move candy thermometer to

one side and wash down any crystals that may have formed on side of pan under the thermometer. Remove saucepan from heat and remove thermometer.

Stir in

1 teaspoon vanilla extract

Pour into the buttered pan without scraping bottom and sides of saucepan. Set aside until just cool enough to hold pan on palm of hand.

Cut candy into rectangles about 2½x1¼ in. Place a pecan half in center of each rectangle. Keeping pecan in center, roll candy over pecan half, forming a pecan kiss.

Wrap kisses in waxed paper. Store in a covered container in a cool dry place.

About 4 doz. kisses

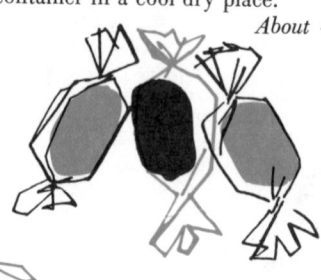

CREAMY TAFFY

▲ **Base Recipe**

Butter a large shallow pan or platter.

Mix thoroughly in heavy saucepan

2¼ cups sugar
1½ cups light corn syrup
4 teaspoons vinegar
¼ teaspoon salt

Cook slowly, stirring constantly, until sugar dissolves. Bring mixture to a boil; add slowly so boiling does not stop

½ cup undiluted evaporated milk

Cook mixture over medium heat, stirring constantly, until temperature of mixture is 248°F (firm ball stage, page 11; remove from heat while testing).

Immediately pour mixture into buttered pan.

When cool enough to handle, pull in cool place, a small portion at a time, (with buttered hands) until candy is light in color and no longer sticky to the touch. Twist pulled strip slightly and place on waxed paper or board. Cut with scissors into 1-in. pieces. Wrap in waxed paper or plastic wrap.

About 2 lbs. taffy

—COCOA TAFFY

Follow ▲ Recipe. Mix ½ cup cocoa with sugar.

PECAN PRALINES I

▲ **Base Recipe**

Pralines have been a distinctive candy of New Orleans ever since the time the city was settled.

Creamy Taffy

Originally made in France using almonds, pralines were named after a famous French Marshall, the Duc de Choiseul-Prasline. He believed that almonds coated in sugar would be more digestible. When Louisiana was settled by French colonists, native pecans were substituted for the almonds of the mother country.

Set out a 2-qt. heavy saucepan and a candy thermometer.

Lay sheets of waxed paper or aluminum foil on baking sheets. If using waxed paper, grease or oil the waxed paper.

Measure and set aside

2 tablespoons butter
1½ cups (about 5½ oz.) pecan halves

Mix in the saucepan

1 cup firmly packed dark brown sugar
1 cup granulated sugar
½ cup cream

Stir over low heat until sugar is dissolved. Increase heat and cook rapidly without stirring. Set the candy thermometer in place. During cooking wash any crystals from sides of pan with a pastry brush dipped in water; move candy thermometer to one side and wash down any crystals that may have formed on sides of pan under the thermometer.

Cook mixture until it reaches 230°F (thread stage, page 11; remove from heat while testing). Stir in butter and pecan halves. Continue cooking, stirring occasionally, until mixture reaches 236°F (soft ball stage, page 11; remove from heat while testing).

Remove mixture from heat and remove candy thermometer. Cool mixture 2 to 3 min. without stirring. Gently stir mixture for about 2 min., or until it becomes slightly thicker and pecans appear well coated with sugar mixture. Quickly drop by tablespoonfuls onto the aluminum foil or greased waxed paper. The candy will flatten. Allow to stand until cool.

When completely cooled, wrap each praline in

waxed paper. Store them in a covered container in a cool dry place.   *About 20 pralines*

—**PECAN PRALINES II**

Follow ▲ Recipe. Substitute **water** for the cream. This praline will be less creamy than Pecan Pralines I.

—**DARK PECAN PRALINES**

Follow ▲ Recipe. Omit granulated sugar, increase dark brown sugar to 2 cups.

—**PEANUT PRALINES**

Follow ▲ Recipe. Omit pecans; add **1½ cups (about 8 oz.) unsalted peanuts.**

—**ALMOND PRALINES**

Follow ▲ Recipe. Omit pecans; add **1½ cups (about 8 oz.) blanched almonds.**

CANDIED CHESTNUTS
(Marrons Glacés)

To Remove Shells and Blanch Chestnuts—Wash and make a slit in both sides of each shell of
1 lb. chestnuts

(Follow either Method 1 or Method 2.)

Method 1: Turn chestnuts into a shallow pan and mix in
1 tablespoon cooking oil
Bake at 450°F 20 min. Cool. Remove shells and all inner skins with a sharp knife.

Method 2: Put chestnuts into saucepan and add water to cover. Boil about 20 min. Drain immediately. Peel off shells and skins.

To Glaze Chestnuts—Turn blanched nuts into saucepan. Cover with boiling salted water. Cover. Simmer 8 to 20 min., or until tender when pierced with a fork. Set aside to drain.

Lightly butter a baking sheet.

Combine in the top of a double boiler with a tight-fitting cover
2 cups sugar
1 cup water
⅛ teaspoon cream of tartar
Stir over low heat until sugar is dissolved.

Chocolate Crinkle Cups

Increase heat to medium and bring mixture to boiling. Cover double boiler top and boil mixture gently 5 min. (This will dissolve any crystals that may have formed on sides of pan.) Uncover and continue cooking without stirring. Using a pastry brush dipped in water, wash down crystals from sides of pan from time to time during cooking. Cook to 300°F (hard crack stage, page 11; remove from heat while testing). Immediately set double boiler top over gently boiling water.

If syrup becomes too thick, place over direct heat until proper consistency. With fork or candy dipper, dip nuts into syrup. Remove when they appear clear. Drain over saucepan for a moment. Dry on prepared baking sheet.
About 1 lb. Candied Chestnuts

CHOCOLATE CRINKLE CUPS

Twelve muffin-pan wells and twelve 2-in. paper baking cups will be needed.

Melt over simmering water
1 pkg. (12 oz.) semisweet chocolate pieces
Remove from heat and stir. With back of teaspoon or small spatula, spread chocolate on inside of baking cups. Set in muffin pan wells. Place in refrigerator and chill until firm, about 1 hr. Carefully peel off paper cups. Fill with pudding, whipped gelatin, candies, sherbet or ice cream. Serve at once.
12 crinkle cups

CHOCOLATE RAISIN CLUSTERS

Line a baking sheet with waxed paper.

Melt (page 10)
1 pkg. (12 oz.) semisweet chocolate pieces
Blend in
1¼ cups (14-oz. can) sweetened condensed milk
Remove from heat and stir in
2 teaspoons vanilla extract
¼ teaspoon salt
2 cups (about 10 oz.) raisins, or 1 cup raisins and 1 cup (about 4 oz.) coarsely chopped nuts
Drop by teaspoonfuls onto paper-lined sheet.

Chill in refrigerator 1 to 2 hrs., or until firm.
About 5 doz. clusters

CHOCOLATE COCONUT CHEWS

▲ Base Recipe

Butter an 11x7-in. pan.

Melt over simmering water, stirring occasionally
48 (¾ lb.) marshmallows
3 tablespoons butter or margarine
2 oz. (2 sq.) unsweetened chocolate

Meanwhile, mix in a buttered large bowl and set aside
4 cups (about 4 oz.) puffed rice or wheat, ready-to-eat oat cereal or corn puffs
1 cup moist flaked coconut

Remove marshmallow mixture from heat. Mix in, stirring well
1 teaspoon vanilla extract
½ teaspoon salt

Slowly pour hot marshmallow mixture over cereal mixture, stirring briskly to coat thoroughly. Turn mixture quickly into pan. Spread and press evenly to corners.

Chill in refrigerator about 1 hr., or until candy is firm. Cut into bars about 2x1-in.
About 3 doz. bars

—**POLKA DOT CHEWS**

Follow ▲ Recipe. Omit chocolate. Mix **1 pkg. (6 oz.) semisweet chocolate pieces** with cereal and coconut.

COCONUT FRUIT BALLS

Place a sheet of waxed paper on a baking sheet.

Chop
1 cup (about 6 oz.) pitted dates
½ cup (about 3 oz.) seedless raisins

Finely blender-chop (page 11)
1¾ cups moist shredded coconut
Combine with dates and raisins in a bowl. Add and beat until well blended
⅔ cup sweetened condensed milk

Shape into 1¼-in. balls. Roll lightly in
Confectioners' sugar
Shake off excess sugar. Place on waxed paper-lined baking sheet.

Chill in refrigerator. *About 2 doz. 1¼-in. balls*

COCONUT KISSES

Line a baking sheet with waxed paper.

Blend in a bowl
½ cup (1 or 2) hot riced or mashed potatoes (somewhat packed in cup)
1 tablespoon butter
Beat in thoroughly
3½ cups (1 lb.) confectioners' sugar, sifted
⅛ teaspoon salt
2 teaspoons vanilla extract

Mix in

3 tablespoons cocoa, sifted, or 1 oz. (1 sq.) unsweetened chocolate, melted (page 10)

Then blend in

3 cups (1 lb.) moist shredded coconut

Drop by teaspoonfuls onto paper-lined sheet. Set kisses in a cool place to harden. Store in tightly covered container.

About 1½ lbs. kisses

TURKISH DELIGHT

Set out a 2-qt. saucepan. Lightly butter an 8-in. square pan; set aside.

Pour into a small bowl

1 cup cold water

Sprinkle over the water

4 env. unflavored gelatin

Set aside until softened.

Meanwhile, combine in a saucepan

3 cups sugar
¼ teaspoon salt
½ cup water

Stir over low heat until sugar is dissolved. Increase heat and bring mixture to boiling; boil 10 min. without stirring. During cooking, occasionally wash crystals from sides of saucepan.

Stir in softened gelatin until completely dissolved. Simmer mixture 10 min. longer, stirring occasionally. Remove from heat and stir in

1 can (6 oz.) frozen orange juice concentrate, partially thawed

Chill until mixture begins to thicken, stirring occasionally.

Meanwhile, drain thoroughly

1 can (8½ oz.) crushed pineapple

When gelatin mixture is of desired thickness, mix in the drained pineapple and turn into prepared pan.

Chill in refrigerator 6 hrs. or overnight.

Cut into 1-in. squares with a sharp knife and roll each square in

Sifted confectioners' sugar

Refrigerate until ready to serve.

About 5 doz. squares

FRUIT-NUT CANDY SQUARES

Lightly grease an 8-in. square pan.

Rinse and put through coarse blade of food chopper

1 cup (about ⅓ lb.) dried figs
1 cup (about 6 oz.) pitted dates
1 cup (about ⅓ lb.) dried apricots

Coarsely chop

½ cup (about 2 oz.) nuts

Combine fruits and nuts with

½ cup moist flaked coconut

and a mixture of

2 teaspoons grated orange peel
3 tablespoons orange juice
½ teaspoon cinnamon

Mix well. Turn into pan and press evenly over bottom. Chill well in refrigerator.

Sprinkle with

Confectioners' sugar

Cut into 1-in. squares. Remove with flexible spatula.

64 squares

CANDIED ORANGE PEEL

Set out a candy thermometer and a heavy 2-qt. saucepan with a tight-fitting cover.

Rinse and carefully remove the peel in large pieces from

3 large oranges (thick peel is preferred)

(Reserve orange pulp for other use.)

Put orange peel into the saucepan and add

1½ cups water
¼ teaspoon salt

Bring to boiling and cook until orange peel is almost tender, about 15 min. Remove from heat and drain well. Return orange peel to saucepan and add

1½ cups water

Bring to boiling Drain immediately. Repeat heating and draining process two more times. After last draining, scrape the white part from the peel. Cut peel into ¼-in. strips.

Mix in the saucepan

1 cup sugar
½ cup water

Stir over low heat until sugar is dissolved. Increase heat and bring mixture to boiling. Cover saucepan and boil gently 5 min. Uncover and set candy thermometer in place. During cooking, wash any crystals from sides of pan with a pastry brush dipped in water; move thermometer and wash down any crystals that may have formed on sides of pan under the thermometer. Continue cooking mixture without stirring until thermometer registers 230 to 234°F (or syrup spins a thread when dropped from spoon; remove pan from heat while testing). Remove thermometer. Add the strips of peel and cook very slowly, stirring frequently, until most of the syrup is absorbed.

Place waxed paper under cooling racks to catch syrup drippings. Remove peel from saucepan

Rum Truffle Balls

and spread over the racks. When peel has cooled slightly, roll, a few pieces at a time, in

Sugar (about ½ cup)

Cool completely. Store in a tightly covered container. *About 2 cups Candied Orange Peel*

RUM TRUFFLE BALLS

▲ *Base Recipe*

Set out

⅓ cup butter or margarine
10 oz. milk chocolate

Grate (page 10) and set aside in the refrigerator 2 oz. (about ¾ cup) of the chocolate. Put remaining chocolate into the top of a double boiler with

¼ cup heavy cream

Heat over simmering water, stirring occasionally, until chocolate is melted. Remove from simmering water and allow mixture to cool slightly.

Divide butter into small pieces and immediately stir all pieces into melted chocolate until butter is melted. Mix thoroughly and blend in until smooth and creamy

2½ teaspoons rum

Chill in freezing compartment of refrigerator about 1 hr., or until firm.

When firm, spoon about 1 teaspoon at a time onto grated chocolate. Quickly work with fingers to form a ball and coat with grated chocolate. *18 to 22 truffle balls*

—LIQUEUR TRUFFLE BALLS

Follow ▲ Recipe. Substitute **1½ teaspoons kirsch** and **1½ teaspoons curaçao** for total amount of rum.

—COFFEE TRUFFLE BALLS

Follow ▲ Recipe. Add **1½ teaspoons instant powdered coffee** to the grated chocolate.

Substitute ½ **teaspoon instant powdered coffee** for total amount of rum.

MARSHMALLOWS

▲ *Base Recipe*

Lightly butter an 11x7x1½-in. pan. Set out a candy thermometer.

Pour into a small saucepan
⅔ cup cold water
Sprinkle evenly over water
2 env. unflavored gelatin
Set saucepan over low heat and stir until gelatin is dissolved.

Heat in a 2-qt. saucepan over medium heat, stirring only until mixture begins to boil
2 cups sugar
½ cup light corn syrup
½ cup hot water
Cover and cook 5 min. (this helps to dissolve any crystals that may have formed on sides of pan). Remove cover and set candy thermometer (page 11) in place. Boil mixture without stirring. During cooking wash any crystals from sides of pan with a pastry brush dipped in water.

Shortly before syrup reaches 248°F (firm ball stage, page 11), put dissolved gelatin into large mixer bowl.

When the syrup reaches 248°F, remove from heat. Immediately, pour syrup in a fine stream onto dissolved gelatin, beating constantly on high speed of electric mixer until thick and lukewarm (about 20 min.).

Blend in
2 teaspoons vanilla extract
Turn marshmallow mixture into pan. If necessary, smooth evenly with spatula.

Let stand uncovered in a cool place on cooling rack (not in refrigerator) until completely cool and set (about 4 hrs.).

Meanwhile, prepare coating.

For Coating—Blender-chop (page 11) any one of the following and set aside
2 cans (10 oz. each) chocolate wafers (about 2½ cups crumbs)
2 pkgs. (about 9 oz. each) macaroon cookies (about 2½ cups crumbs)
2 cans (4 oz. each) moist shredded coconut (about 2 cups, chopped)
8 oz. (about 2 cups) nuts

Note: Coconut may be toasted, if desired.

Measure and combine
1 tablespoon confectioners' sugar
1 tablespoon cornstarch
Sift mixture over cooled marshmallow before removing from pan. Run spatula around sides

of pan and invert on cutting board. Cut marshmallows into squares using knife dipped frequently in warm water. (This prevents sticking.) Immediately roll marshmallows in coating. Or, roll marshmallows in sugar and cornstarch. Allow to stand uncovered overnight.
About 1¼ lbs. marshmallows

—MINT NUT MARSHMALLOWS

Cover bottom of buttered pan with **¼ cup (1 oz.) finely chopped nuts.** Follow ▲ Recipe. For vanilla extract, substitute **1 teaspoon peppermint extract** and **½ teaspoon finely chopped fresh mint leaves.** Coat with chopped nuts.

—TINTED MARSHMALLOWS

Follow ▲ Recipe. Blend in with vanilla extract **1 or more drops desired food coloring.**

—ALMOND MARSHMALLOWS

Follow ▲ Recipe. For vanilla extract substitute **1 teaspoon almond extract.**

—MOCHA MARSHMALLOWS

Follow ▲ Recipe. For vanilla extract substitute **2 teaspoons instant powdered coffee.**

POPCORN BALLS I

If using an electric popper, follow manufacturer's directions. Otherwise, for each pan of popcorn, heat in a heavy skillet or saucepan with a tight-fitting cover
1 tablespoon vegetable shortening, all-purpose shortening, lard or cooking oil
Add enough popcorn to just cover bottom of skillet, and cover tightly. Shake pan over medium heat until popping stops. Turn corn into warm large bowl. In the same way, prepare
10 cups popped corn
Sprinkle over popped corn and mix in
1 teaspoon salt
Set aside.

Mix in a saucepan
1 cup firmly packed brown sugar
¾ cup light corn syrup
1½ teaspoons vinegar
½ teaspoon salt
Cook slowly until sugar is melted. Boil briskly to 280°F (soft crack stage, page 11; remove from heat while testing). Keeping syrup boiling, slowly stir in
½ cup undiluted evaporated milk
Bring to soft crack stage again.

Gradually pour the hot syrup into center of the corn. With a long-handled fork, quickly stir and coat the popcorn with syrup. As soon as it is cool enough to handle, with buttered hands, gather and press the popcorn into firm balls.
10 large or 20 small Popcorn Balls

POPCORN BALLS II

▲ *Base Recipe*

As American as circus day and just as popular.

For Popped Corn—Prepare
3 qts. popped corn
Turn into warm large bowl; set aside and keep popped corn warm.

For Syrup—Combine in a saucepan
1½ cups molasses
¼ cup water
½ cup sugar
1 tablespoon vinegar
½ teaspoon salt
Set candy thermometer in place (page 11). Cook over medium heat, stirring occasionally, until thermometer registers 270°F, or a small amount dropped into very cold water separates into hard but not brittle threads. (Remove from heat while testing.)

Remove from heat and stir in
⅓ cup butter or margarine
1 tablespoon vanilla extract

For Popcorn Balls—Gradually pour hot syrup into center of the corn. With a long-handled fork, quickly stir and coat corn with syrup. With buttered hands, gather and press corn into firm balls. Cool.

Wrap each ball separately in a square piece of waxed paper, drawing the paper around the ball and twisting on top.
About 15 large or 30 small Popcorn Balls

—PIXY POPCORN BALLS

Follow ▲ Recipe. Mix **1 cup (about 5 oz.) salted peanuts** with the popcorn.

—RAISIN POPCORN BALLS

Follow ▲ Recipe or recipe for Pixy Popcorn Balls. Mix **1 cup (about 5 oz.) seedless raisins** with the popcorn.

—CORN-Y LOLLIPOPS

Follow ▲ Recipe or recipe for Pixy Popcorn Balls. Substitute for popped corn, **corn soya**

Popcorn Balls II

Nutty Caramel Apples

shreds or **crisp corn puffs**. Press mixture around one end of wooden skewers to form oval lollipops. Cool on buttered baking sheet.

—AUTUMN POPS

Follow recipe for Corn-y Lollipops. Add ½ **cup corn candy** to cereal before pouring in syrup.

POPCORN RAINBOW

▲ Base Recipe

For Popped Corn—Prepare
    6 cups popped corn
Set popped corn aside and keep warm.

Lay out waxed paper about 24 in. long.

For Wintergreen Popcorn—Combine in a small saucepan
    1 cup sugar
    ½ cup water
    ¼ cup light corn syrup
    1 teaspoon vinegar
Set over low heat, stirring until sugar is dissolved. Increase heat and cook syrup rapidly without stirring.

Put candy thermometer in place (page 11). Cook until thermometer registers 300°F, or a small amount separates into threads which are hard and brittle in very cold water. (Remove from heat while testing.) During cooking wash down crystals from sides of pan with pastry brush dipped in water; move thermometer and wash down crystals that may have formed on sides of pan under the thermometer.

Heat a large bowl by scalding it with boiling water. Dry and set bowl aside to keep warm.

When temperature of mixture reaches 300°F, remove saucepan from heat and stir in
    2 teaspoons wintergreen extract
    ¼ teaspoon green food coloring
Quickly pour syrup into the warm bowl. Add warm popped corn to syrup. With a long-handled fork, *quickly* stir and coat corn with syrup. Dot corn with
    1 tablespoon butter or margarine
Turn coated corn onto the waxed paper and separate kernels. Thoroughly cool coated corn.

Store in a tightly covered container or plastic bag. This will help to prevent sticky corn.
6 cups coated popcorn

—LEMON POPCORN

Follow ▲ Recipe. Substitute **2 teaspoons lemon extract** and **¼ teaspoon yellow food coloring** for the wintergreen extract and green food coloring.

—CINNAMON POPCORN

Follow ▲ Recipe. Substitute **2 teaspoons cinnamon** and **¼ teaspoon red food coloring** for wintergreen extract and green food coloring.

NUTTY CARAMEL APPLES

Grease a baking sheet. Set out eight 4- to 6-in. wooden skewers. Set out a large heavy saucepan.

Chop
    1½ cups (about 6 oz.) nuts
Set aside on waxed paper.

Wash and dry
    8 medium (about 2½ lbs.) apples
Insert skewers in stem ends; set aside.

Combine in the saucepan
    1¼ cups (14-oz. can) sweetened condensed milk
    ½ cup light corn syrup
    ½ cup granulated sugar
    ⅓ cup firmly packed brown sugar
Set candy thermometer in place (page 11). Stirring constantly, cook over medium heat until thermometer registers 234°F, or a small amount forms a soft ball when dropped into very cold water; it flattens when removed from water. (Remove from heat while testing.) Remove from heat and stir in
    1 tablespoon butter or margarine
    1½ teaspoons vanilla extract

Quickly dip and twirl apples in syrup to coat evenly. Immediately roll in chopped nuts. Set on baking sheet (skewers upright) to cool.
8 caramel apples

STUFFED DATES

▲ Base Recipe

Set out a baking sheet.

Set out
    30 (about ½ lb.) plump dates
With a sharp knife, make a lengthwise slit in each date. With tip of knife, remove and discard pits. (If pitted dates are used, open cavities.)

Using ½ to 1 teaspoonful for each date (depending on size), stuff with one of the fillings suggested below. Gently press sides of dates around filling.

Quickly coat one date at a time in a mixture of
    1 egg white, slightly beaten
    2 tablespoons water

Roll dates in
    ½ cup granulated or confectioners' sugar (if desired, add 1 tablespoon cinnamon)
Shake off excess sugar; place on baking sheet to dry slightly.

Store in cool place in a tightly covered container, placing waxed paper between layers of dates.
30 stuffed dates

—STUFFED PRUNES

Follow ▲ Recipe. Substitute **prunes** for dates. Rinse, cover with water and bring to boiling. Cook 10 min. Drain and cool. Remove and discard pits (pits are more easily removed when prunes are slightly warm). Cool on absorbent paper. Proceed with ▲ Recipe, increasing filling to 1 to 2 teaspoons for each prune.

—STUFFED FIGS

Follow ▲ Recipe. Substitute **dried figs** for dates. Rinse. Cover (or wrap loosely in a towel) and steam over boiling water 10 to 15 min., or until fruit is plump. Drain and cool on absorbent paper. Proceed with ▲ Recipe, increasing filling to 1 to 2 teaspoons for each fig.

—FILLINGS FOR DATES

Candied fruit or peel—½ cup (3 to 4 oz.), finely cut. Use one kind or combine several.
Candy bar—1 to 2 (about 2 oz. each) chocolate nut bars, cut in small pieces.
Marshmallows—8 (2 oz.) cut into quarters (page 10). Fill each date with ¼ marshmallow, cut-side up. Before coating with sugar, dip tops into 2 or 3 tablespoons finely chopped nuts. Or, press nut meat into marshmallow.
Nuts—¼ cup (about 1 oz.) plain or salted, whole or halves.
Peanut butter—½ cup (4 oz.). If desired, blend in 1 teaspoon grated orange or lemon peel.
Pineapple—½ cup well-drained crushed pineapple.

Beverages

Nothing quite equals the restorative powers of an ice-chilled beverage in a tall frosty glass served on a warm day. Yet, there are people from many countries where the climate is always hot who know full well the stimulating value of a hot drink—fragrant coffee, refreshing tea, or the spiciness of south-of-the-border hot chocolate. Popular beverages today among Americans include the great variety of malts, shakes and sodas as well as the many fruit "ades" which are easily adaptable to individual tastes. Included here are recipes for beverages of all types, both hot and cold, nonalcoholic and alcoholic, along with those for special-occasion punches and eggnogs.

SUGAR SYRUP

Mix in a saucepan
    2 cups sugar
    2 cups water
Cover, bring to boiling and boil 5 min. Cool; store, tightly covered, in refrigerator.

2½ cups syrup

COCOA SYRUP

▲ *Base Recipe*

Mix thoroughly in a saucepan
    2 cups sugar
    1 cup cocoa
Stir in to make a paste
    ½ cup water
Stir in
    2 cups boiling water
Let boil for 6 min. Remove from heat. Stir in
    ¼ teaspoon salt
Cool syrup. Store in tightly covered jar in refrigerator.   *About 2 cups syrup*

—CHOCOLATE SYRUP

Follow ▲ Recipe. Substitute for cocoa **6 oz. (6 sq.) unsweetened chocolate,** grated. Omit ½ cup water.

—MOCHA COCOA SYRUP

Follow ▲ Recipe. Substitute **double-strength coffee beverage** (page 10) for ½ cup water.

CARAMEL SYRUP

Melt in light-colored heavy skillet over low heat, stirring constantly
    1 cup sugar

When sugar becomes a golden brown syrup, remove from heat. Add carefully and very gradually, stirring constantly
    1 cup boiling water
Return to low heat and continue to stir about 10 min., or until of syrup consistency.

Cool and store tightly covered in refrigerator.

About 1 cup syrup

HOT BEVERAGES

DRIP COFFEE

▲ *Base Recipe*

Preheat coffee maker with boiling water. Drain.

For each standard measuring cup of water, using standard measuring spoons, measure
    2 tablespoons coffee, drip grind
Put into filter section of drip coffee maker. Pour into upper container
    Measured freshly boiling water
Cover. Allow water to drip through coffee grounds, keeping coffee maker over low heat 5 to 8 min., or while coffee is dripping. Do not let coffee boil at any time. Remove coffee compartment; stir and cover the brew. If coffee cannot be served immediately, place coffee maker over low heat. Stir before serving.

—PERCOLATED COFFEE

Use regular grind coffee. Follow ▲ Recipe for amount of coffee to use. Put into strainer basket of coffee maker. Measure freshly drawn cold water into coffee maker. Insert basket into coffee maker. Cover.

Place over heat and when percolating begins, reduce heat to low so that coffee will percolate gently and slowly. Timing varies from 5 to 10 min. after percolation starts. It is wise to experiment to determine exact timing for the amount of coffee usually made. Larger amounts of coffee require the longer timing. Remove coffee basket, cover coffee maker and keep coffee hot over low heat. Do not let coffee boil at any time.

—STEEPED COFFEE

Use regular grind coffee. Follow ▲ Recipe for amount of coffee to use. Put into coffee maker. To clarify this coffee, mix into ground coffee
    1 teaspoon slightly beaten egg for each 2 tablespoons coffee used. Measure and add fresh cold water.

Bring very slowly to boiling, stirring occasionally. Remove from heat at once. Pour ¼ cup cold water down spout to settle grounds.

Let stand 3 to 5 min. without heat. Strain through a fine strainer into a server which has been preheated with boiling water. If necessary to keep hot, let coffee stand over low heat without boiling.

—VACUUM-DRIP COFFEE

Use drip or vacuum grind coffee. Follow ▲ Recipe for amount of coffee to use.

Specific directions for preparing vary according

to type of coffee maker used. Usually, freshly drawn cold water is measured and poured into the decanter or lower bowl of coffee maker. Coffee is measured into upper bowl. Cover. Place coffee maker over moderate to low heat.

When all but a small amount of water below bottom of tube has risen to upper bowl, remove coffee maker from heat. Remove top bowl when the brew has run into decanter. Cover. Serve immediately or keep hot over very low heat. Do not boil at any time.

COFFEE FOR TWENTY (STEEPED)

Thoroughly mix
½ lb. coffee, regular grind
1 egg and crushed egg shell
Tie loosely in fine cheesecloth or put into a lightweight muslin bag. Put into a kettle with
1 gal. (16 cups) freshly drawn cold water
Cover. Place over low heat and bring very slowly to boiling. Boil 3 to 5 min. Taste to test strength. Remove bag when coffee is desired strength. Cover kettle and let stand 10 to 15 min. over low heat without boiling.

20 servings

BLACK COFFEE
(Café Noir)

▲ Base Recipe

Praise for Creole Café Noir begins the instant the bouquet is evident. And that aroma first begins at dawn, returns at breakfast and again after dinner. Café au Lait is served at breakfast and is made by combining equal amounts of Café Noir and hot milk. Creole cooks warn that Café Noir must never be boiled.

Preheat a drip coffee maker by filling it with boiling water. Drain.

For each standard measuring cup of water, using standard measuring spoons, measure
2 to 4 tablespoons drip grind coffee (depending upon strength desired)

Place in filter section of drip coffee maker.

Bring to boiling
Freshly drawn water
Measure and pour boiling water into upper container, about 2 tablespoons at a time. Cover. Allow all of the water to drip through the coffee. Repeat the small additions of boiling water. After four or five additions of water have been made, set coffee maker over very low heat while coffee is dripping. Repeat additions of water until desired quantity of coffee is made. Do not let coffee boil at any time.

Remove coffee compartment; stir and cover the brew. If coffee cannot be served immediately, let stand over low heat without boiling.

Note: Many Creoles prefer a blend of coffee and chicory. This changes the flavor and makes Café Noir darker in color.

—COFFEE WITH MILK
(Café au Lait)

Follow ▲ Recipe, allowing ½ cup of Café Noir for each serving. Scald (page 10) **½ cup milk or cream** per serving. Simultaneously pour hot coffee and hot milk or cream into each cup. Sweeten, if desired.

COFFEE, MACCHINETTA STYLE
(Caffè di Macchinetta)

Set out a macchinetta di caffè (an Italian coffee maker which can be purchased in most department stores).

Place in middle strainer section
3 tablespoons Italian-roasted coffee
To bottom section add
2 cups water
Replace all top sections and place coffee maker over heat. When the water is boiling (steam escapes from a tiny hole in the bottom section of coffee maker) remove macchinetta from heat. Grasping both handles firmly, turn coffee maker upside down. The boiling water will drip through the coffee in a few minutes.

Serve very hot.

This coffee can be served with either **a twist of lemon peel** or with **1 teaspoon rum or anisette** added to each cup.

4 to 6 demitasse cups of coffee

TEA

Fill a teapot with boiling water. When heated thoroughly, pour off water.

Put into pot for each cup of tea to be brewed
1 rounded teaspoon tea or 1 tea bag
For each cup of tea, pour in
1 cup freshly boiling water
Cover pot and let tea brew 3 to 5 min.

Remove tea bags or strain tea into a preheated pot and serve immediately. Serve with any of the following: thin slices or wedges of **lemon,**

Coffee, Macchinetta Style

orange or lime; lemon, orange or lime juice; whole cloves; sprigs of fresh mint; loaf sugar or **simple syrup; cream** or **milk.**

HOT CHOCOLATE

▲ Base Recipe

Mix in a saucepan and cook over low heat, stirring constantly
2 oz. (2 sq.) unsweetened chocolate
¾ cup water
5 to 6 tablespoons sugar
⅛ teaspoon salt

When chocolate is melted, increase heat and boil 3 min., stirring constantly. Reduce heat.

Add gradually, stirring in
3¼ cups milk
Heat to scalding. Do not boil. Stir in
1 teaspoon vanilla extract

6 servings

—HOT COCOA

Follow ▲ Recipe. Substitute **6 tablespoons cocoa** for chocolate. Blend cocoa and sugar before adding water.

—MOCHA CHOCOLATE

Follow ▲ Recipe. Substitute **¾ cup double-strength coffee beverage** (page 10) for ¾ cup of the milk. Add ¼ teaspoon cinnamon, if desired.

—MINT CHOCOLATE

Follow ▲ Recipe. Substitute **8 chocolate-covered peppermint patties** for the chocolate and sugar.

—HONEY HOT CHOCOLATE OR COCOA

Follow ▲ Recipe or Hot Cocoa recipe. Substitute an equal amount of **honey** for the sugar in either recipe.

—QUICK HOT CHOCOLATE OR COCOA

Stir 1½ to 2 tablespoons **Chocolate or Cocoa Syrup** (page 621) into each cup of hot milk.

—CHOCOLATE OR COCOA COOLER

Stir 1½ to 2 tablespoons **Chocolate Syrup or Cocoa Syrup** (page 621) into each glass of cold milk. Add cracked ice, if desired. Serve with a straw.

MEXICAN CHOCOLATE

This deliciously spicy chocolate is so rich that most folks will want very small servings.

Combine in a large heavy saucepan
> **4 oz. (4 sq.) unsweetened chocolate, grated**
> **1 cup double-strength coffee beverage (page 10)**

Heat, stirring until chocolate is melted and mixture is smooth. Cook 2 min., stirring constantly. Mix in
> **1 cup sugar**
> **2 teaspoons cinnamon**
> **Few grains allspice**
> **Few grains salt**

Add gradually, stirring in
> **6 cups milk**

Continue heating until scalding hot.

Remove from heat and blend in
> **1 tablespoon vanilla extract**
> > *About 8 servings*

SPICY CHOCOLATE MOCHA

Any time of the day (or night), sandwiches and cookies taste better with steaming mugs of hearty chocolate mocha, deliciously spiced by a muddler of stick cinnamon. This is another TV special, fine for cold evenings.

Chill a small bowl and beater in refrigerator.

Mix in a medium-size saucepan
> **1½ oz. (1½ sq.) unsweetened chocolate**
> **1 cup hot water**
> **½ cup sugar**
> **¼ cup instant powdered coffee**
> **¼ teaspoon salt**

Spicy Chocolate Mocha

Set over low heat and stir constantly until chocolate is melted. When chocolate is melted, bring rapidly to boiling while stirring gently and constantly. Reduce heat and cook for 3 min., stirring occasionally. Remove from heat. Add gradually, stirring constantly
> **4 cups milk**

Return to heat. Heat to scalding. *Do not boil.*

Meanwhile, beat, using chilled bowl and beater, until cream stands in peaks when beater is slowly lifted upright
> **⅓ cup chilled heavy cream**

Serve chocolate piping hot; top each serving with whipped cream. If desired, sprinkle **nutmeg** over whipped cream.

Put into each mug or cup of beverage
> **Cinnamon stick**
> > *About 6 servings*

HOT MALTED CHOCOLATE

Scald (page 10)
> **2 cups milk**

Rinse an electric blender container with hot water.

Put into blender container
> **½ pkg. (3 oz.) semisweet chocolate pieces**
> **¼ cup malted milk powder**
> **1 teaspoon vanilla extract**
> **Dash salt**

Add about ½ cup of the scalded milk. Cover and blend about 1 min., or until smooth and even colored throughout mixture.

Add remainder of milk and blend about 30 sec. more, or until thoroughly mixed.

Serve immediately.
> *About 2 cups or two 8-oz. servings*

BUTTERSCOTCH BENCHWARMER

Combine in a 2-qt. saucepan
> **4 cups milk**
> **½ cup butterscotch pieces**

Heat until butterscotch pieces are melted, stirring occasionally.

Serve topped with
> **Miniature marshmallows**
> > *About 1 qt. beverage*

CHEERLEADERS' CHOICE

Combine in a 2-qt. saucepan
> **½ cup water**
> **¼ cup red cinnamon candies**
> **¼ cup sugar**
> **2 tablespoons whole cloves**
> **⅛ teaspoon salt**

Simmer over low heat about 5 min., stirring occasionally. Strain and return liquid to saucepan. Add and heat to serving temperature
> **4 cups milk**

Pour into four glasses with handles or mugs. Serve with **cinnamon sticks.**
> *About 1 qt. beverage*

ORANGE HONEY HERO

Combine in a 2-qt. saucepan and heat to serving temperature, stirring occasionally
> **4 cups milk**
> **½ cup instant vanilla pudding mix**
> **6 tablespoons thawed frozen orange juice concentrate**
> **1 tablespoon honey**

Pour into glasses with handles or mugs and garnish with **orange slices.**
> *About 5 cups beverage*

COLD BEVERAGES

ICED TEA

▲ *Base Recipe*

Prepare (for each serving)
> **1 cup double-strength tea**

Fill tall glasses to brim with
> **Crushed ice or ice cubes**

Strain tea while hot and pour over ice.

Serve with any of the following: thin slices or wedges of **lemon, orange or lime; lemon, orange, or lime juice; whole cloves; sprigs of fresh mint; loaf sugar or simple syrup.**

—ICED TEA WITH FRUIT KABOBS

Follow ▲ Recipe. Cut a ½-in. slice from **1 fresh pineapple.** Pare the slice and remove "eyes." Using a sharp knife, remove and discard core section. Cut remaining ring into wedges. Cut a ½-in. slice from center of **1 large orange.** Cut slice into wedge-shaped pieces.

Iced Tea with Fruit Kabobs

Fruit Waters

Thread onto each stirrer (allowing one per glass) **1 fresh strawberry**, rinsed and hulled; **1 slice lime**; **1 red maraschino cherry**, well drained; **2 mint leaves**, rinsed; **1 large seedless grape**, rinsed and stemmed; one wedge of the pineapple ring, and one wedge of the orange slice. Chill in refrigerator. Place a Fruit Kabob in each glass of Iced Tea before serving.

—SPICY ICED TEA

Combine in a saucepan with a tight-fitting cover **1 cup cold water, 1 cup sugar, ⅛ teaspoon salt, ⅛ teaspoon nutmeg, 6 whole cloves** and **4 pieces (2 in. each) stick cinnamon**. Set over low heat; stir until sugar is dissolved. Cover and simmer 20 min. Remove from heat; strain and set aside to cool. Set syrup in refrigerator to chill. Follow ▲ Recipe; prepare 4 cups hot **tea**. Blend in the spiced syrup.

—MINTED ICED TEA

Follow ▲ Recipe. For each 4 cups freshly prepared tea, after straining, add **2 sprigs fresh mint leaves**, bruised, and **3 tablespoons lemon or lime juice**. Let mixture stand ½ to 1 hr.

ICED SPICED COFFEE

Mix together in a 1-qt. heatproof container
   2 tablespoons instant powdered coffee
   6 whole allspice
   4 whole cloves
   2 pieces (2 in. each) stick cinnamon
Pour over coffee-spice mixture
   3 cups boiling water
Cover and set aside for 2 hrs.

To serve, strain and pour over ice cubes or crushed ice in tall glasses. If desired, sweeten with **sugar** and top with **Sweetened Whipped Cream (page 480)**.   *4 servings*

ICED COFFEE

Prepare (for each serving)
   1 cup double-strength coffee beverage (page 10)

Fill tall glasses to brim with
   Crushed ice or ice cubes
Pour hot coffee beverage over ice. Serve with
   Sugar, granulated or confectioners'
   Cream, plain or whipped
If desired, sprinkle with **cinnamon**.

Serve at once.

FRUIT WATERS

On sultry summer evenings, Southerners enjoy a frosty glass of cool fruit water. Simplified modern versions are easily made from commercially prepared fruit syrups or bases.

Concentrated frozen fruit juices such as **orange, orange** and **grapefruit**, or **grape** can be reconstituted with **ginger ale** or **carbonated water** instead of water (1 qt. ginger ale or sparkling water to one 12-oz. can frozen fruit-juice concentrate).

Beverages such as **Lemonade, Orangeade, Limeade** and **Spicy Currant Sparkler** are all fruit waters.

Sugar-frosted glasses are a perfect complement for these delightful coolers. Just brush the rims of the glasses with a portion of slightly beaten **egg white** and dip them into a shallow dish containing **confectioners'** or **granulated sugar**. Or dip rims of glasses into **lemon juice**, then into sugar. Chill the glasses in the refrigerator. Carefully fill glasses with beverage.

Garnish glasses of fruit water with a **lemon, lime,** or **orange slice**, a sprig of **mint**, or a **cherry, strawberry** or other piece of fruit. If desired, serve with gaily colored paper or plastic straws. Even the most weary and warm guest will brighten after such sparkling refreshment!

APRICOT MELON COOLER

Remove seeds and rind; cut into pieces (enough to make 1 cup)
   Melon, cantaloupe or honeydew
Set aside.

Pour into an electric blender container
   1 cup apricot nectar
   2 tablespoons lemon juice
   Dash salt
Cover and turn on motor. Gradually add melon pieces.

Add in order
   4 ice cubes, one at a time
   1 pt. lemon sherbet, by spoonfuls
Blend until thoroughly mixed.

Serve immediately.
   About 3 cups or four 6-oz. servings

CHERRY FRAPPE

Frost and chill 4 tall glasses. (See Fruit Waters, on this page.)

Force through a sieve or food mill contents of
   1 can (16 oz.) pitted red tart cherries
Add to the sieved cherries
   Water (enough to make 3 cups)
   1 cup sugar
Stir until thoroughly mixed. Blend in
   2 tablespoons lemon juice
   ¼ teaspoon almond extract
   Few grains salt
Tint to desired color by blending in one drop at a time
   Red food coloring (about 4 drops)
Pour into refrigerator tray. Freeze until mixture is of mushy consistency, stirring 1 or 2 times.

Serve partially frozen in chilled frosted glasses. Accompany with colored straws.   *4 servings*

SPICY CURRANT SPARKLER

▲ Base Recipe

Set out a small saucepan.

Put into refrigerator to chill, 4 tall glasses and
   1 qt. ginger ale or carbonated water

For Currant Syrup—Rinse, drain, remove and discard stems from
   1 cup fresh currants
Put currants into the saucepan and add
   ¼ cup water
Cover and simmer 10 min. Remove from heat. Force currants through a sieve to remove seeds. Blend into the sieved currants
   ¼ cup sugar
   ⅛ teaspoon cinnamon
Put currant syrup into refrigerator to chill thoroughly.

To Serve—Pour equal amounts of the currant syrup into the four glasses. Fill glasses with the chilled ginger ale or carbonated water and stir.

Garnish each serving with a spray of **currants** and **currant leaves**.   *4 servings*

—SPICY CURRANT FLOAT

Follow ▲ Recipe. Fill glasses about two-thirds full with ginger ale or carbonated water. Float **1 scoop vanilla ice cream** in each glass.

GRAPE SPARKLE

▲ Base Recipe

Four tall glasses will be needed.

Have ready
   1 qt. ginger ale, chilled
Peel and force through a coarse sieve or purée in an electric blender enough bananas, with brown-flecked peel, to yield
   1 cup puréed banana

Add to banana pulp and stir until well blended
   1 cup grape juice
   2 tablespoons confectioners' sugar
Spoon one fourth of banana mixture into each glass. Pour a small amount of the ginger ale into glass and stir to mix intredients. Fill glass with ginger ale.

Serve immediately.   *4 servings*

—PINEAPPLE SPARKLE

Follow ▲ Recipe. Substitute **1 cup pineapple juice** and **2 teaspoons lemon juice** for grape juice.

—CHOCOLATE SPARKLE

Follow ▲ Recipe. Substitute **1 cup softened chocolate or vanilla ice cream** for banana pulp and **½ cup Chocolate Syrup** (page 621) for grape juice. Omit the confectioners' sugar.

—ORANGE SPARKLE

Follow ▲ Recipe. Substitute **½ cup thawed undiluted frozen orange juice concentrate** for grape juice.

—LEMON SPARKLE

Follow ▲ Recipe. Substitute **½ cup lemon juice** for grape juice. Increase confectioners' sugar to ½ cup.

TEXAS SPARKLER

A large pitcher and six tall glasses will be needed.

Have ready
   1 qt. ginger ale, chilled
Set out to thaw
   2 cans (6 oz. each) frozen orange and grapefruit juice concentrate
When ready to serve, pour the thawed juice into the pitcher. Add and stir in
   ¼ cup confectioners' sugar
Add the chilled ginger ale and mix just until blended.

Texas Sparkler

Put one or two ice cubes into each glass. Fill each with ginger ale mixture.

Serve with snacks such as **potato chips** or **salted nuts.**   *6 servings*

PINK LEMONADE

Mix in a large bowl or pitcher
   6 cups cold water
   2 cups lemon juice (about 12 lemons; or use frozen lemon juice, thawed)
   1¾ cups sugar
   ⅓ cup maraschino cherry syrup (drained from one 8-oz. jar maraschino cherries; reserve cherries for other use)
Stir until sugar is dissolved. Set in refrigerator to chill thoroughly.

To serve, pour over crushed ice or ice cubes in chilled glasses and garnish, if desired, with **maraschino cherries.**   *2 qts. lemonade*

FROTHY LEMONADE

Put into an electric blender container, in order
   1 cup water
   ¼ cup lemon juice
   ¼ cup honey
   2 egg whites
   Dash salt
Cover and blend about 30 sec., or until thoroughly blended.

Add, one at a time
   4 ice cubes
Blend until mixed.

Spoon froth over top of drink after pouring liquid into glasses.
            About 3 cups or three 8-oz. servings

LEMONADE OR LIMEADE

▲ Base Recipe

Combine in a saucepan with a tight-fitting cover
   1 cup sugar
   1 cup water
Bring to boiling; stir until sugar is dissolved. Cover and boil 5 min. Remove from heat; cool.

Juice enough fruit to yield
   ¾ cup lemon juice or lime juice
Mix juice, cooled syrup and
   4 cups cold water
Pour over chipped ice or cubes in tall glasses.
            4 or 5 servings

—ORANGEADE

Follow ▲ Recipe. Use ¼ cup lemon juice only. Use **3 cups orange juice** and only 1 cup cold water.

ORANGE BANANA SMASH

Put into an electric blender container
   1 can (6 oz.) frozen orange juice concentrate
   2 cans (1½ cups) cold water
Cover and turn on motor.

Add by pieces
   2 brown-flecked bananas, peeled

Add, one at a time
   4 ice cubes
Blend until thoroughly mixed.
            About 3 cups or three 8-oz. servings

ORANGE JULEP

Combine and stir until sugar is dissolved
   2 cups orange juice
   ¼ cup lime juice
   ½ cup sugar
   3 tablespoons finely chopped fresh mint leaves
   ½ teaspoon grated orange peel
Chill thoroughly in refrigerator.

Just before serving, blend with the orange juice mixture
   2 cups chilled carbonated water
Pour into tall glasses over
   Ice cubes or crushed ice
Garnish with **sprigs of mint.**   *4 servings*

SPICED FRUIT DRINK

Combine in a saucepan and bring to boiling
   ⅓ cup water
   2 tablespoons sugar
   ½ teaspoon grated orange peel
   3 whole cloves
   1 stick cinnamon
Simmer for 10 min. Strain and cool.

Pour over spice mixture
   1⅓ cups pineapple juice
   ⅓ cup orange juice
   2 tablespoons lemon juice
Mix thoroughly. Chill.   *2 cups beverage*

FRUIT FRAPPE

Shave in an electric blender enough to make 1 cup shaved ice
   Ice cubes

Coffee Apricot Milk Drink

Add, while motor is running

1 cup pineapple or orange juice

Blend only until mixed. (Should be the same color throughout.) The mixture will be of spooning consistency and very icy.

Serve immediately in chilled sherbet glasses.

About 2 cups or four 4-oz. servings

FRESH APPLE SHAKE

Wash, quarter, core and set aside

2 medium (about ⅔ lb.) apples

Pour into an electric blender container

¾ cup pineapple juice
2 tablespoons lemon juice

Cover and turn on motor. Add apples by pieces.

Add, in order

1 tablespoon cinnamon candies
3 scoops vanilla ice cream

Blend until thoroughly mixed.

About 2 cups or two 8-oz. servings

APRICOT-RICH MILK

Have ready

¼ cup Sugar Syrup (page 621)

Rinse, halve and pit enough to make 1 cup

About ½ lb. ripe apricots

Set aside.

Pour Sugar Syrup into an electric blender container with

2 cups cold milk
¼ teaspoon almond extract

Cover and turn on motor.

Gradually add apricots with

1 tablespoon lemon juice

Blend about 45 sec., or until slightly thick and smooth and serve immediately.

About 3 cups or four 6-oz. servings

COFFEE APRICOT MILK DRINK

▲ *Base Recipe*

Mix in a large bowl

1½ cups coffee beverage, chilled
1 cup chilled apricot nectar
⅔ cup cold milk

Add and beat until smooth

1 pt. coffee ice cream, softened

Pour mixture into glasses and serve with **nibblers**.

4 servings

—MOCHA-MINT DRINK

Follow ▲ Recipe. Use **double-strength coffee beverage**. Omit apricot nectar; increase milk to 1 cup. Substitute **1 pt. chocolate ice cream** for the coffee ice cream; beat in **¼ teaspoon mint extract**.

BANANA SHAKE

▲ *Base Recipe*

Peel and mash

2 bananas with brown-flecked peel

Blend in

2 tablespoons molasses
½ teaspoon vanilla extract
¼ teaspoon cinnamon
Few grains salt

Add

1½ cups cold milk

Beat with rotary beater or electric mixer until smooth and creamy. Chill.

About 2 cups beverage

—BANANA COFFEELATE

Follow ▲ Recipe. Omit molasses and cinnamon. Add **¼ cup chocolate syrup**, **2 teaspoons sugar** and **2 teaspoons instant powdered coffee** to bananas.

—COCOA SHAKE

Follow ▲ Recipe. Omit bananas and molasses. Add a mixture of **¼ cup water**, **5 tablespoons sugar** and **2 tablespoons cocoa**.

—BERRY MILK DRINK

Follow ▲ Recipe. Omit molasses and cinnamon. Substitute for bananas **1 pt. strawberries or raspberries**, rinsed (imperfect berries discarded). Hull strawberries. Blend into berries **3 tablespoons confectioners' sugar**. (Frozen

sweetened strawberries or raspberries, thawed, may be substituted for the fresh berries.)

—APRICOT MILK DRINK

Follow ▲ Recipe. Omit molasses and cinnamon. Substitute for bananas **⅓ cup cooked drained apricots**. Blend into apricots **3 tablespoons sugar** and substitute **⅛ teaspoon almond extract** for vanilla extract.

BANANA MILK SHAKE

▲ *Base Recipe*

Peel and mash

3 or 4 large bananas with brown-flecked peel

Blend in

2 tablespoons sugar
2 teaspoons vanilla extract

Stir in

4 cups cold milk

Beat vigorously until thoroughly blended.

6 servings

—ORANGE MILK SHAKE

Follow ▲ Recipe. Substitute **1½ cups orange juice** and **1 tablespoon lemon juice** for bananas. Increase sugar to 3 tablespoons. Omit extract. Decrease milk to 3 cups and stir into juices and sugar mixture. Do not beat.

—PEANUT BUTTER MILK SHAKE

Follow ▲ Recipe. Substitute **½ cup peanut butter** for bananas. Mix ½ cup milk with peanut butter, sugar and extract and beat until smooth. Beat in remaining milk.

ICED COCOA

▲ *Base Recipe*

Six tall glasses will be needed.

Mix in a saucepan or top of a double boiler

5 to 6 tablespoons cocoa
5 to 6 tablespoons sugar
¼ teaspoon salt

Blend in slowly

1 cup water

Boil gently 2 min. over direct heat, stirring

until slightly thickened. Reduce heat; stir in
3 cups milk
Heat slowly over low heat or simmering water until scalding hot, stirring occasionally. Remove from heat. Cool; chill, covered, in refrigerator.

When chilled add
1 teaspoon vanilla extract
Beat with rotary beater until foamy.

Fill the glasses to the brim with
Crushed ice or ice cubes
Pour chilled beverage over ice.

Top each serving with
Sweetened Whipped Cream (page 480)
Mint sprigs
Sprinkle each serving lightly with
Cinnamon, nutmeg or ginger

—ICED CHOCOLATE

Follow ▲ Recipe. Substitute **2 oz. (2 sq.) unsweetened chocolate** for cocoa. Break into pieces and combine with sugar, water and salt. Mix and stir constantly over low heat. When chocolate is melted, increase heat and boil 2 min., stirring constantly. Add milk and continue as in ▲ Recipe.

—ICED HONEY COCOA

Follow ▲ Recipe. Substitute **5 to 6 tablespoons honey** for the sugar.

MINTY CHOCOLATE FLIP

Combine and stir until smooth
¼ cup malted milk powder
¼ cup Chocolate or Cocoa Syrup (page 621)
Blend in slowly
2 cups cold milk
1½ teaspoons vanilla extract
½ teaspoon peppermint extract
¼ teaspoon salt

Minty Chocolate Flip

Beat or shake well. Chill in refrigerator. When ready to serve, pour into shaker and add
1 pt. vanilla ice cream, softened
Shake until smooth. Top with **whipped cream.** Sprinkle with **nutmeg.** *6 servings*

BRAZILIAN CHOCOLATE

Combine in a small saucepan
1 oz. (1 sq.) unsweetened chocolate
½ cup double-strength coffee beverage (page 10)
¼ cup sugar
Dash salt
Stir over low heat until chocolate is melted. Bring to boiling, stirring gently. Reduce heat and simmer 3 min. Remove from heat and add gradually, stirring constantly
1½ cups milk
Refrigerate until thoroughly chilled.

When ready to serve, beat until frothy. Pour over **crushed ice** in tall glasses. Top each drink with a dollop of
Sweetened Whipped Cream (page 480)
or whipped dessert topping
About 2 servings

CHOCOLATE MILK SHAKE

▲ Base Recipe

Combine
2 cups cold milk
¼ cup Chocolate Syrup (page 621)
Beat with rotary beater or mix in shaker or electric blender until frothy. Add
2 to 4 scoops softened vanilla ice cream
Beat until well blended. Pour into glasses.
2 servings

—STRAWBERRY OR RASPBERRY MILK SHAKE

Follow ▲ Recipe. Substitute ⅔ **to 1 cup crushed sweetened strawberries or raspberries** for chocolate syrup.

—PINEAPPLE MILK SHAKE

Follow ▲ Recipe. Substitute ⅔ **to 1 cup crushed pineapple** for chocolate syrup.

—BANANA MILK SHAKE

Follow ▲ Recipe. Substitute **2 brown-flecked bananas,** peeled and mashed, for the chocolate syrup.

—APRICOT MILK SHAKE

Follow ▲ Recipe. Substitute ⅔ **to 1 cup sieved apricots and juice** for chocolate syrup.

—DOUBLE CHOCOLATE MILK SHAKE

Follow ▲ Recipe. Substitute **chocolate ice cream** for vanilla ice cream.

Molasses Milk Shake

—MOLASSES MILK SHAKE

Follow ▲ Recipe. Substitute **molasses** for chocolate syrup. If desired, add ⅛ **teaspoon cinnamon** and **a few grains allspice.**

—EGGNOG SHAKE

Follow ▲ Recipe. Substitute a mixture of **2 eggs,** well beaten, and **4 teaspoons sugar** for chocolate syrup. Add ½ **teaspoon vanilla extract** with ice cream. Sprinkle with **nutmeg.**

—MALTED MILK

Follow ▲ Recipe or any variation. Add **2 tablespoons malted milk powder** to milk.

—PEPPERMINT MALTED MILK

Especially delicious with chocolate cookies.

Follow ▲ Recipe. Use 4 cups milk and omit the Chocolate Syrup. Prepare a peppermint syrup by heating the milk and stirring in ½ **cup crushed peppermint stick candy** until dissolved. Cool syrup and chill in refrigerator. To serve, add **6 scoops ice cream** and ¾ **cup malted milk powder.** Beat until blended.
6 servings

CHOCOLATE MINT TINGLE

Pour into an electric blender container
½ cup Chocolate Syrup (page 621)
2 cups carbonated water
Sprinkle over top of liquid
¼ cup instant nonfat dry milk
Cover and blend 1 min., or until thoroughly mixed.

Add in order
6 peppermint sticks (3 in. each), broken
½ pt. vanilla ice cream, by spoonfuls
2 ice cubes
Cover and blend 30 sec. more, or until frothy.

Serve immediately.
About 3 cups or three 8-oz. servings

Note: If desired, top with a blob of whipped cream or a scoop of ice cream and grated chocolate for a super blender-style soda.

CHILLY COFFOLATE

▲ *Base Recipe*

Have ready
  **1 cup cooled double-strength coffee
     beverage (page 10)**
  ¼ cup Chocolate Syrup (page 621)
Pour coffee beverage and syrup into blender
container with
  1 cup cold milk
Cover and blend about 20 sec., or until frothy.
Pour over cracked ice in glasses. If desired, top
with dollops of **whipped cream** dusted with
cinnamon.   *Three 6-oz. servings*

—CHILLY COFFOLATE SHAKE

Follow ▲ Recipe. Add **1 pt. chocolate or
coffee ice cream** by spoonfuls to beverage and
blend about 15 sec. more, or until just mixed.
Do not pour over ice.
          About 3 cups or four 6-oz. servings

—HOT COFFOLATE

Follow ▲ Recipe. Have coffee and milk hot.
Rinse blender container with hot water before
using. Pour Hot Coffolate immediately into
heated mugs and serve with **cinnamon stick
stirrers.**

FROSTED COFFEE SHAKE I

▲ *Base Recipe*

Put into an electric blender container, in order
  2 cups cold milk
  2 tablespoons sugar
  **1 tablespoon instant powdered
     coffee**

Chilly Coffolate

Cover and blend about 10 sec., or until
thoroughly blended.

Add by spoonfuls
  ½ pt. vanilla or chocolate ice cream
Blend until mixed.

Pour into chilled glasses.
          About 3 cups or three 8-oz. servings

—FROSTED COFFEE SHAKE II

Follow ▲ Recipe. Substitute **very cold water**
for milk; sprinkle **½ cup instant nonfat dry
milk** over water and blend as directed in
▲ Recipe.

BLACK COW

▲ *Base Recipe*

For each serving, put into a tall glass
  ¼ cup milk
Fill the glass about one half full with
  Chilled root beer
Stir until blended. Add
  2 scoops vanilla ice cream
Slowly add enough root beer to fill glass.

Serve immediately, accompanied with a straw
and long-handled spoon.

—COLA COW

Follow ▲ Recipe. Substitute **cola beverage**
for root beer.

BANANA NOG

Put into an electric blender container in order
  2 cups cold milk
  1 egg
  1 tablespoon honey or sugar
  Dash nutmeg
Cover and turn on motor. Add by pieces
  1 brown-flecked banana, peeled
Blend until mixed and serve immediately.
          About 3 cups or four 6-oz. servings

FRUIT EGGNOG

▲ *Base Recipe*

Put into an electric blender container
  1½ cups cold milk
  2 eggs
  2 tablespoons sugar

Raspberry Eggnog

Cover and blend about 5 sec., or until mixed

Pour into blender container, while motor is
running
  ½ cup orange, grape or pineapple juice
Continue blending until thoroughly mixed.
          About 3 cups or three 8-oz. servings

—RASPBERRY EGGNOG

Rinse (discarding imperfect berries) **¾ cup
raspberries.** Follow ▲ Recipe. Substitute ½
cup of the raspberries for fruit juice. Pour into
rim-frosted glasses and garnish with remaining
berries.

Note: Frost rims of glasses to make drinks look
even more refreshingly cool. Before preparing
beverage, brush rims of glasses with unbeaten
egg white. Dip the rim of each glass into
sugar. Place glasses in refrigerator to chill.

CHOCOLATE EGGNOG I

▲ *Base Recipe*

*Nutritious eggnog blended with chocolate spells
sheer delight to hungry children and adults, too.*

Beat until thick and lemon-colored
  6 egg yolks

Chocolate Eggnog I

Add, blending well

    6 cups cold rich milk, or one half
        milk and one half cream
    1½ cups Chocolate or Cocoa Syrup
        (page 621)
    1 tablespoon vanilla extract

Beat until rounded peaks are formed

    6 egg whites

Fold beaten egg whites into milk mixture. Serve cold in mugs or in tall glasses. If desired, sprinkle with

    Nutmeg

                    8 servings

—BANANA EGGNOG

Peel and slice **6 brown-flecked bananas** into bowl and beat with hand rotary beater or electric mixer until creamy. Fold in beaten egg white and proceed as in ▲ Recipe.

HONEY EGGNOG

    ▲ *Base Recipe*

Beat together

    4 eggs, well beaten
    ½ cup honey

Beat in

    4 cups cold milk
    4 teaspoons vanilla extract

Pour into glasses. Sprinkle each serving with

    Nutmeg

                4 or 5 servings

—FLUFFY EGGNOG

Follow ▲ Recipe. Separate the eggs. Beat egg yolks with honey or **½ cup sugar** until thick and lemon-colored. Stir in milk and extract. Beat egg whites until rounded peaks are formed. Fold beaten egg whites into egg yolk mixture.

—CHOCOLATE EGGNOG II

Follow ▲ Recipe. Substitute **½ cup chocolate syrup** for honey. Omit nutmeg.

SPICED CURRANT SHAKE

Rinse and stem enough to make 1 cup

    About ½ pt. currants

Put into an electric blender container

    ¼ cup water
    ¼ cup sugar

Add currants and

    ⅛ teaspoon cinnamon

Cover and blend about 45 sec., or until thoroughly blended.

Put through a sieve to remove seeds.

Pour liquid mixture into clean blender container with

    1 cup ginger ale
    ½ pt. vanilla ice cream

Blend about 30 sec., or until thoroughly mixed.

    About 3 cups or three 8-oz. servings

SPICY PEACH FLOAT

Set out an electric blender; chill 2 tall glasses.

Combine in blender container

    ¾ cup milk
    1 cup canned sliced peaches, drained
    1 tablespoon currant jelly
    ⅛ teaspoon cinnamon
    Dash salt

Blend until mixture is smooth. Add

    ¾ cup milk

Mix well and chill thoroughly before pouring into tall glasses. Top each with a large scoop of

    Orange sherbet

                2 servings

PEACHEE MILK DRINK

Whip up this fresh-flavored beverage in a blender in a matter of seconds.

An electric blender will be needed.

Rinse, drain, pare, cut into halves and pit

    4 medium (about 1 lb.) ripe peaches

Cut into pieces and set aside.

Put into blender container

    2 cups cold milk
    ¼ cup sugar
    ⅛ teaspoon almond extract

Cover and turn on motor. Gradually add peaches to blender container while motor is running. Continue to blend about 45 sec., or until smooth and slightly thickened.

Serve immediately.   *About 4 servings*

Note: Be sure to use *ripe* peaches and cold milk. Slightly underripe peaches tend to curdle the milk and make a too-tart beverage.

ICY PEACH PLUM WHIRL

Rinse, pit and cut into pieces (enough to make ½ cup each)

    1 or 2 medium firm ripe peaches
    2 or 3 medium fresh red plums

Put into an electric blender container the peaches, the plums and

    ½ cup sugar
    ½ cup milk
    3 tablespoons lemon juice
    1 cup crushed ice

Cover and turn on motor. Blend until thoroughly mixed. Serve immediately.   *3 servings*

PEPPERMINT MILK

Put into an electric blender container

    2 cups cold milk
    8 peppermint sticks (3 in. each),
        broken in two

Cover and blend about 45 sec., or until thoroughly blended (candy should be completely dissolved).   *2 cups or two 8-oz. servings*

HAWAIIAN MILK TREAT

Have ready

    1 cup pineapple chunks, fresh or
        canned

Put into an electric blender container

    2 cups cold milk
    3 tablespoons brown sugar
    1 teaspoon vanilla extract

Cover and turn on motor. Gradually add pineapple chunks. Blend about 45 sec., or until thoroughly mixed.

    About 3 cups or three 8-oz. servings

RASPBERRY CREAM COOLER

    ▲ *Base Recipe*

Chill for at least three hours

    1 can (16 oz.) raspberries

Pour into an electric blender container

    ⅔ cup cold milk
    ⅔ cup cold cream

Add berries and syrup. Cover and blend about

Homemade Sodas

Blueberry Milk Shake

15 sec., or until thick and smooth. Serve immediately.

About 3½ cups or five 6-oz. servings

—BLUEBERRY MILK SHAKE

Follow ▲ Recipe. Omit raspberries and cream. Add **1 cup chilled, rinsed blueberries** and **½ cup sugar** to blender container with milk. After blending blueberry-milk mixture, add **1 pt. softened vanilla ice cream** by spoonfuls and blend about 15 sec. more, or until well mixed.

STRAWBERRY SODA, BLENDER STYLE

▲ Base Recipe

Rinse (discarding imperfect berries) and hull
    1 pt. strawberries

Pour into an electric blender container
    ¾ cup cold milk or carbonated water
    ½ cup sugar
Cover and turn on motor. Add strawberries and then
    4 large scoops vanilla ice cream
Blend until thick and smooth.

Divide mixture among 8 tall glasses. Fill with
    Carbonated water
Give a quick stir and top each with a scoop of ice cream. *8 tall servings*

—CHERRY COLA SODA, BLENDER STYLE

Follow ▲ Recipe. Use pitted **dark sweet cherries** instead of strawberries. Substitute **cola beverage** for the carbonated water.

HOMEMADE STRAWBERRY OR RASPBERRY SODA

▲ Base Recipe

Blend in a tall glass
    1 small scoop softened vanilla ice cream
    ¼ cup crushed fresh or frozen sweetened strawberries or raspberries
Pour over ice cream mixture
    ½ cup cold milk
    ½ cup carbonated water or ginger ale
Mix thoroughly, but do not shake.

Float in soda mixture
    1 or 2 scoops softened ice cream
Serve immediately, accompanied with a straw and long-handled spoon. *1 serving*

—HOMEMADE PINEAPPLE SODA

Follow ▲ Recipe. Substitute **frozen or canned crushed pineapple** for the strawberries.

—HOMEMADE PEACH SODA

Follow ▲ Recipe. Substitute **⅓ cup mashed ripe fresh or frozen sweetened peaches** for the strawberries.

—HOMEMADE CHOCOLATE SODA

Follow ▲ Recipe. Substitute **2 to 4 tablespoons Chocolate Syrup** (page 621) for strawberries.

STRAWBERRY THICKMALTS

Set out an electric blender; set four tall glasses in refrigerator or freezer to chill.

Rinse and drain
    2 pts. ripe strawberries
Reserve a few whole strawberries to use for garnish. Hull the remaining berries and purée in the blender. Strain through a double thickness of cheesecloth to remove seeds.

Return purée to blender container and add
    1 qt. vanilla ice cream, softened
    ¼ cup malted milk powder
Blend until smooth. Place blender container in freezer for about 1 hr.

Before serving the thickmalts, blend a few seconds until smooth. Spoon into the chilled glasses and serve with long-handled spoons.

Garnish malts with **whole strawberries.**
Four 8-oz. servings

Note: If desired, omit malted milk powder.

STRAWBERRY MELLOW MILK

▲ Base Recipe

Rinse (discarding imperfect berries) and hull
    1 pt. strawberries
Put berries into an electric blender container with
    1⅓ cups cold milk
    ¼ cup sugar
Cover and blend about 30 sec., or until well blended and serve immediately.
About 3 cups or three 8-oz. servings

—STRAWBERRY BUTTERMILK

Follow ▲ Recipe. Substitute **buttermilk** for milk. Increase sugar to 6 tablespoons.

PARTY BEVERAGES

BANANA CHOCOLATE FLOAT

▲ Base Recipe

A punch bowl and glasses will be needed.

Have ready
    1 qt. vanilla ice cream
Peel
    6 bananas with all-yellow or brown-flecked peel
Mash or beat bananas in a large bowl. Blend into puréed bananas
    1 cup Chocolate Syrup (page 621)
    1 teaspoon vanilla extract
    ½ teaspoon almond extract
Using electric mixer, beat in just until smooth
    1 pt. of the vanilla ice cream. Add and beat just until mixed
    4 cups cold milk
Pour mixture into punch bowl. Top with scoops of the remaining ice cream. Or pour into glasses. Top each serving with a scoop of the ice cream or perch rinsed, unpeeled banana slice (which has been brushed with lemon juice) on the rim of each glass.

Serve immediately. *8 servings*

—CHOCOLATE MINT FLOAT

Follow ▲ Recipe. Omit bananas. Substitute

Banana Chocolate Float

½ teaspoon **mint extract** for almond extract. Garnish with **mint sprigs**.

EGGNOG

▲ *Base Recipe*

Beat until very thick and lemon-colored
6 egg yolks
¼ cup sugar
3 tablespoons rum extract
1 teaspoon vanilla extract
Add gradually and continue to beat until blended
1½ cups chilled cream
Set aside.

Beat until frothy
6 egg whites
Add gradually, beating well after each addition
5 tablespoons sugar
Beat until very stiff peaks are formed.

Gently fold egg whites into egg yolk mixture until blended. Chill in refrigerator. Pour into punch bowl and gently mix before serving. Ladle into serving cups and sprinkle lightly with
Nutmeg

About 16 servings

—CRANBERRY NOG

Follow ▲ Recipe. Add **4 cups (2 pts.) cranberry juice cocktail**. Omit rum extract.

CRANBERRY PUNCH

Wash and sort
2 cups firm cranberries
Put into a saucepan with
2 cups water

Cranberry Nog

Cook over low heat until cranberry skins pop, about 5 min. Force cranberries through food mill or sieve. Stir into cranberry purée
¾ cup sugar
1 tablespoon lemon juice
Return to saucepan; bring to boiling and cook 2 min., stirring constantly. Immediately remove from heat, cool and chill thoroughly in refrigerator.

Stir into chilled cranberry mixture
2 cups chilled pineapple juice
½ cup chilled orange juice

About 6 servings

LEMONADE DELIGHT

Eight tall glasses will be needed.

Put into a small saucepan with a tight-fitting cover
1⅓ cups sugar
1 cup water
Stir over low heat until sugar is dissolved. Cover, bring to boiling, and boil 5 min. Remove from heat and set aside to cool.

Prepare, mix, and chill
2 cups lemon juice (about 12 lemons)
1½ tablespoons grated lemon peel
½ cup orange juice (about 2 oranges)

When the syrup is cooled, blend with fruit juices and grated peel. Cover and store in refrigerator until ready to use.

To serve, put into tall glasses
Ice cubes or shaved or crushed ice
Add about ½ cup of the lemon syrup to each glass. Fill glasses with
Cold water
Stir until blended. Garnish with **lemon and/ or orange slices**.

8 servings

PARTY LEMONADE

▲ *Base Recipe*

Squeeze enough lemons to yield
2 cups lemon juice (about 12 medium lemons)
(Or, use 2 cups reconstituted frozen lemon juice concentrate.)

Mix the lemon juice and
6 cups cold water
1½ cups sugar
Stir until sugar is dissolved. Place in refrigerator to chill thoroughly.

Stir and pour over ice cubes or crushed ice.

2 qts. lemonade

—PARTY LIMEADE

Follow ▲ Recipe. Substitute **lime juice** for lemon juice.

—PARTY ORANGEADE

Follow ▲ Recipe. Substitute **6 cups orange juice (about 18 medium oranges)** for lemon

juice. Add **¼ cup lemon juice** (about 2 lemons) and decrease water to 2 cups.

PARTY PUNCH

Set out two large bowls. A punch bowl and serving cups will be needed.

Have ready
1½ qts. ginger ale, chilled
Prepare and pour into a large bowl
5 cups double-strength tea
Set aside to cool at room temperature.

When tea is cool, add to it
2¼ cups sugar
2½ cups orange juice
1½ cups unsweetened grapefruit juice
⅔ cup lemon juice
¼ cup lime juice
Stir until sugar is dissolved. Cover punch and chill in refrigerator. When ready to serve, add the chilled ginger ale. Stir to blend thoroughly.

About 3 qts. punch

To Decorate Punch Bowl—Trim off stems of daisies to 1 in. Secure daisies around edge of bowl with pieces of cellulose tape. Secure two daisies to ladle handle in same way.

For Pink-Frosted Cups—Measure **½ cup sugar** into a shallow pan. Tint sugar the desired pink color by thoroughly mixing in, one drop at a time, a mixture of **red food coloring** and **water** (equal amounts). Set sugar aside to dry. When ready to serve punch, rub rim of each punch cup with the cut surface of a **lemon** or **lime**. Dip each cup into tinted sugar. Decorate each cup handle with a daisy secured with a piece of cellulose tape. Place a decorative ice block in punch bowl. Pour punch into bowl. Ladle punch into Pink-Frosted Cups.

Note: Sweetheart roses or small chrysanthemums may be used in place of daisies.

For Decorative Ice Blocks—Fill a loaf pan or fancy mold one-third full with water. Place in freezing compartment of refrigerator; remove pan or mold when water is partially frozen. Arrange flowers (roses, gardenias, or others), or fruits (small whole, pieces or slices) over the ice. Fill pan or mold with water, covering

Party Punch

South Sea Nectar

flowers or fruit, and freeze. Boiling water before freezing or stirring as it freezes helps to make the ice clear.

For Decorative Ice Cubes—Fill ice-cube tray one-third full with water. Place in freezing compartment of refrigerator; remove ice cube tray when water is partially frozen. Place well-drained **maraschino cherry, mint sprig, pineapple chunk, orange wedge, berry,** or small piece of **fruit** and a **mint leaf** in each cube section. Fill tray with water and freeze.

SPARKLING PINEAPPLE FLOAT

▲ Base Recipe

This refreshing pineapple float is doubly delicious because the beverage and the ice are really "made for each other." Serve with crisp, tender tea cookies or delicate sponge or angel food cake for a dessert party menu that's wonderfully welcome on a hot afternoon.

Set out a refrigerator tray.

Drain, reserving syrup
>   **1 can (20 oz.) crushed pineapple**
>   **(about 1½ cups, drained)**

For Pineapple Syrup—Combine in a saucepan and set over low heat, stirring until sugar is dissolved
>   **2 cups water**
>   **1 cup sugar**

Cover, increase heat and bring to boiling. Boil syrup gently 5 min. Remove from heat.

Blend in the reserved pineapple syrup and
>   **½ cup lemon juice**

Chill ½ cup of syrup mixture for Pineapple Ice. Chill remainder in refrigerator.

For Pineapple Ice—Add the ½ cup chilled syrup mixture to the crushed pineapple and
>   **½ cup cold water**
>   **2 or 3 drops mint extract**

Pour into the refrigerator tray. Freeze until firm, stirring two or three times.

To Serve—Pour the chilled Pineapple Syrup into a large pitcher containing
>   **Ice cubes**

Add and mix gently
>   **3 cups ginger ale**

Pour the beverage into tall glasses, filling each about ⅔ full. Put a spoonful of Pineapple Ice into each glass. Garnish with
>   **Mint sprigs**
>   **Maraschino cherries**

6 servings

—SPARKLING RASPBERRY FLOAT

Set out to thaw **3 pkgs. (10 oz. each) frozen raspberries** (about 3½ cups, thawed). Follow ▲ Recipe. Omit crushed pineapple and mint extract; decrease sugar to ¾ cup. Sieve raspberries and add to the sugar syrup with lemon juice. Use 1 cup of raspberry syrup mixture plus the cold water for the Raspberry Ice. Omit cherries.

SOUTH SEA NECTAR

▲ Base Recipe

To make your guests sit up and take notice, serve any one of these drinks in "Coconut Mugs." Allow one coconut for each mug. Remember, straws are a must with these mugs.

Set in refrigerator to chill
>   **1 can (18 oz.) unsweetened**
>   **pineapple juice (2½ cups)**

Combine in a saucepan
>   **2 cups water**
>   **3 cups (8 oz.) flaked coconut**

Set pan over low heat and bring mixture to boiling, stirring occasionally. Cover and simmer 10 min. Remove from heat and set aside to cool.

Strain through a sieve, pressing coconut with a spoon to extract as much liquid as possible. Chill liquid in refrigerator.

When ready to serve, thoroughly mix the chilled coconut liquid and pineapple juice. Partially fill tall glasses with crushed ice and pour nectar mixture over ice. Garnish with
>   **Lime slices**
>   **Mint sprigs**

Serve with straws. *6 servings*

—APRICOT COCONUT NECTAR

Follow ▲ Recipe. Substitute **2½ cups chilled apricot nectar** for pineapple juice.

—ORANGE COCONUT NECTAR

Follow ▲ Recipe. Substitute **2½ cups chilled orange juice** (fresh or reconstituted frozen) for pineapple juice. Omit lime slices and mint; garnish with one half of an **orange slice.**

To Make a "Coconut Mug"—With an ice

pick, force holes through indentations at one end of
>   **1 medium fresh coconut**

Drain coconut milk from the coconut. Saw off and discard the punctured tip end. Saw off a ring about 1 in. wide (the ring will be used as a holder for the "Coconut Mug"). Chill remaining coconut shell.

Use shell set in ring as a mug for chilled drinks such as Orange Coconut or South Sea Nectar.

RASPBERRY SHRUB

Raspberry Shrub is a classic summertime cooler, with a history generations old. The amount yielded by this recipe will serve a sizable crowd. The syrup may be refrigerated and used as needed.

This syrup must stand for two days before completion.

To Prepare Syrup—(This recipe makes about 2 qts. syrup.) A large heavy saucepot or kettle will be needed for cooking the syrup.

The first day, set out a large bowl.

Sort, rinse and thoroughly drain
>   **4 qts. ripe red or black raspberries**

Put raspberries into the bowl and crush thoroughly. Add, mixing well
>   **1 qt. cider vinegar**

Cover and let mixture stand 48 hrs. in refrigerator or in a cool place, stirring 3 or 4 times to blend well.

The third day, set out the saucepot. Strain the raspberries into the saucepot, using a jelly bag (page 723).

Set the saucepot over medium heat and add, stirring until sugar is dissolved
>   **6 cups sugar**

Increase heat and bring mixture to boiling. Boil mixture uncovered 5 min. Skim off any foam. Remove saucepot from heat and set aside to cool. Store in a covered container in refrigerator.

To Complete Shrub—For each measuring cup of beverage desired, mix together
>   **⅔ cup water**
>   **⅓ cup Raspberry Shrub Syrup**

Serve over ice cubes or crushed ice.

TANGERINE PUNCH

A punch bowl and cups will be needed.

Chill thoroughly
>   **7½ cups tangerine juice (three 18-oz.**
>   **cans or two 6-oz. cans frozen**
>   **concentrate reconstituted)**
>   **1 qt. ginger ale**

Combine chilled ingredients in the punch bowl.

Drop in by tablespoonfuls
>   **1 qt. vanilla ice cream**

Stir thoroughly. Ladle into the punch cups and serve at once. Garnish with **tangerine slices.** *About 3½ qts. punch*

STRAWBERRY PUNCH

A punch bowl and serving cups will be needed.

Chill thoroughly

  2 cans (18 oz. each) unsweetened pineapple juice (4½ cups)
  1 qt. ginger ale

Partially thaw

  2 pkgs. (16 oz. each) frozen sliced strawberries

Shortly before serving time, combine in the

punch bowl the chilled pineapple juice and

  1 cup lemon juice

Add the strawberries and their syrup; stir to blend thoroughly. Add the chilled ginger ale and blend. Add

  Ice cubes or molded ice block

Ladle into the punch cups and serve immediately. *About 3 qts. punch*

ALCOHOLIC BEVERAGES

Alcoholic beverages, when used as refreshers or "coolers," are prepared with more emphasis on their fruit-juice or ginger-ale content than on pure liquor. Sophisticated drinkers, however, usually prefer their cocktails or "apéritifs" quite "dry" or unsweetened, the main ingredient being liquor with only a touch of other flavors.

BARTENDER'S MEASUREMENTS

Jigger—1½ oz.
Pony—¾ oz.
Dash—6 drops
Small cocktail glass—3 to 4 oz.
Large cocktail glass—4 to 6 oz.
Champagne glass—4 to 5½ oz.
Old-fashioned glass—4 to 8 oz.
Sour glass—4 to 5 oz.
Highball glass—8 to 14 oz.
Chimney highball glass—14 oz., tall, thin
Wine glass—3 to 4 oz.

All recipes are for 1 serving unless otherwise indicated.

BEER

Most beer drinkers have their own favorite way of serving beer just as they seem to enjoy their own special brand. Flavor and even texture varies widely, just as does the combination of ingredients and method of brewing. Since those who enjoy beer are inclined to drink a lot of it, it is recommended that the drinker experiment until he finds the particular brand he enjoys most. Here are a few delightful concoctions containing beer as an ingredient.

AMERICAN COLONIAL FLIP
(One Yard of Flannel)

  1 bottle beer
  1 dried lemon peel
  3 or 4 eggs
  1 tablespoon sugar
  ½ teaspoon ginger
  ½ teaspoon nutmeg
  ½ cup rum or brandy

Heat beer with lemon peel. Beat eggs; add

sugar, ginger, nutmeg and rum. When beer is boiling, pour it into a pitcher, and pour rum mixture into another pitcher. Keep pouring from one pitcher to the other until it is as smooth as cream. Reheat in a double boiler. *5 servings*

AMERICAN HALF AND HALF

  ½ cup beer
  ½ cup California champagne

Both ingredients must be very cold. Mix well and serve in a tall glass.

BEER CHAMPAGNE

  2 qts. water
  1½ cups sugar
  2 teaspoons cream of tartar
  5 bottles beer

Mix water and sugar and stir until sugar is dissolved. Add cream of tartar and beer. When mixture is well blended, fill bottles. Cork tightly. Let stand 2 to 3 days. Serve cold. *4 quarts*

BEER CHAUDEAU

  2 eggs
  1 cup domestic sauterne or Rhine wine
  1 bottle beer
  1 tablespoon sugar
  1 cinnamon stick
  1 slice lemon peel

Beat eggs, adding wine slowly. Stir in beer, sugar, cinnamon and lemon peel. Beat constantly over heat until boiling. Remove immediately. Remove cinnamon and lemon peel. Serve hot. *4 servings*

BEER PUNCH
(Hot)

  2 bottles beer
  ½ cup sugar
  1 cinnamon stick
  4 eggs
  ¼ cup rum

Heat beer, sugar and cinnamon. Beat eggs until light, gradually adding rum. Remove beer from heat; remove cinnamon and stir in eggs. Pour mixture into punch glasses and serve hot. *About 5 cups*

BEER PUNCH
(Cold)

  3 bottles beer
  ¼ cup domestic sherry
  ¼ cup domestic brandy
  Dash nutmeg
  1 tablespoon sugar
  3 tablespoons lemon juice
  Few pieces lemon peel

Mix all ingredients and pour over **crushed ice.** *5 cups*

BEER SANGAREE

  1 bottle cold beer
  3 cups cold water
  1 teaspoon sugar
  Dash nutmeg

Mix beer and water in a pitcher. Stir in sugar, pour into glasses and sprinkle with nutmeg. *4 servings*

BRITISH FLIP

  2 bottles beer
  3 lumps sugar
  1 lemon peel
  Small piece stick cinnamon
  6 or 8 egg yolks
  1 tablespoon confectioners' sugar
  Dash nutmeg

Heat half of the beer. Rub lump sugar on lemon peel and add to beer. Add cinnamon. When

beer boils, remove and add remaining beer. Beat egg yolks in a bowl with confectioners' sugar and nutmeg. Pour the two mixtures back and forth until a white froth appears. Chill with finely **chopped ice**. Strain and serve.

4 cups

CHAMPAGNE VELVET
(Black Velvet)

Fill an 8-oz. highball glass half full with **Guinness' stout** and half with **chilled champagne**. Pour very gently so it doesn't overflow. You may prefer to increase the proportion of champagne to stout. Pour the stout in first, or both may be poured simultaneously. Porter ale or beer may be substituted for the stout.

DONALDSON'S BEER CUP

> 1½ cups beer
> 2 cups carbonated water
> 1½ tablespoons noyau
> Peel of ½ lemon
> Dash nutmeg
> 1 teaspoon sugar
> ¼ cup chipped ice

Mix beer, carbonated water and noyau. Add lemon peel, nutmeg and sugar. Add ice and stir vigorously.   *6 servings*

EGG BEER

> 1 egg
> ½ bottle beer
> 1 teaspoon sugar

Beat egg and add beer gradually. Heat and stir. As soon as it foams, remove from heat and add sugar. Grate **nutmeg** over top. Serve cold in summer or warm in winter.

NIGHT CAP

> ½ cup beer
> 1 teaspoon sugar
> 2 tablespoons brandy
> Dash nutmeg

Heat beer. Mix sugar in a glass with the brandy. Add the beer. Top with nutmeg.

BLAZERS

A fine drink for cold weather—a good treatment for a cold, to be taken just before retiring.

BLUE BLAZER

> 2 jiggers rye
> 2 jiggers boiling water

Use two large silverplated mugs with handles; rye in one and water in the other. Ignite the rye. While blazing, mix the two by pouring from one mug to the other four or five times.

Then add **1 teaspoon sugar** and a **twist of lemon peel**.

BRANDY BLAZER

> 2 jiggers brandy
> 1 lump sugar
> Twist of lemon peel
> Twist of orange peel

Stir until sugar dissolves. Ignite while stirring, then strain into an old-fashioned glass.

COBBLERS

Basically a sour drink, cobblers are usually served in a silver goblet or 8-oz. highball glass with finely crushed or cracked ice, garnished with fruit and a sprig of mint. Pour ingredients over the ice into the glass and stir until glass is frosted.

BRANDY COBBLER

> ½ teaspoon fine granulated sugar
>   or Sugar Syrup (page 621)
> 1 teaspoon curaçao
> 2 jiggers brandy

Fill an 8-oz. highball glass three-fourths full with **cracked ice**. Add sugar, curaçao and brandy. Stir until glass is frosted. Decorate with **fresh fruit**.

CHAMPAGNE COBBLER

> ½ teaspoon curaçao
> ½ teaspoon lemon juice
> 1 thin slice orange
> 1 small piece pineapple
> Chilled champagne

Fill highball glass two-thirds full with **cracked ice**. Add curaçao and lemon juice. Stir. Add orange and pineapple. Fill with champagne and stir lightly. Serve with a straw.

GIN COBBLER

> 2 jiggers dry gin
> ¼ teaspoon sugar

Fill an 8-oz. highball glass three-fourths full with **crushed ice**. Add gin and sugar. Fill with **carbonated water** and garnish with **fresh fruit**.

PORT COBBLER

> 1 teaspoon orange juice
> 1 teaspoon curaçao
> Port wine

Fill an 8-oz. highball glass two-thirds full with **cracked ice**. Add orange juice and curaçao. Fill with port wine. Stir until glass is frosted, adding some **sugar** if you like. Decorate with **fresh fruit**.

SHERRY CURACAO COBBLER

> 3 jiggers sherry
> 1 teaspoon curaçao
> 1 thin piece orange peel
> Juice of 1 orange
> 1 teaspoon sugar

Fill a 10-oz. glass three-fourths full with **fine ice**. Add sherry, curaçao, orange peel, orange juice and sugar. Stir well.

RUM COBBLER

> 1 jigger New England rum
> ½ teaspoon curaçao

Fill an 8-oz. glass three-fourths full with **cracked ice**. Add rum and curaçao. Stir well and garnish with a **slice of lemon** and a **slice of orange**.

COCKTAILS

The cocktail is a drink to whet the appetite and not to dull it, to be consumed usually before lunch or dinner; often a drink for social drinking, for gracious gatherings and friendly interchange.

ABSINTHE COCKTAIL

> 1 jigger Pernod or Herbsaint
> 1 pony water
> 1 teaspoon Sugar Syrup (page 621)
> 2 ice cubes

Blend 10 seconds, strain and serve in a cocktail glass with a **twist of lemon peel**.

AFFINITY COCKTAIL

> 1 pony Italian vermouth
> 1 pony French vermouth
> 1 jigger Scotch
> Dash Angostura bitters

Stir well with **ice** and strain into a large cocktail glass or serve on the rocks. Add a **maraschino cherry**.

AIR MAIL COCKTAIL

> Juice of ½ lime
> 1 teaspoon honey
> 1 jigger dark rum
> Chilled champagne

Shake well with **ice**, pour into a large cocktail glass and fill with champagne.

ALASKA COCKTAIL

> 1 jigger dry gin
> 1 jigger yellow chartreuse
> Dash orange bitters
> 2 ice cubes

Blend 6 to 8 seconds, strain into a cocktail glass and serve with a **twist of lemon peel**.

ALBERTINE COCKTAIL

⅓ cherry liqueur
⅓ Cointreau
⅓ yellow chartreuse
½ teaspoon grenadine

Shake well with **ice** and strain into a cocktail glass.

ALEXANDER

1 pony cognac
1 pony crème de cacao
1 pony heavy cream
2 ice cubes

Blend 15 seconds, strain and serve in a 4-oz. glass. Dry gin may be substituted for the cognac.

AMERICANO

This is a very popular drink on the French Riviera.

1 pony Campari Apertivo
1 pony Italian vermouth
Cracked ice
Twist of lemon

Serve with or without **carbonated water** in a cocktail glass.

APOLLO COCKTAIL

One sip and you're on the moon!

1 cube (about 1½ in.) ripe avocado
2 tablespoons beef broth
Dash each salt, pepper, celery salt and Tabasco
5 drops Worcestershire sauce
3 drops lemon juice
1 oz. vodka
1 small scoop crushed ice

Combine all ingredients in an electric blender container. Blend thoroughly and pour into a chilled glass.

AQUEDUCT COCKTAIL

⅓ rye
⅓ curaçao
⅓ lemon juice

Shake well with **ice** and strain into a cocktail glass. Add a **maraschino cherry**.

ARMY AND NAVY COCKTAIL

¼ lemon juice
¼ orgeat
½ dry gin

Stir well with **ice** and strain into a cocktail glass.

ARTILLERY COCKTAIL

Dash Angostura bitters
⅓ Italian vermouth
⅔ dry gin

Stir well with **ice** and strain into a cocktail glass. Add a **twist of lemon peel**.

ASTORIA COCKTAIL

Dash orange bitters
⅔ Holland gin
⅓ French vermouth

Stir well with **ice** and strain into a cocktail glass.

AVALON COCKTAIL

1 piece grapefruit (size of a lime), muddled
½ teaspoon grenadine
1 pony dry gin
1 jigger French vermouth

Shake well with **ice** and strain into a cocktail glass.

BACARDI

1 jigger Bacardi or light rum
½ teaspoon grenadine
Juice of ½ lime

Shake well with **ice** and strain into a cocktail glass.

BELMONT

1 jigger dry gin
1 pony raspberry syrup
1 pony cream
2 ice cubes

Blend 6 to 8 seconds, strain and serve in a cocktail glass.

BENNETT

1 jigger dry gin
½ pony lime juice
½ teaspoon Sugar Syrup (page 621)
Dash Angostura bitters
2 ice cubes

Apollo Cocktail

Blend 6 to 8 seconds, strain and serve in a cocktail glass.

BLUE TRAIN COCKTAIL

1 pony cognac
1 pony mildly sweetened pineapple juice
Chilled champagne

Shake the cognac and pineapple juice carefully with **cracked ice**. Strain into a champagne glass. Fill glass with champagne.

BOUNCER COCKTAIL

⅓ light rum
⅓ French vermouth
⅓ dry gin

Stir well with **ice** and strain into a cocktail glass.

BRANDY COCKTAIL

2 dashes Angostura bitters
½ teaspoon sugar
2 oz. brandy

Stir well with **ice** and strain into a cocktail glass. Garnish with a **twist of lemon peel** and a **maraschino cherry**.

BOURBON COCKTAIL

1 pony Benedictine
1 pony bourbon
½ teaspoon lemon juice
½ teaspoon curaçao
Dash Angostura bitters

Shake well with **ice** and strain into a cocktail glass or serve on the rocks.

BOXCAR COCKTAIL

Sugar
1 jigger dry gin
½ oz. Cointreau
Juice of ½ lime
1 egg white
½ teaspoon grenadine

Frost rim of a cocktail glass with sugar. Shake well with **ice** and strain into the glass.

BROADWAY COCKTAIL

½ rye
½ Italian vermouth
Juice of ½ orange
¼ teaspoon Pernod
¼ teaspoon Angostura bitters

Shake well with **ice** and strain into a cocktail glass.

BRONX COCKTAIL

¼ Italian vermouth
¼ French vermouth
½ dry gin
Juice of ¼ orange

Shake well with **ice** and strain into a cocktail glass.

BUCKINGHAM COCKTAIL

⅔ brandy
⅓ French vermouth
¾ teaspoon Grand Marnier

Shake well with **ice** and strain into a cocktail glass.

CAMPARI AND GIN

½ Campari Aperitivo
½ dry gin

Serve with **ice** in a cocktail or old-fashioned glass.

CANADIAN CLUB COCKTAIL

1½ jiggers Canadian whiskey
1 teaspoon Sugar Syrup (page 621)
Dash Angostura bitters

Stir well with **ice** and strain into a cocktail glass.

CARIOCA COCKTAIL

Juice of 1 lime
½ teaspoon grenadine
1 jigger dry gin
1 jigger Jamaica rum
Dash Angostura bitters

Shake well with **ice** and strain into a cocktail glass.

CASA BLANCA COCKTAIL

Dash Angostura bitters
¾ teaspoon lime juice
¾ teaspoon curaçao
¾ teaspoon maraschino
1½ jiggers Jamaica rum

Shake well with **ice** and strain into a cocktail glass. Add a **maraschino cherry.**

CASA DAY

1 jigger white rum
1 pony Cointreau
½ pony lemon juice
1 egg white
Dash grenadine
2 ice cubes

Blend 12 seconds, strain and serve in a large cocktail glass with a **maraschino cherry.**

CASEY JONES COCKTAIL

1½ jiggers rye
1 oz. grapefruit juice
1 teaspoon peach liqueur
½ teaspoon sugar

Shake well with **ice** and strain into a cocktail glass.

CASINO

1 jigger Old Tom gin
½ teaspoon maraschino
½ teaspoon lemon juice
½ teaspoon orange bitters
2 ice cubes

Blend 6 to 8 seconds, strain and serve in a cocktail glass with a **maraschino cherry.**

CHAMPAGNE COCKTAIL I

1 jigger Southern Comfort
Dash Angostura bitters
1 thin half slice lemon
Chilled champagne

Put Southern Comfort and bitters into an 8-oz. highball glass filled half full with **ice cubes.** Add lemon and fill with champagne.

CHAMPAGNE COCKTAIL II

1 lump sugar
Dash Angostura bitters
1 pony brandy
1 pony Benedictine
1 piece orange peel
1 maraschino cherry
Chilled champagne

Put sugar into a champagne glass and dash over bitters. Add **1 ice cube,** brandy, Benedictine, orange peel and maraschino cherry. Fill with champagne.

CHAMPS ELYSEES COCKTAIL

⅗ brandy
⅕ green chartreuse
⅕ lemon juice
½ teaspoon sugar
Dash Angostura bitters

Shake well with **ice** and strain into a cocktail glass.

CHAPPELLE COCKTAIL

1 pony Italian vermouth
1 pony dry gin
Juice of ½ lime
3 strips fresh pineapple

Shake vermouth, gin and lime juice well and pour into an old-fashioned glass over **ice cubes.** Add pineapple standing upright.

CHARLES COCKTAIL

1 jigger Angostura bitters
½ Italian vermouth
½ brandy

Stir well with **ice** and strain into a cocktail glass.

CHERRY BLOSSOM COCKTAIL

1 jigger cherry liqueur
1 pony brandy
1 teaspoon lemon juice
1 teaspoon curaçao
½ teaspoon grenadine

Shake well with **ice** and strain into a cocktail glass.

CHERRY PORT COCKTAIL

1 jigger port
1 pony cherry liqueur
1 pony French vermouth
Dash orange bitters

Stir well with **ice** and strain into a cocktail glass.

CHURCHILL COCKTAIL

1 jigger Scotch
Juice of ½ lime
1 pony Italian vermouth
1 pony Cointreau

Shake well with **ice** and strain into a cocktail glass.

CLARET COCKTAIL

1 jigger claret
1 jigger Italian vermouth
¾ teaspoon curaçao
Dash Angostura bitters

Stir well with **ice** and strain into a cocktail glass. Add a **maraschino cherry.**

CLOVER CLUB

1 jigger dry gin
½ pony lemon or lime juice
½ pony grenadine
1 egg white
2 ice cubes

Blend 10 seconds and strain into a chilled large cocktail glass.

CONTINENTAL COCKTAIL

Juice of ½ lime
1 pony dry gin
1 pony French vermouth
1 pony Benedictine

Shake well with **ice** and strain into a cocktail glass.

COSSACKS COCKTAIL

1 jigger dry gin
1 pony kümmel
1 pony lemon juice

Stir well with **ice** and strain into a cocktail glass.

COUNTRY CLUB COCKTAIL

1 jigger light rum
1 jigger French vermouth
1 teaspoon curaçao

Shake well with **ice** and strain into a cocktail glass.

CREOLE COCKTAIL

1 jigger rye
1 jigger Italian vermouth
1 pony Benedictine
½ pony Amer Picon

Stir well with **ice** and strain into a cocktail glass. Garnish with a **twist of lemon peel.**

CUBAN COCKTAIL

1 pony apricot liqueur
1 jigger light rum
Juice of ½ lime

Shake well with **ice** and strain into a cocktail glass.

DAIQUIRI

2 jiggers dark rum
¾ teaspoon curaçao
1 teaspoon orange juice
1 teaspoon confectioners' sugar
Juice of ½ lemon or 1 lime

Shake well with **ice** and strain into a cocktail glass.

DAZZLER COCKTAIL

1 pony apricot liqueur
1 pony dry gin
1 pony Scotch
1 teaspoon lemon juice
1 teaspoon orange juice
¼ teaspoon Sugar Syrup (page 653)
1 egg white

Shake well with **ice** and strain into a cocktail glass.

DINNER-AT-EIGHT COCKTAIL

1 jigger dry gin
1 jigger French vermouth
Dash Angostura bitters

Stir well with **ice** and strain into a cocktail glass. Garnish with a **small white onion.**

DIXIE COCKTAIL

1 jigger rye
Dash Angostura bitters
¼ teaspoon curaçao
¾ teaspoon green crème de menthe
¼ teaspoon sugar

Shake well with **ice** and strain into a cocktail glass.

DOCTOR

1 jigger Swedish Punch
1 pony Jamaica rum
½ pony lime juice
2 ice cubes

Blend 8 to 10 seconds and strain into a chilled cocktail glass.

DON Q COCKTAIL

1 pony dry gin
1 jigger Jamaica rum
Dash Angostura bitters
Juice of 1 lime
½ teaspoon grenadine

Shake well with **ice** and strain into a cocktail glass.

DREAM COCKTAIL

1 teaspoon lemon juice
1 jigger light rum
1 teaspoon cream
½ teaspoon sugar
1 egg white
¼ teaspoon grenadine
¼ teaspoon orange flower water

Shake with **ice**; strain into a cocktail glass.

DUBLIN COCKTAIL

1 jigger Irish whiskey
1 teaspoon green chartreuse
1 teaspoon green crème de menthe

Stir well with **ice** and strain into a cocktail glass. Garnish with an **olive.**

DUBONNET AND COGNAC

1 jigger Dubonnet
1 jigger cognac

Stir gently with **ice cubes.** Strain. Serve in a cocktail glass.

DUBONNET COCKTAIL

1 pony dry gin
1 pony Dubonnet
Dash orange bitters
1 ice cube

Blend 6 to 8 seconds. Strain into a cocktail glass.

DUKE OF MARLBOROUGH COCKTAIL

½ sherry
½ Italian vermouth
1 teaspoon raspberry liqueur
Juice of 1 lime

Shake with **ice**; strain into a cocktail glass.

DUNLOP COCKTAIL

Dash Angostura bitters
1 pony sherry
1 jigger light rum

Stir well with **ice** and strain into a cocktail glass.

EMPIRE COCKTAIL

1 pony apricot liqueur
1 pony applejack
1 jigger dry gin

Shake with **ice**; strain into a cocktail glass.

EPICUREAN COCKTAIL

1 jigger brandy
1 pony kümmel
1 pony French vermouth
Dash Angostura bitters

Shake well with **ice** and strain into a cocktail glass.

FINE AND DANDY

1 pony dry gin
½ pony Cointreau
½ pony lemon juice
2 ice cubes

Blend 6 to 8 seconds, strain and serve in a cocktail glass with a **maraschino cherry**.

FIFTY-FIFTY COCKTAIL

Probably the beginning of the Martini.

1 jigger dry gin
1 jigger French vermouth

Stir well with **ice** and strain into a cocktail glass. Add an **olive**.

FROZEN DAIQUIRI

▲ *Base Recipe*

1 jigger white rum
1 teaspoon sugar
1½ teaspoons lime juice
Dash maraschino
4 ice cubes

Put all ingredients into *chilled* blender container. Blend 1 min., or until mixture is the consistency of snow. Strain out any large particles and serve in a saucer champagne glass.

—FROZEN PEACH DAIQUIRI

Follow ▲ Recipe. Add ½ **fresh or frozen peach**.

—FROZEN STRAWBERRY DAIQUIRI

Follow ▲ Recipe. Add ¼ **cup fresh or frozen strawberries**.

GIMLET

1 pony dry gin
1 pony Rose's lime juice
½ teaspoon Sugar Syrup (page 621)
2 ice cubes

Blend 6 to 8 seconds, strain and serve in a chilled cocktail glass.

GIN AND BITTERS

2 dashes Angostura bitters
2 jiggers dry gin

Twirl bitters in a 3-oz. glass so that the glass is thoroughly coated. Pour in gin. *No ice* in this drink.

GIN COCKTAIL

1 jigger dry gin
Dash orange bitters

Stir gently with **ice** and strain into a cocktail glass.

GIN OLD-FASHIONED

Dash Angostura bitters
1 cube sugar
1 jigger dry gin

Dash bitters over sugar in an old-fashioned glass and crush. Add gin and stir. Fill with **cracked ice** and a dash of **carbonated water**. Garnish with a **twist of lemon peel**.

GLOOM CHASER COCKTAIL

As served at the Ermitage, Paris, France.

¼ curaçao
¼ Grand Marnier
¼ grenadine
¼ lemon juice

Shake well with **ice** and strain into a cocktail glass.

GOLDEN BELL COCKTAIL

2 jiggers sherry
1 jigger dry gin
Dash Angostura bitters
Dash orange bitters

Shake well with **ice** and strain into a cocktail glass.

GRASSHOPPER

2 jiggers green crème de menthe
2 jiggers white crème de cacao*
2 jiggers heavy cream
Dash orgeat
4 ice cubes

Blend 15 seconds, strain and serve in 4-oz. glasses.   *3 servings*

*If your crème de cacao happens to be of the chocolate hue, don't worry, your Grasshoppers, tasting just the same, will merely look a little more mellow.

HALF AND HALF COCKTAIL

½ Scotch
¼ orange juice
¼ lemon juice

Shake well with **ice** and strain into a cocktail glass.

HAPPY BOTTOM COCKTAIL

1 jigger rye
1 pony sherry
½ teaspoon peach liqueur

Shake well with **ice** and strain into a cocktail glass. Garnish with a **twist of lemon peel**.

HAVANA COCKTAIL

1 jigger light rum
1 pony pineapple juice
½ teaspoon sugar

Shake well with **ice** and strain into a cocktail glass.

HAWAIIAN COCKTAIL

1 jigger dry gin
1 jigger pineapple juice
1½ teaspoons curaçao
1 ice cube

Blend 10 seconds, strain into a *chilled* cocktail glass.

HEART'S DESIRE COCKTAIL

1 jigger rye
1 pony Italian vermouth
Juice of 1 lemon

Shake with **ice**; strain into a cocktail glass.

HESITATION COCKTAIL

½ teaspoon lemon juice
1 pony rye
1½ jiggers Swedish Punch

Stir well with **ice** and strain into a cocktail glass.

HOLLANDER COCKTAIL

1 jigger apricot brandy
1 pony Holland gin
1 pony grape juice

Shake with **ice**; strain into a cocktail glass.

HONEY COCKTAIL

2 oz. dry gin
1 teaspoon honey
Juice of 1 lime

Shake well with **ice** and strain into a cocktail glass.

HONEY DEW COCKTAIL

½ rye
¼ strained honey
¼ lemon juice
Dash Angostura bitters

Shake well with **ice** and strain into a cocktail glass.

HONEY LAMB

1 jigger cognac
1 pony cream
1 pony crème de mocha
¼ pony lemon juice
1 ice cube

Blend 6 to 8 seconds, strain and serve in a cocktail glass.

HONEYMOON COCKTAIL

1 jigger port
1 pony rye
1 egg
½ teaspoon sugar

Shake well with **ice** and strain into a cocktail glass.

HONOLULU

1 jigger dry gin
Dash orange juice
Dash pineapple juice
Dash lemon juice
Dash Angostura bitters
¼ teaspoon Sugar Syrup (page 621)
2 ice cubes

Blend 6 to 8 seconds, strain and serve in a cocktail glass.

JACK AND JILL COCKTAIL

1 jigger rye
½ teaspoon grenadine
Juice of 1 lemon
1 egg white

Shake well with **ice** and strain into a cocktail glass.

JACK ROSE

1 jigger applejack or Calvados
½ pony lime juice
½ pony grenadine
1 ice cube

Blend 8 to 10 seconds. Strain into a cocktail glass.

JET PILOT

1 pony Scotch
1 pony Pernod or Herbsaint
2 ice cubes

Blend 6 to 8 seconds. Strain into a *chilled* cocktail glass.

JOCKEY CLUB COCKTAIL

1 jigger Italian vermouth
1 jigger rye
¼ teaspoon orange bitters
Dash Angostura bitters
1 teaspoon lemon juice

Shake well with **ice** and strain into a cocktail glass.

JUNE BLOSSOM COCKTAIL

1 jigger dry gin
Juice of ½ lime
½ teaspoon sugar
½ teaspoon Pernod

Shake well with **ice** and strain into a cocktail glass.

KING'S PEG

1 jigger brandy
Chilled champagne

Put **1 ice cube** into a champagne glass. Pour over brandy and fill with champagne.

LENCLAIRE

1 jigger bourbon or rye
½ pony lemon juice
½ pony orgeat
1 egg white
2 ice cubes

Blend 10 seconds, strain and serve in a cocktail glass.

LIBERTY COCKTAIL

½ teaspoon Sugar Syrup (page 621)
1 oz. dark rum
2 oz. applejack

Shake well with **ice** and strain into a cocktail glass.

LONDON COCKTAIL

1 jigger dry gin
Dash orange bitters
Dash orgeat
Dash Pernod
1 ice cube

Blend 6 to 8 seconds. Strain into a chilled cocktail glass. Add a **twist of lemon peel.**

LOVE COCKTAIL

1 jigger sloe gin
1 egg white
¾ teaspoon lemon juice
½ teaspoon grenadine

Shake well with **ice** and strain into a cocktail glass.

MADAGASCAR COCKTAIL

1 jigger light rum
Juice of 1 orange
Juice of 1 lemon

Shake well with **ice** and strain into a cocktail glass. Grate **nutmeg** on top.

MAI-TAI

½ oz. lime juice
½ oz. orgeat
½ oz. curaçao
2 oz. white rum

Pour into a double-size old-fashioned glass half-filled with **finely cracked ice.** Stir gently once or twice. Garnish with a **sprig of fresh mint.** Serve with a straw.

MAIDEN'S BLUSH

¼ teaspoon lemon juice
1½ teaspoons curaçao
1½ teaspoons grenadine
1 jigger dry gin

Stir well with **ice** and strain into a cocktail glass.

MANHATTAN

▲ *Base Recipe*

1 jigger rye or bourbon
1 pony Italian vermouth
Dash Angostura bitters

Stir well with **ice** and strain into a cocktail glass. Add a **maraschino cherry** and a **slice of orange**. This drink may also be served on the rocks in an old-fashioned glass.

—BRANDY MANHATTAN

Follow ▲ Recipe. Substitute **1 jigger brandy** for the rye or bourbon.

—IRISH MANHATTAN

Follow ▲ Recipe. Substitute **1 jigger Irish whiskey** for the rye or bourbon.

—RUM MANHATTAN

Follow ▲ Recipe. Substitute **1 jigger Jamaica rum** for the rye or bourbon.

MAPLE LEAF

  1 pony maple syrup
  1 pony lemon juice
  1 jigger rye

Shake well with **ice** and strain into a cocktail glass.

MARGARITA

  1 jigger tequila
  1 to 1½ oz. triple sec or Cointreau
  Juice of ½ lime or lemon
  Salt

Combine tequila, triple sec and lime juice in a shaker. Add **ice cubes** and shake vigorously. Rub the rim of a small cocktail glass with squeezed lime half. Dip rim in salt. Strain mixture into the glass.

MARTINI
(The Original)

  1 pony French vermouth
  1 jigger dry gin
  ¾ teaspoon orange bitters

Stir well with **ice** and strain into a cocktail glass. Add an **olive**. This drink over the years has undergone much change.

MARTINI
(Today's Style)

  ▲ Base Recipe

  11 parts dry gin
  1 part French or dry vermouth

Stir well (*never shake*) with **ice** and pour into a cocktail glass, or stir ingredients in an old-fashioned glass filled with **ice cubes**. Add an **olive**.

—GIBSON MARTINI

Follow ▲ Recipe. Substitute **3 small pearl white or pink onions** for the olive.

MAYFAIR

  1 pony dry gin
  ½ pony orange juice
  ½ pony apricot liqueur
  Pinch ground cloves
  Dash orange bitters
  1 ice cube

Blend 6 to 8 seconds, strain and serve in a cocktail glass.

MELBA COCKTAIL

  1 pony light rum
  ¾ teaspoon Pernod
  1 pony Swedish Punch
  Juice of ½ lime
  ½ teaspoon grenadine

Shake well with **ice** and strain into a cocktail glass.

MERRY WIDOW

  1 pony dry gin
  1 pony French vermouth
  Dash Angostura bitters
  ¾ teaspoon Pernod
  ¾ teaspoon Benedictine

Stir well with **ice** and strain into a cocktail glass. Add a **twist of lemon peel**.

MILLIONAIRE

  1 jigger dry gin
  1 pony Pernod or Herbsaint
  Dash anisette
  1 egg white
  2 ice cubes

Blend 10 seconds, strain and serve in a large cocktail glass.

NEGRONI COCKTAIL

  ⅓ Campari Apertivo
  ⅓ dry gin
  ⅓ Italian vermouth

Shake well with **ice** and strain into a cocktail glass.

OLD-FASHIONED

  ▲ Base Recipe

  1 jigger bourbon
  Dash Angostura bitters
  ¾ teaspoon orange bitters
  ½ lump sugar, muddled
  1 slice pineapple
  1 slice orange
  1 maraschino cherry

Serve in an old-fashioned glass filled half full with **ice cubes**.

—SCOTCH OLD-FASHIONED

Follow ▲ Recipe. Substitute **1 jigger Scotch** for the bourbon.

OLD IRONSIDES COCKTAIL

  1 jigger sloe gin
  ¾ teaspoon lemon juice
  ½ teaspoon Italian vermouth
  ½ teaspoon New England rum
  ½ teaspoon orange bitters

Shake well with **ice** and strain into a cocktail glass.

OPAL COCKTAIL

  ⅓ dry gin
  ⅓ orange juice
  ⅙ Cointreau
  ⅙ orange flower water

Shake well with **ice** and strain into a cocktail glass.

OPERA COCKTAIL

  ⅙ maraschino
  ⅙ Dubonnet
  ⅔ dry gin

Stir well with **ice** and strain into a cocktail glass. Add a **twist of lemon peel**.

ORANGE BLOSSOM

  1 jigger dry gin
  1 jigger orange juice
  2 ice cubes

Blend 6 to 8 seconds, strain and serve in a cocktail glass.

PADDY COCKTAIL

  ½ Irish whiskey
  ½ Italian vermouth
  Dash Angostura bitters

Shake well with **ice** and strain into a cocktail glass.

PALL MALL COCKTAIL

As served at the Café de Paris, Monte Carlo, Monaco.

  1 teaspoon white crème de menthe
  ½ teaspoon orange bitters
  1 pony Italian vermouth
  1 pony French vermouth
  1 pony dry gin

Shake well with **ice** and strain into a cocktail glass.

Butterscotch Benchwarmer, Cheerleader's Choice and Orange Honey Hero

PARADISE COCKTAIL

1 pony apricot liqueur
1 pony dry gin
1 pony orange juice
¼ teaspoon lemon juice

Shake with **ice**; strain into a cocktail glass.

PICCADILLY COCKTAIL

¼ teaspoon Pernod
¼ teaspoon grenadine
1 pony French vermouth
1 jigger dry gin

Stir well with **ice** and strain into a cocktail glass.

PICON DRY

½ Amer Picon
½ dry vermouth

Stir with **cracked ice** and strain into a cocktail glass. Add a **twist of lemon peel.**

PINK LADY

1 jigger dry gin
1½ teaspoons grenadine
½ teaspoon heavy cream
1 egg white
2 ice cubes

Blend 10 seconds, strain and serve in a 4-oz. cocktail glass.

PLANTATION COCKTAIL

⅓ lemon juice
⅔ Jamaica rum
½ teaspoon sugar
Dash Angostura bitters

Shake well with **ice** and strain into a cocktail glass. Garnish with a **maraschino cherry.**

PREAKNESS COCKTAIL

1 jigger rye
1 pony Italian vermouth
Dash Angostura bitters
¾ teaspoon Benedictine

Stir well with **ice** and strain into a cocktail glass. Garnish with a **twist of lemon peel.**

PRINCE OF WALES

Dash Angostura bitters
1 teaspoon curaçao
1 jigger Madeira
1 jigger brandy

Shake bitters, curaçao, Madeira and brandy carefully with **ice** and pour a jigger of the mixture into a champagne glass. Fill with **chilled champagne** and serve garnished with a **thin slice of orange.**   *2 servings*

Strawberry Thickmalts

QUEEN'S PEG

1 lump sugar
1 jigger dry gin
Chilled champagne

Put the sugar into an 8-oz. highball glass. Add the gin and crush. Add **ice cubes** to half fill the glass. Fill with champagne.

RIALTO COCKTAIL

1 jigger Jamaica rum
1 pony cherry liqueur
¾ teaspoon orange bitters

Shake well with **ice** and strain into a cocktail glass.

ROB ROY

▲ *Base Recipe*

1 pony Italian vermouth
1 jigger Scotch
Dash Angostura bitters
Dash orange bitters

Shake well with **ice** and strain into a cocktail glass. Add an **olive.** This drink may be served on the rocks.

—DRY ROB ROY

Follow ▲ Recipe. Substitute **1 pony French or dry vermouth** for the Italian vermouth.

—PERFECT ROB ROY

Follow ▲ Recipe. Use ½ **pony dry vermouth** and ½ **pony Italian vermouth.**

ROBIN HOOD COCKTAIL

2 oz. bourbon
¾ teaspoon Benedictine
½ teaspoon grenadine
½ teaspoon lime juice

Shake well with **ice** and strain into a cocktail glass. Garnish with a **maraschino cherry.**

ROCK AND RYE

To cure a cold.

2 oz. rye
1 piece rock candy
Juice of 1 lemon

Muddle the candy. Stir well with **ice** until candy dissolves. Serve in an old-fashioned glass.

RON RICO COCKTAIL

2 oz. Jamaica rum
1 oz. dry gin
Dash Angostura bitters
½ teaspoon grenadine
Juice of 1 lime

Shake well with **ice** and strain into a cocktail glass.

ROSE COCKTAIL

1 pony crème de cassis
1 pony kirsch
1 jigger dry gin
Maraschino cherry

Shake well with **ice** and strain into a cocktail glass. Garnish with the cherry.

ROYAL COCKTAIL

1 egg
½ teaspoon sugar
Juice of ½ lemon
1 jigger dry gin

Shake well with **ice** and strain into a cocktail glass.

RUM COCKTAIL

⅗ New England rum
⅕ lemon juice
⅕ Cointreau
½ teaspoon sugar

Shake well with **ice** and strain into a cocktail glass.

RUM AND TRIPLE SEC

1 slice lime
1 pony Triple Sec
1 jigger light rum

Shake well with **ice** and strain into a cocktail glass. Decorate with a **green cherry.**

RUMBA COCKTAIL

1 jigger Jamaica rum
1 pony dry gin
½ teaspoon grenadine

Shake well with **ice** and strain into a cocktail glass.

RUSSIAN COCKTAIL

⅓ crème de cacao
⅓ dry gin
⅓ vodka

Stir well with **ice** and strain into a cocktail glass.

RYE AND PINE COCKTAIL

⅓ rye
⅔ pineapple juice

Shake well with **ice** and strain into a cocktail glass.

SANCTUARY

½ Dubonnet
¼ Amer Picon
¼ Cointreau

Stir gently with **cracked ice.** Strain into a cocktail glass.

SANDER

1 pony dry gin
1 pony Grand Marnier
½ pony orange juice
½ pony lemon juice
2 ice cubes

Blend 8 to 10 seconds. Strain into a *chilled* cocktail glass.

SAZERAC

1 jigger rye
½ teaspoon Peychaud bitters
2 ice cubes

Chill a large old-fashioned glass. Add **Herbsaint** or **Pernod** and twirl the glass to coat thoroughly. Place upside down (letting any excess Pernod run out) until ready to use. Put ingredients into blender container. Blend about 10 seconds and strain into glass. Twist **lemon peel** over the drink, but don't put it into the drink. Serve.

SHAMROCK COCKTAIL

1 jigger Irish whiskey
½ oz. Italian vermouth
½ oz. green crème de menthe
½ oz. green chartreuse

Shake well with **ice** and strain into a cocktail glass. Add a **green olive.**

SHANGHAI COCKTAIL

½ teaspoon grenadine
1 jigger Jamaica rum
Dash Angostura bitters
½ teaspoon maraschino
1 teaspoon curaçao

Shake well with **ice** and strain into a cocktail glass.

SHARPSHOOTER COCKTAIL

2 oz. Irish whiskey
½ teaspoon Pernod
Dash Angostura bitters
½ teaspoon sugar

Shake well with **ice** and strain into a cocktail glass. Garnish with a **twist of lemon peel.**

SEVILLA COCKTAIL

½ teaspoon sugar
1 egg
½ port
½ light rum

Shake well with **ice** and strain into a cocktail glass.

SIDE CAR

1 pony cognac
1 pony Cointreau
1 pony lemon juice
1 ice cube

Run a **piece of lemon** around the rim of a cocktail glass, then dip rim in **confectioners' sugar.** Blend all ingredients 6 to 8 seconds and strain into the glass.

SIGMA CHI COCKTAIL

1 jigger sloe gin
1 pony Benedictine
½ teaspoon orange bitters

Shake well with **ice** and strain into a cocktail glass.

SLOE GIN COCKTAIL

1 jigger sloe gin
Dash orange bitters
1 pony French vermouth

Stir well with **ice** and strain into a cocktail glass.

SNOWBALL COCKTAIL

⅙ Crème Yvette
⅙ white crème de menthe
⅙ anisette
⅙ cream
⅓ dry gin

Shake well with **ice** and strain into a cocktail glass.

SOUTHERN COCKTAIL

1 jigger bourbon
1 lump sugar
Dash Angostura bitters
Dash orange bitters
¾ teaspoon anisette

Stir well with **ice** and strain into a cocktail glass. Garnish with a **twist of lemon peel.**

SPORTSMAN'S COCKTAIL

2 oz. dry gin
1 oz. green crème de menthe
1 egg white
2 oz. orange juice
1 oz. lemon juice
1 teaspoon sugar

Shake well with **ice** and strain into a large cocktail glass.

STINGER

⅓ white crème de menthe
⅔ brandy

Shake well with **ice** and strain into a cocktail glass. Or stir with crushed ice and pour into glass. This drink may also be served on the rocks in an old-fashioned glass.

STUDIO COCKTAIL

1 teaspoon crème de cassis
½ oz. Italian vermouth
1 oz. applejack

Shake well with **ice** and strain into a cocktail glass. Garnish with a **small slice of apple.**

SUBMARINE COCKTAIL

Dash Angostura bitters
¼ French vermouth
¼ dry gin
½ Dubonnet

Stir well with **ice** and strain into a cocktail glass.

TIPPERARY COCKTAIL

1 jigger Irish whiskey
½ oz. Italian vermouth
½ oz. green chartreuse

Shake well with **ice** and strain into a cocktail glass.

TROPICAL COCKTAIL

Juice of 1 lime
¾ teaspoon grenadine
1 teaspoon sugar
1 jigger Jamaica rum

Shake well with **ice** and strain into a cocktail glass. Garnish with **2 slices fresh pineapple.**

TWIN SIX COCKTAIL

1 jigger dry gin
1 pony Italian vermouth
½ teaspoon grenadine
1 egg white

Shake well with **ice** and strain into a cocktail glass. Garnish with a **thin slice of orange.**

UNION JACK

⅓ Crème Yvette
⅔ dry gin

Stir well with **ice** and strain into a cocktail glass.

UPTOWN COCKTAIL

1 teaspoon pineapple juice
1 teaspoon orange juice
1 teaspoon lime juice
1 jigger Jamaica rum
½ teaspoon Cointreau
½ teaspoon grenadine
Dash Angostura bitters

Shake well with **ice** and strain into a large cocktail glass. Garnish with a **maraschino cherry.**

VOLGA COCKTAIL

1 jigger vodka
1 pony orange juice
1 pony lemon juice
Dash Angostura bitters
¾ teaspoon grenadine

Shake well with **ice** and strain into a cocktail glass.

WALDORF COCKTAIL

⅓ rye
⅓ Italian vermouth
⅓ anisette
2 dashes orange bitters

Shake well with **ice** and strain into a cocktail glass.

WEEP NO MORE

⅓ Dubonnet
⅓ cognac
⅓ lime juice
Dash maraschino

Stir gently with **cracked ice.** Strain into a cocktail glass.

WILD WEST COCKTAIL

⅓ Irish whiskey
⅓ Swedish Punch
⅓ French vermouth
Dash Angostura bitters
¼ teaspoon lemon juice

Stir well with **ice** and strain into a cocktail glass.

X.Y.Z. COCKTAIL

½ oz. lemon juice
½ oz. Triple Sec
1 oz. light rum

Shake well with **ice** and strain into a cocktail glass.

YALE COCKTAIL

Dash orange bitters
1 jigger dry gin
1 pony Italian vermouth

Stir well with **ice** and strain into a cocktail glass. Add **carbonated water.**

ZAZA COCKTAIL

1 jigger dry gin
1 jigger Dubonnet

Stir well with **ice** and strain into a cocktail glass. Garnish with a **twist of orange peel.**

COLLINS, COOLERS, RICKEYS, BUCKS AND FIZZES

COLLINS

The collins is a thirst quencher served in the tallest of glasses from 12 to 14 oz. to the drink. It is a sour drink, usually a lemonade spiked with gin, rum, brandy or other hard liquor. To make, shake ingredients with ice, strain into a collins glass, add four or five ice cubes, fill glass with carbonated water and serve.

APPLE COLLINS

1 jigger applejack
Juice of 1 lime
Juice of 1 lemon
2 teaspoons sugar

Mix and serve as directed above. Decorate with **1 maraschino cherry**, a **slice of orange** and a **sprig of fresh mint.**

JOHN COLLINS

Juice of 1 lime
1 teaspoon sugar
1 jigger Holland gin

Mix and serve as directed above.

MINT COLLINS

8 fresh mint leaves muddled with
2 teaspoons sugar
1 jigger dry gin
Juice of ½ lemon

Mix and serve as directed above.

RUM COLLINS

2 oz. Jamaica rum
1 teaspoon sugar
Juice of 1 lime
Dash Angostura bitters

Mix as directed above. Garnish with a **maraschino cherry** and serve.

TOM COLLINS

Juice of 1 lemon
1 jigger dry gin
1 teaspoon sugar

Mix as directed above. Decorate with a **maraschino cherry** and serve.

COOLERS

The cooler is a version of the collins. Serve it in a collins glass. Cut the peel of a lemon or an orange in one continuous spiral and hang it over the edge of the glass so that it spirals through the ice cubes. Pour the ingredients into

the glass and serve. It should be a frosted beauty to behold. If peeling fruit is too difficult, decorate drink with thin slices of lemon or orange.

APRICOT COOLER

Juice of ½ lemon
Juice of ½ lime
¾ teaspoon grenadine
1 jigger apricot brandy

Shake well and pour into a collins glass over peel arranged as above. Fill glass with **carbonated water.**

CHAMPAGNE COOLER

1 jigger cognac
1 jigger Cointreau
Chilled champagne

Pour cognac and Cointreau into an 8-oz. highball glass filled half full with **ice cubes.** Fill glass with champagne and stir gently.

HIGHLAND COOLER

2 oz. Scotch
Juice of ½ lemon
2 dashes Angostura bitters
1 teaspoon sugar
2 ice cubes

Arrange **orange peel** in glass. Shake ingredients well and strain into glass. Fill with **ice cubes** and **ginger ale.**

SEA BREEZE COOLER

Juice of ½ lemon
¾ teaspoon grenadine
1 pony apricot liqueur
1 pony dry gin

Stir ingredients and pour into a collins glass filled with **ice cubes.** Decorate with **2 sprigs fresh mint.**

SLOE GIN COOLER

Juice of ½ lime
½ teaspoon sugar
1 jigger sloe gin
1 pony dark rum

Shake well with ice and pour into a glass filled with **ice cubes.** Fill glass with **lemon-flavored carbonated beverage.**

SUNSET COOLER

Juice of ½ lemon
1 teaspoon sugar
1 jigger sloe gin

Shake ingredients well with **ice** and pour into a collins glass. Fill glass with **ginger ale.** Decorate with a slice of **lemon.**

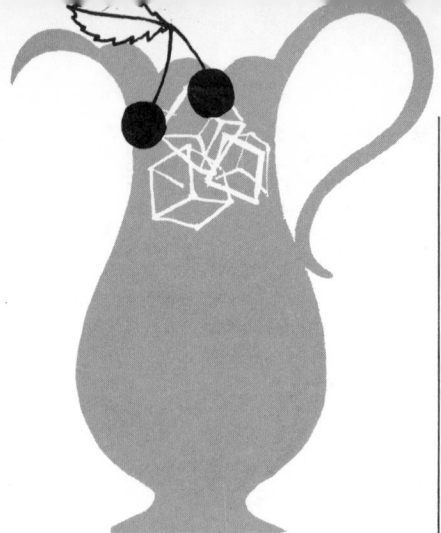

RICKEYS

Always made with lime but with a wide assortment of liquors, a rickey is usually served in an 8-oz. glass—a sort of short collins.

APPLEJACK RICKEY

▲ *Base Recipe*

1 jigger applejack
Juice of 1 lime
3 ice cubes

Combine in a glass. Fill glass with **carbonated water.** Add a **twist of lemon peel.**

—APRICOT RICKEY

Follow ▲ Recipe. Substitute **1 jigger apricot liqueur** for the applejack.

—GIN RICKEY

Follow ▲ Recipe. Substitute **1 jigger dry gin** for the applejack.

—GRENADINE RICKEY

Follow ▲ Recipe. Substitute **1 jigger grenadine** for the applejack.

—IRISH RICKEY

Follow ▲ Recipe. Substitute **1 jigger Irish whiskey** for the applejack.

BOURBON RICKEY

▲ *Base Recipe*

1 jigger bourbon
Juice of 1 lime
1 ice cube

Mix ingredients in an 8-oz. highball glass. Fill glass with **carbonated water.** Add a **twist of lemon peel.**

—SCOTCH RICKEY

Follow ▲ Recipe. Substitute **1 jigger Scotch** for the bourbon.

SLOE GIN RICKEY

2 oz. sloe gin
Juice of 1 lime
1 teaspoon confectioners' sugar
2 ice cubes

Shake well and pour into a glass. Fill glass with **carbonated water.** Add a **twist of lemon peel.**

BUCKS

A member of the collins or rickey family, usually served in a 10-oz. highball glass.

GIN BUCK

Juice of ½ lime or ¼ lemon
2 jiggers dry gin
3 ice cubes

Squeeze shell of lime or lemon and drop into highball glass. Add gin and ice cubes. Fill glass with **ginger ale.**

RUM BUCK

Juice of ½ lemon
2 jiggers dark rum
3 ice cubes
1 piece lemon peel

Put all ingredients in a highball glass. Fill glass with **ginger ale.**

Note: The above drinks may also be made with brandy or bourbon.

FIZZES

Similar to the collins except it is usually served in a smaller (12 oz.) frosted highball glass, generally made from liquor, citrus juices and sugar, shaken with crushed ice and strained into the glass. Fill with carbonated water. There are many variations as you will see below.

ALABAMA FIZZ

    1 jigger dry gin
    1 teaspoon confectioners' sugar
    1 pony lemon juice
    5 mint leaves

Shake well with **ice** and strain into glass. Fill glass with **carbonated water** and stir.

BOURBON FIZZ

    Juice of ¼ lemon
    ½ teaspoon confectioners' sugar
    1 jigger bourbon

Shake well with **ice** and strain into a glass. Add **carbonated water** and stir.

BRANDY FIZZ

    1 egg white
    1 jigger brandy
    Juice of ½ lime
    1 teaspoon confectioners' sugar

Shake well with **ice** and strain into a glass. Add **carbonated water** and stir.

CREAM FIZZ

    1 jigger dry gin
    ½ oz. lemon juice
    ½ teaspoon sugar
    ½ oz. cream

Shake well with ice and strain into a glass. Add **carbonated water** and stir.

GIN FIZZ

    ▲ *Base Recipe*

    1 jigger dry gin
    1 pony lemon juice
    ½ pony Sugar Syrup (page 621)
    2 ice cubes

Blend 15 seconds (don't strain) and pour into an 8-oz. highball glass. Fill with **carbonated water**. Stir gently.

—SLOE GIN FIZZ

Follow ▲ Recipe. Substitute **1½ jiggers sloe gin** for the dry gin.

CRUSTAS

The crusta is made in an old-fashioned or wine glass that has been lined with the spiral peel from half a lemon or orange. Shake the ingredients and pour into the glass filled with ice.

BOURBON CRUSTA

    ▲ *Base Recipe*

    2 oz. bourbon
    1 teaspoon lemon juice
    1 teaspoon sugar
    2 dashes Angostura bitters

Shake well with **ice** and strain into a wine or old-fashioned glass with the rim frosted with **sugar**, and in which there is arranged a spiral of **half a lemon or orange peel**. Decorate with a **maraschino cherry**.

—APPLEJACK CRUSTA

Follow ▲ Recipe. Substitute **1 jigger applejack** for the bourbon; use ½ oz. lemon juice.

—BRANDY CRUSTA

Follow ▲ Recipe. Substitute **1 jigger brandy** for the bourbon; use ½ oz. lemon juice.

—GIN CRUSTA

Follow ▲ Recipe. Substitute **1 jigger Holland gin** for the bourbon; use ½ oz. lemon juice.

DAISIES AND FIXES

The daisy is a sour usually sweetened with grenadine or raspberry syrup, spiced with lemon and served in a highball glass filled with crushed ice which causes the glass to frost. A fix is similar to a daisy. It is usually served in a goblet or glass filled with crushed ice and served with a short straw.

CANADIAN DAISY

    1 pony lemon juice
    ½ pony grenadine
    1 jigger rye

Fill a 12-oz. highball glass with **shaved ice**. Add ingredients and stir until glass is frosted. Garnish with **fresh fruit** and **mint**.

GIN DAISY

    Juice of ½ lemon
    1 teaspoon maraschino
    1 teaspoon sugar
    ½ teaspoon grenadine
    1 jigger dry gin

Fill a highball glass with **shaved ice**. Add ingredients and stir gently until glass is frosted. Fill with **carbonated water**. Decorate with a sprig of **fresh mint**.

RUM DAISY

    2 oz. dark rum
    Juice of ½ lemon
    1 teaspoon yellow chartreuse
    ½ teaspoon grenadine
    1 teaspoon sugar

Shake well with **ice** and pour into a 12-oz. highball glass. Fill with **carbonated water**. Decorate with a **slice of orange** and a **slice of pineapple**.

WHISKEY DAISY

    Juice of ½ lime
    Juice of ¼ lemon
    ½ teaspoon grenadine
    1 jigger rye
    1 teaspoon sugar

Put into a pewter mug with **crushed ice**. Fill with **carbonated water** and stir until frosted. Serve with **fresh fruit, mint leaves** and a straw.

BRANDY FIX

    1 oz. cherry liqueur
    1 oz. brandy
    1 teaspoon sugar
    1 teaspoon carbonated water

Fill glass or goblet with **crushed ice**. Add ingredients and stir slowly. Top with a **slice of lemon**. Serve with a straw.

GIN FIX

    1 teaspoon sugar
    Juice of ½ lemon
    1 jigger carbonated water
    2 jiggers dry gin

Stir ingredients gently. Pour into highball glass or goblet two-thirds full with **crushed ice**. Decorate with **fresh fruit**.

RUM FIX

    1 oz. cherry liqueur
    1 oz. dark rum
    1 teaspoon sugar
    1 teaspoon carbonated water
    Juice of ½ lemon

Put into a highball glass. Fill glass with **crushed ice**. Stir slowly and add **1 slice lemon**. Serve with a straw.

WHISKEY FIX

    ½ teaspoon sugar
    ½ oz. carbonated water
    ½ teaspoon lemon juice
    2 oz. pineapple juice
    2 oz. rye

Stir well with **crushed ice.** Serve as above garnished with a **slice of lemon or orange.**

FLIPS

A kind of eggnog-fizz combination concocted with whole egg, sugar or sugar syrup and liquor, the ingredients shaken with crushed ice and strained into a sour glass, decorated with a dash of nutmeg, if desired.

BLACKBERRY FLIP

▲ *Base Recipe*

1 egg
1 teaspoon confectioners' sugar
1 jigger blackberry liqueur

Shake well with **ice** and strain into a 4- or 5-oz. sour or flip glass. This drink is also made with **1 oz. cream** added.

—CHERRY FLIP

Follow ▲ Recipe. Substitute **1 jigger cherry liqueur** for the blackberry liqueur.

BRANDY FLIP

▲ *Base Recipe*

1 jigger cognac
1 egg
½ teaspoon Sugar Syrup (page 621)
2 ice cubes

Blend 15 seconds, strain into a chilled wine glass and top with **nutmeg.**

—BOURBON FLIP

Follow ▲ Recipe. Substitute **1 jigger bourbon** for the cognac.

—RUM FLIP

Follow ▲ Recipe. Substitute **1 jigger Jamaica rum** for the cognac.

COFFEE FLIP

1 jigger port
1 pony cognac
1 egg
½ teaspoon Sugar Syrup (page 621)
1 teaspoon cream
2 ice cubes

Blend 12 to 15 seconds. Strain into a chilled wine glass.

FRAPPES

To chill a drink to a mushy consistency is to frappé it. It is usually done by serving any liquor over crushed ice.

ABSINTHE FRAPPE

1½ jiggers Pernod or Herbsaint
½ pony Anisette
1 teaspoon Sugar Syrup (page 621)
4 ice cubes

Blend 1½ min., or until ice is of sherbet consistency. Serve in an old-fashioned glass.

CAFE ROYAL FRAPPE

¾ black coffee
¼ brandy

Shake with **crushed ice** until semi-frozen.

CREME DE MENTHE FRAPPE

Fill a cocktail glass with **crushed ice.** Pour over the ice **green crème de menthe.** Serve with a short straw.

HIGHBALLS

Perhaps the most popular American drink. Many liquors are combined with water, carbonated water or other carbonated beverages. Served with or without ice in a highball glass or an old-fashioned glass, the proportions of ice, liquor and mixer may vary to suit the individual taste.

AMERICAN HIGHBALL

1 jigger (or more) rye or bourbon
1, 2 or 3 ice cubes

Put into an 8-oz. highball glass. Fill glass with desired amount of **plain or carbonated water** and stir.

APPLEJACK HIGHBALL

1 jigger applejack
1, 2 or 3 ice cubes

Put into an 8-oz. highball glass. Fill glass with **ginger ale.** Add a **twist of lemon peel.**

CAMPARI SODA

This is how Campari is drunk in Rome.

1 jigger Campari Aperitivo in a
highball glass with a good splash
of carbonated water

Serve very cold.

CUBA LIBRE

2 oz. rum
Juice of ½ lime

Shake well with **ice** and pour into a highball glass. Fill with **cola beverage.**

FORDHAM RAM HIGHBALL

1 oz. sloe gin
2 oz. brandy
½ teaspoon sugar
Juice of 1 lemon

Shake well with **ice** and pour into a 12-oz. glass over **3 ice cubes.** Fill with desired amount of **carbonated water.**

FRENCH "75"

▲ *Base Recipe*

1 jigger dry gin
½ pony lemon juice
1 teaspoon sugar
Chilled champagne

Mix gin, lemon juice and sugar. Pour into an 8-oz. highball glass half full with **ice cubes.** Fill with champagne.

—FRENCH "95"

Follow ▲ Recipe. Substitute **1 jigger Canadian whiskey** for gin.

—FRENCH "125"

Follow ▲ Recipe. Substitute **1 jigger cognac** for gin.

GIN AND TONIC

As served at Shepherd's Hotel, Cairo, Egypt.

1 jigger dry gin
1 thin slice lemon or wedge lime
1, 2 or 3 ice cubes

Put into a highball glass and fill with **quinine water.**

GINGER ALE HIGHBALL

2½ oz. rye
2 ice cubes

Put into an 8-oz. highball glass and fill with **ginger ale.** Add a **twist of lemon peel.**

HORSE'S NECK

Continuous peel of ½ lemon
2 jiggers dry gin
1 teaspoon sugar
1, 2 or 3 ice cubes

Arrange lemon peel in a spiral hooked to the top of a highball glass. Add gin, sugar and ice cubes. Fill glass with **ginger ale.**

RUM HIGHBALL

    1 jigger Jamaica rum
    3 ice cubes

Put rum and ice cubes into an 8-oz. highball glass. Fill glass with **ginger ale.** Add a **twist of lemon peel.**

SLIM JIM HIGHBALL

    Juice of 1 lemon
    2 teaspoons sugar
    2 jiggers dry gin
    2 ice cubes
    1 slice fresh pineapple
    1 maraschino cherry
    1 sprig fresh mint

Put lemon juice, sugar, gin and ice cubes into a highball glass. Fill glass with **carbonated water.** Garnish with pineapple, cherry and mint.

VODKA HIGHBALL

    2 oz. vodka
    3 ice cubes

Put into an 8-oz. highball glass. Add **ginger ale,** or **plain or carbonated water.**

JULEPS AND SMASHES

The julep is a Kentucky drink, usually made with bourbon and mint which has been finely crushed, served in a goblet or frosted glass with crushed ice and garnished with whole mint. A smash is a smaller size julep usually served over ice cubes in an old-fashioned glass.

APPLEJACK JULEP

    1 jigger applejack
    1 pony light rum
    ½ teaspoon maraschino
    1 teaspoon sugar
    2 sprigs fresh mint

Put all ingredients into a highball glass or goblet with **crushed ice.** Stir well and decorate with **fresh mint.**

BRANDY MINT JULEP

    4 sprigs fresh mint
    1 oz. peach liqueur
    2 jiggers brandy
    1 teaspoon confectioners' sugar

Crush mint in a highball glass or goblet. Add remaining ingredients; fill with **cracked ice.** Stir well and decorate with **fresh mint.**

CHAMPAGNE JULEP

    4 sprigs fresh mint
    1 lump sugar
    1 jigger brandy
    Chilled champagne

Crush mint with sugar and 1 teaspoon **water** in an 8-oz. highball glass. Fill half full with **cracked ice** and add brandy. Fill with champagne and decorate with **fresh mint.** Serve with a straw.

SOUTHERN MINT JULEP

    4 sprigs fresh mint
    ¼ teaspoon sugar
    1 teaspoon water
    2 jiggers rye

Crush 2 mint sprigs in a glass. Add sugar, water and rye and stir well. Then fill the glass with **crushed ice.** Stir until frosted. Garnish with remaining mint.

BOURBON SMASH

    ▲ *Base Recipe*

    1 lump sugar muddled with ½
        teaspoon carbonated water and 4
        sprigs fresh mint
    1 jigger bourbon
    Twist of lemon peel
    3 ice cubes

Combine all ingredients in an old-fashioned glass. Fill glass with **carbonated water.** Decorate with an **orange slice.**

—GIN SMASH

Follow ▲ Recipe. Substitute **1 jigger dry gin** for bourbon. Decorate with **fresh fruit.**

BRANDY SMASH

    1 teaspoon confectioners' sugar
    ½ teaspoon water
    2 oz. brandy
    Mint leaves, crushed
    3 ice cubes

Combine all ingredients in an old-fashioned glass. Fill glass with **carbonated water.** Garnish with **fresh fruit.**

SCOTCH SMASH

    1 teaspoon confectioners' sugar
    ½ teaspoon carbonated water
    2 oz. Scotch
    4 sprigs mint, crushed
    3 ice cubes

Combine all ingredients in an old-fashioned glass. Fill glass with **carbonated water.** Decorate with **fresh fruit.**

NOGS

Made with eggs and milk and served in punch cups, mugs or glasses, nogs are usually thought of as holiday drinks, but they may be enjoyed any time of year.

BOSTON EGGNOG

    1 pony cognac
    ½ pony Jamaica rum
    1 jigger Madeira
    1 egg
    ½ pony Sugar Syrup (page 621)
    6 oz. milk
    2 ice cubes

Blend 15 seconds, strain into a highball glass and grate **nutmeg** on top.

Eggnog Distingue

BRANDY EGGNOG

1 egg
1 teaspoon confectioners' sugar
1 jigger brandy
4 oz. milk

Shake well with **ice** and strain into a glass. Grate **nutmeg** on top.

EGGNOG

1 jigger bourbon
1 teaspoon Sugar Syrup (page 621)
1 egg
1 cup milk
2 ice cubes

Blend 12 to 15 seconds, strain into a highball glass and grate **nutmeg** on top.

EGGNOG DISTINGUE

Tea is the distinctive flavor in this unique eggnog.

1 qt. milk
6 eggs, separated
¼ cup sugar
¼ cup orange-and-spice-flavored instant tea
1 cup light rum
¼ teaspoon salt
¼ cup sugar
1 cup heavy cream, chilled

Scald the milk in a heavy 2½- or 3-qt. saucepan.

Set egg whites aside. Beat egg yolks in a large mixing bowl, adding ¼ cup sugar gradually. Continue beating until very thick. Beating constantly, blend in the scalded milk. Return to saucepan. Cook and stir over low heat until mixture coats a metal spoon (do not overcook).

Remove from heat. Blend in the tea. Refrigerate to chill thoroughly.

Then mix in the rum. Add the salt to reserved egg whites and beat until frothy. Adding several tablespoons at a time, beat in the remaining sugar. Continue beating until very stiff peaks are formed. Fold into chilled egg yolk mixture.

Whip the cream until stiff peaks are formed. Fold half of the whipped cream into egg yolk mixture. Turn eggnog into chilled punch bowl and top with dollops of the remaining whipped cream. Sprinkle with additional instant tea.
About 2 qts. eggnog

HOT RUM EGGNOG

1 egg
2 jiggers Jamaica rum
1 teaspoon orgeat
Dash crème de cacao
½ cup milk

Put egg into blender container; heat remaining ingredients to just below boiling. Turn on blender and add liquid slowly to egg. As soon as all liquid is in the blender, turn it off and pour into a heated mug. Grate **nutmeg** on top.

SOUTHERN EGGNOG

10 eggs, separated
1 cup sugar
1½ pts. brandy
1 cup dark rum
2 qts. milk
1 qt. cream

Beat egg yolks with sugar. Mix in brandy and rum, then milk and cream. Beat egg whites until stiff, not dry, peaks form. Fold in. Grate **nutmeg** on top. Serve well chilled in a punch bowl.
About 40 servings

PUNCHES

PARTY PUNCHES

Punches are great for serving large gatherings. They come hot and cold and in great variation. They are usually served from punch bowls and ladled into punch glasses. Usually some of the fruit is included in each serving when fruit is used.

BUTTERED RUM PUNCH

2 qts. cider
½ cup brown sugar
¼ cup butter
1½ cups dark rum

Heat cider until very hot. Add remaining ingredients. Ladle into punch glasses and top with **ground cinnamon**.
12 servings

CARDINAL PUNCH

1 qt. claret
2 oz. brandy
2 oz. Jamaica rum
4 jiggers Italian vermouth
1 lb. confectioners' sugar
1 qt. carbonated water

Combine all ingredients in a punch bowl surrounded by **ice**. Decorate with **fresh cherries, sliced peaches, strawberries, orange slices** or **half slices of lemon** or other fruit. Ladle into punch glasses.
6 to 8 servings

CHAMPAGNE CUP I

½ fresh pineapple, carefully pared and cut into triangles ½ in. wide at center
6 strips cucumber peel
1 pt. fresh strawberries
6 jiggers curaçao
1 pt. chilled carbonated water
2 qts. chilled champagne

Put into a punch bowl containing a **large piece of ice** the pineapple, cucumber peel, strawberries, curaçao and carbonated water. Stir gently. Just before serving, add the champagne and stir again. If upon tasting you feel the combination may be improved or if you need a greater quantity, try adding an additional 2 jiggers curaçao and another quart of chilled champagne.
12 to 16 servings

CHAMPAGNE CUP II

- 2 teaspoons sugar
- 4 jiggers cognac
- 1 jigger curaçao
- 1 jigger maraschino
- 1 jigger Grand Marnier
- 1 orange, thinly sliced
- 2 qts. chilled champagne
- 2 thin slices fresh pineapple, cut in ½ in. wide triangles

Put into a punch bowl containing a **large piece of ice** the sugar, cognac, curaçao, maraschino, Grand Marnier and orange slices. Just before serving, add the champagne and stir gently. Serve in champagne glasses each containing a piece of pineapple and a **maraschino cherry.** Decorate with a sprig of **fresh mint.**

10 to 12 servings

CHAMPAGNE CUP PUNCH

- 1 teaspoon Sugar Syrup (page 621)
- 3 slices orange
- 3 slices lemon
- Peel of 1 lemon
- 1 teaspoon Angostura bitters
- 2 oz. brandy
- 2 oz. maraschino
- 2 oz. curaçao
- 4 oz. sherry
- 1 qt. chilled champagne
- 1 qt. carbonated water

Serve well iced in a punch bowl. Ladle into punch glasses. *6 to 8 servings*

CHAMPAGNE PUNCH I

- 1 pt. chilled carbonated water
- ½ lb. sugar
- 4 jiggers brandy
- 3 jiggers maraschino
- 3 jiggers curaçao
- 3 jiggers lemon juice
- 2 qts. chilled champagne

Mix in a punch bowl the carbonated water, sugar, brandy, maraschino, curaçao and lemon juice. Stir. Add a **block of ice** (or many ice cubes). Pour in the champagne and stir again. Decorate as desired. *10 to 12 servings*

CHAMPAGNE PUNCH II

- Juice of 2 oranges
- Juice of 2 lemons
- ½ cup sugar
- ½ cup light rum
- ½ cup dark rum
- 1 cup pineapple juice
- 2 qts. chilled champagne

Mix in order listed in a punch bowl containing **ice cubes** or a **block of ice** the orange juice, lemon juice, sugar, light and dark rum and pineapple juice. Stir and pour in the champagne. Serve in punch glasses decorated with **fruit.**

12 servings

CHAMPAGNE PUNCH III

- 3 jiggers brandy
- 3 jiggers Cointreau
- 2 qts. chilled champagne

Place a **large piece of ice** in a punch bowl. Add brandy, Cointreau and champagne. Stir gently and serve in champagne glasses.

12 servings

CHAMPAGNE PUNCH IV

- 1½ jiggers maraschino
- 1½ jiggers yellow chartreuse
- 4 jiggers brandy
- 1 pt. chilled carbonated water
- 2 teaspoons sugar
- 2 qts. chilled champagne

Mix in a punch bowl containing a **large block of ice** the maraschino, chartreuse, brandy, carbonated water and sugar. Stir. Just before serving add champagne and stir again. Serve in champagne glasses. *12 servings*

CHAMPAGNE PUNCH V

- 2 jiggers brandy
- 2 jiggers curaçao
- 2 jiggers maraschino
- 2 lemons, thinly sliced
- 2 oranges, thinly sliced
- ½ pt. fresh strawberries or raspberries
- 1 pt. chilled carbonated water
- 2 qts. chilled champagne

Mix in a punch bowl with a **large block of ice** the brandy, curaçao, maraschino, lemon and orange slices and strawberries. Stir gently. Just before serving add the carbonated water and champagne. (Or omit the carbonated water and add 3 qts. champagne.) Stir gently again. Serve in champagne glasses. *12 servings*

CIDER CUP PUNCH

- 1 qt. cider
- 1 pt. carbonated water
- 4 oz. sherry
- 2 jiggers brandy
- Juice of ½ lemon
- 3 twists of lemon peel
- 2 oz. pineapple juice

Stir well with **ice** in a pitcher or punch bowl. Add **sugar** and **nutmeg** to taste. *6 servings*

DRAGOON PUNCH

- 1½ qts. porter ale
- 1½ qts. beer
- 1 cup brandy
- 1 cup sherry
- 1 cup sugar
- 3 lemons, thinly sliced
- 1 pt. chilled carbonated water
- 3 qts. chilled champagne

Mix in a large punch bowl the ale, beer, brandy,

sherry, sugar and lemon slices. Add a **block of ice** and stir. Just before serving add carbonated water and champagne and stir again. Serve in punch glasses. *20 servings*

FLAMING BRANDY PUNCH

- 1 cup water
- ¾ lb. confectioners' sugar
- Peel of 2 lemons
- Pinch cinnamon
- Pinch mace
- Grated nutmeg to taste
- 2 whole cloves
- 1 qt. brandy
- Juice of 2 lemons

Simmer 5 min. the water, sugar, lemon peel and spices; strain. Pour into a punch bowl; add the brandy and lemon juice. Set ablaze and serve in punch glasses while flaming.

20 servings

FRUIT PUNCH

- 1 qt. grapefruit juice
- 1 qt. lemon juice
- 2 qts. strawberry juice
- 2 qts. raspberry juice
- 2 qts. cherry juice
- 1 qt. crushed pineapple
- 8 qts. carbonated water
- 2 lbs. confectioners' sugar
- 8 qts. dark rum

Combine all ingredients and chill. Pour into punch bowls containing **large blocks of ice.** Ladle into punch glasses. Decorate with lots of small fruits such as **cherries, strawberries, peach slices, lemon or orange slices, pineapple cubes,** so that some may be ladled into each serving. *100 servings*

GIN PUNCH

- 4 qts. dry gin
- 4 qts. carbonated water
- Juice of 6 lemons
- Juice of 12 oranges
- 4 oz. maraschino
- ¼ lb. confectioners' sugar

649

Tea-Flavored Champagne Punch

Combine in a punch bowl containing a **block of ice**. Ladle into punch glasses.   *20 servings*

PINEAPPLE PUNCH

1 pony pineapple juice
1 pony grenadine
2 jiggers maraschino
1 jigger dry gin
Juice of 3 lemons
2 teaspoons Angostura bitters
1½ qts. Moselle
1 qt. carbonated water
1 pineapple, cut in small cubes

Combine in a punch bowl surrounded with **ice**. Ladle into punch glasses.   *10 servings*

SWEDISH PUNCH
(Glögg)

A potent beverage guaranteed to warm the heart. Wherever Swedes are at the Christmas season, they raise steaming glasses of Glögg in salute.

1 bottle (25 oz.) Aquavit
1 bottle (25 oz.) claret
1 cup (about 5 oz.) blanched almonds
6 cinnamon sticks, 2½ in. each
1 cup (about 4 oz.) dark seedless raisins
6 pieces candied orange or lemon peel
12 whole cloves
12 cardamom seeds, peeled
1 cup lump sugar

Bring all ingredients except sugar slowly to boiling in a large saucepan. Reduce heat and simmer 10 min. Remove from heat. Put sugar into a large sieve. Place sieve over saucepan. Ladle some of mixture from saucepan over

sugar. Ignite the sugar and continue to ladle the liquid over the sugar until sugar is completely melted. The liquid will be flaming. (If necessary, extinguish the flame by placing cover over pan.) Serve hot in mugs or punch glasses. Be sure there are some raisins and almonds in each serving.   *10 to 15 servings*

Note: Glögg may be prepared days in advance and stored in bottles. When ready to serve, heat thoroughly (do not boil).

TEA-FLAVORED CHAMPAGNE PUNCH

2 qts. water
6 tea bags (orange-and-spice-flavored tea)
3 tablespoons sugar
½ cup brandy, chilled
1 bottle champagne, chilled

Heat the water to boiling in a large saucepan. Add the tea bags, cover saucepan and allow to steep (page 10) 5 min. Remove tea bags and set tea aside to cool.

Measure 1 qt. of cooled tea into a 5½-cup ring mold; if desired, add **orange slices** and **maraschino cherries** (see note). Freeze the ring mold until firm.

Add the sugar to the remaining 1 qt. of tea, stirring until dissolved. Refrigerate to chill. When ready to serve, unmold the ice mold into a chilled punch bowl. Pour in the chilled tea, brandy and champagne.   *About 2 qts. punch*

Note: If using orange slices and maraschino cherries in ice mold, pour cooled tea into the mold to a depth of ¼ in. Arrange fruit in bottom of mold and freeze until layer is partially frozen before adding remaining cooled tea.

WASSAIL BOWL PUNCH

1 qt. warm beer
1 lb. sugar
1 pt. sherry
2 qts. beer
Whole peel of 1 lemon
3 slices toasted bread

Grate **nutmeg** and **ginger** on top of warm beer and sugar in a punch bowl. Mix in sherry, beer and lemon peel. Float toast slices on top.   *12 servings*

WHISKEY PUNCH

1 lb. sugar
1 pt. orange juice
1 pt. lemon juice
2 qts. rye
4 qts. carbonated water
½ pineapple, thinly sliced
3 oranges, quartered
2 lemons, thinly sliced

Serve well iced in a punch bowl. Ladle into punch glasses.   *12 servings*

OTHER PUNCHES

These punches are for only one or two servings, but are punches never the less.

BRANDY MILK PUNCH

3 jiggers cognac
2 dashes Jamaica rum
2 teaspoons Sugar Syrup (page 621)
1 teaspoon curaçao
1 cup milk
4 ice cubes

Blend 10 seconds, strain, serve in highball glasses and grate **nutmeg** on top.   *2 servings*

MILK PUNCH

8 oz. milk
2 teaspoons sugar
2 jiggers rye
1 egg

Shake well with **ice** and strain into small highball glasses. Grate **nutmeg** on top.   *2 servings*

PLANTERS PUNCH

4 jiggers Jamaica rum
1 pony lime juice
1 pony lemon juice
1 pony grenadine
Dash curaçao
4 ice cubes

Blend 25 seconds; pour unstrained into highball glasses, adding ice if necessary to fill, and **slices of lime and lemon**.   *2 servings*

STRAWBERRY PUNCH

12 strawberries, muddled
1 oz. brandy
2 teaspoons sugar
8 oz. milk

Shake well with **ice** and strain into a highball glass. Add a **twist of lemon peel**.

TOM AND JERRY PUNCH

1 egg yolk
¾ oz. Jamaica rum
1 teaspoon sugar
¼ teaspoon allspice
1 egg white, beaten until stiff, not dry, peaks form
1¾ oz. brandy

Mix egg yolk, rum, sugar and allspice; then add egg white and ¼ oz. brandy. Put 1 tablespoon of mixture into a glass and add remaining brandy. Fill glass with **hot milk**. Grate **nutmeg** on top.

Note: Egg mixture is enough for several servings.

WHISKEY PUNCH

> 3 jiggers bourbon or rye
> 1 pony lemon juice
> 1 teaspoon Sugar Syrup (page 621)
> 3 ice cubes

Blend 6 to 8 seconds, strain into highball glasses. Add **crushed ice**, a dash of **cognac**, and fill with **carbonated water**.   *2 servings*

ZOMBIE

> 2 jiggers gold rum
> 1 jigger Jamaica rum
> 1 pony Demerara rum (151 proof)
> 1 pony curaçao
> 1 jigger lemon juice
> 1 pony orange juice
> 1 pony papaya juice
> ¾ pony grenadine
> Dash Pernod or Herbsaint
> 2 ice cubes

Blend 8 to 10 seconds. Pour into a chimney highball glass. Add **cracked ice** if necessary. Serve with a straw.

SANGAREES

A tall old-fashioned without bitters served in an 8-oz. glass. Often served with sherry or nutmeg floated on top.

BRANDY SANGAREE

> 3 ice cubes
> 2 oz. carbonated water
> ½ teaspoon confectioners' sugar
> 2 oz. brandy

Stir well in an 8-oz. glass. Grate **nutmeg** on top and serve.

RUM SANGAREE

> 1 teaspoon confectioners' sugar
>   dissolved in carbonated water
> 2 jiggers Jamaica rum
> 3 ice cubes

Put into an 8-oz. glass. Fill glass with **carbonated water**. Grate **nutmeg** on top.

SHAKES

A sort of "sour" with some ingredients in different proportions, served on crushed ice in an old-fashioned or sour glass.

WHISKEY SHAKE

> Juice of 1 lemon
> 2 jiggers rye
> 2 teaspoons confectioners' sugar

Shake well with **ice** and strain into an old-fashioned or sour glass.

WILSHIRE SHAKE

> 1 jigger New England rum
> 1 pony cherry liqueur
> Juice of 1 lime
> 1 teaspoon maraschino

Combine in an old-fashioned glass. Fill glass with **crushed ice**. Decorate with **pineapple** and **fresh mint**.

SLINGS AND TODDIES

A combination of sweetened fruits, fruit juices, liquor and water. For a hot sling or toddy, fill the glass with boiling water. For a cold sling or toddy, fill the glass with chilled water or carbonated water or with ice cubes. Serve in an old-fashioned glass.

APPLEJACK SLING

> 1 jigger applejack
> ½ oz. grenadine
> Juice of 1 lime
> ½ teaspoon cherry liqueur

Stir gently with **ice** and strain into an old-fashioned glass. Fill glass with **cracked ice**.

BRANDY SLING

> ▲ *Base Recipe*

> 1 teaspoon sugar
> 1 pony carbonated water
> 2 oz. brandy
> 1 piece lemon peel
> 1 piece orange peel

Stir well with **ice** and strain into an old-fashioned glass.

—RUM SLING

Follow ▲ Recipe. Substitute **2 oz. dark rum** for the brandy.

GIN SLING

> 1 teaspoon confectioners' sugar
> 1 pony water
> 1 jigger dry gin
> 1 slice lemon
> 3 ice cubes

Combine in an old-fashioned glass. Fill glass with **carbonated water**.

STRAITS SLING

> ⅔ dry gin
> ⅙ Benedictine
> ⅙ cherry liqueur
> Juice of ½ lemon
> Dash Angostura bitters
> Dash orange bitters

Shake well with **ice** and strain into an old-fashioned glass. Fill glass with chilled **carbonated water**.

WHISKEY SLING

> 1 teaspoon confectioners' sugar
> 1 teaspoon water
> 1 jigger rye
> 2 ice cubes

Muddle confectioners' sugar with water in an old-fashioned glass. Add rye and ice cubes. Fill glass with **carbonated water**.

BRANDY TODDY

> 2 oz. brandy
> ½ oz. apricot liqueur

Shake well with **ice** and strain into an old-fashioned glass. Add **carbonated water**.

BUTTERED RUM TODDY

> 2 oz. New England rum
> 2 oz. boiling water
> ¼ oz. butter

Stir well in an old-fashioned glass or mug and sprinkle **grated nutmeg** on top.

SCOTCH TODDY

> ½ teaspoon confectioners' sugar
> 1 jigger Scotch
> 3 ice cubes
> Twist of lemon peel

Stir well and strain into an old-fashioned glass.

SPICED RUM TODDY

> 1 jigger Jamaica rum
> 2 teaspoons confectioners' sugar
> 2 teaspoons butter
> ½ teaspoon allspice

Combine in an old-fashioned glass or mug. Fill with **boiling water.**

TOM AND JERRY TODDY

- **2 teaspoons confectioners' sugar**
- **1 egg, well beaten**
- **2 oz. Jamaica rum**

Combine in an old-fashioned glass. Fill glass with **boiling water.** Grate **nutmeg** on top.

WHISKEY TODDY

- **1 teaspoon confectioners' sugar**
- **2 jiggers rye**

Combine in an old-fashioned glass. Fill glass with **boiling water.** Top with a **twist of lemon.**

SOURS

GIN SOUR

- **Juice of ⅓ lemon**
- **¼ teaspoon confectioners' sugar**
- **1 jigger dry gin**
- **2 oz. carbonated water**

Shake lemon, sugar and gin well with **ice.** Strain into a sour glass. Add carbonated water and a **thin slice of orange,** a **maraschino cherry** and/or a **pineapple stick.**

RUM SOUR

- **1 teaspoon Sugar Syrup (page 621)**
- **2 oz. Jamaica rum**
- **Juice of ½ lemon**
- **2 oz. carbonated water**

Shake syrup, rum and lemon juice well with **ice.** Strain into a sour glass and add carbonated water. Decorate as for Gin Sour.

SCOTCH SOUR

- **Juice of ½ lemon**
- **½ teaspoon confectioners' sugar**
- **1 jigger Scotch**
- **2 oz. carbonated water**

Shake lemon juice, sugar and Scotch well with **ice.** Strain into a sour glass and add carbonated water. Decorate as for Gin Sour.

WHISKEY SOUR

- **1 teaspoon confectioners' sugar**
- **Juice of ½ lemon**
- **1 jigger rye**
- **2 oz. carbonated water**

Shake sugar, lemon juice and rye well with **ice** and strain into a sour glass. Add carbonated water and decorate as for Gin Sour.

SWIZZLES

An import from the West Indies where the five forked swizzle stick is rapidly twirled to mix the drink, hence the name "swizzle."

NEW ENGLAND SWIZZLE

- **1 jigger New England rum**
- **Juice of ¼ lime**
- **¾ teaspoon Triple Sec**
- **1 pony applejack**

Shake well with **ice** and pour into a tall glass. Fill glass with **carbonated water.** Garnish with **fresh fruit.**

RUM SWIZZLE

- **4 teaspoons sugar**
- **6 sprigs fresh mint**
- **Juice of 6 lemons**
- **1 pt. Jamaica rum**

Mix in a deep jug with **10 ice cubes.** Use swizzle stick until it froths over.   *16 servings*

WEST INDIAN SWIZZLE

- **1 lump sugar**
- **2 oz. carbonated water**
- **2 ice cubes**
- **Dash Angostura bitters**
- **2 oz. West Indian rum**

Swizzle with a stick to froth. Serve in a cocktail glass.

AFTER DINNER DRINKS

POUSSE CAFES

An exciting combination of liqueurs, one floated atop another to create a beautiful effect. Pour each ingredient slowly over a teaspoon, convex side up, so as to float on the previously poured liqueur.

FRENCH POUSSE CAFE

- **½ teaspoon raspberry liqueur (framboise)**
- **½ teaspoon maraschino**
- **½ teaspoon crème de vanille**
- **½ teaspoon curaçao**
- **½ teaspoon yellow chartreuse**
- **½ teaspoon brandy**

Pour into a pousse café glass in the order listed.

L'AMOUR POUSSE CAFE

- **1 teaspoon maraschino**
- **1 teaspoon crème de vanille**
- **1 teaspoon brandy**
- **1 egg yolk**

Pour into a pousse café glass in the order listed.

NEW ORLEANS POUSSE CAFE

- **1 teaspoon brandy**
- **1 teaspoon maraschino**
- **1 teaspoon curaçao**
- **1 teaspoon Jamaica rum**

Pour into a pousse café glass in the order listed.

RAINBOW POUSSE CAFE

- **1 teaspoon crème de cacao**
- **1 teaspoon Crème Yvette**
- **1 teaspoon yellow chartreuse**
- **1 teaspoon maraschino**
- **1 teaspoon Benedictine**
- **1 teaspoon green chartreuse**
- **1 teaspoon brandy**

Pour into a pousse café glass in the order listed.

BRULOTS

CAFE DIABLE

▲ *Base Recipe*

For each cup of hot **black coffee** you will need

- **1 cup brandy**
- **1 slice orange**
- **1 strip lemon peel**
- **2 lumps sugar**
- **2 whole cloves**

Heat all ingredients except coffee in a silver bowl. Lift out a ladleful of the brandy mixture and light. Then lower the ladle into the bowl, lifting it out and pouring it back into bowl to keep it aflame while you continue to pour in the coffee. When the flame dies, pour the mixture into demitasse cups and serve.

—CAFE BRULOT

Follow ▲ Recipe, adding **1 cinnamon stick** per cup. Break the cinnamon into half inch lengths and put into the mixture before heating.

ICED COFFEE AND RUM

    10 oz. iced coffee
    1 oz. New England rum
    ½ oz. cream
    1 teaspoon sugar

Stir well with **ice** and strain into a highball glass.

MORNING-AFTER DRINKS

BLOODY MARY

    3 jiggers tomato juice
    1½ jiggers vodka (100 proof)
    ½ pony lemon juice
    ½ teaspoon Worcestershire sauce
    Pinch salt
    Dash Angostura bitters
    2 ice cubes

Blend 10 seconds; strain into a highball glass. There are many variations of this. Naturally, we think ours the best, but start with tomato juice and vodka, or gin, if you prefer, and concoct your own.

BULL SHOT

    4 oz. chilled beef bouillon
    1 jigger vodka
    ½ lime
    Dash Tabasco
    2 or 3 ice cubes

Pour bouillon and vodka into a shaker. Squeeze juice from lime half into shaker; drop in lime half. Add Tabasco and ice cubes. Shake well and strain into an old-fashioned glass. Garnish with a **cucumber slice.**

COCKTAIL PICK-ME-UP

    1 jigger brandy
    1 pony curaçao
    3 dashes Fernet Branca
    Chilled champagne
    ½ thin slice lemon

Pour brandy, curaçao and Fernet Branca into an 8-oz. highball glass over **1 ice cube.** Stir and fill with champagne. Stir again. Serve with lemon on top.

CORPSE REVIVER

    1 pony Italian vermouth
    1 pony applejack
    1 jigger brandy

Shake well with **ice** and strain into a cocktail glass.

EYE OPENER

    Juice of ½ lime
    1 teaspoon sugar
    1 egg white
    1 jigger rye

Shake well and pour into an old-fashioned glass over **ice.** Fill with **carbonated water.**

FUJIYAMA

    2½ jiggers tomato juice
    1½ jiggers vodka (100 proof)
    ½ pony Escoffier Diable Sauce
    Pinch salt
    1 egg
    2 ice cubes

Blend 15 seconds; strain into a highball glass and watch the horizon clear.

HARVEY WALLBANGER

    Orange juice
    1 oz. vodka
    ½ oz. Galliano

Fill a tall glass with **ice cubes.** Pour in orange juice to fill glass ¾ full. Add vodka and stir. Pour Galliano over top.

PICK ME UP

Hangovers should be suffered in solitary silence.

    1 jigger cognac (or other good brandy)
    1 pony Jamaica rum
    1 egg
    1 teaspoon orgeat or Sugar Syrup
      (page 621)
    Dash Angostura bitters
    Pinch salt
    6 oz. milk
    4 ice cubes

Blend 20 seconds; strain into a tall highball glass. Sprinkle with **nutmeg,** sit down, drink.

PRAIRIE OYSTER COCKTAIL

A nonalcoholic "cure" for a hangover.

    ⅓ teaspoon vinegar
    1 teaspoon ketchup
    1 teaspoon Worcestershire sauce
    Salt
    Pepper
    1 unbroken egg yolk

Stir together in an old-fashioned glass.

SCREWDRIVER

    2 oz. vodka
    2 or 3 ice cubes
    Orange juice

Pour vodka over ice in a 6-oz. old-fashioned glass. Fill with orange juice and stir.

WINE DRINKS

ALFONSO COCKTAIL

    1 lump sugar
    Dash Angostura bitters
    1 jigger Dubonnet
    Chilled champagne

Place **1 ice cube** and the lump of sugar in a champagne glass; dash over the bitters. Add Dubonnet and fill with champagne. Serve with a **twist of lemon.**

CHAMPAGNE COCKTAIL III

    1 lump sugar
    Dash Angostura bitters
    1 thin half slice orange
    1 thin half slice lemon
    Chilled champagne

Place sugar lump in champagne glass and dash over the bitters. Add orange and lemon slices. Fill with champagne.

CHAMPAGNE FIZZ

    Juice of 1 orange
    Chilled champagne

Fill an 8-oz. highball glass two-thirds full with **ice cubes.** Add orange juice. Fill with champagne.

CHAMPAGNE PUNCH VI

    1 pt. lemon ice cream
    1 pt. orange ice cream
    2 qts. chilled champagne

Put ice creams into a punch bowl. Pour over the champagne. Serve in punch glasses.

12 servings

Mulled Wine

CLARET COOLER

4 oz. claret
1 teaspoon sugar
2 thin slices orange
1 thin slice pineapple

Put wine and sugar into a collins glass. Stir well. Fill with **ice cubes** and **carbonated water**. Decorate with the orange and pineapple slices.

CUPID COCKTAIL

2 jiggers sherry
1 egg
1 teaspoon sugar
Pinch cayenne pepper

Shake well with **ice** and strain into a cocktail glass.

DUBONNET DRY

Sometimes called a Mary Garden.

½ Dubonnet
½ dry vermouth
Twist of lemon peel

Stir the wines carefully with **ice cubes**. Strain into a cocktail glass. Top with the lemon twist.

DUBONNET HIGHBALL

2½ oz. Dubonnet
Carbonated water
Twist of lemon peel

Pour Dubonnet into a highball glass with 1, 2 or 3 **ice cubes**. Fill glass with desired amount of carbonated water. Top with the lemon twist.

DUBONNET ON-THE-ROCKS

1½ jiggers Dubonnet
Carbonated water
Twist of lemon peel

Fill an old-fashioned glass with **cracked ice**. Pour over the Dubonnet. Fill with carbonated water. Top with the lemon twist.

DUBONNET ORANGE

1 jigger Dubonnet
Juice of ½ orange

Shake carefully with **cracked ice**. Serve in a cocktail glass.

LONDON SPECIAL

1 lump sugar
Piece of orange peel
2 dashes Peychaud bitters
Chilled champagne

Put **1 ice cube** into a champagne glass with sugar lump, orange peel and bitters. Mix carefully and fill with champagne.

MIMOSA

Juice of ½ orange
Chilled champagne

Put **1 ice cube** into a champagne glass. Add orange juice. Fill with champagne and stir gently.

MULLED WINE

4 cups water
1 cup sugar
Peel from ½ lemon (use yellow layer only)
18 whole cloves
2 cinnamon sticks (3 in. each)
2 bottles (⅘ qt. each) California Burgundy

Combine water and sugar in large saucepan. Add lemon peel, cloves and cinnamon. Boil 15 min. and pour through strainer; discard peel and spices. Add the wine and heat gently (do not boil). Meanwhile, preheat a punch bowl or serving decanter by filling it with warm, then hot, water. When ready to serve, empty punch bowl and dry it. Pour in the mulled wine and serve at once. *20 servings*

To prepare individual servings—Prepare recipe without the wine; store the spicy syrup in refrigerator in a tightly covered container. Preheat mug or glass by rinsing with very hot water. For each drink, use 2 oz. spiced syrup and 5 oz. wine. Heat just to simmering, and pour into preheated mug.

To serve Mulled Wine flaming—Dip **sugar cubes** in **high-proof brandy** and set them afloat on a **slice of orange**. Warm a small

amount of additional brandy and ignite it. Spoon it on the brandy-soaked cubes and they will ignite.

MUSCATEL HIGHBALL

4 oz. muscatel
Juice of ½ lemon
3 ice cubes

Put into a highball glass. Fill glass with **carbonated water**.

ORANGE COOLER

2 jiggers white port
2 jiggers orange juice
2 teaspoons lemon juice
2 teaspoons sugar

Arrange **ice cubes** and a spiral of **orange peel** in a collins glass. Stir wine, juices and sugar well; pour into glass.

ORANGE SHERRY FLIP

▲ *Base Recipe*

1 cup sherry, chilled
1½ cups orange juice, chilled
2 eggs
¼ teaspoon salt

Combine ingredients in an electric blender container and blend until frothy and well mixed. Serve in chilled glasses with **fresh mint sprig** garnish. If very cold drinks are desired, add ½ **cup cracked ice** or **6 ice cubes** just before serving and strain into the glasses. *4 servings*

—CREAM SHERRY FLIP

Follow ▲ Recipe. Blend in ½ **cup cream**.

PEACH BOWL

Put ½ **washed peeled peach** into a champagne glass. Cover it with **chilled champagne**. Puncture the peach several times to blend the flavors and serve. The peach is delicious to eat when the glass is empty.

Orange Sherry Flip

PORT SANGAREE

1 teaspoon confectioners' sugar
4 jiggers port

Shake well with **ice** and strain into an 8-oz. glass. Grate **nutmeg** on top.

RED WINE COBBLER

1 teaspoon finely granulated sugar
Dash maraschino
1 teaspoon lemon juice
Claret

Fill an 8-oz. highball glass half full with **finely cracked ice.** Add sugar, maraschino and lemon juice. Fill with claret wine and stir until glass is frosted. Decorate with **fresh fruit.**

RHINE WINE AND SELTZER

3 ice cubes
½ Rhine wine
½ carbonated water

Put into an 8-oz. highball glass. Stir well and serve.

RHINE WINE COBBLER

1 teaspoon fine granulated sugar
1 teaspoon lemon juice
Rhine wine

Fill a tall 8-oz. highball glass half full with **cracked ice.** Add sugar and lemon juice and stir. Fill with Rhine wine and stir until glass is frosted. Decorate with a **small piece of lemon peel** and **fresh mint.**

RHINE WINE COOLER

Blend chilled **Rhine wine** with an equal part of **lemon-flavored carbonated beverage.** Pour over **crushed ice** in an old-fashioned glass. Garnish with **mint sprigs.**

SAUTERNE COBBLER

1 teaspoon lemon juice
Sauterne
Lemon peel

Fill an 8-oz. highball glass half full with **cracked ice.** Add lemon juice. Stir and fill with sauterne. Garnish with a small piece of lemon peel.

SAUTERNE COOLER

1 teaspoon sugar
4 oz. sauterne
1 orange slice
1 pineapple slice

Arrange **ice cubes** and a spiral strip of **orange or lemon peel** in a collins glass. Mix sugar and

sauterne; pour into glass. Fill with **carbonated water.** Decorate with orange and pineapple slices.

SHERRY COBBLER

1 teaspoon sugar
1 teaspoon orange juice
Sherry

Fill an 8-oz. highball glass half full with **cracked ice.** Add sugar and orange juice. Fill with sherry and stir. Decorate with **fresh fruit.**

SHERRY EGGNOG HIGHBALL

1 egg
2 teaspoons sugar
1 jigger sherry
6 oz. milk

Shake well with **ice** and strain into an 8-oz. highball glass. Grate **nutmeg** on top.

SHERRY EGGNOG PUNCH

1 tablespoon sugar
1 egg
4 oz. sherry
4 oz. milk

Shake well with **ice** and strain into a 10-oz. highball glass. Grate **nutmeg** on top.

SHERRY FLIP

2 oz. sherry
1 egg
1 teaspoon confectioners' sugar

Shake well with **ice** and strain into a 3- or 4-oz. flip or sour glass. This drink may also be made with **1 oz. cream** added.

SHERRY SANGAREE

3 jiggers sherry
½ teaspoon confectioners' sugar

Shake well with **ice** and strain into an 8-oz. highball glass. Grate **nutmeg** on top.

STRAWBERRY WINE PUNCH

1 pt. strawberries
2 cups California rosé
½ cup sugar
1 can (6 oz.) frozen pineapple juice concentrate, thawed
½ teaspoon salt
½ teaspoon almond extract
Grated peel and juice of 1 lemon
1 large bottle chilled California champagne

Wash and hull berries; crush coarsely. Combine with rosé, sugar, pineapple juice concentrate, salt, extract, grated lemon peel and juice

Strawberry Wine Punch

along with empty lemon shell. Cover and refrigerate overnight. Strain liquid, discarding pulp. Pour over **ice** in punch bowl and add champagne just before serving.   *2 qts. punch*

SYLLABUB

All American syllabubs descend from an ancient English recipe brought to Virginia in the early days.

2 cups cream
2 cups milk
½ cup sherry
¼ to ½ cup sugar
Few grains salt

Beat together with a rotary beater until sugar is dissolved and mixture frothy. Serve immediately in punch glasses. Top each serving with a generous sprinkling of **nutmeg.**

About 8 servings

TROCADERO COCKTAIL

Dash orange bitters
½ teaspoon grenadine
½ French vermouth
½ Italian vermouth

Stir well with **ice** and strain into a cocktail glass. Garnish with a **maraschino cherry** and a **twist of lemon peel.**

UPSTAIRS

2 jiggers Dubonnet
Juice of ¼ lemon

Pour into an 8-oz. old-fashioned glass filled with **ice cubes.** Fill with **carbonated water.**

Entertaining

The secret of successful entertaining is to enjoy your own parties. Entertaining should be as much fun for the hostess as it is for the guests—and if you plan carefully, adapting your plans to the special conditions of your home, everything is bound to run along smoothly and result in a wonderful time for everybody—including you.

Some people seem to be born with a knack for entertaining. Good food appears at their parties as if by magic, the guests are relaxed and conversation flourishes. You may be sure, however, that none of this just "happens." The food appears because someone has prepared it; the guests are relaxed because their hostess feels no strain; conversation flows because the hostess is on hand to help it along and not coping with a crisis in the kitchen.

And all of this means that the hostess has planned carefully. She has planned a menu that requires a minimum of attention after the guests arrive, planned and arranged all the details of service, readied the china, linen, glassware and silverware, arranged the flowers and other accessories, set out all the little appurtenances of comfort—coasters, ashtrays, matches, cigarettes. She has probably planned her guest list, too, inviting only persons who will be congenial. And if she is the completely thoughtful hostess, her menu has been planned with due regard for the food likes and dislikes of her guests.

In planning a company menu it is wise to follow the same principles that guide all menu-making. Avoid repetition of foods in the same meal—if fish is an appetizer do not use it for the main dish. Maintain a balance between firm and soft foods. Do not serve too many starches (rice, potatoes and bread at the same meal are not good planning) or too much of any other single food stuff. Avoid a crowd of strong flavors—flavors should harmonize or contrast but not compete. Plan meals with an eye to the overall arrangement, varying foods in color, texture and flavor. Include something sweet and something tart, something hot and something cold in every meal. Delight guests with an occasional surprise, but try out the new recipe on the family first.

LUNCHEONS

All parties are fun, but luncheons are in a class by themselves. They are usually given by women and for women, and so the light and even "fancy" touches which are special fun for the hostess are quite appropriate.

Whether you invite one guest or a dozen, you will summon all the artistry at your command to make the setting of your party beautiful and appropriate. Almost any kind of cloth, table mats or runner is suitable if it harmonizes with the dishes and other accessories, the flowers, and to some extent with the season.

Table decorations, as at any meal, should be kept low, pretty but unobtrusive. Flowers are always appropriate, and so are attractive arrangements of fruits, foliage, handsome vegetables, vines, shells, quaint or beautiful figurines and low-growing plants. Since luncheons are midday affairs, candles are not suitable.

Flatware and crystal are placed as for a dinner party (page 658).

Luncheon for a group may be introduced by cocktails and appetizers in the living room. Choose appetizers from the Appetizer chapter. The luncheon menu itself may include two to four courses, the wise hostess planning it according to what she can handle easily and gracefully. The main dish is often a creamed mixture served in croustades, patty shells, or over split baking powder biscuits. It may be accompanied by salad or not. Particularly if salad is omitted, a nice touch is to garnish the plates with spiced fruit such as spiced crab apples or peaches, watermelon pickles or the like, or with crisp bread-and-butter pickles or preserved kumquats. The dessert should be keyed to the rest of the meal. If the main dish is a rich creamed mixture, serve a light dessert —fruit or a fruit mold or sherbet; if a salad bowl is the main course, a rich and elaborate dessert is in order.

Luncheon Menu I

*Creamed Crab Meat and Mushrooms
in Croustades
Fresh Fruit Salad
with
Tarragon or Orange Fruit Salad Dressing
Sweet Sherry Elegance
Coconut Butter Cookies
Beverage*

Luncheon Menu II

*Turkey à la King over Buttermilk Biscuits
Baked Acorn Squash
Party-Perfect Salad Molds
Angel Food Cake
Beverage*

Luncheon Menu III

*Crimson Soup and Saltines
Trio Salad Plate
Pineapple Sponge Cake
Beverage*

Luncheon Menu IV

*Cranberry Ham Rolls
Shades o' Green Salad
Tiny Tender-Rich Buttermilk Biscuits
Caramel Ice Cream
Meltaway Chocolate Cookies
Beverage*

Sweet Cherry Elegance (page 545)

Cranberry Ham Rolls (page 200)

TEAS

A pleasant and flexible way of entertaining friends or acquaintances is the afternoon tea. There is not very much difference between a formal and an informal tea, except the difference in serving a larger or smaller number of guests. The usual hour for tea is between four and five, but it may be extended if many of the guests are career women, and may start earlier if a large number is expected.

The Informal Tea

Invitations to informal teas are usually extended in person, by telephone or by an informal note, with the time stated. The number invited may vary from five or six to a large number, depending upon the occasion. If a hostess has asked a few friends to drop in for tea, she may serve it in the living room. The tea service should be arranged on an uncovered tray and placed on a low table, spread with a cloth which may barely cover the table or may hang as much as eighteen inches over the sides.

If the hostess has a silver tea service with an alcohol lamp, the tray will contain a kettle of water kept boiling over the flame (which should be lighted only after the tray is safely placed on the table), an empty teapot, creamer and sugar bowl and a plate of lemon slices with a lemon fork, a tea caddy and an empty bowl for tea leaves and for dregs poured from the guests' cups before refilling. In this case the hostess makes the tea in the presence of the guests and serves it with or without additional hot water, according to preference, and with or without cream, sugar or lemon. If the hostess prefers, or if she does not have a tea service with a means of keeping water boiling, the tea may be brewed and strained in the kitchen into a heated teapot, and boiling water poured into a second heated pot to dilute the strong tea as guests request. In this case water should be kept boiling on the range so the supply may be frequently replenished and always hot.

Cups and saucers with teaspoons laid on the saucers to the right of the cups may be placed on the tea tray if it will hold them all, or some may be on the table beside it. Tea plates (7 to 8 inches in diameter) in a stack, and 12-inch tea napkins, are also on the table near the tray. If possible little tables or some other convenient surface should be provided near the chair of each guest to hold plate, cup and saucer. Many hostesses omit saucers entirely, in which case teacup and food are both placed on the tea plate.

The food provided may consist only of strips of cinnamon toast, finger sandwiches spread with whipped butter, cucumber or watercress sandwiches, or tiny hot biscuits with jam. Small crisp cookies or thinly sliced fruitcake, mints and salted nuts may be served too. Only at small intimate teas will hot crumpets or buttered, toasted English muffins be offered in the fashion of a hearty English tea. The serving of these, or of jam, requires spreaders. At formal teas or for a larger group, serve only finger foods.

For a large group, or even in a small group if the hostess knows that some guests prefer it, coffee may be offered as well as tea; and in warm weather there may be some who will like the strong, hot tea or coffee poured over cracked ice in tall glasses. On very hot days a bowl of fruit punch with plenty of ice may replace the tea service altogether.

If the group, even at an informal tea, is quite large, the hostess may ask one close friend to pour the tea for her, another to pour the coffee, and perhaps a third to assist by keeping the serving plates replenished with food, so that she herself may be free to greet her guests. Constant replenishing of the serving plates is necessary to keep the arrangement of the tea table attractive.

The Formal Tea

These large teas are seldom given except for a special occasion—perhaps to introduce a visiting celebrity, or for a club meeting or other official event. Invitations (on a correspondence card or on the hostess's visiting card, with "To meet_____." across the top and the date and hour in a lower corner) are issued about two weeks before the event.

A long table is used for a formal tea, with flowers and tall, white, formal candles (which, if present, should be lighted and should not be present unless needed) in an arrangement which may be higher than for a dinner or luncheon table, since the guests will be standing. The cloth, of formal damask or lace, usually hangs over the table edge from one-quarter to one-half yard. The tea tray, arranged just as for an informal tea, will be at one end of the table. At the other end will be a coffee or chocolate service, or on a warm day, a bowl of iced fruit punch. Only finger foods should be served. Cucumber and watercress sandwiches are traditional at a formal tea. Little cakes such as petits fours, thinly sliced fruitcake, mints and salted nuts also find a place on the formal tea table.

Teacups and saucers with teaspoons laid on the saucer at the right of the cup are usually arranged near each beverage service; additional plates provided for sandwiches and cakes may be stacked (not more than six or eight high) on the table with tea napkins. The foods and the supply of cups, saucers, plates and napkins should be replenished as they are used.

Two intimate friends of the hostess, preferably ladies who are acquainted with most of the guests, should be asked to pour the beverages. They may be replaced by two others at the end of an hour, if the tea is large. Their assistance, and that of a third person to replenish the serving plates and remove the guests' cups and plates as they are emptied, will permit the hostess, together with the guest of honor, to receive her guests.

DESSERT PARTIES

Most exclusively feminine of all forms of entertaining is probably the dessert party. There are a dozen excuses for it, all feminine: a club meeting in the home, an afternoon of bridge, a shower for a bride- or baby-to-be, the introduction of a newcomer in the neighborhood to your friends. It's a gay sort of affair, usually given in the afternoon when the menfolk are away, but occasionally late of an evening when they may possibly be persuaded to participate. And it calls for your most special magic to produce a really superb *pièce de résistance*.

The dessert's the thing—for a dessert party is not and should not be a meal, but merely a gesture of dainty, delectable hospitality. The whole menu served at the dessert party need consist of no more than the dessert itself—eye-appealing, taste-tempting and irresistibly delicious—with, of course, a beverage of distinction. Include nuts and mints if you wish.

Service for the dessert party should be of the simplest. You may have your card table or tables spread with dainty cloths and set with silver and napkins when your guests arrive; this permits your guests to finish eating and you to clear the tables before the business or pleasure of the meeting gets under way. Or finish the business first, and then set the tables, so guests may relax over your dessert masterpiece. The dessert itself may either be served and prettily garnished in the kitchen; or if the dessert is particularly beautiful, by all means display the attractively garnished platter before you serve it with a flourish.

DINNERS

"Company" dinners are classified according to their formality. The majority of dinners the average hostess will give are informal, and the rest are semiformal. The formal dinner is characterized by written or engraved invitations in the polite third person which must be answered in the same way, by full evening dress for both men and women, and by a menu written in French. Preparation and serving of its seven courses (appetizer, soup, fish, meat with vegetables, salad, dessert and fruit, followed by coffee and liqueurs in the drawing room) demand skilled help provided by a trained service staff. The type of service is known as Russian or Continental, and the host and hostess take no part in it.

The Semiformal Dinner

This is the most formal meal most homemakers are likely to give. Invitations may be partially engraved, with names, dates, hours filled in by hand; or they may be extended in an informal letter or by telephone. The time is usually eight or eight-thirty. Men are usually expected to wear dinner jackets, black or, in warm weather, white, rather than business suits; and women usually wear informal evening dress or dinner dresses. The considerate hostess will include a hint of the degree of formality in her invitation.

The dinner itself consists of only four or five courses—soup, fish (usually in the form of a cocktail), meat and vegetables, salad and dessert, and of these either the fish course or the salad is often omitted. After-dinner coffee is usually served in the living room.

Service of a semiformal dinner is what is sometimes known as "compromise" service (a combination of English or family-style and Russian style) and sometimes as American. It is suited to the home with one maid or with a part-time waitress, and means that while the first course, salad and dessert are served by the maid, the host or the host and hostess participate in serving the main course. The host generally carves the meat and places it on plates, which may be passed by the maid or handed down the table by the guests. The hostess sometimes serves the potatoes and vegetables; or the serving dishes may be offered to the guests by the maid. When there is no man of the house, the carving may be done by a close friend; or the hostess may do all the serving.

The Informal Dinner

Invitations to the most frequent and most intimate form of dinner may be issued personally, by telephone or by informal letter. The guests will seldom number more than ten, especially if there is no maid. The guests' dress is dictated by custom; it is perfectly proper for the men to come in business suits and the women to dress accordingly. If the meal is a real "party" on a non-business day, dinner jackets and dinner dresses are quite in order.

The menu may consist of only two or three courses—either soup or fish, meat and vegetables, and dessert; or casserole, salad, and dessert. After-dinner coffee in the living room is still a pleasant custom, but coffee may be served at the table. The "family-style" service may be assisted by a maid, or by a member of the family or a guest, but the hostess will probably do most of the serving. And the hour may be any time from six to eight-thirty.

Table Setting

The hostess's common sense as well as her knowledge of tradition will be called upon in setting the table for dinner. Everything should be correctly planned in an orderly manner.

The first step is to lay the cloth. For a really formal dinner a pure white or pale cream-colored cloth of linen damask is traditional, though a handsome lace cloth may be used. At least 9 inches of overhang should be allowed at each end. For less formal dinners, pastel damask, lace, linen edged with lace, or place mats may be used. A silence cloth or felt is always used under damask or linen.

Next, the dinner plates are placed. These should be spaced equidistant from each other, and one inch from the edge of the table. To allow the guests elbow room, a minimum of twenty inches must be allowed for each place; twenty-five or thirty inches is better.

The flat silver is arranged next. Only pieces actually needed for the food to be served should be put on the table, and these should be arranged in the order in which they will be used, starting from the outside. Forks, except cocktail forks, are placed to the left of the plate, knives, spoons and cocktail forks to the right. All should be parallel to each other and at right angles to the edge of the table, with the handles an inch from the edge. Butter knives are placed on the butter plates, either parallel or at right angles to the table edge. Dessert forks or spoons are usually brought in with the dessert, though at an informal dinner they may be placed on the table.

The water glass is set at the tip of the dinner knife. Other glasses (for wines) are placed to the right and slightly in front of the water glass. The butter plate occupies the position at the tip of the dinner fork. Folded napkins are placed on the dinner plate if it is empty when the guests come to the table, or at the left of the forks; the folding should display the monogram, if there is one, and the open edges should be parallel with the fork and edge of the table and next to the fork. Individual ashtrays with matches and a few cigarettes should be supplied at each place. Iced water should be poured at the last moment; there should be no ice in the glasses.

Any centerpiece should be low enough to permit conversation across the table. Candles should be tall enough to burn above eye level.

Seating of Guests

When dinner is announced, at a semiformal dinner, the hostess leads the way in to the dining room, followed by the ladies and then by the gentlemen, with the host. Only at very formal dinners does the host enter first with the lady guest of honor on his arm; then the hostess goes in last with the gentleman guest of honor. The host is always seated at one end of the table with the lady of honor at his right, and the hostess at the opposite end with the gentleman of honor at her right. If there is no difference in age, rank or distinction among the guests, the lady at the host's right and the gentleman at the hostess's right have the positions of honor. Ladies and gentlemen alternate along the sides of the table, with husbands and wives usually not seated side by side.

A thoughtful hostess will make her seating plan with her guests' interests and tastes in mind, and try to place together those who will find one another interesting and congenial. In a large party, place cards will be helpful, but at a smaller dinner, she may indicate to each guest where he or she is to sit.

Serving Procedure

Whatever the degree of formality, the lady seated at the host's right is always the first to be served. The hostess is never served first, unless she is the only lady present. Nor should the hostess ever be the first to help herself from an untouched serving dish. The classic sequence of serving goes clockwise around the table, starting with the lady guest of honor, but other sequences are also possible and correct; i.e., one course clockwise, the next counterclockwise, so that a different gentleman is last to be served in each case. When several have been served, guests may begin eating without waiting for the hostess, but the considerate hostess will lay her fork on her plate as a signal if she sees that the guests are waiting for her to begin. She should always be the last to finish.

All plates are placed and removed and all serving dishes offered to guests from the left. Ideally, the dishes offered should be held in the waitress's left hand, but in the interest of saving time, she may bring in two dishes at once, or present two dishes on a tray. Water and wine should both be poured from the right, by the waitress's right hand.

Dishes are always removed singly, never "stacked" on the table. When the main course is finished, serving dishes are removed first; then each place is cleared; then the maid takes away the pepper and salt shakers and the breadbasket on a tray, and crumbs the table, using a folded napkin and a clean plate. Dessert plates and silver are then put on the table.

Serving after-dinner coffee in the living room is a practical as well as a pleasant custom. It. may be done in three ways, according to the size and character of the group, the formality of the occasion and the service available. One way is to pour the coffee in the kitchen and have it brought into the living room on a tray by the maid. Another way is to carry in to the living room a tray containing the silver coffeepot, creamer and sugar bowl, and the cups; the hostess then pours and hands the cups to guests who are nearby, or to the host or other member of the family, who will hand them to more distant guests. The hostess may ask each guest for his cream and sugar preference, or they may help themselves. And the third way, perfectly acceptable at informal gatherings, is for the hostess to make the coffee freshly in the presence of the guests, using an electric coffee maker on a coffee tray.

Some Factors in a Successful Dinner

Formal or informal, any dinner party will be more successful if it has been planned in detail. Whether the hostess expects to have a regular or part-time maid for part of the service or to handle it all herself, writing down the work schedule will help prevent last-minute confusion. A maid brought in for the occasion will work more smoothly if time can be given to rehearsal beforehand.

Since the food is still the most important part of the dinner party, its quality should be safeguarded. Hot foods must be piping hot when they are brought from the kitchen, and cold foods should be served very cold. Serving platters and dishes for hot meats and vegetables should be warmed and plates for salads and for refrigerator or frozen desserts, chilled.

More important than the observance of every rule of etiquette is that the dinner party should be enjoyed by everyone, guests and hostess alike. This happy result is most easily attained if the hostess has invited no more guests than she can comfortably seat and serve, and if her planning has been such that everything goes smoothly without visible effort. A dinner is a challenge for any hostess, and it can be fun too.

THE COCKTAIL HOUR

The hour before dinner is, in many homes, the cocktail hour—a pleasant interlude during which guests may relax from the cares of the day and become better acquainted before they dine.

The appetizers that are served with the cocktails should be both delicious and attractive. One or two kinds are enough—perhaps a piquant dip served with crisp crackers or potato chips, and a tiny hot appetizer such as cheese balls. Hot appetizers are better served with before-dinner cocktails than at a cocktail party, because the hostess can be reasonably sure they will be eaten before they cool.

As always, when cocktails are served, a non-alcoholic beverage should be provided for guests who prefer it. It may be a well-seasoned tomato juice, a fruit juice or tart fruit punch.

Dinner Menu I

Broiled Fish Californian with Raisin Sauce
French-Fried Potatoes
Buttered Carrots
Spinach Salad
Hot Rolls
Almond-Stuffed Green Olives
Nutmeg Cake
Coffee

From the sea around us comes this dramatic main course, flavored to perfection, with the drama of the unusual. Everything else—including the hot rolls, which may be Crescent Rolls (page 77) or your own favorite recipe—blends artfully into the harmony of the complete dinner.

Dinner Menu II

Oriental Barbecued Spareribs
Perfection Boiled Rice
Relish Tray or Tossed Green Salad
Hard Rolls
Orange Baked Bananas
Almond Cookies
Tea

Perfect with this exotic meal, which contains a fruit but no vegetable, is a tossed salad of greens, tomatoes and cucumbers with French dressing, or a well-stocked relish tray. Among the relishes on the tray may be crisp carrot sticks, celery stalks or curls, marinated cucumber slices, as well as green and ripe olives,

Molded Pear Ginger Salad (page 377)

pickled peaches, preserved kumquats, artichoke hearts, and cottage cheese mixed with chopped chives. All of these provide pleasing contrast in texture, flavor and temperature with the hot foods and the hard rolls. In harmony with the slightly Oriental character of the menu, tea is the ideal beverage, served from little handle-less teacups if you have them.

Dinner Menu III

Beef Tenderloin with Mushroom Gravy
Heavenly Potato Soufflé
Asparagus Piémontais
Green Salad
Hot Rolls
Nesselrode Pudding
Coffee

The salad of mixed greens needs only your favorite salad dressing to take its place in this sumptuous panorama of fine food, lavishly served.

Dinner Menu IV

Steak à la Diane
Deep-Fried Zucchini or
Best-Ever Brussels Sprouts
Broiled Tomatoes
Molded Pear Ginger Salad
Hot Rolls
Sherry Almond Chiffon Pie
Coffee

For the intimate, informal dinner that everyone finds delightful, here is steak with an outstanding flavor that will please your most fastidious gourmet. And, if you are looking for a main dish that can be cooked at the table, this one will add the touch of drama you desire.

BUFFETS

Buffet service fits perfectly into the relaxed, informal pattern of contemporary living. If you have limited dining space, or if you are a do-it-yourself hostess, buffet service permits you to entertain with more ease than any other type of service, and just as graciously and pleasantly.

Your buffet table may be set against a wall, or in the center of the room. For only six or

eight guests, it is often placed with the long side against a wall; a larger number may need both long sides for sufficient elbow room when serving themselves. Because it presents all the food to the guests at one time and is thus the center of interest, the table should be arranged with care and artistry—and with common sense too, for the buffet table is functional, and its arrangement is as important as its beauty.

The table itself should be dressed as attractively as possible, in lace, linen or pretty place mats. And this is the time for bringing out your beautiful serving trays and plates. Flowers have an important role to play on the buffet table. If the table is against the wall, the flower arrangement may be a background for the foods; if in the center of the room, it will probably be a centerpiece. Since guests will all be standing, there is no need to keep it low. If candles are used for lighting the table, be sure to use plenty of them, placed so they really illuminate.

For the convenience of your guests, plan the arrangement of the table carefully. Confusing traffic plans should be avoided in order to help the serving line progress with ease and speed. Place a stack of large dinner plates at the point where guests are to start—probably at one end of the table. Napkins and silverware should be where they will be picked up last, after the plates are filled. Unless the guests are to eat at small tables, it is customary to serve only foods that can be eaten with a fork, since use of a knife is difficult. Rolls are usually buttered before they are put on the buffet. If you serve a tossed salad, tongs are far more easily handled than the conventional salad fork and spoon, when one hand is occupied by a plate. Since seasoning is so largely a matter of individual preference, individual salt and pepper shakers should be provided on snack tables or other convenient sur-

faces near the guests' chairs rather than on the buffet. A side table may hold a tray with goblets or glasses and a pitcher of iced water.

When guests have served themselves, partially emptied serving dishes should be refilled and empty ones removed from the buffet. Second servings may be passed by the hostess, or she may ask the guests to return to the buffet to serve themselves. When the first course is eaten, the buffet table is cleared, and dessert and the dishes in which it is to be served are then brought out.

The basic pattern of buffet service is varied in many ways. For the most informal type of service, guests may serve themselves with everything, even pouring their own coffee. At a semiformal buffet party, the hostess or a friend may pour the coffee at one end of the table; sometimes another friend may be asked to serve the main hot dish, if it is a casserole. Ornamental trays large enough to hold the plate and coffee cup, napkin and silverware, and water glass may be provided for the guests; the trays may be held on the guests' laps, or they may be mounted on folding legs; if trays are not provided, snack tables or card tables should be provided to set things on while guests deal with their plates on their laps. Plates and silver used in the first course may be returned by the guests (either to the kitchen), if the party is very informal, or to a table set up near the kitchen), or cleared away by the hostess or the host, or a friend. On some occasions, when space allows, a partial buffet may be preferred. Under this arrangement, guests select their food and seat themselves at smaller tables, such as card tables, where a place is set for each one.

Courses for a buffet meal are usually limited to just two—a main course with salad and rolls, and a dessert. Dishes should be chosen that are easy to serve and that stand up well. Casserole dishes are better than delicate soufflés which need to be served immediately. A chafing dish is a great convenience on a buffet table; heat-retaining casseroles are also an aid in keeping hot foods hot. Mixtures should not

be too thin and runny, salads not too juicy. Tossed or molded salads are always good; fruit salad mixtures may be served in lettuce cups which can be transferred to plates.

Remember to consider eye-appeal of foods as well as their taste-appeal. The colors of the foods themselves as well as their arrangement on serving dishes and their garnishings are important, for a buffet meal provides almost the only opportunity for guests to see the whole menu at once. In planning for your party, be sure to estimate quantities generously, for there is something about a buffet which is irresistible to the appetite!

Larger, heartier buffet meals are sometimes served. For one such, a roast turkey may be placed at one end, and a handsomely garnished baked tender ham at the other; both of these may be set out either hot or cold, and sliced or partly sliced beforehand, or else sliced and served by the hostess's helpers. To complete this particular meal, little hot Southern biscuits are delicious, with a big relish tray of carrot sticks, celery curls, olives, cranberry jelly to go with the turkey and spiced crab apples or peaches for the ham, a platter of sliced tomatoes drizzled with French dressing, cauliflower polonaise and lemon meringue tarts. Sumptuous!

MORNING COFFEE

This light and friendly mid-morning party is a type of buffet meal. Almost certain to be an exclusively feminine affair, with the menfolks safely out of the house, it is an easy and informal way of entertaining a few friends cheerfully and easily, or a gracious way to entertain an out-of-town friend when time is limited.

Most informal of all is the impromptu coffee to which neighbors just drift in, and are welcomed by plenty of hot, fragrant coffee and coffee cake, sweet rolls or doughnuts. No special service is required: a bright, sunny kitchen is the pleasantest place possible for such a gathering of a few good neighbors.

When guests are invited for a real morning-coffee "party," usually about 10 or 11 o'clock, more elaborate preparations are in order. Coffee, coffee breads and one or more trays of bite-size relishes of contrasting color and flavor (sweet and sour, bland and savory), may all be arranged on a prettily spread buffet table in living or dining room. The hostess herself will want to pour the coffee for her guests—a hospitable as well as a practical gesture; but a stack of plates on the table, with napkins and teaspoons arranged beside them, will permit

each guest to serve herself to whatever she wants of the other foods provided. The "main course" will be bread, and a good plan is to allow one big, beautiful coffee cake of the good-without-butter kind, already cut for the convenience of the guests, when the party is small; when the group is larger, a selection of delicious sweet rolls should be added.

The relish tray may hold tangy cheese bits, crisp radish roses or celery curls, ripe or green olives, along with fruits such as small clusters of grapes, whole strawberries washed but with hulls intact for finger eating, pineapple chunks, melon balls or hulled berries impaled on picks. An attractive fresh fruit relish bowl can be made by cutting into halves and scooping out a chilled honeydew melon or a fresh pineapple with its spiny crown intact, and heaping with balls or chunks cut from the fruit bowl itself and other fruits, all on wooden picks.

COCKTAIL PARTIES

The cocktail party is a special kind of buffet. The purpose of hors d'oeuvres at this party is a little different from the before-dinner cocktail hour, since no other food is ordinarily to be provided. A variety should be served, allowing at least five or six "pieces" for each guest. Hot hors d'oeuvres should not be attempted unless they can be served piping hot. Tiny and attractively garnished canapés are very much in order. One nonalcoholic beverage should be provided.

In keeping with the delicate and fine quality of cocktail glasses, other serving equipment and the service itself will tend to be formal rather than informal. A beautiful tablecloth, flowers and candles form an attractive background for the hors d'oeuvre trays. Small plates may or may not be provided, but plenty of cocktail napkins should be placed at both ends of the table.

SMORGASBORD

Best-known of all Scandinavian dining customs is the smörgasbord—usually the prelude to the feast, but on some occasions the whole feast itself. In Sweden, where the custom is believed to have originated in the festivities of country people, the smörgasbord is served as a first course. A small number of appetizers, which invariably include herring, are presented buffet-style to guests who relax and nibble, exchange toasts and conversation, and then assemble around the dining table with appetites pleasantly stimulated but unimpaired. In other countries, and especially in America, the character and function of the smörgasbord have altered and it may comprise the principal part of a meal. A munificent variety of fish, meat, cheese, egg and vegetable dishes is arranged on a necessarily commodious buffet or table and guests visit it as often as they please. A dessert (by recommendation simple) and good strong coffee bring the feast to a close.

A time-tried ritual is prescribed for the proper enjoyment of either a small smörgasbord or the full-scale, panoramic affair. First, and always first if one is to observe the Scandinavian spirit of the occasion, the herring! Then one adventures (with clean plate in hand) through dishes in which fish is combined with other ingredients, then cold meats, the delicious hot dishes, the salads and aspics, and finally, for digestion's sake and to soothe a possibly jaded palate, a bit of cheese.

In Norway, the smörgasbord is also called koldt bord. It usually consists of a few appetizers—fish, meat and cheese—but on special occasions may be elaborate and bountiful, including roasts of meat and several kinds of fish. Roast beef tenderloin, for example, and loin of pork served with prunes and apple slices; boiled lobster with mayonnaise, whole baked or boiled salmon with sour cream; and a whole cold ham. Include parsley potatoes in the more elaborate type of smörgasbord. Rum pudding usually rounds out these heroic collations.

A Swedish adaptation of the smörgasbord is the gracious supé—a late supper served after the theater or an evening of dancing. The supé too is governed to some extent by tradition. Hot dishes are always served. They may be croustades with creamed filling, an omelet or soufflé, new potatoes with fresh dill. Breads, especially the fragrant limpa, accompany the dishes. Fish and a relish, such as sliced tomatoes, are included as a matter of course. Amounts served are not lavish. The dishes are kept small, but always garnished with the flair for beauty that characterizes Scandinavian cuisine. Cookies are sometimes included in supé and coffee is always served. To precede a Swedish dinner, a plate of three (it must be three) canapés is placed before each individual. Canapés would not be served with a smörgasbord.

The suggested smörgasbord recipes have been selected with a deep bow to Scandinavian tradition and an understanding nod to some American food preferences: Pickled Herring, Herring Salad, Fish Balls, Rolled Fish Fillets, "Boiled" Salmon, Fish in Aspic, "Boiled" Lobster, Cooked Shrimp, Swedish Meat Balls, Jellied Veal, Smoked Beef Tongue, Rolled Rib Roast of Beef, Roast Ham, Roast Loin of Pork with Prunes, Liver Paste, Stuffed Eggs, Pickled Beets, Hot Potato Salad, Cucumber Salad, Cabbage Salad, Fruit-Filled Gelatin Salad, Macaroni Salad and Tomato Aspic Cream Cheese Salad Ring. The fruit molds, cream-cheese aspics, macaroni and cole slaw salad would probably not be found on a smörgasbord table in Stockholm, except perhaps at the height of the tourist season.

The American homemaker can make a respectable gesture toward a smörgasbord with herring, sardines, anchovies or other small canned fish, a platter of ready-to-serve meats and cheese and a relish or two—all of which may also be included in a much more elaborate buffet.

A word about bread and cheeses: Custom dictates that only the dark breads belong to the smörgasbord and that knackebröd (hardtack

Beef with Green Pepper (page 171), Pineapple Pork (page 188), Broccoli with Beef (page 176) and Chicken with Vegetables (page 253)

in American parlance) should be among them. Cheese may be Swiss, Danish Blue, Edam, goat cheeses or bond ost, but it is never proffered in slices. Guests cut it to individual preference.

Buffet Menu I

Barbecued Spareribs
Beef with Green Pepper
Broccoli with Beef
Chicken with Vegetables
Pineapple Pork
Banana Cake Royale
Tea

The exotic and delicious dishes in this Cantonese meal, like most Oriental foods, are ideal for buffet service. The quantities for each recipe are for six or eight servings.

Buffet Menu II

Turkey Lasagne
Tossed Salad
Garlic Bread
Serve-Yourself Sundaes
Coffee

Buffet Menu III

Beef Stroganoff and Rice
Empress Salad
Hot Rolls
Dessert Superb
Coffee

For a different sort of tossed salad to serve with this buffet, try cubes of cucumber and juicy pear (unpared), and large chunks of juicy watermelon, looking like pink ice. Toss them with escarole and a slightly sweet French dressing made with lemon juice. Call it an Empress Salad, for it's worthy of the name!

Buffet Menu IV

Curried Rock Lobster
Green Beans with Almonds and Mushrooms
Sliced Tomatoes
Hot Rolls
Grape Arbor Pie or Fabulous Cherry Pie
Coffee

661

Holiday recipes

The United States has within its borders people representing many different countries and cultures. To retain some of their old-world traditions and customs, each group takes great pride in the observation of the national and religious holidays which have significance in their lives. Added to these are specifically American holidays which are often celebrated by everyone. Whatever the special observance, it is celebrated with party food served in a festive manner. Here are suggestions for celebrating nine well-recognized holidays.

New Year's Eve Cake

NEW YEAR'S

"Shout out the Old Year! Ring in the New! It's party time!" Buffets, dinners, late suppers, open houses, intimate gatherings—all are means of bringing your family and friends together. Good resolutions will not go astray when you plan your holiday festivities with these recipes.

EGGNOG PIE

Prepare, bake and set aside to cool
    10-in. Pastry Shell (page 485)

Chill hand rotary or electric beater.

Combine and mix thoroughly in top of a double boiler
    1 env. unflavored gelatin
    5 tablespoons sugar
    ½ teaspoon salt

Beat slightly in a mixing bowl
    4 egg yolks
Blend in
    1½ cups milk
Add to the gelatin mixture and place over boiling water in lower part of double boiler. Cook, stirring constantly, until gelatin is completely dissolved, about 5 min.

Dairy Eggnog Pie

Remove from the heat and set aside to cool slightly. Then place in refrigerator to chill. Or set the hot mixture in a bowl of ice and water to chill, stirring occasionally, until it mounds when dropped from a spoon.

Using chilled bowl and beater, beat until cream is of medium consistency (piles softly)
    1 cup chilled heavy cream
Set in refrigerator while egg whites are beaten.

Using clean beater, beat until frothy
    2 egg whites
Add gradually, beating thoroughly after each addition, a mixture of
    ¼ cup sugar
    ½ teaspoon nutmeg
Beat until very stiff peaks are formed.

Fold beaten egg whites and whipped cream into gelatin mixture with
    2 tablespoons rum
    2 teaspoons vanilla extract
Turn into cooled pastry shell.

Sprinkle top evenly with
    ½ teaspoon nutmeg
Chill in refrigerator 2 or 3 hrs.

One 10-in. pie

—DAIRY EGGNOG PIE

Follow ▲ Recipe. Substitute **dairy eggnog** for milk. Omit sprinkling with nutmeg. When ready to serve, whip **½ cup chilled heavy cream** with **2 tablespoons confectioners'**

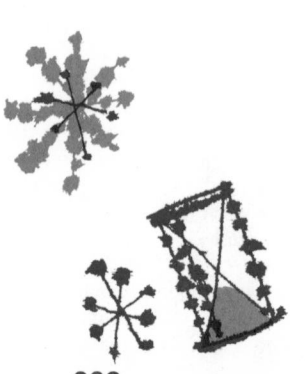

sugar and **1 teaspoon vanilla extract**. Swirl onto top of pie with a spatula. Top with chocolate curls made by pulling **½ oz. (½ sq.) unsweetened chocolate** across a shredder.

NEW YEAR'S EVE CAKE

Prepare
    Cherry Chocolate Cake (page 697)
While cake layers cool, prepare
    Brown Velvet Frosting (page 477)
    White Velvet Frosting (one-third recipe, page 477)
Frost with brown frosting. Force white frosting through pastry bag and No. 3 stem decorating tube to form face of clock.

HOLIDAY EGGNOG

Beat until very thick and lemon-colored
    6 egg yolks
    2 cups sugar
Slowly stir in
    1 pt. bourbon
    1 cup Jamaica rum
    1 cup brandy

Holiday Eggnog

Blend in
3 pts. heavy cream
1 pt. milk
Beat until stiff, not dry, peaks are formed
6 egg whites
Gently fold egg whites into egg yolk mixture. Pour into punch bowl, cover and chill in refrigerator.

Before serving, lightly sprinkle with
Nutmeg

About 25 servings

VALENTINE'S DAY

Remember your first valentine—the lacy-edged heart with silver arrows and pink-cheeked cupids? And all the ones at which you laughed and shyly smiled? And how many have you fashioned from ribbons and red paper? Make another—this time out of sugar, shortening, flour and eggs—Sweetheart Cake, one of the most exciting valentines of all!

RHUBARB STRAWBERRY MOLD

Set out a 1-qt. heart-shape mold or 6 individual molds.

Wash, cut off stem ends and leaves from
1 lb. rhubarb
Peel stalks only if skin is tough. Cut into 1-in. pieces (about 3 cups, cut) and place in saucepan with
¾ cup sugar
¼ cup water
Place over low heat and stir until sugar is dissolved. Cover and cook slowly about 15 min., or until rhubarb is tender.

When rhubarb is tender, drain, reserving hot syrup in a 1-cup measuring cup for liquid. Set rhubarb aside to cool. Add to hot syrup
Boiling water (enough to make 1 cup liquid)
Empty into a bowl contents of
1 pkg. (3 oz.) strawberry-flavored gelatin
Pour hot syrup mixture over gelatin. Stir until gelatin is completely dissolved. Blend in
1 cup cold water

Chill in refrigerator or in pan of ice and water until gelatin mixture is slightly thicker than consistency of thick unbeaten egg white. If placed over ice and water, stir frequently; if placed in refrigerator, stir occasionally.

When gelatin is of correct consistency, blend in cooked rhubarb and
1 cup sweetened sliced fresh strawberries (or one 10-oz. pkg. frozen strawberries, thawed)
Pour into prepared mold. Chill until firm.

Unmold (page 374). Serve with a mixture of
½ cup fruit salad dressing
¼ cup chilled whipping cream, whipped
Garnish with **whole strawberries** sprinkled with sifted **confectioners' sugar.**

6 to 8 servings

Note: One 16-oz. pkg. frozen rhubarb may be substituted for fresh rhubarb. Thaw, following directions on package, drain and reserve drained syrup. Omit sugar and initial cooking of rhubarb. Heat drained syrup and continue as in recipe.

SWEETHEART CAKE

▲ Base Recipe

Prepare (page 10) two 9-in. round or heart-shape layer cake pans.

Sift together and set aside
3 cups sifted cake flour
1 tablespoon baking powder
½ teaspoon salt
Cream together until butter is softened
1 cup butter or margarine
1 tablespoon vanilla extract
Add gradually, creaming until fluffy after each addition
1 cup sugar
Beat until frothy
6 egg whites
Add gradually, beating well after each addition
¾ cup sugar
Continue beating meringue until very stiff peaks are formed.

Measure
½ cup water
½ cup milk
Alternately blend dry ingredients in fourths, liquid in thirds into creamed mixture, beating only until smooth after each addition. (Do not overbeat.) Add the meringue to batter and fold in gently until well blended. Turn batter into pans.

Bake at 350°F 30 to 35 min., or until cake tests done (page 11). Cool and remove from pans as directed (page 11).

Prepare
Pineapple Cream Filling (page 484)
Seven-Minute Frosting (page 474)
White Velvet Frosting (one-third recipe, page 477)
Place one cake layer on cake plate and spread filling over top. Place other cake layer over filling. Frost sides and top of cake with Seven-Minute Frosting.

Tint White Velvet Frosting desired color by blending in one or more drops of
Red food coloring
Force tinted frosting through pastry bag and No. 3 stem decorating tube to write on cake.

To make nosegays, place small **red gumdrops** on wooden picks. Make soft folds in doilies from center to edge. Poke wooden picks down through center of doily and tie in place with red ribbon. Place nosegays around cake. Make one nosegay without ribbon for top of cake.

One 9-in. round or heart-shape layer cake

Note: If round cake layers are used, make heart shape by placing a waxed-paper pattern on layers and cutting around it with a knife.

—CHRISTMAS TREE CAKE

Prepare three 9-in. round cake layer pans. Follow ▲ Recipe, making one and one-half times recipe. Do not prepare filling and Seven-Minute Frosting. Prepare **White Velvet Frosting** (double recipe, page 477). Place one third of frosting in a bowl and tint by blending in one or more drops **green food coloring**. Frost two cake layers with untinted two-thirds of frosting. Cut third layer into a tree shape by cutting around a tree-shape waxed-paper pattern with a knife. Frost tree-shape layer with the tinted frosting and place on top of other two cake layers. Decorate tree with **red cinnamon candies.**

Sweetheart Cake

LINCOLN'S AND WASHINGTON'S BIRTHDAYS

Two famous Presidents, both born in February, deserve grateful tribute on their birthdays. Festivities for George Washington, the father of his country, could appropriately include foods in the Colonial and Southern tradition. Abraham Lincoln, the great emancipator, who was reared on the simple food of the frontier had a special fondness for desserts.

SPARERIBS—RAIL SPLITTER'S ROAST

Prepare
   Apple Stuffing (on this page)
Have ready
   2 sections (about 4 lbs.) spareribs
Place one section on rack in a shallow roasting pan. Mix thoroughly
   1 teaspoon salt
   ¼ teaspoon monosodium glutamate
   ⅛ teaspoon pepper
Sprinkle one half of mixture over spareribs. Spread stuffing on section. Cover with second section of spareribs. Fasten the sections together with skewers. Sprinkle remaining seasoning mixture over top.
Roast at 350°F for 1½ hrs. Remove skewers.

Cut spareribs into serving-size pieces and serve with stuffing. Garnish with **parsley** and rosy **crab apples.** *4 servings*

Note: To keep top section moist, spread with **applesauce** or **sauerkraut.**

APPLE STUFFING

   ▲ *Base Recipe*

Wash, quarter, core, pare, dice and set aside
   1 medium apple (1 cup, chopped)

Melt in a skillet over medium heat
   ¼ cup butter or margarine
Add and cook until tender
   ½ cup (1 medium) chopped onion

Meanwhile, toss together the diced apple and
   2 cups (3 to 4 slices) soft bread crumbs
and a mixture of
   1 teaspoon salt
   1 teaspoon celery seed
   ¼ teaspoon monosodium glutamate
   ⅛ teaspoon pepper
Blend with onion and fat. Toss mixture with
   ¼ cup apple cider (use only enough to barely moisten bread)
   About 3½ cups stuffing

—APPLE STUFFING FOR POULTRY

Prepare three times ▲ Recipe, adding **1 cup chopped celery with leaves.** Spoon stuffing into neck and body cavities—do not pack. Stuff poultry *just before* roasting. Extra stuffing may be placed in a greased baking dish or aluminum foil and baked with bird last hour of roasting time. *Stuffing for 12-lb. bird*

WASHINGTON CHERRY TRICORNS

   ▲ *Base Recipe*

Prepare
   Pastry for Little Pies and Tarts (page 485)
Divide pastry into 2 equal-size balls. Roll each ball ⅛ in. thick; cut each into four 6-in. rounds. Prick each round with a fork.

Cut heavy-duty aluminum foil into the same size (6-in.) rounds. Place one round of pastry on each piece of aluminum foil. Pressing the aluminum foil against the pastry, form a triangular shell. Pinch the aluminum foil together tightly at three equal intervals to form corners.

Bake at 450°F 8 to 10 min., or until pastry is lightly browned. Remove to cooling rack. When cooled, remove aluminum foil molds.

Meanwhile, drain thoroughly, reserving liquid
   2 cans (16 oz. each) pitted red tart cherries (about 3 cups, drained)

Combine in a heavy saucepan
   3 tablespoons cornstarch
   ¾ cup sugar
Add gradually, stirring until smooth
   1 cup reserved cherry liquid
Mix well and bring rapidly to boiling, stirring constantly, until mixture is thick and smooth.

Remove from heat and mix in
   1 teaspoon lemon juice
   ½ teaspoon almond extract
   ¼ teaspoon salt
   8 drops red food coloring
Stir in the cherries. Cool.

Meanwhile, soften
   1 pkg. (3 oz.) cream cheese

Beat in a blend of
   2 tablespoons milk or cream
   ¼ teaspoon almond extract
Whip until light and fluffy.

Fill pastry shells with cherry mixture. Place a rosette of cream cheese forced through pastry bag and No. 27 star tube onto each cherry tricorn. *8 servings*

—WASHINGTON CHERRY PIE

Prepare, bake and set aside to cool **Pastry for 1-Crust Pie** (page 485). Follow ▲ Recipe for cherry filling. Spoon cooled filling into cooled pastry. Top with cheese mixture and **pastry hatchet cutouts.**

LINCOLN LOG

   ▲ *Base Recipe*

Prepare (page 10) a 15x10x1-in. jelly roll pan.

Sift together and set aside
   ¾ cup sifted cake flour
   5 tablespoons cocoa
   ¼ teaspoon salt

Beat until very thick and lemon-colored
   4 egg yolks
   ½ cup sugar
   ¼ cup water
   1½ teaspoons vanilla extract
Gently fold in dry ingredients until well blended. Set aside.

Beat until frothy
   4 egg whites
   ⅛ teaspoon salt
Add and beat slightly
   ½ teaspoon cream of tartar
Add gradually, beating well after each addition
   ½ cup sugar
Continue beating until very stiff peaks are formed. Gently spread egg yolk mixture over egg whites and carefully fold together until

blended. Turn batter into pan and spread evenly to edges.

Bake at 325°F about 30 min., or until cake tests done (page 11).

Immediately loosen edges of cake with a sharp knife and turn onto a clean towel sprinkled with

Sifted confectioners' sugar

Remove paper and cut off any crisp edges of cake. To roll, begin rolling nearest edge of cake. Using towel as a guide, tightly grasp nearest edge of towel and quickly pull it over beyond opposite edge. Cake will roll itself as you pull. Wrap cake in towel and set on cooling rack to cool, about ½ hr.

Meanwhile, prepare

Pineapple Cream Filling (page 484) omit pineapple and increase vanilla extract to 2 teaspoons) Brown Velvet Frosting (page 477)

When ready to fill, carefully unroll cooled cake and spread with the cream filling. Carefully reroll cake. Diagonally cut off tip ends from cake.

Frost sides, ends and top of cake roll with the Brown Velvet Frosting.

Gently draw back tines of a fork lengthwise through frosting. Repeat parallel lines across top and sides of cake roll. Make some lines slightly wavy. (The lines help to make the cake roll resemble a log.)

Chill the cake roll in refrigerator until serving time. (To avoid sogginess, chill roll no longer than 1 hr.)

Garnish top of log with

Stemmed maraschino cherries

or surround base of log with the cherries and top each serving of cake roll with one cherry. With a sharp knife, cut roll into crosswise diagonal slices and serve. *1 cake roll*

—HOLIDAY ROLL

Follow ▲ Recipe or recipe for Jelly Roll (page 458). When baked, rolled and cooled, unroll cake and spread with one half of filling. Reroll and spread top and sides with remaining filling. Garnish with **maraschino cherry halves** and chopped **candied citron**.

For Filling—Prepare **Sweetened Whipped Cream** (double recipe, page 480). Carefully fold in ⅔ cup (8-oz. jar, well drained) chopped **maraschino cherries**, ¼ cup (2 oz.) chopped **candied citron** and ½ cup (about 2½ oz.) **toasted chopped almonds** (page 10).

CHERRY CHOCOLATE CAKE

Prepare (page 10) two 9-in. round layer cake pans.

Melt (page 10) and set aside to cool

2 oz. (2 sq.) unsweetened chocolate

Drain, reserving syrup

1 bottle (6 oz.) maraschino cherries

Finely chop cherries (about ½ cup, chopped) and set aside.

Coarsely chop and set aside

¾ cup (about 3 oz.) black walnuts or pecans

Sift together and set aside

2¼ cups sifted cake flour
2 teaspoons baking powder
¾ teaspoon baking soda
½ teaspoon salt

Cream until softened

½ cup plus 2 tablespoons butter or margarine

Add gradually, creaming until fluffy after each addition

1¼ cups sugar

Add, beating thoroughly

1 egg, well beaten

Stir in chocolate.

Combine

1¼ cups dairy sour cream
¼ cup reserved maraschino cherry syrup

Alternately add dry ingredients in fourths, sour cream mixture in thirds, to creamed mixture. After each addition, beat only until smooth; do not overbeat. Blend in the chopped nuts and cherries.

Turn batter into pans.

Bake at 375°F 30 to 35 min., or until cake tests done (page 11). Cool and remove from pans as directed (page 11).

Two 9-in. round cake layers

—FOURTH OF JULY DRUM CAKE

Frost with **Seven-Minute Frosting** (page 474). Line top and bottom edges of cake to form a rim with **red gumdrops, maraschino** or **candied cherry halves**. On sides, make large X's of red gumdrops or cherries (each X extending from top to bottom of cake). Place **2 sticks peppermint candy** on top for drumsticks.

Irish Scones

ST. PATRICK'S DAY

In the middle of the Lenten season comes this gay holiday when clay pipes, shamrocks, the Blarney Stone and the Wearing of the Green become the order of the day. Celebrated originally in Ireland, this holiday has now become an integral part of our American heritage.

IRISH SCONES

▲ *Base Recipe*

Serve these rich, flaky scones piping hot— split and lavishly spread with butter or margarine.

Set out a baking sheet.

Sift together into a mixing bowl

2 cups sifted all-purpose flour
2 tablespoons sugar
1 tablespoon baking powder
⅛ teaspoon salt

Cut into dry ingredients with a pastry blender or two knives until mixture resembles coarse corn meal

½ cup lard, vegetable shortening or all-purpose shortening

Lightly stir in with a few strokes

½ cup (about 2½ oz.) currants

Make a well in center of mixture and add all at one time, a mixture of

1 egg, well beaten
½ cup cream

Stir with a fork until dough follows fork.

Gently form dough into a ball and put on a lightly oured surface. Knead it lightly with finger tips 10 to 15 times. Roll dough into a round ½ in. thick. Cut into 12 wedges. Place wedges on the ungreased baking sheet.

Bake at 425°F 15 to 20 min., or until golden brown.   *1 doz. scones*

—SUGARED SCONES

Follow ▲ Recipe. Omit currants. Before baking, brush tops of scones lightly with **melted butter or margarine** and sprinkle with **sugar.**

SHAMROCK SANDWICHES

▲ *Base Recipe*

These open-face sandwiches served with Dublin Pineapple Salad spell real eating enjoyment.

For Sandwich Spread—Cream until fluffy
¾ cup butter or margarine
Blend in
3 tablespoons finely chopped chives,
   parsley or watercress
2 tablespoons mayonnaise
¼ teaspoon prepared horseradish
⅛ teaspoon monosodium glutamate
Few grains salt

Add a drop or more of **green food coloring** for a green-colored spread. Set spread aside to let flavors blend.   *About 1 cup spread*

For Shamrocks—Place on a flat working surface
White or whole wheat bread slices
With a shamrock-shape cookie cutter, or a sharp knife and a waxed-paper pattern, carefully cut shamrocks from bread slices. Evenly spread shamrock cutouts with butter mixture.

Garnish each with a sprig of **parsley** or **watercress,** chopped **chives** or a **green olive slice.**

If sandwiches are to be stored in refrigerator until serving time, line a shallow pan with waxed paper, aluminum foil or plastic wrap. Lay sandwiches in pan but do not stack. Cover pan tightly with waxed paper, aluminum foil or plastic wrap, or place in plastic bag and seal tightly.

—LUCKY ST. PAT-WICHES

Follow ▲ Recipe for sandwich spread. Cut out bread horseshoes using waxed-paper horseshoe pattern 2½ in. long. Toast both sides of bread lightly in broiler. Spread with butter mixture. Serve immediately.

IRISH STEW

▲ *Base Recipe*

Set out a large kettle or Dutch oven with a tight-fitting cover.

Have ready
2 lbs. boneless lamb (shoulder)
Cut meat into 2-in. pieces. To coat meat evenly, shake two or three pieces at a time in a plastic bag containing a mixture of
⅓ cup all-purpose flour
2 teaspoons salt
½ teaspoon monosodium glutamate
⅛ teaspoon pepper
Melt in the kettle or Dutch oven
3 tablespoons fat
Brown lamb pieces on all sides in hot fat, over medium heat, turning occasionally. Pour off excess fat. Remove from heat and slowly pour into the kettle
1 qt. hot water
Cover and bring to boiling over high heat. Simmer over low heat about 1½ hrs., or until meat is almost tender.

Plan to add vegetables to cooking mixture about 45 min. before end of cooking period. About 15 min. before adding vegetables to stew, cut off root ends and a thin slice from the stem ends of
6 small onions
Peel, rinse and set aside.

Trim roots, separate stalks, remove blemishes and wash
4 stalks celery with leaves
Cut crosswise into ½-in. slices and set aside.

Wash, scrape and cut into about ½-in. pieces
4 small carrots
Wash, pare and quarter
6 medium (about 2 lbs.) potatoes
1 medium turnip
Add the prepared vegetables to the stew with
1½ teaspoons salt
1 teaspoon monosodium glutamate
⅛ teaspoon pepper
Cover and simmer about 45 min., or until meat and vegetables are tender.

Just before removing meat and vegetables from stew, dissolve in a small amount of hot water
2 teaspoons concentrated meat
   extract

With slotted spoon, remove meat and vegetables from stew to hot dish.

Stir the dissolved concentrated meat extract into the cooking liquid.

To thicken cooking liquid, put into 1-pt. screw-top jar
½ cup cold water
Sprinkle onto water
¼ cup all-purpose flour
Cover jar tightly and shake until mixture is well blended. Slowly pour one half of the mixture into cooking liquid while stirring constantly. Bring to boiling. Gradually add only what is needed of remaining flour-water mixture for consistency desired. Bring mixture to boiling after each addition. Cook 3 to 5 min. Return meat and vegetables to kettle and heat thoroughly.

Garnish stew with **chopped parsley.** Serve immediately.   *8 to 10 servings*

—SAVORY LAMB STEW

Follow ▲ Recipe. Add to meat with seasonings a mixture of ¼ **teaspoon savory,** ¼ **teaspoon basil** and ¼ **teaspoon marjoram.** Omit turnip.

DUBLIN PINEAPPLE SALAD

▲ *Base Recipe*

Set out a 9x5x3-in. loaf pan or a 2-qt. mold. Place a rotary beater and bowl in refrigerator to chill.

Set aside to drain, reserving syrup in a 2-cup measuring cup
1 can (20 oz.) crushed pineapple (about
   1¾ cups, drained)

Pour into a small bowl
½ cup reserved pineapple syrup
½ cup water
Sprinkle evenly over syrup
2 env. unflavored gelatin
Let stand until softened.

Irish Stew

Add to remaining reserved pineapple syrup
**Cold water (enough to make
1½ cups liquid)**
Heat until very hot. Remove from heat and immediately stir in softened gelatin until gelatin is completely dissolved. Add, stirring until sugar is dissolved
**¾ cup sugar
¼ teaspoon salt**

Chill in refrigerator or in pan of ice and water until gelatin mixture is slightly thicker than consistency of thick unbeaten egg white. (If placed over ice and water, stir frequently; if placed in refrigerator, stir occasionally.)

Blend thoroughly
**8 oz. cream cheese, softened
2 teaspoons grated lemon peel
2 tablespoons lemon juice**
Set aside.

When gelatin is about the same consistency as cheese mixture, stir in several tablespoons cooled gelatin. Continue to slowly add gelatin, beating constantly, until well blended.

Using chilled bowl and beater, beat until cream is of medium consistency (piles softly)
1 cup chilled whipping cream
Gently fold whipped cream and crushed pineapple into salad mixture. Turn into prepared pan or mold. Chill in refrigerator until firm. Unmold (page 374).

Garnish with **salad greens** and **"shamrocks."** Slice and serve with **mayonnaise.** *8 servings*

For Shamrocks—Using **green pepper,** cut small shamrocks with shamrock cookie cutter (or trace around cardboard pattern). Use **watercress or parsley stems** for shamrock stems.

—PINEAPPLE RICE DESSERT

Follow ▲ Recipe. Omit cream cheese mixture. Blend with crushed pineapple **1 cup cooked rice,** chilled, and **⅓ cup chopped green cherries.** Continue as in ▲ Recipe. For garnish, drain on absorbent paper additional green cherries with stems. Place cherries around base of mold. Slice mold and serve each slice topped with **Sweetened Whipped Cream** (page 480), tinted green, and a green Cherry.

GREENGAGE PLUM ICE

You'll think they've kissed the Blarney Stone the way they'll praise this cooling, tart ice.

This recipe may be prepared in a dasher-type freezer or in refrigerator. When using refrigerator, set refrigerator control at colder operating temperature if necessary.

Cut into halves, pit and force through a sieve or food mill contents (including syrup) of
**1 can (17 oz.) greengage plums
(about 2 cups purée)**
Set aside.

Easter Egg Bread

Pour into a small cup or custard cup
½ cup water
Sprinkle evenly over water
1 env. unflavored gelatin
Let stand until softened.

Meanwhile, heat until very hot
¾ cup water
Remove from heat and immediately stir in softened gelatin until gelatin is completely dissolved. Add and stir until sugar is completely dissolved
**½ cup sugar
⅛ teaspoon salt**
Set aside to cool.

Combine plum purée with sugar syrup and
**1 cup orange juice
2 tablespoons lemon juice**
To tint ice, mix in one or more drops
Green food coloring
Cool. Pour into refrigerator tray. Freeze until firm (3 to 4 hrs.), stirring two or three times.

Serve in chilled sherbet cups.
1 qt. Greengage Plum Ice

EASTER

A holiday steeped in tradition, Easter Sunday is a day of sunrise church services, gay spring finery and decorated Easter baskets. To the children, these baskets mean the Easter bunny and brightly colored eggs. To the entire family, it means an Easter parade followed by a festive brunch or dinner.

EASTER EGG BREAD
(Pane di Pasqua all 'Uovo)

Sprinkled with brightly colored candies and dotted with multicolored Easter eggs, this bread will add an extra holiday touch to a festive Easter dinner. Traditionally shaped in wreath form, or "corona di nove," many American cooks bake it in the shape of rabbits or fancy Easter baskets.

A 15½x12-in. baking sheet will be needed.

Dip in food dyes to color (follow directions on package) and set aside
5 eggs (uncooked)

Soften
2 pkgs. active dry yeast
in
**½ cup warm water, 105°F to 115°F
(Or if using compressed yeast,
soften 2 cakes in ½ cup
lukewarm water, 80°F to 85°F.)**
Set aside.

Meanwhile, pour into a large bowl
½ cup warm water
Blend in
1½ cups sifted all-purpose flour
Stir softened yeast, and add to flour-water mixture, mixing well. Beat until very smooth. Cover bowl with waxed paper and towel and let stand in warm place (about 80°F) for 1½ to 2 hrs.

Cream until thoroughly blended
**¾ cup shortening
1 tablespoon grated lemon peel
1½ tablespoons lemon juice**
Add gradually, creaming until fluffy after each addition, a mixture of
**¾ cup sugar
1 teaspoon salt**
Add, one at a time, beating thoroughly after each addition
2 eggs
When yeast mixture has doubled in volume, add to creamed mixture, beating thoroughly until smooth.

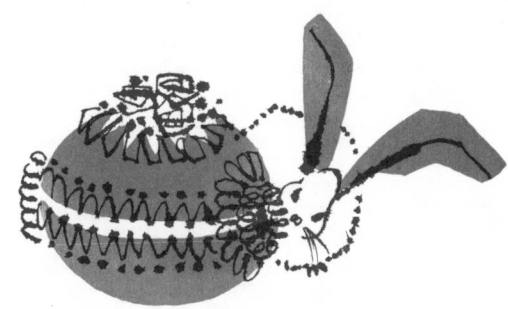

Hot Cross Buns

Measure

3 to 4 cups sifted all-purpose flour

Add about one-half the flour to yeast mixture and beat until very smooth. Mix in enough remaining flour to make a soft dough. Knead (page 10) on a lightly floured surface.

Select a deep bowl just large enough to allow dough to double. Shape dough into a smooth ball and place into greased bowl. Turn dough to bring greased surface to top. Cover bowl with waxed paper and towel and let dough rise until doubled, about 1½ to 2 hrs.

Punch down with fist. Divide dough into two equal balls. Let stand covered for 10 min.

Roll each ball out into a long roll about 26 in. long and about 1 in. thick. Using the two long pieces of dough, form a loosely braided ring, leaving spaces for the five colored eggs. Place on a lightly buttered baking sheet. Place eggs in spaces of braid. Cover with towel. Set dough aside in a warm place until doubled.

Bake at 375°F 10 min.

Brush bread with a mixture of

1 egg yolk

1 tablespoon milk

Sprinkle with

Tiny multicolored candies

Bake 30 to 35 min. or until bread is golden brown. (*Eggs will be hard-cooked*.)

HOT CROSS BUNS

▲ *Base Recipe*

Set out baking sheets.

Coarsely chop

3 oz. candied citron (about ½ cup, chopped)

Mix with the citron and set aside

1 cup currants

Prepare

Yeast Rolls (one-half recipe, page 75; sift 1 teaspoon cinnamon and ¼ teaspoon allspice with the flour. Stir currant mixture in before last addition of flour.)

After punching down, form dough into a roll 2 in. in diameter. Cut crosswise into 1½-in. pieces. Tuck under ends to make smooth, round buns. Place on baking sheet about 1 in. apart. With lightly greased knife or scissors, cut a deep cross in top of each bun. Brush tops with

Melted butter or margarine

Cover with waxed paper and towel and let rise 15 to 25 min., or until nearly doubled.

Bake at 425°F 12 to 15 min., or until buns are golden brown.

While buns are baking, prepare

Confectioners' Sugar Frosting (one-half recipe, page 477)

Remove buns from baking sheet to cooling racks. Cool buns slightly; using a spoon, drizzle frosting into cross on each bun.

1½ to 2 doz. buns

—SAFFRON BUNS

Follow ▲ Recipe. Omit cinnamon and allspice. Before beating eggs, pour **1 tablespoon boiling water** over ¼ **teaspoon saffron**. Cool to lukewarm. Beat into dough with the eggs.

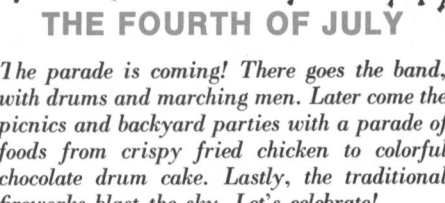

THE FOURTH OF JULY

The parade is coming! There goes the band, with drums and marching men. Later come the picnics and backyard parties with a parade of foods from crispy fried chicken to colorful chocolate drum cake. Lastly, the traditional fireworks blast the sky. Let's celebrate!

CHICKEN IN A BASKET

Set out a Dutch oven or a large heavy skillet with a tight-fitting cover.

Have ready

2 frying chickens, 2 to 3 lbs. each, ready-to-cook weight

(If chickens are frozen, thaw according to directions on package.) Disjoint chickens and cut into serving-size pieces. Rinse and pat dry with absorbent paper.

To coat chicken evenly, shake 2 or 3 pieces at a time in a plastic bag containing a mixture of

1 cup all-purpose flour

2 teaspoons salt

2 teaspoons paprika

1 teaspoon monosodium glutamate

½ teaspoon poultry seasoning

½ teaspoon pepper

Melt in the skillet over medium heat

Fat (or use cooking oil) to at least ½-in. depth

Starting with meaty pieces of chicken, place

Chicken in a Basket and Garden Potato Salad

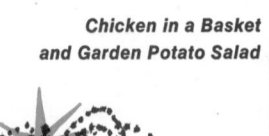

them skin side down in skillet. Put in less meaty pieces as others brown. To brown all sides, turn pieces as necessary with two spoons or tongs. When chicken is evenly browned, reduce heat and add

1 to 2 tablespoons water

Immediately cover skillet. Cook slowly 25 to 40 min., or until thickest pieces of chicken are tender when pierced with a fork. Uncover the last 10 min. to crisp skin.

Place individual servings in baskets lined with paper or cloth napkins. *About 4 servings*

GARDEN POTATO SALAD

▲ *Base Recipe*

Hearty but pretty, with vegetables galore.

Wash, cut into halves and cook covered in boiling salted water to cover

6 medium (about 2 lbs.) potatoes

Cook about 20 min., or until potatoes are tender when pierced with a fork. Drain potatoes. To dry potatoes, shake pan over low heat. Peel potatoes, cut into cubes and put into a deep bowl.

Meanwhile, prepare

2 Hard-Cooked Eggs (page 133)

Slice into bowl with potatoes.

Toss potatoes and eggs lightly with

1 cup chopped celery
½ cup (1 medium) chopped onion
¼ cup chopped green pepper

and a mixture of

1½ teaspoons salt
¼ teaspoon monosodium glutamate
⅛ teaspoon pepper

Add and blend until vegetables are well coated

¼ cup French Dressing (page 410)

Place in refrigerator and chill at least 1 hr.

Gently mix in about

¾ cup Mayonnaise (page 412)

Sprinkle top with **paprika,** finely chopped **parsley** or slice more hard-cooked egg over salad.
4 to 6 servings

—SPECIAL TREAT POTATO SALAD

Follow ▲ Recipe. Omit hard-cooked eggs. Toss in with the vegetables **4 slices Panfried Bacon** (page 190), crumbled, **2 tablespoons drained chopped pimiento** and **8 green or ripe olives,** pitted and sliced.

—KIDNEY BEAN SALAD

Follow ▲ Recipe. Omit potatoes. Toss in with eggs and vegetables **2 cups well-drained canned kidney beans** and **¼ cup chopped sweet pickle.**

—ROSY RING POTATO SALAD

Follow ▲ Recipe. Add with vegetables **6 to 10 cleaned radishes,** thinly sliced, and garnish top of each serving with more radish slices.

JULY FOURTH JELLY ROLLS

Prepare

Jelly Roll (page 458)

As soon as cake is turned onto towel, with longer side nearest you, roll cake (see Lincoln Log recipe, page 664).

When cake is cool, unroll and spread with

Red jelly or jam (cherry, strawberry, raspberry or currant)

Cut cake into thirds lengthwise. Again, with longer side nearest you, roll each section; fasten with wooden picks. Cut each rolled section into thirds. To make firecrackers, insert a **maraschino cherry strip** in the end of each roll for the fuse. *9 rolls*

Note: For Fourth of July Drum Cake, see Cherry Chocolate Cake recipe on page 665.

HALLOWEEN

Halloween "trick-or-treaters" in our country have their counterparts in Britain where All-Hallows Eve is the occasion for English folk to celebrate with cider and sweets. In the 19th century, with the influx of Irish settlers to the United States, came the magic Halloween symbols of black cats, witches, pumpkin heads and pranks, all of which have become a part of our Halloween observance.

HALLOWEEN GARNISHES

Each garnish carries out the holiday theme.

CELERY BROOMS

Cut **celery stalks** into 4-in. lengths. Taper narrow end for broom handle. Cut other end into many fine strips, 1 in. long, for brush part. Chill in ice and water.

DOUGHNUT BALLS

Roll "holes" of **Doughnuts** (page 97) in orange **Colored Sugar** (page 582).

CHEESE PUMPKINS

Shred **sharp Cheddar cheese** and mold into small pumpkin-shape balls. With fork or blunt end of wooden skewer, mark grooves on sides of "pumpkin." Insert strip of **green pepper** into top for stem.

BLACK CATS

Soften **chocolate wafer candies** by placing them on top of hot **cupcakes** (just removed from oven). Wafer forms body of cat. With wooden pick, draw tail, head, ears and whiskers, using melted chocolate from body.

WITCHES' HATS

Small **licorice gumdrops** placed on slices of larger licorice gumdrops make witches' hats for cake decoration.

GOBLIN FRANKS

Your "spooks" will gobble up these franks.

Set out a baking sheet.

Cream thoroughly

¼ cup butter or margarine
1 tablespoon prepared mustard
1 teaspoon prepared horseradish

Prepare

Baking Powder Biscuits (one-half recipe, page 92)

Roll dough ¼ in. thick and spread with creamed mixture. Cut into 8 strips, 1 in. wide. Wrap dough strips around length of

8 frankfurters

Pinch ends of dough to seal. Place on baking sheet. Brush with

Milk

Bake at 425°F about 12 min., or until biscuit rolls are golden brown. *8 servings*

PUMPKIN CUPCAKES

Line with paper baking cups or grease bottoms of eighteen 2½-in. muffin-pan wells.

Sift together and set aside

2½ cups sifted cake flour
1 tablespoon baking powder
½ teaspoon salt
½ teaspoon cinnamon
¼ teaspoon nutmeg
¼ teaspoon ginger

Halloween Popcorn Balls

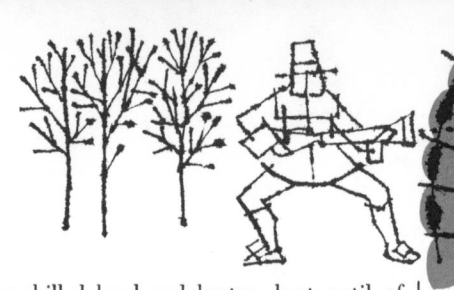

Beat until shortening is softened

½ cup shortening

Add gradually, creaming until fluffy after each addition

¾ cup sugar
¾ cup firmly packed brown sugar

Add in thirds, beating thoroughly after each addition

2 eggs, well beaten

Blend in

¾ cup canned pumpkin

Measure

½ cup milk

Alternately add dry ingredients in fourths, milk in thirds, to creamed mixture. After each addition, beat only until smooth; do not over-beat. Fill paper baking cups or muffin-pan wells one-half full.

Bake at 350°F 15 to 20 min., or until cakes test done (page 11). Cool and remove from muffin wells.

Meanwhile, prepare

Burnt-Sugar Frosting (page 478)

When cupcakes are cooled, frost.

1½ doz. cupcakes

PUMPKIN ICE CREAM

Set bowl and rotary beater in refrigerator to chill.

Melt over simmering water

10 marshmallows, cut (page 9)
1 tablespoon boiling water

Meanwhile, combine in bowl

1 cup canned pumpkin (about one-half 16-oz. can)
⅓ cup firmly packed brown sugar
2 egg yolks, slightly beaten
2 tablespoons orange juice

and a mixture of

1 teaspoon cinnamon
½ teaspoon ginger
½ teaspoon nutmeg
½ teaspoon salt

Blend thoroughly with marshmallows. Cook over simmering water, stirring constantly, about 10 min. Pour into a bowl and set in refrigerator to chill.

Using chilled bowl and beater, beat until of medium consistency (piles softly)

1 cup chilled whipping cream

Fold whipped cream into chilled pumpkin mixture. Pour into 1-qt. refrigerator tray. Freeze until firm. *6 servings*

HALLOWEEN POPCORN BALLS

If using an electric popper, follow manufacturer's directions. Otherwise, for each pan of corn, heat in heavy skillet or saucepan with a tight-fitting cover

1 tablespoon fat or oil

Add enough popcorn to just cover bottom of skillet, and cover tightly. Shake pan over medium heat until popping stops. Turn corn into large warm bowl. In the same way, prepare

10 cups popped corn

Sprinkle over popped corn and mix in

1 teaspoon salt

Set aside.

Combine in a saucepan

1¼ cups light corn syrup
¾ cup light molasses
1 tablespoon vinegar

Boil rapidly to 250°F (hard ball stage, page 11, remove from heat while testing). Remove from heat and stir in

3 tablespoons butter or margarine

Gradually pour hot syrup into center of the corn. With a long-handled fork, quickly stir and coat corn with syrup. With buttered hands, gather and press corn into firm balls.
10 large or 20 small popcorn balls

HOT SPICED CIDER

▲ Base Recipe

Combine in a large saucepan

2 qts. apple cider
¼ cup sugar
12 whole cloves
6 whole allspice
2 3-in. sticks cinnamon

Cover and heat slowly to boiling. Boil 3 to 5 min. Set aside about 30 min. and remove spices.

Serve hot garnished with **orange slices** or rings of unpared **red apple** with whole **cloves** forced through peel. *16 servings*

—TANGY CIDER PUNCH

Omit spices and heating process in ▲ Recipe. Combine chilled cider and sugar with **1 cup orange juice, ½ cup lemon juice** and **1 qt. ginger ale.** Pour over ice cubes or crushed ice in tall glasses. *About 25 servings*

THANKSGIVING

The traditional turkey and pumpkin pie may have their roots in the Thanksgiving Day of the early Pilgrims but the idea of celebrating and rendering homage to the spirits for an abundant harvest is an ancient custom still observed in many lands. For Americans, the holiday is an occasion for a family reunion and enjoyment of a traditional feast.

SPICY CRANBERRY SAUCE

Sort and wash

2 cups (about ½ lb.) cranberries

Combine in a 1-qt. saucepan and stir over low heat until sugar is dissolved

1 cup sugar
1 cup water
1 piece (3 in.) stick cinnamon
⅛ teaspoon salt

Bring to boiling; boil uncovered for 5 min. Add the cranberries. Continue to boil uncovered without stirring, about 5 min., or until skins pop. Cool and remove stick cinnamon.

Serve with meat or poultry.

About 2 cups sauce

INDIVIDUAL PUMPKIN PIES

▲ Base Recipe

Set out eight 4-in. individual pie pans.

Prepare, but do not bake

8 little pie shells (use double recipe, page 485)

Set aside in refrigerator to chill thoroughly.

Meanwhile, combine

2 cups (16-oz. can) canned pumpkin
⅔ cup firmly packed light brown sugar

Individual Pumpkin Pies

Add a mixture of
1 teaspoon mace
¾ teaspoon ginger
¾ teaspoon nutmeg
½ teaspoon cinnamon
½ teaspoon salt
Combine and add to pumpkin mixture, mixing well until smooth
2 eggs, slightly beaten
1 cup cream
1 cup milk
Remove shells from refrigerator. Pour ½ cup filling into each shell. Sprinkle tops with
Nutmeg
Bake at 450°F 10 min. Reduce heat to 350°F and bake 20 min. longer, or until metal knife comes out clean when inserted halfway between center and edge. Remove pies from oven and cool on cooling rack.

Using cookie cutter or waxed-paper pattern and knife, cut turkeys from thin slices of
Cheddar cheese
Place one on top of each individual pie.
8 individual 4-in. pies

—PUMPKIN PIE

Follow ▲ Recipe. Prepare **Pastry for 1-Crust 9-in. Pie** (page 485). Bake 10 min. at 450°F. Substitute **dark brown sugar** for light brown sugar. Omit mace. Increase cinnamon to 1 teaspoon, decrease ginger and nutmeg to ½ teaspoon each and add ⅛ **teaspoon ground cloves.** Omit milk and the nutmeg sprinkled on top. Bake at 350°F 50 to 60 min., or until pie tests done. Omit the cheese cutouts. Serve the pie topped with **Sweetened Whipped Cream** (page 480).

CRANBERRY ICE

Cook in a large saucepan, stirring occasionally, until skins pop
1 lb. (4 cups) cranberries, washed and
    sorted
2 cups water

Pour into a small cup or custard cup
½ cup water
Sprinkle evenly over water
1 env. unflavored gelatin
Let stand until softened.

Force cranberries through sieve or food mill to make a smooth pulp. Immediately stir softened gelatin into hot mixture. Stir constantly until gelatin is completely dissolved. Add and stir until sugar is dissolved
2 cups sugar
Blend in
1¼ cups water
½ cup orange juice
2 teaspoons grated lemon peel
¼ cup lemon juice
Pour into refrigerator tray. Freeze until firm (2 to 3 hrs.), stirring 2 or 3 times.

Serve in chilled sherbet cups.
1 qt. Cranberry Ice

CHRISTMAS

Yuletide is the grand finale of the year. Weeks before are devoted to preparation for the warmest and merriest of holidays. Many other things are afloat, too—aromas that beckon us to the kitchen, mysterious rustles of wrapping behind closed doors, a child's squeal of delight, pleasing harmonies of carolers. We all are heirs to this precious legacy—Christmas.

FRUIT WREATH

With a sharp knife, remove peel and white membrane from
1 grapefruit
Remove sections by cutting on etiher side of dividing membranes; remove section by section, over bowl, to save the juice.

Wash, peel and cut into wedges
1 ripe avocado
Place wedges in bowl with grapefruit so that grapefruit juice covers avocado wedges (this prevents darkening). Place in refrigerator.

Rinse, remove bruised spots on leaves and place in refrigerator to chill
Curly endive
Rinse, make an incision with a sharp knife and peel and remove seeds from
1 pomegranate
Just before serving, make beds of endive on individual salad plates. Overlap avocado wedges and grapefruit sections alternately in a circle to form a wreath on each bed of endive. Sprinkle salads with pomegranate seeds.

Serve with a **fruit salad dressing.**
4 servings

POMEGRANATE STAR MOLD

The pomegranate, a pink or bright red fruit, is really an outsized berry, full of juicy crimson seeds. The juice may be extracted, as in this recipe; or the seeds may be sprinkled over salads and desserts as a garnish. Chunks of pomegranate with their many crimson seeds are a colorful addition to any fruit plate or tray.

Set out a 1½-qt. star-shaped mold.

Cut into halves and remove seeds and juice from
5 pomegranates
Put seeds and juice into a saucepan with
1¾ cups water
2 ¼-in. slices lemon
Bring to boiling, cover and simmer for 15 min., or until the color and flavor of seeds have been absorbed by the water.

Meanwhile, pour into a small bowl
1 cup cold water

Sprinkle evenly over water
3 env. unflavored gelatin
Let stand until softened.

Turn hot mixture into a sieve or food mill set over a saucepan. Discard lemon slices; force pomegranate mixture through the sieve or food mill until all juice has been extracted. Discard the pomegranate seeds.

Reheat the pomegranate juice until very hot. Remove from heat and immediately stir in softened gelatin until gelatin is completely dissolved. Stir in until dissolved
¾ cup sugar
Blend in
2 tablespoons grenadine
½ teaspoon red food coloring
Pour into the mold. Cool; chill in refrigerator until firm.

Unmold (page 374) onto a chilled serving plate. Garnish with **curly endive.**   *8 servings*

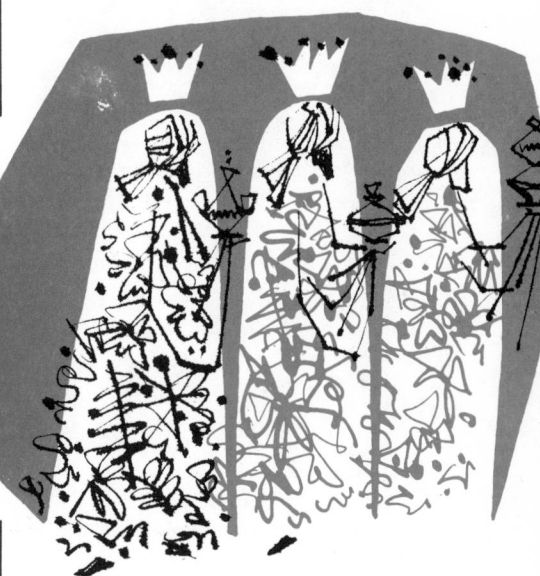

PERSIMMON MOLD

Persimmons are a delicate specialty to tantalize and delight your guests. Persimmons ripen best in a cool, dark place and are ready to eat when soft. Serve well chilled. The persimmon is easily adapted to many variations—in combination with other foods as well as alone.

Set out a 3-cup ring mold.

Empty into a bowl the contents of
1 pkg. (3 oz.) orange-flavored gelatin
Add, stirring until the gelatin is completely dissolved
1 cup very hot water
Blend in
½ cup grapefruit juice
Chill in refrigerator or pan of ice and water until gelatin is slightly thicker than consistency of thick unbeaten egg white. If mixture is placed over ice and water, stir frequently; if placed in refrigerator, stir occasionally.

Wash, remove peel and force through a sieve
1 or 2 ripe persimmons (about 1 cup pulp)
When gelatin is chilled, blend in persimmon pulp and
1½ tablespoons lemon juice
Pour into ring mold. Chill in refrigerator until firm.

Unmold (page 374). Fill center of ring with cut **fruit.** Garnish with **watercress.** *4 to 6 servings*

NORWEGIAN CHRISTMAS BREAD
(Julekake)

In the round of visiting that goes with the Christmas holidays, guests are served this traditional bread and coffee. The use of cardamom is typically Scandinavian.

A 9-in. round layer cake pan will be needed.

Rinse, cut into halves, remove any seeds and force through the medium blade of a food chopper
½ small orange
Set aside.

Bring to boiling
1 cup water
Add, and again bring to boiling
¾ cup (about 4 oz.) golden raisins
Pour off water and drain raisins on absorbent paper. Set aside.

Scald (page 10)
1 cup milk

Meanwhile, soften
1 pkg. active dry yeast
in
¼ cup warm water, 110°F to 115°F (Or if using compressed yeast, soften 1 cake in ¼ cup lukewarm water, 80°F to 85°F.)
Set aside.

Meanwhile, put into a large bowl
½ cup butter
½ cup sugar
1 teaspoon salt
Immediately pour scalded milk over ingredients in bowl. When lukewarm, blend in, beating until smooth, a mixture of
1 cup sifted all-purpose flour
1 teaspoon cardamom
Stir softened yeast and add, mixing well.

Measure
3 to 3½ cups sifted all-purpose flour

Add about one-half the flour to the yeast mixture and beat until very smooth.

Then beat in the ground orange, raisins, and enough remaining flour to make a soft dough. Turn dough onto a lightly floured surface and let rest 5 to 10 min.

Knead dough (page 10).

Form dough into a large ball and place it into a greased deep bowl. Turn dough to bring greased surface to top. Cover with waxed paper and towel and let stand in warm place (about 80°F) until dough is doubled.

Punch down with fist; pull edges of dough in to center and turn dough completely over in bowl. Cover and let rise again until nearly doubled. Punch down and turn dough out onto lightly floured surface.

Lightly grease the layer cake pan.

Shape the dough into a round ball, place in the greased pan and flatten slightly. Cover and let rise about 45 min., or until doubled.

Bake at 350°F 45 min. Remove from oven and brush with
Egg white, slightly beaten
Return to oven and bake 10 to 15 min. longer.

Remove bread from pan and place on cooling rack to cool completely.   *1 loaf bread*

WASSAIL BOWL

Wassail, traditionally a drink for the holiday season, is served hot. Our recipe is made with cider; however, ale, sherry or Madeira may be substituted.

For Baked Apples—Butter two baking dishes and insides of covers.

Wash and core
12 small, firm baking apples (such as Jonathans)
Core by inserting corer in stem end; cut toward blossom end, pushing halfway into apple. Remove corer and insert in opposite end. Make a complete turn with corer in both ends. Remove all the core. Pare about 1-in. strip of peel at the stem end of each apple.

Arrange apples in baking dishes, pared sides up. Fill each with 2 to 3 teaspoons of a mixture of
¾ cup firmly packed brown sugar
¾ teaspoon nutmeg
¾ teaspoon cinnamon
and top each with one-half teaspoon of
2 tablespoons butter or margarine
Combine in a saucepan and bring to boiling
1 cup sugar
1 cup water
Pour over apples in baking dish.

Cover and bake at 350°F 30 to 40 min., or until tender when pierced with a fork. Baste every 5 min. for first 15 min., and then every 15 min.

For Wassail—Stir together in saucepan
2 cups water
1 tablespoon ginger
1 tablespoon nutmeg
6 whole cloves
6 whole allspice
2 sticks (2 in. each) cinnamon
Cover and bring to boiling; boil for 10 min.

Combine in a 6-qt. saucepot
1 gal. apple cider
3 cups sugar
1½ cups firmly packed brown sugar
Simmer over low heat, stirring frequently. Stir in water-spice mixture and continue cooking 5 to 10 min.

Meanwhile, beat until very thick and lemon-colored
12 egg yolks
Beat until rounded peaks are formed
12 egg whites
Slide beaten egg whites into punch bowl. Pour beaten egg yolks over egg whites. Fold together. Add the hot mixture very slowly, stirring constantly. Stir in
1 cup brandy
Float Baked Apples in hot beverage. Serve hot.
About 50 servings

Note: For a Hot Cider Punch, omit Baked Apples, egg yolks and egg whites.

CHRISTMAS CINNAMON STARS

Lightly grease two cookie sheets.

Grate and set aside
2 cups (about ⅔ lb.) unblanched almonds (about 3½ cups, grated)

Beat until stiff, not dry, peaks are formed
3 egg whites
Add gradually, beating constantly
1 cup confectioners' sugar
Continue beating for 5 min. with an electric beater on medium speed. Blend in
1 teaspoon grated lemon peel
¾ teaspoon cinnamon
Set aside ½ cup of meringue for icing.

Fold almonds into remaining meringue mixture. Gently pat or roll out ⅜ in. thick on pastry canvas sprinkled with **granulated sugar.** Lightly sprinkle the top of the dough with more sugar. Cut out stars with a 2- to 2½-in. star-shape cookie cutter dipped in confectioners' sugar. Carefully place stars on cookie sheets. Drop ½ teaspoon of the reserved meringue onto each cookie, drawing meringue out onto each point of the star.

Bake at 325°F 15 to 18 min. Immediately remove cookies from sheets to cooling racks.
About 3 doz. cookies

SUGAR COOKIES

▲ Base Recipe

Lightly grease cookie sheets.

Sift together and set aside
2 cups sifted all-purpose flour
½ teaspoon baking powder
¼ teaspoon salt
¼ teaspoon nutmeg

Cream until shortening is softened
⅔ cup butter or margarine
1½ teaspoons vanilla extract

Add gradually, creaming until fluffy after each addition
1 cup sugar

Add in thirds, beating thoroughly after each addition
2 eggs, well beaten

Stir in dry ingredients in fourths. Blend well. Chill dough thoroughly in refrigerator (1 hr.).

Remove amount of dough needed for a single rolling and return remainder to refrigerator immediately. Roll dough ⅛ in. thick on lightly floured surface. Cut with floured cookie cutter. Sprinkle with sugar.

Bake at 375°F about 10 min. Remove immediately to cooling racks to cool.
About 3 doz. cookies

—SOUR CREAM SUGAR COOKIES

Follow ▲ Recipe. Add ¼ teaspoon baking soda to dry ingredients. Omit nutmeg and 1 egg. Stir in dry ingredients alternately with ⅓ cup dairy sour cream.

Frosted Christmas Trees and Valentine Cookies

—LEMON SUGAR COOKIES

Follow ▲ Recipe. Substitute **1 teaspoon lemon extract** for vanilla extract and add **1 teaspoon grated lemon peel.**

—MAPLE SUGAR COOKIES

Follow ▲ Recipe. Substitute **½ cup firmly packed maple sugar** for one half of the granulated sugar. Decrease vanilla extract to ½ teaspoon.

—CARAWAY COOKIES

Follow ▲ Recipe. Add **2 teaspoons caraway seed** with dry ingredients.

—STANDING TURKEY OR TREE COOKIES

Follow ▲ Recipe. Divide the dough into halves. Cut one rolled portion with turkey- or tree-shaped cookie cutter or cut around waxed-paper pattern with knife. Roll and cut remaining portion of dough with a 2-in. round scalloped cutter. Before baking, make an indentation with spoon (as large as base of turkey or tree cookie) in the center of each scalloped cookie. Bake and cool cookies. Fill indentation with **White Velvet Frosting** (page 477) and stand cookies upright in frosting.

—FROSTED CHRISTMAS TREES

Follow ▲ Recipe. Cut rolled dough with tree-shape cookie cutter or use waxed-paper pattern. Bake and cool cookies. Spread each tree with **Lemon Cream Cheese Frosting** (page 479). Sprinkle **red and green candies** or **sugar** around edge of cookie and tiny **silver dragées** in center.

—VALENTINE COOKIES

Follow ▲ Recipe. Cut heart-shape cookies of three varying sizes. Use heart-shape cookie cutter or cut around heart-shape waxed-paper pattern with a sharp knife. While cookies are baking, prepare **White Velvet Frosting** (page 477). Place one half of frosting in a bowl and tint pink with one or two drops of **red food coloring.** Leave remainder of frosting white. Thinly spread white frosting on bottoms of medium- and small-size cookie hearts. Place on top of large cookies, forming stacks of 2 or 3 cookies, with smallest heart on top. Force tinted frosting through a pastry bag and a No. 2 or 3 decorating tube, forming a loop design around edge of cookies. Force remaining white frosting through pastry bag and No. 14 star tube around base of each stacked cookie.

—HOLIDAY SUGAR COOKIES

Follow ▲ Recipe. Cut rolled dough with star, hatchet, tree, heart or other shape cookie cutter, depending upon holiday, or cut with knife around waxed-paper patterns in decorative shapes. Decorate with **White Velvet Frosting** (page 477) tinted or white, **silver dragées, red or green candies** or **sugar**. For Christmas tree ornaments, make a small hole in top end of each cookie before baking. To hang on tree, run colored yarn or string through hole.

—PLACE CARDS

Follow ▲ Recipe. Cut rolled dough into 3x2-in. rectangles. Bake and cool cookies. Write names on cookies with **decorating frosting** forced through a pastry bag and a No. 2 or 3 decorating tube, and decorate edges. For a base, slit a **marshmallow** or large **gumdrop** halfway down the center so that cookie place card will stand in it.

673

Chafing dish cookery

Back in the glittering 90's, the chafing dish was in high favor as the promoter of many epicurean feasts served in the smart homes and gay restaurants of that period. Then it went into temporary eclipse and only within the last few years has it returned to public favor, this time as a thoroughly utilitarian, as well as attractive piece of household equipment. It is quick and easy to use, versatile, portable, and above all, it glorifies both the cook and the food. The chafing dish remains a symbol of good living, good food and good conversation.

The modern chafing dish consists of three parts—two pans and a frame supporting them over a heat source which may be an electrical unit, an alcohol lamp, or canned heat. The upper pan, or blazer, of the chafing dish may be used alone, as a skillet, directly over the heating unit; the lower pan, which holds simmering water, fits under the blazer to convert it into a double boiler. Chafing dishes are available in various sizes; in the most usual size, the blazer holds about two quarts. (Somewhat similar in appearance to the chafing dish is the warmer which uses a candle as the source of heat. The heat is not sufficient to do any actual cooking, but it does keep hot food warm during serving.)

The chafing dish may be used in several ways, all of them well adapted to making your meal service easier. First, some dishes may be cooked completely in the chafing dish right at the table, before your guests' admiring eyes, and served from it perfectly hot and fresh. Second, part of the cooking may be done in the kitchen and the food transferred to the chafing dish to finish cooking in the dining room at the table or on a buffet. Third, all the cooking may be done in the kitchen ahead of time, in double boiler or skillet, and the mixture reheated in and served from the chafing dish. So however it is used, one can see that it gives the hostess more time to be with her guests.

HOT SPICY MEAT BALLS

The tiny meat balls are an unusually pleasing, hearty appetizer; but the hot sauce alone makes a wonderful dip with the same zestful tang for other appetizer foods too—for example, cocktail franks, Vienna sausage, frankfurters cut into inch-long pieces, and cooked shrimp.

Set out a chafing dish.

For Sauce—Mix in a bowl
   ¾ cup ketchup
   ½ cup water
   ¼ cup cider vinegar
   2 tablespoons brown sugar
   1 tablespoon minced onion
   2 teaspoons Worcestershire sauce
   1½ teaspoons salt
   1 teaspoon dry mustard
   ¼ teaspoon pepper
   3 drops Tabasco
   Few grains cayenne pepper

For Meat Balls—Mix lightly in a bowl with a fork
   ¾ lb. ground beef
   ¾ cup fine dry bread crumbs
   1½ tablespoons finely chopped onion
   ½ teaspoon prepared horseradish
   3 drops Tabasco
   2 eggs, beaten

Add a mixture of
   ¾ teaspoon salt
   ½ teaspoon pepper
Shape mixture into balls ¾ in. in diameter.

To Complete—Melt in the chafing dish blazer
   1 tablespoon butter or margarine
Add the meat balls and brown over direct heat, shaking blazer frequently to produce even browning and keep balls round.

When meat balls are browned, pour off any fat remaining in blazer and pour the sauce over the meat balls. Cover and continue to cook about 10 min., shaking blazer occasionally.

Place over pan of simmering water to keep hot.

Provide wooden picks or fancy cocktail picks to spear the meat balls.

About 3 doz. meat balls

SWISS CHEESE FONDUE

Traditions cluster around a fondue. It is a dish for intimate entertaining of a few friends who can eat literally from the same pot—not for a large group. A perfect fondue should never come in contact with metal. It should be prepared in earthenware over a little cheerful flame to keep the fondue barely bubbling. When the time comes to eat the fondue, all the guests must dunk; and this should be done with cubes of French bread or hard French rolls, cut so that each cube has crust on at least one side. Spear the bread cubes from the soft side, but be sure the fork penetrates the sturdy crust securely, because each dunker must stir the mixture with it as he dips. (Special long-tined fondue forks make the process easier, and are a valuable addition to your silver chest if fondue is a favorite in your home.) Gentle stirring at each dip helps to keep the mixture well blended, and accumulates more on the bread cube at the same time. Lift it out with a twirling motion and eat—quickly! As the feast progresses, some of the cheese will form a brown crust on the bottom of the pan. This is a special delicacy and should be divided among the company when the fondue has been consumed.

Set out a chafing dish.

Cut into bite-size pieces having at least one crusty side and set aside
   1 loaf (1-lb.) French or Italian bread

Shred

1 lb. natural Swiss cheese (about 4 cups, shredded)

Mix in a small bowl and set aside

5 teaspoons cornstarch
2 tablespoons kirsch

Rub the blazer with cut surfaces of

1 clove garlic, cut into halves

Put into the blazer the shredded cheese and a mixture of

¼ teaspoon salt
¼ teaspoon monosodium glutamate
⅛ teaspoon pepper

Pour over the cheese

2 cups Neuchâtel or sauterne

Stirring constantly, cook over direct heat until cheese is melted. Blend in the cornstarch mixture. Continue stirring while cooking 2 to 3 min., or until fondue begins to bubble.

Keep fondue gently bubbling throughout serving time. Serve at the table. Spear bread cubes with a fork; dunk and twirl them in the fondue.

6 to 8 servings

Note: A sprinkling of paprika was added to the fondue in the photo for color contrast.

HOT CURRY DIP

This is the sort of specialty that can make your reputation as a Sunday night hostess—a wonderful hot curry sauce for dipping crisp raw vegetables such as cauliflowerets, carrot sticks, celery and cucumber strips. Try it as a dip for cooked shrimp on a pick, too! If you prefer, this sauce may be cooked ahead of time, and simply reheated in and served from the chafing dish.

Set out a chafing dish.

Heat in the chafing dish blazer over direct heat

¼ cup butter or margarine

Add and cook until onion is tender, stirring occasionally

¼ cup finely chopped onion

Blend in and heat until mixture bubbles

2 tablespoons all-purpose flour

Add and stir to mix well

3 tablespoons chopped crystallized ginger
2 tablespoons curry powder
2 teaspoons salt
1 teaspoon sugar
¼ teaspoon crushed dried mint leaves
4 whole cloves
Few grains cayenne pepper

Remove from heat. Add gradually, stirring in

2 cups milk

Cook rapidly, stirring constantly, until sauce thickens. Place over pan of simmering water. Cook, covered, 30 min., stirring occasionally.

Add and stir in

½ cup (2 oz.) moist flaked or shredded coconut

Cover and cook 10 min. longer.

Add gradually, stirring constantly

½ cup lime juice

Add gradually, stirring constantly

½ cup heavy cream

Continue cooking until sauce is thoroughly heated. *About 3½ cups sauce*

WELSH RABBIT I

▲ *Base Recipe*

If your ideal Welsh rabbit has a special, sharp, piquant flavor, it is natural Cheddar cheese you will want to use, and you must serve the rabbit quite promptly, or else stir it frequently to keep it smooth as velvet. But if you want unfailing smoothness that requires little of your attention while you keep it warm, use a process Cheddar.

Set out a chafing dish.

Have ready

⅔ cup lukewarm beer (measured without foam)

Shred and set aside

1 lb. sharp Cheddar cheese (about 4 cups, shredded)

Melt in chafing dish blazer over the pan of simmering water

1 tablespoon butter

Add cheese all at one time and stir occasionally until it begins to melt. Blend in

½ teaspoon Worcestershire sauce
½ teaspoon dry mustard
Few grains cayenne pepper

As soon as cheese begins to melt, add very gradually, stirring constantly, ½ to ⅔ cup of the beer.

As soon as beer is blended in and mixture is smooth, serve immediately over crisp **toast**.

6 servings

—WELSH RABBIT II

Follow ▲ Recipe. Substitute **milk** for the beer.

—WELSH RABBIT III

Follow ▲ Recipe. Substitute **process Cheddar cheese food** or **process sharp Cheddar cheese** for sharp Cheddar cheese, and **milk** for beer.

—GLORIFIED WELSH RABBIT

Follow ▲ Recipe or either variation. Top each serving with a slice of **tomato**, two slices of **crisp fried bacon**, and a sprig of **parsley**.

Swiss Cheese Fondue

CHEESE TOMATO SUPPER DISH

You may recognize this recipe as the one that parades under such names as Rinktum Ditty, Rum Tum Tiddy or even Rinktumdetty. We've added some hard-cooked eggs and mushrooms for flavor and called it "supper dish" because it is such a perfect choice for a Sunday night supper. Serve it for special occasions or for no particular occasion. Serve it often and call it what you like.

Prepare

6 Hard-Cooked Eggs (page 133)

Peel, cut into quarters lengthwise and set aside.

Meanwhile, shred and set aside

¾ lb. sharp Cheddar cheese (about 3 cups, shredded)

Heat in a chafing pan or in top of double boiler over direct heat

⅔ cup butter or margarine

Add and cook over medium heat, occasionally moving and turning with a spoon, until mushrooms are tender

¼ cup minced onion
1 cup mushrooms, cleaned and sliced (page 9)

With slotted spoon, remove mushrooms to a small bowl. Set aside.

Blend in a mixture of

2 tablespoons all-purpose flour
½ teaspoon dry mustard
¼ teaspoon salt
Few grains cayenne pepper

Heat until mixture bubbles. Remove from heat.

Cheese Tomato Supper Dish

Add gradually, stirring in
>**½ cup milk**
>**½ teaspoon Worcestershire sauce**
>**1 can (10¾ oz.) condensed tomato soup**

Place chafing pan or top of double boiler over simmering water. Add the shredded cheese all at one time. Stir constantly until cheese is melted. Blend in the hard-cooked egg quarters and the vegetables. Garnish with minced **parsley**.

Serve with **toast fingers** or **bread sticks**.

About 8 servings

CREAMED HAM IN POTATO CUPS

Set out a skillet and a chafing dish.

Prepare and keep warm
>**Crispy Potato Cups (page 345)**

Dice and set aside enough cooked ham to yield
>**1½ cups diced cooked ham**

Wipe with a clean damp cloth
>**½ lb. mushrooms**

Remove stems from caps of 8 mushrooms and set the caps aside. Chop the stems and slice the remaining whole mushrooms lengthwise through stems and caps.

Heat in the skillet over low heat
>**3 tablespoons butter or margarine**

Add the mushroom caps to the skillet and cook over medium heat, occasionally moving and turning them with a spoon, until lightly browned and tender. Using a slotted spoon, remove mushroom caps and set aside to keep warm. Add and cook the chopped and sliced mushrooms. Remove from heat and set aside to keep warm.

Heat in the chafing dish blazer over direct heat
>**¼ cup butter or margarine**

Blend in
>**¼ cup sifted all-purpose flour**
>**½ teaspoon salt**
>**½ teaspoon dry mustard**
>**¼ teaspoon celery salt**
>**¼ teaspoon monosodium glutamate**
>**Few grains pepper**

Heat until mixture bubbles. Remove from heat. Add gradually, stirring constantly
>**2 cups milk**

Bring to boiling, stirring constantly; cook 1 to 2 min. longer. Place over the pan of simmer-

ing water. Mix in the ham, mushrooms and
>**1 tablespoon grated onion**
>**1 teaspoon lemon juice**
>**½ teaspoon Worcestershire sauce**

Heat, stirring occasionally, until ham and mushrooms are thoroughly heated. Keep hot over the pan of simmering water.

To serve, spoon creamed ham into the potato cups. Top each cup with one of the mushroom caps. Serve immediately. *8 servings*

CREAMED SWEETBREADS

Set out a large saucepan, a skillet and a chafing dish.

As soon as possible after purchase, rinse with cold water
>**1 lb. sweetbreads**

Put sweetbreads into the saucepan with
>**1 qt. water**
>**2 teaspoons lemon juice**
>**1 teaspoon salt**

Cover and simmer 20 min. Drain and cover with cold water, changing water repeatedly until sweetbreads are cool. Drain. Remove tubes and membranes. Cut sweetbreads into pieces and set aside. (If not to be used immediately, cover cooled sweetbreads and store in refrigerator.)

While sweetbreads are cooking, cut into pieces and set aside enough cooked chicken to yield
>**1 cup cooked chicken pieces**

Cook
>**1 pkg. (9 oz.) frozen green beans**

When beans are just tender, drain if necessary and set aside.

Prepare
>**1 cup quick chicken broth (page 10)**

Set aside.

Clean and slice (page 9)
>**½ lb. mushrooms**

Heat in the skillet over low heat
>**¼ cup butter or margarine**

Add mushrooms and cook over medium heat until delicately browned, occasionally moving and turning with a spoon. Set aside.

Heat in the saucepan over low heat
>**⅓ cup butter or margarine**

Add and cook over medium heat until onion is tender
>**1 tablespoon chopped onion**

Blend in
>**½ cup sifted all-purpose flour**
>**1½ teaspoons monosodium glutamate**
>**¾ teaspoon salt**
>**½ teaspoon savory**
>**½ teaspoon celery salt**
>**Few grains pepper**

Heat until mixture bubbles. Remove from heat. Add gradually, while stirring constantly, the chicken broth and
>**2 cups milk**
>**1 cup cream**

Return to heat and bring rapidly to boiling, stirring constantly; cook 1 to 2 min. longer. Mix in the sweetbreads, chicken, mushrooms and green beans. Reduce heat and stir occasionally until thoroughly heated.

Stir in
>**1 small green pepper, cut in thin strips**
>**2 tablespoons chopped pimiento**

Turn into chafing dish blazer and keep hot over the pan of simmering water.

6 to 8 servings

STUFFED EGGS MORNAY

This recipe and a chafing dish make creamed eggs a glamorous and sophisticated affair.

For Stuffed Eggs—Prepare
>**6 Hard-Cooked Eggs (page 133)**

Cut the peeled, cooled eggs into halves lengthwise. Remove egg yolks to a bowl and set egg whites aside.

Mash egg yolks with a fork. Mix in
>**1 teaspoon lemon juice**
>**½ teaspoon finely chopped onion**

and a mixture of
>**¼ teaspoon salt**
>**⅛ teaspoon pepper**

Set aside.

Drain, remove and discard bony tissue, and separate
>**1 can (6½ oz.) crab meat (about 1⅓ cups)**

Add crab meat to egg yolk mixture and mix with a fork. Blend in, to make a thick, paste-like mixture, about
>**1 tablespoon cream**

Spoon filling into the reserved egg whites, rounding up the tops. Set aside in refrigerator.

For Mornay Sauce—Prepare and set aside
>**¾ cup quick chicken broth (page 10; use 1 chicken bouillon cube and ¾ cup water)**

Heat in chafing dish blazer over direct heat
>**3 tablespoons butter or margarine**

Blend in
>**3 tablespoons all-purpose flour**

Heat until mixture bubbles. Remove from heat and add gradually, stirring constantly, the reserved chicken broth and
>**¾ cup cream**

Return to heat and bring to boiling, stirring constantly; cook 1 to 2 min. longer. Remove

Stuffed Eggs Mornay

from heat and vigorously stir about 3 tablespoons of the hot mixture into

2 egg yolks, slightly beaten

Immediately blend into mixture in blazer and place over simmering water. Cook 3 to 5 min., stirring to keep mixture cooking evenly. Remove from heat.

Add all at one time and stir until thoroughly blended

⅓ cup (about 1½ oz.) grated Parmesan or finely cut Gruyère cheese
1 tablespoon butter or margarine

To Complete—Place blazer over the pan of simmering water. Put Stuffed Eggs into the sauce and spoon some of the sauce over them. Sprinkle with finely chopped **parsley**. Serve over toasted **English muffins**.   *4 servings*

Note: Shrimp, tuna or salmon may be substituted for the crab meat.

CURRIED CHICKEN

▲ Base Recipe

Set out a chafing dish.

Cut into strips and set aside enough cooked chicken to yield

4 cups cooked chicken strips

Coarsely chop and set aside

½ cup (about 3 oz.) toasted unblanched almonds (page 10)

Clean and slice (page 9)

¼ lb. mushrooms

Heat in the chafing dish blazer over direct heat

⅓ cup butter or margarine

Add mushrooms to blazer with

¼ cup finely chopped onion
¼ cup finely chopped celery

Cook until onion is tender and the mushrooms are delicately browned, moving and turning occasionally.

With a slotted spoon, remove vegetables to a small bowl. Blend into butter in skillet

½ cup sifted all-purpose flour
2 teaspoons curry powder
1½ teaspoons monosodium glutamate
1 teaspoon salt

Heat until mixture bubbles, stirring constantly.

Chicken Livers with Pineapple and Almonds

Remove from heat. Add gradually, stirring constantly

2 cups quick chicken broth (page 10)
2 cups cream

Return to heat and bring rapidly to boiling, stirring constantly; cook 1 to 2 min. longer.

Place over the pan of simmering water. Mix chicken and vegetables into sauce. Cook until chicken is thoroughly heated, stirring occasionally. Sprinkle chopped almonds over top.

Serve with curry accompaniments: freshly grated **coconut, golden raisins, Indian chutney** and **broiled bananas.**   *6 to 8 servings*

—CHICKEN A LA KING

Follow ▲ Recipe. Omit curry powder. Add ¼ cup green pepper strips with the mushrooms. Add **2 tablespoons chopped pimiento** with the chicken. Omit curry accompaniments. Serve on split **Baking Powder Biscuits** (page 92), crisp **toast** or **Perfection Boiled Rice** (page 165).

CHICKEN LIVERS WITH PINEAPPLE AND ALMONDS

Here is a fine example of a dish which requires more than one cooking utensil and which may well be prepared ahead of time in the kitchen and attractively served from a chafing dish. A simple warmer with heat provided by a candle is an alternative to a chafing dish used this way.

Set out a medium-size saucepan, a large heavy skillet and a chafing dish or warmer.

Drain, reserving syrup

1 can (20 oz.) pineapple chunks (about 2 cups, drained)

Set aside.

Rinse with cold water, and drain on absorbent paper

2 lbs. chicken livers

(Properly cleaned chicken livers should have no trace of gall, the green substance which might cause a bitter taste.)

Blanch (page 9) and set aside

1 cup (about 5½ oz.) almonds

Mix in the saucepan

¼ cup sugar
¼ cup firmly packed brown sugar
¼ cup cornstarch

Add gradually, while stirring constantly, a mixture of the reserved pineapple syrup and

1½ cups pineapple juice
4 to 6 tablespoons cider vinegar
1 tablespoon soy sauce

Bring rapidly to boiling, stirring constantly. Cook 3 min. longer, stirring occasionally. Set aside and keep hot.

Heat in the skillet over low heat

½ cup butter or margarine

Place livers in skillet; cook about 10 min., or until lightly browned, occasionally moving and turning with a spoon. Add pineapple chunks,

Curried Chicken

almonds and sauce to livers. Cook a few minutes longer, until pineapple is heated, moving mixture gently with a spoon.

Turn mixture into the chafing dish blazer and set over the pan of simmering water to keep warm while serving; or keep warm in the warmer.

Serve over

Perfection Boiled Rice (page 165)

6 to 8 servings

TURKEY ROYAL

▲ Base Recipe

This sumptuous dish glorifies leftover turkey and is, in fact, elegant enough to justify buying and cooking a whole turkey breast just to produce the makin's! Serve it just as is or on toast points, hot biscuits, or fluffy rice. Any way you serve it, it's a regal dish.

Set out a double boiler and a chafing dish.

Cut into bite-size pieces enough cooked turkey to yield

2 cups cooked turkey pieces

Set aside in refrigerator.

Set out

½ cup cooked green peas

Drain, reserving liquid

2 cans (4 oz. each) button mushrooms (about 1¼ cups mushrooms, drained)

Add to mushroom liquid and set aside

Milk (enough to make 1 cup liquid)

Prepare and set aside

¼ cup pimiento strips
1 tablespoon minced parsley
1 tablespoon minced chives
1 tablespoon minced onion

Heat in top of double boiler

¼ cup butter or margarine

Add the minced onion; cook over medium heat, stirring occasionally, until onion is tender. Blend in

6 tablespoons all-purpose flour
1 teaspoon salt
Few grains cayenne pepper
Few grains nutmeg

677

Chicken Royal

Heat until mixture bubbles. Remove from heat and add mushroom liquid and milk gradually, while stirring constantly. Return to heat and cook until mixture thickens, stirring constantly. Cook 1 to 2 min. longer.

Remove from heat and vigorously stir about 3 tablespoons of the hot mixture into

3 egg yolks, slightly beaten

Immediately blend into mixture in double boiler. Cook over simmering water 5 to 10 min., or until thoroughly heated. Stir slowly to keep mixture cooking evenly.

Remove from heat and with a French whip, whisk beater or fork, vigorously stir into hot mixture in very small amounts

2 cups dairy sour cream

Mix in the minced parsley, chives, pimiento strips, peas, mushrooms and turkey pieces.

Cook over simmering water, stirring constantly, 3 to 5 min., or until thoroughly heated.

Turn into chafing dish blazer and keep hot over the pan of simmering water.   *6 servings*

—CHICKEN ROYAL

Follow ▲ Recipe. Substitute **cooked chicken** for the turkey.

OYSTERS A LA NEWBURG

Set out a double boiler and a chafing dish.

Pick over to remove any shell particles and

Shrimp Creole

heat slowly in their own liquor, just until edges curl

1 pt. oysters

Drain and set aside to keep warm.

Blend and set aside

1 teaspoon water
½ teaspoon dry mustard

Heat in top of the double boiler over direct heat

¼ cup butter or margarine

Blend in

2 tablespoons all-purpose flour
1 teaspoon salt
⅛ teaspoon nutmeg
⅛ teaspoon pepper

Heat until mixture bubbles. Remove from heat. Add gradually, stirring constantly

2 cups cream
¼ teaspoon Worcestershire sauce

Blend mustard mixture into sauce. Bring rapidly to boiling over direct heat, stirring constantly; cook 1 to 2 min. longer.

Vigorously stir about 3 tablespoons of the hot mixture into

4 egg yolks, slightly beaten

Immediately blend into mixture in top of double boiler and place over simmering water. Cook 3 to 5 min., stirring slowly to keep mixture cooking evenly. Remove from heat. Blend in

2 tablespoons sherry

Turn into chafing dish blazer and keep warm over the pan of simmering water.

Serve on crisp **toast.**   *6 servings*

SHRIMP CREOLE

Set out a large saucepan, a large heavy skillet and a chafing dish.

Prepare and set aside in refrigerator

1 lb. fresh shrimp with shells (see Cooked Shrimp, page 294)

To Prepare Shrimp Creole—Heat in the skillet
¼ cup butter or margarine

Add and cook over medium heat, stirring occasionally, until vegetables are tender but not soft

½ cup chopped onion
½ cup chopped celery
⅓ cup chopped green pepper

Blend in

3 tablespoons all-purpose flour

Heat until mixture bubbles. Add gradually, stirring constantly

2½ cups canned tomatoes, sieved
1 bay leaf
1 large sprig parsley
1½ teaspoons salt
1 teaspoon sugar
¾ teaspoon Worcestershire sauce
¼ teaspoon freshly ground pepper
2 or 3 drops Tabasco

Cover saucepan and simmer 30 min. Remove bay leaf and parsley. Add shrimp and cook over low heat until heated thoroughly.

To Prepare Rice—Meanwhile, cook following directions on package
1⅓ cups packaged precooked rice

To Serve—Turn Shrimp Creole into chafing dish blazer and keep hot over the pan of simmering water. Turn fluffy rice into a warm bowl and sprinkle with **chopped parsley.** Serve Shrimp Creole over the rice.   *4 or 5 servings*

CHERRIES JUBILEE

Set out a chafing dish or saucepan. Chill desired number of serving dishes in refrigerator.

Set aside to drain thoroughly, reserving syrup

1 can (17 oz.) pitted Bing cherries (about 1½ cups, drained)

Put into the chafing dish over direct heat
Reserved cherry syrup

Stirring occasionally, bring syrup to boiling. Boil about 10 min., or until slightly thicker. Mix in the drained cherries and heat in chafing dish over pan of simmering water (or low heat) until cherries are thoroughly heated. With spoon, gently move cherries in pan occasionally.

When ready to serve, spoon into the chilled serving dishes

1 qt. vanilla ice cream

Heat thoroughly in a small saucepan
⅔ cup brandy

Flame (page 10) and pour over the cherries. Immediately spoon flaming cherries over ice cream and serve while still flaming.

6 to 8 servings

PEACH MELBA

At the close of the 19th century, this famous dessert was created by Escoffier, master of modern French cuisine. The name honored the British operatic soprano, Nellie Melba.

Prepare and chill
Raspberry Sauce (page 580)

Just before dessert is to be prepared, rinse, pare, cut into halves, and pit

3 large (about 1 lb.) firm ripe peaches

To prevent discoloration, brush with
Lemon juice

Mix in chafing dish blazer
1 cup sugar
1 cup water

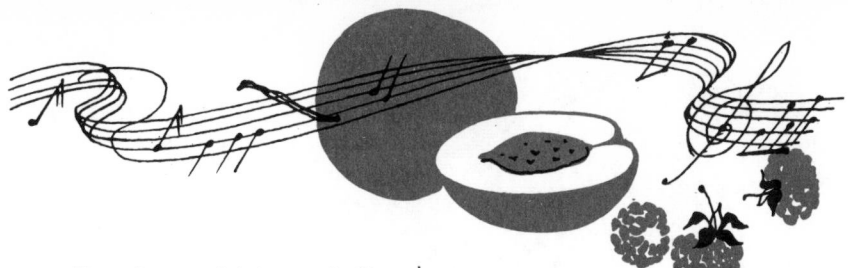

Place over direct heat and bring to boiling, stirring until sugar is dissolved. Cover and boil 5 min.

Stir into hot syrup
1 teaspoon vanilla extract
Add peach halves to syrup and simmer 3 min., or until peaches are heated through.

To serve, spoon into individual serving dishes
1 qt. vanilla ice cream
Arrange warm peaches on ice cream, cut side down. Top with chilled Raspberry Sauce. Serve immediately. *6 servings*

SABAYON SAUCE

▲ Base Recipe

This dramatic and delicious dessert sauce is a French version of the classic Italian dessert, zabaglione. The hot sauce is particularly pleasing over ice cream or cake. Its thickness is regulated by the length of time it is cooked and beaten.

Set out a chafing dish.

In a bowl, beat until thick and lemon-colored
6 egg yolks
½ cup sugar
⅛ teaspoon salt
Add and stir in
1 cup Marsala or white wine
Pour mixture into chafing dish blazer. Set over the pan of simmering water. Beat constantly with rotary beater until mixture is very light and creamy. Add and quickly blend in
1 tablespoon brandy or kirsch
Serve immediately over **angel food or sponge cake**, or **ice cream**. *About 4½ cups sauce*

—ZABAGLIONE

Follow ▲ Recipe. Decrease wine to ⅔ cup and omit brandy or kirsch. Cook, beating constantly, just until mixture foams up and begins to thicken. Immediately spoon into sherbet glasses lined with **ladyfingers**.

CREPES SUZETTE

For Suzette Butter—Cream together until butter is softened
6 tablespoons butter
3 tablespoons orange juice or curaçao
Continue to cream while gradually adding
6 tablespoons confectioners' sugar
Blend thoroughly. If prepared long in advance, cover and store in refrigerator. (Butter should be soft when spread over crêpes.)

For Suzette Sauce—Rub (until flavorful oils are absorbed)
6 cubes of loaf sugar
over
1 lemon peel
1 orange peel
Dissolve sugar in
½ cup orange juice, strained
Set aside.

Cream together
½ cup butter
2 tablespoons confectioners' sugar
Store sweetened orange juice and sweetened butter in refrigerator until ready to use.

For Crêpes—Batter may be prepared hours in advance, stored in a cool place and cooked just before serving. Or crêpes may be cooked in advance and kept warm in a slow oven.

Melt in a 6-in. skillet and set aside
2 tablespoons butter

Sift together into a bowl and set aside
1 cup sifted all-purpose flour
¼ cup sugar
¼ teaspoon salt

Beat together
3 eggs, beaten
1 cup milk
Beat in the melted butter and
1 tablespoon curaçao
1 teaspoon grated orange or lemon peel
Combine egg mixture with dry ingredients and beat with rotary beater until smooth.

Heat skillet moderately hot. Pour in just enough batter to cover bottom. Immediately tilt skillet back and forth to spread batter thinly and evenly. Cook each crêpe over medium heat until light brown on bottom and firm to touch on top.

Loosen edges with spatula. Turn and brown second side. It should be unnecessary to grease skillet for each crêpe.

As each crêpe is cooked, transfer to a hot platter, spread generously with Suzette Butter, and fold in quarters or roll. When all are cooked, set platter in oven to keep warm.

In a chafing dish blazer, over direct heat, melt the butter mixture for Suzette Sauce and blend in the sweetened orange juice. Cook until the liquid is reduced. Add the crêpes, a few at a time, until all have absorbed some of the sauce and are well heated.

Heat thoroughly in a small saucepan
⅓ cup brandy
¼ cup curaçao
2 tablespoons rum or Benedictine

(If preferred, substitute ½ cup curaçao or ½ cup brandy for mixture.) When mixture is hot, ignite it with a match and pour over crêpes. Gently move crêpes in flaming sauce. Serve while sauce is still flaming. Allow 2 crêpes per serving. *16 to 18 crepes*

CAFE BRULOT

Picturesque and dramatic, sophisticated and ceremonious—and most effective in a darkened or softly lighted room.

Prepare and keep hot
3 cups coffee beverage
Mix in chafing dish blazer
1½ cups brandy
2 strips lemon peel (use colored part only; white is bitter)
1 strip orange peel (use colored part only; white is bitter)
8 whole cloves
8 whole allspice
2 pieces (2 in. each) stick cinnamon, broken

Heat thoroughly over direct heat, stirring occasionally.

Meanwhile, set out
8 cubes of loaf sugar
Preheat ladle with boiling water and drain. Remove and discard spices and fruit peel from heated brandy mixture.

Add 7 of the cubes of loaf sugar to the brandy mixture; place remaining cube in ladle. Dip a little of the brandy mixture into the ladle; ignite the liquid with a match. Carefully lower flaming ladle into chafing dish blazer to ignite all the liquid. Stir with the ladle, dipping up and pouring back into the blazer some of the flaming liquid. Continue stirring and ladling until the sugar is dissolved.

While the mixture is still flaming, pour the hot coffee slowly into the chafing dish blazer, against the edge to avoid putting out the flames immediately. Ladle again to blend in coffee. When mixture is no longer flaming, ladle it into demitasse or after-dinner coffee cups. Serve with additional sugar, if desired.
About 16 servings

Crêpes Suzette

Cooking on a grill

Outdoor cookery has become almost a way of life with many American families. Only a few years ago, a cookout meant a simple meal cooked over a small wood fire in the backyard, in the woods, or on the beach. A modern cookout may be far more sophisticated and so is the equipment used to accomplish it. Charcoal or other briquettes have generally supplanted wood for the fuel, and the cooking is done on any of a large variety of grills. Also available are all sorts of other equipment to facilitate the cooking. Outdoor cooking is a man's job and a fine way for him to prove his culinary skills. It is also an enjoyable pastime for people who appreciate good food and all that nature has to offer.

THE EQUIPMENT

You will need a few accessories besides your grill—fuel, a skillet, a long-handled fork and a spoon, an asbestos mitt or heavy pot holder, and metal skewers. Paper napkins or towels—in quantity—are an essential part of outdoor cooking and service, for properly grilled foods are meant to be wonderfully juicy.

THE FIRE

Charcoal lumps or briquettes and hard or fruit woods are the best fuel. Start with a good bed of charcoal, 2 to 3 inches deep. (It should last the entire cooking period.) Sprinkle a charcoal lighter fluid over the fuel and ignite. You'll find plenty to keep you busy while you wait for the coals to burn to a gray color with a ruddy glow underneath. This is your cooking fire which gives a hot, sustained, glowing heat. Allow 30 minutes for your fire to become a bed of coals ready for grilling.

Dampened hickory chips tossed on a charcoal fire just before the meat is placed on the grill create a hickory smoke which gives an added flavor touch.

Another way to start the fire is by beginning the bed with a small amount of paper and kindling. Add a small amount of charcoal and when it is burning, build the entire bed as directed.

Timing of cooking periods will vary with the size of the firebox, degree of heat, amount and direction of wind and type of grill used. Timings and distances given here are only

guides. If dripping fat starts a flare-up, use a baster to douse the flames with sparing applications of water.

GRILLED HAMBURGER FAVORITES

▲ Base Recipe

The all-American favorite enhanced by the wonderful flavor touch from charcoal or hickory chips. Your grill enthusiasts will demand that you double and triple this recipe.

Put into a bowl
  1 lb. ground beef
Mix lightly into the beef a mixture of
  1 teaspoon salt
  ½ teaspoon monosodium glutamate
  ¼ teaspoon pepper
Shape into four patties. Put patties in greased steak broiler or directly onto greased grill at least 5 in. from top of coals. Grill about 4 min., or until browned on one side.

Turn patties and brush with
  Melted butter (or Tangy Marinade, page 685)
Grill patties until second side is browned. Serve on **toasted buns.** Have one or more of the following on hand: **chili sauce, prepared mustard, pickles, olives, onion slices,** or **tomato slices.**

To Toast Buns—Cut buns into halves and brush cut sides with melted butter. Place on grill and toast cut side. Add more melted butter and serve the buns hot. For extra-crispness, toast uncut side a moment before serving. *4 hamburgers*

Note: Chopped dill pickle, chives, toasted nuts, chopped mushrooms or sesame seed blended into the meat mixture offer pleasing variations in flavor. Or, for extra zip blend in ketchup, pickle relish, Worcestershire sauce, chili powder or prepared horseradish.

—CHEESEBURGERS ON THE GRILL

Follow ▲ Recipe. When second side of patties is partially browned, place a **Cheddar cheese slice** on each patty. (The cheese will melt slightly over the burger.)

—SANDWICH-STYLE HAMBURGERS

Follow ▲ Recipe. Shape twice as many patties by making them thinner. Spread 4 patties with a mixture of **2 teaspoons olive oil** and **8 teaspoons Roquefort or blue cheese.** Top with remaining patties and press edges together.

—SURPRISE HAMBURGERS

Follow ▲ Recipe. Shape twice as many patties by making them thinner. Place **1 Cheddar cheese slice** on each of 4 patties. Top cheese slices with remaining patties. Press edges to seal. Wrap **1 slice bacon** around outside edge of each patty and fasten to patty with a wooden pick. Grill as in ▲ Recipe.

—HAWAIIAN BURGERS

Follow ▲ Recipe. Drain **1 can (15¼ oz.) pineapple slices.** Place slices on grill with hamburgers. Brush with **melted butter.** Brown pineapple slices 4 to 5 min. on each side. Top hamburgers with pineapple slices.

—BARBECUED BURGERS

Follow ▲ Recipe. Substitute **Barbecue Sauce** (page 310) for butter. When first side is browned, turn and brush patty with Barbecue Sauce, using pastry brush.

—GRILLED LAMB-BURGERS

Follow ▲ Recipe. Substitute ground **lamb** for

Barbecued Burgers

ground beef. Add ¼ **teaspoon dill seed** or **2 tablespoons chopped mint leaves** to the meat.

GROUND MEAT IN BARBECUE SAUCE

Delicious and hardy—hot from the grill.

*For Barbecue Sauce—*Combine in a 1-pt. screw-top jar

- **1 cup ketchup**
- **½ cup water**
- **2 tablespoons sugar**
- **2 tablespoons prepared mustard**
- **2 tablespoons vinegar**
- **2 teaspoons Worcestershire sauce**

Cover and shake until blended.

*For Meat Mixture—*Heat in skillet on a grill

- **2 tablespoons butter**

Add and cook until onion is tender

- **1 cup (2 medium) chopped onion**

Add, breaking beef apart with spoon or fork

- **2 lbs. ground beef**

and a mixture of

- **2 teaspoons salt**
- **½ teaspoon monosodium glutamate**
- **½ teaspoon pepper**

When meat is browned, blend in sauce. Put skillet on back of grill and cook slowly about 15 min. Spoon meat and sauce into buttered buns.   *4 to 6 servings*

*Note: Sauce may be prepared in advance and stored in refrigerator.

DINNER ON A GRILL

When you prepare this taste-tempting dinner, check cooking time of each food so the entire meal will be piping hot at the same time.

*For Roast Corn—*Select corn with long stem ends for easier handling and turning.

Loosen husks only enough to remove silks and blemishes from

- **4 ears garden-fresh corn**

Dip ears in a deep pail of water. Shake well. Rewrap husks around corn. Plunge in water again and let stand until husks are soaked, about 1 hr. Place ears on grill or in steak broiler over hot coals allowing stem ends to extend beyond end of grill. Roast, turning often, until tender, about 15 min.

Husk and serve with butter.

*For Baked Potatoes—*Wash, scrub, wipe dry

- **4 baking potatoes**

Rub fat over entire surface of potatoes and wrap each loosely in aluminum foil. Seal open ends with a double fold. Place on grill and bake about 1 hr., or until potatoes are soft when pressed with the fingers (protected by pot holder or asbestos gloves). Turn several times for even baking.

Cut cross in top of each potato and pinch open. Place in center of each

- **1 tablespoon butter**

Season each with

- **Few grains salt**
- **Few grains paprika**

Skins and all are edible when potatoes are baked this way.

*For Grilled Onions—*Leave outside skins on

- **4 Spanish or Bermuda onions**

Wet each onion thoroughly. Place on grill; roll onions occasionally while grilling. Onions are done when black on the outside and soft and creamy on the inside, about 50 min.

*For Hamburgers—*Prepare

- **Grilled Hamburger Favorites (page 680) or any variation (omit buns)**

*For Grilled Tomatoes—*Cut into halves crosswise

- **2 large tomatoes**

Brush with

- **Melted butter**

Season with

- **Salt**
- **Pepper**

Place on grill, cut-side up, for about 3 min.
4 servings

Note: Grilled marshmallows are as much fun to prepare for dessert as they are to eat.

BEEF ROAST ON A SPIT

Select

- **1 5-lb. rolled beef rib roast**

(Have a good layer of fat around the outside of roast or an additional layer of suet around it.) Secure meat on spit. Insert barbecue thermometer and place spit in position. Put drip pan under meat to catch drippings. Start motor and roast meat until desired doneness. Allow 15 to 18 min. per lb. for rare meat (140°F), 20 to 25 min. per lb. for medium (160°F), and 30 to 35 min. per lb. (170°F) for well done. (Without a thermometer, test roast for doneness by cutting a slit in meat and noting color.) When using a hand-propelled-type spit, turn meat as it sears, then turn about every 10 min. during roasting.

Baste roast frequently with drippings, **butter,** or **Barbecue Sauce** (page 310).

Carve roast; season with **salt** and **pepper**.
8 to 10 servings

Note: For additional flavor, cut slits in meat before roasting and insert slivers of onion or

Dinner on a Grill

garlic. Then roast. A hood on the grill insures thorough cooking.

CHARCOAL-BROILED STEAK

▲ *Base Recipe*

Mix and set aside

- **1 tablespoon salt**
- **2 teaspoons monosodium glutamate**
- **¼ teaspoon freshly ground pepper**

Rub

- **4 lbs. beef steaks, such as sirloin, porterhouse, tenderloin, T-bone or rib, cut 1½ in. thick**

with cut surfaces of

- **1 clove garlic, halved**

Lightly grease grill with

- **Cooking oil or olive oil**

Place steaks on grill about 3 in. from coals. Grill about 6 min., or until first side is browned. Turn with tongs and sprinkle half of seasoning mixture over top of steaks. Grill second side about 6 min., or until done. To test doneness, slit meat near bone and note color of meat. Season second side of steaks. Remove from grill to serving plates.

Pour over them

- **¼ cup butter or margarine, melted**
4 servings

—GOURMET'S STEAK

Follow ▲ Recipe. Soften ¼ **lb. Blue cheese** and spread on steaks after turning.

—SAUCY STEAK

Follow ▲ Recipe. During grilling baste steaks with **soy sauce** or a favorite **bottled steak sauce**. Serve hot with the melted butter.

—MARINATED STEAK

Follow ▲ Recipe. Place steaks in a shallow pan. Pour over them **1½ cups olive oil** with seasonings and **juice of 1 lemon**. Let stand about 2 hrs. in refrigerator, turning occasionally. When ready to grill remove from marinade.

Variety Kabobs

—ONE-INCH STEAKS

Follow ▲ Recipe. Use steaks about 1 in. thick. Grill about 4 min. on each side about 3 in. from coals.

—STRIP OR CLUB STEAKS

Follow ▲ Recipe. Use strip or club steaks. Grill about 4 min. on each side 3 in. from coals. Season and allow butter to melt over top.

—CUBED STEAKS

Follow ▲ Recipe. Use round, arm, blade or flank steak. Grill about 3 in. from coals about 15 min., total grilling time. Season steaks and pour melted butter over top.

—SANDWICH STEAKS

Have meat dealer prepare "sandwich steaks" by cutting beef tenderloin into pieces and flattening them. Grill about 3 min. on each side 3 in. from coals.

VARIETY KABOBS

Six 8-in. skewers will be needed.

For marinade, prepare and set aside
    Tangy Marinade (page 685) or Zippy Barbecue Sauce (page 686)
Put into a large shallow bowl and pour marinade over
    1½ lbs. boneless sirloin steak or 1½ lbs. lamb such as loin, leg or shoulder, cut in 1-in. cubes
Set in refrigerator to marinate (page 10) for an hour or longer, turning pieces several times if they are not covered with liquid.

Clean
    12 large mushroom caps
Cut into halves
    6 slices bacon
Wrap each mushroom cap with bacon. Clean
    1 large green pepper (or enough to yield 12 1-in. squares)
Set out
    6 cooked small whole onions
    6 plum tomatoes

Remove meat from marinade with slotted spoon and drain. Reserve marinade for basting kabobs during cooking. Arrange meat pieces on the skewers alternately with the mushrooms, green pepper and onions. Put kabob morsels close together for rare kabobs; separate them slightly for well-done kabobs. Brush with marinade.

To Grill Kabobs—Place on greased grill about 3 in. from coals, turning often for even browning. Baste frequently with marinade. Grilling period range is 10 to 20 min., or until meat on kabobs is tender and well-browned.

To Complete Kabobs—Test for doneness by cutting a slit in meat cubes and noting color of meat. During last 3 to 5 min. of cooking, add one of the tomatoes to each skewer. Sprinkle kabobs with a mixture of
    1 teaspoon salt
    ¼ teaspoon monosodium glutamate
    ⅛ teaspoon pepper
Serve at once.   *6 servings*

ROASTED LEG OF LAMB

▲ Base Recipe

Remove spit from hooded grill before building fire so spit will not heat.

Cut slits in
    1 6-lb. boned and rolled leg of lamb roast
Put into slits
    Slivers of garlic or pieces of fresh mint leaves
Insert spit; be sure roast is evenly balanced. Insert thermometer. Set drip pan in place; start motor. Baste with
    Special Barbecue Sauce for Lamb (page 686)
Roast about 25 min. per lb. for medium done (170°F); 30 min. per lb. for well done (180°F).

Carve and serve hot.   *8 to 10 servings*

Note: Boned and rolled lamb shoulder may be used.

—ROASTED LOIN OF LAMB

Follow ▲ Recipe. Use a **4-lb. loin of lamb roast**; cut between each rib three-fourths through. Secure meat lengthwise on spit, directly through center of loin. Place on grill 6 in. from coals. Frequently turn and baste with the sauce. Roast about 1 hr. When done, carve meat into individual "roasts."

GRILLED LAMB CHOPS

▲ Base Recipe

Mix and set aside
    2 teaspoons salt
    1 teaspoon monosodium glutamate
    ⅛ teaspoon freshly ground pepper

Trim most of fat from
    4 lamb chops, such as loin, rib, arm or blade, cut 1 to 1½ in. thick
Rub each side of meat with cut surface of
    ½ clove garlic

Lightly grease grill with
    Cooking oil
Place chops on grill about 4 in. from coals. Grill about 8 min., or until meat is browned. Turn and season with half of seasoning mixture. Grill second side about 8 min., or until done. To test doneness, slit meat near bone and note color of meat. Season other side and serve immediately on hot plates.   *4 servings*

—BARBECUED LAMB CHOPS

Follow ▲ Recipe. Omit garlic and other seasonings. During grilling brush frequently with **Special Barbecue Sauce for Lamb** (page 686).

—CURRIED LAMB CHOPS

Follow ▲ Recipe. Omit garlic and other seasonings. Brush chops with **Curry Basting Sauce** (page 686) during grilling. Serve with some of the condiments usually served with Indian curry, such as **fresh coconut, chopped peanuts, avocado slices,** chopped whites and sieved yolks of **hard-cooked eggs, chopped green pepper, scallions, chives, tomato quarters** and, of course, **chutney.**

CHARCOAL-BROILED HAM SLICE

▲ Base Recipe

Purchase for every 2 or 3 servings
    1 ham slice (½ in. thick)

Grill 3 in. from coals, basting with a mixture of
    ½ cup dairy sour cream
    1½ tablespoons prepared horseradish mustard
Turn and baste often to keep ham moist. Grill until ham is tender, about 10 min.

—GRILLED HAM SLICE WITH BARBECUE SAUCE

Follow ▲ Recipe. Omit sour cream and mustard. Combine ¼ cup ketchup, ¼ cup vinegar, ¼ cup water, ½ teaspoon celery seed and ½ teaspoon dry mustard. Use for basting sauce.

—GRILLED HAM WITH PINEAPPLE SAUCE

Follow ▲ Recipe. Omit sour cream and mustard. Baste with a mixture of ¾ **cup pine-**

apple juice, ½ cup brown sugar, ¼ cup vinegar and 2½ teaspoons dry mustard.

—SKILLET-BROILED HAM SLICE

Purchase ham as in ▲ Recipe. Place ham slice in a heavy skillet. Put skillet on grill. Turn meat occasionally and baste frequently with one of the sauces suggested for Grilled Ham. Cook until meat is tender, about 15 min.

—BREAKFAST HAM SLICE

Follow ▲ Recipe. Omit sour cream and mustard. Brush frequently with **pineapple juice.**

SAUCE-PAINTED SPARERIBS

▲ Base Recipe

Cut into serving-size portions
  4 lbs. spareribs
Partially roast meat (about 30 min.) in oven at 350°F.

Place meaty side down on grill. Slowly grill about 3 in. from hot coals. Turn about every 5 min., brushing with
  Barbecue Sauce (page 310)
Grill until meat is a deep brown and crisp, about 25 min.   *8 servings*

—BARBECUED RIBS, HAWAIIAN

Follow ▲ Recipe. Pour over ribs a mixture of ½ cup **soy sauce**, ¼ cup **cornstarch** and **3 tablespoons chopped preserved or crystallized ginger.** Let stand about 30 min., turning frequently. Roast and grill as usual, brushing with a mixture of ½ cup **pineapple juice**, **3 tablespoons vinegar** and ¾ cup **sugar**.

BARBECUED BOLOGNA ROLL

▲ Base Recipe

Score with ½- to 1-in. cuts, 1 in. apart, side of
  4- to 6-lb. roll of bologna
Secure roll on spit or shish kabob skewer. Spread with a mixture of
  1½ tablespoons prepared mustard
  1½ teaspoons brown sugar
  1 teaspoon prepared horseradish

Attach the spit or place directly on grill about 3 in. from coals. Baste well with a mixture of
  1 cup chili sauce
  3 tablespoons vinegar
Start motor. Grill until roll is thoroughly heated. If placed directly on grill, turn often. Remove spit or skewer; slice.
                    About 16 servings

—BARBECUED BOLOGNA SLICES

Follow ▲ Recipe. Cut bologna roll into 1-in. slices. Double mustard mixture and spread on slices. Secure slices on shish kabob skewer to reshape roll. Grill as in ▲ Recipe.

HOT GRILLED FRANKS

▲ Base Recipe

Place on grill or in hot dog roaster
  2 frankfurters for each serving
Grill, turning frequently, until lightly browned and heated through, about 10 min. Serve on hot toasted **buttered buns.** If desired, spread mayonnaise or salad dressing on buns before toasting. Accompany with **pickle relish, horseradish, mustard, chili sauce and/or ketchup.**

—GRILLED FRANKFURTERS WITH SAUCE

Follow ▲ Recipe. Slit frankfurters lengthwise, almost through. Spread open. Brush with **Barbecue Sauce** (page 310) and grill, starting with cut side down; baste frequently.

—BACON WRAPS

Follow ▲ Recipe. Slit frankfurters almost through, lengthwise. Spread with a **pasteurized process cheese spread**; a mixture of **grated sharp cheese** and **grated onion, pickle relish** or **caraway seed**; or add cheese slices. Starting at one end, wrap **1 slice bacon** around each frankfurter; secure ends with wooden picks. Put these on grill, on skewer, or in hot dog roaster. Grill slowly, until bacon and frankfurters are lightly browned.

—HOT DOGS IN FOIL

Use any of the above variations for frankfurters (except Bacon Wraps). Wrap each frankfurter loosely in aluminum foil. Roast on the grill, about 6 min., turning frequently.

—SKILLET FRANKS

If you prefer using the skillet, brown frankfurters slowly in hot **butter or margarine** at the side of the grill. Turn often. They'll be done in about 7 min. Have ready a Barbecue Sauce made by combining **1 small onion**, finely chopped, **¼ cup finely chopped green pepper, 2 tablespoons brown sugar, 2 tablespoons prepared mustard, 2 teaspoons Worcestershire sauce, 1 teaspoon salt** and **⅔ cup ketchup.** Add to franks in skillet. Simmer 10 to 15 min. Serve franks with sauce.

LIVER STEAKS

Cut into serving-size pieces
  1 lb. calf's or beef liver, ½ in. thick
Brush with
  Melted butter or margarine
Place on a greased grill or in greased steak broiler 3 in. from coals. Turn occasionally. Grill until outside is slightly charred but the inside is still pink and juicy, about 10 min. Sprinkle both sides with a mixture of
  1 teaspoon salt
  ¼ teaspoon pepper
                    4 servings

BACON STEAKS

Arrange on grill about 3 in. from coals
  16 bacon steaks*
Grill over low coals about 20 min., or until evenly crisped and browned. Turn frequently. Have a baster handy filled with water to douse flames as they flare up.   *8 servings*

*Bacon steaks are ½-in. thick slices cut from slab bacon.

GRILLED CANADIAN-STYLE BACON

Allow 2 or 3 slices bacon for each serving.

Place on grill
  Canadian-style bacon slices (½ in. thick)
Grill 3 in. from coals until well browned (about 5 min.). Turn and brown other sides (about 5 min.).

DINNER IN A BOILER

The equipment needed is a clean copper wash boiler and sheets of clean coarse rustproof screen. The screen is used to separate the layers of food. The boiler can be set right on your grill. You'll want plenty of hot coals. The quantities of food used depend upon the size of your boiler, number of guests and the size of their appetites.

First layer—Place a long cake rack on bottom of boiler. Put onto rack
  8 sweet potatoes, washed

Second layer—Remove silk from (do not remove husks)
  8 ears fresh sweet corn

Third layer—Rinse and dry with absorbent paper
  4 broiler chickens, 1 to 1½ lbs. each, ready-to-cook weight
Split each chicken in half lengthwise. If chickens are frozen, thaw following directions on package. Crack joints of drumsticks, hips and wings so chickens can be kept flat. Skewer legs and wings to bodies. Sprinkle each chicken with a mixture of
  1 teaspoon salt
  ½ teaspoon monosodium glutamate
  Dash of pepper
Place each half on a sheet of heavy-duty aluminum foil with
  1 tablespoon butter or margarine
Wrap loosely, closing ends with a double fold.

Fourth layer—Add a layer of
  4 live lobsters, freshly killed (about 1½ lbs. each)
(See Grilled Lobster, page 685, for directions for killing lobsters and cutting into halves.)

Fifth layer—Scrub and wash in running cold water
  1 peck fresh soft clams
Put over all
  1 lb. butter or margarine
  3 large onions, sliced

and a mixture of
>**1 cup lemon juice**
>**⅔ cup (5-oz. bottle) Worcestershire sauce**
>**⅓ cup salt**
>**3 tablespoons pepper**
>**4 bay leaves, crumbled**

Pour over a mixture of
>**3½ qts. boiling water**
>**1 cup wine vinegar**
>**¼ cup sugar**

Place cover on boiler so that some steam can escape. Place on grill and steam slowly about 2 hrs. Serve this meal in courses, layer by layer. Have a bowl of **melted butter** for dipping clams and lobster meat. Then, heap the plates with chicken, sweet potatoes and corn.

8 servings

GRILLED CHICKEN

Rinse and dry with absorbent paper
>**2 broiler-fryer chickens, 1 to 1½ lbs. each, ready-to-cook weight**

Split each chicken in half lengthwise. If chickens are frozen, thaw according to directions on package. Crack joints of drumsticks, hips and wings so chickens can be kept flat during grilling. Skewer legs and wings to bodies. Brush chickens with
>**Lemon Basting Sauce (page 686)**

Place chickens on greased portion of grill or in greased steak broiler. Grill cut side down 3 in. from coals. Turn chickens every 5 min. to brown and cook evenly. Brush frequently with sauce.

Grill about 20 min. (depending on size of chickens), or until chickens test done. They are done when meat on thickest part of drumstick cuts easily and no pink color shows.

Serve with remaining sauce. *4 servings*

CHICKEN ON A SPIT

Remove the spit from hooded grill before you build the fire so it won't heat.

Clean, rinse and dry with absorbent paper
>**1 chicken, about 4 lbs. ready-to-cook weight**

Rub cavity of bird with about
>**2 teaspoons salt**

Grilled Chicken

Wash, quarter, core and pare
>**2 medium apples**

Place in cavity of chicken with
>**1 cup celery leaves, washed**

To close body cavity, sew or skewer and lace with cord. Fasten neck skin to back with skewer. Tie wings to body. Insert spit through chicken. Tie drumsticks to spit by looping cord over tip ends and around spit. Be sure chicken is well balanced. Attach spit; put drip pan in place. Start motor. Baste with
>**Lemon Basting Sauce (page 686)**

Grill about 1½ hrs., or until skin of bird is well browned and begins to split. Baste often to keep skin moist and to add flavor. When using a hand-propelled-type spit, turn bird frequently while roasting.

When done, carve and serve with remaining hot sauce. *4 servings*

DUCKLING ON A SPIT

To prevent its heating, remove spit from grill before building fire.

Clean, rinse and dry with absorbent paper
>**1 ready-to-cook duckling, 5 lbs.**

Rub cavity with about
>**1½ teaspoons salt**

Wash, cut in half, core and pare
>**1 large tart apple**

Wash, core and pare
>**1 medium tart apple**

Place apple halves in cavity of duckling. Insert whole apple in neck opening; fasten neck skin to back with skewers. Insert spit lengthwise through bird. Tie drumsticks to spit by looping cord over tip ends and around spit. Repeat with wings. Be sure duckling is well balanced. Attached spit; place drip pan in position. Start motor and grill about 1½ hrs. When using a hand-propelled-type spit, turn bird frequently while roasting. Baste frequently with
>**1 teaspoon grated orange peel**
>**2 cups orange juice**

When duckling is done, carve; put pieces in orange juice-dripping mixture. Place pan over coals several minutes, basting to glaze meat with mixture. *4 servings*

TURKEY ON A SPIT

Remove the spit from the grill before you build the fire.

Rinse well with cold water and pat dry.
>**1 turkey, 6 to 12 lbs. ready-to-cook weight (allow ¾ lb. per serving)**

Cut off neck at body. Rub cavity of turkey with
>**1 to 2 teaspoons salt**

If desired, fill the body and neck cavities with stuffing. To close the body cavity, sew or skewer and lace with cord. Fasten neck skin to back with skewer. Tie wings to body and legs together. Grease skin thoroughly with
>**Unsalted fat**

Insert spit lengthwise through turkey. Tie drumsticks to spit. Be sure bird is perfectly balanced. Insert thermometer into center of inside thigh muscle or (when turkey is the broad-breasted variety) into center of breast. Thermometer must not touch bone or spit.

Attach spit and place drip pan in proper position; turn on motor. Brush turkey often during roasting with drippings in pan and
>**Melted butter or margarine**

Roast until done, allowing 18 to 22 min. per lb. for hen turkey and 15 to 18 min. per lb. for tom turkey. (Thermometer should register 180°F.-185°F.)

When turkey is done, remove thermometer and take bird from spit; let stand about 10 min. before carving.

Note: A hood on the grill intensifies the cooking heat.

GRILLED FISH STEAKS

▲ *Base Recipe*

Purchase
>**Salmon, halibut or swordfish steaks, about ¾ in. thick**

Allow 1 medium steak for each serving.

Combine in a shallow dish
>**½ cup cooking oil**
>**¼ cup lemon juice**

Place fish steaks in dish. Cover lightly with waxed paper. Let stand about 30 min., turning and basting each steak frequently. Drain fish slightly and place in greased steak broiler. Grill about 3 min., 5 in. from coals. Brush with lemon juice mixture or **melted butter.** Turn fish; brush again. Sprinkle with half a mixture of
>**4 teaspoons salt**
>**1 teaspoon monosodium glutamate**
>**½ teaspoon pepper**

Continue grilling 3 min., or until fish is completely white and flakes easily. Turn and sprinkle with remaining seasonings. Serve hot.

4 servings

Note: Fish fillets can be grilled, fried or cooked in foil in the same way as fish steaks.

—FISH STEAKS IN FOIL

Use fish suggested in ▲ Recipe. Sprinkle each steak with seasonings, top with any vegetable such as **tomato, onion** or **eggplant slices,** or a combination of vegetables. Wrap each steak loosely in heavy-duty aluminum foil, closing ends of foil with double folds. Place on grill about 3 in. from coals. Grill about 12 min.

—FRIED FISH STEAKS

Use fish suggested in ▲ Recipe. Sprinkle steaks with seasonings. Cook until golden brown in skillet containing ¼ **cup hot butter.** Turn steaks carefully with long-handled spatula. Brown second side. Serve at once.

TROUT IN BACON WRAP

▲ *Base Recipe*

Have ready for each serving
    1 dressed small trout (about 10 oz.)
Season each fish with a mixture of
    1 teaspoon salt
    ½ teaspoon monosodium glutamate
    ¼ teaspoon paprika
    ⅛ teaspoon pepper
Wrap each fish completely in
    2 or 3 bacon slices
Fasten with small skewers or wooden picks. Place fish in basket steak broiler. Grill 3 in. from coals, turning once, until bacon is very crisp, about 7 min. Trout will then be cooked.

Serve on warm plates with
    Lemon Butter Sauce (page 686)

—GRILLED TROUT

Follow ▲ Recipe. Omit bacon slices. Baste trout frequently with Lemon Butter Sauce during grilling. Serve on a heated platter with **lemon slices** and the remaining butter sauce.

—PANFRIED TROUT

Follow ▲ Recipe. Roll trout in mixture of **flour** and seasonings. Melt **butter or margarine** in a heavy skillet. Add trout and fry until golden brown (15 to 20 min.). Turn frequently. Serve on a heated platter and accompany with **Cucumber Sauce I** (page 310) in individual cups, if desired.

PERCH KABOBS

Eight 5-in. skewers and a baking sheet will be needed.

Cut into 1½-in. chunks
    2 lbs. frozen ocean perch fillets
Put into a large bowl and set aside.
Prepare
    French Dressing Marinade (on this page)
Pour over fish chunks enough French Dressing Marinade to cover. Let stand 1½ hrs. at room temperature, turning chunks occasionally with fork. Drain marinade from the fish and reserve it for basting.

Set out the skewers and baking sheet.

Cut crosswise into fourths
    4 slices bacon
Cut crosswise into eighths
    2 large dill pickles
To form kabobs, thread onto each skewer a fish chunk, a piece of bacon, and a piece of pickle. Repeat threading, ending with third fish chunk. Place skewers on baking sheet.

To Broil Kabobs—Set temperature control of range at Broil (500°F or higher). Put baking sheet on broiler rack and place in broiler with tops of kabobs 2 in. from heat. Turning frequently and brushing several times with reserved marinade, broil kabobs 12 to 15 min., or until fish flakes easily (page 9).

To Grill Kabobs—Place kabobs on greased grill about 3 in. from bed of coals, turning them almost constantly. Or arrange several in your greased steak or hamburger broiler. Grill until fish flakes easily.

To serve, arrange kabobs on serving platter, garnish with
    Parsley-dipped lemon wedges
Serve immediately.   *6 servings*

GRILLED LOBSTER

Purchase for each serving
    1 live lobster (about 1½ lbs. each)
Live lobsters may be killed and dressed for cooking at the market. If prepared at home, place the lobster on a cutting board with back or smooth shell up. Hold a towel firmly over the head and claws. Kill by quickly inserting the point of a sharp heavy knife into the center of the small cross showing on the back of the head.

Without removing knife, quickly bear down heavily, cutting through entire length of the body and tail. Split the halves apart and remove the stomach, a small sac which lies in the head, and the spongy lungs which lie between meat and shell. Also remove the dark intestinal line running through the center of the body. Crack large claws with a nut cracker or mallet.

Brush meat with
    Lemon Butter Sauce (page 686)
Place shell side down on grill about 5 in. from coals. Grill about 20 min., or until shell is browned. Baste frequently with butter sauce. Serve in shell with remaining sauce.

—BOILED LOBSTER

Boiled lobster may be done on your grill, too— if you have a large kettle.

Follow ▲ Recipe. Plunge live lobster head first in rapidly boiling salted water (1 tablespoon salt per quart of water). Cover and boil about 8 min. (Lobster will turn pink.) Remove with tongs. Slit underside and remove stomach, lungs and vein. Serve lobster with the sauce.

Perch Kabobs

ROCK-LOBSTER TAILS

Thaw
    1 fresh-frozen 12-oz. rock-lobster tail
    for each serving
Snip through and remove thin shell on underside; remove vein. Holding tail in both hands, bend it towards shell side to crack, or insert a skewer lengthwise through meat. This keeps tail flat. (If you can buy fresh rock-lobster tails, your fish dealer may do this for you.)

Place tails shell-side down on grill about 4 in. or more from coals; brush with
    Lemon Butter Sauce (page 686)
Grill about 10 min., or until shell is charred, brushing with sauce occasionally. Be sure not to let the fire get too hot. Turn tails with tongs and continue grilling about 6 min., or until meat is completely white and opaque. Serve with the remaining butter sauce and **lemon wedges** or lots of **melted butter.**

FRENCH DRESSING MARINADE

Put into a screw-top jar
    ¼ cup salad oil
    ¼ cup lemon juice
    2 tablespoons ketchup
    1 teaspoon sugar
    1 teaspoon Worcestershire sauce
    ¾ teaspoon monosodium glutamate
    ½ teaspoon salt
    ¼ teaspoon paprika
    ¼ teaspoon pepper
    ¼ teaspoon dry mustard
    2 drops Tabasco
Cover jar and shake until ingredients are combined thoroughly.

TANGY MARINADE

Mix in a bowl or screw-top jar
    1 tablespoon sugar
    1 teaspoon salt
    1 teaspoon dry mustard
    1 teaspoon paprika
    ¼ teaspoon celery salt

Add
¾ cup salad oil or olive oil
¼ cup cider vinegar, tarragon vinegar or lemon juice
Beat mixture with a rotary beater or shake until well blended. Add
1 clove garlic
Store, covered, in refrigerator. Before using, beat or shake thoroughly; remove garlic.

ZIPPY BARBECUE SAUCE

Mix thoroughly in a saucepan
1 cup water
1 cup ketchup
¼ cup cider vinegar
¼ cup firmly packed dark brown sugar
¼ cup finely chopped onion
1 tablespoon Worcestershire sauce
2 teaspoons dry mustard
1 teaspoon salt
¼ teaspoon pepper
⅛ teaspoon thyme
Bring mixture to boiling; reduce heat and simmer 25 min. *About 2 cups sauce*

Note: Zippy Barbecue Sauce is especially good served with frankfurters, broiled, grilled or cooked in liquid.

SPECIAL BARBECUE SAUCE FOR LAMB

Combine
½ cup water
¼ cup lemon juice
12 fresh mint leaves, crushed
2 cloves garlic, split
2 tablespoons finely chopped onion
1 teaspoon rosemary
Let stand overnight.

Remove garlic and mint leaves. Use sauce for basting lamb chops. *About ¾ cup sauce*

CURRY BASTING SAUCE

Mix in a saucepan
¾ cup salad oil
3 tablespoons lemon juice
2 tablespoons sugar
1 small onion, chopped
1 clove garlic, split
2 teaspoons curry powder
1½ teaspoons salt
½ teaspoon monosodium glutamate
½ teaspoon freshly ground pepper
Cook slowly 10 min. Remove garlic. Use sauce for basting lamb chops. *About 1 cup sauce*

LEMON BASTING SAUCE

Melt
¾ cup butter or margarine

Mix and stir into melted butter
2 teaspoons paprika
1 teaspoon sugar
1 teaspoon salt
½ teaspoon black pepper
¼ teaspoon dry mustard
Few grains cayenne pepper
Blend in thoroughly
½ cup lemon juice
½ cup hot water
Few drops Tabasco
Baste chicken frequently with sauce during grilling. If desired, add **2 tablespoons grated onion** to the sauce. *About 1½ cups sauce*

LEMON BUTTER SAUCE

Heat together in a small saucepan
1 cup butter
2 tablespoons lemon juice
¼ teaspoon salt
⅛ teaspoon pepper
¼ teaspoon paprika
If desired, add
¼ cup chopped parsley
This will make plenty for basting and serving. *About 1 cup sauce*

GRIDDLECAKES ON THE GRILL

▲ *Base Recipe*

Have ready
Griddlecake Batter (below)
(If desired, prepare batter ahead of time and keep it in the refrigerator until ready to use. Or use pancake mix and prepare batter according to directions on package.)

Heat griddle or heavy skillet on grill over low coals until drops of water dance in small beads on surface. Lightly grease griddle with
Butter or margarine
Pour batter from a pitcher or large spoon into small pools about 4 in. in diameter, leaving at least 1 in. between. Turn cakes with a wide turner when they become puffy and full of bubbles. Turn only once. Serve griddlecake stacks immediately with warm **maple syrup** and **butter**. *About 18 griddlecakes*

For Griddlecake Batter—Melt and set aside
2 tablespoons butter or margarine

Sift together
1½ cups sifted all-purpose flour
1 tablespoon sugar
1½ teaspoons baking powder
½ teaspoon salt
Make a well in center of dry ingredients.

Beat together slightly
2 eggs
1⅓ cups milk
Add all at once to dry ingredients. Beat with rotary beater until well blended and smooth. Blend in melted butter. Keep batter in refrigerator until ready to use later the same day.

—BLUEBERRY GRIDDLECAKES

Follow ▲ Recipe. Blend **2 cups fresh blueberries** into batter before baking.

—DESSERT GRIDDLECAKES

Follow ▲ Recipe. Spread griddlecakes with **jam or jelly.** Roll up and dust with **confectioners' sugar.** Or top the griddlecakes with **sweetened crushed berries** and **whipped cream** or **dairy sour cream.** Or generously spread hot griddlecakes with **butter or margarine.** Sprinkle **1 tablespoon brown sugar** and **chopped nuts** over each cake. Roll up.

How to Flip Griddlecakes—Bake griddlecakes one at a time in a heavy skillet. When cake becomes puffy and full of bubbles, it is ready to flip. Shake or loosen from bottom of skillet. Then, to toss, shake the skillet until side of cake away from you touches the edge of the skillet. Toss the far edge of the cake up into the air with a quick motion of the wrist. Catch it in the middle of the skillet when it is upside down. It will sizzle and start to brown on second side. Here practice does make perfect, so try it out before you show off in front of guests.

GRILLED FRENCH BREAD

▲ *Base Recipe*

Make diagonal cuts from ½ to ¾ in. apart almost through
1 loaf French bread
Spread one of the Butters (page 687) on top of bread and between slices. Place loaf on a piece of aluminum foil large enough to cover bread completely. Wrap loosely all around loaf, closing ends with a double fold.

Place on grill about 10 min., or until heated entirely through. Turn frequently for even heating. Serve piping hot.

Garlic Butter—Crush **1 clove garlic** with **¼ teaspoon salt** to form a smooth paste. Blend with **½ cup softened butter or margarine.**

Blue Cheese Butter—Blend to spreading consistency **½ cup softened butter or margarine** and **1 oz. Roquefort or blue cheese,** crumbled.

Poppy Seed Butter—Blend **½ cup softened butter or margarine** with **¼ cup poppy seed.**

Sharp Cheese Butter—Blend **½ cup softened butter or margarine** with **½ cup grated sharp Cheddar cheese, 2 tablespoons finely chopped onion, 1 tablespoon lemon juice** and a **drop of Tabasco.**

Herb Butter—Blend **½ cup softened butter or margarine** with **½ teaspoon tarragon leaves** and **2 tablespoons chopped chives.**

—CHEESE FRENCH BREAD

Follow ▲ Recipe. Spread bread slices with **softened butter** and **prepared mustard.** Place a slice of **Cheddar cheese** and an **onion slice** in each slit. Grill.

—TOASTED FRENCH BREAD

Follow ▲ Recipe. Cut French bread into chunks and toast on the grill or on a stick or fork over low coals. Spread with one of the Butters before and after toasting.

—FRENCH ROLLS

Follow ▲ Recipe. Use French rolls. If desired, places slices of **smoked cheese** in buttered bread slits.

SKILLET COFFEE CAKE

▲ Base Recipe

Thoroughly grease bottom of a Dutch oven or a heavy 10-in. skillet with a tight-fitting cover. Line bottom of skillet with several thicknesses of waxed paper; grease again. Set cover of skillet at edge of grill to heat thoroughly.

For Coconut Topper—Lightly mix and set aside
   ¼ cup biscuit mix
   ¼ cup flaked coconut
   3 tablespoons sugar
   2 teaspoons grated lemon peel
   ½ teaspoon nutmeg

For Coffee Cake—Blend thoroughly
   1½ cups biscuit mix
   ⅓ cup sugar

Beat until thick and piled softly
   1 egg
Add to mix with
   ¼ cup milk
Beat about 100 strokes, or until batter is smooth. (Or, follow directions on biscuit mix package.) Turn into prepared skillet. Sprinkle Coconut Topper on batter. Cover skillet and place over *low* heat at edge of grill. Bake with-

out removing cover 15 to 20 min. Cake is done if a wooden pick comes out clean when inserted in center. *6 to 8 servings*

—JAM-CRESTED COFFEE CAKE

Follow ▲ Recipe. Substitute for topping a mixture of **1 cup bran or wheat flakes, 2 tablespoons brown sugar, ½ teaspoon cinnamon, ¼ teaspoon nutmeg** and **3 tablespoons melted butter or margarine.** Cover batter with topping. Using back of teaspoon, make small hollows at about 2-in. intervals across cake. Fill each hollow with **½ teaspoon fruit jam.**

VEGETABLE KABOBS

▲ Base Recipe

While you prepare the meat, here's a chance for the guests to make and cook their own Vegetable Kabobs. Cook potatoes and onions in advance. Have them ready in bowls with the other vegetables. To make the kabobs all your guests have to do with the vegetables is thread them on a skewer. As you gain skill you will want to experiment with different vegetable combinations of your own, but those listed here can be a beginning.

Wash, pare and cook, covered, in boiling salted water
   6 small potatoes
Cook about 15 min., or until tender.

Wash, peel and cook, uncovered in boiling salted water to cover
   6 small onions
Cook about 10 min., or until tender. (Or, use canned potatoes and onions to eliminate cooking.)

Meanwhile, wipe with a damp cloth and cut off stem ends from
   12 large mushrooms
Wrap each mushroom cap in
   Bacon
Set aside.

Wash, remove pulp and cut into 12 1-in. squares
   Green pepper
Drain potatoes and onions; arrange on 6

skewers with the mushroom caps and green pepper squares. Brush the vegetables with **French Dressing** (page 410) or **melted butter.** Grill until lightly browned, turning often for even browning. Baste frequently. During last 3 to 5 min. of grilling, add to each skewer
   1 small tomato
Sprinkle kabobs with a mixture of
   1 teaspoon salt
   ⅛ teaspoon pepper
Serve hot. *6 kabobs*

—SWEET POTATO KABOBS

Follow ▲ Recipe. Substitute **sweet potatoes** for white potatoes. Do not peel them until after cooking. Cook about 25 min., or just until tender. Alternate pieces on skewer with **pineapple cubes** and **apple wedges.** If desired, put **marshmallows** on skewers about 1 min. before serving.

—VEGETABLE VARIATIONS

Wash, pare and cut **1 medium (about 1 lb.) eggplant** into 1½-in. cubes. Summer squash or zucchini may also be pared and cut for the skewers. Proceed as in ▲ Recipe.

BAKED SQUASH

Split into halves
   Acorn squash (allow 1 half for each serving)
Scoop out seedy centers. Wrap each half loosely in heavy-duty aluminum foil. Double fold open edges to seal. Place squash on grill, cut side down. Grill about 30 min., or until inside of squash is tender.

Put into cavity of each squash half
   1 tablespoon molasses
   1 tablespoon butter
   2 teaspoons brown sugar

ROAST CORN

Loosen husks only enough to remove silks and blemishes from ears of
   Fresh corn
Dip ears in deep pail of water. Shake well. Rewrap husks around corn. Plunge into water again and let stand until husks are soaked.

Place ears on grill over hot coals. Roast, turning often, until tender, about 15 min. Husk and serve.

BUTTER ROASTED CORN

Remove husks, silks and any blemishes from
Ears of fresh corn

For each ear of corn to be served, cream until softened
1 tablespoon butter or margarine
Work in
1 teaspoon minced parsley
¼ teaspoon salt
Dash paprika

Spread on corn. Wrap each ear loosely in aluminum foil, sealing carefully.

Place on grill over hot coals. Roast about 15 min., turning frequently. Partially unwrap and serve corn in the foil.

ROASTED CARROTS

▲ *Base Recipe*

Melt in a heavy skillet
1 or 2 tablespoons butter or margarine
Toss
8 to 10 carrots, cooked (whole, slices or strips)
in a mixture of
1 cup all-purpose flour
1 teaspoon salt
½ teaspoon monosodium glutamate
⅛ teaspoon pepper
Pinch tarragon leaves

Heat carrots in hot butter, turning frequently, until well browned, about 10 min.

4 to 6 servings

Note: If desired, dip whole cooked carrots in butter or margarine and roll in crushed corn flakes. Then place them in steak broiler and grill over hot coals until browned on both sides.

—GLAZED CARROTS

Follow ▲ Recipe. Add **1 or 2 tablespoons sugar** to melted butter in skillet; stir until sugar is dissolved. Add cooked whole carrots or carrot strips and roll in skillet until evenly glazed.

BAKED POTATOES IN FOIL

▲ *Base Recipe*

Wash, scrub and dry
4 baking potatoes
Rub fat over entire surface of potatoes and wrap each loosely in aluminum foil. Seal open ends with a double fold.

Place on grill and bake about 1 hr., or until tender. Turn several times for even baking.

Loosen foil and make a slit in top of potato to see if it is done. Cut cross in top of potato and pinch open. Place in center of each
1 tablespoon butter or margarine
Sprinkle of salt
Sprinkle of paprika
Skins and all are edible when potatoes are baked this way.

4 servings

—CHEESE BAKED POTATOES

Follow ▲ Recipe. When potatoes are tender, cut cross in top and pinch open. Scoop out spoonful of potato. Stuff in **1 cube cheese, 1 tablespoon butter or margarine, ¼ teaspoon salt** and cover with the spoonful of potato. Rewrap in foil. Bake about 10 min. more, or until cheese is melted. Or, sprinkle **1 tablespoon Parmesan cheese** on potato when adding butter.

—HERB BAKED POTATOES

Follow ▲ Recipe. While potatoes are baking, whip butter with **chopped parsley or chives.** Chill and roll into balls. Cut a cross in top of each baked potato and pinch open. Top with herb butter ball and a sprinkle of **paprika.**

—BAKED SWEETS

Follow ▲ Recipe. Substitute **sweet potatoes** for baking potatoes; wrap loosely in aluminum foil. Seal open ends with a double fold. Bake about 45 min. Make a slit in top of each. Place **1 teaspoon *each* brown sugar** and **butter or margarine** in center.

GRILLED PINEAPPLE SLICES

▲ *Base Recipe*

Drain
Canned pineapple slices (1 or 2 for each serving)

Brush with
Melted butter or margarine
Coat both sides with
Brown sugar

Grill until golden brown, turning once. Pineapple slices are also delicious when grilled without the sugar coating.

Note: Peach halves can be grilled in the same way.

—GRILLED FRESH PINEAPPLE

Cut **fresh pineapple** lengthwise into ½-in. slices; pare and core. Generously spread slices with **softened butter** and drizzle **1 to 2 tablespoons honey** over each slice. Grill as directed in ▲ Recipe.

BANANA BOATS

Place on flattest side
Green-tipped or all-yellow bananas, 1 for each serving
Pull back part of upper section of banana peel (do not pull off). Cut a trench the full length of the banana. Poke into trench, along length of banana
Miniature marshmallows
Along side of marshmallows place
Small milk chocolate bar pieces
Pull banana peel back into place over filling. Place banana on grill, flat side down. Roast until skin is black. Pull skin back as you eat banana.

CAMP CARAMEL APPLES

▲ *Base Recipe*

For each serving, wash
1 medium or small tart cooking apple
Spear through stem end on a shish kabob skewer. Lay apple on lightly greased grill or hold over coals. Roast, turning occasionally, until skin breaks and may be easily pulled off. Peel. Dip in a bowl of
Melted butter or margarine
Immediately dip and twirl, covering apple completely, in a deep bowl of
Brown sugar

Hold apple over grill, turning slowly and constantly, until it is covered with a rich caramel coating. Cool slightly before serving.

—NUT-TIPPED APPLES

Follow ▲ Recipe. As soon as sugar is melted on apple, quickly dip top in finely chopped **nuts.**

—TOASTY COCONUT APPLES

Follow ▲ Recipe. Dip peeled apples into **sweetened condensed milk.** Coat with finely chopped **shredded coconut;** toast.

Dishes for two

Cooking just for two should never be an excuse for serving monotonous, poorly balanced everyday meals put together in the quickest way possible. With all the convenient fresh, frozen, and canned items available in the markets today, one can purchase foods in any desired quantity. Besides, the freezer compartment of most modern refrigerators offers every opportunity to prepare one's favorite dishes in normal or even large quantities and freeze unused portions for future use. When cooking for two, it is often wise to plan menus for a week at a time giving careful thought to the nutritional value, to the variety, and to the appetite appeal of the foods included.

THREE CHEESE DIP

Place in an electric blender container
- **2 tablespoons milk or water**
- **½ cup cream-style cottage cheese**
- **½ small clove garlic**

Cover and blend at high speed about 30 sec. Add and blend until smooth
- **1 pkg. (3 oz.) cream cheese, softened at room temperature**
- **1 tablespoon crumbled Roquefort or blue cheese**
- **Few drops Tabasco**

About 1 cup dip

CHICKEN LIVER PATE

Set out an electric blender.

Have ready
- **½ lb. chicken livers**

Heat in a small skillet
- **2 tablespoons butter or margarine**

Add chicken livers (large livers cut in half) and
- **¼ cup chopped onion**

Cook over medium heat until lightly browned, stirring occasionally. Add
- **¼ cup hot chicken broth**

Cook over low heat about 5 min., or until livers are very tender.

Measure into electric blender container
- **1 tablespoon cognac**
- **1 teaspoon Worcestershire sauce**
- **⅛ teaspoon garlic salt**
- **¼ teaspoon curry powder**
- **¼ teaspoon paprika**
- **⅛ teaspoon pepper**

Add livers, about ½ cup at a time, along with liquid in skillet and blend at high speed until mixture is smooth. Beat in gradually
- **3 tablespoons butter or margarine, softened**

Turn pâté into bowl and refrigerate until firm. Serve with **crisp crackers** or small **toast triangles.** *About ¾ cup pâté*

PEANUT CORN SNACKS

Here's an easy-on-the-budget nibbler—crunchy and flavor-appealing—a good go-along with drinks for a casual get-together.

Prepare, following directions on package
- **1 pkg. (about 9 oz.) corn muffin mix**

Spread the batter evenly in a well-greased 15x10x1-in. pan. Sprinkle evenly over surface
- **1 cup salted peanuts, coarsely chopped**
- **½ cup shredded Parmesan cheese**
- **1 teaspoon garlic salt**
- **3 tablespoons butter or margarine, melted**

Bake in 375°F oven about 25 min., or until crisp and lightly browned. Remove from oven and cut into 1- to 1½-in. squares. Cool on wire rack a few minutes before removing snacks from pan. Serve warm.

BEEF VEGETABLE SOUP

Put into a 2½-qt. saucepot or kettle
- **1 to 1½ lbs. beef for soup (including bone)**
- **5 cups water**
- **1 to 1½ teaspoons salt**
- **Several stalks celery with leaves**
- **1 onion, peeled and quartered**
- **1 large carrot, cut in pieces**

Bring to boiling over medium heat. Cover and reduce heat to simmer. Cook about 2 hrs., or until meat is tender.

Remove meat from broth and cut into smaller pieces. Discard bone. Strain broth and combine with the meat. If time permits, chill the broth with meat. Before using, skim fat from surface, then bring broth to boiling. Add a mixture of
- **1½ cups finely cut vegetables (carrots, celery, cabbage, potatoes)**
- **2 tablespoons chopped parsley**
- **½ cup frozen peas or cut beans (optional)**
- **½ cup canned tomatoes (optional)**

Cover saucepot and cook soup gently until vegetables are just tender, 25 to 30 min.

Season to taste with **seasoned pepper.**

2 or 3 servings

FRENCH ONION SOUP

Set out a 1-qt. saucepan.

Peel and thinly slice
- **2 medium onions**

Heat in the saucepan
- **½ tablespoon butter or margarine**

Add onions, and cook over medium heat about 3 min. Add
- **2 cups beef broth**
- **Few drops Worcestershire sauce**

Cook sauce gently until onions are tender. Season to taste with
- **Salt and pepper**

Meanwhile, prepare
- **2 toast rounds**

To serve, ladle soup into 2 heat-resistant soup bowls or individual casseroles. Top with toast rounds and sprinkle with
- **Shredded Parmesan cheese (about 1 tablespoon for each serving)**

Set bowls under broiler about 3 in. from heat and broil until cheese is lightly browned.

2 servings

Dilled Split Pea Soup

ONION SOUP AU VIN

Heat in a 2-qt. saucepot or kettle

1 tablespoon butter or margarine

Add to the heated fat and cook until lightly browned, turning occasionally

3 medium onions, thinly sliced

Stir in and mix well

1 tablespoon all-purpose flour

Add a blend of

2 to 3 teaspoons concentrated beef stock base
3 cups beef broth (2 beef bouillon cubes dissolved in 3 cups hot water)
½ cup Burgundy
Pepper to taste

Cover and simmer over low heat about 30 min.

Top each bowl of soup with **toasted croutons** and sprinkle with **shredded Parmesan cheese**.

2 servings

CREAM OF POTATO ONION SOUP

Cook together in a tightly covered 1-qt. saucepan with only enough salted water to cover vegetables

2 medium potatoes, pared and cut up
1 medium onion, peeled and cut up

When tender, drain and reserve ½ cup cooking liquid. Force vegetables through a food mill or coarse strainer and add the reserved liquid. Set aside.

Heat in the saucepan

2 tablespoons butter or margarine

Stir in and cook over medium heat until bubbly

1 tablespoon all-purpose flour

Add slowly, cooking and stirring until boiling

1½ cups milk

Cook sauce several minutes longer, then combine with potato-onion mixture and add

1 tablespoon snipped parsley
Salt, pepper and celery salt to taste

Heat to serving temperature and serve with toasted **croutons**.

2 servings

DILLED SPLIT PEA SOUP

Set out a small skillet and heavy 1½-qt. saucepan.

Fry slowly in the skillet until crisp

3 slices bacon

Remove bacon to absorbent paper. Measure 2 tablespoons bacon drippings into the saucepan. Add

3 cups boiling water
1½ cups split peas
2 teaspoons salt
¼ cup chopped onion

Cover and cook gently over medium heat 1 hr., adding more boiling water during cooking process (about 1 cup will be needed).

Add

½ teaspoon dill weed

Cover and cook over very low heat 30 min. longer.

Remove from heat and stir in

1⅔ cups (14½-oz. can) evaporated milk
Few grains cayenne pepper

Heat soup to serving temperature. Ladle into soup bowls. Crumble the bacon and sprinkle over each serving.

4 servings

Note: Pour leftover soup into a freezer jar or other container and store in freezer for future use.

FROSTY TOMATO SOUP

Combine, blending thoroughly

1 can (10½ oz.) condensed tomato soup
¼ cup dairy sour cream
¾ cup cold water

Refrigerate to chill thoroughly, at least 4 hrs. Serve in chilled bowls. Garnish with additional sour cream and **chopped chives** or **parsley**.

2 servings

SCOTTISH SCONES

Set out and grease a small baking sheet.

Sift together into a bowl

1 cup all-purpose flour
2 tablespoons sugar
2 teaspoons baking powder
1 teaspoon cream of tartar
½ teaspoon salt

Using a pastry blender or two knives, cut in

⅓ cup butter or margarine

When mixture resembles coarse crumbs, stir in

1 cup rolled oats (quick or old-fashioned, uncooked)

Stir in with a fork, mixing only until dry ingredients are moistened

⅓ cup milk

Turn dough onto floured pastry canvas and pat into an 8-in. round. Divide into 8 pie-shaped wedges and place on prepared baking sheet.

Bake at 425°F about 15 min., or until lightly browned.

Split scones and serve hot with **butter**.

8 scones

Note: If desired, wrap leftover scones for freezing and store in freezer for future use. To serve, split and toast scones. Serve with butter and marmalade.

WHOLE WHEAT CORN MEAL GRIDDLECAKES

Set out a griddle or heavy skillet.

Combine in a large mixer bowl

1 pkg. active dry yeast
¼ cup warm water

Set aside until yeast is softened.

Beat in, mixing thoroughly

¼ cup dark molasses
¼ teaspoon salt
2 eggs (½ cup)
½ cup milk

Add ½ cup at a time, beating only until smooth after each addition

1 cup whole wheat flour
1 cup yellow corn meal

When smooth, blend in

¾ cup milk

Cover and set aside about 20 min., or store, tightly covered, in refrigerator overnight.

When ready to prepare griddlecakes, heat the griddle and add a small amount of

Butter or other shortening

Using about ¼ cup batter for each griddlecake, pour onto hot griddle. Bake until bubbles form and break and griddlecake is lightly browned on bottom. Turn over and bake 1 to 2 min. longer.

Serve immediately with **butter** and **maple syrup** or **honey**. *About 10 large griddlecakes*

Note: Recipe makes about 2½ cups batter. If used for several "bakings" divide batter immediately after mixing and store half in tightly covered container in refrigerator. Store no longer than 2 days. When ready to use,

remove from refrigerator and bake griddle-cakes at once.

SAUSAGE PANCAKES WITH HOT MAPLE BUTTER

Set out a small skillet and a griddle.

Brown in the skillet, draining off the fat
¼ lb. bulk pork sausage

Measure into a bowl
1 cup pancake mix
Combine, blending well
¼ teaspoon baking soda
1 cup buttermilk
Add immediately to pancake mix along with the cooked sausage and
1 egg, slightly beaten
Stir only enough to moisten the dry ingredients. (Do not overbeat.)

Bake on hot, lightly greased griddle. Serve with **Hot Maple Butter** (below).   *About 6 pancakes*

—HOT MAPLE BUTTER

Combine in a small saucepan
½ cup butter
¾ cup maple syrup
Cook and stir over low heat until butter is melted. Serve hot.   *About 1 cup*

CRUMB PANCAKES

Set out a griddle or a heavy skillet.

Prepare coarse crumbs from
1½ slices toasted bread (crusts removed)
Soften crumbs in a mixture of
¾ cup milk, scalded
1 tablespoon butter or margarine
Stir into softened crumbs
1 egg, well beaten
Combine, mixing thoroughly
¼ cup all-purpose flour
1½ teaspoons baking powder
1 teaspoon sugar
¼ teaspoon salt
Stir into crumb mixture along with
½ teaspoon grated lemon peel
Mix thoroughly.

Drop batter from end of spoon onto hot greased griddle, forming pancakes 3 to 4 in. in diameter. Bake until browned on both sides, turning pancakes once.

Serve with **Honey Orange Sauce** (below).
About 6 pancakes

—HONEY ORANGE SAUCE

Combine in a small saucepan
¼ cup butter or margarine
½ cup honey
1 teaspoon grated orange peel
2 tablespoons orange juice
Heat to boiling.   *About ¾ cup sauce*

BRUNCH SCRAMBLE

Combine in a small saucepan
½ can (about ⅔ cup) condensed tomato soup
½ cup coarsely shredded Cheddar cheese
Few drops Worcestershire sauce
Stir over low heat until cheese is melted. Keep sauce hot.

Heat in a small skillet
½ to 1 tablespoon fat
Brown on both sides in the hot fat
4 slices Canadian-style bacon
Remove from skillet and keep warm.

Prepare in the same skillet
Scrambled Eggs (one-half recipe, page 139)
Prepare
4 slices buttered toast
For each serving, arrange 2 slices bacon on a slice of toast; top with one half the scrambled eggs. Spoon hot sauce over egg and garnish with **parsley sprigs**. Cut remaining toast into 4 triangles and place 2 on each individual plate.   *2 servings*

BAKED EGGS

When serving eggs to a large group for a company breakfast or brunch, bake them in muffin-pan wells for convenience.

Set out 6-oz. custard cups or individual ramekins.

Measure into each cup
1 teaspoon light cream
1 teaspoon butter or margarine
Set in a 325°F oven about 10 min. to heat.

Remove from oven and break into each cup
1 large egg (keep yolk intact)
Sprinkle top with
Shredded Parmesan or Cheddar cheese

Bake about 15 min., or until white of egg is just set.

Gently remove egg with a spatula to serving plate, or serve in the custard cup or ramekin.

EGGS TETRAZZINI

Cook, following package directions, in boiling salted water until tender and drain
½ pkg. (about 4 oz.) spaghetti
Prepare
4 Hard-Cooked Eggs (page 133)

Meanwhile, heat in a heavy skillet or saucepan
2 tablespoons butter or margarine
Add to skillet and cook about 3 min.
½ small clove garlic, crushed
½ cup diced celery
1 tablespoon chopped green pepper
Stir in and cook 1 to 2 min.
1 tablespoon all-purpose flour
¼ teaspoon salt
Add gradually, stirring constantly,
1 cup milk
Cook and stir until sauce is thickened.

Add
2 oz. (about ½ cup) coarsely shredded sharp Cheddar cheese
1 teaspoon Worcestershire sauce
2 to 3 teaspoons dry sherry (optional)
Stir until cheese is melted; add hard-cooked eggs, cut in quarters or eighths, reserving several pieces for garnish. Season with **salt and pepper** to taste.

Heat only to serving temperature. (Do not overheat.) Serve over hot spaghetti. Garnish with reserved egg and
2 or 3 pimiento-stuffed olives, thinly sliced
2 tablespoons shredded Parmesan cheese
2 servings

PUFFY OMELET WITH ARTICHOKE HEARTS

Set out a heavy skillet or omelet pan.

Combine in a 1½-qt. saucepan
1 pkg. (9 oz.) frozen artichoke hearts
1 cup boiling water
1½ tablespoons lemon juice
½ to 1 teaspoon garlic salt
Cover and bring quickly to boiling; reduce heat and boil gently until artichoke hearts are just tender, 5 to 10 min. Drain thoroughly.

Puffy Omelet with Artichoke Hearts

Meanwhile, separate

4 eggs

Beat egg yolks in a mixing bowl until very thick. Beat in until blended

2 tablespoons milk
½ teaspoon salt
Dash pepper

Beat egg whites until stiff, not dry, peaks are formed; fold into beaten egg yolks.

Heat in the skillet

3 tablespoons butter or margarine

Tilt skillet to let fat coat sides and bottom. Turn egg mixture into skillet and spread evenly. Cook slowly, turning skillet occasionally to brown omelet evenly. When well puffed and lightly browned on bottom, place in 375°F oven about 4 min. (Omelet is cooked when firm to the touch.)

Meanwhile, finely chop about ⅓ of the cooked artichoke hearts; set aside remainder to use for garnish. Mix with the chopped artichokes

2 tablespoons butter or margarine

Spoon over half of the omelet. Fold omelet over and slide onto serving platter; garnish platter with artichoke hearts. Serve with a sauce.   *2 servings*

Suggested Sauces—Blend enough **milk** with **1 can condensed cream of mushroom or cream of chicken soup** until of pouring consistency; heat. Or serve chilled **dairy sour cream** or a heated mildly seasoned **tomato sauce** with the omelet.

CHEESE FONDUE FOR TWO

Set out and grease two 10-oz. individual casseroles.

Combine in a mixing bowl

½ cup milk, scalded
½ cup small bread cubes (2- to 3-day-old bread)
½ tablespoon butter or margarine
¼ teaspoon salt
Dash dry mustard
Dash pepper

Beat slightly

2 egg yolks

Stir egg yolks into bread mixture along with

½ cup shredded sharp Cheddar cheese

Beat until stiff, but not dry, peaks are formed

2 egg whites

Fold into first mixture and turn equal amounts into the two casseroles.

Bake at 325°F about 30 min., or until firm. Serve at once in the casseroles.   *2 servings*

CHEESE LUNCHEON DISH

Set out a small shallow baking dish.

Remove crusts from

6 slices bread

Arrange 3 slices in bottom of the dish, fitting them in so bottom of dish is entirely covered. Cover the bread with

4 oz. Cheddar cheese, sliced or shredded

Top with remaining bread slices.

Beat in a small mixing bowl

2 eggs

Beat in until blended

1¼ cups milk
¼ teaspoon salt
Dash pepper

Pour over the bread and cheese.

Bake in a 325°F oven about 40 min., or until puffed and browned.   *About 2 servings*

CHEESE RABBIT, HAWAIIAN STYLE

Have ready

1 cup cubed Cheddar cheese
3 slices (rounds) corned beef hash (see note)
3 slices canned pineapple
3 round rusks or toast rounds

Heat in a small saucepan

1 tablespoon butter or margarine

Stir in and cook over medium heat until bubbly

1 tablespoon all-purpose flour

Add slowly, cooking and stirring until boiling

¾ cup milk

Cook several minutes longer, then add Cheddar cheese and

¼ teaspoon salt
¼ teaspoon dry mustard
¼ teaspoon Worcestershire sauce

Continue cooking and stirring until cheese is melted. Set aside and keep hot.

Place corned beef rounds and pineapple slices on broiler rack about 3 in. from the heat and broil until lightly browned.

To serve, place a rusk or toast round on each serving plate, cover with slice of corned beef hash and top with a pineapple slice. Spoon on the cheese sauce and serve at once. *3 servings*

Note: Open both ends of a 15-oz. can corned beef hash and force the contents through can in one whole roll. Using about half of the roll, cut into 3 slices (rounds) ½ to ¾ in. thick. Refrigerate remaining hash for future use.

PARSLEYED CHEESE PUFF

Lightly grease a 1-qt. casserole or baking dish.

Toss together in a bowl

1½ cups small bread cubes (crusts removed)
4 oz. sharp Cheddar cheese, shredded
¼ cup finely chopped parsley
¾ teaspoon celery salt

Separate

2 eggs

Beat egg yolks and combine with

½ cup milk

Stir into mixture in bowl. Beat egg whites until stiff, not dry, peaks are formed; add to first mixture, folding gently until well blended. Turn into casserole.

Pour about 1 in. of hot water into a shallow baking pan and place in a 325°F oven. Set casserole in the pan and bake 40 to 45 min., or until puffy and lightly browned on top. Serve immediately.   *2 or 3 servings*

SHRIMP FRIED RICE

Set out a heavy 10-in. skillet.

Cook, following package directions

½ cup long grain rice

Refrigerate the cooked rice. (Chilling prevents rice sticking to skillet during frying process.)

Meanwhile, clean, devein, and cut in pieces

1 lb. fresh or frozen shrimp

Heat in the skillet

2 tablespoons peanut oil or other cooking oil

Add shrimp and brown slowly over low heat. Add and cook about 2 min.

⅓ cup coarsely chopped onion

Mix in the chilled rice. Sprinkle with

2 to 3 tablespoons soy sauce
Freshly ground black pepper to taste

Cook over low heat about 5 min., or until thoroughly heated. Stir occasionally using a fork to keep rice kernels intact.

Serve garnished with sliced **green onions** with tops or **Julienned Fried Egg** (below).
        2 or 3 servings

—JULIENNED FRIED EGG

Blend in a bowl

1 egg, beaten
1 tablespoon water

Pour egg mixture into a hot lightly greased 6- to 8-in. skillet; cover and cook over low heat until lightly browned and set. Turn the thin "pancake" onto a flat surface and cut into very narrow julienne strips.

FLANK STEAK WITH FILBERT STUFFING

Set out a heavy 8- or 10-in. skillet with tight-fitting cover.

Have ready
1 flank steak (about 1 lb.)

Prepare and set aside in a bowl
2 cups ½-in. bread cubes

Heat in the skillet
2 tablespoons butter or margarine
Add and sauté until lightly browned
¼ cup chopped filberts
Remove nuts with slotted spoon and toss with the bread cubes.

Add to the fat in skillet and cook 3 to 5 min., stirring occasionally.
3 tablespoons chopped onion
½ cup diced celery
Toss with the bread cubes along with
½ teaspoon salt
⅛ teaspoon pepper
¼ to ½ teaspoon poultry seasoning
⅓ to ½ cup hot water
Spread stuffing over flank steak; roll and tie securely. Brown roll well on all sides in the hot skillet with
½ to 1 tablespoon shortening or drippings
Add a small amount of
Beef broth (or hot water)
Cover skillet and simmer until meat is tender, adding additional liquid if needed. Remove meat roll to hot platter and slice to serve. If desired, meat juices in skillet may be thickened for gravy. *2 or 3 servings*

CUBE STEAKS WITH ROQUEFORT TOPPING

Set out a heavy 10-in. skillet with a tight-fitting cover.

Have ready
2 cube (or minute) steaks, cut about ½ in. thick

Combine to form a smooth paste
¼ cup crumbled Roquefort cheese
2 tablespoons butter or margarine
¼ to ½ teaspoon salt
¼ teaspoon lemon pepper marinade
⅛ teaspoon cayenne pepper

Heat in the skillet
1 to 1½ tablespoons olive oil or other cooking oil
Brown the steaks quickly on one side in the hot oil. Remove from heat and turn steaks with browned side up. Spread with cheese mixture and return to heat.

Cover skillet and cook steaks slowly, about 20 min., or until tender. Garnish steaks with **chopped parsley.** *2 servings*

DISTINCTIVE BEEF STEW

Anise seed along with several other spices imparts an unusual flavor to this hearty stew. Served with French fries, it will satisfy the largest appetite.

Set out a 10-in. heavy skillet with a tight-fitting cover.

Have ready
1½ lbs. (about) lean beef stew meat, cut in 1½-in. cubes
Heat in the skillet
1 to 1½ tablespoons cooking oil
Add meat and brown on all sides over medium heat. Remove meat with slotted spoon and add to skillet
1 large onion, cut in wedges
Cook about 5 min. to brown slightly. Return meat to skillet. Add
½ clove garlic, crushed
¾ to 1 cup beef broth
3 to 4 tablespoons tomato paste
½ bay leaf
½ teaspoon anise seed
½ teaspoon salt
⅛ teaspoon pepper
Blend well, cover and cook gently about 1½ hrs., or until meat is tender. *2 or 3 servings*

Savory Stuffed Baked Pork Chops

SAVORY STUFFED BAKED PORK CHOPS

Set out a small saucepan, a heavy skillet and a shallow baking dish.

Set out
2 thick pork chops
Cut a deep pocket in side of each chop and set aside.

Heat in the saucepan
1½ tablespoons fat
Add and cook about 3 min.
1½ tablespoons chopped onion
Combine onion with
2 cups soft bread crumbs
½ teaspoon salt
¼ teaspoon sage
Dash lemon pepper marinade
Toss stuffing ingredients lightly until well mixed and spoon half into pocket of each pork chop. Seal with small skewers or wooden picks.

Lightly coat the chops with a mixture of
1 tablespoon all-purpose flour
¼ teaspoon salt
Heat in the skillet
2 tablespoons fat
Add chops and brown well on both sides over low heat.

Put chops and drippings into baking dish. Pour over chops a mixture of
½ cup condensed tomato soup
⅓ cup water

Bake, uncovered, at 375°F 45 min., or until chops are tender. *2 servings*

SAN JOAQUIN RAISIN HAM

Set out a 1-qt. casserole or baking dish.

Prepare and set aside
1½ cups diced cooked ham

Drain, reserving syrup
1 can (8¾ oz.) pineapple tidbits
Set tidbits aside and combine syrup in a sauce-pan with enough water to make 1 cup liquid. Add and bring mixture to boiling
3 tablespoons vinegar

Meanwhile, mix thoroughly

 ¼ cup firmly packed brown sugar
 1 tablespoon cornstarch
 1 teaspoon dry mustard
 ⅛ teaspoon salt

Add gradually to hot liquid and cook, stirring until mixture thickens. Stir in and set aside

 ½ teaspoon Worcestershire sauce
 1½ teaspoons soy sauce

Spoon ham into casserole. Sprinkle with

 ¼ cup dark or golden raisins

Cover with the drained pineapple and

 ½ medium onion, thinly sliced
 ½ small green pepper, sliced in rings

Pour hot sauce over mixture.

Heat in a 350°F oven about 45 min. Serve with hot **fluffy rice.**   *About 2 servings*

HAM WITH SPICY PEARS

Delicately spiced pears complement baked ham in this attractive easy-to-fix main dish.

Combine in a heavy saucepan and bring to boiling

 ½ cup sugar
 ½ cup water
 ¼ cup vinegar
 1 stick (1½ in.) cinnamon
 2 pieces (½ in. each) gingerroot

Pare, halve, and core

 3 fresh Bartlett or Anjou pears

Add to boiling syrup and cook gently, turning occasionally until fork-tender. Remove from heat; cover and set aside to cool overnight.

Place on a broiler rack

 1 slice (about 1 lb.) center cut
  ready-to-eat ham

Brush surface with some of the cooled syrup. Place under broiler about 3 in. from the heat. Broil until lightly browned on both sides, turning once and basting with syrup.

Stud each pear half with

 Several whole cloves

Arrange around ham slice on a heated platter. Garnish with **parsley.**   *About 2 servings*

Note: If desired, substitute ¼ teaspoon ground cinnamon for the stick cinnamon; substitute ⅛ teaspoon *each* ground ginger and cloves for the gingerroot.

San Joaquin Raisin Ham

LAMB CHOPS WITH MINTED BREAD STUFFING

Set out a small shallow baking dish.

Have ready

 2 loin lamb chops (¾ to 1 in. thick)

Prepare and put into a bowl

 2 cups ½-in. soft bread cubes

Combine with bread cubes, tossing gently to mix well

 ¼ teaspoon salt
 ¾ teaspoon dried mint leaves
 ⅛ teaspoon savory
 1 tablespoon melted butter
  or margarine

Spoon stuffing into the baking dish and top with the lamb chops. Sprinkle chops lightly with **salt** and **seasoned pepper.**

Bake at 350°F 30 to 40 min., or until lamb chops are tender and browned.   *2 servings*

Note: Ground lamb shaped into patties may be substituted for the chops. If desired, add leftover cooked peas to the stuffing and increase the savory to ¼ teaspoon.

VEAL STEAK WITH WINE SAUCE

Set out an 8-in. skillet with tight-fitting cover.

Have ready

 1 lb. veal steak (or veal cutlet,
  cut about 1 in. thick)

Heat in skillet

 1 tablespoon olive oil or other
  cooking oil

Add veal and brown on both sides over medium heat. Reduce heat, cover skillet and cook slowly 20 min., or until meat is tender, turning several times.

While meat is cooking, prepare

 Wine Sauce (below)

When ready to serve, season veal to taste and place on a hot serving platter; pour Wine Sauce over steak and serve at once. *2 servings*

—WINE SAUCE

Heat in a small saucepan

 1 tablespoon butter or margarine

Add and cook 2 to 3 min.

 2 green onions with tops, finely
  chopped

Stir in

 ½ tablespoon all-purpose flour
 ¼ teaspoon salt

Cook and stir until flour browns slightly. Blend in

 ⅓ to ½ cup hot water

Cook until thickened, stirring frequently. Stir in

 1 teaspoon ketchup
 1 to 1½ tablespoons Madeira
 1 tablespoon minced parsley

Cook only until thoroughly heated.
                    About ½ cup sauce

KIDNEY STEW

Set out a 1½-qt. saucepan and a heavy skillet.

Wash, remove membrane and split in halves

 2 lamb or pork kidneys

Remove cores and large tubes from kidney halves. Cover with a blend of

 2 cups cold water
 ½ teaspoon salt
 2 teaspoons vinegar

Set aside about 1 hr.

Rinse kidneys in cold water and cut into ½-in. cubes. Put into saucepan with just enough boiling water to cover; cook gently, tightly covered, over low heat 30 min. Drain.

Dredge kidneys with a mixture of

 3 tablespoons all-purpose flour
 ¼ teaspoon salt
 Dash pepper

Heat in the skillet

 3 tablespoons fat (half bacon drippings
  and half butter or margarine)

Add cubed kidneys and brown slowly on all sides. Stir in

 1 tablespoon chopped onion
 2 tablespoons snipped parsley
 ¼ teaspoon thyme
 ¼ bay leaf

Pour in slowly

 1 cup beef broth

Cook and stir until mixture comes to boiling and thickens. Serve the stew on hot **fluffy rice.**
                         2 servings

TWOSOME MEAT LOAF

Set out a small shallow baking pan.

Combine in a bowl, mixing thoroughly

 ½ lb. lean ground beef
 ¼ cup rolled oats (quick or old
  fashioned, uncooked)
 ½ teaspoon salt
 Few grains pepper
 ⅛ teaspoon dry mustard
 ¼ teaspoon onion powder
 1 egg, beaten
 2 tablespoons sweet pickle liquid
  (or water)

Shape mixture into 2 loaves. Place in baking pan.

Combine and spread over loaves

 3 tablespoons ketchup
 2 tablespoons sweet pickle liquid
  (or water)
 2 teaspoons brown sugar

Bake at 350°F about 30 min., or until loaves are of desired doneness.   *2 servings*

PINEAPPLE-GLAZED CHICKEN

Set out an 8-in. skillet and a shallow baking dish with a cover (or use aluminum foil for cover).

Have ready
   2 boned chicken breasts, halved
Coat the chicken pieces with a mixture of
   ⅓ cup all-purpose flour
   ½ teaspoon monosodium glutamate
   ¼ teaspoon garlic salt
   ¼ teaspoon celery salt
   ⅛ teaspoon nutmeg
Heat in the skillet
   1 to 2 tablespoons butter, margarine, or other shortening
Brown the chicken slowly on all sides in the hot fat. Place in the baking dish. Combine and pour over chicken
   ½ cup heavy syrup drained from 1 can (8¼ oz.) sliced pineapple (reserve pineapple slices)
   ¼ cup soy sauce
   1 tablespoon sugar
Cover dish tightly.

Bake at 350°F about 1 hr., basting chicken several times during baking.

Meanwhile, prepare
   1 cup cooked rice
Heat in skillet
   1 tablespoon butter or margarine
Sauté the pineapple slices in the hot fat.

When chicken is tender, place on heated platter, surround with fluffy hot rice and top with pineapple slices.   *2 servings*

CHERRIED CHICKEN

Set out a heavy 8-in. skillet with tight-fitting cover.

Have ready
   2 large chicken breasts
Dredge chicken with a mixture of
   ¼ cup all-purpose flour
   ½ teaspoon salt
   ¼ teaspoon paprika
   ⅛ teaspoon curry powder
Heat in the skillet
   2 to 3 tablespoons butter or margarine
Brown chicken slowly in the hot fat, turning to brown evenly on all sides. Add to skillet
   ½ cup dry white wine
Cover and cook over low heat about 30 min., or until chicken is tender.

Add to skillet
   ⅔ cup (about) drained canned dark sweet cherries (one-half 17-oz. can)
   ¼ cup drained canned pineapple chunks
Continue cooking over low heat until thoroughly heated.

Arrange chicken with cherries on hot platter; garnish with **sprigs of fresh mint** or **watercress.**   *2 servings*

BAKED CHICKEN SALAD TARTS

Set out two 6-in. pie pans.

Prepare, following package directions
   1 pkg. (about 10 oz.) pie crust mix
Shape into a ball; cover and refrigerate.

Combine, mixing well and set aside
   1 cup diced, cooked chicken
   ½ cup finely diced celery
   3 tablespoons finely diced green pepper
   3 tablespoons toasted, blanched almonds, chopped
   ½ teaspoon Worcestershire sauce
   ½ teaspoon salt
   ⅛ teaspoon tarragon leaves
   Dash nutmeg
   Dash ginger
   ⅓ cup mayonnaise
   ⅓ cup shredded Cheddar cheese

Roll chilled pastry on lightly floured pastry canvas into a round about ⅛ in. thick. Cut two rounds 6 in. in diameter and two rounds 7 in. in diameter. Using a 3-in. cutter, cut out centers from the two 6-in. rounds. If desired, cut scallops around holes. Gently lay solid pastry rounds in the two 6-in. pie pans and fit pastry to the pans without stretching. Trim pastry around edge. Fill each pastry shell with ½ the filling. Moisten edges of bottom crusts with water for a tight seal. Carefully arrange the pastry rings on top of filling. Fold extra pastry under at edge and press edges together with a fork.

Bake at 425°F 20 to 25 min., or until tarts are golden brown.   *Two 6-in. tarts*

"FALL FANCY" CHICKEN

Grease a shallow baking dish.

Have ready
   2 slices unpared eggplant, about ¾ in. thick
   4 slices tomato, about ¼ in. thick
   2 thin slices onion
   2 thin slices Cheddar cheese
   Sliced cooked chicken
   2 slices bacon
Place eggplant slices in the baking dish. Sprinkle with
   Seasoned salt
Top each eggplant slice with 2 tomato slices, 1 onion slice, 1 cheese slice, 1 serving sliced chicken and 1 slice bacon, cut in half.

Place in a 350°F oven 40 min., or until bacon and vegetables are cooked.   *2 servings*

CHICKEN TOKAY

Set out a heavy 10-in. skillet.

Rinse and pat dry
   3 chicken breasts
Sprinkle with
   Salt and pepper

Baked Chicken Salad Tarts

"Fall Fancy" Chicken

Heat in skillet
   2 tablespoons butter or margarine
Add chicken to skillet and brown well on all sides. Add a mixture of
   ¾ cup chicken broth
   Dash allspice
   2 teaspoons lemon juice
Cover and cook gently about 30 min., or until chicken is tender.

While chicken is cooking, rinse, halve and remove seeds from
   1½ cups Tokay grapes
Set aside.

Combine, mixing well
   1½ tablespoons cold water
   2 teaspoons cornstarch
Stir into liquid in skillet and cook until thickened. Add grapes to skillet and cook only until they are heated through. Remove chicken with grapes to heated serving platter and garnish with
   Parsley sprigs
Serve with **hot fluffy rice.**   *3 servings*

CHICKEN LIVERS AND MUSHROOMS

Fry until crisp in a small skillet over low heat
   2 slices bacon, diced

695

Fish Smorrebrod

Remove bacon to absorbent paper. Add to fat in skillet

4 chicken livers, halved or quartered
6 mushrooms, sliced

Cook gently, stirring occasionally, about 5 min., or until livers are lightly browned.

Stir in a blend of

1 teaspoon all-purpose flour
½ teaspoon salt
Dash pepper

Add, cooking and stirring over medium heat until boiling

¼ cup light cream

Add the crisp bacon and

2 tablespoons chopped parsley

Serve immediately on **toast triangles or rounds.** *2 servings*

FISH SMORREBROD

Set out a heavy skillet.

Prepare

Piquant Sauce (below)

Have ready

4 fish fillets (thawed, if frozen)

Dip fillets into

1 egg, slightly beaten

Then dip into

Fine dry bread crumbs

Heat in the skillet until very hot

Vegetable shortening or cooking oil

Add the fish and fry until golden brown.

While fish are frying, fry until crisp and drain on absorbent paper

4 thin slices bacon

Split into halves

2 round buns

Toast halves and spread with

Butter or margarine

To serve, place a fish fillet on each toasted bun half and top with Piquant Sauce and a crisp bacon slice. Garnish each plate with **lemon wedges, sliced tomatoes, lettuce** and **radish roses.** *2 servings*

—PIQUANT SAUCE

Heat in a small saucepan

2 tablespoons butter or margarine

Add and cook about 3 min.

1 tablespoon finely chopped onion

Stir in a mixture of

2 tablespoons all-purpose flour
⅛ teaspoon dry mustard
Dash *each* salt, cayenne pepper,
celery salt, thyme and marjoram

Cook and stir over medium heat until bubbly. Blend in

1 cup milk or light cream

Bring to boiling and cook several minutes, stirring constantly. Mix in a drop at a time

1½ tablespoons lemon juice

Keep hot over simmering water until ready to serve. *1 cup sauce*

SALMON VEGETABLE CASSEROLE

Grease a small casserole and set aside.

Drain and flake (page 9)

1 can (7¾ oz.) salmon

Set aside.

Have ready

½ cup diced potato
½ cup sliced carrot
⅓ cup fresh green peas
1 small onion, chopped

Cook the potato, carrot and peas until tender in a small amount of boiling salted water in a covered saucepan. Drain, reserving ⅓ cup liquid for sauce. Set aside.

Heat in a saucepan

1½ tablespoons butter or margarine

Add the onion and cook until tender. Blend in

1½ tablespoons all-purpose flour
¼ teaspoon salt
Few grains pepper

Heat until mixture bubbles. Add gradually, stirring constantly, the vegetable liquid and

⅔ cup milk

Bring to boiling; stir and cook until thickened. Remove from heat and stir in

1 teaspoon snipped parsley

Arrange alternate layers of vegetables and salmon in casserole. Pour sauce over all.

Prepare and roll or pat out to the size of the casserole

Baking Powder Biscuit dough (one-half recipe, page 92)

Cut small slits in the dough to allow steam to escape and put in place on casserole mixture.

Bake at 450°F 15 to 20 min., or until topping is lightly browned. *2 or 3 servings*

BAKED STUFFED SALMON

Place in a greased shallow baking pan

2 salmon steaks, about ½ in. thick

Sprinkle lightly with **salt** and **pepper** and set aside.

Prepare and set aside in a bowl

1 cup (about) ½-in. soft bread cubes

Heat in a skillet

1 tablespoon butter or margarine

Add and cook 3 to 5 min., stirring occasionally

3 tablespoons chopped celery
1½ tablespoons chopped green pepper

Combine vegetables with bread cubes and add

2 tablespoons chopped pimiento-stuffed olives
½ teaspoon monosodium glutamate
Dash pepper
½ teaspoon paprika

Toss together and add a blend of

2 teaspoons lemon juice
2 to 3 tablespoons hot water

Mix well. Fill the opening formed at the ends

696

of each salmon steak with one-half the stuffing. Bring ends together to hold stuffing in place.

Bake at 400°F 30 to 40 min., or until fish is done. Using a wide spatula, carefully remove steaks with stuffing to serving plates. Garnish with **parsley sprigs** and, if desired, serve with a **lemon butter sauce.** *2 servings*

CREAMED CRAB MEAT ON TOAST

Have ready
> **1 pkg. (6 oz.) frozen Alaska king crab meat, partially thawed**

Heat in small heavy saucepan
> **2 tablespoons butter or margarine**

Blend in until smooth
> **2 tablespoons all-purpose flour**

Cook over medium heat until bubbly and gradually add
> **½ cup milk**

Cook and stir until thickened and smooth.

Add crab meat and
> **2 tablespoons coarsely chopped pimiento**
> **Salt and pepper to taste**

Cook and stir over low heat until crab meat is thawed and the mixture reaches serving temperature. Just before serving, blend in
> **2 or 3 teaspoons dry sherry**

Serve creamed crab meat on **buttered toast triangles.** *2 servings*

CRAB MEAT-FILLED PANCAKES

Set out a heavy 8-in. skillet; lightly grease a shallow baking dish with a cover (or use aluminum foil for cover).

Prepare and keep warm in double boiler top over hot water
> **Creamed Crab Meat (on this page)**

For pancakes, combine in a bowl and beat thoroughly until blended
> **2 eggs, slightly beaten**
> **½ cup buttermilk pancake mix**

Add and continue beating until smooth
> **¾ cup milk**
> **1 tablespoon shortening, melted**

Heat skillet with
> **½ teaspoon (about) shortening or cooking oil**

Pour about ¼ cup batter into hot skillet; quickly tilt skillet to entirely cover bottom with a thin layer of batter. Bake over medium heat until golden brown on both sides, turning pancake once. Repeat process using remaining batter; you will have 7 or 8 thin pancakes. Use 2 pancakes for each serving. (Remaining pancakes may be stacked with waxed paper between them, placed in a plastic container, tightly covered, and stored in refrigerator or freezer for a future meal.)

Spoon some of the crab meat mixture onto the pancakes, roll up and place them, side by side, in the prepared baking dish. Sprinkle with
> **Shredded Parmesan cheese (about 1 tablespoon)**

Cover baking dish and set in a 375°F oven about 15 min., or until pancakes are thoroughly heated. Any leftover creamed crab meat may be spooned over pancakes, if desired.
2 servings

SKILLET CRAB

Set out a large heavy skillet.

Drain
> **1 can (7½ oz.) Alaska king crab meat**

Cut up larger pieces and set crab meat aside.

Heat in the skillet
> **2 tablespoons butter or margarine**

Add and cook until soft, stirring occasionally
> **2 tablespoons sliced green onions with tops**
> **½ cup chopped green pepper**

Stir in
> **1 can (4 oz.) mushrooms (with liquid)**
> **1 can (16 oz.) tomatoes**
> **½ teaspoon salt**
> **Dash pepper**
> **⅛ teaspoon oregano**
> **1 cup uncooked wide egg noodles**

Mix well with a fork, cover skillet tightly and cook mixture gently 8 to 10 min., or until noodles are tender.

Stir in the crab meat along with
> **½ cup shredded Cheddar cheese**
> **¼ cup snipped parsley**

Cover and continue cooking until thoroughly heated. *2 servings*

OYSTERS PARMESAN

Combine in an 8-in. skillet or small saucepan
> **1 cup drained fresh oysters**
> **1 tablespoon chopped onion**
> **½ cup milk**

Cook, covered, over very low heat 10 to 15 min., or until oysters curl slightly at edges.

Meanwhile, heat in a small heavy saucepan
> **1½ tablespoons butter or margarine**

Stir in a blend of
> **2 tablespoons all-purpose flour**
> **¼ teaspoon salt**
> **Dash pepper**
> **¼ teaspoon celery salt**

Cook until bubbly over medium heat. Blend in
> **½ cup milk**

Cook and stir until sauce is thick and smooth. Stir in
> **¼ cup shredded Parmesan cheese**
> **2 teaspoons snipped parsley**

Combine sauce with oyster mixture and heat until very hot. Spoon over
> **2 hard rolls, split in halves, toasted and buttered**
2 servings

ASPARAGUS WITH BLUE CHEESE SAUCE

Wash, cook (page 313) until tender and drain
> **1 bunch asparagus (6 to 8 spears)**

Meanwhile, to prepare sauce, cream until softened in a small heavy saucepan
> **1 pkg. (3 oz.) cream cheese**

Blend in until smooth
> **⅓ cup undiluted evaporated milk**
> **⅛ to ¼ teaspoon salt**

Crumble and mix in (do not beat)
> **1 pkg. (1 oz.) blue cheese**

Place over very low heat until sauce is hot and bubbly, about 3 min., stirring occasionally. Serve over hot asparagus. *2 servings*

BAKED BEAN CASSOULET

Set out 2 individual casseroles.

Combine and spoon into the casseroles
> **½ cup cubed cooked ham**
> **1 can (16 oz.) baked beans**
> **¼ cup drained canned tomatoes**
> **1 tablespoon instant minced onion**
> **¼ teaspoon dry mustard**

Set in a 375°F oven about 30 min., or until thoroughly heated. *About 2 servings*

SKILLET CREOLE CABBAGE

Heat in a heavy 10-in. skillet
> **2 tablespoons butter or margarine**

Add and cook about 3 min., stirring occasionally
> **¼ cup chopped onion**

Baked Bean Cassoulet

Meanwhile, toss with a fork until well mixed

½ cup chopped green pepper
¼ cup sliced celery
1 cup cut-up tomato (1 large tomato)
2 cups finely shredded young green cabbage
½ teaspoon salt
1 teaspoon sugar
Dash pepper

Add mixture to the skillet, cover tightly and cook over high heat until steaming. Stir with a fork; reduce heat to low and cook until cabbage is tender, but not soft (6 to 8 min.).

2 servings

GLOSSY GINGER CARROTS

Set out a heavy 8-in. skillet.

Rinse and pare (or scrape)

6 to 8 small whole carrots (about ½ lb.)

Heat in the skillet

2 tablespoons butter or margarine

Stir in

2 tablespoons thawed frozen orange juice concentrate
1½ teaspoons honey
¼ teaspoon ginger
¼ teaspoon salt

Add carrots; cover tightly and cook over low heat about 20 min., or until carrots are just tender, turning twice. If desired, serve garnished with **fresh mint leaves.**   *2 servings*

BAKED ONIONS IN CHEESE SAUCE

Set out a saucepan, small skillet and a small baking dish.

Peel and cook in saucepan in boiling salted water about 8 min.

2 large onions

Drain onions and when cool enough to handle remove centers, leaving a shell about ¾ in. thick. Set shells aside in the baking dish. Chop onion centers.

Heat in skillet

1 tablespoon butter or margarine

Add chopped onion and cook about 3 min. Combine onion with

1 slice bread (soaked in water a few seconds and squeezed dry)
¼ lb. ground beef
¼ teaspoon salt
Dash pepper
1 egg yolk, slightly beaten
1 tablespoon snipped parsley

Spoon the mixture into onion shells heaping the tops. Set aside.

To prepare cheese sauce, heat in saucepan

1 tablespoon butter or margarine

Stir in and cook until bubbly

1 tablespoon all-purpose flour
¼ teaspoon salt
Dash pepper

Add slowly, cooking and stirring until boiling

¾ cup milk

Cook and stir several minutes longer and add

1 cup cubed sharp Cheddar cheese

Stir until cheese is melted. Pour hot sauce over stuffed onions and sprinkle with

1 tablespoon shredded Parmesan cheese

Set in 350°F oven 40 to 45 min.   *2 servings*

PECAN-STUFFED SWEET POTATOES

Scrub thoroughly and bake at 450°F until tender (35 to 40 min.)

2 medium sweet potatoes

(If desired, bake potatoes at 350°F and increase cooking time.)

Cut a lengthwise slice from top of each potato. Scoop out the inside into a bowl; leave shells intact. Mash hot potatoes with

1 tablespoon butter or margarine
1 tablespoon brown sugar
⅛ teaspoon baking powder
2 tablespoons finely chopped celery
2 tablespoons chopped pecans

Spoon into the potato shells and dot with

Butter or margarine (about 2 teaspoons)

Return to oven and heat about 20 min. longer, or until lightly browned on top.   *2 servings*

POTATOES GATEAU

Set out a 7- or 8-in. skillet.

Pare and thinly slice

2 medium potatoes

Coarsely chop

3 medium onions

Melt in the skillet

2 tablespoons butter or margarine

Pour off ½ tablespoon melted fat and set aside.

In the hot skillet, arrange half the potato slices in an even layer and top with a layer of half the chopped onion. Season to taste with

Salt
Seasoned pepper

Repeat layering and sprinkle over top

¼ cup fine dry bread crumbs

Cook slowly until browned on bottom. Carefully turn potato cake with wide spatula, adding remaining melted fat while turning. Cook until vegetables are tender and potato cake is browned on bottom. Serve at once. *2 servings*

ZUCCHINI AND TOMATOES AU GRATIN

Grease a small baking dish or casserole.

Scrub thoroughly and cut into ½-in. pieces

¼ lb. zucchini

Heat in a small skillet

1 tablespoon butter or margarine

Add and cook 2 to 3 min.

2 tablespoons chopped onion

Add zucchini and cook over low heat about 5 min., stirring frequently. Stir in

½ cup cooked or canned tomatoes
¼ teaspoon salt
Dash pepper

Cover and cook about 5 min. longer. Turn into the baking dish and top with

¼ cup shredded Cheddar cheese

Heat in a 375°F oven about 15 min., or until cheese is melted.   *2 servings*

PINEAPPLE PEPPER SLAW

Combine in a bowl, mixing thoroughly

½ teaspoon dry mustard
2 tablespoons sugar
½ teaspoon salt
¼ teaspoon caraway seed
1 tablespoon vinegar
¼ cup mayonnaise

Add and toss lightly

3 cups shredded green cabbage
½ green pepper, shredded
½ cup pineapple tidbits

Chill before serving.   *About 2 servings*

BOUQUET SALAD

This attractive salad is especially appropriate for a company spring luncheon menu when a bride-to-be is your special guest.

Core, rinse, thoroughly drain and chill

1 head iceberg lettuce

Beat together until blended

1 pkg. (3 oz.) cream cheese, softened
¼ cup mayonnaise
¼ cup dairy sour cream

Blend in

**2 tablespoons chopped chives (fresh
    or freeze-dried)**
Salt and pepper to taste

When ready to serve, drain

1 can (8 oz.) apricot halves

Cut into halves

4 or 5 large slices cooked ham

Cut chilled lettuce crosswise into 4 or 5 rafts (loose slices), saving end pieces to use later in a tossed salad. Place rafts on chilled salad or luncheon plates. Spread with the cream cheese mixture.

Roll the half-slices of ham into conical flower shapes. Place two "flowers" on each lettuce raft with an apricot half inside each. If desired, garnish each plate with **sprigs of parsley** or **watercress**.   *4 or 5 servings*

ITALIAN SALAD BOWL

Set out a salad bowl.

Scrub well, cook until tender, then peel and dice

1 large potato

While potato is cooking prepare salad dressing. Mash together in a bowl, using a fork (or use mortar and pestle)

½ clove garlic
2 or 3 anchovy fillets

Combine with

2 tablespoons olive oil
1½ teaspoons tarragon vinegar
1½ teaspoons lemon juice
½ teaspoon dry mustard
Dash freshly ground black pepper
1½ teaspoons capers

Blend thoroughly and set aside 1 hr.

Meanwhile, drain

**1 can (8 oz.) green beans (about 1
    cup, drained)**

Italian Salad Bowl and Carnival Pineapple Bowl

Toss potato and beans with enough dressing to coat well; chill at least 1 hr. Before serving, toss again.

Line the salad bowl with

Crisp lettuce

Spoon in the potato-bean salad and garnish with

Tomato wedges
Ripe olives
Additional anchovies
                        2 servings

CARNIVAL PINEAPPLE BOWL

Set out and chill 2 individual salad bowls.

Prepare and chill

Rosy Dressing (below)

Combine in a bowl and chill

**4 slices canned pineapple (8½-oz.
    can, drained; reserve syrup)**
¼ cup pineapple syrup
**1 cup melon balls or cubes
    (watermelon or cantaloupe)**

When ready to serve, line the salad bowls with

Chilled crisp greens

Top with mounds of

Cottage cheese

Drain chilled pineapple and arrange 2 slices on each salad. Circle salads with the chilled melon balls and

1 firm ripe banana, sliced

Serve with Rosy Dressing.   *2 servings*

—ROSY DRESSING

Combine in a saucepan and cook and stir over low heat until thickened and smooth

¼ cup pineapple syrup
2 tablespoons water
1 teaspoon cornstarch

Blend in

2 tablespoons lemon juice
¼ teaspoon seasoned salt
½ teaspoon sugar
½ teaspoon prepared mustard
½ teaspoon prepared horseradish
¼ teaspoon paprika
1 tablespoon salad oil
2 tablespoons ketchup or chili sauce
**1 tablespoon finely chopped fresh mint
    (optional)**

Refrigerate. Mix well before using.
                About ¾ cup dressing

FROZEN SEAFOOD SALAD

Set out 2 individual salad molds.

Measure into a custard cup

3 tablespoons cold water

Sprinkle over water

1 teaspoon unflavored gelatin

Let stand until softened, then set over hot water to dissolve gelatin completely.

Combine in a mixing bowl

**1 cup flaked cooked seafood (crab
    meat or lobster)**
⅓ cup ketchup
1 tablespoon lemon juice
1½ tablespoons vinegar
1 teaspoon prepared horseradish
⅛ teaspoon salt

Add and mix thoroughly

¼ cup mayonnaise

Turn mixture into the molds, cover each with aluminum foil and freeze until firm.

Remove molds from freezer about 30 min. before ready to serve to soften slightly. Unmold on **tomato slices** or **crisp greens** on chilled salad plates.   *2 servings*

BAKED BANANAS WITH
CARAMEL TOPPING

Set out a small shallow baking dish or 8-in. pie pan and a small heavy saucepan.

Peel and cut crosswise into halves

2 medium bananas with green tips

Brush bananas generously with

**Thawed frozen orange juice
    concentrate**

Cherries Regalis Sundae

Coat with a mixture of
- **¼ cup packaged corn flake crumbs**
- **1 tablespoon butter or margarine, softened**

Roll pieces in
- **1 egg, slightly beaten**

Coat again with crumbs. Arrange bananas in baking dish.

Bake at 350°F about 10 min., or until just tender.

Meanwhile, prepare topping. Thoroughly heat together in the saucepan
- **½ cup caramel topping (from a jar)**
- **1 tablespoon butter or margarine**

Stir to blend and serve over warm bananas.

2 servings

ORANGE GINGERED BANANAS

Set out a small shallow baking dish.

Combine in a small saucepan
- **¼ cup orange juice**
- **½ teaspoon cornstarch**

Cook and stir over medium heat until boiling. Add a blend of
- **¼ cup orange juice**
- **1½ teaspoons honey**
- **1½ teaspoons chopped crystallized ginger**

Cook and stir until thoroughly heated. Place in the baking dish
- **2 green-tipped bananas, peeled**

Pour the sauce over bananas.

Bake at 350°F about 15 min., or until bananas are tender (but not soft), basting with the sauce several times. *2 servings*

Pears Patricia

CHERRIES REGALIS SUNDAE

Drain, reserving ⅔ cup syrup
- **1 can (17 oz.) dark sweet cherries (use about 1 cup, drained)**

Combine in a saucepan the cherry syrup and
- **¼ teaspoon grated lemon peel**

Stir in a blend of
- **2 teaspoons cornstarch**
- **3 tablespoons sugar**
- **Dash salt**

Cook and stir until mixture comes to boiling; continue cooking until thickened and smooth.

Remove from heat and stir in
- **2 tablespoons brandy**

Mix in drained cherries and cool.

Serve sauce over
- **Vanilla ice cream**

If desired, top servings with
- **Shaved almonds of filberts**

Store leftover sauce in a covered jar in the refrigerator.

PEARS A LA MOUSSELINE

Set out a small heavy skillet and an electric blender.

Pare, halve and core
- **2 firm ripe Anjou or Bartlett pears**

Drain, reserving syrup
- **1 can (8 oz.) apricot halves**

Put apricots in a bowl. Pour syrup into skillet and mix in
- **2 tablespoons sugar**
- **¼ cup water**

Bring to boiling. Add pear halves and cook over low heat about 8 min., turning occasionally in the syrup. Turn into a bowl and stir in
- **2 tablespoons apricot brandy**

Refrigerate until thoroughly chilled.

Turn apricots into electric blender container and add
- **2 tablespoons apricot brandy**

Turn on blender and blend until apricots are puréed. Refrigerate.

When ready to serve, spoon pears and brandied syrup into individual serving dishes. Spoon apricot purée over pears. Top with a dollop of **whipped cream** or **whipped dessert topping** and **slivered salted almonds.** *2 servings*

PEARS PATRICIA

Set out a 1-qt. saucepan. Chill 2 individual serving dishes.

Rinse and dry
- **2 firm ripe Anjou pears**

Leave stems intact.

Combine in saucepan and bring to boiling
- **1 cup water**
- **1 teaspoon vanilla extract**
- **½ cup sugar**

Add pears and poach gently in the syrup until

tender (but still firm). Cool and chill pears in the syrup.

When ready to serve, place in each serving dish
- **1 scoop vanilla ice cream**

Hollow out centers and place a poached pear upright in center of each scoop. Pour over each pear
- **Chocolate sauce, slightly heated**

Sprinkle with
- **Slivered almonds**

2 servings

SPANISH CREAM

Set out a small heavy saucepan and 2 or 3 individual dessert molds.

Combine in the saucepan
- **1 teaspoon unflavored gelatin**
- **2½ tablespoons sugar**
- **Dash salt**

Mix well and add
- **½ cup undiluted evaporated milk**
- **½ cup water**

Stir over low heat until gelatin is dissolved.

Separate
- **1 egg**

Beat egg yolk slightly in a small bowl. Gradually add about ¼ cup of the hot gelatin mixture, stirring constantly. Return to saucepan and cook over low heat until the mixture coats a metal spoon. Remove from heat and stir in
- **½ teaspoon vanilla extract**

Set aside to cool slightly.

Beat the egg white until rounded peaks are formed. Fold into the cooled mixture, blending thoroughly. Turn into the individual molds and chill until set.

Meanwhile, prepare
- **Coffee Sauce (below)**

When ready to serve, unmold desserts onto individual plates and serve with the sauce.

2 or 3 servings

—COFFEE SAUCE

Combine in a small saucepan
- **½ cup sugar**
- **1 cup light corn syrup**
- **1 tablespoon butter or margarine**
- **⅛ teaspoon salt**

Cook and stir over low heat until sugar is dissolved. Increase heat to medium and cook to 230°F or soft-ball stage (page 11); stir frequently. Reduce heat to simmer and cook 15 min. without stirring. Set aside to cool slightly.

Meanwhile, combine
- **⅔ cup (6-oz. can) undiluted evaporated milk**
- **½ teaspoon vanilla extract**

Stir until thoroughly blended and smooth
- **½ tablespoon instant powdered coffee**

Add slowly to the slightly cooled syrup, stirring until blended. *About 1½ cups sauce*

Note: Leftover sauce may be stored in covered jar in refrigerator.

Low-calorie recipes

The secret to a successful diet is not a dramatic change in your eating habits—it's just a little bit less of everything. Of course there are some extravagances you can't afford, like whipped cream-topped chocolate double scoop sundaes. Discretion is the better part of dieting. The information included here is only a guide and is not designed to set a reducing pattern for you. That is a problem to work out with your doctor who will inform you of your calorie requirements for maintaining normal weight.

Once you are overweight and want to reduce, you must regulate the daily intake of calories. Try to learn the number of calories in everything you eat and develop the ability to estimate *portion sizes.* Remember, too, it is quite possible over a period of years for anyone to put on ten or twenty pounds by eating as few as one or two hundred calories too much each day.

The recipes offered here will add enjoyment and excitement to your reducing regimen. Try them—you have nothing to lose but weight. A trim attractive figure is your reward. More important, it can help you enjoy better health and increase your chances of a longer, happier, more active life.

HOW MANY CALORIES DO YOU NEED EACH DAY?

Calories are a measure of the units of energy which any food or beverage supplies when it is taken into the body. From the foods it consumes, the body takes enough calories to make the energy it needs for the day's activities—and that includes breathing and the beating of the heart, as well as work and play and exercise. The calories which are not converted into energy are stored in the body's tissues as fat. The theory behind every reducing diet is to supply the body with *fewer* calories than are needed for its daily energy output, thereby forcing it to spend each day some of its stored calories—its fat. It is safe to take about 500 calories a day from this stored supply. This means that, in general, a safe reducing diet will provide about 500 fewer calories than the body needs for energy.

How many calories is that? The answer is different for each individual. It depends on body weight, body build, and activity. In general, you can calculate your calorie needs very simply. If you are a moderately active person, you need about 15 calories a day to maintain each pound of body weight (slightly more or less depending on activity). Determine (from the chart on page 734) what your own ideal body weight is, for your height and your build. Multiply that, the weight you want to achieve and maintain, by 15. Then subtract 500, the number of calories you want your body to draw from your stored fat reserve every day. The result is the number of calories which should enable you to lose your excess weight at a safe and reasonable rate of about one pound per week.

Here's an example: You are a moderately active homemaker, aged 30 to 35. You are five feet six inches tall in your shoes with medium heels. You have a medium frame—not very small- or very large-boned. Ordinarily dressed, your best weight is about 135 pounds. So—

$$135 \times 15 = 2025 \text{ calories}$$
$$\text{less} \quad 500 \text{ calories}$$
$$\overline{1525 \text{ calories per day}}$$

is the number of calories which should enable *you* to bring your weight down to normal at the rate of one pound a week.

BUT—remember that losing weight is not the only consideration in planning a reducing diet. You also want to maintain your basic health, and you want to feel well while you lose weight. That means that you must choose wisely the foods for your reducing diet—foods which will furnish the building and regulating materials (proteins, vitamins and minerals) that your body needs for health, without providing more than your requirement of calories.

WHAT FOODS DO YOU NEED FOR HEALTH?

There are four basic food groups from which you need some foods every day, whether or not you are reducing.

Milk Group—Use at least 2 glasses of milk daily. (Skim milk, including reconstituted non-fat dry milk and buttermilk supply the same essential nutrients, except fats, and only about one half as many calories as whole milk.)

Meat Group—Use two or more servings daily of meat, poultry, fish, or cheese, and at least 3 to 5 eggs a week.

Vegetables and Fruits Group—Use 4 or more servings daily. Include a dark green leafy or deep yellow vegetable or yellow fruit at least 3 to 4 times a week for vitamin A; a citrus fruit, or tomatoes, or other good source of vitamin C every day.

Breads and Cereals Group—Use 4 or more servings daily of enriched or whole grain products (check labels).

DESIRABLE WEIGHTS

FOR MEN OF AGES 25 AND OVER

HEIGHT		WEIGHT		
with shoes on				
(1-in. heels)		*(in pounds—in indoor clothing)*		
Feet	*Inches*	*Small Frame*	*Medium Frame*	*Large Frame*
5	2	112–120	118–129	126–141
5	3	115–123	121–133	129–144
5	4	118–126	124–136	132–148
5	5	121–129	127–139	135–152
5	6	124–133	130–143	138–156
5	7	128–137	134–147	142–161
5	8	132–141	138–152	147–166
5	9	136–145	142–156	151–170
5	10	140–150	146–160	155–174
5	11	144–154	150–165	159–179
6	0	148–158	154–170	164–184
6	1	152–162	158–175	168–189
6	2	156–167	162–180	173–194
6	3	160–171	167–185	178–199
6	4	164–175	172–190	182–204

FOR WOMEN OF AGES 25 AND OVER

HEIGHT		WEIGHT		
with shoes on				
(2-in. heels)		*(in pounds—in indoor clothing)*		
Feet	*Inches*	*Small Frame*	*Medium Frame*	*Large Frame*
4	10	92– 98	96–107	104–119
4	11	94–101	98–110	106–122
5	0	96–104	101–113	109–125
5	1	99–107	104–116	112–128
5	2	102–110	107–119	115–131
5	3	105–113	110–122	118–134
5	4	108–116	113–126	121–138
5	5	111–119	116–130	125–142
5	6	114–123	120–135	129–146
5	7	118–127	124–139	133–150
5	8	122–131	128–143	137–154
5	9	126–135	132–147	141–158
5	10	130–140	136–151	145–163
5	11	134–144	140–155	149–168
6	0	138–148	144–159	153–173

Courtesy of the Metropolitan Life Insurance Company

COUNT YOUR CALORIES

Food	Quantity	Calories
Almonds		
salted	12 medium	100
shelled	½ cup	420
Anchovies, canned	6 small fillets	40
Anchovy paste	1 tablespoon	42
Apple butter	1 tablespoon	35
Apple juice	½ cup	60
Apples		
baked (with 2 tablespoons sugar)	1 large	200
fresh	1 medium	76
Applesauce		
sweetened	½ cup	92
unsweetened	½ cup	50
Apricot nectar, canned	½ cup	70
Apricots		
canned, syrup pack	4 medium halves and 2 tablespoons syrup	97

Food	Quantity	Calories
canned, water pack	1 cup halves and liquid	77
dried	½ cup small	197
fresh	3 medium	54
Artichoke hearts, canned	5	25
Artichokes, cooked		
French	1 medium	59
Jerusalem	4 small	75
Asparagus		
canned, fresh or frozen	6 spears	15
cooked	½ cup spears (cut)	15
Avocados		
California varieties	½ of a 10-ounce fruit, peeled	185
Florida varieties	½ of a 16-ounce fruit, peeled	195
Bacon		
broiled or fried crisp	1 medium slice, drained	48
Canadian-style, uncooked	1 ounce	65
Bagels	1 medium	165
Bamboo shoots	3½ ounces	27

Food	Quantity	Calories
Bananas, fresh	1 medium (6 x 1½ in.)	100
Barley, pearl, uncooked	½ cup	354
Beans		
baked		
with pork and molasses	½ cup	175
with pork and tomato sauce	½ cup	160
green or wax, cooked	½ cup	15
kidney, canned or cooked	½ cup	115
lima, canned or cooked, drained	½ cup	95
navy, cooked, drained	½ cup	112
soy, dry	½ cup	347
Bean sprouts		
mung, cooked, drained	½ cup	17
soy	½ cup	20
Beef		
chipped or dried	3 ounces	172
chuck, cooked	3 ounces without bone	265
corned, canned	3 ounces, lean	185
hash	3 ounces	155
filet mignon	3 ounces	248
flank, cooked	3 ounces without bone	270
ground, lean, broiled	3 ounces	197
hamburger, broiled	3 ounces	245
porterhouse	3 ounces without bone	293
pot roast	3 ounces	245
rib roast	3 ounces without bone	266
round	3 ounces without bone	197
sirloin	3 ounces without bone	257
stew with vegetables	½ cup	126
T-bone steak	3 ounces	250
tenderloin	3 ounces	248
tongue, cooked	3 ounces	180
Beer (4% alcohol)	12-ounce bottle	150
Beet greens, cooked	½ cup	15
Beets		
fresh, cooked	½ cup, diced	25
pickled	½ cup	28
Biscuits, baking powder	1 (2½-in. diam.)	129
Blackberries		
canned, syrup pack	½ cup	86
fresh	½ cup	41
Blueberries		
canned, syrup pack	½ cup	123
fresh	½ cup	43
frozen, sweetened	½ cup	75
Bouillon		
broth, clear	½ cup	15
cubes	1 cube	5
Brains, all kinds	3 ounces	106
Brazil nuts	4 medium nuts	97
Bread		
Boston brown	1 slice (3 x ¾ in.)	105
cracked wheat	1 average slice	60
Melba toast	1 slice	20
raisin	1 slice	65
rye	1 slice (½-in. thick)	60
white	1 slice (½-in. thick)	70
whole wheat	1 slice (½-in. thick)	60
Bread crumbs, packaged dried	½ cup	170
Broccoli, cooked	3 stalks	100
Brussels sprouts, cooked	6 large	50
Buns, cinnamon	1 (2½-in. square)	200
Butter	1 tablespoon	100
Buttermilk, cultured	1 cup	86
Cabbage		
cooked	½ cup	17
raw	½ cup, shredded	12
Cake		
angel food	⅟₁₂ of 8-in. cake	108
butter, plain	1 cupcake (2¾-in. diam.)	131
frosted	1 cupcake (2¾-in. diam.)	161
chocolate, with chocolate frosting	⅟₁₆ of 9-in. layer cake	235

Food	Quantity	Calories
fruitcake, dark	2 x 2 x ½-in. piece	106
gingerbread	1 2-in. square	175
pound	3 x 2¾ x ⅝-in. piece	130
shortcake, strawberry	average serving	425
sponge	⅟₁₂ of 8-in. cake	117
yellow, without frosting	2-in. wedge of 8-in. cake	205
Candy		
butterscotch	1 ounce	116
caramel, plain	1 ounce (3 medium)	118
chocolate cream	1 ounce (2 or 3 small)	110
chocolate, milk, sweet, with or without almonds	1-ounce bar	150
chocolate mint	1 ounce (1 or 2 patties)	115
fondant	1 ounce	100
fudge, plain	1 ounce	120
gum drops	1 ounce (20 small)	100
hard candy	1 ounce (3 or 4 sourballs)	110
jelly beans	10	66
peanut brittle	1 ounce	125
taffy, salt-water	1 piece	50
Cantaloupe	½ of 5-in. melon	60
Carrots		
cooked	½ cup, diced	22
raw	1 carrot (5½ x 1 in.)	21
Cashew nuts	1 ounce	164
Cauliflower, cooked	½ cup, buds	15
Caviar, pressed	1 ounce	70
Celery		
cooked	½ cup, diced	12
raw	3 small stalks	9
Cereals		
cooked		
farina	½ cup	52
rolled oats	½ cup	65
ready to eat		
bran (100%)	½ cup	100
bran flakes (40% bran)	½ cup	66
corn flakes	½ cup	48
raisin bran	½ cup	100
rice flakes	½ cup	62
rice, puffed	½ cup	28
wheat flakes	½ cup	53
wheat, puffed	½ cup	22
wheat, shredded	1 large biscuit	102
Cheese		
American (pasteurized process)	1 ounce	105
blue or Roquefort	1 ounce	105
Camembert	1 ounce	85
Cheddar	1 ounce (1-in. cube)	115
cottage	½ cup	120
cream	1 ounce	106
Gruyere	1 ounce	115
Limburger	1 ounce	69
Parmesan	1 ounce, grated	130
Swiss (process or natural)	1 ounce	105
Cherries		
canned, tart red	½ cup	61
fresh	½ cup, pitted	47
Chicken		
breast, fried	6.6 ounces	310
broiled (flesh only)	3 ounces	115
canned, boneless	3½ ounces	200
drumstick, fried	2.1 ounces	90
Chicken livers	3 ounces	120
Chicken pie	1 8-ounce	535
Chili con carne, without beans	½ cup	255
Chili sauce	1 tablespoon	15
Chocolate		
candy, sweet milk	1 ounce	143
semisweet	1 ounce	131
syrup	1 tablespoon	42
unsweetened	1 ounce	142
Clams, canned, with liquid	3 ounces	44

Food	Quantity	Calories
Cocoa		
dry, unsweetened	1 tablespoon	21
liquid, with milk	½ cup	118
Coconut		
dried, sweetened	½ cup, shredded	172
fresh	2-in. square	161
	½ cup, shredded	175
Coffee, black	1 cup	5
Cola beverage	1 8-ounce glass	95
Cookies		
animal crackers	1	9
butter	1 3-in. cookie	109
chocolate	1 2-in. cookie	50
fig bar	1 small bar	56
Lorna Doone	2-in. square	35
Corn, cooked	½ cup kernels	84
	1 ear (5 in. long)	70
Corn meal		
cooked	½ cup	60
dry, whole ground	½ cup	210
Corn syrup	1 tablespoon	57
Cornstarch	1 tablespoon	29
Crab meat	3 ounces	89
Crackers		
graham	2 medium	55
matzo	1 6-in. diameter piece	80
oyster	½ cup	60
saltine	2 2-in. squares	34
soda	2 2½-in. squares	50
Cranberries, raw	½ cup	27
Cranberry juice	½ cup	80
Cranberry sauce, sweetened	½ cup	200
Cream		
half and half	1 tablespoon	20
heavy, whipping	1 tablespoon	49
light	1 tablespoon	30
Cucumbers	6 slices	6
Currants, fresh	½ cup	30
Custard, baked or soft	½ cup	164
Dates	½ cup, pitted	253
Doughnuts		
cake-type, plain	1	125
jelly	1	225
sugared	1	175
yeast (raised)	1	125
Duck, roasted	3½ ounces; boned	310
Eggs		
cooked		
fried	1 egg, 1 teaspoon fat	105
hard-cooked	1 medium	77
omelet	2 eggs, 2 teaspoons fat	220
scrambled	1 egg, with milk and fat	110
shirred or poached	1 medium	77
soft-cooked	1 medium	77
raw	1 whole medium	77
	1 white	16
	1 yolk	61
Endive, fresh	½ pound	45
Escarole	½ pound	45
Farina, cooked	½ cup	52
Fats		
butter	1 tablespoon	100
lard	1 tablespoon	125
margarine	1 tablespoon	100
vegetable shortening	1 tablespoon	110
Figs		
canned	3 with 2 tablespoons syrup	129
dried	1 large	57
Fish		
bluefish, baked	3 ounces	135
cod, uncooked	3 ounces	61
fish sticks, breaded, fried	5 average (4 ounces)	200
flounder, uncooked	3 ounces	56
haddock, panfried	1 3½-ounce fillet	158
halibut, broiled	1 4½-ounce steak	228
mackerel, canned	3 ounces	154
perch, ocean, breaded, fried	3 ounces	195
swordfish, broiled	1 4-ounce steak	225
Flour		
all-purpose	½ cup sifted	200
cake	½ cup sifted	183
whole wheat	½ cup sifted	200
Frankfurters	1	155
French toast	1 slice, no syrup	185
Fruit cocktail, canned	½ cup fruit and syrup	90
Fudge, milk chocolate, without nuts	1 ounce	115
Gelatin		
flavored, prepared	3 ounces	324
unflavored	1 tablespoon	35
Ginger ale	8-ounce glass	80
Gingerbread, plain	1 2-in. square	175
Gooseberries, fresh	½ cup	30
Grape juice	½ cup	85
Grapefruit		
canned	½ cup with syrup	91
fresh	½ medium (3¾-in. diam.)	45
Grapefruit juice, fresh or canned		
sweetened	½ cup	65
unsweetened	½ cup	45
Grapes, seedless	½ cup (20 grapes)	51
Gravy, brown meat	2 tablespoons	82
Griddlecakes		
buckwheat	1 cake (4-in. diam.)	55
wheat	1 cake (4-in. diam.)	59
Ham, smoked, cooked	3 ounces	142
Herbs, all kinds		0
Herring		
pickled	3 ounces	190
smoked	3 ounces	160
Honey	1 tablespoon, strained	62
Honeydew melon	1 2-in. wedge	50
Horseradish	1 tablespoon	5
Ice cream, plain	½ cup	145
Ice cream bar, chocolate covered	1	162
Ice cream cone (cone only)	1	45
Ice cream soda, chocolate	1 large glass	255
Ice milk	½ cup	94
Jam	1 tablespoon	55
Jelly	1 tablespoon	50
Kale	½ cup, cooked	15
Ketchup	1 tablespoon	17
Kohlrabi, cooked	½ cup	24
Lamb, cooked		
rib chop	3 ounces without bone	356
roast leg	3 ounces without bone	230
shoulder roast	3 ounces without bone	285
Lard	1 tablespoon	125
Lemon juice	1 tablespoon	4
Lemonade, frozen concentrate, diluted as directed	½ cup	55
Lemons	1 medium	20
Lettuce	1 lb.	68
Lima beans, cooked	½ cup	95
Lime		
juice, fresh	½ cup	32
whole	1 medium	19
Liquors, distilled		
70-proof	1½ ounces (jigger)	85
80-proof	1½ ounces (jigger)	95
86-proof	1½ ounces (jigger)	105
90-proof	1½ ounces (jigger)	110
100-proof	1½ ounces (jigger)	125
Liver, beef, fried	3 ounces	177
Liverwurst	3 ounces	225
Lobster, canned	3 ounces	78

Food	Quantity	Calories
Loganberries		
canned, syrup pack........	½ cup...............	89
fresh.................	½ cup...............	45
Luncheon meat, canned.....	1-ounce slice..........	83
Macaroni		
cooked.............	½ cup...............	80
with cheese..........	½ cup...............	232
Maple syrup, pure.........	1 tablespoon.........	70
Margarine.............	1 tablespoon.........	100
Marmalade.............	1 tablespoon.........	55
Marshmallows.........	1 ounce (4 pieces).........	90
Milk		
buttermilk, cultured........	1 cup...............	86
chocolate-flavored........	1 cup...............	208
condensed, sweetened......	½ cup...............	490
evaporated, undiluted.....	1 cup...............	346
malted (dry powder).....	1 ounce............	115
milkshake, chocolate......	1 cup...............	280
nonfat dry.............	1 tablespoon.........	28
partly skimmed.........	1 cup...............	145
skim, fluid............	1 cup...............	87
whole, dry............	1 tablespoon.........	39
whole, fluid...........	1 cup...............	166
Molasses		
dark.............	1 tablespoon.........	43
light.............	1 tablespoon.........	50
Muffins		
bran.............	1 2¾-in. diam.......	130
corn.............	1 2¾-in. diam.......	150
plain.............	1 2¾-in. diam.......	134
Mushrooms, canned.........	½ cup with liquid......	20
Noodles, cooked...........	½ cup...............	100
Oatmeal, cooked...........	½ cup...............	65
Oil, salad or cooking (includes corn, cottonseed, olive, peanut and soybean)..................	1 tablespoon.........	124
Okra, cooked.............	8 pods............	28
Olives		
green.............	6 medium..........	50
ripe.............	3 large..........	24
Onions		
raw.............	1 tablespoon, chopped.......	4
whole.............	1.............	30
young green.............	6 small, without tops.....	23
Orange juice		
canned		
sweetened.............	½ cup.............	68
unsweetened...........	½ cup.............	60
fresh.............	½ cup.............	55
frozen (diluted as directed)..	½ cup.............	55
Oranges		
sections.............	½ cup.............	45
whole.............	1 medium.........	70
Oysters, raw.............	½ cup.............	80
Pancakes (*see* Griddlecakes)		
Parsnips, cooked...........	½ cup.............	47
Pastrami.............	1 ounce............	100
Pastries (*see also* Cake, Cookies, etc.)		
apple turnover.............	1.............	275
cream puff, cream filling....	1.............	296
Danish.............	1 small............	200
eclair, chocolate icing.....	1.............	316
French.............	1 medium............	225
petit four.............	1.............	150
strudel.............	1.............	200
tart, fruit-filled.............	1.............	200
Peaches		
canned, syrup pack........	½ cup.............	100
canned, water pack........	½ cup.............	33
fresh.............	1 medium............	35
Peanut butter.............	1 tablespoon.............	92
Peanuts, roasted.............	½ cup medium halves........	420
Pears		
canned, syrup pack........	½ cup.............	87
canned, water pack........	½ cup.............	38

Food	Quantity	Calories
fresh.............	1 medium.........	95
Peas		
canned.............	½ cup, drained.............	73
fresh, cooked.........	½ cup.............	56
split, dried, cooked........	½ cup.............	145
Pecans.............	½ cup, shelled.............	370
Peppers		
green, raw.............	1 medium............	16
red, raw.............	1 medium............	20
Pickles		
dill.............	1 large............	15
sweet.............	1 2½-in. long.........	20
Pie crust		
double crust.............	1 9-in. pie.........	1,314
single crust.............	1 9-in. pie.........	651
Pies		
apple.............	⅙ of 9-in. pie.........	410
blueberry.............	⅙ of 9-in. pie.........	387
cherry.............	⅙ of 9-in. pie.........	418
custard.............	⅙ of 9-in. pie.........	327
lemon meringue.........	⅙ of 9-in. pie.........	357
mince.............	⅙ of 9-in. pie.........	434
peach.............	⅙ of 9-in. pie.........	421
pecan.............	⅙ of 9-in. pie.........	668
pumpkin.............	⅙ of 9-in. pie.........	317
raisin.............	⅙ of 9-in. pie.........	325
rhubarb.............	⅙ of 9-in. pie.........	405
strawberry, one crust.......	⅙ of 9-in. pie.........	228
Pineapple		
canned.............	1 large slice and 2 tablespoons syrup..........	95
	½ cup, crushed, with syrup....	102
fresh.............	½ cup, diced.........	37
Pineapple juice, canned.....	½ cup.............	61
Pizza, with sauce and cheese..	⅛ of 14-in. pie......	185
Plums		
canned.............	½ cup with syrup......	93
fresh.............	1 plum (2-in. diam.)......	29
Popcorn, popped, with oil and salt.............	½ cup.............	20
Pork, cooked		
loin chops.............	1 chop, 3.5 ounces......	260
loin roast.............	3 ounces without bone......	284
Potato chips.............	10 medium............	108
Potatoes		
baked.............	1 medium............	97
boiled, peeled.............	1 medium............	105
French fried.............	10 pieces (2 x ½ x ½ in.).....	137
hash browned.............	½ cup.............	235
mashed with milk and butter.............	½ cup.............	93
Pretzels.............	5 small sticks.............	5
Prune juice, canned...........	½ cup.............	100
Prunes		
cooked		
sweetened.............	½ cup with liquid......	200
unsweetened...........	½ cup with liquid......	155
dried.............	4 medium............	73
Pudding		
apple brown betty.........	½ cup.............	211
bread.............	½ cup.............	208
butterscotch.............	½ cup.............	207
chocolate.............	½ cup.............	219
custard.............	½ cup.............	164
rice, with raisins.........	½ cup.............	140
vanilla.............	½ cup.............	152
Pumpkin.............	½ cup.............	38
Radishes.............	4 small............	4
Raisins.............	½ cup, packed......	240
Raspberries		
fresh		
black.............	½ cup.............	50
red.............	½ cup.............	35
frozen, red.............	3 ounces............	84

Food	Quantity	Calories
Rhubarb		
cooked, with sugar	½ cup	192
fresh	½ cup, diced	10
Rice		
brown, uncooked	½ cup	375
precooked, dry	½ cup	210
white		
cooked	½ cup	100
uncooked	½ cup	345
wild, uncooked	½ cup	295
Rolls		
frankfurter	1	120
French	1	100
hamburger	1	120
hard	1	160
onion	1	150
sweet	1	178
yeast, plain	1	118
Rutabaga, cooked	½ cup, cubed	25
Salad dressings		
blue or Roquefort	1 tablespoon	80
cooked	1 tablespoon	30
French	1 tablespoon	60
Italian	1 tablespoon	75
mayonnaise	1 tablespoon	100
Thousand Island	1 tablespoon	75
Salads		
chicken, with celery	½ cup	200
cole slaw	½ cup	50
fruit, fresh	½ cup	65
lettuce and tomatoes	½ cup	13
salmon, with celery	½ cup	195
vegetable combination	½ cup	40
Waldorf	½ cup	140
Salmon		
canned, pink or red	3 ounces	125
fresh cooked	3 ounces	155
Sandwiches (all include 2 regular slices of white bread and an average portion of filling)		
bacon-egg	1	330
bacon-tomato-lettuce	1	282
barbecue beef	1	250
barbecue pork	1	310
bologna	1	350
cheese, Cheddar	1	325
cheese, Swiss	1	325
cheeseburger	1	500
chicken, sliced	1	303
chicken liver	1	310
chicken salad	1	245
club, 3-decker	1	580
corned beef	1	300
cream cheese and jelly	1	368
egg, fried	1	250
egg salad	1	279
frankfurter	1	254
ham and Swiss cheese	1	400
ham, cooked	1	280
ham salad	1	320
liverwurst	1	250
luncheon meat	1	385
pastrami	1	325
peanut butter	1	328
peanut butter and jelly	1	370
pork sausage	1	400
roast beef	1	284
roast beef with gravy	1	429
roast pork	1	288
roast pork with gravy	1	500
salami	1	275
salmon salad	1	375
sardine	1	300
shrimp salad	1	360
sole, fried	1	225

Food	Quantity	Calories
tomato and lettuce	1	160
tongue	1	240
tuna salad	1	278
turkey	1	400
Vienna sausage	1	275
Sardines		
canned, drained	3 ounces	182
in tomato sauce	3 ounces	184
Sauces		
cheese	½ cup	245
cherry	1 tablespoon	25
chocolate	1 tablespoon	50
cranberry	½ cup	200
hard	1 tablespoon	50
Hollandaise	1 tablespoon	45
lemon	1 tablespoon	25
sour cream	1 tablespoon	35
soy	1 tablespoon	7
tartar	1 tablespoon	95
tomato	1 tablespoon	20
white, medium	½ cup	210
Sauerkraut, canned, drained	½ cup	16
Sausage		
bologna	2 ounces	170
liver	2 ounces	175
pork, cooked	1 link (3-in. long, ½-in. diam.)	94
Scallops, cooked	3 ounces	96
Sherbet	½ cup	130
Shortening, solid		
lard	1 tablespoon	125
vegetable	1 tablespoon	110
Shrimp		
canned	3 ounces, drained	108
fried	3½ ounces	225
Soft drinks		
cherry soda	8 ounces	105
cola	8 ounces	95
cream soda	8 ounces	105
ginger ale	8 ounces	80
grape soda	8 ounces	100
lemon soda	8 ounces	95
orange soda	8 ounces	100
root beer	8 ounces	100
Soups (if canned, prepared as directed)		
asparagus, cream of	½ cup	78
barley	½ cup	59
bean with pork	½ cup	85
beef noodle	½ cup	35
bouillon	½ cup	15
celery, cream of	½ cup	100
chicken noodle	½ cup	33
chicken rice	½ cup	25
clam chowder, tomato	½ cup	42
consommé, clear	½ cup	15
minestrone	½ cup	53
mushroom, cream of	½ cup	68
onion, French	½ cup	65
pea, green	½ cup	65
potato	½ cup	93
potato, cream of	½ cup	108
tomato	½ cup	45
tomato, cream of	½ cup	85
vegetable beef	½ cup	40
Spaghetti		
canned	½ cup	121
cooked		
plain	½ cup	77
with meat balls	½ cup	167
with meat sauce	½ cup	218
with tomato sauce	½ cup	130
Spinach, cooked	½ cup	20
Squash, cooked		
summer	½ cup, diced	17
winter	½ cup, mashed	50

Food	Quantity	Calories
Strawberries		
fresh	½ cup	27
frozen	3 ounces	90
Sugar		
brown	1 tablespoon	51
confectioners'	1 tablespoon	31
granulated	1 tablespoon	40
maple	1 1-inch cube	95
Sweet potatoes		
baked	1 medium (5 x 2 in.)	155
candied	1 small (3½ x 2½ in.)	295
Syrup		
chocolate	1 tablespoon	50
corn	1 tablespoon	57
maple	1 tablespoon	50
Tangerine juice, unsweetened	½ cup	48
Tangerines	1 medium	35
Tapioca (quick cooking)	½ cup	274
Tea	1 cup	2
Tomatoes		
canned or cooked	½ cup	23
fresh	1 medium	30
Tomato juice	½ cup	25
Tomato purée	½ cup	45
Tongue	3 ounces	180
Tuna, canned	3 ounces, drained	169

Food	Quantity	Calories
Turkey, roasted		
dark meat	3 ounces	175
light meat	3 ounces	150
Turnips, cooked	½ cup, diced	21
Veal, cooked		
cutlet	3 ounces without bone	184
shoulder roast	3 ounces without bone	230
stew meat	3 ounces without bone	252
Vegetable juice, canned	½ cup	35
Venison, roasted	3½ ounces	146
Vinegar	½ cup	15
Waffles	1 waffle (7-in. diam.)	216
Walnuts, English	½ cup, chopped	395
Watercress, raw	½ lb.	42
Watermelon	½ slice (10 x ¾ in.)	45
Welsh rabbit	½ cup	270
Wheat germ	½ cup	123
Whiskies (*see* Liquors)		
Wine		
champagne	4 ounces	105
dessert	3 ounces	125
table	3 ounces	75
Yeast, active, dry or cake	1 package	20
Yogurt (from part skim, part whole milk)	½ cup	63
Zwieback	1 piece	35

APPETIZERS

COTTAGE CHEESE DIP

253 cal./cup; 16 cal./tablespoon

Put into a bowl
   1 cup (½ lb.) cottage cheese
   2 tablespoons Low-Calorie Salad Dressing (page 750)
Add any one of the following:
   3 tablespoons minced parsley
   2 tablespoons finely chopped onion
   2 tablespoons finely chopped chives
   1 tablespoon prepared mustard
   2 teaspoons crushed mint leaves
   2 teaspoons dill seed
   1 to 2 teaspoons prepared horseradish
   Few drops Tabasco
Beat together until light and fluffy.

About 1 cup dip

Chilled Melon Appetizer

Note: Dip may be served in Green Pepper Shells or Tomato Shells.

CHILLED MELON APPETIZER

51 cal./serving

Chill 4 serving plates.

Set out
   3 medium cantaloupes
Set 2 cantaloupes in refrigerator to chill.

Rinse remaining cantaloupe, cut into halves and scoop out seedy center. Cut meat into balls with a measuring teaspoon or a ball-shaped cutter. Put melon balls into a bowl.

Brush with
   Lemon or lime juice
When ready to serve, remove cantaloupes and melon balls from refrigerator. Rinse cantaloupes, cut into halves and scoop out seedy centers. Place one melon half on each plate. Arrange several melon balls in center of each cantaloupe half.

Garnish with
   Sprigs of mint
If desired, serve with **lemon or lime wedges.**

4 servings

Note: Melon balls may be brushed with any desired liqueur (crème de menthe, kirsch, Cointreau or curaçao).

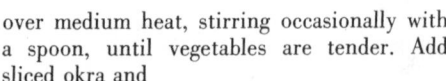

INDIVIDUAL CRAB MEAT APPETIZERS

49 cal./serving

Line six 2½-in. muffin-pan wells with paper baking cups.

Drain, remove and discard bony tissue and separate
1 can (6½ oz.) crab meat (about 1⅓ cups)
Set aside.

Pour into a small cup or custard cup
¼ cup cold water
Sprinkle evenly over cold water
1½ teaspoons unflavored gelatin
Let stand until gelatin is softened. Dissolve softened gelatin completely by placing cup over very hot water.

Meanwhile, mix
3 tablespoons ketchup
2 tablespoons Low-Calorie French Dressing (page 750)
½ teaspoon Worcestershire sauce
½ teaspoon salt
¼ teaspoon paprika
When gelatin is dissolved, stir it and blend thoroughly into the ketchup mixture. Add the crab meat and blend thoroughly. Spoon into the paper baking cups and freeze until firm, about 3 hrs.

Before serving, remove paper cups. Allow appetizers to stand at room temperature for a few minutes to soften very slightly. Serve on plates in **lettuce cups**. *6 servings*

COCKTAILS

(Allow ½ cup juice for each serving)

—VEGETABLE JUICES   *25 cal./serving*

Season chilled **tomato juice** with **celery leaves, onion, salt, pepper, lemon juice, Worcestershire sauce** or **Tabasco**.

Serve vegetable juice combinations chilled or hot, topped with **Whipped Topping** (page 754; 35 cal./serving).

—FRUIT JUICES   *32 to 39 cal./serving*

Serve one or more fruit juices such as **cranberry, orange, grapefruit** or **pineapple juice.** Mix with equal amounts of **ginger ale** or carbonated water, if desired. Serve in juice glasses with cracked ice and **mint sprigs, orange or lemon slices.**

Serve hot juices, such as **apple cider** (*50 cal./serving*) with **cinnamon stick stirrers.**

—SHRUBS   *55 to 65 cal./serving*

Float a small scoop of fruit-flavored sherbet or ice on small servings of fruit juice, using combinations such as **Orange Sherbet** (page 753) on **unsweetened orange or grapefruit juice** or **Grape Sherbet** (page 752) on **unsweetened pineapple juice.**

SOUPS

ONION SOUP   *20 cal./serving*

Clean and thinly slice
3 medium onions
Prepare in a saucepan
3 cups quick meat broth (page 10; use 4 bouillon cubes)
Add the onion rings and
⅛ teaspoon Worcestershire sauce
Cover and simmer about 30 min.

If desired, sprinkle over each serving **1 tablespoon grated Parmesan or sharp Cheddar cheese**; but remember that this will add 28 cal. to each serving. *4 servings*

LOBSTER GUMBO   *106 cal./serving*

Set out a large heavy skillet with a tight-fitting cover.

Wash, cut off and discard stem ends, slice and set aside
¼ lb. okra (about 1 cup, sliced)

Prepare and set aside
½ cup (about 1 medium) chopped onion
¼ cup chopped green pepper
1 clove garlic, minced

Heat in the skillet over low heat
1 tablespoon butter or margarine
Add onion, green pepper and garlic and cook over medium heat, stirring occasionally with a spoon, until vegetables are tender. Add sliced okra and
2 cups (28-oz. can, drained) cooked tomatoes, cut in pieces
½ teaspoon salt
¼ teaspoon pepper
¼ teaspoon monosodium glutamate
¼ teaspoon chili powder
½ bay leaf, crushed
Cover and simmer 20 min., or until okra is almost tender.

Meanwhile, drain and separate
1 can (6½ oz.) lobster meat (about 1 cup, drained)
Add lobster meat to tomato mixture and cook 10 min. longer, or until okra is tender and lobster meat is heated. Remove skillet from heat. Remove about ⅓ cup liquid and mix thoroughly with
1 teaspoon filé powder
Return mixture to skillet and blend thoroughly.
4 servings

Note: Filé powder should always be added after the mixture has been removed from the heat. If cooked, it will make the gumbo stringy and unpalatable.

BOSTON CLAM CHOWDER

61 cal./serving

▲ *Base Recipe*

Potatoes and salt pork have no place in any proper low-calorie soup, but that's no reason for banishing the flavor and nourishment of a good fish chowder from your diet. The really important part of a fish chowder is the fish, and fish is fine low-calorie fare. So are the vegetables that go into chowder.

Set out a 3-qt. saucepan.

Drain, reserving liquid
1 can (10½ oz.) clams (about 1 cup, drained)
Put into the saucepan ½ cup of the clam liquid and
½ cup (about 1 medium) chopped onion
½ cup diced carrots
½ cup water
¼ teaspoon salt
¼ teaspoon white pepper
¼ teaspoon thyme
Cook, covered, over low heat about 20 min., or until vegetables are tender.

Sherry Wine, Dry Martini or Manhattan (3 oz.)	140
Orange Juice (6 oz.)	80
Tomato Juice (6 oz.)	38

50   100   150

Meanwhile, cut clams into halves and set aside.

When vegetables are tender, add the clams to the saucepan. Add gradually, stirring constantly

2 cups skim milk (page 9)

Simmer for 5 min.

Garnish each serving with **chopped parsley**.

6 servings

—OYSTER CHOWDER   *77 cal./serving*

Follow ▲ Recipe. Substitute **oysters** for clams. Drain and pick over oysters to remove any shell particles. Use **oyster liquor** instead of clam liquid.

CHILLED CUCUMBER CHIVE SOUP

77 cal./serving

Nonfat dry milk makes cream soups practicable on low-calorie diets; cucumbers and chives give flavor to this one yet add almost no calories.

Rinse

2 medium cucumbers

Cut twelve ⅛-in. slices from one cucumber for a garnish. Place slices in a small bowl of ice and water and set in refrigerator. Shred enough of the remaining cucumber to yield 2 cups shredded cucumber.

Prepare and pour into top of a double boiler

2½ cups reconstituted instant nonfat dry milk

Sprinkle evenly over milk a mixture of

2 tablespoons all-purpose flour
1 teaspoon salt
½ teaspoon paprika
⅛ teaspoon pepper

Beat with rotary beater until blended. Add

2 bouillon cubes

Cook and stir over direct heat until boiling. Mix in the shredded cucumber and

3 tablespoons chopped chives

Set over simmering water, stirring occasionally, to allow flavors to blend.

Cool, chill in refrigerator about 3 hrs.

Garnish with the cucumber slices.   *6 servings*

Chilled Cucumber Chive Soup and Jellied Consommé Madrilène

CHILLED TOMATO BOUILLON

36 cal./serving

▲ Base Recipe

Prepare in a 2-qt. saucepan

1 cup quick meat broth (page 10; use 2 bouillon cubes)

Add to the broth

3 cups tomato juice
½ cup (1 medium) chopped green pepper
2 teaspoons lemon juice
1 teaspoon Worcestershire sauce
1 teaspoon sugar
½ teaspoon salt
½ teaspoon monosodium glutamate
⅛ teaspoon cloves
Few grains pepper

Cover; simmer 6 to 8 min. Strain. Add

½ clove garlic

Cool; chill in refrigerator about 3 hrs. Remove garlic before serving.   *5 servings*

—JELLIED TOMATO BOUILLON

43 cal./serving

Follow ▲ Recipe. Sprinkle **1 env. unflavored gelatin** over **¼ cup cold water**. Let stand until gelatin is softened; stir into hot tomato bouillon until gelatin is completely dissolved. Cool; chill in refrigerator until set, about 5 hrs. Lightly beat with a fork before serving.

—JELLIED CONSOMME MADRILENE

50 cal./serving

Follow recipe for Jellied Tomato Bouillon. Substitute **chicken bouillon cubes** for beef bouillon cubes and increase water to ½ cup and gelatin to 2 env. Omit Worcestershire sauce, salt, monosodium glutamate, cloves, pepper and garlic. Add the lemon juice and **2 teaspoons aromatic bitters** after straining. Garnish servings with **lemon slices**.

—HOT TOMATO BOUILLON   *36 cal./serving*

Follow ▲ Recipe. Add the ½ clove garlic to the tomato juice mixture before cooking (do not add garlic after straining). Cover, simmer and strain. Serve immediately.

TOMATO MADRILENE   *46 cal./serving*

Put into a saucepan

2½ cups canned tomato juice
¼ cup finely chopped onion
2 tablespoons finely chopped green pepper
2 tablespoons finely chopped celery, with leaves
1 tablespoon lemon juice
¾ teaspoon non caloric sweetening solution or 6 non caloric sweetening tablets (page 9)
½ teaspoon salt
¼ teaspoon paprika
Pinch basil
Pinch rosemary
1 small bay leaf

Cover, bring mixture to boiling and simmer about 20 min., or until vegetables are tender.

Pour into a small cup or custard cup

¼ cup cold water

Sprinkle evenly over the cold water

1 env. unflavored gelatin

Let stand until gelatin is softened.

When vegetables are tender, remove bay leaf and force contents of saucepan through sieve or food mill.

Stir the softened gelatin and add to the hot tomato mixture, stirring until gelatin is com-

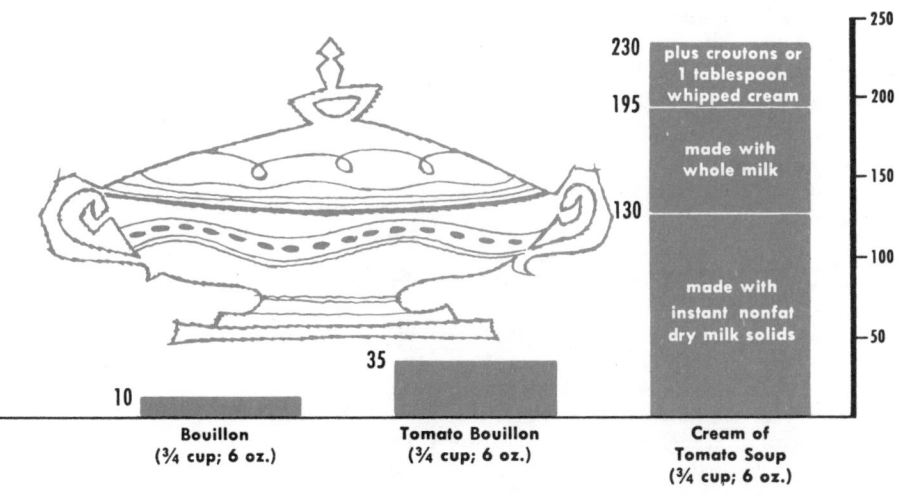

		230 — plus croutons or 1 tablespoon whipped cream
		195 — made with whole milk
		130 — made with instant nonfat dry milk solids
10 Bouillon (¾ cup; 6 oz.)	35 Tomato Bouillon (¾ cup; 6 oz.)	Cream of Tomato Soup (¾ cup; 6 oz.)

pletely dissolved. Cool; put into refrigerator to chill until set.

Lightly beat with a fork before serving.

Garnish with **lemon slices.** *4 servings*

EGGS AND CHEESE

COTTAGE CHEESE ROLL-UPS
285 cal./serving

Mix and set aside
- **2 cups (1 lb.) cottage cheese**
- **1 tablespoon grated onion**
- **1 teaspoon salt**
- **½ teaspoon monosodium glutamate**
- **¼ teaspoon pepper**

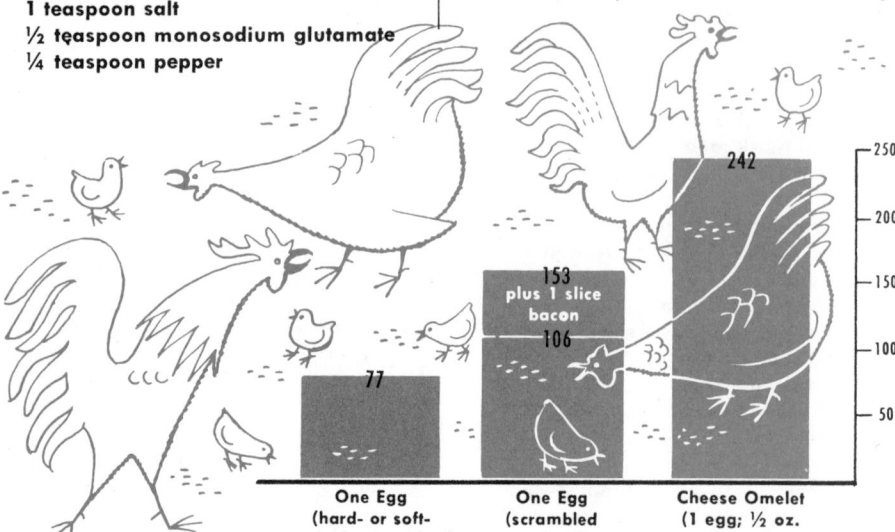

Set griddle or heavy skillet over low heat.

Sift together and set aside
- **1 cup sifted all-purpose flour**
- **1½ teaspoons baking powder**
- **½ teaspoon salt**

Beat together
- **1 egg, well beaten**
- **1½ cups skim milk (page 9)**

Make a well in center of dry ingredients. Add egg mixture all at one time to dry ingredients; beat with a rotary beater until well blended.

Swiss Cheese Soufflé

Blend in
- **1 tablespoon butter or margarine, melted**

Test griddle or skillet; it is hot enough for baking when drops of water sprinkled on surface dance in small beads. Lightly grease griddle or skillet if manufacturer so directs.

Pour batter from a pitcher or large spoon into pools about 4 in. in diameter, leaving at least 1 in. between. Turn pancakes carefully with spatula as they become puffy and full of bubbles, and brown other side; turn pancakes only once.

As each pancake is baked, spread with the cottage cheese mixture and roll up. Serve pancakes immediately. *4 servings*

SWISS CHEESE SOUFFLE
223 cal./serving

▲ Base Recipe

Set out a 1½-qt. casserole; do not grease.

Shred and set aside
- **½ lb. pasteurized process Swiss cheese (about 2 cups, shredded)**

Prepare
- **1 cup Nonfat Thick White Sauce (page 746; add ½ teaspoon nutmeg with seasonings)**

Remove sauce from heat. Add shredded cheese all at once and stir until cheese is melted.

Beat until thick and lemon-colored
- **4 egg yolks**

Add sauce gradually to egg yolks, while stirring vigorously.

Beat until rounded peaks are formed
- **4 egg whites**

Gently spread egg-yolk mixture over beaten egg whites. Carefully fold together until just blended. Turn mixture into casserole. Insert the tip of a spoon 1 in. deep into mixture in casserole, 1 to 1½ in. from edge; run a line around mixture. (Inner part of the mixture will form a "top hat" when baked.)

Salmon Egg Foo Yung

Bake at 325°F about 50 min., or until a metal knife comes out clean when inserted halfway between center and edge of soufflé.

Serve at once (while "top hat" is at its height).
6 servings

—CRAB MEAT SOUFFLE *121 cal./serving*

Follow ▲ Recipe. Omit Swiss cheese and nutmeg. Drain, remove and discard bony tissue and separate **1 can (6½ oz.) crab meat** (about 1⅓ cups). Blend crab meat into the sauce with **2 tablespoons chopped parsley, 2 tablespoons chopped pimiento, 2 tablespoons grated onion** and **1 tablespoon lemon juice.**

EGG FOO YUNG *52 cal./patty*

▲ Base Recipe

Set out a large heavy skillet.

Set aside to drain
- **1 can (16 oz.) bean sprouts**

Finely chop
- **1 medium onion (about ½ cup, chopped)**

Beat together until well blended but not foamy
- **6 eggs**
- **¾ teaspoon salt**
- **⅛ teaspoon pepper**

Heat the skillet until just hot enough to sizzle a drop of water. Melt in skillet
- **2 teaspoons butter or margarine**

Meanwhile, blend the vegetables into the beaten eggs. Pour mixture (about ½ cup for each) into pools to form patties about 4 in. in diameter, leaving at least 1 in. between. Cook until bottoms of patties are browned; turn and brown other side. Drain thoroughly on absorbent paper. Serve with **soy sauce.**
About 14 patties

—SALMON EGG FOO YUNG *86 cal./patty*

Follow ▲ Recipe. Beat eggs with **¼ cup water;** sprinkle **6 tablespoons instant nonfat dry milk** over egg mixture and beat until well blended but not foamy. Mix with vegetables **1 cup (7¾ oz. can, drained) flaked (page 9) salmon.**

—CRAB MEAT EGG FOO YUNG   *65 cal./patty*

Follow ▲ Recipe. Drain, remove and discard bony tissue and separate **1 can (6½ oz.) crab meat** (about 1⅓ cups). Mix into eggs with vegetables.

—BEEF EGG FOO YUNG   *90 cal./patty*

Follow ▲ Recipe. Mix with vegetables **1 cup cooked lean beef strips.**

MEAT, POULTRY AND FISH

BEEF RAGOUT   *206 cal./serving*

▲ Base Recipe

Set out a heavy 10-in. skillet or 3-qt. saucepan with a tight-fitting cover.

Cut into 1-in. pieces
1 lb. round steak
Peel and rinse
3 onions
Cut two onions into quarters, wrap in waxed paper and set aside. Cut the remaining onion into slices.

Heat in the skillet over low heat
2 teaspoons butter or margarine

Add meat pieces and brown slowly on all sides over medium heat. When meat is nearly browned, add the onion slices.

Cook until onion slices are almost tender when tested with a fork; stir the mixture occasionally. When meat is browned, add, pouring in water gradually
    1½ cups hot water
    ½ teaspoon salt
    ½ teaspoon monosodium glutamate
    ¼ teaspoon basil leaves, crushed
    ⅛ teaspoon pepper
    ⅛ teaspoon thyme
Cover and simmer 1½ hrs. If necessary, add more hot water as meat cooks.

Wash, scrape or pare, and cut into ½-in. pieces
    2 medium carrots
Wash, remove ends and cut into 1-in. pieces
    ¼ lb. (about ¾ cup) green beans
Add carrots, green beans and quartered onions, cover and cook 15 to 25 min. longer, or until vegetables are tender. Blend in
    2 tablespoons tomato paste
Garnish ragout with chopped **parsley.** Serve immediately.   *5 servings*

—VEAL RAGOUT   *208 cal./serving*

Follow ▲ Recipe. Substitute **boneless veal shoulder** for round steak. Substitute ½ **teaspoon rosemary leaves**, crushed, and ⅛ **teaspoon cayenne pepper** for basil leaves and thyme. Add **3 tablespoons lemon juice** with

the seasonings. Omit the green beans. Clean **1 medium green pepper** and cut into strips; add to vegetables with **1 cup (8-oz. can, drained) sliced mushrooms.**

—LAMB RAGOUT   *278 cal./serving*

Follow ▲ Recipe. Substitute **boneless lamb shoulder** for round steak. Substitute ½ **teaspoon marjoram** for basil leaves and thyme. Split **1 clove garlic,** insert wooden pick in each half and add with seasonings; remove before serving.

SUKIYAKI   *249 cal./serving*

Low-calorie version of a famed Japanese dish.

Have ready
    1 lb. round steak
Cut into very thin strips about 2 in. long.

Heat in a large heavy skillet over low heat
    1 tablespoon butter or margarine
Add the meat and brown on all sides over medium heat.

Meanwhile, set aside to drain contents of
    1 8-oz. can (about 1 cup, drained) sliced mushrooms
    1 5-oz. can sliced bamboo shoots
Clean
    2 stalks celery
    1 medium onion
Cut the celery into 1-in. pieces and thinly slice the onion. Rinse, cut off root ends and one half of the tops, peel and rinse again
    5 green onions
Cut into ¼-in. pieces. Set vegetables aside.

Prepare
    1 cup quick chicken broth (page 10)
When the meat pieces are well browned, add to the skillet the vegetables, broth and
    ¼ cup soy sauce
    ½ teaspoon salt
    ¼ teaspoon non caloric sweetening solution or 2 non caloric sweetening tablets (page 9)
Cover, bring to boiling and simmer, moving and turning mixture occasionally with a spoon, about 20 min., or until vegetables are partially tender.

Meanwhile, remove and discard tough stems, roots and bruised leaves from
    ¼ lb. fresh spinach
Wash leaves thoroughly by lifting up and down several times in a large amount of cold water. Lift leaves out of water each time before pouring off water. When spinach is free from sand and gritty material, cut the leaves into large shreds. Add the spinach to the meat-vegetable mixture, partially cover skillet and continue cooking, moving and turning pieces occasionally with a spoon, 5 to 10 min., or until spinach is just tender.   *4 servings*

Note: Cooked beef may be used in place of the round steak; add with spinach.

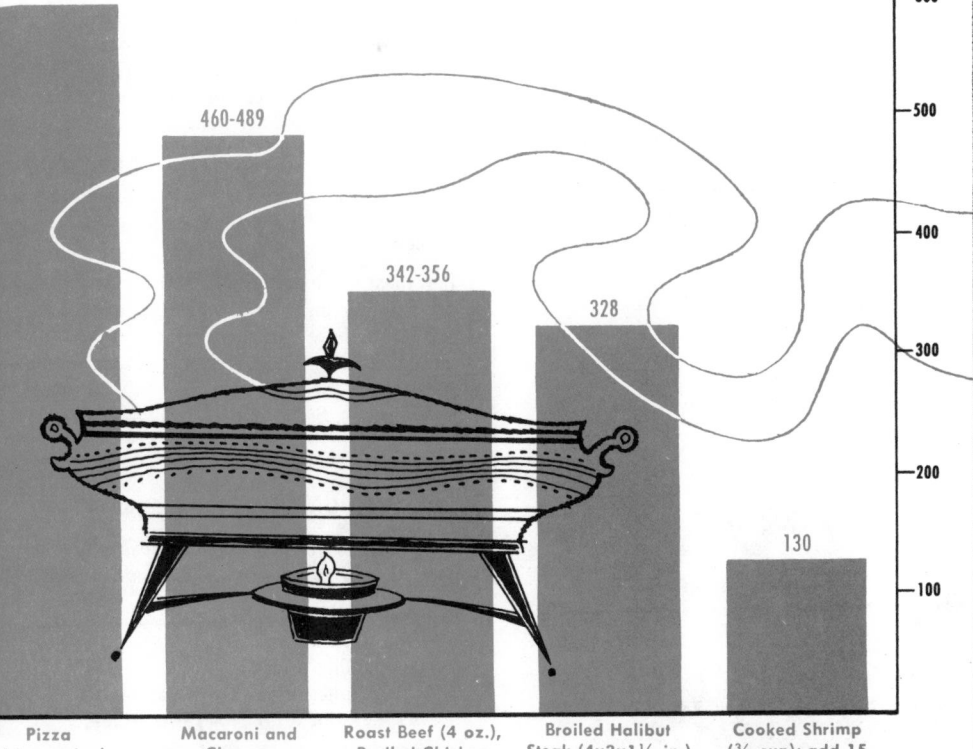

Pizza (4-in. wedge)

Macaroni and Cheese, Chicken à la King (1 cup) or Lobster Newburg (¾ cup) — 460-489

Roast Beef (4 oz.), Broiled Chicken (½ chicken) or Rock Lobster Tail (8 oz.) with 1 tablespoon melted butter — 342-356

Broiled Halibut Steak (4x3x1½ in.) with 1 tablespoon Tartar Sauce — 328

Cooked Shrimp (¾ cup); add 15 cal./tablespoon cocktail sauce; 90 cal./tablespoon Remoulade Sauce — 130

BEEF VEGETABLE LOAF   160 cal./serving

Grease a 9x5x3-in. loaf pan.

Clean and finely chop enough celery, onion and mushrooms to yield
- **½ cup finely chopped celery**
- **¼ cup finely chopped onion**
- **¼ cup finely chopped mushrooms**

Wash, remove ends and finely chop enough green beans to yield
- **¼ cup finely chopped green beans**

Wash, scrape or pare and grate enough carrots to yield
- **¼ cup grated carrot**

Mix together lightly the vegetables and
- **1 lb. lean ground beef**
- **½ cup chopped drained cooked tomatoes**
- **1 teaspoon Worcestershire sauce**
- **2 eggs, beaten**

and a mixture of
- **1 teaspoon salt**
- **¼ teaspoon dry mustard**
- **⅛ teaspoon pepper**
- **⅛ teaspoon oregano**

Pack meat mixture lightly into prepared pan.

Bake at 350°F about 1¼ hrs.

To unmold, loosen meat gently from sides of pan. Pour off any excess juices. Invert onto platter and remove pan. Serve with **Cinnamon Spiced Peaches** (page 421).   *6 servings*

BEEF BURGERS WITH BARBECUE SAUCE   217 cal./serving

▲ *Base Recipe*

Prepare and keep warm
Barbecue Sauce (page 746)

Mix lightly
- **1 lb. lean ground beef**

with a mixture of
- **1 teaspoon salt**
- **½ teaspoon monosodium glutamate**
- **⅛ teaspoon pepper**

Shape into four patties about ¾ in. thick.

Heat a skillet over medium heat. Put patties into skillet and cook until brown on one side. Turn and brown other side. Allow 6 to 10 min. for cooking patties. When patties are browned, place in a shallow baking dish. Pour the sauce over the patties.

Bake at 350°F 20 to 25 min. Baste patties occasionally with the sauce.

Serve patties with the sauce.   *4 servings*

—BROILER BURGERS   184 cal./serving

Follow ▲ Recipe. Omit the Barbecue Sauce. Arrange patties on broiler rack. Set temperature control of range at Broil. Put into broiler with top of patties about 3 in. from heat. Broil 6 to 8 min. When patties are browned on one side, turn and broil second side about 6 to 8 min.

—POTATO BEEF BALLS   286 cal./serving

Follow recipe for Broiler Burgers; do not broil patties. Mix **1 cup grated raw potato** (about 2 medium) with meat and shape mixture into balls about 1½ in. in diameter. Heat **2 tablespoons butter or margarine** in a large heavy skillet. Add potato-beef balls and brown over medium heat, turning occasionally to brown all sides. Add **2 to 3 tablespoons water**, cover and cook over low heat 20 to 25 min., turning occasionally.

PINEAPPLE MEAT LOAF   184 cal./serving

Pineapple does flavor-wonders for meat loaf.

Grease a 9x5x3-in. loaf pan.

Set out
- **3 pineapple slices**

Cut two of the slices into halves. Arrange slices in bottom of pan in an attractive pattern.

Mix lightly
- **1 lb. lean ground beef**
- **½ lb. ground veal**
- **1 cup (about 1½ slices) soft bread crumbs**
- **¾ cup skim milk (page 9)**
- **½ cup (about 1 medium) chopped onion**
- **1 egg, beaten**

and a mixture of
- **1 teaspoon salt**
- **½ teaspoon monosodium glutamate**
- **¼ teaspoon paprika**
- **¼ teaspoon marjoram**
- **⅛ teaspoon thyme**
- **⅛ teaspoon pepper**

Pack meat mixture lightly into loaf pan.

Bake at 350°F about 1½ hrs.

To unmold, loosen meat gently from sides of pan with a spatula. Pour off excess juices; invert onto platter and remove pan. Garnish platter with **radish roses** and **parsley** or as desired.   *8 servings*

CHINESE PORK AND VEGETABLES
393 cal./serving

Set out a heavy skillet with a tight-fitting cover.

Cut into thin strips
- **½ lb. lean pork**

Heat the skillet over medium heat. Add the meat strips and brown, occasionally moving and turning pieces with a fork.

Prepare
- **1 cup quick meat broth (page 10)**

Add to the skillet ½ cup of the meat broth (reserving remainder) and
- **¼ cup soy sauce**
- **1 teaspoon cider vinegar**
- **½ teaspoon monosodium glutamate**
- **¼ teaspoon non caloric sweetening solution or 2 non caloric sweetening tablets (page 9)**
- **1 clove garlic, cut in halves and wooden pick inserted in each half**

Cover and simmer 20 min., or until meat is tender.

Meanwhile, prepare
- **4 stalks celery, cut in 1-in. pieces**
- **3 medium (about ½ lb.) onions, chopped**
- **1 green pepper, cut in bite-size pieces**

Set aside.

Wash (see Sukiyaki, page 711), cut into large shreds
- **¼ lb. spinach**

Set aside.

When meat is almost tender, add to the skillet the remaining meat broth, celery, onion and spinach. Partially cover skillet and cook until meat is tender. Add green pepper and cook about 1 min. longer. (Vegetables will be crisp.) Remove garlic. Serve immediately.   *2 servings*

LIVER AND ONIONS   125 cal./serving

Liver, high in food value, is invaluable for reducers. Add full-bodied flavor with onions.

Clean and thinly slice
- **1 medium onion**

Put into a skillet with
- **½ cup quick meat broth (page 10)**
- **½ teaspoon Worcestershire sauce**
- **¼ teaspoon caraway seed**

Cover and cook over medium heat until onion is almost tender, moving and turning occasionally with a spoon.

Meanwhile, cut away, if necessary, tubes and outer membrane from

4 slices (about 1 lb.) veal or calf's liver, cut about ½ in. thick

Remove the onion slices from skillet with a slotted spoon. Add the liver to the skillet and simmer in the broth about 2 min. Turn pieces and place onion slices on top. Continue cooking about 2 min. longer, or just until liver is tender. *4 servings*

DEVILED VEAL IN SOUR CREAM

323 cal./serving

▲ *Base Recipe*

Set out a medium-size heavy skillet with a tight-fitting cover.

Have ready

2 lbs. veal round steak (cutlet), cut about ½ in. thick

Pound meat until ¼ in. thick; cut into serving-size pieces. Coat with a mixture of

2 tablespoons all-purpose flour
1½ teaspoons paprika
1 teaspoon salt
⅛ teaspoon pepper

Set aside.

Heat in the skillet over low heat

2 tablespoons butter or margarine

Add and cook over medium heat until almost tender, stirring occasionally with a spoon

1 cup (about 2 medium) finely chopped onion

Remove onion from skillet with a slotted spoon;

set aside. In the same skillet, brown veal pieces on both sides. Pour over veal

1½ cups quick meat broth (page 10)

Add chopped onion and

1 tablespoon prepared horseradish
1 teaspoon prepared mustard

Cover and simmer 25 min., or until veal is tender.

Remove meat to a warm serving dish. Add gradually to liquid in skillet, stirring constantly

½ cup dairy sour cream

Spoon over meat and serve immediately.

6 servings

—DEVILED VEAL *282 cal./serving*

Follow ▲ Recipe. Omit sour cream. If desired, spoon liquid over meat before serving.

CHICKEN CREOLE

166 cal./serving

Set out a heavy skillet with a tight-fitting cover.

Set aside to drain

1 4-oz. can (about ½ cup, drained) sliced mushrooms

Clean and chop

1 medium onion (about ½ cup, chopped)
½ small green pepper (about ¼ cup, chopped)

Heat in the skillet over low heat

1 tablespoon butter or margarine

Add onion, green pepper and mushrooms; cook over medium heat until vegetables are tender and mushrooms are lightly browned, stirring occasionally. Add

1 cup quick chicken broth (page 10)
½ cup tomato paste
1 teaspoon salt
¼ teaspoon pepper
¼ teaspoon monosodium glutamate
⅛ teaspoon cayenne pepper

Cover and simmer 30 min.

Cut into strips enough chicken to yield

1 cup cooked chicken strips

Add chicken to skillet and cook 10 min., or until chicken is heated. Occasionally move and turn pieces with a spoon. *4 servings*

SPECIAL STUFFED FISH

177 cal./serving of fish; 91 cal./serving of stuffing

Set out a shallow baking dish.

For Stuffing—Mix in a bowl

3 tablespoons butter or margarine, melted
1 tablespoon lemon juice
½ teaspoon salt
½ teaspoon celery seed
⅛ teaspoon thyme

Add and toss lightly until mixed thoroughly

2 cups (about 3 slices) soft bread crumbs
½ cup minced sweet pickle
1 tablespoon finely chopped onion

Set stuffing aside.

For Fish—Rinse body cavity with cold water, drain well and pat dry with absorbent paper.

3-lb. dressed fish (striped bass or trout or other suitable whole fish available in your market)

Rub the fish cavity with

Salt (about 2 teaspoons)

Lightly pile (do not pack) stuffing into fish. To close cavity, fasten with skewers and lace with cord. Place fish in the baking dish and brush with a mixture of

2 tablespoons butter or margarine, melted
½ teaspoon salt
¼ teaspoon pepper

Bake at 350°F 45 to 50 min., or until fish flakes (page 9).

Remove the skewers and cord from the fish. Carefully remove the fish to a warm serving platter with two wide spatulas. Garnish as desired with **lemon** and **sprigs of parsley**.

6 servings

FILLET OF SOLE WITH MUSHROOMS

192 cal./serving

Grease a 2-qt. shallow casserole with a cover.

Clean and slice

¼ lb. mushrooms

Heat in a skillet over low heat

2 tablespoons butter or margarine

Add mushrooms to skillet. Cook over medium heat, occasionally moving and turning gently

713

with a spoon, until mushrooms are tender and lightly browned. Set aside.

Place in the casserole
1 lb. fillet of sole
(If frozen, thaw as directed on package.)

Spoon mushrooms over fillets. Pour over mushrooms a mixture of
¼ cup dry white wine
2 tablespoons water
2 tablespoons lemon juice
1 tablespoon chopped parsley
½ teaspoon dry mustard
½ teaspoon salt
¼ teaspoon pepper

Cover casserole and bake at 375°F 25 min., or until the fish flakes (page 9).   *3 servings*

Note: Fish fillets such as cod, flounder, haddock, perch or pike may be used instead of fillet of sole.

SHRIMP-STUFFED BAKED TOMATOES

139 cal./serving

▲ *Base Recipe*

Set out a 1-qt. shallow baking dish and a skillet.

Prepare (page 418)
4 large Tomato Shells
Reserve the pulp. Do not chill the Tomato Shells.

For Shrimp Stuffing—Heat in the skillet over low heat
1 tablespoon butter or margarine
Add to skillet and cook over medium heat about 5 min., stirring occasionally
⅓ cup chopped onion
¼ cup chopped celery
2 tablespoons chopped green pepper
Meanwhile, chop
7 oz. (about 1 cup) cooked shrimp
Set aside.

Mix reserved tomato pulp, shrimp, chopped vegetables and
¼ cup soft bread crumbs
¾ teaspoon Worcestershire sauce
and a mixture of
½ teaspoon salt
¼ teaspoon thyme
Few grains pepper

To Complete—Spoon mixture into Tomato Shells, heaping slightly. Place in the baking dish. Evenly cover tops of stuffed tomatoes with
1½ tablespoons shredded Cheddar cheese
Bake at 375°F 15 to 20 min., or until cheese is melted.   *4 servings*

—SHRIMP-STUFFED EGGPLANT

125 cal./serving

Follow ▲ Recipe. Substitute **1 medium (about 1 lb.) eggplant** for tomatoes. Rinse and cut eggplant into halves lengthwise; cook covered in a small amount of boiling salted water about 10 min., or until just tender. Remove from water. With a spoon scoop out pulp, leaving a ½-in. thick shell. Finely chop pulp and mix with chopped shrimp mixture. Bake at 375°F 20 to 25 min.

SAUCES

NONFAT MEDIUM WHITE SAUCE

195 cal.

▲ *Base Recipe*

Pour into a saucepan
1 cup water
Sprinkle evenly over water a mixture of
⅓ cup instant nonfat dry milk
2 tablespoons all-purpose flour
¼ teaspoon salt
¼ teaspoon monosodium glutamate
Few grains pepper
Beat with a rotary beater until blended. Cook over medium heat, stirring constantly, until sauce thickens. Cook 1 to 2 min. longer, stirring constantly.   *About 1 cup sauce*

—NONFAT THICK WHITE SAUCE   220 cal.

Follow ▲ Recipe. Use 3 tablespoons flour. Use in preparation of soufflés.

—NONFAT THIN WHITE SAUCE   170 cal.

Follow ▲ Recipe. Use 1 tablespoon flour. Use as a base for cream soups.

—NONFAT CURRY SAUCE   195 cal.

Follow ▲ Recipe. Add **1 teaspoon curry powder** with seasonings.

MUSTARD SAUCE   438 cal.

Set out
1 cup reconstituted instant nonfat dry milk (use double amount of milk)
Scald ¾ cup of the milk in the top of a double boiler over direct heat; reserve remaining ¼ cup.

Mix in a small saucepan
2 tablespoons dry mustard
2 teaspoons cornstarch
½ teaspoon salt
Blend in the ¼ cup reserved milk and
1½ teaspoons non caloric sweetening solution or 12 non caloric sweetening tablets (page 9)
Add gradually, stirring constantly, the scalded milk. Stirring constantly, bring cornstarch mixture rapidly to boiling over direct heat and cook for 3 min.

Pour mixture into double-boiler top and place over simmering water. Cover and cook 10 to 12 min., stirring occasionally.

Remove cover and vigorously stir about 3 tablespoons of hot mixture into
2 egg yolks, slightly beaten
Immediately blend into mixture in double boiler. Cook over simmering water 3 to 5 min., stirring slowly to keep mixture cooking evenly. Remove from heat. Add gradually and stir in
¼ cup cider vinegar
Serve sauce hot with vegetables or meat.

About 1¼ cups sauce

BARBECUE SAUCE   134 cal.

Mix in a saucepan
½ cup ketchup
¼ cup water
1 tablespoon prepared mustard
1 tablespoon cider vinegar
1 teaspoon Worcestershire sauce
¼ teaspoon non caloric sweetening solution or 2 non caloric sweetening tablets (page 4)
Heat until mixture is hot. Set aside and keep warm until ready to use. Or cool, cover and store in refrigerator.   *About ¾ cup sauce*

VEGETABLES

FLAVORFUL GREEN BEANS

62 cal./serving

Wash, remove ends and french (cut lengthwise into fine strips)
1 lb. (about 3 cups) green beans
Cook (page 313) about 10 min., or until tender. (Frozen or canned green beans may be substituted for fresh beans. Follow directions on package or container for cooking.)

Vegetables in Curry Sauce

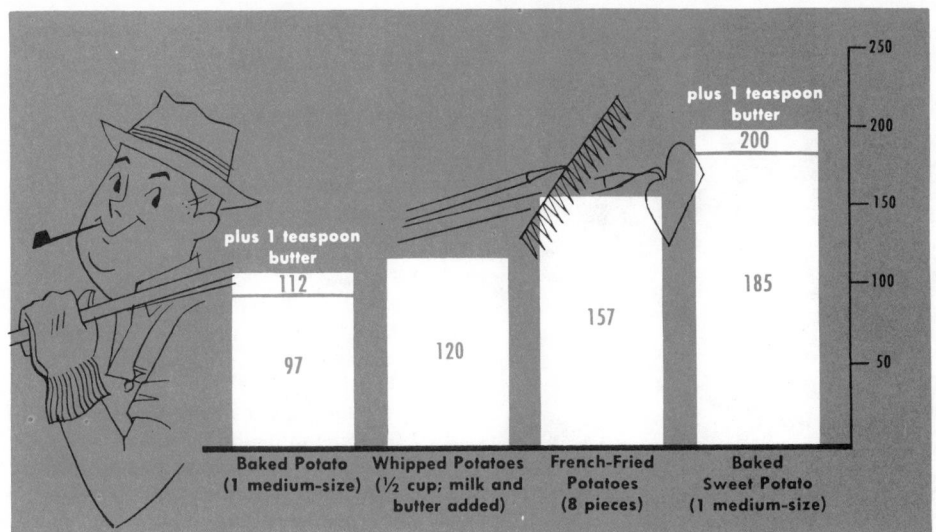

Chart showing calorie counts: Baked Potato (1 medium-size) 97, plus 1 teaspoon butter 112; Whipped Potatoes (½ cup; milk and butter added) 120; French-Fried Potatoes (8 pieces) 157; Baked Sweet Potato (1 medium-size) 185, plus 1 teaspoon butter 200.

Add to the beans

1 tablespoon butter or margarine
¼ teaspoon lemon juice

and a mixture of

¼ teaspoon salt
¼ teaspoon monosodium glutamate
⅛ teaspoon nutmeg

Toss beans gently; serve immediately.

4 servings

BAKED ACORN SQUASH   63 cal./serving

Wash, cut into halves lengthwise, and remove seeds and fibers from

1 medium (about 1 lb.) acorn squash

Place cut side down in a baking pan. Pour boiling water into baking pan to ¼-in. depth.

Bake squash halves at 400°F 25 min. With a fork, turn squash cut side up. Sprinkle over cut surfaces a mixture of

½ teaspoon paprika
½ teaspoon salt
¼ teaspoon pepper

Bake 25 min. longer, or until tender when pierced with a fork.   *2 servings*

VEGETABLES IN CURRY SAUCE

70 cal./serving

Tasty curry sauce adds zest to vegetables.

Have ready

1 cup cooked cauliflowerets
1 cup cooked green beans, cut in pieces
½ cup cooked carrot slices
¼ cup cooked celery pieces
4 cooked small whole onions

Prepare

1½ cups Nonfat Curry Sauce
(1½ times recipe, page 746)

Add vegetables to sauce; thoroughly heat in sauce, occasionally moving and turning vegetables with a spoon. Turn into a warm serving dish and serve immediately.   *6 servings*

COLORFUL VEGETABLE PLATES

(For approximate calorie count see chart)

For eye-appeal and, best of all, for taste-appeal, spark your menus with a tempting array of vegetables arranged on gay plates or platters. Cook the vegetables as directed on page 313. Then add seasonings, using a dash of imagination. Brush lightly, or generously if the calorie total will allow, with melted butter or margarine. Or pour over them a bit of lemon juice. Never forget the flavor thrills that are possible with the use of herbs and spices.

Set a steaming head of **cauliflower** at one side of a large plate. From this radiate cooked vegetables of various shapes, such as small **beets,** French-style **green beans, carrot chunks, asparagus spears** and **green peas.**

Spark another vegetable plate arrangement with **Tomato Broil** (page 350). Add **cauliflower, green beans,** and slices of **carrots**—all cooked to just-tender perfection. Rush to the table while they're piping hot.

SALADS AND SALAD DRESSINGS

CHILLED ASPARAGUS WITH SHARP VINEGAR SAUCE

16 cal./serving; 36 cal./serving with egg

Cook, following directions on package

1 10-oz. pkg. frozen asparagus spears

Meanwhile, prepare

Sharp Vinegar Sauce (below)

When asparagus is tender, drain and put into a bowl. Pour sauce over asparagus and toss lightly to coat thoroughly. Put into refrigerator to marinate (page 10) 12 hrs., or overnight; turn asparagus occasionally.

Before serving, drain asparagus; arrange on **lettuce leaves.**

If desired, garnish with

1 Hard-Cooked Egg (page 133), coarsely chopped

4 servings

For Sharp Vinegar Sauce (8 cal.)—Combine in a screw-top jar

½ cup water
¼ cup cider vinegar
2 teaspoons finely chopped parsley
2 teaspoons finely chopped chives
2 teaspoons finely chopped pimiento
1 teaspoon finely crushed chervil
1 teaspoon capers
1 teaspoon salt
½ teaspoon dry mustard
⅛ teaspoon pepper

Cover jar tightly and shake to blend well. Store in same jar in refrigerator. Before using, shake again.

Use on chilled vegetables such as asparagus.

About 1 cup sauce

TOSSED VEGETABLE SALAD

(For approximate calorie count see chart)

Cut out core and discard bruised and wilted leaves from

1 large head lettuce

Rinse with cold water, drain and pat dry with a soft clean towel or absorbent paper. Store in a plastic bag or in vegetable compartment in refrigerator until chilled.

Other salad greens that can be used, alone or in combination, are **romaine, watercress,** small **dandelion greens, chervil, parsley** or **curly endive.** Wash thoroughly in cold water, drain and pat dry with a soft clean towel or absorbent paper. Store and chill as for head lettuce.

Tossed Vegetable Salad

Peach Blueberry Salad Plate and Salad Bowl Sensation

Prepare and chill in refrigerator
**Low-Calorie French Dressing or
Garlic French Dressing (page 750)**
(It is a wise idea to prepare several dressings and store them in the refrigerator. Make use of them in other food preparation and for variety in tossed salads.)

Just before serving salad, rub a wooden salad bowl with
1 clove garlic, cut in halves
Tear chilled lettuce or other greens into bite-size pieces. Put into salad bowl. Pour about 6 tablespoons dressing over lettuce. Lightly toss the lettuce until it is well coated with the dressing and no liquid remains on the bottom of the bowl.

Other fresh vegetables such as **green pepper strips, tomato chunks, radish, cucumber** and **onion slices** frequently share the limelight with the crisp greens. Chopped **hard-cooked egg** may be used as a garnish.

Cooked vegetables such as **green beans, cauliflower, beets** and **asparagus** are also used for salads, either alone or in combination with fresh vegetables. *6 servings*

CRAB MEAT-STUFFED TOMATOES

103 cal./serving

Prepare
**4 Tomato Shells (page 418) reserve
tomato pulp)**
Mix together the reserved tomato pulp and
**1⅓ cups (1 6½-oz. can) crab meat,
bony tissue removed**
**¼ cup Low-Calorie Salad Dressing
(page 718)**
2 tablespoons chopped celery
2 tablespoons capers
4 teaspoons lemon juice
½ teaspoon salt
¼ teaspoon white pepper

Chill in refrigerator until ready to serve.

To serve, lightly fill Tomato Shells with mixture. *4 servings*

FRUIT SALADS

(For approximate calorie count see chart)

Fruits lend themselves to a multitude of combinations for salad plates or bowls. And they're oh, so pleasing to the eye and palate of that person who is trying to watch the calories. Select for the arrangement fruits which will provide contrast in color, size, shape and texture. Choose from the inspiring variety of fresh and low-calorie canned fruits.

Chill your very prettiest salad plates or bowls, line them with chilled greens and heap with a galaxy of fruit. Add the low-calorie dressing of your choice—and you've a salad worthy of the most discriminating food lover.

PEACH BLUEBERRY SALAD PLATE

Peel juicy ripe **peaches,** cut into halves and brush with a bit of **lemon juice** to prevent darkening. Arrange on a bed of **lettuce leaves** and fill the centers with plump **blueberries.** Add a scoop of **cottage cheese** and top with a sprinkling of **paprika.** Serve with pride to a calorie counter.

SALAD BOWL SENSATION

Fill a large bowl with **lettuce cups.** Halve and seed chilled **grapes.** Break **pomegranates** into chunks or make an incision in them and remove seeds. Core **apples,** cut lengthwise into slices and brush with **pineapple juice.** Heap the apple slices, grape halves and pomegranate seeds or pieces into the lettuce cups. Accompany with your favorite low-calorie salad dressing, homemade or commercial.

PERFECTION SALAD

12 cal./serving

Set out a 1-qt. mold.

Pour into a small cup or custard cup
½ cup cold water
Sprinkle evenly over cold water
1 env. unflavored gelatin
Let gelatin stand until softened.

Meanwhile, heat until very hot
1 cup water
Remove from heat and immediately add softened gelatin, stirring until gelatin is completely dissolved. Add and stir mixture until thoroughly blended
3 to 4 tablespoons cider vinegar
1 tablespoon lemon juice
**¾ teaspoon non caloric sweetening
solution or 6 non caloric sweetening tablets (page 9)**
½ teaspoon salt
Chill until mixture is slightly thicker than consistency of thick unbeaten egg white, stirring occasionally.

Prepare
1 cup diced celery
¾ cup finely cut cabbage
4 teaspoons chopped pimiento

When gelatin mixture is of desired consistency, stir in the prepared vegetables. Turn mixture into the mold. Chill in refrigerator until firm.

To serve, unmold (page 374) onto serving platter. *8 servings*

JELLIED ORANGE CARROT SALAD

35 cal./serving

Set out a 1-qt. mold.

Drain, reserving liquid for use in other food preparation
**2 cans (8 oz. each) low-calorie pine-
apple tidbits (about 1½ cups,
drained)**
Using a sharp knife, cut away peel and white membrane from
1 medium orange
Remove sections by cutting on each side of dividing membrane, working over a bowl to save juice. Remove and discard seeds, if any. Cut into small pieces enough of the orange sections to yield ½ cup orange pieces.

Wash, scrape or pare, and shred enough carrots to yield
½ cup shredded carrot
Set pineapple tidbits, orange pieces and shredded carrot aside.

Pour into a small cup or custard cup
½ cup cold water
Sprinkle evenly over cold water
1 env. unflavored gelatin
Let gelatin stand until softened.

Meanwhile, heat until very hot in a saucepan
½ cup water
Remove from heat and immediately add softened gelatin, stirring until gelatin is completely

dissolved. Add and stir until mixture is thoroughly blended

½ cup orange juice
1½ teaspoons non caloric sweetening solution or 12 non caloric sweetening tablets (page 9)
¼ teaspoon salt

Chill until mixture is slightly thicker than consistency of thick unbeaten egg white, stirring occasionally.

When gelatin is of desired consistency, blend in the pineapple tidbits, orange pieces and shredded carrot. Turn mixture into the mold. Chill in refrigerator until firm.

To serve, unmold (page 374) onto chilled serving platter. *8 servings*

JELLIED PINEAPPLE AND PEAR SALAD

54 cal./serving

▲ Base Recipe

Set out a 1½-qt. mold.

Drain, reserving liquid in a 2-cup measuring cup for liquids

2 cans (8 oz. each) low-calorie pineapple tidbits (about 1½ cups, drained)
Add to pineapple liquid and set aside
Unsweetened pineapple juice (enough to make 1½ cups)
Wash, quarter, core and cut into cubes
3 medium pears
Put pineapple tidbits and pear cubes into a bowl and lightly toss together to prevent discoloration of pears.

Pour into a small bowl
1 cup cold water
Sprinkle evenly over cold water
2 env. unflavored gelatin
Let gelatin stand until softened.

Meanwhile, heat until very hot in a saucepan
1 cup water
Remove from heat and immediately add softened gelatin, stirring until gelatin is completely dissolved. Add and stir in the reserved pineapple liquid and
½ teaspoon non caloric sweetening solution or 4 non caloric sweetening tablets (page 9)
Chill until mixture is slightly thicker than consistency of thick, unbeaten egg white, stirring occasionally.

When gelatin mixture is of desired consistency, stir in the fruit. Turn mixture into the mold. Chill in refrigerator until firm.

To serve, unmold (page 374) onto chilled serving plate. *12 servings*

—JELLIED PINEAPPLE AND APPLE SALAD

49 cal./serving

Follow ▲ Recipe. Substitute **3 medium apples** for the pears.

SHIMMERING EMERALD SALAD

67 cal./serving

This refreshing grapefruit juice mold may also be served as a dessert.

Set out a 1-qt. fancy mold.

Pour into a small bowl
½ cup cold water
½ cup unsweetened grapefruit juice
Sprinkle evenly over cold water
2 env. unflavored gelatin
Let stand until softened.

Heat until very hot in a saucepan
1½ cups unsweetened grapefruit juice

Remove saucepan from heat and immediately

stir in the softened gelatin until gelatin is completely dissolved. Add, stirring until sugar is dissolved
⅓ cup sugar
¼ teaspoon salt
Blend in
¼ cup lemon juice
¼ cup lime juice
Tint to desired color by blending in, a drop at a time
Green food coloring (about 5 drops)
Turn into the mold. Chill in refrigerator until firm.

To serve, unmold (page 374) onto chilled serving plate. Arrange at intervals on plate around sides of mold
Galax leaves
Frosted Grapes (below)

8 servings

For Frosted Grapes—Beat **1 egg white** until frothy. Dip small clusters of rinsed, thoroughly drained **grapes** in the beaten egg white. Shake off excess egg white and dip grapes into **sugar**. Set aside to dry. Chill in refrigerator, if desired.

LOW-CALORIE LUNCHEON PLATTER

207 cal./serving

▲ Base Recipe

Set out 6 individual ring molds.

For Tomato Aspic—Pour into a large saucepan
4 cups tomato juice
Add to tomato juice
⅓ cup chopped celery leaves
⅓ cup chopped onion
1 tablespoon sugar
1¼ teaspoons salt
½ teaspoon monosodium glutamate
½ bay leaf
Stir to blend and cook, uncovered, over low heat about 10 min.

Meanwhile, pour into a small bowl
½ cup cold water
Sprinkle evenly over cold water
2 env. unflavored gelatin
Let stand until softened.

Remove tomato juice mixture from heat. Strain liquid into a large bowl. Immediately add the softened gelatin to tomato-juice mixture and stir until gelatin is completely dissolved. Add and stir well
2½ tablespoons cider vinegar
Pour ⅔ cup of the mixture into each mold. Cool; chill in refrigerator until firm.

Low-Calorie Perfection Salad (½ cup)	20		
Perfection Salad or Tomato Aspic (½ cup)	40		
Tossed Green Salad (½ cup)	30	60	plus 2 teaspoons French dressing
Potato or Waldorf Salad (½ cup)	200		
Avocado (½ medium-size)	285	300	plus 1 teaspoon French dressing
Frozen Fruit Salad (½ cup)	258	350	plus 1 tablespoon dressing

100   200   300   400

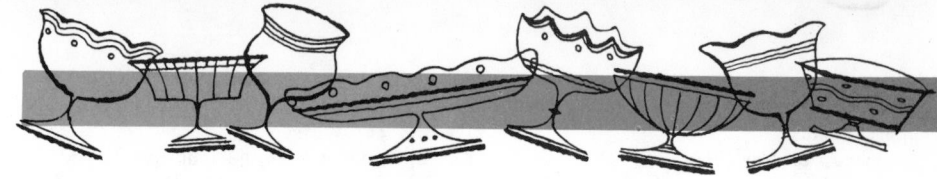

To Serve—Prepare

3 Hard-Cooked Eggs (page 133)

Arrange on a large chilled platter

7 crisp lettuce cups

Unmold (page 374) the aspic rings into six of the lettuce cups. Garnish each ring with

Parsley

Spoon into the remaining lettuce cup

3 cups cottage cheese

Sprinkle with

Chopped chives

Cut the hard-cooked eggs into quarters and pile in center of platter.   *6 servings*

—CHICKEN-TOMATO ASPIC MOLD

115 cal./serving

Follow ▲ Recipe for Tomato Aspic; use a 1½-qt. ring mold. Chop enough cooked chicken to yield **2 cups chopped cooked chicken.** Chill gelatin mixture until it is slightly thicker than the consistency of thick, unbeaten egg white. When gelatin mixture is of desired consistency, stir in the chopped chicken. Turn into mold and chill in refrigerator until firm.

LOW-CALORIE SALAD DRESSING

306 cal.; 19 cal./tablespoon

Much too good to be classed as a "substitute!"

Beat slightly in top of a double boiler

2 eggs

Blend in

½ cup reconstituted instant nonfat dry milk (use double amount of milk)

1 teaspoon monosodium glutamate

½ teaspoon paprika

½ teaspoon dry mustard

2 drops Tabasco

Place over boiling water. Add gradually, stirring in

¼ cup cider vinegar

Cook over boiling water, stirring constantly, until mixture thickens, about 10 min.

Remove from heat. Cool. Store salad dressing in tightly covered jar in refrigerator.

About 1 cup dressing

Note: For a less sharp dressing, decrease vinegar to 2 tablespoons and increase milk to ½ cup plus 2 tablespoons.

LOW-CALORIE FRENCH DRESSING

350 cal.; 18 cal./tablespoon

▲ *Base Recipe*

Mix in a saucepan

¾ cup water

2 teaspoons cornstarch

Bring to boiling over high heat. Reduce heat and cook 5 min., or until mixture is thick and clear. Remove from heat and set aside to cool.

When cool, add

¼ cup lemon juice

¼ cup ketchup

2 tablespoons salad oil

1 teaspoon Worcestershire sauce

¾ teaspoon salt

½ teaspoon monosodium glutamate

¼ teaspoon paprika

¼ teaspoon pepper

¼ teaspoon dry mustard

¼ teaspoon non caloric sweetening solution or 2 non caloric sweetening tablets (page 9)

Beat with a rotary beater until smooth and well blended. Store covered in refrigerator. Shake well before using.   *About 1¼ cups dressing*

—GARLIC FRENCH DRESSING

18 cal./tablespoon

Follow ▲ Recipe. Cut into halves **1 clove garlic** and add to completed dressing. Chill dressing about 12 hrs. to allow flavors to blend. Remove garlic before serving.

DESSERTS

SOFT CUSTARD

55 cal./serving

▲ *Base Recipe*

Set out 6 sherbet glasses.

Scald (page 10) in top of a double boiler

2 cups skim milk (page 9)

Meanwhile, beat slightly

2 eggs

Blend in

1 teaspoon non caloric sweetening solution or 8 non caloric sweetening tablets (page 9)

⅛ teaspoon salt

Stirring constantly, gradually add scalded milk to egg mixture.

Strain mixture into double-boiler top. Cook over simmering water, stirring constantly, until mixture coats a metal spoon. Remove from simmering water at once. Cool to lukewarm over cold water. Blend in

2 teaspoons vanilla extract

Pour into the sherbet glasses and immediately chill in refrigerator. Or chill and use as a sauce.   *6 servings*

—FRUIT CUSTARD

69 cal./serving

Follow ▲ Recipe. Pour custard over **1 cup blueberries** or **1 cup orange sections.** Chill in refrigerator.

—BAKED CUSTARD

55 cal./serving

Follow ▲ Recipe for egg-milk mixture. Strain mixture. Blend in the vanilla extract. Pour into six heat-resistant custard cups and sprinkle each with **nutmeg.** Set filled cups in a baking pan. Pour very hot water into pan to a 1-in. depth. Bake at 325°F 30 to 45 min., or until a knife comes out clean when inserted halfway between center and edge of custard. Serve immediately, or cool and chill in refrigerator.

APRICOT TAPIOCA CREAM

84 cal./serving

▲ *Base Recipe*

Set out a 1-qt. saucepan.

Drain and put into refrigerator to chill

24 low-calorie canned apricot halves

Put into the saucepan

2 egg yolks, slightly beaten

Add gradually, stirring in

3 cups skim milk (page 9)

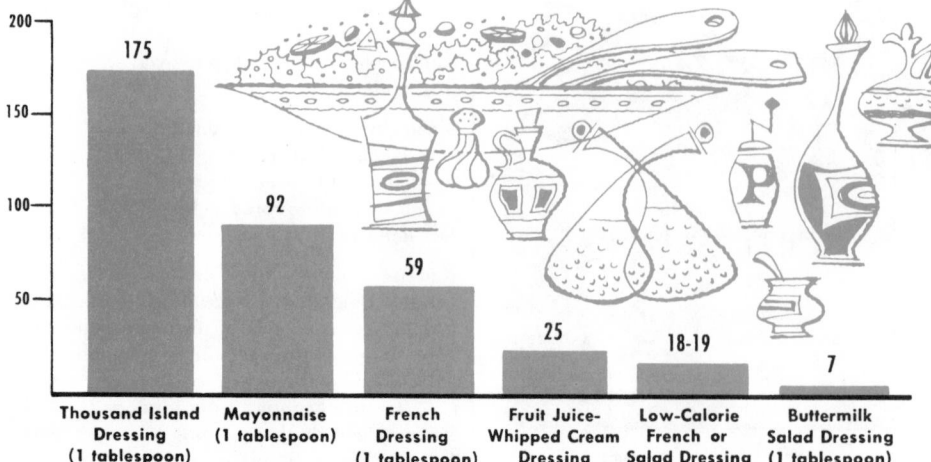

175	92	59	25	18-19	7
Thousand Island Dressing (1 tablespoon)	Mayonnaise (1 tablespoon)	French Dressing (1 tablespoon)	Fruit Juice-Whipped Cream Dressing (1 tablespoon)	Low-Calorie French or Salad Dressing (1 tablespoon)	Buttermilk Salad Dressing (1 tablespoon)

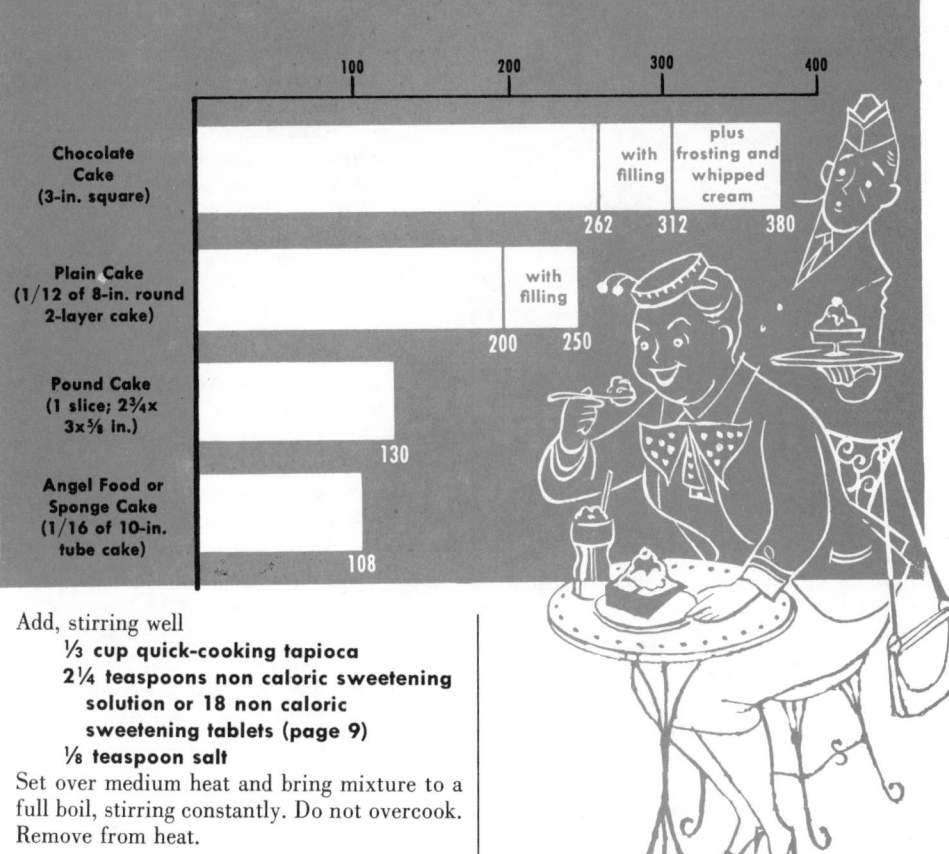

	100	200	300	400
Chocolate Cake (3-in. square)			with filling	plus frosting and whipped cream
			262 312	380
Plain Cake (1/12 of 8-in. round 2-layer cake)		with filling		
		200 250		
Pound Cake (1 slice; 2¾x 3x⅝ in.)		130		
Angel Food or Sponge Cake (1/16 of 10-in. tube cake)	108			

Add, stirring well

⅓ cup quick-cooking tapioca
2¼ teaspoons non caloric sweetening solution or 18 non caloric sweetening tablets (page 9)
⅛ teaspoon salt

Set over medium heat and bring mixture to a full boil, stirring constantly. Do not overcook. Remove from heat.

Beat until rounded peaks are formed

2 egg whites

Add a small amount of the hot tapioca mixture gradually to the egg whites and stir constantly. Then quickly blend in remaining tapioca mixture. Blend in

1½ teaspoons vanilla extract
¼ teaspoon almond extract

Cool, stirring once after 15 to 20 min.

Using parfait glasses, alternate layers of tapioca cream with apricot halves, allowing 3 halves per serving, and beginning and ending with an apricot half.   *8 servings*

—TANGERINE TAPIOCA CREAM
                                    83 cal./serving

Follow ▲ Recipe. Substitute **2 medium tangerines** for apricots. Rinse and chill in refrigerator. When tapioca cream is cooled, peel tangerines, removing white membrane. Line sherbet glasses with tangerine sections; turn tapioca cream into glasses.

—PEACH TAPIOCA CREAM   *83 cal./serving*

Follow ▲ Recipe. Substitute **1 cup drained, low-calorie canned peach slices** for apricots.

—STRAWBERRY TAPIOCA CREAM
                                    81 cal./serving

Follow ▲ Recipe. Substitute **1 cup rinsed drained hulled strawberries** for the apricots. Just before layering dessert, cut strawberries into halves.

APPLE BETTY   *84 cal./serving*

▲ *Base Recipe*

Grease a 1-qt. casserole.

Toss together

2 cups (about 3 slices) soft bread crumbs
1½ teaspoons cinnamon
1 teaspoon grated lemon peel
¼ teaspoon salt

Wash, quarter, core, pare and cut into thin slices

4 medium cooking apples (about 3 cups, sliced)

Spread one third of crumb mixture evenly and lightly over bottom of casserole. Cover with one half of the apples. Repeat. Top with remaining crumb mixture. Drizzle over top a mixture of

¼ cup water
2 tablespoons lemon juice
1½ teaspoons non caloric sweetening solution or 12 non caloric sweetening tablets (page 9)

Bake at 375°F 25 to 30 min., or until apples are tender when pierced with a fork.

Serve warm or cold.   *6 servings*

—PEACH BETTY   *66 cal./serving*

Follow ▲ Recipe. Reduce cinnamon to ¾ teaspoon; add ¼ **teaspoon nutmeg.** Substitute

2 cans (16 oz. each, drained) low-calorie sliced peaches for apples.

APRICOT WHIP   *81 cal./serving*

▲ *Base Recipe*

Put into a saucepan

¾ cup (about 4 oz.) dried apricots
1 cup hot water

Cook apricots, covered, 25 to 30 min., or until fruit is plump and tender when pierced with a fork. Remove from heat. Purée by forcing apricots through a coarse sieve or food mill. Set aside to cool.

When purée is cooled, blend in

1 teaspoon non caloric sweetening solution or 8 non caloric sweetening tablets (page 9)
¼ teaspoon vanilla extract
⅛ teaspoon almond extract

Beat until stiff, not dry, peaks are formed

2 egg whites
⅛ teaspoon salt

Beating constantly, gradually add purée to beaten egg whites. Continue beating until mixture is uniform in color. Spoon into four serving dishes and put into refrigerator to chill thoroughly.

Garnish with **mint leaves** or as desired.

                                    4 servings

—PRUNE WHIP   *78 cal./serving*

Follow ▲ Recipe. Substitute **prunes** for the apricots.

CHERRY FOAM   *30 cal./serving*

Put into a bowl

4 teaspoons low-calorie cherry-flavored gelatin

Add to gelatin

¾ cup hot water

Cherry Foam

Stir until gelatin is completely dissolved. Stir in
1¼ cups ginger ale
1½ teaspoons lemon juice
Chill until mixture is slightly thicker than consistency of thick unbeaten egg white, stirring occasionally.

When gelatin is of desired consistency, beat until rounded peaks are formed
1 egg white
⅛ teaspoon salt
Fold the egg white into the thickened gelatin mixture. Pour mixture into sherbet glasses. Chill until firm.   *5 servings*

CHERRY DESSERT MOLD

66 cal./serving

Set out a 1-qt. mold.

Drain, reserving liquid in a measuring cup for liquids
1 can (16 oz.) low-calorie light
    sweet cherries (about 1 cup, drained)
Put into a bowl
4 teaspoons low-calorie cherry-
    flavored gelatin
Add to reserved cherry liquid
Water (enough to make 1 cup liquid)
Heat until very hot; pour over gelatin, stirring until gelatin is completely dissolved. Stir in
¾ cup water
¼ cup lemon juice
1 teaspoon non caloric sweetening
    solution or 8 non caloric sweet-
    ening tablets (page 9)
Chill until gelatin mixture is slightly thicker than consistency of thick unbeaten egg white, stirring occasionally.

Cut the drained cherries into halves and remove the pits; set aside.

When gelatin mixture is of desired consistency, blend in the cherries. Turn mixture into the mold. Chill in refrigerator until firm.

Unmold (page 374) onto chilled serving plate.

Garnish with grape or galax leaves.

    4 servings

Note: Other flavored gelatins such as raspberry, strawberry or lemon may be substituted for the cherry-flavored gelatin.

COFFEE FLUFF

60 cal./serving

▲ *Base Recipe*

Chill a small bowl and rotary beater in the refrigerator.

Pour into a small cup or custard cup
½ cup cold water
Sprinkle evenly over cold water
1 env. unflavored gelatin
Let stand until softened.

Combine in the top of a double boiler
1¼ cups double-strength coffee
    beverage (page 10)
½ cup skim milk (page 9)
Heat until very hot. Vigorously stir about 3 tablespoons coffee mixture into
2 egg yolks, slightly beaten
Immediately return to mixture in double-boiler top and cook over simmering water, stirring constantly, about 5 min., or until mixture

coats a metal spoon. Remove from heat and add softened gelatin, stirring until gelatin is completely dissolved. Mix in
2 teaspoons non caloric sweetening
    solution or 16 non caloric sweet-
    ening tablets (page 9)
Cool; chill (page 374) until mixture begins to gel (gets slightly thicker).

Meanwhile, pour into the chilled bowl
¼ cup icy cold water
½ teaspoon lemon juice
Sprinkle evenly over the water
¼ cup instant nonfat dry milk
Using the chilled beater, beat until mixture is of medium consistency (piles softly). Sprinkle over the mixture
1½ teaspoons sugar
Quickly beat in the sugar. Set aside in refrigerator.

Using clean beater, beat until rounded peaks are formed
2 egg whites
¼ teaspoon salt
When gelatin mixture is of desired consistency, spread the egg whites and whipped nonfat dry milk over the gelatin mixture and fold together with
1 teaspoon vanilla extract

Chill in refrigerator until firm. Spoon into chilled dessert dishes.   *6 servings*

—CHOCOLATE MOCHA FLUFF

91 cal./serving

Follow ▲ Recipe. Increase skim milk to 1 cup and decrease coffee beverage to ¾ cup. Add **1 oz. (1 sq.) unsweetened chocolate** with coffee and skim milk and heat over simmering water, stirring occasionally, until chocolate is melted.

GRAPE SHERBET

52 cal./serving

▲ *Base Recipe*

Pour into a small cup or custard cup
½ cup cold water
Sprinkle evenly over cold water
1 env. unflavored gelatin
Let stand until softened. Dissolve by setting over very hot water.

Mix together until thoroughly blended
1¾ cups water
2 cups unsweetened grape juice
1 tablespoon grated lemon peel
¼ cup lemon juice
1 tablespoon non caloric sweetening
    solution or 24 non caloric sweet-
    ening tablets (page 9)
¼ teaspoon salt
Blend in the dissolved gelatin. Pour into refrigerator tray and freeze until mixture is mushlike in consistency. Stir mixture 2 or 3 times while in refrigerator.

Meanwhile, set a large bowl in refrigerator.

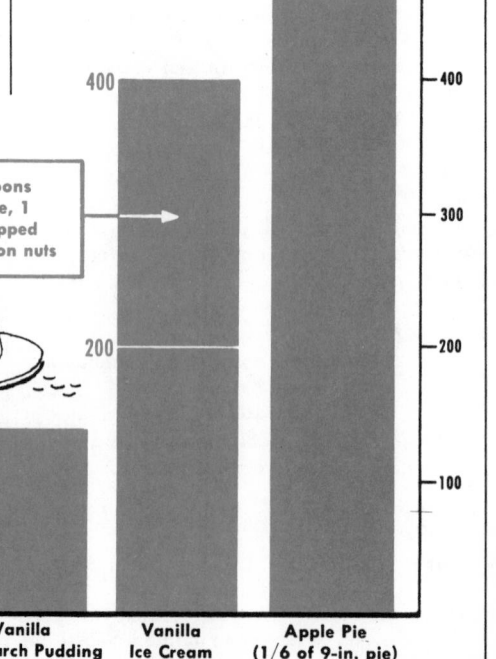

plus 3 tablespoons fruit or 1 tablespoon cream

plus 2 tablespoons chocolate sauce, 1 tablespoon whipped cream, 1 tablespoon nuts

505

4 servings

78 cal./serving

500

400

300

200

138

118

100

77

42

12

| Low-Calorie Flavored Gelatin Dessert (½ cup) | Flavored Gelatin Dessert (½ cup) | Sherbet (½ cup) | Vanilla Cornstarch Pudding (½ cup) | Vanilla Ice Cream (½ cup) | Apple Pie (1/6 of 9-in. pie) |

When mixture is mushlike, beat until stiff, not dry, peaks are formed

2 egg whites

Remove grape mixture to chilled bowl and beat until just smooth but not melted. Add beaten egg whites and beat until smooth. Return to refrigerator tray and freeze until firm.

8 servings

—ORANGE SHERBET   *37 cal./serving*

Follow ▲ Recipe. Substitute **orange juice** for grape juice and **orange peel** for lemon peel.

—PEACH SHERBET   *29 cal./serving*

Follow ▲ Recipe. Omit grape juice. Force **1 can (16 oz.) low-calorie sliced peaches** through a coarse sieve or food mill. Mix with the water-lemon juice mixture.

SUMMERTIME MELON BOWL

(For approximate calorie count see chart)

▲ Base Recipe

Set out

1 medium ripe cantaloupe or honeydew melon

To cut melon, use narrow sharp-pointed knife. Mark points in a sawtooth line at 1-in. intervals around center of melon.

Carefully cut down through marked line to center of melon. Pull halves apart. Remove and discard seedy center. With melon-ball cutter, scoop out balls from melon halves. Wrap shells in waxed paper and put in refrigerator to chill with melon balls.

Prepare and chill in refrigerator

Watermelon balls or chunks, pitted cherries, strawberries, pineapple wedges or any available fresh fruit

To serve, partially fill melon "bowls" with

Watermelon Bowl

Five-Fruit Plate and Sherbet-Topped Grapefruit

chipped ice. Impale the chilled fruit on wooden picks. Heap fruit, picks upright, on top of ice. Sprinkle over fruit

2 or 3 tablespoons lime juice

2 melon bowls

—PINEAPPLE BOWL

Follow ▲ Recipe. Substitute **1 fresh pineapple** for the melon. To prepare, cut whole pineapple into halves lengthwise through crown (spiny top). Wrap one of the halves in waxed paper and place in refrigerator, reserving for use in other food preparation. Cut out and discard core from remaining half. With a grapefruit knife or sharp paring knife, remove pineapple from its shell. Cut pineapple into chunks and use with other fresh fruit pieces. Chill fruit in refrigerator. To serve, fill the pineapple shell with the chilled fruits.

—WATERMELON BOWL

Follow ▲ Recipe. Substitute one half of a large, chilled **watermelon** for the cantaloupe or honeydew melon. Using a ball-shaped cutter, scoop out balls and use with other fresh fruit such as **strawberries, cantaloupe** and **honeydew melon balls**. Chill fruit and the watermelon shell in refrigerator. To serve, fill the watermelon shell with the chilled fruits.

FRUIT PLATES FOR DESSERT

(For approximate calorie count see chart)

Fruit for dessert is a time-honored favorite, and understandably so, for is there anyone who doesn't relish its delicate goodness? Arrangements for fruit plates offer an opportunity to create masterpieces of artistry in refreshment. Select the elements with care, giving thought to color harmony, texture contrast, and flavors—either blending or pleasantly contrasting. Handle the fruit with care and arrange it icy cold on chilled plates. Then serve it with pride!

FRUIT TRIO

A lovely crystal platter is a perfect background for a fruit trio of **low-calorie canned peach halves, grape clusters** and **melon wedges.** A few strategically placed **sprigs of mint** are the perfect garnish.

FIVE-FRUIT PLATE

Slender wedges of **melon,** plump ripe **strawberries,** orange-brushed slices of **banana,** frosty clusters of **grapes** and chunks of **pineapple** make a wonderful dessert-plate combination, especially when accompanied by tall, cool glasses of **iced coffee.**

SHERBET-TOPPED GRAPEFRUIT

Grapefruit with sherbet is a "cool" combination. Wash **grapefruit** and cut into halves. With a grapefruit knife or a sharp paring knife, loosen each section by cutting down and along both sides of dividing membranes and around outer skin. Do not remove fibrous center. Top each half with a scoopful of **Orange Sherbet** (on this page). Serve immediately.

ORANGE FILLING   *145 cal.*

▲ Base Recipe

Mix together in top of double boiler

1½ tablespoons cornstarch
⅛ teaspoon salt

Gradually stir in

¾ cup water
⅓ cup orange juice
1 teaspoon non caloric sweetening solution or 8 non caloric sweetening tablets (page 9)

Stirring gently and constantly, bring rapidly to boiling over direct heat and cook for 3 min. Cover and cook over boiling water 7 min., stirring occasionally. Vigorously stir 2 tablespoons of the hot mixture into

1 egg yolk, slightly beaten

Immediately blend into hot mixture in double-boiler top; stir and cook 3 to 5 min. Remove from heat and blend in

1 teaspoon grated lemon peel
1 tablespoon lemon juice

Cool filling before spreading on cake.

About 1 cup filling

—LEMON FILLING   *131 cal.*

Follow ▲ Recipe. Increase cornstarch to 2 tablespoons, water to 1 cup and sweetening solution to 1½ teaspoons (12 tablets). Substitute **3 tablespoons lemon juice** for the orange juice. Omit additional lemon juice.

WHIPPED TOPPING

314 calories; 10 cal./tablespoon

Chill a small bowl and rotary beater in the refrigerator.

Pour into the chilled bowl
- **½ cup icy cold water**
- **1 teaspoon lemon juice**

Sprinkle evenly over the water
- **½ cup instant nonfat dry milk**

Using the chilled beater, beat until mixture stands in peaks when beater is slowly lifted upright.

Beat in with final few strokes until blended
- **2 tablespoons sugar**
- **¼ teaspoon vanilla extract**

Set in refrigerator if not used immediately.

About 2 cups topping

BEVERAGES

CARROT PINEAPPLE COCKTAIL

42 cal./serving

Wash, scrape or pare, cut into 1½-in. pieces and set aside
- **2 medium carrots**

Put into an electric blender container
- **1 cup unsweetened pineapple juice**
- **1 slice lemon**

Cover and turn on motor. Drop carrots in, piece by piece. Add, one at a time
- **3 ice cubes**

Blend until mixed. Serve immediately.

4 servings

EGGNOG   *164 cal./serving*

▲ Base Recipe

Beat until thick and piled softly
- **2 eggs**

Beat in
- **2 cups chilled skim milk (page 9)**
- **1 teaspoon non caloric sweetening solution or 8 non caloric sweetening tablets (page 9)**
- **2 teaspoons vanilla extract**

Pour into chilled glasses. Sprinkle with
- **Nutmeg**

2 servings

—FLUFFY EGGNOG   *164 cal./serving*

Follow ▲ Recipe. Separate the eggs. Beat egg yolks until thick and lemon-colored. Stir in the milk, sweetening solution and vanilla extract. Beat egg whites until rounded peaks are formed. Fold egg whites into egg yolk mixture.

LEMONADE   *12 cal./serving*

▲ Base Recipe

Mix until blended
- **3 tablespoons lemon juice**
- **½ teaspoon non caloric sweetening solution or 4 non caloric sweetening tablets (page 9)**

Pour into a tall glass. Fill glass with
- **Crushed ice or ice cubes**

Pour in to fill completely
- **Cold water**

Stir until blended. Garnish with **lemon slice**.

1 serving

—LIMEADE   *12 cal./serving*

Follow ▲ Recipe. Substitute **lime juice** for lemon juice.

—ORANGEADE   *31 cal./serving*

Follow ▲ Recipe. Decrease lemon juice to 1 tablespoon and add **3 tablespoons orange juice**.

PEACH PLUM DELIGHT   *47 cal./serving*

Rinse, cut into halves, remove pits and cut into pieces (enough to make ½ cup each)
- **1 medium firm ripe peach**
- **2 medium red plums**

Put into an electric blender container with
- **½ cup skim milk (page 9)**
- **3 tablespoons lemon juice**
- **1 tablespoon non caloric sweetening solution or 24 non caloric sweetening tablets (page 9)**
- **1 cup crushed ice**

Cover and turn on motor. Blend until mixed. Pour into chilled glasses and serve.

3 servings

PINE-CRESS COCKTAIL   *55 cal./serving*

Rinse, drain and pat dry
- **1 bunch (3 oz.) watercress**

Put into an electric blender container with
- **2 cups unsweetened pineapple juice**
- **1 tablespoon sugar**
- **1 tablespoon lemon juice**

Cover and blend about 45 sec., or until watercress is thoroughly blended.

Add, one at a time
- **2 ice cubes**

Blend until mixed. Serve immediately.

6 servings

STRAWBERRY MILK   *80 cal./serving*

▲ Base Recipe

Sort, rinse, hull and drain
- **1 pt. fresh, ripe strawberries**

Force berries through a coarse sieve or food mill. Add
- **1½ cups chilled skim milk (page 9)**
- **1¼ teaspoons non caloric sweetening solution or 10 non caloric sweetening tablets (page 9)**

Mix thoroughly. Pour into chilled glasses and serve immediately.   *3 servings*

—RASPBERRY MILK   *90 cal./serving.*

Follow ▲ Recipe. Substitute **1 pt. fresh red raspberries** for the strawberries.

Coffee or Tea (no cream or sugar)	Skim Milk (8 oz.)	Whole Milk (8 oz.)	Hot Chocolate (8 oz.; made with cocoa or chocolate and whole milk)	Milk Shake (8 oz.)	Malted Milk (8 oz.)
0	87	166	240	279	360

Preserving and pickling

Making pickles and jellies and also preserves might seem like a "labor of love" and quite impractical in these modern days when supermarket shelves are loaded with fine commercial products of every description. Yet, for many homemakers, pickling and preserving is a family way of life, a custom handed down from generation to generation. It is a wonderful convenience to have a generous supply of home-canned, fresh-from-the-garden vegetables and tree-ripened fruits, as well as delicious jellies, piquant preserves and flavorful pickles on hand. With them you can provide appeal and add variety to your menus.

To Make a Jelly Bag

Cut a double thickness of cheesecloth about 36 inches long and fold in half. Dip the cheesecloth into hot water and then wring as dry as possible. Put a large strainer or colander over a large bowl or saucepot and lay the cheesecloth in it. Turn the fruit mixture into the cheesecloth. Gather the four corners of the cloth together and tie firmly. Allow juice to drip through the cheesecloth and strainer; for clear jelly, do not squeeze.

To Make a Spice Bag

Cut a double thickness of cheesecloth about 5 inches square. Put spices in center of cheesecloth and tie corners together.

To Make Jelly Test

Dip spoon into boiling liquid; lift it out and tip it to allow liquid to run over edge. At first, the syrup will run off in a thin stream. When the last two drops in the spoon run together or "sheet," the mixture should be removed from the heat. Remove pan from heat while testing.

To Seal with Paraffin

Melt paraffin in a small saucepan or measuring cup. When ready to seal glasses, immediately pour enough melted paraffin onto top of mixture to make a layer about ⅛ in. thick on each glass. When paraffin has cooled completely, pour enough melted paraffin over first layer to make another layer about ⅛ in. thick. Carefully tilt each glass to distribute paraffin evenly and seal it to the edge of the glass.

GOLDEN JELLY

Set out a heavy 3-qt. saucepan for cooking jelly. Wash and sterilize (page 10) six 8-oz. jelly glasses with lids.

Measure into the saucepan
- **4 cups sugar**
- **2 cups orange juice**
- **3 tablespoons lemon juice**
- **2 tablespoons lime juice**

Cook over medium heat, stirring constantly until sugar is completely dissolved. Increase heat and bring mixture to boiling. Immediately add and stir in
- **½ cup bottled fruit pectin**

Boil rapidly 1 min., stirring constantly. Remove from heat; skim off any foam.

Immediately ladle into the drained jelly glasses, filling to within ½ in. of the tops. Seal with paraffin (on this page); cover with lids.
About six 8-oz. glasses jelly

APPLE JELLY

Set out a large kettle, a heavy saucepan, and four 6-oz. jelly glasses with lids.

Wash and quarter (do not pare or core)
- **4 lbs. tart apples**
Put into kettle with
- **1 qt. water**

Cover and cook gently about 25 min., or until apples are soft.

Ladle the apples into a jelly bag (on this page)

placed in a colander over a large bowl. Let stand until juice is drained from apples. (If desired, use pulp in the bag to make apple butter.)

When ready to make the jelly, wash and sterilize (page 10) jelly glasses and lids.

Measure the drained apple juice and add
- **Sugar (¾ cup sugar for each cup apple juice)**

Cook not more than 4 cups of the juice at a time. Heat to boiling in the saucepan. Add gradually the amount of sugar required and heat to boiling, stirring occasionally. Continue cooking until mixture gives test for jelly (on this page).

Remove from heat, skim off foam and ladle jelly into hot sterilized glasses. Seal with paraffin (on this page); cover with lids.
About four 6-oz. glasses jelly

GRAPE JELLY

▲ Base Recipe

Set out a large heavy saucepot or kettle with a cover for cooking jelly and six 8-oz. jelly glasses with lids.

Make a jelly bag (on this page).

Remove stems, rinse, drain and put into the saucepot
- **3 lbs. Concord grapes**
Crush grapes thoroughly. Add and mix in
- **1 cup water**

Heat to boiling, reduce heat, cover and simmer 15 min. Remove from heat and strain through jelly bag.

Wash and sterilize (page 10) jelly glasses.

When juice has drained through jelly bag, melt over simmering water about
- **¼ lb. paraffin**

Measure 4 cups of juice into the saucepot. Put saucepot over high heat and heat until very hot. Add
- **3 cups sugar**

Stir until sugar is dissolved. Bring to boiling. Continue cooking rapidly until syrup responds to jelly test (on this page). Skim off any foam.

Ladle jelly into hot sterilized glasses. Seal with melted paraffin (on this page); cover with lids.
About six 8-oz. glasses jelly

—CRAB APPLE JELLY

Follow ▲ Recipe. Omit grapes. Rinse, remove stem ends and cut into quarters enough crab apples to yield **3 qts. crab apples** (do not remove cores or peel). Increase water to 3 cups and cook 20 min., or until very tender.

—QUINCE JELLY

Follow ▲ Recipe. Omit grapes. Wash thoroughly, remove stems and cut into pieces enough quince to yield **3 qts. quince** (do not remove cores or peel). Increase water to 6 cups and cook for 25 min., or until very tender. Increase sugar to 4 cups.

—CURRANT JELLY

Follow ▲ Recipe. Substitute **4 lbs. ripe red currants** for the grapes; remove any leaves but do not remove stems. Simmer currant-water mixture for 10 min. Use 4 cups juice and increase sugar to 4 cups.

SPICY GRAPE JELLY

Set out a large heavy saucepot or kettle for cooking jelly and eight 8-oz. jelly glasses with lids.

Make a jelly bag (page 723).

Rinse, discarding stems and imperfect grapes, drain, and put into the saucepot
3 lbs. Concord grapes
Crush grapes thoroughly. Mix thoroughly with the crushed grapes
½ cup cider vinegar
Tie in a spice bag (page 723)
4 cinnamon sticks (3 in. each)
1 tablespoon whole cloves
Add the spice bag and set the saucepot over medium heat. Heat to boiling, reduce heat, cover, and simmer for 10 min.

Remove from heat, remove spice bag; strain grape mixture through jelly bag.

Wash the saucepot for later use.

Wash and sterilize (page 10) the jelly glasses.

Measure 4 cups of juice into the saucepot. Set over high heat and heat until very hot. Add, stirring until dissolved
7 cups sugar
Immediately add and stir in
½ cup bottled fruit pectin
Boil rapidly 1 min., stirring constantly. Remove from heat; skim off any foam.

Immediately ladle into the drained glasses, filling to within ½ in. of tops. Seal with melted paraffin (page 723); cover with lids.
About eight 8-oz. glasses jelly

PEAR LIME HONEY

Set out a 3-qt. heavy saucepot. Wash and sterilize (page 10) about eight ½-pt. jars with covers.

Wash, pare, core and put through fine blade of food chopper
3 lbs. ripe pears (9 cups, ground)
Combine in saucepot with
1 can (13¼ oz.) crushed pineapple, drained
Grated peel and juice of 1 lime
5 cups sugar
Mix thoroughly and cook over low heat until thick, stirring occasionally. (To test for desired consistency, spoon a small amount of jam onto saucer and chill in refrigerator.)

Ladle jam into sterilized jars and seal.
About eight ½-pt. jars jam

MINT HONEY JELLY

Set out a 3-qt. saucepan. Wash and sterilize (page 10) five 6-oz. jelly glasses with lids.

Measure into a small saucepan
2 tablespoons dried mint leaves
¾ cup boiling water
Cover tightly and let stand about 15 min.; strain. Add enough water to make ¾ cup liquid. Combine in large saucepan with
2½ cups strained honey
Heat to boiling and add, stirring constantly
Several drops green food coloring
½ bottle liquid fruit pectin
Bring to full rolling boil. Remove from heat; skim off foam. Ladle into hot sterilized glasses. Seal with melted paraffin (page 723); cover with lids.

Serve as an accompaniment for meat.
About five 6-oz. glasses jelly

GOLDEN APRICOT JAM

Wash and sterilize (page 10) four ½-pt. jars with covers.

Combine in a 2-qt. heavy saucepan and bring to boiling over low heat
½ lb. dried apricots
Grated peel of 1 lemon
3 tablespoons finely grated carrot
1½ cups water
Cover and simmer mixture 25 min., or until apricots are very soft.

Stir in
1½ lbs. sugar (about 3⅓ cups)
Juice of 2 lemons
Bring to boiling and cook 25 to 30 min., or until mixture is glossy and of desired thickness. (To test, spoon a small amount of jam onto a saucer and chill in refrigerator.)

Ladle into hot jars and seal, following manufacturer's directions. *About four ½-pt. jars*

SPICED PEACH JAM

Wash six ½-pt. jars and covers and rinse thoroughly with boiling water.

Cut into halves, pit, peel and put through coarse blade of food chopper
1½ lbs. fully ripe peaches (about 1¾ cups, ground)
Combine peaches in a large bowl or pan with
2 tablespoons lemon juice
¼ teaspoon nutmeg
4¼ cups sugar
Mix thoroughly and set aside.

In a small saucepan mix
¾ cup water
1 box powdered fruit pectin
Bring to boiling and boil 1 min., stirring constantly. Continue stirring about 3 min. (There will be a few remaining sugar crystals.) Quickly ladle jam into hot jars and seal.

When jam is set, store in freezer. If used within 2 or 3 weeks, store in refrigerator.
About six ½-pt. jars jam

RHUBARB PINEAPPLE JAM

A large heavy saucepot or kettle will be needed. Wash and sterilize (page 10) six ½-pt. jars and covers.

Drain
1 can (29½ oz.) crushed pineapple (about 2 cups, drained)
(Pineapple syrup may be reserved for use in other food preparation.)

Put into the saucepot the crushed pineapple and
5 cups frozen rhubarb
2¾ cups sugar
¼ teaspoon salt
Set over medium heat and stir until sugar is dissolved. Bring mixture to boiling; reduce heat and cook slowly about 30 min., stirring occasionally.

Remove from heat and stir in
Red food coloring (about ¼ teaspoon)
Immediately fill the drained jars and seal (page 9). *About six ½-pt. jars jam*

STRAWBERRY RHUBARB JAM

A large heavy saucepan will be needed. Wash and sterilize (page 10) six ½-pt. jars and covers.

Combine in the saucepan
3 cups thinly sliced rhubarb
2 cups sliced fresh ripe strawberries
2 tablespoons grated orange peel
⅓ cup orange juice

Mix well and stir in contents of
1 box powdered fruit pectin
Stir over high heat until mixture comes to a full boil. Immediately stir in
5½ cups sugar
Bring to a full, rolling boil continuing to stir; boil 1 min. Remove from heat and stir the mixture 5 min. Ladle jam into hot sterilized jars; seal. *Six ½-pt. jars jam*

PEAR MARMALADE

Set out a 2-qt. saucepan, a 3-qt. heavy saucepot, and four ½-pt. jars with covers.

Wash and remove peel from
2 oranges
Combine peel in saucepan with
1 qt. water
Bring to boiling and boil 5 min. Drain, discarding liquid. Repeat process, draining orange peel thoroughly in a colander. Put peel and the peeled oranges through coarse blade of food chopper and set aside.

Wash, pare, remove core and cut into small pieces
4 lbs. pears (9 cups, diced)
Combine with ground oranges and
1 can (20 oz.) crushed pineapple, drained
Measure the fruit mixture into saucepot. Add
Sugar (½ cup for each cup of fruit)
¼ cup lemon juice
Mix thoroughly and cook rapidly until almost thick (about 40 min.), stirring occasionally to prevent scorching.

Wash and sterilize (page 10) jars and lids.

Add to thickened marmalade
1 bottle (8 oz.) maraschino cherries, drained and thinly sliced
Cook about 5 min. longer or until marmalade is the consistency desired.

Pour into hot jars and seal, following manufacturer's directions.
About six ½-pt. jars marmalade

PEAR-CHIP PRESERVE

This elegant Southern preserve is delicious with meat, with hot breads and as a topping for ice cream.

Set out a large heavy saucepot or kettle and five 1-pt. jars with covers.

Finely chop enough crystallized ginger to yield
¼ cup chopped crystallized ginger
Wash and thinly slice through peel and pulp, discarding seeds
2 lemons
Rinse, cut into quarters, core, pare and slice thinly
4 lbs. firm pears (Anjou or Comice)
Meanwhile, combine in the saucepot
2 cups water
3½ lbs. (about 7¾ cups) sugar

Stir over medium heat until sugar is dissolved. Increase heat and bring to boiling. Add pears, ginger and lemon to the syrup. Reduce heat and simmer until syrup is thickened, about 2½ hrs.

About 30 min. before preserve is done, wash and sterilize (page 10) the jars and covers.

About 5 min. before preserve is done, stir in
1 cup (about 4 oz.) coarsely chopped pecans
Cook 5 min. longer. Fill and seal jars (page 9). Set jars on cooling racks and cool away from drafts. Label jars; store in a cool dry place.
About 5 pts. preserve

CHERRY TOMATO CONSERVE

Set out a heavy 2-qt. saucepan. Wash and sterilize (page 10) three ½-pt. jars and covers.

Pour boiling water over
4 large ripe tomatoes
Let stand about 1 min., or until skin loosens; remove tomatoes from boiling water, dip into cold water and peel. Chop or cut into small pieces. Combine in the saucepan with
1½ cups sugar
Mix well and set aside 3 hrs., or until sugar is dissolved.

Add and bring to boiling over medium heat
1 medium onion, chopped
1 green pepper, chopped
1 unpeeled lemon, rinsed and thinly sliced
1 teaspoon ginger
Reduce heat and simmer, stirring occasionally, 1½ to 2 hrs., or until conserve is of desired consistency. To test, remove from heat and spoon a small amount of conserve onto a saucer. Chill in refrigerator. If it does not "set" to proper consistency, cook a few minutes longer.

When thickened, stir in
1 jar (8 oz.) red maraschino cherries, drained and chopped
½ cup nuts, chopped
Ladle conserve into sterilized jars and seal, following manufacturer's directions. Store in a cool place (or refrigerator).
About three ½-pt. jars conserve

FRESH ORANGE CONSERVE

Set out a 3-qt. heavy saucepan and three ½-pt. jars with covers.

Rinse thoroughly and thinly slice
3 or 4 oranges (to yield 4½ cups oranges, sliced)
1 lemon
Combine fruit in a bowl and add
2 cups cold water
Cover and let stand 8 hrs. or overnight.

Turn into heavy saucepan and cook gently, uncovered, until citrus peel is tender, about 1½ hrs. Remove from heat and measure the mixture (there should be about 3 cups).

Combine in the saucepan with
3 cups sugar (or use equal parts of sugar and cooked fruit)
Cook over medium heat until thickened, stirring frequently, 1 to 1½ hrs.

Meanwhile, wash and sterilize (page 10) jars and lids.

Add to the conserve 5 min. before end of cooking time
1 teaspoon vanilla extract
½ cup pecans or walnuts, chopped
¼ cup cut-up maraschino cherries
Ladle conserve into hot sterilized jars and seal. *Three ½-pt. jars conserve*

PURPLE PLUM CONSERVE

A heavy 3-qt. saucepot or kettle will be needed.

Wash and sterilize (page 10) twelve ½-pt. jars and covers.

Rinse, quarter and pit
5 to 6 lbs. firm purple plums (enough to yield 3 qts. cut-up plums)
Combine plums in a large bowl with
4 cups sugar
Set aside in a cool place several hours or overnight.

Pour off the syrup which has formed into the saucepot. Add to the syrup and bring to boiling
4 cups sugar
Boil 5 min., stirring constantly.

Add to the saucepot
1 tablespoon grated lemon peel
1 tablespoon grated orange peel
¼ cup lemon juice
½ cup orange juice
Cook over medium heat about 30 min., reducing the heat as the mixture thickens. Stir frequently with a wooden spoon.

Add to the saucepot and continue cooking about 25 min., stirring occasionally
1 lb. seedless raisins
The last 5 min. of cooking, stir in
1 cup walnuts, broken (do not chop)
(To retain the full fruit flavor, avoid overcooking.) To test conserve, quickly chill a spoonful on a chilled saucer. It should be of spreading consistency.

Ladle into hot sterilized jars and seal.
About twelve ½-pt. jars conserve

STRAWBERRY RHUBARB CONSERVE

Set out a heavy 3-qt. saucepan. Wash and sterilize (page 10) five ½-pt. jars and covers.

Combine in saucepan, mixing thoroughly
2 cups diced rhubarb
1 cup seedless raisins
½ cup grated orange peel
1 cup diced orange
3 cups sugar
Set aside 12 hrs.

Add and mix well
2 pts. rinsed and hulled fresh strawberries
Cook over medium heat until boiling and boil 6 min., stirring occasionally.

Stir in
½ cup chopped walnuts
½ bottle liquid fruit pectin (about ⅓ cup)
Remove from heat. Skim, then stir 5 min. to keep fruit in suspension.

Ladle conserve into sterilized jars and seal, following manufacturer's directions.
About five ½-pt. jars conserve

FRESH PEAR CHUTNEY

Set out a large heavy saucepan; wash and sterilize (page 10) five ½-pt. jars with covers.

Rinse, peel, core and finely chop
2 to 2½ lbs. firm, ripe pears (about 3 cups, chopped)
Combine pears in the saucepan with
⅔ cup vinegar
1 cup seedless raisins
⅓ cup chopped onion
¼ cup slivered crystallized or preserved ginger
1 teaspoon allspice
½ teaspoon cloves
½ teaspoon ginger
1 tablespoon salt

Strawberry Rhubarb Conserve

Add to pear mixture and mix thoroughly contents of
1 box powdered fruit pectin
Place over high heat and stir until mixture comes to a brisk boil.

Immediately add
3½ cups granulated sugar
½ cup firmly packed light brown sugar
Stir to blend and bring to a full rolling boil. Boil vigorously, stirring, 5 min. Remove from heat and skim off foam with a metal spoon. Continue stirring and skimming about 10 min. to cool the chutney slightly and prevent floating of the fruit.

Working quickly, ladle hot chutney into hot jars and seal, following manufacturer's directions. (If using jelly glasses, cover the hot chutney immediately with ⅛-in. layer of hot paraffin.)   *Five ½-pt. jars chutney*

APPLE TOMATO CHUTNEY

A deep saucepan or kettle and eight ½-pt. jars and covers will be needed.

Rinse, quarter, core (do not pare) and cut into pieces.
1 lb. tart apples (about 4 cups, cut-up)
Peel and cut into pieces
2 large onions
Put apples and onions through food chopper, using the coarse blade. Combine in the saucepan.

Rinse, peel and coarsely chop
4 medium ripe tomatoes

Add to the mixture in saucepan along with
1 cup dark seedless raisins
1 cup red wine vinegar
6 drops Tabasco
1 tablespoon garlic salt
¼ teaspoon ground cardamom
¼ teaspoon grated gingerroot
¼ teaspoon ground mace
½ cup sugar
½ cup firmly packed brown sugar
Set over low heat and simmer about 1½ hrs., or until thick, stirring occasionally.

Meanwhile, wash and sterilize (page 10) jars and covers.

When chutney is of desired consistency, remove jars from boiling water and drain. Fill jars with hot chutney and seal, following manufacturer's directions.
About five ½-pt. jars chutney

CHILI SAUCE

Spicy and full of zest, this chili sauce is hot enough to be served with seafood cocktails. Try it, too, for a spot of lusty flavor with a roast or with grilled hamburgers.

Set out a 3-qt. heavy saucepot and three 1-pt. jars with covers.

Rinse with cold water
6 lbs. (about 18 medium) ripe tomatoes
Taking a few at a time, dip tomatoes into boiling water for several seconds or until skins split; peel, cut out and discard the seeds. Coarsely chop the tomatoes (enough to yield 9 cups). Set aside.

Prepare and set aside

- **1½ cups coarsely chopped green pepper**
- **1½ cups coarsely chopped onion**
- **1 tablespoon finely minced hot red pepper**

Measure into the saucepot

- **1½ cups vinegar**
- **¾ cup packed brown sugar**
- **1 tablespoon salt**

Tie in a spice bag (page 723)

- **1 teaspoon whole cloves**
- **1 cinnamon stick (3 in.)**

Add spices to saucepot and stir mixture over medium heat until sugar is dissolved. Bring to boiling. Add the chopped vegetables and cook rapidly until thick, stirring frequently to prevent sticking. Length of cooking time will vary with ripeness of tomatoes.

Meanwhile, wash and sterilize (page 10) jars and lids.

When sauce is of desired thickness, skim to remove foam. Ladle into drained hot jars immediately and seal. *About 3 pts. Chili Sauce*

FAVORITE CORN RELISH

Set out a large heavy saucepot or kettle and four 1-pt. jars with covers.

Cut kernels from

- **8 ears fresh corn (about 4 cups corn kernels)**

Prepare

- **2 cups finely chopped young green cabbage (about ½ small head)**
- **1¼ cups diced sweet red peppers (2 medium peppers)**
- **4 cups finely chopped celery (including edible portion of root and tender leaves)**
- **1 cup finely chopped onion (1 large onion)**
- **1 large clove garlic, minced**

Combine vegetables in the saucepot along with a mixture of

- **1 cup sugar**
- **1 tablespoon salt**
- **1 teaspoon monosodium glutamate**
- **1 tablespoon dry mustard**
- **1½ teaspoons celery seed**
- **1 teaspoon turmeric**
- **¼ teaspoon cayenne pepper**

Stir in and mix well

- **2 cups vinegar**

Bring mixture to boiling over medium heat; reduce heat and simmer, uncovered, 15 to 20 minutes. (Avoid overcooking. Celery should be crisp-tender.)

While relish is cooking, wash and sterilize the jars and covers (page 10).

If consistency of relish is too thin after 20 min. of cooking, stir in a smooth blend of

- **2 to 3 tablespoons all-purpose flour**
- **½ cup water**

Cook and stir 2 min., or until relish is slightly thicker.

Quickly ladle into hot sterilized jars and seal immediately, following manufacturer's directions. *4 pts. relish*

PEPPER RELISH

Set out a large heavy saucepot or kettle and six ½-pt. jars with covers.

Chop and combine in the saucepot

- **4 cups chopped pared cucumbers**
- **2 cups coarsely chopped green pepper**
- **1 cup coarsely chopped sweet red pepper**
- **1 cup chopped ripe tomato**

Stir in a mixture of

- **1½ cups cider vinegar**
- **¾ cup sugar**
- **2 tablespoons salt**
- **1 tablespoon celery seed**
- **1 teaspoon ground turmeric**

Tie in a spice bag (page 723)

- **1 tablespoon whole allspice**
- **1 tablespoon whole cloves**
- **3 cinnamon sticks (3 in. each)**

Add to saucepot and stir over medium heat until sugar is dissolved; bring to boiling. Reduce heat and cook gently, uncovered, about 30 min., or until slightly thickened. Stir occasionally to prevent scorching.

Meanwhile, wash and sterilize (page 10) jars and lids.

Ladle the hot relish into hot sterilized jars; seal following manufacturer's directions. *About six ½-pt. jars relish*

PICKLED CRAB APPLES

Set out a large saucepot or kettle and four 1-pt. jars with covers.

Have ready

- **2½ to 3 lbs. crab apples (with stems), uniform in size and free from blemishes**

Wash crab apples and pierce each with a large needle to prevent the fruit from bursting while cooking.

Tie in a spice bag (page 723)

- **2 teaspoons whole allspice**
- **3 cinnamon sticks (2 in. each)**
- **1 tablespoon whole cloves**
- **1 teaspoon whole mace**

Combine in saucepot

- **4 cups vinegar**
- **2 cups water**
- **6 cups sugar**

Add spices and cook, uncovered, over medium heat about 5 minutes. Set aside to cool.

Add crab apples to cooled syrup and heat slowly to prevent bursting of fruit. When thoroughly heated remove saucepot from heat and set aside 12 hrs. or overnight.

Wash and sterilize (page 10) jars and lids.

Pack crab apples in hot jars. Quickly bring the syrup to boiling. Pour syrup over crab apples to within ½ in. of top of jar. Seal jars following manufacturer's directions. Process jars in boiling-water bath 10 min.* Remove from water. *3 to 4 pts. pickles*

*To process jars—Lower filled jars into boiling water (1 in. above jars) onto rack in a water-bath canner, large metal kettle with a tight-fitting cover, or pressure canner with the pet cock left open (no pressure needed). Be sure jars do not touch. Cover; bring water again to boiling. Start the timing after water has reached a full rolling boil. Keep water boiling during processing; add more boiling water if necessary to cover jars.

BRANDIED PEACHES

Set out a 4-qt. kettle and four 1-pt. jars with covers. Wash and sterilize (page 10) jars and covers.

Have ready

- **5 lbs. small firm ripe peaches, uniform in size (about 30)**

Cover peaches with boiling water; let stand 1 min., or until skins loosen. Plunge into cold water. Remove skins and immerse peaches in slightly salted water or lemon water (1 tablespoon salt or lemon juice to 2 qts. cold water). Let stand no longer than 15 min.

Combine in kettle and bring to boiling, stirring occasionally

- **3 cups sugar**
- **2 cups water**

Add a layer of peaches (well drained) and cook gently over medium heat about 10 min., or until just tender (do not overcook).

As peaches are cooked, lift them out of syrup with slotted spoon and pack into hot jars to within ½ in. of top. Cover jars with their lids to keep peaches hot.

When all peaches are cooked and in jars, measure into each jar

2 to 4 tablespoons brandy

Bring syrup in kettle to boiling and pour over peaches to top of jar; seal at once. Let stand at least 2 weeks before using.

About 4 pts. Brandied Peaches

Note: You will have about 1¾ cups syrup leftover. To it, add 4 to 6 tablespoons brandy or rum and use as an ice cream sauce. Or pour syrup over slices of pound cake or sponge cake, top with scoops of ice cream and you will have a quick Baba au Rum or Baba au Brandy.

SLICED CUCUMBER PICKLES

Set out a large kettle and eight 1-pt. jars with covers.

Rinse and thinly slice (do not pare)

6 lbs. cucumbers, about 4 in. long

Finely shred

4 large onions (about 1 qt. shredded)
2 green peppers (about 2 cups shredded)

Combine the vegetables in a large bowl or earthenware crock with

½ cup salt

Cover vegetables with small ice cubes. Cover with a weighted plate and set aside about 3 hrs. Drain in a colander.

Meanwhile, mix thoroughly in a large kettle

5 cups cider vinegar
5 cups sugar
1½ teaspoons turmeric
2 tablespoons mustard seed
2 tablespoons plus 2 teaspoons celery seed
16 whole cloves

Add thoroughly drained vegetables and set over medium heat. Heat thoroughly (keep below boiling point), stirring occasionally with a wooden spoon.

Meanwhile, wash and sterilize (page 10) the jars and lids.

Quickly pack the hot pickles into sterilized jars and seal.   *8 pts. pickles*

GARLICKY DILL BEANS

Wash and sterilize (page 10) three 1-pt. jars with covers.

Rinse and break off ends of

2 lbs. fresh green beans or wax beans

If necessary, trim beans to fit upright in jars. Set aside.

Heat to boiling

4 cups water
1⅓ cups cider vinegar
3 tablespoons coarse salt

Quickly drain the sterilized jars and place in each jar

Large spray of fresh dill
Clove garlic

To Pack Beans in Jars and Seal—Immediately after draining jars, pack beans into the jars. Ladle hot liquid to within ½ in. of top. Insert a knife or narrow spatula along the side of the jar at several places to remove any air bubbles. Add additional liquid if needed. With a clean damp cloth, or a paper towel, remove any liquid that may be on the mouth of the jar. Be sure sealing edge is free of food particles. Seal jars at once, following manufacturer's directions.

Let beans stand 3 months before opening to allow flavors to blend.   *About 3 pts. beans*

MUSTARD PICKLES

These pickles must stand overnight before completion.

A large heavy saucepot or kettle and six 1-pt. jars with covers will be needed.

Break into flowerets

1 small head cauliflower

Wash thoroughly, drain and cut into ¼-in. slices enough 4- to 5-in. cucumbers to yield

6 cups sliced cucumbers (about 12); or use 1 qt. cucumbers and 2 cups whole gherkins

Put slices into a large bowl. Prepare and add to cucumbers

3 cups sliced green peppers (about 6 medium)
2 cups sliced onion (about 4 medium)
2 cups sliced green tomatoes (about 3 medium), rinsed and stem ends cut out

Rinse and drain the flowerets (about 3 cups) and add to vegetables.

Mix together until salt is dissolved

2 qts. water
1 cup coarse salt

Pour over vegetables; cover; set aside overnight.

The following day, wash and sterilize (page 10) the jars and covers.

Put vegetables and brine into a large saucepot and heat to boiling. Reduce heat and simmer 10 min. Remove from heat and turn into a colander to drain thoroughly.

Sift together into top of double boiler

¾ cup sugar
⅓ cup sifted all-purpose flour
2½ tablespoons dry mustard
½ teaspoon turmeric

Mix in

2 teaspoons celery seed

Put over simmering water.

Add slowly, stirring constantly

4 cups white vinegar

Cook about 10 min., or until sauce thickens. Put the drained vegetables in the saucepot and add the sauce, stirring gently. Simmer 5 min.

Fill and seal jars (page 9).

About 6 pts. pickles

SWEET GREEN TOMATO PICKLES

Pickles must stand overnight before completion.

A large heavy saucepot or kettle and four 1-pt. jars with covers will be needed.

Rinse, remove stem ends and slice enough green tomatoes to yield

1 gal. sliced green tomatoes (about 7 lbs. tomatoes)

Measure

1 cup coarse salt

Put one half the tomatoes into a large bowl; add one half the salt. Repeat layering. Cover and set aside overnight.

The following day, wash and sterilize (page 10) the jars and covers.

Drain tomatoes, discarding liquid. Heat to boiling in the pot, stirring until sugar is dissolved

1 qt. cider vinegar
2 cups sugar

*Cherry Tomato Conserve and
Cherry Watermelon Pickle*

Tie together in a spice bag (page 723)

    4 teaspoons whole cloves
    4 teaspoons whole allspice
    **3 pieces stick cinnamon (2 in. each)
    broken**

Add to saucepot with tomatoes; simmer 10 min.

Fill and seal jars (page 9).

About 4 pts. pickles

MINTED WATERMELON PICKLES

Set out a 4-qt. saucepot or kettle and six 1-pt. jars with covers.

Have ready

    Rind of 1 large watermelon

Pare the rind removing the green and pink portions. Cut rind into 1- to 1¼-in. squares. (There should be about 12 cups.) Put rind into a large bowl and cover with a thoroughly blended mixture of

    8 cups cold water
    ¼ cup salt

Set aside 8 hrs. or overnight.

Drain; cover with fresh water and cook, covered, about 1 hr., or until rind is tender. (Do not overcook.) Drain thoroughly in a colander.

Combine in saucepot

    6 cups water
    8 cups sugar
    2 cups vinegar

Cook, uncovered, over medium heat about 8 min. Rinse and thinly slice

    2 lemons

Tie lemon slices in a square of cheesecloth with

    3 pieces stick cinnamon (3 in. each)
    2 teaspoons whole cloves
    2 teaspoons whole allspice

Add to the syrup in saucepot along with the well-drained watermelon rind. Cook, uncovered, about 1 hr., or until rind can be pierced easily with a fork. (Rind should not be soft.)

Meanwhile, wash and sterilize (page 10) jars and lids.

Just before removing rind from the syrup, blend in

    1 tablespoon mint extract
    Several drops green food coloring

Remove rind from syrup with a slotted spoon into hot sterilized jars; add hot syrup to cover rind. Seal jars following manufacturer's directions.

6 pts. pickles

CHERRY WATERMELON PICKLE

Set out a heavy 5- or 6-qt. saucepot or kettle. Wash and sterilize (page 10) three 1-pt. (or six ½-pt.) jars and covers.

Remove green skin and pink flesh portions from

    Rind of ½ large watermelon

Cut rind into 1-in. squares. Put into saucepot and cover with a blend of

    3 qts. cold water
    6 tablespoons salt

Set aside about 4 hrs. Drain, rinse with cold water and drain again. Add fresh water to cover and bring to boiling over medium heat. Continue boiling for 10 min. Remove from heat, drain thoroughly in colander while preparing syrup.

Combine in a saucepot

    6 cups sugar
    2 cups vinegar (white or cider)

Tie in a spice bag (page 723) and add to saucepot

    1 teaspoon whole cloves
    2 sticks cinnamon

Bring mixture to boiling and boil 10 min.

Remove from heat; add drained rind; cool and refrigerate 8 hrs. or overnight. Remove watermelon rind from syrup with slotted spoon. Bring syrup to boiling; add rind and

    **1 jar (8 oz.) red maraschino cherries,
    drained**

Return to boiling and boil 5 min. Remove spice bag.

Pack the pickle in sterilized jars; cover completely with the hot syrup. Seal immediately, following manufacturer's directions. Store in cool place.

About 3 pts. pickle

WATERMELON PICKLES

These pickles require 4 days for completion.

Set out a large heavy saucepot or kettle and a large heat-resistant dish or baking pan. Three 1-pt. jars with covers will be needed.

Set out

    1 large ripe watermelon

Pare and discard outer green rind. Remove pink pulp and set aside for other use. Cut enough of the white rind into 1-in. cubes to yield 9 cups cubed watermelon rind. Put cubes into the saucepot and add

    6 cups boiling water

Simmer until rind is tender when pierced with a fork. Drain thoroughly and turn into the heat-resistant dish.

Combine in a saucepan

    4 cups sugar
    1 cup cider vinegar
    4 sticks cinnamon
    2 teaspoons whole cloves
    1 lemon, thinly sliced

Bring to boiling over high heat, stirring until sugar is dissolved. Pour syrup over rind and set aside to cool. Cover and let stand overnight.

The second day, drain rind, reheat syrup to boiling, and again pour over rind. Cool, cover and set aside overnight.

The third day, repeat.

The fourth day, wash and sterilize (page 10) the jars and covers. Put rind and syrup into saucepot and heat to boiling. Immediately pack pickles into hot drained jars, pour syrup over them, and seal immediately. Cool jars away from drafts. Label jars; store in a cool, dry place.

About 3 pts. pickles

MINCEMEAT

Set out a large heavy skillet.

Put through medium blade of food chopper

    ¼ lb. suet

and enough cooked beef to yield

    1½ cups ground cooked lean beef

Set aside suet and beef.

Wash, quarter, core, pare and chop

    **4 medium apples (about 3 cups,
    chopped)**

Put apples and meat into skillet; add and mix

    1 cup firmly packed brown sugar
    1 cup apple cider
    ½ cup fruit jelly
    ½ cup raisins, chopped
    ½ cup currants
    2 tablespoons molasses

Add a mixture of

    1 teaspoon salt
    1 teaspoon cinnamon
    ½ teaspoon cloves
    ½ teaspoon nutmeg
    ¼ teaspoon mace

Stirring occasionally, simmer uncovered 1 hr., or until almost all of liquid is absorbed. Add

    1 tablespoon grated lemon peel
    1 tablespoon lemon juice

Blend thoroughly.

If mincemeat is not to be used immediately, pack the mixture while hot into sterilized jars (page 10) and seal. Cool away from drafts.

3½ cups Mincemeat

Freezing foods

The availability of frozen foods in many countries is one of the great wonders of our time. The number of families (especially in the United States) who know the convenience of a home freezer stocked with high-quality frozen foods increases yearly. Frozen commercially (and purchased in the market) or frozen in the home, these foods enhance and add variety to modern-day meals.

Commercial processing of frozen foods is truly a twentieth-century miracle. It involves bringing fresh food from farm, orchard, field, stream and sea and quickly freezing it to retain its nourishing and palate-pleasing qualities. The degree to which the food will nourish and please, however, depends upon the way the food is handled and stored after purchase and how it is prepared for serving.

FREEZING AND FROZEN FOOD STORAGE

The object of freezing food is to preserve it in its original state until it is consumed. Nothing in the freezing process can ever improve the quality of that food. Thus, one must select only top-quality products to be frozen, and just as important, a temperature of 0°F or below must be maintained during the period they are stored.

At temperatures above 0°F the foods undergo certain changes—often undesirable changes —in color, texture, flavor or vitamin content. Some strong-flavored foods may develop off-flavors during storage, even though a correct storage temperature has been maintained. To avoid this, omit seasonings such as pepper and other strong spices and herbs during preparation of the dishes. These may be added before reheating the dishes or at serving time.

Fats, after long storage, may develop a rancid flavor, so avoid overstocking the freezer with foods rich in fats, also deep-fried foods.

Crisp toppings for casseroles such as buttered bread crumbs or crushed cereals, chow mein noodles or deep-fried onion rings should be added a few moments before the casserole is removed from oven and before serving. These toppings lose their crispness during freezing.

Vegetables to retain their original crispness may be cooked and added to casserole dishes just before serving.

Preparation for the Freezer—Use clean equipment and keep food covered as much as possible. Handle foods for the freezer as little as possible as bacteria are spread by handling. Be sure that fruits and vegetables are carefully sorted and scrupulously cleaned—but never water-soaked. Cook meats and vegetables until barely tender to avoid mushy textures.

Packaging for the Freezer—Plan to package food in quantities that will be used at a single meal; never plan to refreeze a thawed food. Different shapes and types of food require different containers and wrappings. An ever-increasing variety of freezer containers and wrappings is available to homemakers today, usually in department stores and supermarkets. Choose moisture-vaporproof containers of correct size and shape, and those that seal to air-tightness. Suitable wrappings may prove most economical in food-saving qualities. They include pliable materials such as heavy-duty aluminum foil and moisture-vaporproof plastic-film-type materials.

Pack solidly to keep out air, leaving space at top of container for expansion of soft or liquid foods—about ½ inch in pint containers and about 1 inch in quarts.

Soft foods may be layered in containers to hasten removal and thawing; divide layers of about 1 inch with double thicknesses of a strong pliable material.

Some types of food and dishes (casseroles) are packaged in wrapping material. Care in wrapping demands exclusion of air, a secure drugstore or butcher wrap and tape- or heat-sealing. Here, too, layers of food may be divided to advantage.

Freeze foods in a casserole or other baking dish only if freezer space permits and if the kind of dish used can be subjected to sudden, extreme temperature changes. Put tight-fitting cover over casserole of cooled food and tape-seal the cover to dish, or wrap the entire dish as suggested. Or, cover a top-of-range casserole (after cooling) and freeze. When frozen, remove casserole from freezer and place over very low heat 1 to 2 minutes, or only until contents loosen from sides of casserole; slide onto a large piece of moisture-vaporproof material. Wrap and seal. When a vegetable is to be added to the casserole mixture before serving, package the frozen vegetable and casserole mixture first separately and then together so that the complete casserole dish is in one package.

Labeling for the Freezer—The freezer-storage life of combination or casserole dishes is short; use them within several months (for best flavor, within several weeks). Don't hoard—a rapid turnover of casserole freezer foods is freezer wisdom and freezer economy.

Equip yourself with a freezer pen, pencil or crayon. Write plainly on each package its contents, date of freezing and intended use. Store systematically and conveniently. It's well, too, to keep a handy record near the freezer. List on it that same label information plus any special treatment a food will require when removed from the freezer. Check off foods as they are used. Your future freezing ventures may be even more successful if you'll also calculate lengths of storage periods and resulting quality of the food.

FREEZING DAIRY PRODUCTS

Butter

To store butter, overwrap the original wrap with moisture-vaporproof material and freeze not more than several months.

Cheese

Cottage cheese—Freeze dry cottage cheese in original carton (tightly sealed) or in freezer container. Store about 1 month. Frozen cream-style cottage cheese tends to separate when thawed so freezing is not recommended.

Cream cheese—Freeze in the original wrap with an overwrap of aluminum foil up to 2 months.

Natural and pasteurized process cheeses—Freeze them, for best results, while fresh, preferably in the unopened package (or wrap securely in aluminum foil). Most cheeses, if frozen unopened in original package will retain their good quality up to 6 weeks. After that period some cheeses become crumbly in texture and are suitable only for cooking purposes. Process cheese may be stored in original package up to 4 months.

Cream or Milk

Heavy (or whipping cream)—Freeze cream (whipped and sweetened, if desired) in individual portions such as dollops or rosettes used for dessert toppings. Cream frozen and thawed does not whip satisfactorily.

Dairy sour cream—Freeze sour cream combined with other foods for best results.

Whole milk—Freeze milk in tightly sealed cartons or straight-sided freezer jars (leaving 1-inch space at top for expansion of liquid during freezing).

FREEZING EGGS

Whole eggs—Break the eggs from shells and mix gently only enough to make a fairly homogeneous mass. (Avoid beating in air.) If desired, mix in 1 teaspoon salt or 1 tablespoon sugar or corn syrup for each 2 cups of eggs. Freeze in freezer containers or freezer jars, leaving head space for expansion. To thaw, set containers in refrigerator or in cold water.

Egg whites—Freeze egg whites in freezer cartons or freezer jars, allowing head space for expansion. To thaw, set containers in refrigerator or in cold water. Use as you would unfrozen egg whites.

Egg yolks—Add either sugar or salt to egg yolks for best freezing results, stirring as little as possible to blend. Use 2 teaspoons salt or 2 tablespoons sugar or corn syrup for each 2 cups egg yolks. To thaw, set containers in refrigerator or in cold water. Use within 12 hours after thawing.

FREEZING MEAT

If storing in freezer beyond 1 to 2 weeks, wrap meat (using drugstore or butcher wrap) in moisture-vaporproof material and seal tightly. Freeze the meat at −10°F or lower. Maintain a temperature of 0° or lower during storage. Prepackaged meats should be either rewrapped or overwrapped, using special freezer wrap.

To thaw frozen meat—Keep in original wrapping and thaw in refrigerator, allowing about 5 hours per pound. Or thaw in original package at room temperature, allowing about 2 hours per pound. Hasten thawing of chops, cutlets or small cuts by immersing package (tightly wrapped) in cold water; allow 1 hour per pound.

To cook frozen meat—If thawed, follow the same directions as for meat which has not been frozen.

If meat is cooked from the frozen state, allow one third to one half more time than is required for unfrozen meat.

FREEZING POULTRY

Wrap (raw or cooked) poultry in moisture-vaporproof material and freeze at −10°F. Maintain a storage temperature of 0° or below.

To freeze whole birds—Lock wings and fold neck skin over wing tips. Tie legs and pad ends with paper to prevent puncturing of the wrapping. Wrap birds in moisture-vaporproof material or put into freezer bags. If using plastic bags, press out as much air as possible before sealing tightly.

To freeze disjointed birds—Flatten pieces and place double thickness of wrapping material between pieces for easy separation later. Pad sharp ends of bones. Wrap in freezer material or put into freezer bags or other containers.

Chicken and turkey should be used within 1 year, duck and goose within 6 months.

Package giblets (except livers) separately, since they should be stored no longer than 3 months. Package livers and use within 1 month.

Wrap cooked poultry for the freezer in the same manner as the uncooked. Use cooked poultry dishes within 6 months.

To thaw poultry which was purchased fresh and frozen at home, keep in freezer wrapping and place in refrigerator 1 to 3 days. Or immerse wrapped poultry (tightly sealed) in cold water 2 to 6 hours. Wrapped bird may also be placed in a double paper bag and thawed at room temperature, allowing 1 hour per pound.

To cook frozen poultry—Follow directions on package, if available, when poultry is commercially frozen. Do not thaw commercially stuffed birds before roasting. Thaw unstuffed birds only until flesh is pliable, then cook the same as for fresh poultry.

FREEZING SEAFOOD

Wrap fresh (unfrozen) seafood in moisture-vaporproof material. Seafood and other fish products frozen when purchased should be stored in original package (or plastic bag) and must be kept solidly frozen until ready for cooking. Wrap cooked seafood in moisture-vaporproof material and freeze.

Suggested Freezer Storage Time

Fresh—4 to 6 months
Cooked—2 to 3 months
Salted smoked—does not freeze satisfactorily

Commercially frozen prepackaged seafood usually has adequate cooking directions on the package. In general, breaded fish products should be cooked from the frozen state. Other fish usually requires prior thawing (in refrigerator and not at room temperature). A 1-pound package thaws in 24 hours (about) in the refrigerator; about 1 hour under running cold water.

FREEZING FRUITS

Fruits are prepared for freezing in one of three ways: dry packed (using no sugar); dry sugar packed; packed with a sugar syrup (or a combination of sugar syrup and corn syrup). Frozen fruits as a rule have better texture and flavor if packed with sugar or syrup rather than dry packed. There are a few exceptions: fruits that freeze satisfactorily without sweetening are often used for pies, jams and jellies, and for special diets. Among them are blueberries, cranberries, pineapple, rhubarb and blanched apples.

Dry Pack—Rinse, then drain fruit thoroughly on absorbent paper to prevent it from freezing in a solid mass. For quick freezing, spread fruit in a shallow tray and place in freezer. When frozen solid, pack in freezer containers or plastic-type bags. Seal tightly.

Dry Sugar Pack—For each quart of fruit use ¾ to 1 cup granulated sugar. For a sweeter product, decrease fruit to 3 cups. Sprinkle

sugar over fruit as you put it into the freezer container. Coat the fruit well. Or, if desired, mix fruit and sugar lightly in a bowl before filling the containers.

Syrup Pack—This method of sweetening the fruit is advantageous in that the syrup completely covers the fruit. To prepare the syrup, combine sugar with boiling water and stir to dissolve the sugar. Use syrup thoroughly chilled. Use about 1 cup syrup for 1-pound package or carton of fruit.

Proportions of Sugar and Water for Syrups

Syrup	Cups Sugar	Cups Water
Light (30%)	2	4
Medium (40%)	3 to 3½	4
Heavy (50%)	4 to 5	4

As a general rule, a light syrup is used for mild-flavored fruits; a heavy syrup is used for very tart (sour) fruit.

To improve quality, especially with light-colored fruits, add ½ teaspoon ascorbic acid to each 4 cups of syrup used for covering the fruit. Or for sugar pack, add ¼ teaspoon ascorbic acid dissolved in ¼ cup cold water to each quart of fruit.

Thawing fruits—Thaw fruits in their containers in the refrigerator or at room temperature or under running cold water. Thaw only until pieces of fruit can be separated but are still ice cold.

FREEZING VEGETABLES

Use young, barely mature vegetables (overmature vegetables become starchy and do not freeze well). Wash thoroughly in cold water. Sort, trim and cut vegetables into uniform pieces. Blanch or scald in boiling water (see Timetable for Blanching Vegetables Before Freezing, page 732). Blanch no more than 1 pound of vegetables at a time.

To blanch—Put vegetable into a wire basket, colander, or cheesecloth bag and immerse in rapidly boiling water. Start counting when vegetables are immersed in the water. The water may be used several times for the same kind of vegetable.

Chill vegetables thoroughly by immediately immersing them in ice and water. Cool them about the same length of time as for blanching. Vegetable should be chilled to the very center. Remove vegetable from water and drain thoroughly.

Package vegetable in freezer cartons, plastic-type bags or other suitable containers and seal tightly. Label and place in freezer at once.

For additional detailed information on home freezing, write to The Superintendent of Documents, Government Printing Office, Washington, D.C. 20402.

Do not thaw vegetables before cooking (corn on the cob is an exception). Cook, covered, in a small amount of boiling salted water until just tender. They usually require about one half the time required for the fresh product. The vegetable was partially cooked in the blanching process before the vegetable was packaged.

Vegetables such as squash which have been cooked completely before packaging should be reheated in the top of a double boiler over boiling water or heated in the oven.

FREEZING BREADS

Most yeast breads, if baked and wrapped properly, may be stored in the freezer up to a month with satisfactory results. However, homemakers who like the aroma of newly baked bread permeating their kitchens more often than once or twice a week may accomplish this by freezing the loaves before baking, then baking them as needed. In general, best results are assured with the use of more yeast, fat, and sweetening than used in most recipes, also shaping the dough into smaller loaves.

TIPS ON FREEZING COOKED FOODS

Avoid overcooking foods. Meat should be tender but still firm, vegetables slightly underdone. Reheating before serving will complete the cooking.

Cut the amount of time cooked food is to be exposed to room temperature to a minimum by rapid cooling. Set the dish containing the food in a pan of ice and water, stirring occasionally to hasten cooling. When cool, package and freeze at once.

Avoid using hard-cooked egg whites in food combinations (they become tough); omit cooked potatoes (they become mushy). Mix pieces of hard-cooked eggs and hot cooked potatoes into dishes before serving.

Use as little fat as possible in sauces and gravies to avoid development of a rancid flavor. Fried foods may become rancid in several months.

Use seasonings sparingly in dishes as flavors often become stronger during storage. Seasonings may be added when reheating the food.

Package prepared foods in amounts suitable for serving at one time. Freeze in small casseroles or other containers as much as possible, unless food is thawed completely before reheating.

Do not refreeze cooked foods after thawing or after reheating.

Use most frozen cooked foods within 2 to 3 months.

To save freezer space, cooked rice, spaghetti, macaroni, noodles and other pasta products may be quickly cooked and added to casserole mixtures shortly before serving.

Freeze soup in ice cube trays (using quick-release trays so cubes can be removed without melting). When frozen solid, remove cubes from trays and store in plastic-type bags (3 or 4 cubes for each serving).

Grate or shred a quantity of Cheddar cheese; spread in a shallow pan and freeze. Then turn into freezer containers or bags. Store in freezer. Use as needed for casserole-dish toppings.

Bake more potatoes than are needed for a family meal. Scoop out extras and mash potatoes in a bowl, adding butter, milk and seasonings as desired. Refill shells and sprinkle tops with grated or shredded Cheddar or Parmesan cheese. Cool and place in freezer. When firm, wrap individually in aluminum foil. To reheat at serving time, cut away foil at top of each potato (or turn it back) and reheat at once (do not thaw) in hot oven.

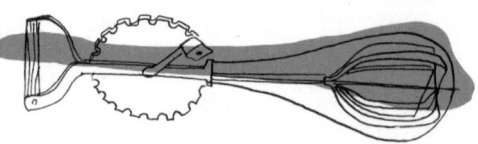

FREEZER RECIPES

FREEZER WHOLE WHEAT BREAD

This whole wheat bread may be frozen before or after baking. If bread is baked immediately only one package of yeast is required.

Generously grease two 8x4x2-in. loaf pans.

Combine in a small saucepan
  1½ cups milk
  ⅓ cup butter or margarine
  3 tablespoons molasses
  ¼ cup honey
  2 to 3 teaspoons salt

TIMETABLE FOR BLANCHING VEGETABLES BEFORE FREEZING

Vegetable*	Heated in Boiling Water (minutes)	Vegetable*	Heated in Boiling Water (minutes)
Asparagus		medium ears (1¼- to 1½-in. diameter)	9
small stalks	2	large ears (over 1½-in. diameter)	11
medium stalks	3	**Corn,** whole kernel and cream style**	4
large stalks	4	**Greens**	
Beans, green or wax	3	beet, chard, kale, mustard, spinach and turnip	2
Beans, lima		collards	3
small beans or pods	2	**Kohlrabi**	
medium beans or pods	3	cubes, ½ in.	1
large beans or pods	4	whole, small to medium	3
Beets		**Okra**	
small	25 to 30	small pods	3
medium	45 to 50	large pods	4
Broccoli, flowerets (1½-in. diameter)	3	**Parsnips,** ½-in. cubes or slices	2
in steam	5	**Peas, black-eyed**	2
Brussels sprouts		**Peas, green**	1½
small heads	3	**Peppers**	
medium heads	4	halves	3
large heads	5	slices	2
Cabbage, shredded or thin wedges	1½	**Pumpkin**	until soft
Carrots		**Rutabagas,** ½-in. cubes	2
whole, small	5	**Squash, summer,** ½-in. slices	3
diced, sliced or strips	2	**Squash, winter**	until soft
Cauliflower, 1-in. pieces	3	**Sweet potatoes**	until almost tender
Celery, 1-in. pieces	3	**Tomato juice** (simmer tomatoes)	5 to 10
Corn, on the cob		**Turnips,** ½-in. cubes	2
small ears (1¼-in. diameter or less)	7		

*For each pound of prepared vegetable use at least 1 gallon of boiling water. After heating the specified time, cool promptly in cold water and drain.
**Time given is for cooking the ears of corn before the kernels are cut off the cob.

Stir over low heat until fat is melted; cool to lukewarm.

Meanwhile, measure into a large mixer bowl

½ cup warm water (105°F to 115°F)

Sprinkle over water

2 pkgs. active dry yeast

Let stand until softened and stir in the milk mixture.

Beat in until thoroughly mixed (dough will be quite sticky)

5 cups whole wheat flour

Turn dough onto a floured pastry canvas using about

½ cup all-purpose flour

Knead dough (page 11) until smooth and not sticky, about 10 min., using more all-purpose flour, if needed.

Divide dough in half and shape into oblong loaves. Place in loaf pans and wrap pans securely using moisture-vaporproof material. Place in freezer at once. If desired, shape dough into 2 round loaves and place on a greased baking sheet. Cover and freeze.

Remove frozen loaves from baking sheet and wrap each in moisture-vaporproof material and return to freezer.

When ready to bake, remove wrapping from loaf pans, cover lightly and let stand at room temperature 2 hrs. to allow dough to thaw. For round loaves, remove wrapping, place loaves on greased baking sheet, and let stand 2 hrs.

Then place loaves, lightly covered, in warm place (about 80° F) until almost doubled, about 2 hrs.

Brush surfaces with

Melted butter or margarine

Bake at 375°F about 30 min., or until bread sounds hollow when tapped. Cool on wire racks. *2 loaves bread*

FREEZER BRAN MUFFINS

This generous easy-to-prepare recipe for light-textured, sweet-flavored muffins will be a boon to the busy homemaker with a large family. The batter may be stored, tightly covered, in the refrigerator up to 3 weeks, instead of being frozen. When ready to use, remove the batter from refrigerator and immediately pour into greased muffin-pan wells and bake.

Measure into a bowl

3 cups whole bran cereal

Pour over bran and set aside until cool

1 cup boiling water

Meanwhile, in a large mixer bowl, beat together until thoroughly blended

½ cup vegetable shortening

1½ cups sugar

Beat in, one at a time

2 eggs

Mix in alternately the soaked bran and

2 cups buttermilk

Sift together and add all at one time

2½ cups all-purpose flour

2½ teaspoons baking soda

½ teaspoon salt

Fold gently until ingredients are thoroughly moistened (do not overmix).

To Freeze Batter—Pour batter into jars or other containers (leave head space), cover tightly and place in freezer for up to 6 weeks.

To Thaw Batter—Remove jars from freezer and thaw in the refrigerator or at room temperature *only* until batter is of pouring consistency.

Pour batter into well-greased 2- to 2½-in. muffin-pan wells, filling each about ⅔ full.

Bake at 400°F 15 to 18 min., or until muffins test done. *About 3 doz. muffins*

Variations—Chopped **raisins, dates** or **nuts** (about ½ cup for each quart of batter) may be folded into batter before baking time.

CHEESE MEAT MACARONI CASSEROLE

Set out and grease a 2-qt. casserole or baking dish.

Cook, following package directions

8 oz. (2 cups) elbow macaroni

Drain and set aside.

Have ready

6 oz. sharp Cheddar cheese, shredded (about 1½ cups)

½ cup finely chopped onion

Heat in a saucepan

2 tablespoons butter or margarine

Stir in a blend of

2 tablespoons all-purpose flour

½ teaspoon salt

½ teaspoon monosodium glutamate

Few grains pepper

¼ teaspoon dry mustard

¼ teaspoon paprika

Heat and stir until bubbly; blend in

2 cups milk

Cook and stir until mixture comes to boiling. Remove from heat and mix in the shredded cheese, onion and

1 teaspoon Worcestershire sauce

Stir until thoroughly blended. Turn one half of the macaroni into the casserole and cover with one half of the cheese sauce. Repeat layers.

To Freeze—Cool casserole, wrap in aluminum foil, and place in freezer.

To Serve—Place wrapped casserole in a 350°F oven about 40 min., or until thawed. Remove wrapping; cover entire top of macaroni mixture with overlapping slices of

Tomato, about 16 thin slices

Luncheon meat (12-oz. can), cut crosswise in 14 slices

Process sharp Cheddar cheese, 8 slices (8 oz.), cut diagonally in halves

Lightly brush with **melted butter or margarine.** Return to oven and continue heating until casserole mixture is very hot and cheese slices are softened and tinged with brown.

About 8 servings

BEEF PINWHEEL PIES

Grease a baking sheet and 8 ramekins or individual casseroles.

Cut into 1-in. cubes

1½ lbs. boneless beef (chuck or round)

To coat cubes evenly, shake a few at a time in a plastic bag containing

¼ cup all-purpose flour

1 teaspoon salt

½ teaspoon monosodium glutamate

⅛ teaspoon pepper

Heat in a large skillet

3 to 4 tablespoons fat

Brown meat cubes on all sides. When meat is browned, pour in

2 cups water

Cover tightly and simmer 1½ to 2 hrs., or until meat is tender. If necessary, add more hot water during cooking.

Meanwhile, heat in a skillet

1 tablespoon fat

Add and separate into small pieces

½ lb. lean ground beef

When almost browned, add and cook about 3 min.

2 tablespoons finely chopped onion

¼ teaspoon salt

Few grains pepper

Remove from heat and mix in

2 to 3 tablespoons chili sauce

Prepare

Baking Powder Biscuit dough (page 92)

Roll into a rectangle ¼ in. thick. Spread ground meat mixture over biscuit dough. Beginning with longer side of rectangle, roll up tightly; pinch edge and ends to seal. Slice into ½-in. pinwheels and place on prepared baking sheet.

Bake at 450°F 10 to 15 min., or until lightly browned. Cool.

Beef Pinwheel Pies

When meat cubes are almost tender, add to skillet and cook about 3 min.

½ cup chopped onion

Remove beef with a slotted spoon; set aside.

Measure liquid in skillet and add enough water to make 3 cups. Return to skillet and add

1 teaspoon Worcestershire sauce

To thicken liquid, put into a 1-pt. screw-top jar

¾ cup water

Add to it a mixture of

⅓ cup all-purpose flour
1 teaspoon salt
½ teaspoon monosodium glutamate
⅛ teaspoon pepper

Cover jar and shake until mixture is well blended. Stirring constantly, slowly add to boiling liquid in skillet. Cook and stir until sauce thickens.

Meanwhile, separate with a fork

2 pkgs. (10 oz. each) frozen green peas

Combine beef, sauce and peas. Proceed as desired.

8 servings

To Freeze—Cool beef mixture, layer in freezer containers separating layers with freezer foil or pliable plastic wrap or turn into ramekins and place in freezer. Package pinwheels in amounts needed for one meal; divide layers by double thicknesses or moisture-vaporproof material. Seal, label and freeze.

To Serve—Remove from freezer the desired amount of pinwheels and number of ramekins or layers of beef mixture. Allow pinwheels to stand at room temperature in wrapping. Heat the beef mixture, stored in containers, about 60 min. (for 1 qt.) in top of double boiler over simmering water. Spoon into ramekins. Remove wrapping from pinwheels. Immediately top mixture in each ramekin with a pinwheel; set in a 375°F oven 10 min. Place any extra pinwheels on baking sheet and heat at the same time.

If meat mixture was stored in ramekins, tightly cover with aluminum foil; set in a 375°F oven about 40 min., or until mixture is bubbling hot in center. Uncover ramekins; top with pinwheels and heat 10 min. longer.

To Complete Without Freezing—Prepare pinwheels and set aside (unbaked). Bring beef mixture to boiling. Turn mixture into ramekins; immediately top each with a pinwheel. Place remaining pinwheels on baking sheet. Bake at 450°F 10 to 15 min., or until pinwheels are lightly browned.

CHOP SUEY EN CASSEROLE

Set out a top-of-range casserole or heavy skillet with a cover.

Heat in casserole

3 to 4 tablespoons fat

Add and brown over medium heat, turning pieces occasionally

1¼ lbs. boneless pork, cut in strips
1 lb. boneless beef, cut in strips
¾ lb. boneless veal, cut in strips

Cover and cook slowly 1 hr.

Stir in

1½ cups coarsely chopped onion
3 cups diagonally sliced celery
1 can (8 oz.) mushrooms, drained; reserve liquid
1 can (16 oz.) bean sprouts, drained; reserve liquid
1 can (5 oz.) water chestnuts, drained and thinly sliced

Add ½ cup *each* of the reserved mushroom and bean sprout liquids and cook gently 20 min. longer.

Combine in a bowl

¼ cup cornstarch
1 teaspoon salt
1 teaspoon monosodium glutamate

Stir in ½ cup of the reserved bean sprout liquid and

½ cup soy sauce
¼ cup bead molasses

Mix well and add to meat mixture, cooking and stirring until boiling; cook 10 to 15 min. longer, occasionally turning mixture with a fork.

To Freeze—Cool, layer in freezer containers (separating layers with freezer foil or pliable plastic wrap) and place in freezer.

To Serve—Separate and remove as many layers as needed; put into the top of a double boiler; cover and heat over simmering water, about 60 min. (for 1 qt.), stirring occasionally.

Meanwhile, cut into slivers and toast

½ cup (about 2 oz.) blanched almonds

Prepare

Perfection Boiled Rice (double recipe, page 165)

Top with almonds and serve with rice.

8 to 10 servings

Note: Almonds and rice are sufficient to serve with complete recipe of chop suey; decrease amounts as desired when reheating smaller amounts of chop suey.

To Complete Without Freezing—Prepare almonds and rice while meat is cooking.

POTATO-CAPPED VEAL CHOPS

Set out a 2-qt. shallow top-of-range casserole with a cover.

Have ready

4 veal chops (shoulder or loin), cut ¾ to 1 in. thick

Coat with a mixture of

¼ cup all-purpose flour
1 teaspoon salt
½ teaspoon monosodium glutamate
⅛ teaspoon pepper

Brown chops lightly and quickly on both sides over medium heat in the casserole containing

2 to 3 tablespoons hot fat

Remove casserole from heat. Combine and pour over meat

1 can (6 oz.) tomato paste
1¾ cups water
¼ cup finely chopped onion
2 tablespoons chopped parsley
1 teaspoon salt
½ teaspoon thyme

Cover and cook in a 300°F oven about 45 min.

To Freeze—Cool casserole, wrap and place in freezer.

To Serve—Set in a 375°F oven 60 to 70 min., or until mixture is bubbling hot in center.

Meanwhile, prepare

Fluffy Whipped Potatoes (one-half recipe, page 339, or prepare instant whipped potatoes)

Cook, following package directions

1 pkg. (9 oz.) frozen green beans

When mixture is bubbling hot, remove casserole from oven. Spread cooked beans over sauce in casserole; press beans down to cover them with sauce. Sprinkle with

3 tablespoons grated Parmesan cheese

Top lightly with mounds of whipped potatoes. Dot mounds with

Butter or margarine

Return to oven; heat, uncovered, 10 to 15 min., or until potatoes are lightly browned.

4 servings

To Complete Without Freezing—Prepare the whipped potatoes and cook green beans while veal is cooking. Complete as directed.

TAMALE PERFECTION

A south of the border inspiration.

Grease a 2-qt. casserole.

Put into a heated large heavy skillet

1 lb. ground beef
¼ lb. bulk pork sausage

Separate into small pieces with a fork or spoon and cook until lightly browned, stirring occasionally. Pour off fat as it collects. When meat begins to brown, add

1 cup finely chopped onion
½ cup finely chopped celery
⅓ cup finely chopped green pepper

Cook until meat is well browned.

Tamale Perfection

Mix in

2¼ cups canned tomatoes, sieved
1½ cups (12-oz. can, drained) whole
    kernel corn

Blend in a mixture of

1 tablespoon salt
2 teaspoons chili powder
½ teaspoon monosodium glutamate
¼ teaspoon pepper

Cover and simmer about 15 min.

Slice enough pitted ripe olives to yield

1 cup sliced ripe olives

Set aside.

Mix well and add gradually to skillet, stirring constantly

1 cup cold water
½ cup yellow corn meal

Cook and stir until thickened. Stir in the sliced olives. Turn into casserole.

Set in a 350°F oven 1 hr.

To Freeze—Cool (do not stir), wrap casserole and place in freezer.

To Serve—Reheat in a 350°F oven about 1 hr. Remove from oven and sprinkle with

¾ cup (3 oz.) shredded sharp Cheddar
    cheese

Return to oven and heat 5 min. longer, or until mixture is thoroughly heated and cheese is melted. Garnish with

Whole ripe olives
Sprigs of parsley

8 servings

To Complete Without Freezing—Top hot tamale mixture with the cheese and heat 5 min. longer.

MEAT BALL MACARONI DINNER

Here's a hearty dish to prepare for the freezer—an excellent emergency meal to use when a dozen or more hungry people are to be fed "on-the-double."

Set out a large heavy skillet, a 2-qt. saucepan and two 3-qt. shallow casseroles or baking dishes.

Prepare

1 lb. zucchini, thinly sliced
½ lb. mushrooms, sliced
1 large onion, chopped (about 1 cup)

Set aside the zucchini, mushrooms and ½ cup of the onion.

Combine in a large bowl the remaining onion and

3 lbs. ground beef
1 tablespoon salt
½ teaspoon lemon pepper marinade

Mix lightly but thoroughly and shape into 36 balls.

Heat in the skillet

1 tablespoon (about) cooking oil

Add half the meat balls and brown well on all sides. Remove balls from the skillet. Add more oil to skillet, if needed, and brown remaining balls. Remove from skillet and keep warm.

Heat in the skillet

2 tablespoons (about) cooking oil
1 clove garlic, crushed

Add zucchini and mushrooms; sprinkle with a mixture of

½ teaspoon salt
¼ teaspoon lemon pepper marinade

Cook and stir gently over medium heat about 3 min.

Meanwhile, heat in saucepan the remaining onion and

3 cloves garlic, crushed
½ teaspoon crushed basil
½ teaspoon crushed oregano
3 cups beef broth
3 cans (6 oz. each) tomato paste
1 can (30 oz.) tomato purée

Cook and stir until mixture comes to boiling and add to vegetables in skillet. Cook gently until zucchini is just tender (do not overcook).

Meanwhile, cook until tender, following package directions

1½ lbs. (about 6 cups) elbow
    macaroni

Drain macaroni in colander and divide equally in the two casseroles. Add the meat balls and tomato mixture in equal amounts. Mix lightly with a fork.

To Freeze—Cool casserole, wrap securely in heavy-duty aluminum foil and place in freezer.

To Serve—Place casserole (do not unwrap or thaw) in a 350°F oven about 1½ hrs. Remove the foil and continue heating about 30 min. Toss mixture gently several times with fork while heating. Sprinkle top of mixture with **grated Parmesan and Romano cheese** a few minutes before removing from oven.

6 to 8 servings/casserole

Note: If desired, the meat ball tomato mixture may be frozen omitting the cooked macaroni. When ready to use, thaw the mixture as directed in recipe. Meanwhile, cook the macaroni until tender; drain and stir into thawed mixture in oven. Continue heating until of serving temperature.

When freezer space is limited, freeze mixture in the following manner: Line two 3-qt. casseroles with large pieces of heavy-duty aluminum foil, leaving ends long enough for a complete wrapping. Add macaroni, meat balls and sauce as directed and seal each package, using drugstore wrap. Freeze until solid, then lift packages from casserole and place packages in freezer. To heat for serving, remove each frozen block from foil, place block in original casserole and heat in a 350°F oven about 2 hrs.

FREEZER CHICKEN A LA KING

▲ *Base Recipe*

Set out a 2-qt. top-of-range casserole.

Clean and slice (page 9)

½ lb. mushrooms

Heat in casserole

⅓ cup butter, margarine or chicken fat

Add mushrooms with

¼ cup chopped green pepper

Cook slowly about 5 min. With slotted spoon lift out vegetables, allowing fat to drain back into casserole; set vegetables aside.

Stir into casserole a mixture of

¼ cup all-purpose flour
1 teaspoon salt
½ teaspoon monosodium glutamate
Few grains pepper

Cook until mixture bubbles. Remove from heat. Stir in

1½ cups cream

Dissolve

2 chicken bouillon cubes

in

1½ cups boiling water

Blend into mixture in saucepan. Bring to boiling; cook and stir 1 to 2 min.

Meanwhile, cut into chunks enough cooked chicken to yield

3 cups cooked chicken

Add to casserole with reserved vegetables and

¼ cup canned pimiento, cut in strips

Cook mixture gently until chicken is thoroughly heated. Proceed as desired. *8 servings*

To Freeze—Cool, layer in freezer containers, separating layers with freezer foil or pliable plastic wrap and place in freezer.

To Serve—Separate and remove as many layers as needed; put into top of double boiler over simmering water, cover and heat about 60 min. (for 1 qt.), stirring occasionally. Serve from a warm casserole.

—CREAMED CHICKEN A LA KING WITH BISCUITS

Follow ▲ Recipe. Omit green pepper and pimiento. Stir in with chicken **½ cup pimiento-stuffed olives**, sliced.

To Freeze and Thaw—See ▲ Recipe. Then turn heated mixture into casserole. Immediately top with **Drop Biscuits** (one-half recipe, page 92). Bake at 450°F 10 to 15 min., or until biscuits are browned.

To Complete Without Freezing—Before preparing casserole, combine biscuit ingredients except for milk. Complete biscuits as chicken mixture heats; immediately drop onto hot mixture and bake.

—CHICKEN PIES

Follow ▲ Recipe. Grease 6 to 8 ramekins or individual casseroles instead of 2-qt. casserole. Add with chicken **1½ cups drained canned whole kernel corn** and **1 cup diced cooked carrots.** Prepare **Pastry Topping** (double recipe,(page 486); roll out dough; cut into size and shape of ramekin tops.

To Freeze—Cool chicken mixture, pour into ramekins or freezer containers and place in freezer. Place pastry cutouts on baking sheet and freeze; when frozen, package in layers divided by freezer foil or other moisture-vapor-proof material. Seal, package, label and return to freezer.

To Serve—Remove pastry cutouts and chicken pie mixture from freezer. Place cutouts on baking sheet. Put the chicken mixture (stored in containers) into double boiler, cover and heat. If stored in ramekins, tightly cover necessary number of ramekins with aluminum foil; heat in oven at 350°F about 30 min. Increase heat to 425°F. Allow time for heat to increase before putting pastry into oven. Prick cutouts with a fork and bake along with ramekins 10 to 12 min., or until cutouts are lightly browned and chicken mixture is bubbling hot in center. Transfer hot pastry tops to ramekins.

To Complete Without Freezing—Turn hot chicken mixture into greased ramekins. Follow directions given with Pastry Topping (page 486) for cutting and fitting pastry. Bake at 425°F 10 to 12 min., or until pastry is lightly browned.

MIXED FRUIT SALAD WITH MAYONNAISE

Set out two 1-pt. round freezer cartons or a 1-qt. mold.

Cut into ½-in. pieces
   1 cup *each* canned apricot and peach halves
   1 cup canned pineapple chunks
Mix thoroughly in a saucepan
   1 env. unflavored gelatin
   ½ cup sugar
Blend in
   ½ cup syrup (drained from canned fruit)
Stir over low heat until gelatin is dissolved. Cool slightly.

Combine in a large bowl the fruit, gelatin and
   3 tablespoons lemon juice
   ¼ cup sliced maraschino cherries
Blend well and chill until slightly thickened.

Meanwhile, whip until soft peaks are formed
   1 cup whipped cream, chilled
Continue to beat while blending in
   1 cup mayonnaise
Mix thoroughly with fruit mixture, then spoon into cartons or mold. Seal tightly and freeze.

When ready to use, remove from freezer about ½ hr. before serving time and place in refrigerator until salad is just firm enough to slice. Remove from cartons (cut away the cartons, if desired) or unmold. Cut into ¾-in. crosswise slices and serve on **crisp salad greens.**

About 8 servings

DEEP-DISH APPLE PIE

Grease a 1½-qt. casserole.

Prepare and set aside
   Cheese Pastry Topping (use Pastry Topping recipe, page 486; decrease shortening to 3 tablespoons and cut in with ¾ cup shredded Cheddar cheese. Omit slit design if pie is to be frozen unbaked.)

Mix thoroughly
   ¾ cup firmly packed brown sugar
   3 tablespoons all-purpose flour
   1 teaspoon cinnamon
   ¼ teaspoon nutmeg
   ½ teaspoon salt
Cut in with pastry blender or 2 knives until mixture is in coarse crumbs
   3 tablespoons butter or margarine
   1 teaspoon grated orange peel
Set aside.

Wash, quarter, core, pare and cut into ⅛-in. slices
   6 to 7 medium firm tart apples (6 cups, sliced)
Put apples into a bowl and drizzle over them a mixture of
   ¼ cup orange juice
   1 tablespoon lemon juice
To coat with the juice, gently turn apples with a fork. Arrange one half of apple slices in casserole. Sprinkle with one half of sugar mixture; repeat. Arrange Pastry Topping on casserole and flute edge. Proceed as desired.

6 to 8 servings

To Freeze Unbaked Pie and Serve—Wrap unbaked pie and seal tightly. To protect crust, set package in a pasteboard box or encircle with pasteboard collar. Label and place in freezer. When ready to bake, remove wrappings and carefully cut slits in crust. Bake at 450°F 15 to 20 min. Reduce heat to 375°F and bake 25 to 35 min., or until crust is golden and apples are tender. Serve warm.

To Freeze Baked Pie and Serve—Bake at 450°F 10 min. Reduce heat to 350°F and bake 25 to 30 min. longer, or until apples are tender and crust is golden. Cool completely, wrap and package for freezer as directed for unbaked pie. To thaw, remove wrappings and loosely cover top of pie with aluminum foil. Set in a 325°F oven 35 to 40 min., or just long enough to thaw and heat to serving temperature.

To Complete Without Freezing—Bake pie as directed. If desired, serve accompanied with **cream, ice cream, sweetened whipped cream** or **whipped dessert topping.**

INDEX

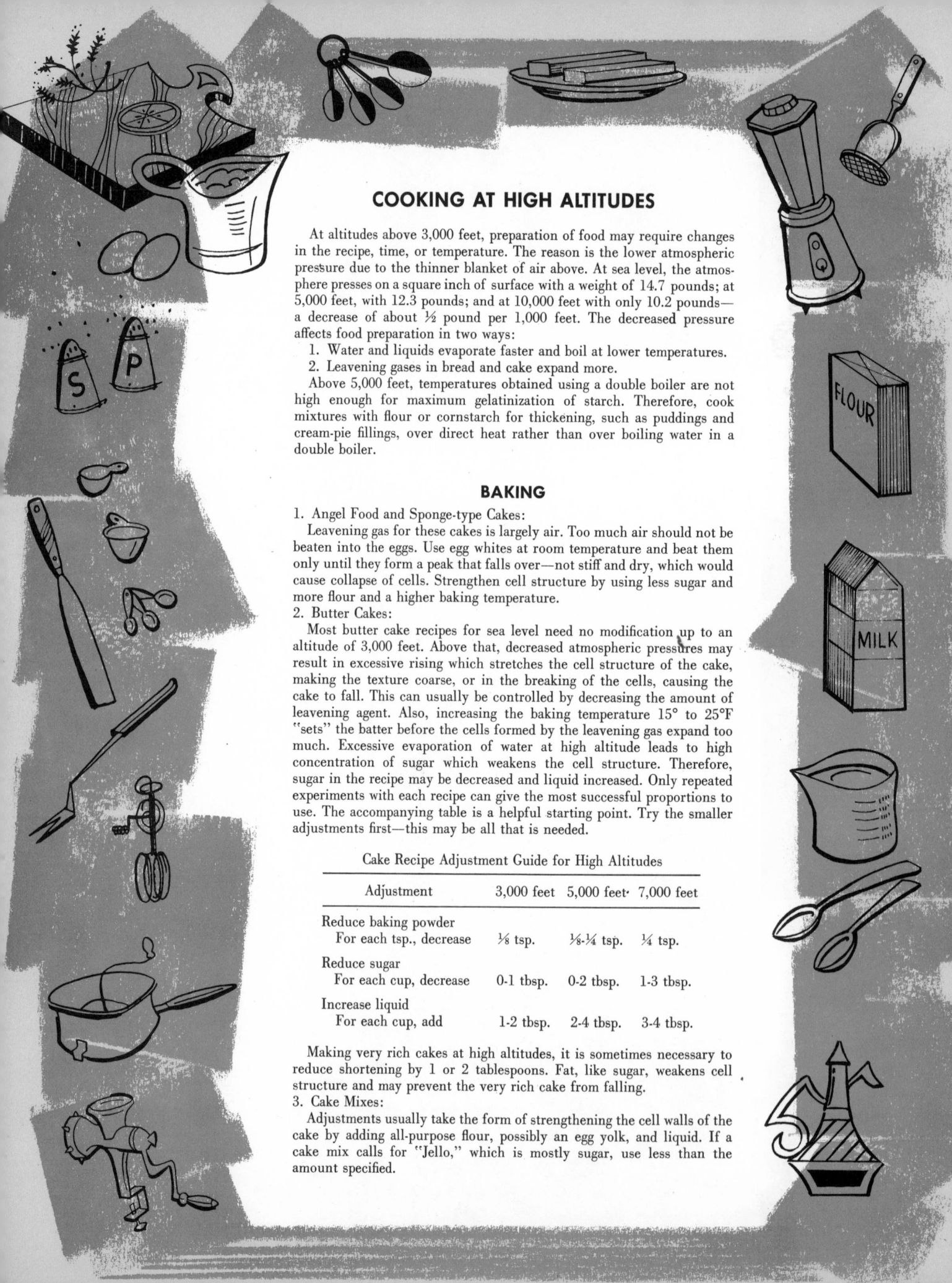

COOKING AT HIGH ALTITUDES

At altitudes above 3,000 feet, preparation of food may require changes in the recipe, time, or temperature. The reason is the lower atmospheric pressure due to the thinner blanket of air above. At sea level, the atmosphere presses on a square inch of surface with a weight of 14.7 pounds; at 5,000 feet, with 12.3 pounds; and at 10,000 feet with only 10.2 pounds—a decrease of about ½ pound per 1,000 feet. The decreased pressure affects food preparation in two ways:

1. Water and liquids evaporate faster and boil at lower temperatures.
2. Leavening gases in bread and cake expand more.

Above 5,000 feet, temperatures obtained using a double boiler are not high enough for maximum gelatinization of starch. Therefore, cook mixtures with flour or cornstarch for thickening, such as puddings and cream-pie fillings, over direct heat rather than over boiling water in a double boiler.

BAKING

1. Angel Food and Sponge-type Cakes:

Leavening gas for these cakes is largely air. Too much air should not be beaten into the eggs. Use egg whites at room temperature and beat them only until they form a peak that falls over—not stiff and dry, which would cause collapse of cells. Strengthen cell structure by using less sugar and more flour and a higher baking temperature.

2. Butter Cakes:

Most butter cake recipes for sea level need no modification up to an altitude of 3,000 feet. Above that, decreased atmospheric pressures may result in excessive rising which stretches the cell structure of the cake, making the texture coarse, or in the breaking of the cells, causing the cake to fall. This can usually be controlled by decreasing the amount of leavening agent. Also, increasing the baking temperature 15° to 25°F "sets" the batter before the cells formed by the leavening gas expand too much. Excessive evaporation of water at high altitude leads to high concentration of sugar which weakens the cell structure. Therefore, sugar in the recipe may be decreased and liquid increased. Only repeated experiments with each recipe can give the most successful proportions to use. The accompanying table is a helpful starting point. Try the smaller adjustments first—this may be all that is needed.

Cake Recipe Adjustment Guide for High Altitudes

Adjustment	3,000 feet	5,000 feet	7,000 feet
Reduce baking powder For each tsp., decrease	⅛ tsp.	⅛-¼ tsp.	¼ tsp.
Reduce sugar For each cup, decrease	0-1 tbsp.	0-2 tbsp.	1-3 tbsp.
Increase liquid For each cup, add	1-2 tbsp.	2-4 tbsp.	3-4 tbsp.

Making very rich cakes at high altitudes, it is sometimes necessary to reduce shortening by 1 or 2 tablespoons. Fat, like sugar, weakens cell structure and may prevent the very rich cake from falling.

3. Cake Mixes:

Adjustments usually take the form of strengthening the cell walls of the cake by adding all-purpose flour, possibly an egg yolk, and liquid. If a cake mix calls for "Jello," which is mostly sugar, use less than the amount specified.